May 6–11, 2017
Denver, CO, USA

Association for Computing Machinery

Advancing Computing as a Science & Profession

CHI'17

Proceedings of the 2017 ACM SIGCHI Conference on Human Factors in Computing Systems

Sponsored by:

ACM SIGCHI

Supported by:

Bloomberg, Facebook, Google, IBM Research, Microsoft, & NSF

Association for
Computing Machinery

Advancing Computing as a Science & Profession

The Association for Computing Machinery
2 Penn Plaza, Suite 701
New York, New York 10121-0701

ISBN: 978-1-4503-4655-9 (Digital)

ISBN: 978-1-4503-5462-2 (Print)

Additional copies may be ordered prepaid from:

ACM Order Department
PO Box 30777
New York, NY 10087-0777, USA

Phone: 1-800-342-6626 (USA and Canada)
+1-212-626-0500 (Global)
Fax: +1-212-944-1318
E-mail: acmhelp@acm.org
Hours of Operation: 8:30 am – 4:30 pm ET

Printed in the USA

CHI 2017 is the premier international conference for the field of Human-Computer Interaction (HCI). This year it was held in Denver, bordering the beautiful Rocky Mountain region in the U.S., and reflected in our logo. The CHI 2017 conference began with two days of workshops and symposia, followed by four days of a technical program with 17 parallel sessions of provocative papers, panels, case studies, SIGs (Special Interest Groups), courses, and the popular student research, design, and game competitions. The growing alt.chi forum, now in its twelfth year, presented stimulating new ideas in HCI. The Interactivity forum showcased cutting-edge technology. For its second year, the CHI Art Exhibit merged art and technology in fascinating ways.

This innovative work can be found in the Proceedings and Extended Abstracts, archived in the ACM Digital Library. For papers, the conference received 2400 submissions which were rigorously reviewed, resulting in 600 accepted papers. To ensure a better fit with reviewers, new subcommittees were created. Across all tracks, CHI received nearly 5000 submissions and accepted over 1000.

Our conference theme this year, *Explore, Innovate, Inspire*, informed our planning process. A new venue held this year was CHI Stories. We generally know little of the personalities that drive the research presented at CHI. CHI Stories is a chance for CHI community members to share personal stories of inspiration, challenge, successes and failures, and grit. We also focused on inclusion this year. Hundreds of CHI attendees volunteered their skills in a Day of Service partnering with non-profit organizations. Inclusion was also manifest throughout the conference, for example, in the Diversity and Inclusion Lunch and by using telepresence robots to enable people with disabilities to participate remotely in the conference. Our keynote speakers were chosen to reflect our conference theme. The speakers were Neri Oxman, who combines computational design, digital fabrication, materials science and synthetic biology; Ben Shneiderman a founder of the CHI conference who, along with some key CHI personalities, gave a perspective on CHI's history and future; Wael Ghonim, credited with starting the Arab Spring and nominated for the Nobel Peace Prize; and best-selling author Nicholas Carr who challenges us to examine the unforeseen impacts of technology, particularly with automation.

The world has experienced a dramatic change this past year. We live in extraordinary times and this calls for extraordinary thinking, something that the CHI community excels at. One of the challenges the community faced this year was responding to a U.S. executive order to ban citizens of certain countries from entering the country to attend CHI. As CHI is committed to inclusion, we decided to hold events at the conference to discuss and plan how we can continue our commitment to inclusion. The conference held a panel to discuss impacts of current political events on science, and hastily organized a panel to promote a conversation of civil liberties in science and a SIG on how the CHI community can participate in change. We are proud to have expanded telepresence options through the use of robots to enable people to participate in the conference remotely if they were physically unable to enter the country. We had a keynote speaker who inspired us on the topic of Internet activism. Our art exhibit, *I'll Be Watching You,* examined the contemporary issue of surveillance.

We are extremely grateful to a legion of volunteers who made CHI 2017 possible, including over 7000 reviewers across all areas of the technical program, 254 senior members of the papers program committee, over 100 members of the CHI 2017 conference organization committee and importantly, the more than 175 student volunteers. We also thank SIGCHI (the Special Interest Group on Computer-Human Interaction of ACM) as well as the ACM itself for its continued support.

Gloria Mark, University of California Irvine, CHI 2017 General Conference Co-Chair

Susan Fussell, Cornell University, CHI 2017 General Conference Co-Chair

Cliff Lampe, University of Michigan, CHI 2017 Technical Program Chair

m.c. schraefel, University of Southampton, CHI 2017 Technical Program Chair

Juan Pablo Hourcade, University of Iowa, CHI 2017 Papers Co-Chair

Caroline Appert, Université Paris-Sud, CHI 2017 Papers Co-Chair

Daniel Wigdor, University of Toronto, CHI 2017 Papers Co-Chair

Loren Terveen, University of Minnesota, President, ACM SIGCHI Executive Committee

Scooter Morris, University of San Francisco, ACM SIGCHI Liaison

Table of Contents

Table of Contents

Table of Contents

Table of Contents

Table of Contents

Table of Contents

Table of Contents

Table of Contents

Table of Contents

Table of Contents

Table of Contents

Table of Contents

Table of Contents

Table of Contents

Table of Contents

Table of Contents

Table of Contents

Table of Contents

Table of Contents

Table of Contents

Table of Contents

Table of Contents

Table of Contents

Table of Contents

Table of Contents

Table of Contents

Table of Contents

Table of Contents

Table of Contents

Table of Contents

Table of Contents

Table of Contents

Table of Contents

CHI 2017 Organization

Conference Chairs
Gloria Mark, University of California, Irvine
Susan Fussell, Cornell University

Assistants to General Chairs
Yiran Wang, University of California, Irvine
Ge Gao, Cornell University

Senior Technical Program Chair
Cliff Lampe, University of Michigan

Technical Program Chair
m.c. schraefel, University of Southampton

Assistant to the Technical Program Chairs
Lindsay Blackwell, University of Michigan

Papers Chairs
Caroline Appert, Univ. Paris-Sud & CNRS
Juan Pablo Hourcade, University of Iowa
Daniel Wigdor, University of Toronto

Assistant to Papers Chairs
Michael Glueck, University of Toronto

alt.chi Chairs
Karrie Karahalios, University of Illinois at Urbana – Champaign
Jessa Lingel, University of Pennsylvania
Janet Vertesi, Princeton University

Case Studies Chairs
Stephen Snow, University of Southampton
Jessica Tsimeris, Google

Courses Chairs
Erik Andersen, Cornell University
Hilary Hutchinson, Google
Max Wilson, University of Nottingham

Demos Chairs
Ido Guy, Yahoo
Stephen Voida, University of Colorado Boulder

Doctoral Consortium Chairs
Anna Cox, University College London
Jeff Bigham, Carnegie Mellon University
Kenton O'Hara, Microsoft Research, UK

Interactive Installations Chairs
Adrian Friday, Lancaster University
Shengdong Zhao, National University of Singapore

Late Breaking Work Chairs
Sharon Ding, Fudan University
Ingrid Erikson, Rutgers University
Bryan Semaan, Syracuse University
Fanis Tsandilas, INRIA

Panels Chairs
Sarita Schoenebeck, University of Michigan
Jude Yew, National University of Singapore

Student Design Competition Chairs
Joonhwan Lee, Seoul National University
Scott Minneman, California College of Arts

Student Game Competition Chairs
Floyd Mueller, RMIT University
Josh Tanenbaum, University of California, Irvine

Student Research Competition Chairs
Jeremy Birnholtz, Northwestern University
Jenn Thom, Spotify

Special Interest Groups Chairs
Lindsay Reynolds, Facebook
Bert Scerbo, Disney

Systems Chairs
Michael Stewart, Virginia Tech
Dorota Filipczuk, University of Southampton

Symposia Chair
Lana Yarosh, University of Minnesota

Video Showcase Chairs
Danyel Fisher, Microsoft Research
Catherine Letondal, ENAC

Workshops Chairs
Duncan Brumby, University College London
Christopher Frauenberger, Vienna University of Technology, Austria
Shamsi Iqbal, Microsoft Research

Art Chairs
Jiffer Harriman, University of Colorado
Andruid Kerne, Texas A&M University
HyunJoo Oh, University of Colorado Boulder
Thecla Schiphorst, Simon Fraser University

CHI Stories Chairs
Nazanin Andalibi, Drexel University
Nick Diakopoulos, University of Maryland, College Park
Andrea Forte, Drexel University
Misa Maruyama, University of Hawaii at Manoa
Scott Robertson, University of Hawaii at Manoa

Career Development Workshop Chairs
Luigina Ciolfi, Sheffield Hallam University
Michael Muller, IBM Research

Journals Chair
Hrvoje Benko, Microsoft Research

Remix Chairs
Susan Dray, Dray & Associates
Amy Voida, University of Colorado Boulder

Student Volunteer Chairs
Patrick Carrington, University of Maryland, Baltimore County (UMBC)
Anna Kötteritzsch, Universität der Bundeswehr München

Video Previews Chair
Carla Griggio, Inria

Awards Chair
Steven Drucker, Microsoft

Accessibility Chairs
Erin Brady, Indiana University – Purdue University Indianapolis
Sean Goggins, Missouri University
Shaun Kane, University of Colorado Boulder

Data Chair
Boyu Gao, Konkuk University
Toni-Jan Keith Monserrat, University of the Philippines Los Baños

Diversity and Inclusivity Lunch Chairs
Anke Brock, Inria Bordeaux
Allison Druin, University of Maryland
Gopinaath Kannabiran, Indiana University, Bloomington

Language Inclusion Chair
Tilman Dingler, University of Stuttgart

Local Arrangements Chairs
Jed Brubaker, University of Colorado Boulder
Tom Yeh, University of Colorado Boulder

Social Impact Chairs
Kathy Baxter, Salesforce
Elizabeth Gerber, Northwestern University
Jill Woelfer, Google

Social Media Chairs
Dan Afergan, Google
Bart Knijnenburg, Clemson University
Vicky McArthur, University of Toronto Mississauga

Telepresence Chairs
Min Kyung Lee, Carnegie Mellon University
Carman Neustaedter, Simon Fraser University

Translations Chairs
Hao-Chuan Wang, National Tsing Hua University
Naomi Yamashita, Nippon Telegraph and Telephone

Design Director
Donghee Yvette Wohn, New Jersey Institute of Technology

Logo Design/Artwork
Jia Zhang, MIT Media Lab

Web Designer
Xiying Wang, Cornell University

Webmaster
Xiying Wang, Cornell University

ACM Liaison
Farrah Khan, ACM

SIGCHI Liaison
Scooter Morris, University of California, San Francisco

Conference Management
Paul Henning, Conference & Logistics Consultants, Inc.
Stacey Ogren, Conference & Logistics Consultants, Inc.
Lois Sarfo-Mensah, Conference & Logistics Consultants, Inc.
Michael O'Connell, Conference & Logistics Consultants, Inc.

Registration
Taylor Vick, Executive Events, Inc.

Sponsorship and Exhibits
Carol Klyver, Foundations of Excellence

Technical Liaison
Sara Drenner, BI WORLDWIDE

Variolite: Supporting Exploratory Programming by Data Scientists

Mary Beth Kery
School of Computer Science
Carnegie Mellon University
Pittsburgh, PA
mkery@cs.cmu.edu

Amber Horvath
Oregon State University
Corvallis, Oregon, USA
horvatha@oregonstate.edu

Brad Myers
School of Computer Science
Carnegie Mellon University
Pittsburgh, PA
bam@cs.cmu.edu

ABSTRACT

How do people ideate through code? Using semi-structured interviews and a survey, we studied data scientists who program, often with small scripts, to experiment with data. These studies show that data scientists frequently code new analysis ideas by building off of their code from a previous idea. They often rely on informal versioning interactions like copying code, keeping unused code, and commenting out code to repurpose older analysis code while attempting to keep those older analyses intact. Unlike conventional version control, these informal practices allow for fast versioning of any size code snippet, and quick comparisons by interchanging which versions are run. However, data scientists must maintain a strong mental map of their code in order to distinguish versions, leading to errors and confusion. We explore the needs for improving version control tools for exploratory tasks, and demonstrate a tool for lightweight local versioning, called Variolite, which programmers found usable and desirable in a preliminary usability study.

Author Keywords

End-User Programming; Version Control Systems (VCS); Exploratory Data Analysis; Variants; Variations

ACM Classification Keywords

D.2.3 Coding Tools and Techniques: *Program editors;* D.2.7 Distribution, Maintenance, and Enhancement: *Version control.*

INTRODUCTION

When programmers write code to design, discover, or explore ideas, there may be no clear requirements for that code at the onset, and there may be a broad space of possible solutions [6][16]. For example, developing a new algorithm for computational biology may take considerable trial-and-error on both the code and the concepts behind it [35]. We call this process *exploratory programming* [32][5], which we define as a programming task in which a specific goal or a means to that goal must be discovered by iteratively writing code for multiple ideas.

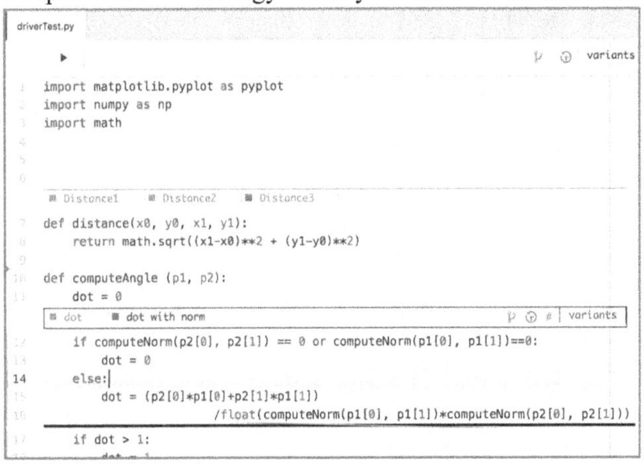

Figure 1. Variolite is a code editing tool that includes local versioning of chunks of code. Here, there are two version boxes. The outer one has three "Distance" versions, and the inner one has two "dot" versions with "dot with norm" currently being used.

Data scientists are a group that does a lot of exploratory programming. The term "data scientist" has a broad [29] and sometimes contested definition [21] but here we use "data scientist" in the simple sense of people who manipulate data to gain insights from it. We specifically target data scientists who write code, which is a large group [29] encompassing people who work with data in domains such as engineering, design, business, and research. One example of when data scientists engage in exploratory programming is "exploratory data analysis," which is a common approach to visualizing and asking questions of data, rather than more straightforward hypothesis testing [12]. Another example is working with data to develop machine learning models or other intelligent systems, which is often a painstaking process of experimenting with different manipulations, parameters, and algorithms [7][14].

CHI 2017, May 06-11, 2017, Denver, CO, USA
© 2017 ACM. ISBN 978-1-4503-4655-9/17/05...$15.00
DOI: http://dx.doi.org/10.1145/3025453.3025626

A great deal of prior work on programming tools, such as live programming tools and development environments like R Studio, has focused on making it easier to quickly prototype ideas [25][24]. Other literate programming tools, such as Knitr [30] or Jupyter notebooks [8] have become popular in recent years for clearly communicating data analysis code, rationale, and output. Yet there is little work on how data scientists manage an abundance of exploratory code over a longer-term project. How do data scientists transition from one data manipulation idea to the next? To what degree do they compare alternative ideas, or revisit older ideas?

Current tools have limited support for variations and versions of ideas. Live programming environments, whose strength is instant feedback, tend to de-emphasize history, which DeLine et al. remarked was an issue their users cared about [25]. Tools like Jupyter notebooks have become immensely popular for data science work [9], however the focus of literate programming tools is to clearly communicate analysis work, so that it can be shared with others and replicated. We found that data scientists frequently try out many less successful paths before cleaning up and condensing their final result into code to publish or share. The linear, narrative style of notebooks gives limited help with the messy and nonlinear path to the final result.

Understanding how humans approach the exploratory process of data science is crucial for improving the usability and accuracy of this kind of work. Patel et al. [14] observed that many difficulties in applying machine learning techniques arose from the "iterative and exploratory process" of using statistics as a software development tool. Patel's interviews with machine learning developers emphasized the *non-linear* progression of this work where "*an apparent dead end for a project was overcome by revisiting an earlier point in their process*" [14]. Others who have studied data science and machine learning developers, such as Hill [7] and Guo [22] have described difficulties even for experts, struggling to create understandable and reproducible models during a process where they attempt many different things. Both Hill and Patel called for advances in software engineering methods and tools for dealing with this kind of programming. Similar arguments have been made in the scientific computing community, where problems of understandability and reproducibility during experimentation with code are often mentioned [13][16][34]. Further, when even experts struggle with an exploratory process, this lowers the accessibility to novices programming in these domains.

To better understand the barriers and opportunities in this area, we conducted semi-structured interviews with 10 data scientists, and then a survey of an additional 60 data scientists, specifically focused on how ideation is carried out at the concrete level of artifacts like source code and files. In summary, we found that data scientists frequently write code for new analysis ideas by repurposing or building off of their code from a previous idea. Due to the sometimes non-linear progression of their exploratory work, participants emphasized reusing code, copying code and keeping code that was sometimes long dead, just in case it became useful later. To facilitate reusing code that overlapped with older analyses while attempting to keep those older analyses intact, many relied on ad-hoc means to version their code. These informal versioning practices took the form of copying files, copying snippets, and comments (sometimes with intricate combinations of code commented on and off).

While these code versioning needs seem like they could use standard software version control systems (VCSs) like Git or SVN, we note: 1) a low usage of VCSs even by participants who actively used one for other kinds of work, and 2) benefits in informal versioning interactions that a conventional VCS does not provide. For example, copying and commenting out code allows for rapid branching and comparison between multiple versions of a single line of code, or any size code of interest, without leaving the code editor. Informal versioning is more transparent than versions of code hidden behind a conventional command line tool, since in that case programmers cannot quickly view and swap among multiple versions of code. However, participants also reported consistent difficulties that arose from informal versioning practices.

We found these ad-hoc interactions are practices individuals had developed for themselves over time and experience. Yet there was considerable overlap in the practices participants reported. Commenting, copying, and keeping code are natural affordances of text programs, and require no new tools. Our studies showed that many people leverage these mechanisms for a variety of purposes, like versioning. By developing a stronger understanding of the workarounds programmers use, we aim to explore what versioning capabilities data scientists need for managing their ideas in a non-linear exploratory process. Through design, we aim to leverage the local interactions that programmers naturally use during exploratory programming, such as versioning arbitrarily sized sections of code.

Our new tool, called Variolite [1](see Figure 1) is an initial probe to test some of these interaction ideas. Variolite, which is a kind of rock structure, here stands for **V**ariations **A**ugment **R**eal **I**terative **O**utcomes **L**etting **I**nformation **T**ranscend **E**xploration. Variolite is built on top of the Atom editor [1], and allows users to directly version code in their editor simply by drawing a box around a section of code and invoking a command. It is a general purpose, programming-language agnostic, versioning tool. We performed an initial usability study that showed that it is usable.

Our work makes contributions in two areas:

[1] Variolite source code https://mkery.github.io/Variolite/

- Our qualitative study showing barriers and requirements of data scientists managing exploratory code.
- A working prototype of a tool to address some of these versioning interaction issues, and a usability study showing its usability.

RELATED WORK

Programming for data analysis or machine learning

Guo previously studied people who program to gain insights from data, whom he called "research programmers" [22]. He noted problems managing a large amount of files produced during exploratory work with data. He also noted a "lack of transparency" in traditional versioning tools, in contrast to the "low-tech" interaction of copying a file and giving it a derivative name (like "file-2"). We expand upon this work by studying a wider range of informal versioning interactions through interviews and through looking at interviewees' project artifacts.

Guo et al. [23] also produced a research system called Burrito, which displays a GUI activity feed of things like outputs, save events, and notes relevant to a given project. While both Burrito and Variolite record history and output provenance information, the Burrito tool collects much more detailed provenance information by working at the operating system level in Linux. Variolite is much more lightweight and is situated in the code editor, but as a trade-off, collects a much simpler link between code and output. Burrito is also intended as a lab notebook approach, like literate programming tools such as Jupyter notebooks [8]. While Variolite certainly could work with added Markdown and other literate programming techniques, our focus in this research is managing ideas during non-linear exploration.

Both Hill et al. [7] and Patel [15] reported that machine learning programmers struggled to reproduce or understand earlier experiments. Patel found that logging experiments was beneficial to return to earlier result, but difficult and time consuming. Patel created a research tool Hindsight, which keeps a history of different parameters used in a programming task for machine learning classification. Hindsight also allows users to combine different alternatives of steps in the classification, such as which data is loaded and which algorithm is used. Hindsight is a GUI based tool specific to classification. Variolite aims to generalize interactions for dealing with alternatives and history to work in a wider range of exploratory tasks.

Dealing with alternatives

Several other research tools have explored interactions for alternatives of code, and also versions of code over time.

Juxtapose [6] is a research tool that provided interaction designers with different alternatives of their code, in order to compare between different parameters of the look and feel of their interface designs. This tool used Linked Editing, a technique for editing two alternative pieces of code simultaneously, previously developed by Toomim et al. [18]. Juxtapose also built off of prior work such as Set Based Interactions [17] and Subjunctive Interfaces [4], which explored general techniques for exploring multiple alternatives in parallel. These were not specific to writing programs.

On the side of professional software engineering, *software product lines* are a method used in industry to adapt one piece of software to be customizable for different clients or devices [20]. Software product line research aims to handle much more complex versions and interdependencies than Variolite, with commensurate complexities in the developer's interface.

Interacting with history

Azurite [33] developed an interaction for selectively undoing past actions in code using a timeline visualization. Other interactions for versioning have been developed for End-user Programmers, such as for Mashups [27]. None of these focused on helping users edit fine grain versions.

METHODOLOGY

Before we approached the design of a tool, we wanted to understand the real needs and barriers faced by data scientists, so we performed two formative studies.

Interview Study

We conducted a series of semi-structured interviews with researchers across multiple universities. Researchers were a convenience sample of our target population: people who do significant exploratory work with data. We recruited individuals who had worked on at least one major exploratory analysis project. Our 10 respondents were a mix of faculty, and graduate and undergraduate student researchers. Eight of interviewees did research in a computer science-related field, one in computational chemistry, and one in computational neuroscience. The gender ratio was 2 females to 8 males. Interviewees worked with a variety of programming languages, with Python and R being the most used. We intentionally oversampled people who were experienced programmers with computer science training in order to better understand the intent of their practices not simply arising from lack of awareness of available tools or lack of skill with software development. Prior work has shown that many scientists are unaware of good software development practices [16].

All participants first signed a consent form. There was no monetary compensation for participation in the study, and participants volunteered their time for a 45-60 minute interview. In the first part of the interview, we asked participants to describe a recent exploratory project at a high level: What were their goals in the project? What high-level steps did they follow to meet those goals? All interviewees discussed projects that had spanned at least several weeks of work. Due to the timespan of significant projects, we chose a retrospective interview methodology rather that direct observation of their work [10]. Next, we asked participants, whenever possible, to show us artifacts from the project, including source code, their folder structure, and data files. During this stage we asked participants to discuss how their high-level ideas had been implemented in code and files.

Each interview was audio recorded and transcribed. Several participants gave us permission to keep and share screenshots of their code and files, and these artifacts were used in our analysis. As the interviews were focused on each participant's research, there were large parts of the transcriptions about an interviewee's general research topic, rather than their work process. To analyze the interviews, two coders first read all interviews and pulled out any quotes related to process, such as plans, code, notes, collaborators, etc. Following an affinity diagramming approach, coders grouped the quotes into higher-level themes, and separated out any quotes that explicitly mentioned a difficulty or complaint.

Survey

We next sought to validate our observations from the interviews on a broader population. Using an online survey, we recruited respondents from several websites for data scientists (e.g., kaggle.com and reddit.com groups for machine learning or data science), as well as emails to acquaintances. A total of 77 people started the survey. However, not all participants answered all of the questions, so here we analyze only the 60 people who answered the questions beyond the demographic information. All 60 self-identified as having experience coding with data in an exploratory way. The average age of participants was 34 (SD = 13), and the gender ratio was 21% females, 74% males. The remaining 5% of participants chose not to disclose their gender.

We structured our survey such that it acted as a quantitative supplement to our interview. Using the interview results, we drafted questions that built upon what issues affected participants most, what design features in a tool they would want to address these concerns, and to see if our findings generalize across a more diverse sample. First, we asked questions to determine the background of our participants, summarized in Figure 2. We then asked questions about coding practices and behaviors. We presented statements such as "I analyze a lot of different questions about the data in a single source file" with a 5-point Likert scale, going from "Never" to "Very Often". We then asked about the problems they encounter, such as "Distinguishing between similarly named versions of code files or output files" with a 5-point Likert scale going from "Not at all a problem" to "A very big problem". We also gave a "don't know / can't answer" option in case participants had never encountered or could not recall encountering such an issue.

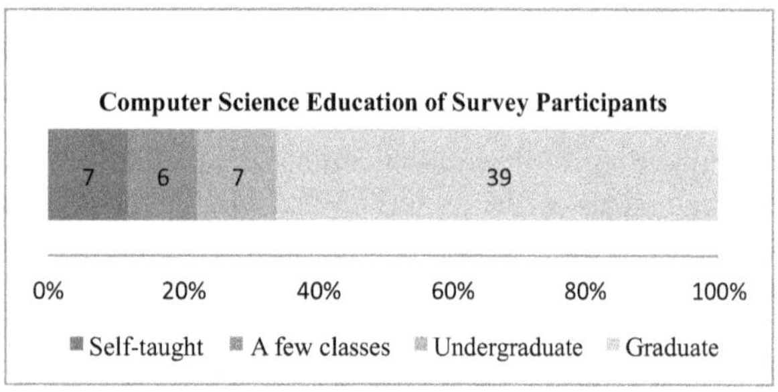

Figure 2. Background statistics about 59 of the survey respondents. Most had graduate degrees in computer science and work in research (one respondent declined to answer).

RESULTS AND DISCUSSION

Interview and survey participants varied widely in their practices, and the kinds of projects they worked on. Despite this, many participants had behaviors and beliefs in common. In the following, participants in the interviews are identified with a "P", and survey responses with percentages for the different answers.

Exploratory Process

The participants mentioned a variety of ways that their programming tasks were exploratory. One of the most salient feelings expressed by participants was the trial-and-error nature of their work, and the risk of investing in an idea that may fail or be discarded:

"I didn't always have a great idea of what would work up front, so I would try a lot of different things and then they wouldn't pan out and then you would disregard most of that work, but maybe still want some of the small processing steps from that work, if that makes sense, to apply to your next statistical model." - P10

Of survey respondents, 43% "Agreed" on a Likert scale that they "prioritize finding a solution over writing high-quality code", while another 33% "Strongly Agreed" (totaling 76%). Although some interviewees were distinctly more messy or meticulous as evidenced by their code artifacts, all mentioned avoiding investment in some way, whether avoiding leaving informational comments in their code, or avoiding taking notes or not using extra software tools beyond the bare minimum needed for their analysis.

"I know how to write code. And I know that I could write functions to reuse functions and I could try to modularize things better, and sometimes I just don't care because why am I going to put effort in that if I'm not going to use it again?" - P6

This sentiment is common to how end-user developers prioritize goals [3]. While "end-user developer" often refers to a programmer without formal training in computer science, many of our participants did have formal training (Figure 2). Ko et al. distinguish end-user developers as having goals where a program is a means to an end, rather than professional developers, whose goals are the code itself as a product [3]. Under this definition, considering data scientists as end-user developers may be fruitful for leveraging existing theories on programmers who write expendable code.

Yet such "throw away" data analysis attempts are often not really thrown away. While all interviewees discussed accumulated failed attempts and earlier analyses that were less informative, they also often talked about *reusing* that code. Interviewees mentioned they often built off code from an earlier attempt in order to try a new method. This is supported by the survey, where 46% of survey participants reported reusing code from the *same* project at least "Often". Similarly, 47% reported reusing code snippets taken from *different* projects at least "Often".

Informal Versioning

Data scientists we interviewed and surveyed faced challenges of trying out multiple alternatives in their code, while trying to judge which code to keep in case that analysis or helper method would be useful again later. Exploration can involve non-linear iteration, so keeping code to backtrack to or to reuse was important to interviewees. 4 of 10 participants discussed actively keeping around old code they were no longer using, just in case some part of that code proved helpful later on. Similarly, 65% of survey respondents reported leaving code snippets they were not currently using in the code at least "Occasionally", and 79% reported commenting out code at least "Often".

Interviewees were cautious about deleting code. Yet this introduced code complexity, as some attempts could not simultaneously exist in the same namespace, or used overlapping code. As quick workarounds, data scientists relied on informal versioning such as commenting:

"I guess this is kind of my own personal version of version control. A lot of times I'll like comment out a whole big section that was there, and then I'll rewrite it so that it's different but I'll keep the original one exactly as is in case the new version kind of sucks." - P9

Code that is commented out does not run. Using comments to store code has been observed in prior studies [6][31]. Ko et al. [2], when studying experienced programmers, found that 60% of edits using comments were for temporarily commenting code during maintenance tasks.

Comments to keep track of attempts

44% of survey takers reported using comments to keep track of what they have tried, and 70% keep commented code to reuse later. This allowed data scientists to keep multiple versions of an idea for reference, with only the relevant one running.

Comments to manipulate execution

Comments were used not only to store chunks of code, but also to mutate the meaning of existing code, sometimes in complex ways. In the survey, 56% of the respondents reported using comments explicitly to control execution.

P3's code, shown in Figure 3, shows an example of this, in which several alternatives for outputting the analysis result are present in the comments. An active chunk of Python code graphs the output, but this code has several commented-out statements. There is a second graphing section of code lower down that is fully commented out.

Duplicating snippets, function and files

Copying code was another popular way of versioning. Shown in Figure 4 is P1's file structure, where many versions of the same script were kept to track major attempts at improving a machine learning model. On average, 72% of the respondents in the survey said they at least "Occasionally" do this, and 58% at least "Often" said they named the new file copies based on the original one. Survey respondents reported making an average of 3-4 versions based on one file. Interviewees also demonstrated multiple versions and copies of functions and smaller code snippets.

```
print "hc policy distribution entropy: \n" + str
#print "2-fold CV Var: \n" + str(CV_variances)

#print "Stdev of (V_M under h^f, avg over states
#print "Stdev of (V_M under h^c, avg over states
#print "Average V_M under h^f: \n" + str(V_M_hf)
#print "Average V_M under h^c: \n" + str(V_M_hc)

fig = plt.figure(figsize=(9,4))
ax = fig.add_subplot(1,1,1)
ax.set_xticks(D_sizes)
plt.plot(D_sizes, [V_star_avgState]*len(D_sizes)
#plt.plot(D_sizes, AvgState_V_hfs)
plt.errorbar(D_sizes,AvgState_V_hfs,yerr=Std_Vs_
#plt.plot(D_sizes, AvgState_V_hcs)
plt.errorbar(D_sizes,AvgState_V_hcs,yerr=Std_Vs_
plt.xlim(0,max(D_sizes))
plt.xlabel('|D|')
plt.ylabel('mean(V)')
plt.grid()
plt.show()

'''
fig = plt.figure(figsize=(10,4))
ax = fig.add_subplot(1,1,1)
ax.set_xticks(D_sizes)
```

Figure 3. Comments used to keep alternatives

Difficulties

As interviewees did not overly invest in notes, comments, or trying to write clear code more than they felt necessary, they had to rely on their mental map of their code to understand it. Here are some difficulties that interviewees mentioned, and responses from the survey that show that these issues are indeed widespread:

Why did I name my file that? Participants discussed having files or methods with ambiguous names or that they often had multiple files with similar names, making it difficult to distinguish between versions (see Figure 4). 7 out of 10 participants expressed confusion when talking about the names they chose for different methods and files. 83% of survey takers reported that closely named artifacts had caused them at least minor problems in their work.

How do I keep track of everything in my project? Participants struggled to keep track of the relationships between files (source code, input data, output data), code snippets, and their analysis progress. 5 out of 10 participants expressed having difficulty in keeping track of the high-level aspects of a project and how it related to the lower-level code. Furthermore, as their code evolved, the code that originally produced a particular result may be changed or obfuscated. 4 out of 10 reported losing track of their mental map of code, especially if the code was messier or had parts commented out.

Interviewees discussed understanding their code in the short term, but having trouble understanding the code when they returned to it later. 85% of survey takers reported that this caused them at least minor problems in their work, with 44% reporting significant problems.

What was I doing in this old project? Participants wanted to go back to old projects to lift code, but had difficulty remembering and understanding the structure and details of these old projects. 5 out of 10 participants expressed difficulty re-orienting themselves with older projects. 67% of survey takers reported that visiting old projects was a significant problem.

What do I do with all this old code? Participants expressed an interest in "hoarding" code through commenting out code snippets and refusing to delete old source code files in case their exploration did not pay off. However, this lead to confusion with keeping track of multiple similar copies as well as commented versus not-commented code.

This file is huge! What's in it? Participants often had large script files that served a variety of purposes, resulting in confusing code dependencies and relationships among various parts of the script. This resulted in an overall difficulty discerning the purpose of a script, which 4 of the 10 participants mentioned. Some reported the problem extending across multiple files, where cluttered directories were composed of confusing relationships between files.

These alternatives are inconsistent! P1 faced problems in which she fixed a bug in one alternative of her code, and then when she needed to backtrack to an earlier alternative, she had lost track of which alternatives had the bug fix, and which did not. 74% of survey takers reported that inconsistent alternatives had caused them at least minor problems, with 35% reporting that this was a significant problem.

Why aren't people using version control systems?

Data scientists face difficulties with informal versioning for multiple overlapping ideas over time. This might seem to be well within the realm of problems that software version control systems are designed to solve. VCSs reduce code clutter by separating out versions. They give order to versions and preserve history, so that older versions and analyses can be reproduced in the future.

However, only 3 out of 10 of interviewees chose to use software version control for their exploratory analysis work, although 9 of 10 *did* actively use VCSs such as Git or SVN for *other* non-exploratory projects they worked on. A benefit of over-sampling from individuals with computer science background in the interview study is that this provides a more nuanced picture than previous work, which has studied version control usage by scientists who lack training in computer science [16]. Nguyen-Hoan et al., in a survey of scientists, found that 30% of their sample used VCS [16]. Despite our over sampling of people with CS backgrounds in our survey (see Figure 2), we found that 48% of participants, just under a half, did *not* use version control for their exploratory data analysis work.

Figure 4. Folder from a data analysis project of P1

A few survey takers did not know how to use software version control, but the most common reasons for not using a VCS were 1) it was too heavy-weight for what they needed, 2) they were not concerned about code collaboration, and 3) they were not concerned about reverting code. This final reason "No need to revert code" was cited by interviewees as well, and appears contradictory to their demonstrated interest in hoarding old code for later reuse. In fact, some interviewees, when pressed to explain, reasoned that because their code was copied and commented in many places, there was no need to "backtrack" or "revert" in the sense that all old code they needed was present in one of their code files.

"I guess because I'm doing like this copy and pasting thing, I also have lots of old versions of stuff everywhere, like other projects and things like that" - P5

It is clear that many data scientists do not perceive VCS as having enough benefit over their current practices to invest effort in using these tools. Furthermore, while using informal versioning can be problematic, we argue there is functionality of these interactions that conventional VCS does not gracefully support:

- Versions are easily accessible and comparable because they are all available in the user's immediate files.
- It is easy to see what code you have available to reuse.
- There is a smaller learning curve, since this should not be much more complicated than the commands it takes to comment or copy something.
- It is easy to temporarily create a version of the code, and then remove the version if not wanted later.
- It is easy to keep alternatives of an *arbitrary size.* While conventional version control operates only at the file level, programmers make use of commenting and copying to version at the level of functions, code snippets, lines, or even single values.

In order to make exploratory programming less prone to confusion, we aim to inform new interactions for software version control tools based on how data scientists naturally use versioning.

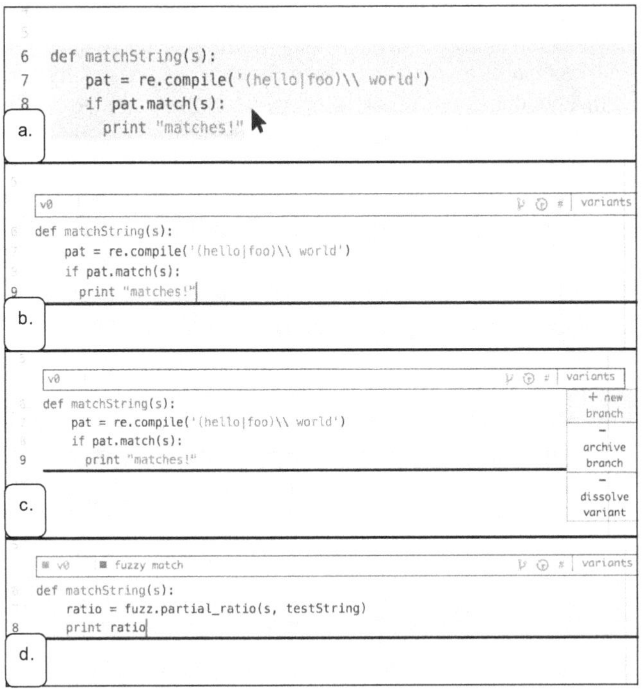

Figure 5. Creating a variant box in Variolite. In (a) the user selects a section of code and selects the command "wrap in variant". In (b) this places a box around the code, which can be used to keep multiple versions of that chunk of code (c, d).

DESIGNING TO SUPPORT LOCAL VERSIONING

To explore this design space, we first sketched a number of possibilities for interacting with versioning within a code editor. We showed these to a convenience sample of 6 data scientists. Between each informal 15-30 minute session we iterated on the drawings based on the open-ended feedback we received.

Based on this feedback, we iteratively designed and implemented a prototype tool called Variolite. Variolite is implemented in CoffeeScript and CSS, using the Atom editor's package framework [1]. Atom is an open-source code editor developed by GitHub, first released in 2015. It has over 1 million active users, and is close in style to other more mature editors such as Sublime Text, which are popular among Python programmers. Although Variolite can be used with any programming language or plain text, here we show examples in Python, as it is a popular language for data science tasks.

Users of Variolite draw "variant boxes" around regions of code, where the code within the box can then be locally versioned or branched (Figure 5). As with commenting, where a user can use the comment symbol as a switch to control execution, users can control which version is run by a simple switch of the active tab on the variant box. This is similar to the tab-based versioning shown in Juxtapose [6]. However, whereas Juxtapose shows alternatives of a file in the code editor, we extend this interaction to encompass any amount of code. A user can draw a variant box to create alternatives of a file, a group of functions, or a single line of code. Multiple variant boxes can exist in a file and they can be nested (Figure 7 b,c). Variant boxes can be created or dissolved back into flat code as needed.

Variolite Use Case

Interviewee P1 was working on developing a machine learning model. To do this, she created many different copies of her Python scripts in order to keep a record of all the variations of the code while trying to achieve the highest predictive accuracy for her model. She also developed an elaborate menu system in her main script, to experiment with different combinations of aspects like algorithms, features, and which features were used in the model.

To illustrate the range of functionality of Variolite, we will describe a fictional use case, based on how P1 might use it. The name "Ellen" and domain in the scenario are fictional:

Drawing a box, version it

Ellen is calculating a new feature for her model. She has a function matchString() and is trying to figure out how to best measure similarity between two pieces of text. She wants to try a new method for doing this. Using Variolite, she selects the code of matchString() with the cursor and selects the command "Wrap in Variant" from the right click menu (Figure 5a). This draws a *variant box* around matchString() (Figure 5b). Now Ellen uses the "new branch" menu item to create a new version of matchString() (Figure 5c), which she titles "fuzzy match". She edits this new version to implement the new algorithm. She can now switch between the two algorithms of matchString() by changing the active tab in the header of the variant box (Figure 5d). Whichever version is showing is the one that is run.

Supporting nonlinear exploration

Like informal versioning, our intention for Variolite is to provide a simple structure that is sufficiently flexible so programmers can leverage versioning in whatever way they need during their exploratory process. As Ellen works, she can vary different aspects of her code. She puts a variant around a single line that changes which machine learning algorithm she is using. She puts variants around different functions that generate features and that control which features are included in the model. Now, by simply interchanging which versions of each of those alternatives are run, she can explore different *combinations* of the different things she has tried. Instead of a purely linear iteration, she can re-try features she used in the past with new versions of the algorithms' parameters. This allows Ellen to more easily explore a problem that can be improved on multiple interrelated dimensions.

Running code

Switching version tabs does introduce a danger of runtime errors if surrounding code that a version was written in has since changed. In future work, this limitation may be addressed using lightweight program analysis, e.g. by at least alerting users to parts of the code that are likely to produce errors.

As Ellen works, she can run her program using the run button at the top (Figure 7a), or a terminal area on the right pane of Variolite (Figure 7e). This will run the entire file at its current state. As with a typical terminal, Variolite displays the command used and output from each run in its terminal pane. By simulating ways to run code within Variolite's interface, we are able to add layers of interaction for dealing with runs. Exploration with data involves not just the code artifact, but also the data and parameters used to produce a certain result. Therefore, each time the code is run, a wrapper script in Variolite records the parameters used, and all inputs/outputs from the run. This provenance data is saved in JSON format separately from the code. However, keeping all outputs can be impractical for space when the output is very large. To mitigate this, users have the option of saving whole data files or simply pointers to those files. Saving only pointers is a trade-off in that Variolite cannot provide accurate provenance information if those data files have changed.

To allow users to revisit past experiments, a commit is also automatically recorded of the entire source code file each time the file is run, as well as a commit for each variant box used in the run. Suppose Ellen would like to review an earlier experiment. She can find the experiment's result in the output pane, or use the search pane to find it if it is out of view (Figure 7d). To help users find interesting results among many runs, a user can provide annotations and tags on versions that are promising, either in the variant box, or in the output panel at the right (Figure 7f).

Double-clicking a given output causes Variolite to set the entire code back to the past version of the file and the past version of each variant box that produced that result. If a new variant box was created later in time after that output, it will not appear in the past. While viewing an earlier commit, Ellen cannot edit the code, but she can re-run it, copy it, or create a new branch from that point in time. Variolite keeps past commits as *immutable* to preserve the output history. If Ellen creates a branch from a past commit, however, she can continue editing from that point.

If Ellen wishes to backtrack a single variant box to an earlier state, she can also navigate its commit data by clicking the clock icon (Figure 6). This activates a timeline slider, where (similar to video editing software) a user can scroll the slider back to view the code at different commits. The user can use this form of time travel both at the file level and with individual variant boxes.

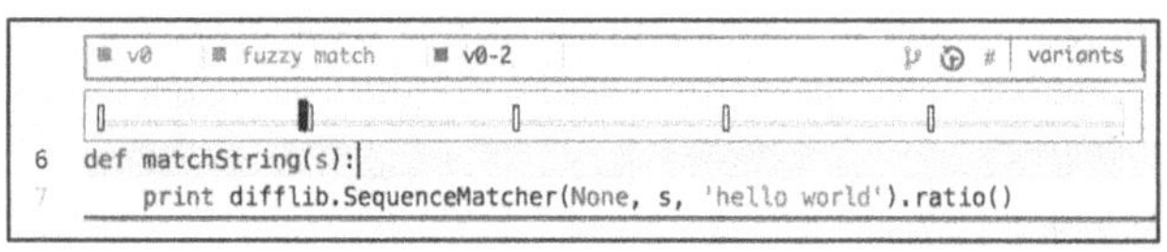

Figure 6. Navigating to a past commit. The orange color of the variant box indicates that the code is showing a past state.

Automatic commits also serve as a safeguard for backtracking. In the earlier example, suppose Ellen decides to keep only the one string-matching algorithm as the best solution. She presses the button "Dissolve Variant" from the box header, which dissolves the variant box around matchString() and returns her code to flat text. However, the variant and the other versions of matchString() are not really gone, since they can be retrieved using undo in the short term. Ellen can also use the commit history of the code to retrieve old versions of matchString() even months later, since that variant box will still exist in earlier commits of the file. This reflects the finding that people do not always know in advance what they will find useful [32].

Modeling alternatives and history

In the same sense as with a normal VCS, creating a new tab in a variant box creates a new *branch* of the code in that box. In a VCS, a *commit* is a copy of source code taken at a certain point in time, and a series of commits are a way to track the history of the software's development. A *branch* allows for multiple concurrent copies of the software's code. In Variolite, each variant box has its own revision tree of commits and branches, like a typical VCS. However, rather than a single revision tree existing for the entire code file, Variolite models the file as one revision tree that points to child revision trees for each variant box in the code. Variolite keeps a revision history for the file, and then links this revision tree to child trees of any variant boxes that are created in the code. Shown as a white header bar at the top of the file (Figure 7a), this top-level variant box wraps the entire file and also acts as a general menu for Variolite, where the user can run the code.

We provide this approach to branches and commits in order to minimize the upfront investment users must take to think about their code's history. In a simple use case, similar to Juxtapose [6], the user does not have to think about versioning more than switching between tabs. However in Variolite we consider that data scientists may work on code over the span of weeks or months. Thus to support long term versioning needs, the full capabilities of a detailed revision tree are available to users if they need it. This is in line with the "low-floor, high-ceiling" principle proposed for creativity support tools [19]. Currently in the prototype of Variolite, all revision data is kept in JSON files separately from the code. This is brittle to external edits, a common round-trip engineering problem. In future work, Variolite can compare between the last recorded version of the file and the one opened by the user, and interact with the user to resolve ambiguities over where to place variant boxes if the annotations are broken. In future work, we will investigate storing the revisions in a way that is consistent with Git.

MANAGING MANY VERSIONS

A chief design concern in creating an automated alternative for informal versioning practices is simply "moving the problem" instead of addressing the difficulties data scientists have with informal versioning. However, unlike informal practices, as programmers scale up the number and complexity of versions they choose to keep, we can use design interventions in a tool to help with these issues.

Figure 7. Variolite with labels for different features. (a) the top level variant box that wraps the entire file and also acts as the tool menu. (b and c) two different variant boxes, one nested within the other. (d) a search bar for finding outputs and versions. (e) the output pane and (f) where the user has given an output and its commit a custom tag.

Code readability

Variolite can improve code readability by reducing the number of loose copies and commented-out sections of code. Yet a design trade-off of situating versioning in the editor is that the GUI components of Variolite must not obstruct code readability. This problem may be amplified when the user has multiple variants throughout their file. We address this problem by styling variants as much as possible like in-line comments. As shown in Figure 7 b and c, variant boxes display a header bar with different controls when the user's cursor is placed within the box. When the cursor is outside, the box is displayed as a line in the same style as a code comment.

Second, the tab layout at the header of a variant box is not manageable to switch among more than 3 to 4 different branches because of the limited space. Still, 3 or 4 branches may be reasonable much of the time, as three is the average number of *file*-copied versions that survey participants reported making. Limiting the space is another design tradeoff for readability. A list of 10 to 20 branches in a variant box may look overwhelming. As a compromise, in Variolite the user can access a larger revision tree showing all the branches of that box (Figure 8), such that they can control which 3 or 4 branches are actively showing.

Distinguishing versions

Although in Variolite, users can name different versions, our study of data scientists suggests that this is not always done, and even if so, they might use similar names which can be hard to distinguish. Furthermore, Variolite cannot force users to pick names that are logical or easy to distinguish. Thus, to address the problem of distinguishing versions, we use metadata to provide users with a variety of different context clues. This decision is informed by prior work by Srinivasa et al. [28] who used an information foraging theory approach to study how programmers distinguish between similar versions. Distinguishing versions can be a difficult task, and participants in that study leveraged a variety of code cues such as file name, output, data, and code features.

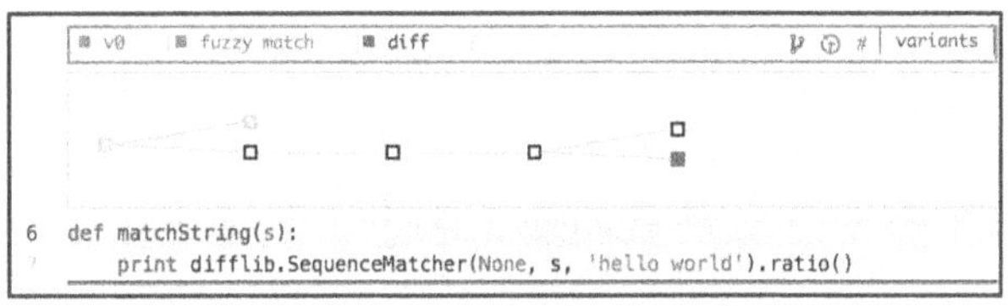

Figure 8. Navigating branches

Some metadata is similar to what is provided by a VCS. For example, a user can name each branch. Each commit and each branch shows a date when it was last edited. Each variant box can show a revision graph, so the user can see the order and relationships among branches. Variolite also gives additional cues:

- The ability to tag any branch or commit with a custom tag, for example "Paper version", "Nice graph!", or something task-specific like "Crows distance" (Figure 7f).
- A snapshot of the latest output for each branch and each commit. Currently, the captured input/output is only

from the console, but capturing pictures, like displayed charts and graphs, are planned as future work.

- The ability to search in past outputs, branches, and commits and not just in the current file (Figure 7d).

Although cues may help, the complexity of interacting with local versions may be a general limitation of a local versioning tool. Variolite may be convenient with smaller scripts that data scientists often use. However we cannot yet claim that it scales to large projects. However, we argue that informal versioning techniques like copying/commenting also do not scale well to large projects. Local versioning is close to Software Product Lines used in industry to mark multiple configurations of code within a code file. These are known for their complexity [20]. The focus of Variolite is using interaction techniques and exploring designs to mitigate this complexity, but having files with variability is a known usability challenge, which we will continue to research.

PRELIMINARY USABILITY STUDY

Our goal at this stage of the design was to create a reasonable alternative for informal versioning interactions, such that in tool form, issues around informal versioning become more tractable to design interventions. Thus, we conducted a pilot usability study. To test the underlying variant box interaction, we limited the Variolite prototype to only variant boxes with tabs (Figure 7b). The additional features reported above were added afterwards using feedback from the usability pilot.

We recruited 10 participants, a mixture of undergraduate and graduate students (7 male, 3 female). Participants had on average 5 years of programming experience and 1.5 years of experience with data analysis. The pilot study was conducted in our lab, using a designated MacBook computer. After signing a consent form, each participant was given a brief tutorial on Variolite, showing how to wrap code in a variant box and create a new version. Next, participants were given an Excel file dataset and a set of "exploratory questions" to answer about the data using the tool and a Python script. We gave participants fixed questions, instead of allowing them freely explore the data, because this allowed us to focus their work on questions that built off of previous questions and required some versioning. After the coding task, each participant filled out an online questionnaire to give feedback on the tool, and was compensated $20 for their time.

9 of 10 participants were able to successfully wrap code in variant boxes, create new versions, and switch between versions during the coding task. The one participant who struggled with the tool became confused when instead of manually selecting all the code in a function, she only selected the function *name* before using the command "wrap in variant". She expected the tool to then wrap the entire function in a variant, but instead it only wrapped that single line. By adding language-specific static analysis checks to Variolite, a future iteration of the tool may include scoping rules such that if the user wraps the line `def foo():` in Python, this would appropriately wrap the whole function.

As recommendations for new features, the participants requested better ways to distinguish different versions. Several mentioned the ability to name their versions was a very useful feature, but more automatic techniques were requested. This motivated some of the features we added to Variolite described above, including ways to navigate and search the branches and commits, and cues such as tags. One participant was concerned with becoming overwhelmed with too many versions of a part of the code, which motivated the branch view (Figure 8).

Overall, 9/10 participants reported on the questionnaire that they liked the tool and found it easy to use. All 10 wrote that they would consider using it in real life, and one participant even emailed us after the study asking when the tool would be released to use.

FUTURE WORK

While we have determined the basic usability of key features of Variolite, a next step is to evaluate the usefulness of all of these interventions together. To do this, we are preparing the tool for longer-term usage by data scientists. A study over days or weeks will allow us to explore how data scientists use versioning, as well as how Variolite's interactions scale and work over time.

CONCLUSIONS

Data scientists must manage complex ideas over time during exploratory programming work. Exploration is iterative and sometimes non-linear. Data scientists often resort to informal methods of versioning, such as commenting out code, in order to keep around old attempts to return to or compare. These informal versioning methods are widespread, and cause difficulties and confusion when the programmer cannot keep a strong mental map of their code. Variolite shows that new interactions for version control can begin to address these difficulties. Creative exploration is key to many kinds of work, as is managing a variety of ideas. By closely studying people's workarounds and how people *want* to use versioning, we can design usable interfaces for software versioning tools for a wider variety of people and a wider variety of tasks. Variolite's lightweight local versioning ideas may also be useful for other creative editing tools, such as text or image editing.

ACKNOWLEDGEMENTS

This research was funded in part by the NSF under grants IIS-1314356, IIS-1644604 and CCF-1560137. Any opinions, findings and conclusions or recommendations expressed in this material are those of the authors and do not necessarily reflect those of the US Government. In addition, we would like to thank Kenneth Holstein and all our participants.

REFERENCES

1. Atom Editor, https://atom.io/
2. Andrew J Ko, Htet Htet Aung, and Brad A Myers. 2005. *Design requirements for more flexible structured editors from a study of programmers' text editing*. In CHI'05 extended abstracts on human factors in computing systems. ACM, 1557–1560.
3. Andrew J Ko, Robin Abraham, Laura Beckwith, Alan Blackwell, Margaret Burnett, Martin Erwig, Chris Scaffidi, Joseph Lawrance, Henry Lieberman, Brad Myers, and others. 2011. *The state of the art in end-user software engineering*. ACM Computing Surveys (CSUR) 43, 3 (2011), 21.
4. Aran Lunzer and Kasper Hornbæk. 2008. *Subjunctive interfaces: Extending applications to support parallel setup, viewing and control of alternative scenarios*. ACM Transactions on Computer-Human Interaction (TOCHI) 14, 4 (2008), 17.
5. Beau Sheil. 1983. *Environments for exploratory programming*. Datamation 29, 7 (1983), 131–144.
6. Björn Hartmann, Loren Yu, Abel Allison, Yeonsoo Yang, and Scott R Klemmer. 2008. *Design as exploration: creating interface alternatives through parallel authoring and runtime tuning*. In Proceedings of the 21st annual ACM symposium on User interface software and technology. ACM, 91–100.
7. Charles Hill, Rachel Bellamy, Thomas Erickson, and Margaret Burnett. 2016. *Trials and Tribulations of Developers of Intelligent Systems: A Field Study*. In 2016 IEEE Symposium on Visual Languages and Human-Centric Computing (VL/HCC). IEEE, 162–170.
8. Fernando Pérez and Brian E Granger. 2007. *IPython: a system for interactive scientific computing*. Computing in Science & Engineering 9, 3 (2007), 21–29.
9. Helen Shen and others. 2014. *Interactive notebooks: Sharing the code*. Nature 515, 7525 (2014), 151–152.
10. Hugh Beyer and Karen Holtzblatt. 1997. *Contextual design: defining customer-centered systems* . Elsevier.
11. John M Carroll and Mary Beth Rosson. 1987. *Paradox of the active user*. The MIT Press.
12. John W Tukey. 1977. *Exploratory data analysis* (1st, ed.). Pearson, New York, NY.
13. Judith Segal. 2007. *Some problems of professional end user developers*. In IEEE Symposium on Visual Languages and Human-Centric Computing (VL/HCC 2007). IEEE, 111–118.
14. Kayur Patel, James Fogarty, James A Landay, and Beverly Harrison. 2008. *Investigating statistical machine learning as a tool for software development*. In Proceedings of the SIGCHI Conference on Human Factors in Computing Systems. ACM, 667–676.
15. Kayur Dushyant Patel. 2013. *Lowering the Barrier to Applying Machine Learning*. Ph.D. Dissertation.
16. Luke Nguyen-Hoan, Shayne Flint, and Ramesh Sankaranarayana. 2010. *A survey of scientific software development*. In Proceedings of the 2010 ACM-IEEE International Symposium on Empirical Software Engineering and Measurement. ACM, 12.
17. Michael Terry, Elizabeth D Mynatt, Kumiyo Nakakoji, and Yasuhiro Yamamoto. 2004. *Variation in element and action: supporting simultaneous development of alternative solutions*. In Proceedings of the SIGCHI conference on Human factors in computing systems. ACM, 711–718.
18. Michael Toomim, Andrew Begel, and Susan L Graham. 2004. *Managing duplicated code with linked editing*. In Visual Languages and Human Centric Computing, 2004 IEEE Symposium on. IEEE, 173–180.
19. Mitchel Resnick, Brad Myers, Kumiyo Nakakoji, Ben Shneiderman, Randy Pausch, Ted Selker, and Mike Eisenberg. 2005. *Design principles for tools to support creative thinking*. (2005).
20. Paul Clements and Linda Northrop. 2001. *Software product lines: Patterns and practice*. Boston, MA, EUA: Addison Wesley Longman Publishing Co (2001).
21. Pete Warden, *Why the term "data science" is flawed but useful: Counterpoints to four common data science criticisms., O'Reilly Radar Data Newsletter,* 3/2011 http://radar.oreilly.com/2011/05/data-science-terminology.html
22. Philip Jia Guo. 2012. *Software tools to facilitate research programming*. Ph.D. Dissertation. Stanford University.
23. Philip J Guo and Margo Seltzer. 2012. *BURRITO: Wrapping Your Lab Notebook in Computational Infrastructure*. In Proceedings of the 12th. USENIX Workshop on the Theory and Practice of Provenance (TaPP 2012) . USENIX, 7–7.
24. R Studio https://www.rstudio.com/
25. Robert DeLine and Danyel Fisher. 2015. *Supporting exploratory data analysis with live programming*. In Visual Languages and Human-Centric Computing (VL/HCC), 2015 IEEE Symposium on. IEEE, 111–119.
26. Robert Hawley. 1987. *Artificial intelligence programming environments*. Intellect Books.
27. Sandeep Kaur Kuttal, Anita Sarma, Amanda Swearngin, and Gregg Rothermel. 2011. *Versioning for Mashups–An Exploratory Study.* In International Symposium on End User Development. Springer, 25–41.

28. Sruti Srinivasa Ragavan, Sandeep Kaur Kuttal, Charles Hill, Anita Sarma, David Piorkowski, and Margaret Burnett. 2016. *Foraging Among an Overabundance of Similar Variants.* In Proceedings of the 2016 CHI Conference on Human Factors in Computing Systems. ACM, 3509–3521.
29. Thomas H Davenport and DJ Patil. 2012. *Data scientist.* Harvard business review 90 (2012), 70–76.
30. Knitr tool, http://yihui.name/knitr/
31. YoungSeok Yoon and Brad A Myers. 2012. *An exploratory study of backtracking strategies used by developers.* In Proceedings of the 5th International Workshop on Co-operative and Human Aspects of Software Engineering. IEEE Press, 138–144.
32. YoungSeok Yoon and Brad A Myers. 2014. *A longitudinal study of programmers' backtracking.* In 2014 IEEE Symposium on Visual Languages and Human-Centric Computing (VL/HCC). IEEE, 101–108.
33. YoungSeok Yoon and Brad A Myers. 2015. *Supporting selective undo in a code editor.* In Proceedings of the 37th International Conference on Software Engineering-Volume 1. IEEE Press, 223–233.
34. Zeeya Merali. 2010. *Computational science: Error, why scientific programming does not compute.* Nature 467, 7317 (2010), 775–777.
35. Ziv Bar-Joseph, Georg K Gerber, Tong Ihn Lee, Nicola J Rinaldi, Jane Y Yoo, François Robert, D Benjamin Gordon, Ernest Fraenkel, Tommi S Jaakkola, Richard A Young, and others. 2003. *Computational discovery of gene modules and regulatory networks.* Nature Biotechnology 21, 11 (2003), 1337–1342.

The Trials and Tribulations of Working with Structured Data - a Study on Information Seeking Behaviour

Laura M Koesten
The Open Data Institute, UK
Univ. of Southampton, UK
laura.koesten@theodi.org

Emilia Kacprzak
The Open Data Institute, UK
Univ. of Southampton, UK
e.kacprzak@theodi.org

Jenifer F A Tennison
The Open Data Institute, UK
jeni@theodi.org

Elena Simperl
Univ. of Southampton, UK
e.simperl@soton.ac.uk

ABSTRACT

Structured data such as databases, spreadsheets and web tables is becoming critical in every domain and professional role. Yet we still do not know much about how people interact with it. Our research focuses on the information seeking behaviour of people looking for new sources of structured data online, including the task context in which the data will be used, data search, and the identification of relevant datasets from a set of possible candidates. We present a mixed-methods study covering in-depth interviews with 20 participants with various professional backgrounds, supported by the analysis of search logs of a large data portal. Based on this study, we propose a framework for human structured-data interaction and discuss challenges people encounter when trying to find and assess data that helps their daily work. We provide design recommendations for data publishers and developers of online data platforms such as data catalogs and marketplaces. These recommendations highlight important questions for HCI research to improve how people engage and make use of this incredibly useful online resource.

ACM Classification Keywords

H.5.2 Information Interfaces and Presentation (e.g. HCI): User-centered design

Author Keywords

Human Data Interaction; Data Search; Data Portal

INTRODUCTION

Structured data, which is data that is explicitly organised, for example in relational databases, spreadsheets and web tables, is becoming critical in every domain and professional role [46]. We use it in various ways - from consulting official statistics to running scientific experiments, finding travel routes, creating maps, predicting elections and designing better products. More and more of it can be accessed or purchased online - a 2011 study by Cafarella et al. found more than one billion structured data resources on the (deep) web (as HTML tables, lists, etc.) [11], while McKinsey estimated two years later that more than one million datasets have been made openly available by governments worldwide [43, 63]. At the same time, the demand for financial, economic and marketing data provided by vendors such as Bloomberg and others continues to increase [10]. And yet, despite its abundance and applications, we still know very little about how people search for data, understand it and put it to use. The tools that support someone's 'data journey' [3] - from specifying a goal and finding the data they need to exploring new resources and assessing their relevance - often do not offer the best user experience [61].

Various scientific communities, including information retrieval (IR), databases, Linked Data, data visualisation and HCI, have looked at such data journeys from different angles. They have proposed new interaction models to engage with a particular species of data, such as graphs [57] or time series [16]; studied information needs and how they are formulated [7]; and developed tools for specific data-related activities, for example statistical analysis [33], visualisation [19], personal information management [31] and teamwork [5].

The scenario we are targeting is slightly different: imagine a data journalist writing an article about the runway expansion at London's main airport in the UK. As part of her research, the journalist will look for factual evidence to substantiate her story, in the form of reports, news on similar topics, as well as data about the economic, social and environmental ramifications of the project, arguing for or against expansion plans at each airport location. A large share of the relevant data is already available online, published by governmental agencies, researchers and other journalists. However, finding and using it is not always straightforward. The journalist could use regular search engines in the same way she does when looking for less structured kinds of information (such as regular Web sites). She might also know of a particular

CHI 2017 May 06-11, 2017, Denver, CO, USA

ACM ISBN 978-1-4503-4655-9/17/05.
DOI: http://dx.doi.org/10.1145/3025453.3025838

data provider, which offers offers access to their data via an online data catalogue. Depending on the tools used to discover the data, this step might involve downloading data files; working with different formats (e.g., CSV, HTML, RDF, relational tables); choosing among several versions of a dataset; alongside sensemaking tasks such as establishing what exactly a dataset covers (its 'attributes' or 'schema') and how accurate, complete, or up-to-date the data is.

In our research we study scenarios like this to inform the design of data tools and technologies that offer the same level of support and quality of user experience that we are used to from the web. On this 'web of data' [6], our data journalist would be able to discover hard facts for her story in the same way she googles the web today - she would tell the data search engine of her choice what she is looking for and the engine would return a ranked list of data sources, or a faceted search interface which would be designed to support her understanding of the data. For each source, the journalist would see a summary of the most important features of the dataset (attributes, descriptive statistics etc.); a sample of the data for easy exploration (perhaps similar to Google's rich snippets); individual data records matching the query; or a visualisation of the data (analogously to the image and video tabs in web search engines). We are still far away from this idea - the web of data currently resembles very much the early ages of the 'traditional' web, when people could access web pages only if they knew where they were located, or via manually crafted directories such as DMOZ [22]. Initiatives such as the Linked Open Data Cloud [6], schema.org [49] and Google's Knowledge Graph [59] show the way forward. They promote the use of interlinked data and vocabularies, which can be easily mixed and re-purposed to make structured data accessible to everyone as easily as any web page today. While this technology vision is slowly coming to life, we need to learn more about how people would engage with it, revisit theories and empirical findings from related literature, and identify data-centric activities that are still challenging to undertake. Just like previous researchers in Human Data Interaction (HDI) and other fields before us [1, 17, 23, 45, 67], our assumption is that, despite many parallels, searching for structured data - whether it is a budget spreadsheet, social network graph, weather measurement or train timetable - will most likely require different tools and interaction models than the ones available for web search.

To study the requirements of our scenario, we followed a mixed-methods approach, combining semi-structured in-depth interviews, thematic analysis and search log analysis from a large open government data portal. The interviews focused on the information seeking behaviour of people who work with data as part of their daily jobs, such as scientists, data analysts, financial traders, IT developers, managers and digital artists. We talked to 20 data practitioners across several domains. The responses showed that people with different skill sets and professional backgrounds follow common workflows when engaging with structured data. Capitalising on these commonalities, we then defined a *framework for human structured-data interaction* with five pillars: *tasks*, *search*, *evaluation*, *exploration* and *use*, extending models in related areas [40, 50]. The proposed framework can help portal providers and data publishers design a better experience for their users. One of the main findings of the interviews was that people often cannot locate the data they need. To understand their problems better, we then looked at one year of search logs of data.gov.uk [18]. We examined the characteristics of more than 100k user queries, which led to 577k dataset downloads, to offer a quantitative view on the common themes of the framework. Finally, we derived design recommendations for data publishers and developers of data catalogs and marketplaces, and identified routes for future research to improve how people engage with and make use of structured data online.

BACKGROUND

Our work is in the broader context of **Human Data Interaction (HDI)**. The term is used by Crabtree and Mortier to refer to how people engage with their personal data and tackle privacy issues [17]. Elmqvist proposed a broader definition that includes the manipulation, analysis and sensemaking of data [23]. In our work, we consider the whole interaction process and its context, covering both people looking for answers to questions, and those interested in a particular dataset or combinations of datasets. For example, someone trying to find the number of schools in a given post code area would need to extract the answer from a larger dataset containing all entries for all schools in a country in 2016. Someone studying how the number of schools across different regions has changed over time would need to process and aggregate several versions of the same data, published year after year. Finally, schools data could be mixed with house prices statistics to understand how one aspect influences the other. All three settings have elements of dataset search, sensemaking and use, which consider different data properties, and our study considers them equally. In the following we explain how our work has been informed by three related fields of inquiry: (1) *data search*; (2) *data sensemaking*; and finally (3) *information seeking*.

Data search presents many challenges, as ideas and tools from web search cannot be (yet) directly applied [53]. Web search engines are designed for documents, not for data [11]. Putting aside the question of links between datasets, which is at the core of algorithms such as Page Rank, established information retrieval technologies are primarily designed to work on (unstructured) documents and less to fulfill the specific needs that people have when looking for data [67]. Keyword-based matching works less well on structured and semi-structured data [42] and a majority of data catalogues online rely on metadata descriptors to discover datasets instead of assessing their content. This metadata often varies in quality and availability, further limiting the user's ability what she needs [2]. Initiatives such as Open Data Monitor [47] and the European Data Portal [51], which build meta-portals with integrated access to multiple data repositories require manually curated mappings between the attributes that describe datasets on each site. Finally, contextual or personalised results are practically non-existent for data search.

In addition to these technology limitations, there is very little research examining data search from a user perspective. Most existing studies have been designed with other requirements in mind and the extent to which they apply to our scenario is yet to be fully investigated. In web search, a common denominator is the differentiation between simple (known-item) and exploratory search (addressing more complex information needs) [1, 8, 21, 44, 55]. Other models distinguish between question answering [64] and document retrieval [29] to emphasise the specific challenges associated with identifying not just the document in which a specific piece of information could be found, but the actual answer to a user's query. We can find some parallels to this in relation to structured data: people searching for data will sometimes need not just to be pointed to the right database, spreadsheet, or list, but to the record that answers their question. This has implications for how data search is implemented, as algorithms that focus on metadata, the de facto standard in existing portals, cannot support this type of query. Closer to our area is the HCI literature on interaction with databases [14, 32, 56]. The focus there has been mostly on how users compose queries and the degree to which these queries can be translated into SQL or similar [14]. Our scenario is much more open in the range of data sources it targets - some of them could be relational databases, but many others will use other formats or will need to be discovered first.

Search log analysis is routinely used to understand the behaviour of users and evaluate search on the web and elsewhere [30, 37, 38, 69], using metrics such as time spent on a page and clickthrough streams, alongside specific activities such as tagging, printing and purchasing [25]. However, their findings are not straightforward to apply to new contexts such as data portals, which, our interviews showed, practitioners routinely used to search for data. Some work has been done in understanding structured queries against online databases such as the Linked Open Data Cloud [4, 48]. However, their aim was to study the popularity of certain parts of the database and query constructs, and not the interaction between users and structured data. In this paper, we take first steps in this direction. To supplement the in-depth interviews, we analyse the logs of a large open government data portal.

Making sense of structured data has mostly been studied in connection to information visualisation, which can help find patterns in data [26, 45]. The visual analytics system built by Stasko et al. [58] was tailored for sensemaking tasks of particular groups of data analysts. In their work on accessing government statistics, the system by Marchionini et al. [45] allowed users to explore data from different perspectives and understand relationships within the data via agile display mechanisms. As the web of data enters mainstream, this type of ideas need to be better integrated into productive environments and data work practice.

Both search and sensemaking are related to the broader area of *information seeking*. Previous research in this space has proposed a series of user-centred models that describe multi-stage and iterative processes of seeking information [7, 24, 40, 66, 68]. They are analysed and compared in [13, 20, 68]. Our study does not put forward a new model of information seeking. Instead, our aim is to investigate how people find, evaluate and explore structured sources of data that meet their information needs and to inform designers and improve the user experience. The information seeking scenario discussed in the introduction is real and increasingly important for various domains and professional roles, but it is not yet well understood and supported by tools and technologies. Existing models are a reasonable starting point, but to be truly useful, they would need to consider the specific search and sensemaking activities people carry out when working with structured data. For example, in Wilson's problem solving model [68], this would mean that at the 'problem resolution' stage the user decides that structured data is needed to solve the problem. We believe this decision affects how the rest of the information seeking process is carried out and the type of support the user requires. Another well-established model in this space is Kulthau's [40]. She defines six stages: task initiation, topic selection, pre-focus exploration, focus formation, information collection and search closure. In contrast to it, we are using the term 'exploration' as a means to understand whether a search result, in our case a dataset, matches an information need. This interpretation is more aligned with data science frameworks such as [50], which is centered around activities to collect relevant data, explore it to make sense of it, and build an analysis model to draw conclusions from it.

Further on, Fidel proposes an ecological approach to information seeking [24], in which the emphasis is on the environment and context in which the search takes place. Similarly, we believe that the design of effective information systems needs to be aware of the complexities of the information space the search draws upon, including types and formats of sources, how reliable they are, how often they change, and whether one or more datasets need to be brought together to complete the user task. Current IR technology focuses on one of these dimensions, - the type of data - and are best suited for unstructured data, such as text or images [1, 17, 23, 45, 67]. Data-centric activities are likely to be dependent on the task people intend to use the data for [34]. Li et al. propose a faceted classification of information seeking tasks, in which one of the facets is the 'product of the task', which can be 'factual information' such as data, facts or similar [41]. We believe that a classification for just data-centric tasks could be useful as a preliminary step to improve the user experience in scenarios such as those discussed in the introduction.

METHODOLOGY

We used a mixed-methods approach, informed by [9], with a focus on qualitative methods in order to improve our understanding of how people work with data. To *expand* our findings [9] around the specific question of dataset search, we also analysed the search logs of a large open data portal quantitatively. We believe that using the logs alongside the qualitative data was meaningful for several reasons: (1) the search logs were relevant to the study, as 17 out of 20 participants cited the data.gov.uk portal as a tool they have used to search for datasets; (2) the analysis of the search logs gave us a less obtrusive way to learn about the behaviour of data search users [36], of which our interviewees are a subset of; and (3) we used the quantitative insights only as a way to add more breadth to our enquiry, without making any claims about any direct links between the two samples.

In-depth interviews

User-system interactions are influenced by factors that are not easily observable or measurable [39]. For this reasons, and given the investigative nature of our research, we focused the study on its qualitative element. We believe the rich data about interaction processes and workflows we were looking for was best provided by in-depth interviews.

Recruitment Our sampling strategy was purposive to include a spread of sectors and a wide range of skill sets and roles. Participants were recruited via targeted emails and social media and asked to fill out an online scoping survey. Emails were sent to preselected relevant participants, namely members of the UK's governmental Open Data User Group (around 15 people). For social media recruitment we used the ODIHQ account (at the time of the study over 31k followers, 5.3k impressions, 90 interactions, 20 retweets). For the interviews we chose only people who use data in their day-to-day work. We tried to cover various domains and professional backgrounds to gain a broad overview and avoid any unintended biases. The scoping survey helped us select the participants in a more targeted way (see additional material). It covered questions about the tools participants used, the type of tasks they performed with data, how often they interacted with new sources of data and whether they searched for data. The respondents identified as relevant at this stage were contacted via email to arrange an interview.

Participants The sample consisted of $n = 20$ data workers (17 male and 3 female), based in the UK ($n = 16$), Germany ($n = 1$), USA ($n = 1$), France ($n = 1$) and globally ($n = 1$). Their roles, as reported by the participants, are shown in Table 1. They used both public (open) and proprietary data in different areas: environmental research, criminal intelligence, retail, social media, transport, education, geospatial information and smart cities. Most interviewees stated that their tasks with data vary greatly and that the number of datasets they interact with - reportedly between two and 50 each week - fluctuates with the nature of their projects. The majority ($n = 17$) reported acquiring the skills to work with data on the job, from colleagues or self taught, by *doing it or experimenting with data (P5)*, though some people also mentioned formal education (in particular on core pre-requisites such as the fundamentals of statistics) and professional training.

Data collection and analysis We used semi-structured, in-depth interviews of circa 45 minutes, which were audio-recorded and subsequently transcribed. They were carried out via Skype or face-to-face for a period of six weeks in summer 2016. The interviews were organised around the participants' data-centric tasks; the search for new data; and the evaluation and exploration of potentially relevant data sources. They were analysed using thematic analysis [54] using Nvivo, a qualitative data analysis package for coding. The coding was done by one researcher, but to enhance reliability two senior researchers checked the analysis for a sample of the data. We applied two layers of coding to be able to look into the data at different levels of generality and from different viewpoints. As a primary layer, we used deductive categories mapping to stages of the data interaction process: what people use data for; what information they need about the data to decide what to select and whether the search results were useful; how and where to search; and how to go about exploring and understanding datasets. For each of these themes we applied a second layer of coding, in which we used an inductive approach [12] to draw out further details. The resulting themes were then used to further categorise tasks and user needs, as we will see in the findings.

P	*G*	*Role*	*Sector*
1	F	Crime and disorder data analyst	Public administration
2	M	Trainer for data journalists	Media&Entertainment
3	M	Data editor & journalist	Media&Entertainment
4	M	PhD researcher, social media analyst	Education
5	M	Senior research scientist	Technology&Telecoms
6	M	Data scientist	Technology&Telecoms
7	M	Lead technologist in data	Technology&Telecoms
8	M	Data consultant and publisher	Technology&Telecoms
9	M	Senior GIS analyst and course director	Geospatial/Mapping
10	M	Research and innovation manager	Public Administration
11	M	Researcher	Transport & Logistics
12	M	Semantic Web PhD researcher	Science&Research
13	F	Project manager	Environment&Weather
14	M	Quantitative trader	Finance&Insurance
15	M	Data manager	Public administration
16	M	Head of data partnerships	Business Services
17	M	Lecturer in quantitative human geography & Computation geographer	Science&Research
18	F	Data artist	Arts,Culture&Heritage
19	M	Associate professor	Health care
20	M	Business intelligence manager	Public Administration

Table 1. Description of participants (P) with gender (G), their profession (Role) and sector they are working in (Sector)

Search logs

The interviews showed that finding data is a major issue for data practitioners. To understand these challenges better, we analysed the search logs of a governmental open data portal in the UK, data.gov.uk [18]. The portal has its own internal search capability and, as of September 2016, contains 39,983 dataset packages, which are collections of datasets (in different formats such as PDF, CSV, RDF etc.), grouped by topics. The portals SERP (search engine results page) shows a ranked list of dataset packages, which resembles the commonly used ten blue-links paradigm. When clicking on a result, the user is taken to a web page that displays dataset metadata, including a textual description and an option for downloading it.

We had access to the search logs generated via Google Analytics (GA) between 01 May 2015 and 30 April 2016 with a total of 100,970 queries, of which 52,824 were unique queries (these were identified by the fingerprint method provided by Open Refine [52], as GA clusters only identical queries). Over 80% of all portal users were identified by GA as being from the UK, with just over 26% of them users being located in London (GA collects this sort of information). These users were responsible for 577,310 dataset downloads in the given time frame. 9.26% of users searched on the site from a mobile device (including tablets) and the rest from a desktop environment (90.74%). In similar web search statistics, more than half of all searches are made from a mobile environment [60]. Google Chrome was the dominant desktop browser used to access the portal (50%) of users, 27% used Internet Explorer,

11% Firefox and Safari with 10%. Again, these results differ from web search, where Chrome is used in more than 70% [65]. Governmental portals like data.gov.uk may be more popular in certain professions, for example with civil servants, who often have restrictions on the usage of new technology; this could be the reason for the high percentage of Internet Explorer users. However, the other differences we observed hint at areas that data tools and technologies providers might want to explore further.

In our analysis we considered the following data, which is readily available in the search log sample: (1) *Landing pages* - pages through which visitors entered the site; (2) *Sessions* - the period of time a user is actively engaged with the page; (3) *Exits* - how often users leave a page after viewing it; (4) *Search refinements* - the total number of times a query is refined within a session; (5) *Time after search* - the amount of time visitors spent on a site after getting the results of their query; and (6) *Search depth* - the number of pages visitors viewed.

Ethics

The interview study was approved by our institution's Ethical Advisory Committees. Informed written consent was given by the participants. Access to Google Analytics to obtain data used for the search log analysis was kindly given to us by data.gov.uk for research purposes. No personal information was used for the search logs analysis.

FINDINGS

In this section we present the findings of our study, which are structured around the themes used in the interviews: tasks, search, evaluation and exploration.

Data-centric tasks

Taxonomy When asked about their activities with data, participants reported a wide range of tasks, spanning from statistical analysis to using data as a material to create something - be that a service, a tool, or an artwork. We categorised these activities into two broad categories: (1) *Process-oriented tasks* - people think of these tasks as doing something transformative with data; and (2) *Goal-oriented tasks* - people think of data as a means to an end. Most participants reported to have engaged in both process- and goal-oriented tasks at some point. Process-oriented tasks include: building tools with data; integrating data in a database; defining predictive statistical models; producing data; publishing data; visualising it, etc. Goal-oriented ones include: seeking the answer to a question; comparing datasets or data items; finding patterns; allocating or managing resources in a data-informed way, etc. While the boundaries between the two categories are somewhat fluid, the primary difference between them lies in what we call the 'user information needs' - that is, the details people need to know about the data in order to interact with it effectively (see also section on information needs). For process-oriented tasks, aspects such as timeliness, licences, updates, quality, methods of data collection and provenance were reported to have a high priority. For goal-oriented tasks, intrinsic qualities of data such as coverage and granularity played a bigger role.

Another way to categorise tasks is based on the specific activities that involve data. Based on feedback from the participants, we identified five activities: (1) *linking*; (2) *time series analysis*; (3) *summarising*; (4) *presenting*; and (5) *exporting*. These categories are not exclusive or exhaustive and the participants reported undertaking one or several of them, both in a process- and goal-oriented task context. As we will see later in the discussion, we believe they lead to different interaction requirements on a system such as a data catalogue or search engine. *Linking* ($n = 14$) is about finding commonalities and differences between two or more datasets. From an interaction point of view, this requires capabilities to view datasets next to each other and be able to spot meaningful relationships. The other classes of activities usually concern only one dataset or datasets that have already been linked. In a *Time series analysis* ($n = 10$), data is ordered by time; the aim is to identify trends, or detect and predict events. [16] looks at ways to carry out such tasks effectively. *Summarising* ($n = 11$) involves creating a more compact, meaningful representation of the data. This could be used to inspect a dataset or as a means to tell a story with data. As elaborated in the next section, data summaries raise questions related to the types of information that is useful in this context, the best approaches to obtain or generate it and the related user experience. *Presenting* ($n = 9$) includes activities that transform data into human-friendly formats, such as visualising them or producing textual descriptions of the data. Finally, *exporting* ($n = 11$) refers to all aspects around producing and publishing a dataset in a given format, including metadata.

Complex tasks A common scenario reported by all interviewees was trying to answer high-level questions with data to explain change, establish causalities or understand behaviour. This is characteristic for the class of goal-oriented tasks introduced earlier. Gaining a better understanding of the problem area and adding different sources together gets people closer to answering their question. This often means breaking it down into more manageable sub-questions, which only become clear after using a particular dataset. The range of activities can be very broad, including all five types discussed in our taxonomy. Examples are understanding why crime in a specific area has risen over the last 10 years or comparing user experience on the internet for people of differing socioeconomic status by considering multiple factors. Participants talked about their journey when searching for data in such cases, which often leads them from one dataset to the next. This is in line with the web of data idea discussed the introduction, which exploits links between datasets to allow people to find and browse structured data in the same way they engage with the web today. For example: one participant discussed a project that aimed to create a map showing the locations of defibrillators in a geographic area, to identify where new defibrillators might be needed. He considered demographic data, as certain age groups are more prone to heart attacks. Furthermore, he tried to consider not only where that population lived, but also where they spend their time during the day. A meaningful interaction with a data catalogue such as data.gov.uk would allow data publishers and users to create links between such related datasets to facilitate browsing and exploration.

The impact of data quality on task outcomes Another aspect that emerged from the interviews was the use of data to increase accountability in decision-making. However, concerns were raised on the role of data quality in the process. It was clear from the interviews that people are often aware that they are not working with the ideal data for a particular task.

> (P15) So although the data is a good quality, it's not really designed for my purpose so actually, for my purposes, there's quite a lot of uncertainty and quite a lot of risk in that, it's still the best data we have but it's that knowledge of how it was and why it was created, against how I want to use it

While this is a well-known challenge, the majority of the participants agreed that, as long as people are aware of the limitations of their data and these limitations are clearly communicated (e.g., through documentation), it can be factored into the decisions being made based on that data. The following comment is indicative of the views of the participants on the matter:

> (P15) In the relationship between the data that's available and the decision that's made, we're saying this is the data we've used to make this decision; we're aware that it's not the best data but it's still the best we have. So there is uncertainty there but are you happy with that level of uncertainty?

For data providers and the publishing platforms they use, this emphasises the importance of data governance and documentation, but also different approaches to data quality (from assessing a given quality dimension automatically, to reviews and other annotations).

Search for structured data

In this section we discuss how people search for datasets. Many participants ($n = 17$) had to regularly search for data in their work. All of these reported experiencing difficulties finding data in the past. Others ($n = 3$) were provided with either external or internally produced datasets or were mostly involved in collecting or publishing data rather than using someone else's. However, all participants had previously tried to search for data online when they did not know whether it existed or not. They reported using: web search engines (e.g., Google); bespoke websites (e.g,. portals, catalogs); recommendations from other people; and Freedom Of Information requests (FOI). More than half ($n = 12$) of the interviewed practitioners said that they regularly struggle when trying to find the data they are looking for.

Searching on the web

A majority of participants ($n = 18$) reported often using Google to find data online, especially when they do not know which institution holds the specific dataset they are interested in. Some reported always using Google as their first search strategy ($n = 7$). When searching for datasets, people most commonly employ a keyword search that is slightly adapted towards data search. Most participants ($n = 17$) mentioned terms such as 'data', 'statistics', 'dataset', alongside keywords describing other aspects of the data, in particular its domain. Some of the respondents ($n = 7$) reported prefering using fewer keywords to make sure that the search engine returns a broad range of (perhaps less accurate) results, which they then filter manually. We discuss below what happens after a query is issued to Google or similar search engines and the user chooses to click on the link of a data portal such as data.gov.uk.

Searching on portals

This section includes insights gained from interviews and analysis of search logs. While 17 of the twenty people interviewed use that particular portal, the two samples do not directly compare. However, there is a clear overlap between our qualitative findings and the user behaviour represented in the log data. The numbers presented here are based on the search log analysis, as explained in our methodology.

Queries Only 2,462 queries out of a total of 100,970 contained the terms such as 'data' or 'dataset', which were mentioned by interviewees. This could point to the importance of specialised data search tools, which allow practitioners to use the same search strategies they are used to from the web. Furthermore, the search box on the portal was labeled *Search for data*. However, the format of the queries had other notable features, which hint at the qualities of data that count for open data portal users. 555 (0.55%) queries mentioned a format - we looked for all structured data formats supported by data.gov.uk: HTML, CSV, WMS, WCS, XLS, JSON, WFS, Esri REST. 5384 queries used a category offered on the portal (5.33%), which were environment, town, cities, city, mapping, government, society, health, governmental spendings, education, business, economy, transport, while a slightly larger share of 8,389 (8.31%) queries contained a location. The latter was determined through keyword matching with lists of towns, counties, regions and countries, which we extracted manually from a subset of those queries issued at least 15 times. Such strategies were mentioned by some of the participants ($n = 8$) in our interview sample:

> (P7) It was somewhat hierarchical [..], like "transport" would be the sector and then I'd put in a specific thing that I'm looking for which could be in he summary or metadata, so "driving licences" and then in this case I included a particular feature that I wanted in the dataset as well, so it was "gender"

The average query length in the logs was 2.44 words. This number refers to 99.9% of all queries - we excluded some outliers because of their length (more than 15 words) and popularity (query frequency less than 10). This length of query matches more or less the situation on the web in 1998 - as search technologies improved, people started writing more detailed queries [62]. The participants in the interview noted using a similar approach for queries via Google. Furthermore, we found 22.09% of queries issued on the portal were subsequently refined, while 80% of sessions with search had only a single query. The majority of users do not refine their queries - either they found what they were looking for, or they are not confident the system can give them the desired result.

Sessions More than half of the search sessions (52.08%) were done by people who landed on the site through Google. Just under a quarter (24.26%) visited the site directly. This backs up some of the comments we received about people preferring to start their search on Google. We believe this may be due to people not knowing that the portal exists before they search; people having the link to a particular dataset preview page already; or a perceived poor search capability of the portal. As noted earlier, the majority of interviewees ($n = 17$) mentioned having experienced difficulties when searching for data on the web either because the data was indeed unavailable or not easy to find with the existing tool support:

> (P17) I often find on most of the websites that provide data [..] often the search function is pretty rubbish, so that's why I often find myself falling back to Google [..] The difference [from searching for web pages] is that it just takes a hell of a lot longer in my experience

In addition, participants ($n = 16$) described finding data as a complex, iterative, process:

> (P17) I would get some things that looked really promising but weren't and then finally, through some kind of mysterious combination of search terms, I suddenly came across the dataset I'd been looking for the entire time

More than half of the search sessions were done by new users. The data contained 58.88% (122,822) new users and 41.12% (85,774) returning ones. Returning users showed a longer session duration (around 10 minutes versus six for newcomers) - we assume those who came back were more familiar with the site content and engaged more with the portal. The time spent on site after search was on average 3.03 minutes and the number of pages viewed after getting results for their query were around 2.39. Just under 23% of users issued a query and left the site immediately after retrieving their search results. From the interviews, we have learned of the complexities of the subsequent steps in evaluating, exploring and eventually deciding to use the data. We assume that the users exiting the site just after landing on the search results page were likely to do so because they could not find what they were looking for.

> (P5) I think I would fall back to like a Google search which is more broad and has a lot better coverage, that someone else would have, I would find a page where someone would have discussed it, mentioned the corresponding dataset

> (P10) I have to do an awful lot of either filtering or sorting through pages to find what I'm looking for

Human recommendation and FOI requests

The other two approaches reported by participants included asking colleagues or directly asking for data from institutions which are likely to hold it, in particular via Freedom of Information (FOI) requests ($n = 3$): requests to a public sector organisation to disclose a particular type of data, by virtue of the The Freedom of Information Act [27].

Obtaining recommendations from colleagues or people working in the respective field who are likely to know about a dataset was very common ($n = 14$). The majority ($n = 15$) reported that they ask other people for data, either in their immediate environment or in public institutions:

> (P13) I'm phoning people and asking them if they could give us their data

> (P15) So generally I tend to go through contacts rather than searches

Another factor that sometimes affects the user experience ($n = 3$), especially in professions which work with official statistics, is the inability to know whether the data they are searching for actually exists or is simply difficult to find. FOI requests were deemed useful to handle such uncertainties.

> (P3) [..] a lot of our articles are FOI based, that's where we get the data from [..] If we actively put out an FOI knowing what we want, we know the data's going to be good because we know what to ask for, we know how to get the information we want

Evaluation and exploration

Once some data of interest is found, participants ($n = 9$) reported spending a considerable amount of effort deciding whether to use it. They reported on a process consisting of two broad stages, each using different methods and data features: (1) a *first look* at the data to get an initial impression ($n = 19$ of participants); and (2) a subsequent more thorough *exploration*. In each of the two stages people seem to use slightly different types of information about the data in question.

Data properties Participants ($n = 16$) reported using different aspects of a dataset in order to decide whether it is useful for them. We grouped them into three categories, as listed in Table 2: (1) *relevance* to the task; (2) *usability*; and (3) *quality*. A number of participants ($n = 9$) raised issues around finding a relevant and usable dataset, e.g., the data might be relevant, but aggregated to an extent that it hides levels of specificity that they were hoping to obtain from it. For example, averaging deprivation of an area might not show pockets of deprivation within that area. Another common theme ($n = 15$) was the struggle with inconsistencies of labelling and a lack of documentation, often even within the same institutions. An example was using multiple datasets because the organisational structure of the local authorities in a country, mean they end up publishing the same data for their respective regions differently. An interviewee noted:

> (P6) Documentation is most frustrating, there's often data without documentation and fishing for this information is the hardest bit

Information about collection methods that would lead to a better understanding of the data was repeatedly mentioned ($n = 11$). Knowing more about the choices that were made in the collection and initial processing was said to enable data practitioners to make a judgment of the impact these core data science activities had on their own analysis of the data and thus help mitigate the risk and uncertainty associated with reusing someone else's data:

> (P10) I spend an awful lot of my time trying to match data with other people's data and in doing that, you may be spend more of the time researching the data than actually using the data

Assess	*Information needed about*
Relevance	context, coverage, original purpose, granularity, summary, time frame
Usability	labeling, documentation, license, access, machine readability, language used, format, schema, ability to share
Quality	collection methods, provenance, consistency of formatting / labeling, completeness, what has been excluded

Table 2. Information needs when selecting datasets

The first look We compiled a list of actions participants reported in Table 3. People make judgments about whether the data is what they expected. They want to evaluate quality, establish trustworthiness and 'understand' the data. Many described *trying to get to know the data* ($n = 16$), by doing a basic visual screening and a resulting sense of relationship with the data they are using:

(P1) [..] look at the column headers and maybe literally read the first two rows of data just to get an idea of what's actually in it

(P10) [..] looking at the nuts and bolts of the very basic concepts of what that data is

First steps of data exploration:
scrolling through / basic visual scan
looking at headers
looking for obvious errors
looking at summarising statistics
filtering relevant data (pivot tables)
visualising to see trends / peaks
looking at schema / format
understanding semantics of the data
looking at documentation / metadata
checking the publication date and provenance
understand the purpose of original dataset

Table 3. What people do to get a first look at a new dataset

At this initial stage, people also reported looking for obvious errors such as missing data, inconsistency, out-of-range values or duplicated unique identifiers:

(P8) I'm looking at [..] the coverage of the data, so does it cover the geographic area I'm interested in? Or the time period that I'm interested in? And does it do that to the level of detail I need?

(P16) Once I've had a quick scroll across, I would then probably look at a couple of records right the way across to see if I can make sense of it

The majority of participants ($n = 18$) had experience of working with datasets they have little information about and were aware of its challenges:

(P17) There are a lot of people who radically underestimate the amount of work that needs to go into understanding the data in the first place, before you can even start doing research

Exploration It emerged that people build a notion of quality and trust of the data during exploration, while being aware of the limitations of the methods they use to assess both:

(P14) Scrolling through the bottom right corner of Excel and going "yeah, that's a lot of data", you haven't done anything. It doesn't actually tell you anything but I would definitely do that.

(P6) It's very difficult first when you download new data, to have a quick idea of what the data represents, a quick summary of the data.

Quality was reported to be associated with *clean* data ($n = 6$). However, several interviewees also mentioned that cleaning data can lead to deleting information that would be relevant for a different task. This is illustrated by one participant discussing a dataset showing the occupancy of local car parks. Due to malfunctioning sensors the car park can appear to be over-full. This can be easily checked (and corrected) by making sure the capacity of the car park is never more than 100%. However, if somebody wanted to use the data to understand the reliability of the sensors, these corrections would remove all relevant data. As discussed earlier, a preferred solution for such challenges is to have access to information about how data was collected and its initial purpose.

(P17) Helping people to understand what's in the data is incredibly useful and also what has been excluded from the data because obviously, a lot of the time, data gets cleaned before it gets put online for other people to work with so what were the cleaning choices? What constitutes a valid record? How did you filter out bad records?

Another critical dimension discussed by the participants was exploration tool support. After finding what looks like a promising dataset, people ($n = 12$) said they often have to download it to establish whether it is actually the data that they were looking for, due to poor description of the dataset:

(*P*17) Even when I've found what looks like the right dataset, I still have to download it and look at it because [..] they often give you a preview of the first few rows and that's like a nice starting point, although it doesn't deal very well with if you've got 24 tabs.

In the financial sector, for instance, data is stored in binary form, but can be easily queried and displayed in human-readable formats. Similar tools that allow users to more easily filter relevant parts of a dataset would make working with data more efficient:

(*P*14) Honestly, if I need data, if I need a data dump in my current job, Bloomberg has a plug-in for Excel and I can get almost everything I want from there

(*P*5) I think it's important to have tools that you let you explore the data in a very automatic way because that's a repetitive task, it will come up again and again

DISCUSSION

In this section we elaborate on the implications of our study. We propose a framework that describes the interaction with structured data alongside design recommendations for data publishers and designers of data platforms such as catalogues and marketplaces.

Framework for Human Structured-Data Interaction

Based on the models described in the background and on insights gained during our study, we understand the process of working with structured data as a five-pillars model: *(1) tasks*; *(2) search*; *(3) evaluation*; *(4) exploration*; and *(5) use*. The process is iterative by design and can involve returning to previous activities at any point - for example, the results of the exploratory data analysis (pillar 4) may lead the 'data workers' [15] to consider evaluating other sources of data (pillar 3), or start a new search attempt (pillar 2). We characterised each pillar based on the descriptions of the participants by defining common categories for data-centric tasks (pillar 1) and identifying which data properties (both intrinsic, such as data attributes, granularity and errors; and extrinsic such as metadata, e.g., release date and licenses) people consider relevant for the subsequent three pillars (search, evaluation and exploration).

Similar to Yi et al. [70], who introduced a taxonomy of tasks in information visualisation, we believe it is critical for system designers in data search to identify user task types in detail, and tailor functionalities accordingly. For this reason we proposed earlier a taxonomy of data-centric tasks with two dimensions - one categorises tasks as either *process* or *goal-oriented*, the other differentiates between five core types of activities: *linking*; *time series analysis*; *summarising*; *presenting*; and *exporting*. This taxonomy, and the broader framework

TASK	SEARCH	EVALUATE	EXPLORE	USE
goal or process oriented linking time series analysis summarising presenting exporting	STRATEGIES: • web search engines • data portals • asking people • FOI request	• relevance[1] • usability[2] • quality[3]	• basic visual scan • obvious errors • summarizing statistics • headers • documentation • metadata	
1: context, coverage, summary, original purpose, granularity, time frame	2: labeling, documentation, licence, access, machine readability, language used, format, ability to share, format		3: collection methods, provenance, consistency of formatting/labeling, completeness, what's been excluded	

Figure 1. Framework for interacting with structured data

it is part of, are aimed to help system designers and publishers of data understand what people do when searching for and engaging with datasets and inform the decisions they make.

For an overview of the workflow through a search for data the framework in Figure 1 can be read from left to right, taking into account that this can be an iterative process. This can be of interest for researchers e.g. in the area of information seeking, interested in the specificities of data search. It can be used as a guidance to structure training for people learning how to find and use data to define how they should be lead through the process. Further individual pillars can be prioritised, and the framework can be used to identify the area of interest within the workflow. For data portals the focus is likely to be pillar 2 and 3 as they might concentrate on the data discovery aspect. Ranking will take into account those metadata attributes that people perceive as relevant for their decisions to use or ignore a dataset. For data publishers pillar 3 can be of particular importance - for example to refine their metadata vocabulary to cover those bits of information that people need in their assessment. If someone is designing data exploration tools pillar 1 and 4 can be of influence for their conceptualisation of user needs. A data catalogue designer will prioritise features such as data summaries and interlinking of datasets higher, as these activities are both common and important for data practitioners (pillar 4), and will consider implementing social sharing and recommendation features (pillar 2).

From interviews and the search logs analysis we learned that people experience difficulties finding datasets and that the information they need to evaluate their fitness of use is not always available or easy to interpret out of context. Looking for data on the web emerged to be more often than not an exploratory search task, involving iterations and complex cognitive processing. In her work on the information seeking process, Kulthau concludes that uncertainty in the exploration stage indicates a space for system designers and intermediaries to intervene [40].

In the following section, we will propose design recommendations for data discovery and exploration tools, as well as for data publishers and providers. We do not claim these to be exhaustive, or equally applicable to all types of data across our taxonomy of tasks and appreciate that in some instances they confirm insights from existing literature. However, our study strongly suggests that this space is by no means standardised and the user experience when interacting with the web of data leaves room for major improvements.

Design recommendations

Data portals We established that in search users need to be supported in evaluating datasets according to their relevance, usability and quality. This could be achieved by providing *visual or textual indicators* of these aspects on the interface, backed up by automatically computed metrics or user-generated reviews and annotations. An interesting direction of future work would be to understand how all this additional information should be spread out across SERP, the dataset preview page and the dataset itself, to avoid overload.

As observed in our findings, data catalogues and similar platforms should allow *additional filtering* for the following types of information: location, provenance, format, licence, time frame and date, publishing date, location of publication and data schema. These filters would allow the user to direct the search process towards more desirable results. In addition, the search capability should be equipped to recognise *specific types of keywords*, such as dates to optimise the accuracy of their results. Providing this information together with search results would also be helpful for time series analysis tasks.

To support relevance assessments, we recommend also displaying information about the *granularity of the data*. One approach would be to display *headers, summarising statistics or previews of the data*, all of which could be provided alongside the search results. Furthermore, having more details on *how the original data was collected* emerged to be critical. While such reproducibility concerns are more common in some data-intensive fields (e.g., science, official statistics), it seems they always aid users develop a notion of trust in the data. While we appreciate that some dimensions of quality cannot be easily calculated automatically, hence creating an overhead for the data publisher in regards to documentation, there are is still room for some easy fixes such as *detecting empty fields and headers* in CSV files, as supported by tools such as Good Tables [35]. This would improve the search experience for users across all types of tasks, in particular for data interlinking and exports.

We noted in our findings that many tasks people perform with data are complex and often span over multiple datasets. Being able to *identify and explore the links* between these datasets would help the user get a better understanding of availability and context. Approaches such as *Linked Data*, alongside tools that would discover relationships between datasets (perhaps available in different formats) would be a very useful addition to the services already offered by data platforms.

When designing tools for data exploration we recommend taking the different types of data-centric tasks into account. Our findings suggest that these result in specific requirements on functionality. For instance, *linking* require tools which allow the comparison of two or more datasets. These should be able to highlight common attributes or visualise datasets side by side to facilitate understanding. Tools which support displaying data in different forms, such as creating interactive visualisations, textual descriptions of the data, or highlighting patterns would be beneficial for *presenting* and *summarising* tasks. For the latter, summarising statistics and representative samples as a preview of the data would be beneficial in allowing a *bird-eye view* (*P5*). One approach for data sensemaking was proposed by Marchionini et al. in their work on relation browsers for statistical information [45]. These are interfaces using facets, containing sets of categories which are displayed graphically, so the user can view the information from different perspectives. Users can choose how the data is represented (e.g., a visualisation, spreadsheet, samples), which means that a wider set of people can potentially use the data. Relation browsers have been shown to work on some forms of structured data, but have a limited number of possible facets. Further research is needed to determine the applicability of the concept for different data-centric tasks.

We learned that people are very interested in a history of the data. That means information about provenance, the processes of data collection, as well as subsequent choices made regarding, for instance, normalisation and cleansing. This is information that could be provided as documentation, capturing the legacy of the data, but also its reuse footprint, which could be displayed in a versioning system. We believe this could enable users who might struggle understanding an uncleaned version of the dataset to use a version which somebody else has already worked on. This would contribute towards the inclusiveness of data interaction tools.

Data publishers Organisations publishing data should aim to support users better in evaluating the data according to its relevance, usability and quality in the context of a particular task. As mentioned earlier in this section, we recommend specific types of information to be made available and stored with the data. Collecting and managing this data should become a core part of the data governance process and the related overhead could be reduced by allowing for *manual annotations and additions* from users, *auto-generating the metadata and other indicators* where possible and *cross-validation*. For example, if a dataset is updated regularly, these updates could be matched with previous versions to provide consistent and machine-readable metadata.

CONCLUSIONS, LIMITATIONS AND FUTURE WORK

This paper investigated how people engage with data in their daily work. By conducting in-depth interviews with data practitioners, we were able to obtain a better understanding of data-centric tasks, as well as about their search, evaluation and exploration strategies and the data qualities that influence these activities. Finding relevant data has emerged as particularly challenging, mostly due to the poor tool support and uncertainties around the availability of a given dataset for public use. To gain a better understanding of the requirements for better data search, we looked at search logs from within one of the largest open government data portal. Our findings and the design framework and recommendations that followed them can inform the development of methods, interfaces and interaction models for core activities such as data search, evaluation and exploration. They can encourage the usage of data by people with different skill sets, for the variety of data-centric activites. Thus our research can be seen as a step towards understanding what usability of data interaction tools means.

Every study, no matter how well it might have been conducted, has limitations. For the interviews, the majority of participants were male ($n = 17$) and working in the UK ($n = 16$). We interviewed a particular type of professional, though working in wide range of sectors and roles. As ours was meant as an initial study into engaging with structured data online, having a large number of participants per sector was less of a priority and some sectors and roles were not covered [15]. However, we were able to find common themes easily in the responses, which supports us in our belief that our sample size reached a saturation which allowed us to get a rich understanding of peoples' interactions with data [28].

Regarding our findings concerning search, we expanded on the breadth of our study by including a second source of data based on a much larger sample. While we did not make any assumption about direct links between the interview and search log samples, the quantitative analysis in itself is novel and representative for a large category of tools people use to find datasets. However, search log analysis also comes with natural limitations: a biased sample of users from a single platform, albeit an important one, with a focus on public sector data, using keyword search (and not, for instance, browsing) to find the data that is right for them. Finally, we recognise the problem with only using one researcher to code and interpret the data; the reliability and diversity of themes might have been different with more researchers. While we could not run any inter-rater reliability tests, we had two senior researchers overseeing the creation of themes in a sample of the data.

There is a large space for future studies extending the current understanding of how people interact with data. Additional research is needed to deepen our understanding of data-centric activites. This could include a direct observation of activities with data, developing an ontology of tasks and investigate the validity of the task taxonomies resulting from this study. An in-depth log analysis, in which a connection between queries and resulting downloads can be made, would support the understanding of user behaviour in dataset search. This can be a step towards modeling the information seeking behaviour of data users. Further studies are needed to develop better methods for automatic validation of structured data and creating additional metadata fields as proposed in our discussion. Advancing state-of-the-art interfaces, tailored for structured data, is not yet fully explored. Determining where in the search process the additional information we specified in our recommendations should be displayed needs to be established based on theoretical and empirical insight. We believe that these contributions can inform the design of data discovery tools, support exploratory assessment of datasets and make the exploration of structured data easier for a wider range of users.

ACKNOWLEDGEMENTS

This project is supported by the European Union's Horizon 2020 research and innovation program under the Marie Skłodowska-Curie grant agreement No 642795. We thank our participants and data.gov.uk for giving us insights and log data.

ADDITIONS

Interview schedule, scoping survey

REFERENCES

1. Michael J Albers. 2015. Human–Information Interaction with Complex Information for Decision-Making. In *Informatics*, Vol. 2. Multidisciplinary Digital Publishing Institute, 4–19.
2. Ulrich Atz. 2014. The tau of data: A new metric to assess the timeliness of data in catalogues. In *Conference for E-Democracy and Open Governement*. 257.
3. Jo Bates, Yu-Wei Lin, and Paula Goodale. 2016. Data journeys: Capturing the socio-material constitution of data objects and flows. *Big Data & Society* 3, 2 (2016).
4. Wouter Beek, Laurens Rietveld, Hamid R Bazoobandi, Jan Wielemaker, and Stefan Schlobach. 2014. LOD laundromat: a uniform way of publishing other people's dirty data. In *International Semantic Web Conference*. Springer, 213–228.
5. Anant Bhardwaj, Amol Deshpande, Aaron J Elmore, David Karger, Sam Madden, Aditya Parameswaran, Harihar Subramanyam, Eugene Wu, and Rebecca Zhang. 2015. Collaborative data analytics with DataHub. *Proceedings of the VLDB Endowment* 8, 12 (2015), 1916–1919.
6. Christian Bizer, Tom Heath, and Tim Berners-Lee. 2009. Linked data-the story so far. *Semantic Services, Interoperability and Web Applications: Emerging Concepts* (2009), 205–227.
7. Ann Blandford and Simon Attfield. 2010. Interacting with information. *Synthesis Lectures on Human-Centered Informatics* 3, 1 (2010), 1–99.
8. Andrei Broder. 2002. A taxonomy of web search. In *ACM Sigir forum*, Vol. 36. ACM, 3–10.
9. Alan Bryman. 2006. Integrating quantitative and qualitative research: how is it done? *Qualitative research* 6, 1 (2006), 97–113.
10. Burton-Taylor. 2015. Demand for financial market data and news. (24 March 2015). https://burton-taylor.com/demand-for-financial-market-data-news-up-4-07-in-2014-highest-since-2011-2/.
11. Michael J Cafarella, Alon Halevy, and Jayant Madhavan. 2011. Structured data on the web. *Commun. ACM* 54, 2 (2011), 72–79.
12. John L Campbell, Charles Quincy, Jordan Osserman, and Ove K Pedersen. 2013. Coding in-depth semistructured interviews problems of unitization and intercoder reliability and agreement. *Sociological Methods & Research* (2013).
13. Donald Owen Case. 2012. *Looking for information: A survey of research on information seeking, needs and behavior*. Emerald Group Publishing.
14. Tiziana Catarci. 2000. What happened when database researchers met usability. *Information Systems* 25, 3 (2000), 177–212.
15. Gabriella Cattaneo, Mike Glennon, Rosanna Lifonti, Giorgio Micheletti, Alys Woodward, Marianne Kolding, Angela Vacca, Carla La Croce, and David Osimo. 2015. European Data Market SMART 2013/0063, D6 - First Interim Report. (October 2015). https://idc-emea.app.box.com/s/k7xv0u3gl6xfvq1rl667xqmw69pzk790.
16. Chris Chatfield. 2016. *The analysis of time series: an introduction*. CRC press.
17. Andy Crabtree and Richard Mortier. September 2015. Human data interaction: Historical lessons from social studies and CSCW. In *ECSCW 2015: Proceedings of the 14th European Conference on Computer Supported Cooperative Work*. Springer, 3–21.
18. Data.gov.uk. 2016. data.gov.uk, Opening up Government. (2016). https://data.gov.uk/
19. William Dilla, Diane J Janvrin, and Robyn Raschke. 2010. Interactive data visualization: New directions for accounting information systems research. *Journal of Information Systems* 24, 2 (2010), 1–37.
20. Jérôme Dinet, Aline Chevalier, and André Tricot. 2012. Information search activity: An overview. *Revue Européenne de Psychologie Appliquée/European Review of Applied Psychology* 62, 2 (2012), 49–62.
21. Abdigani Diriye, Max L Wilson, Ann Blandford, and Anastasios Tombros. 2010. Revisiting exploratory search from the HCI perspective. *HCIR 2010* (2010), 99.
22. DMOX. 2016. Welcome to DMOZ! It's the Web, Organized. (2016). https://www.dmoz.org/
23. N Elmqvist. 2011. Embodied human-data interaction. In *ACM CHI Workshop "Embodied Interaction: Theory and Practice in HCI"*. 104–107.
24. Raya Fidel. 2012. *Human information interaction: an ecological approach to information behavior*. MIT Press.
25. Steve Fox, Kuldeep Karnawat, Mark Mydland, Susan Dumais, and Thomas White. 2005. Evaluating implicit measures to improve web search. *ACM Transactions on Information Systems (TOIS)* 23, 2 (2005), 147–168.
26. George W Furnas and Daniel M Russell. 2005. Making sense of sensemaking. In *CHI'05 extended abstracts on Human factors in computing systems*. ACM, 2115–2116.
27. GOV.UK. 2014. How to make a freedom of information (FOI) request. (November 2014). Retrieved September 05, 2016 from https://www.gov.uk/make-a-freedom-of-information-request/the-freedom-of-information-act.
28. Judith Green and Nicki Thorogood. 2013. *Qualitative methods for health research*. Sage.

29. Shweta Gupta, Sunita Yadav, and Rajesh Prasad. 2016. Document Retrieval using Efficient Indexing Techniques: A Review. *International Journal of Business Analytics (IJBAN)* 3, 4 (2016), 64–82.

30. Ido Guy, Sigalit Ur, Inbal Ronen, Sara Weber, and Tolga Oral. 2012. Best Faces Forward: A Large-scale Study of People Search in the Enterprise. In *Proceedings of the SIGCHI Conference on Human Factors in Computing Systems (CHI '12)*. ACM, 1775–1784.

31. Hamed Haddadi, Richard Mortier, Derek McAuley, and Jon Crowcroft. 2013. Human-data interaction. *University of Cambridge* (2013).

32. Jozef Hvorecký, Martin Drlík, and Michal Munk. 2010. Enhancing database querying skills by choosing a more appropriate interface. In *IEEE EDUCON 2010 Conference*. IEEE, 1897–1905.

33. Ross Ihaka and Robert Gentleman. 1996. R: a language for data analysis and graphics. *Journal of computational and graphical statistics* 5, 3 (1996), 299–314.

34. Peter Emil Rerup Ingwersen. 1992. *Information Retrieval Interaction*. Taylor Graham.

35. Open Knowledge International. 2016. Good Tables. (2016). http://goodtables.okfnlabs.org/

36. Bernard J Jansen. 2006. Search log analysis: What it is, what's been done, how to do it. *Library & information science research* 28, 3 (2006), 407–432.

37. Daxin Jiang, Jian Pei, and Hang Li. 2013. Mining Search and Browse Logs for Web Search: A Survey. *ACM Trans. Intell. Syst. Technol.* 4, 4, Article 57 (October 2013), 57:1–57:37 pages.

38. Steve Jones, Sally Jo Cunningham, Rodger McNab, and Stefan Boddie. 2000. A transaction log analysis of a digital library. *International Journal on Digital Libraries* 3, 2 (2000), 152–169.

39. Diane Kelly. 2009. Methods for evaluating interactive information retrieval systems with users. *Foundations and Trends in Information Retrieval* 3, 1-2 (2009), 1–224.

40. Carol Collier Kuhlthau. 2004. *Seeking meaning: A process approach to library and information services*. Libraries Unltd Incorporated.

41. Yuelin Li and Nicholas J Belkin. 2008. A faceted approach to conceptualizing tasks in information seeking. *Information Processing & Management* 44, 6 (2008), 1822–1837.

42. Jaime I Lopez-Veyna, Victor J Sosa-Sosa, and Ivan Lopez-Arevalo. 2012. KESOSD: keyword search over structured data. In *Proceedings of the Third International Workshop on Keyword Search on Structured Data*. ACM, 23–31.

43. McKinsey Global Institute: James Manyika, Michael Chui, Peter Groves, Diana Farrell, Steve Van Kuiken, and Elizabeth Almasi Doshi. 2013. Open data: Unlocking innovation and performance with liquid information. (2013). http://www.mckinsey.com/business-functions/business-technology/our-nsights/open-data-unlocking-innovation-and-performance-with-liquid-information.

44. Gary Marchionini. 2006. Exploratory search: from finding to understanding. *Commun. ACM* 49, 4 (2006), 41–46.

45. Gary Marchionini, Stephanie W Haas, Junliang Zhang, and Jonathan Elsas. 2005. Accessing government statistical information. *Computer* 38, 12 (2005), 52–61.

46. Viktor Mayer-Schönberger and Kenneth Cukier. 2013. *Big data: A revolution that will transform how we live, work, and think*. Houghton Mifflin Harcourt.

47. Open Data Monitor. 2016. Open Data Monitor. (2016). http://project.opendatamonitor.eu/

48. Mohamed Morsey, Jens Lehmann, Sören Auer, and Axel-Cyrille Ngonga Ngomo. 2011. DBpedia SPARQL benchmark–performance assessment with real queries on real data. In *International Semantic Web Conference*. Springer, 454–469.

49. Peter F Patel-Schneider. 2014. Analyzing schema. org. In *International Semantic Web Conference*. Springer, 261–276.

50. Hanspeter Pfister and Joe Blitzstein. 2015. cs109/2015, Lectures 01-Introduction. https://github.com/cs109/2015/tree/master/Lectures. (2015).

51. European Data Portal. 2016. (2016). https://www.europeandataportal.eu/

52. Jean-Baptiste Pressac. 2016. Open Refine Documentation. (2016). https://github.com/OpenRefine/OpenRefine/wiki

53. Soo Young Rieh, Kevyn Collins-Thompson, Preben Hansen, and Hye-Jung Lee. 2016. Towards searching as a learning process: A review of current perspectives and future directions. *Journal of Information Science* 42, 1 (2016), 19–34.

54. Colin Robson and Kieran McCartan. 2016. *Real world research*. John Wiley & Sons.

55. Daniel E Rose and Danny Levinson. 2004. Understanding user goals in web search. In *Proceedings of the 13th international conference on World Wide Web*. ACM, 13–19.

56. Stefano Spaccapietra and Ramesh Jain. 2013. *Visual Database Systems 3: Visual Information Management*. Springer.

57. Andre Suslik Spritzer and Carla Maria Dal Sasso Freitas. 2008. Navigation and interaction in graph visualizations. *Revista de informática teórica e aplicada* 15, 1 (2008), 111–136.

58. John Stasko, Carsten Görg, and Zhicheng Liu. 2008. Jigsaw: supporting investigative analysis through interactive visualization. *Information visualization* 7, 2 (2008), 118–132.

59. Thomas Steiner, Ruben Verborgh, Raphaël Troncy, Joaquim Gabarro, and Rik Van de Walle. 2012. Adding realtime coverage to the Google knowledge graph. In *Proceedings of the 2012th International Conference on Posters & Demonstrations Track-Volume 914*. 65–68.

60. Greg Sterling. 2015. It's Official: Google Says More Searches Now On Mobile Than On Desktop Company officially confirms what many have been anticipating for years. (May 2015). http://searchengineland.com/its-official-google-says-more-searches-now-on-mobile-than-on-desktop-220369.

61. Monica Swamiraj and Luanne Freund. 2015. Facilitating the discovery of open government datasets through an exploratory data search interface. (2015).

62. Mona Taghavi, Ahmed Patel, Nikita Schmidt, Christopher Wills, and Yiqi Tew. 2012. An analysis of web proxy logs with query distribution pattern approach for search engines. *Computer Standards & Interfaces* 34, 1 (2012), 162–170.

63. Barbara Ubaldi. 2013. Open Government Data. (2013).

64. Ellen M Voorhees and others. 1999. The TREC-8 Question Answering Track Report.. In *Trec*, Vol. 99. 77–82.

65. W3Schools.com. 2016. Browser Statistics. http://www.w3schools.com/browsers/default.asp. (2016).

66. Ryen W White. 2016. *Interactions with search systems*. Cambridge University Press.

67. Max L Wilson, Bill Kules, Ben Shneiderman, and others. 2010. From keyword search to exploration: Designing future search interfaces for the web. *Foundations and Trends in Web Science* 2, 1 (2010), 1–97.

68. Tom D Wilson. 1999. Models in information behaviour research. *Journal of documentation* 55, 3 (1999), 249–270.

69. Lei Yang, Qiaozhu Mei, Kai Zheng, and David A Hanauer. 2011. Query log analysis of an electronic health record search engine. In *AMIA annual symposium proceedings*, Vol. 2011. 915–924.

70. Ji Soo Yi, Youn ah Kang, John Stasko, and Julie Jacko. 2007. Toward a deeper understanding of the role of interaction in information visualization. *IEEE transactions on visualization and computer graphics* 13, 6 (2007), 1224–1231.

Same Stats, Different Graphs: Generating Datasets with Varied Appearance and Identical Statistics through Simulated Annealing

Justin Matejka and George Fitzmaurice
Autodesk Research, Toronto Ontario Canada
{*first.last*}@autodesk.com

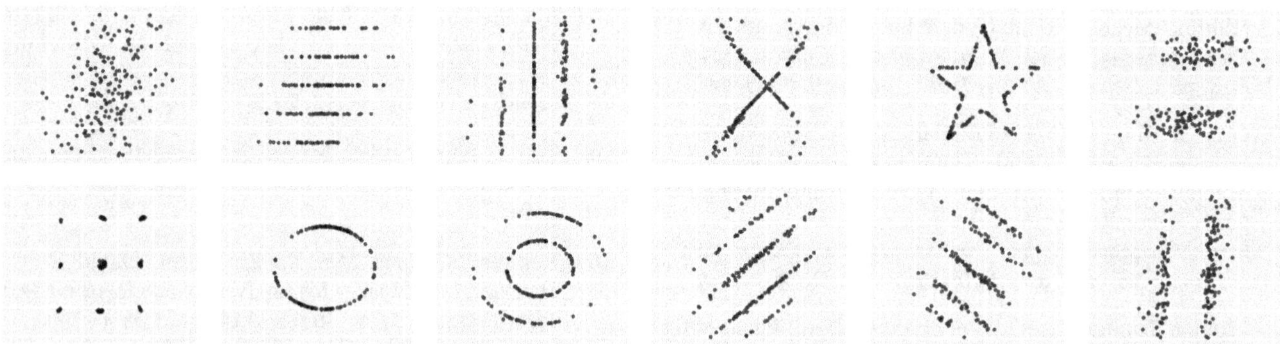

Figure 1. A collection of data sets produced by our technique. While different in appearance, each has the same summary statistics (mean, std. deviation, and Pearson's corr.) to 2 decimal places. (*$\bar{x}$=54.02, $\bar{y}$= 48.09, sd_x = 14.52, sd_y = 24.79, Pearson's r = +0.32*)

ABSTRACT
Datasets which are identical over a number of statistical properties, yet produce dissimilar graphs, are frequently used to illustrate the importance of graphical representations when exploring data. This paper presents a novel method for generating such datasets, along with several examples. Our technique varies from previous approaches in that new datasets are iteratively generated from a seed dataset through random perturbations of individual data points, and can be directed towards a desired outcome through a simulated annealing optimization strategy. Our method has the benefit of being agnostic to the particular statistical properties that are to remain constant between the datasets, and allows for control over the graphical appearance of resulting output.

INTRODUCTION
Anscome's Quartet [1] is a set of four distinct datasets each consisting of 11 (*x,y*) pairs where each dataset produces the same summary statistics (mean, standard deviation, and correlation) while producing vastly different plots (Figure 2A). This dataset is frequently used to illustrate the importance of graphical representations when exploring data. The effectiveness of Anscombe's Quartet is not due to simply having four different data sets which generate the same statistical properties, it is that four *clearly different* and *identifiably distinct* datasets are producing the same statistical properties. Dataset I appears to follow a somewhat noisy linear model, while Dataset II is following a parabolic distribution. Dataset III appears to be strongly linear, except for a single outlier, while Dataset IV forms a vertical line with the regression thrown off by a single outlier. In contrast, Figure 2B shows a series of datasets also sharing the same summary statistics as Anscombe's Quartet, however without any obvious underlying structure to the individual datasets, this quartet is not nearly as effective at demonstrating the importance of graphical representations.

While very popular and effective for illustrating the importance of visualizations, it is not known how Anscombe came up with his datasets [5]. Our work presents a novel method for creating datasets which are identical over a range of statistical properties, yet produce dissimilar graphics. Our method differs from previous by being agnostic to the particular statistical properties that are to remain constant between the datasets, while allowing for control over the graphical appearance of resulting output.

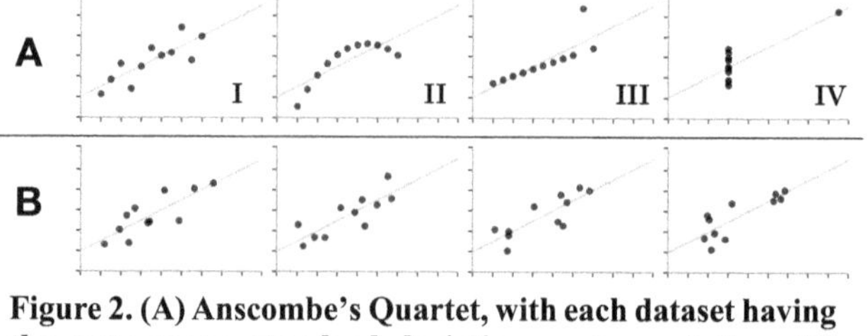

Figure 2. (A) Anscombe's Quartet, with each dataset having the same mean, standard deviation, and correlation. (B) Four *unstructured* datasets, each also having the same statistical properties as those in Anscombe's Quartet.

CHI 2017, May 06 - 11, 2017, Denver, CO, USA

ACM 978-1-4503-4655-9/17/05…$15.00
DOI: http://dx.doi.org/10.1145/3025453.3025912

RELATED WORK

As alluded to above, producing multiple datasets with similar statistics and dissimilar graphics was introduced by Anscombe in 1973 [1]. "Graphs in Statistical Analysis" starts by listing three notions prevalent about graphs at the time:

(1) *Numerical calculations are exact, but graphs are rough;*
(2) *For any particular kind of statistical data there is just one set of calculations constituting a correct statistical analysis;*
(3) *Performing intricate calculations is virtuous, whereas actually looking at the data is cheating.*

While one cannot argue that there is currently as much resistance towards graphical methods as when Anscombe's paper was originally published, the datasets described in the work (Figure 1A) are still effective and frequently used for introducing or reinforcing the importance of visual methods. Unfortunately, Anscombe does not report how the datasets were created, nor suggest any method to create new ones.

The first attempt at producing a generalized method for creating such datasets was published in 2007 by Chatterjee and Firat [5]. They proposed a genetic algorithm based approach where 1,000 random datasets were created with identical summary statistics, then combined and mutated with an objective function to maximize the "graphical dissimilarity" between the initial and final scatter plots. While the datasets produced were graphically dissimilar to the input datasets, they did not have any discernable structure in their composition. Our technique differs by providing a mechanism to direct the solutions towards a specific shape, as well as allowing for variety in the statistical measures which are to remain constant between the solutions.

Govindaraju and Haslett developed a method for regressing datasets towards their sample means while maintaining the same linear regression formula [7]. In 2009, the same authors extended their procedure to creating "cloned" datasets [8]. In addition to maintaining the same linear regression as the seed dataset, their cloned datasets also maintained the same means (but not the same standard deviations). While Chatterjee and Firat [5] wanted to create datasets as graphically dissimilar as possible, Govindaraju and Haslett's cloned datasets were designed to be visually similar, with a proposed application of confidentializing sensitive data for publication purposes. While our technique is primarily aimed at creating visually distinct datasets, by choosing appropriate statistical tests to remain constant through the iterations (such as a Kolmogorov-Smirnov test) our technique can produce datasets with similar graphical characteristics as well.

In the area of generating synthetic datasets, GraphCuisine [2] allows users to direct an evolutionary algorithm to create network graphs matching user-specified parameters. While this work looks at a similar problem, it differs in that it is focused on network graphs, is an interactive system, and allows for directly specifying characteristics of the output, while our technique looks at 1D or 2D distributions of data, is non-interactive, and perturbs the data such that the initial statistical properties are maintained throughout the process.

Finally, on the topic of using scatter plots to encode graphics, Residual Sur(Realism) [11] produces datasets with hidden images which are only revealed when appropriate statistical measures are performed. Conversely, our technique encodes graphical appearance into the data directly.

METHOD

The key insight behind our approach is that while generating a dataset from scratch to have particular statistical properties is relatively *difficult*, it is relatively *easy* to take an existing dataset, modify it slightly, and maintain (nearly) the same statistical properties. With repetition, this process creates a dataset with a different visual appearance from the original, while maintaining the same statistical properties. Further, if the modifications to the dataset are biased to move the points towards a particular goal, the resulting graph can be directed towards a particular visual appearance.

The pseudocode for the high-level algorithm is listed below:

```
current_ds ← initial_ds
for x iterations, do:
   test_ds ← PERTURB(current_ds, temp)
   if ISERROROK(test_ds, initial_ds):
      current_ds ← test_ds

function PERTURB(ds, temp):
   loop:
      test ← MOVERANDOMPOINTS(ds)
      if FIT(test) > FIT(ds) or temp > RANDOM():
         return test
```

INITIAL_DS is the seed dataset from which the statistical values we wish to maintain are calculated. The PERTURB function is called at each iteration of the algorithm to modify the latest version of the dataset (CURRENT_DS) by moving one or more points by a small amount, in a random direction. The "small amount" is chosen from a normal distribution and is calibrated such that >95% of movements result in the statistical properties of the overall dataset remaining unchanged (to two decimal places).

Once the individual points have been moved, the FIT function is used to check if perturbing the points has increased the overall fitness of the dataset. The fitness can be calculated in a variety of ways, but for conditions where we want to coerce the dataset to into a shape, fitness is calculated as the average distance of all points to the nearest point on the target shape.

The naïve approach of accepting only datasets with an improved fitness value results in possibly getting stuck in locally-optimal solutions where other, more globally-optimal solutions are possible. To mitigate this possibility, we employ a simulated annealing technique [9]. With the possible solutions generated in each iteration, simulated annealing works by *always* accepting solutions which improve the fitness, but also, if the fitness is not improved, the solution *may* be accepted based on the "temperature" of the simulated annealing algorithm. If the current temperature is less than a random number between 0 and 1, the solution is accepted even if it the fitness is worsened. We found that using a quadratically-smoothed monotonic cooling schedule starting with a temperature of 0.4 and finishing with a temperature of 0.01 worked well for the sample datasets.

Once the perturbed dataset has been accepted, either through an improved fitness value or from the simulated annealing process, the perturbed dataset is compared to the initial dataset for statistical equivalence. For the examples in this paper we consider properties to be "the same" if they are equal to two decimal places. The ISERROROK function compares the statistics between the datasets, and if they are equal (to the specified number of decimal places), the result from the current iteration becomes the new current state.

Example Generated Datasets

Example 1: Coercion Towards Target Shapes

In this first example (Figure 1), each dataset contains 182 points and are equal (to two decimal places) for the "standard" summary statistics (*x*/*y* mean, *x*/*y* standard deviation, and Pearson's correlation). Each dataset was seeded with the plot in the top left. The target shapes are specified as a series of line segments, and the shapes used in this example are shown in Figure 3.

Figure 3. The initial data set (top-left), and line segment collections used for directing the output towards specific shapes. The results are seen in Figure 1.

With this example dataset, the algorithm ran for 200,000 iterations to achieve the final results. On a laptop computer this process took ~10 minutes. Figure 4 shows the progression of one of the datasets towards the target shape.

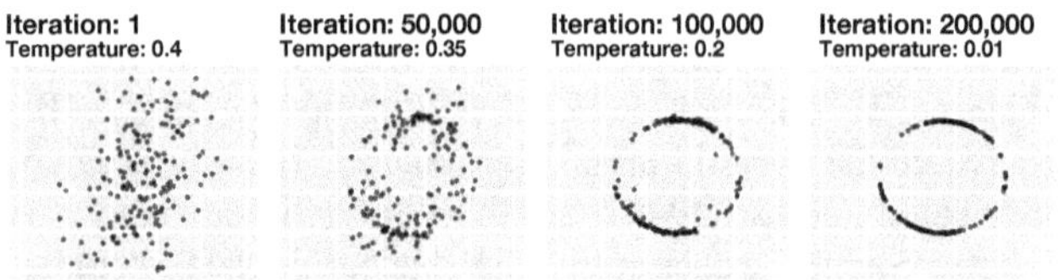

Figure 4. Progression of the algorithm towards a target shape over the course of the cooling schedule.

Example 2: Alternate Statistical Measures

One benefit of our approach over previous methods is that the iterative process is agnostic to the particular statistical properties which remain constant between the datasets. In this example (Figure 5) the datasets are derived from the same initial dataset as in Example 1, but rather than being equal on the parametric properties, the datasets are equal in the non-parametric measures of *x/y median*, *x/y interquartile range (IQR)*, and *Spearman's rank correlation coefficient*.

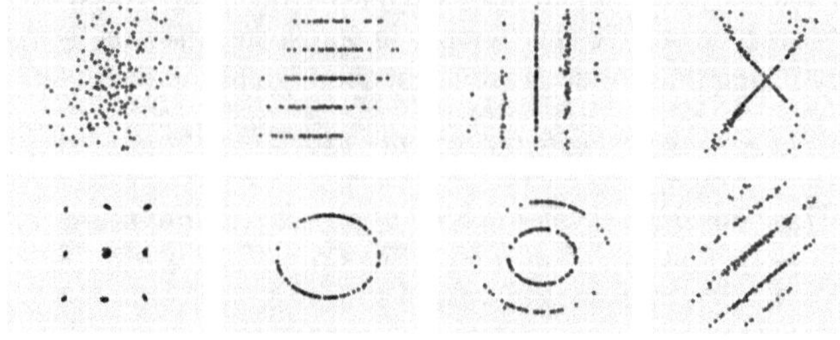

Figure 5. Example datasets are equal in the non-parametric statistics of *x/y median* (53.73, 46.21), *x/y IQR* (19.17, 37.92), and *Spearman's rank correlation coefficient* (+0.31).

Example 3: Specific Initial Dataset

The previous two examples used a rather "generic" dataset of a slightly positively correlated point cloud as the starting point of the optimization. Alternately, it is possible to begin with a very specific dataset to seed the optimization.

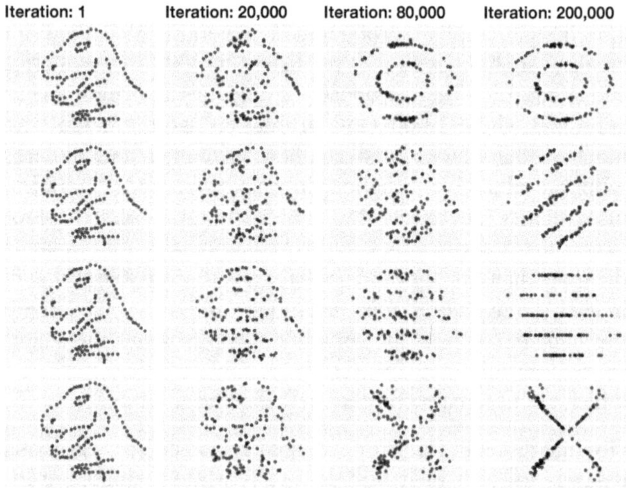

Figure 6. Creating a collection of datasets based on the "dinosaurus" dataset. Each dataset has the same summary statistics to two decimal places: ($\bar{x}$ = *54.26*, $\bar{y}$ = *47.83*, sd_x = *16.76*, sd_y = *26.93*, *Pearson's r* = *-0.06*).

Alberto Cairo produced a dataset called the "Datasaurus" [4]. Like Anscombe's Quartet, this serves as a reminder to the importance of visualizing your data, since, although the dataset produces "normal" summary statistics, the resulting plot is a picture of a dinosaur. In this example we use the "datasaurus" as the initial dataset, and create other datasets with the same summary statistics (Figure 6).

Example 4: Simpson's Paradox

Another instrument for demonstrating the importance of visualizing your data is Simpson's Paradox [3, 10]. This paradox occurs with data sets where a trend appears when looking at individual groups in the data, but disappears or reverses when the groups are combined.

To create a dataset exhibiting Simpson's Paradox, we start with a strongly positively correlated dataset (Figure 7A), and then perturb and direct that dataset towards a series of negatively sloping lines (Figure 7B). The resulting dataset (Figure 7C) has the same positive correlation as the initial dataset when looked at as a whole, while the individual groups each have a strong negative correlation.

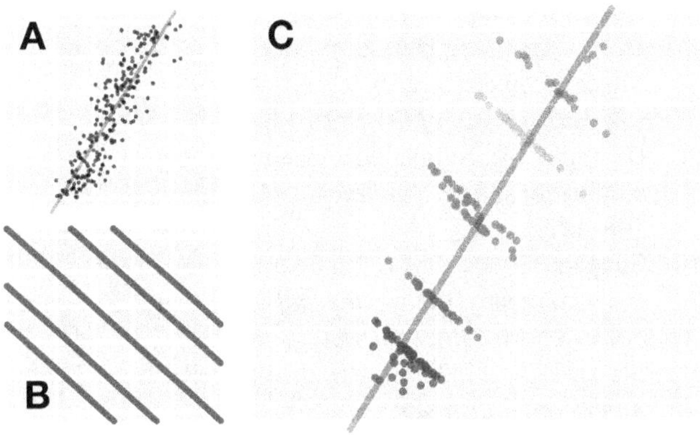

Figure 7. Demonstration of Simpson's Paradox. Both datasets (A and C) have the same overall Pearson's correlation of +0.81, however after coercing the data towards the pattern of sloping lines (B), each subset of data in (C) has an individually negative correlation.

Example 5: Cloned Dataset with Similar Appearance

As discussed by Govindaraju and Haslett [8] another use for datasets with the same statistical properties is the creation of "cloned" datasets to anonymize sensitive data [6]. In this case, it is important that individual data points are changed while the overall structure of the data remains similar. This can be accomplished by performing a Kolmogorov-Smirnov test within the ISERROROK function for both x and y. By only accepting solutions where both the x and y K-S statistic is <0.05 we ensure that the result will have a similar shape to the original (Figure 8). This approach has the benefit of maintaining the x/y means and correlation as accomplished in previous work [8], and additionally the x/y standard deviations as well. This could also be useful for "graphical inference" [12] to create a collection of variant plots following the same null hypothesis.

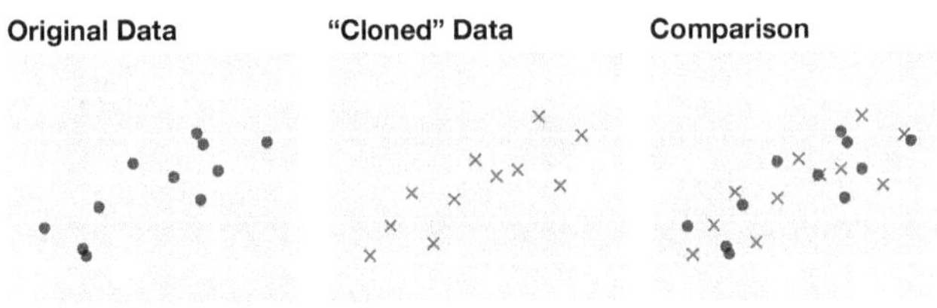

Figure 8. Example of creating a "mirror" dataset as in [8].

Example 6: 1D Boxplots

To demonstrate the applicability of our approach to non 2D-scatterplot data, this example uses a 1D distribution of data as represented by a boxplot. The most common variety of boxplot, the "Tukey Boxplot", presents the 1st quartile, median, and 3rd quartile values on the "box", with the "whiskers" showing the location of the furthest datapoints within 1.5 interquartile ranges (IQR) from the 1st and 3rd quartiles. Starting with the data in a normal distribution (Figure 9A) and perturbing the data to the left (B), right (C), edges (D, E), and arbitrary points along the range (F) while ensuring that the boxplot statistics remain constant produces the results shown in Figure 9.

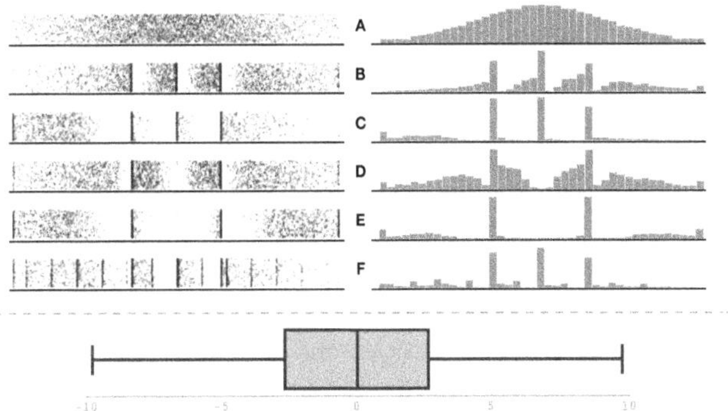

Figure 9. Six data distributions, each with the same 1st quartile, median, and 3rd quartile values, as well as equal locations for points 1.5 IQR from the 1st and 3rd quartiles. Each dataset produces an identical boxplot.

LIMITATIONS AND FUTURE WORK

When the source dataset and the target shape are vastly different, the produced output might not be desirable. An example is show Figure 10, where the data set from Figure 7A is coerced into a star (Figure 10). This problem can be mitigated by coercing the data towards "simpler" patterns with more coverage of the coordinate space – such as lines spanning the grid, or pre-scaling and positioning the target shape to better align with the initial dataset.

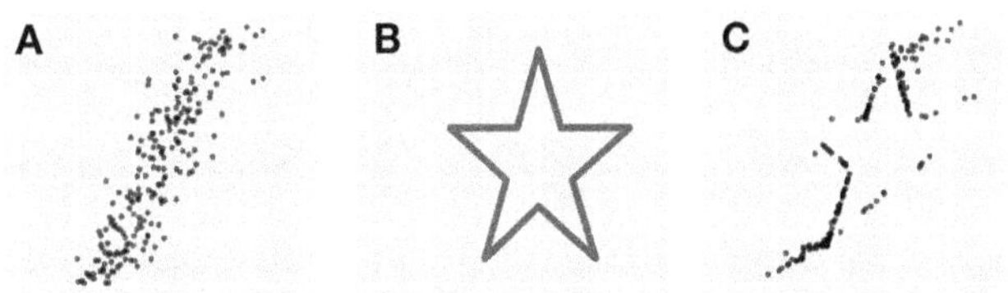

Figure 10. Undesirable outcome (C) when coercing a strongly positively correlated dataset (A) into a star (B).

The currently implemented fitness function looks only at the position of individual points in relation to the target shape, which can result in "clumping" of data points and sparse areas on the target shape. A future improvement could consider an additional goal to "separate" the points to encourage better coverage of the target shape in the output.

The parameters chosen for the algorithm (95% success rate, quadratic cooling scheme, start/end temperatures, etc.) were found to work well, but should not be considered "optimal". Such optimization is left as future work.

The code and datasets presented in this work are available at www.autodeskresearch.com/publications/samestats.

CONCLUSION

We presented a technique for creating visually dissimilar datasets which are equal over a range of statistical properties. The outputs from our method can be used to demonstrate the importance of visualizing your data, and may serve as a starting point for new data anonymization techniques.

REFERENCES

1. Anscombe, F.J. (1973). Graphs in Statistical Analysis. *The American Statistician 27*, 1, 17–21.
2. Bach, B., Spritzer, A., Lutton, E., and Fekete, J.-D. (2012). Interactive Random Graph Generation with Evolutionary Algorithms. *SpringerLink*, 541–552.
3. Blyth, C.R. (1972). On Simpson's Paradox and the Sure-Thing Principle. *Journal of the American Statistical Association 67*, 338, 364–366.
4. Cairo, A. Download the Datasaurus: Never trust summary statistics alone; always visualize your data. http://www.thefunctionalart.com/2016/08/download-datasaurus-never-trust-summary.html.
5. Chatterjee, S. and Firat, A. (2007). Generating Data with Identical Statistics but Dissimilar Graphics. *The American Statistician 61*, 3, 248–254.
6. Fung, B.C.M., Wang, K., Chen, R., and Yu, P.S. (2010). Privacy-preserving Data Publishing: A Survey of Recent Developments. *ACM Comput. Surv. 42*, 4, 14:1–14:53.
7. Govindaraju, K. and Haslett, S.J. (2008). Illustration of regression towards the means. *International Journal of Mathematical Education in Science and Technology 39*, 4, 544–550.
8. Haslett, S.J. and Govindaraju, K. (2009). Cloning Data: Generating Datasets with Exactly the Same Multiple Linear Regression Fit. *Australian & New Zealand Journal of Statistics 51*, 4, 499–503.
9. Hwang, C.-R. Simulated annealing: Theory and applications. *Acta Applicandae Mathematica 12*, 1, 108–111.
10. Simpson, E.H. (1951). The Interpretation of Interaction in Contingency Tables. *Journal of the Royal Statistical Society. Series B (Methodological) 13*, 2, 238–241.
11. Stefanski, L.A. (2007). Residual (Sur)Realism. *The American Statistician*, .
12. Wickham, H., Cook, D., Hofmann, H., and Buja, A. (2010). Graphical inference for infovis. *IEEE Transactions on Visualization and Computer Graphics 16*, 6, 973–979.

Inferring Cognitive Models from Data using Approximate Bayesian Computation

Antti Kangasrääsiö[1], Kumaripaba Athukorala[1], Andrew Howes[2], Jukka Corander[3], Samuel Kaski[1], Antti Oulasvirta[4]
[1]Helsinki Institute for Information Technology HIIT, Department of Computer Science, Aalto University, Finland
[2]School of Computer Science, University of Birmingham, UK
[3]Department of Biostatistics, University of Oslo, Norway
[4]Helsinki Institute for Information Technology HIIT, Department of Communications and Networking, Aalto University, Finland

ABSTRACT
An important problem for HCI researchers is to estimate the parameter values of a cognitive model from behavioral data. This is a difficult problem, because of the substantial complexity and variety in human behavioral strategies. We report an investigation into a new approach using approximate Bayesian computation (ABC) to condition model parameters to data and prior knowledge. As the case study we examine menu interaction, where we have click time data only to infer a cognitive model that implements a search behaviour with parameters such as fixation duration and recall probability. Our results demonstrate that ABC (i) improves estimates of model parameter values, (ii) enables meaningful comparisons between model variants, and (iii) supports fitting models to individual users. ABC provides ample opportunities for theoretical HCI research by allowing principled inference of model parameter values and their uncertainty.

ACM Classification Keywords
H.1.2 User/Machine Systems: Human factors, Human information processing

Author Keywords
Approximate Bayesian computation; Cognitive models in HCI; Computational rationality; Inverse modeling

INTRODUCTION
It has become relatively easy to collect large amounts of data about complex user behaviour. This provides an exciting opportunity as the data has the potential to help HCI researchers understand and possibly predict such user behavior. Yet, unfortunately it has remained difficult to explain what users are doing and why in a given data set.

The difficulty lies in two problems: modeling and inference. The *modeling problem* consists of building models that are sufficiently general to capture a broad range of behaviors. Any model attempting to explain real-world observations must cover a complex interplay of factors, including what users are interested in, their individual capacities, and how they choose to process information (strategies). Recent research has shown progress in the direction of creating models for complex behavior [5, 13, 14, 16, 19, 21, 25, 27, 29, 36]. After constructing the model, we are then faced with the *inference problem*: how to set the parameter values of the model, such that the values agree with literature and prior knowledge, and that the resulting predictions match with the observations we have (Figure 1). Unfortunately, this problem has been less systematically studied in HCI. To this end, the goal of this paper is to report an investigation into a flexible and powerful method for inferring model parameter values, called *approximate Bayesian computation* (ABC) [42].

ABC has been applied to many scientific problems [7, 15, 42]. For example, in climatology the goal is to infer a model of climate from sensor readings, and in infectious disease epidemiology an epidemic model from reports of an infection spread. Inference is of great use both in applications and in theory-formation, in particular when testing models, identifying anomalies, and finding explanations to observations. However ABC, nor any other principled inference method, have, to our knowledge, been applied to complex cognitive models in HCI[1].

We are interested in principled methods for inferring parameter values, because they would be especially useful for process models of behaviour. This is because the models are usually defined as simulators, and thus the inference is very difficult to perform using direct analytical means[2]. Such process models in HCI have been created, for example, based on cognitive science [2, 9, 11, 16, 26, 41], control theory [23], biomechanics [4], game theory [10], foraging [38, 37], economic choice [3], and computational rationality [13]. In the absence of principled inference methods for such models, some approaches

CHI 2017, May 06–11, 2017, Denver, CO, USA
ACM 978-1-4503-4655-9/17/05.
DOI: http://dx.doi.org/10.1145/3025453.3025576

[1]For simpler models, such as regression models (e.g., Fitts' law), there exist well-known methods for finding parameter values, such as ordinary least squares.

[2]In technical terms, such models generally do not have a *likelihood function*—defining the likelihood of parameter values given the observations—that could be written in closed form.

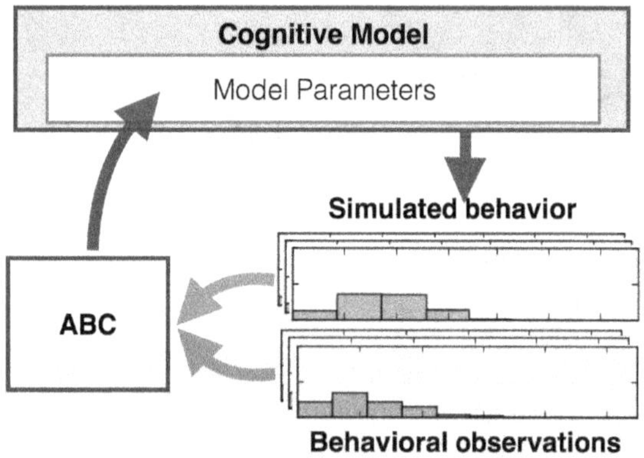

Figure 1. This paper studies methodology for inference of parameter values of cognitive models from observational data in HCI. At the bottom of the figure, we have behavioral data (orange histograms), such as times and targets of menu selections. At the top of the figure, a cognitive model generates simulated interaction data (blue histograms). In this paper, approximate Bayesian computation (ABC) is investigated to identify the model parameter values that yield the best fit between the real data and simulator-generated data, while keeping the parameter values reasonable given prior knowledge.

have included: (1) simplifying models until traditional inference methods are possible; (2) using values adopted from the literature or adjusting them without studying their effect on behavior; or (3) manually iterating to find values that lead to acceptable performance. Compared to this, principled inference methods might reduce the potential for ambiguity, miscalculation, and bias, because model parameter values could be properly conditioned on both literature and prior knowledge, as well as the observation data.

ABC is particularly promising for inferring the values of process model parameters from naturalistic data—a problem that is known to be difficult in cognitive science [31]. The reason is that ABC does not make any further assumptions of the model, apart from the researcher being able to repeatedly simulate data from it using different parameter values. ABC performs inference by systematically simulating user behavior with different parameter configurations. Based on the simulations, ABC estimates which parameter values lead to behavior that is similar to observations, while also being reasonable considering our prior knowledge of plausible parameter values.

As a challenging and representative example, this paper looks at a recent HCI process model class in which behavioral strategies are learned using reinforcement learning [13, 16, 17, 36]. These models assume that users behave (approximately) to maximize utility given limits on their own capacity. The models predict how a user will behave in situations constrained by (1) the environment, such as the physical structure of a user interface (UI); (2) goals, such as the trade-off between time and effort; and (3) the user's cognitive and perceptual capabilities, such as memory capacity or fixation duration. This class of models, called *computational rationality* (CR) models, has been explored previously in HCI, for example in SNIF-ACT [16], economic models of search [3], foraging theory [38], and adaptive interaction [36]. The recent interest in this class is due to the benefit that, when compared with classic cognitive models, it requires no predefined specification of the user's task solution, only the objectives. Given those, and the constraints of the situation, we can use machine learning to infer the optimal behavior policy. However, achieving the inverse, that is inferring the constraints assuming that the behavior is optimal, is exceedingly difficult. The assumptions about data quality and granularity of previously explored methods for this inverse reinforcement learning problem [32, 39, 45] tend to be unreasonable when often only noisy or aggregate-level data exists, such as is often the case in HCI studies.

Our application case is a recent model of *menu interaction* [13]. The model studied here has previously captured adaptation of search behavior, and consequently changes to task completion times, in various situations [13]. The model makes parametric assumptions about the user, for example about the visual system (e.g., fixation durations), and uses reinforcement learning to obtain a behavioral strategy suitable for a particular menu. The inverse problem we study is how to obtain estimates of the properties of the user's visual system from selection time data only (click times of menu items). However, due to the complexity of the model, its parameter values were originally tuned based on literature. Later in Study 1, we demonstrate that we are able to infer the parameter values of this model based on observation data, such that the predictions improve over the baseline, while the parameter values still agree with the literature. To the best of our knowledge, this is also the first time such inverse reinforcement learning problem has been solved based on aggregate-level data.

We also aim to demonstrate the applicability of ABC, and inference in general, in two situations: model development and modeling of individuals. In Study 2, we demonstrate how ABC allows us to make meaningful comparisons between multiple model variants, and their comparable parameters, after they all have been fit to the same dataset. This presents a method for speeding up the development of these kind of complex models, though automatic inference of model parameter values. In Study 3, we demonstrate how ABC allows us to infer model parameter values for individual users. We discover that overall these individual models outperform a population-level model fit to a larger set of data, thus demonstrating the benefit of individual models. As a comparison, it would not be possible to fit individual models based on literature alone, as the information generally only applies on population level.

OVERVIEW OF APPROACH

This paper is concerned with inference of model parameter values from data, which is also called *inverse modeling*. Inverse modeling answers the question: "what were the parameter values of the model, assuming the observed data was generated from the model?" Our goal is to assess the usefulness of approximate Bayesian computation (ABC) [42] to this end.

We now give a short overview of inverse modeling in HCI, after which we review ABC and explain its applicability. We finally provide a short overview of the particular ABC algorithm, BOLFI [18], we use in this study.

Inverse Modeling Approaches for Cognitive Models

For models that have simple algebraic forms, such as linear regression, inverse modeling is simple, as we can explicitly

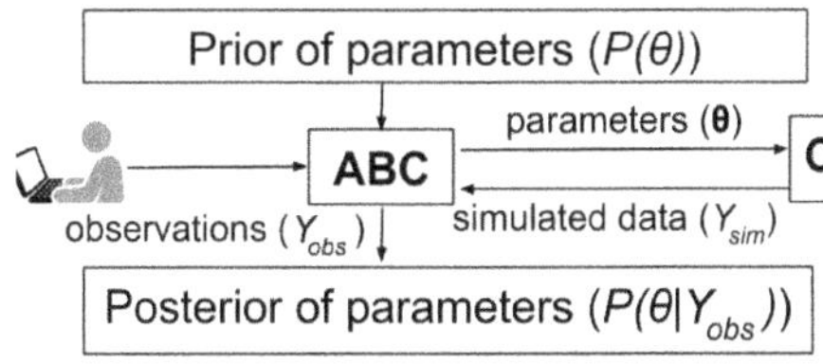

Figure 2. Overview of the ABC inference process for HCI models: Observed user data and priors of the parameters are fed into the ABC algorithm, which then approximates the posterior distribution of the parameter values. The algorithm iterates by choosing values for the parameters of the model (here a CR model) and generating simulated user data. For CR models, generating simulated data requires first training a reinforcement learning agent using the given parameter values.

write down the formula for the most likely parameter values given data. For complex models, such formula might not exist, but it is often possible to write down an explicit *likelihood function*, $L(\theta|Y_{obs})$, which evaluates the likelihood of the parameters θ given the observed data Y_{obs}. When this likelihood function can be evaluated efficiently, inverse modeling can be done, even for reinforcement learning (RL) models [32, 39, 45]. However, this inverse reinforcement learning has been only possible when precise observations are available of the environment states and of the actions the agent took, which in HCI applications is rarely the case.

When the likelihood function of the model can not be evaluated efficiently, there are generally two options left. The traditional way in HCI has been to set the model parameters based on past models and existing literature. If this has not led to acceptable predicted behavior, the researcher might have further tuned the parameters by hand until the predictions were satisfactory. However, this process generally has no guarantees that the final parameters will be close to the most likely values. An alternative solution, which we have not seen used in HCI context before, would be to use likelihood-free inference methods, that allow the model parameters to be estimated without requiring the likelihood function to be evaluated directly. These methods are derived based on mathematical principles, and thus offer performance guarantees, at least in the asymptotic case. ABC is one such method [42], and we will explain it next in more detail.

Approximate Bayesian Computation (ABC)

ABC is a principled method for finding parameter values for complex HCI models, including simulators, based on observed data and prior knowledge. It repeatedly simulates data using different parameter values, in order to find regions of the parameter space that lead to simulated data that is similar to the observed data. Different ABC algorithms differ, for example, in the way in which they choose the parameter values.

The main benefit of ABC for HCI is its generality: the only assumption needed is that the researcher is able to repeatedly simulate observations with different parameter values. Therefore, while in this paper we examine only a particular simulator, the approach is of more general value. To be precise, ABC can be used in the following recurring scenario in HCI:

- **Inputs:** A model M with unknown parameters θ; prior knowledge of reasonable values for θ (for example from literature); observations Y_{obs} of interactive behavior (for example from user study logs)
- **Outputs:** Estimates of likely values for parameters θ and their uncertainty. Likely values of θ should produce a close simulated replication of observed data: $M(\theta) \approx Y_{obs}$, while still being plausible given prior knowledge.

The process of using ABC is depicted in Figure 2. First the researcher implements her model as an executable simulator. Values for well-known parameters of the model are set by hand. For inferred parameters θ a *prior probability distribution* $P(\theta)$ is defined by the researcher based on her prior knowledge of plausible values. The researcher then defines the set of observations Y_{obs} that θ will be conditioned on. Next, the researcher defines a *discrepancy function* $d(Y_{obs}, Y_{sim}) \rightarrow [0, \infty)$, that quantifies the similarity of the observed and simulated data in a way meaningful for the researcher. Finally, an ABC algorithm is run; it selects at which parameter values $\{\theta_i\}$ the simulator will be run, and how the conditional distribution of the parameter values, also known as the *posterior* $P(\theta|Y_{obs})$, is constructed based on the simulations.

BOLFI: An ABC Variant Used in This Paper

This paper employs a recent variant of ABC called BOLFI [18], which reduces the number of simulations[3] while still being able to get adequate estimates for θ. An overview of the method is shown in Figure 3.

The main idea of BOLFI is to learn a statistical regression model—called a Gaussian process—for estimating the discrepancy values over the feasible domain of θ from a smaller number of samples that do not densely cover the whole parameter space. This is justified when the situation is such that small changes in θ do not yield large changes in the discrepancy. Additionally, as we are most interested in finding regions where the discrepancy is small, BOLFI uses a modern optimization method called *Bayesian optimization* for selecting the locations where to simulate. This way we can concentrate the samples to parameter regions that are more likely to lead to low discrepancy simulated data. This approach has resulted

[3]The naive way to use ABC would be to simulate a large amount of samples densely covering the parameter space and keep those that have the lowest discrepancy values. This method is also known as Rejection ABC. However, as in our case the simulations take multiple hours each, this approach has infeasible total computation time.

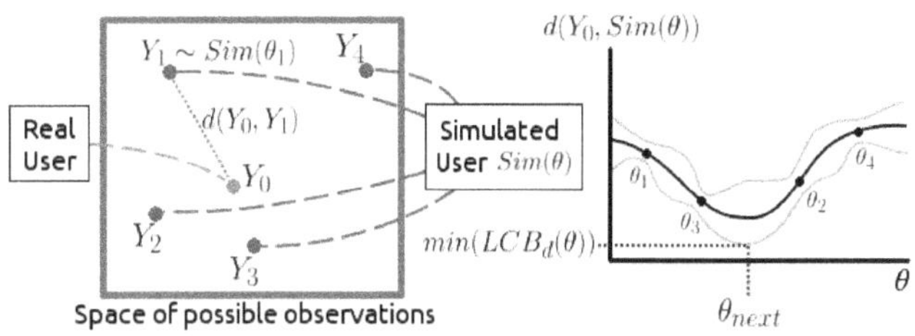

Figure 3. Left: BOLFI finds parameter values that are best able to reproduce empirical observations Y_0 (here the best sample is Y_3, produced by simulating with parameter values θ_3). Right: BOLFI first constructs a statistical regression model for predicting the discrepancy values d associated with different parameter values θ, and then uses Lower Confidence Bound (LCB) values for choosing the next sample location θ_{next}.

in 3–4 orders of faster inference compared with the state-of-the-art ABC algorithms. Details of the method are given in the paper by Gutmann and Corander [18].

CASE: MODEL OF MENU SELECTION

Our case looks at a recent model for visual search of menus, introduced by Chen et al. [13]. The purpose of this model is to predict the visual search behavior (how eyes fixate and move) and task completion times of a person searching for an item from a vertical menu.

This model presents a particularly challenging problem for inference of parameter values because substantial computation is required by the reinforcement learning algorithm to calculate the search behavior policy, given a particular parameter set. The parameters of Chen et al.'s model [13] describe cognitive characteristics of a user, such as the duration of a saccade when searching through the menu. In contrast to Chen et al. [13], where parameters were largely set to values in the literature[4], the inference problem that we study here is to estimate parameter values based on limited behavioral data: click times for menu items. Across the studies, we condition the parameter values of this model, and it's variants, to this type of data in different settings.

Introduction to Computational Rationality

An important property of the model we examine [13] is that it computes computationally rational policies—behavior patterns optimized to maximize the utility of an agent given its bounds and goals [28]. The bounds include limitations on the observation functions and on the actions that the agent can perform. These bounds define a space of possible policies. The use of computationally rational agents to model cognition has been heavily influenced by *rational analysis*, a method for explaining behavior in terms of utility [1, 12, 35], an idea used for example in information foraging theory and economic models of search [3, 38]. Computational rational agents have been used to model a number of phenomena in HCI [36]. Applications relevant to this paper include menu interaction [13] and visual search [20, 30, 34, 44].

[4] For example, the saccade duration parameters were set based on a study by Baloh et al. [6] and the fixation duration parameters based on a study by Brumby et al. [8].

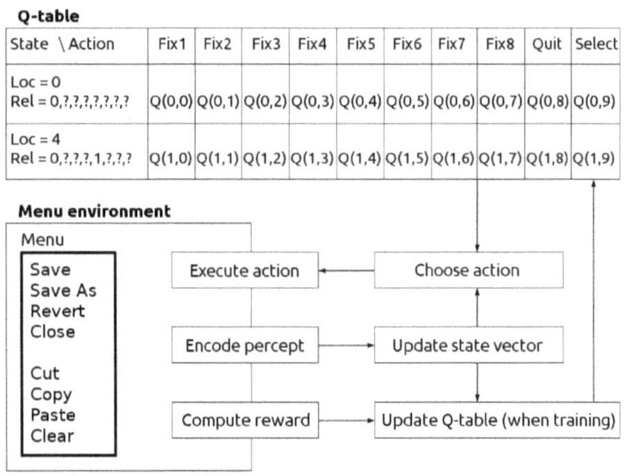

Figure 4. Case model: A simulation process figure of the computational rationality model of user interaction with drop-down menus, adapted from Chen et al. [13]. The Q-table is constructed in the training phase; in the simulation phase it is kept fixed.

CR models use *reinforcement learning* (RL) methods to compute the optimal policies [43]. Applying RL has two prerequisites. First, an environment is needed, which has a state that the RL agent can observe, and actions that the agent can perform to change the state. The environment is commonly a Markov decision process (MDP), and designed to approximate the real-world situation the real user faces. Second, a reward function is required—a mapping from the states of the environment to real numbers—which defines what kind of states are valuable for the RL agent (higher rewards being favorable). The RL algorithm finds the (approximately) optimal policy by experimenting in the environment and updating the policy until (approximate) convergence. The resulting policy—and thus the predicted behavior—naturally depends on the parameters of the environment and of the reward function, which have been set by the researcher.

Overview of Menu Selection Model

We summarize here all key details of the original model of Chen et al. [13] (Fig 4).

The environment is a menu composed of eight items, arranged into two semantic groups of four items each, where the items in each group share some semantic similarity. There are two conditions for the menu: either the item is present in the menu, or absent. At the beginning of an episode the agent is shown a target item. The task of the agent is to select the target item in the menu if it is present, or otherwise to declare that the menu does not contain the target item.

The agent has ten possible actions: fixate on any of the 8 items, select the fixated item or declare that the item is not present in the menu (quit). Fixating on an item reveals its semantic relevance to the agent, whereas selecting an item or quitting ends the episode. After each action, the agent observes the state of the environment, represented with two variables: semantic relevances of the observed menu items and the current fixation location. The agent receives a reward after each action. After a fixation action, the agent gets a penalty that corresponds to the time spent for performing the saccade from the previous location and the fixation to the new item. If the agent performs the correct end action, a large reward is given—otherwise an end action results in a large penalty.

The RL agent selects the actions based on the expected cumulative rewards the action allows the agent to receive starting from the current state—also known as Q-value of the state-action pair in RL terminology. These Q-values are learned in the training phase, over 20 million training episodes, using the Q-learning algorithm. To select an action, the agent compares the Q-values of each action in that state (see the Q-table in Fig 4) and chooses the action with the highest value.

Variants

Above we described one model variant reported in Chen et al. [13]. According to the description of the observation data, no items in the menus had more than 3 letters difference in length

Parameter	Description
f_{dur}	Fixation duration
d_{sel}	Time cost for selecting an item (added to the duration of the last fixation of the episode if the user made a selection)
p_{rec}	Probability of recalling the semantic relevances of all of the menu items during the first fixation of the episode
p_{sem}	Probability of perceiving the semantic relevance of menu items above and below of the fixated item

Table 1. Parameters inferred with ABC in Studies 1-3.

[5]. To comply with this and to reduce the complexity of the state space, we assumed that there is no detectable difference in the length of the items. Thus we used the model variant from Chen et al. [13] where the only detectable feature is the semantic similarity to the target item. In Study 2 reported below, we will explore three additions to the model and their effect on the predictions. All model parameters inferred with ABC, across the studies, are listed in Table 1.

EXPERIMENTS AND RESULTS

In the rest of the paper, we show with three case studies how ABC can be used to improve the current modeling practices. All studies use the Chen et al. model [13], and the core problem in all is *inverse modeling*: Given aggregate observation data (task completion times), find the most likely parameter values θ and their distribution, such that the predictions made by the model agree with the observations.

1. **Study 1. ABC compared to manual tuning**: We demonstrate that ABC can improve model fit by inferring parameter values from data, compared to the common practice of setting them manually based on the literature.
2. **Study 2. ABC in model development**: We demonstrate how ABC helps in improving models, by fitting multiple models to same data, exposing differences and anomalies.
3. **Study 3. ABC in modeling individual differences**: We demonstrate how individual models can be fit with ABC, by conditioning the model to individual data.

We use the same dataset as Chen et al. [13], which is a subset of a study reported by Bailly et al. [5] and based on the study design of Nilsen [33]. In the study, a label is shown and the user must click the correct item in a menu with 8 elements as quickly as possible. Items were repeated multiple times to understand practice effects. Multiple menus were used, and target position and absence/presence of target systematically varied. Eye movement data were collected and processed for fixation and saccade durations. Twenty-one paid participants took part in the study. Further details of the study that produced the data are reported in [5].

We implemented the BOLFI algorithm in Python. Parts of the source code were later published within an open-source library for likelihood-free inference [24]. Running the experiments took around one day each on a cluster computer. Further technical details of the experiments and implementation are described in the Appendix.

Study 1. ABC Compared to Manual Tuning

Our aim in the first study was to analyze how much we can improve the predictions made by the model by conditioning values of key parameters on observation data instead of the standard practice of choosing all of the parameter values manually. The case study was chosen to represent the common setting in HCI research where only aggregate data may be available.

We used the model of Chen et al. [13], and compared the parameter values inferred by ABC to those set based on literature in the original paper [13]. We predicted task completion times (TCT) and fixation durations with both models, and compared them with observation data from [5]. For simplicity, we inferred the value of only one parameter θ with ABC, the *fixation duration* f_{dur}. The rest of the model parameter values were set to be identical with the baseline model. The value of this parameter was conditioned on the observed aggregate task completion times (TCT; combined observations from both menu conditions: target absent—referred to as *abs*, target present—referred to as *pre*). Chen et al. [13] set the value of this parameter to 400 ms based on a study by Brumby et al. [8].

Results

As shown in Figure 5, the parameter value inferred with ABC lead to the model predictions matching better to observation data not used for the modelling. This holds both for TCT and fixation duration. In detail, the ground truth aggregated TCT was 0.92 s (std 0.38 s). The manually fit model predicted 1.49 s (std 0.68 s), whereas the ABC fit model predicted 0.93 s (std 0.40 s). For predictions, we used the maximum a posteriori (MAP) value predicted by ABC, which was 244 ms for fixation duration (detail not shown). This corresponds to values often encountered in e.g. reading tasks [40].

In summary, inferring the fixation duration parameter value using ABC lead to improved predictions, compared to setting the parameter value manually based on literature. The inferred parameter value was also reasonable based on literature.

Observations on the Resulting Models

A closer inspection of predictions made by the models exposed two problematic issues which led to improvements in Study 2. The first issue is that while the aggregate TCT predictions were accurate, and all predictions with ABC were better compared to manual tuning, even ABC-fitted predictions were not reasonable when split to sub-cases according to whether the target was present in the menu or not. This is clearly visible in Figure 5 (rows two and three), where we notice that the predicted TCT when target is absent is actually around four to six times as long as the actual user behavior.

The second issue concerns the search strategies predicted by the model. Chen et al. [13] showed that their model was able to learn a behavior strategy, where the agent would look first at the topmost item, and second at the 5th item, which was

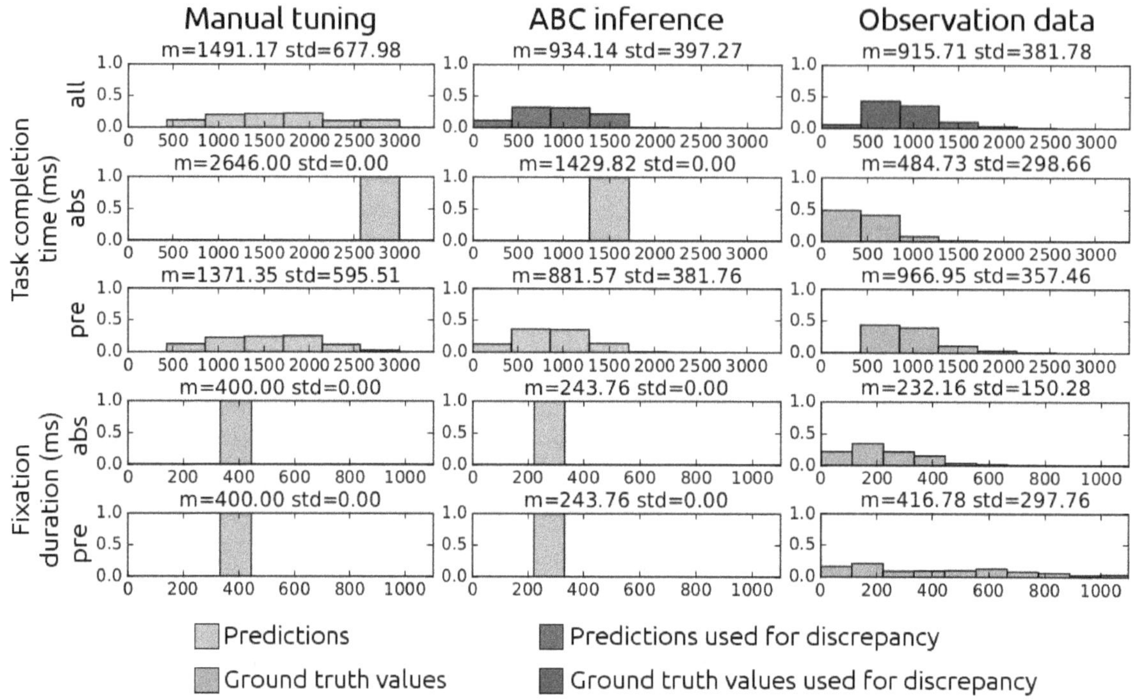

Figure 5. Comparison of manual tuning to ABC inference (Study 1). Predictions made by conditioning parameter values on both aggregate-level observed data and prior knowledge (ABC inference; blue bars in the middle column) agree better with observation data not seen by the model (orange bars on the right column) than predictions made by setting parameter values manually based on literature (Manual tuning; blue bars in the left column). ABC searched for parameter values that resulted in small discrepancy between the model predictions (green) and observed aggregate-level data (brown). ***Left column*****: Manual tuning: all parameter values were set based on literature and manual tuning.** ***Center column*****: ABC inference: the value of f_{dur} has been conditioned on observation data using ABC.** ***Right column*****: Observation data (ground truth) from Bailly et al. [5].** ***All*****: Aggregated data from both conditions.** ***Abs*****: Data from when target was absent from the menu.** ***Pre*****: Data from when target was present in the menu.**

the first item of the second semantic group. This was seen as a clear spike on the fifth item in the "proportion of gazes to target" feature. However, not every attempt to replicate this result succeeded (Fig. 6), and similar variation in predicted strategies was observed with the ABC-fitted model as well[5].

Our conclusion is that there likely exist multiple behavior strategies that are almost equally optimal, and the RL algorithm may then find different local optima in different realizations. This is possible, as Q-learning is guaranteed to find the globally optimal strategy only given an infinite amount of learning samples; with only finite samples, this is not guaranteed. Because of this issue with the inference of the behavioral strategies, we do not discuss in detail the inferred strategies, but only report results that we were able to repeat reliably.

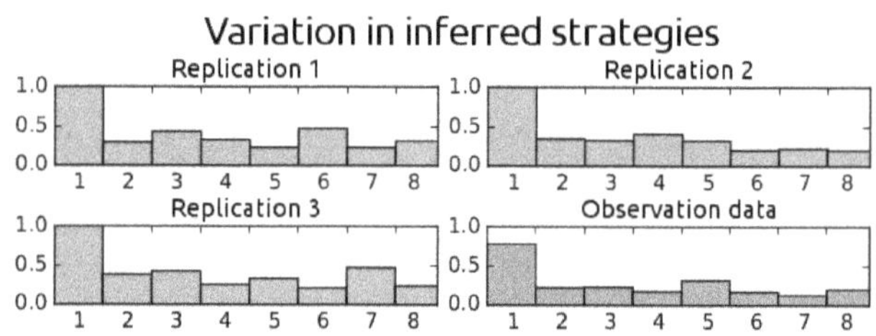

Figure 6. Study 1: Repeated execution of the Chen et al. [13] model yields variations in search patterns. None of the three independent realizations (Replication 1-3) was able to reproduce the noticeable spike on the 5th item (i.e., the first item of the second semantic group) in the Observation data. The bar charts illustrate average proportions of *gazes to target* in search episodes, as a function of the target location. Larger proportions indicate that targets at that location are on average found earlier, as fewer gazes to non-target items are required.

Study 2: ABC in Model Development

We next demonstrate how ABC can be used in the model improvement cycle, where new models are proposed and compared. As a baseline, we start with the model introduced in Study 1, to which we add features to fix the issues we observed in Study 1. We show that with ABC multiple different models can be conditioned to the same observation data, in order to compare their predictions and (compatible) parameter estimates. Doing the same manually would be very laborious.

The model variants we propose are as follows:

- **Variant 1: Chen et al. [13] model + selection latency**: The agent incurs a delay d_{sel} when selecting an item.
- **Variant 2: Variant 1 + immediate menu recognition**: The agent is able to recognize the menu based on the first item with probability p_{recall}.
- **Variant 3: Variant 2 + larger foveated area**: The agent can perceive the semantic relevance of the neighboring

[5] The only technical difference between the original vs. our implementation was that in the original [13] Q-learning was performed on a predetermined set of 10,000 menu realizations, whereas we generated a new menu for every training session. The original implementation thus converged slightly faster, as it explored a smaller part of the state space.

items (above and below the fixated item) through peripheral vision with probability p_{sem}.

Variant 1: We first observed that both the TCT and recorded fixation duration are longer when the target item is present. We hypothesized that the user might have had to spend some time confirming her judgment of the target item and physically making the selection using the pointer. To allow the model to capture this behavior, we added an additional delay, d_{sel}, for the selection action. For example, the mathematical model of Bailly et al. [5] implements a similar selection latency.

Variant 2: We observed that some of the users were able to decide that the target item was not present in the menu just using one fixation on the menu. Our hypothesis was that the users were able to memorize some of the menus, allowing them to naturally finish the task much faster when they recalled the menu layout. To capture this behavior, we allowed the agent to instantly observe the full menu during the first fixation, with probability p_{rec}.

Variant 3: We also observed in Study 1 that the inferred number of fixations was in both cases larger than in the observation data. The models predicted on average 6.0 fixations when the target was absent (ground truth was 1.9) and 3.1 when target was present (ground truth was 2.2). Our hypothesis was that the user might have observed the semantic relevance of neighboring items using peripheral vision, allowing her to finish the task with a smaller number of fixations. The model of Chen et al. [13] had a peripheral vision component but it only applied to size-related information (shape relevance). Our hypothesis is also justified by the experiment setup of Bailly et al. [5], where the neighboring items do fall within the fovea (2 degrees), thus making it physiologically possible for the user to observe the semantic relevance of the neighboring items. To capture this behavior, we allowed the agent to observe the semantic relevance of the items above and below the fixated item in the menu with probability p_{sem} (independently for the item above and below).

Implementation: In order to be able to do inference on these new parameters, we only needed to make small additions to the simulator code: add an interface for setting the values of these new parameters and implement the described changes in the model. On the ABC side, we only described the names and priors of the new parameters, and increased the amount of locations where to simulate. More locations are justified as each new parameter increases the size of the parameter space that needs to be searched. We also noticed in Study 1 that the models were not able to replicate the behavior well in both menu conditions (target present, absent) at the same time. For this reason, we make a small adjustment to the discrepancy function, so that the TCT is compared in both menu conditions separately. This should allow the models to better replicate the full observed behavior. Further details are provided in the Appendix.

Results

The predictions made by the different models, compared to the observation data, are visualized in Figure 7. With increased model complexity, we also see increasing agreement of the predictions with the observation data. This is partly expected, as more complex models are in general able to fit any dataset better. However, with the use of priors, we are able to regularize the parameter values to reasonable ranges, and thus avoid over-fitting the models to the data.

The baseline model was not able to predict the behavior of the user very well on many of the variables. The MAP value for f_{dur} (fixation duration) was 210 ms. The TCTs predicted by the baseline model were [1500 ms (abs), 770 ms (pre)], whereas the ground truth was [490 ms (abs), 970 ms (pre)]. The predicted fixation duration was 210 ms, which is still reasonable, although on the low side, compared to the observed means [230 ms (abs), 420 ms (pre)]. Furthermore, the predicted number of fixations on items on the menu was [6.0 (abs), 3.1 (pre)], whereas the users only performed [1.9 (abs), 2.2 (pre)] fixations.

Variant 1 improved predictions over the baseline. The MAP value for normal f_{dur} was 170 ms and for d_{sel} (selection delay) 320 ms. The predicted TCTs were [1300 ms (abs), 1000 ms (pre)], which is already a very reasonable estimate when target is present, although still far from the truth when the target is absent. The predicted fixation durations (now with the selection delay factored in) were [170 ms (abs), 270 ms (pre)], which is an improvement over the baseline in the present condition, but not on the target absent condition. The predicted numbers of fixations were nearly identical to baseline.

Variant 2 again improved predictions over both the baseline and Variant 1. The MAP value for f_{dur} was 290 ms, for d_{sel} was 300 ms, and for p_{rec} (probability of recall) was 87 %. The predicted TCTs were [570 ms (abs), 980 ms (pre)], which is the first time we have been able to predict a lower TCT for the target absent case. However, the variation in TCT when target is absent is quite large; the predicted standard deviation was 660 ms, whereas the ground truth was 300 ms. The predicted fixation durations were [290 ms (abs), 430 ms (pre)], which is already close to the ground truth in the target present condition. The predicted numbers of fixations were [1.8 (abs), 2.1 (pre)], which is a considerable improvement over previous estimates.

Variant 3 provided still slight improvements over previous results. The MAP value for f_{dur} was 280 ms, for d_{sel} was 290 ms, for p_{rec} was 69 %, and for p_{sem} (the probability of observing the semantic similarity with peripheral vision) was 93 %. The predicted TCTs were [640 ms (abs), 1000 ms (pre)], which is slightly further from the observations than with Variant 2. However, the variation in the distributions is closer to observed values than with Variant 2 (the discrepancy measure led ABC to minimize both the difference in mean and in standard deviation at the same time, details in Appendix). The predicted fixation durations were similar as with Variant 2. The predicted numbers of fixations were [2.0 (abs), 2.2 (pre)], which is slightly better than with Variant 2.

We conclude that we were able to fit multiple model variants to the same observation data, and make meaningful comparisons between the different models because of this. We observed that the quality of the predictions increased when we added our additional assumptions to the model, which was expected

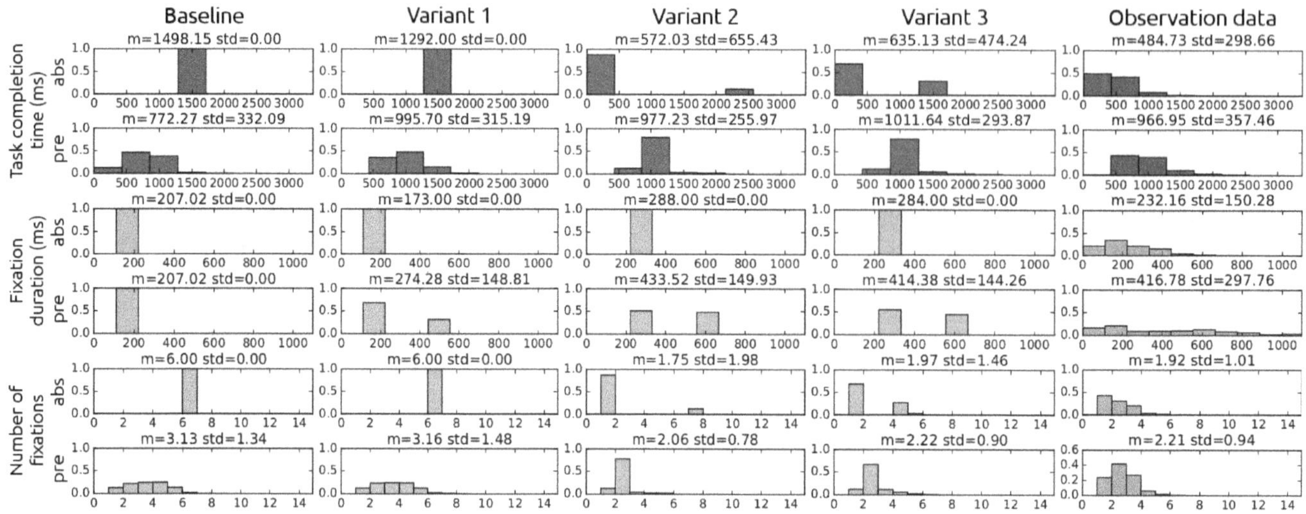

Figure 7. Study 2: ABC exposes how changes to the model (Variants 1-3) result in changes to the predictions when parameter values are conditioned to empirical data. *Baseline*: Same model as in Study 1, but now conditioned on observed behavior in both target conditions (absent, present) at the same time. *Variant 1*: Selection delay feature added to baseline (parameter d_{sel}). *Variant 2*: Menu recall feature added to Variant 1 (parameter p_{rec}). *Variant 3*: Peripheral vision feature added to Variant 2 (parameter p_{sem}). *Observation data*: Same as in Study 1. Reported results are with the MAP parameter values. *Color coding:* Same as in Figure 5. *Abs*: Data from when target was absent from the menu. *Pre*: Data from when target was present in the menu.

as the models became more flexible, but also provided evidence that these features probably reflect actual user behavior as well. Furthermore, ABC was found useful in hypothesis comparison, as we avoided manually trying out a large number of different parameter values manually to find values that lead to reasonable predictions.

Study 3. ABC and Individual Differences

Most modeling research in HCI aims at understanding general patterns of user behavior. However, understanding how individuals differ is important for both theoretical and practical reasons. On the one hand, even seemingly simple interfaces like input devices show large variability in user behavior. On the other hand, adaptive user interfaces and ability-based design rely on differentiating users based on their knowledge and capabilities.

Our final case looks at the problem of individual differences in inverse modeling. In Study 3 we select a group of users and fit an individual model for each of these users. We then compare how good predictions these individual models are able to produce, compared to the same model fit with the data from all of the users in the dataset (population level model).

We selected a representative set of 5 users for Study 3. We first selected all users from the dataset of whom there were 15 or more observations in each menu condition (target absent, present), leaving 11 users. We then ordered the users based on their difference in TCT to population mean, summed from both menu conditions. To get a good distribution of different users, for this experiment we selected the users who were the furthest (S8), third most furthest (S5), and fifth most furthest away (S23) from the population mean – as well as the users who were the closest (S19) and third most closest (S18) to the population mean.

The model we used in this study, for both individual and population level modeling, corresponded to Variant 3 from the previous section. To simplify the analysis, here we only infer the values of two of the parameters for each user, keeping the rest fixed. The inferred parameters were p_{rec} and p_{sem}. Based on the Study 2, it seemed to us that there was less variation in f_{dur} and d_{sel}, whereas the use of memory and acuity of peripheral vision could plausibly vary more between individuals. We fixed the value of f_{dur} to 280 ms and d_{sel} to 290 ms, according to the MAP estimate in Study 2.

For each of the selected users, we collected all of the observations of that user from the dataset, and conditioned the parameter values of the individual model for that user on that small dataset. The parameter values of the population level model were the same as inferred in Study 2 for Variant 3. The accuracy of the predictions made for each user by their individual model was compared with the predictions made by the population level model. In the comparison, we considered the predicted TCTs and numbers of fixations at each condition to the observed values, and report the magnitude (absolute value) of the prediction errors.

Results

The predicted MAP parameter values are collected in Table 2. The individual model parameter values deviate around ± 10 percentage points from the population level model parameter values, which is a reasonable magnitude for individual variation.

We calculated the magnitude of prediction errors for all of the models by taking the absolute difference in model predicted means and observed data means for each feature. The prediction errors of the population level model on the population data and on individual user data are shown in Figure 8. Overall, the prediction errors with a population level model tend to be larger for individual users than they are for the whole population. This shows that population level models that are good for explaining population level dynamics may perform badly

Model	p_{rec}	p_{sem}
S5	61 %	89 %
S8	54 %	87 %
S18	70 %	96 %
S19	76 %	91 %
S23	73 %	92 %
POP	69 %	93 %

Table 2. MAP estimates of parameter values for individual models (S5, S8, S18, S19, S23) and the population level model (POP) in Study 3.

when used for explaining subject level dynamics. Furthermore, as could be expected, prediction errors with a population level model tend to be larger for users who differ more from the population mean. This presents a clear motivation for developing individual models, as they could help to understand subject level dynamics, especially regarding users who differ from the population mean.

The prediction errors of the individual models on individual user data are shown in Figure 9. Overall we observe a rather consistent quality in the predictions made by the individual user models. The only exception is user S8, who was the furthest away from the mean. It is likely that user S8 might have performed the task overall in a very different way from the rest of the users. For example, the number of fixations taken by this user when target was absent was 3.1, but only 2.7 when the target was present. This could indicate that the user was unusually careful in examining the menu before declaring that the target was not present.

Improvements in prediction error magnitude when changing from population level model to an individual model are shown in Figure 10. The overall trend is that individual user models improve prediction quality, although not always in all parts. With most users the prediction errors decreased in at least three of the four predicted features.

We conclude that by using ABC we were able to fit CR models to data from individual users, and that the resulting individual models were able to produce better predictions than a population level model fitted to the whole participant pool. Performing this modeling task would not have been possible with just choosing the values based on literature, as such information tends to only apply for population level models. On the other hand, choosing the parameter values manually for each user would have required a considerable amount of manual labour, which ABC was able to automate. Moreover, inverse modeling helped us expose a behavioral pattern that was not well explained by the model (user S8).

DISCUSSION AND CONCLUSION

We have demonstrated that ABC is applicable for inverse modeling of computationally rational models of complex human behavior based on aggregate behavioural data.

We highlighted advantages ABC has over alternative methods for inferring model parameter values in HCI. First, the method is applicable for a wide range of models, as it relies on only few assumptions. Second, the parameter value estimates are conditioned both on the observation data, as well as any prior

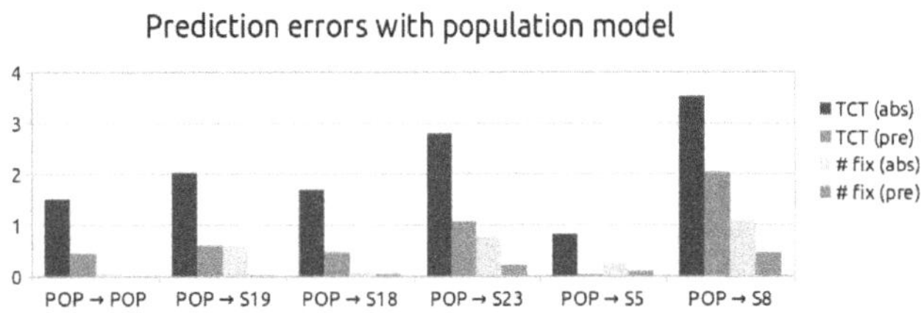

Figure 8. Study 3: *Leftmost:* Prediction error for population level data with population level model (POP). *Right:* Prediction errors for individual users (from most to least similar to population mean) with population level model. Unit of TCT is 100 ms, unit of number of fixations is 1 fixation.

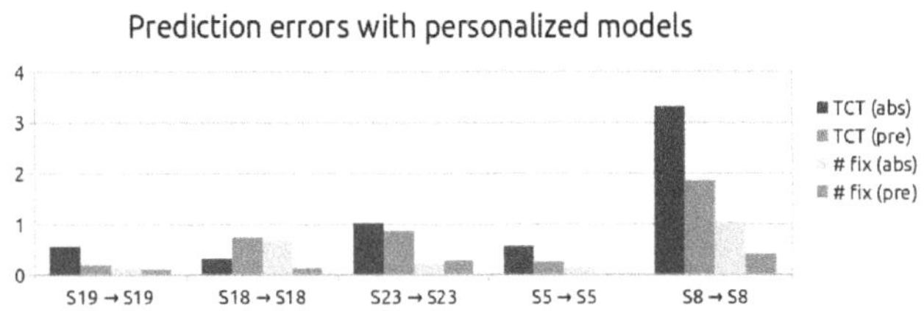

Figure 9. Study 3: Prediction errors for individual users (from most to least similar to population mean) with models conditioned on observations of the individual user. Unit of TCT is 100 ms, unit of number of fixations is 1 fixation.

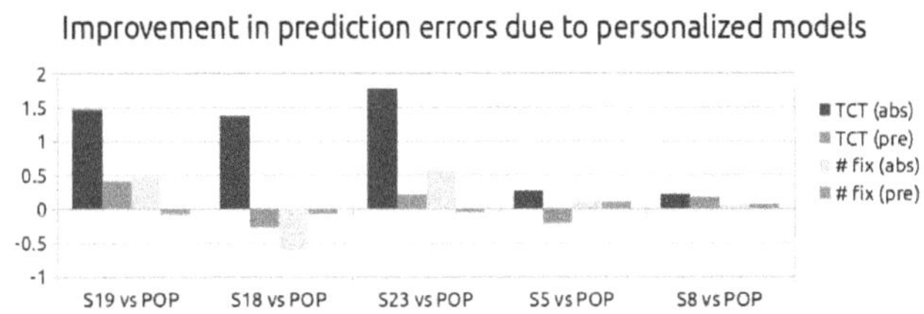

Figure 10. Study 3: Decrease in prediction error when using individual models (Figure 9) instead of the population level model (Figure 8) for individual users (from most to least similar to population mean). Unit of TCT is 100 ms, unit of number of fixations is 1 fixation.

knowledge the researcher might have of the situation. This way over-fitting the model to the observation data may be avoided, which could happen if we had only tried to maximize the ability of the model to replicate the data. Third, the inference process produces a full posterior distribution over the parameter space, instead of only a point estimate, allowing for better analysis of the reliability of the estimates.

In Study 1 we demonstrated that ABC was able to achieve better model fit compared to setting the model parameter value based on literature and manual tuning. We also identified problems with the existing state-of-the-art model for visual search [13], related to both the quality of the predictions and convergence issues.

In Study 2 we demonstrated the applicability of ABC in model comparison by fitting four different models to the same dataset and comparing the resulting predictions and inferred model parameter values. We also proposed improvements to the existing state-of-the-art model, and demonstrated that they resulted in improved quality of predictions.

In Study 3 we demonstrated that with ABC it is possible to fit one of the models from Study 2 to data collected from a single individual, thus creating an individual model. We further demonstrated that the predictions made by the individual models were better compared to a model fit to a large amount of population-level data.

Together, these contributions help address a substantial problem in understanding interactive behaviour that has been evident in HCI and Human Factors for more than 15 years [27]. The problem is how to estimate model parameter values given the strategic flexibility of the human cognitive system [22, 27, 28]. One of the consequences of strategic flexibility has been to make it difficult to test theories of the underlying information processing architecture; because behaviour that is merely strategic can be mistakenly taken as evidence for one or other architectural theory or set of architectural parameters [22]. ABC, and inverse modeling methods in general, addresses this problem by establishing a principled mathematical relationship between the observed behaviour and the model parameter values.

In the future, inverse modeling might provide a general framework for implementing adaptive interfaces that are able to interpret user behavior so as to determine individual preferences, capabilities, and intentions, rather than merely mapping actions directly to effects. In summary, we consider ABC to provide ample opportunities for widespread research activity on both HCI applications, and as a core inference methodology for solving the inverse problems arising in research.

ACKNOWLEDGMENTS

This work has been supported by the Academy of Finland (Finnish Centre of Excellence in Computational Inference Research COIN, and grants 294238, 292334) and TEKES (Re:Know). AH was supported by the EU-funded SPEEDD project (FP7-ICT 619435). AO was funded by the European Research Council (ERC) under the European Union's Horizon 2020 research and innovation programme (grant agreement 637991). Computational resources were provided by the Aalto Science IT project.

APPENDIX: ABC BOLFI IMPLEMENTATION

We implemented BOLFI in Python with the following details. We used a Gaussian process (GP) model from the GPy Python library to model the discrepancy. The kernel was Matern 3/2 with variance 0.01, scale 0.1, and noise variance 0.05. The first N_{init} sample locations were drawn from the quasi-random Sobol sequence (equal to the number of CPU cores allocated for the job). The remaining sample locations were decided as follows. We created a function that computed the lower confidence bound (LCB) for the GP: $LCB(x) = \mu_{GP}(x) - b\sigma_{GP}(x)$. We used $b = 1.0$. For asynchronous parallel sampling, we needed a way to acquire multiple locations that were reasonable, but also sufficiently well apart. For this purpose we created a function that calculated the sum of radial-basis function kernels that were centered at the locations P currently being sampled: $R(x) = \sum_{p \in P} a \exp((x-p)^2/l)$. We used $a = 0.04$, $l = 0.04$. The acquisition function for the next sample location was $A(x) = \min_x[LCB(x) + R(x)]$. Additionally, there was a 10 % chance of the location being drawn from the prior instead of the acquisition function.

Study 1: The model was trained with Q-learning for 20 million training episodes, after which we simulated 10,000 episodes for visualizing the behavior predicted by the trained model. The observation data has the target item absent in 10 % of the sessions, but in the Chen et al. paper [13] it was assumed that it was absent in 50 % of the cases. We tried both splits in training data (10% and 50%), but did not find a large overall difference in the results. In the subsequent experiments, we also used the 10 % split, as it might remove a possible source of bias. Our prior for f_{dur} was a truncated Gaussian distribution with mean 300 ms, std 100 ms, min 0 ms, max 600 ms. The prior was set with the intuition that values between 200 ms and 400 ms should be likely ($\pm$ 1 std), whereas values between 100 ms and 500 ms could still be accepted if the data really supported those values ($\pm$ 2 std). BOLFI computed discrepancy at 100 locations using 40 CPU cores. Of the 10,000 simulated episodes, we only used the first 2,500 for calculating the discrepancy. This was done as it is more sensible to compare datasets of similar size. Altogether the model fitting took 20 h (in wall-clock time), each individual sample taking 6 h. The discrepancy was based on the mean and standard deviation of the aggregate task completion time. It was constructed so that it would fit the mean accurately (L2-penalty) and the standard deviation with lower priority (L1-penalty). The formula was:

$$d = a \times (mean_{obs} - mean_{sim})^2 + b \times |std_{obs} - std_{sim}|,$$

where we used $a = b = 10^{-6}$ for a reasonable scale and the used feature was the aggregate TCT.

Study 2: Our prior for d_{sel} was a truncated Gaussian distribution with mean 300 ms, std 300 ms, min 0 ms, max 1000 ms. 300 ms was selected as our initial best guess for the delay, as the second peak in observed fixation duration when target was present (Figure 5) was around 600 ms and we thought it likely that the normal fixation duration was around 300 ms. However, as we had relatively high uncertainty about this, we chose a quite flat prior. Our prior for p_{rec} and p_{sem} were uniform distributions with [min 0, max 1]. Uninformative priors were used as we were uncertain about the possible true values of these parameters. The discrepancy was the average of $d(TCT_{pre})$ and $d(TCT_{abs})$. As the parameter space sizes varied, we chose the number of samples and CPUs for each case separately. Baseline: 100 samples, 40 CPUs (20 h). Variant 1: 200 samples, 80 CPUs (16 h). Variant 2: 400 samples, 80 CPUs (30 h). Variant 3: 600 samples, 100 CPUs (37 h).

Study 3: The prior for p_{rec} was a truncated Gaussian distribution with [mean 69 %, std 20 %, min 0 %, max 100 %]. The prior for p_{sem} was similar but with mean 93 %. The priors were based on the knowledge gained from Study 2, and thus centered on the MAP estimate of Variant 3, but were reasonably flat to allow for individual variation. The discrepancy was the same as in Study 2. Out of the total 10,000 simulated sessions, we used the first 200 for calculating the discrepancy to match the individual dataset sizes. For each of the users, we computed 200 samples using 60 CPUs (22 h each).

REFERENCES

1. John R. Anderson. 1991. Is human cognition adaptive? *Behavioral and Brain Sciences* 14, 3 (1991), 471–485. DOI: http://dx.doi.org/10.1017/S0140525X00070801
2. John R. Anderson, Michael Matessa, and Christian Lebiere. 1997. ACT-R: A theory of higher level cognition and its relation to visual attention. *Human–Computer Interaction* 12, 4 (1997), 439–462. DOI: http://dx.doi.org/10.1207/s15327051hci1204_5
3. Leif Azzopardi. 2014. Modelling interaction with economic models of search. In *Proceedings of the 37th International ACM SIGIR Conference on Research & Development in Information Retrieval*. ACM, 3–12. DOI: http://dx.doi.org/10.1145/2600428.2609574
4. Myroslav Bachynskyi, Gregorio Palmas, Antti Oulasvirta, and Tino Weinkauf. 2015. Informing the design of novel input methods with muscle coactivation clustering. *ACM Transactions on Computer-Human Interaction* 21, 6 (2015), 30:1–30:25. DOI: http://dx.doi.org/10.1145/2687921
5. Gilles Bailly, Antti Oulasvirta, Duncan P. Brumby, and Andrew Howes. 2014. Model of visual search and selection time in linear menus. In *Proceedings of the 32nd Annual ACM Conference on Human Factors in Computing Systems*. ACM, 3865–3874. DOI: http://dx.doi.org/10.1145/2556288.2557093
6. Robert W. Baloh, Andrew W. Sills, Warren E. Kumley, and Vicente Honrubia. 1975. Quantitative measurement of saccade amplitude, duration, and velocity. *Neurology* 25, 11 (1975), 1065–1065. DOI: http://dx.doi.org/10.1212/WNL.25.11.1065
7. James L. Beck and Ka-Veng Yuen. 2004. Model selection using response measurements: Bayesian probabilistic approach. *Journal of Engineering Mechanics* 130, 2 (2004), 192–203. DOI: http://dx.doi.org/10.1061/(ASCE)0733-9399(2004)130:2(192)
8. Duncan P. Brumby, Anna L. Cox, Jacqueline Chung, and Byron Fernandes. 2014. How does knowing what you are looking for change visual search behavior?. In *Proceedings of the SIGCHI Conference on Human Factors in Computing Systems*. ACM, 3895–3898. DOI: http://dx.doi.org/10.1145/2556288.2557064
9. Michael D. Byrne. 2001. ACT-R/PM and menu selection: Applying a cognitive architecture to HCI. *International Journal of Human–Computer Studies* 55, 1 (2001), 41–84. DOI: http://dx.doi.org/10.1006/ijhc.2001.0469
10. Colin Camerer. 2003. *Behavioral game theory: Experiments in strategic interaction*. Princeton University Press.
11. Stuart K. Card, Allen Newell, and Thomas P. Moran. 1983. *The psychology of human–computer interaction*. L. Erlbaum Associates Inc.
12. Nick Chater and Mike Oaksford. 1999. Ten years of the rational analysis of cognition. *Trends in Cognitive Sciences* 3, 2 (1999), 57–65. DOI: http://dx.doi.org/10.1016/S1364-6613(98)01273-X
13. Xiuli Chen, Gilles Bailly, Duncan P. Brumby, Antti Oulasvirta, and Andrew Howes. 2015. The Emergence of Interactive Behavior: A Model of Rational Menu Search. In *Proceedings of the 33rd Annual ACM Conference on Human Factors in Computing Systems*. ACM, 4217–4226. DOI: http://dx.doi.org/10.1145/2702123.2702483
14. Andy Cockburn, Per O. Kristensson, Jason Alexander, and Shumin Zhai. 2007. Hard lessons: Effort-inducing interfaces benefit spatial learning. In *Proceedings of the SIGCHI Conference on Human Factors in Computing Systems*. ACM, 1571–1580. DOI: http://dx.doi.org/10.1145/1240624.1240863
15. Katalin Csilléry, Michael G.B. Blum, Oscar E. Gaggiotti, and Olivier François. 2010. Approximate Bayesian computation (ABC) in practice. *Trends in Ecology & Evolution* 25, 7 (2010), 410–418. DOI: http://dx.doi.org/10.1016/j.tree.2010.04.001
16. Wai-Tat Fu and Peter Pirolli. 2007. SNIF-ACT: A cognitive model of user navigation on the World Wide Web. *Human–Computer Interaction* 22, 4 (2007), 355–412. http://www.tandfonline.com/doi/abs/10.1080/07370020701638806
17. Samuel J. Gershman, Eric J. Horvitz, and Joshua B. Tenenbaum. 2015. Computational rationality: A converging paradigm for intelligence in brains, minds, and machines. *Science* 349, 6245 (2015), 273–278. DOI: http://dx.doi.org/10.1126/science.aac6076
18. Michael U. Gutmann and Jukka Corander. 2016. Bayesian optimization for likelihood-free inference of simulator-based statistical models. *Journal of Machine Learning Research* 17, 125 (2016), 1–47. http://jmlr.org/papers/v17/15-017.html
19. Tim Halverson and Anthony J. Hornof. 2011. A computational model of "active vision" for visual search in human–computer interaction. *Human–Computer Interaction* 26, 4 (2011), 285–314. DOI: http://dx.doi.org/10.1080/07370024.2011.625237
20. Mary Hayhoe and Dana Ballard. 2014. Modeling task control of eye movements. *Current Biology* 24, 13 (2014), R622–R628. DOI: http://dx.doi.org/10.1016/j.cub.2014.05.020
21. Anthony J. Hornof. 2004. Cognitive strategies for the visual search of hierarchical computer displays. *Human–Computer Interaction* 19, 3 (2004), 183–223. DOI: http://dx.doi.org/10.1207/s15327051hci1903_1
22. Andrew Howes, Richard L. Richard L Lewis, and Alonso Vera. 2009. Rational adaptation under task and processing constraints: Implications for testing theories of cognition and action. *Psychological Review* 116, 4 (2009), 717–751. DOI: http://dx.doi.org/10.1037/a0017187
23. Richard J. Jagacinski and John M. Flach. 2003. *Control theory for humans: Quantitative approaches to modeling performance*. CRC Press.

24. Antti Kangasrääsiö, Jarno Lintusaari, Kusti Skytén, Marko Järvenpää, Henri Vuollekoski, Michael Gutmann, Aki Vehtari, Jukka Corander, and Samuel Kaski. 2016. ELFI: Engine for likelihood-free inference (extended abstract). In *NIPS 2016 Workshop on Advances in Approximate Bayesian Inference*. `https://github.com/hiit/elfi`

25. David E. Kieras and Anthony J. Hornof. 2014. Towards accurate and practical predictive models of active-vision-based visual search. In *Proceedings of the 32nd Annual ACM Conference on Human Factors in Computing Systems*. ACM, 3875–3884. DOI: `http://dx.doi.org/10.1145/2556288.2557324`

26. David E. Kieras and David E. Meyer. 1997. An overview of the EPIC architecture for cognition and performance with application to human–computer interaction. *Human–Computer Interaction* 12, 4 (1997), 391–438. DOI:`http://dx.doi.org/10.1207/s15327051hci1204_4`

27. David E. Kieras, David E. Meyer, James A. Ballas, and Erick J. Lauber. 2000. Modern computational perspectives on executive mental processes and cognitive control: Where to from here? *Control of Cognitive Processes: Attention and Performance XVIII* (2000), 681–712.

28. Richard L. Lewis, Andrew Howes, and Satinder Singh. 2014. Computational rationality: Linking mechanism and behavior through bounded utility maximization. *Topics in Cognitive Science* 6, 2 (2014), 279–311. DOI: `http://dx.doi.org/10.1111/tops.12086`

29. Craig S. Miller and Roger W. Remington. 2004. Modeling information navigation: Implications for information architecture. *Human–Computer Interaction* 19, 3 (2004), 225–271. DOI: `http://dx.doi.org/10.1207/s15327051hci1903_2`

30. Lewis R. L. Howes A. Myers, C. W. 2013. Bounded optimal state estimation and control in visual search: explaining distractor ratio effects. In *Proceedings of the 35th Annual Conference of the Cognitive Science Society*. Cognitive Science Society.

31. Jay I. Myung and Mark A. Pitt. 2016. Model comparison in psychology. In *The Stevens' Handbook of Experimental Psychology and Cognitive Neuroscience (Fourth Edition), Volume 5: Methodology*. John Wiley & Sons. To appear.

32. Andrew Y. Ng and Stuart J. Russell. 2000. Algorithms for inverse reinforcement learning. In *Proceedings of the Seventeenth International Conference on Machine Learning*. 663–670.

33. Erik Nilsen and Jake Evans. 1999. Exploring the divide between two unified theories of cognition: Modeling visual attention in menu selection. In *CHI'99 Extended Abstracts on Human Factors in Computing Systems*. ACM, 288–289. DOI: `http://dx.doi.org/10.1145/632716.632893`

34. Jose Nunez-Varela and Jeremy L. Wyatt. 2013. Models of gaze control for manipulation tasks. *ACM Transactions on Applied Perception* 10, 4 (2013), 20:1–20:22. DOI: `http://dx.doi.org/10.1145/2536764.2536767`

35. Mike Oaksford and Nick Chater. 1994. A rational analysis of the selection task as optimal data selection. *Psychological Review* 101, 4 (1994), 608–631. DOI: `http://dx.doi.org/10.1037/0033-295X.101.4.608`

36. Stephen J. Payne and Andrew Howes. 2013. Adaptive interaction: A utility maximization approach to understanding human interaction with technology. *Synthesis Lectures on Human-Centered Informatics* 6, 1 (2013), 1–111. DOI: `http://dx.doi.org/10.2200/S00479ED1V01Y201302HCI016`

37. Peter Pirolli. 2005. Rational analyses of information foraging on the web. *Cognitive Science* 29, 3 (2005), 343–373. DOI: `http://dx.doi.org/10.1207/s15516709cog0000_20`

38. Peter Pirolli and Stuart Card. 1999. Information foraging. *Psychological Review* 106, 4 (1999), 643–675. DOI: `http://dx.doi.org/10.1037/0033-295X.106.4.643`

39. Deepak Ramachandran and Eyal Amir. 2007. Bayesian inverse reinforcement learning. In *Proceedings of the Twentieth International Joint Conference on Artificial Intelligence*. 2586–2591.

40. Keith Rayner. 1998. Eye movements in reading and information processing: 20 years of research. *Psychological Bulletin* 124, 3 (1998), 372–422. DOI: `http://dx.doi.org/10.1037/0033-2909.124.3.372`

41. David E. Rumelhart and Donald A. Norman. 1982. Simulating a skilled typist: A study of skilled cognitive-motor performance. *Cognitive Science* 6, 1 (1982), 1–36.

42. Mikael Sunnåker, Alberto G. Busetto, Elina Numminen, Jukka Corander, Matthieu Foll, and Christophe Dessimoz. 2013. Approximate Bayesian computation. *PLoS Computational Biology* 9, 1 (2013), e1002803. DOI: `http://dx.doi.org/10.1371/journal.pcbi.1002803`

43. Richard S. Sutton and Andrew G. Barto. 1998. *Reinforcement learning: An introduction*. MIT press.

44. Yuan-Chi Tseng and Andrew Howes. 2015. The adaptation of visual search to utility, ecology and design. *International Journal of Human–Computer Studies* 80 (2015), 45–55. DOI: `http://dx.doi.org/10.1016/j.ijhcs.2015.03.005`

45. Brian D. Ziebart, Andrew Maas, J. Andrew Bagnell, and Anind K. Dey. 2008. Maximum entropy inverse reinforcement learning. In *Proceedings of the Association for the Advancement of Artificial Intelligence Conference on Artificial Intelligence*. 1433–1438.

Effects of Frequency Distribution on Linear Menu Performance

Wanyu Liu[1,2] Gilles Bailly[1,3] Andrew Howes[4]
[1] LTCI, CNRS, Telecom ParisTech, Université Paris-Saclay, Paris, France
[2] LRI, Univ. Paris-Sud, CNRS, Inria, Université Paris-Saclay, Paris, France
[3] Sorbonne Univeristés, UPMC Univ Paris 06, CNRS, ISIR, Paris, France
[4] School of Computer Science,University of Birmingham, Birmingham, UK
wanyu.liu@telecom-paristech.fr, Gilles.Bailly@upmc.fr, HowesA@bham.ac.uk

ABSTRACT
While it is well known that menu usage follows a Zipfian distribution, there has been little interest in the impact of menu item frequency distribution on user's behavior. In this note, we explore the effects of frequency distribution on average menu performance as well as individual item performance. We compare three frequency distributions of menu item usage: Uniform; Zipfian with s=1 and Zipfian with s=2. The results show that (1) user's behavior is sensitive to different frequency distributions at both menu and item level; (2) individual item selection time depends on, not only its frequency, but also the frequency of other items in the menu. Finally, we discuss how these findings might have impacts on menu design, empirical studies and menu modelling.

ACM Classification Keywords
H.5.2 [User Interfaces]: Interaction styles.

Author Keywords
Menus; User performance; Frequency distribution.

INTRODUCTION
Linear menus remain the primary graphical widget in desktop applications and consumer electronics for selecting commands. As a consequence many scientific efforts have been devoted to better understand user's behavior in linear menus[2, 5, 6] and how the menu features impact performance. For instance, several empirical studies described how menu length, menu organization or target position affect performance [4, 21].

Beyond menu features, the behavior of the user is also constrained by, and adapted to, the statistical structure of the environment [22, 23]. One important, but neglected, statistical property of menu use, is that the natural ecology of tasks tends to result in menu items being selected according to a Zipfian distribution, i.e., a highly skewed distribution with the most frequent items tending to be selected far more frequently than the long-tail distribution of low frequency items. While it is well known [6, 8, 9], the consequences of the distribution for behavior have not been systematically investigated. Indeed, many previous studies rely either on a Uniform distribution [2, 4, 5, 16, 20] when comparing selection time, or a variant of a Zipfian distribution [1, 11] when focusing on the average menu selection time. However, it is unclear if these observations hold when given a different, and more ecologically plausible, frequency distribution.

In this note, we investigate the effects of frequency distribution on both individual *Item* selection time and *Menu* selection time[1]. To achieve this, we compare the performance of 2 Zipfian distributions ($s = 1$ & $s = 2$) and the Uniform distribution as a baseline by carefully manipulating the item frequency factor. Our results show that frequency distributions affect user behavior at both the menu level and item level but in an opposite manner. The most surprising result is that individual item selection time does not only depend on its own frequency but also the frequency of other items in the menu. We then discuss how these effects might be of relevance to efforts to design more learnable interfaces and/or training regimes for intermediate skill-level users [3].

THE UNIFORM AND ZIPFIAN DISTRIBUTIONS
While uniform distribution does not reflect menu usage in real worlds [8, 9, 10, 12], it has been used in many menu studies [2, 4, 5, 16, 20] because it is easy to experimentally control. In contrast, Zipfian distribution is more difficult to control in spite of better modelling item frequency distribution in common applications [6, 8, 9]. It describes the fact that few items are selected very frequently while many items are seldom used. A Zipfian distribution is defined as:

$$f(k;s,N) = \frac{1/k^s}{\sum_{n=1}^{N}(1/n^s)} \quad (1)$$

Where N is the number of elements, $k \in [1,N]$ is the rank of the considered element (with $k = 1$ the element with the highest frequency) and s is the value of the exponent characterizing the distribution. For instance, for a menu with 12 items ($N = 12$) and $s = 1$, it means that the most frequent item ($k = 1$) is selected 12 times more often than the least frequent item. Therefore,

[1] We define *Menu* selection time as the average selection time for the whole menu including all the items. *Item* selection time is the selection time for an individual item.

CHI 2017, May 06-11, 2017, Denver, CO, USA

DOI: http://dx.doi.org/10.1145/3025453.3025707

Frequency distribution	*Selection count for 12 items (decreasing order)*	*Distance (R^2) | d*
Uniform	**6**, **4**, 4, 4, 4, 4, 4, 4, **3**, 3, 3, **2**	n/a | 0.26
Zipfian s=1	15, **6**, 5, **4**, **3**, 3, **2**, 2, 2, 1, 1, 1	>0.99 | 0.14
Zipfian s=2	28, **6**, **4**, **3**, **2**, 1, 1, 0, 0, 0, 0, 0	>0.99 | 0.19

Table 1. Distribuions used in the experiment: Names, multiset of item frequencies, the r-squared and pairwise distance. These distributions have 4 item frequencies in common ($C = 4$) marked in bold.

it may trigger some confound effects if the experiment is not delicately designed, e.g., a target item might be faster to select because it is located on the top of the menu or because it is more frequently selected than other items due to practice.

It results that Zipfian distribution was only used when (1) comparing the average menu selection time (rather than item selection time) of different menu techniques, or (2) assuming that the layout is similar enough so that the correspondence between item location in the menu and item frequency do not bias the results. For instance, Cockburn et al. [6] compared the *Menu* performance of four linear menu techniques (e.g., split menus or Morphing menus) with a single Zipfian distribution. Other studies used a *variant* of Zipfian distribution [1, 11] where one frequency corresponds to two items (instead of a single item). While this distribution does not have empirical or theoretical foundations, it reduces the complexity of the experimental design by diminishing the impact of the most frequent items on the total performance of the menu technique.

Finally, Sears and Shneiderman [24] as well as Lee and Yoon [18] used a non-uniform distribution (which is not a Zipfian distribution). They show that the frequency distribution has an impact on the choice of the most effective menu technique. For instance, Split menus and Folded menus are more efficient than traditional linear menus when the two or three most frequent items appear respectively more than 30% and 90% of the time. However, these studies did not use a Zipfian distribution "in order to control experimental complexity" [18] and focused only on the average menu selection time rather than item selection time.

The definition of the frequency distribution thus differs between experiments and is rarely manipulated while this factor might have an impact on performance and menu design.

USER STUDY

In this study we primary investigate the effects of FREQUENCY DISTRIBUTION, ITEM FREQUENCY, on both item selection time and menu selection time, but we also control TARGET LOCATION and PRACTICE. The core aspect of the experimental design is the control of the correspondence between TARGET LOCATION in the menu and ITEM FREQUENCY to compare item selection time. To achieve this, we subtly manipulate FREQUENCY DISTRIBUTION so that each distribution has a a subset of items with the same frequency for comparison purpose. To focus on the main effects, we considered a single menu length with 12 items and a single menu organization (Unordered). We now detail the experimental design.

Frequency Distributions and Item Frequency

FREQUENCY DISTRIBUTION. We considered 3 frequency distributions: two *Zipfian* distributions with $s = 1$ and $s = 2$ as well as *Uniform* distribution as a baseline.

ITEM FREQUENCY. The definition of the item frequency should satisfy some constraints in order to precisely compare item performance:

1. The total duration of the experiment should not exceed one hour. From a pilot study, we estimated that the total number of selections should be limited to 48 per block.
2. Each condition has the same number of selections per block.
3. Item frequency should be adapted so that the item selection count per block is an integer.
4. The distance between the generated and the original distributions should be as close as possible. We used R^2 to measure their similarity as in [6]. We also used *Pairwise distance (d)* as R^2 is not appropriate for *Uniform* distribution. The distance d:
$$d = \frac{1}{N} \times \sqrt{\sum_{i=1}^{N}(G_i - O_i)^2} \quad (2)$$
Where G_i is the generated and O_i is the original frequency distribution. Both distances are given in the table 1.
5. The distributions should maximize the number of item frequencies that they have in common for comparison purpose. This constraint is the most difficult to satisfy and is measured as $C = |Z_{s=1} \cap Z_{s=2} \cap U|$ where Z and U are the sets (without diplactes) of item frequencies for, respectively the *Zipfian* and *Uniform* distribution.

Given the above-mentioned constraints, we generated all possible configurations containing between 35 and 48 selections per block. The optimal number of selection was 45 selections per block with the configurations shown in Table 1. We observe that the above-mentioned constraints are all met and particularly, the generated distributions are very closed from the original distributions as indicated by $R^2 > 0.99$ or $d < 0.5$ and the number of item selection in common (C) is 4.

Item Frequency and Target Location

The ideal design would be to counter-balance all item frequencies and target locations in a way that participants can test all possible configurations. However, the design space is enormous, which is not compatible with a feasible experiment time frame. We reduce the experimental complexity by focusing on a subset of ITEM FREQUENCY and TARGET LOCATION:

- We focused on the item frequencies shared by the three distributions (marked in bold in Table 1): **6**, **4**, **3**, **2**.
- We thus chose a subset of 4 locations: **1**, **4**, **7**, **10**. We did not consider the last item to avoid possible bias related to the last-item effect [2].
- The correspondence between item frequency and item location was counterbalanced across all participants, i.e., each selected item frequency is assigned to each target location an equal number of times.
- The other item frequencies were randomly assigned to the other item locations and participants did not have the most frequent items (*15* in *s=1* and *28* in *s=2*) at the same location across conditions.

Participants and Apparatus

Twenty-four participants (6 females), raging in age 23 to 37 years (median = 26.7, σ = 3.48), were recruited from our institution and received a handful of candies for their participation. All of them were right-handed and interacted with WIMP menus regularly. The experiment was conducted on a Linux desktop at 1280 × 1024 resolution with the use of mouse at the same sensibility and acceleration.

Task, Stimulus and Procedure

Participants were instructed to select the target items as fast and accurately as possible but were *not* informed of the frequency distribution they used. The sequence of action for a trial is the following. The user first moves the cursor above a button located on the bottom of the screen. Then the stimulus appears just above this button and indicates the target item. The user has to click on another button located on the upper part of the screen to open the menu, search the target item and select it. The button to display the stimulus and the one to open the menu was far enough to let enough time for participants to interpret the stimulus before opening the menu. A trial finishes when the target item is selected (i.e., a wrong selection requires the user to reopen the menu to select the target item). The selection time starts when the user opens the menu and finishes when the target item is selected. Participants were forced to take a break between blocks and between conditions, but they could also take a break between trials.

Design

A repeated measures within-subject design was conducted. Each participant tested the three FREQUENCY DISTRIBUTION. The order of frequency distribution was counter-balanced between participants. ITEM FREQUENCY was counter-balanced between TARGET LOCATION. For each condition, participants performed 5 blocks (PRACTICE). In summary, the design was: 24 Participants × 3 FREQUENCY DISTRIBUTION × 5 Blocks × 45 Selections = 16,200 trials.

FINDINGS

We removed trials including wrong selections (4.1%) and outliers (0.5%). The Shapiro-Wilk normality test verified that wrong selections and outliers were randomly distributed across participants, frequency distributions and target locations. Table 2 and 3 summarize the main effects and interaction effects from ANOVA for respectively menu selection time and item selection time. The full table and additional graphs are available in supplementary material. For the following section, we focus on the effects of FREQUENCY DISTRIBUTION and ITEM FREQUENCY effects on *Menu* and *Item* selection time.

Menu Selection time

We used the whole data set (15,455 trials) to analyze menu selection time. Fig.1-Left features an overview of *Menu*

Factors	*df, den*	*F*	*p*
FREQUENCY DISTRIBUTION (F_D)	2, 46	58.4	< 0.0001
PRACTICE (P)	4, 92	98.8	< 0.0001
$F_D \times P$	8, 184	79.2	< 0.001

Table 2. Effects of FREQUENCY DISTRIBUTION **and** PRACTICE **on *Menu* selection time.**

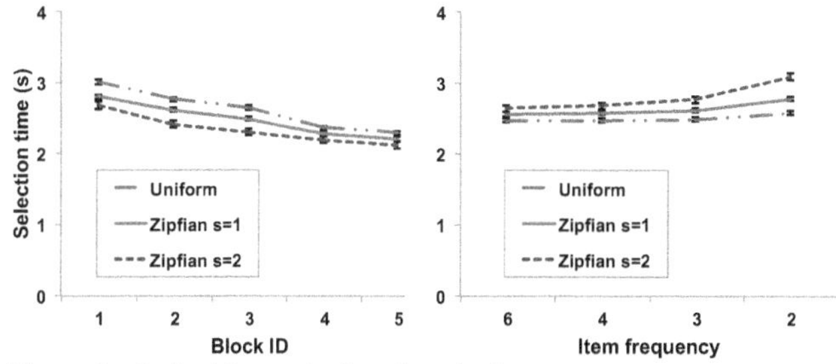

Figure 1. *Left:* *Menu* selection time in 3 FREQUENCY DISTRIBUTION **across blocks. *Right:* Individual *Item* selection time in 3** FREQUENCY DISTRIBUTION**.**

Factors	*df, den*	*F*	*p*
FREQUENCY DISTRIBUTION (F_D)	2, 46	24.1	< 0.001
ITEM FREQUENCY (I_F)	3, 69	12.5	< 0.05
TARGET LOCATION (T_L)	3, 69	11.9	< 0.05
PRACTICE (P)	4, 92	31.2	< 0.001
$F_D \times I_F$	6, 138	18.7	< 0.05
$F_D \times T_L$	6, 138	13.3	< 0.05
$F_D \times P$	8, 184	29.8	< 0.001
$I_F \times T_L$	9, 207	7.8	< 0.05
$I_F \times P$	12, 276	17.5	< 0.001

Table 3. Full factorial ANOVA on *Item* selection time. Only significant effects regarding FREQUENCY DISTRIBUTION **and** ITEM FREQUENCY **are shown here.**

selection time in 3 FREQUENCY DISTRIBUTION across blocks. ANOVA shows a significant effect for PRACTICE with a post-hoc Tukey test confirming that selection time decreases over time. ANOVA also reveals an effect of FREQUENCY DISTRIBUTION. A post-hoc Tukey test shows that *Zipfian* with $s = 2$ (2.31s) is significant faster than *Zipfian* with $s = 1$ (2.52s) which is significantly faster than *Uniform* distribution (2.71s). The FREQUENCY DISTRIBUTION × PRACTICE interaction effect is also significant and shows that FREQUENCY DISTRIBUTION effect decreases with PRACTICE, with no difference between FREQUENCY DISTRIBUTION at the fifth block. This result confirms that using skewed Zipfian distributions reduces the average menu selection time since users only select a subset of items very frequently.

Item selection time

We analyzed the effect of the controlled frequency (6,4,3,2) on item selection time. (This frequency was used in a subset of 5,156 trials.) ANOVA confirmed known effects such as the effects of TARGET LOCATION and PRACTICE (Table 3) on *Item* selection time. More interesting, ANOVA reveals a significant effect of FREQUENCY DISTRIBUTION (FD) and ITEM FREQUENCY (fitemshort) as well as a FD × and IF interaction effect on *Item* selection time which is illustrated in Fig.1-*Right*. Post-hoc Tukey tests show that *Item* selection time increases when ITEM FREQUENCY decreases (**6**: 2.58s; **4**: 2.63s; **3**: 2.69s; **2**: 2.77s) and that *Zipfian* with $s = 2$ (2.82s) is significant slower than *Zipfian* with $s = 1$ (2.67s) which is significantly slower than *Uniform* (2.53s). These results are surprising as they contrast with those obtained for *Menu* selection time (Fig. 1-*Left*) as the performances are in the opposite order. The interaction effect illustrated in Fig. 1-*Right* shows that the difference of *Item* selection time between FREQUENCY DISTRIBUTION increases when ITEM FREQUENCY decreases. Finally, the FREQUENCY DISTRIBUTION

× PRACTICE interaction effect reveals that the difference of *Item* selection time between FREQUENCY DISTRIBUTION increases with PRACTICE. This also contrasts with the results obtained for *Menu* selection time where FREQUENCY DISTRIBUTION shows no difference for overall *Menu* selection time when users are well practized (Fig. 1-*Left*).

DISCUSSION

The main finding is that individual item selection time depends not only on its own frequency but also on the frequency of other items in the menu (i.e. the whole frequency distribution). More precisely, items are selected faster in the Uniform distribution condition than in the skewed distribution (Figure 1-Right). This finding is surprising as it contrasts with average menu selection time illustrated in Figure 1-Left where menus with skewed distribution are faster to select than menus with Uniform distribution.

It is reasonable to expect that the Hick-Hyman Law (HHL) [13, 15] should offer an explanation for this phenomenon, since it demonstrates that human response time is a function of the information conveyed by a particular stimulus. More precisely, HHL indicates that response time is a linear function of H, the weighted surprisal value (also called average uncertainty) [25], $H = -\sum p_i \times log_2(p_i)$ with p_i is the probability of appearance of an item. While HHL may reflect the phenomenon observed for the average menu selection time (i.e. skewed distributions are faster to select), it is unclear how it can be applied to individual item selection time. The original Hick's [13] and Hyman's [15] experiments only concerned the whole distribution, yet later studies [6, 25] have applied HHL to individual item selection time: The former claimed that "decision time depends on the entropy of each item" $T = a + b \times (-log_2(p_i))$ [6] and the latter introduced $-log_2(p_i)$ as "surprisal value for a particular trial" [25]. However, there has been no validation for this application. More importantly, HHL applies only to expert users. In the original experiments [13, 15], participants were trained for more than 8,000 practice trials before starting the test. In contrast, our study involves novice and intermediate users [17].

Instead, the phenomenon might be explained by assuming that users maintain a probability distribution over item locations and that they continually update this distribution, perhaps using Bayes rule, as new evidence is observed. Importantly, this model would not only involve updating the location distribution of the target item but of all items that would be viewed during search for the target item. We refer to this as *incidental learning* because the model would learn about items that are incidental to the target. Importantly, with this model, the location of the small number of frequent target items in a Zipfian distribution would be learnt very quickly but once these locations were learnt, incidental learning would be reduced because the model would move directly to the target without visiting medium and low frequency items. In contrast, the location of items in the Uniform distribution would be learnt more evenly with incidental learning distributed over the location distribution of the entire set of items. This increased use of incidental learning in Uniform distributed menus would give the learning advantage observed in the experiment.

Implications

A correctly parameterized distribution of menu items is essential for ecologically valid investigation of menus. Intuitively, Zipfian distributions lead to faster overall performance, counter-intuitively, they lead to slower performance of individual items with matched probability. These results have implications both for scientists testing theories and for practitioners conducting usability testing. In the former case the validity of a theory of interaction will be questionable in the absence of a parameterized distribution. In the latter case, the validity of the claim that one interface is better than another may depend on the ecologically determined distribution.

Modeling. There is a continuous effort to encapsulate HCI knowledge by building models of users' behavior. Recently, models of menu performance [2, 5, 6] do not only predict average menu selection time, but also item selection time. Our results indicate that we should take frequency distribution into account when modeling menu performance so that the distribution is correctly parameterized and the investigation is ecologically valid.

Menu design. In real life, command selection with radical Zipfian distribution is ubiquitous (i.e., *Copy* and *Paste*). Indeed, analyses of software containing many commands such as AudoCad show that users only use a subset of the available commands [19]. This implies that users' performance is often impaired by not using the appropriate functions, possibly due to the lack of awareness of the menu content [7, 14].

Using a flat frequency distribution might impair short-term performance, but it might also improve long-term performance by favoring the transition from novice to expert behavior. Indeed, when a person uses a menu, they may not only learn about the location of the target item, but also incidentally learn about the locations of non-target items, which are encountered while looking for the target. More such non-target learning will occur when more search is required for the user to find the target. In practice, the way designers assign commands or command shortcuts to software functionalities should be thought so that to improve menu awareness.

Empirical studies. Since empirical studies are essential for both modeling and menu design, we therefore advocate a better consideration of frequency distribution when elaborating experimental designs. While difficult to manipulate, our results show that frequency distribution has an impact on users' behavior and some possible interaction might occur with other factors such as task nature.

In conclusion, this work advances the knowledge of menu selection by a better understanding of the impact of item frequency and frequency distribution on both item and menu selection time. This effect is counter-intuitive but relevant to efforts to design more learnable interfaces.

ACKNOWLEDGMENTS

This research was funded by Labex DigiCosme (ANR-11-LABEX-0045-DIGICOSME), operated by the French Agence Nationale de la Recherche (ANR) as part of the program "Investissement d'Avenir" Idex Paris-Saclay (ANR-11-IDEX-0003-02). We thank reviewers, C. Coutrix and A. Oulasvirta.

REFERENCES

1. Caroline Appert and Shumin Zhai. 2009. Using Strokes As Command Shortcuts: Cognitive Benefits and Toolkit Support. In *Proceedings of the SIGCHI Conference on Human Factors in Computing Systems (CHI '09)*. ACM, New York, NY, USA, 2289–2298. DOI: http://dx.doi.org/10.1145/1518701.1519052
2. Gilles Bailly, Antti Oulasvirta, Duncan P. Brumby, and Andrew Howes. 2014. Model of Visual Search and Selection Time in Linear Menus. In *Proceedings of the SIGCHI Conference on Human Factors in Computing Systems (CHI '14)*. ACM, New York, NY, USA, 3865–3874. DOI: http://dx.doi.org/10.1145/2556288.2557093
3. Suresh K Bhavnani, Bonnie E John, and Ulrich Flemming. 1999. The strategic use of CAD: an empirically inspired, theory-based course. In *Proceedings of the SIGCHI conference on Human Factors in Computing Systems*. ACM, 183–190.
4. Michael D. Byrne, John R. Anderson, Scott Douglass, and Michael Matessa. 1999. Eye Tracking the Visual Search of Click-down Menus. In *Proceedings of the SIGCHI Conference on Human Factors in Computing Systems (CHI '99)*. ACM, New York, NY, USA, 402–409. DOI: http://dx.doi.org/10.1145/302979.303118
5. Xiuli Chen, Gilles Bailly, Duncan P. Brumby, Antti Oulasvirta, and Andrew Howes. 2015. The Emergence of Interactive Behavior: A Model of Rational Menu Search. In *Proceedings of the 33rd Annual ACM Conference on Human Factors in Computing Systems (CHI '15)*. ACM, New York, NY, USA, 4217–4226. DOI: http://dx.doi.org/10.1145/2702123.2702483
6. Andy Cockburn, Carl Gutwin, and Saul Greenberg. 2007. A Predictive Model of Menu Performance. In *Proceedings of the SIGCHI Conference on Human Factors in Computing Systems (CHI '07)*. ACM, New York, NY, USA, 627–636. DOI: http://dx.doi.org/10.1145/1240624.1240723
7. Andy Cockburn, Carl Gutwin, Joey Scarr, and Sylvain Malacria. 2014. Supporting Novice to Expert Transitions in User Interfaces. *ACM Comput. Surv.* 47, 2, Article 31 (Nov. 2014), 36 pages. DOI: http://dx.doi.org/10.1145/2659796
8. Stephen R Ellis and Robert J Hitchcock. 1986. The emergence of Zipf's law: Spontaneous encoding optimization by users of a command language. *IEEE transactions on systems, man, and cybernetics* 16, 3 (1986), 423–427.
9. Leah Findlater and Joanna McGrenere. 2004. A Comparison of Static, Adaptive, and Adaptable Menus. In *Proceedings of the SIGCHI Conference on Human Factors in Computing Systems (CHI '04)*. ACM, New York, NY, USA, 89–96. DOI: http://dx.doi.org/10.1145/985692.985704
10. Saul Greenberg and Ian H Witten. 1993. Supporting command reuse: empirical foundations and principles. (1993).
11. Tovi Grossman, Pierre Dragicevic, and Ravin Balakrishnan. 2007. Strategies for Accelerating On-line Learning of Hotkeys. In *Proceedings of the SIGCHI Conference on Human Factors in Computing Systems (CHI '07)*. ACM, New York, NY, USA, 1591–1600. DOI: http://dx.doi.org/10.1145/1240624.1240865
12. Stephen José Hanson, Robert E Kraut, and James M Farber. 1984. Interface design and multivariate analysis of UNIX command use. *ACM Transactions on Information Systems (TOIS)* 2, 1 (1984), 42–57.
13. William E Hick. 1952. On the rate of gain of information. *Quarterly Journal of Experimental Psychology* 4, 1 (1952), 11–26.
14. Andrew Howes, Stephen J. Payne, and Amelia Woodward. 2000. The Trouble with Shortcuts. In *CHI '00 Extended Abstracts on Human Factors in Computing Systems (CHI EA '00)*. ACM, New York, NY, USA, 267–268. DOI: http://dx.doi.org/10.1145/633292.633448
15. Ray Hyman. 1953. Stimulus information as a determinant of reaction time. *Journal of experimental psychology* 45, 3 (1953), 188.
16. Gordon Kurtenbach and William Buxton. 1993. The Limits of Expert Performance Using Hierarchic Marking Menus. In *Proceedings of the INTERACT '93 and CHI '93 Conference on Human Factors in Computing Systems (CHI '93)*. ACM, New York, NY, USA, 482–487. DOI: http://dx.doi.org/10.1145/169059.169426
17. Roy Lachman, Janet L Lachman, and Earl C Butterfield. 2015. *Cognitive psychology and information processing: An introduction*. Psychology Press.
18. Dong-Seok Lee and Wan Chul Yoon. 2004. Quantitative results assessing design issues of selection-supportive menus. *International Journal of Industrial Ergonomics* 33, 1 (2004), 41–52.
19. Justin Matejka, Wei Li, Tovi Grossman, and George Fitzmaurice. 2009. CommunityCommands: command recommendations for software applications. In *Proceedings of the 22nd annual ACM symposium on User interface software and technology*. ACM, 193–202.
20. Brad Mehlenbacher, Thomas M Duffy, and James Palmer. 1989. Finding information on a menu: linking menu organization to the user's goals. *Human-Computer Interaction* 4, 3 (1989), 231–251.
21. Erik L Nilsen. 1996. *Perceptual-Motor Control in Human-Computer Interaction*. Technical Report. DTIC Document.
22. Stephen J Payne and Andrew Howes. 2013. Adaptive interaction: A utility maximization approach to understanding human interaction with technology. *Synthesis Lectures on Human-Centered Informatics* 6, 1 (2013), 1–111.

23. Peter Pirolli. 2007. *Information foraging theory: Adaptive interaction with information.* Oxford University Press.

24. Andrew Sears and Ben Shneiderman. 1994. Split Menus: Effectively Using Selection Frequency to Organize Menus. *ACM Trans. Comput.-Hum. Interact.* 1, 1 (March 1994), 27–51. DOI: http://dx.doi.org/10.1145/174630.174632

25. Tim Wifall, Eliot Hazeltine, and J Toby Mordkoff. 2015. The roles of stimulus and response uncertainty in forced-choice performance: an amendment to Hick/Hyman Law. *Psychological research* (2015), 1–11.

DemYouth: Co-Designing and Enacting Tools to Support Young People's Engagement with People with Dementia

Roisin McNaney[1], John Vines[2], Jamie Mercer[3], Leon Mexter[3], Daniel Welsh[4] and Tony Young[4]
[1] Lancaster University, Lancaster, UK, r.mcnaney@lancaster.ac.uk
[2] Northumbria University, Newcastle upon Tyne, UK, john.vines@northumbria.ac.uk
[3] Youth Focus North East, Gateshead, UK, {jamie; leon}@youthfocusne.org,uk
[4] Newcastle University, Newcastle upon Tyne, UK, {d.welsh; tony.young}@newcastle.ac.uk

ABSTRACT
There is a growing body of research examining the role of technology in supporting the care of—and relationships surrounding—people with dementia, yet little attention has been given to how this relates to younger family members. We conducted a qualitative study based on a series of 6 co-design workshops conducted with 14 young people who had personal experience with dementia. Initially, our workshops focused on understanding the difficulties that young people face when engaging, interacting and being with people with dementia. Initial analysis of workshop data informed the design of three digital tool concepts that were used as the basis for user enactment workshops. Our findings highlight the young people's desire to be more involved in their family discussions around dementia and a need for them to find new ways to connect with their loved ones with dementia. We offer a set of design considerations for future systems that support these needs and reflect on some of the complexities we faced around engaging young people in this difficult topic of discussion.

Author Keywords
Young people; Dementia; Co-design; Mobile Applications.

ACM Classification Keywords
H.5.m. Information interfaces and presentation (e.g., HCI): Miscellaneous

INTRODUCTION
"Dementia doesn't just affect the person…it affects their whole social circle, their whole family, their whole world" (Jordan, 20)

It is estimated that there are approximately 46 million people living with dementia worldwide [35]. Dementia is an umbrella term which encompasses a range of conditions, with various symptoms, caused by a degeneration of neurons in the brain. It can affect activities of daily living (e.g. money management, cooking, washing, dressing) and cognitive functioning (e.g. memory, reasoning, planning) [4], and can cause fluctuations in, often challenging, behavior. Communication can be especially effected, encompassing difficulties with the expression and comprehension of spoken and written language [38]. Issues range from simple word finding difficulties (such as forgetting the names for people or things) to becoming completely non-verbal in later stages [49]. Unsurprisingly, communication difficulties can equally have a negative influence on relationships between people with dementia and loved ones [10,29,34,38,40,49].

Communicative engagement is vitally important to the quality of life of people with dementia and those around them, but becomes more difficult as the condition develops. This often results in social withdrawal and isolation of people with dementia, and a strain on relationships between family members [52]. There are resources available to help people learn skills and strategies to effectively communicate with their loved ones [e.g. 2,3,53]. However, there has been little study of how intergenerational engagement—between young people and people with dementia—might be meaningfully supported. This is despite estimates that around 250,000 youths in the USA help to provide care for someone with dementia [31]. This brings to light the need for resources to help youths make sense of the multi-faceted, often transient, changes that might be occurring in their loved one.

In this paper we describe work conducted in collaboration with Youth Focus North East (YFNE), a regional charity that supports youths in having a voice within local communities. A key feature of YFNE's work has been in contexts related to youth engagement in health and care services, with a strong focus on supporting those with care responsibilities. Our initial engagement with YFNE involved working together to gather informal feedback from youths on an online toolkit [53] that provides information around strategies for interacting with people with dementia. However, preliminary discussion suggested the advice offered did not always map on to the youths' experiences, highlighting a need to better understand how young people experience this complex condition.

In this paper we describe 6 iterative co-design workshops conducted with 14 youths with personal experiences of dementia. These started by broadly exploring participants' experiences of dementia, identifying common issues to be

CHI 2017, May 06-11, 2017, Denver, CO, USA
ACM978-1-4503-4655-9/17/05.
http://dx.doi.org/10.1145/3025453.3025558

addressed, then generating, refining and finally enacting a number of concepts for new digital tools and services to support youths' engagement with people with dementia. We contribute; 1) new insight into how youths currently engage with dementia, from both a personal and wider family viewpoint; 2) the complexities of designing with this diverse group, particularly in engaging them in sensitive topics; 3) design considerations relating to the development of technologies to support youths be more connected with loved-ones with dementia and enhancing their ongoing care engagement. In providing these contributions our intention is not to present finalized technology designs; rather, we highlight how our co-design techniques elicited empirical insights around the young people's articulated experiences of dementia and the challenges they face, and how these can act as a foundation for future technology design.

BACKGROUND AND RELATED WORK

Youths and dementia care

The United Nations define youths as people between the ages of 15 and 25 [44]. Those with care responsibilities may offer practical or emotional care, conducted alone or in support of primary care responsibilities of another adult [11]. Young carers are less likely to spend as much time in education as their non-caring peers [24], which can negatively impact their academic achievements, social life and the type of employment available to them.

There has been growing interest within the field of HCI over the past decade around the design of technologies for people with dementia to support their care. As a result, an abundance of work has emerged focusing on designing with people with dementia and their adult caregivers [e.g. 5,7,26,27,28,47,48]. This prior work has offered deepened understandings of how to sensitively design with people with dementia and their caregivers, with insight ranging from supporting functional care needs within the family unit (such as wandering [26] and meal times [39]) to enhancing personhood [48]. However, there has been little work setting out to understand how younger family members might be supported as part of the care ecology of older family members with dementia. This is representative of wider concerns that there is a dearth of knowledge on how youths experience dementia in their lives [37].

Engaging youths in discussions around health

It has been noted how youths experience desires for independence and autonomy as they begin to negotiate their individual and social identities. Erikson's seminal work presents a theoretical perspective on the key stages of psychosocial development throughout the life course [13]. He describes how adolescence is pivotal to the formation of identity, as youths begin to explore their belief systems, their personal values and extrapolate their current life experiences (e.g. their studies and friendship groups) onto their future life goals. Over the past decade, as technology and social media use have grown, youths have increasingly been using online platforms to negotiate their identities, blurring the boundaries between their public and private, real and virtual world experiences [18].

Within the field of HCI, youths remain a relatively under-represented group [15,16,17,20,23,32,36,45], particularly in terms of their involvement in design. The complexities of involving youths in design work have been discussed [15,17,45], especially as it relates to the experience of transition between childhood and adulthood. There is an emerging literature around the needs and values of youths in the context of designing personalized health systems [e.g. 20,23,45]. But, there remains little understanding around how we might support them in navigating complexities that arise when changes in their family occur.

Intergenerational communication

While there is limited work that focuses explicitly on the lives of youths in this context, there has been research exploring intergenerational engagement for the purposes of building technology mediated links between older adults and young people. A portion of this work has looked engaging older people in supporting the education of youths [12,18,13], such as the ongoing 'School in the Cloud' project in which retired teachers are supporting learning in rural India over Skype [12]. There has also been work investigating the use of technology to mediate playful interaction between grandparents and their grandchildren who live apart [45].

Another theme within the literature is the use of video based experience sharing as a means to facilitate intergenerational communication [6,30]. For example, Bentley et al [6] describe the 'family stories system', a location based video sharing tool which allows senior family members to record video memories (at home), inspired by specific places, and pin them to a location on a map. Younger family members would then serendipitously be played these stories when in the surrounding area. Although this work was asynchronous in nature, the authors found that use of the system facilitated a sense of connection from younger participants as they learned about their grandparents' lives. It also prompted increased communication between families as they inquired about, and engaged in, the stories been told.

Given that reminiscence is one of the most widely used psychosocial interventions in dementia care, with reported benefits to mood, well-being and quality of life [51], there are certainly applications for this type of technology mediated experience sharing. However, most previous work has focused on cognitively able older people, or adult carers. As such, there remains a gap in the literature around how we might support intergenerational communication between people with dementia and youths. In addition, prior research on the creation of information and support packages for carers and family members of people with dementia has highlighted the need to adapt such resources for younger audiences [52]. In the following we describe our study, which aimed to address this gap by working directly with youths to understand their relationships and engagements

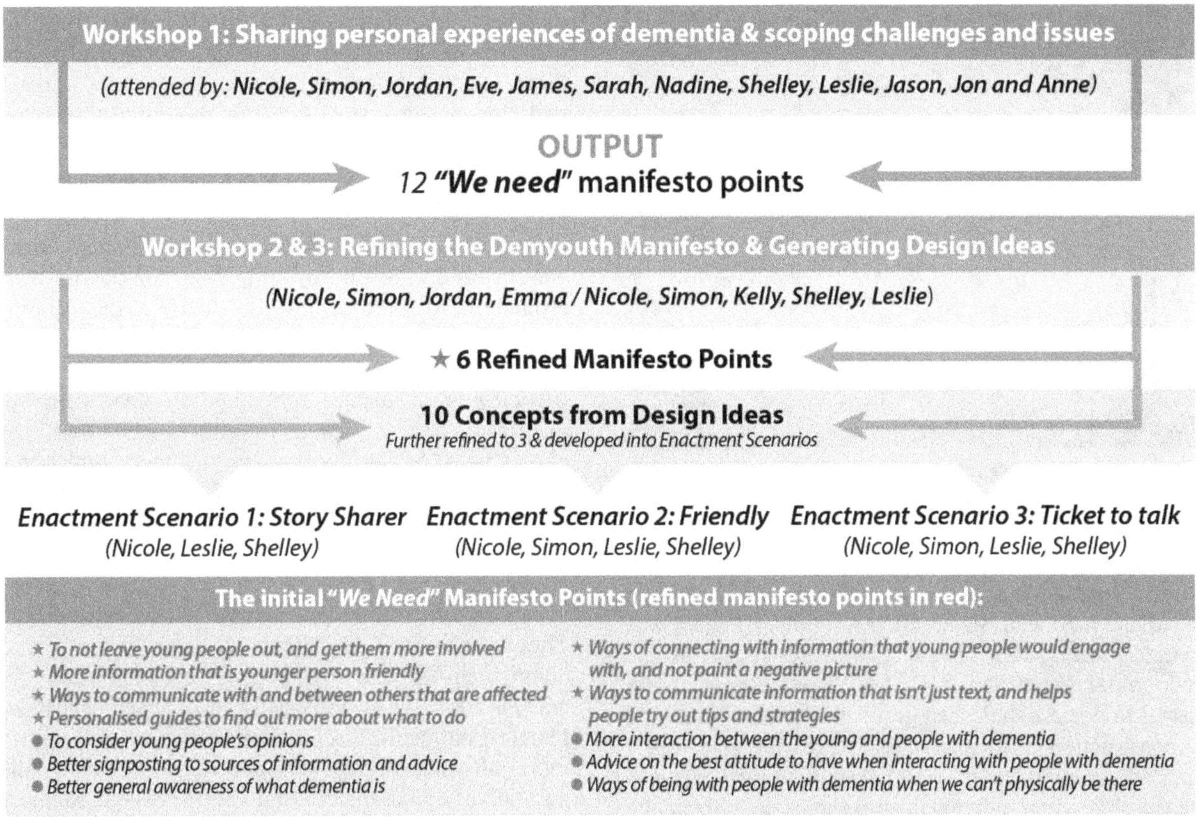

Figure 1. Diagrammatic overview of the DemYouth co-design process.

with people with dementia and the issues, if any, they face within these.

STUDY DESIGN

We approached the research with a view to understanding the care roles that youths were currently undertaking around dementia. In referring to care, we define this broadly; including a grandchild providing company and conversation to a grandparent, a youth who regularly looks after an older family member, or a youth engaging in formal care responsibilities within a care home. Throughout the research we attempted to avoid medicalizing dementia, instead focusing on the youths' experiences of the condition and how they were living with the challenges it brought about. In doing so, we aimed to explore the potential for technology to support youths in engaging meaningfully with people with dementia, through a process of co-designing ideas based on identified challenges and issues.

Participants

A total of 14 youths (9 female) took part in the research. All were involved with YFNE, who facilitated the identification and recruitment of participants, and were aged between 16 and 24. Participants represented a diverse set of experiences and circumstances that motivated them to take part. Nine had family members, primarily grandparents, with dementia who they saw regularly. Two participants (Jordan and Emma) were volunteering in care homes for a day a week, conversing and interacting with residents with dementia. Finally, Nadine, James and Leslie had ongoing care responsibilities for family members with dementia. These participants dedicated significant periods of time each day to caring for their older family members. For 2 of these participants this had involved having to withdraw from upper high school and college education.

Workshop structure

Our co-design activities were conducted across six design workshops. Workshops were divided into two stages of activity. Stage one (workshops 1-3) was focused on broadly exploring personal experiences of dementia and identifying specific issues and challenges to be addressed. Stage two (workshops 4-6) involved an in-depth exploration of three design concepts that were created through a comparative analysis of ideas and discussions from stage one. An overview of the workshop process is provided in Figure 1. The workshops were iterative in nature, with explorations at each stage being drawn from ideas in the last. Workshops lasted approximately 2-2.5 hours each and were held in evenings or at weekends, to accommodate the youths.

All participants were invited to all workshops. However, due to competing schedules (related to school and college work) and care duties, they were not all available for each session. Because of this, the start of each workshop provided a recap of what happened at the previous workshop, which aided reflection and discussion for both those who did and did not attend the previous engagement.

Figure 2. Participants engaging in the design idea generation activity from Workshop 3.

Analysis of the data

Each workshop was audio recorded and transcribed verbatim. Two members of the research team conducted an inductive thematic analysis on the transcripts [9]. Data was summarized with short one or two word codes, at the sentence-to-paragraph level. Codes were compared and contrasted to one-another, then grouped together, which led to the construction of themes that captured the core topics and concerns coming from the data. Analysis of the data was conducted following individual workshops, to inform the design of following workshops, and at the end of each stage. For stage one, this was to inform the refinement of proposed ideas into concepts, and for stage two to understand the responses to, and engagement with, the design concepts than had been created, and to derive considerations for the discussion of our work.

STAGE 1: SCOPING, EXPLORING & DEFINING

In the first stage, we ran three workshops that went through phases of scoping and exploring personal perceptions and experiences of dementia, and then defining specific issues and challenges to be addressed in the project. Figure 1 visualizes the workshop structure across stages 1 and 2.

Workshop 1 (n=12) opened with ice-breaker activities that enabled the young people to introduce themselves and get to know one-another. Following this, we facilitated a series of short activities designed to stimulate talk among participants in relation to perceptions of dementia, with a view to drawing out participants' personal experiences of the condition. The workshop concluded with the creation of a set of 12 *"we need"* points (see figure 1). These were intended to represent a set of problems, ideas and challenges that the participants felt were important for engaging youths in issues relating to dementia. These 12 points acted as a "manifesto" for the project going forward.

Workshops 2 (n=4) and *3* (n=5) focused on refining and prioritizing manifesto points from workshop 1. Participants were split into groups of two or three and asked to discuss, and then rank, the 12 manifesto points in order of significance. After this, they were invited to choose the three manifesto points they felt were most important to take forward. We brought the small groups together to compare their selected priorities; again, after a short discussion participants were asked to refine these into three collective manifesto points. Throughout these activities, participants were given opportunity to combine, refine or edit manifesto points to represent their discussions.

Having selected a set three manifesto points, participants were invited to begin exploring opportunities for designing around these three issues. To scaffold this activity, we introduced the notion of personas to participants. While personas are simplistic, our intention was to engage participants in further reflection on how their selected manifesto points related to either their own personal experiences, or the experiences of other youths and their families. Using a provided template, participants created a persona that, to them, represented people experiencing the types of challenges they identified as priorities in the first activity (e.g. a young person who was struggling to cope with instances where their grandparent forgot who they were). These were then presented to each other, identifying commonalities and differences between the different personas. Finally, we provided a set of ten cards that depicted features and qualities of a combination of well-known, and more obscure, digital services (e.g. a website allowing curation of online material into personalized groups; an app allowing private messaging to specific groups of friends; location based app allowing viewing and posting of anonymous messages to those nearby). Participants worked in small groups to discuss each of these cards. Following this, they individually generated design ideas that combined up to three of the cards and responded to the identified needs of the personas created earlier (see figure 2). The workshops closed with participants sharing their created ideas, elaborating on how the ideas related to the personas and the manifesto points underpinning them.

Findings from stage 1

Trust, fear and confidence

When discussing their experiences of dementia, the youths highlighted the wider impact that it had, not only on them and their relationships with their loved one, but also on the family unit. Where a grandparent was previously seen as someone they were allowed to spend time with, concerns about their perceived abilities as their dementia symptoms gradually progressed was often seen to make parents fearful of letting their children spend time with them alone. For example, Nicole described: *"I've seen a lack of trust leaving kids with my Granddad...when there's a lack of trust from a parent or another relative then the illness has taken away that bond and that's slightly more detrimental than the illness sometimes"*. The youths widely discussed how this fear from parents caused them to become 'left out' of the discussions about, and experiences with, their grandparent. For many, this was a key issue they wanted to address: "[it should be the family] *not saying, "We'll protect the children and keep them out of it" but actually, "Yes, your Granddad's starting to forget things but when he's a bit cross it's mostly because he's frustrated because he can't remember. It doesn't mean he doesn't love you."* (Kelly). However, it was not simply the fear of the person with dementia's ability that was seen to cause relationship breakdowns within the family unit. The youths also felt that their parents had self-doubts around their own abilities to cope with dementia, which in itself caused them to feel a loss of confidence when trying to explain the situation to young family members: *"if the parents are more confident in responding to the condition then they'd be more confident in supporting younger people."* (Kelly). Simon described how upsetting he found it to see his family become frustrated with his great-grandmother *"it's horrible to see everyone getting frustrated with her"*, where Leslie explained how she often took on the role of helping her family members to understand dementia: *"A lot of people, because they don't understand it, think the person is always going to be like that* [violent]. *It's basically just trying to give information proving that isn't always going to the case."*

A further issue related to fear and confidence identified by participants was a general observation that *"you don't see people with dementia out and about much"* (James). There was, for some, a question about whether they could take their grandparents to public places and spaces. This was often framed in relation to personal experiences of family members—like aunts, uncles and parents—inferring that, with dementia, comes an inability to leave the home: *"they don't really want her to go out, just in case something happens"* (Nadine). Leslie further described how she felt her family's unwillingness to engage with her grandmother's dementia had led to her becoming isolated and less independent:

"She's in a home at the minute and the family have just sort of forgot about her... She still remembers about the day centre she used to go to and still talks about going there [...] *She just stays in her little independent flat because she doesn't like going downstairs, so it's kind of taken away her independence really"*

Participants felt that youths were often infantilised by family members when it came to discussing dementia, often due to adults' own fears or lack of understanding. However, they represented themselves throughout the project as strong advocates for their loved ones with dementia, expressing desire to support them to remain independent.

Talking, communicating and relating

There was much discussion around how communication breakdowns between family members and the person with dementia caused frustrations and loss of confidence. Simon described how this led to his family disconnecting from his grandmother altogether: *"everyone was really frustrated* [...] *it got to a point where no one went to visit her or anything, apart from my granddad* [...] *he could talk to her all day really"*. Nicole explained how in her family there was often an onus on one person to be the main communicator: *"you may have one person who can communicate really well but if others can't communicate then it is reliant on that one person to do it all"*. For Emma, it was her younger cousins who struggled with visiting her Grandmother: *"they never really know what to say anymore* [...] *they go because they feel like they should go and see my Nana but they don't really know what to do* [...] *It's quite hard"*. This was echoed by Kelly: *"I find it quite heart-breaking to visit him* [her grandfather] *because I just feel so bad for how confused he is. So it makes it a lot harder because there are very few ways in which we can connect anymore*".

All of the youths, in different ways, highlighted how they sought to find new ways of connecting with their loved ones with dementia. Discussion highlighted a need to find ways to start conversations: *"Like a safe prompt to get things going when it first becomes more daunting"* (Emma). Participants discussed, at length, the concept of using a mobile application to curate information, relevant to the person with dementia, to help initiate talk: *"it will be much easier for* [youths] *to have a conversation* [if] *they talk about things that were interesting for their grandparents"* (Emma). Refining this idea further, the youths suggested the use of different media, such as photographs and songs, as well as having a way to inspire different methods that they could use to encourage engagement with their loved one:

"if the app had somewhere where you could tap for inspiration [...] *if you're at a loss then you've got something like, "Write them a letter about something you've done in the past" or, "Ask them about Uni", or something like that."* (Kelly)

They also described how ideas such as this might act as a way to connect with other family members, who could then subsequently use the content to find new ways to connect with their loved ones by exploring their lives: *So they will get their profile to begin with, originally and then they would branch off with their family member...And then the person will be able to access them to have a look at their life together"* (Simon). This concept of exploring the life course and connecting with people with dementia on a deeper level was seen as important for supporting *"meaningful conversation"* (Emma) about *"something they were able to relate to"* (Simon). This was linked to the idea of seeing the positive in people with dementia: *"reliving the good memories that they are remembering"* (Leslie) and *"not being afraid of them just because of the illness that they've got"* (Shelley). Critically, it was not that participants felt that they needed to, or wished to, learn the *"rules to follow"* (Nicole) when talking to someone with dementia; rather it was that they needed resources to support them in initiating conversation in the first place.

Informing, understanding and personalizing

A further set of issues identified in the workshops related to how the available resources surrounding dementia were inaccessible to youths. Participants described how sifting through multiple web pages was often felt to be overwhelming: *"I have realized that there is so much out there. There is some good information out there, there is good advice, there is good stuff but it is so overwhelming for someone in that situation"* (Jordan). They noted that much of the 'good' information is often very difficult to find: *"Google is good if someone else has searched it before you, if no one else is thinking the same thing you'll not get anything"* (Nicole). Suggestions arose around the use of different media to create more 'young person friendly' information: *"sometimes you don't want to read a load of text sometimes you just want to watch a video or listen to an audio book or whatever"* (Jordan). Nicole also suggested using playful methods: *"Like making a cartoon or a game to mix the information together"*.

The youths described how available information appeared to be highly generic, impersonal and difficult to relate to their own experiences. Initial discussion centered on *"everyone's situation being different"* (Simon) and how *"you can have happy people, sad people, and people with a whole range of different memories"* (Leslie). Nicole for example, reflected on difficulties she faced when trying to relate information she found online to practice: *"it's totally generic* [...] *If you are just going to visit a relative with dementia you want to know some advice on how to speak or deal with that relative"* (Nicole). Simon reflected on his personal experiences of *"being thrown in the deep end"* several years ago when he visited his Grandma soon after she was diagnosed with dementia. He noted that *"there was no information for me out there"*, and that he wouldn't really know *"what to search for"*. One thing that did help was writing notes about the things that seemed to lead to good conversations with his Grandma. From this, he suggested: *"nothing electronic but a pocket guide* [...] *They wouldn't need to carry it round with them, perhaps they could put it in their grandma's biscuit tin or whatever"*. While seemingly a little frivolous, the biscuit tin referred to being able to *"hide it"* but *"know where it is when you need it* [...] *all kids know where the biscuit tin is!"* (Simon).

This discussion highlighted both the desire from the youths to learn more about dementia, and a need for accessible information that would support them to do so. They felt there were several barriers to their access to information: not having the correct language to search for information, being unable/ unwilling to negotiate large amounts of information, and not knowing what online information to trust. While they realized there was a growing wealth of information for them to draw on, they found it difficult to connect with and, most critically, to use in practice.

Sharing, relating and experiencing

It was clear from participants that our workshops provided a very rare opportunity for them to discuss and talk about dementia. There was a recognition that they themselves had rarely discussed the condition with others: *"I think these workshops have been the first time I've chatted it about it really"* (Nicole); and *"Me and Nicole have known each other for years, but we didn't know we both had this in common before we talked about seeing the* [recruitment] *advert."* (Simon). Emma observed that whilst she talked to her cousins about their grandmother's situation, none of them had really talked about it with friends. Leslie further reflected: *"It's hard even when you're caring for someone and you want to talk to others. Where do you go to find them?"*. While there was recognition that professional services did exist, it was felt these were more *"informational"* in nature, and instead there was a desire to seek engagements with people in similar circumstances: *"it's nice to get professional opinion but...it can also be more beneficial to speak to your peers...because they are in the same position as you"* (Nicole).

Perhaps unsurprisingly, many of the participants invoked design ideas that brought the qualities of the workshop environment to online platforms. For example, Nicole created an app that combined *"local chatter"* features with the ability to *"chat instantly"*—allowing her to *"message someone personally"* who lives nearby and is in similar circumstances. Sarah suggested a *"private social network"* that forced you to *"register an account* [...] *to stop trolls"* but then supports *"sharing your stories in an anonymous feature"*. Jordan simply suggested building an online *"community"*.

This process of peer experience sharing was seen as a somewhat cathartic release. Given the already discussed issues the youths described around seeing their parents struggle, peer support was deemed a useful resource for learning about dementia, through experience sharing and learning from one another's mistakes in a supportive way.

STAGE 2: EVOLVING AND ENACTING CONCEPTS

Following our analysis of the initial three workshops, we entered a phase where design concepts were ideated around, and then evolved and refined. These were then used as the basis for a final series of enactments workshops.

Initial analysis provided a range of insights that acted as a starting point for further design. We first identified excerpts from participants where design ideas, or components and features of them, were explicitly articulated. We extracted a total of 23 design ideas, each anchored to data from stage 1. We iteratively filtered these down to 10 design concepts, by combining and refining the ideas that motivated them. This final set of concepts were then more fully realized by writing scenarios depicting the design-in-use, drawing on the language of participants. Through further discussion in design meetings amongst the team (researchers and staff from YFNE) three ideas were taken forward for further exploration with the youths. The final selected ideas were: 1) *StorySharer:* A platform allowing youths to share positive experiences of dementia, in the form of short video and audio clips, which are publically shared, to support advocacy and awareness; 2) *Friendly:* A rate and review platform for local establishments based on their 'dementia friendliness' related to community identified criteria, which can also be used as a learning and training tool for dementia awareness.; 3) *Ticket to Talk:* An application allowing the curation of media related to the life of the person with dementia. Different types of content can be collected and then used as a resource in conversations with the person with dementia.

Enacting DemYouth Design Concepts

We used our 3 selected design concepts as the basis for a further set of workshops with the youths. The design of our workshops was inspired by prior work on user enactments [32]. Odom et al. highlight how user enactments are a productive way of engaging participants in experiencing a snippet of what the future might be like and then engaging in reflection on existing situations, desires and practices in reference to this imagined future. In user enactments, design teams create the conditions for articulating aspects of *'the physical form and the social context of simulated futures, and ask users to enact loosely scripted scenarios involving situations they are familiar with as well as novel technical interventions designed to address these situations'* [32] (p.338). Our approach to enactments deviated from this prior work in some key ways. First, we were less concerned with exploring the physical realization of our design concepts, but instead the ways in which these concepts might act as frameworks for youths to create, share and consume different forms of digital media related to dementia. Second, while the stage 1 workshops were highly insightful, we were still at a stage of exploring the social context surrounding intergenerational engagement and dementia. As such, we designed each of our enactment workshops to take participants through a series of structured scenarios that spoke to the qualities of the underlying design concepts. In doing so, we sought to use these enactments to further probe, elicit talk and reveal insights related to the issues and context we set out to understand and design for.

Enactment 1 (E1) – StorySharer: The first enactment workshop (n=3) revolved around the *StorySharer* design concept, imagined to be accessed on a mobile device. In the concept scenario it inferred people could share short 'video-diaries' or 'vox-pops' that can then be viewed, commented on and used by others. The StorySharer concept also guided users to identify friends, acquaintances and family members who they would capture 'peer interviews' with. As such, the concept explored two key issues from the earlier stages: i) issues around there being no platforms to share and hear other youths' positive stories of dementia, and ii) engaging youths to make visible the hidden commonalities they have with many others in their age group in regards to dementia.

In E1 we took participants through structured activities that explored the potential production of media for StorySharer. We set them a brief, tasking them to collect stories from people they knew who had personal experiences of dementia. Initially, we asked them to generate, as a group, a series of questions they might use to structure a discussion. After this, we asked them to physically map the network of people with whom they might want to share and receive stories about experiences relating to dementia. Each participant was given a set of flags that they could write names on and different colors of string which could be used to add 'connections'. Next, we then asked the group to individually refine the questions that they would like to ask someone about dementia. Finally, everyone at the workshop (including the research team) 'interviewed' one-another for 3 minutes using the developed questions. The session ended with an open discussion on the activities, and reflections on the value of collecting stories around dementia.

Enactment 2 (E2) – Friendly: The second workshop (n=4) revolved around the *Friendly* design concept. This concept invited people to rate local places—such as cafés, restaurants and transport offices—for how accessible and enjoyable they might be for people with dementia. It was imagined that as people rated places, Friendly would prompt them with tips and advice about what to look for, educating both those who completed the ratings, and the establishments that were reviewed through its use. This concept thus explored two issues from the initial workshops: i) engaging youths in a practical way to learn more about the condition; and ii) harnessing the sense of advocacy from the first workshops, focusing on what the person *can* do and ensuring they, their families and their carers can be visible and independent citizens.

In E2 we first asked the youths to define what they felt makes public and social spaces 'dementia friendly'. We prompted them to think about elements related to signage; layout and design of the space; the people who were there; and the general ambience. They were asked to devise a set of 4 criteria for each element, by searching online and drawing from their own experiences, and enter these onto a set of review templates. We then provided them with a small budget to spend in the local town centre. The group were asked to, in pairs, visit a café (to buy a drink or snack), a transport hub (to navigate around and find travel times), a chain store and charity store (to purchase something) and finally a public place to rest (e.g. a street bench or seating area). Once they had returned with their completed reviews, they mapped the places they visited geographically, and discussed the potential dementia friendliness of the local places. Again, the workshop closed with an open and reflective discussion on the activities.

Enactment 3 (E3) – Ticket to Talk: The final workshop (n=4) explored the *Ticket to Talk* concept. The concept posed that a young family member would be guided through finding and collecting media related to a specific period of their loved one's life. It posed that the user would provide basic information related to the person they wished to collect media for. From here, it would prompt them to find clips of songs, movies, TV shows, reports on cultural events and personal photographs from certain periods of time. These could then be used to initiate and guide conversation when meeting or visiting a loved one. This concept explored two issues from the initial workshops: i) it responded to issues relating to a lack of knowing 'what' to talk about with older family members; and ii) it provides a personalized way to document and reflect on what communication approaches were, or were not, working.

In E3, we first presented the youths with the persona of Agnes. Agnes was 74 year old lady with Alzheimer's who they were visiting as volunteers. We posed that Agnes struggled to follow conversation, making seemingly unrelated comments about her brother's visit, but settled in to happily watch a musical, singing along to the songs. We asked participants to identify sections of the scenario where communication breakdowns had occurred, and why they thought these may have happened. From here, we tasked them to create some 'tickets to talk' to bring to their next visit. For this they used media they found online (e.g. photos, YouTube videos, Wikipedia) and the small bits of information they knew of Agnes. Finally, we asked them to, in pairs, role play the scenario again (with the researchers playing Agnes), using the tickets that they had collected. As before, the workshop closed with an open discussion.

Reflections on the DemYouth Enactments

Problems with making things personal

During E1, we asked the youths to visualize the networks of people surrounding them with experience of dementia. They started to earnestly create labels for people; starting with themselves, they mapped out their family members including their loved one with dementia. However, very quickly each participant hesitated and struggled to add more. With some prompting they started to add other people they had met as part of the DemYouth project: *"oh, yes, and there's Jordan, he worked in the care home"* (Nicole). They started to identify some links and connections between one-another: *"Jimmy* [a youth worker] *knows all of us"* (Leslie). However, upon completion, their networks were still rather small, primarily populated with people met from the project or charities in the local town.

It became clear from this activity that the youths had a distinct lack of close peers with whom they could connect with about dementia. Discussion highlighted how they were unable to engage in these types of discussions with their wider circle of friends: *"I don't really know many friends who I could talk to, because I don't really discuss* [dementia] *other than with Simon who said that his family had it"* (Nicole). Because the youths had simply not discussed dementia with friends, they knew of very few people with similar experiences, despite acknowledgement that the condition is *"all around us"* (Nicole). In addition, several participants expressed a reluctance to 'open up' about their experiences of dementia with people that they did not share a close bond with: *"I don't like discussing my own personal issues and situations like that with people I don't really know so it's kind of hard for me to open up about the whole thing"* (Leslie).

In the question generating activity there was a similar reticence to ask personal questions due to concerns around the types of emotions that they might elicit. Reflecting on their own experiences in the early stages of the project they saw *"the benefits of talking to peers"* and the creation of *"private social networks"* to support these discussions. However, this exercise highlighted that, while they were more than happy to share advice and give support, they felt discussion of rich, personal experiences should be reserved for close ties: *"with a family member or something it's more about sharing experiences but with a stranger it's more about asking advice"* (Nicole). The youths felt more comfortable sharing the wealth of advice they had to offer, from signposting resources (e.g. websites and documentaries) and local services they found useful, to sharing small snippets of positivity that they felt would help others, such as: *"remember the person is still there"* (Nicole); and *"it's still your family member at the end of the day"* (Leslie).

Too much unhelpful information

Reflective of earlier discussion around the 'sea of information' surrounding dementia, the youths found it difficult to make sense of online information around dementia friendly places in E2: *"we searched quite a lot of things but didn't get many results. There was a lot of writing on there but not a lot of substance"* (Simon). They felt that much of the information that they did find was simple common sense, and not much use to them: *"I think it was all common sense to be honest, we did find an interesting article on the* [charity] *website but it didn't really lead to much"* (Simon). This activity showed how difficult it was for participants to use online resources to find out specific information about dementia. It also demonstrated a huge reliance on visual examples. For example, one group spent much of this activity looking at images, which made sense considering they were searching for inspiration surrounding physical layout. They only paid limited attention towards reading through long textual resources, and found it challenging to extract the information they wanted. Nicole noted much of the text was *"business speak"* and *"not for a normal person"*.

Despite this, participants managed to select a final set of criteria for rating local places. These related to the physical layout of the establishment (e.g. easy access to a disabled bathroom); how appropriate the atmosphere was (e.g. volume of ambient noise); how easy it was to find their way around using the signs provided (e.g. symbols and written words on signs); and finally, the quality of the interaction they received from staff members (e.g. kindness of staff and willingness to provide help).

Dementia friendly is just friendly for all

While they struggled to find information, participants engaged enthusiastically in visiting local places and 'rating' them for the second part of E2. During their time they described several instances of feeling ignored or devalued by staff when in certain stores. For example, Nicole noted staff at a shop *"didn't come over and offer help and we were walking around like lost souls ... we weren't welcomed"*, and Shelley felt that the cashier in the store she visited *"was miserable"*. They found this lack of attention from staff made places feel *"hostile"* (Nicole). Within the train station they felt staff *"didn't seem very friendly"* (Nicole) and were unapproachable, which might make buying a ticket from a machine particularly difficult. They compared this experience to buying a bus ticket *"you could only buy tickets from the machines, whereas on a bus you've obviously got a driver who could accommodate and help"* (Nicole). However, they appreciated how friendly staff within a sports store smiled and joked with them when playing with the equipment, and felt they would extend this good nature were someone with dementia to make a mistake: *"if something was to happen that you didn't mean to do, then they might not take it too harshly, so if you dropped something they wouldn't tell you off"* (Nicole). In addition, the youths reflected on issues within the places themselves that could cause issues for someone with dementia. Loud music, multiple offers being advertised within the same vicinity and bright lights were seen to be negatives. They also *"found it really cluttered, there were different things everywhere so it was a bit confusing"* (Shelley), while changes in flooring designs *"might give the illusion of a step"* (Simon).

This activity provided the youths with a brief insight into the possible experiences that people with dementia might face on a day to day basis: *"I've never even thought about how a place could be dementia friendly and the impact that could have on someone but it was very interesting."* (Simon). Significantly, what came through here was *"dementia friendly just means friendly for anyone"* (Simon), in regards to the sense that in some places they were ignored or poorly served because they were *"youths"*. In this sense *Friendly* allowed them to connect with people with dementia in a new way, by helping them consider how they might associate their own experiences of exclusion with their loved ones'.

Finding ways in to conversation

The participants initially struggled to enquire into Agnes' situation in E3. The scenario gave only a small glimpse into her life. It inferred that Agnes had someone called "Fred" coming along to visit; but it was ambiguous who he was, whether he was still alive, and when he'd arrive. Nicole and Shelly, for example, both wished to avoid talking about Fred: *"if you start prompting too much about Fred, if he isn't around any longer how do you handle that if she isn't aware that he's not there"* (Nicole); *"or if she suddenly remembered that he'd died and it affected her"* (Shelley). In an attempt to avoid sensitive conversation points, participants focused instead on generating 'tickets' that would speak to things that she might enjoy engaging with; *"we wanted to build up a trust with her, so she felt that she could share her memories with us* (Nicole). Leslie noted the importance of Agnes singing along to a musical in the scenario: *"We'd share with her the musicals that we liked and stuff like that"* (Leslie). Shelly and Nicole also observed this, and searched for and gathered snippets of media related to musicals to share with Agnes: *"we've saved a few photos from the most famous musicals and then we went and looked at the actors that were in them, and saved a few photos of them to see if she recognized them or knew any other films that they were in"* (Shelley). Simon and Leslie also approached the activity by thinking about when she was born and key periods in her life: *"we looked at the years she was remembering, so 1954-1955, the films that were playing around that time and the famous actors and actress"* (Simon).

While this activity allowed the youths to think about how to initiate and support meaningful conversations, it was clear further support would be required to make the realization of this concept successful. We role played the scenario again, asking them to use their tickets to initiate a second conversation with the character (played by a researcher). There were several instances where participants became uncomfortable; not quite sure how to manage digressions from the topic they had introduced or unresponsive instances (typical of many interactions with a person with dementia). Some became over-insistent, asking multiple questions related to their ticket of choice. This highlighted the need for careful scaffolding of such conversational support, so that such communication breakdowns can be repaired as they occur, or avoided in the first place.

DISCUSSION

We have described a co-design enquiry with 14 youths to explore their experiences of dementia and how we might use technology to support them in engaging with the condition. As mentioned, there are approximately 250,000 young people who currently provide care to some degree for people with dementia [44], yet there has been only limited research which has focused on their needs. Our study contributes a deeper understanding around the multifaceted experiences of dementia from a youth perspective; their desire to be more involved within family care relationships and how their information needs are currently not being met. In the following, we offer a set of considerations for future research exploring the development of digital tools and platforms to support youths in their relationships with people with dementia. Whilst we only worked with a small group, the insights provided within this work provide a useful first step towards inciting exploration into this complex design space.

Engaging youths in discussing dementia

We noted many complexities within our design process surrounding engaging youths in discussions of dementia. While participants were willing to open up and share their knowledge and experience within the confines of the research, there was a certain level of discomfort expressed in later stages around sharing very personal experiences. This finding corresponds with previous literature surrounding social support networks, which states that whilst strangers and extended social networks are seen as useful for providing informational support, seeking behaviors surrounding emotional support are reserved for close family and friends [50]. In addition it is worth noting how youths' social identity formation could potentially have a role in this unwillingness to open up; being at a developmental stage of life where social and personal identities are being carefully constructing [13]. The process of describing negative experiences of dementia with friends, a condition known to carry stigma [6], could somewhat hinder their self presentation of themselves as 'cool' [16]. However, more positively, the youths expressed a great desire to promote and advocate around dementia, filling gaps left by unintelligible, generic information. Reflecting on these points, an idea like the *Friendly* app could provide a way for youths to begin thinking about and discussing dementia more openly. By asking people within their existing social networks to engage with Friendly and think about what makes a place suitable for someone with dementia, there is a possibility that they could engage a wider range of people in discussions around the condition, putting the external loci of attention on the surroundings and not their personal experiences per say.

Valuing youths within the family unit

One recurring issue throughout our study was the roles of youths in the ongoing care relationships within the family unit. Many of the youths felt 'left out' and somewhat sheltered by their families in relation to discussions of dementia and the changes that were happening with their loved one. For some, it was a subtle alteration in the way their family members treated the person with dementia; a gradual withdrawal of trust that saw them being restricted in their once prominent roles as caregivers for children. For others it was exposure to the family's frustrations and lack of understanding around the condition that was upsetting. It became clear that the youths wanted to feel supported as valuable actors within the care relationships, whether this be by gaining knowledge and understanding about the condition, to support their inclusion in ongoing conversations, or effective communication skills to support their interactions.

This finding highlights the need for future tools which support the young person's role in the family unit. This involves not seeing them as a separate user group, per say, but finding ways to link the family together around the topic of dementia and support them as a whole. Previous research with youths has focused on supporting their individual identities and the social peer relationships which occur around them, often motivated by the position that youths should be supported in asserting their independence [32]. In our case however there is a need to consider the familial relationships around the youth. In this sense our ticket-to-talk idea, which admittedly was narrowly focused on the youths themselves within the workshop, could be used as a tool to support and structure family interactions. It has the potential to support the creation of shared resources, information and shared learning about the condition, and the building of skills to facilitate interaction with the person with dementia. Throughout our study, the youths brought a level of positivity in their discussions of dementia that could be harnessed within the family. Furthermore, this could lead to the development of novel digital tools which move beyond the functional care aspects of dementia, which have more commonly been focused on in past literature working with adult caregivers [e.g. 26,28,39].

Supporting effective communication

Another issue throughout the study related to finding ways to support conversation, by helping the youths connect with their grandparents in new and meaningful ways. This echoes findings from Strom and Strom [42], who described how many grandchildren report that they do not have a close relationship with the grandparent, despite the grandparents indicating the contrary. The authors suggest that this might be due to contrasting sharing practices among the generations, with youths being more open to sharing their feelings, thoughts and emotions, and older adults remaining guarded in their sharing practices. In this sense, the grandchild is used to being the 'topic' of conversation, with themes of discussion focusing on their lives, achievements and futures. However, with dementia, there is often a need for conversational partners to have a level of pre-existing contextual understanding about the person and their past lives, in order to find 'a way in' to conversation [49], which can be challenging for youths.

In this sense, our *Ticket-to-Talk* idea opened the potential for the young people to learn about and connect with older loved ones in new and interesting ways, using a range of media to do so. However, we found that they displayed a level of uncertainty in relation to managing potentially complex situations (such as the person with dementia displaying issues with topic maintenance). Whilst there is potential for future technologies to provide in-situ support during times that communication breakdowns occur, previous research suggests that these are not always effective and can instead cause additional stress on the conversational partner [21]. In this sense, it is important that future technologies not only facilitate the curation of media and scaffolding of conversation, but also provide a way for youths to shape their practical communication skills. This might be through the provision of practical tips and strategies (e.g. similar to that provided by [53]), or by providing them with a space to reflect on their interactions and the successes and challenges they have faced. Previous work has explored the benefits of collaborative reflection within interpersonal communication in a counseling context [40]. Whilst this is obviously presented within a different context to our work, there is potential for future systems to provide a space for scaffolding collaborative reflection around successful communication strategies, between youths and their family members.

CONCLUSIONS AND FUTURE WORK

Through this study we have offered a deepened understanding of the specific needs and values of youths within the context of engaging with dementia. Our study has reinforced the central role that the initiation and maintenance of conversation, supportive communicative environments, and the recognition of individual personhood, have in supporting intergenerational contact between young people and their loved ones with dementia. The design concepts we created were not intended to be finalized solutions, rather, they served as a tool to facilitate discussion. Future research is required to further scope the design space around digital systems to support youths in connecting with loved ones, through facilitating the initiation and maintenance of meaningful interactions, whilst being appreciative of the complex family relationships that surround youths and people with dementia. There is great potential for future systems to scaffold information and support sharing practices among both peers and individual families.

ACKNOWLEDGEMENTS

This work was funded by the EPSRC Digital Economy Research Centre (EP/M023001/1) and the ESRC-IAA 'Co-production of dementia-care communications technology' project. Data supporting this publication is available under an 'Open Data Commons Open Database License' and is available at: http://dx.doi.org/10.17634/141304-7. Please contact Newcastle University Research Data Service at rdm@ncl.ac.uk for access instructions. We give special thanks to Miriam Sturdee for designing figure 1.

REFERENCES

1. Alm Norman, Richard Dye, Gary Gowans, Jim Campbell, Arlene Jean Astell, and Maggie Ellis. 2007. A communication support system for older people with dementia. *IEEE Computer*. 40, 5: 60-66. DOI: http://dx.doi.org/10.1109/MC.2007.153
2. Alzheimer's Association. Communication. 2016. Retrieved August 21, 2016 from http://www.alz.org/nca/in_my_community_22018.asp
3. Alzheimer's Society. Communicating. 2016. Retrieved August 21, 2016 from https://www.alzheimers.org.uk/site/scripts/documents_info.php?documentID=130
4. American Psychiatric Association. 2013. *Diagnostic and statistical manual of mental disorders* (5th ed.). American Psychiatric Publishing, Arlington, VA.
5. Arlene Astell, Norman Alm, Gary Gowans, Maggie Ellis, Richard Dye, and Phillip Vaughan. 2009. Involving older people with dementia and their carers in designing computer based support systems: some methodological considerations. *Univers. Access Inf. Soc.* 8, 1: 49-58. DOI: http://dx.doi.org/10.1007/s10209-008-0129-9
6. Susan Mary Benbow, David Jolley. 2012. Dementia: stigma and its effects. *Neurodegenerative Disease Management* 2,2:165–172. DOI: http://dx.doi.org/10.2217/nmt.12.7
7. Frank R. Bentley, Santosh Basapur, and Sujoy Kumar Chowdhury. 2011. Promoting intergenerational communication through location-based asynchronous video communication. In*Proceedings of the 13th international conference on Ubiquitous computing* (UbiComp '11). ACM, New York, NY, USA, 31-40. DOI: http://dx.doi.org/10.1145/2030112.2030117
8. Rita Maldonado Branco, Joana Quental, and Óscar Ribeiro. 2016. Playing with personalisation and openness in a codesign project involving people with dementia. In *Proceedings of the 14th Participatory Design Conference: Full papers - Volume 1* (PDC '16), Vol. 1. ACM, New York, NY, USA, 61-70. DOI: http://dx.doi.org/10.1145/2940299.2940309
9. Virginia Braun and Victoria Clarke. 2006. Using thematic analysis in psychology. *Qualitative research in psychology* 3, no. 2 (2006): 77-101. DOI: http://doi.org/abs/10.1191/1478088706qp063oa
10. Louis Burgio, Rebecca Allen-Burge, A. Stevens, L. Davis, D. Marson. 2000. Caring for Alzheimer's disease patients: Issues of verbal communication and social interaction. *The gerontological prism: Developing interdisciplinary bridges*: 231-258.
11. Carer's Trust. What is a young carer? 2012. Retrieved September 21, 2016 from https://www.carers.org/what-young-carer
12. Jill Clark and Ian Hall. The Skype Grannies project final report. Technical report, Newcastle University Centre for Learning and Teaching, 2011. Retrieved September 21, 2016 from http://www.ncl.ac.uk/cflat/news/documents/TheSkypeGranniesProjectupdated110811.pdf
13. Allison Druin, Benjamin B. Bederson, and Alex Quinn. 2009. Designing intergenerational mobile storytelling. In *Proceedings of the 8th International Conference on Interaction Design and Children*(IDC '09). ACM, New York, NY, USA, 325-328. DOI: http://dx.doi.org/10.1145/1551788.1551875
14. Erik H. Erikson. 1968. *Identity: Youth and Crisis*. New York: Norton.
15. Daniel Fitton, and Beth Bell. 2014. Working with Teenagers within HCI Research: Understanding Teen-Computer Interaction. In *Proceedings of the 28th International BCS Human Computer Interaction Conference on HCI 2014-Sand, Sea and Sky-Holiday HCI*, pp. 201-206. BCS, 2014.
16. Daniel Fitton, Janet C. Read, Matthew Horton, Linda Little, Nicola Toth, and Yukang Guo. 2012. Constructing the cool wall: a tool to explore teen meanings of cool. *PsychNology* 10, 2: 141-162.
17. Daniel Fitton, Janet C. Read, and Matthew Horton. 2013. The challenge of working with teens as participants in interaction design. In *CHI '13 Extended Abstracts on Human Factors in Computing Systems* (CHI EA '13). ACM, New York, NY, USA, 205-210. DOI: http://dx.doi.org/10.1145/2468356.2468394
18. Verena Fuchsberger, Julia Nebauer, Christiane Moser, and Manfred Tscheligi. 2012. Design challenges and concept for intergenerational online learning. In *Proceedings of the 11th International Conference on Interaction Design and Children* (IDC '12). ACM, New York, NY, USA, 192-195. DOI=http://dx.doi.org/10.1145/2307096.2307123
19. Fleur Gabriel. 2014. Sexting, selfies and self-harm: young people, social media and the performance of self-development. *Media International Australia,* 151,1: 104-112. DOI: http://dx.doi.org/10.1177/1329878X1415100114
20. Marie Glasemann, Anne Marie Kanstrup, and Thomas Ryberg. 2010. Making chocolate-covered broccoli: designing a mobile learning game about food for young people with diabetes. In*Proceedings of the 8th ACM Conference on Designing Interactive Systems* (DIS '10). ACM, New York, NY, USA, 262-271. DOI: http://doi.acm.org/10.1145/1858171.1858219

21. Kirstie Hawkey, Kori M. Inkpen, Kenneth Rockwood, Michael McAllister, and Jacob Slonim. 2005. Requirements gathering with alzheimer's patients and caregivers. In Proceedings of the 7th international ACM SIGACCESS conference on Computers and accessibility (Assets '05). ACM, New York, NY, USA, 142-149. DOI: http://dx.doi.org/10.1145/1090785.1090812

22. Niels Hendriks, Liesbeth Huybrechts, Andrea Wilkinson, and Karin Slegers. 2014. Challenges in doing participatory design with people with dementia. In *Proceedings of the 13th Participatory Design Conference: Short Papers, Industry Cases, Workshop Descriptions, Doctoral Consortium papers, and Keynote abstracts - Volume 2* (PDC '14), Vol. 2. ACM, New York, NY, USA, 33-36. DOI: http://dx.doi.org/10.1145/2662155.2662196

23. Matthew K. Hong, Lauren Wilcox, Daniel Machado, Thomas A. Olson, and Stephen F. Simoneaux. 2016. Care Partnerships: Toward Technology to Support Teens' Participation in Their Health Care. In *Proceedings of the 2016 CHI Conference on Human Factors in Computing Systems* (CHI '16). ACM, New York, NY, USA, 5337-5349. DOI: http://dx.doi.org/10.1145/2858036.2858508

24. David Hounsell. 2013. Hidden from View: The Experiences of Young Carers in England. The Children's Society. Retrieved September 21, 2016 from http://www.childrenssociety.org.uk/sites/default/files/tcs/report_hidden-from-view_young-carers_final.pdf

25. Amanda Lenhart,, Maeve Duggan, Andrew Perrin, Renee Stepler, Harrison Rainie, and Kim Parker. Teens, social media & technology overview 2015. 2015. Pew Research Centre. Retrieved September 21, 2016 from http://www.pewinternet.org/2015/04/09/teens-social-media-technology-2015/

26. Stephen Lindsay, Katie Brittain, Daniel Jackson, Cassim Ladha, Karim Ladha, and Patrick Olivier. 2012. Empathy, participatory design and people with dementia. In *Proceedings of the SIGCHI Conference on Human Factors in Computing Systems* (CHI '12). ACM, New York, NY, USA, 521-530. DOI: http://dx.doi.org/10.1145/2207676.2207749

27. Julia M. Mayer and Jelena Zach. 2013. Lessons learned from participatory design with and for people with dementia. In *Proceedings of the 15th international conference on Human-computer interaction with mobile devices and services* (MobileHCI '13). ACM, New York, NY, USA, 540-545. DOI: http://dx.doi.org/10.1145/2493190.2494436

28. Maurice Mulvenna, Suzanne Martin, Stefan Sävenstedt, Johan Bengtsson, Franka Meiland, Rose Marie Dröes, Marike Hettinga, Ferial Moelaert, and David Craig. 2010. Designing & evaluating a cognitive prosthetic for people with mild dementia. In *Proceedings of the 28th Annual European Conference on Cognitive Ergonomics* (ECCE '10). ACM, New York, NY, USA, 11-18. DOI: http://dx.doi.org/10.1145/1962300.1962306

29. Joanna Murray, Justine Schneider, Sube Banerjee, & Antony Mann. 1999. EUROCARE: A crossnational study of co-resident spouse carers for people with Alzheimer's disease: II—A qualitative analysis of the experience of caregiving. *International Journal of Geriatric Psychiatry*, 14, 662-667.

30. Toshihiro Nakae, Shiro Ozawa, and Naoya Miyashita. 2010. O-Link: augmented object system for intergenerational communication. *ACM SIGGRAPH 2010 Posters*. ACM, 2010.

31. National Alliance for Caregiving and United Hospital Fund. Young Caregivers in the U.S.: Report of Findings; September 2005. Retrieved September 21, 2016 from www.caregiving.org

32. William Odom, John Zimmerman, Scott Davidoff, Jodi Forlizzi, Anind K. Dey, and Min Kyung Lee. 2012. A fieldwork of the future with user enactments. In *Proceedings of the Designing Interactive Systems Conference* (DIS '12). ACM, New York, NY, USA, 338-347. DOI=http://dx.doi.org/10.1145/2317956.2318008

33. William Odom, John Zimmerman, and Jodi Forlizzi. 2011. Teenagers and their virtual possessions: design opportunities and issues. In *Proceedings of the SIGCHI Conference on Human Factors in Computing Systems* (CHI '11). ACM, New York, NY, USA, 1491-1500. DOI: http://dx.doi.org/10.1145/1978942.1979161

34. J.B. Orange. (1991). Perspectives of family members regarding communication changes. In R.B. Lubinski, J.B. Orange, D. Henderson & N. Stecker (Eds.), Dementia and communication (pp. 168-186). Philadelphia, PA: Mosby.

35. Martin Prince, Anders Wimo, Maelenn Guerchet, et al. 2015. *The Global Impact of Dementia: An analysis of prevalence, incidence, cost and Trends*. Alzheimer's Disease International, London.

36. Janet C. Read, Matthew Horton, Ole Iversen, Daniel Fitton, and Linda Little. 2013. Methods of working with teenagers in interaction design. In *CHI '13 Extended Abstracts on Human Factors in Computing Systems* (CHI EA '13). ACM, New York, NY, USA, 3243-3246. DOI: http://dx.doi.org/10.1145/2468356.2479657

37. Pamela Roach., John, Keady., Penny Bee., Sion Williams. (2013). "We can"t keep going on like this': identifying family storylines in young onset dementia.

Ageing and Society, 34(8), 1397–1426. doi:10.1017/S0144686X13000202

38. Marie Y. Savundranayagam, Mary Lee Hummert, & Rhonda JV Montgomery. 2005. Investigating the effects of communication problems on caregiver burden. *The Journals of Gerontology, Series B: Psychological Sciences and Social Sciences* 60, 1 (2005), S48-S55.

39. Karin Slegers, Andrea Wilkinson, and Niels Hendriks. 2013. Active collaboration in healthcare design: participatory design to develop a dementia care app. In *CHI '13 Extended Abstracts on Human Factors in Computing Systems* (CHI EA '13). ACM, New York, NY, USA, 475-480. DOI: http://dx.doi.org/10.1145/2468356.2468440

40. Petr Slovák, Anja Thieme, David Murphy, Paul Tennent, Patrick Olivier, and Geraldine Fitzpatrick. 2015. On Becoming a Counsellor: Challenges and Opportunities to Support Interpersonal Skills Training. In *Proceedings of the 18th ACM Conference on Computer Supported Cooperative Work & Social Computing* (CSCW '15). ACM, New York, NY, USA, 1336-1347. DOI: http://dx.doi.org/10.1145/2675133.2675190

41. Jeff A. Small, Kathy Geldart, & Gloria Gutman. 2000. Communication between individuals with dementia and their caregivers during activities of daily living. *American Journal of Alzheimer's Disease & Other Dementias*. 15: 291-302.

42. Robert Strom, & Paris Strom. 2013. Grandparents and reciprocal learning for family harmony. In P. Hughes (Ed). A*chieving quality education for all: Perspectives from the Asia-Pacific Region and beyond*. New York, NY: Springer

43. Rachel Thompson. 2011. Using life story work to enhance care. *Nursing Older People* 23 (8): 16-21. DOI: http://dx.doi.org/10.7748/nop2011.10.23.8.16.c8713

44. UNESCO. http://www.unesco.org/new/en/social-and-human-sciences/themes/youth/youth-definition/

45. Frank Vetere, Hilary Davis, Martin R. Gibbs, Peter Francis, and Steve Howard. 2006. A magic box for understanding intergenerational play. In *CHI '06 Extended Abstracts on Human Factors in Computing Systems* (CHI EA '06). ACM, New York, NY, USA, 1475-1480. DOI: http://dx.doi.org/10.1145/1125451.1125722

46. Mary Webster, Emma Foster, Rob Comber, Simon Bowen, Tim Cheetham, and Madeline Balaam. 2015. Understanding the lived experience of adolescents with tyouthse 1 diabetes: opportunities for design. In *Proceedings of the 14th International Conference on Interaction Design and Children*(IDC '15). ACM, New York, NY, USA, 140-149. DOI: http://dx.doi.org/10.1145/2771839.2771854

47. Jayne Wallace, Anja Thieme, Gavin Wood, Guy Schofield, and Patrick Olivier. 2012. Enabling self, intimacy and a sense of home in dementia: an enquiry into design in a hospital setting. In*Proceedings of the SIGCHI Conference on Human Factors in Computing Systems* (CHI '12). ACM, New York, NY, USA, 2629-2638. http://dx.doi.org/10.1145/2207676.2208654

48. Jayne Wallace, Peter C. Wright, John McCarthy, David Philip Green, James Thomas, and Patrick Olivier. 2013. A design-led inquiry into personhood in dementia. In *Proceedings of the SIGCHI Conference on Human Factors in Computing Systems* (CHI '13). ACM, New York, NY, USA, 2617-2626. http://dx.doi.org/10.1145/2470654.2481363

49. Barbara Watson, Lisa Dawn Aizawa, Marie Y. Savundranayagam, & J.B. Orange. Links among communication, dementia and caregiver burden. *Canadian Journal of Speech-Language Pathology and Audiology* 36, 4 (2012), 276-284.

50. Barry Wellman and Scot Wortley. 1990. Different Strokes from Different Folks: Community Ties and Social Support. American Journal of Sociology 96, 3, 558–588

51. Bob Woods, Aimee E Spector, Catherine A Jones, Martin Orrell, and Stephen P Davies. Reminiscence therapy for dementia. *Cochrane Database Syst Rev 2* (2005). DOI: http://dx.doi.org/10.1002/14651858.CD001120.pub2

52. Tony J Young, Chris Manthorp, David Howells, & Ellen Tullo. 2011. Developing a carer communication intervention to support personhood and quality of life in dementia. *Ageing and Society*, 31(6), 1003-1025.

53. Tony J Young, Chris Manthorp, David Howells and John Vines. 2013. DemTalk: Dementia Toolkit for effective communication. Retrieved September 21, 2016 from http://www.demtalk.org.uk/

The Value of Experience-Centred Design Approaches in Dementia Research Contexts

Kellie Morrissey[1], John McCarthy[2], Nadia Pantidi[2]

[1] Open Lab, Newcastle University, Newcastle upon Tyne, UK, kellie.morrissey@newcastle.ac.uk

[2] School of Applied Psychology, University College Cork, Ireland, {john.mccarthy, konstantia.pantidi} @ucc.ie

ABSTRACT
Experience-Centred Design (ECD) has been applied in numerous HCI projects to call attention to the particular and dialogical nature of people's experiences with technology. In this paper, we report on ECD within the context of publicly-funded, long-stay residential dementia care, where the approach helped to highlight aspects of participants' felt experience, and informed sensitive and meaningful design responses. This study contributes an extended understanding of the quality of experience and the means of making sense in dementia, as well as unpicking the potential of ECD to support enriched experience and contextual meaning-making for people with dementia. Finally, we delineate what it is about Experience-Centred Design that differentiates the approach from other often-used approaches in designing in dementia contexts: 1) explorative thinking, 2) working within 'cuttings-out of time and space', 3) careful yet expressive methodology and documentation, and 4) working together to imagine futures. We end with considerations of how the contributions of this research may extend to other experience-centred projects in challenging settings.

Author Keywords
Dementia; Experience-Centred Design; design methods; design approaches; embodiment; experience.

ACM Classification Keywords
H.5.m. Information interfaces and presentation (e.g., HCI): Miscellaneous.

INTRODUCTION
A growing public interest in dementia and in ways of preventing or reversing its effects in recent years has subsequently been mirrored by a growth in the design literature surrounding the condition. This literature tends to find a focus not on prevention, but on helping people with dementia or their carers to live with the condition in ways that are more independent or more meaningful to them. Within the HCI and design community, designing for and with people with dementia (PWD) has also presented opportunities for designing new technologies that can tell us more about the experience of dementia itself.

CHI 2017, May 06-11, 2017, Denver, CO, USA.
 ISBN 978-1-4503-4655-9/17/05…$15.00.
DOI: http://dx.doi.org/10.1145/3025453.3025527

Most design research in the past has focused on addressing these issues by way of designing assistive technologies – e.g., memory aids, GPS tracking devices [4]. For people with dementia (and older people in general), assistive technologies may offer relief and support – particularly in the early stages of dementia, where symptoms are often limited to mild cognitive impairment and where independent living is still possible [3]. However, as the condition progresses, memory problems can be compounded by changes in communication styles, and feelings of frustration, anger and uselessness as independence is curtailed or precipitated by a move into living in care [35]. At this point, designing for technological intervention and the idea of assistive technology becomes a more complex issue.

Experience-Centred Design [ECD - 25, 26, 48] has been applied in studies involving people with dementia as participants [41, 44], as well as when working with people facing difficult circumstances, such as migrant women with experience of domestic violence [8] and women with mental health issues living in institutions [39]. Given the complexity of living with dementia in particular, Experience-Centred Design has been indicated as a way forward in designing for and with people with dementia in order to keep the experience of participants alive and at the forefront of design projects. In a 2016 article in *interactions,* describing the value of ECD in dementia research projects, [18] writes that "*at the heart of Experience-Centred Design is an appreciation for the richness of human experience, a concern for meaning and how people make sense of their experiences, and the mindset that innovation should strive to enhance life, particularly for those who are disenfranchised*" (p. 61).

This paper applies ECD in a context in which lived experience is considered to be far from rich and in which the capacity of the person with dementia to make sense of this experience is considered lost, or greatly diminished [45]. In the process, its major contribution is to extend our understanding of the quality of experience and the means of making sense in dementia, as well as the potential of ECD to support enriching experience and meaning-making in this context. Given the growing prominence of dementia in the design literature, this paper has two key objectives. First, we identify the key elements of an ECD approach in designing for dementia with particular reference to our own design research with people with dementia, and secondly, we delineate key differences in using ECD, when applied to a dementia context. The next section will describe these approaches in more detail.

DESIGN AND DEMENTIA

This section provides a short review of selected extant design literature pertaining to dementia. We have divided these studies into broad themes, and in a final subsection, we describe past ECD design projects that focused on design and dementia, and which offer a contrast to compensation and connection approaches. However, it should be noted that these approaches overlap significantly and cannot be considered as entirely discrete categories.

Compensation and cognition

This subsection describes design research which attempts to enhance or replace cognitive skills that have been seen to have been lost in the progress of a person's dementia. These deficits have often represented seemingly 'fixable' challenges for many designers, even when applied to real-life situations. This sort of design conceptualizes each deficit as a gap that can be bridged with the right design. For instance, the COGKNOW DayNavigator [31] is one such example of a technology that aims to displace some of the issues caused by memory loss in dementia. This is a touchscreen device with computer-mediated controls as well as a mobile device to bring along when going out for the day. Its aim is to remind its users of particular tasks in their day-to-day lives – for instance, when to attend particular appointments and when to eat.

Similarly, some design studies have attempted to solve or ameliorate problems such as wandering in people living with dementia [4, 21]. Wandering is a common symptom of dementia and manifests in different ways – people with dementia who wander may do so either seemingly aimlessly (in nursing homes, for instance, residents may do 'rounds' of the care setting with no clear destination expressed), or with a purpose in mind that is expressed to others (e.g., "I need to find the way out of here"), but eventually forgotten [22]. Wandering in dementia is commonly addressed with the use of a GPS device that is often attached somewhere to the body of the person [4, 21]. Although this may provide peace of mind for the carers, it is easy to imagine why someone with dementia may resist this. Dementia is still stigmatised, and one study of perceptions of stigma by people with dementia describes a tension between seeking medical or community care and, in receiving that help, being marked out as a 'sufferer' [23]. Another study by Hopper, Piasek & Irving [16] indicated that users of assistive technologies for dementia had concerns surrounding their implementation and visibility in home environments.

Looking at participants engaging within an environment, [33] and [46] employ ambient assisted living technologies in a way that helps people with dementia to retain and use skills in an embodied way. The Ambient Kitchen utilizes several sensors in kitchen tools, paneling and flooring as well as cameras and speakers to deliver audio commands to users that guide them through simple cooking tasks such as cooking an omelette or making a cup of tea. This sort of work represents a different approach to designing in dementia – one which makes use of the skills still present in the person themselves and is mindful of the environment in which it is placed.

Although many technological interventions focus on the deterioration of cognitive skills in dementia, people with dementia do not see a total dissolution of these abilities, and many dementia scholars emphasise the interconnectedness of cognition and other aspects of experience:

... many aspects of the cognitive life of people with dementia survive into the moderate to severe stages of the disease. These cognitive abilities include (amongst others) the ability to behave on the basis of the meaning of situations, to experience a range of emotions, to experience and seek to avoid embarrassment, to feel pride and seek to maintain self-respect, to feel concern for others, to communicate effectively with facilitation by others [...], and to display at least implicit short-term and long-term memory. [19:295]

Compensatory approaches are sometimes complicated by their deployment in situations that are politically complex or in "*moments when participation is organised by structures of privilege that deny difference and diversity*" [27] – for instance, while living in care or under the care of family members. A different reading of ability, difference, and experience in dementia may similarly allow us to approach the 'deficits' that come with dementia in a more holistic way. When we seek to compensate in designing for people with dementia, perhaps we might also look at the environment in which the person lives, and the relationships that sustain them therein.

Connection and keeping in touch

This section describes a series of design studies which are primarily interested in keeping people with dementia in touch with their carers and families, or otherwise focusing on the social life of the person with dementia. Social and relational aspects of dementia can impact upon the person as much as the cognitive issues which come with it [34]. In the above-cited paper by [33], participants who had recently received a diagnosis state that people tend to '*stand back from dementia, because it's too heavy*' (p. 33). However, it seems that an active social life in later life can delay or protect against the development of dementia, and may also slow its progression: [46] suggest that the effect may be seen via psychosocial pathways, wherein participation in meaningful activities with others can lend the person with dementia a heightened sense of self-esteem and usefulness.

HCI studies have approached this problem from several different standpoints. [2] focuses on the design of a touchscreen system for the express use of people with dementia, which may help users with dementia and their carers to participate in conversations on a more equal basis. Their prototype, developed with the advice of people with dementia as well as carers, is a touchscreen system that takes for its basis the idea of reminiscence for people with dementia as being potentially useful in stimulating discussion. The evaluation notes that the system allows its users to interact on a '*more or less equal basis*' to others without dementia [2]. The idea that a disconnect between these sets of people rests on differences of *communication* rather than a deficit in *cognition* is one which does not propagate a notion of the person with dementia as 'lesser', and is a promising goal for future work in dementia care.

Other studies in HCI have used the idea of reminiscence and reminiscence therapy as a way to encourage conversation in people with dementia – for example, [20, 37], who both create web-based applications and interactive systems to deliver these services. [37] details the development of a system that delivers 'personalised' reminiscence therapy via a web-based platform. The personalization of this system is carried out via a short questionnaire delivered to users with dementia prior to the system starting up – from then on, the content is personalized to their interests. That the design allows for individualization is likely to be useful for people with dementia and acknowledges the multiplicity of experiences which people with dementia and their families may face in the course of the condition.

One of the most prominent issues in designing within dementia care is the complexity of the effects that are desired – ameliorating conversation, achieving therapeutic effects, or even cognitive rehabilitation. Some studies simply attempt to keep participants with dementia 'in touch' with larger social networks of friends, family and caregivers. [24] describes a social network design which attempts to 'friendsource' unmet needs of people with dementia, both by automatically capturing data from the PWD's smartphone to track their whereabouts, and by providing a private social network group used to 'validate' events in the PWD's life. The paper lists three potential uses of the system as 'reminiscence therapy tool', 'in-situ communication aid', and 'daily routines and reminders'. The system was piloted with staff from a local dementia aid charity, and themes extracted from an interview with the staff member include a need for more balanced tools, the struggle of presenting content, engaging a larger support network, and guarding the right of privacy of people with dementia.

Although most of these papers proceed from a progressive, psychosocial perspective on dementia, many also lack *actual* connection and presence between two or more people – instead, several of these systems intend to automate processes such as choosing material for reminiscence sessions or even conversations (such as Sakai et al's [36] listener agent [chatbot] for people with dementia). This is despite the acknowledgement within these papers that socialization itself is important for people with dementia. If being with others is so important (as evidenced in the clinical literature and the firsthand accounts of families living with the condition [1, 6]), the technologies we design should work to enrich this co-presence rather than provide a facsimile of it.

Working with experience

The following section will unpack ECD not necessarily as an alternative to assistive designs described above, but as a different way of exploring these often deeply personal issues. Dementia is a complex condition that cannot be reduced even to a given set of cognitive, social and emotional issues – in many cases, it is not enough to identify the ways in which participants' lives are lacking and then design to 'cover' those gaps – instead, we should try to understand their lived and felt experience, and position our design as an empathic response to this experience.

Within a context of dementia care, Experience-Centred Design is promising in that it provides a critical approach to design, which "*gives people the chance to have a richer life, to include people who might otherwise feel excluded, to ensure that everybody has a chance to have their say especially those who often feel voiceless*" [47:10]. The approach is a humanistic one to understanding the relationships between people and technology *in felt terms*. It is not an alternative to user-centred design, but "*a different sensibility towards it, a different way of relating to familiar precepts such as know the user, iterative design, and user involvement*" [47:20]. ECD does not disavow the need for user needs and requirements; "*rather the focus is an understanding of individuals, their concerns, desires, aspirations, values, and experience*" [47:20]. Its use in design studies such as Thieme et al's [39] exploration of mental health in women's institutions and Clarke et al's [8] ethnography of a migrant women's centre in the UK is a testament to its suitability to situations where participants are facing significant challenges. In the next subsection, we will discuss its use in dementia research by Wallace et al [43, 44] in particular.

Initial explorations of ECD and dementia

McCarthy & Wright articulate a dialogical ethics which is predicated on aesthetic experience or 'richly seeing' [14], which is integral to keeping the experiences of participants alive. This approach is explored in research for and with people with dementia by Jayne Wallace [43, 44]. For Wallace, this approach helped her to understand the experiences of her participants in a way that made it possible for her to keep their experience alive in the resulting designs. A first project [43], situated in an adult mental health unit which housed people with dementia, featured an interactive art piece entitled *Tales of I*, installed for the use of all residents. The art installation included a wall cabinet which housed a series of globes fitted with RFID tags, and a television unit which facilitated the 'playing' of videos housed within these globes when they were placed upon a certain point on the unit. These globes and videos were 'themed' – e.g., holiday, nature, football – and particular attention is paid to the material and tactile nature of the design engagement:

"*... our use of color, variety of materials and detailed colorful scenes that were captured in resin globes were all intended to catch the eye and provoke curiosity and fascination [...] It was important to us that the piece was well made, interesting and beautiful as we wanted to convey to clients that they were valued and deserved beautiful things*." (p. 2632)

In a paper the following year [44], Wallace et al expanded their work on ECD and dementia care in a paper which described a relationship with Gillian, a woman who had recently received a diagnosis of dementia, and John, her husband, focusing on similar themes of valuing different forms of communication as Gillian's dementia progressed. Our work extends Wallace et al's research in a series of more experientially-impoverished care settings – primarily a publicly-funded, low-resource, and understaffed care centre. Although staff within the home were dedicated, caring and resourceful, the home itself had little funding, and, situated within the grounds of an old hospital, it was clinical-feeling and small – for instance, residents slept in communal dormitories and had relatively little privacy and personal space. Within this project, we focused on themes of participation and community, given an overriding sense of disconnect between residents within the centre. The major contribution of this account is to extend our understanding of the quality of experience in a very different context to those which have gone before, as well as to advance considerations of the means of making sense in dementia.

METHODOLOGY

Our design research for and with people with dementia took place over the course of three years (2013-2016) and was situated in three different care institutions for people with dementia (though this paper reports from engagements from one in particular – St Eithne's). We adopted an ethnographic approach, which saw the first author entering care homes twice a week at the beginning, at first observing daily life in the institutions, before moving to carrying out creative group and one-on-one activities, and, later, design workshops with working prototypes. This research aimed to understand ways in which people with dementia could meaningfully participate in creative activities, with a secondary aim of understanding ways in which this participation might be 'enfolded' into design processes. We were aware that differences in communication may make the expression of residents' experience difficult. As a result, in our observational research, we paid particular attention to bodily forms of communication. We were influenced by Kontos [19], who describes how her participants, people with dementia living in care, would engage in competent and meaningful engagements with their environments and others around them, particularly during embodied activities such as dancing or exercising:

"*Despite their severe cognitive impairment, the residents were not launching their bodies into blind attempts to perform an action. The movements of their bodies were perfectly suited to the circumstances, disclosing a practical competence in their engagement with the world.*" [19: 261]

We took detailed field notes which we expanded later into field texts. These field texts placed a primacy on phenomenological aspects of being within the care centre – on the concrete, visceral and palpable character of experience [25]. Within this, we focused not only on our own experience but on the felt aspect of relations with others.

Reflexivity and dialogicality

The emotional tensions inherent to doing ethnography in dementia care are worth describing. Ethnographers face a number of issues when carrying out what Wacquant [42] dubs 'carnal sociology'; the forms of ethnography which involve deep involvement and participation on behalf of the researcher. These forms of ethnography see the researcher "submit to the fire of action in situ" [42] and can prompt an emotional reaction from the ethnographer which is then detailed in the text produced from the research itself as a part of the action which occurred.

Several researchers have attempted to produce accounts of this empathic approach to navigating and configuring relationships 'in the field'. Wang [47] details her reactions to the formation of relationships during her ethnographic work in an international school in mainland China. Being of closer age to the younger students, she quickly develops relationships with them, which she intermittently refers to as friendships. However, she notes that the intimacy of their relations may have brought her perilously close to 'boundary violations', which have the potential to hurt those who are being researched as a part of the study. For instance, encountering a student-participant one day who was distressed by the behaviour of certain teachers, Wang found that she had to 'check herself' so as not to appear biased towards a certain subset of participants over others:

"*Honestly, I did feel devious at that moment. I could not help questioning myself: were they hurt by my restrained attitude? Were they disappointed in my friendship?*" [47:773]

Navigating relationships within ethnography, Wang concedes, is like navigating between 'falsehood and reality'. In this way, researchers may don a mask of sorts to appear more amenable to talking about participants' lives than really is the case. We straddled a different line between falsehood and reality – suffering from dementia as they did, our participants often believed that we were someone who we were not; a carer, a daughter, a co-worker – and thus our relationship proceeded by way of this 'falsehood', arguably more ethically than it might have, had we chosen reality over falsehood. We will discuss our experiences in navigating this schism responsively and responsibly later in this chapter.

It also bears acknowledging at this point that it is, of course, never possible for us to really *know* the experience of our participants, and this process is one which is even more complicated when there is a great mismatch in the cognitive and linguistic abilities between ourselves and our participants. However, over time (we spent over a year in St Eithne's), and through a dialogical though not necessarily verbally rich process of attentive listening [11], we came to be able to write about participants' experiences with some confidence, and triangulated these experiences with care staff and family members (when available).

Ethics

The research was granted approval by the University College Cork's School of Applied Psychology's research ethics committee, which consists of six senior research psychologists. Proxy consent was sought from families and appointed caregivers; however, the capability of some participants (whose dementia was at early stages) to consent to inclusion in the research was also assessed by medical staff who knew the clients and residents well. In order to ensure ongoing opportunities for participants to question their involvement in the project, we provided them with information sheets for themselves and for family members regarding what it meant to participate in the project. We also introduced the project at the beginning of each visit, and spent time individually with participants to ensure their continued consent. As a matter of course, participants and settings are anonymised throughout this paper.

Grounded Theory in ethnography

Using Grounded Theory (GT) as a method of organising these field notes, we followed Charmaz & Mitchell's [7] guidelines for carrying out qualitative data collection and analysis in ethnographic settings (*"what is the setting of action? What is the distribution of its actors over space and time? What do actors pay attention to?"*). GT is a systematic method of analysing and collecting data which begins with inductive inquiry. The process involves comparing data and analysis against itself in several iterative rounds, and emphasises the interactivity of the method, with the researcher as a kinaesthetically active participant within the analysis. Although GT is often characterised as a fairly rigid data analytic method, Charmaz' own work on chronic illness, which saw her iterative and interpretive collection and analysis of accumulating data, was a model for us as we worked to organise our field texts.

Grounded Theory is often characterised as a method for studying processes [7], making it a sensible choice for our purposes, and beyond this, was chosen early on as a data analytic method for our research due to its openness to all possible theoretical understandings, as well as its inbuilt systematic checks and refinements of major theoretical categories. Our analytic process began with a deep immersion into the data itself (typically a narrative field text), and proceeded with line-by-line coding. As per Charmaz, we coded for processes, actions, and meanings, which helped us to define connections between data. This process of open coding was followed by secondary coding, at which point memos taken from reflective accounts and rough field notes were taken into consideration to begin to build a tentative set of themes (set to change over iterative analyses).

In the below sections, we refer many times to field notes and personal encounters which were almost solely on the behalf of the primary researcher and first author, Kellie – when excerpts refer to 'I', they are extracted from her field notes. This next section expands on four seminal moments in our research process which were either guided by, or embody, certain Experience-Centred Design practices.

DOING ECD IN PUBLICLY-FUNDED, LONG-TERM CARE FOR PEOPLE WITH DEMENTIA

Self and song: Charlie and the songbook

Charlie was a resident who had recently moved from day care to full-time care, and had suffered a decline in his condition at the same time, itself possibly a consequence of the move. Charlie was one of the first residents with whom we connected in our time in St Eithne's – a vibrant, kindly man, he walked with two canes when really he needed only one. Initial field notes in the unit describe him as being *"well-turned out... wearing tweed and carrying a newspaper,"* and we spent a lot of time with him, sitting and talking about his childhood in the locality – fishing in rivers with his father, selling apples from crates in the local market. Charlie spoke to us about these experiences in-depth, chuckling as he recalled grasping the fish, slippery and cool from the river, wistful as he recounted walking the two miles home across fields, even as he was unable to tell us about the food he ate for lunch or the names of his children.

Charlie's home life was becoming increasingly difficult – his wife was very ill (though he couldn't tell us with what, exactly), and nurses told us that his grown family was busy and dispersed through the country. He became a full-time resident, and went from being chatty and fond of telling stories to instead becoming withdrawn, quiet, and relatively isolated as one of the only men in the care unit. Speaking to him now became difficult – he would repeatedly ask if he could leave with Kellie, ask for his car, or instead return to cyclical conversations surrounding a sense of a loss of power he felt. At the same time the unit was understaffed, and new and substitute staff found it difficult to connect with Charlie, of whose life outside the unit they knew quite little.

It was difficult for us to think how we could respond in a designerly way to this situation. The unit in which Charlie was living was one which was low on resources and time, and staff were reluctant for us to initiate contact with family members of people living in the unit (an initial idea was to create digital life story books for people who might be interested). Experience-Centred Design is explicitly interested in how people make sense of themselves in the context of their personal histories and anticipated futures – which is complicated in dementia, where an explicit recollection of past selves can be difficult, and even more difficult when family members are not available to discuss this in more depth with researchers. Most extant design work with people with dementia has involved carers or family members in 'informing' about the person with dementia. Despite these limitations, given Charlie's increasingly difficult experiences as a full-time resident, we knew that a rich response, which expressed something about our own positive relationship with Charlie, who we had come to know as an intelligent, lively and generous man, was warranted.

Our response was to create a simple songbook for Charlie that consisted of songs which we had heard him singing as a day resident (in fact, his performance of one song – The Moonshiner, a humorous Irish song about the illegal alcoholic drink poitín – had recently won him a prize at a local concert). We saw this songbook in use became a balm for the anxiety he felt in the care unit, and singing its songs together provided him a break from his cycle of dehumanising, difficult thinking. Our field notes report that, earlier in the week, prior to this gift-giving, "*he sat far back in his chair, shoulders slack and eyes alternatingly downcast and seemingly glazed over*", but now, "*he leaned forward in his chair, the two of us holding the book open together. The space around us seemed changed.*"

Leaving the unit, the day that we had given him this songbook, he turned to us and said '*My worries are gone. You reminded me I could sing, and I had forgotten that.*' Charlie's sense of his own cognitive decline, coupled with a move into vastly different living circumstances, had been mitigated at least partially by a reminder of aspects of his own self, history and proficiencies which were still very present. As the research process wore on, we saw this small token become an object which Charlie carried with him, and which nurses and staff members used to catch a glimpse of his inner life – for them, it became a 'way in' to Charlie's rich inner experience. Not only was this object a reminder of past experiences, but now something which facilitated a different type of interaction – not the medicalised relationship of professional care, but instead a re-affirmation (which Charlie voiced himself) of his proficiencies. For Charlie, singing meaningful songs was an aesthetic act; mirroring this, McCarthy and Wright write that "*the aesthetic act in daily life involves a reassumption and reconfirmation of one's own place after the other is encountered*" – here, it allowed us to create something which facilitated a positive social positioning of Charlie in the care unit.

Moving together: touch and embodied interaction

We were particularly surprised by the ways in which touch was important to residents of the care units – perhaps given a general change in inhibition in dementia, or to generational differences, many residents would reach out to us, hold our hands, embrace us or kiss us gently on the cheek. Although initially taken aback by this, we came to accept these gestures as being communicative of emotions and experiences which perhaps were not readily expressed in verbal means. This touch seemed to be tied to strong emotion – one resident, Marie, who believed that Kellie was her daughter, would hold her hand tightly and tell her that she loved her very much. It is a strange position for a researcher to be placed into, but Kellie reaffirmed these feelings through her response – not confirming Marie's idea of her as a daughter, but not disrupting it either.

One particular interaction with Marie illustrates the deeply emotional potential of touch in dementia. One day, as Kellie rose to switch the television to a new channel, a resident named Ros "*slapped the hand that* [Kellie] *reached out*":

"*Immediately, Marie is out of her seat and stalking towards the two of us. She grabs Ros's arm tight at the wrist. 'Don't you dare,' she says, hotly, 'touch my daughter. Who do you think you are? Who do you think you are?' The two stand, grappling together for a moment. I attempt to disentangle their hands, urging them to stop.*"

Finally, Ros wrenched free and left the room, wailing. Marie paused for a moment before turning and walking to another section of the room. After some time, Kellie followed her. She stood, looking out at the window. Field notes from Kellie go on to say: "*... she turns to me when she hears me enter, tears in her eyes. 'I'm sorry,' she says. 'I just can't bear anyone doing anything to my family. She's awful. She's awful.' I place my hands on her shoulder, and shortly afterwards we re-enter the parlour.*"

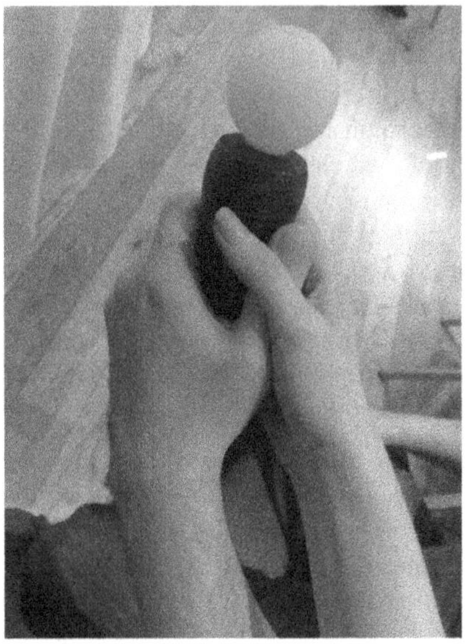

Image 1: SwaytheBand held by two hands at once

Here, different forms of touch (slapping, grabbing, disentangling, wrenching, a hand on the shoulder) provoke deeply felt emotions which are communicative of the relationships between actors within the situation, even when sense-making processes have broken down or changed due to dementia. Responsivity was important for us within these negotiated relationships, as it is in ECD, which describes how we can create the conditions for selfhood through the particulars of our affective and valuational responses to others. Therefore, Kim describes returning the soothing touch that Marie first extended to her in an attempt to make her feel better.

However, touch remains a complicated concept in dementia care. Twigg [40] writes that touch in care is *'structured according to gradations of intimacy and power'* [40:41]; in our interactions, we did not want to remind residents (who were already enduring significant carer intervention into activities such as washing and dressing) of these power imbalances in their current lives. We let them lead by example. One example is that of Valerie, with whom Kim spent an afternoon sitting and swaying gently to music – we detail in earlier publications [29, 30] how, within this interaction Valerie reached for Kim's hand, guiding it, twisting it in time to the music before bringing it gently to her face, rubbing it against her cheek and chin before finally kissing it and laying it down.

These and many other experiences with our participants led directly to several design configurations of our final digital prototype – SwaytheBand, a system of batons which flash to the beat of music to encourage residents to sway and spend time with one another to music (see image 1 for an early prototype using PS Move batons).

We designed the batons to be held by two hands at once, replicating the stretching of arms and touch and grasp of hands which were so prominent during our fieldwork. In this way, we paid particular attention to the sensual nature of explosion; in articulating the sensual thread of experience, McCarthy and Wright hold that this thread is *"concerned with our sensory engagement with a situation which orients us to the concrete, visceral and palpable character of experience... when senses are fully realised, the interaction between person and environment becomes participation and communication"* [25:80]. In working with dementia, the embodied and sensual nature of experience needs to be brought to the fore, not just out of aesthetic concerns, but because a heightened appreciation of this can help people with dementia to communicate in felt and embodied ways.

Making and feeling: absorptions and aesthetics

We carried out numerous small design-centred engagements with people with dementia – these were less like workshops and more like chats which had objects at their centre. For example, one engagement saw Kellie crouched in front of three ladies – Aideen, Teresa and Linda – going through swatches of cloth in an attempt to explore how they felt about the various materials. The end goal would be to use one of the materials in our SwaytheBand prototype, but for now we were simply interested in their ways of interacting with the cloth. To our surprise, the ladies did not give the sort of straightforward feedback we might have expected, but instead talked about the material in terms of the sort of purpose they might have made of it:

"*Aideen refused to touch the furry cap I had brought in, muttering under her breath as I reached out to touch her hand with the fabric, jerking her hand back. Teresa was more receptive. She took the cap, stroking the smooth fur first with the back of her hand, then grasping the fur itself, fingers disappearing into the pelt. She moved to the tail of the cap, which make her laugh. She wagged the tail at the other ladies, and they laughed together. 'I like that,' she said. 'It's lovely.' The ladies began to guess at ideas for what the materials could become. 'For a window,' said Teresa, as we held out a piece of white lace. 'A pyjamas,' said Linda, for a piece of linen.*" [from field text]

Taking the time to engage with materials in this way provided a window into the lives of our participants and allowed them to display and experience past skills. We occasionally brought along a ball of knitting, and, sitting with Máire, Kellie told her about failed attempts to knit a scarf for a sister. Asking Máire for her advice, she was surprised as Máire willingly took the knitting, and then watched Máire's fingers deftly push out row after row of neat stitches atop her own "*large, messy, loops*". Experience, for Dewey as well as McCarthy and Wright, is constituted by the relationship between self and object: feeling people acting and the materials and tools they use. But not only can objects and materials tell us about the people who interact with them: so too can they facilitate aesthetic experiences.

Absorption characterizes aesthetic experience possibly above all else – it is "*a breaking down of barriers between self and object, an outpouring of self into object*". It bears similarity to the notion of "flow", and Killick & Craig [19] use 'flow' to describe an encounter where a participants' engagement with his creative task, and the apparent mastery he displayed, had them wondering if he really had dementia at all. For us, aesthetic experience is defined by absorption, but is also deeply sensual and emotional. In our design workshops which progressively began to incorporate more and more interactions with music, leading to the design of our SwaytheBand prototype, we noticed how people could become absorbed in music when previous art-based engagements would prompt unease and impatience. One resident, Ben, tipped his chair back, closed his eyes, and sang along; another resident would choose to sing the same song over and over, explaining that it was the song her husband used to sing to her early in their marriage. This interpretation of 'material' is one which is loose – here, our materials were songs, sung from memory – but they told us as much about our participants as did engaging with textiles, and much than attempting to sit down with them with paints and pens:

"*Claire had seemed to really dislike the art session, calling herself 'useless' – with a bit of coaxing I got her to shade in part of a beach scene I had drawn, and with a little more coaxing she added some features to the painting, but then slammed her pencil down abruptly.*" [from field text]

Although music may seem like an unconventional way to progress a series of design engagements, for our participants, it made sense. Claire, who slammed her pencil down when we carried out art sessions, '*came alive*' to music. As music played in the background, she would "*... cackle, slide over in her seat towards me and grab my arm, shaking it a little and smiling. Her song would be punctuated by 'woohoos' and 'yoohoos' which garnered many curious looks from other residents; this yelling of hers was, I thought, designed to whip up participation from others.*" [from field text]

Claire would look to others as she shouted, saying 'come on' and gesture to them to begin cheering as well. She would be met with bemusement, but residents would often begin singing once they'd finished laughing. Claire's spectating, we thought, was designed to reach others; designed to spur others on to participation, to make light of the singing and the situation she found herself in and designed to respond not only to the music, but to those around her. Through music, Claire create opportunities to connect and communicate. Her rich engagement with others through music again provided a strong basis for our deployment of SwaytheBand within group settings (see image 2, below).

Anticipating futures: sense-making and improvisation

The final interaction we will describe here concerns the act of sense-making in dementia. McCarthy and Wright articulate this process as consisting of *anticipating* (the notion that our experience is shaped by what has come before), *connecting* (the immediate, prelinguistic sense of a situation), *interpreting* (finding narrative in the encounter), *reflecting* (making judgements on the encounter as it unfolds and placing value on it), *recounting* (considering the encounter in context of other people's experiences), and *appropriating* (relating the experience to past and future experiences – making it our own). We can never be "*outside an experience*", but thinking about processes of sense-making in this way helps to understand processes of meaning-making in dementia in particular.

Living in care for the first time at an advanced age, often experiencing illness beyond dementia, and living with strangers with whom you have nothing else in common, can be very difficult. When this happens, intersecting realities can make for contested space in dementia care. For example, one resident, Gilly, in her early days in the unit, would wander the halls incessantly, searching for a way out. She would then become convinced that she *was* at home, and was confused at the strangers in her house. Gilly would weave behind their seats to open windows in order to ensure her cat, Micky (who she had in fact left at her family home), could get in if he needed to. This caused consternation in the other residents, whose shouts would upset Gilly. Her situation did not make sense to her – in many ways, her wandering, opening of windows and doors, were all attempts at sense-making. For her, the process had broken down.

Over time, Gilly settled into the care unit. However, working with residents' whose processes of sense-making were different to our own was difficult. In one instance, a resident, Fionnuala, highlighted this by turning to Kellie and saying:

"*'I told the doctor about your problem,' she said to me, her eyes flicking to my face.*

'You did?' I asked, again.

'Yes. Did he not give you a call?'" [from field text]

Fionnuala already had an idea of their relationship in her head – one that Kellie was not privy to. She believed she had told the doctor about a problem. If Kellie answered 'incorrectly' here, it might throw the whole conversation off-kilter. When that happened, Fionnuala had a tendency to 'realise' where she was and grow distressed at being unable to leave.

"*'No,' I said. 'He didn't call me yet. Soon though, I hope.' She looked at me a little oddly but then her gaze shifted away. Our relationship, or at least the script of it that she kept running in her mind, was safe for now.*" [from field text]

Again, the ways in which Kellie responded to Fionnuala helped her to preserve a continuous sense of herself. We often wondered as well who *we* were to her in those moments; how she was positioning us. In writing about relationships in dementia, Oppenheimer [34] says that: "*it is the emotional context of these relationships (or their absence) that determine how much the person flourishes or withers, how much his potential for affection, enjoyment, humour, and the vivid communication of feeling, are stifled or expressed*" [34:321]. Our ability to improvise and help to retain Fionnuala's sense of self was brought into play later in the work, as well, where she would seem to have delusions concerning her knowing a famous singer and even believing she was sitting in a concert of his. Although this was unusual and even alarming, we worked with her sense-making processes as well as we could rather than ignore or contradict them.

Image 2: a family using SwaytheBand together

Dementia can make it difficult for people to comprehend a future, which means that many conventional design activities (*"How would you envision using this technology in your future day to day life?"*) are inappropriate. However, dementia doesn't rob them of that future – it simply cuts away the longitudinal ways in which we might construe that future. People with dementia may have fragmented pasts that are unequally buoyed by their rich and intense present, but their futures are still open in that they can be spontaneous, creative; they can improvise, plan at least some seconds into the future.

Improvisational skills are important for designers within this area. Sawyer [38] writing about the nature of improvisation, holds that:

'... *unpredictability and contingency results in performances that, at each moment, have a combinatorial complexity: A large number of next actions is possible, and each one of those actions could result in the subsequent flow of the performance going in a radically different direction.*' [38:33]

The very unpredictability of working with people with dementia itself indicates the vast amount of potential participants might have to offer via their inclusion in design. For now, what is important to take away from our ethnographic work is the value of working within the present moment – with an eye half-open to the future – and that, with participants with a diminished ability to reflect on past experiences, the ethnographer's role should be to 'keep experience alive' via their field notes and other means of data collection.

This brings us to a final point concerning working with rather than against dementia. In an earlier section, we described how many design studies in dementia position the condition as a series of problems to be fixed by the intervention of technology. Although these designs may indeed be useful for many with the condition, it must be tiring and dehumanising to be the object of studies that want to fix you, and which pathologise your symptoms and behaviour as 'wrong'. You may want to be fixed; you may understand that your condition has brought about significant negative change in your life. However, working to create technologies that explore the strengths of people with dementia – the remaining proficiencies, preferences, and passions - is not just ethical; it is likely to produce a design which is more in tune with their lives and likely to enrich their experiences.

DISCUSSION

The above case study contributes an account of Experience-Centred Design 'in action' within the setting of a publicly funded residential care unit for people with dementia. Through illustrated case examples of 1) selfhood being expressed through meaningful song, 2) touch and embodied interaction, 3) absorption in 'making' processes, and 4) sense-making and improvisation, we underline key practices in Experience-Centred Design which helped to 'anchor and capture' the experiences of our participants in a way which then allowed us to create a design response.

Our account differs from existing articulations of Experience-Centred Design in dementia contexts given the very different setting – i.e., a publicly-funded long-stay unit for people with dementia which, during the course of our research, was frequently understaffed and saw little family involvement. Although many people with dementia live in settings which have more resources and can afford richer experiences for them, the truth remains that many people do live within settings where they are dissatisfied. What is more, people can live within these places, often co-habiting with strangers for years at the end of their lives, when they are also possibly sick beyond a diagnosis of dementia. Although we are not suggesting that even the most sensitive digital design can 'fix' these difficult circumstances, we argue that a closely worked and carefully considered account of experience offers opportunities to enrich these experiences.

The picture we are often confronted with of life in nursing homes is grim. Gubrium [13] reflects on his 1975 ethnography of a nursing home to write that life within "*is filled with intimate social ties, the celebration of small accomplishments, agonizing losses, boredom, conspiracies, anger, pride, humiliation, trust, love, hope, despair – in short, all the complexities that occur when a group of people spend their daily lives together*" [12:5]. Writing about life in 'total institutions' like nursing homes, Goffman [12] notes that "*every* [institution] *can be seen as a kind of dead sea which little islands of vivid, encapturing activity appear*" [12:67]. Applying ECD within a dementia care context highlights these moments of 'vivid, encapturing activity' to find their significance within the everyday. The next and final section will highlight how we have delivered our contributions of a) extending our understanding of the quality of experience and the means of making sense in dementia, and b) extending the potential of ECD to support enriching experience and meaning-making in this context.

What does an Experience-Centred Design approach offer?

Experience-Centred Design offers a critical perspective on the design of technologies for people with dementia, but it is worth unpicking what this perspective offers in practical terms. This section delineates four critical points which highlight, for us, some of the particularly important lessons which helped to move our work with people with dementia along creative yet sensitive lines.

1. Explorative thinking vs. solutionist thinking

A critique of solutionism within HCI has risen within recent years, where it has been characterised as actively finding problems to solve, usually with quick fixes, without taking into account the complexity of the overall situation [5]. An explorative, open-ended approach can remain open to where experience takes the research – for example, our choosing to design via musical interactions given our participants' reaction to music, despite a discomfort on the part of the researcher. In ECD, being explorative means to find ways of engaging with and responding to experience, and not necessarily solutions. In this case, it has seen us rely less on language and more on gesture and movement which extended our appreciation of the experience of dementia as different styles of communication which can sometimes painfully pass each other by. This, for us, lead to an emphasis on modalities other than language in which both researchers and people with dementia could come together to make sense of experience.

2. Working within 'cuttings out of time and space'

Experience-Centred Design is frequently situation-specific design, which seeks to understand a person or people in the context of their surroundings. McCarthy & Wright [26] describe this as working within 'cuttings out of time and space', where working within these boundaries helps to keep experience alive within the design process and design interactions.

The notion of working within 'cuttings out' of experience is heightened in dementia, where, as we've described above, you do not simply inhabit a researcher's or designer's reality, but often several at once: consider Marie, who believed the researcher Kim was her daughter, or Fionnuala, who 'called the doctor' on Kim's behalf. We found that, in dementia care, it was more important to re-orient ourselves to our participants' realities than to correct them to the 'right reality' instead. Notions of empathy [23], ambiguity [11], and enchantment [27] are likely to enrich much design research with people with dementia.

3. Careful yet expressive methodology and documentation

Experience-Centred Design is typically centred around the use of qualitative methods such as interviews, ethnography, and diary studies - however, within these methodologies, there is a critical recognition of the researcher as a thinking, feeling tool in the design process. McCarthy and Wright describe ethnography as used in design research as a 'turn away from neutral description' [25:36], and as 'writing others' sense-making in a language that we can understand' [25:6]. Experience in ECD is never finalized, and as such our documentation of this experience is only ever to be understood as a snapshot of a 'cutting out of time and space' – however, doing ECD still requires careful documentation of the researchers' engagement within the world. For our work, it was only when we turned to what it *felt* like to be in the care setting – the scents and textures of care, which so frequently are medical and unfamiliar – that our field notes became rich enough to proceed from. This turn to phenomenological expressions of experience saw us asking how we can be said to understand another's experience when that experience was frequently linguistically incoherent and unlike any experience we have previously had.

4. Working together to imagine futures

Experience-Centred Design is often participative as it engages with people from the ground-up to negotiate a shared understanding of their experience. Moreover, it does this in a way which strives to be on the terms of the participants themselves – for instance, by visiting their homes or other familiar environments, and positioning them as experts in the design process. Although Experience-Centred Design is a research process that involves the elicitation and analysis of the experience of others, it is less a process of translation of experience than a co-negotiated conversation (that is often worked out with design materials). ECD is a process which results in the co-creation of new knowledge, and it is not focused on the representation of past knowledge, but is instead oriented always towards possible futures that are made possible by working together; McCarthy & Wright [26] explain that, in ECD approaches, persons and things are always in a dynamic process of becoming, and are always open to the future – even if that future, in dementia, is one whose horizon may sometimes appear lower than most.

REFLECTIONS ON OUR RESEARCH

This paper has delivered an account of lived experience in dementia care where experience itself is often impoverished and not satisfying, and in which participants' ability to make sense of experience is often vastly different to that of the researchers'. Through an elaborated case study of our own use of the approach within dementia care, this paper's major contribution is to extend our understanding of the quality of experience, and ways of making sense of experience, in dementia. We have also indicated the potential of ECD to support enriching experience and meaning-making in this context.

It is worth considering the scope of research such as this. Our research extended initial work into doing ECD with people with dementia by carrying the work out in experientially impoverished spaces – publicly funded, long-stay units for people with dementia, where family participation was often totally absent. Our application of ECD design principles within a dementia care setting allowed us to open up to new and different ways of communicating with residents in a way which responded to their strengths, interests and values, while being sensitive to the changes which a diagnosis of dementia can bring. ECD, within a dementia care context, allows researchers to focus on certain qualities of experience which are humanizing and sensitizing in working with participants who are non-verbal, yet sometimes extremely expressive via bodily movement, touch, gesture, and facial expression. Beyond this, combined with a flexible, inductive Grounded Theory analytic approach, the dialogical nature of our ECD approach ensured that any design response we created was anchored in the particular expressions of experience of our participants, and therefore lived within the network of relationships which sustained and enriched that same experience.

ACKNOWLEDGEMENTS

We would like to thank the Irish Research Council (GOIPG/2014/341) for funding the larger research project, the Create4Dementia hackathon, Dementia Care and Dave Stevens for providing a space for, as well as invaluable input on, the design of the SwaytheBand system. We would also like to thank our participants, the care staff, and other staff of care institutions, who have made the research possible.

REFERENCES

1. Katherine Abbott and Mark C. Pachucki. 2016. Associations between social network characteristics, cognitive function, and quality of life among residents in a dementia special care unit: A pilot study. *Dementia*, 1 (4): 71-83.
2. Norman Alm, Richard Dye, Gary Gowans, Jim Campbell, Arlene Astell, and Maggie Ellis. 2002. Designing an interface usable by people with dementia. In Proceedings of the 2003 conference on Universal usability (CUU '03). ACM, New York, NY, USA, 156-157. DOI=http://dx.doi.org/10.1145/957205.957237
3. Hamdi Aloulou, Mounir Mokhtari, Thibaut Tiberghien, Jit Biswas, Clifton Phua, Jin Hong Kenneth Lin, and Philip Yap. 2013. Deployment of assistive living technology in a nursing home environment: methods and lessons learned. *BMC Medical Informatics and Decision Making*, 13 (1).
4. Ashok Bharucha, Vivek Anand, Jodi Forlizzi, Mary Amanda Dew, Charles F. Reynolds, Scott Stevens, and Howard Wactlar. 2009. Intelligent assistive technology applications to dementia care: current capabilities, limitations, and future challenges. *The American Journal of Geriatric Psychiatry*, 17(2): 88-104.
5. Mark Blythe, Kristina Andersen, Rachel Clarke, and Peter Wright. 2016. Anti-Solutionist Strategies: Seriously Silly Design Fiction. *In Proceedings of the 2016 CHI Conference on Human Factors in Computing Systems (CHI '16)*. ACM, New York, NY, USA, 4968-4978. DOI: http://dx.doi.org/10.1145/2858036.2858482
6. Froydis Kristine Bruvik, Ingun Dina Ulstein, Anette Hylen Ranhoff, and Knut Engedal. 2012. The quality of life of people with dementia and their family carers. *Dementia and Geriatric Cognitive Disorders*, 34 (1): 7-14.
7. Kathy Charmaz and Rob Mitchell. 2001. Grounded theory in ethnography. In: Atkinson P, Coffey A, Delamont S, et al. (eds) *Handbook of Ethnography*. Thousand Oaks, CA: SAGE, pp. 160–174.
8. Rachel Clarke, Peter Wright, Madeline Balaam, and John McCarthy. 2013. Digital portraits: photo-sharing after domestic violence. In *Proceedings of the SIGCHI Conference on Human Factors in Computing Systems* (CHI '13). ACM, New York, NY, USA, 2517-2526. DOI=http://dx.doi.org/10.1145/2470654.2481348
9. Stefano Federici, Marcia J. Scherer, and Simone Borsci. 2014. An ideal model of an assistive technology assessment and delivery process. *Technology and Disability*, 26 (1): 27-38.
10. Gemma Fiumara. 1990. The Other Side of Language: A Philosophy of Listening, trans. Charles Lambert. London: Routledge.
11. William W. Gaver, Jacob Beaver, and Steve Benford. 2003. Ambiguity as a resource for design. *In Proceedings of the SIGCHI Conference on Human Factors in Computing Systems* (CHI '03). ACM, New York, NY, USA, 233-240. DOI=http://dx.doi.org/10.1145/642611.642653
12. Erving Goffman. 1961. *Asylums: essays on the social situation of mental patients and other inmates.* Doubleday Publishers.
13. Jacob Gubrium. 1975. *Living and dying at Murray Manor*. Charlottesville: University of Virginia Press.
14. Deborah Hicks. 2000. Self and other in Bakhtin's early philosophical essays: Prelude to a theory of prose consciousness. *Mind, Culture, and Activity*, 7 (3): 227-242.
15. Kristine Holbø, Silje Bøthun, and Yngve Dahl. 2013. Safe walking technology for people with dementia: what do they want?. In *Proceedings of the 15th*

International ACM SIGACCESS Conference on Computers and Accessibility (ASSETS '13). ACM, New York, NY, USA, , Article 21 , 8 pages. DOI: http://dx.doi.org/10.1145/2513383.2513434

16. Louise Hopper, Paulina Piasek & Kate Irving. 2015. Ethical Challenges Associated with Technology use with People with Dementia. *International Association of Geriatrics and Gerontology*, Dublin, April 2015.
17. Julian C. Hughes, Stephen J. Louw, Steven R. Sabat. 2006. *Dementia: Mind, Meaning, and the Person.* Oxford University Press.
18. Amy S. Hwang, Khai N. Truong, and Alex Mihailidis. 2016. Expanding design possibilities for life with dementia. *Interactions,* 23 (3), 59-61. DOI=http://dx.doi.org/10.1145/2899380
19. John Killick and Claire Craig. 2011. *Creativity and Communication in Persons with Dementia: A Practical Guide.* London: Jessica Kingsley Publishers.
20. Pia C Kontos, and Gary Naglie. 2006. Expressions of personhood in Alzheimer's: Moving from ethnographic text to performing ethnography. *Qualitative Research*, 6 (3), 301-317.
21. Amanda Lazar. 2014. Using Technology to Increase Meaningful Engagement in a Memory Care Unit. In *Proceedings of the 18th International Conference on Supporting Group Work (GROUP '14)*. ACM, New York, NY, USA, 255-257. DOI=http://dx.doi.org/10.1145/2660398.2660433
22. Ruth Landau and Shirli Werner. 2012. Ethical aspects of using GPS for tracking people with dementia: recommendations for practice. *International Psychogeriatrics*, 24 (3): 358-366.
23. Claudia K. Y. Lai and David G. Arthur. 2003. Wandering behaviour in people with dementia. *Journal of Advanced Nursing*, 44 (2): 173-182.
24. Stephen Lindsay, Katie Brittain, Daniel Jackson, Cassim Ladha, Karim Ladha, and Patrick Olivier. 2012. Empathy, participatory design and people with dementia. *In Proceedings of the SIGCHI Conference on Human Factors in Computing Systems (CHI '12).* ACM, New York, NY, USA, 521-530. DOI=http://dx.doi.org/10.1145/2207676.2207749
25. João Martins, José Carilho, Oliver Schnell, Carlos Duarte, Francisco M. Couto, Luís Carriço, and Tiago Guerreiro. 2014. Friendsourcing the unmet needs of people with dementia. In *Proceedings of the 11th Web for All Conference (W4A '14*). ACM, New York, NY, USA. DOI=http://dx.doi.org/10.1145/2596695.2596716
26. John McCarthy and Peter Wright. 2004. *Technology as Experience*. Cambridge: MIT Press.
27. John McCarthy and Peter Wright. 2015. *Taking [A]part: The Politics and Aesthetics of Participation in Experience-Centred Design*. Cambridge: MIT Press.
28. John McCarthy, Peter Wright, Jayne Wallace, and Andy Dearden. 2006. The experience of enchantment in human–computer interaction. *Personal Ubiquitous Comput.* 10, , 369-378. DOI=http://dx.doi.org/10.1007/s00779-005-0055-2
29. Kellie Morrissey and John McCarthy. 2015. Creative and Opportunistic Use of Everyday Music Technologies in a Dementia Care Unit. In Proceedings of the 2015 ACM SIGCHI Conference on Creativity and Cognition (C&C '15). ACM, New York, NY, USA, 295-298. DOI=http://dx.doi.org/10.1145/2757226.2757228
30. Kellie Morrissey, Gavin Wood, David Green, Nadia Pantidi, and John McCarthy. 2016. 'I'm a rambler, I'm a gambler, I'm a long way from home': The Place of Props, Music, and Design in Dementia Care. In Proceedings of the 2016 ACM Conference on Designing Interactive Systems (DIS '16). ACM, New York, NY, USA, 1008-1020. DOI: https://doi.org/10.1145/2901790.2901798
31. Maurice Mulvenna, Suzanne Martin, Stefan Sävenstedt, Johan Bengtsson, Franka Meiland, Rose Marie Dröes, Marike Hettinga, Ferial Moelaert, and David Craig. 2010. Designing & evaluating a cognitive prosthetic for people with mild dementia. In *Proceedings of the 28th Annual European Conference on Cognitive Ergonomics (ECCE '10).* ACM, New York, NY, USA, 11-18. DOI=http://dx.doi.org/10.1145/1962300.1962306
32. Louise Nolan, Mary McCarron, Phillip McCallion, & Jo Murphy-Lawless. 2006. Perceptions of stigma in dementia: an exploratory study. *Retrieved from: https://www.lenus.ie/hse/handle/10147/299918*, June 17th, 2015.
33. Patrick Olivier, Guangyou Xu, Andrew Monk, and Jesse Hoey. 2009. Ambient kitchen: designing situated services using a high fidelity prototyping environment. *In Proceedings of the 2nd International Conference on PErvasive Technologies Related to Assistive Environments (PETRA '09*). ACM, New York, NY. DOI=http://dx.doi.org/10.1145/1579114.1579161
34. Catherine Oppenheimer. 2006. I am, thou art: Personal identity in dementia. In Hughes, J. C., Stephen J. Louw, Steven R. Sabat. *Dementia: Mind, Meaning, and the Person.* Oxford University Press.
35. Deborah Reed-Danahay. 2006. 'This is your home now!': conceptualizing location and dislocation in a dementia unit. *Qualitative Research*, 1 (1), 47-63.
36. Yoichi Sakai, Yuuko Nonaka, Kiyoshi Yasuda, and Yukiko I. Nakano. 2012. Listener agent for elderly people with dementia. In *Proceedings of the seventh*

annual ACM/IEEE international conference on Human-Robot Interaction (HRI '12). ACM, New York, NY, USA, 199-200. DOI=http://dx.doi.org/10.1145/2157689.2157754

37. Vardit Sarne-Fleischmann, Noam Tractinsky, Tzvi Dwolatzky, and Inbal Rief. 2011. Personalized reminiscence therapy for patients with Alzheimer's disease using a computerized system. In *Proceedings of the 4th International Conference on Pervasive Technologies Related to Assistive Environments (PETRA '11)*. ACM, New York, NY, USA. DOI=http://dx.doi.org/10.1145/2141622.2141679
38. Keith Sawyer. (2003). *Improvised dialogues: Emergence and creativity in conversation.* Greenwood Publishing.
39. Anja Thieme, Jayne Wallace, Paula Johnson, John McCarthy, Siân Lindley, Peter Wright, Patrick Olivier, and Thomas D. Meyer. 2013. Design to promote mindfulness practice and sense of self for vulnerable women in secure hospital services. In *Proceedings of the SIGCHI Conference on Human Factors in Computing Systems (CHI '13)*. ACM, New York, NY, USA, 2647-2656. DOI=http://dx.doi.org/10.1145/2470654.2481366
40. Julia Twigg. 2000. *Bathing: the body and community care.* Routledge Psychology Press.
41. John Vines, Gary Pritchard, Peter Wright, Patrick Olivier, and Katie Brittain. 2015. An Age-Old Problem: Examining the Discourses of Ageing in HCI and Strategies for Future Research. *ACM Trans. Comput.-Hum. Interact. 22, 1, Article 2.* DOI=http://dx.doi.org/10.1145/2696867
42. Loic Wacquant. 2005. Carnal connections: On embodiment, apprenticeship, and membership. Qualitative Sociology, 28 (4), 445-474.
43. Jayne Wallace, Anja Thieme, Gavin Wood, Guy Schofield, and Patrick Olivier. 2012. Enabling self, intimacy and a sense of home in dementia: an enquiry into design in a hospital setting. In *Proceedings of the SIGCHI Conference on Human Factors in Computing Systems (CHI '12)*. ACM, New York, NY, USA, 2629-2638. DOI=http://dx.doi.org/10.1145/2207676.2208654
44. Jayne Wallace, John McCarthy, Peter C. Wright, and Patrick Olivier. 2013. Making design probes work. *In Proceedings of the SIGCHI Conference on Human Factors in Computing Systems (CHI '13).* ACM, New York, NY, USA, 3441-3450. DOI=http://dx.doi.org/10.1145/2470654.2466473
45. Jayne Wallace, Peter C. Wright, John McCarthy, David Philip Green, James Thomas, and Patrick Olivier. 2013. A design-led inquiry into personhood in dementia. In *Proceedings of the SIGCHI Conference on Human Factors in Computing Systems (CHI '13).* ACM, New York, NY, USA, 2617-2626. http://doi.acm.org/10.1145/2470654.2481363
46. Walmsley, Bruce, and Lynne McCormack. 2015. Shame, hope, intimacy and growth: Dementia distress and growth in families from the perspective of senior aged care professionals. *Dementia*, 14 (7) – 121 -130.
47. Xi Wang. 2012. The construction of researcher–researched relationships in school ethnography: doing research, participating in the field and reflecting on ethical dilemmas. International Journal of Qualitative Studies in Education, 26 (7), 763-779.
48. Joe Wherton and Andrew Monk. 2006. Designing cognitive supports for dementia. *SIGACCESS Access. Comput.* 86, 28-31. DOI=http://dx.doi.org/10.1145/1196148.1196155
49. Hui-Xin Wang, Anita Karp, Bengt Winblad, and Laura Fratiglioni. 2002. Late-life engagement in social and leisure activities is associated with a decreased risk of dementia: a longitudinal study from the Kungsholmen project. *American Journal of Epidemiology*, 155 (12): 1081-1087.
50. Peter Wright and John McCarthy. 2010. *Experience-Centred Design.* Cambridge: MIT Press.
51. Huiru Zheng, Chris Nugent, Paul McCullagh, Yan Huang, Shumei Zhang, William Burns, & Richard Davies. 2010. Smart self management: assistive technology to support people with chronic disease. *Journal of Telemedicine and Telecare*, 16 (4): 224-227.

Connecting Those That Care: Designing for Transitioning, Talking, Belonging and Escaping

Kiel Long[1], Lyndsey Bakewell[2], Róisín McNaney[3], Konstantina Vasileiou[4], Mark Atkinson[5], Manuela Barreto[5], Julie Barnett[4], Mike Wilson[2], Shaun Lawson[6], John Vines[6]

[1] Open Lab, Newcastle University, Newcastle upon Tyne, UK, kiel.long@newcastle.ac.uk

[2] Loughborough University, Loughborough, UK, {l.l.bakewell, m.wilson2}@lboro.ac.uk

[3] Lancaster University, Lancaster, UK, r.mcnaney@lancaster.ac.uk

[4] University of Bath, Bath, UK, {k.vasileiou, j.c.barnett}@bath.ac.uk

[5] University of Exeter, Exeter, UK,{m.m.atkinson, m.barreto}@exeter.ac.uk

[6] Northumbria University, Newcastle upon Tyne, UK {firstname.surname}@northumbria.ac.uk

ABSTRACT

Care provision in many nations increasingly relies on the work of informal, or non-professional, carers. Often these carers experience substantial disruptions and reductions to their own sociality, weakened social support networks and, ultimately, a heightened risk of social isolation. We describe a qualitative study, comprised of interviews, design workshops and probes, that investigated the social and community support practices of carers. Our findings highlight issues related to becoming and recognising being a carer, and feelings of being ignored by, and isolated from, others. We also note the benefits that sharing between carers can bring, and routes to coping and relaxing from the burdens of care. We conclude with design considerations for facilitating new forms of digitally mediated support that connect those that care, emphasising design qualities related to transitioning, talking, belonging and escaping.

Author Keywords

Carers; informal care; co-design; qualitative study.

ACM Classification Keywords

H.5.m. Information interfaces and presentation (e.g., HCI): Miscellaneous;

INTRODUCTION

Informal carers are those who provide care and support for another dependent person, often a family member, partner or spouse. These duties are performed outside of, or in support of, organised professional care. As a result of the demands of the care role, carers can experience disruptions to their life due to changes in frequency of contact with family, peers, friends and other social networks [35]. Related to this, it has been noted that informal carers are at heightened risk of experiencing social isolation [1, 22]. Researchers in the field of HCI have identified informal care as a challenging yet valuable space for technology design. Previous work has questioned how carers might, through technology, better manage their own health and wellbeing while still helping others [10, 23]. Others have highlighted how technological social support for carers should be multi-dimensional, providing ways to find others caring for people in similar circumstances, to identify opportunities to seek and share advice, as well as emotional and informational support [41, 42]. Furthermore, carers face specific challenges associated with seeking support in ways that are respectful and sensitive to the person they care for [47] and the complex patterns and routines inherent in caregiving [37]. There is still little concrete understanding of how technologies might sensitively provide support seeking opportunities for carers, however.

We describe a qualitative study that aimed to understand the support seeking practices of carers and the barriers that they face in doing so. First, we conducted semi-structured interviews with 16 carers. These interviews sought to understand the transition to being a carer, and the relationships between carers and those that they care for, as well as any wider support network of friends, family and peers. This was followed by a series of 4 co-design workshops involving 12 carers. These workshops used a range of methods to validate and elaborate on the findings from the interviews, and explored more deeply the qualities and content of channels of support that the carers appreciated and desired.

We contribute to the growing HCI literature on informal care in four ways. Firstly, we extend previous work through synthesis of the experiences of a heterogeneous set of carers, in addition to providing new and deepened understandings of the transition to, and reassurance of, caring. Secondly, we highlight how practices of support that are facilitated by

CHI 2017, May 06-11, 2017, Denver, CO, USA
ACM 978-1-4503-4655-9/17/05.
http://dx.doi.org/10.1145/3025453.3025715

existing technologies fail to address issues related to the experiences of becoming a carer, connecting with other carers, or seeking momentary respite from caring responsibilities. Thirdly, we present opportunities for new technology designs based on the qualities of transitioning, talking, belonging and escaping in relation to care. Finally, we contribute new evidence that socialising strategies of carers differ from that of the general population, and require differently designed technologies to support these.

BACKGROUND

Informal carers[1]—sometimes referred to as family or unpaid carers—can be defined as those who care, unpaid, for family or friends on a full-time basis. Carers are a large and growing population—it is thought there are 44 million informal carers in the United States [8], and informal carers provide 80% of all care in Europe [24].

There is a growing body of research studying the impact that taking on care duties can have on an individual (e.g. [12, 15, 43]). Published literature has broadly highlighted the invisible, and often unrecognised, work of carers, the substantial contributions they make to the economy, and identified a range of health and wellbeing problems they can face. A consistent finding is that many carers feel disconnected from other people, including the person they care for. Carers can have limited opportunities for informal, spontaneous or meaningful socialising with others [37]. Likewise, they can experience a lack of freedom and flexibility, with daily routines generally organised around care duties. Tixier and Lewkowicz [42] examine the social support practices of older carers, noting that they cherish opportunities to talk with others who may be living in similar circumstances. These opportunities to talk were seen as venues to share advice and knowledge with other carers, with informal meet-ups and support group sessions seen as particularly valuable. However, the authors [42] also note that such groups can suffer from limited participation, perhaps again due to the routines and priorities surrounding the care of the family member or friend. The authors also highlight wider social and structural challenges—such as a lack of public places where those with disabilities or health conditions can visit, or a lack of state support for respite care—that further intensify these challenges.

A further challenge is that many people do not necessarily self-identify as carers. Gooberman-Hill and Ebrahim [20] note that this is reflected in how 'informal carers' often express their 'care' duties as simply changes or adaptations to existing relationships with spouses, family or friends. Schorch at al. [37] also note that the experience of becoming a carer can occur over protracted periods of time, requiring negotiation of new roles within the family, which gradually become solidified and accepted. Alongside this, there is an additional sense of becoming the "care expert" over time, which can reinforce views that others do not necessarily understand or appreciate the role of carers [37]. It is also noted that carers experience problems with close friends and relatives not fully understanding a care receiver's situation or condition [42]. This can lead to hesitation around opening up to others, especially relatives or close friends [47]. This web of complex issues—the inability to find like-minded others to speak to, the perceived lack of support from others, or simply a lack of recognition that they are in a caregiving relationship in the first place—can all influence and impact on the support seeking behaviours and opportunities of informal carers.

Technologies to Support Caregiving

Recent work in HCI has highlighted many of the above issues with a view to understanding the role technology might have in mitigating them. One area of research has attended to reducing some of the burdens of care work—such as reminder and information systems to avoid repetitive questioning [21, 47], tools to share information between care receivers and networks of carers [14], remote monitoring and awareness systems [45] and technologies to avoid disruptive sleep [17]. Others have identified how technology can support carers in seeking emotional and informational support. Based on their study of familial carers for people with depression, Yamashita et al. [47] suggest a range of ways that online platforms might provide both social and anonymous spaces to share concerns and seek advice, as well as providing a means for new and experienced carers to share knowledge and skills. In a similar vein, Tixer and Lewkowicz [41] note that online networks for carers should acknowledge the heterogeneity and specificities of carers' situations by connecting those in similar circumstances. They note the importance of storytelling and experience sharing, which can be used as a way of connecting with similar others. Hensely-Schinkinger et al. [23] further note that those in the early stages of caring are more likely to seek support from more experienced carers, while those with more experience provide tips and advice. As such, much of the literature on support seeking strategies by carers echoes that of the literature on online health communities, where involvement in such communities supports the expression of anxieties to others in similar circumstances [32].

Although there is a growing literature on the benefits of online communities and social networks for carers, there have been relatively few studies of the specific ways they might scaffold the expression of concerns and peer-support. An exception to this is Fuentes et al. [18], who developed the Ohana system to aid mothers who caring for a child with terminal cancer document, express, review, and share their emotions. They note the ways that private reflections provide a means for opening up and sharing emotional difficulties with others in similar circumstances. This also echoes work on online health communities, where Chuang and Yang [11]

[1] While this term has its challenges due to assumptions that the care is not as formal as other forms, or of a different standard, we have adopted the term for this paper as our study engages carers who assist their loved ones personally in a number of ways.

noted that changing the modality of communication—for example from a public forum to journals with configurable visibility to others—significantly altered the type of support users looked for. Forums encouraged support of an informational and factual nature, while journals encouraged 'nurturant support'—'expressions that show signs of listening, expressing sympathy, or expressing the importance of relationship' [11, p4]. Likewise, Massimi [33] notes that online social networks are valuable in supporting: connection with others like one's self and offering opportunities to vent; and that persons may find value in offering support to others experiencing challenges they have previously faced themselves. Massimi et al. [34] further highlight the opportunity that such communities provide for 'giving back'; in that they provide a means to 'repay their debt by listening and offering support'.

This previous work highlights the complex nature of technologically-mediated social support networks, requiring provision of factual information, experiential advice and emotional support, alongside opportunities to be heard and to listen. However, while there is a large body of literature that speaks to the potential of online communities and social networking services to support carers, there are very few examples of what these might look like or how they may be used in practice. Furthermore, recent work has highlighted the importance of online activities primarily supporting offline, in-person activities between carers —such as co-ordinating and planning of group meet-ups and joint leisure pursuits [42]. Again, there is still a relative lack of understanding how these might be supported and, critically, the forms and channels of communication through which this support might be provided and desired. The work described in this paper set out to examine these issues, complementing and extending this prior work.

STUDY DESIGN

This work forms part of a larger multi-disciplinary project examining the experiences of social connectivity and support seeking among a range of different populations. This specific study focuses upon understanding the support seeking strategies and experiences of informal carers in the South West of England (UK). It involves researchers with backgrounds in qualitative health research, participatory design, storytelling, social psychology and computer science. The work employs a qualitative lens to explore support seeking, aiming to develop rich, detailed, nuanced, and attentive-to-the-context accounts of the phenomenon of interest. To achieve this comprehensive and rounded examination, multiple sources of evidence are used including interviews, workshop activities and probes. In the following sections we detail our study design, which aimed to: (i) understand the support seeking practices of informal carers; (ii) examine the barriers they face in seeking such support; and (iii) explore the design of technologies, with carers, to address these issues.

Participants

Participant recruitment was conducted in collaboration with a charitable carers centre that provides a range of services for carers living within its vicinity, including information and advice related to access to care services and financial support, counselling services and peer-support groups, and volunteer-run befriending schemes. Many of these services are provided by local volunteers, of whom many have been carers themselves. The centre provided a physical space where adverts for the project could be displayed, and posted invitations on our behalf to carers agreeing to be contacted regarding projects involving the centre[2]. Following this, the qualitative health researcher (who conducted the interviews) arranged a suitable time and location for the interviews. Following the completion of interview, participants informed us if they wished to continue participating in later stages of the study (the workshops).

We recruited 16 participants (11 female, 5 male), with an average age of 63 years old (youngest being 24 and oldest 91). All self-identified as carers. This diverse sample of participants was recruited to represent a heterogeneous informal carer population; nine provided care to a partner or spouse (Anne[3], Barry, Carl, Denise, Edna, Jade, Ken, Lee, Mike) four to a parent (Fiona, Gina, Harriet, Irene), and three to a child with a disability or mental health condition (Penny, Rose, Sue). The participants also represented a diverse set of experiences and expertise with digital technologies; five reported only basic familiarity and use of e-mail and SMS messaging, and five participants made more extensive use of VoIP (e.g. Skype, Apple Facetime) and Facebook. However, six stated that they rarely to never use digital technology. To capture a range of perspectives and reflections on experiences of caring, we employed several methods of data collection with each stage informing the direction and focus of the following stage.

Interviews

Initially, semi-structured interviews were conducted with each participant. These aimed to understand each person's background and experiences of caring. At participants' individual requests, 11 interviews were conducted in the carers' homes, 3 at a local University campus, and 1 at the carers centre. Interviews lasted on average 60 minutes (25 to

[2] Participants interested in taking part contacted the qualitative health researcher, who provided more information upon the aims of the study, where it would be conducted, and the nature of what we would discuss with them. Potential participants were made aware of the possibly sensitive nature of the subject matter of the research, their rights to withdraw at any time, ability to ask us to move away from certain topics, and to take their time. Interested participants were sent a Participant Information Sheet (PIS), and had at least one week to read this and consent to participation. Those interested in taking part in workshops were contacted following the interview and provided a further PIS and consent documents. The researchers conducting the interviews and leading the workshops had received training for conducting qualitative research around sensitive topics, and participants were provided with information regarding advice and support services at debrief if they wished to use them.

[3] Not their real names.

Figure 1: Participants engaging in (from left to right): (a) "hands on" making of magic machines; (b) talking through their probe returns; and (c) creating the front page of their carers newspaper.

90 min) and were divided into two parts. First, participants were invited to discuss how they entered the caring role and what this involved, the main challenges they had faced, the felt impact these had on their life, and the channels of support available to them. Second, they were asked to reflect on their experiences of loneliness and isolation, how they coped with such experiences, and the role technologies held in relation to these.

Co-design Workshops and Cultural Probes

We invited the original participants to a series of design workshops to further explore the issues from the interviews. Due to the intensity of their care routines, or decline in their cared-for's health, 4 of the interview participants chose not to take part in this phase. We thus had a total of 12 carers, split into 2 groups (a group of 5 and a group of 7). Workshops lasted 120 to 180 min, and were held at a local University campus (agreed with participants as the most accessible venue). Each group attended 2 workshops which are now described.

Workshop 1: Scrapbooking and Magic Machines

The first workshops were divided into three activities. Initially, participants introduced themselves to the group and said a little about their personal caring circumstances. After this, participants were provided with prompts to choose from and invited to create a scrapbook page of images, text and material that responded to them. The prompts were derived from statements from the interviews, such as: "Sometimes I need…", "My home is…", "As a wife/father/etc. I want…". Participants were provided with a range of materials such as paper, stickers, coloured pens, etc. and encouraged to respond as they liked and to address as many or as few prompts as they wished. Participants were then asked to share the reflections they felt comfortable talking about with the group. Next, participants were placed into groups of two or three and invited to create 'magic machines' [2, 6]. Following [2, 6], the activity emphasised technology to be a 'magical unknown' and focused participants on material making rather than the feasibility of an idea. We asked the participants to imagine they were transported through time from 2116 to the present day, bringing with them a device used by carers of the future to communicate with one-another. Participants were given a range of materials (cardboard, stickers, shapes, wire and stick on buttons) and asked to assemble their machine (Figure 1a). Once they had created their machine, the researchers questioned them on what it was, asking them to physically demonstrate it to the rest of the group (Figures 2a and 2b).

Cultural Probes

At the end of the first workshop, cultural probes [19, 13] were provided to participants. The probe pack comprised of a customised disposable camera with 14 prompts. In the spirit of past probe studies, the prompts were intentionally ambiguous and open to interpretation, aiming to serve as 'inspiration' for participants [19]. Again, the prompts responded to the insights from the initial interview. For example, one prompt invited the participant to photograph *"something that is a source of comfort"*. Another requested them to take a photo of *"something that helps you"*.

Workshop 2: Radios and Newspapers

The second workshop was divided into three activities designed in response to the discussions from Workshop one. Participants were split into groups of two and three. First, each group viewed their responses to the cultural probe activity and were prompted to choose some of their responses to discuss and compare with one-another (Figure 1b). After this, each group was provided with an image of a blank AM/FM radio and invited to create stations that might feature specifically for carers (Figure 2c). This activity was intended to further probe the 'channels' of support participants may wish to tune in and out of. At the end of this activity, the "radios" were swapped between groups and participants instructed to choose a "station" they found interesting. After this, those who created this station were (to their surprise) asked to role-play the station as though it were real. Finally, participants were invited to create the front page of a newspaper for carers. This included the paper's name, feature stories and regular sections (Figure 1c). Again, this activity was intended to probe the types of information and content that the carers deemed valuable to share with each other. The workshop closed with a short group discussion, reflecting on all of the completed activities.

Data Analysis

All interviews and workshops were audio recorded and transcribed, and material artefacts documented in photos. This data was treated as a corpus upon which we conducted thematic analysis. Following [7], data was coded at the

Figure 2: Completed co-design artefacts (from left to right): (a) Harriet wearing her Digital Bracelet magic machine; (b) Lee demonstrating his Robot magic machine; and (c) Rose's completed carers' radio channels.

sentence to paragraph level and then grouped together into themes. Given the iterative nature of our study, preliminary analyses were conducted following the completion of each of stage of data collection (e.g. following the completion of interviews, first set of workshops etc.) in order to inform the next stage of research. These codes and themes were then iterated, reviewed and extended through the subsequent stages of the study.

FINDINGS

We present our findings of this analysis below. Throughout, pseudonyms have been used to protect the identity of participants, which we append to quotes along with I (for interview) or workshop and group number (e.g. W1G1) to distinguish sources of data.

Becoming a Carer

From the outset of our interviews, participants explained how, on reflection, they drifted into their carer role without necessarily realising it, and thus failed to identify themselves as a carer for some time. Many reported that the nature of the condition of the person they cared for meant that their responsibilities were initially relatively small but grew as ailments progressed: *"over time, the role's just fallen to us, we've just taken on more and more and more"* (Harriet, I). For a smaller number, however, the care role was experienced as being *"thrust upon"* them (Irene, I), often due to a sudden event in the life of a partner or family member. In these cases, there was often a deep-felt unpreparedness for the role: *"there wasn't much warning it was going to happen, or conversation about what it meant for me."* (Denise, I).

The experience of becoming a carer was often marked by adherence to strict routines. Days were reported to be structured around regular tasks (such as bathing, shopping, preparing meals), with periods of inactivity purposely scheduled in to account for unexpected events: *"I have to always leave a lot of time"* (Irene, W2G1). Visits to shops were described as fitting very specific patterns to mitigate against any sort of unpredictability: *"I haven't bothered to go* [there] *because I thought, oh I can't do it in that two hours"* (Anne, I). As such, the transition to identifying oneself as a carer came with a realisation that one's life was becoming more routinised, less flexible and more organised around the schedules of others.

Opportunities to leave the home for anything other than shopping or other routine elements of the day were often very limited, but were appreciated where possible. For example, Barry recounted how he actively sought opportunities to take his wife out, and in doing so benefitted himself by *"bumping into"* people he knows:

"I do take my wife out to lunch as many times as I can because I think the extra stimuli of going out is a good thing for her [...] *and you make a few friends when you go to one place regularly, don't you, or acquaintances, if not actual friends."* (Barry, I).

Barry's story was rather uncommon, however, and typically the routineness and intensity of care work was described as placing significant restrictions on personal freedom. Becoming a carer came with reductions in making spontaneous decisions around doing things, especially out of the home. Opportunities for socialising had significantly reduced for many participants: *"I miss not being able to go out with my friends. I can't just go out and stay out for the day because I can't leave him"* (Anne, I). Offers to meet with friends were often sacrificed to provide care, which led to feelings of loneliness: *"the isolation is increasing because I'm having to drop activities in order to look after* [wife's name]*"* (Lee, I). Even socialising via social media, which might be assumed to be less time invasive an activity, was felt to be difficult to keep up with:

"So having less time means that I've got less time to socialise, and it means that I haven't got time to sit on Facebook chatting to my friends and things like that, so I feel like I'm less in the loop with my friendship group and stuff like that." (Denise, I).

The prioritising of the care role also comes with a feeling of exhaustion that means that when a rare opportunity to see others does occur, participants tend to turn these down: *"I don't do much now. I'm too tired, I can't be bothered"* (Edna, I). Furthermore, in those rare occasions when participants did socialise they reported feelings of anxiety:

"We do make sure we try and get out on a Saturday but the horrible thing is when we come in, our hearts are in our mouths in case something's happened. So all the time we're thinking, "We've got to get back for [father]*"."* (Harriet, I)

It was clear that the experience of becoming a carer was one where the needs of the cared for were felt to be prioritised. The carers' focus was on helping the person they cared for in the *"here and now"* (Lee, W1G1), that it was *"their duty"* (Sue, W1G1) and that all that mattered was *"their comfort"* (Denise, W1G2). Participants had started to feel as though they had lost things in their lives that were important to them; they had stopped working, lost contact with old friends and given up pastimes and hobbies. At the same time, while occasional frustrations surfaced, this was never held against those they care for. Indeed, it was considered normal to have an ever-present concern for their loved one's comfort and welfare, even if this was to the detriment of their own contact with others.

Distancing and Not Being Heard

Many of the participants referred to the ways in which their opportunities to talk to and communicate with others were very limited. Some explicitly referred to the problems they faced talking to the person they cared for, who was typically the person they spent most of their time with. This was a particular challenge for participants who cared for family members with communication difficulties: *"I tell him things and the minute I've told him it seems to have gone. [...]he keeps very quiet. Unless I talk to him he doesn't really make any conversation."* (Anne, I). Similarly, Denise noted that she felt: "*like the only person I get to talk to very much is him* [her partner who she cares for] *a lot of the time he thinks that I'm not a carer and he doesn't have any problems*" (Denise, I). These communication challenges led to additional feelings of isolation: *"I am on my own because she's not relating, there's no conversation other than the weather or the trees, perhaps a bit about the garden, something like that."* (Lee, I). It might be assumed that in light of these challenges, carers may receive more support from family and friends. Indeed, some participants explained how their family provided them with *"wonderful"* (Ken, I) support, frequently phoning them to check in and visiting when possible: *"I have a very supportive family* [...] *obviously, I miss my wife's companionship but I don't think I feel lonely"* (Ken, I). However, the majority reported many barriers to conversing with family about the situation they and the person they care for found themselves in. There was a perceived lack of appreciation of the severity of a situation (e.g. underestimating the impact of illness) or the requirements of the care role (e.g. not understanding the amount of work or effort required by the carer).

It was appreciated that it is difficult for non-carers to understand the challenges carers face: "*It is difficult for him* [her Brother]. *He doesn't understand it at all, like I didn't when I started out"* (Anne, I). Many of the participants explained how they developed strategies to ignore the advice of family members or friends, or found ways to stop having to come into contact with them. Some, such as Denise, felt compelled to keeping in touch with the few people she still spoke to. However, this was experienced as a continued stress and worry for her, as she found it difficult to explain the complexity of her relationship with her partner: *"I feel like people don't understand what's happening with me a lot of the time"* (Denise, I). Views and opinions from outsiders were described as highly draining:

"The other thing that people do, you will say something and they'll make an assumption in their reply and it's wrong. You get to a point where you think I haven't got the strength to say you're wrong because I've got to back and rewind" (Harriet, I).

Therefore, many of the participants found themselves in a situation where those who were their primary means of social contact were also those they often felt most compelled to distance themselves and withdraw from. As Rose explained, this lack of social support distanced her and made her feel "*very empty and numb*" (Rose, I).

Reaching Out for Support and Distractions

Participants also described feelings of loneliness, isolation and even helplessness as a consequence of the limited contact they have with others. A small number of participants felt as though these feelings were inevitable, and did their best to repress them rather than resolve them:

"*I feel lonely quite often but I think I can't do anything about it so just try and shake it off, don't think about it, because that would make me feel really depressed if I keep feeling that I want to do things and want to go out and I can't do it."* (Anne, I)

Most of the participants however described strategies they had developed to prevent feelings of being alone. Denise explained how they would contact friends and family: "*I try and reach out to people. I try and message people and say "I'm feeling really lonely, are you around?"* (Denise, I). However, she went on to say: *"I don't really get a good response on that".* Penny explicitly referred to using Facebook as a means for getting attention from others: *"if I put something on there, someone is going to see it and make a comment or like it, "yeah I'm alive, I'm doing something""* (Penny, I). However, social networks were also seen as causing even greater feelings of isolation. Certain features of sites like Facebook exacerbated negative feelings through indicating people as "online" and available when in reality they were not, just as WhatsApp would show when messages had been read but not responded to; as such, participants described such services as a *"curse"* that can make the experience of *"reaching out"* with no reply more difficult (Harriet, I).

Participants would also try to engage in activities in their home to distract themselves, often temporarily, especially if they were feeling down or lonely. Many of these activities would be seen as ways of *"switching off"* for a short period of time. Carl would, for example, search for funny videos on the Internet: "*if I get really down I'll watch YouTube, dogs and cats and stuff like that, when they're fighting and crazy car parking stuff. Anything that makes me laugh, basically*" (Carl, I). Denise would go to forums and seek help: "*you can post on there saying like "I feel rubbish, can you show me pictures of cats", and people will dutifully send you pictures of cats*" (Denise, I). She would also spend a lot of time on catch-up television, watching *"things that try and cheer me up, so comedy programs and stuff like that*". This sense of being able to temporarily escape through broadcast media was also used by Barry who expressed a *"reliance"* upon his TV.

The use of light-hearted media was echoed during the radio

channel activity in the second co-design workshops. Radio channels were named *"You are good enough FM"* (Denise, W2G2), *"Cheer up AM"* (Denise, W2G2) and *"Saturday live – upbeat and friendly"* (Rose, W2G2), inferring affirmation and support. Humour also featured as a source for participants to move away from their duties as a carer during the newspaper task. Participants suggested ideas like "*Cute corner: Here's a family of meerkats – but one has fallen over! Oh no!*" (Denise, W2G2), a weekly comedy section (Rose, W2G2), funny cartoons (Harriet, W2G1), while Lee (W2G1) dedicated the entire newspaper to carer satire, to the joy of the group. As such, there was a sense that while the newspaper was still seen as a serious endeavour, with many bits of advice and information contained within, it also needed to convey positivity and provide distractions from care as well.

Finding Commonalities with Other Carers

While there were many instances where participants faced barriers to communicating with relations and friends, having opportunities to talk with other carers was greatly appreciated. For example, Sue (I) explained: *"obviously, they're great because they know exactly, their children have got similar things to* [child] *so we're all kind of on the same wavelength"*. The opportunity to meet other carers was described as influencing participants to have a broader, more positive, outlook upon their own role: *"going to groups, talking to people, just the general experience that now I don't feel that everything is a burden"* (Carl, I). There was a recognition of how important it was to have safe spaces to build links with other carers. Mike highlighted this when he reflected on attending a (diverse) carer group event:

"When I did the photography course, one of the guys was looking after his wife and he was having a tough time [...] *it helped him just to be there and relax with other people and because he was in a sort of protective environment, he could say more openly about things or how he was feeling* [...] *everybody there has got some sort of issue and they'll be different but there is a common ground. So there's an immediate camaraderie and bond between you and that's somebody else who hopefully, next time he sees you, feels a little bit of a connection and it's widened out his prospect of support."* (Mike, I)

This sentiment was further evident during the workshops, where it was clear that participants simply appreciated having an opportunity to be with other carers: *"It's nice to be able to talk to other people"* (Anne, W1G1). The participants felt that the workshops had allowed them to share some of their challenges and concerns:

"I think this is incredibly helpful to be with other people in the same situation, even though our situations are different. They're not really, are they? We've all got one common thread that we've always got somebody else on our mind, haven't we? We always all feel responsible for somebody else in some way. I wish we could stay together as a group and meet up." (Penny, W1,G1)

Though many of the participants had rather different care roles and responsibilities, they identified and empathised with the stories of others: *"I'd like to say how much it's easy to relate to all these things, first of all.*" (Irene, W1G1). Moments where participants opened up were met with encouragement and words of advice from other workshop participants. Indeed, these would lead to extended discussions where they reflected on their commonalities, despite their different circumstances (W1G1):

Harriet: *"I struggle between feeling cross, guilty, & loving him."*
Penny: *"Yes. No, it's exactly the same with me and my daughter, and it's the...".*
Harriet: *"Yes, it's the emotions, isn't it that you go through as a carer?"*
Penny: *"It is. It's having an outlet that's really important, isn't it?"*
Harriet: *"Yes."*
Penny: *"This is great, being able to meet other carers."*

These exchanges between participants were free flowing and supportive in nature, with Fiona (W1G1) exclaiming it's "*so lovely to hear other people's confessions*". Harriet (W1G1) elaborated further: *"it's only when you're with people who have the experiences that you feel able to say things*". As such, taking part in the workshops meant she had felt *"safe to actually put things down on paper. I don't normally feel safe to put it on paper, but in this group, I have."*

Sharing Advice and Remotely Connecting

Having opportunities to be with other carers was also found to be valuable for very practical reasons. It was acknowledged by each participant that while there was an abundance of information available online about the types of support and services carers can access, understanding what this information means in practice was very challenging. Harriet (W2G1) explained how *"it's knowing the roots to these things and because if you don't know the routes and the process and the system, you can give up"*. Indeed, Lee (W1G1) exclaimed that much of the practical *"know how"* he had gained was mostly from fellow carers. He noted that when individuals start off as a carer they *"are searching in the dark, really, for these things*", a comment that was affirmed verbally and through nods of agreement from others.

The sharing of practical advice and speaking from experience came through strongly in the radio and newspaper design activities. For example, during the radio activity one of the channels requested to be acted out was *"carers forum"*, which Mike and Harriet (its creators in W2G1) described as *"an information providing service"* (Figure 2c). As they began their improvised role-play, Mike and Harriet introduced the carers forum as a *"phone-in chat show"*. Fiona, who had requested the carers forum idea to be role-played, 'phoned in' and asked for advice about how she could find *"a good care home"* for her elderly Mother —an actual problem she was currently facing. Over the next ten minutes these three participants discussed this situation together—still in chat show guise—while other workshop participants started to also 'phone in' and offer their own advice based on personal experiences. At the end of the activity, Fiona remarked that the advice she received "*sounded so genuine as well*".

The magic machine activities provided further means for participants to explore ways to communicate and express themselves. While this activity was broadly framed around a *"machine to communicate with"*, participants tended to respond with machines that would bring together fellow carers remotely. For example, Harriet, Carl and Penny created a digital bracelet (Figure 2a) that would allow for a continuous link to be established between people: *"carers are often invisible and alone. Even if you've not with people or you're in a room with others who are ignoring you, you're not feeling alone"* (Penny, W1G1). Similarly, Rose suggested her *"walking in other people's shoes machine"* (Rose, W1G2):

"I think we will need to have more empathy... we need to be able to understand other people's feelings, where they're coming from, what makes people tick... it would be able to scan me and work out how stressed I am or scan you and work out whether your cortisol levels are sky high... this could be used for everyday situations but also for our caring situations." (Rose, W1G2)

Others suggested machines that would report to others when your vital signs suggested you were distressed, or a device that allowed people to *"see you portray the emotion that you're going through"* (Lee, W1G1). While provisional and speculative, these ideas illustrated the importance that participants placed on technologies that supported the expression of feelings and new ways of accessing and communicating an individual's circumstances. Particularly notable was that the ideas all supported remote interactions, but in ways that were rich and multidimensional. Indeed, one of the continuing concerns participants expressed in the workshops was that the realities of being a carer meant that physically meeting with other carers —as they did for our study —is effortful, difficult to organise, or often impossible. Therefore, they privileged technologies that would mediate carer interaction, but in ways that were sensitive to the care context and offered greater sincerity than simply sending a message in text.

Finding Space to Relax

Along with the need to feel connected to others, personal time and space was also valued. *"Me time"* was often sought after, enjoyed as a short period of relaxation, and used to provide temporary sanctuary when circumstances become *"too much"*. The nature of this personal time was diverse. Gina (I) would simply have a *"lie down"* and *"go to sleep, [...] I just go and get out of the way of everything."*. Sue (I) explained that she would *"go out to the garden and have a cigarette to calm myself down and then come back in and I feel more able to cope with it*". Others would set aside specific times of the day for a small amount of relaxation: "*I listen to the radio a lot. [...] I don't like lingering in my thoughts before I go to sleep. So, I try and ward off the feelings of loneliness by other voices and other sounds*" (Rose, I).

While escaping and needing time for oneself was viewed as essential, it was also steeped in feelings of guilt: *"I don't know about any of you, but sometimes I just feel incredibly selfish because I just want some time to myself"* (Denise, W1G1). Such feelings would manifest otherwise trivial events as something to be 'deserved': *"Like a cup of tea is not difficult... but I'll just be like "oh, I don't deserve it..."* (Denise, W2G2). These feelings supported self-doubts that to be a good carer you need to be busy all the time. While some participants would be deeply self-critical of their abilities and efforts as a carer, their dedication to their care receiver was clear to see. It is perhaps because of this that participants sought the time and attention of other carers so much; they could be there to provide advice and support, but also to tell them they are doing well, that they are not alone, and that it is acceptable to escape the care role when you need to.

DISCUSSION

While we have divided our findings into distinct themes, many of the issues are deeply entwined. Often, when an individual becomes a carer they experience a reduction in opportunities to socialise as everyday activities fit a care routine. Those meaningful social interactions that do occur become centered on a small number of people—relatives, younger family members, nearby friends. Very often it appears these interactions can, for some, lead to frustration and further withdrawal due to misunderstandings, disagreements or poorly received advice. While carers appear to find fleeting distraction and enjoyment through online and broadcast media, many express a need to talk with other carers. Those that care, often regardless of their specific circumstances, are seen to share values and experiences; belonging to a community of carers comes with opportunities to share stories, difficult experiences and information. It is a chance to feel as though you are not alone. Carers also reaffirm the hard work other carers do, and appreciate the need to escape from this work every now and then. However, opportunities to physically meet with other carers are rare due to the routines and work that promote isolation in the first place. These issues are further compounded as it may take some time for someone to identify as being a carer, and there is guilt associated with thinking about one's own self, health and wellbeing. Therefore, in many respects care needs to be publicly surfaced in order to make connections with others; but it also needs to be experienced in private spaces with those others who appreciate the circumstances one lives within.

We now reflect upon these issues as they relate to the design of future technologies that might connect those that care. We focus our discussion around four design sensitives: *Transitioning*, *Talking*, *Belonging* and *Escaping*.

Designing for Transitioning Into Caring

It was apparent that the experience of becoming a carer was not easily articulated by participants. It was seen to be an ongoing process of self-realisation and eventual self-identification. Identifying with being a carer came with the realisation that daily routines were habitually in support of another. It may also come with significant changes in personal circumstances that result from committing oneself to becoming a carer - such as relocating, retiring, temporarily leaving work, or no longer seeing friends and family or pursuing pastimes and hobbies. It was also clear that transitioning came with a need to learn new skills and navigate complexities related to personal and family finance, state support, and the law. Based on our findings, we consider two areas for future design work to support in relation to transitioning into caring roles:

(a) Supporting making care public: Our findings reflect work in the social sciences on how self-identifying as a carer is a nuanced and dynamic process [25]. Identifying oneself as a carer can be challenging; carers may not see themselves as providers of care but instead helping and supporting a relative or friend [37]. Yet, our participants benefitted in many ways from self-identifying as carers as this enabled them to access otherwise unavailable resources and services. It also enabled them to recognise that there were others doing the same 'work' as them, to join support groups and participate in activities that were articulated as being beneficial. This reveals a challenge to HCI — how can a user-centered discipline reach those who don't (yet) identify as part of a target demographic? Furthermore, how is it possible to reach those experiencing such transitions when they have yet to reach out to support organisations? We suggest that we do not just focus on designing for 'the carer' as a user, but also exploit HCI's potential to 'make things public' and express matters of concern [16]. HCI has emphasised the value of not designing technologies at all [4] and critiquing simplistic solutions to complex and contested issues [6]. In this case, therefore, a direction for future HCI work might be to support advocacy of carers and made visible the work they do [39]. HCI could also be used to contest some of the socio-economic and structural challenges that shape carers' lives. In doing so, we might imagine that raised public visibility of carers would scaffold connections and awareness between those who have yet to self-identify and those who already have.

(b) Supporting mentoring: A significant issue for carers in transition was access to practical advice and information, echoing prior work on informational support for informal and family carers [9, 23, 40, 41]. As Vines et al. [44] note, it is not simply the provision of information that is important; it is the exchange of practical, hands-on know-how. While there may be an abundance of information 'out there', without scaffolding or interpretative support this was seen as having little value. As in [34, 23] our more experienced participants passionately wanted to give back to the carer community. Thus, designing ways that facilitate the mentoring of novice carers by those with practical experience is an important direction for future HCI work. While it may be assumed that traditional online forums might support these activities, such textual interactions would still require significant amounts of interpretation by those in transition. Therefore, we suggest remote mentoring practices be supported via the creation of richer how-to guides where carers talk through processes and experiences of navigating services and protocols. For instance this might be achieved by adopting video-mentoring systems currently used in education (e.g. [30]), or by appropriating video-based narrative and storytelling platforms (e.g. [46]).

Designing for Talking to Other Carers

A finding from our study was the value that participants saw in talking to other carers. This offered respite and opportunity to reflect on their transitions. For those who cared for someone with a communicative difficulty the need for conversation was longed for and expressed not in terms of quantity, but quality. However, as noted in prior work [37, 42], carers have limited opportunities to socialise due to their busy days and short periods of rest. We consider two areas of design to related to this to offer future support:

(c) Support conversation and dialogue: While there was great value placed on conversation, the majority of work in HCI on caring tends to focus on the translation of such in-person talk to online environments (e.g. [10, 42]). It was clear though that, again, participants valued literally being able to talk with others like them. Conversation supported not just being listened to, but being heard and then hearing the experiences of others. The ways such talk supported experience sharing and emotional support was at its clearest in the enactments of radio stations, where personal situations were articulated, politely questioned, elaborated on and responded to. Conversing and going back-and-forth was particularly important as experiences and situations were often difficult to articulate and emotion laden. How these were uttered—with pauses, sighs, and being reworded—were critical in these dialogues and would be entirely lost by most forms of textual expression. Therefore, future systems should support this form of conversational talk, in all its richness—for example by making use of existing real-time IVR (Interactive Voice Response) technologies [27] or social audio [29].

(d) Support asynchronous talk: While talk and conversation is important, the restrictions on their time, opportunities to get out of the home, and individual routines means getting together to talk—even if mediated by digital technologies—would be challenging. Therefore, as well as supporting talk and conversation, we need to support it in asynchronous ways. We might imagine ways of appropriating and extending technologies used to support asynchronous audio messaging in education [26, 36], connect families over distance to receive messages at designated times [28] or recent work on connecting socially isolated elders with their remote families [3]. It is important, however, to considers ways for carers to navigate talk and to express themselves in ways that evoke conversational attributes (a common challenge with asynchronous audio communication [38]).

Designing for Belonging to a Community

There was consensus from the carers that they are "*all kind of on the same wavelength*" (Sue). Simply knowing you are not alone and that others are there for you was deeply appreciated. This has two implications for future work that seeks to support carers:

(e) Support diverse caring communities: The carers in our study self-identified as 'persons who care for another'. In doing so they recognised each other as members of a diverse community. While advocacy and support groups for broad populations of carers do exist, in HCI there is a tendency to focus on specific populations, such as family members with depression [47], parents of high-risk infants [31], and spouses with dementia [21]. This is in contrast to work that, like ours, broadly scopes the experiences of diverse communities of carers [37, 41]. Focusing on specific populations can, of course, lead to clear benefits around the specific support needed for specific conditions. However, doing so comes with an (understandable) preoccupation with that specific care role, rather than the wider forms of support carers may need, and may further restrict opportunities to build awareness and visibility of carers to each other. We suggest there is potential for connecting those who may, at surface level, have limited ways of relating to one-another. We saw that a mother of a child with a disability was able to connect richly with an older carer with a husband with dementia. This reframing might also focus attention towards the carer, rather than just towards the cared-for's ailment.

(f) Support intimacy and ambience: Our findings highlighted that while rich and substantial conversation was important, there were times when subtle forms of support were desired and more appropriate. This included gestures from others that recognised they had been listened to, thought of, or that they were *"alive"*. Indeed, Harriet's magic machine provided a continuous link to other carers to prevent feelings of being alone, yet made a 'callout' when in need of support. Taking this further, we might also imagine ways that activity between carers might be represented to support ambient awareness and presence; or perhaps provide ways of building anticipation to a looked forward to phone call or meet-up. While these forms of support may initially seem superficial they would clearly offer value to people like our participants who, much of the time, could not afford prolonged spells of socialising but longed for expressions of support at critical moments.

Designing for Temporary Escape

Our final discussion points relate to those moments when our participants needed to escape, even if temporarily, from their care duties. Sometimes these were routine; sometimes these were sudden and when a crisis was occurring or some down time was needed. We raise two final directions for future work that might support these moments:

(g) Support safe spaces: Bazarova [5] observes that intimate and honest messages can support relational closeness; however they also have the potential to be misunderstood, considered inappropriate or are problematic if disclosed to third parties. In our case, it was clear that there was a resistance to disclose certain things to family members or friends that participants were comfortable sharing with other carers. Therefore, the provision of safe spaces—which are accessible to only other known carers—could be of great value. Here we do not just advocate creating private, secure and trusted online spaces, but we urge research that explores the ways such spaces are accessed or physically presented in domestic environments (e.g., whether a device to access such spaces is visible on a sideboard, or hidden in a drawer).

(h) Support the person: Making space for sharing stories is important for building connections between people who come together around issues of health and care [11]. While many of our considerations relate to information needs and expressions of empathy and support, there is a need to engage with the 'person' outside of the care duties. Our workshops, while laden with exchanges explicitly related to care, were also successful in supporting participants to chat about upcoming TV shows, a film they'd seen recently or their favourite late night radio show. Although their lives were stressful, our participants still aspired to find periods to relax. Thus, technologies that support carers should offer opportunities for making connections with pleasurable activities people might normally wish to engage in; or find connections between people not based on ailments, but on their own previous biographies, interests or vocations.

CONCLUSION

In this paper, we discussed the practices through which diverse groups of carers connect with and seek support from others. We have surfaced a range of issues that carers face, including problems with finding space to be social, challenges with connecting with relatives and friends, and the joys of being with other carers. Yet we also show that the life of a carer is such that opportunities to seek time with others are limited. We have raised directions for the future design of technologies that seek to connect those that care. By designing to make care more public we may address some of the wider social and structural challenges that mean carers struggle to connect with others in the first place. However, we have also highlighted a range of implications for how digital platforms may support forms of communication that relate well to this group. In doing so, we draw attention to supporting transitions into becoming a carer and the formation of diverse and supportive communities. Future work should specifically address issues of supporting remote talk between carers in ways that do not simply focus on the practical challenges of care but on carers as valued, yet ordinary, individuals that need to escape, vent and be social.

ACKNOWLEDGMENTS

Thank you to our participants for contributing their time and to Selina Sutton for edits and comments on the paper. This work was supported by RCUK grant ES/M003558/1, funded through the Empathy and Trust in Online Communicating (EMoTICON) funding call administered by the Economic and Social Research Council in conjunction with the RCUK Connected Communities, Digital Economy and Partnership for Conflict, Crime and Security themes, and supported by the Defence Science and Technology Laboratory (Dstl) and the Centre for the Protection of National Infrastructure (CPNI).

REFERENCES

1. Ronald Adelman, Lyubov Tmanova, Diana Delgado, Sarah Dion and Mark Lachs. 2014. Caregiver Burden: A Clinical Review. In *JAMA*, 311 (10), 1052-1060. DOI: 10.1001/jama.2014.304.

2. Kristina Andersen. 2013. Making Magic Machines. *10th European Academy of Design Conference-Crafting the Future*. DOI: 10.13140/2.1.1280.1285

3. Ron Baecker, Kate Sellen, Sarah Crosskey, Veronique Boscart, and Barbara Barbosa Neves. 2014. Technology to reduce social isolation and loneliness. In *Proceedings of the 16th international ACM SIGACCESS conference on Computers & accessibility* (ASSETS '14). ACM, New York, NY, USA, 27-34. DOI: http://dx.doi.org/10.1145/2661334.2661375

4. Eric P.S. Baumer and M. Six Silberman. 2011. When the implication is not to design (technology). In *Proceedings of the SIGCHI Conference on Human Factors in Computing Systems* (CHI '11). ACM, New York, NY, USA, 2271-2274. DOI: http://dx.doi.org/10.1145/1978942.1979275

5. Natalya N. Bazarova. 2012. Contents and contexts: disclosure perceptions on facebook. In *Proceedings of the ACM 2012 conference on Computer Supported Cooperative Work* (CSCW '12). ACM, New York, NY, USA, 369-372. DOI: http://dx.doi.org/10.1145/2145204.2145262

6. Mark Blythe, Kristina Andersen, Rachel Clarke, and Peter Wright. 2016. Anti-Solutionist Strategies: Seriously Silly Design Fiction. In *Proceedings of the 2016 CHI Conference on Human Factors in Computing Systems* (CHI '16). ACM, New York, NY, USA, 4968-4978. DOI: http://dx.doi.org/10.1145/2858036.2858482

7. Virginia Braun, and Victoria Clarke. 2006. Using thematic analysis in psychology. *Qualitative research in psychology*. 3 (2). 77-101. DOI: 10.1191/1478088706qp063oa

8. *Caregiving | Family Caregiver Alliance* Retrieved 4-Sept-2016 From: https://www.caregiver.org/caregiving

9. Mary Chambers, A. A. Ryan, and S. L. Connor. 2001, Exploring the emotional support needs and coping strategies of family carers. *Journal of Psychiatric and Mental Health Nursing*, 8: 99–106. DOI: 10.1046/j.1365-2850.2001.00360.x

10. Yunan Chen, Victor Ngo, and Sun Young Park. 2013. Caring for caregivers: designing for integrality. In *Proceedings of the 2013 conference on Computer supported cooperative work* (CSCW '13). ACM, New York, NY, USA, 91-102. DOI: http://dx.doi.org/10.1145/2441776.2441789

11. Katherine Y. Chuang, and Christopher C Yang. 2010. Helping you to help me: exploring supportive interaction in online health community. In *Proceedings of the American Society for Information Science and Technology*, 47(1), 1-10. DOI: 10.1002/meet.14504701140

12. Elizabeth C. Clipp, and Linda K. George. 1990. Caregiver Needs and Patterns of Social Support. *Journal of Gerontology* , 45 (3). 102-111. DOI: 10.1093/geronj/45.3.S102

13. Andy Crabtree, Terry Hemmings, Tom Rodden, Keith Cheverst, Karen Clarke, Guy Dewsbury, John Hughes, and Mark Rouncefield. 2003. Designing with care: Adapting cultural probes to inform design in sensitive settings. In *Proceedings of the 2003 Australasian Conference on Computer-Human Interaction (OZCHI2003)*, pp. 4-13.

14. Matty Cruijsberg, Martijn H. Vastenburg, and Pieter Jan Stappers. 2012. Family Carebook: A Case Study on Designing Peace of Mind for Family Caregivers. In *Ambient Intelligence-Software and Applications.* 129-136. Springer Berlin Heidelberg. DOI: 10.1007/978-3-642-28783-1_16

15. John F. Deeken, Kathryn L. Taylor, Patricia Mangan, K. Robin Yabroff, and Jane M. Ingham. 2003. Care for the caregivers: a review of self-report instruments developed to measure the burden, needs, and quality of life of informal caregivers. *Journal of Pain and Symptom Management.* 26, 4: 922-953. DOI: 10.1016/S0885-3924(03)00327-0

16. Carl DiSalvo, Jonathan Lukens, Thomas Lodato, Tom Jenkins, and Tanyoung Kim. 2014. Making public things: how HCI design can express matters of concern. In *Proceedings of the SIGCHI Conference on Human Factors in Computing Systems* (CHI '14). ACM, New York, NY, USA, 2397-2406. DOI: http://dx.doi.org/10.1145/2556288.2557359

17. Elizabeth H. Ehleringer and Si Jung Kim. 2013. The Wearable Lullaby: Improving Sleep Quality of Caregivers of Dementia Patients. In *CHI '13 Extended Abstracts on Human Factors in Computing Systems* (CHI EA '13). ACM, New York, 409-414. DOI: http://doi.org/10.1145/2468356.2468429

18. Carolina Fuentes, Valeria Herskovic, Jurgen Heysen, and Monica Tentori. 2013. Towards a technology for caregivers' emotional expression and self-reflection. In *International Conference on Ubiquitous Computing and Ambient Intelligence.* 143-150. Springer International Publishing. DOI: 10.1007/978-3-319-03176-7_19

19. Bill Gaver, Tony Dunne, and Elena Pacenti. 1999. Design: Cultural probes. *interactions* 6, 1 (January

1999), 21-29. DOI: http://dx.doi.org/10.1145/291224.291235

20. Rachael Gooberman-Hill and Shah Ebrahim. 2006. Informal Care At Times Of Change In Health And Mobility: A Qualitative Study. In *Age And Ageing*. 35 (3). 261-266. DOI: 10.1093/ageing/afj065

21. Kirstie Hawkey, Kori M. Inkpen, Kenneth Rockwood, Michael McAllister, and Jacob Slonim. 2005. Requirements gathering with alzheimer's patients and caregivers. In *Proceedings of the 7th international ACM SIGACCESS conference on Computers and accessibility* (Assets '05). ACM, New York, NY, USA, 142-149. DOI: http://dx.doi.org/10.1145/1090785.1090812

22. Laura Hayes, Graeme Hawthorne, John Farhall, Brendan O'Hanlon, Carol Harvey. 2015. Quality of Life and Social Isolation Among Caregivers of Adults with Schizophrenia: Policy and Outcomes. *Community Mental Health Journal*, 51 (5), 591-597. DOI: 10.1007/s10597-015-9848-6

23. Susanne Hensely-Schinkinger, Aparecido Fabiano Pinatti de Carvalho, Michael Glanznig, and Hilda Tellioğlu. 2015. The Definition and Use of Personas in the Design of Technologies for Informal Caregivers. In *17th International Conference on Human-Computer Interaction*. 202-213. Springer International Publishing. DOI: 10.1007/978-3-319-20901-2_19

24. Frédérique Hoffmann, and Ricardo Rodrigues. 2010. *Informal carers: who takes care of them?*. Retrieved 4-Sept-2016 From: http://www.euro.centre.org/data/1274190382_99603.pdf

25. Nic Hughes, Louise Locock, and Sue Ziebland. 2013. Personal identity and the role of 'carer' among relatives and friends of people with multiple sclerosis. *Social science & medicine* 96 (2013): 78-85.

26. Philip Ice, Reagan Curtis, Perry Phillips, and John Wells. 2007. Using Asynchronous Audio Feedback to Enhance Teaching Presence and Students' Sense of Community. *Journal of Asynchronous Learning Networks*. 11(2). 3-25.

27. Konstantinos Kazakos, Siddhartha Asthana, Madeline Balaam, Mona Duggal, Amey Holden, Limalemla Jamir, Nanda Kishore Kannuri, Saurabh Kumar, Amarendar Reddy Manindla, Subhashini Arcot Manikam, GVS Murthy, Papreen Nahar, Peter Phillimore, Shreyaswi Sathyanath, Pushpendra Singh, Meenu Singh, Pete Wright, Deepika Yadav, and Patrick Olivier. 2016. A Real-Time IVR Platform for Community Radio. In *Proceedings of the 2016 CHI Conference on Human Factors in Computing Systems* (CHI '16). ACM, New York, NY, USA, 343-354. DOI: http://dx.doi.org/10.1145/2858036.2858585

28. Hyesook Kim, Andrew Monk, Gavin Wood, Mark Blythe, Jayne Wallace, and Patrick Olivier. 2013. TimelyPresent: Connecting families across continents. *International Journal of Human-Computer Studies*. 71(10). 1003-1011

29. Kate Lacey, 2014. Smart radio and audio apps: The politics and paradoxes of listening to (anti-) social media. *Australian Journalism Review*, *36*(2), 77-89

30. Heisook Lee and Sunsook Noh. 2003. Educational Use of E-mentoring to Encourage Women into Science and Engineering. In *Web and Communication Technologies and Internet-Related Social Issues — HSI 2003*. Springer Berlin Heidelberg, 75–84.

31. Leslie S. Liu, Sen H. Hirano, Monica Tentori, Karen G. Cheng, Sheba George, Sun Young Park, and Gillian R. Hayes. 2011. Improving communication and social support for caregivers of high-risk infants through mobile technologies. In *Proceedings of the ACM 2011 conference on Computer supported cooperative work* (CSCW '11). ACM, New York, NY, USA, 475-484. DOI: http://dx.doi.org/10.1145/1958824.1958897

32. Diane Maloney-Krichmar and Jenny Preece. 2005. A multilevel analysis of sociability, usability, and community dynamics in an online health community. *ACM Trans. Comput.-Hum. Interact.* 12, 2 (June 2005), 201-232. DOI: http://dx.doi.org/10.1145/1067860.1067864

33. Michael Massimi. 2013. Exploring remembrance and social support behavior in an online bereavement support group. In Proceedings of the 2013 conference on Computer supported cooperative work (CSCW '13). ACM, New York, NY, USA, 1169-1180. DOI: http://dx.doi.org/10.1145/2441776.2441908

34. Michael Massimi, Jackie L. Bender, Holly O. Witteman, and Osman H. Ahmed. 2014. Life transitions and online health communities: reflecting on adoption, use, and disengagement. In *Proceedings of the 17th ACM conference on Computer supported cooperative work & social computing* (CSCW '14). ACM, New York, NY, USA, 1491-1501. DOI: http://dx.doi.org/10.1145/2531602.2531622

35. Chandylen Nightingale, Barbara Curbow, John Wingard, Deidre Pereira and Giselle Carnaby. 2016. Burden, quality of life, and social support in caregivers of patients undergoing radiotherapy for head and neck cancer: A pilot study. *Chronic Illness*, 12 (3), 236-245. DOI: 10.1177/1742395316644305

36. Jody Oomen-Early, Mary Bold, Kristin L. Wiginton, Tara L. Gallien, and Nancy Anderson. 2008. Using asynchronous audio communication (AAC) in the online classroom: A comparative study. *Journal of Online Learning and Teaching*. 4(3). 267-276.

37. Marén Schorch, Lin Wan, David William Randall, and Volker Wulf. 2016. Designing for Those who are Overlooked: Insider Perspectives on Care Practices and Cooperative Work of Elderly Informal Caregivers. In *Proceedings of the 19th ACM Conference on Computer-Supported Cooperative Work & Social Computing* (CSCW '16). ACM, New York, NY, USA, 787-799. DOI: http://dx.doi.org/10.1145/2818048.2819999

38. Venkatesh Sivaraman, Dongwook Yoon, and Piotr Mitros. 2016. Simplified Audio Production in Asynchronous Voice-Based Discussions. In *Proceedings of the 2016 CHI Conference on Human Factors in Computing Systems* (CHI '16). ACM, New York, NY, USA, 1045-1054. DOI: http://dx.doi.org/10.1145/2858036.2858416

39. Lucy Suchman. 1995. Making work visible. *Communications of the ACM* 38, 9 (September 1995), 56-64. DOI: http://dx.doi.org/10.1145/223248.223263

40. Carl A. Thompson, Karen Spilsbury, Jill Hall, Yvonne Birks, Colin Barnes, and Joy Adamson. 2007. Systematic review of information and support interventions for caregivers of people with dementia. *BMC geriatrics* 7(18) doi:10.1186/1471-2318-7-18

41. Matthieu Tixier and Myriam Lewkowicz. 2015. Looking for Respite and Support: Technological Opportunities for Spousal Caregivers. In *Proceedings of the 33rd Annual ACM Conference on Human Factors in Computing Systems* (CHI '15). ACM, New York, NY, USA, 1155-1158. DOI: http://dx.doi.org/10.1145/2702123.2702563

42. Matthieu Tixier and Myriam Lewkowicz. 2016. "Counting on the Group": Reconciling Online and Offline Social Support among Older Informal Caregivers. In *Proceedings of the 2016 CHI Conference on Human Factors in Computing Systems* (CHI '16). ACM, New York, NY, USA, 3545-3558. DOI: http://dx.doi.org/10.1145/2858036.2858477

43. Michelle Van Ruyn, Sarah Sanders, Katharine Kahn, Courtney van Houtven, Joan Griffin, Sean Phelan, Michelle Martin, Audie Atienza, Deborah Finstad, and Julie Rowland. 2011. Objective Burden, Resources and Other Stressors Among Informal Cancer Caregivers: a hidden quality issue. *Psycho-oncology*. 20, 1. 44-52. DOI:10.1002/pon.1703

44. John Vines, Stephen Lindsay, Gary W. Pritchard, Mabel Lie, David Greathead, Patrick Olivier, and Katie Brittain. 2013. Making family care work: dependence, privacy and remote home monitoring telecare systems. In *Proceedings of the 2013 ACM international joint conference on Pervasive and ubiquitous computing* (UbiComp '13). ACM, New York, NY, USA, 607-616. DOI: http://dx.doi.org/10.1145/2493432.2493469

45. John Vines, Peter C. Wright, David Silver, Maggie Winchcombe, and Patrick Olivier. 2015. Authenticity, Relatability and Collaborative Approaches to Sharing Knowledge about Assistive Living Technology. In *Proceedings of the 18th ACM Conference on Computer Supported Cooperative Work & Social Computing* (CSCW '15). ACM, New York, NY, USA, 82-94. DOI: http://dx.doi.org/10.1145/2675133.2675222

46. Jenny Waycott, Frank Vetere, Sonja Pedell, Lars Kulik, Elizabeth Ozanne, Alan Gruner, and John Downs. 2013. Older adults as digital content producers. In *Proceedings of the SIGCHI Conference on Human Factors in Computing Systems* (CHI '13). ACM, New York, NY, USA, 39-48. DOI: http://dx.doi.org/10.1145/2470654.2470662

47. Naomi Yamashita, Hideaki Kuzuoka, Keiji Hirata, and Takashi Kudo. 2013. Understanding the conflicting demands of family caregivers caring for depressed family members. In *Proceedings of the SIGCHI Conference on Human Factors in Computing Systems* (CHI '13). ACM, New York, NY, USA, 2637-2646. DOI: http://dx.doi.org/10.1145/2470654.2481365.

Designing Game-Based Myoelectric Prosthesis Training

Aaron Tabor[1], Scott Bateman[1], Erik Scheme[1], David R. Flatla[2], Kathrin Gerling[3]
[1]University of New Brunswick, Fredericton, Canada
[2]University of Dundee, Dundee, UK
[3]University of Lincoln, Lincoln, UK
{aaron.tabor, scott.bateman, erik.scheme}@unb.ca, d.flatla@dundee.ac.uk, kgerling@lincoln.ac.uk

ABSTRACT
A myoelectric prosthesis (myo) is a dexterous artificial limb controlled by muscle contractions. Learning to use a myo can be challenging, so extensive training is often required to use a myo prosthesis effectively. Signal visualizations and simple muscle-controlled games are currently used to help patients train their muscles, but are boring and frustrating. Furthermore, current training systems require expensive medical equipment and clinician oversight, restricting training to infrequent clinical visits. To address these limitations, we developed a new game that promotes fun and success, and shows the viability of a low-cost myoelectric input device. We adapted a user-centered design (UCD) process to receive feedback from patients, clinicians, and family members as we iteratively addressed challenges to improve our game. Through this work, we introduce a free and open myo training game, provide new information about the design of myo training games, and reflect on an adapted UCD process for the practical iterative development of therapeutic games.

Author Keywords
Prosthetics; myoelectric; training; games; UCD

ACM Classification Keywords
H.5.m. Info interfaces & presentation (e.g., HCI): Misc.

INTRODUCTION
Amputees, or limb different individuals, are people who are missing a limb due to amputation or a congenital limb difference. A myoelectric-controlled upper-limb prosthesis (myo) is an electrically-powered device that restores some of the missing dexterous movement in the arm and hand, e.g., by providing wrist rotation and hand closing. Myos typically offer greater functionality than passive or body-powered prostheses because they provide improved dexterity, a larger range of movement, a more natural appearance, and enhanced performance of daily tasks [7].

Myos also have drawbacks (including high cost and weight [7,12,22]), which have led to a high rate of abandonment; rejection rates of up to 75% have been reported [7]. Rejection is a complex, multi-factor process, but one of the key contributing factors is poor early myo operation ability arising from inadequate training [12].

Myos work by detecting electrical signals from residual muscle contractions. These signals act as input to control the artificial limb. Precise control and activation of particular muscle groups is required in order for the device to be used effectively. However, due to lack of experience, unfamiliarity, and muscle atrophy, precise activation of specific muscle groups can be very difficult [8].

Occupational Therapists (OTs) employ training activities to improve patients' muscle activation skills, helping them to learn how to operate and adapt to a myo. Learning to use a myo presents a unique challenge; unlike other therapeutic or rehabilitative programs, the goal of myo training is not to relearn forgotten tasks or regain lost functionality (as would be the case with stroke or physical injury rehabilitation), but is instead to learn to operate a device using muscles in a new and unfamiliar way [8].

The experts interviewed in this study agreed that current myo training approaches limit success for three main reasons. First, they are *boring and unengaging*. Training activities are often utilitarian and amount to little more than simple visualizations of muscle signals. Second, they are often *more difficult than using a real prosthesis*. Overly difficult training activities that provide primarily negative feedback are a source of frustration and discouragement. Further, this causes OTs to question the benefit of training given the potential for unintentionally introducing self-doubt. Third, they are *not accessible outside of the clinic*. Commercial training tools cost thousands of dollars, and require professional placement of sensors and interacting with complex software to set up training activities.

Game-based training tools [4,8,11,12,14,25] have been proposed to address the limitations identified above. Games seek to provide a more engaging experience and stronger extrinsic motivation (e.g., rewards, points, leaderboards) to help offset frustration. When coupled with appropriate technology, games can make training more accessible, allowing training to occur at home.

However, previous work has not engaged limb-different patients while designing games; very little work has explored how training games should be designed to best suit the specific needs of trainees and clinicians. While

CHI 2017, May 06 - 11, 2017, Denver, CO, USA

ACM 978-1-4503-4655-9/17/05…$15.00
DOI: http://dx.doi.org/10.1145/3025453.3025676

research considering the needs of end users is prevalent in other therapeutic settings [1,20,21,38], academic efforts towards designing myo training games have focused exclusively on technical issues, and not on the concerns and needs of the people involved (e.g., [4,11,12,14,25]). This direction of focus becomes apparent when considering commercial myo training games, which are widely used [9] but provide few of the motivating elements of game design that create a fun and engaging experience for players [16].

Much like the work of Hernandez et al. [21], our study is a qualitative exploration of game-based myoelectric training, leaving technical and performance issues to future work. First, we developed a prototype based on requirements gathered from previous work, observation of the training process, and discussions with a clinician from a local prosthetics clinic. We then iteratively refined our initial prototype using feedback and observations from a series of adapted user-centered design (UCD) sessions with limb different patients who have previously participated in myoelectric training. We transcribed and thematically analyzed audio recordings of the sessions, which we validated through interviews with subject matter experts. Our themes contribute domain expertise and encode current best practice for the design of future myoelectric training games, as well as therapeutic games in general.

This paper makes four contributions: First, we develop a new game – *The Falling of Momo* – as a starting point for game-based myoelectric training discussions within an adapted UCD process. Second, we present thematic analysis of interview and observation data from limb-different individuals and other stakeholders as a contribution to future work in this area. Third, we outline the process of integrating stakeholder feedback into our iterative game development process. Finally, we discuss the benefits and drawbacks of our adapted UCD process developed for situations when participants are difficult to recruit and follow-up visits are infeasible.

BACKGROUND & RELATED WORK

Myoelectric Control

Myoelectric signals are electrical impulses that occur naturally as we contract our muscles. Myoelectrically-controlled powered prosthetic devices (or myos) read muscle signals (using electromyographic sensors – EMG) from residual muscle tissue, and use them as control for motion [28,29]. The simplest myos open and close based on the presence of inner- and outer-forearm muscle activity (known as flexion and extension, respectively). However, many other control schemes exist and can work in combination, including proportional (adjusting the speed of motion proportionally with the intensity of muscle contractions), mode-switching (to enable selection between different types of movement), and pattern recognition techniques (for more natural control mappings) [17,33]. In this study, we focus specifically on proportionally-

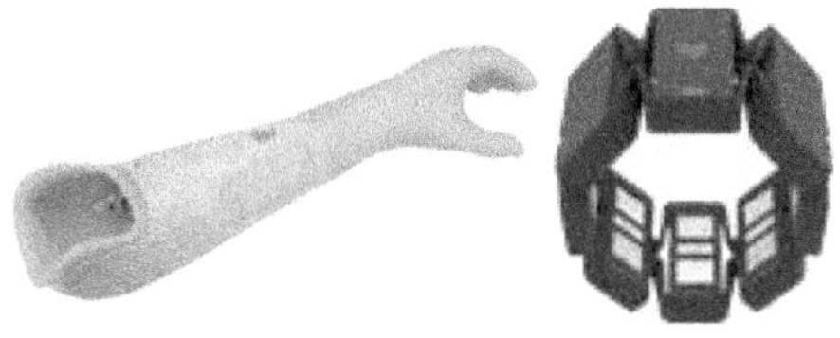

Figure 1. (Left) A myoelectric upper limb prosthesis – myo. (Right) The Thalmic Labs Myo Armband – Myoband.

controlled myoelectric devices (as can be seen in Figure 1), since these are by far the most common type of myo.

Typically, surface sensors are positioned within the sleeve of myos (just visible within the sleeve of the device shown in Figure 1) such that they sit flush against the surface of the skin, directly above the ideal targeted muscle site (identified by the prosthetist or clinician during the fitting process). Accurate placement of these sensors is critical because inconsistency in placement can negatively affect muscle readings [9]. In many myoelectric muscle training tools, the same EMG sensors are used that are employed in prostheses, which are expensive (a training kit for proportional control consisting of 2 sensors and control box costs ~4000USD) making them unfeasible for use outside of the clinical environment [9].

In our study, we work with a consumer-grade EMG sensing armband, the Thalmic Labs Myo Armband (referred to as the 'Myoband' and shown in Figure 1), to assess its viability for use with myoelectric training tools. The Myoband is an off-the-shelf input device that costs under 200USD, and even though the fidelity of its EMG sensors is lower than medical-grade equipment, it is likely more than capable of being used for myo training. Even though the Myoband samples at one-fifth the rate of medical grade devices (Myoband: 200Hz, medical grade: ~1000Hz), the Nyquist theorem states that this is adequate to achieve an accurate representation of the underlying EMG signal [25]. The sensors of the Myoband also sample with a lower signal resolution (Myoband: 8-bit, medical-grade: ~16-bit), but research has shown that such a reduction results in only a marginal loss in control accuracy [31]. Further, there are recent examples of the Myoband being used to successfully operate prostheses in a lab setting (e.g., https://goo.gl/o6p2OE).

Myoelectric Prostheses Training

Traditional Training

The time between amputation and receipt of prosthesis is known as the pre-prosthetic phase, and is recognized as being a crucial period for training [7]. Experts interviewed agreed that building strength in the patient's musculature during this phase, in turn instilling confidence in use of their residual limb is key to ensuring long-term success. While the best training approach for many is direct use of a prosthesis, this is often not initially possible (e.g., post-surgery recovery, insurance processing, fabrication times). To fill this gap, training tools can be used. Many clinics use the Ottobock PAULA [9,27] software, which allows EMG sensors to be affixed directly to the affected limb without the need for a final prosthetic socket. The PAULA suite (Figure 2) provides feedback tools for visualizing raw EMG activity, a virtual hand simulator, and a game involving navigating a car through a series of gaps.

Game-based Training

Past findings related to game-based myoelectric training tools have been conflicting. In one study using the PAULA software suite, it was suggested that game-based training tools are just as effective as traditional techniques, and that training tools could be used interchangeably at the discretion of the clinician or patient [9]. However, a subsequent study suggests that certain training games are no more effective than a total lack of training [13]; the study suggests that while learning may occur within the context of gameplay, these acquired skills might not translate to improved prosthesis use. These conflicting results suggest that the specific challenges associated with designing training games for amputees are not fully understood.

Therapeutic Games

Therapeutic games have recently received a lot of attention, and have been created for people with cerebral palsy [21,40], multiple sclerosis [20], paralysis [34], and who have had a stroke [5,24,32,37]. Findings from research into the participatory design of games for individuals with visual impairment [38] and young people using wheelchairs [19] makes clear that there are no one-size-fits-all solutions for populations that have a wide range of physical capabilities. Balancing the aspects of challenge required for the game to be exciting and effective with the potential vulnerabilities of the intended audience is rarely easy.

While training games should push players to improve their abilities, they should not highlight the player's weaknesses or limitations [18]. To be most effective for therapists, therapeutic games should be easy to start up and configure (ideally, saving configuration settings in a user profile so they can be easily loaded in future sessions), allow the therapist to change difficulty settings on the fly (to adapt to the patient's current needs), easily allow therapist to provide support during gameplay, and track and report patients' performance over time [3].

While myo training games have been created, these have largely focused on technical and performance issues (e.g., [4,11,12,14,25]), and have not involved limb different patients (e.g., [4,11,14]). Very little focus has been given to creating engaging and enjoyable training experiences, and little is known about what game design challenges are unique to myo training games. Despite varying results in past research [6,9,11,18], the experts interviewed expressed that games are important, as they help engage and motivate their patients and can serve as a troubleshooting tool when a patient's prosthesis is behaving unexpectedly.

Game Design Principles

Challenge, theme, reward, and progress are known to be key elements that keep players excited and engaged during gameplay [16]. Throughout the design of our game, we have kept these concepts in mind, and we highlight below how our game incorporates these elements. Further information about our game can be found in [35,36].

Research has also shown that strong game design can lead to more than an increased level of engagement. In a study comparing games for psychoacoustic therapy, it was found that players could detect smaller tone frequency modulations when playing a game that was enjoyable and engaging [1], a task which is believed to involve skills related to genetic ability, and not believed to improve through training.

DESIGNING A MYOELECTRIC TRAINING GAME

To facilitate the exploration of myo training, we designed and implemented a training game [35,36]. This game was shown to participants during playtest-interview sessions (introduced below) and served as a concrete example to stimulate feedback and discussion. As the study progressed, the game allowed us to easily explore the ideas, criticism, and suggestions that surfaced, and was iteratively improved throughout the study. While it is not customary to begin with a full solution in user-centered design, we felt that this choice would allow us to get the most out of our design sessions, given the extremely limited number of participants available. We recognize that this decision can be viewed as limiting, and we emphasize that the game was a starting point meant to stimulate conversation, and was therefore expected to change considerably throughout the study.

Initial Design Requirements

We worked closely with a local prosthetics clinic based at our university. Our main point of contact was an occupational therapist, Linda (pseudonym). Linda specializes in myoelectric prosthetics and training. She works closely with patients first learning to use a myo, and maintains contact with continuing myo users.

Our initial game design was based on requirements

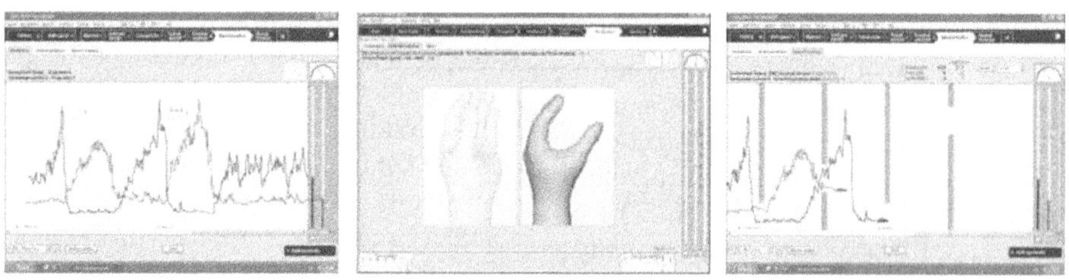

Figure 2: Ottobock PAULA training suite (raw muscle activity, prosthetic hand simulator, and car game, left to right)

gathered through conversations with Linda, in addition to a demonstration of a typical muscle training session with one of her patients. During our initial requirements gathering, we discovered several insights into myo training:

1. Training focuses on specific aspects of muscle control.
2. The "ideal" outcome of training is isolated control over two opposing muscles. However, this is not always achieved in practice, and control strategies exist to accommodate an individual's capabilities.
3. A co-contraction impulse (a quick, simultaneous "burst" with both muscles) is used as a mode switching instruction (e.g., to alternate control between grip aperture and wrist rotation).
4. Existing tools provide primarily negative feedback.
5. Current training tools are inaccessible outside of the clinical environment due to high cost.

We observed that certain aspects of myo training differ from other types of therapy, resulting in unique challenges when designing in this space. Unlike other therapeutic processes, the goal of myo training is not to regain lost functionality, range-of-motion, or bodily control (as is the case in stroke and physical-injury treatments), but is instead to adapt to a new reality. Limb-loss is irreversible, and learning to use a myo involves working with unfamiliar muscles and mastering new control techniques. Furthermore, while other therapeutic programs focus solely on bodily movement, myos use proportional control and require the user to additionally have precise control over the duration and intensity of muscle contractions.

From our observations, it was clear that the training process could be improved through the use of established game design principles. It was also clear that games would need to incorporate the mechanics found in the existing control strategies and provide adjustable difficulty suitable for players with a wide range of skill and ability. Finally, games accessible beyond the clinical environment would allow trainees to continue improving between clinical visits, ultimately achieving "ideal" muscle control more quickly.

Initial Game Design: The Falling of Momo

Our initial design, The Falling of Momo (Figure 3) [35,36], is a casual, survival-style game, where players earn points by descending through a series of rising platforms to avoid being squished by spikes across the top of the screen. Players collect coins that can later be used to purchase new characters, themes and unlockables. We based our design on a casual, familiar style of game because our intended audience spans a wide demographic with varying preferences. The left/right game mechanics were selected because they mapped intuitively to the flexion/extension movements being trained, allowing the desired behavior to be targeted in a natural way.

Gameplay

Players control their avatar using the Myoband, and controls mirror those of typical prostheses. Momo's movements correspond to the intensity (for speed) of forearm flexion and extension (for direction). The player can also jump (to avoid obstacles) by performing a co-contraction impulse. Icy (low-friction) and sticky (high-friction) platforms were added so that players would need to use the full range of proportional control. By providing in-game collectables and unlockable items, we were able to provide replay value and positive feedback while still encouraging the player to train their muscles. The rising platforms (which progressively get faster) introduce a time-pressure mechanic, which creates excitement during game play. While certain guidelines may discourage time-pressure [6,15], Momo incorporates suggestions from past research on accessible action games [21] to ensuring both an exciting and accessible experience.

Game Evolution

The game was iteratively improved throughout the course of the study using observations, feedback, and suggestions collected during playtest-interview sessions (described below). New features were added on an ad hoc basis as issues were discovered or when explicit feature requests were made. The changes that were made throughout the study include crumbling platforms (for practicing muscle quietness), disappearing coins (to encourage quick collection), a bonus level (for game depth and performance assessment), an over-exertion warning (to indicate when muscle contractions are stronger than necessary), and a second screen containing raw EMG visualization (to allow clinicians to better assess muscle signals during gameplay). We include the motivation and details of several of these new features in our Results section as illustrative examples of how the findings of this study have helped shape the game and a full timeline explaining game evolution can be found in supplementary materials. It was interesting to note that the in-game calibration tools evolved as much as the game mechanics throughout the study; a timeline explaining the evolution of calibration tools can also be found in supplementary materials.

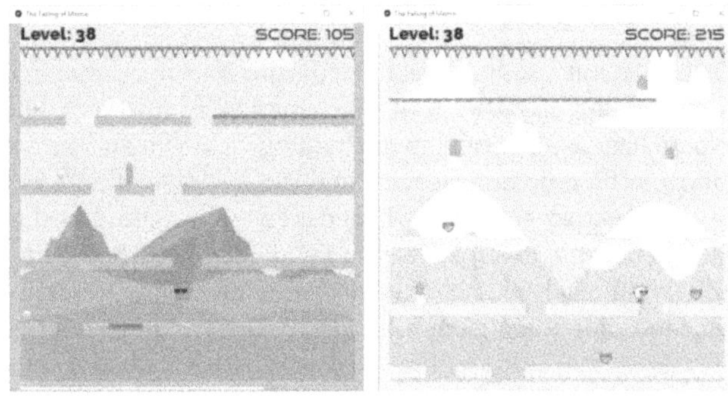

Figure 3: The Falling of Momo myo training game with the default theme (left) and the unlocked cat theme (right).

STUDY METHODOLOGY

To learn more about designing games that provide fun, engaging, and effective myoelectric muscle training, and to assess the viability of the Myoband as a training tool, we conducted a series of 9 playtest-interview sessions with 6 current/past myo users (referred to as patients) and 3 subject matter experts (referred to as experts), each of whom are introduced in Participant Profiles.

Games

Two myoelectric muscle training games were used during playtest-interview sessions: Momo (described above), and a game currently used in our local clinic (referred to as the "car game"), that was developed by the European prosthetics company, Ottobock [27].

The "car game" is part of Ottobock's [9,27] PAULA software training suite (Figure 2) and is controlled using the company's MyoBoy USB peripheral EMG sensors. Players control the height of a red and blue car using flexion and extension contractions, respectively, as the cars drive forward at a constant speed through a course consisting of a series of walls. The game has no score, but keeps a tally of the number of crashes that occur, so the goal of the game can be inferred as minimizing the total number of crashes. The player avoids crashing into walls by aligning each cars height with a gap in the approaching wall. The gaps appearing in the series of walls are positioned in such a way that encourages the player to repeatedly sustain a controlled muscle contraction (to get through a high gap) followed by a brief period of rest (to get through a low gap). If the height of the car is not such to allow it to pass through the gap, a red 'X' and a cartoon crash appear on the screen at the location of the crash, but game-play continues.

The game can be configured so that the player is either responsible for controlling a single car (easier), or for controlling both cars simultaneously as they drive through the course in tandem (harder). Additional configuration options allow the player to adjust the speed at which cars drive forward, the size of gaps in walls, and the duration of time that each round lasts. Feedback is also provided to players by a trail (line) that is drawn from the back of the car (creating a line graph effect).

Procedure

Patients

Each patient session consisted of a semi-structured conversation focused on the patient's history and experience with both myo training and video games followed by a demo of each game (with presentation order balanced across sessions) where patients were introduced to each game and given a chance to play for 10 to 15 minutes. Following each demo, patients were asked a series of questions about the game and were asked to rate it in terms of frustration, effort, fun, and perceived effectiveness. Patients were then given a chance to provide any additional feedback. To conclude the session, patients were asked to compare and contrast their experiences with both games.

All patient sessions occurred in the examination room at the clinic, with Linda present to ensure that patients were comfortable and to help with game setup (e.g., positioning EMG sensors, setup of car game). At least 2 researchers were present for each session, with one researcher leading the session while the other captured detailed notes. Several patients were accompanied by family members or care-givers (specified in "Participant Profiles") and, in these cases, their opinions and feedback were also considered.

Experts

Expert sessions also consisted of a semi-structured conversation followed by a gameplay demo where feedback on both games was collected. Conversation with experts focused on their experience with training in the clinical setting, the ideal and practical outcomes of training, and their views and opinions on game-based training. Experts were given a demo of Momo, but since every expert was already familiar with the car game, no demo was needed. Two expert sessions occurred in person, and in these cases experts were given a chance to play Momo. Due to geographic distance, the other expert sessions occurred over the phone and a video demo providing an overview of the features and mechanics of Momo was used instead (similar to the video-figure accompanying this paper).

Two researchers were present for each expert session, with one leading while the other captured detailed notes. Linda was the subject of one expert session, but was not present during any of the others.

Participants

Linda initiated contact with all participants. Patient participants came from Linda's existing client-base, and were recruited based on availability (i.e., making a visit for unrelated clinical purposes), willingness to participate, and discretion of clinical staff. Expert participants were recruited through Linda's professional contacts.

Participants were not remunerated for their time, and were aware that their participation was voluntary and that they were free to withdraw from the study at any time without implication on their clinical standings. All participants read and signed an ethical consent form (verbal consent was used during expert phone sessions) which explained the purpose, procedure, and voluntary nature of the study. For participants younger than the legal age of consent, a parent read and signed the consent form on their child's behalf, and was present for the duration of the session.

Participant Profiles

A total of 6 patient and 3 expert participants were included in the study. Four of the patients were accompanied by a family member. A brief summary of each participant is provided below. The information is factual, but names have been modified to maintain anonymity.

Kyla is an 11-year-old female who plays video games every day for several hours on her PS4, Xbox, and iPad. Kyla uses two myo arms (not worn while playing games) and a powered wheelchair as the result of an amputation, and has some cognitive deficit. She was accompanied by both her mother and caregiver, who helped answer some of the questions. Kyla's mom told us that since using her myos (~ 1 year) she has been doing much better in school.

Stanley is a 50-year-old male, who has been using a myo for over 30 years. Stanley was born without a right forearm, and believes that his myo has become an integrated part of his body; he uses it very naturally (e.g., twiddling fingers, fidgeting with a pen). Stanley had minimal training when he first received his myo (which was common practice at the time), and does not frequently play video games.

Mark is a 20-year-old male born without a left forearm. Mark used a myo when he was younger, undergoing training with Linda. At the age of 12, he stopped using his myo because the weight of the device made it too difficult to use effectively. Mark casually plays Xbox with his friends without the use of a prosthesis or special equipment. Mark is going to college this year, and is reconsidering using a myo to support independent living. During the interview session, Mark was joined by his father.

Justine is a 24-year-old female who was born without a left forearm, and was accompanied by her boyfriend Jon. Justine underwent training and received her myo as a toddler, but stopped using it at age 11 because she preferred the aesthetics of her passive prosthesis. Justine recently started using a myo again to benefit from the additional functionality it provides her and to alleviate repetitive-use injuries that were sustained in her right arm, and completed further muscle training exercises when she received her new arm. Justine casually plays MarioKart and Donkey Kong with her boyfriend and daughter.

Glen is a 50-year-old male who has been using a myoelectric arm for 32 years. As a result of an accident, Glen had surgery removing his left forearm at the age of 17. Glen trained through practical use, and during his stay in a rehabilitation center following the accident he spent many hours practicing with his new myo arm. Glen enjoys playing cards casually with friends and family, and occasionally plays solitaire on his phone.

Belle is a 10-year-old female (accompanied by her Mom), who was born without a right forearm. She first started using a myo at age 16 months, and continued to use it for several years. Belle more frequently uses a passive arm than her myo, because the weight of the myo is uncomfortable, the passive arm allows her to do physical activity (cheerleading and gymnastics), and she often gets frustrated with her myo because of frequent control problems. Belle casually plays games on her wii and iPad with friends.

Linda is an occupational therapist as described above in the Initial Design Requirements section.

Stuart is a research engineer who has specialized in the field of myoelectric control of prosthetics for 22 years. Stuart's research focuses on using pattern recognition to create more advanced and natural control strategies.

Ruth is an occupational therapist (OT) with 10 years' experience working with two large prosthetics companies. She has also worked in clinics training myo patients, and in teaching prosthetists and other OTs myo training practices.

Data Collection and Analysis

Data collected during each session consisted of a complete audio recording in addition to notes taken during the session capturing the researchers' observations. All patient sessions were transcribed, and then independently coded by two authors. The resulting codes were analyzed with a thematic analysis [10]. To remain patient focused, expert sessions were not included in the thematic analysis, but were instead used to help validate themes identified.

Our thematic analysis adopted a deductive approach where findings were organized around predetermined ideas. The three concepts were based on our initial work with Linda establishing requirements for our game and included: the challenges experienced in training, the role of feedback (positive or negative) on patient/player experience, and the impact play may have on the therapeutic process.

RESULTS

Core Challenges in Training

Most importantly, analysis identified a number of themes that fell into views on and challenges in training, with sub-themes addressing training practices, and patient needs.

Increasing Access to Training

Patients raised issues related to training practices and access to training; a focus also supported by expert feedback.

The most common response within this theme was the **lack of training programs for patients**. Patients reported receiving little to no training, but there was some evidence that they managed to make do with limited opportunities. For example, Stanley had minimal training and has been successfully using his prosthesis for more than 30 years by learning through practical use. However, experts pointed out that a lack of training may sometimes place important limitations on the functionality that is available to a patient or change how they can operate their prosthesis: This was evident in Stanley's gaming session, where we observed his therapist Linda uncover that he had adopted a non-standard control technique. She noticed this by first watching him play the games, and then confirming with muscle signal visualizations. Rather than contracting continuously to create smooth movement of the prosthetic hand or wrist, Stanley had been using a rapid series of pulses (a quick contraction and release) to control his myo. While Stanley used his myo very naturally, Linda commented that this is not strictly correct and could be limiting if he had a newer myo with a different control scheme.

In this context, experts pointed out that ideally **games should be designed to support a pre-prosthetic training phase** (before receiving a prosthesis), in order to make patients aware of how to contract the muscles that will be used to control their prosthesis. Having a broader perspective on the issue of training practices, experts stressed that the actual process can differ greatly depending on the availability of and access to services. At the local clinic, the clinician had a primary role to work with patients in a training and troubleshooting capacity, however many other facilities do not provide this level of service and only introduce patients to basic prosthetic maintenance.

A possible solution that came up in patient feedback and expert interviews alike were **game-based opportunities for out-of-clinic myo training**. Bella's mom explained that training outside of the clinic wasn't an option: *"...we haven't really done any sort of training outside the [clinic]... we tend to come in here and let the professionals do it."*. Experts agreed that learning (and mastering) the use of a myo is something that takes time and substantial training, but training occurs in short, intermittent sessions. Currently, experts don't have anything that they can send home with patients so that they can continue to train their muscles between visits, with Stuart pointing out that *"it's difficult to use one of these [myos] ... improvement comes in stages ... it doesn't all come in the first 3 days..."*. While our work was not directly focused on at-home training, experts were keen on the idea of a robust, low-cost training solution, agreeing that it would be extremely valuable.

Managing Muscle Fatigue

Many patients' responses evolved around the **management of muscle fatigue** and the creation of a positive, empowering player experience. In training, patients are asked to activate and use muscles that they have either never used before (in the case of congenital limb differences), or are vastly different from what they have grown accustomed to (in limb loss due to surgical removal). This poses two specific problems. First, certain patients might need to spend a substantial amount of time exploring methods for creating muscle signals that can be usefully detected by a myoelectric sensor. Second, since these muscles have rarely/never been used or are physically limited, patients can tire quickly.

For example, Justine pointed out that fatigue was challenging for her when playing the car game, *"[...] my muscles would get really, really tired, like tired to the point where I couldn't even do it, like I had to take a break ... I'd have to stop and I couldn't do it for a minute"*, which could negatively affect her experience and therefore engagement with the game in the long run. Likewise, experts voiced the concern that patients would get overly involved in the game and **lose focus on their level of exertion**, straining their muscles more than necessary resulting in premature fatigue.

In order to better make patients aware about when they have reached the maximum input threshold, we added the over-exertion warning, a feature that programmatically draws a red warning around Momo when the player contracts harder than they did during calibration. This was beneficial because it allowed both patient and clinician to identify when over-exertion occurred.

Creating an Empowering, Positive Player Experience

Themes concerning the two games often focused on aspects relevant to therapy and how games could contribute to an empowering positive experience and, most importantly, maintain appropriate levels of difficulty to create an encouraging player experience and broaden the appeal of games through adaptable themes.

Importance of Appropriate Level of Difficulty

A common theme across patients was the importance of **appropriate levels of game difficulty**. Patients clearly found Momo to be easier and, as a result, less frustrating than the car game. For example, Bella's feelings about the car game were made quite clear, *"I don't understand how this is helping me... It's too hard... I keep smashing into the wall, I'm not very good at this game already."*.

While a positive player experience as the result of gameplay that is perceived as easier is generally desirable, this creates some issues with respect to therapeutic goals, but also patient perspectives on the game. Some patients felt that Momo was more suitable for children or younger players. Mark, for example, acknowledged that the game was probably more appealing to a younger audience, *"Umm, maybe not me, but I guess if you were a kid"*. Even when this feeling was expressed, patients still felt that it was an appealing game, with Stanley pointing out that *"In the eyes of a [child]... there's no question, right?... it even brings out the competitiveness in me, right? The old guy."*

A sub-theme that was prominent among experienced myo users focused on **difficulty differences between the games and real life**, stating that playing either of the training games is more strenuous than day-to-day prosthetic use. In terms of training, there are conflicting interests at play. On one hand, practicing more strenuous exercises can help to build strength and stamina, both of which are important for effective prosthetic use. For example, Justine commented that *"[...] it's probably more work than I have to do when I'm doing regular things using my arm, but... it really gets you practicing using the muscles..."*. On the other hand, patients just starting to use a myo may find the strenuous activities discouraging and deter them from further practice, with Glen commenting that *"[...]you're using [your muscles] a whole lot more here [in the game]... for somebody learning, I think that would be very frustrating."*.

This suggests that games must carefully balance creating an appropriate amount of exertion with what is achievable for new patients, and should consider how realistic in-game difficulty maps onto using a myo in the real world.

Adopting Positive Perspectives on Player Performance

A common theme among all patients that was also backed by expert feedback was the importance of **positive perspectives on player performance**. Overall, patients and experts alike found that Momo offered a positive experience, where the car game, in contrast, did not. While the car game doesn't stop after a crash, the simple red 'X' that is displayed seemed to be enough to create negative emotions among players. For example, Glen pointed out that he was *"[...] no good, I [only] got one through... Agh, I crashed again. I'm trying, but they're coming too fast... I'm [just] trying to crash now"*. Yet, other patients didn't seem to mind crashing often because they didn't necessarily see the car game as a game, with Stanley commenting that *"[...] it's no different than going home and doing exercises, right – to get weight off... I would think of it as more of a tool."*. In this context, Linda (expert) pointed out that *"the risk is that [patients] start having a negative opinion about using myo, or that the prosthesis is going to be frustrating too, and then they start with a negative bias"*, underlining the importance of **positive, encouraging player feedback**. In agreement with Abeele [1], this suggests that adding game-like aspects without creating the right experience can be detremental to patients' views of their own abilities to control a myo successfully.

Perceived Self-Efficacy Through Play

Throughout analysis, the importance of providing playful experiences that **allow patients to increase perceived self-efficacy** emerged.

Within the car game, we observed all patients having difficulty sustaining the exact level of muscle contraction that would cause the car to stay at the right level to pass through the gap. Cars would bounce up and down rapidly, because their movement was mapped directly to noisy sensor readings. This caused patients to feel like they had little control, with Stanley pointed out that *"It's hard for me to hit the [gaps] ... I find the longer that I try to maintain the more it goes down"*. Patients identified the speed of the action and the fact that they had to keep track of two cars at once to be overwhelming elements of the car game, with Justine commenting that *"It got overwhelming I feel – I just got so tired and overwhelmed by the 2 cars"*. Furthermore, we observed a challenge related to time-pressure in games previously commented on by Hernandez and colleagues [21] in the context of game accessibility, recommending not to remove action and challenge from games, but to ensure that it is appropriate and manageable: while both games employ time as a central mechanic, players felt less frustrated when playing Momo, suggesting that balancing and maintaining achievable player goals is crucial when leveraging games for prosthesis training. Generally, Momo achieved higher levels of perceived self-efficacy by smoothing in-game representation and reaction to often noisy EMG signals. This highlights an interesting challenge for our project: While Momo's responses to player input are – strictly speaking – less accurate, the game provided a more encouraging overall experience. However, one advantage of the car game is that it explicitly displays muscle signals, which is useful to clinicians during a training session, information which is lost when smoothing EMG input as done in Momo. In response, visualizations to support therapists were added to Momo during design iterations (discussed below), but the simplified control scheme was maintained to preserve player experience.

Increasing Player Engagement Through Flexible Themes

A theme that was frequently touched upon by patient feedback was the desire to **personalize game themes**.

While Momo offers theme elements around monsters, aliens and castles, one patient expressed clearly what she would like to see: *"I want cats... why wouldn't they make cats? ... I really, really, really, really, really, want cats... I love cats! I have 3 cats at my home." (Kyla)*, a change to the game that was also appreciated by other patients.

For others, customization wasn't an important feature, but they still recognized the value in it, for example Glen commenting that *"I guess [it's] not for me personally, but I can see that the options to customize it, to make it fit..."*.

Given the **broad audience of game-based myo training** (e.g., having to accommodate players of different ages and with different levels of gaming experience), we believe that customization should be further explored as a means of maintaining continuous patient engagement through being able to offer individually relevant game themes.

Improving Therapy through Play

The final set of themes that emerged throughout analysis focuses on the improvements that game-based myo training can bring to therapy by making new information available to patients and therapists alike.

Therapy-Relevant In-Game Feedback

Besides encouraging patient engagement with therapy, results suggest that **in-game feedback also offered additional feedback on therapeutic progress**, a feature which was particularly appreciated by patients who otherwise struggle to see little improvements. Stanley explained that the *"...game tells -- tells all of us a little about my control, right? ... I'm learning a little bit about -- about myself, but also about the capabilities of the hand."*. While this effect can also be accomplished through a simple visualization of muscle signals, or using the car game, there were some instances in the use of Momo where its specific mechanics made particular problems more salient. For example, causing Momo to jump in the presence of muscle co-contraction served as an indicator for when patients were having trouble isolating their contractions. This gave a very tangible way for the occupational therapist to convey instructions and feedback, and for the patient to understand what was happening, for example illustrated by a sequence where Linda (expert) pointed out to Justine (patient) that *"When you jump, it usually means that you're using both muscles at the same time... if he's jumping when you don't want him to, just kind of relax, and then try again."*.

Even effective myo users could benefit from feedback as the **games exposed areas where the patients could further improve** their muscle control, and achieve additional/more reliable myoelectric control. For example,

Stanley explained that *"[...] it's good to visually see where you stand and it also tells you if there is room for improvement... I could [only] be at 60% and I wouldn't know, right?"*. Without this feedback, patients would have remained unaware of hidden issues in their muscle control.

Increased Patient Knowledge About Myos

This theme focuses on the increase of **patient understanding of how their prosthesis works** that can be accomplished through the deployment of games. Initially, we had very few feedback mechanisms to allow patients and clinicians to see their calibrated muscle signals in real time. Immediately, we observed that this was problematic when calibration issues arose – minor adjustments to the calibration were important for both Momo and the car game. We added several features to make the calibration and real time muscle signals visible immediately after calibration and selectively available during gameplay. This immediately facilitated calibrating the device and identifying calibration problems, but also changed how the patients worked with their device. The visualization tools helped patients to better understand their device, and we immediately saw patients and clinicians engage in conversation to work out small problems, for example with Justine commenting that *"I feel like this one [sensor] might be a little high *pointing to the on-screen bar growing with muscle contractions*, because he's going that way *points left* when I try to go the other way sometimes"*.

This interaction can be beneficial for patients because it allows them to **get more familiar with how their myo works**, and **engage about it with clinicians in more technical ways**, possibly facilitating troubleshooting and creating a more personalized approach to therapy.

Facilitating Myo Training at Home

Beyond its application in clinics, a theme that emerged from analysis was the potential of the Myoband to **enable patients to carry out prosthesis training in their own homes**. Patients responded well to the idea of using the Myoband as a training device, and expressed comfort when asked about home use, for example with Glen pointing out that *"[...] with the armband, I can slide it on, twist it around to where it needs to be, and do the calibration with some training, but yeah, that would be the way to go."*. At-home training could facilitate the initial adaption to myo use, as underlined by Kyla's mother, who stated that she wished her daughter would have had more training opportunities as it was *"a big challenge for her."*. To this end, the use of more affordable off-the-shelf consumer hardware could enable the wider application of training games such as Momo, adding another layer to the training opportunities currently offered through clinics.

When discussing the home use of the Myoband, one concern expressed by the experts was being able to position sensors appropriately on the arms of all patients, which vary widely in terms of size, shape, and the location of sites used for sensing muscle contractions. Training sessions utilizing Momo showed that our prototypical approach was suitable for all participants, demonstrating that the Myoband can be adapted to be viable for many limb-different patients.

DISCUSSION

We now reflect on our adapted UCD process, the importance of having a positive empowering experience, and the viability of the Myoband as a training tool.

Reflections on our Design Process

We adapted the typical UCD approach for several reasons. Most importantly, we were working with a sensitive population that was difficult to access. Our patients came from a wide geographical area to the clinic for reasons other than our study. As such, our sessions were short (60-90 minutes), with one patient at a time, and there was little opportunity for follow-up. Basing our design sessions on a partially-formed solution proved to be incredibly valuable for both eliciting feedback and encouraging discussion. Having a tangible 'thing' to examine and critique was viewed constructively by our patients and experts, and patients willingly discussed game aspects that were available for them to use, but struggled to conceptualize and reflect on features that were not yet available.

Our adapted design process worked extremely well for us and for our patients. Patients who came later in the process had the benefit of new functionality that allowed them to more quickly address calibration issues, play a more richly-featured game, and receive feedback that ensured their play better aligned with targeted training behavior. While other therapeutic game studies have had the benefit of engaging in a participatory design process and working with a set of patients over an extended period of time (e.g., [18,19]), we feel that this is not practical for many populations such as ours. While more work needs to be done to generalize our approach, we feel that it holds promise as a practical means of balancing the constraints of an understudied population with gleaning meaningful new design knowledge.

Therapeutic Games Need Not Be Unpleasant

Part of the motivation for working with our clinic was that they reported to us the negative feelings that many of their patients have when using previously-developed training tools. While patients usually did not enjoy their training exercises, the clinic still made use of them because they were relatively easy to set up and provided meaningful feedback to both patients and clinicians. However, the experts we spoke with all recognized the potential pitfalls of providing a negative experience to myo patients (hence their focus on facilitating patient success). Part of the reason for this sensitivity to negative feelings is likely due to the extremely high rate of abandonment of myos (up to 75% [7]). While there are many issues that can lead to abandonment (e.g., aesthetics, weight, convenience [22]), frustrations that arise from lack of control over the myo also contribute [12]. While our work does not directly address abandonment, we anticipate that any improvements to the training process will help reduce frustrations due to lack of control, thereby reducing abandonment.

Patients were receptive of Momo for many of the reasons discussed in our results: they felt more in control, negative feedback was minimal, the game started at an appropriate level of difficulty, and it felt more like a genuine game. While both Momo and the car game facilitated practicing the same basic muscle activity, the mechanics of the car game left patients feeling more tired and frustrated. We leave quantitative comparison (e.g., movement precision, training outcomes, abandonment) of Momo to future work, but we are encouraged that both patients and experts felt that Momo provided a better experience.

Myoband Viability and Implications for Home Training

While we started this project assuming that we would only focus on improving Momo's design, we quickly learned that the calibration functionality of our game was of equal importance. Without having easy access to, and meaningful feedback from the calibration, patients would not be able to play our game. Furthermore, without real-time access to performance data, clinicians could miss important information about potential problems with both the calibration settings and a patient's performance. As our tools to calibrate and make use of the Myoband improved, so too did our confidence that it is a viable solution.

As we described earlier, both patients and clinicians were receptive of the Myoband as a training tool. The importance of this finding cannot be understated. Currently, the only other myo training technology costs $4000USD, is more complex, and requires two people to attach (by positioning the electrodes and securing them with a tensor wrap). In contrast, the Myoband, although not designed for this use, has been at least as robust, provides sufficient signals, is easily positioned by a single patient, and costs less than $200USD. Because Momo is free and open source (https://github.com/hcilab/Momo.git), this means that we have a viable training tool at a fraction of the cost of the leading commercial solution. We hope that others will be encouraged to start developing myo training games based on our findings, and that others might use and extend Momo in their own myo training research.

Limitations and Future Work

The adapted UCD process described in this work arose out of the needs of the local clinic and patients. While our process is likely to have confounded some of our findings (as compared to a more traditional approach), it enabled us to introduce quick iterations that maximized the impact of input with a small number of participants and within a short timeframe. We gave careful consideration to the choices in our study design; however, our results must be taken in light of our adapted process. Beginning with a partially developed game may have inadvertently directed/narrowed our exploration of myo training games, and additional results may be found through further exploration.

Likewise, the small number of participants needs to be considered when generalizing our findings. While we believe, our findings can help inform the work of designers along with future research, we are planning to continue our collaboration with the clinic to develop a refined training tool that can be used on an on-going basis with patients.

This study has provided evidence that sending Momo home with patients is an important path forward. In further collaboration with the clinic, we are planning to provide Momo at home on a trial basis to further explore challenges and opportunities associated with home-based myo training. In this context, we plan to investigate pathways to maintain long-term player engagement; e.g., through multiplayer features that could connect patients in remote locations.

CONCLUSION

This paper presents our work on developing a new myo training game, the Falling of Momo. While games for myoelectric training have been previously proposed, research has focused on technical issues, not on the needs of patients and clinicians to provide a positive, empowering experience that targets key training objectives. Our game was initially developed based on requirements gleaned from our interactions with a local prosthetics clinic. Through an adapted UCD process, we then refined Momo to better meet the needs of both patients and clinicians by adding features that 1) facilitate the training process, 2) provide meaningful feedback on target behavior, and 3) increase engagement.

Our findings provide guidance for the design of myo training games and therapeutic games in general. We highlight that patients perceive a felt need for out-of-clinic training tools and that there is a 'fine line' between striving for targeted training behavior and providing a positive, engaging experience. Through play, patients can better understand their progress, both on areas where they can improve and about the device they are training to use.

Our work opens the door for myo training to be more readily available and accessible outside of the clinic by showing the viability of a low-cost input device and an adapted UCD process that focuses on patient needs and experience, while making rapid progress in the development of an engaging training game.

ACKNOWLEDGEMENTS

We would like to thank the Atlantic Clinic for Upper Limb Prosthetics, and especially Wendy Hill, for all the help and guidance that they provided throughout our study. We would like to thanks the patient and expert participants who generously gave time to help with our research. This research was funded through the support of NSERC and New Brunswick Innovation Foundation (NBIF).

REFERENCES

1. Vero Vanden Abeele, Luc Geurts, Jelle Husson, Frederik Windey, Jan Henk Annema, Mathijs Verstraete, and Stef Desmet. 2010. Designing Slow Fun! Physical Therapy Games to Remedy the Negative Consequences of Spasticity. In Proceedings of the 3rd International Conference on Fun and Games (2010): 1-2.
2. Vero Vanden Abeele, Jan Wouters, Pol Ghesquière, Ann Goeleven, and Luc Geurts. 2015. Game-based Assessment of Psycho-acoustic Thresholds: Not All Games Are Equal!. In Proceedings of the 2015 Annual Symposium on Computer-Human Interaction in Play (2015): 331-341.
3. Jan–Henk Annema, Mathijs Verstraete, Vero Vanden Abeele, Stef Desmet, and David Geerts. 2012. Video games in therapy: a therapist's perspective. International Journal of Arts and Technology (2012): 106-122.
4. R. S. Armiger, R. J. Vogelstein. 2008. Air-guitar hero: A real-time video game interface for training and evaluation of dexterous upper-extremity neuroprosthetic control algorithms. In Proceeding of the 2008 IEEE-BIOCAS Biomedical Circuits and Systems Conference (2008): 121–124.
5. Yee Mon Aung, Adel Al-Jumaily. 2011. Development of augmented reality rehabilitation games integrated with biofeedback for upper limb. Proceedings of the 5th International Conference on Rehabilitation Engineering & Assistive Technology (2011): 51-54.
6. BBC - Future Media Standards & Guidelines - Accessible Games Standard v1.0. http://www.bbc.co.uk/guidelines/futuremedia/accessibility/games.shtml. accessed: Jan 3rd, 2017.
7. Elaine A. Biddiss, Tom T. Chau. 2007. Upper limb prosthesis use and abandonment: A survey of the last 25 years. Prosthetics and orthotics international 31, no. 3 (2007): 236-257.
8. Hanneke Bouwsema, Corry K. van der Sluis, Raoul M. Bongers. 2010. Learning to control opening and closing a myoelectric hand. Archives of physical medicine and rehabilitation 91.9 (2010): 1442-1446.
9. Hanneke Bouwsema, Corry K. van der Sluis, Raoul M. Bongers. 2013. Guideline for training with a myoelectric prosthesis. Center for Human Movement Sciences / Department of Rehabilitation Medicine. University Medical Center Groningen, University of Groningen, NLD (2013).
10. Virginia Braun, Victoria Clarke. 2006. Using thematic analysis in psychology. Qualitative research in psychology 3.2 (2006): 77-101.
11. Ryan Clingman, Peter Pidcoe. 2014. A novel myoelectric training device for upper limb prostheses. IEEE Transactions on Neural Systems and Rehabilitation Engineering 22, 4 (2014): 879-885.
12. Michael R. Dawson, Jason P. Carey, Farbod Fahimi. 2011. Myoelectric training systems. Expert review of medical devices 8,5 (2011): 581-589.
13. L. van Dijk, C. van der Sluis, H. van Dijk, and R. Bongers. 2015. Task-oriented gaming for transfer to prosthesis use. IEEE transactions on neural systems and rehabilitation engineering: a publication of the IEEE Engineering in Medicine and Biology Society (2015).
14. A.C. Dupont, Evelyn L. Morin. 1994. A myoelectric control evaluation and trainer system. IEEE Transactions on Rehabilitation Engineering 2, 2 (1994): 100-107.
15. B. Ellis, G. Ford-Williams, L. Graham, D. Grammenos, I. Hamilton, E. Lee, J. Manion, and T. Westin. Game Accessibility Guidelines: A straightforward reference for inclusive game design. http://www.gameaccessibilityguidelines.com. accessed: Jan 3rd, 2017.
16. D.R. Flatla, C. Gutwin, L.E. Nacke, S. Bateman, R.L. Mandryk. Calibration games: making calibration tasks enjoyable by adding motivating game elements Proceedings of the 24th annual ACM symposium on User interface software and technology (2011): 403–412.
17. Anders Fougner, Øyvind Stavdahl, Peter J. Kyberd, Yves G. Losier, Philip A. Parker. 2012. Control of upper limb prostheses: terminology and proportional myoelectric control—a review. IEEE Transactions on neural systems and rehabilitation engineering 20.5 (2012): 663-677.
18. Kathrin Gerling, Conor Linehan, Jonathan Waddington, Michael Kalyn, Adam Evans. 2015. Involving Children and Young Adults With Complex Needs in Game Design. CHI 2015 Workshop on Ethical Encounters in HCI: Research in Sensitive Settings. (2015).
19. Kathrin Gerling, Kieran Hicks, Michael Kalyn, Adam Evans, and Conor Linehan. 2016. Designing Movement-based Play With Young People Using Powered Wheelchairs. In Proceedings of the 2016 CHI Conference on Human Factors in Computing Systems (2016): 4447-4458.
20. Luc Geurts, Vero Vanden Abeele, Jelle Husson, Frederik Windey, Maarten Van Overveldt, Jan-Henk Annema, and Stef Desmet. 2011. Digital games for physical therapy: fulfilling the need for calibration and adaptation. In Proceedings of the 5th international conference on Tangible, embedded, and embodied interaction (2011): 117-124.
21. Hamilton A. Hernandez, Zi Ye, T. C. Graham, Darcy Fehlings, and Lauren Switzer. 2013. Designing action-based exergames for children with cerebral palsy. In Proceedings of the SIGCHI Conference on Human Factors in Computing Systems (2015): 1261-1270.

22. G. H. Kejlaa. 1993. Consumer concerns and the functional value of prostheses to upper limb amputees. Prosthetics and orthotics international. 17,3 (1993): 157-163.
23. Shannon Knights, Nicholas Graham, Lauren Switzer, Hamilton Hernandez, Zi Ye, Briar Findlay, Wen Yan Xie, Virginia Wright, and Darcy Fehlings. 2016. An innovative cycling exergame to promote cardiovascular fitness in youth with cerebral palsy. Developmental neurorehabilitation 19, no. 2 (2016): 135-140.
24. Belinda Lange, Chien-Yen Chang, Evan Suma, Bradley Newman, Albert Skip Rizzo, Mark Bolas. 2011. Development and evaluation of low cost game-based balance rehabilitation tool using the Microsoft Kinect sensor. Annual International Conference of the IEEE Engineering in Medicine and Biology Society (2011): 1831-1834.
25. D. F. Lovely, D. Stocker, R. N. Scott. 1990. A computer-aided myoelectric training system for young upper limb amputees. Journal of Microcomputer Applications 13,3 (1990): 245-259.
26. Myo Gesture Control Armband. Website: https://www.myo.com/ Accessed: May 20th, 2016
27. Ottobock Prosthetics. Website: http://www.ottobock.com/en/ Accessed: July 14th, 2016
28. Philip A. Parker, J. A. Stuller, R. N. Scott. 1977. Signal processing for the multistate myoelectric channel. Proceedings of the IEEE 65.5 (1977): 662-674.
29. Philip A. Parker, Robert N. Scott. 1985. Myoelectric control of prostheses. Critical reviews in biomedical engineering 13.4 (1985): 283-310.
30. Scott Rigby and Richard Ryan. 2007. The Player Experience of Need Satisfaction (PENS): An applied model and methodology for understanding key components of the player experience. Retrieved from immersyve.com/PENS_Sept07.pdf (2007).
31. William Rose. 2011. Electromyogram analysis. Online course material. University of Delaware. Retrieved July 5, 2016 from https://www1.udel.edu/biology/rosewc/kaap686/notes/EMG%20analysis.pdf
32. Sanjay Saini, Dayang Rohaya Awang Rambli, Suziah Sulaiman, Mohamed Nordin Zakaria, Siti Rohkmah Mohd Shukri. 2012. A low-cost game framework for a home-based stroke rehabilitation system. IEEE International Conference on Computer & Information Science (ICCIS) (2012).
33. Erik Scheme and Kevin Englehart. 2011. Electromyogram pattern recognition for control of powered upper-limb prostheses: State of the art and challenges for clinical use. Journal of rehabilitation research and development 48, no. 6 (2011): 643-660.
34. Keisuke Shima, Masaru Okamoto, Nan Bu, Toshio Tsuji. 2006. Novel human interface for game control using voluntarily generated biological signals. Journal of Robotics and Mechatronics 18, no. 5 (2006): 626-633.
35. Aaron Tabor, Alex Kienzle, Carly Smith, Alex Watson, Jason Wurtz, and David Hanna. 2016. The Falling of Momo: A Myo-Electric Controlled Game to Support Research in Prosthesis Training. In Proceedings of the 2016 Annual Symposium on Computer-Human Interaction in Play Companion Extended Abstracts (2016): 71-77.
36. Aaron Tabor, Scott Bateman, and Erik Scheme. 2016. Game-Based Myoelectric Training. In Proceedings of the 2016 Annual Symposium on Computer-Human Interaction in Play Companion Extended Abstracts (2016): 299-306.
37. Boonyarat Viriyasaksathian, Sarawin Khemmachotikun, Panya Kaimuk, Yodchanan Wongsawat. 2011. EMG-based upper-limb rehabilitation via music synchronization with augmented reality. IEEE International Conference on Robotics and Biomimetics (ROBIO) (2011): 2856-2859.
38. Jonathan Waddington, Conor Linehan, Kathrin Gerling, Kieran Hicks, Timothy L. Hodgson. 2015. Participatory design of therapeutic video games for young people with neurological vision impairment. Proceedings of the 33rd Annual ACM Conference on Human Factors in Computing Systems (2015): 3533-3542.
39. Adam W. Wilson, Yves G. Losier, Philip A. Parker, Dennis F. Lovely. 2011. A bus-based smart myoelectric electrode/amplifier—system requirements. IEEE Transactions on Instrumentation and Measurement 60.10 (2011): 3290-3299.
40. Ji Won Yoo, Dong Ryul Lee, Yon Ju Sim, Joshua H. You, Cheol J. Kim. 2014. Effects of innovative virtual reality game and EMG biofeedback on neuromotor control in cerebral palsy. Bio-medical materials and engineering 24.6 (2014): 3613-3618.

Affective Color in Visualization

Lyn Bartram
Simon Fraser University
Surrey, BC, Canada
lyn@sfu.ca

Abhisekh Patra
Simon Fraser University
Surrey, BC, Canada
apatra@sfu.ca

Maureen Stone
Tableau Software
Seattle, WA, USA
mstone@tableau.com

ABSTRACT
Communicating the right affect, a feeling, experience or emotion, is critical in creating engaging visual communication. We carried out three studies examining how different color properties (lightness, chroma and hue) and different palette properties (combinations and distribution of colors) contribute to different affective interpretations in information visualization where the numbers of colors is typically smaller than the rich palettes used in design. Our results show how color and palette properties can be manipulated to achieve affective expressiveness even in the small sets of colors used for data encoding in information visualization.

ACM Classification Keywords
H.5.m. Information Interfaces and Presentation: Misc-Colors

Author Keywords
Affective Visualization; Color Perception; Design

INTRODUCTION
We react emotionally as well as cognitively to visual imagery, and those emotions influence both how we use the information presented to us and how we are affected by its presence in our visual environment [34]. These systems are not independent; emotion can result from cognitive reasoning, and affect influences cognition [34]. Affect matters in visualization for communicative intent, engagement, and storytelling [6, 15]; there is evidence it supports problem solving [13]. While there is a long history of research and practice in how certain visual elements relate to affect, there is yet no framework of affective principles for visualization. The goal of our research is to examine the affective capacity of visual features such as color as part of this emerging framework.

Color palettes play a central role in data visualization where they are frequently used to map categorical attributes for effective discrimination and identification [39, 5]. Principles for using color to represent data in visualization are well established in the field and empirically validated [39, 5]. Designers and artists manipulate color to communicate affect but their knowledge of how to design affective palettes is largely rooted in professional craft and is qualitatively rather than empirically validated. Color psychology has proven the connection between individual colors and affect, but to date there are no studies in how combinations of colors (palettes) may convey different affect in the limited scope used in categorical information visualization.

CHI 2017, May 6-11, 2017, Denver, CO, USA.

ACM ISBN 978-1-4503-4655-9/17/05 ...$15.00.
DOI: http://dx.doi.org/10.1145/3025453.3026041

Unlike the rich palettes available to design applications, mapping colors to categorical data (the most common use of color in visualization) introduces two important constraints. First, the usable scale of the palette is small: typically, 5-10 colors [42]. Second, the colors need to be strongly perceptually distinct [39]. We are interested in validated computational models of how color relates to desired affect in these constrained palettes.

We had two basic research questions. First, can we relate certain affective impressions to properties of a color palette in abstract images such as simple visualizations? And second, what might this mean operationally for the design of affective color palettes that are useful in information visualization? We note an important point here. This work asks: given a desired affect, what palette colors should you choose? It does not answer the broader and much harder question: given an arbitrary palette, what affect does it convey? Our goal is not to absolutely link color and affect for all cases. Instead, we propose that simply being able to recommend statistically likely palettes for a particular affect is useful to visualization practitioners.

In this paper, we report three studies examining how different properties of color palettes were associated with specific affective impressions. Our results show relations between perceptual color properties (hue, chroma and lightness), palette composition (hue clusters, color frequency) and certain types of affect. This research makes the following contributions. First, our results affirm the potential of color for conveying meaning and identify initial palettes that enhance these affective impressions even in the limited space of information visualization palettes. Second, our findings support initial guidelines based on the distribution of hue, chroma and lightness for the affects we studied. Some are very distinct, while others overlap. Third, we propose a new method for modeling palettes using social network analysis that shows some interesting relationships between colors in palettes worth further exploration. These results extend research in design practice and introduce new dimensions of expressivity to visualization.

AFFECTIVE VISUALIZATION

The role of affect in information visualization applications is emerging, as researchers identify its importance in narrative [6, 36], problem solving [13, 33, 16] and contextual framing. The fundamental difference between data and affective visualization is in communicative intent. Information visualization seeks to **represent** data with visual features for effective cognitive interpretation. Affective visualization uses visual features to **evoke** a mood, feeling or impression. These are commonly described by factor-based classifications such as the well-known PAD model of affect [35] that plots them in a dimensional space defined by pleasure (valence) and arousal axes. Valence covers hedonic range, from positive (happiness, pleasure, love) to negative (pain, anger, sadness, fear). Arousal reflects intensity from calm (unaroused, relaxed, sleepy, etc.) to excited (high arousal, stimulated, nervous, alert, etc.). Typical emotions such as surprise, disgust or compassion can be placed in this 2D space; extensive emotion research has defined many more nuanced affects (such as affection or boredom) in this model as well [23].

RELATED WORK

Color psychology examines the interplay between color, cognition, affect and behaviour, considering factors of culture [8, 31], emotional response [40, 21] and behavioural influence (particularly around consumer response) [24, 22, 3]. Various studies show that "warm" colors (red, yellow and orange) are more arousing than "cool" hues of blue and green [32, 3]. Red is considered hot, vibrant and intense across cultures [22, 31, 9], and most likely to induce arousal and anxiety [21]. It is also tightly coupled with semantic cultural meaning, and thus varies in its association with valence. Yellow, orange and brown have less consistency of affective response, although yellow is also considered exciting. A study of website color for e-commerce across cultures found that respondents disliked the yellow scheme, terming it "too showy" and not "appropriately professional" [8]. Studies also associate brown with "sad" and "stale" ratings [31]. Blue, and to a lesser extent green, have positive links to the natural world and are associated with positive content [31, 32, 9, 10]. In particular, blue is strongly associated with peacefulness and calm across cultures [8, 31]. In advertising, blue is associated with trust [8] and competence [22]: it evokes stronger buying impulses than red [3]. Alternately, in room color, blue is more likely to be associated with depression, and red with anxiety [21]. Clearly context is a critical moderating factor in these findings.

Most color psychology has focused on hue rather than chroma and lightness, although recent studies show the influence of lightness and chroma on affective response [24]. High chroma color is exciting and intense; low chroma colors are calmer and less dominant. Greys have been described as "serious" and "professional". Lightness is associated with calm: lighter colors are considered more pleasant, less arousing and less dominant than dark colors [22, 24]. Black is negative and dominant [31, 40]; dark browns are sad. In one study, subjects were less upset when they read about murder on light pink paper than on white [40]. These findings may be useful when hue choice is limited by branding or other assignment, because lightness and chroma can be altered without contravening categorical meaning or desired "personality" [32].

COLOR, AFFECT AND AESTHETICS

Aesthetic principles for palette design are typically based on color harmony, an attempt to model which colors work together visually. This is commonly expressed as geometries with respect to hue wheel, as well as careful control of lightness variation [17, 41]. Itten's qualitatively grounded contrast model formalized the concepts of warm and cool colors, and postulated that tints (light colors) represent the brighter and better aspects of life, while shades (dark colors) represent the darker, sad, and negative forces [17]. Itten contrasts have been used in image analysis of affective colors [30] and aesthetic color selections [29].

Relatively little research has examined color palettes and affect. Madden identified two strategies of color association in logo design (which colors are used together): consistency (colors have a similar meaning) and complementarity (each color is associated with a different meaning) [31]. He found that when blue was used as the designated logo color, it was most often paired with white, green and yellow (largely a consistency strategy). In contrast, when red was the designated main color, respondents preferred a complementary strategy, with the secondary color different across cultures.

PALETTE GENERATION

Foundational work in color naming [4] showed that all cultures have common concepts of a small set of basic colors and their associated verbal names. Heer and Stone built a probabilistic model of color naming [14], showing how it can map between colors and names and measure color similarity. They applied this to compare and evaluate palette design, where minimizing name overlap and maximizing saliency are important for comprehension and memorability [39]. This work was expanded to semantic color design for visualization by Lin et al. [25] and Setlur and Stone [37] for finding appropriate colors associated with categories. These algorithms explore the rich associations grounded in the concept-color relations of objects and identities, but have not been applied to more nuanced terms of emotion, atmosphere or affect.

Color-word associations have long been explored as the basis for palette design using different strategies: manual selection from a predesigned set of colors linked to a particular word or concept, such as the Kobayashi color Image [20] or the Adobe Kuler website; or automatic color extraction and combinations given a set of rules using concepts of color harmony [28, 7]; perceptual contrast [19], keyword-color scales [38] and user pair preferences [11]. Kobayashi's empirically grounded color Image Scale [20] provides 130 basic colors combined in 1170 three-color combinations indexed by 180 keywords such as "provocative" or "romantic," a complex set of expressive concepts. Lindner et. al. used color-word associations and harmonic color themes based on the color wheel for automatic palette generation in which the user described the semantic content and the color extraction algorithm determines the appropriate colors from a precomputed color thesaurus [27] that matches a word to its underlying distribution in HSV [28]. In a small user study they compared their palettes to Adobe Kuler's user-generated palettes and found no significant improvement, concluding that color palette preferences are highly influenced by personal taste. Jahanian et al. [18] took a different approach, using a color extraction method for magazine design palettes based on word association with the concepts in the Kobayashi scale. More recently, researchers have explored automated palette generation for the sparser palettes in visualization. Wijffelaars et al. developed a generalized method based on sampling of a continuous path through color space at uniform intervals [43] with no user input into the generation. In contrast, Colorgorical is an interactive tool for automatic palette generation that uses a sampling based on user discriminability and preferences in which users can customize the sampled selections [11].

COLOR METRICS

Perceptually-based color metrics can be computationally represented as geometries in a three dimensional color space. The common CIELAB representation offers a color distance metric ΔE. This is simply the Euclidean distance between two colors, expressed by their coordinates, L^*, a^*, b^*. Using polar coordinates to represent a^*, b^* creates a more intuitive representation. The radial distance, C^* defines chroma or relative saturation, hue is defined by the hue angle, h°. In this paper, we simplify this notation to L,C,H. We also use the terms 'lightness,' 'chroma' and 'hue' for these quantities. We also use the term 'saturated' and 'desaturated' descriptively to describe high and low chroma colors respectively.

Quantitative measures to represent color palettes are more complex. Lin et al. analyzed them using color distance metrics to extract distinct palettes from images [26]. These included mean, min and max distances between colors in themes. Two quantitative approaches to measuring hue variation are entropy (how distinct the colors are) or saturation-weighted hue dispersion [WHD], which calculates the angular dispersion between hues along the hue wheel, taking saturation into account[12]. When WHD is higher, hues are more concentrated (less dispersed). Methods such as k-means clustering are commonly used to model color associations [25].

MOTIVATION: AFFECT AND COLOR

We were curious whether color and affect would be linked in simple 5-color categorical palettes applied to common visualizations. Are there different groupings of colors that align more consistently to areas in that space? Can the relative differences suggest palette selection based on the desired affect's "location" in the PAD affect space? In other words, if an affect combines **Calm** and **Positive**, would the colors selected for it be similar to colors in palettes selected in both? Our work differs from other concept-color association research in two ways. First, we focus on palettes rather than only single colors. Second, we explore whether color associations along the valence and arousal dimensions map to PAD space such that color selection for other affects reflects their relative influence.

We began by selecting 8 affects. The 4 "core affects" of **Calm, Exciting** and **Positive, Negative** represented the valence and arousal dimensions of the PAD model. We added 4 "pragmatic" affects: **Serious, Playful, Trustworthy** and **Disturbing**. We chose these as examples in a much larger space rather than as definitive "best" options in quantifying exact mappings. These can be considered as combinations of the core affects. **Disturbing** is **Exciting+Negative**; **Playful** is **Exciting+Positive**; **Trustworthy** is **Calm+Positive**; **Serious** is **Calm+ Negative** (although the valence may be less pronounced). We realize that these might not produce exactly equally weighted locations in the affect space, where other emotions such as "Happy" might. But we have a second important design goal: ecological validity. Emotions such as happy or sad may not be of interest in visualization applications, but trust and serious are important affects in business communication [8]. Playful, serious and disturbing are relevant to storytelling, an emerging field in data visualization [6, 15].

APPROACH

We explored color-affect relations in three studies. First (S1), we analyzed the color palettes of tagged images in two large social network databases, Flickr and deviantArt.com. From these results, we generated a set of colors for a design study (S2) in which users selected 5 colors for categorical coloring in simple visualizations to best communicate a specified affect. The results of S2 produced both distinct patterns for color selection and grouping by affect and a new metric of palette weight. We then ran a validation study (S3) in which we generated palettes based on this metric and asked users to rank them for the specified affect. We discuss each in turn.

STUDY 1: IMAGE ANALYSIS

Following [25], we analyzed the palettes of 8608 images. We selected these by searching for images tagged with terms related to our eight affects, and then eliminating all images with humans or human-influenced scenes (such as war images) to avoid conflation with content [23]. Roughly 2/3 of these images were abstract; the remaining 1/3 were landscapes, still-life/object, or nature scenes.

For each image, we calculated mean lightness and chroma. We then computed distribution histograms with a bin size of 10, calculating the percentage of pixels in the image that was in the lightness or chroma range of the bin. We generated 8 sets of 40 distinct hues each using k-means clustering, plus lightness and chromaticity ranges obtained from the image analysis. For each hue, we calculated the probability of a candidate color

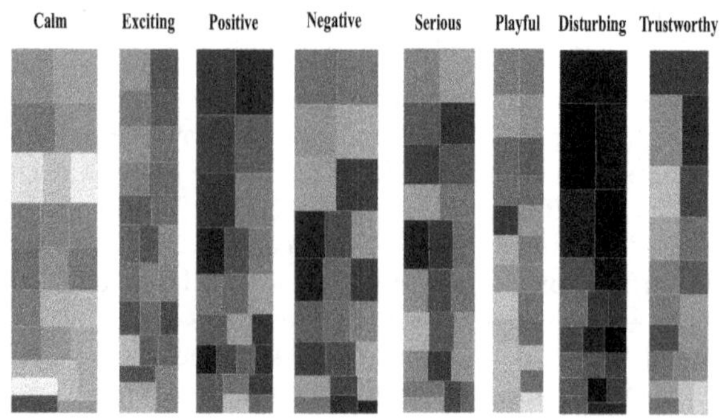

Figure 1. Most common colors by affect in image analysis study (S1)

from the set given an affect value and corresponding image histogram using Lin's algorithm [25]. Each hue was measured against the set of different images that were categorized by affect. We then selected the most commonly used colors in each of the affective image sets (Figure 1).

Results

As our data distribution was marginally non-normal, we used the Kruskal-Wallis test for significance (the rank-based non-parametric equivalent of an ANOVA for multi-factor data). Affect had a significant effect on both lightness X^2 (7, 8607) =199.6250, p<.0001 and chroma X^2 (7, 8607) =387.7106, p<.0001. **Calm, Playful** and **Exciting** images were lighter than **Disturbing** and **Negative**. **Negative** and **Calm** were less saturated than **Playful** and **Exciting**. We see patterns in **Calm** palettes containing a larger concentration of light and desaturated blues and greens. **Trustworthy** also has blues, purples and some greens. **Playful** and **Exciting** use highly saturated colors like reds, vibrant greens and blues with **Exciting** having relatively more dark reds. **Disturbing** has a larger distribution of dark browns, blues, reds and black. **Negative** used more grey and muted browns. With the exception of **Positive**, these results mirror what color psychology would predict. We were surprised by the amount of browns and dark colors in **Positive**.

STUDY 2: USER-DESIGNED PALETTES

We used these results to design colors for a user study. We asked a visualization color expert to design a smaller set for use in our next study. She reduced the set to 36 colors, using a combination of k-means clustering to combine similar colors, and filtering to remove colors that were either too light to offer sufficient contrast with the background or too dark for the hues to be easily visible when small. She then used visual tools and visualizations of the associated color metrics to establish that the resulting colors offered a balanced mix of CIELAB hue, chroma and lightness values.

We ran a pilot study where people with design experience created palettes based on affect. The goal of our study was to see whether they would consistently assign different color sets for each of our 8 affective categories in simple visualization tasks. The results from the pilot showed affect strongly influenced colors chosen, similar to those in Study 1. We then expanded our study to a wider population, to see if the results were specific to designers and to get a larger data sample. We extended the color set to 41 colors, adding more dark, because our results indicated that the original palette did not provide quite enough different colors for some of the darker affects. We show the detailed results for this larger experiment.

Method

Participants completed categorical coloring tasks for two simple visualizations (bar chart or map) using the interface shown in Figure 2 to select palettes of 5 colors for each task from a set of 41. We chose a map and a bar chart as they are familiar information representations. Participants were instructed to select colors to convey an affect from our eight affective categories. They were not told what the data represented other than affective intent. They could additionally modify the palette overall balance by adjusting a slider to control alpha. When

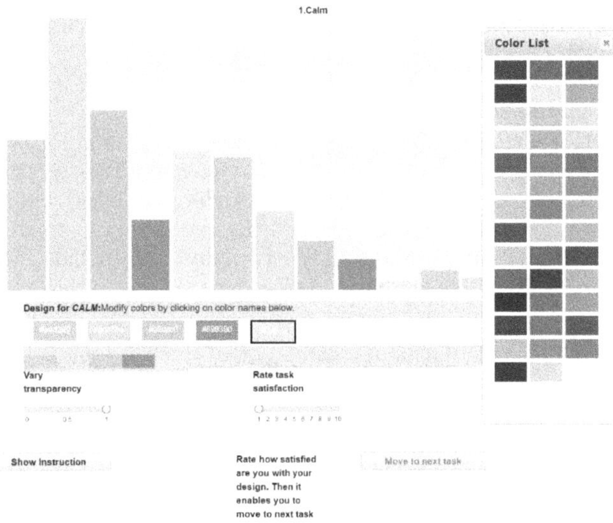

Figure 2. Study 2 interface

the participant was finished with the color selection, s/he rated satisfaction using a slider between 0 and 10 to indicate how successfully s/he felt the colors expressed the concept. At the beginning of each trial the initial alpha value was set to 1 and the visualizations were colored in neutral gray.

Because we were interested in the relative locations of color groups in the PAD space, we paired endpoint tasks of the affect model **(Calm-Exciting, Positive-Negative)** to establish differences (if any), drawing from thc core theoretical work in mapping affect. Similarly, we considered these differences in the pragmatic case **(Serious-Playful)** with clear semantic opposites. Where there was not a clear opposite **(Trustworthy, Disturbing)** we did not pair the tasks but presented them singly. This provided a relative rather than an absolute measure of how palettes might differ with respect to comparative affect. We used this design because we are not expecting to be able to absolutely quantify all possible palettes with respect to affect, but rather to understand what might make a desired affective impression comparatively stronger or weaker. In the cases of Trustworthy and Disturbing (both affects with strong ecological validity that are not clear opposites), we simply sought to see how they might relate to the other affect groupings.

Each affect task was independent and required separate color assignments, alpha and satisfaction rating. Participants could reassign the 5 colors in the palettes until satisfied: they were not constrained to mapping a color to a particular spatial location or size in the visualization. The experiment began with a training task in which participants colored Happy and Sad affects. No time limit was set on training; participants proceeded to the main study when ready. The experiment was hosted on our university web server. People could stop at any time, and login to the system later to complete the study: the system retained state. We report only on results where all tasks were completed.

Factors and metrics

We had two independent variables: Affect (8) and Visualization (2: bar chart, US map). Our raw dependent variables were color metrics (lightness, chroma, hue), alpha, and satisfaction rating.

Hypotheses for Study 2

H1. Affect will influence color choice. Cooler colors will be used for low arousal **(Calm, Serious and Trustworthy)**. High arousal affects **(Exciting, Disturbing, Playful)** will use warmer colors: more reds, browns and oranges. **Positive** affects **(Positive, Playful, Trustworthy)** will include more green. **Negative** will use brown and grey.

H2. Affect will have a significant effect on lightness: **Calm** colors will be lighter, **Negative** ones darker.

H3. Affect will have a significant effect on chroma: high arousal affects **(Exciting, Playful, Disturbing)** will include more saturated colors.

Design

We used a 2-way between-subjects design separated by Visualization type, producing an experiment session of 8 experimental conditions (1 Affect) per group. Trial ordering was randomized and block ordering was counterbalanced. A 76x8 design yielded 608 trials.

Participants

76 persons, roughly distributed by gender, with normal or corrected-to-normal vision, were paid to participate. They were randomly assigned to one of the 2 groups (Bar or Map).

Results

We removed all palettes that were either incomplete or included duplicate colors, giving us 504 palettes that each had 5 unique colors. We then did both visual and statistical analysis. Figure 3 shows the resulting palette colors. Each bubble represents a color that appeared in a palette in the associated affect; the size represents how frequently it was used. Zero frequency values are removed, and each bubble cluster has a slightly different number of bubbles (colors) in it. However, the size scale is the same across all the affects.

We clearly see that colors and color characteristics varied by affect, confirming H1. We used a nonparametric Kruskal-Wallis for significance for all tests. Visualization type had no effect, so we combine the results in subsequent discussion. A statistical analysis on the three perceptual metrics, lightness, chroma and hue, found all were significant. We found significant effects for affect on lightness X^2 (7, 1216) =426.7211, p<.0001 and chroma X^2 (7, 1216) =481.8955, p<.0001. **Calm, Playful** and **Positive** were much lighter than **Disturbing, Serious and Negative**. **Calm** was the least saturated of the affects; **Exciting, Playful** and **Positive** the most colorful (chromatic). While alpha was significant, the effect was very small: it was only applied in **Calm**. Since this effect was small and simply reinforced the already strong pattern of high lightness and low chroma for this affect, we did not use alpha in further analysis. These results statistically confirm our hypotheses H2 that lightness relates to valence **(Calm, Positive, Negative, Playful) Trust** and H3 that arousal influences colorfulness choices **(Exciting, Playful vs Calm, Serious)**. We also saw a combined effect: both valence and arousal influence color choice,

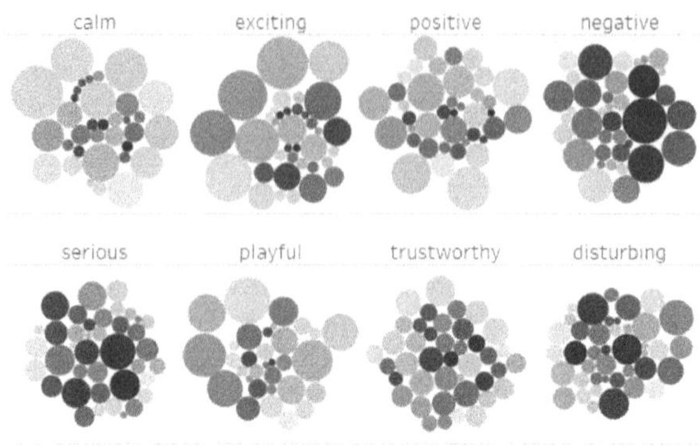

Figure 3. Frequency distribution of colors by affect (S2).

notably in **Calm** which is both lightest and least chromatic. Satisfaction rating was uniformly high and never significant.

Affect was highly significant for hue: X^2 (7, 1216) =93.4. We calculated color dispersion in each palette as saturation-weighted hue dispersion (WHD) and saw significant differences by affect: X^2 (7, 1216) =88.21, p<.0001. Colors in **Exciting, Playful** and **Positive** were most spread out in hue space; **Calm** and **Negative** palettes were the most tightly clustered.

Looking at the core affects, we note some clear patterns. **Calm**, as predicted, makes strong use of cool colors (blues and greens) and is overall high lightness and low chroma. **Exciting** emphasizes warmer and higher chroma colors: more reds and yellows. **Positive**, like **Exciting**, uses strongly saturated hues but incorporates more green. **Negative**, as anticipated, has more browns, dark reds, and greys. These patterns combine in interesting ways when we consider the pragmatic affects. **Playful** is both **Exciting** and **Positive** in affect: its colors are similar to **Exciting**, but included more greens and yellows and fewer reds than **Exciting**. **Serious** shared the greys of **Negative** but used more blue; we would expect that it has aspects of low arousal and **Calm**. Notably, **Serious**, which might be considered both calmer than **Disturbing** and less **Negative**, used fewer red and yellow hues. **Disturbing**, which is clearly **Exciting** and **Negative**, reflects the browns and greys of **Negative** but incorporates more of the reds and yellows of **Exciting**. **Calm** and **Negative** palettes were the most tightly clustered. These findings and the statistical analysis confirm H1.

STUDY 3: USER RANKED PALETTES

We now wanted to validate these results and to assess an algorithmic design metric. We used insights from S2 to design sets of palettes for each affect and ran a study in which people selected the best and worst palette for an affect from a set of 5 choices. To avoid any bias potentially introduced by the pairings in Study 2, affects were presented singly. For each affect, we calculated the weight of each color as how often that color was used in a palette in S2. We then calculated palette weight for each palette in S2 as a sum of its color weights. Given that high palette weight represented the cumulative strongest color combinations for that affect, we conjectured it would be a good predictor of a palette's suitability for a particular affect. We designed palettes for S3 manually based on weight. For each affect, we automatically generated every

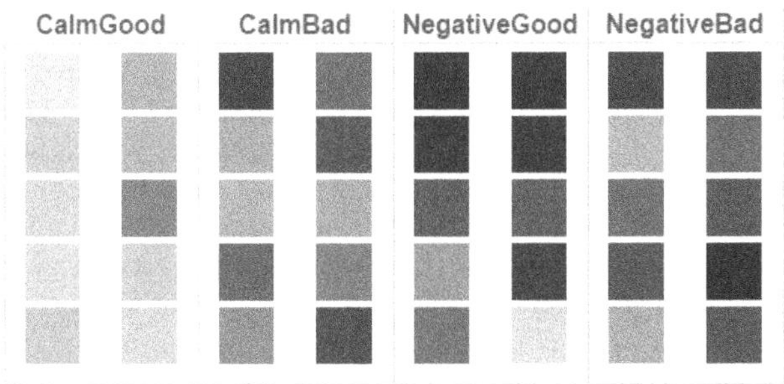

Figure 4. Examples of good (high weight) and bad (low weight) palettes

possible combination of 5 colors (749, 398 sets) and calculated the palette weight of each. We then sorted the list from highest to lowest and manually selected candidate palettes from three relative areas: the top weighted palettes, the lowest weighted palettes and the middle area. We used manual selection to minimize color replication in the palettes, as this was difficult in the highest weighted palettes because there were a few very heavily weighted colors in these: we ensured that no two palettes shared more than 3 colors. Figure 4 shows examples of two good (top weight) and 2 bad (low weight) palettes for each of **Calm** and **Negative**.

Method

In each trial a participant saw 5 spatially identical bar charts, each colored with a different palette (Figure 5). Colors in the palette were randomly assigned to locations in the bar chart. The participant was asked to identify one as Best and one as Worst. There were 8 affective tasks. For each affective category there were 15 possible palettes, binned into 5 "good", 5 "medium" and 5 "bad". These were only used for randomization: in each trial, 2 palettes were randomly selected from the "good" bin, 1 from the "medium" bin and 2 from the "bad" bin. Each participant did 2 repetitions of each affective task (2 Best, 2 Worst). Affect tasks were presented in random order.

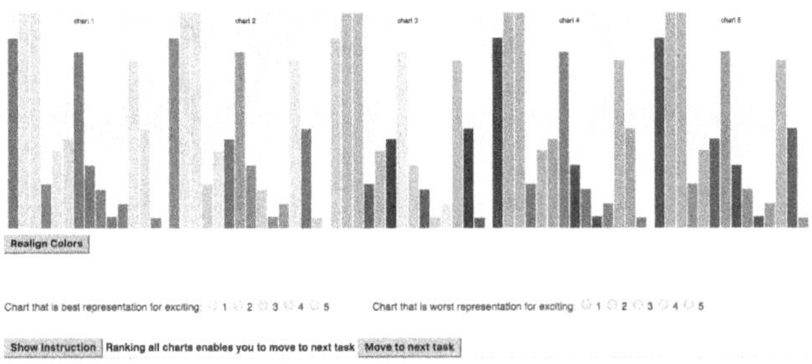

Figure 5. Study 3 Interface: Users ranked the Best and Worst of 5 palettes for each affect in S3.

Metrics

The independent variables were affect and palette weight (PW). The dependent variable was the rating of Best/Worst for each palette. For each palette we thus had the rating, the individual colors in that palette, the frequency weight for each color and the summed palette weight.

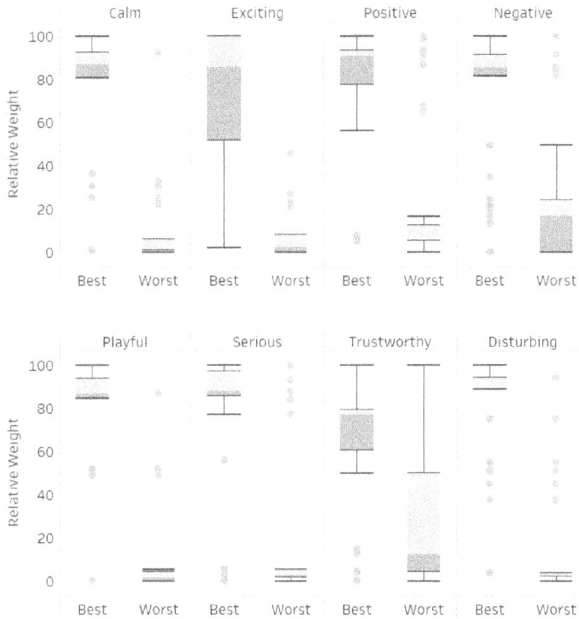

Figure 6. Palette Ranking by relative weight and affect (Study 3)

Hypotheses Study 3

H4. Higher weighted palettes would be more likely to be rated Best than low weighted palettes;

H5. Lower weighted palettes would be more likely to be rated as Worst.

Participants

38 users (and an additional 2 with incomplete data) participated. They were roughly distributed by gender. All had normal or corrected-to-normal vision. Participants were entered into a draw for potential reimbursement. None had taken part in the previous studies.

Results

Figure 6 shows the results of palette ratings by weight and affect. As the palette sets were very different in the **range of weights**, we normalized the weight metric to **relative weight position**: that is, the percentage of the overall range that the weight represented. So, for example, the Calm range was 135 from the lowest weight to the highest weight: a Calm palette with a weight of 109 had a relative weighted position of 80.7. We then used a logistic regression analysis to determine if this would be a significant predictor of Best/Worst choice. The result was extremely significant:X^2 (1, 1218) =1093.32, p<.0001.

These results confirm that palettes are more likely to be ranked better as their weight increases. Conversely, palettes with low weight were more likely to be selected as Worst. These results confirm **H4** and **H5** that palette weight calculated from our previous studies proved a strong predictor of how people ranked it for affect expressivity. More generally, they validate our essential conjectures that even simple palettes of 5 colors can convey different affective impressions, though it can been seen in Figures 3 and 7 that is a stronger finding for some affects than others. In particular, we note that the relative

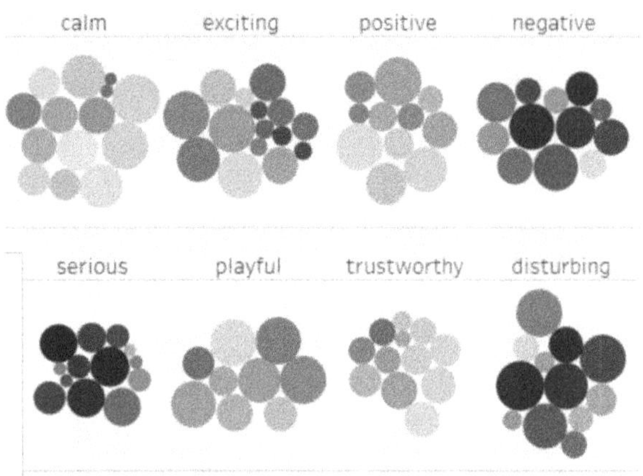

Figure 7. Colors from palettes chosen as "Best" in Study 3

difference between Best and Worst in the more nuanced affect of **Trustworthy** was smaller, and there were more outliers. We surmise this was due to the case that the range of weights in these palettes were smaller: instead of a few highly weighted colors, the preferred colors were more evenly used, and thus the weight ranges were smaller. This raises questions about what else we might need to understand about what contributes to color selection for affective palettes. We calculated the preferred colors for each affect by counting how many times the hues occur in the palettes rated Best for that affect. We then simply selected the colors with the highest count for each affect. Figure 7 shows the preferred colors for each of the affects in Study 3. These strongly reflect the results from S2. If pairing had introduced bias in S2, we would not have seen these confirmatory results in S3, as there were no comparative paired presentations in this study.

PALETTES AS SOCIAL NETWORKS

These results show that there are patterns of color preference by affect. To explore the relationship between colors in palettes, we tried modeling palettes as social networks. Social network analysis provides both a visual and a mathematical analysis of actors (nodes) and relationships (links) to give insight into the various roles and groupings in a network: where are the most influential nodes? What are the strongest connections? Are there clusters? In particular, measures of network centrality identify the most important nodes in the network as a function of how well they are connected to other nodes; models of network structure identify clusters and outliers. While we have no formal results, our analysis was interesting enough that we provide a few examples here.

Using the Gephi library [2],we modeled each palette as a connected subset of 5 colors, where each color Ci was a node in the network of colors and an edge Eij indicated Ci and Cj were used in the same palette. Each of the 8 affect groups was a separate network of our 41 palette colors. This enabled us to see not only the frequency of individual color use but also structural patterns (combinations of colors).

We visualized these palettes as networks using a force-directed layout algorithm. Color frequency is mapped to node size; pairwise frequency (weight) to edge thickness. For clarity, we removed all color combinations with an edge weight less than 3, showing only pairwise combinations used in 3 or more palettes. Figures 8 and 9 show the resulting networks. Node size (frequency of color use) reflects the results of Study 2 and 3. The network structures emphasize which colors are highly connected, which are outliers. Some palettes cluster tightly around a small number of key colors **(Calm, Exciting, Playful)**. Some are more angular and spread out. And then

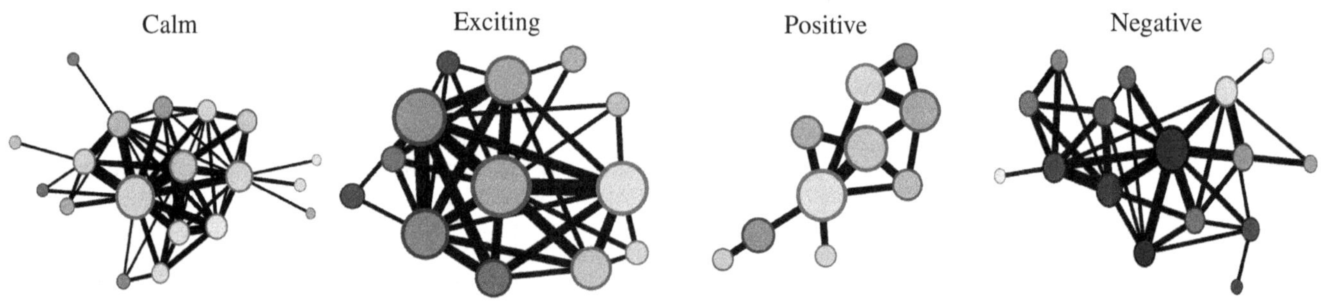

Figure 8. Core Affect Combinations

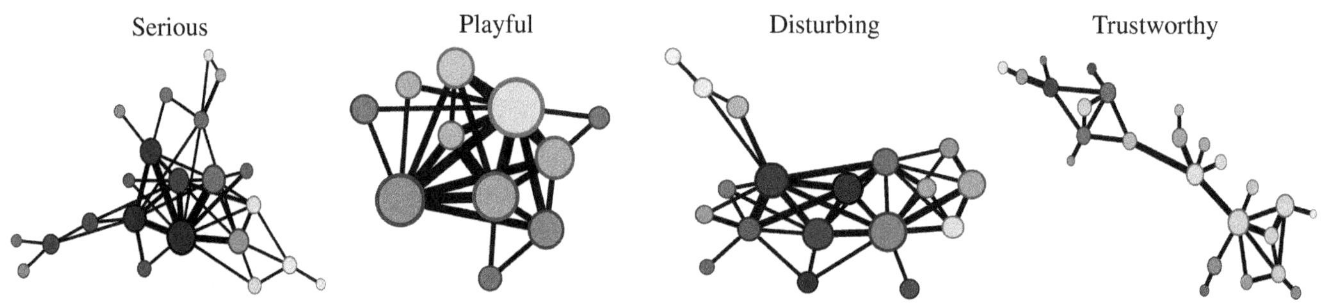

Figure 9. Pragmatic Affect Combinations

there is **Trustworthy**. In the frequency models,**Trustworthy** showed very little structure. It included many colors, fairly uniformly weighted. Here, we see a distinct structure, with two groups linked by yellow. We hope to find further insight by continuing this sort of modeling in the future.

DISCUSSION

What do these results tell us? First and foremost, we are able to reliably associate color and palette properties with affective response even in the limited scope of color selection in simple information visualization representations, extending previous work in individual color-affect relations. Our studies show that both the perceptual properties of small color sets, and the composition patterns of how they are used together, are affectively distinct. From our studies in image analysis (S1) and user-designed palettes (S2), we were able to algorithmically define a simple metric of palette weight based on color frequency use for each affect that proved a reliable predictor of preferred affective palettes in a final validation study (S3).

We see consistent patterns in lightness related to affect across all studies. **Calm, Playful, Positive** and to a lesser extent **Trustworthy** are lightest, while **Serious, Disturbing** and **Negative** are darker. This confirms H1. Similarly, we also saw consistent use of higher chroma colors for **Playful, Exciting, Positive** and **Disturbing**: where **Calm, Serious** and to a lesser extent **Trustworthy** were less saturated. These comparisons are significant, and confirm our hypotheses that lightness and chroma are linked to affect. This indicates that any color set intended for use in expressing these affects must provide enough variation in both lightness and chroma.

One of our primary goals in this is to create guidelines for design and design evaluation simple enough to be programmed, similar to work by Bartram et al. [1]. While these will never replace the skill of an experienced designer, they can reduce the time spent exploring options that simply don't work and provide reasonable starting grounds for further refinement.

Figure 10 summarizes the mapping between affect and color metrics for each affect. Here, each of lightness, chroma and hue have been mapped to a common range, then plotted. For hue, the important metric is whether the colors are warm or cool. We make this easier to see by rotating the hue angle by 60 degrees so that low values are cool, high values are warm. The resulting metrics are labeled (NL, NC, N SH). The box plots show the distributions. Our hypothesis of hue association with affect is supported by these distributions.

Based on the results of study 3, we speculate that if a palette contains colors near the median of L,C,H for a specific affect, then the resulting palette is likely to be judged as matching that affect, especially if the distribution is tight. Some affects have clearer L,C,H "profiles" than others. Of the Core affects, **Calm** is the strongest, requiring high L, low C and cool colors. **Negative** has similar properties for C and H, but dark colors predominate. **Exciting** and **Positive**, however, while distinctly different than **Calm** and **Negative**, are not very different from each other, or from the pragmatic affect **Playful**. The profiles in the other pragmatic affects show similar overlaps, as we might expect. This is why we need more nuanced analysis

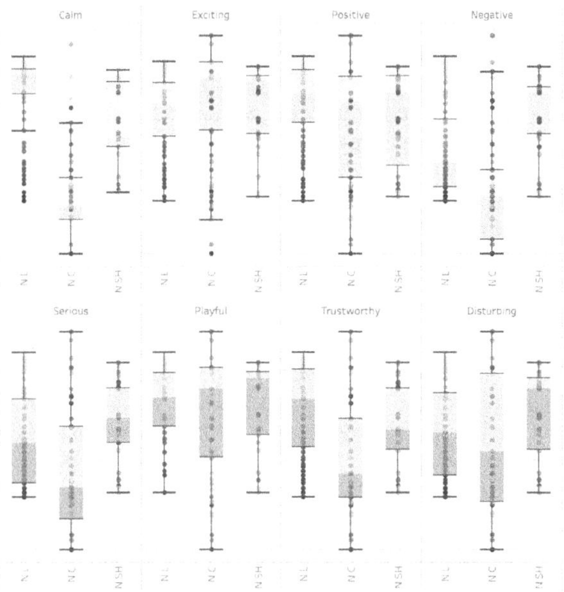

Figure 8. The L,C,H distributions for each affect. Hue is rotated by 60°to group warm and cool colors, all values are normalized to a common range

about which colors go with others, as we are exploring in the network diagrams.

While we cannot reliably profile each affect, even being able to say what colors to avoid for specific affects can be useful. For example, we can say with some authority that highly saturated light colors will NOT be appropriate for **Serious** or **Trust**, or **Calm**; light blues, beiges and greys are never likely to convey **Playful**; dark red and browns are not **Positive**; and light colors, particularly green, do not communicate **Negative** affect.

The network models help us visualize palette composition patterns: groupings that show what colors are likely to be used together. Certain affects showed different palette composition patterns, **Calm, Exciting and Playful** palettes tightly clustered around the main colors, confirming high co-occurrence of these colors in most palettes. In contrast, certain colors in Positive were only used in combination with bright yellow. Greens form an important cluster in **Positive**. **Serious, Negative** and **Disturbing** palettes show loose sub clusters anchored by a central set of core colors. **Trustworthy** shows a clear example of two thematic strategies (blue-gray, green-gray) bridged by a single common color (yellow). In future work, we hope to better understand what these patterns mean and how they might be applied.

We sought to see if there were general color associations with the more abstract dimensions of valence **(Positive-Negative)** and arousal **(Calm-Exciting)** that would translate (lend color elements) to the specific expressions of **Playful, Serious, Trustworthy and Disturbing**. We certainly saw evidence of these crossovers in our limited set of results. Establishing such reliable associations leads to the question of if and how we might algorithmically determine color selection based on the desired affect's location in the PAD affect space. In other words, given a desire to enhance a visualization as more "reassuring", for example, can we quantify where "reassuring" plots between **Calm-Exciting** and **Positive-Negative** and determine the relative hues, chroma and lightness values as a weighted contribution from each? In future work, we plan to explore how the color patterns we see in the core affects may generalize to other pragmatic affects.

LIMITATIONS

While these results indicate the potential for using color to communicate affect, we note several limitations to our studies. We have studied exactly one palette size (5 colors) for a limited set of visualization forms (bar charts and maps), on a white background. While we have confirmed that color and affect can be linked even for these simple, functional cases and speculate that the results have broader value than precisely what we tested, we obviously don't know how far our results can be extended.

Which colors compose an effective palette depends on the size of the features they color. In our studies, all of the features colored were large enough that all of the study colors were easy to perceive and distinguish. The study color set reflected these image constraints. To support fine-grained graphs such as line charts and scatter plots, some of the colors in our study palette would be too light, or would be too difficult to differentiate. We would need a different set of study colors. We hypothesize that we we would see similar palette trends for such graphs, even though the detailed color statistics would be different.

There are many other factors that can influence the affect induced by an image, including cultural color identities, spatial properties such as relative size and juxtapositions, and ultimately, the subject matter. Our work deliberately tries to minimize these influences, as including them would be much more complicated.

We tested only a limited range of affective impressions in abstract contexts. This speaks to the need for more basic research in examining a fuller range of affect, and more applied research in examining the expressive capacity of affective palettes in actual visualization use.

Finally, even within our constraints, our results do not offer unique guidance for each affect as was discussed above. Clearly our current color statistics are not enough. However, the network models do offer some further directions to pursue.

CONCLUSIONS

The first goal of this work was to demonstrate whether color can express affect, even when used as categorical coloring for simple data visualizations. While some may find our results unsurprising, there are many others who expressed skepticism. This study demonstrates clearly that affect is a dimension of categorical color palette design, and motivates extending work in automated palette design to include affective concepts. This brings new dimensions of expressivity and communicative scope to visualization.

Our results show a validated relationship between affect, perceptual color properties (hue, chroma and lightness), and palette composition for the eight categories we measured. This confirms and extends findings in color psychology and design practice to the context of simple information visualization forms and data contexts. While this is not enough to clearly distinguish all affects, it helps limit the design space, which can be of significant practical value. For example, one could extend Colorgorical [11] to include affect by using L, C and H filters.

A more challenging application would be to include affect in the design of palettes where some colors are already defined, especially if they fall outside of the simple L,C,H model of affect. A simple example would be creating a Trustworthy palette for T-Mobile that included its signature bright purple. Here, we would ideally be able to model how to combine that playful colors with others to create an overall **Trustworthy** affect.

In addition, we introduce network modeling as a method to characterize palette composition. We are concerned not with individual color selection per se, but in the much more difficult to quantify sets of colors and how they are combined (the palette). Our network models begin to provide some insight on how single colors that might be individually strong in one affect may still be combined in a palette more suited to another affect (such as the yellow in **Trustworthy**). While preliminary, we believe this approach holds promise for exploring richer design options with color combinations based on more sophisticated social network metrics.

Our work suggests ways to address this that would be interesting to explore further. For example, the psychological dimensions of affect (arousal and valence) are shown to be strongly influenced by lightness and chroma. This indicates that these properties can be used to "tune" palettes of predefined hues to these affects, either by modulating the color itself, or by optimizing these values over the palette as a whole. The work in network modeling suggests, for example, that with a more complete model there may be ways to combine the T-Mobile playful purple with other colors to still convey an overall **Trustworthy** affect.

Finally, we stress that we have approached this research from a perspective of design rather than pure perceptual theory. Our work asks: given a desired affect, what palette colors should you choose? It does not answer the broader and much harder question: given an arbitrary palette, what affect does it convey? To make this distinction concrete, if the goal is a **Calm** affect, our results suggest light, cool, pastel colors. If your goal is to create a **Disturbing** affect, then dark colors, especially reds, are better. Our results cannot reliably tell you whether a palette of pastels plus a vibrant blood red (which might well be **Disturbing** depending on how the red is used) is **Calm** or **Disturbing**. Being able to absolutely relate color to affect for all cases was not our goal: frankly, we don't believe this is possible. However, we do believe that simply being able to recommend validated palettes for a particular affect will prove of interest to those who create and employ visualizations. Clearly, there is much work to be done.

Acknowledgments

This work was supported by the Natural Sciences and Engineering Research Council of Canada. We thank Dr. Peter Gorniak for his assistance in data-mining the image databases.

REFERENCES

1. L. Bartram, B. Cheung, and M. Stone. 2011. The Effect of Colour and Transparency on the Perception of Overlaid Grids. *IEEE Transactions on Visualization and Computer Graphics* 17, 12 (Dec 2011), 1942–1948.
2. Mathieu Bastian, Sebastien Heymann, Mathieu Jacomy, and others. 2009. Gephi: an open source software for exploring and manipulating networks. *ICWSM* 8 (2009), 361–362.
3. Joseph A Bellizzi and Robert E Hite. 1992. Environmental color, consumer feelings, and purchase likelihood. *Psychology & marketing* 9, 5 (1992), 347–363.
4. Brent Berlin and Paul Kay. 1969. *Basic color terms: Their universality and evolution*. Univ of California Press, Berkeley.
5. Cynthia A Brewer. 1994. Color use guidelines for mapping. *Visualization in modern cartography* (1994), 123–148.
6. A. Cairo. 2013. U.S. Gun Deaths and the Challenge of Uncertainty. Peachpit. (2013). `http://www.peachpit.com/articles/article.aspx?p=2036558`
7. Daniel Cohen-Or, Olga Sorkine, Ran Gal, Tommer Leyvand, and Ying-Qing Xu. 2006. Color harmonization. In *ACM Transactions on Graphics (TOG)*, Vol. 25. ACM, 624–630.
8. Dianne Cyr, Milena Head, and Hector Larios. 2010. Colour appeal in website design within and across cultures: A multi-method evaluation. *International journal of human-computer studies* 68, 1 (2010), 1–21.
9. Andrew J Elliot and Markus A Maier. 2014. Color psychology: Effects of perceiving color on psychological functioning in humans. *Annual review of psychology* 65 (2014), 95–120.
10. Timo Elliott and Business Objects. 2008. Why business intelligence projects fail-And what to do about it. In *Bus. Objects User Conf. Europe*, Vol. 2009.
11. Connor C Gramazio, David H Laidlaw, and Karen B Schloss. 2016. Colorgorical: Creating Discriminable and Preferable Color Palettes for Information Visualization. *IEEE Transactions on Visualization & Computer Graphics* 27, 1 (2016), 521–530.
12. Allan Hanbury. 2003. Circular statistics applied to colour images. In *Proceedings of the 8th Computer Vision Winter Workshop*, Vol. 91. Citeseer, 53–71.
13. Lane Harrison, Remco Chang, and Aidong Lu. 2012. Exploring the impact of emotion on visual judgement. In *Visual Analytics Science and Technology (VAST), 2012 IEEE Conference on*. IEEE, 227–228.
14. Jeffrey Heer and Maureen Stone. 2012. Color naming models for color selection, image editing and palette design. In *Proceedings of the SIGCHI Conference on Human Factors in Computing Systems*. ACM, 1007–1016.
15. Jessica Hullman and Nick Diakopoulos. 2011. Visualization rhetoric: Framing effects in narrative visualization. *IEEE transactions on visualization and computer graphics* 17, 12 (2011), 2231–2240.
16. Alice M Isen. 2001. An influence of positive affect on decision making in complex situations: Theoretical issues with practical implications. *Journal of consumer psychology* 11, 2 (2001), 75–85.
17. Johannes Itten. 1974. *The art of color*. Reinhold Pub. Corp, New York.
18. Ali Jahanian, Jerry Liu, Qian Lin, Daniel Tretter, Eamonn O'Brien-Strain, Seungyon Claire Lee, Nic Lyons, and Jan Allebach. 2013. Recommendation system for automatic design of magazine covers. In *Proceedings of the 2013 international conference on Intelligent user interfaces*. ACM, 95–106.
19. Hye-Rin Kim, Min-Joon Yoo, Henry Kang, and In-Kwon Lee. 2014. Perceptually-based Color Assignment. In *Computer Graphics Forum*, Vol. 33. Wiley Online Library, 309–318.
20. Shigenobu Kobayashi. 1981. The aim and method of the color image scale. *Color research & application* 6, 2 (1981), 93–107.
21. Nancy Kwallek, Carol M Lewis, and Ann S Robbins. 1988. Effects of office interior color on workers' mood and productivity. *Perceptual and Motor Skills* 66, 1 (1988), 123–128.
22. Lauren I Labrecque and George R Milne. 2012. Exciting red and competent blue: the importance of color in marketing. *Journal of the Academy of Marketing Science* 40, 5 (2012), 711–727.
23. P Lang and Margaret M Bradley. 2007. The International Affective Picture System (IAPS) in the study of emotion and attention. *Handbook of emotion elicitation and assessment* 29 (2007).
24. Marie-Christine Lichtlé. 2007. The effect of an advertisement's colour on emotions evoked by attitude towards the ad: The moderating role of the optimal stimulation level. *International Journal of Advertising* 26, 1 (2007), 37–62.
25. Sharon Lin, Julie Fortuna, Chinmay Kulkarni, Maureen Stone, and Jeffrey Heer. 2013. Selecting Semantically-Resonant Colors for Data Visualization. In *Computer Graphics Forum*, Vol. 32. Wiley Online Library, Blackwell Publishing Ltd, 401–410.
26. Sharon Lin and Pat Hanrahan. 2013. Modeling how people extract color themes from images. In *Proceedings of the SIGCHI Conference on Human Factors in Computing Systems (CHI '13)*. ACM, 3101–3110.
27. Albrecht Lindner, Bryan Zhi Li, Nicolas Bonnier, and Sabine Süsstrunk. 2012. A large-scale multi-lingual color thesaurus. In *Color and Imaging Conference*, Vol. 2012. Society for Imaging Science and Technology, 30–35.

28. Albrecht Lindner and Sabine Süsstrunk. 2013. Automatic color palette creation from words. In *Color and Imaging Conference*, Vol. 2013. Society for Imaging Science and Technology, 69–74.
29. Peng Lu, Zhijie Kuang, Xujun Peng, and Ruifan Li. 2014. Discovering Harmony: A Hierarchical Colour Harmony Model for Aesthetics Assessment. In *Asian Conference on Computer Vision*. Springer, 452–467.
30. Jana Machajdik and Allan Hanbury. 2010. Affective image classification using features inspired by psychology and art theory. In *Proceedings of the 18th ACM international conference on Multimedia*. ACM, 83–92.
31. Thomas J Madden, Kelly Hewett, and Martin S Roth. 2000. Managing images in different cultures: A cross-national study of color meanings and preferences. *Journal of international marketing* 8, 4 (2000), 90–107.
32. Ravi Mehta and Rui Juliet Zhu. 2009. Blue or red? Exploring the effect of color on cognitive task performances. *Science* 323, 5918 (2009), 1226–1229.
33. Don Norman. 2002. Emotion & Design: Attractive Things Work Better. *interactions* 9, 4 (2002), 36–42.
34. Donald A Norman. 2005. *Emotional design: Why we love (or hate) everyday things*. Basic books, New York.
35. Jonathan Posner, James A Russell, and Bradley S Peterson. 2005. The circumplex model of affect: An integrative approach to affective neuroscience, cognitive development, and psychopathology. *Development and psychopathology* 17, 03 (2005), 715–734.
36. Edward Segel and Jeffrey Heer. 2010. Narrative visualization: Telling stories with data. *IEEE transactions on visualization and computer graphics* 16, 6 (2010), 1139–1148.
37. Vidya Setlur and Maureen C Stone. 2016. A linguistic approach to categorical color assignment for data visualization. *IEEE transactions on visualization and computer graphics* 22, 1 (2016), 698–707.
38. Martin Solli and Reiner Lenz. 2010. Color semantics for image indexing. In *Conference on Colour in Graphics, Imaging, and Vision*, Vol. 2010. Society for Imaging Science and Technology, 353–358.
39. Maureen Stone. 2003. *A field guide to digital color*. AK Peters, Natick, Mass.
40. Patricia Valdez and Albert Mehrabian. 1994. Effects of color on emotions. *Journal of experimental psychology: General* 123, 4 (1994), 394.
41. Lujin Wang and Klaus Mueller. 2008. Harmonic colormaps for volume visualization. In *Proceedings of the Fifth Eurographics/IEEE VGTC conference on Point-Based Graphics*. Eurographics Association, 33–39.
42. Colin Ware. 2008. *Visual thinking for design*. Morgan Kaufmann, Burlington, Mass.
43. Martijn Wijffelaars, Roel Vliegen, Jarke J Van Wijk, and Erik-Jan Van Der Linden. 2008. Generating color palettes using intuitive parameters. In *Computer Graphics Forum*, Vol. 27. Wiley Online Library, 743–750.

Explaining the Gap: Visualizing One's Predictions Improves Recall and Comprehension of Data

Yea-Seul Kim
University of Washington
Seattle, WA, USA
yeaseul1@uw.edu

Katharina Reinecke
University of Washington
Seattle, WA, USA
reinecke@cs.washington.edu

Jessica Hullman
University of Washington
Seattle, WA, USA
jhullman@uw.edu

ABSTRACT
Information visualizations use interactivity to enable user-driven querying of visualized data. However, users' interactions with their internal representations, including their expectations about data, are also critical for a visualization to support learning. We present multiple graphically-based techniques for eliciting and incorporating a user's prior knowledge about data into visualization interaction. We use controlled experiments to evaluate how graphically eliciting forms of prior knowledge and presenting feedback on the gap between prior knowledge and the observed data impacts a user's ability to recall and understand the data. We find that participants who are prompted to reflect on their prior knowledge by predicting and self-explaining data outperform a control group in recall and comprehension. These effects persist when participants have moderate or little prior knowledge on the datasets. We discuss how the effects differ based on text versus visual presentations of data. We characterize the design space of graphical prediction and feedback techniques and describe design recommendations.

Author Keywords
Information visualization; self-explanation; prediction; internal representations of data; mental models

ACM Classification Keywords
H.5.m. Information Interfaces and Presentation (e.g. HCI)

INTRODUCTION
Information visualizations are common in news articles, scientific papers and other forms of digital resources, and serve to inform viewers by engaging with them in ways that text alone cannot. Visualizations often use interactivity, such as filtering, transformation and view navigation, to stimulate viewers' interest and enable user-driven querying of the data. Close studies of visualization comprehension indicate that users' interactions with their *internal representations*—mental models of what they know and are learning about a dataset—of the data are critical to the interpretation process [6, 20, 21, 33, 47]. Asking a person to express their internal representations can enhance critical thinking and prompt changes to existing beliefs to account for new information [16, 24, 46].

CHI 2017, May 06 - 11, 2017, Denver, CO, USA.

ACM 978-1-4503-4655-9/17/05$15.00.
DOI: http://dx.doi.org/10.1145/3025453.3025592

Most visualizations do not provide ways for users to explicitly incorporate their internal representations. The recent New York Times interactive visualization "You Draw It" [2] is a rare exception that attempts to prompt reflection by enabling a user to explicitly incorporate her prior knowledge. The interactive visualization asks viewers to draw their expectation of the data before presenting the observed data alongside their predictions. To prompt reflection on the difference, the interface provides feedback based on the accuracy of a user's expectation. However, it remains unknown whether the reflection on prior knowledge induced by such visualizations can positively impact recall and comprehension of data, or how to design such visualizations for maximal benefit.

We expand on prior work with five contributions: We contribute (1) a set of novel elicitation techniques for eliciting users' prior knowledge in visualization interaction. These include a graphical prediction technique for eliciting users' predictions of data, a feedback technique for presenting personalized feedback on the gap between predictions and observed data, and a self-explanation prompt to explicitly ask participants for self-explanations, which have been found to improve learning from texts and diagrams [1, 11, 12, 10], among others.

We contribute (2) a controlled experiment to test the effect of these techniques on recall and comprehension of data. We find that prompting participants to first predict data, or to self-explain presented data, or to do both, improves data recall and comprehension.

By further contributing (3) replications of our controlled study with datasets that differ in familiarity, we find that these techniques improve recall for datasets for which participants have moderate or little prior knowledge.

We also (4) evaluate how the impact of the techniques differs based on whether the information is presented using text or information visualization. We find that the visualization conditions benefit from predicting the data and viewing the gap between their prediction and the observed data whereas the text conditions do not.

Finally, we contribute (5) a characterization of the design space of data prediction and feedback techniques for information visualization and provide practical design recommendations.

HYPOTHESIS DEVELOPMENT

To generate hypotheses, we survey research in two main areas: (1) studies in cognitive psychology around the role of internal representations in information visualization comprehension, and (2) theories and studies on self-explanation in learning.

Internal Representations of Data in Visualizations

Researchers have developed multiple models describing how people interpret information visualizations (e.g., [30, 38, 44]). Though often overshadowed by research on lower level perceptual processes, "top-down" effects can guide interactions (e.g., eye movements) based on prior knowledge and beliefs, including knowledge about graphs and data analysis [30, 38, 48] and about the content of the data [7].

Studies in graph comprehension indicate that internal representations of relevant knowledge that one already possesses often play a critical role in reasoning with an external static or interactive visualization [20, 31, 33, 47]. Mayer et al. [35] compared well-designed animations to well-designed texts and diagrams for teaching, finding that performance on retention and transfer tests was better among the static media group that relied on internal representations to understand how concepts related. Similarly, Hegarty et al. [23] found that viewers who initially engaged in mental animation of a set of static views, then used an external animated visualization, understood the content better than those who used only the animated visualization. Other studies suggest that externalizing one's internal representations leads to better understanding of visualized information [15, 24, 37, 46]. For example, Stern et al. [46] found that individuals who had to construct a line graph of presented stock data were more accurate on transfer questions involving a new problem with a similar structure than participants who passively viewed a chart of the data. Constructing external representations is believed to help individuals to translate information between different representations, resulting in a more nuanced understanding of the concepts [16, 46]. Building on these results, we contribute various novel interactive elicitation techniques for information visualization that prompt a user to incorporate her prior knowledge in her interaction.

Self-Explanation in Learning

Self-explaining information to oneself is a constructive "metacognitive" learning activity in which a person actively reflects on the mechanism behind a given phenomena [11]. Self-explaining has been elicited by having learners explain the meaning of sentences [10, 11, 12], or diagrams [1], as they study a target domain. When quality self-explanations are generated, such as statements that link concepts from the text using tacit knowledge or attempt to fill in gaps through inferences [10], comprehension tends to be better than without self-explanation [10, 11, 12]. A mental model repair hypothesis is proposed to describe the benefits of self-explaining: by generating inferences to fill in missing information, integrating new information with prior knowledge, and monitoring and repairing faulty knowledge, learners who self-explain develop more accurate internal representations of a concept [10]. In this hypothesis, it is assumed that learners engage more with the process if they identify the discrepancy between their mental model and the presented information [10]. While students who spontaneously generate self-explanations perform better [11, 18, 39, 40, 41], most learners tend not to naturally self-explain [5, 43]. However, even simple prompts [12, 5, 43] have been found to be effective at triggering the self-explanation process [12]. Other studies have shown that immediate feedback on the accuracy of self-explanations can prevent wrong inferences in the explanation process [14, 3, 9]. We develop and test explicit and implicit prompts for self-explanation applied to information visualizations.

Self-explanation techniques have been widely applied in online learning environments, typically to text-based learning materials [13, 14, 3, 4, 40, 25]. A handful of studies have included a combination of diagrams and text [11, 42, 4]. However, studies that attempt to understand how self-explaining of visual representations is different from text are rare. An exception is Ainsworth et al. [1], who compared self-explaining across text and diagrams in a small group (n=20). They find that learners who used diagrams performed better on a comprehension test, generated more self-explanations, and appeared to benefit more from self-explaining than users of texts. We conduct a comparison of the benefits of multiple interactive elicitation techniques, including explicit self-explanation prompting, for data presented through information visualization versus text.

Curiosity theory describes a similar process to self-explanation. A person's curiosity is piqued when she perceives an information gap between her current knowledge and the information she is interested in [34]. Prompting people to guess is thought to be one way to arouse curiosity by making this gap explicit [34]. Awareness of the gap results in an increasing desire to seek knowledge to fill this gap [34], and inspires people to explore more information [29], including in crowdsourcing contexts [32]. We examine whether techniques aimed at implicitly prompt curiosity, such as by having people predict data before they see it, can improve comprehension and recall by enhancing their desire to see the true data.

Formulating Study Conditions & Hypotheses

Based on the previous research in psychology and education, we devise and evaluate several elicitation techniques for information visualization with associated hypotheses.

Study Conditions: Elicitation Techniques

Our techniques are based on three non-mutually exclusive mechanisms for eliciting reflection on prior knowledge and its relationship to presented data in a visualization.

1. Prompting a user to generate self-explanations of the observed data: In a digital setting, prompting a user to type in sentences explaining the data is an *explicit* way to elicit self-explanations [4].

2. Prompting a user to predict the data before seeing it: Asking a user to predict the data has two advantages for prompting reflection on prior knowledge: (1) Prior work showed that asking a user to actively construct an external representation of her prior knowledge about data results in a deeper understanding of the meaning of a dataset and its visual representation [16, 46]. Predicting may also trigger self-explanation [16]. (2) By asking the user to provide predictions

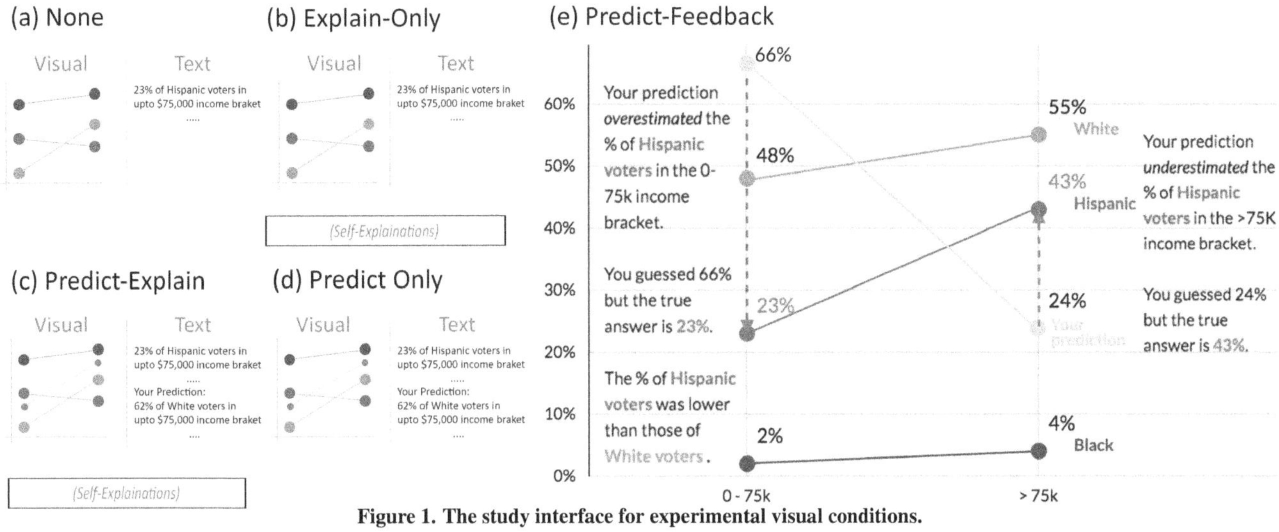

Figure 1. The study interface for experimental visual conditions.

of the data, an interface can then *visualize the gap* between the user's expectations and the observed data. Reviewing the gap may *implicitly* prompt self-regulated learning, in which the user becomes motivated to generate inferences to repair her knowledge [36].

3. Providing the user with feedback on her prediction: Providing direct feedback on the gap between the user's prior knowledge and the observed data may increase the likelihood that a user will recognize the gap and generate inferences to repair her knowledge [14, 3, 9].

Using these three mechanisms, we designed four elicitation techniques and one baseline condition. The observed data is presented using visualization in the visual conditions, and using text in the text condition.:

- **None (baseline)**: The user is prompted simply to examine the observed data (Fig. 1(a)).
- **Explain-Only**: The user is prompted to type self-explanations in a text box as she views the observed data (Fig. 1(b)).
- **Predict-Explain**: The user is shown the observed data, but with some of the data omitted. The user is prompted to predict the omitted data. After her prediction, the user is shown the observed data against her prediction. She is prompted to type in self-explanations about the gap between her prediction and the observed data in a text box (Fig. 1(c)).
- **Predict-Only**:The user is shown the observed data, but with some of the data omitted. The user is prompted to predict the omitted data. After her prediction, the user is shown the observed data against her prediction (Fig. 1(d)).
- **Predict-Feedback**: The user is shown the observed data, but with some of the data omitted. The user is prompted to predict the omitted data. After her prediction, the user is shown the observed data against her prediction. Textual and visual feedback are presented to annotate the difference between her prediction and the observed data to draw her attention to the gap (Fig. 1(e)).

Hypotheses

Since explicitly prompting self-explanations improves comprehension of information in texts and diagrams [1, 12, 11, 10], we expect a similar beneficial effect for data in visualizations:

H1: Participants in the Explain-Only conditions will recall data more accurately than participants in the None condition for visual and text modalities.

Based on the implicit prompting toward reflection by predicting, we expect that:

H2: Participants in the predict conditions (Predict-Explain, Predict-Feedback, Predict-Only) will recall data more accurately than participants in the None condition for visual and text modalities.

While reviewing their predictions and the observed data, participants in the text conditions must actively *seek and infer* the gap as opposed to the visual conditions where the gap is visually available [1]. We therefore expect that effects of predicting will be less pronounced in the text conditions compared to the visualization conditions:

H3: The effects of predicting using text (Predict-Explain-Text, Predict-Only-Text) on recall will be smaller than the effects of predicting using visualizations.

PRELIMINARY SURVEY: CHOICE OF DATASETS

To select a dataset for our main study, we conducted a preliminary survey on Amazon's Mechanical Turk (AMT). We sought a dataset with properties amenable to our elicitation techniques. If a user is extremely familiar with a dataset, prediction or explanation may not offer benefits over her prior knowledge. If a dataset is too unfamiliar, it may be too difficult for a user to make predictions about it. Additionally, our interest in comparing techniques across visualization and text modalities is best supported by a dataset that includes both a higher level relational structure (i.e., trends, which visualizations are often best at depicting) as well as individual data points, which can be remembered with greater numerical accuracy from text [27]. By quantitatively measuring the familiarity of multiple datasets, the preliminary survey also enables us to later test the robustness of our results across datasets of varying familiarity.

We selected datasets with a range of topics from the results of a scientific experiment to the average smart phone price from different manufacturers (all datasets are available in the supplementary materials.) The datasets had the same format, consisting of two categorical dimensions and one continuous measure, resulting in six total data points (Fig. 2). This format is commonly used in the social and physical sciences [8] and allows us to evaluate how well people observe and recall the higher level patterns (e.g., trend lines) as well as how well people observe and recall individual data points. We formulated three measures that approximate prior familiarity with each dataset:

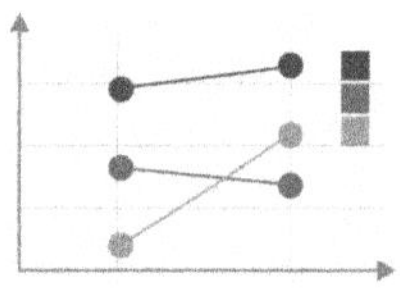

Figure 2. Multivariate data format to allow value and trend estimation.

Perceived familiarity: How familiar participants perceive themselves to be with the data after seeing a short description and a visualization with labeled axes but without data points.

Value familiarity: The absolute error of participants' predictions for each data point. We calculated the absolute difference between the participant's prediction of each data point and the observed data. We normalized the values by dividing by the maximum value on the y-axis to allow for comparison of the value familiarity across the datasets.

Trend familiarity: The difference between participants' predicted slopes and the true slopes for each line in the visualization. We calculated the absolute difference between a participant's slope and the true slope for each of the three groups in each dataset.

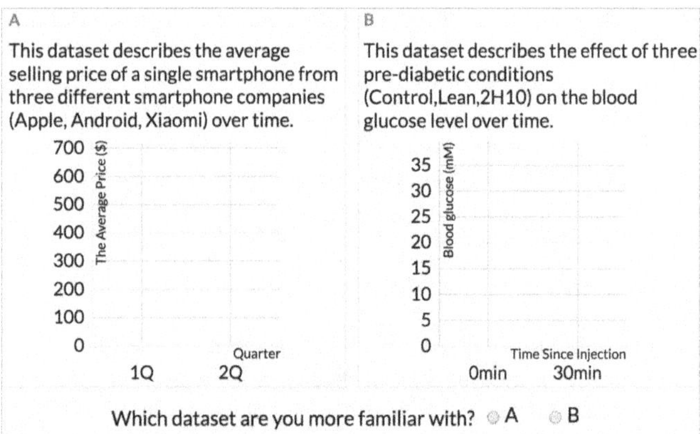

Figure 3. A pair of visualizations with the data omitted. Participants were asked to choose which dataset is more familiar based on labels.

Procedure

The survey consisted of two parts. In the first part, we examined *perceived familiarity* by presenting participants with 15 visualization-pairs (resulting from the pairwise combinations of the six datasets), one at a time in a randomized order (Fig. 3).

The visualizations did not reveal any data; instead, participants only saw labeled axes with a short description of each dataset. Participants were asked to select the dataset that they were more familiar with using a radio button. After watching a short tutorial video on how to enter a data point in a chart, participants were asked to predict the values of all six data points for each of the six datasets (Fig. 4). Each dataset appeared on a separate screen in randomized order. Each screen presented an empty chart area with labels. Three buttons appeared to the right of the chart labeled with each of the three groups for that dataset (e.g., french fries, coke, shake).

The range of the y-axis of the visualizations was set to [0, 1.2*max_data_value]. To input a prediction, participants selected a group by clicking the button for that group, then clicked the chart area to set the position of the two data points for that group. Participants could drag the circles to adjust their prediction for each group.

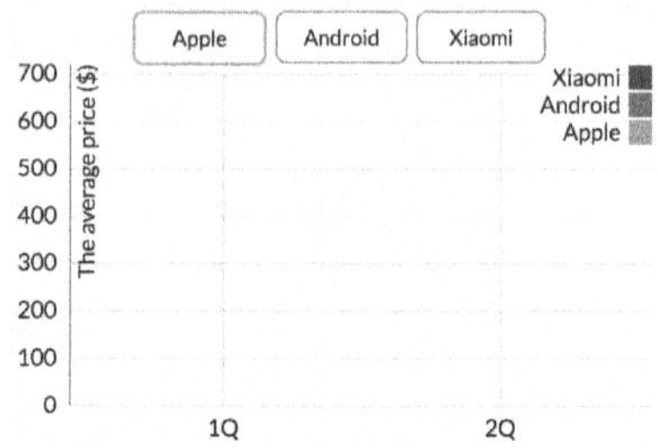

Figure 4. Example of a prediction interface.

Results

We recruited 100 workers from AMT. To calculate the perceived familiarity of each dataset, we summed the number of votes per dataset from the first part of the study.

Table 1 shows the ranking of the datasets by these three measures. While perceived familiarity and value familiarity are highly correlated (Spearman's $\rho = .84$, $p < .001$), perceived familiarity and trend familiarity are more weakly correlated (Spearman's $\rho = .42$, $p < .001$). We see evidence of this in the dataset on median house prices, where participants' perceived familiarity is relatively low (rank 5), but they do well on the prediction tasks (rank 1 for predicting trend). We suspect that various factors might contribute to a difference between perceived familiarity and prediction accuracy. In addition to having prior knowledge specific to the dataset, heuristics may allow participants to guess reasonably accurately because they have some knowledge of the domain. In particular, domain specific knowledge (e.g., the average price of houses is cheaper in Colorado than those in New York), and domain general knowledge (e.g., prices tend to go up over time) may allow participants to make reasonable guesses even when they feel they have little expertise on a topic.

We aggregated the three familiarity rankings and sorted the datasets by the aggregated familiarity (the order of the Table 1). For our main study, we chose the Colorado voting results data, since this dataset was neither clearly familiar nor unfamiliar to participants. To ensure that recalling the data is sufficiently challenging in our main study, we included two visualizations of voting results, for Connecticut and Colorado. We used the more familiar fast food calorie content dataset and the more unfamiliar pre-diabetic experiment dataset to later check the robustness of results from our main study in partial replications.

Table 1. Three familiarity measures for the six datasets. The order of rows in the table is by the mean rank across the three measures. The number indicates the ranking of the dataset with the actual measure in parentheses. Perceived familiarity votes are out of 500 (100 workers * 5 maximum votes per dataset).

	Perceived Familiarity	Value Familiarity	Trend Familiarity
Fast Food Calorie Content	1 (348)	1 (0.14)	2 (0.11)
Smartphone Price	2 (312)	2 (0.15)	3 (0.13)
Median House Price	5 (188)	3 (0.18)	1 (0.10)
Voting Result	3 (297)	4 (0.21)	4 (0.20)
National Budget	4 (283)	5 (0.26)	5 (0.25)
Pre-diabetic Experiment	6 (72)	6 (0.28)	6 (0.36)

STUDY DESIGN

Study Objectives & Experimental Conditions

To understand how different techniques for eliciting prior knowledge with visualization impact data recall and comprehension, we designed a between-subjects factorial study. Participants were assigned to a baseline condition (**None**) or one of four elicitation techniques: **Explain-Only, Predict-Explain, Predict-Only, Predict-Feedback**.

Additionally, to better understand the effects of the elicitation techniques with a visualization, we varied whether a participant interacts with (and makes predictions about) the data using text or visualization (**Text** or **Vis**).

We crossed the elicitation techniques with modality, with the exception of Predict-Feedback, resulting in 9 possible conditions: None-Vis, Explanation-Only-Vis, Predict-Explain-Vis, Predict-Only-Vis, Predict-Feedback-Vis, None-Text, Explanation-Only-Text, Predict-Only-Text, Predict-Explain-Text. We excluded a Predict-Feedback text modality treatment due to the difficulty of generating personalized feedback based on freeform text predictions.

Participants

A prospective power analysis was performed for sample size determination based on the effect size and standard error of each technique and modality in pilots using a mixed effects model. We achieved 0.8 power under $\alpha = 0.05$ with 42 participants per condition. We then recruited 378 participants (42 per condition) from AMT, rewarding their participation with $1.50.

Procedure

Fig. 5 shows an overview of the study procedure. The study started with an *introduction* (Fig. 5(1)), in which we explained the data domain as the percentage of voters of different ethnicities (Hispanic, White, Black) who voted Republican in the 2008 presidential election, for several income brackets and states. To eliminate possible difficulties with the interactive nature of data entry, participants in the visual conditions watched a tutorial video to learn how to set and adjust a value in an related line chart. On the next page, participants in the prediction conditions (Predict-Explain, Predict-Feedback, and Predict-Only) were asked to *predict* the voting percentages for one randomly selected ethnic group across two income levels for each state (Colorado, Connecticut) in randomized order.

To ensure that participants interacted to a similar degree across treatments, participants who were not prompted to predict were asked to *retype* a paragraph about elections in the U.S. (Explain-Only and None condition) (Fig. 5(2)).

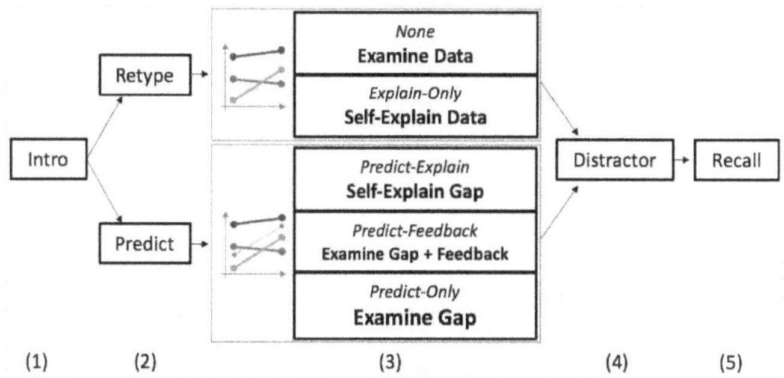

Figure 5. Overview of the study procedure. If participants were not asked to predict, they were asked to retype a general text on elections. If participants were not ask to generate self-explanations, they examined either the data or feedback depending on the condition.

On the next page, all participants *examined* the observed data (Fig. 5(3)), with prompts and feedback varying by condition. Participants in the None conditions were asked to examine the observed data several times (Fig. 1(a)).

Participants in the Explain-Only conditions were asked to generate and type in a few sentences of explanations to help themselves understand the data (Fig. 1(b)).

Participants in the Predict conditions saw their predictions in a lighter color against the observed data in the visual conditions. In the text conditions, the textual predictions that the participant made were shown with the observed data presented in text.

Participants in the Predict-Explain conditions were asked to self-explain the difference between their prediction and the observed data (Fig. 1(c)).

Those in the Predict-Feedback condition saw accuracy feedback based on their predicted values (Fig. 1(e)). Feedback contained 1) the directionality of the participant's error (e.g., "Your prediction *overestimated* the percentage of Hispanic voters."), 2) verbal statements that reiterated the participant's prediction and the observed data (e.g., "You guessed 66%, but the true answer is 23%"), and 3) comparative information that indicated high-level patterns (e.g., Higher portions of white voters vote for John McCain then hispanic voters.), if the participant violated the pattern (e.g., "The percentage of Hispanic voters was lower than those of White voters").

Participants in the Predict-Only condition were asked to examine their predictions and the observed data several times (Fig. 1(d)).

As a distractor task, all participants then completed as many questions on a 10 question digital paper folding test as they could in three minutes [17]. The task also served to gather information on participants spatial visualization abilities, which have been shown to correlate with effective use of internal representations [23, 20, 22], (Fig. 5(4)).

After completing the paper folding test, participants in all conditions were asked to recall the percentage of voters of different ethnicities (Fig. 5(5)). Recall interfaces for each state were provided on separate pages and presented in reverse order from that in which the data was examined. Participants used an interface that matched the modality by which they viewed the data (text or visualization).

Participants were asked to respond to demographic questions, including age, education level, gender, and ethnicity, and were asked about their experience with visualizations.

RESULTS

Data Preliminaries

The average time to complete the experiment was 19.4 minutes (SD=8.4), with no differences in response time across the conditions ($(F(4) = 1.073, p = .37)$ There were no significant differences between participants' demographic responses or relevant experience across the conditions (see supplementary materials for a detailed analysis). We excluded 3 participants that did not specify predictions in the text conditions, and 2 participants who participated multiple times.

Analysis Approach

We used two mixed effects models implemented in R's lme4 package to evaluate H1, H2, and H3. We used the normal approximation to calculate p-values of fixed effects using t-scores produced by lme4. The R code and detailed analyses are available in the supplemental materials [1].

Dependent Variables

We considered two types of error indicating how well participants could recall the observed data. The accuracy in recalling individual data points was measured using the *absolute error*, i.e., the absolute difference between the recalled value and the observed value. To measure accuracy in recalling the higher level structure of datasets (e.g., trends within each group), we calculated the *trend error*, i.e., the absolute difference between the recalled and the actual slope of each line (set of values for an ethnicity) in the visualization.

Model Specification

In each mixed effects model, we included the four elicitation techniques (Explain-Only, Predict-Explain, Predict-Only, and Predict-Feedback), modality, and the interaction terms between modality and the techniques as fixed effects, with the control/baseline condition as the omitted reference condition. We included the participant id and the ethnicity group (e.g., Hispanic, etc.) as random effects. The spatial ability score, calculated as the number of correct answers out of 10 on the paper folding task, was included as a fixed effect. We centered the spatial ability score by its mean so that fixed effects describe a participant of average spatial ability. For easier interpretation, we report the intercepts for each elicitation technique separately for visual versus text with 95% confidence intervals. Coefficients are expressed in terms of the actual units used in the datasets (i.e., percentage).

[1]https://github.com/yeaseulkim/ExplainingTheGap

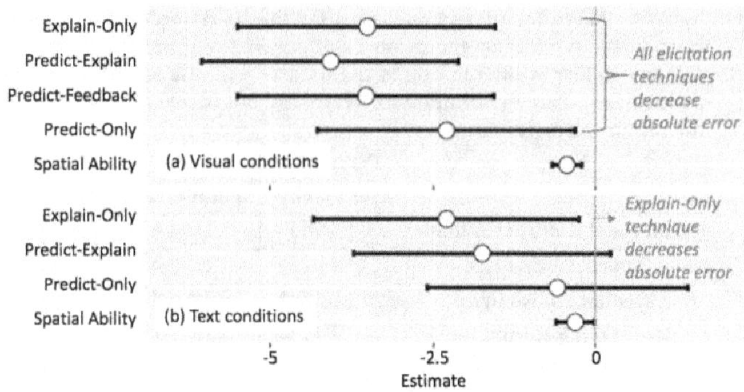

Figure 6. Estimated fixed effect coefficients from analyzing absolute errors for (a) visual and (b) text conditions for the voting result dataset. The error bars indicate 95% confidence intervals. Intervals that do not include include zero imply that we can be reasonably sure that some effect exists.

Core Results

Visual Conditions

Absolute Error: Participants who used one of the four elicitation techniques recalled individual data points more accurately than those in the None-Vis condition (Fig. 6(a)). Proceeding by magnitude of effect, the Predict-Explain-Vis condition had the lowest absolute error relative to the None-Vis condition by -4.08 (i.e., participants in the Predict-Explain-Vis condition were, on any given recalled point out of the 12 total, more accurate at recalling the voting percentage by 4.08% out of 100% compared to the those in the None-Vis condition: $t = -4.02, p < .0001$) The Predict-Feedback-Vis condition had the next lowest effect (-3.54; $t = -3.49, p < .001$), followed by the Explain-Only-Vis condition (-3.52; $t = -3.47, p < .0001$), and the Predict-Only-Vis condition (-2.30; $t = -2.25, p < .05$). Hence, interactive elicitation appears to be reliable way to improve absolute recall of data presented through visualizations, even with variations in how prior knowledge is elicited.

Participants' scores on the spatial ability test also predicted a lower absolute error, as we would predict from prior work indicating the relationship between spatial visualization ability and visualization comprehension [23, 20, 22]. With each additional correct answer in the paper folding task, participants' expected absolute recall error decreased by 0.44 ($t = -3.63, p < .001$).

We observed no difference in absolute error between the four elicitation techniques.

Trend Error: Only participants in the Predict-Explain-Vis and the Predict-Feedback-Vis conditions had a lower trend error compared to the None-Vis condition. Specifically, being in the Predict-Explain-Vis condition lowered errors by -2.06 relative to the None-Vis condition ($t = -2.07, p < .05$), while being in the Predict-Feedback-Vis condition lowered errors by -2.79 relative to the None-Vis condition ($t = -2.80, p < .05$). We observed no effect of the spatial ability score on participants' trend errors ($t = -0.53, p = .596$).

Comparing Effects of Techniques: Visual vs Text

Absolute Error: Overall, we observed 3.76 percentage points (36%) more errors on average per recalled value among visual conditions compared to text. This aligns with prior research indicating that text is better for exact value retention than visualization [27].

In comparing the absolute error between the text conditions, the Explain-Only-Text condition was the only condition that led to lower absolute errors than the None-Text condition, by an average of -2.00 ($t = -2.07, p < .05$). We observed no effect from the Predict-Explain and the Predict-Only techniques in the text modality conditions when we compared them to the None-Text condition (Fig. 6(b)). Text presentations may not provide the same type of natural support for prompting implicit reflection and correction of one's prior knowledge compared to visualizations.

Participants with higher spatial ability scores again had a lower absolute error on recall by 0.31 ($t = -2.04, p < .05$).

Trend Error: Overall, we did not observe differences in average trend errors between visual conditions and text conditions. In comparing the trend error between the text conditions, we found no effect of any of the elicitation techniques (i.e., Explain-Only-Text, Predict-Explain-Text, or Predict-Only-Text) compared to the None-Text condition. We saw no apparent decrease in trend error from spatial ability ($t = -1.30, p = .193$).

Anchoring in the Prediction Conditions

Participants in the Predict-Only-Vis, Predict-Explain-Vis, and Predict-Feedback-Vis conditions may have a tendency to recall aspects of their own prediction due to the deliberate attention required to generate the prediction. We observed a weak positive correlation between the values that participants predicted and the values that they recalled ($R^2 = 0.176$, intercept$= -1.28$, $slope = 0.18$) Additionally, we found that for 75.9% of the data points from participants who were asked to predict, their recalled value showed a bias in the same direction as their predicted value: if they underestimated the value in the prediction phase, they tended to underestimate the value in the recall phrase. The same pattern could be observed when they overestimated. Hence, a slight anchoring effect appears to be present.

Quantity and Quality of Self-Explanations

The quantity and quality of self-explanations have been shown to affect comprehension in prior work [12, 42]. We analyzed the correlation between self-explanation quantity and quality and recall performance for participants in the Explain-Only condition. As a proxy of quantity we counted each sentence as a self-explanation (mean:3.2, range: 1-7). We tallied the total number of self-explanations generated by a participant and regressed the average recall error made by the participant on the sum. We observed no effect of the number of explanations on recall error ($R^2 = 0.001, F = 0.39, p < .533$).

To measure the quality of each self-explanation, we devised criteria informed by Chi's approach to distinguish high and low quality explanations [10]. We differentiated between two factors that characterize the quality of self-explanations: the level of prior knowledge involved in inference (inference with prior knowledge, inference with no prior knowledge, no inference), and the level of detail of the inference (high, low).

Inference without prior knowledge, High detail: "Generally, people with incomes over 75k were less likely to vote for John McCain in 2008. Blacks who made over 75k were slightly more likely to vote for him, but it was a very small increase to 3% meaning not many blacks voted for McCain in any income category."

Inference without prior knowledge, Low detail: "Majority of people no matter ethnicity voted for the Democrats and not Republicans."

Inference with prior knowledge, High detail: "There was a slight increase in the White voting population with the higher income bracket, I could assume that this is due to McCain's policies which benefit the wealthier. "

Inference with prior knowledge, Low detail:"People are more conservative in Colorado."

No inference: "Each colored line is a different race. Each point is a different income bracket."

Two researchers coded the set of 42 explanations ($Cohen\acute{s}\ kappa = 1$). We conducted a two way factor analysis on the average absolute error and the trend error, but observed no effect of either quantity or quality on factors. It may be that the difference between participants' self-explanation quality was smaller overall than in educational studies of spontaneous self-explanation, perhaps due to the incentives to work quickly on AMT. Detailed results are available in the supplemental materials.

Replication on Low & High Familiarity Datasets

We conducted two additional partial replications of our study to evaluate the effect of elicitation techniques on datasets that our preliminary survey identified as more and less familiar on average. We replicated all visual conditions.

Low Familiarity Dataset: Scientific Experiment Results

We created two visualizations depicting results from a scientific experiment on the blood glucose level of various groups of mice after antibody injection [19]. Each visualization differentiated two amounts of time since injection (0 and 30mins, and 60 and 120mins). Each visualization included lines for three groups (Lean, 2H10, and control) similar to the three groups of Hispanics, White, and Black voters in the main study. Hence, the two visualizations replicated the structure of the voting results data across two states.

Absolute Error: We observed a similar pattern of effects of the techniques on decreasing absolute error as for the voting result data, with the exception of the Predict-Only-Vis conditions (Fig. 7(a)). The Explain-Only-Vis condition had lower errors by 1.78 ($t = -3.75, p < .001$), and the Predict-Explain-Vis conditions had lower errors than the None condition by 1.27 ($t = -2.62, p < .01$). The Predict-Feedback-Vis condition had lower errors than the None condition by 1.31 ($t = -2.69, p < .01$). Predict-Only-Vis condition had no effect compared to the None condition ($t = -1.43, p = .152$).

We observed no difference in recall performance between the Explain-Only-Vis, the Predict-Explain-Vis, and the Predict-Feedback-Vis condition.

Trend Error: We also observed no effects of the elicitation techniques on decreasing trend error compared to the None condition.

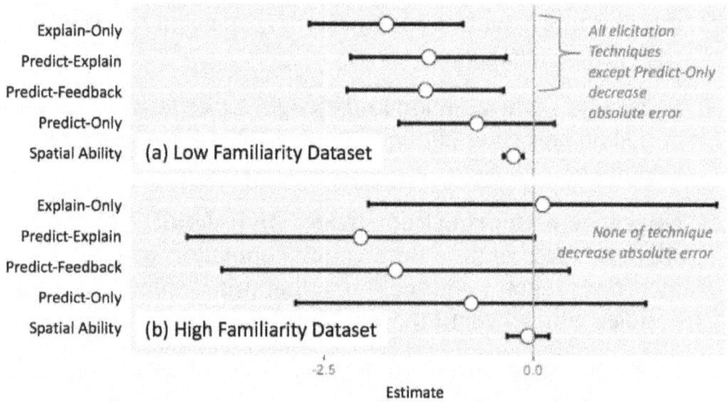

Figure 7. Estimated fixed effect coefficients from analyzing absolute errors for visual conditions (a) for the scientific experiment dataset, and (b) the fast food calories dataset.

High Familiarity Dataset: Calorie Content of Fast Food

We created two visualizations using data on the calorie content of three fast foods (Milkshake, Coke, French fries) for two serving sizes (small, large) at McDonald's and Burger King.

Absolute and Trend Error: Results of the mixed effect model for absolute error (Fig. 7(b)) and trend error indicate no differences between any conditions for the fast food dataset. Detailed results are available in supplemental material.

We conclude from these additional partial replications that prediction, when combined with additional mechanisms like explicit self-explanation or feedback, can lead to lower absolute error even for very unfamiliar data where prediction might be difficult. Perhaps because the data was already too familiar, we saw no replication of effects for any elicitation technique on the high familiarity dataset.

DISCUSSION

Our results suggest the promise of incorporating mechanisms for eliciting prior knowledge in visualization.

First, our work extends prior work on self-explanation by showing that prompting users to self-explain information visualizations can improve their ability to recall specific data points later.

Additionally, our work is the first to show that incorporating prediction tasks, as in our Predict-Explain-Vis, Predict-Only-Vis, Predict-Feedback-Vis also improves users' ability to recall specific data. We hypothesize that predicting focuses a user's attention on their prior knowledge, making them more likely to attend to the gap between their prior knowledge and the observed data when it appears. We expected that predicting would be less effective in the text modality than in the visual modality. In fact, we did not observe an effect of any of the prediction techniques on improving recall in the text conditions. This may be because participants in the visual conditions are shown the gap in a visual form, reducing the deliberative effort required to process the gap in a text format. Using a visualization of the gap is likely to free up participants' cognitive resources in contrast to text, so that they can focus on more meaningful activities [45] such as updating and repairing their mental model.

Except for the Predict-Only-Vis conditions, we were able to replicate the effect of the elicitation techniques for decreasing absolute error with a less familiar dataset, the scientific experiment results. These results suggest that prior knowledge about a dataset is not necessarily required for a user to benefit from prediction, explanation, and feedback techniques. The fact that we were not able to replicate the effects in the Predict-Only condition may indicate that when familiarity is lower, a user needs additional reinforcement to recognize the gap, such as being prompted to explain or being given visual feedback on the gap.

We could not replicate the effects of the elicitation techniques on the high prior familiarity dataset, the calorie content of fast food. One possible reason that we did not see an effect here is that participants were already relatively accurate in estimating the values, such that the initial 'gap' is too small to see much positive impact from the elicitation techniques.

We observed that the Predict-Feedback-Vis and Predict-Explain-Vis techniques decreased the trend error in recalling the visualized trends for the voting results data. However, we did not see similar improvements of trend errors with either of the other datasets. Varying graphical complexity may be one reason for this discrepancy: in the voting results data, two of the lines intersect (thus adding complexity), whereas in the other two datasets all three lines have similar, non-intersecting trends.

We believe that prompting predictions and providing feedback, which we found to reduce both the absolute and relative recall error, would work well when presenting visualizations in practice. Compared to explicitly prompting a user to provide self-explanations, first prompting a user to make predictions is likely to engage a user's curiosity. Once the user has "invested" attention by predicting, they may be more open to feedback that can further direct their attention to needed adjustments in their prior knowledge.

Though we asked participants in the predict conditions to predict only select data points, we observed a decrease in recall error across all data points. In the Predict-Explain-Vis conditions, we see evidence that participants are generating explanations associated with all three ethnic groups despite being prompted to explain only the difference between the predicted group and observed data. For example, participants wrote in the comments:

> "I really overestimated the numbers of black people. I expected more of them to vote than the Hispanics."

> "I may have underestimated the population of Hispanics (and Blacks) in Colorado. I assumed both were minorities who held liberal viewpoints, since traditionally minorities tend to prefer Democratic candidates."

This suggests that a designer need not require a user to predict every data point in the visualization to engage users with the entire dataset.

Task	Detail Task	Manipulation Component	Encoding	Possible Interaction
Predict Continuous (Quantitative) Variable	Predict Data Value	Mark (bar)	Bar chart	Drag up a bar to set height
		Mark (line)	Line chart	Draw a line
		Mark Attribute (color of areas)	Map (choropleth)	Brush on color over an area
Predict Categorical (Nominal, Ordinal) Variable	Predict Categorical Membership	Mark Attribute (color of areas)	Area chart	Brush on color over an area
			Pie chart	Brush on color over a sector
Predict Data Structure and Model	Predict Correlation / Fit	Mark (line)	Scatter plot	Draw a regression line
			Line chart	Draw a line
	Predict Cluster		Scatter plot	Draw a contour
			Dendrogram	Drag and drop element to the cluster
	Predict Connectivity		Node-link diagram	Draw an edge
	Predict Confidence Interval		Box plot	Draw a line to mark confidence interval

Figure 8. Possible tasks.

Design Space for Graphical Prediction & Feedback

Our study shows the benefits of eliciting users' prior knowledge, such as their expectations of data, and prompting them to reflect on how their knowledge relates to the data. However, the design space for applying graphical prediction and feedback techniques to information visualization remains relatively unexplored. In the following, we characterize key considerations in applying these techniques to visualizations.

We informed our elaboration of the design space through several forms of evidence: observations from our studies; examples in the media, primarily from the New York Times [2]; and our own development of prototypes applying the techniques to visualizations like bar charts and line charts.

Based on these experiences, we differentiate three considerations that influence the effectiveness of graphical prediction and feedback applications: the *prediction task and graphical elicitation technique* (for what tasks and in what ways can the user express her prior knowledge?), the *contextualization mechanism* (how does the interface provide clues to constrain the user's prediction?), and the *feedback technique* (how does the interface draw the user's attention to the gap between her predictions and the observed data?).

Prediction Task & Elicitation Technique

A first question in designing a visualization that elicits predictions is "What should the user predict?". A visualization can elicit value predictions for quantitative or nominal (categorical) variables, or the outcome of a model or analysis.

Direct manipulation is a natural way to implement the first one, *value prediction*. For example, a user might click to add a mark, or drag a mark from an axis to set or update its position in a 2D plot like a scatter plot. Other marks require different interactions: a user might drag a bar to set its height or click to position the top of the bar in a bar chart, and use a smooth dragging operations to position a line in a line chart.

Data encoded in the visual attributes of marks, such as color or shape may also be predicted. For example, nominal data (categories) might be encoded by the color hue of marks in a scatter plot. *Predicting categorical membership* can be instrumented with interactions like brushing. For example, some points may remain uncolored in a scatter plot where color encodes the categorical membership of data. The designer can have a user select a color from an interactive legend, and drag across points to assign that category. In The New York Times' elicitation of users' predictions for the 2014 senate election, a user was able to cycle through different binned probability levels for the voting percentage for each party by repeatedly clicking on a state in the map [28].

Similar to categorical membership, the designer of a visualization may ask a user to *predict clusters* in a scatterplot or network diagram. For example, given an interactive network diagram, the user can draw a contour around the nodes or use brushing interactions similar to those described for categorical membership to designate clusters of related nodes. *Predicting connectivity* could also be applied to support edge prediction in a network diagram.

Alternatively, the designer can ask the user to visualize her expectations for the outcome of more complex analyses applied to raw data. For example, graphical prediction techniques could be used to elicit predictions on multivariate correlations, uncertainty, or other results attained through statistical modeling. For example, the New York Times 'You Draw It' interactive prompts the user to *predict a regression line* representing the relationship between parents' income percentile and percent of children who attended college [2]. To facilitate understanding of uncertainty in data, a user might be prompted to *predict a confidence interval or region* given a 2D presentation of bars, points, or lines denoting sample statistics.

Regardless of what is predicted, *the directness of the prediction interaction and degrees of freedom* provided to the user by the interface are important design considerations. Freeform interactions can be used to allow the user greater flexibility in drawing, such as providing a high degree of resolution (i.e., space of possible fits) to users drawing regression lines in 2D visualizations. More constrained forms of interaction can be realized through snapping functions (e.g., snapping a predicted regression line to the nearest grid point). Similarly, a designer may choose to only allow the user to manipulate certain parameters of components (e.g., drag a curve or slider to change line curvature, drag the edge of a circle to increase size while maintaining shape). While more constrained interactions may serve to reduce error and focus user's attention on key parameters (e.g., slope or magnitude alone), they are likely to add abstraction. Our own experimentation with interactive prototypes suggest that many users enjoy the novelty of using an interactive visualization interface to draw with few constraints.

Contextualization Mechanism
Contextualization mechanisms can be used to guide the user's prediction as they form a guess. For example, the amount of effort required for the user to make a guess can differ based on the number of *reference marks* (e.g., dots, bars, lines) that the visualization initially presents. In our study, we presented two of the three ethnic groups by default, which provided cues to guide users' predictions of the remaining group. How much data to reveal through reference marks can be decided based on how familiar users are expected to be with the dataset (less familiar=more reference marks). Or, the reference marks can be selected dynamically through personalization. For example, for datasets that depict regional data, identifying and initially presenting marks depicting the user's region based on their IP address may increase engagement while providing useful context for the user.

Prediction hints provide more direct guidance, either through text or visual annotation, on where a user's prediction should be made, helping educate users about the meaning of the encodings. As the New York Times' visualization "You Draw it" [2] demonstrates, one or more data points can be presented as a hint that the user's prediction line should pass through.

Designers should consider the scale of the x and y-axes in 2D charts. In piloting our preliminary study for choosing a dataset, we observed that users' predictions were quite sensitive to the axis range. When we presented the full 0-100% percentage range for percentage variables (e.g., the percentage of the U.S national budget of health care), users' estimates showed a bias toward the center in the plotting range. This effect was lessened when we trimmed the axis range based on the maximum value of the dataset, suggesting that users implicitly view the axis range as a clue to the data scale.

Feedback Technique
After a user draws her prediction, feedback on how the user's prediction compares to the observed data can help prompt reflection on prior knowledge.

For example, personalized feedback can provide information on the *accuracy of a prediction*, as we provided in our study. Feedback may take the form of aggregated, quantified accuracy information (e.g., "Overall, you were 80% right in guessing the amount of CO_2 emission in U.S") or information on the directionality of biases (e.g., "You over-estimated the overall trend."). Feedback may also occur at a more granular level, encouraging the user to adjust her expectations of individual data points: "Your guess on year 2001 was 6 points off; a little higher and you would be correct."

As users' predictions are collected, *social feedback* may serve to further engage users to think about the data and their own expectations. However, social feedback may also overshadow user's own interpretations; hence social feedback might be withheld until after the user has provided their own prediction [26] The interface can prompt social comparisons by visualizing other users' predictions alongside the user's.

General design considerations affecting feedback include how specific and in what modality feedback is presented (e.g., visual, text, etc.). Based on our study finding that textual presentations are less effective for drawing attention to the gap, we except visual feedback or a combination of visual and text feedback to be more powerful. Animating feedback, such as by dynamically moving marks added by the user to their true positions, or adding textual feedback to prediction errors point by point, may be particularly effective for drawing a user's attention to the gap.

Limitations and Future Work
Our study focused on data with a particular structure, chosen to allow us to examine effects for both absolute data values and trends. We also deliberately chose to test on two sets of visualization with 12 data points to ensure that the recall task was challenging. Future work should evaluate the same techniques applied to other datasets with varying formats and sizes. In our study, all predict conditions predicted one group (e.g., ethnicity) out of three. We did not systematically vary the contextualization mechanism (e.g., number of reference marks provided). However, we suspect that the effects of the techniques can be increased or decreased by adding or removing forms of context.

Elicitation techniques may provide an engaging way to helping novices to learn about data analysis and statistics. Our future work will test whether people are more likely to interact with the interface longer or in more engaged manner, if they prompted to predict and see feedback [32].

Finally, eliciting users' predictions of data opens the possibility for more sophisticated forms of modeling of users' evolving mental conceptions as they use an interactive visualization. As the interface maintains a model of the user's current knowledge, dynamic suggestions can be provided on what content to view next, or on how to correct errors in mental conceptions before continuing to explore data. Developing natural and effective elicitation interfaces and studying how elicitation and feedback can be incorporated into existing visual analysis pipelines are important tasks for future work.

CONCLUSION
Our work began by asking, "What if visualizations integrated users' prior knowledge about the dataset?" Informed by prior work in cognitive and educational psychology, we developed multiple novel elicitation techniques for incorporating users' prior knowledge in visualization interaction. We tested the effects of these techniques, including eliciting users' predictions of data, presenting personalized feedback on predictions, and explicitly prompting self-explanations with a visualization. We observed that providing opportunities for users to interact with their prior knowledge improves recall of data values, and is more powerful when used with visualization than with text. Our findings pave the way for a new paradigm of interactive visualization that enables users to interact with their internal representations to deepen their understanding of data.

REFERENCES
1. Shaaron Ainsworth and Andrea Th Loizou. 2003. The effects of self-explaining when learning with text or diagrams. *Cognitive Science* 27, 4 (2003), 669–681.

2. Gregor Aisch, Amanda Cox, and Kevin Quealy. 2015. You Draw It: How Family Income Predicts Children's College Chances. *The New York Times*, May 28, 2015, *http://nyti.ms/1ezbuWY*,. (2015).
3. Vincent Aleven and Kenneth R Koedinger. 2002. An effective metacognitive strategy: Learning by doing and explaining with a computer-based Cognitive Tutor. *Cognitive science* 26, 2 (2002), 147–179.
4. Vincent Aleven, Octav Popescu, and Kenneth R Koedinger. 2001. Towards tutorial dialog to support self-explanation: Adding natural language understanding to a cognitive tutor. In *Proceedings of Artificial Intelligence in Education*. Citeseer, 246–255.
5. Katerine Bielaczyc, Peter L Pirolli, and Ann L Brown. 1995. Training in self-explanation and self-regulation strategies: Investigating the effects of knowledge acquisition activities on problem solving. *Cognition and instruction* 13, 2 (1995), 221–252.
6. Sally Bogacz and J Gregory Trafton. 2002. Understanding static and dynamic visualizations. In *International Conference on Theory and Application of Diagrams*. Springer, 347–349.
7. Matt Canham and Mary Hegarty. 2010. Effects of knowledge and display design on comprehension of complex graphics. *Learning and instruction* 20, 2 (2010), 155–166.
8. Patricia A Carpenter and Priti Shah. 1998. A model of the perceptual and conceptual processes in graph comprehension. *Journal of Experimental Psychology: Applied* 4, 2 (1998), 75.
9. Andrea Cheshire, Linden J Ball, and CN Lewis. 2005. Self-explanation, feedback and the development of analogical reasoning skills: Microgenetic evidence for a metacognitive processing account. In *Proceedings of the Twenty-Second Annual Conference of the Cognitive Science Society, ed. BG Bara, L. Barsalou & M. Bucciarelli*. Citeseer, 435–41.
10. Michelene TH Chi. 2000. Self-explaining expository texts: The dual processes of generating inferences and repairing mental models. *Advances in instructional psychology* 5 (2000), 161–238.
11. Michelene TH Chi, Miriam Bassok, Matthew W Lewis, Peter Reimann, and Robert Glaser. 1989. Self-explanations: How students study and use examples in learning to solve problems. *Cognitive science* 13, 2 (1989), 145–182.
12. Michelene TH Chi, Nicholas Leeuw, Mei-Hung Chiu, and Christian LaVancher. 1994. Eliciting self-explanations improves understanding. *Cognitive science* 18, 3 (1994), 439–477.
13. Cristina Conati and Kurt VanLehn. 1999. Teaching meta-cognitive skills: Implementation and evaluation of a tutoring system to guide self-explanation while learning from examples. In *Artificial Intelligence in Education*. IOS Press, 297–304.
14. Cristina Conati and Kurt Vanlehn. 2000. Toward computer-based support of meta-cognitive skills: A computational framework to coach self-explanation. *International Journal of Artificial Intelligence in Education (IJAIED)* 11 (2000), 389–415.
15. Leda Cosmides and John Tooby. 1996. Are humans good intuitive statisticians after all? Rethinking some conclusions from the literature on judgment under uncertainty. *cognition* 58, 1 (1996), 1–73.
16. Richard Cox. 1999. Representation construction, externalised cognition and individual differences. *Learning and instruction* 9, 4 (1999), 343–363.
17. Ruth B Ekstrom, John W French, Harry H Harman, and Diran Dermen. 1976. Manual for kit of factor-referenced cognitive tests. *Princeton, NJ: Educational testing service* (1976).
18. Monica GM Ferguson-Hessler and Ton de Jong. 1990. Studying physics texts: Differences in study processes between good and poor performers. *Cognition and Instruction* 7, 1 (1990), 41–54.
19. Carolina E Hagberg, Annika Mehlem, Annelie Falkevall, Lars Muhl, Barbara C Fam, Henrik Ortsäter, Pierre Scotney, Daniel Nyqvist, Erik Samén, Li Lu, and others. 2012. Targeting VEGF-B as a novel treatment for insulin resistance and type 2 diabetes. *Nature* 490, 7420 (2012), 426–430.
20. Mary Hegarty. 2004. Diagrams in the mind and in the world: Relations between internal and external visualizations. In *Diagrammatic representation and inference*. Springer, 1–13.
21. Mary Hegarty and Marcel-Adam Just. 1993. Constructing mental models of machines from text and diagrams. *Journal of memory and language* 32, 6 (1993), 717–742.
22. Mary Hegarty and Sarah Kriz. 2008. Effects of knowledge and spatial ability on learning from animation. *Learning with animation: Research implications for design* (2008), 3–29.
23. Mary Hegarty, Sarah Kriz, and Christina Cate. 2003. The roles of mental animations and external animations in understanding mechanical systems. *Cognition and instruction* 21, 4 (2003), 209–249.
24. Mary Hegarty and Kathryn Steinhoff. 1997. Individual differences in use of diagrams as external memory in mechanical reasoning. *Learning and Individual differences* 9, 1 (1997), 19–42.
25. Dianne E Howie and Kim J Vicente. 1998. Making the most of ecological interface design: The role of self-explanation. *International Journal of Human-Computer Studies* 49, 5 (1998), 651–674.
26. Jessica Hullman, Eytan Adar, and Priti Shah. 2011. The impact of social information on visual judgments. In *Proceedings of the SIGCHI Conference on Human Factors in Computing Systems*. ACM, 1461–1470.

27. Sirkka L Jarvenpaa. 1990. Graphic displays in decision making the visual salience effect. *Journal of Behavioral Decision Making* 3, 4 (1990), 247–262.
28. Wilson Andrews Josh KatZ and Jeremy Bowers. 2014. Elections 2014: Make Your Own Senate Forecast. *The New York Times*, Sep 2, 2014, *http://nyti.ms/1plflyv*,. (2014).
29. Joshua Klayman and Young-Won Ha. 1987. Confirmation, disconfirmation, and information in hypothesis testing. *Psychological review* 94, 2 (1987), 211.
30. Stephen M Kosslyn. 1989. Understanding charts and graphs. *Applied cognitive psychology* 3, 3 (1989), 185–225.
31. Jill H Larkin and Herbert A Simon. 1987. Why a diagram is (sometimes) worth ten thousand words. *Cognitive science* 11, 1 (1987), 65–100.
32. Edith Law, Ming Yin, Kevin Chen Joslin Goh, Michael Terry, and Krzysztof Z Gajos. 2016. Curiosity Killed the Cat, but Makes Crowdwork Better. In *Proceedings of the 2016 CHI Conference on Human Factors in Computing Systems*. ACM, 4098–4110.
33. Zhicheng Liu and John T Stasko. 2010. Mental models, visual reasoning and interaction in information visualization: A top-down perspective. *Visualization and Computer Graphics, IEEE Transactions on* 16, 6 (2010), 999–1008.
34. George Loewenstein. 1994. The psychology of curiosity: A review and reinterpretation. *Psychological bulletin* 116, 1 (1994), 75.
35. Richard E Mayer. 2014. Cognitive theory of multimedia learning. *The Cambridge handbook of multimedia learning* 43 (2014).
36. Danielle S McNamara, Tenaha OâĂŹReilly, Michael Rowe, Chutima Boonthum, and IB Levinstein. 2007. iSTART: A web-based tutor that teaches self-explanation and metacognitive reading strategies. *Reading comprehension strategies: Theories, interventions, and technologies* (2007), 397–421.
37. Hedwig M Natter and Dianne C Berry. 2005. Effects of active information processing on the understanding of risk information. *Applied Cognitive Psychology* 19, 1 (2005), 123–135.
38. Steven Pinker. 1990. A theory of graph comprehension. *Artificial intelligence and the future of testing* (1990), 73–126.
39. Peter Pirolli and Margaret Recker. 1994. Learning strategies and transfer in the domain of programming. *Cognition and instruction* 12, 3 (1994), 235–275.
40. Alexander Renkl. 1997. Learning from worked-out examples: A study on individual differences. *Cognitive science* 21, 1 (1997), 1–29.
41. Alexander Renkl, Robin Stark, Hans Gruber, and Heinz Mandl. 1998. Learning from worked-out examples: The effects of example variability and elicited self-explanations. *Contemporary educational psychology* 23, 1 (1998), 90–108.
42. Marguerite Roy and Michelene TH Chi. 2005. The self-explanation principle in multimedia learning. *The Cambridge handbook of multimedia learning* (2005), 271–286.
43. R Ryan. 1996. Self-explanation and adaptation. *Psychology* (1996).
44. Priti Shah, Richard E Mayer, and Mary Hegarty. 1999. Graphs as aids to knowledge construction: Signaling techniques for guiding the process of graph comprehension. *Journal of Educational Psychology* 91, 4 (1999), 690.
45. Keith Stenning and Jon Oberlander. 1995. A cognitive theory of graphical and linguistic reasoning: Logic and implementation. *Cognitive science* 19, 1 (1995), 97–140.
46. Elsbeth Stern, Carmela Aprea, and Hermann G Ebner. 2003. Improving cross-content transfer in text processing by means of active graphical representation. *Learning and Instruction* 13, 2 (2003), 191–203.
47. J Gregory Trafton, Susan B Trickett, and Farilee E Mintz. 2005. Connecting internal and external representations: Spatial transformations of scientific visualizations. *Foundations of Science* 10, 1 (2005), 89–106.
48. Jeff Zacks and Barbara Tversky. 1999. Bars and lines: A study of graphic communication. *Memory & Cognition* 27, 6 (1999), 1073–1079.

Regression by Eye: Estimating Trends in Bivariate Visualizations

Michael Correll
University of Washington
mcorrell@cs.washington.edu

Jeffrey Heer
University of Washington
jheer@cs.washington.edu

ABSTRACT

Observing trends and predicting future values are common tasks for viewers of bivariate data visualizations. As many charts do not explicitly include trend lines or related statistical summaries, viewers often visually estimate trends directly from a plot. How reliable are the inferences viewers draw when performing such *regression by eye*? Do particular visualization designs or data features bias trend perception? We present a series of crowdsourced experiments that assess the accuracy of trends estimated using regression by eye across a variety of bivariate visualizations, and examine potential sources of bias in these estimations. We find that viewers accurately estimate trends in many standard visualizations of bivariate data, but that both visual features (e.g., "within-the-bar" bias) and data features (e.g., the presence of outliers) can result in visual estimates that systematically diverge from standard least-squares regression models.

ACM Classification Keywords

H.5.2 Information Interfaces and Presentation (e.g., HCI): Evaluation/Methodology

Author Keywords

Information Visualization; Graphical Perception; Regression

INTRODUCTION

An oft-cited example of the power of data visualization is Anscombe's quartet [2]: a set of four bivariate datasets with identical summary statistics, but with qualitatively different patterns when drawn as four scatter plots (Fig. 1). This example relies on the fact that people have the ability to *perceptually* estimate *statistical* quantities of interest. Visualization users regularly perform statistical tasks — including model selection, identification of outliers, and estimation of summary statistics — entirely through visual inspection. Recent work examines the accuracy of visual estimation of means in scatter plots [14] and time series data [10], and speculates on the affordances of visualizations in general for supporting visual estimation of summary statistics [29].

CHI 2017, May 06 - 11, 2017, Denver, CO, USA

ACM 978-1-4503-4655-9/17/05...$15.00
DOI: http://dx.doi.org/10.1145/3025453.3025922

The estimation of trends in bivariate data is an important analytical task, as it is the basis for many factors relevant to decision-making, such as prediction, imputation, and comparison. However, model information is not always explicitly included by visualization designers. When designers do include trend information (for instance, by annotating a scatter plot with a line of best fit), other statistics relevant to the model (such as *r* values or confidence bands) may be absent. Viewers must therefore perform visual estimation to gain a sense of any relevant statistics not provided.

Even if designers include modeling information, the audience may lack the statistical expertise to interpret these values, or may be misled if the data violate modeling assumptions. As a further complication, the form of visual encoding may influence viewers' inferences. For instance, viewers may be more likely to consider trends with line charts, and to compare individual values with bar charts [33]. Visual design choices can also introduce bias, such as the visual asymmetry of bars causing "within-the-bar" bias [27]. Designers would benefit from guidance regarding how accurately viewers make trend estimations by eye, and to what degree different visualization types might bias these estimations.

Knowing the strengths and limitations of such "estimation by eye" is therefore important for designers of data visualizations seeking to communicate statistical quantities, especially to a general audience. On the one hand, visual estimations may be too *inaccurate* for the use cases intended by a designer, or they may be *biased*, leading to systematic over- or under-estimations. On the other hand, while visual estimation lacks the precision of formal statistics, it may be relatively unencumbered by modeling assumptions.

In this work, we describe a series of crowdsourced experiments on the visual estimation of trends in common bivariate visualizations such as scatter plots, area charts, and line graphs. We present the results of three studies investigating estimation of trend slope, trend intercept, and the effect of outliers. We find that, while in most cases viewers accurately estimate trends, area charts introduce systematic under-estimation of trend intercept, and that viewers give low weights to extreme values when estimating trends. These results suggest that there are several areas where human judgments diverge from the fitted models generated by techniques such as Ordinary Least Squares (OLS), and that the design of bivariate visualizations can introduce additional biases in these judgments.

Designers should therefore make an informed decision between designing for regression by eye and the explicit annota-

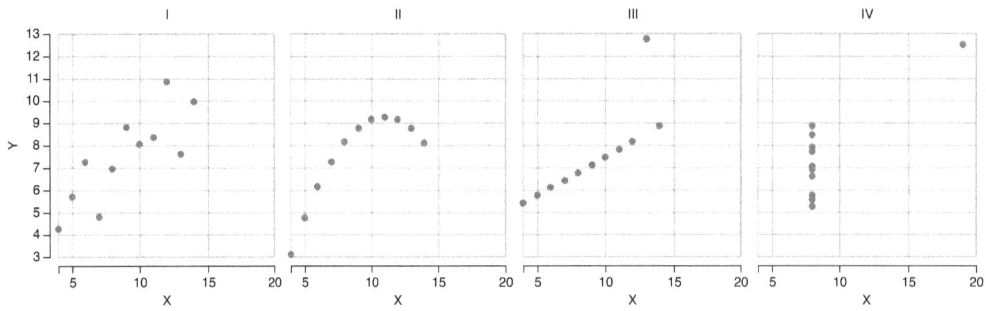

Figure 1. Anscombe's quartet. Each series has nearly identical summary statistics include mean, standard deviation, and linear fit. Yet, through visual inspection, viewers can disambiguate differing patterns and trends. We refer to this visual estimation of trends as "regression by eye."

tion of statistical regression information. Regression by eye affords quick estimations and flexibility in model selections, but is subject to perceptual biases and inaccuracies in estimation. Explicit annotation affords accuracy, but constrains the model space, and adds visual complexity to plots.

RELATED WORK

While there is a great deal of foundational work in visualization and graphical perception dealing with the estimation of individual values in visualizations (such as the height of the bar in a bar chart, or the angle of a line in a line graph), there is comparatively little work on how viewers of visualizations perceive aggregate statistical quantities.

Ariely [3] suggests that, in concert with the perception of individual objects, we also collect information about the *ensemble* properties of visual displays. Szafir et al. [29] note that this *ensemble coding* might afford relatively accurate estimation of *summary statistics* in visualizations. However, visualizations with good performance for summary tasks may not result in good performance at point tasks, and vice versa [1, 13]. A further difficulty is that tasks requiring estimation of values in visualizations (where there is a single correct answer) are qualitatively different from tasks requiring predictions (where differing mental models and priors can result in a multitude of potentially valid responses).

Scatter plots are a standard means of visualizing bivariate data, with a multitude of design parameters that affect their suitability for aggregate tasks [9]. Prior work has confirmed that viewers can make use of scatter plots to perform prediction tasks (which tacitly rely on trend estimation) in ways that are robust to both noise [16] and problem frame [22]. However, the heuristics used to perform these prediction tasks (such as the anchor-and-adjust method [5]) can introduce biases.

Similarly, visual design choices (for instance, the decision to encode class membership with color or with shape) can also impact performance at aggregate tasks [14, 23]. The aspect ratio of graphs can also bias judgments about trends [4]: narrow aspect ratios can result in overestimation in severity of trends, and wider aspect ratios in underestimation of severity. Another bias in prediction tasks is the "within-the-bar" bias [27]: for visually asymmetric visualizations such as bar charts, points contained within the visual area of the bar glyph are perceived as likelier than those outside the glyph.

Recent work in the visualization community has focused on the perception of correlation in scatter plots. Rensink et al. [28] show that viewers can estimate correlation with some accuracy in scatter plots. Harrison et al. [15] extend this finding to other visualization types, and a re-analysis by Kay & Heer [20] indicates that, for many of the more esoteric bivariate visualizations, performance at this task is poor. Estimation of correlation can also be biased by the choice of axis scales [7]: the whitespace changes introduced by expanding the scale of the axes can cause over-estimation of correlation.

Our task of trend estimation combines elements of both prediction and correlation estimation tasks. As with prediction, there is not necessarily an unambiguous correct estimation of trend (different modeling and regression methods can produce different trend lines). As with correlation, viewers must make holistic judgments about the dataset in a way that (as per Harrison et al. [15]) likely relies on a set of visual proxies. That is, while viewers are unlikely to directly estimate correlation *per se*, they are estimating correlation through the perception of visual features such as the envelope of the points, point dispersion, or some other visual feature(s) highly correlated with the statistic of interest.

Prior work in visualization has not directly addressed the capabilities of regression by eye, instead assuming as a given that visual estimates of trend are sufficiently accurate. Work in the perception of summary statistics lends credences to this assumption, but we believe that trend estimation can be biased through conscious or unconscious design choices. For instance, within-the-bar bias may result in under-estimation of trends in bar and area charts, and factors that affect perception of correlation (such as aspect ratio and whitespace) may result in up- or down-weighting of outliers.

GENERAL EXPERIMENTAL METHODS

In order to assess the ability of visualization viewers to estimate trends, we conducted a series of three crowdsourced experiments on Amazon's Mechanical Turk. We designed these experiments to establish a performance baseline for regression by eye, and to examine potential sources of bias. Crowdsourced graphical perception experiments have been found to produce results that are largely in keeping with prior, lab-based work [17, 30]. In this section, we describe experimental design aspects shared across all experiments. Data

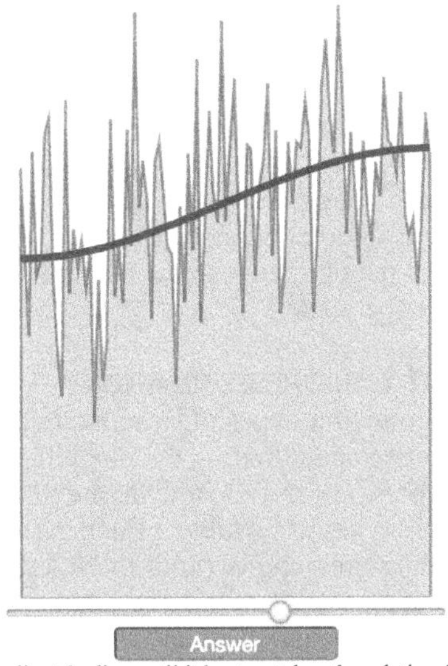

Figure 2. An example estimation task from our experiments. Here, the participant must adjust the amplitude of the purple trigonometric function until it best matches a particular set of bivariate data.

tables, stimuli, and experimental instruments are available online at `https://github.com/uwdata/trend-bias`.

In these experiments, we report effect size using the interquartile mean (or midmean) of absolute error. The interquartile mean discards points in the first and fourth quartiles before averaging, trimming the tails of distributions. Cleveland & McGill [8] used the interquartile mean to provide a more robust measure of central tendency for responses from graphical perception studies, where participant error can create long tailed distributions of error. This is especially the case for crowdsourced studies, where correcting for data quality issues is perceived as more difficult than in laboratory settings [17]. However, the use of interquartile means can violate the assumptions involved in performing null hypothesis significance tests (as sample means can have non-normal distributions). Our statistical analyses were therefore performed using standard group means.

Experimental Interface

We investigated three types of common bivariate visualizations: scatter plots, line graphs, and area charts (see Fig. 3). In each experiment, we presented participants with a visualization and asked them to interactively adjust trend lines to best fit the data. Participants responded using a slider without tick marks, in order to limit anchoring effects [24]. Moving the slider adjusted a purple trend line by modifying its slope (in experiments 1 and 3) or its y-intercept (in experiment 2). Fig. 2 shows an example experimental task. After moving the slider, participants had to confirm their choice of trend line. The primary dependent measure is accuracy (e.g., the difference between the subject-specified slope and the slope of the series if the residuals were removed). We chose this design over a standard binary forced choice design for its greater expressiveness, as well as for the interactive feedback

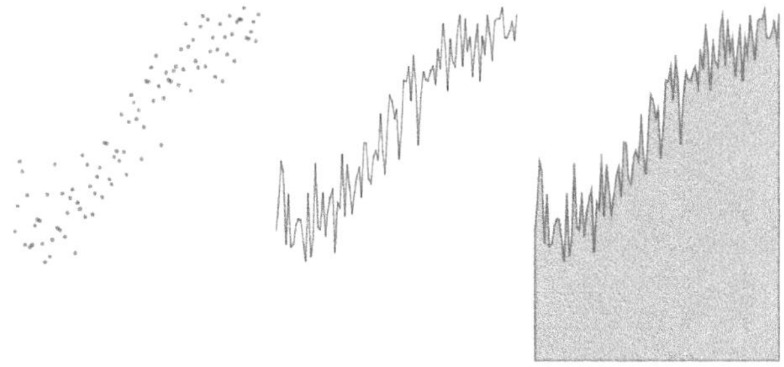

Figure 3. The three types of bivariate visualizations explored in this work: scatter plots, line graphs, and area charts. The density of points made bar charts and area charts visually similar, and so we excluded bar charts from our experiments. Likewise, the error in estimating trends from heatmaps [13] made them unsuitable for the experimental task.

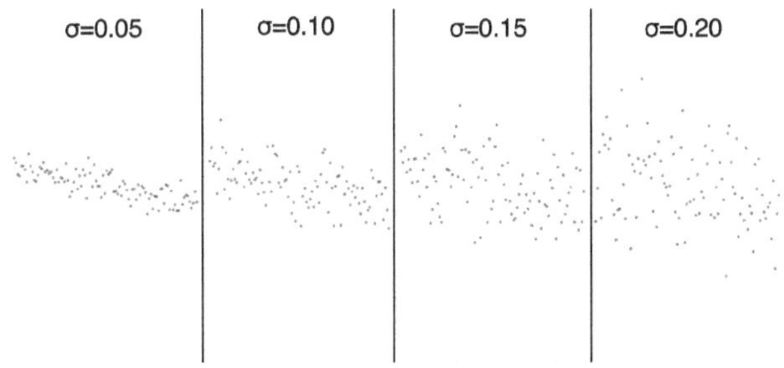

Figure 4. The four different Gaussian bandwidths used to generate residuals in this study. We produced stimuli by creating points on a target trend line (in this case, $f(x) = -0.2x + 0.6$), and then adding residuals drawn evenly from a Gaussian with a given bandwidth σ. Larger bandwidths mean more dispersion and so weaker fits.

of adjusting the fit by hand. While other studies investigate the use of more expressive designs (such as free-form drawing) [21], we sought to disambiguate the model selection task (e.g., the selection of a linear or non-linear model) from the model fitting task (adjusting the parameters of the selected model). Our design also reduces the impact of factors such as noise from motor movements or heterogeneous input devices.

Data Generation

For each stimulus we wished to have precise, independent control over relevant statistics such as noise, slope, and sample size, while maintaining the appearance of a "natural" distribution of points. Existing methods for generating points for related experimental tasks such as estimation of correlations (e.g., Harrison et al. [15]) do not afford independence: e.g., Pearson's r is correlated with the slope, as points with identical residuals but different slopes of their linear fits will have differing r values. We also wished to have a fair comparison between visual estimation and the results of ordinary least squares (OLS) regression. We therefore used the standard model of OLS to generate points, namely that $y = \beta x + \varepsilon$, where ε is a normally-distributed error term.

For each point set, we placed 100 points along a particular trend, regularly spaced in x. This both affords the use of line graphs and area charts for displaying this data (as they require that points be one to one), and aligns well with time series

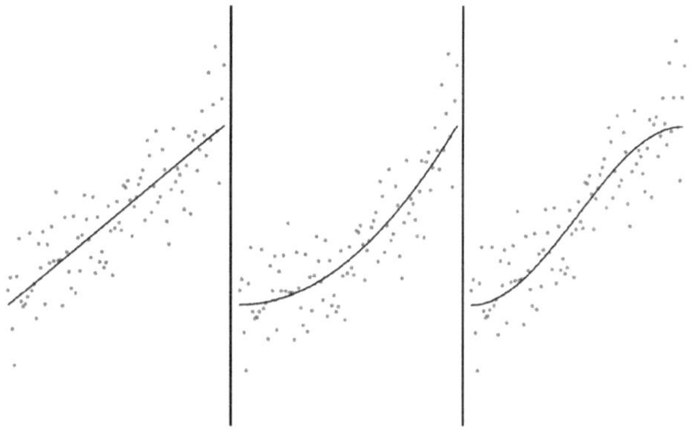

Figure 5. The three different trend types in this study: linear, quadratic, and trigonometric trends. In Experiment 1, participants estimated the slope of the linear fits, curvature of the quadratic fits, and amplitude of the trigonometric fits. In Experiment 2, they estimated the y-intercept of these fits. In Experiment 3, they estimated only the slope of linear fits. Trend lines are displayed here for reference.

data, a common domain for estimating (temporal) trends and relationships. For each point set, we created a set of residual values, sampled evenly from a Gaussian. The bandwidth of this Gaussian controls both goodness of fit and dispersion of points (see Fig. 4). We permuted this set of residuals, and then applied them to the original points. As heteroskedasticity introduced through permutation could alter the trend away from the target trend, we performed rejection sampling to ensure that the slope of the trend of the resulting points was within 10^{-7} of the target. We reused these residuals across all different trend types (linear, quadratic, or trigonometric). Fig. 5 shows these different trend types.

Except where noted, we selected trend lines that were centered in the image: that is, for a horizontal data extent of $[0,1]$, $f(0.5) = 0.5$. In all experiments, we desired control over the direction of the trend. For linear fits, this is the slope of the trend line. For quadratic fits, this was the curvature, as controlled by the coefficient of the second degree term. For trigonometric fits, this was the amplitude of a cosine function (with negative amplitude corresponding to negative slopes). These terms create similar relationships, such that a value of 0 is the line $f(x) = 0.5$, a value of 1 goes from $f(0) = 0$ to $f(1) = 1$, and -1 has the inverse relationship.

Participants

We limited the Mechanical Turk participant pool to subjects from within the United States, with a prior task approval rating of at least 90%. For validation, additional trials, without ambiguities such as outliers or design differences, contained the actual (OLS) trend line, which subjects then needed to simply match. We excluded responses from participants with high average error (greater than 0.2) on these validation stimuli. Across the three reported experiments and pilots, we performed 7 such exclusions. We recruited additional participants to replace these excluded subjects. Based on timings from internal piloting, we paid each participant \$2 for their participation, for a target rate of \$8/hour.

We analyzed data from 48 participants for each experiment (excluding rejections), for a total of 144 participants (98 male, 43 female, 3 who declined to state; $M_{age} = 33.2$, $SD_{age} = 8.8$). Across the subject pool, 10 reported having graduate or professional degrees, 69 college degrees, 40 at least some college, and 25 high school diplomas. After completing the main experimental task, participants were asked to self-assess their familiarity with charts and graphs on a 5 point Likert scale. The plurality (64) rated themselves as "3. Some familiarity," and none rated themselves with the maximum rating of "5. A great deal of experience."

EXPERIMENT 1: SLOPE ESTIMATION

We designed our first experiment to examine how accurate participants were at estimating the magnitude (slope, amplitude, or curvature) of trends in bivariate visualizations. We examined three types of bivariate visualizations: scatter plots, line graphs, and area charts (with the filled area below the line). In addition to linear trends, we examined more complex relationships such as quadratic and trigonometric functions.

We presented participants with a series of bivariate visualizations, who adjusted a slider to fit the perceived trend. The slider parameterized one of three types of trend: linear, quadratic, or trigonometric. For each stimulus, participants adjusted a slider that controlled the slope of a rendered trend line. In the case of quadratic trends, this slope was the curvature; for trigonometric fits, the positive/negative amplitude.

Participants saw one of each combination of 3 chart types (scatter plot, line graph, or area chart), 8 possible slopes $\beta = \pm\{0.1, 0.2, 0.4, 0.8\}$, and 4 bandwidths of Gaussian residuals $\sigma = \{0.05, 0.1, 0.15, 0.2\}$, for a total of 96 stimuli. We also included an additional 4 validation stimuli otherwise excluded from analysis. The type of trend (linear, quadratic, or trigonometric) was a random factor, with 32 stimuli of each factor level randomly assigned.

Hypotheses

We had three hypotheses for the first experiment:

1. **As the bandwidth of the residuals increased, accuracy would decrease**. Increasing the bandwidth of the residuals results in a lower correlation coefficient and higher perceived noise in the bivariate data. Prior work indicates that these related measures correspond to decreased accuracy for aggregate tasks in bivariate visualizations [1, 15].

2. **More complex relationships would result in lower accuracy**. Quadratic and trigonometric relationships are visually more complex than linear relationships, and often require more complex statistical methods to analyze. We anticipated that estimation of these less familiar relationships would therefore be more difficult than the linear case.

3. **Estimations would be unbiased**. That is, there would be no systematic over- or under-estimation of trends.

Results

We performed a three-way analysis of covariance (ANCOVA) of the effect of residual bandwidth, graph type and trend type on error in estimation of trend lines. We included participant ids and the actual slope of the trend line as covariates. We

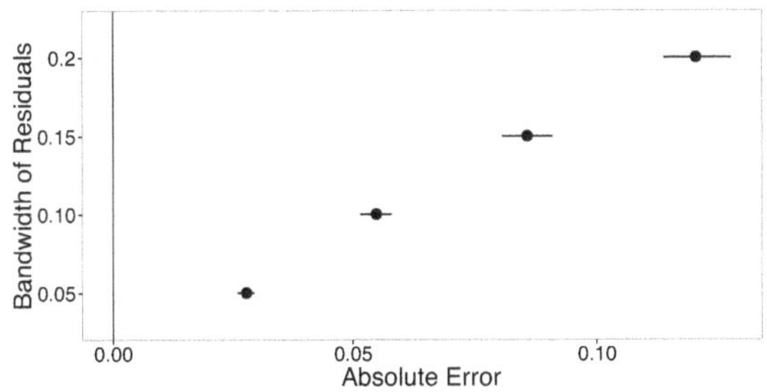

Figure 6. The effect of increased residual bandwidth on error in Experiment 1. See Fig. 4 for example stimuli at each factor level. Absolute error at estimating trend monotonically increases as the goodness of fit decreases. Confidence intervals represent bootstrapped 95% CIs of interquartile means.

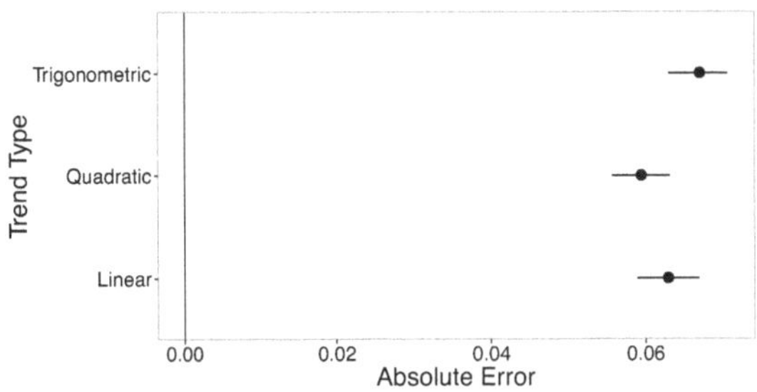

Figure 7. The effect of different trend types on error in Experiment 1. See Fig. 5 for example stimuli at each factor level. Despite the differing complexity of these types of fit, participant estimates were similar, indicating that regression by eye is capable of non-linear estimates. Confidence intervals represent bootstrapped 95% CIs of interquartile means.

defined error as the absolute difference between the slope of the OLS trend line, and the slope of the participant estimate.

Our results support our first hypothesis: **larger residuals result in less accuracy at regression by eye**. We observed a significant main effect for the bandwidth of the Gaussian used to generate residuals ($F(1,4554) = 950$, $p < 0.001$). The interquartile mean of absolute error increased monotonically with this bandwidth, from 0.02 of the actual slope of the trend line when the bandwidth was 0.05, to 0.12 when the bandwidth was 0.20. Figure 6 illustrates this result.

Our results fail to support our second hypothesis: **there was no statistically significant difference in estimation accuracy among linear, quadratic, or trigonometric trends**. Fit type was not a significant main effect ($F(2,4554) = 2.60$, $p = 0.074$), and post-hoc tests (using Tukey's Honest Significant Difference) did not identify any significant pairwise interactions. The interquartile mean of absolute error of was 0.06 for linear and quadratic fits, and 0.07 for trigonometric fits (see Fig. 7). This suggests that the relative unfamiliarity of non-linear trends does not result in poorer performance at regression by eye.

Our results support our third hypothesis: **there was no statistically significant bias in estimations**. Participants saw a balanced set of positive and negative trends. If estimates of these trends were unbiased, we would expect the average signed error to be close to zero. The average signed error was 0.0008, far less than the fidelity of the slider used to input

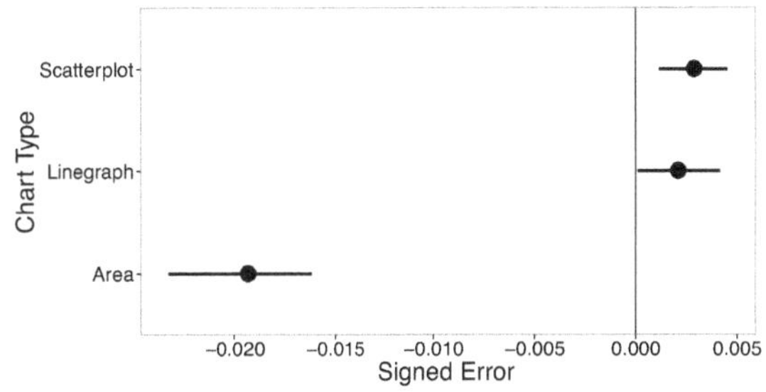

Figure 8. The effect of chart type on signed error in Experiment 2. See Fig. 4 for example stimuli at each factor level. Area charts are visually asymmetric, with the area below the line filled in with a color. This visual asymmetry results in a form of within-the-bar bias [27], where values in the filled region are perceived as likelier than values outside of it. This bias manifests as a consistent under-estimation in the intercept of trend lines. Other chart types we examined do not have this bias. Confidence intervals represent bootstrapped 95% CIs of interquartile means.

guesses ($\Delta = 0.01$). A Student's T-test failed to support the hypothesis that $mu_{error} \neq 0$ ($t(4590) = 0.39$, $p = 0.70$).

Prior work in graphical perception often measures performance as the absolute log error: e.g., Cleveland & McGill [8] calculate their performance metric as $\log_2(|\text{error}| + \frac{1}{8})$. As a point of comparison, the interquartile mean of the absolute log error across all conditions in this experiment was 2.4. Differences in methodology and measurement discourage statistical inferences comparing this value with those in similar experiments. Nevertheless, error rates for regression by eye are at least in the same magnitude as those observed in other graphical perception tasks in both lab and crowdsourced studies. For instance, Heer & Bostock [17] report an absolute log error of 2.5 for proportional judgments in treemaps, and Cleveland & McGill [8] report an absolute log error of 2.4 for proportional judgments in stacked bars (although compare to a log error of estimation of relative lengths of lines of 1.1). This similarity suggests that, despite requiring estimation of aggregate statistical information, regression by eye results in judgments that are accurate enough for many practical purposes, comparable with accuracy in comparing individual values in visualizations.

EXPERIMENT 2: "WITHIN-THE-BAR" BIAS

"Within-the-bar" bias is a known perceptual bias involving bar charts, in which points contained in the visual area of the glyph of the bar are deemed likelier than points outside of the glyph. Newman & Scholl [27] encountered this bias for a sampling task: "how likely is this point to have been drawn from the distribution represented by this bar?" Correll & Gleicher [11] likewise encountered this bias for inferential tasks: "how likely is the population mean to take a particular value, given the sample represented by this bar?"

We hypothesized that this bias would likewise occur in regression by eye when using visually asymmetric visualizations such as area charts: a "within-the-area" bias. The slope estimation task in the previous experiment would not capture this bias, as there is no method for participants to indicate a *uniform* under-estimation in trends; decreasing the slope would cause under-estimation at the beginning of the plot but not the end, and vice versa. We therefore designed this experiment to elicit estimates of the y-intercepts of trends. A within-the-area bias would then appear as systematic under-estimation of intercept in area charts.

As with the previous experiment, we presented participants with a series of bivariate visualizations. However, instead of estimating the *slope* of the points, participants estimated the *y-intercept* of the trend line. For each trial, we added a uniform offset to the points in the bivariate visualization in the data range $[-0.25, 0.25]$. The rendered trend line was initially placed with the correct slope, and such that $f(0.5) = 0.5$ in data space. Participants adjusted a slider controlling the vertical offset of this trend line.

The plots had the same factor levels as the previous experiment, for a total of 96 stimuli per participant, with an additional 4 validation stimuli otherwise excluded from analysis. The uniform offset was an additional random factor for each stimulus.

Hypotheses

We had one hypothesis for the second experiment:

1. **Area charts would be subject to within-the-area bias.** That is, participants would estimate lower values of y-intercepts of trends in area charts, as opposed to line graphs and scatter plots.

Results

We performed a one-way ANCOVA of the effect of graph type on *signed* error. We included residual bandwidth as a covariate, and participant ids as a random factor.

Our results support our first hypothesis: **participants systematically underestimated the intercept of trends in area charts, but not in scatter plots or line graphs**. We observed a significant main effect of graph type on signed error ($F(2, 2431) = 27$, $p < 0.001$). A post-hoc Tukey's HSD confirmed significant differences in error between the area chart and the other two chart types, but not between scatter plots and line graphs. The interquartile mean of the signed error of estimations made with area charts was an under-estimation of -0.02, compared to an interquartile mean of 0.002 for the other two conditions. This under-estimation corresponds to unsigned errors more than twice as large in area charts (interquartile mean of 0.04 for intercepts that ranged from $\{-0.25, 0.25\}$, compared to 0.02 for line graphs and scatter plots). Figure 8 illustrates this result.

EXPERIMENT 3: ESTIMATION INVOLVING OUTLIERS

OLS regression operates under the assumption that there is a unimodal, symmetric distribution of residuals surrounding the line of best fit. Extreme outliers violate this assumption, and can result in trend lines that are substantially different from those produced by more robust methods. Visual inspection can accurately identify certain classes of outliers [1]. Therefore, regression by eye may afford the estimation of both outlier-robust and outlier-sensitive trends. However, cognitive biases [31] such as anchoring (the tendency to overweight the first set of information), availability (the tendency to overweight more recent or extreme information), and the hot-hand fallacy (the tendency to assume that runs of high or low values

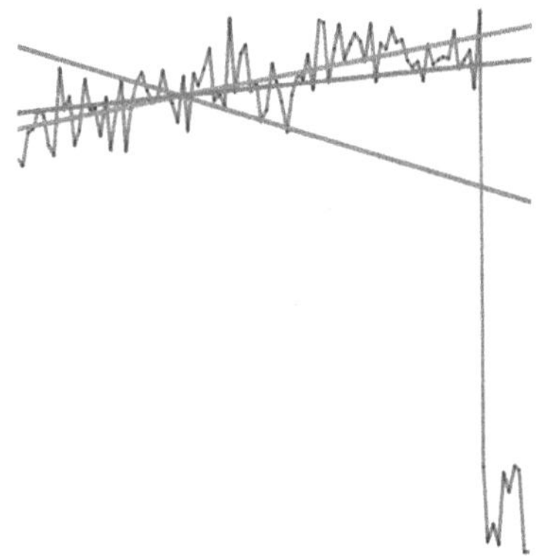

Figure 9. An example stimulus from Experiment 3. We replaced the final 10 points of this dataset with extreme values. The overlaid green trend line represents a robust fit (ignoring the outlier values), while the overlaid orange line represents the standard OLS fit with all points included. The purple line represents the average participant response on this stimulus. In general, participants' estimates of trend lines were closer to the robust than the non-robust trend; regression by eye tends to down-weight outliers compared to OLS.

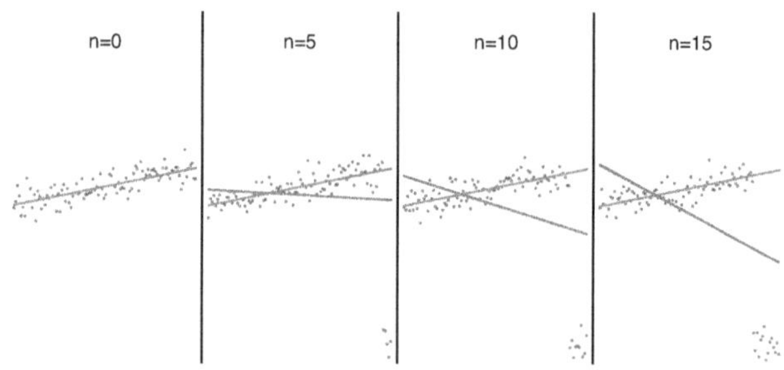

Figure 10. The four different outlier numerosities tested in Experiment 3. The overlaid green trend line represents a robust fit (ignoring the outlier values), while the overlaid orange line represents the standard OLS fit with all points included. More outliers results in larger divergence between these two types of fit.

will continue) can impact how viewers categorize and utilize outliers in prediction tasks [6, 19]. In other words, regression by eye may not uniformly weight outliers, depending on their position in the plot.

This experiment was largely identical to Experiment 1, except we designated 0, 5, 10, or 15 points at the very beginning, first third, or end of the series as outliers. We vertically positioned outliers within the top or bottom 10% of the visual area of the visualization (whichever was farthest from the trend line), and added random jitter. We then calculated the outlier-sensitive line of best fit, as well as the intersection between this new trend line and the original, outlier-less trend line. We refer to the original trend line, estimated without the presence of outliers, as the **robust trend line**. We refer to the re-estimated trend, which takes into account the added outliers, as the **OLS trend line**. Figure 10 shows examples of this process, and the corresponding changes in trend line.

As in Experiment 1, the participants controlled the slope of a rendered trend line with a slider. However, rather than being placed such that $f(0.5) = 0.5$, we offset the trend line to the intersection of the robust (without outliers) and non-robust (including outliers) trend line. This allowed participants to express both types of fit with the same slider interaction, while affording estimations beyond a simple interpolation of both trends. We limited the stimuli to linear fits only, excluding quadratic and trigonometric trends from this experiment.

Participants saw one of each combination of factors: the three graph types, eight slopes, and four Gaussian residual bandwidths. The four outlier quantities $\{0, 5, 10, 15\}$ were an additional factor. To maintain a manageable number of stimuli (piloting showed evidence of fatigue for more than 100 stimuli per trial), both the sign of the trend line (positive or negative), and the location of the outliers (beginning, first third, or end) were random factors, with each level randomly apportioned to half and one third of the stimuli respectively. This resulted in 96 total stimuli, with an additional 4 validation stimuli otherwise excluded from analysis, in line with prior experiments.

Hypotheses

We had three hypotheses for the third experiment:

1. **Participant estimation would hew closer to a robust trend line ignoring outliers, rather than the OLS trend line.** We assumed that in general, participants would ignore or downweight outliers when performing regression by eye.
2. **As the number of outliers increased, estimations would be closer to the non-robust OLS fit.** We speculated on the existence of a "tipping point" of outlier density, beyond which participants would avoid robust fits, and interpolate between the robust and OLS fits.
3. **Outliers at the end of the chart would result in estimations closer to the OLS fit than outliers in other locations on the plot.** Prior work on cognitive biases in predictions suggests that viewers may give more credence to more recent outliers (as indicative as new anchor points, or of an emerging "streak") [12]. We therefore believed that these points would be more heavily weighted, and the resulting estimation closer to the outlier-sensitive OLS line, than outliers "earlier" in the plot.

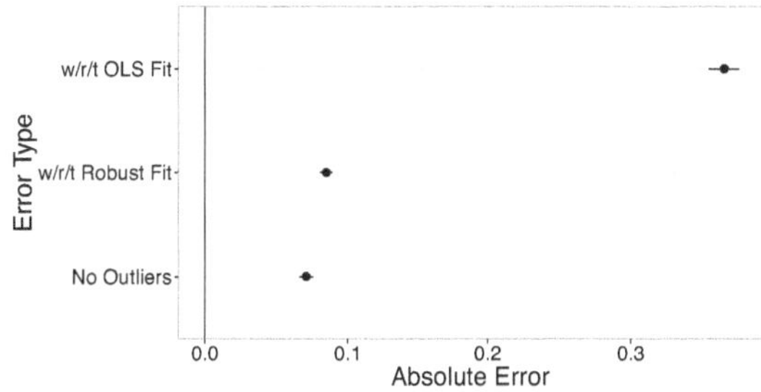

Figure 11. The absolute error of trend estimates in Experiment 3, measured as difference from the OLS slope (which includes outliers, row 1) or from the robust slope (which excludes outliers, row 2). Participants were significantly closer to the robust fit, indicating that they were largely insensitive to outliers. We also include the absolute error for trials with no outliers for reference. Error to the robust line is higher than this standard, indicating that participants were at least performing some interpolation between OLS and robust fits, even if they largely favored the robust fit. Confidence intervals represent bootstrapped 95% CIs of interquartile means.

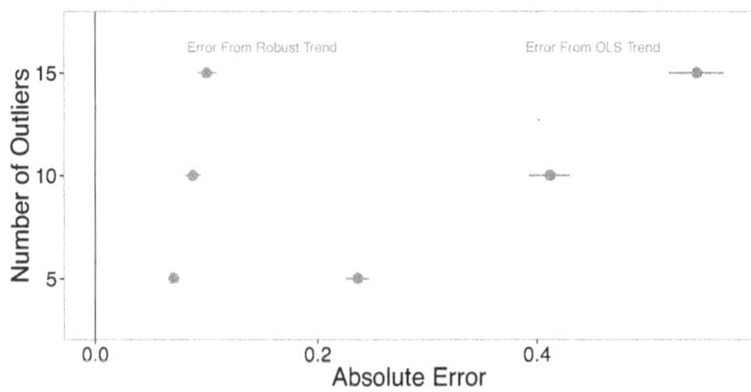

Figure 12. The effect of numerosity of outliers on absolute error in Experiment 3. See Fig. 10 for example stimuli at each factor level. As the number of outliers increases, there is increasing divergence between the robust line of best fit (which ignores outliers), and the standard OLS line of best fit (which is sensitive to outliers). Estimates become increasingly dissimilar to the OLS fit, indicating that participants down-weight outliers when making estimates of trend. However, the increasing error even from the robust trend line indicates that participants still perform some interpolation between the two types of fits. Confidence intervals represent bootstrapped 95% CIs of interquartile means.

Results

Our results support our first hypothesis. **Participant estimates were closer to the robust trend line than the trend line that included outliers**. Excluding conditions with zero outliers (and so the two trend lines would be identical), the interquartile mean of absolute error was over 4 times higher when calculated as a comparison to the OLS trend line (0.36) as opposed to when calculated from the robust trend line (0.08). A Student's T-test confirmed that the error as defined by the OLS line was significantly higher than the robust line ($t(6670) = 43$, $p < 0.001$). However, a Student's T-test found a significant difference in unsigned error when compared to the robust trend line between estimates where no outliers were present, and those with any amount of outliers ($\mu = 0.07$ vs. $\mu = 0.08$, $t(3808) = 9.8$, $p < 0.001$). Figure 11 illustrates this result. This indicates that participants are not entirely ignoring outliers, although the small effect size suggests that participants are giving outliers significantly less weight than OLS regression. Figure 9 shows an comparison of robust, participant, and OLS trend lines.

Our results fail to support our second hypothesis. **While participant estimates diverge from the robust line as the number of outliers increases, the OLS trend line diverges faster than participant estimates**. There was a significant positive interaction between outlier count and absolute error with respect to the robust trend line ($R^2 = 0.02$, $F(1,4591) = 110$, $p < 0.001$). However, there was also a significant positive interaction between outlier count and absolute error with respect to the OLS line ($R^2 = 0.38$, $F(1,4591) = 2800$, $p < 0.001$). Additionally, while the range of errors with respect to the robust line remained small (interquartile means of 0.07 with 0 outliers, monotonically increasing to 0.10 with 15 outliers), absolute error with respect to the OLS line monotonically increased almost 7-fold, from 0.07 with 0 outliers to 0.54 with 15 outliers. These results indicate that, while increased numbers of extreme values may result in participants increasing the weight of these outliers, this increase in weight is slower than the sensitivity of OLS to outliers. Figure 12 illustrates this result.

Our results also fail to support our third hypothesis: **There was no significant impact of outlier location on performance**. There is a confound between outlier location and OLS line: outliers on the ends of the data ranges create larger shifts in slope than outliers in the center, which may only create shifts in intercept. To evaluate our third hypothesis, we therefore defined a parameterized performance function $\frac{\text{Estimated Slope}-\text{Robust Slope}}{\text{OLS Slope}-\text{Robust Slope}}$ that contextualizes a participant estimate as an interpolation between the robust slope (value of 0) and the OLS slope (value of 1). A one way ANCOVA of this interpolation value as an effect of outlier location, with outlier count as a covariate, and participant id as a random factor, found no significant effect of outlier location on interpolative value ($F(2,3441) = 0.63$, $p = 0.53$).

DISCUSSION

In many cases, designers do not explicitly encode regression information. In other cases, viewers may not have the statistical or graphical expertise to interpret such information, even when it is supplied. Yet, our results point to regression by eye as a robust and reasonably accurate method for estimating trends in bivariate data. Participants from a variety of backgrounds and levels of self-reported graphical and statistical expertise were capable of estimating both the slope and intercept of both linear and non-linear trends. That is, viewers of visualization are largely trustworthy when estimating the relationship between two variables in a plot.

However, this general accuracy of trend estimation is not universal. Area charts are visually asymmetrical: the area below the line is filled in, and the area above it is not. We found that this asymmetry creates a "within-the-area" bias: a systematic under-estimation of the intercept of trends, due to the perceived higher likelihood of points in the filled-in area. Designers hoping to rely on regression by eye should avoid such asymmetries in their bivariate visualizations.

Likewise, while viewers do not give the same weight to outliers as OLS regression, they do not ignore them either. For noisy data, this robustness may be beneficial: people can be relied on to perform filtering operations without explicit guidance. In other cases, this insensitivity may be undesirable. For instance, more complicated automatic analytical processes may use OLS regression or other outlier sensitive techniques as part of their calculations, resulting in a disconnect between human and statistical conclusions at later stages of the sensemaking process. Similarly, the human tendency to discount or downweight outliers may result in slow adaptation to new data that does not fit into existing patterns.

Implications for Design

The estimation of trends, both for the prediction of values, and the imputation of missing values, is a common and important task in data analysis. We believe that our results suggest two main recommendations for designers of information visualizations that include time series or bivariate data:

1. *Designers do not need to annotate bivariate visualizations with trend lines in many cases.* Regression by eye, without explicit trend lines, is comparable in accuracy to other types of graphical perception tasks (such as comparison of value), even for a wide class of models. The presence of outliers is an exception to this general advice: human estimation of trends does not give much weight to outliers. For data where outliers are important, and expected to contribute to important trends, designers ought to visualize the outlier sensitive models directly.
2. *Designers should avoid area charts when the perception of trends is important.* The visual asymmetry caused by filling in the area under the line results in a corresponding asymmetry in judgment of trend: an underestimation in perceived trend. This within-the-area bias is undesirable in many cases, but can be countered by visual encodings (such as scatter plots and line charts) that have no such visual asymmetry.

Limitations & Future Work

Our experimental setup was intentionally simple, affording only a single free parameter for each experiment. In actual regression by eye, the viewer may simultaneously engage in multiple types of estimation: choosing a particular type of fit, ignoring outliers, and estimating the parameters of the chosen model. Errors in any one of these steps could compound, resulting in performance worse than our measures, where many of these decisions are fixed *a priori*. It is also likely that there are many visual features, such as the convex hull of points, or the numerosity of point clouds, that are acting as visual proxies for estimation of the trend. Given the unimodal error function and uniform density of our experimental stimuli, these proxies are useful for estimating the trend line. However, in datasets where internal densities of points may be skewed, or the envelope of point clouds non-informative for estimating central tendency, these visual proxies may introduce biases and confounds in visual estimations.

There are also a number of design decisions not considered in this study that could impact regression by eye. For example,

Wood et al. [32] have shown that "sketchiness" in visualizations can result in skepticism of the data and design. It is possible that outliers could receive less visual (and so statistical) weight as a response to this sort of skepticism. Our stimuli likewise contained a sufficient number of points that bar charts were not a feasible choice of visualization. Given the propensity of bar charts to encourage comparison of individual, rather than aggregate quantities [33], it is possible that bar charts of smaller scale bivariate data could promote fitting of local rather than global trends.

Finally, we focused on a simple form of regression, ordinary least squares (OLS), as our standard for measuring accuracy. While our data were constructed to satisfy the assumptions of OLS (with the intentional exception of our outlier experiment), in most real world scenarios OLS is just one tool of many, and analysts must exercise judgment when determining how to fit their data. More complex models may not have ready visual analogues, and data concerning regression by eye may not extend to cover these cases.

Our future work is focused in three areas. First, we wish to examine the impact of annotations relevant to regression (such as confidence bands, error bars, and curve boxplots [26]) on regression by eye. Can sufficient information promote caution in judgments of trend? Second, we wish to examine the impact of different rhetorical framings and presentations on regression by eye. Language from semiotics and rhetoric can provide testable structures for how visualizations are consumed [18]: these framings could similarly impact statistical judgments. For instance, outliers from a credible source could be weighted higher than outliers with more suspect provenance. Likewise, preconceptions about the volatility of data from certain domains may color how experts estimate trends. Lastly, we wish to examine techniques for overcoming bias in regression by eye and similar visual estimations of statistical quantities. Cognitive and perceptual biases are difficult to overcome, and may require exploration of new visualization designs [25].

Conclusion

In this paper, we examine the ability of visualization viewers to perform *regression by eye*: the visual estimation of trends in bivariate visualizations. We show that viewers without statistical training can reliably estimate both linear and non-linear trends in charts such as scatter plots and line graphs. However, area graphs are subject to a "within-the-area" bias, leading to estimated trends with lower intercepts than other bivariate visualizations. Regression by eye is also less sensitive to outliers than standard least-squares regression. This decreased sensitivity results in a divergence between trends estimated by viewers, which do not give much weight to extreme outliers, and those trends calculated by regression methods, that can be heavily influenced by a few extreme values.

ACKNOWLEDGMENTS

This work was supported by a Moore Foundation Data-Driven Discovery Investigator Award.

REFERENCES

1. Danielle Albers, Michael Correll, and Michael Gleicher. 2014. Task-driven evaluation of aggregation in time series visualization. In *Proceedings of the SIGCHI Conference on Human Factors in Computing Systems*. ACM, 551–560.
2. Francis J Anscombe. 1973. Graphs in statistical analysis. *The American Statistician* 27, 1 (1973), 17–21.
3. Dan Ariely. 2001. Seeing sets: Representation by statistical properties. *Psychological science* 12, 2 (2001), 157–162.
4. Vivien Beattie and Michael John Jones. 2002. The impact of graph slope on rate of change judgments in corporate reports. *Abacus* 38, 2 (2002), 177–199.
5. Fergus Bolger and Nigel Harvey. 1993. Context-sensitive heuristics in statistical reasoning. *The Quarterly Journal of Experimental Psychology* 46, 4 (1993), 779–811.
6. Sean D Campbell and Steven A Sharpe. 2009. Anchoring bias in consensus forecasts and its effect on market prices. *Journal of Financial and Quantitative Analysis* 44, 02 (2009), 369–390.
7. William S Cleveland, Persi Diaconis, and Robert McGill. 1982. *Variables on scatterplots look more highly correlated when the scales are increased.* Technical Report. DTIC Document.
8. William S Cleveland and Robert McGill. 1984a. Graphical perception: Theory, experimentation, and application to the development of graphical methods. *Journal of the American statistical association* 79, 387 (1984), 531–554.
9. William S Cleveland and Robert McGill. 1984b. The many faces of a scatterplot. *J. Amer. Statist. Assoc.* 79, 388 (1984), 807–822.
10. Michael Correll, Danielle Albers, Steven Franconeri, and Michael Gleicher. 2012. Comparing averages in time series data. In *Proceedings of the SIGCHI Conference on Human Factors in Computing Systems*. ACM, 1095–1104.
11. Michael Correll and Michael Gleicher. 2014. Error bars considered harmful: Exploring alternate encodings for mean and error. *IEEE transactions on visualization and computer graphics* 20, 12 (2014), 2142–2151.
12. Rachel Croson and James Sundali. 2005. The gamblerâĂŹs fallacy and the hot hand: Empirical data from casinos. *Journal of risk and uncertainty* 30, 3 (2005), 195–209.
13. Johannes Fuchs, Fabian Fischer, Florian Mansmann, Enrico Bertini, and Petra Isenberg. 2013. Evaluation of alternative glyph designs for time series data in a small multiple setting. In *Proceedings of the SIGCHI Conference on Human Factors in Computing Systems*. ACM, 3237–3246.
14. Michael Gleicher, Michael Correll, Christine Nothelfer, and Steven Franconeri. 2013. Perception of average value in multiclass scatterplots. *IEEE transactions on visualization and computer graphics* 19, 12 (2013), 2316–2325.

15. Lane Harrison, Fumeng Yang, Steven Franconeri, and Remco Chang. 2014. Ranking visualizations of correlation using weber's law. *IEEE transactions on visualization and computer graphics* 20, 12 (2014), 1943–1952.
16. Nigel Harvey Teresa Ewart Robert West. 1997. Effects of data noise on statistical judgement. *Thinking & Reasoning* 3, 2 (1997), 111–132.
17. Jeffrey Heer and Michael Bostock. 2010. Crowdsourcing graphical perception: using mechanical turk to assess visualization design. In *Proceedings of the SIGCHI Conference on Human Factors in Computing Systems*. ACM, 203–212.
18. Jessica Hullman and Nick Diakopoulos. 2011. Visualization rhetoric: Framing effects in narrative visualization. *IEEE transactions on visualization and computer graphics* 17, 12 (2011), 2231–2240.
19. Li-Jun Ji, Richard E Nisbett, and Yanjie Su. 2001. Culture, change, and prediction. *Psychological Science* 12, 6 (2001), 450–456.
20. Matthew Kay and Jeffrey Heer. 2016. Beyond Weber's Law: A Second Look at Ranking Visualizations of Correlation. *IEEE transactions on visualization and computer graphics* 22, 1 (2016), 469–478.
21. Yea-Seul Kim, Jessica Hullman, and Katharina Reinecke. 2017. Explaining the Gap: Visualizing OneâĂŹs Predictions Improves Recall and Comprehension of Data. In *Proceedings of the 32nd annual ACM conference on Human factors in computing systems*. ACM. To appear.
22. Stephan Lewandowsky. 2011. Popular consensus climate change is set to continue. *Psychological Science* (2011).
23. Stephan Lewandowsky and Ian Spence. 1989. Discriminating strata in scatterplots. *J. Amer. Statist. Assoc.* 84, 407 (1989), 682–688.
24. Justin Matejka, Michael Glueck, Tovi Grossman, and George Fitzmaurice. 2016. The Effect of Visual Appearance on the Performance of Continuous Sliders and Visual Analogue Scales. In *Proceedings of the 2016 CHI Conference on Human Factors in Computing Systems*. ACM, 5421–5432.
25. Luana Micallef, Pierre Dragicevic, and Jean-Daniel Fekete. 2012. Assessing the effect of visualizations on bayesian reasoning through crowdsourcing. *IEEE Transactions on Visualization and Computer Graphics* 18, 12 (2012), 2536–2545.
26. Mahsa Mirzargar, Ross T Whitaker, and Robert M Kirby. 2014. Curve boxplot: Generalization of boxplot for ensembles of curves. *IEEE transactions on visualization and computer graphics* 20, 12 (2014), 2654–2663.
27. George E Newman and Brian J Scholl. 2012. Bar graphs depicting averages are perceptually misinterpreted: The within-the-bar bias. *Psychonomic bulletin & review* 19, 4 (2012), 601–607.
28. Ronald A Rensink and Gideon Baldridge. 2010. The perception of correlation in scatterplots. In *Computer Graphics Forum*, Vol. 29. Wiley Online Library, 1203–1210.
29. Danielle Albers Szafir, Steve Haroz, Michael Gleicher, and Steven Franconeri. 2016. Four types of ensemble coding in data visualizations. *Journal of vision* 16, 5 (2016), 11–11.
30. Justin Talbot, Vidya Setlur, and Anushka Anand. 2014. Four experiments on the perception of bar charts. *IEEE transactions on visualization and computer graphics* 20, 12 (2014), 2152–2160.
31. Amos Tversky and Daniel Kahneman. 1975. Judgment under uncertainty: Heuristics and biases. In *Utility, probability, and human decision making*. Springer, 141–162.
32. Jo Wood, Petra Isenberg, Tobias Isenberg, Jason Dykes, Nadia Boukhelifa, and Aidan Slingsby. 2012. Sketchy rendering for information visualization. *IEEE Transactions on Visualization and Computer Graphics* 18, 12 (2012), 2749–2758.
33. Jeff Zacks and Barbara Tversky. 1999. Bars and lines: A study of graphic communication. *Memory & Cognition* 27, 6 (1999), 1073–1079.

Evaluating Perceptually Complementary Views for Network Exploration Tasks

Chunlei Chang
Monash University
Melbourne, Australia
chunlei.chang@monash.edu

Benjamin Bach
Monash University
Melbourne, Australia
benj.bach@gmail.com

Tim Dwyer
Monash University
Melbourne, Australia
tim.dwyer@monash.edu

Kim Marriott
Monash University
Melbourne, Australia
kim.marriott@monash.edu

ABSTRACT

We explore the relative merits of matrix, node-link and combined side-by-side views for the visualisation of weighted networks with three controlled studies: (1) finding the most effective visual encoding for weighted edges in matrix representations; (2) comparing matrix, node-link and combined views for static weighted networks; and (3) comparing *MatrixWave*, *Sankey* and combined views of both for event-sequence data. Our studies underline that node-link and matrix views are suited to different analysis tasks. For the combined view, our studies show that there is a perceptually complementary effect in terms of improved accuracy for some tasks, but that there is a cost in terms of longer completion time than the faster of the two techniques alone. Eye-movement data shows that for many tasks participants strongly favour one of the two views, after trying both in the training phase.

ACM Classification Keywords

H.5.m. Information Interfaces and Presentation (e.g. HCI): Miscellaneous;

Author Keywords

Network visualisation, eye tracking, event sequence data, node-link diagrams, sankey diagrams, matrices

INTRODUCTION

The two most commonly used representations for network data are node-link diagrams and adjacency matrices. Studies have demonstrated distinct advantages to each, suggesting a certain complementariness for both visualisations. Similarly, for representing time-varying flows or event-sequences over networks, two complementary representations have been proposed. Sankey diagrams [19] follow the node-link metaphor, showing flows as curved lines between nodes in discrete timesteps; while MatrixWave [26] presents flows through a stacked sequence of matrices.

CHI 2017, May 06-11, 2017, Denver, CO, USA
© 2017 ACM. ISBN 978-1-4503-4655-9/17/05...$15.00
DOI: http://dx.doi.org/10.1145/3025453.3026024

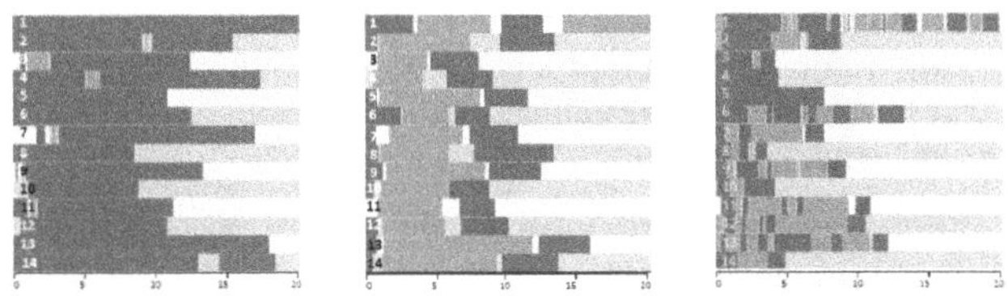

(a) Exclusive use (b) Sequential use (c) Parallel use

Figure 1. Examples of user behaviours while using complementary views. Horizontal bars present study trials for the same user, time running from left to right. Colours indicate the view the participant was looking at.

While node-link diagrams—including Sankey diagrams—suffer from visual clutter when displaying highly-connected (dense) networks, matrix layouts manage to avoid visual clutter by dedicating a predefined space for each link to be shown. However, matrix visualisations seem to be less intuitive and less familiar to most users and especially difficult to use for following paths. The pros and cons of each technique with respect to different tasks suggest that providing users with both views *simultaneously* might improve their performance and satisfaction during the analysis process. However, providing multiple coordinated views comes at the cost of increased visual complexity and requires users to understand when to use which visualisation. This supposed trade-off between complementary effects of simultaneous views versus their additional complexity has not previously been formally studied.

In this paper, we provide evidence from two controlled user studies, each one comparing two sets of visualisations: Node-link versus Matrix and Sankey versus MatrixWave. We consider the combined views to be *perceptually* complementary, as opposed to *informationally* complementary. Informationally complementary views show a different aspect of the data, such as different attributes, times, or levels of detail. Neither view is redundant to the analysis process and it is not possible to generate one view from the other as they contain different information. By contrast, perceptually complementary views show exactly the same information and each is in some sense redundant. Perceptually complementary views may support tasks that require such a redundant but complementary visual encoding, e.g. a clear view of the network topology and a view that more efficiently encodes edge weight.

In investigating perceptually complementary views we seek answers to the following questions:

Q1: Which tasks are better supported for *i)* weighted networks (by Nodelink or Matrix) and for *ii)* event sequences over weighted networks (by MatrixWave or Sankey diagrams)?
Q2: Do side-by-side perceptually complementary views improve or decrease performance (time and error) with respect to the individual views alone?
Q3: How do users use complementary views when provided with two visualisations simultaneously (combined)?

For combined views, our studies show that there is a perceptually complementary effect in terms of improved accuracy for some tasks, but at the cost of longer completion times than the faster of the two techniques alone. Eye-movement data shows that for many tasks participants strongly favour one of the two views, after trying both in the training phase.

Different encodings for edge weight are often seen in practice and in different research on matrix representations of weighted networks but there does not seem to have been any prior formal evaluation of this topic. Since we needed this information for our studies of complementary network visualisation (Studies 2 and 3), we began with an evaluation of edge-weight encodings in matrices (Study 1).

All our datasets, study results, and visualisations of eye-tracking data are available: `http://marvl.infotech.monash.edu/~dwyer/papers/chi2017/`.

RELATED WORK

Our related work describes visualisations and studies on network and event-flow visualisations, as well as the use of complementary views in information visualisation.

Representations of Network Data

Ghoniem and Fekete [10] found that for networks with high link density, various tasks were more easily completed with an adjacency matrix representation, even though matrices were unordered. For sparse directed graphs Keller *et al.* [14] show that finding edges and paths for given nodes is significantly faster with node-link diagrams and they suggest that these are also more intuitive. For networks with weighted edges there appears to be little evidence of how different visualisations are complementary. Alper *et al.* [1] considered different encodings of pairs of edge weights in a single matrix to compare graphs, and found matrices greatly outperform node-link diagrams. However, the context of their study was different and their goal was not to assess complementariness.

Event Sequence Data

Event sequences describe flows of a certain strength between entities at discrete time steps. Formally, these can be considered layered networks with weighted links. Sankey diagrams [19, 24] have become a popular way to show such data, for example, they are supported by a number of visualisation tool-kits including D3 [5] and are offered by Google Analytics for analysis of web clickstream data. Sankey diagrams are easily understood, showing a very literal "pipeline" of flow between nodes at different points in time. However, like other kinds of node-link representations, Sankey diagrams can quickly become cluttered through too many links overlapping and obstructing each other and their readability has not been studied in detail. The only exception of which we are aware is a usability study of a system featuring Sankey diagrams [24] and in which a comparison to alternative visualisations was required for future work.

An alternative technique for visualising event sequence data was recently proposed by Zhao *et al.* [26]. It uses a linked sequence of adjacency matrices in a zig-zag tiling and is, hence, called *MatrixWave*. As with an earlier design for unweighted, levelled directed graphs by Bezerianos *et al.* [4], the design rationale is that adjacency matrices scale better to dense networks than node-link diagrams. MatrixWave was compared to Sankey diagrams by Zhao *et al.* for analysis of click-stream data. This study found distinct advantages of MatrixWave for tasks where participants needed to read precise values of link-weights. However, the study also suggested that Sankey diagrams remained more precise for showing path information. Qualitative feedback indicated that the Sankey diagrams were more intuitive and learnable by participants.

We are not aware of any work that compares the effect of *two representations combined*, i.e. side-by-side. In this sense, our work is the first to investigate such a setup.

Coordinated and Complementary Views

Displaying multiple views on the same data set is common practice in information visualisation [20]. Multiple views have long been used to explore complex data sets [23] and are now standard in visualisation software such as Tableau. Differentiating between *informationally* and *perceptually* complementary views allows us to reason about if and how two views are benefiting the analysis process. Another way of understanding this difference is that informationally complementary views result from "forks" [22] earlier in the visualisation pipeline [6, pg. 17] such that the filters restricting which data is shown in each view differ. Perceptually complementary views result from forks later in the pipeline, after data values have been determined but before the representation has been chosen.

Perceptually complementary views may be beneficial for a different set of tasks than informationally complementary views. This notion, that representations that show the same information in different ways (i.e. that are *isomorphic*) may lead to different understanding, is supported by results in cognitive psychology where it is known as the *representational effect* [25]. Research in information visualisation has shown that, within a single visualisation, redundant encoding of a single data attribute with different visual channels (e.g. colour as well as size of marks) may improve readability [17]. However, the idea that there may be a similar effect across multiple views (e.g. that isomorphic views may be perceptually complementary) has not been formally tested for data visualisations prior to the studies presented in this paper.

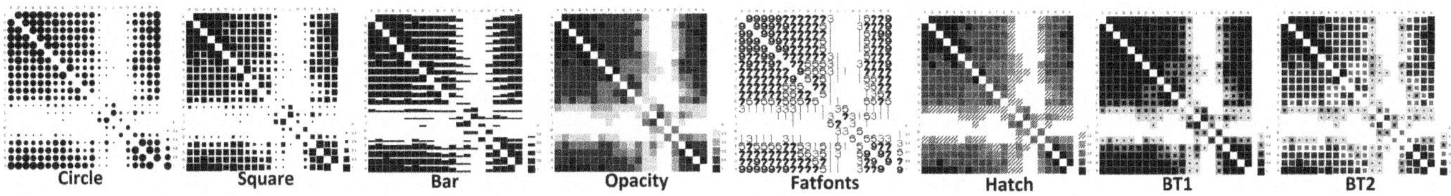

Figure 2. Samples from our encodings used in Study1. (BT = Background Transparency)

It is our view that specification and testing of perceptually complementary visualisation designs is necessary because it is something that has been proposed and tried informally by visualisation designers. For networks, Henry and Fekete proposed MatrixExplorer [11] to explore the potential of combining (coordinated) matrix and node-link visualisation side-by-side in social networks. Potentially, the dual view allows an expert analyst to use the most appropriate representation for the subtask at hand and to move smoothly between the views without loosing their mental model. They might also help novice analysts more quickly learn unfamiliar representations such as the adjacency matrix from familiar representations like a node-link diagram. Of course, this comes at the cost of more screen space, higher coding effort, and the need for the user to aggregate information across both views.

In order to facilitate their parallel usage and aggregate and transfer information between two complementary views, these views are usually *coordinated* or *linked* [16]. Common techniques for linking are brushing-and-linking or visual lines relating data elements (e.g., [7]). In our case, we opted for brushing-and-linking as it is the more flexible and widely used technique to work with coordinated views.

STUDY 1: EDGE-WEIGHTED ENCODING IN MATRICES

Our first study searches for an effective and efficient way to encode edge weights in adjacency matrices. We wanted to find an encoding that would support tasks on two levels: *overview tasks* that include spotting dense regions and finding anomalies, and *detailed tasks* that involve decoding and comparing weights for individual edges. For our study, we selected visual encodings that try to support tasks on both levels.

Encoding Techniques

Links in adjacency matrices are represented by marks in the matrix cells. For overview tasks, to detect patterns quickly within the matrix, an encoding should be pre-attentive. For detailed tasks the encoding should allow the reader to make precise assertions about the encoded value. We assembled eight techniques for our study including both encodings commonly used (e.g., [3, 8, 1, 18]) and a couple that we have not seen used in this context before (*Ff*, *BT2*, see below). The selection of these eight encodings followed discussions and pilot tests and is shown detailed in Figure 2:

- **Circle (Ci):** Edge weight is mapped linearly to the radius of a circle sitting inside matrix cells. In both this encoding and the next, a length-channel encoding is preferred over area following information visualisation standard practice informed by Stevens [21].
- **Square (Sq):** Edge weight is mapped to the size (side length) of a square inside each matrix cell, increasing linearly with edge weight.
- **Bar (Ba):** Similar to *Square*, data values are mapped to the size of the bar. Bars are aligned to the bottom line of the cell and bar height encodes edge weight [3, 18]. Cells with an edge weight of 0 are empty, cells of weight 1 are complete.
- **Opacity (Op)**: Edge weight is mapped to cell opacity between values 0 and 1.
- **Fatfonts (Ff):** Fatfonts encode data redundantly; as numerical value, and by the boldness of the font face that is used to render the numerical value [15]. Larger data values appear as thicker numbers.
- **Hatch (Ha):** Hatching fills the matrix cell with a diagonal line pattern [3, 18]. Similar to fatfonts, hatching can be use for pre-attentive encoding (cell-darkness) and to encode precise values as the number of diagonal lines.
- **Background Transparency 1 (BT1):** This technique is a combination of *Square* and *Opacity* encoding; in addition to square size, edge weight is encoded redundantly in the darkness of the cell-background. It has been used by Alper et al. [1] in a slightly different context. Lower edge weights are represented by a small square in the cell center and a light cell background. Larger values are represented by large black squares and dark cell backgrounds. Edge values of 1 result in entirely dark cells.
- **Background Transparency 2 (BT2):** This encoding is a variation of *Background Transparency 1.* Edge weights larger than 0.5 show a white background. The rational for this encoding is that it may be hard to perceive the size of black squares on a dark background.

Tasks

Detailed task: *edge-weight comparison.* *Given four highlighted cells (two with a blue frame and two with a red frame), which pair has the larger sum of cell weights?* Participants completed this task in four steps: (1) they needed to visually identify all highlighted blue and red cells; (2), they needed to assess the weight of each cell in each colour; and (3) they needed to estimate the aggregated value.

Overview task: *cluster-weight comparison.* *Given two highlighted areas (one marked as blue and one marked as red), which area has the larger sum of cell weights?* Participants completed this task in one step: they needed to estimate which coloured region contained higher aggregated edge weights (in most of our encodings this translated into assessing the overall darkness of a region.)

Both tasks offered the same answer possibilities. Once a participant felt comfortable with the answer, he/she pressed the space-bar; the matrix would vanish, the timing stopped, and participants were presented with a list of possible answers: *blue, red, too difficult, I don't know*. Participants were instructed to vote "too difficult" if they felt their confidence was too low because they could not make proper comparisons. If participants were able to read the encoding but could not make an informed decision, they were told to vote "I don't know", in order to avoid guessing.

Data

We generated data in order to control data characteristics such as edge weights and their distribution. Edge weight varied between 0 and 1, in increments of .2, resulting in 6 levels. We generated networks with a fixed size of 30 nodes and two clusters, as indicated in Figure 2. One cluster was large and homogeneous, the smaller cluster was less homogeneous. For each network, edge weight was altered by a random function.

Participants and Setting

We recruited 19 participants (7 female, 12 male), all with normal or corrected-to-normal vision and without any colour vision impairment. Participants included university students and research staff. 11 participants were familiar with information visualisation, 8 participants where familiar with node-link diagrams. No participant was familiar with matrix visualisations. The study was run on an Intel Core i7 Surface Pro 3 and a 27 inch flat screen (resolution: 3840 $\times$ 2160). The visualisation area was centred in a full size window.

Design

We used a within-subject, full-factorial design: 8 techniques $\times$ 2 tasks $\times$ 18 trials. 18 trials included 3 training trials in the beginning of each condition (technique $\times$ task). The remaining 15 trials contained 3 levels of difficulty (5 $\times$ easy, 5 $\times$ Medium, 5 $\times$ difficult). Difficulty was introduced by edge density, the size of the selection area, and the value difference of selected areas. Each of the 18 trials showed one of the 18 networks, in fixed order and with increasing difficulty. Time per trial was limited to 20 seconds: thus, participants had insufficient time to calculate the sum of edge weights precisely by looking at the legend provided. Rather, they had to compare based on visual impression. For each trial, we measured error and task completion time. After the experiment, participants were asked to rank encodings according to their preference.

Order of techniques was randomised. Before each condition (technique $\times$ task), we instructed participants on the respective task and technique. Then, participants concluded the 3 training trials under supervision and were invited to ask questions. While training was not timed, to limit study duration and participant fatigue, each trial was limited to 20 seconds. After 20 seconds, the matrix was hidden and the participant had to enter his/her response. Excluding training, we resulted in a total of 240 trials per participant.

We had two null-hypotheses for this study:

- H_0: There is no difference in mean error between techniques.

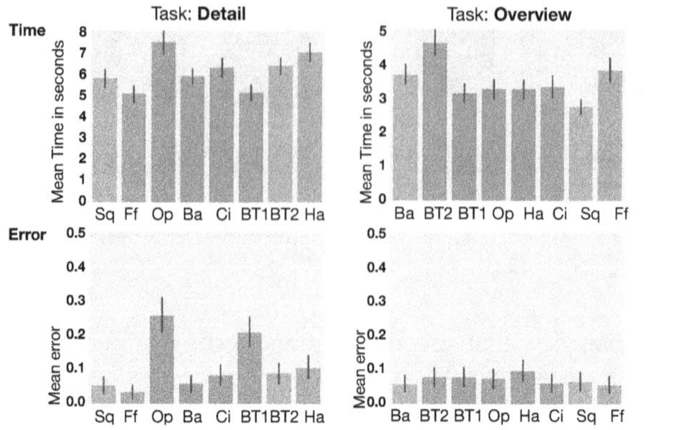

Figure 3. Results for Study 1 (Matrix encoding): task-completion *time* (top) and *error* (bottom). Error bars indicate 95% CI.

- H_1: There is no difference in mean task-completion time between techniques.

Results and Discussion

For the analysis, we removed all samples where participants took less then 1 second, as we considered these samples invalid. This left us with 8908 valid samples (out of 9120 recorded samples, training excluded). Removing samples lead to unequal sample sizes; also, we found that time and error data did not follow a normal distribution and could not be corrected. Therefore, we used the non-parametric *Whitney-Mann-U test* for unequal sample sizes.

***Error*:** Results for error are shown in Figure 3-top. We found significant difference ($p<0.05$) between almost all pairs of techniques, leading us to reject H_0. For the *detailed-task* we found *fatfonts* and *square* to be most accurate (M=0.04 and M=0.06), and *opacity* and *BT1* to be least accurate (M=0.31 and M=0.25). For the *overview-task* we found significant difference only for *hatching*, being the least accurate technique (M=0.11). The most accurate technique on average for this task was *fatfonts* (M=0.06).

***Completion Time*:** Results for completion time are plotted in Figure 3-bottom. We found significances ($p<0.05$) between almost all techniques, rejecting H_1. For the *detailed-task* we found *FatFonts* and *BT1* to be fastest (M=5.0s, SD=3.3 and M=5.0s, SD = 3.5) and *opacity* to be slowest (M=7.7s, SD=4.3). For the *overview-task*, we found *square* and *circle* to be fastest (2.6sec, SD=1.7 and 3.1sec, SD=2.5 no significant difference) and *BT1* and *fatfonts* to be slowest (4.4sec, SD=3.4 and 3.7sec, SD=2.9). The fastest technique (*square*) was 1.57 times faster than the slowest technique (*BT1*).

User preference: Users rated their preference on an 8-point scale ranging from 0 (strongly dislike) to 7 (strongly like). We analysed these ratings using a z-test. We analysed these ratings using a pairwise one-tailed Wilcoxon signed-rank test (with a Bonferroni correction for multiple comparisons) to determine which methods are significantly preferred over the others in the detailed and the overview tasks. We found that in the detailed task, *fatfonts* and *square* are the two most preferred methods. The preference rank changed in the overview task with *square* remaining the top.

Our goal with this study was to find an encoding that performs well across our two tasks (*detailed* and *overview*) with respect to time and error. Results suggest that there is no one encoding scoring best across all tasks but that *square* performed well in all independent measures: *time*, *error*, and *user preference*. Therefore, we decided to use *square* encoding for our two following studies.

STUDY 2: MATRIX AND NODE-LINK DIAGRAM

In a first study on perceptually complementary views, we were interested in the effectiveness of Node-link, Matrix, and a combined side-by-side representation of both Node-link and Matrix, for weighted network exploration.

Techniques

- ***Node-link* (NL):** Nodes are encoded as gray circles and edges as straight lines, laid out using WebCoLa [9]. Edge weight is encoded by line-thickness (Fig. 4 (left)).
- ***Matrix* (M):** According to the results from experiment 1, we use the square encoding to encode edge weight (Fig. 4 (right)). We used optimal leaf ordering to automatically order rows and columns in the matrices.
- ***Combined* (C):** The *Node-link* and *Matrix* views were presented side-by-side, coordinated through brushing-and-linking: i.e. hovering on a circle/row/column/cell/node/link highlights its counterpart element in the complementary view. (Fig. 4)

Tasks

We generated four representative tasks, each aiming to test for different aspects of network data and complementary views.

- ***Two-hop***: *In a train network, find the cheapest route from RED node to BLUE node.* This task translates into finding the path with the lowest overall edge weight between the two highlighted nodes. The target path contained always two hops (2 links) for this task. In *Node-link*, users had to search for narrow lines between nodes, in *Matrix* participants had to find the row with the smallest two squares (summed size) while comparing the two columns representing both highlighted nodes. In *Combined*, we hypothesised participants would search for a set of potentially low-weighted paths in the Node-link view, and then check the path weights in the matrix view. Answers involved a set of candidate paths as well as *"None of the above"* and *"Too difficult"*.
- ***Highest-degree***: *In a social network, find out which person has the most contact with other people.* This task translates into finding the most connected node (highest degree) with the strongest connections. In *Node-link*, participants had to find the node with the thickest lines attached; in *Matrix*, participants had to find the row (or column) with the largest squares (sum of size); in *Combined*, we expected participants to start with one view and check in the other.
- ***Three-hop***: *In a train network, find the cheapest route from RED node to BLUE node.* This task was a variant of *Two-hop*, except that the shortest path included 3 links. In *Matrix*, participants had to search for 2 intermediate nodes by trying different paths. We expected *Matrix* to perform badly and that in *Combined* participants would rely on node-link.

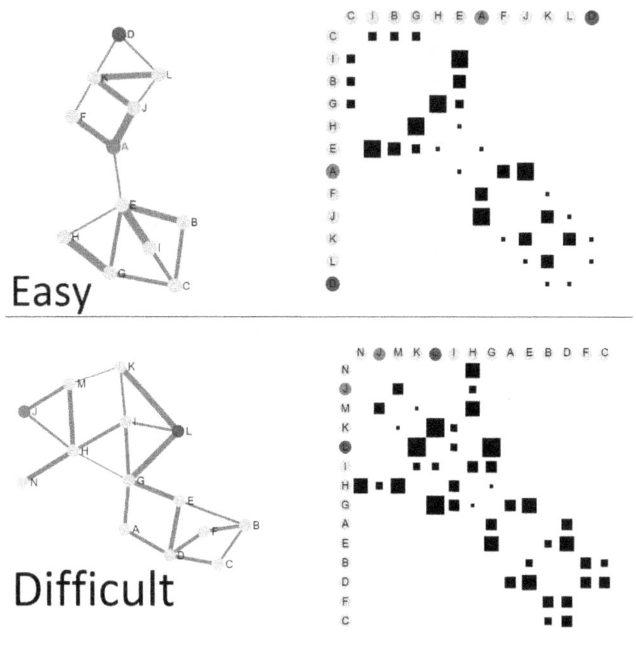

Figure 4. Samples of stimuli used in Study 2. Side-by-side node-link and matrix views with two difficulty levels. Here, participants had to find the path with the lowest cumulative edge weight between the red and blue nodes.

- ***Triangles***: *Count how many triangles are in the network.* In *Node-link*, participants counted all triples of nodes that where connected through lines; in *Combined* users had to check for triangles basically through combinations and the counting of edges. As with *Three-hop*, we expected *Matrix* to perform worse for this task and that in *Combined*, participants would rely on Node-link. Both, this task and *Three-hop* where inserted to test how do participants use complicated visualisations in a combined view setup.

Hypotheses

Based on our initial questions, stated in the introduction, we formulated three specific hypotheses.

- H_0: There is no difference in time and error across techniques, for each task (null-hypothesis).
- $H_{overall}$: *Combined* will be at least as accurate as the best of the two individual techniques *Matrix*and *Node-link*.
- $H_{combined}$: we expected *Combined* to be more accurate for *Two-hop* as participants would spot candidate paths in the node-link view, and verify path strength in the matrix view.

Data

We generated synthetic data in order to ensure the generalisability of our results. All networks had 29 nodes and a density of 5-20%. Networks were generated using Barabasi's preferential attachment method [2]. We created 3 additional datasets for training with a smaller size and density. Similar to Study 1, edge weights had 6 levels. We created 10 datasets for each trial and reused them across tasks containing 2 levels of difficulty (5 × easy, 5 × difficult). To control for difficulty level, the three conditions used the same ten networks. Labels were randomised and layout of matrix and node-link representations were rotated and mirrored differently for every trial to avoid a learning effect. Visualisation size was the same for all visualisations across all conditions. Presentation order was varied to counter-balance the learning effect. Two difficulty levels, *easy* and *difficult*, were introduced by adjusting the density of the data across the ten datasets and the differential in edge weights. Difficult datasets were two times as dense as the easier ones and featured only 10-20% difference between the correct answer the the closest alternative, while the easy datasets featured a difference of 20-60%. Examples of tasks with different difficulty levels are shown in Figure 4.

Participants and Setting

We recruited 29 participants (12 female, 17 male), all with normal or corrected-to-normal vision and without colour vision impairment. Participants included university students and researchers. The study run on an Intel Core i7 surface pro 3 and a 24-inch screen (1920 × 1080). During *Combined*, participants were equipped with a Tobii X3-120 Eye tracker, which was recalibrated at the start of each *Combined* condition. The visualisation area was centred in a full-size window and participants interacted with mouse and keyboard.

Experimental Procedure

We used a within-subject, full-factorial design: 3 techniques × 4 tasks × 13 trials. We counter-balanced the techniques, creating two groups: one group started with *Node-link* and *Matrix* (*trained*), while the other group started with *Combined* (*untrained*). We were interested in usage and performance if users are trained on both views individually, before using the combined views. There were 13 trials including 3 training trials at the start of each condition (technique × task). Each trial showed a different network, increasing in difficulty, and we measured accuracy and task completion time.

Before the controlled experiment, we instructed participants about the visualisations as well as the edge weights used in each trial, making sure none of them had any vision problems. We ask them to complete tasks as accurately and quickly as possible. Before recording the trials, three training trials were provided. Participants were guided to complete the first training task with explanation from the instructor. They answered the remaining training trials on their own unless they had any questions. Order of encoding techniques were randomised. Before each condition (technique × task), we instructed each participant on the respective task and technique. Then, participants concluded the three training trials under supervision and could ask questions. While training was not timed, we limited the time in the remaining 10 trials to 20 seconds (30 seconds for *Three-hop*) in order to avoid participants being too careful in counting and calculating. Participants were notified before the experiment and a timer progress bar was displayed on the top of the screen. To answer the trials, participants pressed the space bar to view the answer options. At that point, the timer stopped and the visualisation disappeared.

Results

For each of our 4 tasks, we obtained 10 trials × 3 techniques × 29 participants = 870 trials (3480 trials in total). We removed 2 trials that had a task-completion time inferior than 1 second as we considered them accidental clicks on the space-bar. We counted the answers '*Too difficult*' and '*None of above*' as error. Reported times are for correct answers only. We decided to keep trials where the participant had hit the time limit for each task as participants were still able to give an answer and we were more interested in accuracy than in completion time. We rerun our analysis removing those turnout-trials but found the results the same with respect to significances and ranking of technique performance.

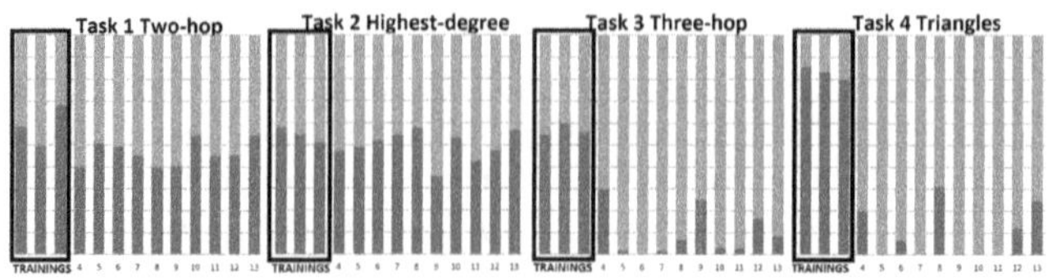

Figure 5. Relative duration (bar-height) spent looking at each view in *Combined*: orange=node-link view, blue=matrix view. Numbers indicate trials. The first 3 trials were training.

Tech.	Measure	*Two-hop*	H.-degree	*Three-hop*	*Triangles*
Time	*Node-link*	***7.8**	***12.6**	***11.4**	***6.2**
	Matrix	*9.9	13.6	*23.7	*18.7
	Combined	*11.2	13.8	*13.5	*7.6
Error	*Node-link*	0.07	*0.20	**0.13**	**0.11**
	Matrix	0.10	**0.11**	*0.40	*0.48
	Combined	0.07	**0.12**	**0.16**	**0.14**

Table 1. Mean results across techniques. Stars indicate values that are significantly different from the other two. Bold values indicate the significantly lowest (best) values.

After cleaning our data, we found time and error measures to be *not* normally distributed and we could not correct this using any standard transformation (Box Cox transformation, log-transformation). We made sure that this was not an artifact of including trials that hit the time-limit. Time and errors were analysed individually for each task. Using the non-parametric FRIEDMANS' TEST for one-way factorial analysis between techniques per test with a significance level of $p < 0.05$. For pair-wise comparison, we used MANN WHITNEY U TEST as removing trials resulted in unequal sample sizes. We did not find any effect of task difficulty on time or error.

In the following, we report on results with a significance level of $p < 0.05$ (*), $p < 0.01$ (**), and $p \leq 0.001$ (***), for each task individually. Numbers in brackets indicate mean values in seconds (time) and mean-errors. Results are summarised in Table 1 and Figure 6.

Eye-tracking data: For each trial in *Combined* we measured the duration spend looking at each view (Figure 5). We also observed eye-tracking data individually for each participant and identified three main strategies (Figure 1): (a) participants sticking to one view to solve the task (exclusive use), (b) participants using both but spending a long time on each view (sequential use) and (c) participants switching frequently between both views (parallel use). We refer back to these strategies, for each task individually.

***Two-hop*:** For *time*, high significance (**) was found between all techniques; *Node-link* was fastest (7.8sec, SD=3.9), *Ma-*

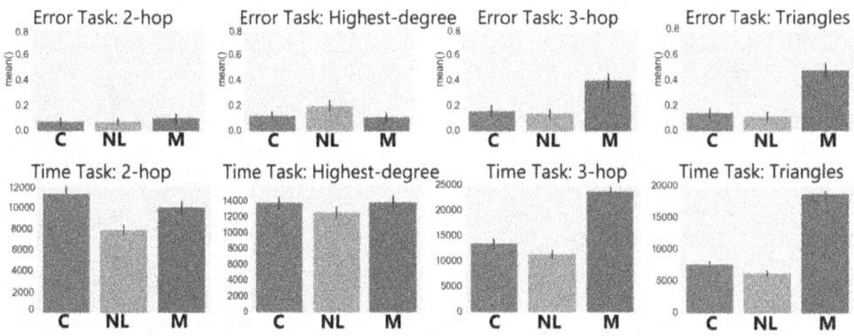

Figure 6. Results for Study 2 (Matrix–Node-link): *error* (top) and *time* (bottom) for all techniques.

trix ranking in the middle (9.9sec, SD=4.4) and *Combined* was slowest (11.2sec, SD=5.5). For *error*, FRIEDMANS' TEST did *not* found any significant difference between *Node-link* and *Combined* both having 0.07 errors on average, and *Matrix* with 0.1 error on average. These results do not support $H_{combined}$, though supporting at least $H_{overall}$. Time was surprisingly higher for *Combined* than for *Node-link*, the fastest individual view for this task. Eye-tracking data suggested that participants spend an equal amount of time looking at each view relying on both strategies: sequential and parallel (Figure 5).

Highest-degree: For *time*, we found *Node-link* to be significantly faster (**), though at a very narrow margin; 12.6sec, SD=5.45 for *Node-link*, and 13.9sec, SD=5.7 for *Matrix* and 13.8sec, SD=5.4 for *Combined*. For *errors*, we found significance (**) for *Node-link* (0.2) being about twice as inaccurate as *Matrix* (0.11) and *Combined* (0.12). Again, we found support for $H_{overall}$ but contradict H_0, with the same result as *Two-hop* that Combined did not increase performance. However, *Combined* was not very much slower than *Matrix*. Surprisingly, participants where faster with *Node-link* but yielded more errors. This may suggest an effect of false confidence in a technique well known by participants. Eye-tracking data shows a similar pattern as for *Two-hop*; participants spend roughly the same time on looking at both views.

Three-hop: For time, we found significance (**) between all techniques; *Matrix* was slowest (23.7sec, SD=6.4), *Node-link* fastest (11.4sec, SD=6.4), and *Combined* (13.5sec, SD=7.7) slightly slower than *Node-link*. With *Matrix*, participants hit the time limit in 35% of the trials (98 out of 280). We conjecture that some participants did this on purpose in order to have more time to solve the task. For *error*, we found *Matrix* (0.4) to be significantly (***) less accurate than *Node-link* (0.13) and and *Combined* (0.16). We expected *Matrix* to be slowest and less accurate due to increased cognitive effort in finding the three hops. Again, our results support $H_{overall}$ and contradict H_0. The eye-tracking data for *Combined* (Figure 5(c)) shows that during training with *Combined* participants spend about the same amount of time on both views. However, after training (trials 1-3), participants mainly decided to work with mostly the Node-link view using an exclusive strategy.

Triangles: For time, we found significance (***) between all techniques: *Node-link* was fastest (6.2sec, SD=3.2), followed by *Combined* (7.6sec, SD=4.7) and *Matrix* was slowest (18.7sec, SD=2.7). Similar to *Three-hop*, we found a high rate of time-turnouts: 39% (111 out of 280) of trials showed participants hitting the time limit. For error, we found *Matrix* (0.48) significantly (***) worse than the other two techniques (*Node-link* 0.11, *Combined* 0.14). Again, these results support $H_{overall}$. During training in *Combined*, participants did spend a larger amount of time on the matrix view, however relying almost exclusively on the node-link view. One participant used the matrix view for the first few trials after training but then switched to node-link and one participant exclusively used the matrix view.

Technique:	*Node-link*	*Matrix*	*Combined*
Percentage using view in *Combined*	44%	5%	53%
User Preference:	34.48%	13.79%	51.72%

Table 2. View usage and user preferences in study 2.

View Use: Based on the eye-tracking data, visualised as shown in Figure 5, we counted the number of participants using both views, and those exclusively using one of the two views. Results are summarised in Table 2. When we compared the actual task performance for each of these user groups, but could not find any significant difference, for no task. Yet, mean-error rate for users actively switching between both views was slightly higher. We also compared strategies of users who started with *Combined* (*trained* group), against those who started with the individual views and were already trained in both views. We found that participants starting with *Combined* had a learning curve to find their strategy. Eventually, participants from this group consistently used both views. However, participants who used *Combined* last had a clear preference and were more likely to stick to one visualisation. In these cases, node-link was generally preferred for task *Three-hop*, and *Triangles* task. Even those participants who generally preferred matrix were more likely to check their guess with node-link.

Overall User Preferences: After the study, we asked each participant which visualisation technique they did most prefer overall. *Combined* was most preferred by half of the participants (51.72%), *Matrix* was the least preferred (13.79%) and *Node-link* ranking in between (34.48%). We can see this as evidence that users felt more comfortable with both views. However, half of the participants where fine with a single view and did not seem to prefer multiple views.

Discussion

Our study aimed to assess for which tasks the individual techniques differ in performance (Q1), what is the effect of showing both views side-by-side (*Combined*) (Q2, $H_{overall}$, $H_{combined}$), and which strategies participants employ while working with two views (Q3). For the two tasks that were comparable to Ghoniem's *et al.* [10] path-following task (two-hop, three-hop) we confirmed their findings. However, our study involves weighted edges, ordered matrices, and both visualisations simultaneous.

Node-link vs. Matrix (Q1) A task-by-task analysis revealed significant differences between techniques for individual tasks, i.e. the choice of technique influences accuracy and time. Thus we can reject H_0. We found there may be general bias towards *Node-link*, being the more familiar visualisation technique. We found each *Matrix* and *Node-link* are each better for different tasks. Yet, overall, we found more positive results and user preferences for *Node-link*. Thus, we conjecture both individual views to be complementary in their overall use.

Performance of Combined (Q2) Half of the participants (51.72%) preferred working with the *Combined* condition. The overall preference for *Combined* and the number of participants using both views, supports this complementariness. For *Combined*, we did not find a significant effect proving that side-by-side views increase error compared to the individual techniques. We can still accept $H_{overall}$ but have to reject $H_{combined}$. Our eye-tracking data suggests that participants use both views when they are provided with the opportunity and in many cases use both views, independent from whether there is one view that is clearly better (e.g. tasks *Three-hop*, *Triangles*). However, in general, if participants found one view is clearly better, they tended to mainly use this view.

User Strategies (Q3) Only half of the participants actively switched between both views, when provided with *Combined* and switching had no effect on the performance. For tasks *Three-hop* and *Triangles*, the eye-tracking data suggests that participants were correctly using the better visualisation (*Node-link* in both cases). We could not observe the same effect for *Highest-degree*, as participants spend the same amount of time on both views, though *Matrix* was significantly more accurate. Though the difference between *Node-link* and *Matrix* was of the amplitude of 2, we have several hypothesis; participants may either: a) not have noticed a difference in accuracy; b) felt more confident with the node-link visualisation; or c) used the second visualisation for cross-checking.

STUDY 3: MATRIXWAVE AND SANKEY DIAGRAM

In our third and last study, we extended our investigations to complementary views for flows between nodes in a networks over several timesteps. We compared two visualisations commonly used for this task; MatrixWave [26] and Sankey diagrams [19]. As in our Study 2, we recorded eye-tracking data for every participant in the *Combined* condition.

Techniques

- ***Sankey*** diagrams visualise the weights of flows between nodes in a network using curved lines between vertical bars (Figure 7-right), Each bar represents a different timestep.
- ***MatrixWave*** is a zig-zag tiling of matrices showing the flow of data. Each cell in the matrix represents the volume of the flow between the corresponding two nodes (Figure 7(left)). Each matrix represents transitions between two timesteps.
- ***Combined*** shows MatrixWave and Sankey side-by-side, coordinated through brushing-and-linking; hovering on a path/rectangle/row/column/cell/node highlighting its counterpart element in both complementary views (Figure 7).

Tasks

We selected four representative tasks for each level-of-detail. We used the scenario of companies and flows of employees to better explain the tasks.

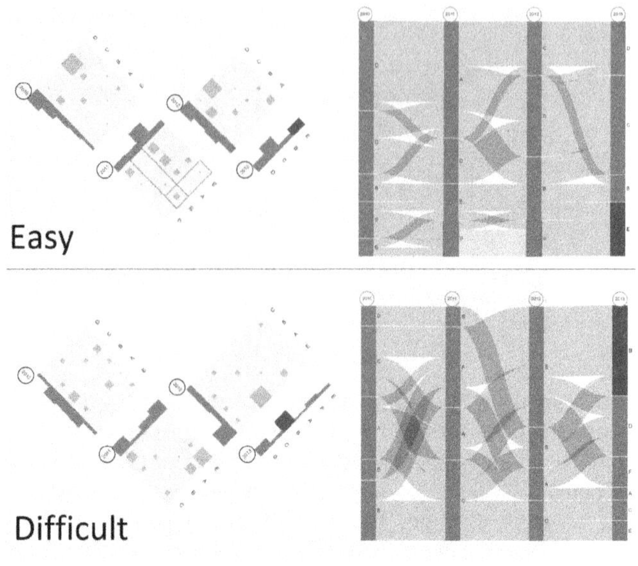

Figure 7. Examples of Easy and Difficult side-by-side view stimuli used in the *Path-following* task for Study 3. Participants need to find the most likely path from red node to blue node. The link is highlighted on both views when the mouse is hovered over any part of it.

- ***Out-link***: *For an employee working in the red organisation in 2010, which organisation are they most likely to be working for in 2013?* This task required participant to identify the largest flow over time; between the red node in the first stage (2010) and any node in the final stage (2013). Participants needed to identify and estimate the possibilities on each stage and summarise in the final stage.
- ***Largest-flow***: *Which is the largest flow in the graph?* In *Sankey*, participants had to find the link with the thickest stroke; in *MatrixWave*, participants need to identify the largest square in any matrices.
- ***Path-following***: *If someone works for the red organisation in 2010 and for the blue organisation in 2013, which organisations are they most likely to have worked at in 2011 and 2012?* This task translates into finding the strongest path between two nodes. Participants needed to locate the source and target nodes, then identify the most possible routes in the middle 2 hops (Figure 7).
- ***Return***: *Which organisation do people leave but never return to?* In this task, participants needed to quickly iterate all the nodes and verify if there is any possible path between the node in the first and last stage.

Hypotheses

Hypotheses were similar to those in Study 2, reflecting our initial questions Q1-Q3.

- H_0: There is no difference across techniques in time and error for each task.
- $H_{combined}$: *Combined* will be at least as accurate as the best of the two individual techniques (*MatrixWave*, *Sankey*).

Participants, Setting, and Data

We recruited 24 participants (9 female, 15 male). Participants were university students and staff; all of normal or corrected-to-normal vision and without any colour vision impairment. The survey equipment configuration was exactly same with

Study 2. Again, data was generated synthetically. In each dataset, there were 4 time steps, each with 4-6 nodes and 5-20 flows for each step. Flow weight was assigned randomly ranging over 6 levels. We introduced two levels of difficulty (6 × easy, 6 × difficult), varying in flow density and value difference. The same twelve graphs were used across conditions with labels and presentation order randomised, and layouts mirrored or rotated in each condition to avoid a memory effect. Visualisation size was the same in all conditions.

Experimental Procedure

We used a within-subject, full-factorial design: 3 techniques × 4 tasks × 15 trials. We counter-balanced techniques in four orders to obtain our 2 groups (*trained, untrained* as in Study 2). 15 trials per condition included 3 training trials in the beginning of each condition (technique x task). Each of the 15 trials showed one of 15 networks, in a fixed order and increasing in difficulty. For each trial, we measured accuracy and task completion time.

Experimental procedure was the same as in Study 2. Before each condition, participants concluded 3 training trials under supervision and could ask questions. While training was not timed, we limited the time in the remaining 12 trials to 20 seconds (30 seconds for *Path-following*). Participants were notified before the experiment that a timer progress bar was displayed on the top of the screen. To answer the trials, participants pressed the space bar.

Results

Similar to our second study, we analysed data for each task individually. We obtained 24 participants × 12 trials × 3 techniques = 864 trials per tasks. We found the time-out rate relatively high for this study, but decided to include these trials since time-out was consistent across techniques and depended on the task only. We repeated our analysis *excluding* these trials, and could not find major differences. Again, we found time and error not normally distributed and used FRIEDMANS' TEST for one-way analysis and MANN WHITNEY U TEST for pair-wise comparisons. Significance levels are indicated as $p < 0.05(*)$, $p < 0.01(**)$, and $p \leq 0.001(***)$. We refer to the results for each task individually, summarised in Table 3 and Figure 8.

For the eye-tracking data, we found the same three strategies as in Study 2 (Figure 1). Duration spent on each view is shown in Figure 9.

***Out-link*:** For time, we found *Sankey* significantly (**) faster (9.8s, SD=5.3s) than any of the other other two techniques (*MatrixWave*: 11.9s, SD=5.5 and *Combined*: 11.2, SD=5.9s). We did not find significant difference for error (0.09, 0.1, 0.08).

***Largest-flow*:** For time, we did not find any significant difference between *Sankey* (7s, SD=3.8) and the other techniques (6.6s, SD=3.8 for *MatrixWave* and 6.7s, SD=4.0 for *Combined*). For error, we found a slight trend (p=0.068) for *Combined* being more accurate (0.05) than *MatrixWave* (0.08) and *Sankey* (0.08). Our results contradict H_0 with respect to time, but confirm it with respect to error. We could not support $H3$. What we did find surprising was the time participants

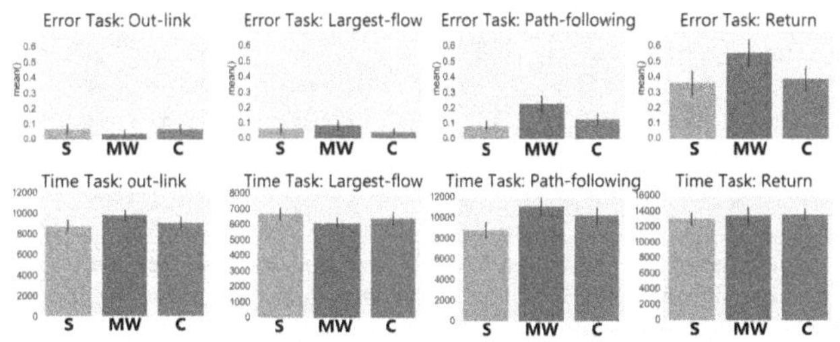

Figure 8. Results for Study 3: MatrixWave (MW), Sankey(S), and combined (D): *error* (top) and *time* (bottom) for all tasks.

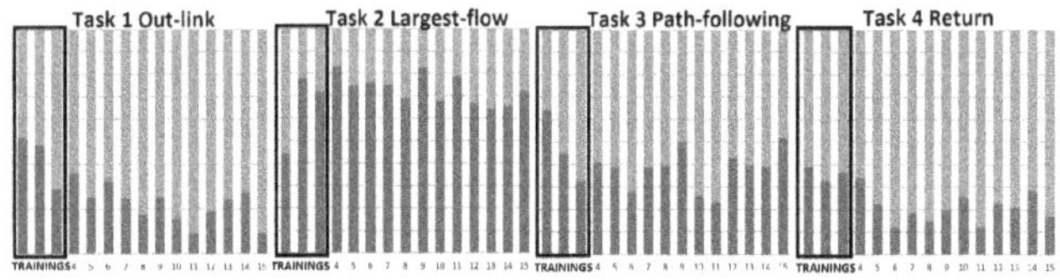

Figure 9. Overall time spent looking at each view in the *Combined* condition: orange=*Sankey*, blue=*MatrixWave*.

spend looking at each view, in *Combined*; despite *Sankey* being about as accurate as *MatrixWave*, overall participants spend much more time looking at *MatrixWave*. Eye-tracking data for *Combined* by participant showed that 4/9 exclusively used *MatrixWave* while briefly gazing over to *Sankey* (similar to Figure 1(a)). Other participants switched between views and were faster in completing the trials. We believe there is a clear advantage to switching between both views.

***Path-following*:** For time, we found significant differences between all techniques: *Sankey* was fastest (9.2s, SD=6.8), *MatrixWave* was slowest (11.6s, SD=6.81) and *Combined* ranking in between (10.8s, SD=7.0). For error, we found *MatrixWave* significantly (***) less accurate (0.24) than *Sankey* (0.09) and *Combined* (0.12). we observed a light trend (p=0.068) between *Combined* and *Sankey*. These results support both hypothesis; H_0 as we did found *Sankey* to be more accurate than *Matrix*, and $H_{combined}$. Individual eye-tracking revealed most participants employing a sequential strategy, 2 used a parallel strategy, and 1 exclusively used *MatrixWave*. We hypothesise that participants searched for the path in MatrixWave and quickly confirmed via Sankey.

***Return*:** For time, we found no significant difference between techniques. We conclude that the time limit was too short and too many participants ran out of time. Though the error rate was generally high for each technique (*Sankey*: 0.36, *MatrixWave*: 0.55, *Combined*: 0.39) we found a significant difference (***) for *Matrix* being most inaccurate, but found no difference between *Sankey* and *Combined*. Again, these results contradict H_0, but support $H_{combined}$. Similar to *Path-following*, the difference in error was high between *Sankey* and *MatrixWave*, but still participants spend some significant amount of time looking at *MatrixWave*. The individual data revealed that all participants used the sequential strategy.

View Use: Comparing the performance of participants in *Combined* by view use (Sankey-exclusive, MatrixWave-exclusive, and both) we did not find any significant difference but

Tech.	Measure	*Out-link*	Larg.-flow	Path-foll.	*Return*
Time	*Sankey*	***9.8s**	7.0s	***9.2s**	16.3s
	MatrixWave	11.9s	6.6s	*11.6s	16.8s
	Combined	11.2s	6.7s	*10.8s	16.5s
Error	*Sankey*	0.09	0.08	**0.09**	**0.37**
	MatrixWave	0.10	0.08	*0.24	*0.56
	Combined	0.08	0.05	0.12	0.40

Table 3. Study 3: mean results across techniques. Stars indicate values that are significant different from the two other. Bold values indicate the significantly lowest (best) values.

Technique:	*Sankey*	*MatrixWave*	*Combined*
User Preference:	54.17%	12.50%	33.33%
Percentage using view in *Combined*	47.6%	28.6%	28.8%

Table 4. View use and user preferences in study 3.

we found consistently lower error rates for those using MatrixWave. Percentages of participants using views exclusively, or relying on both views together, are given in Table 4. When comparing strategies of users starting with *Combined* (*untrained*) to those starting with the individual views (*trained*), we found very similar results to Study 2; *untrained* participants did rely on both views while *trained* participants tend to stick to one of the two views.

Discussion

Sankey vs. MatrixWave (Q1): Compared to Matrix and Node-link in Study 2, complementaryness of *Sankey* and *MatrixWave* was not as strongly evident. We can still reject H_0, and found *MatrixWave* to result in more errors than *Sankey*. In a way, this contradicts the results found in [26]. However, study set-up, tasks, and data sets varied across studies. Our data sets were smaller and their tasks were about comparisons.

Performance of Combined (Q2): We can confirm that *Combined* was always as good as the best of the individual techniques (accepting $H_{combined}$). However, *Combined* was never more accurate than any individual techniques. Similar to Study 2, we did not find any difference in performance for people using both views together or exclusively using one view in the the *Combined* condition.

User Strategies (Q3): Contrary to our findings from Study 2, more participants preferred one of the individual views, than the combined one. *Sankey* was preferred by more than half of the participants, while *Matrix* was ranked last. These results are in accordance with the measures we found for performance. We also think that combing *Sankey* and *MatrixWave* resulted in an increased visual complexity, which for users did not pay off. Still, a combined display attracted much greater preference than a single matrix and most participants used both views in a sequential manner (25/36 cases). Only 6/36 cases used *MatrixWave* exclusively.

SUMMARY AND CONCLUSIONS

We set out to explore the effect of perceptually complementary views for visualising weighted networks and event flows. Within the limits of our tested conditions, we can summarise our findings as follows:

Square and FatFonts are good choices for encoding edge weights in matrices. Both encodings performed well for our tasks and attracted a high user rating. The widely used opacity encodings performed badly for detailed value comparison.

Combined views are not worse than individual views. We found coordinated views as good as individual views and participants did not take longer to work with them. We see this as evidence that participants are able to chose the more performant view. However, we did not find evidence that combined views are more accurate for our tested tasks. More complex and compound tasks may yield different effects. However, studies involving more complex tasks also involve different strategies and require more experienced users. Both may increase result variability.

Trained users tend to stick to the view of their preference. Users new to combined views tend to explore both views and try to solve the task with both views. Users trained in (both) individual views tend to use individual views on a per-task basis. Our participants, though untrained in *each* of our tested visualisations, were quickly able to decide on the better view for a certain task. As we did not obtain bad results about combined views, both for time, error, and user preference, our results generally support the use of perceptually complementary views for network visualisation tasks.

FUTURE WORK

In future, we want to extend our studies towards other perceptually complementary views as well as informationally complementary visualisations, e.g., for tree and hierarchical data and dynamic networks (e.g., views showing topology combined with views showing temporal evolution for dynamic networks).

Future investigation is needed to understand how to measure the degree of perceptual complementariness of two representations. Compressing side-by-side complementary views into hybrid techniques is an interesting direction for future research. There is currently no empirical evaluation of hybrid techniques such as NodeTrix [13] and MatLink [12]. Eventually, we aim to identify tasks where perceptually complementary views actually improve task accuracy and/or completion time.

ACKNOWLEDGEMENTS

This research was supported under Australian Research Council's Discovery Projects funding scheme (project number DP140100077).

REFERENCES

1. Basak Alper, Benjamin Bach, Nathalie Henry Riche, Tobias Isenberg, and Jean-Daniel Fekete. 2013. Weighted graph comparison techniques for brain connectivity analysis. In *Proceedings of the ACM SIGCHI Conference on Human Factors in Computing Systems (CHI)*. ACM, 483–492.
2. Albert-László Barabási and Réka Albert. 1999. Emergence of scaling in random networks. *Science* 286, 5439 (1999), 509–512.
3. Jacques Bertin. 1973. Sémiologie graphique: Les diagrammes-Les réseaux-Les cartes. (1973).
4. Anastasia Bezerianos, Pierre Dragicevic, Jean-Daniel Fekete, Juhee Bae, and Ben Watson. 2010. Geneaquilts: A system for exploring large genealogies. *IEEE Transactions on Visualization and Computer Graphics* 16, 6 (2010), 1073–1081.
5. Michael Bostock. 2012. D3. js. *Data Driven Documents* (2012).
6. Stuart K Card, Jock D Mackinlay, and Ben Shneiderman. 1999. Readings in information visualization: using vision to think. (1999).
7. Christopher Collins and Sheelagh Carpendale. 2007. VisLink: Revealing relationships amongst visualizations. *IEEE Transactions on Visualization and Computer Graphics* 13, 6 (2007), 1192–1199.
8. Antoine de Falguerolles, Felix Friedrich, Günther Sawitzki, and StatLab Heidelberg. 1997. A tribute to J. Bertin's graphical data analysis. *SoftStat* 97 (1997), 11–20.
9. Tim Dwyer. 2016. Constraint-Based Layout in the Browser: WebCoLa. `http://marvl.infotech.monash.edu/webcola/`. (2016). Accessed: 2016-08-08.
10. Mohammad Ghoniem, J-D Fekete, and Philippe Castagliola. 2004. A comparison of the readability of graphs using node-link and matrix-based representations. In *Proceedings of IEEE Symposium on Information Visualization, 2004 (InfoVis)*. IEEE, 17–24.
11. Nathalie Henry and Jean-Daniel Fekete. 2006. MatrixExplorer: a dual-representation system to explore social networks. *IEEE Transactions on Visualization and Computer Graphics* 12, 5 (2006), 677–684.
12. Nathalie Henry and Jean-Daniel Fekete. 2007. Matlink: Enhanced matrix visualization for analyzing social networks. In *IFIP Conference on Human-Computer Interaction*. Springer, 288–302.
13. Nathalie Henry, Jean-Daniel Fekete, and Michael J McGuffin. 2007. NodeTrix: a hybrid visualization of social networks. *IEEE transactions on visualization and computer graphics* 13, 6 (2007), 1302–1309.
14. René Keller, Claudia M Eckert, and P John Clarkson. 2006. Matrices or node-link diagrams: which visual representation is better for visualising connectivity models? *Information Visualization* 5, 1 (2006), 62–76.
15. Miguel Nacenta, Uta Hinrichs, and Sheelagh Carpendale. 2012. FatFonts: combining the symbolic and visual aspects of numbers. In *Proceedings of the International Working Conference on Advanced Visual Interfaces*. ACM, 407–414.
16. Chris North and Ben Shneiderman. 1997. A taxonomy of multiple window coordination. (1997).
17. Lucy Nowell, Robert Schulman, and Deborah Hix. 2002. Graphical encoding for information visualization: an empirical study. In *Information Visualization, 2002. INFOVIS 2002. IEEE Symposium on*. IEEE, 43–50.
18. Charles Perin, Pierre Dragicevic, and Jean-Daniel Fekete. 2014. Revisiting bertin matrices: New interactions for crafting tabular visualizations. *IEEE transactions on visualization and computer graphics* 20, 12 (2014), 2082–2091.
19. Patrick Riehmann, Manfred Hanfler, and Bernd Froehlich. 2005. Interactive sankey diagrams. In *Proceedings of IEEE Symposium on Information Visualization, 2005. (InfoVis)*. IEEE, 233–240.
20. Jonathan C Roberts. 2007. State of the art: Coordinated & multiple views in exploratory visualization. In *Proceedings of International Conference on Coordinated and Multiple Views in Exploratory Visualization, 2007.* IEEE, 61–71.
21. Stanley S Stevens. 1971. Issues in psychophysical measurement. *Psychological review* 78, 5 (1971), 426.
22. Matthew Tobiasz, Petra Isenberg, and Sheelagh Carpendale. 2009. Lark: Coordinating co-located collaboration with information visualization. *IEEE transactions on visualization and computer graphics* 15, 6 (2009), 1065–1072.
23. Michelle Q. Wang Baldonado, Allison Woodruff, and Allan Kuchinsky. 2000. Guidelines for Using Multiple Views in Information Visualization. In *Proceedings of the Working Conference on Advanced Visual Interfaces (AVI '00)*. ACM, New York, NY, USA, 110–119. DOI: `http://dx.doi.org/10.1145/345513.345271`
24. Krist Wongsuphasawat and David Gotz. 2012. Exploring flow, factors, and outcomes of temporal event sequences with the outflow visualization. *IEEE Transactions on Visualization and Computer Graphics* 18, 12 (2012), 2659–2668.
25. Jiaje Zhang and Donald A Norman. 1994. Representations in distributed cognitive tasks. *Cognitive science* 18, 1 (1994), 87–122.
26. Jian Zhao, Zhicheng Liu, Mira Dontcheva, Aaron Hertzmann, and Alan Wilson. 2015. MatrixWave: Visual comparison of event sequence data. In *Proceedings of the ACM SIGCHI Conference on Human Factors in Computing Systems*. ACM, 259–268.

How Design-inclusive UXR Influenced the Integration of Project Activities: Three Design Cases from Industry

Janne van Kollenburg[1,2], Sander Bogers[2,1], Eva Deckers[1], Joep Frens[2], Caroline Hummels[2]

[1] Philips Design,
Eindhoven, The Netherlands
{janne.van.kollenburg,eva.deckers}@philips.com

[2] Eindhoven University of Technology,
Eindhoven, The Netherlands
{s.j.a.bogers, j.w.frens, c.m.m.hummels}@tue.nl

ABSTRACT
In this paper, we discuss how the implementation of design-inclusive User Experience Research (UXR) has influenced the composition of UXR and design activities in the industrial setting of Philips Design. We present three design case studies that were executed in a time span of three years: a baby sleep project; a pregnancy project; and a baby bottle-feeding project. Through a retrospective analysis we conclude that the approach adopted in these cases progressed from complete separation of UXR and design activities to design-inclusive UXR in which design forms an integral part of research. This is reflected by a rearrangement of project activities to *identify*, *envision*, *enable* and *evaluate* user experiences. Previously the UXR (*identify* and *evaluate*) and design (*envision* and *enable*) activities were executed sequentially. Now, these four project activities merge in studying design interventions in context over a prolonged time, to iteratively explore and advance UX design qualities.

Author Keywords
User Experience Research; Design-Inclusive User Experience Research; Design; Activities; Design Processes; Personalized Systems; Case Studies; Design Practice; Philips; Industry.

ACM Classification Keywords
H.5.2. User Interfaces: User Centered Design, Theory and Methods

INTRODUCTION
Over the years, the design space expanded to digitally driven products, services and systems that are interactive and connected. These solutions have the ability to move away from market-segment based solutions [21], that are tailored to a group of people, and become personal solutions [3, 8, 25] that are user, usage and context dependent [24].

CHI 2017, May 06 - 11, 2017, Denver, CO, USA

ACM 978-1-4503-4655-9/17/05...$15.00
DOI: http://dx.doi.org/10.1145/3025453.3025541

An example is Philips Hue [16], a connected light bulb which behavior can be programmed according personal preferences. The interaction can be context dependent (i.e. it can change color according weather conditions), usage dependent (i.e. it can learn about routines) and user dependent (i.e. it can adapt light settings to users in the room). We argue that designing for systemic solutions with high interactivity, context dependency and personalized uniqueness increases complexity. In the remainder of this paper we refer to these solutions as *personalized systems*.

User Experience Research (UXR) is challenged by these personalized systems as they operate in a design space with innate complexity. To cope with this complexity the UXR community articulates a design-inclusive approach to UXR [5, 7, 12, 22, 26]. Design-inclusive UXR proposes an active role for design prototypes as an enabler of experiences and a vehicle for asking questions in the established UXR methods, such as focus groups, questionnaires, contextual experiments and interviews. Following Vermeeren et al [26], design-inclusive UXR is "*UXR where design activities form an integral part of the research, that is, design as a part of, and contributing to UXR*" (p.22). Gaining user experience insights that are directly related to embodied design opportunities (prototypes) has two benefits: firstly, it helps to frame and gain insight into the user experiences which are otherwise hard to grasp, and secondly it iteratively advances the design itself [26].

We recognize the potential of design-inclusive UXR, as introduced by Vermeeren et al., in designing personalized systems and the role design can play in this [26]. However, current literature only lightly touches upon structuring and composing activities in the UXR processes to facilitate design-inclusive UXR. Therefore, we see value in sharing our experience of applying design-inclusive UXR in practice. Exemplified through three cases studies, that were executed at Philips Design over a timespan of three years, we reflect on the changing composition of UXR and design activities. By sharing our retrospective analysis, we set out to the CHI community to, in collaboration, formalize the application and integration of design-inclusive UXR in industry projects.

BACKGROUND & RELATED WORK

In our understanding one can distinguish two perspectives on the integration of design and UXR: (1) research into involving design in UXR and; (2) research that sets out to involve UXR (qualities) in design.

Design in User Experience Research

Over time multiple perspectives arose on what user experiences entail. We follow Hassenzahl and Tractinsky [9] who reflected upon these perspectives and state that *"UX is about technology that fulfills more than just instrumental needs in a way that acknowledges it use as a subjective, situated, complex and dynamic encounter. User experience is a consequence of a user's internal state, the characteristics of the design system and the context within with the interaction occurs"* (p.95). This formulation of user experiences considers a big influence of design next to the user, the context of use and the interaction between those.

In the UXR field Vermeeren et al. [26] further underpin the potential of design in UXR through their design-inclusive UXR approach. They distill opportunities for the UXR discipline to be (more) involved in generative phases of design projects by using design prototypes as vehicles for asking questions over UX design testing in the final phases of the project only.

Van Velsen et al. [25] further highlight design-inclusive evaluation techniques tailored to personalized systems. Their work suggests (1) iterative evaluation of personalized systems by providing users with a version (prototype) of the system and suggests (2) information gathering about the usage through triangulation of subjective (qualitative) evaluation methods and data logging (a video recording of usage) [2, 10, 25, 27]. To embrace complexity, Velsen et al. suggest (3) to execute these evaluation methods in real-life settings with a longitudinal character [11, 25].

User Experience Research in design

From the design perspective a similar movement can be recognized aiming to integrate (qualities of) UXR in design activities. Methods such as co-design [19], co-reflection [23], participatory design [14], living labs [13], and Experiential Design Landscapes [3] are clear examples of this. According Zimmerman, Forlizzi & Evenson [28] the increased complexity present in current design challenges is the reason for design to move towards settings in which user, design and context come together (qualities of UXR). They highlight that complex challenges, which are often named *wicked problems* [24], do not require "*true understanding*" but "*real understanding*" and request the "*right solution*" instead of the objective or "*true solution*". In other words, they set out to find understanding that is situational and build towards a solution that resonates with that user in that context.

Design in User Experience Research and vice versa

It is distinct that design is in need for more situated experiments and explorations as their problems become ungraspable. And UXR wants to embrace complexity of experiences that are, next to the user and context also, design dependent. Therefore, these two disciplines have started to involve (parts of) the other discipline.

The arguments for involving UXR in design and vice versa are clearly expressed. Vermeeren et al. [26] even literally answer the questions why it can be useful to include design in UXR and how UXR outcomes can support the design practice. What could be investigated further is *how* design-inclusive UXR can be carried out in design practice. More specifically we want to reflect how to set up and align UXR and design activities for design-inclusive UXR in an industrial context like Philips Design.

DESIGN AND UXR IN OUR COMPANY

Earlier we deliberately exaggerated the separation of the UXR and the design community to clearly outline how these relate to each other. The relation between these communities is much more blurred with hybrid members being present in both communities. This is not different in industry, but the way these disciplines are organized in our corporate context is distinctive. To clarify, we briefly outline the setup of our groups and teams at Philips.

Philips, a Dutch one-century old multinational, developed itself into a company with multiple businesses, ranging from consumer to professional health related products, services and systems. The company vision is to deliver meaningful solutions that improve people's lives. To do so, we are structured in different businesses (such as Mother and Childcare, Sleep and Respiratory Care, Diagnostic Imaging, Domestic Appliances, etc.) that know the stakeholders' needs, drive sales and manage their product portfolios. Break-through innovations are not solely developed in the separate businesses but are fueled by an overarching innovation group. This group consists of two large departments: a technology/science research department (1200 employees) and a design department (400 employees). These innovations can be picked up by the separate businesses to further develop and introduce to the market.

With a strong industrial design heritage, Philips Design has come to focus on front-end innovation projects next to classical formgiving tasks. To drive people-focused innovation Philips Design has a dedicated UXR of about 30 people worldwide, group. The UXR group is appointed to gain insight in user experiences and to transfer these to designing market-potential products, services and systems that are meaningful and relevant to people. Other design teams within Philips Design take up the challenge to design these meaningful product-service systems. In-house design competences include e.g. interaction design, service design, product design, design strategy and data visualization design.

In the setup of these groups one can recognize a clear split between design and UXR disciplines. It is expected that these groups become experts in their field and bring the best to the table when coming together in multidisciplinary project teams.

At this moment, Philips is going through a radical transformation from a hardware manufacturer to a digital product service company. This requests a different approach and mindset to designing digitally driven products, services and systems, which we earlier introduced as personalized systems. The front-end innovation teams work hard to come to new ways of working that fits this digital transformation.

NAMING ACTIVITIES

Design-inclusive UXR projects that are currently presented in literature [26] do not describe how UXR and design disciplines, represented by different people, need to cooperate to embrace complexity. Neither does it tell us how the distinct design and UXR activities need to be re-arranged. This also makes that there are no activity-labels available helping us to analyze the arrangement of activities in the three case studies.

For categorization of UXR and design activities we build on Schön's *reflective practice design process* [20] steps. We choose this process as a starting point because of its iterative character where, through reflection, design opportunities and knowledge gaining go hand in hand. We recognize this as a good fit for addressing the challenges of personalized systems. This process consists of four activities: (1) *naming* the relevant factors in the situation, (2) *framing* the parameters of the problem, (3) *moving* towards a solution, (4) *evaluating* the moves and framing step. Since we approach these activities from a UXR perspective, we slightly alter the formulation of the activities to (1) *identify*, (2) *envision*, (3) *enable* and (4) *evaluate* user experiences. The *identify*-activity aims to identify opportunities for design, based on existing user experiences. The *envision*-activity has the intention to put these user experience insights in a future perspective; how do we wish to transform them? In the *enable*-activity the focus is on enabling participants to experience envisioned design concepts. In the *evaluate*-activity the earlier activities come together to evaluate the future vision through design prototypes. By renaming the original activities for UXR we aim to give more focus to the understanding of user experiences and designing for these.

CONTEXT OF CASE STUDIES

We present three case studies for which we describe their arrangement of UXR and design activities and their outcomes.From the big pool of internal Philips Design projects, we selected case studies: (a) that were executed in the past three years; (b) that aimed to design for personalized systems and thus faced the earlier outlined complexity challenges; (c) that were executed by a team of which at least one of the authors of this paper was part (to know the activity arrangement and project outcome details); (d) that had an activity arrangement which was representable for a bigger group of projects (unique project setups were excluded).

From the projects that met the inclusion criteria we selected three cases that were all executed in the same application domain (a domain of family care) making it easier to compare the projects.

In the domain of family care Philips aims to deliver health solutions anywhere on the timeline from fertility to two-year-old children. From an experience point of view, the focus is on delivering meaningful experiences, which we try to achieve by making them more personal, continuous and connected. The first project focusses on babies and their sleep, exploring service opportunities for sleep-monitoring technology. The second is a pregnancy project, which aims to design a coaching service that stimulates pregnant women to be more active. The third is a baby-feeding project, which explores how to design for personal and connected feeding experiences.

All three case studies set out to investigate or deliver a personalized system, but the arrangement of UXR and design activities varies. We will reflect upon the different cases to define what characteristics of design-inclusive UXR (earlier described in literature) they employ and what influence it has on the arrangement of design and UXR activities. To recap, design-inclusive UXR is characterized by using design as an enabler of user experiences; having design activities as integral part of research [26]; and considering user, context, design and the interaction between those when studying user experiences [9]. To evaluate design-inclusive UXR in personalized systems we review the case studies on the characteristics described by Velsen et al.: situated testing; combining qualitative methods with data logging; and having a longitudinal character [11, 25].

In a retrospective analysis, we evaluate the outcomes of the case studies through three criteria, of which two were earlier introduced as the benefits of design-inclusive UXR: (1) the level of UX insights and (2) the level to which UX design iteratively advances. We add one evaluation level that is ever present in the industrial context we are in, namely (3) the level to which UX design of the personalized system is scalable. With scalability, we refer to the feasibility and effort needed to make a UX design market-ready.

CASE STUDY 1: BABY SLEEP

The start of this case study was in the research department of Philips, were they developed a new technology that could monitor baby sleep. Based on video analysis, the technology can detect when a baby is in or out of bed and awake or asleep. The request for the design department was to come up with a meaningful product, service or system building on the value of such technology. This design project took place in 2013 and had a lead time of 4 months.

The design team (consisting of two interaction designers, two service designers and a project manager) needed understanding of existing experiences and behaviors of parents in the context of baby sleep. Therefore, they requested two members of the UXR team to *identify* existing user experiences and behavior through desk research (e.g., reading parenting blogs and forums). The resulting insights on parenting dilemmas, limitations and needs were communicated back to the design team in the form of an experience flow [15] and a persona [17].

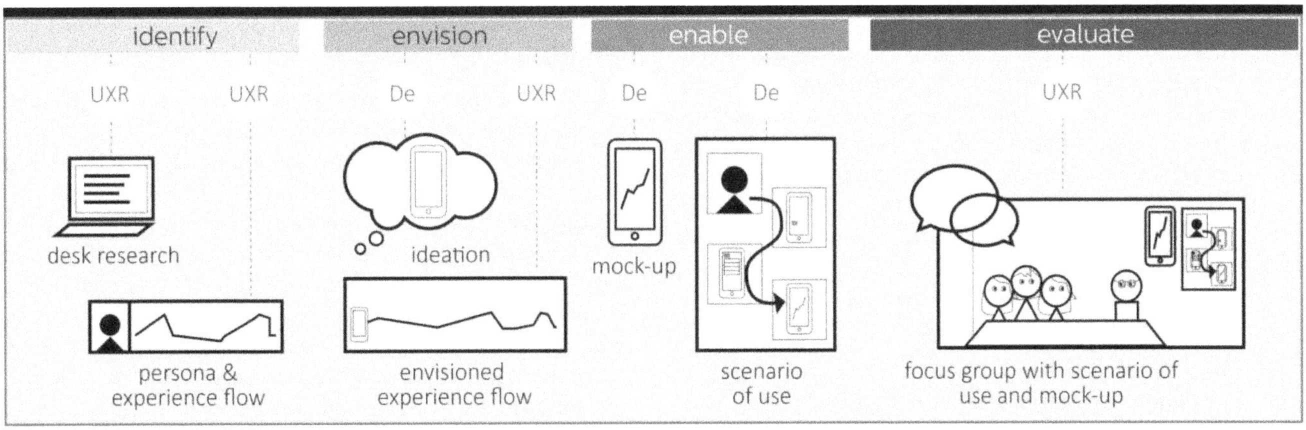

Figure 1: Process overview of activities in the Baby Sleep case. A linear process with separated activities for UXR and design (De).

This user experience knowledge, together with the technical features of the baby sleep algorithm served as input for the design team to further *envision* the service proposition. The design team created an app concept that shows baby sleep data while the baby is in bed (figure 2-left), presents visualizations of baby sleep data over a longer period (figure 2-right), and provides parents with advice, either generated by the system or through online remote expert consultations. When the *envision* activity ended, the UXR was asked to execute a new activity. Namely, to map this 'envisioned' user experience on the original experience flow. This helped the design team to recognize potential areas for novel, meaningful user experiences and showed possible improvements of the concept. With the 'envisioned' user experience flow the design team finalized their concept and created a clickable demo app presenting fictional baby sleep data. The data was neither actual data of the participants' baby, nor real data of any other baby.

To *evaluate* the potential of the design, the two UX researchers were approached again, this time to set up focus groups. Twenty parents participated in two consecutive focus-group sessions, held at the company's venue. During their first visit, the clickable demo app was presented by the UX researchers, accompanied by four scenarios of use (i.e. a parent opens the app while the baby is in bed to see if the baby is sleeping). Participants could respond to these scenarios by using verbal feedback, or by writing/drawing on printouts of the mock-up app screens. Comments of the first focus group were mainly about the look and feel of the product enabling the design team to undertake design updates. The new design was presented (via same means) in the second focus group (with same participants) to notice whether the look and feel suggestions were understood correctly. The insights and conclusions from the *evaluate* activity were captured by the UX researcher and communicated in a digital report to the design team.

After the project a business transfer occurred, meaning that the Mother and Childcare business together with Philips Research continued developing the solution towards a market launch.

Case Study 1: Reflection

Reflecting on the level of design inclusion in UXR activities this project scores low. The *identify* activity did not take any design into account. By contrast, the evaluation activity did involve mock-ups and scenarios aiming to be a vehicle for asking questions. However, the enablers for *evaluation* were presented out of context, contained artificial (i.e. fake) sleep data only and required users to imagine interacting with the system instead of a longitudinal test where users could experience the concept. When comparing these activities with the characteristics of design-inclusive UXR earlier identified in literature, we argue that this project, aiming at designing personalized system, did not follow the design-inclusive UXR approach. Neither in the *identify*, nor in the *evaluate* UXR activities.

Level of insights gained in UX

From a business perspective, the sequential arrangement of activities of this project (see figure 1) and the predefined UXR and design roles seemed a relatively fast way to gain understanding in the user experience and to design for these.

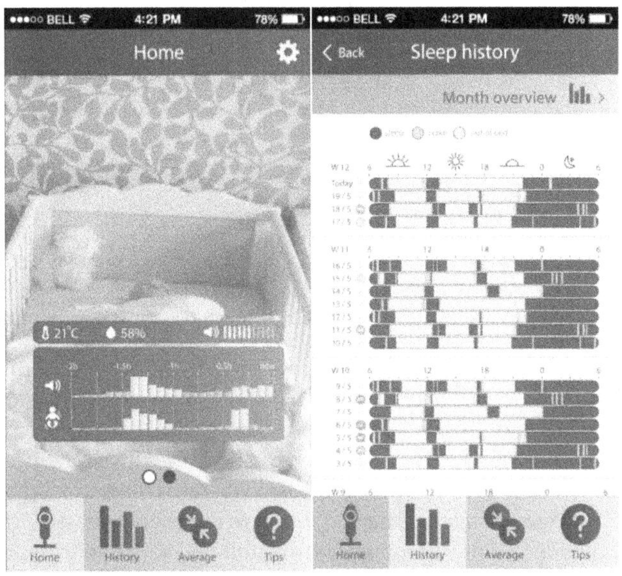

Figure 2: Artificial baby sleep data visualization while the baby is in bed (left) and over a longer period (right)

However, we argue that this setup limited the user experience insights since the feedback of users was based on imagination only (supported by a scenario and mock-up) and did not emerge in interaction of user, context and design. Besides, the design mock-up used artificial data in their representations that may deviate from real data and thus feedback of the user might be based on never existing scenarios. Since participants' feedback was more about the look and feel of the mock-up than the possible added value to their lives, one can question whether this project gained any insight in the experience designed for.

Level to which UX design has iteratively advanced

This case study illustrates a process in which UXR and design roles are separated and in which formal transfer of knowledge and concepts occur. Like how the UXR team handed over experiences flows, capturing the insights from the *identify* activity, to the design team to *envision* possible solutions. This sequential, non-circular arrangement of activities is a result of the limited consultancy role of UXR. Only in the *evaluate* activity the (look and feel of the) design was iteratively advanced through UXR insights.

Level to which UX design of personalized system is scalable

The project outcomes of this case study were picked up by the Mother and Childcare Business Unit fur further development on the roadmap but was delayed at a later stage. Even though the project started with a prototype of the technology at hand, the project missed a nuanced translation of UX insights into a scalable application of the technology. This might be effected by strong simplifications of the concept and mock-up, such as artificial data implementation and not defining how the system could be personalized. In developing mock-up screens for the personalized system, we think we might have required more conscious considerations of the implications of our design decisions and thereby less easy step over the limitations of the technology.

CASE STUDY 2: ACTIVE PREGNANCY

The goal of this project was to design a service that would stimulate pregnant women to walk more during the day, as the Philips Research department had concluded that most pregnant women are not physically active enough for a healthy pregnancy. Philips Design took this as a relevant challenge to design for. The project was executed by a team composed of three UX researchers, an interaction designer, service designer, a research scientist and a project manager. This case study dates from 2014 and took 5 months.

The UX researchers of the team started the project with desk research and interviewing healthcare professionals to *identify* current behaviors and experiences of pregnant women around physical activity. The coaching strategies described by Cialdini [4] appeared to be relevant to the challenge at hand. The UXR team members created an experience flow accompanied by four personas that each matched one of the four coaching strategies of Cialdini. Both the experience flow and personas were *evaluated* and updated based on interviews with six pregnant women and (the same) four professionals.

As a follow-up, the project team, with both UXR and design members, *envisioned* a concept for a mobile application in which pregnant women are coached according coaching strategies inspired by Cialdini. In this concept, users are appointed to a certain coaching strategy and a personal goal (number of steps to take per day). In case this strategy shows not to be effective (i.e., the step count did not increase), the user will either be presented with a different coaching strategy or the goal will be adapted. An experience flow captured the envisioned, dynamic service flow and associated envisioned user experiences of this concept.

To *enable* experiences in context, the project team, again both UXR and design team members, specified functionalities of an experiential prototype. Based on a pre-defined action plan and a list of specifications, an external software development team built a simple Wizard of Oz [6] version of the mobile application. This prototype could collect and visualize the number of steps taken and could display coaching messages. The data analysis, coaching messages and effectiveness monitoring were not automated in the experiential prototype. Instead, data of each walking session was sent to the project team via e-mail. By sending an email back to the experiential prototype, the team could display a so-called coaching message in the app.

In a four-week test with twenty pregnant women the envisioned coaching strategies were *evaluated.* The participants started with a collective introductory meeting to explain the functionality of the app. Participants were not informed about the 'human back-end' of the application that *enabled* the team to explore different predefined ideas during the evaluation. After every week of testing, participants individually filled out intermediate online questionnaires. These online questionnaires aimed to evaluate the pregnant women's perception of her physical activity level and coaching strategy. The test ended with a collective evaluation interview with the pregnant women to reflect upon their experiences of the coaching application.

The project insights on the coaching strategies for pregnant women were captured in a presentation that landed in a behavior change group of Philips Research but the design concept was not picked up yet by a business unit for further development.

Case study 2: reflection

Different from the previous case study this project clearly employs design-inclusive UXR characteristics. In the evaluative activity, it met all design-inclusive UXR requirements. For example, it used the Wizard of Oz prototype as enabler for UXR research and involved design as an integral part to find out what coaching services resonates with pregnant women. Likewise, the experiment was executed in a real-life setting for a period of four weeks and did collect both qualitative (experience) insights as well as data logging (behavioral) insights. However, the design-inclusive UXR characteristics were not present in the *identify* activity; UXR insights were still gained without design involvement.

Different from the first case study, this project was executed by a multidisciplinary team with backgrounds in both design and UXR. To facilitate this cooperative process of UXR and design, prior existing consultancy roles disappeared. This new arrangement of roles prevented formal knowledge transfers and unlocked discussions about UX insights. Besides the project breaks with the strictly linear organization of activities (recognizable in the first case study) as illustrated in figure 3. Namely, an *evaluate* phase follows the *identify* phase. Moreover, there was a large overlap of *enable* and *evaluation* activities towards the end of the project highlighting that the previous design-led *enable* activity overlaps with the originally UXR-led *evaluate* activity.

Level of insights gained in UX

The user experience insights of this project's *evaluation* activity were richer than the previous case study as it enabled participants to experience the concept in their own context, instead of asking participants to imagine an experience out of context. Besides, the quantitative and qualitative data gathering combination allowed to team to gain insight in both user experience and user behavior. Interestingly there was a discrepancy between the two as women thought they were more active (result of interview) than they were (seen in the data) and vice versa. This type of user experience insights sparked ideas for coaching strategies.

The *identify* activity did not involve design to gain insight in the user experience. However, the team tried to find a way to deal with the complexity challenges forwarded by personalization. Namely, they created multiple personas instead of a single persona that need to be the representative of a group.

Level to which UX design has iteratively advanced

The Wizard of Oz prototype allowed for evaluation of real (not imagined) experience in context and over a longer period (four weeks). In this set-up, adjustments could easily be made (change of strategy and/or goals) to explore what resonates with users. Evaluation of these adjustments were informed by both quantitative and qualitative data from participants gathered by enabling the user experiences (number of steps, exercise times and verbal comments). In the change of strategy or goals the team followed the predefined design service flow ('envisioned flow'). Thereby the evaluation considered the dynamic features of the UX design but did not iteratively advance the design service flow itself.

Level to which UX design of personalized system is scalable

The UX design outcomes of this project took the concept of personalization into account but was limited to coaching strategies between which the user could switch (i.e., there was a limited set of options). This was a clever way to design for user experience that might feel tailored and unique but in fact is a multi-pathway service flow.

Unfortunately, the potential to transfer this personalized system and insights to the market was low because the concept did not take any technical feasibilities into account. Namely, the 'human back-end', of the Wizard of Oz prototype, intuitively responded to events. Building an algorithm and system rules with that level of empathy would be very hard. Neither knowing the limitations of an automatic system nor the effect of such artificial equivalent on the user experience questions the business relevance of the obtained UX insights and design from an industrial perspective.

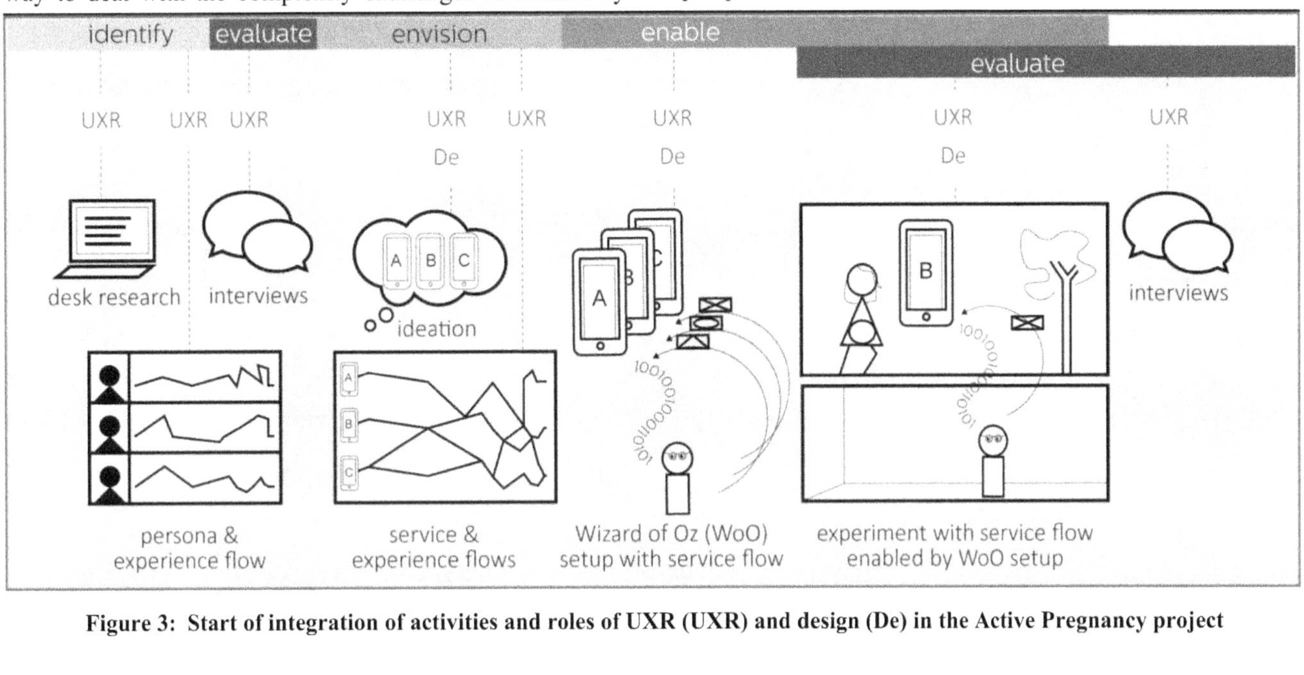

Figure 3: Start of integration of activities and roles of UXR (UXR) and design (De) in the Active Pregnancy project

CASE STUDY 3: BOTTLE FEEDING

The third case study is a Philips Design initiated project that aimed to explore parents' experiences related to baby bottle-feeding. This to recognize opportunities for a personalized service around a 'smart' baby-bottle [1] that might give the baby product business a push towards a more digital portfolio. In 2015, this six-months project ran with a team of two UX researchers, an interaction designer, a service designer, two hardware/software prototype specialists, a project manager and two students from data science and child development studies.

The project (see figure 4) started with desk research to *identify* the existing landscape. More specifically the team gained insight in what was known about bottle feeding (how to prepare a bottle, recommendations from parents, etc), what smart baby products exist (a few) and which datasets (none) are available.

In a workshop facilitated by the UX researchers, the whole team *envisioned* what factors, found in desk research, might be relevant in the user experience of bottle feeding. The team wanted to *evaluate* whether the pre-identified factors of the user experience were indeed relevant in the user experience of bottle-feeding. And they wanted to *identify* other influential factors of which they did not think upfront. To do so, the team set out to quantitatively collect data of bottle-feeding behavior with three sensors (an accelerometer, a temperature sensor and a clock). The so-called data-gathering probe *enabled* the team to gain insight in the existing handling of the bottle through quantitative data gathering. In designing the data-gathering probe it was important to think of unobtrusiveness. Otherwise the probe might interfere with current routines and thus would not reveal existing user behavior and experience.

The team invited five families with babies aging from 2 to 11 months to use the data-gathering probes for two weeks. In addition to the unobtrusive collection of sensor data, the participants were visited by duos of the project team (a UX research accompanied by a soft/hardware prototype expert) for introduction purposes. In that visit the team also handed out a paper diary [2], aiming to collect qualitative insights of the bottle-feeding experiences. During an evaluation session (with a UX researcher accompanied by a designer) at the parents' home, both the diaries and collected data (in the form of simple visualizations) were discussed in an open interview setting. The investigation of existing user experiences and behavior of bottle-feeding concluded with the creation of one experience flow and one profile per family. These flows captured both data gathered with the probe and the qualitative input received from the diaries and interviews. Instead of making a persona from all information available, the team envisioned what factors might be relevant for later personalization purposes.

Consequently, they set out to make a profile which can be (automatically) filled out (through data) for each user that would buy this product in a store. To do so all team disciplines were present in this activity.

From the first user involvement session parents showed interest in viewing their baby-bottle data, since it reveals details otherwise invisible. However, it was not yet clear what a design proposition exactly had to entail to be of value to families. The fact that a personalized system, like such a smart baby-bottle, might have functionalities that are user, usage and context dependent made it even more difficult to define a UX design concept at that moment in time. Therefore, the multidisciplinary team set out to *envision* what direction the concept might go into and on what levels it could tailor to the families.

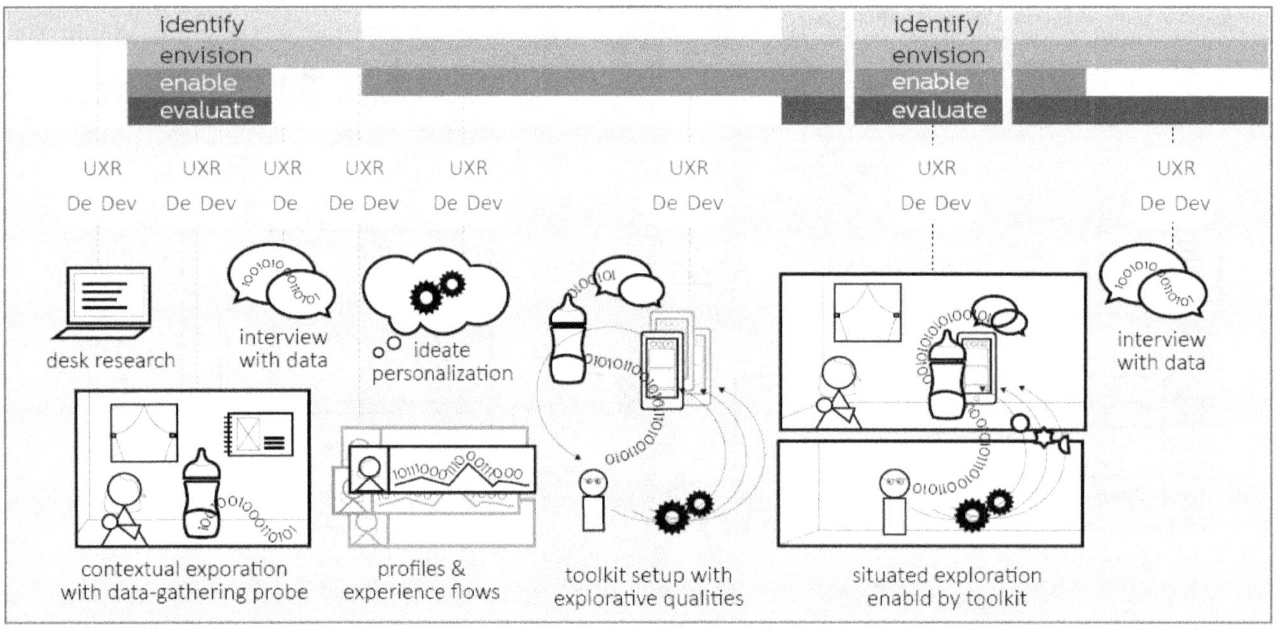

Figure 4: Process overview of activities in bottle feeding project with continuous design-inclusive UXR

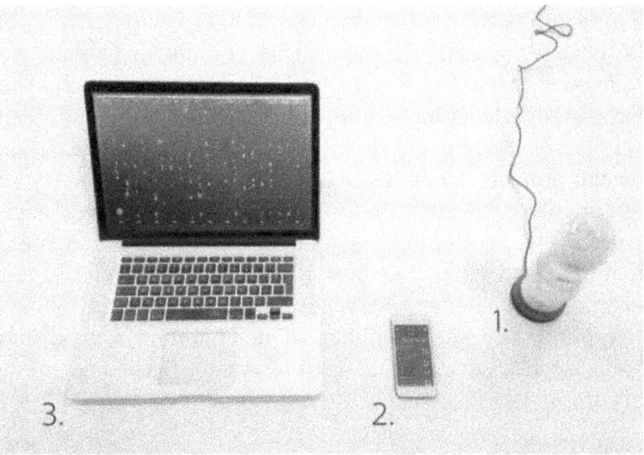

Figure 5. Overview of experiential toolkit elements: (1) Data dashboard, (2) The app and (3) The sensor sleeve.

Instead of predefining a specific service flow (like in the second case study) the team decided to create a toolkit to *enable* exploration of these user experiences. The toolkit (see figure 5) consisted of (1) an updated version of the data-gathering bottle add-on (i.e., light and sound sensors were added as one of the user experience factors not thought of in the first probe). (2) A mobile application for the participants to experience the to-be explored service and to stay in contact with the project team. And (3) a dashboard that visualizes the collected data for the project team.

Building empathy remotely through this combined dataset enabled the project team to act manually as a system. Although, algorithms to automatically detect feeds and update data visualizations were present in the application, all "insights" on the experience were sent manually by the project team. During the field study the team could update the functionalities, data visualizations and the look and feel of the application remotely. Thereby the concept altered from data visualization, to sending the right edcuational information at the right time to personal insights based on correlations between data points indicating a build up of insights and complexity over time.

The toolkit was handed out to nine, not prior participating, bottle-feeding families with babies aging from 2 to 11 months. The three-week situated exploration started with a collective meeting at the company's venue in which participants received the bottle add-on and an iPod with the application installed. Thereby they were *enabled* to experience the concept exploration. The application chat functionality, and weekly online questionnaires facilitated participants to elaborately *evaluate* the concept and thereto related experiences.

At the same time, the whole project team could send questions to the parents (via the app or online questionnaires) to *identify* newly relevant factors and *envision* concept updates. These questions were related to the user experiences, presented functionalities, look and feel, technical errors, and the displayed 'insights'. The situated exploration ended with evaluation interviews executed by the UX team members. In these interviews families reflected upon their participation which helped the team to *evaluate* the iteratively developed design, to *envision* with end-user what improvements could be made and to *identify* topics that benefit more exploration.

The optimistic responses about the user experiences and the positive routine changes, which can be recognized in the data of the participating families, made the business decide to transfer the project and start developing the concept for market launch.

Case study 3: reflection

This third case study clearly illustrates design inclusion in UXR. Where the second case study had design-inclusive UXR characteristics in the evaluative activities only, this project executes design activities (*envision, enable*) as an inherent part of UXR. Ultimately, it even starts to merge the *identify* and *evaluate* activities. In contrast to the second case study, which used a prototype to evaluate the design service flow, this case uses custom created explorative means to identify newly relevant user experience factors. This way the team could directly bring these alive in the design concept, which could then be evaluated with participants.

To be able to do so, the project team was composed of a richer set of disciplines (design, UXR, hardware and software development, data science and psychology expertise) that worked closely and continuously together (one team, one location). Instead of assigning different activities to different disciplines with project sub-goals, the team had a common goal of *identifying*, *envisioning*, *enabling* and *evaluating* user experiences of a personalized system. As decisions made by one discipline could influence the other disciplines, the team had to closely work together and constantly stay aligned. For example, one technical decision about databases could limit data visualization possibilities, means for insight gathering and thus the exploration of "insights" to be send back to the parents. The team ensured a dialogue of decisions through short daily meetings.

Level of insights gained in UX

The method through which the UX insights have been gathered in the third case study can be compared with the second case study. Also, UX insights were gained by enabling 'real' experiences in context over a longer period. Again, by combining qualitative methods with data gathering, insights were not limited to experiences only, but encompassed behavioral patterns too.

New in this case study is the collection of user experiences of multiple users in the same context. This allowed for interesting in-family comparison of behavior and experiences (i.e., we recognized different bottle feeding preparation types due to different believes of 'a good' bottle temperature). Furthermore, the first part of this case study was characterized by the collection of UX insights of the currently existing situation that was not yet influenced by design interventions. Seeing data and hearing about experiences of these often unexpected, 'real' situations fueled many design ideas for the experiment after.

During the first experiment of this case study we collected data for three weeks and presented these in the evaluation interview. There we noticed that participants found it hard to recall details of user experiences that happened in the past. Therefore, the toolkit of the second experiment ensured that we could continuously question and prompt for user experience insights through remote access to the data and remote questioning. Recognizing changes in experiential and behavioral data of gradual design adjustments was a positive effect of this feature.

Level to which UX design has iteratively advanced

The process of this case study is characterized by almost a total overlap of four types of activities and integrates design, UXR and development. Originally, like illustrated in case study one, these activities were separately executed by design and UXR disciplines. Now these come together in an iterative process (figure 4). The dialogue between these disciplines in different activities increased significantly through the data-intensive approach used in this case study. Not only to remotely collect UXR insights, but also to explore UX design and development through remote interventions. This explorative freedom to continuously ask questions, change designs and understand effects, reduced the time of exploration present in the more linear processes.

Level to which UX design of personalized system is scalable

The result (prototype) of the toolkit with high flexible qualities, for quick adjustments and evaluation, was not yet a marketable system. It has automated and integrated its core functionalities, like feeding detection, but it misses algorithms to send personalized data-based insights to the families. Though, this case study differs from the second case study's 'human back-end' that coached pregnant women through data and personal encounters (like getting to know the participant through the introduction session). In this case the information pool of the 'human back-end' was limited to the bottle-feeding data. Thus, choices for sending "insights" were merely made through data insights and did not derive from empathy for the participants. After the study, we sat together with the 'human back-end' and unraveled the logic that occurred in sending out the "insights". That logic is now used as inspiration for building the "insights"-algorithm. So, the gradual steps of design, UXR and development have minimized the next steps to a scalable and meaningful personalized system. The result of the project is not a marketable system but clearly outlines which technical challenges were skipped and development is required.

To live up to the specific demand of industry to deliver UX design that is scalable and can be brought to market, we recognize that design-inclusive UXR was not enough. The case study benefited from hardware, software and data science involvement. Involving these competences in design projects is not new. However, these disciplines were not involved to create a 'working-prototype' of a design concept, like traditionally would happen. Instead they build a toolkit by which the design concept, and technologies affiliated, could iteratively advance. This required a new mindset for these disciplines of not building a rigid and solid system but rather a flexible system that could grew, according UX insights.

DISCUSSION

We presented three case studies, executed in industry, that all aimed to design personalized systems in the domain of Family Care. These projects evolved around very personal topics that were challenged by high complexity, context dependency and conflicting perspectives [18].

The case studies from design industry shows a trend of implementing more design-inclusive UXR characteristics that were earlier defined in academic communities [26]. The first case study showed no design-inclusive UXR characteristics and fully separated design and UXR activities. The second study took advantage of design-inclusive UXR in the evaluation phase of the project but not in the earlier phases. The third case study builds on design-inclusive characteristics from the start and continues the integration of design and UXR over the project.

Re-arrangement of activities and roles

We questioned how the separate UXR and design disciplines, existing in our industrial context, needed to rearrange their (*identify*, *envision*, *enable* and *evaluate*) activities to cope with the complexity challenges forwarded in designing for personalized systems. The case studies have shown a shift of progressively integrating different activities of the UXR and design process that were earlier executed separately by the either design (*envision*, *enable*) or UXR (*identify*, *evaluate*) discipline.

The transition emerged in the quest to setup situated explorations in which insights are gained in 'real' and prolonged situations to iteratively advance UX design. Such UXR cannot go without design involvement as user experiences appear in the interaction between user, design and context. Striving for situated explorations, the UXR and design disciplines transitioned from sequential involvement to a continuous multi-disciplinary approach where they worked intensively together. By activities and working as one team at one table, more continuous and less formal knowledge transfers occurred, reducing the chance of losing nuanced user experience in translation to design.

The integration of project activities and competences has not affected the organizational setup of Philips Design, where competence groups are still clearly split. However, case studies like these have fostered the informal integration of competence groups from bottom-up. Through project experiences and the establishment of virtual horizontal communities, we are keen to advance cross-competence knowledge, methods and approaches.

Categorization of activities

To better understand the user experience components of UXR and design activities in our retrospective analysis, we renamed the four activities of Schön's *reflective practice design process* [20]. Looking back, we notice that Schön's reflective mindset is still embedded in the activities at hand. Namely, with the merge of design and UXR activities, the reflections in the case studies, informing design or UXR decisions, occurred in a blur of activities where reflections from UXR informed design and design reflections informed UXR to gain rich insights (see figure 1, 3 and 4).

Compared to Schön's comprehensive *naming*-activity our focus is more on *identifying* existing user experiences and the opportunities these create. This is different from the approach to clearly formulate a *problem*. Unlike the analytical *framing* activity, the *envision* activity stresses the empathic designerly skills to *envision* how a design prototype can *enable* meaningful user experiences. There is more focus on designing for experiences which can be revealed by the prototype than to make a functional prototype (as described in the Schön's *move* activity) that can only be looked at or solely operated by the design research team. And the *evaluation* activity has much overlap with Schön's description, apart from stressing the value of situated and prolonged experimenting.

Investment of design-inclusive UXR

When reviewing the three case studies one might recognize an increasing trend of lead times and people involved. These design-inclusive UXR projects seem to request a bigger investment to be executed. We affirm that setting up a situated exploration for UXR, design and development increased the preparation time. But once it installed it reduced the time per exploration cycle and ensured iterative explorations of design through user experience insights. Likewise, when we would zoom out and review the innovation process together with the development process (that comes after a business transition) we could argue that these two blur. By taking a feasibility perspective early in the innovation projects we aim to shorten the development track after.

New tools to facilitate design-inclusive UXR

Except from activity rearrangements, changing roles and the involvement of new disciplines, we recognize that UXR methods have changed to cope with the complexity challenges at hand. UXR methods shifted from ad hoc focus groups where participants had to imagine an experience of use, towards prolonged situated explorations of design interventions. Thereby UXR started to combine qualitative user experience insight gathering with data logging about user behavior patterns to iteratively advance UX design.

Another change can be recognized in the use of experience flows and personas. In the first case study the experience flow was described as one journey of one representative persona. In the second case study this converted to multiple persona's and dynamic service flow with associated user experiences. And in the third case study the personas were turned into profiles with data as a fundament to meet personalization scalability.

The three case studies presented here highlight relevant factors of activity integrations but do not give a definite detailed answer to the execution of UXR methods nor what tools are required to facilitate design-inclusive UXR projects in data intensive projects. Therefore, we set out for development of tools that lower the threshold for data-enabled approaches [1] of design-inclusive UXR.

Relevancy of design-inclusive UXR in other fields

Note that the arguments we make for design-inclusive UXR in industry are limited to our experiences within the domain of family care at Philips Design. Although we believe these are relevant for different practices we see a clear need for more cases from other multinationals, SME's and startups. We question the (industrial) UXR community to explore the changing role of UXR and design activities in different product categories and experience domains to build towards a framework for design-inclusive UXR that is both academically rigorous and scalable in practice.

CONCLUSION

The approach adopted in the three industrial case studies at Philips Design progressed from UXR focusing on *identification* and *evaluation* of user experiences to a design-inclusive UXR approach where UXR and design are closely integrated in activities to *identify, envision, enable* and *evaluate* user experiences. The design-inclusive UXR approach is characterized by having design activities as integral part of research and considers user, context, design and the interaction between those. This is achieved in prolonged situated explorations of design interventions where user experience insights iteratively advance UX design and vice versa.

ACKNOWLEDGEMENTS

This paper is built upon a communal effort in the Philips Design community. Therefore we would like to thank all who were involved in execution of the case studies and reflective sessions. This research is supported by the IMPULS perinatology framework.

REFERENCES

1. Bogers S., Frens J., van Kollenburg, J., Deckers, E. and Hummels C. Connected Baby Bottle: A Design Case Study Towards A Framework for Data-Enabled Design. In *Proc. DIS '16*, ACM Press (2016).
2. Bolger, N., Davis, A. and Rafaeli, E. Diary methods: Capturing life as it is lived. *Annual review of psychology 54*, 1 (2003), 579-616.

3. Megens, C., Peeters, M., Hummels, C., and Brombacher, A. Designing for behaviour change towards healthy living. In *Proc. IASDR '13,* ACM Press (2013).

4. Cialdini, R. B. *Invloed-De zes geheimen*. Academic Service, Amsterdam, the Netherlands, 2009.

5. Cockton, G. UCD: Critique via Parody and a Sequel. In *Proc. CHI '12,* ACM Press (2012), 1-10.

6. Dow, S., MacIntyre, B., Lee, J., Oezbek, C., Bolter, J. D. and Gandy, M. Wizard of Oz support throughout an iterative design process. *Pervasive Computing, IEEE 4,* 4 (2005), 18-26.

7. Fallman, D. Design-Oriented Human-Computer Interaction. In *Proc. CHI '03,* ACM Press (2003).

8. Gardien, P. Designing the next step: making meaningful innovation work. Ph.D. Dissertation. University of Technology Eindhoven.

9. Hassenzahl, M. and Tractinsky, N. User experience - a research agenda. *Behaviour & Information Technology 25,* 2 (2006), 91-97.

10. Henderson, R., Rickwood, D. and Roberts, P. The beta test of an electronic supermarket. *Interacting with Computers 10*, 4 (1998), 385–399.

11. Höök, K. Evaluating the utility and usability of an adaptive hypermedia system. In *Proc.IUI '97,* ACM Press (1997).

12. Horvath, I. Differences Between 'Research in Design Context' and 'Design Inclusive Research' in the Domain of Industrial Design Engineering. *Journal of Design Research 7*, 1 (2008), 61–83.

13. Kaasinen, E., Koskela-Huotari, K., Ikonen, V. and Niemeléi, M. Three approaches to co-creating services with users. *Advances in the Human Side of Service Engineering* (2013), *286.*

14. Kensing, F. and Blomberg, J. Participatory design: Issues and concerns. *Computer Supported Cooperative Work (CSCW) 7*, 3-4 (1998), 167-185.

15. Philips Design. 2014. Experience Flows. Retrieved April 13, 2016, from http://www.newscenter.philips.com/main/design/resources/pdf/Inside-Innovation-Backgrounder-Experience-Flows.pdf

16. Philips Lighting B.V. 2016. Meet Hue, Personal Wireless Lighting. Retrieved December 29, 2016, from http://www.meethue.com/

17. Pruitt, J. and Adlin, T. *The persona lifecycle: keeping people in mind throughout product design*. Morgen Kaufmann, 2010.

18. Rittel, H.W.J. and Webber, M.M. Dilemmas in a General Theory of Planning. *Policy Sciences 4,* 2 (1973), 155-66.

19. Sanders, E. B. N. and Stappers, P. J. Co-creation and the new landscapes of design. *Co-design 4,* 1 (2008), 5-18.

20. Schön, D.A. *The Reflective Practitioner: How professionals think in action*. Temple Smith, London, 1984.

21. Smith, W. R. Product differentiation and market segmentation as alternative marketing strategies. *The Journal of Marketing* (1956), 3-8.

22. Stappers, P. J. 2007. *Doing Design as a Part of Doing Research.* Design Research, Birkhäuser, Baser, 2007, 81-91.

23. Tomico, O., Frens, J.W. and Overbeeke, C.J. Co-Reflection: user involvement for highly dynamic design processes. In *Proc. CHI EA '09*, ACM Press, (2009).

24. Van Velsen L., Van der Geest, T. and Steehouder, M., The Contribution of Technical Communicators to the User-Centered-Design Process of Personalized Systems. *Technical Communication 57,* 2 (2010), 182-196.

25. Van Velsen, L., van der Geest, T., Klaassen, R. and Steehouder, M., User-Centered evaluation of adaptive and adaptable systems: a literature overview. *The Knowledge Engineer Review 23,* 3 (2008), 261-281.

26. Vermeeren, A.P.O.S., Roto, V. and Väänänen. Design-Inclusive UX research: design as a part of doing user experience research. *Behavior & Information Technology, 35,* 1 (2016), 27-37.

27. Weibelzahl, S., Jedlitschka, A. and Ayari, B. Eliciting requirements for an adaptive decision support system through structured user interviews. In *Press, Atl '06,* ACM Press (2006).

28. Zimmerman J., Forlizzi J. and Evenson S., Research Through Design as a Method for Interaction Design Research. In *Proc. CHI '07,* ACM Press (2007), 493-50.

Augmented Studio: Projection Mapping on Moving Body for Physiotherapy Education

Thuong Hoang, Martin Reinoso, Zaher Joukhadar, Frank Vetere and David Kelly*
Microsoft Research Centre for SocialNUI, *Melbourne School of Health Sciences
The University of Melbourne, Melbourne, Australia
{thuong.hoang; martin.reinoso; zaher.joukhadar; f.vetere; d.kelly}@unimelb.edu.au

Figure 1. Augmented Studio setup: Left: the 3-sided stage, including scaffolding and 2 projectors with 2 Kinect sensors, set up in a physiotherapy practical classroom; Middle: the stage is captured virtually through projection mapping with a virtual anatomy model; Right: projected virtual anatomy model on a moving body for a physiotherapy practical class

ABSTRACT

Physiotherapy students often struggle to translate anatomical knowledge from textbooks into a dynamic understanding of the mechanics of body movements in real life patients. We present the *Augmented Studio,* an augmented reality system that uses body tracking to project anatomical structures and annotations over moving bodies for physiotherapy education. Through a user and learner centered design approach, we established an understanding that through *augmentation* and *annotation*, augmented reality technology can enhance physiotherapy education. Augmented Studio enables *augmentation* through projection mapping to display anatomical information such as muscles and skeleton in real time on the body as it moves. We created a technique for *annotation* to create projected hand-drawing on the moving body, to enable explicit communication of the teacher's clinical reasoning strategies to the students. Findings from our pilot usability study demonstrate a more engaging learning and teaching experience and increased communication between teacher and students when using Augmented Studio.

CHI 2017, May 06-11, 2017, Denver, CO, USA

DOI: http://dx.doi.org/10.1145/3025453.3025860.

Author Keywords

Projection mapping; spatial augmented reality; annotation; physiotherapy education.

ACM Classification Keywords

H.5.1 [Multimedia Information Systems]: Artificial, augmented, and virtual realities; K.3.0 [Computers and Education]: General

INTRODUCTION

Physiotherapy is currently taught via multiple modalities, such as lectures, tutorials, demonstrations and hands-on training in practical classes. However, physiotherapy students often struggle to translate the anatomical knowledge from textbooks to dynamic understanding of the mechanics of body movements in real life patients. Moreover, one of the critical skills in physiotherapy, and other clinical domains, is clinical reasoning [1]. The students learn to negotiate the complexity of multiple factors, starting with the mastery of strong domain knowledge, such as human anatomy, to form hypotheses through patient inquiry and to test the hypotheses through examination [1]. Clinical reasoning is particularly difficult to teach because it requires students to critically review clinical decisions which are often ephemeral and tacit [2]. The best practice for learning such skills typically involves a class of students observing an expert therapist conducting a consultation with a real patient (or a surrogate patient). However, such settings do not make the therapist's clinical decision making explicitly available to students. One of the major difficulties for the students in learning clinical reasoning is the ability to identify medical cues to develop diagnostic hypotheses [3].

We are interested in the potential of visualization tools such as augmented reality (AR) for physiotherapy education. We aimed to answer the question '*how can augmented reality technology enhance physiotherapy teaching and learning?*', by conducting a focus group and field study with physiotherapy teacher and students. Our findings highlighted the two aspects of AR technology that are valuable to physiotherapy education: *augmentation* and *annotation*. Augmentation is the core strength of AR, which can be used in the context of physiotherapy education to provide augmented visualization for better clinical understanding of human anatomy and musculoskeletal structures. Annotation equips the teacher with the ability to explicitly communicate their experience and clinical reasoning strategies to the students [4].

In this paper, we present *Augmented Studio* (see Figure 1), an augmented reality system that uses body tracking to project anatomical structures and annotations over moving bodies. Augmented Studio enables *augmentation* through projection mapping to turn a human body into a display surface, showing the anatomical information such as muscles and skeleton in real time as the body moves. The moving body of a volunteer student becomes a live canvas for the teacher to illustrate clinical reasoning, through *annotations*, in the form of colored hand drawing on the projected body. The annotations enhance teacher and student communication with the purpose of transferring the real life knowledge and experience of the teacher to a class of students.

The contribution of the paper is the design process, implementation, and pilot usability study of Augmented Studio. We established an understanding of how augmented reality technology can enhance physiotherapy education, through augmentation and annotation. We developed an augmented reality system by combining body tracking with projection mapping to enable augmentation and annotation of anatomical knowledge on a moving body. We created a technique called *annotation sleeve* to enable drawing on the projected anatomical model. We conducted a pilot usability study with graduate physiotherapy students and teachers, by running practical classes in the Augmented Studio environment. All participants unanimously agreed that the system enhanced their learning and teaching experience. Our findings also showed increased communications between the teacher and the students using the annotation capability.

RELATED WORK

The application of augmented reality in medical education has been widely implemented in multiple areas, including anatomy, surgery, and real time visualization [5]. To further understand the needs for AR technologies in this area, we summarized the challenges faced in physiotherapy education. We then reviewed previous work on three types of display technologies for physiotherapy education: head mounted display, screen based, and projection-based AR.

Clinical reasoning and Anatomy in Physiotherapy

Clinical reasoning is identified as one of the top sought-after skills in physiotherapy graduate [6]. Clinical reasoning is defined as the entirety of thinking and decision-making processes related to clinical practice [7]. Learners struggle to learn how to detect key features to generate diagnostic hypothesis and how to integrate different facets of information [3]. A review of teaching approaches highlights the needs for explicit instructions and a focus on understanding of basic science mechanisms [4], which, in most cases, is anatomical knowledge.

A modern curriculum for anatomy education uses multiple pedagogical resources, including cadaveric dissection and virtual simulation [8]. Cadaver lab assists students' understanding of 3D anatomical structures through exploration. However, this resource is often limited due to preservation and maintenance cost. Virtual simulation is described in the following sections, using AR technologies.

Head mounted AR

Augmented reality is an interactive medium in which virtual information is overlaid on real world objects [9]. The power to change the perception of reality lends itself to many applications of information visualization for medical education. Kancherla et al. [10] proposed an AR technology that uses a head mounted display (HMD) to allow the overlay of bones over the body. The initial prototype was limited to a low polygon count model of the elbow joint, which could be scaled to match the patient. In the first stage of the development, the system animated the movements of supination (stretching forearm) and pronation (palm facing down) of the forearm at the elbow joints. Virtual Reality Dynamic Anatomy (VRDA) was an improvement on the previous system [11] to extend to a knee-joint model. The system overlaid the digital knee-bone model using an optical see-through HMD and a complex array of motion sensors located around the knee for alignment of the virtual model [12]. The subjective experience reported from the user was described as being akin to powerful and convincing x-ray vision. Continuing with the development, Rolland et al. [13] presented a tool to train medical practitioners in performing surgical operations, using a dedicated optical tracking system and head mounted projection display.

In addition to HMD, a virtual reality (VR) system built by Sakellariou et al. [14] combines haptic and auditory navigation of a 3D representation of the pelvic and abdominal region through vibrotactile gloves and 3D sound. A comparative user trial with student and expert surgeons was conducted with pre- and post-assessment. The results indicated that the VR system provides better comprehension of the spatial relationships of the anatomical structures, with a strong user preference over traditional teaching methods.

Screen-based AR

Another form of AR system uses a computer screen to display augmented information to the users. Magic Mirror, initially known as mirracle [15], is a system that uses body tracking to show organs and internal human anatomy on the user who stands in front of the screen. The display acts as a mirror that overlays virtual anatomical structures on the body, whose movements are tracked by a depth camera in real time. A survey was conducted with medical students and surgeons to rate the precision, usability and learning potential of the system. The results showed the system provides a helpful visualization for anatomy education.

Projection based AR

Spatial augmented reality [16] uses projection to change the user's perception of the physical environment. An example of projection-based anatomy education system is the Spatial Augmented Reality on Person (SARP) [17], which uses a single projector with Kinect tracking to project muscles, skeleton, and internal organs on the body for anatomy education. The authors built a game called Augmented Anatomy where players need to identify the anatomical structure that are projected on their body. An expert, student, and online survey showed positive comments on engagement and increased interest in the subject. The authors also demonstrated reduced identification errors through successive usage.

Rather than being used in an education context, AnatOnMe [18] is designed to improve doctor and patient communication in a clinical setting. Doctors can project on the patient body pictures of internal organs or bones, by pointing a hand-held projector on the patient's body, to educate the patients of medical concepts relevant to their consultations. A design experiment was conducted to assess patients' preferred projection surface: on wall, on a mannequin model, or on the body. Results did not indicate any significant difference in preference between projection on mannequin model and on-body. An expert review with therapists, however, revealed that the hand-held form factor prevents them from having physical contact with the patient, which is a common work practice in physiotherapy.

Although there has been a large body of work on augmented reality systems for anatomy education, previous works are limited to visualization and identification of anatomical structures. Moreover, existing applications are focused on a single user, which does not translate to a classroom model.

In addition to dynamic visualization of anatomical models during movements, Augmented Studio provides annotation capability to enable virtual hand-drawing on the moving body to illustrate anatomical concepts for teaching purposes. Our system uses large-scale projection mapping that is suitable for a classroom model with multiple students. We applied a user and learner-centered design approach to develop the system, specifically targeting maximum student benefit.

METHODOLOGY

We adopted a user-centered design approach by conducting a focus group and a field study with physiotherapy students and a teacher at the University of Melbourne, to answer the question *'how can immersive technology enhance physiotherapy teaching and learning?'*.

Findings from the study indicated that augmentation and annotation are the strength of augmented reality technology in physiotherapy education. The findings informed the design of *Augmented Studio,* an augmented reality learning system for physiotherapy education. The development of Augmented Studio is guided by learner-centered design approaches [19], focusing on the needs of the learner. One dimension of this approach is an understanding of domain knowledge [20], which is provided by Augmented Studio through the projection of anatomical information directly on the body. The concept of scaffolding in learner-centered design [21] refers to additional support provided for the students to engage in activities that they are learning to master. Augmented Studio allows the teacher to draw virtual information on the body, to illustrate their expert clinical reasoning to the students. The teacher uses this annotation capability as a scaffolding tool to provide additional assistance for student's learning.

We conducted a pilot usability study to evaluate the extent to which Augmented studio benefits physiotherapy teaching and learning. The following sections of the paper provide the details of the focus group, field study and pilot usability study.

USER-CENTERED DESIGN

Focus Group

We recruited eight participants from a cohort of final year graduate physiotherapy students through convenience sampling. The participants were presented with a brief presentation on current examples of immersive technology (virtual and augmented reality) in physiotherapy education. Before the presentation, the participants answered a questionnaire regarding their experience with current physiotherapy education methods, in terms of *confidence, satisfaction, education tools, skills mastery* and *feedback.* After the presentation, the participants answered the same questionnaire to discuss their opinions on the potentials of each technology for physiotherapy education. The answers were recorded on a 5-point Likert scale. One researcher prompted the participants to answer each of the questions, then invited a group discussion on the topic of the question. No statistical analysis was performed on the data, as they were used as a probe to encourage discussion. Another researcher took notes with audio recordings.

The focus group indicated that AR technology can provide an exciting and engaging learning experience. The findings from the focus group highlighted two areas of potential for technological innovations in physiotherapy education: providing tactile sensation and enhancing the understanding of surface anatomy.

Tactile

The participants indicated that the demonstrated motor skill learning is most useful for first and second years of learning.

The participants had reservations about the ability of the technologies to reduce cognitive load and increase their "sense of feel". It was discussed that the sense of feel is assisted by the anatomic understanding of the students.

Anatomy

The study highlighted the need for anatomy education. One participant stated that *"the ultimate product would be an augmented reality that overlays the internal anatomy on a real patient, rather than referring to anatomy textbooks"*.

Field Study

The focus group highlighted the potential of immersive technology to be used for anatomy visualization. We then conducted a pilot field study at the Department of Physiotherapy at the University of Melbourne. The focus of the study was to understand the pedagogical practices in physiotherapy in terms of manual skills teaching, in order to inform the design of a teaching assistant system using immersive technology.

Study Design

We observed six practical classes over the first semester of first year students of the Doctor of Physiotherapy program at the Department of Physiotherapy at our university. The majority of the classes were taught by Daniel (anonymized name) and one class was taught by Mary (anonymized name). Practical classes in the first semester of the physiotherapy program focused on assessment skills. The six classes taught the students manual skills for assessing patients balance, conducting clinical practice, and skills related to different parts of the body, including foot, neck, spinal, and thoracic area.

The duration of the class was two hours. Each class covered a number of assessment skills. For each skill, a student would volunteer to act as a patient, or mock patient. The teacher demonstrated the skills in the role of a therapist on the mock patient while the other students gathered around to observe. After the demonstration, the students broke out in group to practice the skills on each other, or peer-to-peer (P2P) practice. The teacher approached each group to provide feedback. The same process was repeated for each skill. The teaching approach as observed in our study is commonly adopted across multiple institutions [22].

Data collection

We used two methods to collect data: observations and informal conversations. The researchers were introduced by the teacher to the students at the start of the class. During the demonstration, the researchers observed the teacher and the students as well as their interactions. During P2P practice, the researchers followed the teacher as he/she approached each group to provide feedback. The researchers also spent time observing the students' P2P practice. When time permitted, the researchers also undertook informal conversations with the students. The researchers took hand written notes throughout the class. The class required the students to wear tight-fitting sportswear; therefore, neither video nor voice notes were used to respect the students' privacy.

The observation data was coded and we performed an inductive thematic analysis to derive trends and themes, which are presented below.

Anatomical references

Throughout the classes, especially during P2P practice, the students constantly referred to the skeleton mannequin in the practical room to verify skeletal structure. This was noticed especially in the class regarding the foot, when the students were required to identify the cuneiform bones that form the arch of the feet.

Correct anatomical identifications were a major theme extracted from the interactions between the teacher and students during skills demonstrations. Throughout the demonstration, the teacher consistently elicited verbal comments from the students, to identify the part of the skeletal and/or muscular structure that the teacher was performing on.

Informal conversations with the students during P2P practice indicated that they often struggle to translate their anatomical understanding onto the patient's body. This was confirmed by the teacher based on their teaching experience.

Body annotation

In Mary's class focusing on thoracic anatomy, the students were instructed to use crayon to mark and draw the locations of the rib bones and the outline of the lungs. Both Daniel and Mary confirmed that the practice of on-body drawing is common in physiotherapy classes. A study by McMenamin [23] who surveyed students using professional body painting as a tool for anatomy education proved the benefits of such practice in physiotherapy education.

Observation viewpoint

During the demonstration of the manual skills, the teacher needed to regularly move around the mock patient, which lead to reshuffling of the students' positions in the classroom in order to optimize their viewpoints of the demonstrations. Furthermore, the demonstration generally involved fine motor skills. The students needed to come quite close to the teacher to be able to fully observe and understand the demonstration.

Note taking

The students were given a paper or electronic version of a practical handbook, which outlines the structures of each practical lessons for the semester. For each manual task, there was generally one photo or a simple diagram illustrating the skill. The researchers observed the students when they were taking notes during the teacher's demonstration. Some students took notes directly on the paper version. Some students took notes using a computer or tablet, either on the electronic version of the practical handbook or using a separate note taking application. There were three different types of notes, as observed by the researcher and confirmed through informal conversation with the students: A) textual description of the teacher's action; B) comments from the teachers on common mistakes or notes regarding the skills; C) personal notes and observations experienced by the student during P2P practice. Note type A was the most challenging due to the limited time allowed for observation and the extra cognitive load on the student to observe and take notes at the same time, which was proven by cognitive psychology researchers [24].

AUGMENTATION AND ANNOTATION – DESIGN GUIDELINES

The focus group highlighted the need and potential for enhanced anatomy visualization for physiotherapy students. Previous work has demonstrated that the use of 3D display technology in anatomical education has proven beneficial in 74% of the applications [25]. These displays have enhanced communication between teacher-student [25] and doctor-patient [18]. Researchers have found that the use of AR systems for anatomical purposes helps not only spatial interpretation but also student motivation [26].

The findings from the field study strengthened the importance of anatomical knowledge and understanding for students in physiotherapy. Our studies derive the design guidelines for a physiotherapy education support system, to focus on *augmentation* and *annotation*. The potential of augmentation and annotation for physiotherapy education is aligned with the concept of scaffolding in learner-centered design [27]. Scaffolding is defined in educational psychology as the support provided to students for mindful engagement in learning [28], to understand the roots of new concepts and processes, as opposed to rote learning. Learner-centered design [20] places a strong focus on the learner's needs, which include dimensions of domain knowledge and strategic knowledge. In the context of physiotherapy education, domain knowledge relates to anatomical understanding and strategic information is embedded in the teacher's experience and clinical reasoning decisions. We aimed to design an augmented reality learning system that supported augmentation and annotation, with the focus on the learner's needs.

Augmentation is the fundamental strength of augmented reality, which is defined as the capability to overlay virtual objects onto the physical world [9]. AR is typically enabled through 3 main display technologies: head-mounted display (HMD) [29], projection [16] and mobile devices [30]. Of the 3 technologies, projection-based AR is the most suitable for a classroom context, considering that the projection can easily be seen by a group of students. Augmented reality systems enable tracking to align virtual information to the physical world, which provides an opportunity to augment dynamic anatomical information onto the physical body. The interactions between the teacher and the students in a physiotherapy class are focused around the understanding of dynamic anatomical knowledge on a moving body of the patient as well as implicit clinical reasoning, typically illustrated in the form of on-body annotations.

Figure 2. Augmented Studio setup: projected skeleton model on a student volunteer

Annotation is a common application of AR systems to provide contextual information related to a real world object [31, 32]. Annotation is frequently used in physiotherapy education [8], especially in the form of body painting [23], for the teacher to explicitly illustrate their clinical reasoning decisions. Body painting, however, is a time consuming process, which often takes up to 40 minutes to paint a feature or section of the body [23]. In addition, body painting does not allow easy modification or annotation.

AUGMENTED STUDIO

Based on the design principles of augmentation and annotation, we designed and built the initial prototype of the Augmented Studio, to enhance student learning in physiotherapy using spatial augmented reality annotation on moving bodies.

The Augmented Studio provides a stage (approximately 3mx3m, as shown in Figure 3) in which a teacher can interact with a surrogate or student patient in a lecture or practical class setting. Skeletons and muscles models are projected directly onto the patient's body (see Figure 2), and move with the patient, allowing the teacher to explain the movements of muscles, joints and ligaments dynamically.

Spatial learning environment

The Augmented Studio can be set up in a classroom scenario in a lecture theatre or practical room. A patient (or surrogate) stands on the stage and the movements of the patient are mapped to the virtual skeleton or muscle model, which is projected directly on the body of the patient. Anatomical knowledge about human movements come to life on the stage as the teacher asks the patient to perform simple to complex movements to demonstrate the kinesiology understanding of muscles, joints, and bones in the body. The patient's body becomes a live canvas for the teacher to illustrate clinical reasoning. The teacher can draw annotations directly on the virtual body, through mouse input on a desktop system, which are rendered in real time on the patient's body. The annotations are displayed as colored hand drawings on the skeleton or muscle, to identify certain anatomical structures or to illustrate the joints or muscle connections. In a traditional practical class, the teacher uses still photos, figures, and diagrams which do not capture the real time and complex dynamics of the human movements.

Hardware setup

The stage area of the system is made up of four tripods connected with four cross beams, to create a 3x3x3m volume, called the stage. Two projectors and two Microsoft Kinect sensors are mounted on two adjacent beams. Projection screens are dropped from the beams opposite the projectors. White sheets are used to cover the floor. The result is a three-sided stage with two white walls and a floor for projection mapping. The projectors are positioned in way that their projected images cover the entire stage. Current size 3x3 supports group of classroom up to 15 students gathering around the projected body, similar number to traditional class as observed in design process. The design is scalable to larger size with addition of projectors.

The Augmented Studio setup can be deployed easily in existing medical classroom settings. Figure 3 shows the setup in a corner of a physiotherapy practical classroom. To minimize interference with classroom flow, we only use depth cameras to perform skeletal tracking of movements of body segments. Other technologies such as electromyography sensors [33] or embedded textile sensors [34] require intrusive and cumbersome sensors to track detailed muscle activities.

Calibration

Calibration is completed using the Microsoft RoomAlive toolkit [35]. The toolkit uses projectors and Kinects to estimate in real-time the 3D world coordinate of the stage using structured light calibration [16, 36], which enables projection mapping in the entire volume of the stage. In other words, the system can project virtual information on all surfaces within the tracking volume. After the stage calibration, we combine the result with body tracking using Microsoft Kinect to track a moving body within the stage. We developed an application using the Unity3D game engine that combines projection mapping calibration and Kinect body tracking to project onto the patient's body. The result is the ability to project a 3D virtual model, whose movements are controlled by a moving body, directly onto the physical surfaces of the same moving body. Implementing RoomAlive for a large scale is an important contribution to support classroom settings.

Model Preparation and Animation

While previous work adopted a time consuming and expensive process to reconstruct anatomical models from medical imaging [15], we opted for purchasing an off-the-shelf anatomical model which was verified by field experts to determine suitability and accuracy. We purchased a high polygon count muscular system model, including all major deep and external muscles. We invited a physiotherapy lecturer and an anatomy imaging researcher to review the

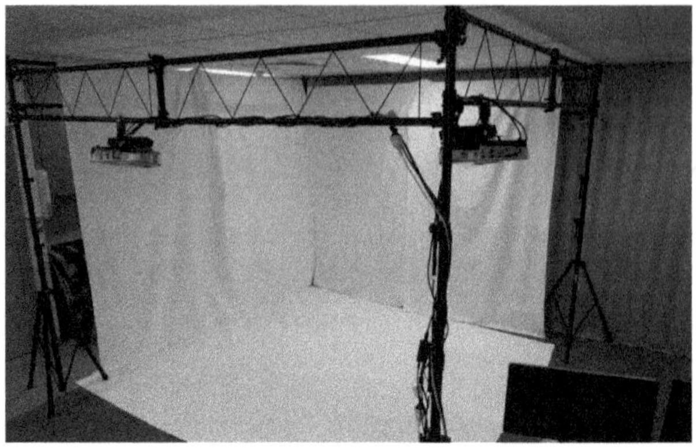

Figure 3. Hardware setup of Augmented Studio: 3x3x3m tracking volume with three sided projection screen and two projectors

model, both of whom validated its accuracy and deemed the model as fit for educational purposes. The model was properly rigged, which is the process that binds the 3D mesh of the model with an internal skeleton structure, for properly articulated animation of the model [37]. We employed the service of a 3D modeling artist to calibrate the rigged skeleton of the model for Kinect skeletal tracking [38], by adjusting the relative locations of the joints to the model to match with positions of the tracked joints relative to the human body, as reported by Kinect skeletal tracking. The model is then scaled to match the size of the human body that it is projected on.

We used a single mesh model containing all the muscles. In order to have realistic muscle animation for anatomical teaching, we applied the process of manual skinning, completed by the 3D modeling artist, with the expert input of a physiotherapy lecturer. Skinning is the process of binding the 3D mesh to the skeleton rig to enable accurate deformation of the mesh during animation [39]. We conducted multiple iterations of skinning and validation via projection on a test subject to achieve maximal animation accuracy for physiotherapy lessons. The validation was completed with an expert lecturer in physiotherapy.

Annotation

Based on our findings from the field study, annotation via hand drawings directly on the body were used as a common learning method, to identify certain anatomical structures or to illustrate the joints and muscle connections. We developed an annotation capability that enabled hand drawings, via mouse input, over the virtual model and the physical body of the students.

Moving annotations

For drawing over the muscles we used an extension on Unity3D called *Paint in 3D*[1]. This extension does not use the classic model for collision detection based on simplified primitives. The extension uses Mesh Colliders[2] in Unity3D, which uses ray casting to draw colors on 3D meshes. The

[1] http://u3d.as/ayF

[2] https://docs.unity3d.com/Manual/class-MeshCollider.html

model we used has a high polygon count, making collision detection a time consuming and resource intensive task. Therefore, real time annotation on a complex model using this method is challenging.

Real time annotations on physical body

Spatial AR requires a physical substrate for projection, which, in Augmented Studio, is the skin surfaces of the human body. In the physiotherapy context, as observed from the field study, there is a need to annotate on both the body and the anatomical structures, such as skeleton and muscles.

When the virtual model and the physical substrate overlaps, for example, the muscular system model, virtual hand drawing annotation can be drawn directly on both the virtual model and the physical body. However, for the skeleton model, the virtual model does not cover the entirety of the body surfaces of the human body. Therefore, we designed a method called *annotation sleeve,* to enable real time hand drawing on both the virtual model and the physical body surfaces. Instead of painting directly on the anatomy model, we created transparent cylindrical convex simple polyhedrons that wrap around the body segments, such as arms, legs or trunks. The sleeve represents the physical body surfaces. The annotation sleeve is a simpler model for calculating collision detection, resulting in a faster performance, as compared to drawing directly on the complex muscular model.

With this solution we can use complex models with high polygon count for real time annotation. We reshaped the annotation sleeve to closely match the muscle mesh while still keeping a low polygon count. The annotation sleeve enables direct hand drawing annotation on complex models (see Figure 4 left) as well as creating a transparent surface to match with the physical substrate for drawing (see Figure 4 right). The low-count polygon with the annotation drawn on it is stretched based on the user's movement. The annotation sleeve is the virtual representation of the body surface, on which the virtual projections reside. Overall, the annotation sleeve bridges the virtual and physical world. Annotation sleeve can be modeled to represent the physical substrate of projection, which is the patient's body. This works particularly well for anatomical models of internal organs or skeletal structures.

User interface

Augmented Studio runs as a standalone Unity3D application (see Figure 6). We used two separate computers for calibration, as each Kinect sensor requires a dedicated computer. After calibration, the system runs on a single machine with multiple display output for the projectors, to which a single Kinect sensor is connected for body tracking.

When the system is running, a student who volunteers to act as a patient can step onto the stage and perform a T position by standing upright, legs together and outstretching both arms horizontally. Once the system detects the T position

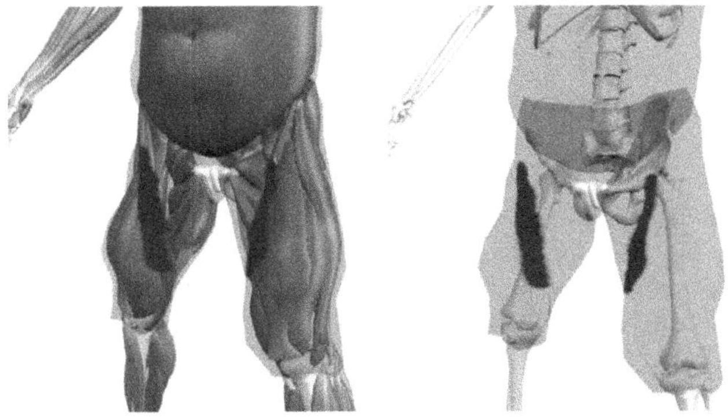

Figure 4. Annotation sleeve (in grey) with drawing in blue to highlight the satorius muscle: Left: on muscular model – the sleeve is modelled tightly around the muscles; Right: on skeleton model, the sleeve acts as a virtual represenation of the body surface for drawing.

(see Figure 2), it will lock the body tracking and projects the virtual model onto the student. The teacher and other students can gather around the volunteer and begin class.

At run time, the system displays the virtual anatomical model in the Unity3D workspace on the computer screen, that captures the movement of the volunteer, while showing the projection on the stage. The workspace allows panning, zooming, and rotation navigation. Currently the annotation capability is completed via a desktop interface using mouse input. The teacher on the stage can perform a gesture to indicate where he/she would like to draw on the volunteer's body, as shown in Figure 5. A student is positioned in front of the computer to draw annotation on the virtual model using mouse input, as indicated. Single point hand tracking can be incorporated in future version of Augmented Studio to enable direct annotation. The system supports three colors blue, green, and red. An eraser is also available. Color and eraser selection is performed via keyboard input.

Benefits

The Augmented studio presents an innovation of novel pedagogical practice delivering benefits to both the teacher and the students. The system aims at enhancing the student learning experience with augmented kinesthetic information and annotated information, provided by the teacher to support interactive observation with augmented visualization, for better clinical understanding of human anatomy and musculoskeletal structures. This will enhance appreciation by students of dynamic change in anatomical configuration of the body through three dimensions.

Compared to previous projection-based systems [17, 18], Augmented Studio provides a tracking volume that allows the volunteer to move freely within the stage without breaking the alignment of the virtual model.

PILOT USABILITY STUDY

We conducted a pilot usability study to evaluate annotation as an original design feature of Augmented Studio. Our hypothesis is that *Augmented Studio enhances the teaching and learning experience for physiotherapy education, through augmentation and annotation.*

Data collection

We recruited graduate physiotherapy students to participate in manual therapy classes, with additional content that was not part of their curriculum, using Augmented Studio. Each class was approximately 15 minutes and was taught by lecturers from the physiotherapy department, who had not been involved with the development of the technology. During class time, the researcher observed and took notes.

After the class, the students completed a questionnaire to evaluate the success of the system for the purpose of physiotherapy education. We adapted DeLone and McLean's model of information system success [40] and another similar approach to evaluate education systems [41] to structure the questionnaire into 5 categories: Learner experience, use intention, system quality, content quality, and overall experience. The participants answered each question in the categories with a 5-point Likert scale (1 for strongly disagree and 5 for strongly agree).

A group discussion with the teacher and participants was conducted at the end to discuss the learning experience, with regards to the communication among the students and towards the teacher. The researcher provided some discussion topics in the form of questions for the students and the teacher. The questions asked about their preferences, comments about performance and limitations, and suggestion for improvements. The participants were encouraged to discuss other topics outside of the provided questions. Video recordings were captured and the researchers took notes during the discussion.

The self-rated questionnaire and discussion enabled us to evaluate the experience of the teacher and students with Augmented Studio, in accordance with our design hypothesis. In this first iteration of the system, we did not aim to evaluate learning benefits in terms of student's performance and/or assessment outcomes.

Participants

Participants were graduate students of physiotherapy from the University of Melbourne. We recruited 9 students (age from 21 to 29, mean 24.7, SD 2.27), 2 teachers and 1 observing teacher. The students were from multiple year levels (2 first years, 3 second year and 4 final year), with 3 males and 6 females. The students and the observing teacher completed the questionnaires. All participants joined the discussion. The participants were recruited through messages posted on the LMS (learning management system) forums of the physiotherapy department.

Task

Each participant attended a 15-minute physiotherapy practical class in a group. The class focused on movement analysis and clinical reasoning skills related to the hip joints. The students were required to understand and be able to analyze a series of movements including kick, squat, single-

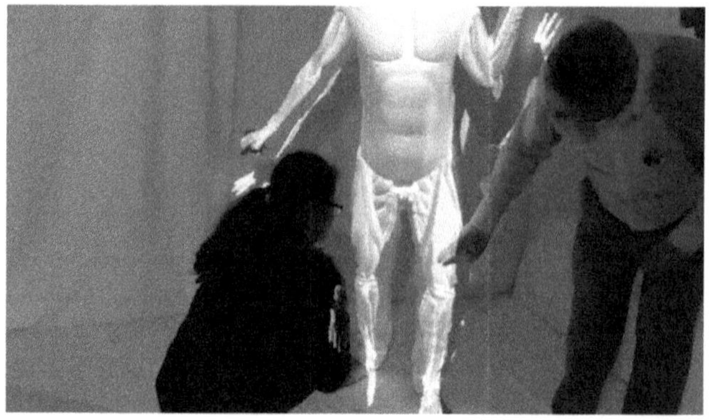

Figure 5. Projected annotation in the form of colored hand drawing on a volunteer's body in a classroom.

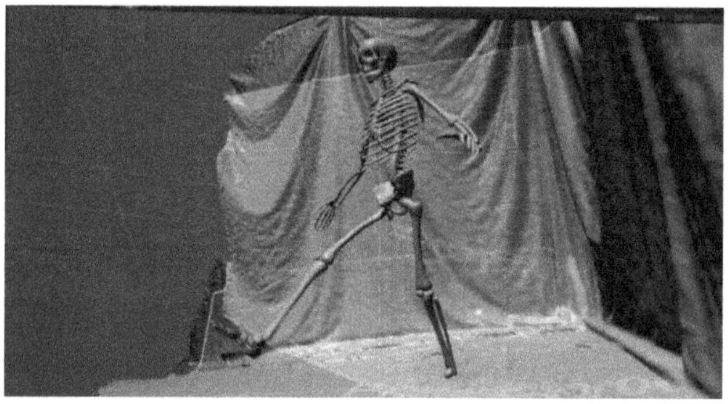

Figure 6. The desktop interface: skeleton model mapped to the volunteer movement on the stage; and the mesh model of the projection sheets that represent the stage

foot squat. The participants then completed the questionnaire and participated in the group discussion. The total time required for each participant was 45 minutes on average. The participants were compensated with a $15 gift voucher.

Procedure

We conducted the classes in one of the practical rooms in the physiotherapy building at our university. We transported all the infrastructure in a section of the practical class the day before. A 3x3x3m stage projection area was set up with two projectors and two Kinect sensors. We ran three classes throughout the day, with an average of three student participants per class. A lab member who is not involved in the development of the system volunteered to participate in the class as the patient. To maximize the projection effect, the volunteer wore a long sleeved white t-shirt and jeans.

Before the class, the participants were briefed with a written plain language statement and a verbal description of the system by the researcher. The class used two virtual anatomy models: skeleton and muscular. As indicated by the teacher during the class, the models were switched, by a researcher at the computer station next to the stage setup. We implemented a partial wizard of oz approach to annotation. The teacher used the annotation feature, by tracing a finger on the projection on the volunteer's body and indicating verbally that the gesture was for annotation. The researcher at the computer station would trace the same path on the virtual model on the screen using a mouse. The teacher could choose between three colors, green, red, or blue, which were also indicated verbally to the researcher. The resulting effect looked as if the teacher drew an annotation directly on the volunteer using their finger. This technique was intended to simulate the future capability of direct annotation for the system. The annotation remained on the body, even when the skeleton and muscle models were switched. Deletion of annotation was completed with a similar process. After the class, the students completed the questionnaires, then re-grouped with the teacher for the group discussion.

Results

We ran descriptive statistics on the questionnaire data. No formal statistical analysis was performed due to the nature of the pilot study. Coded analysis with a theoretical thematic approach [42] was ran on observation notes and group discussion transcript.

Table 1 shows the mean and standard deviation of the questionnaire data. It can be seen that Augmented Studio received a positive response on the majority of factors (mean>4.0). Among the highest scores are satisfaction, enjoyment, improvement with anatomical and kinesiology understanding, useful drawing and visualization, and compelling projection technology.

Such positive responses were also observed during the class. All participants expressed amazement during class, especially when the model switched over and they saw the projected skeleton on the volunteer for the first time. The class started with a muscle model projected on the volunteer.

The teacher also invited students to annotate, using the same method as the teacher, as a way of encouraging participation. During the group discussion, all the participants including teachers unanimously agreed that Augmented Studio enhanced their teaching and learning experience.

DISCUSSION

Overall, the pilot usability of Augmented Studio was a success. The system was greatly complimented by both the teachers and the students. There are two common themes arising from the observation notes and the group discussions. The benefits of Augmented Studio are its ability to enhance the student's learning experience and increased communications between the teacher and the students.

Enhanced experience

Dynamic movements

During the group discussions, all the participants unanimously agreed that their learning had been enhanced in multiple ways. The students found it extremely useful being able to see dynamic movements of anatomical structures. Existing methods of learning anatomy using 3D models only allows viewing a static 3D anatomical model on a computer screen or a pre-recorded animation of movements. The students preferred Augmented Studio because it provides more relevant information with the ability map the 3D model to physical movements.

Category	Description	$\bar{x}$	SD
Overall	Assist learning	4.3	0.48
	Satisfaction	4.1	0.57
	Self-rated success	4.1	0.57
Experience	Better than traditional class	3.9	0.57
	Enjoyment	4.6	0.52
	Fulfil educational needs	3.9	0.74
	Improves communication	4.3	0.67
	Encouraging communication	4.3	0.67
	Efficient	3.7	0.82
	Would recommend to peers	4.8	0.42
	Would use regularly	4	0.67
Use Intention	Teacher proficiency	4.1	0.99
	Improves understanding of: * anatomical structures	4.6	0.52
	* kinesiology	4.1	0.74
	* anatomy movement	3.7	0.95
	Drawing is useful	4.5	0.53
	Visualization is useful	4.6	0.52
System Quality	Projection is compelling	4.5	0.71
	Projection quality	3.9	0.74
	Adaptability	4.4	0.52
	Responsive	3.4	0.84
Content quality	Model quality	4.2	0.42
	Model resolution	3.8	0.42
	Model accuracy	3.8	0.42
	Sufficient annotation details	4.0	0.67
	Model relevance	4.4	0.52

Table 1: Mean and SD values for questionnaire data from students and observing teacher

Scalable tracking volume for tracking and projecting in multiple directions. Current setup has two projectors at 90 angle providing front and side projection on the body. During pilot study, the teacher referred to and annotated on the side of the body in multiple occasions. The volunteer can also move freely around the tracking volume. Previous work [17] only has front view, requires the person to stand still, and does not have the annotation feature.

Cadaver lab

The students compared the experience to cadaver lab, which is proven to help the understanding of 3D anatomical structures for guided dissections by expert demonstrators [8]. The students saw the potential of Augmented Studio to provide similar anatomy learning benefits, with the advantage of seeing the body in movement. A participant commented that even in cadaver lab, you cannot see all the muscles clearly.

Annotations

The annotations on both the skeleton and muscle model helped clarify the attachment of muscles on the body and their functions during movements. One of the students commented that *"I have been to a similar class a thousand times, but for the first time, I understand what the internal rotator muscles do"*, thanks to Augmented Studio.

The students uniformly agreed that the simple annotations of colored lines drawn on the body were exceptionally helpful. Three participants (P1, P2 and P4) commented that at times, just the drawing annotations were enough to illustrate the dynamics of the movements. One student explained that *"seeing (anatomical information) in movement is appealing"* (P1) and *"engaging"* (observing teacher), and that *"the line of pull of the muscle (annotation drawing) helps understand which direction the muscle is going"* (P6).

One student had such a positive experience that they commented that *"I gained more confidence for my upcoming test"*, even though the material covered in the sample class was designed not to overlap with their curriculum.

Increased communication

One observation from the study was that the teacher encouraged the student to perform annotations during class, by tracing their finger on the volunteer's body. The researcher then drew the annotations in real time. Compared to previous notes from the field study, this type of interaction was not observed in the traditional classroom. During the group discussion, both the teacher and the students observed that the annotation capability of Augmented Studio encourages engagement and more interactions between the teacher and the students. Figure 7 captures a moment in the class when the teacher and a student were engaged in the annotations on the volunteer's body. Projection on the white sheets can also help to display other relevant contents for the class, similar to the white board in traditional classrooms. It is important that the system supports large scale projection to match classroom size, where students gather around the teacher and a volunteer mock patient.

By encouraging the students to annotate, the teacher could effectively gauge their understanding of the class content. The observing teacher commented that the normal practical classroom is often very *"dry, and awkward to manipulate the mannequin into the correct posture to illustrate muscle movements"*. The students exclaimed that the annotations were *"very helpful, relevant, and highly interactive"*.

Limitations and Improvements

Despite the positive responses to the Augmented Studio system, participants also highlighted some limitations and suggestions to improve the system. We used two projectors for the study to provide the front and side view of the projections on the volunteer's body. However, it was noted by the teacher and the students that they desired to see the posterior view to illustrate the activities of the hamstring muscle at the back of the leg. Future implementation of Augmented Studio can expand to accommodate more projectors to enable this.

One of the suggestions from the participants was the ability to highlight certain groups of muscles by rendering it in a different color. Another participant commented that they

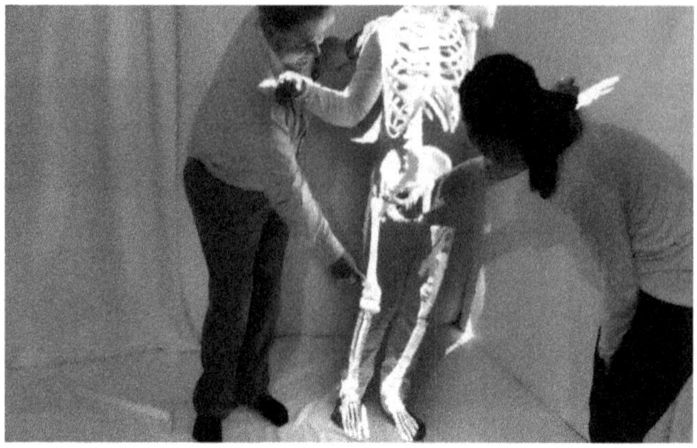

Figure 7. Teacher and student interaction through annotations on a skeleton model

would have liked to visualize different layers of the muscles. Both of those features can be supported through semantic labeling of the anatomical model. Currently the virtual anatomical model used in Augmented Studio does not have any semantic information; in other words, individual muscles are not labelled, therefore, they cannot be identified by the system. The annotation capability of Augmented Studio provides a means to manually highlight muscles using hand-drawing. Future versions of the system will implement a semantic virtual model with labeling.

Tracking issues were also noted by the researcher. However, during the group discussion, participants commented that they were not concerned that tracking did not always present a perfect match between muscles and their relative location on the body, because the anatomical visualization still matched their existing knowledge and understanding.

A final improvement identified during the field study is the requirement for annotations to extend to note taking. The current implementation of the Augmented Studio only allows for hand drawing annotations. There is a potential for future development to incorporate note taking for students during the class. Future study can focus on the advantage and drawbacks of annotations for the students.

CONCLUSION

We have presented the successful application of Augmented Studio to enhance teaching and learning in physiotherapy. We have drawn the connection between physiotherapy education and augmented reality technology through its capability in augmentation and annotation. These findings guided our design and implementation of Augmented Studio, focusing on its features of projection mapping to display virtual anatomical structures on the moving body and projected hand-drawing annotations to illustrate teacher's expert clinical reasoning strategies. Our pilot usability study highlights the true advantage of Augmented Studio to engage the students in a highly interactive communication medium with the teacher, leading to enhanced learning and teaching experiences.

REFERENCES

1. Mark A Jones, Gail Jensen, and Ian Edwards. 2008. Clinical reasoning in physiotherapy. In *Clinical reasoning in the health professions,* (3rd. ed.), Joy Higgs, Mark A Jones, Stephen Loftus, and Nicole Christensen (eds.). Elsevier Health Sciences, 245-256.
2. Vimla L Patel, Jose F Arocha, and David R Kaufman. 1999. Expertise and tacit knowledge in medicine. In *Tacit knowledge in professional practice: Researcher and practitioner perspectives,* Robert J. Sternberg and Joseph A. Horvath (eds.). Psychology Press, 75-99.
3. Marie-Claude Audétat, Suzanne Laurin, Gilbert Sanche, Caroline Béïque, Nathalie Caire Fon, Jean-Guy Blais, and Bernard Charlin. 2013. Clinical reasoning difficulties: a taxonomy for clinical teachers. *Medical teacher*. 35, 3, 984-989.
4. Kevin W Eva. 2005. What every teacher needs to know about clinical reasoning. *Medical education*. 39, 1, 98-106.
5. Carolien Kamphuis, Esther Barsom, Marlies Schijven, and Noor Christoph. 2014. Augmented reality in medical education? *Perspectives on medical education*. 3, 4, 300-311.
6. Joan McMeeken, Gillian Webb, Kerri-Lee Krause, Ruth Grant, and Robin Garnett. 2005. Learning outcomes and curriculum development in Australian physiotherapy education. *Melbourne: The University of Melbourne*.
7. Joy Higgs. 2008. *Clinical reasoning in the health professions.* Elsevier Health Sciences.
8. Kapil Sugand, Peter Abrahams, and Ashish Khurana. 2010. The anatomy of anatomy: a review for its modernization. *Anatomical sciences education*. 3, 2, 83-93.
9. Ronald T. Azuma. 1997. A Survey of Augmented Reality. *Presence: Teleoperators and Virtual Environments*. 6, 4, 355-385. 10.1162/pres.1997.6.4.355
10. Anantha R Kancherla, Jannick P Rolland, Donna L Wright, and Grigore Burdea. 1995. A novel virtual reality tool for teaching dynamic 3D anatomy. In *Computer Vision, Virtual Reality and Robotics in Medicine. Lecture Notes in Computer Science,* N Ayache (eds.). Springer, 163-169.
11. Yohan Baillot and Jannick P Rolland. 1998. Modeling of a knee joint for the VRDA tool. *Studies in health technology and informatics*. 50, 366.
12. Jannick P Rolland and Henry Fuchs. 2000. Optical versus video see-through head-mounted displays in medical visualization. *Presence: Teleoperators and Virtual Environments*. 9, 3, 287-309.
13. Jannick Rolland, Larry Davis, Felix Hamza-Lup, Jason Daly, Yonggang Ha, Glenn Martin, Jack Norfleet, Richard Thumann, and Celina Imielinska. 2003. Development of a training tool for endotracheal intubation: Distributed Augmented Reality. *Studies in health technology and informatics*. 288-294.
14. Sophia Sakellariou, Ben M Ward, Vassilis Charissis, David Chanock, and Paul Anderson. 2009. Design and implementation of augmented reality environment for complex anatomy training: inguinal canal case study. In *Virtual and Mixed Reality. VMR 2009. Lecture Notes in Computer Science, vol 5622,* Shumaker R. (eds.). Springer, Berlin, Heidelberg, 605-614.
15. Tobias Blum, Valerie Kleeberger, Christoph Bichlmeier, and Nassir Navab. 2012. mirracle: An augmented reality magic mirror system for anatomy education. In *IEEE Virtual Reality Workshops (VRW),* 115-116.
16. Oliver Bimber and Ramesh Raskar. 2005. *Spatial augmented reality: merging real and virtual worlds.* CRC press.
17. Adrian S. Johnson and Yu Sun. 2013. Spatial Augmented Reality on Person: Exploring the Most Personal Medium. In *Virtual Augmented and Mixed Reality. Designing and Developing Augmented and Virtual Environments. VAMR 2013. Lecture Notes in Computer Science, vol 8021,* Shumaker Randall (eds.). Springer Berlin Heidelberg, Berlin, Heidelberg, 169-174.
18. Tao Ni, Amy K Karlson, and Daniel Wigdor. 2011. AnatOnMe: facilitating doctor-patient communication using a projection-based handheld device. In *Proceedings of the SIGCHI Conference on Human Factors in Computing Systems,* 3333-3342.
19. Elliot Soloway, Shari L Jackson, Jonathan Klein, Chris Quintana, James Reed, Jeff Spitulnik, Steven J Stratford, Scott Studer, Jim Eng, and Nancy Scala. 1996. Learning theory in practice: Case studies of learner-centered design. In *Proceedings of the SIGCHI conference on Human factors in computing systems,* 189-196.
20. Raven Wallace, Elliot Soloway, Joseph Krajcik, Nathan Bos, Joseph Hoffman, Heather Eccleston Hunter, Dan Kiskis, Elisabeth Klann, Greg Peters, David Richardson, and Ofer Ronen. 1998. ARTEMIS: learner-centered design of an information seeking environment for K-12 education. In *Proceedings of the SIGCHI Conference on Human Factors in Computing Systems,* 195-202. 10.1145/274644.274673
21. Shari L. Jackson, Joseph Krajcik, and Elliot Soloway. 1998. The design of guided learner-adaptable scaffolding in interactive learning environments. In *Proceedings of the SIGCHI Conference on Human*

Factors in Computing Systems, 187-194. 10.1145/274644.274672

22. Stephen Maloney, Michael Storr, Sophie Paynter, Prue Morgan, and Dragan Ilic. 2013. Investigating the efficacy of practical skill teaching: a pilot-study comparing three educational methods. *Advances in Health Sciences Education*. 18, 1, 71-80.
23. Paul G McMenamin. 2008. Body painting as a tool in clinical anatomy teaching. *Anatomical sciences education*. 1, 4, 139-144.
24. Annie Piolat, Thierry Olive, and Ronald T Kellogg. 2005. Cognitive effort during note taking. *Applied Cognitive Psychology*. 19, 3, 291-312.
25. Matthew Hackett and Michael Proctor. 2016. Three-Dimensional Display Technologies for Anatomical Education: A Literature Review. *Journal of Science Education and Technology*. 25, 4, 641-654.
26. J Ferrer-Torregrosa, J Torralba, MA Jimenez, S García, and JM Barcia. 2015. ARBOOK: development and assessment of a tool based on augmented reality for anatomy. *Journal of Science Education and Technology*. 24, 1, 119-124.
27. Kathleen Luchini, Chris Quintana, and Elliot Soloway. 2004. Design guidelines for learner-centered handheld tools. In *Proceedings of the SIGCHI Conference on Human Factors in Computing Systems,* 135-142. 10.1145/985692.985710
28. John D Bransford, Ann L Brown, and Rodney R Cocking. 1999. *How people learn: Brain, mind, experience, and school.* National Academy Press.
29. Paul Milgram, Haruo Takemura, Akira Utsumi, and Fumio Kishino. 1995. Augmented reality: A class of displays on the reality-virtuality continuum. In *Proc. SPIE 2351, Telemanipulator and Telepresence Technologies,* 282-292.
30. Tobias Höllerer and Steve Feiner. 2004. Mobile augmented reality. *Telegeoinformatics: Location-Based Computing and Services. Taylor and Francis Books Ltd., London, UK.* 21,
31. Eric Rose, David Breen, Klaus H Ahlers, Chris Crampton, Mihran Tuceryan, Ross Whitaker, and Douglas Greer. Year. Annotating real-world objects using augmented reality. In *Computer Graphics: Developments in Virtual Environments (Proceedings of CG International'95 Conference),* 357-370.
32. Jason Wither, Stephen DiVerdi, and Tobias Höllerer. 2009. Annotation in outdoor augmented reality. *Computers & Graphics*. 33, 6, 679-689. http://dx.doi.org/10.1016/j.cag.2009.06.001
33. Rachel Nuwer. 2013. Armband adds a twitch to gesture control. *New Scientist*. 217, 2906, 21.
34. J. Meyer, P. Lukowicz, and G. Troster. Year. Textile Pressure Sensor for Muscle Activity and Motion Detection. In *IEEE International Symposium on Wearable Computers (ISWC'06),* 69-72. 10.1109/ISWC.2006.286346
35. Brett Jones, Rajinder Sodhi, Michael Murdock, Ravish Mehra, Hrvoje Benko, Andrew Wilson, Eyal Ofek, Blair MacIntyre, Nikunj Raghuvanshi, and Lior Shapira. 2014. RoomAlive: magical experiences enabled by scalable, adaptive projector-camera units. In *Proceedings of the 27th annual ACM symposium on User interface software and technology,* 637-644.
36. Ramesh Raskar, Greg Welch, Matt Cutts, Adam Lake, Lev Stesin, and Henry Fuchs. Year. The office of the future: A unified approach to image-based modeling and spatially immersive displays. In *Proceedings of the 25th annual conference on Computer graphics and interactive techniques,* 179-188.
37. Marek Teichmann and Seth Teller. 1999. Assisted articulation of closed polygonal models. In *Computer Animation and Simulation'98,* (eds.). Springer, 87-101.
38. Abhishek Kar. 2010. Skeletal tracking using microsoft kinect. *Methodology*. 1, 1-11.
39. Doug L. James and Christopher D. Twigg. 2005. Skinning mesh animations. In *ACM SIGGRAPH 2005 Papers,* 399-407. 10.1145/1186822.1073206
40. William H Delone and Ephraim R McLean. 2003. The DeLone and McLean model of information systems success: a ten-year update. *Journal of management information systems*. 19, 4, 9-30.
41. Sevgi Ozkan, Refika Koseler, and Nazife Baykal. 2009. Evaluating learning management systems: Adoption of hexagonal e-learning assessment model in higher education. *Transforming Government: People, Process and Policy*. 3, 2, 111-130. doi:10.1108/17506160910960522
42. Virginia Braun and Victoria Clarke. 2006. Using thematic analysis in psychology. *Qualitative research in psychology*. 3, 2, 77-101.

Facilitating Development of Pragmatic Competence through a Voice-driven Video Learning Interface

Gabriel Culbertson[1], **Solace Shen**[1], **Malte Jung**[1], **and Erik Andersen**[2]
[1]Department of Information Science, [2]Department of Computer Science, Cornell University
{grc74, solace.shen, mfj28, ela63 }@cornell.edu

ABSTRACT
Authentic foreign language videos are effective for developing pragmatic competence, or sensitivity to meanings expressed by tone and word choice, and the ability to effectively express these meanings. However, established methods for learning from foreign language videos are primarily text-based (e.g. captioning). Using text, learners do not practice aspects of oral performance (e.g. intonation, pausing, and pitch) that are important to pragmatic competence. In this paper we present a voice-driven system where learners practice and learn a foreign language by repeating phrases out loud from any video. Utterances are transcribed and translated and, if captions are available, the system indicates the correctness of the utterance. In an evaluation with 27 participants, we show that participants more frequently used the voice-driven system than a comparison text-based system. Furthermore, in a field study of 130 independent learners, we show potential for community-driven resource collection.

Author Keywords
language learning, pragmatic competence, video learning, speech-recognition

ACM Classification Keywords
K.3.0. Computers and Education: General

INTRODUCTION
Mastering a foreign language requires pragmatic competence, a sensitivity to meanings expressed by tone and word choice, and the ability to effectively express these meanings [18]. Textbooks rarely offer pragmatic input and gaining pragmatic competence through traditional classroom activities is difficult because "classroom discourse is highly conventionalized in ways that severely constrain both the quantity and the quality of learners' participation" [6].

Foreign language videos are an underutilized source of pragmatic input. Sites like YouTube make foreign language videos available that are timely and fit a large variety of topical interests. However, only limited pragmatic competence can be gained from passive video watching [31]. Active engagement with the videos that involve actual practice would lead to more optimal acquisition of pragmatic competence.

CHI 2017, May 06 - 11, 2017, Denver, CO, USA

ISBN 978-1-4503-4655-9/17/05...$15.00
DOI: http://dx.doi.org/10.1145/3025453.3025805

A simple, yet effective, form of active engagement with foreign language videos is repetition. Studies have shown that merely repeating a sentence requires a learner to be able to completely process a language [12]. Existing language learning tools like DuoLingo[1] and Rosetta Stone[2] do not prioritize speaking and existing video learning tools (e.g. [19]) use text rather than speech. Creating tools that focus on repetition of language, and integration of repetition into workflows involving native speaker materials could open new possibilities for language learning tools.

In this paper, we present Seiyuu-Seiyuu, an online video-based learning tool that takes a step towards these goals. Seiyuu means voice actor in Japanese. In Seiyuu-Seiyuu, users suggest videos to watch through a crowdsourced website by linking to YouTube videos. Then, Seiyuu-Seiyuu allows users to repeat utterances they hear in the video, and what's more, to take on the role of an voice actor and speak with paralinguistic cues such as intonation, pitch, etc. Seiyuu-Seiyuu takes advantage of Google Chrome's speech recognition technology to recognize what the user is saying. When using videos for which a transcript has been uploaded, the system allows users to see how much of the video they have correctly repeated.

We present results from an online evaluation study of 27 participants comparing our system to a text-based translation interface. In the study, learners used both the voice and text interface. We found that learners searched 53% more words using the voice interface than the text interface. Furthermore, learners who used voice first conducted more than twice as many total searches with voice and text, indicating an ordering effect from using the voice interface. Furthermore, our qualitative findings support previous research that shows the value of learning with foreign language videos, and suggests that the voice interface is better suited for learning practical conversational skills.

RELATED WORK

Cross-cultural communication
Even with linguistic competence, foreign language learners have difficulty communicating effectively with native speakers. Studies have shown that communication styles largely differ between native and non-native speakers [20, 23] and that these differences impair successful communication. For example, in a lab study, Wong [36] showed that native Mandarin speakers

[1]https://www.duolingo.com/
[2]www.rosettastone.com

had difficulty with repairing misunderstandings in face-to-face communication. Furthermore, in an interview study, Yuan et al. [39] showed that non-native speakers in universities found it difficult to interact with native speakers in part because of lack of common ground and unfamiliarity with informal and idiomatic English. These studies show that understanding the linguistic constructs of a language (e.g. vocabulary and grammar) is not sufficient to communicate effectively, and that communication skills are also important.

Importance of pragmatic competence

"Pragmatics is the study of language from the point of view of users, especially of the choices they make, the constraints they encounter in using language in social interaction and the effects their use of language has on other participants in the act of communication" [10]. Pragmatics is an essential part of communication. Kasper [18] provided the following example: "feed the cat", "can/could/would you feed the cat?", and "the cat's complaining" all communicate the same request, but may have very different impacts on the relationship between the requester and interlocutor. In a study of interpretation of dialogues, Bouton [8] showed that in 27% of cases, non-native speakers with high levels of linguistic competence interpreted the meaning of indirect statements differently from native speakers [18]. Furthermore, the inability to express requests effectively can disadvantage non-native speakers. Bardovi and Hartford [5] showed that in academic advising, non-native speakers were less likely to have their requests fulfilled because of a lack of pragmatic competence.

Some aspects of pragmatic competence learning can be transferred from a learner's first language. However, when norms differ across cultures, this transfer can hurt rather than help learners. In a study of Iranian learners of English, [1] showed that learners with higher proficiency made more pragmatic errors than low-proficiency learners in making refusals because higher proficiency learners tended to transfer more pragmatic knowledge. Because pragmatics differ from language to language, it is important to learn them. This transfer of pragmatic knowledge is nicely illustrated through a classroom exchange between two students that was observed by Hamid and Naeimi [1]. In this exchange, an upper-intermediate Iranian learner of English who plays a teacher responds to a classmate playing a student: "I have been teaching for many years, and I have experienced many paths. I think it's the best way" using formulaic Iranian refusals whereas a native English speaker responded with "Thanks for your suggestion, but we're following a very strict curriculum" [1]. In sum, if a learner wishes to communicate effectively in a second language, pragmatic competence cannot directly transferred from the learner's native language.

Pragmatic competence education

Because of the vast quantity and diversity of contexts that learners may find themselves in, traditional teaching methods that explicitly assign ideal responses to specific scenarios can fail to prepare learners for the real world. In a review of education literature, Kasper [18] writes that pragmatic competence cannot be taught and instead, "[t]he challenge for foreign or second language teaching is whether we can arrange learning opportunities in such a way that they benefit the development of pragmatic competence in L2". The key to teaching pragmatic competence is in giving learners as much experience as possible with as many different scenarios as possible. A later study by Matsumura [21] showed that in Japanese learners, the amount of exposure to English inside and outside of the classroom was more predictive of pragmatic development than English proficiency. Furthermore, other studies have shown that high linguistic competence is not necessary for pragmatic learning. For example, Takehashi and Beebe [28] showed that even early learners can acquire pragmatic competence given enough experience with real scenarios. Furthermore, constructivist views of education suggest that learners must use these scenarios to construct knowledge for themselves [7]. Together, these findings indicate that pragmatic competence is developed independently of linguistic competence and the key factor in pragmatic development is the amount and diversity of language experiences that learners engage with.

Existing language learning tools

There has been a lot of interest in HCI in creating tools for foreign language learning. Some of this work has focused on learning vocabulary, such as MicroMandarin, which uses the user's location to suggest relevant words [14] and Wait Learning, which teaches vocabulary during natural lulls in online conversations [9]. Other systems focused on teaching grammar, such as Ingenium, which provides virtual manipulatives for learning Latin grammar [40]. Finally, video games have been shown to provide a fruitful context for language learning, such as ToneWars, which teaches Chinese tones [17], and Crystallize, a 3D immersive game for learning Japanese vocabulary and grammar [11]. However, in order to learn how to understand speech effectively, learners need to go beyond vocabulary and grammar and listen to a large amount of speech from many different native speakers [15] and in multiple contexts [24].

Learning with foreign language videos

Given the importance of learning language in a variety of contexts, videos are a natural learning resource because they are available across the world and provide many diverse contexts for learning. According to Secules et al. [26], "[v]ideo permits second language learners to witness the dynamics of interactions as they observe native speakers in authentic settings...". Use of video in classrooms has also been shown to improve learner's fluency. For example, Weyers [33] found that the use of Spanish television programs in the classroom improved students' confidence and diversity of words used in communication. Some educators have identified video as an effective tool specifically for pragmatic learning (e.g. [32]).

However, learning directly from authentic foreign language videos can be very challenging for learners. In traditional learning settings, instructors reduce rates of speech and adjust their vocabulary to accommodate learners [3], but in authentic input (such as videos), learners must adapt to the increased rate of speech and more complex word choice and linguistic structure [4]. Because of this, many researchers have studied how to structure activities for learning from videos and developed tools to improve video learning. Foreign language captions are one of the most widely used and studied methods, and have been shown to be more effective for learning than translated subtitles or audio-only video [35, 22]. Others have studied ways to improve over just displaying captions. For example, Kovacs and Miller [19] developed a system for simultaneously displaying the native-language caption along with the English translation and included word-by-word translations upon hovering over individual foreign language words.

Caption generation itself has been explored as a learning method. For example, Williams and Thorne [34] developed a course for subtitle generation and found it to be effective for learning, but it required extensive training in order for learners to participate. A system was developed to make the captioning process more approachable to learners by using a machine-generated transcript as a starting point and providing word-by-word translations [2].

While these systems enable learners to learn from videos, they are all text based, which may limit how deeply learners process speech from the video. For example, Swain and Lapkin [27] argue that learners notice problems with their output during the process of speaking, and then can go on to correct these problems. We therefore see an opportunity for novel language learning systems that draw from a voice-driven approach to learning from videos.

Voice-driven systems

Voice recognition has been explored in several different educational contexts. For example, Yoon et al. [38] developed a system to annotate texts with voice and found it to allow for better expression of complex ideas. Specifically in language learning, applications such as Rosetta Stone[3] incorporate automated pronunciation feedback. However, as noted by Gaur et al. [16], speech recognition systems are often inadequate for producing high-quality text transcripts. Yoon et al. [38] noted similar issues with voice transcription in their system: "participants preferred using the [audio] waveform over transcription because of the detrimental effect of transcription errors". In summary, previous research indicates that voice driven systems have promise in learning tools, but more work needs to be done to determine if current speech-recognition technology is adequate to provide good foreign language learning experiences.

UNDERSTANDING LEARNER USE OF MEDIA DESIGNED FOR NATIVE SPEAKERS

To explore the role of authentic media use in language learners, we conducted a survey with 36 university participants. Participants were between 18 and 25 years old (mean=20), and learned a combined 11 different languages. 55% had spent at least some time learning 2 or more languages. 63% used use native speaker media in their learning. Of the learners that reported using materials designed for native speakers for learning, when asked how they dealt with material they could not understand, many reported using online translation systems such as Google translate (45%). Other strategies included using subtitles (18%), native speaker friends or family (9%) and continuing to listen despite not understanding (9%).

[3]www.rosettastone.com

Motivation for learning	percent
Class	21%
Professional development	12%
Interest in language or culture	19%
Tourism	14%
Broaden world view	16%
Personal Challenge	11%
Communicate with family or friends	7%

Figure 1. Motivations for surveyed learners.

Learning method	percent
Class	59%
Media designed for native speakers	14%
Native speaker friends	10%
Applications	8%
Living abroad	9%

Figure 2. Learning sources for surveyed learners.

Learners were asked to report their biggest challenge in learning a language and results were coded and reported in Figure 3. When asked about the greatest challenge that learners faced, 41% of learners learners reported challenges related to oral competence: 14% said conversation (e.g. *Speaking in conversation as a native would*), 8% said limited interaction with native speakers (e.g. *it was very hard to find other speakers to practice with*), 8% said nuances in language (e.g. *Remembering the correct use of certain words even though they have the same meaning*), 8% said native-like pronunciation (e.g. *Accents to sound natural*), and 3% said listening (e.g. *having to extract what a speaker was saying*). Some learners also indicated difficulty finding resources for improving oral proficiency: one of the most significant challenges was accessing learning resources that allowed me to practice speaking and listening. The reported difficulties with oral proficiency match with the findings of Edge et al. [13]. These findings indicate a need for more effective oral learning tools, specifically those that focus on pragmatic competence.

DESIGN

The most common existing methods for learning a foreign language make use of carefully designed learning materials, which, we argue, fail to provide the breadth of experiences that are necessary to gain situational fluency. Use of authentic materials has been shown to enable pragmatic competence learning. However, using materials designed for native speakers can be incredibly challenging because there are many unfamiliar words and structures in these materials and finding out the meaning of these words and structures is difficult. Therefore, our primary design question was: how can we design to make authentic foreign language materials more accessible?

We observed three key opportunities which inspired the design: (1) the internet is home to countless free authentic foreign language videos, (2) repeating phrases or dialogues from videos is a natural activity and helps improve oral proficiency, and (3) speaking bypasses the need to type which is often very challenging and time consuming in a foreign language.

Challenge	percent
Motivation	17%
Grammar	17%
Conversation	14%
Limited interaction with native speakers	8%
Nuances in language	8%
Reaching native-like pronunciation	8%
Self-confidence	8%
Bad teachers	6%
Lack of time	6%
Listening	3%
Reading	3%
Writing	3%

Figure 3. Greatest challenges faced by learners as identified by our survey. Motivation, grammar and conversation appear to be the most critical.

(1) Freely available videos on YouTube include 76 languages and over 100 million videos[4]. Some countries also have their own streaming video sites (i.e. China - http://www.youku.com/) which can increase the number of videos even further.

(2) Copying words and phrases is how we learn our first language. Videos specifically have been shown to be an important source of learning for infants [25]. In adult learning, many educators use oral repetition as a central learning excercise (e.g. [30]). Furthermore, listening to foreign language before speaking (known as word priming) has been shown to improve recognition and pronunciation of those words [29].

(3) In our survey of authentic material use by foreign language learners, we found that of those that used materials designed for native speakers, 45% reported using a text based tool such as a dictionary or Google translate in order to learn from the material. Furthermore, many learners use videos with flashcard systems such as Anki[5] which requires transcribing text from videos.

Considering these opportunities, we developed an interface for watching any foreign language video while the learner can speak words or phrases to see them transcribed and translated below the video.

Learners use the system by first selecting a video to learn from. For example, a learner of English might choose the television program *Friends*. As the learner watches the program, they listen carefully for words and phrases they can pick out and then repeat them. For example, maybe the learner hears the phrase "Chandler, I sensed it was you." but is unsure of what "sensed" means. The learner would then hold the spacebar to pause the video and repeat the phrase aloud. The speech recognition system would recognize and display the text for the phrase. Below the transcribed text, a translation would appear in the learner's native language. After the learner reads the transcription and translation, they release the spacebar and continue watching the video.

[4]https://www.youtube.com/yt/press/statistics.html
[5]anki.net

The system was implemented using node.js as a backend. Speech recognition was realized using the Speech Recognition Webkit built into Google Chrome. Translation used the Google translate API.

Website

To improve long-term learning and engagement, the web version of the system includes additional features to support existing language learning practices and community building. To support long-term learning, spoken utterances can be saved to a history and edited. A plugin was also developed to allow learners to sync saved phrases with the spaced repetition system Anki[6].

To better engage learners with the system, game features were added. Learners can choose to upload a caption file, which allows the system to check for the accuracy of utterances. When captions are available, learners receive a score based on how much of the video they are able to repeat and learners can watch the same segment multiple times to increase overall progress. Furthermore, a transcript of the video is shown on the side to indicate which words have already been spoken and which words the learner still needs to say. The system is shown in Figure 4.

The website includes a *popular* page where recently viewed YouTube videos are displayed and learners can view their progress as shown in Figure 5. Learners can also choose to add their own video from YouTube or their hard drives. If learners choose a new YouTube video, the video gets displayed on the *popular* page. Videos from users' hard drives videos are not uploaded to the server or displayed on the *popular* page.

EVALUATION

Field study

The site was announced on the reddit LanguageLearning forum[7] as well as individual sub-reddits for Japanese[8] and Spanish[9]. Data was collected through usage logs. A total of 130 participants tried the system and 71 learners spoke 10 or more phrases. Learners that spoke 10 or more phrases spoke an average of 71 utterances. Users uploaded 22 new YouTube videos (in French, Spanish and Japanese) and used 6 unique media from their hard drives. This suggests that the tool can function in the wild.

Furthermore, since some videos may be more effective for pragmatic learning than others, we believe that identifying and sharing effective resources is an important task. Our findings about learner use of our system suggest that the tool could provide motivation for learner-sourced resource evaluation and sharing.

The results indicated that the system has potential to function as an independent learning tool, but we wanted to do a more systematic exploration in order to better understand how the tool compares to existing tools.

[6]anki.net
[7]reddit.com/r/languagelearning
[8]reddit.com/r/LearnJapanese
[9]reddit.com/r/learnspanish

Figure 4. The interface with game features provides feedback when learners sayid phrases correctly (1) over transcribed and translated text (2). A progress bar and text displays how much of the video the learner has correctly repeated (3). Learners can add utterances to their library or remove them using buttons (4), or upload transcripts and adjust how text is displayed through the settings (5). When available, a transcript is also displayed to show how much of the video a learner has repeated, and help learners find new words and phrases to listen to (6). Screenshot taken from *Ode to Joy* on YouTube (https://www.youtube.com/watch?v=4wGpu56WQGQ).

Formal Evaluation

To gain insight into the usability and effectiveness of our system compared to other video learning methods, we conducted an online study with foreign language learners. Originally, the study was available in six languages, but we only had participants use Spanish, French, and Chinese (Mandarin). In our survey of language learners, we found that learners most frequently used Google Translate to learn from native speaker materials. Therefore, to examine the effectiveness of Seiyuu-Seiyuu we developed an interface as a control that allowed learners to type into a textbox upon which translations appeared below using the Google translate API as shown in Figure 7. We used a within subjects design where approximately half of the participants first used the speech interface for video learning and the remaining participants first used the text interface. For all languages, realistic dramas or comedies were chosen for learners to watch. The video was different for each language. This is because culture is an essential element of pragmatic learning, so it was important to us to choose videos coming from cultures where each language was spoken. The videos used are shown in Figure 8.

Participants clicked on a link which redirected them to a webpage where they spoke a test phrase into their microphone in order to verify that speech recognition was working properly. Participants then chose a language and completed a short survey about their prior experience with the chosen language. Next, participants were randomly assigned to either use the speech interface first or the typing interface first. When using the speech interface, text was displayed to indicate that participants should hold the spacebar to pause the video and begin speaking. After pressing the spacebar, the interface would indicate that they should begin speaking as shown in Figure 6. As the participants spoke, their utterances were recognized and translated below the video. In the typing condition, the interface indicated that participants could pause the video by clicking on it, and participants could type words and phrases to see their translations. In each case, the video segment was 10 minutes long. Following the first video segment, participants were asked to rate difficulty, usefulness and enjoyment as well as recall words from the video with their surrounding contexts. Participants then watched a different 10 minute segment of the same video using the interface that they did not use in the first part of the study. Following the second task, participants were asked to report the same information as in the first part. Finally, participants were redirected to a survey where they provided demographic information and were asked to discuss their learning experience and compare the two interfaces.

Participants

Participants were recruited through a campus research system. Participants were compensated either $10 or research credit for participation. Three participants were excluded because they indicated that they were already native speakers of the chosen language or because they skipped parts of the experiment. A total of 27 participants (15 typing first and 12 speech first) were used in the final analysis. 67% of the participants did the study in Spanish, 26% of participants did the study in French and 7% of participants did the study in Chinese.

Figure 5. When visiting the website, learners choose a language (1) and can then view videos that other learners watched in that language (2). Learners can also choose their own video from YouTube or their computer (3). Links to Youtube become visible for all users, but personal videos are only visible to the user who uploaded them.

No significant differences were found in reported measures between languages.

Hypotheses

Given previous research on foreign language learning and voice-driven system design, we set up two hypotheses to explore possible differences between voice-driven and text-driven conditions. First, (H1) learners will try to look up more words in the speaking condition. The cognitive cost of speaking should be less than typing, so we expect learners will be more willing to look up words. Furthermore, previous research on voice-driven learning tools indicates a preference for generating speech over text [38]. (H2) Learners will find the speaking version more useful. Speaking is a goal of many learners, so we expect practicing speaking will be seen as more practical.

Measures

Usage

Usage was measured as the number of times a learner spoke a new utterance or typed a new phrase. This is a numerical score that counts the number of interactions.

Usefulness measure

After each video section, learners were asked to report how useful they found the system using a continuous slider (0 to 100).

Figure 6. In the voice interface used in our evaluation, learners were given instructions on how to use the system (1), and spoken phrases appeared below the video (2) with a translation below the utterance (3). In Japanese and Chinese, pronunciation was displayed beneath the characters. Since the speech recognition was not always accurate, the "more" button (4) could be clicked to show alternatives from the speech recognition system. Screenshot was taken from *Keikon Dekinai Otoko* on YouTube (https://www.youtube.com/watch?v=dX8vYhztrxM).

FINDINGS

Participants' usage frequencies were analyzed using linear mixed regression model. The independent variables were interface type (speech vs. typing) and condition (speech interface first vs. typing interface first). The interface type x condition interaction term was also entered into the model but was non-significant, $F(1,25) = 0.498$, $p = .487$, $\eta^2 = .015$. The within-subject effect of interface type was significant, $F(1,25) = 7.23$, $p = .013$, $\eta^2 = .221$, indicating that participants on average used the speech interface more ($M = 26.52$, $SD = 17.42$) than the typing interface ($M = 18.44$, $SD = 13.95$). The between-subject effect of condition was also significant, $F(1,25) = 29.45$, $p < .001$, $\eta^2 = .541$, indicating that when participants used the speech interface first, they interacted (speech and typing combined) with the system more ($M = 67.00$, $SD = 18.29$) than those participants that used the typing interface first ($M = 27.33$, $SD = 19.32$). Pairwise comparisons of simple effects also revealed the same finding. For the speech interface, participants in the speech interface first condition used it more often ($M = 38.75$, $SD = 12.08$) than participants in the typing interface first condition ($M = 16.73$, $SD = 14.77$), $p < .001$. Similarly, for the typing interface, participants in the speech interface first condition used it more often ($M = 28.25$, $SD = 12.75$) than participants in the typing interface first condition ($M = 10.60$, $SD = 9.23$), $p = .001$.

No significant differences were found in enjoyment, difficulty or reported number of phrases remembered.

Perceived usefulness and usability

A 2x2 mixed ANOVA, with interface type as the within-subject factor and condition as the between-subject factor was performed on participants' perceptions of usefulness. Participants on average found the speech interface more useful ($M = 27.67$, $SD = 22.96$) than the typing interface ($M = 21.41$, $SD = 20.90$). This difference was marginally

Figure 7. In the typing interface used in our evaluation, learners were given instructions below the video (1), could type word or phrases into a text field (2) and translations would appear below after the learner stopped typing (3). Screenshot taken with *Sur Le Fil* on YouTube (`https://www.youtube.com/watch?v=bapP3JM3SZA&t=314s`).

Language	video
Spanish	*Mi Corazón Es Tuyo*
French	*Sur Le Fil*
Chinese (Mandarin)	欢乐颂 *(huan'le'song), Ode to Joy*

Figure 8. Learning sources for surveyed learners.

significant, $F(1,25) = 3.51$, $p = .073$, $\eta^2 = .120$. The main effect of condition as well as interaction effect were non-significant.

However descriptively, when asked on a preference scale (1-7), with 1 being strongly prefer typing interface, 4 being neutral, and 7 being strongly prefer speech interface, most participants found the speech method more useful (63% of participants) than the typing method (15% of participants) and some were neutral (22%).

Although some participants had difficulty with the accuracy of the voice recognition engine (e.g. P6: *"sometimes it could not understand what I was trying to say"*), many participants found speaking was easier than typing (e.g. P18: *"...less cognitive overhead than typing"*, P13: *"...you could just say what you heard [instead of typing]"*). Furthermore, it eliminated the need to worry about spelling (P19: *"The dictionary method was hard because I didn't know how to spell some phrases so it was easier to repeat them."*, P12: *"I was struggling with how to spell the words so that distracted me."*). Other participants indicated that saying words aloud helped with memorization (e.g. P12: *"Saying the words out loud makes me remember them more."*, P15: *"You can pick up on words more quickly by actually saying them out loud."*).

However, some participants preferred the text method because it helped to train spelling (e.g. P5: *"[the voice method] did not help me with placing accents on letters as the program did that for me"*, P7: *"you may be able to hear the words being spoken in conversation but you may not know how to spell them when writing or reading."*). This finding indicates that learner type is important to consider when choosing between text- and voice-driven systems, and perhaps both methods are necessary for comprehensive learning.

While some participants wanted more feedback on pronunciation (e.g. *"I won't know if I pronounce or use these words correctly compared to the method of talking this language with the native speaker."*, P10: *"Saying it out loud doesn't give you a basis for pronunciation so I was saying them incorrectly."*) or blamed their pronunciation for trouble with the speech recognition engine (e.g. P21: *"[The voice interface is] harder if you have terrible pronunciation"*), many participants found the system to be helpful for improving pronunciation (e.g. P15: *"with the voice learning method you can practice speaking the words and sounding them out which is helpful for conversational Spanish."*, P23: *"Voice helped me understand accents more than typing"*).

Furthermore, some participants directly discussed learning pragmatic features with the system (e.g. P22: *"[M]uch better than doing it from a book. This way I know the right way to pronounce things and the context I might use the phrases in."*, P26: *"Voice learning is advantageous to other types of learning because you can hear the emotion in a person's voice. I find that Spanish speakers especially give a lot of clues to what they're saying in the way that they're saying it."*). Furthermore, the system could help learners overcome lack of confidence in pronunciation (e.g. P11: *"[practicing with the voice interface] will not be embarrassing if I pronounce the words badly."*).

Learning with native speaker materials

Using materials designed for native speakers is perceived as difficult by many learners. In the comments, many learners indicated that the speech was difficult to follow. When asked about the materials, 60% of learners indicated that the material was very challenging and learners reported an average of 7/10 points when asked how difficult the material was. For example, P3 wrote *"I found it very difficult to follow along because they were talking so fast"* and P13 wrote *"I may have overestimated my French-speaking ability; but I find it difficult to understand films in which the people are speaking fluidly because of how quickly they talk."*.

However, just because this activity is challenging does not mean it is not worth doing. Many participants indicated that the use of authentic materials made the learning more valuable (e.g. P10: *"I think the materials designed for native speakers is more challenging but it is more original and I believe that I can use it in related situations."*, P22: *"...made me feel like I was learning phrases I would actually use."*). Furthermore, some participants recognized that practice with native speech can can help with communicative goals (e.g. P13: *"[T]his is more real-world applicable. When one speaks to native French speakers; they are not going to enunciate every syllable or speak slowly like we learn in French class."*). We also speculate that the tool raises awareness in learners about the thoroughness of their understanding. It is easy for a learner to think that they understood the phrase adequately, but repeating phrases out loud can highlight the parts they missed.

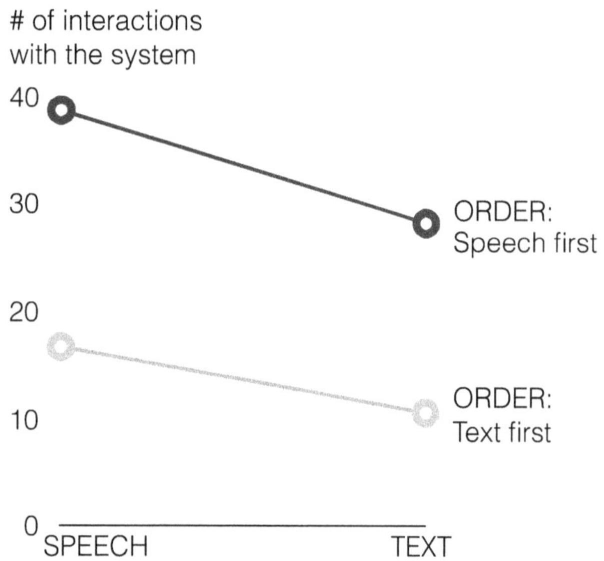

Figure 9. Number of interactions with the system for each interface in each ordering. Learners used the speech interface significantly more than the text interface, and using speech first resulted in more overall interactions.

Our findings also indicate that learners had diverging perspective on how to learn from native speaker materials. Learners were told that they did not need to understand everything, but some learners felt uncomfortable with this learning method (e.g. P18: *"Not as structured. I don't learn the exact grammar. I missed a lot of the dialogue."*, P6: *"It made it a lot harder because they were talking so fast and it was assumed that I could understand when I really had no idea what was going on"*). However, others found this method to be a refreshing change from classroom learning (e.g. P19: *"It felt less intimidating because I knew I wasn't supposed to understand everything. In a classroom; a lot of the material is designed for people at your level to there is more pressure to know exactly what everything means."*, P21: *"...It was also fun to try and repeat the words and trying to see if the translation was correct or made sense."*). Given different perspectives on learning through authentic materials, future work should more closely examine these perspectives and could explore designs to promote or support different learning styles.

Order effect

The linear mixed regression analysis reported above revealed that when participants used the speech interface first, they interacted with the system more through either speaking or typing than those participants that used the typing interface first as shown in Figure 9. We found this to be very interesting, but can only speculate on the reasons for this.

We speculate that the speech activity increased learner engagement or sharpened learners' listening ability. In open-ended comments, of participants that started with text, 40% used the word "fast", "rapid" or "quick" to describe the speech, whereas of those with that started with speech only 25% used one of those words to describe the speech. This could indicate that the speech activity prepared learners for better listening. However, more work needs to be done to explore this area. Regardless of the reason, we find the increased engagement with the video after using the voice interface to be an encouraging sign.

LIMITATIONS

Limitations with speech recognition technology and machine translation

Both speech recognition and machine translation are imperfect technologies. Many participants mentioned that they wished the speech recognition were more accurate. However, we chose to use these technologies over pre-annotated videos because our original design intent was to allow learners to tap into any video or audio resource rather than just those prepared by instructors. By choosing to use raw video and audio, we believe that our findings are more generalizable. Furthermore, despite learners' frustration with inaccuracies, we found that the majority of learners still preferred the speech interface over the text interface.

Furthermore, correctness feedback was not always available. Correctness feedback is beneficial, but there is a tradeoff, as it requires resources that are not available for every video. Our goal was to design a tool that enables users to use any video as a learning resource and we showed that this is possible. Previous literature has shown that even without feedback, learners notice and fix errors when generating second language writing [27]. In another study, novice learners utilized visuals, audio, and narrative understanding to identify errors in foreign language transcripts when provided Google translate [2]. Similarly, we expect users of this tool to be able to identify speech errors using speech recognition output and translation service.

In further exploration we found that 13% of utterances in our study were repeated, suggesting that learners were making corrections during use.

Limitations with videos

In the formal evaluation, participants did not have the option to choose a video, and were only shown specific segments from the video. In real use, we would expect that learners could choose their own videos and choose which parts to watch, as they did in the field study. We would expect that if the videos were better matched to learners' interests and skill level that results would only improve.

Learning limitations

Previous work has shown that interaction with videos can lead to pragmatic competence learning. Therefore our goal was to increase interaction with videos and we did not take quantitative measures of learning. However, we do have qualitative evidence that learners were gaining competence. For example, learners reported the system improving their listening skills, pronunciation, and contextual vocabulary. Furthermore, we asked learners to recall words and phrases along with their contexts and learners reported an average of 2.7 word-context pairs in both the text and voice conditions. This suggests that the video learning activity was leading to contextual learning, but more work will need to be done to improve our understanding of the quantity and quality of learning. Previous work on pragmatic competence learning has used longitudinal studies with durations ranging from a semester to multiple years. In order to perform a qualitative evaluation of our system, future work should perform a longitudinal study of the learning method.

Finally, we wish to point out that language learning is a complex and nuanced activity and, as written by Xiao and Ishii, "traditional HCI methodologies with their focus on optimizing quantifiable metrics risk blinding researchers to the richness and nuance of artistic practices" [37]. Similarly, we fear that a focus on quantifiable metrics in language learning (e.g. vocabulary and grammar) blinds us to essential aspects of foreign language learning, such as pragmatic compotence.

CONCLUSION

The presence of rich context and authentic language makes videos invaluable resources for learning pragmatic competence, but learning with foreign language videos is very difficult. The challenge is to design tools that make the videos more accessible and allow learners to absorb as much as possible from the video materials.

Our results show that using voice is a natural and effective way for learners to engage with videos, and repeating words and phrases from videos can cause learners to engage more with text-based video activities. We found that the tool affords learning through videos that learners enjoy (shown by the variety of cartoons and dramas that learners uploaded during the field study), understanding where phrases might be used (e.g. one participant said: "*This way I know the right way to pronounce things and the context I might use the phrases in.*"), and practicing speech rich in emotion and subtlety (e.g. one participant reflected: "*Voice learning is advantageous to other types of learning because you can hear the emotion in a person's voice*"). To our knowledge, this is the first study to explore using automatic speech recognition to support video learning, and much work remains to be done in interface design to explore other methods for providing feedback, structuring learning within the system, and boosting learner confidence.

Learning with native speaker materials has the potential to be engaging and effective for learning deep language abilities such as pragmatic competence. This tool is a first step in exploring this space, but much work remains to be done to better understand the what can be learned through native speaker materials, and how best to support learners that wish to use these materials.

REFERENCES

1. Hamid Allami and Amin Naeimi. 2011. A cross-linguistic study of refusals: An analysis of pragmatic competence development in Iranian EFL learners. *Journal of Pragmatics* 43, 1 (2011), 385–406.
2. Anatomized. 2017. Have your cake and eat it too: Foreign language learning with a crowdsourced video captioning system. In *Proceedings of the 20th ACM Conference on Computer-Supported Cooperative Work & Social Computing*. ACM. In press.
3. Susan M Bacon. 1992a. Authentic listening in Spanish: How learners adjust their strategies to the difficulty of the input. *Hispania* 75, 2 (1992), 398–412.
4. Susan M Bacon. 1992b. The relationship between gender, comprehension, processing strategies, and cognitive and affective response in foreign language listening. *The modern language Journal* 76, 2 (1992), 160–178.
5. Kathleen Bardovi-Harlig and Beverly S Hartford. 1990. Congruence in native and nonnative conversations: Status balance in the academic advising session. *Language learning* 40, 4 (1990), 467–501.
6. Julie A Belz. 2007. The role of computer mediation in the instruction and development of L2 pragmatic competence. *Annual Review of Applied Linguistics* 27 (2007), 45.
7. Phil Benson. 2013. *Teaching and researching: Autonomy in language learning*. Routledge.
8. Lawrence F Bouton. 1988. A cross-cultural study of ability to interpret implicatures in English. *World Englishes* 7, 2 (1988), 183–196.
9. Carrie J Cai, Philip J Guo, James Glass, and Robert C Miller. 2014. Wait-learning: leveraging conversational dead time for second language education. In *CHI'14 Extended Abstracts on Human Factors in Computing Systems*. ACM, 2239–2244.
10. David Crystal. 2011. *Dictionary of linguistics and phonetics*. Vol. 30. John Wiley & Sons.
11. Gabriel Culbertson, Shiyu Wang, Malte Jung, and Erik Andersen. 2016. Social Situational Language Learning through an Online 3D Game. In *Proceedings of the 2016 CHI Conference on Human Factors in Computing Systems*. ACM, 957–968.
12. P Duff. 2000. Repetition in foreign language classroom. *Second and foreign language learning through classroom interaction* (2000), 109.
13. Darren Edge, Kai-Yin Cheng, Michael Whitney, Yao Qian, Zhijie Yan, and Frank Soong. 2012. Tip tap tones: mobile microtraining of mandarin sounds. In *Proceedings of the 14th international conference on Human-computer interaction with mobile devices and services*. ACM, 427–430.
14. Darren Edge, Elly Searle, Kevin Chiu, Jing Zhao, and James A Landay. 2011. MicroMandarin: mobile language learning in context. In *Proceedings of the SIGCHI Conference on Human Factors in Computing Systems*. ACM, 3169–3178.
15. Maxine Eskenazi. 1999. Using a computer in foreign language pronunciation training: What advantages? *Calico Journal* (1999), 447–469.
16. Yashesh Gaur. 2015. The Effects of Automatic Speech Recognition Quality on Human Transcription Latency. In *Proceedings of the 17th International ACM SIGACCESS Conference on Computers & Accessibility*. ACM, 367–368.

17. Andrew Head, Yi Xu, and Jingtao Wang. 2014. Tonewars: Connecting language learners and native speakers through collaborative mobile games. In *Intelligent Tutoring Systems*. Springer, 368–377.
18. Gabriele Kasper. 1997. Can pragmatic competence be taught. *NetWork* 6 (1997), 105–119.
19. Geza Kovacs and Robert C Miller. 2014. Smart subtitles for vocabulary learning. In *Proceedings of the SIGCHI Conference on Human Factors in Computing Systems*. ACM, 853–862.
20. Han Z Li. 1999. Grounding and information communication in intercultural and intracultural dyadic discourse. *Discourse Processes* 28, 3 (1999), 195–215.
21. Shoichi Matsumura. 2003. Modelling the relationships among interlanguage pragmatic development, L2 proficiency, and exposure to L2. *Applied Linguistics* 24, 4 (2003), 465–491.
22. Holger Mitterer and James M McQueen. 2009. Foreign subtitles help but native-language subtitles harm foreign speech perception. *PloS one* 4, 11 (2009), e7785.
23. Duyen T Nguyen and Susan R Fussell. 2012. How did you feel during our conversation?: retrospective analysis of intercultural and same-culture instant messaging conversations. In *Proceedings of the ACM 2012 conference on Computer Supported Cooperative Work*. ACM, 117–126.
24. Martha C Pennington and Jack C Richards. 1986. Pronunciation revisited. *TESOL quarterly* 20, 2 (1986), 207–225.
25. Mabel Rice. 1983. The role of television in language acquisition. *Developmental Review* 3, 2 (1983), 211–224.
26. Teresa Secules, Carol Herron, and Michael Tomasello. 1992. The effect of video context on foreign language learning. *The Modern Language Journal* 76, 4 (1992), 480–490.
27. Merrill Swain and Sharon Lapkin. 1995. Problems in output and the cognitive processes they generate: A step towards second language learning. *Applied linguistics* 16, 3 (1995), 371–391.
28. Tomoko Takahashi, Leslie M Beebe, and others. 1993. Cross-linguistic influence in the speech act of correction. *Interlanguage pragmatics* 138 (1993), 158–169.
29. Pavel Trofimovich and Elizabeth Gatbonton. 2006. Repetition and focus on form in processing L2 Spanish words: Implications for pronunciation instruction. *The Modern Language Journal* 90, 4 (2006), 519–535.
30. Michio Tsutsui and Masashi Kato. 2001. Designing a Multimedia Feedback Tool for the Development of Oral Skills. *2001). CALL-The challenge of Change: Research & Practice* (2001), 81–88.
31. Robert Vanderplank. 2010. Déjà vu? A decade of research on language laboratories, television and video in language learning. *Language teaching* 43, 01 (2010), 1–37.
32. Gay N Washburn. 2001. Using situation comedies for pragmatic language teaching and learning. *TESOL journal* 10, 4 (2001), 21–26.
33. Joseph R Weyers. 1999. The effect of authentic video on communicative competence. *The modern language journal* 83, 3 (1999), 339–349.
34. Helen Williams and David Thorne. 2000. The value of teletext subtitling as a medium for language learning. *System* 28, 2 (2000), 217–228.
35. Paula Winke, Susan Gass, and Tetyana Sydorenko. 2010. The effects of captioning videos used for foreign language listening activities. *Language Learning & Technology* 14, 1 (2010), 65–86.
36. Jean Wong. 2000. Delayed next turn repair initiation in native/non-native speaker English conversation. *Applied Linguistics* 21, 2 (2000), 244–267.
37. Xiao Xiao and Hiroshi Ishii. 2016. Inspect, Embody, Invent: A Design Framework for Music Learning and Beyond. In *Proceedings of the 2016 CHI Conference on Human Factors in Computing Systems*. ACM, 5397–5408.
38. Dongwook Yoon, Nicholas Chen, François Guimbretière, and Abigail Sellen. 2014. RichReview: blending ink, speech, and gesture to support collaborative document review. In *Proceedings of the 27th annual ACM symposium on User interface software and technology*. ACM, 481–490.
39. Chien Wen Yuan, Leslie D Setlock, Dan Cosley, and Susan R Fussell. 2013. Understanding informal communication in multilingual contexts. In *Proceedings of the 2013 conference on Computer supported cooperative work*. ACM, 909–922.
40. Sharon Zhou, Ivy J Livingston, Mark Schiefsky, Stuart M Shieber, and Krzysztof Z Gajos. 2016. Ingenium: Engaging Novice Students with Latin Grammar. In *Proceedings of the 2016 CHI Conference on Human Factors in Computing Systems*. ACM, 944–956.

Advancing UX Education: A Model for Integrated Studio Pedagogy

Mihaela Vorvoreanu
Purdue University
West Lafayette, IN
mihaela@purdue.edu

Colin M. Gray
Purdue University
West Lafayette, IN
gray42@purdue.edu

Paul Parsons
Purdue University
West Lafayette, IN
parsonsp@purdue.edu

Nancy Rasche
Purdue University
West Lafayette, IN
nrasche@purdue.edu

ABSTRACT
The rapid growth of the UX profession has led to an increased need for qualified practitioners and a proliferation of UX educational programs offered in both academia and industry. In this note, we present the design and initial evaluation of a new studio-based undergraduate program in UX—the first of its kind at a large, research-intensive US university. The program includes several curricular innovations, such as an integrated studio pedagogy in which six topical strands are interwoven across two types of studios. These studios are interconnected and span five semesters of the undergraduate experience. We present the curriculum model and the foundational principles that informed its design. We describe the two types of studios and their interconnection, and present early evaluation data showing that students are building valuable skills. The program described in this note provides a trailblazing model for UX pedagogy at the undergraduate level.

Author Keywords
HCI pedagogy; UX competence; studio education.

ACM Classification Keywords
H.5.m. Information interfaces and presentation (e.g., HCI): Miscellaneous.

INTRODUCTION
The UX profession has experienced rapid growth in recent years, with numerous reports indicating that designers with UX skills are in high demand [1,6,7,34]. For example, in 2015, CNN Money ranked UX designer as the 14th best job in the USA according to levels of growth, pay, and satisfaction [7]—up from the 43rd spot in 2012 [6]. Given the growth of the UX profession, and the increasing demand for qualified professionals, it is important to consider the need for undergraduate UX education.

Early recommendations by SIGCHI suggested that HCI education be kept at the graduate level due to a lack of disciplinary stability [10]. However, some undergraduate programs related to HCI (i.e., UX) have appeared in recent years, primarily in art and design schools [e.g., 4,19,34]. These degree programs complement the multitude of non-academic opportunities for UX education such as those facilitated by General Assembly [24], or certificates offered by both universities and industry organizations [1,34].

The growth of both the profession and UX education makes UX pedagogy a relevant topic for discussion and research. In this note, we describe an integrated studio model for undergraduate UX education. The contribution of this work is twofold: 1) it increases awareness of how HCI scholarship is translated to practice within an undergraduate UX learning experience, laying the groundwork for future research on UX pedagogy; 2) it demonstrates how an integrated studio approach at the undergraduate level activates third-paradigm HCI concerns through learning-by-doing, preparing students for current and future challenges on both technical and critical dimensions of practice.

CHI 2017, May 06 - 11, 2017, Denver, CO, USA

ACM 978-1-4503-4655-9/17/05…$15.00
DOI: http://dx.doi.org/10.1145/3025453.3025726

RELATED WORK
Little scholarship addresses HCI pedagogy in a formal or direct way, and similarly scarce research guides the creation of formal curricula in UX and other emerging areas of HCI practice. Early efforts to consolidate HCI curricula can be found in a 1992 SIGCHI Curriculum Development group report [18], which recommended a range of specific outcomes for graduate education, while discouraging the creation of undergraduate programs due to the lack of disciplinary stability in HCI at the time. In 1992, the major concerns were the “changing nature of the professional role” and the “nature of [HCI] disciplinary knowledge,” with the recommendation to embed HCI within existing disciplinary curricula [18, p.56].

However, a recent report from the SIGCHI Education Project, led by Churchill, Bowser, and Preece [5], has brought renewed attention to HCI pedagogy. While their discussion of HCI education is relatively general, blurring boundaries among interaction design, user experience, and other common strands of practice, this report details concerns and challenges regarding the structure and core knowledge of HCI education. There is a constant tension between keeping curricula current and detailing the types of content and experiences that undergraduate and graduate programs in HCI should include [5,10]. The methods,

Competency Area	Description
Visual & Interactive Representation	Visual and interaction design principles, encompassing the planning, creation, evaluation, and communication of artifacts and design decisions.
Social/Research Methods	Skills in data collection, analysis, and evaluation that span multiple disciplinary perspectives, including qualitative and quantitative approaches.
Design Philosophy	Multiple paradigms of and approaches to design, including the impact of this complexity on a student's development of a personal and independent design identity.
Technical Skill	Development skills related to creating working prototypes, including specific software tools, scripting languages, and physical construction approaches.
Leadership/Teamwork	Project management, entrepreneurship, and professional communication skills.
Global Consciousness	Collaboration skills for a global economy, spanning cultures, time zones, and work contexts.

Table 1. Program-level competency strands.

topics, and subjects mentioned by survey respondents in [5] are truly diverse, paralleling Faiola's [10] call for a broad set of educational focus areas spanning social science, design, business, and computing.

The majority of extant UX pedagogical research relates to the integration of innovative learning approaches, such as studio or critique [1,15,27]. Studio pedagogy refers to a set of practices, largely drawn from art and design education, that encourage the development of expertise through learning-by-doing and reflection on these activities through a formative feedback mechanism known as *critique* [3,20,30,31]. The integration of studio approaches such as critique and constructionist-oriented learning in UX pedagogy have built on third-paradigm approaches to HCI scholarship that bring increased focus on design and criticality. The third paradigm allows a focus on criteria beyond usability and efficiency, addressing the value-laden nature of design activity in HCI [17]. Within this framing, scholars have offered specific approaches to engage the development of design and technical ability [1,10,12,15,36] as well a value-centered approach that incorporates critical dimensions of third-paradigm HCI scholarship [21,33].

Practitioner Expectations of UX Competence

Another important thread of scholarship relevant to UX pedagogy is practitioner self-learning, including the means by which practitioners remain competent over time. Recent studies underscore the importance of understanding HCI practice on its own terms [32], and descriptive studies have outlined important areas of competence that relate not only to technical skill, but also communication and other "soft skills" [13,14,26]. Studies of UX competence [e.g., 13,14] have revealed a range of such skills that are relevant to practice, such as communication, lifelong learning, non-technical representational knowledge, and leadership skills.

INTEGRATED STUDIO PEDAGOGY

The core of the UX pedagogy model we have implemented consists of two types of integrated, interconnected studios. Together, the studios and related areas of coursework support students in achieving mastery in six thematic strands: visual and interaction representation; social/research methods; global conscience; design philosophy; technical skills; leadership/teamwork (Table 1).

The six strands are integrated across the curriculum. One studio experience may include four or more of these strands, resulting in an *integrated studio approach.* This integrated model of studio encourages the development of multiple skills and knowledge simultaneously, in an environment that is grounded in the complexity and reality of UX practice. Integration is achieved through two types of interconnected studios that span five semesters of the students' undergraduate careers. It is further supported by course requirements in related areas that include: psychology, communication, leadership, and global consciousness. The student experience culminates in a year-long capstone project. The following sections provide an overview of the two types of studios and discuss the foundational principles that informed the development of this UX curriculum.

UX Studios

There are two types of studios in our curriculum, which we refer to as Learning Studios (LS) and Experience Studios (ES). Learning Studios are cohort-specific and provide an integrated approach to teaching fundamental and specialized UX skills, while Experience Studios engage multiple levels of students on client projects in an agency-like environment.

Learning Studios (LS)

LS are cohort-specific studios where instruction is structured according to specific learning outcomes. The learning outcomes increase in complexity across five consecutive semesters, with a focus in each semester on the following areas of UX practice: data collection, data analysis, prototyping, evaluation and testing, and theory and history of HCI and design. Students work on team projects and individual exercises, regularly engaging in group critique, peer critique, and reflection as means of formative assessment [29,31]. The projects and assignments are carefully engineered by the teaching team to support student achievement of specific learning outcomes and objectives in an environment that represents a heightened version of practice, where deadlines and constraints intentionally encourage specific types of development. Projects range in duration from two weeks to a full semester, with each experience including primary and secondary data gathering, analysis, problem framing, prototyping, testing, and documentation.

While all LS address user-centered design approaches, methods, and techniques, they differ in complexity and application area. For example, LS1 offers an introduction to the fundamentals of UX and human-centered design, focusing on paper-based deliverables such as sketches and paper prototypes. LS2 is screen-based, adding elements such as visual and interactive design principles, web programming, and high fidelity prototyping. LS3 expands the design space to include physical means of prototyping, and introduction to omni-channel UX. LS4 addresses the integration of UX into business contexts, including concepts such as strategic design and lean UX. Finally, LS5 enables students to continue developing a specific specialization in an aspect of UX, which can also be substituted for an internship experience.

Experience Studios (ES)

As opposed to LS, which are tightly structured around increasingly complex levels of learning outcomes, ES are intended to be a *managed chaos* where the learning is embedded within the experience of doing actual UX work [22]. In ES, students of various levels work together in a diverse team on projects originating from external client sponsors. While LS projects and assignments are written by the teaching team, ES projects and deliverables are specified by the client. Industry, community, and/or university-based partners provide project submissions that specify a problem to be solved. Students apply the skills acquired in LS to solve problems in a real-world consultancy-based experience, acquiring new skills as needed in order to accomplish required tasks, work effectively in a team, and engage in professional communication and project management.

ES learning outcomes of professional communication, project management, teamwork, and UX specialization increase in difficulty across the three levels of ES. For example, teamwork can be assessed differently within one student team, depending on each student's level. Whereas freshmen enrolled in ES1 aim to participate and contribute to teamwork activities, sophomores enrolled in ES2 are expected to be accountable for team activities, and juniors enrolled in ES3 will create and manage team resources and activities. This self-managing team model creates a UX learning community where students engage in peer critique, share knowledge, openly discuss issues, and collaboratively use critical thinking skills to create solutions. [9] The instructor's role is to monitor and coordinate student teams and offer individual guidance as needed. Every team provides weekly updates that are presented and discussed in small peer critique groups that mimic a typical industry environment. The students build metacognitive awareness of their development by engaging in these peer critique opportunities [25], while also the instructor to monitor project management and teamwork goals.

LS and ES are tightly integrated. Their integration, as well as the pedagogical principles that inform the entire curriculum, are explained next.

Foundational Pedagogical Principles

Our UX pedagogy model is informed by a series of foundational pedagogical principles grounded in the studio model of instruction [30,31]: integration, in-context learning, real-world experience, mentorship, multidisciplinarity, and individualized learning.

Integration refers to the integration of several thematic strands at both the curriculum and the course level, and the relationship between the two types of studios. Integration also impacts our approach to *learning in context*, where problem- and project-based learning experiences are used to stimulate connections among concepts and their appropriate application. We apply integration and learning in context within each studio by including multiple areas of UX in each course. For example, students do not take separate courses in research methods or graphic design. Instead, we avoid this artificial separation of topics into courses and instead create holistic learning experiences that require students to engage in multiple aspects of UX work simultaneously. This approach is meant to help students integrate multiple aspects of UX into a comprehensive mental schema. Moreover, it overcomes the transferability problem of traditional approaches to curriculum design, where students often have difficulty making connections among various courses.

Real world experience is ensured through authentic projects in LS and projects sponsored by external clients in ES. Working on client projects ensures that students gain supervised external work experience and are exposed to situations that would not occur otherwise in a classroom. Skills in client communication, professionalism, and UX advocacy are critical for professional success, yet many students are under-prepared in these areas in a traditional undergraduate curriculum [14]. By providing authentic learning experiences, we create opportunities for regular reflection, critique, and mentorship.

Mentorship is integrated at multiple levels through program-wide assignment of peer and faculty mentors. In ES studios, the instructor's function is primarily in a mentoring role, in tandem with student mentorship at multiple levels where advanced students are expected to mentor beginners. Research shows that peer mentorship has numerous benefits, including improving retention rates, fostering a sense of community, building academic and social skills, and increasing learning outcomes [8,28].

By its very nature, UX is a field that draws upon and connects across multiple disciplines. Thus, taking a *multidisciplinary* approach to learning is critical to prepare students for success in their future profession. We integrate multidisciplinarity in studios through team teaching where possible, ensuring that different disciplines (e.g., graphic design, psychology, communication, computer science) are integrated in each studio. Moreover, related areas of coursework are designed to provide students with sufficient background in other disciplines. The related areas emphasize psychology, so that students understand the rationale behind many usability principles, enabling them to create and evaluate solutions with human perception, attention, cognition, and emotion in mind. Technical electives are a second related area that ensures students are conversant in major programming languages, and are able to develop what they imagine. Communication is a related area, not only because of its importance at the interface level, but also because documenting and presenting UX work is a necessary skill. Related areas also include global consciousness and leadership, in addition to free electives.

The last foundational principle is *individualized learning*, and it is directly related to mentorship. Through mentorship and flexible instructional methods, we encourage each student to specialize and pursue her interests. Specialization is supported by choice of courses in related areas, roles on team projects, and a tailored final experience intended to build deep specialized skill in user research, screen-based design, physical computing, or UI design in LS5.

Initial Evaluation

We conducted an initial evaluation of the first semester of the new undergraduate program as a means of quality assurance and alignment across the two studio experiences. Students (n=17; most enrolled in both studios) self-reported their perceived abilities on a seven-point scale. Questions included: defining human-centered design, collecting data from users, finding appropriate problems to solve, defending solutions to stakeholders, and creating compelling prototypes.

	Pre Mean (SD)	Post Mean (SD)
Define design	3.41 (0.93)	5.76 (0.64)
Collect data	3.47 (1.50)	5.76 (0.64)
Frame problems	4.06 (1.39)	5.22 (0.53)
Defend decisions	3.35 (1.33)	5.41 (0.97)
Create prototypes	3.70 (1.52)	5.71 (0.74)

Table 2. Pre/post student survey results.

On all five dimensions, a paired t-test ($df=16$; $p < 0.01$) revealed a significant difference from start to end of LS1.

In addition to the quantitative assessment of learning progress, student reflections and course evaluations also provide insight into the learning experience of the program:

> *"We not only read about theories and methods but we put them to action in the classroom. He gave us a lot of opportunity to use our creative abilities. I also liked how he pushed us getting to know each other and getting comfortable with each other. It made a huge difference when the projects progressed."*

> *"With my experience studio project at [external sponsor], my team has been able to spread what I like to call "The Human Centered Design Manifesto" to many people in a company that is traditionally not equipped or interested in pursuing such endeavors."*

> *"The studio experience really shocked me. I have never been in a course that was so tasking, yet so enjoyable at the same time. It was kind of amazing how excited I was about the content that I was learning and the work I was getting to do day in and day out. That excitement really made the course easier to enjoy and increased my dedication and effort in everything that I did throughout the semester."*

These reflections indicate that students quickly internalize key aspects of UX design and understand the importance of the foundational pedagogical principles. While there are limitations to this initial self-reported course evaluation [11], we expect to see increased gains through multiple measures as students take additional studios and build individual areas of specialization.

FUTURE WORK

Our description of this undergraduate UX program facilitates a broader conversation regarding the state of UX pedagogy in higher education, particularly in a North American context. While many practitioners currently employed in UX or other HCI roles do so without formal training in the discipline [23], the demands of industry require a more substantial focus on educating students explicitly for these careers. This requires the CHI community to invest in the scholarship of teaching and learning as it relates to core HCI knowledge, including identification of pedagogical approaches and curricular models that encompass the broad space of UX, interaction design, and service design practice. While this note is focused on the program level, we also see value in exploring specific course experiences and outcomes in greater detail.

CONCLUSION

In this note, we outlined a model for UX pedagogy, detailing the role of an integrated studio approach in building deep technical and professional competence. This curriculum design lays out a space for research on HCI pedagogy at CHI, expanding on the relevance of translating aspects of core HCI knowledge to learning and practice. This research space ideally ties together recent interests in understanding practice on its own terms [e.g., 13,23,26,32], suggesting that there is substantial benefit in understanding how UX knowledge is created and disseminated within HCI scholarship and practice [16,26], and how this knowledge is acquired via formal and informal means [14].

REFERENCES

1. Martha Andrews. 2015. *The Top Certification Programs for UX Professionals.* https://www.usertesting.com/blog/2014/10/06/ux-certification-programs/
2. Eli Blevis, Yvonne Rogers, Martin Siegel, William Hazlewood, and Amanda Stephano. 2004. Integrating HCI and Design: HCI/d at IUB, a Design Education Case Story. *Workshop position paper, CHI'04.* http://citeseerx.ist.psu.edu/viewdoc/summary?doi=10.1.1.688.3145
3. Elizabeth Boling, Richard A. Schwier, Colin M. Gray, Kennon M. Smith, and Katy Campbell (Eds.). 2016. *Studio Teaching in Higher Education: Selected Design Cases.* Routledge, New York, NY.
4. Diana Buds. 2016. Google Has A Solution For The UX Design Education Gap: Google. https://www.fastcodesign.com/3062640/google-has-a-solution-for-the-ux-design-education-gap-google
5. Elizabeth F. Churchill, Anne Bowser, and Jennifer Preece. 2016. The future of HCI education. *interactions* 23, 2: 70-73. http://doi.org/10.1145/2888574
6. CNN Money. 2012. *Best jobs in America.* http://money.cnn.com/pf/best-jobs/2012/snapshots/43.html
7. CNN Money. 2015. *Best jobs in America.* http://money.cnn.com/gallery/pf/2015/01/27/best-jobs-2015/14.html
8. Janet W. Colvin, and Marinda Ashman. 2010. Roles, Risks, and Benefits of Peer Mentoring Relationships in Higher Education. *Mentoring & Tutoring: Partnership in Learning* 18, 2: 121-134.
9. J. Michael Donovan. 1986. Self-Managing Work Teams—Extending the Quality Circle Concept. *The Quality Circles Journal,* 9, 3: 15-20.
10. Anthony Faiola. 2007. The design enterprise: Rethinking the HCI education paradigm. *Design Issues* 23, 3: 30-45.
11. Jack R. Fraenkel, Norman E. Wallen, and Helen H. Hyun. 2011. *How to design and evaluate research in education.* McGraw-Hill, New York, NY.
12. Guiseppe Getto, and Fred Beecher. 2016. Toward a Model of UX Education: Training UX Designers Within the Academy. *IEEE Transactions on Professional Communication* 59, 2: 153-164. http://doi.org/10.1109/TPC.2016.2561139
13. Elizabeth Goodman, Erik Stolterman, and Ron Wakkary. 2011. Understanding interaction design practices. In *Proceedings of the SIGCHI Conference on Human Factors in Computing Systems* (CHI'11), 1061-1070. http://doi.acm.org/10.1145/1978942.1979100
14. Colin M. Gray. 2014. Evolution of Design Competence in UX Practice. In *CHI'14: Proceedings of the SIGCHI conference on human factors in computing systems*, ACM Press, New York, NY, 1645-2654.
15. Colin M. Gray, and Martin A. Siegel. 2013. Sketching design thinking: representations of design in education and practice. In *DRS // CUMULUS 2013. 2nd International Conference for Design Education Researchers*, HiOA, Oslo, Norway, 2008-2031.
16. Colin M. Gray, Erik Stolterman and Martin A. Siegel. 2014. Reprioritizing the Relationship Between HCI Research and Practice: Bubble-Up and Trickle-Down Effects. In *DIS'14: Proceedings of the 2014 CHI Conference on Designing Interactive Systems*, ACM Press, New York, NY, 725-734. http://dx.doi.org/10.1145/2598510.2598595
17. Steve Harrison, Phoebe Sengers, and Deborah Tatar. 2011. Making epistemological trouble: Third-paradigm HCI as successor science. Interacting with Computers 23, 5: 385-392. http://doi.org/10.1016/j.intcom.2011.03.005
18. Thomas T. Hewett, Ronald Baecker, Stuart Card, Tom Carey, Jean Gasen, Marilyn Mantei, Gary Perlman, Gary Strong, and William Verplank. 1992. *ACM SIGCHI Curricula for Human-Computer Interaction.* Technical Report. ACM, New York, NY.
19. Caroline Hummels, and Diana Vinke. 2009. *Eindhoven Designs: Vol. 2. Developing the competence of designing intelligent systems.* Technische Universiteit Eindhoven, Eindhoven, NL.
20. Helen Klebesadel, and Lisa Kornetsky. 2009. Critique as signature pedagogy in the arts. In *Exploring signature pedagogies: Approaches to teaching disciplinary habits of mind*, R Gurung, N Chick and A Haynie (editors). Stylus Publishing, Sterling, VA, 99-120.
21. Jes A. Koepfler, Luke Stark, Paul Dourish, Phoebe Sengers, and Katie Shilton. 2014. Values & design in HCI education. *CHI'14 Extended Abstracts on Human Factors in Computing Systems*, 127-130.
22. David A. Kolb. 1984. *Experiential learning: Experience as the source of learning and development.* Englewood Cliffs, NJ, Prentice-Hall.
23. Carine Lallemand, Guillaume Gronier, and Vincent Koenig. 2015. User experience: A concept without consensus? Exploring practitioners' perspectives through an international survey. *Computers in Human Behavior* 43: 35-48. http://doi.org/10.1016/j.chb.2014.10.048
24. Mimi Launder. 2016. *Learn UX design: 13 best paid and free UX design courses.* http://www.digitalartsonline.co.uk/features/creative-business/learn-ux-design-13-best-paid-free-courses/

25. Ngar-Fun Liu, and David Carless. 2006. Peer Feedback: The Learning Element of Peer Assessment. *Teaching in Higher Education,* 11, 3: 279-290.
26. Stuart Reeves and Sara Ljungblad. 2015. *Symposium on Connecting HCI and UX.* University of Nottingham, Nottingham, UK. Retrieved from http://www.cs.nott.ac.uk/~pszsr/files/hci-ux-symposium-report.pdf
27. Yolanda Jacobs Reimer, and Sarah A. Douglas. 2003. Teaching HCI design with the studio approach. *Computer Science Education* 13, 3: 191-205.
28. Susan Rodger and Paul F. Tremblay. 2003. The Effects of a Peer Mentoring Program on Academic Success Among First Year University Students. *The Canadian Journal of Higher Education* 33, 3: 1-18.
29. Gordon Rowland, Amy Fixl,and Kenneth Yung. 1992. Educating the reflective designer. *Educational Technology* 32, 12: 36-44.
30. Donald A. Schön. 1985. *The design studio: An exploration of its traditions and potentials.* RIBA Publications Limited, London, UK.
31. Donald A. Schön. 1987. *Educating the reflective practitioner: toward a new design for teaching and learning in the professions.* Jossey-Bass, San Francisco, CA.
32. Erik Stolterman. 2008. The nature of design practice and implications for interaction design research. *International Journal of Design* 2, 1: 55-65.
33. Nicholas True, Jeroen Peeters, and Daniel Fallman. 2013. Confabulation in the Time of Transdisciplinarity: Reflection on HCI Education and a Call for Conversation. In *Human-Computer Interaction. Human-Centred Design Approaches, Methods, Tools, and Environments.* Springer Berlin Heidelberg, 128-136. http://doi.org/10.1007/978-3-642-39232-0_15
34. UT Dallas. 2016. *UX Design Marks Its Spot as Growing Career Path for ATEC Students.* http://www.utdallas.edu/atec/artstechnology/news/2016/09/ux-design-marks-its-spot-as-growing-career-path-for-atec-students
35. Value Colleges. 2016. *Top 50 Alternative UX Design Programs of 2016.* http://www.valuecolleges.com/rankings/best-alternative-ux-design-programs-2016/
36. Mihaela Vorvoreanu, and Patrick E. Connolly. 2015. Using an Experience Design Approach to Curriculum Creation. American Society for Engineering Education, Seattle, WA, 26.1656.1-26.1656.12. http://dx.doi.org/10.18260/p.24992

Bendtroller: An Exploration of In-Game Action Mappings with a Deformable Game Controller

Paden Shorey
Carleton University
Ottawa, Canada
paden.shorey@carleton.ca

Audrey Girouard
Carleton University
Ottawa, Canada
audrey.girouard@carleton.ca

ABSTRACT
We explore controller input mappings for games using a deformable prototype that combines deformation gestures with standard button input. In study one, we tested discrete gestures using three simple games. We categorized the control schemes as binary (button only), action, and navigation, the latter two named based on the game mechanics mapped to the gestures. We found that the binary scheme performed the best, but gesture-based control schemes are stimulating and appealing. Results also suggest that the deformation gestures are best mapped to simple and natural tasks. In study two, we tested continuous gestures in a 3D racing game using the same control scheme categorization. Results were mostly consistent with study one but showed an improvement in performance and preference for the action control scheme.

Author Keywords
Deformable User Interactions; Games; Controller; Novel Input; Bend; Twist

ACM Classification Keywords
H.5.2. User Interfaces – *Interaction Styles*

INTRODUCTION
While new methods of input in games are constantly developed, only a few researchers have looked at deformation gestures in games [5,15,44], focusing solely on bending and twisting without any other form of input. They designed prototypes to allow users to play games on the device themselves [15,44]. As many standard game controllers are separated from the display, we imagine that users might appreciate performing deformation gestures on such stand-alone controllers instead.

We further propose that combining bending and twisting with the standard forms of input, such as buttons and directional pads, could make the experience engaging and more stimulating to players who are used to playing games with standard controllers. Implementing gestures parallel to button input provides users with more input options that are easily accessible without lifting their fingers from buttons. We look into some common game mechanics and evaluate which types of actions will map best to buttons and gestures.

CHI 2017, May 06–11, 2017, Denver, CO, USA
 ISBN 978-1-4503-4655-9/17/05…$15.00
DOI: http://dx.doi.org/10.1145/3025453.3025463

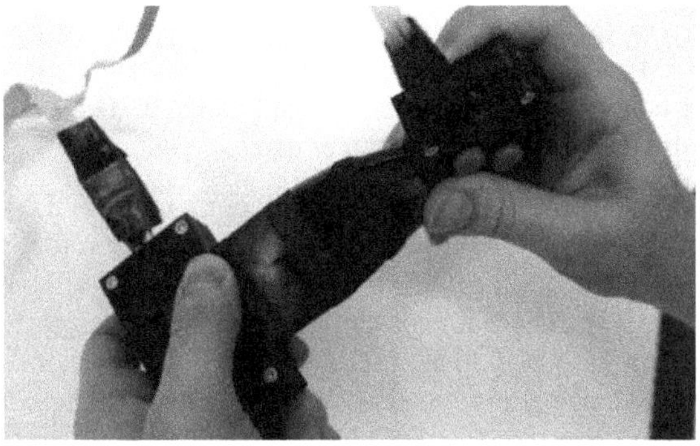

Figure 1. Twist input using our bendable game controller.

To explore these possible mappings, we designed a new controller using six buttons and four deformation gestures (Figure 1). We developed three control schemes, the first using only button input, the other two combining button and deformation gestures, each based on generic in-game mechanics: action and navigation. We first tested three unique, but simple, arcade games with these three schemes. Our second study used continuous gestures in a 3D racing game, as opposed to discrete gestures as used in the first study. Finally, we suggest ways of mapping gestures to in-game mechanics. The main contributions of this paper are (1) proposing the combination of deformation input with standard button input; (2) developing and implementing a stand-alone controller that uses of deformation gestures and button input; and (3) providing empirical evidence that deformation gestures have a place in games, through two studies, with four games and three control schemes.

RELATED WORK
We leveraged prior work exploring deformation interactions from being generic inputs to specific inputs for games, and discuss novel and natural game interactions to create innovative video game controllers.

Deformation Interactions
Deformation is a broad category of interaction that includes bends, twists, wave-forms, and scrunches in the device [1,9]. Researchers have used deformation interaction to perform tasks such as to navigate a smartphone [9,11,32], to create music [39], secure passwords [16], and control a TV as a

remote [14]. Herkenrath et al. [5], with TWEND, were the firsts to look at both bend and twists as interaction techniques for deformable devices, but only implemented bends. With the Kinetic Device, Kildal et al. [9] implemented and evaluated both in a mobile context, noting their worth, but that deformable gestures were not going to replace other methods of input such as touch or buttons, and instead focused on determining the best use for bend and twist gestures. They determined that (1) bend and twist are performed better with two hands, (2) up and down when referring to twist is intuitively different depending on the user's handedness, (3) continuous gestures are better for tasks handling the magnitude of a parameter, and (4) discrete gestures are better used to trigger discrete actions.

Other researchers have looked into combining bend with touch in the front of the device [2,8,28–30,37], in the back [8], or deformation and 3D location tracking [10,36]. For the former, researchers found that these hybrid techniques feel more intuitive than touch on its own, and they demonstrate potential once users are familiar with how the interaction works [8]. Yet, we found no prior work combining gestures with button input for any application, including games.

Deformation Interactions with Games

Most research regarding deformation gestures tends to focus on performance-driven applications such as map navigation [32] or document navigation [42]. Researchers have not thoroughly explored entertainment-driven applications with deformation interaction.

Cobra [44] is an all-in-one deformable handheld gaming system that consists of a flexible board, and a portable shoulder bag supporting a pico-projector. The authors claimed that gestures were dependent on the game being tested as different actions in-game required different methods of input, but did not formally test Cobra. In contrast, Lo and Girouard [15] evaluated deformation input with existing games with their bendable prototype, Bendy. They broke down games into basic tasks and asked users to map bend gestures to them. Users, for the most part, agreed on the gesture mappings. They found that participants had positive reactions to playing games using gesture input, but the inconsistencies in how users held the device led to some issues where participants needed to reposition their hands.

Nguyen et al. created two deformable prototypes, BendID [20] and SOFTii [19] using conductive foam and an array of pressure sensors. However, the authors only informally tested them with 3D games, and did not present any study data. Similarly, Rendl et al. [29] created a transparent flexible film for applications requiring precision with multiple degrees of freedom. They suggest a variety of game mechanics to map to both discrete and continuous gestures already built into FlexSense. They did not, however, test FlexSense with games.

Other researchers integrate games in their studies without making it their focus: one of the tasks in Daliri and Girouard [3] was a simple grid navigation game, while Ahmaniemi et al. [1] asked participants what applications bends would work best with, and reported games where the player controls speed, follows a track, or drops bombs, such as Angry Birds [31] and Tetris [25]. We tested our prototype with simple games based on this body of research. To our knowledge, no prior work has combined buttons with gesture input and performed any formal studies using games.

Novel and Natural Game Interaction

Many researchers such as Villar et al. [41], Ionescu et al. [6], and Smith [35] have tackled novel game interaction, creating adaptable controllers, developing games for controller hybrids, and creating controllers that resemble the main character of the game. This close resemblance to the real world is often said to make interactions more natural. Wigdor and Wixon [43] defined natural as a descriptor "we use to describe a property that is external to the product itself". Skalski et al. [34] separated natural mapping into four distinct categories: directional, kinetic, incomplete tangible, and realistic tangible natural mapping. They determined that natural mapping of a video game controller led to higher spatial awareness and enjoyment when playing games. Naturalness is commonly associated to a positive user experience [20]. Naturally mapped devices offer greater potential for intuitive use, linked to increased experiences for users with less gaming experience or who are familiar with the real-world activity mapped [17]. However, due to their high familiarity with traditional interfaces, expert gamers do not typically experience such an increase in performance with naturally mapped controls.

Some novel controllers attempt to combine traditional input in new ways or with sensors that are new and unique. Ionescu et al. [6] created a system that uses a physical game controller alongside gestures captured by a 3D camera. Users found the interactions natural and immersive as the two types of input provided them with the familiarity of the standard controller combined with the freedom of the hand-movement gestures. Other unique uses for sensors and technology with games include the use of a Rubik's snake to control a samurai sword's shape [7], and a cylindrical motion detecting wand made with two flexible OLED screens [26].

Namco's neGcon controller [45] is the only controller with similar functionality to our intended prototype. Built for a game called Ridge Racer [18], it consists of two rigid halves connected by a dowel that could be twisted relative to each other to turn the car. This 1995 controller only worked with this game, and did not allow for bends.

Our prototype is novel as it combines traditional video game input methods with bend sensors and deformation gestures. We wanted to study the physical gestures alongside buttons, another physical method of input. We attempted to map our control schemes as naturally as possible to maximize fun and easy to use based on this body of work.

Figure 2. Controller Gestures: (1) Bend Up (2) Bend Down (3) Twist Left (4) Twist Right.

PROTOTYPE

We sought to create a game controller to test flexible input combined with binary input for simple video games. We based our prototype on the Nintendo Entertainment System (NES) game pad, the original pad used to play some of the games testing with our prototype. We added a flexible bridge in the middle of the game pad, between the directional buttons and the action buttons, and used the prototype to test PC ports of NES games as well as a PC-based racing game.

Interaction Language

Our controller has ten inputs: 4 deformation gestures and 6 buttons. While prior work discussed over thirty deformation gestures [13], we selected a smaller number so as to not overwhelm our participants. The four gestures are as follows: (1) bend up (2) bend down (3) twist left, and (4) twist right (Figure 2). We define bend up as the bridge arching upwards, and the back of the panels being bent towards each other, similar to Kildal et al. [9]. We define twist left as bringing the top of the left panel away from the user and the top of the right panel towards the user, and twist right as the opposite. Twists were defined that way to simulate how people activate automobile turn signals: rotating your left hand away from your body (flick down) is used to signal left whereas rotating your left hand towards your body (flick up) is used to signal right. Our controller has six buttons, four on the left panel (up, down, left, and right) and two on the right panel (action 1, on the left; action 2, on the right).

Hardware

We built a handheld game controller with rigid side panels connected by a flexible bridge that can bend and twist (Figure 3). We designed the controller to be held with both hands (162 * 75 * 21 mm). We modified the original NES game pad design and dimensions slightly to implement the flexible bridge, and modified the button positions after testing it with multiple hand sizes. We 3D printed the side panels (40 * 75 * 21 mm each) using polylactic acid (PLA) filament which produces a rigid plastic end-product. The flexible bridge (82 * 43 * 6 mm), was made of two 2-inch FlexPoint bend sensors [4] fastened on the rear side of a foam board cutout.

After testing many materials such as plastic, foam and rubber, we selected foam as it was malleable enough to bend and twist in all directions and could retain its shape fairly well, even after excessive use. The internal bend sensors overlap diagonally in the centre of the flexible bridge to accurately distinguish between our four gesture-based input methods. We placed the sensors so they were able to slide.

Figure 3. Front and back view of the prototype.

Wires emerge from the top of either panel, connecting to an external Arduino Leonardo, which in turn connected a MacBook Pro laptop computer via USB. The Arduino has one additional button used to calibrate the controller which we will refer to as the calibration button.

Software

Using Arduino 1.6.7, we analyzed the raw bend sensor data to determine the gesture performed. We implemented a calibration system that set the rest (flat) positions of the bend sensors based on their average input values over a period of ten frames at 66.67 Hz. To minimize accidental input, we used a sensitivity threshold of the value of 80 (sensor values ranging from 0–1024), only above which, from the rest position, a bent gesture will be triggered.

Bend up (or down) was triggered when both sensors read higher (or lower). Twist left (or right) was triggered when the left (or right) sensor read higher (or lower) and the right (or left) sensors read below its rest position. In study one, gestures, like buttons, were triggered discretely, i.e. a gesture cannot be triggered again until the user restored the controller to its rest position. In the second study, gestures were triggered continuously, without the need to go back to their rest position.

In study 1, we used the Arduino virtual keyboard library to simulate key presses with button presses and gesture input to play the game using our prototype. In study 2, participants played a game developed in Unity3D, which read the serial port and parsed the sensor data for use within its scripts. In both studies, the buttons and gestures could be triggered simultaneously.

STUDY 1: BEND INPUT METHODS FOR SIMPLE GAMES

Our primary research goal was to determine if flexible input, combined with binary input, is a satisfying method of input when playing simple video games using our custom-built controller. Our secondary research goal was to determine the differences between various bend control mappings in specific games, which we will assess by looking performance and subjective ratings.

We created two types of mapping between bend gestures and game actions: one that focuses solely on common in-game actions (such as jumping or causing an explosion), and the other on in-game navigation (moving objects in space). This allowed us to generalize the control schemes to give the participants a better immediate idea of what the gestures would be mapped to in each situation.

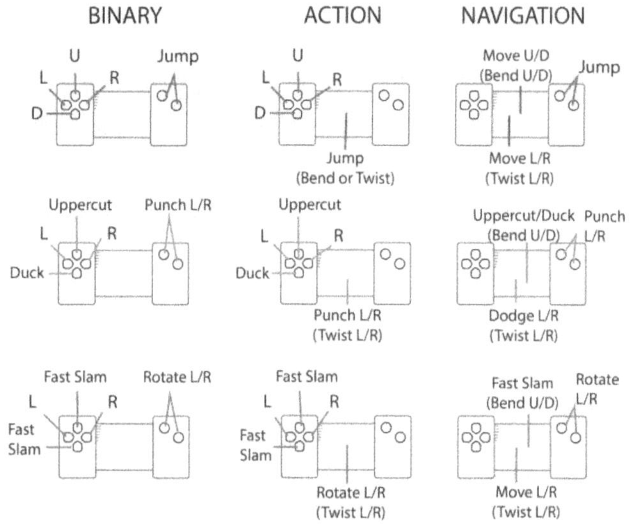

Figure 4. Control Schemes for study one for Donkey Kong (top row), Punch Out (middle), and Tetris (bottom). L=Left, R=Right, U=Up and D=Down.

Games

We selected three games for our study. Donkey Kong [23] is an arcade platformer in which the player avoids obstacles falling down towards him/her (barrels) while climbing up. The player can jump, move left and right, and climb ladders. Punch-Out [27] is an arcade boxing game. The player must punch left, punch right and perform uppercuts. They can also protect their face, duck, dodge left, and dodge right as defensive maneuvers. Tetris [25] is a tile-matching puzzle game. The pieces can be moved and rotated as they fall towards the bottom of the screen. We used OpenEmu [24] to run original NES versions of our games, and users played the games from the first level.

The games were selected on three criteria: our ability to isolate the action and the navigation within the games (for our second goal), the ability to measure performance objectively, and a diversity within gameplay. The latter ensured that the experience with each game was mutually exclusive (learnability did not transfer from one game to another during the study).

Control Schemes

We tested three classifications of control schemes (Figure 4). The first control scheme is only button input, and is representative of the game's original control scheme. We call this scheme **binary** as it only makes use of button input. We include it to provide baseline scores to which we can compare the scores that the gesture schemes receive.

The other two schemes combine binary and gesture input methods. We differentiated these control schemes by the type of in-game mechanic controlled by the gesture input: to control **action** input or to control **navigation** input. We mapped all other necessary inputs to binary controls, and disabled inputs with no direct action in-game.

Methods

We tested the three control schemes with the three games for a total of nine conditions per participant. Each condition consisted of two trials that lasted two minutes each. Each session took about 80 minutes. We presented the games in a counterbalanced order. Within each game, participants played the three control schemes also in a counterbalanced order. We explained each game to participants, and offered them the opportunity to play the game using the keyboard before the trials began, minimizing the measurement of the learnability of the game itself.

We measured performance through raw score for each game. The scores are taken from the games themselves, based on barrels skipped (DK), completed lines at once (Tetris) and type of punch (PO). We measured the user experience using the User Experience Questionnaire (UEQ) [12], an assessment tool used to evaluate an overall user experience with a product or system. It produces results in six categories: attractiveness, perspicuity, efficiency, dependability, stimulation, novelty, further grouped into three categories: attractiveness, pragmatic quality, and hedonic quality. Due to an error creating our survey, we measured the UEQ using a 5-point Likert scale instead of a 7-point. We presented the questionnaire after each game/scheme combination, for a total of 9 times.

After completing all schemes for one game, we asked participants to rank control schemes based on three criteria for each game: most fun and most natural. They had to rank (1–3) all schemes in each category. Finally, we collected demographic data and asked general questions about our flexible controller. This protocol was approved by the Carleton University Research Ethics Board.

Hypotheses

The binary scheme should outperform both the action and navigation schemes (H1). We also predicted that the binary scheme would score higher in pragmatic quality on the UEQ (H2). We believed this would be the case because binary control schemes are already familiar to most players.

However, our third hypothesis was that gesture-based schemes would be more fun and receive higher attractiveness and hedonic scores in the UEQ (H3). Deformation input, being relatively new, would be seen as novel to most participants and using novel input to do something inherently fun, such as playing video games, would likely augment their stimulation levels and sense of enjoyment.

Finally, we predicted that the action scheme would perform better than the navigation scheme across all three games (H4), as the action scheme required less deformation input across all three games compared to the navigation scheme. We also predicted that action would perform better over navigation due to its relative simplicity.

Participants

Our 16 participants (3 female) had a mean age of 22.6 years old (SD=2.7). All were all right-handed. Eleven reported to

Table 1. Statistical results for study one.

Measure	Game	Main effect	Comparison *Binary/Action* *Binary/Navigation* *Action/Navigation*
Score	Donkey Kong	F [1.726, 25.890] = 10.096), $p = 0.001$	$p = 0.032$ $p = 0.001$ not significant
	Punch-Out	F [1.799, 26.969] = 5.397), $p = 0.013$	not significant $p = 0.017$ not significant
	Tetris	F [1.529, 21.410] = 3.930), $p = 0.045$	not significant $p = 0.049$ not significant
Fun	Donkey Kong	not significant	
	Punch-Out	not significant	
	Tetris	not significant	
Naturalness	Donkey Kong	χ^2 (2) = 18.375, $p < 0.001$	$Z = -3.198, p = 0.001$ $Z = -3.666, p < 0.001$ not significant
	Punch-Out	not significant	
	Tetris	χ^2 (2) = 20.933, $p < 0.001$	$Z = -2.399, p = 0.016$ $Z = -3.542, p < 0.001$ $Z = -2.841, p = 0.005$
Attractiveness	Donkey Kong	not significant	
	Punch-Out	not significant	
	Tetris	*F* [1.954, 27.357] = 7.901), $p = 0.002$	not significant $p = 0.007$ $p = 0.021$
Pragmatic Quality	Donkey Kong	*F* [1.830, 27.452] = 16.111), $p < 0.001$	$p = 0.002$ $p < 0.001$ not significant
	Punch-Out	*F* [1.922, 28.824] = 6.487), $p = 0.005$	not significant $p = 0.009$ not significant
	Tetris	*F* [1.999, 27.980] = 6.619), $p < 0.001$	$p = 0.001$ $p < 0.001$ not significant
Hedonic Quality	Donkey Kong	*F* [1.975, 29.628] = 22.247), $p < 0.001$	$p = 0.001$ $p < 0.001$ not significant
	Punch-Out	*F* [1.561, 23.410] = 29.654), $p < 0.001$	$p < 0.001$ $p < 0.001$ not significant
	Tetris	*F* [1.988, 27.827] = 30.639), $p < 0.001$	$p < 0.001$ $p < 0.001$ not significant

play video games for more than three hours weekly. Two had experience using flexible input in a prior study. We presented each participant with a $10 CAN gift card as compensation.

Results & Analysis

We analyzed games individually, as game play, scores and user experiences were not equivalent, and cannot be compared. An overview of the performance statistics can be found in Table 1.

Performance. Every participant played every game with every control scheme apart from one participant who did not play Tetris. We only analyze the values for the second trial, to avoid the initial learnability of the game/scheme combination. We performed a repeated measures ANOVA with a Greenhouse-Geisser correction on the score. For significant main effects, we used post-hoc tests using the Bonferroni correction to investigate pairwise comparisons. Figure 5 presents the mean score for each combination.

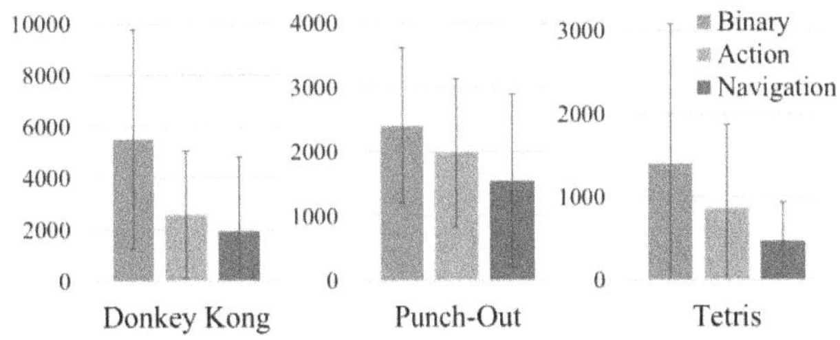

Figure 5. Mean game scores with standard deviation (SD).

Game Experience. We ran a Friedman test to evaluate the main effect of the control scheme for each game on naturalness and fun. For significant main effects, we conducted post-hoc analysis using a Wilcoxon signed-rank test with Bonferroni correction applied ($p < 0.017$). In Donkey Kong, binary was more natural than the other two schemes, while in Tetris, binary was more natural, followed by action, then navigation.

User Experience Questionnaire. We followed the UEQ analysis method and transformed the scores of the 26 ranking questions into values for the three high-level categories (scores between -2 and 2 given our Likert scale error). We evaluated each of the schemes based on these three categories. We performed the same ANOVA as for the performance results. Donkey Kong's mean UEQ scores are displayed in Figure 6.

Post Questionnaire

We asked our participants three questions at the end to get a general sense of their feelings towards the controller. These answers ranged between 1 and 5, 1 being highly disagree and 5 being highly agree (4 and 5 are considered in agreement). 10 participants (63%) agreed that: "the controller was comfortable to use". All participants agreed that: "the controller was fun to use". Finally, 12 participants (75%) agreed that: "I would use this controller to play other games," and only 1 participant disagreed (selected a 1 or 2).

We also asked participants which game they had the most fun playing. Punch-Out was the most popular with 10 votes

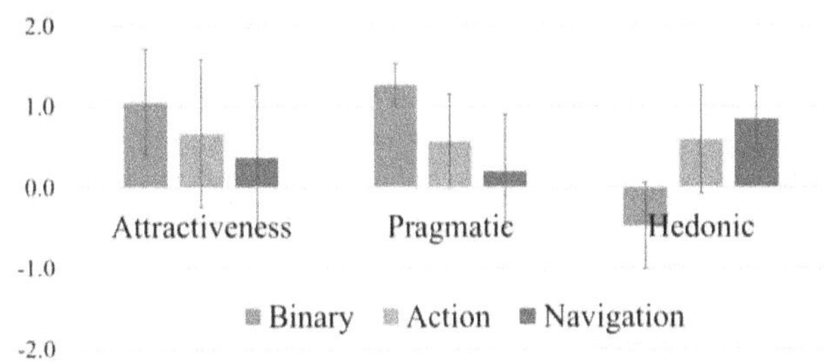

Figure 6. UEQ mean scores for Donkey Kong with SD.

(63%), Donkey Kong was the runner-up with 5 votes (31%) and Tetris only received 1 vote (6%). Participants who chose Punch-Out claimed that the controls felt the most natural and they felt more immersed in the game when using bend/flex controls. Participants who chose Donkey Kong as the most fun game did so because the controls were simple and "didn't impede the gameplay". Finally, the one participant who chose Tetris as their favourite game said it was "less complicated as it involved fewer actions".

We also asked users to describe their overall experience with the controller and which, if any, games they would like to play with bend control schemes. Participants were clear that the controller worked well for some games and not for others and stated that it worked much better with simple actions as opposed to complex input such as navigation in our study. Participant suggestions for potential game genres include: 3D flight games, racing games, 2D platformers, arcade fighting games, rhythm games, and sports games. Five participants commented on the sensitivity and occasional unreliability of the input saying it was too sensitive thus resulting in some unpredictable input.

Discussion

Binary Dominance

Binary consistently outperformed both action and navigation in all games, supporting H1. Binary ranked higher in naturalness than the two gesture-based schemes across all three games. The UEQ displayed higher pragmatic scores for the binary scheme over the gesture-based schemes and consistently outscored those schemes on attractiveness. These subjective results support H2. Our results show that the binary control scheme, across all three games, performed better, ranked better, and required the least amount of work compared to the other two schemes.

We believe that participants' familiarity with standard controllers is the main reason why the binary scheme consistently outperformed and outranked our unique control schemes: all participants were experienced players using standard methods of input, while only two participants had experience, though quite limited, using flexible input methods. Second, the time required to press a button (in place motion) is much lower than that of bending our controller (3D movement). Hence, it took longer for participants to complete their tasks, producing a lower performance overall, which affected their game experience.

Based on this, we conclude that deformable gestures, specifically using our prototype, will not replace binary input for existing games, in part or in whole. However, we introduced the binary scheme in our study mainly to establish a baseline with current game controllers: our real objective with this study is to evaluate two novel control schemes using deformation as input.

Gestures Are Fun

Not only did the gesture schemes outscored the binary scheme in the UEQ for hedonism, participants evaluated action and navigation positively across all three games (the UEQ deems a score of 0.53 or greater as a positive evaluation [12]). The hedonic category averages the stimulation and novelty scores of the UEQ. As this was an introductory study to our prototype, we did not design our tests to negate the novelty effect so this could have an impact on these hedonic scores. However, contrary to the action and navigation schemes, the binary scheme scored negatively in hedonism across all three games. We believe this would be the case regardless of whether or not we tested with the novelty effect in mind. In addition, all three schemes across all three games received similar fun rankings from the game experience survey. This is interesting as the binary scheme significantly outranked gesture-based control schemes in all other categories. While we hypothesized that action or navigation outranked binary in this category (H3), their close values demonstrate that using gestures does not decrease the amount of fun participants had while playing the games.

In addition, we think that the frustration and discomfort the users experienced while using these schemes directly impacted the fun rankings for the gesture schemes. It is possible that by making the controller more comfortable to hold and use, and strengthening the gesture recognition algorithm that the fun rankings will increase.

Participants described their experience using the flexible prototype as "riveting", "innovative", and "immersive". A participant stated that "using the bendable controller made the game more enjoyable compared to the regular button system", and another participant added that the gestures "added another level (to the experience) which I found enjoyable". Every participant agreed that the controller was universally fun to use with three quarters of them claiming that they would like to use bend and twist controls to play other games such as Mario Kart [22], Star Fox [21] and Sonic [38].

Action Scheme Better Than Navigation Scheme

The action scheme, across most criteria for all three games, ranks higher than the navigation scheme as a method of gesture input with our prototype. The performance was not significantly different, which does not support H4. Participants mentioned that "the bending controls were very frustrating to use for navigation". The participant who made the last comment also claimed that the controller was fun when the gestures were used specifically for action.

Action schemes were unique between games, but results show that participants consistently preferred this scheme. In Donkey Kong, bending or twisting in any direction caused Mario to jump in game. Allowing users to move Mario around with the buttons allowed for more precision (necessary in Donkey Kong) and we believe that mapping jump to the gesture input simulates the urgency of jumping in the game. Often times, jumping is reactionary and users jump with little to no preparation in Donkey Kong, which is why we believe gesture input fit so well: participants were able to trigger a jump by simply bending or twisting the controller using the quickest and easiest gesture for them.

A participant stated that "the bending controls were very frustrating to use for navigation, especially when dealing with precision". Another summed up their experience by stating that "bends are better for simple actions" and a third participant chose Donkey Kong as the game they had the most fun with because "jumping with the bend felt quite natural, it was fun to use, and didn't impede the gameplay".

Natural Mapping

Taking into account the gesture schemes only, we noticed that game/scheme combinations that ranked higher for naturalness performed relatively better, and were preferred by participants over the other gesture-based scheme.

Tetris was the only game where there was a significant different in attractiveness between gesture control schemes, with action scoring higher. Action for Tetris also received one of the highest naturalness rankings. Twisting the controller in Tetris rotated the piece in the corresponding direction. We believe that this scheme ranked high in naturalness because the act of twisting is technically a rotation along the x-axis, hence naturally similar to rotating an option in the game. Multiple participants were able to predict how the action scheme would map before it was explained to them, which illustrates its instinctive mapping.

Scheme Consistency & Game Preference

Punch-Out behaved differently from the other two games: we did not find the action and navigation scheme's results to be significantly different in most cases. We also did not find the binary scheme to be significantly different than the other schemes as often. When combined with the fact that 63% of participants chose Punch-Out as the game they had the most fun playing using the flexible prototype, we find this game to be most successful for our novel controller. We believe that Punch-Out's consistency between control schemes is what led most participants to choose it as their preferred experience.

Participant comments support their preference for action due to its naturalness. Participants who chose Punch-Out as the most fun specifically commented on how natural twisting to punch felt. A participant commented that twisting "gave a unique and tangible way to feel more immersed in the actual fight". However, both the action and navigation schemes for Punch-Out received similar scores across all of our evaluations. The act of leaning in either direction with our hands out in-front of us (similar to how boxers hold their hands out) is very similar to the input required to move left and right using the navigation scheme.

In summary, our results revealed that the binary scheme did outperform the gesture-based schemes. Results also showed that the gesture-based schemes were more stimulating and novel, but were not necessarily more fun or attractive. The action scheme received better feedback than the navigation scheme overall. The most naturally mapped the gestures

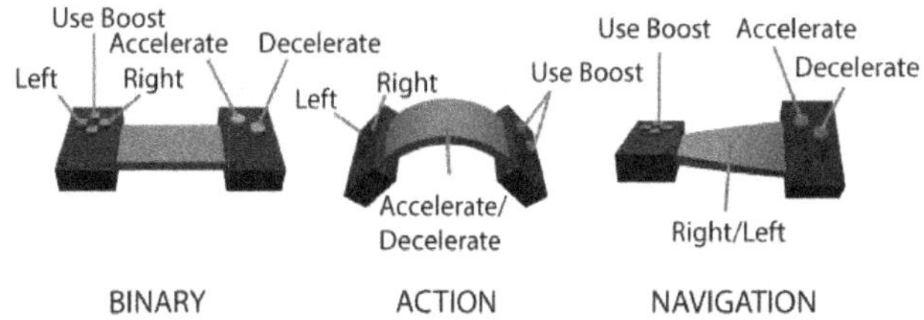

Figure 7. Control schemes for study two

were, the more attractive and appealing they were to participants. Participants suggested using bends and twists for different types of games, like racing games.

STUDY 2: CONTINUOUS BEND INPUT IN RACING GAME

Where in study one we tested discrete gestures, we here explored how continuous gestures could play a role in video game control mapping using bipolar input to control high resolution parameters, as suggested by Ahmaniemi et al. [1]. We evaluated the same prototype, and used the same control schemes categories to see if results would stay consistent. We selected a 3D racing game based on our earlier participants collectively suggesting that a racing game could work well with gesture-based input, given the natural similarities between steering and twisting our prototype. We believed that a racing game has potential to test continuous gestures and new, more advanced, game mechanics.

Game

Participants played a 3D racing game called O.R.B.S. [33]. In O.R.B.S., players race spherical robots from point A to point B. We designed two custom tracks to test two unique mechanics found in racing games: speed, and precision. The speed track has few sharp turns, with 27 power-up platforms scattered, containing a boost that participants can activate at any time. The boost causes the racer to accelerate forward at a faster rate than normal for a pre-determined amount of time. The precision track's sharp turns and obstacles are intentionally placed to force participants to be more precise with the controller. There are no power-up platforms on this track.

We also created a practice arena for users to race around before each trial to get used to each control scheme. This arena is a large square, with no finish line, and is full of obstacles and power-up platforms to practice all required in-game mechanics. They were allowed to practice until they felt comfortable with how the scheme worked.

Control Schemes

Similar to our first study, we used three unique control schemes: binary, action, and navigation (Figure 7). We tested binary again to provide a basis from which to compare performance and different qualities from the UEQ. The action control scheme used the up bend gestures to control the racer's acceleration, and the down bend gesture for deceleration. The greater the magnitude of the bend, the faster the racer will accelerate or decelerate. The navigation scheme uses twisting to turn the racer left and right. The more the user twists the controller, the more extreme the turn.

Table 2. Statistical results for study two.

Track	Measurement	Main Effect	Comparisons *Binary/Action* *Binary/Navigation* *Action/Navigation*
Speed	Time	F [1.127, 19.157] = 13.767, $p = 0.001$	not significant $p = 0.005$ $p = 0.004$
	Collisions	F [1.319, 22.430] = 90.344, $p < 0.001$	not significant $p < 0.001$ $p < 0.001$
	Boosts Used	F [1.605, 27.286] = 21.856, $p < 0.001$	not significant $p < 0.001$ $p < 0.001$
Precision	Time	F [1.232, 20.939] = 29.849, $p < 0.001$	$p = 0.012$ $p < 0.001$ $p < 0.001$
	Collisions	F [1.050, 17.852] = 71.151, $p < 0.001$	not significant $p < 0.001$ $p < 0.001$
Combined	Fun	$\chi^2(2) = 7.741$, $p = 0.024$	$Z = -2.722, p = 0.006$ not significant not significant
	Naturalness	$\chi^2(2) = 24.216$, $p < 0.001$	not significant $Z = -4.354, p < 0.001$ $Z = -3.029, p = 0.002$
	Attractiveness	F [1.933, 67.658] = 4.306, $p = 0.018$	not significant not significant $p = 0.027$
	Pragmatic Quality	F [1.620, 56.685] = 23.143, $p < 0.001$	not significant $p < 0.001$ $p = 0.002$
	Hedonic Quality	F [1.832, 64.112] = 41.447, $p < 0.001$	$p < 0.001$ $p < 0.001$ not significant

Hypotheses

As in study one, we believed that the binary scheme would perform the best across both tracks (H1). We hypothesized that gesture-based control schemes (action and navigation) would score higher for hedonic quality, as well as fun, over the binary scheme (H2). Our third hypothesis was that the navigation scheme would perform better and participants would prefer it over the action scheme (H3) based on the comments participants made in the previous study. Many stated that racing games would make good use of the twisting mechanic as twisting feels very similar to steering.

Methods

Participants answered demographic questions. We tested each control schemes with both the speed and precision tracks for a total of six trials. We counterbalanced by scheme, then counterbalanced the two tracks. Participants first drove in a practice arena before beginning the trials for that scheme. They completed two trials on the track using the current scheme, then answered questionnaires relating to this combination. They then completed the next track with the same scheme, followed by the same questionnaires. This was repeated for all three schemes. After each scheme/track trials, we asked four Likert-style questions regarding

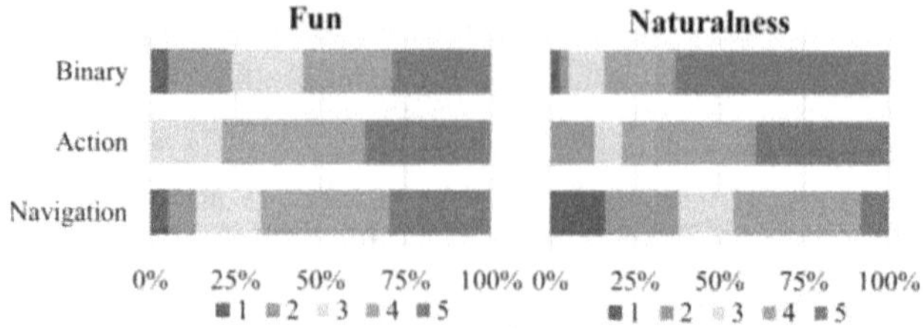

Figure 8. Naturalness and Fun ratings. 1 is negative (very unnatural/boring), 5 is positive (very natural/fun)

naturalness, and fun. Participants also completed the user experience questionnaire. Finally, they answered a post-questionnaire to determine which track-scheme combinations participants preferred. The entire session took approximately 60 minutes. This methodology was approved by the Carleton University Research Ethics Board.

Participants

Our 19 participants (9 female) had a mean age of 23.26 years old (SD=4.4yo). Sixteen were right-handed, two left-handed and one was ambidextrous. Ten reported playing games frequently, eight occasionally and one never. Nine participants had used a flexible method of input, 5 of those participated in our first study. They received a $10 CAN gift card as compensation.

Results & Analysis

The results of the statistical analysis can be found in Table 2.

Performance. We measured time, collisions, and boosts used. Every participant played both tracks with every control scheme apart from one participant who did not play with the navigation control scheme. We analyzed the values for the second trial, to avoid measuring the initial learnability of the track/scheme combinations. We performed a repeated measures ANOVA with a Greenhouse-Geisser correction on each measure for the speed track, and found significant differences between control schemes. We used post hoc tests using the Bonferroni correction to investigate pairwise comparisons.

Trial Experience. We ran a Friedman test on each experience rating, then conducted post-hoc analysis using a Wilcoxon signed-rank test with Bonferroni correction applied ($p < 0.017$) on significant main effects. Results are displayed in Figure 8.

User Experience Questionnaire. We performed the same ANOVA as for the performance data. Overall UEQ scores can be found in Figure 9.

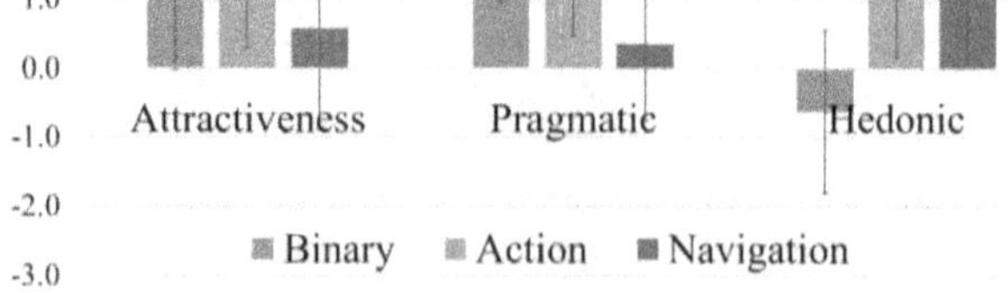

Figure 9. Overall UEQ Scores

Post-Questionnaire
A Friedman test comparing control schemes by rank for the speed track showed no significant preference. For the precision track, navigation ranked lowest (χ^2 (2) = 22.333, p < 0.001). Participants preferred the speed track overall, 33 votes to 24 votes (each participant had three votes as they were asked to choose their preferred track for each of the three schemes). Participants split their track preference for the binary scheme (9 votes to 10 votes), the action scheme weighed more towards the precision track (6 votes to 13 votes), and participants preferred the navigation scheme on the speed track (18 votes to 1 vote).

Participants split the votes for most fun between the two tracks using the action scheme, each receiving 7 votes. The navigation scheme received 4 total votes and the binary scheme only received 1. The navigation scheme on the precision track was voted least fun, receiving a total of 17 votes with other schemes only receiving 1 vote each.

Discussion

Binary is Familiar
We believe that participants' familiarity with binary input in other games made it easier for them to pick up and use more boosts on the speed track, lowering their completion times, similarly to study one. The binary scheme received the highest pragmatic scores and, observationally, took the least time to learn and become comfortable with on the practice track. These results, alongside binary's high naturalness scores, further support H1 in stating that binary is the easiest scheme to pick up and perform well. Multiple participants stated in their comments that "binary was the most predictable" of the three control schemes.

Although participants could learn and perform well with the binary scheme, it was not the most preferred scheme to use. This shows a lack of correlation between performance and interest, fun, or attractiveness. Binary schemes are very familiar to gamers, and that lack of creativity within the scheme might be the cause of its low scores in terms of hedonic quality, attractiveness, and overall preference.

Gestures Are Intriguing
Our results reveal that the gesture-based schemes were more appealing and preferred over the binary scheme overall, confirming our second hypothesis. Action and navigation ranked highest in fun, hedonic quality, and received the most votes for the most fun scheme overall at the end of the study. Hedonic quality includes stimulation and novelty as descriptive factors and participants seem to have found the gesture-based schemes both stimulating and novel based on the results of the questionnaires along with their comments. Participants described gesture-based schemes as "unconventional, but what [they] were hoping for". They also stated that the gesture-based schemes "bring the user more into the actual gaming experience", commenting on their ability to immerse our participants into games such as our racing game O.R.B.S. We believe that these unique control schemes and input methods force users to focus more on what they are doing, possibly immersing them more in the entire experience. The freedom to bend and twist the controller in 3D space provides a natural interaction in terms of how people interact, almost instinctively, with everyday objects (with their hands, in 3D space).

Participants Still Prefer Action
We hypothesized that the navigation scheme would perform well and be preferred based on comments from participants in study one. This hypothesis was not supported: the action scheme performed better was preferred over the navigation scheme. This result is similar to that of the first study.

These results demonstrate that users prefer using gestures to control the racer's speed (action scheme) and describe this scheme as "easy to learn," "more relaxing", and "adding excitement to the tracks". They liked being able to control their speed around corners and near boost pads allowing them to avoid collisions with walls and allowing them to pick up more boosts, which, in turn, lowered their completion time on the speed track.

Navigation is Difficult to Learn and Understand
The navigation scheme performed the worst and ranked the worst overall in study two, although this scheme received some positive feedback in regards to hedonic quality. While we did not focus on the learnability of the gestures in this study, our observations and participant comments led us to believe that there is a steeper learning curve for gesture-based schemes, especially the navigation scheme. We noticed that participants took longer in the practice course with the navigation scheme over the binary and action schemes. We did, however, notice large improvements in completion times and collision counts between their practice trials and recorded trials when using the navigation scheme. This suggests that with practice, their performance could increase, a feature to explore in a separate study.

Consistent Input as a Requirement
Users often have continuous control over their speed and turning in modern racing games such as Mario Kart 8 [22] and Forza Motorsport [40], which helps to slow down around corners and speed up when the track straightens out. It is also critical to have continuous control of the racer's direction to take turns at different angles and be able to precisely navigate through and around obstacles. We did not give participants continuous control over both speed and direction concurrently in our schemes, which participants commented on in both gesture schemes. We found lower performance and pragmatic qualities for gesture-based schemes compared to the binary scheme. We believe that consistent control over speed and direction simultaneously is a necessity to perform well in racing games. A solution might be to implement analogue sticks and triggers into the prototype, providing the ability to control both speed and direction continuously.

One interesting observation is that the binary scheme out-performed both gesture-based schemes, yet did not provide participants with any continuous input. We believe this is due once again to the participants' familiarity with standard control schemes, and the similarity between the speed and direction input, both discrete. This could suggest that control consistency is important in racing games regardless of whether or not it is discrete or continuous control.

GENERAL DISCUSSION AND RECOMMENDATIONS

Overall, participants performed best with the binary scheme. Participants had limited time to familiarize themselves with the control schemes and most participants had not used flexible input methods in the past. Taken into account that most participants frequently played games, this is result consistent with those of McEwan et al. [17], who found that more naturally mapped controls was not linked to an increase in performance compared to traditional controls.

Participants found gesture-based schemes intriguing, they were often excited to pick up and use the gesture-based schemes, even if their performance was not as good. The action and navigation schemes, for the most part, received high hedonic quality scores, and participants often chose them as their favourite. When implementing deformation gestures into current games, we suggest finding game mechanics with natural mappings to bend and twist. We also believe that deformation gestures should only be mapped to key-actions (actions that are critical in terms of game performance) if they represent a natural mapping. If no natural mapping is possible, we suggest to map them to novel in-game actions that increase the fun and enjoyment of the game, but are not critical in terms of performance.

The action scheme outranked and outperformed the navigation scheme in almost all cases. We recommend mapping bends and twists to in-game actions, as opposed to in-game navigation. We also recommend mapping gestures to a minimal number of actions as more gesture mapping make the experience more complex leading to higher levels of frustration and worse performance.

Finally, the ergonomics of the controller and input methods caused a few issues in both studies. We noticed that participants struggled with learning how to twist the controller properly along a middle (invisible) axis, even after explanations. Their lack of understanding and poor twist input caused unexpected reactions in-game which likely lowered their performance and increased their frustration when required to twist. The few participants who did understand how to twist properly ranked the navigation scheme higher and performed better than those who did not Users should be taught how to perform gestures properly and should be shown how their gestures affect the game.

Limitations

Our primary limitation regards the prototype, specifically the unreliability of the bend sensors, and in some cases, the buttons, where the output of the sensors would change over time. We regularly calibrated and applied filters in the second study to compensate, but a better designed controller might improve this issue. Second, while we tested various genres of games using discrete and continuous gestures, we left many genres untouched. We were also not able to test complex game mechanics with our prototype as the prototype itself was quite simple. We believe that with a more complex prototype that implemented input methods such as analogue sticks, left and right triggers, or the ability to sense different degrees of the bend/twist, we could have tested more complex mechanics. Finally, we acknowledge the small sample size in each of our studies.

CONCLUSION

Our goal in this paper was to determine if and where deformation input could fit in with standard gaming input methods. We created a flexible prototype with six buttons and four gesture inputs (bends and twists). We separated the in-game mechanics in terms of actions and navigation and assigned one control scheme to each. We compared them against a traditional control scheme using buttons (binary scheme). We ran two studies, evaluating the schemes with discrete input in arcade games in study one, and with continuous input in a racing game in the second study. We found that the binary scheme performed best and required the least amount of work, but the gesture-based schemes were stimulating and novel. The action scheme performed better than the navigation scheme, and was preferred.

By combining gesture input with standard input in our prototype, we created a user experience that was not only novel, but was stimulating and full of potential. Simple actions, naturally mapped to gestures, tend to be preferred amongst users, and are performed significantly better than more complex and abstract actions. We believe that with sufficient practice, bend gestures will also have the potential to increase performance, in both old and new games alike, but further testing is required. The combination of deformation gestures with standard button input gives users access to more methods of input without requiring them to move their fingers around to reach different buttons. We believe that more advanced and precise functionality can come from combining physical deformation gestures with buttons. Our design recommendations can aid researchers and game developers alike to improve on this hybrid technology to create game experiences where gestures are both preferred and perform well.

For future work, we will look at the learnability of bend gestures in combination with standard methods of input with longer play time. It would be interesting to map continuous input to different mechanics in different genres of games. While we used existing games, it would be worthwhile to investigate games designed specifically for bending and twisting.

ACKNOWLEDGEMENTS

This work was supported and funded by the National Sciences and Engineering Research Council of Canada (NSERC) through a Discovery grant (402494-2011), and a Create grant (465639-2015). We thank Victor Cheung, Alex Eady, Lee Jones and Travis Swan for their help on this paper.

REFERENCES

1. Teemu T. Ahmaniemi, Johan Kildal, and Merja Haveri. 2014. What is a device bend gesture really good for? *Proceedings of the ACM conference on Human factors in computing systems*, 3503–3512. http://doi.org/10.1145/2556288.2557306
2. Jesse Burstyn, Amartya Banerjee, and Roel Vertegaal. 2013. FlexView: an evaluation of depth navigation on deformable mobile devices. *Proceedings of the 7th International Conference on Tangible, Embedded and Embodied Interaction - TEI '13*, ACM Press, 193. http://doi.org/10.1145/2460625.2460655
3. Farshad Daliri and Audrey Girouard. 2016. Visual Feedforward Guides for Performing Bend Gestures on Deformable Prototypes. *Proceedings of Graphics Interfaces 2016*, 209–216. http://doi.org/10.20380/GI2016.27
4. Flexpoint. 2016. http://www.flexpoint.com.
5. Gero Herkenrath, Thorsten Karrer, and Jan Borchers. 2008. Twend: Twisting and Bending as new Interaction Gesture in Mobile Devices. *Proceeding of the twenty-sixth annual CHI conference extended abstracts on Human factors in computing systems - CHI '08*, ACM Press, 3819. http://doi.org/10.1145/1358628.1358936
6. Dan Ionescu, Bogdan Ionescu, Cristian Gadea, and Shahidul Islam. 2011. A multimodal interaction method that combines gestures and physical game controllers. *Proceedings - International Conference on Computer Communications and Networks, ICCCN*: 1–6. http://doi.org/10.1109/ICCCN.2011.6006085
7. Hayato Kajiyama, Akifumi Inoue, and Tohru Hoshi. 2015. SHAPIO : Shape I / O Controller for Video Games. *Proceedings of the 2015 Annual Symposium on Computer-Human Interaction in Play - CHI PLAY '15*, ACM Press, 565–570. http://doi.org/10.1145/2793107.2810318
8. Johan Kildal, Andrés Lucero, and Marion Boberg. 2013. Twisting Touch : Combining Deformation and Touch as Input within the Same Interaction Cycle on Handheld Devices. *Proceedings of the 15th international conference on Human-computer interaction with mobile devices and services - MobileHCI '13*, 237. http://doi.org/10.1145/2493190.2493238
9. Johan Kildal, Susanna Paasovaara, and Viljakaisa Aaltonen. 2012. Kinetic device: Designing Interactions with a Deformable Mobile Interface. *ACM SIGCHI conference on Human Factors in Computing Systems Extended Abstracts*, 1871. http://doi.org/10.1145/2212776.2223721
10. J Konieczny, C Shimizu, G Meyer, and D. Colucci. 2005. A Handheld Flexible Display System. *IEEE Visualization.*, IEEE, 591–597. http://doi.org/10.1109/VISUAL.2005.1532846
11. Byron Lahey, Audrey Girouard, Winslow Burleson, and Roel Vertegaal. 2011. PaperPhone: Understanding the Use of Bend Gestures in Mobile Devices with Flexible Electronic Paper Displays. *ACM SIGCHI Conference on Human Factors in Computing Systems*, 1303. http://doi.org/10.1145/1978942.1979136
12. Bettina Laugwitz, Theo Held, and Martin Schrepp. 2008. Construction and Evaluation of a User Experience Questionnaire. *HCI and Usability for Education and Work*: 63–76. http://doi.org/10.1007/978-3-540-89350-9_6
13. Sang-Su Lee, Sohyun Kim, Bipil Jin, et al. 2010. How users manipulate deformable displays as input devices. *SIGCHI Conference on Human Factors in Computing Systems*, 1647–1656. http://doi.org/10.1145/1753326.1753572
14. Sang-Su Lee, Seungwoo Maeng, Daeeop Kim, et al. 2011. FlexRemote: Exploring the Effectiveness of Deformable User Interface as an Input Device for TV. *HCI International - Poster's Extended Abstracts*, 62–65. http://doi.org/10.1007/978-3-642-22095-1_13
15. Jessica Lo and Audrey Girouard. 2017. Bendy: An Exploration into Gaming with Mobile Flexible Devices. *ACM International Conference on Tangible and Embedded Interaction - TEI*, 10p.
16. Sana Maqsood, Sonia Chiasson, and Audrey Girouard. 2013. Passwords on flexible display devices. *Proceedings of the ACM SIGSAC conference on Computer & communications security*, 1469–1472. http://doi.org/10.1145/2508859.2512528
17. Mitchell McEwan, Alethea Blackler, Daniel Johnson, and Peta Wyeth. 2014. Natural Mapping and Intuitive Interaction in Videogames. *CHI PLAY '14 Proceedings of the First ACM SIGCHI Annual Symposium on Computer-Human Interaction in Play*: 191–200. http://doi.org/10.1145/2658537.2658541
18. Namco. 1993. *Ridge Racer*. Game. (30 October 1993). Namco, Tokyo, Japan.
19. Vinh Nguyen, Pramod Kumar, Sang Ho Yoon, Ansh Verma, and Karthik Ramani. 2015. SOFTii : Soft Tangible Interface for Continuous Control of Virtual Objects with Pressure-based Input. *Proceedings of the Ninth International Conference on Tangible, Embedded, and Embodied Interaction - TEI '15*, ACM Press, 539–544. http://doi.org/10.1145/2677199.2687898
20. Vinh P. Nguyen, Sang Ho Yoon, Ansh Verma, and Karthik Ramani. 2014. BendID: Flexible Interface for Localized Deformation Recognition. *Proceedings of the 2014 ACM International Joint Conference on Pervasive and Ubiquitous Computing - UbiComp '14 Adjunct*, 553–557. http://doi.org/10.1145/2632048.2636092

21. Nintendo. 1993. Star Fox.

22. Nintendo EAD. 2014. *Mario Kart 8*. Game [Wii U]. (29 May 2014). Nintendo, Kyoto, Japan.

23. Nintendo R&D1. 1981. *Donkey Kong*. Game [NES]. (9 July 1981). Nintendo, Kyoto, Japan.

24. OpenEmu. 2013. OpenEmu. Retrieved August 30, 2016 from http://openemu.org/

25. Alexey Pajitnov and Vladimir Pokhilko. 1984. *Tetris*. Game [NES]. (6 June 1984). Nintendo, Kyoto, Japan.

26. Lahiru Lakmal Priyadarshana, Victoria Porter, Juan Pablo Carrascal, Aaron Visser, and Roel Vertegaal. 2016. MagicWand : Exploring Physical Affordances with a Handheld Cylindrical Display Object. *Proceedings of the 2016 CHI Conference Extended Abstracts on Human Factors in Computing Systems - CHI EA '16*, ACM Press, 3762–3765. http://doi.org/10.1145/2851581.2890259

27. Nintendo R&D3. 1987. *Mike Tyson's Punch-Out*. Game [NES]. (18 October 1987). Nintendo, Kyoto, Japan.

28. Raf Ramakers, Johannes Schöning, and Kris Luyten. 2014. Paddle: Highly Deformable Mobile Devices with Physical Controls. *Proceedings of the 32nd annual ACM conference on Human factors in computing systems - CHI '14*, ACM Press, 2569–2578. http://doi.org/10.1145/2556288.2557340

29. Christian Rendl, Michael Haller, Shahram Izadi, et al. 2014. FlexSense: a transparent self-sensing deformable surface. *Proceedings of the 27th annual ACM symposium on User interface software and technology - UIST '14*: 129–138. http://doi.org/10.1145/2642918.2647405

30. Md Riyadh. 2014. Exploring tapping with thumb input for flexible tablets. *Proceedings of the extended abstracts of the 32nd annual ACM conference on Human factors in computing systems - CHI EA '14*, ACM Press, 981–986. http://doi.org/10.1145/2559206.2579422

31. Rovio Mobile. *Angry Birds*. Game. (11 December 2009). Rovio Entertainment, Keilaniemi, Espoo, Finland.

32. Carsten Schwesig, Ivan Poupyrev, and Eijiro Mori. 2004. Gummi: A Bendable Computer. *Proceedings of the 2004 conference on Human factors in computing systems - CHI '04*, 263–270. http://doi.org/10.1145/985692.985726

33. Paden Shorey, Quang Nguyen, Nathan Dubord, Andrew Mukama, and Sunmock Yang. 2014. O.R.B.S. Retrieved August 30, 2016 from http://www.orbsgame.com

34. P. Skalski, R. Tamborini, a. Shelton, M. Buncher, and P. Lindmark. 2011. Mapping the road to fun: Natural video game controllers, presence, and game enjoyment. *New Media & Society* 13, 2: 224–242. http://doi.org/10.1177/1461444810370949

35. Thomas P.B. Smith. 2013. Squidge : An Integrated Game Controller. *CHI '13 Extended Abstracts on Human Factors in Computing Systems on - CHI EA '13*, ACM Press, 2651. http://doi.org/10.1145/2468356.2479486

36. Jürgen Steimle, Andreas Jordt, and Pattie Maes. 2013. Flexpad : Highly Flexible Bending Interactions for Projected Handheld Displays. *Proceedings of the SIGCHI Conference on Human Factors in Computing Systems - CHI '13*, ACM Press, 237. http://doi.org/10.1145/2470654.2470688

37. Aneesh P Tarun, Byron Lahey, Audrey Girouard, Winslow Burleson, and Roel Vertegaal. 2011. Snaplet : Using Body Shape to Inform Function in Mobile Flexible Display Devices. *Proceedings of the 2011 annual conference extended abstracts on Human factors in computing systems - CHI EA '11*, ACM Press, 329. http://doi.org/10.1145/1979742.1979701

38. Sonic Team. 1991. *Sonic The Hedgehog*. Game. (23 June 1991). Sega, Tokyo, Japan.

39. Giovanni Maria Troiano, Esben Warming Pedersen, and Kasper Hornbæk. 2015. Deformable Interfaces for Performing Music. *Proceedings of the 33rd Annual ACM Conference on Human Factors in Computing Systems - CHI '15*, ACM Press, 377–386. http://doi.org/10.1145/2702123.2702492

40. Turn 10 Studios. 2005. *Forza Motorsport*. Game [XBox]. (May 3, 2005). Microsoft Game Studios.

41. Nicolas Villar, Kiel Mark Gilleade, Devina Ramdunyellis, and Hans Gellersen. 2007. The VoodooIO gaming kit. *Computers in Entertainment* 5, 3: 7. http://doi.org/10.1145/1316511.1316518

42. Jun-ichiro Watanabe, Arito Mochizuki, and Youichi Horry. 2008. Bookisheet: Bendable Device for Browsing Content Using the Metaphor of Leafing Through the Pages. *Proceedings of the 10th international conference on Ubiquitous computing - UbiComp '08*, 360. http://doi.org/10.1145/1409635.1409684

43. Daniel Wigdor and Dennis Wixon. 2011. *Brave NUI World: Designing Natural User Interfaces for Touch and Gesture*. http://doi.org/10.1016/B978-0-12-382231-4.X0001-9

44. Zi Ye and Hammad Khalid. 2010. Cobra: Flexible Displays for Mobile Gaming Scenarios. *Proceedings of the 28th of the international conference extended abstracts on Human factors in computing systems - CHI EA '10*, 4363. http://doi.org/10.1145/1753846.1754154

45. 1995. Namco neGcon Controller.

Inner Garden: Connecting Inner States to a Mixed Reality Sandbox for Mindfulness

Joan Sol Roo
Inria, France
joan-sol.roo@inria.fr

Renaud Gervais
Inria, France
renaud.gervais@inria.fr

Jeremy Frey
Univ. Bordeaux, France
jeremy.frey@inria.fr

Martin Hachet
Inria, France
martin.hachet@inria.fr

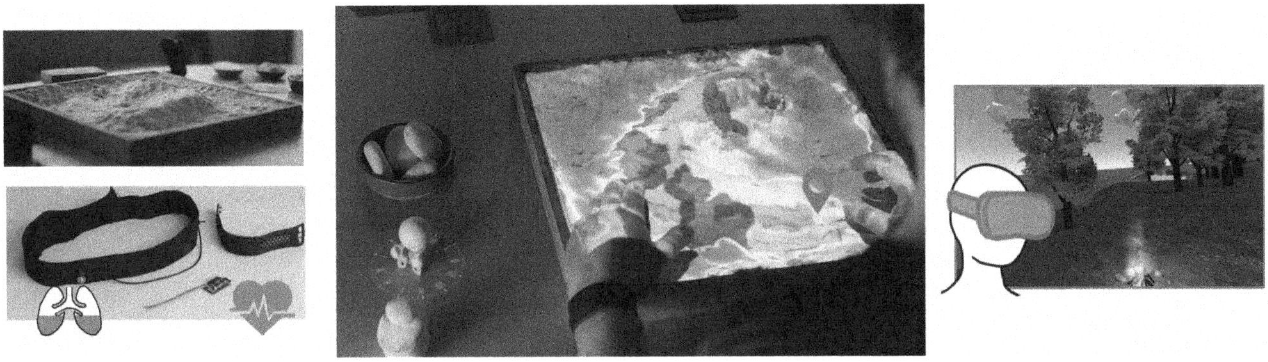

Figure 1. Inner Garden: A sandbox (up left) is connected to physiological sensors (bottom left) to create a mindful interactive experience where the user can shape her own world that evolves according to her breathing and heart rate (center). The user can then decide to be immersed inside this world thanks to a Head Mounted Display (right) for a moment of solitude and meditation.

ABSTRACT

Digital technology has been completely integrated into our daily lives, yet the potential of technology to improve its users' life satisfaction is still largely untapped. Mindfulness, the act of paying a deliberate and non-judgmental attention to the present moment, has been shown to have a positive impact on a person's health and subjective well-being – commonly called "happiness". Based on an iterative process with meditation teachers and practitioners, we designed a new tool to support mindfulness practices. This tool takes the shape of an augmented sandbox, designed to inspire the user's self-motivation and curiosity. By shaping the sand, the user creates a living miniature world that is projected back onto the sand. The natural elements of the garden are connected to real-time physiological measurements, such as breathing, helping the user to stay focused on the body. Moreover, using a Virtual Reality headset, they can travel *inside* their garden for a dedicated meditation session. Preliminary results seem to indicate that the system is well suited for mindfulness and induces a calm and mindful state on the user. The meditation teachers envisioned the use of Inner Garden in their practice.

CHI 2017, May 06 - 11, 2017, Denver, CO, USA

ACM 978-1-4503-4655-9/17/05 $15.00.
DOI: **http://dx.doi.org/10.1145/3025453.3025743**

Author Keywords

Mixed Reality; Tangible Interaction; Spatial Augmented Reality; Virtual Reality; Calm Technologies; Mindfulness

ACM Classification Keywords

H.5.1 Multimedia Information Systems: Artificial, augmented, and virtual realities

INTRODUCTION

The pervasiveness of computational devices found nowadays is getting closer to what was envisioned by Weiser when describing Ubiquitous Computing [54]: we constantly carry with us one or more computers that are always on, and on which we increasingly rely to handle different aspects of our lives. However, there is no evidence that this proliferation of digital technologies in the last 20 years made us any happier [19]. At the cornerstone of Weiser's vision was the sense of *calm* [55] – where technological devices do not compete for the user's attention, but are instead available when required –, putting humane experiences before the efficiency and connectivity. This has not yet seen a widespread adoption in information technologies.

Recently, human-computer interaction (HCI) researchers, designers and technologists started looking at computers not merely as devices to interact with, but as a support of positive changes in their users' lives, aiming to foster subjective well-being, more commonly called "happiness". Examples of this can be seen in the combination of positive psychology [44] – the scientific study of optimal human functioning and flourishing – along with the fields of design [9] and HCI [5, 40]. Subjective well-being is a multifaceted concept often described as a combination of *hedonism* – maximizing pleasure – and *eudaimonia* – developing our human potential [42]. There is a multitude of factors that have been shown to contribute to happiness and could benefit from technology [5], e.g. positive emotions, motivation and engagement, self-awareness, and mindfulness. Among these, this work focuses on *mindfulness* practices.

Mindfulness can be considered as the opposite of mind wandering, which has been demonstrated to cause unhappiness [27]. Kabat-Zinn defines it as "*the awareness that emerges through paying attention on purpose, in the present moment, and non judgmentally to the unfolding of experience moment by moment*" [24]. While mainly used in Buddhist traditions, it has been adapted and brought to a more western audience a few decades ago. It has been empirically tested and proved to be a good tool to train attention [3], for health care, mental illness and education [56]. More specifically, it has been integrated in an eight-week program course – Mindfulness-Based Stress Reduction (MBSR) [23] – to help people cope with stress, pain and depression [15]. More recently, the Mindfulness-Based Cognitive Therapy (MBCT) program has been proposed and has proven effective in treating depression, preventing relapse and promoting well-being [43].

While the mental and physical health benefits of mindfulness have been demonstrated, mindful practices are not easy to integrate into a daily routine. One of the most common said practices is mindfulness meditation. Similar to physical exercises, attention training requires practice and efforts, however, unlike physical activity – for which we can design playful, competitive or compelling settings that contributes to motivate its practice (e.g. sports) [16] –, meditation is a tricky activity to make engaging. Trying to contemplate without judgment or specific goals feels idle, like actively *doing nothing*. For novices, mindfulness meditation can be deceptively hard to practice for more than a few minutes without being distracted, yet involving any external source of motivation would be contradictory with mindfulness itself. The challenge we tackle in this paper is how to design artifacts that are both intrinsically engaging and foster mindfulness practices.

We present Inner Garden, a multi-modal tangible artifact that takes the form of an augmented sandbox depicting a small world (Figure 1), designed to implicitly support mindfulness exercises. The garden combines Physiological Computing [10] with Spatial Augmented Reality [38], Tangible Interaction [20] and immersive Virtual experiences. The Inner Garden's metaphor is anchored in reality using physiological activity and real sand. It is designed both as an ambient display for self-monitoring and as a support for more involved mindfulness exercises: breath and body awareness. The user can shape the terrain with his or her hands or tools, and affect its evolution with his or her internal state. By contemplating and interacting with the garden, the user receives biofeedback (e.g. the breathing controls the waves, changing the sea level and its sound accordingly). This gives a gentle-yet-constant reminder of his or her own bodily activity, providing an anchor to the present moment (Figure 3). Using a head-mounted display, the user can travel *inside* his or her own garden, for a moment of solitude and meditation, still accompanied by the biofeedback.

The three main contributions of this work are: 1) a prototype leveraging Spatial Augmented Reality, Tangible Interaction, Virtual Reality and Physiological Computing for the purpose of supporting mindfulness practices (namely, breath and body awareness), 2) design considerations and takeaways from iterations with experts, and 3) interviews with meditation practitioners that tested the system.

RELATED WORK

The work presented in this paper is at the intersection of different fields: it builds on top of technologies for mindfulness and is implemented using Physiological Computing, Virtual Reality, Spatial Augmented Reality and Tangible Interfaces. A brief introduction to these fields is presented below.

Technologies for Mindfulness

Most technologies that support mindfulness activities rely on guided sessions [18, 46] or leverage social networking features [33], most often delivered through the web or mobile applications. Recently, Virtual Reality (VR) has been used to deliver more immersive experiences, using either guided sessions [6], brain computer interfaces [1] or both [28]; other VR applications provide procedural landscapes based on the user inner activity [49, 7]. Further along the spectrum of reality-virtuality, we find the work of Vidyarthi et al. [52], who proposed Sonic Cradle, where users sit on a hammock in a sound-proof room where their breathing patterns were amplified through sounds. This installation focuses on the embodiment of inner activity to anchor the user into reality, yet it requires a dedicated room, thus it is not part of the user's daily environment.

It is possible to divide the previous technologies into 3 groups: 1) always-available mobile applications, 2) immersive VR sessions, 3) and dedicated rooms with embodied installations. With Inner Garden we propose a middle ground between these options, with a locally-available ambient display which provides an embodied experience, with optional immersive sessions.

Measuring and Displaying Bodily Signals

Mindfulness meditation is based on paying attention to the real world (i.e., what is currently happening, either externally or internally), and it frequently uses the practitioner's inner activity as an anchor (e.g., breath awareness). Nowadays it is possible to monitor in real time some aspects of our physiology. The Quantified Self (QS) [58] is an increasingly popular movement that consists in keeping a log of different metrics related to health or physical activity, which can be used to gain insights about one's own body. Lately, extensions of the QS to cognitive tasks has also been proposed [30]. Different works relate to the tangible and social representations of this data, for example creating a 3D printed object based on a running session [26]. However, the quantification of this data enables comparison – with oneself and others –, which directly leads to striving (and this should be avoided with mindfulness). Bodily signals have been used in the context of calm technologies, for example SWARM [57] is a wearable with sensing capabilities to mediate affect. Similar in spirit with our system is BreathTray [34], an ambient desktop widget that help users to control their breathing patterns. Sonne and Jensen [47] created a game for children suffering from ADHD (Attention Deficit Hyperactivity Disorder) based on slow breathing patterns. Gervais et al. [12] created a toolkit to create tangible animated representations of real-time physiological data. In addition, they used it to create a tangible avatar for a breathing exercise to promote relaxation. However, these systems were not specifically designed for mindfulness.

Spatial Augmented Reality and Tangible Interfaces

Spatial Augmented Reality (SAR) [38] consists in displaying spatially coherent digital information in the environment, either using projectors or screens. Closely related with SAR are Tangible User Interfaces (TUI) [50], which provide physical representation to digital information. In combination, these technologies enable the user to see and interact with digital information using materialized metaphors. SAR has already been used in conjunction with deformable materials. Illuminating Clay [37] has been the first system to combine the two elements. It uses clay to represent a landscape which can be directly shaped with the hands. The result of landscape analysis functions is displayed directly on the clay. In the artistic project *EfectoMariposa* [13], the projected simulated world is alive and evolves on its own – e.g. elements in the mini-world evolve without any user intervention. Dynamic augmented worlds can also be navigated virtually: in MadSand multiplayer game [41], one of the players creates the mini-world using an augmented sandbox and the second one can navigate it in real time using a desktop computer.

Interfaces involving SAR and TUI make abstract topics easier to grasp by enabling the user to experiment hands on [45, 35]. In our case, we present the user their own inner state, giving life to a small world, an embodied meditation metaphor.

INNER GARDEN

Our system is inspired by both the reflective and metaphoric nature of zen gardens as well as the playful and experimental nature of sandboxes. Zen gardens are all about careful placement of elements and are often used for contemplative and meditative purposes. On the other hand, sandboxes call for interaction and experimentation. We purposely used a gardening metaphor to encourage the *continuous practice* of mindfulness; Inner Garden grows with time and with each meditation session a user does. Indeed, mindfulness is not about the quantification of the current experience (e.g. how you performed when watering your garden today), but is instead about the ongoing process of being able to identify a wandering mind and returning it to the present moment (e.g. watering your plants every day). The gardening metaphor puts the user in charge of a living artifact, and it provides a source of relatedness [8].

The garden's sandbox contains polymeric sand (sand with an added polymer that keeps the "wet sand texture"), which can be reshaped at any time using bare hands or tools and determines the topology of the terrain. The real-time simulation handles the generation and evolution of the living mini-world, which is then rendered on the sand using projection. The lowest areas are filled with virtual water, which level is mapped to a breathing sensor attached to the user. Breathing patterns therefore generate waves, producing subtle sound effects audible even when the user is not directing his or her attention on the garden. The user can simply contemplate the mini-world, the sea moving with his or her breathing and the clouds slowly passing by. Finally, the user can decide to go *inside* the mini-world for a moment of solitude [11], selecting a location by placing a mini-avatar in the sandbox (Figure 2), and then using a VR helmet. During the immersive session, the user will find him- or herself sitting at the corresponding location in the garden, facing a campfire that intensifies slightly when the user is breathing out (Figure 1 right). At all times, biofeedback is part of the nature itself, as a gentle reminder to focus on his or her internal state.

The Garden's World

The living mini-world is composed of different elements, each one evolving at a different pace. It consists of the terrain, the sea, life in the mini-world, weather conditions and time. These layers are depicted in Figure 3.

Terrain The sand defines the topology of the mini-world. According to the elevation and slope, sections of terrain with specific properties are defined. For example, if the slope is too steep, no plants will grow; if the terrain is too high, snow will accumulate.

Sea The sea level divides what is above and what is underwater. This level is a fixed value that is set according to the height of the sandbox. Sections of terrain that surround the sea level will not contain flora, having a beach instead.

Life Two types of life form exists in the mini-world: flora and fauna. The flora consists of grass and trees that grow over time. The fauna, while not explicitly made visible in the mini-world, manifests its presence with sounds (birds or crickets).

Weather The weather elements that are simulated in the mini-world include wind and clouds. The wind is one of the central aspects as it is directly linked to breathing. It also impacts other elements of the mini-world. Namely, clouds move according to the wind's speed. In VR, it also directly affects the movement of the trees and the intensity of the campfire.

Time The mini-world has its own internal clock and the passing of time can be made constant (e.g. following the local time) or variable. The clock defines the amount of light and the sun position, which in turn affects how the clouds shadows appear. The day/night cycle also influences the active fauna (birds during the day, crickets during the night).

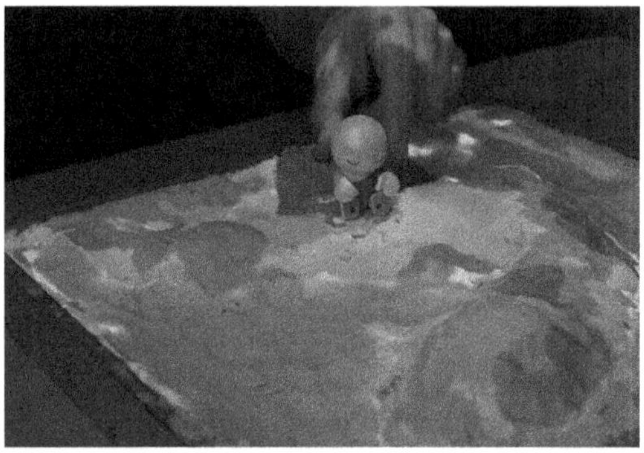

Figure 2. A physical avatar allows the user to choose the location where he or she wants to be immersed in his or her mini-world.

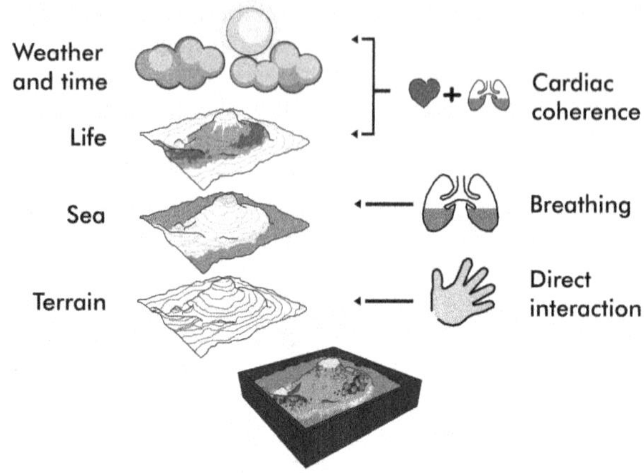

Figure 3. The layers of the Inner Garden and their connection with the user. From bottom to top: the sand is manipulated by hand; the level of the sea is controlled by breathing; vegetation growth and weather depend on cardiac coherence.

Physiological Signals

Inner Garden evolves and reacts to the user's real-time physiological measurements. It acts as both an instant biofeedback device as well as a long term and motivating ambient support. The measured physiological activities and their mapping to the dynamic elements of the mini-world open a wide number of design possibilities. We present the ones we selected and the rationale behind them (Figure 3):

Breathing The oscillating breathing patterns are mapped to the water level (which creates waves), and to the wind strength (creating gusts of wind). These elements are naturally periodic in the real-world, creating a coherent experience. All the experts we interviewed found the water biofeedback interesting since they use similar metaphors in their meditation sessions.

Cardiac coherence (CC) This metric is the positive correlation between the fluctuation of the heart-rate and the breathing cycles, when taking regular, slow and deep breaths. The resulting state has positive impact on well-being [31] and it is associated with a relaxed state. CC is a metric that varies slowly over time, therefore we used it as a subtle indicator of the overall "healthiness" of the garden. When in good health, the amount of clouds reduces, flora's growth speed is increased and sounds caused by the fauna are more present. Note that there is no obvious "unhealthy" state; fauna might hide, but trees will not start dying as a result of a low CC score. This is to avoid the introduction of judgmental effect. CC might be correlated with a relaxed state, but this is not a requirement for practicing mindfulness.

We also considered and discarded two additional sources of feedback:

Heartbeats We avoided direct feedback of the heart beats, since the user cannot control them directly. Moreover, because the rhythm is naturally fast, we considered it could lead to unnecessary discomfort. One of the interviewed experts pointed out that since mindfulness is about acceptance, observing a state like stress should not trigger "negative" biofeedback loops, yet their design should be considered carefully, specially for novice users. We envision the possibility of using heart beats to controls different rhythmic components of the mini-world, such as ambient music.

Electroencephalography (EEG) EEG measures brain activity, and it can detect high level mental states, such as emotional valence and arousal (i.e. if the user is experiencing positive or negative emotions, and how intense they are) [59] or the level of attention. Previous versions of Inner Garden included EEG, but it was excluded from the current version given both the inaccuracy of current methods and the difficulties to equip and calibrate them outside of the lab. In a foreseeable future the detection of high level mental states will be more robust, and EEG electrodes could be embedded in the Head Mounted Displays, enabling its use during immersive sessions, as done in [28].

Designing for Mindfulness

While designing Inner Garden system, we came across different problems and considerations about supporting mindful practices and experiences. As part of the design iterations we tested the system with five experts, either in meditation or medical practitioners initiated in meditation practices. Their diverse backgrounds allowed us to gather feedback from different point of views. Each expert's background is detailed in Table 1.

EXPERT ID	BACKGROUND
E1_Teacher	Transcendental and mindfulness meditation teacher
E2_Psychomotor	Psychologist and psychomotor therapist
E3_MBSR	Head of MBSR center
E4_Psychologist	Psychologist interested in cardiac coherence
E5_Buddhist	Lama of a Buddhist center (Buddhist monk)

Table 1. The experts interviewed along with their backgrounds

Each of the experts was invited for a private session. We described the system and then equipped them with the breathing sensor. After an incremental demonstration of the available features, they were left free to experiment, usually making spontaneous comments in the process. After that, we performed an unstructured interview to know more about their experience and their opinion about the system as a tool for mindfulness. After each session the system was updated taking into account the obtained comments. The resulting design considerations build on the work of Calvo and Peters [5], and are presented below.

Distraction vs Guidance

There are two main approaches to support mindfulness, either provide direct guidance (e.g. external stimuli that point towards the breathing) or to train the required abilities (e.g. requiring focus on the breathing even in the presence of distractions). We chose to include both in a very subtle manner. The sea and wind present aural and visual feedback as a constant reminder of the breathing while animal sounds provide distraction from it. Moreover, since CC is based on consistent and slow breathing cycles, the stop in animal sounds provides a feedback that the breathing frequency is becoming inconsistent.

The pace at which the simulation runs and at which change happens needs to be carefully considered. Like guided meditations, some moments where nothing is happening or heard is required for people to focus, before offering a reminder to come back to the breath. E2_Psychomotor found some of the sounds a little too erratic and distracting while E1_Teacher and E3_MBSR considered these as interesting elements that could provide exercise to train attention. This tends to show that the pace at which events happens should be slow and progressive.

One of the main considerations of E1_Teacher for using Inner Garden in his teaching was how to frame an exercise without any external control. He suggested using the day/night circles to define the length of the exercises, while preventing ending the exercises abruptly (e.g. at nightfall). One interesting aspect for him was the use of naturally occurring events as a timer enabling the user to simply continue with the exercise if desired.

Keeping it Minimalist

A minimalist design can create an environment that has very few distractions, enabling the user to focus. Carefully chosen ambient biofeedback that is thematically built into the system – i.e. nature elements moving on a deserted island – provides a unified minimalist experience. E1_Teacher found the setup visually appealing but sometime hard to focus on. The constantly changing terrain was too detailed and dynamic for him. He suggested more minimalistic textures and slower movements. To address this issue, we reduced the overall speed of the clouds, the range of the sea waves, and the contrast of the textures.

Non-judgment and Non-striving

One of the core aspect of mindfulness is trying to be non-judgmental of your thoughts and adopting a non-striving attitude. We found these aspects were the trickiest part to design for, as one of the main motivation for creating a system supporting mindfulness is in making the activity more attractive and engaging. Usually, to increase engagement, goal-setting is efficient. However, as previously mentioned, it is relatively incompatible with a non-striving attitude. This is why we based its design on exploratory open-ended toys.

One way to get around goal setting is to provide a sense of progression related to the *practice* of the activity and avoid any explicit evaluation of how well a session went. This is also why we consciously avoided any *quantified* data and instead provided *qualified* feedback that is also fleeting – i.e. there is no record of your past breathing patterns or how your cardiac coherence evolved throughout the session. Moreover, to make the practice of mindfulness motivating every day, we added a localized biomass intensifying mechanism. Every time the user chooses to meditate at a specific area in the garden, it acts as a "watering system" for the biomass located there. That is, grass will grow greener and the trees taller, leveraging once again the gardening metaphor. It is based on the completion of an exercise (a given amount of time), and it avoids any negative progression: E1_Teacher insisted that the garden should not dry out if the user misses a day or two of practice – it should simply stay in the same state. This is also backed by the literature, that indicates that positive-only feedback (or progression in our case) is better for novices [17], and would satisfy the eudaimonic personal-growth aspiration [42].

Promoting Acceptance

Exercising acceptance – accepting what is happening, in contrast with the desire or ability to change it – is a key aspect of mindfulness. To train acceptance, the user must acknowledge that the garden will never be complete, and every time he or she modifies the terrain, the life will reset. The user must accept that there are consequences of his or her actions that are out of his or her control. Another way acceptance is exercised is with the immersive session. The user selects where to do the session with a tangible avatar before starting. Then, they can contemplate the surroundings, but cannot navigate the virtual space.

The biofeedback is itself not filtered allowing the user to face his or her own internal states, e.g. if a user starts breathing inconsistently, the water will reproduce this behavior. E3_MBSR considered that the user should exercise the ability to observe negative states (such as stress) without triggering a negative feedback loop, which is related with eudaimonic's self-acceptance aspiration. Even when this seems opposite to what E1_Teacher recommended in the previous section (no negative progression), they are complementary aspects: the user is exposed to both positive and negative states, but only the positive states (daily practice) have a lasting impact on the system.

Promoting Autonomy

This aspect is a core component in both intrinsic motivation and eudaimonic development. It is important to allow the user to control the boundaries of the experience along with when and how the feedback occurs. Ambient information is well suited for this, since it does not impose on the user. Therefore, the user has control over how fine grained he or she needs the information retrieval to be. A more directed attention enables more precise information to be derived while a soft focus will let unconscious mental processes do the monitoring. Moreover, sound is a modality that is easy to either tone down or disable by the way of volume control, if the feedback turns out to be too invasive. When we asked the experts about offering the possibility of controlling the moment of the day in the garden to suit individual preferences in meditation settings, they kept referring to such possibilities as "very ludic", but were concerned that too much control and options will prevent the user from exercising *acceptance*. E1_Teacher and E3_MBSR said that such customization could be useful to define a starting point for the meditation session.

Using Tangible Interaction

A lot of attention-directing exercises leverage the body and its sensation to stay in the present moment (e.g. yoga, guided meditation, tai chi). E5_Buddhist was concerned about the increasingly prevalent disconnection from the body in favor of the world of the mind and thoughts. This expert especially liked the use of the sand in Inner Garden as a tangible, direct and visceral way to reconnect to physical sensations, potentially "bypassing" the mental. E2_Psychomotor and E4_Psychologist found the SAR installation could be particularly useful in physiotherapy, in order to let the patient "get back" to their body. While trying the system, all experts enjoyed doing back and forths between performing modifications on the landscape and periods of contemplation.

Choosing the Right Reality

The use of Virtual Reality (VR) or See-Through Augmented Reality (ST-AR) helmets, such as Oculus Rift [36] and Microsoft Hololens [32] respectively, can provide immersive experiences that can be leveraged in interesting ways for mindfulness purposes, and were used in the past [6, 1, 28] for this objective. For example, these technologies can prove useful when looking for moment of solitude [11], by blocking or tuning out external stimuli. However, completely traveling to an alternate reality seems to go against the "acceptance" of reality described earlier. On this matter, E4_Psychologist also raised concerns on using a VR experience in cases where user has psychological troubles to differentiate what is real and what is not, such as persons suffering from schizophrenia. For these reasons, we made sure that the system was designed around a SAR experience. SAR is interesting because it directly uses the physical world as support and provides a shared experience that does not require users to wear any equipment, unlike ST-AR systems. From this experience anchored in reality, we added a VR modality that allows users to travel to a spot inside their garden. Because of this AR-VR transition, the VR experience is anchored on a real-world element: before the visit, the user built the virtual world with his or her own hands, and placed an avatar on the location they want to travel to. Moreover, even if the virtual world is completely computer generated, the biofeedback is always present, keeping the user aware of his or her own body. For those cases where VR is not recommended, such as with young children, SAR is a very interesting alternative to explore.

During the iterations we experimented with an intermediate Augmented Virtuality modality, where it is possible to see and touch the sand while wearing the VR helmet. This was accomplished by rendering the scene from the user's head position, and using a Leap Motion (attached to the front of the helmet) to provide feedback about the hands position (Figure 4). The resulting hybrid modality mixes both the immersive experience with the tactile feedback from the sand. Experts were concerned that this feature will render the system "too ludic" for mindfulness (i.e., too much playfulness can disperse the user's attention, which is the opposite of the system's objective). This concern might be due to the high degree of interactivity with the virtual elements, that drives away attention from the physically based elements. This modality, while promising, requires further consideration.

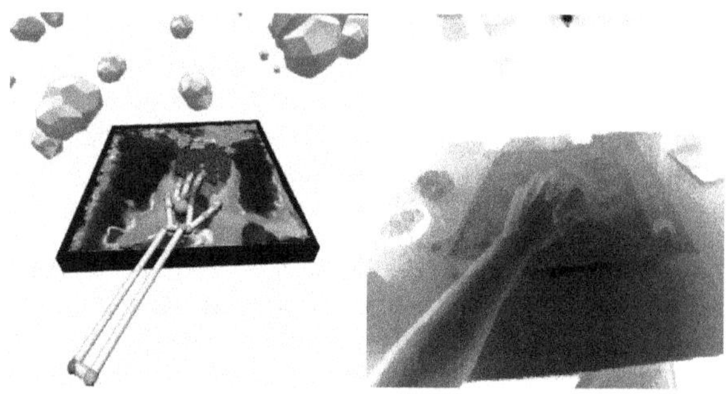

Figure 4. Mixing the SAR and VR experience. Hands are captured by the leap motion. This allows modifying virtual elements (e.g. clouds). A precise mapping between real and virtual allows one to modify physically the sandbox, while being immersed in VR.

Design Overview

The starting point of Inner Garden took inspiration from zen gardens, and it was built on top of existing mindfulness applications, leveraging tangible artifacts. The exchanges with experts either validated or complemented the design considerations we found in the literature, and enabled us through an iterative process to create an engaging artifact for mindfulness. We consider the lessons learned in the process can be of use not just for the reproduction of the system (detailed in the next section), but also when facing the design of novel positive computing artifacts.

SYSTEM IMPLEMENTATION

The final version of the system is composed of five modules: projector-camera calibration, surface scanning, physiological controller, simulation and rendering (Figure 5). The components were implemented using 3 frameworks: vvvv [53], Unity3D v5 [51] and OpenViBE [39]. The whole installation runs on two computers: the graphical pipeline and simulations runs at 80 fps on a Intel i7 Windows 10 desktop computer equipped with a NVidia GTX980Ti graphic card, while the physiological controller runs on a dedicated laptop computer running Kubuntu 14.04 in order to reduce signal acquisition latency.

Projector-Camera Calibration

The SAR setup is comprised of an ASUS short-throw projector to augment the sand and a Microsoft Kinect v1 (Figure 6) to capture the sand's topology. The projector's intrinsic (lens properties) and extrinsics (position and orientation) were calibrated using OpenCV [21] camera calibration tools (2D to 3D calibration), while the Kinect extrinsics were calibrated using the Kabsch algorithm (3D to 3D alignment: rotation

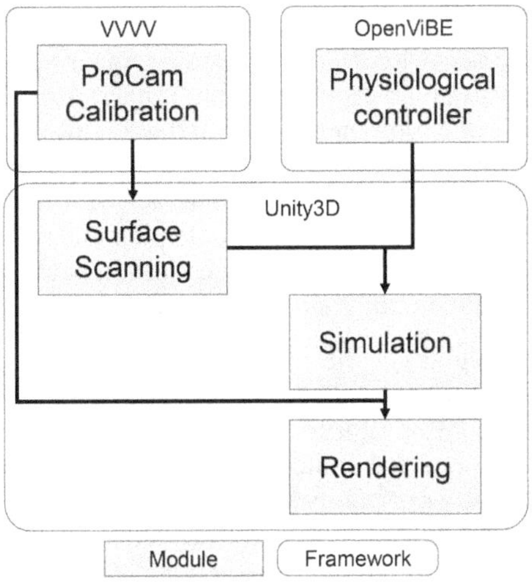

Figure 5. Inner Garden modules. The projector camera-calibration is performed offline, and the physiological controller runs on a dedicated computer. The main application performs the surface scanning, simulation and rendering, and it was implemented using Unity3D.

and translation). The sandbox was used as the common frame of reference. The calibration is performed offline. We used a 40×40×4cm sandbox. Different shapes could be studied, notably in the case of multiple users where circular shapes could ease collaboration.

Surface Scanning

The acquisition of the Kinect information (Figure 7) is performed on a worker thread on the CPU, while the computation of topological information is performed on the GPU. First, the Kinect's depth information is converted into a point-cloud (sparse world positions) using the depth camera's field of view. Then, the Kinect's extrinsic calibration is applied, to obtain the point-cloud in the sandbox referential. Being in the same coordinate system, it is possible to identify the points that are inside of the box, or on areas of interest around it. Then, topological information can be computed: for every point of interest, it is possible to know the height from the base, and the associated normal along with the time from its last modification. Because the Kinect's depth information is noisy, changes under a threshold of 2 cm are ignored.

The detection of the tangible avatar is done using the height information. The avatar can be detected in one of two locations: 1) on a predefined area near the sandbox, or 2) on the surface of the terrain. In the first case, the terrain is updated continuously. The moment the avatar is removed from the preselected position, the update of the terrain geometry is paused. From this point on, significant changes on the heightmap are assumed to belong to the avatar

Physiological Controller

The physiological controller uses the TOBE framework [12], including both the sensors and the signal processing software. In terms of sensors, we used a Mio Fuse smartwatch for measuring heart beats and a homemade belt based on a stretch sensor to measure breathing. The latter is comprised of a

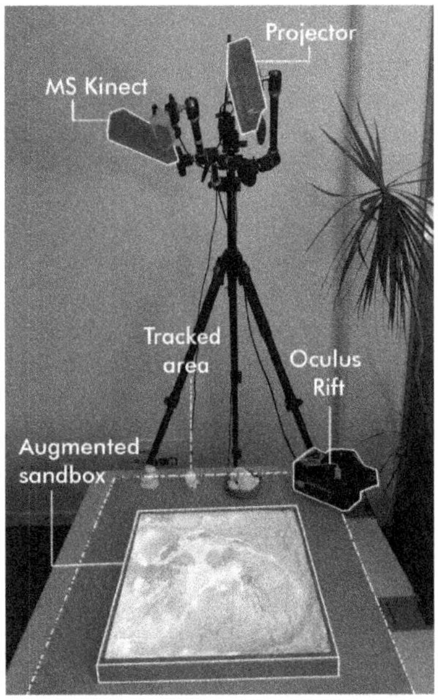

Figure 6. Installation setup: Projector (green), Kinect (blue) tracking the augmented sandbox (purple) and tokens over the table (red zone). The VR headset equipped with a leap motion stands at the back of the table.

conductive rubber band that was mounted as a voltage divider and connected to an instrumentation amplifier. It was then connected to a custom printed circuit board (PCB) that is directly embedded into the breathing belt. The PCB has a Bluetooth 4 module to stream the data to a laptop computer to be processed using OpenViBE, where the value is normalized using a moving window. Finally, the normalized information is sent to Unity3D using the LSL protocol, a network protocol dedicated to the streaming of physiological data[1].

[1] https://github.com/sccn/labstreaminglayer

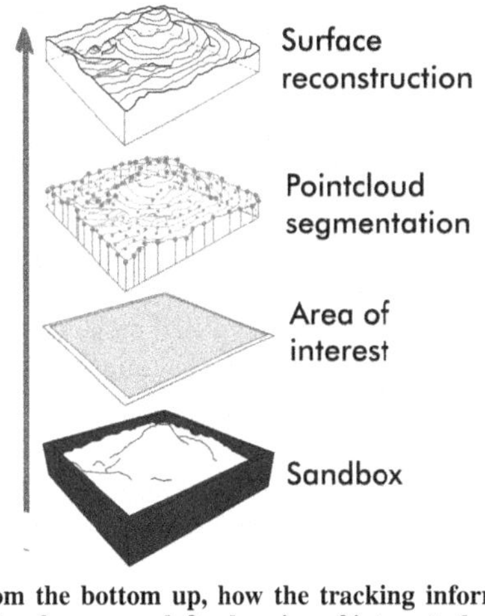

Figure 7. From the bottom up, how the tracking information is performed. Starting from a predefined region of interest, the Kinect point-cloud is segmented, then the per-point height and normal are computed.

Simulation

The simulation handles all the different elements of the garden's world (Figure 3). The generation of the mini-world's topology is created using the result of the surface scanning step. The topological information is used to classify the terrain in different region types (e.g. under water, above water, with snow, too steep to grow life). For each point of the sandbox, the growth of different kinds of vegetation is controlled by the time since its height changed, along with the region type. Therefore, each point will be assigned a color that will result in the terrain texture. Then, assets such as trees are instantiated based on the terrain texture. Finally, virtual elements are added, such as clouds, sun position and stars. These virtual elements are visible while in VR, and they influence the illumination in SAR.

Rendering

Finally, the scene is rendered from the appropriate virtual camera, depending on the output modality (SAR or VR). In the case of SAR, we create a virtual camera using the projector intrinsic and extrinsic parameters obtained previously. The rendering is then display using the projector. In the case of VR, the virtual camera is positioned at the avatar location inside the sandbox, and then visualized using an Oculus Rift DK2.

INTERVIEWS WITH PRACTITIONERS

To complement the feedback from experts, we conducted interviews with meditation practitioners to collect feedback from potential end users. Participants were recruited through the newsletter of a non-profit association that gathers people interested in meditation. 12 females took part in the study, mean age 45 (SD: 11). Most of them (7) practiced meditation regularly – several times a week or every day – but only 3 explicitly mentioned mindfulness practices, in contrast with other meditation practices. The study comprised of 5 stages (Figure 8).

Protocol

The participants entered a dimly lit room and filled out a consent form. Afterwards we introduced the features of the system progressively: shaping the sand, dynamic world, breathing (they were equipped at this moment), and finally the head mounted display. As we explained the breathing, the users could see their breathing projected onto the sand, they were also encouraged to touch it and play for a few moments, in order to see the connection.

After the system introduction, the participants filled several questionnaires so we could know more about their profile. The period during which they filled these questionnaires was used as the breathing baseline. The questionnaires were:

1. A demographic questionnaire
2. The five facet mindfulness questionnaire (FFMQ) [2]: a questionnaire evaluating how "mindful" they are during their everyday life
3. The state-trait anxiety inventory (STAI-YA) [48]: and a questionnaire assessing their present anxiety

Then we instructed the participants about the principles of mindfulness. On par with the instructors we met, we told participants that newcomers to mindfulness meditation could focus their attention on their breathing, taking deep and slow breath. Then the first meditation session occurred, using one of the SAR or VR modality to interact with the system. In the VR condition participants would pick their location using the token (Figure 2); in the SAR condition participants could freely manipulate the sand while meditating.

After 10 minutes – the length suggested by E1_Teacher – we interrupted the meditation exercise and participants filled the Toronto Mindfulness Scale (TMS), a questionnaire assessing how one was mindful during a specific exercise [29]. They had the opportunity to rest for a little while before we prompted them with a second meditation session, using the other interaction modality. Again, after 10 minutes they were interrupted and answered the TMS.

Before the exit questionnaires, participants were invited to use freely the system, without any guidance: they could shape sand, use VR or focus on breathing as they wished. When they finished to do so – usually after 5 min –, they filled three questionnaires:

1. The STAI-YA questionnaire, the same as the beginning of the study
2. The system usability scale (SUS) [4], which, as its name indicates, helps to evaluate the general usability of systems and services
3. Custom questions regarding the acceptability of specific aspects of the system

Finally, we conducted an informal interview with the participants, freely exchanging about the system for 20 to 30 minutes depending on the person.

Questionnaires Results

Concerning the profile of the participants, the FFMQ questionnaire corroborated the meditation practices declared by the participants at the beginning of the study. Regular practitioners scored above the average of our population – on a scale ranging from 39 to 195, the mean of the 5 traits measured by the questionnaire was 146.2 (SD: 14.75). A Wilcoxon Signed-rank test yielded no significant difference ($p = 0.13$) between the two interaction modalities concerning the TMS questionnaire – overall mean: 34.91 (SD: 7.37), scale ranging from 0 to 48. This result may imply that the system induces a mindful state, regardless of the chosen modality. As for the STAI-YA questionnaire given before and after the exposition to the system, the same statistical test showed a significant difference; participants were less anxious at the end of the study (mean: 25, SD: 5.23) as compared to the beginning (mean: 31.50, SD: 10.71), $p < 0.01$ – scores between 20 and 80. Even though mindfulness meditation is not about reducing stress per se, our system may induce calmness. This is reflected by the breathing rate of the participants, that were significantly lower during both mediation sessions, as compared to a baseline recorded at the beginning of the session (9 breaths per minute vs 17). The average SUS score was 80.82

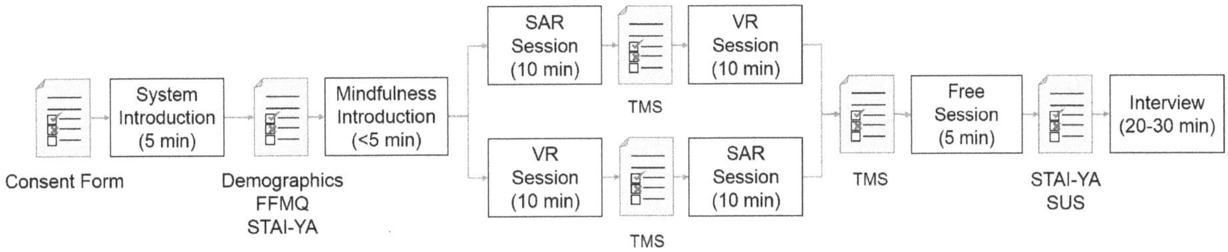

Figure 8. The 5 stages of the study and the questionnaires used. The stages involved: description of the system, two consecutive meditation sessions – SAR and VR, the order of the conditions counterbalanced between participants – , a free session, and finally an informal interview. Various questionnaires, measuring mindfulness and qualities of the system, were given during the study. Overall, a session lasted 1.5 hour.

(SD: 11.78) – scale between 0 and 100. Overall, this indicates that the system has good usability in both its SAR and VR modalities.

Feedback Discussion

The feedback we received was converging around recurring themes: the SAR and VR modalities and the multisensory experience.

VR and SAR

The participants were divided between which modality (SAR or VR) they liked the most – this was not caused for an order effect, since only 7 out of 12 participants preferred the first modality they tried. About half the participants mentioned VR as the best part of the experience, praising the immersion and the sense of control over the environment. Some participants, used to meditate with their eyes closed to fully concentrate, highlighted that the VR world enabled them not to be disturbed by external distractions while having something to look at. The other half of the participants (5/12) mentioned problems related with the heaviness of the VR headset and found the graphics too simplistic. One of the recurring comments was about the limitation of not being able to move in VR and explore the mini-world. This design choice was intentional, in order to prevent both simulator sickness and to foster acceptance, as discussed previously. However, it would be interesting to explore the potential benefits of virtual meditative walks [14]. The fact that the participants were split is a good indicator that providing complementary modalities can be of value to suit personal preferences regarding meditation practices. Interestingly, when asked about the quality of the system's graphics, none of the participants mentioned the augmented sandbox; they only considered the VR as being a graphical display. This indicates that using the physical world as a support can make technology more approachable, if not transparent. This is of special interest given the demographics (middle aged females, two of them explicitly stated their reluctance towards technology before starting the study).

Not all the users saw the SAR and VR components of the systems as parts of a whole. Notably, they saw discrepancies between what they thought they were building in the sandbox and what they witnessed in VR. The users that did see a connection (4/12) found the parts complementary, and highlighted being able to create the virtual world from the real one. The sea was mentioned as the strongest link between real and virtual. Visiting the virtual world can also increase the impact of the projected augmentation: one participant mentioned she could not understand the cloud shadows on the sandbox until she visited VR, and that after she imagined the clouds floating above the real sandbox.

Multisensory Experience

We were interested on how the participants felt about the multisensory aspects of the system, namely the tactile, visual and auditory components.

All the participants enjoyed playing with the sand. They were particularly pleased by the texture of the white polymeric sand. Similar to the experts (E2_Psychomotor, E4_Psychologist, E5_Buddhist), several of them felt that playing with sand had a "grounding" effect, beneficial to their mindfulness. We also had comments about how shaping sand was a freeing activity, reminiscent of when they were children (a known aspect, used in Sandplay [25]). We provided samples of alternative materials. After trying the polymeric sand, the participants were not particularly inspired by the proposed substitutes, even regular sand. On the other hand, they found the idea of using pebbles or rocks an interesting option to create heterogeneous landscapes, such as in traditional zen gardens.

When asked if they were interested in customizing the appearance of the terrain, both the texture or the moment of the day or year, most participants liked the idea, but the ones with experience in mindful meditation were fast to notice that too much customization would be counterproductive for mindfulness, since it would not exercise their acceptance. They instead considered the possibility of an initial parametrization, and then letting the garden evolve slowly. This matches with the opinions gathered from the experts.

The participants were very pleased with the sea sound and being able to control it with the breathing, and felt it was synchronized with their inner state (9/12). They presented mixed emotions regarding the animal sounds: two of the participants, with backgrounds in music, found the overall sound-samples too monotone, and suggested adding a richer variety. This could be addressed using procedurally generated soundtracks.

For the study, the system layout was designed so that the participants sat comfortably on a rigid puff, while facing the sandbox that was placed over a table. Several participants found this position unusual for meditation, and asked if they could sit on the floor, or with their legs crossed. One participant also asked to move to a nearby couch for the VR session. Even when we tried to provide a comfortable environment for the participants, it would be interesting to see the reception of the system in a more ecological context.

Other Comments

Even when sensors we used were not designed for comfort, the participants did not mention them as inconvenient. The breathing belt limited the user's movement, which was not a problem while sitting. This could be still addressed using sensors such as Spire[2].

Finally, some participants confirmed what we observed on the questionnaires: the system created a sense of calm and feeling centered, in particular thanks to the sea and the sand. One of the participants (mindfulness meditation practitioner) sent us an email hours after the session to thank us, and commented she felt more relaxed during her work day. This might be caused simply because we provided a calm context to take a break from their routine, nevertheless we find these results promising.

Study Limitations

Even when the system was designed with novices in mind, the study was conducted with initiated meditators. The rationale behind this decision was that we first wanted to get feedback from practitioners to make sure that our design (and the use of technology) was not antithetical with their practices, to complement the feedback from experts. Even when we used questionnaires to measure the impact of the system, our main interest was to know more about their subjective experience. The preliminary results seem to indicate we are on the right track, laying the bases for a long term study.

Mindful meditation training requires longer periods of time, and measuring the impact of the system would require following novices along the training process. In the future we would like to conduct a long term study with novices, which will include a control condition, in collaboration with the mentioned meditation teachers. This would be vital to determine if the system can help or complement existing mindfulness exercises.

CONCLUSION

We presented Inner Garden, a mixed reality system that leverages Tangible Interaction, Spatial Augmented Reality, Virtual Reality and Physiological Computing in order to support mindful experiences. Our design considerations were based on the literature, complemented and validated with feedback of experts. Finally, we tested the system with meditation practitioners of different levels of experience (from initiated to daily meditators), which found the design engaging while also being well suited for mindfulness. Preliminary quantitative results seem to indicate that the system foster a calm and mindful state on the users.

[2] `https://spire.io/` We contacted the company beforehand, but their API was closed for real time measurements, which is a requirement for our system.

We envision Inner Garden as an ambient device that would both provide a gentle reminder to practice mindfulness in daily life – like a plant that requires watering in an apartment – and a compelling tool to support mindfulness exercises. One of the main challenges will be keeping the system engaging, for example by introducing subtle changes over time such as seasons. Another interesting dimension to study is the potential of such a medium for social interaction around well-being. For example, multiple members of the family could take care of the same garden together, thus taking care of each other in the process. Both E1_Teacher and E3_MBSR perform group meditations as part of their practices and were interested on how it will be extended for multi-users, and explicitly proposed their interest to install the system on their practice. They were especially interested in its use to introduce novices to the practice of mindfulness. In the future we would like to study these aspects with their collaboration.

In the end, Inner Garden was not designed as the sole source of mindful experiences, but as an engaging way to pay attention to foster body and breath awareness. It serves as a first introduction to mindfulness, and ideally leads the users to train and develop a mindful perspective that will extend outside the garden, into their everyday life. For these purposes, tangible interaction is a promising approach. It has this interesting property of not looking like "real" digital technology, being closer to our physical and humane selves. Because of this, we believe that tangible and reality-based interaction [22] provide interesting approaches to the emerging field of positive computing.

ACKNOWLEDGMENTS

This work was supported by the ISAR project ANR-14-CE24-0013. We want to thank Jelena Mladenovic for her help with producing the video, and Thibault Laine for his help with fabrication, in particular the development of the custom physiological PCB.

REFERENCES

1. Amores, J., Benavides, X., and Maes, P. Psychicvr: Increasing mindfulness by using virtual reality and brain computer interfaces. CHI 2016 Video Showcase, 2016.

2. Baer, R. A., Smith, G. T., Hopkins, J., Krietemeyer, J., and Toney, L. Using self-report assessment methods to explore facets of mindfulness. *Assessment 13*, 1 (2006), 27–45.

3. Brandmeyer, T., and Delorme, A. Meditation and neurofeedback. *Frontiers in psychology 4* (2013).

4. Brooke, J. Sus-a quick and dirty usability scale. *Usability evaluation in industry 189* (1996), 194.

5. Calvo, R. A., and Peters, D. *Positive computing: Technology for wellbeing and human potential.* MIT Press, 2014.

6. Cubicle Ninjas. Virtual reality meditation. `http://guidedmeditationvr.com`, 2016. [Online; accessed 22-August-2016].

7. Deep VR. Deep vr. `http://www.exploredeep.com/#about-deep`, 2016. [Online; accessed 21-December-2016].

8. Desmet, P., and Hassenzahl, M. Towards happiness: Possibility-driven design. In *Human-computer interaction: The agency perspective*. Springer, 2012, 3–27.

9. Desmet, P. M., and Pohlmeyer, A. E. Positive design: An introduction to design for subjective well-being. *International Journal of Design, 7 (3), 2013* (2013).

10. Fairclough, S. H. Fundamentals of physiological computing. *Interacting with computers 21*, 1 (2009), 133–145.

11. Fullerton, B. Designing for solitude. *interactions 17*, 6 (2010), 6–9.

12. Gervais, R., Frey, J., Gay, A., Lotte, F., and Hachet, M. TOBE: Tangible Out-of-Body Experience. In *Proceedings of the TEI'16: Tenth International Conference on Tangible, Embedded, and Embodied Interaction*, ACM (Eindhoven, Netherlands, Feb. 2016).

13. Gonzalez, P. Efecto mariposa. `http://patriciogonzalezvivo.com/2011/efectomariposa/`, 2011. [Online; accessed 23-August-2016].

14. Gromala, D., Tong, X., Choo, A., Karamnejad, M., and Shaw, C. D. The virtual meditative walk: virtual reality therapy for chronic pain management. In *Proceedings of the 33rd Annual ACM Conference on Human Factors in Computing Systems*, ACM (2015), 521–524.

15. Grossman, P., Niemann, L., Schmidt, S., and Walach, H. Mindfulness-based stress reduction and health benefits: A meta-analysis. *Journal of psychosomatic research 57*, 1 (2004), 35–43.

16. Hagen, K., Chorianopoulos, K., Wang, A. I., Jaccheri, L., and Weie, S. Gameplay as exercise. In *Proceedings of the 2016 CHI Conference Extended Abstracts on Human Factors in Computing Systems*, CHI EA '16, ACM (New York, NY, USA, 2016), 1872–1878.

17. Hattie, J., and Timperley, H. The power of feedback. *Review of educational research 77*, 1 (2007), 81–112.

18. Headspace inc. Headspace - treat your head right. `https://www.headspace.com/`, 2016. [Online; accessed 22-August-2016].

19. Helliwell, J. F., Layard, R., and Sachs, J. World happiness report. *Earth Institute* (2012).

20. Ishii, H., and Ullmer, B. Tangible bits: towards seamless interfaces between people, bits and atoms. In *Proceedings of the ACM SIGCHI Conference on Human factors in computing systems*, ACM (1997), 234–241.

21. Itseez. Open source computer vision library. `https://github.com/itseez/opencv`, 2015.

22. Jacob, R. J., Girouard, A., Hirshfield, L. M., Horn, M. S., Shaer, O., Solovey, E. T., and Zigelbaum, J. Reality-based interaction: a framework for post-wimp interfaces. In *Proceedings of the SIGCHI conference on Human factors in computing systems*, ACM (2008), 201–210.

23. Kabat-Zinn, J. *Full catastrophe living: The program of the stress reduction clinic at the University of Massachusetts Medical Center*. New York: Delta, 1990.

24. Kabat-Zinn, J. Mindfulness-based interventions in context: past, present, and future. *Clinical psychology: Science and practice 10*, 2 (2003), 144–156.

25. Kalff, D. M. *Sandplay: A psychotherapeutic approach to the psyche*. Temenos Press, 2003.

26. Khot, R. A., Hjorth, L., and Mueller, F. Understanding physical activity through 3d printed material artifacts. In *Proceedings of the 32nd annual ACM conference on Human factors in computing systems*, ACM (2014), 3835–3844.

27. Killingsworth, M. A., and Gilbert, D. T. A wandering mind is an unhappy mind. *Science 330*, 6006 (2010), 932–932.

28. Kosunen, I., Salminen, M., Järvelä, S., Ruonala, A., Ravaja, N., and Jacucci, G. Relaworld: Neuroadaptive and immersive virtual reality meditation system. In *Proceedings of the 21st International Conference on Intelligent User Interfaces*, ACM (2016), 208–217.

29. Koszycki, D., Raab, K., Aldosary, F., and Bradwejn, J. A multifaith spiritually based intervention for generalized anxiety disorder: A pilot randomized trial. *Journal of clinical psychology 66*, 4 (2010), 430–441.

30. Kunze, K., Iwamura, M., Kise, K., Uchida, S., and Omachi, S. Activity recognition for the mind: Toward a cognitive" quantified self". *Computer 46*, 10 (2013), 105–108.

31. McCraty, R., Atkinson, M., Tomasino, D., and Bradley, R. T. The coherent heart: Heart-brain interactions, psychophysiological coherence, and the emergence of system-wide order. *Integral Review 5*, 2 (2009), 10–115.

32. Microsoft. Microsoft hololens | official site. `https://www.microsoft.com/microsoft-hololens/en-us`, 2016. [Online; accessed 23-August-2016].

33. Mindfulnets. Mindfulnets - connecting online from within. `http://mindfulnets.co/en`, 2011. [Online; accessed 22-August-2016].

34. Moraveji, N., Adiseshan, A., and Hagiwara, T. Breathtray: augmenting respiration self-regulation without cognitive deficit. In *CHI'12 Extended Abstracts on Human Factors in Computing Systems*, ACM (2012), 2405–2410.

35. Nakagaki, K., Vink, L., Counts, J., Windham, D., Leithinger, D., Follmer, S., and Ishii, H. Materiable: Rendering dynamic material properties in response to

direct physical touch with shape changing interfaces. In *Proceedings of the 2016 CHI Conference on Human Factors in Computing Systems*, ACM (2016), 2764–2772.

36. Oculus VR. Oculus rift development kit 2 (dk2) | oculus. `https://www3.oculus.com/en-us/dk2/`, 2016. [Online; accessed 23-August-2016].

37. Piper, B., Ratti, C., and Ishii, H. Illuminating clay: a 3-d tangible interface for landscape analysis. In *Proceedings of the SIGCHI conference on Human factors in computing systems*, ACM (2002), 355–362.

38. Raskar, R., Welch, G., and Fuchs, H. Spatially augmented reality. In *IWAR*, Citeseer (1998), 11–20.

39. Renard, Y., Lotte, F., Gibert, G., Congedo, M., Maby, E., Delannoy, V., Bertrand, O., and Lécuyer, A. Openvibe: An open-source software platform to design, test, and use brain–computer interfaces in real and virtual environments. *Presence 19*, 1 (2010), 35–53.

40. Riva, G., Banos, R. M., Botella, C., Wiederhold, B. K., and Gaggioli, A. Positive technology: using interactive technologies to promote positive functioning. *Cyberpsychology, Behavior, and Social Networking 15*, 2 (2012), 69–77.

41. Royal Institute of Technology (KTH). Mad sand. `http://www.csc.kth.se/~lenjons/madsand/`, 2015. [Online; accessed 23-August-2016].

42. Ryff, C. D., and Singer, B. H. Know thyself and become what you are: A eudaimonic approach to psychological well-being. *Journal of happiness studies 9*, 1 (2008), 13–39.

43. Segal, Z. V., Williams, J. M. G., and Teasdale, J. D. *Mindfulness-based cognitive therapy for depression.* Guilford Press, 2012.

44. Seligman, M. E., and Csikszentmihalyi, M. *Positive psychology: An introduction.*, vol. 55. American Psychological Association, 2000.

45. Shaer, O., and Hornecker, E. Tangible User Interfaces: Past, Present, and Future Directions. *Foundations and Trends in Human-Computer Interaction 3*, 1-2 (2009), 1–137.

46. Smiling Mind. Smiling mind - meditation made easy. `http://smilingmind.com.au/`, 2010. [Online; accessed 22-August-2016].

47. Sonne, T., and Jensen, M. M. Chillfish: A respiration game for children with adhd. In *Proceedings of the TEI'16: Tenth International Conference on Tangible, Embedded, and Embodied Interaction*, ACM (2016), 271–278.

48. Spielberger, C. D. *State-Trait anxiety inventory*. Wiley Online Library, 2010.

49. The Mill. Strata: A new vr experiment. `http://www.themill.com/millchannel/862/strata%3A-a-new-vr-experiment`, 2016. [Online; accessed 21-December-2016].

50. Ullmer, B., and Ishii, H. The metadesk: models and prototypes for tangible user interfaces. In *Proceedings of the 10th annual ACM symposium on User interface software and technology*, ACM (1997), 223–232.

51. Unity Technologies. Unity - game engine. `https://unity3d.com/`, 2015. [Online; accessed 23-August-2016].

52. Vidyarthi, J., Riecke, B. E., and Gromala, D. Sonic cradle: designing for an immersive experience of meditation by connecting respiration to music. In *Proceedings of the designing interactive systems conference*, ACM (2012), 408–417.

53. vvvv group. vvvv. `http://vvvv.org`.

54. Weiser, M. The computer for the 21st century. *Scientific american 265*, 3 (1991), 94–104.

55. Weiser, M., and Brown, J. S. Designing calm technology, 1995. *PowerGrid Journal 1*, 1 (1996), 75–85.

56. Williams, J. M. G., and Kabat-Zinn, J. Mindfulness: diverse perspectives on its meaning, origins, and multiple applications at the intersection of science and dharma. *Contemporary Buddhism 12*, 01 (2011), 1–18.

57. Williams, M. A., Roseway, A., O'Dowd, C., Czerwinski, M., and Morris, M. R. Swarm: An actuated wearable for mediating affect. In *Proceedings of the Ninth International Conference on Tangible, Embedded, and Embodied Interaction*, ACM (2015), 293–300.

58. Wolf, G. The data-driven life. *The New York Times 28* (2010), MM38.

59. Yoon, H. J., and Chung, S. Y. Eeg spectral analysis in valence and arousal dimensions of emotion. In *Control, Automation and Systems (ICCAS), 2011 11th International Conference on*, IEEE (2011), 1319–1322.

Providing Haptics to Walls & Heavy Objects in Virtual Reality by Means of Electrical Muscle Stimulation

Pedro Lopes, Sijing You, Lung-Pan Cheng, Sebastian Marwecki, and Patrick Baudisch
Hasso Plattner Institute
Potsdam, Germany
{firstname.lastname}@hpi.de

ABSTRACT
We explore how to add haptics to walls and other heavy objects in virtual reality. When a user tries to push such an object, our system actuates the user's shoulder, arm, and wrist muscles by means of electrical muscle stimulation, creating a counter force that pulls the user's arm backwards. Our device accomplishes this in a wearable form factor.

In our first user study, participants wearing a head-mounted display interacted with objects provided with different types of EMS effects. The *repulsion* design (visualized as an electrical field) and the *soft* design (visualized as a magnetic field) received high scores on "prevented me from passing through" as well as "realistic."

In a second study, we demonstrate the effectiveness of our approach by letting participants explore a virtual world in which all objects provide haptic EMS effects, including walls, gates, sliders, boxes, and projectiles.

Author Keywords
Muscle interfaces; virtual reality; EMS; force feedback.

ACM Classification Keywords
H5.2 [Information interfaces and presentation]: User Interfaces. - Graphical user interfaces.

INTRODUCTION
Recent virtual reality systems allow users to walk freely in the virtual world (aka *real walking* [36]). As the next step towards realism and immersion, many researchers argue that these systems should also support the haptic sense in order to convey the physicality of the virtual world [3,4].

There has been a good amount of progress towards simulating the haptic qualities of *lightweight* objects, such as contact with surfaces [17] or textures [8]. Solutions generally revolve around simulating the tactile qualities of the object, i.e., how the object affects the receptors in the user's skin. These include inflatable pads at the user's fingertips [20], vibro-tactile gloves [5], and glove exoskeletons [17].

CHI 2017, May 06 - 11, 2017, Denver, CO, USA

ACM 978-1-4503-4655-9/17/05...$15.00
DOI: http://dx.doi.org/10.1145/3025453.3025600

Unfortunately, adding haptics to *heavy* objects, such as furniture or walls, has proven substantially more challenging. Even if one simulates the tactile aspects of such objects, the illusion fails as soon as users try to *push* through the object, as their proprioceptive system informs them about the lack of resistance [28].

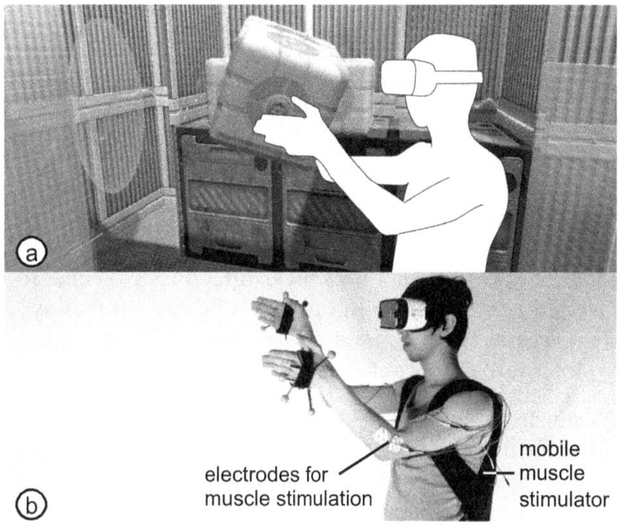

Figure 1: (a) As this user lifts a virtual cube, our system lets the user feel the weight and resistance of the cube. (b) Our system implements this by actuating the user's *opposing* muscles using electrical muscle stimulation.

Traditional approaches to simulating such objects in VR include the use of physical props [15], but even if one reuses props (by means of redirected walking [18] or human actuation [7]) the biggest limitation of this approach remains the size and weight of the props. The other traditional approach is to tether the user's hands (*SPIDAR* [25]). As a first step towards providing such forces to a non-stationary user, Nagai et al. proposed mounting a SPIDAR device into a ~1.5 x1.5 x 1.5 m cage that users carry around (*SPIDAR-W* [26)].

In this paper, we explore how to render heavy objects in VR in a truly wearable form factor.

ELECTRICAL MUSCLE STIMULATION HAPTICS FOR VR
Our main idea is to prevent the user's hands from penetrating virtual objects by means of electrical muscle stimulation (EMS). Figure 1a shows an example. As the shown user lifts a virtual cube, our system lets the user feel the weight and resistance of the cube. The heavier the cube and

the harder the user presses the cube, the stronger a counterforce the system generates. Figure 1b illustrates how our system implements the physicality of the cube, i.e., by actuating the user's *opposing* muscles with EMS.

Figure 2 illustrates the idea in more detail. (a) When the user grabs the virtual cube, the user expects the cube's weight to create tension in the user's *biceps* and the cube's stiffness to create a tension in the user's *pectoralis*. (b) In order to create this sensation, the system actuates the respective *opposition* muscles. In order to put a load onto the user's biceps, it actuates the *triceps* and in order to put a load onto the user's *pectoralis*, it actuates the user's *shoulder muscle*. This creates the desired tension in biceps and pectoralis, thereby creating the desired experience.

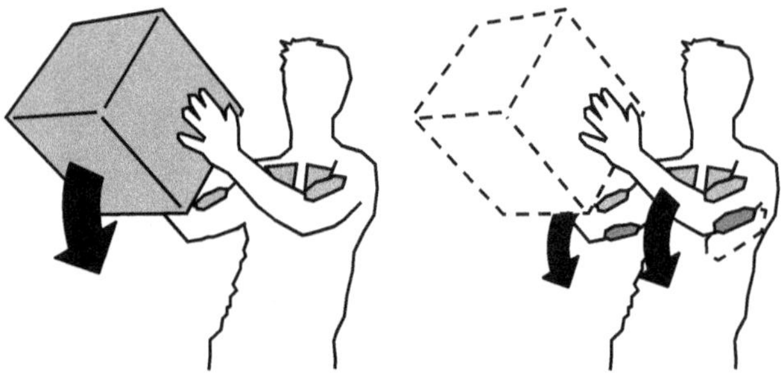

Figure 2: (a) When a user picks up a physical cube, its weight causes tension in the user's biceps. (b) Our system creates this tension by instead actuating the opposing muscles, here the user's triceps and shoulders.

As illustrated by Figure 3, our system stimulates up to four different muscle groups. Through combinations of these muscle groups, our system simulates a range of effects. When pushing a button mounted to a vertical surface, for example, the system actuates biceps and wrist. In the *Example Widgets* section we detail how this allows our system to simulate a wide range of objects, including walls, shelves, buttons, projectiles, etc.

Our system can be worn in a small backpack, as shown in Figure 3. The backpack contains a medical compliant 8-channel muscle stimulator (see also Figure 22 in the Implementation section), which we control via USB from within our VR simulators. We use our system in the context of a typical VR system consisting of a head-worn display (using a Samsung/Oculus GearVR) and a motion capture system (based on eight OptiTrack 17W cameras).

DESIGN

Based on this general concept of using EMS to bring force feedback to VR we can now design the user's experience. Two dimensions have substantial impact on the experience: (1) The intensity pattern we use to actuate the user's muscles and (2) the visuals and sound we present during this haptic event. It turns out that both of these are crucial in that they determine what physical event users will associate with the haptic sensation. These are also crucial for making the experience convincing.

Ideally, a design should fulfill four criteria, presented in order of decreasing importance: (1) *believable:* allow users to buy into the idea of the virtual object causing the experience, (2) *impermeable*: prevent users from passing through the object, (3) *consistent*: visual and haptic sensation should match, and (4) *familiar*: the experience should ideally resemble objects from the real world.

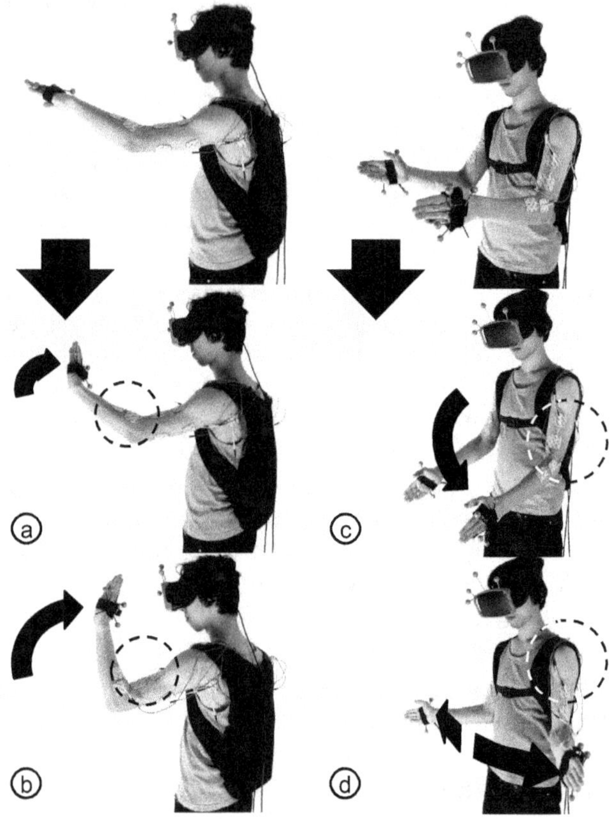

Figure 3: We use up to 8 electrode pairs, actuating (a) wrist, (b) biceps, (c) triceps, and (d) shoulders.

1. The hard object design does not work

Figure 4 illustrates the naïve approach to rendering objects using EMS: (a) From the moment the user's fingertips reach the virtual wall, we actuate the user's hand just strongly enough to prevent it from passing through. We achieve this with a current essentially proportional to the user's force (further details in Implementation).

When we built this version, the results *looked* great. The design prevents the user's hand from passing through the object and thus bystanders observing the scene would typically conclude that the illusion was "working".

However, during piloting it became clear that this design did *not* work. Since the EMS actuation was as long and as strong as the user kept pushing, the EMS signal (a tingling in the respective muscles) could become arbitrarily strong. This would draw the user's attention to the EMS-actuated muscles. These, however, were pointed in the wrong direction, i.e., they were pulling, when the sensation was supposed to be about pushing. One participant in our pilot said this design felt "like a magnet pulling the hand backwards".

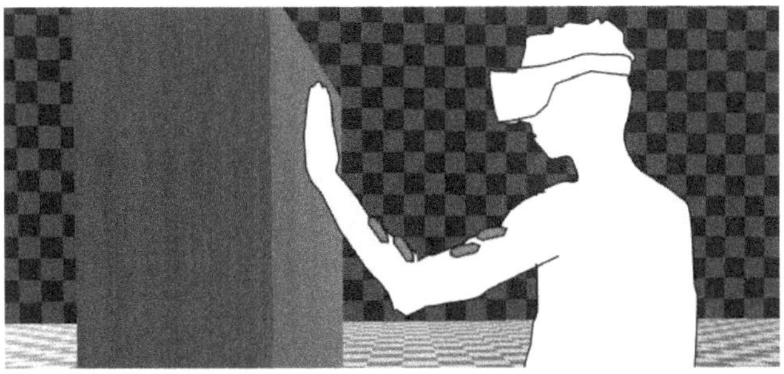

Figure 4: Implementing rigid walls requires stimulating muscles with strong impulses over long periods. This draws undesired attention to the electrical stimulation.

While this design was reasonably *impermeable*, *consistent,* and definitely *familiar*, the strong EMS signal made this design fail with respect to our primary objective: it was not *believable*.

We therefore created two alternative designs with the objective of increasing *believability*. In order to avoid the *long and strong* EMS signal that had made our actuation obvious, we created one design based on a *weaker* signal and one design based on a *shorter* signal.

2. The soft object design

We created our first alternative design by applying a cut-off to EMS intensity. We picked a reasonably low cut-off, allowing users to penetrate objects by about 10 cm. This resulted in a design that produced the impression of *soft* objects.

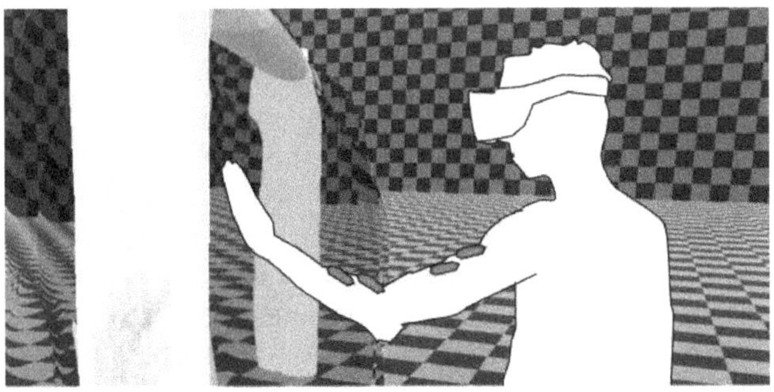

Figure 5: The *magnetic* visuals allow the user's hand to penetrate the surfaces of objects.

Based on this general concept, we explored various visuals, including the soft surface material shown in Figure 1, which is designed to suggest an increasingly solid inside under a soft, permeable surface. This general design became the basis for most of our object designs.

Figure 5 shows the same concept wrapped in visuals suggesting a *magnetic field*, suggesting a magnetic force that carefully pushes the user's hand backwards. In some versions of this design, we attached a block of metal to the back of users' hands to suggest that the magnetic field would apply there in order to affect the hand.

3. The repulsion object design

We created our second alternative design by reducing the *duration* of our EMS signal. This resulted in what we call *repulsion* objects. This design uses a brief EMS pulse (of 200-300 ms, using the user's calibrated maximum intensity) where the EMS propels the user's hand backwards, removing it from the virtual object it is trying to touch. We achieve this with an EMS pulse of still reasonably low intensity, which, like all other EMS signals in our system, is pain free at all times (for EMS pulses of similar intensity see *Impacto* [23]).

Again, we explored various visuals with this haptic design in order to help users rationalize what happens when they touch the object. Figure 6 shows what we call *electro* visuals. This design complements the EMS pulse with a strong white flash which turns the screen white for 100 ms and then fades it back in in 100 ms. At the same time, users hear a loud electrical "bang". To reinforce the effect further, we artificially enlarge the visual appearance of the user's hand movement, making it appear as if it was thrust backwards even further. In some cases, we complemented our EMS pulse with a strong vibration motor mounted to back of users' hands (an eccentric 5V DC motor operated at 12 volts) to suggest an electric flash hitting the user's hand.

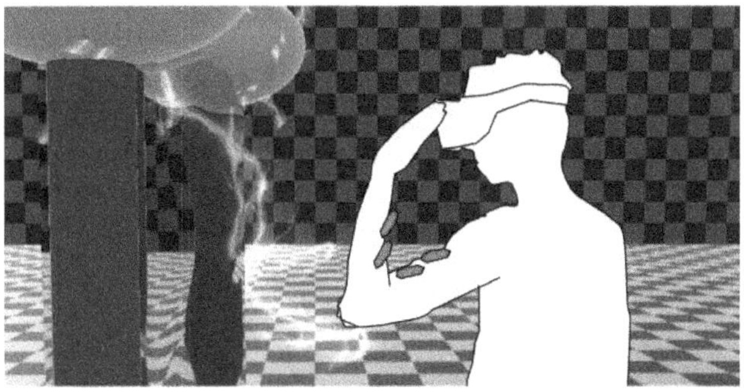

Figure 6: The *electro* visuals.

This gave us two functional designs, i.e., one to represent soft surfaces, as well as the repulsion design, which we would later use as a stand-in for hard surfaces.

FIRST USER STUDY—VALIDATING DESIGNS

We conducted a user study in order to (1) validate our core idea of using EMS as a means for adding haptics to heavy objects in virtual reality and (2) to validate the qualities of our *soft* and our *repulsion* object design. We immersed participants in a simple virtual world that contained nothing but five walls, each featuring a different haptic design. Participants touched all five of them and rated their qualities. We hypothesized that the *soft* and the *repulsion* design would perform best.

Interface conditions

Figure 7 shows the five "walls" arranged in a pentagon with the participant inside.

Each "wall" implemented one of five interface conditions:

1. The *soft* wall used the *magnetic* visuals from Figure 5.

2. The *repulsion* wall used the *electro* visuals (Figure 6).

We also included three additional conditions featuring more conventional visual explanations of a "hard" wall, all of which employed the visuals of a solid wooden wall as depicted in Figure 4.

3. The *soft wood* wall was identical to the *soft* wall, in terms of the EMS feedback, yet depicted a solid wooden wall. We used this condition to validate whether the visual design of the *soft* wall would add to the experience.

4. The *soft vibro wood* wall was identical to the *soft wood* wall, but also actuated the vibrotactile actuator on the back of participants' wrists. We used this condition to test whether vibro tactile would add to the experience.

5. The *vibro only* wall, finally, actuated *only* the vibrotactile actuator on the back of participants' wrists, but did *not* provide any EMS feedback. This condition served as baseline, as vibrotactile is the most common conventional approach to rendering haptic feedback in virtual reality (see our related work section).

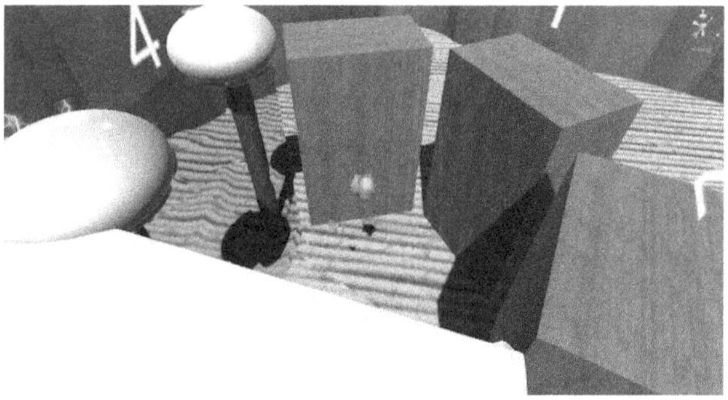

Figure 7: Study participant in the virtual world of the study, here facing the *vibro only* condition.

Apparatus

The apparatus was the prototype described earlier and shown in Figure 22. Participants wore EMS and vibrotactile actuators, one or both of which would be activated according to interface condition.

To reduce setup time, we actuated only *one* of the participants' hands. Also, since the set-up offered only vertical surfaces, we further simplified the set-up and used only two pairs of electrodes: one pair on participants' biceps and another pair on their wrist extensor muscle.

Task and procedure

Participants were prepared and placed into the virtual world shown in Figure 7. For each of five trials, the experimenter instructed the participant, which of the five walls to explore. Walls were labeled with numbers for that purpose. After touching the respective wall design for about 30 seconds, allowing for between 5 to over 20 touches, participants verbally rated this wall, which the experimenter wrote down. The order of the five interface conditions was randomized for all users prior to the start of the study.

Participants

We recruited 13 participants (4 female, 22.4 ±2.1 years). Six participants had previous experience with VR headsets and 5 had previously experienced EMS. With consent of the participants we videotaped the study sessions.

Hypotheses

Our hypotheses revolved primarily around the *repulsion* wall, the *soft* wall, and the *vibro only* baseline. (**H1**) The *repulsion* condition would be perceived as more realistic than the *vibro only* condition. (**H2**) The *soft* condition would be perceived as more realistic than the *vibro only* condition. (**H3**) The *soft* condition would be rated more realistic than the *soft wood* condition. (**H4**) The repulsion condition would be considered more impermeable than the *vibro only* condition.

Results

This section quotes Bonferroni-adjusted *p*-values.

Preference Eleven participants stated a preference for one of the EMS-based interfaces; only to two participants preferred *vibro only*. As depicted in Figure 8, eight participants picked the *repulsion* wall as their favorite. Another three listed this interface as their second favorite.

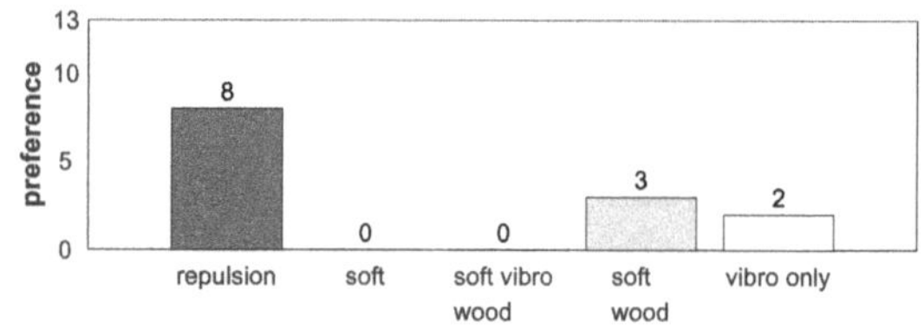

Figure 8: Eight participants picked the *repulsion* wall as their favorite design.

This suggests that our *repulsion* wall was particularly well designed. This raises the question what aspect of the repulsion design caused this preference. One explanation might be found in participants' assessment of the realism of this design.

Realism/consistency. Figure 9 shows how participants rated the five conditions with respect to the question "what I feel matches what I see." A repeated measures ANOVA (as suggested by [27]) found differences between conditions ($F(4,48) = 6.22, p = .000$).

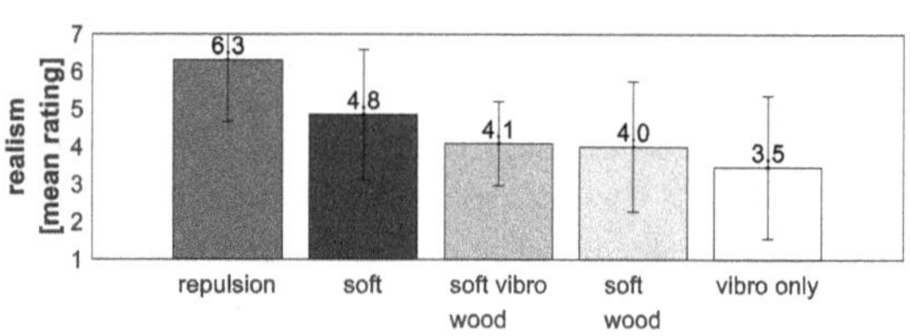

Figure 9: Participants rated the *repulsion* wall the most realistic and the *vibro only* the least realistic.

As expected, the repulsion condition received higher ratings than all other conditions, significantly so for *soft vibro wood* ($t(12) = -5.06, p = .002$) and *vibro only* ($t(12) = 3.71$,

$p = .030$) and with a strong trend with regard to *soft wood* ($t(12) = -3.38$, $p = .055$). This confirms our hypothesis **H1.**

While the *soft wood* condition was rated higher than the *vibro only* condition, this difference was not found to be statistically significant. Hence, **H2** was not supported.

Even though there certainly was a trend, the differences between the *soft* condition and the three conditions that visually display a wooden texture were not found to be statistically significant. We thus found no support for hypotheses **H2** and **H3**.

The second possible explanation for participants' preference for the *repulsion* wall might be found in this design's performance.

Impermeability. Figure 10 shows participants' assessment of "this wall was able to prevent me from passing through". A repeated measures ANOVA found significant differences between conditions ($F(4,48) = 6.68$, $p = .000$). The main finding here is that *repulsion* was rated as more impermeable than *vibro only* ($t(12) = 4.18$, $p = .013$), which confirms our hypothesis **H4**.

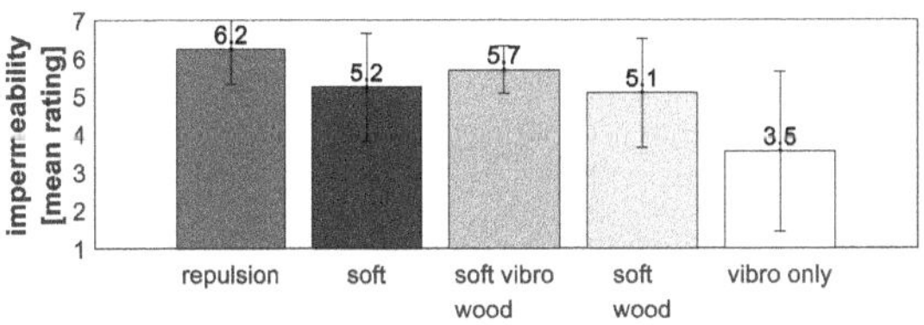

Figure 10: Participants rated any of the EMS conditions more impermeable than *vibro only*.

These responses are backed by our measurements on how deeply participants penetrated into each wall (Figure 11, measured using our optical tracking system *Optitrack 17w*).

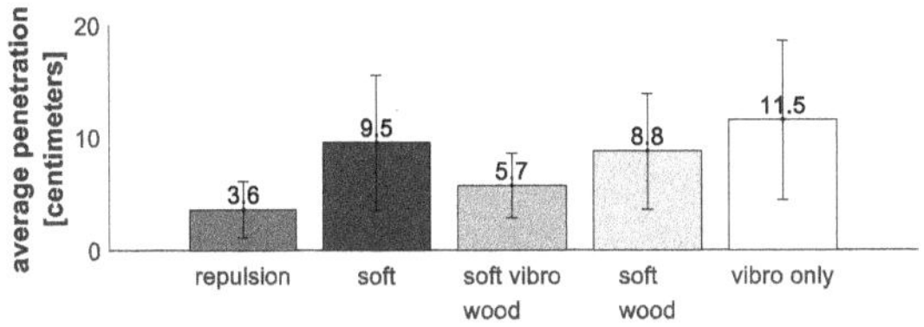

Figure 11: The *repulsion* wall stopped participants' hands on average 3.6 cm (error bars denote std. dev.).

A repeated measures ANOVA found a significant difference between conditions ($F(4, 48) = 7.72$, $p = .000$). The *repulsion* wall stopped participants' hands at only 3.6 cm on average, which is significantly earlier than *vibro only,* as a post-hoc t-test revealed ($t(12) = -3.54$, $p = .040$). This provides additional support for our hypothesis **H4**.

Participants penetrate the *soft* wall significantly deeper than the *repulsion* wall ($t(12) = 3.69$, $p = .031$). This, however, is expected, given that it had been designed to allow for 10 cm penetration.

Data of the average penetration in the virtual barriers was normal according to Shapiro-Wilk tests. The assumption of sphericity was not violated ($\chi2(9) = 14.42$, $p = .11$).

Participants commentaries and open-ended questions

All participants stated that the EMS was fitting the expectation of the "electro wall" visuals and noted its effectiveness in stopping them. P8 added "the pushing effect from these (virtual walls) felt like how a real wall pushes back". Another participant, P1, added, "EMS matched the springiness I expected of the wobbly wall". P5 remarked "it is funny because I feel (the wall's force) it but I know nothing is there".

One participant (P2) emphasized that the "EMS tingles and hence reveals the source of the force", yet, P7 stated "I did not realize how my hand was moving, I could not tell it was the EMS". Furthermore, three participants emphasized that the vibration did not match the expectations of the wooden walls.

Discussion

Our first study confirmed several key hypotheses. First, and maybe most important, it found that *any* of the EMS-based designs performs better than the most commonly chosen haptics option today: vibrotactile feedback.

The *repulsion* design did particularly well. It was rated the most *impermeable*, suggesting that it is suitable wherever virtual world designers have to stop users from passing through. This also recommends the *repulsion* design as a potential stand-in for rigid objects. The *repulsion* design also scored highest in terms of consistency between visuals and haptics. This matches our observation—the optical and acoustic effects behind this design work particularly well at covering up the EMS actuation, especially given that it is brief. Finally, and arguably most important, the majority of participants picked repulsion as their favorite design.

The *soft* design, while clearly not as strong as the repulsive design, demonstrated good "all-round" qualities. Reasonably realistic and reasonably impermeable it clearly outperformed vibrotactile. The combination with vibrotactile does not seem to lower performance, but does not add much either. It therefore seems reasonable to leave vibration out in the future and proceed with the *soft* actuation alone.

BENEFITS AND CONTRIBUTION

Our main contribution is the concept of providing haptics to walls and other heavy objects by means of electrical muscle stimulation. We achieve this in a wearable device, suitable for real-walking virtual reality environments.

Limitations include that users need to wear EMS equipment and that the design space works best for soft and repulsive objects, rather than truly rigid objects. Furthermore, we designed our haptic effects based on eight muscles from both shoulders and arms. These eight muscles alone were sufficient to create our plethora of haptic VR objects and obstacles. While adding more channels would possibly result in more complex haptic effects, it would also require attaching more electrodes and EMS hardware.

EXAMPLE WIDGETS

The *soft* design and the *repulsion* design together allow us to create the haptics for a reasonably wide gamut of virtual objects. In order to illustrate this, we have created a set of example objects and widgets. We combined these widgets into a simple virtual world, which forms the basis for our second user study (see below).

We use the *soft* design for the majority of objects. This design allows users to make physical contact with the object, as the user's hands partially penetrate into the object's interior. This helps maintain physical contact with an object, making it possible drag or carry objects around.

We use the *repulsion* design to complement the soft design and in particular, we use it to implement those walls, doors, and windows that are designed to prevent users from passing through, such as in a jail-like surrounding.

We continued to use electro visuals for the repulsion design. For the soft design we used a multi-layered translucent texture. In order to allow us to apply these designs to arbitrary objects, we implemented their visuals in the form of translucent textures.

We now demonstrate these widgets by giving a walkthrough of the simple virtual experience we designed for the second study. This VR experience consists of three rooms connected by three hallways. Inside this world, everything users can reach is complemented with a haptic effect based on one of the two designs, or based on an interpolation between the two.

Room 1: Repulsion.

We designed the first room so as to primarily illustrate the repulsion design.

Figure 12: The jail cell features "electrified" walls and a gate. Touching any of these repel the user's hand.

Repulsion walls: As illustrated by Figure 12, this room is designed as a jail cell with an "electrified" gate and walls. When touched, these repel the user's hand, which is accompanied by the sound and visuals discussed earlier.

Figure 13: Pushing this soft button opens the gate.

Button: Figure 13: A button allows users to raise the gate. The button is soft, allowing the user's hand to penetrate its surface. The system accompanies this with a sense of increasing counter pressure. The button then tracks with the user's hand and the counter force stays constant until the button is all the way "in", at which point the counter force increases substantially.

Projectiles: As users rush down the hallway, a security system shoots projectiles at them, which they fend up with their hands. The system renders the 12" projectiles using a strong repulsion effect.

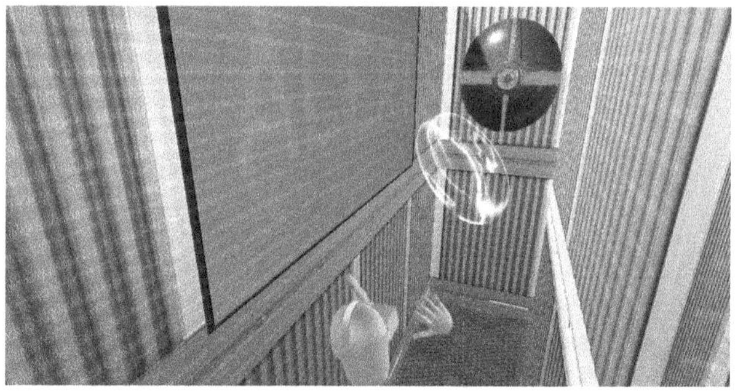

Figure 14: Projectiles based on the *repulsion* effect.

Room 2: Selected widgets

We use this room to illustrate some traditional GUI widgets rendered as interface elements in VR, in particular a slider and an analog rocker switch.

Slider mechanism: As shown in Figure 15, users operate a pair of traditional sliders in order to align the pipeline elements that establish a hydraulic link. The sliders' knobs are based on the soft design. The knobs protrude far enough to allow operation from multiple angles. If users operate the sliders while *facing* the wall, the system primarily actuates their shoulder muscles; if they turn *parallel* to the wall, the system interpolates from shoulder muscle to biceps.

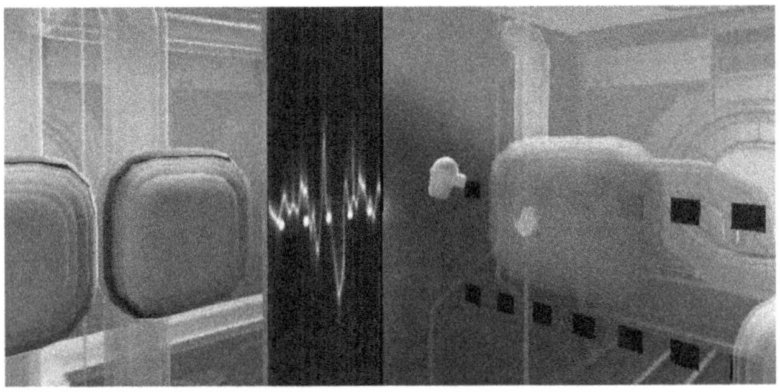

Figure 15: The user is dragging the knob of a slider mechanism. The two buttons on the left form a rocker.

Widgets that push back: Users can now operate the pump to re-establish pressure in the hydraulic system (Figure 15). The device consists of two buttons connected by a rocker mechanism, i.e., as users push one of the buttons in, the button comes out and pushes against their other hand, providing a simple animated haptic response.

Liquids: If users reach into the fish tank shown in Figure 16, their hand is pushed backwards by the water's viscosity. The system renders this by actuating the user's wrist.

Figure 16: Playing with the water in these fish tanks pushes the user's hand backwards.

Room 3: Lifting, punching, and throwing

We use this room to illustrate moveable objects.

Pushing, lifting, and dropping objects: As shown in Figure 17, there are two cubes. As users push the first one towards the adjacent button, they feel haptic feedback. Depending on the angle of attack, the haptic feedback actuates users' biceps, shoulder, or both.

Figure 17: Two cubes that users can push onto the button on the right, or pick up and carry around.

If users *pick up* a cube with both hands (Figure 18), they feel a resistance when their hands come together as to grasp the cube. This happens because their shoulder muscles are stimulated as to open their arms outwards.

Figure 18: The user has picked up a cube and is about to throw it over the glass barrier.

Furthermore, users also feel the weight of the cube in their triceps, as discussed in the introduction. In Figure 18, we see how users pick up the cube and throw it over a glass wall, down a chute, which activates a second button.

Punching objects: Figure 19 shows a third cube that rests on a slide, which leads up to the last of the three buttons. If users push this cube they feel a soft effect in response. However, the contraption requires users to *punch* the cube up the slide in one go. The harder they hit the membrane, the more the system shifts its haptic response from *soft* effect to *repulsion* effect.

Figure 19: Users have to drive this cube up the ramp by punching it. The system responds with a mix between a soft effect and a repulsion effect.

USER STUDY 2: THE EXPERIENCE

Given that our first study was very focused on comparing different wall designs, we now wanted to see what an actual virtual reality experience combined with our EMS prototype would be like. We thus conducted a second study. This time, we gathered only a minimum of Likert scale data, as we were mostly interested in participants' open-ended feedback.

Apparatus

Participants wore the same general type of EMS apparatus as in the first study. However, this time we actuated not only biceps and wrist, but also shoulders. We also considered both hands, for a total of 6 actuation points (compared to 2 in the first study). In exchange, we left out the vibrotactile actuator, which our first study had found to be of only limited usefulness.

Task and procedure

Participants were outfitted with our EMS device and then underwent the same type of interactive calibration procedure as in our first study. We then placed participants into Rooms 1 and 3 of the virtual world previously described.

There were two interface conditions. In the *EMS condition* the EMS equipment was *on*. In the *baseline* condition the EMS equipment was *off*. Participants thus went through the experience twice (in counterbalanced order). After each run, they filled in a questionnaire.

Participants

We recruited 6 new participants from our institution (1 female, 22.0 ±2.09 years old). Five participants had experienced VR headsets before and two had experienced EMS before.

Hypotheses

We hypothesized that our EMS prototype would lead to a better user experience than the control condition without.

Results

As illustrated by Figure 20, the *EMS* condition received substantially higher ratings. As a matter of fact, *all* participants rated *EMS* higher than *baseline*. This confirms our main hypothesis.

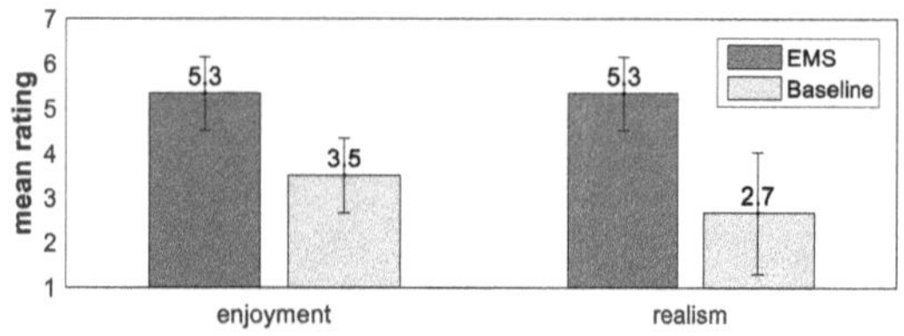

Figure 20: Participants rated their experience in the *EMS* condition higher than in baseline.

Participants also responded to "which object, widget, or effect in the virtual world did you like best and why?" (Figure 21). In the EMS condition, 3 participants preferred the walls ("electrified walls"), 2 participants preferred the cube and one the button. For the control condition, 4 participants preferred the cubes and 2 the button; in the control condition no participant preferred the walls.

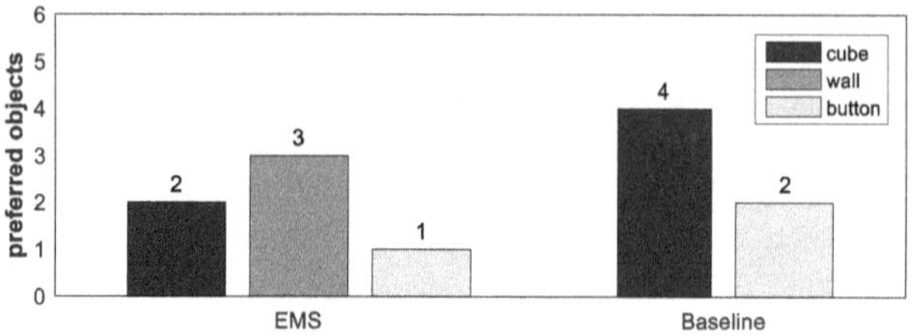

Figure 21: Participants preferred the experience in the *EMS* condition.

We invited participants to comment on their experience. P1 said, regarding the electro wall, "I can't go through this wall", when pointing out the soft walls P2 remarked, "it feels less real (than electro wall) because like this (softer EMS) I can go through". P1 concluded, "I much prefer the sensation *with* EMS—otherwise there is nothing there, just air".

P2 added that the electro walls "added more experience, like better gameplay" and remarked that the "the soft walls were not always necessary, maybe not all switches need it". P2 also added "the cannon (was great) too, but it felt more like a punishment from passing (in front of it)".

P3 stated, "I don't know how VR is supposed to feel but without the EMS it did not seem real at all". Then added, "Also… I could not really grab objects without the EMS, because nothing was there, my hands touched each other". When choosing the button as their favorite object for the baseline condition, P3 remarked, "nothing felt real (without EMS) but at least the button was the only one that was at least kind of realistic". P3 also added that "I immediately felt the difference between an electro wall and a soft wall".

P4 added "The electrified walls worked great—it really felt like touching one. Really surprising." P4 also added "I liked punching the cube at first (without EMS) because it is very (physically) involving, then when I tried it later (with EMS), I felt some impact force; it was great." Later P4 added "the cube is the hardest one to believe, because there are many ways to hold it and it and (the EMS) does not always work that well."

P5 commented with respect to the EMS condition "(The wall) worked great—this was the most realistic element I tried". When P5 experience the same wall without EMS, P5 stated, "oh my… these walls feel really boring". P5's expressed that EMS contributed to simulating walls, buttons, projectile hits, lifting and throwing cubes, but not to punching. P5 explained "I would also like to feel something in my hand, not just the muscles of the arm, it feels misplaced."

P6 stated, "(the) button works great and so do the walls. It feels just right, if I push it, it pushes back and the feeling is continuous". P6 commented about the baseline condition "only the cubes feel right to me because I can manipulate them, the walls and buttons feel wrong". P6 continued "EMS really helped me feel the walls, the button and the projectiles, those really felt strange without EMS, like energy that went nowhere". Lastly, P6 added "the stimulation while operating the cube worked well, but I would have preferred it to push downwards, like pretending to have weight."

Discussion

As expected, EMS added to participants' experience. In particular, participants' responses showed that the "repulsive" wall design using EMS did a good job simulating walls in VR. We also observed, how these walls really stopped participants and participants described them as realistic. In contrast, all participants seemed to agree that walls were *not* realistic in the no-EMS baseline condition. Furthermore, based one participant's feedback regarding the cube ("I would have preferred it to push downwards, like pretending to have weight") we added stimulation to the triceps muscles, hence rendering the cube's weight.

RELATED WORK

The work presented in this paper builds on haptics for virtual reality, in particular tactile stimulation, force feedback, physical props, and electrical muscle stimulation.

Tactile haptics

Vibration is a very common modality in VR because it allows for wearable form factors, such as gloves (e.g., the *CyberTouch* by Virtual Technologies [5]) and vests [21]. It allows conveying the texture of objects [8]. However, it does not allow delivering a *directional* force, which would be required to simulate the force that a virtual object applies to a user's hand.

Other tactile effects besides vibration include skin-stretch [6] and the force feedback illusion created by *Traxion* [30].

Pneumatic Gloves include air pockets that inflate when the user's fingertips touch a virtual object [2]. The *Teleact* glove, for example, featured 30 air pockets around the user's fingers and palm [31]. The technology is also used in surgical manipulators to emulate the experience of touching soft tissue [20]. Another example is *Wearable Jamming Mitten* [32], which locks the user's hand in a clenched position when the user grasps a virtual object. It achieves this by jamming, i.e., by removing all air causing substance inside to interlock (same principle as in [11]).

Passive Haptics in VR

Props. Kohli et al. [18] used props as stand-ins for virtual objects in VR (e.g., to simulate a virtual pedestal in the middle of the room).

Robot arms placing props. Neely proposed using robotic arms for placing props and generating tactile and force feedback for graphics applications [24]. Also, in the system by Yokokohji et al. [37], a robotic arm is used to render the force of pushing against virtual objects in a video-see through reality. Gruenbaum et al. also leverage an industrial robotic manipulator as stands-ins for a control panel of a virtual automobile [12].

Humans placing props. *TurkDeck* [7] employs human actuators to actuate handheld props, including physical walls.

Recently, researchers devised a visual retargeting method for reusing the same prop as a stand-in for different virtual objects [1]. However, this technique only works for similar virtual objects that are closely located.

Forces in VR

Tethers. An approach to providing directional forces is to pull tethers attached to the user (*SPIDAR* [25]). Variations have been used in VR CAVEs to simulate hitting a virtual baseball [16].

Exoskeletons. *Dextrous Hand Master* [14] uses an exoskeleton hand to provide force feedback to the fingers. Other variations of this principle include, for instance, *Dexmo* [13] an exoskeleton for fingers or *FlexTensor* [35], a minimal exoskeleton for the biceps.

SPIDAR-W [26] combines these ideas by mounting a SPIDAR device into a 1.5 x 1.5 x 1.5 m cage that is mounted to the user's body, allowing to scale beyond just fingers.

Also, researchers have combined force-feedback with tactile stimulation. Kron et al. combined a force feedback hand exoskeleton with an eccentric motor on each finger [19]. Similarly, the Data Glove by VPL [10] and Cyber Glove Force by Kramer et al. [17] provide these hybrid force+tactile sensations.

Force feedback using electrical muscle stimulation

EMS originated in the field of rehabilitation medicine where researchers applied electrical impulses to limbs [33]. In Human-Computer Interaction, Tamaki et al. guided users in learning a new instrument (in *possessed hand* [34]) and Pfeiffer et al. used EMS to steer users' while walking [29].

Also, EMS has been used to add force-feedback to mobile devices [22]. Farbiz et al. used EMS on the wrist muscles to render the sensation of a ball hitting a racket in an augmented reality tennis game [9]. Similarly, *Impacto* [23] simulates the sensation of hitting or being hit in VR boxing using a combination of tactile stimuli (a solenoid tapping the skin) and electrical muscle stimulation.

IMPLEMENTATION

To help readers replicate our design, we now provide the necessary technical details.

EMS hardware and calibration

We used the battery-powered, medically compliant 8-channel muscle stimulator (*Hasomed Rehastim*) depicted in Figure 22.

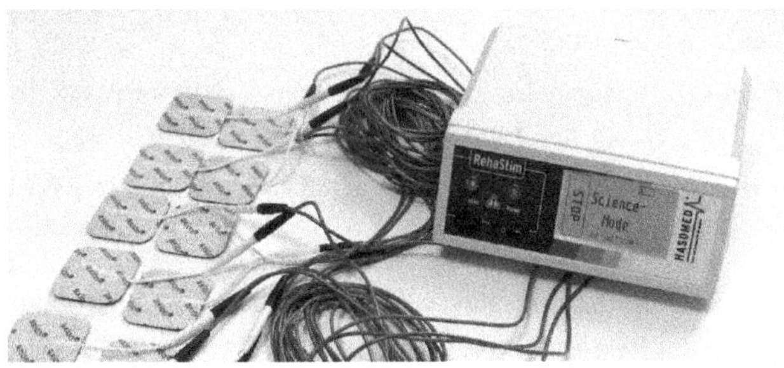

Figure 22: The muscle stimulator we used.

The stimulator is designed for EMS and outputs up to 100 mA per channel. The stimulation is triggered via serial commands using Hasomed's custom protocol, which we generate from inside Unity3D. For each EMS channel, we keep the intensity constant and instead modulate the pulse width (in μs), which we henceforth denote as PWM. This allows us to have greater control (sub-mA) than by varying the current.

Like any haptics system based on EMS, our system requires calibration prior to use. In order to determine what is comfortable for a particular user, we continuously increase the current until we observe a small movement of the targeted muscle. We then let the user calibrate the upper bound that is still comfortable and pain-free. We perform this procedure in the order palm/wrist extensor, biceps, triceps and shoulder rotator muscles.

Electrode placement

Figure 23 depicts the exact electrode placement we used in our prototypes to actuate the user's arm and hand. We placed electrodes on the following muscles: (a) palm and wrist extensors (covering both the *extensor digitorium* and *extensor carpis ulnaris*), (b) biceps, (c) triceps and (d) shoulder external rotators (covering both the *infraspinatus* and *teres major/minor*).

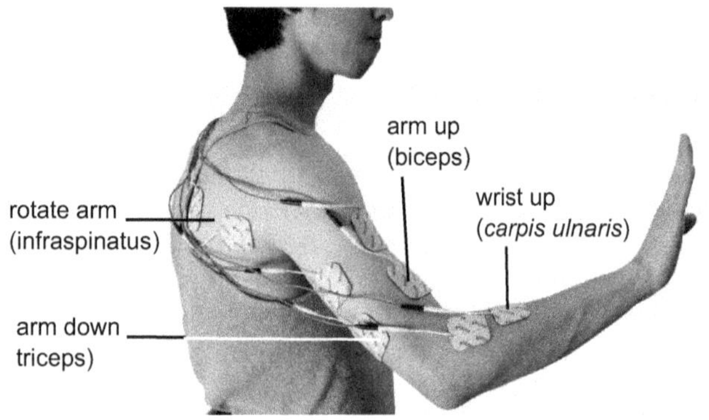

Figure 23: Electrode placement for arm and shoulder.

EMS parameters

Each individual haptic effect, such as the *repulsion* of a wall or the sensation of *picking up* a box has its own specific EMS settings. Values vary across users and should be customized using the calibration procedure described above. Still, here is this data at the example of one of our study participants:

Repulsion wall: palm extensor at 17 mA, 100 µs PWM for 300 ms, biceps at 15 mA and 200 µs PWM for 300 ms.

Soft wall: palm extensor starts at 15 mA and 75 µs PWM, biceps at 15 mA and 70 µs PWM. Here, the stimulation increases linearly as the user presses into the wall or button (function of the distance to the center of object, e.g., a button). The maximum values are 100 µs PWM for the palm extensor and 175 µs PWM for the biceps.

Picking up a box: shoulder muscles at 20 mA and 250 µs PWM and the triceps at 15 mA and 150 µs PWM.

Pushing a box backwards: palm extensor at 15 mA and 100 µs PWM, biceps at 15 mA and 150 µs PWM.

Pushing a box sideways: palm extensor at 15 mA and 200 µs PWM and biceps at 15 mA and 110 µs PWM.

All the aforementioned effects except *repulsion* use a simple linear mapping between the EMS intensity and normalized distance to the object [0=center, 1=surface]. Our intensity-distance mapping is defined as:

$$(\min(\text{intensity}_{\text{maximum}} * (1 - \text{distance}_{\text{normalized}}) * \text{growth}_{\text{factor}}) + \text{intensity}_{\text{offset}},\ \text{intensity}_{\text{maximum}})$$

When *pushing a box backwards* or *sideways*, the applied mapping is steep (hence, growth factor is 2) since the effect should be strong upon contact with the object. However, in the *Soft Wall* the intensity build up is softer, hence the growth factor is kept at 1. When *picking up a box* the growth factor used is also 1; note that on the triceps, the intensity offset is calibrated higher than for the other effects as to constantly simulate the cube's weight as soon as the user grasps it. Lastly, the *Repulsion* effect does not utilize such a mapping because it is only active for 300 ms.

VR engine

We implemented our virtual worlds in *Unity 3D*.

Tracking

We track the user's headset and hands using rigid body optical markers and cameras (8x *Optitrack's Prime 17W*) covering a tracking volume of 4.5 x 4.5 x 3m. When replicating our system, an HTC *Vive* would be equally suitable.

Our system determines collisions between the user's hands and virtual objects using collider objects in Unity. This triggers the respective muscle stimulation patterns by sending a message to a server application that communicates to the EMS device. This allows us to decouple the UI and the EMS hardware, allowing it to run on any device regarding of its serial capabilities.

CONCLUSIONS

In this paper, we presented a new approach to rendering the haptics of heavy and stationary objects, in particular by means of electrical muscle stimulation. This is our main contribution. We also achieve this in a wearable form factor, suitable for real-walking VR environments.

As future work, we plan to explore this approach in *augmented* reality. Since our approach leaves the user's fingertips free to touch physical objects and physical walls, our technology should be a good match for AR.

REFERENCES

1. Mahdi Azmandian, Mark Hancock, Hrvoje Benko, Eyal Ofek, and Andrew D. Wilson. Haptic Retargeting: Dynamic Repurposing of Passive Haptics for Enhanced Virtual Reality Experiences. In *Proceedings of the 2016 CHI Conference on Human Factors in Computing Systems* (CHI '16), 1968-1979. https://doi.org/10.1145/2858036.2858226
2. Mohamed Benali-Khoudja, Moustapha Hafez, Jean-Marc Alexandre, and A. Kheddar. Tactile interfaces: a state-of-the-art survey, In *Proceedings of International Symposium on Robotics* (ISR'04).
3. M. Bergamasco. The GLAD-IN-ART Project. In *Virtual Reality SE-19*, 251–258.

4. Brooks Jr., and P. Frederick. What's real about virtual reality? In IEEE *Computer Graphics and Applications* 19, 6, 16-27, 1999. https://doi.org/10.1109/38.799723
5. Grigore C. Burdea. Haptic Issues in Virtual Environments. In *Proceedings of Computer Graphics International* (GCI '00), 2000. https://doi.org/10.1109/CGI.2000.852345
6. Daniel K. Y. Chen, Iain A. Anderson, Cameron G. Walker and Thor F. Besier. Lower Extremity Lateral Skin Stretch Perception for Haptic Feedback. In *Haptics IEEE Transactions*, 9, 62-68, 2016. https://dx.doi.org/10.1109/TOH.2016.2516012
7. Lung-Pan Cheng, Thijs Roumen, Hannes Rantzsch, Sven Köhler, Patrick Schmidt, Robert Kovacs, Johannes Jasper, Jonas Kemper, and Patrick Baudisch. TurkDeck: Physical Virtual Reality Based on People. In *Proceedings of the 28th Annual ACM Symposium on User Interface Software & Technology* (UIST '15), 417-426. http://dx.doi.org/10.1145/2807442.2807463
8. Heather Culbertson, Juan Jose Lopez Delgado, Katherine J. Kuchenbecker. One hundred data-driven haptic texture models and open-source methods for rendering on 3d objects. In *Proc. IEEE Haptics Symposium,* 2014. https://doi.org/10.1109/HAPTICS.2014.6775475
9. Farzam Farbiz, Zhou Hao Yu, Corey Manders, and Waqas Ahmad. An electrical muscle stimulation haptic feedback for mixed reality tennis game. In *ACM SIGGRAPH 2007 posters* (SIGGRAPH '07), Article 140. https://doi.org/10.1145/1280720.1280873
10. James D. Foley. Interfaces for advanced computing. *Sci. Am.* 257, 4, 126-135, 1987. http://dx.doi.org/10.1038/scientificamerican1087-126
11. Sean Follmer, Daniel Leithinger, Alex Olwal, N. Cheng, and Hiroshii Ishii. Jamming user interfaces: programmable particle stiffness and sensing for malleable and shape-changing devices. In *Proceedings of the 25th annual ACM symposium on User interface software and technology* (UIST '12), 519–528. http://dx.doi.org/10.1145/2380116.2380181
12. P. Gruenbaum, W. McNeely, H. Sowizral, T. Overman, and B. Knutson. Implementation of dynamic robotic graphics for a virtual control panel. In *Proc. Presence'97,* 118–126. http://dx.doi.org/10.1162/pres.1997.6.1.118
13. Xiaochi Gu, Yifei Zhang, Weize Sun, Yuanzhe Bian, Dao Zhou, and Per Ola Kristensson. Dexmo: An Inexpensive and Lightweight Mechanical Exoskeleton for Motion Capture and Force Feedback in VR. In *Proceedings of the 2016 CHI Conference on Human Factors in Computing Systems* (CHI '16), 1991-1995. https://doi.org/10.1145/2858036.2858487
14. J. Hollerbach and S. Jacobsen. Haptic Interfaces for Teleoperation and Virtual Environments. In *Proc. Workshop on Simulation and Interaction in Virtual Environments'95,* 13–15. http://citeseerx.ist.psu.edu/viewdoc/summary?doi=10.1.1.52.978
15. B.E. Insko. Passive haptics significantly enhances virtual environments. *Dissertation at University of North Carolina at Chapel Hill,* 2001. ISBN:0-493-17286-6
16. S. Jeong, N. Hashimoto, and S. Makoto. A novel interaction system with force feedback between real - and virtual human: an entertainment system: "virtual catch ball". In *Proc. ACE'04,* 61–66. http://dx.doi.org/10.1145/1067343.1067350
17. J. Kramer. Force feedback and Texture Simulating Interface device, U.S. Patent 5, 184, 319.
18. Luv Kohli, Eric Burns, Dorian Miller, and Henry Fuchs. Combining passive haptics with redirected walking. In *Proceedings of the 2005 International Conference on Augmented Teleexistence* 57, 4, 253–254. http://dx.doi.org/10.1145/1152399.1152451
19. A. Kron, and G. Schmidt. Multi-fingered Tactile Feedback from Virtual and Remote Environments. In *Proc. HAPTICS'03,* 16–23. https://doi.org/10.1109/HAPTIC.2003.1191219
20. Anthony D. Kurtz. Tactile feel apparatus for use with robotic operations, U.S. Patent 650, 643, filed January 8, 2007, issued July 10, 2008.
21. W. Lindeman, Y. Yanagida, H. Noma, and K. Hosaka. Wearable vibrotactile systems for virtual contact and information display. In *Virtual Reality* 9, 2, 203–213, 2006. http://dx.doi.org/10.1007/s10055-005-0010-6
22. Pedro Lopes and Patrick Baudisch. Muscle-propelled force feedback: bringing force feedback to mobile devices. In *Proceedings of the SIGCHI Conference on Human Factors in Computing Systems* (CHI '13), 2577-2580. http://dx.doi.org/10.1145/2470654.2481355
23. Pedro Lopes, Alexandra Ion, and Patrick Baudisch. Impacto: Simulating Physical Impact by Combining Tactile Stimulation with Electrical Muscle Stimulation. In *Proceedings of the 28th Annual ACM Symposium on User Interface Software & Technology* (UIST '15), 11-19. http://dx.doi.org/10.1145/2807442.2807443
24. A. McNeely. Robotic graphics: a new approach to force feedback for virtual reality. In *Proceedings of the Annual IEEE International Symposium on Virtual Reality,* 336–341, 1999. https://doi.org/10.1109/VRAIS.1993.380761
25. Murayama, J., Bougrila, L., Luo, Y., Akahane, K., Hasegawa, S., Hirsbrunner, B., Sato, M. SPIDAR G&G: a two-handed haptic interface for bimanual VR interaction. In *Proc. EuroHaptics'04,* 138–146.
26. Kazuki Nagai, Soma Tanoue, Katsuhito Akahane, and Makoto Sato. Wearable 6-DoF wrist haptic device

"SPIDAR-W". In *SIGGRAPH Asia 2015 Haptic Media And Contents Design* (SA '15), Article 19. http://dx.doi.org/10.1145/2818384.2818403

27. G. Norman. Likert scales, levels of measurement, and the "laws" of statistics. In *Advances in Health Sciences Education* 15, 5, 625-632, 2010. https://dx.doi.org/10.1007/s10459-010-9222-y

28. K.E. Overvlieta, J.B.J. Smeetsa, and E. Brennera. The use of proprioception and tactile information in haptic search. In *Acta Psychologica* 129, 1, 83–90, 2008. https://dx.doi.org/10.1016/j.actpsy.2008.04.011

29. Max Pfeiffer, Tim Dünte, Stefan Schneegass, Florian Alt, and Michael Rohs. Cruise Control for Pedestrians: Controlling Walking Direction using Electrical Muscle Stimulation. In *Proceedings of the 33rd Annual ACM Conference on Human Factors in Computing Systems* (CHI '15), 2505-2514. http://dx.doi.org/10.1145/2702123.2702190

30. Jun Rekimoto. Traxion: a tactile interaction device with virtual force sensation. In *Proceedings of the 26th annual ACM symposium on User interface software and technology* (UIST '13), 427-432. http://dx.doi.org/10.1145/2501988.2502044

31. William R. Sherman and Alan B. Craig. Understanding Virtual Reality: Interface, Application, and Design. *ed. Morgan Kaufmann, Series in Computer Graphics.*

32. Timothy M. Simon, Ross T. Smith, and Bruce H. Thomas. Wearable jamming mitten for virtual environment haptics. In *Proceedings of the 2014 ACM International Symposium on Wearable Computers* (ISWC '14), 67-70. http://dx.doi.org/10.1145/2634317.2634342

33. P. Strojnik, A. Kralj, and I. Ursic. Programmed six-channel electrical stimulator for complex stimulation of leg muscles during walking. In *IEEE Trans. Biomed. Eng. 26*, 112. https://doi.org/10.1109/TBME.1979.326520

34. Emi Tamaki, Takashi Miyaki, and Jun Rekimoto. PossessedHand: techniques for controlling human hands using electrical muscles stimuli. In *Proceedings of the SIGCHI Conference on Human Factors in Computing Systems* (CHI '11), 543-552. http://dx.doi.org/10.1145/1978942.1979018

35. Dzmitry Tsetserukou, Katsunari Sato, and Susumu Tachi. ExoInterfaces: novel exosceleton haptic interfaces for virtual reality, augmented sport and rehabilitation. In *Proceedings of the 1st Augmented Human International Conference* (AH '10), article 1. http://dx.doi.org/10.1145/1785455.1785456

36. Martin Usoh, Kevin Arthur, Mary C. Whitton, Rui Bastos, Anthony Steed, Mel Slater, and Frederick P. Brooks, Jr. Walking > walking-in-place > flying, in virtual environments. In *Proceedings of the 26th annual conference on Computer graphics and interactive techniques* (SIGGRAPH '99), 359-364. http://dx.doi.org/10.1145/311535.311589

37. Y. Yokokohji, Y. Sugawara, J. Kinoshita, and Yoshikawa T. Mechano-Media that Transmit Kinesthetic Knowledge from a Human to Other Humans. In *Proc. Robotics Research'01,* 499–512. http://dx.doi.org/10.1007/3-540-36460-9_33

"It wasn't really about the Pokémon": Parents' Perspectives on a Location-Based Mobile Game

Kiley Sobel[1], Arpita Bhattacharya[1], Alexis Hiniker[1], Jin Ha Lee[2], Julie A. Kientz[1], Jason C. Yip[2]
[1]Human Centered Design & Engineering, [2]The Information School
DUB Group, University of Washington, Seattle, WA, USA
{ksobel, arpitab, alexisr, jinhalee, jkientz, jcyip}@uw.edu

ABSTRACT
Though prior work shows parents worry about screen media experiences displacing physical activity and time outdoors, this research does not account for location-based mobile games like *Pokémon GO*, which specifically facilitate outdoor activity. To fill this gap in the research, we surveyed and interviewed parents to understand (1) their values and perceptions of this type of gameplay and (2) how they co-play *Pokémon GO* with their children. Our findings provide empirical evidence that, in addition to appreciating the increased exercise and time outdoors, parents valued how play led to family bonding experiences. Furthermore, some traditional concerns about screen time persisted in this context, and new concerns about safety in real-world environments emerged. Parents mitigated these concerns with rules and gameplay choices, such as maintaining control of the mobile device, to ensure children were safe. This work contributes an empirical understanding of families as co-users of technology and offers a generative lens to study and design for joint media engagement among family members where gameplay differs from normative notions of screen time.

Author Keywords
Pokémon GO; location-based mobile games; augmented reality games; joint media engagement; parental mediation; families; children.

ACM Classification Keywords
H.5.m. Information interfaces and presentation (e.g., HCI): Miscellaneous.

INTRODUCTION
As technology becomes ubiquitous in our lives, with an increasing number of adults, teens, and children owning and using mobile devices [26,33,50,60], screen time has become a highly debated and elusive topic for families [56,66,71]. Overexposure to screens has been associated with hostility in children [65]; development of anxiety [77] and attention disorders [78]; risk of obesity, disordered sleep, and other health problems [15,59]; Internet addiction [9], and a myriad of other concerns. As such, the fear that children are displacing other "healthier," more "social," or more "educational" activities by engaging with screen-based media is seemingly omnipresent [67]. In response to these concerns and the fact that digital media is now everywhere, parents have had to take on new roles as mediators of their children's screen time [3,6,16,58].

Yet, with advances in digital technologies and new media comes the knowledge that not all screen time is created equal. Children passively and silently viewing television programming alone is "different" than them talking to grandparents over video chat, actively reading a digital book with a parent, or playing *Dance Dance Revolution* (a dancing game) with a sibling. One way to conceptualize this difference is through *joint media engagement* (JME). JME refers to the experiences of people using media together, which include viewing, playing, searching, reading, contributing, and creating with either digital or traditional media [68]. JME supports learning by providing context and resources for people to co-create meaningful connections among representations, interests, and experiences [68]. Because of how co-engagement leads to social interactions and learning, the American Academy of Pediatrics recommends that families participate with new media together [6,58].

JME is not a static concept though, as the options for how families can co-engage with new media are rapidly evolving. On July 6, 2016, Niantic, Inc. released *Pokémon GO*, a location-based mobile game in which players use their device's GPS capabilities to navigate their avatar in the virtual world by physically moving through real world locations that are meaningful in the game. Then, players can locate, capture, battle, and train virtual characters in the game world called Pokémon ('Pocket monsters') [43]. The game also enables optional augmented reality features that use a mobile device's camera, such that Pokémon appear on the screen as if they were physically co-located in the surrounding area.

As *Pokémon GO* became popular so quickly, with over 500 million downloads in two months [41], it seemed to attract parents and children alike to play together [29,30,49,51]. While other types of similar games exist both commercially

CHI 2017, May 06 - 11, 2017, Denver, CO, USA

ACM 978-1-4503-4655-9/17/05…$15.00
DOI: http://dx.doi.org/10.1145/3025453.3025761

(e.g., *Ingress*) and as research prototypes (e.g., [7,8,35,62]), *Pokémon GO* is the first popularized mainstream location-based mobile game that is available for families to play together. Moreover, unlike *Ingress*, which requires its players to be 13 years or older, *Pokémon GO* has explicit provisions for children under 13 to play with parental consent [44], which are in compliance with laws like the United States' Children's Online Privacy Protection Act [13]. Consequently, the emergence of *Pokémon GO* provided an ideal platform to study how parents are mediating and jointly engaging with their children with a location-based mobile game—a type of screen-based media that, in some ways, flips the normative paradigm of screen time by encouraging more physically grounded experiences that screen time is often perceived to displace. While its usage has declined since the game debuted, the main concern of this paper is not *Pokémon GO* itself per say. Rather, it is about families' experiences with and views of this kind of gameplay from the perspective of parents.

Specifically, in this work, we were interested in understanding parents' experiences, perspectives, and attitudes regarding their children playing location-based mobile games, in particular, *Pokémon GO*. We wanted to learn more about the choices parents and families make on how to play the game, any rules they set about their children's game use and why, how they might jointly engage in this type of gaming with their children, and other relevant experiences. To answer these questions, we administered a qualitative survey to 67 parents (the majority from the U.S.) and conducted interviews with 20 parents in Seattle, Washington, USA from late-July to mid-August 2016. We approached and interviewed all 20 interview participants in a public space where they were already playing or watching their children play *Pokémon GO*.

We found that, in addition to exercise and time outdoors, parents valued how play led to family bonding experiences. This play fit into their lives, coinciding with other important activities (i.e., family walks, dog walks) or as specifically planned *Pokémon GO* time. Additionally, while some traditional concerns about screen time persisted for parents, new concerns about safety in real-world environments emerged. Parents made rules and gameplay choices centered around these concerns that have not be previously reported in literature, which ensured their children were safe. For example, parents reported always accompanying their children while playing and staying in control of the mobile device during gameplay to make sure children were not harmed in the physical environment. These findings both support and bring new light to research on joint family participation and learning with new media.

With this work, we make two main contributions to the HCI community. The first is a new empirical understanding of families as technology users, their values, and perspectives. This understanding can help us reflect on how we may or may not be designing appropriately for this user group. Second, we contextualize families' experiences with *Pokémon GO* within the conditions and processes that Takeuchi and Stevens [68] identify as leading to productive JME. We validate how these conditions have been brought to life by the implementation of *Pokémon GO*, and therefore (as predicted) fostered JME for families. We also bring up new conditions that fostered JME in this distinctive context of playing *Pokémon GO*. Thus, through our discussion, we contribute a generative understanding that promotes studying and designing for JME among family members, where gameplay differs from normative notions of screen time.

RELATED WORK

There has been a significant, growing body of research in family technology and media use within the HCI community [24]. This work has examined the role of technology in family life and how technology supports family interaction and learning through co-use in different ways (e.g., [17,19, 20,22,23,27,28,36,39,70]). We build on this work to expand our notions of HCI in the family context. In the interest of space, in this section we primarily focus on theory and literature in parental mediation and forms of family co-use in relation to games specifically.

Parental Mediation of Children's Digital Media Use

Throughout their long-term collaborative ethnographic study of the everyday digital media practices of children and teens in the United States, Ito et al. [25] found that parents consistently worried about the amount of time their children spent using new media. They were concerned with how their children were spending time online, on their mobile phones, playing video games, using their iPods, and talking to their friends over instant messenger, on social networking sites, and their mobile devices. As shown in other studies (e.g., [16,21,57,76]), these types of concerns are common among parents. According to parental mediation theory, there are three main ways that parents counteract their concerns about screen time. They mediate their children's digital media use through *restrictive mediation, active mediation,* and *social co-viewing or co-use* [10,72].

Parents who make rules, control, and place limits on children's media use, mainly to counteract negative effects, are engaging in *restrictive mediation* [45,72]. Contrasting parents who allow their children to use devices freely without any limits (i.e., *digital enablers*), parents who engage in restrictive mediation to avoid negative side effects of technology use are a known as *digital limiters* [54,55]. In Ito et al.'s [25] study, parents placed restrictions on new media use, such as setting time limits and requiring children to finish schoolwork, chores, and "productive activities" before playing digital games or going on social networks. They also set up specific media areas in the house to be able to monitor their children's digital media use in a more public space [25]. These types of rule setting emerge in many other studies on parental restrictions of children's screen time as well (e.g., [21,34,47]).

As a protective measure, parents also enter dialogues with their children to explain and discuss aspects of new media and its usage, with purposes that are both instructive (e.g., to teach about content in child-friendly language) and evaluative (e.g., to express disapproval). This type of mediation is referred to as *active mediation* [10,72]. Active mediation occurs particularly in families with older children [61] or when parents have positive perceptions about Internet use for younger children [46].

The last type of mediation within parental mediation theory is *social co-viewing* or *co-use* [10,68,72], which has both educational and entertainment purposes [48]. Often, parents who mediate their children's screen time by engaging in it with them are scaffolding the experience [68]. Following Vygotsky [74], they guide or help in areas where their children need support, ultimately enhancing what is good about the experience and allowing their children to learn and grow. In these moments, parents teach, collaborate with, consult on non-technical issues, provide resources to, and even learn from their children [4], which all positively impact children's learning. A middle ground between *digital enablers* and *digital limiters*, parents who both *actively mediate* and *co-use* digital media with their children are known as *digital mentors* [54,55].

One survey of 4,000 families in the U.S. [12] found that 59% of parents of "gamer children" played computer and video games with them weekly. However, parents also imposed time limits on this usage more than on any other form of entertainment [12]. In another study of 3,000 U.S. parents [37], researchers found 92% of parents whose children play video games play with them; and 77% of those parents said it was to spend time together. Still, most parents preferred that children played on game consoles, not computers or mobile devices, because they are easier to monitor.

In the following two sections, we further discuss two forms of co-use (that allow for active, instructive mediation in situ), specifically focusing on gaming together: *hanging out* and *joint media engagement*.

Families 'Hanging Out' with Games

One way that co-use has been conceptualized is as a genre of participation with new media called 'hanging out' [25]. Ito et al. [25] define 'hanging out' as when people engage with new media in the process of spending time together. This is a social experience, and so the digital media itself is not necessarily the central focus. In Ito et al.'s [25] studies, families 'hung' out with new media and viewed this time as a way to facilitate both communication and bonding. This was even true for families who "idealized unplugging," yet still watched television and movies together. In some families, the main way that parents and children connected (especially fathers and sons) was through joint gaming. For others, gaming was still a consistent yet fluid way to spend time together as a family. Therefore, overall, gaming was a particularly important aspect for families 'hanging out' together. Ito et al. [25] note specifically, "'Hanging out' genres of gaming enable people to bridge different forms of gaming expertise and to cross generational and gender divides" (p. 207).

This finding about gaming as a bridge holds across various other studies as well. For instance, Lee et al. [32] found that their gamer interviewees often fondly remembered playing games with family members from as early as four to five years old; thus, gaming was an important part of their childhood. Similarly, in their qualitative study of console gaming, Voida and Greenberg [73] found that these types of games serve as a "computational meeting place," bringing together individuals in families to foster social interactions. Following this research, we wanted to understand if, how, and why this type of 'hanging out' might occur around *Pokémon GO*.

Joint Media Engagement (JME) & Gaming in Families

Another type of parental co-use, which encompasses 'hanging out,' is JME. As mentioned in the Introduction, JME refers to the experiences of people using media together. JME is considered important because of how this engagement supports learning [68]. Through JME, participants can make sense and meaning together in a particular situation and for future situations [63]. However, JME is not limited to solely "educational" media; rather, it concerns studying "all forms of media, especially those that dominate young people's time and experience" [68, p. 5]. Regarding gaming, Stevens et al. [64] claim that collaboration during and around video gameplay provides a positive learning environment; this is because "in-room" (i.e., literally in a room, around gameplay) interactions are social and empowering as players share knowledge and see it successfully used by others. Moreover, boundaries between "in-game," "in-room," and "in-world" (i.e., everyday life) interactions are blurred, facilitating the transfer of knowledge between them [64]. Particularly, "in-room" interactions have complex bidirectional continuities with players' everyday lives [64].

There are a small but growing number of HCI researchers who have studied JME, specifically joint gaming and digital play, within families that include children. While not exhaustive, we discuss some of these studies below. First, researchers have found that parents and children need explicit roles to productively engage with media together. In Brooks et al.'s [5] case study with *Electric Racer*, a computer game specifically designed for two-player intergenerational play, parents and children needed roles within the game clarified, so that parents knew the game's educational goals and how they were supposed to scaffold their children's learning. Second, technology design can also foster JME among siblings (i.e., family members that represent a different co-user group than friends and parents). Ballagas et al. [2] found that their mobile augmented reality and cooperative problem solving game (*Electric Agents*) facilitated physical coordination, physical support, and verbal instructions, clarifications, and communication between older-younger sibling pairs. Third, JME does not require even expertise between co-participants. In Aarsand's [1] ethnographic study, uneven expertise between children and parents about video games fostered joint gaming. When children have more expertise and adults are novices, it allows children to take the lead and disrupt the typical balance of power between children and adults. This can be motivating for sustained joint engagement. Fourth, JME can happen over distances and foster a sense of togetherness. Through a lab study, Follmer et al. [14] found that, for children under seven and their remote family members, playing over video creates a sense of "togetherness" by physically doing something together, as opposed to just talking; that physical objects in play scaffold physical interactions, which lead to discussions; and that story-based content leads to communication and helps scaffold parental guidance. Finally, exergames have been found to be productive for JME. Saksono et al. [53] designed and evaluated *Spaceship Launch*, a task-mastery exergame for parents and children. They found parents viewed in-game competition between players as motivating, which spurred social interactions. Their findings also highlighted the importance of designing systems to help children and parents increase both of their physical activity together.

Moving forward, Takeuchi and Stevens [68] note an important area for future research is studying "the qualities of media design and deliberate use that encourage productive JME" (p. 55). Since JME is not a static issue, it will need to be consistently reassessed as new technology changes and develops over time. Here, we examine the values, practices, interactions, and relationships that occur and develop around the deliberate use of a type of game not currently covered in the family JME literature (*Pokémon GO*) from the point of view of parents. By understanding these perspectives of and experiences with a game that have already pervaded families' lives, which we relate back to the game's design, we follow Takeuchi and Stevens' [68] call for research; ultimately, we help build knowledge about what design can do to foster productive JME.

METHODS

For this study, we targeted surveying and interviewing adult guardians who allowed their children to play location-based mobile games. Initially, our research team conducted non-participant observations of families playing *Pokémon GO* with children in public locations, such as parks, shopping centers, Pokémon events, and a university campus. Our team discussed insights from these observations, which informed our qualitative survey and interview questions. We both piloted and iterated on these protocols before deploying them. We recruited for the survey on online social media platforms such as Facebook, Craigslist, and community mailing lists, which enabled participation from a wider range of people. Even though we encouraged participation from families who played other location-based mobile games with children, every survey respondent reported on playing *Pokémon GO*. Respondents completed the survey in approximately 45 minutes. They were then entered into a US$50 Amazon gift card drawing, which four people received. In parallel, we also conducted 10-minute in-person semi-structured interviews with parents in a local public park, where many people played *Pokémon GO*. Interviewing parents in the context of family gameplay ensured that they could reflect on their gaming process in-situ. We conducted interviews in the afternoon and evening, over two days: 2 weeks (n = 6) and 6 weeks (n = 14) since the release of the game. Parents received small toys for their children for participating in the interview.

The interview and survey included similar open-ended questions to ensure triangulation. Question topics included: (1) perceived benefits of and concerns about the game, (2) their rules for their children playing the game, (3) how the above topics were similar to or different from other games their children played, and (4) descriptions of their most memorable and recent experiences playing the game. All interviews were audio recorded and transcribed. The study was approved by the University of Washington's Human Subjects Division.

Participants

A total of 87 adult guardians (of children under age 18) participated in this research; 67 were survey participants (*S1-S67*) and 20 (*P1-P20*) were interviewees. All but one was a parent (one interviewee was an aunt); thus, we refer to our participants as "parents." Parents' ages ranged from 25 to 65 years old (M = 42; SD = 7.2); 70% identified as female, 28% as male, and 2% as androgynous/other. Parents' children's ages ranged from 2 to 17 years old (M = 9.6; SD = 3.9); 62% of these children were reported as male and 38% as female. Most families lived in the United States, with only two survey participants reporting living elsewhere (i.e., Netherlands and Canada). Of the survey participants, 30% held a master's degree, 25% a bachelor's degree, 24% a doctorate, 7% a professional degree, and 3% an associate's degree; 4% had vocational training, and 4% completed some college but did not hold a degree. These survey participants' household incomes ranged from less than $20,000 to over $200,000 per year with 74% them earning over $100,000 per year.

Data Analysis

We took a joint inductive-deductive approach to the analysis of our qualitative data [11]. Two authors first independently open coded all the survey data, following an inductive approach. They then met to group and iterate on the codes according to consistent themes. Next, the same two coders read through half of the interview transcripts each, and coded them following a similar process. However, for coding interviews, authors looked for similarities across themes in the survey and interview data (a deductive approach) while iterating on and adding new codes as they emerged. Finally, the coders wrote memos, from which they abstracted higher-level themes.

FINDINGS

In this section, we describe the main themes that emerged from our analysis, regarding parents' experiences, values, and perspectives about their children playing *Pokémon GO* and playing *Pokémon GO* together with their children.

Characterization of Family Play

The majority of our participants indicated that they played *Pokémon GO* with their children, as opposed to their children playing independently from them. Seventeen (85%) of our interview participants were at our interview site specifically to play the game together with their children. For our survey participants, 59 (88%) reported that they play *Pokémon GO* together, either with other family members, friends, or just them two. For the other eight participants (12%) who did not play with their children, five participant's children (age 10-17) played with their siblings and/or friends without an adult; and two participants' children (age 8 and 17) played with their other parent. Additionally, 37 survey participants (55%) specified that they play *Pokémon GO* by themselves or with other adults, without any children present.

The families in our study reported that joint *Pokémon GO* gameplay happened both spontaneously, such as on the way to other activities or errands, and as a planned activity. Regarding spontaneous play, parents reported that their children often played when the parents were driving, when they noticed there were Pokémon nearby, or in other situations to "kill time." Some examples reported by parents included seeing Pokémon nearby after having dinner at a restaurant, while waiting for another child to be dismissed from camp, or when having to walk from the car that was parked a half-mile from where they were going.

Yet, other parents talked about how playing *Pokémon GO* became a specific activity that the family planned to do together. In some cases, especially for our interview participants, families decided to go to certain locations because they had heard from their friends, co-workers, or the Internet about these locations being great spots to find Pokémon. At these spots, there were often many other people playing. Specifically, interviewees perceived the experience of seeing crowds (sometimes hundreds) of people out enjoying a similar activity as exciting. However, most survey participants also reported playing *Pokémon GO* in and around the neighborhood and at nearby parks with fewer crowds, which they specifically described as "safe." Furthermore, *Pokémon GO* led to entire extended family and friends playing together. For example, P15 (a 31-year-old mother) brought a group of ten family members (three adults, five children, and two infants) to the interview site to play the game, which is a new and extremely social form of media co-participation.

Parents also appreciated how the game became a motivation for both their children and them to go outside and exercise in ways that were convenient and fit into their lives. Here, we see a shift in screen time usage; families are purposely scheduling time together outside their homes to engage in the game. For instance, S26, a 43-year-old mother who played with her 7-year-old son, said, "*There are times I cannot get out and walk the dogs as my husband works nights and my son just doesn't want to walk. But now I can incite [my son] with the game and he wants to go!!!*" Another mother, S7, a 31-year-old with a three-year-old daughter and another one-year-old, mentioned that her family is walking more because of the game. She noted, "*We go out for nightly long walks as a family... We stop when we see Pokémon and they help to catch them. They get really excited to go out for walks so I love taking them.*" For some participants, this led to walking thousands of more steps a day. A 41-year-old father (P13) said his 11-year-old daughter "*probably lost twelve pounds since she's been playing [the game].*" A popular term participants used for such walks was "Poké-walks," which became dedicated family experiences that parents predictably appreciated for how they were motivation for exercising and going outside.

Turn-Taking & Gameplay Roles

Parents consistently reported on their gameplay practices that involved taking turns and having particular roles during gameplay. In most instances, the family shared one phone to play the game. Some families took turns in specific time intervals; some planned based on gameplay, such as each member catching a specific number of Pokémon, and some let children take turns on one device in ways that were age appropriate and/or matched the child's abilities and interests. For S34, a 35-year-old mother who played with her 2-year-old daughter, this meant that they took turns on the phone because her daughter is learning to share. S34 holds and stays in control of the phone, but "*tell[s] her [daughter] what she needs to do and let[s] her do things that are age appropriate, ie [sic], she can spin, but she's not evolving or transferring Pokémon.*" Other parents set time limits on turns. A 42-year-old mother, S55, and her 6-year-old son each got about five minutes with the phone, passing it back and forth. S6, a 46-year-old mother who plays with her 7-year-old son, said that they set a timer for five minutes each to ensure equal turn-taking. In addition to being a mechanism for imposing rules, some parents were also constrained to a single device due to low memory or compatibility issues, or not wanting to spend money on additional data plans and devices. An interesting work-around to this was tethering a data-enabled device's hotspot with a child's Wi-Fi-only device (which had the added benefit of also keeping them close by).

Nevertheless, other parents reported that each person in the family had their own individual device when playing in the same space. Although parents and children were on separate devices, they were still playing together because of how they ran to catch Pokémon at the same time, took over

Gyms together (a competitive aspect of gameplay, where players battle for ownership of a particular public location), or generally talked about the game. In some cases, having multiple phones still led to sharing the devices. For example, S18, a 50-year-old mother of two sons (the main player being the 12-year-old son), described how she, her sons, and two of their friends played the game in the car while her husband drove them to the pool. She recounted, "*We had 3 phones to play on so we took turns giving each other time to play... We just passed the phones around.*"

Parents also spoke about the ways in which they took on separate roles during gameplay, which often integrated into how they took (or did not take) turns. These roles included parents taking safety roles, such as holding the phone while walking or navigating and suggesting routes. Often, roles were also divided based on skill level or difficulty of the gameplay. A 37-year-old mother (S35) said her 7-year-old daughter played mostly, "*but sometimes she gave [her] the phone for [catching] harder Pokémon.*" Comparably, a 37-year-old mother who plays with her 7-year-old son on her device (S33) described how they decided where to go together but took turns catching Pokémon; she usually caught those, and "*if he didn't capture [one] in 3 tries, he'd give up control to [his mom].*"

Family Bonding

Another theme that emerged from our data was parents feeling that *Pokémon GO* time with their children led to family bonding. Playing together or watching their children play the game was perceived as quality time between parents and children. Parents reported that it even led to them spending more time together and talking more than usual (both about and/or not about the game). For instance, P4, a 45-year-old father who plays *Pokémon GO* with his 42-year-old wife, 15-year-old daughter, and 9-year-old son, stated, "*I think it reinforces that we have common interests and helps us to have a good dialogue as we're sharing this experience.*" Father P13 said that due to the game, he and his daughter "*honestly talk a lot more.*" Parents recounted how they talk about the game itself, beyond playing the game. Additionally, parents spoke about how they enjoyed playing separately from their children and then showing their children what they had accomplished. P16, a 38-year-old mother of two boys (age 7 and 4) whose older son plays *Pokémon GO*, said she sometimes plays for her son and moves him up to the next level; then her son says, "*Yay mom! You're the coolest mom ever*!" Similarly, S35 recounted, "*I love that this is a game we can play together as a family, and I often play a little during the day (alone) so we can talk about my progress at night. My daughter's enthusiasm is turning me into a gamer!*" Being able to play together has encouraged her to play separately so they can talk about it together more.

P14, a 31-year-old father who plays with his 7-year-old daughter, discussed how they talk about the game, feel a sense of camaraderie, and have been brought closer by the experience. He recounted a time when they ran together to find a Pokémon: "*Yeah, we were both running together, and she was looking at me, and she was smiling. It was just a great experience. It turned out it was a Cubone [a type of Pokémon]. I think that was her first Cubone, so that was cool. But it wasn't really about the Pokémon.*" This example shows how, in relation to family bonding, the experience does not necessarily have to do with the game itself but with what the game facilitates and fosters for family interactions and relationships.

As some parents played the game on their own without their children (55% of survey participants) or had played older versions of Pokémon when they were growing up, playing the game together offered a chance for parents to show their expertise to their children and share a similar "growing-up" experience. P12, a 25-year-old father who plays with his 3-year-old son and 5-year-old daughter, indicated he was the most interested in the game out of everyone in the family. When asked about what he learned from playing the game, he said, "*That you can share a game [among all ages]...I grew up on this game. For them to also grow up on it, it's like there's that bond, and I learned that my kids can love something as much as I can. We can both be kids together.*"

Yet, in many instances, there was a shift in expertise: children were the experts in the game and parents were open to learning. Children taught their parents about it and/or parents made efforts to learn about the game, reportedly facilitating bonding. P2, a mother of a 10-year-old boy, relayed how her son has taught her "*a lot about the game,*" which was different from when she "*didn't care*" about engaging with or learning from her son while he was playing *Pokémon* on his Nintendo DS. Along the same lines, P10, a mother who just began playing with her 10-year-old son, said, "*I'm just amazed at how much I learned about this game so I could understand what he's talking about.*" In both examples, parents were making efforts to learn about a game in which their children were interested to facilitate playing and talking about the game together.

Some parents also explicitly mentioned that they thought this type of bonding would not have occurred without the game. S25, a 43-year-old parent who goes out every night with their 16-year-old daughter to play *Pokémon GO* as "*basically her chauffeur and bodyguard,*" said that the game allows them to spend quality time together, and "*as an older teen that's not always something that happens.*" P11, a 27-year-old mother, indicated that the game gave she and her 7-year-old son "*common ground to interact*". A 41-year-old mother (P9) who plays with her 8-year-old son, explained: "*I think it's just helping us find a common thing we can do together as a mom and a boy, and that's really awesome for me. I'm excited about that. I like that he wants to share with me and talk to me about it. As a boy coming home from school, they don't tell you what they ate, or they don't tell you what their teacher said, but now he's telling me this stuff so it's a good way to be communicating. I think hopefully it will keep transcending into him wanting to communicate about more things."* Playing the game together has caused them to talk more, especially (as she points out) as a mother and son. Similarly, fathers expressed the same sentiment about their daughters. Both fathers P13 and P14 noted they were talking more with their daughters since playing *Pokémon GO*.

Concerns & Workarounds

Safety

Unsurprisingly, almost all of our participants had safety concerns for their children in regard to gameplay. These concerns centered around their children being potentially harmed by strangers or getting physically hurt, such as getting hit by a car, due to not paying attention to where they were going. Pointedly, S45, a 39-year-old mother of a 12-year-old son, commented, "*I don't want my kids to be the dumb dumbs who fall off a cliff or [get] run over by a car because they [are] too engaged.*" As the most extreme response about strangers, P19, a father in his 50's with a 10-year-old son, said he and his wife were worried about the crowds and "crazy people." He said, *"Terrorists can also kill people here. Somebody with a gun comes, can easily do a lot of damage... We don't feel safe right now."*

Therefore, many of the rules parents had for gameplay directly related to these concerns. All the parents, not including the few that had older children (i.e., mid- to late-teens), required that they or another adult be with their children while playing. Many explicitly reported that their children were not allowed to speak or play with strangers. For older children who were allowed to play on their own, parents requested that their children always be available by phone and only travel a certain distance from their home. Some also had rules that their older children were not allowed to play at night, unless they were with an adult.

The ways that parents and younger children played together were associated with these concerns as well. First, many of the children only played on their parent's personal device, ensuring that the child could not play without their parent. Most pertinently, parents consistently reported on how they were in control of the phone while walking; parents would either hold the phone or it would stay in their pocket until it vibrated (indicating that a Pokémon was nearby), and then they would hand the phone to their child. Some families took turns looking at the phone, so that one person was always looking at the street while they played. These practices ensured that children (and parents) would not be physically endangered by not looking at their surroundings.

Screen Time

Other concerns of parents related to the concept of screen time. Participants referred to "screen time" broadly and spoke to the idea of balance, using rhetoric like "addiction" and "obsession." For instance, regarding the former, P1 (a 38-year-old mother whose nine-year-old daughter plays) said her main concern about the game was "*just the screen*" because "*it's still screen time.*" She noted, "*I don't know how to... stop it. It's a constant.*" Similarly, P16 said that the game is just adding to "*kids just always wanting to have screen time.*" Similar to other research (e.g., [20]), some parents also noted how it was difficult to get back their mobile devices from their children when they were playing *Pokémon GO*, which sometimes led to conflicts. To counteract these concerns, a few parents had rules (which extended to other forms of screen time) about gameplay. These included setting time limits, shutting down the mobile device if children did not give it back, and parents staying in control of the phone. Many also required that their children had to attend to their other responsibilities and commitments before playing the game. These included chores, homework, reading, drawing, driver's education training, sports, and other similar activities. Some parents also mentioned that they would begin to implement or intensify rules once the academic school year begun.

However, some of these same parents and others also indicated that this type of screen time with the game was "different" than other types of screen time, which changed their rules and perceptions of gameplay. Participants reported this was due to perceived net benefits of getting exercise, spending time outdoors, learning about the neighborhood, spending time with family and friends, and socializing offline. For example, S35 said they break their general solo screen time limit for *Pokémon GO* because it is a family activity. A 36-year-old stepmother of a 9-year-old boy (S66) mentioned, "*[E]ven if it's screen time, it's better than when he's playing Minecraft*" because they are walking around and spending time together. Likewise, a father of a 5-year-old boy and 4-year-old girl whose son mainly plays (P8) was "*less stringent on*" screen time limits because of how the activity was outdoors and physically active. He said, "*I like that. It's less screen time. They're not just buried in [the screen] the whole time.*" Other participants continually identified *Pokémon GO* gameplay as distinct from other forms of screen time, like sitting and playing video and computer games.

Many participants also reported about how playing allowed them and their children to learn more about the neighborhood and surrounding areas. This included learning about how to navigate streets and about specific structures, landmarks, locations, and art in the neighborhood that they did not know about before. A 39-year-old mother of a 12-year-old son (S45) noted, *"There was a giant anchor memorial hidden behind trees that we would never have seen if it weren't for it also being a [PokéStop, an important location in the game]."* Similarly, S9, a 51-year-old mother of a 17-year-old son, said, *"What I like about [the game] is that it points out some of the little things (signs or artwork) that I might normally miss. Like at [a nearby lake] - the benches that are PokéStops are marked with memorials. Most people overlook those – it's kind of cool to stop and read them."*

Finally, parents noted how the game enabled their children to be social with other people outside of the family, including connecting with new friends and even strangers. While most parents had rules that their children were not allowed to play with or talk to strangers, some noted how the game allowed them to see how friendly other players, who they do not know, are. For example, S25 (age 43) said she and her 16-year-old daughter learned how *"in general other [Pokémon GO] players are quite nice and friendly."* P2 explained they were playing one night and her 10-year-old son worked with other players who they did not know on an externally collaborative aspect of the game: *"They were a team. It was really nice, you know, to open up those channels of communication."*

Connecting with new friends outside of the family was particularly important for several participants. This was true for P8's son who was homeschooled and for whom the game enabled him to play and talk with other children; for P13's daughter who has autism spectrum disorder and for whom the game gave her "*something in common to talk to the kids [at camp] about*"; and for S26's son who has attention deficit hyperactivity disorder, sensory issues, and high-functioning autism and for whom the "*game gives him the opportunity to fit in with kids and talk about it.*" Thus, because of how playing was a family, social, outdoor, and/or exercise activity, parents changed their rules and had fewer concerns about screen time.

DISCUSSION

Our findings give us insight into the perspectives, values, and experiences of parents as they relate to screen time, JME, and 'hanging out' while playing *Pokémon GO*. For our parent participants, some traditional concerns about screen time held, namely regarding digital media addiction and obsession. Still, most parents did not seem to be concerned about the displacement of social, physical, and outdoor activities (i.e., normally common concerns for parents regarding screen time) because of how *Pokémon GO* augments and motivates these types of experiences. Additionally, the game sparked learning about the neighborhood because of how it caused them to go to locations that they would not have noticed otherwise. For this reason, parents valued this gameplay as different from normative notions of screen time.

However, new concerns also emerged for parents that focused on safety, namely about their children getting harmed by strangers or getting physically hurt, like walking into the street and getting hit by a car, because of how this type of game can lead players to not pay attention to their surroundings as they travel through space. While not paying attention due to focusing on a screen is a common concern for mobile devices [38], it is more of a focus here because of how the game might encourage players to pay attention to the digital map as they walk.

These types of concerns led to parental mediation practices that are particular to location-based mobile gaming. Livingstone and Helsper [34] refer to differences between mediating personal computer use compared to game console use; our results complement their notion of how changing technology is making restrictions and casual monitoring more difficult [68]. Specifically, parents safeguarded their children by engaging in restrictive mediation (e.g., setting rules for how far older children were allowed to travel), active mediation (e.g., having discussions about where to travel to next), and co-use (e.g., playing together such that a parent takes on the role of always keeping the phone in his or her pocket). This contrasts parents' past preferences for wanting their children to play on consoles [37] and in shared media spaces in the home [25]. Thus, these mediation practices extended beyond typical rule setting, discussions, and co-engagement for screen time because of how normally considered "in-room" activities completely overlap with "in-world" activities. Because it is a location-based mobile game, mediation was mainly about physicality (e.g., physical space, the body, in-person strangers, etc.).

The ways in which families took turns, shared, and/or had specific roles during gameplay supports research in JME as a form of parental mediation that facilitates learning as well. Parents and children playing the game together while taking turns and sharing (and even using timers to scaffold this experience) has the potential to help children learn these skills *in situ*. The fact that parents completed more difficult or less developmentally appropriate aspects of the game for their children, by either stepping in when necessary or taking on specific gameplay roles, is a form of scaffolding for their children to learn how to play the game too. Also, the fact that parents reported that they and their children discovered new things about their neighborhoods and nearby locations while traversing these areas supports research that location-based mobile games are valuable for learning in new ways [31,69].

Furthermore, one child or one parent having expertise or tremendous interest in the game served as motivation to play together and as a form of bonding for families. This occurrence is specific to *Pokémon GO* because of how the franchise has existed since 1995, and the children of 1995 have grown up to become parents themselves. This notion of disparate child/parent knowledge and interest as incentivizing play parallels findings that one-sided expertise in a game is motivation to keep playing together [1].

Finally, our results follow research about joint participation and gameplay as a form of 'hanging out' around new media that leads to family bonding [25]. Contrasting "in-room" activities, *Pokémon GO* fit into families' lives outside of the home and incentivized more "in-world" experiences, which made it a new valuable way to be together. Thus, playing *Pokémon GO* was (both immediate and extended) family time for our participants. Parents appreciated how they learned, talked, and spent time together playing the game. This was particularly important to some of our participants who were parents of older teens, mothers of sons, and fathers of daughters. Our work provides incentive to further study why location-based mobile games might be effective avenues through and around which these different groups can bond. Perhaps this type of bonding and communication among the family can extend long-term to other contexts or continually in this gaming context.

Design Features that Encourage JME and 'Hanging Out'

Using our findings, we can reflect on the conditions and processes surrounding *Pokémon GO* (as a location-based mobile game) that make it productive for family JME and 'hanging out.' First, we use our findings and *Pokémon GO* design features to briefly show how the game facilitates the six conditions [68] that lead to productive JME:

1. ***Mutual engagement*** (i.e., multiple people should be motivated equally to participate; both find it challenging and/or appealing): Families were both able to participate in modes that parents deemed appropriate, whether that be taking turns, parents scaffolding harder elements, or parents mainly watching their children play.
2. ***Dialogic inquiry*** (i.e., should inspire collaboration to make meaning of situations): Parents and children bonded and talked about the game together, even beyond the gameplay setting.
3. ***Co-creation*** (i.e., through co-use, people can create shared understandings, which "provide grounds for communication and learning" [68, p. 43][52,75]): Parents and children learned about the game or taught each other about it. They also learned about their neighborhood and surrounding areas.
4. ***Boundary crossing*** (i.e., it spans times and settings, stimulated by past experiences, and inspiring future activities): The fact that the game motivates parents and children for similar or different reasons (e.g., intergenerational interest in game content, walking, or spending time together) crosses boundaries. Many parents even played this game on their own without their children, facilitating boundary crossing as well.
5. ***Intention to develop*** (i.e., one person should intend to grow through participation, like leveling up): The game involves finding and catching many and rare Pokémon and leveling up. For example, P16 moved her son up to the next level in the game, which excited him and brought them closer. P14 and his daughter had a bonding experience as they ran to catch a new Pokémon.
6. ***Focus on content, not control*** (i.e., technical and user interface features do not distract or take away from partners' interactions or their interactions with the content): The game has simple gameplay mechanics that involve only a few different activities. Thus, parents and children could share in this gameplay in ways that made sense for their family. Additionally, the game does not require players to constantly look at the screen. Rather, parents could put the phone in their pocket as they walked until it was necessary for gameplay.

Additionally, based on this research, we claim that there are other specific qualities about *Pokémon GO* that make it particularly encouraging for productive family JME and 'hanging out.' The first is that, as a location-based mobile game, it hinges on players going outside, walking, and working in teams. Therefore, the game **reconciles some of the issues parents have with screen time** and **fits into the lives of families**, including in their schedules, within various contexts, and during valued activities, while also not tying them to the living room. Because of this, parents may be more likely to accept or promote gameplay or jointly participate with their children.

Next, this type of gameplay depends highly on a **dynamic outdoor context.** For our participants, this led to new forms of learning (i.e., about the neighborhood) that further blurs lines between "in-room" and "in-game" knowledge transfer [31,69]. Providing opportunities for families to learn in new ways is appealing and may lead to more productive JME.

Pokémon GO also facilitated **families and children connecting and being social with other people outside of the family**, sometimes in very large numbers**.** Because the game requires going outside and moving, there is some incentive to interact with people that are not co-engaging in the one instance of gameplay. This added value of diverse, extremely social learning does not occur during games that are bound to a specific place (besides perhaps in collaborative remote games). However, as shown in our findings, this value also comes into conflict with parental concerns about strangers. This tension highlights the importance of parental mediation of children's screen time in this context for families to gain added benefits while mitigating potential dangers.

Finally, while, based on findings of Brooks et al. [5], Takeuchi and Stevens [68] list "differentiation of roles" as a JME design principle (due to how this can ensure all participants are challenged and/or entertained) and also claim, "less structure may fail to elicit dialogic inquiry" (p. 46), no parents reported *Pokémon GO* as being frustrating or causing conflict due to a lack of in-game mechanisms for sharing. Rather, *Pokémon GO* was not designed explicitly for co-use on a single device, but it is still effectively being used as such. Perhaps because **gameplay can be shared differently depending on how parents want to participate**, it is motivation for JME. Some parents wanted to consistently play the game with (and without) their children; others wanted to watch their children play and be their cheerleaders; and some wanted to help when their assistance was necessary. The fact that the roles were *not* prescriptive allowed different types of families to participate together.

Designing Location-Based Mobile Games for Families

Finally, we want to reflect on what our findings may mean for researchers and other practitioners who want to design location-based mobile games for families. What might these designs be disrupting? What might they be enhancing?

In terms of disruptions, we first point to the concerns that parents had about these types of games. It is important to be aware that these types of games, particularly those that are augmented reality games, still cause some worry for parents about the dangers that come along with traveling while looking at a phone. Yet, new hardware like the *Pokémon GO* Plus [42], the Apple Watch [18], Google Glass, or HoloLens, which help players to keep watch of where they are going and still pay attention to the game, could improve safety while navigating. There also may be privacy concerns, which *Pokémon GO* did not elicit, but could be relevant for other location-based mobile games. Depending on the game mechanics, reflecting on issues of tracking and data sharing are especially relevant in this design context. Lastly, it is possible for these types of games to be inaccessible to those who cannot travel outside or in certain areas, and exclusionary to families who live in rural areas and/or who cannot afford large data plans.

In terms of enhancements, it seems that, to parents, the true unique value of location-based mobile games over other games was being outside and physically active and that this could be done *all together*. Some parents even specifically mentioned that they want to see more of these kinds of games produced. There are more opportunities to explore what the integration of other types of content could enhance in terms of family participation and learning as well. Similar yet non-digital versions of these types of games, like geocaching and scavenger hunts, and the research on their effects [40] could help designers understand what new types of features could be integrated to enhance location-based mobile gameplay for families. Overall, it seems that supporting families in jointly participating in new media use together socially, outside, and while exercising poses an exciting new research and design direction that appears to outweigh normative new media concerns.

Limitations & Future Work

In this study, we did not discuss the perspectives or values of parents who do not allow their children to play *Pokémon GO*. Without these perspectives, we cannot make claims about how to potentially engage families in joint gaming who are not doing so already. Future work entails unpacking these parents' values and opinions. We also did not survey or interview children about what they value in this context. It is *extremely* important for future work to consider these co-players' opinions and personal experiences, as their perspectives and values affect how we understand and design location-based mobile games for families.

Furthermore, as our data is highly skewed toward mother participants and sons, future research needs to work toward collecting greater responses from fathers and parents with daughters; then, we can examine if and, if so, how findings may shift according to gender. Along these same lines, our participants also have higher than average income and education levels, which may affect our results' transferability. Future work needs to examine how socio-economic status and other relevant demographic factors influence parents regarding location-based mobile gaming with their children.

Additionally, we only studied this phenomenon in the summer, immediately after *Pokémon GO* was released. The looser screen time rules that some of our participants had for their children correspond to prior work that routines (like structuring time in order to play games) change seasonally, with summers and breaks being less structured [25]. It will be interesting to see how families' rules and the characteristics of gameplay change during the school year, and as the excitement (a type of novelty bias) for *Pokémon GO* wanes. Likewise, studying how and why the usage may have declined for families is important for future research, as it can potentially validate if our findings hold over time and may lead to understandings of what can increase the longevity and benefits of these technologies for families.

Finally, future ethnographic observations of families playing location-based mobile games will triangulate this research, and support (or invalidate) parents' reports of their gameplay practices. New insights could also be gained by seeing how families potentially use the *Pokémon GO* Plus and the Apple Watch to increase safety while playing.

CONCLUSION

For this research, we surveyed and interviewed 87 parents who allow their children (under age 18) to play *Pokémon GO,* a new widely available and popular location-based mobile game. By unpacking parents' values and perceptions of this type of gameplay, we better understand families as co-technology users in a context where common perceptions of screen time appear to be flipped. While parents still had some typical concerns about screen time, the fact that the game motivates outdoor, social, and bonding activities helped mitigate these worries. Parents could alleviate new concerns about safety by accompanying and playing with their children. Because this type of gameplay fit into the lives of families, connected "in-room" and "in-world" experiences, lessened typical screen time worries, allowed for sharing and mixed control, and supported family bonding, this location-based mobile game created a productive platform for JME. Perhaps it was *Pokémon* itself that initially on-boarded families to play, but the valuable experiences of and interactions within families existed and continued to exist beyond the actual content of the game. Without these other important elements, we argue the game's popularity for families would not have been sustained. Through our discussion of these notions and fitting our research into past work in JME [68], we provide a greater generative understanding of what types of contexts and processes support JME. We hope this work will inspire new study and design for families' joint participation with new media where gameplay differs from normative notions of screen time.

ACKNOWLEDGMENTS

Thank you to all our participants and our helpful reviewers!

REFERENCES

1. Pål André Aarsand. 2007. Computer and Video Games in Family Life: The digital divide as a resource in intergenerational interactions. *Childhood* 14, 2 (May 2007), 235-256. DOI: http://dx.doi.org/10.1177/0907568207078330
2. Rafael Ballagas, Thérèse E. Dugan, Glenda Revelle, Koichi Mori, Maria Sandberg, Janet Go, Emily Reardon, and Mirjana Spasojevic. 2013. Electric agents: fostering sibling joint media engagement through interactive television and augmented reality. In *Proceedings of the 2013 conference on Computer supported cooperative work* (CSCW '13). ACM, New York, NY, USA, 225-236. DOI: http://dx.doi.org/10.1145/2441776.2441803
3. Shari Barkin, Edward Ip, Irma Richardson, Sara Klinepeter, Stacia Finch, and Marina Krcmar. 2006. Parental media mediation styles for children aged 2 to 11 years. *Archives of Pediatrics & Adolescent Medicine* 160, 4 (April 2006), 395-401. DOI: http://dx.doi.org/10.1001/archpedi.160.4.395
4. Brigid Barron, Caitlin Kennedy Martin, Lori Takeuchi, and Rachel Fithian. 2009. Parents as learning partners in the development of technological fluency. *International Journal of Learning and Media* 1, 2 (May 2009), 55-77. DOI: http://dx.doi.org/10.1162/ijlm.2009.0021
5. Mindy Brooks, Ashley Fenwick-Naditch, and Erica Branch-Ridley. 2011. Electric Racer: An intergenerational gaming experience designed to promote literacy. In *The New Coviewing: Designing for Learning through Joint Media*, 30-33.
6. Ari Brown, Donald L. Shifrin, and David L. Hill. 2015. Beyond 'turn it off': How to advise families on media use. *AAP News* 36, 10 (October 2015).
7. Adrian David Cheok, Kok Hwee Goh, Wei Liu, Farzam Farbiz, Siew Wan Fong, Sze Lee Teo, Yu Li, and Xubo Yang. 2004. Human Pacman: A mobile, wide-area entertainment system based on physical, social, and ubiquitous computing. *Personal and Ubiquitous Computing* 8, 2 (May 2004), 71-81. DOI: http://dx.doi.org/10.1007/s00779-004-0267-x
8. Luca Chittaro and Riccardo Sioni. 2012. Turning the classic snake mobile game into a location–based exergame that encourages walking. In *International Conference on Persuasive Technology*, Springer Berlin Heidelberg, 43-54. DOI: http://dx.doi.org/10.1007/978-3-642-31037-9_4
9. Dimitri A. Christakis. 2010. Internet addiction: A 21st century epidemic? *BMC Medicine* 8, 1 (2010). DOI: http://dx.doi.org/10.1186/1741-7015-8-61
10. Lynn Schofield Clark. 2011. Parental mediation theory for the digital age. *Communication Theory* 21, 4 (October 2011): 323-343. DOI: http://dx.doi.org/10.1111/j.1468-2885.2011.01391.x
11. Juliet Corbin and Anselm Strauss. 2015. *Basics of Qualitative Research* (4th ed.) SAGE Publications, Inc.
12. Entertainment Software Association. 2015. *Essential Facts about the Computer and Video Game Industry*. Retrieved September 15, 2016 from http://www.theesa.com/wp-content/uploads/2015/04/ESA-Essential-Facts-2015.pdf.
13. Federal Trade Commission. Children's Online Privacy Protection Rule ("COPPA"). Retrieved on September 16, 2016 from https://www.ftc.gov/enforcement/rules/rulemaking-regulatory-reform-proceedings/childrens-online-privacy-protection-rule.
14. Sean Follmer, Hayes Raffle, Janet Go, Rafael Ballagas, and Hiroshi Ishii. 2010. Video play: playful interactions in video conferencing for long-distance families with young children. In *Proceedings of the 9th International Conference on Interaction Design and Children* (IDC '10). ACM, New York, NY, USA, 49-58. DOI: http://dx.doi.org/10.1145/1810543.1810550
15. Michelle M. Garrison, Kimberly Liekweg, and Dimitri A. Christakis. 2011. Media use and child sleep: The impact of content, timing, and environment. *Pediatrics* 128, 1 (June 2011), 29–35. DOI: http://dx.doi.org/10.1542/peds.2010-3304
16. Douglas A. Gentile, Amy I. Nathanson, Eric E. Rasmussen, Rachel A. Reimer, and David A. Walsh. 2012. Do you see what I see? Parent and child reports of parental monitoring of media. *Family Relations* 61, 3 (June 2012): 470-487. DOI: http://dx.doi.org/10.1111/j.1741-3729.2012.00709.x
17. Janet Go, Rafael Ballagas, and Mirjana Spasojevic. 2012. Brothers and sisters at play: exploring game play with siblings. In *Proceedings of the ACM 2012 conference on Computer Supported Cooperative Work* (CSCW '12). ACM, New York, NY, USA, 739-748. DOI: http://dx.doi.org/10.1145/2145204.2145316
18. Mark Hachman. 2016. Pokémon Go is coming to Apple Watch to get you outside and on the go. *Macworld*. Retrieved September 15, 2016 from http://www.macworld.com/article/3117338/ios-apps/pokmon-go-is-coming-to-apple-watch-to-get-you-outside-and-on-the-go.html.
19. Megan K. Halpern, Max Evjen, Dan Cosley, Michael Lin, Stephen Tseou, Erica Horowitz, Tejaswi Peesapati, and Geri Gay. 2011. SunDial: embodied informal science education using GPS. *MedieKultur: Journal of Media and Communication Research* 27, 50 (June 2011), 48-65. DOI: http://dx.doi.org/10.7146/mediekultur.v27i50.3341
20. Alexis Hiniker, Kiley Sobel, Hyewon Suh, Yi-Chen Sung, Charlotte P. Lee, and Julie A. Kientz. 2015. Texting while Parenting: How Adults Use Mobile Phones

while Caring for Children at the Playground. In *Proceedings of the 33rd Annual ACM Conference on Human Factors in Computing Systems* (CHI '15). ACM, New York, NY, USA, 727-736. DOI: http://dx.doi.org/10.1145/2702123.2702199

21. Alexis Hiniker, Hyewon Suh, Sabina Cao, and Julie A. Kientz. 2016. Screen Time Tantrums: How Families Manage Screen Media Experiences for Toddlers and Preschoolers. In *Proceedings of the 2016 CHI Conference on Human Factors in Computing Systems* (CHI '16). ACM, New York, NY, USA, 648-660. DOI: http://dx.doi.org/10.1145/2858036.2858278
22. Tom Hope, Yoshiyuki Nakamura, Toru Takahashi, Atsushi Nobayashi, Shota Fukuoka, Masahiro Hamasaki, and Takuichi Nishimura. 2009. Familial collaborations in a museum. In *Proceedings of the SIGCHI Conference on Human Factors in Computing Systems* (CHI '09). ACM, New York, NY, USA, 1963-1972. DOI: http://dx.doi.org/10.1145/1518701.1519000
23. Hilary Hutchinson, Wendy Mackay, Bo Westerlund, Benjamin B. Bederson, Allison Druin, Catherine Plaisant, Michel Beaudouin-Lafon, Stéphane Conversy, Helen Evans, Heiko Hansen, Nicolas Roussel, and Björn Eiderbäck. 2003. Technology probes: inspiring design for and with families. In *Proceedings of the SIGCHI Conference on Human Factors in Computing Systems (CHI '03)*. ACM, New York, NY, USA, 17-24. DOI: http://dx.doi.org/10.1145/642611.642616
24. Sara Isola and Jerry Alan Fails. 2012. Family and design in the IDC and CHI communities. In *Proceedings of the 11th International Conference on Interaction Design and Children* (IDC '12). ACM, New York, NY, USA, 40-49. DOI: http://dx.doi.org/10.1145/2307096.2307102
25. Mizuko Ito, Sonja Baumer, Matteo Bittanti, danah boyd, Rachel Cody, Becky Herr, Heather A. Horst, Patricia G. Lange, Dilan Mahendran, Katynka Martinez, C.J. Pascoe, Dan Perkel, Laura Robinson, Christo Sims, and Lisa Tripp. 2010. *Hanging Out, Messing Around, and Geeking Out.* MIT Press.
26. Hilda K. Kabali, Matilde M. Irigoyen, Rosemary Nunez-Davis, Jennifer G. Budacki, Sweta H. Mohanty, Kristin P. Leister, Robert L. Bonner Jr. 2015. Exposure and use of mobile media devices by young children. *Pediatrics* 136, 6 (November 2015), 1044-1050. DOI: http://dx.doi.org/10.1542/peds.2015-2151
27. Jofish Kaye, Matti Nelimarkka, Riitta Kauppinen, Sini Vartiainen, and Pekka Isosomppi. 2011. Mobile family interaction: how to use mobile technology to bring trust, safety and wellbeing into families. *In Proceedings of the 13th International Conference on Human Computer Interaction with Mobile Devices and Services* (MobileHCI '11). ACM, New York, NY, USA, 721-724. DOI: http://dx.doi.org/10.1145/2037373.2037497
28. Konstantinos Kazakos, Elizabeth Bales, Carman Neustaedter, Svetlana Yarosh, Joseph 'Jofish' Kaye, and David Kirk. 2013. Exploring the diversity of families: designing technologies for the contemporary family life. In *CHI '13 Extended Abstracts on Human Factors in Computing Systems* (CHI EA '13). ACM, New York, NY, USA, 3255-3258. DOI: http://dx.doi.org/10.1145/2468356.2479660
29. John Keilman. 2016. ‘Pokemon Go’ can bring families together. *The Chicago Tribune*. Retrieved on August 20, 2016 from http://www.chicagotribune.com/news/columnists/ct-pokemon-go-keilman-column-hf-0720-20160714-column.html.
30. Brian Koerber. 2016. ‘Pokémon GO’ is actually bringing families together. *Mashable*. Retrieved on August 20, 2016 from http://mashable.com/2016/07/11/pokemon-go-family-bonding-dad/#sDU4uQJMIZqz.
31. Kevin M. Leander, Nathan C. Phillips, and Katherine Headrick Taylor. 2010. The changing social spaces of learning: Mapping new mobilities. *Review of research in Education* 34, 1 (March 2010), 329-394. DOI: http://dx.doi.org/10.3102/0091732x09358129
32. Jin Ha Lee, Rachel Ivy Clarke, and Yea-Seul Kim. 2015. Video game information needs and game organization: differences by sex and age. *Information Research* 20, 3 (September 2015), 1-24.
33. Amanda Lenhart. 2015. A Majority of American Teens Report Access to a Computer, Game Console, Smartphone and a Tablet. *Pew Research Center*. Retrieved September 6, 2016 from http://www.pewinternet.org/2015/04/09/a-majority-of-american-teens-report-access-to-a-computer-game-console-smartphone-and-a-tablet/.
34. Sonia Livingstone and Ellen J. Helsper. 2008. Parental mediation of children's internet use. *Journal of Broadcasting & Electronic Media* 52, 4 (November 2008): 581-599. DOI: http://dx.doi.org/10.1080/08838150802437396
35. Kate Lund, Paul Coulton, and Andrew Wilson. 2011. Free All Monsters!: a context-aware location based game. In *Proceedings of the 13th International Conference on Human Computer Interaction with Mobile Devices and Services* (MobileHCI '11). ACM, New York, NY, USA, 675-678. DOI: http://dx.doi.org/10.1145/2037373.2037482
36. Leilah Lyons, David Becker, and Jessica Roberts. 2010. Analyzing the affordances of mobile technologies for informal science learning. *Museums & Social Issues* 5, 1 (April 2010), 87-102. DOI: http://dx.doi.org/10.1179/msi.2010.5.1.87

37. Frank N. Magid Associates, Inc. 2015. *Family Gaming Study*. Retrieved September 15, 2016 from http://v.magid.com/video/mmf/Magid_Family_Gaming_Study_October_2015.pdf.
38. Joe Marshall and Paul Tennent. 2013. Mobile interaction does not exist. In *CHI '13 Extended Abstracts on Human Factors in Computing Systems* (CHI EA '13). ACM, New York, NY, USA, 2069-2078. DOI: http://dx.doi.org/10.1145/2468356.2468725
39. Carman Neustaedter, Tejinder K. Judge, Steve Harrison, Abigail Sellen, Xiang Cao, David Kirk, and Joseph Kaye. 2010. Connecting families: new technologies, family communication, and the impact on domestic space. In *Proceedings of the 16th ACM international conference on Supporting group work* (GROUP '10). ACM, New York, NY, USA, 363-366. DOI: http://dx.doi.org/10.1145/1880071.1880152
40. Carman Neustaedter, Anthony Tang, and Tejinder K. Judge. 2013. Creating scalable location-based games: lessons from Geocaching. *Personal and Ubiquitous Computing* 17, 2 (February 2013), 335-349. DOI: http://dx.doi.org/10.1007/s00779-011-0497-7
41. Niantic, Inc. 2016. Heads up! Retrieved September 18, 2016 from http://pokemongo.nianticlabs.com/en/post/headsup/.
42. Niantic, Inc. 2016. Pokémon GO Plus. Retrieved September 18, 2016 from http://www.pokemongo.com/en-us/pokemon-go-plus/.
43. Niantic, Inc. 2016. Pokémon GO Support. Retrieved September 15, 2016 from https://support.pokemongo.nianticlabs.com/hc/en-us.
44. Niantic, Inc. 2016. Pokémon GO Safety FAQs. Retrieved September 15, 2016 from https://support.pokemongo.nianticlabs.com/hc/en-us/articles/226389207-Safety-FAQs.
45. Peter Nikken and Jeroen Jansz. 2006. Parental mediation of children's videogame playing: A comparison of the reports by parents and children. *Learning, media and technology* 31, 2 (June 2006): 181-202. DOI: http://dx.doi.org/10.1080/17439880600756803
46. Peter Nikken and Jeroen Jansz. 2013. Developing scales to measure parental mediation of young children's internet use. *Learning, Media and Technology* 39, 2 (March 2013), 250-266. DOI: http://dx.doi.org/10.1080/17439884.2013.782038
47. Peter Nikken, Jeroen Jansz, and Sanneke Schouwstra. 2007. Parents' interest in videogame ratings and content descriptors in relation to game mediation. *European Journal of Communication* 22, 3 (September 2007), 315-336. DOI: http://dx.doi.org/10.1177/0267323107079684
48. Peter Nikken and Marjon Schols. 2015. How and why parents guide the media use of young children. *Journal of child and family studies* 24, 11 (February 2015), 3423-3435. DOI: http://dx.doi.org/10.1007/s10826-015-0144-4
49. Mary Emily O'Hara. 2016. Meet the Pokémoms: Obsession with playing Pokémon Go has brought families closer together. Retrieved August 20, 2016 from http://www.salon.com/2016/08/14/meet-the-pokemoms-ob_partner/.
50. Pew Research Center. Device Ownership Over Time. Retrieved September 6, 2016 from http://www.pewinternet.org/data-trend/mobile/device-ownership/.
51. Andy Robertson. 2016. The best way to enjoy Pokémon Go? Keep it in the family. *The Telegraph*. Retrieved August 20, 2016 from http://www.telegraph.co.uk/gaming/what-to-play/the-best-way-to-enjoy-pokemon-go-keep-it-in-the-family/.
52. Barbara Rogoff. 1990. *Apprenticeship in thinking: Cognitive development in social context*. Oxford University Press.
53. Herman Saksono, Ashwini Ranade, Geeta Kamarthi, Carmen Castaneda-Sceppa, Jessica A. Hoffman, Cathy Wirth, and Andrea G. Parker. 2015. Spaceship Launch: Designing a collaborative exergame for families. In *Proceedings of the 18th ACM Conference on Computer Supported Cooperative Work & Social Computing* (CSCW '15). ACM, New York, NY, USA, 1776-1787. DOI: http://dx.doi.org/10.1145/2675133.2675159
54. Alexandra Samuel. 2015. Parents: Reject Technology Shame. *The Atlantic*. Retrieved September 15, 2016 from http://www.theatlantic.com/technology/archive/2015/11/why-parents-shouldnt-feel-technology-shame/414163/.
55. Alexandra Samuel. 2015. What kind of digital parent are you? *@AlexandraSamuel*. Retrieved on September 15, 2016 from http://alexandrasamuel.com/parenting/what-kind-of-digital-parent-are-you.
56. Jeremy Sarachan. 2011. Limiting Screen Time Is Not the Key to Parenting in the Digital Age. *International Journal of Learning and Media* 3, 4 (September 2011), 1-5. DOI: http://dx.doi.org/10.1162/ijlm_a_00082
57. Kelly L. Schmitt. 2000. *Public policy, family rules and children's media use in the home*. Annenberg Public Policy Center of the University of Pennsylvania.
58. Donald Shifrin, Ari Brown, David Hill, Laura Jana, and Susan K. Flinn. 2015. Growing up digital: Media research symposium. *American Academy of Pediatrics* (October 2015), 1-7.
59. Aric Sigman. 2012. Time for a view on screen time. *Archives of disease in childhood* 97, 11 (October

2012), 935-942. DOI: http://doi.org/10.1136/archdischild-2012-302196

60. Aaron Smith. 2015. U.S. Smartphone Use in 2015. *Pew Research Center*. Retrieved September 6, 2016 from http://www.pewinternet.org/2015/04/01/us-smartphone-use-in-2015/.
61. Nathalie Sonck, Peter Nikken, and Jos de Haan. 2013. Determinants of internet mediation: A comparison of the reports by Dutch parents and children. *Journal of Children and Media* 7, 1 (February 2013), 96-113. DOI: http://dx.doi.org/10.1080/17482798.2012.739806
62. Kevin G. Stanley, Ian Livingston, Alan Bandurka, Robert Kapiszka, and Regan L. Mandryk. 2010. PiNiZoRo: a GPS-based exercise game for families. In *Proceedings of the International Academic Conference on the Future of Game Design and Technology* (Futureplay '10). ACM, New York, NY, USA, 243-246. DOI: http://dx.doi.org/10.1145/1920778.1920817
63. Reed Stevens and William R. Penuel. 2010. Studying and fostering learning through joint media engagement. In *Principal Investigators Meeting of the National Science Foundation's Science of Learning Centers*, 1-75.
64. Reed Stevens, T. Satwicz, and L. McCarthy, L. 2008. In-game, in-room, in-world: Reconnecting video game play to the rest of kids' lives. *The ecology of games: Connecting youth, games, and learning,* 41-66. MIT Press.
65. Victor C Strasburger. 2010. Media education. *Pediatrics* 126, 5 (September 2010), 1012-1017. DOI: http://doi.org/10.1542/peds.2010-1636
66. Victor C. Strasburger, Barbara J. Wilson, and Amy B. Jordan. 2009. *Children, adolescents, and the media.* Sage.
67. Lori Takeuchi. 2011. *Families Matter: Designing Media for a Digital Age.* The Joan Ganz Cooney Center at Sesame Workshop, New York.
68. Lori Takeuchi and Reed Stevens. 2011. *The New Coviewing: Designing for Learning through Joint Media Engagement.* The Joan Ganz Cooney Center at Sesame Workshop, New York.
69. Katie Headrick Taylor and Rogers Hall. 2013. Counter-mapping the neighborhood on bicycles: Mobilizing youth to reimagine the city. *Technology, Knowledge and Learning* 18, 1-2 (April 2013), 65-93. DOI: http://dx.doi.org/10.1007/s10758-013-9201-5
70. Michael Tscholl and Robb Lindgren. 2016. Designing for learning conversations: How parents support children's science Learning within an immersive simulation. *Science Education* 100, 5 (April 2016), 877-902. DOI: http://dx.doi.org/10.1002/sce.21228
71. Sherry Turkle. 2011. *Life on the Screen.* Simon and Schuster.
72. Patti M. Valkenburg, Marina Krcmar, Allerd L. Peeters, and Nies M. Marseille. 1999. Developing a scale to assess three styles of television mediation: "Instructive mediation," "restrictive mediation," and "social coviewing." *Journal of Broadcasting & Electronic Media* 43, 1 (January 1999): 52-66. DOI: http://dx.doi.org/10.1080/08838159909364474
73. Amy Voida and Saul Greenberg. 2009. Wii all play: the console game as a computational meeting place. In *Proceedings of the SIGCHI Conference on Human Factors in Computing Systems* (CHI '09). ACM, New York, NY, USA, 1559-1568. DOI: http://dx.doi.org/10.1145/1518701.1518940
74. Lev S. Vygotsky. 1980. *Mind in society: The development of higher psychological processes.* Harvard University Press.
75. Lev S. Vygotsky. 1987. Thinking and speech. In L. S. Vygotsky, R. W. Rieber (Series Eds.), and A. S. Carton (Vol. Ed.), *The collected works of L. S. Vygotsky. Vol. 1: Problems in general psychology* (N. Minick, Trans.). New York: Plenum.
76. Ellen A. Wartella and Nancy Jennings. 2000. Children and computers: New technology. Old concerns. *The future of children* 10, 2 (2000), 31-43. DOI: http://dx.doi.org/10.2307/1602688
77. Barbara J. Wilson. 2008. Media and children's aggression, fear, and altruism. *Future of Children* 18, 1 (2008), 87–118. DOI: http://dx.doi.org/10.1353/foc.0.0005
78. Frederick J. Zimmerman and Dimitri A. Christakis. 2007. Associations between content types of early media exposure and subsequent attentional problems. *Pediatrics* 120, 5 (November 2007), 986–992. DOI: http://dx.doi.org/10.1542/peds.2006-3322

Placing and Recalling Virtual Items on the Skin

Joanna Bergstrom-Lehtovirta, Sebastian Boring, Kasper Hornbæk
University of Copenhagen, Denmark
{joanna, sebastian.boring, kash}@di.ku.dk

ABSTRACT
The human skin provides an ample, always-on surface for input to smart watches, mobile phones, and remote displays. Using touch on bare skin to issue commands, however, requires users to recall the location of items without direct visual feedback. We present an in-depth study in which participants placed 30 items on the hand and forearm and attempted to recall their locations. We found that participants used a variety of landmarks, personal associations, and semantic groupings in placing the items on the skin. Although participants most frequently used anatomical landmarks (e.g., fingers, joints, and nails), recall rates were higher for items placed on personal landmarks, including scars and tattoos. We further found that personal associations between items improved recall, and that participants often grouped important items in similar areas, such as family members on the nails. We conclude by discussing the implications of our findings for design of skin-based interfaces.

Author Keywords
Skin input; recall performance; interface design

ACM Classification Keywords
H.5.m. Information Interfaces and Presentation (e.g. HCI): Miscellaneous

INTRODUCTION
Touching the skin can be used as input for smart glasses [17], televisions or other remote displays [2, 12], mobile phones [11], and auditory interfaces [6, 14]. These interfaces do not display touch targets directly on the skin – users need to learn and recall where targets are located. We refer to such targets as *virtual items*.

Landmarks on the skin (such as joints, bumps, wrinkles, tattoos, and veins) can improve input performance with virtual items [2, 6, 8, 11, 14, 17]. For instance, users can tap more accurately on the fingertips of the index finger and thumb [5] and on the elbow and wrist [11] than on areas between those. However, previous work has examined only a small number of landmarks on local parts of the body (e.g., the palm in [2, 13], the forearm in [3, 11], and the fingertips in [5]). Therefore, it is unclear which kinds of landmarks across the hand and forearm can be used for placing virtual items, and what the recall performance of item locations on the skin is.

The skin and landmarks on it are highly personal. Scars, birthmarks, and tattoos can be associated with individuals' personal lives and memories (Figure 1). Research in HCI and memory has shown that users create personal semantics when placing items on physical locations, suggesting that these associations have positive effects on recall [15]. Studies on user-designed layouts on the skin, however, have used familiar interfaces and abstract items, such as numbers [11], keyboards [17], or directional keys [2]. These may limit creation of personal associations and encourage consistency with familiar layouts. Thus, personal strategies for placing items on the skin – including the use of landmarks and establishing associations between items and locations – have remained unexplored, as have their effects on recall.

We collected in-depth data in a study where participants placed 30 virtual items on their hand and forearm, and attempted to learn and recall the locations of those items. We interviewed the participants to analyse strategies used in placing the items; collected touch data of mapped items across the skin area to identify frequently used locations; and captured images of hands and arms to examine the types of landmarks at different item locations. We also investigated recall performance across the locations and the items. This paper contributes empirical data of mapping and recall performance on the skin, and discusses implications for designing skin-based interfaces.

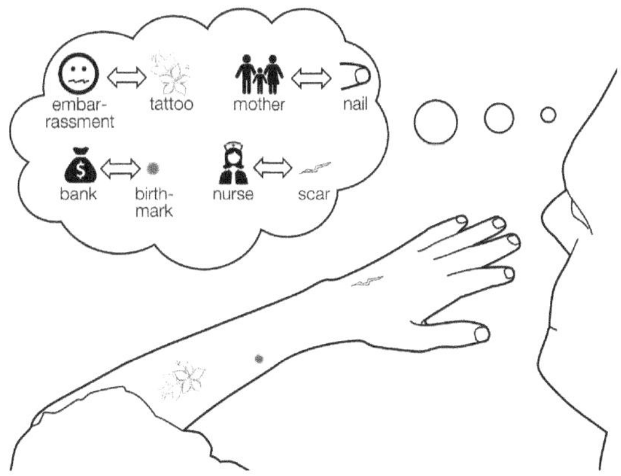

Figure 1: Some associations between the virtual items and locations on the skin that participants created in our study.

CHI 2017, May 6-11, 2017, Denver, CO, USA.

ACM ISBN 978-1-4503-4655-9/17/05 ...$15.00.
http://dx.doi.org/10.1145/3025453.3026030

RELATED WORK

The related work on skin-based interfaces consists of several studies using virtual items. Users can, for instance, browse through an audio-based mobile phone's menu by sliding a finger across invisible items on the fingers and palm [5], or type blind-folded on a personalized QWERTY-layout to give input for smart glasses [17]. Previous research has developed technologies to track touch input, measured touch accuracy on item locations, and examined how users design item layouts, such as what kind of landmarks they use on the skin.

Technologies for Tracking Touch on the Skin

Touch on bare skin can be estimated through optical tracking [1, 2, 7, 9, 10, 16, 17] or by tracking signal propagation on the skin surface [8, 12]. Motion capture systems [7] and tracking of acoustic signals [8, 12] allow sensing touches across the entire forearm and hand areas. Infrared sensors are used locally for sensing touches; for instance, on the palm [9, 10, 17]. These technologies enable input on virtual items on the skin, with few restrictions on item layouts or the size of the interactive area. Therefore, it is important to examine where to place virtual items on both the forearm and hand.

Touch Performance on Virtual Items

Related work on skin input suggests that touch performance on virtual items is better when those items are located at landmarks on the skin, rather than on areas with fewer landmarks. For example, Gustafson et al. [5] used an imaginary grid layout with anchoring points on the thumb tip, the index fingertip, and the point where the thumb and index join, and showed that participants pointed most accurately on anchor points, while pointing error significantly increased the farther the target was from these landmarks. In another paper about imaginary interfaces, Gustafson et al. [6] demonstrated that in the absence of visual feedback from a palm interface, allowing users to see their bare hands still resulted in twice as fast target acquisition speed as in a blind-folded condition. Lin et al. [11] showed significantly higher tapping accuracies on locations at the elbow and wrist compared to three other locations along the forearm. These studies used a small number of targets, because their focus was on examining touch accuracy on the skin without visual feedback. To our knowledge, earlier studies have not measured recall performance of virtual item locations on the skin.

Mapping Items on the Skin

Related research has used landmarks to create interface layouts that fit the shape of the skin surface. Gustafson et al. [6], for instance, mapped mobile phone menu items on the hand and fingers using a layout similar to that on the phone. Instead of grid layouts that might suit such imaginary [5] or projected interfaces [7], researchers have also asked users to decide on or design virtual item layouts. For example, Lin et al. [11] asked participants to place a small number of targets (six to nine) on their forearm; Dezfuli et al. [2] asked participants to map TV remote control buttons on the palm side of the hand and fingers; and Wang et al. [17] asked participants to design a QWERTY -keyboard layout and adjust its key shapes for the palm side of the hand and fingers.

The virtual item placements participants made in these studies, however, may have been influenced by using existing, pre-defined layouts. For example, the directional keys of a TV remote control [2], and most keys of the QWERTY -keyboard [17] remained in similar locations in relation to each other on the palm and in the reference interfaces. Moreover, mapping abstract items – such as the numbers from 1-6 [11], or alphabetical keys [17] – can limit the creation of personal associations between the items and the skin, encouraging to maintain a familiar ordering between the items.

Landmarks Around the Hand and Forearm

Related work mentions various kinds of landmarks on the skin, such as freckles, fingertips, fingers, finger joints, tattoos, veins, elbow, wrist, and higher and lower points on the skin (e.g., [2, 3, 13]). For example, Oh and Findlater [13] found that strategies participants used in creating on-body gestures included using specific parts of the hands – such as fingertips and palm – as landmarks. A system by Gannon et al. [3] allows incorporating individual landmarks, such as knuckles, freckles, veins, and tattoos, in calibrating gestures (which travel through those). Participants found these useful when both hands were engaged in skin input. Dezfuli et al. [2] reported that participants found nine landmarks on the palm side of the hand (five convex and concave areas on the palm and four digit fingers) which they believed they could easily touch without looking. However, these studies focus on landmarks in local areas of the skin (the palm in [2, 13] and the forearm in [3]). We could not find previous research that addressed a comprehensive set of the mentioned landmarks over the hand and forearm.

STUDY

We conducted an in-depth study where participants placed 30 virtual items on their hand and forearm and tried to recall their locations. The overall purpose of the study was to examine:

1. Where participants place items on the hand and forearm?
2. What kind of landmarks they use?
3. What their recall performance will be?
4. What type of strategies participants use when placing items on their skin?

Items

The 30 items that were used in this study as virtual items were everyday things, collected by searching Wikipedia, and various vocabulary sites, with four categorical words (*emotions, buildings and places, occupations,* and *family members*) [1]. We used these everyday items for two reasons. First, we aimed to enable creation of personal associations between items and the skin, because when placing virtual items in physical surroundings, creation and use of associations is suggested to improve recall of item locations [15]. Furthermore, people often have personal associations with their computer's

[1]The items were: Disgust, Embarrassed, Hopeful, Irritated, Melancholy, Panic, Surprise, Teacher, Actor, Dentist, Farmer, Lawyer, Nurse, Police, Aunt, Brother, Cousin, Daughter, Father, Mother, Nephew, Sister, Bank, Hospital, House, Library, Museum, Park, Restaurant, Supermarket.

contents, such as the mobile phone contact list and applications menu. Second, in order to identify what types of landmarks are used, and to find personal differences in their usage, we aimed to induce creative use of landmarks on the skin. Using items from a particular application, or item groups with an explicit, discrete, or linear order (such as numbers or alphabets), might influence how participants organize the items, limiting the generalizability of the results to other applications.

It was necessary to use an adequate number of items to allow us to examine a variety of placements across the skin. With 30 items, we aimed to induce the participants to use multiple areas and multiple types of landmarks on the hand and forearm, as well as inventive strategies in placing the items. Furthermore, the number needed to be high enough to allow measurement of recall performance and possible learning effects after repetition of recall tasks without ceiling. In Perrault et al. [15], the participants were already in the first phase able to recall nearly all (in average 47.5 out of 48) physical locations of virtual items they had placed in a room. We first piloted the setup with 60 items, but recognized that the experiment's duration extended to over 1.5 hours, and that recall rate was low. We aimed to keep the experiment short enough to prevent fatigue, which might reduce participants' motivation to try their best to create placement strategies that would result in effective recall. We therefore piloted the experiment again using 36 items and two participants; recall rates suggested that, with 30 items, participants would be unlikely to achieve full recall of the locations on the skin.

Participants

Data were collected from 16 right-handed participants (9 females and 7 males, with a mean age of 26.7 years). All of them used a touchscreen mobile phone daily (9 of them frequently throughout the day), and 10 participants used a touchscreen tablet device daily. We recruited participants from three different nationalities and five occupations. Participants were instructed to wear a shirt that left the skin bare below the elbow, and to remove all jewelry and watches when participating in the experiment. The experiment lasted approximately an hour, and participants received gifts as compensation for their time.

Study Setup and Implementation

The purpose of the study was to examine (1) placement of items on the hand and forearm, (2) landmarks on the skin at item locations, (3) recall performance of these locations, and (4) participant strategies for item placement. Therefore, we required three types of data: touch locations on the skin, pictures of the skin features, and interview recordings. Pictures were taken with a camera, and interviews recorded on a mobile phone. Table 1 summarizes the phases of this study, the tasks or actions conducted in each phase, and the purpose or the data collected in those.

To capture the touch locations on the skin, we designed a setup that provided us both real-time finger coordinates, and a representation of the skin surface that enables relating the coordinates to it post hoc. The coordinates needed to be processed in real-time to provide participants with feedback about their recall performance during the tasks – that is, whether they had touched the location at which they had placed an item earlier on. The representation of the skin's surface allowed us to use the finger coordinates to infer actual touch points.

Tracking Touch Locations

We used an OptiTrack motion-capture system consisting of eight Flex13 cameras with 56 degrees field of view to track the index finger (Figure 2) and deliver the fingertip coordinates to an experimental software. This motion capture system tracked the IR reflective markers on the finger with a 120Hz sampling rate, and with less than 0.3mm spatial accuracy in 3D space.

We designed and 3D-printed a rigid body (a rigid piece of plastic on which reflective markers are attached) for the index finger (Figure 2). This rigid body was designed to allow

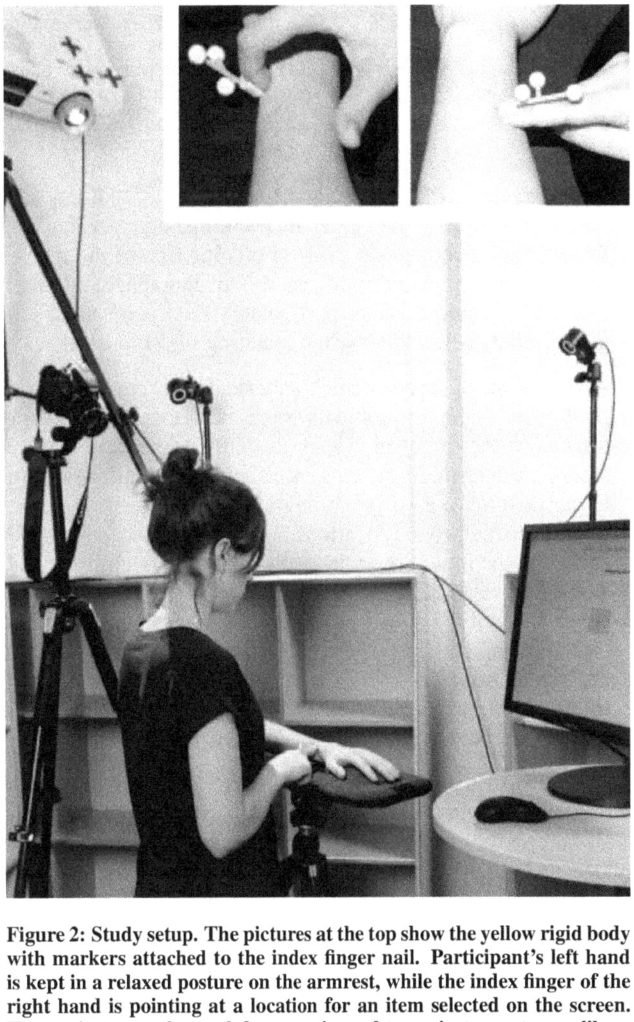

Figure 2: Study setup. The pictures at the top show the yellow rigid body with markers attached to the index finger nail. Participant's left hand is kept in a relaxed posture on the armrest, while the index finger of the right hand is pointing at a location for an item selected on the screen. The projector on the top left corner is used to project a posture calibration grid on the arm. The OptiTrack motion capture system with eight cameras (two of those visible in the picture) is placed around the participant, tracking the rigid body attached to the index finger and delivering its coordinates. A Canon EOS camera placed above and to the left of the user captures pictures of the hands.

Table 1: Experimental phases, tasks, and data collection.

Steps	Phase	Task	Purpose and Data Collection
1	Posture Calibration	The experimenter sets the armrest to support a relaxed posture, then draws the projected grid with a UV marker.	To mark the posture so that the same posture can be adapted for all phases. Needed for evaluating whether recall was successful.
2	Mapping Phase	The participant places 30 virtual items on the skin.	Location coordinates of items from motion capture data of the finger, and pictures of the hands placing the items from a camera. For examining placement of items and landmarks on the skin.
Before each phase 3-8	Break	The participant adapts the posture to match the UV marker lines and the projected grid before beginning the next phase.	Short breaks help the participant to keep still during the phases.
3, 5	Learning Phases	The participant tries to recall the locations of 30 virtual items on the skin.	Giving participants feedback of recall performance to induce learning. Recall performance measures from finger coordinates.
4, 6	Recall Phases	The participant tries to recall the locations of 30 virtual items on the skin.	No feedback given of recall performance. Recall performance measured from finger coordinates.
7	Random Recall	The participant tries to recall the locations of 6 randomly chosen virtual items on the skin.	Recall performance measures from finger coordinates. Recall in a random order without showing the order used in previous phases. Allows us to determine whether this affected recall performance.
8	Capturing the skin surface	The experimenter captures 15 000-20 000 coordinates across the hand and forearm which represent the skin surface in a posture that was used in the experiment.	To relate the location coordinates of the index finger to the actual skin surface in a posture it was kept during the phases.
(2), 9	Interviews	Think-aloud motivations for placements of items in phase 2. Semi-structured interview after the experiment.	Voice records to gain insights about placement strategies, and personal associations between the items and the skin.

robust tracking of participants' fingertip in 3D space, allow natural posture of the finger in pointing, and yet leave the fingertip uncovered. We avoided placing one of the markers on the nail, because due to the size of the sphere (diameter 14mm), it would obscure participants' vision of small landmarks (such as freckles) when touching the skin nearby.

A minimum of three of such spherical markers on the rigid body were needed to robustly track the orientation and coordinates of the finger in 3D space. This orientation was necessary to determine the fingertip's precise location, because finger posture (e.g., orientation in relation to the skin surface) varies between touch locations across the hand and arm. For example, the index finger is extended when touching the near side of the arm (Figure 2, top right) because flexion would cause the nail to touch, whereas the finger is flexed when touching the far side of the arm (Figure 2, top left). Without orientation, varying approaching angles of touches (e.g., tilting the finger) at a single point would have been mistakenly interpreted as different touch coordinates.

The head of the rigid body was curved similarly to a nail so that it attached tightly to the nail with double-sided adhesive. Attaching the rigid body to the nail left all of the index finger skin on the palm side uncovered, allowing participants to also feel the skin of the left hand when placing items.

Images of the Skin

A Canon EOS 600D camera was used to capture high-resolution pictures of the hands. The pictures were used in analysing landmarks on the skin, and also displayed to participants during the experiment after false touch locations. The camera was placed above the participant to the left (Figure 2) so as to cover the entire left forearm and hand, providing a first person view when these images were displayed as feedback during the experiment. The purpose of a first-person view was to help participants relate displayed touch locations to their skin. The camera was controlled by an experimental software.

Software

The software developed for this study streams OptiTrack data to log touch coordinates, processes touch data, controls the camera to capture images, and serves as a user interface in the experimental task.

The interface displayed 30 buttons, each labeled with an item name in a randomised order. The button list was randomised to encourage participants to place the items in an order of their choice instead of a pre-defined order. The list stayed the same throughout the experiment, allowing participants to find items they wanted to select without remarkable effort.

Participants selected items to place or recall by clicking them with a mouse. When touching the skin on the location they selected for an item, the experimenter pressed the space bar and the software captured a picture with the camera and logged the coordinates of the index finger tip from the OptiTrack.

When placing the items, the software ensured that the location did not overlap with any of the previously placed items; if it did overlap, the interface turned the button red so that the participant could select a new location for it. To evaluate recall performance, the software calculated the nearest item from the location of touch to determine if the selection corresponded to the location where the item that was selected on the screen was placed earlier. If the location corresponded to that item, the recall was logged as successful.

Interpreting Touch Locations on the Skin

Physical IR-trackable markers (such as those provided by OptiTrack and used on the rigid body on the index finger) would have provided the participants with additional landmarks on the left hand and arm, imposing a risk of bias in the usage of skin-based landmarks. Therefore, the OptiTrack was used only for tracking the coordinates of the index finger. Because a representation of the skin surface was needed, the posture of the left hand and arm had to be consistent throughout the experiment. The participants were instructed to keep their hand still during all phases; the location and shape of the hand were then captured in a separate calibration phase after the experimental phases.

We also built an armrest to assist participants in keeping their hand and arm relaxed and still during the experiment (Figure 2). The armrest was shaped from foam, and contained two prominences on both sides of the arm, one under the wrist, and one hemispherical under the palm. With the design of the armrest we aimed to not provide any extra landmarks around the hand and arm, and therefore also covered the armrest with black fabric. The armrest was placed on a tripod to enable adjusting it according to the participant's height.

To calculate the nearest items based on index finger coordinates only, it was necessary for participants to adapt precisely the same posture each time. Before initiating the experiment, a grid (Figure 3) was projected on the left hand and forearm and its lines were drawn on the skin with a UV marker invisible in normal light. Before each experimental phase, the projector and a blacklight torch making the UV marker visible were turned on, and the posture was adapted until the lines matched and maintained throughout the next phase.

To relate the OptiTrack data of the index finger to the skin, we build a 3D mesh representing the skin surface of each participant. After the tasks, the experimenter used another rigid body to capture points (coordinates) on the skin. The experimenter then "drew" the outlines of the hand and arm and "colored" across the entire skin surface with a rigid body marker. By tracking the marker that traveled on the skin surface, we collected approximately 15-20 000 coordinates on each participant's skin. We exported this point cloud from OptiTrack to MatLab, and performed a Delaunay triangulation to create a mesh representing the skin surface. The index finger coordinates were then plotted on this mesh (see examples of these meshes in the Results section), allowing us to analyse touch locations on the skin.

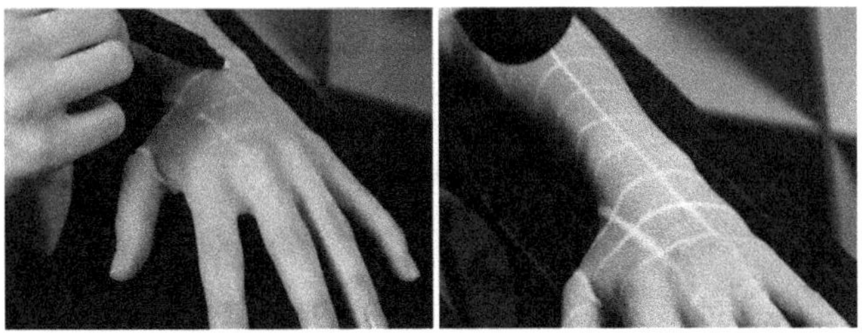

Figure 3: Picture on the left shows the experimenter drawing the projected grid with UV marker invisible in normal light. Picture on the right shows the participant adapting her posture to match the blue UV marker lines and the projected grid before starting the next recall phase.

Task

The task was to place 30 virtual items on the surface of the hand and forearm (skin and nails), and then recall their locations. Participants were free to choose the order in which they placed and recalled these items.

The participants placed and recalled the items one by one by first clicking an item button of their choice with a mouse, and then touching the selected location on the skin using their index finger (Figure 2). The selection's coordinates were captured when the participant told the experimenter to confirm the location (e.g., saying "there"). This verbal command was used to avoid any additional body movements of participants and possible errors in tracking precise touch locations caused by those. Moreover, this allowed participants to view and feel their skin before making a selection; this would not be possible with, for instance, a capacitive touch sensor on the fingertip.

Procedure

The experiment consisted of six phases, including mapping, learning, recall, and a random recall phase (see Table 1). The mapping phase was performed first, in which the participants placed the items onto the skin. In the learning phase participants trained this mapping with a recall task by receiving feedback on their selections. In the recall phase participants attempted to recall all locations without any feedback on their performance. These learning and recall phases were performed twice to reveal possible learning effects. Finally, we performed a short random recall test presenting six items, one after the other. The purpose of this recall test was to examine whether recall order had any effect on recall performance by preventing participants from following a self-chosen sequential and spatial order and forcing them to follow a random one instead.

Posture Calibration

Participants were instructed to keep their hand in the same fixed but relaxed posture throughout the phases. This posture was calibrated at the beginning of the experiment by adjusting the armrest to a height where the arm and hand were fully supported, and where participant felt relaxed. The projected lines were then drawn on the skin, and before each phase this posture was re-adapted.

Mapping Phase

In the mapping phase participants were instructed to place the items anywhere on the visible skin or nails between the elbow and the fingertips. After successful placement of an item, that item's button was disabled so that the participant saw which items remained for placement. Once an item was selected and placed, no further changes to the mapping were allowed. Therefore, participants were instructed to take their time while proceeding through the item list, and to try to be inventive with their choice of locations so that they could more easily recall them later on. We also asked the participants to 'think aloud' while mapping to gain insights on their strategies. Their voices were recorded during the mapping phase so as to capture these thoughts.

To separate successful recalls from false ones by calculating the nearest items, we needed to prevent overlapping item placements. If the item distance to the nearest item placed earlier during mapping phase was smaller than the 8mm threshold, the item button turned red, and the participant could place the item elsewhere. The threshold was twice the mean error (4mm) of touches in a pilot in which a participant pointed to 10 visual targets marked on the skin. The 8mm threshold also coincides with approximately half of the width of an average adult index finger tip [4].

Learning Phases

In the learning phase participants were shown the same items in the same order as in the mapping phase. The learning phase consisted of a recall task with feedback. Using the recall task allowed performance to be measured, while simultaneously inducing learning. The items and their location were selected in a similar procedure to that used in the mapping phase, by clicking the item button with a mouse and touching its recalled location on the skin.

Recall was considered to be correct if the nearest point (Euclidian distance in 3D space) from the 30 locations determined in the mapping phase was the location of the selected item and the distance to that was within 20mm. When the recalled location was correct, the item button turned grey (i.e., was disabled).). If the location was incorrect, an image of the participant's hand and the finger touching the selected location (captured in the mapping phase) was displayed on the screen (see an example of such image in Figure 5). With this visual guidance, the participant then reattempted to select the correct location.

Recall Phases

In the recall phases the task was similar to the learning phase. However, participants received no feedback as to whether the recalled location was correct or not. After selection, the button was disabled.

Random Recall

The random recall phase consisted of six randomly selected items from the item list used in the experiment. The interface displayed the items one at a time centered on the computer's display. This prevented participants from using the item's position on the display, or the sequential order of items, to aid recall. Otherwise, the task was similar to the one used in the recall phase.

Interviews

After the recall tasks, we interviewed participants using a semi-structured approach. For the interview, participants were shown the same list of items they had seen during the experiment. They were then asked to describe their strategies for item placement on the skin. The experimenter also asked first, whether the participant grouped the items and if so, how; second, how they chose the locations on the skin, and whether they had used any landmarks there; and finally, were some item locations easier or more difficult to recall and if so, why.

RESULTS

Touch data and pictures were used for examining where the participants placed items on the hand and forearm. Based on the meshes and the associated touch coordinates, we coded touch locations on physical areas and anatomical landmarks, such as bones, joints, and nails. The pictures complemented the touch data – which does not extend to purely visual features, such as tattoos or pigments – and also helped to resolve uncertainties regarding touch locations. Touch data was used to calculate participants' overall recall performances, as well as recall performances per items. The coding of landmarks was used for calculating recall performances on specific areas and landmarks. Finally, voice recordings from mapping phases and interviews were used for exploration of personal associations between items and locations on the skin, as well as strategies used to organize and place the items.

The total duration of the experimental phases from the beginning of the mapping phase to the end of random recall was 42 minutes, on average. The mapping phase took an average of 10.8 min, the first learning phase 7.1 min, the first recall 4.1 min, the second learning phase 5.3 min, the second recall 3.0 min, and the random recall 31.9 seconds.

Placement of Items

We coded the placement of items from the touch coordinates plotted on the meshes of hand surfaces together with the pictures taken during the mapping phase. Examples of these two data for P2 are depicted in Figure 5. Coding was conducted by examining the plots and images, and creating new landmark types when they emerged.

We began the coding by dividing the skin to five areas: Fingers, Hand, Wrist, Arm, and Elbow. Out of all items, 39.4% were placed on fingers, 16.5% on the hand, 6.0% on the wrist, 35.2% on the arm, and 2.9% on the elbow. We then coded

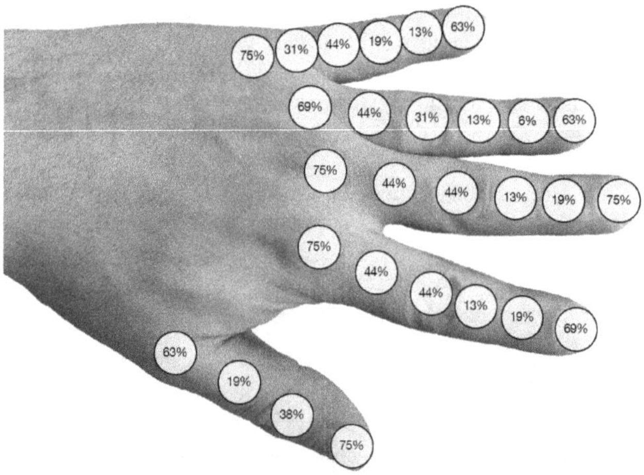

Figure 4: Location frequencies by a percentage of participants who placed an item there. We coded six locations from the nail to knuckle: 1. Distal phalanx (nail), 2. Distal interphalangeal (DIP) joint , 3. Intermediate (middle) phalanx, 4. Proximal interphalangeal (PIP) joint, 5. Proximal phalanx, and 6. Metacarpophalangeal (MCP) joint (knuckle). The thumb lacks an intermediate phalanx, and therefore has no DIP joint.

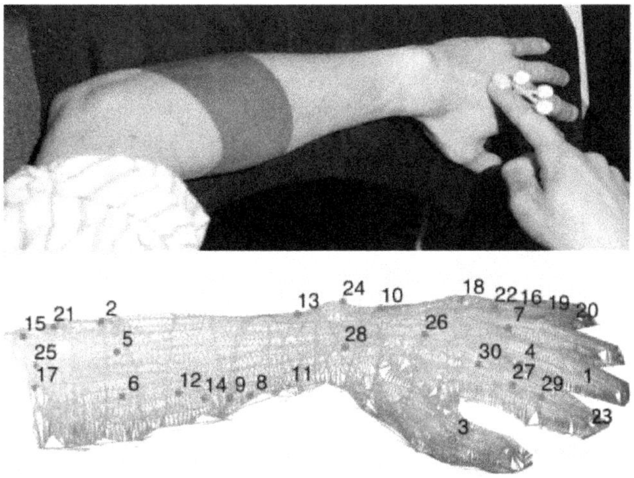

Figure 5: An image of the skin and the mapped item locations plotted on the mesh of P2. P2 is selecting a location on a vein on the back of the hand. The three item IDs (2, 5, and 6) placed over the midline of the tattoo are plotted on the mesh, and correspond to 'Embarrassed', 'Melancholy', and 'Panic', respectively.

the item locations on the fingers for each finger separately by dividing it into joints and phalanges. (Phalanges are the fingerbones between the joints). Most participants placed items on nails (fingertips) and knuckles (ranging between 63% and 75% in each case), whereas on other joints and phalanges the frequencies were more distributed (Figure 4). The participants never placed more than 6 items on a finger, each on a separate bone or joint. Therefore, no other landmarks were recognized on the fingers.

We found seven additional landmark types outside the fingers. One type is close to the fingers; a soft area on the hand between the carpometacarpal bones of the thumb and index finger. Out of all items, 1.9% were placed there. About 1.25% of all items were placed on the pisiform (the bone on the wrist visible on P2 in Figure 5). Another anatomical landmark was the wrinkle or line at the anterior side of the elbow, which is visible when the elbow is flexed. Out of all items, 3.5% were placed here. Birthmarks, moles, or freckles were used for 7.1% of the items. Tattoos were used for 2.3%, veins for 1.0%, and scars for 0.2% of the items.

Items on Specific Locations

We also examined the frequency of items on landmarks and areas on the skin. Family members were most often (69.5%) placed on fingers. Most participants (81.3%) placed 'Father' on fingers and 75.0% also placed 'Mother' and 'Daughter' there. Emotions and places were often placed on the forearm. For example, most participants placed 'Melancholy' (81.3%) and 'Embarrassed' (62.5%) there. Separating specific landmarks within these areas, we found that almost half of the participants (43.8%) placed 'Mother' and 'Father' on the fingernails, and 31.3% also 'Brother' and 'Sister'. Three participants had tattoos and all of them placed 'Melancholy' on those. Most of the items placed on tattoos (88.9%) were emotions.

Recall Performance

The average performance in the first recall phase was 19.8 (.95 CI $\pm$2.8) items and in the second recall phase 21.2 (.95 CI $\pm$3.0) items. Although a slight trend of increased performance after learning phases can be seen (Figure 6), there was no significant improvement after repetition.

Learning

Visual guidance (images shown after erroneous selection in learning phases) helped in learning; 60.6% of the cases in the first learning phase and 52.8% of the cases in the second learning phase resulted in the correct selection when retrying. However, when participants did not recall the location even after receiving visual help (when retrying), in most cases they were not able to recall the locations of these items in later phases either (72.3% of the fails after visual help in the first learning phase were failed in the first recall phase, and 64.7% of the fails in the second learning phase also failed in the second recall phase). Similarly, when participants succeeded after help, they also recalled well in later phases, that is, learnt the items they recalled. This suggests that using landmarks is important for performing well in recall; even when people are shown where their finger pointed, they still cannot find the exact location without having some form of reference point on the skin.

Random Order

There were no significant difference between participants' average recall performance in the random recall phase (where 67.7%, .95 CI $\pm$14.3% of item locations were recalled correctly) and in four learning and recall phases (where 68.1%, .95 CI $\pm$9.2% of item locations were recalled correctly). Thus, there is no evidence that sequential ordering of item selections in the experiment (which the participants were free to choose) and the spatial layout of items on the display (which was randomized) have affected recall performance. This suggests that usage of landmarks, item locations on the skin, and personal strategies in mapping the items might influence recall more than selection order or layout of the reference interface.

Items

Each item category contained items that were easier to recall than others. Among the emotion items, the location of 'Hopeful' was recalled significantly more often (79.7%, .95 CI $\pm$11.1%) than the locations of 'Embarrassed' (65.6%, .95 CI $\pm$16.0%), 'Irritated' (60.9%, .95 CI $\pm$15.4%), and 'Melancholy'(62.5%, .95 CI $\pm$16.9%). Among occupations, 'Nurse' resulted in significantly better recall performances (78.1%, .95 CI $\pm$11.8%) than 'Lawyer' (59.4%, .95 CI $\pm$18.1%). In the family category, the location of 'Mother' was significantly more often recalled (78.1%, .95 CI $\pm$16.8%) than 'Daughter' (56.3%, .95 CI $\pm$19.2%). Among places, 'Hospital' (76.6%, .95 CI $\pm$12.4%) and 'House' (76.6%, .95 CI $\pm$14.2%) were recalled significantly more often than 'Bank' (60.9%, .95 CI $\pm$17.5%) and 'Library' (57.8%, .95 CI $\pm$18.0%). Although these differences were found between single items, there were no difference in recall between item categories. This suggests that regardless of the types of items, personally important ones, which the users can associate with, are recalled better.

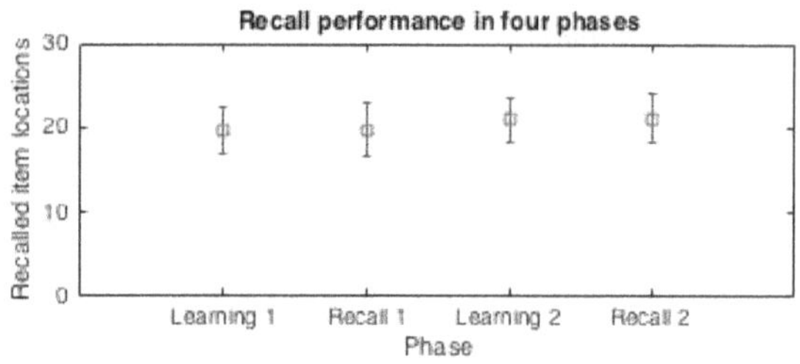

Figure 6: Recall performance in four phases.

Locations

Item locations in the second recall phase were recalled worse on the arm (63.3%, .95 CI ±12.6%) than on the fingers (73.5%, .95 CI ±14.9%), hand (75.6%, .95 CI ±23.9%) wrist (75.9%, .95 CI ±38.5%), and elbow (85.7%, .95 CI ±52.2%). However, as the variations were large, these differences are not significant.

The recall rate of item locations on the nails was 78.0% (.95 CI ±34.1%) and on the knuckles 64.7% (.95 CI ±31.4%). Items placed on scars and on the pisiform (the bone on the wrist) were recalled in the second recall phase at a rate of 100%, on tattoos at a rate of 82%, on the spot between index and thumb at a rate of 77.8%, and on pigments at a rate of 73.5%. Use of these landmarks, however, was so rare among our participants that statistical significances of recall performances cannot be evaluated.

Qualitative Insights on Placing and Recalling Items

Table 2 shows a summary of 177 interview snippets. From these, we extracted comments about strategies for placing and recalling items to create groups. As the intention with this data was to complement the image and touch location data, we ignored comments and strategies that would be bettered covered by those sources of data (e.g., where the items were placed, or how groups were placed together).

Selecting Overall Mapping

The snippets revealed four strategies participants used to lay out their overall mappings between items and their arm and hand. A mapping works as a principle for relating one or more items to the hand and arm. Most participants combined multiple mappings, either because different categories required different mappings or because one mapping stopped working (e.g., running out of space on a finger).

First, 10 participants speak about absolute *spatial* features and how these work to structure item placement. They mentioned creating lines and super imposing them on their arms (4 participants); as one person explained, "I had lines in many places, like imaginary lines. So I had partly tattoos, injury, knuckles, and then partly imaginary lines." (P16). Four other participants discussed distances "I tried to put things next to each other and to kind of equal distances." (P10). Some participants also spoke about creating a "mental map", a "grid", or a "spatial ordering". In all cases, space rather than landmarks was the guiding principle.

Second, 6 participants decided to map particular groups of items to particular *areas*. Those areas could be anatomical (e.g., "I'm trying to keep the emotions on the fingers," P1), easy to access ("The front of my arm, the first part, is kind a handy, easy access, so I picked the places I like the most," P7), or importance (e.g., "And the thumb I choose for important stuff, like hospital or being sick, like you have to call a dentist or nurse." P8). All of these give a clear mapping of items to particular areas.

Third, two participants used the *sense of touch on its own*. One of them explained: "So, I kind of went on feeling that I could remember the touch, like where I touched my skin. And that kind of helped too, so it was a mix of like an emotional or image association, and if it felt right, if it felt like the right place to touch." (P13).

Fourth, all participants on at least one occasion proceeded with an *anchor and association* mapping, meaning that they chose one item to serve as an anchor and then proceeded to place items around that anchor. P9 started from a birthmark: "Museum, let's check this birthmark. So museum.. Library. Supermarket here. Park right next to it. So I have this tiny square right next to my birthmark."

Relating Items to Each Other

In both placing and recalling items, participants took care to relate items to other items. As mentioned above (in anchoring), some participants derived the bulk of their mapping in this way. Next we summarize the different ways of doing so; typically these do not relate to landmarks or skin features.

First, participants mentioned many principles of *ordering*. These included alphabetical ordering, and ordering based on size or age. One participant also used a process order (P16): "Then the food stuff, I kind a drew line across my arm. And I grouped those in a process order, so first there is a farm and then a supermarket."

Second, three participants talked about creating *stories* when placing or recalling items. For instance, one participant placed items while making up a story (P14): "Okay, so once upon a time there was a house (to index finger nail), and the house was located in a park (proximal joint). And there lived a farmer (index finger's knuckle). Who was very embarrassed (middle finger's knuckle), because he bought all his groceries in a supermarket (proximal joint) and sold those to a restaurant (middle finger nail)."

Third, a number of different types of personal *associations* also served as ways of relating items within an area. For example, P2 used a perceived order of value: "Like I placed the bank on the tip because that's most prestigious and rich and going down to the supermarket."

Coupling Items to Skin Features

One key tactic in item placement is the association of a particular item with a feature of the skin. We differentiate skin features that are personal (e.g., a scar) from those that are shared (e.g., knuckles). An orthogonal dimension, then, depends on whether the reason for coupling an item to a feature is objective or based on a personal experience. This provides

Table 2: Grouping of the interview data, the number of participants who mentioned these strategies, description of the strategies, and example quotes from snippets.

	N	Explanation	Examples
Finding layout			
Spatial mapping	10	Using mental maps, imaginary lines, and distances along those.	"I used distances also to remember where I put items. Like spatial ordering." (P7)
Mapping onto an area	6	Deciding to place a group of items on an area.	"Well basically I started with family members because family is important so I used them as in the primary part of the hand like fingernails." (P4)
Feeling a way forward	2	Touching the skin and finding locations by touch.	"I also used finger structure, so I was trying to feel bones and spaces between those." (P11)
Anchoring to a point	16	Finding a starting location and moving forward in an ad hoc fashion.	"Then I had like mental buttons. I made a grid. I started from the birthmark as a corner and then from there. It made easy to remember." (P14)
Organizing items			
Common	4	A commonly used ordering, e.g., alphabetical ordering, or ordering based on size.	"Alphabetical order I used for emotions, because only hopeful was remotely good so I couldn't group those like good and bad feelings, so then I just didn't see any way to differ between various bad feelings. So the alphabetical order worked just fine for me." (P7)
Stories	9	Fictional and personal stories.	"So mum was a nurse so nurse next to it. And my dad is in the hospital, so I put hospital above him. Then next to them my sister, and my sister is a lawyer, so that above her. And then my brother. And he wanted to be a policeman so that's above him." (P14)
Associations	6	Ordering based on personal perception of a hierarchy.	"Then I had the family group, which I put close family on one finger in some kind of hierarchy with mother on top and the sister in the bottom because thats how my family is." (P2)
Coupling Items to Skin			
Shared feature and personal experience	10	Connecting a personal experience to a shared landmark, such as to a knuckle.	"The reason why I placed the dentist towards my elbow, is because when I went to the dentist once, I hit my elbow and we made fun with the dentist about that." (P9)
Personal feature and personal experience	8	Connecting a personal story to a personal feature, such as to a tattoo or birthmark.	"Tattoo is like a mourning band for me so I put melancholy there." (P2)
Shared feature and common experience	5	Common connections, such as cultural associations.	"Disgust: Disgust I'll place here. Because if you are disgusted you might give someone the finger." (P3)
Personal feature and common experience	4	Connections other people could make, but to a personal landmark.	"Irritated: Irritated because I have an injury on my arm, and it's very irritated right there." (P3)

four main groups of reasons for coupling items to skin features.

The most common of these was the association of a *shared feature with a personal experience* (10 participants). Reasons for placing the item mother include "Put it here because the wrist is my favorite part of my arm and it's the one that I touch the most. And if this would be to call my mother, this would be the easiest one," (P1); "There, I'm placing mother on the index finger, because she's to me, mother to me is very, she's given me directions. Sort of like pointing me the right direction," (P13); and "I place mother here, because it's like a very soft spot on my arm and I like to connect that with mother." (P3). These, and many other associations, centered on using a personal story (such as P2's: "The ring finger is for the wedding ring and sometimes the proposal is a surprise") to connect common features (e.g., ring finger) with items (e.g., surprise).

The *personal story is often linked to a personal feature* (8 participants), such as a vein, tattoo, or birthmark. Emotions were linked to veins in three comments, for instance, "I'm gonna start with panic, and I'm gonna click right under my index finger, and it's because I have a little vein there," (P6); "Panic: I place panic here, because I have a big vein here and if I panic it might be like irritated," (P3); and the same participant continuing with "Embarrassed: Because when you are embarrassed you get like hot and I get very sweaty. And I have a vein there who always bumps when I get embarrassed."

Common stories can be linked to common features, such as areas on the hand. Two participants mentioned a connection between thumbs and positive feelings, and two linked negative feelings to the middle finger. For example, "Irritated I put on the bad finger, which you can signal to people that you are irritated with them," and "Hopeful: Hopeful I will put on my thumb. Thumbs up is a kind of positive feeling," (P2).

Finally, *common connection can also be linked to a personal feature*. For instance, "Hospital... Well that should go to some scar tissue as well, that makes sense" (P12).

Summary of Findings

We found that participants frequently placed virtual items on both the fingers (39.4%) and the forearm (35.2%). Participants recalled locations of 21.2 items in average (out of 30, 70.7%) when they were allowed to place items themselves, both when traversing a list of all items and when recalling items at random. No significant effect was found between item locations on recall rates, but locations on the arm appear to be harder to recall than on other areas. Item locations on fingernails were well recalled (78%), but certain personal landmarks helped to achieve better recall rates, such as scars (100%) and tattoos (82%). The findings from the effects of visual guidance suggest that landmarks are important for recall even when visual feedback about the item location is given on external display. However, most of the participants used also mental grids alongside other mapping strategies.

DISCUSSION

We have presented a study of placing and recalling virtual items on the skin that combines data from motion tracking, images of the skin, and interviews. The results show the complexity and inventiveness of user-generated layouts of items on the skin. While earlier studies have allowed users to place items on their own, the item sets have had natural orderings (e.g., numbers [11], alphabet [17], or directional keys [2]). In the present study, we used everyday items that enabled finding a variety of mapping strategies between and within items and landmarks. We also coupled the use of landmarks to recall performance and showed how particular areas of the hand (e.g., nails) helped participants to achieve higher recall performance.

Implications for Skin Interfaces

Our study has implications for skin interfaces beyond providing basic knowledge about recall rates. Most importantly, participants used an overwhelming variety of mapping strategies and landmarks; while not all of these would likely be used with an actual interface, recognition of their existence can be beneficial in interface design.

First, our findings on learning effects suggest that using landmarks in mapping is important for recalling item locations on the skin, because without landmarks the exact locations are difficult to retrieve even when visual guidance is provided. These results are in line with previous research: Gustafson et al. [5], for instance, showed that touch accuracy decreases the futher the target is located from a landmark. Our results, however, also suggested frequent use of mental grids. These can be efficient when the items are not located too closely together. The number of items in mental grids per anchor point may also affect recall performance of exact item locations. Therefore, interface designs should allow enough landmarks on the skin to act as anchoring points, and enough distance between virtual items when anchors are absent or mental grids are preferred.

Second, the findings provide insight into the many strategies that are used in coupling items to skin. We found couplings between shared features and common experiences similar to those identified in earlier work. Weigel et al. [18], for instance, have previously reported findings regarding the use of the thumb for positive emotions (because of "thumbs up"), or anterior side of the forearm for personally significant items due to that location's physical proximity to the body. We found that personal experiences can also be connected with common landmarks, and common experiences with personal landmarks. While common landmarks can be used in interface design, the layouts cannot rely on personal ones, such as on tattoos, because not all users will have them. However, many of the personal landmarks are also common among people, such as veins, although these are located on different places on the skin. Therefore, it is important for interface design to recognize which landmarks should be embedded as item locations, and to allow flexible locations for these landmarks.

Third, our results indicate the touch locations participants most frequently used for virtual items. These touch locations can inform technological development of sensors tracking touch input on the skin. For example, our findings suggest frequent use of the fingers and forearm for virtual items, while previous work on gestures [18] have found more frequent usage of the forearm than of the fingers (50% vs. 7.3%). These findings may imply the importance of tracking touch on both the fingers and forearm, while tracking the forearm appears to be more important for gesture input on the skin. Motion capture systems [7] and some systems sensing acoustic signals propagating on the skin [8, 12], have already demonstrated their ability to track touches across the hand and arm, and might therefore be suitable for skin interfaces with virtual items.

Limitations and Methodology

In studies of recall of items (e.g., [15]) the type and number of items placed is a key decision. The number of 30 items were based on pilot studies to avoid ceiling (perfect recall) or floor effects. Future work should study how to increase that number; for instance, by explicitly training participants in the mapping strategies identified in this study.

Recall may also depend, in a non-linear way, on the number of items: as a participant is required to place more items, recall can decrease progressively, for instance because of interference. Thus, we are not suggesting that the average recall of 70.7% would scale to other numbers of items, but merely observing that in the present setup participants were able to recall around 21 items out of 30, much more than most studies of skin input have investigated [2, 6, 5, 7, 11, 12, 13, 14].

The instructions for recall can have a large effect on performance; we used the approach from [15] of showing an item list and having participants to place and recall while the list was visible. Our empirical approach and the selecetion of items aimed not to restrict the usefulness of results to any particular technology for tracking input, or to any existing interface design that could be mapped to the skin. In the random recall phase, in which participants recalled items without the cue of the list, they performed as well as with the list. For us, this clears up the potential methodological confound that the list may help recall (by associations between its spatial structure and the locations of items, and also by the sequence of recalls).

We recommend that future work addresses item placement around the hand and forearm and allow participants to move their arm (which they will in real recall circumstances); unfortunately, technical limitations prevented this setup for our study. In addition, we only investigated discrete touches; the use of gestures on the skin [18] may enable other recall strategies.

ACKNOWLEDGMENTS

This project has received funding from the European Research Council (ERC) under the European Union's Horizon 2020 research and innovation program (grant agreement 648785). The work was supported by KAUTE Foundation and Ulla Tuominen Foundation.

REFERENCES

1. Chan, L., Chen, Y.-L., Hsieh, C.-H., Liang, R.-H., and Chen, B.-Y. Cyclopsring: Enabling whole-hand and context-aware interactions through a fisheye ring. In *Proceedings of the 28th Annual ACM Symposium on User Interface Software & Technology*, ACM (2015), 549–556.
2. Dezfuli, N., Khalilbeigi, M., Huber, J., Özkorkmaz, M., and Mühlhäuser, M. PalmRC: leveraging the palm surface as an imaginary eyes-free television remote control. *Behaviour & Information Technology 33*, 8 (2014), 829–843.
3. Gannon, M., Grossman, T., and Fitzmaurice, G. Tactum: A Skin-Centric Approach to Digital Design and Fabrication. In *Proceedings of the 33rd Annual ACM Conference on Human Factors in Computing Systems*, ACM (2015), 1779–1788.
4. Garrett, J. W. The adult human hand: some anthropometric and biomechanical considerations. *Human Factors: The Journal of the Human Factors and Ergonomics Society 13*, 2 (1971), 117–131.
5. Gustafson, S., Bierwirth, D., and Baudisch, P. Imaginary interfaces: spatial interaction with empty hands and without visual feedback. In *Proceedings of the 23nd annual ACM symposium on User interface software and technology*, ACM (2010), 3–12.
6. Gustafson, S. G., Rabe, B., and Baudisch, P. M. Understanding palm-based imaginary interfaces: the role of visual and tactile cues when browsing. In *Proceedings of the SIGCHI Conference on Human Factors in Computing Systems*, ACM (2013), 889–898.
7. Harrison, C., Benko, H., and Wilson, A. D. OmniTouch: wearable multitouch interaction everywhere. In *Proceedings of the 24th annual ACM symposium on User interface software and technology*, ACM (2011), 441–450.
8. Harrison, C., Tan, D., and Morris, D. Skinput: appropriating the body as an input surface. In *Proceedings of the SIGCHI Conference on Human Factors in Computing Systems*, ACM (2010), 453–462.
9. Knibbe, J., Martinez Plasencia, D., Bainbridge, C., Chan, C.-K., Wu, J., Cable, T., Munir, H., and Coyle, D. Extending interaction for smart watches: enabling bimanual around device control. In *CHI'14 Extended Abstracts on Human Factors in Computing Systems*, ACM (2014), 1891–1896.
10. Lim, S.-C., Shin, J., Kim, S.-C., and Park, J. Expansion of Smartwatch Touch Interface from Touchscreen to Around Device Interface Using Infrared Line Image Sensors. *Sensors 15*, 7 (2015), 16642–16653.
11. Lin, S.-Y., Su, C.-H., Cheng, K.-Y., Liang, R.-H., Kuo, T.-H., and Chen, B.-Y. Pub-point upon body: exploring eyes-free interaction and methods on an arm. In *Proceedings of the 24th annual ACM symposium on User interface software and technology*, ACM (2011), 481–488.
12. Mujibiya, A., Cao, X., Tan, D. S., Morris, D., Patel, S. N., and Rekimoto, J. The sound of touch: on-body touch and gesture sensing based on transdermal ultrasound propagation. In *Proceedings of the 2013 ACM international conference on Interactive tabletops and surfaces*, ACM (2013), 189–198.
13. Oh, U., and Findlater, L. Design of and subjective response to on-body input for people with visual impairments. In *Proceedings of the 16th international ACM SIGACCESS conference on Computers & accessibility*, ACM (2014), 115–122.
14. Oh, U., and Findlater, L. A Performance Comparison of On-Hand versus On-Phone Nonvisual Input by Blind and Sighted Users. *ACM Transactions on Accessible Computing (TACCESS) 7*, 4 (2015), 14.
15. Perrault, S. T., Lecolinet, E., Bourse, Y. P., Zhao, S., and Guiard, Y. Physical Loci: Leveraging Spatial, Object and Semantic Memory for Command Selection. In *Proceedings of the 33rd Annual ACM Conference on Human Factors in Computing Systems*, ACM (2015), 299–308.
16. Prätorius, M., Valkov, D., Burgbacher, U., and Hinrichs, K. DigiTap: an eyes-free VR/AR symbolic input device. In *Proceedings of the 20th ACM Symposium on Virtual Reality Software and Technology*, ACM (2014), 9–18.
17. Wang, C.-Y., Chu, W.-C., Chiu, P.-T., Hsiu, M.-C., Chiang, Y.-H., and Chen, M. Y. PalmType: Using palms as keyboards for smart glasses. In *Proceedings of the 17th International Conference on Human-Computer Interaction with Mobile Devices and Services*, ACM (2015), 153–160.
18. Weigel, M., Mehta, V., and Steimle, J. More than touch: understanding how people use skin as an input surface for mobile computing. In *Proceedings of the SIGCHI Conference on Human Factors in Computing Systems*, ACM (2014), 179–188.

FLIPPIN' : Exploring a Paper-based Book UI Design in a Public Space

Koichi Yoshino[1] **Koichi Obata**[1] **Satoru Tokuhisa**[2]

Toppan Printing Co., Ltd.[1]
Bunkyo-ku, Tokyo, Japan
{koichi.yoshino, koichi.obata}@toppan.co.jp

Yamaguchi University [2]
Yamaguchi-city, Yamaguchi, Japan
dangkang@yamaguchi-u.ac.jp

Figure 1a. "Flip and Touch the Hokusai Manga" evaluation exhibition using FLIPPIN' UI system (left); Figure 1b. Touch point operation (center); Figure 1c. FLIPPIN' UI device designed to realize a reading experience comparable to a traditional book (right).

ABSTRACT

Digital information systems are increasingly being used in public spaces such as museums. Such systems should be easily accessible, arouse interest and offer useful information, and be easy to use. We present FLIPPIN' user interface (UI) system, which mimics the look, feel, and usability of traditional books. We explored how the paper-based book UI is designed to improve the usability problems in a public space while creating the prototypes with the aim of introducing Japanese cultural assets and conducting a field evaluation to compare the proposed system to a touch panel UI. The results of evaluation indicated the positive effects of the system, especially in terms of the usability and user's active appreciation derived from a physical book interaction. In addition, we present design guidelines derived from our findings. The suggested design guidelines are expected to facilitate the future development of effective interactive digital information systems in public spaces.

Keywords

Paper computing; book user interface; tangible; digital information system; public space; interaction design

ACM Classification Keywords

H.5.2. Information Interfaces and Presentation (e.g. HCI): User Interfaces

CHI 2017, May 06-11, 2017, Denver, CO, USA
© 2017 ACM. ISBN 978-1-4503-4655-9/17/05…$15.00
DOI: http://dx.doi.org/10.1145/3025453.3025981

INTRODUCTION

People increasingly obtain information via digital devices rather than traditional paper-based books. However, digital devices have usability problems, particularly with respect to reading. These problems are caused by a lack of physical book interaction with the device. With e-books (e.g., Amazon's Kindle and Apple's iBook), users interact by swiping and touching the digital display to perform various functions such as moving to the next page, bookmarking or highlighting an important section, and determining their position in the book. With paper-based books, users perform physical operations such as turning pages, folding a page and making notes. In addition, they can determine their reading position by simply looking at the book or touching piled page-papers of the book [1, 2, 3].

The superiority of such physical interactions has been clarified by studies that explore the optimal interaction design of e-books. For example, in a study that compared reading paper and on-line documents, O'Hara et al. found that reading speed and comprehension are superior with a physical book [4]. Liesaputra et al. analyzed the features associated with reading a paper-based book and created a 3D virtual book application with features similar to those of a paper-based book. They found that the usability of a paper-based book was superior to that of an e-book used to read digital documents such as PDF files [5]. Based on these findings, we assume that digital devices that emulate paper-based books may resolve e-book usability problems.

The results of studies that compare the usability of paper-based and digital books have enabled development of a new reading experience by combining the feel and usability of a traditional book with the advantages of digital technologies in terms of information retrieval and flexible representation [6]. Several studies have assumed the use of digital books for reading in a personal space such as a home or classroom and expected to support users' immersive reading for enjoying the depth of content as well as their learning activities [7, 8].

Digital devices that present reading material are also used in public spaces. Such devices are used to present guidebooks, annotation boards, and pamphlets in a public facility, e.g., a museum, and urban areas. The use of such digital information systems has rapidly increased in recent times. In the near future, digital information systems are expected to have a wide range of applications, e.g., interactive guidance systems that use stationary touch panel devices and information systems that use personal mobile devices. However, the following three issues must be considered for information systems in a public space.

Issue 1. How easily can UI devices be accessed or used by all visitors.
In a public space, operating a touch-panel user interface (UI) within a limited period tends to impose an inconvenient level of effort for visitors. As a result, people sometimes leave the facility without engaging the provided information systems.

Issue 2. How the system stimulates user interest via content.
In a public space, information systems are expected to provide both essential and supplemental information. Therefore, such systems should efficiently encourage visitors to find information that is relevant to their interests. However, it is difficult for visitors with various tastes to actively obtain such information within a limited period.

Issue 3. How digital systems are designed to solve the reading usability problem.
When reading an e-book, for example, when using a touch-panel UI, it is difficult to grasp the entire content quickly and know where you are in the book. In a public space, this usability problem is notable because the number of pages in a virtual book or the amount of hyper-text content can increase due to the presentation capabilities of digital devices, and many visitors will not spend the time required to find the desired information.

We expect that the usability of traditional paper books will help solve the e-book usability problem in public spaces. With respect to studies targeting applications in public spaces, their paper-based UI devices play crucial roles in digital information system in a public space, e.g., art exhibition using books [9] or posters [10] in a museum. However, few studies have targeted public space applications.

Thus, to address these issues, we examine the design of a paper-based book UI for information systems in public spaces. We created prototype systems, evaluated them in a field, and attempted to create design guidelines for future information systems in public spaces.

PREVIOUS WORKS

We focus on the usability of paper-based books in digital device. The challenge is to enable unobtrusive paper-based input sensing while preserving the lightweight, feel of paper and operational stability, thereby enabling effective interaction between users and the content using a paper-based UI device.

Regarding sensing techniques for turning pages, several studies have investigated the possibility of embedding soft sensors and electronics in paper. Watanabe et al analyzed reader's paging actions and developed an interface system by attaching a light-dependent resistor (LDR) and a bend sensor to each sheet [3]. This system realized feedback by sensing a subtle bending when turning pages of a book. Back et al. adopted the method of reading radio frequency identification (RFID) tags on each page of the exhibition installation “Listen Reader” [9]. This novel technique enabled the device to work without a battery. However, this method of attaching an electronic component to each page is unsuitable for a book comprising many pages even though these components are inexpensive. Several studies have adopted Augmented Reality (AR) techniques, e.g., reading an AR marker printed on a page [8, 11, 12]. Although such methods constrain a user's reading-environment conditions, such as device position and lighting, it has the advantage of being easy to implement on books because it is only necessary to print a marker on each page. Regarding the ease of implementation, there are methods for printing electronic circuits onto pages using conductive ink [7, 13, 14]. Though simply sensing and actuation mechanism only are built at this time, these methods allow to implement on books by printing or drawing the wiring patterns.

In addition, several studies have examined information presentation methods using a paper-based book UI. An information presentation method where the user operates a book UI and images or text are projected onto its pages or the reading environment has been used [15, 16, 17]. This method enables users to see superimposed book information and projected content. However, this method imposes some limitations on the environmental lighting and viewer position. In addition, liquid-crystal display (LCD) systems have been used [18]. Such systems expand presentation environment possibilities; however, the user is forced to view information in a book and a display device simultaneously. Figueiredo et al. created systems that comprise a display device and an adjacent book UI device, and they clarified the roles of each device by outputting synchronized content to both devices [19].

DESIGN

Field configuration and limitations

We selected the Knowledge Capital Association's "ACTIVE Lab." in the Grand Front Osaka shopping mall near Osaka station [20] (Figure 2) for our evaluation. The exhibition facility comprises 12 areas and introduces new technologies and activities sponsored by corporations, universities and other institutions in a way that is fun and easy to understand for everyone. More than 700,000 people visit the lab each year, with an average of approximately 1,900 visitors per day. We conducted the evaluation in an area where artwork and cultural assets are introduced using near-future media.

The advantages of this location are as follows. (1) This is a public space. A variety of visitors attend because admission is free and the facility is located near hotels and Osaka station. (2) This facility allows research to be conducted; thus, it is easy to collect data from interviews, observations, and user-behavior logs using camera-based sensors.
However, the following constraints exist. (1) The system should be designed such that users can operate it without instruction. (2) The hours of operation are from 10 AM to 9 PM, seven days a week, and the evaluation period is expected to last from April 15, 2016 to March, 2017. Therefore, the durability and robustness of the exhibition apparatus should be appropriate because many visitors attend this location. (3) There is limited floor space (2.5 m × 2.5 m) and lighting conditions should not interfere with nearby exhibitions. We exhibit Japanese cultural assets to raises awareness of Japanese culture. Note that we target adults in terms of stakeholder requirements.

Figure 2. Toppan Printing Booth in "ACTIVE Lab." (The Grand Front Osaka).

Content configuration and limitations

We chose to exhibit *the Hokusai Manga*, which is a collection of sketches of various subjects by Japanese artist Katsushika Hokusai (1760–1849) (Figure 3). *The Hokusai Manga*, which comprises nearly 4,000 sketches in 15 volumes, was one of the best-selling publications at the time. *The Hokusai Manga* is considered to be the Edo period encyclopedia. Hokusai's influence stretched to western contemporaries. A more direct influence was "Japonism" in 19th century Europe. We selected *the Hokusai Manga* because it is available in high-quality digital form and the content can be edited flexibly.

The exhibition's purpose is to introduce visitors to *the Hokusai Manga*, which includes a variety of drawings and various woodblock printing techniques in small sketches.

Figure3. "The Hokusai Manga" by Katsushika Hokusai, from the Uragami collection.

FLIPPIN' design

We considered four design specifications. The first is to design a system with which the user interacts with the content on an LCD using a book UI device to represent Hokusai's precise drawing under bright lighting conditions, enable the sharing of information among multiple users, and attract the interest of visitors near the exhibition.

The second is to assign the roles of the book UI device and the display device. The book UI device is a controller that operates the software. In addition, the book UI guides the reading experience based on user interest. The display device visualizes various operations, such as switching sketches, scaling, and providing additional information about sketches. We assign these roles to each device to avoid user confusion while appreciating the content.

The third is to set the basic manipulations of the book UI, i.e., "flipping pages" and "touching the touch-sign on paper" to mimic how a real book is read compared to the swipe and touch operations of a touch-panel UI.

The fourth is to reproduce the usability of a paper-based book while preserving the system's operational stability and robustness. In consideration of previous studies [7, 8, 9, 13], we adopted the following implementation methods: (1) a page-sensing function embedded in the book device that does not require radio frequency (RF) or camera-based recognition technologies to enhance the robustness of the UI; (2) a wiring and sensing-pad pattern on paper using a thin conductive film or conductive ink to retain the look and feel of a real book.

Additionally, our paper-based book UI system was named FLIPPIN'.

PROTOTYPE

System configuration

The exhibition-installation system was named *Flip and Touch the Hokusai Manga*. It comprises an 80-inch LCD (SHARP PN-H801: resolution, 3,840 × 2,160 pixels), a camera sensor (Microsoft Kinect v2), a PC (HP Z840) with the content application (developed with Unity 3D 5.3 in wireless communications) installed on its hard drive, and FLIPPIN' UI device (Figure 4). This device is operated by flipping pages or touching specified points on a page, and the input signals are sent to the content application. Then, the application displays enlarged images of sketches or guidance information. Simultaneously, to collect the log data, the users' behavior is recorded frame-by-frame using Kinect.

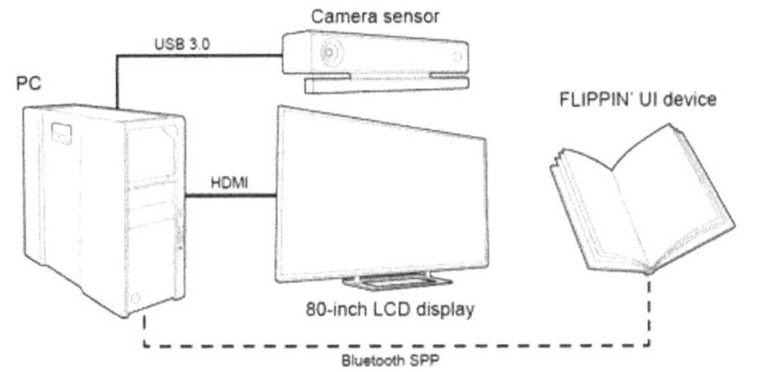

Figure 4. "Flip and Touch the Hokusai Manga" System Configuration.

FLIPPIN' UI device configuration

We implemented and bound FLIPPIN' UI device in the following way. Electronic components such as an Arduino microcontroller, a capacitance touch-sensor controller (MPR121 × 4), an accelerometer module, a Bluetooth module (RN-42), and a Li–Po battery were integrated into the inside of the face cover (Figure 5). Sensor pads and wiring patterns were printed on each page using conductive ink (Agic). For page detection, the sensor controllers detect the variation of capacitance as sensor pads come closer to each other, and the PC application determines whether the page opens or closes according to the resulting values.

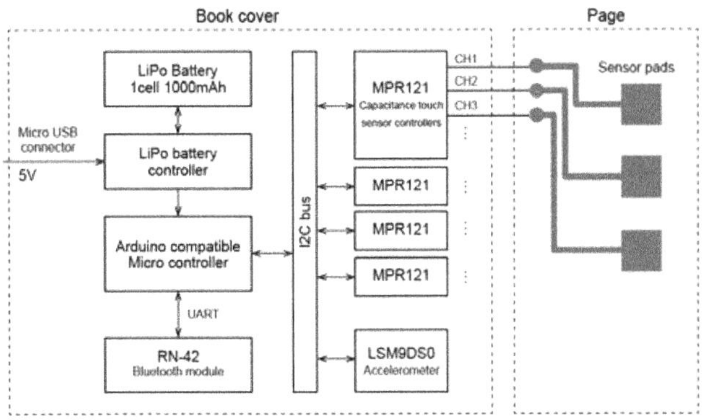

Figure5. "FLIPPIN'" System Configuration.

Each page has a dual-layer structure comprising a conductive-ink-dedicated paper for electronic wiring and a Japanese paper for printing content such that the electronic wiring pattern does not affect the content on the pages (Figure 6). The reason for using Japanese paper is to provide a soft, slightly rough feel similar to a real page of *the Hokusai Manga*. In this way, FLIPPIN' UI device was bound with 22 pages (Figure 1c).

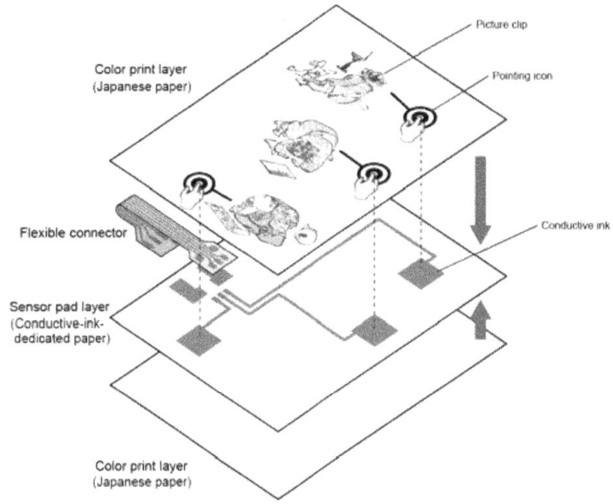

Figure 6. Wiring on a paper by conductive ink.

The content configuration

The content of *Flip and Touch the Hokusai Manga* comprises the following three sections. Section 1 offers commentary on how to operate the book, who Katsushika Hokusai was, and the nature of *the Hokusai Manga*. Section 2 presents the Manga (sketch) collection, which comprises 66 selected sketches classified into categories such as jobs, daily life, eating, and animals. Each category comprises 6 sketches in facing pages. The user turns a page of the Manga collection. Then, 8 or 10 sketches including 6 sketches printed on FLIPPIN' UI device are displayed on the large display in front of him/her. The user touches a pointing icon on the page. Then, the sketch is enlarged, animated with sound effects and additional information is presented on the display. Section 3 presents a quiz game in which silhouettes of images in the sketches are presented, and the user must match these to the corresponding sketch in Section 2.

Prototype 1

We created three prototypes with different design patterns to explore the design of a presentation installation using a book UI system.

In Prototype 1, the content on the display progresses with the content of the sections based on a preset time. Prototype 1 was designed so that users could experience all sections. In addition, we expected to gradually stimulate user interest according to the order of all sections.

The system flow of Prototype 1 is as follows (Figure 7). First, the user moves in front of the exhibition and a commentary movie about *the Hokusai Manga* is played automatically on the display. Second, FLIPPIN' UI device is picked up and an instructional video is played. Third, the Manga collection starts to play, and the user freely appreciates *the Hokusai Manga* for 2 minutes. Fourth, two silhouette-matching questions are asked in a quiz game.

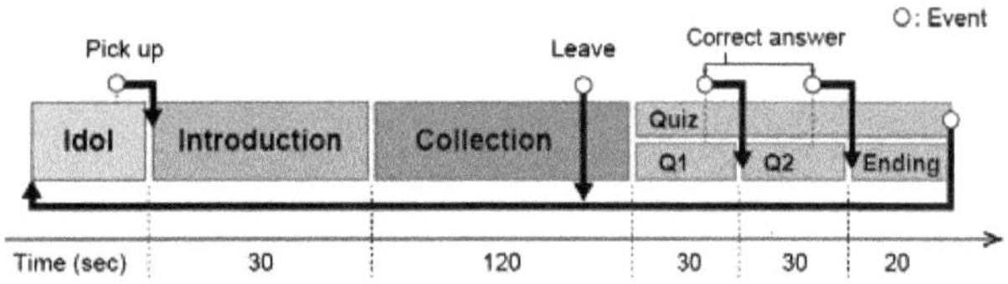

Figure 7. System flow of Prototype 1.

Prototype 2

Prototype 2 was designed so that users could access each section freely by turning pages to experience the content at their pace according to their interests, which was expected to encourage appreciation of the content.

The system flow of Prototype 2 is as follows (Figure 8). FLIPPIN' UI device in which the content is edited, including the commentary, Manga collection, and quiz sections, is picked up, and the title is shown on the display device. In the introduction section, the user reads the commentary on FLIPPIN' UI device. If the user touches a pointing icon in the commentary, additional information (such as Hokusai's chronology table and sketches) is displayed on the display device. In the collection section, in response to the user's turning of pages or touching of an icon, the categories of sketches is changed, and the selected sketch is enlarged and moved with additional information on the display. Furthermore, if the user turns the quiz section page and touches an icon, then a question appears on the display.

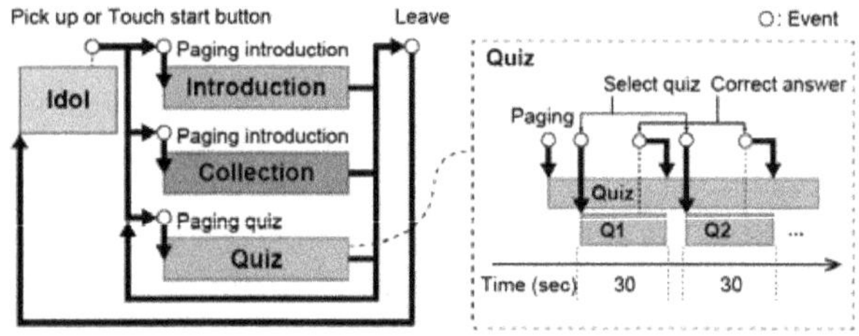

Figure 8. System flow of Prototypes 2 and 3.

Prototype 3

Prototype 3 was designed to compare the usability of physical paging using FLIPPIN' UI device and swipe paging using a touch-panel UI device (GeChic on-Lap, 15 inch) (Figure 9). We expected physical paging to be superior to swipe paging. The virtual book application installed on a PC (HP ZBook 15) for the touch-panel UI.

This virtual book was edited the same as that of the content of the book in Prototype 2. The system flow of Prototype 3 is shown in Figure 8. In Prototype 3, flipping and touching operation in Prototype 1 and 2 replaces swiping and touching operation on a touch-panel display.

Figure 9. Touch-panel UI device and Prototype 3 content.

EVALUATION

Method

Focused evaluation of FLIPPIN' was conducted on July 28 and 29, 2016; August 13 and 14, 2016; and September 3 and 4, 2016, at the Grand Front Osaka, ACTIVE Lab. The purpose of this evaluation was to evaluate general users' experiences of using FLIPPIN' (including the touch-panel UI system of Prototype 3) and to acquire design insights. We used the previously described three prototypes for this evaluation.

The subjects of this evaluation included all visitors who came to our booth at the ACTIVE Lab. They were not informed that they were participating in an evaluation during their experience of using FLIPPIN'; however, the people who were interviewed were made aware of their participation.

Two types of log data were acquired: the operational log of the users operating FLIPPIN' and the behavioral data obtained from the users around and within the booth. The first dataset includes the number of users, duration of their experience, number of paging, number of pointing, duration spent on each page, and duration spent on each section. The second dataset includes participation ratios. If a person entered a certain area and Kinect detected his/her body, the system counts the person as a user. Based on the number of recognized persons and the number of users as per the operative log data, the system calculates the ratio of participation.

We observed the users who had experienced FLIPPIN'. The method of observation was semi-constructive and included factors such as sex, external characteristics, age, behavior, facial expression, comments, the scale of watching between the main display and the book interface, and the scale of interest between the system and the contents. The same two persons observed the participants during the evaluation.

We obtained consent and conducted interviews with users who experienced FLIPPIN' for more than 1 minute. The interview method was semi-constructive and included several factors, such as age, occupation, nationality, knowledge of the content, proficiency with IT devices (e.g., tablets and smartphones), a detailed explanation about their behaviors, facial expressions and comments during the experience, negative and positive opinions about the UI and user experience, the ratio between focusing on the main display and the book interface, and changes in interest in the content before and after FLIPPIN' experience. Note that the same interviewer conducted all interviews.

The results of evaluation

In total, there were 161 users for Prototype 1, 242 for Prototype 2, and 183 for Prototype 3. We conducted observations for 41 groups and 84 users, 34 groups and 73 users, and 62 groups and 104 users for Prototype 1, 2, and 3, respectively and then interviewed 8 groups and 15 users, 10 groups and 21 users, and 4 groups and 8 users for Prototype 1, 2, and 3. In this case, a "group" means a unit of the users who simultaneously experienced FLIPPIN'.

Figure 10 compares the durations of experience for the three prototypes on the basis of their operative log data. The average experience-durations on Prototype 2 and 3 were 104.8 s and 89.7 s, respectively. Since Prototype 1 has a restriction upon the maximum duration of the experience, the comparison is only effective between Prototypes 2 and 3 in this case.

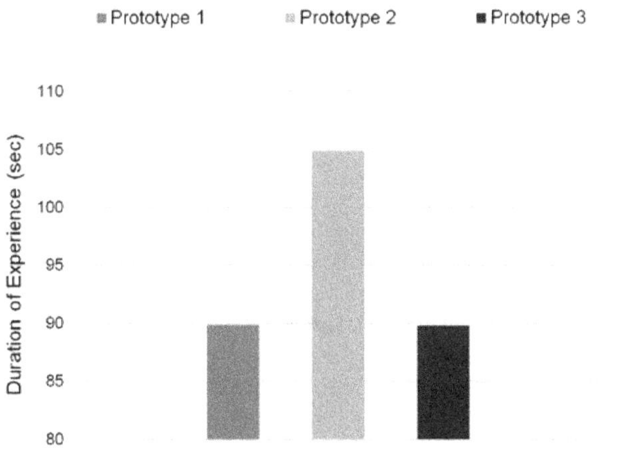

Figure 10. Comparison between experience duration for the three prototypes. [1]

Figure 11 compares the number of paging among the three prototypes. The average numbers of paging on Prototype 2 and 3 were 16 and 12.7, respectively. In addition, the average numbers of pointing on Prototype 2 and 3 were 18.6 and 10.8, respectively.

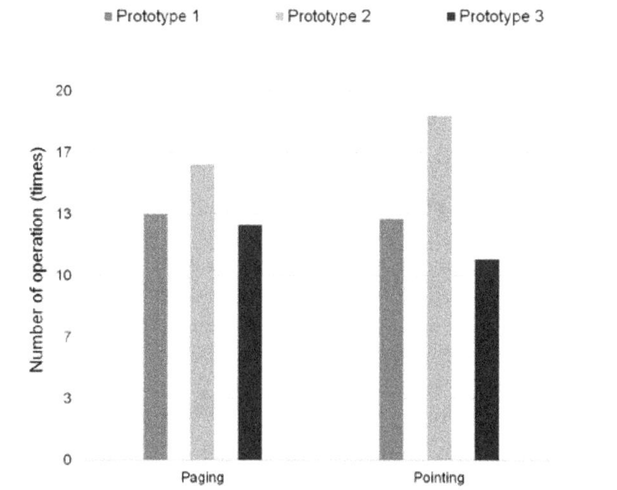

Figure 11. Comparison of the number of paging and pointing operations among the three prototypes. [2]

Table 1 compares the durations spent on examining each section of the three prototypes. For Prototype 1, the largest duration was spent on the introduction section on condition that this section automatically proceeds within 30 seconds, whereas for Prototype 2, the largest duration was spent on the collection section.

	Introduction (sec)	Collection (sec)	Quiz (sec)
Proto1	**26.5534732**	72.62271676	10.54081277
Proto2	9.82202276	**79.24832416**	**10.61679307**
Proto3	9.214661261	66.91787819	5.197089071

Table 1. Comparison of duration spent examining each section with the three prototypes.

We obtained four main concepts from our observations of the users.

Observation 1: "Smooth participation"
With each prototype, the users instantly touched the UI device, started operating the device, and understood how to operate it through actual operation.

Observation 2: "Multiuser cooperation"
With Prototypes 1 and 2, more users cooperated compared to Prototype 3. For example, a user was trying to look at

[1] Proto1-2: p=9E-09, Proto1-3: p=1.2E-05, Proto2-3: p= 0.0528 (F Test)

[2] Proto1-2: p= 2.12571E-05, Proto1-3: p= 1.0103E-14, Proto2-3: p= 0.00045 (F Test). Pointing, Proto1-2: p= 3.33067E-15, Proto1-3: p= 4.11815E-08, Proto2-3: p= 0.059994602 (F Test)

other pages while another user was reading a page on the book UI. This is related to the first design specification mentioned in FLIPPIN' design.

Observation 3: "Transition of interest from interface to content"
Prototype 1 and 2 users showed decreasing interest in the interface itself and mutual conversation within a few minutes of using the system. The main topic of conversation changed to interactions with contents, such as image scaling, animation, and sound effects. In particular, Prototype 2 user spent more talking about content than the users of the other two prototypes. This may be related to the third design specification in FLIPPIN' design. On the other hand, Prototype 3 users showed less interest in the content after they became accustomed to the interface.

Observation 4: "Easy comprehension of the content"
Most users attempted to comprehend the content at the beginning of their experience while they learned how to operate the system through actual operations. Prototype 1 and 2 users spent less time comprehending the content compared to Prototype 3 users, and many Prototype 3 users quit during their experience.

Implications

Repair and Robustness

The first version of FLIPPIN' UI device needed to be replaced every few days because the flexible connecter part became disconnected. The copper foil tape on the connecter part became disconnected after users had repeatedly opened and closed a page. This problem was solved by exchanging the copper foil tape with conductive cloth tape. Moreover, due to influence from the local radio environment, the wireless Bluetooth communication was sometimes disable. In addition, we selected a wired USB cable to enhance operational stability after one week.

Improvement of experience duration

The interface increased the experience duration of users in the public space. Figure 10 shows that Prototype 3 had lower experience duration than Prototype 2. This was because touch panels and tablets are already widely used, and the users were uninterested in the proposed interface. Thus, long durations could not be maintained unless the users were interested in the content.

Improvement of interest in content

The interface increased user interest in the content. Through interviews, it was found that 11 users out of the 10 groups and 21 people observed with Prototype 2 commented that interest in the content had improved. List.1 shows typical examples of user comments. Note that only one user out of the four groups and eight people observed with Prototype 3 gave similar comments.

"Yes, I think that it was easier to get interested in the contents in comparison to reading a normal book. Indeed, I pushed them, and then some characters were animated. This is why I feel it was easier to understand or somehow more attractive." (20's/female/student)

"I got a feeling that I'd like to see other paintings as well as the contents, and I feel that I want to experience it again." (40's/female/housewife)

"Touching the contents made me feel more interested than just looking at them." (40's/male/manufacturing industry)

List.1: Examples of improvement in interest toward the contents displayed through the novel interface.

Figure 11 shows that Prototype 2 had the largest numbers of paging and pointing. This result supports the idea that the novel interface increases users' interest in the content.

User-experience design to encourage social interaction

All the prototypes prompted social interaction in cases where multiple users played the game. For example, the following phenomena were observed:

A user pointed out a character in the Manga collection section, and another user left comments about it.

A user was in charge of paging, and another user was in charge of pointing.

Based on these findings, if a specific function and user experience could be designed for multiple users, their satisfaction could be further increased.

Scenario design based on the interests of the users

Prototype 1 adopted a single-thread scenario that showed the introduction section to the users via the main display, presented the Manga collection section for 2 min, and then automatically moved to the quiz section. As a result of interviews and observations, the users who were interested in the book interface tended to miss the introduction section because they had to see two different areas, namely, the main display and the book interface. Additionally, the users who were interested in the content had to stop their experience because the collection stopped after 2 min. Some users attempted to replay the content two or three times after the quiz section.

Based on these results, Prototype 2 adopted a multithread scenario that showed the introduction section to the users via the book interface, thereby allowing users to freely experience the introduction, collection, and quiz sections. As a result of this update, the average experience-duration on Prototype 3 increased by about 15 s than the experience-duration on Prototype 1. However, the users of Prototype 1 and 3 watched the introduction section for about 26 s and 9 s, respectively, on an average.

Thus, we concluded that the best scenario is a hybrid one that shows the introduction section first and then allows users to freely experience the collection and quiz sections. In this case, the system should have a function to skip the introduction section for users who would repeatedly experience the system. In addition, the book interface shows an alert for the users to look at the main display during the introduction section; this will avoid the problem of users missing this section.

DISCUSSION

In this section, based on our evaluation results, we discuss how an information system using FLIPPIN' could solve the three issues described previously.

Issue 1. How easily can UI devices be accessed or used by all visitors.

With respect to this issue, we presume that FLIPPIN', which employed in Prototype 2, changed the quality of usability. From user observation 1, "Smooth participation," users showed a tendency to immediately begin exploring operation methods while actually handling the system with all prototypes. However, in consideration of the experience duration (Figure 10), the number of operations (Figure 11), and the implication that duration experience was improved by the interface, it can be assumed that Prototype 2 encouraged users to continue interacting with the system.

Issue 2. How the system stimulates user interest via content.

From the implications that the interface contributes to improvements, Prototype 1 and 2 could improve user interest in the content. All the prototypes influenced to encourage the users to have conversations among them and to stimulate their interest. It is considered that both the UI device and a large display make it easier to share the content. Furthermore, in consideration of observation 2, "Multiuser cooperation," it was easier to share the UI device with Prototypes 1 and 2 compared to Prototype 3.

On the other hand, from a hypothetical perspective, FLIPPIN' could help build an interaction mental model. We assume that phenomena associated with observation 3, "Transition of interest from interface to content," were caused by immediately building an interaction mental model because turning pages is directly related to progressing through the content. In contrast, when reading an e-book using a touch-panel display, he/she could not automatically operate the system and focus on the content.

Issue 3. How digital systems are designed to solve the reading usability problem.

The exhibition design using FLIPPIN' has suggested clues to solve the reading usability problem of digital information systems in public spaces. This is supported by observations 2 and 4, i.e., "Multiuser cooperation" and "Easy comprehension of the content." The phenomenon was derived by a physical book interaction, and it demonstrated the superiority of FLIPPIN'.

From the above mentioned section, we presume that FLIPPIN' improved three issues. In particular, the novelty and the usability derived from a physical book interaction provided a positive effect on our information system. However, this does not mean that our system sufficiently solves the reading usability problem because it has some limitations, such as the number of pages and unchangeable content, compared to existing digital devices.

CONCLUSION

Here, based on the evaluation results and the stated implications, we formulate design guidelines for information systems using a paper-based book UI in public spaces. In particular, the guidelines will help designers and engineers guide to design an interactive information system that has the limitations and needs as the same as that of ACTIVE Lab where we conducted the evaluation.

The design guidelines are divided into two categories.

Paper-based book UI device design:

1. Mimicking real books.

Users tended to recognize a paper-based book UI device as a novel device. In public spaces, novelty is an important factor that encourages users to use information systems. For practical application, it is even more important to mimic the look, feel, and usability of a real book in order to provide users novelty. To realize a novel device, FLIPPIN indicated the effective implementation method of combining usability of a real book and digital technologies with robustness.

2. Paper-based book UIs should allow simultaneous users.

This is related to the implication, "User-experience design to encourage social interaction" and observation 2, "Multiuser cooperation" in evaluation section. The interaction affordance of book encourages to immediately build user's interaction mental model and to share the operation method and the content.

3. Paper-based book UIs should be edited to be able to read from anywhere based on user's interest.

This is related to the implication, "Scenario design based on the interests of the users", and our observation that Prototype 2 is superior to Prototype 1. Prototype 2 is edited so that users could access each section freely based on their interest. We observed that some users began with the quiz section, and then continued to enjoy the collection section.

Content design:

1. Content progression should not be limited by preset times.

Content progression with preset time leads to user frustration. As mentioned in the implication, "Scenario design based on the interests of the users", with Prototype 1, users who were attracted to *the Hokusai Manga* were forced to stop viewing after a predetermined duration, and some users restarted and continued their appreciation.

2. It is desirable that explanatory information is presented as the feedbacks from user's operation.

Users tended to not read the introduction section that the explanatory information is written nearly 150 words in terms of English, in Prototype 2. On the other hand, from the user interviews, the users indicated that more comments are required when enlarging a sketch. From the findings, it is inferred that even if explanatory information is provided for users in a public space, the active reading is encouraged by easy input operation and immediate feedbacks based on the user's interest.

3. The easiness of creating system image should be leveraged for the instruction.
In all prototypes, most users immediately understood the system's operations when first handling the device. In such systems, an easily understood and effective system image should be created. We observed the tendency of disturbing the handling by a one-sided interaction such as 30-seconds instructional video of Prototype 1. Therefore, the instruction description of the operation should be kept to a minimum.

4. Device roles should be clearly identified.
In this study, users were sometimes unable to decide whether to look the book content or the display content. Thus, more specific device roles are required for such systems. For example, Figueiredo et al. attempted to guide the user's visual line by identifying the role of each device by synchronizing the contents of book and display device according to these positions [13].

The present study has demonstrated the practicality of the interactive information system with our paper-based book UI, FLIPPIN', through a field evaluation. In addition, design guidelines for interactive information systems in public spaces have been suggested. FLIPPIN' allows easy access to information by mimicking the look, feel, and usability of traditional books with robustness and arouses interest in content through social interactions. If the technical limitations of producing paper-based book UIs are solved in future, such interactive information systems could become convenient alternatives to actual paper guidebooks or pamphlets in public spaces.

ACKNOWLEDGEMENTS
We would like to thank all the participants, Mitsuru Uragami of the Uragami Sokyudo, Naruo Shigeta, Kazuaki Morisawa, Yuichi Uchiyama of Toppan Printing Co., Ltd. and The Grand Front Osaka, the Knowledge Capital, ACTIVE Lab.

REFERENCES
1. Marshall, C. and Bly, S. Turning the page on navigation. In Proc. ACM/IEEE Joint Conference on Digital Libraries, ACM Press (2005), 225–234. https://dx.doi.org/10.1145/1065385.1065438
2. Rosner, D. K., Oehlberg, L., and Ryokai, K. 2008. Studying paper use to inform the design of personal and portable technology. In Extended Abstracts of CHI'08. Work In Progress Submission. ACM Press (2008), 3405-3410. https://dx.doi.org/10.1145/1358628.1358865
3. Watanabe, J., Mochizuki, A., and Horry, Y. Bookisheet: Bendable device for browsing content using the metaphor of leafing through the pages. In Proc. Ubicomp 2008, ACM Press (2008), 360–369. https://dx.doi.org/10.1145/1409635.1409684
4. O'Hara, K., and Sellen, A. A comparison of reading paper and on-line documents. In Proc. CHI '97, ACM Press (1997), 335-342. https://dx.doi.org/10.1145/258549.258787
5. Liesaputra,V and Witten, I. H. Seeking Information in Realistic Books: A user study. In Proc. Joint Conf. of Digital Libraries (2008), 29-38. http://dx.doi.org/10.1145/1378889.1378896
6. Freed, N, Qi, J, Sylla, C, and Branco, P. Beyond the binding: exploring the future book. In Proc. C&C '11, ACM Press (2011), 445-446. https://dx.doi.org/10.1145/2069618.2069742
7. Qi, J and Buechley, L. Sketching in circuits: designing and building electronics on paper. In Proc. CHI '14, ACM Press (2014), 1713-1722. https://dx.doi.org/10.1145/2556288.2557391
8. Zhao, Y., Qin, Y., Liu, Y., Liu, S. and Shi, Y. QOOK: A New Physical-Virtual Coupling Experience for ActiveReading. In Proc. UIST 2013 Adjunct, ACM Press (2013), 5-6. https://dx.doi.org/10.1145/2508468.2514928
9. Back, M., Cohen, J., Gold, R., Harrison, S., Minneman, S. Listen Reader: An Electronically Augmented Paper-Based Book, In Proc. CHI '01, ACM Press (2001), 23-29. https://dx.doi.org/10.1145/365024.365031
10. Thorn, E., Rennick-Egglestone, S., Koleva, B.,Preston, W., Benford, S., Quinn, A and Mortier, R, Exploring Large-Scale Interactive Public Illustrations, In Proc. DIS 2016, the ACM conference on Designing Interactive Systems, ACM(2016). 17-27. https://dx.doi.org/10.1145/2901790.2901826
11. Grasset, R., Dünser, A., Billinghurst, M. & Seichter, H. The Mixed-Reality Book: A New Multimedia Reading Experience. In Proc. CHI '07 Extended Abstracts on Human Factors in Computing Systems, ACM Press (2007), 1953 - 1958. https://dx.doi.org/10.1145/1240866.1240931
12. Grasset, R., Dünser, A., and Billinghurst, M. Edutainment with a mixed reality book: a visually augmented illustrative children's book. In Proc. of the 2008 Intl. Conf. on Advances in Comp. Entertainment Tech. ACM Press (2008). 292-295. https://dx.doi.org/10.1145/1501750.1501819
13. Qi, J and Buechley, L. Electronic popables: exploring paper-based computing through an interactive pop-up book. In TEI '10. ACM Press (2010). 121–128. https://doi.org/10.1145/1709886.1709909
14. Li, H., Brockmeyer, E., Carter, E.J., Fromm, J., Hudson, S.E., Patel, S.N., Sample, A. (2016). PaperID:

A technique for drawing functional battery-free wireless interfaces on paper. In Proc. CHI'16, ACM Press (2016), 5885-5896. https://dx.doi.org/10.1145/2858036.2858249

15. Yamada, H. SequenceBook: Interactive Paper Book Capable of Changing the Storylines by Shuffling Pages. Ext. Abstracts CHI 2010, ACM Press (2010), 4375-4380. https://doi.org/10.1145/1753846.1754156
16. Dumesny, J. Tomitsc, M. Reconciling Paper and Tablets: Interaction Mappings for Linking Physical Information with Digital Documents, In Proc. OzCHI 2014, ACM Press (2014), 184-193. https://dx.doi.org/10.1145/2686612.2686641
17. Schafer,G. Green, K. Walker, I. Fullerton, S. Lewis, E. An Interactive, Cyber-Physical Read-Aloud Environment: Results and Lessons from an Evaluation Activity with Children and their Teachers. In Proc. DIS 2014, the ACM conference on Designing Interactive Systems, ACM Press (2014), 865-874. https://dx.doi.org/10.1145/2598510.2598562
18. Wijnen, J. and van den Hoven, E. Connected Sketchbook: Linking Digital Files to Physical Pages. In Proc. DESIRE 2011, ACM Press (2011), 43-46. http://dx.doi.org/10.1145/2079216.2079221
19. Figueiredo, A. C., Pinto, A. L., Branco, P., Zagalo, N., and Coquet, E. Bridging book: a not-so-electronic children's picturebook. In Proc. IDC '13. ACM Press (2013), 569- 572. https://dx.doi.org/10.1145/2485760.2485867
20. The Grand Front Osaka, the Knowledge Capital, ACTIVE Lab. https://kc-i.jp/en/facilities/the-lab/active-lab/

Designing Interactive Advertisements for Public Displays

Hasibullah Sahibzada, Eva Hornecker, Florian Echtler, Patrick Tobias Fischer
Bauhaus-Universität Weimar, Bauhausstr. 11, 99423 Weimar, Germany
first.middle.lastname@uni-weimar.de

ABSTRACT
Although public displays are increasingly being deployed in everyday situations, they are still mostly used as auto-active information sources. Adding interactivity can help to attract and engage users. We report on the design and in-the-wild evaluation of an interactive advert for a public display in a tourist information center. We evaluate and compare 3 different variants – non-interactive, interaction using body tracking, and interaction using personal mobile devices – with respect to attracting the attention and interaction from passersby. We further compare these variants with an iterated version of the body tracking system with an extended tracking area. Our findings include an unexpected reluctance of passersby to use their mobile device in public, and the increased interactive area for body interaction resulting in increased engagement and spontaneous multi-user interaction, while removing the so-called 'landing effect'. Based on our findings, we suggest guidelines for interactive adverts on public displays.

ACM Classification Keywords
H.5.m. Information Interfaces and Presentation (e.g. HCI): Miscellaneous

Author Keywords
public display; advertisements; full-body interaction; mobile devices; Kinect; in-the-wild study

INTRODUCTION
Traditional advertisements present content in a static form (posters) or as linear video, passively exposing the consumer to product information [5]. But people tend to ignore adverts and public displays [7, 21, 16]. Interactive adverts hold the potential to increase attractiveness and attention levels [15, 2]. Both body/gesture-based interaction and mobile phone-based input [21, 22, 27, 24] have been suggested as suitable modalities, but it is not clear which is most effective, in particular for a public situation, and how to optimize attraction levels and ease of use.

Our research investigates how interactive elements can increase attraction of adverts, how to increase the attention levels of passersby and how to motivate users to engage in subsequent stages of interaction, from first attention over implicit and explicit interaction to follow-up action. Our interactive advert promotes the Bauhaus walks, a guided tour by students from our university of its historical buildings in the town. The tour is currently taken by around 5000 visitors per year. The core idea of the advert is that users move across a map of the town and trigger short information snippets on top of historic sites. They have a time window in which to explore 5 sites, and then are shown a brief video providing information on when and where to find the walks. We developed 4 system variants in a user-centered design process in collaboration with the Bauhaus walk guides and deployed and evaluated these in our local tourist information center.

CHI 2017, May 06 - 11, 2017, Denver, CO, USA

ISBN 978-1-4503-4655-9/17/05...$15.00
DOI: http://dx.doi.org/10.1145/3025453.3025531

Figure 1. Hardware setup in field study at tourist information center.

We compare a non-interactive advert (a video showing the same information as the other versions) serving as baseline, with a Kinect-based version where users' body movements are translated into their silhouette moving across the map, and a mobile interaction version where users use their phone as controller to navigate across the map. In addition, we developed and deployed a second version of the body interaction system with an extended tracking angle. These 4 versions were evaluated in a field study in the Weimar tourist information office where they were deployed for 5 days each, respectively 3 days for the second body interaction version. We evaluated for commonly used measures of success of adverts and pervasive displays, such as the number of glances received, the number of people taking attention and interacting, the overall length of engagement, and how many people transitioned from each stage of engagement to the next [23, 4, 19, 24, 27].

Our study revealed that for our specific design decisions and application scenario, the mobile phone interaction mode was

Figure 2. Screenshots of the non-interactive advert with start screen, map, pictures of sites appearing over the map and final information on the walks.

not successful, creating too large a threshold for interaction for our context and user population. We demonstrate the utility of a silhouette display in a multi-user scenario and explore how to increase its effectiveness. Extending the tracking angle of our display removed the landing effect and resulted in higher attention rates. Our observations further show that advert content needs to be tightly integrated into the interaction process in order to be taken notice of and that a match between content and interaction mode supports this.

RELATED WORK

When pervasive computing technology is used for advertisement, this is termed *pervasive advertisement* [18]. Examples include Bluescreen [26], which selects and displays ads on detecting users and allows them to choose and manipulate content by positioning themselves to the display, and the Prospero project [9]. Many auto-active digital displays are already used by the advertisement industry and increasingly, companies experiment with interactive adverts, such as games where players can win a coupon [11], or awareness campaigns [12].

A well known issue is display blindness; people tend to ignore advertisements [7, 21]. Huang et al [16] found that many factors, such as display position, eye-catching content, and size influence this along with viewers' expectations. People often intentionally ignore displays [16, 21] because of information overload, as they expect only uninteresting content. Interactive ads hold the potential to increase attractiveness, attention levels and recall [15, 2]. More research is needed on which interaction modalities are best. Direct feedback on body movement has been found effective for prompting attention and interaction [20, 24]. But more (physically demanding) movement can negatively influence recall from large interactive screens, and non-interactive screens sometimes even outperform interactive scenarios [23]. She et al [27] argue for the effectiveness of smart mobile devices, as they enable personal and discrete interaction, sharing and storing of information, and can be used from a distance. While studies of mobile interaction with public screen adverts have shown that users like this [30, 22], these tend to be proof of concept and to use an experimental study setup, even when run in 'real' locations. The question thus remains whether mobile input is effective in-the-wild.

A common measure in public display research for how much attention a display garners is the number of glances from passersby who turn their head towards the display [14, 16, 21] in relation to how many ignore it. Advertisers are interested in the conversation rate (conation step [27]), that is, how many viewers take the intended follow-up action. With internet ads, this can be automatically tracked via cookies and logfiles, but for public displays it is much harder to discern. A common approach to model effectiveness of advertisement is the *conversion funnel* [4]. This begins with viewer's attention, as higher attention benefits the recall of factual content of ads [15, 25] and is seen as first phase of engagement. Attention then leads to interest and motivation, desire (e.g. to own the product) and finally action (buy it) [13]. The funnel metaphor indicates that at each step less people continue.

In research on public displays, various models of the user interaction process can be found. Besides of Vogel's [28] zones of interaction model (ambient display, implicit, subtle and personal interaction) and Brignull and Roger's [6] interaction phase model (from peripheral over focal awareness to participation and direct interaction) the most relevant for our work is Müller et al's [19] *audience funnel* model. It relates to the *conversion funnel*, as its first phase is attention, where passersby notice the display, react to it, and become motivated to interact. The audience funnel model assumes a reactive display that draws people in via subtle indirect interactions (e.g. reacting to users' proximity to the display) before they engage in direct (e.g. touch) interaction. Once a user interacts, others might join, and finally they leave and might engage in follow-up actions. Effectiveness of public displays is measured via several factors, including how many passersby glance at the display [14, 16, 21], how many started interacting [20, 14], and for how long they engaged.

In our analysis, we build on the conversion funnel model, and adapt this to the behavior we can reliably observe, taking inspiration from the audience funnel model. This concerns indicators of interest and viewers' involvement in terms of them interacting with the advert and its content.

SYSTEM DESCRIPTION

Our system was installed in the local tourist information center. Its main components in the final iteration are a 32 inch screen, situated at eye level (~1.60 m) on a counter next to the central info desk (see figure 1), and three Kinect cameras arranged below the screen to detect and track people. Both components are connected to a Windows 10 computer and a local WiFi network used in the mobile condition (described below).

The non-interactive version of the advert (see figure 2) shows the start screen (without a call-to-action), followed by a map of Weimar with blinking dots on selected points of interest. Pictures of these locations are successively shown as miniatures on the map, followed by a short video giving information on the walks and how to participate.

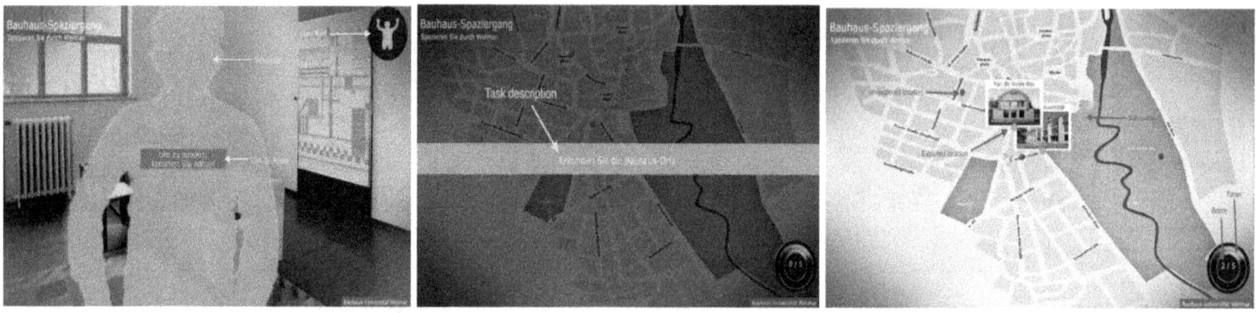

Figure 3. The body interaction initial attention grabbing phase with the 'come closer to play' prompt then transitions to the map game interface with instructions while scaling down the silhouette. Users need to walk around in front of the screen to move their silhouette around the map.

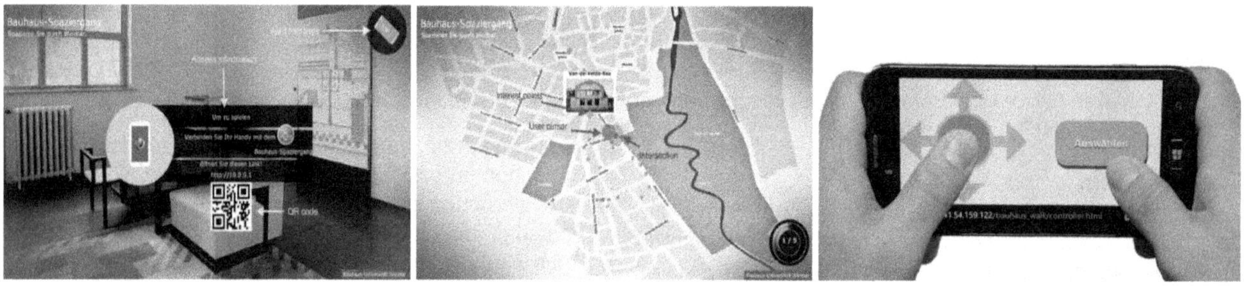

Figure 4. Initial Screen for the Mobile Interaction Modality (here, silhouette feedback is provided), Map Interface and Mobile Controller Interface.

For the interactive versions, the same pictures are revealed on the map (with name tag and short description) when their location is hit by the user. For each round of interaction, 5 locations are selected at random (as incentive for further exploration) and indicated by colored dots on the map. Once all locations are explored, the final information video is shown.

Body Interaction

The initial iteration of the body interaction variant used only a single, front-facing Kinect camera. When people pass by the screen, their silhouette is shown as an overlay on the start screen (a strategy found effective in previous work [20, 24, 30]) and the *call-to-action* prompt says 'to play come closer' (see figure 3 left). In addition, in the top right corner an alert icon appears if the user moves out of camera range. The system can detect up to 7 people and project their silhouettes, each in a different colour.

While people are far away or in the non-central area of the tracking range, this corresponds to the 'implicit interaction' phase of the audience funnel model [19]. Once they enter the central area and face the display (so they can read the call-to-action), they enter the subtle interaction phase. If they are near the screen for more than 3 seconds, the system transitions to the map interface and scales the silhouettes down to fit with the map, while fading the map in over the previous image (figure 3). Users can move around in front of the screen to navigate their silhouettes on the map, and a point of interest is activated by contact with any part of a silhouette. Interaction finishes once all five points of interest are explored or a 40 second timer runs out. To emphasize the gaming aspect, a progress icon in one corner displays this information (n/5 and a timer running down). Finally, the information video advert is shown.

Mobile Interaction

The mobile variant also uses the silhouette representation on the start screen to attract attention and then guides the user to use their phone as controller. While technologies such as Bluetooth and NFC may be utilized to attract attention, these are not yet supported by a majority of devices (or might not be switched on). We thus sought to maximize the reach of this attention-grabbing phase using the silhouette representation.

In this variant, the call-to-action instructs the user to connect to the local WiFi network and open a specific website shown as a QR code (see figure 4 left). Once the user has connected via the QR code (or typed in the IP address) and turned their phone into landscape mode as instructed, the interface transitions, representing the users' cursors with differently coloured circles on the map. The interface on the mobile is a simple HTML5 page which displays a cursor that can be moved around to navigate the map and a select button. The mobile interface uses WebSockets to ensure low latency for interaction and is based on the MMM framework by Weissker et al. [29].

Body Interaction with Wide Angle of Tracking

Based on observations from the first phase of in-situ evaluation and an initial analysis of data, an improved version of the body interaction system was developed that aimed to increase the attention and interaction levels. We had observed that people often walked past the screen due to its positioning alongside a path of travel (cf. figure 7) and were often distracted by the book desk opposite (turning their head away) or looked straight onward. Consequently, when the screen lay still in their field

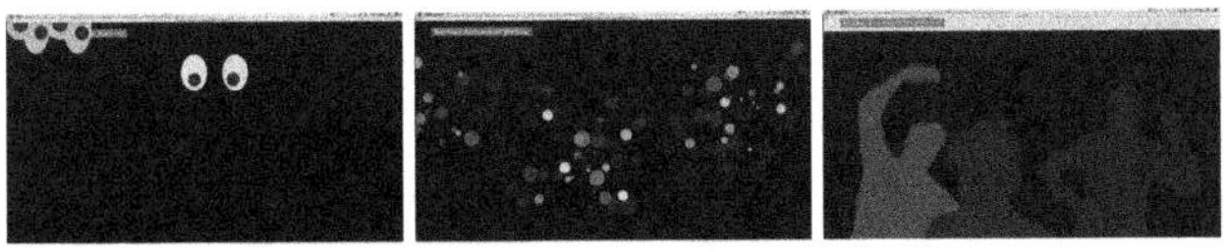

Figure 5. Following eyes, fireworks animation and silhouette representation for the initial 'attention grabbing' study.

of view, they had not yet entered the Kinect's tracking area (and thus received no visual feedback).

The main impetus of our design iteration was thus to increase the angle of view. We accomplished this by using two additional Kinect cameras facing at an angle outwards. As we relied on the standard Kinect data interpretation toolkit (Microsoft SDK), data from each camera is interpreted individually, i.e. not merged into a single tracking space. As it would have been confusing to have silhouettes switch colour when passing a tracking boundary, we used only a single colour for all silhouettes. All other interactions with the system were the same as in the initial body interaction variant.

THE SYSTEM DESIGN PROCESS

Our system design is based on an iterative user-centered design process and insights from the literature. The idea for the advertisement was developed in a co-design process with guides from the Bauhaus Walks and the system design was iterated with repeated user tests of prototypes.

Pre-Study

We compared 3 simple visualizations (figure 5) that react to people's proximity (Kinect-based tracking) to determine the best attention-grabber for our advert. Whenever a person is detected, (1) a pair of eyeballs appears on-screen and follows the person, (2) coloured animated fireworks appear at their rough location, (3) a coloured silhouette appears (similar to [20], who found this to be more effective as representation of the users' body than an abstract avatar or video image). For our study, we utilized a 14" screen installed above eye level in the entrance area of our university canteen that shows local adverts. As baseline we used a static advert shown by default.

Over four days, for 2 hours each, the visualisations were shown and one person counted glances of passersby. Only 7.6 % looked at the traditional advert (9 out of 118 passersby) whereas the silhouette attracted 15.82 % glances (from 139 passersby). The following eyes were less effective (12.98 %) followed by fireworks (10.1 %). A X^2 test revealed that the silhouette attracts significantly more glances than the non-interactive display (X^2, (1, N=257)=4.046, $p < .05$ (p=.04)). No significant difference was found for the other visualisations. This confirmed the effectiveness of a silhouette display for attracting attention compared to more abstract representations.

Focus Groups and Iterative Development

We ran two focus group sessions with Bauhaus Walk guides, one to determine the target group and develop initial ideas, and one for feedback on two alternative designs that had emerged (moving Bauhaus-design chess pieces and walking across a map). The map idea was considered more suitable for the

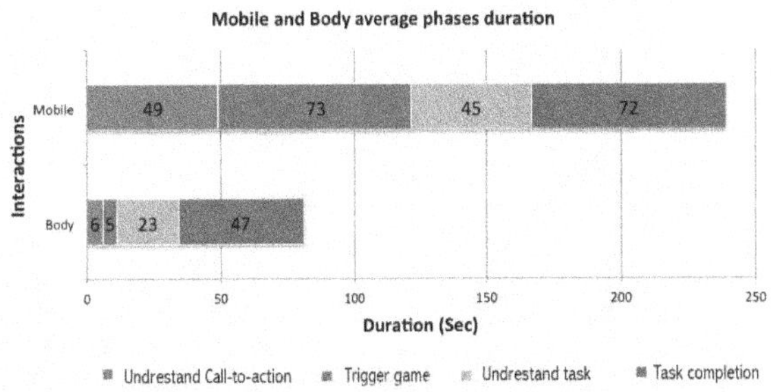

Figure 6. Comparison of body and mobile interaction duration for each phase in the high fidelity prototype evaluation study.

advert content of a guided walk and easier to understand. Participants further suggested that the advert should allow for multi-user interaction (also considered important in the literature on interactive adverts [27]).

An early paper prototype was tested (for mobile and silhouette-body) with 5 participants in WOz manner, with a researcher moving a paper body silhouette across a display in response to participant actions. This resulted in design changes and simplifications. This test indicated difficulties for mobile interaction, e.g. understanding that one needs to scan a QR code to get started, and to turn the phone into landscape mode. It further appeared not to be as 'natural' to move around a map (on a 2nd display) by navigating with the finger across a screen.

A functional prototype of both interface versions was tested with 12 participants using a think-aloud approach. We investigated how long each phase of interaction took (understanding the 'call-to-action' screen, getting started, understanding the map navigation task, and the interaction itself) (figure 6). This user test revealed that mobile interaction overall took about 3 times as long, mostly due to understanding what to do and managing to start the game. All phases of interaction took much longer, including map navigation (on average 72 seconds in the mobile modality versus 47 with body interaction). Participants took 6 seconds to react to the call-to-action in the body interaction modality, but 49 seconds for mobile interaction. Comments from participants indicated that seeing their own body represented on the map provided a strong clue of 'walking' that made it easy to grasp the interaction method. Some participants suggested that movement interaction might be too embarrassing in public, and that mobile phone interaction would be better suited, even though most preferred the body interaction system. This test resulted in further iteration of the system design, in particular, simplifying the start phase of the mobile version.

IN-SITU EVALUATION

The final system was evaluated in-the-wild, in the Weimar tourist information center. As baseline condition, the non-interactive advert consisting of a video provided the same information as could be gained from the interactive version. The non-interactive, body interaction and mobile version were deployed for five days each in three consecutive weeks. The improved, wide-angle version of the body interaction system was deployed for three days, a few weeks later.

Figure 7. Setup in our tourist information center, with the display at the right hand side next to the information counter.

All four versions of the advert system were deployed at the exact same location and without any changes to the surroundings. Figure 7 shows the setup of our installation in the tourist center. The building entrance is just visible at the top right end of the photo. Visitors first pass by the counter, which is shaped as a half circle. Two tables with books surround the counter. Our display was placed on a desk in the adjacent space to the counter, which opens up to a larger open area (at bottom of photo). The 32 inch screen was set up at eye level (~1.60 m). Visitor levels were fairly consistent over the entire time period. From our observations, around 60 % of passersby were elderly and 15 % children.

Data Collection and Measures

In the context of our project, it was logistically not feasible to measure the actual conversion rate, which would have required questioning all participants of the Bauhaus walks in the weeks following the in-situ deployments and identifying which system condition they had been exposed to. Therefore, we limit our study to the initial phases of the conversion funnel, i.e. attention (or attraction and awareness [27]) and further engagement with the advert.

A researcher spent 2 hours of in-situ observation on each day of observation and manually counted people glancing at the display (turning head towards the display for up to 3 seconds) vs. the number of people who ignore it.

In addition, we analysed the Kinect depth data recorded over the entire deployment. Due to space and processing limitations, only a 2D colored silhouette image was stored once per second. These images were analysed alongside logfiles (which provide accurate time stamps). This data was analysed by one of the authors and three people trained to count our measures of engagement. We measured engagement as defined by attention paid (stopping in front of the display for at least 3 seconds) and overall engagement duration, based on the Kinect data. We further measured the number and duration of interactions, also based on Kinect data, as well as how many people viewed the final video advert (the first step of conation [27]). From the Kinect silhouette images we further identified incidences of the honeypot effect (where interacting people attract bystanders who later also want to interact, creating a social buzz) [6] and landing effects [20], where a person passes by the display and, having noticed the interactive response after passing, walks back to explore this.

Furthermore, a researcher took notes of passersby behaviour for 2 hours per day. In addition, we interviewed a subset of people after they interacted with the display or watched the non-interactive video version. These interviews were audio recorded and transcribed.

Due to our design iteration, there are two phases of data collection. The first phase covers one week each for the non-interactive, mobile and body-interaction prototype. This enables us to compare our measures over an identical number of hours and days across these 3 conditions. The second phase of data collection is based on 3 days of deployment of the second wide-angle body interaction prototype. Besides of using an identical setup, we were lucky for the weather to be very similar on these days.

FINDINGS

In the following, we first focus on quantitative measures related to the conversion funnel, i.e. glances, attention and interaction, and the number of honeypot effect and landing incidences. Then we discuss further findings.

We ran statistical tests based on the manual counting of passersby in the Kinect image data to verify that the number of overall passersby for each interface condition was similar, in order to compare between conditions for interface effects. In the first study phase, 1031 people passed the non-interactive prototype, 995 went past the body interaction system and 852 passed the mobile interaction version (this is much higher than the average numbers of participants for lab and field studies reported in Alt et al's survey [3]). An ANOVA revealed no significant difference (F2,5)=0.8873, p>0.05 (p=0.437). We calculated the η^2 effect size index for this to be 0.18 (18 % difference in number of passersby). For the second stage of analysis, data from three days of deployment (the same weekdays) each was considered, resulting in lower overall numbers (629 for non-interactive, 597 for body interaction, and 679 for the iterated body interaction version). An ANOVA revealed no significant difference ((F2,3)=0.1449, p=0.868).

Comparison of Glance Counts

Based on our manual in-situ count (2 hours on 5 days each), 71.17% (274 of 385 passersby) ignored the non-interactive advert display (cp. figure 8), and only 28.83% glanced at it, whereas 34% glanced at the mobile interaction version (from 237) and 41.4% glanced at the body interaction version (106 of 256 passersby). A X^2 test reveals a difference between conditions (X^2(2, N=878)=10.863, p < .05 (p=0.4376)).

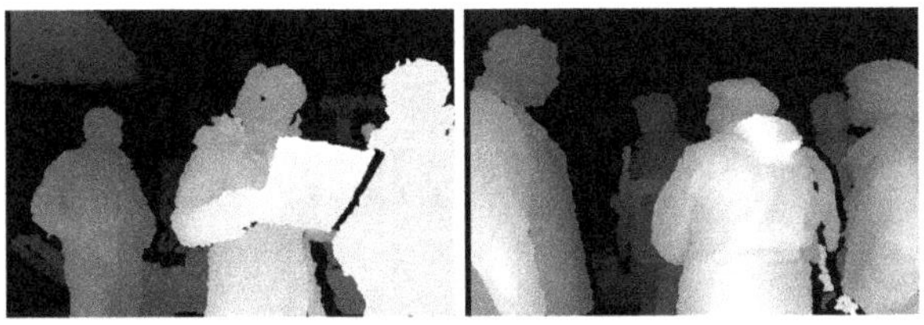

Figure 8. Display Blindness at the non-interactive version.

A pair-wise comparison reveals a significant difference between the body interaction and the non-interactive version (X^2(N=641)=10.863, p < .05 (p=.00437)), but none between mobile and non-interactive or body interaction version.

We furthermore compared the number of glances at the non-interactive and the body interaction adverts with glances manually counted over three days deployment of the wide-angle body interaction version. From 225 passersby for this iterated version, 51,11% (115) glanced at the display. The number of glances thus increased by almost 10% compared to the first body interaction version This difference is statistically significant (X^2(1, N=481)=4.5413, p < .05 (p=.033086)). Moreover, the wide-angle body system increased attention in terms of glances highly significantly compared to the non-interactive version (X^2(1, N=610)=30.2247, p < .001 (p=.0)).

Comparison of Engagement and Interaction Measures

Our measures of engagement and interaction are related to the conversion funnel discussed earlier. Here, we aim to study the conversion rate between each level of engagement with the display (engage/attention, interaction, viewing video). Since the manual glance count was only done for 2 hours each day, we here rely on a different measure indicating attention being paid, that is people stopping in front of the display for at least 3 seconds. This information was extracted from the Kinect data. Further measures include overall engagement duration, the number of interactions (based on Kinect data) and duration of the different interaction phases, and how many people viewed the final video advert.

We first compare five days each of non-interactive, mobile and body interaction. Engagement for the non-interactive advert varied between 5 to 100 seconds, on average 34 seconds. Only 79 from 1031 passersby (7.66%) were categorized as engaged (standing in front of the screen for more than 3 seconds).

With the body interaction system, people spent between 10 and 200 seconds in different stages of engagement, on average 42 seconds. Some left in the middle of the interaction and some people only stared at the screen without triggering the map game, and a few repeated the interaction. On average it took 20 seconds to react to the call for action and to trigger the map. Map interaction lasted on average 18 seconds. Most users left when the advert video started, while those that remained appeared to only wait in order to play again. Among 995 passersby, 115 were categorized as engaged, that is 11.56%. Of these, 51 interacted with the system (5.1% of passerby), and 34 persisted to view the video advert (3.4% of passerby), the last stage of the conversion funnel considered here.

For the mobile interaction modality, engagement duration (22 seconds) was only half as long as for the body interaction version (42 seconds), and fared even worse than the non-interactive advert (34 seconds). People did react to the attention-grabbing start screen, seeing their silhouette on the screen, and engaged with it. Based on Kinect images, 77 from 852 passersby were identified as engaged, that is 9%. But they then did not proceed to use their mobile phone. Only two people pulled out their phone and took a photo of the QR code, but did not proceed further. Overall, none of the passersby interacted with the mobile version, and thus none saw the video advert. In terms of the audience funnel, none entered the direct interaction stage.

A one-way ANOVA indicates a significant difference in the number of engaged passersby between the three conditions ((F2,5)=11,20, p <.05 (p=.002)). A post-hoc Tukey test (critical value Q of 5.0430) shows a strongly significant difference between non-interactive and body interaction system (Q=5.6337, p=.0047509) and between body and mobile interaction version (Q=5.9467, p=.0032197), but none between mobile and non-interactive system. The η^2 effect size is 0.8, that is 80% of variance is accounted for by conditions.

We also compared tracking-based data from 3 days each of the non-interactive and the body interaction system with the iterated body interaction version with its wider angle of tracking. There were 45 engaged passersby over three days for the non-interactive system, 69 for body interaction and 104 for the improved body interaction system (of which 61 interacted with the map game and 27 viewed the final video). An ANOVA reveals a significant difference in engagement between conditions ((F2,3)=20.4154, p < 0.05 (p=0.0021)). A post-hoc Tukey's HSD test reveals no difference between non-interactive and original body interaction version (possibly because of the smaller numbers based on 3 days instead of 5), and a strong significant difference between the non-interactive version and the iterated body version (critical value Q of 6.325 and found Q of 8.9627, p<.01, p=.001744) and a significant difference between the original body version and the iterated body interaction version (critical value Q of 4.3341 and found Q of 5.3169, p<.05, p=.0218582). The revised body interaction version thus increased the number of engaged passersby. An effect size η^2 of .89 was calculated, that is 89% of variance is accounted for by conditions. Furthermore, a larger proportion (58.6%) of engaged users continued on to play the map game compared to the initial body interaction system (43x%), although the difference is not statistically significant.

Regarding the conversion funnel, we saw little overall conversion to the final step of viewing the video advert. From observation and the behaviour observable in the Kinect image data, it is clear that most people that stayed for the video did so because they wanted to interact again (and were not genuinely interested in the video). Of 51 interacting users (body interaction version), 17 ignored the advert video entirely by leaving the display, standing at one side, or turning around to talk with others until the video was over to then start over the game. The video was viewed by similar numbers of people in both body interaction conditions, 3.97% in the wide-angle setup

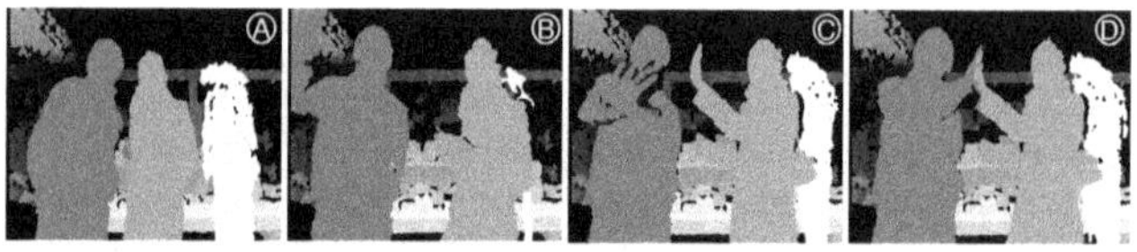

Figure 9. Playing with the silhouettes.

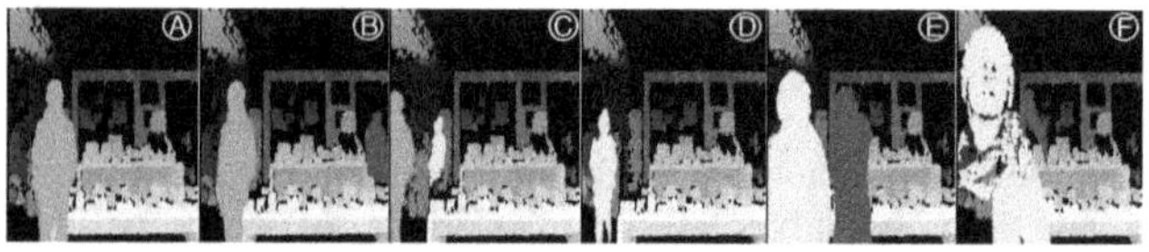

Figure 10. Honeypot effect (mobile version) – the yellow person is attracted to the display after having seen the green person's silhouette.

and 3.41% in the initial setup with a narrow tracking angle. This indicates that video content cannot be simply added at the end, but needs to be integrated into the interactive sequences.

Further Findings and Observations

Well known behaviours from the literature on public displays include the landing effect [20] and the honeypot effect [6]. In the following, we describe our findings for these behaviours as well as other interactions.

From observation, passersby behaviour around the non-interactive advert was calm and passive, with little curiosity towards the display and advert content. Most only viewed short fragments of the advert video. Very often the display was neglected (display blindness effect) even though people stood right in front of it, e.g. reading a leaflet, turning their back to it or talking with their group members (cf. figure 8).

However, this was different for the body interaction version. Here people were frequently playing with their own silhouette and engaging in various ways. Figure 9 shows two people who play with their silhouettes and the colour effect. From the observations during the field study, we conclude that the simple prompt to 'come closer to play' was well understood once users had realized the display was interactive and were close enough to read. Similarly, the metaphor of walking around a map appeared to worked well. The silhouette display triggers the landing effect as desired, and also attracts bystanders.

Out of 51 who played the game in the body interaction mode, four repeated the interactive game twice and two people thrice. Interestingly, this number was reduced for the second system version with a wide angle of tracking. Here, overall numbers increased (61), but only one person played twice. The numbers are not big enough though for statistical comparison.

Honeypot Effect

The mobile version was the least effective in triggering a honeypot effect, with only two occurrences. The non-interactive video advert resulted in seven and the body interaction version in 15 incidences. An ANOVA ((F2,5)=12.29, p=.001) and subsequent post-hoc Tukey HSD test shows that the body interaction version created significantly more honeypot incidences than the non-interactive version (Q=4.2762, p=.0264780) and strongly significantly more than the mobile version (Q=6.9488, p=.0010053). The effect size η^2 is 0.47 for non-interactive versus body interaction conditions and 0.64 for for body versus mobile interaction.

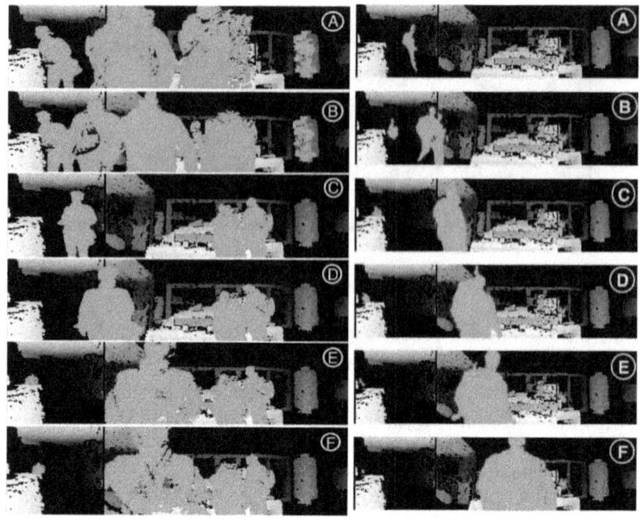

Figure 11. (Left:) Honeypot effect in the iterated body version. Two men interact for a while (frame A). A women is busy at the help desk at the left, but often looks toward the engaged pair, apparently curious. The two men leave (frame B). The woman at the left is alone and watches herself on-screen (frame C). She approaches (frame D), comes closer and starts interacting (frames E, F). (Right:) The wider tracking area means users notice the interactivity much earlier due to early visual feedback

The number of incidences for three days of deployment remained identical for the original and the iterated body interaction system (10 each, 5 for the non-interactive version). An ANOVA revealed no significant difference between conditions.

Figure 11 (left) shows a honeypot effect occurring from the iterated body interaction version where two men interact and attract a woman that interacts once they have left. Figure 10 exemplifies a honeypot effect from the mobile condition.

Landing Effect

Interestingly, during analysis of the Kinect image data from the non-interactive advert (it was used for data collection), we found incidences of the landing effect, where passersby went past the screen and turned back as they reached the other side, beginning to look at the display. These were not frequent, but over five days, four incidences occurred. This was also the case for the honeypot effect (seven incidences). These effects thus are not limited to interactive or reactive systems. For the mobile version, four landing effects were found, and with body interaction, a total of twelve.

An ANOVA ((F2,5)=7.5294, p <.05 (p=.0076)) and subsequent post-hoc Tukey's HSD test revealed that the body interaction advert led to a significantly higher number of landing effect incidences than either the non-interactive (Q = 4.7527, p=.0144554) or mobile interaction version (Q=5.9467, p=.014454) (with a critical Q value of 3.7711). The effect size η^2 for non-interactive versus body interaction conditions was 0.66; for body versus mobile interaction, this also was 0.66.

Figure 12. Landing Effect (left: non-interactive, right: body interaction)

Figure 12 shows two examples of the landing effect from the non-interactive and the initial body interaction setup (left, a person coming from the right turns back just after approaching the left end of the screen; right, two people coming from the left stop and return just as they reach the right hand side). We were initially surprised to find a much lower number of landing effects for the second version of the body interaction system with its wider angle of tracking. Over three days, there were six incidences, compared to seven with the original body interaction version. With data from three days (identical weekdays from the field study for non-interactive and original body interaction), an ANOVA was run, which revealed no significant difference.

But this should be interpreted positively, indicating that our design iteration was effective. With the revised version, people notice the interactivity much earlier, before they have passed through the middle of the interaction zone, and thus do not need to turn back. Figure 11 (right) exemplifies this, showing a passersby who notices himself as he enters the focal area of the screen (frame D, E) and then begins to interact. The landing effect thus could be considered a side-effect of a public display's spatial setup and its interaction zone size in relation to human walking speed. It takes people around 1.2 seconds to react to their silhouette when walking past it [20]. For a setup where people approach the screen from the front, there is more time and focal attention. But for a setup such as ours, where people walk past the screen, the display reaction can easily go unnoticed.

Other Observations

From our impressions during observation, users showed the most fun and joy in both body interaction conditions. Passersby were attracted quickly and showed signs of curiosity, waving their hands or moving about explicitly to learn about the interactivity. People also frequently called their friends over to jointly play with the coloured silhouettes. Figure 15 (left) shows an example of a lady calling her friend, who joins

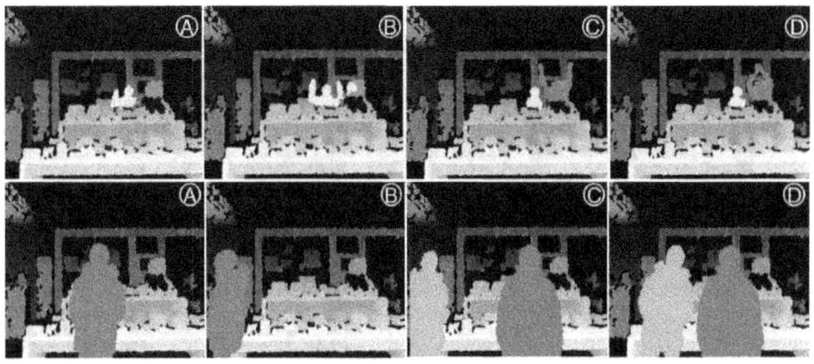

Figure 13. (Top): Noticing interactivity from afar. (Bottom): Calling each other: in frame (A) a person is engaged with the display and then moves out. In frame (C), the person calls a friend to join. In frame (D), both are engaged.

her in the iterated version of the body interaction system and figure 13 (bottom) shows a similar incidence from the initial body interaction variant.

The enhanced version with 3 Kinects covering a wider angle allowed for more people to interact simultaneously than the first version. People standing towards the side of the screen who would not come to the fore were still able to interact. Figure 15 (right) illustrates this kind of bystander interaction.

This resulted in more group interaction, with far more people (almost two thirds) interacting in groups (versus on their own) with the enhanced version (41 from 61 people over three days, in a total of 19 groups) compared to the first version where around half interacted in groups (27 from 51 interacting users over five days, in overall 11 groups). The size of groups remained similar, with most people interacting in pairs, and occasionally with three people, maximally four.

For both versions of the body interaction system, recall in subsequent interviews with people who had interacted was good, as they all remembered that the advert was for a walk or tour and related to the Bauhaus.

DISCUSSION

Our findings confirm that a silhouette display mirroring users' movements is effective in attracting people to a public display (cf. [20, 30, 24]). It was very effective for the body interaction system and also worked as attention grabber for the mobile version (but did not support further transitioning to mobile phone interaction). Moreover, in our pre-study in the canteen, from three interactive feedbacks (silhouette vs. following eyes vs. fireworks) only the silhouette received significantly more attention in terms of glances than the traditional static advert.

Different to Müller's study, our study investigates three modalities, and also an extended version of the body-tracking setup.

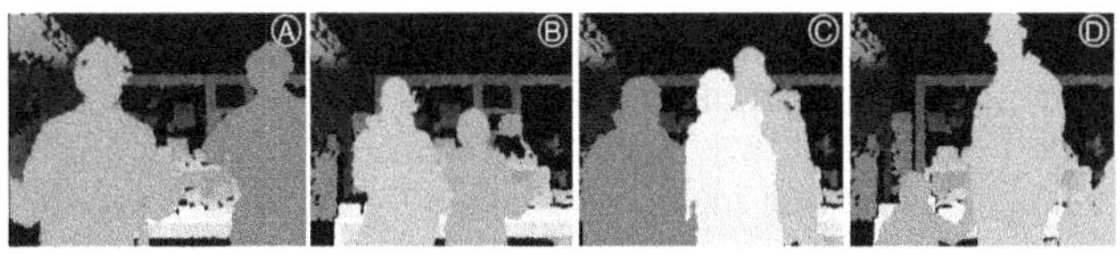

Figure 14. Group interactions with the body interaction version (4 different groups).

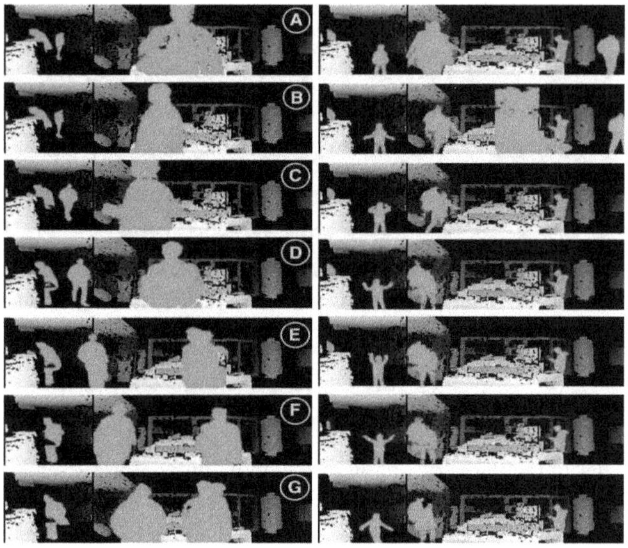

Figure 15. (Left) Calling others. A lady engages with the screen for a while (frame A). She turns and calls her friend, who is further away, looking at books (B). Her friend approaches. The lady is back at the screen (D), makes space for her friend (F), who finally also starts interacting (frame G). (Right) The enlarged tracking area increases opportunities for bystander interaction. A girl stands with her parents at the information desk. She recognizes herself on-screen, waving her hand to confirm, and starts to play with her silhouette, but remains at a distance.

Moreover, our interactive advert consists of different phases including a final video, and we study conversion rates between these phases. Previous studies (e.g. [21]) have largely focused on a younger audience due to their setting on university premises; however, given demographic developments, we consider our older user group to be a strength of our study.

While some authors argue vehemently for the effectiveness of mobile phones to interact with adverts [27] and this has been explored in experimental studies with proof-of-concept applications [22], our in-the-wild study revealed that people hesitated to use their phones. While this may be due to the usage context (cf. [1]) it provides evidence against She's claims [27] that mobile devices are ideal for the attraction stage and provide conveniences of personal and discrete interaction. In addition, if passersby are unwilling to pull out their phones in the first place, then other means of mobile interaction (e.g. iBeacons, QR codes or NFC) will also be ineffective.

Our mobile variant also reveals a dilemma for system designers - while a reactive silhouette display might be most effective for attracting initial attention, it did not motivate users sufficiently to then switch interaction mode to mobile interaction (which might improve retention due to being less physically demanding (cf. [23])). The prompt to pull out a phone might clash with expectations. It remains an open question whether other forms of inciting people to pull out their mobile may be more successful (e.g. a non-verbal prompt by a mirrored silhouette of the user that morphs into a figure holding a mobile).

In comparison to other in-the-wild studies our results for the body interaction system are encouraging. Parra et al [24] had 10.84% reacting to their mirror image in a busy train station, only at most 3% interacting (5.1% in our case), and only a small fraction watched a final video.

Isssues with Mobile Interaction

We found that our implementation of mobile phone interaction had too high a threshold, especially for an older audience beyond teenagers and university students. We interviewed some people that had been looking at the display after they left the area. This revealed that many consider their phone to be private and do not like to use it in public, and in general were sceptical of using it in this context. Some did not own a smartphone. This is surely influenced by the user group in our setting, with primarily middle-aged and older visitors attending the tourist office. Uptake levels in other settings with younger visitors might be higher. Our pre-study of the hi-fi prototype showed that getting started (and understanding what to do) takes far longer and is more difficult to convey than with the body interaction variant. Even though we acknowledge that the mobile interaction process could be improved (no dedicated WiFi network, no prompt for a name), the fact that only 2 people went as far as pulling out their phones and tried to scan the QR tag shows that the initial hurdle was too big.

Effects of Wide-Angle Body Interaction

The increase of attention for the revised body interaction advert can be traced to several factors. With wide angle tracking, people can see themselves on the screen when approaching from all sides and have a chance to do so when walking past the entire area around the screen. This increases exposure time to the reactive image, in which people's attention is caught and they can begin to understand how to interact (cf. [24]). Other studies found that it takes around 1.2 seconds to understand interactivity with a silhouette display on a large screen [20].

This, interestingly, removes the landing effect. It only occurs when the time span for passing along the interactive zone is just within the range of recognition time (1.2 seconds) so that people still have time to react, but are already past the central zone. Thus the landing effect is frequently an artifact of the size of the interactive zone and of visual flow/path.

Contrary to expectations, the wide-angle body version did not result in more honeypot effects. This is possibly because people in a tourist center do not stay around for long and thus the number of people who can get involved in a honeypot is limited. Furthermore, people may be hesitant to approach when strangers are already interacting with the system, and may prefer to wait until the system is free.

Design Recommendations

From our study, a number of design recommendations emerge. It should be noted that these are based on one study in a particular context (cf. effects of space and place [1] and audience). Limitations of our study are discussed in a following section.

Positioning and path matter. Where people don't walk towards the display but tangential to it and are focused on what is in front of them, they might not notice system feedback as easily.

Extending the interactive area resulted in prolonged exposure time to the system. This increased noticing by 10% and resulted in an increase in engagement and interaction.

Mirrored silhouette feedback works well: Our study confirms findings from previous work [20] on the effectiveness of a silhouette display as visual feedback to attract passersby attention and interest, and provoking playful interaction.

Multi-user interaction. She et al [27] mention multi-user interaction as research challenge for interactive adverts. In our case, simultaneous interaction worked well, people even explored the map together on occasion and often called a partner to come closer and share the interaction. Sometimes bystanders would interact from a distance. We recommend to enable people to collaborate in a simple, non-conflicting way.

Avoid media breaks and interaction modality switches. The video advert at the end of the game constitutes a media break, and wasn't successful. The switch from an attention grabber via silhouette feedback to phone input in the mobile condition did not work, and rather appeared to confuse people. If such a switch is inevitable, it needs to be more fluid in order to influence expectations.

Integrate advert content into the interaction. We found that the final video broke off engagement (similar to [24]). People left or just waited for the end of the video to replay the game, mostly ignoring the video. This means advert content should be integrated into the interaction, or the video needs to be very attractive and provide surprises or some kind of gratification (e.g. different video depending on how well you did, integrating your silhouette into the ad etc.) .

Content and interaction modality fit. The content greatly influences usage of public displays [23]. We received positive feedback in our early evaluations of prototypes on bodily interaction with the map, the interaction (moving about) being a direct match, without much metaphorical translation, to the task of exploring a map. Moreover, the advert content of a guided walk was considered a good fit. Such direct translation will not always be as evident, but this should be considered when generating and deciding between design alternatives.

Mobile phone input needs to be extremely low threshold and only works in contexts where people are apt to use their mobile: Mobile interaction was revealed as problematic, especially at a site where people do not have extended time on their hands, and populated mostly by an older age group that is not comfortable and/or familiar with QR codes. This implies that phone interaction needs to be as instantaneous as body interaction, to utilize apps that people have already installed as part of longer-term brand engagement, with a long-term narrative, or to provide added benefit (e.g. storing information, immediate purchases, cp. [27, 22]). It might require situations/locations with a younger audience, and where people people spend considerably more time, might be bored, and might take their phones out to kill time.

Limitations of Our Study

Many factors are known to influence attention and user engagement, from display location and size [16], orientation [17] to the environmental context [8, 10, 1]. A display in a cafe or train station will have different outcomes than one in a library or workplace. In our case, we tested effectiveness for a tourist information center. Furthermore, we only tested one design for an interactive advert.

Counting of glances was done manually in observation and might have missed some incidences. For the analysis of depth-images of passersby we were unable to determine whether one person might have passed the display twice, creating an error margin for our calculation of numbers of passersby.

The type of engagement in the three conditions is different. In the non-interactive mode, engagement means the user watches the advert, but does not need to do anything. In the mobile mode, engagement encompasses the initial silhouette feedback phase and the actual mobile phone use for the map game – but people did not go beyond the first phase of interacting with the silhouette. In the body-interaction mode, people did interact with the map game. An open question is whether a different attraction mechanism for mobile interaction might result in improved levels of engagements. The iterated wide-angle version of the body interaction system did not utilize multiple colours of silhouettes. This may have reduced the attractiveness of the display and resulted in less group play. It is likely that a multi-colour silhouette display in the wide-angle body version would be even more successful. This system was furthermore only tested for three days, resulting in less statistical power.

CONCLUSION

We presented a multi-part study on interactive advertisements. Our initial analysis confirmed previous findings that a silhouette is effective in attracting users. Based on this data, we designed an interactive advert experience with focus groups, Wizard-of-Oz and high-fidelity prototypes. Several variants of this interactive system were deployed in a public location. Our observations allow us to conclude that in our scenario, a simple prompt to 'come closer to play' in conjunction with the users' silhouette was well understood, as was the metaphor of walking around a map. On the other hand, having initially engaged people switch to use their mobile phone to play was not well received. We found that although prior research [23] indicates that movement-based interaction can reduce recall compared to other interaction modes that require less physical effort and some researchers [27] argue that it has severe limitations compared to mobile interaction with adverts, it received the most attention and active engagement, constituting a trade-off that designers of interactive adverts need to be aware of. As the silhouette representation attracts bystanders, the final iteration of our setup used an increased tracking area to attract users even earlier when passing by the display. This iteration was successful in increasing engagement levels further and attracting more group interaction, but interestingly, due to enhanced exposure time, removed the landing effect. Finally, we provided a number of design recommendations for the design of interactive advertisements.

ACKNOWLEDGMENTS

We thank all volunteers who helped with the design process as well as video and data analysis, all visitors who participated in the study and the very helpful tourist center staff.

REFERENCES

1. Imeh Akpan, Paul Marshall, Jon Bird, and Daniel Harrison. 2013. Exploring the Effects of Space and Place on Engagement with an Interactive Installation. In *Proceedings of the SIGCHI Conference on Human Factors in Computing Systems (CHI '13)*. ACM, New York, NY, USA, 2213–2222. DOI: http://dx.doi.org/10.1145/2470654.2481306
2. Florian Alt, Stefan Schneegass, Michael Girgis, and Albrecht Schmidt. 2013. Cognitive Effects of Interactive Public Display Applications. In *Proceedings of the 2Nd ACM International Symposium on Pervasive Displays (PerDis '13)*. ACM, New York, NY, USA, 13–18. DOI: http://dx.doi.org/10.1145/2491568.2491572
3. Florian Alt, Stefan Schneegaß, Albrecht Schmidt, Jörg Müller, and Nemanja Memarovic. 2012. How to Evaluate Public Displays. In *Proceedings of the 2012 International Symposium on Pervasive Displays (PerDis '12)*. ACM, New York, NY, USA, Article 17, 6 pages. DOI: http://dx.doi.org/10.1145/2307798.2307815
4. Abraham Bagherjeiran, Andrew O. Hatch, and Adwait Ratnaparkhi. 2010. Ranking for the Conversion Funnel. In *Proceedings of the 33rd International ACM SIGIR Conference on Research and Development in Information Retrieval (SIGIR '10)*. ACM, New York, NY, USA, 146–153. DOI: http://dx.doi.org/10.1145/1835449.1835476
5. A. Bezjian-Avery, B. Calder, and D. Iacobucci. 1998. New media interactive advertising vs. traditional advertising. *Journal of Advertising Research* 38, 4 (1998), 23–32. https://www.scopus.com/inward/record.uri?eid=2-s2.0-0002101166&partnerID=40&md5=ad6a4696560529a4e9f71f460bf7ede8
6. Harry Brignull and Yvonne Rogers. 2003. Enticing People to Interact with Large Public Displays in Public Spaces. In *Human-Computer Interaction INTERACT '03: IFIP TC13 International Conference on Human-Computer Interaction, 1st-5th September 2003, Zurich, Switzerland*, Matthias Rauterberg, Marino Menozzi, and Janet Wesson (Eds.). IOS Press.
7. Moira Burke, Anthony Hornof, Erik Nilsen, and Nicholas Gorman. 2005. High-cost Banner Blindness: Ads Increase Perceived Workload, Hinder Visual Search, and Are Forgotten. *ACM Trans. Comput.-Hum. Interact.* 12, 4 (Dec. 2005), 423–445. DOI: http://dx.doi.org/10.1145/1121112.1121116
8. Elizabeth F. Churchill, Les Nelson, and Laurent Denoue. 2003. *Multimedia Fliers: Information Sharing With Digital Community Bulletin Boards*. Springer Netherlands, Dordrecht, 97–117. DOI: http://dx.doi.org/10.1007/978-94-017-0115-0_6
9. Ben Congleton. 2007. Prospero - A 'Visual Commons' Framework for Community-Aware Public Displays. (2007).
10. Nicholas S. Dalton, Emily Collins, and Paul Marshall. 2015. Display Blindness?: Looking Again at the Visibility of Situated Displays Using Eye-tracking. In *Proceedings of the 33rd Annual ACM Conference on Human Factors in Computing Systems (CHI '15)*. ACM, New York, NY, USA, 3889–3898. DOI: http://dx.doi.org/10.1145/2702123.2702150
11. ddbsthlm. 2011. Mc Donalds Pick 'n' Play. Video. (30 May 2011). Retrieved September 8th, 2016 from https://www.youtube.com/watch?v=7u0ij9D5S4Y.
12. Brendan Fitzgibbons. 2014. Powerful billboard lets you stop child abuse. (2 December 2014). Retrieved September 8th, 2016 from https://www.dramafever.com/news/powerful-billboard-lets-you-stop-child-abuse-/.
13. Anthony G Greenwald and Clark Leavitt. 1984. Audience Involvement in Advertising: Four Levels. *Journal of Consumer Research* 11, 1 (1984), 581–92. http://EconPapers.repec.org/RePEc:oup:jconrs:v:11:y:1984:i:1:p:581-92
14. John Hardy, Enrico Rukzio, and Nigel Davies. 2011. Real World Responses to Interactive Gesture Based Public Displays. In *Proceedings of the 10th International Conference on Mobile and Ubiquitous Multimedia (MUM '11)*. ACM, New York, NY, USA, 33–39. DOI: http://dx.doi.org/10.1145/2107596.2107600
15. Robert Heath, David Brandt, and Agnes Nairn. 2006. Brand relationships:strengthened by emotion, weakened by attention. *Journal of Advertising Research* 46, 4 (December 2006), 410–419. http://opus.bath.ac.uk/11844/
16. Elaine M. Huang, Anna Koster, and Jan Borchers. 2008. *Overcoming Assumptions and Uncovering Practices: When Does the Public Really Look at Public Displays?* Springer Berlin Heidelberg, Berlin, Heidelberg, 228–243. DOI: http://dx.doi.org/10.1007/978-3-540-79576-6_14
17. Junko Ichino, Kazuo Isoda, Tetsuya Ueda, and Reimi Satoh. 2016. Effects of the Display Angle on Social Behaviors of the People Around the Display: A Field Study at a Museum. In *Proceedings of the 19th ACM Conference on Computer-Supported Cooperative Work & Social Computing (CSCW '16)*. ACM, New York, NY, USA, 26–37. DOI: http://dx.doi.org/10.1145/2818048.2819938
18. Jörg Müller, Florian Alt, and Daniel Michelis. 2011. Pervasive advertising. In *Pervasive Advertising*. Springer London, 1–29.
19. Jörg Müller, Florian Alt, Daniel Michelis, and Albrecht Schmidt. 2010. Requirements and Design Space for Interactive Public Displays. In *Proceedings of the 18th ACM International Conference on Multimedia (MM '10)*. ACM, New York, NY, USA, 1285–1294. DOI: http://dx.doi.org/10.1145/1873951.1874203
20. Jörg Müller, Robert Walter, Gilles Bailly, Michael Nischt, and Florian Alt. 2012. Looking Glass: A Field Study on Noticing Interactivity of a Shop Window. In *Proceedings of the SIGCHI Conference on Human Factors in*

Computing Systems (CHI '12). ACM, New York, NY, USA, 297–306. DOI: http://dx.doi.org/10.1145/2207676.2207718

21. Jörg Müller, Dennis Wilmsmann, Juliane Exeler, Markus Buzeck, Albrecht Schmidt, Tim Jay, and Antonio Krüger. 2009. Display Blindness: The Effect of Expectations on Attention Towards Digital Signage. In *Proceedings of the 7th International Conference on Pervasive Computing (Pervasive '09)*. Springer-Verlag, Berlin, Heidelberg, 1–8. DOI:http://dx.doi.org/10.1007/978-3-642-01516-8_1

22. Masafumi Muta, Soh Masuko, Keiji Shinzato, and Adiyan Mujibiya. 2015. Interactive Study of WallSHOP: Multiuser Connectivity Between Public Digital Advertising and Private Devices for Personalized Shopping. In *Proceedings of the 4th International Symposium on Pervasive Displays (PerDis '15)*. ACM, New York, NY, USA, 187–193. DOI: http://dx.doi.org/10.1145/2757710.2757732

23. Philipp Panhey, Tanja Döring, Stefan Schneegass, Dirk Wenig, and Florian Alt. 2015. What People Really Remember: Understanding Cognitive Effects When Interacting with Large Displays. In *Proceedings of the 2015 International Conference on Interactive Tabletops & Surfaces (ITS '15)*. ACM, New York, NY, USA, 103–106. DOI:http://dx.doi.org/10.1145/2817721.2817732

24. Gonzalo Parra, Joris Klerkx, and Erik Duval. 2014. Understanding Engagement with Interactive Public Displays: An Awareness Campaign in the Wild. In *Proceedings of The International Symposium on Pervasive Displays (PerDis '14)*. ACM, New York, NY, USA, Article 180, 6 pages. DOI: http://dx.doi.org/10.1145/2611009.2611020

25. Josh Schwartz. 2013. How Engaged Time Affects Brand Recall. (20 May 2013). Retrieved September 12th, 2016 from http://blog.chartbeat.com/2013/05/20/how-engaged-time-affects-brand-recall/.

26. Matthew Sharifi, Terry Payne, and Esther David. 2006. Public Display Advertising Based on Bluetooth Device Presence. In *Mobile Interaction with the Real World (MIRW 2006) in conjunction with the 8th International Conference on Human Computer Interaction with Mobile Devices and Services*. Espoo, Finland. http://www.hcilab.org/events/mirw2006/pdf/mirw2006_sharifi.pdf

27. James She, Jon Crowcroft, Hao Fu, and Flora Li. 2014. Convergence of Interactive Displays with Smart Mobile Devices for Effective Advertising: A Survey. *ACM Trans. Multimedia Comput. Commun. Appl.* 10, 2, Article 17 (Feb. 2014), 16 pages. DOI: http://dx.doi.org/10.1145/2557450

28. Daniel Vogel and Ravin Balakrishnan. 2004. Interactive Public Ambient Displays: Transitioning from Implicit to Explicit, Public to Personal, Interaction with Multiple Users. In *Proceedings of the 17th Annual ACM Symposium on User Interface Software and Technology (UIST '04)*. ACM, New York, NY, USA, 137–146. DOI: http://dx.doi.org/10.1145/1029632.1029656

29. Tim Weissker, Andreas Berst, Johannes Hartmann, and Florian Echtler. 2016. The Massive Mobile Multiuser Framework: Enabling Ad-hoc Realtime Interaction on Public Displays with Mobile Devices. In *Proceedings of the 5th ACM International Symposium on Pervasive Displays (PerDis '16)*. ACM, New York, NY, USA, 168–174. DOI: http://dx.doi.org/10.1145/2914920.2915004

30. Matthias Wölfel and Luigi Bucchino. 2014. Increasing Customers' Attention Using Implicit and Explicit Interaction in Urban Advertisement. In *Proceedings of the 16th International Conference on Multimodal Interaction (ICMI '14)*. ACM, New York, NY, USA, 204–207. DOI: http://dx.doi.org/10.1145/2663204.2663268

Don't Talk Dirty to Me: How Sexist Beliefs Affect Experience in Sexist Games

Jason T. Bowey, Ansgar E. Depping, and Regan L. Mandryk
Department of Computer Science, University of Saskatchewan
Saskatoon, SK, Canada
{firstname.lastname}@usask.ca

ABSTRACT

Research on sexism in digital games has suggested that women self-select out of playing sexist games; however, assuming a homogenous gender-based response does not account for the diversity of identities within a gender group. Gender-incongruent responses to recent events like #gamergate implies that the gender of the participant is not paramount to experience, but that their beliefs about gender roles are. To explore the role of sexist beliefs on experience in sexist games, we created three versions of a game that were identical except for the presence of sexist imagery and/or dialogue. We show that enjoyment of sexist games is not predicted by player gender, but by the player's pre-existing beliefs about gender. Furthermore, avatar identification is the pathway through which enjoyment is facilitated. Finally, sexist dialogue does not improve the play experience for anyone – rather it harms experience for players of all genders who do not hold sexist beliefs.

Author Keywords

Digital games; play experience; sexism; #gamergate

ACM Classification Keywords

K.8.0. General: Games

INTRODUCTION

Sex sells. In the context of digital games – which is a $100 billion industry worldwide [24, 65] – this translates into many popular games that portray female characters as hypersexual (e.g., Red Dead Redemption [77]) or portray male characters as hypermasculine (e.g., Gears of War [25]). Female characters are often treated as rewards to be obtained (e.g.,The Witcher [15]), as damsels in distress who need to be rescued (e.g., Legend of Zelda [67]), as a prop in service of the male protagonist's character development – often referred to as "woman in the refrigerator" (e.g., God of War [82], Fable 2 [55]), or simply as background decoration (e.g., Hitman: Absolution [44]) [83,84]. And even when the main character is a strong female with a developed personality and attributes, her body and clothing (or lack thereof) is often hypersexual (e.g., Lara Croft [19], Bayonetta [70]). Previous literature has argued that sexist character roles can be attractive and useful in fostering avatar identification [46,43]; however, other literature suggests that female players are offended by highly sexualized female characters and high levels of violence [40,97], may be irritated by sexist design choices intended to target male gamers [17], and in many cases may make an active choice to not play games with sexist content [28,51].

Feminist game critics have long criticized the game industry for catering to the presumed straight male player [14,49,83,84]. The vitriolic response from a group of mostly male gamers escalated into threats of rape, violence, and even death against women who spoke out against sexism in games and the game industry [8,63,95]. The debate around sexism in the games industry got massive public exposure through the recent #gamergate and #notyourshield controversies, which helped to shed light on many aspects of sexism within games and the game industry, including how players – particularly women – experience sexist game content [16]. Discussions around sexist game content sometimes suggest an 'us vs them' dynamic between male and female gamers [13]; however, the issue is not as simple as one of pitting men against women. For example, many men oppose the sexist rhetoric of #gamergate supporters [92] – an open letter in support of diversity in the game community was started by a male feminist and was quickly signed by 2500 people in response to #gamergate [98]. Conversely, there are women who challenge the idea of women being offended by sexist games and support #gamergate as a fight for masculinity and for male spaces in games [9,86,87]. That men and women do not react to rhetoric around sexism in games as two distinctly homogenous groups is not surprising, as feminist scholars have long suggested that it is a mistake to divide men and women into two *dichotomous* groups and assume corresponding attitudes, rather than allowing them to choose and perform their own individual identity and beliefs that might include a *dualistic* balance of the masculine and feminine [12,21,51,88].

As applied to an understanding of play experience, this all suggests that it may not be as simple as suggesting that women self-select out of playing games with sexist content, imagery, or themes [29,51]. We propose in this paper that the gender of the participant is not paramount to game

CHI 2017, May 06 - 11, 2017, Denver, CO, USA

ACM 978-1-4503-4655-9/17/05…$15.00
DOI: http://dx.doi.org/10.1145/3025453.3025563

experience, but that their *beliefs about gender roles and sexism* are. To explore the relationships between gender, sexist beliefs, and sexism in games, we conducted an experiment to determine how people who hold a range of sexist beliefs respond to games that contain sexist content.

We created a short role-playing game based on a prologue, 3 playable levels with a single common mechanic in each (i.e., fighting, infinite runner, shooting), and an epilogue. We created a game (rather than adapting an off-the shelf game) so that we could completely control and isolate the source of the sexist content in the game. To create sexist game versions, we added sexist imagery – i.e., characters that visually reinforced sexist stereotypes (helpless damsel, sexualized harlot, hyper-masculine barbarian, manly hero) – in one version and both sexist imagery and dialogue – i.e., through using gendered pronouns, sexual innuendo, diminutive nicknames, and objectification – in another.

Participants played one game version and answered several questionnaires about their beliefs around gender roles, sexist beliefs, and play experience. As it has been suggested that sexist characters can aid in avatar identification [43,46], and that avatar identification facilitates game enjoyment [43], we measured avatar identification and resulting game enjoyment. We have four main findings.

- The gender of the player does not predict avatar identification; however, their beliefs about gender roles and benevolent sexism do predict avatar identification.
- Lower avatar identification translates into less game enjoyment.
- Sexist dialogue harms play experience: adding sexist dialogue harms experience for people who do not hold sexist beliefs, and also does not improve experience for those who do.
- Including visually sexist character stereotypes does not harm identification and enjoyment; however, sexist character stereotypes reinforced through both imagery and dialogue harms both identification and enjoyment.

Our work explores player response to sexist characters and behaviours in a role-playing game. We refute the notion that men and women form distinct groups that respond in a predictable manner to sexist content in games. Player response is determined not by their gender, but by the beliefs about gender that they hold.

RELATED WORK

We use *sex* to refer to the biological sex of a character or player, and *gender* to refer to their identification as male, female, or other [69]. Because we asked participants their gender, rather than their sex, we refer to the players as having genders. *Gender roles* describe beliefs about appropriate behavior based on gender [34,71] and *sexist beliefs* refers to beliefs that are based on sex and/or gender.

Sexist content in games can be derived from multiple sources, including from graphics, interactions, narratives, or themes. The presence of sexual content does not by definition make a game sexist; we use sexism to refer to content (sexual or otherwise) that promotes gender inequality [7,75] between male and female characters or players. Gender inequality is generally derived from sex-based differences in power (i.e., the ability to influence the behavior of another person), violence (i.e., behavior intended to harm another person who tries to avoid being harmed), or objectification, which either emphasizes someone's instrumentality (i.e., treating someone as a tool for achieving one's own goals) or dehumanizes (i.e., denying that people have thoughts and feelings) them [53]. As such, we use *sexism* similarly to [29] to refer to *attitudes and actions that are based on gender and/or sex and promote inequality between men and women.* Although sexism is often of a hostile nature (e.g., violence toward women), sexism is also often of a benevolent nature; for example, the view that women are more helpful, empathetic, or intimacy-seeking than men or that women require paternal protection [34]. Although framed in subjectively positive traits, this benevolent form of sexism is an attitude of inequality based on gender or sex [34] and is sexist as it places women on a pedestal while simultaneously reinforcing their subordination [89].

Gender Roles and Sexism in Games

Male characters are represented in games much more often than female [23,45,94]. When female characters are portrayed in video games, they are often depicted in sexualized ways such as partially nude, with an unrealistic body image, or wearing sexually revealing clothing or inappropriate attire [11,23,45]. This tendency towards sexualizing women in video games has repeatedly led to criticism of the game industry for only catering towards presumed straight male players [28,36,84]. Research on the consequences of sexualized imagery indicates that men show a greater likelihood to harass women after play [22,96]. The harassment towards female users are usually sexist remarks ranging from traditional sexism (e.g., "get back in the kitchen.") to sexual harassment (e.g., "show me your tits.") [28]. Fox and Tang [29] conclude that sexualized imagery therefore might promote the growing problem of harassment of women in games. In addition to this, research suggests that female users experience diminished self-efficacy [1] and increased self-objectification [27,28] after play. The effect that sexualized imagery of women has on both men and women has led to the conclusion that, when exposed to these portrayals, women may self-select out of such environments [28], which in turn reinforces the idea of games being a "man's world" dominated by masculine disclosure [81].

Issues of masculinity in games and the games industry have been explored by feminist scholars for several decades [49]. A common perspective focuses on how to make games more gender-inclusive to be attractive to girls as a leisure activity [14,49]. Based on the notion that games provide early exposure and comfort with digital technologies, the arguments often center around how the male-centric games industry disadvantages girls from gaining that early exposure to STEM topics [13,35] and from the stealth-learning that digital games provide [48]. Books, such as Graner Ray's *Gender Inclusive Game Design: Expanding the Market* (2004) [73] present arguments on how to design games that appeal to the playstyle and preferences of female players. Cassell and Jenkins's *From Barbie to Mortal Kombat* (1998) [14] similarly focused on the emergence of the 'girls game' movement, albeit with a more inclusive perspective of gender preferences.

Beyond this foundational work on female gamers, literature on sexism in games can be distilled into three main trends. First, the majority of the research focuses on how women experience sexism in games differently than men. The distinguishing variable that influences the effect of sexist content in games is almost always gender conceptualized as the binary "men vs. women" [23,28,94]. This dichotomous approach asserts that 'women' are a group with a set of similar characteristics and beliefs that is fundamentally different from the group 'men'. Contemporary theories about gender might argue that this dichotomous distinction is reinforcing a deterministic view of gender relations in which people are divided into clear-cut groups, i.e., women and men [12], rather than a dualistic distinction in which people embody varying amounts of the masculine and feminine, regardless of their biological sex [51]. Furthermore, it may be more relevant to distinguish players who adhere to the concepts of gender that sexist games elicit (e.g., strong, dominant men and sexualized, helpless women) from those who don't. Adherence to these more traditional concepts of gender might be a better predictor for who is bothered by sexist game content and who is not.

Second, most studies investigated sexualized imagery [23]. While the visual depiction of female characters is certainly a powerful example of how games depict genders differently, there are other aspects of games that are, while being more subtle, just as sexist. Though imagery is an important part of games, it should not be the only factor considered when examining sexist content. In particular, the structure of a game's narrative, or the story trope, is crucial because of its power to objectify male and female characters [54]. In addition to the structure of tropes, language itself can have a powerful effect on sexism. Swim et al. [89] considered the role of sexist language and how it relates to subtle sexism. McConnel et al. [61] showed that adding male suffixes to occupation titles led perceivers to interpret a social target's personality as more masculine. Finally, language is a dominant means by which stereotypes are defined, communicated, and assessed [58], so language and dialogue in media should not be overlooked when it comes to sexist content and the effects it can have.

Third, to our knowledge, all studies investigating the effect of sexist content in games considered consequences in areas like tolerance for sexual harassment [22], beliefs about benevolent sexism [96], and agreement with gender attitudes and stereotypes [1], rather than directly examining the effects of sexism on game experience. In our work, we propose to examine the role of sexist game content on player experience, as it is the driving factor behind game enjoyment and greatly influences purchasing decisions.

Player Experience

Research in understanding the experience of players draws from traditions in psychology, games user research, and human-computer interaction. The most prevalent model that explains player experience is the satisfaction of needs during play [80], which is part of the broader context of self-determination theory [79]. Self-determination theory suggests that we are intrinsically motivated to engage in an activity because of our pure desire to do it, outside of the context of any external rewards [78] and has been shown to describe the experience of people playing games [80].

Intrinsic motivation is comprised of our interest-enjoyment in an activity, the effort-importance we invest on the activity, our perceived competence with the activity, and how much tension-pressure we feel during the activity [60]. Measurement of motivation is accomplished using the Intrinsic Motivation Inventory (IMI) [60]. The satisfaction of our need for competence autonomy, and relatedness – i.e., mastering challenges under our own volition, while feeling connected to others – work together to foster intrinsic motivation [78]. This relationship has been shown in a range of domains, including video game play [90]. As such, these constructs are often used in evaluating game experience, including the experience of different types of people during game play [5,50,72], of different game mechanics [32], or of different game input devices [4,85,93]. Measurement of need satisfaction is often accomplished using the Player Experience of Need Satisfaction Scale (PENS) [80].

In translating research on need satisfaction to the play context, Ryan et al., [80] added two additional constructs of particular relevance to game play. Intuitive controls describe control of the game that feels natural, whereas immersion/presence describes the experience of being transported into the digital environment [47]. Other researchers have described immersion as being comprised of three components [2]: transportation [39] – i.e., narrative engagement, loss of awareness, and flow; identification – i.e., identifying with a character's virtual personality and representation [18]; and telepresence – i.e., feeling present inside of a virtual world [56]. Because the immersive aspects of transportation and identification are particularly relevant to the experience of sexism in games [43,46], we describe them in more detail.

Transportation and Identification

Transportation is often described using a traveler metaphor, in which an audience member becomes absorbed and lost in the world created by a piece of media. [33] The audience member loses their sense of self as mental systems become

Figure 1: Level 1 with fighting mechanic (left), Level 2 infinite runner (centre), Level 3 with shooting mechanic (right).

focused on the narrative, excluding attention to the outside world. Similar to transportation, transportability is a personality trait defined as an individual's susceptibility to be transported into a narrative. [20] Previous work has confirmed that transportability predicts transportation [20], as well as enjoyment [3]. In addition, transportation has been shown to be a causal factor in increased identification with story characters [20]. Identification is a cognitive process through which audience members experiencing a piece of media adopt the point of view of a particular character. The process of identification has been described as a process in which the audience member loses awareness of self to be temporarily replaced with emotional and cognitive connections to a particular character [18].

The process begins with the audience member either: adopting a character's perspective, feeling fondness towards a character, or realizing some similarity between themselves and the character. As the narrative progresses, the audience member adopts the goals of the identified character and empathizes with the events of the narrative. Previous work has shown that higher identification with a character in a game leads to higher levels of enjoyment [43]. Also, greater time spent engaging with a story has been shown to result in stronger identification [74].

It has been previously hypothesized that narratives could be used in persuasion [2] and identification has been proposed as an important candidate to be effective at creating persuasive narratives [52]. In particular, identification could be used in persuasion by manipulating the source of a message, rather than the message itself, to make the message more attractive and palatable. [18] In addition, it has been shown that higher identification leads to increased activation of trait characteristics and increases the chance of mimicking behavioural tendencies displayed by the identified character, suggesting that experiencing strong identification with a character for long periods of time could have lasting effects on an individual's beliefs and values. As such, it is plausible that identifying with a character who displays sexist behavior could affect the experience and beliefs of players of sexist games.

EXPERIMENT DESIGN

We conducted an online study in which we presented three different versions of a simple role-playing game (RPG) that varied in their degree of sexism. We measured individual traits and player experience using several validated scales.

Game

We designed a 10-minute 2.5D game that was comprised of a prologue, three levels, and an epilogue. The prologue was a simple cut-scene to set up the narrative's conflict, the levels were each designed around a single straightforward game mechanic, and the epilogue was an interactive conversation between the player and one of the characters in the game (see Figure **1**).

Game Narrative and Mechanics

The main conflict in the game's narrative was based around the 'damsel-in-distress' trope. Players were informed that the Kingdom's Royal Heir has been captured by a dark wizard and must be rescued. Along the way, the player would encounter obstacles, opponents, and dilemmas in order to reach their goal [30].

The prologue was a short cut-scene showing the Royal Heir running in a field with a looming dragon shadow overhead.

In the first level, we employed a side-scrolling fighting mechanic. The player had to progress through a forest – using the 'A' and 'D' keys to move left and right respectively – fighting barbarians they encountered, using the left mouse button to attack. Eventually, the player reached a clearing where a barbarian was watching over a cage with a prisoner. The player is told the prisoner is to be sold to slavers, and challenges the barbarian to a fight. After defeating the barbarian, the prisoner promises to help the player rescue the Royal Heir once all of the barbarians have been defeated. Several more barbarians attack and the player must defeat them all. Having defeated all of the barbarians, the player finds a key to the cage and releases the prisoner. The prisoner tries to go back on their promise to help the player and runs off, forcing the player to follow.

In the second level, we employed an infinite runner mechanic. The player chased the prisoner down a forest path, avoiding obstacles by jumping or swerving left or right by pressing 'W', 'A', and 'D' respectively, trying to reach the prisoner and get the promised information regarding the Royal Heir. The player slowly catches up to the prisoner, until the prisoner finally admits defeat and leads the player to their village.

Figure 2: Gendered (left) and neutral (right) characters. From left to right: Harlot, Knight, Barbarian, Princess.

In the third level, we used the shooting mechanic. The player and the prisoner arrived at the village, but was under attack by barbarians. The player found a crossbow and had to shoot twenty barbarians, while avoiding shooting the villagers, to scare the invaders away and earn the promised information. Pressing the left mouse button would slow down time so the player could be more accurate with their shot, and releasing the mouse button fired the crossbow.

Finally, in the epilogue, the prisoner led the player to the Dark Wizard's castle, only to discover that 'The Princess had been taken to another castle'. The player then had to choose what to do with the prisoner to end the game.

Game Versions

Depending on their assigned condition, participants played one of three versions of the game: Gender Neutral, Sexist Imagery, and Sexist Imagery plus Dialogue. Although the game mechanics did not vary across versions, we manipulated the graphics of the characters (see Figure 2) and the sexism present in the dialogue.

Gender Neutral. All four characters were androgynous in appearance, each identical in body type, face, and hair, varying the hair colour, skin colour, and shirt colour to differentiate them. All dialogue in the game was generic and non-gendered, following the 'damsel-in-distress' narrative trope as loosely as possible while maintaining the overall story structure. All gendered pronouns were removed and characters were referred to generically by their titles (Royal Heir, Prisoner, Bandit, Player).

Sexist Imagery. All four characters were highly gendered in their appearance to conform to the Damsel-in-Distress Trope. The Player looked like a knight (masculine), the Bandit looked like a barbarian (masculine), the Heir looked like a princess (feminine) and the Prisoner looked like a harlot (feminine). Character models were custom designed to reinforce sexist stereotypes (helpless damsel, sexualized harlot, hyper-masculine barbarian, and manly hero). The gender-neutral dialogue was also used in this version. To confirm that our characters were perceived by participants in the intended way, we conducted two pre-studies (see Appendix). Our male characters were perceived as highly masculine, our female characters as highly feminine, and our neutral characters as neutral (see Figure 2).

Sexist Imagery plus Dialogue. We used the sexist imagery, but also reinforced gender roles through the use of sexist dialogue. First, the dialogue used gendered pronouns (he, she). Second, the dialogue was systematically edited in four ways to reinforce sexist stereotypes, inspired by the tropes and dialogue typically used in modern games and by theories of objectification and instrumentality [68]. We reinforced the idea that women are weak and men are strong, e.g., "That is a frightening weapon!" vs "One of them dropped a crossbow, use that". We included sexual innuendo in reference to the Harlot, e.g., "Wow! You really know how to handle a sword." vs "Amazing, your skill with a blade is impressive". We added diminutive nicknames in reference to the Harlot, e.g., "Darling, Sweetie". We also reinforced the idea that women are interchangeable [68], e.g., "She is ours. Go get your own." vs "This is our prisoner". We did not change the plot or add new narrative concepts in any way; the variations were intended to reinforce sexism in the game through dialogue. We did not do additional studies to confirm that the dialogue was perceived as sexist; however, we can be assured that it had the intended effect based on the "bug report" responses of participants who played this version (participants were under the pretense that they were playtesting a game under development), e.g., "Make it not a chauvinistic sexist game" "Remove misogyny", "I would change the rampant sexism of the game", and "I feel like I need a shower".

Cover Story

Participants were told they would be playing a short game and evaluating it for enjoyment. After completion of the experiment, participants were informed of the true purpose of the study and presented with a manipulation check that confirmed they read and understood the debriefing.

Measures

We collected both subjective and behavioural measures.

Individual Traits

Transportability. We assessed transportability, which is a personality trait that determines an individual's susceptibility to being transported or immersed into a narrative, using the Transportability Scale of 20 items [20] (Cronbach's alpha = .91).

Male Role Attitudes. We assessed pre-existing sexist beliefs by gathering the Male Role Attitudes Scale (MRAS), which measures masculine ideology through 8 items, such as "It bothers me when a guy acts like a girl" and "A young man should be physically tough, even if he's not big" [71] (Cronbach's alpha = .79).

Benevolent Sexism. We also assessed pre-existing sexist beliefs by gathering the benevolent sexism subscales of the Ambivalent Sexism Inventory (ASI), which measures protective paternalism (e.g., "Women should be cherished and protected by men"), complementary gender differentiation (e.g., "Women have a superior moral sensibility"), heterosexual intimacy (e.g., "Despite accomplishment, men are incomplete without women"), and a combined level of general benevolent sexism through 11 items [34] (Cronbach's alpha = .91).

Player Experience

Enjoyment was measured using interest-enjoyment subscale of the Intrinsic Motivation Inventory (IMI) [60], which measures how much the player enjoyed the game through five items (Cronbach's alpha = .94). We chose to use IMI instead of PENS [79] to measure Player Experience because we were more interested in exploring enjoyment, rather than focus on the building blocks that lead to enjoyment, which is what PENS measures.

Identification

Identification was measured using the Player Identification Scale (PIS) [57]: similarity identification, embodied identification, and wishful identification combine to give a general measure of avatar identification through 17 items (Cronbach's alpha = .97).

Participants and Deployment Platform

We recruited 439 participants to participate in the study through Amazon Mechanical Turk (MTurk), which has been shown to be a reliable research tool [59] in the context of games research [6,10]. To exclude participants who did not take care in answering the survey questions, we identified noncompliance by response time, response patterns and consistency metrics, as suggested by Meade & Craig [62]. We removed participants who spent less than 1.5 seconds/question on 2 or more questionnaires (N=50). We also detected the variance of responses for each individual susbscale and excluded participants with more than 3 standard deviations above the mean on more than 3 subscales (N=36) – this process excluded participants who consistently did not pay attention to reverse-coded items. This left 353 participants (161 self-identified as female) in our analyses. Ethical approval was obtained from the behavioural research ethics board of our university, and participants provided informed consent. To comply with ethical guidelines, the experiment was only available to workers in the USA who were older than 18. Participants were compensated with $3 USD; the entire task took approximately 20 minutes.

Procedure

At the beginning of the experiment, participants were assigned to one of three conditions which determined which version of the game they would play: gender-neutral dialogue and visuals (*neutral*) (N=122, 52 female), gender-neutral dialogue with gendered graphics (*sexist imagery*) (N=122, 66 female), and gendered dialogue with gendered graphics (*sexist imagery plus dialogue*) (N=109, 43 female). Other than the different versions of the game, participants all experienced the same experiment protocol.

First, participants were presented with the cover story and asked to provide informed consent to their participation in the study. Next, they provided basic demographic information and completed the Transportability scale.

Participants then played their assigned version of the game in a between-subjects design. Immediately after playing the game, participants were asked to fill out the player experience questionnaires (Identification and Enjoyment) and a questionnaire about sexist beliefs (ASI). Participants were provided with several open-answer questions asking for comments about the game and general feedback. Finally, participants were debriefed on the purpose of the study and were asked to confirm which version of the game they experienced.

Follow-Up Study

Approximately one week after their participation in the study, participants were sent an email inviting them to participate in a follow-up study. Participants were given five days to respond and were compensated $1 USD for their participation. In total we received follow-up data from 362 participants (82% response rate).

The purpose of the follow-up study was to measure participant's **pre-existing sexist beliefs** without potential influence or priming caused by the game. The follow-up study included only two questionnaires: the ASI and the MRAS as measures of sexist beliefs. The individual traits were gathered after the main experiment to not prime participants as to the nature of the manipulations prior to play; we waited several days before the follow-up study to ensure that the experimental conditions no longer affected participants' baseline answers.

Data Analyses

Collected data was analyzed using SPSS 24, with the Process macro for SPSS [42]. We had 353 participants in our full sample, and we had pre-existing sexist belief data for 287 of these participants from our follow-up study. We first checked for group differences in the individual traits to ensure that random assignment generated groups that did not differ on our traits of interest. One-way ANOVAs revealed that the groups were comparable in terms of transportability ($F_{2,352}$=.95, p=.388), and pre-existing benevolent sexism ($F_{2,286}$=2.16, p=.118).

RESULTS

Our research questions center around the relative roles of gender and sexist beliefs in the play experience of games that contain sexist imagery and dialogue. We first present results regarding the translation of identification into enjoyment, followed by the relative contributions of gender and sexist beliefs to play experience, and the role of sexist imagery or dialogue in experience.

Gender and Sexist Beliefs

Before presenting the effects of sexist content, we first show the relationship between gender and sexist beliefs. We used a linear regression to determine whether gender predicted sexist beliefs; however gender does not significantly predict benevolent sexism (β=.182, p=.238) or MRAS (β=.002, p=.988). Figure 3 shows the distribution of benevolent sexism and MRAS by gender.

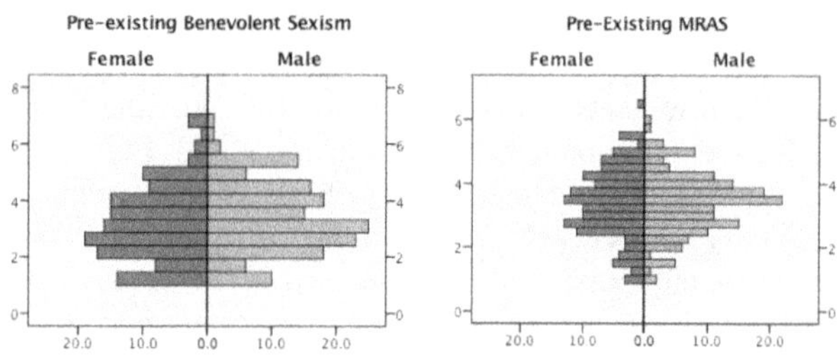

Figure 3. Distributions of sexist beliefs by player gender.

The Role of Identification in Predicting Enjoyment

We first investigate effects of identification on enjoyment because literature suggests that identification with characters in narratives and games leads to enjoyment [43].

Identification predicts enjoyment

Linear regressions revealed that avatar identification predicts enjoyment in all three versions of the game (Neutral: β=.568, p<.001; Imagery: β=.667, p<.001; Dialogue: β=.672, p<.001). So regardless of whether the game contained sexist imagery or dialogue, identifying with the characters significantly increases game enjoyment.

The Role of Gender and Sexist Beliefs on Identification

Previous literature on sexist games has suggested that women self-select out of playing games with sexist imagery or themes because they don't find it enjoyable to play them [17]; however, previous work has argued against the effectiveness of looking for differences between men and women [26], which suggests that it may not be as simple as assuming that men enjoy sexist themes while women do not. Perhaps men who don't identify with the sexist themes also self-select out of playing while women who do identify with these themes enjoy the games. To determine the relative roles of gender and sexist beliefs on play experience of sexist games, we computed several models.

Predicting identification from gender

We first tested whether a player's gender predicted how much they identified with the protagonist in the different versions. Linear regressions revealed that gender did not significantly predict avatar identification in either the neutral (β=-.254, p=.279), sexist imagery (β=-.244, p=.330) or sexist dialogue (β=.079, p=.792) conditions.

Sexist beliefs predict identification

We next tested whether a player's index of benevolent sexism or affiliation with male role models (MRAS) predicted how much they identified with the game's protagonist. Linear regressions revealed that neither benevolent sexism nor MRAS predicted avatar identification in the neutral condition (Ben: β=.109, p=.252; MRAS: β=.158, p=.208). However, both constructs predicted identification in the sexist imagery (Ben: β=.293, p=.009; MRAS: β=.296, p=.044) and sexist dialogue (Ben: β=.542, p<.001; MRAS: β=.536, p<.001) conditions.

The beta values presented above suggest that sexist beliefs is a more salient predictor of identification in games with sexist dialogue and imagery than with sexist imagery alone. In the game with sexist imagery, a one-point increase on the benevolent sexism scale translates into an increase in identification of one-third of a point. However, in the game with sexist imagery and dialogue, an increase of one point in benevolent sexism translates into an increase of over half a point in identification (see Figure 4).

Sexist imagery is helpful, but sexist dialogue and imagery together is harmful

Figure 4 shows the relationship between sexist beliefs and identification in the different conditions. Identification with the character is similarly high in both sexist games for those with a high level of benevolent sexism; however, the imagery plus dialogue condition translated into less identification for those low in benevolent sexism. As such, overall, adding sexist dialogue to sexist imagery can be considered to be harmful for identification.

On the other hand, when we consider the effect of adding sexist imagery alone, we see a different pattern emerge. Figure 4 shows the relationship between sexist beliefs and identification for the neutral condition. For those low in benevolent sexism, there is no difference in identification between the neutral or sexist imagery versions of the game; however, identification increases with increased benevolent sexism in the sexist imagery game. Interestingly, sexist graphics alone actually aid with identification for people who hold sexist beliefs over a neutral version of the game.

The pattern that sexist imagery aids identification, but sexist imagery and dialogue harm identification is also demonstrated by looking at the overall levels of identification in the different games. A one-way ANOVA shows a significant effect of game version on avatar identification ($F_{2,350}$=4.88, p<.008). Post-hoc comparisons (Tukey's HSD) show that players in the sexist imagery condition identify more than players in the neutral condition (p=.045) and that players in the sexist imagery plus dialogue condition identify less than those who played with sexist imagery alone (p=.010).

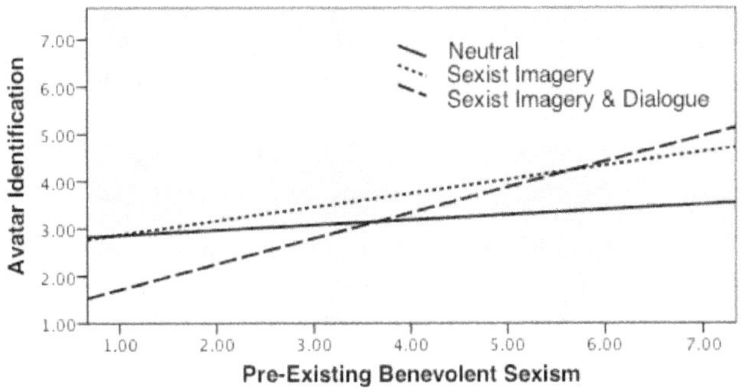

Figure 4. Linear regression lines showing the prediction of sexist beliefs on avatar identification for the three versions.

The Role of Sexist Beliefs in Predicting Enjoyment

Our results show that identification predicts enjoyment in each game, but that people who do not hold sexist beliefs identify less in the sexist versions of the game. So, do the sexist beliefs of players that affect identification in sexist games translate into enjoyment of those games?

The prediction of identification by sexist beliefs in the sexist game translate into enjoyment

We conducted a moderated mediation [41] for the two sexist versions of the game only. The full model is significant (R=.638, p<.0001). The prediction of benelovent sexism on enjoyment is fully mediated by identification (p<.001), and the mediation is significant for both the game with sexist imagery and the game with sexist imagery and dialogue (the bootstrapped confidence intervals do not contain zero in either case [41]: imagery: .016 - .372; dialogue: .213-.541). As such, our results suggest that sexist beliefs affect the enjoyment of sexist games because of the resulting identification with the character.

Women enjoy the games more, regardless of game version

Finally, we conducted a 2 (gender) by 3 (game version) ANOVA on game enjoyment, and found a significant effect of gender ($F_{2,347}$=31.5, p<.0001), in which women rated their enjoyment as higher than men. However, there was no significant interaction of gender with game version ($F_{2,347}$=1.54, p=.798) showing that this result did not vary with the presence of sexist imagery or dialogue.

DISCUSSION

We summarize our findings, situate results in the context of underlying theory, and address limitations and future work.

Summary of Findings

We show results of the relative roles of gender and beliefs about gender on player experience of sexist games.

First, the gender of the player does not predict avatar identification; however, their beliefs about gender roles and sexism do. Second, the differences in avatar identification as a result of the sexist content translated into game enjoyment. Third, the sexist imagery and dialogue harmed avatar identification (and resulting enjoyment) for those players who do not hold sexist beliefs; it did not aid avatar identification over sexist imagery alone for those who do. And fourth, sexist character stereotypes reinforced through graphic representations increased identification and enjoyment; however, sexist character stereotypes reinforced through both graphics and dialogue harms identification and enjoyment.

Explanation of Findings

In this section we will explain our findings and contextualize them in terms of the underlying theory.

Why Identification?

Avatar identification is a key component of becoming immersed in a narrative for various types of media [64]. The importance of identification likely is explained by the act of playing a game. In text-based media, such as a novel, identification is created through the point of view of a narrating character. The reader finds a connection with the character to facilitate this identification [18] but it heavily depends on the quality and delivery of the work itself. Similarly, in film, identification is primarily created by leveraging the perspective through which the viewer experiences the media, namely the camera. This has been theorized to be a weaker and more difficult connection to forge for cinema-style viewing [18] and extremely difficult for a viewing experience situated in front of a television [18]. In games, however, the player has control over many aspects of the character – from controlling the character, moving and controlling the camera perspective, and in many cases, customizing the character's visual appearance. For these reasons, it would be fair to argue that avatar identification would indeed play a large and important role in the way players experience games. Furthermore, while games likely facilitate stronger identification than other forms of media, it would also make sense for identification to be greatly reduced if there is a divergence between the player's beliefs and the beliefs and actions displayed by the character when outside of the player's control.

Why do Sexist Visuals Help Identification?

There are several possibilities why the sexist visuals increased avatar identification. One possibility is that the Knight character's appearance was more attractive and interesting than the androgynous character, which may have led to players liking the Knight more, leading in turn to stronger identification [18]. Second, most players are used to playing as a male knight character, regardless of their own gender, because most games have male protagonists [23]. Positive previous experience with a character can lead to an increased fondness for that particular character, which enables easier identification in similar situations in the future [18], so many players would more easily identify with a character if they have fond memories of other games where they played as a similar character. Third, knight characters are traditionally seen as noble or paragon: they are an ideal to strive for. As such, players who strive to be a better person may identify with the Knight character in a wishful way, forging a connection with him that they wish they could be. Previous literature has suggested that tropes can facilitate immersion and enjoyment through familiarity [2], so it is not surprising that adding gender-stereotypical visuals aids identification and enjoyment.

Why is Sexist Dialogue Harmful to Identification?

Language is an important factor in perpetuating sexism [58,61], which means players can easily interpret sexist ideas when they are conveyed through language. Also, for those who do not hold sexist beliefs, a sexist character would be less likable, which is detrimental to the process of identification [18]. Similarly, a sexist knight may be seen as less noble, which may reduce the previously mentioned desire players may have to be similar to him.

Why is Identification Harmed for Those who do not Hold Sexist Beliefs?

The process of identification requires an individual to feel connection or similarity with a character [18]. For someone who does not hold sexist beliefs, a sexist character would not be one that that individual would relate to or want to be similar to. Thus, they would experience less identification with the character than someone who shares similar beliefs.

Why Does Identification not Increase with Sexist Dialogue for those Who Hold Sexist Beliefs?

We likely did not observe greater identification when sexist dialogue was added because of the asymmetry between creating identification and breaking it. The act of breaking identification can occur easily, from external stimuli such as the phone ringing, to stimuli brought by the story such as changing narrative perspective [18]. Conversely, forming identification is more involved and must be maintained for the audience member to feel identified. This asymmetry would explain why people who do not hold sexist beliefs were more easily turned off by the sexism, and why the opposite does not seem to be true for people who hold sexist beliefs. The sexist dialogue is just one more factor on top of several others that would forge identification for people with sexist beliefs (e.g., agency through controlling the character, relating to the knight visually).

Which Beliefs Matter for Identification and Enjoyment?

We measured two constructs to gather information on the participants' preexisting beliefs about gender: benevolent sexism and male role acceptance. For both constructs, we assumed they might differentiate between players whose experience was harmed by sexist content and players who didn't mind the sexist content. While male role acceptance showed similar trends to benevolent sexism, our empirical results are stronger for benevolent sexism. We believe this trend is due to the relationship between the occurring themes in the game and the nature of the preexisting beliefs that were examined. The male role acceptance scale measures beliefs about masculinity and does not include gender excitations for women. Benevolent sexism includes some ideas about masculinity, e.g., "Despite accomplishment, men are incomplete without women"; however, focuses mostly on beliefs about women, e.g., "Women should be cherished and protected by men". Our game, while also prompting traditional concepts of masculinity (i.e., the strong, dominant and aggressive hero), mostly caters to sexist ideas about women (i.e., the scantily-dressed seductive, yet helpless harlot, the pure and innocent princess in distress). Benevolent sexism was likely the stronger predictor in our data because it more accurately speaks to the kind of sexism that is portrayed in our game.

This opens up the interesting follow up question: Would we find the same results with a different game as an example? We interpreted our results as exemplary to how preexisting beliefs influence the experience of a game. Benevolent sexism is most likely not always the distinguishing trait to determine who is affected by sexist content and who is not. Sexist content can take on many forms, from overtly misogynistic violence towards women (e.g., Grand Theft Auto [76]) to subversively embedded ideas of traditional gender roles (e.g., Princess Peach in Super Mario Bros. [66], God of War [82]) It is reasonable to assume that there is a set of different constructs that can become relevant depending on the "brand" of sexism portrayed in the game.

Shooting games, for example, often provide a militarized narrative structure that emphasizes hypermasculine traits such as dominance, violence, and lack of emotional expression (e.g., Gears of War [25]). These types of games are likely more affected by preexisting ideas of masculinity, than benevolent sexism. Similarly, games that portray highly sexualized and objectified female avatars are likely highly affected by a preexisting propensity to sexualize and objectify women. (e.g., Duke Nukem [31], Dead or Alive Xtreme Beach Volleyball [91]) and may be more affected by existing ideas about women as sexual objects. Finally, games that contain high levels of aggression toward women are probably affected by a tendency to normalize and justify harassment and physical violence towards women (e.g., Grand Theft Auto [76], God of War [82]), as is measured through scales of hostile sexism [34].

How Do Our Results Fit with Existing Literature?

As presented in the related literature section, there is a significant body of work on gender and games that makes research contributions using a range of methodological approaches – in particular, through qualitative contributions (e.g., [21,48,49]) or through quasi-experimental approaches (e.g., [29,51]). We approached the issue of sexism in games from an empirical perspective, looking at the effects of a particular experimental manipulation on player experience. There are many potential problems that arise from playing sexist games – e.g., hostility towards women [22,28], long-term effects in society [28,29], and issues of gender equality and representation [23,45,94] – that our results do not address; however, our work is in line with the body of work on gender in games that suggests that sexism in games is harmful to play experience for a large proportion of gamers. Our work takes the literature a step further by identifying that the harm of sexist games is not specific to female players, but that sexism in games negatively affects the enjoyment of both female and male players.

Limitations and Future Work

Although we carefully controlled our design and analyses, there are limitations that can be addressed in future work.

First, our game was relatively short (10 minutes) compared to the way that games – especially role-playing games – are normally played. These short play times likely help to explain our small effect sizes. If players spent longer interacting through and with the characters, we would likely observe greater identification through increased interaction [74]. We would like to explore the role of sexist beliefs on identification in games with longer play times and depth.

Second, we introduced sexist dialogue almost immediately. Identification is a cognitive process in which players are less likely to question their own beliefs by being immersed in the story [18]; however, in our game, the players were immediately faced with sexist dialogue, giving no chance to first identify with the knight. Our results may have been different if the sexism was added after the player had already undergone the process of identification. For example, a game in which a player builds a strong connection and empathy with a character early on may be less likely to alienate players if the character suddenly began displaying behaviours that went against the player's own personal beliefs because the process of identification was already underway. In this way, game designers could leverage identification in a persuasive manner to force a player to see something from a different perspective, with their defensive shields down and more willing to listen to points of view contrary to their own. We would like to explore the persuasive aspects of character identification.

Third, we focused on the effects of sexist games on player experience and avatar identification. We would like to extend the empirical control we used to the exploration of how sexist elements in games normalize sexist thoughts and behaviors [1,96] by unpacking how sexist content from different sources (i.e., graphics, dialogue) influence participants' sexist beliefs in the short term.

Fourth, we focused on a particular type of sexism – the objectification of female characters alongside their helplessness and interchangeability. We would like to further explore the role of hypermasculine characters on game experience for players who hold different beliefs.

Fifth, the characters in the sexist imagery condition had light skin; two of the characters in the neutral version had blue skin. We did not examine how sexist depictions interact with race of the character or player and would be interested in exploring the interaction of sexist imagery with unfavorable depictions of other marginalized groups.

Finally, the characters in our game were assigned, rather than created by the players. Increasing player agency in the game may allow the players to construct the character's persona more similarly to their own, which is likely to increase identification. We would like to explore how increasing player agency affects the experience.

CONCLUSION

Research on sexism in digital games has suggested that women self-select out of playing sexist games; however, we suggest based on literature that the gender of the participant is not paramount to experience, but that their beliefs about gender roles are. To explore the role of sexist beliefs on experience in sexist games, we created three versions of a game that were identical except for the presence of sexist imagery or sexist imagery and dialogue. We conducted an experiment with 353 players and showed that enjoyment of sexist games is not predicted by the gender of the player, but by pre-existing beliefs about gender that the player holds. In addition, we demonstrate that avatar identification is the pathway through which enjoyment is facilitated for players who hold different sexist beliefs. Furthermore, we show that adding sexist dialogue to sexist games harms experience for people who do not hold sexist beliefs, but does not improve experience for those who do. Finally, we show that including visually sexist character stereotypes can aid in identification and enjoyment; however, sexist character stereotypes that are reinforced through both imagery and dialogue harms identification and enjoyment.

Our work explores player response to sexist characters and behaviours in a role-playing game. We refute the notion that men and women form distinct groups that respond in a predictable manner to sexist content. Player response is not about gender, but is determined by the beliefs about gender roles that players hold.

ACKNOWLEDGEMENTS

We thank our participants, the Interaction Lab for support, and NSERC SWaGUR for funding.

APPENDIX

We conducted two pre-studies to determine that our character designs indeed matched the gender tropes we were trying to match. In the first study (N=80), we tested the gendered characters and several neutral designs, asking participants to rate the character on a continuous sliding scale from masculine (-1.0) to feminine (1.0). One-sample t-tests (comparing to neutral) showed that the knight (M=-.82, SD=.4, t_{78}=-18.0, p<.001) and barbarian (M=-.89, SD=.3, t_{78}=-27.1, p<.001) were perceived as significantly masculine; the harlot (M=.89, SD=.3, t_{78}=23.5, p<.001) and princess (M=.89, SD=.3, t_{78}=25.4, p<.001) were perceived as significantly feminine. The initial neutral characters were perceived as more masculine, thus we iterated on the model and hairstyles, conducting a follow-up study (N=40). We selected our neutral characters based on the two designs that were perceived as most neutral (M=-.11, SD=.6, t_{39}=-1.1, p=.260; M=-.14, SD=.6, t_{39}=-1.4, p=.169); see Figure 2.

REFERENCES

1. Elizabeth Behm-Morawitz and Dana Mastro. 2009. The Effects of the Sexualization of Female Video Game Characters on Gender Stereotyping and Female Self-Concept. *Sex Roles* 61, 11-12: 808–823. http://doi.org/10.1007/s11199-009-9683-8
2. Helena Bilandzic and Rick W. Busselle. 2008. Transportation and Transportability in the Cultivation of Genre-Consistent Attitudes and Estimates. *Journal of Communication* 58, 3: 508–529. http://doi.org/10.1111/j.1460-2466.2008.00397.x
3. Helena Bilandzic and Rick W. Busselle. 2011. Enjoyment of films as a function of narrative experience, perceived realism and transportability. *Communications* 36, 1. http://doi.org/10.1515/comm.2011.002
4. Max Birk and Regan L. Mandryk. 2013. Control your game-self. *Proceedings of the SIGCHI Conference on Human Factors in Computing Systems - CHI '13*. http://doi.org/10.1145/2470654.2470752
5. Max V. Birk, Dereck Toker, Regan L. Mandryk, and Cristina Conati. 2015. Modeling Motivation in a Social Network Game Using Player-Centric Traits and Personality Traits. *Lecture Notes in Computer Science User Modeling, Adaptation and Personalization*: 18–30. http://doi.org/10.1007/978-3-319-20267-9_2
6. Max V. Birk, Cheralyn Atkins, Jason T. Bowey, and Regan L. Mandryk. 2016. Fostering Intrinsic Motivation through Avatar Identification in Digital Games. *Proceedings of the 2016 CHI Conference on Human Factors in Computing Systems - CHI '16*. http://doi.org/10.1145/2858036.2858062
7. Kathleen M. Blee and Mary R. Jackman. 1994. The Velvet Glove: Paternalism and Conflict in Gender, Class, and Race Relations. *Contemporary Sociology* 23, 6: 792. http://doi.org/10.2307/2076034
8. Blog death threats spark debate. Retrieved December 21, 2016 from http://news.bbc.co.uk/2/hi/technology/6499095.stm
9. Janet Bloomfield. 2015. #GamerGate is fundamentally a fight for men, for masculinity and for male spaces. *judgybitch*. Retrieved from http://judgybitch.com/2015/09/16/gamergate-is-fundamentally-a-fight-for-men-for-masculinity-and-for-male-spaces/
10. Jason T. Bowey, Max V. Birk, and Regan L. Mandryk. 2015. Manipulating Leaderboards to Induce Player Experience. *Proceedings of the 2015 Annual Symposium on Computer-Human Interaction in Play - CHI PLAY '15*. http://doi.org/10.1145/2793107.2793138
11. Melinda C. R. Burgess, Steven Paul Stermer, and Stephen R. Burgess. 2007. Sex, Lies, and Video Games: The Portrayal of Male and Female Characters on Video Game Covers. *Sex Roles* 57, 5-6: 419–433. http://doi.org/10.1007/s11199-007-9250-0
12. Judith Butler. 1990. *Gender trouble: feminism and the subversion of identity*. Routledge, New York.
13. Justine Cassell and Henry Jenkins. 1998. Chess for girls? Feminism and computer games, *From Barbie to Mortal Kombat: gender and computer games*.
14. Justine Cassell and Henry Jenkins. 1998. From Barbie to Mortal Kombat: gender and computer games. MIT Press, Cambridge, MA.
15. CD Projekt RED. 2007. The Witcher. Game [Microsoft Windows, Mac OS]. (26 October 2007). Atari.
16. Shira Chess and Adrienne Shaw. 2015. A Conspiracy of Fishes, or, How We Learned to Stop Worrying About #GamerGate and Embrace Hegemonic Masculinity. *Journal of Broadcasting & Electronic Media* 59, 1: 208–220. http://doi.org/10.1080/08838151.2014.999917
17. Katheryn R. Christy and Jesse Fox. 2016. Transportability and Presence as Predictors of Avatar Identification Within Narrative Video Games. *Cyberpsychology, Behavior, and Social Networking* 19, 4: 283–287. http://doi.org/10.1089/cyber.2015.0474
18. Jonathan Cohen. 2001. Defining Identification: A Theoretical Look at the Identification of Audiences With Media Characters. *Mass Communication and Society* 4, 3: 245–264. http://doi.org/10.1207/s15327825mcs0403_01
19. Core Design. 1996. *Tomb Raider*. Game[Sega Saturn, PlayStation, MS-DOS]. (25 October 1996). Edits Interactive.
20. Sonya. Dal Cin, Mark P. Zanna, Geoffrey. T. Fong. Narrative persuasion and overcoming resistance. *Resistance and persuasion*. http://doi.org/10.1037/e633872013-232
21. Suzanne De Castell and Mary Bryson. 1998. Re-tooling play: Dystopia, dysphoria, and difference. *From Barbie to Mortal Kombat: gender and computer games*: 232-261.
22. Karen E. Dill, Brian P. Brown, and Michael A. Collins. 2008. Effects of exposure to sex-stereotyped video game characters on tolerance of sexual harassment. *Journal of Experimental Social Psychology* 44, 5: 1402–1408. http://doi.org/10.1016/j.jesp.2008.06.002
23. Edward Downs and Stacy L. Smith. 2009. Keeping Abreast of Hypersexuality: A Video Game Character Content Analysis. *Sex Roles* 62, 11-12: 721–733. http://doi.org/10.1007/s11199-009-9637-1
24. Christopher Dring. 2015. More money is spent on games than movies and music combined, says IHS. *The Market for Computer and Video Games*. Retrieved

from http://www.mcvuk.com/news/read/more-money-is-spent-on-games-than-movies-and-music-combined-says-ihs/0151059

25. Epic Games. 2006. Gears of War. Game [Xbox 360, Microsoft Windows]. (7 November 2006). Microsoft Game Studios.
26. O. E. Favreau. 1997. Sex and Gender Comparisons: Does Null Hypothesis Testing Create a False Dichotomy? *Feminism & Psychology* 7, 1: 63–81. http://doi.org/10.1177/0959353597071010
27. J. Fox, R. A. Ralston, C. K. Cooper, and K. A. Jones. 2014. Sexualized Avatars Lead to Women's Self-Objectification and Acceptance of Rape Myths. *Psychology of Women Quarterly* 39, 3: 349–362. http://doi.org/10.1177/0361684314553578
28. Jesse Fox, Jeremy N. Bailenson, and Liz Tricase. 2013. The embodiment of sexualized virtual selves: The Proteus effect and experiences of self-objectification via avatars. *Computers in Human Behavior* 29, 3: 930–938. http://doi.org/10.1016/j.chb.2012.12.027
29. Jesse Fox and Wai Yen Tang. 2014. Sexism in online video games: The role of conformity to masculine norms and social dominance orientation. *Computers in Human Behavior* 33: 314–320. http://doi.org/10.1016/j.chb.2013.07.014
30. Tracy Fullerton. 2014. *Game design workshop: a playcentric approach to creating innovative games.*
31. Gearbox Software. 2011. *Duke Nukem Forever.* Game [Microsoft Windows, Mac OS X, PlayStation 3, Xbox 360]. (10 Jun 2011). 2K Games.
32. Kathrin Maria Gerling, Matthew Miller, Regan L. Mandryk, Max Valentin Birk, and Jan David Smeddinck. 2014. Effects of balancing for physical abilities on player performance, experience and self-esteem in exergames. *Proceedings of the 32nd annual ACM conference on Human factors in computing systems - CHI '14.* http://doi.org/10.1145/2556288.2556963
33. Richard J. Gerrig. 1993. Experiencing narrative worlds: on the psychological activities of reading. *Yale University Press*, New Haven.
34. Peter Glick and Susan T. Fiske. 1996. The Ambivalent Sexism Inventory: Differentiating hostile and benevolent sexism. *Journal of Personality and Social Psychology* 70, 3: 491–512. http://doi.org/10.1037/0022-3514.70.3.491
35. Joanna Goode, Rachel Estrella, Jane Margolis. 2006. Lost in translation: gender and high school computer science. Women and Information Technology: Research on Underrepresentation, eds J. M. Cohoon & W. Aspray, *MIT Press*, Cambridge, MA, pp. 89–114.
36. K. L. Gray. 2012. Deviant bodies, stigmatized identities, and racist acts: examining the experiences of African-American gamers in Xbox Live. *New Review of Hypermedia and Multimedia* 18, 4: 261–276. http://doi.org/10.1080/13614568.2012.746740
37. Melanie C. Green and Timothy C. Brock. 2000. The role of transportation in the persuasiveness of public narratives. *Journal of Personality and Social Psychology* 79, 5: 701–721. http://doi.org/10.1037/0022-3514.79.5.701
38. Melanie C. Green and Timothy C. Brock. 2000. The role of transportation in the persuasiveness of public narratives. *Journal of Personality and Social Psychology* 79, 5: 701–721. http://doi.org/10.1037/0022-3514.79.5.701
39. Melanie C. Green, Timothy C. Brock, and Geoff F. Kaufman. 2004. Understanding Media Enjoyment: The Role of Transportation Into Narrative Worlds. *Commun Theory Communication Theory* 14, 4: 311–327. http://doi.org/10.1111/j.1468-2885.2004.tb00317.x
40. Tilo Hartmann and Christoph Klimmt. 2006. Gender and Computer Games: Exploring Females' Dislikes. *Journal of Computer-Mediated Communication J Comp Mediated Comm* 11, 4: 910–931. http://doi.org/10.1111/j.1083-6101.2006.00301.x
41. Andrew F. Hayes. 2013. Introduction to mediation, moderation, and conditional process analysis: a regression-based approach. *The Guilford Press*, New York.
42. Andrew F. Hayes. 2012. PROCESS: A versatile computational tool for observed variable mediation, moderation, and conditional process modelling. Retrieved from http://www.afhayes.com/public/process2012.pdf
43. Dorothée Hefner, Christoph Klimmt, and Peter Vorderer. Identification with the Player Character as Determinant of Video Game Enjoyment. *Entertainment Computing – ICEC 2007 Lecture Notes in Computer Science*: 39–48. http://doi.org/10.1007/978-3-540-74873-1_6
44. IO Interactive. 2012. *Hitman: Absolution.* Game [PlayStation 3, Xbox 360, Microsoft Windows, Mac OS] .(20 November 2012). Square Enix.
45. James D. Ivory. 2006. Still a Man's Game: Gender Representation in Online Reviews of Video Games. *Mass Communication and Society* 9, 1: 103–114. http://doi.org/10.1207/s15327825mcs0901_6
46. J. Jansz. 2005. The Emotional Appeal of Violent Video Games for Adolescent Males. *Communication Theory* 15, 3: 219–241. http://doi.org/10.1093/ct/15.3.219
47. Charlene Jennett, Anna L. Cox, Paul Cairns, et al. 2008. Measuring and defining the experience of immersion in games. *International Journal of Human-Computer Studies* 66, 9: 641–661. http://doi.org/10.1016/j.ijhcs.2008.04.004

48. Jennifer Jenson and Suzanne de Castell. 2011. Girls@ Play. *Feminist Media Studies* 11, 2: 167-179. http://doi.org/10.1080/14680777.2010.521625
49. Jennifer Jenson and Suzanne de Castell. 2008. Theorizing gender and digital gameplay: Oversights, accidents and surprises. *Eludamos: Journal for Computer Game Culture* 2, 1: 15–25.
50. Daniel Johnson and John Gardner. 2010. Personality, motivation and video games. *Proceedings of the 22nd Conference of the Computer-Human Interaction Special Interest Group of Australia on Computer-Human Interaction - OZCHI '10.* http://doi.org/10.1145/1952222.1952281
51. Kamala O. Norris. 2004. Gender Stereotypes, Aggression, and Computer Games: An Online Survey of Women. *CyberPsychology & Behavior* 7, 6: 714-727. Web. http://doi.org/10.1089/cpb.2004.7.714
52. Herbert C. Kelman. 1961. Processes of Opinion Change. *Public Opinion Quarterly* 25, 1: 57. http://doi.org/10.1086/266996
53. Marleen J. E. Klaassen and Jochen Peter. 2014. Gender (In)equality in Internet Pornography: A Content Analysis of Popular Pornographic Internet Videos. *The Journal of Sex Research* 52, 7: 721–735. http://doi.org/10.1080/00224499.2014.976781
54. L. Kruse, E. Weimer, and F. Wagner. 1988. What Men and Women are Said to Be: Social Representation and Language. *Journal of Language and Social Psychology* 7, 3-4: 243–262. http://doi.org/10.1177/0261927x8800700407
55. Lionhead Studios. 2008. *Fable II.* Game [Xbox 360, Xbox One]. (21 October 2008). Microsoft Game Studios.
56. Matthew Lombard, Robert D. Reich, Maria E. Grabe, Cheryl C. Bracken, and Theresa B. Ditton. "Presence and television." Human Communication Research 26, no. 1 (2000): 75-98.
57. Jan Van Looy, Cédric Courtois, Melanie De Vocht, and Lieven De Marez. 2012. Player Identification in Online Games: Validation of a Scale for Measuring Identification in MMOGs. *Media Psychology* 15, 2: 197–221. http://doi.org/10.1080/15213269.2012.674917
58. C. Neil. Macrae, Charles Stangor, and Miles Hewstone. 1996. Language and stereotyping. In *Stereotypes and stereotyping*. Guilford Press, New York.
59. Winter Mason and Siddharth Suri. 2011. Conducting behavioral research on Amazon's Mechanical Turk. *Behav Res Behavior Research Methods* 44, 1: 1–23. http://doi.org/10.3758/s13428-011-0124-6
60. Edward Mcauley, Terry Duncan, and Vance V. Tammen. 1989. Psychometric Properties of the Intrinsic Motivation Inventory in a Competitive Sport Setting: A Confirmatory Factor Analysis. *Research Quarterly for Exercise and Sport* 60, 1: 48–58. http://doi.org/10.1080/02701367.1989.10607413
61. A. R. Mcconnell and R. H. Fazio. 1996. Women as Men and People: Effects of Gender-Marked Language. *Personality and Social Psychology Bulletin* 22, 10: 1004–1013. http://doi.org/10.1177/01461672962210003
62. Adam W. Meade and S. Bartholomew Craig. 2012. Identifying careless responses in survey data. *Psychological Methods* 17, 3: 437–455. http://doi.org/10.1037/a0028085
63. O Moore. 2012. Woman's Call to End Video Game Misogyny Sparks Vicious Online Attacks. *The Globe and Mail.*
64. David Morley. 1992. *Television, audiences, and cultural studies*. Routledge, London.
65. Newzoo. Global Games Market Will Reach $102.9 Billion in 2017. Retrieved from: http://www.newzoo.com/insights/global-games-market-will-reach-102-9-billion-2017-2/
66. Nintendo. 1985. *Super Mario Bros.* Game [NES]. (13 September 1985). Nintendo.
67. Nintendo Entertainment Analysis & Development. 2006. The Legend of Zelda: Twilight Princess. Game [Wii, GameCube]. (19 November 2006). Nintendo.
68. Martha C. Nussbaum. 1995. Objectification. *Philosophy Public Affairs Philosophy & Public Affairs* 24, 4: 249–291. http://doi.org/10.1111/j.1088-4963.1995.tb00032.x
69. Susan P. Phillips. 2005. Defining and measuring gender: A social determinant of health whose time has come. *International Journal for Equity in Health.*
70. Platinum Games. 2009. *Bayonetta.* Game [PlayStation 3, Xbox 360]. (29 October 2009). Nintendo.
71. Joseph H. Pleck, Freya L. Sonenstein, and Leighton C. Ku. 1994. Attitudes toward male roles among adolescent males: A discriminant validity analysis. *Sex Roles* 30, 7-8: 481–501. http://doi.org/10.1007/bf01420798
72. Andrew K. Przybylski, Netta Weinstein, Richard M. Ryan, and C. Scott Rigby. 2009. Having to versus Wanting to Play: Background and Consequences of Harmonious versus Obsessive Engagement in Video Games. *CyberPsychology & Behavior* 12, 5: 485–492. http://doi.org/10.1089/cpb.2009.0083
73. Sheri Graner Ray. 2004. Gender inclusive game design: expanding the market. Charles River Media, Hingham, MA.
74. Eva A. Van Reijmersdal, Jeroen Jansz, Oscar Peters, and Guda Van Noort. 2013. Why girls go pink: Game character identification and game-players' motivations.

Computers in Human Behavior 29, 6: 2640–2649. http://doi.org/10.1016/j.chb.2013.06.046

75. Cecilia L. Ridgeway. 1992. *Gender, interaction, and inequality*. Springer-Verlag, New York.
76. Rockstar North. 2013. *Grand Theft Auto V*. Game [PlayStation 4, PlayStation 3, Xbox One, Xbox 360, Microsoft Windows]. (17 September 2013). Rockstar Games.
77. Rockstar San Diego. 2010. *Red Dead Redemption*. Game [PlayStation 3, Xbox 360]. (18 May 2010). Rockstar Games.
78. Richard M. Ryan and Edward L. Deci. 2000. Intrinsic and Extrinsic Motivations: Classic Definitions and New Directions. *Contemporary Educational Psychology* 25, 1: 54–67. http://doi.org/10.1006/ceps.1999.1020
79. Richard M. Ryan and Edward L. Deci. 2000. Self-determination theory and the facilitation of intrinsic motivation, social development, and well-being. *American Psychologist* 55, 1: 68–78. http://doi.org/10.1037/0003-066x.55.1.68
80. Richard M. Ryan, C. Scott Rigby, and Andrew Przybylski. 2006. The Motivational Pull of Video Games: A Self-Determination Theory Approach. *Motivation and Emotion Motiv Emot* 30, 4: 344–360. http://doi.org/10.1007/s11031-006-9051-8
81. Anastasia Salter and Bridget Blodgett. 2012. Hypermasculinity & Dickwolves: The Contentious Role of Women in the New Gaming Public. *Journal of Broadcasting & Electronic Media* 56, 3: 401–416. http://doi.org/10.1080/08838151.2012.705199
82. Santa Monica Studio. 2005. God of War. Game [PlayStation 3, PlayStation 2, PlayStation Vita]. (22 March 2005). Sony Computer Entertainment.
83. Anita Sarkeesian. 2011. Tropes vs. Women:#2 Women in Refrigerators. *Feminist Frequency*. Retrieved from https://feministfrequency.com/video/tropes-vs-women-2-women-in-refrigerators/
84. Anita Sarkeesian. 2014. Women as Background Decoration (Part 1). *Feminist Frequency*. Retrieved from https://feministfrequency.com/video/women-as-background-decoration-tropes-vs-women/
85. P. Skalski, R. Tamborini, A. Shelton, M. Buncher, and P. Lindmark. 2010. Mapping the road to fun: Natural video game controllers, presence, and game enjoyment. *New Media & Society* 13, 2: 224–242. http://doi.org/10.1177/1461444810370949
86. Christina Hoff Sommers. 2014. What critics of GamerGate get wrong. *Youtube*. Retrieved from https://www.youtube.com/watch?v=5rvlcvbd21w
87. Christina Hoff Sommers. 2015. The war on gamers continues. *Youtube*. Retrieved from https://www.youtube.com/watch?v=ymw39mckmzy
88. Spence, J.T., & Helmreich, R.L. (1978). *Masculinity and femininity: their psychological dimensions, correlates, and antecedents*. Austin, TX: University of Texas Press.
89. Janet K. Swim, Robyn Mallett, and Charles Stangor. 2004. Understanding Subtle Sexism: Detection and Use of Sexist Language. *Sex Roles* 51, 3/4: 117–128. http://doi.org/10.1023/b:sers.0000037757.73192.06
90. Ron Tamborini, Nicholas David Bowman, Allison Eden, Matthew Grizzard, and Ashley Organ. 2010. Defining Media Enjoyment as the Satisfaction of Intrinsic Needs. *Journal of Communication* 60, 4: 758–777. http://doi.org/10.1111/j.1460-2466.2010.01513.x
91. Team Ninja. 2003. *Dead or Alive Xtreme Beach Volleyball*. Game [Xbox]. (22 January 2003). Tecmo.
92. 2014. Thoughts on #GamerGate | Game/Show | PBS Digital Studios. *Youtube*. Retrieved from https://www.youtube.com/watch?v=ezrt--qvz04
93. Diane Watson, Mark Hancock, Regan L. Mandryk, and Max Birk. 2013. Deconstructing the touch experience. *Proceedings of the 2013 ACM international conference on Interactive tabletops and surfaces - ITS '13*. http://doi.org/10.1145/2512349.2512819
94. D. Williams, N. Martins, M. Consalvo, and J. D. Ivory. 2009. The virtual census: representations of gender, race and age in video games. *New Media & Society* 11, 5: 815–834. http://doi.org/10.1177/1461444809105354
95. Brianna Wu. No skin thick enough: The daily harassment of women in the game industry. Retrieved December 22, 2016 from http://www.polygon.com/2014/7/22/5926193/women-gaming-harassment
96. Mike Z. Yao, Chad Mahood, and Daniel Linz. 2009. Sexual Priming, Gender Stereotyping, and Likelihood to Sexually Harass: Examining the Cognitive Effects of Playing a Sexually-Explicit Video Game. *Sex Roles* 62, 1-2: 77–88. http://doi.org/10.1007/s11199-009-9695-4
97. Nick Yee, Nicolas Ducheneaut, Han-Tai Shiao, and Les Nelson. 2012. Through the azerothian looking glass. *Proceedings of the 2012 ACM annual conference on Human Factors in Computing Systems - CHI '12*. http://doi.org/10.1145/2207676.2208683
98. Andreas Zecher. 2014. Open letter to the gaming community. *Medium*. Retrieved from https://medium.com/@andreaszecher/open-letter-to-the-gaming-community-df4511032e8a#.f1heon42t

Understanding Gaming Perceptions and Experiences in a Women's College Community

Orit Shaer, Lauren Westendorf, Nicholas A. Knouf
Wellesley College
Wellesley, MA
{oshaer, lwestend, nknouf}@wellesley.edu

Claudia Pederson
Wichita State University
Wichita, KS
claudia.pederson@wichita.edu

ABSTRACT
Recent trends in gaming diversification have shown that women are both an increasingly significant pool of consumers and game producers, and regular victims of misogynistic harassment. Such observations stress the importance of investigating the complex relationships of women and gaming. In this paper, we draw upon perspectives from Feminist HCI to extend the current knowledge of issues in gaming that are specific to women. We present results from a mixed-methods study with 327 participants who are students and alumnae of a women's college. Our findings shed light on the complex relationships of women with games, with other gamers, and with gaming culture and industry. The results also indicate that in some cases gender-related negative experiences of gaming have lasting impact on the participation and self-confidence of young women. We conclude by discussing the implications of our findings for the design of games, game development education, and for the study of gaming.

ACM Classification Keywords
H.5.m. Information Interfaces and Presentation (e.g. HCI): Miscellaneous

Author Keywords
Feminism, Gender, Video Games

INTRODUCTION
While the gaming community has, for many years, been assumed to consist of primarily young men, recent developments suggest a significant shift underway. In fact, the most up-to-date survey by the industry's largest trade group, the Entertainment Software Association, shows that 41% of the game-playing population are female, and that women age 18 or older now represent a significantly greater portion of the game-playing population (31%) than boys age 18 or younger (17%) [43]. Examining the actual composition of the game-playing population suggests that we need to further our understanding of who is a gamer as well as to broaden the composition of subject pools in our studies of gamers.

Recent efforts of some women, men, and transgender individuals to have greater representation and diversity in gaming show that gaming is no longer a boys' "club house" [64]. Such a shift, however, is not taking place without resistance. Consider "GamerGate", an organized action targeting the media critic Anita Sarkeesian and the game developer Zoe Quinn, among others, for their critiques of misogynistic representations and behavior in the broader gaming community [14, 28, 72, 83]. While those participating in GamerGate argued that their aim was to protect "ethics" in videogame journalism, their actions evinced an anti-feminist stance.

The most recent developer surveys show a gaming industry dominated by men, with only 22% of game developers identifying as female and only 2% as transgender or non-binary. Diversity in sexual orientation, race, and ethnicity in the mainstream industry is similarly low [43]. However, new alternative platforms, such as Twine, are gaining popularity with female and transgender gaming communities, enabling new types of narratives to be explored with minimal capital and technical investment [1, 52, 66, 67].

Consequently, gaming is emerging as a significant site for expanding our understanding of the intersections of gender and technology. After all, it is often through games that girls and young women today have some of their first encounters with technology [48]. Early experiences with games inform not only how young women participate in games and gaming culture, but also how they view their own potential role within this field. However, while literature on the subject of women and games often focuses on issues of representation, gaming research is primarily done on mixed subject or male dominated subject pools [19, 49, 76, 78]. Thus, we know very little about the gaming behavior, perceptions, and experiences of women. Moreover, we have limited understanding of how young women envision themselves as part of this male-dominated field and perceive a potential career in games.

The GamerGate controversy has certainly highlighted the rampant sexism, misogyny, and physical threats that women and transgender individuals face when playing games or discussing representation in games [7, 54, 68]. While the importance of these observations cannot be understated, we believe that the gaming experiences of women cannot be reduced to the perva-

CHI 2017, May 06-11, 2017, Denver, CO, USA
©2017 ACM. ISBN 978-1-4503-4655-9/17/05...$15.00
DOI: http://dx.doi.org/10.1145/3025453.3025623

sive misogyny that some gamers face. We are thus interested in exploring the complicated relationships women have with gaming in general, gaming with others, and the gaming industry as a whole.

In this paper, we present results from a study with a sample of 327 students and alumnae of a women's college that contributes to extending the knowledge about young women's perceptions and experiences of gaming, gaming culture and the gaming industry. We examine participants' experiences with same- and mixed-gender players, their motivation for gaming, their experiences (or not) of harassment, and their perception of careers in game development. We triangulate these experiences through the lenses of their self-professed engagement with gaming, their major, as well as their (self-reported) race and ethnicity. Our results show that the experiences of the participants in our sample are incredibly complex, unable to be simply categorized in gendered fashion. We also find evidence that in some cases online harassment and toxicity have long-term impact on the participation and confidence of young women in online gaming, and on their view of their own potential role within this growing industry. At the same time, we found that positive experiences could help women to persist, participate, and develop a sense of belonging to gaming culture and communities.

We begin by exploring why the context of a women's college should be of interest to the broader CHI community. We then explore related work and describe our study methodology and our quantitative and qualitative results. We conclude by outlining how these results inform game design, game development education, as well as further studies of games.

Studying a Women's College Community

Our work draws upon and contributes to recent activities of Gender and Feminist HCI [2, 3, 4, 6, 39, 57, 71] as well as to broader currents of feminist science and technology studies [36, 37, 38, 82]. In particular, we draw on Sandra Harding's elaboration of "standpoint epistemology" for science and technological fields, which emphasizes the importance of moving away from an "essentialized" standpoint of marginalized groups [38]. Instead of assuming that there is a singular women's experience of gaming, as implied by the GamerGate reports, we seek to understand the diversity of perspectives within the varied standpoints of women. This allows us to counter essentialized views of women's experiences in gaming and of a particularly "feminine" way of playing.

Our choice to study gaming behaviors, attitudes, and experiences at a women's college was influenced by our observation that, on the heels of GamerGate reporting, more attention is being given to women-only spaces in computer science and in technology more broadly. These include women-only hackathons, hackerspaces, and groups such as FemTechNet [29, 32, 60], which were created to foster the participation of women in gaming and computing. A women's college is another example of such a space, where gender issues and participation of women in computing and media are paramount.

A women's college is therefore a prime site for applying HCI feminist methodology [3], which emphasizes an empathic relationship with research participants, co-construction of the research activities and goals, and self disclosure of researchers' perspectives. Two of the authors teach in a women's college where discussions inside and outside of class often examine gender representation and participation in depth. Another author teaches a course on game design from a feminist art history perspective. The goals of this study and the research questions explored were co-constructed with students of a women's college who participated in a course and research group about games. We approached these research questions from a feminist perspective, arguing for considering not only the experiences of women playing games but also their perceptions and aspirations of developing games. The fourth author is an alumna who participated in the research group.

A women's college is, of course, not representative of society or women as a whole. However, studying this population provides several advantages to HCI researchers seeking to understand the relationship of women and gaming in detail. First, a women's college environment reduces stereotypes about women in computing and STEM [51], increasing the likelihood of student engagement in activities that are traditionally considered masculine. In addition, women's colleges currently enroll a more racially and ethnically diverse population of students than other liberal arts colleges [73]. As such, only 45.4% of our study participants identify themselves as White. Thus, while our sample is not representative of the general population, it does provide a more diverse data set than in many previous studies, which enables us to investigate not only gender and gaming but also racialized aspects of gaming. Finally, while existing studies are often confined to a particular game, set of games, or self-contained gaming community, ours is not limited by these boundaries, but instead represents a condensed cross-section of a women's college community in gaming culture. As such, we can investigate diversity of experiences in gaming.

RELATED WORK

Partly as a result of GamerGate, and partly as a result of shifts in gaming more broadly, there has been a growing body of work on the intersection of gaming and gender, perhaps most easily indexed in the popular media by a syllabus on "Gaming and Feminism" produced by *The New Inquiry*, an online publication devoted to critical analyses of contemporary culture [62]. As a result, it is impossible to cite all of the relevant and important work in this area. Rather, we focus mostly on work that directly intersects with HCI and the immediate concerns of this paper.

The intersection of gender and gaming has been of wide interest to computing scholars since the landmark *From Barbie to Mortal Kombat: Gender and Computer Games*, a text that has been recently updated in *Beyond Barbie and Mortal Kombat: New Perspectives on Gender and Gaming* [13, 49]. A sampling of recent works examines modding communities in The Sims 2 [85], intimacy in World of Warcraft [63], marriage in the online game Audition [33] and gaming motivation in the "pink game" GoSupermodel [81]. The latter study is illustrative of what has become a common critique against these "pink games", namely that they reify assumptions regarding gender, suggesting that women gamers are "naturally" drawn to certain types of games [78]. Other researchers have suggested that any future research on women and games needs to take this realization into account, arguing that the task is to "find out how to identify differences in game play without naturalizing them into an underlying truth of gender" [45, pg. 176], while drawing upon salient allied research in theories of gender, queerness, and postcoloniality [44]. Also important is the need to recognize that who is and who is not considered a "gamer" is open to question, as playing games intersects with many other identities and varies in different social contexts [75].

Research also shows that gaming is at time most inhospitable for women [31, 40, 46]. Conformance with masculine norms and higher scores on social dominance scales predicted higher scores on a video game sexism scale [30]. Harassment is not limited to female gamers, as female-passing chatbots experienced more sexual language and more sexist stereotypes directed at them than male-passing chatbots [10]. Online harassment, and in particular of young women, is also prevalent beyond games [26].

Finally, the intersection of computer science and gaming—game development—is also often inhospitable to women [17, 77]. While the composition of game players in terms of gender and race has changed dramatically over the past decade, approaching parity with the wider population, the composition of game developers has not [43, 74]. More broadly, women remain underrepresented within the world of computer science and programming due to a number of issues, including preexisting biases, implicit sexism, and lack of support, even if the situation is much improved compared to the days of women as literal computers [21, 57, 67]. Women have been shown to still parrot these negative stereotypes [15], and continue to leave computing in greater numbers than men [59, 65, 70]. Yet, encouragement by family members and friends combatting some of these stereotypes was found to be an important factor in girls' decisions to take computer programming classes in high school [5]. This potentially carries over to gaming. While there is equivocal evidence as to whether or not an interest in gaming is correlated with an interest in computer science [25], it has been found that storytelling activities, in the context of game development, can encourage middle school girls to become interested in programming [50].

STUDY

Goals and Research Questions

The goal of our study is to examine the gaming experiences and attitudes of members of a women's college community. We seek to unpack the experiences of women with games and to examine assumptions of who is a gamer, what is the impact of gender and race on game playing, and how women perceive the qualities required for a career in game development. More specifically we seek to answer the following questions:

Q1: What are the gaming attitudes and habits of participants: how often do they play, what do they play, and why do they play?

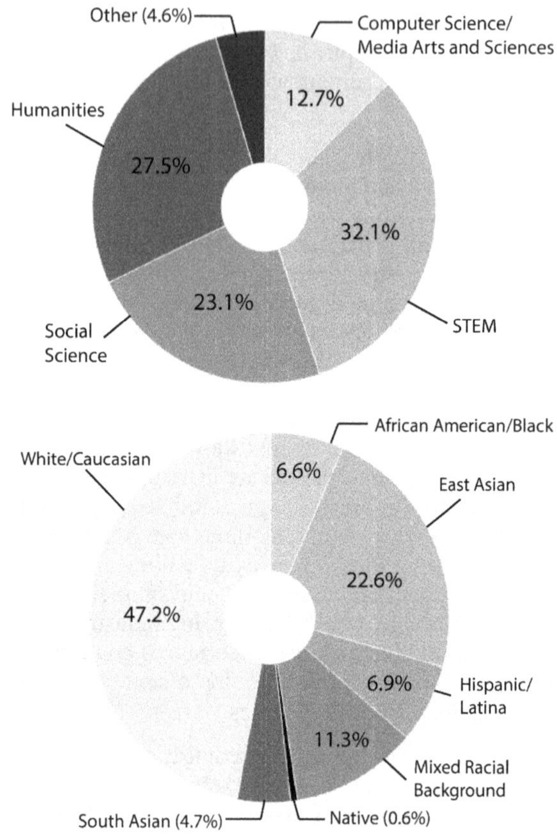

Figure 1: Participants by primary major (upper) and race/ethnicity (lower)

Q2: What are memorable experiences participants have had from playing with others (with same-gender players and with different-gender players)?

Q3: What (if any) negative experiences did participants have while playing that are related to their gender and what was the impact of such experiences?

Q4: What (if any) negative experiences did participants have from playing that are related to their race and ethnicity and what was the impact of such experiences?

Finally, Q5: How do participants perceive the qualities required for a game development career and do they envision themselves seeking opportunities in this field?

Methods

Participants

We recruited participants using online public mailing lists limited to students and alums of Wellesley College, a liberal arts college for women. The invitation read: "Take our survey on gaming behaviors and perceptions. Even if you only play a few games on your phone, your responses are important. . . ." Participation was voluntary and no compensation was given in exchange for participation, but all participants were offered a chance to win an Amazon Kindle device. 327 students and alumnae from the college completed this study. Of these,

313 participants self-identified as women, and 14 participants self-identified a gender other than male or female (e.g. genderqueer, genderfluid, non-binary). Of these 327 participants, the average age was 20.9 years old (SD=4.0), and 23.8% were alumnae. Our sample, while not representative of the general population, is representative of Wellesley College's population in terms of ethnic/racial and major diversity (Figure 1) [84].

Procedure
Participants completed an online questionnaire available only to the college community.

Questionnaire
The questionnaire was designed to collect both quantitative and qualitative data. It was comprised of the following measures and indicators:

Gaming habits were surveyed through multiple-choice questions about platforms used to play games, favorite genres, and time per week playing games. We also asked participants about what age did they start playing video games.

Attitude was assessed using the question *how important is gaming for you* (5-point Likert scale where 5 is very important).

Gaming motivation was assessed using the Gaming Motivation Scale (GAMS) [56]. We chose this scale because it is validated, multidimensional, and goes beyond online gaming. GAMS was designed to assess *intrinsic motivation*, four types of *extrinsic motivation*, as well as *amotivation*. Intrinsic motivation is the desire to perform an activity for itself [22, 23]: players who play because they enjoy exploring the game, improving their skills for the thrill of the game. Extrinsic motivation refers to engaging in an activity as a means to an end. GAMS identifies four types of extrinsic motivation including: *external regulation*, which refers to behavior regulated through external means such as rewards and competition; *introjected regulation*, which refers to regulation through internal pressures such as anxiety and guilt; *identified motivation*, where people engage in a behavior based on its perceived meaning or relation to personal goals; and *integrated regulation*, which entails engaging in an activity out of choice that is part of the person's sense of self [80]. Finally, amotivation refers to the relative absence of motivation either intrinsic or extrinsic.

Gender-related experiences were surveyed through open questions. We inquired whether and why a participant felt uncomfortable in online gaming because of their gender, whether a participant self reported a different gender in online games and why, and whether a participant ever received a gender related comment in online games and how were they impacted by such comments.

Similarly, race/ethnicity related experiences were surveyed through open questions. We inquired whether a participant felt uncomfortable in online gaming because of their race or ethnicity, whether a participant self-reported different race or ethnicity in online games, as well as whether a participant ever received race or ethnicity related comments and how they were impacted by such comments.

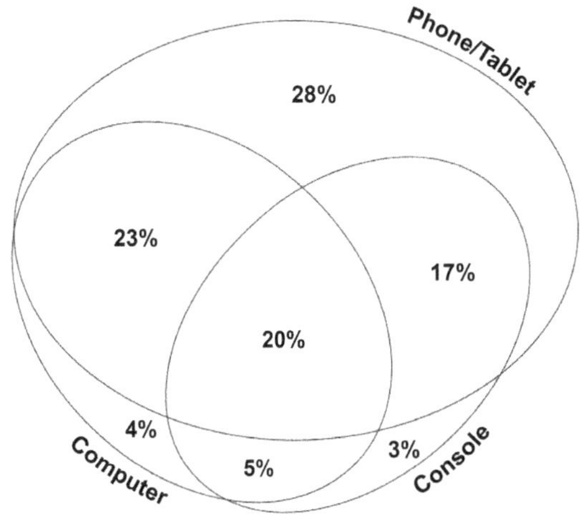

Figure 2: Venn diagram of percentage of participants per platform used.

Interaction with other players was studied by asking users to describe a memorable experience with a player of other gender, and another memorable experience with a player of the same gender.

Perceptions of career in gaming were investigated by quantifying how many participants have considered a career in gaming, and how many know a female game developer. We also asked participants to describe the skills they believe are required for a career in game development.

Data Analysis
We analyzed quantitative data using IBM SPSS Statistics, Version 22. All multiple choice responses were coded numerically and all mean comparison was done using independent samples t-tests. Responses to open questions averaged 26.2 (SD=23.3) words per answer per user. We analyzed the qualitative data using content analysis methods. First-level codes were developed from preliminary review of the data by two independent coders and were then collapsed into advanced categories based on frequency. Categories were analyzed for the identification of themes. Inter-coder reliability based on 100% of the data was good with 87% agreement.

RESULTS

Gaming Habits
On average, participants spend 5 to 10 hours a week playing games. The average age reported for starting to play digital games was 8.6 (SD=3.3). While 22% of the participants only play on their phone, 45% of the participants play on a console, and 51% play using a computer. The distribution of players per gaming platform is described in Figure 2. These results stand in contrast to an image long held that women are not interested in or are not actually playing computer games [78]. Many of our participants play puzzle games (34.3%), however, a significant portion are involved with role playing (13.8%),

Genre	Frequency
Puzzles	112 (34.3%)
Role Playing	45 (13.8%)
Strategy	25 (7.6%)
Adventure	24 (7.3%)
Simulation	18 (5.5%)
Trivia	16 (4.9%)
Word	15 (4.6%)
Action	14 (4.3%)
Independent	10 (3.1%)
Arcade	10 (3.1%)

Table 1: Favorite genre by number and percentage of participants

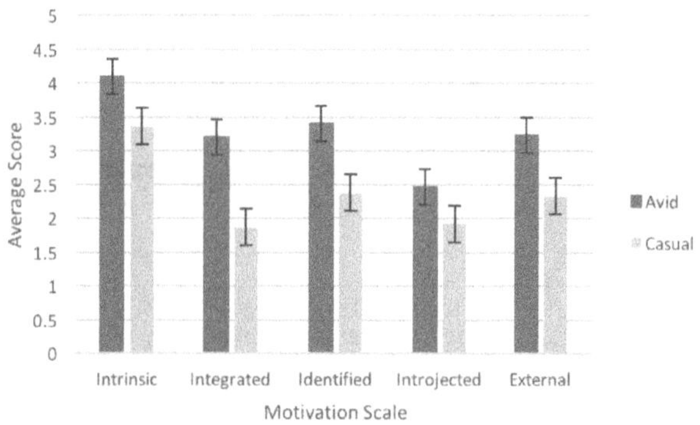

Figure 3: Average motivation scores for avid and casual gamers

strategy (7.6%), and adventure (7.3%) games. The top ten favorite genres reported are detailed in Table 1. These results differ from the notion that women are naturally drawn to casual and/or "pink" games [53, 69].

Gaming Attitude

19.3% (63/327) of participants responded "Important" or "Very Important" when asked "How important is gaming to you?" These participants reported significantly more time spent gaming than other participants, with 76% playing regularly more than 5 hours a week. They were less likely to play on their phone and more likely to play on a computer or a console. We thereby labeled them as avid gamers. The remaining 264 participants were classified as casual gamers [18, 47].

Motivation

Both avid and casual gamers reported higher levels of intrinsic motivation than extrinsic motivation—playing because they enjoy exploring and mastering the game. Avid gamers scored significantly higher on all five motivation scales than casual gamers using Bonferroni adjusted alpha levels of .01 per test ($p < .001$, see Figure 3). Notably, avid gamers reported moderate to high external and integrated motivation, which indicate competitive game orientation. Such competitive orientation is often overlooked as a motivating factor for women [78].

Time, Attitude, and Motivation

Time spent gaming, importance of gaming, and all five measures of motivation significantly correlated with each other for all participants ($p < .001$). The alpha coefficients for each motivation scales were as follows: intrinsic (.626), integrated (.890), identified (.829), introjected (.690), external (.771).

Gender and Gaming

Overall, 22.6% (74/327) of the participants reported that they received gender-related comments about or while gaming. Of the 178 participants who had visited an online game room 48% (85/178) reported feeling uncomfortable because of their gender. Participants who had received gender related comments were less likely to play on their phone for gaming and more likely to play on the computer or a console. Avid gamers reported more gender- and race-based comments than did their casual gamer counterparts, χ^2 (2, N = 327) = 11.82, p =.001.

Gender-related comments

To better understand the nature of gender-related comments, we analyzed participant open responses. We identified several core themes including: sexualized comments and slurs; comments about women's lack in skills; and division of value between boy and girl games, avatars, and characters. About 22% (16/74) reported sexualized comments. In the voice of one participant: "While I was in a public voicechat server, a random gamer who wasn't even playing with us joined the server and started saying sexual things to me after he heard my voice." Another participant reported "I've been called a whore, told to go make people sandwiches, I've been targeted during attacks (Call of Duty)." Many of these comments included unwelcomed invitations such as: "Someone asked to date me. They were persistent." Or, "My sister, then 13, and I offered to help a new player if he needed advice. He asked us if we were girls, and when we confirmed it, he asked for our phone numbers and generally was extremely abrasive."

23% of these participants (17/74) reported comments indicating that women lack in skills. For example, one participant described, "Boys make fun of me for being bad because I'm a girl, friends included." Another participant wrote, "People would act surprised if I played well because I was a girl. They'd act more humiliated as if it was a degrading thing to get beaten by a female." Participants also reported that when attempting to respond to comments they were often dismissed: "It was clearly based on the presumption that I was a less talented gamer due to my gender. It further was based on me being 'too sensitive' due to my response that his behavior was not OK."

18% (13/74) reported comments that expressed surprise that a gamer is a woman. In the words of one participant: "Whenever I use it [a microphone] people always ask if I'm a little boy or a girl. Often are shocked to hear I am a girl." Similarly, a console player shared: "When I connect my console to the Internet I can play with a wider community. Sometimes they notice that I have a more feminine voice. As a result, they either want to place me in a more defensible/safer position b/c they doubt my ability. Or they respond with surprise and then leave me alone after the initial realization that there is a girl on their team."

10.8% (8/74) described comments that highlight division of value between boy and girl games, avatars, or characters. For example, "I make a point of avoiding situations and groups that aren't pointedly female-friendly to avoid gender-related comments, but when I do get these comments, it's often just to tell me that my interests even within open-ended games (like Skyrim or MMOs, or even girlier sims like Animal Crossing or Harvest Moon) are 'frilly' or 'girly' in the sense that they are not the intended experience of games, and that I am somehow playing them all wrong." Finally, 10.8% (8/74) reported targeted attack that excluded them from a game: "I used pink spray paint to play counter strike and got called out for likely being female, when I responded that I was booted out."

Impact of gender-related comments
Of the 74 participants who received some sort of gender-related negative comments, 53% (39/74) reported that these comments affected their attitude toward gaming negatively. Avid gamers received significantly more gender related comments and were more likely to report losing interest in online gaming based on a gender related comment. From analyzing participant open responses, we identified several themes of negative impact including: negative perception of gaming culture, losing interest or avoiding online gaming, losing interest in a game-related career, loss of confidence, and hesitancy to show gender. Many participant comments integrated more than one theme.

Sharing their perception of gaming, participants expressed their frustration and sense of being excluded from the community (13/74). One participant wrote: "I'm frustrated sometimes because ideally I would feel like participating more in the greater community if it wasn't full of racist, sexist dudebro who make me feel unwanted and/or unsafe. I also sometimes feel like I need to hide the fact that I play videogames because it is something gross."

Participants also described losing interest or avoiding online gaming (25/74): "I have found certain games that allow me to play as a woman without prejudice, ie I never got serious about multiplayer online games but instead started playing simulation games in single player mode."

Participants also described losing interest in pursuing a career in gaming (4/74): "When I was younger, I thought it would be interesting to go into game design. I now refuse to enter that field due to the misogyny and unsafe environment for women that exists." Another participants described: "I grew up playing video games. By the time I was truly considering career options, this thought was long gone, mostly due to the sexism that exists in game development."

In several cases participants described sensitivity to gender related judgment, internalization of stereotypes, and lose of confidence (5/74). In the words of one participant: "I stopped playing regularly because I should do more feminine things. I have constant guilt for getting a game console, and also regret for not playing." Another participant shared: "I'm afraid to play because of my lack of skill in games I enjoy."

Finally, participants described changing their behavior and hiding their identity in online gaming (6/74). One participant described: "I'm always so paranoid and uncomfortable when I meet a male gamer for the first time, even if my friends are there. I usually never join voicechat-required games without a good friend with me."

Taken together, these findings indicate that gender-related comments in online gaming do have a significant negative impact that in some cases results in alienating women from gaming, gaming culture, and industry.

Self-reporting gender
Previous studies found that players take advantage of the freedom for making avatar choices in virtual worlds to recreate their gendered identities and to explore human relationships mediated by these sociotechnical systems [11, 33, 42]. We sought to investigate socio-cultural contexts that cause players to self-report a different gender in online games. Gender reporting is not always consistent with avatar choice.

12% (38/327) of all participants shared that they self-reported a different gender in online games. From participant responses, we identified several reasons for self reporting a different gender, including: to be treated with respect; to not being scrutinized for own abilities; to blend in; dissatisfaction with female characters; for fun, new experiences, or as a social experiment; because of gender fluidity; and for privacy. Many participants refer to more than one of these reasons in their response.

Some participants emphasized hostility towards women. For example, "Super toxic communities. It was easier to be mistaken as a teenage boy undergoing puberty than a female." Similarly, "On games such as Call of Duty, male players seem to target and seek out female players on occasion more than other players." Other participants sought to avoid unfair scrutiny and judgment: "You don't get judged as harshly for the same level of skill."

Participants also expressed dissatisfaction with female characters, the economy surrounding female characters, and with how female characters are treated by other players. In the words of one participant: "The male characters have more clothes and people treat them with more respect. I always worry that when I start a new game like when I joined WoW that people would be more judgmental if I identified as a girl." Another player describes, "I tried an MMORPG once and the culture was very misogynistic. Even the virtual economy was very biased to favor male players." Other participants mentioned exploration and experimentation as a reason for self-reporting a different gender: "I wanted to know if it was any different being a guy. It wasn't." Similarly, "I thought it would be fun to play that way and have the other players assume I was a male." Finally, participants mentioned lack of flexibility in avatar and gender reporting choices: "I wanted to have a male avatar and was restricted to only female if reporting female." Another participant wrote: "People are less likely to make rude/sexist comments if I say I'm male. Also, I'm genderfluid, so generally there's no possible way to self-report my actual gender."

Race, Ethnicity, and Gaming

As previous research highlights, gender is not an identity category that exists separately from other considerations such as age, race, class, and ethnicity [12, 16, 27]. Our ethnically and racially diverse sample (see Figure 1), enables us to investigate racialized aspects of gaming in addition to gender related issues.

A much smaller proportion of the participants felt uncomfortable in online gaming rooms because of race or ethnicity (15/327 of all participants) compared to those who felt uncomfortable because of their gender. 13 of these participants reported that they experienced race/ethnicity-related comments.

Participant responses revealed comments targeting Asian, black, or Jewish gamers. For example, "not bad for an Asian girl", "people like to use the n-word that rhymes with 'figure'", and "one of my online friends would call me a Chink (I'm Chinese)". In the words of a participant, "racist and anti-Semitic comments abound."

Of the respondents who have played online games, four participants shared that they self reported a different race/ethnicity. Among the reasons for self reporting different race or ethnicity, participants listed avoiding harassment and fear of racist reactions: "When you're a black person on an anonymous forum, the best option is usually to not disclose [your race]. Going around saying 'hey guys, guess who's black!' is a great way to get unwanted attention."

Also, similarly to gender reporting, participants mentioned lack of flexibility in avatar choices: "Well, I'm a complicated race/ethnicity. 'Other' on the census form...", and "For games that ask you to choose a character, the characters usually do not have different ethnicities apart from caucasian or black."

Impact of race/ethnicity related comments

Of the 13 individuals that reported race related comments, 46% (6/13) reported that such comments affected their attitude toward gaming in a negative way. In the words of one participant: "Sometimes the negativity gets to me, but I'm actively working on improving my overall attitude." A different participant wrote: "Another reason I don't play with strangers." And "It just disgusts me on a certain level that human beings can be so casual with racial slurs."

Interaction with Other Players

Interactions with players of a different gender

Only 23% (75/327) responded to the questions about sharing memorable interactions with players from a different gender. Of the participants who responded, 75% (56/75) shared positive experiences, and 30% (21/75) shared negative experiences.

Positive experiences included bonding with and making new friends (including romantic connections), finding support, teaching and helping, and connecting with family members.

Many participants described making and strengthening relationships with other players. One participant shared: "In middle school, I used online gaming as a way to make friends with the boys in my class. The first time I got asked out on a date was while online gaming." Participants also described relationships they developed through online gaming: "I had this really good friend, we actually met in real life a few times. It was interesting because he didn't friend me for my gender but for my gaming skills."

Some participants described experiences of teaching, helping to develop a skill, or experimenting together. For example, "I remember my male friend helping me play a shooting game and being encouraging despite my ineptitude", or in the words of a different participant, "My male friend always chose a female character and I always chose a male character." Other participants described support they received from male friends against gender-based harassment: "One of my teammates heard another gamer making comments about my gender and spoke up saying that gender has nothing to do with skill."

The negative experiences center around gender-based comments with similar themes to those discussed earlier in the paper. In the words of one participant: "I used to play Runescape when I was 10/11 years old, but stopped after a male player propositioned me for cyber sex in exchange for making me new armor in the game. This came after another male player two years older than me asked me to be his in-game girlfriend and a boy I knew from school tried to trick me into 'marrying' him."

Interactions with players of the same gender

Only 20% (66/327) of participants answered the question about sharing memorable interactions with players of the same gender. Interestingly, one participant that did not share a memorable interaction wrote: "Only elaborating here because I just realized I never interacted with a girl on the online games I've played." Of the participants that did share a memorable experience, 89% (59/66) shared positive experiences including sharing passion, finding support, making new friends, and bonding with family members and friends. For example, one participant described, "My mom has been a gamer for a long time too." Another participant shared: "My wife and I both like gaming and play together—it's a lot of fun." Also, "My sister and I used to compete on video games. I also taught several older family members about some of the games I liked to play."

Other participants shared a memorable experience playing with a close friend. "My female best friend and I played several online fantasy games together in middle school. Having a friend play with me made me feel like less of an outsider, especially because all the other people I knew who played the games were male." Participants also described bonding with other female gamers, sometime extending their friendship beyond the game: "A female gamer picked me up in a car in GTA Online and went on a mission with me." Another participant described: "One of my teammates is a girl and we've listened to each other rant and supported each other when anything, even not-gaming related, goes too negative." A different participant shared:

> I guess I've had a lot of "memorable interactions" with gamers of the same gender as I specifically seek

> out mixed-gender or solely non-male groups in online games/groups. It's not even talking about the experience in such a sexist atmosphere, it's knowing that friendliness/help is not coming from ulterior motives. That you are more likely to be viewed as a person, not a girl conforming to/subverting stereotypes about girls playing videogames. Just talking in conversational styles that are comfortable/natural for me with someone who will not judge me weirdly for doing so, is sometimes a breath of fresh air.

Only 11% (7/66) of the responders shared negative experiences, mostly due to gender-based comments from female friends. One participant described: "Quite a few girls in my year in high school (I went to high school in Hong Kong if that matters) are pretty heavy gamers. A lot of them throw the same gendered insults about gaming towards their friends/other gamers, e.g. 'xx game is so girly', etc."

Views on Game Development Careers

Career in gaming

Despite the evidence that our study participants play and enjoy a large range of games, only 21% (69/327) of participants have considered a career in gaming. These participants were significantly more likely to be avid gamers (χ^2 (2, N = 327) = 22.18, p <.001). They were also more likely to be a Computer Science (19.0%), Media Arts and Science (6.3%), or English majors (11.1%) and less likely to be a Science or Social Science majors. There were no significant differences in race/ethnicity for the two groups. Interestingly, participants considering a career in gaming were more likely to know a female game developer than those who had not, χ^2 (2, N=327) = 7.69, p = .006. Overall, 11% (36/327) of the participants reported to know a female game developer. Most of these participants knew a female game developer through their social or professional network. Others heard about famous game developers through the media or through classes.

Perceptions of game development

To gain insight into how our participants perceive the loosely defined position of a game developer, we asked participants about the skills they think a game developer should have. About 21.1% (69/327) of participants view game developers as "Renaissance" people holding both strong artistic skills and technical skills: "Creative. Coding. Artistic. Technical abilities." Another 19.6% (64/327) of participants view game development as requiring "analytical skills, problem solving, and intellect". These views are in line with a common stereotypical image of game developers, thought to be responsible for all aspects of the game including development, design, art, and sound [41, 58, 61, 79]. Noticeably, 14.7% (48/327) of participants described qualities such as determination, "thick skin", strong will, and the ability to work long hours, which perhaps reflect the harsh reality of female game developers as portrayed by the media. This view is also in line with the traditional portrayal of game development, which emphasizes long hours and deadlines [41]. Finally, 17.4% (57/315) of participants mentioned cultural, racial, and gender sensitivity as required skills: "Someone who has the technical skills/creativity to develop a game, but who also has the awareness/empathy to reach wider audiences, and be cognizant of the social impact their game (or certain tropes within the game) might have, especially for minority audiences." This reflects a desire to make games more inclusive and the view that game developers can potentially lead to a positive change in the industry.

DISCUSSION

In this study, we expanded on existing work that aims to understand the experiences of women in gaming, by presenting findings from a study that goes beyond a particular game, set of games, or self-contained gaming community, to examine a condensed cross-section of women in gaming culture. Our results show that the experiences of the participants in our sample are complex, and cannot simply be categorized as either feminine or masculine, and thus requiring a nuanced analysis that takes into account the complicated ways in which identity and gaming intersect. This study thereby contributes to calls by others to understand how gaming amongst women is not homogeneous and relates to other identities [44, 75, 76]. In particular, this study contributes to Sandra Harding's call to move away from an "essentialized" standpoint of marginalized groups [44, 75, 76].

Our findings show that there is no singular "women's" experience of gaming, but rather a diversity of perspectives within the varied standpoints of members of a community. Women who participated in our study enjoy a large variety of game genres on different platforms. Within our participant population, we identified both casual and avid gamers, and found that participants are motivated mostly by intrinsic factors, though avid gamers are also motivated by extrinsic factors including competition. Taken together, our findings undermine the stereotypical view of who is a gamer, are in contrast to the notion that women are naturally drawn to casual and/or 'pink' games, and show that competitive orientation can be a major motivating factor for women. These findings are supported by previous research [78].

In many ways, we found that our participants play games in spite of barriers to entry. To play online, our participants needed to navigate unfriendly and sometime unsafe spaces, while being offered limited options of female characters with often dull economy of accessories and objects. About 23% of the participants reported that they received gender-related comments about gaming. Of the participants who had visited an online game room, about half reported feeling uncomfortable because of their gender. Participants reported incidents of blunt sexualized comments, harassment, being targeted while playing, demeaning comments about their skills, harsh judging, and exclusion from participation. While most comments came from male players, a small number of participants reported negative gender-related comments from female players or friends. In some cases participants reported long lasting negative impact on the perception of gaming and on participation in online gaming. Some women who had hostile experiences reported that they were less likely to pursue a career in the game industry. This finding is consistent with findings from a recent study by Fox and Tang [31].

However, the experiences of the participants are complex and cannot be reduced to simply facing pervasive misogyny. Many participants shared positive memorable experiences of playing with other players, male and female. Such experiences highlight the increasing relevance of videogames and game spaces as spaces of profound sociability for women, where connections are strengthened and formed, and gender relations are negotiated and contested. Also, positive experiences with gaming, such as bonding among female players, could help women to persist and participate in gaming as well as foster a sense of belonging to gaming communities or culture.

Only one out of five of our participants have considered a career in gaming, reflecting the current reality in the field [43]. We argue that women who face barriers to entry for playing games find it difficult to envision themselves in this field. These results are consistent with findings from a number of studies on female presence, or lack of it, in the gaming industry [43], which show that the male dominated environment, the gendered perception of gaming, and the lack of information about careers in gaming pose barriers for women to enter the industry. Notably, participants who know other game developers are more likely to consider career in gaming. This highlights a need to expose more women to role models as well as to provide information about opportunities in the field. Our participants mostly view game development as an interdisciplinary endeavor, including both technical skills of programming, but also skills more related to the humanities, such as training in the arts, media and cultural acumen, and the ability to tell coherent and engaging narratives. A large number of our participants suggested the importance of gender and racial sensitivity for game developers, indicating a desire to increase inclusion and improve representation in games.

Implications for Design

Our findings have implications for the design of games, game development education, and studies about gaming. In the design of games, our participants commented on thinly drawn female characters present in many mainstream games and on the limited economy around female characters. This raises a need to increase and diversify the representation of female characters while making the economy around them as equally rich and intriguing as around male characters. Also, our findings indicate a need for supporting more gender fluidity—the ability to smoothly move between genders beyond the binary of male/female—as a key aspect of the game experience. This could be achieved by providing more freedom in choosing characters and in reporting a player's gender. Applying a more complicated understanding of gender and identity to the representation of characters in games could result in environments that are not only inviting to diverse populations but are also more intriguing and enjoyable. Beyond representation, fostering civility in a gaming community can increase the participation of women. Game designers can apply various techniques and systems for monitoring communication between players, encouraging positive behavior, and punishing negative behavior. Online forums have had varying levels of success with flagging and human moderation [20, 34, 35]. Advances in machine learning offer opportunities for automatic identification and response to exclusion, harassment and verbal toxicity [8, 9, 24, 55, 58].

In the design of courses about gaming and game production, our findings identify opportunities for humanities, arts, and engineering collaborations that are based on the observation that those participants who want to become game developers are interested in storytelling as much as in the technology. In addition, to extend the skills of game developers to include awareness about gender and racial representation there is a need to educate students on how representations of any kind (including games and game developers) reflect the social context in which they are embedded. This requires joint effort between science and humanities fields, so that courses in art history, visual culture, cinema and media studies, women's and gender studies, in addition to math and computing, can be a requirement in training new game developers. In addition, the wide diversity of gaming experiences and interests highlighted in our findings suggests offering students more diverse options in terms of assignments and content to encompass a variety of game genres and cultures that enable students to learn about and experiment with different forms of representation. By diversifying our classroom materials and activities we increase the likelihood of inviting female students to engage with gaming culture and development. Furthermore, considering the impact of role models and of friendships with other female players and developers, it is important to consider the development of women-only spaces for game studies. Examples include classes, workshops, hackathons, etc. Such spaces have already proven effective in computing education, and could empower girls and women to engage in gaming, and to pursue an active role shaping the direction of the field.

Finally, while existing studies of gaming are often confined to a small number of women playing a particular game, a set of games, or a part of a self-contained gaming community, our study demonstrates that it is also important to conduct studies that are not limited by these boundaries, but instead represent a condensed cross-section of a gamer population. This study, focusing on a detailed investigation of a population of women that are students and alumnae of a women's college, shows tremendous variation rather than homogeneity. Our results demonstrate that the experiences of the women in our sample cannot simply be categorized in a gendered fashion. In the spirit of standpoint epistemology [38], we believe that findings from this study could be useful when studying other populations in gaming, and together demonstrate the need to broaden studies on gaming to further diversify our knowledge of experiences and behaviors in gaming.

Limitations and Future Work

There are a number of limitations to this study that should be considered in future research. First, our study utilized an online survey, which collects a one-time data point from self-selected participants. Our future work will expand on this work using interviews for a more in depth examination of life experiences related to gaming and to particular game platforms and communities. Second, although our sample included 14 gender non-conforming individuals, we focused mostly on issues specific to female players. Future work will expand on issues specific to gender non-conforming individuals' in gaming. Third, our research focused on women that are students and alumnae of a women's college. While we described the advantages that this user population provides for HCI research, our study population is not representative of women as a whole. Other studies should focus on different populations of women and girls, including intergenerational populations. Fourth, our research indicates that race and ethnicity play an important factor in the gaming experience; future studies should expand upon this area. Finally, the responses to our open-ended questions about experiences with same and other genders were fascinating, highlighting a range of behaviors, from support to harassment, both within and across genders. Further studies should delve into this area in more detail, not only to learn about these dynamics, but also to potentially develop strategies across genders to combat misogynistic behavior wherever it is found.

CONCLUSION

As gaming rapidly diversifies in terms of market and culture, women are both discussed as an increasingly significant pool of consumers, critics, and producers of video games, as well as victims of misogynistic aggression. In the interest of broadening perceptions, our study draws upon perspectives from Gender and Feminist HCI, to expand on existing work aiming to understand the experiences of women in gaming. Our goal of this paper is not to make definitive statements but rather to make a descriptive contribution–rigorously documenting and assessing the prevalence of different types of women's experiences with games, yielding richer data about diversity in games that others can build on.

Our findings highlight games as a space of social and professional possibility for women where participation is affected by certain barriers. The hostility many women face while playing does have, in some cases, a long-lasting impact on the participation of women in gaming. Some women who experienced hostility also reported on decreased interest in pursuing career in gaming. Our findings also suggest that positive experiences with gaming such as bonding among female players, could result in positive impact, helping women to persist and participate as well as fostering a sense of belonging to a game community, or more broadly to gaming culture. Thus, to reduce hostility and to pursue potential benefits of positive experiences we suggest advantages to pursuing parallel changes both in game design, and in game development education. Finally, our study indicates the urgency of elaborated and nuanced exploration of women and gaming.

ACKNOWLEDGMENTS

We thank Sheridan Sunier, Elizabeth Stowell, and the students of CAMS 272 for their contributions. We would also like to thank all of the anonymous respondents for taking the time to complete the survey.

REFERENCES

1. Anna Anthropy. 2012. *Rise of the Videogame Zinesters: How Freaks, Normals, Amateurs, Artists, Dreams, Dropouts, Queers, Housewives, and People Like You Are Taking Back an Art Form*. Seven Stories Press, New York.
2. Shaowen Bardzell. 2010. Feminist HCI: Taking Stock and Outlining an Agenda for Design. In *Proceedings of the SIGCHI Conference on Human Factors in Computing Systems (CHI '10)*. ACM, New York, NY, USA, 1301–1310. DOI: http://dx.doi.org/10.1145/1753326.1753521
3. Shaowen Bardzell and Jeffrey Bardzell. 2011. Towards a Feminist HCI Methodology: Social Science, Feminism, and HCI. In *Proceedings of the SIGCHI Conference on Human Factors in Computing Systems (CHI '11)*. ACM, New York, NY, USA, 675–684. DOI: http://dx.doi.org/10.1145/1978942.1979041
4. Shaowen Bardzell, Elizabeth Churchill, Jeffrey Bardzell, Jodi Forlizzi, Rebecca Grinter, and Deborah Tatar. 2011. Feminism and Interaction Design. In *CHI '11 Extended Abstracts on Human Factors in Computing Systems (CHI EA '11)*. ACM, New York, NY, USA, 1–4. DOI: http://dx.doi.org/10.1145/1979742.1979587
5. Brigid Barron. 2004. Learning Ecologies for Technological Fluency: Gender and Experience Differences. *Journal of Educational Computing Research* 31 (2004), 1–36. Issue 1.
6. L. Beckwith and M. Burnett. 2004. Gender: An Important Factor in End-User Programming Environments?. In *Visual Languages and Human Centric Computing, 2004 IEEE Symposium on*. 107–114. DOI: http://dx.doi.org/10.1109/VLHCC.2004.28
7. Elena Bertozzi. 2008. 'You Play Like a Girl!': Cross-Gender Competition and the Uneven Playing Field. *Convergence* 14, 4 (2008), 473–487. DOI: http://dx.doi.org/10.1177/1354856508094667
8. Max V. Birk, Benjamin Buttlar, Jason T. Bowey, Susanne Poeller, Shelby C. Thomson, Nicola Baumann, and Regan L. Mandryk. 2016. The Effects of Social Exclusion on Play Experience and Hostile Cognitions in Digital Games. In *Proceedings of the 2016 CHI Conference on Human Factors in Computing Systems (CHI '16)*. ACM, New York, NY, USA, 3007–3019. DOI: http://dx.doi.org/10.1145/2858036.2858061
9. Jeremy Blackburn and Haewoon Kwak. 2014. STFU NOOB!: Predicting Crowdsourced Decisions on Toxic Behavior in Online Games. In *Proceedings of the 23rd International Conference on World Wide Web (WWW '14)*. ACM, New York, NY, USA, 877–888. DOI: http://dx.doi.org/10.1145/2566486.2567987
10. Sheryl Brahnam and Antonella De Angeli. 2012. Gender Affordances of Conversational Agents. *Interacting with Computers* 24, 3 (May 2012), 139–153. DOI: http://dx.doi.org/10.1016/j.intcom.2012.05.001
11. Robert Alan Brookey and Kristopher L. Cannon. 2009. Sex Lives in Second Life. *Critical Studies in Media Communication* 26, 2 (2009), 145–164. DOI: http://dx.doi.org/10.1080/15295030902860260
12. Judith Butler. 1999. *Gender Trouble: Feminism and the Subversion of Identity*. Routledge.

13. Justine Cassell and Henry Jenkins (Eds.). 1998. *From Barbie to Mortal Kombat: Gender and Computer Games*. MIT Press, Cambridge.
14. Shira Chess and Adrienne Shaw. 2015. A Conspiracy of Fishes, or, How We Learned to Stop Worrying About #GamerGate and Embrace Hegemonic Masculinity. *Journal of Broadcasting & Electronic Media* 59, 1 (2015), 208–220. DOI: http://dx.doi.org/10.1080/08838151.2014.999917
15. Kaylene L. Clayton, Liisa A. von Hellens, and Sue H. Nielsen. 2009. Gender Stereotypes Prevail in ICT: A Research Review. In *Proceedings of the Special Interest Group on Management Information System's 47th Annual Conference on Computer Personnel Research (SIGMIS CPR '09)*. ACM, New York, NY, USA, 153–158. DOI: http://dx.doi.org/10.1145/1542130.1542160
16. Patricia Hill Collins. 2000. *Black feminist thought : knowledge, consciousness, and the politics of empowerment*. Routledge, New York.
17. Mia Consalvo. 2008. Crunched by Passion: Women Game Developers and Workplace Challenges. In *Beyond Barbie and Mortal Kombat: New Perspectives on Gender and Gaming*, Yasmin B. Kafai, Carrie Heeter, Jill Denner, and Jennifer Y. Sun (Eds.). MIT Press, Cambridge, 177–191.
18. Mia Consalvo. 2009. Hardcore Casual: Game Culture Return(s) to Ravenhearst. In *Proceedings of the 4th International Conference on Foundations of Digital Games (FDG '09)*. ACM, New York, NY, USA, 50–54. DOI:http://dx.doi.org/10.1145/1536513.1536531
19. Hilde G. Corneliussen and Jill Walker Rettberg (Eds.). 2008. *Digital Culture, Play, and Identity: A World of Warcraft® Reader*. MIT Press, Cambridge.
20. Kate Crawford and Tarleton Gillespie. 2016. What is a flag for? Social media reporting tools and the vocabulary of complaint. *New Media & Society* 18, 3 (2016), 410–428. DOI: http://dx.doi.org/10.1177/1461444814543163
21. Janet Davis. 2012. GHC Spotlight: Jane Margolis, Unlocking the Clubhouse 10 Years Later. *SIGCSE Bulletin* 44, 4 (Oct. 2012), 3–3. DOI: http://dx.doi.org/10.1145/2398328.2398329
22. Edward L. Deci and Richard M. Ryan. 1985. *Intrinsic Motivation and Self-Determination in Human Behavior*. Plenum, New York.
23. Edward L. Deci and Richard M. Ryan. 2000. The "What" and "Why" of Goal Pursuits: Human Needs and the Self-Determination of Behavior. *Psychological Inquiry* 11, 4 (2000), 227–268. DOI: http://dx.doi.org/10.1207/S15327965PLI1104_01
24. Karthik Dinakar, Birago Jones, Catherine Havasi, Henry Lieberman, and Rosalind Picard. 2012. Common Sense Reasoning for Detection, Prevention, and Mitigation of Cyberbullying. *ACM Transactions on Interactive Intelligent Systems* 2, 3, Article 18 (Sept. 2012), 30 pages. DOI:http://dx.doi.org/10.1145/2362394.2362400
25. Betsy James DiSalvo and Amy Bruckman. 2009. Questioning Video Games' Influence on CS Interest. In *Proceedings of the 4th International Conference on Foundations of Digital Games (FDG '09)*. ACM, New York, NY, USA, 272–278. DOI: http://dx.doi.org/10.1145/1536513.1536561
26. Maeve Duggan. 2014. Online Harassment. Pew Internet Project, Washington, DC. (22 Oct. 2014). Retrieved December 30, 2016 from http://www.pewinternet.org/2014/10/22/online-harassment/.
27. Karen Dugger. 1988. Social Location and Gender-Role Attitudes: A Comparison of Black and White Women. *Gender and Society* 2, 4 (1988), 425–448.
28. Cara Ellison. 2014. Games, Noir and the 17%: Where Are the Women? (Feb. 2014). Retrieved December 30, 2016 from http://www.pastemagazine.com/articles/2014/02/games-noir-and-the-17.html.
29. FemTechNet. 2015. Welcome to FemTechNet! (2015). Retrieved December 30, 2016 from http://femtechnet.org/.
30. Jesse Fox and Wai Yen Tang. 2014. Sexism in Online Video Games: The Role of Conformity to Masculine Norms and Social Dominance Orientation. *Computers in Human Behavior* 33 (April 2014), 314–320. DOI: http://dx.doi.org/10.1016/j.chb.2013.07.014
31. Jesse Fox and Wai Yen Tang. 2016. Women's experiences with general and sexual harassment in online video games: Rumination, organizational responsiveness, withdrawal, and coping strategies. *New Media & Society* (2016). DOI: http://dx.doi.org/10.1177/1461444816635778 OnlineFirst.
32. Sarah Fox, Rachel Rose Ulgado, and Daniela Rosner. 2015. Hacking Culture, Not Devices: Access and Recognition in Feminist Hackerspaces. In *Proceedings of the 18th ACM Conference on Computer Supported Cooperative Work & Social Computing (CSCW '15)*. ACM, New York, NY, USA, 56–68. DOI: http://dx.doi.org/10.1145/2675133.2675223
33. Guo Freeman, Jeffrey Bardzell, Shaowen Bardzell, and Susan C. Herring. 2015. Simulating Marriage: Gender Roles and Emerging Intimacy in an Online Game. In *Proceedings of the 18th ACM Conference on Computer Supported Cooperative Work & Social Computing (CSCW '15)*. ACM, New York, NY, USA, 1191–1200. DOI:http://dx.doi.org/10.1145/2675133.2675192
34. R. Stuart Geiger and Aaron Halfaker. 2013. When the Levee Breaks: Without Bots, What Happens to Wikipedia's Quality Control Processes?. In *Proceedings of the 9th International Symposium on Open Collaboration (WikiSym '13)*. ACM, New York, NY, USA, Article 6, 6 pages. DOI: http://dx.doi.org/10.1145/2491055.2491061

35. James Grimmelmann. 2015. The Virtues of Moderation. *Yale Journal of Law & Technology* 17 (2015), 42–109.

36. Donna J. Haraway. 1991a. A Cyborg Manifesto: Science, Technology, and Socialist-Feminism in the Late Twentieth Century. In *Simians, Cyborgs, and Women: The Reinvention of Nature*. Routledge, New York, 149–181.

37. Donna J. Haraway. 1991b. Situated Knowledges: The Science Question in Feminism and the Privilege of Partial Perspective. In *Simians, Cyborgs, and Women: The Reinvention of Nature*. Routledge, New York, 183–201.

38. Sandra Harding. 2001 [1991]. Feminist Standpoint Epistemology. In *The Gender and Science Reader*, Muriel Lederman and Ingrid Bartsch (Eds.). Routledge, London, 145–168.

39. Steve Harrison, Phoebe Sengers, and Deborah Tatar. 2011. Making Epistemological Trouble: Third-paradigm HCI As Successor Science. *Interacting with Computers* 23, 5 (Sept. 2011), 385–392. DOI: http://dx.doi.org/10.1016/j.intcom.2011.03.005

40. Michael James Heron, Pauline Belford, and Ayse Goker. 2014. Sexism in the Circuitry: Female Participation in Male-dominated Popular Computer Culture. *SIGCAS Computers and Society* 44, 4 (Dec. 2014), 18–29. DOI: http://dx.doi.org/10.1145/2695577.2695582

41. Richard Hill-Whittall. 2015. *The Indie Game Developer Handbook*. Focal Press, Burlington, MA.

42. Searle Huh and Dmitri Williams. 2010. Dude Looks like a Lady: Gender Swapping in an Online Game. In *Online Worlds: Convergence of the Real and the Virtual*, William Sims Bainbridge (Ed.). Springer London, London, 161–174. DOI: http://dx.doi.org/10.1007/978-1-84882-825-4_13

43. International Game Developers Association. 2015. Developer Satisfaction Survey 2015: Summary Report. (2015). Retrieved December 30, 2016 from https://www.igda.org/resource/collection/CB31CE86-F8EE-4AE3-B46A-148490336605/IGDA%20DSS%202015-SummaryReport_Final_Sept15.pdf.

44. Jennifer Jenson and Suzanne de Castell. 2010. Gender, Simulation, and Gaming: Research Review and Redirections. *Simulation & Gaming* 41, 1 (Feb. 2010), 51–71. DOI: http://dx.doi.org/10.1177/1046878109353473

45. Jennifer Jenson and Suzanne de Castell. 2011. Girls@Play: An ethnographic study of gender and digital gameplay. *Feminist Media Studies* 11, 2 (2011), 167 – 179.

46. Jennifer Jenson and Suzanne de Castell. 2013. Tipping Points: Marginality, Misogyny and Videogames. *Journal of Curriculum Theorizing* 29, 2 (2013), 72–85.

47. Jesper Juul. 2010. *A Casual Revolution: Reinventing Video Games and Their Players*. MIT Press, Cambridge.

48. Yasmin B. Kafai and Quinn Burke. 2014. Beyond Game Design for Broadening Participation: Building New Clubhouses of Computing for Girls. In *Proceedings of Gender and IT Appropriation. Science and Practice on Dialogue - Forum for Interdisciplinary Exchange (Gender IT '14)*. European Society for Socially Embedded Technologies, Siegen, Germany, Germany, Article 21, 21:21–21:28 pages. http://dl.acm.org/citation.cfm?id=2670296.2670301

49. Yasmin B. Kafai, Carrie Heeter, Jill Denner, and Jennifer Y. Sun (Eds.). 2008. *Beyond Barbie and Mortal Kombat: New Perspectives on Gender and Gaming*. MIT Press, Cambridge.

50. Caitlin Kelleher and Randy Pausch. 2007. Using Storytelling to Motivate Programming. *Commun. ACM* 50, 7 (July 2007), 58–64. DOI: http://dx.doi.org/10.1145/1272516.1272540

51. Jillian Kinzie, Robert Gonyea, George D. Kuh, Paul Umbach, Charlie Blaich, and Ali Korkmaz. 2007. The Relationship Between Gender and Student Engagement in College. In *Paper presented at the 32nd annual conference of the Association for the Study of Higher Education*.

52. Merritt Kopas (Ed.). 2015. *Videogames for Humans*. Instar, New York.

53. Ralph Koster. 2005. *A Theory of Fun for Game Design*. Paraglyph Press, Scottsdale, AZ.

54. Jeffrey H. Kuznekoff and Lindsey M. Rose. 2013. Communication in multiplayer gaming: Examining player responses to gender cues. *New Media & Society* 15, 4 (2013), 541–556. DOI: http://dx.doi.org/10.1177/1461444812458271

55. Haewoon Kwak, Jeremy Blackburn, and Seungyeop Han. 2015. Exploring Cyberbullying and Other Toxic Behavior in Team Competition Online Games. In *Proceedings of the 33rd Annual ACM Conference on Human Factors in Computing Systems (CHI '15)*. ACM, New York, NY, USA, 3739–3748. DOI: http://dx.doi.org/10.1145/2702123.2702529

56. Marc-André K. Lafrenière, Jérémie Verner-Filion, and Robert J. Vallerand. 2012. Development and validation of the Gaming Motivation Scale (GAMS). *Personality and Individual Differences* 53 (2012), 827–831. Issue 7.

57. Ann Light. 2011. HCI As Heterodoxy: Technologies of Identity and the Queering of Interaction with Computers. *Interacting with Computers* 23, 5 (Sept. 2011), 430–438. DOI: http://dx.doi.org/10.1016/j.intcom.2011.02.002

58. B. Maher. 2016. Can a video game company tame toxic behaviour? *Nature* 531 (March 2016), 568–571. DOI: http://dx.doi.org/10.1038/531568a

59. Jane Margolis and Allan Fisher. 2002. *Unlocking the Clubhouse: Women in Computing*. MIT Press, Cambridge.

60. Microsoft Research. 2014. International Women's Hackathon 2014. (25 April 2014). Retrieved September 7, 2015 from http://research.microsoft.com/en-us/events/womens-hackathon2014/.
61. National Careers Service. 2015. Computer games developer. (2015). Retrieved December 30, 2016 from https://nationalcareersservice.direct.gov.uk/advice/planning/jobprofiles/Pages/computergamesdeveloper.aspx.
62. The New Inquiry. 2014. TNI Syllabus: Gaming and Feminism. (2 Sept. 2014). Retrieved September 7, 2015 from http://thenewinquiry.com/features/tni-syllabus-gaming-and-feminism/.
63. Tyler Pace, Shaowen Bardzell, and Jeffrey Bardzell. 2010. The Rogue in the Lovely Black Dress: Intimacy in World of Warcraft. In *Proceedings of the SIGCHI Conference on Human Factors in Computing Systems (CHI '10)*. ACM, New York, NY, USA, 233–242. DOI: http://dx.doi.org/10.1145/1753326.1753361
64. Simon Parkin. 2014. Gamergate: A Scandal Erupts in the Video-Game Community. (17 Oct. 2014). Retrieved December 30, 2016 from http://www.newyorker.com/tech/elements/gamergate-scandal-erupts-video-game-community.
65. Elizabeth Patitsas, Michelle Craig, and Steve Easterbrook. 2014. A Historical Examination of the Social Factors Affecting Female Participation in Computing. In *Proceedings of the 2014 Conference on Innovation & Technology in Computer Science Education (ITiCSE '14)*. ACM, New York, NY, USA, 111–116. DOI: http://dx.doi.org/10.1145/2591708.2591731
66. Porpentine. 2012. Creation Under Capitalism and the Twine Revolution. (25 Nov. 2012). Retrieved December 30, 2016 from http://nightmaremode.thegamerstrust.com/2012/11/25/creation-under-capitalism/.
67. Porpentine. 2013. Parasite. (25 June 2013). Retrieved September 6, 2015 from http://thenewinquiry.com/features/parasite/.
68. Rabindra A. Ratan, Nicholas Taylor, Jameson Hogan, Tracy Kennedy, and Dmitri Williams. 2015. Stand by Your Man: An Examination of Gender Disparity in League of Legends. *Games and Culture* 10, 5 (2015), 438–462. DOI: http://dx.doi.org/10.1177/1555412014567228
69. Sheri Graner Ray. 2004. *Gender Inclusive Game Design: Expanding the Market*. Charles River Media, Hingham, MA.
70. Madeleine R. H. Roberts, Tanya J. McGill, and Peter N. Hyland. 2012. Attrition from Australian ICT Degrees: Why Women Leave. In *Proceedings of the Fourteenth Australasian Computing Education Conference - Volume 123 (ACE '12)*. Australian Computer Society, Inc., Darlinghurst, Australia, Australia, 15–24. http://dl.acm.org/citation.cfm?id=2483716.2483719
71. Jennifer A. Rode. 2011. A Theoretical Agenda for Feminist HCI. *Interacting with Computers* 23, 5 (Sept. 2011), 393–400. DOI: http://dx.doi.org/10.1016/j.intcom.2011.04.005
72. Anita Sarkeesian. 2015. Gender Breakdown of Games Showcased at E3 2015. (22 June 2015). Retrieved December 30, 2016 from http://feministfrequency.com/2015/06/22/gender-breakdown-of-games-showcased-at-e3-2015/.
73. Linda J. Sax, Jennifer Berdan Lozano, and Colleen Quinn Vandenboom. 2015. Who Attends A Women's College? Identifying Unique Characteristics and Patterns of Change, 1971-2011. (2015). http://womenscolleges.org/sites/default/files/report/files/main/students_at_womens_colleges_final_report.pdf Published by the Women's College Coalition.
74. Amber Settle, Monica M. McGill, and Adrienne Decker. 2013. Diversity in the Game Industry: Is Outreach the Solution?. In *Proceedings of the 14th Annual ACM SIGITE Conference on Information Technology Education (SIGITE '13)*. ACM, New York, NY, USA, 171–176. DOI: http://dx.doi.org/10.1145/2512276.2512283
75. Adrienne Shaw. 2012. Do you identify as a gamer? Gender, race, sexuality, and gamer identity. *New Media & Society* 14, 1 (2012), 28–44. DOI: http://dx.doi.org/10.1177/1461444811410394
76. Adrienne Shaw. 2014. *Gaming at the Edge: Sexuality and Gender at the Margins of Gamer Culture*. University of Minnesota Press, Minneapolis.
77. Penelope Sweetser, Peta Wyeth, Nicole McMahon, and Daniel Johnson. 2013. Female Game Developers Wanted: Low pay, long hours, inflexible work environments. In *Proceedings of the 5th International IEEE Consumer Electronic Society Games Innovation Conference*. 243–249.
78. T. L. Taylor. 2006. *Play Between Worlds: Exploring Online Game Culture*. MIT Press, Cambridge.
79. Kristine Tucker. 2015. Qualifications for a Video Game Designer. (2015). Retrieved December 30, 2016 from http://work.chron.com/qualifications-video-game-designer-5484.html.
80. Robert J. Vallerand. 1997. Toward a hierarchical model of intrinsic and extrinsic motivation. *Advances in experimental social psychology, Vol. 29* (1997), 271–360. DOI: http://dx.doi.org/10.1016/S0065-2601(08)60019-2
81. Eva A. Van Reijmersdal, Jeroen Jansz, Oscar Peters, and Guda Van Noort. 2013. Why Girls Go Pink: Game Character Identification and Game-players' Motivations. *Computers in Human Behavior* 29, 6 (Nov. 2013), 2640–2649. DOI: http://dx.doi.org/10.1016/j.chb.2013.06.046
82. Judy Wajcman. 2004. *TechnoFeminism*. Polity, Cambridge.

83. Sarah Wanenchak. 2014. "The Consumption Palace": Gamers, misogyny, and capitalism. (10 Aug. 2014). Retrieved December 30, 2016 from http://thesocietypages.org/cyborgology/2014/09/01/the-consumption-palace-gamers-misogyny-and-capitalism/.

84. Wellesley College. 2016. Class of 2020 Admission Statistics. (1 Sept. 2016). Retrieved December 30, 2016 from http://www.wellesley.edu/admission/facts.

85. Hanna Wirman. 2014. Gender and Identity in Game-Modifying Communities. *Simulation & Gaming* 45, 1 (Feb. 2014), 70–92. DOI: http://dx.doi.org/10.1177/1046878113519572

Ways of Spectating: Unravelling Spectator Participation in Kinect Play

Burak S. Tekin
Department of Linguistics and Literature
University of Basel
burak.tekin@unibas.ch

Stuart Reeves
Mixed Reality Lab
School of Computer Science
University of Nottingham
stuart@tropic.org.uk

ABSTRACT
We explore spectating on video game play as an interactional and participatory activity. Drawing on a corpus of video recordings capturing 'naturally occurring' Kinect gaming within home settings, we detail how the analytic 'work' of spectating is interactionally accomplished as a matter of collaborative action with players and engagement in the game. We examine: spectators supporting players with continuous 'scaffolding'; spectators critiquing player technique during and between moments of play; spectators recognising and complimenting competent player conduct; and spectators reflecting on prior play to build instructions for the player. From this we draw out a number of points that shift the conversation in HCI about 'the spectator' towards understanding and designing for spectat<u>ing</u> as an interactional activity; that is, sequentially ordered and temporally coordinated. We also discuss bodily conduct and the particular ways of 'seeing' involved in spectating, and conclude with remarks on conceptual and design implications for HCI.

Author Keywords
Spectatorship; spectating; Kinect; video gaming; participation; ethnomethodology; conversation analysis.

ACM Classification Keywords
H.5.m. Information interfaces and presentation (e.g., HCI): Miscellaneous.

INTRODUCTION
Spectator experience, and its relevance for the design of interaction with devices and systems, has been of interest to HCI for some time. This interest has developed as encounters with technologies such as large screen displays, mobile devices, and sensing systems have become increasingly common in our everyday lives—interactions with which routinely take place in front of others. In response, HCI has developed a range of empirical and conceptual accounts (e.g., design frameworks), for instance, [3, 45, 46, 8, 57]. HCI research now supplies plentiful instances of spectatorship as a matter of public interaction, often with interactive displays of varying sizes, e.g., [27, 38, 43]. Frequently these are coupled with body-based interfaces or so-called 'natural'[1] user interfaces of some form that leverage gaze, gestural or whole-body interactions in order to render them more readily accessible as public displays, e.g., [56].

CHI 2017, May 06 - 11, 2017, Denver, CO, USA

ACM 978-1-4503- 4655-9/17/05...$15.00
DOI: http://dx.doi.org/10.1145/3025453.3025813

The role of *spectating in collocated gaming* has recently attracted attention (e.g., [23, 7]), yet there are few *naturalistic* studies of this pervasive aspect of video gaming (excepting Harper and Mentis's study of Kinect play in the home [16] and Lin and Sun's exploration of spectating in arcade gaming [29]). This seems very unusual given the mainstream uptake of spectating on gaming more broadly (e.g., Twitch.tv [14]). Specifically we point to a lack of *praxeological* accounts of how the activities of people playing and watching are accomplished. To help remedy this, we offer a detailed study of collocated spectator-player interactions by examining the social organisation of body-based (Kinect) gaming in households.

We note that body-based interfaces typically produce a greater availability (e.g., visibility) of user actions (i.e., they are "revealed" in the terminology of [45]). Therefore, *as novel spectator interfaces,* body-based interfaces also present new experiences for those spectating and therefore offer us a rich site for deepening our understanding of spectatorship in HCI and what spectating looks like as an *organised*, *participatory* activity. In other words, by looking at the practical details of play in these settings, we seek to emphasise the importance of recognising spectat<u>ing</u> as an interactional accomplishment beyond HCI's current conceptual emphasis on identifying 'the spectator' or

[1] We share strong reservations about the 'naturalness' or a given 'intuitiveness' of these interfaces [43, 16, 15, 40], and the notion that comes along with this designation as interfaces that somehow do *not* need the development of particular practices.

audience as a specific role or class of roles (e.g., as "orchestrators, managers, coaches, directors, puppeteers, commentators, hecklers" etc. [8]).

To do this, we draw upon a series of fragments of video-recorded Kinect play in home settings, which let us see some of the ways in which those watching play conduct their participation in the game in a range of interactionally coordinated, interwoven, and organised ways. Our video data lets us get a closer look at what it means to 'do' spectating, showing the broad range of participatory activities that this can involve. Specifically, we explore how spectating involves activities including: 'scaffolding' play as it happens by instructing players in a timely way, critiquing play by closely analysing the bodily conduct of players and providing assessments of this (e.g., to finesse gaming technique), recognising and complimenting displays of player skill and expertise, and reflecting on the game by drawing on practical experience with the game being played and gaming in general.

The inquiry pursued in this paper is organised around three sections. Firstly, we review HCI research on spectator experience in video gaming, and the connection with body-based interfaces. Then, we introduce our approach—ethnomethodology and conversation analysis, or EMCA—and the phenomenon, and present some fragments drawn from our corpus of video data. Finally, we discuss the implications of our study for understandings of the role of spectating on interaction in HCI.

SPECTATORSHIP IN VIDEO GAME PLAY

There has long been a ready characterisation of spectating and spectators—often also termed audiences, viewers, or third parties—as 'passive' in contrast with the 'active' user, performer, or in the case of this paper, player [50]. As interest in the role of spectatorship has increased in HCI, so there has been a definite maturation of this view towards understanding spectators as participants that are implicated in interaction with technology in various possible ways. In this paper while we are partly concerned with this broader literature on spectators, passers-by, and bystanders who happen to be implicated in interactive systems (e.g., [41]), our primary interest is in how this relates to the activity of video gaming. Contrary to assumptions around gaming practices being largely solitary affairs, it has been argued within HCI that there is a strong *sociability* to gaming [54]. This sociability necessarily means that *watching* gaming is a key component of play, thus gaming has recently developed as a venue for HCI researchers to better understand the nature of spectating more broadly.

Yet initially we must also distinguish *different forms* of spectating on play. Perhaps the most readily recognisable form of spectating is found in 'e-sports', where crowds watch large screen displays of players competing against one another [5, 51]. For spectators, this form of watching play involves similar activities to sports spectating: clapping, cheering, talking with other spectators, listening to commentators, and so on. E-sports events are often broadcast online, and form part of a wider phenomenon of streaming gameplay using platforms such as Twitch.tv where spectators can also interact directly with the player and other users watching via chat features. These have been subject to analyses of audience composition [24] as well as accounts of the community practices viewers [14].

However, mass spectating is only one form. Arguably a more mundane and likely more pervasive form—taking place commonly in households but not exclusive to them—is *collocated gaming*. This has received less focus in HCI although recently the topic has begun to be addressed. For example, Downs et al. [7] used a series of lab experiments to discover the relationship between the physicality of video game play with accounts reported by participants watching players, as well as the anticipatory effects of taking one's turn at the game. Interventions have also been performed, for example Maurer et al. [31] developed a system to support gaze-based interactions by spectators in order to support players. Yet our work substantially differs from this by looking at spectating practices from the perspective of participants in naturalistic settings.

Our paper also offers some conceptual distinctions that can contribute to theoretical developments on spectatorship in gaming. Building on prior design frameworks for spectatorship (e.g., [3, 46]), HCI researchers studying gameplay have developed various extensions. For instance, Downs et al. describe a spectrum of participation in play for spectators ranging between low to high "levels" [8], while Maurer et al. conceive of this as active and passive [31]. Downs et al. also develop further typologies of spectatorship that provide classificatory frameworks for spectatorship in games and beyond. In doing this, Downs et al. discuss subdivisions of spectator roles that can be used to describe the changing circumstances of play—thus producing a set of "durable roles" ("bystanders", "audience" and "players") and momentary "ephemeral roles" that spectators might take on so that they may do other things "beyond just waiting for a turn" such as commenting, coaching, directing, or heckling. This idea of a typology of spectatorship has also been operationalised experimentally, by comparing the effects on players of different spectator 'types' such as the negative, positive and neutral spectators of [23]. While our study in some sense does offer examples of, say, practices that seem similar to "coaching" [8], our concern is to articulate these activities as interactionally-negotiated, interactionally-produced matters (i.e., a joint, ongoing *achievement* between players and spectators) rather than 'states' that someone is 'in'.

Our final point of connection with the HCI literature relates to body-based interfaces, which have received considerable interest in HCI recently, including applications in surgery [43], and dance and performance [32] to name a few. Most relevant for us, however, is body-based gaming [19, 16]. The 'naturalness' or a given 'intuitiveness' of these interfaces might lead us to imagine that somehow body-based interfaces do not need the development of particular practices—or "specialist techniques" [43]—in order to engage in their use. Yet, interaction with the Kinect, like many body-based interfaces, necessarily involves learning particular kinds of body movements and gestures [16], which itself suggests *new kinds of experiences* for potential spectators beyond more typical methods of interaction with video games (e.g., via handheld controller). Body-based interfaces like the Kinect provide opportunities for this in that they transform readily witnessable bodily conduct (such as gestures, arm swings, foot movements, etc.) into machine-relevant actions. Research on body-based gaming in general often draws attention to the *potential for spectacle* to be produced [19], yet stops short of providing detailed studies of its interactional production. Accordingly, body-based interfaces like the Kinect have featured strongly in HCI work that directly addresses or at least touches upon spectatorship and gaming (e.g., [23, 31, 8, 16, 39]). As Nansen et al. put it, "the Kinect creates a shared and interactive relationship between the player and the audience" [39]. It is *this* relationship that we seek to explicate in more detail in this paper, while at the same time offering us a site for nuancing existing understandings of movement-based gaming [19].

WATCHING AND PLAYING KINECT AT HOME

In contrast with much existing HCI literature that examines spectatorship in physical play and video gaming, we take an approach informed by ethnomethodology and conversation analysis—an established orientation at CHI (e.g., see recent work [44, 48]). We investigate the organised, methodical ways in which social action is ordered and achieved [9, 49], and how these achievements are *endogenously* negotiated and produced, arising from members' practices. For studying Kinect play, this means that we are interested in the ways in which players and those watching play *work* to make their activities readily intelligible and accountable to the organisation of play. Thus, we are concerned with the detailed ways that the activity of video game playing unfolds moment-by-moment as a matter of orderly action between players and those watching (who may have recently been players themselves).

As a brief adjunct to our literature review above, here we note that spectating features in EMCA oriented research, but not as a focal topic of investigation. For instance, spectators may be in adjacent rooms, as in [30] where dentistry students follow live video broadcasts of a dentist performing endodontic treatments, or in a large auditorium, as in [37] where an audience of trainees inspect a team of surgeons doing surgical operations through live video transmission. Likewise, spectating does not have a central place in the EMCA work on video games (see, for example, [47] for a review of such studies). This may possibly stem from the likelihood that the presence of spectators normatively points to a more 'central' activity (e.g., playing video games) which tends to attract greater analytic focus for researchers entering such settings. However, while it has been suggested by others that EMCA approaches have struggled to gain purchase on 'playful' activities [53], examining such activities is not new for EMCA (e.g., [20, 28]), although this literature remains fairly sparse as pointed out by Tolmie and Rouncefield [53]. Nevertheless, EMCA interest in play extends to video games (e.g., see [47]), which, briefly, has studied on-screen actions [2], players' talk, and bodily conduct 'in' and 'out' of games [34]. Yet this work also rarely discusses spectating. Thus our paper also offers a novel contribution to the EMCA literature in providing a study of spectating *on video gaming activities*.

Turning now to the practical details of our study, to examine spectating as an interactional phenomenon we draw upon a large corpus of video recorded data of Kinect play in naturalistic settings, based on fieldwork conducted by one of the authors over the course of four months in various household environments sited in Turkey (resulting in 19 hours of video from 12 different homes). A variety of games were played, but the data we present focuses on the Kinect Sports Rivals games, specifically its climbing, tennis, and bowling games. A critical feature of the video captured in these settings is that they often involve the presence of people watching a current player's bodily engagement with the game in some ways (and perhaps also awaiting their own turn). Therefore, this setting presents a *perspicuous setting* [10] for studying spectating practices, and spectator participation.

Our corpus presents us with a wide range of spectating phenomena. In this study, we focus on four prevalent practices of spectating in order to provide a rounded picture of the diversity of spectating represented in our corpus. In this sense, our fragments present a selective and partial view on spectating that omits some features—for instance, while players and those watching *did* joke with one another [16], we found that more often than not they treated play as 'serious'. Fundamentally, our selection was guided by an interest in illustrating some of the distinct ways in which spectating is intersubjectively accomplished by *both* parties (i.e., as a collaborative endeavour). Thus we selected fragments that show something of the range *different* forms of participation frameworks [13] that spectating is tied to. Our selection lets us explore how spectating involves working to inspect gameplay as it happens (e.g., establishing visual and bodily alignments), and formulating next actions in ways that are sensitive to the game on-screen and the bodily conduct of player(s). In this way our fragments range across just some of many possible forms: spectators 'scaffolding' play moment-by-moment, critiquing play technique, producing recognitions and compliments of player competence, and reflecting on their own play.

Our fragments are transcribed using Jefferson notation [21] (widely used in EMCA). This highlights the sequential and temporal organisation of turns at talk, and the details of their prosodic delivery. We also employ additional transcription features drawn from Mondada [36] in order to include bodily conduct. Fragment 1 contains annotations (in red) of the meaning of various symbols and aspects of these transcription systems. Turkish utterances are in bold type, with English translations below in italics. Relevant stills from the video recordings are inserted where appropriate with indications of the moments in time they appear with a '#' in the transcripts, and with figure numbers overlaid on the stills. In all fragments, we use the term 'player' to refer to participant(s) *directly* interacting with the Kinect (labelled **PL**, or **PL1**, **PL2**, etc.), other participants we consider to be 'spectating' and we refer to as 'spectators' (labelled **SP**, or **SP1**, **SP2**, etc.)—note that labels in lower case (i.e., '**pl**', '**sp**', etc.) indicate non-verbal actions.

'Scaffolding' play

One of the most prevalent things that spectators do during Kinect gaming is to seek to display continuous engagement with the player (particularly when the player is 'in' the game [34]). While in some sense all of our fragments exhibit this as a feature of the way spectators organise their participation in the game, here we examine a very clear example of this. In this fragment, the player (PL)—a young child—is participating in a climbing game, and is watched by two others—another child (who is silent for the duration of the fragment) and their grandmother (SP). To progress, the player needs to 'grab' holds and move between them, which he achieves with various gestures and larger bodily movements (e.g., physically jumping).

```
             PL                                        SP
01        (1.2)          temporal gaps in seconds      bodily conduct of pl
02        *(1.0)* *(0.7)* (0.8) *(0.6)*                delimited by matching
                                                       symbols (*, +, %, etc.)
   pl     *jumps* *grabs*       *grabs*
03        (0.2)
04 SP     tut
          grab
05        (1.8)
06        *(1.1)* *(1.0)*
   pl     *jumps* *grabs*
07 SP     i*yi tut
          grab tight
   pl      *jumps ->
08        (0.5)*
   pl        ->*
09        (0.2)
10        *(0.2)*
   pl     *grabs*
11 SP     tut ● (.) ● >↑tut  tut  t+ut  tut<
          grab          grab grab grab grab
   sp                          +looks twrd PL ->
12        (0.2)+ *(0.2)    '↑' indicates rising pitch
   sp        ->+           '>' '<' indicates words spoken faster
   pl            *grabs ->
```

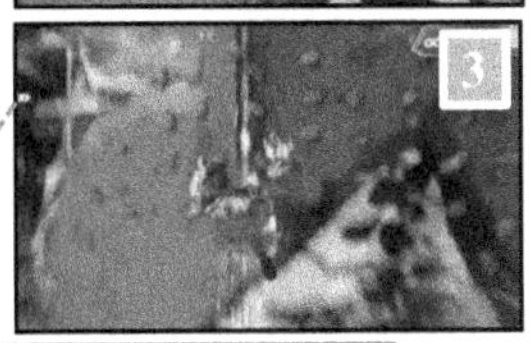

```
13 SP     tut*ma*dıı:n*       one or more ':' indicate extensions of sound
          you did not grab
   pl      ->*   *grabs*
14        (2.9)
15 PL     tüh  kötü ol[du      '[' indicates overlapped talk
          damn it was bad
16 SP                 [neyse *başlıyo
                whatever it is starting
   pl                         *jumps ->
17        ha*di süren dolmadan                 indicates
          come on before your time is up       continuation of
   pl     ->*                                  action by pl
```

Fragment 1: Scaffolding play (transcript legend in red)

Fragment 1 shows how SP adapts her actions to the temporality of the game in finely tuned ways. When PL is 'in' the game, SP produces timely instructions to him (lines 04, 07, 11). The first instruction takes the form of a bare imperative ("grab", line 04); this is uttered precisely at a time when it is relevant and necessary to grab one of holds (not doing so of course resulting in PL's avatar falling down). SP then issues another instruction, this time formatted as an 'imperative + adverb' combination ("grab tight", line 07). SP, displaying an orientation to the temporal urgency of the game and the need for PL to take action, then produces repeated imperatives ("grab (.) grab grab grab grab", line 11). This is done as the avatar reaches the next hold, but then starts to fall down (Figures 2 and 3). SP produces these utterances in a way that is again carefully timed with the trajectory of the jump. The first "grab" in line 11 occurs at the jump's apex but it becomes visible that the avatar is actually falling down. The repeated imperatives point to the urgency to grab—for this particular game, the avatar *can* escape from falling down if the player manages to get it to grab one of the holds during the fall. In line 13 the game then suspends before PL's avatar is respawned again. During this suspension, SP shifts to an assessment of what just happened moments ago in the form of a negatively formulated utterance (line 13) which places responsibility of the fall on the player ("you did not grab"). After a pause, PL utters his own assessment (line 15), but as a next move he neither accepts nor rejects responsibility, but rather deflects via attributing blame with an ambiguous utterance, "it was bad". In this way, while this assessment by PL acknowledges the failure, it does not build in any particular agent as responsible. In overlap with this assessment (line 16), SP rejects this deflection of responsibility ("whatever"), while at the same time projecting the restart of the game ("it is starting"), and coupling this with an encouragement that also foregrounds the game's temporality once again ("come on before your time is up", line 17).

It is significant to note that SP's gaze is for the most part directed towards the TV screen (Figure 1). Only towards the end of repeated imperatives does she briefly direct her gaze towards PL. This shows that she uses the game actions displayed on the screen as a resource to instruct PL. While we cannot easily say whether SP's seated position allows her to simultaneously also keep track of PL's bodily conduct (which is also important for this kind of activity), we examine spectating as 'seeing' in detail later.

That said, as a broader matter of SP's participation in play and her 'scaffolding' of the courses of action of PL, we can see how she engages in the provision of a range of timely instructions, assessments and encouragements that on the whole demonstrate a keen sensitivity to the *temporality* of the game. Specifically, the ways she formats her instructions at particular moments (bare imperatives, 'imperative + adverb' combinations, repeated imperatives) reflect this temporal sensitivity towards the contingencies in the game. SP's actions here, particularly her continuous instructions to PL as the play unfolds, can be characterised as doing "live" or perhaps "online" coaching (see [18]), while also bearing similarities to what Downs et al. [7] gloss as "coaching and directing" players. This kind of engagement can also be found in Mondada's studies of console gaming [34, 35], where football game players begin to instruct their co-player at moments when that co-player's activities are more consequential for the game (related to who has possession of the ball).

Critiquing play technique

Playing different kinds of games necessarily results in quite different temporalities to play. In this fragment we examine bowling, which introduces a very different pace of game. In our fragment we examine some of the more detailed analytic work of spectating, looking at the way players' gaming movements with the Kinect may be inspected and assessed. While we will see a 'critical' kind of spectating here, later in Fragment 3 we will see more 'complimentary' forms. Nevertheless, opportunities to perform such assessments are provided particularly when a current spectator is awaiting their turn, i.e., when they are not so much a 'permanent' spectator (as in the previous fragment) but rather 'the next player'.

Here we join two friends playing bowling together (PL and SP). Our fragment is divided into two parts, showing the first and second of two consecutive bowls by the current player. To perform a successful bowl, the player must adjust their bodily position and arm swing using an indicator on-screen that shows the coordination of the throw and therefore future trajectory of the ball (Figure 4).

Figure 4: Triangular indicators in-game

```
01       *(4.2) + (3.0)#*
   pl    *steps left, forwards, right, then back*
   sp            +reclines ->
   fig                      #fig.5
02       *(2.2)*
   pl    *bowls*
03       ^(1.7)^
         ^knocks down four pins^
04       (0.2)+ (0.4) *(0.6) #
   sp      ->+
   pl                 *turns towards sp ->
   fig                             #fig.6
05 SP    o dengeyi* nasıl sağlıcaz
         how will we maintain that balance
   pl            ->*
06       (0.4)
07 PL    ortaya kendisi şeyapıyo
         it is doing itself towards the centre
08       ayarı kendisi veriyo
         it is adjusting itself
```

Fragment 2a: Spectator 'leaning in' to troubleshoot play

As we see in Fragment 2a, to make the first throw, PL initially adjusts his body spatially by making small steps left, forward, right and then slightly back, tracing out a circle of sorts. As he does this, SP lays down on the couch (Figure 5, line 01). This generates a different visual alignment for SP in his perspective on PL and their actions with respect to the game as it unfolds on-screen. PL performs a small step forwards as he then bowls (line 02), knocking down four pins out of ten. After this, the game is temporarily suspended to show the scoreboard, whereupon SP straights up somewhat, and PL moves slightly to the side, turning towards him (line 04). This establishes a new interactional space [26, 33] between them (Figure 6). Within this new arrangement, SP produces a question regarding the coordination of an appropriate bowling position (determined by the bodily position of the player) and the swing performed (SP describes this coordination as "balance" and positions this as a matter for both of them, i.e., the pronoun ending associated with the person plural, line 05, or "we"). There is a brief pause, after which PL assumes the next turn-at-talk, hearing the question as a criticism—i.e., he attributes responsibility for his performance to the Kinect as the agent managing the coordination between bowling position and swing (lines 07 and 08). PL then continues with the next bowl.

```
09       (4.0)
10       *(1.4) + (5.4)#*
   pl    *steps left, forw, pause, right, and left*
   sp            +reclines ->
   fig                     #fig.7
11       *(1.9)*
   pl    *bowls with stationary feet*
12       ^(2.0)^+
         ^knocks down remaining six pins^
   sp          ->+
13 PL    çok güzel
         very nice
14       *(0.4) #(0.4)
   pl    *gazes towards sp ->
   fig          #fig.8
15 SP    atarken de bo*zuluyo ama
```

```
        but it is going wrong while throwing
   pl              ->*
16      (0.7)
17 PL   bozulsun o
        it does not matter if it goes wrong
18      ben köşeye doğru vurdum zaten
        I already threw it towards the corner
19      (0.6)
20 PL   çizdim bak
        look I drew ((the line))
21      (0.2) *(0.6) +(0.8)+ (0.3)*
   pl         * looks towards sp  *
   sp               +nods +
```

Fragment 2b: continuation of Fragment 2a

In Fragment 2b, we see a similar organisational structure to Fragment 2a. PL searches for a particular bodily-spatial positioning (line 10) while SP reclines to secure a visual alignment between PL and screen (Figure 7). However, it is notable that PL's movements in line 10 do not simply repeat his prior action from line 01. This time PL swings his arm and bowls with stationary feet, knocking the remaining six pins down, followed by a replay of the throw then a display of the scoreboard. As this happens SP straightens slightly, with PL—who starts to gaze back at SP—moving into a similar spatial arrangement once again (Figure 8). As PL does this, SP this time produces an utterance ("but it is going wrong while throwing", line 15), with which he problematises the coordination of PL's bowling position and throw. This is also related to his previous question in Fragment 2a (line 05). Before, PL attributed responsibility to the Kinect, but here SP pursues his earlier critique nevertheless, in effect dismissing PL's claim that there is some deficiency in the Kinect's sensing capabilities and / or the game's design. PL then in turn dismisses this 'extension' of the critique from SP (lines 17 and 18), and points to the scoreboard displayed on the screen ("look I drew", line 20), and referring to his success of achieving a spare nevertheless (represented with '/' on the scoreboard and which PL also traces in the air with his hand).

As we now turn to a deeper analysis we note that this fragment, like Fragment 1, involves SP producing utterances (lines 05 and 15) that themselves follow a delicate temporal placement, where both are uttered sequentially after PL bowls. In other words, SP demonstrates sensitivity to the temporality of play as he deploys questions and assessments. Yet there is more happening here that is of interest. Thus we now pick up on three points to develop our analysis: the critical nature of the assessments being done; SP's analysis of PL's bodily actions; and bodily action conducted by SP himself.

On the first point we note the following. In the first bowl (which knocks down four pins out of ten), SP questions the general coordination, and in the second one (which knocks down the remaining six pins and thereby makes a spare), he makes a further negative assessment. SP works to inspect play by attending to and drawing upon various resources that are available to and continuously unfolding in front of him. Furthermore, though PL's second bowl actually achieves the best possible result in the circumstances (i.e., knocking down all the remaining pins), SP *still* does not produce a compliment at this moment (i.e., a normatively expected place). Instead, SP builds his assessment of the play of the game. Here we can thus see how a sense of SP's conduct as 'critique' emerges.

On the second point, SP's analysis of the player's body is central to forming these assessments. After the first bowl, the question SP utters deals with the coordination (or "balance" in the spectator's own words) between the body of PL and the "body's double" [25], i.e., that which is represented in the game. In doing this SP is at the same time indicating a need for PL to adjust and position his body in space in particular ways. However, after this, as we saw, SP deflects any critique of his bodily movements towards a failure of the Kinect's recognition, although interestingly in his second bowl, his preparatory movements (line 10) *are* indeed different. What is interesting here is that SP raises the issue of the PL's adherence to a particular kind of "bodily discipline" [52] imposed by the Kinect sensor. We note that these are *not* just "ordinary gestures" [22] in the sense that physical movements may be routinely produced in front of screens yet also pertain to what they show. Instead, as Harper and Mentis describe, the bodily discipline of the Kinect player involves the discovery of a "regime of body movements and gestures" [16]. Being able to *see and remark* on this discipline becomes relevant for the spectator in doing critiquing.

On the final point, we note that SP also repeatedly arranges his own body in a reclined way as PL prepares to swing his arm. In doing so, SP can visually align himself in regard to the bodily movements of PL, and the corresponding actions sensed by the Kinect—and of course the resultant sensing of those actions as represented on-screen (e.g., by the indicator in Figure 4). This is a kind of 'dual vision', one might say, which then becomes a resource for SP both in his initial question about coordination (line 05) and subsequent critical assessment of the trouble with the player's swing (line 15).

Recognising and complimenting competence

As well as involving critiques of player conduct, spectating also involves doing positive assessments of play (as "supporters" [8]). The following fragment is part of a larger sequence in which two players are competing at tennis (PL1, PL2) while one spectator watches (SP). As we join the action in Fragment 3, PL1 and PL2 are engaging in a rally, with PL2 having just returned the ball to PL1.

```
01        (0.8)
02        *(1.8)*
    pl1   *hits the ball*
03        (0.3)
04        §(1.3)§
    pl2   §fails to return the ball§
05        (0.7)
06 SP     bayağ +sert vuruyon # haa:
          you are hitting quite powerfully
    sp          +gazes towards pl1 ->
    fig                          #fig.9
07        top gi*derken # bile +ses *şey yapıyo
          even while the ball moves it is
          making a sound
    pl1         * gazes towards sp   *
    sp                           ->+
    fig                    #fig.10
08 PL1    vururum kan[*ka
          I hit it mate
    pl1               *serves for next game ->
09 SP                 [iyice ayıktın sen duruma
         you really have understood the situation
10        (0.7)* (1.1)
    pl1      ->*
```

Fragment 3: A spectator complimenting a player

We see in line 02 that PL1 hits the ball back to PL2, with PL2 failing to return the shot, which results in PL1 gaining a point in the game (line 04). On completion of this rally, SP produces a positive assessment about the technique of PL1 ("you are hitting quite powerfully", line 06). This assessment, during which SP gazes towards PL1 (figure 9), integrates an account of the player's bodily conduct and gains its appreciative character from its timely production sequentially, i.e., positioned directly after winning the point. SP continues, elaborating this assessment as PL1 returns his gaze (Figure 10, line 07). In doing so SP also draws upon the audio-visual properties of the game—particularly the sound 'generated' by PL1's rapid, powerful arm swing as he hits the ball—in order to build on his appreciative, positive account of the player's conduct. PL1 immediately follows this with a confirmatory account of his action ("I hit it mate", line 08). In doing this, PL1 acknowledges SP's assessment and then starts to serve the ball for the next opening shot. Finally SP generalises his assessment of the player's competence (line 09).

SP's recognition and appreciation of PL1's gameplay help to 'position' his spectating activities in two ways. Firstly, SP displays himself as a keen, competent observer of the game, who is actively interested in the proceedings of play even though he is currently 'just' watching (in that sense we could say he is being a 'good spectator'). Secondly, in complimenting the competence of PL1, SP is also displaying an ability to recognise 'good play'. That is to say, the very recognition of skilled play can speak of a spectator's *own* competences in the game—i.e., as someone who possesses sufficient practical game knowledge and stock of play experiences so as to be able to see, assess, and produce appropriate judgements of the skilled embodied performances of other players.

Reflecting on play

The forms of spectating in our fragments up to this point have been quite tightly tied to what is happening at any given moment in the game 'now'. In contrast we now examine a moment where spectating involves reflection on past play, built into the organisation of current play. As a matter of occasioning this reflection, we join the same group as Fragment 3—albeit playing bowling now—where a spectator is 'in transition' between being an active player to someone watching play. Our fragment begins as one member of the setting (SP1) is sitting down the couch having just played a turn, while the another (PL) is getting ready for his turn, stepping forwards. During this, another spectator (SP2) is still sitting waiting for his turn.

```
01        *+(1.6)+ (2.8)
    pl    *>>steps forwards, prepares for bowl ->
    sp1    +>>sits down+
02 SP1    yürüyerek atınca
          when you throw while walking
03        biraz daha sanki şey
          it is a bit like
04        hız[lı gidiyo
          it is as if it goes faster
05 SP2       [hızlı gidiyo öyle
          it goes faster like that
06        (0.3)* *(0.2)
    pl       ->* *bowls ->
07 SP2    şu enerji*yi felan varsa
          that energy and so if available
    pl            ->*
08 SP2    onu kullandırıyor
          it makes you use that
09        (1.8)
10 SP1    s[s:-
11 SP2     [∞hatta %şu *bov%ling hareketi var ya
          actually you know that bowling movement
    sp2     ∞gazes towards pl ->
    sp2             %,,,,,,,,%moves feet ->
    pl                   *gazes towards sp2 ->
12 SP2    a#yak    # hareketi%
          the foot movement
    sp2                   ->%
    fig    #fig.11 #fig.12
13 SP2    onu* ya∞parsan daha da şey
          if you do it it is even greater
    pl     ->*
    sp2        ->∞
14        (1.2)
```

Fragment 4: Reflecting on play

Here, while PL is preparing himself (lines 01-06), SP1 produces an observation about the relationship between physical mobility and bowling speed, i.e., that the bowling ball in the game "goes faster" if you "throw while walking" as opposed to using a stationary swing of the arm, thus potentially improving play. SP2 joins in (line 05) displaying agreement with SP1. After a brief pause just as PL bowls (line 06), SP2 continues the conversation by building on the reflections of SP1, introducing the notion of in-game energy (power-up), by which the participants are referring to special features (i.e., 'super' bowls) which become available to players by using the bodily techniques under discussion (lines 07-08). Just after PL's bowl has knocked down all but two pins, SP2 starts gazing at PL and shares another reflection regarding foot movement (lines 11-13). His utterance embeds a claim that performing this foot movement while bowling makes the bowl more powerful. As he utters this, SP2 raises his feet, keeps them up for a while and moves them mid-air with a 'peddling' motion, demonstrating [8] the foot movement (Figures 11 and 12). SP2 performs this *as* he secures the player's gaze (line 11), gradually raising his legs during PL's turn towards him. PL attends to SP2's commenced demo in a momentarily similar interactional space to Fragment 2.

What we see in this fragment is how SP1 topicalises having recently been a player, and that this observation acts as a 'reflection' on his activities. Becoming a spectator, transitioning from player to spectator [3, 46, 1], makes it *relevant* to comment upon previous play—SP1's utterance gains its sense as a reflection by being done at this particular place in the sequence of interaction, i.e., by its sequential positioning after the end his turn-at-play and coordinated with his sitting down (just as a greeting is done at the opening of an encounter and gains its sense as a greeting in-and-through that [17]). Having just had a turn-at-play affords a sense of 'authority' about being able to 'speak' about the details of performing game actions (such as the motion of one's body and feet).

Over the course of the fragment, SP2 essentially transforms the reflection by SP1 into an instruction directed at PL's play. This is achieved because SP1's reflection also tacitly provides an instruction to the other participants in the game—that they adopt a different kind of bodily engagement with the Kinect that is more mobile and less stationary during a bowling swing. In overlap with this, SP2 produces an assessment (line 05). This overlap is affiliative and claims and confirms a similar knowledge and experience to SP1 [12]. SP2 then further develops the reflection of SP1, and produces two different instructions in the form of assessments (lines 07-08, and 11-13) regarding bodily conduct in-game.

This final part of the fragment also further reveals the ways in which the timing of talk and bodily actions of the spectators here are carefully oriented around the player's actions, and help us further unpack what SP2 is doing. Briefly prior to SP2's utterance on line 11, SP2 and SP1 have been conversing with one another. This temporally coincides with a natural moment of pause for PL as he has just bowled. In line 11, SP2 gazes at PL as he starts to produce his utterance and moves his feet slightly up. After receiving PL's gaze, SP2 launches into "that bowling movement" and simultaneously performs his demonstration with his feet, with his body still reclined somewhat on the couch. The careful timing of this interaction is used to manage and configure the intertwined participation frameworks between the three of them [13] in spite of the bowling game engaging only one player at a time directly. On this last point we also note that offering instructions and instructive demonstrations to others in a *competitive* gaming environment further reflects the spectators' orientation towards collaboration.

DISCUSSION

In its broadest framing, our study has sought to draw a distinction between 'being a spectator' and 'doing spectat*ing*'—while HCI research has explored the former extensively, we are more interested in the latter, which we have argued can be understood as an interactional phenomenon that is negotiated, managed and achieved moment-by-moment between participants in a game. The primary contribution of this paper has been to provide a detailed study in a naturalistic setting of the complex analytic work of spectating and the organised ways in which spectators *participate* in interaction with players (cf. [42]). This also builds upon preliminary examinations of Kinect play [16]. In some sense our use of the term 'work' is literal as well as metaphorical—spectatorship isn't always a smooth road and really has to be continuously *worked at*. In many ways the detail of this analytic work is the stuff of enjoyment in video game play [4].

Our discussion here is structured in the following way. First, we review the salient findings of our study. Then, we use these to refine some concepts of spectator roles and spectating in HCI. Subsequently, we conclude with a consideration of some possible implications for designing the spectator experience in HCI.

Spectating in and around gameplay with Kinect

A theme that has been repeatedly foregrounded by our analysis is the idea that **spectating is strongly temporally-oriented** towards both the organisation of the game being played and the organised conduct of players (and of course any other spectators, such as the pair found in Fragment 4). In Fragment 1 we see this very clearly with the spectator's production of timely imperatives such that they are tightly interwoven with the conduct of the player and the game on-screen. Spectating also involves structuring the form of participation in play around projected moments. In Fragment 2 the temporal organisation of turn-taking in bowling is used by the spectator to project and locate appropriate slots to produce assessments of the player's recent actions and provide an opportunity for the player to produce revised actions when the game resumes. Fragment 3 involves the spectator producing a compliment about the player at the end of a rally, while in Fragment 4, we see a similar moment that one of the spectators takes as an opportunity to provide a demonstration to the player.

Secondly, we have uncovered some of the **interactional resources involved in spectating** that are employed in the course of their analytic work. This includes resources that are more immediately 'obvious' such as deployments of particular forms of talk (e.g., assessments, Fragment 3), and bodily conduct (e.g., shifting one's body to develop certain visual perspectives on the player and screen, Fragment 2). It also includes more subtle features such as adjustments of gaze (e.g., waiting for opportune moments to complement a player, Fragment 3, or to establish an interactionally and temporally appropriate moment to perform a demonstration, Fragment 4). Spatial aspects are also crucial resources, such as the establishment of common interactional spaces via bodily arrangements of players and spectators as we see in Fragments 2, 3 and 4.

Thirdly, a significant but perhaps underexplored element of spectatorship is **spectating as 'seeing'**. This is particularly the case for seeing certain kinds of bodily conduct by players, the "ambiguity of movement" and its relationship to the sensor [19]. Although spectating on Kinect gaming do not involve a *professional* commitment to seeing as in, say, the seeing of particular kinds of movement qualities in performance practices [32]—and it would also be incorrect to characterise their activities as "professional vision" [11]—our fragments show that spectating nevertheless *does* often involve careful scrutiny of player activities (including what is available on-screen). However, our study also finesses this point. Seeing is embedded in practical courses of action and here it is no different. This means that 'seeing' done as a matter of spectating is not *only* about observing the movement of a player's feet (Fragment 4) or that a player is performing hand grabbing actions (Fragment 1). Rather, it is about *seeing that there are interactional implications of these*, i.e., "in circumstances where they are relevantly to be seen" [6, p. 260]. For instance, this means seeing that the player didn't move their feet forwards in such-and-such a way within a broader bowling activity, or seeing that a hand grabbing action must continue as a temporally-sensitive matter as the player's avatar begins to fall. In this sense spectating means also drawing on a 'dual vision'; that is, seeing the player(s) and the screen as one, as a gestalt—although we note that certain spatial arrangements may enable or hinder this dual vision.

Fourthly we want to underline the importance of **spectating as bodily work** in conjunction with seeing work—a feature of spectating within our study which is perhaps most clearly tied the Kinect sensor itself and the bodily discipline of players. Seeing is not purely 'ocular' but practically embedded in spectators' own bodily courses of action. Perhaps most obviously spectators are bodily engaged in particular comportments and arrangements on couches in all fragments so as to provide particular visual possibilities. But, bodily work in spectating is also sequentially organised; hence in Fragment 2 we see how the spectator coordinated his own posture in a way that supported his ability to see particular alignments between the player's body and screen at particular sequentially-relevant moments during bowling. There are of course other kinds of bodily work, such as in Fragment 4 where the movement of the spectator's feet offer a demonstration in order to finesse the bodily conduct of the player.

This leads to our final point about the **'authority' of spectating**. Doing spectating provides participants with rights, and sometimes obligations, to instruct, assess, compliment, critique, etc. the players and their conduct. To produce such actions necessitates the spectators to understand and draw upon the game-related actions players perform and the disciplined bodies they adopt, which are required so as to be 'seen' by the Kinect. The kind of authority in question here is mainly related to not being the agent for the activity. Spectators are not directly controlling the game (be it avatars or other in-game representations of the players), meaning that it is relatively easier for them to talk about, for instance, what needs to done in the cases of failures in gaming space. This is the case in Fragment 1, where the spectator produces continuous instructions for the player via a series of imperatives. A further layer of the authority of spectating is based on having just recently had a turn in game, as we see in Fragment 4. In that fragment, SP1, and subsequently SP2, build upon their prior game experiences to discuss their current approaches to play. SP2 even demonstrates the foot movement that he claims lead to better outcomes in game. In short, doing spectating is connected to having a measure of authority, and this authority is itself often 'at play' in the game as it unfolds.

Spectators and spectating in HCI research and design

Next we turn to consider the conceptual implications of our study for existing characterisations of spectating and spectators in the HCI literature, particularly for video games.

Firstly, our study has identified a diverse range of spectating practices. Here we point to Harper and Mentis's prior accounts of Kinect play in the home, which has emphasised the "fostering [of] laughter" and moments of "ridicule and mockery" as key characterisations of the social organisation of Kinect play [16]. However, while the broader corpus of our video recordings certainly presented moments that reflected this, our fragments also show a much greater range of participatory forms of spectating. This has included instructing, critiquing, complementing, reflecting, and so on. Importantly, we have unpacked these in detail, thus locating such spectating practices as deeply endogenous concerns of the setting which are interactionally achieved between player and spectator.

Secondly, as we have noted before, spectator experiences have often been formalised in various design frameworks, in terms spectrums of passive to active participation [23], and as part of constellations of discrete roles such as player, spectator, or bystander, which are transitioned between by members of a setting [8, 46]. In these frameworks, spectatorship may itself involve further subdivisions or personas that finesse these distinctions [8], such as spectators acting as "assistants" to players [5]. Our paper offers two contributions in this regard. As noted above, our study provides an enriched account of the diverse activities of spectators that in many senses builds detail around those of [8]. At the same time, the highly participatory nature of spectating that we have articulated might give us pause when considering assignments of particular and distinct 'roles' to them (also see [29]). Spectating in our study is an interactional matter, i.e., it is achieved moment-by-moment as a matter of participation with the current player. Who is and who is not a spectator is sometimes a moot point [55]; rather, for design in HCI we might perhaps consider what *courses of action* does spectating involve? Equally it leads us to ask at what point the terminology of 'spectators' and 'players' no longer necessarily helps us analytically understand settings and circumstances (and therefore might even cloud design understanding)? While we would not suggest abandoning distinctions or avoiding the assignments of the category of 'spectator' to members of a setting for the purposes of interaction design, at the same time we are left wondering what the end-game from a design point of view is for developing more and more gradations of spectator 'states' in terms of roles and subroles.

Design possibilities for spectating in HCI

Finally, based on the main contribution of our findings, we consider more specific design implications for HCI. Explorations of ways to support the spectator as participant in play have emerged in HCI recently (e.g., [31]). Our study has presented opportunities to think about spectating as a participatory activity in play and how this is achieved by diverse methods. In a broad sense it confirms that spectators do indeed play a role in *assisting* players, yet the ways they do so is more collaborative and complex than previously reported. This leads us to three design possibilities

1. Spectating involves complex analytic work, both in seeing the player, and seeing the game (i.e., 'dual vision'). This alternative perspective to the active player invites game designers to consider offering game elements that are *only* available to the perspective of spectating but which contribute to the game in some way.
2. What spectators can do analytically during play may range between continuous engagement in 'scaffolding' through to offering post-hoc reflections on their own play. This suggests an equally broad range of temporal modes of participation that could be supported by any given game. There is a substantial difference between spectating on a game that is continuous compared with spectating on one where play is suspended at particular moments.
3. Whole body interaction supported by sensors like the Kinect prevent the spectator from engaging in certain forms of physical participation, particularly in things like demonstrations. This leads to technical challenges for sensing systems that (perhaps counterintuitively) detect the player yet *ignore* the spectator in order to enable greater participation [8].

CONCLUSION

In this paper we have presented a close and detailed look at spectating in the home around Kinect gaming, examining how such spectating practices are sequentially ordered and temporally coordinated with players and the game in play. To the best of our knowledge, our empirical study seems to be the first of its kind in exploring—in a detailed, naturalistic way—spectating in collocated gaming settings where body-based interfaces act as game controllers. In doing so we have demonstrated that, by examining the local sequential organisation of conduct by spectators and those they are watching, we may better understand the dynamic interactional and participatory nature of spectating, and its implications for HCI's understanding of spectatorship and spectating.

ACKNOWLEDGMENTS

We are grateful to Lorenza Mondada for feedback on this paper, Joe Marshall, and the EMCA data session group at MRL for discussion of the fragments. Burak S. Tekin's work is supported by Hermann Paul School of Linguistics (HPSL); Stuart Reeves acknowledges the support of EPSRC (EP/M02315X/1 & EP/K025848/1).

Data access statement: Due to ethical concerns and consent restrictions of our corpus, supporting research data (collected by Tekin) cannot be made openly available.

REFERENCES

1. Steve Benford, and Gabriella Giannachi. 2011. *Performing Mixed Reality*. Cambridge: The MIT Press.
2. Ulrika Bennerstedt, and Jonas Ivarsson. 2010. Knowing the way: Managing epistemic topologies in virtual game worlds. *Computer Supported Cooperative Work* 19, 201-230.
   http://dx.doi.org/10.1007/s10606-010-9109-8
3. Harry Brignull, and Yvonne Rogers. 2003. Enticing people to interact with large public displays in public spaces. In *Proceedings of INTERACT'03*, 17-24.
4. Barry Brown, and Oskar Juhlin. 2015. *Enjoying Machines*. Cambridge: MIT Press.
5. Gifford Cheung, and Jeff Huang. 2011. Starcraft from the stands: Understanding the game spectator. In *Proceedings of CHI'11*, 763-772.

http://dx.doi.org/10.1145/1978942.1979053

6. Jeff Coulter, E. D. Parsons. 1990. The praxiology of perception: Visual orientations and practical action. *Inquiry* 33, 251–72.
http://dx.doi.org/10.1080/00201749008602223
7. John Downs, Frank Vetere, Steve Howard, Steve Loughnan, and Wally Smith. 2014. Audience experience in social videogaming: effects of turn expectation and game physicality. In *Proceedings of the SIGCHI Conference on Human Factors in Computing Systems* (CHI'14). ACM, New York, NY, USA, 3473-3482. http://dx.doi.org/10.1145/2556288.2556965
8. John Downs, Frank Vetere, and Wally Smith. 2015. Differentiated participation in social videogaming. In *Proceedings of OzCHI'15*, 92-100.
https://doi.org/10.1145/2838739.2838777
9. Harold Garfinkel. 1967. *Studies in Ethnomethodology*. Englewood Cliffs: Prentice Hall.
10. Harold Garfinkel. 2002. *Ethnomethodology's Program*. New York: Rowman and Littlefield.
11. Charles Goodwin. 1994. Professional vision. *American Anthropologist* 96(3), 606-633.
http://dx.doi.org/10.1525/aa.1994.96.3.02a00100
12. Charles Goodwin, and Marjorie Harness Goodwin. 1987. Concurrent operation on talk: Notes on the interactive organization of assessments. *IPRA Papers in Pragmatics* 1, 1-54.
http://dx.doi.org/10.1075/iprapip.1.1.01goo
13. Charles Goodwin, and Marjorie Harness Goodwin. 2004. Participation. In *A Companion to Linguistic Anthropology*, Alessandro Duranti (Ed.). Oxford: Blackwell, 222-244.
14. William A. Hamilton, Oliver Garretson, and Andruid Kerne. 2014. Streaming on Twitch: Fostering participatory communities of play within live mixed media. In *Proceedings of CHI'14*, 1315-1324.
http://dx.doi.org/10.1145/2556288.2557048
15. Lone Koefoed Hansen, and Peter Dalsgaard.2015. Note to self: Stop calling interfaces "natural". In *Proceedings of 5th Decennial Aarhus Conference on Critical Alternatives*.
http://dx.doi.org/10.7146/aahcc.v1i1.21316
16. Richard Harper, and Helena H. Mentis. 2013. The mocking gaze: The social organization of Kinect use. In *Proceedings of CSCW'13*, 167-180.
http://dx.doi.org/10.1145/2441776.2441797
17. John Heritage. 1984. *Garfinkel and Ethnomethodology*. Cambridge: Polity Press.
18. John Heritage, and Tanya Stivers. 1999. Online commentary in acute medical visits: A method of shaping patient expectations. *Social Science and Medicine* 49, 1501-1507.
http://dx.doi.org/10.1016/S0277-9536(99)00219-1
19. Katherine Isbister, and Florian Floyd Mueller. 2015. Guidelines for the design of movement-based games and their relevance to HCI. *Human-Computer Interaction* 30(3-4), 366-399.
http://dx.doi.org/10.1080/07370024.2014.996647
20. Jonas Ivarsson, and Christian Greiffenhagen. 2015. The organization of turn-taking in pool skate sessions. *Research on Language and Social Interaction* 48(4), 406-429.
http://dx.doi.org/10.1080/08351813.2015.1090114
21. Gail Jefferson. 1984. Transcript notation. In *Structures of social action: Studies in conversation analysis*, J. Maxwell Atkinson, and John Heritage (Eds.). Cambridge: Cambridge University Press. ix–xvi.
22. Oskar Juhlin, and Elin Önneval. 2013. On the relation of ordinary gestures to TV screens: General lessons for the design of collaborative interactive techniques. In *Proceedings of CHI'13*, 919-928.
http://dx.doi.org/10.1145/2470654.2466118
23. Dennis L. Kappen, Pejman Mirza-Babaei, Jens Johannsmeier, Daniel Buckstein, James Robb, and Lennart E. Nacke. 2014. Engaged by boss and cheers: The effect of co-located game audiences on social player experience. In *Proceedings of CHI PLAY'14*, 151-160.
http://dx.doi.org/10.1145/2658537.2658687
24. Mehdi Kaytoue, Arlei Silva, Loïc Cerf, Wagner Meira Jr., and Chedy Raïssi. 2012. Watch me playing, I am a professional: A first study on video game live streaming. In *Proceedings of WWW'12*, 1181-1188.
http://dx.doi.org/10.1145/2187980.2188259
25. Elizabeth Keating. 2008. Space shifting: New technologies, new opportunities. *Texas Linguistic Forum* 52, 70-79.
26. Adam Kendon. 1990. *Conducting interaction*. Cambridge: Cambridge University Press.
27. Maurice Ten Koppel, Gilles Bailly, Jörg Müller, and Robert Walter. 2012. Chained displays: configurations of public displays can be used to influence actor-, audience-, and passer-by behavior. In *Proceedings of the SIGCHI Conference on Human Factors in Computing Systems* (CHI'12). ACM, New York, NY, USA, 317-326.
http://dx.doi.org/10.1145/2207676.2207720
28. Kenneth Liberman. 2013. *More studies in Ethnomethodology*. Albany: State University of New York Press.

29. Holin Lin and Chuen-Tsai Sun. 2011. The Role of Onlookers in Arcade Gaming: Frame Analysis of Public Behaviours. *Convergence* 17(2):125-137, Sage (May 2011).
http://dx.doi.org/10.1177%2F1354856510397111

30. Oskar Lindwall, and Gustav Lymer. 2014. Inquiries of the body: Novice questions and the instructable observability of endodontic scenes. *Discourse Studies* 16(2), 271-294.
http://dx.doi.org/10.1177%2F1461445613514672

31. Bernhard Maurer, Ilhan Aslan, Martin Wuchse, Katja Neureiter, and Manfred Tsceligi. 2015. Gaze-based onlooker integration: Exploring the in-between of active player and passive spectator in co-located gaming. In *Proceedings of CHI PLAY'15*, 163-373.
https://doi.org/10.1145/2793107.2793126

32. Helena M. Mentis, and Carolina Johannson. 2013. Seeing movement qualities. In *Proceedings of CHI'13*, 3375-3384.
http://dx.doi.org/10.1145/2470654.2466462

33. Lorenza Mondada. 2009. Emergent focused interactions in public spaces: A systematic analysis of the multimodal achievement of a common interactional space. *Journal of Pragmatics* 41, 1977-1997.
http://dx.doi.org/10.1016/j.pragma.2008.09.019

34. Lorenza Mondada. 2012. Coordinating action and talk-in-interaction in and out of video games. In *The appropriation of media in everyday life*, Ruth Ayass & Cornelia Gerhardt (Eds.). Amsterdam: John Benjamins, 231-270.

35. Lorenza Mondada. 2013. Coordinating mobile action in real time: The timed organization of directives in video games. In *Mobility and Interaction*, Pentti Haddington, Lorenza Mondada, and Maurice Nevile (Eds.). Berlin: De Gruyter, 300-341.

36. Lorenza Mondada. 2014. Conventions for multimodal transcription. https://franz.unibas.ch/fileadmin/franz/user_upload/redaktion/Mondada_conv_multimodality.pdf (retrieved 21/09/16)

37. Lorenza Mondada. 2014. Instructions in the operating room: How the surgeon directs their assistant's hands. *Discourse Studies* 16(2), 131-161.
http://dx.doi.org/10.1177/1461445613515325

38. Jörg Müller, Robert Walter, Gilles Bailly, Michael Nischt, and Florian Alt. 2012. Looking glass: A field study on noticing interactivity of a shop window. In *Proceedings of CHI'12*, 297-306.
http://dx.doi.org/10.1145/2207676.2207718

39. Bjorn Nansen, Frank Vetere, Toni Robertson, John Downs, Margot Brereton, and Jeannetter Durick. 2014. Reciprocal habituation: A study of older people and the Kinect. *ACM Transactions on Computer-Human Interaction,* 21(3).
http://dx.doi.org/10.1145/2617573

40. Donald A. Norman. 2010. Natural user interfaces are not natural. *interactions* 17, 3 (May 2010), 6-10.
http://dx.doi.org/10.1145/1744161.1744163

41. Kenton O'Hara, Maxine Glancy, and Simon Robertshaw. 2008. Understanding collective play in an urban screen game. In *Proceedings of CSCW'08*, 67-78.
http://dx.doi.org/10.1145/1460563.1460576

42. Kenton O'Hara, Abigail Sellen, and Richard Harper. 2011. Embodiment in Brain-Computer Interaction. In *Proceedings of CHI'11*, 353-362.
http://dx.doi.org/10.1145/1978942.1978994

43. Kenton O'Hara, Richard Harper, Helena Mentis, Abigail Sellen, and Alex Taylor. 2013. On the naturalness of touchless: Putting the "interaction" back into NUI. *ACM Transactions on Computer-Human Interaction,* 20(1).
http://dx.doi.org/10.1145/2442106.2442111

44. Hannah R.M. Pelikan and Mathias Broth. 2016. Why That Nao?: How Humans Adapt to a Conventional Humanoid Robot in Taking Turns-at-Talk. In *Proceedings of the 2016 CHI Conference on Human Factors in Computing Systems* (CHI'16). ACM, New York, NY, USA, 4921-4932. DOI:
https://doi.org/10.1145/2858036.2858478

45. Stuart Reeves, Steve Benford, Claire O'Malley, and Mike Fraser. 2005. Designing the spectator experience. In *Proceedings of CHI'05*, 741-750.
http://dx.doi.org/10.1145/1054972.1055074

46. Stuart Reeves. 2011. *Designing interfaces in public settings*. London: Springer.
http://dx.doi.org/10.1007/978-0-85729-265-0

47. Stuart Reeves, Christian Greiffenhagen, and Eric Laurier. 2016. Video gaming as practical accomplishment: Ethnomethodology, conversation analysis, and play. *Topics in Cognitive Science* (2016).
http://dx.doi.org/10.1111/tops.12234

48. Sean Rintel, Richard Harper, and Kenton O'Hara. 2016. The Tyranny of the Everyday in Mobile Video Messaging. In *Proceedings of the 2016 CHI Conference on Human Factors in Computing Systems* (CHI'16). ACM, New York, NY, USA, 4781-4792. DOI:
https://doi.org/10.1145/2858036.2858042

49. Harvey Sacks. 1992. *Lectures on conversation.* Oxford: Blackwell.

50. Nicholas Taylor. 2015. Play to the camera: Video ethnography, spectatorship, and e-sports. *Convergence* 22(2): 115-130, Sage (April 2016).

http://dx.doi.org/10.1177%2F1354856515580282

51. T. L. Taylor. 2012. Chapter 8, Spectatorship and Fandom. In *Raising the Stakes: E-Sports and the Professionalization of Computer Gaming*. Cambridge: The MIT Press.

52. Burak S. Tekin. 2015. Embodied manipulations of controllers and manipulating the bodies as controllers. In *Proceedings of The International Institute for Ethnomethodology and Conversation Analysis* (IIEMCA) conference, August 2015, Kolding, Denmark.

53. Peter Tolmie, and Mark Rouncefield. 2013. *Ethnomethodology at Play*. Surrey: Ashgate.

54. Amy Voida, and Saul Greenberg. 2009. Wii All Play: The console game as a computational meeting place. In *Proceedings of CHI'09*, 1559-1568.

http://dx.doi.org/10.1145/1518701.1518940

55. Dirk vom Lehn, Jon Hindmarsh, Paul Luff, and Christian Heath. 2007. Engaging constable: revealing art with new technology. In *Proceedings of the SIGCHI Conference on Human Factors in Computing Systems* (CHI'07). ACM, New York, NY, USA, 1485-1494.

http://dx.doi.org/10.1145/1240624.1240848

56. Robert Walter, Gilles Bailly, and Jörg Müller. 2013. StrikeAPose: revealing mid-air gestures on public displays. In *Proceedings of CHI'13*, 841-850.

http://dx.doi.org/10.1145/2470654.2470774

57. Niels Wouters, John Downs, Mitchell Harrop, Travis Cox, Eduardo Oliveira, Sarah Webber, Frank Vetere, and Andrew Vande Moere. 2016. Uncovering the Honeypot Effect: How Audiences Engage with Public Interactive Systems. In *Proceedings of DIS'16*, 5-16.

https://doi.org/10.1145/2901790.2901796

Expanding Video Game Live-Streams with Enhanced Communication Channels: A Case Study

Pascal Lessel
DFKI GmbH
Saarland Informatics Campus
pascal.lessel@dfki.de

Alexander Vielhauer
Saarland University
Saarland Informatics Campus
s9alviel@stud.uni-saarland.de

Antonio Krüger
DFKI GmbH
Saarland Informatics Campus
krueger@dfki.de

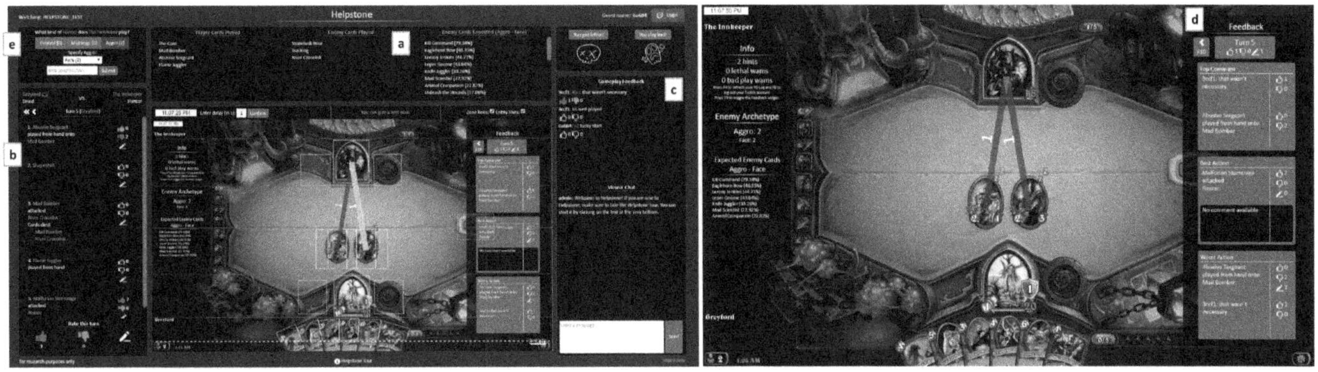

Figure 1. User interfaces of Helpstone. Left: Overview of the viewer's web page with the stream embedded in the middle and widgets around it. Right: Streamer's view of Blizzard's game Hearthstone with overlays, showing aggregated/filtered viewers' inputs. Figure 2 shows enlarged widgets (a-e).

ABSTRACT
Live-streaming of video games is a recent phenomenon. One driving factor is the direct communication between the streamer and the audience. Currently, besides the platform-integrated options such as text chats, streamers often use external sources to let their community better articulate their opinions. In this paper we present a case study with our tool Helpstone, a live-streaming tool for the card game Hearthstone. Helpstone provides several new communication channels that allow for a better viewer-streamer interaction. We evaluated the tool within a live-streaming session with 23 viewers using Helpstone, and interviewed the streamer. The results indicate that not every implemented interactivity option is relevant. However, in general, new communication channels appear to be valuable and novel influence options are appreciated.

ACM Classification Keywords
H.5.m. Information Interfaces and Presentation (e.g. HCI): Miscellaneous

Author Keywords
Twitch; Hearthstone; audience influence; streaming

CHI 2017, May 06-11, 2017, Denver, CO, USA
© 2017 ACM. ISBN 978-1-4503-4655-9/17/05...$15.00
DOI: http://dx.doi.org/10.1145/3025453.3025708

INTRODUCTION
Streaming platforms such as Twitch allow for distributing user-generated live video content and host large online communities [12]. During a stream, streamers are able to communicate with their audience. This direct communication channel might be one reason why this form of content production attracts so much attention: In 2014, Twitch was one of the top five internet traffic generators in the US [5]. Twitch's core focus is on gaming, i.e., video games or board games are streamed, which attracts a large audience [8, 20]. The direct communication medium of Twitch is a text chat in which the audience can communicate with each other. Their messages can also be read (and thus commented on) by the streamer. Especially in large channels (>10,000 viewers) it becomes nearly impossible for the streamer and the viewers to get all the relevant information through the chat, even if only a small portion of the viewership uses this medium. Many streamers use third-party software to introduce further means of interactivity, such as the polling software StrawPoll [10], which is used to find out what the majority of the audience wants. However, this has shortcomings, as a streamer needs to explicitly set up a poll and wait for votes. Thus it is cumbersome to sketch the audience's opinion—especially while playing a game. Novel streaming platforms, such as Beam.pro [9], try to refine interactivity by providing more sophisticated, built-in real-time interaction options to enhance the communication channels. Even though interactivity was shown to be relevant for certain viewer groups [4], it is currently unclear how viewers perceive and use such sophisticated features. We contribute to this question by conducting a case study within a live-streaming

environment. A system is designed on top of the basic stream features (i.e. game window live-stream and chat) to extend the state-of-the-art approaches with new interaction options. We used the popular game *Hearthstone: Hereos of Warcraft* [6] as a game to be streamed and implemented *Helpstone*, a tool which offers a set of novel communication channels on top of this game. An investigation in a live-streaming setting with 23 viewers revealed differences in the perception of features among the viewers, which game designers and researchers can build upon. It also showed that additional communication channels are valuable to the audience—partly because of the influence they can exert on the streamer by using them.

RELATED WORK

Live-streaming platforms have been investigated recently. In his study about community building, Postigo discusses the importance of integrating viewer opinions [17]. Smith et al. analyzed the viewer personas of [4] with respect to video game streams and showed that certain personas can be better engaged in streams when more interaction options are offered [20]. Kow and Young investigated StarCraft streams and found that learners use them as a primary source of knowledge [13], which was also reported for chess players [7]. All this work hints that tools which allow streamers and viewers to better articulate and discuss the game-related content seem reasonable. TwitchViz [16] is a tool to analyze chat messages of viewers (currently without a real-time capability) after a streaming session. This can provide valuable insights to a streamer for upcoming sessions. The World Cupinion application [19] shows that it is beneficial to provide feedback options to the viewers and present the provided feedback in an aggregated form to all the viewers, as this increases fun and perceived connectedness. The research done on live-streaming systems revealed issues that, in our opinion, are important when new communication channels are considered: Live-streaming platforms have a (technically-caused) video delay ("lag") between streamer and viewers. For Twitch it is at least 12 seconds (usually more) and varies between viewers [23]. Chat messages have nearly no delay, requiring the streamer to think back to his previous actions to understand the meaning of the messages correctly. Hamilton et al. [8] reported that communication with an audience of $\geq$ 150 viewers is hard to maintain and leads to information overload. Thus, work on input aggregation becomes relevant as well [14, 18]. Another issue is that viewers can join a channel at any time and will have missed important elements; hence, they need on-demand information about the current game state [2] to make well-informed inputs. These issues show that the offered chat as primary communication channel, especially for game-related aspects, seems insufficient and more sophisticated options are necessary, which we explore in this work.

HEARTHSTONE AND HELPSTONE

Hearthstone: Heroes of Warcraft [6] was released in 2014 by Blizzard Entertainment and is a round-based video card game. Players build their deck from a number of cards and play against other players. Every turn a player has a limited amount of resources (more resources become available every round). A player wins as soon as the other player has less than 1 hit point. Damage can be done through special powers or through the cards themselves. For example, played minions (also having hit points and attack values) can directly attack the other player or minions of that player, allowing for tactics. One turn is limited to 75 seconds but can be ended prematurely by the player. [21] provides the complete rules of the game. Hearthstone was chosen for this study, as it is among the most popular games streamed on Twitch [11], is round-based (thus, providing time to react), offers a log file for all game actions, and many streamers discuss their options in the game with their audience already; therefore, dedicated communication channels seem to be beneficial.

Helpstone has the goal to provide more sophisticated communication channels in which game-related feedback and hints can be easily given by the viewers and are presented in an easy-to-analyze way for the streamer. The system consists of two parts: the viewers have access to a web page embedding the Hearthstone live-stream as well as different widgets. The streamer uses the Overwolf [15] plug-in system, an HTML-based framework which can be used in game windows and allows for interactions (see Figure 1 for the viewer's and streamer's interface). Real-time game state information is parsed from the Hearthstone log and then used in Helpstone. In the system design we needed to cope with issues mentioned in the related work section. To ensure that all information presented to the viewers relates to the in-game situation shown by the live-stream, users can compare and adjust a clock on their website with a clock live-streamed by the streamer. By that, Helpstone widgets are synchronized with the video live-stream. The widgets follow the concept of "ballot box communication" [22], i.e., we limit the options viewers have and aggregate these inputs. Only the aggregations are then visualized, to reduce information overload. Finally, elements providing historical information are available as well. Helpstone widgets are described in the following:

- **Stream Overlay**: To simulate natural game interaction for the viewers and get sophisticated visualization of hints, viewers can draw lines on the video stream. These lines are directly shown to the streamer via a transparent fullscreen Overwolf widget (see middle elements in Figure 1). For the viewers, areas of interest are visualized by rectangles; only here, lines can start or end. When in the same zones, lines of different viewers are aggregated and become thicker to make popular moves visible at a glance for the streamer. Whenever the streamer performs an in-game action, the lines are cleared.
- **Archetype Voting**: To speculate about the enemy's strategy together with the streamer, the opponent's play style ("archetypes") can be classified (similar to openings in chess). Viewers can vote on the three main existing play styles. As many card deck variants exist for every archetype, we also allow viewers to vote on a specification (see Figure 2e). The most-voted specification and the number of votes for every archetype are shown to the streamer.
- **Cards Tracker**: For historical information, played cards are tracked and allow the viewers (including ones who joined later) to get an overview of the current match. With a mouse-over, the original game cards with all details are

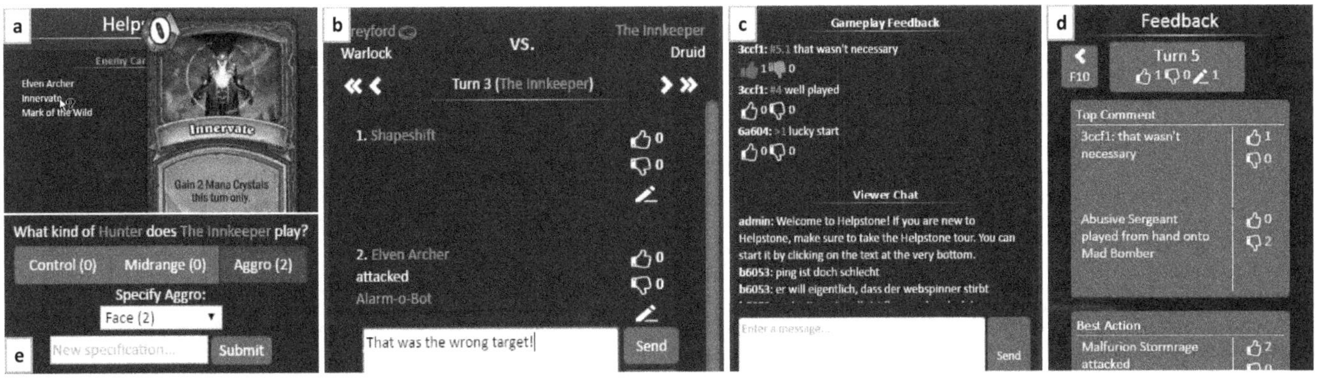

Figure 2. A selection of different widgets. For the overall screen composition see Figure 1. a) Shows a part of the Cards Tracker, with a mouse-over event, b) the History, c) the Chat with the History comments at the top, d) part of the History overview for the streamer, e) the Archetype Voting.

shown (see Figure 2a). Together with the Archetype Voting, this widget helps viewers to make informed decisions. We also show card predictions, based on past games and previously seen cards, for the most-voted archetype/specification.

- **History and Chat**: For historical information, all turns with details on every action and involved cards (see Figure 2b) are accessible to the viewers. Similar to the Cards Tracker, the cards can be inspected via mouse-over. Viewers can rate actions and turns (thumbs up and down) and can also provide a comment. These are then visualized in a dedicated chat area (see Figure 2c), in which comments can also be up-/down-voted and are sorted accordingly. Besides these specific elements, the chat works similarly to an IRC. The streamer can toggle a specific overview (see Figure 2d): The best-rated comment is shown, and the best/worst rated action in this turn, as well as the comment that was rated best for these actions. This should allow streamers to discuss the important points with their audience in a structured way.
- **Emergency Buttons**: As quick and easy-to-analyze feedback, viewers have the option to indicate, by a simple button press (see Figure 1, left, top-right corner), that the current situation can be considered as a "bad play" or that the streamer could win the game ("has lethal"). The streamer always sees the number of bad play and lethal hints for his current turn. When a threshold is reached ($max(0.05 * viewercount, 5)$), the widget starts to blink red.

USER STUDY

Helpstone was evaluated with the goal to receive insights on how viewers perceive the enhanced communication channels.

Method

We recruited a German streamer (25-year-old experienced male Hearthstone player, streaming since November 2015) who usually has 20 to 50 viewers. At the beginning, a 4-minute tutorial video was shown in the live-stream to provide the viewers with a tutorial on Helpstone. Additionally, a tour on the web page explained all elements for viewers who joined later. The streamer played against a simple computer opponent to let the viewers and himself get familiar with the system (the system has also been explained to the streamer beforehand). Thereafter, the streamer played against a strong computer opponent (without time pressure) and one round against one of his viewers. The viewers were encouraged to use Helpstone; all interactions were logged. After these matches, the stream was ended and a link to an online questionnaire consisting of demographic data questions, a SUS questionnaire [3] (to measure the overall usability of Helpstone) and statements on the use, usability and the perception of every widget was provided. Respondents had to express their agreement with these statements on a 5-point scale ranging from disagree (1) to agree (5). These statements were introduced to make the widgets comparable and receive specific insights into each of them. Free-text answers were also allowed for every widget and the overall system. The streamer was interviewed in a semi-structured way by two of the authors to receive insights into his perception of the system and options for the audience.

Results

23 viewers visited our Helpstone website. 10 (8 male; 1x <18, 4x 18-25, 5x 25-30 years old) completed the questionnaire. Half of them were regular viewers and 9 respondents reported being at least moderately skilled in playing Hearthstone.

Helpstone subjectively raises the audience activity level and perceived influence: The viewers enjoyed Helpstone (M=4.4, SD=0.52) and by using it reported being more active while watching the live-stream (M=4.5, SD=0.71). Some participants also reported that Helpstone helped them to better interact with the streamer (M=3.8, SD=1.23) and the majority of the viewers had the feeling of exerting influence on him (M=4.5, SD=0.53). The streamer also reported the feeling that he had been influenced, even though he played in "his style".

Helpstone increases game-related interactions: Before the experiment, we tracked the viewer's activity for this channel for three consecutive Hearthstone matches (which took 12 minutes in total) and found that 30 to 40 viewers were watching. Out of those, seven wrote 22 chat messages; none of them was game-related. A later tracking of an one-hour footage of this channel with a similar audience size showed that only 18 of 144 chat messages (12.5%) were game related. In the interview, the streamer stated that he also thinks that more social than game-related conversation happens on his channel. Further, he states that his viewership indeed provides hints—especially when he plays badly—and that he sometimes asks his viewers game-related questions, thus making Helpstone reasonable for his channel. The two matches in our experiment lasted 26 minutes in total, thus revealing that Helpstone will

Element	1st match	2nd match	Total
Drawing lines	61 (16)	43 (12)	104 (20)
Player up-/down-votes	50 (9)	23 (7)	73 (12)
Opponent up-/down-votes	20 (7)	10 (5)	30 (12)
Bad play warnings	11 (5)	7 (7)	18 (10)
Comments on player action/turns	8 (5)	10 (6)	18 (8)
Archetype votes	-	10 (10)	10 (10)
Up-/down-votes on comments	2 (2)	11 (5)	13 (7)
Comments on opponent action/turns	2 (2)	1 (1)	3 (3)
Lethal warnings	0 (0)	1 (1)	1 (1)
Total interactions	154 (16)	116 (13)	270 (22)

Table 1. Number of interactions per match and element; () = number of unique users using it. Note: The Archetype Voting is not supported against computer opponents. The 1st match took 14 and 2nd 12 minutes.

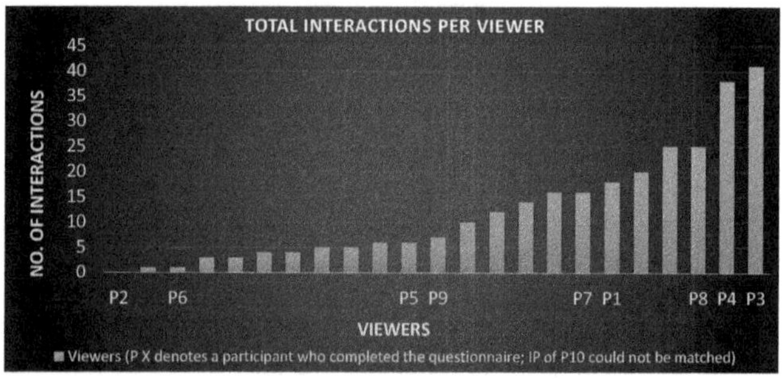

Figure 3. Number of interactions per viewer.

prolong matches, to give the audience room for suggestions. Table 1 shows the number of interactions with the Helpstone elements and Figure 3 shows the interaction count per participant. Both indicate that through Helpstone more game-related interactions happen. The artificial situation and the novelty effect might have had a strong influence, but especially the numbers of drawn lines and the up-votes (the two most often used features) indicate that viewers' game-related interactions might increase if a tool enables sophisticated input methods.

Helpstone offers relevant features, even for passive viewers: Table 2 shows that not all new features were perceived as relevant; thus, not every option for more interaction should be offered unconditionally. Research needs to investigate, whether interaction options in a stream that are not perceived as relevant are harmful. By considering Table 1 and Table 2, we could follow that the stream overlay was perceived as the most important element, even though usability flaws were reported (see next result). It seems that the direct interaction with the video stream and the immediate feedback are promising for such systems. Rating game actions (cf. Table 2) and presenting the results in an aggregated fashion was appreciated by the viewers (M=4.2, SD=0.63) and explicitly approved by the streamer. We conclude that interactive features which provide more discussion options for the streamer are thus important. Finally, it seems that for functions providing general information on the game state, easy-to-verify ground-truth information (lethal warnings), is preferred over subjective or ambiguous ones (bad play warnings).

Considering the interaction count of the viewers who provided answers to our questionnaire (see Figure 3), we see that some only made a few interactions. The assessment of the different features in Table 2 shows that these (passive) users also had positively rated the interactive features; otherwise, the mean

I think it is relevant...	Mean (SD)
... to suggest actions to the streamer (by drawing lines)	4.5 (0.50)
... that viewers can vote for comments (thumbs up/down)	4.2 (0.98)
... that viewers can rate actions (thumbs up/down)	4.2 (0.98)
... to be able to warn the streamer of lethal situations	4.1 (0.94)
... that viewers can comment on actions	4.1 (1.22)
... that viewers can suggest new specifications	3.9 (0.94)
... that viewers can comment on turns	3.9 (1.51)
... to see a prognosis of the remaining opponent's cards	3.7 (1.10)
... that viewers can rate turns	3.7 (1.42)
... to be able to vote for archetypes	3.4 (1.28)
... to be able to warn the streamer of urgent bad play	2.9 (1.30)

Table 2. Relevance statements for the different system elements.

values would have been worse (t-tests between viewers with low (≤ 10) and high (> 10) numbers of interactions did not reveal any significant differences for the different ratings). This hints that viewers who want to watch rather than to interact see usefulness in the new communication channels.

Helpstone's usability can be further improved: The SUS score was M=70.25 (SD=13.46). According to [1], this is acceptable, but leaves room for improvements. Usability issues were reported: The History always advances to the next turn, which sometimes causes viewers to rate or comment on the wrong turn. The Stream Overlay needs refinement to be more suitable for Hearthstone matches (to suggest chains of actions). The streamer also reported that the Stream Overlay interferes with in-game information (e.g. card texts). However, both widgets were seen as relevant and were used.

DISCUSSION AND CONCLUSION

The case study revealed that Helpstone can improve the communication, give the audience a feeling of influence, and raise their activity level, and may also be interesting for more passive viewers who simply want to watch the stream. To our knowledge, we are the first to contribute an investigation of such a setup that allows a better direct interaction between viewer and streamer. However, the results should not be overgeneralized, as we had only a relatively small sample size, only one streamer and focused on a round-based game only. We deem these limitations acceptable for a first exploration of this topic and we showed that research on further interactive options for live-streams is worthwhile. As not every function offered seems equally relevant to viewers and more and more approaches become available (either built-in or third party), it seems necessary to have rules to know what works in which situations. Further research can build upon our concepts and results, especially "ballot box communication" and direct interactions on the video stream, as these seem promising for novel interactive streaming tools. Our concepts are applicable to other turn-based games with a fixed camera, such as chess or poker. Continuous game play and a moving camera add complexity and should be analyzed next. Nonetheless, even here, our concepts can be used: For example, for first person shooters, comments and up-votes could show which weapons to use next, while for role-playing games, dialogue options to be selected by the streamer could be made interactive for the viewers on the video stream. Work on such tools could create completely novel experiences for streamers and viewers. Future work should also focus on the streamers' perspective, e.g., whether they want to give their audience so much control.

REFERENCES

1. Aaron Bangor, Philip Kortum, and James Miller. 2009. Determining What Individual SUS Scores Mean: Adding an Adjective Rating Scale. *Journal of Usability Studies* 4, 3 (May 2009), 114–123. http://dl.acm.org/citation.cfm?id=2835587.2835589
2. James Bonner and Clinton J. Woodward. 2012. On Domain-Specific Decision Support Systems for e-Sports Strategy Games. In *Proceedings of the 24th Australian Computer-Human Interaction Conference (OzCHI '12)*. ACM, New York, NY, USA, 42–51. DOI: http://dx.doi.org/10.1145/2414536.2414544
3. John Brooke. 1996. SUS: A Quick and Dirty Usability Scale. In *Usability Evaluation in Industry*, P. W. Jordan, B. Weerdmeester, A. Thomas, and I. L. McClelland (Eds.). Taylor and Francis, London, 189–194.
4. Gifford Cheung and Jeff Huang. 2011. Starcraft from the Stands: Understanding the Game Spectator. In *Proceedings of the 29th Conference on Human Factors in Computing Systems (CHI '11)*. ACM, New York, NY, USA, 763–772. DOI: http://dx.doi.org/10.1145/1978942.1979053
5. Matthew DiPietro. 2014. Twitch is 4th in Peak US Internet Traffic. (2014). https://blog.twitch.tv/twitch-is-4th-in-peak-us-internet-traffic-90b1295af358, last accessed: 06/01/2017.
6. Blizzard Entertainment. 2014. Hearthstone: Heroes of Warcraft. (2014). http://eu.battle.net/hearthstone/de/, last accessed: 06/01/2017.
7. Stephen R. Foster, Sarah Esper, and William G. Griswold. 2013. From Competition to Metacognition: Designing Diverse, Sustainable Educational Games. In *Proceedings of the 31st Conference on Human Factors in Computing Systems (CHI '13)*. ACM, New York, NY, USA, 99–108. DOI: http://dx.doi.org/10.1145/2470654.2470669
8. William A. Hamilton, Oliver Garretson, and Andruid Kerne. 2014. Streaming on Twitch: Fostering Participatory Communities of Play Within Live Mixed Media. In *Proceedings of the 32nd Conference on Human Factors in Computing Systems (CHI '14)*. ACM, New York, NY, USA, 1315–1324. DOI: http://dx.doi.org/10.1145/2556288.2557048
9. Beam Interactive Inc. 2017a. Beam.pro. (2017). https://beam.pro, last accessed: 06/01/2017.
10. Curse Inc. 2017b. StrawPoll. (2017). https://strawpoll.me, last accessed: 06/01/2017.
11. Twitch Inc. 2015. 2015 Retrospective. (2015). https://www.twitch.tv/year/2015, last accessed: 06/01/2017.
12. Mehdi Kaytoue, Arlei Silva, Loïc Cerf, Wagner Meira, Jr., and Chedy Raïssi. 2012. Watch Me Playing, I Am a Professional: A First Study on Video Game Live Streaming. In *Proceedings of the 21st International Conference on World Wide Web (WWW '12 Companion)*. ACM, New York, NY, USA, 1181–1188. DOI: http://dx.doi.org/10.1145/2187980.2188259
13. Yong Ming Kow and Timothy Young. 2013. Media Technologies and Learning in the Starcraft Esport Community. In *Proceedings of the 2013 Conference on Computer Supported Cooperative Work (CSCW '13)*. ACM, New York, NY, USA, 387–398. DOI: http://dx.doi.org/10.1145/2441776.2441821
14. Walter S. Lasecki, Kyle I. Murray, Samuel White, Robert C. Miller, and Jeffrey P. Bigham. 2011. Real-time Crowd Control of Existing Interfaces. In *Proceedings of the 24th Annual ACM Symposium on User Interface Software and Technology (UIST '11)*. ACM, New York, NY, USA, 23–32. DOI: http://dx.doi.org/10.1145/2047196.2047200
15. Overwolf Ltd. 2017. Overwolf. (2017). http://www.overwolf.com, last accessed: 06/01/2017.
16. Rui Pan, Lyn Bartram, and Carman Neustaedter. 2016. TwitchViz: A Visualization Tool for Twitch Chatrooms. In *Extended Abstracts on Human Factors in Computing Systems (CHI EA '16)*. ACM, New York, NY, USA, 1959–1965. DOI: http://dx.doi.org/10.1145/2851581.2892427
17. Hector Postigo. 2016. The Socio-Technical Architecture of Digital Labor: Converting Play Into YouTube Money. *New Media & Society* 18, 2 (2016), 332–349. DOI: http://dx.doi.org/10.1177/1461444814541527
18. Nguyen Quoc Viet Hung, Nguyen Thanh Tam, LamNgoc Tran, and Karl Aberer. 2013. An Evaluation of Aggregation Techniques in Crowdsourcing. In *Web Information Systems Engineering (WISE 2013)*, Xuemin Lin, Yannis Manolopoulos, Divesh Srivastava, and Guangyan Huang (Eds.). Lecture Notes in Computer Science, Vol. 8181. Springer Berlin Heidelberg, 1–15. DOI: http://dx.doi.org/10.1007/978-3-642-41154-0_1
19. Alireza Sahami Shirazi, Michael Rohs, Robert Schleicher, Sven Kratz, Alexander Müller, and Albrecht Schmidt. 2011. Real-time Nonverbal Opinion Sharing Through Mobile Phones During Sports Events. In *Proceedings of the 29th Conference on Human Factors in Computing Systems (CHI '11)*. ACM, New York, NY, USA, 307–310. DOI: http://dx.doi.org/10.1145/1978942.1978985
20. Thomas Smith, Marianna Obrist, and Peter Wright. 2013. Live-streaming Changes the (Video) Game. In *Proceedings of the 11th European Conference on Interactive TV and Video (EuroITV '13)*. ACM, New York, NY, USA, 131–138. DOI: http://dx.doi.org/10.1145/2465958.2465971
21. Hearthstone Wiki. 2017. Advanced Rulebook. (2017). http://hearthstone.gamepedia.com/Advanced_rulebook, last accessed: 06/01/2017.
22. Mu Xia, Yun Huang, Wenjing Duan, and Andrew B. Whinston. 2009. Ballot Box Communication in Online Communities. *Communications of the ACM* 52, 9 (Sept. 2009), 138–142. DOI: http://dx.doi.org/10.1145/1562164.1562199

23. Cong Zhang and Jiangchuan Liu. 2015. On Crowdsourced Interactive Live Streaming: A Twitch.Tv-based Measurement Study. In *Proceedings of the 25th ACM Workshop on Network and Operating Systems Support for Digital Audio and Video (NOSSDAV '15)*. ACM, New York, NY, USA, 55–60. DOI: http://dx.doi.org/10.1145/2736084.2736091

"These are not my hands!": Effect of Gender on the Perception of Avatar Hands in Virtual Reality

Valentin Schwind[a], Pascal Knierim[a], Cagri Tasci[b], Patrick Franczak[b], Nico Haas[b], Niels Henze[a]
VIS, University of Stuttgart
Stuttgart, Germany
[a]{firstname.lastname}@vis.uni-stuttgart.de
[b]{firstname.lastname}@studi.informatik.uni-stuttgart.de

ABSTRACT
Rendering the user's body in virtual reality increases immersion and presence – the illusion of 'being there'. Recent technology enables determining the pose and position of the hands to render them accordingly while interacting within the virtual environment. Virtual reality applications often use realistic male or female hands, mimic robotic hands, or cartoon hands. However, it is unclear how users perceive different hand styles. We conducted a study with 14 male and 14 female participants in virtual reality to investigate the effect of gender on the perception of six different hands. Quantitative and qualitative results show that women perceive lower levels of presence while using male avatar hands and male perceive lower levels of presence using non-human avatar hands. While women dislike male hands, men accept and feel presence with avatar hands of both genders. Our results highlight the importance of considering the users' diversity when designing virtual reality experiences.

ACM Classification Keywords
H.1.2 User/Machine Systems: Human factors; I.3.0 Computer Graphics: General

Author Keywords
virtual reality; presence; uncanny valley; immersion; avatars

INTRODUCTION AND BACKGROUND
A core challenge of virtual reality (VR) is transporting people to another place and inducing the illusion of 'being there'. The subjective experience of 'being there' as well as the ability to 'act there', even when one is physically situated in another place, is known as *presence* [5, 21]. Relating to the perception of VR, authors define presence as "the sense of being in an environment" [3] or "the outcome or a direct function of immersion" [17]. VR systems and applications are usually designed to maximize the experience of presence and often make use of virtual body representations of users, also known as their *avatars*, to provide a realistic and familiar interface between the own body and the virtual environment.

CHI 2017, May 06-11, 2017, Denver, CO, USA
© 2017 ACM. ISBN 978-1-4503-4655-9/17/05...$15.00
DOI: http://dx.doi.org/10.1145/3025453.3025602

Previous work shows that realism and appearance of avatars have an effect on experiencing presence in VR. The effect on presence using different levels of realism was examined by Vinayagamoorthy et al. [20]. While in a VR cave, participants reported that the lowest degree of presence was caused by more realistic characters. Similarly, Lugrin et al. measured a lower degree of body ownership using more realistic avatars in VR [10]. Authors of both works assume that their results might be the outcome of the *Uncanny Valley* phenomenon coined by Mori [12]. Mori's hypothesis predicts that imperfections of appearance and motion of very human-like characters (e.g. robots [11] or animated CGI characters [7]) lead to an uncanny sensation by human observers.

Experiencing presence in VR depends on individual factors that should be considered when creating very immersive applications (cf. Lombard and Ditton [9]). It has been shown that there can be gender-related differences between men and women: For example, Felnhofer et al. suggest that regardless of age, men generally experience higher levels of presence than women in VR [4]. Schmidt et al., however, conclude that women feel higher levels of technology-related immersion and anxiety in VR [16]. Changes in interpersonal attitudes caused by using VR were found by Peck et al. [13]. The authors conclude that embodying light-skinned people in a dark-skinned virtual body can decrease participants' implicit racial bias.

Displaying the user's hand as the primary body part for interaction enables natural user interactions with the virtual world and has different effects on interaction (cf. [14, 2]). For example, Argelaguet et al. found that hand realism has an influence on the sense of agency, which is stronger for less realistic virtual hands [1]. The sense of ownership is increased for human virtual hands, which was confirmed by Lin and Jörg [8]. However, it is unclear whether and how the human-likeness of user controlled virtual hands influence the perceived sensation of presence in VR. Furthermore, it is unknown if virtual hands are perceived differently by men and women, especially when avatar hands from another gender are used.

In this exploratory study, we investigate the effect of different hands and gender on presence experienced by men and women in immersive virtual environments through a first-person VR experiment. Gender-related differences caused by violated expectations of how the own avatar have to look like would have consequences for designers and developers of immersive VR applications and games. We contribute with design implications for human avatar hands in immersive VR applications.

METHOD

The aim of our study is to investigate the effect of human and non-human virtual hands on presence perceived by men and women in VR. We use a mixed factorial design with the within-subjects variable *virtual hand* and the between-subjects variable *gender*. Participants answered quantitative questionnaires in VR and provided further feedback by thinking-aloud while performing three different tasks.

Stimuli

We used three realistic and three artificial hand models (see Figure 2). Male and female hand models were taken from the Leap Motion SDK. The male model has a haired skin texture and a muscular appearance. The female hands model has glossy nail textures and dainty fingers. An androgynous hand was created through an equal blending of meshes and textures from the male and female hands. We selected an abstract, cartoon, and robot hand as artificial hand models. The abstract hand model was extracted from the Leap Motion SDK and was equipped with white cylinders as bones and gray spheres as joints. For the cartoon model we smoothed the mesh topology of the androgynous hand and replaced the texture by a skin-colored toon shader with a black outline. Model and textures of the robot hands were extracted from the Genesis Bot model for the DAZ3D software application using a rigid skinning for the hand skeleton.

Apparatus and Tasks

Our apparatus consists of an Oculus Rift DK2 head-mounted display (HMD), a Leap Motion sensor, and an application developed in Unity3D. Our application uses the hand tracking of the Orion beta SDK provided by Leap Motion for VR support on HMDs. The Leap Motion sensor is mounted on the front of the Oculus Rift using a 3D-prined frame. Our experiment was running on a Windows PC with an Intel i7-6700, 16GB RAM, and a Nvidia GTX980. According to the refresh rate of the Oculus DK2 HMD, we set the target frame rate in Unity3D to 60 frames per second (fps). To ensure that the fps remains constant we designed a simple scene in Unity3D. To ensure that the tracking quality was throughout the same for all hands, we used throughout the same tracking system provided by Leap and the same configuration of bones.

We developed three different tasks which were used to ensure that the hands are present in the field of view of the participant and facilitate an immersive VR-experience: (1) in the *keyboard task* participants operate with a virtual keyboard to enter "I love VR" into a text display. (2) In the *draw task* participants paint curves and lines into the virtual space while moving their hands and performing a pinch gesture. Their task was to draw "Hello World" in 3D space. (3) In the *pyramid building task*, participants generate blocks on a virtual table by pressing a virtual button and built a small pyramid of at least 6 blocks. All scenes were blended using black fading. The application provides auditory feedback to confirm button presses through loudspeakers.

Measures

Post-test questionnaires are the most frequently used measures of presence in previous work. One disadvantage of post-test questionnaires is that they rely on subjects' memories, which reflect an inconsistent and incomplete picture of the VR-experience. We, therefore, developed a *VR questionnaire* which appears in front of the participant within the virtual environment. Thus, participants filled the virtual questionnaire using the virtual hands whose influence we measured (cf. suggestions by Frommel et al. [6] to avoid interruptions in immersive games). We decided to use the 32-item presence questionnaire by Witmer & Singer [21] due to following reasons: (1) it addresses related factors as involvement, naturalness, and interface (avatar) quality, (2) the presence questionnaire does not include any question that can not meaningfully be answered within the VR, and (3) the questionnaire has been used in a large number of studies (cf. [15, 19, 23]). In line with Schwind et al. [18] and according to our assumption that there are avatar-related factors that influence presence in VR, we asked for the perceived likeability, attractiveness, naturalness, and eerieness of the virtual hands on a 7-point Likert scale. We would like to remark that the direct measure of perceived naturalness could be a potential confound of the naturalness subscale in the presence questionnaire. Due to inconsistent or inconclusive outcomes of previous work, psychophysiological measures for presence as heart-rate, skin conductance, or electromyography (EMG) were not used.

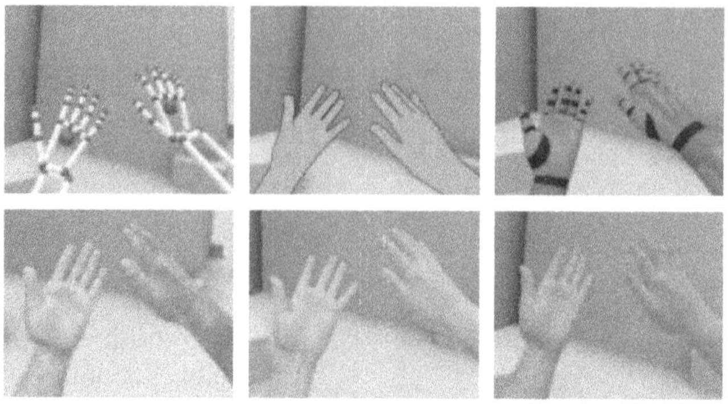

Figure 2. 1st row: screenshots of non-human hands: abstract, cartoon, robot; 2nd row: human hands: male, female, androgynous

Participants

Our sample was drawn from students and employees of our university. 14 male and 14 female participants from Central Europe with light skin tones took part in our experiment. The mean age was 26.07 years ($SD = 7.99$). Students received a compensation of 10€. Seventeen participants stated to have no VR experience at all, 11 had limited VR experiences.

Procedure

After signing the consent form, the participant was asked to take a seat in the middle of our VR-laboratory. We presented all devices and explained the procedure of the study. The direction of the virtual space was aligned according to the speakers placed in front of the participant. After setting up the HMD, a participant was familiarized with the first virtual hand and the first task. The participant could finish the task by pressing a button or showing a thumbs-up gesture. After each task, participants had to rate how they liked the task using a 7-point Likert item on a virtual panel presented in VR. Since not all questions could be displayed at once, a virtual wall containing four questions per page was presented. The

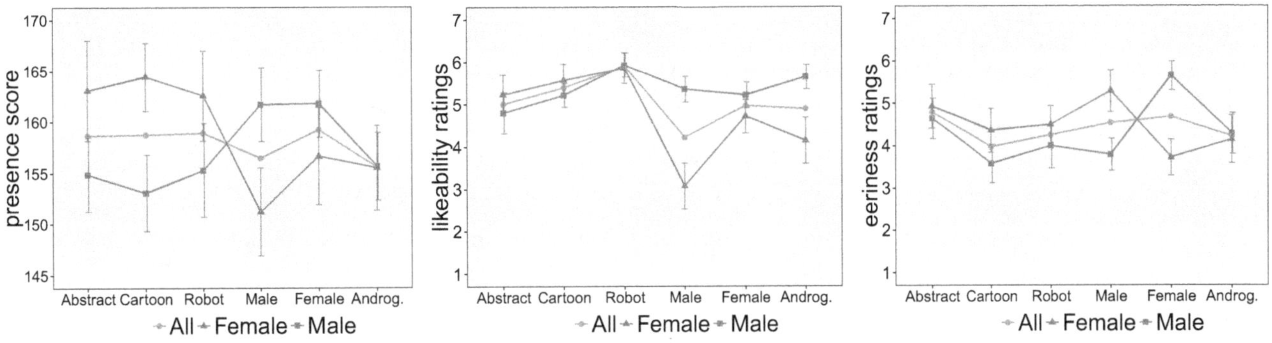

Figure 1. Gender related differences of presence (l.), likeability (c.), and eerieness (r.) between the avatar hand models. Virtual hands are sorted by mean naturalness ratings of all participants (not depicted). Presence scale ranges from 145 to 170. All error bars show standard error of the mean (SE).

participant could navigate through the questionnaire by pressing "next" and "back" buttons. As long as participants asked for no break, they remained in VR for all hands, tasks, and questions. Using thinking-aloud, we asked the participants to describe their thoughts, issues, and concerns. After finishing all questions the participant repeated the procedure using the next virtual hands. After leaving the VR, we handed out a questionnaire on a sheet of paper. We asked for comments about their concerns, what they would like to improve, and which hand they finally prefer.

RESULTS

On average, participants spent 58.6 minutes ($SD = 18.1$ min) in VR. Thus, the average time each participant used a virtual hand pair was 9.76 minutes.

Quantitative Results

Virtual hand style and gender of the participants were used as factors in a multi-factorial analysis of variance of aligned rank transformed data as introduced by Wobbrock et al. [22]. All pairwise cross-factor comparisons are Bonferroni corrected. Level of the significance level α is at .05.

We found no significant effect of hands $[F(5,130) = .345, p = .884]$ or gender $[F(1,26) = .272, p = .606]$ on perceived presence. However, the hands×gender interaction was significant $[F(5,130) = 3.898, p < .001]$. Pairwise cross-factor comparisons of gender and virtual hand revealed significant differences between the abstract and male hand ($p = .047$), male and robot hand ($p = .034$), as well as male and cartoon hand ($p = .003$). Other pairwise comparisons of presence showed not significant differences (all $p > .05$).

Hands had a significant effect on likeability $[F(5,130) = 5.903, p < .001]$ but we found no significant effect for gender $[F(1,26) = 3.549, p = .071]$. We found an interaction effect of hands×gender on likeability $[F(5,130) = 5.951, p < .001]$. Pairwise cross-factor comparisons revealed significant differences between the following hands: abstract and male ($p < .001$), abstract and androgynous ($p = .044$), male and robot ($p = .008$), male and cartoon($p < .001$), and cartoon and androgynous ($p = .043$) hands. Other pairwise comparisons of likeability ratings were not significant (all $p \geq .178$).

We found no significant effect of hands $[F(5,130) = 1.181, p = .322]$ or gender $[F(1,26) = .472, p = .498]$ on ratings of eeriness. However, the hands×gender interaction was significant $[F(5,130) = 4.157, p < .001]$ again. Pairwise cross-factor comparisons of gender and virtual hand revealed significant differences between male and female hands ($p < .001$) and female and cartoon hands ($p = .011$) hands for the eeriness ratings. Other pairwise comparisons of eeriness ratings showed no significant differences (all $p > .05$).

To understand which avatar-related factors influence presence, we conducted a multiple linear regression using the enter method. Ratings of likeability, eeriness, naturalness, and attractiveness were used as independent variables. The regression equation was significant $[R^2 = .441, R^2_{Adj.} = .195, SE = 19.138, F(4,163) = 9.854, p < .001, d = .784]$ for β-coefficients of naturalness ($\beta = -.159, p = .047$) and eerieness ($\beta = -.336, p < .001$). We found no significant effects on presence for likeability ($\beta = -.154, p = .171$) and attractiveness ($\beta = -.036, p = .755$). The scatterplot (not illustrated) of standardized residuals indicated that the data met the assumptions of homogeneity of variance, linearity, and homoscedasticity of the regression analysis. Assuming that the factors are independent, eeriness would explain 11% of the variance of the mean presence.

In the final questionnaire, presented after a participant had left the VR, we asked for demographics and which virtual hand they would like to use again in VR: 8 (5 male/3 female) participants would use the robot hand again, 7 participants (1 m./6 f.) the female hand, 5 (3 m./2 f.) the cartoon hand, 4 (3 m./1 f.) the androgynous hand, and 3 (1 m./2 f.) the abstract hand. One male would use the male hand again. Participants were also asked which hand they never would like to use again: 10 (3 m./7 f.) never would like to use the male hand again, 6 male the abstract hand, 6 (3 m./3 f.) the female hand, 3 female the cartoon hand, and 3 (2 m./1 f.) the androgynous hand.

Qualitative Results

Qualitative feedback was collected through think-aloud protocols to gain deeper insights into participants' perception. Participants' comments were transcribed, annotated, and analyzed. Through open coding, we analyzed why the avatar hands affect the experience of presence. Two researchers went through all transcribed notes to check each other's coding and to establish consistency in the assignment of codes to the same phenomena. A list of categories from the raw data was identified through underlining the key concepts. We found that participants' presence in VR was affected by three different deviations from their own hands:

(1) Deviations from human appearance were mostly mentioned using the non-human hands. Participants emphasized that too abstract styles are not uncanny but not familiar enough to feel present. Participants mentioned, for example, that they feel very uncomfortable using the abstract hands: "It's a completely unnatural arm – like a prosthesis. It distracts" (P8, m.); and "[...] too much abstraction feels unnatural and that abstraction is not really acceptable" (P6, m.). One participant was confused due to the shading of the cartoon hands. "I don't see how I should hold my hand correctly" (P25, f.). We found that female participants accept non-human hands when they consider them as "gloves" (P25, f.) or "a costume" (P20, f.).

(2) Deviations from one's gender were perceived while using virtual human hands. Especially women reacted negatively when interacting with male hands. One female participant nearly wanted to end the VR when starting to use the male hands: "I can't do that. This is so creepy!" (P23, f.). In particular hair on the male arms evoke very uncomfortable feelings: "This is so disgusting, greasy, chunky, hairy – I just want to have a shaver and wash my hands" (P20, f.). In contrast to male participants who regarded female hands as "very realistic" (P13, f.) or "unusual, but very attractive" (P10, m.).

(3) Deviations from the own body were noticed when participants used virtual human hands. For example, female participants draw direct comparisons with themselves when using female hands: "Where are my freckles?" (P19, f.), "I hadn't French manicure! These are not my hands!" (P22, f). "Proportions of these hands make it clear that these are not my own." (P8, m.). Deviations from the movement of their own hands were especially criticized by male participants. The quality of the tracking was criticized using virtual human hands, although the same tracking was used for all virtual hands: "The tracking of this [male] hand is significantly worse. [...] The abstract hand has the best tracking" (P2, m.).

We identified **habituation** and **excitement** (of being in VR) as factors with a positive effect on feeling presence while using virtual hands. Especially participants that had no VR experience were strongly involved as soon as they started a task. We observed, for example, a female participant starting with female hands and without VR experience who was immediately highly involved in the task. She naturally interacted fast and without any comments. On request, she explained that she did not even notice the hands because it "is self-explanatory to interact with them in this way". Furthermore, just being in another body was often considered positively and as exciting: "I love it! It's fun. It's so different to be another character, another type of sense and appearance" (P26, f.).

DISCUSSION AND CONCLUSION

In this paper, we investigated how virtual hands influence the perception of presence in VR. Using questionnaires integrated into VR we found that presence is perceived by men and women differently. Our results show that there are significant interaction effects of gender and hands on presence. Women, in particular, feel less presence and perceive more eeriness using virtual male hands. Women feel higher levels of presence using non-human hands. In contrast to men, who feel a higher level of presence using human hands including virtual female hands. We measured lower ratings and a significant difference between ratings of female's likeability for male hands in contrast to the male's likeability for female hands. Using regression analyzes we found that the perceived eeriness and naturalness of virtual hands have a significant effect on perceived presence.

Qualitative feedback provided by think-aloud protocols reveals potential reasons for the quantitative results. We found three levels of deviation from real hands which affect the feeling of presence: Deviations from common human appearance, the own gender, or the own body. We found that deviations from the own gender were perceived negatively by female participants. Women were averse to the hair on virtual male arms and feel disgusted and were distracted. They feel comfortable when they used non-human hands and regarded them as gloves or costumes. Men highlighted the perceived realism and the hand tracking quality and feel more present with human hands.

We conclude that women have increased expectations for their representation. However, eeriness ratings show that both women and men feel discomfort, when using hands of the other gender. An overall decrease of presence or likeability as predicted by the Uncanny Valley was not found. Lacking coherence between the perception and actual projection of the own presence as well as violations of a gender-specific appearance are potentially caused by an induced gender dysphoria – a negatively perceived mismatch of the actual (biological) sex and the perceived gender. We suggest that deviations from the own gender and the own self in VR should be investigated by further research.

Our findings have wide implications for designers: We suggest to avoid gender-swapping in very immersive VR applications and to provide male and female hands if human avatars are desired. An androgynous model without noticeable characteristics is a compromise while using human hands model. Suits, costumes, gender-neutral styles, or abstract avatar hands are rather preferred by women. The robot style seems the best trade-off between men and women for non-human avatars.

Effects of age, ethnicity, or the own skin tone were not investigated in our study and we can not draw conclusions about populations with other skin melanation, which should be investigated in further research. For example, previous work indicates that there are ethnicity-related changes in VR [13], which could also be investigated using different avatar styles. We also want to highlight that being accustomed to the VR experience probably means that the avatar is faded out by the user. Due to our positive experiences with questionnaires in VR, which do not only rely on a participant's memories, we suggest to use this measuring to collect subjective data in VR for future research. Source code and assets used in this experiment are available at github[1].

ACKNOWLEDGMENTS

This work was supported by the German Research Foundation (DFG) through project C04 of SFB/Transregio 161 and by the German Federal Ministry of Education and Research as part of the project Be-greifen (Grant No. 16SV7527).

[1] https://github.com/valentin-schwind/selfpresence

REFERENCES

1. Ferran Argelaguet, Ludovic Hoyet, Michaël Trico, and Anatole Lécuyer. 2016. The role of interaction in virtual embodiment: Effects of the virtual hand representation. *Proceedings - IEEE Virtual Reality* 2016-July (2016), 3–10. DOI:http://dx.doi.org/10.1109/VR.2016.7504682
2. Mahdi Azmandian, Mark Hancock, Hrvoje Benko, Eyal Ofek, and Andrew D. Wilson. 2016. Haptic Retargeting: Dynamic Repurposing of Passive Haptics for Enhanced Virtual Reality Experiences. In *Proceedings of the 2016 CHI Conference on Human Factors in Computing Systems (CHI '16)*. ACM Press. DOI: http://dx.doi.org/10.1145/2858036.2858226
3. Frank Biocca and Mark R. Levy. 2013. *Communication in the Age of Virtual Reality*. L. Erlbaum Associates Inc., Hillsdale, NJ, USA. 416 pages.
4. Anna Felnhofer, Oswald D Kothgassner, Nathalie Hauk, Leon Beutl, Helmut Hlavacs, and Ilse Kryspin-Exner. 2013. Physical and social presence in collaborative virtual environments: Exploring age and gender differences with respect to empathy. *Computers in Human Behavior* 31 (2013), 272–279. DOI: http://dx.doi.org/10.1016/j.chb.2013.10.045
5. Gary Fontaine. 1992. The Experience of a Sense of Presence in Intercultural and International Encounters. *Presence: Teleoperators and Virtual Environments* 1, 4 (1992), 482–490. DOI: http://dx.doi.org/10.1162/pres.1992.1.4.482
6. Julian Frommel, Michael Weber, Katja Rogers, Julia Brich, Daniel Besserer, Leonard Bradatsch, Isabel Ortinau, Ramona Schabenberger, Valentin Riemer, and Claudia Schrader. 2015. Integrated Questionnaires: Maintaining Presence in Game Environments for Self-Reported Data Acquisition. In *Proceedings of the 2015 Annual Symposium on Computer-Human Interaction in Play (CHI PLAY '15)*. ACM Press, 359–368. DOI: http://dx.doi.org/10.1145/2793107.2793130
7. Jari Kätsyri, Meeri Mäkäräinen, and Tapio Takala. 2016. Testing the âĂŸuncanny valley' hypothesis in semirealistic computer-animated film characters: An empirical evaluation of natural film stimuli. *International Journal of Human-Computer Studies* (sep 2016). DOI: http://dx.doi.org/10.1016/j.ijhcs.2016.09.010
8. Lorraine Lin and Sophie Jörg. 2016. Need a Hand?: How Appearance Affects the Virtual Hand Illusion. In *Proceedings of the ACM Symposium on Applied Perception (SAP '16)*. ACM, New York, NY, USA, 69–76. DOI:http://dx.doi.org/10.1145/2931002.2931006
9. Matthew Lombard and Theresa Ditton. 1997. At the Heart of It All: The Concept of Presence. *Journal of Computer-Mediated Communication* 3, 2 (1997). DOI: http://dx.doi.org/10.1111/j.1083-6101.1997.tb00072.x
10. Jean-Luc Lugrin, Johanna Latt, and Marc Erich Latoschik. 2015. Anthropomorphism and Illusion of Virtual Body Ownership. In *Proceedings of the 25th International Conference on Artificial Reality and Telexistence and 20th Eurographics Symposium on Virtual Environments (ICAT - EGVE '15)*. Eurographics Association, 1–8. DOI: http://dx.doi.org/10.2312/egve.20151303
11. Karl F. MacDorman, Robert D. Green, Chin Chang Ho, and Clinton T. Koch. 2009. Too real for comfort? Uncanny responses to computer generated faces. *Computers in Human Behavior* 25, 3 (may 2009), 695–710. DOI: http://dx.doi.org/10.1016/j.chb.2008.12.026
12. Masahiro Mori, Karl F MacDorman, and Norri Kageki. 1970/2012. The Uncanny Valley [From the Field]. *Robotics & Automation Magazine, IEEE* 19, 2 (1970/2012), 98–100. DOI: http://dx.doi.org/10.1109/MRA.2012.2192811
13. Tabitha C. Peck, Sofia Seinfeld, Salvatore M. Aglioti, and Mel Slater. 2013. Putting yourself in the skin of a black avatar reduces implicit racial bias. *Consciousness and Cognition* 22, 3 (sep 2013), 779–787. DOI: http://dx.doi.org/10.1016/j.concog.2013.04.016
14. Mamy Pouliquen, Alain Bernard, Jacques Marsot, and Laurent Chodorge. 2007. Virtual hands and virtual reality multimodal platform to design safer industrial systems. *Computers in Industry* 58, 1 (2007), 46–56. DOI: http://dx.doi.org/10.1016/j.compind.2006.04.001
15. Patrice Renaud, Joanne L Rouleau, Luc Granger, Ian Barsetti, and Stéphane Bouchard. 2002. Measuring sexual preferences in virtual reality: A pilot study. *CyberPsychology & Behavior* 5, 1 (2002), 1–9. DOI: http://dx.doi.org/10.1089/109493102753685836
16. Mareike Schmidt, Johanna Xenia Kafka, Oswald D. Kothgassner, Helmut Hlavacs, Leon Beutl, and Anna Felnhofer. 2013. *Why Does It Always Rain on Me? Influence of Gender and Environmental Factors on Usability, Technology Related Anxiety and Immersion in Virtual Environments*. Springer International Publishing, Cham, 392–402. DOI: http://dx.doi.org/10.1007/978-3-319-03161-3_29
17. Thomas Schubert, Frank Friedmann, and Holger Regenbrecht. 2001. The Experience of Presence: Factor Analytic Insights. *Presence: Teleoperators and Virtual Environments* 10, 3 (2001), 266–281. DOI: http://dx.doi.org/10.1162/105474601300343603
18. Valentin Schwind, Katrin Wolf, Niels Henze, and Oliver Korn. 2015. Determining the Characteristics of Preferred Virtual Faces Using an Avatar Generator. In *Proceedings of the 2015 Annual Symposium on Computer-Human Interaction in Play (CHI PLAY '15)*. ACM Press, 221–230. DOI: http://dx.doi.org/10.1145/2793107.2793116
19. Kay M. Stanney, Kelly S. Kingdon, David Graeber, and Robert S. Kennedy. 2002. Human Performance in Immersive Virtual Environments: Effects of Exposure Duration, User Control, and Scene Complexity. *Human*

Performance 15, 4 (2002), 339–366. DOI: http://dx.doi.org/10.1207/S15327043HUP1504_03

20. Vinoba Vinayagamoorthy, Andrea Brogni, Marco Gillies, Mel Slater, and Anthony Steed. 2004. An investigation of presence response across variations in visual realism. In *The 7th Annual International Presence Workshop*. 148–155.

21. Bob G. Witmer and Michael J. Singer. 1998. Measuring Presence in Virtual Environments: A Presence Questionnaire. *Presence: Teleoperators and Virtual Environments* 7, 3 (1998), 225–240. DOI: http://dx.doi.org/10.1162/105474698565686

22. Jacob O. Wobbrock, Leah Findlater, Darren Gergle, and James J. Higgins. 2011. The Aligned Rank Transform for Nonparametric Factorial Analyses Using Only Anova Procedures. In *Proceedings of the SIGCHI Conference on Human Factors in Computing Systems (CHI '11)*. ACM Press, 143–146. DOI: http://dx.doi.org/10.1145/1978942.1978963

23. Christine Youngblut and Odette Huie. 2003. The relationship between presence and performance in virtual environments: results of a VERTS study. In *IEEE Virtual Reality, 2003. Proceedings.*, Vol. 2003-Janua. IEEE Comput. Soc, 277–278. DOI: http://dx.doi.org/10.1109/VR.2003.1191158

Looking Inside the Wires: Understanding Museum Visitor Learning with an Augmented Circuit Exhibit

Elham Beheshti, David Kim, Gabrielle Ecanow, Michael S. Horn
Northwestern University
Evanston, USA
beheshti@u.northwestern.edu

ABSTRACT
Understanding electrical circuits can be difficult for novices of all ages. In this paper, we describe a science museum exhibit that enables visitors to make circuits on an interactive tabletop and observe a simulation of electrons flowing through the circuit. Our goal is to use multiple representations to help convey basic concepts of current and resistance. To study visitor interaction and learning, we tested the design at a popular science museum with 60 parent-child dyads in three conditions: a control condition with no electron simulation; a condition with the simulation displayed alongside the circuit on the same screen; and an augmented reality condition, with the simulation displayed on a tablet that acts as a lens to see into the circuit. Our findings show that children did significantly better on a post-test in both experimental conditions, with children performing best in the AR condition. However, analysis of session videos shows unexpected parent-child collaboration in the AR condition.

Author Keywords
Electrical circuits; multiple representations; augmented reality; agent-based modeling; design; interactive surfaces; museum learning.

ACM Classification Keywords
H.5.2 Information Interfaces and Presentation: User Interfaces - Interaction styles

INTRODUCTION
Understanding the flow of current in electrical circuits can be challenging for learners of all ages [17, 28, 36, 39]. Research in Learning Sciences has documented a variety of mental models that novices rely on as they struggle with concepts like resistance, current, and voltage drop. One stream of studies has shown that novices have an insufficient understanding of what happens at the level of atoms and electrons in a circuit [9, 30, 34]. For example, learners might think of current as something like water in a pipe that flows out of the battery and encounters each component in turn [30]. Or, they might think of current as a substance that gets consumed by things like lightbulbs and resistors. And, while these models have some value for understanding electrical phenomena, they differ from the scientific understanding in ways that makes it difficult to predict things like the relative brightness of lightbulbs in a series circuit (e.g. Figure 5).

One promising strategy to help learners understand circuits is to provide dynamic visual representations of electrical concepts [15, 34]. For example, Frederiksen et al. explored different ways of visualizing the concept of voltage for learners by relating it to the distribution of charged particles in a circuit [15]. In another example, Sengupta and Wilesnky [34] created an *agent-based* representation of current based on Drude's model. In this model, a cloud of free electrons has a net movement through a circuit when a potential difference is applied. Simple kinetic interactions between free electrons and ions in conductive materials result in emergent properties that approximate Ohm's law (see [34]). Research has shown that this kind of electron-level representation along with structured curriculum can help students develop more sophisticated understandings of simple circuits [35].

In this paper, we present the design and evaluation of *Spark*, an augmented circuit exhibit for science museums (Figures 1-3). *Spark* combines a virtual circuit building environment with a simulation of current flow based on Sengupta and Wilensky's instantiation of Drude's model. Visitors drag and connect circuit components (wires, batteries, resistors, and

CHI 2017, May 06-11, 2017, Denver, CO, USA

ISBN 978-1-4503-4655-9/17/05...$15.00
DOI: http://dx.doi.org/10.1145/3025453.3025479

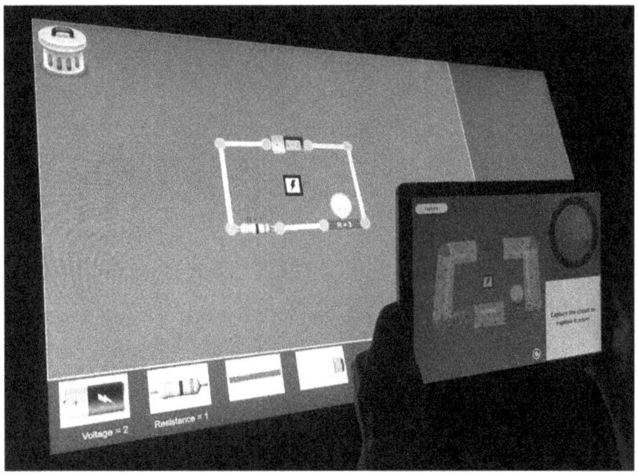

Figure 1. *Spark* interactive tabletop exhibit.

lightbulbs) on a multi-touch tabletop display. As they make changes to their circuit, they can explore an electron simulation that gets updated in real time. In one version of the exhibit (Figure 2a), the simulation is displayed alongside the circuit on the same display. In another version (Figure 2b), we use an AR Toolkit [42] to display the simulation on a tablet computer that visitors hold above the table. This creates the illusion of peering inside the circuit (Figure 1). *Spark* enables visitors interact with electrical circuits at two levels. At one level, visitors can create and test a variety of circuits by wiring together the circuit components (circuit model). At another level, visitors can inspect a simulation of electrons moving through these components (electron simulation).

The primary goal of our design is to enhance children's understanding of electrical current and resistance by enabling them to develop meaningful connections between the two representations. Prior research suggests that using multiple representations can improve learning but that they are difficult to design [1, 16]. If two representations of a scientific concept are not appropriately linked, learners can misinterpret the connections between representations based on unrelated surface features instead of scientific concepts. One important design consideration of a multi-representational simulation environment is how to support *translation* between the two representations [1]. In this study, we aim to investigate different ways to *dynamically link* the circuit representation with the electron simulation to support an effective translation between the representations.

To study visitor interaction and learning, we recruited 60 parent-child dyads at the Museum of Science and Industry in Chicago to participate in three conditions: a control condition with no electron simulation (condition C1); a condition with an electron simulation displayed on the same screen as the circuit model (C2); and an augmented reality condition with the electron model displayed on a separate handheld tablet device (C3). Our research questions are: does the combination of the two circuit representations enhance children's learning? And, are there differences in the two experimental conditions? Second, we were interested in how parent-child dyads interacted with the exhibit and made sense of circuits in each condition.

We discuss findings from our investigation of visitor interaction and learning in each condition. Our findings have implications for design of interactive exhibits with multiple representations and considerations for improving the family experiences with interactive tabletop exhibits.

BACKGROUND

Existing Learning Environments

There are several computational environments and activities that allow children to investigate simple circuits. Examples include the Circuit Construction Kit from the PhET project, which simulates the behavior of simple circuits [14]; and LightUp [8], which uses augmented reality to project a simple representation of current flow on top of an image of the physical circuit. NIELS [34] is an example of an agent-based modeling environment that shows how electrical concepts such as current and resistance emerge from the interactions between electrons and ions in a conductive material. NIELS directly inspired the design of electron simulation in *Spark*.

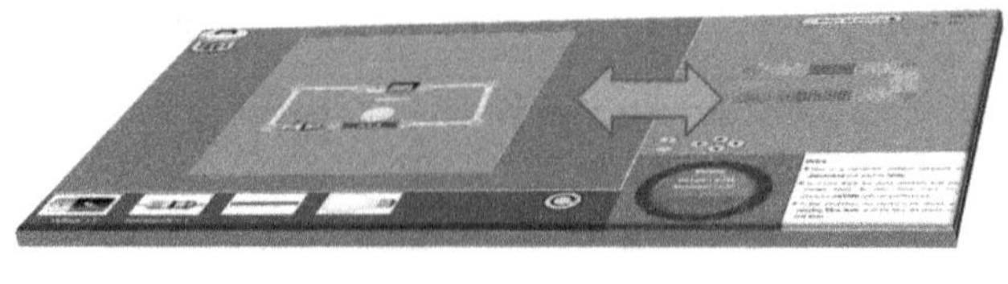

(a) Single-display condition

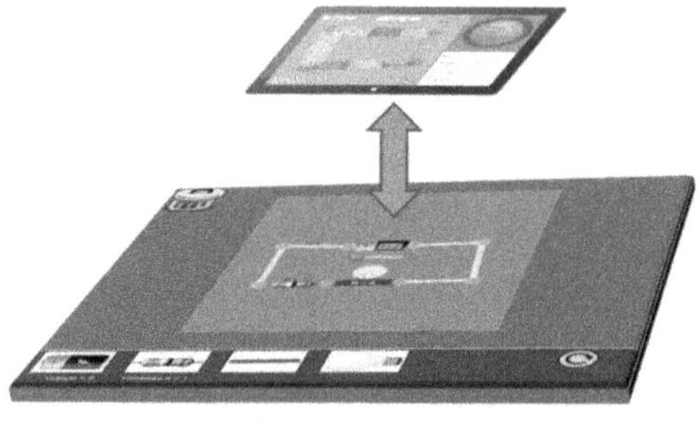

(b) AR condition

Figure 2. Linking two representations of a circuit (a) side-by-side on one display and (b) with AR on a second display.

Museum Learning

Research in museums and other informal settings has shown that it is possible to increase learner interest and engagement around scientific phenomena [19, 23, 41]. Recent studies suggest that interactive exhibits containing novel technology can be attractive to visitors, promote enhanced understanding of content [2], and engage people for extended periods of time [31]. Other studies highlight the potential that museums have in changing individuals' conceptual understandings of scientific ideas and processes of science [13].

Researchers have also explored factors that facilitate or hinder collaborative family learning in museums [2, 7]. This work has revealed that factors such as the height of displays and the accessibility of interactive elements to multiple family members can impact enjoyment, depth of engagement, and learning behaviors like identifying, describing, and interpreting information [22]. Other studies explored how increasing the visibility of different types of information can affect the authority and accountability of family visitors [24].

Learning with Multiple Representations

Even though the idea of combining multiple representations in one learning environment seems promising, studies have demonstrated that learners fail to gain from multiple representations if they are not carefully designed [1, 16, 21].

Ainsworth [1] suggests that multiple representations require learners to understand each individual representation, a complex process in its own right, in addition to the relationship between representations. Moreover, learners tend to treat representations in isolation and find it difficult to integrate information from more than one resource [1, 16]. These studies suggest that it is critical to support a fluid and meaningful transition among the representations in a learning environment.

Affordances of AR in Learning

Recent studies have investigated the affordances of augmented reality for learning in different settings [11, 27, 37, 40, 41]. Augmented reality can enable learners to see the world around them in novel ways and engage with dynamic processes within contexts in which they are already familiar [11]. Furthermore, augmented reality fosters interactivity, which provides users with control over their learning and thus tailors to the need of each learner [33].

Museums have also started to explore the use of augmented reality; however, much of the research has been focused on usability rather than learning outcomes [12]. The few existing studies have promising findings. For example, Yoon and colleagues conducted several studies finding that the addition of digital augmentation resulted in significant learning gains [40] and lead to increased engagement and group participation [41]. Asai and colleagues found that their augmented reality lunar surface navigation system helped facilitate collaborative interactions between parents and children in an informal environment [3]. AR interfaces have also been shown to aid in capturing visitor interest: Hall and Bannon found that interest and engagement increased when children interacted with digitally augmented museum artifacts [18], and Szymanski and colleagues demonstrated that visitors of a historic house were more likely to explore augmented objects [38]. One of our primary goals in the current study is to study the use of AR to help families make meaningful connections between representations.

DESIGN OF SPARK

Through a three-year iterative design process [5, 6], we developed an interactive exhibit that enables visitors to construct circuits and then see a simulation of electrons moving through the various components. The system consists of four components (Figure 3): a DC circuit simulator, an agent-based model of current flow, a virtual multimeter, and a brief textual description of basic concepts on electricity. We briefly describe each of these parts.

Circuit Simulator

In *Spark*, visitors can build simple electrical circuits by dragging and connecting components from a toolbox menu on a multi-touch display. Each component has three variables: voltage drop, current, and resistance. The lightbulb has a fourth variable of brightness factor. The voltage of batteries and resistance of resistors can be changed adjusting with a slider. We calculate current and voltage drop for each component every time a visitor makes a change to the circuit.

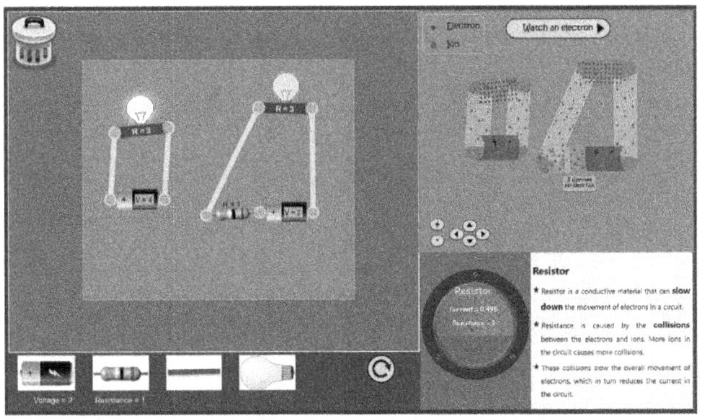

Figure 3. Snapshot of *Spark* system in the single-display condition.

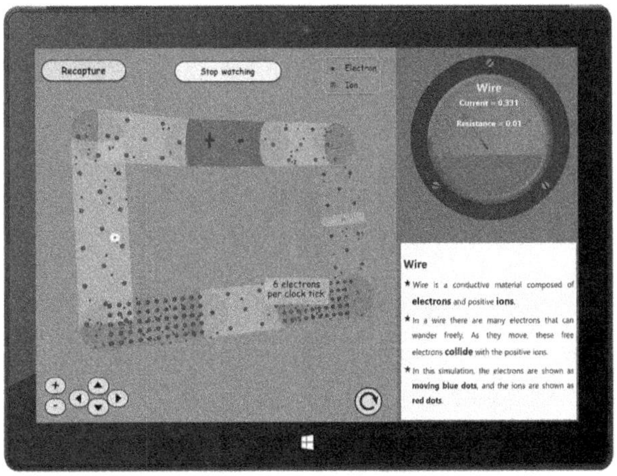

Figure 4. Electron model display in the AR condition. The blue dots are moving electrons and the red dots represent ions in conductive materials. Resistors have higher ion densities than wires.

Electron Model

We developed a 3D visualization of current flow using Three.js [43], a browser-based JavaScript library based on WebGL. *Spark* electron model is inspired by NIELS simulation environment [34] and is based on Drude's free electron theory in which electrical current and resistance can be thought of as phenomena that emerge from simple kinetic interactions between electrons and ions in the conductive materials. Here, resistance is modeled by the collisions between the electrons and ions. Thus, more ions in the circuit cause more collisions resulting in higher resistance (see the example in Figure 4). These collisions slow the overall movement of electrons, which in turn reduces the current in the circuit.

The model is updated every time a visitor makes a change to the circuit. Visitors can tap on a "watch an electron" button to track the movement of a random electron through the circuit (see Figure 4). Visitors can also tap on a component to see its electrical measures, a textual description about the component, and also a counter that shows the "electrons per clock tick" rate. This measure indicates how many electrons pass by the cross section of the component over a certain

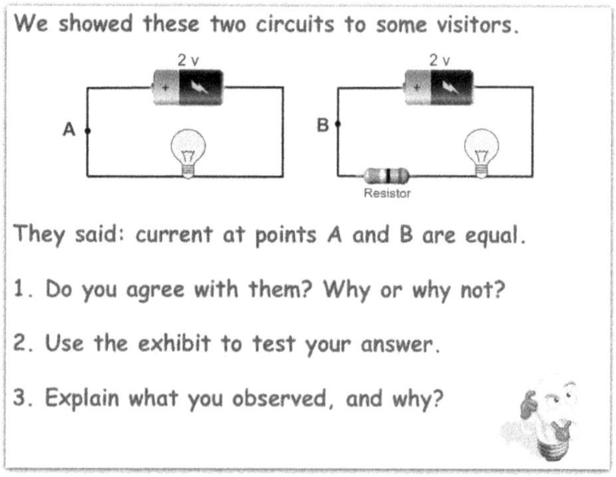

Figure 5. Final task (task 3) in the series of tasks.

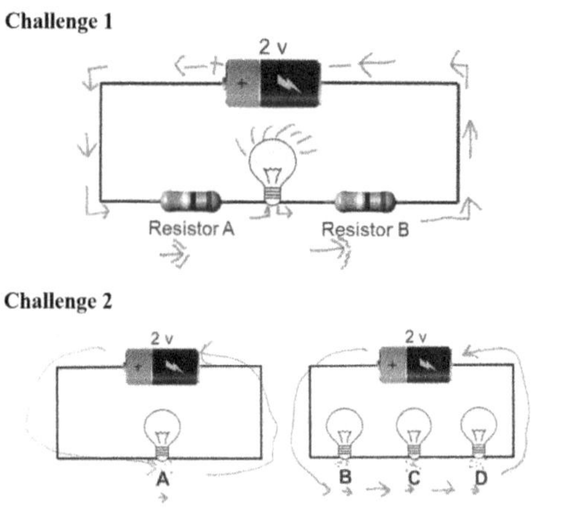

Figure 6. Post-interview questions and two examples of children's drawings to show the flow of current.

time, which is directly proportional to the measure of current in that component. Finally, visitors can zoom and pan the display using direct touch interaction or buttons in a toolbar.

Multimeter

The third component of the exhibit is a multimeter that shows the variables (current, voltage, resistance) of each component. These variables are updated every time there is a change in the circuit.

Information Window

The last component of the exhibit is a window that contains brief textual descriptions of the underlying concepts of an electrical circuit, such as current and resistance. Four short scripts are provided for each component type to describe what is inside a wire, what a battery does, what is current, and what is a resistor. The descriptions provide simple explanations of the concepts based on the electron model and do not include any explicit notion of circuit equations or laws such as Ohms law (V = IR).

METHODS

Conditions

We recruited 60 parent-child dyads who were visiting the science museum to participate in one of three conditions.

Condition 1: Control Condition

In the control condition visitors could create circuits, use the multimeter, and read textual descriptions. But the simulation of electrons flowing through the circuit was not visible. Visitors could drag a magnifying glass icon over a component to see its measures.

Condition 2: Single-display Condition

In condition 2, we introduced the electron simulation. The simulation was shown alongside the circuit on the same display (see Figure 3). With every change to the circuit, the electron simulation was updated in real time.

Condition 3: AR Condition

In condition 3, we displayed the electron simulation on a separate handheld tablet device using the JSARToolKit library [42]. The tablet's rear-facing camera was used to track the position of an AR tag displayed on the tabletop. This created the illusion that the tablet was a lens that could peer into a circuit. Visitors could zoom in to focus on a specific segment of circuit or zoom out to have a view of electrons moving around the whole circuit. Visitors used a capture button to pause and resume tracking of the AR tag. When paused, visitors could explore the simulation by tracking an electron or tapping on a component to see its electrical measures and textual description.

Apparatus

We used a 21×12-inch multi-touch monitor as the tabletop screen. The monitor was placed flat on a table and connected to a laptop that ran the simulation. For the AR condition, we used a Microsoft Surface Pro 4 with a 12×8-inch display to run the electron model. This display size allowed us to keep the size of the electron simulation consistent across both experimental conditions.

Participants

We tested each condition with parent-child dyads who were visiting the Museum of Science and Industry in Chicago. For each of the three conditions in the study, we recruited 20 parent-child dyads (a total of 60 families) with children between the ages of 10 and 14 years old. We approached any group of visitors (with minors within the target age range) who passed the exhibits nearby the space where our design was setup and asked them if they were interested in participating in the study. The study sample was generally representative of the museum population, which is predominately white (Caucasian). Based on the self-report data driven from the demographic questionnaire, in condition 1, 6 of the families reported non-white ethnicity, whereas 2 families for each of condition 2 and condition 3 reported non-white ethnicity. The median education level of families in all conditions was 4-year college degree, and the distribution of education level across the three conditions was not statistically different. We also asked parents how much they knew about electrical circuits and how much they thought their children knew about electrical circuits. There were no significant differences on either of these measures across conditions.

We used matched sampling to balance boy/girl ratios across our three conditions. There were 37 boys and 23 girls in the study (12 boys and 8 girls in condition 1; 12 boys and 8 girls in condition 2; and 13 boys and 7 girls in condition 3). These ratios reflected the visitor population as a whole; around 65% of children who visit the museum are boys. The age of children in the study ranged between 10 and 14 years (M=11.85 and SD=1.42 for condition 1; M=11.65 and SD=1.27 for condition 2; and M=11.75 and SD=1.41 for condition 3).

Procedure

The study took place over 8 weeks of summer. To avoid distractions from other museum visitors, we set up our exhibit in a relatively quiet activity room and recruited families who passed nearby. After introducing the study and obtaining informed consent, we invited dyads to use the interface for their condition. Before using the interface, the researcher gave a one-minute demo of the interface to make sure that all the families are aware of the different features of the design. Our intention was to limit the effect of prior experience with touch screens. The researcher then asked families to use the exhibit to complete a series of tasks. We asked participants to pretend the researchers were not in the room and to use our design as they would use any other exhibit. We also asked participants to talk out loud while interacting with the system. Upon the completion of this phase, we interviewed the child about electricity understanding while the parent filled out a demographic questionnaire. Participants were compensated with a $10 gift certificate to the museum store. Sessions were video recorded from two different camera angles. In total, the sessions took around 25 minutes to complete.

Tasks

We asked families to use the interface to complete a series of tasks (e.g. Figure 5). The tasks were printed on paper cards and were handed to families one at a time. We designed the tasks as a way to focus families' attention to certain target concepts, such as the idea that current is the same throughout a simple series circuit, or that adding resistance decreases the current. To make sure that all families knew how to make a complete circuit, we first asked them to make a simple circuit to turn on a lightbulb. If families could not complete this task after 2 minutes, we handed them a hint card that instructed them on how to make a complete circuit. This warm-up task was followed by three additional tasks. Each of the tasks had three parts: it opened with a statement about the circuit in question and asked families to agree or disagree with the statement (prediction); then to test their answers (exploration); and finally, to explain what they observed (explanation).

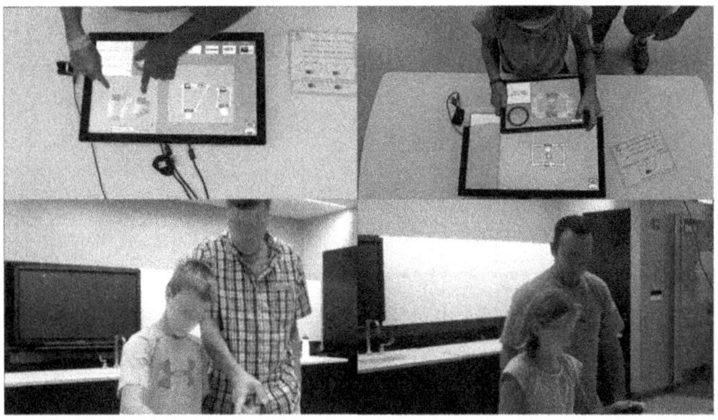

Figure 7. Snapshots of parent-child dyads using the exhibit in the single-display condition (left) and the AR condition (right)

The first task involved comparing the relative measure of current before and after a lightbulb. The second task asked families to compare the brightness of two bulbs in series. The third task explored the effects of adding a resistor to a circuit. The focus in task 3 was on the concept of resistance, and the relationship between resistance and current in a circuit (see Figure 5). Task 3 was the most difficult task for families to complete, as it required comparing two circuits and understanding the relationship between current and resistance. If families constructed a better understanding of current in the first two tasks, they were more likely to offer a correct prediction for task 3. It took families 13:06 minutes on average to complete all the tasks in condition 1, 13:16 in condition 2, and 16:24 in condition 3.

Post-Test Interviews

To assess the effect of exhibit on children's conceptions of electric current and resistance, we interviewed children in all conditions with a set of two challenges (Figure 6). In the first challenge we asked children to predict the effect of changing the resistance of two resistors on the brightness of a lightbulb placed between them. We also asked children to use a pen to draw the current flow on the circuit. The second challenge involved comparing the brightness of four lightbulbs in two series circuits. We designed the challenges to help us understand mental models that children evoke in their explanations and whether there is a difference in these models across the conditions. Children's responses to the challenges were transcribed and coded.

Data

Data took the form of video recordings from families' interactions with the interface, children's post-interview responses, and field notes. We used two camera angles, to capture both the parents and children body expressions and gestures and the families' interactions with the interface including touch interactions, points, and gestures. We also recorded the screen of the interface. Figure 7 illustrates two snapshots of the synchronized video recordings.

	Code	Description
Current Path Models	No current in return path	Current leaves one terminal of battery and is completely consumed by the circuit and no current remains in the return path
	Clashing currents	Current travels from both terminals of battery and clashes at the bulb or resistor
	Bidirectional currents	Current flows around the circuit in both clockwise and counter-clockwise directions
	Unidirectional current	Current flows in one direction around the circuit
Current Flow Causal Relationships	Sequential model	Current travels from point to point and affects each component in turn as it is encountered with the circuit (domino-like effect)
	Traffic jam model	Similar to sequential model, current travels point to a point, but can be slowed down by traffic congestion ahead
	Cyclic model	Current travels around the circuit in repeated cycles
	Concurrent model	The effect of a change in the circuit affects the circuit as a whole. In other words, a local change causes a global effect which affects the entire circuit simultaneously
Current Lowering Models	Consumption model	Current is consumed in components of the circuit
	Slow-down model	Current is slowed down in components of the circuit

Table 1. Coding scheme for children conceptions of current and resistance.

RESULTS

In this section, we first report on children's conceptions of current and resistance in the post-interviews. We then examine videos of parent-child interaction with the exhibit.

Post-Test Interviews

To analyze children's interviews, we first transcribed video recordings and then coded for the presence or absence of target concepts about electricity. We inductively developed the coding scheme based on literature [17, 28] (Table 1). We identified three main dimensions for children's mental models: (1) current path models dealing with the direction of current flow; (2) models that attempt to explain cause and effect relationships in a circuit; and (3) current lowering models that include thinking of current as a substance being consumed or as a flow that is slowed down. Table 1 shows the list of codes for each dimension.

One researcher conducted the majority of the coding. Two assistants coded 20% of the transcripts to establish inter-rater reliability. We achieved an agreement of 94% for the first research assistant (Kappa = 0.78), and 93% for the second research assistant (Kappa = 0.72).

Current Path

To assess children's understanding of current path, we grouped the first three codes together (Table 1); these three models are considered incorrect or non-scientific, whereas the fourth model, unidirectional current, is considered correct. We did not see any instances of the first incorrect model (no current in return path). This was likely because the diagrams in the challenge questions provide a hint that one needs two wires to have a circuit. Figure 8 shows the differences in usage of incorrect and correct conceptions for current path in each condition. We found that 6 children in control condition evoked an incorrect conception of current path, compared to one participant in each of the experimental conditions. A chi-square test showed that the two experimental conditions differed significantly from the control condition ($p = 0.027$). This was not surprising as the electron simulation shows current flowing in one general direction when the circuit is closed.

Current Flow Mechanism

We then studied children's conceptions of the underlying mechanism of current flow (second dimension of the coding scheme). We identified four different models in this category based on our review of the literature and inductive coding of children's responses in our study. The models in this category seem to suggest a sequence of conceptions that progress towards a more scientific understanding of causal relationships in circuit. The first model (*sequential*) views current as a substance that fills up an initially empty circuit one component at a time. Children who hold this model think that a component placed in a circuit after the bulb cannot affect the brightness of bulb. Second, in the *traffic jam* model, current can be jammed behind a resistor after a lightbulb and hence the resistor can increase the brightness of lightbulb (in reality it decreases the brightness). Third, the *cyclic model* is a progression from sequential model towards concurrent model; it includes a reasoning that current flows in the circuit in a cycle. As a result, a change in circuit after a bulb can still affect the bulb in the next cycle through the circuit. But, there is still a temporal relationship between cause and effect. Fourth, the *concurrent* model is the correct model in this category. This model indicates a non-sequential relationship: a change in any part of the circuit affects the whole circuit instantaneously, and there is no real beginning or ending.

We considered the cyclic model as an intermediate model towards the correct model. In addition, in some cases it was unclear whether the child is using a cyclic model or a concurrent model. For these two reasons, we grouped these two models together as progressed conceptions. For both

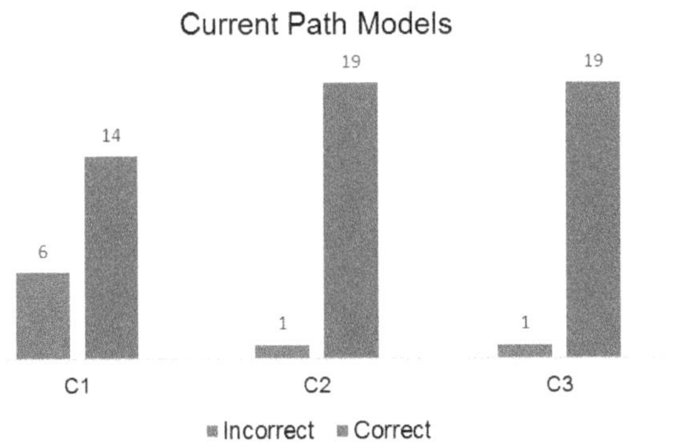

Figure 8. Children's mental models of current flow path in control condition (C1); single-display condition (C2); and AR condition (C3).

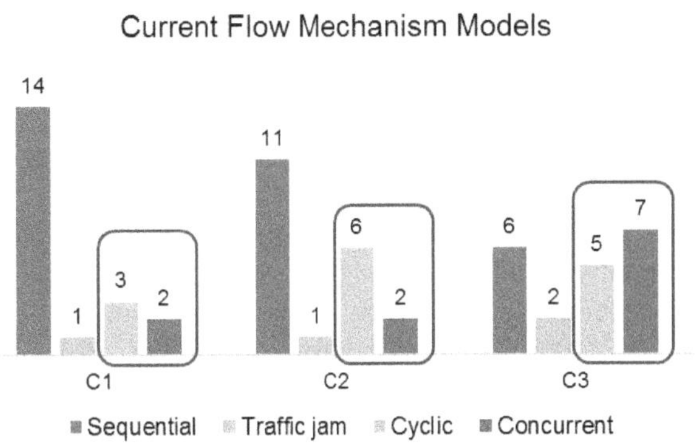

Figure 9. Children's mental models of mechanism of current flow with cyclic model and concurrent model grouped as "progressed" conceptions.

experimental conditions, we observed an increase in number of times that children used either of the progressed models (Figure 9). Children in control condition mostly used a sequential model to reason about circuits. A chi-square test shows that this increase is significant from condition 1 to condition 3 ($p = 0.025$), but not significant from condition 1 to condition 2.

We then reviewed the interviews and compared the completeness of responses qualitatively. Our observations show that children's explanations increased in completeness for both experimental conditions, with most complete responses in condition 3 (AR). In condition 3, children were more likely to provide an elaborate explanation for their responses. The following excerpt demonstrates a child's conception of current in the AR condition:

[Researcher shows the circuit in Challenge 1]
Researcher: In this circuit, if I increase the resistance of resistor A [the resistor before the lightbulb], what do you think happens to the brightness of lightbulb?
Participant: Um, I think it's going to get less bright. It's gonna get dimmer.
Researcher: Can you tell me why?
Participant: Because it slows the amount of electrons going through, with more collisions, so they [electrons] slow down and then that's less electricity going through every second, so then it would be dimmer.
Researcher: And what happens if I increase the resistance of resistor B?
Participant: Well, based on what we saw [reference to experience with the exhibit] where the resistor kind of affects all the way through the circuit [kid motions his hand in circles around the circuit diagram], I think the same effect would happen with what happens with resistor A, where it would slow down the amount over the whole circuit.
Researcher: And so does it make the lightbulb dimmer or brighter?
Participant: dimmer.

In this excerpt, the child relies on his experience with the exhibit and provides a relatively complete explanation of how a resistor affects the circuit as a whole (concurrent model). Moreover, we observed that children in this condition used electron-based language more frequent than children in single-display condition. For example, we observed that children in the AR condition used the concept of electrons being slowed down due to collisions with ions more frequently than children in single-display condition (11 and 6 times, respectively).

Current Lowering Models

Previous studies suggest that children commonly think of current as a substance that is being used up by the components in circuit (*consumption* model) [17, 30]. In this model, adding more resistance to a circuit makes the current weaker by decreasing its quantity. However, a more scientific model describes current as a flow that can be slowed down by the resistive materials in the circuit (*slow-down* model). In this model, the focus is on rate.

We coded the interviews with regard to these two models. We observed that some children used both models in their explanations for different parts of the interview. In other cases, children did not evoke either model. Therefore, for this measure we counted the number of times that each code was used across all interview responses.

We found a similar pattern across all the three conditions: children in control condition used the consumption model 9 times and the slow-down model 12 times (57% use of slow-down model). This ratio was 10 to 13 for condition 2 (57% use of slow-down) and 9 to 17 for condition 3 (65% use of slow-down). There was no significant difference across the conditions.

Parent-Child Learning and Interaction

We analyzed videos of visitor sessions to investigate how families learned from and interacted with the exhibit. We examined discourse, physical interaction, and the shifting roles of parents and children in the activity. We share findings that focuses on understanding how families learned about the concepts of electricity using the exhibit.

Assessment of Dyad Learning

To assess learning with the exhibit, we examined the prediction part of task 3. In task 3 (Figure 5), families are shown two circuits; the first circuit has one lightbulb, and the second circuit has one resistor and one bulb after the resistor (assuming a counter-clockwise direction of current flow). The question asks visitors to agree or disagree with a comparative statement about two points on these two circuits placed before the resistor and bulb: the current at points A and B is equal. The correct answer is that current is greater at point A because the resistor in the second circuit slows down the current in the whole circuit. Applying a sequential model results in concluding that the currents at points A and B are equal because the current has not yet encountered the bulb or resistor.

We chose to examine task 3 to assess the learning process for two reasons: first, when starting task 3, families have had several minutes of interaction time with the exhibit. Second, task 3 was the most difficult task as it required families to construct a relatively complete understanding of current to predict the correct answer. Therefore, we saw performance on the prediction part of the final task as a good gauge for the quality of dyads' explorations of circuits.

We coded families' verbal and nonverbal actions while predicting the answer for task 3 and categorized the sessions into three separate groups: (1) incorrect prediction; (2) correct prediction with no explanation; and (3) correct prediction supported with some explanation. Depending on parents' engagement in the prediction task, answers (and explanations) were offered by the child, parent, or after dialogue between parent and child. One family in the control condition did not offer a prediction, and one family in condition 3 gave conflicting predictions: the parent gave an incorrect answer while the child disagreed with her by predicting the answer correctly. We coded this instance with correct prediction since we consider children as the primary users of the interface. Figure 10 shows the number of incorrect and correct predictions in each condition.

We found that families in condition 2 performed significantly better than the other two groups. We applied chi-square tests for the number of correct (with or without explanation) versus incorrect predictions and found a significant difference between condition 1 and 2 ($p = 0.002$) but no significant difference between condition 1 and 3. We also found a significant difference between the two experimental conditions ($p = 0.005$).

These findings suggest that families in the AR condition did only slightly better than families in control condition. On the other hand, most of the families in single-display condition predicted the answer correctly. This was surprising for us as our earlier analysis on post-test interviews suggested that children in the AR condition perform better than the other two groups and significantly better than the control condition.

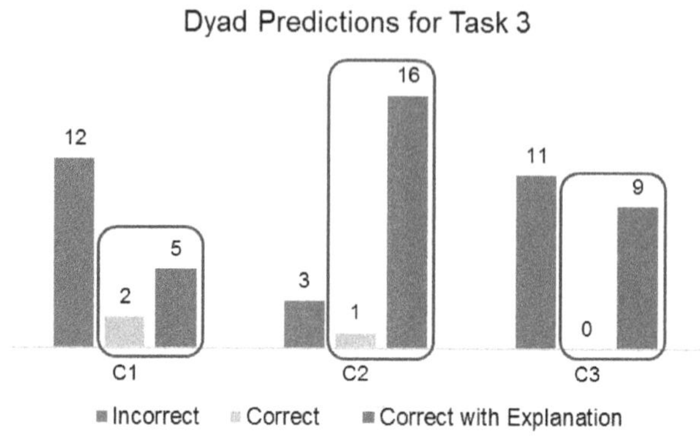

Figure 10. Parent-child dyad predictions for task 3.

To make sense of this trend, we re-examined the videos of families' predictions for task 3, however this time we focused our attention on the process through which the predictions were formed. We observed that parents in the control condition and single-display condition frequently let their child to come up with an answer by prompting questions and leading a conversation to assist the child. Parents in these two groups were less likely to tell what they believed the correct answer was. However, unlike the other two groups, parents in the AR condition actively articulated ideas and conceptions, and were more likely to offer what they thought. This change in behavior led to an increase in number of incorrect answers, as parents actively influenced the process. We found three different scenarios for the influence of parents resulting in incorrect answer: (1) after reading the question, the parent offered an answer before letting the child express his opinion. The child said nothing and started on building the circuit to test his parent's answer (one case); (2) the child initially predicted correctly, but then the parent offered an incorrect answer and thus the child changed his/her mind to comply with the parent's opinion (3 cases); (3) the child was trying to come up with the answer and the parent directed the child's attention to a misleading conceptualization of the circuit in question (2 cases). The following episode illustrates an example of the second scenario:

Child: [after reading the question] I don't think that A and B is equal, because one has a resistor and one doesn't.
Dad: but I am going to say they will be equal because the resistor is after, if it is flowing this way [motions a counter-clockwise path from the positive end of battery]. Should we test it?
Child: what?
Dad: should we try it?
Child: [keeps looking at the question]
Dad: See, I think because there is a resistor that lowers [the current] and so if it is flowing this way [counter-clockwise], point B is before the resistor. So, I think B and A will be the same.
Child: Oh!
Dad: but if you were to measure the [brightness of] lightbulbs those will be different.
Child: [nods head] yeah, yeah, B and A will be the same then.

Dad: should we try it? [dad and child start building the circuit together.]

In this vignette, the child starts her articulation with a correct answer but then her father immediately disagrees with her and offers his idea about comparing the two circuits. He provokes a sequential model and thinks that current affects the circuit point by point. The child seems to be confused by her father's explanation at first, but after the second time that her father articulates his idea, the child finally agrees with him.

It is important to note that the parents' active engagement did not always result in an incorrect prediction. In two cases, the parent initiated the prediction by providing the correct answer and the child either said nothing, or agreed with the parent. In two other cases, parent's engagement resulted in a conversation between parent and child to come up with correct reasoning.

Shift in Parental Engagement

To further investigate parental engagement, we extended our video analysis to look at family interaction while completing task 2. We were interested in finding out whether a similar pattern could be observed for a shift in parents' engagement in the AR condition. For this purpose, we narrowed our analysis to the two experimental conditions. We first open-coded the videos for all the families in both groups and formed a coding scheme with four distinct parental roles (see Table 2). We then coded the session video. The primary researcher worked with one of the two research assistants. Each of the researchers coded the video sessions separately and then compared the codes and resolved disagreements.

For each family, we identified the dominant role for parents. In some cases, we could identify a secondary role for parents, but for this analysis we only looked at the primary role of parents in the session. Figure 11 illustrates the distribution of parental roles in each group. As demonstrated in the graph, we found that parents in single-display conditions mostly took the role of *educator* or *observer*. On the other hand, parents in the AR condition, were commonly engaged in a collaborative learning process. Chi-square tests show a significant relationship between the type of interaction and parental role ($p = 0.001$). This observation is consistent with our earlier analysis for shift in parents' engagement in the final tasks predictions. In sum, we observed that parents were acting more collaboratively in the AR condition, leading to more incorrect predictions in task 3.

DISCUSSION

Our findings show that children did significantly better on a post-test in both experimental conditions, with children performing best in the AR condition. Moreover, our analysis of both the video sessions and post-test interviews suggest that children in the AR condition were more likely to attend to the electron simulation and the behavior of electrons moving in the circuit. This finding is in agreement with previous studies that suggest AR can enhance learning in various ways

Code	Description
Absent	Parent has no interaction with the exhibit or content of tasks
Observer	Parent has some interaction, but the extend of interaction excludes learning
Educator	Parent tries to teach the child by prompting questions, directing child's attention, and providing explanations
Co-learner	Parent is engaged in the learning process with the child and offers ideas

Table 2. Coding scheme for parental roles

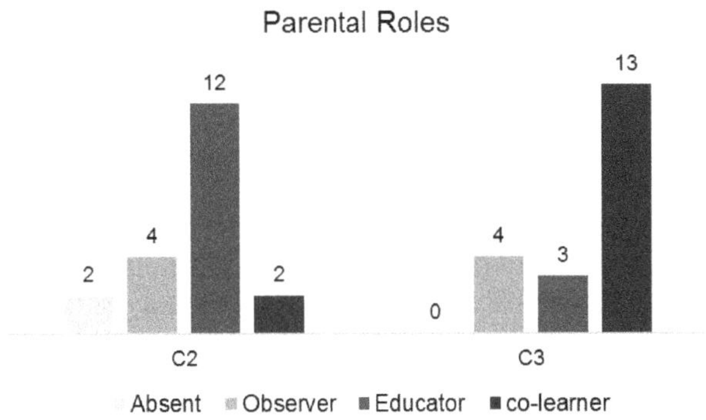

Figure 11. Different types of parental roles in task 2 in the single-display condition (C2) and the AR condition (C3).

[40, 41]. Here, one affordance of AR on learning is that it can support a better transition between the two representations, as it allows visitors to naturally inspect the circuit components using the tablet as a lens that sees *through* the circuit. In other words, it can enhance the coupling between the two representations. On the other hand, visitors have the option to ignore the tablet display allowing them to physically decouple the two representations, possibly making exploration less confusing for novice learners.

We also examined parent-child interactions with the exhibit in the single-display condition and the AR condition. Extensive museum studies show that parents often take on the role of educators during the museum visit and use specific mediating behaviors [10, 29]. These studies suggest that teaching occurs as a fundamental aspect of interactions of family members in science museums. In accordance with these studies, we observed that parents in the single-display condition commonly took the role of educator while using the exhibit; they instructed their children by means of three common actions: prompting questions; directing child's attention to components of the exhibit; and explaining how circuits work. However, we observed that parents in the AR condition were significantly less likely to take on the role of educator and instead acted as a co-learner.

This was an interesting finding for us. We have two plausible explanations; the first argument is that due to the novelty in technology being used in the AR condition, parents became less comfortable with their role as educators. A 2009 study by Barron and her colleagues identifies seven different types of roles that parents play to support their children with activities that involve computers and new technologies, "Teacher" and "Collaborator" being two of these roles [4]. This study suggests that most of these roles did not require parents to have greater technical expertise than the child. We observed that, when being introduced to the exhibit, parents made comments about the technology, saying "*this is the type of things that you [child] know better than me*". In other words, inclusion of AR technology might have affected the parents' level of comfort leading to a more collaborative role.

Second, holding the tablet device might result in a perception for child that he/she has control over the interaction with the exhibit. In other words, the tablet acts as a tool that allows the child to control the experience with the exhibit; In most cases, the child is responsible for holding the tablet, capturing the electron model, and then interacting with the model. Having control over the investigation could have raised the child's status or power in parent-child interaction. This explanation aligns with [24], which suggest that appropriating different resources and making different types of information visible can help children claim authority over their activity in a museum environment.

CONCLUSION AND FUTURE WORK

In this paper, we presented the design and evaluation of a science museum exhibit that enables visitors to make circuits on an interactive tabletop and observe a simulation of electrons flowing through the circuit which conveys basic concepts of current and resistance. Our findings show that having access to the electron simulation could benefit children to better understand the concepts of electricity. We also observed that coupling the electron simulation through augmented reality significantly enhanced the learning benefits of the exhibit. Moreover, an analysis of session videos shows an interesting shift in parents' engagement. We observed that parents in the AR condition no longer acted as an educator and instead toke the role of co-learner. These findings raise the question for us that what factors could account for this shift in parental engagement. We will continue our research to further investigate this question.

Moreover, we are interested in studying the effects of working with physical circuit components (tangibles) instead of a digital circuit simulator. Research has shown that physical manipulatives can support science learning [26, 32]. Recent museum studies also suggest that physical manipulative are more inviting than their virtual counterparts [20, 25]. We are currently working on designing and testing a tangible prototype of the system (Figure 12). In the future, we will recruit family visitors to examine the effect of tangibles on parent-child learning and interaction.

Working Prototype

The design of physical components is inspired by the work of Chan and colleagues on LightUp [8]. Similar to LightUp, the electronic components of the circuit are attached to each other with magnetic connectors. The physical components

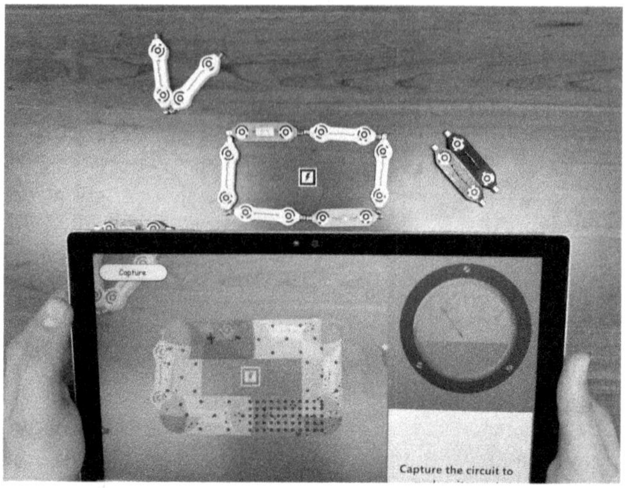

Figure 12. A demonstration of Tangible *Spark*.

include wires, batteries, resistors, and lightbulbs (Figure 12), similar to the digital circuit simulator. To detect the circuit components and render the corresponding electron simulation of circuit, we use Top-Code markers [44] on both ends of each component. We use a Microsoft Surface Pro 4 for running the computer vision code and then rendering the electron simulation. The computer vision code analyzes the capturing video stream and uses a series of algorithms to detect the components in the frame along their corresponding connections. This data is then passed to the electron simulation that runs on the tablet.

ACKNOWLEDGMENTS

We thank the Museum of Science and Industry in Chicago, and its Manager of Evaluation and Research, Aaron Price, for their valuable help and allowing us to conduct this research in their facilities. Thanks to Uri Wilensky and Anne Marie Piper who provided us with insightful comments on this work. We also thank the members of TIDAL lab and CCL lab at Northwestern University.

REFERENCES

1. Shaaron Ainsworth. 2006. DeFT: A conceptual framework for considering learning with multiple representations. *Learning and Instruction* 16, 3: 183–198. https://doi.org/10.1016/j.learninstruc.2006.03.001
2. Sue Allen. 2004. Designs for learning: Studying science museum exhibits that do more than entertain. *Science Education* 88, S1: S17–S33. https://doi.org/10.1002/sce.20016
3. Kikuo Asai, Yuji Sugimoto, and Mark Billinghurst. 2010. Exhibition of Lunar Surface Navigation System Facilitating Collaboration Between Children and Parents in Science Museum. In *Proceedings of the 9th ACM SIGGRAPH Conference on Virtual-Reality Continuum and Its Applications in Industry* (VRCAI '10), 119–124. https://doi.org/10.1145/1900179.1900203
4. Brigid Barron, Caitlin Kennedy Martin, Lori Takeuchi, and Rachel Fithian. 2009. Parents as Learning Partners in the Development of Technological Fluency.

International Journal of Learning and Media 1, 2: 55–77. https://doi.org/10.1162/ijlm.2009.0021
5. E. Beheshti, A. Aljuhani, and M.S. Horn. 2014. Electrons to light bulbs: Understanding electricity with a multi-level simulation environment. In *2014 IEEE Frontiers in Education Conference (FIE)*, 1–8. https://doi.org/10.1109/FIE.2014.7044047
6. Elham Beheshti, Mmachi Obiorah, and Michael S. Horn. 2015. "Let's Dive into It!": Learning Electricity with Multiple Representations. In *Proceedings of the 14th International Conference on Interaction Design and Children* (IDC '15), 263–266. https://doi.org/10.1145/2771839.2771892
7. Minda Borun, Margaret B. Chambers, Jennifer Dritsas, and Julie I. Johnson. 1997. Enhancing Family Learning Through Exhibits. *Curator: The Museum Journal* 40, 4: 279–295. https://doi.org/10.1111/j.2151-6952.1997.tb01313.x
8. Joshua Chan, Tarun Pondicherry, and Paulo Blikstein. 2013. LightUp: An Augmented, Learning Platform for Electronics. In *Proceedings of the 12th International Conference on Interaction Design and Children* (IDC '13), 491–494. https://doi.org/10.1145/2485760.2485812
9. Michelene T. H Chi, Rod D Roscoe, James D Slotta, Marguerite Roy, and Catherine C Chase. 2012. Misconceived Causal Explanations for Emergent Processes. *Cognitive Science* 36, 1: 1–61. https://doi.org/10.1111/j.1551-6709.2011.01207.x
10. Judy Diamond. 1986. The Behavior of Family Groups in Science Museums. *Curator: The Museum Journal* 29, 2: 139–154. https://doi.org/10.1111/j.2151-6952.1986.tb01434.x
11. Matt Dunleavy, Chris Dede, and Rebecca Mitchell. 2008. Affordances and Limitations of Immersive Participatory Augmented Reality Simulations for Teaching and Learning. *Journal of Science Education and Technology* 18, 1: 7–22. https://doi.org/10.1007/s10956-008-9119-1
12. Committee on Learning Science in Informal Environments, Board on Science Education, Center for Education, Division of Behavioral and Social Sciences and Education, and National Research Council. 2009. *Learning Science in Informal Environments: People, Places, and Pursuits*. National Academies Press.
13. John Howard Falk and Susan Foutz. 2007. *In Principle, in Practice: Museums as Learning Institutions*. Rowman Altamira.
14. N. D. Finkelstein, W. K. Adams, C. J. Keller, P. B. Kohl, K. K. Perkins, N. S. Podolefsky, S. Reid, and R. LeMaster. 2005. When learning about the real world is better done virtually: A study of substituting computer simulations for laboratory equipment. *Physical Review Special Topics - Physics Education Research* 1, 1: 10103. https://doi.org/10.1103/PhysRevSTPER.1.010103
15. John R. Frederiksen, Barbara Y. White, and Joshua Gutwill. 1999. Dynamic mental models in learning science: The importance of constructing derivational linkages among models. *Journal of Research in Science Teaching* 36, 7: 806–836. https://doi.org/10.1002/(SICI)1098-2736(199909)36:7<806::AID-TEA5>3.0.CO;2-2
16. Susan R. Goldman. 2003. Learning in Complex Domains: When and Why Do Multiple Representations Help? Commentary. *Learning and Instruction* 13, 2: 239–44.
17. Tina A Grotzer and Margot Sudbury. 2000. Moving Beyond Underlying Linear Causal Models of Electrical Circuits. In *annual meeting of the National Association of Research in Science Teaching*, New Orleans, LA.
18. T. Hall and L. Bannon. 2006. Designing ubiquitous computing to enhance children's learning in museums. *Journal of Computer Assisted Learning* 22, 4: 231–243. https://doi.org/10.1111/j.1365-2729.2006.00177.x
19. Michael Horn, Zeina Atrash Leong, Florian Block, Judy Diamond, E. Margaret Evans, Brenda Phillips, and Chia Shen. 2012. Of BATs and APEs: An Interactive Tabletop Game for Natural History Museums. In *Proceedings of the SIGCHI Conference on Human Factors in Computing Systems* (CHI '12), 2059–2068. https://doi.org/10.1145/2207676.2208355
20. Michael S. Horn, R. Jordan Crouser, and Marina U. Bers. 2011. Tangible interaction and learning: the case for a hybrid approach. *Personal and Ubiquitous Computing*. https://doi.org/10.1007/s00779-011-0404-2
21. Robert B. Kozma. 1994. Will media influence learning? Reframing the debate. *Educational Technology Research and Development* 42, 2: 7–19. https://doi.org/10.1007/BF02299087
22. Gaea Leinhardt, Kevin Crowley, and Karen Knutson. 2003. *Learning Conversations in Museums*. Taylor & Francis.
23. Gaea Leinhardt, Karen Knutson, and Kevin Crowley. 2003. Museum Learning Colloborative Redux. *The Journal of Museum Education* 28, 1: 23–31.
24. Leilah Lyons, Michael Tissenbaum, Matthew Berland, Rebecca Eydt, Lauren Wielgus, and Adam Mechtley. 2015. Designing Visible Engineering: Supporting Tinkering Performances in Museums. In *Proceedings of the 14th International Conference on Interaction Design and Children* (IDC '15), 49–58. https://doi.org/10.1145/2771839.2771845
25. Joyce Ma, Lisa Sindorf, Isaac Liao, and Jennifer Frazier. 2015. Using a Tangible Versus a Multi-touch Graphical User Interface to Support Data Exploration at a Museum Exhibit. In *Proceedings of the Ninth International Conference on Tangible, Embedded, and Embodied Interaction* (TEI '15), 33–40. https://doi.org/10.1145/2677199.2680555
26. Taylor Martin and Daniel L. Schwartz. 2005. Physically Distributed Learning: Adapting and Reinterpreting Physical Environments in the Development of Fraction

Concepts. *Cognitive Science* 29, 4: 587–625. https://doi.org/10.1207/s15516709cog0000_15

27. Tom Moher, Brian Uphoff, Darshan Bhatt, Brenda López Silva, and Peter Malcolm. 2008. WallCology: Designing Interaction Affordances for Learner Engagement in Authentic Science Inquiry. In *Proceedings of the SIGCHI Conference on Human Factors in Computing Systems* (CHI '08), 163–172. https://doi.org/10.1145/1357054.1357082
28. Roger Osborne. 1983. Towards Modifying Children's Ideas about Electric Current. *Research in Science & Technological Education* 1, 1: 73–82. https://doi.org/10.1080/0263514830010108
29. Sasha Palmquist and Kevin Crowley. 2007. From teachers to testers: How parents talk to novice and expert children in a natural history museum. *Science Education* 91, 5: 783–804. https://doi.org/10.1002/sce.20215
30. Miriam Reiner, James D. Slotta, Michelene T. H. Chi, and Lauren B. Resnick. 2000. Naive Physics Reasoning: A Commitment to Substance-Based Conceptions. *Cognition and Instruction* 18, 1: 1–34. https://doi.org/10.1207/S1532690XCI1801_01
31. Cody Sandifer. 2003. Technological novelty and open-endedness: Two characteristics of interactive exhibits that contribute to the holding of visitor attention in a science museum. *Journal of Research in Science Teaching* 40, 2: 121–137. https://doi.org/10.1002/tea.10068
32. B. Schneider, J. Wallace, P. Blikstein, and R. Pea. 2013. Preparing for Future Learning with a Tangible User Interface: The Case of Neuroscience. *IEEE Transactions on Learning Technologies* 6, 2: 117–129. https://doi.org/10.1109/TLT.2013.15
33. Stephan Schwan and Roland Riempp. 2004. The cognitive benefits of interactive videos: learning to tie nautical knots. *Learning and Instruction* 14, 3: 293–305. https://doi.org/10.1016/j.learninstruc.2004.06.005
34. Pratim Sengupta and Uri Wilensky. 2009. Learning Electricity with NIELS: Thinking with Electrons and Thinking in Levels. *International Journal of Computers for Mathematical Learning* 14, 1: 21–50. https://doi.org/10.1007/s10758-009-9144-z
35. Pratim Sengupta and Uri Wilensky. 2011. Lowering the Learning Threshold: Multi-Agent-Based Models and Learning Electricity. In *Models and Modeling*, Myint Swe Khine and Issa M. Saleh (eds.). Springer Netherlands, Dordrecht, 141–171.
36. D. . Shipstone. 1984. A study of children's understanding of electricity in simple DC circuits. *European Journal of Science Education* 6, 2: 185–198. https://doi.org/10.1080/0140528840060208
37. Kurt Squire and Eric Klopfer. 2007. Augmented Reality Simulaions on Handheld Computers. *Journal of the Learning Sciences* 16, 3: 371–413. https://doi.org/10.1080/10508400701413435
38. Margaret H. Szymanski, Paul M. Aoki, Rebecca E. Grinter, Amy Hurst, James D. Thornton, and Allison Woodruff. 2007. Sotto Voce: Facilitating Social Learning in a Historic House. *Computer Supported Cooperative Work (CSCW)* 17, 1: 5–34. https://doi.org/10.1007/s10606-007-9067-y
39. A. Tarciso Borges. 1999. Mental models of electricity. *International Journal of Science Education* 21, 1: 95–117. https://doi.org/10.1080/095006999290859
40. Susan A. Yoon, Karen Elinich, Joyce Wang, Christopher Steinmeier, and Sean Tucker. 2012. Using augmented reality and knowledge-building scaffolds to improve learning in a science museum. *International Journal of Computer-Supported Collaborative Learning* 7, 4: 519–541. https://doi.org/10.1007/s11412-012-9156-x
41. Susan A. Yoon and Joyce Wang. 2013. Making the Invisible Visible in Science Museums Through Augmented Reality Devices. *TechTrends* 58, 1: 49–55. https://doi.org/10.1007/s11528-013-0720-7
42. *JSARToolKit library*. Retrieved from https://github.com/artoolkit/jsartoolkit5
43. *Three.js library*. Retrieved from http://threejs.org/
44. *TopCode library*. Retrieved from http: //users.eecs.northwestern.edu/~mhorn/topcodes/

Log it While It's Hot: Designing Human Interaction with Smart Thermostats for Shared Work Environments

Stephen Snow
University of Southampton
Southampton, UK
s.snow@soton.ac.uk

Frederik Auffenberg
University of Southampton
Southampton, UK
fa1c12@ecs.soton.ac.uk

m.c. schraefel
University of Southampton
Southampton, UK
mc@ecs.soton.ac.uk

ABSTRACT
Smart thermostats offer impressive scope for adapting to users' thermal comfort preferences and saving energy in shared work environments. Yet human interactions with smart thermostats thus far amount to an assumption from designers that users are willing and able to provide unbiased data at regular intervals; which may be unrealistic. In this paper we highlight the variety of social factors which complicate users' relationships with smart thermostats in shared work environments. These include social dynamics, expectations, and contextually specific factors that influence motivations for interaction with the system. In response we outline our framework towards a *Smarter Thermostat*: one which better accounts for these messy social inevitabilities, is equipped for a decline in user feedback over time and one which augments rather than attempts to replaces human intelligence- thereby ensuring a smarter thermostat does not create dumber humans.

Author Keywords
Smart thermostat; thermal comfort; shared work environments; office; reciprocity; participatory sensing

ACM Classification Keywords
H.5.2 User Interfaces: User-centered design

INTRODUCTION
Ongoing issues of climate change and peak demand provide a strong case for reducing building energy use. Given that Heating, Ventilation and Air Conditioning (HVAC) accounts for over 40% of a commercial building's energy consumption [8], improving the efficiency of HVAC systems through smart technology, offers advantages in terms of sustainability and running costs.

Smart thermostats which learn and adapt to users' thermal preferences, offer a promising solution to balancing a reduction of HVAC energy use while retaining thermal satisfaction for users [1, 3, 10, 18, 21]. In order to achieve this, machine learning algorithms for smart thermostats tend to be grounded in a generalized model of thermal comfort (e.g. [7] or [11]), with an added capacity to learn peoples' preferences for certain parameters through user-input into the system. However, assumptions made about how humans can or should interact with such systems can limit their suitability in practice. Further, relatively less smart thermostat-related research concentrates on field deployments in shared work environments (e.g. offices) as opposed to in the home.

In shared work environments, participatory sensing mechanisms designed to assist smart thermostats in calculating peoples' thermal comfort thus far amount to an assumption that users are willing and able to engage with the system at regular intervals over extended time periods [10, 18, 23, 25, 27]. These assumptions contradict social research which finds everyday life to be messy and unpredictable [31] and that engagement with personal informatics tends to wane over time [15, 29, 33]. More fundamentally, if the notion of "smart" represents a system learning users' preferences and progressively absolving them from responsibility for regulating their thermal comfort, do we run a risk of smart thermostats creating humans who are less connected to the outdoor environment and less adaptable to thermal fluctuations?

In this paper, we describe the variety of social and interactional issues we encountered during our deployment of a novel participatory sensing system which allowed users to log their thermal comfort. Using a human-centred approach to understanding thermal comfort in work environments, our findings highlight a number of social and context-specific factors which can affect the use of such a system. We found that interaction with the system was motivated by user discomfort, was affected by pre-existing relationships with building managers and was characterized a decline in usage over time.

Based on these findings, we highlight the limits of relying on users as reliable and autonomous sensors. Participatory sensing systems for smart thermostats require careful consideration in design in order to account for the human factors which such systems will inevitably encounter in real-world deployments. Finally, we consider how these systems may reciprocate the input provided by their users. These factors shape our vision for a *Smarter Thermostat*,

CHI 2017, May 06-11, 2017, Denver, CO, USA
 ISBN 978-1-4503-4655-9/17/05…$15.00
DOI: http://dx.doi.org/10.1145/3025453.3025578

one which: (1) Leverages the messy social inevitabilities that we highlight in our deployment and is equipped to handle changes in user engagement, and; (2) Augments, human intelligence through reciprocity and actionable information.

While these considerations for design have been developed in the specific context of smart thermostats in shared work environments, we expect they may potentially be generalizable to designers of smart systems more broadly.

Background: Refining smart thermostat operation through human input

A smart thermostat is a computer-based agent to control temperature via HVAC systems in the home or office. Two typical aims of smart thermostats are to: (1) reduce HVAC energy consumption by simplifying interactions between the human and the thermostat [3, 22] and (2) for the thermostat to provide agreeable thermal comfort to occupants by learning their heating schedules [32] or thermal comfort preferences [10, 18]. Machine learning approaches to thermal comfort modelling for smart thermostats involve extracting user-specific information from existing thermal comfort models, (e.g. the Static [11] or Adaptive [7] models) and learning these parameters through user input. User feedback is used to train and refine the thermal comfort model in order for the system to adjust for individual users' preferences. As such, designing for human involvement in smart thermostat systems is equally fundamental to the accuracy of the model to which it is grounded.

The necessity of human input into smart thermostat operations make it a problem well suited to HCI. Existing HCI work on thermal comfort extends to wearable sensors for personal thermostat control [12] and for sensing thermal comfort [5, 16]. Compact wrist-wearable pulse and skin temperature sensors can provide accurate real-time physiological thermal comfort information from multiple users [5, 16]. Such systems provide accurate per-individual information on thermal comfort at the individual level, however, given the transient occupation and higher numbers of users in shared work environments, their practicality for use here may be limited.

Literature on smart thermostat deployments in the home suggests that the value of human participation in smart thermostat systems has been compromised in the past by factors related to usability and the machine's inability to sense the intent of user input [32]. Smart thermostat deployments in the home thus far have had limited success in leveraging human input into their operations. In contrast to their common goal of energy saving, some have in fact increased energy use in the past [9]. Alan et al. [1] found users' expectations of the function of their smart thermostat did not always match the thermostats capabilities. The Nest home thermostat adapted heating schedules learned from users' interactions with the system. However the ability of the thermostat to learn preferences was complicated by too much or too little input from users, which led to a mutual misunderstanding between the users and the system [32].

Beyond the home: Smart thermostats in shared work environments

Shared work environments such as offices represents a relatively under-explored context for smart thermostat research in HCI, with thermal comfort sensing and modelling work thus far constrained to the fields of artificial intelligence and machine learning [3, 10, 13, 18, 21, 23, 25, 26, 27]. Shared work environments provide a unique set of challenges for smart thermostats as distinct from the home. It is far easier for a system to learn the thermal comfort preferences of a family of 2-4 than it is an office of 20-40 people. Factors affecting use in the home such as cost/comfort trade-offs (e.g. [21]) are not applicable in shared work environments, given office workers or library visitors do not pay the buildings' utility bills.

Recent work suggests that the potential for participation in activities related to thermal comfort in offices can be influenced by social factors [28]. Workers in naturally ventilated offices were found to willingly tolerate thermal discomfort before requesting a window be opened or a heater adjusted, either out of consideration for other co-workers or simply not wanting to make a fuss [28]. In climate controlled buildings, achieving acceptable thermal comfort for a larger number of people can be equally complicated by the variety of personal preferences concerning how a thermostat "should" be controlled (i.e. set and forget versus adaptive control) [6]. An objective of this line of research is to understand comfort in offices in a broader context than individual thermal comfort alone, given that expectations and experiences of comfort are shaped in part by culture and conventions [4]: *"Rather than figuring out more efficient ways of maintaining 21-23° in the face of global warming, society should be embarking on a much more searching debate about the meaning of comfort and the ways of life associated with it"* [4 pp.39]. We re-visit this call-to-action later in the paper.

Mathur et al. [19, 20] visualized environmental variables in an office as part of a "Quantified Office" technology probe. Data on air quality, noise, self-reported mood and activity were collected and visualized on a screen in a break-out space. The project is somewhat unique, not only because it deployed shared informatics in a novel context, but that it represents one of the few studies of this nature to take a bottom-up approach, asking the question *"what information do employees find useful themselves?"* rather than assuming this first [19]. The authors suggest office-situated deployments should provide "actionable" quantifications- i.e. information upon which users can act [19].

Does it actually work? Validation of smart thermostats in-the-wild

Unlike the home, where smart thermostats have been observed in-the-wild [1, 32], the same is not true for smart thermostat deployments in shared work environments.

Various thermal comfort models and participatory sensing systems for office-based smart thermostats exist [3, 10, 13, 18, 23, 25, 26, 27], however the validation and practical implementation of these models does not always extend to in-the-wild user trials [10, 18, 25, 27].

Recent participatory sensing approaches for thermal comfort in offices include affording users the ability to influence the set-point of their offices' thermostat via a mobile [10, 18, 25] or PC application [27]. In each of these studies, users select their thermal comfort level between 'Cold' to 'Hot' on a scale. Initial user trials hint at the potential for considerable HVAC energy savings of 10% [10] to 18% [18]. Yet some potential difficulties remain regarding the applicability of such platforms to represent a human interface for smart thermostat over the long term. Lam et al. [18] for example requires input for the gender, height and weight for occupants; information some occupants may not feel comfortable disclosing. Some systems utilize human participation only in the training stage of their model and then rely solely on the model to provide thermal comfort from this baseline user data [13, 18]. This does not allow the system to adapt for a change of occupancy or user preferences over time. On the other hand participatory sensing systems such as [10, 23, 25, 27] all rely on regular user input over longer timescales, which may not be realistic given the tendency for user engagement in situated technology to evolve over time to less frequent interactions, or diminish all together [14, 15, 33].

Designing for "Resource Man"?

Notable in the design of several examples above, is the assumption that users will be sufficiently interested and engaged with the thermal comfort of their home or office to provide the system with regular and accurate data over extended timeframes. Such assumptions have been highlighted as problematic [30, 31]. Strengers [30] highlights the tendency of designers of smart technology to assume (wrongly) that every user is a "Resource Man"- i.e. a technically-minded rational consumer; who is aware of the factors affecting their personal informatics and willing and able to respond to fluctuations in price-signals with economically rational decisions. In reality everyday life is messy and unpredictable [31]; and many users are simply uninterested in the quantification of their personal informatics. Although the provocation of *"Are you Designing for Resource Man?"* is created for the purpose of highlighting the problematic assumptions made by energy utilities of their consumers [30, 31], the stereotype is applicable more broadly to human-machine interfaces such as smart thermostats. In particular, in the design of systems requiring human engagement or input, it is important to understand how social contexts and everyday life may influence or interrupt use [15, 29, 31]. In this paper, we outline our vision for how these assumptions of rationality may be avoided in the design of smart thermostats.

METHODS

Background

The method undertaken in this paper is usefully understood in the context of our previous work. In response to the practical limitations in applying existing thermal comfort models (i.e. Static [11], or Adaptive [7]) to smart thermostats, we proposed our own personalized thermal comfort model which only requires easily obtainable inputs from the user and utilizes Bayesian networks to adapt to individual users' preferences. This model, further described in [3] offers up to 23% more accurate predictions of users' actual comfort levels than previous models. Previously, however, the model had only been tested on training data from the ASHRAE RP-884 project [2] and requires further validation in the wild if it is to be incorporated into a smart thermostat. The motivation for this paper originated from our attempts to validate this model in the wild, using a novel means of user input which we explain here.

Experimental design and deployments

The original intent of this research was to determine people's definitions of acceptable temperatures and whether these fall within the values predicted by our model [3]. We developed a poster inviting people to log how they are feeling in relation to the temperature. We made 172 unique posters in total to be placed at various locations around (1) a university library and (2) several offices on one floor of a naturally ventilated office building in Southampton, UK.

The purpose of the deployment was two-fold. First, to validate the accuracy of our model in-the-wild with real users and in doing this, to gather an idea of the range of human factors that we anticipated such a deployment might encounter. Each poster featured the title "How's the temperature?" and a large QR code and a URL address unique to each poster (Figure 1 below).

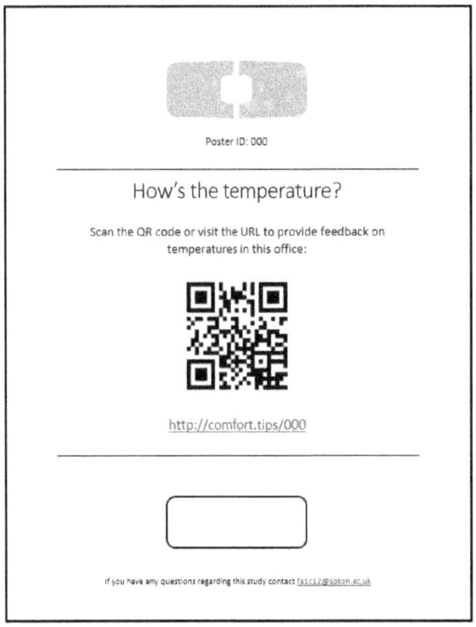

Figure 1: Poster

Scanning the QR code or entering the poster's unique URL into a browser linked the user to a portal where thermal comfort could be logged by means of moving two sliders up or down and optionally selecting buttons representing different reasons for potentially sub-optimal thermal comfort (i.e. "Heat from radiators", "Cold draft" etc). Refer Figure 2 below. The website was designed to be as simple as possible, for use from both PC's and mobile devices. All votes to the system were anonymous and the website stored only a unique identifier for each login, simply to be able to identify peoples' consecutive votes and to determine how many times and to which poster people had voted.

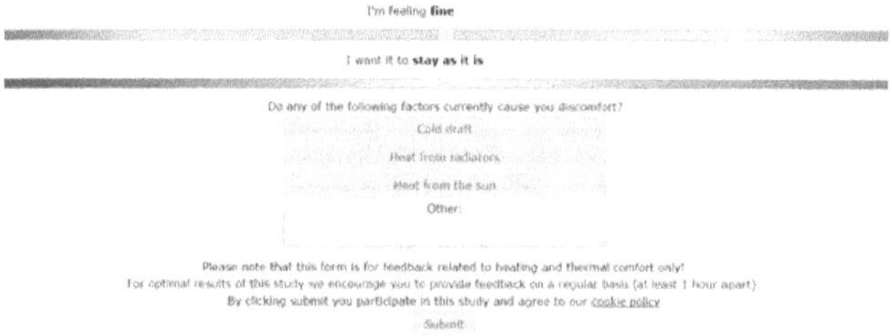

Figure 2: Web interface

The intention was to have the posters as physical reminders for people to register their thermal comfort with the system, in contrast to [10] and [18] who required users to open a mobile app and then select their location from a menu. On the bottom of each poster, we attached a small portable Joulo temperature logger which was pre-programmed to record the time, date and ambient temperature every 10 minutes for the university library deployment and every 4 minutes for the office deployment. This continuous logging allowed correlation of the ambient temperature at the time that each thermal comfort observation was recorded.

Library deployment: We positioned 143 posters over all 5 floors of a large university library. The library, originally built in 1914 and extended/modified in the 1930's, 1950's, 1990's and 2000's respectively, represents a patchwork of building extensions and HVAC arrangements. Heating is primarily by conventional radiators. Ventilation arrangements vary throughout the library; the majority is ventilated by forced mechanical ventilation, however some areas are naturally ventilated with user-openable windows and an area of the archives is air conditioned. In our deployment we aimed for a balance between representative geographic coverage for temperature measurements and choosing sufficiently public locations such that the posters achieved a presence in the library. Additionally 3 humidity sensors were attached to 3 of the posters in order to provide an indication of humidity across the library. Of the 143 posters deployed, 85% were placed in open spaces and 15% in bookable meeting rooms. The deployment of the posters lasted 5 weeks between May and June 2016. Adhering to ethical restrictions of the study and the wishes of the library, we did not approach students for qualitative interviews following the deployment and relied instead on the comments box of the user interface for qualitative feedback (Figure 2).

Office deployment: In this deployment we positioned 29 posters and the three humidity sensors in 8 offices and 3 hallway locations around a single floor of a naturally ventilated office building. The offices where the posters were deployed ranged in occupancy from 2 people (one office) 3-10 people (4 offices) and three large open plan offices each with more than 20 occupants. The offices were populated with university administrative workers involved with finance, student services, human resources and legal. The posters remained in place for the two-week deployment between February and March 2016. All offices were naturally ventilated via occupant-controlled windows and were heated via conventional radiators. A glass-roofed atrium had been retrofitted to one side of the building some years prior. This connected two previously separate naturally ventilated buildings, compromising the ability of both buildings to ventilate. The smaller offices in our study with windows opening to the atrium featured portable, manually controlled air conditioning units which had been introduced owing to complaints about the heat in summer.

In each office we visited to deploy the posters we made a short address to the employees present, to explain the purpose of the posters and how to log their thermal comfort votes. We asked people to vote as often as they liked, but to ideally space votes at least one hour apart. We also instructed office members to pass on the information about the trial and extend our invitation to other office members who were not present during our visit. Wishing to replicate achievable real world conditions beyond the novelty phase, unlike [25] and [27], we did not remind people to vote. Instead we placed the posters in visible and accessible locations around the offices and corridors, so as to encourage the type of opportunistic interaction which may be sustainable over longer timescales.

Interviews

Following the office deployment, we invited participation in semi-structured interviews related to the deployment. Sampling for the interviews was restricted to those employees who worked in an office where one or more poster was deployed and who had logged their thermal comfort on one or more of the posters at least once throughout the deployment.

Semi-structured interviews averaging 30 minutes in length were carried out with 14 participants, which represented approximately 15% of the total workers in all of the offices where the posters had been deployed, and 23% of the total number of users who had logged at least one thermal comfort vote throughout the deployment. Participants comprised 13 females and 1 male. Ages ranged between 26 and 57 with a mean of 39. All participants worked for the university in administrative roles including human resources, financial services, student services and legal. The gender bias of the interview participants is reflective of the majority female occupancy observed in the offices.

Discussions in the interviews related to the participants' work environment, the different factors affecting their thermal comfort, social dynamics around thermal comfort decisions such as opening or closing windows, symptoms they felt in the office and ways they improved their thermal comfort if it was poor. The second part of the interviews related to the usability of the system, motivations for accessing the system and potential improvements.

Analysis

Temperature data: At the end of the deployment, we collected all the Joulo temperature loggers and downloaded the logged temperature data. In the library deployment, 17 of the 142 loggers had either disappeared (12), stopped working (2) or had been configured wrongly (3). For feedback provided to these loggers, we interpolated temperature data from the nearest three loggers. We used thin plate interpolation to calculate an approximation of the temperature between the loggers for the visualization of the heat map created from the data (Figures 3A and 3B).

Feedback from user interface: Data from the "Comments Box" of the thermal comfort interface was downloaded to a spreadsheet. These were read individually and assigned into four categories and later quantified: (1) heat-related (2) cold-related (3) ventilation/stuffy/humidity-related (4) other.

Interviews: All interviews were transcribed verbatim and read by the research team. Initially, responses were aligned to the different key questions asked. Following this, a second read of the transcripts was used in a thematic analysis where transcripts were read independently of the question asked and responses were manually coded according to themes emergent from the data.

FINDINGS

The findings from both the library and office deployment are presented in terms of (1) an overview of the quantitative findings from both deployments, (2) a discussion of the key motivations for users to record their thermal comfort, (3) reflections on usability aspects of the system from both deployments and (4) social factors and office politics observed.

Overview: Temperature

The average temperature across all Joulos over the study periods of both deployments were 24.67°C in the Library and 22.13°C in the Office. As can be seen in Figures 3A and 3B, however, this temperature was not evenly distributed geographically.

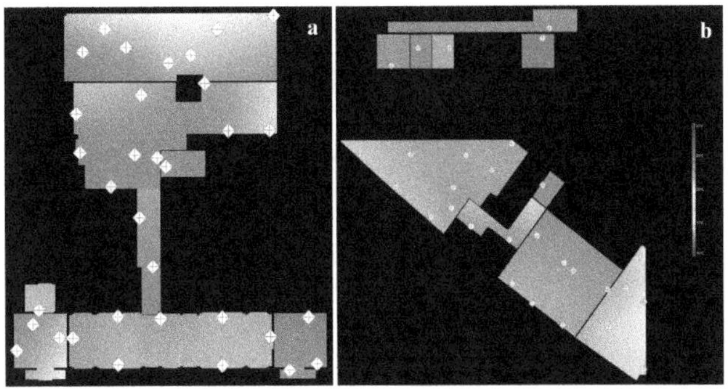

Figures 3A and 3B: Averaged geographic temperature distribution across the library (3A) and office deployment (3B)

Figures 3A and 3B show the temperature distribution across the top floor of the Library (3A) and across the entire deployment across the single floor of the Office (3B).

In the Library, we offer no explanation for the distribution of the temperature, as the building represents a patchwork of retrofits and HVAC situations. The relatively high average temperature during the library deployment was due to one unusually warm week in early May coinciding with the winter heating not yet turned off. The temperatures varied slightly less in the office deployment, with the warmest offices being those with windows that opened out to the enclosed atrium (Figure 3A and 3B).

Overview: Votes logged

Both deployments received a substantial number of votes throughout the respective deployments (refer Table 1). Votes were relatively well distributed between posters, however some posters located in quieter areas of the library received none. Table 1 (below) shows the distribution of the votes between the two deployments.

	Library	Office
Total votes logged	990	167
Total users who voted	688	57
Av no. votes per user	1.44	2.93
Av no. votes per poster	6.92	5.76

Table 1: Distribution of votes

Finally, Figures 4 and 5 below show the temporal distribution of votes over the course of the two deployments

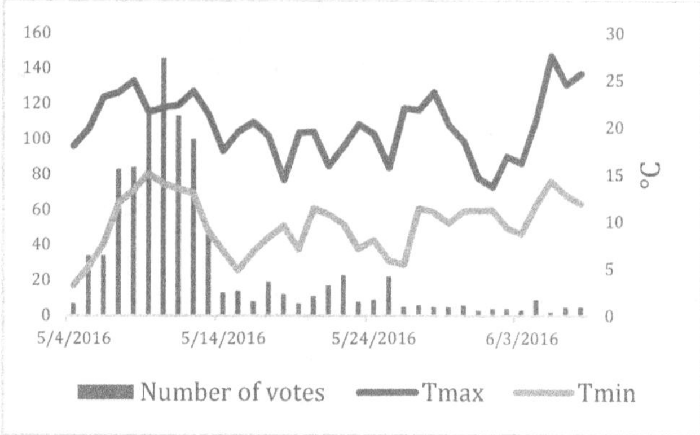

Figure 4: Number of votes plotted against min and max outdoor temperature: Library deployment

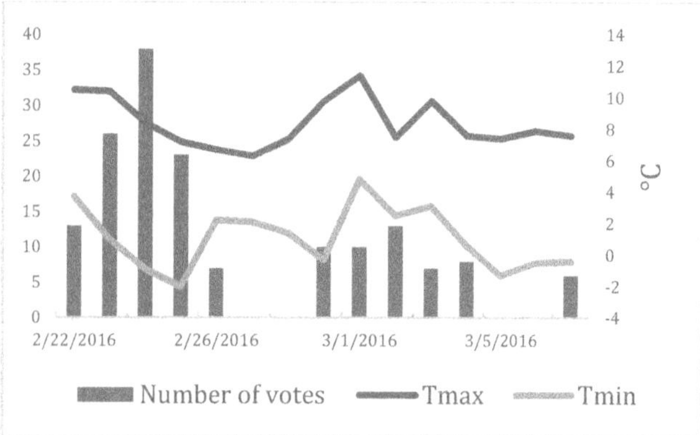

Figure 5: Number of votes plotted against min and max outdoor temperature: Office deployment

Figures 4 and 5 both show a pronounced drop in the number of votes recorded per day following an initial peak. The pronounced novelty affect described above was validated in the qualitative interviews, where five participants recalled being too busy or forgetting to log their thermal comfort on the system in the second week of the deployment: *"[I was] busy and kept forgetting. It was only when I felt like, 'Oh god! It's too hot!'" (P7)*. In the Library (Figure 4), as mentioned, a warm week in May occurred while the heating was still active, overheating areas of the library and prompting a large number of votes. As such it is unclear in Figure 4 (library) as to whether the drop in votes correspond to a novelty effect or simply a return to more reasonable temperatures in the library once the weather cooled and the heating was turned off.

Far more significant than the timing of votes, however, was the nature of the votes recorded in terms of thermal comfort. Figure 6 shows the distribution of all temperatures logged by the Joulos throughout the office deployment (blue) and the normalized distribution of votes per temperature logged (red).

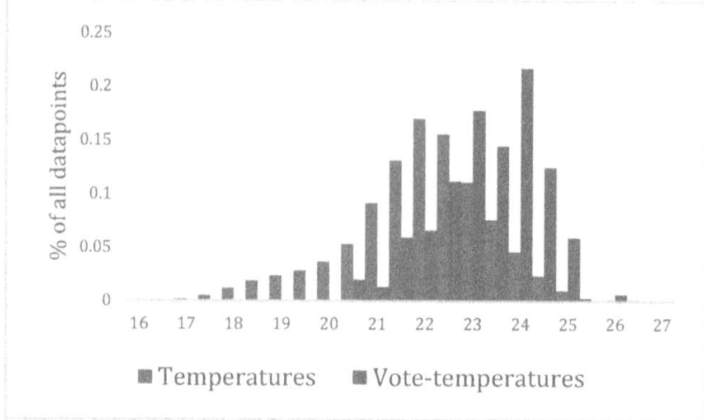

Figure 6: Distribution of indoor temperatures and votes per temperature

What can be seen here is the marked tendency for people to log it while it's hot- i.e. the vast majority of votes were placed when the temperature was higher.

In the library, of the 990 total votes cast over the four-week deployment. 88.4% corresponded to people feeling warm or hot with only 7.96% registering a 'neutral' vote and 3.64% wanting it to be cooler. This pattern was repeated in the office, with only 15% of all the votes correlating to employees wanting it to be cooler and less than 10% of all the 167 votes cast corresponded to people feeling neutral. In this respect, our system was essentially used as a digital complaints box.

Due to the single-sided nature of the votes recorded in our study as described above, we were unable to validate our comfort model on this data. To accurately learn user preferences, the model requires votes in a range of different conditions. Having only 'too hot' votes in a steadily hot environment causes the model to be biased towards predicting 'too hot' in any case, regardless of the actual thermal conditions.

Motivations for use- Heat

It emerged that motivation for recording thermal comfort votes in the systems was primarily related to the temperature in the office. Of the 303 comments entered into the comments box of the user interface from the library deployment, 251 were concerned with the heat or being too hot, compared to only 5 relating to being too cold. *"Too hot on Level 1", I'M MELTING!!!", "Can't concentrate"*. Lack of ventilation, high humidity and stuffiness were also commonly reported alongside temperature complaints.

In the interviews following the office deployment, eight of the 14 participants recalled being reminded to vote only when they felt uncomfortable, i.e. too hot or cold and did not, or simply forgot, to interact with the system when they felt comfortable:

"I think you're more likely to remember to vote if you are feeling cold or hot or warm. It was just a reminder in your mind, 'Ooh, we need to log these things,' rather than when you were feeling just comfortable with anything" (P4)

"[Voted mainly]... near the beginning of the trial, mainly because it was that was when it was hotter and I wanted to comment on it and then later in the week it cooled down. [laughter]" (P11)

This shows how discomfort acted as a key reminder to interact with the system and users were less likely to remember to interact with such a system if they were feeling comfortable. Despite our purposeful placement of certain posters in thoroughfares, while several of our interviewees reported opportunistic interactions with the system, (i.e. being reminded by walking past a poster) this reminder appeared ultimately insufficient to retain peoples' engagement with the system into the second week of the deployment (Figures 4 and 5). Contrary to our expectations, social motivations did not feature prominently. Only one participant mentioned being socially motivated to vote. In this case, P12 would vote together with another colleague, typically on the way to or from a tea break.

Motivations- Fighting for a cause

What the quantitative results for temperature and thermal comfort in the office deployment do not illuminate, is the long history of negotiations between occupants and building managers ("Estates and Facilities") around the issue of overheating and ventilation. The thermal comfort of the building was an on-going cause of frustration among participants and resulted in a persistent tension between building occupants and the Estates and Facilities department. Interviewees related the different work-arounds employed over the recent years to attempt to improve thermal comfort in the building:

"They've installed some extra ventilation things to try and help with the ventilation and the temperatures in those rooms, but I don't know if it works (P1)

"During the summer, they issued everyone with a little bottle of water so that they could spray themselves because it was that hot. That was the only way they could think of trying to cool people down" (P8)

Despite this, it was felt these work-arounds were ultimately unhelpful and participants continued to feel unsatisfied with their office environment, yet powerless to improve their situation.

Unhappiness with the thermal performance of the building (at least in summer) represented an exceptionally strong theme in the first interview (P1). Based on this, we then asked P1 and each subsequent participant specifically about whether they believe they would have engaged with the system less if they knew the data would not be shared with anyone who could make a difference. Nine of the 14 participants agreed this to be true for them. Participant 14 summed this up: *"I would probably just say, 'Oh, well what's the point then?'"*. These comments were made in full knowledge of the fact that we were researchers and were not connected to the Estates and Facilities department.

Despite this, when also asked specifically whether they might have exaggerated their responses (i.e. voted "hot" when feeling neutral) in pursuit of generating a more extreme outcome, none of the participants agreed they had exaggerated their votes. This shows that despite participation with the system being influenced by the wish to have their voices heard, that participants still voted truthfully about their thermal comfort and did not exaggerate their responses.

Usability of the system

Being HCI researchers, we were particularly interested in the usability of the poster and the web interface, and asked a number of questions to these ends in the qualitative interviews. Interestingly however, usability did not emerge as a specific issue in any of the interviews and none of the 303 comments written in the Comments Box of the library deployment related to usability. Interview participants reported the interface easy to access through both the QR code and the URL, despite one participant noting she needed to be taught how to download and use a QR scanner on her phone by another colleague. Two participants mentioned that they would like to have been able to list the adaptive measures they had already taken before voting, e.g. Removed cardigan (✓) removed shoes (✓), turned on desk fan (✓)" and *still* feeling "hot".

Although usability was not flagged as a problem, when asked, several participants agreed they would like to have more quantification of the conditions in the office. Six of the 14 participants mentioned they would have liked a quantification of how stuffy it was in their office. The sentiments of the majority of participants was summed up by P4: *"We feel like the air quality is low, but nothing to show any measurements for that" (P4).* Towards this, two participants, had already brought their own thermometers in from home and we found that one of the digital humidity sensors we had originally deployed in a corridor had been moved into an office. P11 explained that "one of the guys" from the office next door had done this, so they could press the button on the logger and read the temperature and humidity in the office.

Social factors around air quality

A key part of the interview process was to gather qualitative data on the social context of thermal comfort and air quality in offices. We observed that negotiations around thermal comfort were mostly polite and amiable. However, we found ample evidence suggesting that social factors such as politeness and empathy can serve to complicate otherwise rational actions towards improving one's satisfaction with thermal comfort conditions in the office. People would not always speak up if they were unhappy with the air quality in the office, out of not wanting to cause a fuss, or discomfort to their co-workers. The fact that the adequate ventilation of certain offices relied on opening windows was problematic in the winter:

"I might want the window open which will then cause a cold draught to somebody... Yeah, I'd like to open a window but that might not be right... So I'll turn my fan on [instead]" (P11)

Participant 4 believed a number of people in her office elected to put up with air quality they were unhappy with, purely out of consideration for others.

Interviewer to P4: *"Do you think that there's a lot of people who suffer in silence, who'd like the window to be open but don't want to disturb others?"*
P4: *"Oh, definitely at this point of the year, yeah, you will find that in the office.... [Later]: I think people will sort of, before they give their own opinions, will look at everybody else first, and then they'll go along with the consensus"*

This was the case for P7 who put consideration for others before her own thermal (dis)comfort in relation to desk fan use. Although her fan caused her discomfort, she turned it on anyway out of consideration for others:

"I wear contact lenses, so if I have the fan on directly in my face, then it dries them [my eyes] out. I do struggle with that, but I tend to keep quiet in the summer because I know how bad it is in there" (P7)

It can be seen here how consideration for others can be placed before personal comfort, resulting in participants not taking advantage of very simple measures to make themselves more comfortable.

P3 and P5 who worked in one of the three large offices both noticed a marked discrepancy in their office between people who feel the cold versus people who feel the heat. P3 related this as: "two factions" in the office- *"people who are permanently hot no matter what the temperature is and some who are really, really cold"* (P3). This did not affect social relations in the office and both participants mentioned the negotiations around thermal comfort in the office were almost always agreeable:

"I'm sitting there watching them and layers come off and then the fan goes on and the window goes open. And it is generally warm. The other faction are permanently walking around with neck scarves and jackets on, so they make it fairly... [obvious]" (P3)

These findings highlights that the agreeable and polite negotiations around thermal comfort do not necessarily equate to satisfaction with thermal comfort, nor satisfaction with ways that others achieve their own personal comfort. What also becomes particularly clear in these findings is the variety of ways that social factors in offices can impact thermal comfort and air quality and that access to means of adjusting thermal comfort (i.e. windows, radiators, fans), does not mean they will be used in ways that might be rationally expected.

DISCUSSION: TOWARDS A SMARTER THERMOSTAT

In this paper we have argued that designing for human interactions with smart thermostats is just as important as the accuracy of the thermal comfort model to which they are grounded. Results show that contrary to our expectations that interactions with the system would be largely opportunistic, motivations for interacting were in fact much more complex. People tended to vote only when they were uncomfortable and many interactions in the office deployment took place in the hope that the resultant data might provoke actions by building managers to improve conditions in the building. In this way the system was used as something of a digital complaints box and the lack of neutral or cold votes negated our ability to validate our model on this data.

Given evidence that females are more likely to express dissatisfaction than males in equal thermal conditions [17], it might be tempting to conclude that the gender bias in our interviews is indicative of females' exhibiting a higher thermal sensitivity than males. While we acknowledge the gender bias, we do not wish to speculate here on the possible influence of gender, given: (1) the existing female-weighted gender balance of the offices; (2) the user-feedback system not recording input for the gender of contributors; and (3) the possibility that the females who volunteered for our interview were simply more pro-active in volunteering for the interviews than their male counterparts, rather than being more thermally sensitive.

Overall, participation in the study was characterized by a decline in engagement over the course of the deployment (Figures 4 and 5) with participants reporting being busy or simply forgetting. This finding is consistent with literature on personal informatics and eco-feedback, where engagement with situated systems has also been found to decline over time or transition to less frequent forms [14, 15, 29, 33]. Additionally, we found that polite and amiable negotiations around adjustments of windows, radiators or desk fans did not necessarily equate to satisfaction with thermal comfort. These findings echo those of previous research [28]. These various and bespoke social factors affecting use are not yet well represented in the literature on smart thermostats in shared work environments. We have also demonstrated the limits of assuming humans to be reliable sensors for thermal comfort, willing and able to provide accurate data at regular intervals. In this way we have shown how the falsity of the "Resource Man" stereotype [30] extends from the home to shared work environments.

Our findings suggest that we need to eschew the assumption that humans will act as regular and reliable sensors for thermal comfort. A move is necessary towards design seeking to take advantage of when a person actually wants to interact with a thermostat- or any such technology-rather than expecting people will interact (and continue to interact) with a system out of altruism or obligation. From these findings we have synthesized design considerations towards a *Smarter Thermostat* for shared work environments; one which: (1) Leverages the messy social inevitabilities that we have highlighted in our deployment so they are, by design, equipped to handle changes in user engagement, and; (2) Augments human intelligence through reciprocity and actionable information. We discuss these in turn below.

Leveraging the Digital Complaints Box: Equipped to handle diminishing user engagement

Existing models for participatory sensing of thermal comfort in shared work environments operate either by: (a) learning user input only during an initial training phase; thereby being less adaptable to changes in occupancy [13, 18], or (b) requiring relatively high and sustained levels of human input into the system in order to function [23, 25, 27] which may not be sustainable in the long term. In our study, despite aiming for opportunistic engagement, the average number of votes per user was only 1.44 and 2.93 in the library and office deployments respectively, and overall engagement with the system declined over time.

For this reason, we believe a *Smarter Thermostat* is one which is equipped to handle diminishing user engagement; and which is capable of operating within the constraints of users' tendency to only log their thermal comfort when they are uncomfortable. As such, we envisage a *Smarter Thermostat* utilizing user input to instead determine users' *limits of comfort.* Precisely, the thermostat determines to what extent it can mimic the outdoor temperature before complaints begin to be registered. In the training phase, this would involve the thermostat operating within a purposefully large temperature range and narrowing this range based on users' feedback if and when the environment is uncomfortable.

In this way, the thermostat operates within the largest acceptable range for a given office. Given a key goal of smart thermostats is saving energy [1, 9, 21], the energy saving implications for an HVAC system maintaining the temperature in an office between (for example) 20 and 25°C are far greater than the same system attempting to keep the temperature within a narrower range of 21-22°C as conventional thermostats often attempt to. This in turn encourages human adaptability to fluctuations in temperature [7] and maintains a better connection to outdoor conditions. Encouraging adaptation in this way holds the potential to broaden office occupants' understandings and expectations of comfort beyond ubiquitous mechanical intervention [4]. Pragmatically, a *Smarter Thermostat* is not affected by the likely decline in user engagement over time attributed to other situated interfaces [14, 15, 29, 33], but it still provides users with the ability to log their thermal (dis)comfort, should they become dissatisfied with it. This simply means maintaining an interface for human input as we did throughout our deployments, such that the system may continue to respond to changes in occupancy, such as employee turn-over or visitors with different thermal comfort preferences.

Augmenting human intelligence: Ensuring smarter thermostats = smarter humans

A common feature of smart thermostat design is their ability to learn occupants' temperature preferences and then autonomously provide user-optimal temperatures with minimal further input [18, 27, 32]; gradually reducing the need for users to interact with the system. However we are not convinced such a rationale for design is necessarily in the best interests of users. We share an unease expressed by Rogers [24] with the tendency of "smart" technology to take responsibility away from humans; reducing the need for them to think for themselves or engage with the issue at hand. We argue that such a rationale runs the risk of creating users who are less adaptable to changes in temperature [7] and less engaged with the smart technology designed to support them.

Indeed, although engagement in our system was variable, we found ample evidence that the quality of the indoor environment was of keen interest to many of our participants. Two had brought thermometers in from home to measure the temperature, four had engaged directly with Estates and Facilities and six of the 14 participants noted how they would have liked a quantification for how stuffy it was in the office. Thus we see it as important that smart technology aims to foster this engagement [24]

We argue a *Smarter Thermostat* is one which aims to augment intelligence, not absolve responsibility. Rather than users entering data into a black box which is supposed to improve their thermal comfort- as is currently the case- we draw from Mathur [19] and suggest a *Smarter Thermostat* could reciprocate user input, by offering users information they can act upon themselves. An example of what this could look like in practice is Figures 3A and 3B in our findings, where we have provided a thermal-map from both the office and library deployment. Users would be able to use such maps to choose (or even be recommended) warmer, cooler, fresher, i.e. more personally suitable locations to work in a library or open-plan office. Such a system supports the various personal preferences of users that we identified (i.e. preferences for cool or warmth) and how these preferences may change over time, for example new arrivals to a country becoming acclimatized, or due to personal circumstances such as menopause (P12), pregnancy (P10) or other health conditions (P14).

Yet we have demonstrated that maintaining thermal comfort in the workplace is not an isolated personal adjustment. It is a negotiated, social activity. Smarter Thermostats incorporating a form of situated display as we have advocated above, allows reflection on how individual and group actions impact upon others. For example being able to see how the opening of a certain window causes a cold spot over an adjacent colleague. We envisage Smarter Thermostats contributing to shared understandings of thermal cause-and-effect within offices; contributing to comfort being managed and negotiated as a team, rather than only by individuals taking individual actions, as is currently the case. We echo Chappels and Shove's call to promote debate around definitions of comfort itself, rather than concentrating only on how to maintain a narrow comfort range more efficiently [4]. Thermostat design of the nature we describe here may be a starting point for this.

Beyond the office, there is the potential to augment the intelligence of external parties such as building managers or health and safety officers. This is important given the propensity for these parties to act at times as "gate keepers" for ceiling vents, heating boilers or external windows [28]. Providing these groups with more granular and immediate information on conditions within different offices allow for a quicker response time to open vents or adjust settings if conditions become sub-optimal. This type of information could also provide useful feedback on the thermal performance of recent retrofits, space planning, or identifying malfunctions in HVAC performance.

Considerations for future work

Finally, we briefly outline privacy as a concern for future work in this space. Although privacy was not a primary focus in our interviews, we anticipate that privacy concerns have the potential affect the use of smart thermostats in shared work environments. Our interview findings suggest an inclination for users to put up with a considerable level of thermal discomfort rather than speak up, so as not to cause a fuss. Thus despite many potential benefits of thermal visualizations as we have described above, we do not believe that users' votes should feature in this information. Even if displayed in an aggregated form (for example thermal maps based on user votes rather than ambient temperature), this may still affect use. As an example, aggregated data can easily become attributable if surrounding colleagues are absent. Certain people may elect not to vote in order to maintain the status quo, in precisely the same way that some participants did not vocalize their opinions in our study. Further research is warranted into how a *Smarter Thermostat* might best reciprocate user participation without affecting their inclination to participate in the first place.

CONCLUSIONS

Considering the performance of smart thermostats in shared work environments is contingent upon human input into the system, it is surprising the current deficit in human-centred approaches to design. The research described above represents a contribution to the literature to address this gap, in offering a tested, novel means of gathering thermal comfort information from users in shared work environments. Based on our results, we have argued that the design of the human interaction with smart thermostats is just as important as the accuracy of the thermal comfort model to which it is grounded. Towards this, we outlined two key considerations for the design of a *Smarter Thermostat* concerned with; (1) coping with the messy reality of user engagement; and (2) augmenting human intelligence rather than absolving responsibility.

This work offers several contributions to the literature on smart thermostats in shared work environments:

First, using a bottom-up approach to understanding thermal comfort, our findings demonstrate a multitude of individual, social and contextual factors affecting the use of participatory sensing systems. These include use of the system being influenced by discomfort, pre-existing relationships with building managers and a novelty affect with usage over time. These aren't yet well accounted for in the existing literature on smart thermostats in shared work environments.

Second, we highlight the limits of relying on users as reliable and autonomous sensors. Our findings foreground the need for smart thermostats to be capable of providing thermal comfort and energy efficiency within the realistic constraints of the type and frequency of human data they are likely to receive.

Third, we have highlighted the possibility and value of reciprocity in smart technology; opportunities for smart systems to augment human intelligence- rather than absolve responsibility- by providing users with actionable information. The value of such information may extend beyond individual users to foster a more shared understanding of comfort in offices and the creation of thermal datasets for use by building managers, energy auditors and potentially policymakers. Yet further research is warranted into users' expectations and preferences for privacy disclosure.

Although much further work is necessary, we anticipate this rationale for smart thermostats has relevance to the design of smart systems more generally. Namely, that any smart technology might benefit from design which equips it to deal with changes in use that arise from the messy nature of everyday life; and that might enable a more empowering experience by reciprocating its user input with useful information.

ACKNOWLEDGMENTS

This work is funded by the Engineering and Physical Sciences Research Council, UK, under the Challenging Engineering scheme. The ReFresh Project: Remodeling Building Design and Sustainability from a Human Centered Perspective (grant number EP/K021907/1). The Joulo temperature loggers were developed with the assistance of: University of Southampton Carbon Management Plan project - 'CMP165 - Joulo Temperature & Light Logging and Analysis of Offices and Laboratories' - awarded to Prof. Alex Rogers and Dr. Reuben Wilcock.

REFERENCES

1. Alan, A. T., Shann, M., Costanza, E., Ramchurn, S. D., & Seuken, S. 2016. It is too Hot: An In-Situ Study of Three Designs for Heating. In *Proceedings of the 2016 CHI Conference on Human Factors in Computing Systems*, pp. 5262-5273. ACM.
2. ASHRAE 55, 2010. Thermal Environmental Conditions for Human Occupancy (ANSI Approved), 2010.
3. Auffenberg, F., Stein, S., Rogers, A. 2015 A personalised thermal comfort model using a Bayesian network, *Proceedings of the 24th International Conference on Artificial Intelligence*, p.2547-2553, July 25-31, 2015, Buenos Aires, Argentina.
4. Chappells, H., & Shove, E. 2005. Debating the future of comfort: environmental sustainability, energy consumption and the indoor environment. *Building Research & Information*, 33(1), 32-40.
5. Chin, J. 2015. Design and implementation of an adaptive wearable thermal comfort data acquisition prototype. In Adjunct *Proceedings of the 2015 ACM International Joint Conference on Pervasive and Ubiquitous Computing and Proceedings of the 2015 ACM International Symposium on Wearable Computers* (pp. 585-590). ACM.
6. Clear, A., Friday, A., Hazas, M., & Lord, C. 2014. Catch my drift?: Achieving comfort more sustainably in conventionally heated buildings. In *Proceedings of the 2014 conference on Designing Interactive Systems (DIS),* pp. 1015-1024. ACM.
7. de Dear, R.J., and Brager, G.S. 1998. Developing an adaptive model of thermal comfort and preference. In *ASHRAE Transactions*, volume 104, pp. 145–167. ASHRAE.
8. Department of Industry, Innovation and Science. (2016) Heating, Ventilation and Air Conditioning High Efficiency Systems Strategy. Available at: http://industry.gov.au/Energy/EnergyEfficiency/Non-residentialBuildings/HVAC/FactSheets/Documents/HVACFSEnergyBreakdown.pdf. Accessed: 18/9/16
9. EPA. Summary of research: Findings from the programmable thermostat market. Washington, DC: 2004.
10. Erickson, V.L. and Cerpa, A.E. 2012. Thermovote: Participatory sensing for efficient building HVAC conditioning. In *Proceedings of the Fourth ACM Workshop on Embedded Sensing Systems for Energy-Efficiency in Buildings*, pp. 9–16.
11. Fanger, P.O. 1970 Thermal comfort. Analysis and applications in environmental engineering. In *Thermal comfort. Analysis and applications in environmental engineering*, pp.244.
12. Feldmeier, M., & Paradiso, J. A. 2010. Personalized HVAC control system. In *Internet of Things (IOT), 2010*, pp. 1-8. IEEE.
13. Ghahramani, A., Jazizadeh, F., & Becerik-Gerber, B. 2014. A knowledge based approach for selecting energy-aware and comfort-driven HVAC temperature set points. *Energy and Buildings*, 85, pp.536–548.
14. Gulotta, R., Forlizzi, J., Yang, R., & Newman, M. W. 2016. Fostering Engagement with Personal Informatics Systems. In *Proceedings of the 2016 ACM Conference on Designing Interactive Systems (DIS)* (pp. 286-300). ACM.
15. Hargreaves, T., Nye, M., Burgess, J. 2013. Keeping energy visible? Exploring how householders interact with feedback from smart energy monitors in the longer term. *Energy Policy* 52, pp. 126-134.
16. Huang, C.C., Yang, R., Newman, W.W. 2015. The potential and challenges of inferring thermal comfort at home using commodity sensors. In *Proceedings of UbiComp '15*. ACM, pp.1089-1100.
17. Karjalainen, S. 2012. Thermal comfort and gender: a literature review. *Indoor air*, 22(2), 96-109.
18. Lam, A.H., Yuan, Y., and Wang, D. 2014. An Occupant-participatory approach for thermal comfort enhancement and energy conservation in buildings: Categories and subject descriptors. In *Proceedings of the fifth International Conference on Future Energy Systems (ICFS)*, pp. 133–143.
19. Mathur, A., Broeck, M. Van Den, Vanderhulst, G., Mashhadi, A., Kawsar, F., & Laboratories, B. 2015. Tiny habits in the giant enterprise : Understanding the dynamics of a quantified workplace. *Proceedings of the ACM International Joint Conference on Pervasive and Ubiquitous Computing (UbiComp '15)*, pp.577–588.
20. Mathur, A., Broeck, M. V. D., Vanderhulst, G., Mashhadi, A., & Kawsar, F. 2015. Quantified workplace: Opportunities and challenges. In *Proceedings of the 2nd workshop on Workshop on Physical Analytics*, pp. 37-41. ACM.
21. Panagopoulos, A. A., Alam, M., Rogers, A., & Jennings, N. R. 2015. AdaHeat: A General Adaptive Intelligent Agent for Domestic Heating Control. In *Proceedings of the 2015 International Conference on Autonomous Agents and Multiagent Systems* (pp. 1295-1303)
22. Pisharoty, D., Yang, R., Newman, M. W., & Whitehouse, K. 2015. Thermocoach: Reducing home energy consumption with personalized thermostat recommendations. In *Proceedings of the 2nd ACM International Conference on Embedded Systems for Energy-Efficient Built Environments*, pp. 201-210. ACM.

23. Purdon, S., Kusy, B., Jurdak, R., & Challen, G. 2013. Model-free HVAC control using occupant feedback. In *Proceedings - Conference on Local Computer Networks, LCN*, pp. 84–92.
24. Rogers, Y. 2006. Moving on from weiser's vision of calm computing: engaging ubicomp experiences. In *Proceedings of the 8th international conference on Ubiquitous Computing (UbiComp'06),* Paul Dourish and Springer-Verlag, Berlin, Heidelberg, pp.404-421.
25. Sarkar, C., Nambi, A. U., & Prasad, R. V. 2016. iLTC: Achieving Individual Comfort in Shared Spaces. In *International Conference on Embedded Wireless Systems and Networks* (EWSN 2016), pp. 65–76.
26. Shann, M., and Seuken, S. 2013. An Active Learning Approach to Home Heating in the Smart Grid. In *Proceedings of the Twenty-Third International Joint Conference on Artificial Intelligence (IJCAI '13).* AAAI Press, pp. 2892–2899
27. Shetty, S. S., Chinh, H. D., & Panda, S. K. 2015. Strategies for Thermal Comfort Improvement and Energy Savings in existing Office Buildings using Occupant Feedback. In *2015 IEEE International Conference on Building Efficiency and Sustainable Technologies*, pp. 23–27.
28. Snow, S., Soska, A., Chatterjee, S. K., schraefel, m.c. 2016. Keep calm and carry on: Exploring the social determinants of indoor environment quality. In Proceedings of the *2016 CHI Conference Extended Abstracts on Human Factors in Computing Systems*, pp. 1476-1482.
29. Snow S., Buys L., Roe P., Brereton, M. 2013. Curiosity to cupboard: self-reported disengagement with energy use feedback over time. In: *Proceedings of the Australian Conference on Human-Computer Interaction (OzCHI 2013).* ACM, pp. 245–254
30. Strengers, Y. 2014. Smart energy in everyday life: Are you designing for resource man? *Interactions* 21.4 pp. 24-31.
31. Strengers, Y. 2013. Smart energy technologies in everyday life: Smart Utopia? Springer.
32. Yang, R and Newman, M. W. 2013. Learning from a learning thermostat: Lessons for intelligent systems for the home. *Proceedings of the 2013 ACM international joint conference on Pervasive and Ubiquitous Computing (UbiComp '13)*, pp. 93–102.
33. Yang, R., Newman, M. W., & Forlizzi, J. 2014. Making sustainability sustainable: challenges in the design of eco-interaction technologies. In *Proceedings of the SIGCHI Conference on Human Factors in Computing Systems*, ACM pp. 823-832.

Community-Empowered Air Quality Monitoring System

Yen-Chia Hsu, Paul Dille, Jennifer Cross, Beatrice Dias, Randy Sargent, Illah Nourbakhsh
The Robotics Institute, Carnegie Mellon University, Pittsburgh, U.S.A.
{yenchiah, pdille, jcross1, mdias, rsargent, illah}@andrew.cmu.edu

ABSTRACT

Developing information technology to democratize scientific knowledge and support citizen empowerment is a challenging task. In our case, a local community suffered from air pollution caused by industrial activity. The residents lacked the technological fluency to gather and curate diverse scientific data to advocate for regulatory change. We collaborated with the community in developing an air quality monitoring system which integrated heterogeneous data over a large spatial and temporal scale. The system afforded strong scientific evidence by using animated smoke images, air quality data, crowd-sourced smell reports, and wind data. In our evaluation, we report patterns of sharing smoke images among stakeholders. Our survey study shows that the scientific knowledge provided by the system encourages agonistic discussions with regulators, empowers the community to support policy making, and rebalances the power relationship between stakeholders.

ACM Classification Keywords

H.5.m. Information Interfaces and Presentation (e.g. HCI): Miscellaneous

Author Keywords

Citizen science; sustainable HCI; adversarial design; participatory design; community engagement; data visualization; air quality

INTRODUCTION

Air pollution is a critical environmental issue for people who live near industrial sites. To address this problem, it takes communities a great effort to gather scientific evidence at a large spatial and temporal scale, which requires the assistance of information technology in collecting, curating, and visualizing various types of data. In our case, 70,000 residents near Pittsburgh suffer from air pollution caused by a coke (fuel) plant. Under some unusual situations, the coke plant leaks hazardous smoke irregularly, known as fugitive emissions (see Figure 1), into the atmosphere. The resulting toxic emissions with fine particulates pose risks to health and have negative impacts to living quality [26, 46].

CHI 2017, May 6-11, 2017, Denver, CO, USA.
 ISBN 978-1-4503-4655-9/17/05 ...$15.00.
http://dx.doi.org/10.1145/3025453.3025853

Figure 1. This figure shows different types of fugitive emissions.

To address air pollution, residents formed the ACCAN (Allegheny County Clean Air Now) group. In several community meetings, residents mentioned that adults and children developed respiratory problems because of exposure to coke oven gas. In addition, residents must close windows at night because of irritating burning smells. They also said that the air quality was so poor that they could not exercise outside. To pursue environmental justice, the community took a series of actions, such as gathering evidence of violations and filing petitions to the government. They envisioned that these actions could raise public awareness about air quality issues and pressure the government to deal with air pollution problems.

To advocate for themselves in improving the local air quality, the community needed to gather convincing evidence in communicating with stakeholders. Traditionally, the community collected scientific data manually, which was time-consuming, error-prone, and offered limited scientific validity. The community lacked technological fluency and required the assistance of experts in setting up an automatic system to collect and archive data from various sources. Starting in January 2015, we aided the community to set up outdoor air quality sensors and live cameras pointed at the coke oven where smoke usually occurred. We also created an electronic process for capturing smell reports. To visualize hybrid data (sensor readings, smell reports, real-time high resolution imagery, and wind information), we developed a web-based air quality monitoring system. Community members could use the system to manually search for smoke in timelapse videos and use a thumbnail generator to create animated images. But searching and documenting all smoke emissions required manpower and took an impractical investment of time. Therefore, we implemented a computer vision tool to detect smoke and produce

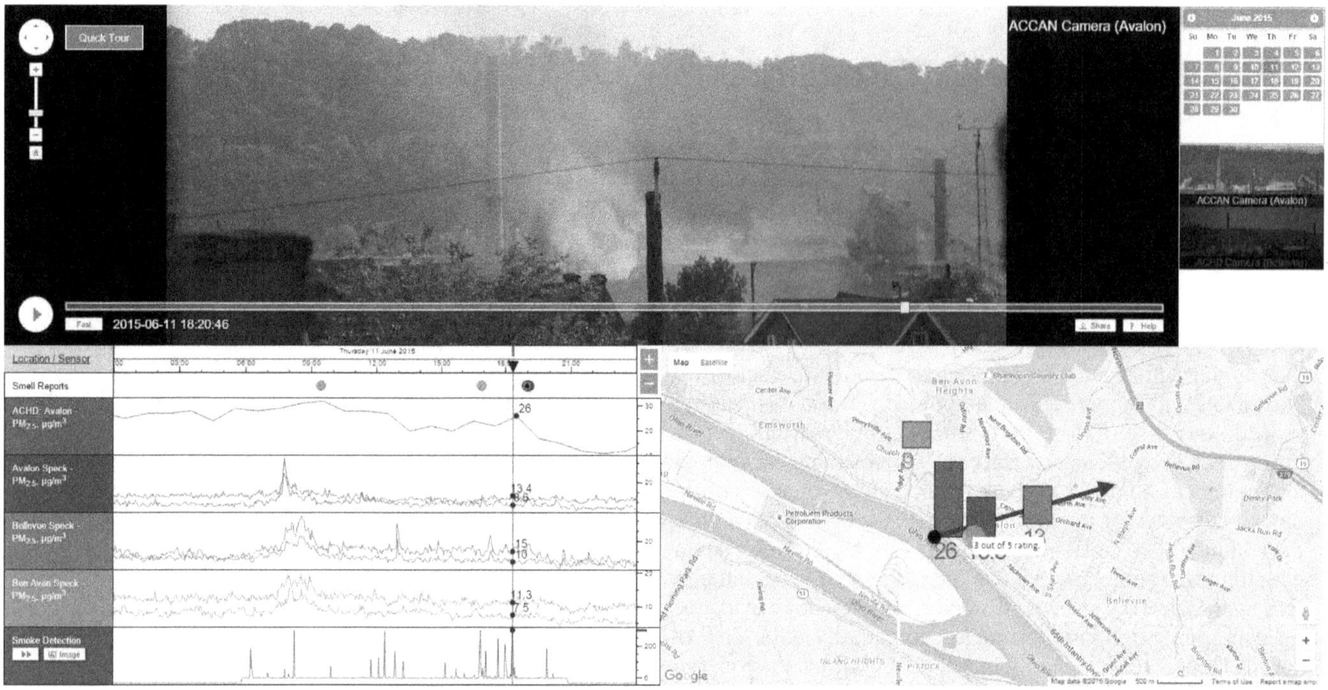

Figure 2. The user interface of the web-based air quality monitoring system. The top-left part is a zoomable and pannable viewer which shows the timelapse video. The bottom-left charts visualize crowdsourced smell reports, PM2.5 sensor readings, and automatic smoke detection results. The blue line shows readings from the sensor operated by the local health department. The purple, green, and orange lines shows readings from six sensors that we deployed in the community. The bottom-right map indicates wind speed (length of the blue arrow), wind direction (orientation of the blue arrow), and sensor locations (bar charts). The colors and heights of bar charts on the map correspond to the colors and readings on the line charts respectively.

corresponding animated images (see Figure 4), which could then be curated in online documents and shared on social media. With the monitoring system, community members could tell stories with concrete scientific evidence about what happened (using animated smoke images) and how these events affected the local neighborhood (using sensor readings, smell reports, and wind information).

To evaluate community engagement, we analyzed the server logs, which store HTTP requests of thumbnails from August 2015 to July 2016. In addition, we conducted a survey study with the research question: does interacting with the air quality monitoring system increase community engagement in addressing air pollution concerns? We anticipated that the intervention of the system increases awareness, self-efficacy [1, 7], and sense of community [40], which are the three dependent variables in our survey study. Awareness means participants know a problem exists and has impact on daily lives. Self-efficacy means the strength of participants' belief in their ability to successfully reach the community's goal. Sense of community means participants feel they have influence in the community and a sense of belonging. We form three corresponding hypotheses: interacting with the system improves the ability to perceive air quality problems, strengthens the belief that the ACCAN community can reach its goal of improving air quality, and makes people think that they are influential and fit in the community. The independent variables are involvement, age range, and education level. Involvement is the level of participation, such as exploring, documenting, and sharing data from the system.

In this paper, we explore the formation and use of scientific knowledge in citizen empowerment via the intervention of information technology. Our design principle is to stimulate critical discussions and confront the current unbalanced power relation between stakeholders. We begin by explaining the research scope and reviewing similar projects. Then, we describe the design process and the implemented web-based air quality monitoring system. In addition, we discuss the results of smoke image usage from server logs and survey study. Finally, we provide insights in developing systems to empower data-driven community action and conclude with limitations. Our contributions are:

- Detailed documentation of a worked example which used scientific data from heterogeneous sources to critically reveal, question, and challenge environmental conditions.
- Analysis of community behavior changes after the intervention of information technology and participatory design.
- Analysis of how the community uses smoke images over a long-term participation period (12 months).
- Insights for researchers to develop environmental monitoring systems that combine politics, community, and information technology.

RELATED WORK

Citizen science [24, 10] and sustainable human-computer interaction [14, 18, 6, 2, 38] are growing trends in addressing community concerns around local specific problems, such as air pollution. The core idea is to empower amateurs and professionals to produce scientific knowledge through public engagement [50, 39], which is different from conventional communication methods, such as newsletters or public hearings. Scientific knowledge can contribute to the well-being of communities and has two major values: science education [10, 41, 52, 4, 11], which increases public understanding of science by spreading knowledge among common people, and participatory democracy [24, 20, 61, 55, 25], which promotes the idea that citizens can participate in policy-making using scientific evidence. Our work focuses on the latter.

Citizen science has various participation levels [3, 60, 21, 51]. They include defining problems, developing plans, providing data, analyzing data, and making decisions. Consider participation along a spectrum from citizens as tools to citizens as scientists. At one end, scientists treat volunteers as tools that provide or interpret data, which is also called crowdsourcing. One typical example is Galaxy Zoo [37], where participants classify a large amount of galaxies online. At the other end, scientists treat volunteers as collaborators over the entire project life cycle. Our work takes the concept of citizens as scientists, where volunteers and scientists establish a strong partnership through collaboration and engagement.

Citizen science can be led by a central organization, multiple stakeholders, or a community. These correspond to three governance structures respectively: top-down, multi-party, and bottom-up [9]. One example of the top-down approach is The Neighborhood Networks Project [17, 16], a participatory design practice which uses sensing technology to engage residents in collecting environmental data and making critical discussions about local environmental issues. The project is led by researchers from an academic institution with pre-designed public engagement procedures. In contrast, we collaborated with the community via the bottom-up approach, where communities themselves initiate, organize, and lead grassroots movements about local specific issues. An example of the bottom-up approach is the Bucket Brigade project [42], which provides a low-cost device for citizens to measure their local air quality. During our collaboration with the community, besides applying the concept of citizens as scientists, which asks what common people can do for professional scientists, we emphasize the importance of scientists as citizens [24, 61, 55, 21], which asks what professional scientists can do for common people. Our work explores how scientists can engage in social and ethical issues that are promulgated by citizens.

Modern citizen science projects gain scientific knowledge at a large spatial and temporal scale. This requires the investment of information technology to collect, curate, and visualize data from heterogeneous sources, such as video, sensors, and crowds [4, 44]. Developing interactive computational tools to improve technological fluency among citizen scientists and to foster communication for participatory democracy is an ongoing challenge [5, 39]. This research focuses on empowering local communities in pursuing environmental justice collaboratively through the intervention of information technology, which falls into the field of designing computational tools to support democratizing scientific knowledge. The largest limitation in prior work is that they often focus on either video, sensor, or crowdsourced data. However, in our context, communities need to interpret the cause and effect of emissions from an identified pollution source. This requires collecting, curating, visualizing, comparing, and making sense of hybrid scientific data, which include live imagery, sensor readings, image recognition results, smell reports, wind direction, and wind speed. We are unaware of the existence of systems that can tackle the complexity of data required for this task.

Understanding Video Data Using Crowdsourcing

There are tools which focus on understanding video data using crowdsourcing. SynTag [23] is a real-time collaborative tagging system for labeling presentation videos. Audiences can tag "good", "question", or "disagree" during or after the presentation. These tags are shown on a line chart, which provides indices for video segments. Glance [35] is a video coding tool which asks crowdworkers on Mechanical Turk to label small clips in parallel. Without searching the entire video, users can use the aggregated crowdsourcing labels to quickly identify events. Further extending this concept, Zensors [34] is an image recognition tool using cameras on mobile devices, which combines crowdsourcing and computer vision to answer user defined questions. Initially, answers are provided by workers on Mechanical Turk. The tool then uses these answers as labels to train a computer vision classifier, which takes the image recognition task when its accuracy reaches a threshold for a certain period. These tools provide us with the concept that using other data sources to index archived videos can help users in making sense of video content efficiently.

Gathering and Managing Sensor Data

Other work focuses on gathering and managing sensor data. Kuznetsov et al. in 2011 [30] developed a monitoring system which involves low-cost air quality sensors and web-based visualizations. In 2013, Kuznetsov et al. [31] designed a bio-electronic soil sensor to detect bacterial activities and visualized the data by using LED matrices and an LCD screen on a wooden enclosure. Kuznetsov et al. in 2014 [32] presented a low-tech and low-cost paper sensor for collecting particulate pollution in the air. Kim et al. [28] described an indoor air quality monitoring system in domestic environments. Tian et al. [59] implemented a low-cost wearable sensor to measure airborne particles and a mobile application for visualizing the air quality data. These works emphasize studying the impact after deploying sensors on multiple communities by analyzing changes of user behaviors and ways that users interact with technology. User studies show that sensing technology with well-crafted visualizations can engage local communities to participate in political activism using concrete scientific evidence.

Collecting and Curating Crowdsourced Data

Several works focus on collecting and curating crowdsourced data. Creek Watch [29] is a monitoring system which enables collecting water flow and trash data in creeks via cameras on mobile devices. EOL (Encyclopedia of Life) [48] is a platform for curating biological content. Participants can comment and make "trust," "untrust," or "hide" decision on data. Content providers can then improve the data based on the collaborative feedback. Sensr [27] is a framework for creating data collection and management applications on mobile devices without programming skills. Project managers can use the tool to create a campaign website around a specific issue, such as air quality, and community members can report data, such as images, via a mobile application. eBird [56, 57] is a crowdsourcing tool for birdwatchers, scientists, and policy makers to collect, store, visualize, and analyze bird data. These works demonstrate that, beyond collecting data, it is important to understand what data stakeholders need, how to make data useful, and how to effectively deliver data. They consider tools as an integrated system, which supports different levels of participation, rather than individual and separate components.

DESIGN PROCESS AND CHALLENGES

Our main goal is to use information and communication technology to democratize scientific knowledge by empowering citizens to collect and interpret data as evidence in taking political action. This falls in the context of design for democracy [12], which has in general two opposing approaches: consensus and agonism. The design principle of consensus is to support structured deliberation. One project that uses the consensus approach is eBird [56, 57], which is a tool for birdwatchers, scientists, and policy makers to collect, visualize, and analyze bird data collaboratively. Another example is the Community Resource Messenger [36], which applies ubiquitous computing at a shelter for homeless mothers to facilitate the communication between staff and residents. In contrast, our design principle is adversarial design [13], which is based on agonism [43]. Adversarial design promotes critical political discussions and challenges the current unbalanced power structure between citizens, governments, and businesses. One project that uses adversarial design is Feral Robot [33], which is a low-cost mobile sensor for grassroots communities to collect, map, and present chemical pollution data in a local park. Our design purpose is not to support the mechanism and procedure of governance, but to improve the condition of society. The information technology is not used to solve the environmental problem, but to provide technology affordance [19] for seeking and revealing the condition (form, function, economy, and time [45]) of the problem.

We began by participating in monthly community meetings to understand the context of air pollution issues. The community was taking a series of actions, such as reporting industrial smells and filing petitions to the local health department and the EPA (Environmental Protection Agency). Our roles were as supporters, which use information technology to assist the citizen-led grassroots movement around local air quality issues, and as researchers, which study the effect of the technological intervention.

The successfulness of the intervention of information technology is highly dependent on community engagement [54], the involvement of citizens in local neighborhoods. During initial discussions with the community, we found that the most significant gap in community engagement is the lack of scientific evidence. For instance, it was difficult for residents to report the exact time when an air quality violation occurred and its environmental impact to government regulators. Therefore, we proposed building an air quality monitoring system, which could afford exploring, archiving, presenting, and sharing scientific evidence among stakeholders.

The problem that the community dealt with is in nature wicked [47, 8]. One characteristic of a wicked problem is that it cannot be fully observed, which means that solving a subset of a wicked problem reveals new ones. Based on this idea, we argue that our work requires an iterative design approach to handle and solve design challenges step by step. Thus, we adopt the community-based participatory design approach [15]. It is iterative in the sense that citizens and developers explore design options collaboratively.

We collaborated closely with the community and implemented system features based on iterative feedback from community members. There were two major design challenges in setting up the monitoring system. First, the community did not have sufficient technological fluency. Our system had to curate and visualize data in a way that users could easily perceive and document the seriousness of smoke emissions and their impacts to local neighborhoods. Second, this work had a timing issue, where residents had to form and use strong scientific evidence to convince regulators on a planned community meeting with the local health department and the EPA. These challenges served as constraints that affected our design decisions.

SYSTEM

We now explain system components together with three design iterations, which naturally emerged during the design process. The number of iterations depends on the complexity of the wicked problem [47, 8] that the community tackles. Each iteration contained system features which were implemented based on the challenges revealed iteratively.

First Iteration:

Interactive Web-based Timelapse Viewer

Starting in January 2015, we installed a live camera which was oriented towards the coke plant from a volunteer home. The live camera takes a high quality image every 5 seconds for a total of 17,000 each day. We streamed the time-series imagery to our servers and used an open source tool developed by Sargent et al. [49] to process these images into multi-resolution video tiles. The tool was implemented in JavaScript/HTML and provided an **interactive web-based timelapse viewer** (top-left part of Figure 2) where users could search for fugitive emissions by panning, zooming, and playing the video. The viewer loaded and showed the video tile corresponding to the zoom and pan level. Users could share a particular view or use the thumbnail tool to generate sharable animated images (see Figure 3). After we developed the web-based viewer, community members were excited and shared screenshots with each other via emails. At that time, the community pointed out two major challenges. Static images such as screenshots could not represent the dynamics and persistent time quality of smoke

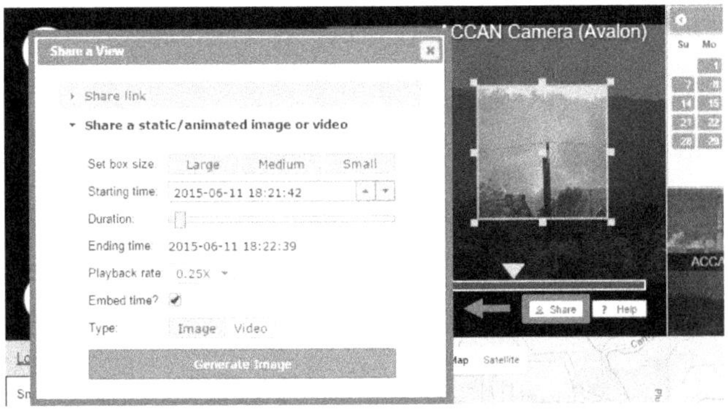

Figure 3. Clicking the share button on the timelapse viewer on the main user interface (see Figure 2) shows the thumbnail tool, which is used for generating sharable animated images. Users can edit the image size by resizing the green box on the viewer. The dialog window provides adjustable parameters, such as starting time and duration of the animated image.

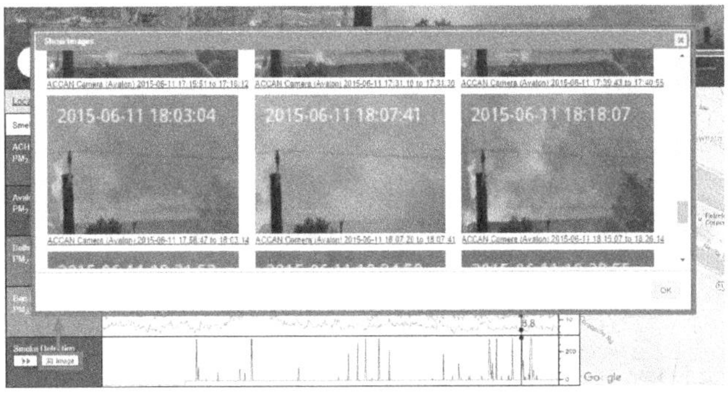

Figure 4. Clicking the image button on the line charts on the main user interface (see Figure 2) shows web links and animated images produced by the smoke detection algorithm. Users can quickly select representative images and insert them into an online document. Users can also click on a peak of a spike on the line chart to seek to a video frame with fugitive emissions.

emissions. In addition, although smoke images indicated the source of air pollution, they did not show the impacts to local air quality. These challenges led to the next design iteration.

Second Iteration:

Thumbnail Generator and Sensor Data Visualization

To address the emergent challenges, we implemented a **thumbnail generator**, which allowed community members to create and document animated smoke images as visual evidence. We also visualized $PM_{2.5}$ (particle pollution) data from a sensor station operated by the local health department. In addition, we visualized smell reports which were collected via a Google Form, only available to community members. In the form, we asked community members to rate the severity of the pollution odors from 1 to 5, with 5 being the worst. The form was disseminated to the community via a Google Groups email and phone calls. The **visualization of air quality data and smell reports** showed how smoke emissions affected the living quality of the community. With these new features, residents could compare smoke images together with sensor and crowdsourced data to identify correlations. We recorded a tutorial video and taught residents how to use these features during community meetings. The community was using the tool to find, generate, and share animated smoke images. However, searching smoke emissions manually from a large amount of time-series imagery was laborious and time-consuming. Moreover, the government-operated sensor station reported data only once per hour, which had difficulties in identifying air quality changes over a shorter time period. Furthermore, the lack of visualized wind data and sensor locations hindered the ability to determine how pollutants affected the air quality hyperlocally. These challenges again led to another design iteration.

Third Iteration:

Citizen Sensors, Computer Vision Tool, and Map Visualization

To account for the challenges from the previous iteration, we deployed **six commercial air quality sensors** [53, 58] in local areas with finer time resolutions. These sensors reported $PM_{2.5}$ data to our server via wireless Internet once per minute. The location of sensors and the Internet services were provided by community volunteers. Furthermore, we developed a **computer vision tool** based on an existing smoke detection algorithm [22] for finding fugitive emissions automatically. The algorithm identified the number of smoke pixels for each video frame at daytime (bottom chart in Figure 4) and automatically produced corresponding sharable animated images (see Figure 4). We also added a **map visualization** for showing wind direction, wind strength, and sensor locations (bottom-right part of Figure 2). All sensor data and smoke detection results were plotted on multiple charts (bottom-left part of Figure 2). Users could use the charts as indicators for finding unusual events such as fugitive emissions. Clicking on a smell report or a peak of a spike on the chart jumped the video to the corresponding time. Users could also click on the image button near the smoke detection chart to bring up a dialog box with animated smoke images, which could be shared via social media or archived into a Google Doc.

The final design enabled community members to fully explore and compare data from heterogeneous sources (animated smoke images, finer air quality data, crowdsourced smell reports, and wind information). When residents noticed industrial smells like sulfur, they could use the timelapse viewer to check if the coke plant emitted smoke at a specific time. They could then compare sensor readings, smell reports, and wind data to verify if the emission came from the coke plant and affected the local air quality. With the system, the community could form and share convincing narratives grounded with scientific evidence aggregated from hybrid data.

EVALUATION

Google Analytics evaluation of our website shows that from August 2015 to July 2016 there were 542 unique users, which contributed 1480 sessions. The average session duration was three minutes. We now discuss the image usage study for identifying how community members used animated images. Then we present the results of the survey study.

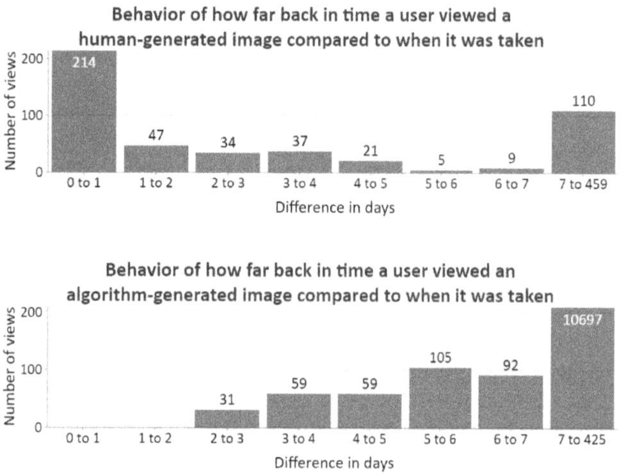

Figure 5. Behavior of how far back in time a user viewed a human-generated or algorithm-generated image compared to when it was taken. The x-axis is the difference in days (denote *D*) between the dates that an image was viewed and taken. Image views with small or large *D* mean they are used for verifying if an event, such as fugitive emissions happened (e.g. fugitive emission) or reviewing previous events respectively. While human-generated images were often viewed in less than one day after events occur, algorithm-generated images were usually viewed at least a week after the events.

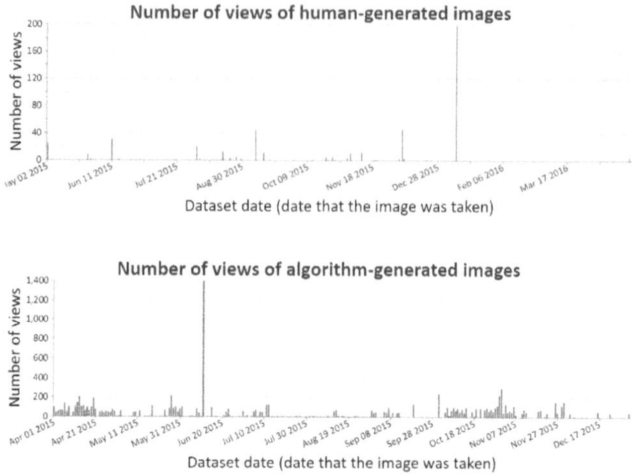

Figure 6. Number of views of human-generated or algorithm-generated images which are aggregated by dataset date. From these two graphs, we can see that the views of algorithm-generated images are more distributed across datasets, which means that users tend to use algorithm-generated images to explore events in different dates.

Image Usage Study

We evaluated the usage patterns of animated smoke images by parsing server logs. The logs stored HTTP requests of images from our server over an 11-month period from August 2015 to July 2016. Each request contained the source IP address, requested date, image URL, and browser type. Each image URL indicated its bounding box, size, time, and dataset. We first excluded all IP addresses from our research institute. Then for each HTTP request, we subtracted the requested date from the image taken date to get *D*, the difference in days, which indicated how far back in time a user viewed an image compared to when the image was taken. Table 1 shows summary statistics of animated images and users. The number of views of algorithm-generated images greatly exceeds the ones of human-generated images. Next we discuss two sub-studies which focus on images and users.

# of unique and viewed HG images	135
# of views of all HG images	477
# of unique and viewed AG images	6745
# of views of all AG images	11043
# of total views	11520
# of users who created HG images	32
# of users who viewed HG images	85
# of users who viewed AG images	75
# of total users	141

Table 1. Summary statistics of animated smoke images and users. The "HG" and "AG" abbreviations mean "human-generated" and "algorithm-generated" respectively. The "#" sign means "number of". We can see that the number of views of algorithm-generated images greatly exceeds the ones of human-generated images.

Image-based Sub-study

For the image-based sub-study, we separated images into two sets: created by human or created by the computer vision tool. Then for each set, we aggregated the number of images, views, viewed datasets, and users based on three criteria: viewing date (date that the image was viewed), dataset date (date that the image was taken), and *D* (difference in days). We now present three interesting findings.

First, while human-generated images were suitable for initiating community engagement, algorithm-generated images were useful for maintaining community engagement. In Figure 5, we aggregated number of views based on *D*, difference in days. The top graph in Figure 5 showed that a large portion of views of human-generated images had small *D*, which indicated a short period between when a user viewed an image and when the image was taken. This suggested that our users tended to create animated images manually by using the thumbnail generator after a recent event (e.g. smoke emission), which showed the purpose of initiating community engagement. However, most of the views of algorithm-generated images had high *D* (see the bottom graph in Figure 5). This showed that community members tended to use images generated automatically by the computer vision tool to review events occurring well beforehand, which demonstrated the objective of maintaining community engagement.

Second, the computer vision tool encouraged community members to explore more datasets. In Figure 6, we aggregated the number of views based on dataset date, the time that the image was taken. The top and bottom graphs in Figure 6 show results for human-generated and algorithm-generated images respectively. By comparing these graphs, the number of views of algorithm-generated images were more distributed across datasets than the ones of human-generated images, which were concentrated on specific days.

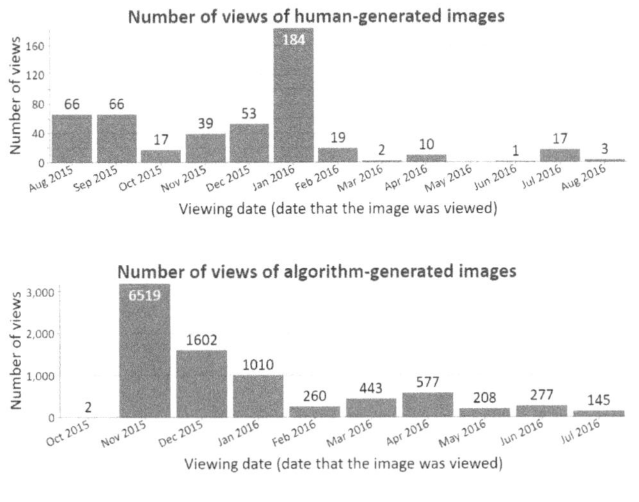

Figure 7. Number of views of human-generated or algorithm-generated images which are aggregated by viewing date. There is a significant decrease after January 2016, which was when the coke plant was closed.

Third, the existence of the coke plant was significant in motivating the community to interact with the monitoring system. In Figure 7, we aggregated the number of views based on viewing date, the time that image was viewed. The figure shows that community members viewed much less human-generated and algorithm-generated images after Jan 2016, which was the time that the coke plant was closed.

User-based Sub-study

For the user-based sub-study, we aggregated the number of images, views, and viewed datasets based on unique IP addresses to obtain a series of vectors. To find relationships, we computed the correlation matrix of five vectors into the number of: created human-generated images, viewed human-generated images, viewed datasets in human-generated images, viewed algorithm-generated images, and viewed datasets in algorithm-generated images. We now summarize two findings.

First, there were strong correlations within the usage of human-generated images. Community members who created more images by using the thumbnail generator also viewed more human-generated images (Pearson's R Correlation = 0.91) and explored more datasets (Pearson's R Correlation = 0.89). Moreover, community members who viewed more human-generated images also explored more datasets (Pearson's R Correlation = 0.8).

Second, it appeared that there was no obvious relationship between the usage of human-generated and algorithm-generated images. Community members who created or viewed more human-generated images did not necessarily view more algorithm-generated images (Pearson's R Correlation = 0.13 and 0.07 respectively). Furthermore, there were no strong correlations within the usage of algorithm-generated images. Community members who viewed more algorithm-generated images did not necessarily explore more datasets (Pearson's R Correlation = 0.35). The rhetorically compelling power of human-generated data should not be underestimated.

	18-24	25-34	35-44	45-54	55-64	64-74	75+	Sum
No degree	0	0	0	0	0	1	0	1
Bachelor	1	1	1	0	2	2	0	7
Master	0	0	2	2	2	3	0	9
Doctor	0	0	0	0	0	0	1	1
Sum	1	1	3	2	4	6	1	18

Table 2. Age and education level for the participants of 18 valid survey responses. Participants have a high education level in general.

Survey Study

We now discuss the survey study for evaluating changes in the community's attitude after the intervention of our system.

Participants

ACCAN members were the primary users of the air quality monitoring system. Adult volunteers (age 18 and older) were recruited from these users through a Google Groups email. The email described the research purpose and included a link to an online survey. Paper surveys were also provided at a community meeting. All responses were kept confidential and there was no compensation. There was a brief consent script to review before taking the survey. We received 24 responses in total from 83 community members on the Google Groups (29% response rate). One invalid response which contained inconsistent answers and five incomplete ones were discarded. Most of the participants had a high education level and were over the age of 35 (see Table 2 for demographics).

Procedure and Materials

Participants filled out a survey. The survey was expected to take less than 30 minutes and contained three question types. The first type measured participants' involvement in the community action, such as exploring, documenting, and sharing data on the system. The second type measured community engagement, which included Likert scale questions related to the dependent variables: awareness, self-efficacy [1, 7], and sense of community [40]. The third type asked demographics, such as age range and education level. The range of the Likert scale was from 1 to 5, with 5 being the highest attitude.

Analysis

In the survey, participants answered three questions about how they explored, documented, or shared data by using the system. These three questions contained 5, 3, and 4 choices respectively. We summed up the number of choices that were selected by participants in each question to obtain participation levels (see Figure 8). We also asked questions about the frequency (from 1 to 5, with 5 being the highest frequency) of browsing the data in the system after noticing bad smells, number of people that a participant discussed the system with, and number of monthly meetings (from 0 to 12) attended in 2015 (see Table. 3).

For a dependent variable, participants answered a question set twice based on the time before (denote S_i^b) and after (denote S_i^a) they learned about the air quality monitoring system. Each question set had two Likert scale questions. We then averaged the Likert scales in set S_i^b and S_i^a to obtain a pair of scores. Figure 9 showed the difference of scores for each dependent variable. Positive values indicated increases, and vice versa.

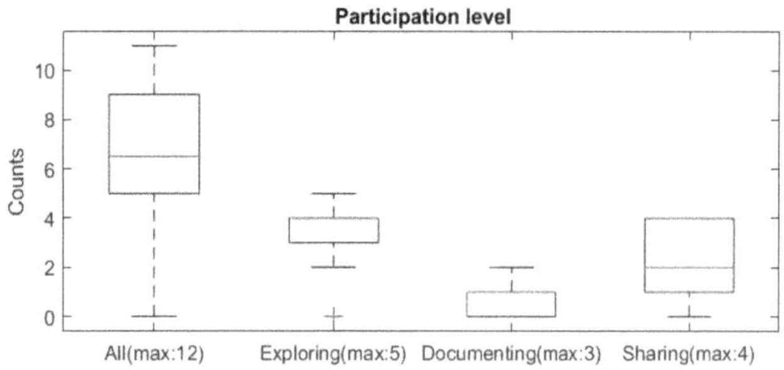

Figure 8. The boxplot of the participation level. We asked three multi-choice questions related to how users explore, document, and share the data provided by the system (the x-axis). These three questions had 5, 3, and 4 choices respectively. We summed up the number of choices that were selected by participants in each question to obtain participation levels (the y-axis). In general, the users had high participation levels.

	Browsing (V_b)		People discussed (V_d)		Meetings (V_m)	
μ | σ	2.94	1.35	22.28	21.85	7.83	3.60

Table 3. The mean (μ) and standard deviation (σ) of other independent variables. V_b is the frequency (from 1 to 5, with 5 being the highest) of browsing the data in the system after noticing bad smells. V_d is the number of people that a participant discussed the system with. V_m is the number of monthly community meetings (from 0 to 12) attended in 2015. In general, participants were active in the community.

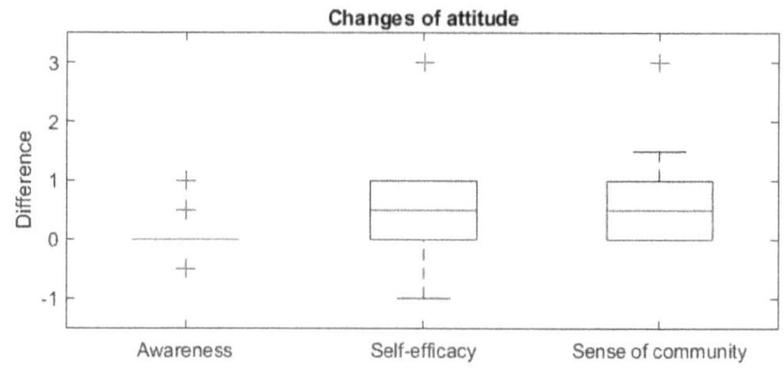

Figure 9. The boxplots of the changes of mental states among all participants after interacting with the monitoring system. The x-axis indicates dependent variables. The y-axis is the differences in Likert scale. Positive values mean increases, and vice versa.

	Awareness	Self-efficacy	Community sense
p-value	0.2500	0.0042	0.0010
CI	0.08±0.15	0.53±0.40	0.56±0.38

Table 4. The p-value of right-tailed Wilcoxon signed-rank test and the confidence interval on the differences of paired samples. CI indicates 95% confidence interval. Gray cells indicate statistical significance ($p < 0.05$) or the confidence interval which does not contain zero.

Our directional null hypotheses were that the community did not have significant increases in awareness, self-efficacy, and sense of community. Since the differences of our paired samples did not follow a normal distribution (see Figure 9), we performed a right-tailed Wilcoxon signed-rank test, a nonparametric version of paired t-test. Table 4 showed the p-values and confidence interval.

Results

According to the analysis (see Table 4), the result favored the alternative hypotheses, which claimed there were significant increases ($p < 0.05$) in self-efficacy and sense of community after interacting with the system. The average increases in these two dependent variables were 0.53 and 0.56 respectively in Likert scale. However, we retained the null hypothesis, which stated there was no significant increase in awareness, since $p > 0.05$ and the confidence interval contained zero.

Open-ended answers in surveys showed that the monitoring system could encourage agonistic discussion with regulators and empower the community in supporting local policy making. With the system, community members could report concrete scientific evidence of fugitive emissions to the local health department, such as animated smoke images and the exact time of emissions, instead of vague reports.

> *"I **made screenshots** of the [system name] dashboard at different times/days when wind was strong and in the direction of my community. I inserted these screenshots into Powerpoint slides. I **shared printed versions of these slides** with my Township commissioner when asking for assistance in reducing emissions."*

> *"I **continually spoke** at regional meetings, City, County, Health Department, Clairton, Lawrenceville, etc. Wrote numerous letters to the editor, most did get published, not all."*

> *"I reported specific emissions from [coke plant name] to ACHD. I was able to **provide specific times** so that ACHD could review the exact episodes that I was reporting."*

> *"I **shared web links** to the [system name] when I submitted complaints to the health department"*

> *"Confronted ACHD staffers repeatedly with **'uncomfortable' info**."*

> *"I **e-mailed images** to others, including regulators."*

Moreover, others mentioned that their confidence in taking action was significantly improved after interacting with the system. One important reason was that integrating heterogeneous data (smoke images, air quality data, smell reports, and wind information) formed strong scientific evidence, which was powerful in communicating with regulators and thus changed the power relationship between citizens and the government.

> *"I felt that the more information/proof that I made available might help justify my concern and spur action. **I felt** that my concerns with what I was experiencing were **grounded in actual imagery, wind data and spatial data.**"*

> *"I **believe** that the [system name] was very important in helping us **get the attention of regulators** (ACHD and EPA) and get them to take our concerns seriously."*

> *"The [system name] was one of the most important tools the community has in holding the plant accountable. I **believe** that images presented at the Nov. 2015 EPA ACHD ACCAN meeting **provided a tipping point for the plant's shutdown.**"*

	μ	σ
The timelapse video	4.81	0.54
Zooming in and out of the video	4.50	0.73
Sharing a web link of a view and time	4.43	0.85
Smell reports	4.38	0.81
Line charts showing sensor readings	4.31	0.87
The map showing sensor values	4.44	0.73
The thumbnail tool	4.19	0.83
The automatic smoke detection tool	4.31	0.70
Smoke images shown on the meeting with EPA	4.94	0.25

Table 5. The mean and standard deviation ($\mu|\sigma$) of the importance rating of features on the air quality monitoring system. In general, participants rated all features important.

> *"**I believe** that the [system name] images shown at the November 2015 community meeting 'tipped the balance' for the EPA and may have resulted directly in the closing of [coke plant name]. In fact, **without those images, it may have taken years to close the plant.**"*

In addition, several community members specifically identified the political and educational values of the monitoring system. In addition, they showed a desire of reproducing the monitoring system on other neighborhoods.

> *"Background as a **environmental law paralegal.**"*

> *"Fantastic **educational** tool."*

> *"I would like to see **similar monitoring of other pollution sites** in Pittsburgh, ie. the [other coke plant name] and others mentioned in the Toxic Ten listing."*

DISCUSSION

The community that we collaborated with has fought for decades to resolve the air pollution problem, which existed since 1999. The monitoring system was launched in Fall 2015. In November 2015, the community held a meeting at their local church with government officials from the ACHD (Allegheny County Health Department) and the EPA. During the meeting, as information technology supporters, we demonstrated the system and the visualization. In addition, the community projected hundreds of animated smoke images generated by the system on a large screen in front of ACHD and EPA regulators. Community members described how their living quality was affected by the air pollution together with animated smoke images, air quality sensors, crowdsourced smell reports, and wind data. The scientific knowlege demonstrated how heavy air pollution flowed into the neighborhood. The community successfully combined personal experiences and scientific evidence into a story to convince regulators. The story showed that the pollution source was the coke plant, and its fugitive emissions acturally affected the local air quality. This forced regulators to respond to the air quality problem publicly. The acting director of the EPA from the Region III Air Protection Division in Philadelphia pointed at the screen and said: *"But what I see in the video, is totally unacceptable."* In addition, the local air quality problem became available for further debate and investigation. The administrator agreed that the EPA would continue to review the coke works' compliance with the 2012 federal consent decree. Furthermore, on December 2015, the parent company of the coke works announced the closure of the plant, which was the ultimate goal that the community had tried to achieve for decades.

Insights

Based on the major community meeting described in the previous paragraph and the results presented in the previous section, we now summarize our findings into three key insights and offer suggestions to future researchers.

Use a Flexible and Iterative Design Process

We encourage using a flexible and iterative procedure instead of a single and prescribed one. This practice is also mentioned by DiSalvo et al. [16] as community co-design, a process which involves community members when designing a system that supports citizen empowerment. Often there are attempts to duplicate successful systems in another similar real-world context. However, this is unlikely to succeed because the environmental problem that the community deals with is wicked [47, 8]. Every wicked problem has no clear formulation, is unique, and cannot be fully observed. Therefore, like the experience we describe in the design process and system sections, we recommend scheduling multiple design phases to reveal unique challenges and to apply specific solutions on these challenges iteratively. In the survey study, participants rate the importance of features of the system (see Table 5). The rating scale is from 0 to 5, with 5 being the most important. The average ratings are all above 4, which verifies that the iterative design process help develop altogether useful system features to the community.

Initiate and Maintain Community Engagement

It is critical to initiate and maintain community engagement via actual participation in using the system. We recommend combining manual and automatic approaches, which are the thumbnail generator and the computer vision tool respectively in this work, to serve two different purposes in citizen participation. First, a manual approach can initiate citizen participation and lead to follow-up interactions. The image usage study shows that community members use the thumbnail generator to manually create images after they notice unusual events (see Figure 5), such as industrial smell or hazardous smoke. Correlation analysis of image usage indicates that users who create more images also view more images and explore more datasets (see the User-based Sub-study subsection). Second, an automatic approach can encourage community members to participate in a long temporal horizon. Smoke images generated automatically by the computer vision tool are used for reviewing fugitive emissions (see Figure 5). The computer vision tool encourages community members to explore more datasets (see Figure 6). However, it appears that there are no clear correlations between the manual and automatic approach (see the User-based Sub-study subsection). How to integrate these two approaches seamlessly to open up and maintain citizen participation remains an important research question.

Enable the Formation of Scientific Knowledge via Hybrid Data

Data requires being interpreted into scientific knowledge to be impactful in changing unbalanced power relations between citizens and governments. Besides collecting data, providing affordance for citizens to make sense of the relationship among various types of data is key to generating scientific knowledge. We suggest integrating image, sensor, and crowdsourced data from both human and machines into such a system. Analysis in the survey study is limited by the small sample size of total users, and this should be taken as a caveat in regards to analysis of statistical significance. Nonetheless, Figure 9 shows the changes of participants' attitudes and Table 4 includes statistical significance findings in self-efficacy and sense of community. Open responses in the survey show that with scientific knowledge, citizens can present data in meaningful ways to regulators who have the power to make policy changes. At the meeting in November 2015, the community successfully influenced the attitude of the government after presenting the evidence. Scientific knowledge gives citizens power to advocate for their living quality and to influence other stakeholders.

Limitation

Measuring information and communication technology (ICT) interventions in community advocacy is generally challenging. Community advocacy has the ultimate goal of policy change, yet it is difficult to causally prove how critical to a successful policy change the communities' actions have been. Such projects succeed not only when policy goals are achieved, but in how the relationship between citizens, policy makers, and businesses evolves. This work shows that making scientific data transparent to stakeholders can foster sustainable relationships among them. It is sustainable in the sense that the system promotes a healthy and balanced power structure for democracy in the long term. We believe patterns of scientific data usage and changes of mental state among community members are useful proxies for evaluating the effectiveness of such projects. To better understand usage patterns, we suggest tracking the usage of data in the system. Future research about how to evaluate ICT interventions is still needed. For instance, qualitative research, like in-depth interviews, will be needed to identify key factors for successful collaboration between stakeholders and to understand changes of power dynamics among citizens, scientists, developers, and regulators. Moreover, forming scientific knowledge about the relationship between the smoke emissions and the severity of the air pollution by using the monitoring system currently relies on human interpretation. Additional future research involves enhancing the knowledge by analyzing the correlations between various types of data. The analysis can explain how these data reinforce or conflict with each other, which provides strong statistical scientific evidence.

Another limitation is that the sample size of participants in the survey study is too small and the statistical analysis conclusion (see subsection Results) is weak. Participants only represent a fraction of the population in the neighborhood near the coke works. They have high education (see Table 2) and involvement levels (see Table 3 and the left-most boxplot in Figure 8), which includes interacting with the system, discussing the system with others, and attending monthly community meetings. Most of them have strong activation before learning about the monitoring system, which causes the failure to reject the null hypothesis related to awareness (see Table 4). The strong activation may also result in the high correlation between community members who created and viewed smoke images (see subsection User-based Sub-study). Nevertheless, one alternative explanation of this limitation is that without high awareness, it would be impossible to support community advocacy with ICT interventions. In other words, high awareness may be a necessary condition for successful citizen empowerment. How attitude may change among people with low education or low involvement level after interacting with the air quality monitoring system still remain an open research question.

Furthermore, the smoke detection algorithm used in the system is tuned to operate in our settings. Currently, the algorithm uses a heuristic method and has too many tuning parameters, which is not robust enough for similar contexts for other communities. One approach to generalize the system is to collect crowdsourced labels via mobile or online platforms, which requires deeper citizen participation. These labels can then be used to train a smoke image classifier using machine learning. Moreover, it appears that the existence of the coke plant is the major source of motivation (see Figure 7). This crowdsourcing approach may provide extra motivations to the community. Besides collecting labels, organizing the hybrid scientific data collected in the system into a comprehensive dataset can potentially assist future academic research related to environmental problems.

CONCLUSION

This paper presents a web-based air quality monitoring system which integrates image, sensor, and crowdsourced data. It is an instance of adversarial design [12, 13] which critically reveals, questions, and challenges a real-world environmental problem. The system provides technological affordance for forming strong scientific evidence. We discuss the iterative participatory design process that leads to decisions of system features with the community. We describe our evaluation, which includes an image usage study from server logs and a survey study. The survey study indicates statistically significant increases in self-efficacy and sense of community among users after interacting with the system. Open responses in the study show that the system promotes critical discussions with policy makers and empowers citizens to participate in community actions. Based on the evaluation, we offer three key insights about using an iterative design process, encouraging community engagement, and forming scientific knowledge. Finally, we mention limitations and future research directions related to evaluating the intervention of information technology, studying user behavior of community members with low participation level, and generalizing the smoke detection algorithm by collecting crowdsourced labels. We hope that this work can inspire other researchers to contribute towards developing innovative information technology that supports citizen empowerment.

ACKNOWLEDGMENTS

The Heinz Endowments, Allegheny County Clean Air Now, and all other participants. The authors thank Yen-Chi Chen for the advice in statistical analysis.

REFERENCES

1. Albert Bandura. 1977. Self-efficacy: toward a unifying theory of behavioral change. *Psychological review* 84, 2 (1977), 191.

2. Eli Blevis. 2007. Sustainable Interaction Design: Invention & Disposal, Renewal & Reuse. In *Proceedings of the SIGCHI Conference on Human Factors in Computing Systems (CHI '07)*. ACM, New York, NY, USA, 503–512.

3. Rick Bonney, Heidi Ballard, Rebecca Jordan, Ellen McCallie, Tina Phillips, Jennifer Shirk, and Candie C Wilderman. 2009a. Public Participation in Scientific Research: Defining the Field and Assessing Its Potential for Informal Science Education. A CAISE Inquiry Group Report. *Online Submission* (2009).

4. Rick Bonney, Caren B. Cooper, Janis Dickinson, Steve Kelling, Tina Phillips, Kenneth V. Rosenberg, and Jennifer Shirk. 2009b. Citizen Science: A Developing Tool for Expanding Science Knowledge and Scientific Literacy. *BioScience* 59 (2009), 977–984. Issue 11.

5. Rick Bonney, Jennifer L. Shirk, Tina B. Phillips, Andrea Wiggins, Heidi L. Ballard, Abraham J. Miller-Rushing, and Julia K. Parrish. 2014. Next Steps for Citizen Science. *Science* 343, 6178 (2014), 1436–1437.

6. Hronn Brynjarsdottir, Maria Håkansson, James Pierce, Eric Baumer, Carl DiSalvo, and Phoebe Sengers. 2012. Sustainably Unpersuaded: How Persuasion Narrows Our Vision of Sustainability. In *Proceedings of the SIGCHI Conference on Human Factors in Computing Systems (CHI '12)*. ACM, New York, NY, USA, 947–956.

7. John M. Carroll, Mary Beth Rosson, and Jingying Zhou. 2005. Collective Efficacy As a Measure of Community. In *Proceedings of the SIGCHI Conference on Human Factors in Computing Systems (CHI '05)*. ACM, New York, NY, USA, 1–10.

8. Jeff Conklin. 2005. *Dialogue Mapping: Building Shared Understanding of Wicked Problems*. John Wiley & Sons, Inc., New York, NY, USA.

9. Cathy C. Conrad and Krista G. Hilchey. 2011. A review of citizen science and community-based environmental monitoring: issues and opportunities. *Environmental Monitoring and Assessment* 176, 1 (2011), 273–291.

10. Janis L. Dickinson and Rick Bonney. 2012. *Citizen Science: Public Participation in Environmental Research* (1 ed.). Cornell University Press.

11. Janis L Dickinson, Jennifer Shirk, David Bonter, Rick Bonney, Rhiannon L Crain, Jason Martin, Tina Phillips, and Karen Purcell. 2012. The current state of citizen science as a tool for ecological research and public engagement. *Frontiers in Ecology and the Environment* 10, 6 (2012), 291–297.

12. Carl DiSalvo. 2010. Design, Democracy and Agonistic Pluralism. In *Proceedings of the design research society conference*. 366–371.

13. Carl DiSalvo. 2012. *Adversarial Design*. The MIT Press.

14. Carl DiSalvo, Kirsten Boehner, Nicholas A. Knouf, and Phoebe Sengers. 2009. Nourishing the Ground for Sustainable HCI: Considerations from Ecologically Engaged Art. In *Proceedings of the SIGCHI Conference on Human Factors in Computing Systems (CHI '09)*. ACM, New York, NY, USA, 385–394.

15. Carl DiSalvo, Andrew Clement, and Volkmar Pipek. 2013. Participatory Design For, With, and By Communities. In *International Handbook of Participatory Design*, Jesper Simonsen and Toni Robertson (Eds.). Routledge, 182–209.

16. Carl DiSalvo, Marti Louw, Julina Coupland, and MaryAnn Steiner. 2009. Local Issues, Local Uses: Tools for Robotics and Sensing in Community Contexts. In *Proceedings of the Seventh ACM Conference on Creativity and Cognition (C&C '09)*. ACM, New York, NY, USA, 245–254.

17. Carl DiSalvo, Illah Nourbakhsh, David Holstius, Ayça Akin, and Marti Louw. 2008. The Neighborhood Networks Project: A Case Study of Critical Engagement and Creative Expression Through Participatory Design. In *Proceedings of the Tenth Anniversary Conference on Participatory Design 2008 (PDC '08)*. Indiana University, Indianapolis, IN, USA, 41–50.

18. Carl DiSalvo, Phoebe Sengers, and Hrönn Brynjarsdóttir. 2010. Mapping the Landscape of Sustainable HCI. In *Proceedings of the SIGCHI Conference on Human Factors in Computing Systems (CHI '10)*. ACM, New York, NY, USA, 1975–1984.

19. William W. Gaver. 1991. Technology Affordances. In *Proceedings of the SIGCHI Conference on Human Factors in Computing Systems (CHI '91)*. ACM, New York, NY, USA, 79–84.

20. Bernard Greaves and Gordon Lishman. 1980. The Theory and Practice of Community Politics. A.L.C. Campaign Booklet No. 12. (1980). http://www.rosenstiel.co.uk/aldc/commpol.htm.

21. Muki Haklay. 2013. Citizen Science and Volunteered Geographic Information: Overview and Typology of Participation. In *Crowdsourcing Geographic Knowledge: Volunteered Geographic Information (VGI) in Theory and Practice*, Daniel Sui, Sarah Elwood, and Michael Goodchild (Eds.). Springer Netherlands, Dordrecht, 105–122.

22. Yen-Chia Hsu, Paul S Dille, Randy Sargent, and Illah Nourbakhsh . 2016. *Industrial Smoke Detection and Visualization*. Technical Report CMU-RI-TR-16-55. Robotics Institute, Pittsburgh, PA.

23. Yen-Chia Hsu, Tay-Sheng Jeng, Yang-Ting Shen, and Po-Chun Chen. 2012. SynTag: A Web-based Platform for Labeling Real-time Video. In *Proceedings of the ACM 2012 Conference on Computer Supported Cooperative Work (CSCW '12)*. ACM, New York, NY, USA, 715–718.

24. Alan Irwin. 1995. *Citizen science: A study of people, expertise and sustainable development*. Psychology Press.

25. Alan Irwin. 2001. Constructing the scientific citizen: Science and democracy in the biosciences. *Public Understanding of Science* 10, 1 (2001), 1–18.

26. Marilena Kampa and Elias Castanas. 2008. Human health effects of air pollution. *Environmental Pollution* 151, 2 (2008), 362 – 367. Proceedings of the 4th International Workshop on Biomonitoring of Atmospheric Pollution (With Emphasis on Trace Elements).

27. Sunyoung Kim, Jennifer Mankoff, and Eric Paulos. 2013a. Sensr: Evaluating a Flexible Framework for Authoring Mobile Data-collection Tools for Citizen Science. In *Proceedings of the 2013 Conference on Computer Supported Cooperative Work (CSCW '13)*. ACM, New York, NY, USA, 1453–1462.

28. Sunyoung Kim, Eric Paulos, and Jennifer Mankoff. 2013b. inAir: A Longitudinal Study of Indoor Air Quality Measurements and Visualizations. In *Proceedings of the SIGCHI Conference on Human Factors in Computing Systems (CHI '13)*. ACM, New York, NY, USA, 2745–2754.

29. Sunyoung Kim, Christine Robson, Thomas Zimmerman, Jeffrey Pierce, and Eben M. Haber. 2011. Creek Watch: Pairing Usefulness and Usability for Successful Citizen Science. In *Proceedings of the SIGCHI Conference on Human Factors in Computing Systems (CHI '11)*. ACM, New York, NY, USA, 2125–2134.

30. Stacey Kuznetsov, George Davis, Jian Cheung, and Eric Paulos. 2011. Ceci N'Est Pas Une Pipe Bombe: Authoring Urban Landscapes with Air Quality Sensors. In *Proceedings of the SIGCHI Conference on Human Factors in Computing Systems (CHI '11)*. ACM, New York, NY, USA, 2375–2384.

31. Stacey Kuznetsov, Will Harrigan-Anderson, Haakon Faste, Scott E. Hudson, and Eric Paulos. 2013a. Community Engagements with Living Sensing Systems. In *Proceedings of the 9th ACM Conference on Creativity & Cognition (C&C '13)*. ACM, New York, NY, USA, 213–222.

32. Stacey Kuznetsov, Scott E. Hudson, and Eric Paulos. 2013b. A Low-tech Sensing System for Particulate Pollution. In *Proceedings of the 8th International Conference on Tangible, Embedded and Embodied Interaction (TEI '14)*. ACM, New York, NY, USA, 259–266.

33. G. Lane, C. Brueton, D. Diall, D. Airantzis, N. Jeremijenko, G. Papamarkos, G. Roussos, and K. Martin. 2006. Community-based public authoring with mobile chemical sensor networks. In *Intelligent Environments, 2006. IE 06. 2nd IET International Conference on*, Vol. 2. 23–29.

34. Gierad Laput, Walter S. Lasecki, Jason Wiese, Robert Xiao, Jeffrey P. Bigham, and Chris Harrison. 2015. Zensors: Adaptive, Rapidly Deployable, Human-Intelligent Sensor Feeds. In *Proceedings of the 33rd Annual ACM Conference on Human Factors in Computing Systems (CHI '15)*. ACM, New York, NY, USA, 1935–1944.

35. Walter S. Lasecki, Mitchell Gordon, Danai Koutra, Malte F. Jung, Steven P. Dow, and Jeffrey P. Bigham. 2014. Glance: Rapidly Coding Behavioral Video with the Crowd. In *Proceedings of the 27th Annual ACM Symposium on User Interface Software and Technology (UIST '14)*. ACM, New York, NY, USA, 551–562.

36. Christopher A. Le Dantec, Robert G. Farrell, Jim E. Christensen, Mark Bailey, Jason B. Ellis, Wendy A. Kellogg, and W. Keith Edwards. 2011. Publics in Practice: Ubiquitous Computing at a Shelter for Homeless Mothers. In *Proceedings of the SIGCHI Conference on Human Factors in Computing Systems (CHI '11)*. ACM, New York, NY, USA, 1687–1696.

37. Chris J. Lintott, Kevin Schawinski, AnÅ¿e Slosar, Kate Land, Steven Bamford, Daniel Thomas, M. Jordan Raddick, Robert C. Nichol, Alex Szalay, Dan Andreescu, Phil Murray, and Jan Vandenberg. 2008. Galaxy Zoo: morphologies derived from visual inspection of galaxies from the Sloan Digital Sky Survey. *MNRAS* 389 (2008), 1179–1189.

38. Jennifer C. Mankoff, Eli Blevis, Alan Borning, Batya Friedman, Susan R. Fussell, Jay Hasbrouck, Allison Woodruff, and Phoebe Sengers. 2007. Environmental Sustainability and Interaction. In *CHI '07 Extended Abstracts on Human Factors in Computing Systems (CHI EA '07)*. ACM, New York, NY, USA, 2121–2124.

39. Duncan C. McKinley, Abraham J. Miller-Rushing, Heidi L. Ballard, Rick Bonney, Hutch Brown, Daniel M. Evans, Rebecca A. French, Julia K. Parrish, Tina B. Phillips, Sean F. Ryan, Lea A. Shanley, Jennifer L. Shirk, Kristine F. Stepenuck, Jake F. Weltzin, Andrea Wiggins, Owen D. Boyle, Russell D. Briggs, Stuart F. Chapin III, David A. Hewitt, Peter W. Preuss, and Michael A. Soukup. 2015. Investing in Citizen Science Can Improve Natural Resource Management and Environmental Protection. *Issues In Ecology* (2015). Issue 19.

40. David W. McMillan and David M. Chavis. 1986. Sense of community: A definition and theory. *Journal of Community Psychology* 14, 1 (1986), 6–23.

41. Abraham Miller-Rushing, Richard Primack, and Rick Bonney. 2012. The history of public participation in ecological research. *Frontiers in Ecology and the Environment* 10, 6 (2012), 285–290.

42. Global Community Monitor. 2016. Bucket Brigade. (2016). http://www.gcmonitor.org/communities/start-a-bucket-brigade/.

43. Chantal Mouffe. 2000. *The Democratic Paradox*. verso.

44. Greg Newman, Andrea Wiggins, Alycia Crall, Eric Graham, Sarah Newman, and Kevin Crowston. 2012. The future of citizen science: emerging technologies and shifting paradigms. *Frontiers in Ecology and the Environment* 10, 6 (2012), 298–304.

45. William M. Pena and Steven A. Parshall. 2012. *Problem Seeking: An Architectural Programming Primer*. Wiley; 5 edition (February 28, 2012).

46. C Arden Pope III and Douglas W Dockery. 2006. Health effects of fine particulate air pollution: lines that connect. *Journal of the air & waste management association* 56, 6 (2006), 709–742.

47. Horst W. J. Rittel and Melvin M. Webber. 1973. Dilemmas in a general theory of planning. *Policy Sciences* 4, 2 (1973), 155–169.

48. Dana Rotman, Kezia Procita, Derek Hansen, Cynthia Sims Parr, and Jennifer Preece. 2012. Supporting content curation communities: The case of the Encyclopedia of Life. *Journal of the American Society for Information Science and Technology* 63, 6 (2012), 1092–1107.

49. Randy Sargent, Chris Bartley, Paul Dille, Jeff Keller, and Illah Nourbakhsh. 2010. Timelapse GigaPan: Capturing, Sharing, and Exploring Timelapse Gigapixel Imagery. In *Fine International Conference on Gigapixel Imaging for Science*.

50. Bristol Science Communication Unit, University of the West of England. 2013. Science for Environment Policy Indepth Report: Environmental Citizen Science. *Report produced for the European Commission DG Environment* (December 2013). http://ec.europa.eu/science-environment-policy

51. Jennifer L Shirk, Heidi L Ballard, Candie C Wilderman, Tina Phillips, Andrea Wiggins, Rebecca Jordan, Ellen McCallie, Matthew Minarchek, Bruce V Lewenstein, Marianne E Krasny, and others. 2012. Public participation in scientific research: a framework for deliberate design. *Ecology and Society* 17, 2 (2012), 29.

52. Jonathan Silvertown. 2009. A new dawn for citizen science. *Trends in Ecology and Evolution* 24, 9 (2009), 46–471.

53. Speck Air Quality Sensor. 2015. (2015). https://www.specksensor.com/.

54. M. Stevens, M. Vitos, J. Altenbuchner, G. Conquest, J. Lewis, and M. Haklay. 2014. Taking Participatory Citizen Science to Extremes. *IEEE Pervasive Computing* 13, 2 (Apr 2014), 20–29.

55. Jack Stilgoe. 2009. *Citizen Scientists: reconnecting science with civil society*. Demos London.

56. Brian L. Sullivan, Jocelyn L. Aycrigg, Jessie H. Barry, Rick E. Bonney, Nicholas Bruns, Caren B. Cooper, Theo Damoulas, AndrÃľ A. Dhondt, Tom Dietterich, Andrew Farnsworth, Daniel Fink, John W. Fitzpatrick, Thomas Fredericks, Jeff Gerbracht, Carla Gomes, Wesley M. Hochachka, Marshall J. Iliff, Carl Lagoze, Frank A. La Sorte, Matthew Merrifield, Will Morris, Tina B. Phillips, Mark Reynolds, Amanda D. Rodewald, Kenneth V. Rosenberg, Nancy M. Trautmann, Andrea Wiggins, David W. Winkler, Weng-Keen Wong, Christopher L. Wood, Jun Yu, and Steve Kelling. 2014. The eBird enterprise: An integrated approach to development and application of citizen science. *Biological Conservation* 169 (2014), 31 – 40.

57. Brian L. Sullivan, Christopher L. Wood, Marshall J. Iliff, Rick E. Bonney, Daniel Fink, and Steve Kelling. 2009. eBird: A citizen-based bird observation network in the biological sciences. *Biological Conservation* 142, 10 (2009), 2282 – 2292.

58. MD Taylor and IR Nourbakhsh. 2015. A low-cost particle counter and signal processing method for indoor air pollution. *Air Pollution XXIII* 198 (2015), 337.

59. Rundong Tian, Christine Dierk, Christopher Myers, and Eric Paulos. 2016. MyPart: Personal, Portable, Accurate, Airborne Particle Counting. In *Proceedings of the 2016 CHI Conference on Human Factors in Computing Systems (CHI '16)*. ACM, New York, NY, USA, 1338–1348.

60. A. Wiggins and K. Crowston. 2011. From Conservation to Crowdsourcing: A Typology of Citizen Science. In *2011 44th Hawaii International Conference on System Sciences (HICSS)*. 1–10.

61. James Wilsdon, Jack Stilgoe, and Brian Wynne. 2005. *The public value of science: or how to ensure that science really matters*. Demos London.

The Catch(es) with Smart Home – Experiences of a Living Lab Field Study

Timo Jakobi[1,2], Corinna Ogonowski[2], Nico Castelli[1,2], Gunnar Stevens[1,2], Volker Wulf[2,3]
[1]Bonn-Rhein-Sieg University of Applied Science, Sankt Augustin, Germany
[2] University of Siegen, Siegen Germany
[3]Fraunhofer Institute for Applied Information Technology, Sankt Augustin, Germany

ABSTRACT
Smart home systems are becoming an integral feature of the emerging home IT market. Under this general term, products mainly address issues of security, energy savings and comfort. Comprehensive systems that cover several use cases are typically operated and managed via a unified dashboard. Unfortunately, research targeting user experience (UX) design for smart home interaction that spans several use cases or covering the entire system is scarce. Furthermore, existing comprehensive and user-centered long-term studies on challenges and needs throughout phases of information collection, installation and operation of smart home systems are technologically outdated. Our 18-month Living Lab study covering 14 households equipped with smart home technology provides insights on how to design for improving smart home appropriation. This includes a stronger sensibility for household practices during setup and configuration, flexible visualizations for evolving demands and an extension of smart home beyond the location.

Author Keywords
User Experience, Smart Home, Living Lab, Design, Qualitative Study

ACM Classification Keywords
H.5.2 [Information interfaces and presentation (e.g., HCI)]: User Interfaces --- User Centered Design; H.5.m Miscellaneous

INTRODUCTION AND BACKGROUND
The smart home seems to be the exemplar *par excellence* of possibilities inherent in the Internet of Things. Currently, both established companies such as Apple, Samsung and Google, and newcomers are positioning their own smart home products in the market. The idea of the smart home is not new and several researchers have already investigated challenges of making homes smart from a feasibility [34,45] and user interaction [22] point of view and highlight the substantial 'work to make a network work' [27] for users. However, in recent years, advancing technology (i.e. the introduction of mobile and ubiquitous computing devices paired with low-power wireless communication protocols) has massively changed the way smart homes can be, and are, equipped and interacted with. For example, Harper's study [28], which dates back more than ten years, took place at a time when wireless affordances were not available, and where interconnected devices were rare.

This evolution has sparked more recent 'in the wild' smart home research that focusses on identifying challenges which smart home users face [10,41]. Mennicken et al. [44] provide an overview of the literature and conduct an interview study with 22 participants, concerning themselves in the main with the relationship between user concerns and those of system builders. What we need, according to Mennicken et al. [42] is to '…stimulate both actionable insights and design artifacts that better capture the evolutionary nature of users and their home contexts'. Some challenges for users, then, are identified, though perhaps not in any great contextual detail. There remains, that is, something of a research gap. We aim, then, to report on the appropriation processes associated with smart home technology, covering the whole customer journey of system setup, installation and configuration, use, reconfiguration and extension, as a first step.

We therefore ask: how do smart home systems perform under real-life conditions? What are current challenges for successfully embedding the smart home into households' everyday practices, both from the system's and the users' perspective? While these questions have been raised in a user-centered manner, so far, there has been no recent long-term study on the smart home, one which actually accompanies households in their struggle to make their homes smart for a longer period of time.

The remainder of the paper is structured as follows. We first further motivate our research question by outlining related work and the current smart home product landscape. Subsequently, the methods and the smart home research artefact are introduced. The results from a case study with 14 households based on qualitative data from interviews, workshops, regulars' table meetings and mobile feedback application input collected in the past 18 months are then presented. Finally, we discuss design guidelines to help

CHI 2017, May 06 - 11, 2017, Denver, CO, USA

ACM 978-1-4503-4655-9/17/05...$15.00
DOI: http://dx.doi.org/10.1145/3025453.3025799

non-expert users to be able to manage their smart home adequately. Based on our findings, we suggest three main strategies: (a) To further hide technological detail in systems and instead make systems visible in a way that reflects how users construct their demands to make installation and configuration more user-friendly. (b) To acknowledge the individuality of users' information demands and provide flexible visualization solutions for evolving needs. (c) To support flexibility for extending smart homes beyond the home as a place.

RELATED WORK

Researching the smart home has a long, if slightly technology-driven, history. Several commercial and research-driven projects have explored various use cases and the potential of technologies for smart homes [28,31,34,37,45] from a feasibility point of view. In the following, we introduce design-oriented research for the home. Thus, we outline the concept of appropriation for informing smart home design and point towards a lack of long-term appropriation studies of technology in this context.

Informing Smart Home Interface Design

Studies relating to technology design for the home deal with a large number of different issues. For instance, in recent years, smart energy systems have received attention in research [2,62], with a lively community studying smart metering, and with considerable efforts also focussing on privacy [13,49]. In Sustainable Interaction Design [7], much research has focused on how to design energy monitoring systems from a user perspective [3,26,50]. It typically aims at making the consumption of the abstract resource "energy" – mostly electricity – visible and understandable as feedback to the consumer. Those working on Ambient Assisted Living technologies (AAL) [15] are very active in supporting comfortable and independent living for older people [18,30,39]. Amiribesheli et al. [4], for example, present a literature review for AAL and conclude with general design guidelines, supposedly also applicable when designing smart home technology. The role of security for the home has also been researched, e.g. within the field of access control [54] Ur et al. [59], for example, have shown that many smart home systems feature their own login system, thus fragmenting user flow and hindering a positive UX. Yet another issue identified is that of designing eco-feedback. For example, Froelich et al. stress, 'it is critical for the HCI community to step back and define an approach and theoretical foundation for the design and evaluation of eco-feedback technology' [26]. Strengers [55] also critiques the models underpinning eco-feedback systems and argues for an approach embedded in daily life. Such positions, as we argue below, have wider ramifications. Other studies focus on single aspects of a smart home, such as automation [14], activity recognition [56], privacy implications [16,36,58] or certain parts of smart home user interfaces, such as the use of calendars [43].

Smart home systems, however, promise to include a multitude of uses, including but not limited to the ones outlined above. For these complex systems, user-centered research deals, at least to some extent, with challenges posed, drawn from interviews with experts or people living with a smart home. For example, Brush et al. [10] have investigated the user acceptance factors of home automation technology. They identify high costs, inflexibility, bad usability and security issues as the most important barriers to the success of smart home platform systems. Similarly, Mennicken have found barriers to succesful smart home integration, identifying a better support for routines as one central aspect [44].

Understanding the User: Designing for Appropriation

A more comprehensive view on the use of technology can be developed by researching its appropriation in everyday life. This process is understood to include not only interaction with technology itself but also collecting information about it, envisioning possible use cases and developing an overall attitude towards it [11]. Generally, designing for appropriation means taking into account that users will make use of technology in unanticipated or even unintended ways in their everyday life. Design of technology thus should support flexibility in terms of adaptability to different environments, evolving (user) needs and environment as well as ownership [19]. In this vein, Carroll et al. [11,12] have investigated what younger people do with technology, especially mobile phones. Stevens et al. [53] suggest ways of designing for individualized use of software engineering tools. Similarly, Dourish [21] outlines guidelines for supporting appropriation of document management systems in terms of important features to be included within a solution.

When aiming at reducing barriers to the appropriation of smart home platform systems, it likewise stands to reason that a broader view on a product's lifecycle, ranging from the system setup phase, over installation and routinization to reconfiguration can be beneficial. Such an comprehensive approach calls for long-term in-situ investigation into how users ascribe meaning to smart home technology and how this technology evolves in association with social practice and vice versa [52].

However, our inquiries reveal no recent long-term studies, investigating different phases of smart home interaction. As a notable exception, and as mentioned, Harper and colleagues [28] specifically researched the home from the users' perspective, looking closely at the appropriation of technology in the social space of the home. One chapter [48] specifically focuses on what it is like to live with and in a smart home, outlining design guidelines and possible futures. In contrast to most other research, the people in that research actually lived in a smart home, thus entailing a longer term approach to technology appropriation. However, as we have pointed out, the setup had limitations. Participants were not actually living in their own homes and technology at that point did not encompass cloud systems, smartphones, or new low-power wireless protocols, which allow battery-powered sensors and actors to become independent of wall sockets and thus to be installed more flexibly in unelectrified areas of the home. Therefore, more than ten years after Harper's study, it seems reasonable to revisit the appropriation of smart home technology.

BACKGROUND ON SMART HOME SYSTEMS

In principle, smart home systems have existed ever since computers found their way into the home during the 1980s. At that time, hobbyists put huge effort into wiring up their homes. Such "wired homes" [28] were highly customized and characterized more as individual solutions rather than ones with the quality and scalability of a commercial product. Recent advances in low-power wireless communication protocols as well as miniaturization and decreasing costs of hardware have turned smart homes into a main stream and lifestyle product, and they are considered as soon becoming the next digitalized part of daily-life. Currently, in addition to established home automation solution providers, many other IT companies, illumination manufacturers, telcos or even power supply companies are positioning their own smart home products, not to mention start-ups' attempts at gaining a market share.

Under the general term smart home, products vary greatly in terms of the technology used and the use cases covered. For our purpose, we distinguish between smart home systems along two dimensions, similar to Brush et al. [10]. First, there are products that only serve a single use case, such as smart thermostats, and second, platform solutions spanning across use cases and allowing greater flexibility. The latter systems either call for expert installation or are do-it-yourself solutions based on the principles of plug and play.

Single Product vs. Platform Systems

While there are no limits to the heterogeneity of hardware offered for the smart home, components can generally be categorized by use cases supported. Here, four trends can be identified. (1) Systems for supporting comfort, such as by sensing temperature, daytime or brightness and automating shutters, light, and air conditioning, entertainment and related appliances. (2) Increasing security in the home by installing internet-linked or networked cameras, motion detection, sirens, remote control of lights for simulating presence and control as well as alarm notifications via text messages or push notifications on mobile devices. (3) Monitoring and saving energy by avoiding standby consumption, automated switching off of devices and appliance-based measurement of energy consumption as well as visualization of consumption. Here, generally, smart plugs are used, placed between the device's plug and the power outlet. (4) , enabling more sustainable self-determined living through AAL technologies.

While smart home products may consist of only one sensor, platform providers, offering a set of hardware and software, are becoming more popular. These systems typically feature a hardware gateway and address more than one of the aforementioned main use cases with their set of sensors and actors. The multitude of protocols and vendors, however, make the current market highly fragmented. Interoperability between the devices of different vendors is rarely supported even when they use the same protocol. Some systems, however, have a whitelist of products using the same protocol; others allow for extending their system with dongles to enable other protocols to be used.

Smart home systems have three main ways of interacting with and controlling the system. First of all, many systems enable basic interactions via the hardware interfaces of their sensors and actors. For example, simple on-/off switches are provided. Moreover, there are switches dedicated to triggering predefined actions on other actors. More sophisticated controls are sometimes provided by dedicated displays. In most cases, however, smart home platform vendors provide controlling and monitoring mechanisms via mobile or desktop applications. Here, dashboard-styled control dominates, allowing direct manipulation of sensors and actors. Furthermore, these interfaces typically support (1) gaining an overview of the current and past state of the home (2) managing existing and adding new devices, and (3) managing automation rules and groupings.

Expert Installation vs. Plug and Play

For a long time, smart home systems required wired connections between control panels and sensors or actors. Installing and configuring such systems is often accomplished by professionals, and users without expert knowledge can only perform basic configurational settings. Wired connections for the smart home have several benefits. Typically, flush-mounted, they are well integrated into the home and can be almost invisible. Additionally, wired connections guarantee a good connection to control and monitoring stations. On the other hand, using wired connection makes "smartness" very inflexible in relation to evolving demands. Additionally, including a wired smart home into a building – be it new or retro-fitted – requires complex planning and significant investment.

More recent products in the smart home rely on low power wireless communication protocols. Emphasizing their plug and play character, these systems are surface-mounted and battery-powered and thus can be positioned in remote sites within the home. This way, such systems are more flexible in terms of being adaptable for users. They are less cost intensive than wired systems and easier to integrate into existing home infrastructures. However, the burden at present is on the user to setup and manage rules and configurations.

SETTING UP THE SMART HOME LIVING LAB

Against the backdrop of quickly evolving technology, we believe it is appropriate to investigate the appropriation of smart home technologies in everyday life. Following Stevens et al. [53] and Wulf et al. [61], we seek to inform the design of smart home systems through understanding user behaviours throughout the process, thus informing UX design in future smart home products.

The work described in this paper was conducted as part of a 3-year research project focusing on the development of new concepts and strategies for smart home systems with a specific focus on UX. We applied a Living Lab approach [23,25,46] to address the complexity and situatedness of these systems over different stages, namely (1) system setup (2) installation and configuration, (3) use and embedding into practice and (4) extension and reconfiguration in real life environments. Living Labs allow different stakeholders from research and design to be brought together with users and technology in an open-ended design process in real life environments [25] as far as possible, given that they are predicated on the introduction of new technology into the environment in question, Living Labs are intended to be 'naturalistic'. Such frameworks are specifically suited to supporting long-term cooperation, co-design and collaborative exploration among researchers, users and other stakeholders. Involving users in the design process from the very beginning in sensing, prototyping, validating and refining complex solutions in multiple and evolving real life contexts allows a continuous formative evaluation of the designed artefacts and uncovers appropriation phenomena at early stages in the technology life cycle [6]. The advantages of the Living Lab approach lie in its flexibility, allowing for creative spaces for discussions on new concepts, long-term observational studies and, where necessary, lab-based interventions, designed to assess the long-term appropriation of new IT-artefacts [46].

Recruitment and User Sample

We recruited our user sample through a four-staged selection process. From November 2014 to January 2015 (see Fig. 1), we placed information about the study in the local press and via radio stations. We did not offer any compensation for participation. The only incentive we provided was the free provision of a smart home system used as the central research artefact and active participation in the project. Via an online platform, interested people had to provide basic information concerning their households' technical infrastructure, motivation for participation and expectations of the project. At this stage, more than 100 households applied to participate in the project.

Second, we checked all applications in terms of accuracy of fit for our project's demands. We decided to only include households within the postcode of the city of Siegen, Germany. This restriction allowed us to get in touch with them easily, e.g. for home visits, interviews and roundtables. As technological requirements, we defined two more criteria, which we believe are not critical but are worth mentioning. First, only households with a reliable internet connection with at least 2 kbit/s download according to the carrier contract were included. Second, due to budget constraints, only households in possession of at least one smartphone could participate, so households could be provided with tablets.

In a third stage, telephone interviews with each of the remaining 63 households were conducted to gather an impression of the motivation for participation, willingness to actively participate in the project and technical- and smart home-related foreknowledge. Additionally, these interviews served to get to know participants' self-reflectiveness, articulateness and understanding of the character of soft- and hardware prototypes compared to products.

Finally, we characterized all households and chose a sample, varying in terms of age, sex, household size, rented or owned home, house or flat, rural or urban residential area and tech-savvyness as well as educational level. Finally, 14 households with 23 participants were selected. The sample consists of two single-person households, five multi-person households without children and five multi-person households with children. Four households lived in flats, while ten were owner occupied. Participants were aged between 27 and 61 years. Motivation varied, ranging through dissatisfaction with existing smart home systems, technological interest, to curiosity about being part of a research endeavor. Based on this qualitative user sample, we started the longitudinal Living Lab study.

Study Design and Data Collection

In March 2015, we first conducted a kick-off event to brief households regarding our overall research agenda. This was the first opportunity for households to get to know each other. Following this event, we set up an exploratory on-site study with a semi-structured interview guideline. We mainly aimed at a better understanding of the participants' homes, their daily routines and habits as well as their ideas for using a smart home. We also used the initial interviews to get to know each other and to establish trusting relationships. At this point, we also distributed wish-lists for smart home equipment. Households were allowed to pick any combination of available sensors and actors. To avoid a mental overload and to help participants to start thinking 'small', we suggested equipping only one room at the beginning and decided to set a maximum of ten hardware components. However, some households were allowed to order more than ten components if they were able to explain which use cases and scenarios they wanted to realize and what they wanted to achieve with them.

Based on these wish-lists, we provided an out-of-the-box plug and play smart home platform system released on the German market in May 2015 to the households. The installation and configuration process was either observed and video-recorded by researchers on-site (seven households) or self-reported by participants (seven households). To subsequently collect experiences in-situ and maintain a close relationship to households, a mobile feedback application was provided and integrated into the companion app of the smart home system. An informal regulars' table and an instant messenger group were initiated and maintained to foster exchange of experiences, ideas, problems and their solutions between users and researchers. More formal communication about invitations to design workshops, technical announcements or updates about the project`s progression was carried out via email by a university staff member who was responsible as central contact person for participating households and was a communication node between all project members. After this initial setup phase, households used their smart home over 15 months and participated in four design workshops focusing on information collection and interface design for new smart home concepts.

As a first evaluative intervention, in September 2015, after three months of use, we conducted a second interview study gathering experiences, demands and limitations when using the system. We focused on ways of appropriating the system into everyday life and reflections on the installation and usage routines in terms of usability und UX problems. We also asked for examples of best practice and implemented use cases. In August 2016, after 15 months of use, a third interview study was conducted where we asked again for best practices and desired or implemented use cases but also for changes in system configuration based on changed user needs or seasonal influences or based on the integration of new third-party components. We also noted changes within routines and daily habits in the course of using the system. All interviews, workshops and home visits were audio-recorded and videotaped where it was deemed to be helpful for data collection.

Smart Home Infrastructure

We chose a Z-wave based smart home platform system from a German provider. It is marketed as a plug and play solution with surface-mounted components only. Apart from manual control, the system also allows for automated control: setting up rules (if this, then that), scenes (setting a defined state for a number of components) and timers. Devices also can be grouped, for example, by room or by any other custom aggregation. A customizable dashboard serves as a homescreen where all chosen components are presented in widget-style fashion. Additionally, a weather-widget and a text-based home logbook are included. The latter provided information regarding the system state (starting and stopping the gateway, connection to cloud, updates etc.) and listed every event (sensed motion, input, changed settings, triggered switches, rules, scenes or timers) of the smart system.

The sensors and actors were organized via a gateway, which was connected to the home router and thus the vendor's cloud. All existing settings were executable without internet connection, but changing settings and – naturally – remote control out of the home network depended on an internet connection. Controlling the system was possible via sensors and actors themselves (switches, remote control, thermostats and smart plugs), a companion app and a web portal.

While third-party sensors were not officially supported, there were user-generated whitelists in forums. When the project started, the smart home product included the following sensors and actors which households could pick: room thermostats (14 picks), radiator thermostats (31), motion and brightness detection (14), door-/window contacts sensing openness or closedness (29), smart plugs for measuring electricity consumption and switching appliances (45), remote controls (6), freely positionable switches supporting two or four different positions (11) and a smoke detector (10). While the product is offered in typical starter sets and sets focusing on a certain use case, such as heating, we allowed households to freely choose a constellation of sensors and actors for their smart home.

Data Analysis

To identify challenges and experiences of smart home from a user perspective, our analysis is based on all data (interviews, workshops, field notes from home visits and regulars' table, text histories from instant messenger group) collected during the 18-month period of the Living Lab research. All audio-taped material was transcribed. Each document was processed by two researchers individually using thematic analysis with an inductive coding process [9]. After each empirical phase, the codes were consolidated and developed iteratively. We discussed gained insights internally with researchers who were not involved in the project as well as with our industrial partners in the consortium.

For the analysis, we searched for common patterns and categories related to how participants find and select appropriate smart home solutions, how they used smart home components (sensors and actors) as well as looking at software design, interactions and information provided through the system and how households tried to include smart home components into their lives and how everyday life changed through the smart homes. The analysis enabled us to identify four central categories relevant to the successful appropriation of smart home technology within four stages of use. Based on Silverstone and Haddon [52] we have ideal-typically organized these categories into four phases of smart home appropriation: (1) system setup, (2) installation and configuration, (3) routinized use and (4) demands of reconfiguration and extension. All quotes used in our findings section were translated from German by the authors.

FINDINGS: UX CHALLENGES FOR THE SMART HOME

In this section, we present results of our qualitative Living Lab study. We broadly assigned them into the phases of system setup, installation and configuration, routinized use and demands for reconfiguration and extension.

System Setup: Choosing hardware components

Product innovation literature shows that there can be a considerable mismatch between the functionalities on offer and the expectations of consumers (i.e. [40,63]). Our initial interviews showed that most of the households already had informed themselves about smart homes via the internet or magazines. However, participants planning to include smart home technology in their newly built or modernized home were overwhelmed by the number of existing products and their implications for future interoperability. Most common reasons for abandoning the search were a lack of market transparency and helpful information about use cases and best practices as well as an overly technical presentation of smart homes. Here, especially different communication protocols raised uncertainties. A male participant from a more tech-savvy multi-person household describes the assessment of existing smart home technologies as follows:

"I haven't decided on anything yet because I know there are many solutions. It is well known that [product A] is pretty expensive. [product B] is more for hobbyists [...]. Maybe those plug and play systems are better. [...] Investing hours of time reading through forums, writing scripts – which I cannot do myself – or programming something via copy and paste, I simply don't have the nerves for that right now."

While smart home technology is evolving fairly quickly, as far as the integration into home infrastructure goes, items need to be future proof, especially (but not only) when flush-mounted and thus more permanently installed. Additionally, the variety of more sophisticated product packages, and varying payment models requiring considerable financial investment, further discouraged households from deciding to buy.

When households were picking components for setting up their future smart home, it became obvious that many had very little knowledge of the various features of sensors and actors, as well as of their potential for combination. Except for tech-savvy households, participants had problems in articulating their needs and translating them into use cases or more complex scenarios with several hardware components beyond the ones that had sparked the interest in a smart home. Here, households often oriented towards use cases that researchers or other households provided e.g. via the instant messaging group or the regulars' table meetings. This complexity problem for the smart home user is reflected in several comments from participants, such as the case of a couple with grown-up children who have already moved out of the house:

"It has got to stay easy. Not everyone has daily contact with IT. We have seen people standing in [a consumer market] in front of smart home products, and I literally saw the question marks in their eyes."

The core problem our participants had in making their choices was to be able to identify routines to be supported and then map how the system might support a certain use case. While, in respect of hardware, this was unproblematic for use cases where only a single (kind) of sensors was needed, such as heating, the complexity grew strongly with the number of different sensors included in a scenario. Moreover, sensors often have secondary features, such that a motion detector, for instance, also senses brightness. These hidden features made it very hard for households to actually understand what possibilities existed.

Installation and Configuration

In the phase of installation and configuration, households came in first contact with hard- and software. The system setup which households chose needed the hardware components to be installed and paired with the gateway. Additionally, households had to register with their email addresses to gain access to the vendor's cloud portal. Components were used to define rules and relationships on a software level. The installation routine was either accompanied by a researcher or self-reported by the provided in-situ feedback function of the companion app. Even so, households ran into problems getting the system running without considerable support from researchers or the vendors' support channels (hotline and live chat support).

The most common problem touched on that of pairing devices with the gateway – a necessary step for Z-wave based components. The whole process raised serious issues and was a task many participants felt uneasy accomplishing.

"For me, installation was very ... complicated. I mean you always think its like plug and play. Meaning: I will just try bevore reading the instructions. And that didn't work at all. Then I read the manual and thought I had understood it. But this still wasn't the case and looking closer to the manual, you found half a sentence you missed and then it worked." (multi-person household)

Moreover, the reason for having to undergo the process was unclear to participants unfamiliar with the technology; they expected the smart home to be plug and play compatible.

"Retrospectively, I would prefer to simply put the devices where they should be and then they should make themselves visible automatically somewhere and then you just ascribe them instead of having to wait and do all these steps." (multi-person household)

Introductory screens and overlays, described with highlights, arrows and text boxes, were deemed not especially helpful. The overlays were often quickly removed and, in fact, not read at all. When the overlays' informative character was subsequently described, reactions were more positive:

"If you haven't ever done this before and you don't know [how to], you would probably search, search, search. In this way, it is prescribed to you: Oh yes, you have to click

here, to start the timing. I think that actually is quite okay." (multi-person household)

For pairing devices, in ordert to include them into the system, rules for automated behavior in an if-this-then-that style needed to be defined by users. Identifying these concrete procedures necessitated considerable reflection:

P1: "I find it especially hard to set up rules...And setting them the way I want them to work. I don't manage to do this myself."

Interviewer: "So what did you do?"

P2: "I always try. Let's look [into the system]. A rule is for example: In case the thermostat measures 23 degrees Celsius, shut down the heating. That's a rule, right?"

P1: "If one thing happens, the other thing must follow. That's a rule. I never manage to do this."

P2: "When the window is open, I get an email. We tested this down here: opening and closing. Then I tried to include that it would only write an email after 10 minutes or so, because we only need a reminder when we have forgotten it. And I dind't find it and eventually gave up. "

Noticeably, households typically defined rules in a step-by-step manner. For example, when wanting a light to switch on depending on sensed movement: First, coupling the motion sensor with the smart plug was set and tested as a rule by moving in front of the sensor. After success, the period of time where the light was to remain turned on was set and tested again. Finally, the restriction that light should only be turned on when ambient light is low was added. In one case, darkness was simulated by putting the sensor under a cushion or covering it with a hand to get immediate results. This example makes two challenges explicit: First, users had a need for immediately testing rules due to either lack of trust in their own accurate understanding of rules or in the system's interpretation. In other instances, automatic timers were defined to trigger certain actions during testing. Households explicitly used fake times to get feedback about whether their idea of implementing the rule was correctly reflected in the system. Second, and more importantly, the problem of thinking about daily routines in algorithmic structures is not an everyday task for many households, resulting in inconveniently having to set up rules incrementally to make them work and fit actual needs.

„But the rule, such that I can say: 'The door sensor measures certain brightness and it should turn on the lights.' I still don't know how to get there. But I have followed the chat in the group and Dave is really good at this." (multi-person household)

Tech-savvy households with basic experience in configuring IT-systems and pairing processes often figured out troubleshooting for themselves and supported others, for instance, by setting up rules or suggesting use cases, with hints in meetings and within the instant messaging chat group.

Domestification and Daily Use

In the following months, participants used their individually configured smart home in more routinized ways. Within this phase, participants reported a considerably reduced interaction on the software interface level, due to having found their optimized configuration.

Regular and permanent home awareness demands

Despite households' general desire for background automation, we also found various demands for explicit information and awareness. In particular, permanent demand for historical data was mentioned. One household, for instance, which already manually kept track of gas and electricity consumption on sheets of paper wanted to digitalize and improve monitoring:

"For example, when I have invested let's say into my heating, I want to know: Does it pay off? Or when changing my heating settings. [..] I want a conclusion: Did it pay off or not? Therefore, I need to measure. If I don't, I can't change anything. I am not a control freak, but I want to know." (multi-person household)

This permanent home awareness mechanism targeted not only support consumption optimization, but also security aspects regarding the whole home:

"When I'm on vacation or just gone for a week, then you want to know what has happened." (multi-person household)

In particular, instead of having an interest in every single event, households tended to look for groups of events, which they were able to identify as a "normal" amount or sequence. Identifying patterns such as activities and times of absence, one could assess whether everything was okay at home or not.

Coming or leaving home were two very common scenarios in which households wanted to check on things or set devices to a certain state. For example, the same household with cats had installed a safety mechanism for their pets:

"It is dangerous for our cats if we let the window open when we leave the house because they could get hurt by getting stuck in a partly opened window." (multi-person household)

For this purpose, they connected a small light to a smart plug next to the entrance door which switched the light on when windows are open. Similarly, another households set up an awareness system for the dryer which was positioned in the basement, by connecting a smart plug to the machine and defining a rule that a smart plug in the living room should make a light blink when power consumption of the dryer dropped. After presenting his idea at a regulars' table meeting, this solution was adopted by others, too. Other demands for information related to security issues, such as checking for open windows or making sure all electronics were switched off.

A second kind of permanently demanded information related to system awareness:

"I check the system to see if something has failed, like my heating control at the beginning?" (multi-person household)

Related to system awareness, users showed relatively little concerns in privacy, though some users wanted to know what information was being transferred to the vendor (or 3rd parties). That is, they demanded a degree of awareness:

"For now, I don't see any way of misusing my data that could turn out to be my downfall. [...] It would be nice, however, to see what data is transferred or stored. If I can control this, its on me to decide what may be transferred or used." (single-person household)

Moreover, we found that most households did not understand the potential of information that could be deduced by third parties analysing data. However, if users understood, e.g that smart home logs provide strong hints as to whether anyone was at home at a given time, awareness and caution grew:

"After looking at the diary widget, I realized what information the smart home collected. Especially, in terms of motion profiles, because these are safety-critical information." (multi-person household)

One-time and temporal home awareness demands

During summer, in particular, a set of temporal or seasonal information demands became apparent. With longer daylight and higher temperatures during the summer season there was simply less to be managed in the house and interest in checking the temperature for heating was less sought. During the summer, however, a two-person household with cats for example wanted to check the room temperature whilöe they were abroad:

"[..] We could control if it was too hot for the cats at home." (two-person household)

Several information demands were limited to a special event or timespan. This could be due to activities of members of the households or due to a change of infrastructure: for example, to gain an understanding how much energy the new washing machine consumed. After tracking the machine for a while, there was no further interest in a long-term consumption evaluation.

Controlling the home

The physical smart home switch was considered a great way of controlling the home, and many households appreciated the possibility of simply positioning switches whenever a smart home command was used regularly. For example, several households positioned a switch, which was supposed to be put on a wall, on their living room table to change light settings when sitting on the sofa despite aesthetic considerations. The switch was only available in white, since it was built for wall mounting, and was seen as intruding on the interior decoration.

Although also a frequently used interface when at home, the mobile application was primarily used abroad. Here, use cases serving a demand for security awareness prevailed. Simulating presence by switching on and off lights manually was especially considered a benefit. While traditional timers were already used by some participants, their static programmable time slots were perceived as a limitation and easily detectable by potential burglars. Either random timers or randomized timeslots were mentioned as possible solutions.

While core use cases seemed to be identified, the routinization phase points towards the complexity and heterogeneity of households' ecosystems. Even though comfort, security and energy savings might motivate households to have an interest in a smart home on a global level, concrete use cases are highly individual and changed noticeably depending on seasonal factors, changing infrastructure or (irr-)regular events and households' evolving routines. Many use cases only arose in a later phase after households had the systems installed.

Becoming an Expert: Reconfiguration and Extension

In our first reflective interviews after four months of smart home use, participants told us about having integrated their smart home into their households to varying extents. Upon asking about the system's cost and its relation to the market price, however, the smart home was valued more as an expensive 'nice to have' gadget, rather than as a vital part of the home. However, no household took the offer to remove the system; they all wanted to participate further.

With households getting used to the system, its limitations became more evident. These, in part, stemmed from the sensors and actors not included within the system. For example, flush mounted switches or IP cameras were not available. While disappointing in principle, households understood that the product was still new and its landscape was to be extended. Other limitations of the smart home, however, were less anticipated and less accepted.

First, many users perceived Z-wave as a strictly standardized protocol and thought that any Z-wave-based sensor or actor was supposed to work with the system, too. Therefore, as an alternative to missing sensors and actors in the system, more technology-experienced households themselves tried to include third-party devices into the system. In most cases, and to varying extent, this failed due to differing interpretation of the communication standard. One participant found a third-party device that included several sensors which he wanted to be shown on his dashboard. Athough compliant to the Z-wave standard, including the sensor was hard work and only partially worked:

"Well this (...) small bowl [I got] (...) It was kind of a jack of all trades device including earthquake sensor, motion detection and temperature (...). After four weeks, I managed [to include] it, but it only offered me the motion detection function." (multi-person household)

The only way to know whether a product would work, even within the same standard, was to either find out by word-of-mouth or by trial and error. Thoughout the smart home market official whitelists are seldom to be found.

Second, users found limits in the product itself, posing a barrier for their intended use. For example, some configurations of includable sensors were not possible, e.g. defining the sending rate of a light detector was not possible because of the vendor's battery saving intentions. This however, limited adaptability and led to feelings of helplessness and frustration:

"I guess you have to think twice whether it is the right component to fulfill your wish? [..] But I think it is kind of an issue, when expectations of users differ from what the vendor was thinking." (single-person household)

Users also naively thought that other systems they used would be interoperable with a smart home, especially the ones promising "smartness". For example, some households had smart meters installed, which they thought would easily go with a smart home system – in fact they were considered a vital part of it. Similarly, other smart systems such as smartphones or audio systems were expected to be able to have an interface for sensors and actors, such that e.g. the smart home would be able to react to the GPS of the phone or the battery of an electric vehicle.

DISCUSSION AND CONCLUSION

In the 18-month Living Lab study, we identified 3 potential ways of fostering appropriation of smart home technology. We provide significant empirical detail, showing not only that users experience certain kinds of barriers but also *in what circumstances and when* they are likely to do so. Secondly, the extensive qualitative research undertaken demonstrates how these barriers are significant at particular stages of the appropriation process and suggests that designers need be mindful of this evolving set of conditions. Thirdly, we have shown, in and through the Living Lab study, that the various barriers to use should not be treated as separate matters, but need to be addressed in a holistic manner. In particular, the heterogeneous ways in which households demanded configuration forms, and the degree of knowledge required in order to do so, was identified. Throughout the study, the most common and severe problems arose in the fields of (a) a disconnect between users' expression of demands and the systems' capability to understand and process them. This became visible in the system setup phase and during installation and configuration, (b) maintaining awareness in routine use and and finding suitable visualizations for feedback demands, and (c) system extension beyond the home as a place. We discuss these practice-based phenomena and outline promising ways of addressing these issues.

Setup and configuration with practices and routines

Despite being interested in buying a smart home product, all households in our Living Lab mentioned having experienced problems identifying a suitable solution. The market is evolving quickly, and new products are being continually offered, making it hard to gain an overview. Most importantly, a smart home system was understood to be a significant investment, thus requiring it to be extendable in the future [10]. Here, the implications of choosing a particular system were not transparent in relation to future extensibility of the communication protocols and third-party sensors or actors. In this regard, our observations here were similar to Mennicken et al. [41]. Our findings go further, however, in highlighting that households actually did have ideas of what a smart home is supposed to provide, but often failed to map their interest to suitable technological setups. When asking, what could be improved or automated in the home, households often came up with what smart homes already offer. However, the step towards choosing the right technology was where our households reported feeling undecided and lost. We believe that orienting towards practices, routines and use cases to be supported will help users better understand what kind of technological setup they might need.

This disconnect between what users desired and how to map this to the system also was a major theme during installation and configuration, too. Although in the past even experts struggled to get distributed digital systems to work [57], new interfaces and web technologies promise plug and play even for "ordinary" users. This is in line with several attempts to make the smart home plug-and-play compatible [1,8,35,47]. Taking into account the individuality of user demands, End-User-Development (EUD) is known to pose a promising strategy for making complex systems work for non-experts, and should be relevant to the smart home [32,60].

We now argue that it is especially useful to support the operationalization of behavior and routines into events measurable for sensors. Smart homes, we argue, should be sensitive to local and changing, routines by affording more obvious and flexible (re-)configuration possibilities [44]. The typically proposed if-this-then-that style posed major challenges to households not familiar with algorithms in their everyday life. Reflecting on household practices in such a way that they could be matched to technology behavior was a serious challenge. Here, systems could more actively support users, e.g. by being pre-paired and preconfigured [47]. For example, products could be adapted to users during the buying decision by them reporting about routines. This way, the workload of algorithmically reflecting about daily routines would be transferred into a non-technological language, while still allowing rules and dependencies to be deduced and use cases to be suggested.

This would allow the vendor to include rules into the system upfront, thus relieving the user of a task and fostering the plug and play character.

Design for evolving visualization demands

During sustained and routine use, households checked up on their smart home, in the main for three reasons: (a) Maintaining control and awareness of what has been going on in the home and how it performs (i.e. in terms of energy consumption), (b) system check (i.e. whether the smart home does what it should), and (c) for temporary or specific event-driven information demands. Although, generally, the system worked in the background autonomously, usable means for maintaining sovereignty in the home were demanded. Regardless of the reason the concrete requirements on what exactly households wanted to check were highly individual and changed over time. In the field of energy consumption, these are known phenomena [51], calling for software to allow for continuous change and adaptability [32,33]. EUD [5,38] could support the users' journey from a novice to an expert user by allowing for adaptable information dashboards and information widgets for evolving or temporary demands.

Extending the 'home'

After getting used to their system, some households explicitly tested boundaries or came up with new use cases that included other electronic devices, such as smart meters, photovoltaic systems, smartphones, IP-based gardening equipment, cameras or car-mounted GPS-sensors. The isolation of these smart systems was counterintuitive to users and often led to frustration when different smart systems were not interoperable. This separation was not reduced to single appliances and protocols [10], but rather spanned across ecosystems. On a UX and usability level, the single access points to the systems lacking coherence in wording, style and control.

Households increasingly perceived their smart home interface as the central point for managing their home and wanted a single management system that also included e.g. their garden electronics and connection to external sensors and actors such as the smartphone. In this regard, the home is more than a location [17]. One promising solution is unified dashboards and control centers of distributed information sources from cyber-physical systems in household environments, similar to what Few [24] describes for business dashboards. For respective measures to be effective, this also calls for action on the middleware level [20]. If respective APIs and interfaces for protocols are provided, user interfaces may make use of them.

Limitations

Our findings might in part be due to system peculiarities. Even so, having conducted a market analysis and lab-based test of several platform-based systems we believe that most findings are not bound to a specific product. For smart home systems, Z-wave is a widespread standard, as are dashboards and IFTTT mechanisms for rule definition. All of which have implications for setup, running and maintenance that our system shares with many others. Also, market complexity and limitations in interoperability are not product-related. More sensors might have improved the smart home experience. However, at least for surface-mounted solutions, an evolving growth of the smart home system better represents the actual way of buying such systems. Moreover, most inexperienced participants ran into major problems making their smart home work with about ten existing sensors. In limiting the amounts of sensors, we supported a steady appropriation and found newly developed use cases over time. Finally, our research was of a qualitative nature, which also sparks typical limitations. For further evaluating validity and classifying the relevance of each problem dimension identified, further quantitative research could and should be conducted.

CONCLUSION

Our Living Lab-based case study has identified design guidelines addressing challenges during the process of smart home appropriation. Overall, we argue that smart home so far has targeted the home primarily as a technological space, rather than a a place formed by routines and interaction [29]. By becoming more sensitive to the routines and practices of users, four challenges could be addressed: Regarding the challenges of setting up and configuring the smart home, we stress the importance of daily routines as a metaphor which households can cope with, in contrast to technical detail or algorithmic patterns. For supporting operation and maintenance of a smart home, evolving visualization demands call for flexible user interfaces, adaptable to both temporary and permanent information demands on home and system awareness. Finally, smart home systems could unlock more of their potential when going beyond typical place-related boundaries, incorporating floating and interweaving practices which are not limited to the home as a building.

ACKNOWLEDGMENTS

This work was funded by the German Federal Ministry for Economic Affairs and Energy (Grant Number: 01MU14001). We warmly thank all contributing households for participation and cooperation in this study. We also thank Dave Randall for his helpful comments and linguistic revisions.

REFERENCES

1. Bessam Abdulrazak and A. Helal. 2006. Enabling a Plug-and-play integration of smart environments. In *2006 2nd International Conference on Information & Communication Technologies*, 820–825. Retrieved December 26, 2016 from http://ieeexplore.ieee.org/xpls/abs_all.jsp?arnumber=1684479
2. Wokje Abrahamse, Linda Steg, Charles Vlek, and Talib Rothengatter. 2005. A review of intervention studies aimed at household energy conservation. *Journal of Environmental Psychology* 25, 3: 273–291. https://doi.org/10.1016/j.jenvp.2005.08.002

3. Wokje Abrahamse, Linda Steg, Charles Vlek, and Talib Rothengatter. 2007. The effect of tailored information, goal setting, and tailored feedback on household energy use, energy-related behaviors, and behavioral antecedents. *Journal of Environmental Psychology* 27, 4: 265–276. https://doi.org/10.1016/j.jenvp.2007.08.002
4. Mohsen Amiribesheli, Asma Benmansour, and Abdelhamid Bouchachia. 2015. A review of smart homes in healthcare. *Journal of Ambient Intelligence and Humanized Computing* 6, 4: 495–517.
5. Barbara Rita Barricelli and Stefano Valtolina. 2015. Designing for End-User Development in the Internet of Things. In *End-User Development*. Springer, 9–24. Retrieved March 21, 2016 from http://link.springer.com/chapter/10.1007/978-3-319-18425-8_2
6. Regina Bernhaupt, Marianna Obrist, Astrid Weiss, Elke Beck, and Manfred Tscheligi. 2008. Trends in the living room and beyond: results from ethnographic studies using creative and playful probing. *Computers in Entertainment (CIE)* 6, 1: 5.
7. Eli Blevis. 2007. Sustainable interaction design: invention & disposal, renewal & reuse. *Proceedings of the SIGCHI conference on Human factors in computing systems - CHI '07*: 503–512. https://doi.org/10.1145/1240624.1240705
8. Raja Bose, Jeffrey King, H. El-Zabadani, S. Pickles, and A. Helal. 2006. Building plug-and-play smart homes using the atlas platform. In *Proceedings of the 4th International Conference on Smart Homes and Health Telematic (ICOST), Belfast, the Northern Islands*. Retrieved December 26, 2016 from http://citeseerx.ist.psu.edu/viewdoc/download?doi=10.1.1.83.1562&rep=rep1&type=pdf
9. Virginia Braun and Victoria Clarke. 2006. Using thematic analysis in psychology. *Qualitative research in psychology* 3, 2: 77–101.
10. A. J. Brush, Bongshin Lee, Ratul Mahajan, Sharad Agarwal, Stefan Saroiu, and Colin Dixon. 2011. Home automation in the wild: challenges and opportunities. In *Proceedings of the SIGCHI Conference on Human Factors in Computing Systems*, 2115–2124. Retrieved February 23, 2016 from http://dl.acm.org/citation.cfm?id=1979249
11. Jennie Carroll, Steve Howard, Frank Vetere, Jane Peck, and John Murphy. 2001. Identity, power and fragmentation in cyberspace: technology appropriation by young people. *ACIS 2001 Proceedings*: 6.
12. Jennie Carroll, Steve Howard, Frank Vetere, Jane Peck, and John Murphy. 2002. Just what do the youth of today want? Technology appropriation by young people. In *System Sciences, 2002. HICSS. Proceedings of the 35th Annual Hawaii International Conference on*, 1777–1785. Retrieved September 4, 2016 from http://ieeexplore.ieee.org/xpls/abs_all.jsp?arnumber=994089
13. Ann Cavoukian and Alexander Dix. 2012. *Smart Meters in Europe: Privacy by Design at its Best.* Information and Privacy Commissioner of Ontario, Canada. Retrieved October 20, 2014 from http://www.ipc.on.ca/images/Resources/pbd-smartmeters-europe.pdf
14. Diane J. Cook, G. Michael Youngblood, Edwin O. Heierman III, Karthik Gopalratnam, Sira Rao, Andrey Litvin, and Farhan Khawaja. 2003. MavHome: An Agent-Based Smart Home. In *PerCom*, 521–524. Retrieved July 18, 2016 from https://www.researchgate.net/profile/G_Youngblood/publication/4011271_MavHome_An_Agent-Based_Smart_Home/links/5451065f0cf2bf864cba8691.pdf
15. Ricardo Costa, Davide Carneiro, Paulo Novais, Luís Lima, José Machado, Alberto Marques, and José Neves. 2009. Ambient assisted living. In *3rd Symposium of Ubiquitous Computing and Ambient Intelligence 2008*, 86–94. Retrieved July 18, 2016 from http://link.springer.com/chapter/10.1007/978-3-540-85867-6_10
16. Karen L. Courtney and others. 2008. Privacy and senior willingness to adopt smart home information technology in residential care facilities. *Methods Inf Med* 47, 1: 76–81.
17. Scott Davidoff, Min Kyung Lee, Charles Yiu, John Zimmerman, and Anind K. Dey. 2006. Principles of smart home control. In *International Conference on Ubiquitous Computing*, 19–34. Retrieved September 13, 2016 from http://link.springer.com/10.1007%2F11853565_2
18. George Demiris, Marilyn J. Rantz, Myra A. Aud, Karen D. Marek, Harry W. Tyrer, Marjorie Skubic, and Ali A. Hussam. 2004. Older adults' attitudes towards and perceptions of "smart home"technologies: a pilot study. *Medical informatics and the Internet in medicine* 29, 2: 87–94.
19. Alan Dix. 2007. Designing for appropriation. In *Proceedings of the 21st British HCI Group Annual Conference on People and Computers: HCI... but not as we know it-Volume 2*, 27–30. Retrieved August 12, 2016 from http://dl.acm.org/citation.cfm?id=1531415
20. Colin Dixon, Ratul Mahajan, Sharad Agarwal, A. J. Brush, Bongshin Lee, Stefan Saroiu, and Victor Bahl. 2010. The home needs an operating system (and an app store). In *Proceedings of the 9th ACM SIGCOMM Workshop on Hot Topics in Networks*, 18. Retrieved September 20, 2016 from http://dl.acm.org/citation.cfm?id=1868465
21. Paul Dourish. 2003. The appropriation of interactive technologies: Some lessons from placeless documents. *Computer Supported Cooperative Work (CSCW)* 12, 4: 465–490.
22. W. Keith Edwards and Rebecca E. Grinter. 2001. At home with ubiquitous computing: Seven challenges. In *Ubicomp 2001: Ubiquitous Computing*, 256–272.

Retrieved January 27, 2016 from http://link.springer.com/10.1007/3-540-45427-6_22
23. Mats Eriksson, Veli-Pekka Niitamo, and Seja Kulkki. 2005. *State-of-the-art in utilizing Living Labs approach to user- centric ICT innovation - a European approach.* Lulea University of Technology, Sweden, Lulea. Retrieved from www.vinnova.se/upload/dokument/verksamhet/tita/stateoftheart_livinglabs_eriksson2005.pdf
24. Stephen Few. 2006. *Information Dashboard Design: The Effective Visual Communication of Data*. O'Reilly Media, Beijing ; Cambride MA.
25. Asbjørn Følstad. 2008. Living labs for innovation and development of information and communication technology: a literature review. *The Electronic Journal for Virtual Organizations and Networks* 10, 7: 99–131.
26. Jon Froehlich, Leah Findlater, James Landay, and Computer Science. 2010. The design of eco-feedback technology. In *Proceedings of the 28th international conference on Human factors in computing systems - CHI '10*, 1999–2008. https://doi.org/10.1145/1753326.1753629
27. Rebecca E. Grinter, W. Keith Edwards, Mark W. Newman, and Nicolas Ducheneaut. 2005. The work to make a home network work. In *ECSCW 2005*, 469–488. Retrieved December 24, 2016 from http://link.springer.com/chapter/10.1007/1-4020-4023-7_24
28. Richard Harper. 2006. *Inside the smart home*. Springer Science & Business Media. Retrieved February 17, 2016 from https://books.google.de/books?hl=en&lr=&id=3J0MBwAAQBAJ&oi=fnd&pg=PA1&dq=smart+home+design&ots=zmhCkGdioy&sig=A8nrOE8gwY6Z1apSygIHpdUBFlE
29. Steve Harrison and Paul Dourish. 1996. Re-place-ing space: the roles of place and space in collaborative systems. In *Proceedings of the 1996 ACM conference on Computer supported cooperative work*, 67–76. Retrieved December 26, 2016 from http://dl.acm.org/citation.cfm?id=240193
30. OA Blanson Henkemans, K. E. Caine, W. A. Rogers, A. D. Fisk, and M. A. Neerincx. 2007. Medical monitoring for independent living: user-centered design of smart home technologies for older adults. In *Proc. Med-e-Tel Conf. eHealth, Telemedicine and Health Information and Communication Technologies*, 18–20. Retrieved February 17, 2016 from http://ii.tudelft.nl/pub/olivier/Med-e-Tel_BlansonHenkemansetal..pdf
31. Stephen S. Intille. 2002. Designing a home of the future. *IEEE pervasive computing* 1, 2: 76–82.
32. Timo Jakobi and Tobias Schwartz. 2012. Putting the user in charge: end user development for eco-feedback technologies. In *Sustainable Internet and ICT for Sustainability (SustainIT), 2012*, 1–4. Retrieved December 14, 2013 from http://ieeexplore.ieee.org/xpls/abs_all.jsp?arnumber=6388020
33. Timo Jakobi, Gunnar Stevens, and Tobias Schwartz. 2011. EUD @ Smart Homes Smart refurbishment of rented apartments to improve energy efficiency.
34. Julie A. Kientz, Shwetak N. Patel, Brian Jones, E. D. Price, Elizabeth D. Mynatt, and Gregory D. Abowd. 2008. The georgia tech aware home. In *CHI'08 extended abstracts on Human factors in computing systems*, 3675–3680. Retrieved March 2, 2016 from http://dl.acm.org/citation.cfm?id=1358628.1358911
35. Ji Eun Kim, George Boulos, John Yackovich, Tassilo Barth, Christian Beckel, and Daniel Mosse. 2012. Seamless integration of heterogeneous devices and access control in smart homes. In *Intelligent Environments (IE), 2012 8th International Conference on*, 206–213. Retrieved December 26, 2016 from http://ieeexplore.ieee.org/xpls/abs_all.jsp?arnumber=6258524
36. Andreas Kirmse. 2012. Privacy in Smart Homes. *ComSys Seminar: Advanced Internet Technology SS2012*. Retrieved from http://kirmandi.rumeln.net/data/paper-Privacy.in.Smart.Homes.pdf
37. Tiiu Koskela and Kaisa Väänänen-Vainio-Mattila. 2004. Evolution towards smart home environments: empirical evaluation of three user interfaces. *Personal and Ubiquitous Computing* 8, 3–4: 234–240.
38. Henry Lieberman, Fabio Paternò, Markus Klann, and Volker Wulf. 2006. End-user development: An emerging paradigm. In *End user development*. Springer, 1–8. Retrieved November 22, 2013 from http://link.springer.com/chapter/10.1007/1-4020-5386-X_1
39. Suzanne Martin, Greg Kelly, W. George Kernohan, Bernadette McCreight, and Christopher Nugent. 2008. Smart home technologies for health and social care support. *Cochrane Database Syst Rev* 4. Retrieved February 17, 2016 from http://onlinelibrary.wiley.com/doi/10.1002/14651858.CD006412.pub2/pdf/
40. Peter Mayer, Dirk Volland, Frédéric Thiesse, and Elgar Fleisch. 2011. User Acceptance of'Smart Products': An Empirical Investigation. Retrieved December 24, 2016 from https://www.alexandria.unisg.ch/145231/
41. Sarah Mennicken and Elaine M. Huang. 2012. Hacking the natural habitat: an in-the-wild study of smart homes, their development, and the people who live in them. In *International Conference on Pervasive Computing*, 143–160. Retrieved December 21, 2016 from http://link.springer.com/chapter/10.1007/978-3-642-31205-2_10
42. Sarah Mennicken, Amy Hwang, Rayoung Yang, Jesse Hoey, Alex Mihailidis, and Elaine M. Huang. 2015. Smart for Life: Designing Smart Home Technologies that Evolve with Users. In *Proceedings of the 33rd*

Annual ACM Conference Extended Abstracts on Human Factors in Computing Systems, 2377–2380. Retrieved December 24, 2016 from http://dl.acm.org/citation.cfm?id=2702631

43. Sarah Mennicken, David Kim, and Elaine May Huang. 2016. Integrating the Smart Home into the Digital Calendar. In *Proceedings of the 2016 CHI Conference on Human Factors in Computing Systems*, 5958–5969. Retrieved July 10, 2016 from http://dl.acm.org/citation.cfm?id=2858168
44. Sarah Mennicken, Jo Vermeulen, and Elaine M. Huang. 2014. From today's augmented houses to tomorrow's smart homes: new directions for home automation research. In *Proceedings of the 2014 ACM International Joint Conference on Pervasive and Ubiquitous Computing*, 105–115. Retrieved December 21, 2016 from http://dl.acm.org/citation.cfm?id=2636076
45. Michael Mozer. 2004. Lessons from an adaptive house. Architectural Engineering. Retrieved March 2, 2016 from https://www.researchgate.net/profile/Michael_Mozer/publication/266594221_Lessons_From_An_Adaptive_House/links/55b90cdb08aed621de085fd9.pdf
46. Corinna Ogonowski, Benedikt Ley, and Jan Hess. 2013. Designing for the living room: long-term user involvement in a living lab. *Proceedings of the SIGCHI Conference on Human Factors in Computing Systems*. Retrieved from http://dl.acm.org/citation.cfm?id=2466205
47. Ogonowski Ogonowski, Philippe Hennes, and Maximilian Seiffert,. 2016. Shop&Play Erlebnis im Smart Home: Nutzung statt Installationschaos. Workshop Usability für die betriebliche Praxis.
48. Dave Randall. 2006. Living inside a smart home: A case study. In *Inside the smart home*. Springer Science & Business Media, London, 227–246.
49. Alfredo Rial and George Danezis. 2011. Privacy-preserving smart metering. In *Proceedings of the 10th annual ACM workshop on Privacy in the electronic society*, 49–60. Retrieved September 2, 2014 from http://dl.acm.org/citation.cfm?id=2046564
50. Tobias Schwartz, Gunnar Stevens, Timo Jakobi, Sebastian Denef, Leonardo Ramirez, Volker Wulf, and Dave Randall. 2014. What People Do with Consumption Feedback: A Long-Term Living Lab Study of a Home Energy Management System. *Interacting with Computers* 26, 3: iwu009. https://doi.org/10.1093/iwc/iwu009
51. Tobias Schwartz, Gunnar Stevens, Leonardo Ramirez, and Volker Wulf. 2013. Uncovering Practices of Making Energy Consumption Accountable: A Phenomenological Inquiry. *ACM Trans. Comput.-Hum. Interact.* 20, 2: 12:1–12:30. https://doi.org/10.1145/2463579.2463583
52. Roger Silverstone and Leslie Haddon. 1996. Design and the domestication of ICTs: technical change and everyday life. *Communicating by Design: The Politics of Information and Communication Technologies*: 44–74.
53. Gunnar Stevens, Volkmar Pipek, and Volker Wulf. 2009. Appropriation infrastructure: Supporting the design of usages. In *End-user development*. Springer, 50–69. Retrieved March 23, 2016 from http://link.springer.com/chapter/10.1007/978-3-642-00427-8_4
54. Gunnar Stevens and Volker Wulf. 2009. Computer-supported access control. *ACM Transactions on Computer-Human Interaction (TOCHI)* 16, 3: 12.
55. Yolande Strengers. 2011. Negotiating everyday life: The role of energy and water consumption feedback. *Journal of Consumer Culture* 11, 3: 319–338.
56. Emmanuel Munguia Tapia, Stephen S. Intille, and Kent Larson. 2004. *Activity recognition in the home using simple and ubiquitous sensors*. Springer. Retrieved February 17, 2016 from http://link.springer.com/chapter/10.1007/978-3-540-24646-6_10
57. Peter Tolmie, Andy Crabtree, Stefan Egglestone, Jan Humble, Chris Greenhalgh, and Tom Rodden. 2009. Digital plumbing: the mundane work of deploying UbiComp in the home. *Personal and Ubiquitous Computing* 14, 3: 181–196. https://doi.org/10.1007/s00779-009-0260-5
58. Daphne Townsend, Frank Knoefel, and Rafik Goubran. 2011. Privacy versus autonomy: a tradeoff model for smart home monitoring technologies. In *Engineering in Medicine and Biology Society, EMBC, 2011 Annual International Conference of the IEEE*, 4749–4752. Retrieved July 17, 2014 from http://ieeexplore.ieee.org/xpls/abs_all.jsp?arnumber=6091176
59. Blase Ur, Jaeyeon Jung, and Stuart Schechter. 2013. The current state of access control for smart devices in homes. In *Workshop on Home Usable Privacy and Security (HUPS)*. Retrieved December 15, 2014 from http://cups.cs.cmu.edu/soups/2013/HUPS/HUPS13-BlaseUR.pdf
60. Jong-bum Woo and Youn-kyung Lim. 2015. User experience in do-it-yourself-style smart homes. In *Proceedings of the 2015 ACM International Joint Conference on Pervasive and Ubiquitous Computing*, 779–790. Retrieved December 28, 2016 from http://dl.acm.org/citation.cfm?id=2806063
61. Volker Wulf, Markus Rohde, V Pipek, and G Stevens. 2011. Engaging with practices: design case studies as a research framework in CSCW. *Proceedings of the ACM 2011 conference on Computer supported cooperative work*: 505–512.
62. Tomoki Yoshihisa, Naotaka Fujita, and Masahiko Tsukamoto. 2011. HEMS toolkit: A toolkit for constructing a home energy management system. *2011 IEEE Consumer Communications and Networking*

Conference (CCNC): 822–823. https://doi.org/10.1109/CCNC.2011.5766612

63. Paschalina Lilia Ziamou, Stephen Gould, and Alladi Venkatesh. 2012. "Am I Getting It or Not?" The Practices Involved in "Trying to Consume" a New Technology. *Journal of Product Innovation Management* 29, 2: 216–228.

A Social Media Based Index of Mental Well-Being in College Campuses

Shrey Bagroy
Precog
IIIT-Delhi
shrey14099@iiitd.ac.in

Ponnurangam Kumaraguru
Precog
IIIT-Delhi
pk@iiitd.ac.in

Munmun De Choudhury
College of Computing
Georgia Tech
munmund@gatech.edu

ABSTRACT
Psychological distress in the form of depression, anxiety and other mental health challenges among college students is a growing health concern. Dearth of accurate, continuous, and multi-campus data on mental well-being presents significant challenges to intervention and mitigation efforts in college campuses. We examine the potential of social media as a new "barometer" for quantifying the mental well-being of college populations. Utilizing student-contributed data in Reddit communities of over 100 universities, we first build and evaluate a transfer learning based classification approach that can detect mental health expressions with 97% accuracy. Thereafter, we propose a robust campus-specific Mental Well-being Index: MWI. We find that MWI is able to reveal meaningful temporal patterns of mental well-being in campuses, and to assess how their expressions relate to university attributes like size, academic prestige, and student demographics. We discuss the implications of our work for improving counselor efforts, and in the design of tools that can enable better assessment of the mental health climate of college campuses.

Author Keywords
college mental health; Reddit; social media; transfer learning

ACM Classification Keywords
H.5.m. Information Interfaces and Presentation (e.g. HCI): Miscellaneous

INTRODUCTION
College students confront many challenges in pursuit of their educational goals [51]. When such experiences are perceived as negative for a prolonged period of time, they can have an adverse effect on students' well-being [1, 3, 66]. Beyond implications for personal health, the Federal Bureau of Investigation has reported that mental health concerns on college campuses can pertain directly to episodes of violence [22].

Yet few university students seek help related to mental illness. Only 18% of students with a past-year history of poor mental wellness are known to seek counseling, therapy or treatment [9]. This arises due to a variety of barriers: limited health insurance coverage, paucity of knowledge about psychiatric services, social stigma, and lack of time [1, 57].

It is recognized that campus-wide support measures, coping strategies, and mitigation programs might decrease the negative effects of mental illness in college students [3, 54, 66]. However, employing all of these interventions necessitates adequate assessment of the "mental health climate" within a university campus. Currently, such assessments are challenged due to the paucity of adequate and accurate data on students' well-being. Local data is gathered through visits to the campus counseling center. However these services are often only availed by students when their mental well-being takes a downward turn [27]. Complementarily, many universities conduct periodic surveys [5] to gauge mental health challenges of students and supplement clinical data on students' mental health [35, 9]. However the large temporal gaps across which these measurements are made, the retrospective nature of recalling past experiences, and limited consistency of survey findings across multiple campuses make it difficult for authorities to act upon such information and influence campus mental health intervention programs.

In this paper, we aim to bridge this gap by utilizing social media as an unobtrusive "lens" to gauge mental health expressions of students in university campuses. Our motivation stems from two observations. First, recent advances in HCI and social computing research has provided promising evidence that content shared on social media, especially its linguistic characteristics, can enable accurate inference, tracking, and understanding of mental health states [19, 14, 60]. Second, over 90% of young adults, or individuals of college going age, use social media [40]. In fact, many college students are appropriating these platforms to meet a variety of their needs, such as for self-disclosure, support seeking and social connectedness [30]. How can we build on these methodological advances and the pervasive use of social media by students to gauge their mental well-being? To answer this question, we focus on the following research aims:

- **Aim 1:** Building and validating a machine learning methodology to identify mental health expressions of students in campus-geared online communities.
- **Aim 2:** Analyzing the linguistic and temporal characteristics of the above inferred mental health expressions of students in different university campuses.
- **Aim 3:** Developing an index of collective mental well-being in a campus, and examining its relationship to at-

CHI'17, May 06-11, 2017, Denver, CO, USA

http://dx.doi.org/10.1145/3025453.3025909

tributes of the university, including academic prestige, enrollment size, and student demographic distribution.

To accomplish these research aims, we use large-scale, passively gathered, longitudinal data shared in over 100 campus-geared communities on the social media Reddit. We then show that an inductive transfer learning approach [49] can help to detect mental health expressions in student populations with high precision and accuracy (97%). Analyzing these expressions over time, we find that they show a monotonically increasing trend through the academic year. However these expressions demonstrate a decreasing trend during the summer months. Alarmingly, we also observe that the relative proportion of these expressions have shown a 16% increase between 2011 and 2015. Then, we demonstrate that our transfer learning based classification approach can be used to develop a novel metric of college campus well-being, known as "Mental Well-being Index" (MWI). MWI enables us to discover both established as well as previously underexplored differences across college campuses. We find MWI to be lower in public universities with large undergraduate student bodies and female students; counter-intuitively, it is not lower in colleges with higher academic prestige.

To the best of our knowledge, we present the first large-scale multi-campus study of college student mental health by leveraging social media data of over 100 campuses. Our findings bear implications for improving mental health support and counseling efforts within campuses. We conclude by discussing design considerations for technologies that enable unobtrusive, real-time tracking of collective mental health of college student populations.

RELATED WORK

Mental Health of College Campuses

Clinical and Epidemiological Assessments

There is a rich body of work in psychology, health policy, epidemiology, and public health around assessing and understanding mental health concerns of college students [31, 45, 59]. While some of these works focus on identifying the underlying factors that impact college students' mental health [59], the bulk focuses on assessing the mental health of students who seek help at college counseling centers [31]. Most college counseling centers persistently collect local data from students seeking their services on individual campuses, such as through survey instruments validated against the Diagnostic and Statistical Manual of Mental Disorders (DSM) [45]. However it has been noted that these data are rarely shared nationally. Further, Soet and Sevig [56] argued that college students who do not come to counseling centers need to be investigated to examine similarities and differences between clinical (those who seek mental health treatment) and non-clinical populations. By focusing on content shared on university campus social media communities, we are able to identify an alternative mechanism to gather information about mental health challenges in college campuses, including of those who may be unwilling or unable to seek professional help.

Noting the challenges of solely focusing on clinical student populations, many universities have adopted a survey conducted by the American College Health Association [6]. The survey includes limited questions on mental health issues such as medication use, depression, and suicide. However these studies are limited in temporal granularity and involve significant resource commitment to conduct.

To overcome limitations of survey approaches, researchers have employed wearable sensing technologies and experience sampling methods to obtain a variety of physiological and psychological signals in a continuous fashion from college student populations [62, 28, 65, 64]. However most of these works have been done in a controlled lab setting or supervised real-life setting. Exception is the recent work of Wang et al [62], who used smartphone sensing to validate attributes of campus life, including academic conduct, lifestyle, socialization, depression, stress, and mood [13, 63, 10].

Although these approaches capture rich, dense sensing data about people's behaviors, activities and moods, they need considerable cooperation, intervention, and compliance from participants. This challenges conducting longitudinal, repeatable studies on student mental health spanning large populations. Social media data, on the other hand, can be passively collected, and therefore can scale to multiple campuses easily. Thus it can be more useful for longitudinal tracking of a specific university's mental health climate.

Differences Across Academic and Student Attributes

Various research studies have explored how mental health of college students relates to demographic and social factors [7]. Racial and ethnic minority students are reported to underuse mental health services, even while reporting more distress [67]. Further, studies report gender differences in psychological distress among young adults and students [45]. Therefore, it is posited that a focus on reaching diverse groups of college students, such as gender or racial minorities in specific campuses, is needed [24].

However, there has been limited research examining the manifestation of mental health concerns among students in the light of the academic setting, such as enrollment size, competitiveness, prestige, supportiveness of academic personnel, and field of study [56]. Hunt and Eisenberg [32] argued that the risk factors for mental disorders among students must be understood in the context of not only their vulnerabilities, but also how they interact with external factors in college. Our work attempts to fill this gap by analyzing the relationship between social media derived mental well-being of students, and a range of attributes of the corresponding institutions, such as the size and demographics of their student body, and academic prestige.

Social Media and Mental Health

General Population. An emergent body of work in HCI and related disciplines has examined the relationship between mental well-being and self-disclosure on social media [18, 2]. De Choudhury and De [18] explored individuals who appropriated the Reddit platform to express a variety of emotional and mental distress, and how these expressions are characterized by disinhibiting behavior. Andalibi et al. [2] qualitatively characterized the variety of emotional expressions that are shared on Instagram via the hashtag "#depression". In other work, social media content analysis, specifically of linguistic cues and conversational patterns, has enabled novel mechanisms to predict risk to mental health concerns, ranging from depression [19], substance abuse [47, 41], loneliness [36], eating disorders [12], and other mental health disorders [14, 60]. We extend this body of work by developing an automated machine learning method that can detect mental health expressions in social media, specifically in the context of college student populations.

College Students. There is limited work on college students' social media use and their mental well-being. Ellison et al. [26], in a seminal study, found that there is a positive relationship between college students' Facebook use and the maintenance and creation of social capital. Similarly, Manago et al. [42] found that social networking sites helped college students satisfy enduring human psychosocial needs. Other work has found that social media use may foster the development of intimate relationships, including supportive friendships among college students [52]. Moreover, the communication with friends that occurs on these platforms may help college students resolve key issues present during this transitional phase of life [44]. Given the pervasiveness of social media use among college students and its relationship with psychological well-being [30, 43, 61], we examine how data gathered from these platforms may lend insights into the collective mental well-being of college campuses.

Macro-Scale Mental Well-Being With Social Media

Leveraging social media, researchers have also sought to develop quantifiable indices of emotional and mental well-being of large populations [46, 34, 29]. Kramer [37] developed a "Gross National Happiness" index with Facebook posts, whereas Dodds et al. [21] developed a "happiness index", a hedonometer, based on textual content shared on Twitter. More recently, Schwartz et al. [55] adopted more sophisticated methods like topic models to study the patterns of county-specific levels of well-being and life satisfaction using Twitter data. Utilizing clinical self-reported information about depression, De Choudhury et al. [17] also developed a Twitter-based state-level index of depression. Our contributions in this paper build on these investigations and methodologies. We examine how unobtrusive data gathered from students' social media use may inform the development of a quantifiable index that tracks collective mental well-being of students in different college campuses.

DATA

University Data

We first obtained a list of 150 ranked major universities in the United States by crawling the US News and World Report website [48]. This list is constructed based on the Carnegie classification, employed extensively by higher education researchers, and using a set of 16 indicators of academic excellence, defined by US News. The list includes a variety of universities spread across the US in different settings (e.g., urban, rural), and with a wide range of student enrollment sizes. Figure 1(a) shows their geographic distribution. As a part of this crawl, we also obtained university metadata: gender distribution of students, average tuition and fees, and academic calendar (semester/quarter).

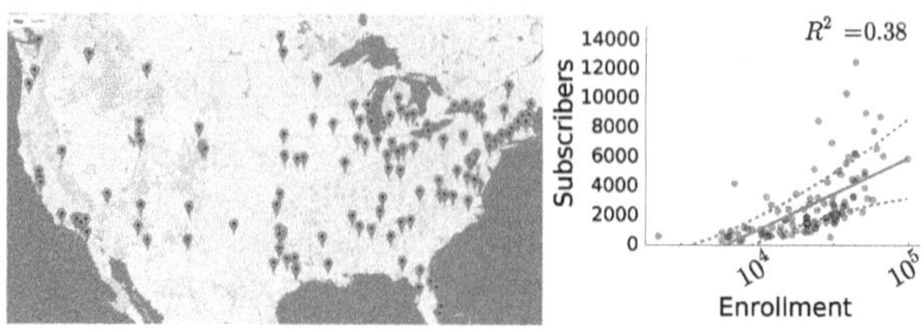

(a) (b)

Figure 1: (a) Geographical distribution of the 150 ranked universities used in this paper. (b) University subreddit size over student enrollment, (as of July 2016).

To obtain further information about the nature of the student body, we crawled the Wikipedia pages of all of the 150 universities. From these pages, we extracted the size of student enrollment, type (public/private), and setting (rural/suburban/urban/city) at every institution. These definitions come from a formal categorization scheme used by the US Department of Education. The student body enrollment sizes ranged from 2,255 to 97,494, with 98 public and 52 private universities. 50 universities were reported to be urban, 47 city, 39 suburban, and 13 rural.

Finally, we obtained information on racial diversity of the universities from a website known as Priceonomics [58]. The website calculates the Herfindahl-Hirschman Index (HHI), by combining the race/ethnicity distribution of student bodies at different universities, with data given from the Department of Education. HHI ranges from 1 (the least diverse: a population of all one type) to $1/N$ (the most diverse), where N is the number of different racial categories being analyzed.

Social Media Data of Universities

Next we obtained social media data of the above universities. Specifically, we focused on the social media Reddit.

Why Reddit? Reddit is known to be a widely used online forum and social media site among the college student demographic [23]. Due to its forum structure, it is extensively used for both content sharing, as well as for obtaining feedback and information from communities of interest. Reddit harbors a variety of communities known as "subreddits", including many dedicated to specific university campuses. This allows a large sample of posts shared by students of a university to be collected in one place. Our preliminary manual inspection of university subreddits (e.g., r/gatech or r/KState) revealed that these subreddits are appropriated by students to discuss college topics (Table 1). Focusing on these public Reddit communities also does not require explicit data collection efforts to be coordinated at each of the 150 university sites. Although more students are likely to use Facebook, due to its largely privately shared content, it is challenging to obtain access to a large dataset of a university's students. Next, while Twitter is also widely adopted, without explicit self-reported information, it is challenging to identify college student accounts. Finally, prior work [2, 18] notes that semi-anonymity of Reddit enables candid self-disclosure around stigmatized topics like mental health.

What constitutes a "good" GPA? I'm currently entering my third quarter as a CS major and realize today that I've no idea what's considered a "good" (or even "average") GPA here
Not getting calculus I have a 3.7 GPA and I made an A in both [class A] and [class B], so I know I'm not dumb. I don't know what the hell is wrong with me cause I sure feel dumb.
Need a little help please I'm not doing very well, I don't mean academically I mean in my head. I really don't think I can continue with this quarter.

Table 1: Example (slightly paraphrased) subreddit posts identified to be written by university students.

By utilizing Reddit's subreddit search functionality, we crafted various search queries using names and acronyms of the university names in our above list. We were able to identify the public subreddit pages of 146 out of the 150 above identified universities. Thereafter we employed a multi-step approach to secure posts and associated metadata shared in these 146 subreddits:

Initial Data Acquisition. We leveraged the archive of all of Reddit data made available on Google's BigQuery [11]. BigQuery is a cloud based managed data warehouse, that allows third parties to access large publicly available dataset through simple SQL-type queries. Our queries grabbed all posts ranging between June 2011 and February 2016 available in the Reddit data archive. This included 424,984 posts from 153,378 unique users across all of the 146 universities, with a mean of 2,910.8 posts ($\sigma = 4329.6$) and 1,050 unique users ($\sigma = 1407$) per subreddit.

Filling the Gaps in Subreddit Data. The second step of our data collection process focused on identifying subreddits with insufficient data, and supplementing them through additional alternative data collection. Through Reddit's official API (https://www.reddit.com/dev/api/), we obtained the most recent number of subscribers in the 146 university subreddits (as of July 2016). Then to investigate if and to what extent some subreddits may have had unusually low data as given in step 1, we determined the median unique user to subscriber ratio in each subreddit. This allows us to capture the subreddits where the subscriber count is high, however the data obtained is not sufficiently representative. For subreddits with unique user to subscriber ratio under median (.42) (73 in all), we performed a one-time data collection using the Reddit API. This gave us a set of (at most) 1000 most recent posts for each subreddit, with a total of 39,824 posts added to the data obtained in step 1, following de-duplication. We note that this procedure did not skew the yearly distributions of data across the subreddits: The skew (yearly rate of change) before and after data filling were 4.86 and 5.05 respectively, which were found to be statistically equivalent based on a two-sample equivalence test ($p = .013$, $p = .025$), a test that uses two one-sided t-tests on the before-after yearly rates of change from both sides of a chosen difference interval $[-1, 1]$.

Correcting for Under-Adoption of Reddit. Based on the Reddit data we collected, from Figure 1(b) we observe high positive correlation between a university's size of student body (enrollment) and the number of users subscribing to the corresponding subreddit ($R^2 = .38; \rho^2 = .6; p < .05$). For subreddits deviating from trend, it would imply that the associated university's student body was under or over-represented on Reddit. We therefore devised a method to identify these subreddits, to correct especially for under-adoption bias. We first calculated the ratio between the number of subreddit subscribers to student enrollment for each subreddit and the corresponding university. If, for a subreddit, this ratio was less than the expected adoption of Reddit for the same demographic group (4-8% as of 2016[1]), we assumed that Reddit was under-adopted by the students in the corresponding university. We thus removed subreddits where this ratio was <4%. This brought down our subreddits from 146 to 109. In these 109 subreddits, the mean Reddit adoption was 8.6% (σ =1.3), which is close to the highest adoption reported by Pew.

The final dataset employed in our ensuing analyses included 446,897 posts from 152,834 unique users (mean posts per subreddit: 4,100; mean users per subreddit: 1,402). Figure 2(a) gives a distribution of the volume of crawled posts over the years. Figure 2(b) gives the final distribution of subreddits over the unique user to subscriber count ratio. Figure 2(c-d) gives distribution of the posts and unique users across the final 109 subreddits.

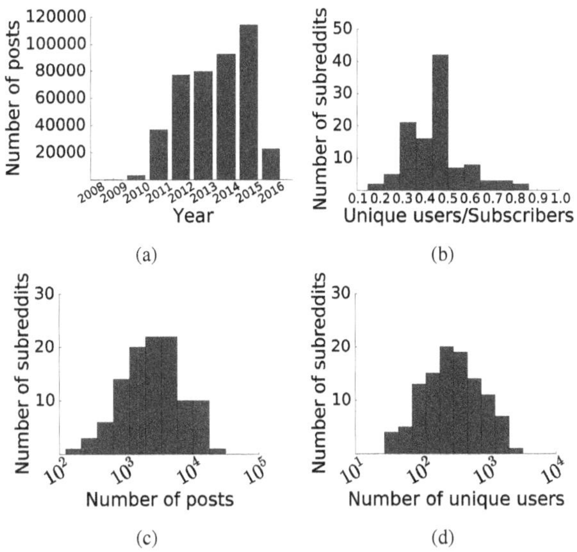

Figure 2: (a) Volume of posts over time, from the final 109 university subreddits. (b) Distribution of subreddits over unique user to subscriber count ratio. (c) Distribution of subreddits over total number of posts. (d) Distribution of subreddits over the number of unique users.

Demographic Representativeness

We note, it is possible that the type of students who frequent the university subreddits could be consistently different from the student body at the same university. To examine the representativeness of our university subreddit data, we employed a random sample of 500 posts, distributed across the subreddits and the years, for manual examination of demographics. Two researchers then independently coded these posts

[1] http://www.journalism.org/2016/05/26/news-use-across-social-media-platforms-2016/

for self-reported gender, race, or academic stage (undergraduate/graduate). For instance, from the post *"I'm a junior transfer and this will be my second semester"*, the researchers identified the post author to be an undergraduate, whereas from *"Hi all! I'm a new grad student (male, 22) here*, the gender of the author can be inferred to be male. We found the interrater agreement to be high: Cohen's $\kappa = .84$.

The relative ratios between the gender, race, and academic stage distributions of the coded posts and the university student body (obtained based on our methodology in the subsection "University Data") showed significant positive correlation: The mean undergrad/grad ratio in our labeled data was 2.9, while it was 2.6 in the universities. A two-sample test of equivalence gave p-values of .016 and .011 respectively, with respect to the difference interval $[-.4, .4]$. The sex (male/female) ratio for our labeled data was 1.6, also observed to be statistically equivalent to that of the student body, 1.1 ($p = .02$, $p = .03$, w.r.t. the difference interval $[-.5, .5]$). This establishes the validity of our acquired Reddit data as a representative data source for studying mental health disclosures in university campuses.

METHODS

We now present a methodology of identifying posts shared in university subreddits that that are likely to be mental health expressions. Note that, our Reddit data does not contain any gold standard information around whether a post shared in a university subreddit is about one's mental health experience or condition. Our proposed method overcomes this challenge by employing an inductive transfer learning approach [16].

First, we include (as ground truth data) Reddit posts made on various mental health support communities. Prior work has established that, in these communities, individuals self-disclose a variety of mental health challenges explicitly [50]. Parallelly, we utilize another set of Reddit posts, made on generic subreddits unrelated to mental health, to be a control. Next, we build a machine learning classifier to distinguish between these two types of posts. Then we learn features that could detect whether an post shared in a university subreddit could be an expression of some mental health concern. We discuss these steps in detail in the following subsections.

Mental Health and Control Data

We gained access to a sample of 63,485 public posts from 35,038 unique users, shared between 2014 and 2016, in a variety of mental health subreddits—this repository of posts has been used in prior work to study mental health self-disclosure and support seeking manifested in social media [18, 50, 39, 20]. This dataset includes posts and associated metadata spanning 14 mental health related subreddits, such as r/depression, r/mentalhealth, and r/traumatoolbox, r/bipolarreddit. From this corpus, we excluded posts that contained only a title without a post body. This gave us 21,734 posts. We refer to these posts as MH posts.

Our control data also relied on a dataset compiled and utilized in prior work [50]; it contains posts from subreddits such as r/WorldNews, r/food, and r/AskReddit. We randomly sampled an equal number of posts (21,734) as the MH posts above for our control dataset. We refer to these posts as CL posts.

Automatic Identification of Mental Health Expressions

In order to automatically identify posts relating to mental health expressions, we adopted an inductive transfer learning approach [49]. As described above, we utilized the dataset of MH and CL posts as positive and negative examples in a binary classification framework. We utilized this data to train and test different classification techniques, including random forests, Ada Boost, Support Vector Machines (SVM), and Logistic Regression. We also adopted k-fold cross validation to evaluate the optimality and robustness of the approach, and included as features the linguistic content of the posts (stopword eliminated uni-, bi-, and tri-grams).

Mental Well-being Index of Universities (MWI)

Can the ability to predict whether or not a Reddit post involves an individual's mental health expression provide the basis for an accurate, reliable, fine-grained model of mental well-being manifested in various university subreddits? To this end, we use our above developed machine learning classifier to *automatically* label the corpus of posts shared in the 109 university subreddits. Thereafter, we define a metric called the "Mental Well-being Index" (MWI). At a time t and for a university U, we define it as the standardized difference between the frequencies of users sharing non-mental health expression posts $f_n(t, U)$ observed until t in the subreddit of U, and that of the users sharing mental health expressions until t in the same subreddit ($f_p(t, U)$):

$$\text{MWI}(t, U) = (f_n(t, U) - \mu_n)/\sigma_n - (f_p(t, U) - \mu_p)/\sigma_p \quad (1)$$

where μ_p (correspondingly μ_n) and σ_p (correspondingly σ_n) are the mean and standard deviations of the frequencies of mental health expression (correspondingly non-mental health expression) posts. Note that we consider separate terms for the two classes of posts. This allows mental health expression and other expressions in posts to be weighted equally (since their relative volumes are likely to be different in a subreddit). This way, we also focus on variation in each class separately. That is, even if per one's behavior, some individuals dramatically under-express mental health concerns in their posts, the relative non-mental health expression compared to mental health expression will be informative.

RESULTS

Aim 1: Evaluating the Mental Health Expression Classifier

Model Performance

First, we evaluate our transfer learning based classifier for detecting mental health expressions in Reddit posts. We split up our corpus of 43,486 posts shared on the MH and CL communities into a training set (on which 5-fold cross validation is applied) and a validation set, with 80% posts for training and 20% for validation. Following 5-fold cross validation with different classification approaches, we found our logistic regression model to

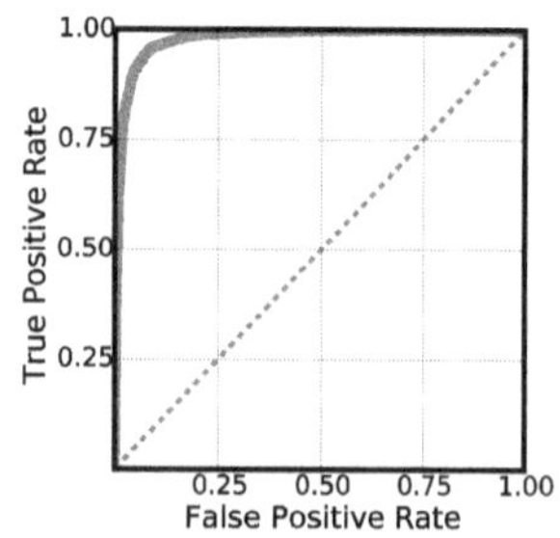

Figure 3: ROC curve in classifying mental health (MH) and control (CL) posts.

	Val. set	Test set
Acc.	93.4%	96.8%
Prec.	0.93	0.98
Rec.	0.93	0.97
AUC	0.98	0.97
F1	0.93	0.97

Table 2: Classifier performance on validation (8,692 MH and CL posts) and test sets (500 annotated university subreddit posts).

	Predicted	
Actual	CL	MH
CL	4080	266
MHD	308	4038

Table 3: Confusion matrix classifying posts in the validation set for mental health (MH) and control (CL) posts.

yield the highest accuracy: 93.4%, with an average precision, recall, and F-1 score of .93 each (refer to the column on "Validation set" Table 2 for these metrics). Table 3 presents the confusion matrix corresponding to classification on this validation set. We also note the area-under-curve (AUC) value for this classifier, corresponding to the receiver operating characteristic (ROC) curve, to be high: .98 (see Figure 3). AUC is a widely used metric because it shows the tradeoff between true and false positive rates. Figure 3 shows that with only about 5% of FPR, we can achieve TPR of over 90%, illustrating high performance.

We also evaluate this best performing logistic regression in terms of its explanatory power in the validation set over an equivalent `Null` model. We find that the difference between the deviance of the `Null` model and the deviance of our model approximately follows a χ^2 distribution, with degrees of freedom equal to the number of additional predictor features in the latter model: $\chi^2(250,000, N = 8692) = 123076 - 98476 = 2.46 \times 10^4, p < 10^{10}$. Summarily, our model results in significant reduction of deviance in classifying MH and CL posts.

Examining Significant Predictive Features

Which n-gram features given by the logistic regression model are the most predictive of a post being classified to be MH or CL? To answer this question, we present, in Table 4, the 30 predictor features with positive β coefficient weights (i.e., they are correlated with MH posts), and another 30 predictor features with negative β coefficient weights (i.e., they are correlated with CL posts). We illustrate the context of use of a sample of these features to understand their relationship to classification outcomes.

Vast majority of the coefficients associated with positive weights pertain to expressions of a variety of different mental health challenges ("bpd", "bipolar", "ptsd", "suicide", "depressed", "mental health"). Some of the other features with positive coefficients include mentions of stress and anxiety ("anxiety", "anxious", "nervous"), some of the known concomitants of mental health concerns. Other features appear to be calls for help and support seeking on Reddit ("help", "talk", "request"). Some features also appear in discussions of treatment, coping strategies and outcomes ("meds", "therapy", "medication", "diagnosed", "psychiatrist", "recovery"). Finally, a set of features with positive coefficients also include manifestation of negative emotions, hopelessness and dejection, pain, and even extreme thoughts of harming and killing oneself ("kill", "tired", "suicidal", "die", "worse").

n-gram	β	n-gram	β	n-gram	β	n-gram	β
bpd	10.5	manic	4.3	reddit	-9.7	favorite	-2.5
anxiety	9.8	don know	4.1	tifu	-7.2	movie	-2.5
bipolar	7.8	tired	4.1	dae	-6.0	did	-2.4
ptsd	7.7	going	4.1	eli5	-5.7	muscle	-2.4
suicide	7.6	fucking	4.0	lpt	-5.6	gym	-2.4
feel	7.3	hate	4.0	ysk	-5.6	edit	-2.4
depressed	6.6	mental health	4.0	women	-4.8	guy	-2.3
help	6.4	diagnosed	4.0	redditors	-4.6	pregnant	-2.2
sa	6.1	psychiatrist	3.9	men	-3.7	squat	-2.1
just	5.8	social	3.8	sex	-3.4	pill	-2.1
mental	5.8	suicidal	3.8	workout	-3.2	song	-2.1
talk	5.7	today	3.8	trp	-3.2	thread	-2.1
meds	5.6	dbt	3.8	baby	-3.1	story	-2.1
therapy	5.5	request	3.7	discussion	-3.0	nsfw	-2.0
kill	5.4	years	3.7	dad	-3.0	curious	-2.0

Table 4: Selected top 60 predictor features and their most positive/negative β coefficients from our logistic regression classifier. We show features corresponding to both mental health disclosure and control posts.

On the other hand, the predictor features with large negative β coefficients span a diverse range of topics, ranging from events and experiences ('christmas", 'pregnant"), lifestyle ("workout", "gym"), sports ("game"), community participation and usage practices ("lpt request", "want know", "curious"), to Reddit specific topics ("reddit", redditors", "edit").

In summary, we observe that our transfer learning based classifier is able to robustly detect and characterize MH expressions in Reddit posts with high accuracy.

Expert Evaluation of MH Expressions in University Subreddits

Using the above trained and validated MH-CL post classifier, we then examined its performance in identifying mental health (henceforth MH) expressions in the posts belonging to the 109 university subreddits. For the purpose, we first employed two raters to annotate a random sample of 500 university subreddit posts (balanced across the two classes) to be about MH expressions or not. We used this annotated sample as a test set on which we applied our trained classifier.

Our qualitative annotation task proceeded as follows. Adopting an inductive semi-open coding approach, first, two raters, one a clinical psychologist and another a social media expert independently assigned binary annotations (MH expression or not) to a sub-sample of 100 posts. To arrive at these rules, they referred to prior work on qualitative and quantitative studies of mental health disclosures on social media [8, 2], and literature in psychology on markers of mental health expressions [53, 15, 33]. Following this initial rating exercise, the raters got together to resolve differences and constructed a final rulebook. Per this rulebook, a post had to satisfy one of more of these criteria to be annotated to be a MH expression:

- Explicit expressions of first hand experience of psychological distress or mental health concerns ("i get overwhelmingly depressed", "i get into a negative spiral", "I think I am on the verge and feel like it's the end").
- Explicit expressions of support, help, or advice seeking around difficult life challenges and experiences ("are there

Unigrams	Bigrams	Trigrams
health	to talk	feel like i
care	my life	course an intro
worried	my parents	was doing great
family	dont think	but i feel
problems	really dont	the jobs i
feeling	just need	only one homework
guess	my story	feel like im
hate	can help	really dont want
exhausted	the people	i really need
talking	killing myself	to make friends
cheated	people i	im just not
depression	life isnt	want to live
honestly	though i	doing poorly in
issues	mental health	issues with depression
fucking	social life	could help me
strangers	up late	go into debt
ruin	worried about	to deal with
psychiatric	suicidal thoughts	dont know where
experiences	need help	to hang out
alone	isnt fair	i need help

Table 5: Top 20 uni-, bi-, and tri-grams that appear uniquely in university subreddit posts detected by our classifier to be about mental health disclosures.

any resources I can use to talk to someone about depression?", "I have been going to therapy for 2 days a week every week for my anxiety").

Using this rulebook, the raters then annotated the larger sample of remaining 400 posts. The final agreement was found to be high (Cohen's $\kappa = .83$).

We then applied our trained classifier to this annotated test set of 500 posts. We found our classifier to demonstrate consistent performance as before, in the task of distinguishing between university subreddit posts that are related to MH expressions and those that are not. We achieved a mean accuracy of 96.8%, with AUC of .97 (see the second column on "Test set" in Table 2). We, therefore, proceeded with using this classifier in machine labeling all of the 446,397 other university subreddits posts. Our classifier identified 13,914 posts (3.1%) to be MH expressions, whereas the rest of the 432,483 posts were marked not about the topic. This corresponded to 9010 unique users out of a total of 152,834 (mean=5%, std. dev.=1.5% across the 109 subreddits).

Aim 2: Analyzing MH Expressions in Universities

As per our next research aim, we present analytical observations given by the above classification of university subreddit posts—specifically we seek to: 1) identify what linguistic constructs (n-grams) characterize posts predicted to be MH expressions, and 2) understand the temporal manifestations of MH expressions in the context of different universities.

Linguistic Characteristics of MH Expressions

In Table 5 we present the top 20 uni-, 20 bi-, and 20 tri-grams that appear uniquely in university subreddit posts identified to be MH expressions. For qualitative inspection of the context of use of these n-grams, we randomly sampled a set of 100 MH posts that contained at least one of these top n-grams. We performed qualitative semi-open coding on this sample, employing the same two raters as above. The rating task discovered various topical contexts in which these n-grams were used in the university subreddit posts:

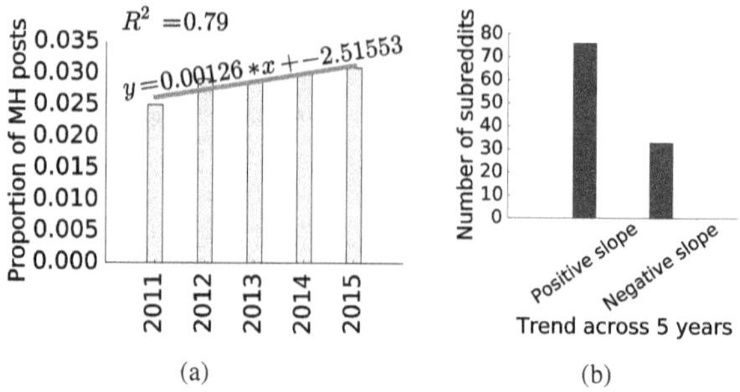

Figure 4: (a) Yearly trend of the proportion of mental health (MH) posts aggregated across all of the university subreddits. (b) Distribution of university subreddits over their respective positive or negative slopes of linear least squares fit to (a).

We find that students appropriate the Reddit communities to converse on a number of college, academic, relationship, and personal life challenges that relate to their mental well-being ("go into debt", "doing poorly in", "only one homework", "course an intro", "up late", "the jobs i"):

> I'm lost and overwhelmed. [...] I feel sick to my stomach because it made me *go into debt* and I can't seem to bring myself to go out there and find a job.

The n-grams also indicate that certain posts contain explicit mentions of mental health challenges ("psychiatric", "depression", "killing myself", "suicidal thoughts"), as well as the difficulties students face in their lives due to these experiences ("life isnt", "issues with depression", "was doing great", "ruin", "cheated"):

> New Fall transfer here. Can I use `[some service]` to get *psychiatric* help, including a diagnosis and meds IF necessary? There's definitely some psychological issues I've been carrying around with me my entire life.

Finally, some of the n-grams indicate that students tend to vent on the different subreddits about challenges of college life, or to share their personal stories, feelings, and experiences ("exhausted", "isnt fair", "my story", "im just not"):

> [...] Since it's too late to apply to any colleges for the fall semester, and since my entire social life is here at `[some university]`, I would prefer to stick around here rather than going home. So that's basically *my story*. Can anyone recommend me a mental health professional?

Some of the top n-grams are also used in the context of seeking support ("need help", "i really need", "could help me"):

> Anyone willing to help me with `[some course]` preparing for the final? I *need help*, this semester has been extremely stressful due to development of clinical depression and anxiety.

Putting it together, this analysis help us validate that our classifier is able to reveal markers of mental health challenges in college students that are known to relate to their academic, personal or social lives [31, 45, 59].

Temporal Characteristics of MH Expressions

Next, we present an analysis of how the identified MH expressions in different university subreddits change over time. First, we compute the proportion of MH posts for each of

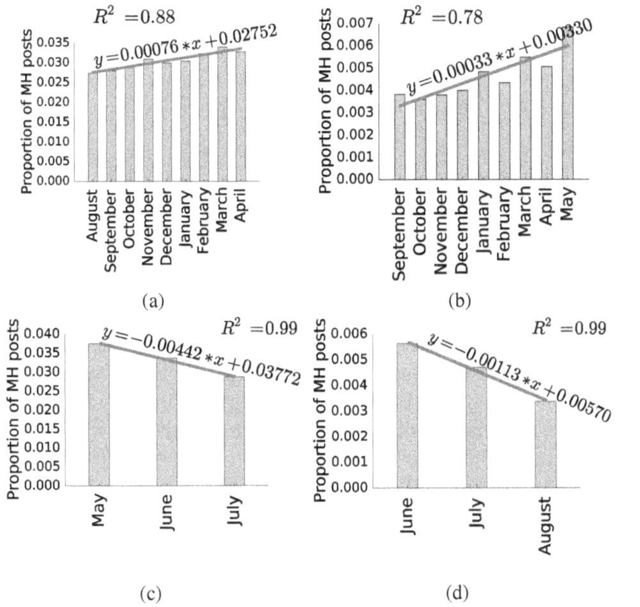

Figure 5: MWI during (a) the academic year for universities with the semester system; (b) the academic year for universities with the quarter system; (c) the summer for universities with the semester system; and (d) the summer for universities with the quarter system.

the 109 subreddits. Aggregating this fraction over each of the years in our datasets[2], we study the relative temporal change in expression of mental health in the university subreddits under consideration. In Figure 4(a), we show this trend, along with a corresponding linear least squares model fit ($R^2 = .79, p < .05$). We observe that, the proportion of posts with MH expressions has been on the rise—there is 16% increase in 2015, compared to that in 2011. Further, identifying groups of subreddits with strictly positive or negative slopes per their least square fits (Figure 4(b)), we find that although there are some university subreddits with negative slopes (i.e., they show a decreasing trend over the years), for the vast majority (71% of the 109 subreddits), there has been a continual increase over time.

Next, we examine how MH expressions in university subreddits change over the course of a typical academic year. Since academic years differ in universities adopting the semester and the quarter system, we compare differences in the trends of MH expressions across these university groups as well. From Figure 5(a-b) we find that over the course of a typical academic year, the proportion of MH posts of universities in both the semester and quarter system show a monotonically increasing trend. Note the positive slopes of the two linear least squares model fits: $R^2 = .88, p < .05$ and $R^2 = .78, p < .05$ respectively. Between August and April, for the universities in the semester system, we observe an 18.5% increase in MH expression ($p < .05$); this percentage is much higher: 78% for those in the quarter system, when compared between September and May ($p < .05$). On the other hand, during the summer months (Figure 5(c-d)), for

[2]We exclude 2016 since we don't have complete data for the year.

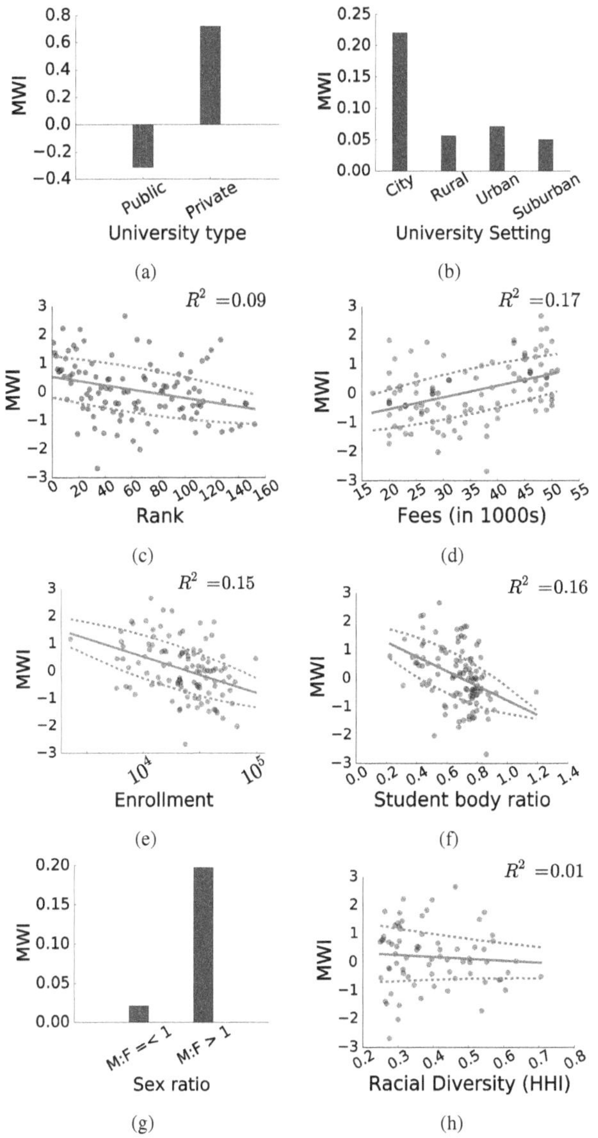

Figure 6: Scatterplots of MWI vs (a) university type, (b) university setting, (c) rank, (d) fees, (e) enrollment, (f) student body ratio, (g) sex ratio, and (h) Racial Diversity (HHI).

both semester system and quarter system universities, we observe a reverse trend for the proportion of MH posts, i.e., a trend with a negative slope: $R^2 = .99, p < .05$ for both university groups.

Aim 3: Relating MWI to University Attributes

For our final investigation (aim 3), we compute the MWI metric for each of the 109 university subreddits. We examine the relationship between the MWI of each university subreddit and the corresponding university's attributes.

We glean several interesting observations from Figure 6(a-h). From Figure 6(a) we find that MWI of the 66 public universities we consider, is lower, relative to that in the 43 private universities, by 332%. This difference is found to be statistically significant based on an independent sample t-test

($t = 7.38, p < .05$). Examining universities by their setting (Figure 6(b)), we find that MWI is lower in the 7 rural and 33 suburban universities by 40-266% compared to others ($p < .05$), while it is the highest in the 31 universities categorized to be in cities (by $29 - 77\%; p < .05$). Next, Figure 6(c) and (d) show the relationship between MWI of the universities, and their academic prestige and tuition fees. We observe a negative slope in the scatter plot of the former ($R^2 = .09; p < .05$), while a positive slope in case of the latter ($R^2 = .17; p < .05$). In essence, universities with higher academic prestige (or low absolute value rank) and higher tuition tend to be associated with higher MWI.

Now we discuss the relationship of MWI of the universities with four attributes of their student body. Both Figure 6(e) and Figure 6(f) show that universities with larger student bodies (enrollment) as well as greater proportion of undergraduates in their student bodies tend to be associated with lower MWI ($R^2 = .15; p < .05$ and $R^2 = .16; p < .05$ respectively). Finally, examining two demography related attributes of student bodies, we find from Figure 6(g) and (h) that MWI tends to be lower in universities with more females (or sex ratio, male to female ≤ 1) by 850% ($p < .01$). Further, although our data shows a marginally lower MWI in universities with greater racial diversity, we did not find statistical significance to support this claim ($R^2 = .01; p = .2$).

DISCUSSION

Theoretical Implications of the Findings

Mechanisms for collective assessment of mental health challenges in college populations are highly valued in the literature [56, 6], however they are rare in practice. By proposing an index of mental well-being in campuses that is derived from passively acquired social media data of students, we believe our work makes a contribution to close this gap. As our results have shown, with this kind of measurement, we are able to glean previously established as well as new insights into students' mental well-being in different universities and types of student bodies.

MH expressions of universities have been increasing over the years. A notable finding of our analysis is the monotonically increasing trend of (normalized) MH expressions across university campuses—there was a 16% rise between 2015 and 2011. This finding aligns with observations from nationwide surveys on mental health of college students. In a 2008 national survey of directors of campus counseling centers, 95% of directors reported a significant increase in severe psychological problems among their students [4]. While our findings do not extrapolate to the same set of universities or the same timeframe, same directionality of the trend provides some validation of our MH expression detection method.

MH expressions show increase during the academic year, but decrease over the summer. We also observe that the MH expressions consistently increase through the academic year, while consistently decrease during the summer. There is prior work that situates academic pressure as a notable contributing factor of mental health challenges in students [31, 45]. We hypothesize that as the academic year advanced, the accumulating academic pressure may be one reason behind the monotonically increasing trend of MH expressions. On the other hand, students may have identified the summer months to be a time to unwind and relax, hence likely lowering the expression of MH challenges. However we suggest caution in deriving causal claims from these findings.

MWI is lower for large, public universities with large undergraduate student bodies. Next, in relating student body attributes to a university's MWI, we are able to confirm some known facts about college student mental health. The campuses most challenged by mental health issues tend to be public universities which have large student bodies and a greater proportion of undergraduate students. It is reported that the student bodies of these campuses include many who are the first in their families to attend college and therefore carry intense pressure to succeed [32]. Further, undergraduate students especially are known to be at an elevated risk [35, 7]. We conjecture these prior findings may provide some explanation behind the observed low MWI in universities with large undergraduate student bodies.

MWI is higher in high prestige universities. Further, we observe that there is a positive correlation with higher academic prestige (in terms of ranking) of a university and MWI. Despite reports of mental health challenges being more prevalent in top ranked colleges [25], our results reveal an opposite trend. In a high prestige university, it is likely the student body is self-selected, in that they perhaps already have internalized the need to deal with the academic pressure and rigor needed for success. Therefore they might be unlikely to express being overwhelmed mentally and emotionally on a public social media community like Reddit.

MWI is higher in universities with higher tuition. Relatedly, the other somewhat surprising finding is the positive relationship between a university's tuition fees and its MWI. Financial stress is identified to be a major factor behind college students' mental health issues [31]. Our finding deviates from this expected behavior. We conjecture it might be explained by the socio-economic support structure that many of the students at high tuition universities may come with—those who get admitted are likely to have friends, family, and a sound financial backbone that may be mediating their risk to well-being challenges [24].

MWI is lower in universities with a larger female student body. As a final observation, our results indicate that there is greater expression of mental health challenges in universities that have a larger proportion of female students over male. As noted in our literature review, female college students tend to seek mental health help more frequently compared to male students [45]. Hence it can be presumed that they also tend to be more expressive about their mental health challenges in social media, thereby explaining our finding for MWI.

Taken together, through this paper, we introduced social media, for detecting campus-specific mental health expressions of students. This has enabled us to obtain a variety of insights, like the ones discussed above, into the mental well-being of a campus in a granularity and scale not possible before. Moreover, with our approach, it is possible to gather these insights through unobtrusive, inexpensive means, with little intrusion. Thus our work can expand and complement current survey-based efforts of assessing student mental health and its relationship to attributes of the university or the student body. Broadly, we contribute to the emergent body of HCI research that leverages naturalistically shared population data on social media for mental health measurement [19]: We are able to identify a variety of college-student specific linguistic markers of mental health challenges by employing a novel data source of university-specific Reddit communities.

Implications for Design

We believe that our work can enable technology design that promotes population-centric reflection of mental well-being in college campuses in ways not possible before. This can be accomplished in the following ways:

Technologies for Improving Counseling Efforts. Our work shows that when college students appropriate social media to express their mental health challenges, our method can accurately identify and measure such expressions. This observation and methodology can be incorporated into interactive applications for campus counselors. The application could surface specific linguistic attributes highly correlated with the mental health expressions of students on social media, as well as the temporal manifestations of these attributes in different student groups. This information can be highly beneficial to campus counseling centers and other campus health service providers in understanding the pervasiveness of mental health expressions, and the variety of topics that student attribute in these communities to be related to mental health challenges. They could act on this information to allocate their services and strategies to better reach and serve students.

Technologies for Assessing Campus Morale. Our method and findings bear implications for the design of novel student mental well-being tracking interfaces, visualizations, and systems for use by campus administrators. These interfaces could provide stakeholders with an interactive way to identify temporally and in a near real-time fashion, the ebbs and highs of mental well-being, during a typical academic year as well as over extended periods of time. This information can then be utilized for routine assessments of campus morale, as well as to understand the impacts of academic events like examinations, regulations and policy decisions in campus life. Further, it can also contribute to improved preparedness in campus in case of an emergency and assessing mental resilience of the student body in response to adverse events that affect mental well-being of student. Finally, these systems can also empower campus administrators with collective information about students given by the students themselves, to identify how to proactively employ, allow and manage campus specific resources, mental health awareness and mitigation programs in order to best cater to the needs of the students, and improve campus mental well-being.

Limitations and Future Work

Diagnostic Claims, Causality, and Generalizability. We note that the Mental Well-being Index is not meant to be a diagnostic tool to assess who is at risk of mental illness. Thus we caution against appropriating the index as a mechanism to identify specific college students who could be suffering from mental health concerns. However, as future work, it will be worthwhile to examine to what extent MWI's assessments of mental health challenges correlate with psychometric assessments obtained via instruments like the Patient Health Questionnaire (PHQ) [38]. We also caution against deriving causal claims between various university attributes and manifested MWI. Further, we only studied 150 ranked universities in the US. We caution against arbitrary generalizations.

Prevalence. We found that the percentages of mental health expression users in Reddit were slightly lower (5%) than reported national statistics of college students with significant mental health concerns (7%) [6]. We hypothesize a couple of reasons behind this difference. 1) Students, due to the stigma of mental illness, may be underreporting their mental health concerns on a public platform like Reddit. 2) Students who appropriate social media for mental health needs may be ones who do not (or are not able to) seek professional help, accounting for the discrepancy.

Evaluation. Although our validation approach for MWI derived trends that align with some known patterns of college students' mental health challenges, one of the limitations of our work is more rigorous evaluation. Which are the campuses with the most mental health challenges, and does our MWI metric correlate with those statistics? Answering this question requires access to the normalized levels of mental health concerns in the universities studied here, which is not available for public use [56]. Moreover, university administrators may be hesitant to share such statistics more widely due to the stigma it may bring to a university student body. However, as we showed, MWI can be adopted to compare across subgroups of campuses that share similar attributes.

Alternative Data Sources. Finally, we leveraged data from Reddit. While this social media is very popular in the college student demographic, it is likely that a variety of other social media are also used with data volunteering efforts of students, such as Instagram, Twitter, and Snapchat, as noted earlier. Future research could examine how data from these various platforms may be integrated to improve the assessment of mental health expressions in campuses.

CONCLUSION

Many college students are appropriating online social platforms for mental health disclosure and support seeking needs. We used student-geared Reddit communities of over a hundred universities to build and evaluate a transfer learning based classification approach that can detect mental health expressions with 97% accuracy. Leveraging this classifier, we then developed a Mental Well-being Index (MWI) to evaluate the collective mental health status of over 100 university campuses in the US. We then showed the relationship between various attributes of the universities and their student bodies, and MWI. We believe our work can enbale technology design to tackle mental health challenges in college populations.

ACKNOWLEDGMENTS

We thank Gregory Abowd and other members of the Georgia Tech CampusLife team for valuable feedback. We also thank members of Precog for their valuable inputs; special thanks to Niharika Sachdeva. De Choudhury was partly supported through NIH grant #1R01GM11269701.

REFERENCES

1. Reda Abouserie. 1994. Sources and levels of stress in relation to locus of control and self esteem in university students. *Educational psychology* 14, 3 (1994), 323–330.
2. Nazanin Andalibi, Pinar Ozturk, and Andrea Forte. 2015. Depression-related Imagery on Instagram. In *Proc. CSCW'15 Companion*. 231–234.
3. Aaron Antonovsky. 1979. Health, stress, and coping. (1979).
4. American College Health Association and others. 2009. American College Health Association-National College Health Assessment Spring 2008 Reference Group Data Report (abridged): the American College Health Association. *Journal of American college health: J of ACH* 57, 5 (2009), 477.
5. American College Health Association and others. 2012. American College Health Association-National College Health Assessment II: Reference Group Data Report Spring 2012. *Linthicum, MD: American College Health Association* (2012).
6. American College Health Association and others. 2013. National College Health Assessment II: Reference Group Executive Summary Fall 2012. *Hanover, MD: American College Health Association* (2013).
7. Roger C Bailey and Christy Miller. 1998. Life satisfaction and life demands in college students. *Social Behavior and Personality: an international journal* 26, 1 (1998), 51–56.
8. Sairam Balani and Munmun De Choudhury. 2015. Detecting and Characterizing Mental Health Related Self-Disclosure in Social Media. In *Proceedings of the 33rd Annual ACM Conference Extended Abstracts on Human Factors in Computing Systems*. ACM, 1373–1378.
9. David H Barlow, Paul M Lehrer, Robert L Woolfolk, and Wesley E Sime. 2007. *Principles and practice of stress management*. Guilford Press.
10. Dror Ben-Zeev, Emily A Scherer, Rui Wang, Haiyi Xie, and Andrew T Campbell. 2015. Next-Generation Psychiatric Assessment: Using Smartphone Sensors to Monitor Behavior and Mental Health. (2015).
11. Google BigQuery. 2015. Reddit Archive on Google BigQuery. `https://bigquery.cloud.google.com/table/fh-bigquery:redditposts.fullcorpus201512?pli=1`. (2015). Accessed: 2016-09-03.
12. Stevie Chancellor, Zhiyuan Lin, Erica L Goodman, Stephanie Zerwas, and Munmun De Choudhury. 2016. Quantifying and Predicting Mental Illness Severity in Online Pro-Eating Disorder Communities. In *Proceedings of the 19th ACM Conference on Computer-Supported Cooperative Work & Social Computing*. ACM, 1171–1184.
13. Fanglin Chen, Rui Wang, Xia Zhou, and Andrew T Campbell. 2014. My smartphone knows i am hungry. In *Proceedings of the 2014 workshop on physical analytics*. ACM, 9–14.
14. Glen Coppersmith, Mark Dredze, and Craig Harman. 2014. Quantifying mental health signals in twitter. In *ACL Workshop on Computational Linguistics and Clinical Psychology*.
15. Paul C Cozby. 1973. Self-disclosure: a literature review. *Psychological bulletin* 79, 2 (1973), 73.
16. Wenyuan Dai, Qiang Yang, Gui-Rong Xue, and Yong Yu. 2007. Boosting for transfer learning. In *Proceedings of the 24th international conference on Machine learning*. ACM, 193–200.
17. Munmun De Choudhury, Scott Counts, and Eric Horvitz. 2013a. Social media as a measurement tool of depression in populations. In *Proceedings of the 5th Annual ACM Web Science Conference*. ACM, 47–56.
18. Munmun De Choudhury and Sushovan De. 2014. Mental Health Discourse on reddit: Self-disclosure, Social Support, and Anonymity. In *International Conference on Weblogs and Social Media (ICWSM)*.
19. Munmun De Choudhury, Michael Gamon, Scott Counts, and Eric Horvitz. 2013b. Predicting depression via social media. In *AAAI Conference on Weblogs and Social Media*.
20. Munmun De Choudhury, Emre Kiciman, Mark Dredze, Glen Coppersmith, and Mrinal Kumar. 2016. Discovering shifts to suicidal ideation from mental health content in social media. In *Proceedings of the 2016 CHI Conference on Human Factors in Computing Systems*. ACM, 2098–2110.
21. Peter Sheridan Dodds, Kameron Decker Harris, Isabel M Kloumann, Catherine A Bliss, and Christopher M Danforth. 2011. Temporal patterns of happiness and information in a global social network: Hedonometrics and Twitter. *PloS one* 6, 12 (2011), e26752.
22. Diana A Drysdale, William Modzeleski, Andre B Simons, Janet Napolitano, Mark Sullivan, Arne Duncan, Kevin Jennings, Eric Holder, Robert S. Mueller III, and others. 2010. Targeted Violence Affecting Institutions of Higher Education. `https://www.fbi.gov/stats-services/publications/campus-attacks`. (2010). Accessed: 2010-09-30.
23. Maeve Duggan and Aaron Smith. 2013. 6% of Online Adults are reddit Users. `http://www.pewinternet.org/2013/07/03/6-of-online-adults-are-reddit-users/`. (2013). Accessed: 2016-09-03.
24. Daniel Eisenberg, Ezra Golberstein, and Sarah E Gollust. 2007. Help-seeking and access to mental health care in a university student population. *Medical care* 45, 7 (2007), 594–601.

25. Daniel Eisenberg, Justin Hunt, and Nicole Speer. 2013. Mental health in American colleges and universities: variation across student subgroups and across campuses. *The Journal of nervous and mental disease* 201, 1 (2013), 60–67.

26. Nicole B Ellison, Charles Steinfield, and Cliff Lampe. 2007. The benefits of Facebook "friends": Social capital and college students' use of online social network sites. *Journal of Computer-Mediated Communication* 12, 4 (2007), 1143–1168.

27. Robert P Gallagher and Al Gill. 2004. National survey of counseling center directors. *Alexandria, VA: International Association of Counseling Services* (2004).

28. Martin Gjoreski, Hristijan Gjoreski, Mitja Lutrek, and Matja Gams. 2015. Automatic detection of perceived stress in campus students using smartphones. In *Intelligent Environments (IE), 2015 International Conference on*. IEEE, 132–135.

29. Scott A Golder and Michael W Macy. 2011. Diurnal and seasonal mood vary with work, sleep, and daylength across diverse cultures. *Science* 333, 6051 (2011), 1878–1881.

30. Keith Hampton, Lauren Sessions Goulet, Lee Rainie, and Kristen Purcell. 2011. Social networking sites and our lives. *Retrieved July 12, 2011 from* (2011).

31. Suzanne Hudd, Jennifer Dumlao, Diane Erdmann-Sager, Daniel Murray, Emily Phan, Nicholas Soukas, and Nori Yokozuka. 2000. Stress at college: Effects on health habits, health status and self-esteem. *College Student Journal* (2000).

32. Justin Hunt and Daniel Eisenberg. 2010. Mental health problems and help-seeking behavior among college students. *Journal of Adolescent Health* 46, 1 (2010), 3–10.

33. Sidney M Jourard. 1959. Healthy personality and self-disclosure. *Mental Hygiene. New York* (1959).

34. Sepandar D Kamvar and Jonathan Harris. 2011. We feel fine and searching the emotional web. In *Proceedings of the fourth ACM international conference on Web search and data mining*. ACM, 117–126.

35. Martha Anne Kitzrow. 2003. The mental health needs of today's college students: Challenges and recommendations. *NASPA journal* 41, 1 (2003), 167–181.

36. Funda Kivran-Swaine, Jeremy Ting, Jed R Brubaker, Rannie Teodoro, and Mor Naaman. 2014. Understanding Loneliness in Social Awareness Streams: Expressions and Responses.. In *ICWSM*.

37. Adam DI Kramer. 2010. An unobtrusive behavioral model of gross national happiness. In *Proceedings of the SIGCHI Conference on Human Factors in Computing Systems*. ACM, 287–290.

38. Kurt Kroenke, Robert L Spitzer, and Janet BW Williams. 2001. The Phq-9. *Journal of general internal medicine* 16, 9 (2001), 606–613.

39. Mrinal Kumar, Mark Dredze, Glen Coppersmith, and Munmun De Choudhury. 2015. Detecting Changes in Suicide Content Manifested in Social Media Following Celebrity Suicides. In *Proceedings of the 26th ACM Conference on Hypertext & Social Media*. ACM, 85–94.

40. Amanda Lenhart, Kristen Purcell, Aaron Smith, and Kathryn Zickuhr. 2010. Social media and young adults. *Pew Internet & American Life Project* 3 (2010).

41. Diana MacLean, Sonal Gupta, Anna Lembke, Christopher Manning, and Jeffrey Heer. 2015. Forum77: An Analysis of an Online Health Forum Dedicated to Addiction Recovery. In *Computer-Supported Cooperative Work and Social Computing (CSCW)*.

42. Adriana M Manago, Tamara Taylor, and Patricia M Greenfield. 2012. Me and my 400 friends: the anatomy of college students' Facebook networks, their communication patterns, and well-being. *Developmental psychology* 48, 2 (2012), 369.

43. Gloria Mark, Yiran Wang, Melissa Niiya, and Stephanie Reich. 2016. Sleep Debt in Student Life: Online Attention Focus, Facebook, and Mood. In *Proceedings of the 2016 CHI Conference on Human Factors in Computing Systems*. ACM, 5517–5528.

44. M Kyle Matsuba. 2006. Searching for self and relationships online. *CyberPsychology & Behavior* 9, 3 (2006), 275–284.

45. Rumi Matsushima and Kunio Shiomi. 2003. Social self-efficacy and interpersonal stress in adolescence. *Social Behavior and Personality: an international journal* 31, 4 (2003), 323–332.

46. Gilad Mishne and Maarten De Rijke. 2006. Capturing Global Mood Levels using Blog Posts.. In *AAAI spring symposium: computational approaches to analyzing weblogs*. 145–152.

47. Elizabeth L Murnane and Scott Counts. 2014. Unraveling abstinence and relapse: smoking cessation reflected in social media. In *Proceedings of the 32nd annual ACM conference on Human factors in computing systems*. ACM, 1345–1354.

48. US News. 2015. US News University Rankings. `http://colleges.usnews.rankingsandreviews.com/best-colleges`. (2015). Accessed: 2016-09-03.

49. Sinno Jialin Pan and Qiang Yang. 2010. A survey on transfer learning. *IEEE Transactions on knowledge and data engineering* 22, 10 (2010), 1345–1359.

50. Umashanthi Pavalanathan and Munmun De Choudhury. 2015. Identity Management and Mental Health Discourse in Social Media. In *Proceedings of the 24th International Conference on World Wide Web Companion*. International World Wide Web Conferences Steering Committee, 315–321.

51. Leonard I Pearlin. 1999. Stress and mental health: A conceptual overview. (1999).

52. Tiffany A Pempek, Yevdokiya A Yermolayeva, and Sandra L Calvert. 2009. College students' social networking experiences on Facebook. *Journal of applied developmental psychology* 30, 3 (2009), 227–238.

53. James W Pennebaker, Matthias R Mehl, and Kate G Niederhoffer. 2003. Psychological aspects of natural language use: Our words, our selves. *Annual review of psychology* 54, 1 (2003), 547–577.

54. Andrea Dixon Rayle and Kuo-Yi Chung. 2007. Revisiting first-year college students' mattering: Social support, academic stress, and the mattering experience. *Journal of College Student Retention: Research, Theory & Practice* 9, 1 (2007), 21–37.

55. Hansen Andrew Schwartz, Johannes C Eichstaedt, Margaret L Kern, and Lukasz et al. Dziurzynski. 2013. Characterizing Geographic Variation in Well-Being Using Tweets. In *Proc. ICWSM*.

56. Johanna Soet and Todd Sevig. 2006. Mental health issues facing a diverse sample of college students: Results from the College Student Mental Health Survey. *NASPA journal* 43, 3 (2006), 410–431.

57. C Ward Struthers, Raymond P Perry, and Verena H Menec. 2000. An examination of the relationship among academic stress, coping, motivation, and performance in college. *Research in higher education* 41, 5 (2000), 581–592.

58. Priceonomics Data Studio. 2016. Ranking the Most (and Least) Diverse Colleges in America. `https://priceonomics.com/ranking-the-most-and-least-diverse-colleges-in/`. (2016). Accessed: 2016-09-03.

59. Lynn C Towbes and Lawrence H Cohen. 1996. Chronic stress in the lives of college students: Scale development and prospective prediction of distress. *Journal of youth and adolescence* 25, 2 (1996), 199–217.

60. Sho Tsugawa, Yusuke Kikuchi, Fumio Kishino, Kosuke Nakajima, Yuichi Itoh, and Hiroyuki Ohsaki. 2015. Recognizing Depression from Twitter Activity. In *Proceedings of the 33rd Annual ACM Conference on Human Factors in Computing Systems*. ACM, 3187–3196.

61. Patti M Valkenburg, Jochen Peter, and Alexander P Schouten. 2006. Friend networking sites and their relationship to adolescents' well-being and social self-esteem. *CyberPsychology & Behavior* 9, 5 (2006), 584–590.

62. Rui Wang, Fanglin Chen, Zhenyu Chen, Tianxing Li, Gabriella Harari, Stefanie Tignor, Xia Zhou, Dror Ben-Zeev, and Andrew T Campbell. 2014. StudentLife: assessing mental health, academic performance and behavioral trends of college students using smartphones. In *Proceedings of the 2014 ACM International Joint Conference on Pervasive and Ubiquitous Computing*. ACM, 3–14.

63. Rui Wang, Gabriella Harari, Peilin Hao, Xia Zhou, and Andrew T Campbell. 2015. SmartGPA: how smartphones can assess and predict academic performance of college students. In *Proceedings of the 2015 ACM International Joint Conference on Pervasive and Ubiquitous Computing*. ACM, 295–306.

64. Jun-ichiro Watanabe, Saki Matsuda, and Kazuo Yano. 2013a. Using wearable sensor badges to improve scholastic performance. In *Proceedings of the 2013 ACM conference on Pervasive and ubiquitous computing adjunct publication*. ACM, 139–142.

65. Jun-Ichiro Watanabe, Kazuo Yano, and Saki Matsuda. 2013b. Relationship between physical behaviors of students and their scholastic performance. In *Ubiquitous Intelligence and Computing, 2013 IEEE 10th International Conference on and 10th International Conference on Autonomic and Trusted Computing (UIC/ATC)*. IEEE, 170–177.

66. Anna Zajacova, Scott M Lynch, and Thomas J Espenshade. 2005. Self-efficacy, stress, and academic success in college. *Research in higher education* 46, 6 (2005), 677–706.

67. Kara Zivin, Daniel Eisenberg, Sarah E Gollust, and Ezra Golberstein. 2009. Persistence of mental health problems and needs in a college student population. *Journal of affective disorders* 117, 3 (2009), 180–185.

When Fitness Meets Social Networks: Investigating Fitness Tracking and Social Practices on WeRun

Xinning Gui [1] **Yu Chen** [1] **Clara Caldeira** [1] **Dan Xiao** [2] **Yunan Chen** [1]

[1] Department of Informatics
University of California, Irvine
Irvine, CA, United States
{guix, ychen25, claram, yunanc}@uci.edu

[2] School of Animation
Shenzhen Polytechnic
Shenzhen, Guangdong, China
xiaodan10@szpt.edu.cn

ABSTRACT
The last two decades have seen growing interest in promoting physical activities by using self-tracking technologies. Previous work has identified social interactions in self-tracking as a crucial factor in motivating users to exercise. However, it is unclear how integrating fitness features into complex pre-existing social network affects users' fitness tracking practices and social interactions. In this research, we address this gap through a qualitative study of 32 users of WeRun—a fitness plugin of the widely adopted Chinese mobile social networking service WeChat. Our findings indicate that sharing fitness data with pre-existing social networks motivates users to continue self-tracking and enhances their existing social relationships. Nevertheless, users' concerns about their online personal images lead to challenges around privacy. We discuss how our study could advance understanding of the effects of fitness applications built on top of pre-existing social networks. We present implications for future social fitness applications design.

Author Keywords
Behavior change; fitness; motivation; personal informatics; physical activity; privacy; self-tracking; social influence; social interaction; social network; sharing; wearable; WeChat; WeRun.

ACM Classification Keywords
H.5.m. Information interfaces and presentation (e.g. HCI): Miscellaneous; J.3 Life and Medical Sciences, Health, Medical Information Systems.

INTRODUCTION
In recent years, personal informatics and fitness tools have gained popularity. Personal informatics practices such as fitness tracking have evolved with fitness tools, from pedometers to more advanced gadgets like wearable devices, and smartphones that leverage built-in sensors. Using data from devices that track users' physical activities, many fitness applications attempt to motivate users to exercise through a variety of features, such as goal-setting [35], games [30], virtual rewards [11], and social influence [14].

Studies have shown promising effects of integrating social influence into fitness applications on increasing users' activity levels [11,14,30]. Social influence primarily involves sharing fitness data with other users [4], competing or collaborating [11,30], and keeping others accountable to their fitness goals [34]. Stressing the power of social influence, prior work has focused on scenarios where fitness data from standalone trackers are shared on social networking sites such as Facebook and Twitter. (e.g. [17,24,35,37,42]). However, these scenarios reportedly led to limited peer support and reciprocity [35] and even negative reactions from non-trackers [19,35], because contacts in users' pre-existing networks might not share similar interests in self-tracking or fitness, and sharing with small groups might not provide enough support [35]. Therefore, we ask the following question: *how might users experience fitness data sharing with a large group of pre-existing contacts who are mutually interested in tracking and sharing in a social network?*

We investigate this question by studying *WeRun*, a fitness plugin built in *WeChat*, the largest mobile social networking application in China. Like Facebook, WeChat supports a wide and complex spectrum of social relationships, ranging from strong offline connection to strangers [16,46]. Different from standalone fitness tracking tools that allow users to share data within the fitness community, WeRun is embedded in WeChat and built upon pre-existing complex social relationships on WeChat. As opposed to the many fitness applications that allow users to share their data within their social networks to both trackers and non-trackers, WeRun automatically shares real-time fitness data with all contacts who signed up with WeRun. Therefore, WeRun is an ideal site to investigate the effects of sharing fitness data with pre-existing contacts who also track.

We conducted a qualitative study with 32 participants who had used WeRun for at least two months to understand their fitness tracking and social practices. In this paper, we use **fitness tracking practices** to refer to fitness data tracking, reflecting, and sharing behaviors of our users. We chose to

CHI 2017, May 06-11, 2017, Denver, CO, USA
© 2017 ACM. ISBN 978-1-4503-4655-9/17/05$15.00
DOI: http://dx.doi.org/10.1145/3025453.3025654

study long-term users, aiming to offer insights into the impact of a large pre-existing social network on the user experience and retention of fitness applications in the real world context. We found that participants chose WeRun over other social fitness applications because it allowed automatic, mutual sharing of fitness data with pre-existing contacts. They cared less about the accuracy of tracked data, and were motivated to sustain fitness tracking because of an active social environment instead of competing with others. On the other hand, our participants reported inferring others' activities and lifestyles from shared fitness data, and were aware of how others might infer their own lifestyle. Participants found that their fitness tracking practices helped enhance social interaction and closeness with their WeRun contacts. However, being able to interpret other's lifestyles also raised privacy concerns under certain circumstances.

Our study contributes to the HCI community by extending existing knowledge on social influence on fitness practices and investigating the effects of fitness applications built on top of pre-existing social networks in a natural setting. More specifically, we present the mutual impact of social practices and fitness practices on each other. Finally, we offer implications for the design of self-tracking tools that balance social influence and privacy, and that benefit both fitness practices and maintaining social relationships.

RELATED WORK

Social influence plays a crucial role in fitness tracking [14]. Two common modes of soliciting social influence in existing fitness applications are sharing fitness data among peer users such as a fitness community built around a tracking device, and broadcasting fitness data on social networking platforms to both trackers and non-trackers.

Many systems allow users to connect with peers who also track fitness data. Prior work on social influence in peer-based fitness applications aim to help users who share similar goals [2,44] to form teams who can exercise together [3,10,30], to compete [3] or cooperate with others [30], and to be accountable for fitness goals [11]. These social features not only promote users' physical activities, but also provide benefits such as enjoyment and enhanced interpersonal relationships within the group [30,32]. These studies mainly examined the impact of peer support of fitness practices among small groups and relatively homogeneous social relationships, such as among family members, at schools and universities [3,32], in the workplace [30], in small groups of friends, or among strangers who have similar fitness goals [2]. Sharing fitness data among strangers with similar goals can provide instrumental support, but lacks emotional support; sharing among a small group of known contacts can provide emotional support, however it can be ineffective due to the incompatibility of capabilities in physical activities [11]. Furthermore, these fitness tools are usually standalone applications and devices, and the impact of social influence is studied within a short period of time. The long-term effects of leveraging social influence for fitness tracking in pre-existing complex social networks is understudied.

A second model of soliciting social influence in fitness applications is to encourage users to post their fitness data on social networking platforms such as Facebook and Twitter. For example, MyFitnessPal [37] users can share several types of fitness-related data on Twitter, such as calorie intake and exercise logs. Studies have investigated users' sharing of physical activities on Twitter [24,42], analyzing the posts' content [42], and identifying the characteristics associated with more retweets and favorites [19]. Park and Weber [37] have found that the development of implicit social influence through a sustained network of users interested in fitness correlates with long-term fitness data-sharing. In these studies, users shared fitness data as regular posts, or tweets, on social networking platforms; the fitness tracking tools themselves were standalone. However, studies have pointed out a few limitations of broadcasting fitness data on social networking sites, such as receiving limited peer support and reciprocity [35] and even negative reactions from non-trackers [19,35], as only a few people in these pre-existing networks had similar fitness interests. To the best of our knowledge, there has been no study on integrating fitness features as part of a widely adopted social networking platform, in which users can mutually share their fitness data.

When evaluating systems that facilitated behavior change, researchers emphasized the importance of investigating users' experiences with the technology in order to design effective fitness systems [26]. Previous studies about technologies that promote physical activities have mainly focused on how social influence facilitates fitness-related activities, but less on how these technologies influence social relationships. As Lupton argues, "*the reasons why a person may choose to take up self-tracking and the meanings she or he gives to the practice are socially enculturated. Self-tracking as a phenomenon has no meaning in itself. It is endowed with meaning by wider discourses on technology, selfhood, the body and social relations that circulate within the cultural context in which the practice is carried out.* "[31]. Coupled with the nature of social influence, people's fitness-tracking practices have a significant and inseparable social dimension that is worth investigating.

In summary, with the shown promises of integrating social influence in fitness applications, previous research has mainly investigated standalone tools that allowed users to share fitness data among peer users or broadcast data on social networking platforms. Each of the above models has limitations. Another model – building fitness applications on pre-existing social networks with fitness interests – has yet to be studied. Further, while previous work mainly evaluates the unidirectional impact of social influence on fitness practices, how pre-existing social networks and fitness tracking practices mutually impact each other is understudied. Our study fills the gap by examining social fitness application users' fitness practices alongside their social behavior. In our study, in addition to examining how building a fitness application upon a pre-existing complex social network may impact the uses and outcomes of self-tracking applications, we also study how fitness tracking practices affect social relationships. To build upon previous studies that were largely based on short-term experimental settings [20], we used a long-term and naturalistic usage setting to study fitness tracking and social practices in a fitness application built upon pre-existing social networks.

WERUN: FITNESS TRACKING BUILT ON PRE-EXISTING SOCIAL NEXTWORKS

WeRun is a social fitness plugin built on WeChat, China's most popular mobile social networking application. Launched in 2011, as of April 2016 WeChat has reached over 700 million monthly active users [9]. WeChat's fundamental functions include multiple forms of instant messaging, such as text messages, voice messages, sending photos, sharing locations, and group chats. Users can also post updates to their networks using *Moments* –similar to Facebook's Wall.

Because of WeChat's pervasive and multi-functional characteristics, Chinese people use it to communicate with close friends and families, as well as with less familiar contacts such as coworkers, acquaintances, and strangers without previous offline connections. WeChat only allows one personal account per mobile device, making it inconvenient for users to simultaneously use different accounts to manage diverse social networks. Each user's WeChat contacts usually include both strong and weak ties, personal and professional contacts. With public and private social spaces collapsing into a single social-technical system, WeChat is characterized by its complex social networks [46].

Launched in February 2015, WeRun is a fitness-tracking function and one of the most used features of WeChat [45]. WeRun imports fitness data from compatible fitness tracking tools and automatically shares fitness data within users' WeRun social networks. WeRun can import fitness data from smartphones that provide built-in fitness tracking functions. It is also compatible with many popular fitness tracking apps and wearable devices. Since WeRun imports and displays only users' daily number of steps, this paper uses fitness data and the number of steps interchangeably.

Built upon WeChat networks, WeRun supports multiple social functions. The prominent social feature is WeRun *Ranking*, which automatically ranks the daily steps of users and their WeChat contacts who also use WeRun (Figure 1 (a)). WeRun rewards the top-ranking user by displaying his/her WeChat cover photo at the top of the Ranking, also known as "*setting the cover.*" In Figure 1(a), for example, the cover photo of the Ranking page is the leader's cover photo, i.e., the blue sky. Since each user has a unique WeChat network, the members in each user's Ranking are unique. Users can *like* each other's steps. They can also *follow* other users' steps, meaning that WeRun prioritizes the display of specified users' steps, e.g., friends or loved ones (Figure 1 (b)). Users can also send their fitness data in a message to specific friends or post it to their Moments (Figure 1(b)).

WeRun does not have privacy controls. The fitness data shared can only be seen by users' WeChat contacts who also use WeRun, but users have no control over who cannot see it. Because users' WeRun contact lists are formed by pre-existing complex social relationships, their fitness data are shared to strong ties, weak ties, and even strangers, and among both personal and professional relationships. This complex yet natural setting makes WeRun an ideal application to study the mutual influences of pre-existing complex social relationships and fitness tracking practices.

METHODOLOGY

From April to July 2016, we conducted 32 semi-structured, audiotaped interviews with WeRun users in order to understand their usage and attitudes "in the wild" [38]. We recruited our participants with two methods: direct contact and snowball sampling. At the time of writing this paper, four of our authors had used WeChat for at least two years, and WeRun for at least five months. We first interviewed 10 direct WeChat contacts who used WeRun, and then invited them to refer their friends who are also WeRun users. We found 22 participants through snowball sampling.

Our participants had diverse demographic backgrounds; the 14 female and 18 male participants ranged in age from 19 to 63 and lived in 15 different cities in Mainland China. All of the participants' native language was Mandarin Chinese. Their educational backgrounds ranged from high school to doctorate. Their occupations included office worker, government official, public service worker, student, retiree, manager, teacher, freelancer, psychological consultant, IT practitioner, and engineer. At the time of the interviews, 28 participants had used WeRun for more than a year, and the other 4 had been using WeRun for more than two months by the time of the interviews. Although 15 out of 32 participants

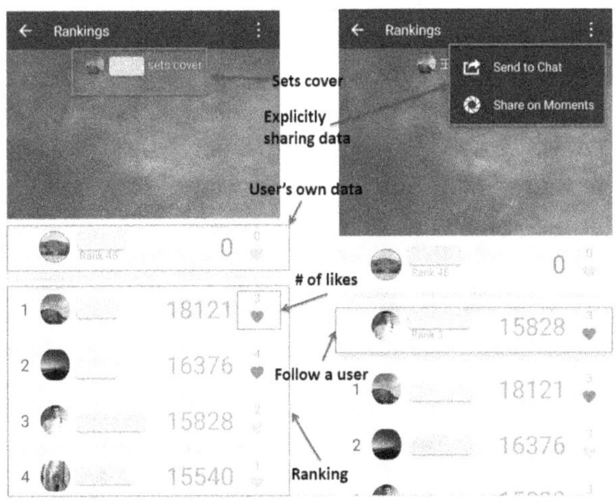

(a) (b)

Figure 1. WeRun interfaces: (a) ranking, setting the cover, and liking; (b) following a user and other sharing options

used tracking devices or applications other than built-in smartphone sensors to feed data to WeRun, such as *Le Dong Li (乐动力) and Mi Band*, all of our participants checked data only on WeRun.

During the semi-structured interviews, which lasted between 30 minutes and two hours, we asked participants what kinds of fitness applications they used, their reasons for using the application(s), what factors made them use WeRun instead of other fitness applications, what shortcomings of WeRun they had observed, how they used WeRun data, whether they self-reflected on the data, and whether, where, with whom, and why they shared the data. We conducted interviews online through Skype, phone call, or WeChat Video Call, audio-recorded them, and then transcribed them in Chinese.

All participants were added as WeChat contacts by at least one author. With participants' permissions, we collected screenshots of WeRun that our participants shared with us. Institutional Review Board approval was obtained prior to the beginning of data collection.

We employed a grounded theory approach [15] to analyze our data. We conducted memoing and theoretical sampling [15] during and after each interview. We read all interview transcripts and used our initial understanding to generate a starting list of codes. We then returned to the data to conduct a systematic axial coding [15] and identify the emergent themes. To validate the codes, the first and second authors double-coded the data and compared the results. The first author also went back and compared the codes against the interview data to make sure the codes fits with the data [15]. After several iterations of coding, we identified and categorized themes that emerged naturally, which we present in our findings. We then returned to our transcripts to find related quotes and later translated them into English. When we report quotes from interviews, we retain original punctuation. To protect our participants' identities, we use pseudonyms to anonymize them. When we use screenshots, we blur identifiable information.

FINDINGS

In this section, we report on the mutual influence between pre-existing complex social relationships and users' fitness tracking practices.

Pre-existing Complex Social Relationships Impacted Fitness Tracking Practices

All participants in our study had over 100 WeChat contacts, which represented different kinds of relationships, including friends, families, colleagues, superiors, business partners, and even strangers. It was common for participants to add someone whom they recently met or had never met as a WeChat contact, for business, professional, and information-seeking purposes. Participants emphasized the complex pre-existing social relations among their contacts who used WeRun (reported between 40 and over 100). The following subsections uncover how such social relationships may impact fitness tracking practices.

Choosing WeRun over other applications

Many of our participants chose to use WeRun over other fitness applications because the real-time, automatic sharing feature of WeRun enabled them to effortlessly share data and view others' fitness data. For instance, Min, a 53-year-old government official who had been using WeRun for over one year, explained:

> *I mainly use WeRun. WeRun is actually a fitness network of WeChat contacts. It does not directly track my physical activities, since it has to be connected to a tracking app and synchronize data from the app... I prefer WeRun because I can automatically share my data and also observe my friends and family members' data. For example, it enables me to automatically report how many steps I have to my son and daughter-in-law who live overseas... There are many other fitness apps, such as Yuedongquan (悦动圈). However, they just track and record my own physical activities. Yuedongquan indeed allows me to see other users' data within the same city, but I do not care about that. So I stopped using them... Sharing data with friends and family and looking at their data is more fun than comparing with strangers.*

From Min's perspective, compared with other fitness applications he tried, WeRun's main merit is that its instant and automatic sharing allows him, his family members, and his friends to easily check each other's fitness data. He preferred sharing fitness data with pre-existing social networks than with strangers. Min further emphasized WeRun's convenience:

> *I often check my WeChat for messages anyway. So it's convenient for to check my own and others' fitness data (on WeRun) within WeChat.*

Built on a popular social networking application, users can, as Min pointed out, check fitness data on WeRun whenever they check messages and updates on Moments on WeChat. There was no additional cognitive demand to check fitness data that is needed on a standalone fitness application. In his evaluation of fitness applications, Min considered data-sharing within existing social networks and the convenience of checking fitness data as part of social media use more valuable in comparison with other features.

Participants also chose WeRun over other fitness apps with more comprehensive health features. Nan, a 35-year-old psychological consultant who had been using WeRun for six months, told us:

> *My smartphone also has a built-in health app, which has more fitness related functions than WeRun. For example, the app can suggest daily exercise goals and estimate the calories burned based on my age, weight, and height. Despite of more comprehensive functions, [...] I only use that app to feed fitness data into WeRun so that it can be shared in my social networks... It's not just about tracking myself. It's simply because my friends are there (on WeRun), so I can see how they are doing.*

Nan chose WeRun over other applications because of the presence and awareness of her friends' fitness data. From Nan's point of view, sharing data within pre-existing social networks was more important than comprehensive functions.

Some participants expressed that they were particularly interested in seeing fitness data from people they cared about. Xun, a 30-year-old doctoral student, commented,

> *If I am not interested in someone, even if he/she exercises a lot, unless I were a sport maniac, I will not care about his/her fitness data.... So it truly depends on whom I care about, who is sharing the data, how is our relationship.... Between fitness and social networks, social networks must come first. Only based on the social relationships do people really care about each other's fitness data.*

Xun was only interested in the fitness data of people in his social circles; for him, building upon pre-existing social relationships was the prerequisite and motivation for sharing data on fitness applications.

Accuracy is nonessential

As opposed to previous literature that has demonstrated the crucial role of accuracy in fitness tracking tools [18,20,23,47], our participants did not place much value on the accuracy of fitness tracking data. In fact, many of them reported that the tracked data shown on WeRun was not very accurate, speculating that: 1) WeRun may stop synchronizing fitness tracking data when there is no Internet connection; and 2) activity sensors embedded in smartphones and other fitness tracking devices may not accurately detect physical activity. For example, Lei, a 49-year-old government official, reported:

> *The data shown on WeRun is not that accurate. For example, when I'm on the bus or on the train, my phone considers me as walking even when it is the train or bus that is vibrating. I was on a business trip in the past few days. After getting off from the train, I already had more than 4,000 steps. My phone considers the vibration of the train as a sign of walking.*

Lei understood that his phone's built-in sensors could not precisely detect physical activities, and, consequently, that the data automatically reported on WeRun were inaccurate.

Even though the tracked data shown on WeRun were sometimes inaccurate, our participants reported that inaccuracy did not affect their fitness tracking activities or the choice of application. For instance, Cai, a 55-year-old female retiree, reported:

> *I don't think the data are accurate... The main feature that interests me is that we are aware of each other's fitness status within WeRun and can "like" each other.*

Cai did not deem inaccuracy a problem, because she valued awareness of each other's data and resulting social interactions more than self-tracking. The fact that WeRun supports mutual awareness of fitness activities and social interactions within pre-existing social networks increased our participants' tolerance of inaccuracy.

Many participants felt that they no longer needed to track daily physical activities, as they had become capable of estimating their activity levels after having used WeRun for a period of time. For example, Jun, a 63-year-old retiree who had been using WeRun for over a year, said,

> *I have very regular lifestyle and routine walking routes. I walk my grandson to and back from school every day. I go out to folk dance every evening in the park. Thus, I can estimate how many steps I have by walking on those regular routes (based on my previous tracking history).*

Despite having gained enough self-knowledge to estimate their daily activities, our participants continued to use WeRun because it allowed them to share fitness data with a pre-existing social network. For example, Ping, a 52-year-old engineer told us,

> *I don't track my fitness any more. I can already estimate how many steps I have walked within a certain amount of time or on some familiar routes... But I check WeRun every day, even when I don't exercise some days... I will "like" my friends who have more than 10000 steps. I also check whether someone has "liked" me.*

Checking friends' fitness data and interacting with them led Ping to continue using WeRun. For these types of users, the social functions based on pre-existing social networks sustained their interests and WeRun usage.

Acknowledging individual differences instead of competing

Ranking features are by nature designed for comparison and competition. WeRun ranks users by their daily number of steps. As an incentive, the Ranking page displays the cover page with (Figure 1 (a)) that of the top-ranking user, i.e., "setting the cover." However, for most participants, competition was not a primary motivation for fitness tracking.

Since they were formed on top of pre-existing social relationships instead of fitness goals, WeRun users' contacts are usually diverse in terms of occupation, age, health status, and lifestyle. Our participants acknowledged the diversity, considering it more reasonable to evaluate their individual situation before comparing steps. For example, Min told us this during the interview:

> *I seldom "set the cover." It doesn't matter.... Don't compete for ranking, as it may end up with over-exercise or even disease likes synovitis. We should exercise according to our own physical conditions.*

Min emphasized that there was little basis for competing on WeRun, since everyone had different physical conditions.

Given that participants already knew some of their WeRun contacts very well, they were familiar with their lifestyle differences, such as how they commute. Xun commented,

> *I used to compete with my best friend. But he had natural advantages: he got many steps by commuting on foot. I usually sit in office and live near my office. So I stopped competing. Our situations are not comparable.*

Age difference was another factor that led participants to consider that competing with WeRun contacts was not realistic. Wu, a 50-year-old government official, said,

> *... It's hard to set the cover. Usually you need about 26,000 steps to be No.1. I am older than many friends on WeRun. I don't think I can compete with them. As long as I reach my own daily goal —10,000 steps—I'm satisfied.*

Wu was uninterested in competing with others because he saw his younger contacts as naturally more active. For him, setting his own goal was enough to motivate him.

Considering individual differences, rather than competing with others, is a theme present in all of our interviews. Previous studies have shown that it is essential to consider the comparability of competing members when designing social fitness applications features intended to motivate users [11]. However, our findings showed that users who shared pre-existing social relationships had enough knowledge about themselves and their WeRun contacts to judge their comparability. More importantly, fitness goals, such as competing with peers, were not the primary motivation among WeRun users. Thus, people were not demotivated if they were unable to attain first place.

Rather than using WeRun to compete with others, participants used the ranking feature as a reminder to exercise. For instance, Hu, a 46-year-old male manager, explained how WeRun motivated him to exercise more routinely:

> *It's like when kids do homework together, they will be more motivated, as there's an atmosphere of learning. Similarly, I see some friends exercise a lot on WeRun. The atmosphere of exercising reminds me that I haven't exercised today.*

Rather than motivating users through competition, the feeling of being surrounded by physically active contacts incentivized our participants to maintain their daily exercises.

Fitness Tracking in Pre-existing Social Networks Impacted Social Practices

Users' fitness tracking and sharing practices influenced social interactions in multiple ways, which we present in the following subsections.

Beyond self-reflection: social reflection

Many prior studies have emphasized how reflecting on fitness data on the individual level enables users to compare personal information at different times and discover trends and patterns [28]. In our study, we found that participants also reflected on others' fitness data displayed on WeRun and used the insights they gained to speculate on the potential impression their fitness data might make on others.

Most of our interviewees mentioned that they often inferred their contacts' ongoing activities or daily habits through shared fitness data on WeRun. For example, Zhong, a 52-year-old IT manager commented,

> *Some people usually have zero steps at 7 am, while some already have 100 steps at 5:30 am and 2,000 steps at 6:00 am. Having several hundred steps means that this person is probably just walking at home, like drinking water and doing some household work. But if it's 1,000 steps or more, it means this person has started exercising. Based on the temporal changes of steps during the day, I can get a sense of their living habits.*

Although the speculation based on fitness data may not always be accurate, many participants felt that the fitness data helped them better understand their WeRun contacts.

Fan, a 63-year-old retiree explained,

> *If someone only has dozens of steps one day, I can tell that this person probably just stays at home all day long. If someone has 20,000 steps or so, I can tell that this person is probably having fun outdoors or traveling. Most of the time, my guess was proved correct after seeing them uploading photos on WeChat Moments.*

For Fan, sometimes she could better infer other's activities by considering their fitness data alongside updates on WeChat Moments.

Inferring others' activities and lifestyle through fitness data often served as a way of initiating communication or group activities. For instance, Nan said,

> *I often guess my friends' activities based on their fitness data on WeRun and then chat with them. For example, once I noticed Mr. Wang was still walking after 10 pm, as his fitness data was continuously increasing... So I messaged him through WeChat, "Why are you walking so late?" ... I am often curious when my friend's fitness data suddenly increase or decrease. I will ask what they have been doing that day.*

Similarly, Ying, a 45-year-old female public service worker, often joined her friends after noticing that they were exercising,

> *When I see some friend's fitness data is rapidly increasing, I will call her or message her on WeChat, asking: "Where are you running?" She will tell me her location, then I will join her to run. It is not easy to schedule a workout together as plans often change, but by knowing whether others are running or not through their steps, it's much easier to join each other's workout.*

For our participants, checking others' data and inferring their activities was also a way of caring for their loved ones. Many interviewees reported that they often checked whether their friends were doing well after noticing unusual data, and then reminded their friends to exercise. They were also often monitored and reminded by their friends. Wu, a 50-year-old male public service worker, told us,

> *We chat a lot after inferring each other's fitness data... when I see someone who usually has 10,000 steps only had 3,000 yesterday, I messaged him asking whether he went out drinking and didn't exercise last night. Others also ask me when they see I had much fewer steps than usual. We often remind each other that we should exercise more. When I only have 3,000 or 4,000 steps one day, some friends will say, "You are lazy again! Don't drink! Don't play poker! Don't drive that much!"*

Our interviewees recognized that others could infer their activities and lifestyles in the same way, which they considered a form of caring and communicating. Nevertheless, due to the complexity of social relationships on WeRun, our interviewees also acknowledged that fitness data played a role in influencing their online images. Sometimes, they might speculate the impression their data might have on others, especially among co-workers with whom they maintain a professional relationship. For example, an interviewee who was a business owner said,

> *Doing physical activity is a good thing that's worth sharing. It can cause positive effects. It's different from showing off a luxury bag... I love physical exercises and sharing my fitness data. It shows I am diligent. If I am physically active for a long term, people will feel I must also be energetic and persistent when I work.*

The interviewee perceived being physically active as an indication of his diligent personality, and believed that sharing it could benefit his professional reputation.

Participants showed mixed feelings about the privacy issues about the possibilities of speculating their lifestyles based on sharing fitness data. Dong, a 32-year-old project manager, considered fitness data important for personal image, and not a worrisome privacy issue.

> *It's not a privacy concern, but it's about others' impression of me. Because of my work, I often need to walk among different project sites every day. When I walk a lot before getting off work, my superiors who are also on my WeRun contact list can see that. Sometimes they praised me that "You are so hardworking! You have walked so much today!" My colleagues often commented on each other's fitness data as well. For example, we ask each other, "You walked so much yesterday. You must have been working hard."*

While some participants did not consider sharing data a privacy issue, others had concerns. For most participants, whether exposing fitness data on existing social networks raises privacy issues depends on the social relationships with their contacts on WeRun and their occupations. Zheng, a 30-year programmer, expressed his concern,

> *... in some cases, exposing my fitness data is not good. I am a programmer, so I am supposed to be sitting in front of computer at office most of time. It will be unusual if I have many steps on weekdays... if my boss notices that, he may doubt my working attitude.*

For most participants, whether they have privacy concerns for sharing fitness data mainly depends on their occupations and who they share it with. On WeRun, many participants reported cases of self-presentation [8] with fitness data among co-workers.

Beyond fitness: promoting social interactions

When asked whether they have become more physically active after using WeRun, few participants reported significant changes in their number of steps: most people did not report making an effort to increase their steps after using WeRun; some felt they were already active enough, thus there was no need to exercise more; and others did not have time to exercise more due to their busy lifestyles.

However, most participants mentioned that WeRun promoted social interaction with their WeRun contacts. First, "liking" each other's data on WeRun helped them express care toward each other, regardless of the physical distance between them. Liking each other's fitness data served as a communication channel to express care and encouragement for others' physical activities. For example, Cai shared her experience,

> *Some of my friends live far away from me. When I find out from WeRun that some friend does not walk enough today, I will give him a "like", which represents my care towards him. It's also a form of social interaction, as he will also "like" me back. Although there is no direct communication, we can feel the connection and friendship. Fitness becomes a communication medium.... We can feel that we care about each other's fitness activities, which strengthens our friendship.*

Compared to WeChat Moments, which also allows people to "like" each other's posts, WeRun's specific focus on physical activities means that "liking" shows special care for one another's fitness. Older users like Cai did not update their status on WeChat Moments often, whereas on WeRun they could "like" each other's fitness data every day. Fitness data became a facilitator of expressing care towards each other, which resonates with previous research findings that "liking" on Facebook maintains interpersonal relationships [40].

Second, fitness data shared within pre-existing social networks carried a quality of playfulness. In the study, we found many participants played with the numbers for fun, which led to increased communication among their WeRun contacts. Most of our participants reported the experience of manipulating and sharing their step numbers in an entertaining way. For example, Feng reported,

> *WeRun itself is entertaining. You can observe how others play with their data, and you can share your manipulated data to others. Playing numbers is very funny and can*

actually increase closeness. For example, one time I intentionally reached 250 steps and put my phone on table to stop tracking. Then my friends screenshot it and sent it to me, joking that I was a silly billy that day.

Besides its numerical meaning, 250 is a Mandarin slang term meaning being silly. When manipulating the numbers, our participants' goal was to create playful interactions with their contacts, rather than to prevail in competitions.

Third, sharing data within existing social networks created topics for people to talk about on WeChat, and thus increased communication opportunities. For instance, Yue, a 60-year-old retiree who moved to another city after retirement, found that through sharing fitness data on WeRun, both his old friend in his hometown and his new friend in the current city frequently communicated with him about his fitness data. Yue felt that sharing fitness data facilitated communication and thus strengthened his social ties. He told us proudly, "*Some people directly message me on WeChat, praising me for doing exercise or asking me how I can walk so much.*"

Some participants also appreciated that sharing data on WeRun increased online communication. Meanwhile, they wished for more interaction channels. For instance, Quan, a 49-year-old government official, commented,

We can only "like" each other (on WeRun). We do often talk about each other's data and encourage each other through WeChat messaging. ... WeChat enables users to form groups, but WeRun doesn't support that. If WeRun allows us to comment, send message, share playlists for workout, form fitness groups, and discuss about fitness within the groups, it would be much better.

While previous research and fitness applications have leveraged existing social relationships as a way of promoting fitness, for our participants, social interaction around fitness data was also a means to strengthen their existing social relationships and convey a sense of caring to each other.

Overall, we found that the combination of fitness tracking and pre-existing social networks on WeRun benefitted both fitness and social practices. It provided motivation for users to sustain their use of WeRun, and created new opportunities for social interactions among pre-existing social contacts.

DISCUSSION

We have reported the findings of WeRun users' fitness tracking and social practices. Sharing fitness data within a pre-existing complex social network was one important factor that sustained our participants' interest in fitness tracking. The fitness practices also benefited users' social interactions, but there were instances of privacy concerns regarding how others interpreted their behavior. Next, we discuss how our study could advance understanding of integrating fitness tracking into social networking platforms.

Sustaining Fitness Tracking Practices

We found that WeRun, by leveraging pre-existing WeChat contacts, facilitated our participants' fitness tracking practices. Previous research has shown that users stopped using tracking devices after a period of time due to having learned enough from fitness data about daily routines and fitness plans, lacking a cross-platform tool that allows users of different tracking systems to compare and compete, and inaccuracy of tracking data [13,19,23,27]. Our study showed that most participants had already learned enough about their lifestyles, used a diverse range of tracking tools, and were aware that some of their fitness data were not accurate. Despite these circumstances, our findings indicated that the combination of sharing fitness data within existing social networks, the social interactions facilitated by sharing fitness data, and the convenience provided by WeRun was helpful in participants' sustained interest in fitness tracking. Given that participants were long-term users, we cannot determine how our findings may explain early abandonment or adoption. Our contributions lie in pointing out the factors that lead to the sustained use during the maintenance phase when the initial user interest and excitement has faded.

First, the pre-existing social network provided our participants with a supportive environment and created an atmosphere of caring about each other's physical wellness. Previous studies have addressed the importance of peer influence in fitness applications [11], such as sending encouragement and reminders, and liking each other's progress. However, sharing fitness data with strangers even with similar exercise goals can fall short in providing emotional support commonly found among friends and family members [34]. Sharing fitness data among a small group of friends or family members with incompatible exercise capabilities sometimes might de-motivate users [11]. Studies have also found obstacles in sharing fitness data on social networking sites. For example, the lack of a supportive exercising community on Facebook made people feel uncomfortable sharing fitness data [36], and Twitter users may consider posting fitness data as bragging [19].

In contrast, in our study, a closed fitness community naturally formed out of a large pre-existing social network, rather than being deliberately designed or initiated. WeRun provided a collective atmosphere of fitness. WeRun users self-tracked and observed their contacts' data, which made sharing fitness data a natural and motivating activity. Even though participants reported disinterest in competition, seeing their friends' active updates on WeRun motivated them to exercise and achieve their own goals. The community of WeRun contacts created social facilitation, an increase in interests in fitness caused by observing others doing the same task [21]. Compared to posting fitness data on existing social networking services such as Facebook and Twitter, WeRun contacts served as a supportive fitness community as a subset of the WeChat network, where members could mutually support each other. Only users who joined the fitness service could see the fitness data. WeRun network became a fitness community that helped maintain users. All WeRun members self-track and share fitness data, and at the same time know and care about one another. Thus, our study suggests that having a large fitness-tracking group within a user's social network could potentially support long-term fitness tracking practices.

Second, WeRun's incorporations of fitness data from multiple tools also facilitated its users' sustained usage and fitness tracking practices. Previous studies have found that an inability to compare data with friends who use different self-tracking tools is a major reason that users stop self-tracking [6,13,23]. Although our participants and their contacts used different kinds of self-tracking tools, WeRun's integration of various sources of fitness data allowed these users to form a large fitness community.

Third, the convenience brought by natively integrating fitness data into an existing popular social networking service instead of a standalone fitness application is another important characteristic that contributed to sustained fitness tracking practices. According to a recent report in 2016, WeChat is highly pervasive, as 94% of WeChat users use it daily, and 61% open WeChat more than 10 times per day [45]. Thus, WeRun users can easily check fitness data when they use WeChat without switching or remembering to check data in a separate application. This is also reflected in the study of Zhao et al. [48], which showed that when designing new social systems, it is useful to extend a user's existing ecology of social networking systems to provide convenience and reduce unnecessary switching costs.

In summary, WeRun motivated our participants to continue their fitness tracking practices, primarily due to a naturally formed virtual fitness community that provided support from preexisting contacts who were also conducting fitness tracking practices. The ability to choose from a wide range of compatible self-tracking tools facilitated establishing such communities. Furthermore, building features in an already widely adopted app reduced user effort compared with using a standalone application. Thus, we propose the following design implication:

Consider building cross-platform fitness applications on pre-existing social networks to facilitate long-term fitness tracking practices and exercising.

Balancing Awareness and Privacy Concerns

In our study, we found that our participants easily and frequently inferred their friends' activities and lifestyles from WeRun data. Some participants also mentioned inferring others' activities using fitness data combined with WeChat Moments posts (similar to Facebook updates).

Fitness data is usually considered less sensitive than location and audio recordings [25]. However, a recent study [17] found that some participants preferred to keep fine-grained fitness data private, or to only share them with friends or interested contacts. Another study about a workplace fitness campaign showed that over time participants developed more privacy concerns about being able to infer each other's private life through daily steps [22]. In the study, participants logged their steps on a website, and shared within the workplace. Most participants did not continue after the 21-day campaign ended due to privacy concern. In our study, the WeRun networks were mixed with friends, family members, co-workers, and strangers. Users' fitness data were automatically shared on WeRun Ranking in real time. As our findings reveal, our participants' attitudes towards fitness data sharing were nuanced. Many participants reported enjoying inferring friends' activities from shared fitness data. They also often appreciated having their own activities inferred by others, seeing it as a way of caring and communicating, rather than an invasion of privacy. However, at times they did have privacy concerns, which depended on who could see their data, their occupations, and timing, especially among co-workers. For example, they perceived that a programmer should not have many steps during working hours, while a project manager should have active workdays. On the other hand, when they felt their fitness data could create a positive self-image, such as being diligent and hardworking, they wanted others to see it.

Privacy issues in data sharing have been widely studied [39]; location [43] in social media and genomic information in the health domain [5] have led to serious concerns. Sharing fitness data, especially without locations, is usually considered safe [25]. As a previous study [22] has shown, revealing daily step count could provide information of participants' private life on a daily scale. Our study indicates that by sharing real-time steps within one's own network, users could even infer others' activities in real time. Combining users' fitness data with their updates on WeChat Moments may lead to further privacy concerns. While previous research has found that users want to control who can access their data [20], an opt-in approach of selecting a group of friends has not provided satisfactory social support [35]. Because the large group of contacts in WeRun seems fundamental to forming a fitness community within one's pre-existing social network and promoting sustained fitness tracking practices, we propose that an opt-out approach might be better able to balance social influence and privacy control. Thus, we suggest a second design implication:

Consider designing features that allow users to control how, when, and whom with not to share fitness data to balance social awareness and privacy concerns.

Increasing Social Interactions and Closeness

Previous research has investigated how to leverage social interactions to promote physical activities [14]. In this study, we found that fitness practices could also create opportunities to enhance social interactions, particularly among users who are interested in fitness. Our participants perceived increased closeness with WeRun contacts due to being aware of their physical activities and lifestyles, "liking" each other's fitness data, manipulating their data to joke with friends, and communicating about fitness topics. The above findings shed light on three aspects of how social fitness could promote social interactions and increase closeness between users and their WeRun contacts.

First, providing mutual awareness of fitness data improves users' knowledge about their contacts' activities and lifestyles. In our study, participants who lived far away from their friends felt more connected when their friends could infer that they were physically active, even though they were not explicitly communicating with each other. This indirect and implicit caring supports previous findings that awareness of *seemingly trivial* information, (e.g. location [7] or online game activities [12]), could trigger users to think about and imagine the life of their friends and family members, and thus lead to an increase in perceived closeness.

In addition, social interactions such as liking and chatting create opportunities for participants to directly communicate with others and participate in group activities. Participants reported that actively "liking" others' fitness data was an easy way to express that they cared about their contacts on WeRun. Since WeRun provides automatic fitness data updates, participants can easily use the liking function to send the "caring" signal to friends.

Besides using WeRun's social features, participants also found creative ways to interact with their contacts, such as sending screenshots of their step count with specific meanings to their friends and joking to create joyful social experience. Although this is not a design feature of WeRun, users' voluntary social interaction reflects playfulness [41]. Previous studies have indicated that playfulness positively influences users' intention to use social fitness applications [1]. In this study, we found that users' spontaneous play with fitness data could also enhance social interaction. Therefore, we propose a third design suggestion:

Consider providing social interaction features in fitness applications to promote social relationships.

Contributions

This work contributes to our understanding of how pre-existing social networks could help sustain fitness tracking practices, and how fitness tracking practices could reinforce social interactions. In the following, we highlight how our work advances current knowledge of social fitness applications, comparing our findings with prior research.

First, previous research has suggested that leveraging social influence [13,19,23], particularly comparing and competing with others [19,23], might address abandonment issues in fitness tracking. Our empirical study of long-term users show that, the ability to integrate a wide variety of tracking devices into WeRun facilitated the emergence of large supportive fitness communities within each user's pre-existing social network. The fitness community built around pre-existing social relationships motivated our participants to continue using WeRun despite having reached the maintenance phase [29] , being aware of data inaccuracy, and not interested in competition. One future research direction is to further investigate how WeRun's characteristics affect abandonment factors through comparative studies with both short-term and long-term users.

Second, previous studies have shown that sharing fitness data with unknown peers may provide limited social support [35], sharing with friends and family members with diverse exercise goals may demotivate users [11], and sharing on large social networking sites raises concerns about over-sharing [33]. In contrast, we did not observe these concerns among our participants. A potential explanation is that WeChat does not support fitness data sharing with unknown peers, and only supports sharing with mostly known contacts, such as friends, coworkers and family members. Hence, WeRun's unique social fitness network allowed us to obtain additional insights regarding social sharing of fitness data beyond previous studies.

Third, we raise a potential privacy issue in social fitness applications. By studying the effects of sharing fitness data without privacy controls, our study identified the potential risk of inferring others' activities from their data, especially in a network with diverse types of social relationships, including strangers and co-workers. This privacy issue is further aggravated when combining users' fitness data with their status updates and uploaded photos.

Finally, we examined the role of sharing fitness data in enhancing social interactions. In addition to promoting physical exercises and fulfilling fitness goals, we found that simply viewing fitness data and basic interactions around it, – such as "like" chatting around fitness data, and playing with numbers – could enhance social interactions and social relationships.

CONCLUSION

Previous research has argued that integrating social features in fitness tracking can promote physical activities, but little is known about the impact of mutual sharing of fitness data on pre-existing complex social networks. We report a qualitative study with 32 users of WeRun, a fitness data sharing plugin of the pervasive social networking app WeChat. We have found that WeRun's social features motivated participants to continue fitness tracking practices in the long term, and that fitness tracking practices created new opportunities for social interactions among contacts. These findings indicate that integrating fitness data sharing functionalities into widely adopted social networks could potentially help promote long-term fitness tracking by leveraging a pre-existing social network. Further, our findings suggest that sharing fitness data could raise privacy concerns, while benefitting social interactions and relationships among users.

ACKNOWLEDGEMENTS

We are grateful to our study participants for their dedication. Many thanks to our labmates for insightful comments, and to our anonymous reviewers for their insightful feedback. This work was partially supported by the US National Science Foundation under grant HCC-1219197 and Swiss National Science Foundation under the grant P2ELP2_158933.

REFERENCES

1. Aino Ahtinen, Pertti Huuskonen, and Jonna Häkkilä. 2010. Let's All Get Up and Walk to the North Pole: Design and Evaluation of a Mobile Wellness Application. In *Proc. of NordiCHI 2010*, 3–12. https://doi.org/10.1145/1868914.1868920
2. Aino Ahtinen, Minna Isomursu, Muzayun Mukhtar, Jani Mäntyjärvi, Jonna Häkkilä, and Jan Blom. 2009. Designing social features for mobile and ubiquitous wellness applications. *Proc. of the 8th International Conference on Mobile and Ubiquitous Multimedia*: 1–10. https://doi.org/10.1145/1658550.1658562
3. Noor Ali-hasan. 2006. Fitster : Social Fitness Information Visualizer. In *Proc. of CHI EA 2006*, 1795–1800.
4. Ian Anderson, Julie Maitland, Scott Sherwood, Louise Barkhuus, Matthew Chalmers, Malcolm Hall, Barry Brown, and Henk Muller. 2007. Shakra: Tracking and Sharing Daily Activity Levels with Unaugmented Mobile Phones. *Mobile Networks and Applications* 12, 2–3: 185–199. https://doi.org/10.1007/s11036-007-0011-7
5. Erman Ayday, Emiliano De Cristofaro, Jean-Pierre Hubaux, and Gene Tsudik. 2015. Whole Genome Sequencing: Revolutionary Medicine or Privacy Nightmare? *Computer* 48, 2: 58–66. https://doi.org/10.1109/MC.2015.59
6. Amid Ayobi, Paul Marshall, and Anna L Cox. 2016. Reflections on 5 Years of Personal Informatics : Rising Concerns and Emerging Directions. In *Proc. of CHI EA 2016*, 2774–2781. https://doi.org/10.1145/2851581.2892406
7. Elizabeth Bales, Kevin A. Li, and William Griwsold. 2011. CoupleVIBE: Mobile Implicit Communication to Improve Awareness for (Long-Distance) Couples. In *Proc. of CSCW 2011*, 65–74. https://doi.org/10.1145/1958824.1958835
8. Roy F. Baumeister. 1989. Motives and costs of self-presentation in organizations. In *Impression Management in the Organization*, Robert A. Giacalone and Paul Rosenfeld (eds.). Lawrence Erlbaum Associates, Inc., Hillsdale, NJ, 57–71.
9. BI Intelligence. 2016. WeChat breaks 700 million monthly active users. *Business Insider*. Retrieved from http://www.businessinsider.com/wechat-breaks-700-million-monthly-active-users-2016-4
10. Taj Campbell, Brian Ngo, and James Fogarty. 2008. Game Design Principles in Everyday Fitness Applications. In *Proc. of CSCW 2008*, 249–252. https://doi.org/10.1145/1460563.1460603
11. Yu Chen and Pearl Pu. 2014. HealthyTogether: Exploring Social Incentives for Mobile Fitness Applications. In *Proc. of Chinese CHI 2014*, 25–34. https://doi.org/10.1145/2592235.2592240
12. Yunan Chen, Jing Wen, and Bo Xie. 2012. "I communicate with my children in the game": Mediated Intergenerational Family Relationships through a Social Networking Game. *The Journal of Community Informatics* 8, 1.
13. James Clawson, J. Pater, A. Miller, E. Mynatt, and Lena Mamykina. 2015. No Longer Wearing: Investigating the Abandonment of Personal Health-Tracking Technologies on Craigslist. In *Proc. of UbiComp 2015*, 647–658. https://doi.org/10.1145/2750858.2807554
14. Sunny Consolvo, Katherine Everitt, Ian Smith, and James A. Landay. 2006. Design Requirements for Technologies that Encourage Physical Activity. In *Proc. of CHI 2006*, 457–466. https://doi.org/10.1145/1124772.1124840
15. Juliet Corbin and Anselm Strauss. 2015. *Basics of Qualitative Research Techniques and Procedures for Developing Grounded Theory*. SAGE Publications, Inc.
16. N. B. Ellison, C. Steinfield, and C. Lampe. 2011. Connection strategies: Social capital implications of Facebook-enabled communication practices. *New Media & Society* 13, 6: 873–892. https://doi.org/10.1177/1461444810385389
17. Daniel A. Epstein, Alan Borning, and James Fogarty. 2013. Fine-Grained Sharing of Sensed Physical Activity : A Value Sensitive Approach. In *Proc. of Ubicomp 2013*, 489–498. https://doi.org/10.1145/2493432.2493433
18. Daniel A. Epstein, Monica Caraway, Chuck Johnston, An Ping, James Fogarty, and Sean A. Munson. 2016. Beyond Abandonment to Next Steps: Understanding and Designing for Life After Personal Informatics Tool Use. In *Proc. of CHI 2016*, 1109–1113. https://doi.org/10.1145/2858036.2858045
19. Daniel A. Epstein, Bradley H. Jacobson, Elizabeth Bales, David W. McDonald, and Sean A. Munson. 2015. From "nobody cares" to "way to go!": A Design Framework for Social Sharing in Personal Informatics. In *Proc. of CSCW 2015*, 1622–1636. https://doi.org/10.1145/2675133.2675135
20. Thomas Fritz, Elaine M. Huang, Gail C. Murphy, and Thomas Zimmermann. 2014. Persuasive Technology in the Real World: A Study of Long-Term Use of Activity Sensing Devices for Fitness. In *Proc. of CHI 2014*, 487–496. https://doi.org/10.1145/2556288.2557383
21. Geri Gay. 2009. Context-Aware Mobile Computing: Affordances of Space, Social Awareness, and Social Influence. *Synthesis Lectures on Human-Centered Informatics* 2, 1: 1–62.

https://doi.org/10.2200/S00135ED1V01Y200905HCI004

22. Nanna Gorm and Irina Shklovski. 2016. Sharing Steps in the Workplace: Changing Privacy Concerns Over Time. In *Proc. of CHI 2016*, 4315–4319. https://doi.org/10.1145/2858036.2858352
23. Daniel Harrison, Paul Marshall, Nadia Bianchi-Berthouze, and Jon Bird. 2015. Activity Tracking: Barriers, Workarounds and Customisation. In *Proc. of UbiComp 2015*, 617–621. https://doi.org/10.1145/2750858.2805832
24. Logan Kendall, Andrea Hartzler, Predrag Klasnja, and Wanda Pratt. 2011. Descriptive Analysis of Physical Activity Conversations on Twitter. In *Proc. of CHI EA 2011*, 1555–1560. https://doi.org/10.1145/1979742.1979807
25. Predrag Klasnja, Sunny Consolvo, Tanzeem Choudhury, Richard Beckwith, and Jeffrey Hightower. 2009. Exploring Privacy Concerns about Personal Sensing. In *Proc. of Pervasive 2009*, 176–183. https://doi.org/10.1007/978-3-642-01516-8_13
26. Predrag Klasnja, Sunny Consolvo, David W McDonald, James a Landay, and Wanda Pratt. 2009. Using Mobile & Personal Sensing Technologies to Support Health Behavior Change in Everyday Life: Lessons Learned. In *Proc. of AMIA 2009 Symposium*, 338–342.
27. Amanda Lazar, Christian Koehler, Joshua Tanenbaum, and David H. Nguyen. 2015. Why We Use and Abandon Smart Devices. In *Proc. of UbiComp 2015*, 635–646. https://doi.org/10.1145/2750858.2804288
28. Ian Li, Anind Dey, and Jodi Forlizzi. 2010. A Stage-Based Model of Personal Informatics Systems. In *Proc. of CHI 2010*, 557–566. https://doi.org/10.1145/1753326.1753409
29. Ian Li, Anind K. Dey, and Jodi Forlizzi. 2011. Understanding My Data, Myself: Supporting Self-Reflection with Ubicomp Technologies. In *Proc. of Ubicomp 2011*, 405. https://doi.org/10.1145/2030112.2030166
30. James J. Lin, Lena Mamykina, Silvia Lindtner, Gregory Delajoux, and Henry B. Strub. 2006. Fish'n'Steps: Encouraging Physical Activity with an Interactive Computer Game. In *Proc. of UbiComp 2006*, 261–278. https://doi.org/10.1007/11853565_16
31. Deborah Lupton. 2014. Self-tracking cultures: towards a sociology of personal informatics. In *Proc. of OZCHI 2014*, 77–86. https://doi.org/10.1145/2686612.2686623
32. Andrew D. Miller and Elizabeth D. Mynatt. 2014. StepStream: A School-based Pervasive Social Fitness System for Everyday Adolescent Health. In *Proc. of CHI 2014*, 2823–2832. https://doi.org/10.1145/2556288.2557190
33. Sean A. Munson, Debra Lauterbach, Mark W. Newman, and Paul Resnick. 2010. Happier Together: Integrating a Wellness Application into a Social Network Site. In *Proc. of PERSUASIVE 2010*, 27–39. https://doi.org/10.1007/978-3-642-13226-1_5
34. Sean A Munson, Erin Krupka, Caroline Richardson, and Paul Resnick. 2015. Effects of Public Commitments and Accountability in a Technology-Supported Physical Activity Intervention. In *Proc. of CHI 2015*, 1135–1144. https://doi.org/10.1145/2702123.2702524
35. Sean Munson and Sunny Consolvo. 2012. Exploring Goal-setting, Rewards, Self-monitoring, and Sharing to Motivate Physical Activity. In *Proc. of PervasiveHealth 2012*, 25–32. https://doi.org/10.4108/icst.pervasivehealth.2012.248691
36. Mark W. Newman, Debra Lauterbach, Sean A. Munson, Paul Resnick, and Margaret E. Morris. 2011. "It's not that I don't have problems, I'm just not putting them on Facebook": Challenges and Opportunities in Using Online Social Networks for Health. In *Proc. of CSCW 2011*, 341–350. https://doi.org/10.1145/1958824.1958876
37. Kunwoo Park, Ingmar Weber, Meeyoung Cha, and Chul Lee. 2016. Persistent Sharing of Fitness App Status on Twitter. In *Proc. of CSCW 2016*, 183–193. https://doi.org/10.1145/2818048.2819921
38. Yvonne Rogers. 2011. Interaction Design Gone Wild: Striving for Wild Theory. *interactions 18*, 58–62. https://doi.org/10.1145/1978822.1978834
39. Norman Sadeh, Jason Hong, Lorrie Cranor, Ian Fette, Patrick Kelley, Madhu Prabaker, and Jinghai Rao. 2009. Understanding and capturing people's privacy policies in a mobile social networking application. *Personal and Ubiquitous Computing* 13, 6: 401–412. https://doi.org/10.1007/s00779-008-0214-3
40. Lauren Scissors, Moira Burke, and Steven Wengrovitz. 2016. What-s in a Like? Attitudes and behaviors around receiving Likes on Facebook. In *Proc. of CSCW 2016*, 1499–1508. https://doi.org/10.1145/2818048.2820066
41. Deb Sledgianowski and Songpol Kulviwat. 2009. Using Social Network Sites: The Effects of Playfulness, Critical Mass and Trust in a Hedonic Context. *Journal of Computer Information Systems* 49, 4: 74–83.
42. Rannie Teodoro and Mor Naaman. 2013. Fitter with Twitter: Understanding Personal Health and Fitness Activity in Social Media. In *Proc. of the 7th International Conference on Weblogs and Social Media.*

43. Eran Toch, Justin Cranshaw, Paul Hankes Drielsma, Janice Y. Tsai, Patrick Gage Kelley, James Springfield, Lorrie Cranor, Jason Hong, and Norman Sadeh. 2010. Empirical Models of Privacy in Location Sharing. In *Proc. of UbiComp 2010*, 129–138. https://doi.org/10.1145/1864349.1864364

44. Tammy Toscos and Anne Faber. 2006. Chick Clique : Persuasive Technology to Motivate Teenage Girls to Exercise. In *Proc. of CHI EA 2006*, 1873–1878.

45. WalktheChat. 2016. *WeChat impact report 2016: all the latest WeChat data*. Retrieved from http://walkthechat.com/wechat-impact-report-2016/

46. Yang Wang, Yao Li, Bryan Semaan, and Jian Tang. 2016. Space Collapse: Reinforcing, Reconfiguring and Enhancing Chinese Social Practices through WeChat. *Proc. of the 10th International Conference on Weblogs and Social Media*.

47. Rayoung Yang, Eunice Shin, Mark W. Newman, and Mark S. Ackerman. 2015. When Fitness Trackers Don't "Fit": End-User Difficulties in the Assessment of Personal Tracking Device Accuracy. In *Proc. of UbiComp 2015*, 623–634. https://doi.org/10.1145/2750858.2804269

48. Xuan Zhao, Cliff Lampe, and Nicole B. Ellison. 2016. The Social Media Ecology: User Perceptions, Strategies and Challenges. In *Proc. of CHI 2016*, 89–100. https://doi.org/10.1145/2858036.2858333

"Be Grateful You Don't Have a Real Disease": Understanding Rare Disease Relationships

Haley MacLeod, Grace Bastin, Leslie S. Liu, Katie Siek, Kay Connelly
School of Informatics & Computing
Indiana University
Bloomington, IN, USA
{hemacleo, gkbastin, lsliu, ksiek, connelly}@indiana.edu

ABSTRACT

We characterize how people with rare diseases consider their support needs as being met or neglected by different sources. After a 22-week study with 11 participants, we found that people with rare diseases identify strongly with their conditions but demonstrate a range of outlooks on their condition (positive, negative, and accepting). We found that participants think of themselves as being in a separate "Rare World" from the "normal" people in their lives and that relationships with friends and family members are strained. On the other hand, online communities were described as valuable sources of many forms of support, but do not adequately compensate for the lack of *tangible* support in offline relationships. We propose an approach to facilitating tangible support that leverages existing research on social matching, towards facilitating support among people with *different* rare diseases to overcome geographic and symptomatic challenges of coordinating support between people with the *same* rare disease.

ACM Classification Keywords

H.5.m. Information Interfaces and Presentation (e.g. HCI): Miscellaneous; J.3 Life and Medical Sciences: Health

Author Keywords

Rare disease; chronic illness; online health communities; timebanking; social matching; social support.

INTRODUCTION

HCI researchers have explored challenges and solutions in many different health domains, focusing on health concerns on social media sites [13, 30, 42, 72], patient communities [45, 59, 64], mobile technology [8, 31, 38, 57], and other platforms. This research has focused primarily on common health concerns impacting a large number of people. Those conditions have very specific sets of symptoms that are generally well understood in medical literature, making it possible to design tailored solutions for maximum effectiveness.

CHI 2017, May 06–11, 2017, Denver, CO, USA

ACM 978-1-4503-4655-9/17/05...$15.00
DOI: http://dx.doi.org/10.1145/3025453.3025796

Rare diseases have not been as widely studied in HCI, and there is an opportunity here to better support the experiences of this unique population. Rare diseases are conditions that, by definition, impact an extremely small number of people. In the US, rare diseases are those that impact less than 200,000 people (or 0.06% of the population) [78]. While each individual disease is rare, it is estimated that 10% of people world wide have one of the approximately 7,000 different known rare diseases [78]. These conditions can be very challenging to diagnose – it takes an average of five (in the UK) to seven (in the US) years to receive a diagnosis, and patients are misdiagnosed an average of two or three times before receiving a final diagnosis [78]. This process requires visits to many different primary care physicians and specialists. There is also a heavy emotional toll of living with a rare disease; people with rare diseases have reported experiencing depression (75%), anxiety (86%), isolation from friends/family (65%), and less interaction with friends/family (70%) [78].

Although rare diseases have not been widely studied in HCI, our previous work [61, 62] examined the needs of people with rare diseases, and how they are similar to or different from the needs of people with common chronic illnesses (i.e., diseases like diabetes, asthma, or arthritis that impact large numbers of people). We found that people with rare diseases face a unique set of challenges because they have diseases that few have even heard of, let alone understand.

In [61] we described the experiences of people with rare diseases; here we build on this work by focusing specifically on *relationships* between people with rare diseases and their friends and family. We invited people with rare diseases to join a private Facebook group and provided the 11 participants with 10 activities over 22 weeks. We identified ways in which people with rare diseases felt that their support needs were being met or neglected. In this work we describe:

1. The perspective of people with rare diseases on family and friend relationships.
2. An approach to reducing reliance on external support, in favor of support between people with rare diseases.
3. A proposal to encourage support between people with *different* rare diseases, focusing on the experience of "rarity" rather than the symptoms, and leveraging different skills and abilities for supportive matching.

RELATED WORK

Our work towards understanding the support needs and relationships of people with rare diseases draws from several different areas of prior work. First, we discuss types of social support and their presence in online health communities and other sociotechnical interventions. Understanding these types of support allows us to examine if/how the support needs of people with rare diseases are met (or not). In our study, we are interested in the sources of support (i.e., from friends and family vs. from other people with rare diseases and online communities) and the areas where support is lacking. Second, we discuss theories of help seeking and expectations of support in different types of relationships. This helps to understand barriers to seeking and providing support to explain some of those areas where social support is lacking. Understanding how those norms vary by relationship is helpful to better contextualize the differences in sources of different types of support. Finally, our related work concludes with a discussion of the differences in providing support voluntarily or through a caregiving obligation. We draw from work suggesting a shift towards peer support (and away from traditional caregiving models) which we suggest is a valuable lens for thinking about support for people with rare diseases.

Social Support

Social support is defined as *"verbal and nonverbal communication between recipients and providers that reduces uncertainty about the situation, the self, the other, or the relationships, and functions to enhance a perception of personal control in one's experience"* [2]. Social support can be beneficial when used appropriately, but when misused, or provided in the wrong context, it can have a negative impact [56] depending on the nature of the relationship between the provider and recipient [27, 43], the timing of the support [48], the personality of the recipient [43, 55], the nature of the stress [21, 26], and the spontaneity of the support [27, 32, 36, 54].

While several authors have suggested taxonomies of support behaviors, in this paper we rely on Cutrona and Suhr's five categories of social support [28]:

- **Informational support:** *"advice ('I think you should tell your supervisor'); factual input ('If you don't treat the infection quickly, it will get worse'); and feedback on actions ('You shouldn't have told her so bluntly')."*
- **Emotional support:** *"expressions of caring ('I love you'), concern ('Are you feeling better?'), empathy ('You must have been really hurt by his coldness'), and sympathy ('I'm so sorry you're upset')."*
- **Network support:** *"a sense of belonging among people with similar interests and concerns ('We'd like you to join our support group')."*
- **Esteem support:** *"expressions of regard for one's skills, abilities ('I know you'll do a good job') and intrinsic value ('Losing your job doesn't mean you're worthless')."*
- **Tangible aid:** *"offers to provide needed goods (e.g., money, food, books) and services (e.g., baby-sitting, transportation, housework)."*

Cutrona and Suhr [28] classify these support types into two categories: ***action-facilitating support*** (informational, tangible) and ***nurturant support*** (emotional, network, esteem). Action-facilitating is intended to eliminate a problem, whereas nurturant support focuses on comforting or consoling without directly addressing the problem.

In the case of rare diseases, where people are geographically dispersed, online health communities and social networks are valuable sources of support [3, 5, 24, 33, 40, 61, 75, 78]. This is particularly true for informational support; Braithwaite et al. [10] hypothesize that the asynchronous nature of online communities make it easier to provide informational support, because supporters can take time to look up information instead of having to respond immediately off the top of their head. Posting a request for information online also means it will be read by a larger audience than just one person, thereby increasing the likelihood of a useful response.

Online communities are also known as places for a high volumes of emotional support, especially for people with rare diseases [3, 5, 33, 40, 75]. This is somewhat intuitive, as these communities represent a place where people can connect with people who might better understand what they are going through (because they are going through similar things).

Esteem, network and tangible support have not been the object of support messages on online communities to the same extent [1, 10, 24]. Of particular interest to our study is tangible support; the low volume of tangible support messages in studies of online health communities is to be expected, as most of these behaviors require collocation between partners. In many cases, this support need is attended to by collocated family and friends (as in [80]). Our findings here have shown that this support is not provided in the same way to people with rare diseases, and we suggest there is an important opportunity to better facilitate tangible support.

Support Relationships and Help Seeking

Clark and Mills have extensively studied expectations of support and norms around seeking support in different kinds of relationsips [16, 17, 18, 19, 20]. They draw a distinction between two different types of relationships:

The first are ***exchange relationships***, where support is given *"with the expectation of receiving a comparable benefit (or benefits) in return"* [17]. Receiving support from an exchange partner incurs an obligation to provide an equivalent benefit in return. People keep track of how much they owe and are owed [18], and even conduct a brief cost-benefit analysis before choosing to enter into the relationship [34]. These tend to be relationships between acquaintances or strangers.

The second is a ***communal relationship***, typically found in close friends, family members, or romantic partners (with some exceptions). In these relationships, support is given without any expectation of repayment. The support recipient may still feel motivated to similarly provide support in the future should the opportunity arise, and the support provider may still *"hope that the recipient will be similarly responsive to his or her needs as they arise"* [17], but there is no expectation that these benefits come with a price tag.

In both kinds of relationships, people prefer support that is offered spontaneously over having to ask for it explicitly, and struggle to ask for help when they need it. In communal relationships [27], if a person does not provide support until asked, this causes their partner to doubt the quality of the relationship. If help is provided unsolicited, this reinforces perceptions of the helper as attentive to the needs of their partner and strengthens the intimacy of the relationship. Spontaneous support is also preferred in exchange relationships because support seekers feel embarrassed or inadequate when asking for help [32, 54, 85], underestimate the willingness of others to comply with requests for help [36], feel they are imposing on their exchange partner [36], and worry about incurring a debt they might not be able to repay [17, 27, 32].

This suggests that communal relationships are filled with challenging dynamics at the best of times if people do not ask for support when they need it but expect people to provide support without being asked. Our study shows this is certainly the case for people with rare diseases, who do not feel their support needs are being met by their communal partners. While there3 may be opportunities to overcome these barriers in communal relationships, in this work we turn to exchange relationships as an alternative source of support and focus on ways of reducing barriers to support in exchange contexts.

Prosocial Behavior vs. Caregiver Burden

There is a substantial difference between obligatory and voluntary support. Voluntarily engaging in prosocial behaviors (via volunteering or peer support groups) provides positive benefits to the support provider [6, 12, 68, 76, 50]. Cialdini et al. [15] propose that adults are more likely to help others when they feel bad, as a way of improving their mood [7]. This has been validated numerous times: Wilson et al. [50] found volunteering is beneficial for one's health, Schwartz et al. [76] found quality of life increased when people provided emotional support to others, and Brown et al. [12] found reduced mortality from providing instrumental support.

On the other hand, when caregiving is an obligation (e.g., caring for an ailing family member) the literature describes both objective (practical consequences) and especially subjective (emotional) burdens [14, 39, 70]. Unfortunately, caregivers deal with these burdens largely in isolation; they feel they cannot vent to someone more vulnerable (i.e., the person they are caring for) [14], especially if expressing their frustrations may exacerbate symptoms (as in depression [86]). Caregivers often lose their own social connections through the caring process [86], and develop depression and anxiety; the strongest predictors of depression/anxiety in caregivers are subjective and objective burdens [39]. There have been a few sociotechnical approaches to addressing this issue of caregiver burden:

1) Supporting Caregivers with Technology: There are a few examples of technology designed for caregivers, and often these are centered around communication, coordination, or providing information [29, 57, 74, 82]. For example, the Estrellita system [57, 82] aims to make things easier for parents of high risk infants by facilitating communication between parents and the medical team. Chen et al. [14] argue against these kind of systems, because they may unintentionally increase the burden on caregivers by making it easier to do even more work. Hwang et al. [47] similarly found that caregivers were concerned that these systems would add to their burden because they would additionally have to manage the technology on top of existing caregiving tasks. Instead, Chen et al. [14] and Tixier et al. [84] both suggest that systems for caregivers should include room for personal tasks to bring more balance to the caregiver's life. Fuentes et al. [37] designed the Ohana Bear, which focuses more on the emotion work and reflection necessary for caregivers.

2) Expanding the Care Network: Chen et al. [14] noted that caregivers often felt that others did not appreciate the volume of work they were doing. One approach to reducing this burden is to expand what Consolvo et al. [23] call the care network, distributing the volume of work across more caregivers. Hong et al. [44] leverage this idea in SocialMirror, a device for young adults with autism that allows them to seek advice from a trusted network. Similarly, Consolvo et al.'s [23] CareNet prototype, Paganelli et al.'s [74] ERMHAN system, and Skeels et al.'s Helping Quilt [80] all aim to coordinate care between network members. Chen et al. [14] propose a system that maps out the entire workload a caregiver routinely undertakes and allows other people to offer help, as a way of increasing the visibility of the workload and reducing it.

3) Shifting Towards Peer Support: Arreola et al.'s [4] older adult participants relied more heavily on their peer group for support (e.g., running errands) and hesitated to ask their adult children for help. The authors argue for a shift from the one-caregiver-to-one-older-adult model to a peer support model where older adults help care for each other: *"By replacing the individual caregiver with a peer group, each older adult has more eyes watching for them in case there is a problem. There is also less social stigma associated with asking about the day-to-day business of peers. This allows for less friction in terms of communication and may enhance activity within a community."* [4]

Stroomer et al.'s study found this shift towards peer support to be a successful strategy, stating *"people may be willing to provide support within their community, proving the barriers are lowered in asking for support. The field trial demonstrated that a social network service could be used to lower barriers towards asking for help."* [81]

Research around supporting caregivers or expanding the care network provides thoughtful solutions in cases where there is one or more overburdened caregiver. Our findings here have shown that people with rare diseases currently face so much isolation that a prerequisite step (prior to adapting those solutions for this context) would be determining ways of repairing those relationships or preventing them from breaking down in the first place. Thus, in the interim, we propose that the shift away from a caregiving model towards a peer support model makes sense for people with rare diseases as a way of more urgently addressing their unmet support needs. Participants in our study speak much more positively about the emotional and informational support they receive from online health communities; we suggest a way of extending this peer support model to also include tangible support.

Disease Name	Description
Avascular Necrosis (AVN) (aka Osteonecrosis)	AVN is the death of bone tissue due to a lack of blood supply. Pain can be mild or severe and develops gradually.
Ehlers Danlos Syndrome (EDS)	EDS affects connective tissue, primarily the skin, joints, and blood vessel walls. Symptoms include overly flexible joints that can dislocate, and skin that's translucent, elastic, and bruises easily. In some cases, there may be dilation and even rupture of major blood vessels.
Hereditary Angioedema (HAE)	HAE causes episodes of extremely painful swelling that often inhibits normal routines. Gastrointestinal attacks involve excruciating pain, nausea, vomiting, and diarrhea. Some patients undergo unnecessary surgery during abdominal attacks because the symptoms mimic a surgical emergency. Laryngeal swelling can close the airway and cause death.
Inclusion Body Myositis (IBM)	IBM is a progressive weakness in the muscles of the wrists and fingers and those at the front of the thigh. Trouble with gripping, such as a shopping bag or briefcase, and frequent stumbles are common. About a third of people with IBM have some weakness of the swallowing muscles. Most people with IBM remain able to walk, although some require a wheelchair full time.
Kallmann Syndrome (KS)	KS is characterized by a failure to go through puberty. People with KS have no sense of smell or very weak ability to smell. Males have undescended testes, a small penis, and simultaneous movement of both hands. Menstruation never starts in women.

Table 1: Rare Disease Descriptions

METHOD

We used the Asynchronous Remote Communities (ARC) method [1] [60] to understand the needs and experiences of people with rare diseases with a particular focus on relationships and support needs. We invited participants to join a private Facebook group specific to the study and provided participants with 10 activities over the course of 22 weeks. These activities were:

1. **Diary.** Participants tracked interactions with others about their disease and documented who they talked to, how they communicated, what they discussed, and how they felt.
2. **Circles.** Participants used small objects to illustrate their comfort level sharing information with different people by drawing circles with themselves at the center and placing people at different distances from the center.
3. **Questions.** Participants made a list of questions they wished their friends/family would ask about their disease.
4. **Problems.** Participants ranked a list of problems generated from their previous posts in order of how much each was a problem for them personally.
5. **Solutions.** Participants discussed strategies or solutions they used to address these problems.
6. **Photo Elicitation.** Participants took photos around a theme and commented on each other's photos.
7. **Mad Lib.** Participants created a mad lib, detailing the more humorous aspects of conversations they have surrounding their conditions.
8. **Movie Script.** Participants wrote scripts for the movie of their life.
9. **Rant Line.** Participants called, texted, or sent photos to a "Rant Line," a Google Voice number, anytime they needed or wanted to rant about something.
10. **Personas.** Participants critiqued two personas and discussed how representative they were of their own lives.

In addition to these activities, participants independently started new conversations amongst themselves - these posts are included in our analysis. This study was approved by our Institutional Review Board (IRB).

Participants

We recruited adults with a rare disease from Facebook support groups, since Facebook is actively used by people with rare diseases as a way of connecting with each other [61] and providing a sense of support. We did not recruit from other sources because we did not want to create additional privacy risks by encouraging people to share their data on Facebook who were not already doing so.

There were 11 active participants in our study. These participants had one of five different rare diseases (Table 1). We relied on the National Institutes of Health's list of rare diseases [2] to determine inclusion criteria. Participants ranged in age from 32–68 (mean=48.9). Ten participants identified as female and one as male. All participants were from the US, except one from Australia. Two participants were employed full time, while the rest were either unemployed, receiving disability payments, or retired at the time of the study. They were each offered a $50 honorarium for their participation in the study, regardless of their level of activity.

[1] We developed the ARC method specifically for this study so we could conduct group-based research with this dispersed population. We have reported in detail on the method, the data collected in each activity, and the response rates over the course of the study in [60] and encourage readers with additional questions about the methods used in this study to consult that paper.

[2] https://rarediseases.info.nih.gov/gard

Code Name	# of Participants	Total Instances
Outlook & Self-Image		
Identity - Acceptance	7	16
Identity - Positive	9	20
Identity - Negative	7	17
Mourning One's Old Life	4	11
Adjusting Expectations*	4	6
Expectations to Feel a Certain Way*	4	6
Jealousy*	3	4
Relationships Outside Rare World		
Absence of Relationship	6	23
Emotional Distance from Others	9	34
Belief/Validation	8	43
Listening	9	25
Passive Disinterest	8	28
Active Denial	6	22
Unhelpful Comments	9	32
Practical Support	7	28
Recognizing Limitations	8	16
Guilt/Burden*	4	4
Wanting an Apology*	2	2
Relationships Within Rare World		
Support from Other Groups	7	15
Comments about Other Participants	5	8

Table 2: Summary of codes used in analysis. Number of participants refers to participants who made at least one comment during the study that was classified as that code. Total instances is the number of comments classified as that code. Codes with asterisks (*) are not discussed in this paper.

Analysis

We iteratively coded all data from the study. Three researchers participated in the coding process, ultimately converging on an inter-rater reliability (Cohen's Kappa) score of 0.72. A summary of our codes are provided in Table 2. In this paper, we do not discuss codes with low prevalence (i.e., where they were only discussed by a small number of participants) or where there was a heavy skew towards a single participant (i.e., where a topic was discussed extensively by one participant, but rarely by others).

Because of the highly sensitive nature of this research topic and the high re-identification risks associated with rare diseases, we have removed any potentially identifying information from quotes included in this paper, including disease names (a summary of the diseases present in this study are provided in Table 1). Additionally, all participants were given the chance to review this paper before publication to ensure they were comfortable with the content.

Limitations

We did not recruit any participants' friends or family members as part of our study. Although it would have been interesting to study these relationships from both perspectives, many of the relationships of people in our study had broken down, resulting in estrangement or divorce. We focus our analysis on the perspective of people with rare diseases, rather than on the perspectives of their loved ones.

Additionally, we made the choice to recruit participants solely from rare disease Facebook support groups so that we would not expose participants to additional privacy risks by encouraging them to share information about their condition on Facebook if they were not already doing so. We recognize that this means that our findings may not be representative of people who are less engaged, or do not have access to online rare diseases support communities (either because none exist for their conditions or because they do not have access to the necessary technology).

FINDINGS

Our previous work [61] broadly described the experiences of people with rare diseases and a phenomenon called "Rare World." People with rare diseases face additional challenges as a result of a rare disease diagnosis, which influences their perspective on the world around them. We found this concept pervasive in our data in this study as well. We define "Rare World" as meaning that people with rare diseases compare themselves to the "normal" people in their lives (i.e., healthy people or people with common chronic illnesses), leaving them with a feeling of isolation or inadequate support.

We begin with a brief description of the outlook and self-image of participants from our study (bolstering findings from [61]). We then extend this work to focus specifically on people with rare diseases' perspectives on their relationships with people outside of "Rare World". Finally, we discuss the relationships people build and the support they receive from within Rare World (from others with a rare disease).

Outlook & Self-Image

We found that having a rare disease was a significant part of a participant's identity. They made comments like *"I told [my son] we [the participant and another family member with the same condition] were sharing about a main feature in our lives and something we were proud of"*(P8). This echoes findings from [61] that people with rare diseases think of themselves *"as ambassadors, as if they could not be understood apart from their medical conditions."* Given the work that goes into living with a rare disease (navigating the medical system, staying up to date with research, raising awareness of the condition, advocacy initiatives, etc.) as well as the severity and persistence of some of these conditions, it is understandable that it becomes an easy thing upon which to fixate. Participants even agreed with this characterization, and wished it was not the case:

> *"I tried not talking about my disease at all or how I feel or what's happening to me medically, because when I respond to their questions of "how are you doing?" with honesty, their next comment is always that I am dwelling on my illness and I need more activities in my life. To which I always agree. And feel discounted every time it happens"*(P7).

Even within this sense of identifying with the condition, we saw variance in the *valence* of participants' outlooks on their conditions. Although previous research found that people with chronic illnesses have different needs and outlooks based on their illness trajectory [35], participants in our study did not fall into a particular mindset based on the progression of their disease (i.e., someone who had been diagnosed with a disease for years did not necessarily feel more accepting of it than someone who was newly diagnosed). They even shifted between these mindsets over the course of the 22 week study; of the 11 participants who were active throughout the entire study, we observed a range of outlooks in all them (see codes for positive, negative, and accepting identities in Table 2).

We observed some participants who managed to reach a stable point in their lives, maintaining an attitude of doing the best that they could and acknowledging their limitations without being defined by them. When faced with insulting or unhelpful comments, accepting participants laughed it off and made a joke of it. They were not necessarily "proud" of their condition, but had learned to deal with it and accept it.

Other participants demonstrated a more positive mindset, not only accepting that they were dealing with a new normal, but also wanting to go beyond acceptance by helping others who were struggling, raising awareness or advocating for the condition, conducting research about the condition, and engaging in other proactive and positive behaviours.

Finally, we saw that some participants saw their disease as a factor that isolated them from the rest of their family and friends, and saw the disease as having *"pretty much destroyed my whole world"*(P4). These participants seemed to adjust poorly to the limitations their disease now placed on their daily activities, as they were sometimes jealous of those who were healthy and often mourned the loss of their old life:

> *"I used to have all the nice crap. I owned a condo full of antiques, I drove a brand new BMW, I had amazing jobs, a million friends, NOW, 3 years later, I had to declare bankruptcy, my parents are kicking me out of their basement after this surgery"*(P1).

Relationships Outside of Rare World

Some participants had family members that were supportive, especially in cases of hereditary conditions where a participant's parent also had the condition (e.g., *"[My friends and family] have been good. Though they kind of understand that Dad passed this to me :("*(P5)). For the most part however, participants described wanting support out of those relationships and did not feel those support needs were being met.

In many cases, participants' relationships had broken down and many participants attributed this to the rare disease experience. They commented, *"I've been abandoned by most of my friends. Nobody comes visit, nobody calls me. It gets very lonely and very depressing"* (P10) or *"Being sick all the time has ruined family relationships, friendships, and put a severe strain on my marriage"* (P8). Sometimes this isolation was something participants did to themselves, stating, *"I have gone through times where I have insulated and isolated myself because I have felt so different from others"* (P9).

Nurturant Support

Participants discussed a lack of emotional, esteem, and network support. They regularly felt people simply did not care about them, lamenting, *"How about someone in my family actually asking and remembering the name of my disease? And how about just one of them wants to know what it is, how it affects me, what it's trajectory is, what is likely to happen to me, and is it hereditary? None of those questions have ever been asked of me the past 11 years"*(P8).

One participant theorized that their friends or family members found it hard to face these health concerns, explaining that *"'Normal' people don't really want to hear about sad things and from people who have a health problem because it makes them feel 'down' or guilty that they are well."*(P8)

Other times, participants attributed this lack of support to a lack of understanding, feeling that people generally wanted to be helpful but sometimes made comments that may have been intended as caring and supportive, but came across as minimizing or unhelpful. Participants described how family and friends would suggest, *"Let go and let God."*(P10) or *"try eating healthier, acupuncture etc"*(P3). Participants found these comments to be minimizing, lamenting, *"...face palm. 'Friends' and I air quote because they are proving themselves to be less and less, downsize it and say things like they never heard of it and it can't be thaatttt badd. Omg if I hear that one more time!"*(P3).

Comparisons to cancer were especially common (e.g., *"You ought to be grateful you don't have a real disease like cancer"*(P7)). Participants expressed frustration with these comparisons, stating *"It's minimizing, [t]hose kind of comments, especially the first, 'at least you do not have something serious, like cancer.' [Cancer], not minimizing it at all, is not the only financially, emotionally, physically, mentally devastating disease. But it is the only [one] [t]hat many have heard of. It has a face."* (P2) Some participants went as far as wishing they *did* have cancer stating, *"actually I think I would have a better chance of survival with some forms of cancer"* (P7) or *"If I shaved my head I would bet they wouldn't think twice about asking me"* (P10).

Participants felt others did not believe they were sick, believed they were sick but not with a rare disease, or thought they were exaggerating their symptoms (*"my mom is in denial and tells me I am not disabled"*(P1)). Participants regularly commented that doctors, friends, and family members alike all accused them of being hypochondriacs (*"I get treated as if I'm a know it all and a hypochondriac sometimes too"*(P3)). Additionally, they heard accusations of making up the disease to get attention (*"If I had a nickel for every time that I over heard people saying that I was just seeking attention (that one really hurts)"*(P2)). Others expressed that their family members felt that because the disease was rare, the participant probably didn't have it: *"It's a very rare disease so you can not have it...Why [don't you] go to another doctor and find out what's really wrong with you?"*(P7).

Participants sought to combat this disinterest or lack of understanding with education; they were very active in seeking out and distributing information about their condition to their friends and family members. One participant described how they *"TRIED to send email links about [disease name], [disease name], etc., I have TRIED to send letters from DOCTORS stating that [disease name] is HEREDITARY and the risks and how they should be tested, I HAVE TRIED to personally educate, I have TRIED to take people to dinners and Dr appointments, NONE OF IT HAS HELPED."*(P8)

Some participants sent articles to friends and family members that were more detailed (*"I have sent medical journal articles to my relatives to read that talk about the disease in some detail"*(P7)), while others looked for materials that were easier to understand (*"I've searched the internet and tried to find easy info for my family to read and research."*(P1)). Regardless of how the information was presented, it did not appear to make a difference to the reception of the information (*"but that seems to have had really no effect at all"*(P7) and *"Not sure if they don't want to face it, or if they are scared, which leads to them not wanting to believe me"*(P1)).

Action Facilitating Support

Participants also wished friends and family members would be more understanding of their physical limitations (e.g., trouble gripping objects or moving around) or other sorts of tangible support needs (e.g., needing a place to live or financial support). When we asked participants what kinds of questions they wished their family and friends would ask, many of these were centered around practical, instrumental support:

- *"Are there any projects you could use help on?...Could I pick up anything for you at the store?"*(P8)
- *"What kind of routine household chores do you need help with?"*(P2)
- *"What kind of limitations does XXX cause you? What can I do to help you with those limitations?"*(P11)

This tangible support was generally not present. Participants provided anecdotes like their parents kicking them out of the house or a relative refusing to come inside when picking up his daughter from the participant's house. Participants had to adjust their practical need expectations based on what they could and could not get done in a given day. One participant said, *"I prioritize what I must get done today over what I'd like to get done, because I might not have the energy for both"* (P8). Definitions of "busy" or "getting a lot done" had to change: *"I had a 'busy day' today. I was able to shower and go to the grocery store with my mom."* (P1)

In our study, participants did not discuss informational support as being something they expected or wanted from friends and family members. This type of support is something they generally expected more of from other sources (e.g., medical professionals, "Dr. Google", or other patients).

Relationships within Rare World

People with rare diseases connect with each other via support groups [61, 75]. In cases of other kinds of chronic conditions, research has shown that supporting each other may alleviate some of the need for outside help and even act as a form of self-therapy [58].

We observed that if there is support needed that is not currently being provided by friends and family members, people with rare diseases turn to each other for support. Participants reported that this was the case for the Facebook groups they were a part of (*"the [online] support groups are where I find the best support"*(P5)), and even within our study group we observed participants engaging in discussions with each other outside of the formal study activities. Often, these discussions involved a participant describing some experience or challenge they were going through while other participants offered empathy or emotional support. Participants regularly posted updates on their life, such as recent or upcoming medical visits. Sometimes these were topics not directly related to their medical condition, but around notable things going on they wanted to share. They regularly exchanged resources or information with one another. One participant shared a link to their blog and other participants were curious about how to start one, so they began exchanging instructions. Similarly, a participant experiencing financial stress received suggestions about applying for disability insurance and where to find an appropriate lawyer. An international participant asked about health insurance while travelling in the US.

Most participants were either retired, unemployed, or receiving disability payments and some even considered managing their disease as being their job now: *"I am on disability so I spend my time learning and keeping up on research for my disease so I can keep my doc informed. Sad isn't it? lol"* (P5). They discussed how they contributed to their other groups and communities (i.e., not our study group but the Facebook groups we recruited from) by sharing research they found. *"I subscribe to Google scholar for research on [disease name] as soon as it's published. I don't always understand the biochem information, but I share the research paper with Facebook [disease name] group and there is usually someone who can put the information into understandable English for me LOL"*(P7).

In this work, we created a group for participants with *different* rare diseases to come together. We found that they were interested in learning from one another and were curious about each other's conditions. Although there was a certain amount of clustering by disease, participants expressed empathy towards each other and were appreciative of the support they received. Despite the difference in symptoms, the shared experience of living in "Rare World" provided much common ground. *"I am glad that I got to be a part of this experience. I learned a lot about other people and their conditions, and that we are ALL basically fighting the same battles..."*. They expressed an appreciation for the support they received from each other,

> *"PUT ON YOUR PARTY HATS AND GET OUT THE NOISEMAKERS, MY HUSBAND GOT A JOB!! Let me tell you, after years of disappointments and tears and fears, learning how to feel again is different. I'm numb...The thing is, that most of you didn't know that you supported us; BUT YOU DID! Thank you all."*(P2)

Participants even expressed that that this diversity of diseases gave them a different perspective on their own experience, *"I came to the conclusion from being in this group that most of you are far worse off than people with [my condition]"*(P8).

IMPLICATIONS FOR DESIGN

We saw that people with rare diseases often do not feel they are getting the support they need from their friends and family members. There may be opportunities for designers and HCI researchers to support the relationships between people with rare diseases and their friends and family, but further study of these challenges from the perspective of these friends and family members would be necessary to properly understand the barriers.

Instead, we suggest there are opportunities for people with rare diseases to support *each other*, instead of relying as much on people outside of Rare World. While existing rare disease support groups excel at providing informational, emotional, network, and esteem support, there are barriers to facilitating tangible support within these communities. We propose overcoming these barriers using social matching to facilitate support among people with *different* rare diseases. We conclude by providing three example scenarios of this *networked peer support* approach.

Peer Support

People in our study described receiving better support from similar others [53, 69] (i.e., people who also had a rare disease who were more familiar with their experiences and better able to empathize). Arreola et al.'s [4] argument for shifting away from a caregiving model towards a peer support model allows people to tap into much richer, more diverse ecosystems for support and reduce the burden on a traditional informal caregivers. Adopting a similar mindset of empowering people with rare diseases to support *each other* may reduce some of the reliance on friends and family members.

Helping each other would not only address gaps in the support needs of people with rare diseases, but could also serve as a useful distraction from the challenges of living with a rare disease, or self-reported "dwelling" on one's illness. Being empathetic and helping someone else with a rare disease would allow people to continue to live in "Rare World" without as much negativity. As was the case in our study, this might also provide some perspective on what others may be experiencing. This idea is also supported by previous work in psychology and sociology, showing that individuals derive a number of mental and physical health benefits from helping others [7, 12, 15, 49, 50, 68, 73, 76].

Support Between People with Different Rare Diseases

Peer support between people with rare diseases already happens to a certain extent within disease-specific support groups, especially for informational, emotional, network, and esteem support. These groups provide people with a sense of community and belonging they do not feel they are getting elsewhere.

An interesting new opportunity for HCI designers and researchers is to consider how we might extend work on social matching [51, 65, 66, 83] towards more *tangible* forms of support. The low prevalence of specific rare diseases makes any sort of in-person practical or tangible support currently challenging to coordinate (i.e., if there is no one with the same condition in an individual's geographic area). Additionally, some of the tasks participants described needing help with are things that would be challenging for someone with the same condition to provide; if a person requires help with groceries because their condition makes lifting the grocery bags challenging, it is likely that someone with the same disease might have similar support needs, rather than being able to help out.

We propose extending research on social matching by focusing on abilities, skills, and expertise instead of (or in addition to) demographic characterstics, interests, and preferences. We distinguish between abilities, skills, and expertise as follows: *abilities* are tied to physiological capabilities or symptomatic limitations (e.g., being able to see, hear, walk, lift something); *skills* are acquired abilities, learned through experience or through study (e.g., cooking, programming, knowing a different language); *expertise* is acquired through formal education, certification, or regulated professional experience (e.g., practicing law, real estate, skilled trade)

We suggest that approaches to matching based on abilities, skills, and expertise be applied to help a person with a rare disease connect with people with *different* rare diseases. Mayer et al. [67] introduce the concept of *match moderators* in social matching, which help determine which simliarities are most useful in matching people. They suggest that the *rarity* of a similarity, or how many other individuals have the same attribute in either the local or broader social context, is an important match moderator. Our research here reinforces findings [61, 62] that despite the differences in diseases and symptoms, there are many experiences, challenges, and perspectives in common between people with different rare diseases and that these are unique from people with common chronic illnesses or no health afflictions at all. We hypothesize that these common social experiences of rarity may serve as appropriate common ground, while coordinating support among *different* rare diseases may help overcome the symptomatic and geographic limitations of trying to coordinate tangible support between people with the same condition.

Networked Peer Support in Rare World

Although it might be possible to facilitate one-on-one exchanges of tangible support, we suggest this would be more effectively achieved using a pay-it-forward mentality. Research on timebanking [9, 22, 41, 52, 77] uses the idea of "time dollars." We suggest that a person with a rare disease would gain time dollars for help they provide to others that they could then redeem for help with their own needs.

Here we provide three example scenarios of how social matching based on skills, abilities, and expertise might facilitate this type of cross-disease support. In all scenarios, we will refer to the "support provider" and the "support recipient" for clarity, but we note that people with rare diseases would shift between these two roles at various times, earning and spending time dollars as they go.

It is also possible a "support provider" in a given scenario could be a friend or family member, in a case where there *are* friends or family members that want to be supportive and helpful. This would be particularly useful in a case where the friend or family member does not live near the person with the rare disease, but still wants to be helpful. The support provider could bank time for their remote friend or family member while helping someone locally.

Scenario 1: Coordinating Support by Abilities
Several participants had conditions with severe physical symptoms. For example, the primary symptom of IBM is progressive muscle weakening. For other conditions, the physical limitations might not be persistent, but rather temporary debilitating flareups, such as in the swelling episodes associated with HAE.

One task participants specifically mentioned as an example was carrying groceries. Although there are an increasing number of grocery delivery services available, these do not take care of the tasks of gripping the bags, carrying the heavy items into the house, and lifting them into the fridge or cupboards. We imagine that if a support provider in the neighbourhood was going grocery shopping, they could take the support recipient with them, helping them bring the groceries inside at the end of the trip. Alternatively, if the support recipient is not up for the trip to the store, they could give the support provider a shopping list to be filled independently.

To facilitate this kind of match, it would be ideal to know information about the location and grocery habits (schedule, location, mode of transport, etc.) of both parties. Speaking more generally about matching based on abilities, it may be possible to infer various abilities (or the lack of these abilities as exclusion criteria) from online behaviour. For example, Morris et al. [71] found that it was possible to identify accounts on Twitter belonging to blind users, even if there was no explicit mention of blindness. While Morris et al. [71] discuss this primarily as a potential privacy risk, there might be value in being able to detect different kinds of abilities towards facilitating matches.

Scenario 2: Coordinating Support by Skills
One conversation that took place in our study was around how to start a blog. This was something that one participant mentioned doing as a way of sharing their experiences and educating the public about the condition. Other participants in the study found this interesting and considered starting their own, but had questions about how to do so.

We imagine that a support provider who is comfortable with technology, familiar with blogging platforms, or maybe skilled with web programming could help a support recipient who is less skilled in this way to put together and/or maintain their own blog.

Notably, this scenario relies on skills that might be picked up formally (e.g., through some computing education program), but could also be self-taught (e.g., having taught oneself to put together a personal blog). This example also does not require geographic proximity. To facilitate this kind of match, it would be useful to know details about the skill set of the support provider. Where these skills are related to education programs, employment, or hobbies, there may be clues in one's online profile from which skill sets can be inferred.

Scenario 3: Coordinating Support by Expertise
Another conversation that took place in our study group was around the process for a claim for disability payments. One participant was experiencing financial hardship, and another participant described their experience through the process and provided advice on how to find a lawyer to help them.

We propose extending this informational support scenario even further to the tangible next step: What if the support provider *was* a disability lawyer? While it may initially seem like an infrequent combination to find a disability lawyer who also has a rare disease, research suggests that people often choose a career path to which they have some personal connection, especially when it comes to health topics [11, 25].

As a second example, it is possible that someone with a strong background in certain sciences or medicine could help interpret or explain the medical jargon often used in research papers that are of interest to a support recipient.

In this kind of matching scenario, it would be important to know not only the support provider's area of expertise (as in Scenario 2), but also their credentials and qualifications. This is a critical step in preventing bad legal advice or incorrect medical advice (as discussed in [46, 63]). This is especially important because potential support providers might not always be aware of their own limitations. For example, Siek et al. [79] described how people with end-stage renal disease had a sense of being smarter than others, even when they were describing information that was incorrect. Our previous research [61] similarly found that people with rare diseases were quick to point out whatever experience they *did* have with medicine or research, listing everything from a past career in phlebotomy, working as a nurse, or teaching professional development to science teachers. They felt that these experiences made them better equipped than an average person to understand medical information.

CONCLUSION

In this work, we provided insight into the support needs of people with rare diseases and their perspective on their relationships with friends and family with respect to these needs. We saw that people with rare diseases live in a separate world from their non-rare disease counterparts, and experience numerous challenges and barriers to receiving support from outside of this Rare World bubble.

We proposed not only matching people with rare diseases for the sake of facilitating peer support within Rare World, but in particular matching people with *different* rare diseases to help overcome geographic and symptomatic barriers to tangible support that may exist within disease specific communities. Where existing research on social matching aims to match people with similar demographic characteristics or interests, we propose additionally considering people's complimentary abilities, skills, and expertise.

This notion of networked support has shown some initial success in older adult communities (e.g., [4]), but has not yet been explored as a way of facilitating support between people with *different* chronic conditions. We see this approach as having potential benefits for rare disease communities, for whom tangible support is limited and difficult to coordinate.

The possibility of extending this approach to more common chronic conditions as well is an interesting area of future study; while these conditions might not have the same barriers to receiving support, existing research on caregiver burden [86] suggests that there may still be value in expanding the care network [23] and reducing demands on existing caregivers by empowering people with chronic illnesses to support each other.

ACKNOWLEDGMENTS

This work is supported by CLEAR Health Information and by the Center of Excellence for Women in Technology (CEWIT). We also thank Kim Oakes for her help in moderating the study, and Prianka Rayamajhi and Katie Spoon for their help with analysis. Finally, we thank the participants of this study for their time and contributions.

REFERENCES

1. Phil Adams, Eric PS Baumer, and Geri Gay. 2014. Staccato Social Support in Mobile Health Applications. In *Proceedings of the SIGCHI Conference on Human Factors in Computing Systems (CHI '14)*. ACM, New York, NY, USA, 653–662. DOI: http://dx.doi.org/10.1145/2556288.2557297
2. Terrance L. Albrecht and Mara B. Adelman. 1987. *Communicating social support*. Sage Publications, Newbury Park, California.
3. Tawfiq Ammari and Sarita Schoenebeck. 2015. Networked Empowerment on Facebook Groups for Parents of Children with Special Needs. In *Proceedings of the 33rd Annual ACM Conference on Human Factors in Computing Systems (CHI '15)*. ACM, New York, NY, USA, 2805–2814. DOI: http://dx.doi.org/10.1145/2702123.2702324
4. Ingrid Arreola, Zan Morris, Matthew Francisco, Kay Connelly, Kelly Caine, and Ginger White. 2014. From Checking on to Checking in: Designing for Low Socio-economic Status Older Adults. In *Proceedings of the 32Nd Annual ACM Conference on Human Factors in Computing Systems (CHI '14)*. ACM, New York, NY, USA, 1933–1936. DOI: http://dx.doi.org/10.1145/2556288.2557084
5. Ségolène Aymé, Anna Kole, and Stephen Groft. 2008. Empowerment of patients: lessons from the rare diseases community. *The Lancet* 371, 9629 (June 2008), 2048–2051. DOI: http://dx.doi.org/10.1016/S0140-6736(08)60875-2
6. C. Daniel Batson and Adam A. Powell. 2003a. Altruism and Prosocial Behavior. In *Handbook of Psychology*, Irving B. Weiner (Ed.). John Wiley & Sons, Inc., Hoboken, NJ, USA. DOI: http://dx.doi.org/10.1002/0471264385.wei0519
7. C. Daniel Batson and Adam A. Powell. 2003b. Altruism and Prosocial Behavior. In *Handbook of Psychology*, Irving B. Weiner (Ed.). John Wiley & Sons, Inc., Hoboken, NJ, USA. http://doi.wiley.com/10.1002/0471264385.wei0519
8. Eric P.S. Baumer, Sherri Jean Katz, Jill E. Freeman, Phil Adams, Amy L. Gonzales, John Pollak, Daniela Retelny, Jeff Niederdeppe, Christine M. Olson, and Geri K. Gay. 2012. Prescriptive Persuasion and Open-ended Social Awareness: Expanding the Design Space of Mobile Health. In *Proceedings of the ACM 2012 Conference on Computer Supported Cooperative Work (CSCW '12)*. ACM, New York, NY, USA, 475–484. DOI: http://dx.doi.org/10.1145/2145204.2145279
9. Victoria M.E. Bellotti, Sara Cambridge, Karen Hoy, Patrick C. Shih, Lisa Renery Handalian, Kyungsik Han, and John M. Carroll. 2014. Towards Community-centered Support for Peer-to-peer Service Exchange: Rethinking the Timebanking Metaphor. In *Proceedings of the 32Nd Annual ACM Conference on Human Factors in Computing Systems (CHI '14)*. ACM, New York, NY, USA, 2975–2984. DOI: http://dx.doi.org/10.1145/2556288.2557061
10. Dawn O. Braithwaite, Vincent R. Waldron, and Jerry Finn. 1999. Communication of Social Support in Computer-Mediated Groups for People With Disabilities. *Health Communication* 11, 2 (April 1999), 123–151. DOI: http://dx.doi.org/10.1207/s15327027hc1102_2
11. Alyssa T. Brooks, Shakira Washington, Bradley O. Boekeloo, Brian Gilchrist, and Min Qi Wang. 2013. Relationship of Personal Health Experiences with Interest in Health Careers Among Youth from an Underserved Area. *Journal of allied health* 42, 3 (Fall 2013), 135–40.
12. Stephanie L. Brown, Randolph M. Nesse, Amiram D. Vinokur, and Dylan M. Smith. 2003. Providing Social Support May Be More Beneficial Than Receiving It: Results From a Prospective Study of Mortality. *Psychological Science* 14, 4 (July 2003), 320–327. DOI: http://dx.doi.org/10.1111/1467-9280.14461
13. Stevie Chancellor, Zhiyuan Lin, Erica L. Goodman, Stephanie Zerwas, and Munmun De Choudhury. 2016. Quantifying and Predicting Mental Illness Severity in Online Pro-Eating Disorder Communities. In *Proceedings of the 19th ACM Conference on Computer-Supported Cooperative Work & Social Computing (CSCW '16)*. ACM, New York, NY, USA, 1171–1184. DOI: http://dx.doi.org/10.1145/2818048.2819973
14. Yunan Chen, Victor Ngo, and Sun Young Park. 2013. Caring for Caregivers: Designing for Integrality. In *Proceedings of the 2013 Conference on Computer Supported Cooperative Work (CSCW '13)*. ACM, New York, NY, USA, 91–102. DOI: http://dx.doi.org/10.1145/2441776.2441789

15. Robert B. Cialdini, Betty Lee Darby, and Joyce E. Vincent. 1973. Transgression and altruism: A case for hedonism. *Journal of Experimental Social Psychology* 9, 6 (Nov. 1973), 502–516. DOI:http://dx.doi.org/10.1016/0022-1031(73)90031-0
16. Margaret S. Clark and Judson R. Mills. 1979. Interpersonal attraction in exchange and communal relationships. *Journal of Personality and Social Psychology* 37, 1 (1979), 12–24. DOI:http://dx.doi.org/10.1037/0022-3514.37.1.12
17. Margaret S. Clark and Judson R. Mills. 2011. A Theory of Communal (and Exchange) Relationships. In *Handbook of Theories of Social Psychology: Volume Two*, Paul A. M. Van Lange, Arie W. Kruglanski, and E. Tory Higgins (Eds.). SAGE.
18. Margaret S. Clark, Judson R. Mills, and David M. Corcoran. 1989. Keeping Track of Needs and Inputs of Friends and Strangers. *Personality and Social Psychology Bulletin* 15, 4 (Dec. 1989), 533–542. DOI:http://dx.doi.org/10.1177/0146167289154007
19. Margaret S. Clark, Judson R. Mills, and Martha C. Powell. 1986. Keeping track of needs in communal and exchange relationships. *Journal of Personality and Social Psychology* 51, 2 (1986), 333–338. DOI:http://dx.doi.org/10.1037/0022-3514.51.2.333
20. Margaret S. Clark and Carolyn Taraban. 1991. Reactions to and willingness to express emotion in communal and exchange relationships. *Journal of Experimental Social Psychology* 27, 4 (July 1991), 324–336. DOI:http://dx.doi.org/10.1016/0022-1031(91)90029-6
21. Sheldon Cohen and Thomas A. Wills. 1985. Stress, social support, and the buffering hypothesis. *Psychological Bulletin* 98, 2 (1985), 310–357. DOI:http://dx.doi.org/10.1037/0033-2909.98.2.310
22. Ed Collom. 2008. Engagement of the Elderly in Time Banking: The Potential for Social Capital Generation in an Aging Society. *Journal of Aging & Social Policy* 20, 4 (2008), 414–436.
23. Sunny Consolvo, Peter. Roessler, Brett E. Shelton, Anthony LaMarca, Bill. Schilit, and Sara Bly. 2004. Technology for care networks of elders. *IEEE Pervasive Computing* 3, 2 (April 2004), 22–29. DOI:http://dx.doi.org/10.1109/MPRV.2004.1316814
24. Neil S. Coulson, Heather Buchanan, and Aimee Aubeeluck. 2007. Social support in cyberspace: A content analysis of communication within a Huntington's disease online support group. *Patient Education and Counseling* 68, 2 (2007), 173–178. DOI:http://dx.doi.org/10.1016/j.pec.2007.06.002
25. H. L. Crimlisk and I. C. Mcanus. 1987. The effect of personal illness experience on career preference in medical students. *Medical Education* 21, 6 (Nov. 1987), 464–467. DOI:http://dx.doi.org/10.1111/j.1365-2923.1987.tb01403.x
26. Carolyn E. Cutrona. 1990. Stress and Social Support in Search of Optimal Matching. *Journal of Social and Clinical Psychology* 9, 1 (March 1990), 3–14. DOI:http://dx.doi.org/10.1521/jscp.1990.9.1.3
27. Carolyn E. Cutrona, B. Beth Cohen, and Surria Igram. 1990. Contextual Determinants of the Perceived Supportiveness of Helping Behaviors. *Journal of Social and Personal Relationships* 7, 4 (Nov. 1990), 553–562. DOI:http://dx.doi.org/10.1177/0265407590074011
28. Carolyn E. Cutrona and Julie A. Suhr. 1992. Controllability of Stressful Events and Satisfaction With Spouse Support Behaviors. *Communication Research* 19, 2 (1992), 154–174.
29. Sara J. Czaja and Mark P. Rubert. 2002. Telecommunications Technology as an Aid to Family Caregivers of Persons With Dementia:. *Psychosomatic Medicine* 64, 3 (May 2002), 469–476. DOI:http://dx.doi.org/10.1097/00006842-200205000-00011
30. Munmun De Choudhury, Scott Counts, Eric J. Horvitz, and Aaron Hoff. 2014. Characterizing and Predicting Postpartum Depression from Shared Facebook Data. In *Proceedings of the 17th ACM Conference on Computer Supported Cooperative Work & Social Computing (CSCW '14)*. ACM, New York, NY, USA, 626–638. DOI:http://dx.doi.org/10.1145/2531602.2531675
31. Mary Beth Deline, Eric P.S. Baumer, and Geri Gay. 2012. Normative Communication Processes and Associated Emotion in Mobile Health Groups. In *Proceedings of the ACM 2012 Conference on Computer Supported Cooperative Work Companion (CSCW '12)*. ACM, New York, NY, USA, 75–78. DOI:http://dx.doi.org/10.1145/2141512.2141546
32. Bella M. DePaulo, Gregory L. Brittingham, and Mary K. Kaiser. 1983. Receiving competence-relevant help: Effects on reciprocity, affect, and sensitivity to the helper's nonverbally expressed needs. *Journal of Personality and Social Psychology* 45, 5 (1983), 1045–1060. DOI:http://dx.doi.org/10.1037/0022-3514.45.5.1045
33. Maya Doyle. 2015. Peer Support and Mentorship in a US Rare Disease Community: Findings from the Cystinosis in Emerging Adulthood Study. *The Patient - Patient-Centered Outcomes Research* 8, 1 (Feb. 2015), 65–73. DOI:http://dx.doi.org/10.1007/s40271-014-0085-9
34. Richard M. Emerson. 1976. Social Exchange Theory. *Annual Review of Sociology* 2 (1976), 335–362.
35. Jordan Eschler, Zakariya Dehlawi, and Wanda Pratt. 2015. Self-characterized illness phase and information needs of participants in an online cancer forum *(AAAI Conference on Web and Social Media)*. 101–109.
36. Francis J. Flynn and Vaness K. Lake. 2008. If you need help, just ask: underestimating compliance with direct requests for help. *Journal of personality and social psychology* 95 (2008), 128.

37. Carolina Fuentes, Valeria Herskovic, Jurgen Heysen, and Monica Tentori. 2013. Towards a Technology for Caregivers' Emotional Expression and Self-reflection. In *Ubiquitous Computing and Ambient Intelligence. Context-Awareness and Context-Driven Interaction*, Gabriel Urzaiz, Sergio F. Ochoa, José Bravo, Liming Luke Chen, and Jonice Oliveira (Eds.). Lecture Notes in Computer Science, Vol. 8276. Springer, 143–150.

38. Andrea Grimes, Martin Bednar, Jay David Bolter, and Rebecca E. Grinter. 2008. EatWell: Sharing Nutrition-related Memories in a Low-income Community. In *Proceedings of the 2008 ACM Conference on Computer Supported Cooperative Work (CSCW '08)*. ACM, New York, NY, USA, 87–96. DOI: http://dx.doi.org/10.1145/1460563.1460579

39. Eva Grunfeld, Doug Coyle, Timothy Whelan, Jennifer Clinch, Leonard Reyno, Craig C. Earle, Andrew Willan, Raymond Viola, Marjorie Coristine, Teresa Janz, and Robert Glossop. 2004. Family caregiver burden: results of a longitudinal study of breast cancer patients and their principal caregivers. *Canadian Medical Association Journal* 170, 12 (June 2004), 1795–1801. DOI: http://dx.doi.org/10.1503/cmaj.1031205

40. Tonje Gundersen. 2011. 'One wants to know what a chromosome is': the internet as a coping resource when adjusting to life parenting a child with a rare genetic disorder: Parenting children with a rare genetic disorder. *Sociology of Health & Illness* 33, 1 (Jan. 2011), 81–95. DOI: http://dx.doi.org/10.1111/j.1467-9566.2010.01277.x

41. Kyungsik Han, Patrick C. Shih, Victoria Bellotti, and John M. Carroll. 2015. It's Time There Was an App for That Too: A Usability Study of Mobile Timebanking. *Int. J. Mob. Hum. Comput. Interact.* 7, 2 (April 2015), 1–22. DOI: http://dx.doi.org/10.4018/ijmhci.2015040101

42. Andrea L Hartzler, Megan N Taylor, Albert Park, Troy Griffiths, Uba Backonja, David W McDonald, Sam Wahbeh, Cory Brown, and Wanda Pratt. 2016. Leveraging cues from person-generated health data for peer matching in online communities. *Journal of the American Medical Informatics Association* (2016).

43. Stevan E. Hobfoll, Arie Nadler, and Joseph Leiberman. 1986. Satisfaction with social support during crisis: Intimacy and self-esteem as critical determinants. *Journal of Personality and Social Psychology* 51, 2 (1986), 296–304. DOI: http://dx.doi.org/10.1037/0022-3514.51.2.296

44. Hwajung Hong, Jennifer G. Kim, Gregory D. Abowd, and Rosa I. Arriaga. 2012. Designing a Social Network to Support the Independence of Young Adults with Autism. In *Proceedings of the ACM 2012 Conference on Computer Supported Cooperative Work (CSCW '12)*. ACM, New York, NY, USA, 627–636. DOI: http://dx.doi.org/10.1145/2145204.2145300

45. Jina Huh. 2015. Clinical Questions in Online Health Communities: The Case of "See Your Doctor" Threads. In *Proceedings of the 18th ACM Conference on Computer Supported Cooperative Work & Social Computing (CSCW '15)*. ACM, New York, NY, USA, 1488–1499. DOI: http://dx.doi.org/10.1145/2675133.2675259

46. Jina Huh and Wanda Pratt. 2014. Weaving Clinical Expertise in Online Health Communities. In *Proceedings of the 32Nd Annual ACM Conference on Human Factors in Computing Systems (CHI '14)*. ACM, New York, NY, USA, 1355–1364. DOI: http://dx.doi.org/10.1145/2556288.2557293

47. Amy Hwang, Khai Truong, and Alex Mihailidis. 2012. Using participatory design to determine the needs of informal caregivers for smart home user interfaces. In *Pervasive Computing Technologies for Healthcare (PervasiveHealth), 2012 6th International Conference on*. IEEE. DOI: http://dx.doi.org/10.4108/icst.pervasivehealth.2012.248671

48. David E. Jacobson. 1986. Types and Timing of Social Support. *Journal of Health and Social Behavior* 27, 3 (1986), 250–264.

49. R. Jay Turner John Taylor. 2001. A Longitudinal Study of the Role and Significance of Mattering to Others for Depressive Symptoms. *Journal of Health and Social Behavior* 42, 3 (2001), 310–325. http://www.jstor.org/stable/3090217

50. Marc Musick John Wilson. 1999. The Effects of Volunteering on the Volunteer. *Law and Contemporary Problems* 62, 4 (1999), 141–168. http://www.jstor.org/stable/1192270

51. Hyunggu Jung, Victoria Bellotti, Afsaneh Doryab, Dean Leitersdorf, Jiawei Chen, Benjamin V. Hanrahan, Sooyeon Lee, Dan Turner, Anind K. Dey, and John M. Carroll. 2016. 'MASTerful' Matchmaking in Service Transactions: Inferred Abilities, Needs and Interests Versus Activity Histories. In *Proceedings of the 2016 CHI Conference on Human Factors in Computing Systems (CHI '16)*. ACM, New York, NY, USA, 1644–1655. DOI: http://dx.doi.org/10.1145/2858036.2858263

52. Judith Lasker, Ed Collom, Tara Bealer, Erin Niclaus, Jessica Young Keefe, Zane Kratzer, Lauren Baldasari, Ethan Kramer, Rachel Mandeville, Julia Schulman, Danielle Suchow, Abby Letcher, Anne Rogers, and Kathy Perlow. 2011. Time Banking and Health: The Role of a Community Currency Organization in Enhancing Well-Being. *Health promotion practice* 12, 1 (2011), 102–115.

53. Paul F. Lazarsfeld, Robert K. Merton, and others. 1954. Friendship as a social process: A substantive and methodological analysis. *Freedom and control in modern society* 18, 1 (1954), 18–66.

54. Fiona Lee. 1997. When the Going Gets Tough, Do the Tough Ask for Help? Help Seeking and Power Motivation in Organizations. *Organizational Behavior and Human Decision Processes* 72, 3 (Dec. 1997), 336–363. DOI: http://dx.doi.org/10.1006/obhd.1997.2746

55. Herbert M. Lefcourt, Rod A. Martin, and Wendy E. Saleh. 1984. Locus of control and social support: Interactive moderators of stress. *Journal of Personality and Social Psychology* 47, 2 (1984), 378–389. DOI: http://dx.doi.org/10.1037/0022-3514.47.2.378

56. Darrin R. Lehman, John H. Ellard, and Camille B. Wortman. 1986. Social support for the bereaved: Recipients' and providers' perspectives on what is helpful. *Journal of Consulting and Clinical Psychology* 54, 4 (1986), 438–446. DOI: http://dx.doi.org/10.1037/0022-006X.54.4.438

57. Leslie S. Liu, Sen H. Hirano, Monica Tentori, Karen G. Cheng, Sheba George, Sun Young Park, and Gillian R. Hayes. 2011. Improving Communication and Social Support for Caregivers of High-risk Infants Through Mobile Technologies. In *Proceedings of the ACM 2011 Conference on Computer Supported Cooperative Work (CSCW '11)*. ACM, New York, NY, USA, 475–484. DOI: http://dx.doi.org/10.1145/1958824.1958897

58. Leslie S. Liu, Jina Huh, Tina Neogi, Kori Inkpen, and Wanda Pratt. 2013. Health Vlogger-viewer Interaction in Chronic Illness Management. In *Proceedings of the SIGCHI Conference on Human Factors in Computing Systems (CHI '13)*. ACM, New York, NY, USA, 49–58. DOI: http://dx.doi.org/10.1145/2470654.2470663

59. Diana MacLean, Sonal Gupta, Anna Lembke, Christopher Manning, and Jeffrey Heer. 2015. Forum77: An Analysis of an Online Health Forum Dedicated to Addiction Recovery. In *Proceedings of the 18th ACM Conference on Computer Supported Cooperative Work & Social Computing (CSCW '15)*. ACM, New York, NY, USA, 1511–1526. DOI: http://dx.doi.org/10.1145/2675133.2675146

60. Haley MacLeod, Ben Jelen, Annu Prabhakar, Lora Oehlberg, Katie Siek, and Kay Connelly. 2016. Asynchronous Remote Communities (ARC) for Researching Distributed Populations. In *10th EAI International Conference on Pervasive Computing Technologies for Healthcare*. ACM. DOI: http://dx.doi.org/10.4108/eai.16-5-2016.2263322

61. Haley MacLeod, Kim Oakes, Danika Geisler, Kay Connelly, and Katie Siek. 2015. Rare World: Towards Technology for Rare Diseases. In *Proceedings of the 33rd Annual ACM Conference on Human Factors in Computing Systems (CHI '15)*. ACM, New York, NY, USA, 1145–1154. DOI: http://dx.doi.org/10.1145/2702123.2702494

62. Haley MacLeod, Shuo Yang, Kim Oakes, Kay Connelly, and Sriraam Natarajan. 2016. Identifying Rare Diseases from Behavioural Data: A Machine Learning Approach. In *Connected Health: Applications, Systems and Engineering Technologies (CHASE), 2016 IEEE First International Conference on*. IEEE. DOI: http://dx.doi.org/10.1109/CHASE.2016.7

63. Lena Mamykina, Elizabeth D. Mynatt, and David R. Kaufman. 2006. Investigating Health Management Practices of Individuals with Diabetes. In *Proceedings of the SIGCHI Conference on Human Factors in Computing Systems (CHI '06)*. ACM, New York, NY, USA, 927–936. DOI: http://dx.doi.org/10.1145/1124772.1124910

64. Michael Massimi, Jackie L. Bender, Holly O. Witteman, and Osman H. Ahmed. 2014. Life Transitions and Online Health Communities: Reflecting on Adoption, Use, and Disengagement. In *Proceedings of the 17th ACM Conference on Computer Supported Cooperative Work & Social Computing (CSCW '14)*. ACM, New York, NY, USA, 1491–1501. DOI: http://dx.doi.org/10.1145/2531602.2531622

65. Julia M. Mayer, Starr Roxanne Hiltz, Louise Barkhuus, Kaisa Väänänen, and Quentin Jones. 2016. Supporting Opportunities for Context-Aware Social Matching: An Experience Sampling Study. In *Proceedings of the 2016 CHI Conference on Human Factors in Computing Systems (CHI '16)*. ACM, New York, NY, USA, 2430–2441. DOI: http://dx.doi.org/10.1145/2858036.2858175

66. Julia M. Mayer, Starr Roxanne Hiltz, and Quentin Jones. 2015. Making Social Matching Context-Aware: Design Concepts and Open Challenges. In *Proceedings of the 33rd Annual ACM Conference on Human Factors in Computing Systems (CHI '15)*. ACM, New York, NY, USA, 545–554. DOI: http://dx.doi.org/10.1145/2702123.2702343

67. Julia M. Mayer, Sara Motahari, Richard P. Schuler, and Quentin Jones. 2010. Common Attributes in an Unusual Context: Predicting the Desirability of a Social Match. In *Proceedings of the Fourth ACM Conference on Recommender Systems (RecSys '10)*. ACM, New York, NY, USA, 337–340. DOI: http://dx.doi.org/10.1145/1864708.1864781

68. Elizabeth Midlarsky. 1991. Helping as Coping. In *Prosocial behavior*, Margaret Clark (Ed.). US: Sage Publications, Inc., Thousand Oaks, CA, 238–264.

69. James M. Cook Miller McPherson, Lynn Smith-Lovin. 2001. Birds of a Feather: Homophily in Social Networks. *Annual Review of Sociology* 27 (2001), 415–444. http://www.jstor.org/stable/2678628

70. R. J. V. Montgomery, J. G. Gonyea, and N. R. Hooyman. 1985. Caregiving and the Experience of Subjective and Objective Burden. *Family Relations* 34, 1 (Jan. 1985), 19. DOI: http://dx.doi.org/10.2307/583753

71. Meredith Ringel Morris, Annuska Zolyomi, Catherine Yao, Sina Bahram, Jeffrey P. Bigham, and Shaun K. Kane. 2016. "With Most of It Being Pictures Now, I Rarely Use It": Understanding Twitter's Evolving Accessibility to Blind Users. In *Proceedings of the 2016 CHI Conference on Human Factors in Computing Systems (CHI '16)*. ACM, New York, NY, USA, 5506–5516. DOI:http://dx.doi.org/10.1145/2858036.2858116

72. Mark W. Newman, Debra Lauterbach, Sean A. Munson, Paul Resnick, and Margaret E. Morris. 2011. It's Not That I Don't Have Problems, I'm Just Not Putting Them on Facebook: Challenges and Opportunities in Using Online Social Networks for Health. In *Proceedings of the ACM 2011 Conference on Computer Supported Cooperative Work (CSCW '11)*. ACM, New York, NY, USA, 341–350. DOI:http://dx.doi.org/10.1145/1958824.1958876

73. Allen M. Omoto and Mark Snyder. 1995. Sustained helping without obligation: Motivation, longevity of service, and perceived attitude change among AIDS volunteers. *Journal of Personality and Social Psychology* 68, 4 (1995), 671–686. DOI:http://dx.doi.org/10.1037/0022-3514.68.4.671

74. Federica Paganelli, Emilio Spinicci, and Dino Giuli. 2008. ERMHAN: A Context-aware Service Platform to Support Continuous Care Networks for Home-based Assistance. *Int. J. Telemedicine Appl.* 2008 (Jan. 2008), 4:1–4:13. DOI:http://dx.doi.org/10.1155/2008/867639

75. Naveen Pemmaraju, Vikas Gupta, Ruben Mesa, and Michael A. Thompson. 2015. Social Media and Myeloproliferative Neoplasms (MPN)—Focus on Twitter and the Development of a Disease-specific Community: #MPNSM. *Current Hematologic Malignancy Reports* 10, 4 (2015), 413–420.

76. Carolyn E Schwartz and Rabbi Meir Sendor. 1999. Helping others helps oneself: response shift effects in peer support. *Social Science & Medicine* 48, 11 (June 1999), 1563–1575. DOI:http://dx.doi.org/10.1016/S0277-9536(99)00049-0

77. Patrick C. Shih, Victoria Bellotti, Kyungsik Han, and John M. Carroll. 2015. Unequal Time for Unequal Value: Implications of Differing Motivations for Participation in Timebanking. In *Proceedings of the 33rd Annual ACM Conference on Human Factors in Computing Systems (CHI '15)*. ACM, New York, NY, USA, 1075–1084. DOI:http://dx.doi.org/10.1145/2702123.2702560

78. Shire Human Genetic Therapies. 2013. *Rare Disease Impact Report: Insights from patients and the medical community*. Technical Report. Shire Human Genetic Therapies.

79. Katie A. Siek, Kay H. Connelly, and Yvonne Rogers. 2006. Pride and Prejudice: Learning How Chronically Ill People Think About Food. In *Proceedings of the SIGCHI Conference on Human Factors in Computing Systems (CHI '06)*. ACM, New York, NY, USA, 947–950. DOI:http://dx.doi.org/10.1145/1124772.1124912

80. Meredith M. Skeels, Kenton T. Unruh, Christopher Powell, and Wanda Pratt. 2010. Catalyzing Social Support for Breast Cancer Patients. In *Proceedings of the SIGCHI Conference on Human Factors in Computing Systems (CHI '10)*. ACM, New York, NY, USA, 173–182. DOI:http://dx.doi.org/10.1145/1753326.1753353

81. Bas Stroomer, Martijn H. Vastenburg, and David V. Keyson. 2011. *CommunityNet: Mediating Care at the Local Community Level*. Springer Berlin Heidelberg, Berlin, Heidelberg, 275–284. DOI:http://dx.doi.org/10.1007/978-3-642-25167-2_37

82. Karen Tang, Sen Hirano, Karen Cheng, and Gillian Hayes. 2012. Balancing Caregiver and Clinician Needs in a Mobile Health Informatics Tool for Preterm Infants. In *Pervasive Computing Technologies for Healthcare (PervasiveHealth), 2012 6th International Conference on*. IEEE. DOI:http://dx.doi.org/10.4108/icst.pervasivehealth.2012.248716

83. Loren Terveen and David W. McDonald. 2005. Social Matching: A Framework and Research Agenda. *ACM Trans. Comput.-Hum. Interact.* 12, 3 (Sept. 2005), 401–434. DOI:http://dx.doi.org/10.1145/1096737.1096740

84. Matthieu Tixier and Myriam Lewkowicz. 2016. "Counting on the Group": Reconciling Online and Offline Social Support Among Older Informal Caregivers. In *Proceedings of the 2016 CHI Conference on Human Factors in Computing Systems (CHI '16)*. ACM, New York, NY, USA, 3545–3558. DOI:http://dx.doi.org/10.1145/2858036.2858477

85. Karen B. Williams and Kipling D. Williams. 1983. Social inhibition and asking for help: The effects of number, strength, and immediacy of potential help givers. *Journal of Personality and Social Psychology* 44, 1 (1983), 67–77. DOI:http://dx.doi.org/10.1037/0022-3514.44.1.67

86. Naomi Yamashita, Hideaki Kuzuoka, Keiji Hirata, and Takashi Kudo. 2013. Understanding the Conflicting Demands of Family Caregivers Caring for Depressed Family Members. In *Proceedings of the SIGCHI Conference on Human Factors in Computing Systems (CHI '13)*. ACM, New York, NY, USA, 2637–2646. DOI:http://dx.doi.org/10.1145/2470654.2481365

When Personal Tracking Becomes Social: Examining the Use of Instagram for Healthy Eating

Chia-Fang Chung[1], Elena Agapie[1], Jessica Schroeder[2], Sonali Mishra[3], James Fogarty[2], Sean A. Munson[1]
[1]Human Centered Design & Engineering, [2]Computer Science & Engineering, [3]The Information School
DUB Group, University of Washington
{cfchung, eagapie, jesscs, srmishra, jaf1978, smunson}@uw.edu

ABSTRACT
Many people appropriate social media and online communities in their pursuit of personal health goals, such as healthy eating or increased physical activity. However, people struggle with impression management, and with reaching the right audiences when they share health information on these platforms. Instagram, a popular photo-based social media platform, has attracted many people who post and share their food photos. We aim to inform the design of tools to support healthy behaviors by understanding how people appropriate Instagram to track and share food data, the benefits they obtain from doing so, and the challenges they encounter. We interviewed 16 women who consistently record and share what they eat on Instagram. Participants tracked to support themselves and others in their pursuit of healthy eating goals. They sought social support for their own tracking and healthy behaviors and strove to provide that support for others. People adapted their personal tracking practices to better receive and give this support. Applying these results to the design of health tracking tools has the potential to help people better access social support.

Author Keywords
Self-Tracking; Personal Informatics; Social Support; Health; Social Media; Food Journals.

ACM Classification Keywords
H.5.m. Information interfaces and presentation (e.g., HCI).

INTRODUCTION
Many people use social media and online communities to support healthy behavior change [31] and chronic disease management [43,53]. Some seek emotional support, accountability, motivation, and information from others on these platforms [43]. Others keep track of illness-related symptoms, hoping these data could lead to better diagnoses and treatments [53]. However, user concern about how health information may affect their image influences what and with whom they are comfortable sharing.

Since the launch of Instagram in 2010, the mobile photo- and video-based social media app has rapidly increased its user base to over 600 million people [47]. Food photos are particularly prevalent [37], and the popularity of food photos has drawn attention from HCI and CSCW researchers. Using Instagram as a food photo database [38], researchers were able to identify food deserts [11] and associate eating habits with locations [36]. Researchers have also examined how the platform is used to promote eating disorder behavior [9,45].

Some people post food photos to Instagram to support their health goals, using it as an everyday tracking tool as they pursue healthy eating choices. Understanding why and how people appropriate Instagram to track and share food data has the potential to inform system design to support healthy eating. We look at people's practices through different stages of tracking: their choice of Instagram among other tracking tools, their tracking and reflection practices, and their lapses of tracking. To answer the following research questions, we conducted an interview study with 16 people who frequently record and share what they eat on Instagram:

- Why and how do people keep track of their food on Instagram to support their health goals?
- How does social interaction affect their health tracking decisions and tracking behavior on Instagram?

We found that people track their food on Instagram with a mix of co-existing goals: recording what they eat, receiving social support, and providing social support. We use the lived informatics model [21] as a lens to examine different phases participants experience regarding tracking and sharing what they eat on Instagram. The lived informatics model extends other personal informatics models (e.g., [29]) to describe the decision to track, tool selection, and lapsing and resumption of tracking. Using this model supported our analysis of how and why participants choose Instagram for food tracking among other tools; how they iteratively track and act on these food posts (collecting data, integrating it, and reflecting on it); and how they intentionally or unintentionally lapse and resume tracking. We found that participants adapt their personal tracking behavior in every tracking stage to receive and provide better social support.

CHI 2017, May 06 - 11, 2017, Denver, CO, USA

ACM 978-1-4503-4655-9/17/05...$15.00
DOI: http://dx.doi.org/10.1145/3025453.3025747

Building upon prior work on health information sharing in online communities, we discuss how participants use Instagram features to help receive social support while maintaining their needs for impression management. We also reflect on these findings to discuss how social needs could be integrated into personal informatics models and inform the design of future health tracking tools.

BACKGROUND

Our study of how people appropriate Instagram to track and share their food was informed by prior research on technologies to support healthy eating and how people share their health tracking data with other people. To situate sharing of food posts on Instagram within broader research on online health information sharing, we also draw upon prior research on health information sharing in online communities.

Self-tracking and Personal Informatics Models

People use a myriad of self-tracking tools to collect and reflect on their personal information. To understand how people use these tools and the information they collect, Li et al. developed the five-staged personal informatics model [29]: *preparation*, *collection*, *integration*, *reflection*, and *action*. They later expanded the reflection stage to *maintenance* and *discovery* phases [30].

Rooksby et al. proposed "lived informatics" to describe the intertwined roles of self-tracking plays in people's everyday life [49]. They also described various goals people have while adopting self-tracking practices, such as behavior change, curiosity, or instrumental purposes (having a record, receiving incentives, and maintaining a relationship). Epstein et al. later developed the lived informatics model [21] to better describe people's tool selection choices, the concurrent and iterative nature of collection, integration, and reflection, as well as the lapse or resumption of tracking. The lived informatics model has three major stages: (1) *Deciding and selecting*: In this stage, people make decisions about tracking and choose the tools they want to use. (2) *Tracking and acting*: People *collect* data about themselves, *integrate* that data (sometimes across several tools or data sources), and *reflect* on the data they collected. (3) *Lapsing and resuming*: People periodically forget, intentionally skip, or suspend tracking.

Prior studies of self-tracking to support healthy eating goals have examined ways to ease the burden of *collection* and to include social features to encourage *collection*, *reflection* and *action*. In this study, we provide an in-depth understanding of how people appropriate social media for personal tracking. Our findings add to the current personal informatics models and inform various ways social needs influence personal tracking decisions and practices.

Technologies to Support Healthy Eating Goals

Traditional methods for tracking food to support healthy eating have relied on associating ingredients with calories (e.g., MyFitnessPal); tracking food with app-computed scores (e.g., Weight Watchers Smart Points, a food scoring system used by Weight Watchers based on calories, saturated fat, sugar, and protein); or scanning food barcodes to avoid the need to enter ingredients (e.g., the Weight Watchers app). These food journals usually rely on food databases, which are not comprehensive: they usually only contain common food items and recipes, and they do not account for variability of ingredients in the actual food people eat [17]. Furthermore, people using such databases often start eating more packaged food, because it is relatively easy to track foods with barcodes or that are otherwise mass-produced. This nudge is often at odds with their healthy eating goals. Even if a comprehensive database existed, item-by-item tracking is tedious and difficult to perform in certain social contexts, which makes it difficult to develop a reliable, long-term habit of food tracking.

Researchers have investigated approaches to enhance the tracking experience and address these issues, such as making tracking easier and more engaging through photo-based journals [16,35], participating in food challenges [20], recording voice memos of food experiences [23], or automatically taking photos of food [4,51]. These lightweight journaling methods can support people's health goals and increase their awareness of their eating habits, including unhealthy eating [6,16,42,55]. In particular, photo-based food journals make it easier to collect data, assess progress, and track failures such as unintended larger meals [16]. However, photo-based tracking also generally means a lack of caloric data relevant to many health goals, and many people still forget to track their food. In a similar tradeoff, fully automated solutions can make information capture easier, but they have also been found to reduce the mindfulness that people gain from food tracking [54].

Previous food tracking systems have often been designed to help people improve their behaviors. Researchers have also called for more research and design focusing on positive interactions and experiences with food, such as aspects of family connectedness, food as gifting, creativity, and pleasure or nostalgia in creating food [24].

Health Tracking with Social Sharing

Prior research has explored how social features can help engage people with self-tracking technologies and encourage behavior change [32,46,48]. The addition of social features can help users consistently meet their health goals [6,15], can help people receive support through social interactions, and can encourage a feeling of accountability to others [18]. People also often value understanding other's emotions in relation to their food experiences [23].

Baumer et al. introduced *VERA*, a photo-based system in which a user posted a picture of a "health-related" decision they made and others could comment [5]. By leaving the definition of "healthy" to each user's interpretation, people could decide for themselves what constituted a healthy lifestyle. In a follow-up study, they found that users who interacted with others who shared their goals stayed more engaged on VERA [2]. *Community Mosaic*, another photo-based system, allowed users to send messages of food photos to a local community server with explicit goals to help community members improve their healthy diet practice. These photos were later shared anonymously in a public kiosk where other community members could rate whether the photo was inspirational [44]. By thinking about how to provide helpful food photos, users reflect on their own food choices and preparation processes.

Although social features can motivate people to use self-tracking technologies, they can also introduce impression management concerns for their users [15], especially when the tracking technology appropriates existing social media platforms. In an online experiment, automatically posting announcements of their weekly physical activity goals on Facebook decreased people's willingness to set goals [40]. Furthermore, systems that allow people to share their progress on Facebook can cause anxiety about cluttering friend news feeds or appearing boring [41].

Sharing Health Information in Online Health Communities

According to a 2013 survey, 72% of US internet users search for health information online [22]. Many people also turn to online groups for social support as they pursue lifestyle change goals [31] or manage illnesses [27]. People find guidance and motivation in the day-to-day experiences of people with similar health challenges or similar health goals [13,26,27,31]. They also pursue emotional support in these online health communities. People were able to find and develop a strong sense of community with people who had similar experiences [28,33,34] and receive emotional support to help them move through difficult recoveries or struggles to adopt lifestyle changes [26,31,43].

People have appropriated social media, such as Facebook and Twitter, for searching, sharing health information, and seeking social support from pre-existing relationships [11,43]. People with potentially stigmatized illnesses, such as anorexia or depression, approach Tumblr and Instagram for recovery support [8]. Although these sites can help people struggling with such illnesses, they can also introduce new challenges, such as exposure to pro-anorexic sentiment [8] or negative comments [3]. People trade off these concerns and benefits, along with the needs for impression management [43], to decide where and with whom they share health information.

We studied food journaling on Instagram to understand how people combine photo-based food journaling and social interactions in public Instagram communities to support their healthy eating goals. We found people chose Instagram as a self-tracking tool because of opportunities to both receive and provide social support. They also weigh tradeoffs between consistent tracking, social support, and impression management to make ongoing decisions about what to track, whether and how to act, and when to lapse.

METHODS

We conducted semi-structured interviews with 16 participants who self-identify as using Instagram to support their healthy eating and/or fitness goals. We recruited participants through a pre-screening survey shared via researcher social networks, direct messages to Instagram users who use specific food tracking hashtags (#fooddiary and #foodjournal) and use English in their posts, and snowball sampling via interview participants. Each interview participant was compensated with a $10 gift card. Participants were primarily located in the US, with two from the UK (I09 and I11, Table1).

We asked participants why they decided to use Instagram to pursue their health goals and what their Instagram practices and experiences were regarding healthy eating. We also asked whether and how they interacted with other Instagram users, as well as what role Instagram played in supporting their health goals in relation to other self-tracking

Participant Number	Age	Instagram Experience (months)	Food Posting Experience (months)	Number of Followers	Number Following	Health Goals	Self-Identified Community	Occupation
I01	25-34	> 12	6	198	81	Conscious eating	None	N/A
I02	25-34	> 12	6	462	857	Ketogenic diet	Keto Diet	N/A
I03	18-24	> 12	6	362	536	Eating disorder recovery	None	Student
I04	18-24	> 12	6-12	260	66	Healthy cooking and eating	None	Student
I05	25-34	6-12	6-12	377	323	Weight loss	None	Video games
I06	25-34	6	6	323	415	Weight loss	Weight Watchers	Stay-home Mom
I07	25-34	6-12	6-12	218	224	Weight loss	None	Homemaker
I08	18-24	> 12	6-12	9721	1377	Healthy eating and fitness	Bikini Body Guide	Eating disorder center worker
I09	18-24	> 12	6-12	1991	388	Weight loss	MyFitnessPal	Caretaker in children's home
I10	25-34	6-12	6	3345	133	Weight loss	Weight Watchers	N/A
I11	25-34	> 12	> 12	3005	1081	Ketogenic Diet	Keto Diet	YouTube content creator
I12	25-34	> 12	> 12	98	158	Conscious Eating	None	Student
I13	25-34	> 12	6-12	1066	548	Fitness	Bikini Body Guide	Victim advocate
I14	18-24	> 12	> 12	1276	673	Fitness	Bikini Body Guide	Marketing
I15	25-34	> 12	> 12	6646	144	Weight loss	Weight Watchers	N/A
I16	25-34	> 12	6-12	3455	288	Weight loss	Weight Watchers	Event planner & space coordinator

Table 1: Interview participant demographics, health goals, and community affiliations.

tools, social media, and online communities. The interviews lasted 45 to 77 (M = 60) minutes. All interviews were audio-recorded and transcribed for further analysis.

We adopted a mix of inductive and deductive approaches to analyze the data. Four researchers first each coded two transcripts and discussed the emergent codes, organizing the codes via affinity diagramming and creating a code book based on our original research questions, the lived informatics model [21], and a prior study on adopting online communities and social media to support health [43].

Prior research on food journaling and other personal informatics domains has shown that tool selection is important for later tracking and action; that data collection, reflection, and action are often concurrent or iterative; and that both short term lapses and abandonment are common. We chose to use the lived informatics model to inform our analysis because it best captures these characteristics.

People share health information in online health communities to seek emotional support, motivation, accountability, and information [43]. We analyzed our data based on these social support needs to understand whether and how they influence participants in their choice to use Instagram and in their tracking and sharing behaviors on Instagram.

We then recoded the same two transcripts using the code book, augmenting with codes that emerged through the process. After discussion, the code book was updated with the emerging codes and used to code the remaining transcripts.

WHY AND HOW DO PEOPLE TRACK WHAT THEY EAT ON INSTAGRAM TO SUPPORT HEALTHY EATING?

Our participants use Instagram because it allows them to keep a record of activities relevant to their health goals, while obtaining and providing social support and information to communities with which they identify. People primarily record what they eat and cook. We use the lived informatics model [21] to describe personal tracking in stages. Understanding why people use Instagram for healthy eating goals and how they use Instagram in each of these stages can provide insights about people's evolving goals and unmet needs. Because reflection happened both concurrently with collection and integration (as suggested by the lived informatics model) and on its own at a later time, we discuss reflection separately from collection and integration.

Through the lens of the lived informatics model, we describe health, instrumental, and social-support goals of participants. Many participants sought to improve their health behaviors, while others tracked for instrumental goals such as building an audience or educating others. These goals were not mutually exclusive. Some participants also sought social support through their tracking behavior. We relate the pursuit of receiving and providing social benefits to the type of tracking activities participants perform. We discuss how these themes manifest in the different stages of the lived informatics model.

Deciding to Track and Selecting Tools

The lived informatics model suggests people select tracking tools based on features, aesthetics, and conveniences [21]. Our participants chose to use Instagram because it provided an easier, more fun, and more social way to track what they eat. Contrary to the individual focus of the lived informatics model, they also often wanted to motivate and encourage others to maintain their health. Many participants had experience with or were concurrently using other tools to record calories and nutrient details in addition to recording food photos on Instagram, such as *MyFitnessPal* (I01, I02, I05, I06, I07, I09, I11, I14), the official *Weight Watchers* app (I06, I16), *iTrackBites* (I15), or *YouFood* (I15). Others also used *Fitbit* (I04, I07, I08, I13) or *Polar watch* (I12, I14) to track their physical activities and posted screenshots or photos of those activities on Instagram.

Photo-based food tracking is perceived as fun

Participants considered tracking and sharing food photos on Instagram as an engaging experience, which helped them sustain their interests and keep a record of what they ate. Food photos feel closer to people's experiences than text descriptions: "*I think the fact that Instagram is much more visually stimulating [than MyFitnessPal], really makes the people more real, or it makes the goals more real.*" (I07). I05 described how this increased engagement helped her maintain food journaling not just on Instagram, but also on MyFitnessPal: "*I have a streak on MyFitnessPal since February (over five months at the time of interview). Before I would just use MyFitnessPal for maybe two weeks and then be like, this is too hard and I stop. ... It's really helpful to have all the photos because if I forget to enter it in or if I'm busy during the day, I can enter it at the end of the day and I have an accurate log of what I ate.*"

Photo-based food tracking is perceived as socially appropriate

Consistent with prior evaluations of mobile-based food journaling [16], participants considered using photos to record what they eat easier and more socially appropriate than a traditional mobile food journal: "*If I was out with friends or something, then a quick snapshot of the food would be easier than saying, 'Hold on guys, I need to pull up MyFitnessPal and put everything down and the right serving size'*" (I07). As a result, some participants believed tracking with photos better supported their health goals because they could easily take a photo whenever they ate rather than entering all food entries at the end of the day or when they are free: "*[I'd rather] post frequently throughout the day and have short little posts [on Instagram] than do big long posts and do them once a day [using other tools]*" (I15).

Instagram helps people find community support

Many participants chose Instagram for the social support they can gain through the many people using Instagram for healthy eating goals. Participants discovered these communities through prior experiences using Instagram for general use (I01, I02, I03, I04, I07, I09, I11), friend recommendations (I05, I12), or other health communities such as Weight Watchers (I06, I10, I15, I16) or Bikini

Body Guide (I08, I13, I14). Many participants found Instagram users more supportive than users of other social media platforms. For example, I05 did not think Facebook was a proper place to share her everyday diet and workout: "*A lot of my friends on social media are acquaintances or old coworkers ... they have some connection to you but not enough so that they care about actually supporting you.*"

To find communities, participants often augmented their posts with hashtags. They decided which hashtags to use based on other people's posts or popular food hashtags from Instagram's autofill features. They also learned new hashtags by noting ones that were used concurrently with the ones they knew. After determining whether the hashtag caught the attention of people they wanted to attract (e.g., people belonging to specific communities, such as #weightwatchers), they gradually settled on a fixed set of hashtags used for most of their posts. I07 explained: "*I think the hashtags [help] us find each other .... If I was just posting these photos to an empty wall, there was no way that I'd be connected to others with similar goals to me.*" Hashtags are especially useful for people following a specific program or participating in an event. I08 met other women participating in the same health challenge through hashtags (e.g., #oneperfectweek) and would use such tags to find updates from others at a similar stage of progress. Many participants also use hashtags to find people across communities. For example, participants who investigated hashtags like "#caloriecounting" or "#weightloss" often encountered Instagrammers who subscribed to alternate diet plans. Through this exploration, they discovered different diet and exercise routines.

Instagram allows people to motivate and educate others

Some participants chose Instagram because it gave them a way to share their experience with, motivate, and educate other people. I06 mentioned that she started posting food and workouts on Instagram because she wanted her weight loss experience to motivate others: "*Like people that are trying to lose weight and get healthy and might need some extra motivation or just feel stuck or maybe discouraged. I had hoped they would find me, and I could help inspire and motivate them in some way.*" Similarly, I04 started to share her cooking on Instagram to help friends who wanted to improve their cooking skills to eat healthier. These cooking posts often led to comments, messages, and even phone calls from friends wanting food preparation details: "'*What flour did you use, and how did you get it? Can you come and teach me?' Then we just had this discussion about the same thing or maybe you should try it this way*" (I04).

Collection and Integration

In our analysis, *collection* occurs when participants post about their food or fitness on Instagram. We define *integration* as incorporating other information related to their health goals in the photos or captions. The lived informatics model suggests people collect and integrate data differently depending on their motivation for tracking. For example, people who track to change their behavior usually track frequently, while instrumental trackers collect data when the benefits outweigh the costs. Participants also integrate data when integration generates insight. Our participants tracked for a mix of behavior change and instrumental goals. Receiving and providing social support motivated them to collect data consistently, and it sometimes motivated them to integrate data from multiple tracking tools.

Accountability: Tracking to keep one and others accountable

Participants frequently said that Instagram supported their health goals by giving them a sense of accountability. Social accountability refers to sharing one's progress to support their continued pursuit of their health goals [35]. Participants described collecting and integrating data on Instagram to stay accountable to themselves and others.

Participants felt that sharing their food photos and having people follow their posts helped them remain accountable for their tracking and health goals. For this reason, participants described feeling a need to honestly record everything: "*I'd post everything even if that's not super healthy*" (I06). I07 would sometimes 'cheat' on MyFitnessPal by leaving out small treats, but would post everything on Instagram, which held her accountable to her goal: "*before [when using MyFitnessPal] I would have a small snack pack that was a bag of chips and be like, 'Oh, that doesn't really count because it's just a little tiny bag.' But I think with Instagram, it helped me because I was taking a picture of it - It's real and it exists and it does count towards what I was eating. And then putting a visual image of it up really helped me stay honest.*" This accountability is important because missing entries commonly results in abandonment [17].

Emotional Support: Sharing tracked data for support

Participants posted and shared what they ate to receive emotional support. By finding others interested in similar diet options, having the same goals, or going through the same weight loss processes, many participants felt better supported by Instagram than by their friends and families: "*It makes me feel like I'm then around other people that feel the same, that have the same goals as me, and it can support me in that; whereas I don't particularly have that with my friends and family just because they're not particularly interested anymore*" (I09).

Participants often posted particularly difficult moments, hoping to receive emotional support. Participants generally perceived Instagram users as being open about sharing bad days and encouraging to each other: "*people are acknowledging that I'm trying*" (I02) and "*there were people rooting for me.*" (I15). Sharing failures (i.e., behaviors conflicting with the individual's health goals) helped them get the emotional support they needed to accept their failures and move on. I15 described a motivational quote she posted when she had a bad day: "*Some of my followers, and people who I follow as well, commented and wished me well and sent me love. It didn't make my day any better but it did make me feel better about everything.*"

Participants also used captions to attract support from others by helping others relate to their experience. Over time, I01 found that adding more personal messages in captions helps her to get more reactions from followers: "*To be a little less objective, a little more personal, to share more of what I'm feeling versus just stating [in the caption]. ... I find that people respond better to that. People will comment more. It almost feels as if they're encouraging me because people want to support each other.*"

Participants strove to make the photos they posted visually appealing because they felt that more attractive photos get more attention from other Instagram users. This attention helped increase their motivation for posting and sharing: "*I notice that when I had something that looked tasty and healthy, I would get more people liking the photo... I think I really used that as motivation too*" (I07). Participants had various strategies for taking proper food photos. They would adjust layout and lighting or use various filters or third-party apps. These strategies sometimes affected their food choices: "*[I started to make and eat more vegetarian food] because I think a lot of vegetarian food and vegan food that I make has a lot of green stuff in it and it's very attractive to people*" (I05). Participants also considered timing of posts strategically to get social interactions from other users: "*I've kind of figured out certain times during the day that more people seem to be active on Instagram*" (I03).

Motivation: Tracking to motivate oneself and others

Participants posted about accomplishments and experiences to motivate themselves and others. Some participants posted accomplishments, such as reaching weight or fitness goals. For example, I06 posted a day when she reached a large number of steps: "*I had a really good day, and I had gotten 16,000 or more steps, then I feel like I want to share my progress and everything with everyone.*" (I06).

Others posted on Instagram to provide motivation to others. I06 thought that "*show[ing] others what I was going through and eating and everything would help inspire and motivate them.*" I15 mentioned that she kept posting her food even after she reached her goal weight because she wanted to become a "*source of motivation and inspiration for people;*" she thought that continuing to share her previous and current habits would help encourage others.

Information: Posting to share information and ideas

Participants also commonly posted what they eat on Instagram to share knowledge about and ideas for healthy eating to others. For example, I01 wanted to convey that dieting does not require giving up flavorful food: "*I just wanted to show people that you can eat food that tastes good and still meets it. It has all the protein and the carbohydrates and the healthy fats, I still hit within the caloric range that I'm aiming for, but it tastes good. It doesn't feel like I'm eating broccoli and chicken*" (I01).

To make food posts useful for others, participants supplemented food photos with informative comments and hashtags. Many participants included recipes and food preparation information in their posts. Since it is difficult to include URLs in comments on Instagram, participants posted full recipes inside the comment instead. Some used hashtags to represent the ingredients to make it easier for others to search for the recipe: "*If I used a particular ingredient or method, I would sometimes use that as a hashtag. An example of that is, you can make kind of fake spaghetti noodles out of zucchini using a spiralizer and they're called zoodles, so I would use the hashtag for zoodles if I made something with that*" (I13).

Some participants integrated information from other tools into their food posts to provide more details. I11 shared her Instagram posts on Tumblr, where she could include more details, and provided the Tumblr link in her Instagram profile: "*If I post a picture on Instagram and then they go to the blog to see the entire recipe then they can actually click on the links.*" I06 would calculate Smart Points and add that to her photos: "*It helps because a lot of people that might be using Weight Watchers usually are saying like how many Smart Points is in whatever they are eating. ...That helps when you see people posting stuff like that so then you can kind of get ideas on what to eat.*" Others also often manually incorporated caloric information in their text descriptions, hashtags (e.g., #200calories), or photos using photo-editing tools to help others and themselves reflect and search for previously cooked foods based on calories.

Participants also considered what post content and timings would be most appropriate and useful for their followers. For example, I01 would deliberately make variations of the same food or perform easier workouts so others can follow more easily. I11 once wanted to share a coffee with sugar-free syrup, but decided to post at a time when the content would be more appropriate for her followers: "*I took the picture and then I was like, 'Is it good to post a picture with coffee at 10:00 in the evening UK?'*"

Reflection

Participants often reflected on their decisions of eating and tracking by reading their old posts and by reading and commenting on other people's posts. The lived informatics model suggests that people who track to change their behavior usually review their data more often than instrumental trackers. Our participants saw reflection as a way to receive and provide social support, and thus were motivated to reflect on their data and that of others.

Accountability: Reflecting on old posts to stay accountable

Participants maintained accountability by reviewing and reflecting on what they had done in the past. Participants found that looking back at their posts made them aware of how well they were maintaining their desired diet and helped keep them accountable. One participant noted how much she had eaten out in the past week and decided to cook more meals at home: "*if I've posted a lot of pictures of food from restaurants, it also kind of tells me, 'Hey, you haven't had anything that's been homemade in a while.*

You've been eating out a lot. Maybe you should make a salad for yourself.'" (I03). Another participant decided to pack her lunches at night after noticing she was eating out too much: *"One trend that I've noticed is that I definitely need to take the time to pack a lunch at night before work because if I don't ... I'm going to eat a burrito ... I'll take a photo with a burrito in my hand in the car. It's helpful for me to see that and look back at the different days"* (I13).

Participants also checked other people's posts to keep others accountable to their goals. I08 mentioned she checked in with other women participating in the same healthy eating challenge to make sure they are making progress: "*We are finishing up day 2 of this one perfect week so I'm just checking in, seeing how they are doing and asking how their day went. This is also a photo to show like, 'Oh, this is what I had for dinner.' I tagged them and then asked for them to tag me in any of their photos.*"

Emotional Support: Reading and commenting for support
Participants read comments from other people and reviewed the 'likes' their posts received to gain emotional support. I01 described what kind of feedback she got and how she was encouraged: *"People will send a combination of emoticons in kind of encouragement. You'll see people that say 'nice', or 'good job', 'keep it up'. You'll have like clapping hands, you'll have smiley faces or thumbs up kind of thing. It's really fun to have that kind of nice little, even emoji feedbacks, it's super positive for me."*

Participants also felt that giving emotional support back to the community was important. To provide this support, they proactively looked for other people's posts to comment on. They commented on posts by their usual followers, people they follow, and people who use the same hashtags: *"I'll still go to these certain hashtags and scroll through and comment and encourage other people on some posts if they need encouragement or anything like that ... not just 'like' other pictures just to get my Instagram handle out there but to actually add to the community*" (I14).

Motivation: Reading and commenting for motivation
Participants found looking back at their feed motivating, particularly during weeks when they were not performing as well towards their goal: "*I felt like I'm stuck, and I wasn't losing weight or anything. I had a bad couple of weeks, so I wanted to go back and see what was I eating a few weeks ago where I was feeling really good and doing good just to refresh my mind and re-motivate myself*" (I06).

Seeing posts from other people was also inspiring and motivating. Many participants, such as I12, described being motivated by seeing what others do: "*There's this picture [another Instagram user] posted today: 'Look at me doing tuck jumps. I couldn't do tuck jumps when I started.' It probably would have killed her. She can do it and I see her ... It's like, 'I guess I can do it.'*"

People also found motivation by motivating others. I03 described how she commented on posts from other women struggling with eating disorder recovery: "*I want to motivate those other girls that are struggling to say, 'Hey, I'm in recovery, too, and look what I'm eating.' Like, I've had to go over the same kind of fears, of different fear-foods and stuff. I kind of use it as more of a motivation.*"

Information: Reviewing posts for inspiration and information
To help make day-to-day decisions that support their health goals and to find inspiration, participants often looked for ideas and information in their old posts. Participants browsed old posts to find ideas about what to eat or make: "*if I'm wondering what I should make for the week, I like looking through my posts to see other things I cooked before*" (I07). This reflection was particularly useful when they wanted to replicate previous successes: "*when I hit a plateau, going back and seeing, 'Oh, I remember that that week there was a sudden loss. Let's go and see exactly what I ate.' It's very easy to track and replicate*" (I11).

Reviewing other people's food posts also helped our participants obtain ideas and knowledge about food, which was useful to sustain their eating behavior change. As I06 described, new ideas kept her motivated about maintaining her diet goal: "*if I get kind of bored with stuff I'm eating, I can kind of look and see maybe what other people are eating to give me some of the ideas.* "

Lapsing and Resuming Tracking
The lived informatics model categorizes four types of lapsing: forgetting, upkeep, skipping, and suspending. Our participants did not report lapsing because of forgetting or upkeep. They did sometimes intentionally skip or suspend tracking for reasons related to themselves and others. They often received social support when they lapsed.

Accountability: Lapsing when accountability needs change
Participants often lapsed when their goals shifted and caused their accountability needs to change. Some participants were rigorous about tracking when they were trying to change their behavior but relaxed when they were satisfied with it (I03, I04, I07). I03 described how her level of tracking loosened when she reached a goal: *"I'm on a vacation, then I eat out ... Suddenly I come back on Monday. I eat at home the whole time because I have to make up for eating out. 'I'm going to keep track until Friday,' and then I'm like, 'Okay, so now I'm back on track, so I don't have to keep tracking anymore.'"*

Other participants lapsed because they wanted to help others keep accountable to their goals and worried that certain posts could negatively affect the behavior of their followers. I13 decided that she would not post certain food photos that could cause negative behavior in others: "*I just don't want to post too many potentially triggering photos because they have no way of opting out of seeing them.*"

The goal of accountability was also sometimes at odds with impression management, and participants sometimes lapsed to preserve their image. For example, some were reluctant to post food perceived as undesirable, and I04 worried about her parents seeing posts that showed her drinking: *"If I take pictures of something that I've been drinking, I don't share it with my parents because they don't like me drinking ... that's to share with friends"* (I04).

Alternatively, some participants felt uncomfortable lapsing because of their perceived accountability to others. They felt the need to explain their behavior because they did not want to disappoint others. I09 described one instance when she went traveling and did not have a reliable internet connection for three days. Concerned that her followers were waiting for her posts, she explained her connectivity issues to her followers in her first post after her return. I11 similarly felt that her followers were *"looking at [her] as the UK keto guide"*. Because of this perceived accountability, she felt she needed to justify actions that did not befit a role model: *"why I've eaten bad that day."*

Emotional Support: Lapsing triggered additional support

Participants mentioned that their lapses sometimes lead to additional emotional support from others, which could help them resume tracking. After being sick and not posting on Instagram for a while, I12 found others left encouraging comments when she resumed posting: "*The girls are like, 'Yeah, see that's good. You're still eating healthy. At least you're doing it.'*" Some participants even received in-app messages from others when they had not posted for a while (I06, I10, I12): *"I had someone message me, and I had no idea who it was, and she had like commented in some of my pictures, and she messaged me to see me if I'm okay because I hadn't posted anything in a couple of days, and I was like 'Wow.' I'm like 'Thanks.' ... it made me feel good and kind of got me motivated that like someone that I don't even know takes the time to send me a message to make sure everything was okay"* (I06). These comments and messages made participants feel they were cared for and supported, with messages helping them go through difficult time and resume their everyday tracking activities.

Information: Lapsing when photos lacked useful information

Participants whose primary goal on Instagram was to provide knowledge to others were more selective about their posts, intentionally posting about food or workouts to be informative rather than posting all the food they ate or exercises they did (I04, I11, I15). For example, I04 only shared food she had not previously posted because she did not think reposting the same food would be useful for other people: *"I will post maybe once a week or twice a week. Then I won't repeat my posts. I wouldn't post something that I already posted ... I post something that's interesting."*

DISCUSSION

People track their food on Instagram with the intertwined goals of supporting healthy eating and providing and receiving social support. The lived informatics model and other personal informatics models may be strengthened by the inclusion of social interaction and other social roles in the model. As seen among our participants, use of Instagram for food journaling can support both health and social goals, but this use requires people to make tradeoffs between consistent tracking and social needs. Designs can better support people in making these decisions.

Including Social Roles in Personal Informatics Models

Our findings show that people's interactions with others can influence personal tracking behaviors. Prior research established that others, such as health care providers [12,35] or family members [25,50], influence people's tracking and health decisions and can help them maintain their health. Involvement of others can offer accountability and guidance on how to track as well as how to interpret and act on tracked data. Although the importance of others in health behaviors and in self-tracking decisions is well-established, the models the HCI community uses to understand and design for self-tracking tools [21,29] still focus on the individual.

Our study of Instagram for food tracking offers an in-depth understanding of the many ways others can influence tracking decisions and related behaviors. Participants chose to use Instagram in their food tracking for many of the same reasons people share health information in other forums: to receive accountability, motivation, emotional support, and information from others. But they also chose to use, or continue using, Instagram for their food tracking so they could offer this social support to others.

This motivation carried through to the collection stage of tracking. Our participants created and curated posts to make them desirable, motivating, inspirational, and informative for themselves and others. Our participants also reflected on data collected both by themselves and others, which differs from the emphasis of personal informatics on reflecting primarily on one's own data. Prior work has demonstrated that reflecting on family member's tracking data [50] and receiving prompts from health experts [35] can address challenges that arise in reflection.

The desire to pursue or provide social support can also have negative consequences, triggering lapsing and resumption in tracking. For example, only posting informative photos can leave tracking data incomplete for later reflection on behavior change goals. However, people might have other goals for reflection, and some recent studies (e.g., [19]) have begun to examine how to make incomplete tracking data useful to support such reflection. By understanding why people lapse and resume, and how these reasons conflict with their goals for reflection, systems can also make people aware of these decisions. Systems can also help people make informed decisions that accommodate tradeoffs between social needs and reflection, such as the frequency or the type of posts.

Updating personal informatics models to more explicitly help designers and researchers consider the different roles and influences people may have in self-tracking could lead to new design opportunities. Below, we discuss some of those opportunities in the food tracking domain.

Using Hashtags to Reveal Myriad Communities

Previous work has suggested that hashtags can induce a sense of ad hoc community [3]. Our findings suggest that this function of hashtags was an important reason users select Instagram for food tracking. The ability to use multiple hashtags allowed users to easily find similar others and to discover and enter new communities. This exposure to new communities helped them find ideas for new exercise and diet options (e.g., new ingredient options to try) and develop their own recipes or exercise regimen.

Prior work in online communities [3,31,43] and health tracking [14,52] has shown the value of social support from similar others. Most online communities and social media platforms also provide features to support people in finding others with the same interests or goals, such as discussion boards with specific topics, Facebook groups, or subreddits. However, commenters with different conditions or illnesses can still share related experiences and provide emotional support [28]. Similarly, strangers on online communities can also provide accountability and information support [43]. Our findings confirm that both similar others and people who are quite different can provide support. Our participants were inspired by users who shared similar healthy eating goals but whose lives were quite different from their own (e.g., students vs. stay-at-home moms). They could also explore new ingredients that are different from their usual choices, but still within their diet restrictions or preferences (e.g., fresh food vs. artificial food substitutes).

However, in Instagram's current form, user discovery of new hashtags depends on serendipity. To better support this type of exploration, systems can show users commonly co-occurring hashtags. Systems can also help users navigate through different communities whose norms they are not familiar with by exposing in-group norms [9] and exposing information that is desirable across different communities.

Managing Tensions between Goals and Social Needs

Using Instagram both for tracking one's own health behaviors and for engaging others creates a tension between personal tracking goals and social goals. This tension can cause people to adjust their behaviors to reconcile the two goals. Sometimes this adjustment leads to behaviors that are both better for the user's health and more engaging for others, but sometimes people prioritize one goal over the other, even to the detriment of their own health behaviors.

Tracking change when supporting social needs

Membership in the Instagram community influenced how our participants collected information. Previous research has also found that participants wanted to post interesting rather than routine content [41,43], including photos [5]. Findings in other online communities [43] and family journaling [25] also show that people strove to engage and inform their audience with the content they posted, even when this conflicted with personal goals.

Our findings emphasize an underlying conflict in this preference: the desire to keep an Instagram feed interesting and engaging poses a challenge to users who want to record their day-to-day meals. Because of this conflict, all but two participants created separate accounts to prevent over-sharing. To maintain an interesting feed, some participants also lapsed in tracking, which in turn limited their ability to review and reflect on past behavior, such as preventing people from identifying personal antecedents of a negative outcome (e.g., undesired weight gain). One design opportunity could be to support different content lifespan for sharing and reflection. For example, systems could support ephemeral sharing, similar to Instagram Stories, to fulfill people's social needs while maintaining the content privately for future reflection. Designers of tracking systems should also consider supporting reflection according to what people try to learn from their or other people's behavior. For example, when people seek inspiration from past behavior, systems could highlight weeks when the user ate healthy or diversified meals, even given an incomplete record. When reflecting to understand personal behavior, the system could highlight the weeks most representative of food patterns and emphasize when the data might be incomplete.

Behavior change when supporting social needs

The conflict between Instagram norms and someone's personal health goals also affects user behaviors, in positive and negative ways. In some cases, social norms influenced participants to act in ways more consistent with their own health goals. For instance, some participants mentioned eating fewer snacks (I12), more vegetables (I03, I05), or more diverse food (I10, I15) because they did not want to disappoint their followers and wanted to stay accountable to them. Their healthy behavior choices were often reinforced by reading other people's posts to learn healthy eating strategies and by receiving feedback from followers. Similar to Community Mosaic users, our participants also made healthier choices so they would not have and then share experiences that might negatively influence others [44].

However, in other cases social pressure made participants less likely to engage in healthy behaviors: I01 swam less frequently because the workout was less accessible to her followers. Increases in negative behaviors and outcomes have occurred in other Instagram communities, such as depression in eating disorder recovery communities [7]. Content can also influence people who run across the posts but are not part of the community, such as people who find pro-anorexia content by searching for fitness or health-related hashtags [45]. As suggested by research on depression online [10], designers or facilitators of online communities should consider creating awareness by proposing community norms for positive behavior. Systems can promote this awareness by supporting people to reflect on their long-term trend in relation to a community's overall behavior. Systems can also involve health experts to moderate negative posts or promote educational material to increase awareness of positive behavior.

Appropriating Multiple Tools for Social Personal Tracking

Munson et al. [39] describe how repurposing social media platforms for health can be a first-order approximation —a "*tractable solution that partially solves specific problems with known trade-offs*" [1]— that can help individuals attempting to manage different aspects of their health. Using Instagram as a social, photo-based food journal, is one such approximation: it provides features to support food photo collection, reflection on old posts, and finding community support. Instagram was not designed for personal tracking, and does not include common self-tracking features, such as summaries designed to support reflection. As Instagram was not designed to support a focus on healthy eating, it also lacks features to support recording or sharing detailed food information or recipes. The lack of these features might be challenging for people who seek to appropriate Instagram as a personal food tracking system.

However, our findings suggest that participants with varied health goals could appropriate Instagram's features to fit with their needs. Some participants would glance chronologically through the color and content of food photos to find trends and awareness. Others felt more engaged with their tracking without entering all the details. Some of Instagram's flexibility derives from it not being designed for food tracking, and so it does not impose a designer's notion of how people should track food. This allows people to use the photos and text fields as needed to meet their goals.

People also use Instagram alongside other tools to support particular tracking needs, such as I15 who used YouFood for detailed food tracking while also posting photos to Instagram for social support. I05 also use Instagram photos as a reminder of what she had eaten for the day and then used MyFitnessPal for calorie counting. While participants often found tracking different information using several apps useful, they also discussed a need to integrate information from several sources to help them reflect on their holistic health goals. Helping users easily integrate additional information with the right level of detail into their food posts could support their reflection on their behaviors in more detail. Future systems should also consider allowing importing and exporting data from different tools with customized levels of disclosure. In this way, users can select tools that best fit their needs.

LIMITATIONS AND FUTURE WORK

We searched for users using #fooddiary or #foodjournal at various times of day to recruit participants across different time zones who were posting food photos at different times of day. However, we only encountered one male in over 200 Instagram users we contacted, who did not respond to our interview invitation. We specifically looked for males in snowball sampling. Participants also commented on male scarcity. As a result, participants were all female and 18 to 34 years old, leaving us unable to describe experiences of Instagram users more broadly.

We were also only able to recruit participants who were actively using Instagram to support healthy eating behavior, because hashtag searching on Instagram only shows results from the most current hashtag use. Therefore, although our study includes participants who had previously lapsed, it does not describe the experiences of people who abandoned food tracking on Instagram.

While we strove to understand a range of uses and experiences, including participants with varied numbers of followers and in different stages of pursuing healthy eating, we did not collect socioeconomic status (e.g., education or income). Future research should examine the experiences of people of diverse socioeconomic status. In addition, while our participants had diverse goals and follower counts, our sample size was small. Future, larger-scale research is needed to provide nuanced insight into differences between user groups.

CONCLUSION

Building on prior knowledge of how people appropriate social media for the pursuit of health goals, we describe lived experiences of personal food tracking in a social environment. We use the lived informatics model to describe how people's tracking activities were shaped by their intent to receive and provide social support on Instagram. Goals of managing one's impression, receiving and providing social benefits, and keeping track of behavior are intertwined and influence each other.

Designers wanting to support personal tracking in social contexts should consider features that help users pursue social benefits. For example, systems can help users access communities for specific health goals and diverse exploration as well as providing strategies to navigate through different communities. Also, systems can support users in integrating information from different apps that are better fit to various aspects of their health goals.

For personal informatics researchers, the personal informatics models should be further developed to account for social influence. Researchers should reflect on how social needs affect people's decisions about and behavior surrounding the acts of selecting tools, collecting, integrating, and reflecting on data, and lapsing and resuming.

ACKNOWLEDGMENTS

We thank Laura Pina, Daniel Epstein, Lucas Colusso, Arpita Bhattacharya, and reviewers for thoughtful feedback on the earlier version of this paper. This study is funded in part by the National Science Foundation under awards IIS-1553167 and SCH-1344613, the Agency for Healthcare Research and Quality under award 1R21HS023654, a University of Washington Innovation Research Award, and Microsoft.

REFERENCES

1. Mark Ackerman. 2009. The Intellectual Challenge of CSCW: The Gap Between Social Requirements and Technical Feasibility. *International Journal of Human Computer interaction* 24, July 2014: 37–41. http://doi.org/10.1207/S15327051HCI1523
2. Phil Adams, Eric PS Baumer, and Geri Gay. 2014. Staccato Social Support in Mobile Health Applications. *Proceedings of the SIGCHI conference on Human Factors in Computing Systems (CHI 2014)*: 653–662. http://doi.org/10.1145/2556288.2557297
3. Nazanin Andalibi, Pinar Ozturk, and Andrea Forte. Sensitive Self-disclosures, Responses, and Social Support on Instagram: the Case of #Depression. *Proceedings of the ACM Conference on Computer Supported Cooperative Work (CSCW 2017).* http://doi.org/10.1145/2998181.2998243
4. Lenore Arab, Deborah Estrin, Donnie H Kim, Jeff Burke, and Jeff Goldman. 2011. Feasibility Testing of an Automated Image-Capture Method to Aid Dietary Recall. *European Journal of Clinical Nutrition* 65, 10: 1156–1162. http://doi.org/10.1038/ejcn.2011.75
5. Eric PS Baumer, Sherri J Katz, Jill E Freeman, Phil Adams, Amy L Gonzales, John Pollak, Daniela Retelny, Jeff Niederdeppe, Christine M Olson, and Geri K Gay. 2012. Prescriptive Persuasion and Open-Ended Social Awareness: Expanding the Design Space of Mobile Health. *Proceedings of the ACM Conference on Computer Supported Cooperative Work (CSCW 2012)*: 475–484. http://doi.org/10.1145/2145204.2145279
6. G Bird and P C Elwood. 1983. The Dietary Intakes of Subjects Estimated From Photographs Compared with a Weighed Record. *Human nutrition. Applied nutrition* 37, 6: 470–473. http://europepmc.org/abstract/MED/6662734
7. Stevie Chancellor, Zhiyuan Lin, Erica L Goodman, Stephanie Zerwas, and Munmun De Choudhury. 2016. Quantifying and Predicting Mental Illness Severity in Online Pro-Eating Disorder Communities. *Proceedings of the ACM Conference on Computer-Supported Cooperative Work and Social Computing (CSCW 2016)*: 1171–1184. http://doi.org/10.1145/2818048.2819973
8. Stevie Chancellor, Tanushree Mitra, and Munmun De Choudhury. 2016. Recovery Amid Pro-Anorexia: Analysis of Recovery in Social Media. *Proceedings of the SIGCHI Conference on Human Factors in Computing Systems (CHI 2016)*: 2111–2123. http://doi.org/10.1145/2858036.2858246
9. Stevie Chancellor, Jessica Annette Pater, Trustin Clear, Eric Gilbert, and Munmun De Choudhury. 2016. # thyghgapp: Instagram Content Moderation and Lexical Variation in Pro-Eating Disorder Communities. *Proceedings of the ACM Conference on Computer-Supported Cooperative Work & Social Computing (CSCW 2016)*: 1201–1213. http://doi.org/10.1145/2818048.2819963
10. Munmun De Choudhury, Emre Kiciman, Mark Dredze, Glen Coppersmith, and Mrinal Kumar. 2016. Discovering Shifts to Suicidal Ideation from Mental Health Content in Social Media. *Proceedings of the SIGCHI Conference on Human Factors in Computing Systems (CHI 2016)*: 2098–2110. http://doi.org/10.1145/2858036.2858207
11. Munmun De Choudhury, Sanket Sharma, and Emre Kiciman. 2016. Characterizing Dietary Choices, Nutrition, and Language in Food Deserts via Social Media. *Proceedings of the ACM Conference on Computer-Supported Cooperative Work & Social Computing (CSCW 2016)*: 1157–1170. http://doi.org/10.1145/2818048.2819956
12. Chia-Fang Chung, Kristin Dew, Allison Cole, Jasmine Zia, James Fogarty, Julie A Kientz, and Sean A Munson. 2016. Boundary Negotiating Artifacts in Personal Informatics: Patient-Provider Collaboration with Patient-Generated Data. *Proceedings of the ACM Conference on Computer-Supported Cooperative Work & Social Computing (CSCW 2016)*: 770–786. http://doi.org/10.1145/2818048.2819926
13. Andrea Civan-Hartzler, David W McDonald, Chris Powell, Meredith M Skeels, Marlee Mukai, and Wanda Pratt. 2010. Bringing the Field into Focus: User-centered Design of a Patient Expertise Locator. *Proceedings of the SIGCHI Conference on Human Factors in Computing Systems (CHI 2010)*: 1675–1684. http://doi.org/10.1145/1753326.1753577
14. Sunny Consolvo, Katherine Everitt, Ian Smith, and James A Landay. 2006. Design Requirements for Technologies that Encourage Physical Activity. *Proceedings of the SIGCHI Conference on Human Factors in Computing Systems (CHI 2006)*: 457–466. http://doi.org/10.1145/1124772.1124840
15. Sunny Consolvo, Predrag Klasnja, David W McDonald, and James A Landay. 2012. Designing for Healthy Lifestyles: Design Considerations for Mobile Technologies to Encourage Consumer Health and Wellness. *Foundations and Trends in Human–Computer Interaction* 6, 3–4: 167–315. http://doi.org/10.1561/1100000040
16. Felicia Cordeiro, Elizabeth Bales, Erin Cherry, and James Fogarty. 2015. Rethinking the Mobile Food Journal. *Proceedings of the SIGCHI Conference on Human Factors in Computing Systems (CHI 2015)*: 3207–3216. http://doi.org/10.1145/2702123.2702154
17. Felicia Cordeiro, Daniel A Epstein, Edison Thomaz, Cordeiro, Elizabeth Bales, Arvind K Jagannathan, Gregory D Abowd, and James Fogarty. 2015. Barriers and Negative Nudges: Exploring Challenges in Food Journaling. *Proceedings of the SIGCHI Conference on Human Factors in Computing Systems (CHI 2015)*: 1159–1162. http://doi.org/10.1145/2702123.2702155

18. Daniel A Epstein, Bradley H Jacobson, Elizabeth Bales, David W McDonald, and Sean A Munson. 2015. From "nobody cares" to "way to go!": A Design Framework for Social Sharing in Personal Informatics. *Proceedings of the ACM Conference on Computer Supported Cooperative Work & Social Computing (CSCW 2015)*: 1622–1636. http://doi.org/10.1145/2675133.2675135

19. Daniel A Epstein, Jennifer H Kang, Laura R Pina, James Fogarty, and Sean A Munson. 2016. Reconsidering the Device in the Drawer: Lapses as a Design Opportunity in Personal Informatics. *Proceedings of the 2016 ACM International Joint Conference on Pervasive and Ubiquitous Computing (UbiComp 2016)*: 829–840. http://doi.org/10.1145/2971648.2971656

20. Daniel A Epstein, Felicia Cordeiro, James Fogarty, Gary Hsieh, and Sean A Munson. 2016. Crumbs: Lightweight Daily Food Challenges to Promote Engagement and Mindfulness. *Proceedings of the SIGCHI Conference on Human Factors in Computing Systems (CHI 2016)*: 5632–5644. http://doi.org/10.1145/2858036.2858044

21. Daniel A Epstein, An Ping, James Fogarty, and Sean A Munson. 2015. A Lived Informatics Model of Personal Informatics. *Proceedings of the 2015 ACM International Joint Conference on Pervasive and Ubiquitous Computing (UbiComp 2015)*: 731–742. http://doi.org/10.1145/2750858.2804250

22. Susannah Fox and M Duggan. 2013. Health online 2013. *Health*: 1–55. Retrieved from http://www.pewinternet.org/~/media/Files/Reports/PIP_HealthOnline.pdf

23. Andrea Grimes, Martin Bednar, Jay D Bolter, and Rebecca E Grinter. 2008. EatWell: Sharing Nutrition-related Memories in a Low-income Community. *Proceedings of the ACM Conference on Computer Supported Cooperative Work (CSCW 2008)*: 87–96. http://doi.org/10.1145/1460563.1460579

24. Andrea Grimes and Richard Harper. 2008. Celebratory Technology : New Directions for Food Research in HCI. *Proceedings of the SIGCHI Conference on Human Factors in Computing Systems (CHI 2008)*: 467–476. http://doi.org/10.1145/1357054.1357130

25. Andrea Grimes, Desney Tan, and Dan Morris. 2009. Toward Technologies that Support Family Reflections on Health. *Proceedings of the ACM 2009 International Conference on Supporting Group Work (Group 2009)*: 311–320. https://doi.org/10.1145/1531674.1531721

26. Andrea Hartzler and Wanda Pratt. 2011. Managing the Personal Side of Health: How Patient Expertise Differs From the Expertise of Clinicians. *Journal of Medical Internet Research* 13, 3. http://doi.org/10.2196/jmir.1728

27. Jina Huh and Mark S Ackerman. 2012. Collaborative Help in Chronic Disease Management. *Proceedings of the ACM conference on Computer Supported Cooperative Work (CSCW 2012)*: 853. http://doi.org/10.1145/2145204.2145331

28. Jina Huh, Leslie S Liu, Tina Neogi, Kori Inkpen, and Wanda Pratt. 2014. Health Vlogs as Social Support for Chronic Illness Management. *ACM Transactions on Computer-Human Interaction (TOCHI)* 21, 4: 23. http://doi.org/10.1145/2630067

29. Ian Li, Anind Dey, and Jodi Forlizzi. 2010. A Stage-Based Model of Personal Informatics Systems. *Proceedings of the SIGCHI Conference on Human Factors in Computing Systems (CHI 2010)*: 557–566. http://doi.org/10.1145/1753326.1753409

30. Ian Li, Anind Dey, and Jodi Forlizzi. 2011. Understanding My Data, Myself: Supporting Self-Reflection with Ubicomp Technologies. *Proceedings of the 13th International Conference on Ubiquitous computing (UbiComp 2011)*: 405–414. http://doi.org/10.1145/2030112.2030166

31. Victor Li, David W McDonald, Elizabeth V Eikey, Jessica Sweeney, Janessa Escajeda, Guarav Dubey, Kaitlin Riley, Erika S Poole, and Eric B Hekler. 2014. Losing it Online: Characterizing Participation in an Online Weight Loss Community. *Proceedings of the 18th International Conference on Supporting Group Work (Group 2014)*: 35–45. http://doi.org/10.1145/2660398.2660416

32. James J Lin, Lena Mamykina, Silvia Lindtner, Gregory Delajoux, and Henry B Strub. 2006. Fish'n'Steps: Encouraging Physical Activity with an Interactive Computer Game. *Proceedings of the 2006 International Conference on Ubiquitous computing (UbiComp 2006)*: 261–278. http://doi.org/10.1007/11853565_16

33. Leslie S Liu, Jina Huh, Tina Neogi, Kori Inkpen, and Wanda Pratt. 2013. Health Vlogger-Viewer Interaction in Chronic Illness Management. *Proceedings of the SIGCHI Conference on Human factors in Computing Systems (CHI 2013)*: 49–58. http://doi.org/10.1145/2470654.2470663

34. Diane Maloney-Krichmar and Jenny Preece. 2005. A Multilevel Analysis of Sociability, Usability, and Community Dynamics in an Online Health Community. *ACM Transactions on Computer-Human Interaction (TOCHI)* 12, 2: 201–232. http://doi.org/10.1145/1067860.1067864

35. Lena Mamykina, Elizabeth Mynatt, Patricia Davidson, and Daniel Greenblatt. 2008. MAHI: Investigation of Social Scaffolding for Reflective Thinking in Diabetes Management. *Proceedings of the SIGCHI Conference on Human Factors in Computing Systems (CHI 2008)*: 477–486. http://doi.org/10.1145/1357054.1357131

36. Yelena Mejova, Sofiane Abbar, and Hamed Haddadi. 2016. Fetishizing Food in Digital Age: #foodporn Around the World. *Tenth International AAAI Conference on Web and Social Media (ICWSM 2016).*

37. Hannah K Menefee, Morgan J Thompson, Thomas M Guterbock, Ishan C Williams, and Rupa S Valdez. 2016. Mechanisms of Communicating Health Information Through Facebook: Implications for Consumer Health Information Technology Design. *Journal of Medical Internet Research* 18, 8. http://doi.org/10.2196/jmir.5949

38. Anders K Munk, Andreas Birkbak, and Morten K Petersen. 2016. (Re-) Appropriating Instagram for Social Research: Three Methods for Studying Obesogenic Environments. *Proceedings of the 7th 2016 International Conference on Social Media & Society*: 19. https://doi.org/10.1145/2930971.2930991

39. Sean A Munson, Hasan Cavusoglu, Larry Frisch, and Sidney Fels. 2013. Sociotechnical Challenges and Progress in Using Social Media for Health. *Journal of Medical Internet Research* 15, 10: 1–14. http://doi.org/10.2196/jmir.2792

40. Sean A Munson, Erin Krupka, Caroline Richardson, and Paul Resnick. 2015. Effects of Public Commitments and Accountability in a Technology-Supported Physical Activity Intervention. *Proceedings of the SIGCHI Conference on Human Factors in Computing Systems (CHI 2015)*, 1135–1144. http://doi.org/10.1145/2702123.2702524

41. Sean A Munson, Debra Lauterbach, Mark W Newman, and Paul Resnick. 2010. Happier Together: Integrating a Wellness Application into a Social Network Site. In *International Conference on Persuasive Technology (PERSUASIVE 2010)*: 27–39. http://doi.org/10.1007/978-3-642-13226-1_5

42. Michael Nelson, M Atkinson, and S Darbyshire. 1996. Food Photography II: Use of Food Photographs for Estimating Portion Size and the Nutrient Content of Meals. *The British Journal of Nutrition* 76, 1: 31–49. http://doi.org/10.1079/BJN19960007

43. Mark W Newman, Debra Lauterbach, Sean A Munson, Paul Resnick, and Margaret E Morris. 2011. "It's not that I don't have problems , I'm just not putting them on Facebook": Challenges and Opportunities in Using Online Social Networks for Health. *Proceedings of the ACM Conference on Computer Supported Cooperative Work (CSCW 2011)*: 341–350. http://doi.org/10.1145/1958824.1958876

44. Andrea Grimes Parker. 2014. Reflection-Through-Performance: Personal Implications of Documenting Health Behaviors for the Collective. *Personal and Ubiquitous Computing* 18, 7: 1737–1752. http://doi.org/10.1007/s00779-014-0780-5

45. Jessica Pater, Oliver Haimson, Nazanin Andalibi, and Elizabeth D Mynatt. 2016. "Hunger Hurts but Starving Works": Characterzing the Presentation of Eating Disorders Online. *Proceedings of the ACM Conference on Computer-Supported Cooperative Work & Social Computing (CSCW 2016)*: 1185-1200. http://doi.org/10.1145/2818048.2820030

46. Josée Poirier and Nathan K Cobb. 2012. Social Influence as a Driver of Engagement in a Web-based Health Intervention. *Journal of Medical Internet Research* 14, 1: 1–9. http://doi.org/10.2196/jmir.1957

47. Instagram Press. 600 Million and Counting. http://blog.instagram.com/post/154506585127/161215-600million

48. Caroline R Richardson, Lorraine R Buis, Adrienne W. Janney, David E Goodrich, Ananda Sen, Michael L Hess, Kathleen S Mehari, Laurie A Fortlage1, Paul J Resnick, Brian J Zikmund-Fisher, Victor J Strecher, and John D Piette. An Online Community Improves Adherence in an Internet-Mediated Walking Program. Part 1: Results of a Randomized Controlled Trial. *Journal of Medical Internet Research* 12, 4: e41. http://doi.org/10.2196/jmir.1338

49. John Rooksby, Mattias Rost, Alistair Morrison, and Matthew Chalmers Chalmers. 2014. Personal Tracking as Lived Informatics. *Proceedings of the SIGCHI Conference on Human Factors in Computing Systems (CHI 2014)*: 1163–1172. http://doi.org/10.1145/2556288.2557039

50. Chris Schaefbauer, Danish Kahn, Amy Le, Garrett Sczechowski, and Katie Siek. 2015. Snack Buddy: Supporting Healthy Snacking in Low Socioeconomic Status Families. *Proceedings of the ACM Conference on Computer Supported Cooperative Work & Social Computing (CSCW 2015)*: 1045–1057. http://doi.org/10.1145/2675133.2675180

51. Edison Thomaz, Aman Parnami, Irfan Essa, and Gregory D Abowd. 2013. Feasibility of Identifying Eating Moments from First-Person Images Leveraging Human Computation. *Proceedings of the 4th International SenseCam & Pervasive Imaging Conference*: 26–33. http://doi.org/10.1145/2526667.2526672

52. Tammy Toscos, Anne Faber, Shunying An, and Mona Praful Gandhi. 2006. Chick Clique: Persuasive Technology to Motivate Teenage Girls to Exercise. *CHI '06 Extended Abstracts on Human Factors in Computing Systems* 31, 3: 1873–1878. http://doi.org/10.1145/1125451.1125805

53. Paul Wicks, Michael Massagli, Jeana Frost, Catherine Brownstein, Sally Okun, Timothy Vaughan, Richard Bradley, and James Heywood. 2010. Sharing Health Data for Better Outcomes on Patientslikeme. *Journal of Medical Internet Research* 12, 2: 1–12. http://doi.org/10.2196/jmir.1549

54. Mary H Wilde and Suzanne Garvin. 2007. A Concept Analysis of Self-monitoring. *Journal of Advanced Nursing* 57, 3: 339–350. http://doi.org/10.1111/j.1365-2648.2006.04089.x

55. Lydia Zepeda and David Deal. 2008. Think before You Eat: Photographic Food Diaries ss Intervention Tools to Change Dietary Decision Making and Attitudes. *International Journal of Consumer Studies* 32, 6: 692–698. http://doi.org/10.1111/j.1470-6431.2008.00725.x

Participatory Media: Creating Spaces for Storytelling in Neighbourhood Planning

Jennifer Manuel, Geoff Vigar, Tom Bartindale & Rob Comber
Open Lab
Newcastle University
Newcastle upon Tyne, UK
{j.manuel2@ncl.ac.uk/geoff.vigar@ncl.ac.uk/ tom@bartindale.com/rob.comber@ncl.ac.uk}

ABSTRACT
Neighbourhood planning devolves power to communities to create their own planning policy but traditional forms of participation are still relied upon. And despite the ubiquitous nature of technology in society, digital participation methods are rarely used. In this paper, we outline fieldwork with two neighbourhood planning groups who used participatory media technology to improve engagement though the art of storytelling. We focus on the configuration of participatory media as a way to widen participation and enable story creation and sharing amongst citizens. We highlight that storytelling using media technology can provide a model *of* and a model *for* the way we 'do' neighbourhood planning whilst emphasising the challenges of ensuring processes are linked to tangible actions and encouraging the multiplicity of stories.

Author Keywords
Participatory media; new media; neighbourhood planning

ACM Classification Keywords
H.5.m. Information interfaces and presentation (e.g., HCI): Miscellaneous

INTRODUCTION
Neighbourhood planning in the UK was created by the Localism Act 2011 [37] which gave new rights to citizens. It was a way to devolve power away from local and central government to local people at the lowest level [85]. The aim is to empower citizens to organise together to produce their own planning policy which will shape the future development of their area and will be officially adopted by the local authority [9, 42]. Citizen engagement in planning has been promoted for a number of years, but neighbourhood planning provides the first opportunity for citizens to have direct power to decide what development they do and do not want in their neighbourhood [9].

The move from local government shaping agendas to communities influencing their own neighbourhood coincides with the 'story turn' in planning which advocates for the narratives of everyday experiences to be combined into political processes [65]. This is not always realised in practice, particularly as citizen participation in political matters remains fairly low [60, 80] and traditional engagement methods restrict the type of responses in consultations [5, 17].

CHI 2017, May 06-11, 2017, Denver, CO, USA
ACM 978-1-4503-4655-9/17/05.
http://dx.doi.org/10.1145/3025453.3025745

Particularly in neighbourhood planning, finding new approaches to allow citizens' stories to be shared and heard is essential, especially as the process relies on community input. Neighbourhood planning requires citizen participation to organise together to begin the process; to gain input from the wider public; and to enable the plan to pass a community referendum at the end of the process. Neighbourhood planning could be a futile endeavour if participation does not take account of the need for a multiplicity of citizens' stories.

In this paper, we explore the process of sharing and listening to citizen stories in the neighbourhood planning process through the method of participatory media. Through a two-part process, we used storyboarding as a way to share individual's stories and create new community stories before using the Bootlegger platform as a participatory media commissioning tool to capture these citizen narratives through video. We highlight the need for new, creative digital methods of engagement to widen participation and include new stories in neighbourhood planning. Through the discussion of our deployment, we demonstrate that i) participatory media storytelling can contribute to a model *of* and a model *for* neighbourhood planning; ii) the production of a video can highlight missing stories; and iii) synchronous participatory media technology opens a space for a multiplicity of citizen stories. Our reflections from the fieldwork highlight new possibilities for future participatory media technology as a conduit for storytelling that leads to authentic policy creation in neighbourhood planning.

RELATED WORK
Neighbourhood planning still relies upon traditional participation methods to engage citizens resulting in a multitude of issues as to whose stories are told and heard in the process. With a turn in HCI towards technologies for civic participation [7, 16, 30, 38, 68, 82], there is a huge potential to introduce new methods and, therefore, bring new voices into neighbourhood planning.

Neighbourhood Planning Participation and Storytelling
The UK town planning system was built on a foundation of representative democracy with elected councillors

representing the views of their community [75]. As the demand for more citizen participation grew, the requirements placed on consultation also grew [85]. Despite this, the methods and approaches used have a limited ability to reach out to the whole community and gather the stories of all actors in the process [14]. Town hall meetings, forums and formal events are still the common methods used along with the addition of drop-in events [5]. These can be seen as the legitimate way to participate [14] and do not account for more informal methods and individual and community storytelling. These traditional methods and formal planning processes require comments and input from citizens to relate to 'material planning considerations': a set of prescribed criteria which are the issues that are taken into when making planning decisions in the UK [62].

The 'story turn' in planning literature advocates for the representation of "space, life and languages" of a city through the use of narratives [67]. Narratives are seen as essential to the planning system as a way to promote change, show the origins of communities and to form the basis of policy [67]. By accounting for storytelling in the engagement of citizens, there would be increased opportunity for identities and meaning to be created by communities themselves [26], however, this has not been fully explored in planning practice on a day-to-day basis.

Considering the formal participation methods and the failure to take everyday stories into account, those who do participate are often of a certain demographic and background. The formal mode of communication suits and attracts citizens from a middle class, retired, professional backgrounds who have the time and resources to tell their stories [56]. Compounding this factor, is that the complexities of neighbourhood planning mean that 'expert' citizen activists from those backgrounds are most likely to participate [85] and are able to express their stories in the most appropriate format to suit the planning system.

Bearing these issues in mind, there is, therefore, a reliance on a rational choice model based on the self-interest of individuals [34]. This means that during decision-making, individuals will always prefer options that will benefit themselves rather than their community as a whole [34], making the bonding of individual and community stories difficult to achieve.

Although the issues above are true of the wider planning system, there is an argument to show neighbourhood planning suffers from the same problems [85] which can cause real challenges for a process which relies on citizen participation. One of the key issues, then, is the way in which engagement is carried out and how stories are captured. In his 2002 speech Robin Cook, the chair of the Government's Cabinet Committee, said "There is a connection to be made between the decline in democratic participation and the explosion in new ways of communicating" [57] and there has been little done to improve the situation since. By considering this, it is possible to turn the self-interest model around to create a more open one by thinking about the ways citizens want and are able to engage and share their stories in a political debate [34].

Aside from the traditional forms of citizen participation, there has been an increase in the use of digital technologies as a form of communication. These digital methods have aimed to involve a wider range of citizens and increase our interactions with one another [34, 28]. Digital technology has been seen to offer an opportunity to empower citizens and act as a democratisation of complex, elitist processes [19]. It has also been seen to be able to overcome 'physical, temporal and spatial limits' of traditional processes such as the benefits of reduced cost and increased access [4, 28]. Despite the advantages that have been heavily cited in literature [4, 28], there is a school of thought which shows that digital methods can still be exclusive and elitist [19, 5]. Digital technology provides alternative opportunities for those engaged in the process to share their stories [61] but struggle to reach those disengaged. Regardless of the benefits and disadvantages, digital technologies do provide new approaches to engaging citizens in neighbourhood planning that has not yet been explored. Rather than seeing digital technologies as the solution, it should be considered one method of a set of tools that include traditional methods to provide multiple communication channels by which to engage citizens in story creation and sharing [52].

HCI and Citizen Participation

There has been a growth of work in HCI for civic participation and community agendas to support citizens "on their own terms" [48]. Indeed, a wealth of research has focused on activism [1, 24, 49], opinion gathering [44, 77, 82], facilitating discussion and debate [8, 23], and action [59, 70] as well as the recognition of civic crowdsourcing for collective knowledge feeding into political decisions [32].

Of particular emphasis is the need for decentralized online forums as a way to engage non-activists and attract a broader demographic [39]. For example, *AmericaSpeaks 21st Century Town Meeting* [50] was an attempt to engage citizens virtually to allow them to participate in a way of their choosing. In addition, the appropriation of social media for the same purposes has also been explored [22] as well as GPS place-based mapping tools [32, 79] with a spatial focus on how to reproduce and represent urban spaces [24]. However, there has also been work which explores the notion of the difference between space and place which can draw an important distinction for the design of technologies in this area. With many applications relying on the spatial element of the everyday world, technology can often assume that citizens' behaviour and interactions are also spatial when, in fact, sense of place and identity is essential to everyday experiences and interactions [33]. Technology which supports the everyday experiences "of and in physical space" is paramount and, therefore, research which builds relationships with local citizens to be able to work in their 'everyday' is also essential [38, 77].

Technology situated in the everyday world of citizens such as *Viewpoint* [38, 77] which takes the decision-making processes to the sites where everyday talk occurs, have provided the opportunity to gather feedback from citizens to support political decision-making. In addition, *Discussions in Space,* a project to engage with Brisbane residents, encourages discussions and questions about civic issues via a publicly visible screen [58]. It encourages "collective expression and public discourse" in place to engage citizens [58]. Other such technologies offer the possibility to communicate through mundane means yet have activist possibilities [34, 65, 66].

There has also been further work which specifically focuses on the need for citizens' stories to be told, shared and heard. *StoryTrek* [40] enabled individuals to create a narrative through real-time, location-aware stories which are created whilst moving through physical space. It enabled citizens to use agency in creating their narrative whilst allowing them to consider alternative perspectives, reflect on their stories and, when used with other citizens, create a shared experience [40]. In addition, *I'm Your Body* [45] also used a location-based mobile storytelling platform to share thoughts and feelings about a place as a political tool. It was found that the inclusion of emotion behind political debates and arguments is key to understanding points of view.

Even those applications designed for storytelling still have a heavy focus on spatial applications rather than place and identity. There is a need to design technologies that allow for space and place to be represented whilst recognising the two characteristics are fundamentally different [33] and that citizen stories are crucial in civic participation.

Participatory Media and Citizen Participation

New media technology has become ubiquitous with citizens increasingly making use of multimedia communication channels in everyday life [52]. Considering the use of video, in particular, as a tool for community engagement, it has been found that it can provide "immediate and authentic feedback" and can strengthen and empower communities [35, 68]. Leading from this, participatory media emerged from the *Fogo Process* initiated by the National Film Board of Canada in the late 1960s which "pioneered the use of documentary for community development" [83].

Participatory video can be a tool for positive social change which provides the opportunity for deeper engagement [51, 65] and it allows the revelation of "hidden social relations and provoke[s] collective action" [54, 79]. It can provide a catalyst for community dialogue that wouldn't otherwise occur, is easily accessible for most people and it can help with the formation of communities around particular issues or causes [6, 66]. Within political processes, such as neighbourhood planning, participatory video could be invaluable particularly as there has been a democratisation of mobile and web technologies as a way to produce, edit, distribute and communicate video [53, 72].

Examples of work which have focused on citizen story creation and sharing through participatory media include *Vox Populi* [7] which aimed to create community narratives; *Civic Life Online* [63] where youth publicly communicated issues they care about; and *Interactive Design Documentaries* [30] which facilitated encounters and exchanges across public and online spaces to catalyse community dialogues around specific issues. Further to this, *Collect Yourselves!* [74] and the development of a *MultiMedia Narrative* application [27] were developed to empower citizens to create digital narratives through web-based and mobile-based applications. However, both enabled the use of photography and audio but did not support the sharing of video which has been shown to be "an invaluable tool for showing spaces and places and people moving around in them...conveys emotions, body language and relationships in a way that photographs simply cannot" [68]. The ability to convey that emotion allows the capture of lived experience of place rather than simply showing a geographical space [68]. In addition, a narrative resource kit has been developed to support "stakeholder debate; animate community engagement; and develop and display community narratives" [26]. Not only did this seek to capture vernacular experiences by the citizens themselves, it enabled virtual engagement by interested citizens, new ways to capture lived experience and provided a way to contribute to the development of planning policy. Other work [29, 43] has shown that such methods can maximise participation and offer the opportunity for shared community narratives and histories.

From this previous work, it has been shown that providing a tool that communities can be in control of to create their own narratives in a way that suits them is essential. *Bootlegger* [5] was developed as a response to the need for footage that is captured in a more structured way and of an aesthetically higher quality than crowd sourced video. Originally developed for community commissioning of local event videos, the platform allows the use of templates and graphic overlays to plan what the community should capture. *Bootlegger* has been proven to support the creativity of citizens whilst engaging their inherent media literacy in the film making process to produce high quality videos. We see scaffolding the process of narrative capture as key in engaging citizens in neighbourhood planning [6].

STUDY DESIGN

We deployed the Bootlegger platform with two neighbourhood planning groups in North East England to capture their stories with video. This section will describe the field sites and the approach to the research as well as the methods used to engage participants in using the technology.

Bootlegger

Bootlegger [6] is a media commissioning platform that uses an easy to use camera style mobile app which connects to a central web platform to commission and aggregate video content. The tool supports "community contributors to democratize both the commissioning and capture process, whilst retaining the core values of shot quality and content" [6]. Templates are used to define what each contributor should capture, and are fully customisable, allowing the community organiser to define various sets of videos that should be captured. Graphic overlays are used to help define visual elements of what to capture, whilst descriptions and length limitations help guide the creation of content. To initialise the process, we defined the initial set of shoot parameters in a template. Subsequently, citizens were able to change this to better represent what they wanted to capture.

Field Sites

The two neighbourhood planning groups involved in this study are at different stages in the neighbourhood planning process. The two areas also differ greatly in terms of the issues they face but, despite their differences, the use of Bootlegger as a participatory media tool could fit into a number of stages of the neighbourhood planning process (see Fig 1.). Testing the use of the app in both locations gave a broader view of how it could be used.

Fig. 1 – Neighbourhood Planning Process of which each stage can take up to 4-5 months

The first location is Kingston Park. Predominantly a residential area, Kingston Park also has a large retail park and the Newcastle Airport Industrial Estate. The area is under significant pressure with several large housing developments being built on the edge of the area. The neighbourhood planning group was established through the creation of a neighbourhood forum made up of 21 members of the community (as per the regulations). However, around 6-8 people attend the core steering group regularly all of whom are residents apart from one local councillor. The Chair of the steering group is an active citizen within the voluntary and community sector. The group are at the very early stages of the neighbourhood planning process and are beginning an initial community consultation.

Berwick-upon-Tweed is a coastal town in Northumberland. The neighbourhood planning group is formed through the Town Council and has a core steering group of around 14 members. The citizens who attend are a mixture of residents, councillors, business-owners and workers, and all are active 'expert' citizens. They are currently at the working group stage of the process where they work to gather evidence about key planning topics (e.g. housing, tourism and built environment) before forming planning policy.

The lead author's involvement with both groups began through discussions with planning officers and the neighbourhood planning Chairs in both areas. Both areas were keen to engage the wider community as much as possible, involving as many citizens in their neighbourhood as they can. Both groups also recognise that to do so, new methods and ways of engaging the community are required, particularly using digital technologies. In Kingston Park, they are keen to consider this from the early stages and Berwick have identified they are missing a range of voices in their past consultation processes but are keen to rectify this moving forward. Both groups would like to explore the use of digital technologies to reach populations that may otherwise not engage in such processes.

Method

In both communities, we used workshops as a way to engage the steering groups, allowing citizens to explore the use of Bootlegger whilst we were there for support and facilitation. As the two groups were at different stages of the neighbourhood planning process, two different workshops were developed.

Fig. 2 - Kingston **Park Workshop – Example of material at each station**

We ran one workshop with the steering group from Kingston Park. The video footage recorded as part of this workshop will be used as part of their initial consultation process. During the workshop, we provided a demonstration of Bootlegger before handing the technology over to small groups of the citizens. There was a small icebreaker to enable the groups to feel comfortable and familiarise themselves with Bootlegger. The main activity consisted of six stations around the room each focusing on a different planning topic: retail, housing, leisure, community, transport and growth (see Fig. 2). Each station provided some planning policy information from the city policy as well as some photographs of the area to provide inspiration. There were a set of questions at each station and the groups would interview one another about their thoughts and opinions of their area.

In Berwick, we ran 6 workshops with 6 of the 7 working groups: tourism, transport, housing, built environment, natural environment and youth. The aim of these films would be to use in the wider community engagement in the future, but also as a way to communicate the progress of the neighbourhood plan. The workshops were an iterative process designed to capture media for whatever stage the working groups were at. We met in a café in Berwick to create a storyboard using post-it notes and pens focusing on capturing the key issues they would like to show in a story format (see Fig. 3). Once completed, we provided a demonstration of the app before handing the technology to the citizens. We then travelled around Berwick to film places and spaces that they had planned as part of the storyboard.

Fig. 3 Built Environment Working Group Storyboard

Data Collection and Analysis

We took a participatory action research (PAR) approach based on the foundation of action research which challenges the positivistic view that research must be objective and value-free and that, as researchers, our work is already embedded into a system of values [15]. Action research encourages those values to be recognised and considered. PAR is a "collaborative process of research, education, and action, explicitly oriented toward social change" [41]. It is a form of research which radically challenges how we collect data, what kind of knowledge we generate and what impacts it has [41].

Commonly, the process of PAR can be chaotic and 'messy' requiring the researcher to be flexible in their approach and recognise that the participants are experts in their own lives and communities [15]. It is generally a cyclical process of research, action and reflection by the researchers and participants so both can learn from their experiences [41]. Ethically, it also requires the researcher to be part of the process rather than independent and so must have an "evolving and adaptive awareness" of the power positions that exist [66].

The involvement of both areas came about through discussions with the Chairs of the respective groups. Through the lead author's experience of working in the field of neighbourhood planning, they became embedded in the community and, therefore, the research, helping the groups wherever possible as well as carrying out the study. This involved attending steering group meetings, building relationships and becoming more familiar with the area and the issues faced. This enabled the lead author to observe, contribute and interpret the interactions in this research. As in many PAR projects, after attending any of the neighbourhood planning group meetings or workshops, reflexive field notes were written. The participants also provided feedback during the workshops through informal conversations made possible through the relationship that had been developed with the lead author. This feedback was then included in the field notes.

FINDINGS

A total of 52 video clips were recorded at the Kingston Park workshop of which 9 were from the icebreaker activity. As the groups could choose which stations and questions they answered, it is clear from Table 1 that some topics were more interesting to the participants than others.

Working Group	No. of clips
Community	11
Housing	1
Leisure	10
Neighbourhood Growth	18
Retail	3

Table. 1 Number of clips per topic

From the 6 workshops in Berwick, a total of 330 video clips were generated. The amount of footage captured by each of the working groups differed greatly (see Table 2). The groups that recorded less footage had made decisions quite early in the participatory media process about locations, key messages and choosing to record the audio at a later stage. Groups with more footage, although they had created a storyboard, had made fewer decisions and were unsure about the narrative they wanted to create.

Working Group	No. of clips
Built environment	128
Natural environment	32
Transport	15
Youth	26
Tourism	33
Housing	95

Table. 2 Number of clips per working group

The average length of the clips for all of the footage recorded in Berwick was 27 seconds. As well as the meta-data collected from Bootlegger, we carried out a thematic analysis [10] to explore the qualitative data from field notes and considered the design implications for participatory media technologies.

Creating Spaces for Storytelling

The participatory media activities had a democratising effect, both in Berwick and Kingston Park. In the workshops in both areas, participants discussed the key issues that mattered to them. In each workshop there were one or two actors that were either from a planning background previously or were heavily involved in wider community activities, including activist causes. These 'expert' citizens often had strong views and tended to dominate the conversations by sharing their own stories. Through the use of the storyboarding activity and the process of filming, these actors' voices were diminished slightly allowing the stories of other citizens to be genuinely heard and considered in the process.

For example, in Berwick, P5 was keen to portray their experience: *"I think we should stay focused on the streetscape on the main street, it's too busy."*. When others made suggestions, P5's response was often negative: *"No, it's pointless suggesting that. I know the businesses wouldn't agree to that, they'd fight against it so it's pointless to consider it."*. P5 often positioned their own narrative above those of others in the group, however, by the end of the workshop, there were open discussions considering the stories of all citizens and the possibility of all ideas. In addition, P2 who is usually dominant in voicing their own agenda in steering group meetings and was initially dominant in the workshop, quieted his views to allow a more open space for storytelling to take place with other participants.

The discussions captured through the storyboarding, and the views and opinions captured during the filming would usually be discussed amongst a small group of citizens and would not be visible to the wider public. The use of participatory media opened the space for the stories developed during such activities to be out in the open, available to the wider group and to the public in future consultations. For example, in Berwick, citizens were beginning to discuss new ideas for the town that could be included in policy. Such ideas would not usually be available to discuss until the policy itself had been developed. In Kingston Park, videos were shared via social media at a very early stage which began to open the space for storytelling beyond the steering group with the wider public. Not only did the activities allow for the creation of a space for storytelling for all citizens involved, it also enabled hidden stories to be told within this space.

In both areas, the space for storytelling allowed citizens to reflect on their individual stories and consider what they meant when put together as a collection of narratives. Deciding what should and should not be included in the filming and, once situated in the neighbourhoods, what they did and did not film (which was often different to the initial plan) helped individuals consider the importance of bonding stories as a community as well as identifying that their own stories were often based on bias and assumptions.

In particular, P8 and P9's stories were framed around their everyday practices of cycling and walking. This led their focus for filming to be on the need for sustainable transport in Berwick with one of the participants stating *"We need more bike routes that are safe and we need to encourage people to walk into the town centre. Like the people who work in the centre, a lot of them could walk from home to work but they choose to bring the car"*. As the discussion continued, the sharing of stories together enabled reflection that allowed them to realise that their views were heavily biased because of their everyday experiences. P9 began to speak about other modes of transport: *"We do still need to consider cars and lorries. We need a way for lorries to get into the centre for deliveries. Plus, we said we want to encourage people to come here from further afield so we need to make sure they can come here by car"*. This began the formation of a new, more inclusive, community narrative, made possible by the creation of space for storytelling.

The same kind of situation occurred at Kingston Park where participants were discussing issues and stories framed from their own perspectives without much thought for others. Through the discussion, they began to change the conversation to think about transport networks for older citizens or young families, for example. There was a key difference between the two areas in that the space created for storytelling in Berwick using the structure of the storyboarding exercise promoted the reframing of individual opinions whereas the more unstructured space in Kingston Park meant the chance to think from other perspectives was only prompted on an ad hoc basis.

Finally, the space for storytelling also allowed the citizens to question the truth of the stories in a safe environment. When forming a more inclusive community story, created from individuals' vernacular experiences, not all citizens would agree on others' points of view. The ability to challenge and question all stories to decide on a shared story became a vital part of the process. For example, one working group in Berwick had formed their community narrative based on the stories of actors present in the workshops which resulted in a strong focus on the town centre of Berwick. They began to realise this:

P6: We need to be careful about what we're saying and how we're saying it. Think about it, if we're sharing this with people, they'll think we've ignored their neighbourhood.
P7: Yes, we have to remember that we're supposed to be looking at the whole neighbourhood planning boundary. What do we want to include about that?
P5: I don't think we have much information about the rest of the boundary.
P7: We don't so what do we do? People will think we're too focused on the town centre and we're neglecting everywhere else.

This conversation highlights the questioning of the collective story they had already formed and, through this, they began to recognise that there were more stories to collect and consider to form a full picture from other citizens who were not present.

Content Creation

In Berwick, the initial storyboarding activity was a way to elicit individual stories to begin to construct one, shared story. The creation of new stories is important to neighbourhood planning which looks to develop new, imagined futures. What became apparent was the difference between what the citizens planned to capture and what they actually captured once out filming the area. The discussion often created a shared story which citizens were satisfied with, however, once filming, citizens felt there were parts of the story missing or issues that had not been captured. In Kingston Park, there was less structure to plan the filming, however, the same was found in that citizens felt there was often something missing from the filming.

During the filming, P2 stated *"I don't think we've covered everything, I think we need to go away and think more about this"* to which P3 responded *"I think we should get the rest of the group to have some input"*. This conversation took place after 1 hour of planning the filming and 2 hours filming in various locations around the town and was typical of instances from other workshop groups. They felt that the clips captured told the shared story they had planned but parts of the narrative were missing and this meant the story did not feel coherent to the citizens. They recognised that they had only captured part of the story and would like to gather more voices before completing the final, shared story they were aiming for whilst acknowledging that the video captured thus far was still valuable.

The content creation through the filming and, to some extent, the storyboarding activity helped the citizens to imagine a new future with a new story for their neighbourhood. The more creative method of participation meant that the citizens were more imaginative and told their stories in a more animated and interesting way which conveyed emotion and lived experience. For example, in Berwick, the tourism working group spoke of the town's history as a way to frame the new imagined future for the town's tourism. In another instance, the youth working group often became excited about the potential for the imagined future with P10 stating: *"There's so much potential! There's loads of space we could use for facilities for youth – they could have a skate park, music studios, dance studios, youth group facilities...there's so many possibilities!"*. The citizens also recognised that the stories they create could be imaginative yet would still feed into planning policy. The content produced during this project can be directly linked to the reports from the working groups which will be used to draft planning policy. They were able to express their stories creatively without the restrictions of other formal methods.

The graphic overlays in Bootlegger were used by all citizens to help them capture higher quality footage with P10 stating *"Oh, that's good. So I can just line up the landscape with the overlay? That'll be helpful to make sure what I'm doing is okay then"*. In addition, the shorter clips were favoured as *"they're less daunting"* (P8). In Kingston Park, the graphic overlays were crucial to the citizens in supporting the media capture with many participants unfamiliar with capturing video on a mobile phone. The media literacy support enabled the citizens to focus on creating the creative content, rather than the additional stress of training to be able to capture video.

There had been strong reservations by some citizens about using a creative method that was not usually associated with planning but they still chose to attend and tell their story. Some citizens expressed hesitancy in using the technology with most stating *"I'm not very good with technology"* or *"I'm not very tech-savvy"*. Despite this, almost all participants became comfortable in using Bootlegger by the end of the workshop. In Berwick, the confidence of participants grew and by the end of each workshop, at least one member of each group was fully sufficient in using the app. P4 said *"Can I download this onto my own phone? Just I'd like to film some of the landscapes when I'm walking the dogs at sunrise"* and P10 said *"This is great. Now that I've had plenty of practice with you there, I'll download it and get some more footage of the area. I'll get others from the working group that couldn't come today to do it as well"*. All of the working groups in Berwick said they would like to film more footage on their own, of which four groups have done so thus far.

At the end of the workshop, P5 who was reluctant to take part in such an '*unusual*' way said *"Thank you for this. It was really good. I thought it would be pointless and I couldn't see what difference it would make. I'm used to the older ways of planning that I used to do but it was really good"*. The creative methods did begin to break down some of the barriers once citizens were creating content, both in relation to using technology and using video as a useful method for neighbourhood planning.

Widening Participation

In Berwick, the workshops allowed people that would otherwise not get involved in neighbourhood planning to take part in a different, more creative, way to share their story. However, due to timescales, Kingston Park were only able to involve the steering group with a view to involving the wider community in the coming months which shows the future potential.

When first organising the workshops in Berwick, speaking with the Chair and members of the steering group, one participant was particularly keen to take part. P10, along with the Chair, thought that this particular method of filming and using mobile technology would be appealing to young people. This was also a factor that the steering group initially mentioned when the lead researcher was getting to know the area in that they felt that digital technologies would help them to involve a younger generation.

The youth working group, in one workshop, engaged

approximately 15 young people in the neighbourhood plan through the filming process. This included musicians, BMX bikers and army cadets, all of whom provided their stories of Berwick. This brought new perspectives to the shared community story that would otherwise have gone unheard. The lived experience of being a young person in Berwick was different to what other, older citizens had imagined. In addition, the young people were comfortable with this method of participation with P10 stating *"I think they [young people] were comfortable with being filmed. That first girl, the musician, she did it in one take. She's used to all this technology, though."*.

Although these were the only instances of widening engagement at this stage, the participants in both areas recognised the need to involve more people in the process. Initially the groups were keen to engage a wider demographic and had specifically said this during prior discussions. However, it became apparent that they were unsure what widening engagement meant, what it would involve and why it was actually necessary. Through the participatory media workshop, they recognised they were not necessarily the 'experts' and they would need to engage and include stories from the whole community. One participant in particular who had previously dominated conversation with strong opinions said *"I think we need to use this media as a way to ask other people what they think and what they know. We've focused too much on the centre and the people that live in the other neighbourhoods will know more than we do. We could use the video as a way to ask them their opinions"*. Similarly, the transport working group recognised that the group members in attendance were keen cyclists but they should use the filming as an opportunity to invite stories from car users.

In Kingston Park, they recognised the value of the participatory media and were keen to include this in their initial three-month consultation with the wider community to invite new participation: *"We should hold some workshops with different groups to build up more interest and to get people's opinions. It'd be particularly good for youth groups or schools even"*. Subsequently, this has been accounted for in the group's engagement strategy.

The widening of participation and recognition of the need for more participation by the citizens, enabled hidden parts of the neighbourhood to be made visible as well as hidden issues that would otherwise not be discussed. Particularly in Berwick with the addition of youth engagement, areas of the town which had not been discussed were brought to the forefront of the discussion. For example, when speaking to the young musicians, they said *"There's nowhere for us to play and sing and record. We go to the youth centre, but that's not just about music. There's a tiny little place we can go to record, but that's it and it's not ideal. We really want to record more of our own music but there's nowhere to practice either"*. Highlighting the lack of places in the town that were suitable, the young people brought the current facilities into discussion: facilities which would otherwise not have been discussed.

On the other hand, places in the town that were often discussed by citizens were often thought about through a different lens by the young people. For example, the BMX bikers stated *"There's nowhere to go on our bikes. People don't like us hanging around here [the Quay] but there's nowhere else"*. The Quayside had been discussed on a number of occasions by the citizens involved but the stories of other, minority groups had not been considered previously. However, through the participatory media and, in particular, the filming aspect, the young people were able to tell their story and contribute to a re-imagination of the future of the spaces and places in discussion.

Despite the positive aspects that storytelling brought to neighbourhood planning participation, the process of storytelling and content creation relied upon facilitation. The activities were facilitated through this research and, in many cases, citizens were reliant on the mediation and input of the researcher during discussions. This was particularly true when a new bonded community story was being developed:

Field notes: There had already been a long, detailed discussion about the issues in the town centre.
P5: We could use the film to showcase the town centre and we could even show what it was like before from some old photographs.
P6: I am a little concerned that we're too focused on the town centre still.
Researcher: Let's go back to the purpose of the film. What will it show? Do you want to show something from the whole area or do you want to use it as a way to say to the community, we need your help?
P6: We could. We could showcase the town centre and then ask for responses about other parts of the neighbourhood.

There was also the need to prompt the sharing of stories and help to configure the space so citizens felt comfortable sharing amongst a group. In addition, the facilitation also supported the citizens in making decisions about the stories that would be shared and how to create a new, shared story.

DISCUSSION

The use of Bootlegger as a participatory media technology in neighbourhood planning reveals a method of participation which can create spaces for storytelling to generate a more inclusive narrative. In the next section, we discuss how participatory media technology can contribute to a model *of* and a model *for* storytelling in neighbourhood planning and how, through the creation of a 'thing', stories can be debated and elaborated by citizens. We highlight the possibility for participatory media technology to allow for a multiplicity of citizen stories in neighbourhood planning and wider democratic practice.

Participatory Media as a Model *of* and *for* Neighbourhood Planning

A model *of* and a model *for* the way we 'do' planning

through storytelling has been previously developed [81]. The premise for storytelling as a model *of* neighbourhood planning focuses on the current planning practice whereby citizens' formal and informal interactions in their everyday lives could inform policy, but only by chance [11, 81]. Policy documents, in themselves, tell their own stories but they are often not representative of the communities they are referring to. Local government often represents places in policy as "clichéd…dry as dust…emotion has been rigorously purged" leading to documents that are "misleading at best, (dishonest at worst), about the kinds of problems and choices we face in cities" [67]. As citizen's stories are not prioritised on a day-to-day basis in planning practice, it is unlikely that they will link to policy outcomes [81]. In instances where these everyday stories do link to policy, the stories are often re-represented by planning officers who make assumptions about the meaning behind the narrative and filter the issues through the restrictive 'material planning considerations' that the UK planning system hinges on [62].

On the other hand, a model *for* storytelling in planning shows the way citizens' stories *could* be used to improve planning practice [81]. This focuses on creating spaces for citizens themselves to tell stories of their own "everyday vernacular experiences and practices" [43]. This would make participation more inclusive and democratic and those facilitating such processes have an important role in configuring the space to accommodate minority groups [67]. The importance of storytelling in the model *for* neighbourhood planning centres on stories as 'special', however even when the space for this is created, there is still a disconnect between stories and policy [67, 81].

The use of participatory media in this study provides a bridge in the gap between stories and their relationship to policy outcomes, and, therefore, a bridge between a model *of* and a model *for* storytelling in neighbourhood planning. This was highlighted through the example of the media in Berwick directly relating to the working group reports which will be used to form policy. A further three phases of citizens in Berwick and Kingston Park using the technology highlights the bridging of the models.

Firstly, the initial storyboarding exercise created that 'special' democratic space which was able to open up the discussion of citizens' stories. During the workshops in Berwick, citizens could contribute their stories one at a time, resolve conflicting views and make decisions about the creation of a shared understanding. Not only does this fit into the model *for* neighbourhood planning, it also encourages the move away from a self-interest model whereby citizens are only concerned about their own needs to more of a community-based approach [67]. Secondly, when citizens moved on to capture their stories through video, the technology was in the hands of the citizens themselves. In both Berwick and Kingston Park, citizens felt comfortable and confident with the technology to be able to film both during the workshop and afterwards without support. This enabled citizens to create a representation of their own stories rather than being re-represented by planning officers. Finally, once the video was captured by citizens, it created a tangible outcome which linked to the formation of policy. The video in Berwick has lead directly on to policy formation in the next stage of the neighbourhood planning process and, in Kingston Park, it provides initial ideas of where policy could be focused in future.

The model *of* and model *for* storytelling in neighbourhood planning were never meant to be mutually exclusive, however, in current planning practice they often are [81]. However, by creating the space for a model *for* storytelling in neighbourhood planning, it also creates a new model *of*. The models are then reconceptualised using participatory media technologies which bridges the gap between the two.

Participatory Media to Create a 'Thing'

The media produced from the video capture creates an object which aims to represent the story of the citizen who created it. However, the final object highlighted missing stories and made those citizens *not* included in the process visible. In both Berwick and Kingston Park, the recognition by participants that their own knowledge was not sufficient and the realisation that other citizens would need to counter and add to their stories, highlighted those missing narratives and was key to this project. With this in mind, the video as the object has a common function to represent stories and, when this breaks down, we are left with a 'thing' [12, 13]. The 'thing' exists because it evokes conflicting political issues from different interest groups and, in this case, the counter stories or missing stories from citizens [46]. The 'thingness' portrays a multitude of different values, principles and opinions [46] that highlight who is assembled around it and, importantly, who is *not*.

Rather than creating a final object through debate and decision-making with a select group of citizens, the media is created at an earlier stage in the neighbourhood planning process. The participatory media enables the creation of the media to support earlier deliberation with a wider group of citizens. In both Berwick and Kingston Park, the 'thing' will be debated during further engagement with the public.

The media allows citizens to recognise these missing stories earlier in the neighbourhood planning process and question the truth of what is represented, a challenge which is familiar to others in how we can use digital tools to "make the invisible visible" [69]. For example, the built environment working group in Berwick created an initial story based on the town centre, but then began to question the truth of the narrative they were (re)presenting. The issue here, then, is one of representation: we can see that not only is it important to "rerepresent what is the object of concern" but also to "gather the legitimate people around" [46]. Although stories in planning literature are often presented as positive in and of themselves, when the spaces created for storytelling aren't inclusive, community-focused or, in other words, representative, they accept exclusivity in participation [81].

Now that the 'thingness' of the video has been recognised, the story that is represented can be built upon by those missing actors. By continuing to engage the public more inclusively and reflect on the representativeness of the citizens involved, the media can become more representative of the issues at play in that community. Storytelling, in a more subtle sense, is also common in everyday experiences of citizens through commenting, building or elaborating on the stories that already exist, providing conflicting accounts or adding to the detail [81]. In Berwick and Kingston Park, the citizens involved at this stage are keen to have the wider public add to the narratives and build upon the stories told thus far.

Synchronous Story Capture

We have shown that participatory media bridges the gap between the model *of* and model *for* storytelling in neighbourhood planning and that the creation of a 'thing' highlights missing stories, however, the focus in both cases remains very much on individual citizen stories. The debate, discussion and decision-making about individual's stories leads to the production of one shared story. This creates a multitude of problems: which story is dominant; what makes one story more worthy than another; and which stories are told, heard and carry weight [67, 81]?

During this research, the use of the storyboarding exercise created the safe, democratic space that is recognised as important to share citizens' stories [67, 81] but it became focused on individual narratives. It was counterproductive in promoting a *multiplicity* of stories by forcing citizens to share their stories one person at a time and make decisions about what should and should not be included in the video capture. As an example, in Berwick, the transport group shared their narratives of sustainable transport which they then began to question based on the recognition of missing stories. Rather than being able to include the narrative of sustainable transport and the stories of others, the group was forced to make a decision about what should and should not be included. This reverts back to traditional participation methods with discussion, debate and committee-like decision-making that promotes individual contributions in a model of consensus democracy and does not suit the process of storytelling [2, 78].

Participatory media technology can avoid the acceptance of individualistic narratives. It can go further to promote a multiplicity of citizen stories for neighbourhood planning through synchronous story capture by many people at the same time. The shared narrative was created through this process and represents different actors allowing for "differences in perspective, storyline and focal point" within the collective story [29].

This would allow the model *of* and *for* storytelling in neighbourhood planning to be realised more inclusively by opening the 'special' space for storytelling to be much broader. In other words, it provides the space where people can participate *together*, rather than simply as individuals, in something that is defined. This focuses on citizens interacting as a group rather than as individuals. It also then enables citizens' to question the truth of their own and others' stories recognising they could be both true and false for different actors in different circumstances as "transparent, unmediated, undisputable facts" are almost 'beyond reach'. The result is a shared story in which "coherence was not a product of an integrated plan, but rather an emergent quality of a nationwide collection of plurivocal narratives" [29]. This supports inclusivity and encourages the idea of agonistic pluralism which supports contestation between citizens' stories as well as revealing the power influences at play [24].

The possibility for capturing synchronous stories through participatory media could not only benefit neighbourhood planning, but could contribute to other democratic processes where citizen's views are important. Encouraging the agonistic model of democracy in civic participation more broadly through participatory media would allow 'things' to "become the centre of our attention" as a way to support (dis)agreement.

CONCLUSION

We presented the use of participatory media technology as a way to capture citizen stories to contribute to neighbourhood planning participation. Through deployments with two neighbourhoods we captured a total of 382 videos which together create multiple narratives of community stories. We have shown that the ability to capture citizen stories can provide a model *of* and a model *for* neighbourhood planning participation which can create media that reveals of missing stories. We argue that digital methods of participation should promote synchronous story capture to support inclusivity and the multiplicity of narratives not only in neighbourhood planning but in wider democratic processes. Future work will focus on the use of participatory media with other neighbourhood planning groups to continue to explore this area at different points in the neighbourhood planning process and more closely explore the link to policy.

ACKNOWLEDGMENTS

I would like to thank Berwick Neighbourhood Planning Steering Group and Kingston Park Neighbourhood Forum for allowing me to become part of their community and for taking part in this study. This research was funded through the EPSRC Centre for Doctoral Training in Digital Civics (EP/L016176/1). 'Data supporting this publication is openly available under an 'Open Data Commons Open Database License'. Additional metadata are available at: http://dx.doi.org/10.17634/154300-35. Please contact Newcastle Research Data Service at rdm@ncl.ac.uk for access instructions.

REFERENCES

1. Nader Afzalan and Jennifer Evans-Cowley. 2015. Planning and social media: Facebook for planning at the neighbourhood scale. *Planning Practice & Research*. 30, 3:270-285.

2. Phil Allmendinger and Graham Haughton. 2012. Post-political spatial planning in England: a crisis of consensus?. *Transactions of the Institute of British Geographers*, 37, 1: 89-103.
3. Sherry R. Arnstein. 1969. A Ladder of Citizen Participation. *Journal of the American Institute of Planners.* 35, 4:216-224.
4. Mariam Asad and Christopher A. Le Dantec. 2015. Illegtimate civic participation: supporting community activists on the ground. In *Proceedings of the 18th ACM Conference on Computer Supported Cooperative Work & Social Computing.* 1694-1703.
5. Mark Baker, Jon Coaffee and Graeme Sherriff. 2007. Achieving successful participation in the new UK spatial planning system. *Planning Practice & Research.* 22, 1:79-93.
6. Tom Bartindale, Guy Schofield and Peter Wright. 2016. Scaffolding Community Documentary Film Making using Commissioning Templates. In *proceedings of the 2016 CHI Conference on Human Factors in Computing Systems.* 2705-2716.
7. Janak Bhimani, Toshihiro Nakakura, Ali Almahr, Masaki Sato, Kazunori Sugiura and Naohisa Ohta. 2013. Vox populi: enabling community-based narratives through collaboration and content creation. In *Proceedings of the 11th European conference on Interactive TV and video.* 31-40.
8. Erling Björgvinsson, Pelle Ehn, and Per-Anders Hillgren. 2010. Participatory design and "democratizing innovation". *In Proc. PDC 2010*, 41-50.
9. Quintin Bradley. 2015. The political identities of neighbourhood planning in England. *Space and Policy.* 19, 2:97-109.
10. Virginia Braun and Victoria Clarke. 2006. Using thematic analysis in psychology. *Qualitative research in psychology.* 3, 2:77-101.
11. Jeffrey C. Bridger. 1997. Community stories and their relevance to planning. *Applied Behavioral Science Review.* 5, 1: 67-80.
12. Bill Brown. 2003. A sense of things: the object matter of American literature. *University of Chicago Press.*
13. Bill Brown. 2014. Things. *University of Chicago Press.*
14. Sue Brownhill and Juliet Carpenter. 2007. Increasing participation in planning: Emergent experiences of the reformed planning system in England. *Planning Practice & Research.* 22, 4: 619-634.
15. Mary Brydon-Miller, Davydd Greenwood and Patricia Maguire. 2003. Why action research? *Action research.* 1, 1:9-28.
16. Nien-Tsu N. Chen, Fan Dong, Sandra J. Ball-Rokeach, Michael Parks and Jin Huang. 2012. Building a new media platform for local storytelling and civic engagement in ethnically diverse neighbourhoods. *New Media & Society.* 14, 6:931-950.
17. Maria Conroy and Steven Gordon. 2004. Utility of interactive computer-based materials for enhancing public participation. *Journal of Environmental Planning and Management.* 47. 19-33
18. Marit Kathryn Corneil. 2012. *Citizenship and Participatory Video*. AltaMira Press, USA.
19. William J. Craig, Trevor Harris and Daniels Weiner.2002. *Community participation and geographical information systems.* CRC Press.
20. Clara Crivellaro, Rob Comber, Martyn Dade-Robertson, Simon J. Bowen, Peter Wright, and Patrick Olivier. 2015. Contesting the City: Enacting the Political Through Digitally Supported Urban Walks. In *Proceedings of the 33rd Annual ACM Conference on Human Factors in Computing Systems.* 2853-2862.
21. Clara Crivellaro, Alex Taylor, Vasillis Vlachokyriakos, Rob Comber, Bettina Nissen and Peter Wright. 2016. Re-Making Places: HCI, 'Community Building' and Change. In *Proceedings of the 2016 CHI Conference on Human Factors in Computing Systems.* 2958-2969.
22. Clara Crivellaro, Rob Comber, John Bowers, Peter Wright and Patrick Olivier. 2014. A pool of dream: Facebook, politics and the emergence of a social movement. In *Proceedings of the SIGCHI Conference on Human Factors in Computing Systems.* 3573-3582.
23. Carl DiSalvo. 2012. Adversarial Design (Design Thinking, Design Theory). The MIT Press.
24. Carl DiSalvo, Illah Nourbakhsh, David Holstius, Ayca Akin, and Marti Louw. 2008. The Neighborhood Networks project: a case study of critical engagement and creative expression through participatory design. In*Proceedings of the Tenth Anniversary Conference on Participatory Design 2008.* 41-50.
25. Jennifer Evans-Cowley and Justin Hollander. 2010. The New Generation of Public Participation: Internet-based Participation Tools. *Planning Practice & Research.* 25, 3:397-408.
26. Marcus Foth, Helen Klaebe and Greg Hearn. 2008. The role of new media and digital narratives in urban planning and community development. *Body, Space & Technology.* 7:2.
27. David Frohlich, Simon Robinson, Kristen Eglinton, Matt Jones and Elina Vartiainen. 2012. Creative cameraphone use in rural developing regions. In*Proceedings of the 14th international conference on Human-computer interaction with mobile devices and services.* 181-190.
28. Rina Ghose. 2001. Use of Information Technology for Community Empowerment: Transforming Geographic

Information Systems into Community Information Systems. *Transactions in GOS.* 5, 2:141-163.

29. Bruce E. Goldstein, Anne T. Wessells, Raul Lejano and William Butler. 2015. Narrating resilience: Transforming urban systems through collaborative storytelling. *Urban Studies.* 52, 7:1285-1303.
30. David Green, Clara Crivellaro and Jimmy Tidey. 2015. Interactive Design Documentary as a method for Civic Engagement. In *Proceedings of the ACM International Conference on Interactive Experiences for TV and Online Video.* 161-166.
31. Derek L. Hansen, Jes A. Koepfler, Paul T. Jaeger, John C. Bertot, and Tracy Viselli. 2014. Civic action brokering platforms. *Proceedings of the 17th ACM conference on Computer supported cooperative work & social computing - CSCW '14.* 1308–1322.
32. Mike Harding, Bran Knowles, Nigel Davies, and Mark Rouncefield. 2015. HCI, Civic Engagement & Trust. *Proceedings of the 33rd Annual ACM Conference on Human Factors in Computing Systems - CHI '15.* 2833–2842.
33. Steve Harrison and Paul Dourish. 1996. Re-P1ace-ing Space: The Roles of Place Collaborative Systems and Space in Collaborative Systems. In *Proceedings of the 1996 ACM Conference on Computer Supported Coopertative Work.* 67-76.
34. Gerard Hauser and Chantal Benoit-Barne. 2002. Reflections on Rhetoric, Deliberative Democracy, Civic Society, and Trust. *Rhetoric & Public Affairs.* 5, 2:261-275.I mi
35. Chris High, Namita Singh, Lisa Petheram and Gustav Nemes. 2012. Defining participatory video from practice. *Handbook of participatory video*, 35-48.
36. HM Government. 2010. Decentralisation and The Localism Bill: an essential guide. HMSO, London.
37. HM Government. 2011. Localism Act 2011. HMSO, London.
38. Ian Johnson, John Vines, Nick Taylor, Edwad Jenkins, and Justin Marshall. 2016. Reflections on Deploying Distributed Consultation Technologies with Community Organisations. In *Proceedings of the 2016 CHI Conference on Human Factors in Computing Systems*, 2945-2957.
39. Andrea Kavanaugh, Manuel A. Perez-Quinones, John C. Tedesco, and Willian Sanders. 2009. Toward a virtual town square in the era of Web 2.0. In *International Handbook of Internet Research.* pp. 279-294.
40. Rilla Khaled, Pippin Barr, Brian Greenspan, Robert Biddle and Elise Vist. 2011. StoryTrek: experiencing stories in the real world. In *Proceedings of the 15th International Academic MindTrek Conference: Envisioning Future Media Environments.* 125-132.
41. Sara Kindon, Rachel Pain and Mike Kesby. 2008. Participatory action research. *International encyclopedia of human geography.* 90-95.
42. Ben Kisby. 2010. The Big Society: Power to the People? *The Political Quarterly.* 81, 4:484-491.
43. Helen G. Klaebe, Marcus Foth, Jean E. Burgess and Mark Bilandzic. 2007. Digital storytelling and history lines: Community engagement in a master-planned development. In *Proceedings of the 13th International Conference on Virtual Systems and Multimedia: Exchange and Experience in Space and Place, VSMM 2007.*
44. Lisa Koeman, Vaiva Kalnikaité, and Yvonne Rogers. 2015. "Everyone Is Talking about It!" *Proceedings of the 33rd Annual ACM Conference on Human Factors in Computing Systems - CHI '15*, ACM Press, 3127–3136.
45. Matthias Korn and Jon Back. 2012. Talking it further: from feelings and memories to civic discussions in and about places. In *Proceedings of the 7th Nordic Conference on Human-Computer Interaction: Making Sense Through Design.* 189-198.
46. Bruno Latour. 2005. From realpolitik to dingpolitik. *Making things public: Atmospheres of democracy*, 14-44.
47. Christopher A. Le Dantec. 2012. Participation and publics: supporting community engagement. In *Proceedings of the SIGCHI Conference on Human Factors in Computing Systems.* 1351-1360.
48. Christopher A. Le Dantec and Sarah Fox. 2015. Strangers at the gate: Gaining access, building rapport, and co-constructing community-based research. In *Proceedings of the 18th ACM Conference on Computer Supported Cooperative Work & Social Computing.* 1348-1358.
49. Yu-Hao Lee and Gary Hsieh. 2013. Does slacktivism hurt activism? *Proceedings of the SIGCHI Conference on Human Factors in Computing Systems - CHI '13*, ACM Press, 811.
50. Carolyn J. Lukensmeyer and Steve Brigham. 2002. Taking Democracy to Scale: Creating a Town Hall Meeting for the Twenty-First Century. *National Civic Review.* 91, 4:351-366.
51. Nick Lunch and Chris Lunch. 2006. *Insights into participatory video: A handbook for the field.* InsightShare.
52. Linda Macphersoon. 1999. Joystick not included: new media technologies are ideal tools for gaining stakeholder interest, acceptance. *Water Environment & Technology.* 11, 9:51-53.
53. Lev Manovich. 2001. What is new media. *The language of new media.* 18-48.

54. E-J Milne. 2016. Critiquing participatory video: experiences from around the world. *Area.*
55. Claudia Mitchell, Naydene de Lange and Relebohile Moletsane. 2014. Me and my cellphone: constructing change from the inside through cellphilms and participatory video in a rural community. *Area.*
56. John Mohan. 2011. Mapping the big society. *Third Sector Research Paper.* Working Paper 62. Retrieved from http://www.birmingham.ac.uk/generic/tsrc/documents/tsrc/working-papers/working-paper-62.pdf
57. Giles Moss and Stephen Coleman. 2014. Deliberative manoeuvres in the digital darkness: e-democracy policy in the UK. *The British Journal of Politics and International Relations.* 16, 3:410-427.
58. Nancy Odendaal. 2006. Towards the digital city in South Africa: Issues and constraints. *Journal of Urban Technology.* 13, 3:29-48.
59. Sissel Olander, Tau Ulv Lenskjold, Signe Lousie Yndigegn and Maria Foverskov. 2011. Mobilising for Community Building and Everyday Innovation. *Interactions.* 18, 4: 28-32.
60. Gavin Parke. 2008. Parish and community-led planning, local empowerment and local evidence bases: An examination of 'good practice' in West Berkshire'. *Town Planning Review,* 79. 61-85.
61. Lindsay Pettingill. 2008. Engagement 2.0? How the New Digital Media Can Invigorate Civic Engagement. *Snovis Journal.* 8:155-161.
62. Planning Aid. 2016. Material Planning Considerations. Retrieved from http://www.rtpi.org.uk/media/686895/Material-Planning-Considerations.pdf
63. Howard Rheingold. 2008. Using participatory media and public voice to encourage civic engagement. *Civic life online: Learning how digital media can engage youth.* 97-118.
64. Matt Rogers. 2014. Problematising participatory video with youth in Canada: the intersection of therapeutic, deficit and individualising discourses. *Area.*
65. Leonie Sandercock. 2010. From the campfire to the computer: An epistemology of multiplicity and the story turn in planning. In *multimedia Explorations in Urban Policy and Planning.* 17-37.
66. Leonie Sandercock and Giovanni Attilli. 2010. Digital ethnography as planning praxis: An experiment with film as social research, community engagement and policy dialogue. *Planning Theory & Practice.* 11, 1:23-45.
67. Leonie Sandercock. 2003. Out of the closet: The importance of stories and storytelling in planning practice. *Planning Theory & Practice.* 4, 1: 11-28.
68. Wendy Sarkissian. 2010. The Beginning of Something: Using Video as a Tool in Community Engagement. In *Multimedia Explorations in Urban Policy and Planning.* 151-165.
69. Ronald Schroeter and Marcus Foth. 2009. Discussion in space. *Proceedings of the 21st Annual Conference of the Australian Computer-Human Interaction Special Interest Group: Design: Open 24/7.* 381-384.
70. Bryan Semaan, Heather Faucett, Scott P. Robertson, Misa Maruyama, and Sara Douglas. 2015. Designing Political Deliberation Environments to Support Interactions in the Public Sphere. *Proceedings of the 33rd Annual ACM Conference on Human Factors in Computing Systems - CHI '15.* 3167–3176.
71. Rachel Silcock. 2001. What is E-government? *Parliamentary Affairs.* 54, 1:88-101
72. Bailey Socha and Barabara Eber-Schmid. 2014. What is new media? Retrieved from New Media Institute http://www.newmedia.org/what-is-new-media.html
73. Jocelyn Spence, David Frohlich and Steven Andrews. Live Digital Storytelling.
74. Jocelyn Spence. 2015. Performing digital media design. In *Proceedings of the 2015 ACM SIGCHI Conference on Creativity and Cognition.* 401-402.
75. John Sturzaker and Dave Shaw. 2015. Localism in practice: lessons from a pioneer neighbourhood plan in England. *Town Planning Review.* 86, 5:587-609.
76. Nick Taylor, Keith Cheverst, Peter Wright, and Patrick Olivier. 2013. Leaving the wild. *Proceedings of the SIGCHI Conference on Human Factors in Computing Systems - CHI '13*, 1549-1558.
77. Nick Taylor, Justin Marshall, Alicia Blum-Ross, Justin Marshall, Alicia Blum-Ross, John Mills, Jon Rogers, Paul Egglestone, David M. Frohlich, Peter Wright and Patrick Olivier. 2012. Viewpoint. *Proceedings of the 2012 ACM annual conference on Human Factors in Computing Systems - CHI '12.* 1361.
78. James A. Throgmorton. 2003. Planning as persuasive storytelling in a global-scale web of relationships. *Planning Theory.* 2, 2: 125-151.
79. Alain Touraine. 1981. *The Voice and the Eye: An Analysis of Social Movements.* Cambridge University Press, Cambridge.
80. Christopher Twitchen and David Adams. 2011. Increasing levels of public participation in planning using web 2.0 technology. *Centre for Environment and Society Research working paper series.*
81. Merlijn Van Hulst. 2012. Storytelling, a model of and a model for planning. *Planning Theory.* 299-318.
82. Vasilis Vlachokyriakos, Rob Comber, Karim Ladha, Nick Taylor, Paul Dunphy, Patrick McCorry and Patrick Olivier. 2014. PosterVote: expanding the action

repertoire for local political activism. In *Proceedings of the 2014 conference on Designing interactive systems*. 795-804.

83. Peter K. Wiesner. 1992. Media for the people: The Canadian experiments with film and video in community development. *American Review of Canadian Studies*. 22, 1; 65-99.

84. Katharine Willis, Gianni Corino and Karen Martin. 2012. Developing a neighbourhood locative media toolkit. In *Proceedings of the 4th Media Architecture Biennale Conference: Participation.* 75-78.

85. Jane Wills. 2016. Emerging geographies of English localism: The case of neighbourhood planning. *Political Geography.* 53:43-53.

Block Party: Synchronized Planning and Navigation Views for Neighbourhood Expeditions

Huiyuan Zhou , Aisha Edrah , Bonnie MacKay , Derek Reilly
Department of Computer Science, Dalhousie University, Halifax, Canada
{hzhou, edrah, bmackay, reilly}@cs.dal.ca

ABSTRACT
Mobile wayfinding and guide apps have become indispensable tools for navigating unfamiliar urban spaces. Such applications address targeted, "just-in-time" queries, but are not optimally designed for multi-point expeditions that can quickly build route and survey-level familiarity with a neighbourhood. We first conducted an experimental simulation involving a homebuying scenario to assess the usefulness of a popular mobile wayfinding and search application (Google Maps) for exploring a neighbourhood. We then designed a prototype application called Block Party that addresses a number of limitations of Google Maps for this purpose, and evaluated it in a second replica study. The results suggested that application designs that facilitate switching among distinct but synchronized navigation views such as Block Party might support more efficient usage and the selection of task-appropriate views, leading to better overall spatial awareness.

Author Keywords
Neighbourhood expeditions; itinerary planning; wayfinding; Google Maps; mobile guide

ACM Classification Keywords
H.5.2. Information interfaces and presentation: User Interfaces.

INTRODUCTION
Exploring unfamiliar urban neighbourhoods is a common activity for both locals and visitors to a city: homebuyers/renters might do this to build familiarity with a potential neighbourhood, local retailers when they are planning a new store location, new students when they arrive on campus, and tourists or professionals when they arrive at a new location for an extended stay. Exploring neighbourhoods close to home is also part of locative games like Pokémon Go.

Urban neighbourhoods can be difficult to penetrate. What may appear to an outsider as just another busy street is often the focal point of a community, who conduct a good portion their day-to-day lives within a set of city blocks. Services like daycares, schools, grocery stores, vets, fitness clubs, dog walkers are linked through physical proximity and community networks. It is not enough to become familiar with the physical space when exploring urban neighbourhoods; we also want to build an appreciation of the neighbourhood as *place*. The potential resident wants to sample their prospective day-to-day, the retailer wants to understand how the neighbourhood ebbs and flows and how to integrate with existing stores, and the visitor wants to experience the local culture.

CHI 2017, May 06 - 11, 2017, Denver, CO, USA

ACM 978-1-4503-4655-9/17/05…$15.00
DOI: http://dx.doi.org/10.1145/3025453.3026035

Mobile applications provide a variety of data about neighbourhoods including local stores and reviews, attractions and places of interest, real estate listings and prices, local news and events, transit schedules, even crime statistics. Such apps often offer spatial views and some navigation support. In the case of tourism, some even support multi-point itineraries [26], but in a manner that is highly tailored for short tourist visits. Wayfinding apps such as Google Maps are optimized for targeted search and navigation from point A to B. Google Maps has only offered support for multi-point itineraries very recently, and there again is optimized for the navigation task, rather than for exploring an area and updating an itinerary *in situ.*

Some mobile recommender systems research does consider serendipitous exploration and adaptive itinerary planning [12]. For example, Magitti models user behavior and other contextual information to recommend leisure activities [6]. TramMate is a route planning tool which suggests routes based on contextual data, planned activities (e.g., appointments), and public transport system details [17]. Where these studies emphasize route planning algorithms and context inference, our work explores basic interface designs for *user-driven* planning and exploration, to support goal-driven *expeditions* (e.g., explore amenities near a potential home): this middle ground between strict planning and free exploration is underexplored in the literature.

While many mobile map and guide applications provide multiple spatial views, most mobile maps research has compared views rather than explore how they work together to support an activity. The intuition driving our work is that neighbourhood expeditions would benefit from a flexible Coordinated and Multiple Views (CMV) approach [33,40], involving several lightweight spatial views, each supporting different wayfinding and discovery tasks, and by making it simple to switch views while keeping them synchronized. To the best of our knowledge ours is the first work that considers how a CMV approach can be applied to support neighbourhood expeditions.

We conducted a field assessment of a widely-used mobile wayfinding tool (Google Maps) using a homebuying scenario, to establish a need for more targeted application designs for neighbourhood expeditions, and as a baseline comparison for our CMV approach. We found that views were often dictated or their selection impeded by design, support for multi-location itineraries was minimal, and that switching views required significant interaction with the app and sometimes restarts, interrupting the main task. We present a prototype application called *Block Party* we designed to address these limitations. Block Party provides synchronized views supporting navigation, orientation, and planning, single click transitions between views, and support for multi-point itineraries and in situ itinerary modifications. A replica field evaluation provides evidence that the synchronized view design promotes fewer, but more purposeful transitions, serendipitous and dynamic activity modifications, and better overall spatial awareness.

We contribute to the mobile guide and wayfinding research by addressing a gap in current wayfinding mobile apps specifically designed for people exploring a new neighbourhood. We challenge the sequential, point-to-point design assumptions embedded in widely used pedestrian wayfinding apps and demonstrate how a design based on coordinated multiple spatial views providing compatible detail can improve flexibility. This opens up new design opportunities for such apps. We provide evidence that the CMV approach encourages heightened spatial awareness, benefitting new residents and others who wish not only to get a flavor for a neighbourhood but also to know its layout.

RELATED WORK

Mobile Information Needs

Location and activity can impact a user's information needs, for both familiar and unfamiliar places [9,28,36]. Users often search for information related to their current location, for routes and directions, or to find places close to their final destinations [9,37].

Information needs for pedestrians are also different than those in vehicles. While drivers use turn-by-turn directions when navigating, pedestrians often need more route context such as instructions with visual landmarks (e.g., turn left at the library) [24]. Pedestrians are interested in points of interest (POIs) close to their current location, and they use mobile apps to find information about their environment while locating desired services [36].

In their classification of location-based services, Zipf and Jost [42] distinguish primary services (such as maps, navigation, and search support) from secondary services (e.g., mobile guide content, commerce features). Our study emphasizes primary services in support of neighbourhood expeditions, but secondary services would be integrated in implementations tailored for specific needs.

Spatial Cognition and Navigation

Spatial awareness affects how people build knowledge of the location of landmarks or POIs within the environment [10]. Work by Tversky [38] and others on spatial mental models suggests that people use landmarks to help identify locations and remember how to get back to them. In contrast to the pure landmark-route-survey (LRS) model [21], which suggests that survey knowledge is the ultimate organizing mental spatial representation, Tversky argues that both route and survey like descriptions are used when describing where landmarks are situated. Pedestrians in urban areas often use landmarks rather than street names, numbers and distances as navigational cues and apply specific details to landmarks (e.g., Starbucks instead of coffee shop) [22]. Kallioniemi and Turnuen [16] found that pedestrians chose landmarks that were unique, close to the route (e.g., within 200 metres) and could be clearly seen *en route* to help navigation.

In Block Party, we provide survey (map), route (map, list), and egocentric landmark-focused (AR) views, all of which highlight and connect the same set of POIs. By making it straightforward to switch between views, and by marking the same landmarks on each, we hope to reinforce spatial relationships and encourage the formation of useful spatial mental models.

Mobile Maps, Map Views and Navigation Guides

Much work has considered how people use maps on mobile devices. Agrawala and Stolte [1] identified readability, clarity, completeness, and conveniences as design goals for information displayed on electronic route maps. Navigation and interactions are also important when designing map-based mobile applications [5,7,15,29,30,31], as is presenting information that helps users find a route or search for a POI [5,15,34].

Partala et al. [27] compared three spatial views (road maps, satellite maps, and street images) for pedestrian navigation. Participants preferred road maps for navigation, and thought street images were effective for displaying landmarks but required more time to compare them with their environment. Goh et al. [13] compared three views (list, map, and augmented reality) for searching. Participants took a similar amount of time to perform searching tasks with all three views, but preferred the list view for presenting search results. The map view was slowest for general browsing tasks. Vatinnen et al. presented CityScene [39], an app using a street view form of navigation. It was found useful for pedestrians to browse and explore their surroundings and to confirm arrival at their destination. They recommend that image-based systems allow simple switching between navigation views.

Augmented reality can also be used to provide spatial views. Applications use AR for a variety of reasons, including supporting navigation (e.g., [32]), searching for POIs (e.g., Yelp), and providing museum tours (e.g., [34]). AR has been found to be more advantageous than the street view approach for driving by keeping the driver's attention on the road [23]. AR views need to consider contexts of use (e.g., task and information needs) to help reduce clutter and information overload [13]. Just-for-Us used augmented panoramic photographs to exploit cues (e.g., color of buildings) in the physical surroundings [18], and integrated these with complementary activity-specific views. Mulloni et al. provided seamless switching between egocentric AR and exocentric (top-down) map views to promote contextualization [25].

In addition to the easy transition between spatial views and the effective use of AR or image-based views, studies have identified the need for other features similar to those in Block Party. These include the ability to develop routes with multiple POIs, the ability to divert from the recommended route, and to personalize routes [3, 8, 19]. For example, Hornecker et al. [14] designed a serendipitous city guide that encouraged flexible, unexpected discovery while ensuring visitors would not be missing nearby places of interest with vibration alerts.

PRELIMINARY WORK

We began by interviewing 2 recent homebuyers and 2 real estate professionals, to build an understanding of the neighbourhood expedition activities that homebuyers undergo. This allowed us to derive scenarios for our study, and to design a first mobile application concept.

To explore how effective current tools were in helping people explore neighbourhoods, we ran a pilot study with 4 participants in Riverdale, a neighbourhood in Toronto, Canada. We asked participants to use Google Maps and other apps of their choice while they performed home-buying scenario tasks. Participants were asked to find a set of POIs in the neighbourhood and to build their own route involving a subset of the POIs before navigating. We also asked them to establish their location relative to a prospective home at certain stages. At the end of the study, we asked participants for feedback on the suitability of the preliminary app design for this and similar activities. Observational data and qualitative feedback were collected.

When first searching for POIs and planning routes, participants used Google Maps search (4 participants), Yelp (2), and a branded coffeeshop app (1). The star feature in Google Maps was useful to plan and to keep track of progress on a simple route. When mobile participants used Google Maps exclusively. The default Map View was helpful to find the closest POI (e.g., a nearby market). In addition, 3 tried the navigation support, and 4 used Street View at certain POIs and for short bursts, to reorient or identify places that were not easy to locate. Importantly, no single feature was sufficient to support all 4 participants when exploring Riverdale. Moreover, while multiple services and application features were used, it was up to the participants to integrate information coming from these different sources. These shortcomings for neighbourhood expedition warranted further study.

GOOGLE MAPS FIELD EVALUATION

Building on this initial work, we recruited 10 participants to explore two neighbourhoods using Google Maps. We were interested in further exploring: 1) which map view(s) benefit spatial awareness when on neighbourhood expeditions 2) when and why participants switch map views 3) the limitations of a point-to-point navigation app (i.e. Google Maps) for neighbourhood expeditions, and 4) impressions of our initial CMV-inspired prototype.

Setting and Tasks

Participants were told to imagine that they were looking to purchase a home, had identified two, and wanted to explore the neighbourhood each home was located in (the Waterfront and Downtown Dartmouth neighbourhoods of the city of Halifax, Canada). The Waterfront and Downtown Dartmouth are connected by ferry, and have condos or family style homes intermixed with restaurants, cafes, parks, etc. We selected a more familiar (Waterfront) and less familiar (Dartmouth) neighbourhood to explore the impact of familiarity on participant behaviour.

Individual participants conducted similar tasks at both locations including: locating POIs (search for a set of distinct places and service categories they are likely to visit near the potential home); route planning (build a multi-point itinerary visiting a subset of POIs); navigation (walk to each POI in the route); periodically noting the distance and orientation of their starting point or other key landmark; serendipitous discovery (making notes of interesting places encountered); and route modification (needing to change plans midway, or add a new POI). While the tasks do not span *all* neighbourhood expedition activities (e.g., attending local events, learning about a neighbourhood's history), they were designed to simulate the experience of discovering walkable urban neighbourhoods.

Map Views

Participants were introduced to all features of Google Maps and told they could use whichever features they wanted to complete the tasks. We divided the views into main categories (see Figure 1): Map (A, B), Navigation (C, D) and Street (E, F) views. The default Map view is a 2D top down map. Selecting a transportation icon (e.g., the walking man in A) displays a route to the selected destination (B). Clicking the "start" arrow transitions to Navigation view. The Satellite option can be selected for Map or Navigation based views (e.g., C). Step by step textual directions can also be selected from Navigation view (D). Voice guidance can be enabled during navigation. Clicking on a search result or a location from the Map brings up a hybrid view containing a smaller scale Map view, information about the location, and a clickable Street View snapshot (E). Street view shows a panoramic image of the buildings and other landmarks as you see on the street (F). The view can be

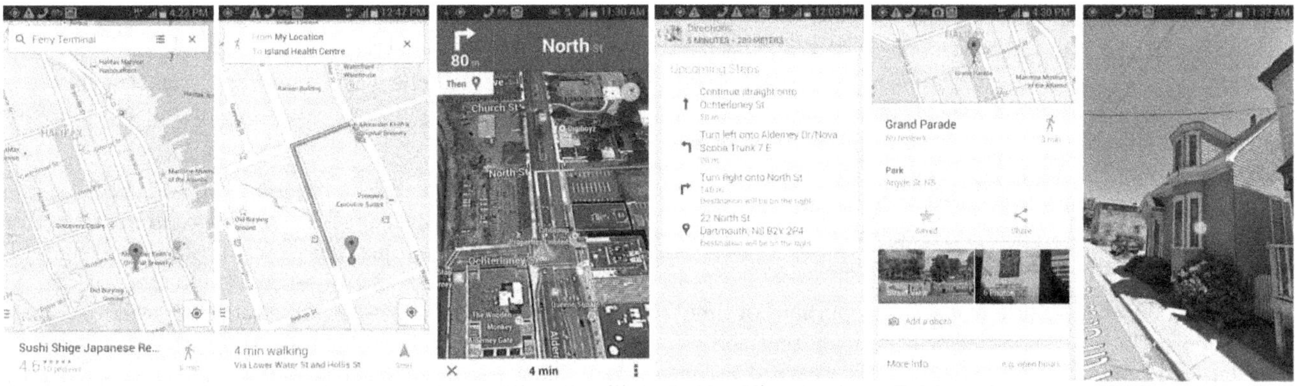

A. Map View B. Map with route C. Nav View (Satellite) D. Nav View (text) E. Map + Street F. Street View

Figure 1. Map, Navigation and Street views in Google Maps.

controlled using swiping gestures or can be synchronized with the phone's orientation sensors.

Study Process

Participants (6 male, 4 female) were recruited from the Dalhousie University community. Nine were between 18-35 years old and one was over 50. Participants' self-reported sense of direction was on average 4.6 out of 7 (SD=0.6) on the Santa Barbara Sense of Direction Questionnaire (SBSOD). All of the participants rented their current home. We asked for their familiarity with each neighbourhood on a scale of 1 to 5. Average familiarity was 3.6 out of 5 (SD=0.7) for Waterfront, 1.9 out of 5 (SD=0.7) for Dartmouth, thus participants were more familiar with Waterfront ($Z=-2.86$, $p<.01$). When finding their current residences, 9/10 used online sources and two used mobile maps. While we didn't recruit prospective home buyers, all participants were familiar with finding new accommodations. No participant lived in the neighbourhoods used in the study. Even in the Waterfront, most POIs were unfamiliar to the participants.

Prior to the study, participants gave consent and filled in the background and SBSOD questionnaires. Two researchers then met the participants at a meeting point and provided them with a Samsung Galaxy Note II smartphone. We demonstrated the features of Google Maps during a training session that involved walking to the location of their potential home using each view at different stages. We emphasized that the training session was not to suggest a "best" way to use the app, but to build familiarity with the features. Participants performed a set of tasks in each neighbourhood, using the ferry to travel between them. The study order was counterbalanced (5 participants started in Waterfront, 5 in Dartmouth). From the training session onward, we videotaped the participants, screen captured the smartphone, and took hand written observation notes.

Once at the starting point (prospective home), participants entered a planning phase. They were given a list of generic destinations (e.g., dentist, bank) to search for using Google Maps. When possible, we personalized the destinations to boost realism (e.g., visit their bank or favorite type of restaurant). Participants searched for matching POIs close to the house and starred them. One common destination was included so all participants would reach the same location at some point. Once a set of POIs was determined, participants planned a multi-point itinerary.

Participants conducted the neighbourhood expedition by going to each destination in the itinerary in sequence, identifying it to the facilitators on arrival before moving to the next POI. At three points we asked participants to stop and point in the direction of a landmark (e.g., the house). We also asked participants to look out for other places of interest to them, and to star them on the map. When participants arrived at the pre-set common destination, an itinerary change was initiated: we asked them to search for and to go to three specific destinations in turn. For example, for Waterfront the premise was that friends wanted to meet somewhere, but once the participant arrives the friends called and changed the meetup location. The participants were asked to visit a third location on the way to the new meetup point. Although wayfinding was a main activity in the tasks, we introduced several mechanisms to support exploratory goals: participants selected their own items and built their own multipoint itinerary; POIs used were customized in part by participants' preferences; an unexpected change to the itinerary was introduced; participants were asked to take note of interesting places encountered along and way and to periodically reflect on relative orientations and distances between POIs.

Participants completed a neighbourhood familiarity test to assess their spatial awareness and recollection of the area after exploring each neighbourhood. We also performed a post-study interview, asking participants to reflect on how they used the app. We then demonstrated our Block Party prototype and elicited their feedback on the design and its suitability for neighbourhood expeditions.

Data Analysis

Video and screen capture data were synchronized in Adobe Premiere, and played side by side for coding. One researcher annotated a subset of video data in a freeform way. All researchers then reviewed the annotations to arrive at a coding scheme. Using this the video was formally coded to determine when participants searched (e.g., at the beginning of a task, while navigating, etc.), which map views were used and when, when map view switches occurred, and when device rotation occurred in a first pass. Other interesting behaviours such as when participants were lost were annotated in a second pass. The interview data and the video analysis data were organized into major themes using an affinity diagramming approach.

Using the coded data, we also compiled proportions of time spent using each view across each participant and across each start/end point. We further split each start/end point into a *planning* phase (beginning when participants began to prepare to go to their next destination) and an *on-path* phase (from when participants began to walk to when they identified the destination, or gave up).

Results

Participants took around 2.5 hours to complete the field visits. Even though 8/10 participants used Google Maps for navigation in their daily lives, participants experienced a range of issues with switching views, multitasking, searching and route planning.

View Usage

Participants used different map views to accomplish different tasks. We measured the average time proportion participants spent on each view across tasks. During the planning phase, participants spent 90% of their time on Map, 4% on Navigation and 6% on Street View; while en route, they spent 56%, 40%, and 4% of time on Map, Navigation, and Street views, respectively; when asked to point in the direction of landmarks and estimate their distance, they used Map 97% of the time (the remaining 3% was Navigation View).

Map view was used almost exclusively when planning to go to the next destination, but once on-path usage was diverse: 6 participants mainly used the Navigation view (5 with voice guidance, 4 with Satellite view enabled), 3 used the Map view with the route on it, and 1 used Map Only most of the time.

Cost of Switching Views in a Sequential Workflow

Google Maps' application design assumed a sequential pattern of view access: target identification on Map view, followed by the route display, sometimes followed by Navigation mode. Street View can only be accessed from Map view. However, users have wide variations in view access flows. For example, when getting close to the destination, 9 participants switched to Street View from whichever view they were on to see what the destination point looked like. P3 commented: "*now I am having trouble using Street View when it is doing navigation*". When 8 participants had difficulty identifying the destinations, they switched to any other view (e.g., Map, Street, Navigation, Satellite) that might help them. Participants had to go through a series of redundant views (1-5 extra clicks) to find the target view that 3 of them closed the app to break away from the current flow. This observation suggests designs that facilitate easy, non-linear switches between different views might better suit the varying workflow of navigation tasks.

Many other unintended switches happened because the system did not behave consistently across different types of views. For example, operations such as searching, starring, accessing the name and distance information of starred locations can only be performed on the Map view. 5 participants had to switch from Navigation view back to Map view for these reasons. Allowing for synchronized operations on different views could improve this unnecessary switching.

Cost of Multitasking in a Sequential Workflow

We introduced additional tasks during navigation to simulate the variety of activities people might engage in during expedition such as pointing landmarks (e.g., where is my house in relation to where I am now), diversion tasks (e.g., have to go somewhere else first), and serendipitous discovery (e.g., star a restaurant to check up later). We observed that these tasks often interrupted the workflow of current navigation tasks. For example, while P2 and P4 were using the navigation view and they found places they were interested in (e.g., café), they weren't able to save or search it without going back to the Map view. Then they lost the current location and progress and had to start over. When asked to point to the direction of a landmark or estimate the distance, most of participants would go back to the Map, search for the place, retrieve and information and start again. Being able to multitasking without losing the current history or status could be useful for more complicated contexts than simple navigation tasks.

Spatial Awareness

The neighbourhood familiarity test was designed to assess participants' spatial knowledge acquired including route/ procedural (a sequence of points), landmark (a single point) and survey (spatial relation of at least two points) knowledge [2]. We asked participants to use paper, 2D maps to a) draw routes between two locations, b) to mark the locations of landmarks that they would have viewed while on route (e.g., a dentist office), and to mark where an image of a landmark (e.g., an image of corner flower shop) belonged on the map, c) to draw arrows from a marked landmark to the direction of an unmarked landmark (e.g, if you were standing at the starting house, what direction is the vet). On average participants drew 1.1/2 routes, marked 4.3/7 locations, labeled 2/10 images and drew 2.2/3 directions correctly across the neighbourhoods. We found there was a marginal difference for the labelling score ($Z=-1.845$, $p=0.065$), with lower scores in Dartmouth, which may be due to the lower familiarity in that neighbourhood.

Getting Lost, Reorienting, and Street View

Participants got lost (i.e. disoriented as to where they are or what direction they are heading) 3 times on average during the entire study. The main reasons were missing / poor signage (e.g., a dentistry inside a building), inaccurate or vague location data (e.g., a dry cleaner that has moved), and destinations that didn't match expectations (e.g., a museum looked like an ordinary house). The voice guidance reminder, the addresses, the GPS arrow and the map all helped participants to get back on track.

7/10 participants switched to Street View as a strategy for reorienting, but found it not helpful if it showed multiple buildings but not the exact destination (4 participants), the images are outdated to reflect the reality (3) or users were not familiar with the place (2). An AR view is similar to Street View in some ways, but provides real-time visuals and visible markers for a destination or other POI.

Star-based Route Planning

In terms of multi-stop route planning, the star feature was thought to be helpful in saving locations for future use and aiding spatial visualization. For example, P7 noted: "*You can visually see where all the points are and create a route*." However, no explicit itinerary for multiple stars led to extra checking the names of the stars and not remembering the itineraries. 5 participants suggested having a list of all saved points by name or number. Also some participants failed to plan an efficient itinerary that they had to backtrack or revise the planned route. 2 participants complained they couldn't "*letter*" or "*number*" the stars to create a route connecting all the different points to avoid backtrack. 3 participants wanted the application to show the optimal route "*in terms of time or of priority on my choice*" (P8).

BLOCK PARTY DESIGN

Using the outcomes of the prior two studies and the feedback provided by participants on our early prototypes, we designed Block Party to support: 1) easy switching among distinct views that support diverse tasks 2) synchronized data/operations among views. 3) a directory-based list of POIs. 4) explicit support of planning, creation, and modification of multi-point itineraries.

Coordinated Multiple Views

Block Party uses three distinct types of views (see Figure 2): Map, List and Immersive views toggled with the bottom menu to facilitate easy switch among different ways to view the data. Each view has a Select and a Plan+go mode toggled with the tab bar in the top right corner to *select* POIs from a number of potential locations and *plan* an order of visiting the selected POIs. The Map view is a top down 2D map display with points shown as markers (A) or numbered points connected with a highlighted route (B) to provide a big picture of the area. The List view displays location information (i.e., name & address) in a list (C) or ordered list of points with textual turn-by-turn directions between any two points (D) to support navigation from one point to another. To give a sense of where clusters of services are located and visualize relative location of the next destination, the Immersive view uses an augmented reality view with the camera stream and displays the name, address, and distance from the current location of a point in a box when the user holds their camera in the direction of the point (E), or multiple ordered points (F).

We maintained constant states across the three views such that when one location was selected in one view (e.g, Map), it was automatically selected in the other two views; when a particular order was planned for multiple points in one view, the data was updated for the other two views. The synchronized data was designed to support expedition tasks that might require multiple views at different stages. In Google Maps, same data (e.g., address) is often available in one view (e.g., Map) but not in another (e.g., Navigation).

Directory-based locations and Annotation

In addition to searching, we mocked up a directory-based location database to facilitate discovery of unfamiliar areas. Selecting a location and a category (see Figure 3, A) from the home page would generate a list of curated POIs in all three views. The services under each category are pre-defined by the researchers for the purpose of evaluating the prototype. When users find places of interests on the way, they can click on the Map view and type the name and description of the location in the popped up window (Figure3, C). A pink marker will be added to the map and the point can be selected or planned as existing locations.

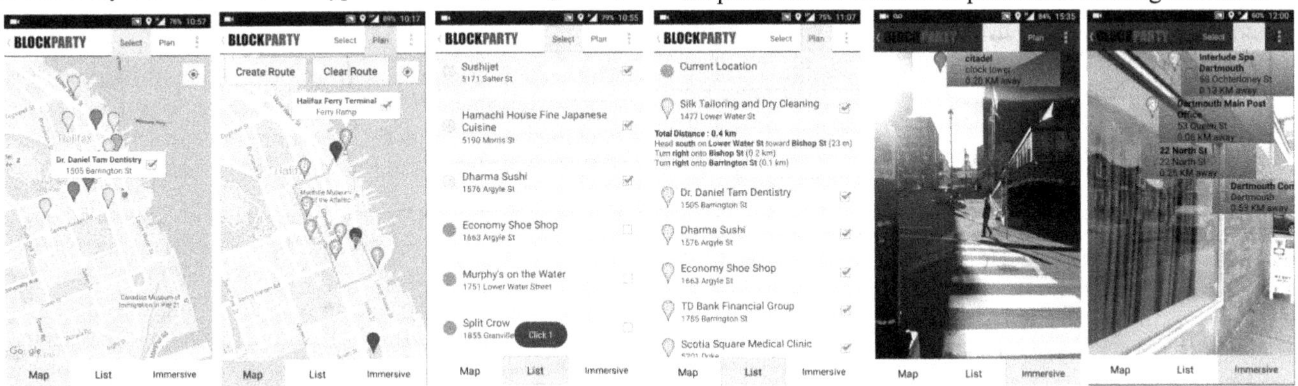

A. Map (select) B. Map (plan+go) C. List (select) D. List (plan+go) E. Immersive (select) F. Immersive (plan+go)

Figure 2. Map, List and Immersive views with both Select and Plan+go modes in Block Party.

Multi-point Route Planning

Once the user has selected a category (e.g., bank), a list of POIs shows on the Select mode of the Map view as red markers by default. By clicking on the wanted ones and select with checkmarks, the markers will change to green and appear in the Plan+go mode as blue markers. The user can keep selecting new POIs from other categories (Figure 3, B). All the selection history will be saved in the Plan+go mode as blue markers. As the user click each location in the Plan+go mode in a desired order, the markers are numbered in turn and an itinerary was created. Being able to transition between Select and Plan+go mode allows for checking, adding other locations (in Select Mode) without breaking the existing itinerary (in Plan+go Mode) thus the ability of performing multiple activities in expedition.

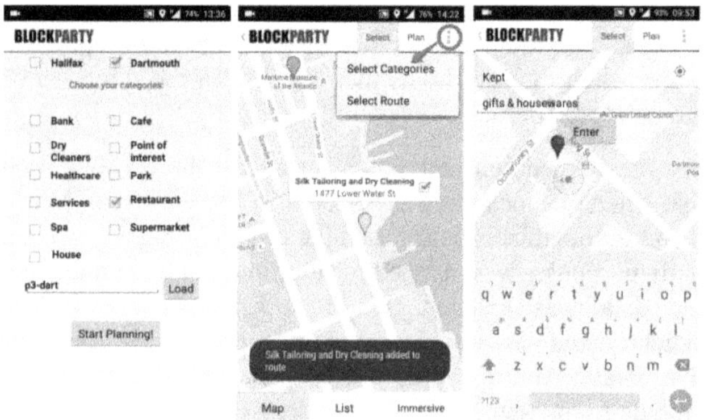

A.Categories B.Select categories C.Annotation

Figure 3. Location selection and annotation in Block Party.

Implementation

Block Party is an Android application using the phone's GPS, camera and orientation sensors, the Google Maps API and a third party augmented reality API. The multipoint route in the Map view was determined through calls to the Google Maps API.

By demonstrating the concept and prototype of Block Party in the preliminary and Google Maps studies, participants imagined the AR view would be beneficial for people who are poor at translating map and world orientations or easy to get lost. We considered all feedback and made a number of revisions such as adding select and plan+go modes to all views, and avoiding overlapping POIs in the AR view. We further evaluated Block Party through an adapted version of the Google Maps study.

BLOCK PARTY FIELD EVALUATION

We recruited 10 new participants for Block Party, and replicated the study design and analysis methodology of the Google Maps evaluation for comparison with the following differences: 1) the location database had a few different destinations (e.g., dry cleaners) that participants could choose from due to business changes since the prior study. Most POIs remained the same. 2) two images in the familiarity test were updated due to business changes or city renovation. 3) we logged the view usage data (e.g., view, mode, timestamp) and one researcher collated the data with video/screen capture and assigned the tasks participants performed on each view. All other differences in the study protocol result from the design differences between Google Maps and Block Party (e.g., directory selection vs. search, Block Party's annotation feature).

Recruitment

Participant demographics were similar to those of the previous study: participants (5 male, 5 female versus 6 male, 4 female) were recruited from the Dalhousie University community, between the ages 18-38 (Median = 26). Participants had average self-reported sense of direction, scoring 4.6 (SD=0.8) on the SBSOD Questionnaire, which was not different from the previous study (M=4.6, SD=0.6, p=.38). The average familiarity score was 3.8 (SD=0.4) with Waterfront and 2.7 (SD=0.9) with Dartmouth. As before, participants were more familiar with Waterfront (Z=-2.5, p=.013). 9 participants were students from a diverse background (e.g., health, art, law) and one was a professional. 8 participants rent and 2 own their current home/apartment. When finding their current residences, 9/10 participants used online sources, 4 used real estate agents/companies and 2 used mobile maps.

RESULTS

On average participants took 2 hours to complete the study, with mainly less time on wayfinding (e.g., search POIs, navigation, get lost) compared to the prior study (2.5h). Participants used diverse combinations of views both among different tasks and within the same task. With Block Party, participants made less switches during navigation, had less interruption when rerouting during expedition, and retained more route and direction knowledge than with Google Maps. Multi-stop itinerary planning was useful in neighbourhood expedition.

View Usage

We compared the proportion of total time participants spent on each view for each type of task between Google Maps and Block Party (see Figure 4).

While participants mainly relied on the Map View to plan an itinerary with Google Maps, those with Block Party behaved differently: 6 participants mainly used the Map whereas 4 participants used a combination of Map and List – List to select POIs among many options (rather than clicking each POI on the map to retrieve descriptions), and moving to Map to visually figure out an order.

For pointing to POIs, participants relied on directions of the arrow on the Map in Google Maps to orient themselves. With Block Party, most people chose a combination of Map and AR view, 8 people spent more than 70% of time on AR view as it's "*a lot easier*" (P1) to point and check distances information. Map was used to select POIs and sometimes as a means of confirmation or to roughly identify directions.

For navigation from between POIs, 6 participants spent more than 75% of their time on Map and the rest with AR or List view, 3 used equal or more time on List than Map, and 1 used Map mostly. A common pattern was to use the AR view to establish the general direction of the next POI before departing and then switching to Map or List. The AR view was also used to confirm that they were approaching their destination. With Google Maps, more participants used Navigation view. Using Map to get the lay of the land first, follow Navigation, and confirm with Street view when nearby the destination was typical.

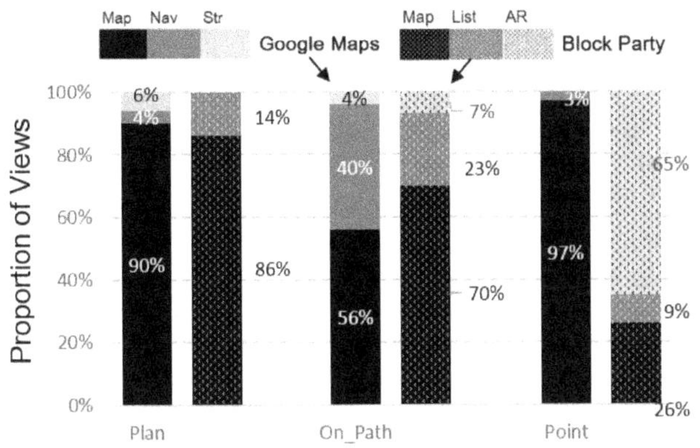

Figure 4. Proportion of view usage comparison on task type.

Coordinated Multiple Views & Easy Switching

In addition to participants switching views to begin a new subtask better supported by another view, there were also cases when participants switched views during a task. We summarized three main reasons for this.

Cross-checking information. 6 participants switched to AR view when they were disoriented, couldn't find or weren't sure about the destinations. 4 switched to others when the directions of List were confusing.

Serving complementary purposes. For example, for planning a route, List allowed users to look for specific names to pick while Map provided visualization of where all the locations are. For navigation, some used Map or AR to confirm being on the right track, and List for turn-by-turn directions. P1 said: "(with Map) *I couldn't know which direction I am to start with. Immersive complements that…It's almost like combining it.*" For pointing a location, some participants first looked at the map to get a sense of "*whether it's in front of me or behind me*" (P8), and then switched to AR view for precise directions.

Extra information. Sometimes information in a different view can be easier to use or unique. For example, participants switched from Map to List to easily see addresses or the destination is on which side of the road.

As the walking phase saw the most diverse usage of views, we compared the total number of switches between Google Maps and Block Party when walking. We found across all the participants, the median number of switches using Google Maps is 33 and Block Party 13 during walking. Participants in two studies switched views for similar reasons, but the result shows Block Party might be able to reduce the number of switches required among different views with designs to support easy switch among coordinated views.

7 participants liked the concept of easily switching between different views. P8 commented: "*the list and the immersive were useful for different tasks, and it was nice if you could switch quickly between them.*" Similarly, P4 noted: "*I really like how quickly it was to switch between map, list and immersion…I would flip them back and forth so frequently.*" P6 found it less distracting if all the information is not on the same screen. However, people didn't necessarily like switching *per se* as it was extra interaction. For example, P5 liked "*the separation between everything and the immersive view, immersive being its own kind of thing*" but wanted map and list to be "*compact in one*", whereas P1 liked "*condensing*" list and immersive "*so that you just have to switch between two (views) instead of three*".

Multitasking Support & Rerouting

While participants saved 36 POIs in total (twice as many as the 18 POIs bookmarked using Google Maps) for future use and pointed to 12 POIs on the way, none of them have to abandon the current route to perform those tasks. For the 4 diversion tasks (e.g., go to somewhere outside the planned route), 6 participants recreated 2 routes on average: 1 rerouted every time a diversion happened and others only recreated a route when they were unsure of the destinations or the route looked complicated with lots of turns. 4 participants didn't recreate routes at all, as P5 said, "*so that we don't disturb our route*". Being able to add new locations to the map via Select mode without changing the history in the Plan+go mode supported flexible multitasking and easier returning to the current workflow. The cost being additional within-view switches and added complexity to use the interface. On average, participants transitioned between the Select and Plan+go mode within the same views 16 times across the study: 7 times in plan phase, 6 in walking and 3 in pointing. In a few cases, participants couldn't find the intended locations in one mode (e.g., Plan+go), which were supposed to appear in the other mode (e.g., Select) only.

Improved Spatial Awareness

On average participants drew 1.8/2 routes, drew 2.7/3 directions, marked 6/7 locations and labeled 4.3/10 images correctly with Block Party. Similarly, there were difference for the marking locations score (Z=-2.271, p=.023), with lower scores in the Dartmouth. Using Spearman's correlation test, participants with higher familiarity with the areas tend to rank higher on marking scores (r_s=.49, p=.03) and labeling scores (r_s=.56, p=.01) while self-reported sense of direction has non-significant correlation with test scores.

After adjusting the impact of the two changed images for labeling test (the average score for one image is higher than the original one), we compared the number of correct answers for the familiarity test between Google Maps and Block Party (see Figure 5). Mann-Whitney U tests indicated that participants performed better with Block Party than Google Maps on all the tests: route (Z=-2.4, p=.016), direction (Z=-1.98, p=.048), marking (Z=-2.56, p=.01) and labeling (Z=-2.74, p=.006). As the overall familiarity with both locations is slightly higher in the current study (3.3 vs 2.8, Z=-1.8, p=.073), we compared the test score in Waterfront only because the familiarity in both studies has no difference (3.6 vs 3.8, p=.335). The results were similar: all the test scores were higher than in the Google Maps study (p=.022, .053, .012 & .029). Ruling out the potential impact of the familiarity difference with the study locations, the results suggest Block Party might at least increase the route and direction awareness comparing to Google Maps.

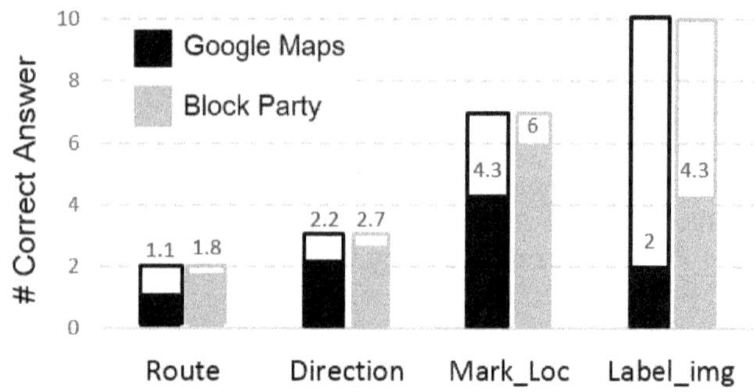

Figure 5. Familiarity test performance comparison.

Directory-based Location Selection and Annotations

6 participants thought the directory-based selection system was quite useful because of the recommendation of specific types of places (e.g., "this category gives me the whole picture of the city", P10), no prior knowledge assumed (e.g., "*I don't know how people call it [to search for it]*", P8), and limited selections in each category (e.g., "*you don't have to sift through much information, it's already curated*", P3). In general, participants wanted more fine-grained filters to narrow down their options such as displaying locations by distance (e.g., < 200 meters) or more specific categories (e.g., split different types of doctors). Other issues include missing categories and having to guess the categorization when selecting POIs.

9 participants saved serendipitous locations during their journeys that reflected diverse personal interests (e.g., shops, services, tourist attractions). The varied descriptions they used were general (e.g., "food", "restaurant") or specific (e.g., "pizza", "Lebanese", "dinner").

Multi-point Route Planning

All participants created highlighted multi-point routes. Participants cited their convenience ("*instead of having to go back, erase and type in the next stop*"-P5), efficiency ("*it was useful to...create a route that would go as much in a circle or square to save your time*"-P1), and support for in situ changes ("*especially if there is more than one place, it's very useful that I add it into the route...it would be easier for me to follow*"-P8).

DISCUSSION

General Feedback on Neighbourhood Expedition

Most participants had positive overall experience with Block Party. P4 thought it was a fun tour and commented: "*Just check on places and add to my itinerary. It's more of a tourist tool in my mind.*" P2 liked how Block Party "*assumes you are walking...I'm here, what are things around me*". P5 found "*it was actually very entertaining...It had more options to use than just a map and directions.*" Participants suggested features beyond planning and navigation for neighbourhood expeditions, including supporting in-situ experiences such as interactions with people, places, and events, providing recommendations for local establishments and services, and general descriptions of the neighbourhood itself.

Differences in View Usage and Familiarity Tests

Dünser et al. found a combination of Map and AR interface was preferred over single views because of more choices and no best view could suit varied situations [11]. Similarly, Block Party allow for more diversified usage of combinations of views. For example, when given the options, participants added List in planning and AR in pointing tasks instead of relying on a single view.

Participants using Block Party did better in all spatial awareness questions. Familiarity with the neighbourhood certainly played a role, but couldn't fully explain the difference. As users may often understand their data better if they can view it through different representations [33], the convenience to crosscheck, access complementary or additional information in our CMV design might have facilitated memory of route, direction etc. Another possible reason is that participants using Google Maps paid less attention due to less workload required by the forward-up navigation view [41] or more interrupted workflow dictated by Google Maps' design. Also Street View might require more time while AR was "*really fast*" (P8) in telling exactly where things were. Further investigations with stricter control and larger sample size would be useful.

Feedback on Spatial Views in Block Party

Map View was favoured by most participants. Combining survey, route, and landmark information facilitated understanding and recollection. As P8 said: "*When I see it on the map and I see it in reality, the two kinds of memories go together and it helps it stay in my mind*". In accordance with prior research, 3 participants had trouble figuring out directions with the north-up map orientation. 2 participants wanted to see distance information on the map in a manner similar to List and AR.

List View's instructions provided useful information such as street names, distance to the next turn, and which side of the road the destination will be on. However, 3 participants found it hard to orient using only the textual "west" or "east". Others felt they wanted more context ("*you have to know where streets are*", P2). ("*I feel in a vacuum because I just have street name, I don't know...what should be* *around me.*", P7). One participant suggested adding a compass to show the relative direction of each street.

AR View received positive feedback from almost all participants. It was useful to get "*a general sense of direction*" (P1) to orient and confirm they were on the right track. It helped "*figure out where things are instinctively*" (P4). Half of the participants complained about instable location labels due to the signal fluctuation. 2 felt awkward holding the phone vertically while walking in public, and 2 mentioned that the view became cluttered with POIs at certain points. P4 suggested adding route detail ("*...paint the blue line down the road.*"), and P8 wanted access to more detail (e.g., names, pics, reviews) so she could "*stand on the street and scan*" her immediate environment.

Participants suggested that in addition to keeping views *synchronized*, they should be made as *consistent* as is reasonable. Several recommended providing estimated time and distance to a selected POI on all three views. Kjeldskov et al. found route planning information should be based on users' current time and location, and key information such as walking distance and travel time should be easily accessible [17], which are in line with our findings.

Getting Lost, Reorienting, and AR View

Participants got lost on average 2 times across the study using Block Party. The reasons were similar to the Google Maps study: poor signage, a moved business, issues with GPS updates and accuracy. From the human error side, the common cases were that participants went to the opposite direction or thought the destination was on the opposite side of the road. Participants used addresses/ distance information, Map, natural landscape such as water as reference, and the AR view to reorient themselves. But the error occurred mainly because of the difficulty of mental rotation and manipulation of the Map view. As P8 noted: "*to look at the map then transfer that to reality and know which direction to go would be hard for me, and it would take me a while that I really think it through*". P10 said "*I tried to reverse directions in my mind*" but reversed left and right a couple of times.

Furthermore, during both studies 7 people reoriented the mobile phone, the map, and themselves at multiple points for various tasks: to make turning decisions, find directions, or mentally generate a route. This showed the mental rotation consumes significant cognitive resources and that people relied on physical rotation to facilitate comparison. Seager et al. showed that physical rotation is the most effective and preferred navigation assistance [35]. AR view is such an ego-centric view that saved users' work of mental rotation and had the additional benefit of translating the cartographic representations to the real world.

Limitations and Future Work

The current work is limited in terms of study design and interface design. For study design, while 10 participants in each study is a relatively small sample to compare the two designs, we combined quantitative and qualitative insights obtained through multiple test settings to strengthen our conclusions. In addition to homebuying scenario, other neighbourhood expedition scenarios should be considered in future work. For example, tourists might differ with home buyers in having less prior knowledge (e.g., of street names) and may get lost more easily. By leveraging the user's visual context, an AR view might be more useful than a List view in this case. The study tasks were designed around planned excursions with emphasis on navigation which do not represent a full picture of learning about a neighbourhood. However, this focus was derived from the limitations of the point to point design of Google Maps and used as inspiration for Block Party's design. While we identified a need for locative annotation and added this to Block Party, a full consideration of how annotation support integrates with locative information retrieval for neighbourhood expedition is left for future work.

For interface design, additional views (e.g., street view, ego-centric navigation views) could be integrated to complement the current design. A hybrid system with both searching and directory-based selection might be more useful. A more controlled comparison between coordinated synchronized views and a compact view which combines different views on one screen would be interesting. Community built itineraries and annotations can be further explored as a means to build neighbourhood awareness and community.

Aporta and Higgs distinguish technology that "physically and socially" engages from technology "that reduces engagement with experience of the land, people, and local knowledge" [4]. Leshed et al. [20] argue that GPS-based wayfinding apps can detach people from physical and social interactions, and suggest redesigning GPS interfaces with environmental engagement as goals. How mobile guides might be designed to help discover, understand and appreciate the physical world, and enhance social engagement with other pedestrians or social networks remains a key research challenge.

CONCLUSION

We presented the design and comparative field evaluation of an application called Block Party with a popular point-to-point navigation and search application (Google Maps) in support of neighbourhood expeditions. With a design emphasis on synchronized, lightweight spatial views, curated directory-based POIs and explicit support for multi-stop itinerary planning, Block Party was found to improve the efficiency of the wayfinding workflow, and better establish spatial awareness in the visited neighbourhoods.

ACKNOWLEDGEMENTS

We thank the reviewers for their recommendations, they have improved the paper considerably. This research was funded by NSERC and Boeing.

REFERENCES

1. Agrawala, M., & Stolte, C. (2000, March). A design and implementation for effective computer-generated route maps. In *AAAI symposium on smart graphics* (pp. 61-65).
2. Alawadhi, A., Chandrasekera, T., & Yang, C. (2011). The effect of spatial knowledge on sense of belonging in university/academic environments. *Considering Research: Reflecting Upon Current Themes in Architectural Research*, 337.
3. Aoki, P. M., Grinter, R. E., Hurst, A., Szymanski, M. H., Thornton, J. D., & Woodruff, A. (2002, April). Sotto voce: exploring the interplay of conversation and mobile audio spaces. In *Proceedings of the SIGCHI conference on Human factors in computing systems* (pp. 431-438). ACM.
4. Aporta, C., Higgs, E., Hakken, D., Palmer, L., Palmer, M., Rundstrom, R., ... & Higgs, E. (2005). Satellite culture: global positioning systems, Inuit wayfinding, and the need for a new account of technology. *Current Anthropology*, *46*(5), 729-753.
5. Baus, J., Cheverst, K., & Kray, C. (2005). A survey of map-based mobile guides map-based mobile services—theories, methods and implementations, chap. 13 (pp. 193-209). Meng/Zipf.
6. Bellotti, V., Begole, B., Chi, E. H., Ducheneaut, N., Fang, J., Isaacs, E., ... & Rasmussen, P. (2008, April). Activity-based serendipitous recommendations with the Magitti mobile leisure guide. In *Proceedings of the SIGCHI Conference on Human Factors in Computing Systems* (pp. 1157-1166). ACM.
7. Burigat, S., & Chittaro, L. (2012). Mobile Navigation and Information Services for Disabled Students in University Buildings: a Needs Assessment Investigation. In *Proceedings of the 2nd Workshop on Mobile Accessibility, MOBILE HCI 2012 Conference*.
8. Cheverst, K., Mitchell, K., & Davies, N. (2002). Exploring context-aware information push. *Personal and Ubiquitous Computing*, *6*(4), 276-281.
9. Church, K., & Smyth, B. (2009, February). Understanding the intent behind mobile information needs. In *Proceedings of the 14th international conference on Intelligent user interfaces* (pp. 247-256). ACM.
10. Draper, M. (1995). Exploring the influence of a virtual body on spatial awareness. *Context*, *10*, 35.
11. DüNser, A., Billinghurst, M., Wen, J., Lehtinen, V., & Nurminen, A. (2012). Exploring the use of handheld AR for outdoor navigation. *Computers & Graphics*, *36*(8), 1084-1095.
12. Gavalas, D., Konstantopoulos, C., Mastakas, K., & Pantziou, G. (2014). Mobile recommender systems in tourism. *Journal of Network and Computer Applications*, *39*, 319-333.
13. Goh, D. H. L., Lee, C. S., & Razikin, K. (2011, October). Comparative evaluation of interfaces for presenting location-based information on mobile devices. In *International Conference on Asian Digital Libraries* (pp. 237-246). Springer Berlin Heidelberg.
14. Hornecker, E., Swindells, S., & Dunlop, M. (2011, August). A mobile guide for serendipitous exploration of cities. In *Proceedings of the 13th International Conference on Human Computer Interaction with Mobile Devices and Services* (pp. 557-562). ACM.
15. Kaasinen, E. (2003). User needs for location-aware mobile services.*Personal and ubiquitous computing*, *7*(1), 70-79.
16. Kallioniemi, P., & Turunen, M. (2012, December). Model for landmark highlighting in mobile web services. In *Proceedings of the 11th International Conference on Mobile and Ubiquitous Multimedia* (p. 25). ACM.
17. Kjeldskov, J., & Paay, J. (2006, November). Indexical interaction design for context-aware mobile computer systems. In *Proceedings of the 18th Australia conference on Computer-Human Interaction: Design: Activities, Artefacts and Environments* (pp. 71-78). ACM.
18. Kjeldskov, J., & Paay, J. (2010). Indexicality: Understanding mobile human-computer interaction in context. *ACM Transactions on Computer-Human Interaction (TOCHI)*, *17*(4), 14.
19. Kuflik, T., Stock, O., Zancanaro, M., Gorfinkel, A., Jbara, S., Kats, S., ... & Kashtan, N. (2011). A visitor's guide in an active museum: Presentations, communications, and reflection. *Journal on Computing and Cultural Heritage (JOCCH)*, *3*(3), 11.
20. Leshed, G., Velden, T., Rieger, O., Kot, B., & Sengers, P. (2008, April). In-car gps navigation: engagement with and disengagement from the environment. In *Proceedings of the SIGCHI Conference on Human Factors in Computing Systems* (pp. 1675-1684). ACM.
21. Mark, D., Freksa, C., Hirtle, S., Lloyd, R., and Tversky, B. Cognitive models of geographic space. International Journal of Geographical Information Science 13, 8 (1999), 747–774.
22. May, A. J., Ross, T., Bayer, S. H., & Tarkiainen, M. J. (2003). Pedestrian navigation aids: information requirements and design implications. *Personal and Ubiquitous Computing*, *7*(6), 331-338.
23. Medenica, Z., Kun, A. L., Paek, T., & Palinko, O. (2011, August). Augmented reality vs. street views: a driving simulator study comparing two emerging navigation aids. In *Proceedings of the 13th International Conference on Human Computer*

Interaction with Mobile Devices and Services (pp. 265-274). ACM.

24. Millonig, A., & Schechtner, K. (2007). Developing landmark-based pedestrian-navigation systems. *IEEE Transactions on Intelligent Transportation Systems*, *8*(1), 43-49.
25. Mulloni, A., Dünser, A., & Schmalstieg, D. (2010, September). Zooming interfaces for augmented reality browsers. In *Proceedings of the 12th international conference on Human computer interaction with mobile devices and services* (pp. 161-170). ACM.
26. Naismith, L., Sharples, M., & Ting, J. (2005). Evaluation of CAERUS: a context aware mobile guide. In *mLearn 2005*.
27. Partala, T., & Salminen, M. (2012, May). User experience of photorealistic urban pedestrian navigation. In *Proceedings of the International Working Conference on Advanced Visual Interfaces* (pp. 204-207). ACM.
28. Rao, B., & Minakakis, L. (2003). Evolution of mobile location-based services. *Communications of the ACM*, *46*(12), 61-65.
29. Reilly, D., & Chen, H. (2006). Mobile lenses: a hybrid approach to direct interaction with maps and kiosks. In *Proc. of 2nd intl workshop on pervasive mobile interaction devices (PerMID'06).*
30. Reilly, D., Mackay, B., & Inkpen, K. (2008). How mobile maps cooperate with existing navigational infrastructure. In *Map-based Mobile Services* (pp. 267-292). Springer Berlin Heidelberg.
31. Reilly, D., Mackay, B., Watters, C., & Inkpen, K. (2009). Planners, navigators, and pragmatists: collaborative wayfinding using a single mobile phone. *Personal and Ubiquitous Computing*, *13*(4), 321-329.
32. Reitmayr, G., & Schmalstieg, D. (2004). Collaborative augmented reality for outdoor navigation and information browsing. In *Proceedings from LBS 2004: The 1st International Symposium on Location Based Services and TeleCartography* (pp. 31-41).
33. Roberts, J. C. (2007, July). State of the art: Coordinated & multiple views in exploratory visualization. In *Coordinated and Multiple Views in Exploratory Visualization, 2007. CMV'07. Fifth International Conference on* (pp. 61-71). IEEE.
34. Schmalstieg, D., & Wagner, D. (2005). A handheld augmented reality museum guide. In *In Proc. IADIS International Conference on Mobile Learning.*
35. Seager, W., & Fraser, D. S. (2007, April). Comparing physical, automatic and manual map rotation for pedestrian navigation. In *Proceedings of the SIGCHI conference on Human factors in computing systems* (pp. 767-776). ACM.
36. Sohn, T., Li, K. A., Griswold, W. G., & Hollan, J. D. (2008, April). A diary study of mobile information needs. In *Proceedings of the SIGCHI Conference on Human Factors in Computing Systems* (pp. 433-442). ACM.
37. Teevan, J., Karlson, A., Amini, S., Brush, A. J., & Krumm, J. (2011, August). Understanding the importance of location, time, and people in mobile local search behavior. In *Proceedings of the 13th International Conference on Human Computer Interaction with Mobile Devices and Services* (pp. 77-80). ACM.
38. Tversky, B. (1993, September). Cognitive maps, cognitive collages, and spatial mental models. In *European Conference on Spatial Information Theory* (pp. 14-24). Springer Berlin Heidelberg.
39. Vaittinen, T., Salminen, M., & Olsson, T. (2013, August). City scene: field trial of a mobile street-imagery-based navigation service. In *Proceedings of the 15th international conference on Human-computer interaction with mobile devices and services* (pp. 193-202). ACM.
40. Wang Baldonado, M. Q., Woodruff, A., & Kuchinsky, A. (2000, May). Guidelines for using multiple views in information visualization. In*Proceedings of the working conference on Advanced visual interfaces* (pp. 110-119). ACM.
41. Wen, J., Helton, W. S., & Billinghurst, M. (2013, September). A study of user perception, interface performance, and actual usage of mobile pedestrian navigation aides. In *Proceedings of the Human Factors and Ergonomics Society Annual Meeting* (Vol. 57, No. 1, pp. 1958-1962). SAGE Publications.
42. Zipf, A., & Jöst, M. M. (2011). Location-based services. In *Springer Handbook of Geographic Information* (pp. 417-421). Springer Berlin Heidelberg.

Designing for Cohabitation: Naturecultures, Hybrids, and Decentering the Human in Design

Nancy Smith
Indiana University
Bloomington, IN, USA
smithnae@indiana.edu

Shaowen Bardzell
Indiana University
Bloomington, IN, USA
selu@indiana.edu

Jeffrey Bardzell
Indiana University
Bloomington, IN, USA
jbardzel@indiana.edu

ABSTRACT

Recent research in urban informatics has presented the city as both a complex technological center and a diverse cultural, social, and political entity. However, there has been little research into the changing role that nature plays in urban space, particularly when it comes to understanding how animals have adapted to life in technological and networked cities. In the wake of urbanization, new kinds of cohabitation, including increased interactions between humans and animals, has resulted in new challenges for those working in urban informatics. We leverage key concepts in the Anthropocene—naturecultures, hybrids, and decentering the human in design—to unpack the entanglements of animal-human-computer interaction in two design cases: The Big Cat Behavioral Tracking Initiative and The Phenology Clock. We contribute to urban informatics and HCI research by reflecting on ways in which design can promote new forms of cohabitation and support a broader conception of the city that sees animals as an essential part of the urban landscape.

Author Keywords

Animal-Computer Interaction; Urban Informatics; Cohabitation; Posthumanism; Anthropocene

ACM Classification Keywords

H.5.m. Information interfaces and presentation (e.g. HCI): Miscellaneous.

INTRODUCTION

Cities are often described as technological hubs, full of shining skyscrapers, dense networks, flows of people, and home to a diverse range of cultural, social, and political structures. Missing from such a conception of the city are elements such as plants, trees, mountains, water, and animals—the natural world—which has long been conceived of as something relegated to designated spaces such as parks, or more broadly as something "out there" or apart from urban space. However, given the rapid course of urbanization, cities and natural spaces have become geographically entangled—not only do we see more common animals such as our domestic pets, birds, and squirrels in our neighborhoods, but as cities around the world continue to encroach on animal habitats, there is an increasing chance that we may encounter cougars, foxes, monkeys, wolves, or what we might call urban wild things [30]. It is likely that interactions between humans, animals, and technologies will only grow in frequency and complexity in the future, and we see a need for those working in HCI to identify both the ways in which urban animals may be affected by design, as well as the ways these animals may inform interaction design.

Urban informatics research has explored not only the physical and technical characteristics of cities [25, 61] but also the increasingly complex social and cultural aspects [59, 11, 34] of urban spaces. Additionally, recent research in HCI has been conducted on such things as the influence of climate patterns in everyday urban life [60], growing food in the city [41], and even an asocial hiking app [51], all of which have implications for how we think about the relationship between nature and cities. However, there has been little research on the role that animals play in urban space.

As we enter the Anthropocene—the proposed geological epoch in which we now find ourselves—we see new avenues with which we can develop more robust theoretical foundations and actionable design practices regarding the role of animals in cities. Not only does the Anthropocene bring to the fore pressing issues such as climate change and mass extinction, but the Anthropocene, as part of a posthuman discourse, also compels a vision of the world that includes the so-called *end of nature* [52]. Consequently, we see a need to develop new urban design processes that are more equitable for all species; if we are to survive in the conditions of this new epoch, adapting perspectives that decenter the human from design practice will promote new conceptions of cohabitation that help both humans and nonhumans thrive in the future. What is at stake here is not only animal welfare or simply an ethical obligation to support urban wild things, but rather we are presented with an opportunity to build interactive systems that are more sensitive to the environmental and cultural capacities of different cities around the world.

CHI 2017, May 06 - 11, 2017, Denver, CO, USA

ACM 978-1-4503-4655-9/17/05…$15.00
DOI: http://dx.doi.org/10.1145/3025453.3025948

We situate our work in the intersection of urban informatics and animal-computer interaction to make the following contributions: First, we introduce scientific and cultural research on the Anthropocene and motivate the uptakes for HCI researchers and designers concerned with cities and animal-centered designs. Second, we present a critical analysis of two design cases to explore the productive role the Anthropocene discourse plays in urban informatics/ACI research; in particular, concepts such as *naturecultures, hybrids, and decentering the human* surface issues surrounding the design of behavioral tracking technologies for animals and sensitize us to our role as inhabitants of and actors in technologized cities with other creatures. And finally, we reflect on design and HCI in the Anthropocene, seeing roles for citizen science, everyday design, and a revision of concepts of the city, culture, and design itself.

ANIMAL-COMPUTER INTERACTION

Animals, though not a prominent part of the design discourse, have recently emerged as an important player within HCI. Animal-computer interaction (ACI) is defined as the explicit and systematic application of design principles that place the animal at the center of an iterative development process as a legitimate user and design contributor [43]. ACI researcher Clara Mancini has called for interaction designers to be more explicit in considering animals in their work. She writes, "The negative effects of this lack of animal perspective become obvious when, for example, the behavior and welfare of seals fitted with bio-logging tags and satellite transmitters are significantly affected and data gathered during costly conservation studies risks invalidation, or when cows who do not engage with milking systems are culled and farmers suffer capital losses. But risk mitigation aside, what about the things we could gain from a shift in perspective? What would it allow us to learn about and achieve with interactive technology? How would it influence our reflection on usability, adaptation, appropriation, methodology, and ethics, to name but a few aspects? [44]" In the Anthropocene, these questions are particularly relevant in urban informatics because more than fifty percent of the population now live in cities. Global cities are increasingly entangled human-nonhuman spaces that open up the possibilities for increased interactions among diverse groupings of species. This trend indicates a need to consider alternative understandings of cohabitation and to develop ways in which those working in urban informatics might adopt and promote practices that support the goals of ACI.

Interaction design related to animals generally falls into several key categories: 1) Designing *for* animals 2) Designing technology to *mimic* animal behavior 3) Designing tools to *study* animals 4) Designing animal-technology interactions *for humans*. Designing *for* animals accounts for devices that are created specifically for animal use, such as service dogs who need light switches and door handles that are more paw-friendly. Designing technology to *mimic* animal behavior has become a popular aim within the field of robotics. For example, a team at Harvard has recently developed a robotic bee that may aid in worldwide pollination after the death of millions of bees over the past decade [54]. Designing tools to *study* animals accounts largely for scientific and cultural projects that aim to capture animal behavior. Designing animal-technology interactions that primarily *benefit* humans accounts for a large part of interaction design work related to animals, especially in such fields as farming and medicine. However, we also see novel uses of interaction design, such as HeroRat, a project that trains and utilizes rats to detect land mines that would otherwise pose a danger [1].

In urban informatics, we see significant overlaps in the potential aims of ACI because designing *for* animals in cities is likely benefit humans as well. However, as [44] observes, "The animal perspective has seldom informed the design of animal computing applications, whose development has so far been driven by academic disciplines other than computer science or by other industrial sectors. The design of these technologies remains fundamentally human-centered, and the study of how they are adopted by or affect their users remains fundamentally outside the remit of user-computer interaction research." There are promising opportunities for designers to engage with animal perspectives, and the practical aims of developing technological interventions in urban space require a theoretical foundation upon which to build such design practices. The idea of the Anthropocene, which has not been extensively adopted in HCI, provides a productive resource because it readily suggests new ways of thinking about global change that offer generative possibilities to support the aims and processes of those working in urban informatics.

THE END OF NATURE

The Anthropocene, originally conceived of as a geological epoch in which humans have irreparably changed the Earth, has become a prominent concept in a variety of fields, from the sciences to the humanities [17]. Anthropologist Xuemei Bai and colleagues define the Anthropocene as signifying, "1) the novelty of the time period in which humans find themselves as a result of this [irreparable change]; 2) the novel challenges, opportunities, and uncertainties that awareness of this global potency brings; and 3) the new perspectives required to deal with them [3]." This conception of the Anthropocene suggests a need for those in urban informatics to interrogate the foundations and implications of global change, so that we are better positioned to design systems that support cohabitation in urban contexts.

One of the key concepts associated with the Anthropocene is the so-called *end of nature*. What this means is not that the natural world has ceased to exist, but rather the social construction of "nature" as a concept is no longer tenable in light of human influence in the world. Environmental law professor Jedediah Purdy has captured this phenomenon, arguing, "The natural and the artificial have merged at every scale. Climate change makes the global atmosphere, its chemistry and weather systems, into Frankenstein's monster—part natural, part made. The same is true of seas, as carbon absorption turns oceans acidic and threatens everything that lives in them. The planet's landscapes, its forests and fields, along with the species that inhabit them, are a mélange of those we have created, those we have cultivated and introduced, and those we let live… […] If Nature were a place, we could not find it. It Nature were a state of mind, we could not attain it. We are something else, and so is the world" [52]. The notion that we are designing after nature has implications in areas of critical making [53], sustainability [57], and collapse informatics [56] among others. We see broad application of these ideas across the field, but in this paper, we will focus in particular on drawing out the connections between the Anthropocene and urban informatics because urbanization is a particularly challenging design concern. In what follows, we highlight three concepts—naturecultures, hybrids, and decentering the human in design—and explore the implications for designing for cohabitation in the city.

Naturecultures

Within urban informatics, cities are often construed as entities that are apart from, or at odds with, nature, as if nature is some green (or brown or blue) space that exists miles outside of urban areas. However, city dwellers are deeply entangled with natural elements, including plant life, animals, dirt, water, and so forth. At the same time, what we tend to think of as "pristine wilderness" is hardly pristine; conserved lands are highly managed by humans. Historian William Cronon has written significantly on the problem with wilderness: "[We must] abandon the dualism that sees the tree in the garden as artificial—completely fallen and unnatural—and the tree in the wilderness as natural—completely pristine and wild. Both trees in some ultimate sense are wild; both in a practical sense now depend on our management and care. We are responsible for both, even though we can claim credit for neither [16]." In the Anthropocene, there is no place on Earth that remains "untouched" by humans; even the pollution we have projected into the air has made its way into the furthest reaches of the planet.

Rigidly distinguishing between natures and cultures poses several problems for designers. First, these foundational perspectives affect the ways in which knowledge is produced in our field; setting up research based in this dualism is unlikely to produce useful conceptions of urban space because cities cannot be separated neatly into natural and cultural elements. Naturecultures, as both a term and a concept, not only provides a useful frame with which to prevent faulty knowledge production, but it also gives us a way to talk about the interconnectedness between natural and cultural elements in an urban setting.

Second, this dualism prohibits us from seeing and understanding the entangled nature of cities because under such a divide, the individual elements of a city are seen as unattached from one another. Urban technologies are deeply embedded in these entanglements. Consider, for example, an interactive kiosk at a bus stop. This tool may provide information for people riding the bus, or for tourists who need to consult a map. But it does not stand alone with a unified function apart from the nonhuman elements of the city. The structure may provide a home for birds (or may perhaps disrupt a previous home for birds). The light from the screen may affect moths and other nocturnal creatures. The kiosk could be designed to support water collection or to allow for a plant to grow on or in it to foster a more harmonious relationship among animals, humans, and technology. There are numerous, and many yet unknown, interactions that may occur at these intersections between technology, humans, and animals. We can see this evidenced in the numerous effects that are currently being uncovered as technology makes its way outside the human world. For example, electrosmog has disrupted orientation in migratory birds [22]. Another consideration within urban informatics, informed by the Anthropocene, is the animal-technology relationship, which may or may not involve humans at all.

In writing about the concept of *natureculture* (a term coined by Donna Haraway) Science and Technology Studies (STS) researcher Joanna Latimer suggests that the term works as "a provocation for collapsing and transgressing the dominant metaphysics that dichotomizes nature and culture, and through which culture and all that is human is constituted as discontinuous with the rest of the world. As Haraway points out, nature cannot stand outside of culture, just as culture cannot stand outside of nature. This is because the meaning of nature—what we identify as natural—is not just determined by culture but is also the result of specific historical, material and political conditions of possibility. [38]." The term natureculture, then, provides us with a useful concept with which to think about design in urban informatics because a shift in thinking towards naturecultures will support a foundation for those in HCI who aim to integrate a wider range of perspectives in practice (both in generating empirical and theoretical work on the topic). By breaking away from this perceived divide between urban space and nature, we are better positioned to investigate cities, not only as technological centers, consisting of buildings, infrastructures, and networks, but as vibrant, living things, teeming with a diverse range of plant and animal life.

Hybrids

One of the perspectives that opens up with the turn to naturecultures is that of *hybridity*. Design researcher and STS scholar Laura Forlano argues that "hybridity offer[s] a way of enabling designers to think and act more critically about their responsibility to design more ethical ways of living and working in cities given socio-technical complexity [24]." The notion of hybridity helps us to reimagine, in the words of anthropologist Jamie Lorimer, the *category* animal, in order to "recognize the multiple forms of difference it subsumes, and to take seriously the ways in which humans and animals are shaped by their interactions [40]." The implication for HCI research is that such conceptual openings help attune us better to ways that technology does and/or might mediate animal-human interactions. Additionally, hybridity has the capacity to inspire new methodological approaches in urban informatics that promote such attunement and make visible these human-nonhuman interactions.

It has been suggested that the most complex design challenges we face are those related to environmental change [33] and thus, this pathway into HCI is already beginning to happen: methods such as multispecies ethnography, first developed in cultural anthropology [36] have been taken up in HCI to investigate human-dog relationships [42]. Multispecies ethnography advocates for thinking beyond the human and aims to understand the complex ways in which different beings affect one another. Similarly, thing ethnography [23] articulates a nonanthropocentric way of understanding design from a material objects' perspective.

Hybrid worlds also acknowledge nature as what Haraway might call a *relational achievement* [27]. Lorimer articulates this notion with an example that is productive for us to think with. He refers to Sri Lanka's elephants as archetypal companion species and suggests that we can "trace their diverse entanglements within multispecies histories and geographies. Elephants have coevolved with people over millennia. Their genetics, anatomies, behaviors, feelings, social groupings, and wider ecologies all bear a human signature. At the same time, the language, culture, religions, agricultures, and economies of their human coinhabitants carry a pachyderm trace. These relations are unequal and frequently fraught and cut across species divides" [40]. Conceiving of humans and animals in a relational perspective prevents us from defining humans as the dominant force, which has been a problematic narrative throughout the proposed time of the Anthropocene.

Decentering the human in design

Naturecultures and hybridity can help us to *decenter* the human from design. This is a crucial shift in thought if we are to develop new technologies for cohabitation because it will help us reframe HCI from a human-centered field and towards holistic practices that are more environmentally and culturally sensitive to global cities. There have been a number of recent proposals advocating for the decentering of the human within HCI [18, 19, 24, 32, 35] and we further this aim by identifying the ways in which engaging with the Anthropocene supports this goal. Those in STS, particularly within the tradition of posthumanism, have long held that human exceptionality is problematic, arguing that humans and nonhuman actors necessarily create intersubjective worlds, where both human and nonhuman perspectives shape interactions [29]. Forlano has recently argued for the decentering of humans in the development and design of cities: "Designers are increasingly engaged in projects that go beyond crafting individual graphics or products and toward the design of services, organizations, systems, platforms, and experiences. As designers take on these roles, they are engaged in the active creation and curation of complex socio-technical networks, constituencies, and alliances that come together around problems, issues, and controversies that have distinct politics, values, and ethics" [24]. As designers are now faced with developing technology that exists within these complex socio-technical networks, new challenges have arisen that require a shift in thinking from traditional design practices that focus on human wellbeing, to more inclusive practices that emphasize a multiplicity of perspectives.

Decentering the human, it should be noted, does not mean *excluding* human perspectives; nor does it mean placing animal, or other, perspectives at the center of design thinking. Rather, a decentering of the human in design blurs the boundaries between people and things, emphasizing the interconnectedness that is inherent in human/nonhuman assemblages; a decentering would promote news ways of approaching technology development that accounts for multiple and heterogeneous standpoints within urban spaces.

REIMAGINING URBAN INFORMATICS IN THE ANTHROPOCENE

One of the issues with the way the Anthropocene is conceived in the natural sciences is as a series of phenomena that has led to global climate change, which is often talked about as a neutral set of occurrences, such as increased global temperatures, ozone depletion, ocean acidification, and decreased biodiversity. On the other hand, those in the humanities rightly call for a need to situate this phenomenon in historical and cultural contexts [46]. For example, it has been demonstrated that climate change is primarily caused by wealthy nations, and disproportionally affects poorer individuals, especially those who rely on the earth for their livelihoods [13]. In other words, climate change cannot be addressed independent of social justice, so design interventions in the one are tied to the other. The kinds of questions this raises for those working in urban informatics include: What kinds of systems or tools might designers develop to address this disparity? How can we conceive of the global nature of technology use and development as something that is tremendously unbalanced across and within different nations? And, most relevant to the present project, how does a broader understanding of issues related to the Anthropocene help designers to conceive of more equitable ways of incorporating other species in the development of urban technologies?

According to [3], "while the concept "Anthropocene" reflects the nature, scale and magnitude of human impacts on the Earth, its societal significance lies in how it can be used to explore and guide attitudes, choices, decisions and actions that will reverberate far into the future." The Anthropocene is useful to designers, not only as a way to understand the physical changes occurring on Earth, but also as a bridging concept that helps us to engage with issues such as global inequalities, power dynamics, interspecies relationships, and historically and culturally situated systems. [3] continue, "The Anthropocene thus implies a fundamental reconceptualization of the role of individual and collective human agency and its relation to structures, systems and inputs." The implication for urban informatics is evident: It means a fundamental shift in how we conceive of cities, as well as a shift in thinking towards design as an inherent and dynamic part of all naturecultures.

Animals, as part of an urban ecosystem, contribute in surprising (and yet unknown) ways. As Haraway observes, "The constant question when considering systemic phenomena has to be, when do changes in degree become changes in kind, and what are the effects of bioculturally, biotechnically, biopolitically, historically situated people (not Man) relative to, and combined with, the effects of other species assemblages and other biotic/abiotic forces? No species, not even our own arrogant one pretending to be good individuals in so-called modern Western scripts, acts alone; assemblages of organic species and of abiotic actors make history, the evolutionary kind and the other kinds too [28]." Here, again, we can see an articulation of the relationship between animals and humans that moves away from dualism and supports a more ecological perspective. No species, as Haraway suggests, acts alone. The same can be said of technology, which always already exists within and among other urban elements.

DESIGNING FOR COHABITATION

We critically analyze two examples of interaction design to further illustrate how engaging with the Anthropocene can play a productive role in urban informatics research and identify ways this idea can be more robustly integrated into practice in order to promote design for cohabitation. We present analysis of two design cases informed by Bardzell's conception of interaction criticism [5]. Interaction criticism entails "rigorous interpretive interrogations of the complex relationships between (a) the interface, including its material and perceptual qualities as well as its broader situatedness in visual languages and culture and (b) the user experience, including the meanings, behaviors, perceptions, affects, insights, and social sensibilities that arise in the context of interaction and its outcomes." It has also been argued that knowledge is unfolded in the interpretation of objects. Importantly, for our purposes, this takes seriously the idea that "reading and interpretation of complex design objects provides resources to support research through design. Designers are tasked with understanding the relationships between present and near-future technological possibility and future ways of being, such that design solutions can be introduced" [4]. Methodologically, this allows us to critically examine these designs and place them within socio-technical systems with the aim of identifying the characteristics of non-human centered design and the ways in which designers can explicitly develop work that supports animal life. Such criticism enhances our sensitivities to how particular design decisions, materials, and processes can help us realize our values and goals.

We selected two design cases—the Big Cat Behavioral Tracking Initiative and the Phenology Clock Project—primarily because they point towards novel conceptions of cohabitation in urban space, revealing and also proposing ways of understanding urban wild things in order to design systems that support complex city entanglements. Additionally, they represent tremendous diversity in terms of their functionality and aesthetic qualities. We see these two designs as operating at different ends of the spectrum in terms of what cohabitations might mean, but they compliment one another because they both highlight different needs that designers may have when considering animal-human-technology interactions.

The Quantified Cat

Tracking the behavior of animals in urban space has a long history in fields related to animal science, such as biology and ecology, as well as in fields such as anthropology and cultural studies, which are interested in understanding the social and cultural implications of animal behavior in relation to human life [50]. Digital technologies allow us new ways of tracking, observing, and learning about animal movement, patterns, interactions, and lifestyles. These technologies have been applied extensively in the context of domestic pets, such as The Paw Tracker [47], PetPace [48], Nuzzle [45] and others, but we are especially interested in the way these tracking tools are used to study urban wild things, and what implications this data has for developing future cohabitation technologies.

In support of conservation efforts, tracking devices, such as GPS collars are often used to follow the movements of big cats, such as leopards, jaguars, lions, and tigers. These tracking devices provide scientists, conservationists, and NGO workers insight into big cat behavior and habitat needs. For example, the Snow Leopard Trust, a conservation organization that has been conducting long-term ecological study on snow leopards since 2008, utilizes tracking devices and research cameras to gain insight into questions such as: How much space does a snow leopard typically use? Where do snow leopards hunt and find water? Where are the biggest threats to snow leopards located [55]? This data reveals aspects of how snow leopards cohabit with humans, including conflicts with mining companies whose land acquisition often cuts through snow leopard territory, and local herders whose cattle sometimes become snow leopard prey.

To capture this information, GPS-enabled trackers are implanted in collars that are attached to the leopards (the leopards are not harmed during this process) and the collars are programmed to release one to two years after placement so that researchers can collect them. The data captured in these trackers includes location information and have been deployed in long-term studies in China, Mongolia, India, Pakistan, and Kyrgyzstan [55]. Snow Leopards are shy, often elusive animals, and tracking devices helps researchers to gain valuable insight into their lives. That said, as human development encroaches on animal habitats, big cats have begun to lose their shyness around humans in order to adapt to urban life, as increasingly common news stories about cougars in Los Angeles attest.

Sub-Saharan Africa and India are home to the two largest populations of leopards in the world, and in cities such as Mumbai, with a population of 21 million, leopards can be found living alongside the expansive neighborhoods of the city. About 35 leopards are known to live in Sanjay Gandhi National Park, 40-square-miles of green space in central Mumbai. Environmental writer Richard Conniff, who specializes human and animal behavior, has explored this phenomenon and he observes: "That's an average of less than two square miles of habitat apiece, for animals that can easily range ten miles in a day. These leopards also live surrounded by some of the world's most crowded urban neighborhoods, housing 52,000 people or more per square mile. (That's nearly twice the population density of New York City.) And yet the leopards thrive. Part of their diet comes from spotted deer and other wild prey within the park. But many of the leopards also work the unfenced border between nature and civilization. While the city sleeps, they slip through the streets and alleys below, where they pick off dogs, cats, pigs, rats, chickens, and goats, the camp followers of human civilization. They eat people too, though rarely [15]." As cities grow, one of the ways in which humans have tried to address urban wild things is simply to remove them from cities. As the thinking goes, we worry that leopards might attack humans, so we tranquilize them, take them to areas that are far outside the limits of the city center with the hope that they will not pose a danger to people. However, recent studies have suggested that this can actually cause *more* human attacks because the cats are dropped off in an unfamiliar location, which can be disorienting and alarming for the cat, who finds itself in a rural area with little food and water. When the cat does come across a rural family, they are more likely to attack than they would have if they had simply been left free to roam in the city where they have ample access to other food sources [2].

The cohabitation of humans and big cats in major cities around the world presents us with a concrete example of hybridity described earlier; in particular that ecosystems are relational achievements. This has both technical and ethical implications for urban informaticists: From a human-centered perspective, in which only people have interests and value, the meaning we create is subjectively based on *our* perception, however we are not the only ones that perceive the world around us and create meaning. Purdy argues, "This exclusively human-centered outlook would wipe out a great swath of experience, perception, and relationships—to places, other living things, and practices such as wilderness pilgrimages and eco-pastoral farming—that would have formed environmental imagination. The obliteration would take away, make unsayable, much of what has mattered in powering environmental politics, and seems likely to matter just as much or more in Anthropocene politics [52]." A posthumanist perspective encourages alternative conceptions of possible ways of being, beyond the human-defined sense of existence. To put that another way: when we begin to think like a leopard, we can also design environments that support leopard behavior. Technologies such as trackers, which give us insights into their behavior, help us do this work.

One such design intervention that has resulted in the data gathered from both observation, and later tracking devices, is the *Wildlife Crossing*, a commonly used design solution that provides alternative paths for animals to cross high-traffic roads [8, 21, 39].

Figure 1. Wildlife Crossing, Alberta, Canada. ©Maggie Tacheny

Wildlife Crossings are designed to functionally support the movement of animals, while minimizing the chance of accidents from moving vehicles. If a road runs through a cohabitated area, between areas of shelter and access to water, for example, a wildlife crossing supports animals' abilities to safely cross to access a water source. Wildlife Crossings take numerous shapes and sizes; they may go over, under, or around a road, and generally aim to utilize natural elements, such as grasses, trees, and plants that already exist in the area. This encourages animals to move through the crossing, rather than to cross the road because the environment is more familiar to them.

Wildlife Crossings exemplify the posthuman hybrid notion that we are not entities but ecologies [10]. Humans, it is argued, are made up of more nonhuman than "human" material including significant amounts of bacteria and other kinds of matter. We see this idea reflected in the environment as well; it is a complex entanglement of human and nonhuman elements, impossible to divide into neat categories. The bridge creates a path that benefits both animals and humans without disrupting the ecosystem, but at the same time it breaks down the perceived divide between nature and culture. It is, quite literally, human-designed nature, and it is based on the cultural norm of protecting both animal and human life from highway accidents. Is a Wildlife Crossing a cultural artifact or a natural one? We would be hard-pressed to define it as either one, and urbanization suggests that this kind of design will necessarily become more common as a result of increased cohabitation between humans and animals.

Tracking the movements and behavior of big cats helps us to develop design interventions such as the Wildlife Crossing. This is just one example of what may emerge from the collection of this kind of data, and it suggests that quantification will be an increasingly important tool for understanding animal behavior and its changes in the Anthropocene.

The Phenology Clock

Quantified cat initiatives show how technology helps conservationists develop new awareness of how humans and apex predators already cohabit, where the points of friction are (e.g., highways that cut through territory and rural herders whose livelihoods become prey animals), and new ways of "thinking like a leopard." But humans are not only acquiring new facts about apex predators; we are also changing our self-understanding as inhabitants of and actors on planet Earth. Designs that support reflection are one means of doing this work [9]. We turn now to a design that arguably does such work: the Phenology Clock.

Phenology is the centuries-old practice of tracking and identifying the natural rhythms of the planet—when birds migrate, when cherry trees blooms, when bears hibernate, and so forth. We could say that phenology is the study of the Earth's calendar. This "calendar" is deeply affected by climate change and as we move away from stable Holocene conditions into the yet unknown conditions of the Anthropocene, phenology allows us a way to track, monitor, and record the inevitable changes in natural phenomena. Recent advances in technology have advanced the capabilities of this practice; what was once done by careful human observation can now be augmented with remote sensors that can track air, water, soil, and other natural conditions.

The London Phenological Clock (part of The Phenology Clock Project [49]) designed by Natalie Jeremijenko's Environmental Health Clinic, is a clock that displays when local plants and animals emerge, bloom, or migrate throughout the year. This design was originally displayed as part of the "All of This Belongs to You Exhibition" at the Victoria and Albert Museum, and also functions as an interactive website that can be publically accessed. The clock displays data recorded in London from 2000-2014. The data was collected and managed by the Woodland Trust as part of its Nature's Calendar project run in partnership with the Centre for Ecology and Hydrology. This data is gathered by citizen scientists, or volunteers, who are interested in observing and recording phenomena in their neighborhood; it is then collected by The Centre and can be used as a way to understand natural phenomena and as evidence of the effects of climate change.

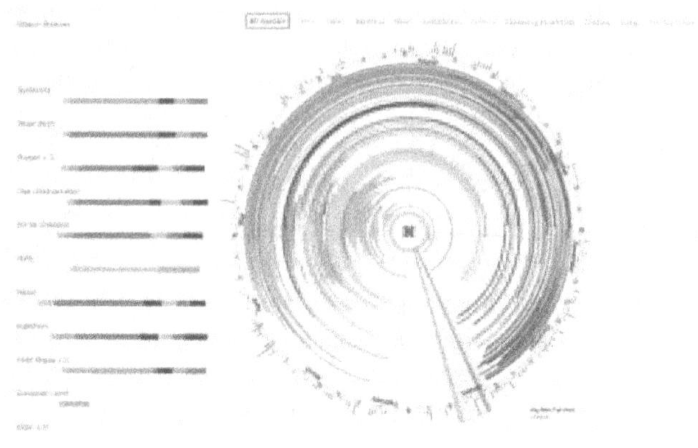

Figure 2. The London Phenological Clock ©Natalie Jeremijenko, Jake M Richardson, Tega Brain, and Blacki Li Rudi Migliozzi

The Phenology Clock (see Figure 2) visually alludes to a traditional clock—round with a face, dials, and hands that reflect information. However, it is more complex than a clock that keeps track only of time. In the Phenology Clock we see not only the information displayed in a central circular infographic, but it sits atop an X-Y axis—the X displays the different species that have been tracked: trees, plants, mammals, birds, amphibians, flowering perennials, grasses, fungi, and soil microbes. The Y-axis displays the individual species within a given category. For example, if you select trees, the vertical axis will reflect: Oak, Sycamore, Silver Birch, Rowan, Chestnut, Holly, Hazel, and so forth. There is an option to choose "all species" which will reflect data from all of the categories. Spans of time are selected by rotating the "hands" of the clock to choose specific dates; time selections include aggregated information during each of the tracked months over the course of 2000-2014.

The clock allows for a tremendous amount of data to be efficiently and elegantly visualized and organized by assigning specific colors to each species; hovering over trees illuminates a ring of different shades of green, while hovering over birds shows us a variety of pinks, light and dark, depending on which species appear in the data set. At the same time, we can drill even deeper into the data by hovering over a specific colored ring in the clock. For example, Figure 3 shows data for Bramble, also known as Rubis Fruitcosus. There were 1,721 observations of the first ripe fruit between October and June, which gives us an accurate sense of when this fruit first appears. In order to understand ecological connections, other animals who may eat the berries, such as birds, may also be tracked during the same period to see if they appear around the Bramble. There are some challenges in interacting with this design in part because of the constraints of a screen, which limits the amount of data that can be seen at once. Additionally, some of the connections between animals and plants are not as intuitive as might be suggested. For example, it is unclear *which* animals might feed off certain fruits or plants and how we might know this without trial-and-error clicking.

Based on the data presented in the Phenology Clock, there are numerous interpretive possibilities for developing technologies that work in consort with the natural phenomena that occurs in urban space. The clock inherently accounts for a wide variety of species and their diverse entanglements, and it visualizes data that would be otherwise unavailable to laypersons who don't study animals. Not only is it a tool for capturing data about the planet, but, if we consider this a tool to help us think about natural patterns, it also works as a pedagogical tool for those interested in environmental design. We can also imagine alternative expressions of the phenology clock, such as one that that also tracks the human-based patterns of a city, including light, noise, traffic, and pollution.

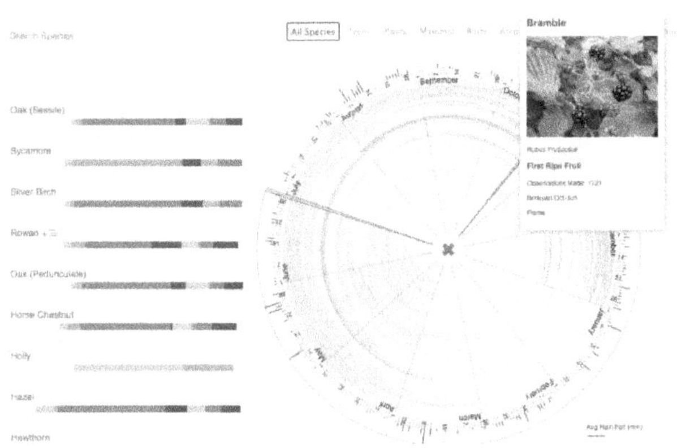

Figure 3. The London Phenological Clock, Bramble. ©Natalie Jeremijenko, Jake M Richardson, Tega Brain, and Blacki Li Rudi Migliozzi

Whereas the Wilderness Crossings present an example of concrete intervention inspired by collected data on animal movement, the Phenology Clock works as an object for us to think with and a learning device that helps us to plan and shape such interventions. The Phenology Clock has important implications in the Anthropocene because we are currently undergoing a time of great change in which Holocene conditions are irreparably damaged. But the exact nature and scale of the changes are difficult to grasp, and designs like the Phenology Clock propose different *rhetorics*—self-led, interactive, graphic—than what we more standardly experience in the media (e.g., statistics and verbal warnings from scientists). This design has the capacity to inspire those interested in learning about the natural world to go out and explore their own neighborhoods and observe and track the phenomena in their own backyards.

Moreover, a phenology clock could help us to record and learn about these emerging patterns in a more participative way than traditional science affords. One thing we do know is that there is no possible return to the conditions of the Holocene [26]. This means that we will have to conceive of a future world that has conditions—climate, temperature, air quality, biodiversity, and so forth—that are significantly different than any that came before. This design not only accounts for those changes, but also has the potential to help future designers to create with these planetary shifts in mind. Consistent with the reasoning in collapse informatics regarding designing for scarcity, [56] this also supports the idea of developing designs that are more adaptive to the changing blooming or migrating patterns of the various plants and creatures on the planet, rather than fixed designs that function the same way year-round.

We can see in this design one of the requirements of living in this new geological epoch, or what has been articulated to as "the ability to think and act beyond human experience [26]." The Anthropocene forces us to reconsider the role that humans play in shaping the Earth. No longer can we see ourselves as exceptional, but in this new geological era we are confronted with a need for hybrid thinking that helps us to learn how to work with and for other experiences on the planet. The Phenology Clock promotes nonhuman understanding by illustrating the behaviors, characteristics, and patterns of plant and animal life in a given place. It suggests that as humans increasingly experience life in cohabitation with urban wild things, we can develop digital tools that give us insight into the lives of these other creatures.

What might some of those design interventions look like? We see three key characteristics promoted by the Phenomenology Clock: biodiversity, time, and location specificity. Design in the Anthropocene requires us to carefully consider each of these factors, and one challenge for urban informaticists is that we don't necessarily have the tools or abilities to investigate and understand the biodiversity that exists in a given city. One option is to draw from other fields such as biology and ecology, which can help shape our knowledge development; the other option is to develop technologies that gather this kind of data and make it accessible to those without advanced environmental scientific training—which, incidentally, includes most designers. (This is also fundamental to the quantified self movement, which allows non-experts to collect and analyze data on their own bodies.) At the same time, this clock critiques traditional notions of time that humans have constructed and lived with for centuries. Although we have calendars based on the seasons and the path of the Earth around the sun, animals don't necessarily adhere to these demarcations in the way that humans do. This is especially true as we consider global cities with natural environments that are as wide ranging as hot, humid Mumbai summers and the icy winters of St. Petersburg. Similarly, we now must contend with artificial light that upends our associations to the patterns of the sun. Of particular importance to those working in urban informatics is the need to understand not only global patterns of urbanization, but also the situated, idiosyncratic characteristics within each city and region in the world. The Phenology Clock advocates for such a sensibility because the data presented within can be specific to individual cities, although it has broader global implications for understanding climate change.

Design in the Anthropocene

Critiquing these particular designs helps us to ground the theoretical concepts that we have explored in order to highlight possible ecological interventions. Big Cat Tracking presents us with an example of how data collection tools are used to study animals; in turn, this data can be used to support cohabitation as evidenced by the emergence of Wildlife Crossings. The creation of the Wildlife Crossing, as something that employs natural elements, has proven to be significantly more effective than other animal bridges that simply emulate human bridges (e.g. those made of cement and steel), as animals are less likely to cross. Informed by the concept of hybridity, and explicitly situated in the Anthropocene, we can see the Wildlife Crossing as an example that supports cohabitation because it purports to design from an animal perspective.

Similarly, in the Phenology Clock, we are able to engage with the concept of natureculture in a way that grounds the theory in a functional design. This design captures information that is vital to designing spaces of cohabitation, but it does more than simply capture and present data; it also engages information in a way that challenges typical presentation of global change phenomena. Our engagement with these designs in combination with key concepts from the Anthropocene are likely to lead to more appropriate design solutions in the future because they promote a non-human centered approach, and we can see concrete takeaways informed by notions such as naturecultures and hybridity. Big Cat Tracking and the Phenology Clock are unique in their approaches towards animal technology. The Big Cat Tracking Initiative is one example of a larger class of projects related to data tracking, while the Phenology Clock is a singular, more artistically-driven instance and in both of these designs, we see material trajectories for future work in developing technologies for cohabitation.

DESIGNING [WITHIN/FOR] COHABITATION

Within Urban Informatics, we see a vision of the city that has evolved from a more technology-centered hub towards a more socio-cultural conception with unique manifestations in different global cities. At the same time, we can see that research across the natural and social sciences has identified the Anthropocene as a locus for research related to global change phenomena, including climate change, mass extinction, loss of biodiversity, air and water pollution, and other concerns related to urbanization. Key concepts, such as naturecultures and hybridity, inform our understanding of the Anthropocene have been explored here with the aim of decentering the human from design and promoting new forms of urban cohabitation. If the Anthropocene brings about the *end of nature*, we can no longer think of culture and nature as separate entities, but rather as deeply entangled concepts that shape our urban experiences. Given that HCI agendas are increasingly taking responsibility for urban experiences, and given that the end of nature is shaping such experiences now, then it follows that this shift in our conception of nature is, or should be, part of HCI's concern. Cohabitation both describes the present and anticipatable future, and also is a goal—yet a goal that HCI as a field has not yet systematically pursued.

Current research in ACI has tended to focus on animals such as pets, guide dogs, and farm animals; however, if we are to extend the practices of ACI into urban informatics, we see a need to include urban wild things in this agenda. Animals of all kinds inhabit all cities around the world, even apex predators such as leopards that many of us tend not think about as urban animals. Moreover, we have seen that all different kinds of animals are needed for a healthy ecosystem, urban or otherwise. By considering big cats, we have shed light on the kinds of animals that tend to be neglected in the ACI discourse. At the same time, considering big cats can also help us to think about the overall species diversity of any major city. The existence of cougars in Los Angeles presents unique concerns for the inhabitants of that area, whereas, the presence of cougars in Boise or Denver may present other needs and opportunities for design interventions. Similarly the presence of leopards in Mumbai makes visible yet *another* set of concerns for the residents of that city. While we can see connections across world cities in the work we have presented here, more precise data captured in individual locations will reveal that animal-human interactions are idiosyncratic in each locale—shaped by the numbers and behaviors of relevant animal species, urban geographies, and human cultures. Such a conception is in-line with and contributes towards the arguments already prevalent in urban informatics that challenge the notion of "the city" as a monolithic concept.

One of the implications surfaced by the present work is an increased understanding of how global change might be addressed in the future by those who have no scientific training. Although the Anthropocene exhibits natural phenomena that is observed, measured, and studied by those in the natural sciences, we will require design sensibilities and approaches from those who have little or no scientific training at all. As shown earlier, the data gathered for the Phenology Clock was collected by ordinary citizens who tracked the plant and animal behavior in their own backyards. Similarly, the Snow Leopard Trust relies on crowd-sourced data analysis to sift through the huge amount of images collected through camera traps. In both cases, it is not only highly trained scientists who are involved in such initiatives, but anyone who is concerned with conservation and the environment. Addressing issues such as climate change and mass extinction necessitates the collaboration of all—policymakers, government officials, researchers, designers, technologists, and citizens alike—towards possible solutions. This raises important questions about how knowledge is generated and who has the capacity to contribute towards addressing climate change. The two designs we have explored in this paper reveal ways different stakeholders with varying expertise can work in concert with one another for interventions.

Designs like the Phenology Clock are useful as a way to make data accessible to anyone interested in engaging with ecological data related to the natural patterns of the earth, but through our analysis we can see that it does *more* than simply present information. It challenges basic human assumptions about time and space. The information presented in the Phenology Clock assumes the entangled nature of space in that it accounts for a multitude of species and recognizes the fact that none of these species exists on its own without the others. The Clock also promotes a time scale that may be at odds with human-defined time. One of the challenges with developing urban technologies is the fact that all the creatures in a given city don't adhere to the same structures of time, nor to the same patterns of movement. Designs like the Phenology Clock make this multiplicity visible and inspire a design approach that necessarily privileges the notion of cohabitation as a guiding characteristic of the city.

CONCLUSION

Urban informatics/urban computing has been evolving from a techno-centric vision of the city (i.e., a city with sensors) towards a physical-social-cultural assemblage. In the meantime, research in the natural sciences helps us understand the emergence of the Anthropocene—climate change, mass extinction, and the fact that cities have grown to a scale that they now encroach on what was previously considered animal habitat. Indeed, the long-held nature-culture dualism is fast collapsing. The Anthropocene has become a key concept of our time because it has captured a strong sense of urgency around what humans have done to the Earth; however, the Anthropocene, and its associated concepts and concerns, is only just beginning to be taken up into HCI.

As shown in our analysis of two design cases, the Anthropocene challenges us to rethink our conceptions around the relationship between animals and humans and the different ways in which we perceive and act in the world. Moving forward, we can build on the implications of the Anthropocene to develop design strategies that refigure human-animal relations to support cohabitation and presumably even redefine cohabitation. As the transdisciplinary research agenda around the Anthropocene continues to develop, there are opportunities for further dialogues between HCI researchers and designers interested in issues of global change, and especially those concerned with urbanization and animal-centered designs, which are also of concern to both scientific and cultural scholars of the Anthropocene.

ACI researcher Mancini (cited earlier) challenges us to shift our animal perspective and provocatively asks what would happen if we did. The Phenology Clock revealed the ways that our conceptions of time—which we think of as objective and external—are actually human-defined and human-centric. A similar distinction is made between space and place, where the one is said to be external and objective and the other is human-meaningful. Perhaps designing for cohabitation might decenter the human in our conceptions of space, helping us perceive and therefore design for new spatialities.

Purdy's reflections on Anthropocene futures leads him to conclude, "Whatever innovation brings, people will continue to shape the earth by inhabiting it, changing everything from its atmospheric cycles to its soils and habitats. It is much too late to imagine that any technology could enable humanity to 'stop disturbing' the earth. Instead, every technology will become part of the joint human-natural system in which we make and remake the world just by living here [52]." That joint human-natural system might be our greatest—and most urgent—design challenge.

REFERENCES

1. Apopo: https://www.apopo.org
2. Athreya, Vidya, Morten Odden, John DC Linnell, Jagdish Krishnaswamy, and K. Ullas Karanth. "A cat among the dogs: leopard Panthera pardus diet in a human-dominated landscape in western Maharashtra, India." *Oryx* 50, no. 01 (2016): 156-162.
3. Bai, Xuemei, Sander Van Der Leeuw, Karen O'Brien, Frans Berkhout, Frank Biermann, Eduardo S. Brondizio, Christophe Cudennec et al. "Plausible and desirable futures in the Anthropocene: a new research agenda." *Global Environmental Change* (2015).
4. Bardzell, Jeffrey, Shaowen Bardzell, and Lone Koefoed Hansen. "Immodest proposals: Research through design and knowledge." In *Proceedings of the 33rd Annual ACM Conference on Human Factors in Computing Systems*, pp. 2093-2102. ACM, 2015.
5. Bardzell, Jeffrey. "Interaction criticism: An Introduction to the Practice." *Interacting with computers* 23, no. 6 (2011): 604-621.
6. Bardzell, Shaowen. "Feminist HCI: taking stock and outlining an agenda for design." In *Proceedings of the SIGCHI Conference on Human Factors in Computing Systems*, pp. 1301-1310. ACM, 2010.
7. Bardzell, Shaowen. "Utopias of participation: design, criticality, and emancipation." In *Proceedings of the 13th Participatory Design Conference: Short Papers,*

Industry Cases, Workshop Descriptions, Doctoral Consortium papers, and Keynote abstracts-Volume 2, pp. 189-190. ACM, 2014.

8. Barrueto, Mirjam, Adam T. Ford, and Anthony P. Clevenger. "Anthropogenic effects on activity patterns of wildlife at crossing structures." *Ecosphere* 5, no. 3 (2014): 1-19.
9. Baumer, Eric PS. "Reflective informatics: conceptual dimensions for designing technologies of reflection." In *Proceedings of the 33rd Annual ACM Conference on Human Factors in Computing Systems*, pp. 585-594. ACM, 2015.
10. Braidotti, Rosi. *The Posthuman*. John Wiley & Sons, 2013.
11. Brewer, Johanna, and Paul Dourish. "Storied spaces: Cultural accounts of mobility, technology, and environmental knowing." International Journal of Human-Computer Studies 66.12 (2008): 963-976.
12. Brondizio, Eduardo S., Karen O'Brien, Xuemei Bai, Frank Biermann, Will Steffen, Frans Berkhout, Christophe Cudennec et al. "Re-conceptualizing the Anthropocene: A call for collaboration." *Global Environmental Change,* 2016.
13. Carney, Megan. The biopolitics of 'food insecurity:' towards a critical political ecology of the body in studies of women's transnational migration. *Journal of Political Ecology*. 2014;21:1-8.
14. Carrington, Damian. "The Anthropocene epoch: scientists declare dawn of human-influenced age" *The Guardian*. 20 August 2016.
15. Conniff, Richard. "Learning to Live With Leopards." *National Geographic. 2015.*
16. Cronon, William. "The Trouble with Wilderness," in Uncommon Ground: Rethinking the Human Place in Nature. Ed. William Cronon. W.W. Norton, New York. 1995. p. 80.
17. Crutzen, Paul J. "Geology of Mankind." *Nature* 415, no. 6867 (2002): 23-23.
18. DiSalvo, Carl and Jonathan Lukens, "Nonathropocentrism and the Nonhuman in Design: Possibilities for Designing New Forms of Engagement with and through Technology," in *From Social Butterfly to Engaged Citizen: Urban Informatics, Social Media, Ubiquitous Computing, and Mobile Technology to Support Citizen Engagement,* Marcus Foth et al., eds., Cambridge, MA: MIT Press, 2011.
19. DiSalvo, Carl and Jonathan Lukens, "Seeing the City through Machines: Non-Anthropocentric Design and Youth Robotics," in *Digital Cities 6: Concepts, Methods and Systems of Urban Informat-ics,* Marcus Foth, Laura Forlano, and Hiromitsu Hattori, eds., State College: Penn State University Press, 2009.
20. Dourish, Paul. "HCI and environmental sustainability: the politics of design and the design of politics." In *Proceedings of the 8th ACM Conference on Designing Interactive Systems*, pp. 1-10. ACM, 2010.
21. Downs, Joni, Mark Horner, Rebecca Loraamm, James Anderson, Hyun Kim, and Dave Onorato. "Strategically locating wildlife crossing structures for Florida panthers using maximal covering approaches." *Transactions in GIS*18, no. 1 (2014)
22. Engels, Svenja, Nils-Lasse Schneider, Nele Lefeldt, Christine Maira Hein, Manuela Zapka, Andreas Michalik, Dana Elbers, Achim Kittel, P. J. Hore, and Henrik Mouritsen. "Anthropogenic electromagnetic noise disrupts magnetic compass orientation in a migratory bird." *Nature* 509, no. 7500 (2014): 353-356.
23. Giaccardi, Elisa, Nazli Cila, Chris Speed, and Melissa Caldwell. "Thing Ethnography: Doing Design Research with Non-Humans." In *Proceedings of the 2016 ACM Conference on Designing Interactive Systems*, pp. 377-387. ACM, 2016.
24. Forlano, Laura. "Decentering the Human in the Design of Collaborative Cities." *Design Issues* 32, no. 3 (2016): 42-54.
25. Foth, Marcus, Jaz Hee-jeong Choi, and Christine Satchell. "Urban Informatics." In *Proceedings of the ACM 2011 conference on Computer supported cooperative work*, pp. 1-8. ACM, 2011.
26. Hamilton, Clive, Christophe Bonneuil, and François Gemenne. "Thinking the Anthropocene." *The Anthropocene and the Global Environmental Crisis*(2015): 1-14.
27. Haraway, Donna Jeanne. *The companion species manifesto: Dogs, people, and significant otherness*. Vol. 1. Chicago: Prickly Paradigm Press, 2003.
28. Haraway, Donna. "Anthropocene, Capitalocene, Plantationocene, Chthulucene: Making Kin" in *Environmental Humanities*, vol 6, 2015, pp. 159-165.
29. Hayles, N. Katherine. *How we became posthuman: Virtual bodies in cybernetics, literature, and informatics*. University of Chicago Press, 2008.
30. Hinchliffe, Steve, Matthew B. Kearnes, Monica Degen, and Sarah Whatmore. "Urban Wild Things: A Cosmopolitical Experiment." *Environment and planning D: Society and Space* 23, no. 5 (2005): 643-658.
31. Ingold Tim. *The perception of the environment: essays on livelihood, dwelling and skill.* Psychology Press; 2000. p. 51.
32. Jenkins, Tom, Christopher A. Le Dantec, Carl DiSalvo, Thomas Lodato, and Mariam Asad. "Object-Oriented Publics." In *Proceedings of the 2016 CHI Conference on Human Factors in Computing Systems*, pp. 827-839. ACM, 2016.

33. Jeremijenko, Natalie. "Creative Agency and the Space Race of the 21st Century: Towards a Museum of Natural Futures." In *Proceedings of the 2016 ACM Conference on Designing Interactive Systems*, pp. 3-4. ACM, 2016.
34. Johnson, Rose. "Using technology to reveal the politics of the built environment." Proceedings of the 2013 ACM conference on Pervasive and ubiquitous computing adjunct publication. ACM, 2013.
35. Jönsson, Li, and Tau Ulv Lenskjold. "A Foray Into Not-Quite Companion Species: Design Experiments With Urban-Animals as Significant Others." *Artifact* 3, no. 2 (2014): 7-1.
36. Kirksey, Stefan, and Stefan Helmreich. "The emergence of multispecies ethnography." *Cultural anthropology* 25, no. 4 (2010): 545-576.
37. Kohn, Eduardo. *How forests think: Toward an Anthropology Beyond the Human*. Univ of California Press, 2013.
38. Latimer, Joanna, and Mara Miele. "Naturecultures? Science, Affect and the Non-human." *Theory, Culture & Society*, 2013.
39. Lister, Nina-Marie, Marta Brocki, and Robert Ament. "Integrated adaptive design for wildlife movement under climate change." *Frontiers in Ecology and the Environment* 13, no. 9 (2015): 493-502.
40. Lorimer, Jamie. *Wildlife in the Anthropocene*. University of Minnesota Press, 2015.
41. Lyle, Peter, Jaz Hee-jeong Choi, and Marcus Foth. "Growing food in the city: design ideations for urban residential gardeners." In *Proceedings of the 7th International Conference on Communities and Technologies*, pp. 89-97. ACM, 2015.
42. Mancini, Clara, Janet van der Linden, Jon Bryan, and Andrew Stuart. "Exploring Interspecies Sensemaking: Dog Tracking Semiotics and Multispecies Ethnography." In Proceedings of the 2012 ACM Conference on Ubiquitous Computing, pp. 143-152. ACM, 2012.
43. Mancini, Clara. "Animal-computer interaction (ACI): changing perspective on HCI, participation and sustainability." In *CHI'13 Extended Abstracts on Human Factors in Computing Systems*, pp. 2227-2236. ACM, 2013.
44. Mancini, Clara. "Animal-Computer Interaction: A Manifesto." *Interactions* 18.4 (2011): 69-73.
45. Nuzzle: http://hellonuzzle.com
46. Palsson G, Szerszynski B, Sörlin S, Marks J, Avril B, Crumley C, Hackmann H, Holm P, Ingram J, Kirman A, Buendía MP. "Reconceptualizing the 'Anthropos' in the Anthropocene: Integrating the social sciences and humanities in global environmental change research" *in Environmental Science & Policy*. 2013
47. Paw Tracker: https://www.thepawtracker.com
48. PetPace: http://petpace.com
49. Phenology Clock: Design and concept by Natalie Jeremijenko, Jake M Richardson, Tega Brain, & Blacki Li Rudi Migliozzi http://environmentalhealthclinic.net/phenologics
50. Philo, Chris. "Animals, geography, and the city: Notes on inclusions and exclusions." *Environment and planning D: Society and space* 13, no. 6 (1995): 655-681.
51. Posti, Maaret, Johannes Schöning, and Jonna Häkkilä. "Unexpected journeys with the HOBBIT: the design and evaluation of an asocial hiking app." In *Proceedings of the 2014 conference on Designing interactive systems*, pp. 637-646. ACM, 2014.
52. Purdy, Jedediah. *After nature: a politics for the Anthropocene*. Harvard University Press, 2015.
53. Ratto, Matt. "Making at the end of nature." *interactions* 23, no. 5 (2016): 26-35.
54. Robobees: http://robobees.seas.harvard.edu
55. Snow Leopard Trust: http://www.snowleopard.org
56. Tomlinson, Bill, Eli Blevis, Bonnie Nardi, Donald J. Patterson, M. Silberman, and Yue Pan. "Collapse informatics and practice: Theory, method, and design." *ACM Transactions on Computer-Human Interaction (TOCHI)* 20, no. 4 (2013): 24.
57. Verbeek, Peter-Paul. *What things do: Philosophical reflections on technology, agency, and design*. Penn State Press, 2010.
58. Wildlife Crossing Photo: CC by Maggie Tacheny
59. Williams, Amanda, Erica Robles, and Paul Dourish. "Urbane-ing the city: Examining and refining the assumptions behind urban informatics."*Handbook of research on urban informatics: The practice and promise of the real-time city* (2009): 1-20.
60. Ylipulli, Johanna, Anna Luusua, Hannu Kukka, and Timo Ojala. "Winter is coming: Introducing climate sensitive urban computing." In *Proceedings of the 2014 conference on Designing interactive systems*, pp. 647-656. ACM, 2014.
61. Zheng, Yu, et al. "Urban computing: concepts, methodologies, and applications." ACM Transactions on Intelligent Systems and Technology (TIST) 5.3 (2014): 38.

Stranger Searching in a Strange Land: The Impact of Familiarity on Local Search

Isaac Johnson
Northwestern University
Evanston, USA
isaacj@u.northwestern.edu

Victoria Schwanda Sosik
Google, Inc.
Mountain View, USA
victoriasosik@google.com

Kacey Ballard
Google, Inc.
Mountain View, USA
kaceyballard@google.com

ABSTRACT
Local search entails looking for places, such as restaurants or hotels, in a geographically-constrained region. Within local search, it has been observed that an individual's familiarity with their environment (i.e. how well they know the area in a query of the form "{places} in {area}") impacts which places they are most interested in visiting. Less well-understood though is how people's information preferences differ during 1) different phases of the search process and 2) based on their level of familiarity. Through a series of surveys in the domain of dining, we explore how familiarity moderates what level of information is useful to an individual about restaurant location when choosing a place to visit. We further examine how these preferences vary between regions and phases of local search (deciding on a restaurant or determining how to go). We contribute an understanding of people's information preferences during search, building on prior research of how offline context impacts online needs.

Author Keywords
Local search; dining; familiarity; localization.

ACM Classification Keywords
H.5.m. Information interfaces and presentation (e.g., HCI): Miscellaneous;

INTRODUCTION
Though exact numbers vary, local search queries (e.g., "restaurants near me") comprise a large proportion of search volume at major search engines [15,17]. For queries such as "restaurants near me", it has been shown that whether an individual is interested in going to a quick chain restaurant or a bustling, well-known place that serves a local specialty is mediated by characteristics such as the individual's familiarity with the area in which they are searching for restaurants [6,12]. Familiarity also has been shown to mediate the aspects of an area (e.g., parks, streets, neighborhoods) that an individual can recall [2].

CHI 2017, May 06-11, 2017, Denver, CO, USA
ACM 978-1-4503-4655-9/17/05.
http://dx.doi.org/10.1145/3025453.3025705

Missing from our understanding of how familiarity impacts local search though is *how the varying needs and recall patterns of users with different levels of familiarity translate into different information preferences.* We focus on the domain of dining and conduct a series of surveys that explore an important information need in local search, the restaurant's location. For example, while specific, actionable information like the address of a restaurant might be most useful to a long-term resident who already knows the area, a restaurant's proximity to a well-known park might be more useful to an unfamiliar individual despite the lack of information that it provides about the specific location.

Because there are multiple phases to local search with different goals [5,8], we also examine how the type of information needed regarding a restaurant's location varies between two phases of local search: 1) deciding upon a restaurant, and, 2) determining how to get to a restaurant. Finally, we target our surveys at seven different cities because it is known that there are regional differences in how people orient themselves [11].

In summary, we focus on two primary research questions:

- **RQ1:** How does an individual's familiarity with an area impacts their information preferences regarding a restaurant's location?
- **RQ2:** How does the phase of local search impact these information preferences?

FAMILIARITY AND LOCAL SEARCH
Local search online covers a wide variety of topics [17] and is impacted by many characteristics of individuals and their offline context [1,12,14,15]. There can be multiple phases to this decision-making process online [8], individuals can have very different needs [5], and, in many cases, the decision-making process is followed by a visit to the place that is found [15].

An individual's familiarity with the area is known to be highly important not just in local search but in general for how one relates to the places around them. Wu et al. [13] showed that the salient landmarks to an individual in an area differ greatly depending on that individual's familiarity with the area. Locals (i.e. presumed high familiarity) tend to focus on restaurants and places that are associated with more daily

Q1: Have you heard of The Feisty Lamb restaurant in Portland, OR? [Single-response]

- Yes, and I have been there
- Yes, but I have never been there
- No

Q2: Each answer below accurately describes the location of The Feisty Lamb in different terms. Which is most useful in determining whether you **would want to go**? [Single-response]

- At W Burnside St and SW King Ave [Cross-streets]
- 0.4 miles from Providence Park MAX Station [Transit Station]
- Near Washington Park [Landmark, Area-based]
- 2174 W Burnside St [Address]
- In Goose Hollow [Neighborhood]
- 0.8 miles from the Portland Japanese Garden [Landmark, Point-based]
- Other [open-text]

Q3: Why was that description the most useful? [Open-ended]

Q4: How many times have you been to the **Goose Hollow** neighborhood in Portland, OR? [Single-response]

- Never
- Once or twice
- Several times
- Many times
- Other [open-text]

Figure 1. Example survey questions. Details in brackets are for annotation and were not in the actual survey. Q2 answers randomly ordered. Q1, Q4 randomly reversed.

needs while non-locals (i.e. presumed lower familiarity) focus on tourist attractions and shopping areas. Bentley et al. [2] found that the aspects of cities that a person can recall vary based on their familiarity, with long-term residents mentioning neighborhoods while tourists tended to focus on landmarks. Salimian et al. [9] found that more familiar individuals explored larger areas in a map-based news visualization while less familiar individuals zoomed into the few areas that they knew.

Furthermore, we see different patterns in the search and visit behavior of locals as compared to non-locals. White and Buscher [12] examined Microsoft Bing logs and found that locals tend to reserve tables at higher-rated restaurants and have different cuisine preferences from non-locals. Han and Yamana [6] found in an analysis of Foursquare check-ins that individuals with high familiarity tend towards less popular restaurants and "slower" food while low-familiarity individuals tended towards trendier restaurants and chains.

LOCATION INFORMATION SURVEY

We developed a survey to determine whether there are differences in what types of location context (e.g., street address, proximity to a landmark, neighborhood) are useful to an individual based upon their familiarity with an area. We built 14 variants of this survey to cover seven cities and two contexts for each city as described below. We focus on the domain of restaurants, a common domain in which to study local search [e.g., 7,12] that comprises a significant proportion of local search volume [16].

Each survey followed the same basic structure (see Figure 1 for an example). The respondent was shown a restaurant and asked whether they had heard of the restaurant and had ever been. They then selected which of six location descriptions (or in two cases, seven, when the restaurant was contained in a named building) was most useful to them. Respondents then described in an open-text field why they had selected that location option to provide insight into what information needs their choice fulfilled. Finally, they were asked how many times they had visited the neighborhood in which the restaurant was located to estimate their familiarity with that area.

We localized the survey to seven cities (one restaurant per city) across four countries and distributed it to Android mobile users through the Google Consumer Survey (GCS) platform because GCS provides the ability to easily target a survey at different regions in a variety of countries (e.g., individual states within the United States). We deployed local language surveys in Washington, DC, Portland, OR, Chicago, IL, Manhattan, NY, London, UK, Tokyo, Japan, and Brasília, Brazil. We also varied the intent, providing them either with the task of *deciding whether they would want to go to a restaurant* or *determining how to get to a restaurant*. These two intents correspond with a decision-making phase (i.e. "Decide", similar to informational queries [3]) and action phase (i.e. "Go", similar to transactional queries [3]) in local search. The GCS platform has been shown to provide representative sample populations comparable to large-scale survey panels [10]. Each survey received approximately 100 responses for a total of 1405 respondents (respondents were given only one survey each).

Restaurants were chosen by searching "restaurants in <city>" on Google and selecting a result that was near a few landmarks but was neither overly expensive nor a large chain. Attempts were made to choose restaurants in neighborhoods that were also not the most touristy or visited neighborhoods in the city, though some degree of arbitrariness was unavoidable.

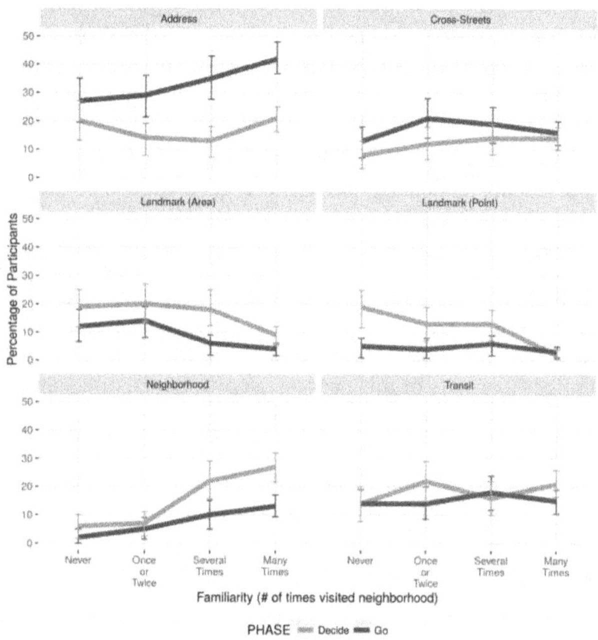

Figure 2. Percentage of respondents who selected each location text option (with 95% CI for proportions), sliced by familiarity and search phase. If the two lines in a graph do not intersect, phase likely is important. A monotonic trend indicates that familiarity likely is important.

The types of location strings shown as options in the survey have all been observed as important in prior research or are found in common restaurant search apps. We used the address (e.g., Google Search, Yelp, [4]), cross-streets (e.g., Yelp, Foursquare, [4]), proximity to a larger transit station (e.g., TripAdvisor), proximity to a landmark such as a park (i.e. POI that is a large area) [11], proximity to a landmark such as a building (i.e. POI that is a point) [11], and neighborhood (e.g., Yelp, Zomato).

Survey Analysis

We first examine broad trends from the survey. We then model each type of location response with logistic regression to determine which factors actually have a significant effect on selection of location text response after controlling for region and demographic factors. We run a regression for each location text option (e.g. Address) where each model includes the following independent variables: neighborhood familiarity (ordinal variable), search phase (binary variable), city (nominal), gender (binary), age (ordinal), and population density (ordinal). Wald's test is used to test for significance of ordinal variables. Finally, one researcher used an open-coding procedure to identify key themes from the open-ended text responses to better understand what information needs the selected location text options fulfilled.

The GCS platform estimates demographics based on respondents' browsing histories, and we find a good balance in age, gender, and income of respondents across all surveys. We see respondents skew towards being familiar with the restaurants' neighborhoods, with the following distribution: 18% (*Never*), 19%, 21%, and 41% (*Many Times*). Respondents most often had never heard of the specific restaurant (69%), while 22% had heard of it and 9% had been there.

RESULTS AND DISCUSSION

Several trends are apparent when examining Figure 2, which depicts the percentage of respondents across all cities who selected each type of location text when sliced by search phase and familiarity. Overall, respondents vary greatly in which type of location text is preferable. The importance of familiarity can be judged by examining whether the percentage of respondents who selected an option changes monotonically as familiarity increases on the X-axis from "*Never*" to "*Many times*". The importance of search phase can be judged by examining whether the type of location text is consistently preferred in one phase over another (i.e. there is a complete gap between the two lines in a graph).

Impact of Familiarity

For both types of landmarks, increased familiarity corresponds with decreased preference by respondents. This is verified by the logistic regressions, which show that an increase in neighborhood familiarity (e.g., from "*Never*" visited to visited "*Once or twice*") decreases the odds of a respondent selecting a landmark as the most useful description by 30% ($p<0.01$). Inversely, with neighborhoods, increased familiarity leads to an increased preference for this type of location information (66% increase in odds with each step up in familiarity, $p<0.001$). Address, cross-streets, and transit stations all have mixed responses to increased familiarity in the graphs.

The tendency for landmarks to be favored by low-familiarity individuals is also supported by the open-text responses. We see that lower familiarity respondents, despite never or rarely having visited the neighborhood, often mention being familiar with the landmark. Responses like "*Landmark everyone is familiar with*" and "*Near tourist site im familiar with*" indicate that landmarks can provide context even to those who have not visited the area. Unfamiliar respondents also often spoke about the opportunity to pair the landmark with eating out (e.g., "*Because the museum is somewhere I would visit and its nice to know what is close*"). Equally common among all respondents was viewing the landmark not just as a chance for additional activities but as a reference point for the restaurant's location (e.g., "*I know the museum and gives me an indication of where the location is*").

Among those who chose the neighborhood, familiar respondents often mention the additional context the neighborhood provides (e.g., "*Because it gives an indication of the character of the restaurant as well as a description of the location*") and that neighborhoods matched up with their mental map of the city (e.g., "*I live in DC and neighborhoods are the most useful geographic marker for me*"). References to mental maps were also made by familiar individuals for transit stations (predominantly in London, which we return to later) and the road network.

These results also provide evidence that the differences in recall [2,13] and needs [5] between individuals of varying familiarity do translate into different preferences for what information is presented.

Impact of Search Phase

For addresses, user preference is consistently higher in the *Go* phase as opposed to the *Decide* phase (per regression, odds of selecting address are 183% higher, p<0.001). Cross-streets follow a similar pattern, but the effect is smaller (odds increase by 46%, p<0.05). Both types of landmarks as well as neighborhoods are preferred in the *Decide* phase (for each, odds of selecting them in the *Go* phase is 60% less likely, p<0.001). Transit is not clearly preferred in either phase.

Examining the open-text responses provides insight as to why these trends emerge. For address and cross-streets, a large proportion of respondents mention that they are precise or clear descriptions and could be used to get directions (e.g., "*Specific and can put it into GPS*"). Respondents who selected cross-streets also note that this information allows them to picture where the restaurant is whereas the address itself meant little to them (e.g., "*Those are two streets that I recognized. I do not have any clue where it is if you give me the number.*"). For individuals who chose the neighborhood or landmarks, they often mention that this provides context about the area in which the restaurant is located (e.g., "*Because I know what it's by*"), which would be more useful when deciding whether to go to that particular restaurant.

It would seem surprising that the usefulness of transit stations is not considerably higher in the *Go* phase. Some respondents mentioned that their mental map of the city corresponded with the transit station (e.g., "*I use tube stops to orientate myself*"), or that the transit stations acted as reference points to figure out the area in which the restaurant is (e.g., "*Distance and known landmark*"). More common though was some mention of the transit stations as being useful for deciding whether it would be easy to get to the restaurant and therefore they would like to go (e.g., "*I knew how easy it would be to get there + more less where it is*"). As such, transit stations can be used as reference points in different ways, some that support getting to a place, and some that support deciding whether to go there.

In the *Decide* version of the Manhattan survey, 29% of respondents selected "*Near Central Park*" despite the fact that this description could refer to a very large area of the city. An additional 10% of respondents selected "*In the Upper West Side*", which is a neighborhood that stretches 51 blocks north-to-south. This illustrates that for many people, it is not the specific location but the surrounding area that is the primary information need when deciding on whether to go to a particular restaurant. When an initial choice has been made though and an individual is determining how they might actually get to the restaurant, their information needs change from broader, contextual information to specific details about the location upon which they can act.

Localization

Though our survey results cannot support robust conclusions about how information needs vary by city, they do offer some insight into how large the differences can be. For instance, with transit stations, 41% of Tokyo respondents chose the transit station followed by London at 28% and Washington, DC, at 20%. Large city effects are also seen for cross-streets, where 33% of respondents in the Manhattan survey chose them, while Portland was next highest at 19%. Other studies have also seen city-specific effects on what is considered important by people when they navigate their city (e.g., [11]). This suggests that future work should continue to explore how the structure of cities can impact people's information needs throughout the local search process.

LIMITATIONS AND FUTURE WORK

Respondents' familiarity was observed and correlates with residency and demographics. Further research could directly manipulate an individual's familiarity to better isolate the effects of familiarity. Because this was a survey, the tasks are contrived and lack some of the context and motivation usually part of local search.

Future work could explore other types of context about a restaurant's location that would best support varying information needs in local search. Other user contexts (e.g., size-of-group) and common aspects of the local search experience (e.g., types of photos, important aspects of reviews) could also be explored.

CONCLUSION

In summary, through a series of surveys, we examined how familiarity moderates information preferences regarding restaurant's location in local search. We found that while all individuals are looking for location descriptions that they recognize, familiar individuals tend to prefer references to the area (e.g., neighborhood name) whereas unfamiliar individuals tend towards landmarks that are recognizable and also provide ideas of other activities in the area. We also demonstrated that the phase of local search matters greatly, with broader information being important when deciding on a restaurant but specific information such as the address or cross-streets being the most helpful for deciding how to get to the restaurant. These findings suggest that information preferences of individuals during local search vary depending on their familiarity with the area and intent.

ACKNOWLEDGMENTS

We would like to thank our reviewers for their valuable feedback. I also would like to thank Google and the Local Search team for the internship opportunity.

REFERENCES

1. Linas Baltrunas, Bernd Ludwig, Stefan Peer, and Francesco Ricci. 2012. Context relevance assessment and exploitation in mobile recommender systems. *Personal and Ubiquitous Computing* 16, 5: 507–526.
2. Frank Bentley, Henriette Cramer, William Hamilton, and Santosh Basapur. 2012. Drawing the city: differing perceptions of the urban environment. In *Proceedings of the SIGCHI Conference on Human Factors in Computing Systems*, 1603–1606.
3. Andrei Broder. 2002. A taxonomy of web search. In *ACM SIGIR forum*, 3–10.
4. Jaewoo Chung and Chris Schmandt. 2009. Going my way: a user-aware route planner. In *Proceedings of the SIGCHI Conference on Human Factors in Computing Systems*, 1899–1902.
5. Karen Church and Henriette Cramer. 2015. Understanding Requirements of Place in Local Search. 1857–1862. https://doi.org/10.1145/2702613.2732871
6. Jungkyu Han and Hayato Yamana. 2015. Why people go to unfamiliar areas?: analysis of mobility pattern based on users' familiarity. In *Proceedings of the 17th International Conference on Information Integration and Web-based Applications & Services*, 28.
7. Jon Pearce, Shanton Chang, Basil Alzougool, Gregor Kennedy, Mary Ainley, and Susan Rodrigues. 2011. Search or explore: do you know what you're looking for? In *Proceedings of the 23rd Australian Computer-Human Interaction Conference*, 253–256.
8. Jens Riegelsberger, Michelle Lee, and Scott Lederer. 2012. A room with a view: understanding users' stages in picking a hotel online. In *CHI'12 Extended Abstracts on Human Factors in Computing Systems*, 713–716.
9. Mohamad H. Salimian, Stephen Brooks, and Derek Reilly. 2013. Examining the impact of regional familiarity and design characteristics on use of a map-based news visualization. 24–29. https://doi.org/10.1145/2534931.2534943
10. Victoria Schwanda-Sosik, Elie Bursztein, Sunny Consolvo, David A. Huffaker, Gueorgi Kossinets, Kerwell Liao, Paul McDonald, and Aaron Sedley. 2014. Online microsurveys for user experience research. 889–892. https://doi.org/10.1145/2559206.2559975
11. Fernando Torre, Yanjie Liu, Zhengjie Liu, and Loren G. Terveen. 2013. Local Knowledge Matters for Crowdsourcing Systems: Experience from Transferring an American Site to China. In *ICWSM*.
12. Ryen White and Georg Buscher. 2012. Characterizing local interests and local knowledge. In *Proceedings of the SIGCHI Conference on Human Factors in Computing Systems*, 1607–1610.
13. Shaomei Wu, Shenwei Liu, Dan Cosley, and Michael Macy. 2011. Mining collective local knowledge from google mymaps. In *Proceedings of the 20th international conference companion on World wide web*, 151–152.
14. Jeonghee Yi, Farzin Maghoul, and Jan Pedersen. 2008. Deciphering mobile search patterns: a study of yahoo! mobile search queries. In *Proceedings of the 17th international conference on World Wide Web*, 257–266.
15. 2014. Understanding Consumers' Local Search Behavior. *Think with Google*. Retrieved from https://www.thinkwithgoogle.com/research-studies/how-advertisers-can-extend-their-relevance-with-search.html
16. 2015. I-Want-to-Go Moments: From Search to Store. *Think with Google*. Retrieved from https://www.thinkwithgoogle.com/articles/i-want-to-go-micro-moments.html
17. 2016. How to Build Your Mobile-Centric Search Strategy. *Think with Google*. Retrieved from https://www.thinkwithgoogle.com/articles/build-your-mobile-centric-search-strategy.html

Ambiotherm: Enhancing Sense of Presence in Virtual Reality by Simulating Real-World Environmental Conditions

Nimesha Ranasinghe[1], **Pravar Jain**[1], **Shienny Karwita**[1], **David Tolley**[1], **Ellen Yi-Luen Do**[1,2]
Keio-NUS CUTE Center, Interactive & Digital Media Institute, National University of Singapore[1]
School of Industrial Design & School of Interactive Computing, Georgia Institute of Technology[2]
{nimesha, pravar, shienny, dtolley, ellendo}@nus.edu.sg, ellendo@gatech.edu

ABSTRACT
In this paper, we present and evaluate Ambiotherm, a wearable accessory for Head Mounted Displays (HMD) that provides thermal and wind stimuli to simulate real-world environmental conditions, such as ambient temperatures and wind conditions, to enhance the sense of presence in Virtual Reality (VR). Ambiotherm consists of a Ambient Temperature Module that is attached to the user's neck, a Wind Simulation Module focused towards the user's face, and a Control Module utilizing Bluetooth communication. We demonstrate Ambiotherm with two VR environments, a hot desert, and a snowy mountain, to showcase the different types of simulated environmental conditions. We conduct several studies to 1) address design factors of the system and 2) evaluate Ambiotherm's effect on factors related to a user's sense of presence. Our findings show that the addition of wind and thermal stimuli significantly improves sensory and realism factors, contributing towards an enhanced sense of presence when compared to traditional VR experiences.

ACM Classification Keywords
H.5.1. Information Interfaces and Presentation (e.g. HCI): Multimedia Information Systems: Artificial, augmented, and virtual realities

Author Keywords
Presence; Ambient Temperature; Virtual Wind; Virtual Reality; Multimodal Interaction

INTRODUCTION
Simulating environmental conditions by utilizing multisensory stimuli is essential to providing sensory-rich experiences and enhancing immersion in Virtual Reality (VR). However, despite ongoing research and development, the majority of existing VR systems utilize interfaces that do not provide users with multisensory feedback that accurately mirrors their experiences of environmental conditions in the real-world. This lack of additional environmental feedback restricts potential

CHI 2017, May 06-11, 2017, Denver, CO, USA
© 2017 ACM. ISBN 978-1-4503-4655-9/17/05...$15.00
DOI: http://dx.doi.org/10.1145/3025453.3025723

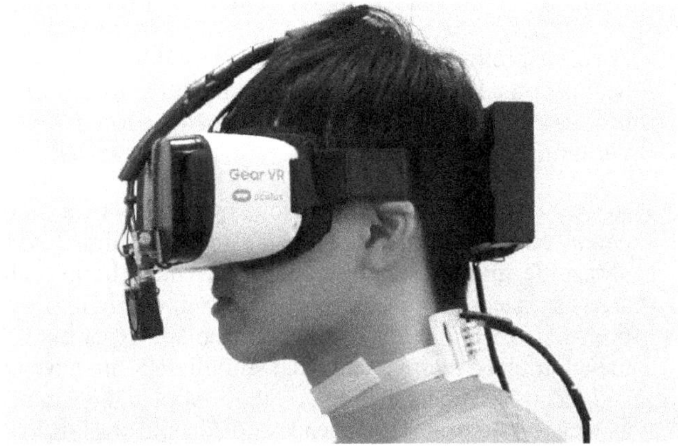

Figure 1. A participant is using the Ambiotherm system with a Samsung™ Gear VR HMD. The control module is attached behind the neck.

immersive features which, in turn, can have severely negative effects on a user's sense of presence within a VR experience and their ability to interact with respective virtual environments [40]. Although the inclusion of visual and auditory stimuli is key to providing users with an enhanced sense of immersion and presence in VR experiences, there are many other forms of multisensory stimuli whose capabilities for conveying environmental factors are yet to be as thoroughly investigated in the same context.

For example, several research works in human-environment psychology have suggested that both thermal and wind stimuli can have strong impacts on the way in which people perceive their environmental surroundings [2, 3, 23, 36]. Whilst there has been a relatively limited amount of research performed regarding the utilization of thermal and wind feedback, existing studies have suggested that the inclusion of these stimuli within VR applications can provide users with an enhanced sense of presence by enabling greater multisensory engagement and increasing users' perceived immersion and involvement within VR experiences [17, 34]. In addition to these beneficial capabilities, several studies have also highlighted that thermal and wind stimuli can be used as a tool to increase a user's performance during location, orientation and memory-based tasks in VR [8, 9].

In this paper, we present Ambiotherm: a novel accessory for existing VR Head Mounted Displays (HMDs) that incorporates both thermal and wind stimuli into traditional VR experiences. Ambiotherm is a wearable solution that aims to increase users' sense of immersion and presence in VR experiences by simulating real-world environmental conditions such as ambient temperatures and wind patterns. To achieve this functionality, as shown in Figure 1, the system is equipped with 1) an Ambient Temperature Simulation Module that utilizes Peltier elements to provide heating and cooling sensations (worn on the neck) and 2) a Wind Simulation Module that utilizes multidirectional fans focused towards the user's face.

In summary, the main contributions of this paper are:

- A proof-of-concept prototype of Ambiotherm that provides thermal and wind stimuli, enabling the simulation of real-world environmental conditions within VR experiences.
- A set of preliminary studies that are used to address key design considerations made prior to the implementation of the system. Here, aspects including the location, intensity, duration and relative comfort of stimuli are analyzed.
- A user evaluation that compares key aspects of a user's perceived sense of presence when using a traditional HMD alongside multiple configurations of Ambiotherm. This study suggests that 1) Ambiotherm significantly improves both sensory and realism factors of the VR experience, 2) the addition of thermal and wind stimuli does not have any significant detrimental effects on the control and distraction aspects of the user's experience and 3) wind stimuli, comparative to thermal stimuli, are more easily identified and perceived as realistic environmental sensations.

BACKGROUND AND RELATED WORK

Interdisciplinary by nature, Ambiotherm draws on concepts from several fields including VR, telepresence, and human thermoception. In this section, we first define the meaning of presence in VR and the ways in which this can be enhanced through multisensory stimuli. Following this, we provide a review of related thermal and wind stimuli research to highlight the key capabilities and limitations of existing simulation methods for environmental conditions.

Enhancing Presence in VR

Witmer and Singer [40] define presence as the experience of being in one place or environment, even when one is physically situated in another. In terms of VR, sense of presence occurs when experiencing a computer generated environment as opposed to the physical real-world environment that it represents. As expressed by Sheridan [34], presence is an extremely subjective sensation. Due to the fact that presence in VR is dependent on both the physical interface and the user's individual experience [17], it cannot be easily measured through objective definitions.

Improving a user's sense of presence in VR is an inherently challenging issue due to the multiple factors that can affect a user's perception during a VR experience. In related literature, it is noted that aspects such as the immediacy and mode of control, the presentation and consistency of multimodal information, the user's awareness of the interface device and the personal meaningfulness of the VR experience [11, 17, 25, 34] may have a notable impact on a user's sense of presence.

However, one concept that is consistently predominant in related research is that, in order to achieve an optimum sense of presence in VR, a user must be provided with a broad and coherent range of multisensory stimuli [11, 25, 40]. As described in [37], this is due to the fact that the human perceptual system has been trained for the perception of real-world multisensory stimuli through the process of evolution and that it is crucial to appeal to these perceptual mechanisms. With regards to generating a perceived sense of presence based on multisensory stimuli, both Witmer and Singer [40] and McGreevy [25] share similar arguments in that presence depends on the ability to focus on one meaningful VR stimulus set, where the experience of presence is based on attention to the continuities, connectedness and coherence of the stimulus flow.

Studies in Thermal and Wind Stimulation

In 2009, Gooch [13] developed and tested a device that was able to significantly increase feelings of social presence through thermal feedback. In 2010 Iwasaki [20] et al. constructed a prototype system that uses galvanic skin response (GSR) measurements to detect one user's emotional state and then displays this information to another user via temperature changes on the back panel of a mobile handset. Similarly, Lee & Lim [24] discuss the prospect of using thermal feedback to display information within the context of a messaging platform, highlighting the concepts of using thermal feedback to change user's emotions. In 2015, Song et al. [35], developed a wrist-worn device that provides thermal and pressure cues for the purpose of non-visual notifications. Although pressure cues were easily recognized, thermal cues had a high recognition error rate due to latency and users' thermal sensitivity. In studies by both Hannah et al. [16] and Nakashige et al. [31], a set of visual stimuli were coupled with congruent thermal stimuli (e.g. Images of hot soup and ice cream paired with warm and cold sensations respectively), which, in certain cases, was able to enhance the emotional reactions of users.

As the majority of aforementioned studies are proofs of concept for specific applications of thermal feedback, none of these studies thoroughly investigate the mapping between thermal stimuli and corresponding changes in environmental perception and emotions experienced by the user. Studies by both Wilson et al. [39] and Salminen et al. [33] examined responses to thermal cues using methods such as gathering subjective feedback about the comfort and intensity of thermal sensations and by taking physical measurements of the user's skin conductance response (SCR). Although the findings of these studies indicate that thermal feedback may be used to evoke certain emotions, they only investigate the effects of thermal feedback as an isolated stimulus.

With respect to research on wind stimuli, the majority of existing studies have only focused on the human ability to detect wind speed and direction [1, 32], the types of wind conditions that can affect human motion [19] and the acceptability of wind conditions for human comfort in and around buildings [26]. As is the case with thermal stimuli, this field still lacks research that thoroughly assesses the effects of wind stimuli on human emotions and environmental perception.

Employment of Thermal and Wind Stimuli in VR

Despite there being limited research that explores the direct effects of thermal and wind stimuli on human environmental perceptions, continuous advances in VR technologies have generated increased interest in utilizing wind and thermal stimuli to enhance immersion in VR experiences.

One of the earliest examples of an immersive, multisensory VR system, "Sensorama Simulator" [29], featured wind, vibration and olfactory environmental feedback that was presented alongside stereoscopic film to enhance viewer's sense of presence. In 1997, Dionisio [10] created VR Thermal Kit; a system for simulating environmental thermal conditions by utilizing a set of convectors, infrared lamps and Peltier elements to influence whole-body and localized thermal sensations, respectively. Initial testing of this system suggested that a level of environmental thermal perception was achievable by relatively simple technical means.

More recently, in 2014, Hülsmann et al. [18] performed a comprehensive analysis of software and hardware requirements for simulating wind and warmth sensations for Cave Automatic Virtual Environments (CAVE). Based on this analysis, Hülsmann et al. created a three-sided CAVE system, including projectors, a camera system for user tracking, an 8.1 surround sound speaker configuration and an array of infrared lamps and fans for simulating thermal and wind sensations. Pilot studies of this system suggested that users experienced a strong sense of presence within the VR environment, although the authors recommended further studies to quantify presence and collect significant results.

With regard to the incorporation of wind stimuli in VR systems, attempts to simulate environmental wind conditions can be categorized based on the positioning of stimuli relative to the user. In systems such as WindCube [28], VR Scooter [8] and Verlinden's sailing simulator [38], arrays of static fans are positioned at different angles facing towards the user in order to simulate wind from different directions. In studies performed on these systems, participants reported an increased sense of presence when experiencing wind sensations and, in studies that measured task performance, achieved faster performance times than when performing tasks without wind stimuli. However, similarly to the VR Thermal Kit and Hülsmann's CAVE system, all these systems consist of heavy and expensive equipment that require large operational spaces.

As stated by Minakuchi [27], systems that employ arrays of static fans can suffer from stimuli latency and intensity issues based on the distance between each fan and the user. To address this issue, Cardin et al. [6] developed a head-mounted wind generation system that utilizes a set of 8 fans which are positioned in a ring and worn by the user. Although initial studies of this system suggested that participants were able to correctly detect wind direction and experienced an enhanced sense of presence, stimuli latency and the physical weight of the system were still notable issues that required further study.

Overall, the studies discussed in this section outline 1) the potential for creating more immersive multisensory experiences by simulating thermal and wind sensations as part of existing VR systems and 2) the inherent physical and performance challenges related to developing a system of this manner. By designing Ambiotherm as a wearable multisensory accessory to existing HMD devices, we aim to form a VR system that simultaneously utilizes the immersive capabilities of thermal and wind stimuli whilst countering issues experienced by these reviewed works.

STIMULI DESIGN CONSIDERATIONS

This section discusses key multisensory stimuli design considerations that were identified prior to the implementation of the prototype system. Here, notable design considerations include the delivery method, the location and intensity of thermal and wind stimuli. It should be noted that the points discussed in the following subsections focus on multisensory stimuli design and that many other design aspects such as the device's physical form were also considered during development.

Delivery Method

Similar to [12], we established a set of stimuli requirements to ensure that appropriate environmental sensations were provided within the context of Ambiotherm: 1) not pose any significant safety risks to the user, 2) be controlled in real-time to produce low-latency stimulation, 3) provide multi-directional stimulations of wind, heating, and cooling, and 4) be available in a form that does not affect the portability of the system.

Based on these requirements, Peltier elements were used to generate thermal stimulation. Unlike devices such as radiant heaters or infrared heat lamps [18], Peltier elements are well-suited to this application as they are compact lightweight components that can produce both heating and cooling sensations. As they require direct contact with the skin, Peltier elements avoid some of the thermal latency issues that affect other forms of non-direct thermal stimuli. Due to their capabilities for being controlled with low-latency, the thermal sensations produced by Peltier elements can be easily maintained within a controlled range of temperatures that are safe for contact with human skin.

Wind stimulation is achieved by incorporating two small fans into the system. Unlike air conditioning or large scale fan configurations [28, 8, 38] that are too heavy for portable applications, these compact fans can be fitted to low-power servo motors to facilitate controllable multi-directional wind stimulation. Although using pressurized air can be another low-latency alternative to using fans, incorporating pressurized air storage components into the system would have a detrimental effect on both its safety and portability.

Location, Intensity, and Comfort

Since different parts of the human body have varying levels of thermal and cutaneous wind sensitivity, selecting an appropriate location and respective intensity range for stimuli was crucial for effectively simulating environmental sensations in Ambiotherm. To elicit effective wind perception, two fans are positioned to direct wind onto the user's face, a location with a high density of sensitive somatosensory receptors [14]. Although using a larger array of fans was considered, this type of setup, as stated in [6], can add significant weight to a system and is not effective for users with long hair.

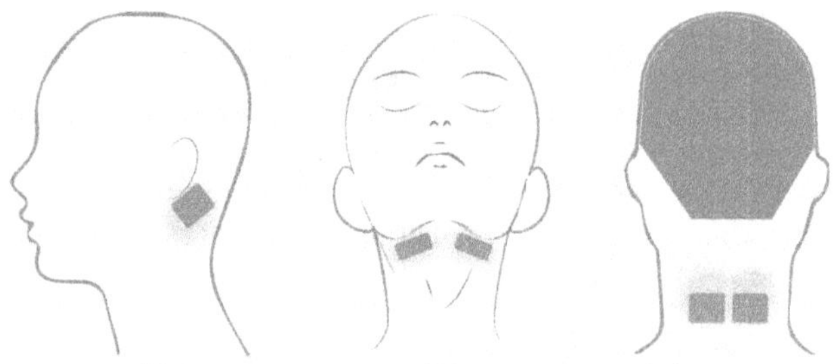

Figure 2. Different locations selected for delivering thermal stimuli: (A) Behind The Ear, (B) On The Throat, and (C) Behind The Neck.

With respect to thermoception, three of the main factors that are known to affect the human ability to detect changes in temperature are the site of stimulated skin, the amplitude of the temperature change and the rate of temperature change [22]. Based on these factors, the following studies were performed to identify the optimum locations and intensities for providing thermal stimulation via Peltier elements. The studies and their findings are discussed in the following subsections.

Selection of Location for Thermal Stimuli

Three locations: 1) Behind The Neck (BTN), 2) On The Throat (OTT) and 3) Behind The Ear (BTE), as shown in Figure 2, were chosen for the study due to their proximity to the thermoregulatory centre of the central nervous system [15]. A user experiment was conducted with 15 participants (12 males and 3 females, average age = 26.4, SD = 3.99) and they were asked to rate the different locations based on sensation of the applied thermal stimuli (HR4, HS10, CR8 and CS10 stimuli as in Table 1). These sensations were recorded on a continuous sensation scale containing intervals ranging from "very cold" to "very hot", based on an adaptation of the ASHRAE 7-point scale of thermal comfort by Arens et al. [4]. They were subsequently asked to rank the locations based on the degree of comfort. For each participant, the order of the locations was randomized. The study was conducted using Peltier elements in a room with controlled temperature (24°C) and no air circulation.

(i) Selection of Location Based on Sensation:

A repeated measures ANOVA with sphericity-assumed determined that mean sensitivity to heating at the three locations differed statistically significantly ($F_{2,118} = 38.4$, $p < 0.001$). Post hoc tests using the Bonferroni correction further revealed that BTN (M = 0.86, SD = 0.09) was significantly different to OTT (M = 0.73, SD = 0.19) ($p < 0.001$), as well as to BTE (M = 0.63, SD = 0.18) ($p < 0.001$). A significant difference was also observed between OTT and BTE ($p < 0.001$). Therefore, we concluded that BTN is most sensitive to the heating stimuli (Figure 3 (A)). Repeated measures ANOVA with sphericity-assumed determined that mean sensitivity to cooling at the three locations differed statistically significantly ($F_{2,118} = 4.68$, $p < 0.05$). Post hoc tests using the Bonferroni correction further revealed that there was no significant difference between OTT (M = 0.22, SD = 0.17) and BTE (M = 0.2, SD = 0.14) ($p > 0.05$) as well as between OTT and BTN (M = 0.28, SD = 0.20) ($p > 0.05$). However, BTE was significantly different to BTN ($p < 0.05$) with the lowest average thermal score. Therefore, we concluded that BTE was relatively more sensitive to the cooling stimuli (Figure 3 (B)).

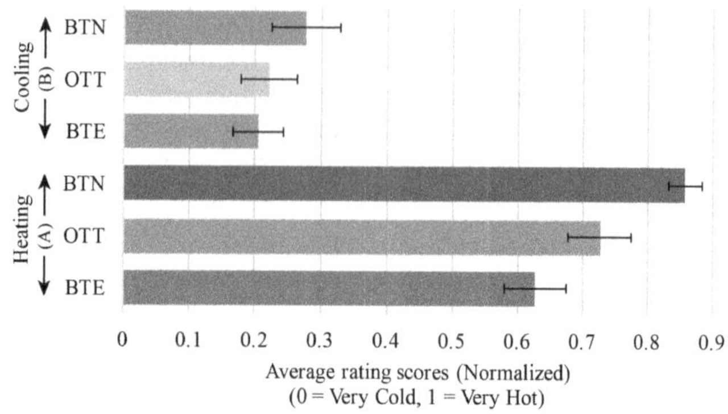

Figure 3. Normalized average rating scores: (A) heating sensation at three locations and (B) cooling sensation at three locations. (Error bars represent 95% CI, n = 15).

(ii) Selection of Location Based on Comfort:

87% of the participants selected BTN as their first preference while 13% chose BTE and 0% chose OTT. 100% of the participants who chose BTE or OTT as their first preference, listed BTN as their second preference.

Although BTN was found to be most sensitive to the heating stimuli, it was not the most sensitive to the cooling stimuli. However, BTN was still selected as the location for thermal stimulation in our system, primarily due to three reasons: 1) high levels of comfort based on participant's preference, 2) provides a perception of overall temperature change (similar to the effects of induced hypothermia [21]) and, 3) can be used to augment heat loss or heat gain whilst, at the same time, not competing with thermoregulatory needs [30]. Using this location also mirrors the effects of familiar practices, such as wearing a scarf or opening a collar to preserve or release body heat, respectively.

Selection of Thermal Stimuli

The same 15 participants were then asked to rate the different thermal stimuli applied at the BTN location based on sensation. These sensations were recorded on a continuous sensation scale containing intervals ranging from "Very Cold" to "Very Hot", based on an adaptation of the ASHRAE 7-point scale of thermal comfort by Arens et al. [4]. They were also asked to rate the different stimuli based on comfort, with a continuous comfort scale, ranging from "Very Uncomfortable" to "Very Comfortable", based on Arens et al. [4]. For each participant, the order of the thermal stimuli presented was randomized. Details of the set of thermal stimuli used are provided in Table 1. This study was also conducted using Peltier elements in a room with controlled temperature (24°C) and no air circulation.

(i) Selection of Stimuli Based on Sensation:

In order to compare the sensation scores of the four heating stimuli (HR2, HR4, HS6, and HS10), a one-way repeated measures ANOVA was conducted with sphericity-assumed. A significant difference in the sensation scores of the four heating stimuli ($F_{3,42} = 8.6$, $p < 0.001$) was observed. Post

Label	Type	Mode	Duration (seconds)	Approximate Temperature Change (°C)
HR2	Heating	Rapid	2	+2
HR4	Heating	Rapid	4	+4
HS6	Heating	Slow	6	+3
HS10	Heating	Slow	10	+5
CR4	Cooling	Rapid	4	-3
CR8	Cooling	Rapid	8	-6
CS5	Cooling	Slow	5	-2.25
CS10	Cooling	Slow	10	-4.5

Table 1. Details of the set of thermal stimuli used in the study.

hoc tests using the Bonferroni correction revealed that HR4 ($M = 0.93$, $SD = 0.08$) was significantly different to HR2 ($M = 0.8$, $SD = 0.09$) ($p < 0.005$) as well as to HS6 ($M = 0.83$, $SD = 0.08$) ($p < 0.001$). No significant difference was observed between: 1) HR4 and HS10 ($M = 0.87$, $SD = 0.1$) ($p > 0.05$), 2) HR2 and HS6 ($p > 0.05$), 3) HR2 and HS10 ($p > 0.05$) and 4) HS6 and HS10 ($p > 0.05$) (Figure 4 (A): sensation scores). Participant's comments, as well as prior studies, indicate that a rapid change in temperature can generate a sense of pain and may, in turn, affect the degree of immersion [7]. Hence, HR4 was not selected as a potential heating stimulus.

Similarly, to compare the sensation scores of the four cooling stimuli (CR4, CR8, CS5, and CS10), a one-way repeated measures ANOVA was conducted with sphericity-assumed. A significant difference in the sensation scores of the four cooling stimuli ($F_{3,42} = 5.2$, $p < 0.01$) was observed. Post hoc tests using the Bonferroni correction revealed that CR8 ($M = 0.18$, $SD = 0.21$) was significantly different to CS5 ($M = 0.37$, $SD = 0.15$) ($p < 0.05$). No significant difference was observed between: 1) CR4 ($M = 0.24$, $SD = 0.24$) and CS10 ($M = 0.32$, $SD = 0.17$) ($p > 0.05$), 2) CR4 and CS5 ($p > 0.05$), 3) CR4 and CR8 ($p > 0.05$), 4) CR8 and CS10 ($p > 0.05$) and 5) CS5 and CS10 ($p > 0.05$) (Figure 4 (B): sensation scores). Due to the aforementioned effects of pain produced by rapid temperature changes, CR8 was not selected for further analysis or as a potential cooling stimulus.

(ii) Selection of Stimuli Based on Comfort:

A one-way repeated measures ANOVA with sphericity-assumed was conducted to compare the comfort scores of the four heating stimuli (HR2, HR4, HS6, and HS10). A significant difference in the sensation scores of the four heating stimuli ($F_{3,42} = 12.68$, $p < 0.001$) was observed. Post hoc tests using the Bonferroni correction revealed that HR4 ($M = 0.29$, $SD = 0.27$) was significantly different to HR2 ($M = 0.68$, $SD = 0.2$) ($p < 0.05$) as well as to HS6 ($M = 0.6$, $SD = 0.23$) ($p < 0.05$). No significant difference was observed between: 1) HR4 and HS10 ($M = 0.52$, $SD = 0.2$) ($p > 0.05$), 2) HS6 and HS10 ($p > 0.05$), 3) HR2 and HS10 ($p > 0.05$) and 4) HS6 and HS10 ($p > 0.05$) (Figure 4 (A): comfort scores). Confirming previous findings, HR4 was found to be the most uncomfortable stimulus with the lowest average score.

Similarly, to compare the comfort scores of the four cooling stimuli (CR4, CR8, CS5, and CS10), a one-way repeated

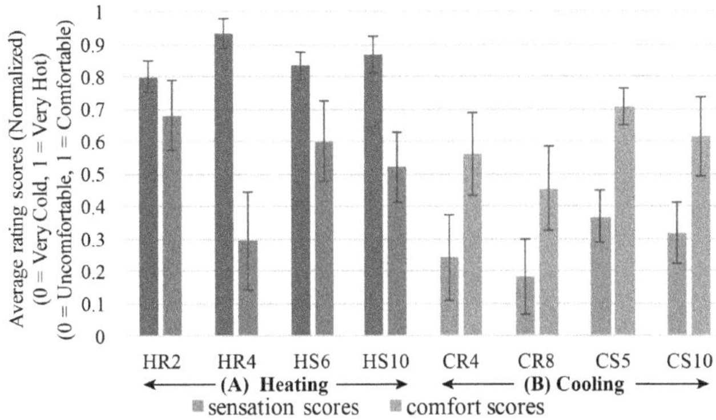

Figure 4. Normalized average sensation and comfort scores: (A) four heating stimuli and (B) four cooling stimuli. (Error bars represent 95% CI, n = 15).

measures ANOVA was conducted with sphericity-assumed. A statistically significant difference in the sensation scores of the four cooling stimuli ($F_{3,42} = 4.93$, $p < 0.01$) was observed. Post hoc tests using the Bonferroni correction revealed that CR8 ($M = 0.45$, $SD = 0.23$) was significantly different to CS5 ($M = 0.7$, $SD = 0.1$) ($p < 0.05$). No significant difference was observed between: 1) CR4 ($M = 0.56$, $SD = 0.23$) and CS10 ($M = 0.61$, $SD = 0.22$) ($p > 0.05$), 2) CR4 and CS5 ($p > 0.05$), 3) CR4 and CR8 ($p > 0.05$), 4) CR8 and CR10 ($p > 0.05$) and 5) CS5 and CS10 ($p > 0.05$) (Figure 4 (B): comfort scores). Again, confirming previous findings, CR8 was found to be the most uncomfortable stimulus with the lowest average score.

These studies indicate that there is no statistically significant difference based on sensation as well as comfort between the three heating stimuli HR2, HS6 and HS10 and also between the three cooling stimuli CR4, CS5 and CS10. The results of these user studies allow us to choose either of the stimuli from the respective groups without affecting the degree of sensation or comfort. Based on our application to simulate environmental conditions of real-world, stimuli HS10 and CS10 were chosen for heating and cooling respectively to ensure a subtle and continuous change in temperature.

SYSTEM IMPLEMENTATION

As shown in Figures 5 and 6, the system consists of three primary modules: 1) Head Mounted Display (HMD), 2) Control Module and 3) Environment Simulation Module. The Environment Simulation Module comprises of 3a) Wind Simulation Module and 3b) Ambient Temperature Module.

Head Mounted Display (HMD)

Both the Control Module and Environment Simulation Modules were mounted on the Samsung Gear VR[1] HMD, and an application for VR simulation was built on Unity 3D using Unity's Android SDK. In order to connect the VR application with the Control Module, we developed a separate API that triggers and controls wind and thermal stimuli. Based on the VR environment, the application wirelessly triggers stimuli and controls parameters such as direction, speed, and sweep speed for wind stimuli, and type, intensity, and duration

[1] Consumer Edition SM-R322

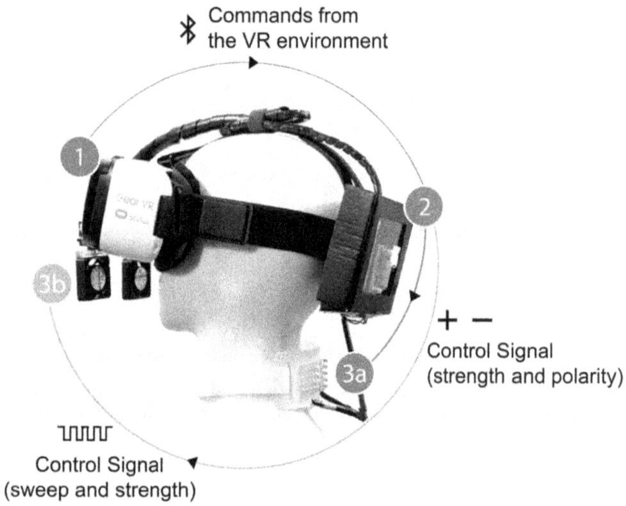

Figure 5. Operational procedure of Ambiotherm: (1) VR environment (Android Application) sends commands to (2) control module that actives (3a) thermal module and (3b) wind module.

for thermal stimuli. These commands are sent to the control module via Bluetooth using the developed Ambiotherm serial command protocol.

Control Module

A DFRobot Bluno Nano BLE-enabled microcontroller connected to the Samsung Galaxy Note 5 of the HMD interprets the received commands and generates control signals in real-time. It drives the Wind Simulation Module using the technique of Pulse Width Modulation (PWM), and controls factors such as wind intensity and wind direction (using the servo motors) in accordance with the VR environmental conditions. Similarly, thermal stimuli factors such as type, intensity and duration are controlled by varying the magnitude and polarity of the current supplied to the Ambient Temperature Module using PWM via a full H-Bridge MC33926 motor driver carrier, capable of delivering up to 3A of current continuously.

Environment Simulation Module

The Wind Simulation Module, mounted on the HMD panel, consists of two 5V fans (each of dimensions 40 x 40 x 10 mm) mounted on micro servo motors facing the user's cheeks. The Ambient Temperature Module, worn on the neck of the user, consists of two Peltier elements that draw up to 13W and are mounted on heatsinks for efficient temperature control.

EVALUATION

We developed two distinct VR environments (as an Android application) to showcase Ambiotherm's capabilities for simulating real-world environmental conditions within VR experiences. Here, the user experiences a desert environment (Figure 7 (A)) and a snowy mountain environment (Figure 7 (B)) for 30 seconds each, presented in a randomized order. The user follows the virtual guide on her path and is provided with a first-person view of the virtual environment. The user is also provided with auditory feedback that represents the virtual guide's footsteps and the wind blowing. Although the user is able to look around the 3D virtual environment using

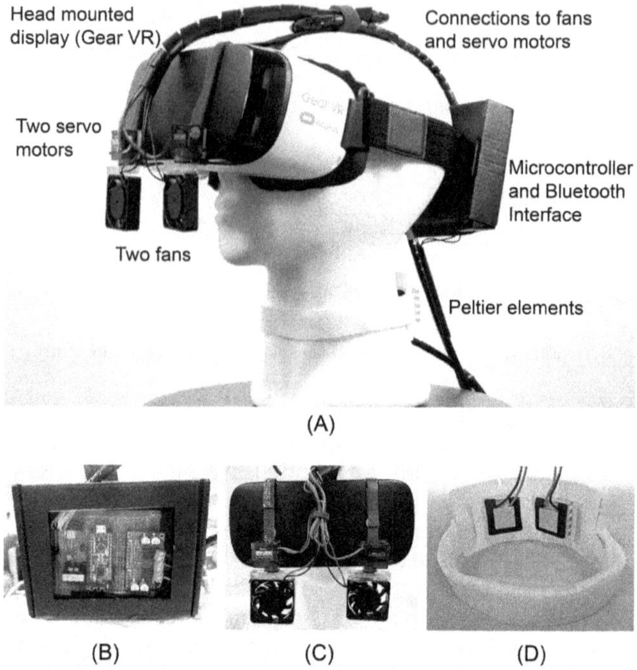

Figure 6. Ambiotherm: (A) Main components, (B) Control Module, (C) Wind Simulation Module, and (D) Ambient Temperature Module.

the HMD's head-tracking system, no additional interactions were added to this version as interactive factors were not the main focus of this study.

Instrumentation

The HMD that was used in this study was a Samsung Gear VR with a Samsung Galaxy Note 5 mobile phone running the demo application. To provide auditory feedback from the mobile device, a pair of Samsung Wired earphones[2] were used. The following section describes a pre-study experiment that was performed to prevent any detrimental impacts of stimuli latency on the users' experience by ensuring that wind and thermal stimuli were correctly synchronized with visual and auditory stimuli from the VR HMD.

Synchronization of Thermal and Wind Stimuli with Visual and Auditory Stimuli

By applying randomized heating and cooling thermal stimuli, mentioned in Table 1, to 10 participants (5 males and 5 females, average age = 24.4, SD = 1.17) via Peltier elements behind the neck, it was indicated that the average time to perceive the selected heating stimuli was 3 seconds, and the average time to perceive selected cooling stimuli was 2 seconds.

Based on these response times, the following thermal and wind synchronization timings were chosen to be examined with respect to the timings of visual and auditory stimuli produced by the demo application running on the HMD:

- Thermal: Cooling stimuli triggered 2 seconds before scene starts (C-2), triggered simultaneously with scene start (C0), and triggered 2 seconds after scene starts (C+2). Heating

[2]Model No: HS3303

Figure 7. User's first-person view following the virtual guide in (A) the hot desert and (B) the snowy mountain virtual environments.

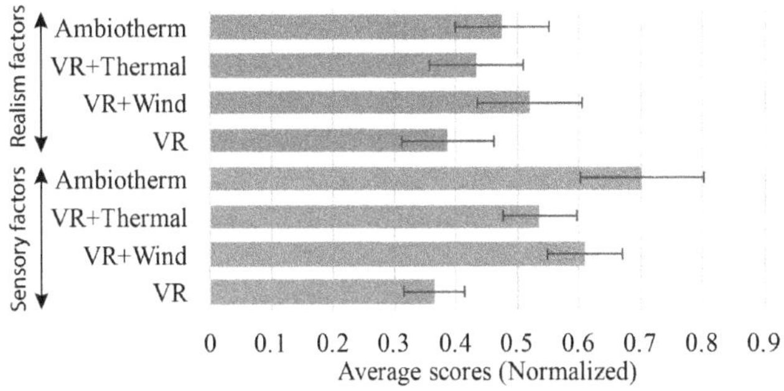

Figure 8. Normalized average Sensory and Realism Factors scores for four stimuli configurations (Error bars represent 95% CI, n = 20).

stimuli triggered 3 seconds before scene starts (H-3), triggered simultaneously with scene start (H0), and triggered 3 seconds after scene starts (H+3).

- Wind: Wind stimuli triggered 2 seconds before wind audio (W-2), triggered simultaneously with wind audio (W0), and triggered 2 seconds after wind audio (W+2).

Again, 10 participants (5 males and 5 females, average age = 24, SD = 1.24) were randomly selected and asked to rate how much they felt that these stimuli configurations (randomized) were disconnected with their respective visual or auditory stimuli. These ratings were recorded on a continuous scale ranging from "Strongly Disagree" to "Strongly Agree". The results of a one-way repeated measures ANOVA with sphericity-assumed indicated that the conditions C-2, C0 and C+2 have no significant difference ($F_{2,18} = 0.66$, $p > 0.05$) with 76% of participants not feeling any disconnect with respective visual and auditory stimuli across the three conditions. However, results of a one-way repeated measures ANOVA with sphericity-assumed indicated that the conditions H-3, H0 and H+3 have a significant difference ($F_{2,18} = 4.73$, $p < 0.05$). Post hoc tests using the Bonferroni correction further revealed that H+3 (M = 0.55, SD = 0.23) was significantly different to H0 (M = 0.8, SD = 0.16) ($p < 0.05$). No significant difference was observed between: 1) H+3 and H-3 (M = 0.8, SD = 0.26) ($p > 0.05$) and 2) H0 and H-3 ($p > 0.05$). Further confirming these statistical findings, 30% of participants reported a disconnect with H+3 and the audio-visual stimuli, 10% of participants reported a disconnect with H-3 and 0% with H0. The results of a one-way repeated measures ANOVA with Greenhouse-Geisser correction indicated that the disconnect between wind and auditory stimuli within conditions W-2, W0 and W+2 have no significant difference ($F_{1.15,10.36} = 1.64$, $p > 0.05$). Based on these results, conditions C0, H0 and W0 were chosen for the user study that is described in the following sections.

Procedure

20 participants (11 males, 9 females, average age = 25.45, SD = 4.98) were recruited for this study. All 20 participants had experienced VR systems prior to the study and were aware of HMD and VR technology. Prior to each new participant using the system in this study, earphones used to provide auditory stimuli were sanitized using alcohol swabs and the straps of the HMD were tightened to ensure that the device was both secure and comfortable on the participant. Before using the system, participants were also asked to provide basic demographic information (gender and age).

During the study, participants were asked to experience the demo application with four different system configurations: 1) via the HMD without the addition of thermal or wind stimuli (VR only), 2) via the HMD with only thermal stimuli (VR+Thermal), 3) via the HMD with only wind stimuli (VR+Wind), and 4) via the HMD with both thermal and wind stimuli (VR+Wind+Thermal = Ambiotherm). For each participant, the order of the four trials (aforementioned configurations) was randomized to avoid any effects that may occur from a set sequence of experiences.

Following each trial with the system, participants were asked to complete a questionnaire evaluating different aspects of their experience with respect to their sense of presence in the virtual environment. This questionnaire consisted of 21 questions that were adapted from Witmer and Singer's [40] presence questionnaire. As stated in [40], these questions each focused on one of four presence related factors; sensory factors, control factors, realism factors and distraction factors.

As user interactions and user-specific tasks were not the focus of this study, questions that relate to interaction and task-based aspects from Witmer and Singer's Presence Questionnaire were not included. Furthermore, questions pertaining to involvement were adapted to assess both thermal and wind aspects of the system.

Here, each question was answered on a continuous scale based on the semantic differential principle, adapted from [5], where each item is anchored at the ends by opposing descriptors. By doing so, data sets were collected that represent sensory, control, realism and distraction factors for each configuration of Ambiotherm compared to that of a standard HMD experience. The overall time taken by each participant per session, including instructions and completing all four questionnaires, was approximately 20 minutes. This study was conducted in an air conditioned room (24°C) with no air circulation.

Results

In this section, we present and discuss the results from the analysis of the user studies in terms of sensory, realism, distraction and control factors, all of which are associated with sense of presence within the VR experience [40].

Evaluation of Sensory Factors

A one-way repeated measures ANOVA, with Greenhouse-Geisser correction was conducted using the average sensory

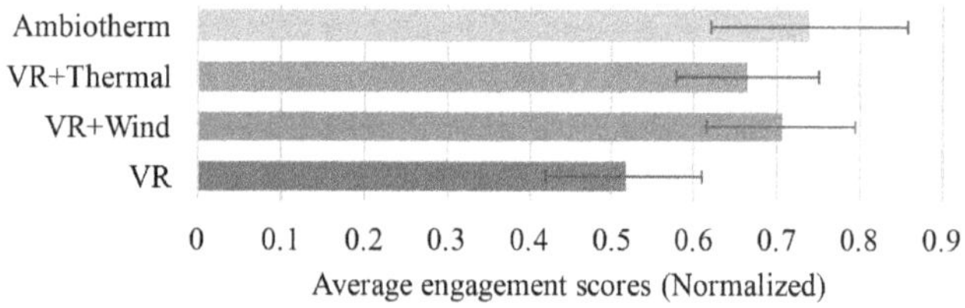

Figure 9. Normalized average engagement scores for four stimuli configurations (Error bars represent 95% CI, n = 20).

factor scores given for each of the four stimuli configurations (VR, VR+Wind, VR+Thermal, and Ambiotherm). There was a significant difference in the scores ($F_{1.7,32.44} = 27.1$, $p < 0.001$) with Ambiotherm having the highest average score (M = 0.70, SD = 0.21), as seen in Figure 8. Post hoc tests using the Bonferroni correction revealed that Ambiotherm (M = 0.7, SD = 0.21) was significantly different to: 1) VR (M = 0.37, SD = 0.11) ($p < 0.05$) and 2) VR+Thermal (M = 0.54, SD = 0.13) ($p < 0.05$), but not to VR+Wind (M = 0.61, SD = 0.13) ($p > 0.05$). Also, significant differences were observed between: 1) VR+Thermal and VR ($p < 0.05$) and 2) VR+Wind and VR ($p < 0.05$), but not between VR+Wind and VR+Thermal ($p > 0.05$). Following are the summarized results:

i) A significant difference was observed in the engagement scores of the four setups (Greenhouse-Geisser correction, $F_{2.15,40.97} = 6.07$, $p < 0.005$) with Ambiotherm having the highest engagement, as seen in Figure 9. Post hoc tests using the Bonferroni correction revealed that Ambiotherm (M = 0.74, SD = 0.26) was significantly different to VR (M = 0.51, SD = 0.2) ($p < 0.05$) but not to 1) VR+Wind (M = 0.71, SD = 0.19) ($p > 0.05$) or 2) VR+Thermal (M = 0.66, SD = 0.19) ($p > 0.05$). Also, a significant difference was observed between: 1) VR+Thermal and VR ($p < 0.05$) and 2) VR+Wind and VR ($p < 0.05$). However, no significant difference was observed between VR+Wind and VR+Thermal ($p > 0.05$).

ii) As expected, no significant difference was observed in the involvement due to visual aspects (Greenhouse-Geisser correction, $F_{1.72,32.76} = 2.32$, $p > 0.05$) and auditory aspects (Greenhouse-Geisser correction, $F_{2.1,39.88} = 0.83$, $p > 0.05$), as these were identical across the four configurations.

iii) A significant difference was seen in the involvement scores due to the thermal aspects (sphericity-assumed, $F_{3,57} = 36.76$, $p < 0.001$), where, as expected, Ambiotherm and VR+Thermal had higher scores (as shown in Figure 10). Post hoc tests using the Bonferroni correction revealed that Ambiotherm (M = 0.64, SD = 0.28) was significantly different to: 1) VR (M = 0.07, SD = 0.17) ($p < 0.05$) and 2) VR+Wind (M = 0.24, SD = 0.32) ($p < 0.05$), but not to VR+Thermal (M = 0.65, SD = 0.24) ($p > 0.05$). Also, statistically significant difference was observed between: 1) VR+Thermal and VR ($p < 0.05$) and 2) VR+Thermal and VR+Wind ($p < 0.05$), but no significant difference was observed between VR+Wind and VR ($p > 0.05$).

iv) Similarly, a significant difference was noted in the involvement scores due to the wind aspects (sphericity-assumed, $F_{3,57} = 31.67$, $p < 0.001$) with Ambiotherm and VR+Wind having higher scores as seen in Figure 10. Post hoc tests using the

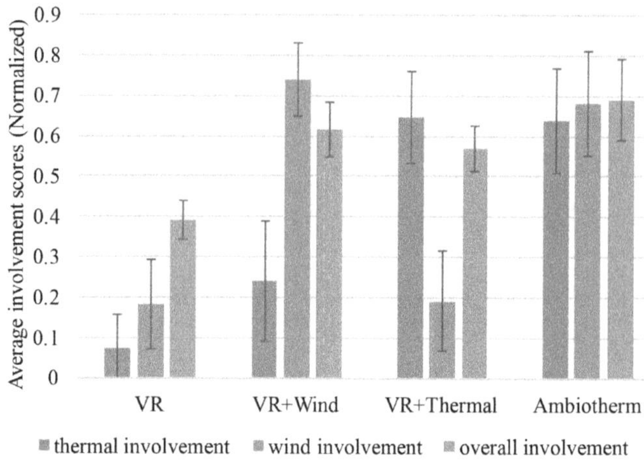

Figure 10. Normalized average thermal, wind, and overall Involvement scores for four stimuli configurations (Error bars represent 95% CI, n = 20).

Bonferroni correction revealed that Ambiotherm (M = 0.68, SD = 0.28) was significantly different to: 1) VR (M = 0.18, SD = 0.23) ($p < 0.05$) and 2) VR+Thermal (M = 0.19, SD = 0.27) ($p < 0.05$), but not to VR+Wind (M = 0.74, SD = 0.2) ($p > 0.05$). Also, a significant difference was observed between: 1) VR+Wind and VR ($p < 0.05$) and 2) VR+Wind and VR+Thermal ($p < 0.05$), but no significant difference was observed between VR+Thermal and VR ($p > 0.05$).

v) A significant difference was observed in the overall involvement (visual, auditory, thermal and wind stimuli combined) scores (Greenhouse-Geisser correction, $F_{1.75,33.25} = 17.85$, $p < 0.001$) with a notable improvement in Ambiotherm from the traditional VR experience, as seen in Figure 10. Post hoc tests using the Bonferroni correction revealed that Ambiotherm (M = 0.69, SD = 0.22) was significantly different to VR (M = 0.39, SD = 0.1) ($p < 0.05$), but not to 1) VR+Wind (M = 0.62, SD = 0.14) ($p > 0.05$) and 2) VR+Thermal (M = 0.57, SD = 0.12) ($p > 0.05$). Also, a significant difference was observed between: 1) VR+Wind and VR ($p < 0.05$) and 2) VR+Thermal and VR ($p < 0.05$), but no significant difference was observed between VR+Wind and VR+Thermal ($p > 0.05$).

vi) Lastly, even with the addition of extra multisensory stimuli, no significant difference in the delay between the modalities was noticed (Greenhouse-Geisser correction, $F_{2.07,39.23} = 0.61$, $p > 0.05$), thereby validating selected synchronization settings.

This study also revealed that 95% of the participants were able to identify the thermal stimuli delivered using Ambiotherm, of which, 73% perceived the thermal sensation as part of the ambient environment. However, only 50% of these participants perceived the thermal sensation as an overall body experience. This highlights a potential limitation of the system and suggests that methods to decrease this localized perception of thermal stimuli should be explored in future work. Furthermore, 90% of the participants were able to identify the wind stimuli delivered using Ambiotherm, out of which 94% perceived the wind sensation as part of the ambient environment. Additionally, a paired-samples t-test, conducted to compare the degree to which the sense of moving was compelling, re-

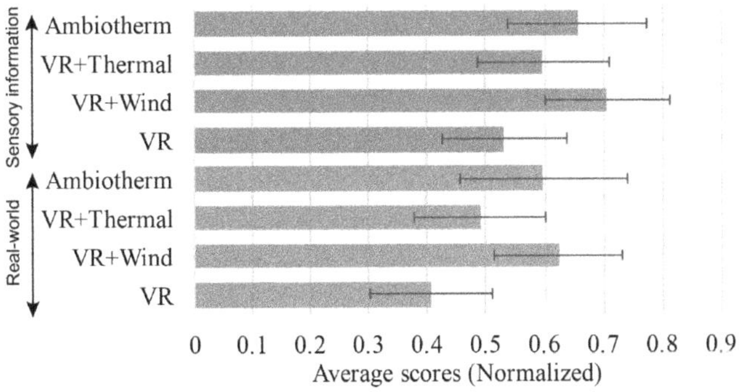

Figure 11. Normalized average consistency scores of VR Environment compared to Real-World and consistency scores for sensory information for four stimuli configurations (Error bars represent 95% CI, n = 20).

vealed a significant improvement ($t(19)=-4.16$, $p < 0.05$) in Ambiotherm (M = 0.72, SD = 0.23) when compared to the traditional VR experience (M = 0.55, SD = 0.19).

Evaluation of Realism Factors

A one-way repeated measures ANOVA, with Greenhouse-Geisser correction was conducted using the average realism factor scores given for each of the four stimuli configurations. There was a significant difference in the scores ($F_{2.07,39.4} = 6.53$, $p < 0.05$) with Ambiotherm having an average score significantly higher than the traditional VR experience, as shown in Figure 8. Post hoc tests using the Bonferroni correction revealed that Ambiotherm (M = 0.48, SD = 0.16) was significantly different to VR (M = 0.39, SD = 0.16) ($p < 0.05$) but not to 1) VR+Wind (M = 0.52, SD = 0.18) ($p > 0.05$) or 2) VR+Thermal (M = 0.43, SD = 0.16) ($p > 0.05$). Also, a significant difference was observed between VR+Wind and VR ($p < 0.05$), but no significant difference was observed between 1) VR+Thermal and VR ($p > 0.05$) or 2) VR+Wind and VR+Thermal ($p > 0.05$). Although there was no significant difference in the realism factor scores between Ambiotherm and VR+Wind, we believe that the difference in score may be due to the relatively localized nature of thermal stimuli which are present in the Ambiotherm configuration.

A one-way repeated measures ANOVA, with sphericity-assumed, was conducted to compare how consistent the VR environment was in comparison with the participants' experiences of the real-world. Results for the four stimuli configurations revealed a significant difference in scores ($F_{3,57} = 8.26$, $p < 0.001$), with Ambiotherm (M = 0.6, SD = 0.3) and the VR+Wind (M = 0.62, SD = 0.23) having higher average scores, as shown in Figure 11. Post hoc tests using the Bonferroni correction revealed that Ambiotherm was significantly different to VR (M = 0.4, SD = 0.22) ($p < 0.05$) but not to 1) VR+Wind ($p > 0.05$) or 2) VR+Thermal (M = 0.49, SD = 0.23) ($p > 0.05$). Also, a significant difference was observed between VR+Wind and VR ($p < 0.05$), but no significant difference was observed between 1) VR+Thermal and VR ($p > 0.05$) or 2) VR+Wind and VR+Thermal ($p > 0.05$). Similarly, results of a one-way repeated measures ANOVA, with sphericity-assumed, indicate a significant difference in the scores for consistency of information coming from the various senses ($F_{3,57} = 4.19$, $p < 0.05$), where Ambiotherm and VR+Wind have higher average

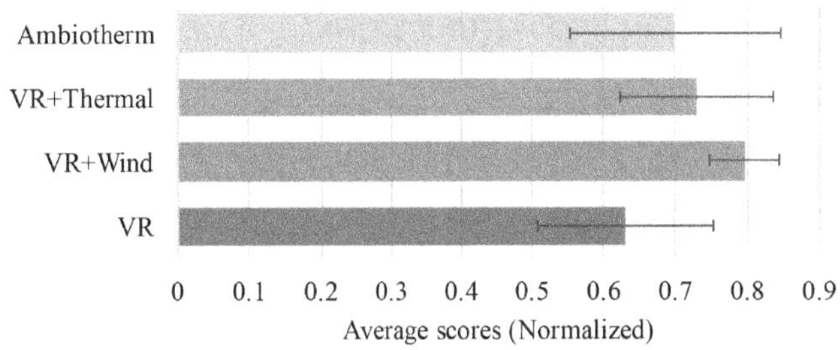

Figure 12. Normalized average scores assessing the quickness to adjust to the VR Environment with four stimuli configurations (Error bars represent 95% CI, n = 20).

scores, as seen in Figure 11. Post hoc tests using the Bonferroni correction revealed no significant difference between: 1) Ambiotherm (M = 0.66, SD = 0.26) and VR (M = 0.53, SD = 0.23) ($p > 0.05$), 2) Ambiotherm and VR+Wind (M = 0.70 SD = 0.23) ($p > 0.05$), 3) Ambiotherm and VR+Thermal (M = 0.6, SD = 0.24) ($p > 0.05$), 4) VR+Wind and VR+Thermal ($p > 0.05$) and 5) VR+Thermal and VR ($p > 0.05$), however a significant difference was observed between VR+Wind and VR ($p < 0.05$). Furthermore, the participants indicated that they did not feel disoriented after any trials during the study.

Evaluation of Control Factors

On conducting a one-way repeated measures ANOVA, with Greenhouse-Geisser correction, no significant difference in the control factor scores for the four different stimuli configurations was found ($F_{2.13,40.55} = 1.01$, $p > 0.05$). These results matched our expectations, as the developed VR environments in the demo application did not include any responsive interactions other than changes in visual stimuli based on head-tracking. Interestingly, a significant difference was observed from the results of a one-way repeated measures ANOVA, with sphericity-assumed, in the rate of adjustment to the VR environment in the four configurations ($F_{3,57} = 4.8$, $p < 0.05$) with VR+Wind being found to have an average score (M = 0.79, SD = 0.10) higher than the other three configurations as shown in Figure 12. Post hoc tests using the Bonferroni correction revealed no significant difference between: 1) Ambiotherm (M = 0.73, SD = 0.25) and VR (M = 0.63, SD = 0.26) ($p > 0.05$), 2) Ambiotherm and VR+Wind (M = 0.79, SD = 0.1) ($p > 0.05$), 3) Ambiotherm and VR+Thermal (M = 0.73, SD = 0.23) ($p > 0.05$), 4) VR+Wind and VR+Thermal ($p > 0.05$) and 5) VR+Thermal and VR ($p > 0.05$), however a significant difference was observed between VR+Wind and VR ($p < 0.05$).

Evaluation of Distraction Factors

The results of a one-way repeated measures ANOVA, with sphericity assumed, indicates no significant difference in the scores of distraction factors for the four different stimuli configurations ($F_{3,57} = 1.18$, $p > 0.05$). This validates the settings of the selected thermal and wind stimuli as they do not cause any additional notable distractions to the user's experience in the VR environment. However, it should be noted that Ambiotherm was unable to address the distractions caused due to real-world conditions and the physical device, such as its weight, which remain a common issue with all existing HMDs.

DISCUSSION AND FUTURE WORK

This work was our first attempt to understand how a combination of wind and thermal stimuli can be utilized to enhance the sense of presence in VR. The study also explored several aspects of human multisensory perception, utilizing information from visual, auditory, and haptic sensations, and addressed several issues including design factors for multisensory stimuli. Here, we discuss a number of interesting findings from our studies, highlighting limitations and proposing further studies of this technology in the future.

Within this study, one of our primary observations is that, despite both performing equally well in many aspects, Ambiotherm outperformed VR+Wind in terms of thermal involvement. We speculate that, due to the relatively localized nature of the thermal stimuli presented by Ambiotherm, a marginal drop in scores was observed for aspects such as consistency in sensory information (Realism Factor) and speed of adjustment to the VR environment (Control Factor), when compared to VR+Wind. Another notable observation is that VR+Wind consistently outperformed VR+Thermal in nearly all recorded aspects. We speculate that this may be due to differences in the raw impact of the two stimuli. Unlike the relatively subtle thermal stimuli behind the neck, the wind stimuli on the face were perceived more intensely due to the number of somatosensory receptors within the face (physiologically), and as humans are generally more aware of activities occurring near the face (psychologically).

Future implementations of Ambiotherm may be improved by integrating heating and cooling mechanisms within the fans, with the aim of controlling the temperature of the wind stimuli. We also believe that developing this functionality may provide additional benefits as this will 1) form a single module that can generate both thermal and wind stimuli, 2) enable Ambiotherm to more accurately simulate real-world environmental conditions and 3) enable thermal stimulation to be applied in multiple locations (both on the face and back of the neck). Furthermore, additional modalities such as smell as well as other haptic sensations, including vibration and humidity (vaporized water), will be integrated in the future to simulate additional environmental conditions.

Besides multisensory stimuli considerations, there are several other aspects that may be improved in future work. For example, this study does not include interactions between the user and the virtual environment. As stated by Witmer and Singer [40], interaction is a key factor that can affect the sense of presence, thus, we intend to extend our studies to compare the passive and interactive VR experiences. In addition, when using a questionnaire to evaluate a subjective experience such as the sense of presence, participants tend to interpret each question differently, based on prior experiences. In future research, other objective physiological measurements, for example, participant's heart rate and skin responses will also be incorporated into our studies. Furthermore while conducting the analysis, we observed that some datasets, such as degree of sensation to thermal stimuli, had high variances, suggesting a need for larger sample sizes in future studies.

Through the synchronization study we observed that the overall latency of stimuli perception is reduced when all modalities of Ambiotherm are combined. We believe that, by engaging multiple modalities, Ambiotherm appeals to many of the same perceptual mechanisms that a user employs when experiencing the real-world, in turn, potentially enabling users to process multisensory stimuli more efficiently than in traditional VR experiences [37].

Moreover, as an extension of the synchronization study, potential cross-modal effects between stimuli should be explored in future work. Results from these studies will further help to refine the stimuli design and protocol to facilitate the creation of more compelling virtual experiences. Although the stimuli used during this study had consistent characteristics for all user experiences, future work may also look towards developing individual calibration methods that alter stimuli parameters based on users' sensitivity or preferences.

Aside from making the electronics more compact and enhancing the system's power efficiency, we are developing Ambiotherm as a platform that is integrated with VR development environments, such as Unity, where developers may directly utilize its capabilities. By further studying and refining these multisensory stimuli, a taxonomy may be established for future VR developers.

Finally, as noted by Witmer and Singer [40], it is not clear how appropriate weightage can be assigned to signify the influence of each factor on the overall sense of presence. This is mainly due to the fact that the concept of sense of presence is both multi-faceted and subjective. Due to this, we have presented the results of our analysis, and our conclusions, under these separate factors without constructing an overall score to compare the four different system configurations.

CONCLUSION

We have developed the Ambiotherm system to simulate the sensory aspects of different environmental conditions such as wind and ambient temperature in VR environments, with the aim of enhancing the users' sense of presence within VR experiences. We have conducted multiple experiments to optimize fundamental aspects such as location, level of comfort and intensity of stimuli. Furthermore, a formal study was conducted to evaluate the effectiveness of the prototype system. In summary, a significant improvement in scores for sensory and realism factors of the VR experience was observed in Ambiotherm when compared to a traditional VR configuration. Secondly, the addition of thermal and wind stimuli via Ambiotherm did not cause notable distractions during the users' VR experiences. Lastly, compared to the relatively localized thermal stimuli, the wind stimuli had a more significant effect on users' sense of presence when simulating realistic environmental wind conditions.

ACKNOWLEDGMENTS

This research is supported by the National Research Foundation, Prime Minister's Office, Singapore under its International Research Centres in Singapore Funding Initiative.

REFERENCES

1. Duzgun Agdas, Gregory D Webster, and Forrest J Masters. 2012. Wind speed perception and risk. *PloS one* 7, 11 (2012), e49944.
2. Khandaker Shabbir Ahmed. 2003. Comfort in urban spaces: defining the boundaries of outdoor thermal comfort for the tropical urban environments. *Energy and Buildings* 35, 1 (2003), 103–110.
3. Henrique Andrade, Maria-João Alcoforado, and Sandra Oliveira. 2011. Perception of temperature and wind by users of public outdoor spaces: relationships with weather parameters and personal characteristics. *International journal of biometeorology* 55, 5 (2011), 665–680.
4. Edward Arens, Hui Zhang, and Charlie Huizenga. 2006. Partial-and whole-body thermal sensation and comfort-Part I: Uniform environmental conditions. *Journal of thermal Biology* 31, 1 (2006), 53–59.
5. Bettina A Babbitt and Charles O Nystrom. 1989. *Questionnaire construction manual*. Technical Report. DTIC Document.
6. Sylvain Cardin, Daniel Thalmann, and Frederic Vexo. 2007. Head mounted wind. In *proceeding of the 20th annual conference on Computer Animation and Social Agents (CASA2007)*. 101–108.
7. Ian Darian-Smith and Kenneth O Johnson. 1977. Thermal sensibility and thermoreceptors. *Journal of Investigative Dermatology* 69, 1 (1977), 146–153.
8. Leonidas Deligiannidis and Robert JK Jacob. 2006. The vr scooter: Wind and tactile feedback improve user performance. In *3D User Interfaces (3DUI'06)*. IEEE, 143–150.
9. Huong Q Dinh, Neff Walker, Larry F Hodges, Chang Song, and Akira Kobayashi. 1999. Evaluating the importance of multi-sensory input on memory and the sense of presence in virtual environments. In *Virtual Reality, 1999. Proceedings., IEEE*. IEEE, 222–228.
10. José Dionisio. 1997. Virtual hell: A trip through the flames. *IEEE Computer Graphics and Applications* 17, 3 (1997), 11–14.
11. Gary Fontaine. 1992. The experience of a sense of presence in intercultural and international encounters. *Presence: Teleoperators & Virtual Environments* 1, 4 (1992), 482–490.
12. Chauncey Frend and Michael Boyles. 2015. Programmable immersive peripheral environmental system (PIPES): a prototype control system for environmental feedback devices. In *SPIE/IS&T Electronic Imaging*. International Society for Optics and Photonics, 939209–939209.
13. D Gooch. 2009. *An Investigation into Communicating Social Presence With Thermal Devices*. Ph.D. Dissertation. MSc Dissertation.
14. Barry G Green and Barbara Gelhard. 1987. Perception of temperature on oral and facial skin. *Somatosensory research* 4, 3 (1987), 191–200.
15. HT Hammel, DC Jackson, JAJ Stolwijk, JD Hardy, and SB Stromme. 1963. Temperature regulation by hypothalamic proportional control with an adjustable set point. *Journal of Applied Physiology* 18, 6 (1963), 1146–1154.
16. David Hannah, Martin Halvey, Graham Wilson, and Stephen A Brewster. 2011. Using multimodal interactions for 3D television and multimedia browsing. In *Proceddings of the 9th international interactive conference on Interactive television*. ACM, 181–184.
17. Richard M Held and Nathaniel I Durlach. 1992. Telepresence. *Presence: Teleoperators & Virtual Environments* 1, 1 (1992), 109–112.
18. Felix Hülsmann, Julia Fröhlich, Nikita Mattar, and Ipke Wachsmuth. 2014. Wind and warmth in virtual reality: implementation and evaluation. In *Proceedings of the 2014 Virtual Reality International Conference*. ACM, 24.
19. JCR Hunt, EC Poulton, and JC Mumford. 1976. The effects of wind on people; new criteria based on wind tunnel experiments. *Building and Environment* 11, 1 (1976), 15–28.
20. Ken Iwasaki, Takashi Miyaki, and Jun Rekimoto. 2010. AffectPhone: A Handset Device to Present User's Emotional State with Warmth/Coolness. In *B-Interface*. 83–88.
21. Claus Jessen. 2012. *Temperature regulation in humans and other mammals*. Springer Science & Business Media.
22. Lynette A Jones and Michal Berris. 2002. The psychophysics of temperature perception and thermal-interface design. In *Haptic Interfaces for Virtual Environment and Teleoperator Systems, 2002. HAPTICS 2002. Proceedings. 10th Symposium on*. IEEE, 137–142.
23. Igor Knez and Sofia Thorsson. 2006. Influences of culture and environmental attitude on thermal, emotional and perceptual evaluations of a public square. *International journal of biometeorology* 50, 5 (2006), 258–268.
24. Wonjun Lee and Youn-kyung Lim. 2010. Thermo-message: exploring the potential of heat as a modality of peripheral expression. In *CHI'10 Extended Abstracts on Human Factors in Computing Systems*. ACM, 4231–4236.
25. Michael W McGreevy. 1992. The presence of field geologists in Mars-like terrain. *Presence: Teleoperators & Virtual Environments* 1, 4 (1992), 375–403.
26. W. H. Melbourne. 1978. Criteria for environmental wind conditions. *Journal of Wind Engineering and Industrial Aerodynamics* 3, 2-3 (1978), 241–249.
27. Mitsuru Minakuchi and Satoshi Nakamura. 2007. Collaborative ambient systems by blow displays. In *Proceedings of the 1st international conference on Tangible and embedded interaction*. ACM, 105–108.

28. Taeyong Moon and Gerard J Kim. 2004. Design and evaluation of a wind display for virtual reality. In *Proceedings of the ACM symposium on Virtual reality software and technology*. ACM, 122–128.
29. Heilig Morton. 1962. Sensorama simulator. (Aug. 28 1962). US Patent 3,050,870.
30. Mayumi Nakamura, Tamae Yoda, Larry I Crawshaw, Momoko Kasuga, Yuki Uchida, Ken Tokizawa, Kei Nagashima, and Kazuyuki Kanosue. 2013. Relative importance of different surface regions for thermal comfort in humans. *European journal of applied physiology* 113, 1 (2013), 63–76.
31. Mutsuhiro Nakashige, Minoru Kobayashi, Yuriko Suzuki, Hidekazu Tamaki, and Suguru Higashino. 2009. Hiya-Atsu media: augmenting digital media with temperature. In *CHI'09 Extended Abstracts on Human Factors in Computing Systems*. ACM, 3181–3186.
32. Joost P Pluijms, Rouwen Cañal-Bruland, Wouter M Bergmann Tiest, Fabian A Mulder, and Geert JP Savelsbergh. 2015. Expertise effects in cutaneous wind perception. *Attention, Perception, & Psychophysics* 77, 6 (2015), 2121–2133.
33. Katri Salminen, Veikko Surakka, Jukka Raisamo, Jani Lylykangas, Johannes Pystynen, Roope Raisamo, Kalle Mäkelä, and Teemu Ahmaniemi. 2011. Emotional responses to thermal stimuli. In *Proceedings of the 13th international conference on multimodal interfaces*. ACM, 193–196.
34. Thomas B Sheridan. 1992. Musings on telepresence and virtual presence. *Presence: Teleoperators & Virtual Environments* 1, 1 (1992), 120–126.
35. Sunghyun Song, Geeyoung Noh, Junwoo Yoo, Ian Oakley, Jundong Cho, and Andrea Bianchi. 2015. Hot & tight: exploring thermo and squeeze cues recognition on wrist wearables. In *Proceedings of the 2015 ACM International Symposium on Wearable Computers*. ACM, 39–42.
36. Theodore Stathopoulos, Hanqing Wu, and John Zacharias. 2004. Outdoor human comfort in an urban climate. *Building and Environment* 39, 3 (2004), 297–305.
37. Jonathan Steuer. 1992. Defining virtual reality: Dimensions determining telepresence. *Journal of communication* 42, 4 (1992), 73–93.
38. Jouke C Verlinden, Fabian A Mulder, Joris S Vergeest, Anna de Jonge, Darina Krutiy, Zsuzsa Nagy, Bob J Logeman, and Paul Schouten. 2013. Enhancement of presence in a virtual sailing environment through localized wind simulation. *Procedia Engineering* 60 (2013), 435–441.
39. Graham Wilson, Martin Halvey, Stephen A Brewster, and Stephen A Hughes. 2011. Some like it hot: thermal feedback for mobile devices. In *Proceedings of the SIGCHI Conference on Human Factors in Computing Systems*. ACM, 2555–2564.
40. Bob G Witmer and Michael J Singer. 1998. Measuring presence in virtual environments: A presence questionnaire. *Presence: Teleoperators and virtual environments* 7, 3 (1998), 225–240.

Multi-Moji: Combining Thermal, Vibrotactile & Visual Stimuli to Expand the Affective Range of Feedback

Graham Wilson & Stephen A. Brewster
Glasgow Interactive Systems Section, School of Computing Science
University of Glasgow, G12 8QQ UK
{first.last}@glasgow.ac.uk

ABSTRACT

This paper explores the combination of multiple concurrent modalities for conveying emotional information in HCI: temperature, vibration and abstract visual displays. Each modality has been studied individually, but can only convey a limited range of emotions within two-dimensional valence-arousal space. This paper is the first to systematically combine multiple modalities to expand the available affective range. Three studies were conducted: Study 1 measured the emotionality of vibrotactile feedback by itself; Study 2 measured the perceived emotional content of three bimodal combinations: vibrotactile + thermal, vibrotactile + visual and visual + thermal. Study 3 then combined all three modalities. Results show that combining modalities increases the available range of emotional states, particularly in the problematic top-right and bottom-left quadrants of the dimensional model. We also provide a novel lookup resource for designers to identify stimuli to convey a range of emotions.

Author Keywords

Emotion; thermal feedback; vibration; visual feedback

ACM Classification Keywords

H.5.2. Information interfaces and presentation (e.g., HCI): Haptic I/O

INTRODUCTION

Emotional experience plays a central role in social communication, motivation and memory, so it is important to support effective emotional expression in HCI. Human displays of emotion are complex and multifaceted, including facial expressions [14], vocal elements [9], body movements [4], tactile (touch, push, squeeze) and thermal (hug, hold hands) sensations [19]. In the absence of physical presence during digital communication, emotion needs to be conveyed through different means. In synchronous communication, facial expressions can be conveyed through video and voice through audio, but these signals are limited and devoid of tactile cues, and people with visual or hearing impairments miss out on cues. During asynchronous communication, such as text-based messaging, emotion is frequently conveyed using stylized pictorial expressions such as "emoji" (Figure 1), but these are difficult to interpret [26] and unsuitable for visual impairments. They are also different to real affective signals, lacking body movement, sound, touch and temperature.

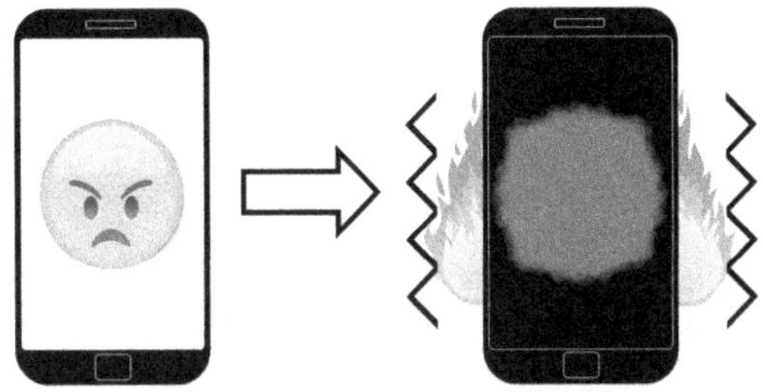

Figure 1: We expand existing ways of conveying emotion in digital communication with multimodal feedback.

The fields of *social signal processing* and *multisensory input* attempt to *detect* user emotion through the complex signals in facial expressions, voice and movements. However, little research has gone into *conveying* emotional states to users, for the purposes of digital communication (e.g., social media), enhancing media (audio, video) or conveying signals to people with sensory impairments. As people of all ages spend increasing amounts of time using digital devices and communicating online [28], it becomes more important to facilitate realistic social expressions.

Research in HCI has looked at how certain individual modalities can convey affective information, including thermal feedback [33,34,49], vibration [27,36,53], force feedback [6,37,52] and abstract visual displays [43,44,51]. Unfortunately, research shows that the individual modalities are only capable of conveying a limited range of emotional meaning by themselves. In most cases, emotion/affect is measured using the common *valence* (pleasantness) and *arousal* (excitedness) scales from Russell's circumplex model [31]. Thermal [49] and abstract visual [51] feedback have similar emotional ranges, while vibrotactile feedback is largely limited to highly arousing or "excited" emotions [36,53], limiting the applicability of these channels in communication. As emotion is multimodal, it is important to study how multiple modalities might combine to provide a wider range of emotional expressivity and so support better emotional communication in HCI (illustrated in Figure 1). The word *emoji* comes from the Japanese words *e* ("picture") and *moji* ("character"). Here we discuss *multi-moji*: multimodal characters for conveying emotional information.

CHI'17, May 06 - 11, 2017, Denver, CO, USA

ACM 978-1-4503-4655-9/17/05...$15.00
DOI: http://dx.doi.org/10.1145/3025453.3025614

To systematically explore the space, this paper presents three studies which measured the perceived emotional meaning, in terms of valence and arousal, conveyed by four different combinations of modalities: 1) vibrotactile + thermal, 2) vibrotactile + visual, 3) visual + thermal and 4) all three modalities together. We build upon existing feedback designs for each individual modality for a more robust comparison and to identify the effect of combining modalities on the perceived emotional meaning. Study 1 recreated previous research on the perceived emotional meaning of vibrotactile stimuli [53] to provide a baseline. Study 2 then measured the perceived emotion being conveyed from all three bimodal combinations. Finally, Study 3 combined all three modalities (visual, vibrotactile, thermal) together. The results from the multimodal combinations were compared to the perceived emotionality of the individual channels, to determine if combining cues facilitates a wider range of affective expression.

RELATED RESEARCH

To improve emotional communication in HCI, researchers have looked at the expressive capabilities of a range of visual and non-visual feedback designs. Our discussion focuses on the three feedback channels most studied in affective HCI: tactile, thermal and visual feedback. It mostly discusses research that has taken valence and arousal measurements of cues, as our aim is to compare the affective ranges of individual modalities to those of multimodal feedback, to determine how to expand affective expression.

Figure 2: Original mapping of emotions to a circumplex along valence (x-axis) and arousal (y-axis) dimensions (from [31]).

Measuring and Classifying Emotion

The most common conceptualization of emotion is the two-dimensional *valence* (V; emotional pleasantness) and *arousal* (A; emotional activation/excitation) model [31]. Additional axes include dominance (feeling of control) and potency (the intensity of the emotion), but most of the variance in emotional experience is described by only valence and arousal. Using these scales allows us to avoid the ambiguous definitions of discrete emotional labels (e.g., fear) and point to the underlying characteristics on continuous scales. By taking subjective V-A ratings, researchers can measure the emotional response elicited within an individual (e.g., after viewing pictures [22]) or record the perceived emotion being conveyed (e.g., in digital communication [27,37,49]). These ratings are then plotted within a two-dimensional space to compare the ratings of different stimuli and, potentially, attribute discrete emotional labels, e.g., *happy, sad, angry*, etc. Russell's circumplex model of affect [31] (Figure 2) is the most commonly used for associating V-A ratings to discrete emotions, dividing the two-dimensional space into four quadrants: *calm, pleasant* emotions (lower-right); *excited, pleasant* emotions (top-right); *excited, unpleasant* emotions (top-left) and *calm, unpleasant* emotions (lower-right).

Haptic and Actuated Feedback

Research has looked at devices that move or act against an individual for conveying emotion, but they tend to use qualitative analysis, making it harder to integrate these cues with our own and those discussed below. Research has looked at conveying emotion through a user's movement of a force-feedback arm, such as PHANToM devices [6], or actuated knobs [37]: one user encodes an emotional state by moving the device, and the movement is "played back" to a second user to interpret the emotion. However, even with a small list of possible emotion labels to choose from, accuracy only reached up to 63% for 4 emotions using a knob [37] or 50% for 7 emotions using a PHANToM [6]. Yohanan & MacLean [52] encoded the affective expression of a non-human creature via the movement of its ears and breathing and the use of purring sounds. The chosen emotion labels did not match those intended, but V-A ratings were more congruent, highlighting the issues in using labels rather than dimensions.

The emergence of deformable devices has led researchers to investigate conveying emotion through devices that are capable of changing shape e.g., bending or flexing different parts of the device [13,23,38] or devices that can react to user approaches (e.g., recoil or reach out) [18,29]. However, these studies are largely explorative, in terms of identifying what kinds of deformation are possible, or describing the movement along multiple scales, of which emotionality is only one, providing few clear feedback design guidelines.

Tactile Affective Feedback

Given the ubiquity of vibration motors in mobile and consumer devices, most research looking at conveying emotion non-visually has used vibration. In summary, short or rapid vibrotactile pulses, or longer overall patterns, are viewed as highly arousing [27,36,53]. The carrier frequency and intensity of the vibration both influence V and A simultaneously, with increases in either parameter increasing both V and A [3,27,36,53]. Producing vibrations of different texture, e.g., by increasing "roughness" [36] increases A and decreases V [53]. Yoo *et al.* [53] systematically analysed the V-A ratings of a range of vibrations for use in interpersonal communication. The parameters they investigated were five acceleration *amplitudes* (from 0.12 to 1.4g), *frequency* (60, 100, 150, 200 & 300Hz), *duration* (50, 100, 300, 500, 1000, 2000ms) and *envelope frequency* (0, 1, 2, 4, 8, 16Hz). They found that most vibrations are perceived as being highly arousing, a common finding in HCI research. There is also a narrow valence range, with more stimuli on the "unpleasant" side.

A very small number of studies have measured how the addition of vibration modulates the perceived affective content in media. Salminen *et al.* [32] found that combining positive and negative speech samples with the vibrotactile waveform of that speech made it seem more arousing and dominating. Akshita *et al.* [3] found that vibration made IAPS images [22] more arousing, but did not influence their valence.

Thermal Affective Feedback

There are inherent links between thermal sensation and emotion, such as the need for physical warmth for psychosocial development of infants [10,17], or the associations of words such as "loving" to "warm" personalities [5,15]. HCI researchers have started to measure the perceived emotional meaning of warm and cool sensations to improve interfaces for media or communication. Qualitative research has observed that participants consistently attribute opposite meaning to warm and cold: positive experiences and emotions are attributed to warm stimuli and unpleasant ones are attributed to cool [24,39,40,48]. Thermal feedback can also influence the emotional response to images, increasing the subjective enjoyment [25] or increasing (through warmth)/decreasing (through cold) the valence of images [2,16]. Research has also taken V-A ratings of thermal stimuli, to precisely measure emotional content/responses. Salminen *et al.* [34] recorded participants' emotional response to thermal feedback and found that warm stimuli resulted in lower valence (unpleasant) and higher arousal responses than cool stimuli. The larger the change (2 to 6°C), the more unpleasant and arousing the response.

Wilson *et al.* [49] expanded on this research by also measuring the effect of the rate of temperature change on V-A ratings and mapping the responses to two different models of emotion. In contrast to Salminen, the participants were asked to rate the perceived emotion being conveyed by the thermal feedback, rather than their own response. Potentially due to this difference in framing, Wilson *et al.* found that warm stimuli represented more pleasant emotions than cold, however, other patterns were similar: increasing either the extent of temperature change or the speed of change led to simultaneous increases in the perceived arousal (i.e., more excited) and decrease in the perceived valence (i.e., more unpleasant). The distribution of stimuli in V-A space is shown in panel G of Figure 5, and is quite limited in its range.

There is a degree of variability in the interpretation of thermal feedback across studies. In some, cooling changes are pleasant or positive valence (and warming changes unpleasant/negative valence) [33,34,50], while other studies have found the opposite, that warming changes are pleasant/positive and cooling is unpleasant/negative [48,49]. We believe the differences are at least partly due to task framing: what meaning is attached to the stimulus, such as its effect on one's own emotional state [33,34], describing the stimulus itself [50,53] or the emotion being conveyed by another [49]. Our paper uses the same framing as the studies we take stimuli from [49,51], so we believe interpretations will persist.

Visual Affective Feedback

Outside of emoji ambiguity [26], research has looked at minimalist or abstract visual feedback designs, leveraging correlates of facial activity [44] or inherent psychological associations of colour to affective judgements [1,30,42,45]. Research has also identified hedonic perceptions of shape and contour, finding that people have a consistent preference for curved over pointed objects [7,30], possibly due to the inherent "threat" of sharp objects [8] (see summary in [51]).

Valtchanov & Hancock [43] used this research to design abstract visual feedback to convey to users the affective valence (pleasant/unpleasant) of photography scenes. They gained subjective views on an affective "pulsing amoeba", a circular shape that regularly expanded/contracted, coloured green to convey pleasant scenes, white for neutral and red for unpleasant scenes. The amoeba changed from rounded contour and slow pulse (pleasant) to jagged contour and fast pulse (unpleasant). While a more explicitly informative bar-based design was easier to use, the amoeba was successful in creating affective responses, as it was "captivating" and "responsive", with the jagged shape being "threatening".

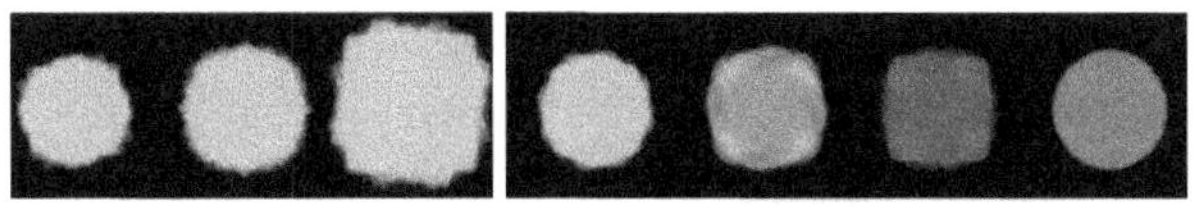

Figure 3: Example abstract visual feedback. Left: jagged "pulsing amoeba" [51] of different size (starting size, small increase and large increase). Right: coloured smooth amoeba.

Wilson *et al.* [51] extended this research, analysing how each individual visual design parameter in Valtchanov & Hancock's pulsing amoeba influenced the perceived emotion being conveyed, individuating *contour* (jagged, smooth), *pulse size* (small, large), *pulse rate* (slow, fast) and *colour* (green, red, blue and grey; see Figure 3). They found that blue and green colours were more pleasant (higher valence) than red/grey, and that higher pulse rates or larger pulse sizes were more arousing and more unpleasant. The full distribution of stimulus V-A ratings is shown in panel F of Figure 5.

Limitations & Research Contribution

Sound is an important part of expressing many emotions, and psychologists have identified characteristics of vocal expressions that convey emotional states [9]. They validated a set of "affective bursts" (short non-verbal expressions) but they can only convey a limited number of discrete emotions and with widely varying accuracy [9]. Little HCI research has studied how to create a range of affective sound cues, and so sound was not included in the current research.

There is a significant lack of truly *multi*modal affective feedback, where more than one modality is used simultaneously. Some research has studied the modulation of an emotional response to one modality, through the simultaneous presentation of another [2,3,16,32]. However, these studies only ask participants to focus on and rate the one modality, with those ratings potentially altered by the second. The signals are not being treated holistically by participants.

Real human emotional displays are multimodal, yet HCI research has not explored how multiple feedback channels might combine to convey emotion. This is especially important given the limited range of emotions that visual [51], vibrotactile [36,53] and thermal feedback [34,49] are capable of conveying individually. Panel H in Figure 5 shows the individual distributions for the three modalities overlaid on a single graph, and several limitations are clear: 1) the modalities convey similar ranges of emotions, 2) most points are fairly near the centre and 3) there are very few points in the top-right (pleasant excited emotions) and bottom-left (unpleasant calm emotions) quadrants. This paper addresses these limitations and provides the following contributions: 1) *the first systematic measurement of combining two and three modalities on the perceived emotional meaning*; 2) *the first comparison of the perceived emotional content in multimodal stimuli to that of individual modalities*. We use the vibrotactile stimuli from Yoo *et al.* [53], the thermal stimuli from Wilson *et al.* [49] and the visual stimuli from Wilson *et al.* [51], as they provide the widest range of V-A ratings on which to base feedback designs and compare results.

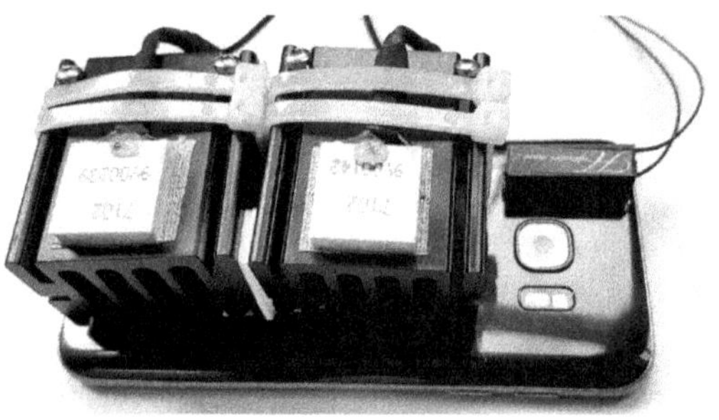

Figure 4: Phone with two 2cm^2 Peltier modules and a Haptuator Mk II on the back. Device rested in (stimulated) the palm.

EXPERIMENTAL APPARATUS

The same hardware was used for all three Studies and experimental software ran on a MacBook Pro laptop. The thermal and vibrotactile cues were presented from stimulators attached to the back of an Android mobile phone (see Figure 4). A phone was chosen as it represents a common interaction form factor that fits well with the study framing (conveying emotion in digital communication), and has been used in previous research [47,53]. We used a mains-powered Peltier-based thermal stimulator [49] that connected to the laptop over Bluetooth. The Peltiers were attached to metal heatsinks and the base of the heatsinks were stuck to the phone with double-sided adhesive tape. They were positioned so that the Peltiers made good contact with the palm as the device rested on the hand. The Haptuator Mark II was also stuck to the back, above the Peltiers, using double-sided adhesives. The Haptuator was put in the same y-axis orientation as Yoo *et al.*, as orientation affects intensity [20], and was driven by sound files played over a 3.5mm cable from the laptop, via an amplifier. White noise was played through headphones to mask any noise from the vibrations.

During all three studies, participants sat at a desk with the device resting in the palm of their non-dominant hand so that the Peltiers made good contact. The haptuator vibrated the entire device so participants felt the vibrations through the Peltiers, collocating both sensations. Visual feedback, and valence/arousal scales, were shown on the screen of a laptop.

STUDY 1: BASELINE VIBROTACTILE STIMULI

To be able to reliably compare our results to previous research it was important to use the same feedback cues, to produce the same affective interpretations. This was more straightforward for the thermal and visual cues, as they were reproduced using the same Peltier equipment and visual designs as the original authors [49,51]. We could produce the same vibration parameters as Yoo *et al.* [53], however, we were unable to obtain the same Haptuator they used; we were limited to the newer Haptuator Mark II [41]. The specification details for each model shows they have different characteristics, most notably in terms of the rated frequency bandwidth (50-500Hz for the original vs. 90-1000Hz for Mark II) and the reference acceleration (gravity @ 3V input, 125Hz input): 3.0g (original) vs. 7.5g (Mark II).

Parameter	Values
Amplitude	A1, A2, A3
Frequency (Hz)	90, 200, 300
Duration (ms)	100, 1000

	A1	A2	A3
90Hz	1.7g	3.3g	4.3g
200Hz	0.6g	1.0g	1.3g
300Hz	0.9g	1.2g	2.2g

Table 1: Vibrotactile stimuli used to measure affective ratings from Haptuator Mark II; and Amplitude values (*g* = gravity).

Therefore, we measured the perceived affectivity (valence and arousal ratings) of some of Yoo *et al.*'s stimuli using our Mark II, to ensure that we used affectively similar stimuli to them and to provide a baseline for comparing to the combined modalities in Studies 2 and 3. As we would only be using a small number of stimuli for each modality in Study 2 and 3, we tested only a subset of 18 of Yoo *et al.*'s stimuli, shown in Table 1. To avoid damaging the device and producing invalid results from an ostensibly unsupported frequency, we did not use 60Hz, opting for 90Hz instead (the nearest frequency), giving three frequencies (labelled F): 90Hz (F1), 200Hz (F2) and 300Hz (F3). We identified three amplitude values (labelled A1-A3, measured in gravitational acceleration, *g*) which were subjectively similar in intensity across the three carrier frequencies (see Table 1). Durations (D) of 100ms (D1) and 1000ms (D2) were used, as they had significantly different V-A scores [53]. The stimuli were therefore labelled e.g., F1A1D1 to mean 90Hz, amplitude 1, 100ms.

Participants

12 University staff/students (4 F, 8 M) aged 24 to 32 (mean = 28.3) took part in the study, which lasted 15 minutes.

Experimental Design

The experimental design used throughout this paper closely followed that of previous unimodal research studies [34,36,49,51,53], to maximise the validity of comparisons. Each of the 18 stimuli were presented twice in a random order, with each presentation consisting of three repetitions of the stimulus at 1.5-second intervals. Participants were not able to replay stimuli. Once the stimulus had been presented to the hand, 7-point *valence* ("unpleasant" to "pleasant") and *arousal* ("low arousal" to "high arousal") ratings were gained from two dialogue boxes on the laptop screen and the next random stimulus played after three seconds. The Independent Variables were: *Amplitude*, *Frequency* and *Duration*, and the Dependent Variables were: *Valence* and *Arousal*, with the 7-point Likert values converted to -3 to +3.

Results

The full distribution of average V-A ratings for each stimulus is shown in panel E of Figure 5 with means for each parameter listed in Table 2. As in Yoo *et al.* [53], Valence decreased as Amplitude increased (Duration made little difference) and arousal increased as Amplitude, Frequency or Duration increased. In contrast, we found that increasing Frequency decreased Valence. The distribution of stimuli has a roughly equal split in the number of stimuli in the top (excited) and bottom (calm) halves. Slightly more stimuli rest in the left (unpleasant) than in the right (pleasant) but there are large differences between the populations of each quadrant. The top-left and bottom-right quadrants have several stimuli, with few in the top-right and bottom-left, and those in the bottom-left are very close to the centre of the graph.

	Amplitude			Frequency (Hz)			Duration (ms)	
	1	2	3	90	200	300	100	1000
Valence	0.15	-0.37	-0.62	0.79	-0.30	-1.33	-0.20	-0.36
Arousal	-0.40	0.29	0.97	-0.50	0.41	0.96	-0.56	1.13

Table 2: Mean Valence and Arousal ratings (-3 to 3) for each level of the vibrotactile parameters in Study 1.

There are some differences to the results in Yoo *et al.* [53]. We found a wider but less symmetrical valence range and we found the opposite effect of Frequency: Yoo *et al.* found increasing Frequency led to *increasing* valence. These differences could be due to the different actuator responses, or cultural factors (European vs. South Korean participants), and suggest that affective ratings are sensitive to experimental variability. Studies 2 and 3 use the same stimuli, equipment and experimental framing as previous research, maximising the validity, comparability and generalisation of results.

STUDY 2: TWO-MODALITY COMBINATIONS

Multimodal Feedback Designs

This section describes the stimuli chosen to represent each of the three modalities in Studies 2 and 3. Because of the large number of stimuli available in the tactile [53], thermal [49] and visual [51] modalities, and the huge number of potential multimodal combinations, we used only four stimuli for each modality: one that represented each quadrant of the V-A model (all stimuli are shown in Table 3).

Vibrotactile Feedback

The four vibrotactile signals came from Study 1, and provide a spread of all three frequencies and both durations, as well as two of the three amplitudes: 1) *90Hz, A1, 100ms* (*F1A1D1*), 2) *90Hz, A3, 1000ms* (*F1A3D2*), 3) *200Hz, A2, 100ms* (*F2A2D1*) & 4) *300Hz, A3, 1000ms* (*F3A3D2*).

Thermal Feedback

The thermal stimuli were based on the dimensional distribution from Wilson *et al.* [49] (Figure 5, panel G) and all changed from a neutral starting skin temperature of 30°C: 1) *cool down 8°C at 3°C/sec* (shortened to "*c83*"), 2) *warm up 4°C at 3°C/sec* ("*w43*"), 3) *cool down 4°C at 3°C/sec* ("*c43*") and 4) *warm up 2°C at 1°C/sec* ("*w21*"). This provided a balanced set of stimuli: two warm and two cool; two slow and two fast; and three different temperature deltas. The thermal distribution is concentrated in the bottom-right and top-left quadrants, resulting in an uneven representation, which multimodal combinations may help to expand.

	Arousal
Vibration: 300Hz, A3, 1000ms (*F3A3D2*) **Visual**: Red-Jagged-Large-Fast (*RJLF*) **Thermal**: -8°C @ 3°C/sec (*c83*)	**Vibration**: 90Hz, A3, 1000ms (*F1A3D2*) **Visual**: Blue-Jagged-Small-Fast (*BJSF*) **Thermal**: +4°C @ 3°C/sec (*w43*) *Valence*
Vibration: 200Hz, A2, 100ms (*F2A2D1*) **Visual**: Grey-Smooth-Large-Slow (*GSLS*) **Thermal**: -4°C @ 3°C/sec (*c43*)	**Vibration**: 90Hz, A1, 100ms (*F1A1D1*) **Visual**: Blue-Smooth-Small-Slow (*BSSS*) **Thermal**: +2°C @ 1°C/sec (*w21*)

Table 3: Stimuli chosen to represent each quadrant in the *valence* (y-axis)-*arousal* (x-axis) model of affect in Study 2.

Visual Feedback

The visual stimuli were chosen from the distribution in Wilson *et al.* [51]. The four animated "amoebas" (Figure 3) used were: 1) *Blue-Jagged-Small-Fast* (shortened to *"BJSF"*), 2) *Blue-Smooth-Small-Slow (BSSS)*, 3) *Grey-Smooth-Large-Slow (GSLS)* and 4) *Red-Jagged-Large-Fast (RJLF)*. Small amoeba increased in size by 20%, large ones increased by 40%. Slow amoebas took 10 secs to grow, fast ones took 1 sec. Like the thermal stimuli, the distribution (Figure 5, panel F) is concentrated in the bottom-right and top-left quadrants, so these are better represented than the top-right/bottom-left.

Combining Stimuli

When combining two modalities, all possible stimulus combinations were used: four from the first modality were each combined with all four from the second modality, giving 16 stimuli per bimodal combination. This allowed us to measure the effect of both *complimentary* (stimuli from same quadrant) and *conflicting* combinations (from opposing valence/arousal values) on the perceived emotionality.

Participants

18 students (10 F, 8 M) aged 19-53 (mean = 24.6) were paid £10 for both Study 2 (~45 minutes) and 3 (~15 minutes).

Experimental Design & Procedure

The experimental design was the same as Study 1, except it consisted of three Sub-studies, one for each bimodal combination, with different stimuli and different sets of valence and arousal data. All participants took part in all three Sub-studies in a counterbalanced order and each Sub-study consisted of a single block where all 16 stimuli were presented twice in a random order. Each stimulus lasted for seven seconds. If vibration was presented, it was done in the same way as Study 1: played three times at intervals of 1.5 seconds. If visual feedback was presented, a 7-second animation of the pulsing amoeba was shown on the laptop screen. If thermal feedback was presented, the Peltiers were set to a common starting temperature of 30°C throughout the Sub-study so that the skin rested at a neutral temperature [21,48]. During a stimulus, the Peltiers changed by the given extent and rate of change over the 7 seconds, before returning to 30°C for 10 seconds before the next trial.

Following each stimulus, the same 7-point Likert scales as in Study 1 were presented on the laptop screen and the participants used a mouse to make their choices. Once all 32 stimuli had been presented, participants were given a 5-minute break before starting the next Sub-study. The Independent Variables were the *Vibration*, *Temperature* and *Amoeba* stimuli shown in Table 3 (depending on the combination), while the Dependent Variables were *Valence* and *Arousal*. All Sub-studies were separately analysed in two steps: 1) a two-way repeated-measures MANOVA with Valence and Arousal as combined dependent variables; 2) two 4 x 4 repeated-measures ANOVA, one on the Valence data and one on Arousal, to determine effects on individual measures (effect sizes are shown as η_p^2). To measure participants' internal reliability of ratings between the two presentations of the same stimulus, we compared the mean ratings using paired-samples T-tests (including Pearson's correlation *r*). The full dimensional distributions for each bimodal combination are shown in Figure 5 (panels A-C), alongside the distributions for each modality individually (panels E-G), for comparison.

Sub-study 1: Vibrotactile & Thermal Feedback

The MANOVA found significant main effects of both Vibration ($F_{(6, 208)} = 24.15$, p<0.001; Wilks' $\Lambda = 0.347$, $\eta_p^2 = 0.41$) and Temperature ($F_{(6, 208)} = 7.03$, p<0.001; Wilks' $\Lambda = 0.69$, $\eta_p^2 = 0.17$) on the combined DVs. Individual ANOVAs found a significant main effect of Vibration on Arousal ($F_{(3, 105)} = 62.27$, p<0.001, $\eta_p^2 = 0.64$), with all Vibrations conveying significantly different Arousal levels from each other. There was no effect of Temperature on Arousal, and no interaction. There was a significant main effect of Temperature on Valence ($F_{(3, 105)} = 11.34$, p=0.001, $\eta_p^2 = 0.24$): c83 conveyed significantly lower Valence than all other Temperatures, and c43 significantly lower than w21. There was no effect of Vibration on Valence, and no interaction. There were no significant differences in an individual's ratings of same stimuli in either Valence (t = -0.52, *r* = 0.67) or Arousal (t = -1.67, *r* = 0.68), suggesting internal reliability of ratings.

As Panel A in Figure 5 shows, combining thermal and vibrotactile feedback results in a fairly narrow Valence range but a relatively wide Arousal range. Vibration appears to be largely responsible for the perceived Arousal: increasing either amplitude or frequency increased arousal, the same as in Study 1 and in Yoo *et al.* [53]. Temperature appears largely responsible for the perceived Valence, with cool stimuli having negative/unpleasant valence and warm temperatures having positive/pleasant valence, as found in [49]. The lack of any interaction effects suggests there were no differences between combining complimentary (same quadrant) vs. conflicting (different quadrant) stimuli across modalities.

Sub-study 2: Vibrotactile & Visual Feedback

The MANOVA found significant main effects of both Vibration ($F_{(6, 208)} = 24.53$, p<0.001; Wilks' $\Lambda = 0.343$, $\eta_p^2 = 0.41$) and Amoeba ($F_{(6, 208)} = 16.47$, p<0.001; Wilks' $\Lambda = 0.46$, η_p^2

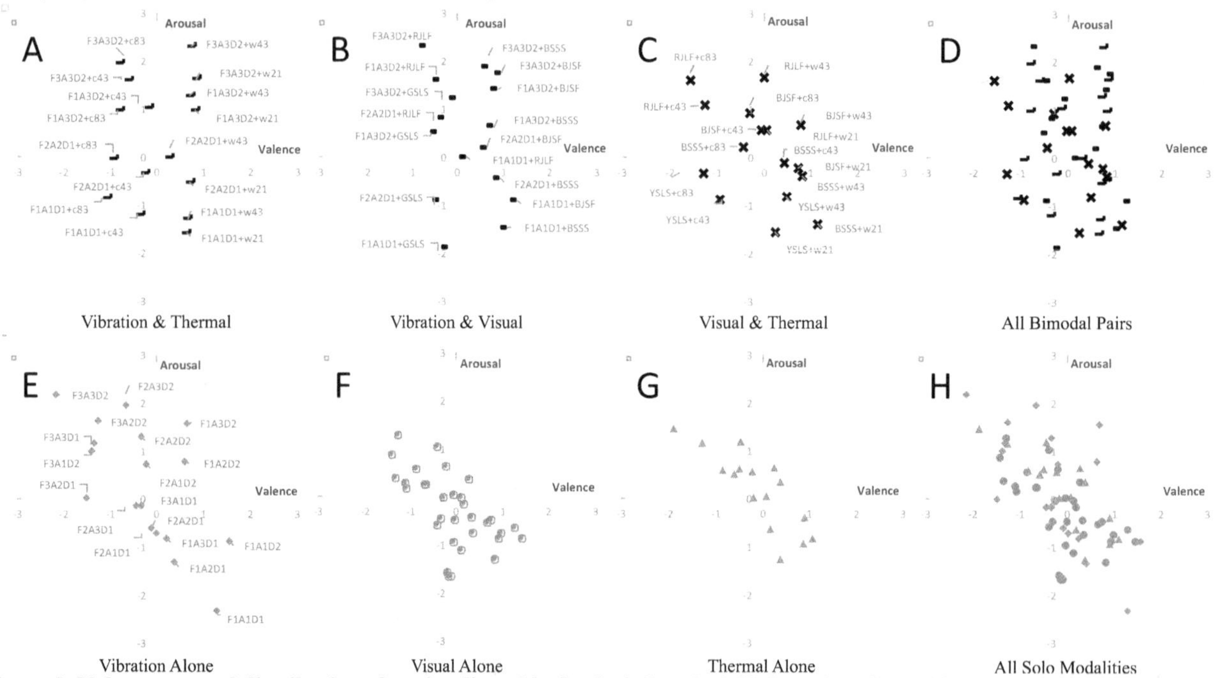

Figure 5: Valence-arousal distributions for stimuli used in Study 2. Panels A-E show data from this paper: Sub-study 1 (A), Sub-study 2 (B), Sub-study 3 (C), Sub-studies 1-3 combined (D) and Vibrotactile stimuli from Study 1(E). Panels F (thermal stimuli from [49]) and G (visual stimuli from [51]) are from previous research. Panel H shows panels E-G combined.

= 0.32) on the combined DVs. Individual ANOVA found a significant main effect of Vibration on Arousal ($F_{(3, 105)}$ = 64.45, p<0.001, η_p^2 = 0.65), with all Vibrations conveying significantly different Arousal levels from each other. There was also a significant main effect of Amoeba ($F_{(3, 105)}$ = 23.26, p<0.001, η_p^2 = 0.40), as all amoebas conveyed significantly different Arousal levels. There was no interaction effect. There was a significant main effect of Amoeba on Valence ($F_{(3, 105)}$ = 10.44, p<0.001, η_p^2 = 0.23): BJSF and BSSS conveyed significantly higher Valence than RJLF and YSLS. There was no effect of Vibration and no interaction. There were no significant differences in an individual's ratings of same stimuli in either Valence (t = 0.92, *r* = 0.70) or Arousal (t = -0.15, *r* = 0.66), suggesting consistent ratings.

The results were similar to the combination of Vibration with Thermal feedback, as there is a narrow Valence range with a wider Arousal range. Both Vibration and the form of the Amoeba influenced Arousal: Vibration did so in the same way as Sub-study 1 (increasing frequency/duration led to increased Arousal), and the blue Amoeba conveyed Arousal levels between the red and grey Amoebas, the latter being the only one conveying calm Arousal. Rounded Amoeba had lower Arousal, while jagged ones had higher, in line with previous research [51]. The Visual design also predominantly dictated that Valence ratings, with the blue shapes having positive/pleasant Valence and the red and grey having similarly negative/unpleasant Valence (as in [51]). The lack of interaction effects again shows there were no differences between complimentary and conflicting combinations.

Sub-study 3: Thermal & Visual Feedback

The MANOVA found significant main effects of both Amoeba ($F_{(6, 208)}$ = 16.70, p<0.001; Wilks' Λ = 0.46, η_p^2 = 0.32) and Temperature ($F_{(6, 208)}$ = 9.95, p<0.001; Wilks' Λ = 0.60, η_p^2 = 0.22) on the combined DVs. Individual ANOVA found a significant main effect of Temperature on Arousal ($F_{(3, 105)}$ = 9.61, p<0.001, η_p^2 = 0.21): all conveyed significantly different Arousal levels (w43 only differed from w21). There was also a significant main effect of Amoeba ($F_{(3, 105)}$ = 26.07, p<0.001, η_p^2 = 0.43), with all conveying significantly different Arousal levels. There was no interaction.

There was a significant effect of Temperature on Valence ($F_{(3, 105)}$ = 10.95, p<0.001, η_p^2 = 0.24): all conveyed significantly different Valence values from each other, except when comparing the two warming stimuli. There was also a significant effect of Amoeba on Valence ($F_{(3, 105)}$ = 9.33, p<0.001, η_p^2 = 0.21): BJSF led to higher ratings than RJLF, and BSSS led to higher ratings than both RJLF and YSLS. There were no significant differences in the ratings of same stimuli in Valence (t = 1.62, *r* = 0.75) or Arousal (t = 0.52, *r* = 0.67).

The distribution is different to the other Sub-studies: when vibration is not included there is a wider Valence range and a smaller Arousal range, and the points are more dispersed. Also, both modalities influence both dimensions, rather than each dictating one, as was more common in the other combinations. Again, cool, red or grey stimuli had negative Valence, while warm or blue stimuli had positive Valence. There were no interaction effects, showing no difference between complimentary vs. conflicting combinations.

Discussion: Comparing to Individual Modalities

The top row of Figure 5 shows the valence-arousal distributions for each bimodal combination in Sub-studies 1 to 3 (panels A to C), as well as all 3 overlaid on top (D), to show the range of emotional meaning that can be conveyed. The bottom row shows the distributions for each modality by itself (vibration in panel E from Study 1, visual in F [51], and thermal in G [49]), as well as all three solo modalities overlaid (panel H). Combining two modalities (A-C) can convey a wider range of emotion, mostly in the top-right (excited pleasant emotions) and bottom-left (calm unpleasant emotions) quadrants. There is also a roughly even number and spread of stimuli in each of the four quadrants, although the bottom-left remains slightly sparser. These results are significant and promising, as the top-right and bottom-left quadrants have proven difficult to access in other research [3,49,51,53], and no other research has found such an even spread of stimuli throughout the model.

It is also clear that combining modalities has different effects on the range of arousal vs. valence that can be conveyed: combining modalities facilitates a slightly wider arousal range but a similar, and sometimes more contracted, valence range. The distributions for combinations involving vibration (panels A and B in Figure 5) are notable for being tall and thin: in the presence of vibration, it appears to be difficult to convey strong pleasantness or unpleasantness. Vibration was primarily responsible for varying arousal in Sub-studies 1 and 2, so it may be that vibration dominates perception/interpretation over temperature or abstract visual feedback.

When temperature and visual feedback are combined (panel C), there is a smaller available arousal range than when vibration is present, but there is a wider valence range in return. The distribution for vibrotactile feedback alone (panel E) actually has a wider valence range than the two combinations (A, B), which raises the question: why would a combination attenuate the valence of a vibration? There are two factors which go some way to answering this, and they also help explain why we have not seen a wider valence range in general, compared to the individual modalities. The first is that participants appear to *average* the perceived emotional meaning from two modalities, rather than *sum* it; and the second factor is the influence of *individual differences*.

Emotionality is Averaged, Not Summed

To inspect the effects of combining modalities more closely, we took each individual stimulus used in Sub-studies 1 to 3 and compared its V-A values when presented in isolation to the values from each time it was combined. This would show the effect of adding each individual vibrotactile, thermal or visual stimulus (depending on Sub-study) on the perceived emotional meaning. For example, comparing the values for BSSS from [51] and F1A1D1 from Study 1, we can see

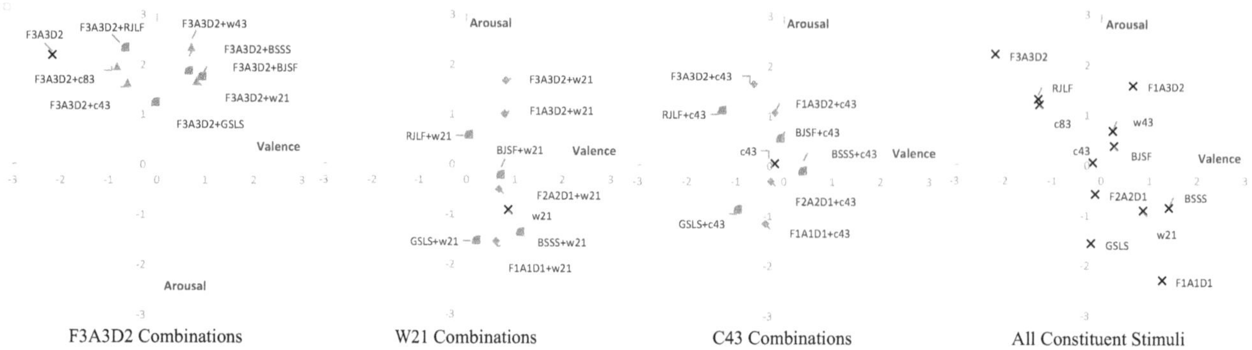

Figure 6: Examples of how perceived emotionality of individual stimuli (black cross) is affected by adding another modality: visual (circle), thermal (triangle), vibration (diamond). Right: valence-arousal values for individual stimuli used in combinations.

where BSSS+F1A1D1 sits relative to those. As this paper is the first to do in-depth analysis of how modalities combine to convey emotion, there was no prior knowledge from which to predict *how* the combined ratings would differ from the individual ones. The pleasantness and calmness of both BSSS and F1A1D1 could have combined to convey an even calmer and more pleasant emotion. Or the use of two modalities could make the emotion more arousing, as there is greater sensory stimulation.

However, it appears that, for most combined stimuli, the perceived emotion was simply *averaged* across the two modalities. The perceived valence/arousal when combined were somewhere between the valence/arousal values of the individual stimuli. Examples of this are shown in the middle panels of Figure 6, where the reference individual stimulus is shown (black cross) and the combinations it was included in are shown around it. The distribution on the far right shows the locations of each individual stimulus, for comparison. This averaging of values seems to have contributed to the lack of a wider valence range than individual modalities, as there would always be two stimuli 'pulling' on each other.

This effect appears to be weaker on the range of perceived arousal, which is not contracted when combining modalities. But this is only the case when vibration is present, suggesting that the strength and dominance of vibration over arousal has the benefit of maintaining arousal across combinations, but with the detriment of overpowering the second modality that is required to influence valence. Therefore, the "attenuation" of vibrotactile valence, comparing the single modality (panel E, Figure 5) to the combinations (panels A & B), comes from averaging the valence with the thermal or visual stimulus.

There are a few notable exceptions where there *does* appear to be an additive effect, rather than averaging, particularly when combining F3A3D2 with thermal or visual stimuli. In isolation, F3A3D2 was rated as highly arousing and very low valence. However, the far left of Figure 6 shows all the combination stimuli that contain F3A3D2, and two effects have occurred: all the combinations have much higher valence than F3A3D2 by itself, but the vibration has also greatly increased the arousal of the non-vibration stimulus. For example, w21, BSSS and GSLS all have calm arousal by themselves, but higher arousal for their combinations with F3A3D2. The combinations in the far left of Figure 6 are all examples of the arousal of F3A3D2 being *added* to the valence of the other modality (thermal/visual).

Other examples primarily involve an additive effect on only one dimension (see Figure 6): valence *or* arousal. Combining w21+BSSS produces a calmer (but averaged valence) emotion than either individually; combining w43+RJLF leads to a higher arousal (but averaged valence) emotion than individually; and combining GSLS+c43 results in lower valence (but averaged arousal) emotion than individually.

Averaging (and adding) opens up interesting opportunities for interface designers: for a given stimulus type (e.g., vibration), designers can effectively move it around the V-A space by adding other cues, opening a trimodal *palette* for creating, and adjusting, affective cues. If a user inputs an emoji or otherwise indicates a desired emotion, a system using our results can identify where in the dimensional model it sits and choose appropriate stimuli to convey that emotion.

Individual Differences Have A Strong Effect

Seifi & Maclean [36] also found quite large individual differences in their participants' affective ratings of vibrations. The valence values for all of our 48 combination stimuli had standard deviations of more than 1.2 (up to 2.2, with an average of 1.7). Panels A to C in Figure 5 show that the average valence was little more than ±1, meaning nearly all stimuli were perceived as conveying both pleasant and unpleasant emotions, depending on the participant. These then cancel each other out to produce a more central mean value. We looked at how often each stimulus was rated as "pleasant" (valence of >= 1) vs. "unpleasant" (valence <= -1), to identify which might be more reliable in their interpretation across users, as feedback designs need to rely on predictable interpretation. Research on the interpretation of audible affective bursts [9] found reliability (i.e., accuracy) values of between 56% and 86%, and research into the identification of multimodal feedback, such as Earcons [11], Tactons [12] and thermal icons [46] considered identification rates of >75% to be acceptable. Therefore, we considered 75% as the threshold to deem a stimulus reliably "pleasant" or "unpleasant" if 75% or more of the subjective valence ratings were >= 1 or <= -1, respectively.

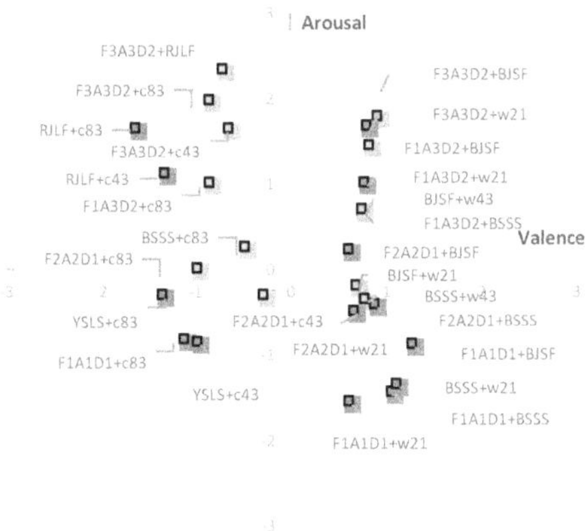

Figure 7: Distributions for reliably interpreted (>75%, green) and moderately reliable (65-74%, yellow) stimuli.

Only 14 out of the 48 stimuli (shown in green in Figure 7) met the threshold: five from Sub-study 1 (vibration + thermal), four from Sub-study 2 (vibration + visual) and five from Sub-study 3 (visual + thermal). A further 17 had reliability of 65-74% (Figure 7, yellow), leaving 17 stimuli whose pleasantness interpretation sits near chance level (50%). Examining the reliable vs. unreliable stimuli does not show particularly clear or predictable patterns. In Sub-study 1, warm stimuli are generally more reliably interpreted (in this case as pleasant) than cool stimuli, but this varies with vibration (e.g., F1A1D1 + c83 was reliably unpleasant at 79%). However, this pattern is mirrored in Sub-study 3, as the reliable (unpleasant) stimuli involved cooling, but only when combined with the (also unpleasant) RJLF or GSLS amoebas. In Sub-study 2, stimuli with blue amoeba were more reliably interpreted (as pleasant). It should be noted, however, that each participant had strong *internal reliability* in interpretation, rating the same stimulus similarly across the two presentations in a Sub-study, and our affective ratings closely match those in [49,51], suggesting a level of subjective consistency across studies and across/within people.

Summary

Overall, the results from Study 2 are promising. Combining modalities expands the available range of emotions that can be conveyed into previously hard-to-reach areas, and the manner in which combinations are interpreted (averaging/adding) can be leveraged to potentially access *any* position in the V-A space, provided it is between, or near, two known stimulus positions. However, emotional averaging, and individual differences, mean it remains challenging to reliably convey a *full* range of emotions.

STUDY 3: THREE-MODALITY COMBINATIONS

Having measured the effects of combining two modalities, Study 3 then combined stimuli from all three to investigate how that would influence the emotional range. The method for combining stimuli in Study 2 was systematic: the four stimuli that best represented each of the four quadrants in one modality were taken and combined with all four stimuli of the other modality. This was done to test the effects of combining complimentary and conflicting meaning, to see if it led to ratings otherwise impossible with only one modality. The lack of any significant interaction effects and the apparent averaging of emotionality observed in Study 2 led us to a more selective method for choosing trimodal combinations, to maximise the potential range.

	Arousal
F3A3D2+RJLF+c83 F1A3D2+RJLF+c43 F1A3D2+BJSF+c83	F3A3D2+BJSF+w43 F3A3D2+BSSS+w21 F1A3D2+BJSF+w43 Valence
F2A2D1+GSLS+c83 F1A1D1+GSLS+c43 F1A3D2+GSLS+c43	F1A1D1+BSSS+w21 F1A1D1+BJSF+w43 F2A2D1+BSSS+w43

Table 4: Trimodal vibrotactile, visual and thermal stimuli.

We first identified the bimodal stimuli from each Sub-study that sat furthest into each quadrant and then added a component from the 3rd modality (e.g., adding a visual component to a bimodal vibration+thermal pair). The component chosen was that which most frequently appeared in other pairs far into quadrants. The most common components in each quadrant were: F3A3D2, F1A3D2, c83, c43, RJLF & BJSF (top-left); F3A3D2, F1A3D2, w43, w21, BJSF & BSSS (top-right); F1A1D1, F2A2D1, w43, w21, BJSF & BSSS (bottom-right); F2A2D1, F1A1D1, c83, c43 & YSLS (bottom-left). These were then used to create the trimodal stimuli shown in Table 4, in the manner of: F3A3D2+c83 (Sub-study 1) plus F3A3D2+RJLF (S-s. 2) plus RJLF+c83 (S-s. 3) = F3A3D2+RJLF+c83.

Experimental Design & Procedure

Study 3 was completed by 12 of the same participants (9 female, 3 male) as Study 2, in a session carried out one week later. The hardware and experimental design were the same as Study 2, except that only one condition was completed (~15 minutes). Due to the selective nature of the stimulus set, there were uneven numbers of individual stimuli, meaning we could not carry out a balanced statistical analysis.

Results

The distribution for the trimodal stimuli is shown on the left of Figure 8. The values do not show a markedly different valence or arousal range compared to two-modality combinations, although the bottom-right stimuli sit slightly outside the bimodal range, as does one in the bottom-left. The arousal range is also slightly smaller, despite the presence of vibration; it may be that the dominance vibration exerts over one other modality is lessened when two other modalities are present. The three stimuli in each quadrant are the three stimuli chosen to represent each quadrant, so our selective approach has limited the pulling effects of stimuli far apart in valence/arousal, although averaging (this time between the positions of bimodal stimuli) was still seen. Combining three modalities did not lead to any additive effects on perceived emotionality. Anecdotally, some participants said it was confusing to process three modalities at once, and in our future research we will look at the processing, and relative impact, of each part of a trimodal stimulus.

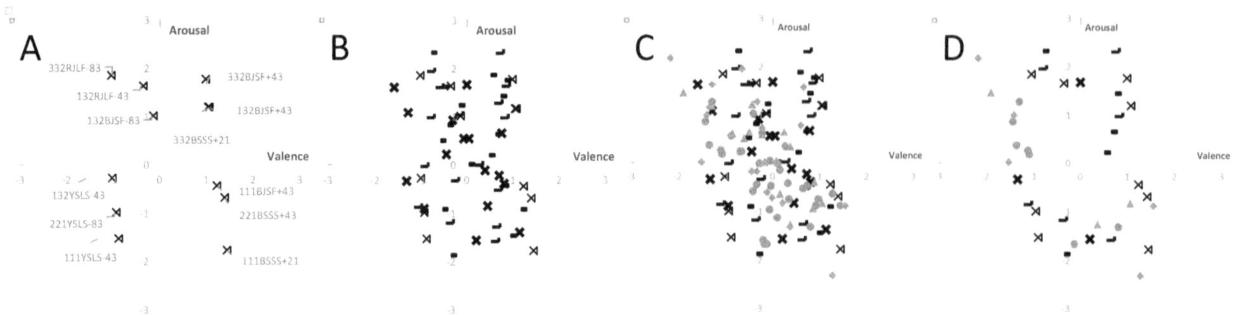

All Trimodal Stimuli (Study 3) | All Bimodal (Study 2) + Trimodal | All Stimuli (Study 2 and 3) | Approximated Circumplex

Figure 8: Panel A: distribution for trimodal stimuli. Panel B: trimodal stimuli overlaid with all bimodal distributions (Panel D in Figure 5). Panel C: All stimuli from this paper (Panel B overlaid on individual modality distributions (Figure 5, panel H). Panel D: Isolating stimuli around outside of range in an approximate circumplex [31].

GENERAL DISCUSSION

Our multimodal combinations, or *multi-moji*, have led to a wider range of conveyable emotional states than individual modalities are capable of, mostly in the top-right and bottom-left quadrants of the valence-arousal model [31], which have traditionally been the areas most poorly covered by feedback in HCI [3,49,51,53]. This means that UI designers now have a much richer set of possible emotional cues to use, to expand the affective range of feedback. Combining stimuli appears to complicate the interpretation of signals and, in the case of the averaging of emotionality, combining stimuli may act to *reduce* the emotional range, compared to individual stimuli. However, averaging also provides designers with a *multi-modal palette*: a method to convey potentially *any* emotional state, as long as it is positioned between known stimuli.

In general, vibration is limited to influencing the perceived arousal and, while thermal or visual feedback influence valence, their ability to do so may be hindered by the dominance of the vibrotactile sensation. Combining three modalities expands the total affective range over what is possible with two, again in the problematic top-right, bottom-left quadrants, and it appears to reduce the dominance of the vibrotactile stimulus, maintaining a better valence range.

Feedback Design Guidelines

We have synthesised and distilled the results from Studies 1 to 3, and their comparisons to previous unimodal research, to produce guidelines for how to best convey affective states using different feedback modalities.

Distributions as Lookup Tables

The distributions in this paper can be used as 'lookup tables' for designers wishing to convey particular emotional meaning through multimodal feedback e.g., by matching the position (or angle) of an emotion on the circumplex to the position of a stimulus, or simply choosing the stimulus that sits closest to a desired level of pleasantness/excitedness. Because of the multiple modalities, stimuli can be chosen based on the technology available or the capabilities of the user.

Combining Modalities Increases Affective Range

Through a trimodal *palette*, combining two or three modalities can increase the available affective range of a display, in comparison to single modalities, particularly in terms of arousal and in accessing 1) excited pleasant and 2) calm unpleasant emotional states. The modalities chosen can be tailored based on what state is required, as vibration expands the arousal range, while thermal/visual expands valence.

Three Modalities Temper Vibration, But Could Confuse

When vibration is presented with another modality, it can dominate the overall interpretation, potentially contracting the available valence. Combining three modalities appears to temper this dominance, allowing for a more balanced valence and arousal range. However, presenting three concurrent modalities may be perceptually taxing on users.

Averaged Emotionality Can Be Leveraged

When combining modalities, the emotionality of the constituent elements is generally averaged. While this can act to limit the accessible range compared to additive effects, it also means that a desired emotional state can be conveyed by combining two adjacent stimuli.

Individual Differences Should Be Considered

People are in favour of customizing their affective notifications [35] and so, given the range of interpretations, it is recommended that a system utilising multimodal affective feedback should provide an initial calibration phase. Participants can either rate example stimuli, or choose ones to fit an affective state, to tailor the feedback to their views.

CONCLUSIONS

The research in this paper represents the first systematic investigation into the effects of combining two and three modalities on the perceived emotion of stimuli, as a way of expanding the affective bandwidth of interfaces in HCI. Combining modalities led to a larger affective range than individual modalities, particularly in areas of the valence-arousal model that have previously been poorly covered. Vibration mostly influences arousal, while thermal and visual feedback mostly influence valence, but combining all three modalities together tempers the dominating influence of vibration. Our research provides a novel and flexible resource for designers to look up how they can convey a range of emotional states using different combinations of available modalities.

ACKNOWLEDGEMENTS

This work was funded by the EC ABBI project (#611452).

REFERENCES

1. Francis Adams and Charles Osgood. 1973. A Cross-Cultural Study of the Affective Meanings of Color. *Journal of Cross-Cultural Psychology* 4, 2: 135–156. http://doi.org/0803973233
2. Moses Akazue, Martin Halvey, Lynne Baillie, and Stephen Brewster. 2016. The Effect of Thermal Stimuli on the Emotional Perception of Images. *Proceedings of the SIGCHI Conference on Human Factors in Computing Systems (CHI '16)*, 4401–4412. http://doi.org/10.1145/2858036.2858307
3. Akshita, Harini Sampath, Bipin Indurkhya, Eunhwa Lee, and Yudong Bae. 2015. Towards Multimodal Affective Feedback : Interaction between Visual and Haptic Modalities. *Proceedings of the SIGCHI Conference on Human Factors in Computing Systems (CHI '15)*, 2043–2052. http://doi.acm.org/10.1145/2702123.2702288
4. Betsy App, Daniel N McIntosh, Catherine L Reed, and Matthew J Hertenstein. 2011. Nonverbal channel use in communication of emotion: how may depend on why. *Emotion* 11, 3: 603–617. http://doi.org/10.1037/a0023164
5. Solomon E Asch. 1946. Forming impressions of personality. *Journal of abnormal psychology* 41: 258–290. http://doi.org/10.1037/h0060423
6. Jeremy N Bailenson, Nick Yee, Scott Brave, Dan Merget, and David Koslow. 2007. Virtual interpersonal touch: expressing and recognizing emotions through haptic devices. *Human-Computer Interaction* 22: 325–353. http://doi.org/10.1080/07370020701493509
7. Moshe Bar and Maital Neta. 2006. Humans prefer curved visual objects. *Psychological Science* 17, 8: 645–648. http://doi.org/10.1111/j.1467-9280.2006.01759.x
8. Moshe Bar and Maital Neta. 2007. Visual elements of subjective preference modulate amygdala activation. *Neuropsychologia* 45, 10: 2191–200. http://doi.org/10.1016/j.neuropsychologia.2007.03.008
9. Pascal Belin, Sarah Fillion-Bilodeau, and Frédéric Gosselin. 2008. The Montreal Affective Voices: a validated set of nonverbal affect bursts for research on auditory affective processing. *Behavior research methods* 40, 2: 531–539. http://doi.org/10.3758/BRM.40.2.531
10. John Bowlby. 1969. *Attachment and Loss*. Hogarth Press, London.
11. Stephen A. Brewster, Peter C. Wright, and Alistair D.N. Edwards. 1995. Experimentally derived guidelines for the creation of earcons. *Adjunct Proceedings of HCI 1995*, 155–159.
12. Lorna Brown, Stephen Brewster, and Helen Purchase. 2006. Multidimensional Tactons for Non-Visual Information Presentation in Mobile Devices. *Proceedings of the International Conference on Human-Computer Interaction with Mobile Devices and Services (MobileHCI '06)*, 231–238. papers://c80d98e4-9a96-4487-8d06-8e1acc780d86/Paper/p79
13. Jessica Dawson, Oliver Schneider, Joel Ferstay, et al. 2013. It's alive!: exploring the design space of a gesturing phone. *Proceedings of Graphics Interface 2013*, 205–212. http://dl.acm.org/citation.cfm?id=2532164
14. Paul Ekman. 1993. Facial Expression and Emotion. *American Psychologist* 48, 4: 376–379.
15. Susan T. Fiske, Amy J.C. Cuddy, and Peter Glick. 2007. Universal dimensions of social cognition: warmth and competence. *Trends in Cognitive Sciences* 11, 2: 77–83. http://doi.org/10.1016/j.tics.2006.11.005
16. Martin Halvey, Michael Henderson, Stephen A. Brewster, Graham Wilson, and Stephen A. Hughes. 2012. Augmenting Media with Thermal Stimulation. *Proceedings of International Workshop on Haptic and Audio Interaction Design (HAID '12)*, 91–100. http://dx.doi.org/10.1007/978-3-642-32796-4_10
17. Harry F. Harlow. 1958. The Nature of Love. *American Psychologist* 13: 673–685.
18. Fabian Hemmert, Matthias Löwe, Anne Wohlauf, and Gesche Joost. 2013. Animate mobiles. *Proceedings of the 7th International Conference on Tangible, Embedded and Embodied Interaction - TEI '13*: 267. http://doi.org/10.1145/2460625.2460669
19. Matthew J Hertenstein, Rachel Holmes, Margaret McCullough, and Dacher Keltner. 2009. The communication of emotion via touch. *Emotion* 9, 4: 566–573. http://dx.doi.org/10.1037/a0016108
20. Inwook Hwang, Jongman Seo, Myongchan Kim, and Seungmoon Choi. 2013. Vibrotactile perceived intensity for mobile devices as a function of direction, amplitude, and frequency. *IEEE Transactions on Haptics* 6, 3: 352–362. http://doi.org/10.1109/TOH.2013.2
21. L Jones and M Berris. 2002. The Psychophysics of Temperature Perception and Thermal-Interface Design. *Proceedings of the International Symposium on Haptic Interfaces for Virtual Environment and Teleoperator Systems (HAPTICS)*, 137–142. papers://c80d98e4-9a96-4487-8d06-8e1acc780d86/Paper/p591
22. Peter J Lang, Margaret M Bradley, and BN Cuthbert. 2008. *International Affective Picture System (IAPS): Technical Manual and Affective Ratings*. Gainesville, FL.
23. Jung Min Lee, SY Jeong, and Ju DY. 2015. Emotional Interaction and Notification of Flexible Handheld Devices. *Proceedings of the SIGCHI Conference on Human Factors in Computing Systems (CHI '15)*, 2025–2030.
24. Wonjun Lee and Youn-kyung Lim. 2012. Explorative

research on the heat as an expression medium: focused on interpersonal communication. *Personal and Ubiquitous Computing* 16: 1039–1049. http://dx.doi.org/10.1007/s00779-011-0424-y

25. Markus Löchtefeld, Nadine Lautemann, Sven Gehring, and Antonio Krüger. 2014. ambiPad – Enriching Mobile Digital Media With Ambient Feedback. *Proceedings of the International Conference on Human-Computer Interaction with Mobile Devices and Services (MobileHCI '14)*, 295–298.
26. Hannah Miller, Jacob Thebault-Spieker, Shuo Chang, Isaac Johnson, Loren Terveen, and Brent Hecht. 2016. "Blissfully happy" or "ready to fight": Varying Interpretations of Emoji. *Proceedings of ICWSM 2016*.
27. Marianna Obrist, Sriram Subramanian, Elia Gatti, Benjamin Long, and Thomas Carter. 2015. Emotions Mediated Through Mid-Air Haptics. *Proceedings of the SIGCHI Conference on Human Factors in Computing Systems (CHI '15)*, 2053–2062. http://doi.acm.org/10.1145/2702123.2702361
28. Ofcom. 2015. Time spent online doubles in a decade. *Media Use and Attitudes 2015*. Retrieved September 18, 2016 from http://consumers.ofcom.org.uk/news/time-spent-online-doubles/
29. Esben W Pedersen, Sriram Subramanian, and Kasper Hornbæk. 2014. Is My Phone Alive?: A Large-scale Study of Shape Change in Handheld Devices Using Videos. *Proceedings of the SIGCHI Conference on Human Factors in Computing Systems (CHI '14)*: 2579–2588. http://doi.org/10.1145/2556288.2557018
30. AT Poffenberger and BE Barrows. 1924. The Feeling Value of Lines. *Journal of Applied Psychology* 8, 2: 187–205.
31. James A Russell. 1980. A Circumplex Model of Affect. *Journal of Personality and Social Psychology* 39, 6: 1161–1178. http://dx.doi.org/10.1037/h0077714
32. Katri Salminen, Veikko Surakka, Jani Lylykangas, et al. 2012. Tactile modulation of emotional speech samples. *Advances in Human-Computer Interaction* 2012. http://doi.org/10.1155/2012/741304
33. Katri Salminen, Veikko Surakka, Jukka Raisamo, et al. 2011. Emotional Responses to Thermal Stimuli. *Proceedings of ICMI 2011*, 193–196. http://doi.acm.org/10.1145/2070481.2070513
34. Katri Salminen, Veikko Surakka, Jukka Raisamo, et al. 2013. Cold or hot? How thermal stimuli are related to human emotional system? *Proceedings of International Workshop on Haptic and Audio Interaction Design (HAID '13)* 7989: 20–29. http://doi.org/10.1007/978-3-642-41068-0_3
35. Hasti Seifi, Chamila Anthonypillai, and Karon E. Maclean. 2014. End-user customization of affective tactile messages: A qualitative examination of tool parameters. *IEEE Haptics Symposium, HAPTICS*: 251–256. http://doi.org/10.1109/HAPTICS.2014.6775463
36. Hasti Seifi and Karon E. Maclean. 2013. A first look at individuals' affective ratings of vibrations. *Proceedings of World Haptics 2013*, 605–610. http://doi.org/10.1109/WHC.2013.6548477
37. Jocelyn Smith and Karon MacLean. 2007. Communicating emotion through a haptic link: Design space and methodology. *International Journal of Human-Computer Studies* 65: 376–387. http://www.sciencedirect.com/science/article/pii/S1071581906001911
38. Paul Strohmeier, Juan Pablo Carrascal, Bernard Cheng, Margaret Meban, and Roel Vertegaal. 2016. An Evaluation of Shape Changes for Conveying Emotions. *Proceedings of the SIGCHI Conference on Human Factors in Computing Systems (CHI '16)*, 3781–3792. http://doi.org/10.1145/2858036.2858537
39. Katja Suhonen, Sebastian Muller, Jussi Rantala, Kaisa Vaananen-Vainio-Mattila, Roope Raisamo, and Vuokko Lantz. 2012. Haptically Augmented Remote Speech Communication: A Study of User Practices and Experiences. *Proceedings of the Nordic Conference on Human-Computer Interaction (NordiCHI '12)*, 361–369. http://doi.acm.org/10.1145/2399016.2399073
40. Katja Suhonen, Kaisa Väänänen-Vainio-Mattila, and Kalle Mäkelä. 2012. User experiences and expectations of vibrotactile, thermal and squeeze feedback in interpersonal communication. *Proceedings of the Annual BCS Interaction Specialist Group Conference on People and Computers (BCS-HCI '12)*, 205–214. http://dl.acm.org/citation.cfm?id=2377916.2377939
41. TactileLabs. Haptuator Mark II Specification. Retrieved August 16, 2016 from http://tactilelabs.com/wp-content/uploads/2012/07/TL002-09-A_v1.01.pdf
42. Patricia Valdez and Albert Mehrabian. 1994. Effects of color on emotions. *Journal of Experimental Psychology* 123, 4: 394–409. http://doi.org/10.1037/0096-3445.123.4.394
43. Deltcho Valtchanov and Mark Hancock. 2015. EnviroPulse : Providing Feedback about the Expected Affective Valence of the Environment. *Proceedings of the SIGCHI Conference on Human Factors in Computing Systems (CHI '15)*, 2073–2082.
44. Hanna Venesvirta, Veikko Surakka, Yulia Gizatdinova, et al. 2015. Emotional Reactions to Point-Light Display Animations. *Interacting with Computers*, 1973: iwv028. http://doi.org/10.1093/iwc/iwv028
45. T W Whitfield and T J Wiltshire. 1990. Color psychology: a critical review. *Genetic, social, and general psychology monographs* 116, 4: 385–411. http://www.ncbi.nlm.nih.gov/pubmed/2289687
46. Graham Wilson, Stephen Brewster, Martin Halvey, and

Stephen Hughes. 2012. Thermal Icons: Evaluating Structured Thermal Feedback for Mobile Interaction. *Proceedings of the International Conference on Human-Computer Interaction with Mobile Devices and Services (MobileHCI '12)*, 309–312. papers://c80d98e4-9a96-4487-8d06-8e1acc780d86/Paper/p9328

47. Graham Wilson, Stephen Brewster, Martin Halvey, and Stephen Hughes. 2013. Thermal Feedback Identification in a Mobile Environment. *Proceedings of International Workshop on Haptic and Audio Interaction Design (HAID '13)*, Article 2. papers://c80d98e4-9a96-4487-8d06-8e1acc780d86/Paper/p9329

48. Graham Wilson, Gavin Davidson, and Stephen Brewster. 2015. In the Heat of the Moment : Subjective Interpretations of Thermal Feedback During Interaction. *Proceedings of the SIGCHI Conference on Human Factors in Computing Systems (CHI '15)*, 2063–2072. http://doi.acm.org/10.1145/2702123.2702219

49. Graham Wilson, Dobromir Dobrev, and Stephen A Brewster. 2016. Hot Under the Collar: Mapping Thermal Feedback to Dimensional Models of Emotion. *Proceedings of the SIGCHI Conference on Human Factors in Computing Systems (CHI '16)*, 4838–4849.

50. Graham Wilson, Martin Halvey, Stephen A Brewster, and Stephen A Hughes. 2011. Some Like it Hot? Thermal Feedback for Mobile Devices. *Proceedings of the SIGCHI Conference on Human Factors in Computing Systems (CHI '11)*, 2555–2564. http://doi.acm.org/10.1145/1978942.1979316

51. Graham Wilson, Pietro Romeo, and Stephen A Brewster. 2016. Mapping Abstract Visual Feedback to a Dimensional Model of Emotion. *Proceedings of the SIGCHI Conference on Human Factors in Computing Systems (CHI '16) Extended Abstracts*.

52. Steve Yohanan and Karon E. MacLean. 2011. Design and assessment of the haptic creature's affect display. *Proceedings of Human-robot interaction 2011*, 473. http://doi.org/10.1145/1957656.1957820

53. Yongjae Yoo, Taekbeom Yoo, Jihyun Kong, and Seungmoon Choi. 2015. Emotional Responses of Tactile Icons : Effects of Amplitude , Frequency , Duration , and Envelope. *Proceedings of World Haptics 2015*, 235–240. http://dx.doi.org/10.1109/WHC.2015.7177719

The Heat is On: A Temperature Display for Conveying Affective Feedback

Jordan Tewell
City, University of London
London, United Kingdom
jordan.tewell.1@city.ac.uk

Jon Bird
City, University of London
London, United Kingdom
jon.bird@city.ac.uk

George R. Buchanan
University of Melbourne
Melbourne, Australia
george.buchanan@unimelb.edu.au

ABSTRACT
Previous research has investigated whether temperature can augment a range of media including music, images and video. We describe the first experiment to investigate whether temperature can augment emotion conveyed by text messages. A challenge in prior work has been ensuring users can discern different thermal signals. We present an improved technique for thermal feedback that uses an array of three thermal stimulators. We demonstrate that the Thermal Array Display (TAD) increases users' ability to identify temperatures within a narrower range, compared to using a single thermal stimulator. While text messages dominate valence in the absence of context for temperature, the TAD consistently conveys arousal, and can enhance arousal of text messages, especially those that are emotionally neutral. We discuss potential applications of augmenting text with temperature.

Author Keywords
Thermal feedback; thermal haptics; affective computing

ACM Classification Keywords
H.5.2. User Interfaces – Haptic IO.

INTRODUCTION
An emerging trend in CHI research is using temperature to augment. Recent studies have examined temperature conveying qualities, such as emotion, activity level, and social distance [18][40][26].

Human performance in perceiving temperature and its rate of change potentially limits the application of this approach. Cutaneous sense of temperature is carried on nerve endings with slow response times [23] and incorrect perception of temperature results in sensory illusions such as 'synthetic heat' as illustrated by placing a hand on interlaced warm and cool bars [5]. Thermal signals must be sufficiently intense, otherwise they may be difficult for users to perceive correctly, if at all [42]. Along with human factors are limitations of thermal electric coolers (TECs), the technology used in thermal feedback research. Depending on which TECs are used, they can have high power consumption, high latency, and low accuracy.

We demonstrate latency can be mitigated using an array of TECs. The Thermal Array Display (TAD) is a device worn on the arm that displays patterns of warm, cool, and neutral temperatures using three TEC stimulators. Individually, the TECS are heated and cooled over a small thermal range, but as a group, they signal a wide temperature span. Multiple stimulators also increase stimulated skin area, easing perception of the thermal signal for users.

There are three contributions in this paper. First, we conducted a pilot study to detect if participants could identify warm and cool patterns on their arm. The difficulty of discerning patterns led to investigating if the TAD could instead increase user discrimination of temperature. Results showed participants could identify thermal cues signalled with an array of TECs better compared to the case where only one TEC was used. Second, we conducted another study to demonstrate how thermal cues signalled with the TAD can communicate arousal. Lastly, we proceed to demonstrate that, while text messages dominate valence in the absence of context for temperature, the TAD consistently affects arousal, especially arousal of more emotionally neutral text messages.

BACKGROUND
While vibrotactile feedback (VTF) research is more common to convey information, Suhonen *et al.* reported instances where VTF was misunderstood emotionally [32]. Alternatively, they claimed that temperature could communicate emotional meanings with warmth and coolness, thanks to its bi-directional and continuous advantage over VTF.

HCI literature has investigated whether thermal cues can convey qualities, such as social presence and proximity, [10][26], supporting behaviour such as musical performance, [25] and therapy [35]. AffectPhone [18] mapped arousal to temperature on the recipient's phone, and Lovelet [8] conveyed situation by sensing body temperature and sending it to the other partner. These examples, however, focused on output form novelty and lacked extensive, empirical studies to verify hardware design or the feedback. As noted in the Introduction, human

CHI 2017, May 06-11, 2017, Denver, CO, USA
© 2017 ACM. ISBN 978-1-4503-4655-9/17/05...$15.00
DOI: http://dx.doi.org/10.1145/3025453.3025844

physiology limits effectiveness of thermal communication, and a more detailed examination is needed.

Thermal Feedback System Design

A direction thermal HCI has taken is examining specifics of designing effective sensory output systems. Wilson *et al.* [42] noted 1°C/sec rates of change were appropriate for thermal displays and did not produce stimuli more difficult to detect than 3°C/sec or greater changes. 1°C change magnitudes, on the other hand, were harder to detect than 3°C and 6°C changes and resulted in longer time-to-detections. Users found it harder to detect thermal changes in a mobile setting than when they were seated [42], when wearing stimulators over clothes instead of directly on the skin [15], and when using stimulators outdoors due to ambient temperature interference [13]. Wilson *et al.* combined thermal cues with VTF [39] and examined practical uses of thermal feedback, such as assigning temperatures to activity levels and reviewing restaurants [40]. While results revealed users could detect different levels of temperature, it was not clear, indeed doubtful, if those levels could be discriminated accurately.

Problems of discrimination are primarily due to nonlinear temperature effects that occur when areas of skin in close proximity are exposed to differing temperatures. Due to the low ability of people to discern detailed spatial resolution of the skin's sense of heat, adjacent stimulations affect one other, creating perceptual temperature illusions. These physiological limitations create potential barriers to the effective use of thermal displays.

A key physiological phenomenon in thermal feedback design is *referral*. This occurs when stimulation at one point on the skin is experienced at another location. Green [11] demonstrated this when participants placed their index, middle, and ring fingers on three TECs set to hot and cold patterns. He noted strong sensations outweighed weak ones. Participants found the middle sensation strongest when adjacent stimulators were the same temperature – a form of referral. Referral also occurred when stimulation of the ring and index finger created a sense of temperature applied to the middle finger. When adjacent stimulations mixed hot and cold, users had a (mild) burning sensation termed *synthetic heat.*

Oron-Giland *et al.* [27], created a thermal display comprised of three TEC stimulators worn on the arm. They investigated synthetic heat and primarily looked at spatial configurations of two stimulators turned on in pairs of hot and cold. They found great variance in detection times among participants, and that the thermal detection threshold varied more for hot temperatures than cold. However, their use of multiple TECs only focused on synthetic heat, and they did not examine potential of three-stimulator feedback to communicate thermal patterns to invoke emotion.

Other researchers have used multiple stimulators to explore thermal sensitivity of different body locations. Watanbe *et al.* [36] used two stimulators mounted on a surface that the user's arm rested on. They sent mixed pairs of hot (40°C), cold (20°C), and neutral (33°C) temperatures to participants, who reported the sensations at each stimulator. A major discovery was that extent of referral increases for warm sensations nearer the elbow, or towards the body centre, and cold stimulation has greater referral distance near the hand, or towards the periphery. Participants could judge correctly when both stimulators were set to the same temperature, but had trouble distinguishing if one was set to neutral because of referral. Synthetic heat was also perceived asymmetrically- the wrist does not perceive it, or more generally, thermal referral, as well as if the stimulation occurred nearer the elbow. Thus, stimulator location influences user detection accuracy and perception for hot, cold, or synthetic temperatures.

Multiple stimulators have also been used to address the problem of the time it takes users to discern temperature stimuli. Sato and Maeno [31] found that, although distinguishing thermal stimuli patterns is difficult, multiple stimulators can reduce latency. They created a device consisting of a small 2x2 matrix of TECs that participants placed their fingertips on that exploited the skin's low spatial resolution. Participants could only identify TEC positions at 50% chance levels, but could guess correctly whether the stimulus was hot or cold. Sato and Maeno also demonstrated that patterns of all hot or all cold lowered detection response times compared to mixed patterns. Akiyama *et al.* [1] used two TECs side by side, placed under the hand to 'prime' the skin before sending a hot and cold stimulus. They claimed this reduced detection times up to 28% and 24% for hot and cold, respectively.

Affective Thermal Feedback

Giving someone the cold shoulder or giving them a warm welcome are popular metaphors for communicating abstract concepts that humans harbour toward each other. Concrete experiences, such as sensing temperature, ground such concepts when they are co-experienced, such as affection. This demonstrates a "systemic inter-dependence among language, perception, and social proximity" [17, pp 1214].

Because of this, temperature could be used to alter one's physical state to regulate underlying emotions. Thermoception has both enteroceptive and affective aspects, as both temperature and emotion are processed in the limbic system. Medical studies utilizing PET and fMRI imaging of the brain have shown cooling a patient's right hand linearly correlates with activity in the insular cortex, which regulates internal feelings such as panic, anxiety, sadness, and sexual arousal [6]. Warm stimulation activates distributed regions of the brain associated with affective responses and could induce subjective awareness, such as inner body feelings and emotionality [33].

Social perception involves physical and perceptual content. Lawrence and Bargh described 'Psychological Warmth' to influence a first impression of others. They primed participants by asking them to hold warm and cold beverages before meeting a stranger. Participants primed with warm beverages perceived the stranger more positively than those who held cold beverages [37]. A similar experiment demonstrated that warm beverages induced greater social proximity, and warm, ambient temperatures enabled participants to describe social events more concretely [17]. Subsequently, 'Psychological Cold' influences social exclusion, [43] as excluded participants gave lower estimates of room temperature and craved hotter foods than those not excluded in their study.

As discussed earlier, thermal stimulator prototypes have been used in HCI research to invoke emotional responses, but few have examined the effect of temperature on emotion thoroughly. Salminen *et al.* examined two methods for conveying temperature to invoke emotional responses [30]. In both methods, warming up was sensed as more arousing, dominating, and motivational. Temperature did not affect ratings in pleasantness (valence) and acceptability. Lee and Lim [21] [22] asked participants to investigate information conveyed with wrist worn thermal devices. They found thermal feedback only has meaning in context, but has a unique emotional value which allows for an unobtrusive, casual method of communicating. Heat worked better on a visceral, unconscious level than cognitive, as humans have no legacy for communicating information with heat. Wilson *et al.* [41] examined thermal responses on valence, arousal, and domination. They found useful parameters for temperature to elicit emotional responses but only few emotions were elicited from temperature alone. However, they did not look at thermal augmentation.

Research utilizing thermal augmentation has been used on images and movies, but have only focused on novelty with no significant work relating specific emotions with the stimuli. Hannah *et al.* [16] augmented videos displayed on a television by heating a remote device during happy scenes and cooling it for sad ones. They proposed information could be embedded within the metadata of a movie file for more practical applications. AmbiPad [24] was an Android tablet modified with coloured lighting around the frame and TECs on the back to enhance contents of the screen when it played a movie.

The most intensive research in augmentation was carried out by Halvey *et al.* [12]. They studied the effect of temperature on subjective perceptions of images and music to evoke emotional responses. Images were selected from the International Affective Picture System, and music was selected based on audio dynamics and volume levels. They found temperature could significantly enhance or dampen affective experiences with images. However, no significant differences were found pulsing temperature dynamically with music. They only used three temperatures, and only varied the rate of change as a parameter.

No similar research has augmented text with temperature. Though Thermal Hug Belt [10] examined how temperature could mediate a sense of social presence when subjects used IM chat, they did not examine how temperature could elevate or decrease emotion, as text was not controlled.

To summarize the literature review, research has shown that temperature can effectively communicate meanings, such as emotional state. [32][18][8] demonstrated temperature eliciting such reactions from participants. Furthermore, studies have examined key parameters for designing thermal feedback, such as Wilson *et al.*'s work, [42][15][13][39][40]. Green [11], Oran-Giland *et al.* [27], Watanabe *et al.* [36], Sato and Maeno [31], and Akiyama *et al.* [1] incorporated multiple stimulators into their work to investigate perceptual aspects of temperature. However, they focused on physiological aspects and were not necessary HCI related. Thus, gaps in the knowledge remain:

- Can multi-stimulator thermal devices relay more complex patterns akin to vibrotactile patterns [3]?
- Can users' thermal sensory acuity be boosted further than previous work [31][1]?
- Can temperature augment emotion when paired with social media messages?

HARDWARE OVERVIEW

We constructed the Thermal Array Display, or TAD, to investigate these knowledge gaps. First, we examined how accurately users could distinguish thermal patterns. The TAD device, shown in Figure 1, is worn on the arm and can signal thermal patterns using three stimulators.

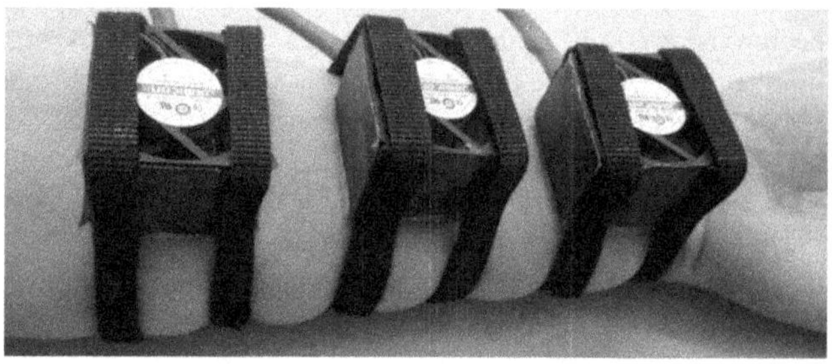

Figure 1. The Thermal Array Display

Most modern thermal output systems use TECs: flat, rectangular, thermoelectric components that cool down and heat up on either side depending on how current is applied. By varying voltage using Pulse Width Modulated (PWM) signals from a micro-controller, one can control how much heat is transferred from the cool side to the warm side, depending on rise time of the signal. When polarity is reversed to a TEC, the heat transfer direction reverses, allowing either side to warm up or cool down. This behaviour can be moderated using an H-Bridge circuit, which is implemented in motor drivers. By using a Proportional-Integral-Derivative (PID) controller, one can set the temperature of the TEC by reading current temperature using a thermistor and appropriately updating output and direction of the current to the TEC.

In our system, an Arduino Mega 2560 is used to control three TECs independently. Each TEC (MCPE1-01708NC-S, Multicomp) is connected to a thermistor (MC65F103A, Amphenol Sensors) that is polled in the Arduino main loop. As Arduino pins are rated at only 40 mA, the TECs are driven by a motor driver (MC33926, Pololu), which draws power from a 6V, 10A mains supply. Each TEC is connected in series with an inductor to 'smooth' the PWM signal from the motor driver to appear as a DC current source. This signal is pulsed at 490 Hz, as it produced the most stable temperature behaviour compared with other frequencies attainable on the Arduino.

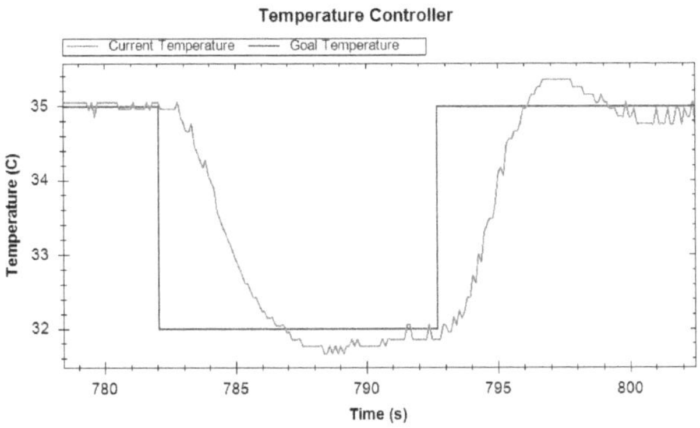

Figure 2: Temperature Plot

Maintaining a fixed rate of change is difficult using a PID controller. After careful tuning, we achieved, on average, 1°C/s rates of change using tuning parameters of K_p=50, K_i=2, and K_d=0, the proportional, integral, and derivative constants, respectively. Figure 2 shows a time plot of temperature changes using the system, first cooling from 35°C to 32°C and then warming up back to 35°C.

Figure 3 shows the stimulator pad construction. Design is based Oron-Giland *et al.*'s device [27], the only instance of an arm-worn, three-stimulator display in literature. Each stimulator consists of a TEC, attached to a heat sink (BGA-STD-115, ABL) using double-sided thermal tape. A 5V DC fan is attached on top of the heat sink by gorilla tape. Fans are driven from an external power supply using BD137 NPN transistors. Both heat sinks and the fans are needed to extract heat away from the TECs. Otherwise, the efficiency of the TECs decreases as they heat up, potentially posing a safety hazard. The participant was insulated from the heat sink using a panel of cardboard and Styrofoam glued together. Double-sided Velcro was glued to both sides of the heat sink, which allows users to wear the stimulators by strapping them around the arm.

Oron-Giland *et al.* used a thin, 3mm thick, metal plate at the point of contact between the skin and the TEC itself. This involved drilling a hole in one of the plate's four lateral surfaces to insert the temperature probe into. This is an alternative to mounting the sensor directly on top of the TEC, as is done in most systems reported and allows the stimulator to be comfortably worn. It also protects the sensor from exposure to the ambient environment, which may result in less reliable readings. Instead of using aluminium for the plate however, we used C101 copper due to its superior heat transfer properties. Before inserting the probe, the hole was filled with thermal grease (MX-4, Artic). After insertion, it was sealed with epoxy.

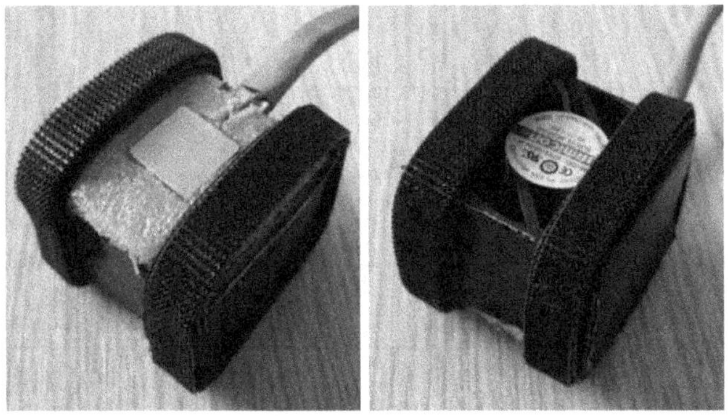

Figure 3: A Single Stimulator- Bottom (Left) and Top (Right)

Software consists of Arduino firmware and a PC user interface. The Arduino monitors temperature from the thermistors, connected as part of a voltage dividing circuit that feeds into the Arduino's analog pins. This raw voltage input is converted into degrees Celsius using the Steinhart-Hart thermistor equation. The PC software interfaces with the Arduino using the USB serial library CMDmessenger [7]. The basic functionality sets the temperature of each TEC separately, monitors safety, reads parameters from files, and logs participant data in real-time.

PILOT STUDY

The initial aim of the TAD was developing a pattern-based, thermal-tactile language. We conducted a short pilot to see if users could identify patterns of three stimulators set to warm, cool, or neutral temperatures.

- Participants wore the TAD and were shown visual representations of eight thermal patterns.
- Participants were instructed to select one they believed was 'displayed' to them.
- Each pattern was used twice.

Oron-Giland *et al.* [27] proposed patterns of three alternating thermal stimuli but no study was conducted. Wilson discussed the ideas of area stimulation and 'thermal waves' [38], like unidirectional vibro-tactile rhythms [3]. However, he did not pursue it due to perceptual problems and technological issues. This research carried out a pilot study to investigate this further.

As the TAD uses three stimulators, 27 patterns are achievable with warm, cool, and neutral temperatures. A taxonomy was devised to categorize such patterns. Each had a 'mechanical' device setting and a 'perceived' effect derived from physiological illusions [11] and the anticipated spatial direction the temperature would travel [36]. Two parameters were used: the temperature direction (hot, cold, and neutral) and TEC arm positioning, (elbow, middle of the forearm, and wrist). Table 1 illustrates a few of these.

Mechanical	Description	Perceived
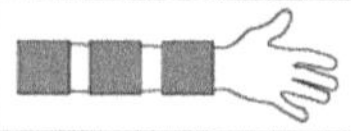	Enhanced Hot	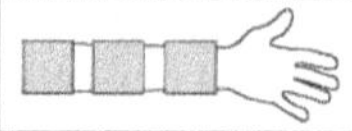
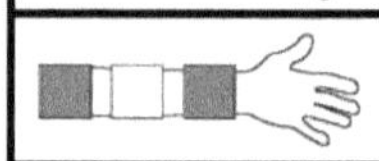	Inward Referred Hot	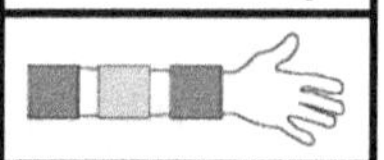
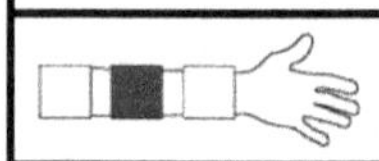	Outward Referred Cold	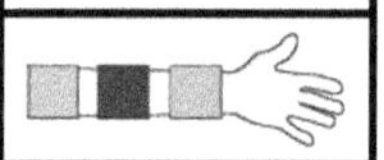
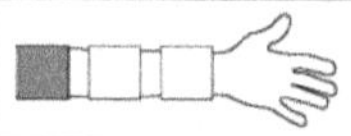	Proximal Referred Hot	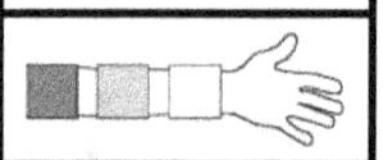
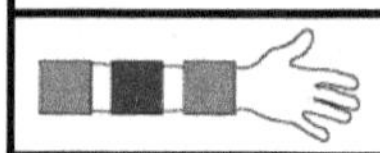	Synthetic Heat	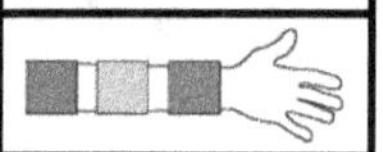
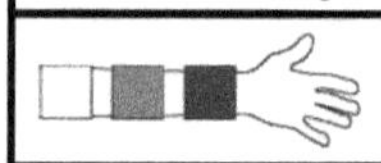	Distal Optimal Synthetic Heat	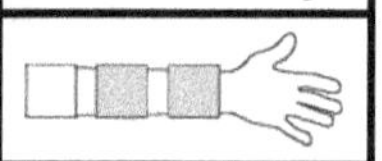

Table 1: Thermal Patterns

Pilot studies revealed similar findings to Sato and Maeno [31]: participants could not easily identify temperature of the individual TECs when presented simultaneously. We therefore investigated whether the TAD could improve ability of users to accurately identify single temperature states. The TAD increases the skin area that is stimulated which could potentially enhance signal intensity, making perception of temperature easier to discriminate.

Two further studies were conducted with the TAD. The first compared two methods of signalling temperature with three stimulators and compared accuracy of users' responses to the case where only one stimulator was used. Participants recorded responses on a 7-point Likert scale (Figure 4), where each point, illustrated as a radio button, corresponded to a temperature state of the TAD (Table 2). The second study investigated if thermal cues could convey emotion by measuring valence and arousal when participants viewed positive, neutral, and negatively rated Facebook messages on-screen with temperature.

EXPERIMENT 1

Participants were asked to identify seven thermal stimuli using three methods: Single, where only one stimulator was used, Amplification, where all stimulators were set to the same temperature, and Quantification, where the target temperature was represented by setting one, two, or all three stimulators to the warmest or coolest temperature.

- The Single, Amplification, and Quantification tests were presented in random order.
- Each test had a calibration session beforehand to acquaint participants with stimuli.
- During each test, seven temperature stimuli were presented three times each, and the skin temperature returned to neutral before each was presented.
- Participants made selections on a 7-point Likert scale.
- There was a five-minute break in between each test.

Stimuli Design

Three parameters were considered when designing the temperature stimuli: neutral temperature; temperature range; and the temperature difference between stimuli. We discuss each in this section and then describe how we signalled temperature using the TAD.

Since skin adapts to stimulation, consideration was made which temperature to use as the neutral stimulus or baseline temperature. This neutral temperature varies from person to person, but it is thought to be in the range of 20°C - 40°C [19]. Within this range, skin will adapt slowly to reduce the sensation of stimulation until full re-adaptation has taken place and the user no longer perceives any sensation. Temperatures closer to the middle of this range are easier to adapt than at the extremes [14]. Beyond this range, temperatures feel persistently cold or hot [20]. Such extreme temperatures are not commonly used as they are uncomfortable and painful. We chose a conservative temperature of 32°C as was used in Wilson and Halvey *et al.*'s work [39][42][13][25].

The use of wide temperature ranges requires more time to reach the extreme temperatures. This results in longer latencies, the time between temperature changes. It is paramount to use as small a range that can be detected to reduce time taken for the TECs to change temperature, and thereby reduce the time to communicate a temperature state. Limiting the number of thermal scale points and the temperature difference between them minimizes the total temperature range needed for a feedback system.

Wilson *et al.* used a temperature range of 22°C-38°C with 2°C as the smallest difference between two stimuli [40]. Within this range is a safe and comfortable zone of temperatures appropriate for thermal feedback. In contrast, we chose a narrower range of 29°C - 35°C and reduced the step between stimuli to 1°C. These two changes reduced the time to signal different temperature states. More importantly, smaller step changes make it more difficult to discern neighbouring states. This forms a better apparatus for testing fine stimuli discriminability with multiple TECs.

Table 2 shows how temperature was signalled in each test. Squares represent stimulators, where the left, middle, and right squares represent the wrist, middle, and elbow stimulators, respectively. Colours denote whether the stimulus was warm, cool, or neutral using red, blue, and white, respectively. Colour saturation indicates stimuli intensity. There are three intensities for warm and cool.

Single Test

This test used only the middle stimulator. The middle stimulator was chosen to prevent biasing effects from using either the elbow location, which would have made warm sensations stronger [36], or the wrist, which is the direction cold sensations spread better towards. Other stimulators were not worn as it eliminated the decision of whether to leave them on (at neutral) or off. Participants were asked to identify which of the seven stimuli was presented. Stimuli differed by 1°C increments with neutral at 32°C. Hence, warm was 33°C, warmer was 34°C, and warmest was 35°C. Cool was 31°C, cooler was 30°C, and coolest was 29°C.

Amplification Test

This method represents intensity by setting all stimulators to the same temperature. All three stimulators were worn, and the participants were asked to identify the combined stimulus. As with the single test, temperature states differed by 1°C increments with neutral at 32°C, applied to all three stimulators, using the temperatures from the Single test.

Quantification Test

Participants were asked to discriminate cues wearing all stimulators, however, this approach used only 29°C for cool stimuli and 35°C for warm stimuli. It is the number of active stimulators that determines the intensity rather than indicating intensity by temperature. Thus, warm set one stimulator to 35°C, warmer set two stimulators to 35°C, and warmest set all stimulators to 35°C. Cool set one stimulator to 29°C, cooler set two stimulators at 29°C, and coolest set all three stimulators to 29°C. Stimulators that are not set to either 29°C or 35°C were left at 32°C, neutral.

Name	Single	Amplification	Quantification
Coolest			
Cooler			
Cool			
Neutral			
Warm			
Warmer			
Warmest			

Table 2: Experiment 1 Stimuli

Procedure

Twelve participants, ten males and two females, were recruited from the engineering school of a UK university. While gender differences are a debatable subject in thermal perception studies, the most recent paper by Wilson *et al.* [41] showed no differences in perceiving temperature. Each participant received £10 for their time, in line with standard practices at the institution, and the experiment was approved by the school ethics board in advance.

To ensure both wellbeing of participants and efficacy of the study, exclusions were made. Individuals could not participate if they had medical problems that could impede temperature perception, such as over-sensitive skin, or where exposure to temperature causes discomfort or harm.

Participants wore the TAD on their non-dominant arm, following the practice of previous studies [40]. Each participant took approximately one hour to complete the experiment, including induction and completion of all tests. There was no time limit imposed on participants, thus the duration lasted until they submitted their selections for each trial. Participants, however, were instructed not to dwell on answers and to move on as quickly as they could.

The entire experiment was automated. Tests were separated by five-minute breaks to allow participants to relax their arms. Participants were told to read the instructions on screen and complete the tests by recording their perception of the signalled temperature on a 7-point Likert scale, shown in Figure 4. Each point denotes one of the states, colour coded from 'Coolest' to 'Warmest', with 'Neutral' in the middle. The seven stimuli were presented three times, in random order for each test. The order of the three tests was also randomized by counterbalancing beforehand.

Preceding each test was a calibration session to familiarize participants with the stimuli presented and the user interface. This session was nearly identical to the real tests that followed, but the Likert scale was pre-selected with the correct response. Additional color-coded graphics depicted the position of stimulators on the arm, with instructions on navigating the interface, and the displayed name of the selected stimulus, e.g. 'Warmest' or 'Neutral'.

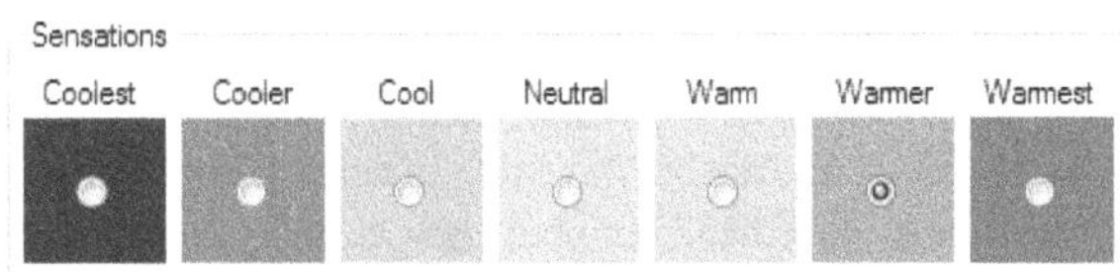

Figure 4: User Interface

Between each stimulus was a short delay to allow the skin temperature to re-adapt back to neutral. This process, discussed in the Stimuli Design section, ensured participants could discern the next trial without bias from the proceeding stimulus. It also serves to establish the reference temperature for judging subsequent stimuli. Previous studies used delays between ten seconds [40] to two minutes [15] for re-adaptation. We chose the shortest time of ten seconds due to time constraints of the study. Our temperature range was even smaller than the range used in [40], so this time was deemed acceptable. After re-adapting, the next stimulus was presented for three seconds and then the scale was displayed on screen for selection.

Results

We first tested the error rate (frequency) for all three presentations, using a chi-squared test. This produced $\chi^2 = 10.89$, df=2, p=0.004. The Single method provided the worst outcome, with 34.9% correct judgments, while Amplification and Quantification produced 49.2% and 44.4% correct ratings, respectively.

We also tested the degree of error, the absolute difference between the target and actual values. The degree of error was measured separately from error rate as non-significance in either test would lead to rejecting the alternate hypothesis. A Kruskall-Wallis test on the degree of error produced H=22.59, df=2, $p < 0.001$. Again, the multi-stimulator approaches both proved superior to the single stimulator. The alternative test for the population distribution of errors using chi-squared also proved significant (from errors of 1 to 5, calculated from the error formula above) and produced χ^2=20.55, df=8, p=0.001. The multi-stimulator methods gave more accurate detections, and resulted in lower degrees of error. As the data was not normally distributed, ANOVA was not used.

Subsequent testing for the precision of the two methods produced a clear advantage for the amplification method in terms of exact ratings (χ^2= 4.51, df=1, p=0.036), but there was no difference in the relative degree of error. This suggests that Amplification is the most promising method for signalling thermal states, but as the advantage over Quantification was low-power, both multi-stimulator approaches are more accurate alternatives to the traditional single stimulator method and merit further study.

EXPERIMENT 2

We examined how temperature could be used as an augmenting modality for Facebook post messages. The experiment consisted of two studies: a pilot study that selected appropriate media from an existing corpus of Facebook messages and thermal stimuli; and a main study which combined the messages and thermal stimuli in pairs to investigate whether temperature could augment the emotion communicated by the Facebook posts.

For both studies, twelve participants were selected from the engineering school of a UK university. Like the previous experiment, each participant received £10 for his or her time, and the same exclusions rules were applied. Nine males and three females were used in the pilot, which took about 40 minutes to complete. For the main study, which took about an hour to complete, twelve new participants comprised of four males and eight females were used.

Pilot Study

A two-part pilot was conducted to verify messages and thermal stimuli appropriate for the main study. First, participants evaluated valance and arousal of messages from a previous study [28]. Next, participants rated valance and arousal of the thermal stimuli from Experiment 1.

- In Part 1, participants rated twenty-five messages, each repeated three times.
- In Part 2, participants rated seven temperatures using Amplification, repeated three times each.
- Participants were given written instructions for both parts and a five-minute break in between.
- Participants reported valance and arousal selections on two 5-point SAM scales.

Stimuli Selection

Augmentation of text messages using temperature could be studied by examining impact of valence and arousal. Research investigating text messages and emotion such as [9] have demonstrated agreement between expert trained users and naïve (non-emotion expert) users when rating emotions from the Russell circumplex model [29]. Though databases of such messages exist [34], early pilots revealed difficulty of obtaining suitable messages that our non-expert participants agreed were happy or unhappy and excited or calm. Instead, we utilized results of a recent study [28] that rated Facebook posts by psychological trained annotators based on valence and arousal traits.

Similar to Halvey *et al.* [12] we selected messages for each emotional state: high valance/high arousal, high valence/low arousal, low valence/high arousal, low valence/low arousal, and neutral valence/neutral arousal. As the study in [28] rated messages on 9-point scales, any message rated 1-3 by both experts in the study was selected as a candidate for either low arousal or low valance. Messages rated 7-9 were candidates for high arousal or high valance. Messages that were rated 5 for both valance and arousal were candidates for the neutral stimulus. We used these criteria as there were only few instances of messages that had either 1 or 9 ratings for valence and arousal that were consistent across the reviewers. Neutral messages with ratings of 5 were abundant, and we did not have to extend their score range to 4-6 for inclusion. Along with the text messages, the thermal stimuli described in the Amplification section were also evaluated emotionally.

A 5-point Self-Assessment Manikin (SAM) technique [2] was employed to capture participants' valence and arousal reactions to both the temperature and message stimuli. In light of the experience of participants in the first study we aimed to simplify the effort required to rate signals. For this reason, we did not use the 9-point SAM scale used in the Facebook study, nor did we use the 7-point scale from Experiment 1 as we were not measuring discrimination of the seven thermal stimuli.

Procedure

To ensure consistency across participants, stimulator positions were marked on the arms before the study. Elbow distance to the wrist was measured; the midpoint was marked for placement of the middle stimulator to compensate for differing forearm lengths. Furthermore, participants were given a brief 'calibration' session where they were presented the warmest and coolest stimuli to ensure they could detect these temperatures and to allow themselves to become familiarized with the TAD.

After the setup, participants completed the two parts of the study. In Part 1, they rated the Facebook messages. They were instructed to read the message that appeared at the top of the screen and were given the context to imagine it was sent from a close friend on Facebook. Participants rated valence and arousal using the SAM as shown in Figure 5.

After completion, the TAD device was then attached to their non-dominant arm and they proceeded to rate the thermal stimuli. Unlike the messages, the temperatures were not given a context in the instructions, and participants were instructed to just rate how the temperatures made them feel while perceiving them. Like Experiment 1, ten seconds was used to re-adapt the skin to return to a baseline temperature in between trials. All stimuli for both parts were repeated three times in a random, counter-balanced order unknown to either the participant or the lab monitor until after the test. Like before, there was no time limit to making selections.

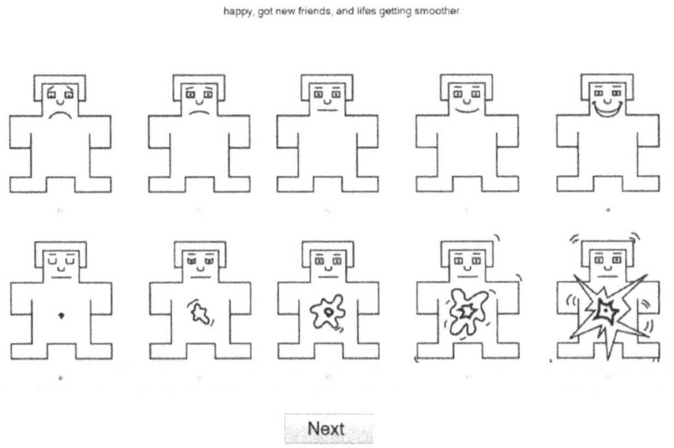

Figure 5: SAM Interface. The small text at the top is the Facebook message post.

Results – rating message valence and arousal

Participants could differentiate messages per valance and arousal. Table 3 shows the five messages selected for the main study, with mean valance and arousal scores. As a 5-point scale was used, neutral scores are 3. Message 1 was selected as the high valence/high arousal text, Message 2 as high valence/low arousal, Message 3 as low valence/low arousal, Message 4 as low valence/high arousal, and Message 5 as the neutral message.

ID	Message	V	A
1	Blessed with a baby boy today	3.6	3.5
2	life is beautiful	3.7	2.3
3	SICK AGAIN !!!! HATE IT !!!!!	2.3	2.4
4	At least 15 dead as israeli forces attack Gaza aid ahips!!!!!!! i hhhhhhate israil	1.4	3.8
5	And one careless match can start a forest fire but it takes a whole damn box to get a campfire going!	3.1	2.8

Table 3: Selected Messages

Figure 6 shows the valence and arousal means from Table 3 in a scatterplot, with the horizontal axis denoting the valence scale and the vertical axis denoting the arousal scale. Quadrants above the horizontal axis denote messages with high arousal and the bottom two quadrants denote messages with low arousal. Messages to the right of the vertical axis are high valence (happy), and messages to the left of the vertical axis are low valence (unhappy). The selected messages fall within their respective quadrants showing appropriateness for their valence and arousal traits.

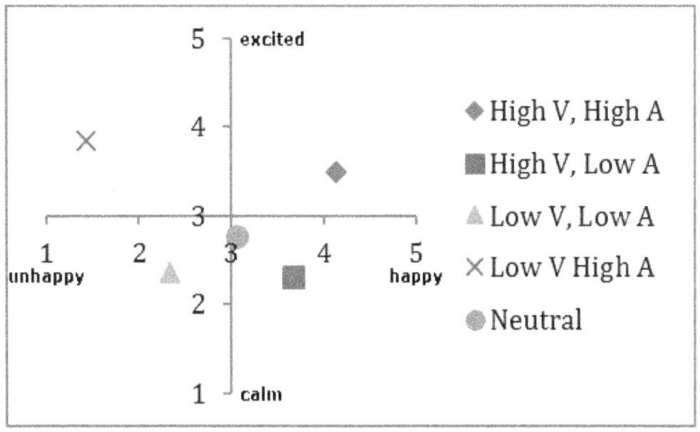

Figure 6: Selected message mean valence and arousal scores

Results – rating temperature valence and arousal

Participants disagreed which temperatures had a high or low valence. Six participants interpreted cool stimuli as high valence and warm as low valence. Two did the opposite: rating warm stimuli as high valence and cool stimuli as low valence. The remainder rated either all stimuli as low valence or only certain scales of warmth or cool as high valence. This was surprising, as [21] reported participants rating warm as high valence and cold as low valence. However, they only assessed this using qualitative data. Salminen *et al.* [30] on the other hand, concluded temperature did not affect pleasantness (valence) ratings and that it only affected arousal and dominance. Some research has been mixed. Halvey *et al.* [12, pp. 95] reported warm stimuli were given higher valence ratings than cool stimuli "with some exceptions", though they did not explain why neutral temperatures had higher valence ratings than warm stimuli.

On the other hand, there was general agreement amongst participants perceiving more intense stimuli as more arousing. Participants found scales of warm to be more arousing than cool scales. This may have depended on how intense they perceived the stimuli as some participants remarked warm stimuli felt more intense than the cool ones. Our findings here agree with prior literature.

The mean time to rate the messages was 6.82 sec (sd = 1.5 sec). The mean time to rate thermal cues was 6.84 sec (sd = 0.8 sec). This suggests that, despite latency of thermal cues, they require no more cognition than reading text messages.

Main Study

We proceeded to examine interaction between text messages and thermal stimuli. As discussed, research has examined emotions and thermal stimuli separately, as well as using temperature to augment images and music. However, it has yet looked at whether thermal cues can augment emotions communicated in text messages.

- The study consisted of 96 trials that were comprised of 48 unique stimuli that were each used twice.
- 12 trials were message-only stimuli. 72 were pairs of a message and temperature, 12 were temperature alone.

- The 12 message trials were tested together either before or after the other 84 trials.
- The 84 thermal trials were split into 3 blocks with 5 minute breaks between them.
- For all 96 trials, the participants reported valence and arousal on two 9-point SAM scales.

SAM scales were increased to nine points from five points. This was done as almost every participant in the pilot rated temperature using only the 2-, 3-, or 4-point selections and some participants remarked they would have preferred a wider range of choices. It should be emphasised that the stimuli chosen from the pilot were re-tested again in the manner they were presented alone in the pilot- results of the 5-point and 9-point scales were not 'mixed'.

The seven thermal stimuli were combined into pairs with one of the five message types or a blank message (for the temperature only condition) and displayed to the participant. Each pair was presented to the participant twice during the test, resulting in 84 trials. As before, there was a ten second re-adaption period between each trial. The order of all trials was randomized and divided into three blocks, with five-minute breaks between blocks to prevent fatigue.

Conditions where either the messages were displayed without temperature or thermal cues were displayed alone were tested again, due to the switch from 5-point SAM scales in the pilot to 9 points used in the main study. As it would have been difficult to detach the thermal device each time the message only stimulus was presented, they were tested separately from the rest of the thermal stimuli trials. To prevent ordering effects resulting from this, participants were split into two groups. The first group rated the messages and then proceeded to rate the other 84 thermal trials, and the second group rated the 84 thermal trials and then proceeded to rate the messages.

Results

We first tested the distribution of the participants' ratings of valence and arousal. Researchers have previously raised concerns on the validity of using ANOVA on Likert data, but when data is normally distributed, ANOVA is appropriate [4, p. 126] and can test for interaction effects.

To test for normality of the data, we used Shapiro-Wilkes tests for the data set as a whole, and then separated the data by message and thermal stimuli to ensure that all subsets were also normally distributed. All results produced $W>0.975$, and exceeded the critical values at $p<0.01$. This confirmed the normality of the data, and permitted the use of ANOVA.

The ratings for valence had a global mean of 4.8 and a standard deviation of 1.9; while arousal had a mean of 4.7 and standard deviation of 1.6. To again test for the validity of ANOVA on the data, we obtained standard deviations for the subsets of thermal and message stimuli, with valence ranging between 1.1 and 1.7, and arousal from 1.8 to 2.1. The level of variance in standard deviations was within the tolerances expected of a two-factor ANOVA.

Two tests allowed us to check for experimental effects from wearing the apparatus. First, we tested the temperature-only stimuli results against the trials that paired thermal signals with a neutral message. Second, the message-only responses were tested versus the same messages with a neutral thermal signal. Any positive result would indicate an undesirable substantial experimental effect. Using ANOVA, F values varied between 0.07 ($p>0.85$) and 1.5 ($p>0.20$). For the main effects, scores were at or above $F=8.5$ ($p<0.005$) Thus, we could discount the likelihood of a significant side effect from wearing the device.

The global descriptive data suggests that arousal responses were diffuse and inconsistent, whereas valence responses were more concentrated and consistent. As such, valence will be addressed first before proceeding to testing arousal.

We first tested valence using the message and thermal stimuli as the two variables. The ANOVA result was $F(2,385) = 118.45$ ($p < 0.001$) for the messages dimension, but the thermal dimension yielded $F = 0.43$, and interaction produced $F=0.29$, both very far from significant. While messages substantially influenced the perceived valence, thermal signals had no discernible effect.

For arousal, the ANOVA result was $F(2,385)=3.62$ ($p<0.05$) for message effect and 3.41 ($p<0.05$) for thermal effect, with the interaction producing $F=0.20$ ($p>0.80$). There is again no evidence of an interaction effect. Both the message and the thermal stimulus had a similar and reliable effect, but neither was as marked as the impact of the message on valence.

Thus, for valence and arousal, the message content had a reliable main effect. The effect was much more powerful in valence than arousal. In contrast, thermal stimulation had no reliable effect on the valence, but had a similar level of efficacy to the message for arousal levels.

Discussion

Figure 7 shows the plots of the mean valence and arousal scale responses (y-axis) as a function of temperature change (x-axis) for each category of message and thermal pairings. Plot (a) shows the pairing with a blank message for testing temperature only. The bottom of the y-axis denotes ratings of 1 on the valence and arousal scales (unhappy and calm), and the top of the y-axis denotes ratings of 9 on the scales (happy and excited). The far right of the x-axis denotes the coolest temperature setting and the far left denotes the warmest setting, with neutral at the position of the y-axis.

Arousal is marked by the red lines in each plot. As expected, as temperature increases, arousal ratings generally tend to move upward. Except for plot (c), arousal ratings tend to be negative for cooler temperatures and only cross the x-axis when warmer stimuli are applied. For all categories, temperature had a reliable main effect on arousal, including plot (f).

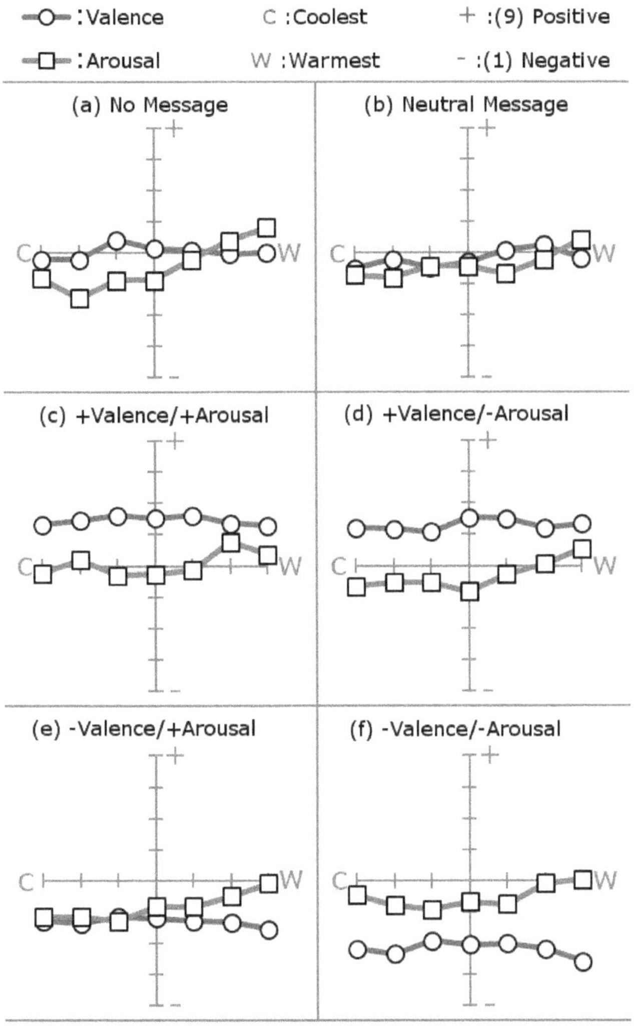

Figure 7: Message and temperature pairing mean plots for valence and arousal

Valance is marked with the blue line. As discussed in the Results section, temperature had no reliable effect. As plots (c), (d), (e), and (f) illustrate, the valance of the message clearly dominated, with the lines clearly above or below the x-axis. These lines remained relatively straight, regardless of thermal stimulus applied. For plot (a), where only temperature was displayed with no message and plot (b), where temperatures were paired with the neutral message, the means remained close to neutral. Plot (a) illustrates pilot test findings with no thermal valence effect.

Why did we not observe a thermal effect on valence? Lee and Lim offer some clues. They reported environmental factors could influence thermal expression, as humans tend to feel safe from factors that change body temperature [21]. We did not control this, and though thermal feedback recommendations still hold in varying ambient temperatures [13], it may influence thermal expression of valence. [21, p. 4235] also reports "heat seems to have hardly any meaning by alone without its context". As we instructed participants to "rate how the temperature made you feel" this context may have been ambiguous, as we did not ask them to interpret it in a context like with the messages. Future research should address the effect of context on the affective perception of thermal cues in different environments, including a control condition where temperature is sent ambiguously.

We can conclude that temperature itself consistently generates arousal responses. In a temperature-augmented message, strong textual valence will dominate the emotion communicated to the user. For all messages, but particularly if the message is neutral, temperature significantly influences the emotional arousal communicated.

CONCLUSION

Users find it hard to identify the physical position of TECs when they are placed in patterns. However, the TAD enabled more accurate discrimination with smaller temperature differences between thermal signals, reducing time for user identification of thermal state changes. In our test of single- versus multi-TEC methods, the single-TEC method had the worst error rate and degree of error. We deployed two multi-TEC methods: Amplification set all TECs to the same temperature, with the temperature indicating the system state; Quantification used the number of TECs set to hot or cold to indicate the state. The error rate and degree of error for Amplification were significantly lower than the Single method. Quantification was superior to the Single method but had higher error rates than Amplification. However, there was no significant difference in degree of error between the two multi-TEC methods.

Temperature without a message context gave arousal reactions but did not provide valence. Warm temperatures were perceived as more arousing than cool temperatures. For valence, message content was highly effective, and heat was ineffective. Temperature exerted a discernable and reliable effect on arousal when paired with neutral messages. This effect was also seen when paired with low and high arousal messages, providing a similar influence on arousal to text. No reliable interaction effect was found between temperature and message for arousal.

Thermal signals portrayed emotional arousal to participants as effectively as text. We suggest two areas where this feedback may be useful. Those with cognitive impairments, such as Autism, which impede their sense of emotional message content, could potentially benefit. Thermal cues could allow them to sense that a message is, for example, intended to excite them. Another possible application is education, where language learning could be reinforced by augmenting foreign sentences with temperature, which are mapped to intended emotional meanings of words.

REFERENCES

1. Shimon Akiyama, Katsunari Sato, Yasutoshi Makino, and Takashi Maeno. 2012. Presentation of thermal sensation through preliminary adjustment of adapting skin temperature. In *Haptics Symposium* (HAPTICS '12), 355-358.
2. Margaret M. Bradley and Peter J. Lang. 1994. Measuring emotion: the self-assessment manikin and the semantic differential. *Journal of behavior therapy and experimental psychiatry* 25, 1: 49-59.
3. Lorna M. Brown, Stephen A. Brewster, and Helen C. Purchase. 2006. Multidimensional tactons for non-visual information presentation in mobile devices. In Proceedings of the 8th conference on Human-computer interaction with mobile devices and services (MobileHCI '06). ACM, New York, NY, USA, 231-238.
4. Paul Cairns and Anna L. Cox. 2008. Research Methods for Human-Computer Interaction (1st ed.). Cambridge University Press, New York, NY, USA.
5. Arthur. D. Craig and M.C. Bushnell. 1994. The thermal grill illusion: unmasking the burn of cold pain. *Science* 256, 5169: 252-255.
6. Arthur D. Craig, Chen Kewei, D. Bandy, and Eric M. Reiman. 2000. Thermosensory activation of insular cortex. *Nature neuroscience* 3, 2: 184-190.
7. CMDMessenger Library. Retrieved March 22, 2016 from http://playground.arduino.cc/Code/CmdMessenger
8. Hidenori Fujita and Kazushi Nishimoto. 2004. Lovelet: a heartwarming communication tool for intimate people by constantly conveying situation data. In *CHI '04 Extended Abstracts on Human Factors in Computing Systems* (CHI EA '04), 1553-1553.
9. Alastair J. Gill, Darren Gergle, Robert M. French, and Jon Oberlander. 2008. Emotion rating from short blog texts. In *Proceedings of the SIGCHI Conference on Human Factors in Computing Systems* (CHI '08), 1121-1124.
10. Daniel Gooch, and Leon Watts. 2010. Communicating social presence through thermal hugs.
11. Barry G. Green. 1977. Localization of thermal sensation: An illusion and synthetic heat. *Perception & Psychophysics* 22, 4: 331-337.
12. Martin Halvey, Michael Henderson, Stephen A. Brewster, Graham Wilson, and Stephen A. Hughes. 2012. Augmenting media with thermal stimulation. In *International Conference on Haptic and Audio Interaction Design*, 91-100.
13. Martin Halvey, Graham Wilson, Stephen Brewster, and Stephen Hughes. 2012. Baby it's cold outside: the influence of ambient temperature and humidity on thermal feedback. In *Proceedings of the SIGCHI Conference on Human Factors in Computing Systems* (CHI '12), 715-724.
14. Martin Halvey, Graham Wilson, Stephen A. Brewster, and Stephen A. Hughes. 2013. Perception of thermal stimuli for continuous interaction. In *CHI '13 Extended Abstracts on Human Factors in Computing Systems* (CHI EA '13), 1587-1592.
15. Martin Halvey, Graham Wilson, Yolanda Vazquez-Alvarez, Stephen A. Brewster, and Stephen A. Hughes. 2011. The effect of clothing on thermal feedback perception. In *Proceedings of the 13th international conference on multimodal interfaces* (ICMI '11), 217-220.
16. David Hannah, Martin Halvey, Graham Wilson, and Stephen A. Brewster. 2011. Using multimodal interactions for 3D television and multimedia browsing. In *Proceedings of the 9th international interactive conference on Interactive television* (EuroITV '11), 181-184.
17. Hans IJzerman, and Gün R. Semin. 2009. "The thermometer of social relations mapping social proximity on temperature." *Psychological science* 20, 10: 1214-1220.
18. Ken Iwasaki, Takashi Miyaki, and Jun Rekimoto. 2010. AffectPhone: a handset device to present user's emotional state with warmth/coolness. In *Proceedings of the 1st International Workshop on Bio-inspired Human-Machine Interfaces and Healthcare Applications*, 83-88.
19. Lynette A. Jones, and Michal Berris. 2002. The psychophysics of temperature perception and thermal-interface design. In *Proceedings of the 10th Symposium on Haptic Interfaces for Virtual Environment and Teleoperator Systems* (HAPTICS '02), 137-142.
20. Dan R. Kenshalo and Harley A. Scott. 1966. Temporal course of thermal adaptation. *Science* 151, 3714: 1095-1096.
21. Wonjun Lee and Youn-kyung Lim. 2010. Thermo-message: exploring the potential of heat as a modality of peripheral expression. In *CHI '10 Extended Abstracts on Human Factors in Computing Systems* (CHI EA '10) 4231-4236.
22. Wonjun Lee and Youn-kyung Lim. 2012. Explorative research on the heat as an expression medium: focused on interpersonal communication. *Personal and Ubiquitous Computing* 16, 8: 1039-1049.
23. Michael W. Levine and Jeremy M. Shefner. 2000. *Fundamentals of Sensation and Perception* (3rd. ed.). Oxford University Press.
24. Markus Löchtefeld, Nadine Lautemann, Sven Gehring, and Antonio Krüger. 2014. ambiPad: enriching mobile digital media with ambient feedback. In *Proceedings of the 16th international conference on Human-computer*

interaction with mobile devices & services (MobileHCI '14), 295-298.

25. Homei Miyashita and Kazushi Nishimoto. 2004. Thermoscore: a new-type musical score with temperature sensation. In *Proceedings of the 2004 Conference on New Interfaces for Musical Expression* (NIME '04), 104-107.
26. Takuji Narumi, Akagawa Tomohiro, Young Ah Seong, and Michitaka Hirose. 2009. Characterizing the Space by thermal feedback through a wearable device. In *Virtual and Mixed Reality*, Randall Shumaker (ed.). Springer Berlin Heidelberg, 355-364.
27. Tal Oron-Gilad, Yael Salzer, and Adi Ronen. 2008. Thermoelectric tactile display based on the thermal grill illusion. In *Haptics: Perception, Devices and Scenarios*, Manuel Ferre (ed.). Springer Berlin Heidelberg, 343-348.
28. Preotiuc-Pietro, D., Schwartz, H.A., Park, G., Eichstaedt, J.C., Kern, M., Ungar, L. and Shulman, E.P., 2016. Modelling Valence and Arousal in Facebook posts. Proceedings of the Workshop on Computational Approaches to Subjectivity, Sentiment and Social Media Analysis (WASSA), NAACL.
29. James A Russell. 1980. A Circumplex Model of Affect. *Journal of Personality and Social Psychology* 39, 6: 1161–1178.
30. Katri Salminen, Veikko Surakka, Jukka Raisamo, Jani Lylykangas, Johannes Pystynen, Roope Raisamo, Kalle Mäkelä, and Teemu Ahmaniemi. 2011. Emotional responses to thermal stimuli. In *Proceedings of the 13th international conference on multimodal interfaces* (ICMI '11), 193-196.
31. Katsunari Sato and Takashi Maeno. 2012. Presentation of sudden temperature change using spatially divided warm and cool stimuli. In *Haptics: Perception, Devices, Mobility, and Communication*, Poika Isokoski and Jukka Springare (eds.). Springer Berlin Heidelberg, 457-468.
32. Katja Suhonen, Sebastian Müller, Jussi Rantala, Kaisa Väänänen-Vainio-Mattila, Roope Raisamo, and Vuokko Lantz. 2012. Haptically augmented remote speech communication: a study of user practices and experiences. In *Proceedings of the 7th Nordic Conference on Human-Computer Interaction: Making Sense Through Design* (NordiCHI '12), 361-369.
33. Eun-Jung Sung, Seung-Schik Yoo, Hyo Woon Yoon, Sung-Suk Oh, Yeji Han, and Hyun Wook Park. Brain activation related to affective dimension during thermal stimulation in humans: a functional magnetic resonance imaging study. 2007. *International Journal of Neuroscience* 117, 7: 1011-1027.
34. Caroline Tagg. 2009. *A corpus linguistics study of SMS text messaging*. Ph.D Dissertation. The University of Birmingham, Birmingham, UK.
35. Cati Vaucelle, Leonardo Bonanni, and Hiroshi Ishii. 2009. Design of haptic interfaces for therapy. *In Proceedings of the SIGCHI Conference on Human Factors in Computing Systems* (CHI '09), 467-470.
36. Ryuji Watanabe, Ryuta Okazaki, and Hiroyuki Kajimoto. 2014. Mutual referral of thermal sensation between two thermal-tactile stimuli. In *Haptics Symposium* (HAPTICS '14), 299-302.
37. Lawrence E. Williams, and John A. Bargh. 2008. Experiencing physical warmth promotes interpersonal warmth. *Science* 322, 5901: 606-607.
38. Graham Alasdair Wilson. 2013. *Using pressure input and thermal feedback to broaden haptic interaction with mobile devices.* Ph.D Dissertation. University of Glasgow, UK.
39. Graham Wilson, Stephen Brewster, Martin Halvey, and Stephen Hughes. 2012. Thermal icons: evaluating structured thermal feedback for mobile interaction. In *Proceedings of the 14th International Conference on Human-Computer Interaction with Mobile Devices and Services* (MobileHCI '12), 309-312.
40. Graham Wilson, Gavin Davidson, and Stephen A. Brewster. 2015. In the heat of the moment: subjective interpretations of thermal feedback during interaction. In *Proceedings of the 33rd Annual ACM Conference on Human Factors in Computing Systems* (CHI' 15), 2063-2072.
41. Graham Wilson, Dobromir Dobrev, and Stephen A. Brewster. 2016. Hot Under the Collar: Mapping Thermal Feedback to Dimensional Models of Emotion. In *Proceedings of the 2016 CHI Conference on Human Factors in Computing Systems* (CHI '16), 4838-4849.
42. Graham Wilson, Martin Halvey, Stephen A. Brewster, and Stephen A. Hughes. 2011. Some like it hot: thermal feedback for mobile devices. In *Proceedings of the SIGCHI Conference on Human Factors in Computing Systems* (CHI '11), 2555-2564.
43. Chen-Bo Zhong and Geoffrey J. Leonardelli. 2008. Cold and lonely does social exclusion literally feel cold?. *Psychological Science* 19, 9: 838-842.

Exploring Novice Approaches to Smartphone-based Thermographic Energy Auditing: A Field Study

Matthew Louis Mauriello[1], Manaswi Saha[1], Erica Brown[2], Jon E. Froehlich[1]
Makeability Lab | Human-Computer Interaction Lab
Department of Computer Science[1], Department of Bioengineering[2]
University of Maryland, College Park
{mattm401, manaswi, ebrown17, jonf}@umd.edu

ABSTRACT
The recent integration of thermal cameras with commodity smartphones presents an opportunity to engage the public in evaluating energy-efficiency issues in the built environment. However, it is unclear how novice users without professional experience or training approach thermographic energy auditing activities. In this paper, we recruited 10 participants for a four-week field study of end-user behavior exploring novice approaches to semi-structured thermographic energy auditing tasks. We analyze thermographic imagery captured by participants as well as weekly surveys and post-study debrief interviews. Our findings suggest that while novice users perceived thermal cameras as useful in identifying energy-efficiency issues in buildings, they struggled with interpretation and confidence. We characterize how novices perform thermographic-based energy auditing, synthesize key challenges, and discuss implications for design.

Author Keywords
Thermography; Mobile Devices; Formative Inquiry; Field Study; Sustainable HCI; Energy Efficiency

ACM Classification Keywords
H.5.m. Information interfaces and presentation (e.g., HCI)

INTRODUCTION
Improving energy efficiency in the built environment is an important global concern [54]. In the United States, for example, buildings account for 41% of primary energy consumption—more than any other sector—and contribute an increasing portion of carbon dioxide emissions (33% in 1980 *vs.* 40% in 2009) [38]. To reduce consumption and emission levels, the U.S. Department of Energy (DOE) recommends conducting energy audits to help identify sources of inefficiencies and make recommendations for renovations and retrofits. Home energy audits typically identify improvements that lead to 5-30% reductions in utility use [64]. Energy audit requirements are increasingly becoming part of city legislation [4] and building

CHI 2017, May 06-11, 2017, Denver, CO, USA
© 2017 ACM. ISBN 978-1-4503-4655-9/17/05...$15.00
DOI: http://dx.doi.org/10.1145/3025453.3025471

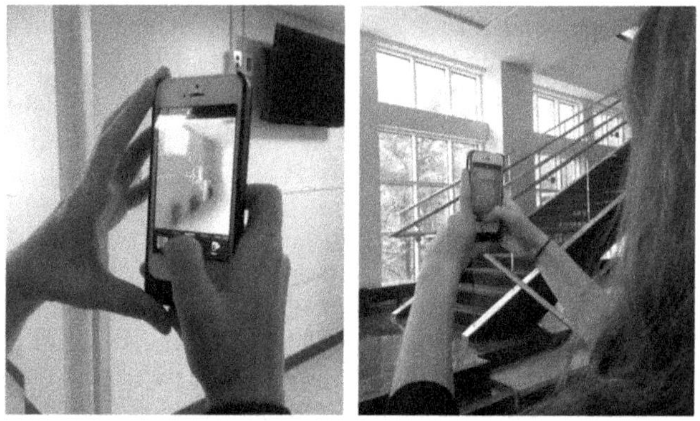

Figure 1: Smartphone-based thermal cameras present an opportunity to engage novice users in thermographic energy auditing activities, which could increase engagement in efficiency initiatives.

certification programs [37,62]. In response, interest in professional energy auditing has increased [35,52].

Professional energy auditors assess buildings using an array of diagnostic tests. With improvements in handheld infrared sensors and falling costs, auditors have been increasingly using *thermography* during energy audits [5,9,21,42]. Thermographic-based energy auditing is a data collection and a visual analytics technique that uses thermal cameras to help detect, diagnose, and document energy issues such as building defects and air leakage that produce thermal signatures (*e.g.,* areas of missing insulation) [47,51]. Prior work has shown that including thermal imagery, or *thermograms*, in end-user reports positively influences (homeowner) retrofit decisions and conservation behaviors [29,51]. However, despite technological advances, thermographic-based energy audits remain a laborious activity requiring training and expertise [47].

Recently, thermal camera attachments have emerged for smartphones, which have begun to broaden the adoption of this technology (Figure 1) [70,71]. Marketing materials suggest diverse use, including for DIY energy audits, art and electronics projects, and outdoor recreation (*e.g.,* see [72]). The release of smartphone-based thermal camera attachments—and even fully integrated smartphone thermal cameras [74]—has prompted the development of an increasing number of mobile apps that use and support thermography [22]. While still early, these trends foreshadow a future in which thermal cameras are ubiquitous—integrated into commodity electronics and part of a range of services and applications.

In this paper, we conduct the first qualitative field study of thermal camera use by novices. As formative work, our research questions include: *How do novice users of thermal cameras assess the built environment? What attributes of the built environment do they focus on, learn about, and discover? What challenges do they encounter? What benefits do they perceive?* To explore these questions, we recruited 10 novice participants to take part in a four-week field study of smartphone-based thermal camera usage. Participants were asked to use their thermal cameras whenever and however they wanted. To help guide their auditing activities, participants were also asked to complete weekly thermographic "missions" with specific themes: the home, the workplace, commercial buildings, and the community. At the end of each week's mission, participants submitted their thermal imagery and completed a survey about their activities. The study concluded with semi-structured debrief interviews with participants.

Our findings suggest that novice users can use thermal cameras to document energy-efficiency issues in buildings and to find previously unknown problems. Our participants also reported a general heightened awareness of electrical energy use and a greater likelihood of engaging in energy conservation practices (complementing findings of [29,51]). However, participants had difficulty gauging the severity of the issues they uncovered making it difficult to determine the impact of energy-efficiency improvements. Reflecting on our findings, we discuss barriers to novice thermographic energy auditing as well as design implications for both Sustainable HCI and public auditing of the built environment.

In summary, the contributions of this work include: (i) the first study of how novices approach using thermal cameras within the context of energy auditing; (ii) a synthesis of key challenges novices experience when collecting and interpreting thermal imagery; and (iii) a discussion of implications for future thermographic systems. Our work should be of interest to Sustainable HCI researchers, designers, and those working energy auditing.

BACKGROUND AND RELATED WORK

We provide background on energy auditing, trends in thermographic research, and links between thermography and Sustainable HCI. We also describe work relevant to thermal cameras as tools for public energy initiatives.

Energy Auditing and Thermographic Assessment

Energy audits are performed for many reasons including to verify that buildings are operating efficiently and/or to identify sources of inefficiencies [64]. Audits frequently begin with a walkthrough inspection to collect information about a building's construction, on-site appliances, safety, and environmental comfort. This information is combined with historical utility data and may be used to predict the expected financial return on investment on efficiency recommendations.

As noted in the introduction, thermographic-based energy audits are becoming more common due to the increased availability of thermal cameras and their decreased cost. Thermal cameras work by detecting the electromagnetic radiation emitted by all objects above absolute zero [27]. The thermal data is automatically combined with images from a conventional camera to produce a contextualized thermal image or *thermogram*. Energy auditors use thermal cameras to measure surface temperatures in walls, roofs, ceilings, and other parts of a building's envelope while looking for inconsistent patterns, discontinuities, and other anomalous heat signatures that may indicate the presence of an efficiency issue [9,42].

While thermographic scanning can be beneficial during energy audits (*e.g.,* to detect the location of air leakages), there are limitations to the technique that impact data accuracy such as wind and intensity of sun. According to ISO standards, thermal scans should be conducted only when a minimum temperature differential of 14°C between a building's interior and exterior can be established [36,65]. Additionally, blower doors, a type of door-mounted fan, are often helpful to intensify airflow and increase the visibility of thermal signatures during data collection [21,63]. Beyond the need to assess or configure the environment, data collection and analysis is often a subjective process relying on the training and experience of the auditor [46]. This subjectivity has led to calls for developing more quantitative methods and tools for collecting and analyzing thermal imagery [65].

While novice users now have increased access to thermal cameras, there has been no examination of how they approach using this technology or what challenges they face when interpreting thermal imagery. Due to the subjective nature of thermographic energy auditing, it is unclear whether novices can perform thermographic energy audits, especially in absence of tools designed specifically with them in mind. In our work, we explore how novices use thermal cameras within the context of thermographic energy auditing and how their participation impacts their understanding of energy use and the potential for building energy efficiency improvements.

Thermograms as Eco-Visualizations

In addition to being a diagnostic tool, another primary reason for capturing thermal imagery during energy audits is that it serves as an effective *eco-visualization,* helping to reveal otherwise invisible information about energy flow [55]. Prior work has found that persons who reviewed thermal imagery from their household audits were nearly five times more likely to make retrofit decisions [29] and that viewing thermal imagery encourages energy conservation behaviors [51]. One explanation for these findings is that thermal imagery provides a "particularly compelling" reason to consider retrofit recommendations and behavior changes by surfacing invisible issues and making them seem more tangible [35]. However, these studies have been performed in the context of larger interactions between professional auditors and clients [35,47]. Thus, it is currently unclear how beneficial novice end-users will find their personally collected and interpreted imagery without professional guidance, which this study begins to address.

Trends in Thermographic Research

While using thermography during energy auditing activities is viewed as beneficial by professional auditors, collecting and analyzing thermal imagery is typically seen as laborious and costly [47]. Thus, researchers have explored ways to both scale-up collection and improve human interpretation of the data. For example, using automatic [7,16,43] and semi-automatic [44] robotic systems as data collection platforms to scalably audit urban areas. Touted advantages include manual labor reductions, increases in the volume of data, which can enable new types of analyses, and the ability to safely survey inaccessible or potentially hazardous areas (*e.g.,* building rooftops) [43,44]. However, professional auditors argue that these approaches, while scalable, are not able to configure an environment for capture, tend to capture only partial views of exterior building facades, and analysis of the collected imagery remains time consuming [47]. Closer to our work is the development of human-oriented solutions such as hand-held and wearable data collection tools [49,50,66], augmented reality devices [15], and thermographic analysis software [31]. Our work explores the potential for novices to perform DIY thermographic energy audits via emerging smartphone-based thermal cameras, which would scale thermography along a new dimension: end-users.

Sustainable HCI

Since its emergence at CHI in 2007 [6], a large portion of Sustainable HCI literature has centered on curbing CO2 emissions through the design of *eco-feedback* [25] and *persuasive* [23] technologies (see surveys [10,19,41]). These technologies frequently focus on monitoring resource consumption (*e.g.,* electricity [2], water [26]) or promoting sustainable practices (*e.g.,* use of public transportation [24], recycling [14]) that can influence emission rates. Looking specifically at home energy consumption, research has shown that technology-based interventions can reduce energy consumption by 4-12% [20]. Commodity thermal cameras and their interactive capture and analysis software offer building occupants a potential new resource to learn about energy use and inefficiencies, particularly for otherwise overlooked areas like detecting poor insulation and window/door sealing. As Gardner and Stern note [28], humans place a disproportionate focus on *curtailment behaviors*, which involve forming new routines to reduce environmental impact (*e.g.,* turning off lights when leaving a room), rather than one-time behaviors such as upgrading insulation, which provide a lasting impact and are far more significant to improving efficiency. Thermal cameras can uniquely aid in the latter, especially in cases where occupants have the ability to make changes to their environment [10,40].

Our specific interest is to explore the use of thermal cameras as an empowerment technology that allows users of varying skill to investigate, analyze, and report building energy efficiency issues [40]. As formative work, our research shares similar aims to other qualitative Sustainable HCI studies (*e.g.,* [18,30,68]): to understand how this technology is used and identify what role HCI may play.

Smartphone-based Public Auditing

One long-term research focus is investigating how commodity thermal cameras may be used to engage end-users in citizen science initiatives—for example, in using thermography to help audit largescale infrastructures in cities. However, to date there have been only limited attempts to engage the public in energy auditing tasks [1,33]. Smartphones, our focus, are often used by the public to perform volunteer audits on a range of topics, including noise pollution [59], air conditioning use [57], potholes [48]. Smartphones are particularly attractive tools for public auditing projects because they are relatively accessible, provide lightweight computing capabilities to support task completion, and generate easily shareable data. Similar to *SeeClickFix*, a smartphone app for capturing and reporting infrastructural issues to city governments [69], our work begins to explore the idea that thermographic energy audits can be performed by the public across use-contexts (*e.g.,* home, workplace) [55].

FIELD STUDY: NON-PROFESSIONAL THERMOGRAPHY

To investigate how novices use thermal cameras for energy auditing and how they interpret thermal imagery, we conducted a four-week field study with 10 participants during the winter months of 2015. Each participant was provided a *FLIR ONE* thermal camera attachment (Figure 2) for their personal smartphone and told to explore freely throughout the study. To help guide their auditing activities, participants were also asked to complete weekly

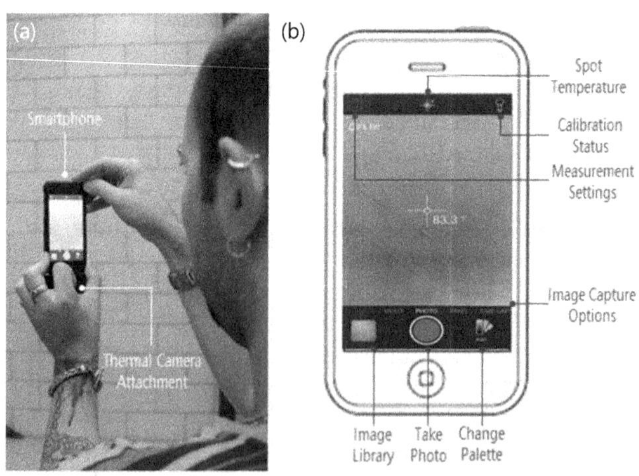

Figure 2: (a) A thermal camera attached to an iPhone 5. **(b)** A close-up of the standard FLIR ONE camera application that ships with the attachment.

thermographic "missions" (adapted from the prompting method in [58]). Missions were included to scaffold and motivate data collection across a range of use-contexts: home, work, and two public spaces. Prior work informed our study design [47] as did our pilot studies [45] where we found that missions helped structure auditing activities and think more broadly about places to capture thermal imagery. To help us understand participant activities, participants answered an online questionnaire and uploaded their thermograms weekly. At the end of the study, participants were debriefed via a semi-structured interview and compensated with $100.

Field Study Equipment

The FLIR ONE thermal camera attachment is widely available—sold at Apple Stores and online—and fits a wide range of iPhone models. As shown in Figure 2a, the thermal camera attaches to the iPhone's Lightning port. For our study, participants used the FLIR ONE thermal camera application, which looks and largely functions like a conventional camera application with a "Take Photo" button in the center and a list of image capture options (Figure 2b). The display updates in real-time; photos can be taken at any time but the camera works best in a stable position. The user can change how the camera colorizes the thermal data (*i.e.*, the "Change Palette" button). In the example shown, the "Iron" palette is used which displays colder regions in the image in shades of purple and warmer regions in shades of orange. The icons on the top menubar allow users to change measurement settings, display a temperature measurement tool (*i.e.*, average temperature in in the crosshairs), and see when the camera is calibrating.

Field Study Method

Participants

We recruited 10 participants (5 female) from the general population using local mailing lists and community message boards (Table 1). Our recruitment ad specified that we were interested in studying smartphone-based thermal cameras for energy auditing. Potential participants completed a short eligibility questionnaire. We screened for adults (ages 18+) and compatible smartphones. Participants were enrolled on a first-come, first-served basis.

To collect demographic information and understand attitudes toward environmental sustainability, participants completed a short, pre-study questionnaire. In general, our

ID	Age	Gender	Education	Profession	iPhone
P1	22	Female	Bachelor's	Public Affairs Specialist	6
P2	25	Female	Bachelor's	Graduate Student	6
P3	30	Male	Master's	Graduate Student	5s
P4	58	Female	Doctorate	Research Scientist	5s
P5	31	Female	Master's	Higher Education Professional	6s
P6	56	Male	Master's	Government Scientist	5
P7	28	Male	Master's	User Experience Designer	6s
P8	53	Male	Master's	Marketing Coordinator	5
P9	34	Female	High School	Education Coordinator	6
P10	40	Male	Master's	Educator	6

Table 1: A summary of the participant's demographic information.

Concern	Average
Climate Change	6.5 (SD=0.8, Mdn=7.0)
Home	5.3 (SD=1.2, Mdn=5.5)
Community	5.2 (SD=1.5, Mdn=5.5)
Workplace	4.8 (SD=1.5, Mdn=4.5)

Table 2: The pre-study survey asked participants how concerned they were about climate change and the energy efficiency of specific contexts in their daily lives.

Week	Mission
Home	Investigate your home with your thermal camera for signs of energy inefficiencies and comfort issues; collect at least 25 photos that highlight aspects of your investigation.
Workplace	Investigate your workplace to help inform new policies on energy conservation and comfort; collect at least 25 photos that highlight aspects of your investigation.
Commercial	As if you were a building inspector, investigate a commercial location (e.g., a café) for potential issues based on your previous experience; collect at least 25 photos that highlight aspects of your investigation.
Community	As if you were a municipal inspector, investigate your local downtown or community area; collect at least 25 photos that highlight aspects of your investigation.

Table 3: Weekly mission descriptions were sent to participants via email along. Lightweight feedback about the previous week was also provided.

participants were eco-conscious and concerned about the environment. Using 7-point Likert scales ordered from *very unconcerned* (1) to *very concerned* (7), participants reported being very concerned about climate change, concerned about the energy efficiency of their homes and their local community, but less concerned about their workplace—see Table 2. Additionally, half (*N*=5) reported regularly engaging in conservation behaviors (*e.g.*, turning off lights) and making minor efficiency modifications in their homes (*e.g.*, upgrading light fixtures). Some (3) reported making large efficiency improvements (*e.g.*, installing solar panels). A few (2) reported making minor changes to solve winter comfort issues (*e.g.*, sealing drafty windows with plastic). Participants reported no previous experience with thermal cameras; however, a few (3) previously had professional energy audits of their homes; two included thermography.

Procedure

Introductory briefings were held in our lab or in a local café, depending on participant preference. Upon arrival, a research assistant discussed the study plan, obtained consent, provided the thermal camera and accessories (*e.g.*, manufacturer's documentation), and reviewed a 4-page custom training document (see Supplementary Materials). The document was synthesized from thermal smartphone applications [22], how-to guides from manufacturers [73], and DOE materials [63,64] by a research team member with a professional thermography certification; it covered key elements of a successful thermographic investigations.

Participants were encouraged to freely explore objects, their environment, or anything that struck their interest with their thermal cameras. To help structure and motivate their explorations, we also provided them with weekly energy-themed missions. The missions ranged from home inspections to community explorations; see Table 3. All participants received missions in the same order. At the end of each week, participants uploaded their photos and completed an online questionnaire about their experience.

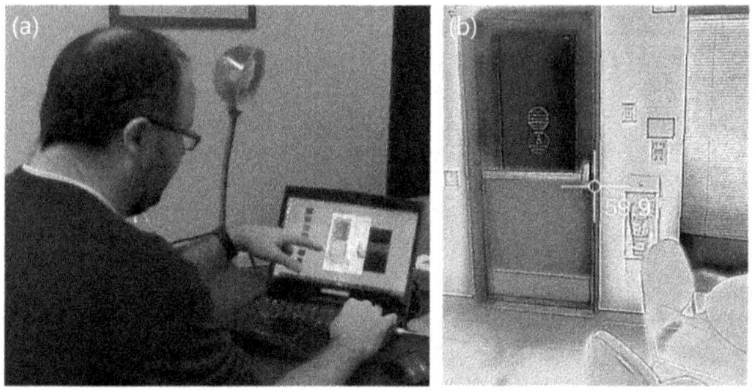

Figure 3: **(a)** A participant describes an air leakage issue found while auditing his workplace during the post-study debrief interview. **(b)** A close-up of the actual thermal image being discussed.

At the end of week four, participants participated in an in-person, semi-structured interview with a photo-elicitation component [13]. During the photo-elicitation, participants used their thermogram collection as a visual aid to help recall and describe experiences (Figure 3). Except where the interviewer had marked a photo for discussion, participants chose which photos to discuss. After the photo-elicitation, participants described their experiences over the four-week study, including discussions about how current thermal cameras could be used by non-professionals and improved to better support them in the future.

Data and Analysis

Images and interviews were qualitatively coded. Counts and descriptive statistics were calculated for survey data.

Images. In total, participants took 1,991 thermographic images; however, 83 of these images (4.2%) were invalid because either the thermal camera was calibrating when the image was taken or the image was indecipherable (*e.g.,* a thumb blocking the camera lens). To determine what participants were taking pictures of, the remaining 1,908 images were analyzed through an iterative coding method using both inductive and deductive coding [8,34]. Multiple codes could be applied to the same image. We first selected and coded a random participant's image dataset (*total images*=139). The initial codebook was composed of a list of expected objects and contexts (*e.g.,* window, outdoor) and a miscellaneous code that allowed researchers to tag unforeseen yet significant elements within the images (*e.g.,* pet). Two researchers independently coded each image. Cohen's Kappa (κ) was used to measure inter-rater reliability (IRR). IRR on the first iteration of the codebook was κ=0.57 (*SD*=0.23) suggesting it required iteration [67]. The two researchers met, resolved disagreements, and updated the codebook accordingly. Both researchers then coded a second, randomly selected participant's image collection and achieved an IRR of κ=0.80 (*SD*=0.20) with codes ranging from *strong* to *near perfect* agreement. Our final codebook included 19 codes grouped into four categories: *subjects* (*e.g.,* electrical device), *context* (*e.g.,* indoor), *biologic* (*e.g.,* animal), and *misc.* (*e.g.,* clutter). The remaining images were then split between the two researchers and coded independently. The final codebook is included in our Supplementary Materials.

Weekly Surveys. The weekly surveys captured feedback on each mission such as: a description of what participants found during their assessment activities and recommendations, if any, that they might have to improve building performance. The surveys also asked for procedural details such as the date and duration of their audit activities. Finally, participants filled Likert-scale questions about their experience using the thermal camera. The survey took approximately 30 minutes to complete.

Debrief Interviews. The semi-structured interview sessions lasted an average of 75 minutes (*SD*=18.2). Interviews were audio recorded and professionally transcribed. Similar to the image analysis, we pursued an iterative coding approach using a mixture of inductive and deductive codes. Two researchers explored the interview transcript of a randomly selected participant using an early codebook developed based on research literature, our study protocol, and discussions amongst the research team. The final codebook included 12 codes grouped into three categories: *experiential* (*e.g.,* exploratory behavior), *design ideas & challenges* (*e.g.,* design idea), and *broader impact* (*e.g.,* potential benefit). The unit of analysis was the response to a single question or image. IRR on the first iteration of the codebook was κ=0.51 (*SD*=0.21). Again, the two researchers met and resolved disagreements. This was repeated with randomly selected transcripts three times achieving an overall IRR of 0.87 (*SD*=0.08); remaining transcripts were split and coded. Again, the final codebook is included in Supplementary Materials.

Field Study Results

We first provide an overview of the field study activities. Next, we review each mission based on the weekly survey responses and captured images. After presenting the field study results, we address our research questions through thematic analysis of the entire corpus of study data. Finally,

WEEKLY MISSION	IMAGE TOTALS	AVG. IMAGES PER PARTICIPANT	AVG. TIME SPENT (MINS)	AVG. # AUDIT SESSIONS	AVG. MISSION DIFFICULTY	THERMAL CAMERA HELPED W/ LEARNING	THERMAL CAMERA HELPED W/ IDENTIFICATION
Home	572	57.2 (*SD*=52.27)	34.9 (*SD*=15.02)	1.9	5.3 (*SD*=1.25, *Mdn*=6.0)	5.9 (*SD*=1.19, *Mdn*=6.0)	5.4 (*SD*=0.66, *Mdn*=5.5)
Workplace	405	40.5 (*SD*=18.02)	32.0 (*SD*=14.59)	2.0	4.4 (*SD*=1.26, *Mdn*=4.5)	5.4 (*SD*=0.32, *Mdn*=6.0)	5.2 (*SD*=0.32, *Mdn*=5.5)
Commercial	415	41.5 (*SD*=9.72)	28.7 (*SD*=16.77)	1.7	4.2 (*SD*=1.39, *Mdn*=3.5)	6.3 (*SD*=0.67, *Mdn*=6.0)	5.9 (*SD*=1.19, *Mdn*=6.0)
Community	516	51.6 (*SD*=26.73)	29.7 (*SD*=13.69)	2.1	4.5 (*SD*=1.26, *Mdn*=4.5)	5.5 (*SD*=0.84, *Mdn*=5.5)	5.0 (*SD*=1.05, *Mdn*=5.0)

Table 4: An overview of participant behavior and survey responses. Average time spent was calculated by adding the total minutes spent across all data collection sessions in a given week based on participant's self-report data. For Likert questions, we used a 7-point scale ordered from *strongly disagree* (1) to *strongly agree* (7); 4 was neutral. We report median (*Mdn*=X) and standard deviation (*SD*=X). For mission difficulty, higher is easier.

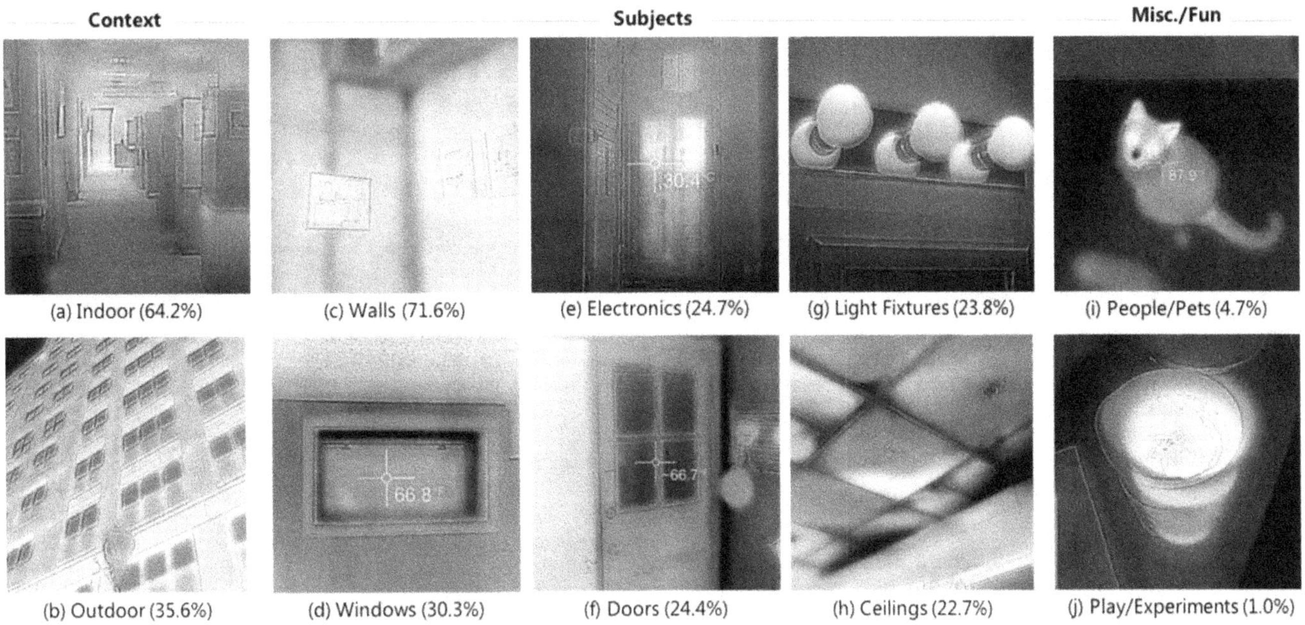

Figure 4: Examples of the image contexts, subjects, and non-mission photos as well as the percentage of the dataset that includes these features.

we present participant design considerations for future thermographic tools. Participant quotes are attributed using a 'P' followed by their identification number (*e.g.,* P1).

Overview of the Four Auditing Missions

To characterize participant activities during the missions, we examined: what participants took pictures of, how much time participants spent performing their auditing activities, and the perceived utility of the thermal camera. For the latter, participants reported how helpful they felt the thermal camera was for learning about and identifying energy-related issues during audits. Table 4 presents specific details for each mission, which we summarize next.

Data Collected. Participants took 47.7 photos per mission, most commonly containing walls (71.6% of images), windows (30.3%), doors (24.4%), and electrical devices (23.7%). Participants concentrated on interior inspections (64.2 %) rather than outdoors. See Figure 4 for examples.

Time Spent. Participants typically spent 1.2 hours completing each mission, which was often divided across multiple days (usually 2). Participants reported spending 30 minutes capturing thermal imagery and another 30 minutes on reporting (*i.e.,* completing the weekly survey). The remaining time was spent planning (*i.e.,* what building to audit) and uploading imagery to the research team.

Thermal Camera Utility. Overall, the thermal camera was deemed helpful in identifying and learning about potential problems in buildings, particularly for the first three missions (Home, Workplace, and Commercial).

Individual Auditing Missions

In each of the four missions, participants were asked to explore a different location. Here we briefly describe results from each mission before discussing pervasive themes.

Home Mission. In this mission, participants investigated their homes looking for potential energy inefficiency issues. Half of the participants (5) investigated single-family homes, three investigated town homes, and the remaining two investigated apartment units. In the post-mission survey, all participants (10) reported checking for window, door, and insulation issues. Most participants (8) started with pre-existing comfort issues (*e.g.,* rooms that were not adequately heated or cooled). A few (3) explored electrical appliances (*e.g.,* dryer) due to a safety concern. Additionally, a few (2) investigated a friend's home.

Based on their auditing activities, several participants (4) concluded that the windows in their homes needed minor repairs (*e.g.,* improved air sealing), a few (3) reported insulation issues, one was motivated to contact an electrician, and the rest (2) did not report finding any issues. As a positive example, in the post-mission survey, P7 reported exploring a pre-existing thermal comfort problem and that the thermograms made him "*very confident about missing insulation issues, especially in the ceilings of that room*" (Figure 4a). Thus, the participant decided, "*I would like to share this image with my landlord,*" to see if this issue could be addressed.

Workplace Mission. In the second mission, participants explored energy use in their workplaces. Most participants (7) investigated office buildings, two investigated university buildings, and another investigated a local grocery market. Like the Home Mission, all participants (10) reported looking for leaky windows, doors, and noted interest in the heat signatures produced by electronics. Two participants did not report finding any energy efficiency issues. Three reported finding leaky windows and doors, and five reported finding electronic devices using phantom energy (Figure 4b). As P4 explained:

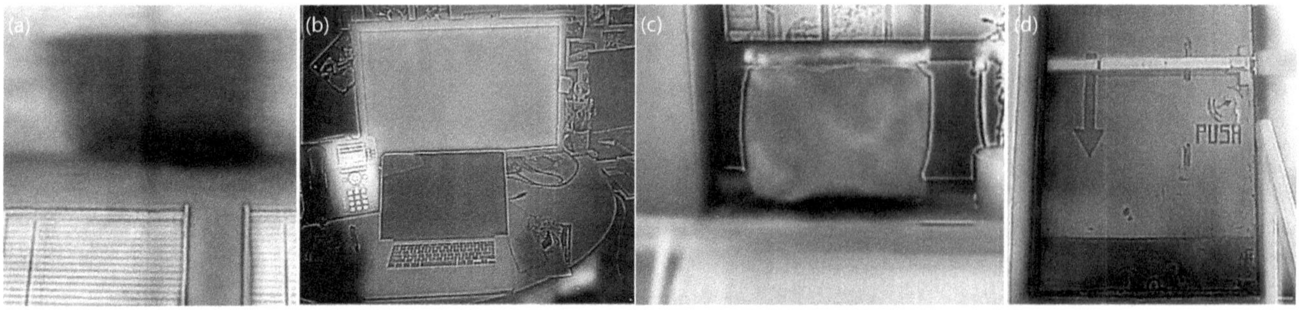

Figure 5: Example imagery from participant investigations: (**a**) insulation issue in roof of a residential home, (**b**) observing power consumption of computer equipment in an office, (**c**) gathering evidence of insufficient winterization procedure of window air conditioning units in a university building, and (**d**) documenting the need to repair weather stripping around an emergency exit door at a community theater.

> *"I was stunned to realize that my monitor doesn't completely turn off when it goes to sleep. It was unused for the weekend but still appeared hot. So I turned it off when I went to lunch and when I came back and it was indeed cooler." –P4*

As in the Home Mission, two participants used thermal comfort as motivation to explore their workspace. For example, due to this mission being conducted in the winter season, P5 noted that many offices in her building were cold and that she used the thermal camera to confirm her suspicion: *"I found that most of the ceiling vents were colder which leads me to believe they might still be pumping out cool air."* Thus, P5 concluded that her workplace's air conditioning settings might need to be adjusted. P10 described a similar shared concern about how drafty his workplace became because of insufficient air conditioning unit winterization procedures and used his thermal camera to investigate (Figure 5c). Based on his imagery, he concluded:

> *"The situation with the window A/C units is absurd. Honestly, they should be removed in the fall and reinstalled in the spring since it is so hard to insulate them and they are only needed during the summer. Having that much air getting through in the summer is also a problem, we just don't realize it and continue running the units." –P10*

At the time of the debrief interview, P10 reported that he was considering sending the imagery to his facilities management to help evaluate the problem.

Commercial Mission. The third mission asked participants to explore a commercial building. Participants investigated a wide range of establishments from restaurants to hardware stores. Seven participants did not report finding any evidence of potential efficiency issues. Unlike the previous missions, participants were not able to use their knowledge and experience of a place to guide their explorations (*e.g.,* where cold drafts were located). Most participants (9) investigated equipment such as storage, food preparation, and serving areas found in commercial cafés or markets. One participant found potential evidence of moisture damage in a restaurant. Two reported finding evidence of leaky windows and doors. For example, P8 investigated a community theater and reported finding air leakage issues prompting a discussion with the operators (Figure 4d):

> *"The theatre underwent went a major renovation in 2014-15 where it was closed for several months. ...In speaking with the operator, she indicated that although there were all new exteriors doors and windows on the main level, the upstairs office windows and fire doors were original." –P8*

P8 reported sharing his thermal photographs with the operators, who planned to send the images to city officials to show the need for further repairs.

Community Mission. The final mission was open ended; participants were asked to investigate their local community, which they mostly did outdoors. Nine participants did not report finding any issues but did describe finding and learning about utility infrastructure in their community such as water lines and electrical equipment (Figure 6a). P4 additionally explored a local makerspace and reported (Figure 6b):

> *"The makerspace was a treasure trove: clear differences between new and old windows, where patches of the walls were made (cold sources), evidence of water damage (confirmed by renter of the space), and old pipes creating cold spots on the walls and ceiling." –P4*

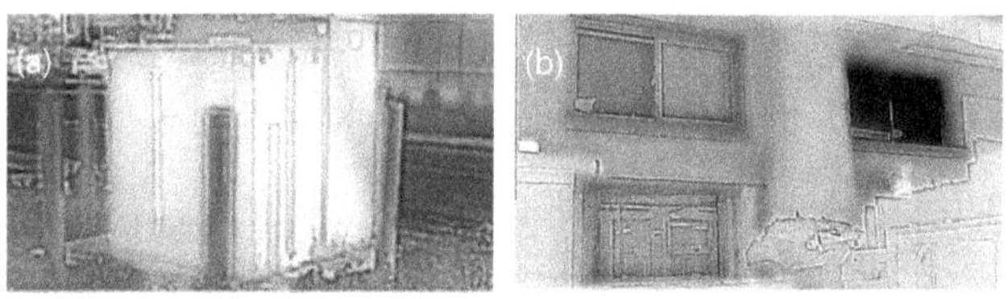

Figure 6: During the community mission, participants learned about utility infrastructure **(a)**; one explored a makerspace **(b).**

Summary. During the first three missions, participants primarily investigated buildings for missing insulation, air leakage issues, and understanding phantom energy use. In the home, participants seemed comfortable drawing conclusions about the need for repairs. In each mission, a small number of participants indicated that they wanted to address discovered problems by contacting a landlord, an electrician, or building owners/operators. In the final mission, participants used their cameras to explore their community and, most did not find concerning issues; however, they mostly took exterior pictures of buildings.

Major Themes Across Missions

While the previous section characterized participant behavior on a per-mission basis, we now turn toward describing themes that emerged across our four-week study, including: how participants collected and interpreted thermal imagery, what they learned, and what influenced their ability to act on their findings.

Data Collection. Rather than following any specific plan or procedure as an expert auditor might do [61], all participants (10) described their investigations as random walks through the interior of buildings. Participants occasionally followed their interior walk with another around the building's exterior, and participants who were aware of pre-existing issues tended to start in those areas. This was especially true during the home and workplace missions. With no pre-existing issues in mind, participants described their activities as exploratory, often using the camera as an augmented reality lens into otherwise invisible energy flows. As P1 said:

> *"I was mostly just looking through the lens of the camera. I wasn't looking at my surroundings and then putting a camera up. I was holding the camera up and taking photos." – P1*

When looking through the live view of the thermal camera, if participants discovered what they perceived as an anomalous heat signature, they would then take two-to-three images from slightly different positions or angles to ensure adequate capture. Even if they did not find anything of interest, participants would still take one or two wide-angle photographs to help them record areas that they investigated. Due to the time it took to attach the camera and load the thermal app, most participants did not report taking many photos outside of the mission scenarios.

Interpretation. When asked about interpreting thermal imagery, participants described how they appraised an image and things that made this task challenging. To determine if an anomalous heat signature was an issue, all (10) participants described looking for areas of high contrast in the images. Participants believed they could readily identify air leakages around windows and doors as well as the heat signatures from electronics; however, participants also described capturing imagery that they did not understand such as the cause of a warm spot on a wall that did not have any obvious source. While participants were not always able to describe what made interpreting a thermal signature difficult, most participants (8) attributed difficulties to the presence of confounding objects (*e.g.*, heating elements), materials (*e.g.*, metals), and other environmental factors (*e.g.*, sunlight). For example, referring to an image P3 said:

> *"This is all glass, so it's reflective. It's not clear to me if it's really that much warmer on the inside of this building than the outside." –P3*

All (10) participants said that at times they lacked confidence in their ability to draw appropriate conclusions from the thermal images. Most participants (6) found it difficult to determine the severity of issues they found and the potential impact repairs would have on the efficiency of the building. As P2 described, *"I don't know how much [the issue] really affects the energy use of my apartment."* Additionally, half (5) of the participants suggested that a lack of information about a building (*e.g.*, age) and/or its construction (*e.g.*, type or rating of insulation used) limited their ability to draw confident conclusions.

Knowledge Gains. Through their use of the thermal camera, all participants (10) reported learning to identify hidden structures or common issues in the built environment such as hot water pipes or leaky windows. Many participants (6) also stated that they learned about how materials had different conductive or reflective properties. P3 said: *"I certainly learned about the thermal reflectance of common surfaces, that's something that I had not known before."*

Awareness of Energy Efficiency. In the debrief interviews, seven participants described how their perspective on the way buildings are used and maintained had changed. We classified these perspectives into two categories, related to *energy consumption* (5) and *building maintenance* (2). participants frequently mentioned that seeing the easily recognizable thermal signatures from electronic devices forced them to consider electrical use and conservation. For example, P10 found that thermal images were a helpful reminder to turn off devices that are left on standby (and consuming phantom energy [56]):

> *"It's one of those things that I'm aware of in theory: when you leave things plugged in there is still some energy use, but seeing it like this reminds me about it." –P10*

However, a few participants also pointed out that there are many "*always on*" devices that do not have a convenient way to manage their energy consumption (reaffirming [12]), including their internet routers at home or the phone systems common in office environments. Two participants noted that their perspective on building maintenance had changed. P6, for example, had come to believe that inspections and building efficiency maintenance should be an ongoing practice, like with a car:

> *"It's one of these things you've got to keep working at to incrementally find, you know, I can do something more efficiently here, turn this off more, or fix that problem."* –P6

Perceived Value of Thermography. All (10) participants perceived value in having a tool that helped them investigate potential energy-related problems in buildings. Most (8) suggested that thermal imagery could provide supporting evidence to building owners and or others in charge of building maintenance. For example, P3 stated *"I've been meaning to contact my landlord with these images and say, look, there seems to be a clear issue here that I think you should address."* Two participants suggested thermography might be useful for community related improvements. As P2 described:

> *"It would be interesting to go and do this in the local high school and see if it's built well, that we're not wasting energy*

> *and resources that we could be using for something else... I feel like if there are ways that we could save on energy by repairing things, then that would be beneficial." –P2*

Locus of Control. Two main issues were raised about making energy improvement decisions: lack of control and apathy. Some participants (4) who rented or lived in housing cooperatives were concerned that if they found evidence of a problem that they would not be in a position to make retrofit decisions. As P5 stated, *"If I took a picture that showed an insulation issue, I don't necessarily think the owner would get on top of fixing it."* In missions outside the home, one participant expressed that it was not clear who they should talk to if they discovered an issue. In response to performing a mission in a local café, P2 asked:

> *"If I find an issue, who am I going to tell and are they really going to care? My biggest concern is what if something is wrong and they don't want to do anything about it." –P2*

While locus of control issues are non-trivial, especially in residential buildings where asymmetric power relationships may exist with landlords (*e.g.*, [10,60]), thermal cameras may play a unique advocacy role for tenants to highlight otherwise difficult-to-observe problems or provide continued evidence of an unresolved issue.

Participant Design Considerations

At the end of the debrief interview, participants were asked for suggestions to improve smartphone-based thermography tools. Participants discussed support for automation, privacy, and general usability improvements.

*Automated Assistance.*_Similar to our findings with professional auditors [47], most participants (8) suggested adding "intelligent" mechanisms that would help them collect and analyze thermographic data. For example, participants wanted the live camera view to automatically identify anomalous thermal signatures as well as provide an estimate of problem severity and the amount of money saved if addressed. P9 summarized:

> *"You want to make sure that you are in a very energy efficient area, so that you're not wasting and not spending too much money. Does making a change really help save energy costs? These are things I am interested in learning." –P9*

Privacy. While three participants had no concerns, half of participants (5) indicated they would adopt their normal digital photograph sharing practices for the thermograms. Two participants who had investigated the homes of others during the study considered those thermograms to be potentially sensitive, and felt that they would need to ask for permission to share. P3 summarized:

> *"All the photos from Missions 2, 3, and 4, I have no problem sharing. The ones from my friend's house I wouldn't want to share period; it's not my house to share. The ones from my house I'd be fine sharing online." –P3*

Usability. Most participants (9) wanted the thermal camera to be fully integrated with their smartphones due to the perceived tediousness of retrieving and connecting the attachment. Participants speculated that this change would make them more likely to perform explorative activities.

DISCUSSION

As the first qualitative, human-centered inquiry into novice approaches to smartphone-based thermographic energy auditing, our findings demonstrate that novice users with minimal training can use thermal cameras to detect potential energy efficiency issues in the built environment; however, that they often lacked confidence in correctly interpreting thermographic imagery and understanding the severity of problems they identified. Furthermore, our findings described: (i) how novice users collect and interpret thermal imagery, (ii) challenges that impede their auditing activities, and (iii) design considerations that could guide the development of future thermographic systems. Below we reflect on our findings, suggest future work, and discuss limitations.

Reflection on Method: Mission Structure

In this study, we asked novices to freely explore their environment using a thermal camera as well as complete structured weekly missions (adapted from [58]). While the mission structure may have prompted certain behaviors that would otherwise not have been observed, they also allowed participants to explore different scenarios, motivated data collection, and helped keep participants engaged over the four-weeks. We believe that these methods enabled us to extract meaningful data, and would be appropriate for studying similar technologies in the future within specific use scenarios like ours. Follow-up work may want to explore completely unstructured thermal camera use in the wild.

Barriers to Novice Thermographic Energy Auditing

While novice users perceived value in their use of thermal cameras, they also highlighted several potential barriers to utilization of this data, which we discuss here.

Knowledge and Experience. Future systems designed for novice use will need to consider how to assist them with performing thermographic inspections and interpreting thermal imagery. As noted by [47], professional thermographers suggested that knowledge of building materials, construction practices, and thermographic measurement procedures (*e.g.*, ISO standards) are critical to performing a good thermographic scan. Future applications could provide the needed scaffolding during data collection activities (*e.g.*, via on-screen prompts). Tools that support novice analysis of thermographic data could help generate recommendations with assistance from automation, social networks, or professionals; this might help reduce the experiential gaps between thermographers.

Decision Making. With the emergence of low-cost thermography tools, end-users will likely play an increasingly active role in energy auditing activities. Participants observed that thermal cameras were useful for detecting problems (*e.g.*, air leakage around windows or doors) and, as others have noted [47,52], to perceive energy use in buildings. However, participants also expressed concern about not always knowing what to do with the information they obtained from their audits. Particularly in cases where users have the locus of control necessary to implement changes, it will be important to understand how to bridge the gap between information and action (*e.g.*, through actionable recommendations) [32]. Future, more longitudinal work should investigate how likely novice auditors are to implement their self-generated recommendations, particularly in the home, and if energy efficiency improvements are achieved.

Locus of Control. It is important to consider the limits of a user's ability to effect change outside of their immediate locus of control (or use-contexts [43]). The barriers to effecting change expressed by our participants are consistent with the findings of other researchers who examined the role of social factors in energy consumption and building maintenance [12,13]. In contrast to a professional energy auditor whose services are requested unless the user is the owner or operator of the building, it may be difficult for them to make changes—particularly structural upgrades, improved insulation, and the purchase of energy-efficient appliances. As building energy efficiency is increasing as a priority [4,37,62], authorities may give more credence to issues with sensor-based evidence such as that from a thermal camera. Future work should investigate how to assist end-users with verifying their sensor-based recommendations and advocating for having issues addressed.

Privacy and Sharing. Thermal images can contain identifiable and sensitive information. Participants expressed concern about sharing thermal images (similar to those raised about conventional photographs [2]) and considered the social implications—questioning their right to share imagery that contained data they considered owned by others—and about who else the data would be shared with. These concerns also mirror those raised by professional energy auditors [35]. Our work suggests that future thermographic systems should investigate anonymization and privacy protection.

Implications for Public Auditing

With the increasing availability of thermal cameras, our work begins to explore scenarios in which motivated citizenry can use thermography to audit public infrastructure—perhaps, to increase transparency and accountability. Our findings suggest that novice auditors will likely perform best in scenarios that have clearly defined goals (*i.e.*, Missions 1–3) and that their approach will likely focus on recording potential issues rather than the lack thereof—though both are important. This finding is consistent with other novice data collection communities (*e.g.*, citizen science [39,53]). Given emerging examples of citizens using thermal cameras in energy and pollution monitoring contexts as a form of whistleblowing [11,17], novice thermography use for social causes is a potentially rich area for future Sustainable HCI research.

Limitations

Our study had four primary limitations, which should be addressed in future work. First, our participants were eco-conscious and highly educated, which may have influenced their perceptions and interpretations of thermography as well as their willingness to suggest taking actions. However, our participants likely represent early adopters making their feedback and experiences valuable. Second, as our participants were involved in a semi-structured study, our findings may not translate to general, unguided use of these tools. Third, while a trained thermographer reviewed participant data, we did not attempt to systematically verify or study the accuracy of participant diagnoses based on their thermal images. Finally, some participants discussed making retrofit decisions or conversing with building operators (*e.g.*, landlords) based on their thermographic findings; however, we did not conduct follow-ups, so we do not know what (if any) actions took place.

CONCLUSION

This paper contributes the first qualitative investigation of novice approaches to smartphone-based thermographic energy auditing. Through a four-week field study of end-user behavior, we assessed the efficacy of novice thermographic energy auditing activities across different use-contexts. Our findings indicate that participants perceived thermal cameras as effective diagnostic tools and suggests that novice imagery could be an impactful form of Eco-Visualization. Through our semi-structured interviews, we identified important challenges and potential benefits of engaging novices in thermographic energy auditing. Our findings have implications for both the design of future thermographic tools and for Sustainable HCI researchers working in energy efficiency. Cheap, emerging thermal cameras have the potential to broadly impact the way we interact with and understand our built environment—from residential homes to commercial buildings [3].

ACKNOWLEDGMENTS

This research was partially funded by the UMD Office of Sustainability. Erica Brown worked with us through the *National Socio-Environmental Synthesis Center (SESYNC)* Summer Internship Program.

REFERENCES

1. Bilal Abdulkarim, Rustam Kamberov, and Geoffrey Hay. 2014. Supporting Urban Energy Efficiency with Volunteered Roof Information and the Google Maps API. *Remote Sensing* 6, 10: 9691–9711.

2. Alper T Alan, Enrico Costanza, Sarvapali D Ramchurn, Joel Fischer, Tom Rodden, and Nicholas R Jennings. 2016. Tariff Agent: Interacting with a Future Smart Energy System at Home. *ACM Trans. Comput.-Hum. Interact.* 23, 4: 25:1--25:28. https://doi.org/10.1145/2943770

3. Hamed Alavi, Denis Lalanne, Julien Nembrini, Elizabeth Churchill, David Kirk, and Wendy Moncur. 2016. Future of Human-Building Interaction. In *Proceedings of the 34rd Annual ACM Conference Extended Abstracts on Human Factors in Computing Systems.*
4. Association of Energy Engineers. 2014. Certified Energy Auditor. Retrieved from http://www.aeecenter.org/i4a/pages/index.cfm?pageid=3365
5. C.A. Balaras and A.A. Argiriou. 2002. Infrared thermography for building diagnostics. *Energy and Buildings* 34, 2: 171–183.
6. Eli Blevis. 2007. Sustainable Interaction Design: Invention & Disposal, Renewal & Reuse. In *Proceedings of the SIGCHI Conference on Human Factors in Computing Systems* (CHI '07), 503–512. https://doi.org/10.1145/1240624.1240705
7. Dorit Borrmann, Andreas Nüchter, Marija Đakulović, Ivan Maurović, Ivan Petrović, Dinko Osmanković, and Jasmin Velagić. 2014. A mobile robot based system for fully automated thermal 3D mapping. *Advanced Engineering Informatics.*
8. Virginia Braun and Victoria Clarke. 2006. Using thematic analysis in psychology. *Qualitative Research in Psychology* 3, 2: 77–101.
9. Peter Brooks. 2007. Testing Building Envelopes with Infrared Thermography: Delivering the "Big Picture." *Interface, the Technical Journal of RCI* July. Retrieved from http://www.rci-online.org/interface/2007-07-brooks.pdf
10. Hronn Brynjarsdottir, Maria Håkansson, James Pierce, Eric Baumer, Carl DiSalvo, and Phoebe Sengers. 2012. Sustainably Unpersuaded: How Persuasion Narrows Our Vision of Sustainability. In *Proceedings of the SIGCHI Conference on Human Factors in Computing Systems* (CHI '12), 947–956. https://doi.org/10.1145/2207676.2208539
11. Chesapeake Bay Foundation. 2011. Infrared Video of Drilling Air Pollution. Retrieved January 1, 2015 from https://youtu.be/d-ybofaO9wI
12. Marshini Chetty, A J Bernheim Brush, Brian R Meyers, and Paul Johns. 2009. It's Not Easy Being Green: Understanding Home Computer Power Management. In *Proceedings of the SIGCHI Conference on Human Factors in Computing Systems* (CHI '09), 1033–1042. https://doi.org/10.1145/1518701.1518860
13. Marisol Clark-Ibáñez. 2004. Framing the social world with photo-elicitation interviews. *American behavioral scientist* 47, 12: 1507–1527.
14. Rob Comber and Anja Thieme. 2013. Designing beyond habit: opening space for improved recycling and food waste behaviors through processes of persuasion, social influence and aversive affect. *Personal and Ubiquitous Computing* 17, 6: 1197–1210. https://doi.org/10.1007/s00779-012-0587-1
15. Saverio Debernardis, Michele Fiorentino, Antonio E Uva, and Giuseppe Monno. 2016. A System to Exploit Thermographic Data Using Projected Augmented Reality. In *International Conference on Augmented Reality, Virtual Reality and Computer Graphics*, 489–499.
16. Girum G Demisse, Dorit Borrmann, and Andreas Nuchter. 2013. Interpreting thermal 3D models of indoor environments for energy efficiency. In *Advanced Robotics (ICAR), 2013 16th International Conference on*, 1–8. https://doi.org/10.1109/ICAR.2013.6766550
17. Tomas DiFiore. 2014. Fugitive Emissions And Methane Loading Of The Atmosphere. Retrieved February 4, 2015 from https://youtu.be/UVviIKw3V6g
18. Tawanna Dillahunt, Jennifer Mankoff, and Eric Paulos. 2010. Understanding Conflict Between Landlords and Tenants: Implications for Energy Sensing and Feedback. In *Proceedings of the 12th ACM International Conference on Ubiquitous Computing* (Ubicomp '10), 149–158. https://doi.org/10.1145/1864349.1864376
19. Carl DiSalvo, Phoebe Sengers, and Hrönn Brynjarsdóttir. 2010. Mapping the Landscape of Sustainable HCI. In *Proceedings of the SIGCHI Conference on Human Factors in Computing Systems* (CHI '10), 1975–1984. https://doi.org/10.1145/1753326.1753625
20. Karen Ehrhardt-Martinez, Kat A Donnelly, Laitner Contributors, Dan York, Jacob Talbot, and Katherine Friedrich. 2010. Advanced Metering Initiatives and Residential Feedback Programs: A Meta-Review for Household Electricity-Saving Opportunities. Retrieved January 8, 2017 from http://aceee.org/sites/default/files/publications/researchreports/e105.pdf
21. Energy.gov. 2012. Blower Door Tests. *U.S. Department of Energy*. Retrieved from http://energy.gov/energysaver/articles/blower-door-tests
22. FLIR Inc. 2016. FLIR Approved Applications. Retrieved August 8, 2016 from http://www.flir.com/flirone/display/?id=69356
23. B J Fogg. 2002. *Persuasive Technology: Using Computers to Change What We Think and Do*. Morgan Kaufmann Publishers Inc., San Francisco, CA, USA.
24. Jon Froehlich, Tawanna Dillahunt, Predrag Klasnja, Jennifer Mankoff, Sunny Consolvo, Beverly Harrison, and James A Landay. 2009. UbiGreen: Investigating a Mobile Tool for Tracking and Supporting Green Transportation Habits. In *Proceedings of the SIGCHI Conference on Human Factors in Computing Systems* (CHI '09), 1043–1052. https://doi.org/10.1145/1518701.1518861
25. Jon Froehlich, Leah Findlater, and James Landay. 2010. The Design of Eco-feedback Technology. In *Proceedings of the SIGCHI Conference on Human Factors in Computing Systems* (CHI '10), 1999–2008. https://doi.org/10.1145/1753326.1753629
26. Jon Froehlich, Eric Larson, Elliot Saba, Tim Campbell, Les Atlas, James Fogarty, and Shwetak Patel. 2011. A Longitudinal Study of Pressure Sensing to Infer Real-World Water Usage Events in the Home. Springer Berlin Heidelberg, 50–69. https://doi.org/10.1007/978-3-642-21726-5_4
27. Rikke Gade and Thomas B. Moeslund. 2013. Thermal cameras and applications: a survey. *Machine Vision and Applications* 25, 1: 245–262.

28. Gerald T. Gardner and Paul C. Stern. 2008. The Short List: The Most Effective Actions U.S. Households Can Take to Curb Climate Change. *Environment: Science and Policy for Sustainable Development* 50, 5: 12–25. https://doi.org/10.3200/ENVT.50.5.12-25
29. Julie Goodhew, Sabine Pahl, Tim Auburn, and Steve Goodhew. 2014. Making Heat Visible: Promoting Energy Conservation Behaviors Through Thermal Imaging. *Environment and Behavior*: 0013916514546218-.
30. Maria Håkansson and Phoebe Sengers. 2013. Beyond Being Green: Simple Living Families and ICT. In *Proceedings of the SIGCHI Conference on Human Factors in Computing Systems* (CHI '13), 2725–2734. https://doi.org/10.1145/2470654.2481378
31. Youngjib Ham and Mani Golparvar-Fard. 2013. Calculating the Cost of Heating and Cooling Loss for Building Diagnostics Using EPAR (Energy Performance Augmented Reality Models). In *ASCE International Workshop on Computing in Civil Engineering*.
32. Hanna Hasselqvist, Cristian Bogdan, and Filip Kis. 2016. Linking Data to Action: Designing for Amateur Energy Management. In *Proceedings of the 2016 ACM Conference on Designing Interactive Systems* (DIS '16), 473–483. https://doi.org/10.1145/2901790.2901837
33. Geoffrey J Hay, Christopher Kyle, Bharanidharan Hemachandran, Gang Chen, Mir Mustafizur Rahman, Tak S Fung, and Joseph L Arvai. 2011. Geospatial Technologies to Improve Urban Energy Efficiency. *Remote Sensing* 3, 7: 1380. https://doi.org/10.3390/rs3071380
34. Daniel J. Hruschka, Deborah Schwartz, Daphne Cobb St.John, Erin Picone-Decaro, Richard A. Jenkins, and James W. Carey. 2004. Reliability in Coding Open-Ended Data: Lessons Learned from HIV Behavioral Research. *Field Methods* 16, 3: 307–331. https://doi.org/10.1177/1525822X04266540
35. Aaron Ingle, Mithra Moezzi, Loren Lutzenhiser, Zac Hathaway, Susan Lutzenhiser, Joe Van Clock, Jane Peter, Rebecca Smith, David Heslam, and Richard C. Diamond. 2013. Behavioral Perspectives on Home Energy Audits: The Role of Auditors, Labels, Reports, and Audit Tools on Homeowner Decision Making. 1–396. Retrieved from http://www.escholarship.org/uc/item/1323m27r
36. ISO. 2012. *ISO 6781:1983: Thermal Insulation -- Qualitative detection of thermal irregularities in building envelopes -- Infrared method.* Retrieved from http://www.iso.org/iso/catalogue_detail.htm?csnumber=13277
37. ISO. 2014. *ISO 50002:2014: Energy audits -- Requirements with guidance for use.* Retrieved from https://www.iso.org/obp/ui/#iso:std:60088:en
38. Jordan D. Kelso. 2011. *Buildings energy data book.* Retrieved from http://buildingsdatabook.eren.doe.gov/
39. Sunyoung Kim, Christine Robson, Thomas Zimmerman, Jeffrey Pierce, and Eben M Haber. 2011. Creek Watch: Pairing Usefulness and Usability for Successful Citizen Science. In *Proceedings of the SIGCHI Conference on Human Factors in Computing Systems* (CHI '11), 2125–2134. https://doi.org/10.1145/1978942.1979251
40. Bran Knowles, Lynne Blair, Paul Coulton, and Mark Lochrie. 2014. Rethinking Plan A for Sustainable HCI. In *Proceedings of the 32Nd Annual ACM Conference on Human Factors in Computing Systems* (CHI '14), 3593–3596. https://doi.org/10.1145/2556288.2557311
41. Bran Knowles, Lynne Blair, Mike Hazas, and Stuart Walker. 2013. Exploring Sustainability Research in Computing: Where We Are and Where We Go Next. In *Proceedings of the 2013 ACM International Joint Conference on Pervasive and Ubiquitous Computing* (UbiComp '13), 305–314. https://doi.org/10.1145/2493432.2493474
42. Angeliki Kylili, Paris A. Fokaides, Petros Christou, and Soteris A. Kalogirou. 2014. Infrared thermography (IRT) applications for building diagnostics: A review. *Applied Energy* 134: 531–549.
43. Susana Lagüela, Lucia Diaz-Vilarino, David Roca, and Julia Armesto. 2014. Aerial oblique thermographic imagery for the generation of building 3D models to complement Geographic Information Systems. In *12th International Conference on Quantitative Infrared Thermography (QIRT 2014).*
44. Rob Matheson. 2015. Drive-By Heat Mapping. *MIT News*. Retrieved from http://newsoffice.mit.edu/2015/startup-essess-heat-mapping-cars-0105
45. Matthew Louis Mauriello, Matthew Dahlhausen, Erica Brown, Manaswi Saha, and Jon Froehlich. 2016. The Future Role of Thermography in Human-Building Interaction. In *Proceedings of the 34rd Annual ACM Conference Extended Abstracts on Human Factors in Computing Systems.*
46. Matthew Louis Mauriello and Jon E Froehlich. 2014. Towards Automated Thermal Profiling of Buildings at Scale Using Unmanned Aerial Vehicles and 3D-reconstruction. In *Proceedings of the 2014 ACM International Joint Conference on Pervasive and Ubiquitous Computing: Adjunct Publication* (UbiComp '14 Adjunct), 119–122. https://doi.org/10.1145/2638728.2638731
47. Matthew Louis Mauriello, Leyla Norooz, and Jon E. Froehlich. 2015. Understanding the Role of Thermography in Energy Auditing: Current Practices and the Potential for Automated Solutions. In *Proceedings of the 33rd Annual ACM Conference on Human Factors in Computing Systems*, 1993--2002. https://doi.org/10.1145/2702123.2702528
48. Ines Mergel. 2012. Distributed democracy: Seeclickfix. com for crowdsourced issue reporting. *Com for Crowdsourced Issue Reporting (January 27, 2012).* Retrieved from http://papers.ssrn.com/sol3/papers.cfm?abstract_id=1992968
49. Peyman Moghadam and Stephen Vidas. 2014. HeatWave: the next generation of thermography devices. In *SPIE Sensing Technology + Applications*, 91050F. Retrieved September 18, 2014 from http://proceedings.spiedigitallibrary.org/proceeding.aspx?articleid=1875668
50. Omar Oreifej, Jason Cramer, and Avideh Zakhor. 2014. Automatic Generation of 3D Thermal Maps of Building Interiors. *ASHRAE transactions.* Retrieved from http://www.eecs.berkeley.edu/~oreifej/papers/Thermal_2014.pdf

51. Sabine Pahl, Julie Goodhew, Christine Boomsma, and Stephen R J Sheppard. 2016. The Role of Energy Visualization in Addressing Energy Use: Insights from the eViz Project. *Frontiers in psychology* 7.
52. Karen Palmer, Margaret Walls, Hal Gordon, and Todd Gerarden. 2012. Assessing the energy-efficiency information gap: results from a survey of home energy auditors. *Energy Efficiency* 6, 2: 271–292. Retrieved September 3, 2014 from http://link.springer.com/10.1007/s12053-012-9178-2
53. Eric Paulos, R Honicky, and Ben Hooker. 2008. Citizen science: Enabling participatory urbanism. *Urban Informatics: Community Integration and Implementation.*
54. Luis Pérez-Lombard, José Ortiz, and Christine Pout. 2008. A review on buildings energy consumption information. *Energy and buildings* 40, 3: 394–398. Retrieved from http://www.sciencedirect.com/science/article/pii/S0378778807001016
55. James Pierce, William Odom, and Eli Blevis. 2008. Energy Aware Dwelling: A Critical Survey of Interaction Design for Eco-visualizations. In *Proceedings of the 20th Australasian Conference on Computer-Human Interaction: Designing for Habitus and Habitat* (OZCHI '08), 1–8. https://doi.org/10.1145/1517744.1517746
56. James Pierce and David Roedl. 2008. COVER STORY: Changing Energy Use Through Design. *interactions* 15, 4: 6–12. https://doi.org/10.1145/1374489.1374491
57. Chris Preist, Elaine Massung, and David Coyle. 2014. Competing or Aiming to Be Average?: Normification As a Means of Engaging Digital Volunteers. In *Proceedings of the 17th ACM Conference on Computer Supported Cooperative Work & Social Computing* (CSCW '14), 1222–1233. https://doi.org/10.1145/2531602.2531615
58. Rita Shewbridge, Amy Hurst, and Shaun K Kane. 2014. Everyday Making: Identifying Future Uses for 3D Printing in the Home. In *Proceedings of the 2014 Conference on Designing Interactive Systems* (DIS '14), 815–824. https://doi.org/10.1145/2598510.2598544
59. Matthias Stevens and Ellie D'Hondt. 2010. Crowdsourcing of pollution data using smartphones. In *Workshop on Ubiquitous Crowdsourcing*. Retrieved from http://soft.vub.ac.be/Publications/2010/vub-tr-soft-10-15.pdf
60. Yolande Strengers. 2013. Smart energy technologies in everyday life: Smart Utopia?
61. Yolande Strengers. 2014. Smart Energy in Everyday Life: Are You Designing for Resource Man? *interactions* 21, 4: 24–31. https://doi.org/10.1145/2621931
62. U.S. Green Building Council. 2016. *LEED v4 for BUILDING OPERATIONS AND MAINTENANCE*. Retrieved from http://www.usgbc.org/resources/leed-v4-building-operations-and-maintenance-current-version
63. US Department of Energy. 2012. Thermographic Inspections. Retrieved from http://energy.gov/energysaver/articles/thermographic-inspections
64. US Department of Energy. 2014. #AskEnergySaver: Home Energy Audits. Retrieved from http://energy.gov/articles/askenergysaver-home-energy-audits
65. V. P. Vavilov. 2011. A pessimistic view of the energy auditing of building structures with the use of infrared thermography. *Russian Journal of Nondestructive Testing* 46, 12: 906–910.
66. Stephen Vidas and Peyman Moghadam. 2013. HeatWave: A handheld 3D thermography system for energy auditing. *Energy and Buildings* 66: 445–460.
67. Anthony J Viera, Joanne M Garrett, *et al.* 2005. Understanding interobserver agreement: the kappa statistic. *Fam Med* 37, 5: 360–363. Retrieved from http://www.stfm.org/FamilyMedicine/Vol37Issue5/Viera360
68. Allison Woodruff, Jay Hasbrouck, and Sally Augustin. 2008. A Bright Green Perspective on Sustainable Choices. In *Proceedings of the SIGCHI Conference on Human Factors in Computing Systems* (CHI '08), 313–322. https://doi.org/10.1145/1357054.1357109
69. SeeClickFix. Retrieved June 1, 2015 from http://seeclickfix.com/apps
70. 2014. FLIR Systems Introduces First Thermal Imager Designed for Smartphones. *FLIR Inc.* Retrieved January 7, 2014 from http://investors.flir.com/releasedetail.cfm?releaseid=817445
71. 2014. Seek Thermal Announces It Will Bring Next-Generation Thermal Imaging To Mass Market. *Seek Thermal Inc.* Retrieved May 1, 2016 from http://www.thermal.com/press-releases/2015/2/12/seek-thermal-announces-it-will-bring-next-generation-thermal-imaging-to-mass-market
72. 2015. How Thermal Imaging Works: A Closer View. *FLIR Inc.* Retrieved May 1, 2016 from http://www.flir.com/flirone/Press/FLIR-ONE-Android-iOS-How-It-Works.pdf
73. 2015. FLIR One: At Home. *FLIR Inc.* Retrieved January 1, 2016 from http://www.flir.com/flirone/content/?id=62915
74. 2016. CAT S60 ANNOUNCED AS WORLD'S FIRST SMARTPHONE WITH INTEGRATED THERMAL CAMERA. *Caterpillar Inc.* Retrieved March 21, 2016 from http://www.catphones.com/en-us/news/press-releases/cat-s60-announced-as-worlds-first-smartphone-with-integrated-thermal-camera

"People Are Either Too Fake or Too Real": Opportunities and Challenges in Tie-Based Anonymity

Xiao Ma
Jacobs Institute, Cornell Tech
New York, NY, USA
xiao@jacobs.cornell.edu

Nazanin Andalibi
College of Computing and Informatics, Drexel University
Philadelphia, PA, USA
naz@drexel.edu

Louise Barkhuus
The IT University of Copenhagen
Copenhagen, Denmark
barkhuus@itu.dk

Mor Naaman
Jacobs Institute, Cornell Tech
New York, NY, USA
mor@jacobs.cornell.edu

ABSTRACT
In recent years, several mobile applications allowed individuals to anonymously share information with friends and contacts, without any persistent identity marker. The functions of these "tie-based" anonymity services may be notably different than other social media services. We use semi-structured interviews to qualitatively examine motivations, practices and perceptions in two tie-based anonymity apps: Secret (now defunct, in the US) and Mimi (in China). Among the findings, we show that: (1) while users are more comfortable in self-disclosure, they still have specific practices and strategies to avoid or allow identification; (2) attempts for de-identification of others are prevalent and often elaborate; and (3) participants come to expect both negativity and support in response to posts. Our findings highlight unique opportunities and potential benefits for tie-based anonymity apps, including serving disclosure needs and social probing. Still, challenges for making such applications successful, for example the prevalence of negativity and bullying, are substantial.

Author Keywords
Anonymity; social media; self-disclosure; CMC; Secret; Wumii; Mimi

ACM Classification Keywords
K.4.3 Computer-supported collaborative work

INTRODUCTION
From masquerade balls to online forums and popular systems like Reddit and 4chan, the design of anonymity functions has affected social interactions and dynamics in offline and online environments [11, 27]. Anonymity allows people to feel less constrained by the expectations of their everyday identities [3, 25], which in turn allows more candid and honest self-expressions [1, 43]. Anonymity also leads users to disclose more information [52], which may result in positive emotional outcomes for the person disclosing [45]. On the other hand, the lack of attribution and responsibility in anonymous environments can encourage malicious behaviors such as trolling [33] and cyberbullying [5, 6, 34]. It is no wonder that society in general, and HCI researchers in particular, have been fascinated with the topic of anonymity.

While early Internet platforms traditionally defaulted to anonymity or pseudonymity, the last decade has witnessed a "real-name", complete-identity push by some social media platforms like Facebook, Google+, and LinkedIn. Over the last few years, though, a number of new systems have emerged that adopt a new model of anonymity that we call *relation-based* anonymity. These applications often build on mobile device affordances such as persistent user identification and metadata such as location, as well as information about one's social ties through linkage to real-name social media platforms.

Most notably, *relation-based* anonymous applications such as Secret, Mimi, Whisper, Rumr and Yik Yak all provide mobile services to anonymously share content with people related to them, for example by physical proximity (*proximity-based*) or social affinity (*tie-based*) [37]. Secret, now defunct, was a *tie-based* mobile application when first launched in 2013: it allowed users to "share with friends, anonymously". Yik Yak, on the other hand, adopted the *proximity-based* model that allows users to see anonymous posts within a 10-mile radius or within a given university campus. Notably, in all these services, individual posts by the same contributor cannot be linked to each other[1]. The combination of relationship and

[1]In March 2016 (two years after launch), Yik Yak introduced "handles"—permanent pseudonyms that users can choose to post with.

CHI 2017, May 06 - 11, 2017, Denver, CO, USA

ACM 978-1-4503-4655-9/17/05...$15.00.
DOI: http://dx.doi.org/10.1145/3025453.3025956

lack of persistent identity resulted in this new and interesting model of anonymity, and presents a wide set of new research questions within HCI.

While HCI research has extensively studied the topic of anonymity, we here extend that literature by providing a qualitative examination of *tie-based* anonymous applications. Past HCI research includes broad examinations of anonymity perceptions and practices across multiple services and systems (e.g., [28, 44]), as well as studies of anonymity on specific platforms [29]. In the latter category, HCI research has examined various platforms, including for instance anonymity on social media [12, 28]; fully anonymous persistent-identity topic-based forums [26, 40, 47, 59]; community ad-hoc discussion threads [1, 30, 31, 35]; proximity-based anonymity services [29]; platforms that allow selective anonymity such as Ask.fm [18]; and anonymity in open collaboration projects such as Wikipedia [20]. Most of these platforms feature anonymity models significantly different from our model of interest here, likely resulting in different dynamics and affordances than tie-based anonymity services. The fact that contributors are aware that their readers are within their friend (and friend-of-friend) circle, provides a different foundation than, for example, pseudononymous social media.

To explore people's practices and perceptions around this new anonymity model, we posed the following research questions:

RQ1. What type of interactions do tie-based anonymous social networks afford according to regular users?

RQ2. What benefits and affordances do users of tie-based anonymous social networks experience?

RQ3. What are the perceived drawbacks and negative experiences by users of tie-based anonymous social networks?

To this end, we conducted a qualitative interview study with users of two apps: the US-based (and now defunct) Secret, and the China-based Mimi (now known as Wumii[2]). We conducted semi-structured interviews with users of these applications, and followed up with interviewees seven months later, after a period of significant change in both apps. In particular, during that period, Secret had changed from a tie-based to a proximity-based anonymous sharing model, and subsequently (after we concluded our research) shut down.

We present our results organized around five key themes. First, we present participants' motivations and general practices in using these services. Second, we illustrate how identity management *does* play a role, even within these anonymous, no-persistent-identity applications. Third, we discuss participants' widely used de-anonymization activities where they attempted to expose the identity of others on these services. Fourth, we show how the services provided some degree of intimacy and social support. In a fifth theme we consider the negativity and bullying aspects of these services. In addition to these themes, we consider the much-reduced use of the services after a period of six to seven months and the reasons for the usage drop-off. Finally, the discussion section addresses a key goal of this work: providing an overview of the opportunities and challenges of tie-based applications exposed by this research, to inform the design of future platforms and services that support this model.

[2] `https://www.wumii.org/`

BACKGROUND AND RELATED WORK

The HCI community has long been interested in anonymous platforms and services, and how identity practices affect community and social dynamics. In particular, we discuss various types or models of anonymity that were studied in the field, including persistent identity systems, anonymity in ad-hoc discussion threads and mixed anonymity models. Before we expand on the specific types of anonymity, we briefly review literature on self-disclosure.

Self-disclosure in social network environments can be seen as driven by an extended functional process [10] that takes into account audience perceptions and identity representation, balancing benefits and risks. People try to maximize the rewards brought by self-disclosure (e.g., social validation and self-expression) [9, 14] and minimize the risks (e.g., concerns about sensitive information shared with third parties) [10, 16]. Under the condition of anonymity, people have been found to disclose personal information more freely, potentially because they feel less constrained by the expectations of others or perceive less associated risks of social sanction [3, 25]. Anonymity also allows people to share sensitive intimate narratives, and seek and provide support in stigmatized contexts such as sexual abuse or mental illness [1,2], and explore aspects of their identity that otherwise would have been impossible [12, 56]. Most recently, an interview study of adolescents who use Ask.fm—a platform that allows selective anonymity—found that by strategically using selective anonymity, young people can build from social processes and work towards key developmental goals [18]. Particularly, this study argues that selective anonymity allows for higher levels of perceived authenticity, bypassing social expectations, learning about one's self, managing identity, and initiating and growing relationships [18].

On the other hand, the lack of attribution and responsibility associated with anonymity can also encourage malicious behaviors such as trolling, hostile commenting [33], deception [24], and cyberbullying [5, 6, 34]. Research suggests, for example, that lack of eye contact is a contributing factor to disinhibition and one of the reasons for online negativity [33], where other research points out that positive attitudes towards cyber-bullying increase later tendencies of this behavior in anonymous fora [6].

Next, we briefly report on the different models of anonymous platforms and services that have been studied in HCI, including recent research on relation-based anonymous platforms.

Models and Dynamics of Anonymous Services

One model of anonymity is persistent identity systems—services in which the identity of the poster may be unknown to others but still consistent from one post to another. This includes network-based systems like Twitter, where the posters can choose whether to use their "real name" or not, as well as topic-based systems (e.g., online forums, discussion groups, etc.) where participants have a persistent identity that may be pseudonymous. Previous studies on topic-based anonymous platforms for example, looked into how identity design impact communication dynamics on the platform [17]. Research has also addressed social support, most often through topic-based anonymous forums, from early studies of interaction practices on forums [47] to more recent studies of limitations to online medical support [26, 59]. Many of these studies illustrate that the anonymity within these forums affords more self-disclosure and emotional support [27]. At the same time, the posting dynamics there express higher accountability and somewhat more risk than the more ephemeral anonymity services.

Most systems with non-persistent identities are content-based, for example 4chan, Reddit and others. As one 4chan study showed [11], 90% of the posts made in the network are anonymous and cannot be linked to other submissions by the same individual. Such submissions arguably allow individuals to express themselves more freely, but result in increased negativity or need for moderation [32]. A significant issue in anonymous systems with non-persistent identities is the issue of source evaluation and credibility; in 4chan, the /b/ community uses shared context expressed in language and images that helps established credibility [11]. Trammell goes further to argue that the validation and approval practices on 4chan make it equivalent in some ways to a persistent user identity community [55].

A few recent examples mixed anonymity models by bridging persistent- and ephemeral-identity platforms. Recent research points out how "throwaway accounts" on otherwise single-identity pseudonymous social media forums enable users to switch identity temporarily [35] to be able to disclose particular information without repercussion. For instance, Andalibi et al. discuss the nuances of anonymity and suggest that sexual abuse survivors are more likely to use the anonymity afforded by throwaway accounts to disclose their experiences and seek support, and men are more likely to do so due to more stigma in the context of abuse [1]. Another recent study [12] looked at the support seeking and response behavior in a mixed anonymous/real-name forum: Facebook confessions boards. On these systems, people post anonymously (via a mediator) but receive replies by identifiable Facebook users. This dynamic lead to little negativity and an appropriate forum for discussing taboo topics and stigmatized identities [12].

As services that support a relation-based anonymity model are quite new, only recently research had started examining these platforms. Kang et al. conducted a qualitative study of users of these new services and emphasized how important it was for their participants to get social validation even from anonymous strangers, echoing early research on Usenet [29]. However, only four of their eighteen participants were Secret users, and the remaining were Whisper and Yik Yak users, services that rely on a proximity relation rather then a set of existing social connections (i.e., being connected through other social networks) [29]. Other recent studies have quantitatively examined data from the proximity-based anonymity service Whisper: One study compared Whisper's and Twitter's different anonymity models and found that users use anonymity to express their wants, needs, and wishes [15]. Another empirical study using 24 million posts on Whisper looked into structures of user interaction, user engagement, and network stickiness [58].

To summarize, in this paper we investigate tie-based anonymity services, where the perceived affordances, benefits and risks of participation are different than those of more traditional social media services, including anonymous ones.

TIE-BASED ANONYMOUS SOCIAL APPS

The tie-based anonymous social applications have several characteristics that set them apart from previous anonymous chat rooms and forums. Where traditional online forums and chat rooms are most often *topic-based* and support forum-wide identity, ephemeral identity systems make use of some sort of relationship between poster and reader, such as proximity or existing digital social ties. In this work we focus on the unique category of tie-based anonymous applications, where the anonymous application uses data from another social network where social ties are articulated, for example Facebook, or the phone's address book. With this social network information available to the application, it can mark content as posted by "friend" or "friend of friend"—based on a match done by the application but not exposed to the user.

Secret, available from December 2013 to April 2015, was a mobile application that allowed users to share information anonymously with Facebook friends and friends listed in the user's telephone contacts. Based on the friends list, the app displayed a stream of posts shared by the user's friends, friends of friends, as well as popular posts by non-friends. Users would see a list of reverse chronologically ordered posts that include text on top of a solid background or attached picture, with the source identified as "friend" or "friend of friend" when appropriate. In addition to these posts, users could also view popular posts using the "Explore" tab on the application, providing a list of popular and nearby posts by non-friends.

In this version of Secret, users could "like" any post by clicking on the heart-shaped button but only comment on posts from their friends or friends of friends. Comments were anonymous as well, and commenting users were assigned a colored icon consistent within the context of a single post. As a result, there was no built-in mechanism to identify posts or comments made by the same user beyond a single post and discussion thread.

The Secret app changed functionality and look during its lifetime and our study. In December 2014, the app transitioned from tie-based to proximity-based model. Like the popular app Yik Yak, Secret showed anonymous posts from people nearby, rather than from friends. In April 2015, shortly after our last follow-up interview, Secret had shut down.

A Chinese app called Mimi ("secret" in Chinese) was launched in late March 2014. The Mimi app is very similar to the earlier version of Secret, to the point of being considered a clone. Despite this similarity, Mimi did include additional functions such as private messaging, allowing users to send direct messages to the original author of a post. At the time of writing, Mimi is still available and active under the name Wumii. It is important to note that we included Mimi in the study to increase the generalizability of our findings, rather than to explicitly study cultural differences.

METHOD

Our study was based on in-depth, semi-structured interviews with users of Secret and Mimi, conducted in August and September 2014, with follow-up interviews six to seven months later. Our aim was to investigate uses and practices around the applications, as well as attitudes towards content and anonymity in these new tie-based platforms. We asked questions about participants' current experiences within and around these applications, with the goal of documenting examples of posts and reactions to these posts. We asked about types of content and types of interactions taking place as well as how they thought anonymity affected their interactions on the platform. Seven months after the first round of interviews, we followed up with a subset of participants via short interviews or email correspondence (we approached all but only a subset responded). By then, Secret had changed the posting mechanism to focus on showing nearby posts ("proximity-based"). The second-round interviews focused on the changes to the participants' practices through the past seven months, in particular given the changes to the app in the case of Secret.

Participants

We interviewed 15 participants: six users of the Chinese app Mimi (three men, three women) and nine users (six men, three women) of the US-based app Secret. Participants' ages ranged from 21 to 27 for Mimi, and 22 to 37 for Secret. Participants held a diverse set of jobs, from pre-school teacher and digital manager to advertisement agent and public relations. The Chinese participants all lived in China and Secret users were located in the US. To recruit the participants, we posted fliers at coffee shops in a major American metropolitan area, performed snowball sampling through social networking sites, and approached users who posted about these apps on Twitter and the Chinese-language weChat (through direct messaging and forwarding recruiting messages). The interviews with the Chinese participants were conducted with a Chinese interviewer (one of the authors, a native Chinese speaker) in Chinese and were translated to English by the same person. Participants had to have used the applications for at least two weeks at the time of the interview; most had used it for several months when we conducted the first round of interviews. The first round of interviews lasted 30–60 minutes. The participants were compensated $20 for their time. All interviews were conducted over the phone due to geographical distance.

When approaching the participants again seven months later, we were able to conduct follow-up interviews with five of the Secret users, and received five written responses from the Mimi users. For the remaining four Secret users, three did not respond and one declined to be interviewed again. The second round interviews with Secret users lasted 10–40 minutes depending on if they still used the application or not; from the participants who responded, only one was still using the application, four were not, but all reported using the app for months after the first interview. As the Mimi app did not change as significantly, we limited the interaction with the Mimi participants to an email inquiry where we asked if and how they were still using the application. In Mimi's case, two participants were still using the application, but four were not, citing that they have used it for a number of months after the first round of interviews.

The recruitment process and study protocol were reviewed and approved for the inclusion of human subjects by an Academic Institutional Review Board (Protocol #1406004763). All the names of our participants were anonymized for analysis. In the results we identify quotes with a code indicating the app used, gender and age of the participant. For example, SF36 is a Secret user, female, who was 36 years old.

Analysis

The analysis of the data was conducted through qualitative categorization and thematic analysis. After the interviews were transcribed and translated into English (when needed), one researcher independently coded all interviews for major categories. Then a second researcher conducted more detailed analysis using sub-categorization and constant comparison [53]. Based on our research questions, we then highlighted relevant mentions in the transcripts, and grouped these categories into major sub-categories iteratively. Comparing the original categories and the sub-categories to each research question, we determined the most important findings that we elaborate on in the following sections. The follow-up interviews were coded and analyzed later but in close connection to the corresponding original interview.

Due to the similarities in terms of functionality of the Chinese app Mimi and the majorly US-based app Secret, we analyzed the two sets of interviews collectively. Our interest was not in cultural differences per se, but rather to sample across two cultures. We closely watched out for potential cultural differences emerging from the interviews. In the end, we only observed minor differences. We therefore continue to describe our findings collectively, and only point out the few subtle cultural differences in the later part of the paper.

RESULTS

We now discuss the results from the first set of interviews. After briefly describing the general motivations and uses of the two services, we explore five themes: Motivations and general uses; the need for identity management in this type of anonymous social media; the de-anonymization that in fact took place; how the app fostered intimacy, support and encouragement; and finally, how users dealt with conflicts inside the app.

Motivations and Uses

This first set of findings echos and enforces the findings of Kang et al.'s investigation of relation-based anonymity apps, which focused on location-based platform but included some users of a tie-based platform (Secret) [29]. We report on these findings briefly below, to focus on angles and findings specific to tie-based platforms which were not highlighted in earlier research.

One major motivating factor participants cited for using the apps was entertainment: five participants mentioned checking the app when bored as a kind of distraction and mostly glanced over it for locating humorous and funny posts. One user reported that *"it's sort of my morning routine. I wake up and check my phone; I look at my email, check Twitter, and then I'd go to Secret"* [SM24]. Despite the very different model for anonymity, interviewees sometimes described their motivations in relation to other anonymous social media such as Reddit. One participant talked about Reddit being *"completely different"* in terms of the motivation for using the platform: *"Secret... connects you with friends, and it's more personalized type of secrets that people are uploading"* [SF36].

A key motivation was illustrated through participants describing the platform as a place where people can "let it out" without having their names attached. *"It allows and enables you just say that stuff that's on your mind. It may not make everyone happy"* [SM27] or *"things that I would like to tweet, but I don't want my name attached to it because people might have judgments about that"* [SM24]. One interviewee specifically mentioned anonymous apps as a platform for self-disclosure that avoids social sanction: *"I think everyone has the desire to self-disclose. They want to express the most indecent side of themselves, things that your society doesn't recognize or value [...] Indicating that you are good at sex is a positive image for you; but you cannot say, I am asexual (on social media) [...] These things can only be posted on anonymous communities"* [MM21]. Other participants reported being able to post untrue content. When asked the reason behind that, one participant responded: *"to see what would happen... and what kind of responses I would get, or what kind of comments or what kind of reaction I could elicit"* [SF36]. The curiosity of the reactions to extreme posts sometimes trumped the social norm of posting "real" secrets and made this type of social probing fairly common.

Several of the participants indicated that posting to these apps allowed them to avoid complications from their friends while still gaining the benefits from social interaction and validation. One participant reported posting a secret that received around ten likes: *"I met my ex boyfriend a few days ago. I got an email from him just now. I deleted it, without reading"* [MF24]. One of the reasons she did not post a particular post on her real-name social networks was that she only wanted to post to release her feelings but did not want anyone to know it was her. Posting under real-name would have led to her friends asking what happened and to "overthink". These statements illustrate previous findings on the benefits of self-disclosure [16,45] and earlier findings in the study of Kang et al. [29]. We return to this theme in the discussion.

Motivations for recurring use grew together with the size of the participant's Secret network. Some participants commented on how the size of their network determined the visibility and readership of posts, and hence significantly affected their experience on the platform (and the motivation for using the app). As one participant put it, *"If you don't have a lot of friends, your post is only getting read by however many people in that circle... "* [SF36]. The enjoyment of consumption was also limited with a smaller network, for example: *"[In the beginning] I would go on maybe once a week just because there wasn't very many updated posts for me to see, so there wasn't much action happening"* [SM24]. While the value of the network grew with the size of it, it was not simple to "recruit" friends to use the app, precisely due to the app's anonymous nature, but participants still reported occasionally asking their friends if they were using the app or not.

Identity Management

Six of the participants explicitly stated that the reduced need for identity management was something that made the application in question different. One person for example reported that *"on social networks where people know your identity, [...] you will have a drive to construct your self-image, and intentionally post things that are beneficial [...], that adds to your high-end image construction"* [MM21]. Other participants differentiated the identity aspects of Secret from other anonymous services: *"on [other anonymous social media], you have an identity on the entire site, or multiple identities if you're logging in with multiple accounts. But no matter what you do [there], no matter what the thread is, it's the same identity"* [SF22]. Participants reported that the ephemeral identity on the Secret app helped them to not be concerned about identity management since there was no pressure to live up to their "real self" as represented on other social media. This freedom did not necessarily mean that the users presented a false image. SF24, for example, explained how she felt she was representing her true self on Secret: *"I think I've never pretended to [...] be anything that I wasn't or anyone that I wasn't, and I feel like I guess I'm the most myself on Secret"*.

Interestingly, identity considerations still applied in some cases as participants used the text of the post to hint at, or further obscure, their identity. Interviewees reported crafting their posts carefully, based on their desired audiences: sometimes explicitly targeting their friends or expecting friends to be able to identify them, and at other times making sure to avoid identification by friends. One participant for example explained *"when I'm feeling depressed [...] I don't want people to know who I am, so I intentionally hide my speech habits. For [other types] I don't really care so I don't change anything in particular"* [MF22]. In doing that, these participants took full advantage of the non-persistent nature of identities where different posts cannot be associated with the same author: *"If you present yourself as the same in your daily life, like funny or hilarious, [...] it's very easy for friends to guess who this is; but if you post something that no one knows about, they couldn't guess who that is, even if you post a lot of secrets"* [MF24]. In summary, participants were articulate about identity management still being important to a certain degree, perhaps because they were aware of the possible process of de-anonymization, a practice we discuss next.

De-Anonymization

We identified two types of "identity hacking" that participants were aware of. We name them "hard-hacking" (i.e., using technical approaches) and "soft-hacking" (de-anonymization via social engineering and manual procedures). Most participants had no concern for hard-hacking, saying for example: *"I've read their articles about how they sort of anonymize things, and so I feel very comfortable with sort of the technical aspects behind things, and how they set up their system"* [SM24]. However, eight participants reported concerns or at least an awareness of "soft hacking", for example saying that *"some friends could easily figure things out by thinking about it for more than half a second"* [SM24].

Actual practices of soft-hacking by participants were prevalent as well. Seven of the participants expressed how it was "half the fun" or even a game to figure out who was the poster of an item. They used guessing, their knowledge of their friends, or language and speech cues to do so. A participant said he *"knew exactly who it was because six months prior..., my friend said the exact same quote to me... "* [SM24]. Participants also practiced de-anonymization, with fairly sophisticated practical methods. Participants reported, for example: (1) trying to figure out who in their contact list was using the app; (2) sharing screenshots to others via text messaging or other social media; (3) comparing (and triangulating) friend lists with other friends who used the app. In contrast, several participants were not motivated, saying that *"while it's not very difficult to identify who posted the secret, no one has the extra time to actually do this, and nobody would believe it anyway"* [MM21]. When asked if there were any differences between a post from a "friend" or a "friend of a friend", MF24 responded: *"Of course, I definitely care more about my friends' posts [...] If it's something shocking from a friend, I am definitely interested in figuring out who that was."*

Intimacy, Support and Encouragement

As noted above, participants certainly observed and reported posting more intimate content, due to the disinhibition effect of anonymous platforms [54]. Moreover, participants understood (and often reported witnessing) the benefits of such disclosures. One participant for example commented: *"Those things that people are too shy to discuss in real life but truly want to know more about, not involving attacking others, are actually beneficial"* [MF23]. Others said that they would not share the posted content with friends in person if they were worried about being judged. Relatedly, one user described the anonymous sharing as *"almost like gossiping without the negative effects of it landing specifically on someone... "* [SF36].

Ten of the participants described finding encouragement and validation for the sentiment shared on Secret or Mimi, for themselves or for others. One participant for example reported that she posted on Secret about being afraid to go to the gynecologist because of a past sexual assault, something she could not talk openly about. She received several comments and said: *"I think most of them were friends, and they said something encouraging along the lines of 'it's important for your health, and I'm really sorry that that all happened. We're here for you if you reach out to somebody to go with you.' Just trying to help, ease my fear, more or less."* She also received more likes than comments, and attributed that to *"they don't really know what to say, but they're just trying to show support or affirmation of some kind"* [SF24].

A more subtle benefit of the tie-based anonymity was a better understanding of attitudes and opinions among one's social ties, or at least a perception of such understanding. In eight of the interviews, participants reported that they were able to gain a better understanding of their collective group of friends, which in effect influenced their face-to-face social behavior. One participant told us how he had no idea that some of his friends were in fact questioning their sexual orientation: *"For example, [...] I had no idea that some people in my friend network questioned their sexual orientation. And they're afraid to talk about it in person, but they're okay with talking about it in sort of this anonymous aspect. [...] so I think it's great for me to understand my group of friends better as a whole and maybe next time when I'm in a social gathering, I won't make any comments about people's sexual orientation or anything like that. Big [...] friendship strategy decisions on my end"* [SM24].

Sometimes, the experienced benefit was to learn about an agreement with others within the anonymous tie-based network. Some very popular posts had a shared sentiment of surprising recognition, for example as described by one participant: *"[...] you can find someone who says some random things, and you'll realize [...] (s)he feels the same or is also like this! This is very interesting and very unique"* [MM27]. Another participant reported that one of his posts got three thousand likes and four hundred comments in a few days, saying it really must have *"struck a chord"* [SM27]; he reported receiving comments like *"yep, I do the same thing."*

People reported being motivated to explicitly provide support. One participant for example said that *"if it can help others, giving one or two sentences and be the audience of that person's thoughts wouldn't be a bad thing. After all, they are friends, or your friends of friends. If someone has problems, it's nice if you can comfort or cheer them up a bit"* [MM27]. On the other hand, this knowledge of ties, even remote, can make negative comments even more hurtful. One user reported stopping posting secrets after receiving very negative responses from several of her quite emotional posts, a topic we now turn to.

Debates, Conflicts and Bullying

As may be expected, postings and comments on these services often lead to debate and conflict. Participants reported that highly contentious topics could lead to non-supportive and judging comments: *"[...] these battles [can be really] drawn out and obnoxious to a certain point because both of them are just on such extremes that no one was really having a really worthwhile debate"* [SM27]. Another participant described: *"When there are two different opinions on certain things, and some people are just not very tactful in the way they say things. So if somebody posts something about being cheated on, then there will be commenters who will come in and say, 'oh you always deserve a second chance', and some others would say 'no, once a cheater, always a cheater'. And then some of the commenters will fight back and forth about their opinions."*

Although participants did not admit to bullying or directly contributing to conflicts, as expected with a fairly self-selected set of participants, some confessed commenting in an impulsive way, saying things they did not really mean. One participant explicitly admitted commenting un-constructively when he was not in a good mood. Overall, though, participants often claimed that they defended attacked posters from their attackers, and that they reported or called out offenders when inappropriate content was posted.

Participants were exposed to and well aware of negativity in these apps, and were often unsurprised when it occurred, recognizing the anonymity dynamics. *"Whenever you don't have to be held accountable, I think, unfortunately that there are other people who will use that to hurt people. [...] You tend to lean towards doing something that you probably wouldn't if you could be held accountable"* [SM37]. This behavior is often referred to as "trolling" behavior, such as degrading and objectionable comments in response to others' content. Participants were all well aware of trolling on these services, with thirteen of them mentioning the negative characteristics of some of the posts. One participant for example told us about comments that *"say really nasty, negative things"* [SF36]. Another participant specifically mentioned threads bashing an identified person on Secret: *"It's like a train wreck... it's a disaster when you look because you just can't believe that people are this terrible"* [SF22]. Participants reported flagging and reporting posts and comments, as well as calling out people within the social network.

Finally, the negativity on the platforms can lead to decreased engagement and disclosure through the platform. According to one participant, *"Most of the times there were rumors, scandals, made up stories and especially this abusing others or something like that. We say in Chinese 'negative energy'. It makes people frustrated and disappointed sometimes. [...] So yes after one or two uncomfortable experience I chose not to post on Mimi"* [MF21].

Revisiting: Persistence of Use and Changes in App Functionality

As we mentioned earlier, we contacted participants for a second interview during a period between six to seven months after the first interview. We were primarily interested in changes to the the participants' practices during the past months, particularly in respect to the changes in the applications. This allowed us to get a longer term perspective of use of tie-based anonymous applications. Between the first and the second interview, the Secret app had gone through significant changes: it transformed into a primarily proximity-based app (much like Yik Yak). Mimi, on the other hand, kept the original tie-based concept, but had added a few new features, such as eliminating the option to see if a post came from friends or friends of friends.

For the second round of interviews, all of the Secret participants reported a radical change of content over the last months where bullying and name calling had become prominent alongside adult content, reinforcing the findings of Kang et al. [29] with longitudinal evidence. One participant mused that it was *"a sad commentary about humanity that as soon as we get to be anonymous we abuse it"* [SM37]. Participants reported increased abusive and bullying behavior on the app, and one recalled a heated conflict within her own circle of friends that had taken place between the two interviews. Several participants reported incidents involving posters identifying others *within* the posts. Only one of the five participants we talked to was still using Secret; the other four particularly reported the reason for having left to be the negative and bullying postings. One participant described how she kept seeing her friends post unpleasant content, starting to specifically name others and how, even if she called them out on it, they continued. She said she gradually stopped using Secret until one day she just simply deleted the application from her phone.

Two of the participants mentioned they were initially enthusiastic to have the app change its feed logic to not only proximity-based but also letting them peek at other cities. A participant who were still using the app, for example said *"I like that there is more on the app, there weren't much, [I] got bored before. Now it is much better and allows us to chat directly, it makes it a lot more interesting. I just think the entire concept behind Secret... now I can see what people are thinking"* [SF36]. She felt that the New York and the San Francisco feed were more interesting than her local Miami feed, which seemed a bit "childish."

One of the main changes in the Mimi app was that the app no longer showed explicitly whether posters were friends, or just friends of friends, thus making de-identification more difficult. All but two of our six participants reported having given up using the app with different reasons: Two felt the application did not provide enough content and entertainment. Two others tied their disengagement to the anonymity change: not being able to distinguish between friends and friends of friends, the de-anonymization was limited and the app was not as fun.

DISCUSSION

Before our discussion, we note a few cultural differences in relation to tie-based anonymity systems—differences that were not readily apparent from our study. As an investigation into this topic, we included Chinese and US participants in order to be comprehensive rather than to be comparative. Indeed, we analyzed the data with an eye for differences in how the themes were expressed by participants of different cultures but no such differences emerged. Of course, the fact that the Mimi app is still active, versus the disappearance (and preceding adaptation) of Secret from the US market, may by itself suggest cultural differences, but these are a matter of another, more targeted investigation.

We now turn to our discussion where we highlight opportunities and challenges for tie-based anonymity applications. We use these opportunities and challenges to motivate several ideas and implications for future tie-based anonymity platforms. We acknowledge that some of the opportunities we identified *can* also be problematic depending on the specific implementation, and that finding ways to design for the trade-offs between the benefits and risks of tie-based anonymity is a fruitful area for future work.

Opportunity: Self-disclosure

Based on our findings, we believe the self-disclosure opportunities with tie-based anonymity goes beyond what is afforded by other anonymous services, particularly due to the connection with friends.

As recognized by past research on self-disclosure, the disclosure itself may provide significant benefits [16, 45]. As is also known, under the condition of anonymity, users tend to disclose more, a phenomena known as the disinhibition effect [54], which we also identified in our participants' remarks. Furthermore, our interviews suggest that free from identification concerns, participants perceive less associated risks of social sanction or issues of self-representation, similar to earlier findings [3, 25]. As is the case for other anonymous systems [12, 29], tie-based systems thus allow greater self-disclosure than other social applications, as well as provide grounds for self-expression and relief.

The core value, we believe, lies in the potential reward for self-disclosure in tie-based applications, which is potentially more substantial than in other anonymous applications. Self-disclosure is a function of both risk and reward [10, 41] where rewards may include, for example, social validation and self-expression [14]. As mentioned above, the opportunity for self-disclosure in tie-based anonymity applications is strengthened through the reduced risks of being identified. Importantly, it is also strengthened through the heightened reward (compared to other anonymous platforms) given that the post is likely to be seen by a subset of one's social ties; despite trends of negativity and mean behavior, participants reported being able to receive support and encouragement based on their disclosure. In other words, while anonymity in general allows people to explore aspects of their identity that otherwise would have been impossible [40,56], tie-based systems allow one to do that *in the context of their social ties*. Or, in Goffman's terms [22], tie-based anonymity may allow backstage-like performance in a front stage-like context.

Opportunity: Extending Social Behavior

Beyond self-disclosure, our findings highlight an opportunity for extending social behavior through tie-based anonymity services, providing social affordances that go beyond identifiable media and other types of anonymous systems. It was clear from our participants that they, or others on these tie-based services, were engaging in social behavior and extracted social insights about their social ties in a way that is not readily attainable from other services or classic social networks.

First, the opportunity to perform social probing, with little risk, and in the context of friends, is a powerful and unique affordance of tie-based anonymous services. Our findings suggest that users can go beyond self-disclosure to post messages, whether true or false, that are intended to elicit reactions or "test the waters" with their group of social ties. This opportunity is available in anonymized settings, where an individual is not at risk by posting the information, and by replying to it with honest attitudes. Furthermore, only in tie-based anonymized settings people can post such message to get feedback from and exposure to friends and social ties. Prior work on identity transition has similarly found a need for people to be able to test out aspects of their identities that they may feel vulnerable about in online spaces [23]. In doing such posting, it may fill a social probing role similar to one of humor [19]; relatedly, tie-based applications allow radical ideas to be tested in social settings. Even here, the expression can take a slant that is sometimes playful and more tentative.

Second, and relatedly, is the opportunity for an individual user of tie-based anonymous services to develop a better understanding of their group of friends and social ties using information shared on the application, even without explicit probing activities. Some participants in our study hinted at a potential for a better window into their friends' attitudes, opinions, and perhaps even actions due to the properties of the tie-based services, aligned with the fundamental human need to belong [7]. Note that these impressions may or may not be warranted (e.g., as only a minority of most participants' friends were active on these services), and the understanding may not even be accurate (e.g., as participants themselves noted, information may be untrue). Nevertheless, the opportunity to be—or merely to feel—more informed about one's social ties is significant. We emphasize that this affordance is unique to tie-based systems. Social information processing theory [57] has long considered how people slowly develop mutual impressions and understanding over computer-mediated communication. Here, the learning is not about a specific connection, and definitely not an identified one, but rather about a set of social ties. A critical difference from other types of anonymous groups is the tie-based setup, where each individual is connected to their own social ties, as opposed to the topic- and content-based, or location-based anonymous groups or communities in other anonymity models.

Opportunity: Anonymity at Will

Finally, an opportunity that has yet to be widely utilized within social networks is the new mechanism for "anonymity at will". We saw from our interviews the users' ability to construct their posts in relation to who would be reading them, thus providing the level of anonymity that they wanted each post to have. Sometimes they were able to be completely anonymous, but they felt they could craft posts to signal identity to some subset of readers or all. Ellison et al. suggest that particularly for adolescents, being able to selectively engage in anonymous interactions with a group of known peers has, key implications for identity and social development [18].

Social steganography [39] refers to a practice of hiding secret messages in plain sight, where unwanted parties are not aware of their existence, or are unable to penetrate their actual meaning. This sharing practice is not uncommon in other social media, where for example location is revealed but only to the level of detail that an inside circle of friends would understand [4,36], or posts are "coded" through culturally specific references, inside jokes and other linguistic tools [13].

In a slightly different way, tie-based anonymity services create new avenues for people to transmit sensitive messages to friends: here the content is exposed but the *identity* of the poster may be only known to some specific target set of individuals through the crafting of the message. We term this practice "identity steganography". As such, any new avenue for communication could serve an important social role [13]. For example, users can use identity steganography to seek social support while preserving privacy, especially in tie-based anonymity as friends who have the relevant context may know the identity of the original poster and reach out privately.

We discussed opportunities and potential benefits, but of course, there are darker sides to tie-based anonymity. Next, we discuss some of the key challenges.

Challenge: Negativity and Bullying

As is the case in other anonymous platforms, negativity and bullying are a significant challenge. Throughout the life of anonymous or pseudo-anonymous networks (i.e., site-wide user names, nick-name based networks), "trolling" can significantly curb participation and constructive contributions [33, 34]. Participants in our study also described widespread negativity, getting even worse later on in the lifetime of the Secret application. This negativity increase could potentially be due to the fact that anonymity accentuate the interchangeability of group members, making trolling behavior "catch on" and converge to become the social norm [46]. While our results do not explicitly hint at that, there is a further risk of particular forms of abuse when the negativity is expressed by a friend, from the comfort of their anonymity cover. As shown in our findings and by Kang et al. [29], this negative behavior is likely the reason for a decline of the use of these applications over time.

While participants reported "flagging" certain posts and otherwise trying to prevent abuse in the platform, this issue remains a challenge for services that would require significant resources to address. A sliver of hope lies in the fact that in mobile-based applications (which relation- and tie-based anonymity services tend to be), a robust user identifier is available to the service (i.e., an identifier of the mobile device used to access the app) and it is hard for users to create a new access avenue. This feature makes banning users, at least theoretically, more plausible than for other anonymous services, for example on the Web. However, given the amount of potential interactions, moderating, flagging and banning content is likely to remain a challenge for any popular tie-based anonymity platform.

Challenge: Rumors and Gossip

Beyond negativity, the lack of accountability also transforms tie-based anonymous services into places where rumor and gossip can be spread easily. Through our interviews we also uncovered a general perception by our participants that the two secret apps were rife with rumors and gossip. It has been long argued that gossip has a social function [21,42]; gossip provides ways of making sense to help us cope with uncertainty and anxiety [49,50], and can serve to convey information about the society and culture [8,60]. Interestingly, "gossip tends to have an 'inner-circleness' about it, in that it is customarily passed between people who have a common history or shared interests" [51], aligning gossip outcomes well with tie-based anonymous applications.

On the other hand, social psychology defines rumors as "a statement whose truth-value is unverifiable or deliberately false" [48]. Rumors thrive in secret environments, and often has significant negative outcomes [50]. The challenge of controlling the spread of rumors on social media platforms has been substantial. Even with real-name or persistent identity on social media, where one can verify or identify the source of information, rumor practices is an open issue and an active research area [48]. In tie-based anonymous applications, this evaluation is much harder or impossible. Even worse, individuals run little risk in spreading rumors on these platforms. Participants felt that to be engaging, the content needed to be believable but as we pointed out above, the tie-based services often offered content that was "too fake or too real". The uncertainly, and inability to evaluate content, could be a challenge for adoption and continued use.

Adding to the challenge is the fact that due to the unverifiable nature of rumors, hurtful rumors and gossiping may be harder to moderate than negativity and bullying, which are more often immediately identifiable.

Challenge: Critical Mass

One challenge for any social media application is critical mass and adoption [38]. Many social media services rely on known ties and existing social networks for diffusion, for example via mechanisms to invite friends to join. To have enough compelling content from one's friend, tie-based anonymity services also need to reach scale in adoption. This presents a significant challenge for these systems, as they cannot rely on traditional diffusion techniques: an individual cannot reveal their own identity to invite people to join the service. Of course, due to the anonymity and lack of persistent identity, one cannot create ties directly on these platforms either, as one would for example on Facebook or Twitter. As a result, tie-based anonymous platforms could find it hard to grow the network, and hence limit the available tie-based content and audience for any single user. This challenge had direct impact on the participants in our study, whom could not get enough content to keep them entertained and engaged in the apps. While proximity-based anonymous services could simply expand content by extending the radius of relevant posts, in tie-based services it is unclear whether the context (i.e., social radius) can be extended meaningfully (one might not care to read updates from a friend-of-friend-of-friend). All in all, without the ability to directly invite one's friends or create new ties on a tie-based anonymity service, the availability of content on the platform would be quite sparse.

Design Implications

We provide several design implications and considerations for providing tie-based anonymity services. Importantly, some of these suggestions are not for stand-alone tie-based services, but instead argue for inclusion of similar features in other social media platforms.

Anonymity flashes. One way to allow for the benefits listed above while perhaps circumventing some of the challenges is to directly build tie-based anonymity features into the experience of identity-based social network services like Twitter or Facebook. For example, Facebook could allow users to post one anonymous post per day (an "anonymous flash") that would be broadcast—without attribution—to the user's network. Deep integration into such social network service can allow comments and replies to the post to be identified (for instance as described in [12]) or similarly anonymous, each option provides different benefits.

Guessing game. Given the magnitude of de-anonymization attempts, tie-based services or functions may consider including a formal mechanism where, via private messages, individuals can be queried and admit (or perhaps prove) that they posted any specific content item ("Alice, is that you?" queries Bob). In "pure" tie-based anonymity services even the fact that individuals participate in the system is obscure, which would make such mechanism difficult to implement. However, such mechanism would be easier to implement if the tie-based system is integrated into a persistent identity platform like Twitter or Facebook.

Minimize de-identification risks. To make it harder for users to engage in "contact list hacking", future applications should make permanent the app content shown to the user, and not dependent on the user's current set of followees. In other words, once a user sees a post, it always remains on their list, preventing the option of hacking your contact list by removing contacts one-by-one to figure out who made one specific post.

Curbing negativity. Given that anonymity and loose social norms can quickly cause tie-based anonymity services to degenerate into a hostile and negative environment, it is critical to offer more comprehensive support to battling this type of content. Immediate flagged content removal (delete-then-verify) and other more proactive techniques may be a better approach. One can perhaps consider that users posting negative comments slowly lose their privileges (e.g., their anonymity) on the service, essentially circumventing outright banning but limiting the opportunity for negative postings by any one user. Note that the main enablers of these tie-based systems—the fact that they are tied to a specific ID, often a mobile phone identifier, and even when it is not exposed in the service—-should be useful for banning and restricting users, compared to other anonymous services like news commenting, or online forums.

CONCLUSION

In this paper we provided a qualitative in-depth examination of user practices in tie-based anonymity services, and showed why the affordances provided by these services form a new model of anonymity in computer-mediated communication. Such tie-based systems offer opportunities for self-disclosure that are not available in "real-name" networks or persistent-identity anonymous networks. Furthermore, these services can provide an environment where people can test the waters with their friends, exploring attitudes and possible reactions for complicated situations in their lives. We also highlighted a set of challenges for tie-based anonymity systems. Without having to rule whether tie-based anonymity services have any merit or potential for broad appeal and mass adoption as stand-alone applications, we believe our design considerations may be useful for providing the benefits of such services in the future in various settings.

ACKNOWLEDGMENTS

This research was funded by AOL through the Connected Experience Lab. We would like to thank Raz Schwartz and Funda Kivran-Swaine for conducting interviews with Secret users, as well as all the participants for their time.

REFERENCES

1. Nazanin Andalibi, Oliver L Haimson, Munmun De Choudhury, and Andrea Forte. 2016. Understanding social media disclosures of sexual abuse through the lenses of support seeking and anonymity. In *Proceedings of the 2016 CHI Conference on Human Factors in Computing Systems (CHI '16)*. ACM, New York, NY, USA, 3906–3918. DOI: http://dx.doi.org/10.1145/2858036.2858096
2. Nazanin Andalibi, Pinar Ozturk, and Andrea Forte. 2017. Sensitive self-disclosures, responses, and social support on Instagram: The case of #depression. In *Proceedings of the 20th ACM Conference on Computer-Supported Cooperative Work & Social Computing (CSCW '17)*. ACM, New York, NY, USA. DOI: http://dx.doi.org/10.1145/2998181.2998243
3. John A Bargh, Katelyn YA McKenna, and Grainne M Fitzsimons. 2002. Can you see the real me? Activation and expression of the "true self" on the Internet. *Journal of Social Issues* 58, 1 (2002), 33–48. DOI: http://dx.doi.org/10.1111/1540-4560.00247
4. Louise Barkhuus and Juliana Tashiro. 2010. Student socialization in the age of facebook. In *Proceedings of the SIGCHI Conference on Human Factors in Computing Systems (CHI '10)*. ACM, New York, NY, USA, 133–142. DOI: http://dx.doi.org/10.1145/1753326.1753347
5. Christopher P Barlett and Douglas A Gentile. 2012. Attacking others online: The formation of cyberbullying in late adolescence. *Psychology of Popular Media Culture* 1, 2 (2012), 123–135. DOI: http://dx.doi.org/10.1037/a0028113
6. Christopher P Barlett, Douglas A Gentile, and Chelsea Chew. 2014. Predicting cyberbullying from anonymity. *Psychology of Popular Media Culture* 5, 2 (2014), 171–180. DOI: http://dx.doi.org/10.1037/ppm0000055
7. Roy F Baumeister and Mark R Leary. 1995. The need to belong: desire for interpersonal attachments as a

fundamental human motivation. *Psychological Bulletin* 117, 3 (1995), 497–529. DOI: http://dx.doi.org/10.1037/0033-2909.117.3.497

8. Roy F Baumeister, Liqing Zhang, and Kathleen D Vohs. 2004. Gossip as cultural learning. *Review of General Psychology* 8, 2 (2004), 111–121. DOI: http://dx.doi.org/10.1037/1089-2680.8.2.111
9. Natalya N Bazarova. 2012. Public intimacy: Disclosure interpretation and social judgments on Facebook. *Journal of Communication* 62, 5 (2012), 815–832. DOI:http://dx.doi.org/10.1111/j.1460-2466.2012.01664.x
10. Natalya N Bazarova and Yoon Hyung Choi. 2014. Self-disclosure in social media: Extending the functional approach to disclosure motivations and characteristics on social network sites. *Journal of Communication* 64, 4 (2014), 635–657. DOI: http://dx.doi.org/10.1111/jcom.12106
11. Michael S Bernstein, Andrés Monroy-Hernández, Drew Harry, Paul André, Katrina Panovich, and Gregory G Vargas. 4chan and/b: An analysis of anonymity and ephemerality in a large online community. In *Proceedings of the 5th International AAAI Conference on Weblogs and Social Media (ICWSM '11)*.
12. Jeremy Birnholtz, Nicholas Aaron Ross Merola, and Arindam Paul. 2015. "Is it weird to still be a virgin": Anonymous, locally targeted questions on Facebook confession boards. In *Proceedings of the 33rd Annual ACM Conference on Human Factors in Computing Systems (CHI '15)*. ACM, New York, NY, USA, 2613–2622. DOI: http://dx.doi.org/10.1145/2702123.2702410
13. danah boyd. 2014. *It's complicated: The social lives of networked teens*. Yale University Press.
14. Nancy L Collins and Lynn Carol Miller. 1994. Self-disclosure and liking: A meta-analytic review. *Psychological Bulletin* 116, 3 (1994), 457–475. DOI: http://dx.doi.org/10.1037/0033-2909.116.3.457
15. Denzil Correa, Leandro Araújo Silva, Mainack Mondal, Fabrício Benevenuto, and Krishna P Gummadi. The many shades of anonymity: Characterizing anonymous social media content. In *Proceedings of the 9th International AAAI Conference on Weblogs and Social Media (ICWSM '15)*.
16. Valerian J Derlega, Barbara A Winstead, and Kathryn Greene. 1997. Self-disclosure and starting a close relationship. *Handbook of Relationship* (1997), 153–174.
17. Judith S Donath. 1999. Identity and deception in the virtual community. In *Communities in Cyberspace*. 29–59.
18. Nicole B Ellison, Lindsay Blackwell, Cliff Lampe, and Penny Trieu. 2016. "The question exists, but you don't exist with it": Strategic anonymity in the social lives of adolescents. *Social Media + Society* 2, 4 (2016). DOI: http://dx.doi.org/10.1177/2056305116670673
19. Hugh C Foot and May McCreaddie. 1997. Humour and laughter. In *The Handbook of Communication Skills*. Routledge, 259–285.
20. Andrea Forte, Nazanin Andalibi, and Rachel Greenstadt. 2017. Privacy, anonymity, and perceived risk in open collaboration: A study of Tor users and Wikipedians. In *Proceedings of the 20th ACM Conference on Computer-Supported Cooperative Work & Social Computing (CSCW '17)*. ACM, New York, NY, USA. DOI:http://dx.doi.org/10.1145/2998181.2998273
21. Max Gluckman. 1963. Papers in honor of Melville J. Herskovits: Gossip and scandal. *Current Anthropology* 4, 3 (1963), 307–316.
22. Erving Goffman. 1959. The presentation of self in everyday life. (1959).
23. Oliver L Haimson, Anne E Bowser, Edward F Melcer, and Elizabeth F Churchill. 2015. Online inspiration and exploration for identity reinvention. In *Proceedings of the 33rd Annual ACM Conference on Human Factors in Computing Systems (CHI '15)*. ACM, New York, NY, USA, 3809–3818. DOI: http://dx.doi.org/10.1145/2702123.2702270
24. Jeffrey T Hancock, Jennifer Thom-Santelli, and Thompson Ritchie. 2004. Deception and design: The impact of communication technology on lying behavior. In *Proceedings of the SIGCHI Conference on Human Factors in Computing Systems (CHI '04)*. ACM, New York, NY, USA, 129–134. DOI: http://dx.doi.org/10.1145/985692.985709
25. Erin E Hollenbaugh and Marcia K Everett. 2013. The effects of anonymity on self-disclosure in blogs: An application of the online disinhibition effect. *Journal of Computer-Mediated Communication* 18, 3 (2013), 283–302. DOI: http://dx.doi.org/10.1111/jcc4.12008
26. Jina Huh. 2015. Clinical questions in online health communities: The case of "see your doctor" threads. In *Proceedings of the 18th ACM Conference on Computer Supported Cooperative Work & Social Computing (CSCW '15)*. ACM, New York, NY, USA, 1488–1499. DOI:http://dx.doi.org/10.1145/2675133.2675259
27. Jina Huh, Rupa Patel, and Wanda Pratt. 2012. Tackling dilemmas in supporting 'the whole person' in online patient communities. In *Proceedings of the SIGCHI Conference on Human Factors in Computing Systems (CHI '12)*. ACM, New York, NY, USA, 923–926. DOI: http://dx.doi.org/10.1145/2207676.2208535
28. Ruogu Kang, Stephanie Brown, and Sara Kiesler. 2013. Why do people seek anonymity on the Internet?: Informing policy and design. In *Proceedings of the SIGCHI Conference on Human Factors in Computing Systems (CHI '13)*. ACM, New York, NY, USA, 2657–2666. DOI: http://dx.doi.org/10.1145/2470654.2481368

29. Ruogu Kang, Laura Dabbish, and Katherine Sutton. 2016. Strangers on your phone: Why people use anonymous communication applications. In *Proceedings of the 19th ACM Conference on Computer-Supported Cooperative Work & Social Computing (CSCW '16)*. ACM, New York, NY, USA, 359–370. DOI: http://dx.doi.org/10.1145/2818048.2820081
30. Lee Knuttila. 2011. User unknown: 4chan, anonymity and contingency. *First Monday* 16, 10 (2011). DOI: http://dx.doi.org/10.5210/fm.v16i10.3665
31. Cliff Lampe and Erik Johnston. 2005. Follow the (slash) dot: Effects of feedback on new members in an online community. In *Proceedings of the 2005 International ACM SIGGROUP Conference on Supporting Group Work (GROUP '05)*. ACM, New York, NY, USA, 11–20. DOI: http://dx.doi.org/10.1145/1099203.1099206
32. Cliff Lampe and Paul Resnick. 2004. Slash(dot) and burn: Distributed moderation in a large online conversation space. In *Proceedings of the SIGCHI Conference on Human Factors in Computing Systems (CHI '04)*. ACM, New York, NY, USA, 543–550. DOI: http://dx.doi.org/10.1145/985692.985761
33. Noam Lapidot-Lefler and Azy Barak. 2012. Effects of anonymity, invisibility, and lack of eye-contact on toxic online disinhibition. *Computers in Human Behavior* 28, 2 (2012), 434–443. http://dx.doi.org/10.1016/j.chb.2011.10.014
34. Danielle M Law, Jennifer D Shapka, Shelley Hymel, Brent F Olson, and Terry Waterhouse. 2012. The changing face of bullying: An empirical comparison between traditional and internet bullying and victimization. *Computers in Human Behavior* 28, 1 (2012), 226–232. http://dx.doi.org/10.1016/j.chb.2011.09.004
35. Alex Leavitt. 2015. "This is a throwaway account": Temporary technical identities and perceptions of anonymity in a massive online community. In *Proceedings of the 18th ACM Conference on Computer Supported Cooperative Work & Social Computing (CSCW '15)*. ACM, New York, NY, USA, 317–327. DOI: http://dx.doi.org/10.1145/2675133.2675175
36. Jessica Lingel, Aaron Trammell, Joe Sanchez, and Mor Naaman. 2012. Practices of information and secrecy in a punk rock subculture. In *Proceedings of the ACM 2012 Conference on Computer Supported Cooperative Work (CSCW '12)*. ACM, New York, NY, USA, 157–166. DOI: http://dx.doi.org/10.1145/2145204.2145230
37. Xiao Ma, Jeffery T Hancock, and Mor Naaman. 2016. Anonymity, intimacy and self-disclosure in social media. In *Proceedings of the 2016 CHI Conference on Human Factors in Computing Systems (CHI '16)*. ACM, New York, NY, USA, 3857–3869. DOI: http://dx.doi.org/10.1145/2858036.2858414
38. M. Lynne Markus. 1987. Toward a "critical mass" theory of interactive media: Universal access, interdependence and diffusion. *Communication Research* 14, 5 (1987), 491–511. DOI: http://dx.doi.org/10.1177/009365087014005003
39. Alice E. Marwick and danah boyd. 2011. The drama! Teen conflict, gossip, and bullying in networked publics. A Decade in Internet Time: Symposium on the Dynamics of the Internet and Society. Available from SSRN. (2011). http://ssrn.com/abstract=1926349
40. Mark W. Newman, Debra Lauterbach, Sean A. Munson, Paul Resnick, and Margaret E. Morris. 2011. It's not that I don't have problems, I'm just not putting them on Facebook: Challenges and opportunities in using online social networks for health. In *Proceedings of the ACM 2011 Conference on Computer Supported Cooperative Work (CSCW '11)*. ACM, New York, NY, USA, 341–350. DOI: http://dx.doi.org/10.1145/1958824.1958876
41. Julia Omarzu. 2000. A disclosure decision model: Determining how and when individuals will self-disclose. *Personality and Social Psychology Review* 4, 2 (2000), 174–185. DOI: http://dx.doi.org/10.1207/S15327957PSPR0402_05
42. Robert Paine. 1967. What is gossip about? An alternative hypothesis. *Man* 2, 2 (1967), 278–285. DOI: http://dx.doi.org/10.2307/2799493
43. W Babnett Pearce and Stewart M Sharp. 1973. Self-disclosing communication. *Journal of Communication* 23, 4 (1973), 409–425. DOI: http://dx.doi.org/10.1111/j.1460-2466.1973.tb00958.x
44. Sai Teja Peddinti, Keith W. Ross, and Justin Cappos. 2014. "On the Internet, nobody knows you're a dog": A Twitter case study of anonymity in social networks. In *Proceedings of the Second ACM Conference on Online Social Networks (COSN '14)*. ACM, New York, NY, USA, 83–94. DOI: http://dx.doi.org/10.1145/2660460.2660467
45. James W Pennebaker. 2012. *Opening up: The healing power of expressing emotions*. Guilford Press.
46. T Postmes, R Spears, and M Lea. 2000. The formation of group norms in computer-mediated communication. *Human Communication Research* 26, 3 (2000), 341–371. DOI: http://dx.doi.org/10.1111/j.1468-2958.2000.tb00761.x
47. Jenny Preece. 1999. Empathic communities: Balancing emotional and factual communication. *Interacting with Computers* 12, 1 (1999), 63–77. DOI: http://dx.doi.org/10.1016/S0953-5438(98)00056-3
48. Vahed Qazvinian, Emily Rosengren, Dragomir R Radev, and Qiaozhu Mei. 2011. Rumor has it: Identifying misinformation in microblogs. In *Proceedings of the Conference on Empirical Methods in Natural Language Processing (EMNLP '11)*. Association for Computational Linguistics, Stroudsburg, PA, USA, 1589–1599.

49. Ralph L Rosnow. 1988. Rumor as communication: A contextualist approach. *Journal of Communication* 38, 1 (1988), 12–28. DOI: http://dx.doi.org/10.1111/j.1460-2466.1988.tb02033.x

50. Ralph L Rosnow. 2001. Rumor and gossip in interpersonal interaction and beyond: A social exchange perspective. In *Behaving badly: Aversive behaviors in interpersonal relationships.*, Robin M. Kowalski (Ed.). American Psychological Association, Chapter 8, 203–232. DOI: http://dx.doi.org/10.1037/10365-008

51. Ralph L Rosnow and Eric K Foster. 2005. Rumor and gossip research. *Psychological Science Agenda* 19, 4 (2005).

52. William B Stiles. 1987. "I have to talk to somebody". In *Self-Disclosure: Theory, Research, and Therapy.* Springer US, 257–282. DOI: http://dx.doi.org/10.1007/978-1-4899-3523-6_12

53. Anselm Strauss and Juliet M Corbin. 1997. *Grounded theory in practice.* Sage.

54. John Suler. 2004. The online disinhibition effect. *Cyberpsychology & behavior* 7, 3 (2004), 321–326. DOI: http://dx.doi.org/10.1089/1094931041291295

55. Matthew Trammell. 2014. User investment and behavior policing on 4chan. *First Monday* 19, 2 (2014). DOI: http://dx.doi.org/10.5210/fm.v19i2.4819

56. Sherry Turkle. 1995. *Life on the screen: Identity in the age of the Internet.* Simon & Schuster Trade.

57. Joseph B Walther. 1996. Computer-mediated communication: Impersonal, interpersonal, and hyperpersonal interaction. *Communication Research* 23, 1 (1996), 3–43. DOI: http://dx.doi.org/10.1177/009365096023001001

58. Gang Wang, Bolun Wang, Tianyi Wang, Ana Nika, Haitao Zheng, and Ben Y Zhao. 2014. Whispers in the dark: Analysis of an anonymous social network. In *Proceedings of the 2014 Conference on Internet Measurement Conference (IMC '14).* ACM, New York, NY, USA, 137–150. DOI: http://dx.doi.org/10.1145/2663716.2663728

59. Yi-Chia Wang, Robert Kraut, and John M. Levine. 2012. To stay or leave?: The relationship of emotional and informational support to commitment in online health support groups. In *Proceedings of the ACM 2012 Conference on Computer Supported Cooperative Work (CSCW '12).* ACM, New York, NY, USA, 833–842. DOI: http://dx.doi.org/10.1145/2145204.2145329

60. Sally Yerkovich. 1977. Gossiping as a way of speaking. *Journal of Communication* 27, 1 (1977), 192–196. DOI: http://dx.doi.org/10.1111/j.1460-2466.1977.tb01817.x

Environment-Scale Fabrication: Replicating Outdoor Climbing Experiences

Emily Whiting[1] **Nada Ouf**[2] **Liane Makatura**[1] **Christos Mousas**[1]
Zhenyu Shu[3] **Ladislav Kavan**[4]
Dartmouth College[1] University of Pennsylvania[2]
Ningbo Institute of Technology, Zhejiang University[3] University of Utah[4]

ABSTRACT

Despite rapid advances in 3D printing, fabricating large, durable and robust artifacts is impractical with current technology. We focus on a particularly challenging environment-scale artifact: rock climbing routes. We propose a prototype fabrication method to replicate part of an outdoor climbing route and enable the same sensorimotor experience in an indoor gym. We start with 3D reconstruction of the rock wall using multi-view stereo and use reference videos of a climber in action to identify localized rock features that are necessary for ascent. We create 3D models akin to traditional indoor climbing holds, fabricated using rapid prototyping, molding and casting techniques. This results in robust holds accurately replicating the features and configuration of the original rock route. Validation was performed on two rock climbing sites in New Hampshire and Utah. We verified our results by comparing climbers moves on the indoor replicas and original outdoor routes.

ACM Classification Keywords

I.3.5 Computer Graphics: Computational Geometry and Object Modeling

Author Keywords

Fabrication; rapid prototyping; 3D reconstruction; terrain modeling; rock climbing; sports technologies.

INTRODUCTION

Fabrication at the scale of natural environments is typically out of scope for rapid prototyping technology. Although 3D printing with concrete has recently become feasible [14], the material and extrusion methods limit the ability to produce fine detail. Traditional FDM 3D printers have been used experimentally to produce house-sized structures [5], but require enormous time and financial investments. In this paper, we propose a strategic approach to fabricating large-scale environmental sites by taking advantage of how users will interact with the final structure.

CHI 2017, May 06 - 11, 2017, Denver, CO, USA

ISBN 978-1-4503-46559/17/05... $15.00

DOI: http://dx.doi.org/10.1145/3025453.3025465

Figure 1. We capture the crux of an outdoor rock climbing route (left), fabricate the key holds and mount them in an indoor climbing wall (right). Our replica mimics the climbing experience of the original outdoor route.

We focus on outdoor rock climbing routes. In addition to representing an object which is very challenging to fabricate, rock climbing is an increasingly popular sport. Outdoor climbing areas are usually scarce and fragile and their extensive use for sport or recreational purposes represents environmental concerns. 3D printing an entire rock face would be prohibitively expensive and time consuming. We make the fabrication problem tractable by focusing only on the key aspect: how climbers interact with the site. The set of requirements for creating the same sensorimotor experience are well defined: a) configuration of the climbing holds must have the same geometry as the outdoor site; b) graspability of the contact areas (for hands and feet) must be the same; c) friction characteristics should be mimicked.

We replicate the most challenging part of an outdoor climbing route (the "crux"), starting by taking several hundred photos of the crux region and performing multi-view 3D reconstruction of the rock wall. Because fabricating the entire crux region would be prohibitively expensive, we find only the key rock features which are necessary for ascent. We do this by analyzing a video of a climber ascending the outdoor route, localizing the regions where the climber's hands or shoe sole was supported by the rock. We isolate these parts of the rock wall geometry and turn them into physical climbing holds, similar to those used in indoor climbing walls, but replicating the 3D geometry of our outdoor wall. Fabricating accurate and durable climbing holds is a challenge and we experimented with several possibilities, ultimately choosing a rapid prototyping of physical models of the holds, followed by a molding and casting procedure. Finally, we mount the holds on the gym wall, optimizing for the best possible reconstruction accuracy subject to the constraints imposed by the indoor wall (such as given configuration of pre-installed bolt fasteners). Our current workflow assumes the route has approximately constant, vertical slope, deferring more complex rock geometries or overhanging routes to future work.

We validated our method by replicating cruxes of two rock climbing routes with differing geological features. The first route is a schist rock formation located at Rumney, New Hampshire. The second route is part of a sandstone crag near St. George in Southern Utah. Both routes are vertical face climbs suitable for our approach. We validated our results by comparing video recordings of climbers in action on the original outdoor routes and their indoor replicas. As shown in Figure 1, the moves executed by a climber on the outdoor route are similar to the moves needed to scale our replicated climbs.

We believe that replication of outdoor rock climbing problems will enhance the indoor training experience of novice climbers and experts alike, while openings new opportunities. Competitive climbers may appreciate the possibility of measuring their forces on accurate replicas of some of the world's hardest rock climbing routes. Further, setting indoor climbing routes currently relies on the skill and creativity of often professional route setters, who craft new climbing problems much like a painter creates a painting. In this light, our approach represents the analogue of photography, because we capture and "develop" climbing problems crafted by nature.

In a broader context, our contribution is a complete system for fabrication of large-scale structures which would be difficult and impractical to produce directly by 3D printing. We focus not only on the structures and their geometries, but also on how humans interact with them. While our current project focuses on replication of rock climbing experiences, we believe that the lessons learned would be applicable more generally and we provide some specific ideas in the Conclusion section.

RELATED WORK

Replicating outdoor climbing

Outdoor climbing routes serve as a natural source of inspiration for developing training tools. For example, the "Campus board," is an inclined board with thin horizontal slats that was invented by Wolfgang Güllich in 1988. Today, the Campus board can be found in many climbing gyms or even private homes. More recently, Matyas Luzan created an accurate replica of Action Directe (5.14d route in Frankenjura, Germany) in a local climbing gym [22]. Luzan sculpted hold replicas from wood, finished with varnish to replicate the texture of the rock. After 16 months and 200 training sessions, Matyas managed to climb the outdoor Action Directe on April 2015. In addition to serving as an excellent training tool, the replica spares the rock from deterioration due to frequent contact with human skin, climbing chalk, and sole rubber.

Technology for rock climbing

Indoor climbing gyms cater to climbers of all levels. Setting indoor routes of various difficulty grades is a craft which takes years to master and commercial gyms often employ a team of route setters [3]. To facilitate this process, Pfeil et al. [23] proposed an interactive system for creating routes using a simulated virtual climber. A different approach was explored by Phillips et al. [24], who generate new climbing routes from examples using machine learning and mathematics of chaos. More recent augmented reality approaches promise to revolutionize the indoor climbing experience via projectors displaying information directly on the climbing walls [12].

Another emerging technology is wrist-worn motion sensors which track the climber in action [13, 17, 18, 20]. The biomechanics of rock climbing has also been studied using instrumented indoor walls, i.e., with artificial holds equipped with built-in force sensors [2, 25]. Measuring forces on natural rock walls would require invasive installations, therefore we focus on kinematics which can be inferred from video.

3D reconstruction of terrain

Our approach has been enabled by advances in multi-view 3D reconstruction and their robust implementations [10, 11, 9]. Among recent exciting applications are Hyper-lapse videos [16], which stabilize raw video sequences captured, e.g., by a helmet-mounted camera while climbing. Aerial imagery has been successfully used to create 3D maps of famous mountain terrains such as the Eiger North Face [8] and Matterhorn (senseFly corporation). The GIS community also developed photogrammetric solutions designed specifically for vertical walls [15].

Large-scale fabrication

Scaling up fabrication technology for building-sized or environment-scale prototypes has seen recent progress. Additive fabrication of cement was made possible with the introduction of extrusion nozzles combined with contour crafting [14], but the system is targeted for construction applications where fine detail is not needed. Autodesk's Project Escher is a software solution allowing multiple extruders to collaborate in parallel for increased print speed [4]. However both these systems require a large CNC gantry. To avoid gantries, some alternative approaches employ hand-held dispensers ejecting a stick-glue composite [27] or tubes of adhesive tape [1]. In contrast to these approaches, we seek to maintain product-scale resolution using commonly available technology, while massively reducing required print volume.

ROUTE ACQUISITION

In the following sections we describe our pipeline covering the process from scanning outdoor rock walls to creating 3D polygonal models of our holds which are ready for fabrication. We aim for a technique accessible to casual users, and therefore we assume that only a conventional digital camera is used for data acquisition.

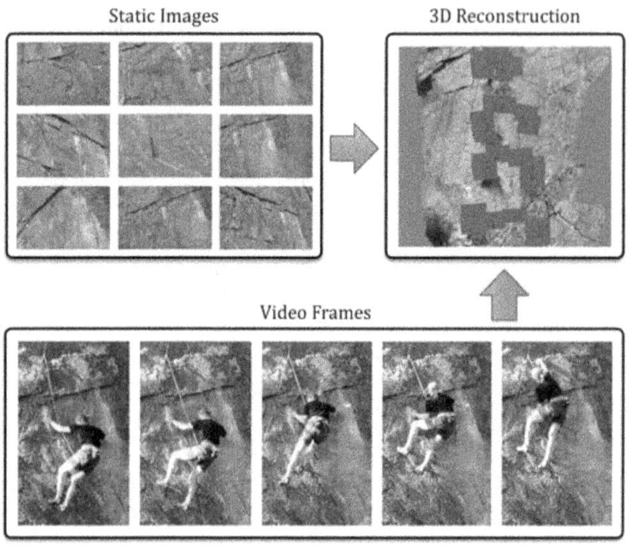

Figure 2. Close-up photos of the rock wall together with video frames are converted into 3D reconstruction using multi-view stereo.

Rock wall reconstruction

The first part of the process is to identify the "crux" region of a rock climbing route which will be the subject of our reconstruction. The size of the crux region is typically approx. 1 by 2 meters, containing the most difficult climbing moves. In our experiments, we rig the route with a top rope anchor, which facilitates close-up photography. With the assistance of a belay partner, a climber is lowered (rappelling) while taking photos of the rock wall from multiple viewpoints using a regular digital camera. This process requires only elementary rappelling skills. It is particularly important to choose viewpoints covering all of the rock features, including concavities which may be critical for climbing. For each crux, we obtain 200-500 photos with sufficient overlaps. We also capture several photos showing the rock wall along with a calibration marker which will be used to scale the resulting 3D reconstruction. Additionally, we take photos of a free hanging rope to determine the gravity direction $\mathbf{g}_{crag}$ R^3. Although we currently assume vertical rock walls (as opposed to overhanging or inclined), the gravity vector is important to correctly orient the fabricated route.

In addition to photos, we capture video of the climber ascending the route. The individual video frames are treated as additional images and will be used in the next step of the pipeline to determine which rock features the climber used during the ascent. We submit all images to AgiSoft PhotoScan which produces a 3D reconstruction (polygon mesh) along with extrinsic camera parameters for each image (Fig. 2). We used only one climber for each of our experiments, however, it would be possible to capture ascents of the same route by multiple climbers. In some cases, climbers of different physiques may use different holds, and this way we would be able to replicate all climbable features.

Climbing sequence analysis

The next step is to find the rock features the climber used during the ascent, which we determine by analyzing recorded video of the climber in action. We start by tracking the skeletal motion of the climber applying sum-of-gaussians motion capture algorithm [26]. We are using only a monocular RGB video stream which means the motion capture problem is ill-posed. Fortunately, we can leverage a strong, rock-climbing-specific prior: the climber's body is in close contact with the rock wall. As we already computed a 3D reconstruction of the rock wall and corresponding camera extrinsics, we can extract the missing depth information by projecting the climber's body onto the reconstructed rock wall mesh (Fig. 3). Though the climber is not two-dimensional the approximate depth information provides sufficient accuracy for our pose estimations. See Figure 4 for an example pose sequence.

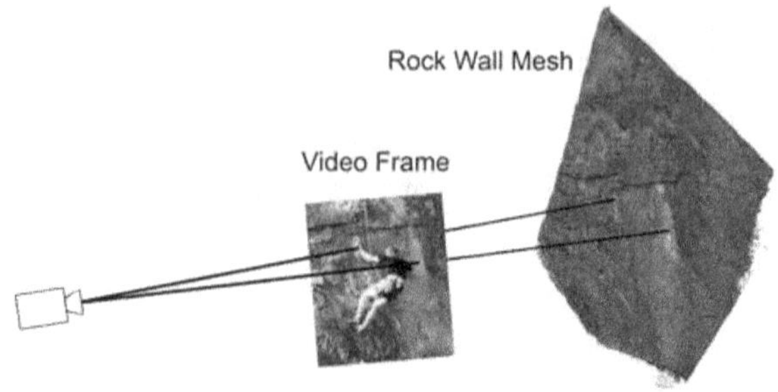

Figure 3. Multi-view stereo produces camera extrinsics which allow us to project from the image plane to the 3D scene.

Contact regions

The result of the motion-capture process is a 3D skeletal animation sequence, aligned with the rock wall reconstruction, see Figure 4. The key information is the position of the climber's hands and feet. We detect motion-less phases [21] of each of the extremities (both hands and feet). We assume that during these static phases, the extremity is in contact with the rock wall and being used to support the body weight of the climber. Though this will not always be true, e.g., a limb can be static even when hanging loosely in the air, this is rare in rock climbing moves, a loose extremity typically quickly moves towards the next available hold.

The 3D positions of the detected contact points tell us approximate locations of the key rock features the climber was using for her ascent. However, there is even more we can extract from the 3D skeletal poses: we can roughly estimate the direction of the forces, $\mathbf{f}_c$ R^3, acting between the climber's body and the rock wall. We experimented with two methods: first, we defined the approximate directions as vectors from the hip joint to each of the extremities. The second approach is to assume the force directions are aligned with the axial directions of the forearm and shin bones. We found the latter approach more accurate in our experiments since it takes into account the orientation of the limbs, rather than only considering contact points and center of mass of the climber. Fig. 5 (left) shows the contact force directions for the TATAN route. Scenarios exist where the limb directions will not align with the contact forces, but in most cases we found this to be a useful approximation.

To find the contact regions, i.e., the rock features the climber was grasping with her hands or stepping on, we calculate the dot product between our estimated contact force directions $\mathbf{f}_c$ and the surface normals $\mathbf{n}_c$ of the 3D reconstruction: $d_c = \mathbf{f}_c \ \ \mathbf{n}_c$. Values close to $d_c = 1$ mean the normals are parallel to our estimated contact forces and in compression, indicating foot holds. Similarly, d_c close to -1 indicate hand holds (contact forces acting against the normal, pulling on the rock). The most common climbing technique generally dictates that applied forces are well aligned with the surface normal to minimize opportunities for sliding failure. Therefore, we find the contact patches by executing flood fill on the triangle mesh (treating triangles as nodes, with adjacent triangles connected with edges), initialized at the contact point. The flood fill stops where d_c lies outside of our interval of interest (i.e., too low or too high d_c, depending on whether we are detecting hand or foot holds). This process terminates with a connected set of triangles which form the resulting estimate of the contact region. This contact region is inspected by the user and, if necessary, edited using a 3D painting interface. We found that this semi-automatic process provides effective guidance and considerably improves user experience compared to a fully manual pipeline. It is often challenging to locate contact regions manually, since many rock features look alike. Note that accurate measurement of contact forces is unfeasible without additional sensors, e.g., using instrumented artificial holds [2, 25].

Our current approach does not consider certain types of climbing technique such as *flagging*, where one leg hangs in the air and is used only as counter-balance, or *smearing*, where there is no prominent rock feature and the climber relies mainly on friction. In our current pipeline we labeled such moves manually and excluded them from contact region detection.

ROUTE MODELING

The resulting contact regions correspond to the 3D geometry we need to replicate in the indoor climbing experience. The next stage is to generate fabricatable 3D models which will be mounted on the gym wall.

Plane fitting

First, we determine the location and orientation of a plane representing the artificial indoor wall. This plane should be a best fit to the contact regions (to minimize the volume of material for fabrication) without intersecting any of the contact regions, which could negatively affect the climbability of the route. Let us denote the vertices of all contact regions as

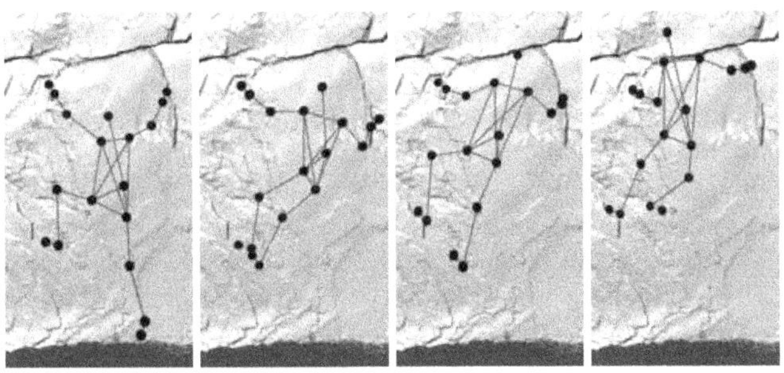

Figure 4. Rock climbing motion capture: skeletal poses estimated from a video of a climber in action.

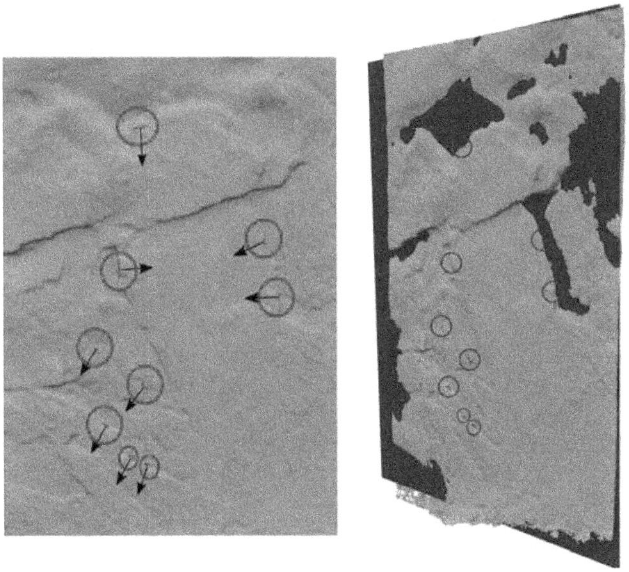

Figure 5. (Left) Contact regions and approximate contact force directions. (Right) Gym-wall plane (blue): the target for the route replica.

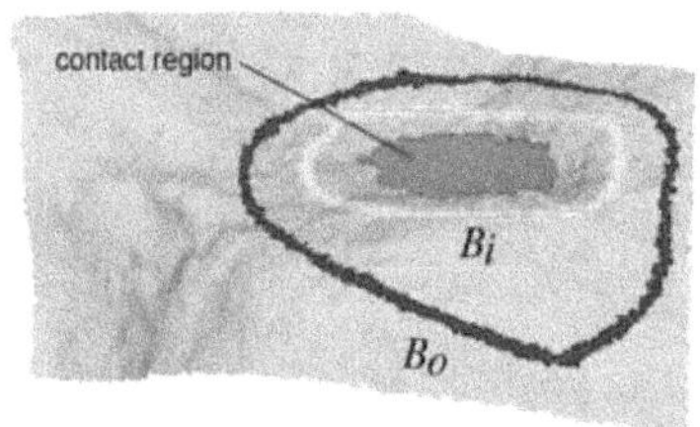

Figure 6. Estimated contact region (red) where the rock is grasped. When modeling the climbing hold, the area inside boundary B_i is unaltered. Outer boundary B_o is projected to the wall plane.

$\mathbf{v}_1, \ldots, \mathbf{v}_n \quad \mathsf{R}^3$ and the gravity vector as $\mathbf{g}_{\texttt{crag}} \quad \mathsf{R}^3$. If our plane is defined using a point $\mathbf{p} \quad \mathsf{R}^3$ and normal vector $\mathbf{n} \quad \mathsf{R}^3$, we can find the optimal plane by solving the following constrained optimization problem:

$$\begin{aligned} \underset{\mathbf{p},\mathbf{n}}{\text{minimize}} \quad & \sum_i (\mathbf{n}^T(\mathbf{v}_i - \mathbf{p}))^2 \\ \text{subject to} \quad & \ \mathbf{n}\ ^2 = 1, \mathbf{n}^T \mathbf{g}_{\texttt{crag}} = 0, \mathbf{n}^T(\mathbf{v}_i - \mathbf{p}) \quad 0. \end{aligned} \tag{1}$$

This is a non-convex optimization problem with inequality constraints. The inequality constraints are essential to ensuring that none of the contact region vertices gets clipped by the resulting plane, i.e., all contact regions remain intact. We solve this problem using the `fmincon` routine in MATLAB with a variety of starting points in order to increase the likelihood of finding a global optimum. Even though other optimization methods would also be possible, we found the `fmincon` approach easy to implement and fast due to the low number of unknowns.

Hold modeling

Having defined a suitable fitting plane and contact regions, the following step is to create fabrication-suitable pieces akin to traditional indoor climbing holds. Many constraints and objectives are involved in creating fabricatable holds. We attempt to minimize material use, and at the same time the boundaries must be large enough to allow for a drilled hole that doesn't block the grasping area. Most critically, the added geometry must not alter the way the hold will be grasped, for example, introducing sharp curvature may add a graspable ledge that reduces the difficulty of the route.

We create one piece for each contact region. For each piece, we manually design an inner and outer boundary (see Fig. 6). The outer boundary, B_o, specifies the entire volume of the hold; triangles of the 3D reconstruction outside of the outer boundaries can be discarded. The inner boundary, B_i, encloses the contact region, i.e., the part of the hold which is grasped and must not be altered. The outer boundary is projected to the gym-wall plane while the inner boundary is fixed. We edit the geometry between B_i and B_o to create a smooth transition to the gym-wall plane without modifying the contact region.

To construct our prototypes we performed the editing using Sculptris. Deformation through automatic methods is an opportunity for future research, e.g., Botsch and Kobbelt [6] address the geometric aspects of this modeling problem but not the grasping, fabrication, or structural stability constraints.

HOLD FABRICATION

From the reconstruction and modeling stages we have high resolution geometry of the rock contact regions used by the climber. The modeling phase provides us with a set of discrete holds. The goal of the fabrication pipeline is to create physical prototypes from the hold geometry so they may be mounted in a climbing gym using standard hardware. In this section we detail our fabrication pipeline.

Overview

Fabrication of climbing holds presents unique challenges. Material strength must be high enough to support the body weight of a climber. The applied forces from the climber can be observed under a variety of directions and locations, as a hold could be used for both hand or foot contacts at various phases of the climb. Additionally, emulating the friction properties is essential for reproducing a realistic route. Climbers often have miniscule surface area to grasp onto, sometimes barely larger than the width of a finger. The difference between a rough or polished surface can determine whether a route is climbable or not.

Our fabrication pipeline consists of several stages:

1. We rapid prototype the 3D digital models of the holds. Our experiments used both 3D printing and foam cutting with a CNC router.

2. A flexible silicone mold is made from the initial prototype. The final solid hold is then cast from the mold.

3. Holes are drilled for mounting on a gym wall.

A summary of materials is given in Table 1. The following sections discuss fabrication methods.

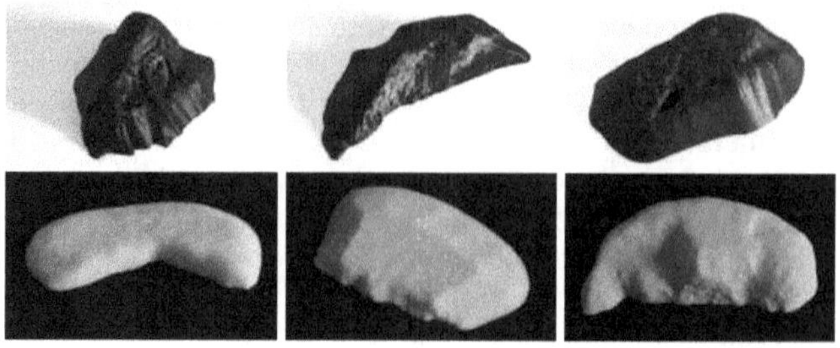

Figure 7. 3D printed holds. Geometry generated by reconstructions from natural rock formations. (Top) "Pilgrimage" route. (Bottom) "TATAN" route.

Rapid Prototyping

The first stage of the pipeline is to create a physical replica of the digital model for each climbing hold.

3D printing: To 3D print each climbing hold, we used a Stratasys Titan Fused Deposition Modeling (FDM) 3D printer with ABS plastic material. In order to conserve material, only the exterior shell is printed with sparse interior fill. See Fig. 7 for sample holds. It can be seen that the 3D prints capture natural features of the rock. To achieve texture resembling actual rock we roughen the surface by adhering sand to the surface of the print. The mold process captures these granular details.

Foam cutting: As an alternative prototyping method we created physical replicas from foam using a CNC Router. The primary motivation was improved friction: a sandy texture is inherent to the foam material, avoiding the extra step of adhering sand to surface. We used a Shopbot CNC Router with a 5/16" bit and 3-10% stepover depending on the geometry of the hold. Fig. 8 shows example holds. Compared to 3D printing, the router approach offers significant time savings – an entire piece can be cut in as little as 10 minutes (foot hold) compared to several hours for 3D printing. A limitation is in the range of geometry that can be carved. Undercuts are not feasible without a 4-axis or 5-axis machine, which tend to have smaller volume capacity and incur higher expense.

The next step is to create holds robust enough for mounting on the gym wall. Foam does not have sufficient rigidity, and 3D prints lack the surface quality to match the friction of rock. FDM printer resolution is insufficient to print a granular surface, and further, layering in FDM prints may create planes of weakness prone to fracture. Alternative materials are available for 3D printing but have disadvantages: plaster-based prints match the texture of rock but are structurally brittle. Photo-polymer prints approach the resolution of granular rock, but incur impractical high expense.

Creating the mold

Given a rapid prototyped climbing hold, the next stage is to create a mold (negative of the final product). Molds are frequently used in manufacturing commercial climbing holds. However, these practices are generally considered trade secrets and are not disclosed.

Our molds consisted of a 2-part pourable silicone rubber, Smooth-On OOMOO R 25 & 30. A bounding box is created

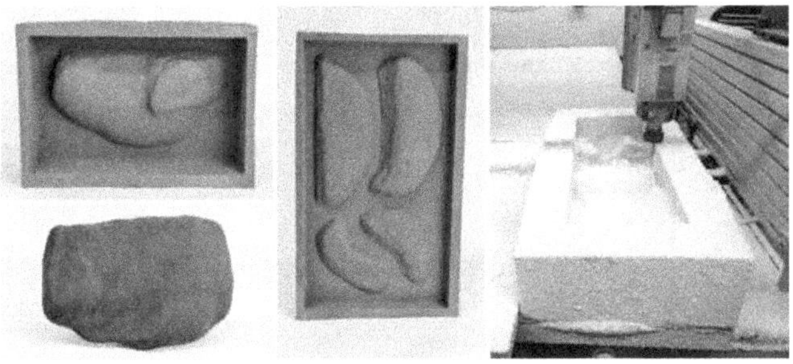

Figure 8. Foam holds carved with a CNC Router. Holds from "TATAN" route shown.

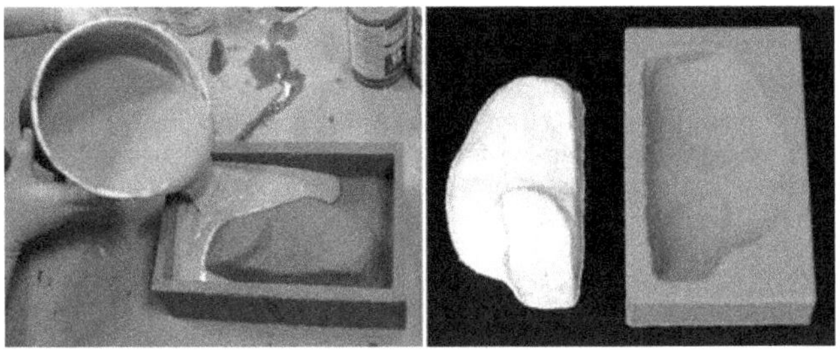

Figure 9. Molding & casting process. (Left) Silicone rubber poured over foam prototype to create the mold. The curing process requires 3-6 hours. (Right) Final cast climbing hold alongside its mold. Cast uses low viscosity resin which completes in under 5 minutes. The surface texture of the original foam is retained.

around the hold to limit the material volume. The silicone rubber is flexible, which allows use of a single-piece mold despite slight concavities, i.e. it was not necessary to consider problems of assembly/disassembly that would be relevant for rigid molds. The mold materials are straightforward to use: convenient 1:1 mixing ratio by volume for the liquid components and no degassing mechanism was required to remove air bubbles. The silicone material captured surface textures of the rapid prototyped hold (foam or 3D print with adhered sand), and was sufficiently resilient when used for multiple casts. The process is shown in Fig. 9.

Casting the hold

Once the mold is prepared, we create the final hold through a casting procedure. We use Smooth Cast R 300 series liquid plastic, which is a low viscosity casting resin. The fully cured plastic has high durability and toughness, rated at 4000 psi compressive strength, 3000 psi tensile strength, and 4500 psi flexural strength making it suitable for supporting applied forces from a climber. Similar to molding, casting involves mixing a 2-part pourable set of liquids in a convenient 1:1 volume ratio. Degassing is not necessary for removal of air bubbles.

Mounting the holds

As a final step, the fabricated holds must be mounted on the gym wall. We drill a bolt hole in each climbing hold so that it can be attached using standard T-nut fasteners, commonly found in climbing gyms with plywood walls. For safety precautions and to allow tightening, the bolt is sunken so that it lies below the exterior surface. See Fig. 10 for an example.

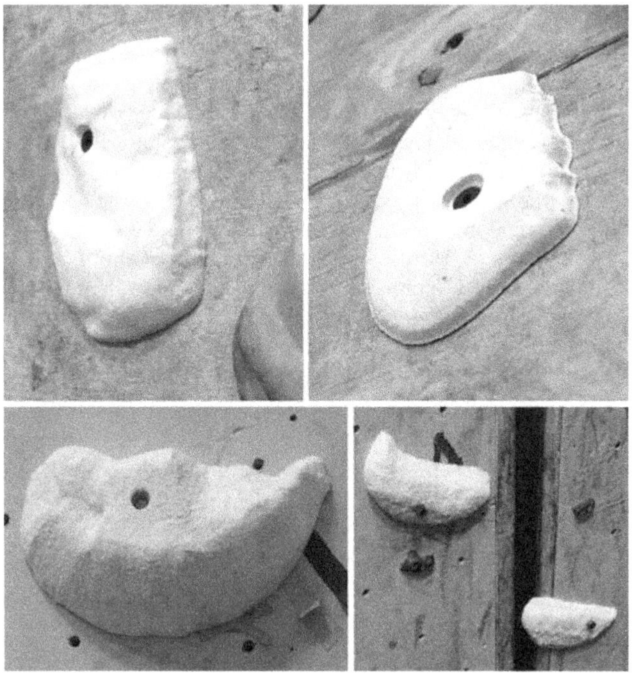

Figure 10. Fabricated holds mounted on the gym wall.

An additional challenge in the mounting process is determining hold placement on the wall. A given wall may consist of hundreds of T-nuts, and optimal positioning is a key component in replicating the original route. We generate a visual guide, as displayed in Fig. 11, which aids in constructing the final route. Our method for determining hold placement is discussed in the *Indoor Con guration* Section.

Overall, the molding & casting procedure is effective in both structural properties and cost, since molds can be re-used. The mold incurs only moderate expense ($20/hold on average), while the cast material is relatively cheap. The mold requires 3-6 hours to set, while casting completes in approx. 15 min. Compared to 3D printing each hold (upwards of 10 hours and $50-100 per print), the cost and time benefit grows the more holds produced.

INDOOR CONFIGURATION

From the previous steps, we have 3D models of suitable pieces, resembling traditional indoor climbing holds. We also know the location of the gym-wall plane. The last step is to determine *where* to drill the holes in the fabricated pieces so that they can be attached to the gym wall to resemble the 3D geometry of the original outdoor crag as closely as possible.

Process	Material
3D Printing	ABS thermoplastic
CNC Router	High density shaping foam
Mold	Smooth-On OOMOO R 25 & 30 silicone rubber
Cast	Smooth Cast R 300 series liquid plastic
Wall Mount	3/8" socket head bolt with hex drive

Table 1. Summary of fabrication materials

T-nut positions acquisition

Gym walls are equipped with T-nuts which serve as attachment points for the holds. The holds are attached using bolts and can be easily mounted and dismounted. However, the configuration of the T-nuts is fixed and cannot be changed without major construction efforts. Some gym walls have T-nuts arranged in a regular grid, but other gyms - such as ours - feature randomly perturbed positions. To find the coordinates we start by capturing a 3D reconstruction of the gym wall, following the same process as with outdoor walls, including estimation of the gravity vector and scale. We assume that our chosen gym wall is vertical and planar. In this plane we define a 2D coordinate system by picking an arbitrary origin O (typically at the base of the climb) and defining an "up vector" $\mathbf{y}$ by projecting the negative gravity vector $\mathbf{g}_{\texttt{gym}}$ to the plane. Because we assume the wall is vertical, $\mathbf{g}_{\texttt{gym}}$ should be almost parallel to the plane. The $\mathbf{x}$-vector of the basis is given by rotating $\mathbf{g}_{\texttt{gym}}$ around $\mathbf{n}$ by 90 degrees.

Our next task is to find the coordinates of the centers of the T-nuts with respect to the $(O, \mathbf{x}, \mathbf{y})$ coordinate system. First, we identify the T-nuts in the gym-wall photos using the circular Hough transformation (function `imfindcircles` in MATLAB), taking advantage of the fact that each T-nut has the same radius, which we can easily measure. Analogously to our motion capture pipeline, we cast a ray from the camera center though the center of each T-nut. The intersection of the ray with the gym-wall plane gives us a point which we express in terms of our coordinate system $(O, \mathbf{x}, \mathbf{y})$.

Positioning on the indoor wall

Having defined 2D coordinates of each hole in the gym-wall plane, the last step is to determine where to place the ensemble of our fabricated holds. At this stage, we only need to work with projections of the holds to the 2D plane, reducing the problem to two dimensions. Typical indoor climbing walls feature many T-nuts and therefore, there are many possibilities where to attach our holds. We aim to reproduce the 3D geometry of the original outdoor crux as closely as possible. First, we rotate all of the pieces in order to align $\mathbf{g}_{\texttt{crag}}$ with $\mathbf{g}_{\texttt{gym}}$, i.e., the climbing problem is oriented the same way with respect to gravity. Determining suitable translation of the ensemble is slightly more complicated. Let us denote the ideal position of the hole in each piece as $\mathbf{c}_j \in \mathsf{R}^2$, typically at the center of each piece to maximize structural stability after drilling the hole. We want to find a translation vector $\mathbf{t} \in \mathsf{R}^2$ such that each $\mathbf{c}_j + \mathbf{t}$ would get as close as possible to *some* T-nut. This leads to the following optimization problem:

$$\underset{\mathbf{t} \in \mathcal{T}}{\text{minimize}} \quad \sum_j \lambda_j \left\| \mathbf{c}_j + \mathbf{t} - P(\mathbf{c}_j + \mathbf{t}) \right\|^2 \tag{2}$$

where $\mathcal{T}$ is a set of allowed translations (user-defined rectangle in our case), $\lambda_j > 0$ are user-selected weights, and $P : \mathsf{R}^2 \rightarrow \mathsf{R}^2$ is a function which projects an input point to the closest T-nut. For a given initial guess of $\mathbf{t}$, we can minimize the problem (2) by alternating between two steps, similarly to local-global solvers [7]. In the first (local) step, we assume that $\mathbf{t}$ is fixed and we compute the closest T-nut $P(\mathbf{c}_j + \mathbf{t})$. In the second (global) step, we assume the projections $P(\mathbf{c}_j + \mathbf{t})$ are fixed and we solve a simple convex quadratic minimization problem to obtain the optimal $\mathbf{t}$. These steps are iterated until the closest T-nuts are no longer changing, at which point we found a local minimum. To increase the chances of finding a global minimizer, we sample the entire region $\mathcal{T}$ and run the above described optimization from many different initial guesses. Generous sampling is not difficult due to the low dimensions of $\mathcal{T}$ (subset of R^2). The result for our TATAN route can be seen in Figure 11. Note that our route can naturally coexist with traditional indoor climbing routes. We can evaluate the accuracy of the fit of each hold by computing the positioning error $e_j = \left\| \mathbf{c}_j + \mathbf{t} - P(\mathbf{c}_j + \mathbf{t}) \right\|$ for each hold j.

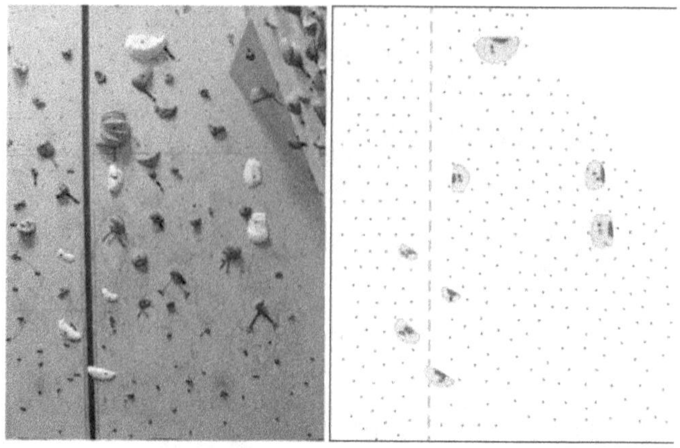

Figure 11. (Left) White holds forming our replicated route were positioned by finding optimal matching against T-nuts permanently installed in the gym wall. (Right) T-nut positions are shown as blue circles. Red circles correspond to hold centers and crosses correspond to the optimal T-nut match.

Building our prototype routes revealed that in future work it may be advantageous to augment the objective in Eq. 2. The most common failure mode of a hold attachment is rotation around the bolt due to high applied torque. We could penalize hole positions which lead to large torques under the expected loadings; note that a single hold is frequently used both as a foot *and* hand hold in different phases of the climb, so it is necessary to find an effective compromise. Another requirement is robustness. After tightening the bolt, the hold must be able to withstand large loads without fracturing. One possibility would be to study internal stresses using Finite Element Analysis. With a realistic friction model for the hold/wall interface, it would also be possible to calculate the optimal range of tightening torque, which needs to be high enough to prevent spinning, but not so high the hold would fail.

RESULTS

The poses a climber uses to ascend a route are highly constrained by the geometry and placement of the holds. As such, we chose to perform user studies as an indicative method for validating our results. We compare the corresponding poses of the same climber on 1) the original outdoor crux and 2) our indoor replica. In studies of two example routes – TATAN and Pilgrimage – we demonstrate a close visual match between the climbers poses on the original and replicated route. Both routes are vertical face climbs suitable for our approach.

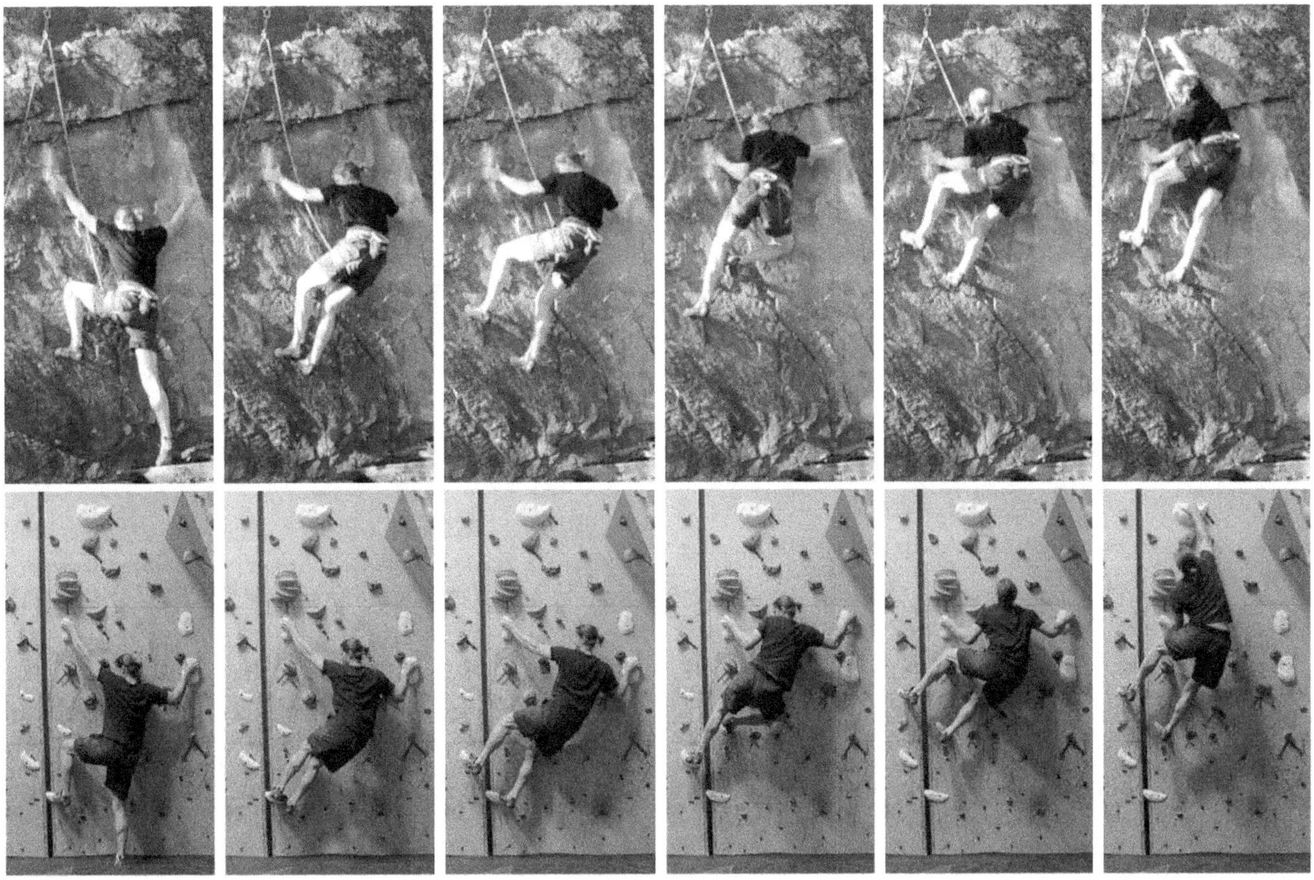

Figure 12. TATAN route: Pose by pose comparison of climber A between the original outdoor route, and our indoor replication.

Theoretically, an ideal way to evaluate the climbing experience (and route difficulty) would be by measuring time-varying forces in the musculoskeletal system, e.g., muscle activations. Electromyographics studies of muscle activations during climbing have been performed before [19], however this seems feasible only in a controlled lab environment.

TATAN

The TATAN route is a schist rock formation, graded 5.12a. It is located at Rumney, New Hampshire, a popular climbing destination in the Northeast USA. We fabricated 8 holds for the crux region and replicated the route in a climbing gym. The minimum positioning error ($\min_j e_j$) was $1.1cm$ and the maximum ($\max_j e_j$) was $5.8cm$.

We obtained informal feedback from four adult male rock climbers. All four of the test climbers (A, B, C, D) had prior experience climbing the corresponding outdoor route. Our route reconstruction was based on climber A's ascent (Fig. 12) and, as shown in the accompanying video, his ascent of the replica indeed closely matches his ascent of the outdoor route. Climber B used slightly different footholds on the outdoor route and therefore his ascent of our replica was not identical (see the accompanying video and Fig. 13). This could be improved by manufacturing additional holds. We did not have reference outdoor video of climbers C and D.

All four climbers unanimously agreed on the similarity between the outdoor route and our indoor replica. Feedback included that it was a close match and in particular that "the movement feels similar." As criticism, one user stated that the slope of the wall is slightly steeper making the indoor climb more challenging than the original.

Pilgrimage

The second route, "Pilgrimage," is graded 5.12a and is part of a sandstone crag near St. George in Southern Utah. We fabricated 6 holds to replicate the crux. The minimum positioning error ($\min_j e_j$) was $4.17cm$ and the maximum ($\max_j e_j$) was $12.4cm$. We had three adult male rock climbers (F, G, H) ascend our replication for the study. With our indoor climbing gym being located in New Hampshire, we did not have access to the original climber (E) in the reference videos or any climbers familiar with the Pilgrimage route. Instead, we show a comparison between static poses with two different climbers, see Fig. 14. The poses are similar but do not match as well as in the TATAN example, especially in the beginning of the crux because we omitted the reconstruction of the initial footholds, relying on features pre-installed on the indoor climbing wall. Also, the vertical positioning of the right foot in the last move (columns 3 and 4 in Fig. 14) has a different relative alignment from the outdoor climb. When finding the optimal T-nuts, the left foothold was moved down and the

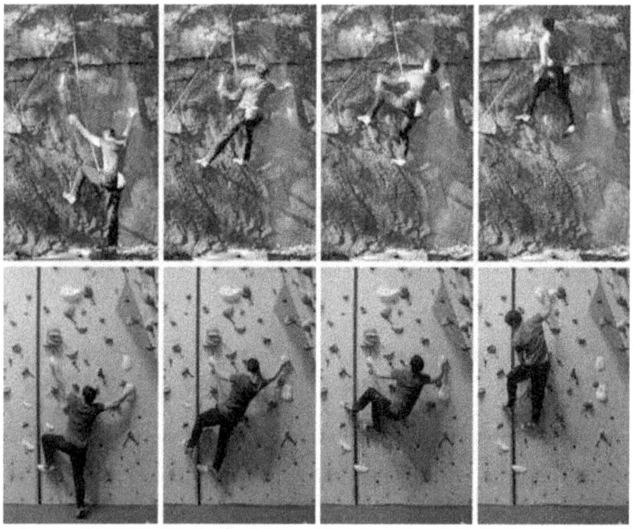

Figure 13. Pose by pose comparison for climber B on the TATAN route.

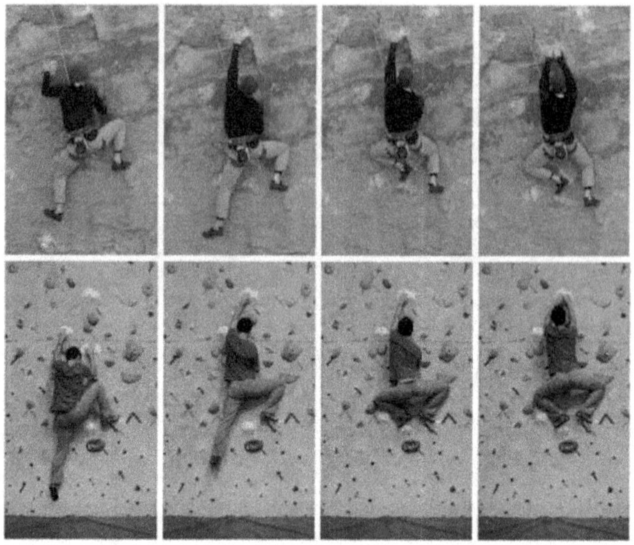

Figure 14. Pilgrimage route: Pose by pose comparison between the original outdoor route (climber E), and our indoor replication (climber F).

right up, resulting in compounding of the error. In the future it may be desirable to alter the optimization objective (2) to explicitly account for *relative* errors, as opposed to the current global error.

Generally, the climbers were excited by the idea of being able to climb a replica of a route from a location more than 2000 miles away. Overall we were pleased that test climbers immediately demonstrated an interest in using the routes for training and to experience remote locations. Note the Pilgrimage route replication was accomplished in a purely digital way, i.e., no physical artifacts were transported from Utah to New Hampshire, only data (specifically, photos and videos). This "route teleportation" may prove useful in the future when attempting to replicate routes from hardly accessible areas, e.g, high mountains in foreign countries, where already reaching the base of the climb requires non-trivial logistics.

Climb analysis

We analyzed video recordings of corresponding outdoor and indoor climbs, see Table 2. The indoor time reduction for TATAN was due to the climbers' familiarity with the climbing sequence; less time was spent in each static pose, determining the next move. This was not the case with Pilgrimage, since our climbers never climbed its outdoor counterpart. On the outdoor TATAN route climber B used 5 different holds compared to climber A, but 3 out of the 5 were still present at our replicated holds (closer to the center of the crux as B was shorter than A). In the indoor TATAN replica, climber B used one extra foothold compared to climber A's ascent of the indoor TATAN, compensating for the fact that we have not replicated the bottom portions of the route. All of the crux moves were completed using the fabricated holds.

	Climb	Climber	Time	Poses	Extra Holds
TATAN	Outdoor	A	22s	6	0
	Indoor	A	15s	6	0
	Outdoor	B	27s	9	5
	Indoor	B	15s	6	1
Pilg.	Outdoor	E	6s	4	0
	Indoor	F	8s	4	0

Table 2. Results of video analysis of the climbs. Time is the total climb time measured from the start of the rst static pose to the start of the last static pose.

Surface texture

In addition to testing climbing poses on the replicated routes, we gathered feedback on texture properties of the fabricated holds. We presented climbers with pairs of holds having identical geometry, but fabricated with the alternative techniques of 3D printing and foam cutting. We asked users to comment on which felt more like natural rock. The study involved 9 adult climbers, all experienced in outdoor climbing. Note that we tested the final cast holds, but refer to the alternatives as "foam" or "3D printed" to indicate the intermediate rapid prototyping method.

Seven out of nine climbers agreed the foam holds felt more like real rock. One preferred foam for a more pleasant climbing experience but did not have an opinion about realism. The last user had no stated preference. Zero users preferred the 3D printed holds. Five users specifically remarked that the foam holds felt like sandstone (matching the Pilgrimage route rock). Users appreciated that the foam holds felt more homogeneous and would maintain their friction over time. The main criticism of the 3D printed holds covered with glued sand was that they are too abrasive.

We conclude that foam is the better option for rapid prototyping, considering both realistic friction and longevity. However, since few users noted similarities to Rumney's schist rock, we are interested in continuing to analyze the factors that contribute to the natural feeling of rock varieties. In the future, it may be possible to measure the friction properties of the rock quantitatively and replicate them using fine-scale fabrication techniques.

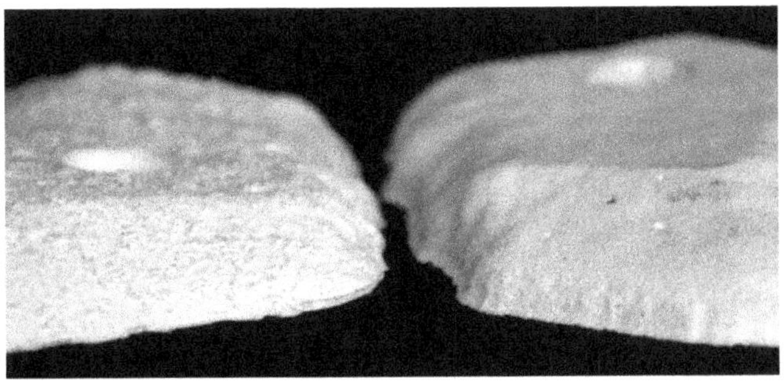

Figure 15. Comparison of surface texture in fabricated holds. (Left) Cast from a 3D printed hold with adhered sand. (Right) Cast from a porous foam hold.

Limitations and Future Work

Our route replication workflow currently assumes climbing routes have constant inclination. Replicating the 3D architecture of rock – where planar wall approximations are insufficient – is a major challenge for future work. In the gym, our holds could be extended using e.g. wood boxes bolted to the wall (a.k.a. climbing volumes). An automatic technique to determine the box geometry and positioning would expand the range of routes we can reproduce. Another human-specific consideration is the effect of gradual muscle burnout and fatigue, critical especially with long routes. In the future, it would be possible to design training routines focusing on stamina.

Our current acquisition pipeline assumes that a climber capable of leading the route is available. In the future, we would like to explore route acquisition using e.g. drone photography to remove this restriction. Carefully planned flight paths will be essential to capturing all of the rock features including concavities. Another challenge will be the lack of reference climbing video recordings, which would be replaced e.g. by biomechanic simulations determining which climbing moves are feasible.

The problems of fabrication of large-scale artifacts are not restricted to rock climbing. Future applications might include:

Replicating cave paintings in a museum setting. To save cost it may be preferable to reconstruct only sparse areas of interest of the cave environment. The geometric configuration of the individual paintings should be retained, as it may tell a story or reflect aspects of early human cultures.

Reconstructing crime scenes for Forensic analysis. Physical evidence requires high detail, and relative placement may represent critical cues for understanding interrelationships between components in the scene.

VR environments, replicating geometry of objects that invite interaction to provide tactile feedback. Virtual and Augmented Reality experiences combined with climbing are already starting to be explored in the videogame industry (e.g. *The Climb* developed by Crytek for Oculus Rift).

CONCLUSION

Our work explores a new and unusual problem in large-scale fabrication, specifically, replication of outdoor climbing walls. We focus on recreating the sensorimotor experience of the user while interacting with our replica. The main challenge of this project consisted in discovering the appropriate techniques from various disciplines (HCI, computer vision, CAD, and fabrication) and determining how to connect them to obtain a complete system capable of environment-scale fabrication.

We believe that replicating outdoor routes could impact the indoor climbing gym industry and inspire future research in environment-scale fabrication as well as related scientific and technological questions. For example, how to measure and replicate friction properties of natural materials, combining large-scale physical artifacts with Augmented or Virtual Reality, studying biomechanics of human locomotion in challenging conditions, or 3D capture of environments not accessible by regular vehicles or on foot.

Acknowledgments

Thank you to our dedicated rock climbers: William Braasch, Wayne Norse, and Patrick Xu; the Dartmouth College Thayer Machine Shop for fabrication resources; the anonymous reviewers for their feedback; and our colleagues Kevin Chen, Elaine Cohen, Perttu Hämäläinen, Jaakko Lehtinen, and Frieder Wittmann for insightful discussions. This material is based upon work supported by the National Science Foundation under Grant Numbers 1464267, 1617172 and 1622360. We also gratefully acknowledge the support of Activision.

REFERENCES

1. Harshit Agrawal, Udayan Umapathi, Robert Kovacs, Johannes Frohnhofen, Hsiang-Ting Chen, Stefanie Mueller, and Patrick Baudisch. 2015. Protopiper: Physically Sketching Room-Sized Objects at Actual Scale. In *UIST 15*. ACM, 427–436.
2. Rami Aladdin and Paul G. Kry. 2012. Static Pose Reconstruction with an Instrumented Bouldering Wall. In *VRST*. 177–184.
3. Louie Anderson. 2004. *The Art of Coursesetting*.
4. Autodesk. 2016. New Advancements in 3D Printing to Improve Speed and Scale. Online: `http://spark.autodesk.com/blog/`. (March 2016).
5. Robert Bogue. 2013. 3D printing: the dawn of a new era in manufacturing? *Assembly Automation* 33, 4 (2013), 307–311.
6. Mario Botsch and Leif Kobbelt. An intuitive framework for real-time freeform modeling. In *ACM Transactions on Graphics*.
7. Sofien Bouaziz, Sebastian Martin, Tiantian Liu, Ladislav Kavan, and Mark Pauly. 2014. Projective Dynamics: Fusing Constraint Projections for Fast Simulation. *ACM Trans. Graph.* 33, 4, Article 154 (July 2014).
8. M. Buchroithner. 2002. Creating the virtual Eiger North Face. *Journal of Photogrammetry and Remote Sensing* (2002).
9. S. Fuhrmann and M. Goesele. 2014. Floating Scale Surface Reconstruction. *ACM Trans. Graph.* (2014).

10. Yasutaka Furukawa and Jean Ponce. 2010. Accurate, Dense, and Robust Multi-View Stereopsis. *IEEE Trans. on Pattern Analysis and Machine Intelligence* 32, 8 (2010), 1362–1376.
11. Michal Jancosek and Tomas Pajdla. 2011. Multi-view reconstruction preserving weakly-supported surfaces. In *CVPR*.
12. Raine Kajastila and Perttu Hämäläinen. 2014. Augmented climbing: Interacting with projected graphics on a climbing wall. In *CHI 14*.
13. Avinash Kalyanaraman, Juhi Ranjan, and Kamin Whitehouse. 2015. Automatic Rock Climbing Route Inference Using Wearables. In *UbiComp/ISWC 15*. 41–44.
14. Behrokh Khoshnevis. 2004. Automated construction by contour craftingrelated robotics and information technologies. *Automation in Construction* 13, 1 (2004), 5–19.
15. Natalia Kolecka. 2012. High-resolution mapping and visualization of a climbing wall. In *True-3D in Cartography*.
16. Johannes Kopf, Michael F. Cohen, and Richard Szeliski. 2014. First-person Hyper-lapse videos. *ACM Trans. Graph.* 33, 4 (2014), 78:1–78:10.
17. Felix Kosmalla, Florian Daiber, and Antonio Krüger. 2015. ClimbSense: Automatic Climbing Route Recognition Using Wrist-worn Inertia Measurement Units. In *CHI 15*. 2033–2042.
18. Felix Kosmalla, Frederik Wiehr, Florian Daiber, Antonio Krüger, and Markus Löchtefeld. 2016. ClimbAware: Investigating Perception and Acceptance of Wearables in Rock Climbing. In *CHI 16*. ACM, 1097–1108.
19. TD Koukoubis, LW Cooper, RR Glisson, AV Seaber, and JA Feagin Jr. 1995. An electromyographic study of arm muscles during climbing. *Knee Surgery, Sports Traumatology, Arthroscopy* 3, 2 (1995), 121–124.
20. Cassim Ladha, Nils Y Hammerla, Patrick Olivier, and Thomas Plötz. 2013. ClimbAX: skill assessment for climbing enthusiasts. In *UbiComp*.
21. Sergey Levine, Christian Theobalt, and Vladlen Koltun. 2009. Real-time Prosody-driven Synthesis of Body Language. *ACM Trans. Graph.* 28, 5, Article 172 (Dec. 2009), 10 pages.
22. Matyas Luzan. 2015. On the Path to Action Directe 9a. Online: `http://luzanmatyas.blogspot.com/`. (2015).
23. Jonas Pfeil, Jun Mitani, and Takeo Igarashi. 2011. Interactive climbing route design using a simulated virtual climber. In *SIGGRAPH Asia 2011 Sketches*. ACM, 2.
24. Caleb Phillips, Lee Becker, and Elizabeth Bradley. 2011. Strange Beta: An Assistance System for Indoor Rock Climbing Route Setting Using Chaotic Variations and Machine Learning. *CoRR* abs/1110.0532 (2011). `http://arxiv.org/abs/1110.0532`
25. M. Simnacher, R. Spoerri, G. Rauter, R. Riener, and P. Wolf. 2012. Development and Application of a Dynamometric System for Sport Climbing. *Journal of Biomechanics* (2012).
26. Carsten Stoll, Nils Hasler, Juergen Gall, Hans-Peter Seidel, and Christian Theobalt. 2011. Fast articulated motion tracking using a sums of gaussians body model. In *ICCV*.
27. Hironori Yoshida, Takeo Igarashi, Yusuke Obuchi, Yosuke Takami, Jun Sato, Mika Araki, Masaaki Miki, Kosuke Nagata, Kazuhide Sakai, and Syunsuke Igarashi. 2015. Architecture-scale Human-assisted Additive Manufacturing. *ACM Trans. Graph.* 34, 4 (July 2015), 88:1–88:8.

Why Tangibility Matters: A Design Case Study of At-Risk Children Learning to Read and Spell

Min Fan[1] **Alissa N. Antle**[1] **Maureen Hoskyn**[2] **Carman Neustaedter**[1] **Emily S. Cramer**[1]

School of Interactive Arts & Technology[1]
Simon Fraser University
250-13450 102 Avenue
Surrey, B.C. Canada V3T 0A3

Centre for Research on Early Child Health and Education[2]
Simon Fraser University
8888 University Drive
Burnaby, B.C. Canada V5A 1S6

[minf, aantle, mhoskyn, carman, ecramer]@sfu.ca

ABSTRACT

Tangibles may be effective for reading applications. Letters can be represented as 3D physical objects. Words are spatially organized collections of letters. We explore how tangibility impacts reading and spelling acquisition for young Anglophone children who have dyslexia. We describe our theory-based design rationale and present a mixed-methods case study of eight children using our PhonoBlocks system. All children made significant gains in reading and spelling on trained and untrained (new) words, and could apply all spelling rules a month later. We discuss the design features of our system that contributed to effective learning processes, resulting in successful learning outcomes: dynamic colour cues embedded in 3D letters, which can draw attention to how letter(s) position changes their sounds; and the form of 3D tangible letters, which can enforce correct letter orientation and enable epistemic strategies in letter organization that simplify spelling tasks. We conclude with design guidelines for tangible reading systems.

Author Keywords

Tangible user interfaces; dyslexia; children; embedded interaction; reading acquisition; mixed-methods.

ACM Classification Keywords

H.5.2. Information interfaces and presentation: User Interfaces. K.3.2. Computers and education: Miscellaneous.

INTRODUCTION

Success in early reading acquisition requires learning phonological awareness (PA), which is the ability to identify and manipulate units of oral language (e.g. the sounds that groups of letters make) and learning the alphabetic principle, which is that letters represent sounds which form words according to predictable relationships or rules that link letters and spoken sounds. If a child understands these kinds of letter-sound associations then s/he will be able to learn to read and spell words [6,26,30]. However, in English-speaking countries, approximately 10% of children have difficulties in learning to read and spell [17]. This specific learning difficulty is referred to as "dyslexia" [26]. Dyslexia can result in tremendous social, emotional and economical costs for children, their families and society. Recent research has suggested the potential of tangible user interfaces (TUIs) in supporting learning to read for children, particularly for children with dyslexia [9,13]. Despite these suggestions, few TUIs have been designed for children with dyslexia (for exceptions, see [23,24]). Few empirical studies have evaluated if, and how such systems support children in learning to read (for an exception, see [13]). No systems have been designed that explicitly address and evaluate early reading acquisition targeting PA and the alphabetic principle.

We address this opportunity and knowledge gap by presenting the theory-based design and evaluation of a tangible reading system called PhonoBlocks. Our goal was to create a system to help 7 to 8 year old children at risk for dyslexia to learn six letter-sound rules required to read and spell many words in English, which they had been unable to learn with classroom instruction. We targeted PA and the alphabetic principle as critical phases in early reading because children with dyslexia struggle with these concepts, which all children must master. The design of PhonoBlocks, in particular its two core design features, dynamic embedded colour cues and 3D tangible letters, were developed based on theories of causes of dyslexia and analysis of non-computational multi-sensory reading interventions, which are effective but resource intensive. We used a mixed-methods approach to investigate *if* and *how* our system might help Anglophone children at risk for dyslexia to learn to read and spell a set of English alphabetic rules.

In this paper, we present an analysis of eight individual cases who each received a total of 12 x 20 minute training sessions with PhonoBlocks. We provide a summary of quantitative results of children's reading and spelling gains, and then provide a detailed analysis of the qualities of interactions and behaviours that PhonoBlocks enabled in order to better understand how tangible design elements may facilitate learning to read and spell. Our results provide empirical

CHI 2017, May 06 - 11, 2017, Denver, CO, USA

ACM 978-1-4503-4655-9/17/05…$15.00
DOI: http://dx.doi.org/10.1145/3025453.3026048

evidence that indicates two unique features of tangibility were effective in supporting children at risk to learn to read and spell. Our results may be generalizable to TUI systems designed to support second (foreign) language learners who face similar challenges to the students in our study, and because all children must learn PA and the alphabetic principle, to TUI early reading systems for typical children.

BACKGROUND

Theories of Dyslexia

Dyslexia is a specific learning difficulty that affects children's language acquisition skills such as learning to read and spell. Although dyslexia is heterogeneous, the most direct cause is suggested to be impairment in phonological awareness, the ability to hear sounds that make up words in spoken language. This includes recognizing when words rhyme, judging if words begin or end with the same sounds and understanding that sounds can be manipulated to create words [26,30]. Phonological deficits impede children's acquisitions of the alphabetic principle and the subsequent mastery of language. In addition, dyslexia often co-occurs with attentional deficits [25]. Learning to read English poses particular challenges for children with dyslexia due to its inconsistent letter-sound mappings in its orthography (referred to as an "opaque" language) [6,28]. Therefore, helping children with dyslexia to improve their phonological awareness and cueing attention to the alphabetic principle are extremely important during the acquisition of "opaque" languages.

Multisensory Instruction

Although dyslexia is a lifelong condition, children with dyslexia can learn to read and spell under proper instruction [6]. Research suggests that explicit, intense, and highly structured phonics-based instruction, which stresses the acquisition of the alphabetic principle and its use in reading and spelling, has been effective, particularly for children with dyslexia [15,26]. Phonics-based training also helps children learn PA because it focuses on the reciprocal relationship between PA (focus on sounds) and the alphabetic principle (focus on letters) [18]. One widely used phonics-based approach is the multisensory approach in which visual, auditory, tactile, and kinaesthetic representations are linked to help children understand letter-sound associations [15]. Other approaches, like the Montessori method, which may use multi-sensory materials, have produced inconsistent results and remain under-studied.

The Orton-Gillingham (O-G) program is one example of multisensory instruction [27]. The O-G program is often conducted with a trained tutor supporting a child with dyslexia [15]. The tutor directs the activity and uses a phonics-based approach to explicitly teach the child letter-sound correspondences using multiple forms of representations [15]. For example, physical letter tiles or coloured beads, which may be put into sequences, are often used in the O-G program [3]. One important sensory activity in the O-G program is having children trace letters to develop an understanding of how they feel [3]. Like typical readers, dyslexic children also have problems distinguishing mirrored letterforms [6]. The letter tracing activity can help dyslexic children to learn similar letterforms [3,6]. Handling letters while sounds are played may improve dyslexic children's attention to letter-sound correspondences [10,20] as well as helping them learn, remember and apply spelling rules [2]. During such interventions, tutors may also use other cues such as pictures [8] and colours (e.g. *pat*, *rat*, *bat*) [4,14] to attract children's attention to and improve memory of letter-sound correspondences. However, one limitation of this approach is that it is extremely resource intensive. Most O-G programs do not involve computational materials and rely on highly trained tutors who provide many one-to-one sessions with structured guidance and feedback.

Tangible Reading Systems for At-Risk Children

Researchers have highlighted the potential of computer-based methods for reading instruction. Some potential advantages are: cost-effectiveness [9,22]; digital feedback; playful learning through multimedia (e.g. text, images, sounds, and objects); and motivational game-mechanisms [21]. Compared to graphic user interfaces (GUIs), the physical and spatial qualities of TUIs may be beneficial because the letters can be represented as tangible objects that can be interacted with more easily than printing letters, can be traced, and are easily organized into related groups and/or linear sequences of words. There are many tangible reading prototypes (e.g. [7,11,16,29]) and several commercial products (Tiggly[1], Osmo[2]). Few are specifically designed for children with reading difficulties and most focus on a whole-word approach which is ineffective for children struggling with PA and the alphabetic principle [6]. Therefore, tangible reading systems designed for typical children, particularly those focusing on the whole-word approach, are likely to be ineffective for children at risk for dyslexia.

We identified two systems specifically designed for children with dyslexia [23,24] and one designed for non- or hardly speaking toddlers [13]. SpellBound is a tangible system that supports dyslexic children to learn letter-sound correspondences [23]. SpellBound allows children to construct 2D letters by using a set of flat wooden shapes that can be used to form letters (e.g. the crossbar of a *t*, or tail of a *q*). Then, each 2D letter can be placed onto a platform to trigger the letter sound and associated picture of the word. However, this prototype was only sketched out; it has not been developed yet. Also, SpellBound focuses on letter forms and individual sounds rather than the complex rules of letter-sound correspondences in words.

Tiblo uses Lego-like blocks to represent words, numbers, or phonemes, which are distinct sounds (e.g. *a, th, ex*) [24]. Children with dyslexia can draw the concept on a piece of

[1] https://www.tiggly.com

[2] https://www.playosmo.com

paper, attach it to a block, and record the sound for the concept. A set of blocks can then be connected in a certain order to represent a word, narrative or any other concepts. Apparently, the typical user scenario of Tiblo is not the acquisition of letter-sound correspondences. Furthermore, the researchers only evaluated the usability of this prototype but not its effectiveness in supporting children learning to read.

Hengeveld and colleagues developed LinguaBytes, a tangible system aimed at stimulating language development for non- or hardly speaking toddlers aged 1-4 years [12,13]. LinguaBytes consists of a digital display, a physical control panel, and a wide range of tangible input materials such as story booklets, 3D tangible letters, and programmable RFID labels. This prototype can support a variety of activities including exercises related to phonological awareness, semantics, and story reading. In the phonological activity, toddlers learn letter sounds by placing one 3D tangible letter on the platform. Audiovisual feedback is provided on the digital display, including 2D words and sounds starting with the same letter. The 3D tangible letters of LinguaBytes enable letter tracing and organization of letters in space. The coupling between the 2D word and sound on the display and the 3D tangible letter enables toddlers to learn letter-sound correspondences by using multiple senses. However, the design of LinguaBytes is limited in only allowing toddlers to learn basic one-to-one letter and sound associations rather than the rules of often inconsistent letter-sound mappings in words. The researchers used a research-through-design approach to iteratively design and evaluate the prototype. They argued that tangible interaction offers more opportunities for collaboration between the therapist and the child and promotes engagement that can consequently lead to more opportunities for learning.

In summary, previous research has suggested that TUIs may have the potential to help children to learn to read and spell. However, current tangible reading systems do not focus on helping children at risk for dyslexia learn PA or the alphabetic principle. Nor do they fully leverage the use of TUI features suggested by multisensory instruction (e.g. 3D tangible letters, dynamic colour cues). Lastly, few empirical studies have evaluated if and how such systems support children learning to read. We address all three of these knowledge gaps in our work.

SYSTEM DESCRIPTION

The theories of the causes of dyslexia and best practices of multisensory instruction suggest that the system should satisfy the following key requirements:

- The phonological deficit theory of dyslexia [26,30] and the opaque orthography of English [6,28] suggest that the learning goal should focus on letter-sound correspondences within word contexts (***Req1***).
- The phonological deficit theory [26], attentional challenges [25] and successful multisensory interventions [15] suggest the potential of using multiple cues such as colour [4,14] and pictures [8] to help children notice the common patterns within words while learning of letter-sound correspondences (***Req2***).
- Multisensory interventions suggest the importance of the tutor's role during the learning process [15] (***Req3***), although we would like the children to also be able to practice on their own with feedback to reduce resources.
- The importance of letter-tracing [3] and manipulation [2,10,20] suggests the inclusion of letterforms in the design of physical representations in TUIs (***Req4***).

Based on these four requirements, we present the design of a tangible reading system called PhonoBlocks designed for 7 to 8 year old children at risk for dyslexia to support their learning of six rules that are part of the alphabetic principle in English (***Req1***). PhonoBlocks is comprised of a touch-based laptop display, a word-making platform with seven slots, and 46 lowercase "hand-sized" 3D tangible letters (duplicates for common letters, e.g. *a, e, d, t*) (***Req4***). Children learn letter-sound correspondences by placing one or more 3D tangible letters on the platform. Visual feedback is embedded in the 3D letters using LED strips that change colour to indicate sound changes as letters are added or removed (***Req2***) (e.g. Figure 1). Visual and audio feedback are also provided on the digital display using coloured 2D letters and playing associated letter sounds (***Req2***).

PhonoBlocks contains the following basic features (1) displays a picture related to the word meaning so that children can use pictorial cues to consolidate their memory of letter-sound correspondences (***Req2***) [8]; (2) provides a both tutor and child modes, which offers the freedom for tutors to teach each activity and/or allow a child to practice on their own through a set of games (***Req3***)[15,21]; (3) offers a word history list that displays all words made so far, so that children can compare new and previous words (and see their progress) (***Req3***) [15]; and (4) incorporates a function that enables children to blend letters into a whole word by swiping right across the word to trigger the whole word sound and display letters in a single colour (purple) or decode a word into individual letters and sounds by swiping left across the word to display separate letter colours and clicking a button to trigger individual letter sounds. This function enables children to practice blending and decoding skills (***Req1***) [30].

In addition to the general features, PhonoBlocks has two novel design features: embedded dynamic colour and 3D tangible letters.

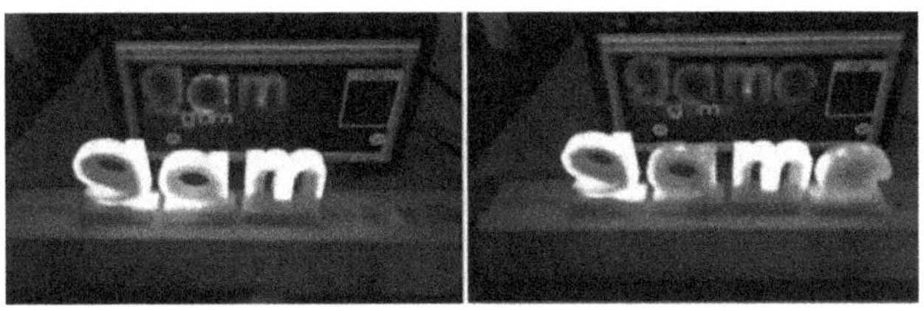

Figure 1. Magic-e activity: the colour of "*a*" changes from yellow to red to illustrate the sound change from short to long.

Embedded Dynamic Colour Cues

We use dynamic colour embedded in the 3D letters to cue (attract) children's attention to the moment when adding new letter(s) changes sound(s) and, in doing so, *explicitly* show them the letter-sound correspondences in different word contexts (***Req1&2***). Each of the six rules has a unique dynamic colour cue design. For example, in the consonant blends activity, the letter *f* and letter *l* change to green to indicate they make a blended sound together. In the magic-e activity, the vowel letter changes from yellow to red to indicate the vowel sound changes from short to long when a trailing *e* is added (Figure 1). We also use flashing colours to draw attention to changes. For example, in the magic-e lesson, when the vowel is placed, the letter flashes three times before staying yellow (short sound). After an *e* is added, both the *e* letter and the vowel letter flash three times, then change to red together. The specific dynamic colour cue design for each rule can be found in Table 1.

3D Tangible Letters

We use sturdy, hand-sized 3D tangible letterforms to facilitate letter tracing and manipulation activities (***Req4***). We use physical constraints: a notch in each letter, to help children learn the orientation of mirrored letters (e.g. *p*, *d* or *b* can only be placed correctly due to the physical notch constraint). Embedded colours are only displayed when letters are placed on the platform; on a table letters are offline, encouraging manipulation.

Learning Activities: Six Spelling Rules	Examples
1. **Consonant Vowel Consonant (CVC)**: CVC patterns	bet pet jet
2. **Consonant Blends:** two consonants make a blended sound in which you can hear two parts to the sound	f → fl → flag
3. **Consonant Digraphs:** two consonants make one sound	t → th → thin
4. **Magic-e Rule**: vowel sound changes from short to long when an *e* is added at the end of word	gam → game
5. **Vowel Teams**: two vowels make one sound	e → ea → eat
6. **R-Controlled Vowels**: r-controlled vowel sounds in which different vowel-r combinations sound the same	er → stern ur → turn

Table 1. Six spelling rule-based activities and colour-coding schemas (black text = white LED light; grey text = LED off).

STUDY METHODOLOGY

The overarching goal of this study was to explore the effectiveness of PhonoBlocks, and to evaluate how design features impacted learning. Our research questions are:

- ***RQ1***: *Do children improve word reading and spelling accuracy after instruction with PhonoBlocks on trained words, new words, and on both after a month?*
- ***RQ2***: *What are the key design factors in PhonoBlocks that benefit children in learning to read and spell?*
- ***RQ3***: *What do children like and dislike about the system?*
- ***RQ4***: *Do children's individual characteristics influence learning performance, behaviours, and/or likes/dislikes?*

We used a case study design to address these research questions for two main reasons: (1) it is critical to evaluate the system in the real life context. It is not feasible to find two "matched" groups of children at risk for dyslexia in a school context due to the variety of children's backgrounds and learning challenges; (2) understanding the relationship between children's learning performance (reading and spelling scores on pre-, post- and follow-up tests), interactional behaviours with the system, preferences and individual characteristics (e.g. attentional challenges, motivation, temperament) requires mixed data sources and detailed examination of evidence, an approach supported in case-by-case analysis. We also interviewed teachers about each child's challenges and any changes they noticed over the course of our study.

Participants

The resource teacher recruited eight children, 7-8 years old, studying at a public elementary school in an urban city in Canada to participate in our study. The teacher identified them as at risk for dyslexia. There were five boys and three girls with an average age of 7.3±0.5 years old. We assessed each child's current knowledge of English to ensure they knew letter names and basic sounds but had minimal knowledge of how to read and spell words using our six rules.

Tasks

The learning tasks were six rule-based lessons, including: Consonant-Vowel-Consonant (CVC), Consonant Blends, Consonant Digraphs, Magic-e Rule, Vowel Teams, and R-Controlled Vowels lessons (Table 1). Children learned each of the six rules in two x 20 minute individual sessions, for a total of 12 sessions. We developed the lesson plans and word lists based on previous research [4] and following suggestions of an educational psychologist and the school's resource teacher who specialize in teaching children with dyslexia. We chose these rules because they are appropriate for 7 to 8 year old children and teachers often spend hours/weeks teaching them. We also verified that the words and rules used in our study were not being taught in class during the time of our study. Children worked with the facilitator to learn three words in each session (e.g. *bet, dad, tin*, called the "trained words"), for a total of 36 trained words over 12 sessions. In addition, children practiced the rule by themselves by building three new *variation* words, (e.g. *dad-bad, tin-bin, bed-ted*).

In order to examine whether the children remembered trained words, we tested their reading and spelling accuracies on 36 trained words for reading and 12 trained words for spelling. In order to examine if they could transfer the rules to other similar words we tested 36 (new) untrained words for reading and 12 untrained words for spelling that followed the same rules in a post-test. In order to examine if children could remember the rules and apply them in other contexts we examined "maintenance" by conducting a follow-up test on trained and untrained words one month after the post-test.

Procedure

Prior to using PhonoBlocks the children received a pre-test for baseline assessment (see details under Data Collection and Analysis below). All tests were individually administered by a research facilitator in a quiet room at the school, taking 30 minutes for each child. Then each child was taken out of class three times a week to receive the 12 one-to-one training sessions facilitated by a single trained research facilitator in a quiet room at the school. The facilitator was trained by the educational psychologist and they then co-developed the teaching protocol. Each session lasted about 30 minutes, including 15 minutes of instruction with the facilitator, five minutes of the child practicing with the system, five minutes for a reading test (not reported in this paper), and five minutes for transition. During instruction, the facilitator used a teaching protocol that followed an explicit phonics-based approach to teaching the letter-sound associations [4]. The facilitator was allowed to answer the participants' questions, re-direct their attention, and provide help when the children were stuck during instruction. However, during practice time, the children had to complete the spelling tasks for new words using the system by themselves. The facilitator only provided technical support if needed (e.g. making sure a letter was clicked into its slot).

The post-tests were conducted immediately after all the sessions. Each child's word reading and spelling accuracies were assessed individually by the facilitator. The entire post-test assessment took approximately 30 minutes for each child and was conducted over two days. After the post-test, each child was individually asked a set of closed (Likert-scale) and open questions pertaining to their preferences about the system. The facilitator read the questions and wrote down the answers (since the children cannot read or write reliably). The teachers of the children were also interviewed about the challenges for each child (e.g. attentional, learning, social, emotional), other characteristics (e.g. temperament, visual-spatial skills, motivation, curiosity, competitiveness) and whether they had seen any change over the one month study. The follow-up maintenance test was conducted one month after the post-test. The procedure was similar to that of the post-test.

Data Collection and Analysis

Our mixed-methods approach involved collecting and analyzing multiple sources of data. During the pre-test, the participants were asked to read the list of 36 words they were going to learn. The words were presented on a computer screen. They were asked to spell 12 words they were going to learn on paper. The raw accuracy scores for reading and spelling were recorded (e.g. 8/36, 3/12). During the post- and maintenance tests, the participants were asked to read the same 36 (now trained) and 36 (new) untrained words presented on a computer screen and to spell 12 trained and 12 untrained words on paper. The accuracy scores were recorded. Children and teachers were asked open and closed questions after all the sessions (as above).

After the sessions children were asked to rate their preferences on a variety of questions. They were asked to rate how much they liked/disliked the system, how easy the system was to use, how much they would like to continue using the system and how much they liked the dynamic colour cues and 3D tangible letters. We used a 4-point scale suitable for young children, including *Not at all, A little, Some* and *Very much*. We assigned a value 1 (*Not at all*) to 4 (*Very much*). We also asked teachers about children's challenges (learning, attention), skills (visual-spatial), and temperament (extroverted, curious).

We also collected data about the children's interactional behaviours using video recording and structured observational note sheets. Notes were taken by the facilitator and a second researcher who operated the video camera and helped with transitions.

We used quantitative methods to address ***RQ1** (effective)*, including using correlated *t*-tests to determine the differences of the means of the raw scores[3] of reading and spelling accuracies on trained and untrained words between the pre and post, and post and follow-up tests. We conducted participant level analysis to ensure that individuals did not unduly account for affects. We used thematic analysis to address ***RQ2** (design elements)*, including identifying common and interesting patterns of interaction from the video and from observational notes. We used both quantitative and qualitative methods to address ***RQ3** (preference)*, including analyzing 4-point Likert scales questions (e.g. How much did you like using the system?) with descriptive statistics and analyzing children's responses to the open-ended questions looking for interesting and common themes. We also used both quantitative and qualitative methods to address ***RQ4** (individual characteristics)*. We first re-coded data about individual characteristics to binary (e.g. attention issues) or ordinal (e.g. introvert/mixed/extrovert to -1, 0, 1), and ran the appropriate correlational tests between children's learning gains, preferences and individual characteristics. We also supplemented these findings with observations and teacher interviews. One child (P7) was absent for a prolonged period and so we could not administer the maintenance test.

RESULTS

Reading and Spelling Accuracy

For *reading*, correlated *t*-test results showed that there was a statistically significant increase at the $p<0.01$ level in participants' raw accuracy scores on trained word reading accuracy between the pre- and post- tests, increasing from 19.4±9.6 words to 34.9±0.8 words out of 36 trained words in total ($t(7)=4.808, p=0.002, d=1.7$). The participants transferred some of their new reading knowledge to the untrained words. Results showed that there was a statistically significant increase at the $p<0.01$ level in participants' scores

[3] Raw scores = each word was scored 1 score for a correct word and 0 score for an incorrect word.

between the pre-test trained words and the post-test (new) untrained words ($t(7)$=4.335, p=0.003, d=1.5). The mean of children's scores increased from 19.4±9.6 to 33.1±1.6 words out of 36 trained/untrained words. There was a statistically significant difference at the p<0.01 level on the post-test reading improvement between the trained and untrained words ($t(7)$=4.249, p=0.004, d=1.5).

For *spelling*, results showed a statistically significant increase at the p<0.01 level in participants' scores on trained word spelling between the pre- and post-tests, increasing from 5.8±3.1 to 10.0±1.9 words out of 12 trained words ($t(7)$=4.937, p=0.002, d=1.8). The participants transferred some of their new spelling knowledge to the untrained words. Results showed a statistically significant increase at the p<0.01 level in participants' scores between the pre-test trained words and the post-test (new) untrained words ($t(7)$=3.851, p=0.006, d=1.4). The mean of raw scores increased from 5.8±3.1 to 8.9±2.0 words out of 12 trained/untrained words. Results also showed a statistically significant difference at the p<0.05 level on the post-test spelling improvement between the trained and untrained words ($t(7)$=2.826, p=0.026, d=1.0).

For *reading accuracy maintenance* results showed no statistically significant difference between participants' raw scores on trained word reading accuracy ($t(6)$=0.281, p=0.788) and on untrained word reading accuracy ($t(6)$=1.179, p=0.283) between the post- and follow-up test. Participants (without P7) maintained both trained and untrained word reading after one month. For *spelling accuracy maintenance* results showed no statistically significant difference of participants' raw scores on trained word spelling accuracy ($t(6)$<.0001, p>.99) and on untrained word reading accuracy test ($t(6)$=1.508, p=0.182) between the post-test and follow-up tests. Participants (without P7) maintained the observed effects of trained word spelling after one month.

In summary, our instruction with PhonoBlocks was effective in helping participants to learn 6 rules (from the alphabetic principle) used in reading and spelling, and took about 20 minutes per rule, which is significantly less resource intensive than approaches used by the tutors we interviewed.

Beneficial Design Features

Dynamic Colour Cues Embedded in Tangible Letters

Most participants were attracted to and engaged with the flashing dynamic colour cues. We saw this when children (1) asked questions about the meaning of the colours; (2) wanted to try out other words to see if the colours would stay or change; (3) asked about what colours would appear in new lessons; and/or (4) made comments about the colour cues after the colour change flashed. For example, when P1 first used the blend/decode function, he was very excited and asked: "Now it's all purple! Why it's all purple?" In the consonant diagraph session, P6 wanted to know what would happen if he switched the two consonant letters in the consonant digraph *sh*: "I am wondering what will happen if I switch them (*sh*) around. Is it still green?" P6 often asked how the dynamic colour cue would work in the next session: "What's the colour for the magic-e?" or made comments about it "I like purple!" "You should change this (the blended colour) to blue." "It's cool!" These verbalizations indicated that children's attention and interest was drawn to the dynamic colour cues.

The participants were able to understand or quickly learn what the dynamic colour cues represented. For example, in the r-controlled vowel lesson, when making the word *car* P8 saw that the *ar* pair changed red together. She guessed and said: "The red colour means they (the *a* and *r* letters) go together," even before the facilitator explained the meaning of the colour. She automatically focused on the red *ar* pair rather than the letter *c* (which was in white).

We also asked whether children understood what colour changes meant. For example, in the consonant blends lesson, when the facilitator asked: "How come it (*st*) was supposed to be green?" P1 answered: "They make a blended sound." In response to same question, P2 said: "Because it's supposed to be blended together." In the consonant digraphs activity, P3 and P7 said green letters meant the two letters were working together. In the magic-e activity when the facilitator asked: "What does the red mean?" P2 said: "The magic *e* makes the (vowel) letter to say its name (pointing to the vowel letter)." The facilitator said: "If I take out the letter *e*, what colour will *a* be?" P2 said: "yellow".

Some children noticed patterns of colour change without being asked by the facilitator. For the magic-e rule P1, P5, and P6 all spontaneously described the colour change when the trailing *e* was added. P5 said: "Oh, it's a pattern, blue (blue-ish-white), red, blue, red." P6 pointed at each letter and said: "…white, red, white, red.". Similarly, in the r-controlled vowel lesson, even before the facilitator explained the colour change, when P8 saw the *ar* change to red when making the word *car*, she said "The red colour means they (the *a* and *r* letters) are together." These verbalizations provide evidence that most children understood how the letter colours and sounds changed for each rule.

The colour flash is also important because it draws attention to the moment when placing a letter(s) changes a sound (s). For example, we observed that the yellow and red vowel flashes encouraged the children to notice the vowel sound changes from short to long when an *e* was added in the magic-e rule.

The participants noticed "unexpected" changes in colours and used them to detect spelling errors. In the magic-e activity, P2 misspelled the word *late* as *latb*. She noticed that the expected colour change pattern did not happen (white-red-white-red). She tried placing the same letters again, realized her mistake and changed the letter from *b* to *e*. When asked how she knew she had made a mistake, she explained: "Because it (the vowel letter) wasn't turning red." In the vowel teams lesson, when the facilitator asked P1 to make the word *heat*, P1 placed the letters *ie* and said: "They are not red." He then changed the vowel letters to the correct ones (*ea*), which turned to red.

3D Tangible Letters

The participants used the physical constraints (notch) to determine correct letter orientation. For example, many participants (P2, P3, P6, P7, and P8) looked at the bottom of the tangible letters where the notch was to determine the correct orientation of the letters. The participants also realized that the orientation mattered for some letters more than others. For example, P6 said: "The *o* can be put in this way or that way." In the CVC lesson, P4 was asked to make the word *bad*. He picked up the letter *d* and placed it onto the first slot on the platform. He then stared at the letter *d* and said to himself "Is it the other way around?" After thinking for a while, he switched the orientation but found it did not match to the opening for the notch in the slot. Eventually, he put *d* down and picked up the letter *b* and put it onto the first slot of the platform correctly.

The participants compared mirror letter shapes side-by-side to determine correct letter orientation. Several participants (P2, P6, and P8) made comparisons by physically holding the two similar tangible letters side-by-side when making the words that contained the mirrored letters *b*/*d* (Figure 2). For example, in the CVC lesson, when the facilitator asked P2 to make the word *bad*, P2 was not sure about *b*/*d*, so she held the letter *d* in her hand and compared it with the other letter *b* on the platform. After she had confirmed that the letter in her hand was *d*, she placed it onto the platform. The 3D tangible letter forms enable children to easily compare mirrored letter shapes by seeing, touching or even tracing these letters. Comparing and rotating physical letters is a form of complementary action which may simplify the task by shifting a mental task to a visual-physical task (i.e., cognitive offloading) [1]. This strategy may explain why many participants' spelling accuracy on words with *b*/*d* letters on paper were worse in the post- and follow-up tests compared to that during practice with the system. Practicing spelling with 3D tangible letters enables strategies that simplify determining the correct orientation of mirrored letters. This may help a child attend to the rules of spelling rather than focusing on writing a letter in the correct orientation.

Figure 2. P2, P6, and P8 compared *b* and *d* letters.

Many participants developed spatial organization strategies to simplify spelling tasks. Children used space to organize the physical letters in three ways. First, some participants (P1, P4, P5, P6) placed the tangible letters in a line, which appeared to help them visually and physically find certain letters. P1, P4, and P5 often lined them up in alphabetic order so they could quickly find the letters they needed.

Second, several participants (P4, P5, P8) picked up tangible letters they were going to use later and held all of them or placed them aside in a group (Figure 3). For example, when making the word *trip*, P5 first picked up all four letters, held them in his hands, and then placed them one by one onto the platform. When building the word *bet*, P8 first selected all the letters she needed to use, placed them in front of her, and then put them onto the platform. Similarly, P4 and P8 often picked up letters and placed them on the desk first. P5 often held letters in her hands before placement.

Third, P8 developed strategies to manage the letters differently for each learning activity. In the CVC activity, she placed all the vowel letters to one side. In the vowel teams activity, she placed all the vowel letters on the right side and all the consonant letters on the left side. In the r-controlled vowel lesson she changed her strategy and put all the vowel letters *a*, *u* and *o* together followed by the letter *r* (Figure 4). Our design enabled children to organize tangible letters on the desk space to make their tasks easier to solve later (called epistemic actions [1]).

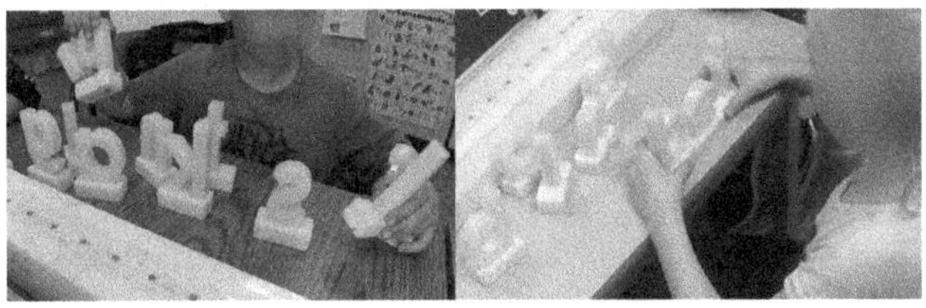

Figure 3. P5 held the letters in *flop* in his hands (*left*); P8 placed the letters for *bet* grouped in front of her (*right*).

Figure 4. Vowel teams rule: vowel letters on the right side and consonant letters on the left side (*top*); r-controlled vowel rule: all the vowel letters together with followed by *r* letter (*bottom*).

Participants' hand actions mirrored their understanding of how letters make sounds. We noticed that some participants placed letters one by one when they were learning a rule, but then later placed pairs of letters with two hands (e.g. for blends) once they understood the rule. Most participants (P2, P4, P5, P6, and P8) switched from this kind of one- to two-handed interaction as they learned rules. For example, when P4 was asked to make the word *chin*, he first placed the letter *h* in the second slot, thought for a while, and then placed the letter *t* in the first slot (*th* not *ch*). This suggested that he was confused about the *ch* and the *th* sounds and used a single hand to place each letter of the consonant digraph. However, when he made the *sh* pair in the word *shop*, he picked up the letters *s* and *h* simultaneously using two hands, showing his understanding of their blended sound. We noticed this pattern frequently with P2, P4, P5, P6 and P8 when they were making words that contained consonant blends, consonant digraphs, vowel teams, and r-controlled vowel pairs.

We also noticed that the participants (P4, P5, and P8) sometimes crossed their hands to place the tangible letter pairs when they were extremely sure about their answers (Figure 5). For example, P4's verbalizations show that he quickly remembered the *sh* pair. For example, P4 said, "I can memorize the word *shop,* I need *s* and *h.*"). In this case, since the letters were on the desk in reverse order, P4 picked them up by crossing his arms-hands to put the letters into the correct order to make *sh* in the word *shot.* P5 did the same thing to make the *ea* pair for the word *beat.* P8 also used this crossed action when making the *oa* pair for the word *coat.* It seems that as children become more certain of the rules, they take a shortcut, moving letters into the correct order as they move them through the air into place, rather than organizing them first on the desk space and then moving them in slots.

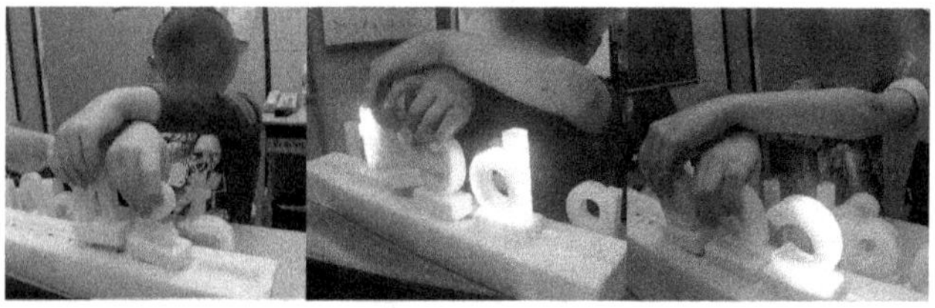

Figure 5. Shortcut: Ordering letters in the air on route to placing them: consonant digraph (*sh*) & vowel teams (*ea*, *oa*).

Other Important Design Features

The pictures associated with words aroused the participants' interest in learning with the system and may have promoted associative learning. The video and observational data showed that the participants always checked the picture for each word. They smiled or made comments about the pictures. For example, P8 smiled when she saw the picture of the word *pup* and said: "It's so cute!" The pictures also allowed the participants to associate different but related words with the one depicted in the picture. For example, When P1 saw the picture of the word *jar*, he said: "It's jelly jar! Delicious!" "Both the words *jelly* and *jar* start with the same letter *j.*"

The participants enjoyed playing on their own in practice mode. For example, during the instruction, P1 always asked "Can I do the challenges (practice mode) now?" P6: "When can I play the game?" Our video data also showed that the participants were excited to hear the rewarding sounds and pictures when successfully completing the tasks. P1 showed the victory gesture and said "Yeah!" when he correctly completed the spelling tasks. P3, P6, and P8 smiled when they heard the rewarding sounds.

Many participants (P1, P3, P4, P5, P7, and P8) often used the word history list. The word history list contained all the words children had made. They could touch a word to trigger its sound or visually compare common patterns between the words. For example, when making the new vowel team words (*beat* and *load*), P4 and P5 checked the words they already had in the word history list (*eat, boat*) and compared the common vowel team patterns.

The blend/decode function was frequently used during the instruction and practice parts of sessions. We observed that all the participants clicked the button to listen to the individual letter sounds (letters are coloured based on their sounds) and the blended word sound (when letters are coloured all purple). When the letters were all purple in the blending mode the children tended to focus on the whole word by sounding out the whole word. However, when the letters were in various colours in the decoding mode, the children tended to focus on the different coloured parts by sounding out the individual phonemes. We observed that P1, P3, P4, P6, P7, and P8 often used this function after they created a word - they listened to the blended sound of the whole word when the colours changed to purple. They then clicked the button again to hear the individual letter sounds and to see the colours change back. After instruction in the tutor mode, most of the participants practiced the blend/decode function on their own. We could see them attend to the whole word and individual letter sounds when using this function. Some participants (P2, P4, P7, and P8) also used this function to check if they had spelled a word correctly before submitting it. When P2, P7, and P8 expressed doubt about their spelling they often clicked the button to check the individual sounds before submitting their answers to the system.

Children's Preferences

The results of the preference ratings (1-4 scale) showed that most participants really liked the system (mean=3.8±0.7), thought the system was easy to use (mean=3.8±0.5) and said they would like to continue using the system (mean=2.9±1.4). We interpret this cautiously due to the novelty effect and researcher-child power difference. We asked children who said they did not want to continue for their reasons. P8 said she did not want to miss gym time. P1 did not give a reason. However, we observed that he often looked engaged in the class he was in at session time, and was often resistant to leaving that class. We infer that sometimes when children were taken out of classes they enjoyed it reduced their motivation to use our system, which in turn may have impacted learning, but could be overcome when our system is used in a normal (non-research study) classroom context.

The participants were also asked how much they liked the dynamic colour cue feature. The results showed that all participants really liked this feature (mean=4.0±0.0). This was also consistent with our observations. Participants showed interest and curiosity through the questions they asked (reported above). When asked how much they liked the 3D tangible letters, results showed that most participants really liked them (mean=3.8±0.5). We also observed that most children held, played with, and manipulated the 3D tangible letters for most of the session time. P1 even said, "I got more babies today!" when new letters were added.

How Individual Characteristics Affect Learning Gains

Attentional Challenges

The teachers reported that P1, P4, and P8 had attentional challenges during learning. Based on the teachers' feedback, we assigned 1 (Yes) and -1 (No) to represent whether a participant had attentional deficits. The results of a point-biserial correlation test showed a significant correlation at the level $p<0.05$ between the participants' attentional challenges and their learning gains ((post-test score – pre-test score)/(full score-pre-test score) [19]) on trained word reading (r_{pb} (6)=0.730, p=0.040), with the participants who had no attentional challenges achieving more learning gains on trained words reading (1.0±0.2 versus 0.9±0.3).

Of the children with attentional challenges, we found that P1's gains on reading and spelling were larger than those of P4 and P8. We suggest that this is because P1 was distracted by features of system related to the task at hand (the pictures) but the others were distracted by letters not in use for the task (not related to the task at hand). Based on our observations, P4 and P8 frequently played with the 3D tangible letters while the facilitator taught them the rules. This may have reduced the amount of attention they could devote to listening and learning. However, P1 was distracted in ways that were more related to the task and so it was easy to redirect him. For example, P1 often made associations based on the current word or picture. When he saw the picture for the word *bait*, he left the seat and pretended to swim like a fish. He also closed his eyes and tried to look for letters through feeling and touching. "Where is the letter *i*?" Enacting scenarios including learned words may have been distracting or it seems possible that it may improve learning through association of multiple representations of words, which is in line with O-G practices.

Motivation

Based on the teachers' feedback and our observation, we assigned 1 (Yes) and -1 (No) to represent whether a participant had great motivation in learning or exploring new things. The results of a point-biserial correlation test showed that there was a significant correlation at the level $p<0.01$ between the motivation and the learning gains on trained word spelling (r_{pb} (6) =0.887, p=0.003), with the participants who had greater motivation achieving more personal learning gains on trained words spelling (0.8±0.1 versus 0.4±0.1).

The teachers reported that P2 and P8 had little motivation for exploring new things in general. This was consistent with the results from the questionnaire that showed P2 and P8 had less motivation compared to others (e.g. P2 chose "some" and P8 chose "not at all" when asked if they would like to continue using the system). We also noticed that P5 was interested at the beginning of a session but he lost his motivation during the middle stage when he knew that he had to receive a reading test and he could not play with the system as he wanted (e.g. building the words he liked). Lower motivation may be related to inattention and is related to lower learning gains. Our observations showed that unmotivated children had trouble maintaining focus for the duration of a session.

How Individual Characteristics Affect Preferences

Temperament

The results of a Spearman's ranking-order correlation test showed a strong correlation at the level $p<0.05$ between children's temperament (extrovert/mixed/introvert) and their preference on 3D tangible letters. The participants who were more extroverted liked 3D tangible letters more (r_s (6) =0.800, p=0.017). We also noticed that more extroverted children liked to ask questions related to the 3D tangible letters more. For example, P5: "Is there any lights inside the letters?" P6: "How does the letter connect to the computer?" The results of the questionnaire also showed that the children who were extroverted liked the 3D tangible letters more than the children who were introverted.

DISCUSSION

Our results suggest that scripted instruction with PhonoBlocks was effective in supporting the children at risk for dyslexia in learning to read and spell six common rules. Based on our findings we suggest four design recommendations for TUI systems designed to teach the alphabetic principle. We suggest that our recommendations will also benefit typical children because all children follow the same learning process, although dyslexic children have greater challenges hearing sounds and attending to how letter position changes sounds. Another group who may benefit are children who learn English as a second/foreign language (ESL/EFL) (e.g. Chinese) because they often have poor PA and limited knowledge of the alphabetic principle. [5,31].

1 Use dynamic colour cues embedded in tangible letters to draw attention to letter-sound correspondences

Using dynamic colour cues embedded in tangible letters, which flash to draw attention to the moment when letters' sounds change, appears more effective than using static letter colours, as seen in other reading acquisition systems (e.g. [4,14]). Our results showed that flashing a colour within a letter(s) helped children notice that something had happened. They either immediately understood the meaning, asked about it, or expressed understanding when it was explained. Some changes were easier to understand (e.g. adding *e* in magic-e rule) than others (blends). When expected colour changes did not happen, children used this information to correct their spelling errors during their practice sessions.

Many reading systems use different colours for each letter, or for vowels and consonants (e.g. Tiggly and Osmo). In our approach we use only a small number of colours to highlight parts of words (groups of letters), which helps draw attention to the letters that are important in each rule. Specifically, we use the colours to represent key elements of the rules and use white to represent the other parts of the word. We use flashing colours to highlight the moment of change. This design approach helps the children to focus on the part of the word relevant to the rules rather than on the whole word or on individual letters.

2 Create 3D tangible letters forms and workspace to enable epistemic actions, which simplify spelling and reading tasks
Epistemic actions are actions used to change external elements in the world in order to simplify a task [1]. Previous research has suggested that TUIs may encourage more epistemic actions compared to similar GUIs [1]. Our results showed that the 3D tangible letters enabled several types of epistemic actions. In order to support children's epistemic actions in learning to read and spell, the following design elements of 3D tangible letters need to be considered: (1) they should be an appropriate size and crafted with robust and safe (e.g. no wires) materials so that children can easily pick up or hold groups of them with their hands. The appropriate size here also means that there is enough space on the table to place all the letters with room to group and sort them; (2) letters should be able to stand up on their own so children can easily organize them in space; and (3) they should have both physical constraints (e.g. on the bottom) and visible marks (e.g. on top) that enable children to quickly recognize each letter and orient it correctly in space (e.g. *d*, *b*, *p*, *q*).

3 Use 3D forms and tasks that enable hands-on interaction, which improves attention and makes learning visible
The stand-alone letters should also be light, pleasant to touch, and easy to move, organize and handle. Providing a small subset of letters for each learning task and encouraging both tutor and child to handle them (e.g. place in slots) helps focus attention to the letters. This is consistent with the previous theories that showed the use of kinaesthetic/tactile modalities could improve learners' attention and memory [10,20]. If letters are light and robust, letters not in use can easily be moved away with an arm swipe. If letters are easy to handle, children can use single and two-handed interactions, which reflects their understanding of letter-sound structures and enables a facilitator to see learning happening in real time, and provide appropriate feedback.

4. Provide blend/decode function to enable children to learn how individual letters combine into blended sounds in words
The blend/decode function enabled children to construct whole words by hearing whole word sounds (swipe right) and then deconstructing words into individual letter colours and their sounds (swipe left). This function can help children practice their PA and decoding skills by seeing and hearing the changing letter colours and corresponding sounds.

LIMITATIONS

The main limitation of our study is the small sample size. Although we examined the participants' reading and spelling gains, due to the limited number of participants and the nature of a case study (without a control group), we cannot make a strong claim about the effectiveness of our system. However, our quantitative results are encouraging. In terms of design, our qualitative analysis of video and observational data enabled us to provide evidence for key design features that enabled behaviours we know contribute to, or are correlated with, learning. Based on our mixed-methods results we suggest generalizable guidance about specific design features which may be useful for others to explore and evaluate. In the future a more wide-scale controlled experiment would enable us to make stronger claims about the effectiveness of our entire system. In addition, a study that separates the effects of different elements of tangibility would contribute to design knowledge about why and how tangibility matters. Both are needed.

CONCLUSION

We present the design and evaluation of a tangible reading system for children at risk for dyslexia. Our system is the first to leverage tangible features of embedded dynamic colour cues in hands-on 3D tangible letters, alongside features shown to be important in other reading systems (e.g. linked representations, blend/decode function). Our system focuses on at-risk readers who are challenged to master PA and the alphabetic principle. The results of our case study showed that all eight children achieved significant gains in reading and spelling on trained and untrained words after instruction with our system and they maintained learning one month later. These results combined with our qualitative analysis of the ways the children interacted with the system suggest that the core design features of TUIs positively impacted learning. In addition, we discovered that children's individual characteristics influenced their learning gain and preferences. Based on our results we proposed four recommendations.

Our work suggests that tangibility matters because reading is, in part, spatial. Letters can be represented as objects that have spatial-visual properties. Words are linear sequences of letters. The position of letters in the words dictates the sounds in the words. Tangible letters make it easy for children to position the letters and hear associated sound changes. Because computation can be embedded in these tangible letters they can also change their colour in response to their position in the word, drawing a child's attention to the moment where one letter changes the sound of the rest of the word. Tangibility also matters because the physicality of tangible letters means children can use epistemic strategies, such as pairing and ordering, to make the task of spelling words easier than if they were printing words on paper. The act of spelling is separated from the act of printing. Taken together, embeddedness and physicality mean that children's letter manipulation, attentional focus and use of epidemic strategies makes the task of learning basic spelling rules easier. Over time children will learn and memorize these foundational spelling rules and the tangible system will no longer be necessary. Our work contributes to design recommendations which are applicable to the design of reading TUIs for typical, dyslexic, and ESL/EFL children.

ACKNOWLEDGMENTS

We should like to thank our funders: SSHRC and CSC, the tutors at the Kenneth Gordon Maplewood School, and teachers and children at Montecito Elementary School.

REFERENCES

1. Alissa N. Antle. 2013. Exploring how children use their hands to think: An embodied interactional analysis. *Behaviour & Information Technology* 32, 9: 938–954.
2. Alissa N. Antle. 2013. Research opportunities: Embodied child–computer interaction. *International Journal of Child-Computer Interaction* 1, 1: 30–36. https://doi.org/10.1016/j.ijcci.2012.08.001
3. Florence Bara, Edouard Gentaz, and Pascale Colé. 2007. Haptics in learning to read with children from low socio-economic status families. *British Journal of Developmental Psychology* 25, 4: 643–663. https://doi.org/10.1348/026151007X186643
4. Virginia W. Berninger, Robert D. Abbott, Dori Zook, Stacy Ogier, Zenia Lemos-Britton, and Rebecca Brooksher. 1999. Early Intervention for Reading Disabilities Teaching the Alphabet Principle in a Connectionist Framework. *Journal of Learning Disabilities* 32, 6: 491–503. https://doi.org/10.1177/002221949903200604
5. Pauline Daphne Bunce. 2007. Alphabet headaches Hong Kong's English literacy challenge. Retrieved January 29, 2016 from http://espace.cdu.edu.au/view/cdu:6542
6. Stanislas Dehaene. 2009. *Reading in the Brain: The New Science of How We Read.* Penguin.
7. Amnon Dekel, Galit Yavne, Ela Ben-Tov, and Yulia Roschak. 2007. The Spelling Bee: An Augmented Physical Block System That Knows How to Spell. In *Proceedings of the International Conference on Advances in Computer Entertainment Technology* (ACE '07), 212–215. https://doi.org/10.1145/1255047.1255092
8. Linnea C. Ehri. 2014. Orthographic Mapping in the Acquisition of Sight Word Reading, Spelling Memory, and Vocabulary Learning. *Scientific Studies of Reading* 18, 1: 5–21. https://doi.org/10.1080/10888438.2013.819356
9. Min Fan, Alissa N. Antle, and Emily S. Cramer. 2016. Design Rationale: Opportunities and Recommendations for Tangible Reading Systems for Children. In *Proceedings of the The 15th International Conference on Interaction Design and Children* (IDC '16), 101–112. https://doi.org/10.1145/2930674.2930690
10. Arthur M. Glenberg, Megan Brown, and Joel R. Levin. 2007. Enhancing comprehension in small reading groups using a manipulation strategy. *Contemporary Educational Psychology* 32, 3: 389–399. https://doi.org/10.1016/j.cedpsych.2006.03.001
11. Wooi Boon Goh, L. L. Chamara Kasun, Fitriani, Jacquelyn Tan, and Wei Shou. 2012. The i-Cube: Design Considerations for Block-based Digital Manipulatives and Their Applications. In *Proceedings of the Designing Interactive Systems Conference* (DIS '12), 398–407. https://doi.org/10.1145/2317956.2318016
12. Bart Hengeveld, Caroline Hummels, Hans van Balkom, Riny Voort, and Jan de Moor. 2013. Wrapping Up LinguaBytes, for Now. In *Proceedings of the 7th International Conference on Tangible, Embedded and Embodied Interaction* (TEI '13), 237–244. https://doi.org/10.1145/2460625.2460664
13. Bart Hengeveld. 2011. Designing LinguaBytes: A tangible learning system for non-or-hardly speaking toddlers. Thesis. Retrieved December 31, 2016 from http://repository.tue.nl/715535. https://doi.org/10.1145/1226969.1227002
14. Sara J. Hines. 2009. The Effectiveness of a Color-Coded, Onset-Rime Decoding Intervention with First-Grade Students at Serious Risk for Reading Disabilities. *Learning Disabilities Research & Practice* 24, 1: 21–32. https://doi.org/10.1111/j.1540-5826.2008.01274.x
15. Kathleen Kelly and Sylvia Phillips. 2011. *Teaching Literacy to Learners with Dyslexia: A Multi-sensory Approach.* SAGE.
16. Jonathan Kleiman, Michael Pope, and Paulo Blikstein. 2013. RoyoBlocks: An Exploration in Tangible Literacy Learning. In *Proceedings of the 12th International Conference on Interaction Design and Children* (IDC '13), 543–546. https://doi.org/10.1145/2485760.2485861
17. Ricardo Baeza-Yates Luz Rello. 2013. Frequent Words Improve Readability and Short Words Improve Understandability for People with Dyslexia. https://doi.org/10.1007/978-3-642-40498-6_15
18. Diane McGuinness, Carmen McGuinness, and John Donohue. 1995. Phonological training and the alphabet principle: Evidence for reciprocal causality. *Reading Research Quarterly*: 830–852.
19. Allen Menlo and M. C. Johnson. 1969. Percentage Gain: An Alternative Approach to the Measurement of Change. Retrieved August 22, 2016 from http://eric.ed.gov/?id=ED021259
20. James Minogue and M. Gail Jones. 2006. Haptics in Education: Exploring an Untapped Sensory Modality. *Review of Educational Research* 76, 3: 317–348. https://doi.org/10.3102/00346543076003317
21. D. Mioduser, H. Tur-Kaspa, and I. Leitner. 2000. The learning value of computer-based instruction of early reading skills. *Journal of Computer Assisted Learning* 16, 1: 54–63. https://doi.org/10.1046/j.1365-2729.2000.00115.x
22. Roderick Nicolson, Angela Fawcett, and Margaret Nicolson. 2000. Evaluation of a computer-based reading intervention in infant and junior schools. *Journal of Research in Reading* 23, 2: 194–209. https://doi.org/10.1111/1467-9817.00114
23. Sumit Pandey and Swati Srivastava. 2011. SpellBound: A Tangible Spelling Aid for the Dyslexic Child. In *Proceedings of the 3rd International*

Conference on Human Computer Interaction (IndiaHCI '11), 101–104. https://doi.org/10.1145/2407796.2407813

24. Sumit Pandey and Swati Srivastava. 2011. Tiblo: A Tangible Learning Aid for Children with Dyslexia. In *Proceedings of the Second Conference on Creativity and Innovation in Design* (DESIRE '11), 211–220. https://doi.org/10.1145/2079216.2079247
25. Franck Ramus. 2004. Neurobiology of dyslexia: a reinterpretation of the data. *Trends in Neurosciences* 27, 12: 720–726. https://doi.org/10.1016/j.tins.2004.10.004
26. Gavin Reid. 2013. *Dyslexia: A Practitioner's Handbook*. John Wiley & Sons.
27. Kristen D. Ritchey and Jennifer L. Goeke. 2006. Orton-Gillingham and Orton-Gillingham-Based Reading Instruction: A Review of the Literature. *The Journal of Special Education* 40, 3: 171–183. https://doi.org/10.1177/00224669060400030501
28. Margaret J. Snowling and Joy Stackhouse. 2013. *Dyslexia, Speech and Language: A Practitioner's Handbook*. John Wiley & Sons.
29. Ja-Young Sung, A. Levisohn, Ji-won Song, B. Tomassetti, and A. Mazalek. 2007. Shadow Box: an interactive learning toy for children. In *The First IEEE International Workshop on Digital Game and Intelligent Toy Enhanced Learning, 2007. DIGITEL '07*, 206–208. https://doi.org/10.1109/DIGITEL.2007.43
30. Frank R. Vellutino, Jack M. Fletcher, Margaret J. Snowling, and Donna M. Scanlon. 2004. Specific reading disability (dyslexia): what have we learned in the past four decades? *Journal of Child Psychology and Psychiatry* 45, 1: 2–40. https://doi.org/10.1046/j.0021-9630.2003.00305.x
31. Min Wang, Keiko Koda, and Charles A. Perfetti. 2003. Alphabetic and nonalphabetic L1 effects in English word identification: Lexical and visual-orthographic processes. Retrieved March 20, 2016 from http://philpapers.org.proxy.lib.sfu.ca/rec/WANAAN-3

WeBuild: Automatically Distributing Assembly Tasks Among Collocated Workers to Improve Coordination

C. Ailie Fraser[1,2], Tovi Grossman[1], George Fitzmaurice[1]
[1]Autodesk Research
{tovi.grossman, george.fitzmaurice}@autodesk.com
[2]Design Lab, UC San Diego
cafraser@cs.ucsd.edu

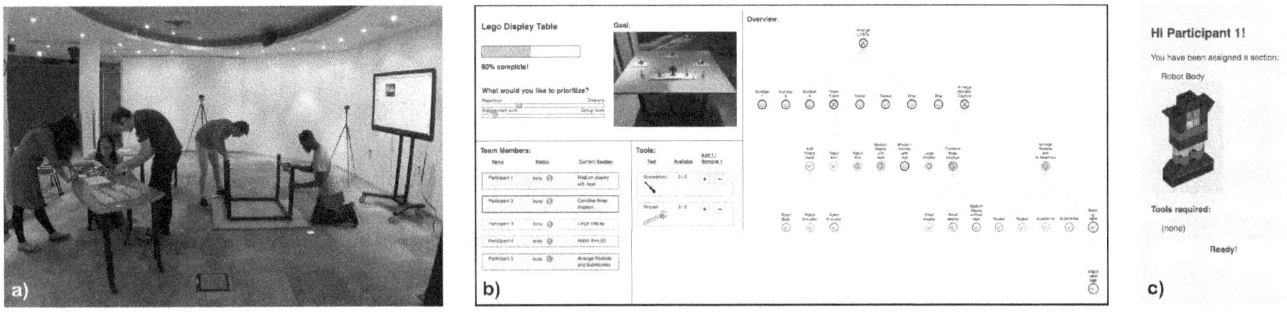

Figure 1: WeBuild helps collocated groups coordinate tasks. a) A group completes our study task with the help of WeBuild. b) A shared dashboard display provides a task overview. c) Each user views personalized step-by-step instructions on a mobile phone.

ABSTRACT
Physical construction and assembly tasks are often carried out by groups of collocated workers, and they can be difficult to coordinate. Group members must spend time deciding how to split up the task, how to assign subtasks to each other, and in what order subtasks should be completed. Informed by an observational study examining group coordination challenges, we built a task distribution system called WeBuild. Our custom algorithm dynamically assigns subtasks to workers in a group, taking into account factors such as the dependencies between subtasks and the skills of each group member. Each worker views personalized step-by-step instructions on a mobile phone, while a dashboard visualizes the entire process. An initial study found that WeBuild reduced the start-up time needed to coordinate and begin a task, and provides direction for future research to build on toward improving group efficiency and coordination for complex tasks.

Author Keywords
Task distribution; collaboration; coordination; assembly instructions

ACM Classification Keywords
H.5.3. Information interfaces and presentation (e.g., HCI): Group and Organization Interfaces.

CHI 2017, May 06-11, 2017, Denver, CO, USA
© 2017 ACM. ISBN 978-1-4503-4655-9/17/05...$15.00
DOI: http://dx.doi.org/10.1145/3025453.3026036

INTRODUCTION
Physical building tasks, such as building construction, furniture assembly, and toy kit construction, are often carried out by groups of collocated workers. With the exception of professional settings that involve a dedicated manager, the coordination amongst workers can be a challenge. The workers must spend time dividing and assigning tasks, locating and sharing tools, and figuring out how to execute instructions. As a result, the time spent actually completing the task may only be a fraction of the total time taken [44].

Traditional assembly instructions rarely indicate how multiple workers should collaborate (Figure 2a, b) or how the task can be efficiently subdivided (Figure 2c). While aids for physical assembly have been studied, they are often developed for a single user scenario (e.g. [5, 17, 18, 34, 38, 43, 45]). Multiple users have been considered, but typically with an expert providing remote assistance (e.g. [21, 23, 25, 33, 36]). With the exception of recent Crowdsourced Fabrication research [26], little work has looked at how to provide dynamic assistance to a team of collocated workers.

Our work aims to bring the known benefits of task management systems [27, 29, 39] and interactive instructions [1, 5, 17, 24] to the scenario of collocated group construction and assembly. We introduce WeBuild, a system that automatically distributes subtasks among workers, taking into account the workers' skills, the dependencies between subtasks, and the availability of tools, with the goal of improving group efficiency and coordination (Figure 1). WeBuild continuously adapts to the progress of the group to ensure an efficient distribution of tasks. An initial study found that WeBuild reduced the start-up time to coordinate and begin a task by 88%, and though further formal validation is needed, our findings suggest that such a system can improve group efficiency and satisfaction.

Figure 2: Instructions from an IKEA cabinet [46] (a) and a JYSK shelf [47] (b) both show a 2-person requirement at the beginning, but do not show where or how the second person should help. c) Instructions for a microwave [48] show a second person helping for one step but no indication as to what this additional person should do for the rest of the task.

The main contribution of our work is the design and implementation of WeBuild. We also contribute a back-end model for representing and subdividing physical task instructions, and an adaptive on-the-fly algorithm for distributing subtasks among workers. Finally we contribute observations and insights gathered from two studies, the first being an observational study of group coordination challenges, and the second being a preliminary evaluation of WeBuild as compared to a baseline condition of paper instructions. Our studies and implementations look at smaller-scale static tasks, such as toy building and furniture assembly, so we conclude by discussing how WeBuild could generalize to larger scales and more dynamically changing tasks, such as architectural construction and disaster relief.

RELATED WORK

Our work has been guided and inspired by previous research in the domains of physical task assistance, collaborative task aids, and automatic task distribution.

Real-time Assistance for Physical Tasks

Static instructions such as online tutorials and paper manuals are a popular resource for physical tasks. However, the burden is on the user to keep track of their progress and evaluate whether they are following the instructions correctly. Dynamic, context-sensitive assistance has been shown to help with these challenges by detecting user progress and stepping through instructions accordingly, and providing real-time feedback to ensure that users complete each step correctly [5, 17, 34, 43].

Researchers have explored several different modalities for displaying such real-time assistance for physical tasks. Wearable hands-free displays such as smartwatches have been found to be promising for providing short, relevant instructions [1, 26, 45]. Augmented reality, provided through projections or head-mounted displays, can further help to guide users through complex tasks [17, 18, 38, 43]. Alternatively, Knibbe et al. used a tabletop display to provide contextually relevant instructions for DIY tasks [24]. Our work similarly leverages both mobile devices and large displays, but adapts these concepts to a multi-user scenario.

In terms of what type of task to use for evaluating such assistive systems, Funk et al. proposed standardized benchmark tasks in two high-level categories: "pick-and-place" (e.g. LEGO) and "industrial assembly" (e.g. using screws and nails) [13]. The task used in our study is heavily based on these benchmarks but is designed specifically for a group of workers. Like Funk et al. [13, 14], we include our full task instructions as supplementary material to similarly serve as a potential benchmarking task or inspiration for future group assembly work.

Collaborative Task Aids

Most research examining collaboration on physical tasks has focused on improving *remote* collaboration, often between a worker and a remote expert [21, 23, 25, 33, 36]. For example, a remote helper's presence can be improved by displaying their hand gestures in 3D [36] or 2D video [23, 33], and hands-free technology can help users communicate while actively working on the task [21]. Our work focuses instead on *collocated* collaboration within a group of users, none of whom may be an expert at the task.

There are few examples of aids for collocated collaborative physical tasks. TurkDeck projects instructions onto the environment for a group of people arranging props in a haptic virtual reality scene [10]. Lafreniere et al.'s work on Crowdsourced Fabrication [26] advanced this to more complex tasks, where a crowd of workers assembled a large pavilion structure with dynamic assistance via smartwatches. However, the system had each worker complete the exact same task independently. This was done approximately two hundred times, with little required coordination or collaboration. Our system considers tasks comprising many different subtasks, each of which may involve different tools and require different numbers of people.

Collocated group collaboration has also been studied for other types of tasks such as brainstorming [11], decision-making [6], problem solving [9, 20, 37, 41], and software development [7]. While the main need of remote teams tends to be improved communication [7], collocated teams have been shown to mainly have need for improved task structuring and scheduling [8, 11], documentation of progress [7], and awareness of others' progress and overall task status [9, 32, 41]. Our work, informed by these findings, mainly focuses on task coordination and structuring, by automating the distribution and management of subtasks.

Task Distribution

The general problem of task distribution is found in many different domains, and it involves balancing a set of defined constraints, dependencies, and goals, the specifics of which depend on the domain at hand.

For example, with resource scheduling in operating systems, fair allocation is an important goal, and so randomized algorithms have been shown to work well [40]. For software development and release planning, there are often many different potentially conflicting criteria to optimize, such as the various stakeholders' opinions [16]. Greer & Ruhe [16] presented a flexible algorithm that re-calculates the optimal plan after each increment is complete, thus adapting smoothly to changing circumstances.

Theoretically, this problem is known as the "resource-constrained project scheduling problem", and has been widely researched (e.g. [4, 31]). For example, Artigues showed that this problem can be framed as a combinatorial optimization problem [4]. Our work differs slightly in that we do not know the execution times of each subtask beforehand, but our formalization of the task model is similar.

In the industrial domain, physical assembly tasks are often carried out by groups of robot workers. A large body of work has focused on algorithms to optimally allocate tasks (e.g. [15, 35, 39]). Human workers tend to be less predictable, so these algorithms do not translate directly, though our own task model and algorithm were inspired by those used in the robotic task planning literature.

In summary, despite the extensive research on aids for physical assembly tasks, little work has been done to understand and aid in the challenges associated with coordinating a group of collocated workers for completing such tasks.

OBSERVATIONAL STUDY

To improve our understanding of the current challenges groups face and the strategies they use when collaborating on physical tasks, we conducted an exploratory observational study. To avoid constraining our findings and design goals to one specific task, we used two different tasks: two groups built a Meccano Tower Bridge set [49], and two groups built an IKEA cabinet [50].

Participants

We recruited 16 participants from our organization (4 female, ages 18 - 54) and split them into groups of four. All participants had at least some experience working with hand tools (mean 3.75/5, *SD* 0.86, where 1 = never used, and 5 = use all the time). Participants had limited experience working with IKEA and Meccano specifically: IKEA participants' mean experience was 2.63/5 (*SD* 0.74), and Meccano participants' mean was 1.25/5 (*SD* 0.46). In each group, some participants knew each other well, while others had never met.

Procedure

Each group was given four copies of the instruction booklets for their task. All of the required tools were provided, with enough tools for four people to work simultaneously on any individual step if they chose to do so. The IKEA task required screwdrivers and a hammer, and the Meccano task required a small wrench and a screwdriver.

Groups were told to accomplish as much of the task as they could within one hour. An experimenter took notes and observed group dynamics. After the session, each participant completed a questionnaire reflecting on how the session went and how they felt it could have been improved, as well as providing demographic information and details about their prior building experience. Observations and participant responses were analyzed to highlight recurrent themes and behaviours.

Observations

Task Distribution

All groups spent several minutes of initial "start-up time" figuring out how the different components of the task fit together and deciding how to split up the task. In both Meccano groups, each person worked on one of the four main towers. Both IKEA groups initially divided into two pairs, one building the cabinet body, and one building the four drawers (Figure 3). Once these main IKEA components were finished, additional time was spent figuring out which of the remaining components to do next. The distribution of the remaining subtasks varied between the two groups, as the optimal order to complete them in was not obvious.

Task distribution and collaboration strategies also varied between pairs. For those working on the IKEA drawers, one pair opted to build each drawer together one at a time, while the other opted to build the first drawer together, and the next two in parallel. The former group was more successful, as in the latter group, one participant worked ahead on their drawer while the other got stuck on an earlier step. Some time was lost before the first participant noticed and helped the second.

In the IKEA task, a few steps required two people to work together (e.g. lifting and positioning the large cabinet walls). However, we noticed that having two people work on a single-person subtask was often advantageous. For example, participants building the cabinet body would simultaneously screw in screws on opposite sides of the cabinet, eliminating the need for one participant to move around to both sides after completing each step.

Figure 3: A group in our observational study split into pairs to build the IKEA cabinet.

In general, once a person had completed a step or subtask once, they were able to do it again faster and more easily. Sometimes the group would recognize this and delegate a subtask to someone who had done it already. Several participants mentioned afterward that an "assembly line" setup might have been more efficient, as each group member could become a "specialist" at certain subtasks. However, figuring out how to distribute the tasks in this way would have taken longer as it would require a deeper understanding of the required subtasks from the onset.

Communication

Overall, communication was strong within pairs but weaker across the group. Participants working on the same subtask communicated frequently, asking each other questions, helping each other complete tricky steps, and gathering tools and parts for each other. There was less communication across the entire group, and several participants mentioned afterward that they wished they had been more aware of the status of the other pair on their team. This could potentially have helped with the challenge of task distribution, as not knowing what stage the other pair was at made it more difficult to decide what subtask to do next.

Prior Experience

Some participants seemed to be naturally suited for certain types of tasks. In some cases, this was due to prior experience (e.g. knowing how IKEA locking screws work). However, in other cases users exhibited inherent skills. One participant with smaller hands was better at a particularly finicky Meccano step. Another participant with no prior IKEA experience was better at assembling drawers than other participants who had some experience, which could be due to exceptional problem-solving or spatial reasoning skills.

DESIGN GOALS

Our observational study validated our belief that coordinating physical tasks in a group can be challenging and thus an automatic task distribution system would be useful. Based on our observations, and guided by our review of the literature, we derived a set of design goals for an intelligent task distribution system.

D1. Continuously Adapt to the Situation and Workers

While task allocation systems for robot workers can generate optimal distribution plans before the task has begun [39], a system for human workers must account for the unpredictability and individual differences of humans. It should therefore continuously adapt to the group's progress rather than determine a global schedule. For example, if one worker is faster at a certain subtask, the system should assign future similar subtasks to that worker. The system should also account for users' prior experience [27].

D2. Provide a Task Overview and Promote Awareness

Several participants mentioned a desire for more knowledge of the overall context of their current subtask, as well as more awareness of other group members' progress. This need for task and group awareness has also been well documented in the literature [8, 9, 41].

D3. Display Step-by-Step Instructions to Each Worker

As the literature on software tutorials (e.g. [12]) and physical task assistance (e.g. [24, 26]) has shown, it is beneficial for participants to see instructions one step at a time, to help them stay on track and know what is next without having to hunt through an instruction booklet.

D4. Support Adaptive Teamwork

Participants in our study frequently grouped into pairs, as having someone to talk to and compare work with was often helpful. An intelligent task distribution system should therefore support dynamic formation of sub-teams. The system should be aware of which subtasks should be done individually, and which can be aided by multiple workers, and assign subtasks accordingly.

WEBUILD: SYSTEM DESCRIPTION

Guided by the above design goals, we built a task distribution system called WeBuild. The goal of the WeBuild system is to help groups complete physical assembly tasks more efficiently, and to alleviate some of the coordination challenges that may otherwise be present. WeBuild takes in the step-by-step instructions for a task as input, including details about step dependencies, required tools, and associated skills, and it automatically assigns subtasks to workers. The algorithm works adaptively, only assigning the next subtask once a previous one is complete. The task instructions and details must be manually entered; our work assumes such information would be available, allowing us to focus on the system design and behaviour.

Range of Tasks Supported

WeBuild is designed to support assembly tasks that can be represented with *static* step-by-step instructions. These include group furniture building (e.g. assembling an IKEA kitchen), large art installations (e.g. pavilions), controlled construction projects (e.g. building a prefabricated house), or high-quantity manual tasks (e.g. circuit board assembly). It does not currently support *dynamic* tasks where the end goal may change or there are external uncontrollable variables (e.g. disaster relief and volunteer habitat building), though we aim to provide the groundwork for future research to explore these possibilities.

WeBuild is usable by both groups of workers who are familiar with each other, and groups of strangers. We predict that WeBuild will be particularly useful in situations where groups do not know each other (e.g. [26]) and are likely to find collaboration more challenging.

System Overview

WeBuild comprises a central server, a dashboard display, and a mobile smartphone for each group member (Figure 4). The central server can be any laptop or desktop in the work area. The system can scale to any number of workers, and can adapt to workers entering or exiting mid-task. The dashboard displays the overall process and structure of the task, to help support group awareness. Each worker's mobile phone displays instructions for their current subtask.

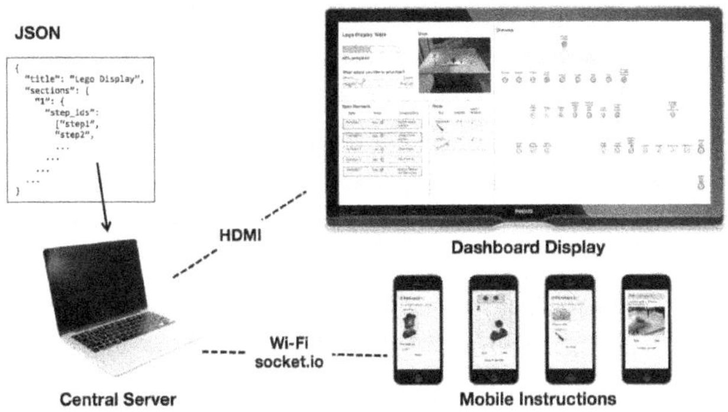

Figure 4: The WeBuild system architecture.

Task Initialization

Before the task can begin, a group member must specify how many of each required tool the group has available on the central server. Clicking "Start" begins the task, at which point the system begins allocating subtasks to all users.

Dashboard Display

The dashboard display provides high-level task information to promote group awareness (D2) (Figure 1b).

The left side displays a progress bar, parameter sliders, a photo of the final goal, and information about each user and tool (Figure 5). The "Team Members" section shows the names and statuses of all users, including which section of the task they are currently working on. The "Tools" section displays the tools required for the task, how many of each are in use or available, and buttons to update their quantity.

The right side of the dashboard displays the task overview in a tree representation, broken down into sections (Figure 6). The tree is structured by dependencies, with the root at the top being the final section, and the child nodes being the sections required for a parent node to be started.

Individual User View

Each group member uses a mobile phone to access an individual view (Figure 7). We chose mobile phones over smartwatches [1, 26] because of their ubiquity and larger screen real estate for displaying graphical instructions.

Each user connects to the IP address of the server, and logs in by entering their name, choosing a colour to be represented by, and rating their prior experience at each needed skill. Our algorithm uses this information to ensure that users are more likely to be assigned to tasks they are familiar with (D1).

The device informs the user when they are assigned to a section, and displays a photo of the section and its required tools (Figure 7a). Once the user has collected the tools and pressed the confirmation button, the instructions are shown one step at a time (Figure 7b). Users proceed through the steps manually using the "Next" and "Back" buttons (D3). Once the user completes the last step of the section, the system prompts them to confirm that they are finished, and displays a photo of the completed section to check their work against (Figure 7c).

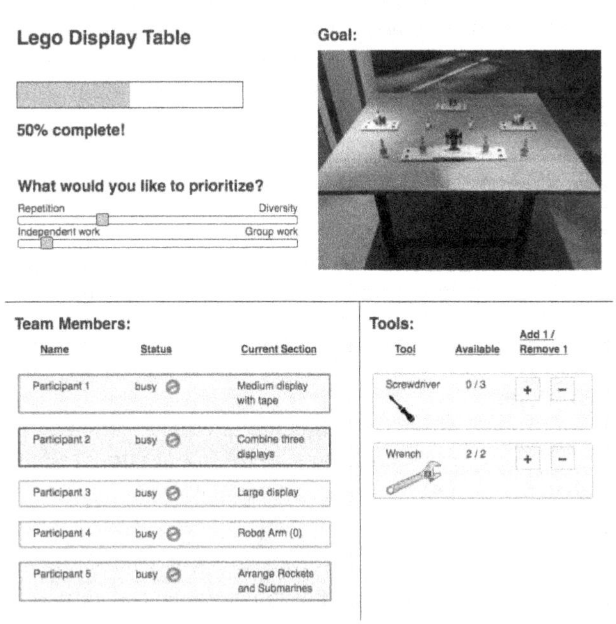

Figure 5: The left side of the dashboard displays a progress bar, parameter sliders, a photo of the final goal, and information about each user and the available tools.

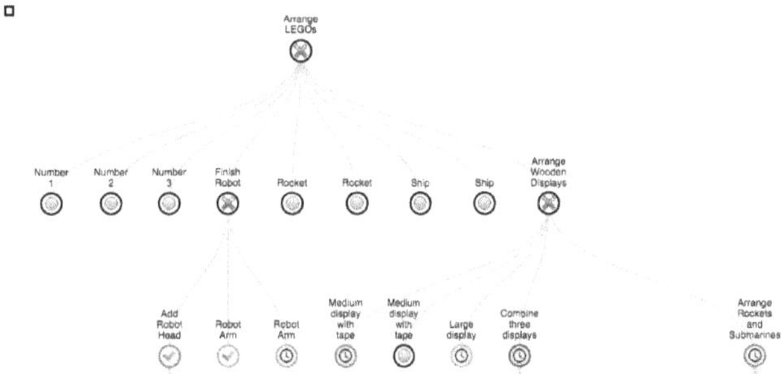

Figure 6: The right side of the dashboard displays a tree representation of the task. Green nodes have no dependencies and are therefore ready to be assigned. Red X nodes are waiting on their dependencies and therefore cannot be assigned yet. Completed nodes and nodes in progress show the colour(s) of the assigned worker(s).

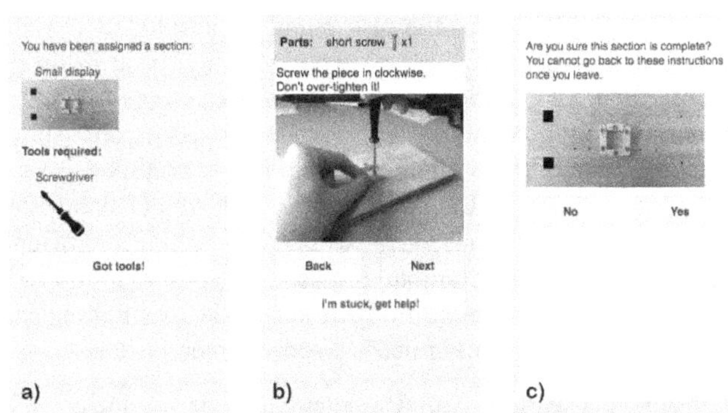

Figure 7: The WeBuild mobile interface. a) The user has been assigned a section and must gather the tools to start. b) The user is working on a section, and views each step one at a time. c) The user has finished their section, and must confirm it is complete.

When multiple users are assigned to work on a section together, the display shows who is on their sub-team and instructs them to find each other. Once one of the users presses the confirmation button to begin the section, all of the sub-team members' screens are synchronized to show the same step. For added validation, all members of the sub-team must confirm when the subtask has been completed.

If a user or group is stuck during a section, they can ask for help (Figure 7b). The next available user will then be assigned to join that section. At any time, a user can click "Exit" to leave the task entirely, at which point the system logs them out and reassigns the task they were working on.

Task Model

A prerequisite of our system is that a representation of the task already exists within the system. In our current implementation, this information is entered manually.

We developed a novel task representation based on similar models in the literature [4, 19, 27, 39]. A task T can be formally defined by the sets of sections, tools, and skills it is composed of:

$T = \{Sections, Tools, Skills\}$, where:

$Sections = \{S_1, S_2, ..., S_n\}$
$Tools = \{T_1, T_2, ..., T_m\}$
$Skills = \{K_1, K_2, ..., K_p\}$

Each Section S_i is a subtask, and is further defined by a sequence of steps from the task instructions ($Steps_i$), the tools required by each participant ($Tools_i$), the type of skills required ($Skills_i$), the minimum (Min_i) and maximum (Max_i) number of people that can work on the section, and the sections that must be complete for this section to begin ($Dependencies_i$):

$S_i = \{Steps_i, Tools_i, Skills_i, Max_i, Min_i, Dependencies_i\}$, where:

$Steps_i = \{step_{1i}, step_{2i}, ..., step_{qi}\}$
$Tools_i[j] = \{x \mid \text{Tool } T_x \text{ is required by the } j^{th} \text{ user for section } S_i\}$
$Skills_i = \{y \mid \text{Skill } K_y \text{ is required for section } S_i\}$
$Dependencies_i = \{z \mid \text{Section } S_z \text{ is a dependency of section } S_i\}$

The skills required for the task could be defined at a high level, such as experience with woodworking, or at a lower level, such as experience with specific tools. Min_i is the minimum required number of people for a section, while Max_i is the maximum number of people that could be a useful addition (D4). The set of tools for each step ($Tools_i$) is a set of sets, as each subsequent worker may require a different set of tools. For example, if a second worker is required to hold a block while the first worker screws something in, then only the first worker needs a screwdriver.

For any two sections, we also calculate their similarity as a value between 0 and 1. In our current implementation, similarity is based on the number of common tools between the sections, to a maximum of 0.5, and is equal to 1 only if the sections are equivalent:

$$Similarity(i,j) = \begin{cases} 1, if\ S_i \stackrel{\text{def}}{=} S_j, \\ 0.5 \dfrac{\|Tools_i \cap Tools_j\|}{Max(\|Tools_i\|, \|Tools_j\|)}, otherwise. \end{cases}$$

Task Distribution Algorithm

Our task distribution algorithm works on-the-fly: every time one or more users become available, it looks for the best section to assign to each available user (D1).

Algorithm Parameters

The algorithm includes two parameters whose values can vary between 0 and 1: these are *task diversity* and *group priority*. Both of these values can be adjusted with sliders on the dashboard at any time during the task.

If *task diversity* is 1, the system prioritizes giving users a variety of subtasks, which can increase engagement, produce higher quality work, and prevent repetitive strain [19, 29]. If *task diversity* is 0, workers are more likely to repeat the same or similar subtasks, which can help them learn specific skills and become more efficient [30].

If *group priority* is 1, the system biases towards assigning multiple workers to a section. If it is set to 0, the system prioritizes working individually. In cases where team building is particularly important, prioritizing group work may be preferred. In cases where it is important for workers to stay focused and quiet, individual work may be preferred.

Each time the algorithm is triggered, it prioritizes diversity with a probability equal to the value of the *task diversity* parameter. Otherwise, it prioritizes repetition. Similarly, it prioritizes group work with a probability equal to *group priority*. Otherwise, it prioritizes individual work.

Section Assignment Algorithm

The section assignment algorithm is triggered any time there is a free user. This happens when the task is started, when a new user joins, and when any section is completed. A detailed example of the values calculated by this algorithm is included in the Appendix. The algorithm generates a list of available users $U = \{u_1, u_2, ..., u_n\}$ who are not currently assigned to a section, and a list of available sections $A = \{S_1, S_2, ..., S_m\}$. A section is considered available if its required tools are available, it is currently unassigned or in progress with less than its maximum number of workers, and all its dependencies are complete. For each free user u_i, we build several lists P_i of priority values $\{p_{i1}, p_{i2}, ..., p_{iq}\}$ where p_{ij} is the priority value for assigning user u_i to section S_j. We build one list for each of the following criteria:

- **Tree depth (P_D):** $P_D[j]$ is the depth of section S_j in the task tree. Sections with larger depth are prioritized because the further a section is down the task tree, the more sections that are potentially waiting on it to be completed.
- **Group (P_G):** If individual work is being prioritized, $P_G[j]$ is 1 for all unassigned sections (as these do not yet have anyone working on them) and 0 for all sections in progress (where the user would be joining an existing team). Otherwise, the opposite values are set.

- **Prior Experience (P_E):** $P_E[j]$ is the user's self-rated experience (a value between 1 and 5) at the skill required by section S_j. If S_j requires multiple skills, it is the average of the user's experience ratings at those skills.

If the user has just completed a section S_c, we also create lists for the following criteria:

- **Next section (P_N):** $P_N[j]$ is 1 if section S_j is the next section after S_c (it is its parent node), and 0 otherwise. This prioritizes overall continuity of assignments.
- **Repetition or diversity (P_R):** If repetition is being prioritized, $P_R[j]$ is the similarity value *Similarity(j,c)*. Otherwise, $P_R[j]$ is set to 1 - *Similarity(j,c)*.
- **Speed (P_S):** This list prioritizes sections the user has already excelled at. For each available section S_j, we calculate the average time all users have taken on all completed sections weighted their by similarity to S_j, and the average time the current user has taken. $P_S[j]$ is the difference between these two averages.

To calculate the overall priority values P_{itotal} for each user u_i, we normalize each list above and add the values together element-wise.

$$P_{itotal} = P_{iD} + P_{iG} + P_{iE} + P_{iN} + P_{iR} + P_{iS}$$

We then use a greedy algorithm to make the section assignments: we find the single highest priority value in all of the P_{total} lists across every user, and assign that user to the corresponding section. We then recalculate the list of available sections and repeat the above process for the remaining free users, until all users have been assigned.

Initial Assignments
When the task is first started, we can only consider the first three criteria above, as no sections have been completed:

$$P_{itotal} = P_{iD} + P_{iG} + P_{iE}$$

However, we can still account for the *task diversity* slider value, by planning ahead. If repetition is being prioritized, we narrow down the list of available sections to a list of *unique* available sections, so that all users will be assigned to a different section, and thus more likely to repeat their section again later. Otherwise, we assign as many of the same section as possible to the available users so that each user will be less likely to repeat their section later.

Asking for Help
When a user presses the "get help" button, the section they are currently working on is added to a global list of sections that need help. The next time the algorithm runs, only sections in this help list are considered available. Each free user's priorities are calculated as above, and the user with the highest priority is assigned to help with that section.

Adapting to Users and Tools
Our algorithm provides the flexibility for users to join or leave the task at any point, by logging in or exiting from the mobile interface. The system can also adapt to tools being added or removed from the work environment, for example if more tools are found or a tool breaks. To do this, a user must update the number of tools on the dashboard display.

Implementation
WeBuild is implemented as a Node.js application running on a local server. Task information is stored on the server in JSON format. The application uses web sockets to communicate with each mobile phone, implemented using the socket.io module. Any device with a web browser can join by navigating to the server's IP address.

STUDY
To gain insights and an initial understanding of the impact of using WeBuild on a collaborative task, we conducted a between-subjects experiment comparing WeBuild to traditional paper manuals. Participants worked in groups of 5 on a custom designed task that combined LEGO assembly and simple woodworking. This served as an abstraction of a medium-sized task with a range of tools, materials, and required skills. We hypothesized that WeBuild would help groups complete the task more efficiently, and that it would reduce start-up time at the beginning of the task and coordination time between subtasks.

Participants
We recruited 40 participants (19 female, ages 18 - 54) from our institution and external recruitment lists. When signing up, participants were asked to rate their prior experience with LEGO and with hand tools (such as screwdrivers, wrenches, and hammers) from 1 (no experience) to 5 (very experienced). Participants were split into 8 groups of 5, with 4 groups in each condition. We balanced gender and prior experience across conditions and within each group (see Table 1 for a breakdown).

Most participants had never met, however in 4 of the 8 groups, two or three participants knew each other with varying degrees of familiarity (3 Control groups, 1 WeBuild group).

	Female	Male	LEGO Experience	Tools Experience
Control	8	12	3.2	3.45
WeBuild	11	9	3.25	3.45
Total	**19**	**21**	**3.23**	**3.45**

Table 1: Participants' gender and experience by condition.

The Task
LEGO tasks are frequently used in assembly task research studies [2, 13, 23, 33] due to their relatively clear instructions and simple assembly procedure. However, we also wanted our task to include physical tools to diversify the required skills. As such, we created a custom task that combines Funk et al.'s "pick-and-place" and "industrial assembly" task types [13]: it consists of several small LEGO models, several wooden displays of varying sizes, and a large table to hold the entire display (Figure 8). Building the wooden displays involves using a screwdriver, and building the table involves using a wrench. The table requires two people to lift it once assembled.

Figure 8: The final goal of the task used in our study.

We used the manufacturer's instructions for the LEGO models, and created our own step-by-step instructions for the table and displays. For the Control condition, the final instructions combined into a single booklet, which we have included as supplementary material for reference. For the WeBuild condition, the same instructions were entered into the system, along with the additional task information as previously described. We fixed the *task diversity* and *group priority* parameters to 0 for this study based on our knowledge of the task and the main goal of efficiency. We also disabled the "get help" feature as this task involved relatively small groups working in close quarters.

Procedure

At the start of each session, the experimenter explained the task to the group, and showed them a picture of the final goal. Participants were told to "work together to complete the task". In the Control condition, each participant was given a copy of the full instruction booklet. Participants were given a brief overview of how the booklet was organized. In the WeBuild condition, each participant was given an iPhone 5C with WeBuild loaded. The experimenter gave a brief explanation of the dashboard display, and showed participants a quick example task to explain the mobile interface. Participants in the WeBuild condition were then asked to log in, and rate their prior experience with the two skills involved in this task: LEGO and hand tools. Once all participants were ready, they were told to begin the task. When the entire group was satisfied that the task was complete, it was marked as finished. Participants then filled out a post-task questionnaire.

Measures

Our metrics were in part informed by those used in other related studies [6, 21, 33, 42].

In both conditions, we computed the overall completion time from start to finish. We also computed start-up time as the time from when the group was told to start until all five participants had begun working on something. We also computed the start and end time for each section. WeBuild saved this information directly, and in the Control condition it was determined later by watching and coding video recordings of the sessions.

From this data, we were able to compute the fraction of the total time each person spent working on sections vs. not working (i.e. waiting or coordinating with others). From the video recordings, we also computed the amount of time the group spent working in silence, to see if the amount of conversation differed between conditions.

We also measured the amount of parallel activity in each session using a similar calculation as Birnholtz et al. [6]: we split each session into 10-second time intervals and counted how many users were actively working during each interval (0-5). For each session, we averaged these scores across all intervals to determine the average amount of parallelism.

In the post-task questionnaire, participants rated the overall success of their group, as well as their group's efficiency and communication. Participants were also asked how aware they were throughout the task of their other team members' progress. Participants in the WeBuild condition also provided feedback on the system.

RESULTS

Given the scale of this study, we did not expect to formally validate our approach, however the following summary will be useful in guiding further evaluations and improvements.

Quantitative Results

For all measures, an independent t-test was used to compare the means between conditions. On average, groups in the WeBuild condition completed the task faster (23m13s) than groups in the Control condition (24m38s), however this was not significant. Figure 9 shows the progress of all eight groups over time. There appears to be more variation in the progress of Control groups. Given our small sample size such results should be considered cautiously.

The most significant observed difference between conditions was in the start-up times: WeBuild groups took an average of 24 seconds to start up, while Control groups took an average of 204 seconds ($t(6) = -5.64$, $p < 0.01$) (Figure 10a). WeBuild groups also spent a significantly higher fraction of their total time working (86%) than Control groups (72%) ($t(6) = 3.95$, $p < 0.01$) (Figure 10b). Accordingly, WeBuild groups also exhibited significantly more parallel activity (mean 4.48) than Control groups (mean 3.77) ($t(6) = 3.98, p < 0.01$).

On average, WeBuild groups spent more of their total time in silence (44%) than Control groups (25%), however this was not significant ($t(6) = 1.59$, $p = 0.16$) and may have also been influenced by the specific social dynamics of each group, including whether members knew each other.

Participants' answers to the post-task questions regarding success, efficiency, and communication did not differ significantly across conditions (all had averages greater than 4.5/5). However, there was a significant difference in awareness: WeBuild participants rated themselves as *less* aware (mean 3.35/5) than Control participants (mean 4.3/5) ($t(38) = -3.45, p < 0.01$).

Overall, participants in the WeBuild condition responded positively to the system. The mean rating of WeBuild's overall usefulness was 4.1/5 (*SD* 0.97). Participants felt WeBuild did a good job assigning tasks (mean 4.05/5, *SD* 0.76), and that being able to step through instructions one by one was useful (mean 4.55/5, *SD* 0.69). However, ratings were mixed on the usefulness of the dashboard display (mean 2.85/5, *SD* 1.42).

Qualitative Results

Observed Challenges

Based on our observations, the Control groups seemed to have more confusion regarding which wooden pieces were for which display boards, and participants spent some time flipping back and forth in the instructions comparing different sections.

Overall, there were no major coordination issues, though in one Control session two participants ended up accidentally switching tasks, because one thought that the other had started working on their task when in fact they had not.

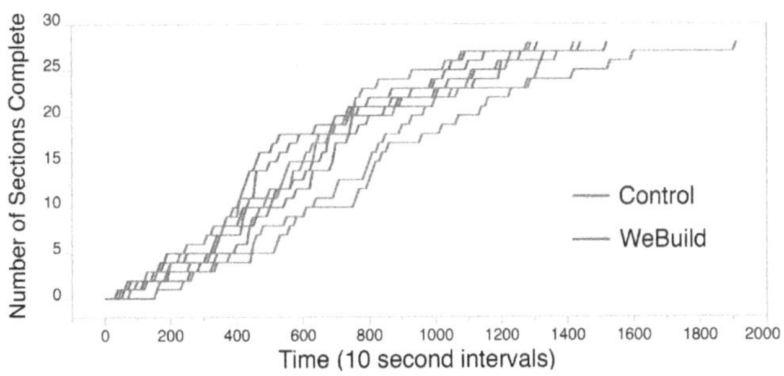

Figure 9: The progress of each group, shown as the number of sections complete in every 10-second time interval.

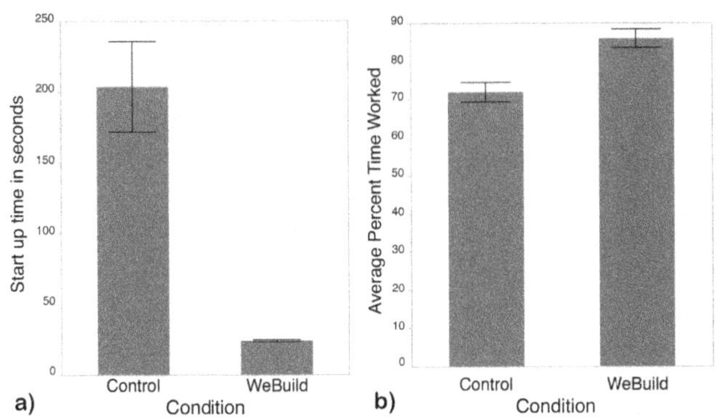

Figure 10: a) Task start-up time was significantly faster in the WeBuild condition. b) Groups in the WeBuild condition spent a larger fraction of their overall time working on the task (as opposed to waiting or coordinating). Error bars show 1 standard error from the mean.

In the WeBuild groups, participants were sometimes assigned to join sections already in progress, especially near the end of the task when there were only a few sections left. This required additional coordination as the person already working on the section had to explain what they had done to the person joining. In several cases, the first person was almost finished, and so the second person was not able to help at all.

Participant Feedback

Most participants felt their group communicated effectively. When asked how it could have been improved, participants in the Control condition suggested things like having one person be the "supervisor" to oversee group progress, and more explicit sharing of progress with each other. Several WeBuild participants answered that communication was not necessary as the system managed the task for them.

When asked how efficiency could have been improved, several Control participants mentioned that having more of an overall understanding of the task or spending more time talking through the instructions before starting would have been beneficial. WeBuild participants mentioned that sometimes having two people work on a task was unnecessary, and that when certain group members took longer than others, there was time spent waiting at the end.

Many WeBuild participants mentioned that the system was helpful as it allowed them to get started right away. As one participant stated, *"You don't need to think about the overall plan as much - you just focus on the task and assume it all works in the end"*. Suggested improvements to the system included giving participants who are waiting for a section something to do, such as help out others or provide encouragement to the group; and providing more overview information on the phone itself, as participants tended not to look away from their phones to check the dashboard.

DISCUSSION

The results from this study highlight the potential for a task distribution system to help groups coordinate physical tasks. We observed positive results overall, but it is important to note that due to the scale of our study and task, these results are suggestive rather than definitive. Our results should be treated with caution, and further formal evaluation is needed.

We predict that overall times did not differ as significantly as start-up times because once participants knew what section to do, individual section completion times were similar across conditions. Since groups spent the majority of time working on the task, the effect of the coordination improvements were most apparent at the start, but dampened across the entire session. For larger tasks where more coordination is necessary, we predict these benefits may be stronger.

Most of the non-working time spent in the WeBuild condition was near the end of the task, when participants were waiting on one or two team members to finish their final section. This could potentially be reduced with an improved scheduling algorithm that estimates section completion times. Future implementations should also avoid assigning people to join tasks in progress unless assistance has been requested, as participants mostly found this inconvenient.

An interesting result from the study was that workers had less overall awareness in the WeBuild condition, but did not seem to mind. Participants rarely looked at the dashboard display, with most looking at it only when they had nothing else to do. This demonstrates that the system successfully eliminated any required decision-making, and workers had faith in the sections they were assigned. It would be interesting to study whether similar effects would be found for larger groups and real-world tasks where group members are likely more emotionally attached to the quality of the outcome.

The overall positive response we received from WeBuild participants was promising. It is likely that by isolating individual sections, the task distribution system reduced the need for a global understanding of the task. This allowed participants to focus on their current section without worrying about the rest, whereas Control participants had to spend time building an understanding of the overall task.

One interesting topic our work raises is that there are more dimensions to group efficiency than task completion time. For example, our system provides the option of prioritizing repetition vs. diversity, each with its own trade-offs. Essentially, this is an issue of division of labour which has a longstanding philosophical background: Marx believed that too much division and specialization would make workers less skilled overall and less motivated [28]. On the other hand, Kant believed this allowed workers to develop skills specific to their specialization and thus complete the work better [22]. We leave this choice to the users, so they can tailor the system to best fit their needs. Similarly, efficiency may not always be the main goal; for example product quality may be more important, in which case having someone rate the quality of each section could be a more useful criterion than speed.

LIMITATIONS AND FUTURE WORK

In the future we hope to test the system with more complex tasks and larger groups. For such tasks, manual coordination would likely break down as the task and group size increased. In particular, we believe our system could be adapted to large-scale efforts such as architectural construction [26] and volunteer disaster relief [27]. The main challenge of adapting to such scenarios would be creating an accurate task model.

This issue points towards one of the main areas for future improvement. The system currently requires task information and instructions to be manually entered. For each step of the instructions, an admin must enter an image of the step, information about the tools and people needed, and its dependencies. We have written a script that uses this information to segment the task into sections that can be completed independently. A simple interface for entering these inputs could aid with this process, by providing a fillable form that requests each type of information, and displays the previously entered steps for selecting dependencies. Given the rapidly growing amount of instructional content that is represented electronically, and the increasing structure in online content (e.g. instructables.com), some of this information could potentially be extracted automatically instead. In addition, prior research on generating assembly instructions automatically [2] could be extended to generate the required information for our task model.

Another limitation is that our task model assumes the task can be represented as a tree, namely that every child node has one parent. However in some tasks, several different sections could be dependent on the same child section. A more general graph representation like those used in other related work [19, 39] could handle these cases.

Regarding the distribution algorithm, it would be interesting to consider global optimizations in addition to our step-by-step algorithm. Additional prior information such as estimated completion times and more details about participants' skills could help lead to an optimal task schedule. Furthermore, our algorithm currently weighs all criteria equally when making assignments. Tweaking the weight distribution could significantly impact the outcome.

In terms of the user experience, WeBuild currently requires workers to manually advance through instructions. More adaptive support could be added by taking advantage of existing context-aware systems for automatically advancing instructions [3, 12, 34] and providing real-time error detection [17]. It would also be interesting to consider delivery of instructions through wearable devices such as smart watches [1, 26, 45] or head mounted displays [21, 38].

Our current system could also have the limitation that by reducing the amount of communication and awareness, group members find the process less enjoyable and social. Though none of our study participants mentioned this as a disadvantage, future work could consider allowing users the option to choose whom to collaborate with or which subtask to join. Other features such as the "get help" button could also be disabled as it was in our study to encourage more spontaneous collaboration.

CONCLUSION

Our initial study showed promising indications that WeBuild can help groups coordinate tasks. In addition to our suggestive results, we have contributed the design and implementation of an intelligent task distribution system that can potentially scale to larger complex tasks with an arbitrary number of workers. We also contributed a model for representing tasks and the information needed in order to make informed assignments of subtasks. We believe this research will serve as important groundwork for future efforts in coordinating collocated workers for physical tasks.

REFERENCES

1. Mario Aehnelt and Bodo Urban. 2014. Follow-Me: Smartwatch Assistance on the Shop Floor. In *HCI in Business*. Springer International Publishing, 279–287. http://doi.org/10.1007/978-3-319-07293-7_27
2. Maneesh Agrawala, Doantam Phan, Julie Heiser, et al. 2003. Designing effective step-by-step assembly instructions. *ACM SIGGRAPH 2003 Papers on - SIGGRAPH '03*, ACM Press, 828. http://doi.org/10.1145/1201775.882352
3. Stavros Antifakos, Florian Michahelles, and Bernt Schiele. 2002. Proactive Instructions for Furniture Assembly. In *UbiComp 2002: Ubiquitous Computing*. Springer Berlin Heidelberg, 351–360. http://doi.org/10.1007/3-540-45809-3_27
4. Christian Artigues. 2008. The Resource-Constrained Project Scheduling Problem. In *Resource-Constrained Project Scheduling*, Christian Artigues, Sophie Demassey and Emmanuel Nron (eds.). ISTE, London, UK, 21–36. http://doi.org/10.1002/9780470611227
5. A. Bannat, A. Bannat, F. Wallhoff, et al. 2008. Towards optimal worker assistance: A framework for adaptive selection and presentation of assembly instructions. *Proc. 1st Int. Workshop on Cognition for Technical Systems, Cotesys*.
6. Jeremy P. Birnholtz, Tovi Grossman, Clarissa Mak, and Ravin Balakrishnan. 2007. An exploratory study of input configuration and group process in a negotiation task using a large display. *Proceedings of the SIGCHI conference on Human factors in computing systems - CHI '07*, ACM Press, 91. http://doi.org/10.1145/1240624.1240638
7. Bruno Campagnolo, Cesar A. Tacla, Emerson C. Paraiso, Gilson Y. Sato, and Milton P. Ramos. 2009. An architecture for supporting small collocated teams in cooperative software development. *2009 13th International Conference on Computer Supported Cooperative Work in Design*, IEEE, 264–269. http://doi.org/10.1109/CSCWD.2009.4968069
8. John M. Carroll, Dennis C. Neale, Philip L. Isenhour, Mary Beth Rosson, and D.Scott McCrickard. 2003. Notification and awareness: Synchronizing task-oriented collaborative activity. *International Journal of Human-Computer Studies* 58, 5: 605–632. http://doi.org/10.1016/S1071-5819(03)00024-7
9. Y.-L. Betty Chang, Stacey D. Scott, and Mark Hancock. 2014. Supporting Situation Awareness in Collaborative Tabletop Systems with Automation. *Proceedings of the Ninth ACM International Conference on Interactive Tabletops and Surfaces - ITS '14*, ACM Press, 185–194. http://doi.org/10.1145/2669485.2669496
10. Lung-Pan Cheng, Thijs Roumen, Hannes Rantzsch, et al. 2015. TurkDeck: Physical virtual reality based on people. *Proceedings of the 28th Annual ACM Symposium on User Interface Software & Technology - UIST '15*, ACM Press, 417–426. http://doi.org/10.1145/2807442.2807463
11. Andrew Clayphan, Judy Kay, and Armin Weinberger. 2014. ScriptStorm: Scripting to enhance tabletop brainstorming. *Personal and Ubiquitous Computing* 18, 6: 1433–1453. http://doi.org/10.1007/s00779-013-0746-z
12. Mira Dontcheva, Robert R. Morris, Joel R. Brandt, et al. 2014. Combining crowdsourcing and learning to improve engagement and performance. *Proceedings of the 32nd annual ACM conference on Human factors in computing systems - CHI '14*, ACM Press, 3379–3388. http://doi.org/10.1145/2556288.2557217
13. Markus Funk, Thomas Kosch, Scott W. Greenwald, and Albrecht Schmidt. 2015. A benchmark for interactive augmented reality instructions for assembly tasks. *Proceedings of the 14th International Conference on Mobile and Ubiquitous Multimedia - MUM '15*, ACM Press, 253–257. http://doi.org/10.1145/2836041.2836067
14. Markus Funk, Thomas Kosch, and Albrecht Schmidt. 2016. Interactive worker assistance. *Proceedings of the 2016 ACM International Joint Conference on Pervasive and Ubiquitous Computing - UbiComp '16*, ACM Press, 934–939. http://doi.org/10.1145/2971648.2971706
15. B. P. Gerkey and Maja J. Matarić. 2004. A Formal Analysis and Taxonomy of Task Allocation in Multi-Robot Systems. *The International Journal of Robotics Research* 23, 9: 939–954. http://doi.org/10.1177/0278364904045564
16. D Greer and G Ruhe. 2004. Software release planning: An evolutionary and iterative approach. *Information and Software Technology* 46, 4: 243–253. http://doi.org/10.1016/j.infsof.2003.07.002
17. Ankit Gupta, Dieter Fox, Brian Curless, and Michael Cohen. 2012. DuploTrack: A realtime system for authoring and guiding Duplo block assembly. *Proceedings of the 25th annual ACM symposium on User interface software and technology - UIST '12*, ACM Press, 389. http://doi.org/10.1145/2380116.2380167
18. Steven J. Henderson and Steven K. Feiner. 2011. Augmented reality in the psychomotor phase of a procedural task. *2011 10th IEEE International Symposium on Mixed and Augmented Reality*, IEEE, 191–200. http://doi.org/10.1109/ISMAR.2011.6092386
19. S.J. Hu, J. Ko, L. Weyand, et al. 2011. Assembly

system design and operations for product variety. *CIRP Annals - Manufacturing Technology* 60, 2: 715–733. http://doi.org/10.1016/j.cirp.2011.05.004

20. Petra Isenberg, Danyel Fisher, Meredith Ringel Morris, Kori Inkpen, and Mary Czerwinski. 2010. An Exploratory Study of Co-located Collaborative Visual Analytics around a Tabletop Display. *Proceedings of Visual Analytics Science and Technology (VAST)*, IEEE Computer Society.
21. Steven Johnson, Madeleine Gibson, and Bilge Mutlu. 2015. Handheld or handsfree?: Remote collaboration via lightweight head-mounted displays and handheld devices. *Proceedings of the 18th ACM Conference on Computer Supported Cooperative Work & Social Computing - CSCW '15*, ACM Press, 1825–1836. http://doi.org/10.1145/2675133.2675176
22. Immanuel Kant. 1785. *Groundwork of the metaphysics of morals*.
23. David Kirk, Tom Rodden, and Danaë Stanton Fraser. 2007. Turn it this way: Grounding collaborative action with remote gestures. *Proceedings of the SIGCHI conference on Human factors in computing systems - CHI '07*, ACM Press, 1039. http://doi.org/10.1145/1240624.1240782
24. Jarrod Knibbe, Tovi Grossman, and George Fitzmaurice. 2015. Smart Makerspace: An immersive instructional space for physical tasks. *Proceedings of the 2015 International Conference on Interactive Tabletops & Surfaces - ITS '15*, ACM Press, 83–92. http://doi.org/10.1145/2817721.2817741
25. Robert E. Kraut, Mark D. Miller, and Jane Siegel. 1996. Collaboration in performance of physical tasks: Effects on outcomes and communication. *Proceedings of the 1996 ACM conference on Computer supported cooperative work - CSCW '96*, ACM Press, 57–66. http://doi.org/10.1145/240080.240190
26. Benjamin Lafreniere, Tovi Grossman, Fraser Anderson, et al. 2016. Crowdsourced Fabrication. *Proceedings of the 29th Annual Symposium on User Interface Software and Technology - UIST '16*, ACM Press, 15–28. http://doi.org/10.1145/2984511.2984553
27. Faisal Luqman and Martin Griss. 2010. Overseer: A mobile context-aware collaboration and task management system for disaster response. *2010 Eighth International Conference on Creating, Connecting and Collaborating through Computing*, IEEE, 76–82. http://doi.org/10.1109/C5.2010.10
28. Karl Marx. 1844. Wages of Labour. In *First Manuscript, Economic and Philosophical Manuscripts*.
29. G. Michalos, S. Makris, N. Papakostas, D. Mourtzis, and G. Chryssolouris. 2010. Automotive assembly technologies review: Challenges and outlook for a flexible and adaptive approach. *CIRP Journal of Manufacturing Science and Technology* 2, 2: 81–91. http://doi.org/10.1016/j.cirpj.2009.12.001
30. Allen Newell and Paul S. Rosenbloom. 1981. Mechanisms of skill acquisition and the law of practice. In *Cognitive skills and their acquisition*, John Robert Anderson (ed.). Lawrence Erlbaum Associates, Inc., Hillsdale, NJ, 1–55.
31. Linet Özdamar and Gündüz Ulusoy. 1995. A survey on the resource-constrained project scheduling problem. *IIE Transactions* 27, 5: 574–586. http://doi.org/10.1080/07408179508936773
32. David Pinelle and Carl Gutwin. 2008. Evaluating teamwork support in tabletop groupware applications using collaboration usability analysis. *Personal and Ubiquitous Computing* 12, 3: 237–254. http://doi.org/10.1007/s00779-007-0145-4
33. Abhishek Ranjan, Jeremy P. Birnholtz, and Ravin Balakrishnan. 2007. Dynamic shared visual spaces: Experimenting with automatic camera control in a remote repair task. *Proceedings of the SIGCHI conference on Human factors in computing systems - CHI '07*, ACM Press, 1177. http://doi.org/10.1145/1240624.1240802
34. Eldon Schoop, Michelle Nguyen, Daniel Lim, Valkyrie Savage, Sean Follmer, and Björn Hartmann. 2016. Drill Sergeant: Supporting physical construction projects through an ecosystem of augmented tools. *Proceedings of the 2016 CHI Conference Extended Abstracts on Human Factors in Computing Systems - CHI EA '16*, ACM Press, 1607–1614. http://doi.org/10.1145/2851581.2892429
35. Onn Shehory and Sarit Kraus. 1998. Methods for task allocation via agent coalition formation. *Artificial Intelligence* 101, 1: 165–200. http://doi.org/10.1016/S0004-3702(98)00045-9
36. Rajinder S. Sodhi, Brett R. Jones, David Forsyth, Brian P. Bailey, and Giuliano Maciocci. 2013. BeThere: 3D mobile collaboration with spatial input. *Proceedings of the SIGCHI Conference on Human Factors in Computing Systems - CHI '13*, ACM Press, 179. http://doi.org/10.1145/2470654.2470679
37. Desney S. Tan, Darren Gergle, Regan Mandryk, et al. 2008. Using job-shop scheduling tasks for evaluating collocated collaboration. *Personal and Ubiquitous Computing* 12, 3: 255–267. http://doi.org/10.1007/s00779-007-0154-3
38. Arthur Tang, Charles Owen, Frank Biocca, and Weimin Mou. 2003. Comparative effectiveness of augmented reality in object assembly. *Proceedings of the conference on Human factors in computing systems - CHI '03*, ACM Press, 73.

http://doi.org/10.1145/642611.642626

39. C. Del Valle and E.F. Camacho. 1996. Automatic assembly task assignment for a multirobot environment. *Control Engineering Practice* 4, 7: 915–921. http://doi.org/10.1016/0967-0661(96)00089-5
40. Carl A. Waldspurger and William E. Weihl. 1994. Lottery scheduling: Flexible proportional-share resource management. *Proceedings of the 1st USENIX conference on Operating Systems Design and Implementation*, USENIX Association, 1.
41. James R. Wallace, Stacey D. Scott, Eugene Lai, and Deon Jajalla. 2011. Investigating the Role of a Large, Shared Display in Multi-Display Environments. *Computer Supported Cooperative Work (CSCW)* 20, 6: 529–561. http://doi.org/10.1007/s10606-011-9149-8
42. James R. Wallace, Stacey D. Scott, Taryn Stutz, Tricia Enns, and Kori Inkpen. 2009. Investigating teamwork and taskwork in single- and multi-display groupware systems. *Personal and Ubiquitous Computing* 13, 8: 569–581. http://doi.org/10.1007/s00779-009-0241-8
43. Giles Westerfield, Antonija Mitrovic, and Mark Billinghurst. 2013. Intelligent augmented reality training for assembly tasks. . Springer Berlin Heidelberg, 542–551. http://doi.org/10.1007/978-3-642-39112-5_55
44. Gwen M. Wittenbaum, Sandra I. Vaughan, and Garold Strasser. 2002. Coordination in Task-Performing Groups. In *Theory and Research on Small Groups*, R. Scott Tindale, Linda Heath, John Edwards, et al. (eds.). Kluwer Academic Publishers, Boston, 177–204. http://doi.org/10.1007/0-306-47144-2_9
45. Jens Ziegler, Sebastian Heinze, and Leon Urbas. 2015. The potential of smartwatches to support mobile industrial maintenance tasks. *2015 IEEE 20th Conference on Emerging Technologies & Factory Automation (ETFA)*, IEEE, 1–7. http://doi.org/10.1109/ETFA.2015.7301479
46. LILLÅNGEN Wall cabinet. Retrieved from http://www.ikea.com/ca/en/catalog/products/80240789/
47. LANDON Shelf. Retrieved from https://www.jysk.ca/furniture/home-office-furniture/bookcases/landon-narrow-shelf.html
48. ME16K3000AS Over the Range Microwave. Retrieved from http://www.samsung.com/ca/consumer/home-appliances/cooking-appliances/microwave-ovens/ME16K3000AS/AC
49. Tower Bridge Set. Retrieved from http://www.meccano.com/product/p10940/tower-bridge-set
50. SEKTION High cabinet w/door & 4 drawers, white Förvara, Häggeby white. Retrieved from http://www.ikea.com/ca/en/catalog/products/S29044659/#/S89044680

APPENDIX

In this section we provide a detailed walkthrough for one iteration of our task distribution algorithm, using a simplified example task. We show the values calculated at each step of the algorithm to illustrate how the next assigned section is chosen. In this example, we assume that *task diversity* and *group priority* are both set to 0, as they were for our full study task. Assume we have two workers, X and Y. X is currently working on the Robot Body section, and Y has just finished the first Robot Shoulder section. The section assignment algorithm is triggered so that Y can be assigned a new section.

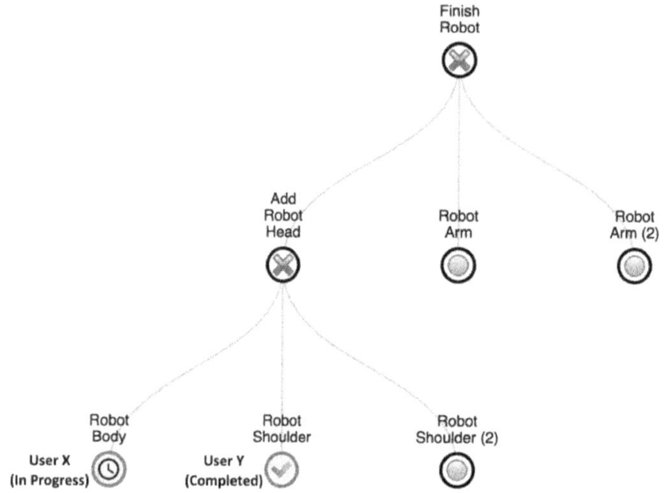

We calculate the lists U of available users and A of available sections:
$U = \{Y\}$
$A = \{$Robot Body, Robot Shoulder (2), Robot Arm, Robot Arm (2)$\}$

Note that Robot Body is included as an available section even though there is already a user working on it. This is because the maximum number of people that can work on this section (Max_i) is set to 2, so a second user could potentially join.

Now, for user Y, we build a priority list for each criterion with priority values corresponding to each section in A:

Tree Depth: $\boldsymbol{P_D} = \{3, 3, 2, 2\}$ since the first two sections (Robot Body and Robot Shoulder (2)) are at a depth of 3 in the tree, and the next two (Robot Arm and Robot Arm (2)) are at a depth of two.

Group: $\boldsymbol{P_G} = \{0, 1, 1, 1\}$ since individual work is being prioritized, and Robot Body is the only section already in progress.

Prior Experience: Assume user Y has an experience level of 3/5 with LEGO. Then $\boldsymbol{P_E} = \{3, 3, 3, 3\}$, since all sections require the LEGO skill. Since this list will be normalized later, prior experience in this case has no effect on the assignment.

Next Section: $\boldsymbol{P_N} = \{0, 0, 0, 0\}$ since the parent section of Robot Shoulder (which Y just completed) is not included in A, as it is still waiting on some other dependencies.

Repetition or diversity: Since we are prioritizing repetition in this example, we set each value $P_R[j]$ to *Similarity(j, c)* where section S_c is the one Y just completed (Robot Shoulder). Therefore, $\boldsymbol{P_R} = \{0.5, 1, 0.5, 0.5\}$ since the second section (Robot Shoulder (2)) is an exact copy of Robot Shoulder, and all other sections require the same number of tools as S_c (no tools).

Speed: For this example, speed does not affect the section assignment. This is because the only completed section so far is Robot Shoulder, and it has only been completed once by user Y. Therefore, the difference between the average time all users have taken and the average time user Y has taken will be zero (since these times are the same). Therefore, $\boldsymbol{P_S} = \{0, 0, 0, 0\}$.

To calculate the overall priority value P_{Ytotal}, we normalize each list above and add the values together element-wise:

$$\begin{aligned} P_{Ytotal} &= P_D + P_G + P_E + P_N + P_R + P_S \\ &= \{0.3, 0.3, 0.2, 0.2\} + \{0, 0.3, 0.3, 0.3\} + \{0.25, 0.25, 0.25, 0.25\} + \{0, 0, 0, 0\} + \{0.2, 0.4, 0.2, 0.2\} + \{0, 0, 0, 0\} \\ &= \{0.75, 1.25, 0.95, 0.95\} \end{aligned}$$

The highest priority value in this list is the second one (1.25), so it corresponds with the second section in A: Robot Shoulder (2). User Y is therefore assigned to Robot Shoulder (2) as the next section. This is a sensible choice given the parameters we set, since we are prioritizing for repetition and this section is identical to the one user Y just completed. We can see that its higher value came primarily from P_R, but also from P_D and P_G, since it is at the largest depth possible in the tree, and it is not already in progress and therefore will be completed individually.

Pressure-Based Gain Factor Control for Mobile 3D Interaction using Locally-Coupled Devices

Lonni Besançon
Univ. Paris Saclay & Inria
Orsay, France
lonni.besancon@gmail.com

Mehdi Ammi
Limsi CNRS
Orsay, France
mehdi.ammi@limsi.fr

Tobias Isenberg
Inria
Orsay, France
tobias.isenberg@inria.fr

ABSTRACT

We present the design and evaluation of pressure-based interactive control of 3D navigation precision. Specifically, we examine the control of gain factors in tangible 3D interactions using locally-coupled mobile devices. By focusing on pressure as a separate input channel we can adjust gain factors independently from other input modalities used in 3D navigation, in particular for the exploration of 3D visualizations. We present two experiments. First, we determined that people strongly preferred higher pressures to be mapped to higher gain factors. Using this mapping, we compared pressure with rate control, velocity control, and slider-based control in a second study. Our results show that pressure-based gain control allows people to be more precise in the same amount of time compared to established input modalities. Pressure-based control was also clearly preferred by our participants. In summary, we demonstrate that pressure facilitates effective and efficient precision control for mobile 3D navigation.

ACM Classification Keywords

H.5.2. User Interfaces: Input devices and strategies

Author Keywords

Pressure input; tangible interaction; TUI; 3D navigation.

INTRODUCTION

We present the design and the evaluation of a prototype that adds pressure-based input sensing to the back of a mobile device. Pressure or isometric force is a continuous form of input that is increasingly used in HCI systems. The recent release of devices equipped with *3D-touch*[1] may well encourage an even higher number of manufacturers to provide to equip their systems with this input channel—so our research enables future developers to design pressure-based control effectively.

We use pressure as an input channel to provide users with a manual control of the gain factor associated with the tangible manipulations of 3D content shown on the device. Gain factors (also called control-display gain, CD gain; [8, 36, 56]) play an important role in interaction. Hinckley et al. [25] even state that one of the major hurdles with 3D interaction is to be able to "provide an interface which effectively integrates rapid, imprecise [...] object placements with slower but more precise object placement, while providing feedback that makes it all comprehensible." Past work has focused on techniques to set the CD gain for mouse or tactile interaction (e. g., [6, 13, 36, 56]), but some work for direct 3D input [30, 31] and interaction in VR [22] exists as well. In the special case of tangible manipulations, different gain factor for the same interaction mapping can make a manipulation extremely exhausting and frustrating (e. g., when the gain factor is low and the user has to make many different arm/hand/shoulder movements) or really frustrating (e. g., when the gain factor is high and the manipulation not precise enough).

Previous work in the context of 3D manipulations [7] has shown that tactile manipulation of a slider widget during tangible manipulation was not appropriate: even though users could precisely set the gain factor, they did not want to stop their current interaction to reset the gain factor. With our pressure-based control we present a new approach to control the gain factor independently from the other input modalities.

Our contributions are thus threefold. First, we present the design of a back-of-device pressure-sensing system controlling the gain factor associated with tangible manipulation of a mobile device. Second, we study the pressure-based control of gain factors to learn which interaction mapping is preferred by participants and used most efficiently by them. Finally, we compare this pressure-based form of gain control with established mappings including velocity-based, slider-based, and rate control. Our evaluation comprises performance workload and fatigue measures as well as subjective preferences. Our results show that pressure-based control was not only clearly preferred but also that pressure-based gain control allows people to be more precise in the same amount of time compared to established input modalities.

RELATED WORK

Work related to our own comes from one of three major fields: interaction with the back of (mobile) devices, the use of pressure as an input modality, and the use of pressure to augment other input techniques. We discuss these aspects next.

[1] https://developer.apple.com/ios/3d-touch/

ACM ISBN 978-1-4503-4655-9/17/05 ...$15.00.
http://dx.doi.org/10.1145/3025453.3025890

Back-of-Device Interaction

Several research projects have investigated interaction on the back of the device as a way to eliminate on-screen occlusion. For instance, systems like *BehindTouch* [26] and *BlindSight* [34] use a 12-key pad on the back of a mobile device. In particular for small devices, occlusion is one of the biggest usability issues. In the context of very small screens, Baudisch and Chu [5] as well as Wigdor et al. [52] thus propose to combine back-of-device interaction with a see-through effect to improve pointing. Liang et al. [35] also propose to use a secondary mobile device attached to the the back of the first one to facilitate tactile input above and under the mobile device and thus support task such as rotation, translation, stretching or slicing. Similarly, Shen et al. [47] propose a set of gestures for 3D interaction with back-to-back devices. In addition, back-of-device interaction has been used on larger devices. For instance, Wigdor et al. [53] propose to use a two-sided interactive touch table to add a new dimension of input for co-located collaborative work. Finally, back-of-device interaction has also been used combined with other types of input; e. g., with stylus input on a PDA [49] or to detect bending using a position sensor on the back of the Gummi device [45]. We build on the general approach of back-of-device input to provide easily accessible pressure control when interacting while holding a tablet.

Pressure as an Input Modality

Pressure input is a continuous input data [12, 14, 43, 48] that has been shown in the literature to be usable as a primary modality for a variety of tasks. Early work conducted by Buxton et al. [12] includes an example of a drawing application. Buxton et al. map continuous pressure data to a continuous scale that varies the width of the painting brush, allowing users to control both width and path with a single finger. Brewster et al. [9], for instance, use pressure to control text entry. They map the pressure input to two discrete states: a light pressure will be mapped to lowercase letters while a strong pressure will be mapped to uppercase letters. Similarly, Mclachlan et al. [38] and Wilson et al. [54] use pressure-based menu selection on mobile devices. Ren et al. [44] use pressure values of pen-based interfaces to control the continuous size of a circular cursor (or its contexts) to assist users for selection tasks. Other non-touch-enabled devices also make use of pressure as a primary input. For instance, Issartel et al. [29] use pressure input to realize a grasping metaphor on a tangible volume. In their case, pressure controls a state representing whether the user is trying to grasp—for pressure larger than a given threshold—or release a virtual object. In our work we map the pressure input to a continuous range of gain-factor values.

Pressure input can be captured by means of force-sensing resistors (FSRs) [38] or can be indirectly captured on touch screens. One of the techniques used for this purpose builds on the fact that a higher pressure on a point leads to a wider point of contact between the finger and the surface [11] and was implemented by Forlines and Shen [21] or Benko et al. [6]. Arif and Stuerzlinger [2], for instance, use it to create a technique to bypass incorrect word predictions of text entries on a tactile device. While this indirect sensing of pressure on touch-screen is promising, in our work we only consider sensor-captured pressure. Indeed, even though our prototype has a touch screen, we take advantage of back-of-device pressure sensing which is easier to achieve with simple FSRs.

A vast majority of studies conducted on pressure in the HCI community have focused on determining how many distinct levels of pressure can be applied by users. Early work conducted by Herot and Weinzapfel [24] already suggested that accuracy with pressure input methods is achievable with a continuous and real-time visual feedback. With the presence of a visual feedback, pressure-based interaction has been proven to be highly accurate. For instance, Cechanowicz et al. [14] proved that users could differentiate between 64 modes on a dual-pressure augmented mouse, while Wilson et al. [54] showed that users could distinguish accurately up to 10 levels of pressure with adequate feedback on a mobile device. The value obtained in the former is high enough for us to consider it as a virtual continuous scale. The value obtained in the latter can still be seen as close to continuous for our purposes. Indeed, participants in our study had to use pressure input to vary the gain factor from 0.3 to 3 (i. e., by a factor of 10).

Pressure as Augmentation

Pressure can be a direct and primary way to interact on mobile devices and thus can replace touch interaction. We are investigating, however, the use of isometric force as a supplementary, auxiliary input that could augment or complete other input technique. Touch and pressure input have been combined in the past, for example, by Arif et al. [1] to increase the security of conventional digit-lock of recent smartphones. McLachlan et al. [37] investigated this characteristic of the pressure input in the context of bimanual interactions on mobile devices. They could not find evidence that would suggest that the pressure input had effects on the accuracy of the dominant-hand performing touch inputs. Similarly, McLachlan and Brewster [38], demonstrated that the ability to perform simultaneous pressure inputs and touch gestures depended on the complexity of the gesture. Tangible 3D manipulations are regarded as natural since they are based on skills people have developed through their everyday interactions [27]. We thus hypothesize that these results may be generalizable to tangible 3D manipulations of a mobile devices and that thus the pressure input facilitates an additional and independent form of control to be used to adjust the gain factor in 3D interactions. Ramos and Balakrishnan [42] proposed such a combination of pressure and touch input. The first modality is used to provide a fluid integrated manipulation of the scale while the touch input is used to provide parameter manipulation within the pressure-obtained scale. Similarly, Ramos et al. [43] combined position (obtained via touch input) and continuous pressure input (obtained from a stylus) to provide Pressure Widgets on mobile devices. Our design builds on their ideas but we use pressure to adjust the gain factor, while 3D navigations are still carried through physical manipulation of the tablet.

PROTOTYPE

To test this interaction concept we used an existing mobile device as a locally-coupled[2] tangible 3D exploration tool and

[2] A locally-coupled device is both display and input device [30, 41].

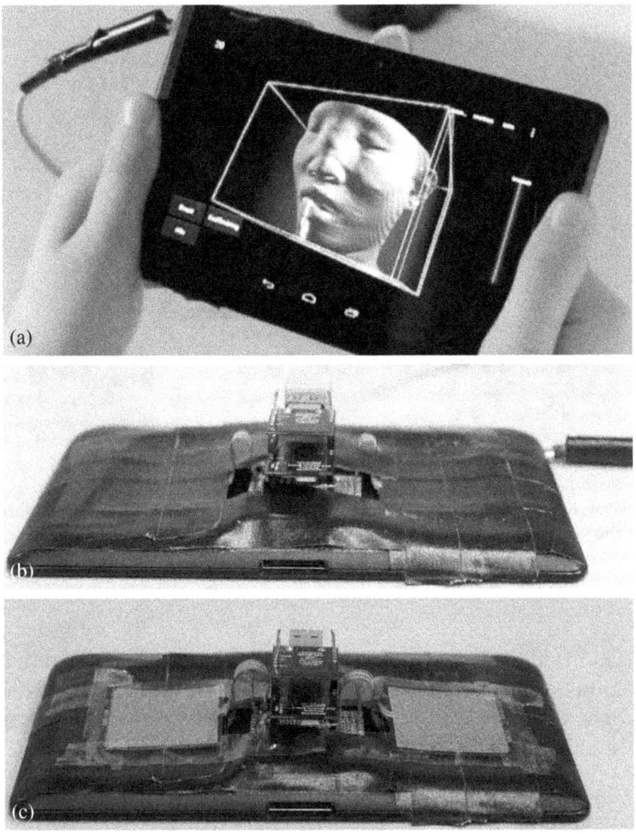

Figure 1. Interaction prototype: (a) prototype in use, (b) electronics installation on the back with taped pressure sensors, and (c) mock-up of the arrangement of the pressure sensors (hidden by the tape in (b)).

fitted it with pressure sensors (see Fig. 1). We used a Google Tango tablet[3] as it provides both a tactile screen and a position-aware mechanism that facilitates tangible manipulations. We then augmented the tablet with back-of-device pressure FSR sensors that are located right under users' fingers on the back of the tablet. The FSR sensors are often used in pressure-sensing prototype [37] and we coupled them to a RFDuino board, each one of them with a 3.3kΩ resistance. The sensitivity of the FSRs depends on the value of the resistance and a pilot study with six participants allowed us to determine that 3.3kΩ was ideal in our case. To keep the prototype fully portable, the RFDuino board is powered by a cable that connects it to the micro-USB port of the tablet. The pressure values are computed by the RFDuino board and sent over Bluetooth Low Energy (BLE) to the tablet. Clutching is achieved by putting/removing the fingers from the pressure sensors Fig. 2. While we first wanted to realize the clutching through touches on the screen, another pilot study showed us that it was easier for people to clutch with the pressure sensors. Because previous work [14, 48, 54, 55] has shown that pressure input is made more precise with the help of visual feedback, a cursor (aka slider) was added to the GUI on the tablet to reflect the gain-factor value obtained with pressure input. This kind of visual feedback has been used before in various studies and setups such as the ones used by McLachlan et al. [37, 38].

[3]https://get.google.com/tango/

EXPERIMENT 1: CHOICE OF FORCE MAPPING

We conducted a first study to compare two possible pressure-based gain factor adjustment techniques. The first technique (P1) maps the pressure of the sensors directly to the gain factor: a high pressure results in a higher gain factor, i. e., to larger/stronger motions. The metaphor for this mapping is that the stronger pressure forces are equivalent to stronger and larger motions, and that lower pressure thus yields a more precise control. The second technique (P2) does exactly the opposite: a high pressure results in a lower gain factor, i. e., to more precise motions. The metaphor of this second technique is that with stronger pressure the interacting person holds on more tightly to be able to better control a precise manipulation. Our goal with this experiment was to determine whether one of these two technique yield better results and/or is preferred by users and thus to to determine which mapping we should use in our follow-up experiment.

Participants

For this first study we recruited 12 unpaid participants (2 female; ages 21–39, mean = 26.75, med = 26, SD = 5.01). Six of them had at least university degree, while the remaining six had at most an A-level equivalent. Five of of the participants were used to 3D manipulation through the extensive use of video games or 3D software. All participants were right handed and had normal or corrected-to-normal vision.

Procedure and Task

We first presented participants with the tablet device and told them they would have to perform translation and rotations in a 3D virtual world. We presented them the application and showed how the clutching was achieved. An initial docking target was already present during this training phase of the experiment. We asked participant to try and use the tablet so as to match the target docking. The purpose of the training was twofold. First, as highlighted by Issartel et al. [28], we wanted to assert whether the participant preferred allocentric or egocentric mapping.[4] Because our docking task was similar to the first environment used by Issartel et al. [28] which showed a 70% preference for the egocentric mapping, we set the initial mapping to egocentric. However, this initial training could be used to set it to allocentric if participant felt that they could not use the mapping correctly. Four participants did so and set their mapping to allocentric. Second, the gain factor was set by the experimenter for the initial training once to both a high value (i. e., 3) and to a low value (i. e., 0.3)—to let our participant understand the need for a manual control of the gain factor. Achieving a precise positioning was almost impossible with the high gain factor because it was too sensitive, while it took more than a minute for participant to do

[4]These two notions are frequently discussed in the literature [10, 32, 40]. In general, the egocentric term seems to be associated with the idea of the viewing perspective, and the allocentric term with the idea of a fixed, external reference point. In other words, when the manipulated object is being moved in the same direction as the tablet, the mapping is allocentric. When the manipulated object moves in the opposite direction of the tablet, the mappings is egocentric.

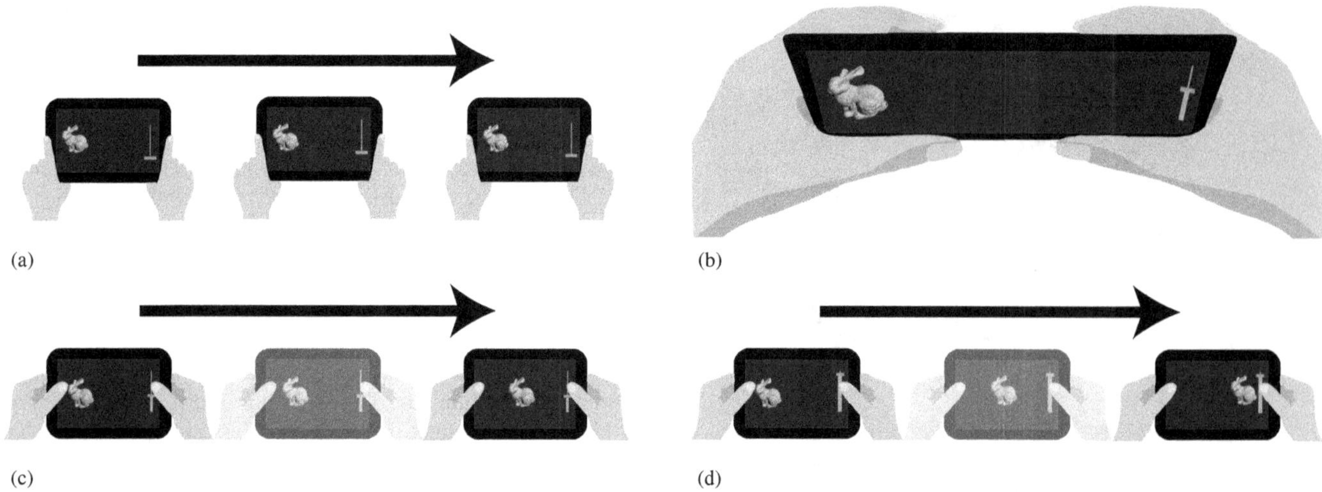

Figure 2. Illustration of the clutching mechanism: (a) fingers are not on the pressure sensors, thus movements sensed by the tablet are not propagated to the virtual object; (b) the force applied to the pressure sensors is mapped to the slider such that movements are now propagated to the virtual object; (c) if the pressure is low the slider value and the gain factor value are low such that the virtual object is translated only by a little; (d) if the pressure is high the slider value and the gain factor value are high such that the virtual object is translated more than in (c).

it with a low gain factor. Each participant thus experienced both extreme gain factors, in a counter-balanced order. During training, participants had an unlimited time to get used to the manipulation of the tablet and the purpose of the docking task.

Once they expressed to be familiar with the interaction techniques and task type, the experimenter launched the actual experiment. Participant were asked to complete 20 docking tasks for each technique (i. e., a total of 40 docking tasks), for each of which they had a maximum of 30 seconds. The order of technique was counter-balanced to avoid learning biases. The pool of possible docking targets had been manually created ahead of time to ensure that participants had to frequently manually change the gain factor. For each trial, the target was randomly picked from this pool and then removed from the pool. At the end of the experiment, each participant's preference was asked by the experimenter and a semi-structured interview was conducted to determine whether participant could use the technique properly.

Hypotheses

We hypothesized, based on previous work [37, 38], that (**H1**) the use of pressure as an input modality to control the interaction gain factor would not endanger the use of tangible control of 3D manipulations using the mobile device. We also hypothesized that (**H2**) it would be more natural for users to use P2 than it is to use P1 and that P2 would thus outperform P1—due to our own observations that people playing video games often put a lot of effort in being precise and, as they perform these precise interactions, tend to squeeze their game controller.

RESULTS OF EXPERIMENT 1

We collected a total of 480 docking trials from our 12 participants, i. e., 240 per technique. In addition, we recorded the answers of the participants in the semi-structured interview and analyzed our participants' subjective preferences and a comparison of their subjectively rated intuitiveness. First, to analyze our hypothesis H1, we specifically asked our participants during the semi-structured interviews about whether the additional pressure-input was harmful to their 3D manipulations. None of them reported so. We thus fond no evidence that would refute H1, making the pressure-based gain factor manipulation a viable option for tangible 3D interaction.

To assess the docking precision and thus to analyze H2, we then compared the Euclidean distance of and the angular difference between the manipulated object and the docking target.[5] We first discuss the Euclidean and the angular distance to the target, for both technique. The Euclidean distance is computed as the distance between the centers of the two objects. The angular difference d_a is computed as

$$d_a = 2 \cdot arccos(q_{d\omega}) \; ; \quad q_d = q_o^{-1} \cdot q_t \tag{1}$$

with q_o being the quaternion of the manipulated object, q_t being the quaternion of the target, thus q_d being the difference quaternion, and q_ω being the ω component of an $\omega + xi + yj + zk$ quaternion with $i^2 = j^2 = k^2 = ijk = -1$. We then aggregated and averaged both the angular and the Euclidean distances per participant. The distribution is not normal, so we estimated population means using 95% bootstraped confidence intervals (CIs). Fig. 3 clearly shows that there is no evidence of a better performance of P2 over P1 for both the Euclidean distance and the angular distance to the target.

Even though we found no evidence of a performance difference between the two techniques, there were differences in

[5]Data from HCI experiments has often been analyzed by applying null hypothesis significance testing (NHST) in the past. This form of analysis of experimental data, however, is increasingly being criticized by statisticians [4, 16] and within HCI [18, 19]. Therefore, we report our analysis using estimation techniques with effect sizes and confidence intervals (i. e., not using p-values) as recommended by the APA [51]. The term *effect size* here simply refers to the measured difference of means—we do not make use of standardized effect sizes [15] because their use is not generally recommended [3]. While we make use of estimation techniques, a p-value-approach reading of our results can be done by comparing our CIs spacing with common p-value spacing as shown by Krzywinski and Altman [33].

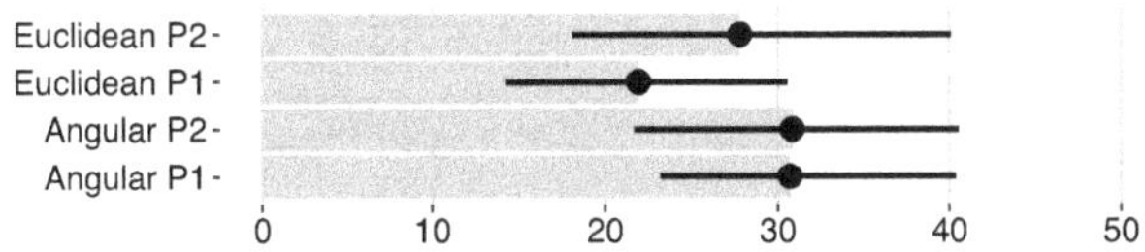

Figure 3. Euclidean and angular distance to the target for both P1 and P2. Error bars are 95% bootstrapped confidence intervals.

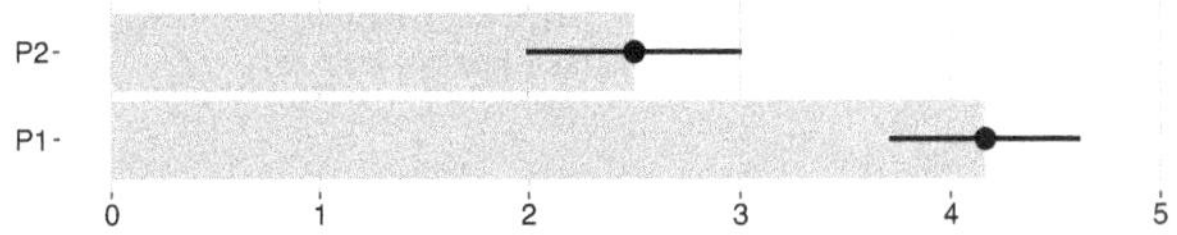

Figure 4. Likert scale score of intuitiveness for each technique. Error bars: 95% bootstrapped CIs.

preference. Fig. 4 shows aggregated ratings of the intuitiveness of each technique on a five-point Likert scale, and 11 out of our 12 participants reported that their favorite technique was P1 which maps a strong pressure input to a high gain factor. They all explained during the semi-structured interview that it felt more logical to have such a mapping. The remaining participant had no overall preference but stated that P1 also seemed more logical. Furthermore, four participants reported that P1 was less tiring than P2 and another six stated that P1 was easier to use. Finally, three participants reported a higher exit error issue—often found in tactile interaction [50]—with P2. Indeed, when leaving a state of high pressure to release the fingers and clutch, the gain factors gets from a very low value to a high value and any involuntary movement of the tablet at that time is thus followed by a relatively big movement of the manipulated object in the virtual world. For all the above reasons, we thus refuted hypothesis H2 and decided to use P1 as the primary mapping for the following experiment.

EXPERIMENT 2: USABILITY OF GAIN FACTOR CONTROL

Our second study used the same prototype and task as Experiment 1. However, we asked participants to perform the docking task with one of four different techniques to compare our pressure-based technique to three established mappings: slider-based control, velocity-based control, and rate control. The first one used a touch-based slider on the dominant hand's side of the screen that allows users to manipulate the gain factor. Arguably, sliders are the most commonly used ways to provide values within a specific range in regular interfaces and, in contrast to keyboard input, are effective on mobile devices. We told each participant that they could change the placement of the slider to the left or right side regardless of their dominant hand. The second technique used the velocity of the tablet's movements (rotations and translations) to derive the gain factor—similar to mouse-based gain factor control [13, 20, 22]. The third technique used a rate-control approach: the further the tablet was translated/rotated away from its initial position, the higher was the gain factor for translation/rotations. However, because rate-control has been proven to be inappropriate for devices without a self-centering mechanism [57], we compensated by adding a centering mechanism based on clutching. Still, rate-control is frequently used for 3D games with remote controls or joysticks so we deemed it an appropriate candidate for a comparison with the added centering mechanism. For the sake of fairness, the value of the gain factor was represented on the (potentially inactive slider in all cases. We also note that the gain factor ranges were identical for all conditions. We used the pilot studies to find appropriate (linear) mappings from the available input value ranges of these three techniques to the range of gain factors.

Participants

For this study, we recruited 24 new unpaid participants (9 female; ages 20–53, mean = 31.6, med = 26.5, SD = 11.1). Twelve of them had at least a university degree (bachelor or equivalent), while the remaining half had at most an A-level equivalent. Half of them were experienced with 3D manipulation through extensive use of video games (9×) or 3D modeling software (3×). Two participants were left-handed and all participants had normal or corrected-to-normal vision.

Procedure and Task

This experiment was largely based on the precudure of Experiment 1, using the same docking task. Participants were first greeted and introduced to the tablet device, before being told that they would perform translations and rotations with it. We explained the clutching mechanism and made them perform the docking with the high and low gain factors to allow them to understand the necessity of a manual gain factor control. We asked participants to complete 20 docking tasks with each of the mentioned 4 different techniques (total of 80 docking tasks). For each docking task we allowed participants up to 20 seconds, a time span that is based on the average time of 19.2 seconds it took participants to complete the task in Experiment 1. The second experiment thus lasted a bit more than 26 minutes overall.

Similar to Experiment 1, the second study also used an egocentric mapping but participants could change it during this training phase. Eleven participants stated that this mapping was not completely natural for them and switched to an allocentric mapping. In between each technique, participants were asked to fill in a questionnaire to assess their workload and their fatigue. For the former, we used NASA's Task Load Index (TLX).[6] For the latter, we created our own questionnaire based on Shaw's approach [46]. To avoid seemingly random choices made in the second part of the TLX (which were often seen as confusing by participants in our pilot studies) that would lead to inconclusive or even incorrect results, we removed the second part of the TLX questionnaire. We thus performed a *RAW TLX* (RTLX) which, according to Hart's survey [23], is equally well suited as a regular TLX. Finally, at the end of the experiment—and following Nielsen's [39] recommendation for the evaluation of subjective preferences—we asked participants to rank each technique based on their preferences and we conducted semi-structured interviews.

To avoid participant response bias [17], we told our particpants that all the techniques were state-of-the-art techniques, that none of them was invented by us, and that we simply wanted to evaluate how they performed with each of them. Our participant number of 24 ensured that each sequence of conditions was tested exactly once in a counter-balanced fashion).

[6] http://humansystems.arc.nasa.gov/groups/tlx/downloads/TLXScale.pdf

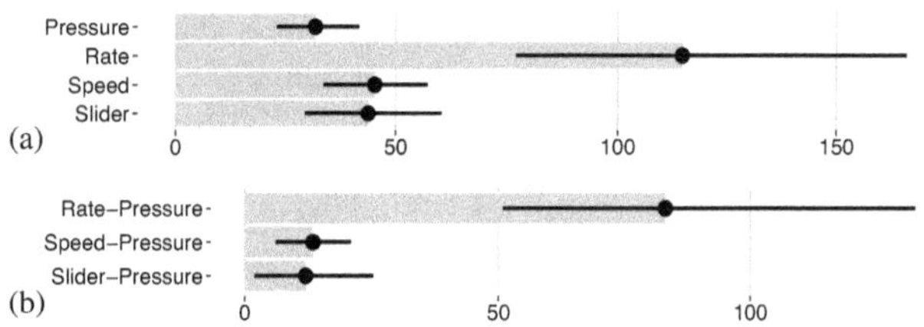

Figure 5. Euclidean distance to the target: (a) absolute values and (b) pair-wise differences. Error bars: 95% bootstrapped CIs.

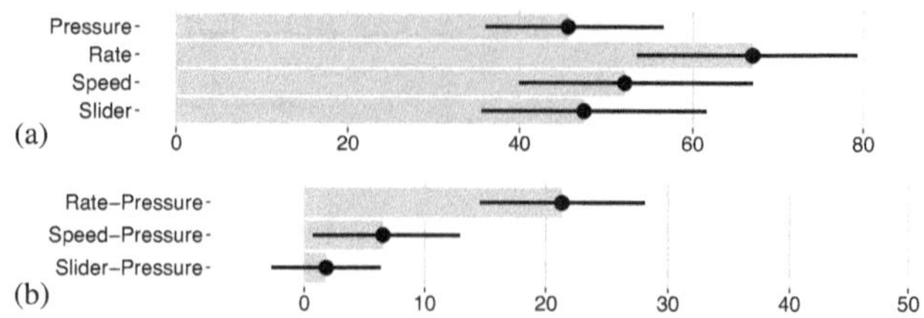

Figure 6. Angular distance to the target: (a) absolute values and (b) pair-wise differences. Error bars: 95% bootstrapped CIs.

Hypotheses

Based on pilot studies and previous work results, we formulated a number of hypotheses:

H3 Even with the clutching mechanism to reset the interaction center, participants' performances using rate control will be poor and it will not be preferred by our participants. The reason is that, even with an added clutching for re-centering [57], on locally-coupled devices the interaction will not be natural due to the conflict of the rate control for the gain factor with the tangible position-based control of the 3D manipulation and it will thus not be understood correctly by most participants.

H4 Pressure-based control will have a higher performance (accuracy) than the three other techniques because it facilitates gain factor manipulation using a separate input channel that does not disrupt the tangible manipulation.

H5 Pressure-based control, however, will cause a higher fatigue in participants' fingers due to the additional force that is necessary compared to the other interaction techniques.

H6 Speed-based control will be the cause of a high overall fatigue and physical demand, even though the mental demand would be low compared to other techniques—we noticed that participants in our pilot studies tended to resort to overly fast movements to ensure that the gain factor will be high, causing sore arms and shoulders.

RESULTS OF EXPERIMENT 2

We now discuss the measured performance values in form of the Euclidean and the angular distance to the target. We also present participants' subjective preferences as well as their self-assessed fatigue, and workload. Similar to Experiment 1 we report our results using simple effect sizes.

Euclidean and Angular Distances

We collected a total of 1920 trials from our 24 partcipants, 480 per technique. We averaged our distance observations per participant and computed population means using 95% bootstrapped confidence intervals.

The Euclidean distances to the target for all four techniques is shown in Fig. 5(a). These results show strong evidence for a better performance of pressure-based, speed-based, and slider-based control compared to rate control. There is also weak evidence for a better performance of pressure-control over the slider-based and speed-based methods. To assess this difference in detail, we looked at the difference between pressure-control and the three other condition as shown in Fig. 5(b). The fact that none of the confidence intervals for these differences overlaps with zero supports our finding of pressure-based control of the gain factor being more accurate than the other techniques: it leads to 3.6 smaller Euclidean distances than rate-control, 1.4 smaller than speed-based control, and 1.3 smaller than slider-based control.

The angular distances to the target for all four techniques are shown in Fig. 6(a). Again, there is a strong evidence that rate control is outperformed by all three other techniques. While there is no evidence for a difference in performance between speed-based and slider-based control or pressure-based and slider-based control, there is slight evidence that pressure-based control may also perform better than speed-based control for rotational distances. Similar to the analysis of the Euclidean distance, we computed the pair-wise differences between pressure-based control and the other techniques and show them in Fig. 6(b). These values confirm that pressure-based control of the gain factor allowed participants to obtain a better angular accuracy than rate-control and speed-based controls The confidence interval of the difference between slider-based and pressured-based control, however, overlaps 0 so that we claim a difference between these two modalities.

Workload

The individual results of the TLX questionnaire are shown in Fig. 7. Fig. 7(a) suggest that strong evidence exists of speed-based control being physically more demanding than slider-based control, but we cannot make any further conclusion with respect to the other techniques. Fig. 7(b), however, shows strong evidence of rate control being approximately 1.5 times more mentally demanding that the other three techniques. Fig. 7(c) exhibits strong evidence of rate control being temporally more demanding than pressure-based, speed-based, and slider-based control. We conjecture that this observation results from participants being more stressed with a technique that they did not master, thus suggesting that rate control does not give them the level of control they wanted. This hypothesis is further reinforced by the confidence intervals shown in Fig. 7(d) which provide strong evidence for rate control giving a much higher (at least twice and almost three times as much when compared to pressure-based control) perceived performance than the other three conditions. Fig. 7(d) also provides strong evidence of a better perceived performance for pressure-based control than for the slider-based or speed-based conditions. While there is no evidence for an difference in effort between rate control, speed-based, or slider-based control, Fig. 7(e) provides strong evidences of pressure-based control being less effort-demanding than the three other techniques.

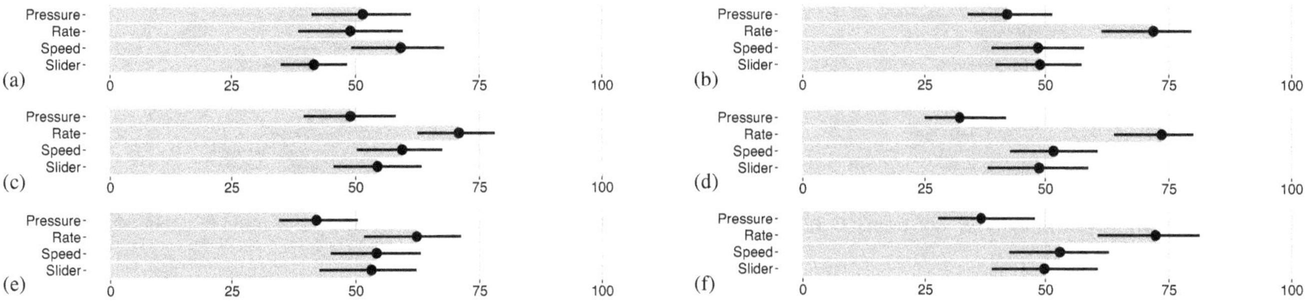

Figure 7. Workload measurement in NASA TLX units (∈ [0, 100]) with respect to (a) physical demand, (b) mental demand, (c) temporal demand, (d) performance (lower is better), (e) effort, and (f) frustration. Error bars: 95% bootstrapped CIs.

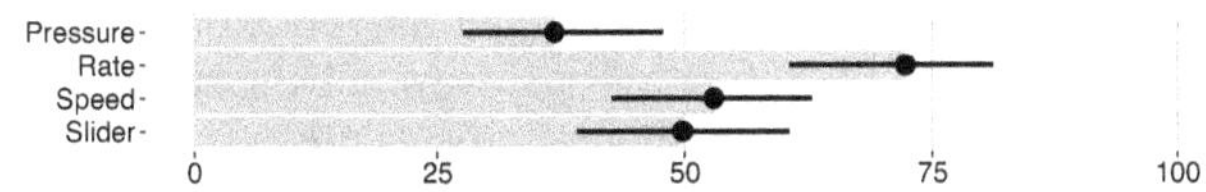

Figure 8. Total workload per factor. Error bars: 95% bootstrapped CIs.

Similarly, Fig. 7(f) has strong evidence that pressure-based control is less frustrating by a factor of two than rate control, and strong evidence for speed-based and slider-based control to be less frustrating than rate control.

The overall TLX workload is shown in Fig. 8. There is strong evidence for a higher workload of the use of rate-control compared to the other techniques. While we cannot find evidence for differences in workload between speed-based and slider-based control, there is evidence that pressure-based control is overall less demanding than all the other techniques.

Fatigue

Fig. 9 presents the results of the fatigue questionnaire that each participant filled in after each condition. We used a 11-point Likert scale (0 meaning no fatigue at all and 10 meaning extreme fatigue) for fingers, hands, arms, and shoulders. Fig. 9(a) suggest that there is strong evidence of the pressure-based control being slightly more tiring (between 1.3 and 1.5 times) for the fingers than the other three techniques. It appears, however, that the overall finger fatigue caused by a pressure-based control is still not too high. We also can see in Fig. 9(b) that all techniques result in a similar hand fatigue. Fig. 9(c) and Fig. 9(d) provide strong evidence of speed-based control causing more arm and shoulder fatigue than pressure-based and slider-based control. However, there is no evidence of a fatigue difference between rate control and the other three conditions for arms and shoulder. The total fatigue measurements are shown in Fig. 10. Fig. 10(a) treats all four fatigue aspects equally and derives the total fatigue measurements as a sum of the individual factors. From these sums we cannot find evidence for a difference in the overall fatigue measure between the different technique. However, the different fatigue aspects may be more or less important to people, so we also asked our participants about the importance of the individual fatigue aspects and derived a weighted aggregated fatigue rating in Fig. 10(b). The mean weighted aggregated fatigue rating is lowest for pressure-based control, with weak evidence of it being different from speed-based control.

technique	*median*	*mean*	*SD*	#1st	#2nd	#3rd	#4th
pressure	1.0	1.5	0.8	15	7	1	1
rate	4.0	3.4	1.0	3	0	3	18
speed	3.0	2.6	0.8	3	8	12	1
slider	2.5	2.4	0.9	3	9	8	4

Table 1. Participants' preferences between their most favorite (1) and least favorite (4) technique to control the gain factor.

Preference and Qualitative Feedback

After the experiment, we asked participants to rank the technique from their preferred (1) to their least preferred (4) method for which we present the results in Table 1. The pressure modality was most preferred 15× and the slider-based control, the speed-based control, and the rate-control were most preferred by 3 participants each. These results show a strong preference for the pressure-based control of the gain-factor. Similarly, we found that most participants did not like the rate control technique. It is more difficult, however, to state a definite difference between speed-based and and slider-based control. To better analyze this result, we determined the number of times each technique was picked as the favorite with simultaneous confidence intervals (that are applied on a multinomial distribution) and show the result in Fig. 11. The non-overlapping confidence interval of pressure-based control with all three other techniques allows us to infer that pressure-based control is likely to be the preferred technique by a vast majority of the population.

Participants also voiced interesting comments during the study. Two participants stated that the pressure-based control gave them a better feeling of precision and of being in control, thus "eliminating all the temporal pressure of the experiment." Two other participants also reported that, although the "speed-based control [was] interesting," it was difficult to evaluate and find the correct speed needed to achieve what they wanted. Three participants who picked the slider as their favorite technique stated at the end of the experiment that it was "easy to use" and that it gave "the more precise control of the gain factor."

DISCUSSION

Based on these results we now discuss our most relevant and interesting findings. Our ultimate goal in this work is to find a modality that is suitable for gain factor control for 3D tangible manipulations of a locally-coupled device.

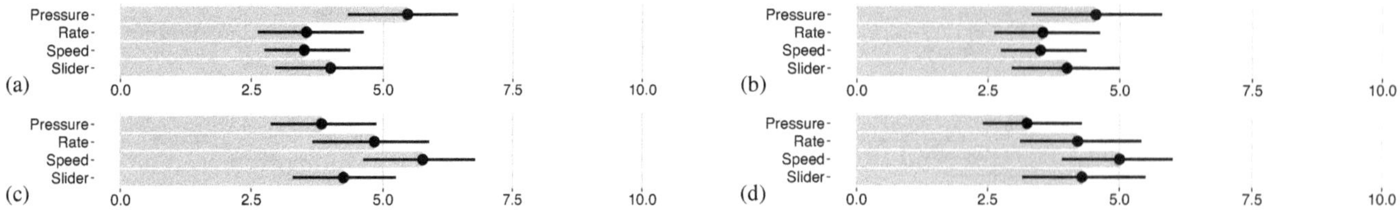

Figure 9. Fatigue measurement on a scale from 0 to 10 for (a) fingers, (b) hands, (c) arms, and (d) shoulders. Error bars: 95% bootstrapped CIs.

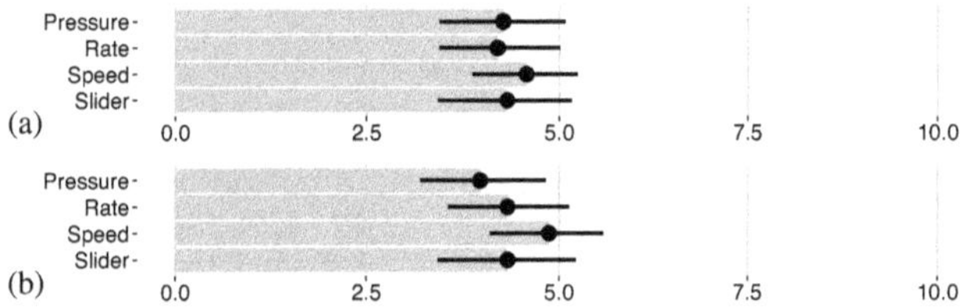

Figure 10. Aggregated fatigue measurements: (a) non-weighted and (b) weighted, both from 0 to 10. Error bars: 95% bootstrapped CIs.

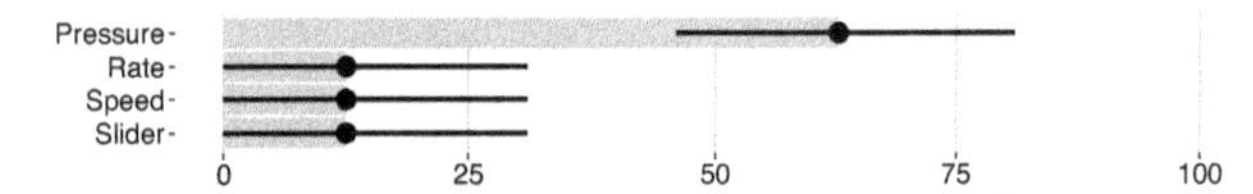

Figure 11. Percentage of times of each technique to be named the number one favorite. Error bars: 95% bootstrapped CIs.

Performance

Support for our hypothesis H3 comes from the poor performance of rate control compared to the other three techniques. For both Euclidean and angular distances, rate control exhibits performance results that do not make it a viable technique for gain factor manipulations. One of the reasons for this finding is likely the lack of self-centering mechanism [57]. However, an interaction technique based on rate control is also an indirect and joystick-like manipulation which contrasts the direct manipulations otherwise offered by the tablet. This contrast may also contribute to the poor performance of rate control we observed with our participants.

For both Euclidean and angular distances, our study did not reveal a difference between speed-based and slider-based control. Both techniques also performed noticeably better than rate control. Pressure-based control, however, clearly provided better performances in terms of Euclidean distances—even though this difference could not be found for the angular distances. We can thus partially confirm our hypothesis H4: the overall performance obtained by pressure-based control is better than the three other conditions, but the difference (compared to slider-based and speed-based control) is small and only noticeable for Euclidean distances.

Fatigue

We can confirm our hypothesis H5: pressure-based control caused more fatigue in participants' fingers than the other three interaction techniques. However, for hand, arm, and shoulder fatigue the pressure-based control caused only as much fatigue or less compared to the other techniques we tested. Hypothesis H5 should thus be treated in a nuanced way. This point is further reinforced by the overall and weighted overall fatigue ratings we showed in Fig. 10 that exhibit no evidence for pressure-based control causing more fatigue than the other techniques overall. We can thus conclude that fatigue considerations do not prevent us using pressure-based control. Moreover, we conjecture that finger fatigue could have been reduced with if the pressure sensors were better integrated in the device: In our study the participants pressed their fingers on a bare and hard pressure sensor attached to the tablet. The use of memory foam or other visco-elastic components above the pressure sensors could probably reduce the finger fatigue.

We can, however, dismiss our hypothesis H6. Not only was the mental workload of the speed-based control similar to that of the other techniques (or smaller than that of rate control), but also the overall fatigue it caused was not higher than the fatigue of the other techniques—except potentially compared to pressure-based control in the weighted average.

Workload

While the individual workload aspects may each be slightly different, the overall workload is lower for pressure-based control than for all the other techniques. This result only further supports our conclusion about the performance measurements and fatigue ratings, showing that pressure-based control is not only a viable contender but an ideal choice for the adjustment of the gain factor. Moreover, the perceived performance (Fig. 7(d)) was best with pressure-based control. This specific result means that our participants were not only more precise with this technique but also had the highest confidence in their results in this experimental condition.

Preferences

In addition to all these measured benefits, our experimental results also allow us to conclude that pressured-based control was clearly the favorite technique to adjust the gain factor among our 24 participants. Indeed, 15 of them reported that it was their preferred technique. Such a ratio allows us to generalize our results beyond the pool of our 24 participants: overall, people will likely prefer the pressure-based control over the other tested techniques.

Design Guidelines and Recommendations

While pressure-based control thus has clear benefits to controlling the gain factor, it is sometimes also necessary to set a well-defined gain factor value. Such control is difficult with pressure input, but is easily facilitated by a slider or text widget as highlighted by three participants. So while we advocate the use of pressure input in general, it may be useful to integrate it with a way to set an explicit value though a slider or otherwise, for example for expert users or in professional tools. In fact, nothing prohibits the implementation of all four techniques, with a possibility to set the main technique based on personal preferences. Yet, we still recommend to use pressure-based control as the default due to its discussed performance benefits.

Limitations

Despite our careful experimental design there are some limitations to be mentioned. In particular, there may be a bias towards the novelty of the pressure-based control—after all, it has only recently been introduced to mobile device interaction for the general public. We also argue, however, that the overall tangible manipulation was new as well to our participants and that, therefore, the novelty effect of pressure-based manipulation was likely not too large. While no participant reported being tired or feeling any particular fatigue in our first study which exposed them to pressure manipulation for 20 minutes, we—for the sake of performance evaluation—reduced the interaction time for each technique to approximately 6 minutes. This reduction implies that further work is needed to check the influence of each technique on fatigue or physical demand with a longer exposition time. In addition, the task we asked our participant to carry out was a generic 3D manipulation task. While it is used in many 3D studies, it may not completely resemble the 3D interaction tasks needed for specific 3D interaction scenarios. Pressure-based control should thus also be evaluated in the context other application domains, including those that rely on less abstract tasks than 3D docking.

CONCLUSION

With our design and evaluation of a pressure-based interactive control of the gain factor for 3D navigation we identified an appropriate channel for such manipulations—one that is independent from the otherwise dominant channels such as tactile and tangible input. Our first experiment guided our interaction design and the specific pressure mapping we used, while the second experiment provided clear evidence for the advantages of the new design over other types of input.

One of the most important insights we derive from our experiments is that the use of pressure input allowed our participants, in particular, to focus on their 3D manipulation task without the need to constantly reflect the interaction mapping (as it was the case for speed-based and rate control) and without the need to constantly change their interaction focus to be able to interact with a separate widget on the display (like it was necessary for slider-based control). We argue that our participants were thus more effective in their interaction (better performance), without pressure-based control causing any additional cost on workload or fatigue.

In our work we used a specific back-of-device design to enable pressure-based interaction. While we believe that this setup has advantages with respect to the ergonomics of the interaction with the tablet and the use of screen real estate, the general use of pressure as an input channel for gain factor control does not require the use of such a back-of-device design. Input could thus also be provided on the front of the device—and there are already commercially available devices that offer such display-based pressure sensing. Moreover, due to the specific character of the gain factor control that only requires the input of differences—and not of precise, absolute input values—it is also possible to use existing pseudo-pressure sensing [1, 2] which could be explored in the future.

Our work thus provides guidelines to implement gain factor control for 3D manipulations and other forms of interaction, for a variety of mobile devices. Our results, however, may also be generalizable to the control of other scalar values where only relative changes are important and constant visual feedback is provided.

REFERENCES

1. Ahmed Sabbir Arif, Ali Mazalek, and Wolfgang Sturzlinger. 2014. The use of pseudo pressure in authenticating smartphone users. In *Proceedongs of the International Conference on Mobile and Ubiquitous Systems: Computing, Networking and Services*. ICST, Brussels, 151–160. DOI: http://dx.doi.org/10.4108/icst.mobiquitous.2014.257919
2. Ahmed Sabbir Arif and Wolfgang Stuerzlinger. 2013. Pseudo-pressure detection and its use in predictive text entry on touchscreens. In *Proceedings of the Australian Computer-Human Interaction Conference: Augmentation, Application, Innovation, Collaboration*. ACM, New York, 383–392. DOI: http://dx.doi.org/10.1145/2541016.2541024
3. Thom Baguley. 2009. Standardized or simple effect size: What should be reported? *British Journal of Psychology* 100, 3 (Aug. 2009), 603–617. DOI: http://dx.doi.org/10.1348/000712608X377117
4. Monya Baker. 2015. Statisticians issue warning over misuse of P values. *Nature* 531, 7593 (March 2015), 151. DOI:http://dx.doi.org/10.1038/nature.2016.19503
5. Patrick Baudisch and Gerry Chu. 2009. Back-of-device interaction allows creating very small touch devices. In *Proceedings of the SIGCHI Conference on Human Factors in Computing Systems*. ACM, New York, 1923–1932. DOI: http://dx.doi.org/10.1145/1518701.1518995
6. Hrvoje Benko, Andrew D. Wilson, and Patrick Baudisch. 2006. Precise selection techniques for multi-touch screens. In *Proceedings of the SIGCHI Conference on Human Factors in Computing Systems*. ACM, New York, 1263–1272. DOI: http://dx.doi.org/10.1145/1124772.1124963
7. Lonni Besançon, Paul Issartel, Mehdi Ammi, and Tobias Isenberg. 2017. Hybrid tactile/tangible interaction for 3D data exploration. *IEEE Transactions on Visualization and Computer Graphics* 23, 1 (Jan. 2017), 881–890. DOI: http://dx.doi.org/10.1109/TVCG.2016.2599217
8. Renaud Blanch, Yves Guiard, and Michel Beaudouin-Lafon. 2004. Semantic pointing: Improving target acquisition with control-display ratio adaptation. In *Proceedings of the SIGCHI Conference on Human Factors in Computing Systems*. ACM, New York, 519–526. DOI:http://dx.doi.org/10.1145/985692.985758

9. Stephen A. Brewster and Michael Hughes. 2009. Pressure-based text entry for mobile devices. In *Proceedings of the SIGCHI Conference on Human Factors in Computing Systems*. ACM, New York. DOI: http://dx.doi.org/10.1145/1613858.1613870

10. Neil Burgess, Hugo J. Spiers, and Eleni Paleologou. 2004. Orientational manoeuvres in the dark: Dissociating allocentric and egocentric influences on spatial memory. *Cognition* 94, 2 (Dec. 2004), 149–166. DOI: http://dx.doi.org/10.1016/j.cognition.2004.01.001

11. Bill Buxton. 2007. Multi-touch systems that I have known and loved. Website. (Jan. 2007). http://www.billbuxton.com/multitouchOverview.html Updated last on June 12, 2014, visited in March 2016.

12. William Buxton, Ralph Hill, and Peter Rowley. 1985. Issues and techniques in touch-sensitive tablet input. *ACM SIGGRAPH Computer Graphics* 19, 3 (July 1985), 215–224. DOI: http://dx.doi.org/10.1145/325165.325239

13. Géry Casiez, Daniel Vogel, Ravin Balakrishnan, and Andy Cockburn. 2008. The impact of control-display gain on user performance in pointing tasks. *Human–Computer Interaction* 23, 3 (2008), 215–250. DOI: http://dx.doi.org/10.1080/07370020802278163

14. Jared Cechanowicz, Pourang Irani, and Sriram Subramanian. 2007. Augmenting the mouse with pressure sensitive input. In *Proceedings of the SIGCHI Conference on Human Factors in Computing Systems*. ACM, New York, 1385–1394. DOI: http://dx.doi.org/10.1145/1240624.1240835

15. Robert Coe. 2002. It's the effect size, stupid: What effect size is and why it is important. In *Proceedings of the Annual Conference of the British Educational Research Association*. http://www.leeds.ac.uk/educol/documents/00002182.htm

16. Geoff Cumming. 2014. The new statistics: Why and how. *Psychological Science* 25, 1 (Jan. 2014), 7–29. DOI: http://dx.doi.org/10.1177/0956797613504966

17. Nicola Dell, Vidya Vaidyanathan, Indrani Medhi, Edward Cutrell, and William Thies. 2012. "Yours is better!" Participant response bias in HCI. In *Proceedings of the SIGCHI Conference on Human Factors in Computing Systems*. ACM, New York, 1321–1330. DOI: http://dx.doi.org/10.1145/2207676.2208589

18. Pierre Dragicevic. 2016. Fair statistical communication in HCI. In *Modern Statistical Methods for HCI*, Judy Robertson and Maurits Kaptein (Eds.). Springer International Publishing, Cham, Switzerland, Chapter 13, 291–330. DOI: http://dx.doi.org/10.1007/978-3-319-26633-6_13

19. Pierre Dragicevic, Fanny Chevalier, and Stéphane Huot. 2014. Running an HCI experiment in multiple parallel universes. In *Extended Abstracts on Human Factors in Computing Systems*. ACM, New York, 607–618. DOI: http://dx.doi.org/10.1145/2559206.2578881

20. James D. Foley, Victor L. Wallace, and Peggy Chan. 1984. The human factors of computer graphics interaction techniques. *IEEE Computer Graphics and Applications* 4, 11 (Nov. 1984), 13–48. DOI: http://dx.doi.org/10.1109/MCG.1984.6429355

21. Clifton Forlines, Chia Shen, and Bill Buxton. 2005. Glimpse: A novel input model for multi-level devices. In *Extended Abstracts on Human Factors in Computing Systems*. ACM, New York, 1375–1378. DOI: http://dx.doi.org/10.1145/1056808.1056920

22. Scott Frees and G. Drew Kessler. 2005. Precise and rapid interaction through scaled manipulation in immersive virtual environments. In *Proceedings of the IEEE Conference on Virtual Reality*. IEEE, 99–106. DOI: http://dx.doi.org/10.1109/VR.2005.1492759

23. Sandra G. Hart. 2006. NASA-task load index (NASA-TLX); 20 years later. *Proceedings of the Human Factors and Ergonomics Society Annual Meeting* 50, 9 (Oct. 2006), 904–908. DOI: http://dx.doi.org/10.1177/154193120605000909

24. Christopher F. Herot and Guy Weinzapfel. 1978. One-point touch input of vector information for computer displays. *ACM SIGGRAPH Computer Graphics* 12, 3 (Aug. 1978), 210–216. DOI: http://dx.doi.org/10.1145/965139.807392

25. Ken Hinckley, Randy Pausch, John C. Goble, and Neal F. Kassell. 1994. A survey of design issues in spatial input. In *Proceedings of the Annual ACM Symposium on User Interface Software and Technology*. ACM, New York, 213–222. DOI: http://dx.doi.org/10.1145/192426.192501

26. Shigeo Hiraoka, Isshin Miyamoto, and Kiyoshi Tomimatsu. 2003. Behind touch, a text input method for mobile phones by the back and tactile sense interface. In *Proceedings of Interaction*. Information Processing Society of Japan, Tokyo, 131–138.

27. Hiroshi Ishii and Brygg Ullmer. 1997. Tangible bits: Towards seamless interfaces between people, bits and atoms. In *Proceedings of the SIGCHI Conference on Human Factors in Computing Systems*. ACM, New York, 234–241. DOI: http://dx.doi.org/10.1145/258549.258715

28. Paul Issartel, Lonni Besançon, Florimond Guéniat, Tobias Isenberg, and Mehdi Ammi. 2016a. Preference between allocentric and egocentric 3D manipulation in a locally coupled configuration. In *Proceedings of the ACM Symposium on Spatial User Interaction*. ACM, New York, 79–88. DOI: http://dx.doi.org/10.1145/2983310.2985750

29. Paul Issartel, Lonni Besançon, Tobias Isenberg, and Meryem Ammi. 2016b. A tangible volume for portable 3D interaction. In *Proceedings of the International Symposium on Mixed and Augmented Reality*. IEEE Computer Society, Los Alamitos.

30. Paul Issartel, Florimond Guéniat, Tobias Isenberg, and Mehdi Ammi. 2016c. *Analysis of locally coupled 3D manipulation mappings based on mobile device motion.*

arXiv.org preprint 1603.07462. http://www.arxiv.org/abs/1603.07462

31. Jeroen Keijser, Sheelagh Carpendale, Mark Hancock, and Tobias Isenberg. 2007. Exploring 3D interaction in alternate control-display space mappings. In *Proceedings of the IEEE Symposium on 3D User Interfaces*. IEEE Computer Society, Los Alamitos, 17–24. DOI: http://dx.doi.org/10.1109/3DUI.2007.340769

32. Roberta L. Klatzky. 1998. Allocentric and egocentric spatial representations: Definitions, distinctions, and interconnections. In *Spatial cognition*, Christian Freksa, Christopher Habel, and Karl F. Wender (Eds.). Springer, Berlin/Heidelberg, 210–216. DOI: http://dx.doi.org/10.1007/3-540-69342-4_1

33. Martin Krzywinski and Naomi Altman. 2013. Points of significance: Error bars. *Nature Methods* 10, 10 (Oct. 2013), 921–922. http://dx.doi.org/10.1038/nmeth.2659

34. Kevin A. Li, Patrick Baudisch, and Ken Hinckley. 2008. Blindsight: Eyes-free access to mobile phones. In *Proceedings of the SIGCHI Conference on Human Factors in Computing Systems*. ACM, New York, 1389–1398. DOI: http://dx.doi.org/10.1145/1357054.1357273

35. Hai-Ning Liang, Cary Williams, Myron Semegen, Wolfgang Stuerzlinger, and Pourang Irani. 2013. An investigation of suitable interactions for 3D manipulation of distant objects through a mobile device. *International Journal of Innovative Computing, Information and Control* 9, 12 (Dec. 2013), 4737–4752. http://www.ijicic.org/apchi12-291.pdf

36. I. Scott MacKenzie and Stan Riddersma. 1994. Effects of output display and control-display gain on human performance in interactive systems. *Behaviour & Information Technology* 13, 5 (1994), 328–337. DOI: http://dx.doi.org/10.1080/01449299408914613

37. Ross McLachlan, Daniel Boland, and Stephen Brewster. 2014. Transient and transitional states: pressure as an auxiliary input modality for bimanual interaction. In *Proceedings of the SIGCHI Conference on Human Factors in Computing Systems*. ACM, New York, 401–410. DOI: http://dx.doi.org/10.1145/2556288.2557260

38. Ross McLachlan and Stephen Brewster. 2015. Bimanual input for tablet devices with pressure and multi-touch gestures. In *Proceedings of the International Conference on Human-Computer Interaction with Mobile Devices and Services*. ACM, New York, 547–556. DOI: http://dx.doi.org/10.1145/2785830.2785878

39. Jakob Nielsen. 1993. *Usability Engineering*. Morgan Kaufmann, San Francisco. DOI: http://dx.doi.org/10.1016/B978-0-08-052029-2.50001-2

40. Ivan Poupyrev, Suzanne Weghorst, Mark Billinghurst, and Tadao Ichikawa. 1998. Egocentric object manipulation in virtual environments: Empirical evaluation of interaction techniques. *Computer Graphics Forum* 17, 3 (Sept. 1998), 41–52. DOI: http://dx.doi.org/10.1111/1467-8659.00252

41. Mahfuz Rahman, Sean Gustafson, Pourang Irani, and Sriram Subramanian. 2009. Tilt techniques: investigating the dexterity of wrist-based input. In *Proceedings of the SIGCHI Conference on Human Factors in Computing Systems*. ACM, 1943–1952.

42. Gonzalo Ramos and Ravin Balakrishnan. 2005. Zliding: Fluid zooming and sliding for high precision parameter manipulation. In *Proceedings of the Annual ACM Symposium on User Interface Software and Technology*. ACM, New York, 143–152. DOI: http://dx.doi.org/10.1145/1095034.1095059

43. Gonzalo Ramos, Matthew Boulos, and Ravin Balakrishnan. 2004. Pressure widgets. In *Proceedings of the SIGCHI Conference on Human Factors in Computing Systems*. ACM, New York, 487–494. DOI: http://dx.doi.org/10.1145/985692.985754

44. Xiangshi Ren, Jibin Yin, Shengdong Zhao, and Yang Li. 2007. The adaptive hybrid cursor: A pressure-based target selection technique for pen-based user interfaces. In *Proceedings of the IFIP Conference on Human-Computer Interaction*. Springer, Berlin/Heidelberg, 310–323. DOI: http://dx.doi.org/10.1007/978-3-540-74796-3_29

45. Carsten Schwesig, Ivan Poupyrev, and Eijiro Mori. 2004. Gummi: A bendable computer. In *Proceedings of the SIGCHI Conference on Human Factors in Computing Systems*. ACM, New York, 263–270. DOI: http://dx.doi.org/10.1145/985692.985726

46. Christopher D. Shaw. 1998. Pain and fatigue in desktop VR: Initial results. In *Proceedings of Graphics Interface*. CIPS, Toronto, 185–192. DOI: http://dx.doi.org/10.20380/GI1998.23

47. Erh-li Early Shen, Sung-sheng Daniel Tsai, Hao-hua Chu, Yung-jen Jane Hsu, and Chi-wen Euro Chen. 2009. Double-side multi-touch input for mobile devices. In *Extended Abstracts on Human Factors in Computing Systems*. ACM, New York, 4339–4344. DOI: http://dx.doi.org/10.1145/1520340.1520663

48. Craig Stewart, Michael Rohs, Sven Kratz, and Georg Essl. 2010. Characteristics of pressure-based input for mobile devices. In *Proceedings of the SIGCHI Conference on Human Factors in Computing Systems*. ACM, New York, 801–810. DOI: http://dx.doi.org/10.1145/1753326.1753444

49. Masanori Sugimoto and Keiichi Hiroki. 2006. HybridTouch: An intuitive manipulation technique for PDAs using their front and rear surfaces. In *Proceedings of the International Conference on Human-Computer Interaction with Mobile Devices and Services*. ACM, New York, 137–140. DOI: http://dx.doi.org/10.1145/1152215.1152243

50. Philip Tuddenham, David Kirk, and Shahram Izadi. 2010. Graspables revisited: Multi-touch vs. tangible input for tabletop displays in acquisition and manipulation tasks. In *Proceedings of the SIGCHI Conference on Human Factors in Computing Systems*. ACM, New York, 2223–2232. DOI: http://dx.doi.org/10.1145/1753326.1753662

51. Gary R. VandenBos (Ed.). 2009. *Publication Manual of the American Psychological Association* (6th ed.). American Psychological Association, Washington, DC. http://www.apastyle.org/manual/

52. Daniel Wigdor, Clifton Forlines, Patrick Baudisch, John Barnwell, and Chia Shen. 2007. LucidTouch: A see-through mobile device. In *Proceedings of the Annual ACM Symposium on User Interface Software and Technology*. ACM, New York, 269–278. DOI: http://dx.doi.org/10.1145/1294211.1294259

53. Daniel Wigdor, Darren Leigh, Clifton Forlines, Samuel Shipman, John Barnwell, Ravin Balakrishnan, and Chia Shen. 2006. Under the table interaction. In *Proceedings of the Annual ACM Symposium on User Interface Software and Technology*. ACM, New York, 259–268. DOI:http://dx.doi.org/10.1145/1166253.1166294

54. Graham Wilson, Craig Stewart, and Stephen A. Brewster. 2010. Pressure-based menu selection for mobile devices. In *Proceedings of the International Conference on Human-Computer Interaction with Mobile Devices and Services*. ACM, New York, 181–190. DOI: http://dx.doi.org/10.1145/1851600.1851631

55. Graham Alasdair Wilson. 2013. *Using pressure input and thermal feedback to broaden haptic interaction with mobile devices*. Ph.D. Dissertation. University of Glasgow, Scotland. http://theses.gla.ac.uk/id/eprint/4363

56. Aileen Worden, Nef Walker, Krishna Bharat, and Scott Hudson. 1997. Making computers easier for older adults to use: Area cursors and sticky icons. In *Proceedings of the SIGCHI Conference on Human Factors in Computing Systems*. ACM, New York, 266–271. DOI: http://dx.doi.org/10.1145/258549.258724

57. Shumin Zhai. 1998. User performance in relation to 3D input device design. *ACM SIGGRAPH Computer Graphics* 32, 4 (Nov. 1998), 50–54. DOI: http://dx.doi.org/10.1145/307710.307728

The Effect of Peripheral Micro-tasks on Crowd Ideation

Victor Girotto[1] **Erin Walker**[1]
[1] School of Computing, Informatics, and Decision Systems Engineering
Arizona State University
Tempe, AZ, USA
{victor.girotto, erin.a.walker}@asu.edu

Winslow Burleson[2]
[2] Rory Meyers College of Nursing
New York University
New York, NY, USA
wb50@nyu.edu

ABSTRACT
Research has explored different ways of improving crowd ideation, such as presenting examples or employing facilitators. While such support is usually generated through peripheral tasks delegated to crowd workers who are not part of the ideation, it is possible that the ideators themselves could benefit from the extra thought involved in doing them. Therefore, we iterate over an ideation system in which ideators can perform one of three peripheral tasks (rating originality and usefulness, similarity, or idea combination) on demand. In controlled experiments with workers on Mechanical Turk, we compare the effects of these secondary tasks to simple idea exposure or no support at all, examining usage of the inspirations, fluency, breadth, and depth of ideas generated. We find tasks to be as good or better than exposure, although this depends on the period of ideation and the fluency level. We also discuss implications of inspiration size, homogeneity, and frequency.

Author Keywords
Crowdsourcing; ideation; creativity; microtasks.

ACM Classification Keywords
H.5.3. Group and Organization Interfaces: Computer-supported cooperative work.

INTRODUCTION
With the advent of crowdsourcing, people can now collectively accomplish a wide range of tasks that could not otherwise be done by a single human or computer. One approach to crowdsourcing that has stood out is the use of micro-task markets such as Amazon's Mechanical Turk (MTurk) [14]. In this approach, many workers perform small tasks that together approximate the quality of experts. Using micro-task markets, researchers have been able to achieve good results on a wide variety of tasks [2,5].

CHI 2017, May 06-11, 2017, Denver, CO, USA
 ISBN 978-1-4503-4655-9/17/05…$15.00
DOI: http://dx.doi.org/10.1145/3025453.3025464

In our work, we leverage a similar micro-tasks paradigm to achieve creative solutions in response to complex problems. Creativity thrives on diversity and exploration. It is about creating something that is both novel, breaking away from common knowledge or practices, but at the same time being appropriate or useful [11]. From designing T-shirts (www.threadless.com) to solving tough technical challenges (www.innocentive.com), there are many examples of the crowd performing tasks that rely on their creativity.

Why explore the creativity of the crowds? The first reason is that a great number of people will generate a great number of ideas. Furthermore, the heterogeneity of the crowd can increase the potential of ideas being sparked that otherwise wouldn't [8]. However, there are also issues that need to be carefully considered in a system that tries to tap into the crowd's creativity. Issues such as cognitive interference or social loafing can increase together with the number of ideators [8]. Therefore, crowd ideation needs to be carefully designed in order to improve, not hinder the creative output.

A popular method used for generating ideas is typically brainstorming, which seeks to increase the number of ideas generated by encouraging intensive exploration of ideas while restricting criticism [25]. In the crowd context, just like in smaller groups, people have tried to enhance idea generation during brainstorming sessions in different ways, many times employing other individuals or workers, outside of ideation, to do tasks whose output will benefit ideators. We call these tasks *peripheral tasks*. The result of their work is then presented in some way to crowd ideators. For example: Yu et al. [31] had workers generate problem schemas, and subsequently used them to enhance ideation performance of other workers in a subsequent study. However, the extra cognitive effort that is required to perform these tasks could potentially benefit ideators as much as just using their results.

This paper, therefore, examines the effect that performing peripheral tasks has on ideation. More specifically, it embeds three types of peripheral tasks—rating, similarity, and combination—into an online brainstorming session. We explore the following questions:

1. How does performing peripheral micro-tasks affect ideation performance?
2. Do different types of peripheral tasks affect ideation differently? If so, how?

Exploration of these questions could allow ideation systems to move from passive to active forms of inspiration and support, resulting in more data collection during an ideation session, aiding in convergent tasks such as idea selection. A similar approach has been explored by Siangliulue and colleagues through the IdeaHound system [28]. IdeaHound allows users to physically cluster semantically related ideas together in a virtual workspace. This organization enables the system to infer a semantic model of the ideas. Our approach differs in that it makes this data collection explicit rather than implicitly building it in the UI interactions of the system. In other words, rather than inferring semantic relatedness by examining how ideators cluster ideas together, we explicitly ask them to judge the similarity of two ideas. Our focus, however, is on how doing these tasks affects ideation performance, rather than examining their result.

In the remainder of this paper, we review literature related to creativity and crowdsourcing. We then describe a system built to allow ideators to perform small tasks during ideation, and describe metrics for its evaluation, including a tree-based representation of individual ideators' performance. We then describe four experiments, evaluating how their combined results answer the questions above. Generally, we find that tasks are just as useful as simple idea exposure, with rating and combination tasks even outperforming it in certain situations. We also explore how inspiration size, frequency, and homogeneity affects ideation.

RELATED WORK

Creativity: Convergent and Divergent Processes

Creativity can be defined, at the most basic level, as the production of something original and appropriate [11]. While there are many different theories of the underlying nature of creative processes and products [17], our specific interest is in the dichotomy between divergent and convergent processes. Divergent processes are those that generate a wide variety of ideas, thus increasing the solution space [6,17]. On the other hand, convergent processes are those that involve the selection of a particular number of the best ideas, seeking to reduce ambiguity and the size of the possible solution space [6,17]. Both processes are necessary for creativity: generating variability (divergence) without effectively exploring and evaluating your ideas (convergence) can lead to lost opportunities or disastrous changes [6].

Brainstorming

Much of the effort in research and practice in improving creativity has focused on supporting divergent processes through brainstorming. Brainstorming was popularized by Osborn in the 1950's, and consists of a few simple rules, such as holding back on criticism and building on the ideas of others [25]. There are in fact benefits to this approach, as attending to the ideas of others can be inspiring [19,23]. But it is vulnerable to factors such as evaluation apprehension, free riding, or perhaps more influentially, production blocking—that is, not being able to share or generate new ideas while someone is sharing theirs [9].

By moving from interactive co-located groups to electronic communication media, production blocking and other issues can be lessened [7]. For example, individuals in an ideation group that uses an instant messaging channel for collaboration don't have to wait their turn to speak, and can choose to attend to others' ideas as they desire. Furthermore, as communication technologies advance and the world grows increasingly connected, ever increasing group sizes become more feasible and the possibility of synergy between the participants' ideas can also increase [7,8]. In other words, by being exposed to more ideas, it becomes more likely that users will see concepts that may spark new ideas.

One common feature of group brainstorming sessions is to hear ideas developed by others and build on them. Exposure to other ideas may have different effects depending on the type of exposure, with the possibility of either stimulating or hindering creativity. On the one hand, exposure to a diverse set of ideas can increase breadth of ideation, while exposure to a homogenous set of ideas can increase the depth of exploration within each semantic category [24]. On the other hand, exposure to ideas might lead to conformity and fixation effects, where ideators take the main concepts of the ideas they were exposed to and use them in their solutions [13,19,30]. This cognitive interference may affect the exploration of the solution space, causing answers to be more like each other. There is evidence that the nature of the external influence as well as *how* you attend to it defines its effect on you. Paying too much attention to the superficial details of the example ideas may lead to fixation [13,19], while a higher-level view of ideas, possibly in the form of analogies or schemas, can improve idea generation [31,32].

Perhaps the clearest way to understand the effect of external stimuli comes from the Search for Ideas in Associate Memory (SIAM) model [23,24]. This model assumes the existence of two kinds of memory: a low-capacity short-term memory, i.e. working memory (WM) and a high-capacity long-term memory (LTM). It proposes that idea generation involves these two memories in two stages: first, an ideator retrieves a concept along with its features from LTM into the WM (e.g. the concept *hotel* has the feature "has rooms" [23]), and then generates ideas based it. When the ideator continuously fails at generating new ideas based on the current concept, he or she may activate another concept from the search queue and try again. This queue is comprised of items such as the problem definition or previously generated ideas. When an idea is shown to an ideator, it can be added to the search queue if it is sufficiently attended to [24]. Therefore, it can be said that an ideator had a great *breadth* of ideation if he or she explored many concepts and great *depth* if he or she developed many ideas within a concept.

Peripheral Ideation Tasks

Much of the support for crowd ideation sessions comes from peripheral tasks done by other MTurk crowd workers. These tasks can be classified along four main categories: rating, combination, inspiration design, and problem abstraction. In crowd ideation contexts, workers outside of the ideation are typically tasked with performing them. However, we argue that these tasks have promise for improving the quality of brainstorming when executed by the ideators themselves. We now review the rating and combination tasks, which are explored in depth in this paper. They were chosen due to their simplicity and for their usage of external ideas, allowing for a cleaner comparison with simple idea exposure. We leave the remaining two categories for future work.

Rating

Rating an idea or artifact on one or more dimensions is one of the most common forms of peripheral tasks. We are concerned with two types of rating: the nature of the idea (originality and usefulness), or its similarity to other ideas. Rating can support ideation by, for example, presenting the most creative or diverse sets of ideas as inspiration to other ideators [24]. Comparisons are either relative—rate ideas in terms of each other—or absolute—rate ideas individually on a given scale. For example, Siangliulue et al. [27] looked into rating ideas based on their similarity in two different ways: for the first, they presented workers with three ideas, asking them to choose which of two ideas was more similar to another. They also tasked workers with rating 30 pairs of ideas on their similarity, using a 7-point scale. Other ways ratings tasks have been performed are to ask workers to rate ideas in terms of novelty and quality (or similar dimension), both on a 7-point scale [4,28,32].

What could be the effect of performing rating tasks on an ideator's performance? By rating others' ideas, ideators would be exposed to a small number of raw ideas which, as we have already reviewed, may produce either stimulation or fixation effects. These tasks would require users to think critically about the examples in order to rate them in terms of their similarity, usefulness, or originality. Attending to the stimuli provided by external ideas is a requirement for the idea to influence ideation [10]. In fact, the SIAM model proposes that an idea will only be added to the search cue if sufficiently attended to [23]. Therefore, having users actively engage in analyzing other ideas may promote a larger effect—either of stimulation or interference—than if just passively being exposed to them. But this may depend on the nature of the idea and how it is displayed [24,29], as rating others' ideas may positively affect the creativity, diversity, depth, and quantity of ideas generated.

A negative effect may come from engaging in criticism or judgment during brainstorming, which usually discourages criticism as it may lead to evaluation apprehension. However, there is evidence that this effect does not account for most productivity loss in brainstorming [9]. In fact, criticism has even been found to improve performance [21]. Furthermore, while rating an idea's originality and usefulness may produce such effect, other rating tasks such as rating the similarity may not yield such effects due to their non-judgmental nature.

Combination

Combination tasks revolve around combining characteristics of two ideas, with the goal of generating a third idea. Combination engages divergent processes that can produce better, more diverse ideas [16]. In a study by Yu & Nickerson [33], for example, workers were presented with two different ideas, generated by other workers, for the design of a chair. Their task was to design a new chair that combined aspects of the two other ideas. The resulting design was then passed to a different set of workers for further processing. Combinations could also employ higher representations of ideas—schemas—as explored by Yu, Kittur, & Kraut, who used them in both exploration and generation of ideas [31,32]. Schemas can facilitate analogical reasoning when combining ideas, focusing ideators on the core principles of an idea rather than on its surface features.

While, to our knowledge, there are no other examples of combination tasks in crowdsourced ideation within a microtask platform such as MTurk, the microtasks literature provides other instances of similar tasks, which demonstrate the feasibility of assigning workers to combine two or more different objects. On a general level, the CrowdForge framework [15] defines three types of tasks: partition, in which tasks are broken up in smaller pieces; map, in which a task is processed by one or more workers; and reduce, in which the result of multiple worker's tasks are merged into a single output. One of their examples demonstrates how workers could write an article by breaking it down into an outline, assigning workers to write down facts for each topic in an outline, and having workers merge those facts into paragraphs. In the case of ideation tasks, the merge step could be defined as combining two ideas. More specifically, however, combination of results from different workers is a common feature in MTurk workflows, generally for quality assurance purposes (e.g. [2,5]).

Thus, our hypothesized effect of combination tasks on ideation relates to that of rating: users are exposed to new ideas and have to attend to them to perform the combination. However, unlike the rating tasks, this is not an entirely convergent process, but also includes a divergent step of generating a new idea [16]. This may counterbalance any fixation that can happen while attending to the ideas that are to be combined. On the other hand, the depth of the produced ideas might decrease due to this increased divergence.

SYSTEM AND WORKFLOW

We developed an online ideation system that enables the creation of timed asynchronous ideation sessions, as well as a mechanism for seeing other people's ideas upon request via an inspiration button, thus allowing ideators to *pull* inspirations whenever they choose to do so. This is in line with previous approaches (e.g. [4,29]). An alternative to this approach would be to *push* inspirations at regular time intervals. This would ensure that every ideator was exposed to the same number of inspirations, allowing a clearer comparison of the effect of the different types of tasks.

However, one of our goals was to see if embedding tasks into inspirations would detract from users' interest in using the inspiration mechanism or decrease performance. A push approach would hinder us from exploring this. Furthermore, the SIAM model predicts that pushing inspirations could negatively affect performance [22], since it could interrupt a users' train of thought. In fact, Siangliulue et al. found issues with fluency using a push approach [29]. Therefore, we allowed users to request inspirations on demand.

The system is comprised of four main parts (Figure 1). Although the figure depicts the system in its final iteration, its overall structure as described in this section was maintained throughout the sessions, with a few incremental differences that will be pointed out in each experiment's section. At the top (A), the system displays instructions, the problem definition, and a timer. On the left is the ideation panel. It consists of a form for entering an idea along with a list of user defined tags associated with it (B), and a list of the user's previously submitted ideas and tags (C). On the right side is the inspiration panel (D). When the button is clicked, the user is presented with a set of ideas and depending on their condition, a task associated with them. This mechanism draws randomly from a pool of ideas generated in previous experiments.

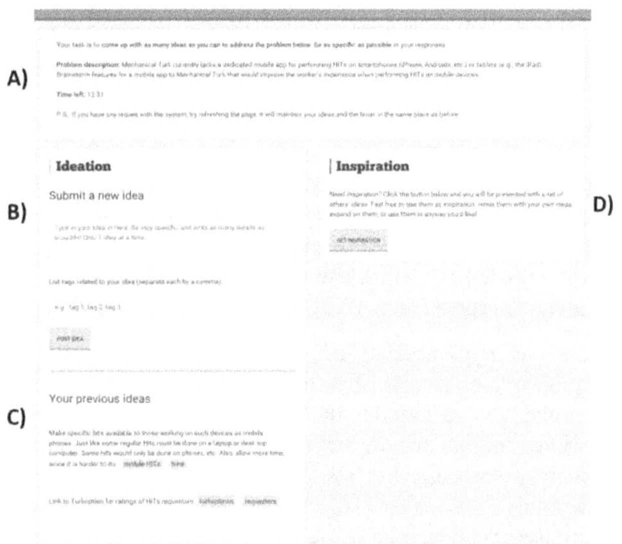

Figure 1. Screenshot of the ideation system as used in the final experiment, comprised of the following parts: A) Problem description and timer; B) idea submission input; C) list of the users' submitted ideas; D) inspiration panel.

When users access the system, they first see a page stating how much time the session lasts, and asking them to move forward only if absolutely sure that they can commit their full attention for the specified amount of time. Following that, users would see another page describing the system, including the inspiration mechanism (if any), and how to use it. Upon finishing the instructions, users begin the ideation session. After the timer is done, the system presents users with a thank you message, a user ID (used for payment), and a link to a short post-session survey.

For every study in this paper, the problem that ideators were tasked to ideate on was: "*Mechanical Turk currently lacks a dedicated mobile app for performing HITs on smartphones (iPhone, Androids, etc.) or tablets (e.g., the iPad). Brainstorm N features for a mobile app to Mechanical Turk that would improve the worker's experience when performing HITs on mobile devices. Be as specific as possible in your responses.*" This task, suggested by Krynicki [18], was chosen because it has been successfully used in previous studies [3,18] and MTurk users have knowledge about the issue and may be motivated to contribute to it, as it could increase their opportunities for engaging with HITs and improving their income. Both motivation and knowledge are key to creativity [1].

METRICS

For each study, we report the following metrics:

- *Fluency*: number of ideas generated by the user.
- *Number of inspirations*: number of times the user clicked the inspiration button.
- *Inspiration influence*: a user's average similarity between an idea and the most similar of its preceding inspirations.

More central to our interests, however, are metrics of *breadth* and *depth*, which we extracted from an *ideation tree*, described below. Tree representations have been previously suggested to measure or visualize ideation outcome [12,20], and the semantics of the different branches of a tree can reflect the usual discrete categorization of ideas traditionally used in creativity research [26], while their depth can represent the notion of ideation within one category [23]. This tree is built from a chronological list of user actions—they either add a new idea or request an inspiration. In the tree, similarity between ideas is measured using Latent Semantic Analysis (LSA) [3]. For this paper, our LSA corpus was built on 5640 ideas generated to solve the same problem that we explore in this paper. This corpus comes both from our own studies (2115 ideas) and the corpus shared by the authors of [4] (3525 ideas). Figure 2 shows the tree and idea pool in five different points in time during a user's ideation:

1. We add the first user idea as the child of a dummy node;
2. For the second user generated idea, we compare it either with every node that is already in the tree, or with every inspiration previously seen. If the LSA similarity to any of those is greater than a given threshold (we used 0.5), we add it as a child of the most similar node. In this point in time, idea 2 was most similar to idea 1, and is added as its child;
3. At the third point in time, the user has generated a third idea. Again, we compare it to every node already in the tree. In this case, none of the similarities exceeded the threshold, so this idea is added as a new child of the root node, representing an estimated new category of ideation.

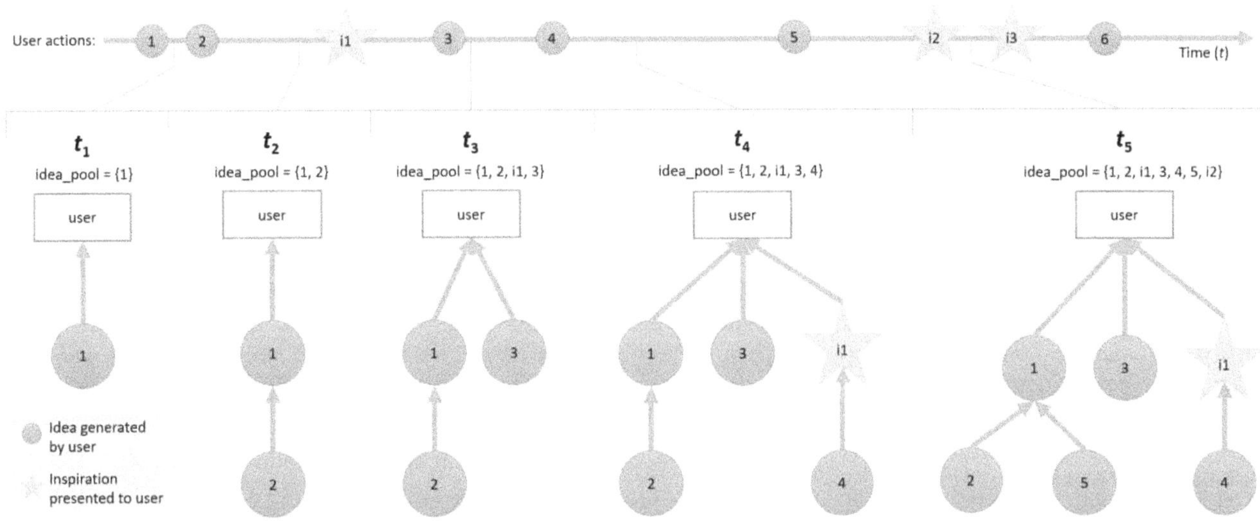

Figure 2. Snapshots of the ideation tree and idea pool in five different points of time in a given user's ideation.

Also note that between t_2 and t_3 the ideator has requested an inspiration, which is added to the idea pool but not to the tree;

4. The user's 4th idea is compared to every node in the idea pool. In this case, a previously seen inspiration is the most similar. Therefore, we add it as a child of the inspiration node, which we then add as a new child of the root node;
5. Finally, another idea has been generated by the user. It is compared to previous ideas and inspirations, and is added as a child to the most similar node, which is the first one.

From this tree, we extract the two metrics:

- *Breadth*: the number of children in the root node. These were the ideas that, at the time they were added, were not similar enough to be considered a continuation of another idea, therefore creating a new branch of ideas. For example, in Figure 2 at t_5, the breadth would be 3.
- *Depth*: the number of nodes in the branch with the most number of nodes. For example, in Figure 2 at t_5, the depth would be 3.

As a check on this measure, we additionally calculated the metrics described by Chan et al. [4], also built using Latent Semantic Analysis (LSA). In [4], breadth was the mean distance between each pair of ideas generated by a user. Depth was the maximum similarity between the ideas generated by a user. Our metrics are significantly correlated with these, at $r = 0.650$, $p < 0.001$ for breadth, and $r = 0.564$, $p = 0.001$ for depth. And while there may be concerns relative to the metric's sensitivity to the threshold value, we have found that threshold changes in either direction do not result in drastic changes in the results. For example, changing it to 0.7 resulted in a mean difference of 2.3 (SD=2.2) in breadth. Therefore, we believe that this metric is both valid and capable of more accurately representing the notions of breadth and depth.

EXPERIMENT 1: RATING TASK

For the first experiment, we chose to start our exploration with rating tasks. Due to their simplicity, they can easily and quickly be done by any worker, and they are very effective for supporting convergence processes. We used an earlier version of the system than the one described in the system section, which differed as follows: the input box for the idea was on the top panel, along with the problem description; users did not have to input tags for their ideas; Lastly, the inspiration box did not have any instructions regarding how inspirations could be used. This study had three conditions:

1. **Control**: This condition is equivalent to a nominal group in typical brainstorming settings. There is no inspiration panel, and thus no external stimulus. Users type their ideas, and can see the list of their own ideas.
2. **Exposure**: In this condition, the inspiration panel is visible. When the inspiration button is clicked, it displays one idea from the pool of past ideas, without any task associated with it. The idea disappears when the user clicks the "done" button.
3. **Rating**: This condition is similar to the exposure condition. However, when the inspiration button is clicked, in addition to the idea, users also received a task prompting them to rate the inspiration idea in 2 dimensions: originality and practicality (Figure 3). After submitting the rating, the idea disappears.

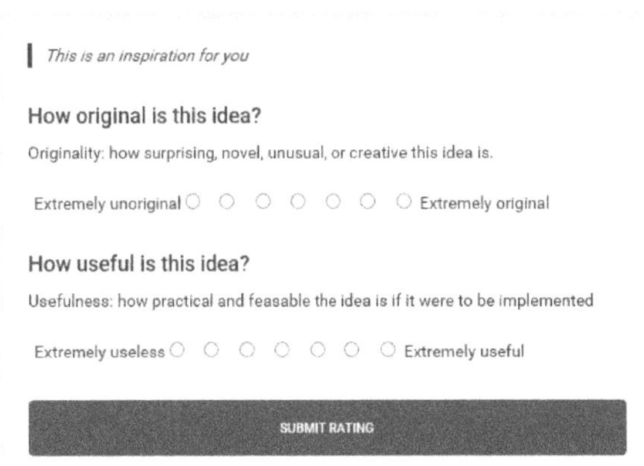

Figure 3. Rating task interface.

We published a MTurk HIT that directed workers to our system. 60 workers participated in this study (at least 1000 completed HITs, approval > 95%, US only), but 1 (exposure condition) was excluded from the analysis due to an abnormal number of inspirations requested (142). In total, 559 ideas were generated. Each worker ideated for 18 minutes, filled out a small survey at the end of the session, and was compensated $2. Workers also received an ideation qualification on MTurk (awarded after every experiment). Subsequent experiments reported here required workers to not have this qualification, thus ensuring participants were unique for each session.

Results

Condition	Workers	Ideas / Worker	Insp. / Worker
Baseline	19	10.37 (4.16)	-
Exposure	19	9.53 (4.62)	12.16 (10.64)
Rating	21	8.62 (5.02)	6.67 (6.80)

Table 1. Fluency and inspiration metrics for experiment.

Tables 1 and 2 summarize the metrics across the different conditions. A one-way ANOVA test shows no significant difference in fluency, $F(2,56) = 0.713$, $p = 0.495$. There was a marginally significant difference in number of inspirations requested across the two conditions, $F(1,38) = 3.855$, $p = 0.057$. We do, however, find a difference in inspiration influence between the exposure and rating conditions, $F(1,38) = 9.855$, $p = 0.003$.

Condition	Breadth	Depth	Influence
Baseline	5.37 (2.54)	4.74 (3.69)	-
Exposure	6.40 (3.20)	3.25 (1.74)	0.23 (0.90)
Rating	5.10 (2.70)	3.29 (1.52)	0.12 (0.12)

Table 2. Breadth, depth, and influence for experiment 1.

We calculated a Mixed Generalized Linear Model (GLM) with breadth as outcome variable, condition as factor, and the fluency as covariate. We included the interaction between condition and fluency in the model. We found a marginally significant interaction effect between condition and fluency, $F(2, 56) = 3.078$, $p = 0.054$, and no main effect of condition on breadth, $F(2,56) = 1.374$, $p = 0.262$.

As the depth of user ideas followed a negative binomial distribution rather than a normal distribution, we conducted a negative binomial regression with depth as outcome, condition as factor, and fluency as covariate. The interaction between fluency and condition was included in the model. We found no significant interaction effect or main effect of condition on depth, Wald Chi-Square = 4.099, $p = 0.129$.

Discussion for Study 1

While we see only a marginal effect of the interaction between condition and fluency on breadth, we find no clear advantage in any condition. The fact that breadth seemed to be more affected than depth may spring from inspirations being randomly drawn from the pool of ideas, which will likely create a heterogeneous set of examples. Past work has shown that a heterogeneous set of examples will improve diversity of ideas [24,27]. Having no clear advantage could mean a problem either in the intervention (e.g. it is too simple) or in how users performed it (e.g. they did not attend to it). There may also have been confusion on how users should use the ideas in the rating task. For example, a user declared feeling that the inspiration they got would invalidate using that idea: "*I think it hindered me more than it helped because it just provided an example that I then couldn't use*". Perhaps guidelines might be effective in helping users better use the inspirations.

EXPERIMENTS 2A & 2B: SIMILARITY CHOICE TASK

In experiment 1, we found no clear advantages over the baseline, even though there was a larger influence in the exposure condition. Given these results, we decided to change the task to similarity comparison, the number of ideas displayed, and to add a clarification on how they could use the inspirations (see the text at the top of Figure 4).

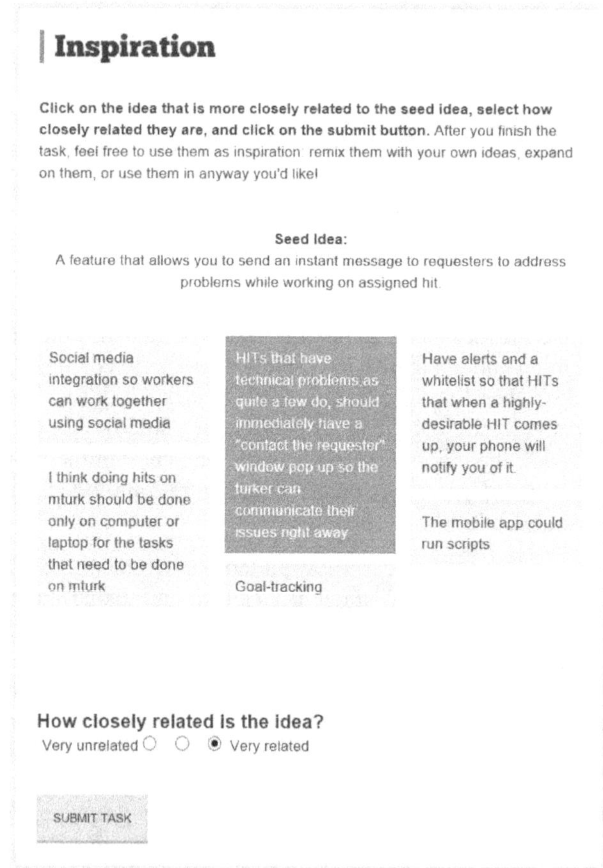

Figure 4. The task panel for condition 3. Users were shown a seed idea along with 6 other ideas, and were asked to click on the most similar one (in this case, the user clicked on the dark blue idea), as well as rating their degree of relationship.

Experiment 2A

In this experiment, the task condition presents the user with one seed idea along with 6 other ideas, asking him or her to choose the most similar to the seed (Figure 4). The number of ideas was chosen to maximize the possibility of similar ideas being shown, as well as to explore the result of a more dramatic increase in the number of ideas shown per inspiration. We expected this to yield a stronger influence on ideators' breadth, as they would be exposed to more ideas. We also hypothesized that similarity comparisons would force to user to think more abstractly about the ideas in order to find common features between them, thus reducing fixation and possibly improving breadth.

This second experiment followed the same method as the first, with the two key differences above. 60 workers participated in this study (at least 1000 completed HITs, approval > 95%, US only). In total, 492 ideas were generated. Each worker ideated for 18 minutes, filled out a small survey at the end of the session, and was paid $2.

Results

Condition	Workers	Ideas / Worker	Insp. / Worker
Baseline	20	7.45 (5.51)	-
Exposure	22	8.50 (4.34)	2.00 (2.19)
Similarity	18	8.61 (2.87)	2.28 (1.77)

Table 3. Fluency and inspiration metrics for experiment 2A.

Tables 3 and 4 summarize the metrics for this experiment. A one-way ANOVA test shows no difference in fluency, $F(2,57) = 0.416$, $p = 0.661$, or number of inspirations requested between the exposure and task conditions, $F(1,28) = 0.261$, $p = 0.612$. Finally, similarly to the last study, we found a difference in inspiration influence. This time, however, the task condition displayed a higher influence than the exposure, $F(1,28) = 4.59$, $p = 0.039$ (see Table 4) .

Condition	Breadth	Depth	Influence
Baseline	4.90 (3.43)	2.40 (1.31)	-
Exposure	6.36 (2.95)	2.05 (0.785)	0.11 (0.03)
Similarity	5.78 (2.15)	2.28 (0.82)	0.13 (0.03)

Table 4. Breadth, depth, and influence for experiment 2A.

We calculated a Mixed GLM with breadth as outcome variable, condition as factor, and fluency as covariate, finding no significant difference, $F(2,57) = 1.962$, $p = 0.150$. As in the last study, we conducted a negative binomial regression for depth. With condition as factor and number of ideas as covariate, we found no significant difference, Wald Chi-Square = 2.108, $p = 0.348$.

Discussion for study 2A

Unlike the first study, the task condition yielded a significantly higher influence than the exposure condition, but this did not translate into an improvement in ideation breadth or depth. In general, all three conditions appeared to be very similar with respect to breadth and depth, despite the small but significant difference in influence. This is not so surprising when you consider the low number of inspirations requested for both inspiration conditions—close to 2. It is likely that the great number of ideas per inspiration either overwhelmed users or provided them with what they judged to be enough inspiration for a long stretch of time.

Experiment 2B: Smaller Inspirations, Controlled Pool

In experiment 2A, we found no meaningful difference across conditions, likely due to the very small number of inspirations requested in both experimental conditions. Therefore, we reduced the number of ideas per inspiration to 3. We also controlled the pool of ideas. One of the authors went through the existing idea pool and generated 40 different groups of 3 ideas. The goal was to create sets of ideas that shared similar elements, making the choice task easier, while at the same time having different features. For example, the idea "*Notifications such as sound or vibration when a new hit is available*" was grouped with "*sounds effects so people know when to do the surveys and also tools to see how well they are doing*" and "*The app would have alarms, bells, or sounds to notify of particular work or requesters*". The three ideas in the group would always come together, but in random order.

The method for this experiment changed in one significant way: we increased ideation time from 18 to 25 minutes, to collect more data on how ideation changes as fluency increases. We also increased the target number of users per condition (see Table 5). 89 workers participated in this study (at least 1000 completed HITs, approval > 98%, US only. In total, 863 ideas were generated. Workers also filled out a small survey at the end. Each worker was paid $3.50.

Condition	Workers	Ideas / Worker	Insp. / Worker
Baseline	35	8.43 (4.74)	-
Exposure	27	9.53 (5.95)	12.59 (12.29)
Similarity	27	9.15 (5.11)	5.74 (5.18)

Table 5. Fluency and inspiration metrics for experiment 2B.

Tables 5 and 6 summarize the metrics for this experiment. A one-way ANOVA shows a significant difference in fluency, $F(2,86) = 3.528$, $p = 0.034$. A post hoc Tukey test shows a significant difference between baseline and exposure conditions, $p = 0.031$, but no difference between baseline and task ($p = 0.854$) or exposure and task ($p = 0.139$). There was also a significant difference in number of inspirations between the exposure and similarity conditions, $F(1,52) = 7.119$, $p = 0.01$. However, this time no significant differences were found in inspiration influence, $F(1,47)$ 2.019, $p = 0.162$.

Condition	Breadth	Depth	Influence
Baseline	5.31 (2.99)	3.17 (2.62)	-
Exposure	8.07 (3.79)	3.33 (1.68)	0.14 (0.04)
Similarity	6.33 (3.75)	2.78 (1.45)	0.16 (0.04)

Table 6. Breadth, depth, and influence for experiment 2B.

We calculated a Mixed GLM with breadth as outcome, condition as factor, and fluency as covariate, including the interaction between condition and fluency. We found a marginally significant interaction between condition and fluency, $F(2,83) = 2.88$, $p = 0.062$, but no main effect of condition on breadth, $F(2,83) = 1.269$, $p = 0.286$.

For depth, a negative binomial regression with condition as factor, fluency as covariate, and including the interaction between fluency and condition found a significant interaction between fluency and condition, Wald Chi-Square = 10.003, $p = 0.007$, but no significant main effect of condition, Wald Chi-Square = 4.550, $p = 0.103$. A pairwise comparison shows a difference only for high fluency ideators (1 SD above the mean). In this case, those in the control condition (M=6.31, SE=0.850) performed significantly above both exposure (M=3.84, SE=0.425, $p = 0.009$) and similarity (M=3.35, SE=0.584, $p = 0.004$) conditions.

We also divided both halves of the ideation and analyzed their breadth and depth separately. This was done since the effect of inspirations on users is likely not constant across the session, as they will likely be able to generate more ideas by themselves at the beginning of the session than at the end, when inspirations may be more useful. Thus, looking at the metrics over the entire session may wash out some effects.

A Mixed GLM with breadth for the first and second halves (run separately) as outcome variables, with condition as factor, and fluency as covariate yielded no main effect of condition on the first half breadth, $F(2,85) = 2.704$, $p = 0.073$. On the second half, however, it yielded a main condition effect, $F(2,83) = 3.527$, $p = 0.034$, as well as a significant interaction on condition and fluency, $F(2,83) = 6.957$, $p = 0.03$. In pairwise comparisons, a difference was seen for low fluency ideators (1 SD below the mean), where the control condition (M=1.54, SE=0.322) was significantly superior to the task condition (M=0.38, SE=0.381, $p = 0.022$), but was not significantly different than the exposure condition (M=1.06, SE=0.447, p=0.386).

For the first half depth metric, a negative binomial regression with condition as factor, fluency as covariate, and including the interaction between condition and fluency yielded a significant main effect, Wald Chi-Square = 6.48, $p = 0.039$, and a significant interaction between condition and number of ideas, Wald Chi-Square = 7.46, $p = 0.024$. For low fluency ideators (1 SD below the mean), we see the exposure condition (M=1.99, SE=0.348) significantly outperform the control condition (M=1.05, SE=0.22, $p = 0.042$), but it was not significantly different to the task condition (M=1.74, SE=0.409, p=0.638). No pairwise differences were seen for high fluency ideators. The second half presented no significant interaction or main condition effect, Wald Chi-Square = 3.362, $p = 0.186$.

Discussion for study 2B

To summarize this study, we found a significant difference in fluency only between the exposure condition over control. The exposure condition also saw more inspiration requests. We also found baseline high fluency ideators outperforming the others in overall depth, low fluency baseline outperforming task in 2nd half breadth, and low fluency exposure outperforming baseline in 1st half depth. In other words, the inspirations not only did not help, but actually hindered the depth of high fluency ideators. It is possible that the closely related nature of the inspirations promoted fixation for them, thus detracting from their second half depth. Finally, for low fluency ideators, we see exposure helping them in first half depth, but we see tasks detracting from their second half breadth.

EXPERIMENT 3: COMPARISON ACROSS TASK TYPES

We conducted a final study in order to compare the two previous task types with a new one: combination. Combination tasks involve not only convergent processes, but also a divergent one—the generation of the new, combined idea [16]. While this can happen naturally during ideation, this task explicitly forces it to happen. Therefore, we expect a positive impact of combination on breadth. We also reverted back to completely random inspiration retrieval. The method remained the same as the one employed in experiment 2B, with the difference being that there are five conditions (control, exposure, 3 task types).

150 workers participated in this study (at least 1000 completed HITs, approval > 98%, US only), but 7 workers were not included in the analysis, as they either wrote unrelated ideas (n=1), generated unrelated tags (e.g. "tags 1", n=4), or didn't complete the post session questionnaire (n=2). In total, 1480 ideas were generated. Workers ideated for 25 minutes, and filled out a small survey at the end of the session. Each worker was paid $3.50.

Condition	Workers	Ideas / Worker	Insp. / Worker
Baseline	29	11.38 (7.178)	-
Exposure	28	10.57 (6.143)	7.70 (6.92)
Rating	27	8.48 (4.136)	4.28 (4.86)
Similarity	31	11.52 (6.45)	8.77 (5.36)
Combine	28	9.57 (5.647)	3.16 (2.51)

Table 7. Fluency and inspiration metrics for experiment 3.

Tables 7 and 8 summarize the metrics for this experiment. A one-way ANOVA shows no significant difference in fluency across conditions, $F(4,142) = 1.276$, $p = 0.283$. A one-way ANOVA for number of inspirations between conditions shows a significant difference in the number of inspirations requested, $F(3,110) = 8.022$, $p < 0.001$. A post hoc Tukey test shows that the exposure and similarity conditions were significantly higher than the rating and combination conditions ($p < 0.05$), but not from each other. As for influence, a one-way ANOVA shows no significant difference, $F(3,105) = 1.285$, $p = 0.283$.

Condition	Breadth	Depth	Influence
Baseline	7.86 (4.086)	3.28 (2.52)	-
Exposure	8.00 (4.830)	2.61 (1.52)	0.14 (0.05)
Rating	6.48 (3.887)	2.56 (1.76)	0.15 (0.07)
Similarity	8.74 (4.289)	2.58 (1.52)	0.12 (0.04)
Combine	8.07 (4.48)	2.07 (1.15)	0.13 (0.05)

Table 8. Breadth, depth, and influence for experiment 3.

A Mixed GLM with breadth as outcome variable, condition as factor, fluency as covariate, and including the interaction between condition and fluency yielded a significant interaction of condition and number of ideas on breadth, $F(4,133) = 3.736$, $p = 0.006$, but no main effect of condition, $F(4,133) = 1.823$, $p = 0.128$. For average fluency ideators (10 ideas), a pairwise comparison shows a significant difference between the control (M=7.20, SE=0.39) and combine (M=8.38, SE=0.39) conditions, $p = 0.037$. There are also significant differences for high fluency ideators (1 SD above the mean, fluency = 16 ideas), in which the control condition was outperformed by all other conditions ($p_{exposure} = 0.018$, $p_{rating} = 0.010$, $p_{similarity} = 0.046$, $p_{combine} < 0.001$), but they were not significantly different among themselves. Figure 5 depicts the regression lines for the different conditions.

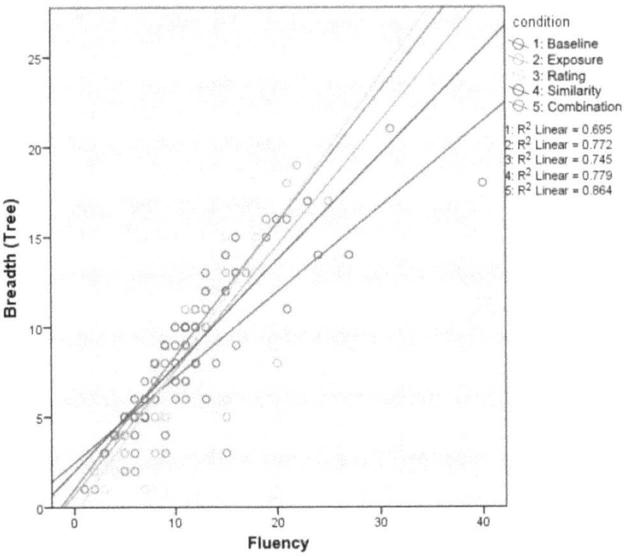

Figure 5. Regression lines for breadth by fluency.

Again, we calculated the breadth metric for each half, and found that a Mixed GLM with first half breadth as outcome variable, condition as factor, and fluency as covariate yielded no significant effect of condition, $F(4,137) = 1.342$, $p = 0.257$. However, using the second half breadth as outcome variable and including an interaction between condition and fluency yields a significant interaction between condition and fluency, $F(4,133) = 7.197$, $p < 0.001$, and a main effect of condition, $F(4,133) = 2.725$, $p = 0.032$. Figure 6 shows the marginal means for second half breadth across the different conditions, with fluency fixed at 1 SD below (4 ideas) and 1 SD above the mean (16 ideas). No significant difference is seen for low fluency ideators. For high fluency ideators, however, we see that that the three task conditions significantly outperformed the baseline ($p < 0.001$). When compared to the exposure condition, however, only the rating and combination conditions significantly outperformed it.

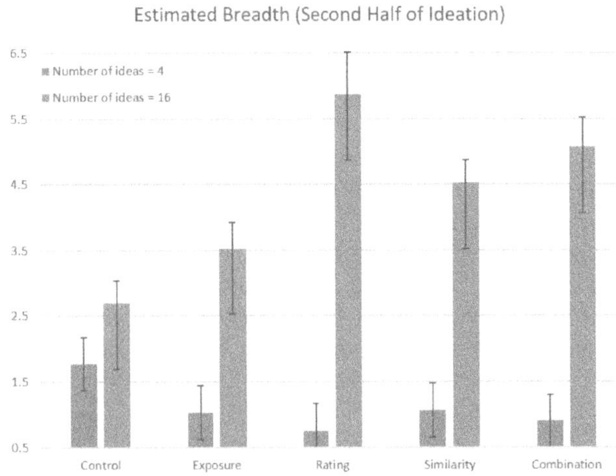

Figure 6. Marginal means and std. error for breadth (when fluency is 4 and 16) during the second half of ideation.

For overall depth, the control condition trended higher than the others, but a negative binomial regression with depth as outcome variable, condition as factor, and fluency as covariate found no effect of condition, Wald Chi-Square = 5.456, $p = 0.244$. The same model, but separately testing first and second half depth as outcome variables also yielded no significant differences, 1st half Wald Chi-Square = 1.469, $p = 0.832$, 2nd half Wald Chi-Square = 3.422, $p = 0.49$.

DISCUSSION

Through four experiments, we explored the integration of peripheral microtasks as part of an ideation session. Experiment 1 compared the rating task with simple exposure, finding very little influence. Experiments 2A and 2B increased the number of ideas and evaluated similarity tasks, pointing to limitations with quantity and homogeneity of inspiration ideas. Finally, experiment 3 compared all three task types together. We now discuss the main points from the combined results.

Tasks Performed as Good as Exposure, Outperforming it in Some Cases

Experiment 3 shows combination tasks outperforming the baseline for average fluency ideators. As for high fluency ideators, we find all conditions outperforming the baseline. However, when we isolate the second half of ideation, we find significant differences between the types of inspiration. The rating and combination tasks significantly outperformed the exposure condition, while similarity significantly outperformed control. One explanation for this difference is that these tasks were more cognitively demanding than the similarity and exposition inspirations. But unique characteristics of the tasks may explain them further. While usual brainstorming rules discourage criticism of ideas [25], there is evidence that criticism may foster exploration [21], which could partially account for the better performance of the rating task. Alternatively, it is possible that the rating scales provided users with a structure that guided them in generating ideas or evaluating inspirations. As for the combination task, this result was in line with our expectation, as the task also involves a divergent step [16], which could foster breadth of exploration.

Fewer Effective Inspirations May Be Better than Many Ineffective Ones

It is interesting to note that the two most effective conditions had the lowest number of inspiration requests. This may lead to the conclusion that the cognitive load of an inspiration may be more important than the number of times it is used. In other words, fewer but more effective inspirations can be better than having many less effective inspirations. An alternative explanation is that since these users requested fewer inspirations, they had more time to ideate, thus increasing breadth. However, since the fluency was not different across conditions, this is an unlikely explanation.

Inspiration Effects Depend on Timing and Fluency

The studies, especially experiment 3, highlight that inspirations may influence different users at different times. On experiment 3, for example, we see significant differences only for average or high fluency ideators. This is not surprising, as low fluency ideators may simply not be engaged enough to attend to the task or the inspirations, regardless of condition. Furthermore, results were mainly seen on the second half of ideation. This is intuitive, since at later points in time ideators are more likely to be running out of ideas [23], and thus may be more susceptible to the inspirations. This suggests that a "one size fits all" approach does not work. It may prove useful for crowd ideation support systems to restrain inspirations for a latter phase of ideation, or to initially target fluency improvement. Research that looks into adaptive support could prove fruitful.

Very Simple or Complex Inspirations Have no Effect

Studies 1 and 2A, while exploring two different types of tasks, shed light on lower and upper limits when concerning the number of ideas that can be presented for each inspiration. With both one (experiment 1) and seven (experiment 2A) ideas per inspiration, we see no significant difference between conditions. On the lower end, this lack of effect happened despite a considerable number of inspiration requests. This could be due to the simplicity of the inspirations not fostering attention to the ideas, or to users not knowing how to use the inspirations, as previously discussed. On the higher end, the lack of effect likely happened due to the low number of requests. At the end, we have found better effects with inspirations containing three ideas each. This could, however, vary depending on the inspiration type (e.g. a combination task of size 6 could be considerably more demanding than a similarity task of size 6), or even nature of ideas (homogenous idea sets may be less cognitively demanding, allowing more ideas per inspiration).

The Homogeneity of Idea Sets Can Influence the Effects

While most results were seen in breadth, we see a different pattern in experiment 2B, where the inspiration idea sets were manipulated to be more homogenous. In it, we see exposure outperforming control in first half depth, and control outperforming task in second half breadth. This could be explained partially by the homogenous nature of the ideas, as previously discussed. This indicates that the nature of the inspiration sets is highly influential in the outcome [27]. Therefore, the effect of different levels of homogeneity and task types should be explored in future work.

Some limitations of this investigation must be noted, with the first being the metrics. While the tree-based metric is consistent with previous practices and results, it needs further evaluation. A comparison with similar trees built by human experts would shed light on its performance. Alternatively, graph-based metrics could also be devised in order to better represent the inherent uncertainties in automated textual analysis (e.g. ideas could be linked to more than just one parent idea, with edge weights representing their similarity). Furthermore, we do not explore measures of creativity, whereas past research has used MTurk workers to do that [3,29,33]. However, we found workers to have very low degrees of agreement among themselves, and therefore do not report these measures. There are also limitations to the pull approach. While it allowed us to compare the performance in a natural setting, the numerical differences in inspiration requests limit our ability to clearly determine the effects of the different tasks. Finally, we do not explore the results of the tasks (e.g. the quality of the ratings). While this exploration is outside of the scope of this paper, past results are encouraging in the potential of peripheral crowd work to yield useful outcomes such as a semantic model of ideas [28].

CONCLUSION

In this paper, we have analyzed the effect of performing three different types of tasks normally done by other crowd workers: rating, similarity, and combination. We ran four subsequent experiments on MTurk to evaluate how they compare to idea exposure or individual ideation. Using breadth and depth metrics based on an ideation tree, we found the performance of task inspirations to be as good or better than simple idea exposure. We also found that the effect of inspirations depends on the fluency of ideators and the period in which it is used. Finally, we saw indications that the homogeneity of inspirations influences the outcome. Therefore, this paper provides some support and guidance in explicitly embedding microtasks into ideation, which will not only be generating information useful for convergent processes, but will also aid ideators in improving the divergence of their idea generation.

ACKNOWLEDGMENTS

The authors would like to thank all of the Mechanical Turk workers who participated in the studies. This research was funded by the CAPES Foundation, Ministry of Education of Brazil, Brasília - DF 70040-020, Brazil.

REFERENCES

1. Teresa M. Amabile. 1983. The social psychology of creativity: A componential conceptualization. *Journal of personality and social psychology* 45, 2: 357.
2. Michael S. Bernstein, Greg Little, Robert C. Miller, Björn Hartmann, Mark S. Ackerman, David R. Karger, David Crowell, and Katrina Panovich. 2010. Soylent: a word processor with a crowd inside. In *Proceedings of the 23nd annual ACM symposium on User interface software and technology*, 313–322. Retrieved January 11, 2016 from http://dl.acm.org/citation.cfm?id=1866078
3. Joel Chan, Steven Dang, and Steven P. Dow. 2016. Comparing Different Sensemaking Approaches for Large-Scale Ideation. Retrieved March 11, 2016 from http://joelchan.me/files/2016-chi-sensemaking-ideation.pdf
4. Joel Chan, Steven Dang, and Steven P. Dow. 2016. Improving Crowd Innovation with Expert Facilitation.
5. Lydia B. Chilton, Greg Little, Darren Edge, Daniel S. Weld, and James A. Landay. 2013. Cascade: Crowdsourcing taxonomy creation. In *Proceedings of the SIGCHI Conference on Human Factors in Computing Systems*, 1999–2008. Retrieved January 11, 2016 from http://dl.acm.org/citation.cfm?id=2466265
6. Arthur Cropley. 2006. In praise of convergent thinking. *Creativity research journal* 18, 3: 391–404.
7. Alan R. Dennis and Joseph S. Valacich. 1993. Computer brainstorms: More heads are better than one. *Journal of applied psychology* 78, 4: 531.
8. Alan R. Dennis and Mike L. Williams. 2003. Electronic Brainstorming: Theory, Research, and Future Directions. In *Group creativity: Innovation through collaboration*. Oxford University Press.
9. Michael Diehl and Wolfgang Stroebe. 1987. Productivity loss in brainstorming groups: Toward the solution of a riddle. *Journal of Personality and Social Psychology* 53, 3: 497–509. https://doi.org/10.1037/0022-3514.53.3.497
10. Karen Leggett Dugosh, Paul B. Paulus, Evelyn J. Roland, and Huei-Chuan Yang. 2000. Cognitive stimulation in brainstorming. *Journal of Personality and Social Psychology* 79, 5: 722–735. https://doi.org/10.1037/0022-3514.79.5.722
11. Beth A. Hennessey and Teresa M. Amabile. 2010. Creativity. *Annual Review of Psychology* 61, 1: 569–598. https://doi.org/10.1146/annurev.psych.093008.100416
12. Alex Ivanov and Dianne Cyr. 2006. The Concept Plot: a concept mapping visualization tool for asynchronous web-based brainstorming sessions. *Information Visualization* 5, 3: 185–191. https://doi.org/10.1057/palgrave.ivs.9500130
13. D. G. Jansson and S. M. Smith. 1991. Design Fixation. *Design Studies* 12, 1: 3–11.
14. Aniket Kittur, Ed H. Chi, and Bongwon Suh. 2008. Crowdsourcing user studies with Mechanical Turk. In *Proceedings of the SIGCHI conference on human factors in computing systems*, 453–456. Retrieved August 17, 2015 from http://dl.acm.org/citation.cfm?id=1357127
15. Aniket Kittur, Boris Smus, Susheel Khamkar, and Robert E. Kraut. 2011. Crowdforge: Crowdsourcing complex work. In *Proceedings of the 24th annual ACM symposium on User interface software and technology*, 43–52. Retrieved August 4, 2015 from http://dl.acm.org/citation.cfm?id=2047202
16. Nicholas W. Kohn, Paul B. Paulus, and YunHee Choi. 2011. Building on the ideas of others: An examination of the idea combination process. *Journal of Experimental Social Psychology* 47, 3: 554–561. https://doi.org/10.1016/j.jesp.2011.01.004
17. Aaron Kozbelt, Ronald A. Beghetto, and Mark A. Runco. 2010. Theories of creativity. *The Cambridge handbook of creativity*: 20–47.
18. Filip Krynicki. 2014. Methods and models for the quantitative analysis of crowd brainstorming. Retrieved April 5, 2016 from https://uwspace.uwaterloo.ca/handle/10012/8347
19. Richard L. Marsh, Joshua D. Landau, and Jason L. Hicks. 1996. How examples may (and may not) constrain creativity. *Memory & cognition* 24, 5: 669–680.
20. Brent A. Nelson, Jamal O. Wilson, David Rosen, and Jeannette Yen. 2009. Refined metrics for measuring ideation effectiveness. *Design Studies* 30, 6: 737–743. https://doi.org/10.1016/j.destud.2009.07.002
21. Charlan J. Nemeth, Bernard Personnaz, Marie Personnaz, and Jack A. Goncalo. 2004. The liberating role of conflict in group creativity: A study in two countries. *European Journal of Social Psychology* 34, 4: 365–374. https://doi.org/10.1002/ejsp.210
22. Bernard A. Nijstad, Michael Diehl, and Wolfgang Stroebe. 2003. Cognitive Stimulation and Interference in Idea-Generating Groups. In *Group Creativity: Innovation Through Collaboration*. Oxford University Press.
23. Bernard A. Nijstad and Wolfgang Stroebe. 2006. How the group affects the mind: A cognitive model of idea generation in groups. *Personality and social psychology review* 10, 3: 186–213.
24. Bernard A. Nijstad, Wolfgang Stroebe, and Hein FM Lodewijkx. 2002. Cognitive stimulation and interference in groups: Exposure effects in an idea generation task. *Journal of experimental social psychology* 38, 6: 535–544.
25. Alex F. Osborn. 1963. *Applied imagination; principles and procedures of creative problem-solving*. Scribner, New York.
26. Jonathan A. Plucker and Matthew C. Makel. 2010. Assessment of Creativity. In *The Cambridge Handbook of Creativity*, James C. Kaufman and Robert J. Sternberg (eds.). Cambridge University Press, Cambridge, 48–73. Retrieved November 29, 2016 from http://ebooks.cambridge.org/ref/id/CBO9780511763205A013
27. Pao Siangliulue, Kenneth C. Arnold, Krzysztof Z. Gajos, and Steven P. Dow. 2015. Toward Collaborative Ideation at Scale: Leveraging Ideas from Others to Generate More Creative and Diverse Ideas. 937–945. https://doi.org/10.1145/2675133.2675239
28. Pao Siangliulue, Joel Chan, Steven P. Dow, and

Krzysztof Z. Gajos. 2016. IdeaHound: Improving Large-scale Collaborative Ideation with Crowd-Powered Real-time Semantic Modeling. 609–624. https://doi.org/10.1145/2984511.2984578

29. Pao Siangliulue, Joel Chan, Krzysztof Z. Gajos, and Steven P. Dow. 2015. Providing Timely Examples Improves the Quantity and Quality of Generated Ideas. 83–92. https://doi.org/10.1145/2757226.2757230

30. Steven M. Smith. 2003. The constraining effects of initial ideas. In *Group creativity: Innovation through collaboration*, Paul B. Paulus and Bernard A. Nijstad (eds.). Oxford University Press, New York, NY, US, 15–31.

31. Lixiu Yu, Aniket Kittur, and Robert E. Kraut. 2014. Distributed analogical idea generation: inventing with crowds. 1245–1254. https://doi.org/10.1145/2556288.2557371

32. Lixiu Yu, Aniket Kittur, and Robert E. Kraut. 2014. Searching for analogical ideas with crowds. 1225–1234. https://doi.org/10.1145/2556288.2557378

33. Lixiu Yu and Jeffrey V. Nickerson. 2011. Cooks or cobblers?: crowd creativity through combination. In *Proceedings of the SIGCHI conference on human factors in computing systems*, 1393–1402. Retrieved October 12, 2015 from http://dl.acm.org/citation.cfm?id=1979147

Respeak: A Voice-based, Crowd-powered Speech Transcription System

Aditya Vashistha
University of Washington
adityav@cs.washington.edu

Pooja Sethi
University of Washington
psethi17@cs.washington.edu

Richard Anderson
University of Washington
anderson@cs.washington.edu

ABSTRACT
Speech transcription is an expensive service with high turnaround time for audio files containing languages spoken in developing countries and regional accents of well-represented languages. We present *Respeak* — a voice-based, crowd-powered system that capitalizes on the strengths of crowdsourcing and automatic speech recognition (instead of typing) to transcribe such audio files. We created *Respeak* and optimized its design through a series of cognitive experiments. We deployed it with 25 university students in India who completed 5464 micro-transcription tasks, transcribing 55 minutes of widely-varied audio content, and collectively earning USD 46 as mobile airtime. The *Respeak* engine aligned the transcript generated by five randomly selected users to transcribe Hindi and Indian English audio files with a word error rate (WER) of 8.6% and 15.2%, respectively. The cost of speech transcription was USD 0.83 per minute with a turnaround time of 39.8 hours, substantially less than industry standards. Using a mixed-methods analysis of cognitive experiments, system performance and qualitative interviews, we evaluate *Respeak*'s design, user experience, strengths, and weaknesses. Our findings suggest that *Respeak* improves the quality of speech transcription while enhancing the earning potential of low-income populations in resource-constrained settings.

ACM Classification Keywords
H.5.m. Information Interfaces and Presentation (e.g. HCI): Miscellaneous

Author Keywords
HCI4D, Crowdsourcing, Speech, Transcription, India

INTRODUCTION
Speech transcription — including general, medical and legal transcription — fuels a massive industry; medical transcription alone is expected to reach USD 60 billion globally by 2019 [10]. Transcription of recorded audio is demanded for a wide variety of content, including public speeches, movies, songs, television programs, advertisements, news, interviews, recorded lectures, online videos, and telephone calls. Manual transcription via typing is both slow and expensive. The advent of crowdsourcing has resulted in the rise of crowd-powered transcription organizations, such as CastingWords [3] and SpeechPad [15]; these businesses typically charge USD 1 – 6 per minute of recording and require a one-week turnaround time for the cheapest pricing alternative. Existing automatic speech recognition (ASR) based transcription solutions, like Nuance Dragon, work satisfactorily but only for individual use of well-represented languages, such as English and Spanish, and require respeaking to transcribe audio files. However, no crowdsourcing platform or ASR system currently supports transcription of audio files in languages spoken in developing countries and localized accents of well-represented languages. Though online services like Quick Transcription [11] and Scripts Complete [14] support such transcription using a fleet of transcribers, their transcription cost starts at USD 5 per minute.

The emergence of crowd-powered speech transcription platforms has demonstrated the potential to provide additional earning opportunities to low-income people. However, several inclusion criteria — a minimum typing speed of 40 words per minute (WPM) [15], an active PayPal account connected to a banking institution [3, 12, 15, 16, 17], and access to an Internet-connected computer [3, 12, 15, 16, 17] — makes it difficult for many in developing regions to receive benefits of these platforms. Other crowdsourcing platforms, such as Samasource [13] and MobileWorks [37], designed especially for people in developing countries require workers to have acceptable typing skills: an acquired skill for English language and onerous for local languages like Hindi.

Our primary contribution is the design, deployment and evaluation of *Respeak*: a voice-based, crowd-powered speech transcription system that combines the benefits of crowdsourcing with ASR to transcribe audio files containing local languages like Hindi and localized accents of well-represented languages like English. *Respeak* lets people use their speaking rather than typing skills to transcribe audio files with a low WER, turnaround time, and transcription cost. The *Respeak* engine works by segmenting an audio file into utterances that are each three to five seconds long. Each audio segment is sent to multiple *Respeak* smartphone application users who then listen to the segment and re-speak what they heard into the application in a quiet environment. The smartphone application uses Google's Android speech recognition API to generate an instantaneous transcript for the segment, albeit with some errors. The user then submits this transcript to the *Respeak*

CHI 2017, May 6-11, 2017, Denver, CO, USA.
Copyright © 2017 ACM ISBN 978-1-4503-4655-9/17/05 ...$15.00.
http://dx.doi.org/10.1145/3025453.3025640

engine. For each segment, the *Respeak* engine combines the output transcripts obtained from users into one best estimation transcript by using multiple string alignment and majority voting. Each submitted transcript earns *Respeak* users a reward of mobile airtime depending on the similarity between the transcript they submitted and the best estimation transcript. Finally, the engine concatenates the best estimation transcript for each segment to yield a final transcript of the original audio file.

We conducted a series of cognitive experiments with 24 university students to obtain key design insights into the segmentation process, ordering of tasks, and comparison of speaking and typing skills of potential users. We then seeded *Respeak* with 21 audio files in Hindi and Indian English containing 55 minutes of widely-varied content and deployed the *Respeak* application for one month with 25 university students in India. The *Respeak* engine segmented these audio files to obtain 756 short segments and presented them as micro-transcription tasks to the application users. Collectively, *Respeak* users performed 5464 tasks with an individual average WER of 23.7%, and earned USD 46. The *Respeak* engine aligned the transcripts generated by five randomly selected users to reduce the transcription WER to 10.6%. *Respeak* was particularly effective for Hindi and produced transcriptions with an average WER of 8.6%. The cost of speech transcription was USD 0.83 per minute, and the turnaround time was 39.8 hours, substantially less than the industry standard of USD 5 per minute for Hindi and Indian English transcription. In addition to providing users mobile airtime, with an expected payout of USD 1.16 per hour of usage, *Respeak* also provided them instrumental benefits, such as improved vocabulary, pronunciation and oral skills, a new-found interest in content, and a fun cognitive exercise. We discuss the lessons learned from the cognitive experiments and deployment, strengths and weaknesses of *Respeak*, and the implications for the future of voice-based crowdsourcing marketplaces.

RELATED WORK

Manual transcription, while efficient, is an expensive process with a high turnaround time. Manual transcribers are trained to type faster, understand different accents and languages, differentiate speakers, and tune out ambient noise, making manual transcription a specialized as well as expensive service. The cost of manual transcription service varies from USD 1–4 per minute depending on several parameters, including the language, quality of speech, length of audio file, ambient noise, number of speakers in the audio file and their accent, requested turnaround time, and verbatim versus non-verbatim transcription.

The advent of crowdsourcing has had a profound effect on the speech transcription industry. Several service providers — such as SpeechPad [15], CastingWords [3], TranscribeMe [17], Rev [12], CrowdSurf [5], and Tigerfish [16] — are capitalizing on the strengths of crowdsourcing and manual transcription. However, most of these providers support only popular accents of English, and none of them support any local language spoken in developing countries. Moreover, their cost varies from USD 1–6 per minute depending on several parameters noted earlier. Workers also transcribe files that can be up to several hours long, making transcription a high cognitive load exercise. Moreover, inclusion criteria noted previously severely limit the adoption of these platforms in developing countries. In India alone, 47% of the 15+ year population does not have a bank account [2] making it hard to compensate them for their work, 97% of households do not have access to a computer connected to the Internet [1], and the typing speed, even of college students, is around 29.5 WPM (more details in the next section). Though several online non-crowdsourcing portals [11, 14, 18] transcribe content in languages spoken in developing regions (like Hindi, Marathi, Urdu and Indian English) using a fleet of transcribers, the cost of transcription starts at USD 5 per minute.

Recent years have seen the rise of several crowdsourcing marketplaces specifically designed to bring additional earning opportunities to low-income people in resource-constrained settings. mClerk [24] and MobileWorks [37] let low-income people transcribe picture SMS sent to their feature mobile phones or perform optical character recognition tasks; TxtEagle lets basic phone users answer survey questions and perform translation tasks using text messages [21]. The rapidly decreasing cost of smartphones and Internet access is helping many of those with low-income and limited technology skills gain access to low-end smartphones and Internet. Jana [9] capitalizes on this trend by transferring mobile airtime to their users who watch videos produced by brands and download smartphone applications. Samasource [13] maintains a dedicated workforce of low-income people who perform varied tasks, including categorization, data mining and transcription. However, the transcription tasks on these platforms require workers to have acceptable typing skills in English and other local languages. *Respeak*, on the other hand, lets low-income people perform speech transcription by listening to the audio and speaking back into an ASR system, which is more natural and usable than typing.

Prior speech transcription research has designed editing tools to improve transcripts generated by an ASR system [20, 26, 41, 44], built speech acquisition systems using Mechanical Turk to expand language corpora [27, 29, 32], and used gamification for speech labeling, identifying accents and prosody annotations [19, 22, 23, 31]. Parent and Eskenazi [38] and Lee and Glass [30] used a two-stage, crowd-powered speech transcription process, where audio files were broken into short segments to reduce cognitive load on workers. Parent and Eskenazi requested that workers first label each utterance and corresponding transcript generated by ASR as understandable/non-understandable and correct/incorrect. The workers were then asked to transcribe understandable but incorrect segments by typing them. A majority vote on the output generated by three workers for each utterance was used to attain the final transcription with a WER of 8.1% without controlling workers' quality. Similarly, Lee and Glass requested workers to type transcriptions for short segments; once each segment was transcribed by one worker, the short transcripts were combined to create the final transcript by using performance estimation and filtering to attain a WER of 10.2%. Lasecki et al. [28] designed a real-time captioning system where non-expert crowd workers transcribed overlapping segments of audio by typing; these segments were merged in real-time by multiple string alignment and majority voting [36] to yield a WER of 45% when attributes were balanced to achieve 66% coverage and 88% precision. *Respeak* draws on existing research by using a two-stage process that segments a large audio file into smaller utterances and then merge transcripts generated for the utterances using multiple string alignment and majority voting. However, unlike other systems, *Respeak* users speak the content into a standard built-in speech recognition engine rather than typing it. Using speaking skills rather than typing skills makes *Respeak* easy and natural to use, especially for people with no or low typing skills.

Prior research exploring re-speaking [25, 39, 42] requires significant data to generate speaker dependent acoustic models and domain dependent language models, making these solutions expensive and untenable at scale. *Respeak*, on the other hand, uses an off-the-shelf generic ASR system and combines transcripts generated by multiple users to reduce ASR errors. Rather than relying on high-skilled re-speakers that have undergone an intensive training of several months and capable of handling multiple hours of captioning without break in a controlled environment [39], *Respeak* rely on multiple unskilled crowd workers to perform micro re-speaking tasks in their everyday environment. Lastly, *Respeak* provides transcription for resource-constrained languages and accents that yield lower ASR accuracy than the well-represented languages and accents, such as English and Japanese, used in prior works.

RESPEAK PROCESS OVERVIEW

Respeak — a voice-based, crowd-powered speech transcription system — combines the benefits of both human intelligence and ASR systems while mitigating their weaknesses by using a five-step process, as follows:

1. **Segmentation:** The *Respeak* engine segments a large audio file for transcription into short utterances that are easier for *Respeak* smartphone application users to remember.

2. **Distribution to Crowd Workers:** Each segment is sent to multiple *Respeak* smartphone application users.

3. **Transcription by Crowd Workers using ASR:** *Respeak* users listen to the segment and repeat the same words into the application in a quiet environment. The application uses the Android ASR API to obtain a transcript for the spoken segment and displays it to the user. The transcript thus produced is expected to have a high WER. The user submits the transcript for the current segment and then receives a new micro-transcription task.

4. **First-stage Merging:** For each segment, the *Respeak* engine combines multiple users' output transcripts into one best estimation transcript using multiple string alignment (MSA) and majority voting. If the errors in the output from the ASR system are randomly distributed, merging the transcripts from different users reduces the overall WER as the correct word is recognized for the majority of users. The transcript sent by the user is compared to the best estimation transcript obtained using MSA and majority voting to determine the reward. Once the cumulative reward amount earned by a user reaches INR 10[1], a mobile airtime credit of INR 10 is sent to the user by the *Respeak* engine.

5. **Second-stage Merging:** The *Respeak* engine concatenates all best estimation transcripts from first-stage merging into one large file to yield the final transcription.

In the following section, we discuss the cognitive experiments we conducted to understand key questions that affect the user interface design of *Respeak*.

COGNITIVE EXPERIMENTS FOR INTERFACE DESIGN

We considered several issues when designing the *Respeak* interface. One key issue pertains to the process of partitioning large audio file into small segments that are easier to retain and re-speak. A simple algorithm could segment a file based on the occurrence of natural pauses in speech. Because such pauses are natural transition points, the segments so obtained might be easier to remember. However, these segments could be long, making them difficult to retain for re-speaking. Moreover, detecting natural pauses in audio files with high ambient noise or music poses a non-trivial problem. Another segmentation approach could split the file into short, fixed-length segments. Though shorter segments would be easier to retain, their abrupt beginnings and endings could impose a high cognitive load for retention. Another main design issue involves identifying how segment length and order of micro-task presentation affects retention. Finally, evaluating the benefits and limitations of re-speaking versus typing significantly affects design choices. Thus, we conducted three cognitive experiments to evaluate:

1. How audio segment length affects content retention and cognitive load experienced by a *Respeak* user.

2. How segment presentation order (sequential vs. random) affects content retention and cognitive load.

3. Whether speaking is indeed more efficient and usable output medium for transcription than typing.

Methodology for Cognitive Experiments

We conducted a within-subjects design study to evaluate the first experiment. We randomly selected 14 audio segments from a televised English news broadcast in India. Two segments each were selected with a length of 1–7 seconds. The average speaking rate in the segments was 160 WPM. Participants performed 14 tasks; in each task, they played a randomly selected segment multiple times on a laptop and re-spoke the content once they memorized it.

We conducted a between-subjects design study to evaluate the second experiment. We randomly selected a one-minute segment from a televised Indian English news broadcast with a speaking rate of 137 WPM. We used a fixed-length segmentation scheme to obtain 15 segments, each of which was four-second long. Participants were randomly partitioned into two groups. The first group listened to the segments in a random order, while the second listened to the segments sequentially. Participants performed 15 tasks, one for each segment. They

[1] In this paper, we use an exchange rate of USD 1 = 66 INR.

	Very good	Good	Average	Bad	Very bad
English speaking	4	14	6	0	0
English typing	4	13	7	0	0
Hindi speaking	4	11	9	0	0
Hindi typing	0	0	5	3	16

Table 1. Self-assessment of participants' language skills.

played the selected segment multiple times and then re-spoke the content once they memorized it.

We conducted a within-subjects study to evaluate the third experiment. We randomly selected a 100-word English news article from a newspaper in India. Participants had to do three tasks: type the article on their computer, type the article on their phone, and read the article out loud. We chose a written article than recorded material since we believed that listening and then typing/re-speaking would also test retention skills in addition to typing/speaking skills. We randomized and balanced the order in which participants completed the tasks.

We recorded and manually transcribed the content re-spoken by participants for each task in all experiments. We measured the WER of re-spoken content and the task completion time. For the first and second experiment, we also measured the number of times participants listened to the segment. We conducted semi-structured interviews after participants finished tasks in all three experiments. The interviews were recorded, transcribed, and analyzed using open coding.

Cognitive Experiments Participants' Demographics

We used a campus-wide email list from a university in India to invite participation and randomly selected 24 respondents. Seventeen participants were male, and seven were female. The average age of participants was 24.4 years. Eight participants were summer interns at the university; five were hired as project staff; four were pursuing a bachelor's, four a master's, and three a Ph.D. degree. Twenty participants were from the engineering disciplines and four were from the humanities. All but one participants owned a smartphone with Internet access. The average daily phone and computer usage was reported to be around 5.5 hours and 10 hours, respectively. Nine participants knew about crowdsourcing platforms, but only two had used them previously. As Table 1 shows, the majority of participants assessed their Hindi typing skills as being very bad.

Findings of Cognitive Experiments

While WER predicts the performance of content retention, task completion time and number of listens predict the cognitive load experienced by participants.

Experiment 1: Impact of Segment Length on Retention

Figure 1 compares the WER, time taken to retain and re-speak segments, and number of times segments were listened in the first experiment. A repeated measures ANOVA with a Greenhouse-Geisser correction determined a statistically significant difference (at $p<.001$) in the three parameters for the segments that were 1–7 seconds long. Table 2 highlights the parameters that significantly differ (at $p<.05$) on a pairwise comparison of the segments of different lengths. The WER and time taken were much higher for segments exceeding five

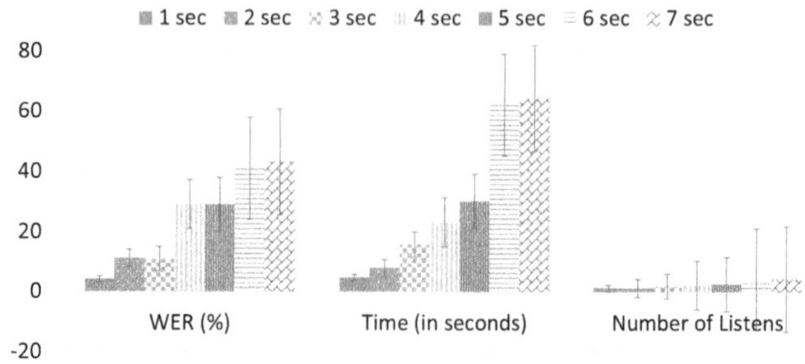

Figure 1. Comparison of varying length segments on several parameters.

	1s	2s	3s	4s	5s	6s	7s
1s	-	T	TL	WTL	WTL	WTL	WTL
2s	T	-	TL	WTL	WTL	WTL	WTL
3s	TL	TL	-	WT	WTL	WTL	WTL
4s	WTL	WTL	WT	-	T	WTL	WTL
5s	WTL	WTL	WTL	T	-	WTL	WTL
6s	WTL	WTL	WTL	WTL	WTL	-	-
7s	WTL	WTL	WTL	WTL	WTL	-	-

Table 2. Significant difference in WER (W), completion time (T) and number of listens (L) on pairwise comparison of varied length segments.

seconds. Our interviews also revealed that several participants could not retain such segments because of complicated sentence constructions and the excessive number of concepts to remember. Thus, using such segments in *Respeak* could result in a poor accuracy speech transcription and put significant cognitive load on users. Eleven participants used synonyms or missed articles while re-speaking content. Three participants found it difficult to retain segments containing an incoherent word. Another three participants found it challenging to retain unfamiliar proper nouns. Four participants found content retention to depend on their familiarity with subject matter rather than on duration. One of them stated:

> *If you present segments on cricket to a cricket enthusiast, he will easily remember the content irrespective of how long it is. But if the same person has to remember content related to military strategies, they may not remember it.*

Twelve participants found it difficult to retain segments containing partial sentences. Abrupt cuts resulting in an incomplete or incoherent word made it substantially more difficult to retain the segment. A participant stated:

> *The segments that started or ended with a clipped word were very distracting. My mind got stuck on the clipped words, making it impossible for me to retain the content.*

Nine participants suggested using natural pauses rather than abrupt cuts to split a long sentence in multiple segments. Eleven participants found a 3–4 second length optimal for content retention. These findings prompted us to design a segmentation scheme that splits an audio file based on the occurrence of natural pauses. If the individual segments so obtained exceeded a predefined length, the segments were recursively divided into smaller chunks of the desired length.

Experiment 2: Impact of Segment Ordering on Retention

We conducted independent samples t-test to analyze the effect of segment ordering on content retention. We found a significant difference in the WER when segments were played

	Time Taken (seconds)			WER (%)		
	CT	PT	S	CT	PT	S
M	211.7	370.3	37.8	4.5	5.0	3.1
SD	44.8	285.9	5.5	4.4	4.6	4.1

Table 3. Mean (M) and standard deviation (SD) for computer typing (CT), phone typing (PT) and speaking (S) tasks.

sequentially (M = 16.59, SD = 3.85) rather than randomly (M = 32.27, SD = 13.18); $t(22) = 3.96$, p=.001. We did not find a difference in task completion time or the number of times participants listened to segments. These results suggest that content retention is much higher when segments are presented sequentially. In the interviews, five participants specifically mentioned that sequential ordering increased their understanding of context, making it easier to estimate incoherent and clipped words. One of them stated:

> *When I hear the second segment after the first, I am able to connect it and even predict some of the words. Hearing segments in contiguous order makes cognition very easy.*

Experiment 3: Speaking versus Typing

Table 3 shows descriptive statistics for the tasks in the third experiment. The average speed of computer typing, phone typing, and speaking was 29.5, 19.3, and 161 WPM, respectively. A repeated measures ANOVA with a Greenhouse-Geisser correction determined a statistically significant difference in task completion time, $F(1.03, 23.74) = 25.41$, p<.001. Post hoc tests using the Bonferroni correction also revealed a significant difference (p<.05) in task completion time, even for pairwise comparisons of all three tasks. Though the average WER for speaking was lower than for typing, we did not find any statistical evidence to substantiate this.

We also requested participants to rate the three tasks on a ten-point scale for NASA TLX parameters to assess subjective workload. As seen in Figure 2, participants found that speaking caused the least mental demand, physical demand, effort, and frustration. Moreover, they perceived their performance for the speaking task to be higher than for the typing tasks. A participant explained the ease of speaking vs. typing content:

> *Speaking is better as it comes naturally to us. It does not require any gadgets. Typing is something external.*

A repeated measures ANOVA with a Greenhouse-Geisser correction determined a statistically significant difference in mental demand (p<.001), physical demand (p<.001), performance (p=.001), effort (p<.001) and frustration (p<.001) for the three tasks. A pairwise comparison of the three tasks revealed a statistically significant difference (p<.05) in all five parameters for computer typing vs. phone typing, and phone typing vs. speaking. We also found a statistically significant difference (p<.05) in mental and physical demand for computer typing vs. speaking. These results suggest that speaking is a more efficient and easier output medium than phone or computer typing. We believe these results would be more significant and extreme if the participants were non-engineering students.

In summary, our cognitive experiments revealed that audio files should be partitioned by detecting natural pauses to yield segments of less than six seconds in length. These segments should be presented sequentially to ensure higher retention and less cognitive load on users. The users should complete micro-transcription tasks by speaking rather than typing.

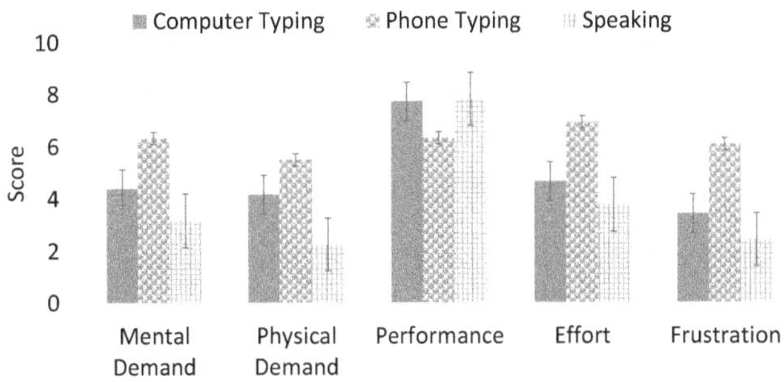

Figure 2. Evaluation of output modes on NASA TLX parameters.

FIRST-STAGE MERGING USING CROWDSOURCING

Respeak's speech transcription efficiency depends on the performance of the multiple string alignment (MSA) algorithm, and the majority voting process that is the core of first-stage merging. For each segment, the *Respeak* engine combines the transcripts submitted by *Respeak* users to produce a best estimation of actual word sequence in the segment. The MSA algorithm in our implementation uses word as the individual atomic unit rather than character or phoneme. We adapted and implemented the multiple sequence alignment algorithm proposed by Naim et al. [36] that uses the A* search algorithm to reduce the search space of multi-dimensional lattice. Any ties during majority voting are broken randomly. Let us assume that first-stage merging takes as input transcripts generated by K users by repeating the same phrase in the *Respeak* mobile application. If the ASR errors are uncorrelated across users, then the WER of the hypothesized word sequence should decrease as K increases. Let P be the average accuracy of speech recognition for individual users. The WER then is $1-P$. Assuming that the errors are randomly distributed across users, the accuracy of the alignment of segments (P_{final}) for N users computed using majority voting is:

$$1-\binom{N}{N}(1-P)^{N}-\binom{N}{N-1}(1-P)^{N-1}P.....-\binom{N}{K}(1-P)^{K}P^{N-K}, K\geq N/2 \quad (1)$$

Figure 3 depicts the estimated improvement in accuracy achievable by aligning the transcripts generated by one, three, five and seven users for several values of P.

To test the feasibility and performance of first-stage merging, we designed, built and deployed a simple smartphone application to collect data from 29 university students in India who volunteered to take part in the experiment. The participants were requested to read the short segments rather than memorize and re-speak them. The speech-to-text output was instantly displayed on the application using the built-in Google ASR engine. There were 25 short segments in Indian English and ten short segments in Hindi. The average number of words were 13 (min=5, max=33, SD=8.08) for English segments and 15 (min=9, max=27, SD=5.6) for Hindi segments. Seventeen participants collected data for English and twelve for Hindi.

Participants had different WERs due to a variety of factors, such as differing background noise, accents, and speaking

Ground truth:	it	is		strong	in	the	market
Transcript 1:	it	is	BLANK	BLANK	from	the	market
Transcript 2:	it	is	BLANK	strong	in	the	market
Transcript 3:	it	is	a	strong	in	the	market
Majority voting:	it	is	BLANK	strong	in	the	market
Reconstructed segment:	it	is		strong	in	the	market

Table 4. Alignment of segment using MSA and majority voting on transcripts obtained from 3 speakers.

Users (K)	Expected WER	Actual WER
1	33%	33%
3	26%	25%
5	21%	17%
7	18%	19%

Table 5. Word error rates (WERs) after MSA and majority voting.

rate. The best speaker had a WER of 11%, the worst had a WER of 58%, and the average WER was 33%. To measure the degree of improvement in transcription by using MSA and majority voting, we varied the number of speakers used to align transcripts. Table 4 illustrates the alignment of the segment *"it is strong in the market"* from three speakers. The ASR transcript contained an error for all three speakers. However, combining the transcripts generated by ASR for all three speakers mitigated the errors made by individual speakers. Table 5 reports the WERs averaged over ten runs of experiments where K speakers were randomly selected from the pool of 29 participants for each run. The WER of the alignment using seven speakers exceeded that for 28 participants and was comparable to the theoretically estimated improvement. The field evaluation validated our hypothesis that aligning transcripts generated by multiple users decreases the WER when ASR errors are randomly distributed.

FIELD DEPLOYMENT IN INDIA

Since many university students have smartphones connected to the Internet and also have financial constraints that might motivate them to earn mobile airtime, we sent an email inviting students in a university in Mumbai, India to participate in our controlled deployment. We randomly selected 25 respondents as users and conducted a face-to-face orientation session with them to install the *Respeak* application on their personal smartphones, show them how to use the application, and collect demographic information.

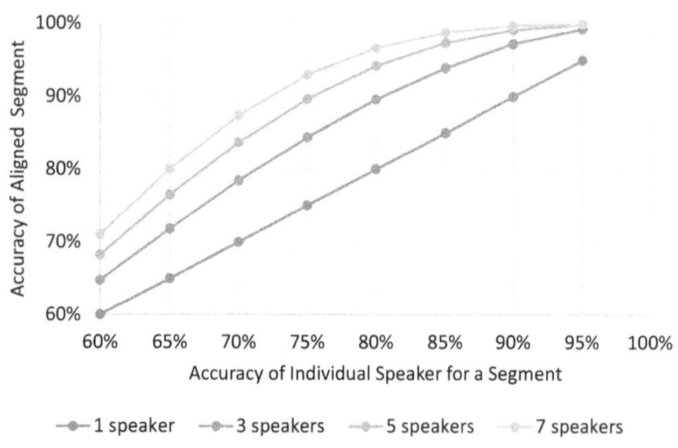

Figure 3. Improvement in accuracy by using MSA and majority voting.

Tasks

We submitted thirteen Hindi and eight English audio files to the *Respeak* engine for transcription. To stress test *Respeak*, we selected audio files that had ambient noise and heavily localized Hindi or English accents. The files contained varied content, including public speeches, telephone conversations, news, television advertisements, songs, interviews, YouTube content, and online lectures. The total duration of the Hindi and English files was 43 minutes and 12 minutes, respectively. The *Respeak* engine partitioned Hindi files into 499 segments and English files into 257 segments to yield 756 unique micro-transcription tasks (see Table 6). The threshold length for the segmentation scheme was based on the speaking rate in the audio file: the length for public speeches and songs was 5–6 seconds, news and YouTube videos was 4 seconds, and interviews and phone calls was 3 seconds. The collective download size of all tasks was 85 MB and the cost of downloading them was roughly 20 INR (USD 0.30) on a 3G connection. Each task could be performed by a maximum of ten users who could see a high-level overview of their transcription accuracy, amount earned, payment processed, and completed tasks.

Payment Scale

The *Respeak* reward structure was designed to keep the cost of transcription below USD 1 per minute. Each transcription task was assigned a reward equal to 0.2 INR multiplied by segment length in seconds. We hypothesized that for each segment, if we aligned the transcripts generated by five users and if all of them performed the task with a high accuracy, the maximum transcription cost would still be USD 0.92 per minute. Each time a user submitted a transcript for a segment, we compared their output with the pre-computed ground truth. If the transcript's accuracy was $\geq 80\%$, we added the entire task reward to the user' earning. If the accuracy was $\geq 50\%$, we added a proportionate percentage of the task reward to the user' earning. A user received no reward if the accuracy was $< 50\%$. This reward structure gave users the incentives to produce speech transcription with more than 80% accuracy, gave proportionate returns to average performers, and penalized poor performers. Once the cumulative earnings of a user reached 10 INR, we processed a mobile airtime credit of the same value to them. The maximum amount a *Respeak* user could earn by doing Hindi tasks was 514 INR (USD 7.80) and by doing English tasks was 152 INR (USD 2.30). The reward structure could also be designed differently to satisfy other optimization goals.

Ideally, the transcripts submitted by *Respeak* users should be evaluated by comparing them to the best estimation transcript generated in first-stage merging. However, at the time of experiment we were unsure about how and when people would use the application, forcing us to use the pre-computed ground truth for comparison. We ran the comparison module every

	Interview			Song			TV ad			News			Public speech			Phone call			YouTube video			Lecture		
	File	Task	Len	File	Task	Len	File	Task	Len	File	Task	Len	File	Task	Len	File	Task	Len	File	Task	Len	File	Task	Len
English	2	177	494	-	-	-	1	10	40	1	10	30	1	15	60	-	-	-	2	35	105	1	9	27
Hindi	-	-	-	3	77	431	-	-	-	1	17	51	5	313	1760	3	37	111	1	54	216	-	-	-
Total	2	177	494	3	77	431	1	10	40	2	27	81	6	328	1820	3	37	111	3	89	321	1	9	27

Table 6. Number of files, tasks and length of files (in seconds) used for each category of transcribed content by language.

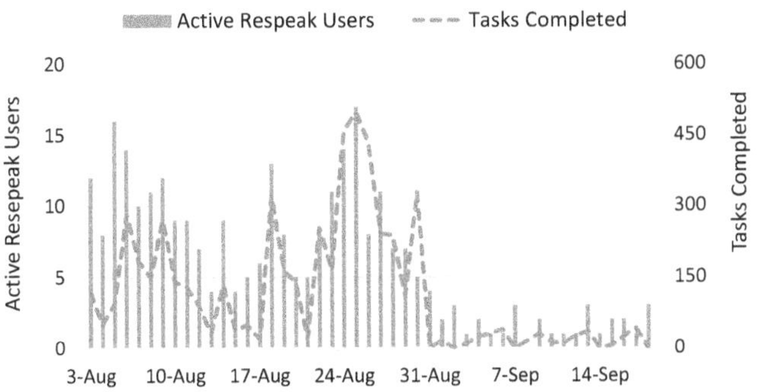

Figure 4. Time series analysis of active users and tasks completed.

15 minutes to balance the desire of users to receive immediate feedback and the need to simulate a delay that would occur awaiting transcripts generated by others for MSA and majority voting process.

Methodology to Evaluate Deployment

We used a mixed-methods approach spanning quantitative analyses of performance, cost, and turnaround time, and qualitative interviews to evaluate *Respeak*. We conducted in-depth, semi-structured, face-to-face interviews with 20 *Respeak* users at the end of deployment. Each interview lasted around 40 minutes and covered several themes, including information on the general technology use, user experience and usability, conception of *Respeak*, and benefits and limitations of the *Respeak* application. The interviews were conducted by the first author (male, 29 years old, Hindi speaking) and were recorded, transcribed, and analyzed using open coding.

FINDINGS

The *Respeak* application was deployed for a month with 25 users. Figure 4 depicts the time series analysis of the number of tasks completed by active *Respeak* users. The low activity between August 10–20 corresponded to an intermittent campus-wide Internet outage at the university where we deployed *Respeak*. Though the deployment ended on August 31, some users continued using the application for another 20 days. 756 audio segments were presented as 5464 micro-tasks to the users, who transcribed the segments successfully with an individual average WER of 23.7%. On average, *Respeak* users listened to segments 2.7 times and re-spoke them 2.1 times before moving on to the next task. The median time for task completion was 36 seconds, and the cost of transcription was USD 0.83 per minute. Collectively, *Respeak* users spent 39.8 hours using the system and earned 3036 INR (USD 46). The expected payout for an hour of their time was 76 INR (USD 1.16), one-fourth of the average daily wage rate in India [7]. The *Respeak* engine combined the transcripts generated by five users for each segment, reducing the average WER to 10.6%. The best alignment yielded a WER of 6.8%.

Respeak Users Demographics

Fifteen *Respeak* users were male and ten were female. Fourteen were students, six were contractual staff, and five were summer interns. Twenty users were from varied engineering departments, and five from the humanities. Eighteen users had or were pursuing a bachelor's degree, six had or were pursuing a master's degree, and one was pursuing a Ph.D. Fifteen users did not have any scholarship, stipend, or salary and were supported by their families. The average monthly income of employed users was USD 293, and their average monthly family income was USD 1557.

All users owned an Android smartphone, had cellular Internet access, and used their phones for an average of 5 hours a day. Despite heavy and ubiquitous phone usage, 17 participants had a shoestring budget for mobile airtime and data, and relied on the free WiFi provided by the university. Like participants in the cognitive experiments, all users rated their English language skills and Hindi speaking skills highly. However, 22 users reported their Hindi typing skills to be bad. Sixteen of them did not even know how to type in Hindi. Sixteen users were unaware of crowdsourcing systems, and only three had used them previously. After we explained crowdsourcing to them, they expressed an interest in using such systems to earn money (N=14), gain knowledge (N=13), help others (N=6), and spend their copious time productively (N=3).

Efficiency of Speech Transcription

The average WER of the transcription generated by ASR engine for individual *Respeak* users was 23.7%. We performed a series of experiments to measure the improvement in transcription using MSA and majority voting. For each segment, we conducted ten runs of experiments. In each run, the transcripts generated by three randomly selected *Respeak* users were used for MSA and majority voting in first-stage merging. The WERs obtained in each of the ten runs were averaged for evaluation. By aligning the transcripts generated by 3 speakers, the WER dropped to 15.1% — an improvement of 36.3%. We used the same setup to align transcripts generated for each segment by 5 randomly selected *Respeak* users, and the WER dropped further to 13.2% — an improvement of 44.3%.

A closer inspection of users' transcripts and the ground truth revealed interesting cases that were registered as errors by the comparison module but were semantically correct. The application's Google ASR engine transcribed several words in English and Hindi differently for different speakers. In English, the words were often contracted or abbreviated (e.g., it is vs. it's; Doctor vs. Dr.), and the numbers were transcribed either in numeric or textual format (e.g., 3 vs. three) for different speakers. In Hindi, multiple spellings with minor variations were output for the same word depending on the stress, intonation and nasality used by speakers (see Figure 5).

Word	Spelling 1	Spelling 2	Spelling 3
उन्होंने	उन्होने	उंन्होंने	उन्होन
भाइयों	भाईयों	भाइयो	
छोड़ा	छोडा		

Figure 5. Different spellings generated by Google ASR engine for words in Hindi.

The manual correction of such corner cases in *Respeak* user transcripts lowered the average WER for individual users from 23.7% to 21.9%. We recomputed the set of experiments where transcripts generated by multiple users were aligned, and the WER dropped to 12.5% and 10.6% when transcripts generated by 3 and 5 randomly selected users were aligned, respectively. Thus, the alignment of transcripts generated by five randomly selected users reduced the average WER by 55.3%. For future deployments, we recommend using existing dictionaries or building a customized dictionary to resolve these corner cases automatically in the comparison module.

To evaluate the effect on WER and cost as more transcripts are used for alignment and majority voting, we randomly selected 50% of 391 tasks that were each completed by ten *Respeak* users. We conducted ten runs of experiments; in each run, we used the transcripts generated by *K* randomly selected *Respeak* users. We varied the value of *K* from 1–9 and averaged the WER obtained for each value of *K* over ten runs of experiments. The cost of transcription was calculated using the rate of 0.2 INR per second of transcription per user — an overestimate that assumed that users would receive the entire reward amount promised for each task. As depicted in Figure 6, the WER decreased as *K* increased, and the cost of speech transcription linearly increased with *K*.

To compare *Respeak* with a state-of-the-art speech recognition engine, we submitted the original audio files to the Google Cloud Speech API [4] after noise reduction. The API yielded transcription with the overall WER of 50% — 4.72 times higher than the WER obtained by *Respeak*. The WER for Hindi audio files was 54% — 6.3 times higher than the WER obtained by *Respeak*. These results suggest that *Respeak* capitalized on the benefits of re-speaking and crowdsourcing to outperform transcription generated by the state-of-the-art speech recognition engine.

Tables 7 and 8 report the WER of transcription obtained for different languages and content types by aligning transcripts generated by K *Respeak* users during first-stage merging. Our

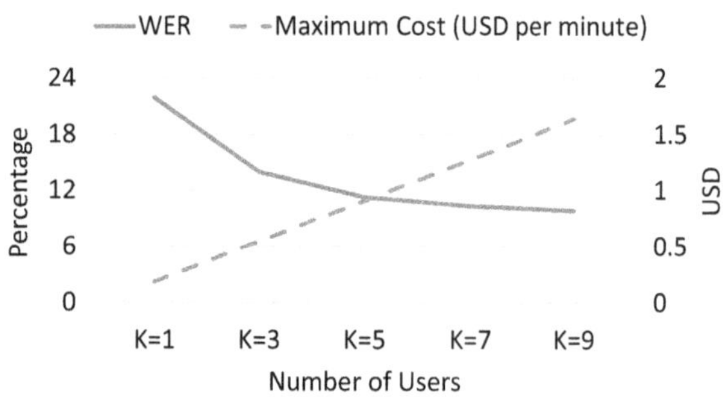

Figure 6. Effect of number of users on WER and cost.

Language	WER (%) before correction			WER (%) after correction		
	K=1	K=3	K=5	K=1	K=3	K=5
English	26.9	19.8	16.7	26.2	18.1	15.2
Hindi	19.9	13	11.7	17.1	10	8.6
Both	23.7	15.1	13.2	21.9	12.5	10.6

Table 7. WER obtained by *Respeak* for English and Hindi languages.

Content Type	WER (%) before correction			WER (%) post correction		
	K=1	K=3	K=5	K=1	K=3	K=5
Interview	27.8	21.2	18	27.2	19.1	16.4
Song	22.9	13.2	10.3	20.2	10.9	7.8
TV ad	31.2	26	24.3	29.1	23.8	19.7
News	23.2	14	9.8	20.6	10.7	8.3
Public speech	20.1	13.2	12	17.4	10.3	8.8
Phone call	25.9	18.8	17.4	22.8	15.2	12.8
YouTube video	16.9	11.2	10.2	14.9	8.9	7.8
Online Lecture	17.4	13.2	10.7	16.5	11.3	9.8

Table 8. WER obtained by *Respeak* for different content categories.

interviews revealed that six users found it easier to do Hindi tasks, and four found it easier to do English tasks. The language preference existed either because of better language skills or faster recognition from the ASR engine in their preferred language. Seven users found it easiest to re-speak song segments while others found interviews (N=3), speeches (N=2), news (N=1), lectures (N=1) and poems (N=1) the easiest. Six users found it very difficult to understand the segments containing an interview of a former president of India, three found it hardest to retain the advertisement segments because of the audio's unclear accent, and the other three found it difficult to re-speak Bollywood song segments because of the *"cheesy"* lyrics. The remaining users found no difference in the difficulty level of tasks based on content type. Three users sang the segments containing songs rather than merely re-speaking them. A user explained how he had to remain aware of his surroundings while re-speaking song segments:

> *Singing songs was difficult as I had to speak cheesy lines like, "My heart is beating for you". My parents overheard me re-speaking this and asked me, 'Who are you talking to; what is going on?' It was awkward to explain.*

Five users found it useful that the segments of an audio file were presented in a sequential order as tasks. However, three users found it monotonous to do tasks continuously for the same audio file. They suggested an alternate scheme where small blocks from different files could be randomly presented, where each block could have segments from the same audio file presented sequentially. Four users found it challenging to do tasks with clipped words either at the beginning or end; they were unsure whether to re-speak or ignore such words.

Figure 7 plots the average WER for segments of varying word lengths. Surprisingly, the WER for individual users did not vary significantly as the number of words in segments increased. However, the improvement in WER by aligning transcripts from 5 users rather than 3 users decreased as the number of words in a segment increased. Though the randomness in errors increased with the increase in number of words in a segment, the errors were sparsely distributed reducing the performance improvement gained by MSA and majority vote.

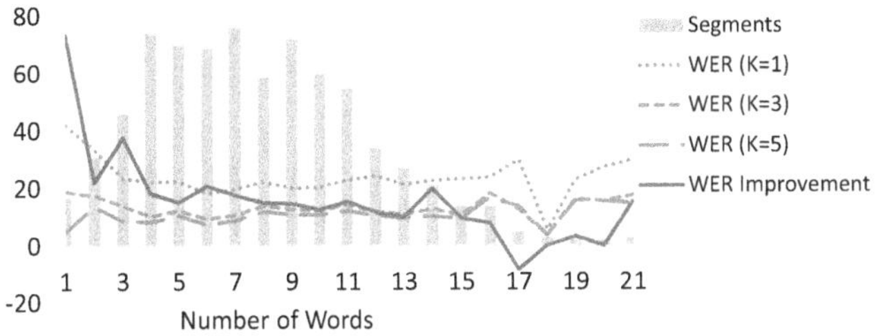

Figure 7. WER for segments of varying word length.

Amount Earned (INR) ≤	*Respeak* Users
100	15
200	5
300	1
400	0
500	3

Table 9. Amount earned by *Respeak* users.

Payments

We processed mobile airtime of 3040 INR (USD 46) to 24 users. The top 3 users earned 44% of the total payments, while the top 20% and 50% users earned 60% and 87%, respectively (see Table 9). Ten users earned more than their monthly phone expense. Several users reported that using the application for ten minutes daily was sufficient to subsidize their phone expenses. *Respeak* became a portal to transfer mobile airtime to their phones. A user reported:

> *I exhausted my phone balance while chatting with a friend. I did not have money to refill my phone online. I quickly did some tasks on* Respeak *using free WIFI, received a top-up, and then called him.*

All but one users were happy to receive the amount earned as mobile airtime. Some users suggested payments in the form of food coupons (N=6), Amazon gift coupons (N=5), and top-ups of higher value that results in the equivalent mobile airtime [2] (N=3). Two users emphasized the need to process a 10 INR mobile airtime for immediate gratification. A user stated:

> *There is not much you get for 10 INR in market other than mobile airtime. If the amount when payment is processed is higher, many people may stop using the application. even before they reach that number.*

Eight users found that their efforts using *Respeak* were commensurate with the amount they earned. Six users found that the money they earned exceeded their efforts, while six others felt the opposite way.

Instrumental Benefits

Seven *Respeak* users reported receiving instrumental benefits from the application use. Three found that *Respeak* improved their language and oral skills. While re-speaking audio segments, they focused on pronouncing the words correctly for faster recognition by the ASR engine. Often, they searched online for the meaning and pronunciation of unfamiliar words, thereby expanding their vocabulary. *Respeak* provided them with the opportunity to speak English aloud *"without being judged by others."* One user reported a new-found interest in the content he transcribed, viz., an old Bollywood song on YouTube. Another found *Respeak* to be a challenging yet fun exercise that improved his cognitive abilities. Two users reported acquiring new knowledge while doing the tasks and found some of the speeches inspiring. One of them stated:

> *Receiving a mobile recharge was good. However, listening to speeches and interviews increased my general knowledge. Most importantly, the application improved my pronunciation as I was focusing to pronounce words better so that they get recognized.*

Feedback on Respeak

Figure 8 presents average user ratings for NASA TLX parameters on a ten-point scale. Users enjoyed *Respeak* for a wide variety of reasons, including earning mobile airtime (N=8), excitement to see their speech recognized (N=6), ability to track their accuracy (N=4), easy-to-use interface (N=4), listening to interesting content (N=1), the opportunity to practice speaking English out loud (N=1), and the chance to compare their accuracy to others (N=1). Even before our interviews, we received user emails describing their enthusiasm for *Respeak*. One such enthusiastic user wrote: *"Respeak is cool. Got a little excited with the top-up I just received."*

Nine users found Internet usage to be a barrier to using the application. Seven users found it difficult to get their speech recognized and four faced challenges in getting ASR engine to recognize people's names. Though users voluntarily signed-up to participate in the deployment, four reported time constraints that limited their application use. Eight users suggested gamification to make the application more entertaining. Five wanted functionality to skip tasks for unclear or difficult-to-retain segments. Two suggested including a feature that let users type to edit the transcript generated by the ASR engine after multiple unsuccessful re-speaking trials. Three users wanted the ability to filter tasks by language. One each suggested incorporating graphs to track improvement in user accuracy, a leaderboard, and a feature to regulate playback speed.

The users considered the ideal *Respeak* demographic to include: students (N=15), unemployed people (N=4), home makers (N=2), people spending long hours commuting (N=2), and those interested in learning oral skills (N=1). After the deployment, eleven participants expressed an interest in using the application daily, primarily to earn mobile airtime and

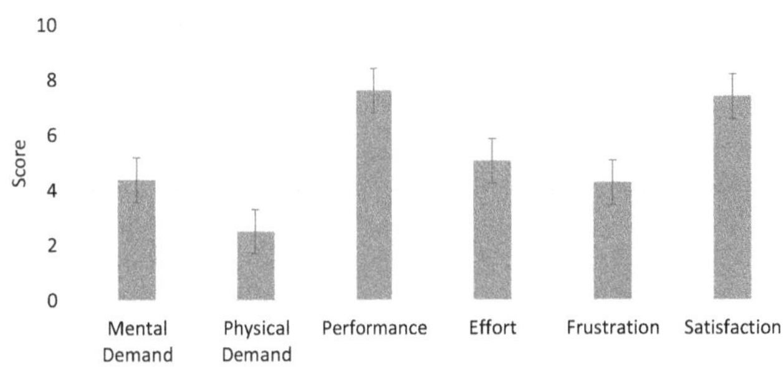

Figure 8. Average ratings by *Respeak* users for several parameters.

[2]A top-up of 10 INR gave 7.8 INR in airtime. The lowest top-up that gave full mobile airtime is around 100 INR for different providers.

improve their language skills; six stated that they would use it sparingly when they need mobile airtime; three stated that the lack of time would inhibit their application use in the future.

DISCUSSION AND CONCLUSIONS

Respeak was successful in producing efficient and cost-effective speech transcription with a low turnaround time for widely-varied Hindi and Indian English audio files. Our cognitive experiments were instrumental in designing *Respeak*; they revealed that audio files should be partitioned by detecting natural pauses to yield segments of less than six-second length and presented sequentially to increase retention and decrease cognitive load. In the deployment with 25 university students in India, *Respeak* produced speech transcription with an accuracy of 89.4% and turnaround time of 39.8 hours. The average WER decreased from 21.9% to 12.5% (three users) and further to 10.2% (five users) when the transcripts generated by multiple users were aligned using MSA and majority voting to reduce randomly distributed ASR errors. *Respeak* transcribed audio content in Hindi and Indian English with a WER of 8.6% and 15.2%, respectively. The WER for Hindi tasks was much lower than that for English tasks because of users' better listening and speaking skills in Hindi. *Respeak* produced high-accuracy transcription even for audio files with high ambient noises like songs (WER=7.8%) and telephone calls (WER=12.8%) as humans are better than ASR systems at ignoring ambient noise and interpreting unclear speech. Since the cost of transcription using *Respeak* (USD 0.83 per minute) is only one-sixth of the industry standard of USD 5 per minute for Hindi and Indian English content [11, 14, 18], it is feasible to increase the worker payout rate of USD 1.16 per hour in future iterations to make *Respeak* more lucrative for workers.

One key strength of *Respeak* is its voice-based implementation: *Respeak* let users generate transcripts by speaking rather than typing. Though our deployment had technology-savvy users who were engineering students, the majority did not know how to type in Hindi, and those who knew had poor Hindi typing skills. *Respeak* capitalized on users' speaking skills rather than typing skills that are scarce for languages that do not use Latin script. Though several technologies, like Google Input Tools [6] and India Typing [8], take Latin script input and produce Devanagari script output using transliteration, speaking was much easier for *Respeak* users since voice is a natural and accessible medium of interaction. The reliance on speaking skills makes *Respeak* more inclusive of people with no or poor typing skills.

Respeak has some limitations, however. Its users were unsure what words to re-speak when multiple people simultaneously spoke in a segment. Moreover, the *Respeak* engine did not distinguish speakers in transcription for audio files with multiple speakers. Future versions could consider an improved segmentation scheme that is cognizant of speakers in an audio file containing multiple speakers. Further, the transcription generated by *Respeak* lacked punctuation marks. Though punctuation marks could be added automatically based on the identification and length of natural pauses, a better algorithm is needed when it would be difficult to detect natural pauses due to ambient noise. One possible solution could be to send an audio segment and corresponding transcript generated by *Respeak* to users, who are then asked to identify speakers and place punctuation marks.

Respeak users were primarily driven to use the application for earning mobile airtime. Some users found *Respeak* to be monotonous and less enjoyable towards the end of the deployment. To make it more interesting, seven users created informal leaderboards to compete with each other on accuracy of speech transcription and the number of tasks they completed. They conducted these discussions over emails and WhatsApp groups. Future work could use gamification to increase user retention and entertainment value. Several users reported receiving instrumental benefits, such as improved vocabulary and pronunciation skills, access to new information and knowledge, and a new-found interest in content. Though we did not have any quantitative measure of these indicators, future work could capitalize on language learning aspects to re-design and evaluate *Respeak*.

One of the most direct ways to empower low-income communities in resource-constrained settings is to provide them with additional earning opportunities. Recent years have seen rapid increase in penetration and decrease in cost of smartphones and Internet in developing countries [34, 33]. *Respeak* provides a definite step forward in realizing a smartphone- and voice-based crowdsourcing marketplace. *Respeak* was the first crowdsourcing platform for 88% of its users, who were technology-savvy university students. Fifteen users were financially dependent on their family members, and ten others earned USD 9.76 per day through their job. The amount earned by using *Respeak* was significant for many technology-savvy low-income literate people in our deployment, and we believe *Respeak* has potential to be transformative for other marginalized communities including low-literate and visually impaired people. Our immediate next step is to conduct more deployments with these populations to investigate the external validity of our findings.

Respeak could also be used to subsidize the cost of participation of low-income, low-literate people on voice-based social computing platforms, such as CGNet Swara [35], Sangeet Swara [43], and Polly [40]. More work is needed to adapt *Respeak* to basic mobile phones, where users could call-in to an interactive voice response system, listen to a short segment, re-speak it, and earn mobile airtime. In doing this work, we confront several interesting challenges, such as ensuring reasonable accuracy of ASR systems on telephone lines, providing immediate feedback on transcripts generated by ASR systems, and managing the overhead cost of voice calls. The *Respeak* call-in service could have a high potential to provide additional earning opportunities through crowdsourcing marketplaces to billions of low-literate people with access to a basic phone.

ACKNOWLEDGMENTS

We are grateful to Gaetano Borriello, Aaron Jaech, Ganesh Ramakrishnan, Bill Thies and the anonymous reviewers for their helpful suggestions. This work is funded by a grant (#AID-OAA-G-14-00014) from USAID.

REFERENCES

1. 2012. *Press Note on Release of Data on Houses, Household Amenities and Assets, Census 2011*. Technical Report. Ministry of Home Affairs, Government of India. http://censusindia.gov.in/2011census/hlo/Data_sheet/India/HLO_Press_Release.pdf
2. 2014. *Global Findex 2014 - Financial Inclusion*. Technical Report. World Bank. http://datatopics.worldbank.org/financialinclusion/country/india
3. 2016. CastingWords. (2016). https://castingwords.com/.
4. 2016. CLOUD SPEECH API: Speech to text conversion powered by machine learning. (2016). https://cloud.google.com/speech/.
5. 2016. CrowdSurf. (2016). http://crowdsurfwork.com/.
6. 2016. Google Input Tools. (2016). https://www.google.com/inputtools/.
7. 2016. India Average Daily Wage Rate Forecast 2016-2020. (2016). http://www.tradingeconomics.com/india/wages/forecast.
8. 2016. India Typing. (2016). http://indiatyping.com/.
9. 2016. Jana. (2016). https://www.jana.com/.
10. 2016. *Medical Transcription Services Market - Global Industry Analysis, Size, Share, Growth, Trends and Forecast, 2013 - 2019*. Technical Report. Transparency Market Research.
11. 2016. Quick Transcription Service. (2016). http://www.quicktranscriptionservice.com/Hindi-Transcription.html.
12. 2016. Rev. (2016). https://www.rev.com/.
13. 2016. Samasource. (2016). http://www.samasource.org/.
14. 2016. Scripts Complete. (2016). http://scriptscomplete.com/Hindi-Transcription-Services.php.
15. 2016. SpeechPad. (2016). https://www.speechpad.com/.
16. 2016. Tigerfish. (2016). http://tigerfish.com/.
17. 2016a. TranscribeMe. (2016). http://transcribeme.com/.
18. 2016b. Transcription Services Us. (2016). http://www.transcription-services-us.com/Language-Transcription-Rates.php.
19. Rio Akasaka. 2009. *Foreign accented speech transcription and accent recognition using a game-based approach*. Ph.D. Dissertation. Swarthmore Department of Linguistics.
20. Floraine Berthouzoz, Wilmot Li, and Maneesh Agrawala. 2012. Tools for Placing Cuts and Transitions in Interview Video. *ACM Transaction of Graphics* 31, 4 (2012).
21. Nathan Eagle. 2009. Txteagle: Mobile Crowdsourcing. In *Proceedings of HCI International*. Springer-Verlag.
22. Keelan Evanini and Klaus Zechner. 2011. Using crowdsourcing to provide prosodic annotations for non-native speech. In *Proceedings of Interspeech*.
23. Alexander Gruenstein, Ian McGraw, and Andrew Sutherland. 2009. A Self-Transcribing Speech Corpus: Collecting Continuous Speech with an Online Educational Game. In *Proceedings of SLaTE*.
24. Aakar Gupta, William Thies, Edward Cutrell, and Ravin Balakrishnan. 2012. mClerk: Enabling Mobile Crowdsourcing in Developing Regions. In *Proceedings of CHI*.
25. Toru Imai, Atsushi Matsui, Shinichi Homma, Takeshi Kobayakawa, Kazuo Onoe, Shoei Sato, and Akio Ando. 2002. Speech recognition with a re-speak method for subtitling live broadcasts. In *Proceedings of ICSLP*.
26. Jennifer Lai and John Vergo. 1997. MedSpeak: Report Creation with Continuous Speech Recognition. In *Proceedings of CHI*.
27. Ian Lane, Alex Waibel, Matthias Eck, and Kay Rottmann. 2010. Tools for Collecting Speech Corpora via Mechanical Turk. In *Proceedings of the NAACL HLT*.
28. Walter Lasecki, Christopher Miller, Adam Sadilek, Andrew Abumoussa, Donato Borrello, Raja Kushalnagar, and Jeffrey Bigham. 2012. Real-time Captioning by Groups of Non-experts. In *Proceedings of UIST*.
29. Jonathan Ledlie, Billy Odero, Einat Minkov, Imre Kiss, and Joseph Polifroni. 2010. Crowd Translator: On Building Localized Speech Recognizers Through Micropayments. *SIGOPS Oper. Syst. Rev.* 43, 4 (Jan. 2010).
30. Chia-ying Lee and James Glass. 2011. A Transcription Task for Crowdsourcing with Automatic Quality Control. In *Proceedings of Interspeech*.
31. Ian Mcgraw, Er Gruenstein, and Andrew Sutherl. 2009. A Self-Labeling Speech Corpus: Collecting Spoken Words with an Online Educational Game. In *Proceedings of Interspeech*.
32. Ian Mcgraw, Chia-ying Lee, Lee Hetherington, Stephanie Seneff, and Jim Glass. 2010. Collecting Voices from the Cloud. In *Proceedings of LREC*.
33. Mary Meeker. 2015. *2015 Internet Trends*. Technical Report. KPCB. http://www.kpcb.com/blog/2015-internet-trends
34. Mary Meeker and Liang Wu. 2014. *2014 Internet Trends*. Technical Report. KPCB. https://www.kpcb.com/insights/2014-internet-trends
35. Preeti Mudliar, Jonathan Donner, and William Thies. 2012. Emergent Practices Around CGNet Swara, A Voice Forum for Citizen Journalism in Rural India. In *Proceedings of ICTD*.
36. Iftekhar Naim, Daniel Gildea, Walter S. Lasecki, and Jeffrey P. Bigham. 2013. Text Alignment for Real-Time Crowd Captioning. In *Proceesings of HLT-NAACL*.

37. Prayag Narula, David Rolnitzky, and Bjoern Hartmann. 2011. MobileWorks: A Mobile Crowdsourcing Platform for Workers at the Bottom of the Pyramid. In *In Proceedings of HCOMP*.

38. G. Parent and M. Eskenazi. 2010. Toward better crowdsourced transcription: Transcription of a year of the Let's Go Bus Information System data. In *Proceedings of SLT*.

39. Ales PrazÃąk, Zdenek Loose, Jan Trmal, Josef V. Psutka, and Josef Psutka. 2012. Novel Approach to Live Captioning Through Re-speaking: Tailoring Speech Recognition to Re-speaker's Needs.. In *Proceedings of Interspeech*.

40. Agha Ali Raza, Farhan Ul Haq, Zain Tariq, Mansoor Pervaiz, Samia Razaq, Umar Saif, and Roni Rosenfeld. 2013. Job Opportunities Through Entertainment: Virally Spread Speech-based Services for Low-literate Users. In *Proceedings of CHI*.

41. Venkatesh Sivaraman, Dongwook Yoon, and Piotr Mitros. 2016. Simplified Audio Production in Asynchronous Voice-Based Discussions. In *Proceedings of CHI*.

42. Matthias Sperber, Graham Neubig, Christian Fugen, Satoshi Nakamura, and Alex Waibel. 2013. Efficient Speech Transcription Through Respeaking. In *Proceesings of Interspeech*.

43. Aditya Vashistha, Edward Cutrell, Gaetano Borriello, and William Thies. 2015. Sangeet Swara: A Community-Moderated Voice Forum in Rural India. In *Proceedings of CHI*.

44. Dongwook Yoon, Nicholas Chen, FranÃğois GuimbretiÃÍre, and Abigail Sellen. 2014. RichReview: Blending Ink, Speech, and Gesture to Support Collaborative Document Review. In *Proceedings of UIST*.

Subcontracting Microwork

Meredith Ringel Morris[1], Jeffrey P. Bigham[2], Robin Brewer[3], Jonathan Bragg[4], Anand Kulkarni[5], Jessie Li[2], and Saiph Savage[6]
[1]Microsoft Research, Redmond, WA, USA
[2]Carnegie Mellon University, Pittsburgh, PA, USA
[3]Northwestern University, Evanston, IL, USA
[4]University of Washington, Seattle, WA, USA
[5]University of California, Berkeley, CA, USA
[6]West Virginia University, Morgantown, WV, USA
merrie@microsoft.com, {bigham, jessieli}@cs.cmu.edu, rnbrewer@u.northwestern.edu, jbragg@cs.washington.edu, anandk@berkeley.edu, savage@mail.wvu.edu

ABSTRACT
Mainstream crowdwork platforms treat microtasks as indivisible units; however, in this article, we propose that there is value in re-examining this assumption. We argue that crowdwork platforms can improve their value proposition for all stakeholders by supporting *subcontracting* within microtasks. After describing the value proposition of subcontracting, we then define three models for microtask subcontracting: *real-time assistance*, *task management*, and *task improvement*, and reflect on potential use cases and implementation considerations associated with each. Finally, we describe the outcome of two tasks on Mechanical Turk meant to simulate aspects of subcontracting. We reflect on the implications of these findings for the design of future crowd work platforms that effectively harness the potential of subcontracting workflows.

Author Keywords
Crowdsourcing; microwork; subcontracting; human computation; task selection; task design.

ACM Classification Keywords
H.5.3. Group and Organization Interfaces.

INTRODUCTION
Microwork, small tasks performed on crowd work platforms (e.g., Amazon's Mechanical Turk, Upwork, LeadGenius, SamaSource, and many others [37]), is an increasingly important form of digital labor, representing both a valued, flexible job opportunity for workers [39] and a viable means of accomplishing work at scale for businesses [17, 31], scientific enterprises [10, 11], and community or volunteer ventures [5]. Mainstream crowdwork platforms treat microtasks (also called human intelligence tasks or HITs) as indivisible units; however, we propose that there is value in re-examining this assumption. We argue that crowdwork platforms can improve their value proposition for all stakeholders by supporting *subcontracting* within microtasks, i.e. outsourcing one or more aspects of a microtask to additional workers.

After describing the value proposition of subcontracting, we then define three models for subcontracting microtasks: *real-time assistance*, *task management*, and *task improvement*, and reflect on potential use cases and implementation considerations associated with each. Finally, we describe the outcome of two tasks on Mechanical Turk meant to simulate aspects of subcontracting; these simple HITs demonstrate the potential of subcontracting for improving aspects of crowdwork such as making workers and/or requesters aware of accessibility bugs, and for better matching task components to workers' skills and interests. We reflect on the implications for the design of future crowd work platforms that effectively harness the potential of subcontracting workflows.

Value Proposition
We propose that enabling subcontracting of microwork, if properly implemented, can enhance crowdwork processes and outcomes. Subcontracting can provide value from the perspective of requesters, workers, and platform owners.

Value for Workers
From the perspective of a subcontracting-enabled crowd platform, there are two classes of workers, whom we will refer to as the *primary worker* (the original worker accepting a task, who may initiate subcontracting), and *secondary workers* (the workers who perform the subcontracted microwork).

Microtaskers performing primary worker roles in a subcontracting-enabled system would have added responsibilities that bring opportunities to begin to learn new

CHI 2017, May 06 - 11, 2017, Denver, CO, USA

ACM 978-1-4503-4655-9/17/05…$15.00
DOI: http://dx.doi.org/10.1145/3025453.3025687

skills, such as management and task design, providing scaffolding for career growth, a dynamic currently lacking from most mainstream crowd platforms [20]. The added responsibility associated with the role of primary workers should result in increased wages for these roles, in an economically fair system [1]. Subcontracting also fundamentally enables new work types within platforms, such as task labeling, headhunting, management, etc.; these roles might encourage more diverse audiences to engage with crowd work by offering tasks that better match their skills and/or interests.

Secondary (subcontracted) work can offer low-reputation workers (e.g., platform newcomers, workers lacking skills with tasks of certain categories, etc.) a path to building skills and reputation. Secondary work can also lower the barrier for novice or casual workers by allowing them to invest less time and effort in task selection, by instead following a trusted primary worker or by benefiting from task decomposition and metadata added by other secondary workers.

Value for Requesters

One potential benefit of a subcontracting-based system for task requesters is that it may allow them to reduce the time and effort necessary for optimizing the deconstruction of tasks into microtasks, or of adding metadata or instructions to tasks, as such tasks may be delegated to workers themselves through the subcontracting structure (see the "Models of Subcontracting" section for more in-depth explanations of these processes).

Additionally, for requesters the addition of a layer of indirection through subcontracting mitigates the risk and workload involved in working with a full crowd of potentially unreliable or untrusted workers, as some of this risk is now delegated to primary workers. This benefit is analogous to the benefit of using a contracting or temp agency in the traditional economy – the temp agency manager is analogous to the primary worker, while individual temps map to secondary workers.

Value for Platforms

Subcontracting can benefit platform operators by enabling a more efficient and productive work system. Via subcontracting's potential to enhance task design, better match workers with tasks, and reduce rates of partially-completed tasks, platforms can expect to see better throughput and higher-quality work outcomes. By empowering workers and offering them more flexibility and initiative within their work, platforms may also see enhanced employee productivity and reduced turnover.

MODELS OF SUBCONTRACTING

In this section, we unpack the concept of subcontracting as it might apply to microtasking platforms, identifying three primary models of subcontracting work in this context: *real-time assistance*, *task management*, and *task improvement*.

Note that it is not necessarily the case that subcontracting crowd work results in workers interacting with sub-components of an original microtask/HIT (e.g., working on a component that has been doled out by a primary worker in the task management model). For instance, in some cases secondary workers might simply support a complete, original HIT (e.g., in the real-time assistance model). Subcontracting could even enlarge the original HIT to be more than it first embodied (e.g., the addition of metadata in the task improvement model).

While not explicitly focused on the need for subcontracting, several prior systems and studies illustrate scenarios in which one or more of our three subcontracting models may be useful and/or have implemented a specific workflow that exemplifies these different types of subcontracting. We discuss this prior work in the context of each of the three subcontracting models.

Real-Time Assistance

Real-time assistance encompasses a model of subcontracting in which the primary worker engages one or more secondary workers to provide real-time advice, assistance, or support during a task. Such interactions might occur with the integration of widgets for real-time assistance, and might include easy integration of video-conferencing, screen sharing, VOIP calls, live-streaming, instant-messaging, or other types of real-time communications for task sharing.

For instance, Kobayashi et al. [21] and Brewer et al. [6] postulate IM or video chat interactions with experienced crowd workers during HIT execution may be necessary for supporting older adults (or other novice or less tech-savvy workers) in understanding complex task interfaces or workflows. Such chat support would constitute a type of real-time assistance subcontracting, since the support-giver is not the original worker who accepted the HIT, but is facilitating its completion. Similarly, real-time assistance could help facilitate task completion (or better task quality) by connecting workers with people with whom they can discuss and clarify interpretations of task instructions, or with people who may have domain expertise or other skills relevant to completion of a task.

Zyskowski et al. [39] noted that some crowd workers with disabilities have to leave tasks incomplete due to difficulties encountered mid-way through (e.g., a blind participant discovering that one sub-component of a task requires examining an uncaptioned image). Real-time assistance could allow a worker with disabilities to connect with someone who has the capabilities to assist with a specific component of a task, as an alternative to the status quo practice of task abandonment in such situations.

Prior work on seeking assistance online has shown how crowd workers form informal or formal communities to offer and receive help from others [15, 18, 27]. A community assistance model, such as the real-time assistance subcontracting we propose, could be a compelling avenue to explore with subcontracting, but asking for and receiving help remains a challenging task. Prior work shows how people do not know how to ask for help and may prefer automated recommendations, particularly if they develop trust with the system [2, 9, 33]. Further, trust plays a role in less automated forms of help, as prior work suggests microworkers may ask for and receive assistance but may be more trusting of responses they get from people they know [29]. This suggests that an important component of implementing real time assistance within a platform is to provide context about the helpers (e.g. their helper rating, their profession, skills, or other aspects of demographics or reputation, etc.); the capability to request assistance from a specific, known worker may also be valued.

Task Management

Task management subcontracting applies to situations in which a primary worker takes on a meta-work role for a complex task, delegating components to secondary workers and taking responsibility for integrating and/or approving the products of the secondary workers' labor. Headhunting work (i.e., identifying workers with specific talents or skills appropriate for aspects of a complex task) is another component of task management subcontracting.

Task management work may offer desired career growth opportunities for experienced workers [20]. Headhunting may be particularly valued by both requesters and workers, as finding tasks that are a good match for a worker's skills is an unresolved problem in mainstream crowd work platforms, currently addressed somewhat inefficiently through informal backchannels [15, 18].

Leadership via task management by the primary worker may be helpful for efficient task completion, but online leadership is challenging, particularly for leaders of multiple projects who can feel overburdened, resulting in failed or unfinished projects [25]. Using the theory of distributed leadership, tools have been designed for leadership redistribution [25], a concept that could be used within a task management subcontracting model. Pipeline is one such tool, that focuses on decentralization for sharing leadership responsibilities and automation through a trusted member system to improve task completion speed and efficiency [25]. Pipeline allowed workers to self-select microtasks to complete, yet for larger and varied projects, it may be beneficial for leaders to assign tasks similar to [35].

The Atelier system has explored a mentorship/internship crowdwork model where novice workers are assigned more experienced mentors to help them complete tasks [35]. These mentors not only provide feedback to the interns, but also help to structure the tasks into manageable milestones and answer questions, thus illustrating examples of both real-time assistance and task management subcontracting styles; the Atelier model also illustrates how different subcontracting styles may be used in an integrative fashion.

Task Improvement

Task improvement subcontracting entails allowing a primary worker to edit task structure, including clarifying instructions, fixing user interface components, changing the task workflow, and adding, removing, or merging sub-tasks. Clarifying instructions and fixing user interface components in particular would help to address the first two of seven main risk factors for workers identified by McInnis et al. [28]. Task improvement may also involve adding metadata to tasks (or creating meta-tasks that instruct secondary workers to add metadata), such as metadata that might help workers better identify the skills or abilities required to complete a task, its difficulty level, compliance with accessibility guidelines [39], etc. These improved tasks and sub-tasks can then be assigned to or discovered by secondary workers. Task improvement can make a task more accessible to a larger pool of workers, less risky, faster to complete, and/or more likely to generate quality output.

Current metadata about tasks is limited to subjective ratings [18] or implicit feedback [7, 16] related to pay and interactions with the requester. Information on other task aspects, such as usability or accessibility, may be available in an unstructured form through forum discussions or reviews [15, 18]. However, workers who are unable to find this information may choose to assume unnecessary risk by attempting the task or avoiding the task altogether, resulting in market inefficiency.

Some task improvements can be handed off entirely to workers, but others may require interaction with the requester. Kulkarni et al. [22] had workers decompose tasks into subtasks, enabling a kind of distributed workflow specification. One could also imagine assigning this managerial role to a smaller set of skilled workers, who could perhaps make use of tools originally designed for requesters [19, 32]. On the other hand, subcontracting tasks like clarifying instructions may require occasional feedback from the requester to ensure that the instructions align with the requester's desired work product and evaluation criteria.

Task improvement roles address the fact that many requesters, due to inexperience, time pressure, disinterest, or other reasons, do a poor job in decomposing and specifying their tasks [30]. Allowing workers to iteratively improve task instructions, decompositions, and workflows (rather than merely giving such requesters and tasks low ratings on external forums like Turkopticon [18]) may be a valued service to requesters. Experimental platforms like Stanford's Daemo [34] enable requesters to create "prototype tasks" in order to iterate on and improve task design – task improvement subcontracting takes task prototyping one step further, by placing the power to iterate and make changes in the hands of primary workers, rather than with requesters alone.

IMPLEMENTATION CONSIDERATIONS

Subcontracting of microwork fundamentally alters many of the assumptions currently underlying crowd work platforms, such as economic incentive models and the efficacy of some prevailing workflows. However, subcontracting also legitimizes and codifies some existing informal practices that currently take place off-platform [15]. While addressing the challenges of introducing formal subcontracting support may be complex, the benefits offered in terms of moving some unofficial activity into a legitimate and structured realm, as well as the potential benefits to workers, requesters, and platform operators mentioned in the Introduction, makes grappling with these challenges a worthwhile endeavor. Here, we identify five key issues crucial to creating a successful subcontracting structure, and reflect on design alternatives for each: *incentive models*, *reputation models*, *transparency*, *quality control,* and *ethical considerations*.

Incentive Models

Developing a fair and understandable compensation model for primary and secondary workers is integral to the success of any subcontracting scheme for crowdwork. Three possible design alternatives are job-based, flat-rate and altruistic.

Job-based compensation is the most flexible model, in which the economic arrangement for how the initial wage offered per HIT will be flexibly divided amongst primary and secondary workers and is based on the properties of the work. One possibility is that the primary worker will have the ability to negotiate the HIT wage with the requester, which may be relevant in cases such as task improvement subcontracting, wherein significant work beyond what the requester initially envisioned is required to improve the quality of a task. Given a set wage for the original HIT, another possibility is that platforms provide infrastructure for secondary workers to negotiate subcontracting wages with primary workers.

Flat-rate compensation avoids negotiation; instead, either the platform or the requester can specify fee splits for different types of subcontracting arrangements (e.g., real-time assistance = 50% of the initial HIT wage multiplied by the percent of the HIT duration for which the assistance lasts).

Altruistic compensation schemes may apply to particular subcontracting scenarios, in which workers may volunteer their services in a subcontracting capacity through intrinsic motivation [29]. Workers may complete microtasks for causes they care about (e.g., a worker interested in disability rights may voluntarily fix HITs to make them more accessible to screen reader users). Some secondary workers may want to enhance the experience of fellow workers whom they care for (exchanging social capital rather than cash). Research on unpaid volunteers contributing to open source projects show how people volunteered based on the concept of *generalized exchange* in which they helped other people because others helped them before, and they would want someone to do the same if they encountered a problem in the future [23]. Or, some secondary workers may be motivated to complete subcontracting tasks for non-monetary rewards, such as to build reputation within a system or learn new skills.

Reputation Models

Reputation models are an important component of existing crowd platforms. The introduction of formal subcontracting systems may necessitate changing current reputation models, as current models typically award reputation points to a worker based on the outcome of a given HIT; however, if multiple workers are able to contribute to a single HIT via subcontracting, the allocation of reputation becomes less straightforward.

One possibility is that primary workers may take on the reputation risk of work done by secondary workers to whom they subcontract work, which may help create strong incentives for careful choice of when and with whom to engage in subcontracting relationships and incentivize quality-checking of subcontracted work outcomes by primary workers.

If secondary workers directly earn reputation for their work, one consideration is whether they should be rated by the primary worker or by the original task requester (or by a third party, such as peer-comprised Crowd Guilds [38]). The transparency of the subcontracting relationship (see next section) may influence the choice in this regard.

Alternately, there could be new and different categories of reputation within crowd work platforms, such as separate reputation point systems for different task types, including meta-tasks associated with new subcontracting forms such as assisting other workers, metadata creation, task restructuring, etc.

The worker community strongly advocates for formal reputation models for requesters, and as many platforms do not yet support requester rating, this is often done unofficially on third-party sites like Turker Nation and Turkopticon [18]. In platforms supporting requester rating, workers taking on the primary worker role may need to earn reputation both as requesters (as rated by the secondary workers they recruit) as well as having worker reputation (as rated by the original HIT requester).

Transparency

Transparency concerns the extent to which parties need to be aware of subcontracting practices. Two key design choices are the degree of transparency of subcontracting to requesters and the degree of transparency to workers. To some extent, transparency choices are interrelated with choices regarding reputation and incentive models.

If work quality is unchanged from non-subcontracting systems (or improved, as we postulate it may be in many cases), then requesters may not need or desire transparency regarding any subcontracting arrangements. However, in some cases it may be important for requesters to know whether subcontracting has occurred, or even to be able to prevent subcontracting on certain tasks (perhaps by setting a special flag within the system). For example, some academic research HITs, such as psychology studies, may have the fundamental assumption that a single worker is completing a questionnaire (although even without formal subcontracting infrastructure in place, such assumptions may be invalid due to informal, offline worker practices of collaboration and information sharing [15]).

It may also be beneficial in some cases for requesters to understand if and why subcontracting has occurred, such as task improvement work – this may help the requester to create better tasks themselves in the future, or to be alerted to any unintended changes in the nature of the HIT that may result from well-intentioned task improvement subcontracting. In addition to passing back the final HIT result to the original requester, it may also be valuable to allow primary workers to pass back additional meta-information, including information about why subcontracting may have been needed, what improvements (if any) were made to the task design, perhaps even re-usable templates for replicating that design in the future. Requesters may also wish to give bonus payments to primary or secondary workers who enhance the outcomes of their tasks through high-quality assistance, task management, or task improvement labor. On the other hand, if task improvement work actually results in low quality secondary HITs – as has been observed in some task decompositions performed by workers [22] – transparency may protect requesters from negative reviews that could damage their reputation and affect their ability to recruit future workers.

It may also be desirable to include a system flag that specifically lets requesters indicate a wish to have certain types of subcontracting work (such as task improvement) performed for their HIT, such as in instances where requesters are piloting a new task or are unsure of how to best design or break down work or of how to advertise to the right worker set.

Determining whether secondary workers need to know whether they are taking on a HIT from an original requester versus a subcontracted HIT from a primary worker is another key design decision. In general, we recommend transparency to secondary workers, to help avoid worker exploitation. It may also be important to task outcome/quality for secondary workers to understand their role within a larger task structure.

Quality Control

Requesters submit work for crowd workers to complete because they assume they will receive quality responses in return. The quality of these responses is already a concern when task workflows are more direct and one person is working on one task [20]; paradigms such as replication + majority vote or embedding of gold-standard tasks are fairly standard for quality control in status quo microtasking environments [8, 24]. However, subcontracting can lead to multiple people collaborating on the same task, adding more uncertainty to the system and thereby making quality control become a more pressing, or at least more complex, issue. Prior work has examined this issue by comparing different types of quality control techniques [20] and how workers give feedback on task submissions [12].

Correctness is only one part of quality control. Requester feedback has also been shown to improve result quality [12, 26]. Further, prior work shows that when comparing self- and expert-generated feedback on submitted tasks, there was no difference in worker performance. However, workers who received expert feedback did revise their work more [12] and thought the feedback improved their work [26]. Regardless of the type of feedback and correctness checks, any system using a subcontracting model would need some form of quality control because multiple workers contributing to the same task may have different perceptions of completion quality.

Ethical Considerations

While subcontracting has the possibility of making crowd work more interesting and challenging for primary workers, it may carry the risk, depending upon implementation, of creating even more menial, micro-microtasks for secondary workers. While such tasks may be desired by some workers, extreme levels of task decomposition may dehumanize and deskill work to inappropriate levels. Our proposed models of subcontracting (real-time assistance, task management, and task improvement) aim to support improved workflows overall rather than promote extreme task decomposition for decomposition's sake; however, the possibility for subcontracting to move crowdwork further along the piecework continuum is an ethical consideration to be aware of, and to attempt to prevent through careful platform design.

The economic model of subcontracting also warrants ethical consideration; fair pay continues to be a problem for many crowd workers who struggle to earn an hourly wage that meets the legal standards set in the U.S. for traditional forms of labor [3, 13]. It may be important for platforms to include checks against efforts to game the system, such as a primary worker merely reposting a task, unaltered, to secondary workers at a very low wage, thereby taking a large cut of pay without having contributed value.

There is the risk that secondary workers could be an even further de-valued type of laborer than today's crowd workers, particularly if secondary work is not well-designed (e.g., extreme deskilling) or is not fairly paid. To avoid such ethical pitfalls, it may be important that platform designers implement features to safeguard against such possibilities rather leaving the mechanics of subcontracting completely in the hands of task requesters or primary workers, whose incentive models may not produce behavior that aligns with a platform operator's ethical standards (better legal protections for crowd workers would, of course, also be of benefit). For instance, platform features to enable reporting and adjudication of unfair pay practices may help address some of these concerns, as would legal rules to establish and enforce fair pay guidelines for microwork. Of course, striking an appropriate balance between the autonomy afforded requesters and workers versus the controls put in place by the platform may itself present an additional ethical issue.

Zyskowski et al [39] suggested that real-time assistance subcontracting may be vital to supporting the full participation of people with disabilities in crowd work. The United Nations' Convention on the Rights of Persons with Disabilities [36, Article 27] affirms that people with disabilities have the right to work and that labor markets and work environments should be "open, inclusive, and accessible to persons with disabilities." The potential for subcontracting workflows to expand participation in this emerging form of digital labor to diverse, under-represented, and under-served populations is also an important ethical consideration.

SUBCONTRACTING IN PRACTICE

To explore the idea of subcontracting, we released two tasks on Amazon Mechanical Turk. The first was designed to explore the feasibility of one type of task improvement subcontracting (HIT metadata creation), and the second aimed to provide insight into task management by exploring worker motivations and decision-making when provided the chance to outsource components of a task to other workers.

Task Improvement HIT

We designed and released a HIT on Mechanical Turk to explore one type of task improvement subcontracting, labeling other HITs with metadata about task properties. Our HIT took the form of a survey asking workers to accept a *different* HIT (not ours) to work on simultaneously in another browser tab, and then to answer several questions about that HIT in our survey. These questions included providing descriptive tags about the topic of the task, indicating what abilities or technical skills the task required, and identifying any accessibility issues that might make it difficult for people with disabilities to complete the task (a category inspired by Zyskowski et al. [39] and Brewer et al. [6]). Note that this HIT is designed to illustrate (within the constraints of a status quo platform) the potential benefit of task improvement workflows and the feasibility of having workers label tasks for this purpose (i.e., can workers identify inaccessible tasks); however, this HIT does not necessarily represent an ideal task improvement workflow, which might include additional subcontracted tasks to identify relevant metadata categories, evaluate the efficacy of the added metadata, etc. Figure 1a gives an overview of the HIT's workflow.

We recruited 100 workers to complete our HIT, which took less than 5 minutes on average paid \$0.95 USD (about \$11/hour). In practice, the time and cost could likely be optimized by asking fewer, more targeted questions; optimizing templates and workflows for task improvement work is an important area for further study.

All workers were able to finish our HIT and provide feedback about another microtask. Worker labels indicated that a substantial portion of tasks may have accessibility concerns for certain user groups, a finding consistent with prior, qualitative work [6, 39]. For instance, 76% of tasks labeled by workers dong our HIT were reported as containing visual material that would not be accessible to a blind worker, and 13% necessitated listening to audio materials that would not be accessible to a worker who was deaf or hard of hearing.

If a platform were designed to support collecting and using task labels such as those gathered in our example HIT, this could offer several benefits; for instance, workers could use these labels to more easily search and filter HITS to find work that is a good match for their skills, interests, and abilities, and task requesters could use these labels to gain insight into improvement areas for their tasks (in our example, the labels identify accessibility issues that requesters should be interested in rectifying in order to attract a larger worker base, improve task outcome quality, and/or comply with potential future legal regulations regarding the accessibility of digital labor).

Of course, platform support for task improvement microtasking could also allow better, more integrated interfaces for task labeling than the method employed for our exploratory task. Note also that we did not provide any training for workers in our labeling task (nor did we verify the accuracy of their labels); for straightforward labeling tasks such as HIT topic, such training is likely unnecessary, but more nuanced labels such as our example of identifying accessibility bugs might necessitate selecting workers with existing expertise (or willing to take training), and/or implementing other quality control measures.

Task Management HIT

Our second HIT was designed to give workers on Mechanical Turk a chance to engage in task management, since due to the platform's capabilities and the existing norms around task types and workflows on mTurk, most existing HITs are so decomposed as to not be suitable for task management subcontracting.

In our HIT, we presented a task with three components: (1) watching a one-minute video (excerpted from a TED talk) and captioning it by transcribing its audio track, (2) writing a 100-word response to the video, and (3) reading the 100-word response aloud and uploading that recording. We felt this task was especially well-suited for exploring subcontracting because each subtask would require several

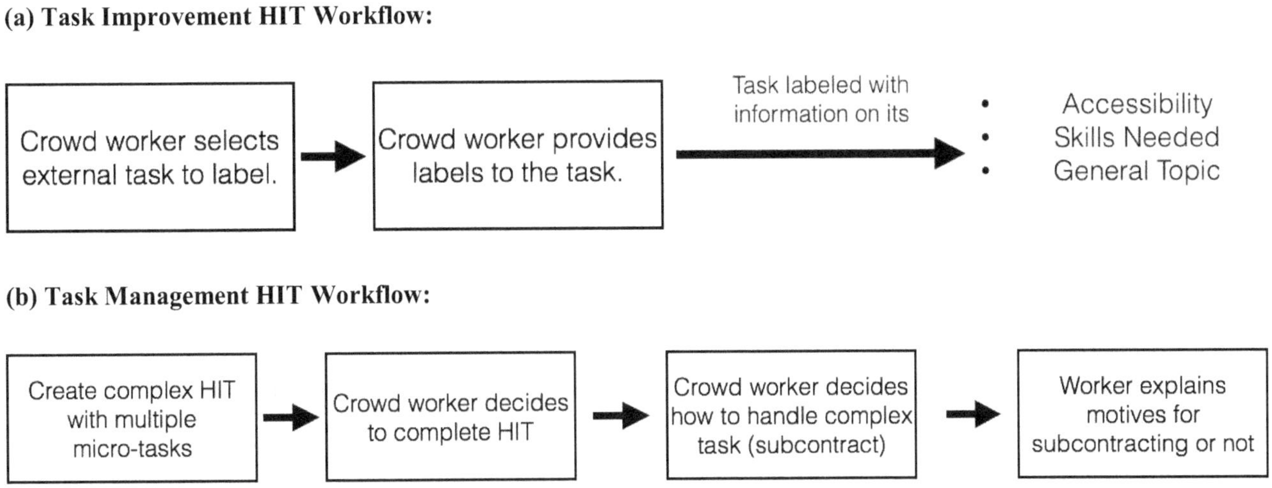

Figure 1. (a) Overview of our Task Improvement HIT workflow, aimed at assessing the feasibility of workers adding valuable content to pre-existing HITs. (b) Overview of our Task Management HIT workflow, aimed at exploring whether workers would choose to engage in subcontracting decomposed tasks, and assessing their motivation behind this choice. These sample HITs are meant to give initial insights into the feasibility and appeal of subcontracting workflows rather than to exemplify ideal subcontracting HIT design.

minutes to complete. Furthermore, each subtask required substantially different skills, which may appeal to different workers, and also may require special equipment (speakers to play back audio, a microphone to record it, etc.).

Workers were offered \$0.50 USD for the base task and were randomly assigned to one of three bonus conditions (\$0.50, \$1.00, or \$2.00 USD) for each of the three components they chose to complete; primary workers could therefore earn up to a total of \$2.00, \$3.50, or \$6.50 depending on their pay condition assignment. Because the Mechanical Turk platform does not offer subcontracting support, workers could not actually assign any of the three task components to a secondary worker; instead, we simulated subcontracting capabilities by telling workers that they could either earn money by doing each task themselves (the bonuses), or indicate to us which (if any) of the sub-tasks they'd prefer we reassign to other workers. Workers were required to complete at least one of the three sub-tasks themselves. We also asked workers to fill in a brief free-response box indicating why they did or did not choose to carry out each subtask. 200 workers completed this HIT. Figure 1b gives an overview of this task's workflow.

We hypothesized that offering different monetary incentives would affect workers' decisions about whether or not to subcontract. However, a chi-square test of independence did not find a statistically significant effect on bonus price for subcontracting any of the three subtasks at the 0.05 significance level (χ^2 (2, N = 200) = 1.77, p = .41) for the captioning subtask; χ^2 (2, N = 200) = 1.19, p = .55) for the writing subtask; and χ^2 (2, N = 200) = 0.15, p = .93) for the audio recording subtask). Thus, the remainder of our analysis considers the aggregate data from all three bonus-price conditions. The following qualitative analysis suggests that other factors dominated the variation in bonus amount that we offered.

72% of workers chose that they would want to subcontract at least one of the three sub-tasks. 11% of workers marked the captioning task for subcontracting, 23% wanted to subcontract the written response, and 65% indicated they would subcontract creating the audio recording. Below, we explore workers' motivations for these choices, by using Latent Dirichlet Allocation (LDA) topic models [4] to extract keywords from the open-ended responses and cluster them into themes, then manually reviewing and interpreting these clusters; through this analysis, we identified three primary themes (skills, money, and interests) that influenced workers' choices. The relative prevalence of these motivating factors is summarized in Figure 2.

Choosing to Subcontract

Skills: 22% of the choices to subcontract sub-tasks were because workers did not have the necessary skills or technology to execute that portion of the task. For instance, some workers did not have a microphone to record audio; others did, but were unfamiliar with how to use it ("*I don't know how to record and upload voice files*"). One expressed that a speech disability made him choose not to record audio, noting, "*I do not like my voice, and I have a slight speech impediment. I thought the recording would not turn out well, and it would ruin the impact of my written critique...*" Another worker expressed not having the right skill-set to effectively complete the critique-writing portion of the task: "*I didn't think I could come up with a 100-word critique of the video. She had presented scientific evidence [in the video], and there wasn't much I could say to either back it* *up or refute it, as I have limited knowledge of brain science...*"

Money: When choosing to subcontract part of a task, 38% of the time workers mentioned that they felt the time a subtask would take was not worth the money they would earn for that portion of the task. For example, one worker noted that a task he subcontracted "*would have taken more time than I thought it was worth.*" Another worker noted that he had a microphone, but that the time to configure it for the audio recording task would have changed the time/earnings tradeoff for him.

Interests: For 40% of subcontracting choices, workers indicated that personal interests and preferences impacted their choice to subcontract portions of our HIT. For example, one noted, "*I didn't feel like thinking and writing a critique*"; another said, "*I don't like writing non-fiction.*"

Choosing Not to Subcontract

Skills: In 9% of cases where workers chose to complete a task themselves, they referred to their skills as being a reason not to subcontract out a particular task, noting that they felt they were particularly strong at certain types of tasks and therefore it made sense to perform them themselves. For example, "*[I decided not to subcontract the recording part because] I have done HITs with my microphone before and already had the software installed in order to do it.*"

Money: In 64% of cases where workers did not choose to outsource a subtask, they noted that money was the main influence in deciding not to subcontract; in these cases, the workers chose to do the work themselves so that they would not have to share earnings with others. "*I wanted $2 [bonus],*" one noted. Another said, "*I'm currently trying to earn enough money to buy an expensive DSLR camera that I want really badly... and this task paid extra money [that I need].*"

Interests: Finally, in 27% of cases of not subcontracting, workers indicated that personal interests influenced their choice of completing sub-tasks on their own, specifically that they enjoyed doing certain types of work. For instance, one worker said, "*I like recording stuff,*" and another said, "*I love English, so I wanted to express [myself].*" Some workers in this category specifically noted how doing certain task types would benefit them by helping them acquire needed skills; for instance, one chose to do the video captioning himself because "*I love doing transcription tasks. It helps me in learning the art to type or write faster while listening.*" Another felt that watching and responding to the video would benefit them educationally because "*I also generally enjoy TED talks presentations... I believed I would further enjoy performing the task while I, hopefully, learned something new.*"

Reflection

These findings indicate that money was not the only factor in whether primary workers chose to complete subtasks versus mark them as being for subcontracting; rather, our findings show that workers chose to assign tasks to others based on their *interests* or disinterest in different components of a task (and desire to grow their interests and knowledge) and on their *skills* or lack thereof (in this case, having or lacking audio equipment, being strong in English or science, or even having disabilities). This supports the idea that subcontracting (if implemented in a manner mindful of the considerations we identified relating to incentives, reputation, transparency, quality, and ethics) can be an important route to realizing Kittur et al.'s [20] vision of a more engaging, meaningful, and challenging future of crowd work, as well as supporting broader participation in crowd work by people with varying technical, physical, or cognitive capabilities [6, 39].

Figure 2. Overview of the motives crowd workers reported for their decisions to subcontract or not subcontract portions of the larger HIT. Sacrificing income was one of the main motives for not subcontracting.

DISCUSSION

In this paper, we synthesized a set of work styles and user needs articulated in prior research in order to formalize the concept of subcontracting as it applies to microwork, identifying three distinct classes of subcontracting (real-time assistance, task improvement, and task management), and reflecting on the potential advantages and challenges associated with this style of work. We also presented two sample HITs that offered some initial insights into the feasibility and motivation issues likely to impact subcontracting's success. In the "Implementation Considerations" section, we discussed several topics (incentive models, reputation models, transparency, quality control, and ethical considerations) that must be addressed in the instantiation of subcontracting. Implementing and exploring the parameter space of these concepts is a key area for future research. Building platforms that support subcontracting workflows in an intentional manner will enable the crowdwork research community to evaluate the efficacy of these choices and further refine this concept. We particularly stress the importance of the ethical considerations component, as our intent in introducing and formalizing concepts related to subcontracting microwork is to facilitate more inclusive, satisfying, efficient, and high-quality work, rather than to facilitate extreme task decomposition strategies that may result in deskilling or untenable wages.

Our two example tasks illustrated that some limited styles of subcontracting may be feasible to retrofit onto status quo platforms (though we advocate for intentional feature support within platforms as a preferred implementation), and that many workers have interest in subcontracting work. However, these example HITs are merely first steps in evaluating this style of microwork. Larger, longer-term, and more varied evaluations are necessary to understand the nuance and efficacy of each of the three types of subcontracting. Measuring the impact of subcontracting workflows on variables such as worker satisfaction, requester satisfaction, work efficiency and quality, impact on worker reputation and pay, factors influencing worker participation in various subcontracting roles, etc. are important topics for future investigation. Employing multiple methods (e.g., surveys and interviews to gain insight on stakeholder perspectives; design, building, and testing of new platform features; and/or execution of HITs exemplifying different subcontracting algorithms) will be key to understanding this emerging topic.

It is also important to note that our proposed model of subcontracting may be incomplete. Indeed, the process of building and deploying platforms that explicitly support or even encourage subcontracting will likely shed light on unconsidered nuances of this work style that we were unable to anticipate based on our experiences with status quo platforms and tasks. For example, what should be done if a primary worker drops out of a task before it is complete – should they be replaced with an entirely new worker, or perhaps should one of the secondary workers be elevated to fill their place? What should the cascading impact be on any agreements (i.e., regarding pay allocation) that the now-absent primary made with any secondary workers? The relative pros and cons of such choices remain hypothetical in the absence of concrete implementations and scenarios.

CONCLUSION

In this paper, we proposed that *subcontracting*, i.e. outsourcing one or more aspects of microtasks from a primary worker to one or more secondary workers, is a work model that has potential to benefit crowd workers, task requesters, and platform operators. We defined three subcontracting styles: real-time assistance, task improvement, and task management, and drew on crowd work literature to identify sample scenarios suited to each approach. However, current microtasks and microwork platforms are not necessarily designed in ways that facilitate subcontracting; we identified important considerations, such as incentive models, reputation models, transparency, quality control, and ethics that should be taken into account when implementing subcontracting support. We also presented the results of two microtasks deployed on Mechanical Turk that explored aspects of subcontracting. These task outcomes lend support to our arguments regarding the feasibility and desirability of subcontracting microwork. This work contributes a practical foundation on which to design new platforms and workflows that can facilitate new forms of engagement for all members of the crowdwork ecosystem. The ideas and findings in this work also set the stage for a rich body of future research on subcontracting microwork, such as building subcontracting support into platforms, testing the outcomes of different incentive structures, reputation models, transparency policies, or quality control workflows, and measuring the impact of subcontracting-related practices on metrics such as output quality, platform efficiency, and worker and requester satisfaction.

REFERENCES

1. Bederson, B.B., Quinn A.J. Web workers unite! Addressing challenges of online laborers. *Proceedings of CHI 2011.*
2. Belkin, N.J. Helping People Find What They Don't Know. *Communications of the ACM*, 43(8), August 2000, p. 58 – 61.
3. Berg, J. Income Security in the On-Demand Economy: Findings and Policy Lessons from a Survey of Crowdworkers. *Comparative Labor Law & Policy Journal, Vol. 37, No. 3, March 2016.*
4. Blei, D., Ng., A., and Jordan, M. 2003. Latent Dirichlet Allocation. *The Journal of Machine Learning Research*, 3, 993-1022.
5. Brady, E., Morris, M.R., and Bigham, J.P. Gauging Receptiveness to Social Microvolunteering. *Proceedings of CHI 2015.*
6. Brewer, R., Morris, M.R., and Piper, A.M. "Why would anybody do this?": Older Adults' Understanding of and Experiences with Crowdwork. *Proceedings of CHI 2016.*
7. Callison-Burch, C. Crowd-Workers: Aggregating Information Across Turkers To Help Them Find Higher Paying Work. *HCOMP 2014 Extended Abstracts.*
8. Callison-Burch, C. Fast, cheap, and creative: evaluating translation quality using Amazon's Mechanical Turk. *Proceedings of EMNLP 2009.*
9. Chilana, P.K., Ko, A.J., and Wobbrock, J.O. LemonAid: Selection-Based Crowdsourced Contextual Help for Web Applications. *Proceedings of CHI 2012.*
10. Clery, D. Galaxy Zoo Volunteers Share Pain and Glory of Research. *Science*, July 2011.
11. Cooper, S., Khatib, F., Treuille, A., Barbero, J., Lee, J., Beenen, M., Leaver-Fay, A., Baker, D., Popovic, Z., and Foldit Players. Predicting Structures with a Multiplayer Online Game. *Nature* (2010).

12. Dow, S.P., Kulkarni, A., Klemmer, S.R., and Hartmann, B. Shepherding the Crowd Yields Better Work. *Proceedings of CSCW 2012*.
13. Dynamo Wiki. "Fair Payment". Retrieved December 12, 2016 at http://wiki.wearedynamo.org/index.php?title=Fair_payment
14. Flanagan, J. The critical incident technique. *Psychological Bulletin,* 51:327-358, 1954.
15. Gray, M.L., Suri, S., Ali, S.S., Kulkarni, D. The Crowd is a Collaborative Network. *Proceedings of CSCW 2016*.
16. Hanrahan, B.V., Willamowski, J.K., Swaminathan, S., and Martin, D.B. TurkBench: Rendering the Market for Turkers. *Proceedings of CHI 2015*.
17. Ipeirotis, P.G. Analyzing the Amazon Mechanical Turk Marketplace. *ACM Crossroads*, 17(2), Winter 2010, p. 16 – 21.
18. Irani, L. and Silberman, M.S. Turkopticon: Interrupting Worker Invisibility in Amazon Mechanical Turk. *Proceedings of CHI 2013*.
19. Kittur, A., Khamkar, S., André, P., and Kraut, R. CrowdWeaver: Visually Managing Complex Crowd Work. *Proceedings of CSCW 2012*.
20. Kittur, A., Nickerson, J.V., Bernstein, M., Gerber, E., Shaw, A., Zimmerman, J., Lease, M., and Horton, J. The Future of Crowd Work. *Proceedings of CSCW 2013*.
21. Kobayashi, M., Ishihara, T., and Itoko, T. Age-Based Task Specialization for Crowdsourced Proofreading. *Proceedings of HCII 2013*.
22. Kulkarni, A., Can, M., and Hartmann, B. Collaboratively Crowdsourcing Workflows with Turkomatic. *Proceedings of CSCW 2012*.
23. Lakhani, K.R. and von Hippel, E. How Open Source Software Works: "Free" User-to-User Assistance. *Research Policy*, 32, 2003, p. 923-943.
24. Lasecki, W.S., Murray, K.I., White, S., Miller, R.C., and Bigham, J.P. Real-Time Crowd Control of Existing Interfaces. *Proceedings of UIST 2011*.
25. Luther, K. Fiesler, C., and Bruckman, A. Redistributing Leadership in Online Creative Collaboration. *Proceedings of CSCW 2013*.
26. Luther, K., Tolentino, J., Wu, W., Pavel, A., Agrawala, M., Bailey, B., Hartmann, B., and Dow, S. Structuring, Aggregating, and Evaluating Crowdsourced Design Critique. *Proceedings of CSCW 2015*.
27. Martin, D., Hanrahan, B.V., O'Neill, J., and Gupta, N. Being a Turker. *Proceedings of CSCW 2014*.
28. McInnis, B., Cosley, D., Nam, C., and Leshed, G. Taking a HIT: Designing around Rejection, Mistrust, Risk, and Workers' Experiences in Amazon Mechanical Turk. *Proceedings of CHI 2016*.
29. Morris, M.R., Teevan, J., and Panovich, K. What Do People Ask Their Social Networks, and Why? A Survey Study of Status Message Q&A Behavior. *Proceedings of CHI 2010*.
30. Papoutsaki, A., Guo, H., Metaxa-Kakavouli, D., Gramazio, C., Rasley, J., Xie, W., Wang, G., and Huang, J. Crowdsourcing from Scratch: A Pragmatic Experiment in Data Collection by Novice Requesters. *Proceedings of HCOMP 2015*.
31. Plante, C. Doritos and the Decade-Long Scame for Free Super Bowl Commercials. *The Verge*, Feb 3., 2016.
32. Rzeszotarski, J. and Kittur, A. CrowdScape: Interactively Visualizing User Behavior and Output. *Proceedings of UIST 2012*.
33. Singh, V., Twidale, M. B., Rathi D. Open Source Technical Support: A Look at Peer Help-Giving. *Proceedings of HICSS 2006*.
34. Stanford Crowd Research Collective. Daemo: A Self-Governed Crowdsourcing Marketplace. *UIST 2015 Extended Abstracts*.
35. Suzuki, R., Salehi, N., Lam, M.S., Marroquin, J.C., and Bernstein, M.S. Atelier: Repurposing Expert Crowdsourcing Tasks as Micro-internships. *Proceedings of CHI 2016*.
36. United Nations. Convention on the Rights of Persons with Disabilities. December 2006.
37. Vakharia, D. and Lease, M. Beyond Mechanical Turk: An Analysis of Paid Crowd Work Platforms. *Proceedings of iConference 2015*.
38. Whiting, M. et al. Crowd Guilds: Worker-led Reputation and Feedback on Crowdsourcing Platforms. *Proceedings of CSCW 2017*.
39. Zyskowski, K., Morris, M.R., Bigham, J.P., Gray, M.L., and Kane, S. Accessible Crowdwork? Understanding the Value in and Challenge of Microtask Employment for People with Disabilities. *Proceedings of CSCW 2015*.

Scalable Annotation of Fine-Grained Categories Without Experts

Timnit Gebru[1], Jonathan Krause[1], Jia Deng[2], Li Fei-Fei[1]
Stanford University[1], University of Michigan[2]
{tgebru, jkrause, feifeili}@cs.stanford.edu, jiadeng@umich.edu

ABSTRACT
We present a crowdsourcing workflow to collect image annotations for visually similar synthetic categories without requiring experts. In animals, there is a direct link between taxonomy and visual similarity: e.g. a collie (type of dog) looks more similar to other collies (e.g. smooth collie) than a greyhound (another type of dog). However, in synthetic categories such as cars, objects with similar taxonomy can have very different appearance: e.g. a 2011 Ford F-150 Supercrew-HD looks the same as a 2011 Ford F-150 Supercrew-LL but very different from a 2011 Ford F-150 Supercrew-SVT. We introduce a graph based crowdsourcing algorithm to automatically group visually indistinguishable objects together. Using our workflow, we label 712,430 images by $\sim 1,000$ Amazon Mechanical Turk workers; resulting in the largest fine-grained visual dataset reported to date with 2,657 categories of cars annotated at $1/20^{th}$ the cost of hiring experts.

ACM Classification Keywords
Algorithm Information Interfaces and Presentation (e.g. HCI): Miscellaneous

Author Keywords
Fine-grained dataset; crowdsourcing; human computation

INTRODUCTION
To automatically detect cancer, an image recognition system has to be able to distinguish between cancerous and noncancerous cells which look almost identical. This system needs to perform what is called fine-grained image classification: distinguishing between highly similar objects [9, 13, 1, 2, 19]. Recently, deep learning based classification models have been shown to distinguish between similar categories of objects (e.g. birds) with greater than 92% accuracy if trained with enough labeled data [10]. Thus, the first step in creating any such image classification system is gathering sufficient annotated data where each image is labeled with the correct category.

Existing large scale visual datasets, such as ImageNet, were constructed using crowdsourcing to label the object instances in images [5]. These objects range from animals like cats or dogs to synthetic artifacts like airplanes and cars. A worker annotating images for this dataset only needs to be able to distinguish between very dissimilar categories, like cats and dogs or cars and airplanes. This allows any non-expert worker to label images in ImageNet with no prior training. On the other hand, a non-expert cannot accurately distinguish between fine-grained categories like cancerous and non-cancerous cells or 2011 GMC Sierra-1500 extended cab sle and 2011 GMC Sierra-1500 extended cab work truck (Figure 1). Thus, building fine-grained datasets is prohibitively expensive because hiring experts to annotate images costs a conservative average of 16 cents per annotation (assuming a wage of $10 per hour at an annotation speed of 1 image per minute). For instance, there are over 2,500 visually distinct types of cars manufactured since 1990 alone [7], and typical large scale image classification systems require over 1,000 annotated training instances per category [16]. To build a comprehensive fine-grained car classification system, we would need to collect a dataset with over 2 million annotations, a process which would cost over $300,000 using experts. Thus, inexpensively collecting large fine-grained datasets requires a methodology that is able to utilize non-expert workers.

Figure 1. Fine-grained car categories look very similar to a non-expert. Here, a 2011 GMC Sierra-1500 extended cab sle (left) and a 2011 GMC Sierra-1500 extended cab work truck (right) look almost identical. However, the second car has a small opening on the metal bumper whereas the first one does not. Our fine-grained object grouping methodology correctly assigns these cars to different categories.

In this paper, we present a crowdsourcing workflow to collect visual datasets of synthetic fine-grained categories without requiring experts. The first and most difficult step in our workflow consists of creating a class list, i.e. grouping visually indistinguishable objects into the same category. For a dataset of all cars manufactured since 1990, this step consists of examining 15,213 different types of cars and grouping those that have the same appearance together. This step is especially difficult for fine-grained datasets where different categories look very similar. In our case, care must be taken to ensure that cars with slight visual distinctions (such as those in Figure 1) are not grouped into the same class. We introduce a graph based crowdsourcing algorithm to cluster visually indistinguishable categories of cars. First, we construct a tree using existing car

CHI'17, May 6–11, 2017, Denver, CO, USA
Copyright © 2017 ACM. ISBN 978-1-4503-4655-9/17/0...$15.00
DOI: http://dx.doi.org/10.1145/3025453.3025930

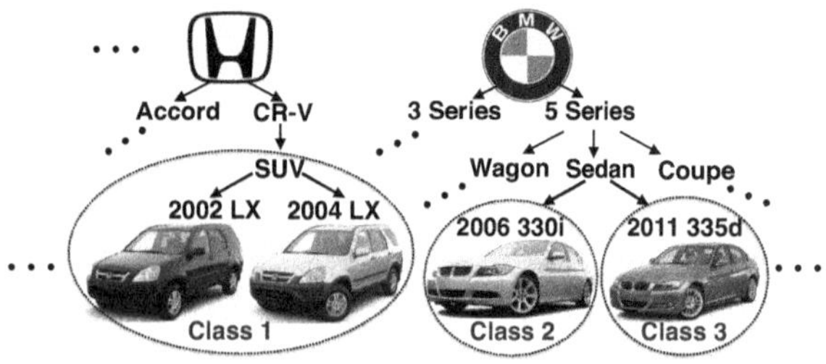

Figure 2. Cars follow a taxonomic hierarchy which can be interpreted as a tree. At the root node is the make of the car, e.g. Honda vs BMW, followed by the model, body type (e.g. sedan, wagon, coupe, SUV), year and trim (e.g. LX, 330i). All nodes under one make tree (e.g. BMW) are visually different from all nodes under another make tree (e.g. Honda). But nodes under the same tree can be visually the same or different. In this example, the two cars at the BMW leaf node have slight visual differences and are grouped into two different classes. Conversely, those under the Honda leaf node are grouped into the same class.

taxonomy where the leaves correspond to different categories. We then use binary tasks to iteratively merge pairs of leaves moving up the tree in a bottom-up-breadth-first search order. After iteratively merging car categories, we use connected component analysis [8] to arrive at our final groupings of cars.

Finally, we use our generated class list to collect images for all the car categories by querying craigslist.com and cars.com – websites where people sell their cars along with images and detailed description of the car's make and model. For each type of car, we use text processing methods to parse cragislist.com and cars.com posts and find vehicles that match our query. We then download all images for that post and use an Amazon Mechanical Turk (AMT) verification task to filter out images that do not have cars. Each image contains one car and is annotated by its corresponding category from our constructed class list. Our result is a fine-grained car dataset with $2,657$ categories and $712,430$ images with a precision of 96.6%. It was labeled by over a thousand AMT workers and cost only $\$6,000$ instead of an estimated $\sim \$119,000$ had we hired experts. We evaluate our visual taxonomy creation algorithm on a subset of the dataset consisting of all Honda Accord sedans manufactured since 1990, and show comparable accuracy with an expert.

RELATED WORK

A number of fine-grained datasets have been released for image classification. The most widely used one, CUB-200, consists of 200 species of birds with 30 images per category [20]. Recently, larger datasets of birds have been constructed by crowdsourcing the task to experts [14, 1]. To date, the largest fine-grained dataset of synthetic objects is CompCars consisting of $214,345$ images of $1,687$ car models [22]. However, its use in fine-grained image classification is limited because all cars for one model are grouped into the same category, in spite of their visual differences. For instance, a 2005 Toyota Corolla looks very different from a 2015 Toyota Corolla but is categorized into the same class in the CompCars dataset.

Our proposed workflow draws inspiration from prior work in decreasing image labeling cost through crowdsourcing while

Figure 3. Unlike existing fine-grained image annotation methods, we cannot rely on taxonomy to group cars into visual categories. For instance, a 2011 Ford F-150 Supercrew HD (left) looks the same as a 2001 Ford F-150 Supercrew LL (right) but very different from a 2011 Ford F-150 Supercrew SVT (middle).

maintaining high annotation precision. Previous works have explored methods to speed up binary annotation tasks by minimizing penalties for worker errors [11]. Others have exploited relationships between categories for efficient multi-label annotations [6]. Methods to acquire expert level labels through crowdsourcing have also been extensively studied by investigating the use of multiple noisy workers to annotate data [21, 15]. In all these works, crowdsourcing has proved to be a reliable technique to obtain labels with expert level accuracy [17].

Our work is also related to previous techniques in class list generation and categorization [4, 3]. These methods use crowdsourcing algorithms to generate taxonomies for textual data [4], and a collaboration between humans and machine learning algorithms to cluster text [3]. Here, we want to group visually indistinguishable objects together regardless of their textual taxonomy. Thus, we cannot rely on textual data to create our class list of cars. Our task also differs from taxonomy creation in that category names are known beforehand. Thus, crowd workers only have to answer questions regarding objects' visual similarity. They are not required to create category names for objects. The objects we consider might also have very small visual distinctions making the categorization prone to errors by non-experts. Thus, we introduce a new crowdsourcing algorithm to create a visual taxonomy of synthetic fine grained categories.

APPROACH

Constructing the class list

While current fine-grained datasets [20] rely on object taxonomy to create groupings of visually indistinguishable objects, we cannot use the same methodology to construct our class list of cars. For example, species of birds with the same name (like Bobolink) can be classified into one visual category whereas those with different names (like Bobolink and Cardinal) are visually different and belong in separate classes. However, different synthetic object categories are not necessarily correlated with their visual similarity. As seen in Figure 3, objects with different names can look the same (e.g. 2011 Ford F-150 Supercrew HD and 2001 Ford F-150 Supercrew LL) or different (2011 Ford F-150 Supercrew HD and 2001 Ford F-150 Supercrew SVT). We present a graph based crowdsourcing approach to creating this class list, distilling the crowdsourcing task to one simple binary question: "Are these two cars the same?".

Cars follow a taxonomic hierarchy visualized in Figure 2 where the root node of each tree in the forest is the make of the

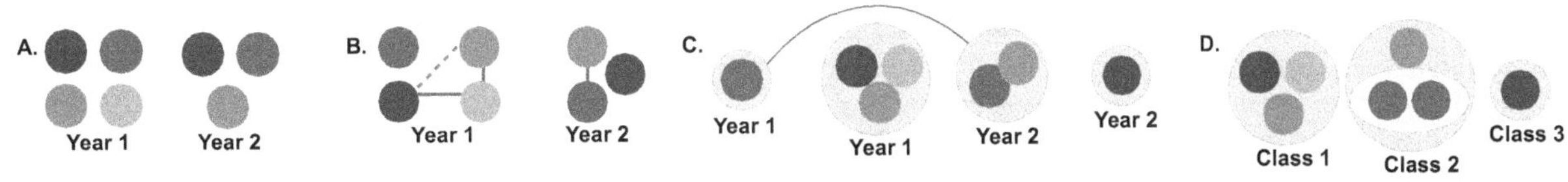

Figure 4. A simple example illustrating our procedure to cluster car categories. A. A graph with each circle representing a node. Different colors indicate distinct trims under the same make, model, body type and year of a car. We query whether all pairs of trims in Year 1 should be merged and do the same for Year 2. B. The resulting graph structure with an edge (in grey) connecting trims with the same appearance. A dashed line between red and green trims shows an edge that would have been present if the merging procedure for red, green and yellow trims in Year 1 were correct. After detecting that edges between red, green and yellow trims do not form a clique, we repeat the query for those nodes. C. The merging process for the same trims in different years. An edge is added between trims in Year 1 and Year 2 due to their indistinguishable visual appearance. D. The cars are grouped into 3 classes because there are 3 connected components in C.

Figure 5. Examples of images for 2008-2010 Chevrolet Malibu sedan ls,lt,base,fleet showing intra class variation in our dataset. In addition to variations in color, background, lighting and pose, doors and trunks can be open or closed and cars can be occluded.

car (e.g. Honda vs. BMW). We know all nodes in one tree to be visually different from all nodes in a different tree. Under the make node is the model (e.g. 3 Series, 5 Series etc. for BMW). Under the model is the body type (e.g. sedan, wagon etc.) and manufactured year and trim (e.g. 330i, 335d, etc.). As noted earlier, nodes under one body type can look the same or different. Each type of car can be visualized as a leaf node in this tree.

We group visually indistinguishable cars using a bottom-up clustering approach combined with a binary crowdsourcing task. Starting at the leaf nodes, we recursively query whether or not to combine pairs of child nodes, moving up the tree in a reverse breadth-first-search fashion. We represent each distinct car category as a node in a graph (V, E) with zero edges. In our implementation, we start with 15,213 types of cars listed in edmunds.com corresponding to 15,213 nodes in our graph. Each car category is accompanied by example images. To query whether two types of cars should be merged, we show example images and ask AMT workers if the two cars are the same. Each task has 6 such binary questions with 2 gold standards, inserted in random order for quality control. Every time a "yes" answer is returned from a task, we add an undirected edge between the two car nodes. Once all edges are queried, we use connected components [8] to form clusters of nodes resulting in our final set of categories.

Figure 4 further describes the process with an example. We start with the graph in Figure 4A. where each node is a car with a specific make, model, year and trim (leaf nodes in the car taxonomy tree). We query whether trim 1 and trim 2 of the same make, model and year should be merged. If yes, we add an undirected edge between them (Figure 4B). We repeat this process comparing all trims within the same make, model and year adding edges as necessary. For quality control, we make use of the fact that all edges need to form cliques. That is, if car 1 and car 2 are determined to look the same, and car 2 and car 3 are also grouped together, then cars 1 and 3 should also be merged. We repeat the querying process for nodes that do not have this correct edge structure.

Once we cluster all trims of cars in the same year, we arrive at the graph structure in Figure 4B. We repeat this process, comparing trims with the same name across different years and adding edges where necessary (Figure 4C). The output of this step is a graph where each node consists of merged car categories and each edge connects cars whose appearance has not changed throughout the compared years. We use connected components to get our final list of category groupings (Figure 4D), where the number of connected components corresponds to the number of classes.

Although we used our methodology to collect annotated images for a car dataset, it is generalizable to other synthetic fine-grained domains with certain characteristics. Our workflow is effective because an exhaustive list of car classes is available to start the clustering process and there are image repositories (craigslist.com, cars.com) that can be queried with object names. Thus, our methodology is useful in other domains where such class lists and repositories are also available. These domains include most objects sold online like clothes (shoes, shirts, etc.), or other retail items such as those sold on Amazon (phones, etc.).

Large Scale Fine-Grained Dataset

To automatically obtain car images with fine-grained labels, we leverage e-commerce websites like craigslist.com and cars.com. The images on these websites are uploaded by people hoping to sell their cars. Thus, they are likely to be labeled with the car make, model, body type, year and trim information allowing us to obtain labels for free. For each of the 15,213 types of cars in our dataset, we construct a query by concatenating the make, model, body type, year and trim of the car. We enter each query into cars.com and craigslist.com and use regular expressions to analyze all returned posts. Finally, we download images associated with posts whose titles contain all the words in our query. We cleanup our dataset by crowdsourcing binary tasks, filtering out images that do not contain cars and using our implementation of [15] for quality control. We gathered a total number of 712,430 annotated images for a total cost of only $5,000.

Figure 5 shows example images highlighting our dataset's intraclass variability. All images have a single car that occupies most of the pixel space. In addition to variations in pose, lighting and resolution, some cars in the same class are occluded and others are deformed (due to accidents). They can also have open or closed doors, backs of trucks that are covered or uncovered, and additional ornaments.

EXPERIMENTS

We now estimate the accuracy of our constructed class list as well as the precision of our dataset. Then, we use it to train a fine-grained car classifier, publishing results that can serve as baselines for future researchers using our dataset.

To measure the accuracy of our constructed class list, we hired an expert to manually group all 92 types of Honda Accord sedans in our dataset into visually indistinguishable sets of cars. Then, for each type of car in this set, we measured the intersection between vehicles placed in the same group as the car by our algorithm and by the expert. We divide the intersection by the union of other vehicles grouped with the car by both methods.

Specifically, for each car type c, let S_{exp} be the set of cars grouped into the same category as c by the expert, and S_{alg} be the set of cars grouped with c by our method. We calculate

$$(S_{exp} \cap S_{alg}) / (S_{exp} \cup S_{alg}) \quad (1)$$

to measure our level of agreement with the expert in grouping each car. Averaging this number over the 92 selected cars gives us an estimate of 81.09% agreement with the expert across all categories in question.

To estimate the precision of our dataset, we look at 100 random images for 170 classes of cars, investigating a total of 17,000 images. 96.6% of the investigated images were of cars belonging to the right category verifying that our dataset has a high precision. To put this number into context: CUB 2011 [20], a standard fine-grained dataset today, has an accuracy of 96% and ImageNet's fine-grained categories have a higher annotation error [18]. An in-depth analysis by [18] shows that a 5% annotation error minimally affects fine-grained classification accuracy when the number of categories approaches 1000.

Finally, we trained a fine-grained car classification model following the method of [12], and tested it on all 2,657 classes in our dataset. We obtained an accuracy of 67.60% verifying that we have constructed a challenging fine-grained dataset with categories that are difficult to visually distinguish. The same method achieves a similar classification accuracy of 61.3% on CUBS 2011 [20]. This low baseline shows that our dataset will be useful in training and benchmarking algorithms that seek to improve fine-grained classification accuracy. Table 1 summarizes our results.

Experiment	Result
Class list accuracy	81.09%
Dataset precision	96.60%
Fine-grained classification accuracy	67.60%

Table 1. Experimental results measuring the accuracy of our constructed class list, the precision of our dataset and fine-grained car classification accuracy of a model trained with, and tested on our dataset.

CONCLUSION

We have presented a workflow to construct a dataset of visually similar synthetic objects – in this case, cars – without using experts. We used our workflow to construct a large-scale fine-grained dataset consisting of 712,430 images of 2,657 car categories comprising all cars manufactured since 1990 and annotated at a fraction of the cost ($6,000) of hiring experts. Central to our approach is a graph based crowdsourcing algorithm to group different types of cars into visually distinct categories. This is an important and often difficult step because taxonomic divisions do not correspond to visual similarity in synthetic objects. What types of differences count must also be predefined by creators of the dataset, and communicated to crowd workers. Workers are asked to compare cars with no differences of interest, or differences that are very subtle. Thus, errors are mostly in recall rather than precision: if the worker indicates a difference, there usually is one. However, workers can miss subtle differences and indicate that 2 objects are visually the same. We suggest future work investigating the use of our workflow to gather a richer dataset. For instance, instead of only answering whether two types of cars are visually the same, workers can indicate differences by drawing boxes on car parts.

ACKNOWLEDGMENTS

We thank Ranjay Krishna whose continuous help and encouragement made this paper possible, and Olga Russakovsky and Danaë Metaxa-Kakavouli for their valuable feedback. This research is partially supported by an NSF grant (IIS-1115493), the Stanford DARE fellowship (to T.G.) and by NVIDIA (through donated GPUs).

REFERENCES

1. Thomas Berg, Jiongxin Liu, Seung Woo Lee, Michelle L Alexander, David W Jacobs, and Peter N Belhumeur. 2014. Birdsnap: Large-scale fine-grained visual categorization of birds. In *2014 IEEE Conference on Computer Vision and Pattern Recognition*. IEEE, 2019–2026.
2. Steve Branson, Grant Van Horn, Serge Belongie, and Pietro Perona. 2014. Bird species categorization using pose normalized deep convolutional nets. *arXiv preprint arXiv:1406.2952* (2014).
3. Joseph Chee Chang, Aniket Kittur, and Nathan Hahn. 2016. Alloy: Clustering with Crowds and Computation. In *Proceedings of the 2016 CHI Conference on Human Factors in Computing Systems*. ACM, 3180–3191.
4. Lydia B Chilton, Greg Little, Darren Edge, Daniel S Weld, and James A Landay. 2013. Cascade: Crowdsourcing taxonomy creation. In *Proceedings of the SIGCHI Conference on Human Factors in Computing Systems*. ACM, 1999–2008.
5. Jia Deng, Wei Dong, Richard Socher, Li-Jia Li, Kai Li, and Li Fei-Fei. 2009. Imagenet: A large-scale

hierarchical image database. In *Computer Vision and Pattern Recognition, 2009. CVPR 2009. IEEE Conference on*. IEEE, 248–255.

6. Jia Deng, Olga Russakovsky, Jonathan Krause, Michael S Bernstein, Alex Berg, and Li Fei-Fei. 2014. Scalable multi-label annotation. In *Proceedings of the SIGCHI Conference on Human Factors in Computing Systems*. ACM, 3099–3102.
7. Edmunds. 2016. edmunds.com. (2016). `http://www.edmunds.com/`.
8. John E Hopcroft and Robert E Tarjan. 1971. Efficient algorithms for graph manipulation. (1971).
9. Aditya Khosla, Nityananda Jayadevaprakash, Bangpeng Yao, and Li Fei-Fei. 2011. Novel dataset for fine-grained image categorization: Stanford dogs. In *Proc. CVPR Workshop on Fine-Grained Visual Categorization (FGVC)*, Vol. 2.
10. Jonathan Krause, Benjamin Sapp, Andrew Howard, Howard Zhou, Alexander Toshev, Tom Duerig, James Philbin, and Li Fei-Fei. 2015. The Unreasonable Effectiveness of Noisy Data for Fine-Grained Recognition. *arXiv preprint arXiv:1511.06789* (2015).
11. Ranjay Krishna, Kenji Hata, Stephanie Chen, Joshua Kravitz, David A Shamma, Li Fei-Fei, and Michael S Bernstein. 2016. Embracing error to enable rapid crowdsourcing. *arXiv preprint arXiv:1602.04506* (2016).
12. Alex Krizhevsky, Ilya Sutskever, and Geoffrey E Hinton. 2012. Imagenet classification with deep convolutional neural networks. In *Advances in neural information processing systems*. 1097–1105.
13. Jiongxin Liu, Angjoo Kanazawa, David Jacobs, and Peter Belhumeur. 2012. Dog breed classification using part localization. In *European Conference on Computer Vision*. Springer, 172–185.
14. Pietro Perona. 2010. Vision of a Visipedia. *Proc. IEEE* 98, 8 (2010), 1526–1534.
15. Victor S Sheng, Foster Provost, and Panagiotis G Ipeirotis. 2008. Get another label? improving data quality and data mining using multiple, noisy labelers. In *Proceedings of the 14th ACM SIGKDD international conference on Knowledge discovery and data mining*. ACM, 614–622.
16. Karen Simonyan and Andrew Zisserman. 2014. Very deep convolutional networks for large-scale image recognition. *arXiv preprint arXiv:1409.1556* (2014).
17. Rion Snow, Brendan O'Connor, Daniel Jurafsky, and Andrew Y Ng. 2008. Cheap and fast—but is it good?: evaluating non-expert annotations for natural language tasks. In *Proceedings of the conference on empirical methods in natural language processing*. Association for Computational Linguistics, 254–263.
18. Grant Van Horn, Steve Branson, Ryan Farrell, Scott Haber, Jessie Barry, Panos Ipeirotis, Pietro Perona, and Serge Belongie. 2015. Building a bird recognition app and large scale dataset with citizen scientists: The fine print in fine-grained dataset collection. In *Proceedings of the IEEE Conference on Computer Vision and Pattern Recognition*. 595–604.
19. Catherine Wah, Steve Branson, Peter Welinder, Pietro Perona, and Serge Belongie. 2011. The caltech-ucsd birds-200-2011 dataset. (2011).
20. P. Welinder, S. Branson, T. Mita, C. Wah, F. Schroff, S. Belongie, and P. Perona. 2010a. *Caltech-UCSD Birds 200*. Technical Report CNS-TR-2010-001. California Institute of Technology.
21. Peter Welinder, Steve Branson, Pietro Perona, and Serge J Belongie. 2010b. The multidimensional wisdom of crowds. In *Advances in neural information processing systems*. 2424–2432.
22. Linjie Yang, Ping Luo, Chen Change Loy, and Xiaoou Tang. 2015. A large-scale car dataset for fine-grained categorization and verification. In *Proceedings of the IEEE Conference on Computer Vision and Pattern Recognition*. 3973–3981.

The Effect of Performance Feedback on Social Media Sharing in Volunteer-Based Online Experiment Platforms

Bernd Huber
Harvard University
Cambridge, MA, USA
bhb@seas.harvard.edu

Katharina Reinecke
University of Washington
Seattle, WA, USA
reinecke@cs.washington.edu

Krzysztof Z. Gajos
Harvard University
Cambridge, MA, USA
kgajos@eecs.harvard.edu

ABSTRACT
As an alternative to online labor markets, several platforms recruit unpaid online volunteers to participate in behavioral experiments that provide personalized feedback. These platforms rely on word-of-mouth sharing by previous participants for recruitment of new participants. We analyzed the impact of performance feedback provided at the end of an experiment on 81,131 participants' sharing behavior. We show that higher performing participants share significantly more. We also show that self-verification has a moderating effect: people who expected to do poorly are not affected by a high score, but people who expected to do as well as others or better, are. In a second experiment, we evaluate three distinct social comparison designs for the presentation of the results. As expected, the design that most emphasized participants' relative success led to most sharing. Contrary to our expectations, people who expected to do poorly benefited from the most optimistic social comparison more than participants who expected to do better than others.

ACM Classification Keywords
H.5.m. Information Interfaces and Presentation (e.g. HCI): Miscellaneous

Author Keywords
Social comparison; Volunteer-based Online Experiments; Self-Evaluation

INTRODUCTION
Volunteer-based online behavioral research platforms, such as TestMyBrain.org [9], Project Implicit [1], or LabintheWild.org [13], offer people feedback on their traits and skills in return for participation in experiments. Unlike conventional laboratory studies or those conducted on Amazon Mechanical Turk, where participants are frequently motivated by monetary compensation, volunteer-based platforms rely on participants' interest in receiving personalized results at the end of each study. To provide participants with engaging feedback, the personalized results are often presented using social comparison (e.g., "You scored better than the average participant"). The original social comparison theory explains how people compare themselves to others in order to evaluate their own abilities and opinions, which assumes that people have an inherent drive to gain accurate self-evaluation [8]. The feedback in online experiments is thought to motivate participants to exert themselves; previous work has found that participants provide reliable data and that experiments conducted on volunteer-based experiment platforms can accurately replicate laboratory study results [13, 9]. In addition, prior work found that this social comparison feedback is one reason why people share their behavioral experiment results on social networking sites such as twitter [13]. It therefore plays a key role in the recruitment of participants.

CHI 2017, May 06 - 11, 2017, Denver, CO, USA.

ACM 978-1-4503-4655-9/17/05...$15.00 .
DOI: http://dx.doi.org/10.1145/3025453.3025553

Despite the vital role of social comparison feedback in volunteer-based online experiments for data quality, motivating participation, and spreading the word, little is known how to present this feedback most effectively. Previous work demonstrates that social comparison interventions can increase participant contribution in online communities, in which contribution is a direct result of participant's effort [5, 12]. The effort of newcomers to online communities seems to be particularly receptive to social learning [4]. The goal of online experiment designers is not solely to increase participant's effort, but rather to increase engagement with the experiment results. Hence, social comparison may affect the way participants interpret them, ultimately influencing their sharing behavior. To find out why people share their results, we conducted two studies in the context of the Social Intelligence Test (rebranded Reading the Mind in the Eyes Test [3]). We implemented the test on LabintheWild.org, a popular volunteer-based online experiment platform. Participants taking this test have the option to share the experiment by clicking on social media buttons on the feedback page at the end of the test, which is the measure we used to estimate share rates (see Figure 1b).

In our first study, we analyzed sharing behavior when participant scores were communicated with the global average score as a reference point (see Figure 1b). We found that both participants' scores and the interaction between participants' self-conceptions and their actual scores affected their probability of sharing. Our results show that most people who take the test are attempting to make themselves feel good about themselves by receiving a positive evaluation of their social intelligence (a motivation that researchers have called "self-enhancement" [18]). The motivation for self-verification [17], i.e., people's desire to confirm their own judgements of their social intelligence, plays a moderating role.

In our second study, we tested three different designs to communicate the results to participants. We used social downward and upward comparison to emphasize that one's performance is better or worse than others, respectively. Both kinds of comparisons can motivate people, but not in all circumstances: For example, downward comparison can make people feel better because it might elevate the self-regard [10]. On the other hand, upward comparison may lead to the hope of self-improvement in some cases, but may be discouraging in others [16, 6]. Consistent with the results from Study 1, we found that more positive score communication led to more shares. These findings further suggest that participants in the *Social Intelligence Test* may be primarily driven by self-enhancement. Surprisingly, in this study people who expected to do poorly benefited from the most optimistic social comparison more than participants who expected to do better than others.

STUDY 1: WHAT MOTIVATES PARTICIPANTS?

To identify which of the three self-evaluation motives plays the greatest role, we studied how likely people were to share their results given a particular score, and how this is affected by their self-conceptions. The core assumption behind social comparison theory is that people have an inherent drive to gain an accurate self-evaluation [8]. The original theory explains how people compare themselves to others in order to evaluate their own abilities and opinions [8]. Subsequent research identified three distinct possible motivations for engaging in self-evaluation activities, such as completing skill or trait tests: (1) The *self-enhancement* motive to improve the positivity of one's self-concept [18], (2) the *self-assessment* motive to have an accurate and objective evaluation of the self [14], and (3) the *self-verification* motive to verify one's pre-existing self-conceptions [17]. These three motivations result in three distinct predictions about participants' likelihood of sharing their results depending on the feedback that they receive at the end of a study:

Self-enhancement predicts that the higher the score a participant receives, the more likely they will be to share.

Self-assessment predicts that the score will have no impact on the likelihood of sharing.

Self-verification predicts an interaction between the pre-existing self-conceptions with respect to the social intelligence, and the actual score: People whose score confirms pre-existing self-conceptions will be more likely to share than those who receive a score that contradicts their self-conceptions.

Participants

Our participants in this study were 75,120 online volunteers (aged 11–70, 42.7% male, 48.7% female, 2.3% other, the rest declining to answer). No financial compensation was given.

Task

Participants took the Reading the Mind in the Eyes test [3] (advertised as *Social Intelligence Test*) on LabintheWild.org [13], a volunteer-based online experiment platform. The test was originally developed in the context of autism research, but it has also been used to measure theory of mind (the ability to attribute cognitive and emotional states to others) in general

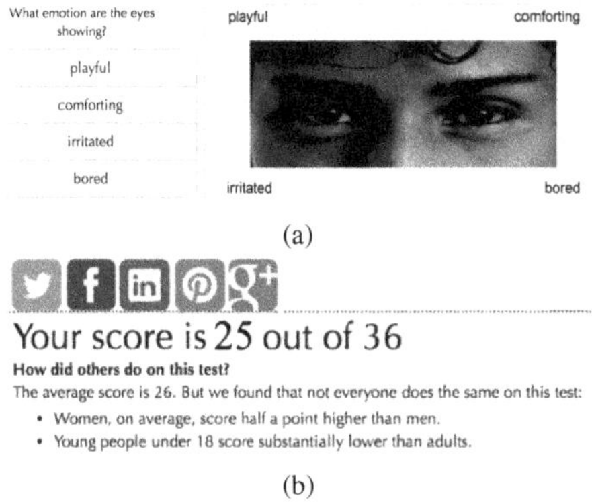

Figure 1: (a) During the test, participants choose emotions the person in the photograph is expressing. (b) At the end of the test, participants are presented with their own score, and information other participants' performed.

population and it has been demonstrated to be a strong predictor of success on team-based problem-solving tasks [19, 7]. This is why we decided that renaming it as a Social Intelligence Test was justified and better communicated its relevance to the general population. During the test, participants were presented with 36 images depicting the eyes of different people and were asked to tell what emotion the person in the image was expressing (see Figure 1a). The possible scores ranged between 0 and 36.

Procedure

Participants arrived at the experiment site organically. Logs indicate that approximately 30% arrived at the test from social media sites or referrals. The landing page included test title, a tag line ("Test how well you can read emotions of others just by looking at their eyes") and a brief explanation of the test. Participants who clicked through were first presented with an informed consent statement, followed by a brief demographics questionnaire. The demographics questionnaire also included a question on participants' pre-existing self-conceptions with respect to social intelligence, phrased as "Compared to your family and friends, how good are you at reading people's emotions?". Participants were asked to answer this question on a 5-point Likert scale (1 = much worse, 5 = much better). All demographics questions were optional. Completing the actual test took 10 minutes on average. Before being presented with their results, participants were asked if they cheated in any way, experienced technical difficulties or had any other comments. The results page then showed the participant's score, the average score over all participants as a reference point, and background information on how to interpret the score (see Figure 1b). The results page also included links for sharing the test on social networking sites.

Design and Analysis

We conducted one analysis with 75,120 participants to analyze the effect of the score on the probability that a participant would share the test on a social networking site. We conducted a follow-up analysis with a subset of 7,068 additional participants to look for an interaction effect between pre-existing self-conceptions and the score. The self-conception question was added several months after the experiment was launched

(a)

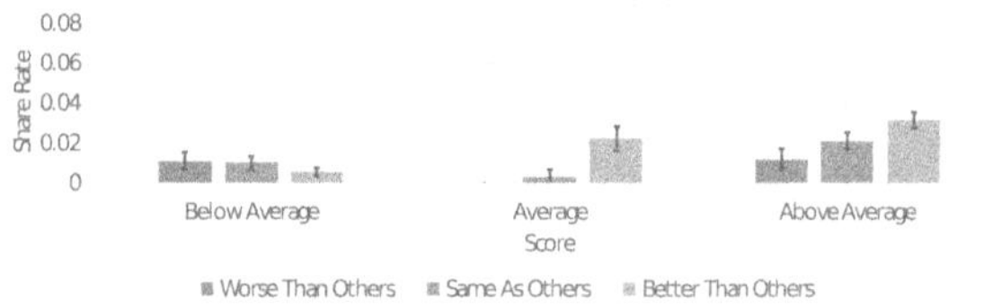

(b)

Figure 2: Participants' scores on the *Social Intelligence Test* vs. share rates on social media. Error bars show standard errors. (a) There is a significant main effect of score on the probability that participants share. (b) There is a significant interaction between score and self-conception. Scores were binned for better visualization.

and answering that question was optional, which resulted in fewer participants in the second analysis of this study.

The share rate was calculated using the mean of the binomial variable share/not share across all participants per condition. Score was modeled as a continuous variable and pre-existing self-conception was treated as an ordinal variable with three levels (worse than others, same as others, better than others). To analyze the data, we used logistic regression (generalized linear model with binomial distribution). For better interpretation, we also include results of pairwise correlation analyses.

Prior to the analysis, we excluded participants who reported having taken the test before, having cheated, or having experienced technical difficulties. We also removed extreme outliers with respect to the score, that is, participants whose score was more than two standard deviations from the mean (i.e., participants with scores of 15 or lower). Self-conception responses were bucketed in *worse*, *equal* and *better* than others.

Results

We observed a significant main effect of score on the likelihood of participants sharing the test with their peers ($\chi^2_{1,N=75120} = 426.56, p < .0001$), with participants receiving a higher score being more likely to share (see Figure 2a and Table 1 for complete results).

We also observed a significant interaction between score and self-conception ($\chi^2_{2,N=7068} = 7.81, p < .05$). People who thought they were worse than others at reading emotions were not any more likely to share if they received a high score ($\chi^2_{2,N=1135} = 3.38, p = .18$; $r(19) = -.12, p = .62$), but people who thought they were better than others were significantly more likely to share the higher the score they received ($\chi^2_{2,N=3620} = 40.21, p < .0001$; $r(19) = .91, p < .0001$). These results indicate that self-enhancement plays a major role in participants' motivation, and that this effect is strongest for participants with high self-conception.

Predictor	β	SE β	Walds χ^2	df	p	e^β
Main Effect						
Intercept	-8.47	0.24	1815.08	1	<.0001	NA
Score	0.16	0.008	426.56	1	<.0001	1.17
Interaction Effect						
Intercept	6.68	0.74	90.14	1	<.0001	NA
Score*Self-Conception[worse]	0.08	0.05	3.13	2	.077	1.08
Score*Self-Conception[equal]	0.009	0.04	0.01	2	.90	1.009

Table 1: Logistic regression table for Study 1: The model predicts the likelihood for a participant sharing the experiment. e^β is the odds ratio, i.e., the odds of the variable having an effect.

STUDY 2: EFFECT OF RESULT PRESENTATION

Results of the first study indicated that people taking the Social Intelligence Test were primarily motivated by the desire to improve the positivity of their self-concept (the self-enhancement motivation) with self-verification playing a smaller role. Given that volunteer-based online experiments rely on participants' sharing behavior (and thus, recruiting others), the goal of our second study was to find out how those with lower scores could be encouraged to share if their scores were presented differently. The three designs were:

Upward Comparison "Your score is lower than XX% of all participants."

Downward Comparison "Your score is higher than YY% of all participants."

Downward/Equal Comparison "Your score is equal or higher than ZZ% of all participants."

The difference between how Downward and Downward/Equal comparisons are perceived may be large, as one more point may make up to 10% of participants. For example, the score of 25 is *higher than 35% of all participants*, but *equal or higher than 45% of all participants.*

Given that our participants are primarily motivated by self-enhancement, we hypothesized that presenting the results in the most positive light (the Downward/Equal Comparison) would result in more sharing than either Upward Comparison (negative framing of feedback) or Downward Comparison (lower apparent magnitude of the participant's achievement).

We additionally hypothesized an interaction effect between self-conception and comparison presentation: while participants with a more positive self-conception would prefer Downward/Equal Comparison, participants with more negative self-conceptions would prefer Upward Comparison.

Participants

Participants were 6,011 online volunteers (aged 11–70, 45.7% male, 45.3% female, 1.6% other, the rest declining to answer). No financial compensation was given.

Experiment Design and Procedure

Task and procedure were the same as in Study 1 with the exception that for this study, we randomly assigned participants to one of the three result presentation conditions. Hence, we used a between-subjects design with one factor: presentation of the results.

Analysis

As in Study 1, we used logistic regression to analyze the data with presentation of the results and self-conception as the two

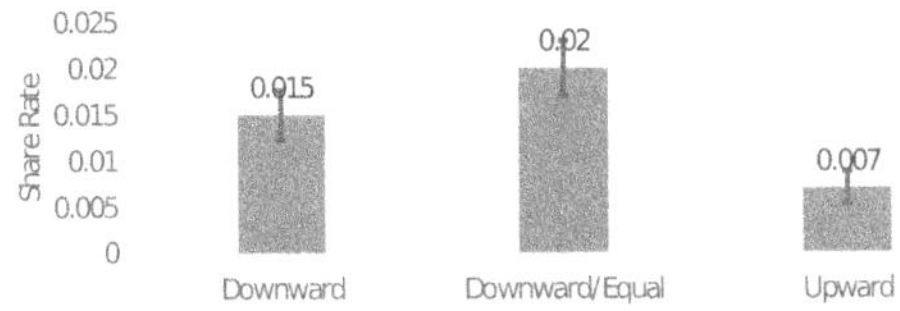

(a)

(b)

Figure 3: (a) Share rates for Downward, Downward/Equal and Upward comparison of 6,011 participants. Share rate is the fraction of participants that shared their results with others. (b) Share rates for Downward, Downward/Equal, and Upward, for different self-conceptions.

independent variables. The share rate was calculated the same way as in Study 1. In this study, we additionally controlled for score by including it as a covariate. We used the same exclusion criteria as in Study 1.

Results

We observed a significant main effect of the way the score was communicated on the likelihood of participants sharing the test with their peers ($\chi^2_{2,N=6011} = 14.00, p < .001$). Post hoc pairwise comparisons with Bonferroni correction showed that participants receiving Upward comparison (M=0.007) were significantly less likely to share than participants receiving Downward Comparison (M=0.015, $\chi^2_{1,N=4324} = 6.60, p < .05$) or participants receiving Downward/Equal Comparison (M=0.02, $\chi^2_{1,N=4397} = 14.22, p < .001$). There was no significant difference between participants receiving Downward/Equal or Downward Comparison ($\chi^2_{1,N=4407} = 1.44, p = .45$).

We also observed a significant interaction effect between self-conception and the way the score was communicated ($\chi^2_{4,N=6011} = 9.63, p < .05$). This effect was different from what we expected: People who expected to do poorly benefited more from the most optimistic presentation of the results than people who expected to do well.

DISCUSSION AND FUTURE WORK

In this work, we asked the question how to get people to share more often their results on online behavioral experiment platforms. To answer this question, we investigated whether people on volunteer-based online experiment platforms are driven by self-evaluation, self-enhancement or self-assessment. To do this, we analyzed participants' sharing behavior through the lens of social comparison theory in the context of the Social Intelligence Test. In Study 1, we observed a main effect of a participant's score on the probability that the participant would share the test on a social networking site. We also found an interaction effect between score and self-conception. These findings suggest that people taking the Social Intelligence Test are mostly driven by self-enhancement with some self-verification motives.

Predictor	β	SE β	Walds χ^2	df	p	e^β
Intercept	-9.71	1.41	58.69	1	<.0001	NA
Score	0.17	0.05	13.93	1	.0002	1.18
Presentation[Down]	-0.25	0.73	0	1	1	0.78
Presentation[Down/Equal]	1.60	0.59	13.94	1	.0002	4.95
Self-Conception[Low-Medium]	0.29	0.60	0.64	1	.42	1.34
Self-Conception[High-Medium]	0.77	0.27	9.97	1	.0016	2.16
Presentation[Down]*Self-Conc.[Low-Medium]	0.57	.79	0	1	1	1.77
Presentation[Down]*Self-Conc.[High-Medium]	-.13	.35	0.10	1	0.76	0.88
Presentation[Equal/Down]*Self-Conc.[Low-Medium]	-1.60	.67	9.07	1	.0026	0.20
Presentation[Equal/Down]*Self-Conc.[High-Medium]	0.35	.37	0.79	1	0.37	1.42

Table 2: Logistic regression table for study 2: The model predicts the likelihood for a participant sharing the experiment.

Given that volunteer-based online experiments rely on participants' sharing behavior (and thus, recruiting others), we conducted Study 2, in which we manipulated the presentation of participants' individual results. We found that the most positive social comparison condition resulted in the highest share rates, but this time we did not observe the expected moderating effect of pre-existing self-conception: Surprisingly, people with lower self-conception were more (rather than less) likely to share in the most positive social comparison condition. In contrast, the *self-verification* motive — partially supported by the results of the first study — would have predicted that lower self-conception might have led to higher sharing rates in the case of more negative score presentation [17]. Finding out why the self-conception had an opposite effect in our two studies will be an interesting further research direction.

Overall, these results show that high-performers are more likely to share their results, which could bias the participant pool if, for example, an online social network mainly consisted of other high-performers (there is ample evidence of homophily in social networks along many dimensions, including cognitive abilities [11]). Our results imply that we could manipulate the presentation of the results not just to increase the overall sharing rate, but also to reduce the difference in sharing rates between high and low performers. By personalizing participant feedback for self-conception and participant performance using social comparison, designers can significantly improve share rates and therefore might increase the overall impact and quality of their online experiment. For example, the feedback for participants with a low self-conception could emphasize the positivity of the results.

A limitation of our study is that we did not measure whether participants believed that their ability to read the emotions of others was a fixed trait or a skill that could be improved. Another limitation of our approach is that we did not measure the actual reasons for sharing. Measuring and understanding the role of the participant's need for self-affirmation, i.e. the need for projecting a certain image to others, might be a promising direction, as self-affirmation has been shown to be an important motive for sharing information with others [2]. These directions might affect the impact of social comparison [15] and should be considered in future work.

Acknowledgements. The authors would like to thank Ofra Amir for helpful comments and suggestions.

Online Appendix. The data used in this work can be found at `http://iis.seas.harvard.edu/resources/`.

REFERENCES

1. 2016. Implicit Association Test. https://implicit.harvard.edu/implicit/. (2016). Accessed: 2016-12-22.
2. Aliosha Alexandrov, Bryan Lilly, and Emin Babakus. 2013. The effects of social-and self-motives on the intentions to share positive and negative word of mouth. *Journal of the Academy of Marketing Science* 41, 5 (2013), 531–546.
3. Simon Baron-Cohen, Sally Wheelwright, Jacqueline Hill, Yogini Raste, and Ian Plumb. 2001. The Reading the Mind in the Eyes test revised version: A study with normal adults, and adults with Asperger syndrome or high-functioning autism. *Journal of child psychology and psychiatry* 42, 2 (2001), 241–251.
4. Moira Burke, Cameron Marlow, and Thomas Lento. 2009. Feed me: motivating newcomer contribution in social network sites. In *Proceedings of the SIGCHI conference on human factors in computing systems*. ACM, 945–954.
5. Yan Chen, F Maxwell Harper, Joseph Konstan, and Sherry Xin Li. 2010. Social comparisons and contributions to online communities: A field experiment on movielens. *The American economic review* 100, 4 (2010), 1358–1398.
6. Rebecca L Collins. 1996. For better or worse: The impact of upward social comparison on self-evaluations. *Psychological bulletin* 119, 1 (1996), 51.
7. David Engel, Anita Williams Woolley, Lisa X. Jing, Christopher F. Chabris, and Thomas W. Malone. 2014. Reading the mind in the eyes or reading between the lines? Theory of mind. 12 (2014). DOI: http://dx.doi.org/10.1371/journal.pone.0115212
8. Leon Festinger. 1954. A theory of social comparison processes. *Human relations* 7, 2 (1954), 117–140.
9. Laura Germine, Ken Nakayama, Bradley C Duchaine, Christopher F Chabris, Garga Chatterjee, and Jeremy B Wilmer. 2012. Is the Web as good as the lab? Comparable performance from Web and lab in cognitive/perceptual experiments. *Psychonomic bulletin & review* 19, 5 (2012), 847–857.
10. Frederick X Gibbons. 1986. Social comparison and depression: Company's effect on misery. *Journal of Personality and Social Psychology* 51, 1 (1986), 140.
11. Miller McPherson, Lynn Smith-Lovin, and James M Cook. 2001. Birds of a feather: Homophily in social networks. *Annual review of sociology* (2001), 415–444.
12. Petromil Petkov, Felix Köbler, Marcus Foth, and Helmut Krcmar. 2011. Motivating domestic energy conservation through comparative, community-based feedback in mobile and social media. In *Proceedings of the 5th International Conference on Communities and Technologies*. ACM, 21–30.
13. Katharina Reinecke and Krzysztof Z Gajos. 2015. LabintheWild: Conducting large-scale online experiments with uncompensated samples. In *Proceedings of the 18th ACM Conference on Computer Supported Cooperative Work & Social Computing*. ACM, 1364–1378.
14. Constantine Sedikides. 1993. Assessment, enhancement, and verification determinants of the self-evaluation process. *Journal of personality and social psychology* 65, 2 (1993), 317.
15. Diederik A Stapel and Willem Koomen. 2000. Distinctiveness of others, mutability of selves: Their impact on self-evaluations. *Journal of personality and social psychology* 79, 6 (2000), 1068.
16. Jerry Suls, Rene Martin, and Ladd Wheeler. 2002. Social comparison: Why, with whom, and with what effect? *Current directions in psychological science* 11, 5 (2002), 159–163.
17. William B Swarm Jr. 1983. Self-verification: Bringing social reality into harmony with the self. *Social psychological perspectives on the self* 2 (1983), 33–66.
18. Joanne V Wood. 1989. Theory and research concerning social comparisons of personal attributes. *Psychological bulletin* 106, 2 (1989), 231.
19. Anita Williams Woolley, Christopher F Chabris, Alex Pentland, Nada Hashmi, and Thomas W Malone. 2010. Evidence for a collective intelligence factor in the performance of human groups. *science* 330, 6004 (2010), 686–688.

Toward Realistic Hands Gesture Interface: Keeping it Simple for Developers and Machines

Eyal Krupka[1] Kfir Karmon[1] Noam Bloom[1]
Daniel Freedman[1] Ilya Gurvich[1] Aviv Hurvitz[1]
Ido Leichter[1] Yoni Smolin[1] Yuval Tzairi[1]
Alon Vinnikov[1] Aharon Bar Hillel[2]
[1] Microsoft Research
{eyalk, kfirk, t-noblo, danifree, ilyagu, avivh, idol, yonis, yutzairi, alvinn}@microsoft.com
[2]Ben-Gurion University, Israel
barhille@bgu.ac.il

ABSTRACT
Development of a rich hand-gesture-based interface is currently a tedious process, requiring expertise in computer vision and/or machine learning. We address this problem by introducing a simple language for pose and gesture description, a set of development tools for using it, and an algorithmic pipeline that recognizes it with high accuracy. The language is based on a small set of basic propositions, obtained by applying four predicate types to the fingers and to palm center: direction, relative location, finger touching and finger folding state. This enables easy development of a gesture-based interface, using coding constructs, gesture definition files or an editing GUI. The language is recognized from 3D camera input with an algorithmic pipeline composed of multiple classification/regression stages, trained on a large annotated dataset. Our experimental results indicate that the pipeline enables successful gesture recognition with a very low computational load, thus enabling a gesture-based interface on low-end processors.

ACM Classification Keywords
H.5.2. User Interfaces: Input devices and strategies, Prototyping; I.5.4. Pattern Recognition applications: Computer vision; I.4.9. Image processing and Computer Vision: Applications

Author Keywords
Hand gesture recognition; Hand gesture NUI development

INTRODUCTION
Hand gestures are a natural communication mode for humans, and a promising direction for a human-computer interface. Scenarios of interest range from personal computers to mobile devices and to emerging virtual and augmented reality platforms[4, 8]. In addition, advances in depth camera imaging and computer vision have made such an interface possible in recent years [27, 14, 15, 16, 17, 26]. However, a practical gesture-based interface still faces severe difficulties, due to conflicting demands on both the development and run-time environments. Development of a rich gesture-based interface is currently a considerable effort requiring long development cycles with teams skilled in computer vision and machine learning. A common alternative is to use a mature tuned system (like [14] or [1]), but these typically offer a small predefined set of gestures to choose from, thus limiting the uniqueness and richness of the experience. In the run-time environment, the dilemma is between system accuracy and its computational demands. Several recent articles describe systems that already achieve real time performance using multi-core CPUs. However, a useful system should utilize only a fraction of the CPU power, so it does not disturb other running applications, yet maintain accuracy and responsiveness. These contradicting demands are exacerbated in low-power, low-end CPUs used in mobile devices.

Figure 1. The camera and user setting we address - providing a gesture-based user interface for common laptop and desktop experiences.

We propose to address these difficulties by introducing a simple language for the definition of poses and gestures, and by developing a set of tools and algorithms demonstrating that the language is practical for both development and algorithmic recognition. Our contribution is three-fold. First, we propose a language. In its design, our primary guideline was to keep it simple enough so that development is easy, yet expressive enough to enable most of the gestures coming to one's mind. Second, we developed a set of tools that enable natural development of a gesture-based interface, without prerequisite knowledge in algorithms or machine vision. These tools enable gesture definition using code, XAML files or an editing GUI, and include visualization and verification tools.

CHI'17, May 6–11, 2017, Denver, USA.

DOI http://dx.doi.org/10.1145/3025453.3025508

Third, and most important, we have developed an algorithmic pipeline which enables recognition of the defined gestures from a 3D camera stream, with high accuracy. This pipeline includes many extremely fast predictors, operating in multiple stages, and trained on a large annotated data corpus. With this pipeline, we achieve real time performance with a single thread, using only a small fraction of the CPU.

The language we propose is based on four basic predicates which are naturally used to describe hand poses, applied to the six main interest points of the hand: the five fingertips and the palm center. The predicates are: pointing direction ('the thumb points up'), relative location ('the index is above the middle'), fingertip touching ('the ring finger touches the thumb') and finger flexion ('the pinky is folded'). Using these predicates, 102 basic propositions are created, which serve as the basic binary building blocks of the calculus. A hand pose (sometimes termed 'posture') is defined mainly as a conjunction of the basic propositions, with disjunctions partially allowed in certain cases. A gesture, in turn, is defined plainly as a sequence of hand poses. Defining a gesture in this language is fairly straightforward, due to its proximity to pose description in natural language, and the gesture developer is not asked to state continuous parameters like distances or angles. Despite its qualitative nature, the language is very expressive. For example, it can express without difficulty the basic signs in the American Sign Language (ASL) phonology [24], and the basic poses used in several current commercial systems. See figure 2 for some examples.

Based on the proposed language, a gesture based interface can be built using several possible tools. For a *C#* programmer, a pose class can be defined in a few lines of code, and a gesture class can be constructed once all of its constituent poses are defined. Above the code interface, additional layers are added to enable gesture definitions by non-programmers. We developed a simple text parser which enables definition of poses and gestures using XAML code. The parser then creates the appropriate *C#* classes. In addition, we have designed a visual gesture editor displaying the poses as states in a sequence. The editor enables pose manipulations using context sensitive menus, and its output can be exported into XAML format. For visualizing the edited poses in real time we developed a fast inverse kinematics algorithm, utilizing the language's simplicity. The algorithm produces a pose satisfying the chosen propositions, which is then rendered using a generic hand model. Finally, this system aids in identifying non-valid hand definitions.

The algorithmic pipeline which recognizes the language has to resolve the accuracy versus speed tension mentioned earlier. To ease this tension, we use Convolutional Table Ensemble (CTE) classifiers and regressors [14, 3]. These are extremely fast predictors, typically processing an image in less than a millisecond. As shown in [14], the CTE architecture enables trading training sample size for speed and accuracy, that is: by using larger sample size at the training stage, the run-time predictor can be made faster while keeping the same accuracy. The pipeline includes several stages, each employing a set of CTEs. In the first stage, the position of the hand center is found and the image is centered around it. Then the global hand orientation is found, framed as a classification problem into 16 discrete pose clusters, and is then refined. At a third stage the location and direction of fingertips are found, by applying a cluster-specific regressor. This regressor in turn includes several stages of regressing the fingertip location, centering the image around the tip and regressing again for refinement. Finally, the truth value of the basic 102 language propositions is inferred from the fingertips and palm center locations.

In order to obtain the speed and accuracy benefits from the CTE architecture, a large dataset is required for training. In our proposed system, however, this training is a one time event and no machine learning effort is required from the gesture developer. We collected more than $360,000$ annotated images for the pipeline training, using a custom-built dome-shaped structure equipped with multiple cameras. Since the target camera uses IR, colors which are IR-invisible were used to mark interest points on the hands of the subjects. Some annotation was then automatically collected using a set of surrounding RGB cameras, while another portion, like exact fingertip locations, required manual tagging.

We evaluated the accuracy of our algorithm on several levels: estimation of fingertip locations, recognition of the language propositions, and recognition of full gestures. Hand pose estimation is usually evaluated in the literature by considering statistics of the distance between fingertips position and their algorithmic estimates. We evaluated our algorithm using these metrics in two publicly available datasets, NYU [27] and Dexter [22]. Using NYU, which is the larger and more challenging dataset, our method is comparable to the best method, and using Dexter it is ranked third among nine methods. This accuracy is obtained in 14 millisecond per image on a single CPU thread - roughly an order of magnitude faster than any other method of similar accuracy. This degree of accuracy and speed enables a practical, real-time, gesture-based interface in a variety of scenarios. Moreover, unlike other leading methods, we recognize the hand pose without using temporal information (single frame), which makes the measured accuracy robust to fast pose changes and short gestures.

Beyond fingertip localization errors, for real gesture recognition using a language of the type we define here, the important statistics are the probabilities of correctly detecting basic propositions and full gestures. We estimated our capabilities for recognition of the basic propositions using a test set of $61,397$ images containing random hand poses. Our system is able to recognize basic propositions 92% of the time with a false positive rate lower than 1.4%. For full gestures, we tested our system using a set of 12 selected gestures, performed multiple times by 10 different persons, and an additional set of non-gesture hand activity clips for false alarm rate estimation. Our pipeline achieves an average detection rate of 96% for users after a few minutes of practice.

RELATED WORK

Our contribution is in language and development tools for hand gesture interface, as well as in the hand pose estimation

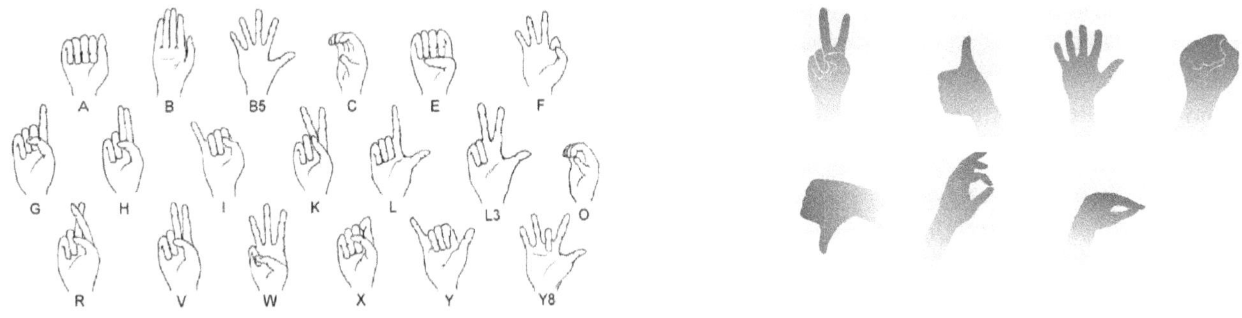

Figure 2. Pose dictionaries: (Left) The hand shapes found in a phonemic analysis of ASL. According to the analysis, these (together with location and motion elements) were found to be basic patterns characterizing the symbolic vocabulary of the language. Each of these hand poses can be well characterized, and distinguished from the others, using a few basic propositions utilizing our four base predicates: finger/palm direction, finger folding state, finger tangency and relative direction. (Right) The hand shapes used in the static gestures of a popular commercial system [1]. These can also be naturally described using our simple language.

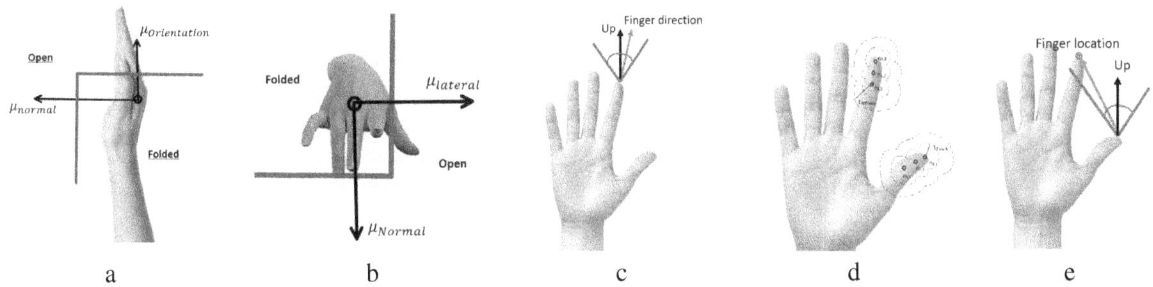

Figure 3. Predicate operational definitions: (a) A non-thumb finger is considered folded if its tip resides in the marked quarter, defined by planes whose normal is the palm direction and palm orientation. (b) The folding region of the thumb (c) A finger is pointing 'up' if its direction is in a cone with the base placed at the fingertip. An analogous definition is given for the other 5 directions. (d) Touching and not-touching relations are determined by the intersection of multiple balls around the distal phalanges of the two fingers (e) Relative directions are determined using a cone whose axis is aligned with canonical direction. Here the index is above the thumb because it falls in this cone for 'up' direction.

algorithm. Here we briefly refer to the relevant literature in these two domains.

Gesture language and development tools: In [19] the advantages of using a declarative gesture language compared to procedural gesture programming are elaborated, but in the context of full body and touch gestures. Three such advantages are mentioned: easier feedback providing during the gesture, avoiding code division among components (termed 'spaghetti code' there), and convenient treatment of compositionality and gestures with partial overlap. Among these, our method enjoys the two latter advantages, but does not currently address user feedback during a gesture - an action is performed only at the end of the poses sequence.

The Gesture Description Language (GDL), presented in [11], uses a context free grammar to define a language describing full body gestures. The primitive joints relate to large body entities, but not to hand parts or fingers, and the language is recognized using a Microsoft Kinect system followed by an inference engine. Unlike in our methodology, describing gestures requires the developer to state numerical parameters and relations like exact angles or distances between joints. Another context free grammar for full body gesture specification is presented in [10]. The goal of the suggested language is not to ease interface development, and no actual recognition engine for the language is suggested. Instead the focus is on privacy, security and reliability: verifying that the gestures suggested are valid, not empty, there are no collisions between registered gestures, etc. Most similar to our method in spirit, the 'Proton++' system [13] includes a language and a recognition algorithm for multi-touch gestures. Like in our language, they describe a gesture as a sequence of basic elements (finger strokes) characterized using a small set of propositions. A basic stroke is defined by its type (finger up/down/move), the finger index, and several stroke attributes (movement direction, pressure, etc.). Like in our system, a state machine handles the recognition and disambiguation of multiple gestures.

More related to hands-based interface, in [5] a stochastic context free grammar is suggested for the composition of single poses into gestures. This grammar assigns probabilities to gestures given an input sequence of detected primitive poses, and so it enables gesture detection in cases of non-accurate execution. However, the language does not include description of general poses - instead a set of only 4 primitive poses is used (fist, open hand, one or two fingers raised). In another work [7] hand gestures based on hand motion are described as compositions of 14 primitive motion elements known from the ASL phonemic decomposition [24]. This work is orthogonal to ours, as hand internal pose is not addressed at all -

the hand is assumed to be rigid. In [20] the dexterity and independence properties of the different fingers are examined, and an efficient language for text dictation via finger folding is devised.

Hand pose estimation algorithms: A lot of work [15, 16, 12, 27, 17, 26, 22, 21, 14, 25, 6, 2] has been done in recent years. See [9] for a review. We compare our results to many of these methods. There are several quite different approaches to the hand pose estimation problem. One line of work uses a 3*D* hand model and addresses the problem as model-based tracking [17, 2, 26]. These methods are usually accurate, but require high computational effort. Another direction uses ensembles of trees or ferns for pose estimation from a single frame [12, 14, 25, 18]. The advantages are the ability to run with a low computational budget and to comprehend fast motion. Specificlly in [18] a method based on multi-stage random forest was used to successfully discriminate between 6 pre-defined poses on smartphones with a simple RGB camera. Our work belongs to this algorithmic family, and significantly improves its accuracy. Some work is based on combining modules from model-based tracking and single-frame fast detection, such as [22, 21]. Finally, several groups have used Convolutional Neural Networks (CNN) [27, 15, 16] with increasing degrees of sophistication and accuracy over time.

LANGUAGE

The language we propose is based on a set of qualitative basic propositions, such as "the index and middle are not touching". These propositions are close to gesture descriptions in natural language, and thereby enable easy pose characterization for the developer. To contrast, quantitative descriptions such as "keep the Index and Middle tips 3cm away from each other" include parameters that are hard for the developer to estimate as they often do not have good intuition for their values. Moreover, even when they do estimate such values well for their own hands, the result is not likely to generalize well to people with different hand size or different morphology/flexibility. We believe tuning these parameters is better left for the system.

Basic propositions

The propositions are obtained by applying two one-argument predicates (direction, flexion) and two two-argument predicates (relative direction, tangency) to one or two of six interest points on the hand: the fingertips and palm center. Direction and direction relationships are quantized to 6 canonical values: "Left (of the subject)","Right", "Up", "Down", "Forward" and "Backward". The other two predicates, flexion and tangency, are naturally binary. Here are the basic propositions in detail:

- **Palm pose**:
  - Palm direction: This is the direction of the normal of the palm, pointing out of the forehand. 6 propositions of the form "the palm points in direction X" are defined, for the 6 canonical directions.
  - Palm orientation: The direction pointing from the wrist to the base of the middle finger. Again 6 propositions are defined.

  The operational definition of '*pointing toward a canonical direction*' is that the pointing direction has a small angle with the canonical direction. However, the parameter, as any other parameter in the system, is not exposed to the developer. See figure 3.a for visualization of the palm direction (μ_{normal} in the figure) and orientation ($\mu_{Orientation}$) concepts.

- **Fingers**:
  - Finger direction: For each finger we define the 6 propositions of pointing in the canonical directions, for a total of 30 propositions. (See figure 3.c) for the direction operational definition.
  - Finger flexion: For each finger two states are defined, as '*open*' and '*folded*', giving 10 propositions. A non-thumb finger is declared folded if its tip is in the quarter of the space near the hand, as defined by two planes (See figure 3.a). A similar characterization is given to the thumb. (See figure 3.b).
  - Finger tangency: For each of the 10 possible finger pair combinations, an '*a is touching b*' proposition is defined, as well as an '*a is not touching b*', for a total of 20 propositions. To evaluate these propositions, we define the distance between fingers as follows: *K* points, *d* millimeters apart from each other, are defined along the ray starting from the tip and pointing in the opposite of the finger direction. Two fingers are considered touching if the minimal distance between a point on one finger and the tip of the other is lower than a threshold (See figure 3.d), and 'not touching' when this minimal distance is higher than a different, greater threshold, such that '*not touching*' and '*touching*' are not a simple negation of each other: typically there are cases where neither of them applies.
  - Finger relative position: For each finger pair, a proposition is defined stating that '*a is in direction C from b*' where C is one of the 6 canonical directions. Since propositions like '*middle is above the thumb*' and '*thumb is below the middle*' are equivalent, this yields altogether 30 propositions. A proposition is satisfied if point a is in a cone whose base is at point b and its central axis is in the direction C (See figure 3.e).

Poses and gestures

Static hand poses are defined as conjunctions of propositions, where a proposition is either one of the basic 102 propositions, or a '*direction-disjunction*' over them. A *direction disjunction* is a statement such as '*the thumb points either left or up*', that is: the disjunction is over several basic propositions differing only in the direction stated. A static hand pose can be detected from a single frame. Gestures are defined simply as sequences of poses in time. To complete a gesture, the user has to go through the sequence of defined poses, with the time interval between the poses no longer than a threshold parameter.

DEVELOPMENT TOOLS

Based on the proposed language, we have created a set of development tools to enable easy hand gesture interface development. Gestures can be programmed in *C#* using a set of

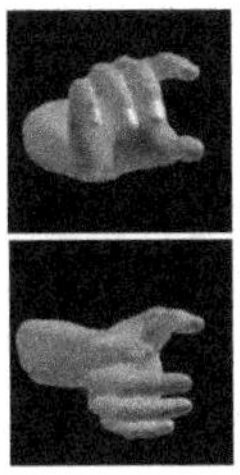

a

```csharp
public SingleHandPose CreateIndexThumbPointPose(string name, FingersRelativeLocation indexThumbRelation)
{
    var indexThumbPointPose = new SingleHandPose(name);
    indexThumbPointPose.PoseConstraints.Add(new[] { Finger.Thumb, Finger.Index },
                                            FingerFlexion.Open, PoseDirection.Forward);
    indexThumbPointPose.PoseConstraints.Add(Finger.Index, indexThumbRelation, Finger.Thumb);
    indexThumbPointPose.PoseConstraints.Add(Finger.Index, FingersTangency.NotTouching, Finger.Thumb);
    return indexThumbPointPose;
}

public Gesture CreateRotateGesture()
{
    var rotateGesture = new Gesture("RotateGesture");
    rotateGesture.AddSegment(CreateIndexThumbPointPose("LockObjectPose", FingersRelativeLocation.Above));
    rotateGesture.AddSegment(CreateIndexThumbPointPose("RotateObjectPose", FingersRelativeLocation.Right));
    rotateGesture.ConnectSegments(rotateGesture.IdleGestureSegment);
    return rotateGesture;
}
```

b

```xml
<Gesture Name="RotateGesture">
    <Gesture.Segments>
        <IdleGestureSegment Name="Idle"/>
        <SingleHandPose Name="LockObjectPose">
            <FingersPose Context="Thumb, Index" Flexion="Open" Direction="Forward"/>
            <FingersLocalityRelation Context="Index" LocalityRelation="Above" OtherContext="Thumb"/>
            <FingersTangencyRelation Context="Index" TangencyRelation="NotTouching" OtherContext="Thumb"/>
        </SingleHandPose>
        <SingleHandPose Name="RotateObjectPose">
            <FingersPose Context="Thumb, Index" Flexion="Open" Direction="Forward"/>
            <FingersLocalityRelation Context="Index" LocalityRelation="Right" OtherContext="Thumb"/>
            <FingersTangencyRelation Context="Index" TangencyRelation="NotTouching" OtherContext="Thumb"/>
        </SingleHandPose>
    </Gesture.Segments>

    <Gesture.SegmentsConnections>
        <SegmentConnections From="Idle" To="Idle, LockObject"/>
        <SegmentConnections From="LockObject" To="RotateObject"/>
        <SegmentConnections From="RotateObject" To="Idle"/>
    </Gesture.SegmentsConnections>
</Gesture>
```

c

Figure 4. Gesture description in formal language: (a) A 'Rotate Right' gesture is composed of the two shown poses, starting with the index above the thumb, and ending with the index right of the thumb (from the user's perspective). (b) *C#* code that generates a 'Rotate Right' gesture object. The two comprising poses are defined using a single method 'CreateIndexThumbPointPose()' accepting the required index-to-thumb relation as input argument. 'Rotate Right' is then defined as a short sequence of the two poses. (c) 'Rotate Right' gesture defined in XAML format. The same propositions are applied, but without the *C#* syntax.

classes, or text-edited by non-programmers. On top of these tools, we have devised a visual gesture builder tool, allowing gesture editing with a graphical user interface. The builder includes a visualization tool, which renders hand poses based on their definition in the language.

The runtime environment

Our suggested hand pose estimation algorithm (described in the next section) is an efficient routine running on the user's machine. In order to work with it, the developer builds and registers a *Gesture* object, which includes a gesture definition and a pointer to a callback function. Upon frame arrival, the runtime system computes the relevant basic propositions - a subset of the 102 propositions that is relevant for currently registered gestures. The execution of each registered gesture is tracked using a simple finite-state machine, monitoring which of the poses were already executed and what pose is expected next. Upon execution of the last pose, the callback function registered with the gesture is called. The direct interface for gesture building is programming in *C#*, and linking to the runtime library.

A *C#* interface

Writing a new pose class is done by inheriting the new class from an abstract *SingleHandPose* class, and adding the actual propositions content of the pose using predefined enum types. A gesture class is then defined by concatenating a predefined set of pose classes into a sequence. An example of a '*Rotate Right*' gesture written in *C#* is shown in figure 4, including two poses. Since the two poses are similar, they are defined in a single method, accepting as parameter the direction relation required between the thumb and the index. The gesture is defined in a few lines of code, and the lines describing the poses are fairly intuitive, reflecting the tight relation to natural language descriptions.

XAML text interface

The programming interface is the most straightforward, but it requires programming skills in *C#* and it mixes the programming work with gesture design, while the two tasks require different expertise and are usually performed by different people. Hence we consider an option to write gesture definitions in an XAML format, which is independent of a specific programming language. '*Rotate Right*' written in an XAML format is shown in figure 4.c. These files are easier to write, and provide a convenient middle layer for the next design level: a visual gesture builder.

A Visual Gesture Builder

A more natural way for building gestures is using a visual editor, providing immediate visual feedback. We have developed such a tool for gesture design in the suggested language. The gesture is presented as a visual sequence of poses (see figure 5). Once a pose is selected, the developer can choose one of the six areas of interest - the palm or one of the fingers - and edit it using a context menu. This menu allows choosing the item's direction and its flexion state (for fingers). For fingers there are four additional items in the menu, allowing one to choose a second finger and establishing the required relation between the two fingers. These relations are chosen from a second-level context menu, and allow specifying fingertip touching and directional relations between the chosen fingers.

When a menu item choice changes, the gesture builder calls a quick inverse kinematics algorithm to find a pose (a vector of joint angle values) which meets the new set of constraints, and renders it instead of the previous pose. When conflicting constraints exist, the inverse kinematics fails to find a valid pose satisfying the constraints, and a warning message is issued. For example, this happens if the thumb and index are instructed to point forward, but the ring is instructed to point left (see figure 5.d(bottom)). The developer may rotate the camera view of the hand at any time by dragging the mouse inside the pose circle, to better understand the finger locations in complex, partially occluded poses. Once editing is done, the gesture is saved as a XAML file, from which classes representing the new gesture are automatically generated. This tool enables trial and error experimentation in the space of pose definitions, and can significantly accelerate gesture development.

The inverse kinematics algorithm mentioned above has to solve a hard satisfaction problem including non-convex constraints, and do it immediately to enable real time feedback. We use a coarse-to-fine greedy approach, starting from a base-

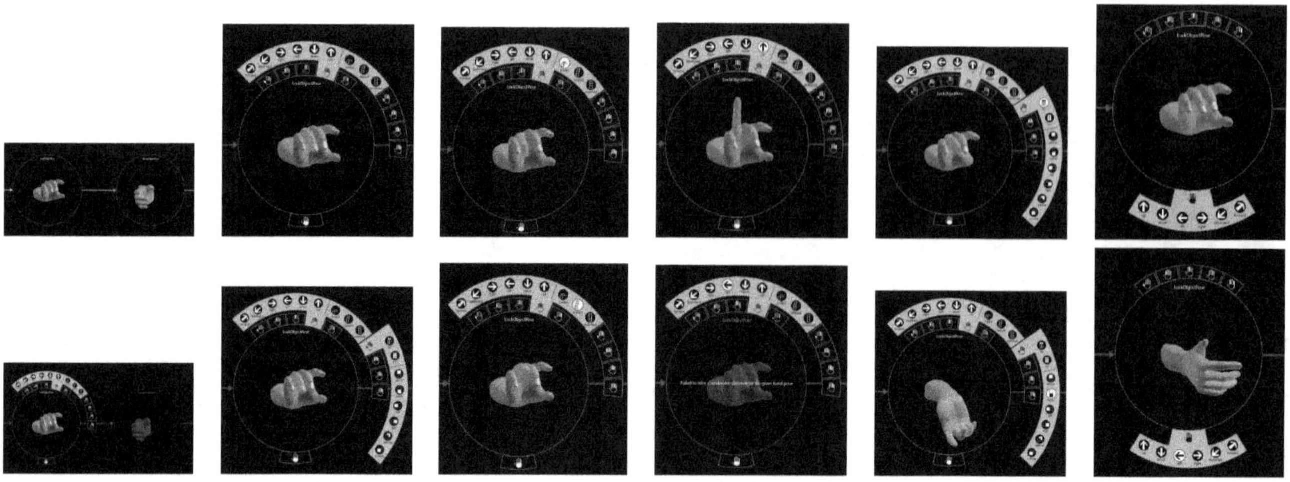

a b c d e f

Figure 5. Visual gesture builder: (a) The builder presents the poses of the gesture as a sequence (top) and allows the developer to choose a pose to edit using a mouse click (bottom). (b) A selected finger is marked in blue, and opens a context menu (top), from which a second menu enables choosing a second finger, marked in red (bottom). (c) A selected finger can be constrained to be in folded (top) or open (bottom) state. (d) Finger direction can be chosen, up in the example (top), but if it cannot be reconciled with current constraints an alert message is displayed instead (bottom). (e) When two fingers are marked, relations of tip touching (top) and relative locations (bottom) can be stated. (f) the palm can be marked, then rotated to a different direction.

Algorithm 1 Ferns Ensemble computation

Input: An image I of size $S_x \times S_y$,
Classifier parameters $\{\Theta^m, A^m, W_c^m, \beta_c\}_{m=1,c=1}^{M,C}$
$\Theta^m = \{\delta_k^{1,m}, \delta_k^{2,m}, t_k^m\}_{k=1}^{K}$, $A^m \subset \{1,..,S_x\} \times \{1,..,S_y\}$, $W_c^m \in \mathbb{R}^{2^K}$, $\beta_c \in \mathbb{R}^C$
Output: Class scores vector *Score*
Initialization: For $c = 1,..,C$ $Score[c] = -\beta_c$
For all ferns $m = 1,..,M$
    For all pixels $p \in A^m$
        Compute a k-bit index b_p^m
        For $c = 1,..,C$ $Score[c] = Score[c] + W_c^m[b_p^m]$
Return *Score*

line pose and enforcing constraint families one at a time. First we look for a pose satisfying the palm direction and relative finger direction constraints, as these two constraint types put strong limitations on the global hand orientation. Then finger flexion, finger direction and finger tangency constraints are enforced, in that order. In most cases, this process successfully finds a pose satisfying all the constraints if there is one.

HAND POSE ESTIMATION ALGORITHM

Our practical hand pose estimation algorithm is based on two high level ideas: multiple stage problem breakdown, and prediction based on clever memorization. The pose estimation task is broken into several stages, each with a small scope problem to solve. At each stage we use a set of very fast predictors (the CTE family) whose activation essentially amounts to indexing a set of tables. These tables, created during training, memorize hand pose information and enable fast answer prediction by gathering the votes across an ensemble.

Convolutional Table Ensembles (CTE)

A CTE predictor extracts codeword indices from multiple positions in the image, and uses them to index multiple tables. The tables' votes are combined linearly to predict the output of interest. At [14] these classifiers were introduced in which the codeword indices are extracted using a set of independent questions, in which case the index computing structure is called a *'fern'*, and the classifier is termed a Discriminative Ferns Ensemble (DFE). We also use some of the improvements suggested in [3], except that for codeword computation we use ferns rather than trees, as ferns are faster.

The ferns ensemble predictor operates on an image patch I, consisting of P pixels. For a single fern and pixel location $p \in \mathbb{N}^2$, a local descriptor for p's neighborhood is computed using a set of $k = 1,..K$ binary questions of the form

$$b_k = \sigma(I[p+\delta_k^1] - I[p+\delta_k^2] - t) \tag{1}$$

where $\delta_k^1, \delta_k^2 \in \{-s,...,s\}^2$ are location offsets, $t \in \mathbb{R}$ is a threshold, and $\sigma(\cdot)$ is the Heaviside function. These are simple and computationally-light questions, comparing the difference between two pixels to a threshold. For fern m, location p and question k denote the bit obtained by $b_{p,k}^m$. Concatenating the K bits together, a K-bit codeword b_p^m is obtained at for every fern and pixel location.

Histogram of Bit Vectors: In order to obtain translation invariance a spatial histogram of codewords over pixel locations is computed. Denote the histogram for the mth fern by $H^m(I)$. An entry $b \in \{0,1\}^K$ of H^m is defined by

$$H_b^m = \sum_{p \in A^m} \delta(b_p^m - b) \tag{2}$$

where δ is a discrete delta function, and $A^m \subset \{1,..,P\}$ is the spatial aggregation region for fern m. Note that H^m is a sparse vector, with at most P non-zero entries.

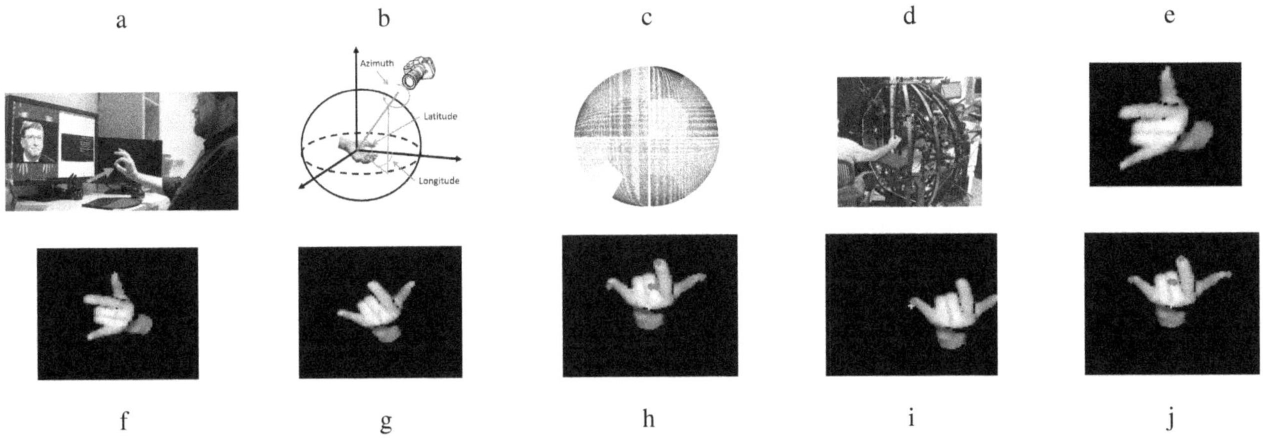

Figure 6. Hand estimation pipeline: (a) in the user setting we address the hand is typically the dynamic object closest to the camera in the direction shown. (b) Latitude, longitude and azimuth in a hand-centered coordinate system. (c) The clusters we use on the (latitude, longitude) sphere, viewed from the right axis in b. (d) The iron dome used for data gathering. (e) A segmented hand patch. (f) The hand patch after centering. Estimated hand center marked in green. (g) The hand after coarse (latitude, longitude) finding and azimuth correction. (h) The hand after global hand pose refinement and initial fingertip location regression. (i) A finger-centered image sent for finger refinement. (j) The final fingertip locations estimation.

Histograms concatenation: The final output is computed by a linear classifier or regressor applied to the concatenation of the M fern histograms.

$$f(I) = W^T H(I) = \sum_{m=1}^{M} \sum_{b\in\{0,1\}^K} w_b^m H_b^m - \beta \qquad (3)$$

with $H(I) = [H^1(I), \ldots, H^M(I)] \in \mathbb{N}^{M2^K}$, a weight vector $W = [W^1, \ldots, W^M] \in \mathbb{R}^{M2^K}$, and a bias term $\beta \in \mathbb{R}$. When multiple outputs are required (as in multiclass classification), C weight vectors and biases $\{W_c, \beta_c\}_{c=1}^{C}$ are trained and used to obtained C output scores using the same set of ferns.

Run time classifier/regressor: Algorithm 1 describes the operation of a DFE at test time. The pipeline is extremely simple. For each fern and each pixel in the fern's aggregation region we compute the codeword index, and access the tables of all classes with this index to get the codeword's score contribution. The complexity is $O(M\bar{A}(K+C))$ where $\bar{A}$ is the average number of pixels per aggregation region.

CTE training: As described in [14, 3], a CTE is trained by iterating between adding a fern and training a global predictor over the current set of ferns' features. The global optimization is done with SVM when classification is handled, and an SVR loss when regression is required. Adding a fern, which adds 2^K features to the predictor, requires optimization over the bit function parameters Θ^m, and the aggregation area A^m. These are chosen greedily so that the added features align well with the gradient of the current predictor. Following [3], beyond bit functions comparing two pixels, we use also bit functions comparing one pixel to a threshold, as well as spatial bits providing information regarding the pixel location.

Hand Pose Estimation Pipeline

The algorithmic pipeline consists of multiple stages: hand segmentation, hand centering, global orientation classification, global pose refinement, fingers pose estimation, and finally, estimation of basic propositions truth values. The main stages (hand pose and finger pose estimation) rely on CTE predictors.

Hand segmentation: Hand finding is based on two assumptions: hand movement and hand proximity to the camera. We start by dropping pixels far from the camera and static pixels, using a fast background subtraction method. Among the remaining pixels, the pixel with lowest projection on the 3D direction $(0, -1, 2)$ is chosen as the hand's '*anchor pixel*', reflecting the relative position of the camera and user in our setting (see figure 6.a). The hand is then segmented by taking the set of pixels whose $3D$ distance from the anchor pixel is smaller than a threshold (See figure 6.e).

Hand centering: The hand center of mass in $3D$ is found and a $3D$ transformation is computed so as to rotate it about the shortest rotation direction onto the camera principal axis. This transformation, together with affine scaling, is then applied to all the hand pixels, and the hand is re-rendered. This process maps all hands to frame center and roughly equal size, thus reducing variation due to perspective projection and distance from camera (see figure 6.f).

Global hand orientation classification: We term the following 6 parameters by 'global hand pose': the $3D$ palm center location and $3D$ hand orientation. Hand orientation is a main source of variance in hand pose estimation: hands seen from different viewpoints have very different appearances of the palm, the fingers and their mutual occlusion patterns. Therefore we consider the coarse global orientation determination as a classification problem, and the pipeline in the next stages is split to different paths according to the classification decision. Instead of thinking about the hand as rotating, we fix it in a canonical pose at $(0, 0, 0)$, and consider the possible camera positions and rotations on the viewing sphere (See figure 6.b). The camera longitude and latitude determine its position on the unit sphere, and the azimuth is related to the camera rotation around its principal axis (in-plane rotation). Viewpoints in which the hand is seen from the arm direction (first person) are not considered, since they rarely occur in our scenario.

We treat longitude/latitude and azimuth differently in our classification. The viewing half-sphere is divided into 16 (latitude, longitude) clusters (See 6.c), and the azimuth is independently divided to 8 equidistant clusters centered at rotations of $0°, 45°, ..315°$. During training we use the ground truth hand rotation to assign an image to one of the $16 \times 8 = 128$ possible labels. A single CTE classifier is learned with 16 classes, where output i is trained to discriminate images with azimuth cluster 0 and (latitude, longitude) cluster i from all other images. At test time, the image is rotated 8 times in $45°$ intervals, and submitted to the classifier in each rotation. Since the classifier was trained to discriminate images from a single rotation, 7 of the rotated images are expected to get low scores in all their 16 outputs, and only the correct rotation gets a high i-th output. The highest scoring class among the 128 outputs determines the (latitude, longitude) orientation cluster, and the azimuth cluster. The hand image is then rotated so as to cancel out the predicted azimuth. (see figure 6.g).

Global hand pose refinement: This stage refines the coarse hand orientation and location (known from orientation classification and hand centering stages respectively). The refinement is done in two regression stages, each with 6 outputs. At each stage, the hand image is re-centered and re-rotated using the current estimates. Then the residual difference between the current estimates and true (center, orientation) values is regressed. During training, two such consecutive stages are trained for each (longitude, latitude) cluster, for a total of $16 \times 2 = 32$ CTE-regressors. However, when testing only 2 regressors corresponding to the chosen cluster are activated.

Fingers regression: This part of the pipeline includes 3 regression stages (see figure 6.h-j) trained separately for each (longitude, latitude) cluster. The first stage operates on the rotated and centered hand image and regresses the rough location of the 5 fingertips. Following that, two finger refinement stages take place for each finger separately. At each stage, the image is translated to have the finger of interest centered according to the current estimation, and the residual translation of the real finger is regressed. At the second stage, the position of the distal finger joint is also regressed, in order to get the finger direction by subtracting it from the fingertip. Overall there are $1 + 2 \times 5 = 11$ regressors activated at this stage, and $11 \times 16 = 176$ regressors are trained for all clusters.

Basic propositions truth value: As described earlier, each of the 102 propositions has an operational definition in terms of global palm direction, fingertip locations or fingertip directions. Given the estimations of the latter, the truth value of the relevant basic propositions can be readily estimated.

Overall, the estimation system contains 209 CTE predictors, but only 21 CTE activations are performed at test time per frame. Such a multi-classifier approach is possible due to the very low computational cost of CTE predictors. For example, a classifier with $m = 20$ ferns, $C = 10$ class, $K = 12$ bits and an aggregation area of 64×64 pixels runs at $550\mu S$ on a single thread of an $i7 - 3720QM$ CPU@$2.6GHz$ processor.

Data and annotation gathering

In the CTE framework, gathering a large annotated dataset is the key for test time speed, since a larger data set allows usage of larger tables (larger K) and therefore fewer ferns (lower M) - see [14] for the details. Our data was gathered using Intel's RealSense SR300 camera [1], providing 640×480 depth and IR images using coded light technology. In order to get a large dataset, we constructed an iron dome, with up to 23 affixed Intel cameras and 8 high definition RGB cameras, all pointing toward the dome center (See figure 6.d). All of the cameras were jointly calibrated and synchronized (synchronization is required due to the active nature of the cameras, which may cause interference). Using this construction, a hand pose in the center of the dome provides 23 depth images, and annotation obtained can be readily propagated between them.

The RGB cameras are used to obtain the annotation needed: global hand pose, as well as location of fingertips and distal finger joints. We marked the positions of key joints on each subject's right hand using colors not seen by the IR cameras. Specifically, 3 points and one short line were marked on the back of the hand, for determination of the global hand pose. When the hand is placed at the dome's center, each such point is seen by at least 2 RGB cameras, so its $2D$ image position was automatically detected, and its $3D$ point location was found by triangulation. In this manner, the global pose annotation is found automatically. For fingertips and other joint locations we could not achieve this automatic annotation due to marker confusion and occlusion problems, and so we resorted to manual annotation.

Altogether $89,333$ images were collected and automatically tagged for global hand pose training. To this we added virtual samples, created from the original samples using in-plane rotation. For fingertips detection $274,068$ images were manually annotated. This large a sample is required since 16 different fingertip detection pipelines are trained, one per (longitude, latitude) cluster, using mutually exclusive sub-samples.

In addition to the training data, two datasets were gathered for evaluation purposes. The first includes $61,397$ fully annotated images of random hand poses, used for estimation of fingertip location accuracy and basic proposition estimation. A second dataset includes 507 clips of 12 gestures, performed multiple times by 10 different subjects. A $3,500$ random subset of the first dataset, and the entire second dataset are made publicly available[1]. Prior to recording, the subjects were allowed to train on the 12 gestures for three minutes, to simulate the steady state of experienced users. Clips were annotated with tags marking the temporal intervals in which poses of interest were maintained. In addition, 17 minutes of intensive non-gesture hand activities were recorded. This dataset is used for estimation of gesture-detection statistics: detection and false alarm rates. See the appendix for a more detailed description.

EMPIRICAL RESULTS

In most of the hand pose estimation literature [27, 15, 16, 17, 26, 25], system performance is measured using statistics of $3D$ deviations between true finger locations and their estimates.

[1] https://aka.ms/atli-hands-chi2017

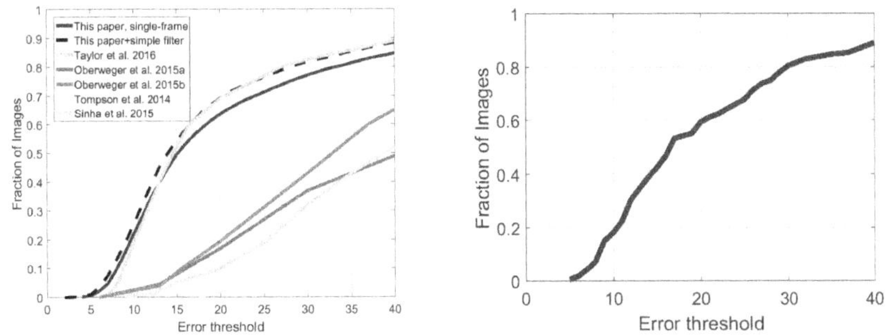

Method	Error (mm)
Taylor et al. 2016 [26]	9.5
Tagliasacchi et al. 2015 [2]	9.8
This paper, simple filter	12.7
This paper, single frame	14.8
Sharp et al. 2015 [17]	15.0
Sridhar et al. 2015 [21]	19.6
Sridhar et. al 2014 [23]	24.1
Choi et al. 2015 [6]	25.3
Sridhar et al. 2013 [22]	31.8
Tang et al. 2014 [25]	42.4

Figure 7. Joint deviation results: (Left) Max deviation CDF results on NYU dataset. See text for explanation. (Center) Max deviation CDF on a random subset of our test data, consisting of $3,500$ images. (Right) Average error rates on Dexter data for our method and alternatives. Our accuracy is obtained in 14 millisecond per image on a single CPU thread - roughly an order of magnitude faster than any other method of comparable accuracy. Our pose recognition is based on single-frame. When adding even a simple temporal median filter on adjacent frames, the accuracy increases (see Method "This paper, simple filter"), demonstrating further potential for improvements.

We report our results using these measures on our test data, and compare to other methods on two publicly available datasets. However, for practical gesture recognition performance beyond deviation statistics should be measured. We measure the accuracy of our system on two higher level tasks: estimating the truth value of our 102 basic propositions, and detecting actual gestures phrased in our language.

3D finger deviations - comparison to state of the art

We experimented with two publicly available datasets: NYU [27] and Dexter [22]. NYU is a large dataset with $N = 8252$ test images including challenging poses. Dexter is a smaller ($N = 2931$) and easier dataset, where the hand is frontal in most of the poses and all fingertips are usually visible. We use the methodology of [26] to map the output joints of our method to ground truth joints of the specific dataset. In both these datasets, the hand movement is often relatively slow compared to natural gestures and the importance of temporal information is emphasized. On the contrary our method, which is a single-frame algorithm designed to cope with fast gestures, does not use temporal information at all. To make the comparison fair, we show our results both for the pure algorithm, and for the algorithm after applying a simple temporal median filter independently for each joint location, with a window of 5 frames.

In figure 7.Left we compare our NYU results to several alternatives. The graph shows a CDF of maximal deviation in a frame: for each joint the deviation in millimeters between estimated and true location is computed, and the graph shows the fraction of frames in which the maximal deviation is smaller than a threshold. The table in figure 7.Right lists the average fingertip estimation error in millimeters on Dexter dataset for our algorithm and alternative methods. Figure 7.Center shows the maximal deviation CDF on a subset of our own test set. This set contains diverse, random hand poses taken from the covered half of the viewing sphere.

The comparison to alternatives shows that our method is comparable to the state-of-the-art method [26] on NYU, and slightly lower on Dexter. The higher relative ranking on NYU indicates that our strength is mostly with hard poses, where finger occlusion is prevalent. When comparing to [26] several points should be noted: First, our method runs in $11.5ms$ on a single thread (laptop with i7-4810MQ @2.8GHz), while the method of [26] is reported to consume most of the CPU on an 8-core, 16-thread machine. Our method is therefore at least one order of magnitude faster. This is also true regarding the methods accurate on Dexter [17, 2], which run on GPU. Second, unlike these alternatives our method inferences using a single frame, and is therefore more robust for fast and abrupt hand motions which are prevalent in natural gesturing.

Basic proposition accuracy

We tested the algorithm in the task of estimating the truth value of the 102 basic language propositions, using our test set of $61,397$ images. For each image the basic proposition's truth value was computed using the algorithm estimations, and compared to the truth value computed using the ground truth joint locations. Since we quantize continuous hand orientation angles into discrete directions, we allowed margin of +/-15 degrees between positive and negative zones, and ignore borderline cases with such low margins. In addition, for finger posture propositions, we excluded cases where the palm direction is away from the camera. For example, if a pose is defined with the palm backward, it does not make sense to add a fingertip touching condition, as fingers are occluded. This does not factor out all types of occlusions, as one finger may occlude other fingers. However, our hand pose recognizer can deal with most of these types of occlusion. Detection and false alarm rates for families of basic propositions are reported in figure 8.Left. Among the basic proposition types, finger tangency and finger relative location are the hardest to detect, since successful detection requires accurate estimation of two fingertip locations, both of which may be occluded.

Gesture recognition accuracy

Detection rates on the new gestures dataset are shown in figure 8.(Right). Most gestures are detected well, with detection rates above 90%, with the 'Swipe down' gesture as an exception with a detection rate of 78%. We found that one of the main reasons for failures is that subjects do not perform a gesture as intended, even after it is shown to them. This highlights the importance of a real time feedback mechanism

Propositions	Detection	False Alarm
Palm direction	0.99	0.001
Finger direction	0.96	0.006
Finger flexion	0.91	0.043
Finger tangency	0.86	0.019
Finger non-tangency	0.98	0.005
Finger relative location	0.87	0.018
Overall	0.92	0.014

Gesture	Detection Rate	Gesture	Detection Rate
Hang Up	1.00	Explode	1.00
Swipe Up	1.00	Mute	0.97
Like	1.00	Shoot	0.94
Lock	1.00	Flute	0.92
Bloom	1.00	Tap	0.91
Rotate Right	1.00	Swipe Down	0.78

Figure 8. (Left) Detection and false alarm rate for basic propositions. (Right) Detection rates for 12 gestures using our new data set. The average detection rate is 96%.

as part of the user experience. More generally, the system needs to understand the users' intent, not just what they do.

The false alarm rate in real-usage scenario is very low, since in realistic scenarios the users keep their hands down most of the time. In addition, most of the gestures are registered only in a specific context (for example, when a certain window is in focus), so they are active only for a fraction of the activity time. Modeling the realistic hand activity distribution is hence very inefficient as it would require gathering many hours of mostly irrelevant data. Instead, our data includes 17 minutes of intensive non-gesture hand activity, on which the false alarm rate is 1.21 (false alarms)/minute.

DISCUSSION

Our method can be measured using several different metrics:

- Can a non-expert define poses and gestures? How long does it take?
- How expressive is the proposed language?
- What is the gesture recognition accuracy?

Regarding the first question above, we have shared the gesture buidling tools with 5 software engineers and designers, with no experience in computer vision. They were all able to learn from sample code, and define poses and gestures on their own in a few minutes. Nevetheless, a more comprehensive study is required in order to estimate finer distinctions, like the preference between visual and text-based gesture definition. Regarding language expressivity, we believe an evidence for the strength of the coverage is that ASL poses are covered almost entirely, as well as standard commercial gestures.

The issue of gesture recognition accuracy is complex to estimate, and may be seperated into two levels: the accuracy at recognizing poses and gestures performed according to the formal definitions, and the accuracy at understanding user intent. As can be seen in figures 7,8.(Left), the algorithmic pipe has state of the art accuracy in finger location, and high recognition rates of the language's basic propositions. Despite being multi-staged, the system is very robust, mainly because solving for the palm global parameters, which is done in the first stages, is much easier than fingertip location done later. Specifically, the accuracy of the first stages, including palm orientation detection is very high, with 98.6 of the cases ending with very low deviations.

Understanding and interpreting correctly the user intent is more involved. For 11 of 12 defined gestures we achieve high detection rate ($> 90\%$, see Table 8). The main cause of false negatives is that some subjects performed the gesture not as the developer intended. Bridging the gap between ideal definition of a gesture and the way different subjects actually perform it, is challenging and requires expertise. Our approach conceals this complexity from the developer. For this purpose, we collected gestures from multiple subjects and tuned tolerance parameters. Still, more work is needed to improve it.

FUTURE WORK

Our language enables a rich scope of hand gestures based on varying the hand pose, but currently it lacks motion elements. Adding such elements to the language as additional basic propositions is an important route to follow. The development tools we presented here can also be improved, e.g. the current XAML representation can gain from a mechanism to avoid repeating lines of code when describing two similar poses that have a minor difference. The gesture builder lacks a clear presentation of the currently chosen basic propositions, as choices are often hidden in non-visible context menus.

In terms of interface usefulness, our work shows that general detection of certain hand poses is still challenging even with state-of-the-art hand pose estimation accuracy. Specifically, propositions of fingertip relations may benefit from additional accuracy improvements. With the current accuracy some care has to be taken to choose sets of gestures which are different enough from each other, and gesture registration is better limited to predefined contexts to avoid excessive false alarms.

There are several clear avenues for increased pose estimation accuracy in our system. One direction is the incorporation of temporal information and/or a generative 3*D* model, as in [26, 2]. This reasoning is highly complementary to the single-frame discriminative reasoning currently used in our system. Another element with a significant potential for improvement is adding a fingertip detection module to complement the currently used regression stages. This can improve accuracy for the cases where the fingertips are visible.

CONCLUSIONS

We presented a simple language for the design of a hand-gesture-based user interface, and a set of tools enabling rapid development. The algorithmic pipeline, based on fast CTE classifiers, is able to combine high speed with state of the art accuracy, and enables recognition of general gestures expressed in the proposed language. We believe the system represents an important step forward in the development and employment of general and practical gesture-based interfaces, accessible to any developer.

REFERENCES

1. 2016. Intel RealSense SDK Design Guidelines. https://software.intel.com/en-us/articles/intel-realsense-sdk-ux-design-guidelines. (2016).

2. Tagliasacchi A., Schroder M., Tkach A., Bouaziz S., Botsch M., and Pauly M. 2015. Robust articulated-ICP for real-time hand tracking. In *Computer Graphics Forum.*

3. Aharon Bar-Hillel, Eyal Krupka, and Noam Bloom. 2016. Convolutional Tables Ensemble: classification in microseconds. *CoRR* abs/1602.04489 (2016). http://arxiv.org/abs/1602.04489

4. Henry Chen, Austin S. Lee, Mark Swift, and John C. Tang. 2015. 3D Collaboration Method over HoloLens™and Skype™End Points. In *Proceedings of the 3rd International Workshop on Immersive Media Experiences*. 27–30. http://doi.acm.org/10.1145/2814347.2814350

5. Qing Chen, Nicolas D. Georganas, and Emil M. Petriu. 2007. Real-time Vision-based Hand Gesture Recognition Using Haar-like Features. In *IMTC*.

6. Chiho Choi, Ayan Sinha, Joon Hee Choi, Sujin Jang, and Karthik Ramani. 2015. A Collaborative Filtering Approach to Real-Time Hand Pose Estimation. In *ICCV*.

7. Konstantinos G. Derpanis, Richard P. Wildes, and John K. Tsotsos. 2004. Hand Gesture Recognition within a Linguistics-Based Framework. In *ECCV*.

8. Parth Rajesh Desai, Pooja Nikhil Desai, Komal Deepak Ajmera, and Khushbu Mehta. 2014. A Review Paper on Oculus Rift-A Virtual Reality Headset. *International Journal of Engineering Trends and Technology (IJETT)* 13 (2014). https://arxiv.org/ftp/arxiv/papers/1408/1408.1173.pdf

9. Ali Erol, George Bebis, Mircea Nicolescu, Richard D. Boyle, and Xander Twombly. 2007. Vision-based hand pose estimation: A review. *Comput. Vis. Image Underst.* 108, 1-2 (2007), 52–73.

10. Lucas Silva Figueiredo, Benjamin Livshits, David Molnar, and Margus Veanes. 2016. Prepose: Privacy, Security, and Reliability for Gesture-Based Programming. In *IEEE Symposium on Security and Privacy*.

11. Tomasz Hachaj and Marek R. Ogiela. 2014. Rule-based approach to recognizing human body poses and gestures in real time. *Multimedia systems* 20 (2014), 81–89.

12. Cem Keskin, Furkan Kirac, Yunus Emre Kara, and Lale Akarun. 2012. Hand pose estimation and hand shape classification using multi-layered randomized decision forests. In *ECCV*. 852–863.

13. Kenrick Kin, Bjarn Hartmann, Tony DeRose, and Maneesh Agrawala. 2012. Proton++: a customizable declarative multitouch framework. In *The 25th annual ACM symposium on User interface software and technology (UIST)*. 477–486.

14. Eyal Krupka, Alon Vinnikov, Ben Klein, Aharon Bar Hillel, Daniel Freedman, and Simon Stachniak. 2014. Discriminative Ferns Ensemble for Hand Pose Recognition. In *The IEEE Conference on Computer Vision and Pattern Recognition (CVPR)*.

15. Markus Oberweger, Paul Wohlhart, and Vincent Lepetit. 2015a. Hands Deep in Deep Learning for Hand Pose Estimation. In *Proc. Computer Vision Winter Workshop (CVWW)*.

16. Markus Oberweger, Paul Wohlhart, and Vincent Lepetit. 2015b. Training a Feedback Loop for Hand Pose Estimation. In *Proceedings of the International Conference on Computer Vision*.

17. Toby Sharp, Cem Keskin, Duncan Robertson, Jonathan Taylor, Jamie Shotton, David Kim, Christoph Rhemann, Ido Leichter, Alon Vinnikov, Yichen Wei, Daniel Freedman, Pushmeet Kohli, Eyal Krupka, Andrew Fitzgibbon, and Shahram Izadi. 2015. Accurate, Robust, and Flexible Real-time Hand Tracking. In *CHI*.

18. Jie Song, Gabor Soros, Fabrizio Pece, Sean Ryan Fanello, Shahram Izadi, Cem Keskin, and Otmar Hilliges. 2014. In-air Gestures Around Unmodified Mobile Devices. In *The ACM Symposium on User Interface Software and Technology*.

19. Lucio Davide Spano, Antonio Cisternino, Fabio Paterna, and Gianni Fenu. 2013. GestIT: a declarative and compositional framework for multiplatform gesture definition. In *The ACM SIGCHI symposium on Engineering interactive computing systems (EICS '13)*. 187–196.

20. Srinath Sridhar, Anna Maria Feit, Christian Theobalt, and Antti Oulasvirta. 2015a. Investigating the Dexterity of Multi-Finger Input for Mid-Air Text Entry. In *The ACM Conference on Human Factors in Computing Systems*. 3643–3652.

21. Srinath Sridhar, Franziska Mueller, Antti Oulasvirta, and Christian Theobalt. 2015b. Fast and Robust Hand Tracking Using Detection-Guided Optimization. In *Proceedings of Computer Vision and Pattern Recognition (CVPR)*. http://handtracker.mpi-inf.mpg.de/projects/FastHandTracker/

22. Srinath Sridhar, Antti Oulasvirta, and Christian Theobalt. 2013. Interactive Markerless Articulated Hand Motion Tracking Using RGB and Depth Data. In *ICCV*.

23. Srinath Sridhar, Helge Rhodin, Hans-Peter Seidel, Antti Oulasvirta, and Christian Theobalt. 2014. Real-time Hand Tracking Using a Sum of Anisotropic Gaussians Model. In *Proceedings of the International Conference on 3D Vision (3DV)*. 8. http://handtracker.mpi-inf.mpg.de/projects/ellipsoidtracker_3dv2014/

24. W.C. Stokoe, D. Casterline, and C. C. Croneberg. 1965. *A Dictionary of American Sign Language*. Linstok Press, Washington, DC.

25. D. Tang, H. J. Chang, A. Tejani, and T.-K. Kim. 2014. Latent regression forest: Structured estimation of 3d articulated hand posture. In *CVPR*. 3786âĂŞ3793.

26. Jonathan Taylor, Lucas Bordeaux, Thomas Cashman, Bob Corish, Cem Keskin, Toby Sharp, Eduardo Soto, David Sweeney, Julien Valentin, Benjamin Luff, Arran Topalian, Erroll Wood, Sameh Khamis, Pushmeet Kohli, Shahram Izadi, Richard Banks, Andrew Fitzgibbon, and Jamie Shotton. 2016. Efficient and Precise Interactive Hand Tracking Through Joint, Continuous Optimization of Pose and Correspondences. *ACM Trans. Graph.* 35, 4 (July 2016), 143:1–143:12.

27. Jonathan Tompson, Murphy Stein, Yann Lecun, and Ken Perlin. 2014. Real-Time Continuous Pose Recovery of Human Hands Using Convolutional Networks. *ACM Trans. Graph.* 33, 5 (2014).

Memory in Motion: The Influence of Gesture- and Touch-Based Input Modalities on Spatial Memory

Johannes Zagermann, Ulrike Pfeil, Daniel Fink, Philipp von Bauer, and Harald Reiterer
HCI Group, University of Konstanz,
{johannes.zagermann,ulrike.pfeil,daniel.immanuel.fink,philipp.bauer,harald.reiterer}@uni-konstanz.de

Figure 1. Our three different input modalities PAD, TOUCH, and MOVE used on LARGE

ABSTRACT

People's ability to remember and recall spatial information can be harnessed to improve navigation and search performances in interactive systems. In this paper, we investigate how display size and input modality influence spatial memory, especially in relation to efficiency and user satisfaction. Based on an experiment with 28 participants, we analyze the effect of three input modalities (trackpad, direct touch, and gesture-based motion controller) and two display sizes (10.6″ and 55″) on people's ability to navigate to spatially spread items and recall their positions. Our findings show that the impact of input modality and display size on spatial memory is not straightforward, but characterized by trade-offs between spatial memory, efficiency, and user satisfaction.

ACM Classification Keywords

H.5.2. User Interfaces: Input devices and strategies (e.g., mouse, touchscreen). Evaluation/methodology

Author Keywords

spatial memory; input modality; output device

INTRODUCTION

Spatial memory is a crucial aspect for successful interaction design as it takes advantage of users' ability to memorize object locations to ease navigation and search processes. Interfaces that harness users' spatial memory can profoundly reduce cognitive and physical load, support fluid interaction, and free resources to allow for better task performance [24]. Spatial memory is a fundamental component of HCI design across a wide span of everyday interactive systems. For example, it can be utilized in desktop applications to support menu navigation and icon search [21, 24]. In particular, spatial memory is an important aspect for interfaces consisting of a large digital landscape that extends the visible display space (e.g. pan and zoom interfaces in public displays, overview + detail interfaces in navigation systems). In regular use, spatial memory eventually reduces visual search leading to automatic navigation and freeing cognitive resources for the task [24].

Previous research has shown that the display size and the input modality impact on users' spatial memory and navigation performance [11, 20, 23, 24, 27, 28]. Yet, these studies investigated in- and output modalities separately, making it difficult to apply the results to real world scenarios. We believe that we need to consider the interplay of different in- and output modalities to provide valuable insights on spatial memory for everyday interactive systems (e.g. desktop applications, navigation systems, or public displays). In our work, we thus focus on the combination of in- and output modality that map current off-the-shelf interactive systems (e.g. tablets, laptops, and tabletops supporting input via trackpad, direct touch as well as gesture). Also, previous work suggests that different aspects of embodiment (e.g. touch vs. mouse [11, 28], body vs. touch panning [13], body movement [22], direct vs. indirect touch [20]) positively affect spatial memory performance. However, existing studies mostly compare input modalities that differ profoundly in their interaction techniques, not explaining how the underlying aspects of embodiment influence spatial memory. Applying the findings to settings beyond the specific conditions used in these studies is difficult. Understanding how aspects of embodiment (e.g. haptic feedback, kinesthetic cues, or direct interaction) influence spatial memory can help system designers to apply the findings to the in- and output modalities of their specific setting. Furthermore, previous research has focused on navigation path length and object location when investigating spatial memory. However, for designers to be useful, it is important to understand how spatial memory relates to aspects of usability. Looking at the definition of usability, which is divided into the aspects effectiveness, efficiency, and user satisfaction [7], we argue

CHI 2017, May 06–11, 2017, Denver, CO, USA
©2017 ACM. ISBN 978-1-4503-4655-9/17/05...$15.00
DOI: http://dx.doi.org/10.1145/3025453.3026001

that current methods can be mapped to effectiveness (e.g. how well users perform a task). However, the relations of spatial memory to efficiency and user satisfaction are unclear. In real-life scenarios, spatial memory is not detached from usability, but designers have to gauge these aspects depending on the context and the task at hand (e.g. prefer efficiency in desktop application or user satisfaction in leisure activities). In these cases, relating spatial memory to aspects of usability facilitates the incorporation of spatial memory into system design.

Our work contributes a detailed understanding of how the combination of different in- and output modalities impact on spatial memory. We also investigate the role of embodiment (e.g. kinesthetic cues, haptic feedback, direct interaction) in these effects. Analysing the influence of these aspects of embodiment not only on spatial memory but also on efficiency and user satisfaction, we tackle the question to what extent these measurements lead to coherent results. Our multi-faceted analysis accounts for complex combinations of in- and output modalities. Thus, results can be mapped onto real-world scenarios and implications can explain user behavior and support navigation and search processes in interactive systems.

RELATED WORK

In this section, we first define our understanding of spatial memory, especially in the context of HCI. Further, we summarize related studies regarding the impact of in- and output modalities on spatial memory. We explain how existing studies informed our work and led us to our research questions.

Spatial Memory

Spatial memory is described as the aspect of human cognition that enables us to acquire spatial information, for example the location of objects and places and the way to navigate to them. Once this spatial information is successfully learned and stored, spatial memory can be harnessed in order to perform navigation and search tasks with low cognitive effort [1, 24].

The prospects of a more fluid interaction when spatial memory is harnessed can also be applied to HCI. Here, spatial memory can support a user's interaction with a system by easing the cognitive effort required for navigating and manipulating an information space. Giving an extensive review of spatial memory in HCI research, Scarr et al. [24] distinguish between the components of navigation and object location memory. Interfaces that support spatial memory make use of people's ability to memorize object locations and navigation paths spatially which allows them to increase their interaction performance.

Influence of Input Modality

We identified previous studies investigating the impact of input modality on users' spatial memory. Tan et al. [28] focused on the influence of touch vs. mouse interaction on users' spatial memory. They asked 28 participants to perform a memorization task on a 18.1″ screen with an invisible grid and concluded with a 19% increased memorization accuracy for touch input. Building on this work, Jetter et al. [11] investigated the effect of multi-touch vs. mouse input on participants' navigation performance and object location memory in *panning* and *panning & zooming* interfaces. Results show that multi-touch results in better spatial memory and navigation performance for *panning* interfaces but not for *panning & zooming* interfaces. Palleis and Hussmann [20] distinguished between the influence of kinesthetic cues and direct interaction on spatial memory and navigation performance. Results show that neither of these aspects influences spatial memory, but a smaller touch input surface in the indirect touch condition resulted in a better navigation performance.

Focusing on whole body movements, Klinkhammer et al. [13] compared users' spatial memory for panning using single touch vs. body panning on a horizontal user interface. Although body panning did not result in an increased navigation performance, participants performed better with regard to object location memory. Similarly, Rädle et al. [22] investigated the effect of egocentric movements in peephole navigation of zoomable peephole interfaces, concluding with a positive effect of egocentric body movements on spatial memory.

The above mentioned studies indicate that users' spatial memory can be positively influenced by a suitable input modality, however, results on the characteristics of the optimal input modality are contradicting. Conditions that used touch performed better than mouse [11, 28]. However, when replacing the mouse with an indirect touch modality, findings show no difference in spatial memory and an improvement for navigation performance for the indirect interaction on a small input surface [20]. Conditions including whole body movement (e.g. body panning, egocentric body movements) performed better than those with less movement [13]. Our goal is to build on this existing research to further understand the influence of different aspects of embodiment (kinesthetic cues, haptic feedback, direct interaction) on spatial memory including not only touch-based but also gesture-based input modalities.

Influence of Output Modality

Previous research investigated how different visualization techniques influence spatial memory. For example, fisheye lenses [25], peephole navigation [12, 16, 23] and systems that allow for an overview [8] or focus and context view [3, 19] have been analysed to further understand how these techniques impact on navigation and object relocation. Visualizations like grids and structural alignments of items on a landscape have been found to positively effect spatial memory [15, 24].

Analyzing the influence of screen properties on spatial memory has shown that large displays lead to a greater sense of presence and a higher level of immersion which positively influences users' spatial memory performance [26, 29]. For example, Tan et al. [26, 27] showed that physically large displays increase performance on spatial tasks such as 3D navigation, mental map formation and memory tasks. Further, they found that the benefit of using a large display strongly depends on the kind of tasks performed on it: The benefit of large screens was found to be restricted to tasks in which users have to take on an egocentric strategy [26]. However, this finding could not be replicated by Tyndiuk et al. [29] who found that large displays are beneficial for both, ego- and exocentric tasks.

Tan et al. [27] also investigated users' spatial memory performance when navigating a virtual environment. Results show that users perform better in mental map formation and memory tasks on a large display because they feel more immersed into the environment compared to a small screen. Tyndiuk et al. [29] investigated the influence of display size on spatial memory and showed that not all users benefit from the use of large displays as only users with high visual selective attention abilities performed better on large displays. Rädle et al. [23] focused on peephole navigation and analyzed the effect of peephole size on users' map navigation behavior, navigation performance, and task load. They confirmed a sweet spot of a tablet-sized peephole where learning speed, navigation speed, and task load were improved.

We believe that the contradicting findings concerning the influence of display size on spatial memory performance might be due to the different input modalities that participants of previous studies worked with. Thus, we analyze the influence of display size in relation to the input modality to further understand their combined influence on spatial memory.

RESEARCH QUESTIONS

The goal of our study was to better understand how aspects of embodiment influence spatial memory. In addition, we were interested in the relation of these measures to the efficiency of task completion and user satisfaction. To this end, we defined input modality and display size as independent variables. In order to address our dependent variables, we focused on spatial memory, efficiency, and user satisfaction resulting in the following three research questions:

RQ1: How do different levels of embodiment influence spatial memory? (measured in the navigation performance and object location memory performance)

RQ2: How do different levels of embodiment influence the efficiency of task completion? (measured in navigation speed and task completion time)

RQ3: How do different levels of embodiment influence the user satisfaction? (measured in perceived task load and user experience)

Concerning the input modality we defined the three conditions (1) **PAD** (using a trackpad), (2) **TOUCH** (using direct single touch), and (3) **MOVE** (using a gesture-based motion controller). We chose these three conditions as they constitute three types of state-of-the-art input modalities: Trackpads are common features of laptops and can replace the use of a mouse especially to provide mobility. Touch technology can be seen as the main input modality for mobile devices, tabletops, and public displays. As the number of consumer devices that allow for gesture-based interaction either using additional sensing hardware like controllers (e.g. Sony PlayStation 3 Move motion controller or Nintendo's Wii Remote) or based on computational image processing (e.g. Microsoft Kinect or laptops with built-in Intel RealSense cameras) increases, we chose gesture-based interaction as a third input modality. In addition to off-the-shelf devices that allow for the individual use of the named input modalities, there is also a growing market of devices like e.g. laptops that enable all three input modalities to be used in sequence or even in combination, bringing up the question when to use which of them. We tested several arrangements and carefully considered comparable conditions to make sure that participants can handle the conditions equally well to ensure comparability and prevent problems with target acquisition. Regarding **MOVE**, we decided for an additional sensing hardware as the controller showed a higher accuracy and robustness for panning operations compared to the computational detection of a hand's position. This was also the case when dealing with arbitrary and task-dependent movements like panning or clutching. The activation of the panning-mode was more robust using the trigger of the controller compared to the detection of an additional finger gesture.

	PAD	TOUCH	MOVE
Kinesthetic Cues	–	×	×
Direct Interaction	–	×	–
Haptic Feedback	×	×	–
Activation	Touch	Touch	Trigger

Table 1. Comparison of the three different input modalities

Table 1 shows an overview of the characteristics of the three different input modalities with respect to embodiment. Our choice of input modalities allows to compare them on the basis of four aspects: (1) *kinesthetic cues* – an awareness of body's (or parts of it) position with respect to itself or to the environment [28]. For our study, we describe *kinesthetic cues* as the extent to which the user's arm movement corresponds to the actual path length, (2) *direct interaction* – here we distinguish between direct panning manipulations (TOUCH) and indirect panning manipulations using a mediator (PAD and MOVE), (3) *haptic feedback* – we consider this as direct feedback to panning a specific surface, and (4) *activation* – switching the mode between arbitrary and task-oriented movements.

The independent variable *input modality* is a within-subjects variable allowing for inner-subjects ratings of comparisons and preferences.

Concerning the output modality, we define the conditions (1) **SMALL** (display size: 10.6″, a typical size for a personal device) and (2) **LARGE** (display size: 55″, a typical size for a tabletop/public display) to account for two different scales to exhaust the respective level of embodiment. This independent variable is a between-subject variable. We expect that especially the positive influence of kinesthetic cues will result in greater spatial memory performance on the LARGE condition compared to the SMALL condition.

EXPERIMENT

This section provides an overview of the employed methods, including the apparatus, the task, participants and the procedure that we followed in our experiment.

Apparatus

Figure 1 shows the setting of our study with LARGE and the three input modalities PAD, TOUCH, and MOVE. We chose two differently sized output devices: a 10.6″ Microsoft Surface 2 Pro and a 55″ Microsoft Perceptive Pixel. Both devices had the same display resolution of 1920×1080 pixels to guarantee for a higher internal validity of the study. In the condition with the 10.6″ display, the device was placed on top and in the center of the 55″ display as our pre-test showed that it eased interaction with MOVE and TOUCH (people stepped back when placing the tablet closer). Also, this placement ensured that participants' postures were comparable for both display sizes. Next to the display, we placed a small mobile desk, which could be easily reconfigured by participants depending on their handedness. This desk was used to fill out questionnaires and to place the input devices on.

In the **TOUCH** condition, participants used the output device specific touch capabilities. For our study, we asked participants to use single touch only to ensure comparability between the three conditions. We used a Logitech T650 trackpad for the **PAD** condition, adjusting it in three ways: from a hardware perspective, we limited the area where participants could interact with it to a 16:9 ratio. This allowed us to have the same ratio of participants' movements in all conditions as the displays have the same ratio. We did this by placing an overlay on top of the trackpad itself. From a software perspective, we changed the control-display-ratio. Panning from the outer-most left position of the trackpad to its outer-most right position was equivalent to the same panning operation using TOUCH resulting in a 1:1 mapping with the output device. We adjusted the trackpad to work without additional pressing to have a comparable haptic feedback with TOUCH. These three design decisions regarding the trackpad led to a better comparability between the three conditions.

For the **MOVE** condition, we used a Sony PlayStation 3 Move motion controller (weight: 277g). We attached a PlayStation Eye Camera in bird's-eye-view directly above the display and adjusted the distance to the display to allow for an interaction space corresponding to the size of the display, which allowed us to have a comparable movement range to the TOUCH condition. The camera detected the position of the visual marker of the controller, and participants were able to pan the canvas by pulling and holding a trigger at the backside of it.

Task

We used a well-established and validated task [11, 13, 15, 16, 17, 22] consisting of a navigation phase and a subsequent object location memory phase (see the video in supplemental materials). Using one of the input modalities, a canvas could be navigated using panning operations. The canvas itself contained a 24×18 grid with a spatial configuration of 18 items in total. In the default position, a 8×6 section of the grid was visible – containing no items.

In the navigation task, the system started at the default position in the center of the canvas where no items were located. In the middle of this default position, a semi-transparent overlay of the item to be searched was shown. Participants had to find this item on the canvas and pan to its position using the condition-specific panning possibilities. Items to be searched were auto-selected as participants panned to their position with a tolerance of 100px to their center. After the item was found, the task continued at the default position with the next item. For each input modality, participants had to find 8 out of 18 items. The same sequence was repeated 6 times (6 blocks), resulting in 48 search trials. In total, each participant had three of these 48 search trials (one per input modality), resulting in 144 trials per participant and 4032 trials over all sessions.

To avoid possible learning effects, we used several item sets: (1) a demo item set containing 12 letters of the alphabet, (2) an exercise item set containing 18 symbols, and (3) three task item sets containing 18 symbols each. All item sets were exclusive without overlaps. Additionally, the items were divided equally between the different item sets with respect to their complexity and theme (devices, animals, vehicles, etc.). Also, the position of the different items and thus the total optimal navigation path length was taken into consideration with a similar length in all item sets (16729px, 16125px, and 15956px) with a randomization factor of +-3% to prevent possible influencing factors like symmetry or memorization of specific areas.

In the second phase – the object location phase – participants had to locate the presented items on their specific position on the canvas. In this phase, the entire canvas was shown, with no need for panning interaction. To locate the items, participants used the arrow keys of a keyboard to avoid influences of the specific input modality (cf. [11]). After placing an item to its position, the specific item was invisible to avoid possible mental constructs. We provide the application with all item sets and a supplemental video online.[1]

Participants

28 participants (12 female) were recruited for the experiment. As a precondition, we only invited participants that had German as their mother tongue. By this, we avoided possible influences on the memorization of the items due to different linguistic representations of foreign languages similar to [11, 15]. The mean age was 24.57 years (SD = 3.62, aged 18-32). All participants were right-handed and had normal or corrected to normal eye-sight, consequently they had no problems with the employed size of items. 21 participants were undergraduate students, 4 PhD students and 3 university employees. Participants had a mixed background ranging from computer science, to psychology, biology, educational science, and law. All participants were familiar with touch interfaces and 18 participants reported to already have used gesture-based input modalities, for example Nintendo's Wii Remote. To recruit participants, we used postings and flyers looking for people who are interested in playing games like Memory/Pairs[2], which helped us to find participants who were motivated by our chosen task. We assigned 14 participants to each display size.

Procedure

At the beginning of the study, each participant was asked to fill out a demographic questionnaire including questions about tech-savviness and eye-sight. Then, each participant received an introduction into the navigation and object relocation phases with their first input modality and a demo item set. Participants were given time to explore the functionalities of the system and input modality with an exercise data set until they felt comfortable using it. After that, participants were asked to start the navigation phase with the first input modality with the remark to navigate to the required items as fast as possible. After that, participants were asked to fill in a NASA TLX [6] and User Experience Questionnaire (UEQ) [14]. Then, participants had to relocate the position of all items on the canvas as precisely as possible. This sequence was the same for all three input modalities. In order to avoid

[1] http://hci.uni-konstanz.de/trr161

[2] https://www.ravensburger.de/start/memory/index.html

learning effects, we counterbalanced the order of input devices and the assignment of item sets by using a random selection of 14 out of 36 possible combinations for each output modality. Finally, each participant filled out a post-questionnaire concerning subjective preferences. Each session lasted about one hour in total, and participants were compensated for their time.

ANALYSIS

We chose a 2×3 factor split-plot counterbalanced study design consisting of a between-subjects part with the display size as independent variable with two conditions (SMALL and LARGE) and a within-subjects part with the input modality as independent variable with three conditions (PAD, TOUCH, and MOVE)

Data collection

We employed several data collection methods in order to investigate our research questions:

RQ1 - Spatial Memory: We focused on the task-dependent aspect of spatial memory: Navigation performance and object location memory performance. For the navigation performance, we calculated the ratio between users' actual navigation path to the shortest possible path (excluding the first search block as results for this are influenced by the randomness of initial navigation trials, cf. [11]). For the object location memory, participants were asked to position items on an empty canvas at the correct position. Here, we logged the position and calculated the Euclidean distance to its actual position in pixels.

RQ2 - Efficiency: In order to analyze the efficiency of task completion, we logged the duration participants needed to find the specific items (e.g. the task completion time in seconds for each item) and the navigation speed (pixels per second) that participants operated at.

RQ3 - Satisfaction: To analyze the user satisfaction for the investigated conditions, we used three questionnaires in total: a NASA TLX [6] was used to measure the perceived task load. The UEQ [14] provided information on the experience using the system in the different conditions. Additionally, we asked participants at the end of the experiments to rank the three input modalities and justify their preferences.

RESULTS

In this section, we report our findings in relation to our three research questions. In particular, we focus on the differences across the three different input modalities (PAD, TOUCH, and MOVE) and output devices (SMALL and LARGE) with respect to participants' spatial memory (RQ1), their efficiency (RQ2), and their subjective satisfaction (RQ3). As the data violated the assumption of normal distribution, we decided to use a non-parametric approach to analyse the data statistically. For the overall tests on statistical significance concerning the three different input modalities, we used a Friedman test. If this test showed statistical significant differences, we employed a Wilcoxon signed-rank test as a post-hoc analysis including Bonferroni correction. Additionally, a Mann-Withney-U-test was used to test for statistical significant differences between the two different display sizes.

RQ1: Spatial Memory

For spatial memory, we differentiate between navigation path and object location memory.

Navigation Path Length

Mean values for *Navigation Path Length* are shown in Table 2. Results show a statistically significant difference in the navigation path length depending on the input modality, $\chi^2(2)=6.929$, $p<.05$, irrespectively of the display size. However, a Wilcoxon signed-rank test showed no statistical significant effect between pairs after applying Bonferroni correction. A Friedman test showed no statistically significant differences on the levels of SMALL and LARGE for the three input modalities.

A Mann-Whitney-U-Test showed a statistical significant difference for the display size when comparing navigation path length for TOUCH ($U = 55.0$, $p<.05$) and MOVE ($U = 52.0$, $p<.05$).

Focusing on the navigation path across blocks, Figure 2 shows that participants performance increased over time with all input modalities. Whereas with PAD and MOVE, the navigation path seems to level off in block 5, this was found to occur earlier in TOUCH as here, the curve already bends in block 4. In addition, the lines indicating the decrease in mean navigation path length per block differ for TOUCH and MOVE when comparing SMALL and LARGE.

	PAD	TOUCH	MOVE
M_{TOTAL}	2.65 (1.10)	2.11 (0.85)	2.43 (0.97)
M_{SMALL}	2.74 (1.07)	2.43^* (0.93)	2.69^* (0.75)
M_{LARGE}	2.56 (1.17)	1.78^* (0.64)	2.18^* (1.13)

Table 2. Mean navigation path length (1.0 = optimal path length). Standard deviation (SD) is shown in brackets, statistically significant differences are indicated via asterisks (for between).

Object Location Memory

Mean values for *Object Location Memory* are shown in Table 3. Results show no statistically significant difference in the object location memory depending on the input modality ($\chi^2(2)=3.429$, $p>.05$), irrespectively of the display size. However, there was a statistically significant difference in the object location memory for LARGE, ($\chi^2(2)=7.429$, $p<.05$) – but no difference for SMALL. A Wilcoxon signed-rank test showed a statistically significant difference for a pairwise comparison of PAD and MOVE for LARGE ($Z=-2.919$, $p<.016$).

A Mann-Whitney-U-Test showed no statistically significant difference for the display size when comparing object location memory.

	PAD	TOUCH	MOVE
M_{TOTAL}	1175.12 (457.97)	1075.80 (352.63)	1059.50 (534.19)
M_{SMALL}	1107.45 (521.41)	1156.96 (399.52)	1250.64 (638.24)
M_{LARGE}	1242.79^g (392.26)	994.64 (290.61)	868.36^g (326.53)

Table 3. Mean Euclidian distance in pixels. SD is shown in brackets, statistically significant differences are indicated via raised letters (for within).

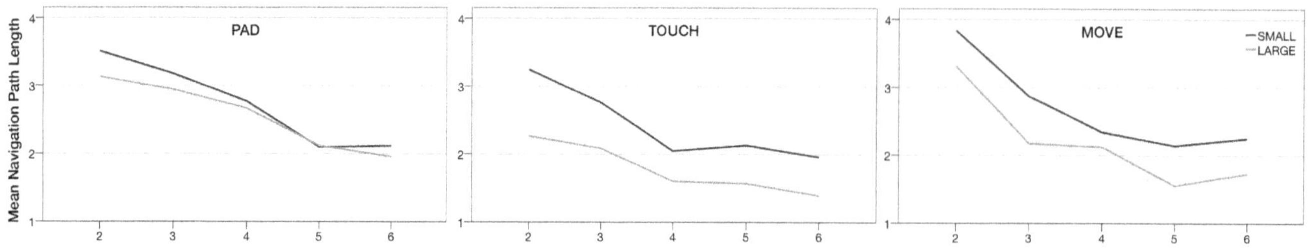

Figure 2. Mean Navigation Path Length for PAD, TOUCH, and MOVE per block. Optimal navigation path length: 1.0

RQ2: Efficiency

To provide a nuanced description of efficiency, we differentiate between navigation speed (in pixels per second) and average task completion time for each item search (in seconds).

Navigation Speed

Mean values for *Navigation Speed* are shown in Table 4. There was a statistically significant difference in the navigation speed depending on which type of input device was used, $\chi^2(2) = 30.071$, $p < .05$, irrespectively of the display size. A Wilcoxon signed-rank test showed that the navigation speed among all three input modalities was statistically significantly different: PAD-TOUCH: ($Z = -3.575$, $p < .016$), PAD-MOVE: ($Z = -4.486$, $p < .016$), TOUCH-MOVE: ($Z = -4.144$, $p < .016$).

Results show statistically significant differences in the navigation speed across the input modalities for SMALL ($\chi^2(2) = 9.000$, $p < .05$) and for LARGE ($\chi^2(2) = 24.571$, $p < .05$). A Wilcoxon signed-rank test showed that the navigation speed using SMALL was statistically significant different for pairwise comparisons of PAD and MOVE ($Z = -2.919$, $p < .016$) and for TOUCH and MOVE ($Z = -2.982$, $p < .016$). A Wilcoxon signed-rank test showed that the navigation speed on LARGE was statistically significant different for all three pairwise comparisons of input modalities: PAD-TOUCH: ($Z = -3.296$, $p < .016$), PAD-MOVE: ($Z = -3.296$, $p < .016$), TOUCH-MOVE: ($Z = -2.982$, $p < .016$).

A Mann-Whitney-U-test showed a statistical significant difference for the display size when comparing navigation speed for TOUCH ($U = 2.0$, $p < .05$) and MOVE ($U = 1.0$, $p < .05$).

	PAD	TOUCH	MOVE
M_{TOTAL}	$1421.96^{a, c}$ (456.62)	$1159.53^{b, c}$ (394.74)	$967.79^{a, b}$ (327.92)
M_{SMALL}	1499.03^{d} (581.62)	$1474.18^{e, *}$ (299.29)	$1224.72^{d, e, *}$ (266.30)
M_{LARGE}	$1344.89^{g, h}$ (286.30)	$844.89^{g, i, *}$ (144.30)	$710.87^{h, i, *}$ (101.20)

Table 4. Mean navigation speed (in pixels per second). SD is shown in brackets, statistically significant differences are indicated via asterisks (for between) or raised letters (for within).

Task Completion Time

Mean values for *Task Completion Time* for single items are shown in Table 5. Results show a statistically significant difference in the task completion time depending on the input modality, $\chi^2(2) = 22.071$, $p < .05$, irrespectively of the display size. A Wilcoxon signed-rank test showed that task completion time using MOVE was statistically significantly longer than using PAD ($Z = -4.099$, $p < .016$) and TOUCH ($Z = -2.755$, $p < .016$). There was no statistically significant difference between PAD and TOUCH.

Results also show a statistically significant difference in the task completion time depending on the input modality – for SMALL ($\chi^2(2) = 15.857$, $p < .05$) and for LARGE ($\chi^2(2) = 9.000$, $p < .05$). A Wilcoxon signed-rank test showed that the navigation time on SMALL was statistically significantly different for pairwise comparisons of PAD and MOVE ($Z = -2.480$, $p < .016$) and for TOUCH and MOVE ($Z = -2.480$, $p < .016$). A Wilcoxon signed-rank test showed that only the pairwise comparison for the task completion time using LARGE for PAD and MOVE are statistically significantly different ($Z = -3.233$, $p < .016$).

A Mann-Whitney-U-Test showed a statistically significant difference for the display size when comparing navigation time for TOUCH ($U = 55.0$, $p < .05$).

	PAD	TOUCH	MOVE
M_{TOTAL}	3.71^{a} (1.21)	3.90^{b} (1.54)	$5.31^{a, b}$ (2.17)
M_{SMALL}	3.56^{d} (0.89)	$3.37^{e, *}$ (1.14)	$4.48^{d, e}$ (1.02)
M_{LARGE}	3.87^{g} (1.48)	4.43^{*} (1.74)	6.13^{g} (2.70)

Table 5. Mean task completion time (in seconds). SD is shown in brackets, statistically significant differences are indicated via asterisks (for between) or raised letters (for within).

RQ3: User Satisfaction

For user satisfaction, we differentiate between participants' task load, their user experience and the subjective preferences of input modalities.

Task Load

Mean values for *Task Load* are shown in Table 6. Results show a statistically significant difference in the task load measured by the NASA TLX questionnaire depending on the input modality, $\chi^2(2) = 14.721$, $p < .05$, irrespectively of the display size. A Wilcoxon signed-rank test showed that the task load using MOVE was statistically significantly higher than for PAD ($Z = -3.952$, $p < .016$) and for TOUCH ($Z = -3.063$, $p < .016$). There was no statistically significant difference between PAD and TOUCH ($Z = -0.445$, $p > .016$).

Results also show a statistically significant difference when comparing the overall task load for the three different input modalities on the level of SMALL, $\chi^2(2) = 10.145$, $p < .05$. Here, a Wilcoxon signed-rank test revealed statistically significant differences for a pairwise comparison of PAD and MOVE ($Z = -3.077$, $p < .016$). However, no statistically significant difference was found on the level of LARGE.

A Mann-Whitney U-test revealed no statistically significant differences between the two display sizes.

	PAD	TOUCH	MOVE
M_{TOTAL}	31.15[a] (15.36)	32.13[b] (12.91)	44.96[a, b] (19.46)
M_{SMALL}	32.44[d] (15.76)	33.37 (9.35)	46.45[d] (19.88)
M_{LARGE}	29.87 (15.43)	30.88 (15.99)	43.46 (19.65)

Table 6. Mean user task load. SD is shown in brackets, statistically significant differences are indicated via raised letters (for within).

Analysis of mean values in the TLX subscales showed statistically significant differences for *physical demand* ($\chi^2(2)=22.691, p<.05$), *effort* ($\chi^2(2)=16.074, p<.05$), and *frustration* ($\chi^2(2)=15.340, p<.05$). Table 7 shows the mean values for these subscales.

A Wilcoxon signed-rank test showed that the *physical demand* was statistically significantly higher for MOVE when compared to PAD ($Z=-4.251, p<.016$) and TOUCH ($Z=-3.354, p<.016$). The *effort* was also statistically significantly higher for MOVE when compared to PAD ($Z=-3.321, p<.016$) and TOUCH ($Z=-3.153, p<.016$). The level of *frustration* was statistically significantly higher for MOVE when compared to PAD ($Z=-2.909, p<.016$) and TOUCH ($Z=-2.791, p<.016$). Subscales that indicated statistically significantly different mean values are shown Table 7.

A Mann-Whitney-U-Test showed a statistically significant difference for display size when comparing the subscale *performance* (U = 54.0, $p<.05$). For MOVE, participants rated their performance better on LARGE with $M_{LARGE}=33.57$, (SD = 28.04) and $M_{SMALL}=49.86$, (SD = 20.29).

	PAD	TOUCH	MOVE
Physical Demand	19.89[a] (15.76)	31.57[b] (23.56)	53.50[a, b] (24.58)
Effort	33.54[a] (21.55)	35.07[b] (19.75)	50.54[a, b] (19.94)
Frustration	23.54[a] (20.88)	22.82[b] (17.38)	39.21[a, b] (25.41)

Table 7. TLX subscales. SD is shown in brackets, statistically significant differences are indicated via raised letters (for within).

User Experience

User Experience was evaluated based on the subscales of the UEQ [14]: *attractiveness*, *perspicuity*, *efficiency*, *dependability*, *stimulation*, and *novelty*.

Irrespectively of the display size, results show no statistically significant difference in *attractiveness* depending on the input modality, $\chi^2(2)=3.448, p>.05$. However, we found statistically significant differences in *perspicuity* ($\chi^2(2)=14.673, p<.05$), *efficiency* ($\chi^2(2)=12.250, p<.05.$), *dependability* ($\chi^2(2)=18.780, p<.05.$), *stimulation* ($\chi^2(2)=6.928, p<.05.$), and *novelty* ($\chi^2(2)=21.189, p<.05.$). Mean values for these subscales are shown in Table 8.

A Wilcoxon signed-rank test showed that the *perspicuity* was ranked better for PAD compared to MOVE ($Z=-2.916, p<.016$), and for TOUCH compared to MOVE ($Z=-3.078, p<.016$). Also, the *efficiency* was evaluated likewise with $Z=-3.623, p<.016$ for the comparison of PAD with MOVE and $Z=-3.180, p<.016$ for the comparison of TOUCH and MOVE. The *dependability* was ranked higher for PAD in comparison to MOVE ($Z=-3.746, p<.016$) and for TOUCH in comparison to MOVE ($Z=-3.993, p<.016$). The post-hoc analysis showed no statistically significant differences for the scale of *stimulation* after Bonferroni correction. The *novelty* was ranked highest for MOVE and lowest for PAD. Pairwise comparisons showed statistically significant differences between PAD and TOUCH ($Z=-2.502, p<.016$), PAD and MOVE ($Z=-3.695, p<.016$), and TOUCH and MOVE ($Z=-3.182, p<.016$).

Additionally, a Mann-Whitney U-test showed a statistically significant difference for display size when comparing *novelty* for PAD (U = 48.5, $p<.05$, with M_{LARGE} = 0.57, (SD = 0.89) and M_{SMALL} = −0.30, (SD = 0.84)), and TOUCH (U = 47.5, $p<.05$, with M_{LARGE} = 1.00, (SD = 0.73) and M_{SMALL} = 0.09, (SD = 1.02)). In these two conditions, LARGE led to a more novel impression of PAD and TOUCH.

	PAD	TOUCH	MOVE
Perspicuity	1.87[a] (1.16)	2.12[b] (0.78)	1.21[a, b] (1.21)
Efficiency	1.23[a] (0.92)	1.16[b] (0.88)	0.21[a, b] (1.04)
Dependability	1.65[a] (0.76)	1.81[b] (0.56)	0.69[a, b] (1.15)
Novelty	0.13[a, c] (1.27)	0.55[b, c] (0.99)	1.29[a, b] (1.12)

Table 8. Subscales of the UEQ. SD is shown in brackets, statistically significant differences are indicated via raised letters (for within). Semantic Differential: Min: −3, Max: 3.

Subjective Preferences

Concerning the subjective preferences of input modalities, we asked participants to rank them. For analysis, we gave input modalities scores based on their ranked position (e.g. 1 for the input device ranked best, 2 for the one ranked second, and 3 for the least preferred input modality). Table 9 shows the mean scores based on the given ranks.

	PAD	TOUCH	MOVE
M_{TOTAL}	1.71 (0.71)	1.68 (0.77)	2.61 (0.63)
M_{SMALL}	1.79 (0.70)	1.50 (0.76)	2.71 (0.47)
M_{LARGE}	1.64 (0.74)	1.86 (0.77)	2.50 (0.76)

Table 9. Subjective Preferences. SD is shown in brackets.

Results show that participants preferred PAD and TOUCH compared to the MOVE condition. PAD was rated best by 12 participants. Concerning the PAD, participants specifically preferred the "quick, efficient and easy interaction" (P14) and the possibility for "fast navigation" (P19). In addition, participants liked the fact that it required "less movement" (P10) than the other conditions. Fourteen participants rated TOUCH as their favourite input modality. Concerning TOUCH, participants specifically liked the "intuitive interaction" (P20) and the "direct manipulation" (P4) that allowed for a "good overview over the canvas" (P28) and a "direct way of navigating towards the items" (P11). Out of 28 participants, 19 ranked MOVE to be the least preferred input device. Reasons for that were mostly the "cumbersome" (P32) interaction as participants often felt that navigation was "jerky" (P9). In particular, the use of the trigger was perceived as "disruptive" (P15).

DISCUSSION

In our discussion, we address the three research questions (RQ1 - RQ3) regarding the aspects of spatial memory, efficiency, and user satisfaction.

Spatial Memory

Regarding the performance of spatial memory, we measured the navigation performance (ratio of actual navigation path and shortest possible path) and participants' object location memory (distances of the placed items to the correct location in the reconstruction task). Our results concerning the two measurements match, however they contradict the results regarding the efficiency of task completion.

Our results show that the display size has a positive impact on the navigation performance in the conditions TOUCH and MOVE. With these two input modalities, participants performed statistically significantly better in the LARGE condition. These findings are similar to previous research that a larger display positively influences spatial memory [27], however our findings show that this is only the case for interaction modalities that provide kinesthetic cues (TOUCH and MOVE), suggesting that this effect only occurs when arm movements are sufficiently large. We could also observe that TOUCH resulted in a steeper learning curve for navigation path length across the blocks, levelling off earlier than those for PAD and MOVE (see Figure 2). Our findings are in line with previous research that kinesthetic cues and direct interaction improve navigation performance in panning interfaces [11, 28].

Results regarding the object location memory go even further, showing more accuracy for MOVE. This effect was statistically significantly different between PAD and MOVE for LARGE. However, differences between TOUCH and PAD were not statistically significant. This finding resonates with [20] as spatial memory was not found to be influenced by direct interaction in touch-based interaction. Nonetheless, the statistically significant improvement for MOVE in LARGE suggests that kinesthetic cues in gesture-based interaction indeed positively impact on spatial memory.

In summary, we conclude that embodiment impacts on the performance of spatial memory, as kinesthetic cues in the LARGE condition lead to better navigation performance when working with TOUCH and MOVE. In addition, object location memory performance is increased when interacting with MOVE suggesting that – in gesture-based interaction – the involvement of kinesthetic cues does not only lead to a better navigation performance but also positively influences object location memory. This finding could not be replicated for touch-based interaction.

Efficiency

Regarding the efficiency, we were particularly interested in how the different aspects of embodiment impact on participants' navigation speed and task completion time. Although, we assumed that these two measurements should be correlated, our results showed unexpected differences regarding these two measurements between the different input modalities and display sizes.

As expected, PAD resulted in statistically significantly higher navigation speed compared to TOUCH and MOVE. We believe that this result is due to the 1:1 mapping of PAD to the display size. Thus, kinesthetic cues can hamper efficiency by forcing the user to engage in larger arm movements. Interestingly, there was also a statistically significant difference in navigation speed between TOUCH and MOVE, showing that TOUCH was statistically significantly faster. This finding is interesting as the difference in motor activity between these conditions is marginal. However, in addition to the arm movement, participants had to handle MOVE (e.g. pull the trigger) which might have caused them to move at a slower speed. In the TOUCH condition, there was no such device interference. In addition, MOVE required participants to lift their arms, which might have caused fatigue as another possible reason for slower navigation speed.

Our results show that display size positively influences spatial memory when using TOUCH and MOVE, as a smaller display increased the navigation speed for these modalities. This finding was expected as SMALL requires less motor activity. This was not the case for PAD which allowed for equally fast interaction across SMALL and LARGE.

The increase of navigation speed was only partially transferred into task completion time. Although interacting with PAD still resulted in faster task completion time, TOUCH reached similar results and the statistically significant difference found between these input modalities concerning navigation speed diminished when measuring task completion time. This is in line with previous research who did not find statistically significant differences in task completion time between direct and indirect touch input [20]. In our study, PAD and TOUCH resulted in statistically significant faster task completion times than MOVE. These results suggest that the haptic feedback in TOUCH allowed for similar task completion times by compensating for the slower navigation speed. We suspect that it might be a more accurate way of navigating to the item that allowed participants using TOUCH to reach similar task completion times than participants using the PAD. Alternatively, another interpretation might be that PAD allowed for navigation at such a fast speed that users were not able to keep up with. This resulted in the fact that the headstart in navigation speed could not be held concerning the task completion time.

MOVE resulted in statistically significant longer task completion times than both, PAD and TOUCH. This shows that participants were not able to apply a strategy that compensated for the slower navigation speed resulting in correlating results of slower navigation speed and slower task completion time for MOVE. We suspect that they had to focus on the interaction with the device when using MOVE, which negatively affected both, the navigation speed and task completion time.

In summary, we conclude that embodiment also affects the efficiency of task completion, as larger motor activities result in slower navigation speed. However, we also showed that parts of the slower navigation speed can be compensated for in TOUCH but not in MOVE. This suggests that haptic feedback allows participants to compensate for slower navigation speed resulting in faster task completion times.

User Satisfaction

Regarding the user satisfaction, we were particularly interested in users' subjective rating of their task load (measured with the NASA TLX [6]) and their user experience (measured with the UEQ [14]). Results of these two questionnaires show that irrespectively of the display size, participants rated MOVE differently compared to PAD and TOUCH.

Results of the NASA TLX show that there are statistically significant differences regarding the task load across the three input modalities. Post-hoc tests revealed that MOVE resulted in a statistically significantly higher task load. Looking at the subscales, MOVE was rated with a statistically significantly higher task load onto the user with respect to *physical demand*, *effort*, and *frustration*. Physically handling the device in addition to the kinesthetic movement might have caused the physical demand. We believe that the novel way of interaction required users to put more effort into using the device and problems during usage might have caused frustration. When looking at the results of the UEQ, we can observe similar patterns: Here, TOUCH and PAD scored statistically significant better in the subcategories *perspicuity*, *efficiency*, and *dependability*, reflecting the benefits of the approved and long-learned interaction modalities. As MOVE was also rated to be statistically significantly more novel than the other two modalities, we believe that it might be due to this novelty, that it was scored lower on the other scales of user experience. As expected, the display size did not profoundly impact on the user satisfaction, as the only difference was that PAD and TOUCH were rated statistically significant more novel in the LARGE condition.

In summary, we conclude that both TOUCH and PAD are rated equally well, both regarding the subjective task load, and the user experience. However, MOVE was perceived to acquire a higher task load and resulted in a lower user experience. Although this is in line with our findings regarding the efficiency of interaction, it contradicts our findings regarding spatial memory. Higher efficiency and user satisfaction for PAD and TOUCH was not reflected in the spatial memory performance.

LIMITATIONS

The accuracy and the general behavior of the different input modalities might have influenced participants when solving the task: The 1:1 mapping of PAD and thus the resulting possible navigation speed might have been unfamiliar to participants as most of them are used to classic control-display ratios of off-the-shelf laptops. Also, the novelty and unfamiliar experience using MOVE might have influenced participants' interaction behavior. The visual representation of items, which differed in their size regarding the two display sizes, can be seen as another possible influence. The perceived visual representation of items on LARGE was larger in contrast to SMALL, which might have biased the memorization of items.

IMPLICATIONS FOR DESIGN AND RESEARCH

Summarizing, our results show that embodiment indeed impacts on spatial memory, however not in a straightforward way. Our measurements regarding efficiency showed that larger kinesthetic cues (arm movements) resulted in slower navigation speed which also negatively influenced the overall task completion time. However, TOUCH (with its direct interaction and haptic feedback) mediated this effect by guiding towards a more accurate way of interaction. We name this phenomena the *Efficiency vs. Spatial Memory* trade-off. The longer it took participants to use the modality and complete the task, the more they engaged with the items and remembered them resulting in better spatial memory performance. In addition, our results also showed that embodiment as implemented in MOVE (gesture-interaction with additional device) was rated quite negatively with regard to user experience and task workload. However, it also had a positive impact on the performance of spatial memory (maybe due to the inconvenience of the interaction). We name this phenomena the *User Satisfaction vs. Spatial Memory* trade-off.

In the following sections, we discuss how the two trade-offs can be exploited to influence users' interaction patterns with regard to spatial memory. We discuss the implications of our results for practitioners and show how they can be used to inform design decisions.

Efficiency vs. Spatial Memory

This trade-off is especially reflected in the strategy employed when working with PAD. For PAD, participants made use of the increased interaction speed, resulting in fast interaction and short task completion times. However, this high speed came at a cost regarding spatial memory performance, as users seemed to be less accurate when navigating towards an item and performed less accurate in object relocation. Regarding navigation performance, Figure 3 (participants had to navigate to the item at the left) exemplifies that participants using PAD tended to overshoot and diverted from the optimal path towards the end (when they could already see the item). This suggests that with PAD, participants were less careful to navigate accurately. Contrary to that, participants working with TOUCH and MOVE interacted in a slower pace, however being more careful in their navigation precision (compare Figure 3 in the middle and on the right). Working with TOUCH, this precision led to surprisingly fast task completion times. Working with MOVE, it resulted in high object location memory.

Regarding the display size, participants working with TOUCH and MOVE benefit from larger kinesthetic movements and thus a larger display as it improves their navigation performance, however no statistically significant differences between the two display sizes could be found regarding the object location memory. Using PAD, no benefits could be gained when working on a larger display.

For designers, knowing about the trade-off between efficiency and spatial memory can bear important implications: Depending on the task and context, designers need to account for the specific input modality. For example, desktop applications (especially for laptops) are often designed for the interaction with a trackpad. Knowing that this modality scores high on efficient interaction, designers are encouraged to compensate for the flipside of the coin: a lower performance in spatial memory. As the indirect mapping of this input leads to more speed, long navigation distances can be easily compensated for. However, this comes at the cost of a less accurate navigation and a lower accuracy in object relocation. Thus, great care should be taken to support spatial memory from an application perspective, for example by easing target acquisition (e.g. with iceberg targets [31, p. 76], accounting for low accuracy) or

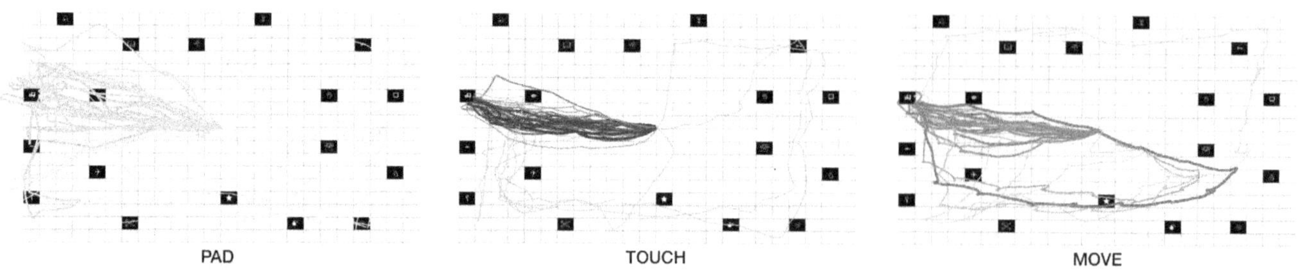

Figure 3. Visualizations of navigation paths for the subset of participants navigating to the same item on LARGE using PAD, TOUCH and MOVE. The thickness of the paths visualize the sequence of trials. Early trials are thinner.

by providing additional visual cues like e.g. landmarks [30], Halos [2], or Wedges [5], accounting for lower object location memory performance.

On the other hand, when designing systems for large interactive surfaces in public settings (e.g. in a museum or in a tourist information store), touch interaction is often chosen to allow for direct manipulation. Our findings show that such a direct mapping of input and output leads to slower navigation speed, especially for large displays. On the other hand, we could also show that the haptic feedback in TOUCH supports a high precision in navigation performance. We therefore encourage designers to compensate for the slower navigation speed. We recommend to allow for interaction on different levels of detail to increase the efficiency of task completion (e.g. by using interactive overview + detail visualizations [4]).

User Satisfaction vs. Spatial Memory

This trade-off is best reflected in the interaction patterns with MOVE. Interacting with MOVE not only resulted in a low efficiency but also led to frustration. The novelty of the device hampered user interaction, and caused the user to focus more on the device than on the task. This led to slower task completion times and lower user satisfaction. Although using MOVE on LARGE led to even lower efficiency (slower navigation speed and longer task completion time), it had a positive impact on spatial memory (navigation path length and object location memory). Especially when working on LARGE, the combination of kinesthetic cues and additional effort to interact with the device led to a shorter navigation path and better object location memory. This discrepancy in our findings between user satisfaction and spatial memory performance is in line with the "performance-preference dissociation" [9, 10, 18] that states that "people are not necessarily performing best with the interfaces they prefer" [10]. Although spatial memory performance was best when interacting with MOVE, participants clearly rated this input modality lowest.

We strongly recommend designers to carefully take into account the trade-off between user satisfaction and spatial memory in the design of interactive systems. Especially in use cases that work with gesture input (e.g. in-car settings or in sterile environments like the operating theatre), care has to be taken to make use of the high spatial memory performance in order to alleviate the low subjective rating concerning task load and user experience. We therefore suggest to allow for the customization of the interface by the user as this increases satisfaction [24] but also nurtures spatial memory due to conscious and explicit individual configuration activities.

Our findings show that especially with gestural input, participants can well remember the navigation path to get to an item as well as the absolute position of that item on a digital landscape. However, the complexity of the input procedure itself was considered to be cumbersome and frustrating. The realization of a gesture should therefore place as little effort as possible to the user [24] to allow for easy and smooth interaction. Future research could also focus on the role of performing gestures without an additional device.

CONCLUSION

In this paper, we studied the effects of different levels of embodiment on participants' spatial memory, from different perspectives that formed our research questions: spatial memory performance, efficiency, and user satisfaction. We conducted an experiment using a well-established task and item set and studied individuals working on three different input modalities and two output devices. In detail, we focused on aspects like navigation paths and object location memory (spatial memory), navigation speed and task completion time (efficiency), and subjective preferences, user experience and task load (user satisfaction).

We were able to identify effects of different combinations of off-the-shelf in- and output modalities, which helped us to come up with a nuanced description of the influences of different aspects of embodiment. Relating traditional measurements for spatial memory to additional, usability-based measurements provides a first step towards interactive systems that rely on both: Exploitation of a user's spatial memory while providing efficient and satisfying interaction.

Rather than rating interaction modalities and display sizes with respect to their impact on spatial memory, our findings show that participants engage in different interaction strategies when working in different conditions. Depending on the interaction modality and the display size, we identified two trade-offs: The *Efficiency vs. Spatial Memory* trade-off shows that navigation speed negatively correlates with the navigation and spatial memory performance, and the *User Satisfaction vs. Spatial Memory* trade-off shows that a subjective user satisfaction score negatively correlates with the performance of spatial memory. Thus, the interrelation of user satisfaction, efficiency, and spatial memory leads to different usage patterns that participants take on to fulfil the task at hand.

ACKNOWLEDGMENTS

We thank the German Research Foundation (DFG) for financial support within project C01 of SFB/Transregio 161.

REFERENCES

1. Gary L Allen. 2004. *Human spatial memory: Remembering where*. Psychology Press.
2. Patrick Baudisch and Ruth Rosenholtz. 2003. Halo: A Technique for Visualizing Off-screen Objects. In *Proceedings of the SIGCHI Conference on Human Factors in Computing Systems (CHI '03)*. ACM, New York, NY, USA, 481–488. DOI: http://dx.doi.org/10.1145/642611.642695
3. Simon Butscher and Harald Reiterer. 2016. Applying Guidelines for the Design of Distortions on Focus+Context Interfaces. In *Proceedings of the International Working Conference on Advanced Visual Interfaces (AVI '16)*. ACM, New York, NY, USA, 244–247. DOI: http://dx.doi.org/10.1145/2909132.2909284
4. Andy Cockburn, Amy Karlson, and Benjamin B. Bederson. 2009. A Review of Overview+Detail, Zooming, and Focus+Context Interfaces. *ACM Comput. Surv.* 41, 1, Article 2 (Jan. 2009), 31 pages. DOI: http://dx.doi.org/10.1145/1456650.1456652
5. Sean Gustafson, Patrick Baudisch, Carl Gutwin, and Pourang Irani. 2008. Wedge: Clutter-free Visualization of Off-screen Locations. In *Proceedings of the SIGCHI Conference on Human Factors in Computing Systems (CHI '08)*. ACM, New York, NY, USA, 787–796. DOI: http://dx.doi.org/10.1145/1357054.1357179
6. Sandra G. Hart and Lowell E Staveland. 1988. Development of NASA-TLX (Task Load Index): Results of empirical and theoretical research. *Human mental workload* 1, 3 (1988), 139–183.
7. Kasper Hornbæk. 2006. Current Practice in Measuring Usability: Challenges to Usability Studies and Research. *Int. J. Hum.-Comput. Stud.* 64, 2 (Feb. 2006), 79–102.
8. Kasper Hornbæk, Benjamin B. Bederson, and Catherine Plaisant. 2002. Navigation Patterns and Usability of Zoomable User Interfaces with and Without an Overview. *ACM Trans. Comput.-Hum. Interact.* 9, 4 (Dec. 2002), 362–389. DOI: http://dx.doi.org/10.1145/586081.586086
9. Kasper Hornbæk and Effie Lai-Chong Law. 2007. Meta-analysis of Correlations Among Usability Measures. In *Proceedings of the SIGCHI Conference on Human Factors in Computing Systems (CHI '07)*. ACM, New York, NY, USA, 617–626. DOI: http://dx.doi.org/10.1145/1240624.1240722
10. Mikkel R. Jakobsen, Yvonne Jansen, Sebastian Boring, and Kasper Hornbæk. 2015. *Should I Stay or Should I Go? Selecting Between Touch and Mid-Air Gestures for Large-Display Interaction*. Springer International Publishing, Cham, 455–473. DOI: http://dx.doi.org/10.1007/978-3-319-22698-9_31
11. Hans-Christian Jetter, Svenja Leifert, Jens Gerken, Sören Schubert, and Harald Reiterer. 2012. Does (Multi-)Touch Aid Users' Spatial Memory and Navigation in 'Panning' and in 'Zooming & Panning' UIs?. In *Proceedings of the International Working Conference on Advanced Visual Interfaces (AVI '12)*. ACM, New York, NY, USA, 83–90. DOI: http://dx.doi.org/10.1145/2254556.2254575
12. Bonifaz Kaufmann and David Ahlström. 2013. Studying Spatial Memory and Map Navigation Performance on Projector Phones with Peephole Interaction. In *Proceedings of the SIGCHI Conference on Human Factors in Computing Systems (CHI '13)*. ACM, New York, NY, USA, 3173–3176. DOI: http://dx.doi.org/10.1145/2470654.2466434
13. Daniel Klinkhammer, Jan Oke Tennie, Paula Erdoes, and Harald Reiterer. 2013. Body Panning: A Movement-based Navigation Technique for Large Interactive Surfaces. In *Proceedings of the 2013 ACM International Conference on Interactive Tabletops and Surfaces (ITS '13)*. ACM, New York, NY, USA, 37–40. DOI: http://dx.doi.org/10.1145/2512349.2512822
14. Bettina Laugwitz, Theo Held, and Martin Schrepp. 2008. Construction and evaluation of a user experience questionnaire. In *Symposium of the Austrian HCI and Usability Engineering Group*. Springer, 63–76.
15. Svenja Leifert. 2011. The Influence of Grids on Spatial and Content Memory. In *CHI '11 Extended Abstracts on Human Factors in Computing Systems (CHI EA '11)*. ACM, New York, NY, USA, 941–946. DOI: http://dx.doi.org/10.1145/1979742.1979522
16. Jens Müller, Roman Rädle, Hans-Christian Jetter, and Harald Reiterer. 2015. An Experimental Comparison of Vertical and Horizontal Dynamic Peephole Navigation. In *Proceedings of the 33rd Annual ACM Conference on Human Factors in Computing Systems (CHI '15)*. ACM, New York, NY, USA, 1523–1526. DOI: http://dx.doi.org/10.1145/2702123.2702227
17. Jens Müller, Roman Rädle, and Harald Reiterer. 2016. Virtual Objects As Spatial Cues in Collaborative Mixed Reality Environments: How They Shape Communication Behavior and User Task Load. In *Proceedings of the 2016 CHI Conference on Human Factors in Computing Systems (CHI '16)*. ACM, New York, NY, USA, 1245–1249. DOI: http://dx.doi.org/10.1145/2858036.2858043
18. Jakob Nielsen and Jonathan Levy. 1994. Measuring Usability: Preference vs. Performance. *Commun. ACM* 37, 4 (April 1994), 66–75. DOI: http://dx.doi.org/10.1145/175276.175282
19. Kenton O'Hara, Abigail Sellen, and Richard Bentley. 1999. Supporting Memory for Spatial Location While Reading from Small Displays. In *CHI '99 Extended Abstracts on Human Factors in Computing Systems (CHI EA '99)*. ACM, New York, NY, USA, 220–221.
20. Henri Palleis and Heinrich Hussmann. 2016. Indirect 2D Touch Panning: How Does It Affect Spatial Memory and Navigation Performance?. In *Proceedings of the 2016 CHI Conference on Human Factors in Computing Systems (CHI '16)*. ACM, New York, NY, USA, 1947–1951. DOI: http://dx.doi.org/10.1145/2858036.2858334

21. Kathrin Probst. 2016. *Peripheral Interaction in Desktop Computing: Why It's Worth Stepping Beyond Traditional Mouse and Keyboard*. Springer International Publishing, Cham, 183–205. DOI: http://dx.doi.org/10.1007/978-3-319-29523-7_9

22. Roman Rädle, Hans-Christian Jetter, Simon Butscher, and Harald Reiterer. 2013. The Effect of Egocentric Body Movements on Users' Navigation Performance and Spatial Memory in Zoomable User Interfaces. In *Proceedings of the 2013 ACM International Conference on Interactive Tabletops and Surfaces (ITS '13)*. ACM, New York, NY, USA, 23–32. DOI: http://dx.doi.org/10.1145/2512349.2512811

23. Roman Rädle, Hans-Christian Jetter, Jens Müller, and Harald Reiterer. 2014. Bigger is Not Always Better: Display Size, Performance, and Task Load During Peephole Map Navigation. In *Proceedings of the SIGCHI Conference on Human Factors in Computing Systems (CHI '14)*. ACM, New York, NY, USA, 4127–4136. DOI: http://dx.doi.org/10.1145/2556288.2557071

24. Joey Scarr, Andy Cockburn, and Carl Gutwin. 2012. Supporting and exploiting spatial memory in user interfaces. *Interaction* 6, 1 (2012), 1–84.

25. Amy Skopik and Carl Gutwin. 2005. Improving Revisitation in Fisheye Views with Visit Wear. In *Proceedings of the SIGCHI Conference on Human Factors in Computing Systems (CHI '05)*. ACM, New York, NY, USA, 771–780. DOI: http://dx.doi.org/10.1145/1054972.1055079

26. Desney S. Tan, Darren Gergle, Peter Scupelli, and Randy Pausch. 2003. With Similar Visual Angles, Larger Displays Improve Spatial Performance. In *Proceedings of the SIGCHI Conference on Human Factors in Computing Systems (CHI '03)*. ACM, New York, NY, USA, 217–224. DOI: http://dx.doi.org/10.1145/642611.642650

27. Desney S. Tan, Darren Gergle, Peter G. Scupelli, and Randy Pausch. 2004. Physically Large Displays Improve Path Integration in 3D Virtual Navigation Tasks. In *Proceedings of the SIGCHI Conference on Human Factors in Computing Systems (CHI '04)*. ACM, New York, NY, USA, 439–446. DOI: http://dx.doi.org/10.1145/985692.985748

28. Desney S. Tan, Randy Pausch, Jeanine K. Stefanucci, and Dennis R. Proffitt. 2002. Kinesthetic Cues Aid Spatial Memory. In *CHI '02 Extended Abstracts on Human Factors in Computing Systems (CHI EA '02)*. ACM, New York, NY, USA, 806–807. DOI: http://dx.doi.org/10.1145/506443.506607

29. F. Tyndiuk, G. Thomas, V. Lespinet-Najib, and C. Schlick. 2005. Cognitive Comparison of 3D Interaction in Front of Large vs. Small Displays. In *Proceedings of the ACM Symposium on Virtual Reality Software and Technology (VRST '05)*. ACM, New York, NY, USA, 117–123. DOI: http://dx.doi.org/10.1145/1101616.1101641

30. Norman G. Vinson. 1999. Design Guidelines for Landmarks to Support Navigation in Virtual Environments. In *Proceedings of the SIGCHI Conference on Human Factors in Computing Systems (CHI '99)*. ACM, New York, NY, USA, 278–285. DOI: http://dx.doi.org/10.1145/302979.303062

31. Daniel Wigdor and Dennis Wixon. 2011. *Brave NUI World: Designing Natural User Interfaces for Touch and Gesture* (1st ed.). Morgan Kaufmann Publishers Inc., San Francisco, CA, USA.

EarFieldSensing: A Novel In-Ear Electric Field Sensing to Enrich Wearable Gesture Input through Facial Expressions

Denys J.C. Matthies[1], Bernhard A. Strecker[1,2], Bodo Urban[1]
[1] Fraunhofer IGD Rostock, Germany, {denys.matthies, bodo.urban}@igd-r.fraunhofer.de
[2] University of Cologne, Germany, bernhard.strecker@uni-koeln.de

ABSTRACT

EarFieldSensing (EarFS) is a novel input method for mobile and wearable computing using facial expressions. Facial muscle movements induce both electric field changes and physical deformations, which are detectable with electrodes placed inside the ear canal. The chosen ear-plug form factor is rather unobtrusive and allows for facial gesture recognition while utilizing the close proximity to the face. We collected 25 facial-related gestures and used them to compare the performance levels of several electric sensing technologies (EMG, CS, EFS, *EarFS*) with varying electrode setups. Our developed wearable fine-tuned electric field sensing employs differential amplification to effectively cancel out environmental noise while still being sensitive towards small facial-movement-related electric field changes and artifacts from ear canal deformations. By comparing a mobile with a stationary scenario, we found that *EarFS* continues to perform better in a mobile scenario. Quantitative results show *EarFS* to be capable of detecting a set of 5 facial gestures with a precision of 90% while sitting and 85.2% while walking. We provide detailed instructions to enable replication of our low-cost sensing device. Applying it to different positions of our body will also allow to sense a variety of other gestures and activities.

Author Keywords

Electric field sensing, body potential sensing, facial expression control, wearable computing, hands-/eyes-free.

ACM Classification Keywords

H.5.2. [User interfaces] – Input devices and strategies.

INTRODUCTION

In Human-Computer Interaction, wearables become increasingly important, which is indicated by the prevalence of smart devices such as glasses or watches. Their tendency to engage the center of attention still hinders the interaction to become truly mobile, though. Therefore, one should reconsider how to access and to interact with technology.

CHI 2017, May 06 - 11, 2017, Denver, CO, USA

ACM 978-1-4503-4655-9/17/05…$15.00
DOI: http://dx.doi.org/10.1145/3025453.3025692

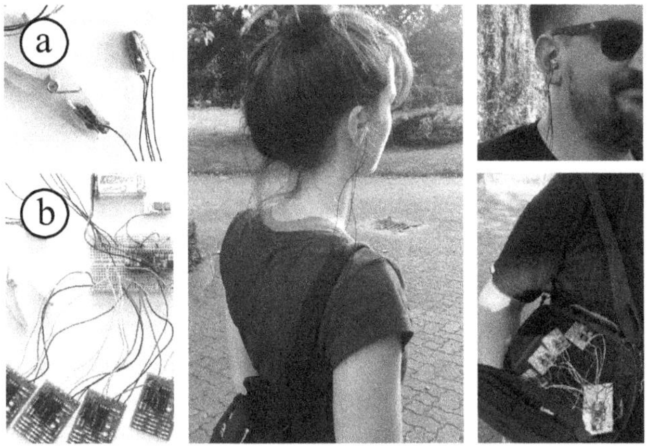

Figure 1. *EarFS* is a wearable electric field sensing device which enables to sense mobile facial-related gestures. It consists of a) an ear plug plus a reference electrode (a clothes peg that has to be attached to the ear lobe), and b) four sensing shields that are connected to an Arduino which runs on a 9V battery supply and transmits data via Bluetooth.

In 1998 already, Steve Mann stated that wearables should be: »*Unmonopolizing of the user's attention:* […] *One can attend to other matters while using the apparatus,* [while it should be] *unrestrictive to the user.*« [23]

Mann envisions wearable computers to provide situational benefits while not obstructing the user and enabling him for subtle multitasking. In contrast, most of the current interaction concepts still do not provide these qualities. Users are often distracted by current smart devices, such as mobile phones, as they usually require the user's full attention while involving the user's *hands* and *eyes*. For instance, rejecting a phone call or switching between songs on a music player forces the user to take out the device, which unnecessarily demands visual attention and occupies at least one hand. However, *EarFS* enables the user to have these interaction channels available for a potential primary task. This is especially relevant for critical tasks, such as when being involved in traffic. Therefore, we make use of a facial expression control in the manner of microinteractions »*...because they may minimize interruption; that is, they allow for a tiny burst of interaction with a device so that the user can quickly return to the task at hand.*« – Ashbrook [1]

While some facial gestures are also subtle, we potentially enable a shifting of microinteractions to the periphery of our attention [16], which matches the described affordances sketched by Mann. In this paper, we demonstrate such *hands-free* and *eyes-free peripheral microinteractions* with:

- a broad gesture set based on facial expressions, which has been evaluated with various in-ear electrode setups using different wearable technologies (EMG, CS, EFS, *EarFS*);
- a differential amplification EFS (*EarFS*), applicable for wearable computing, that is sensitive enough towards very small changes in electric fields of the human body to detect micro-gestures, such as facial expressions.

RELATED WORK

Facial-expressions, have been widely investigated in the area of affective computing [29]. Affective computing can be described as a system being able to recognize, interpret, process, and simulate human affects. Human affects can be expressed through our faces, which has been extensively investigated starting in the 1970s by Paul Ekman. In one of his fundamental works, he established a facial action coding system (FACS) which is still the ground-truth database for all facial movements and their associated emotional states [8]. Nowadays, we are able to use facial-expressions to determine the frustration level of a user. In terms of technology, two different major setups exist: (1) contact electrodes, which are attached to the face, such as electromyography (EMG) [17] or piezoelectric sensing [36], and (2) proximity sensing, which is often vision-based [13]. Still, utilizing facial expressions for gesture input has not been extensively investigated yet, as we will illustrate.

Facial Expression Control in Medical Context

A major field for application in a medical context is the support of patients, such as those suffering from locked-in syndrome [37]. A common solution is eye tracking (mostly based on vision/camera [20] or electrooculography (EOG) [11]), which can be considered as a facial expression approach. These solutions often include a displayed software keyboard on which the user focuses his vision on in order to enter text [20]. Other use cases include steering a wheelchair by gaze, as already demonstrated by Gips [12], who distributed several EOG electrodes onto the face around the eyes. Furthermore, eye blinks can be used as a binary input in order to provide locked-in patients who are unable to control their eye movements with the ability to communicate. Eye blinks can be detected with several technologies, such as electroencephalography (EEG) [39], or in an optical way [2]. Those text-input systems usually combine a typical P300 speller in scanning mode.

Sensing Technologies for Facial Activity

Technology-wise, there are various ways to detect facial expressions. In the following, we provide a rough overview:

Optical Sensing

The most commonly used technology is a vision-based camera tracking of facial expressions [10]. Obvious expressions, such as frowning, mouth movements, head movements, etc. are detectable with high precision [3,6]. Although visual processing presents one of the most effective techniques, it yields drawbacks: cameras are quickly affected by bad lighting conditions, camera-based systems are usually bulky or stationary, and very small movements, such as tongue gestures, cannot be detected sufficiently.

Electromyography (EMG)

The most rudimentary action is a binary on/off-switch, which can be achieved by measuring an emerging action potential, such as caused by contracting muscles. This has been demonstrated by San Agustin with an EMG headband that detects a frowning or a tightening of the user's jaw [34]. In TongueSee [40], 8 EMG electrodes have been attached to the cheeks and throat to detect tongue muscle movements. This setup enables the user to perform 6 different tongue gestures with an average accuracy of 94%.

Electroencephalography (EEG)

With EEG we usually measure neuro-activity on the cortical surface or within the brain by so called Brain-Computer Interfaces (BCIs). We can use BCIs as a control in two ways: by either utilizing a clean data stream or by using "artifacts" which are created through muscle activity, such as by nose wrinkling, eye blinks, and other facial expressions [27]. Matthies et al. [25] utilize eye winking, ear wiggling, and head gestures, such as nodding and shaking to control a handheld with Emotiv's mobile EEG headset. Since an EEG headset is bulky and hardly applicable in realistic scenarios, an in-ear headset consisting of a hacked NeuroSky EEG system and two gyroscopes was presented, which enables the same gesture set [24]. A similar setup, a foam earplug with two electrodes, has recently been used to classify sleep stages [28]. In our opinion, an ear-plug form factor is the least obtrusive setup.

Electrooculography (EOG)

With EOG Glasses, eye gestures, which are basically tracked eye-movements, could control smart environments such as suggested by Bulling et al. [4]. Other researchers, such as Ishimaru et al. [19], used EOG goggles to roughly identify chewing, talking, eating, and reading with an accuracy of 70%. Manabe et al. attached EOG sensors to a pair of headband headphones [21] and to an in-ear headset [22] in order to sense eye gestures. We believe that placing electrodes into an in-ear headset is rather unobtrusive and apparently offers great sensing potential.

Capacitive Sensing (CS)

Rantanen et al. [30] presented a capacitive sensing glass which is capable of detecting a frowning and a lifting of eyebrows to execute click-events with an average accuracy of 82.5%. In 2013, Rantanen et al. [31] furthermore introduced a face-hugging device which consists of 12 electrodes. They found the activation of four different muscle groups to be detectable with a proximity sensing. While these results are impressive, wearing a face-hugger is rather obtrusive since it almost covers the whole face.

Electromagnetic Sensing

In 2006, Fagan et al. [9] placed seven magnets on the lips, teeth and tongue that cause a significant change in the magnetic field when performing mouth-movements. 6 Dual axis magnetic sensors were mounted on a prepared pair of glasses, which enabled a detection of 13 phonemes with an accuracy of 94%, and 9 words with an accuracy of 97%. Even though the physical setup is quite bulky and obtrusive, the results are impressive. In 2014, Sahni et al. [32] attached only one magnet onto the tongue and utilized the built-in 3 axis magnetometer of Google Glass plus an in-ear piece measuring the optical ear canal deformations in order to detect tongue and jaw movements. They report to be capable of distinguishing 11 sentences with 90.5%.

Prior research reveals that we face a trade-off between having an obtrusive hardware setup providing quite meaningful features versus unobtrusive hardware setups that are limited in features and recognition precision. However, we believe that it is possible to find a more advantageous solution compared to those presented before – a device that is unobtrusive (such as an in-ear plug) and that still provides a reasonable feature set.

EARFIELDSENSING

We present *EarFieldSensing (EarFS)*, an improved electric field sensing device capable of sensing electrical changes in the ear canal by an in-ear electrode setup. We think, hiding a sensing device in a subtle ear plug is less obtrusive than other approaches demonstrated in literature. Also, using facial expressions for input enables for *hands-free* and *eyes-free* interaction, which is safe when operating devices, such as a smartphone, while being involved in traffic.

Contribution

As an essential part of this work, we developed an improved electric field sensing for which we provide technical details to enable reproduction of our sensing technology.

To gain insights into the performance level, we conducted a lab study to compare previous technologies with a gesture set of 25 facial-related gestures. Compared technologies:

- Electromyography – EMG (*Shimmer3*[1]),
- Capacitive Sensing – CS (*FDC2214 Texas Instruments*[2]),
- Electrical Field Sensing – EFS (*hacked OpenCapSense* [14]),
- Improved Electrical Field Sensing – *EarFS*.

A comparison of technologies in a stationary setup can reveal theoretical performance differences, but does not reflect reality, such as when the user freely moves around. Therefore, we conducted a second study in which we present more insights into performance differences in a mobile context. As a result, we found *EarFS* (*see Figure 1*) to outperform other evaluated electrical sensing technologies when it comes to the recognition of facial-related gestures in mobility while walking.

[1] Shimmer3 EMG Unit: http://www.shimmersensing.com/images/uploads/docs/Shimmer3_ECG_EMG_Specification_Sheet_Revision_1.7.pdf

[2] Texas Instruments FDC2214: http://www.ti.com/lit/ds/symlink/fdc2214.pdf

Background

In this subsection, we describe the reason of being able to sense various facial muscle movements and head gestures by placing a sensor piece into the ear canal.

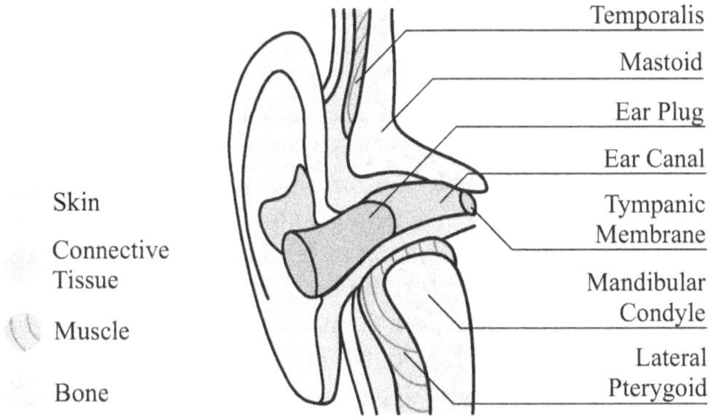

Figure 2. An ear plug enables the experience of deformations and changes in an electrical field while resting in the ear canal.

When talking of the ear canal, we mean the tunnel between Mastoid and Mandibular Condyle (*see Figure 2*). Facial expressions, such as yawning, cause an opening of the mouth which is triggered by a contraction of the Lateral Pterygoid. This process causes the Mandibular Condyle to slide forward and thus a tiny void is created, which is then filled with the surrounding tissue. A change in volume and deformed tissue creates a very different electrical field, which is detectable. Even eye movements and head movements are perceivable, although the electrical change is comparably small. As we quickly figured out, movements of the jaw are quite easily perceivable. Other muscle activities, such as raising eye brows, are apparently triggered by other muscle groups (e.g. Frontalis) located on the forehead. Still, we can sense these activities in the ear, because many facial muscles are connected with the Temporalis, the biggest muscle of the head, which forwards mechanical and electrical artifacts towards the ear canal.

Performing a manual self-test: putting the pinky inside our ear, while executing facial expressions, lets us sense these deformations.

Nature of Signals

In a spot so small as the ear canal, we measure compound electrical activity (white sensor noise, environmental noise, potential changes from muscle activity, characteristic signal peaks from ear canal deformations, and very tiny signals from neural activity such as from brainwaves). As mentioned before, ear canal deformations inducing changing electrode-skin contact play a major role. As a matter of fact, increasing skin-contact gradually decreases the electrode input impedance and leads to a transition in signal contributions, e.g. the action potentials' share of the total signal increases.

Mobile Sensing of Facial Expressions

The application of facial expression recognition via an in-ear-positioned electric field sensing is challenging and far more delicate than just recognizing hand/arm gestures. This is due to the electric field changes that are brought upon by facial muscle movements, which are much smaller in magnitude. Especially in a mobile situation, artifacts caused by walking are crucial. Nevertheless, we envision a facial gesture recognition in mobile scenarios that works independently from side-actions, such as walking, running, biking, jumping and sitting. For the example activity of walking, the user's body experiences a periodically changing capacitive coupling to ground, which substantially impacts an electric field sensing on any part of the human's body. Unfortunately, it is hard to anticipate the frequency of the signal caused by walking or running since speed levels are likely to change when the user, for example, hurries to catch a bus. Therefore, it is hard to target specific frequencies for filtering out. Moreover, these frequencies are rather low and can typically range from anywhere in between 1 to 5 Hz, which are the same frequencies that carry information of facial gestures.

Technical Solution

The first step of *EarFS* is to isolate electric field changes brought upon by facial gestures as effectively as possible while simultaneously reducing environmental artifacts, such as caused by walking. As mentioned before, an option would be to filter out periodical signals which are reappearing over a longer period of time. However, this does not solve the problem since parts of the unwanted artifacts may also overlap with signals stemming from facial expressions. A simple filtering of artifacts would possibly erase signals of facial gestures as well, because they are too marginal in amplitude in comparison to the artifacts' signal strengths. In fact, as long as artifacts occur on the signal we cannot amplify these comparably small facial gestures. Otherwise, the operational amplifiers would saturate and low magnitude facial gestures are prone to disappear in the signal. Therefore, we eliminate these high magnitude artifacts early on by isolating them beforehand and subtracting them from the original signal with a dual electrode approach as described next.

Differential Amplification using a second Electrode

Our solution uses a second "reference" electrode that needs to be placed relatively far away from the face. We then feed a difference / instrumentation amplifier with the two signals, the one gathered from the reference electrode, and the other from the in-ear electrode. This way, common-mode signals stemming from walking artifacts, which are similar on the whole body, are likely to be filtered out or at least substantially reduced. It is important to note that the placement of the reference electrode is crucial, because any limb movements may affect signals. By attaching the reference electrode to the waist, for example, the arm would create a change in electrical field while nearing or passing the reference electrode when the user walks. An ideal place

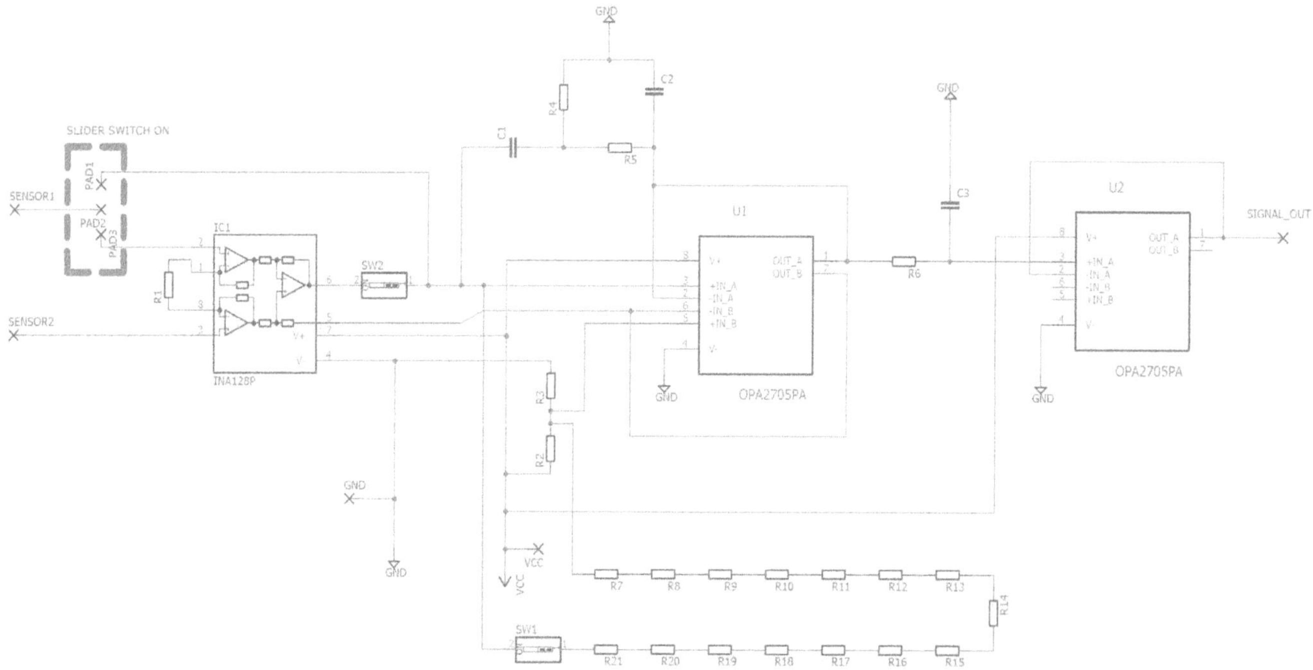

Figure 3. Schematic of the *EarFS* prototype, supporting both (1) single electrode and (2) differential electrode mode. In single electrode mode, to cover electric field changes of both polarities, a large pull-up/-down resistor is used to elevate the signal level of the earplug-electrode to half the supply voltage. We use fifteen 10 MΩ resistors (R7-21; 10 MΩ resistors are more common than 150 MΩ ones) in series between a simple voltage divider (|R2|=|R3|) and the signal path in order to pull slowly enough for detecting electric field changes. In differential mode, the INA128P instrumentation amplifier filters out environmental noise by common-mode rejection. The difference in voltage between the earplug- (SENSOR1) and earlobe-reference (SENSOR2) electrodes is expected to be rather small, so it is amplified by a factor of 5001 (R1 = 10 Ω), which is well within the gain-range of the INA128P (10k is max). Also the output signal of the INA128P is elevated to half the supply voltage. A band-pass filter (C1 = C2 = 4.7 nF, R4 = 1.8 MΩ, R5 = 390 kΩ) reduces power-hum (50 or 60 Hz) by negatively feeding it back into the signal. Based on application context, C3 & R6 can be used to implement a low-pass filter of choice. Please note: band-pass- & low-pass-filtering are not compulsory.

of the reference electrode would be a relatively stationary position that is far away from the face to get a significantly different electric potential sensing compared to the electrode placed in close proximity to the face. As a matter of fact, the electric field strength declines exponentially with distance, so the reference electrode can also be placed close to the face, such as at the backside of the neck, spine, shoulders, or at the ear lobe. While both electrodes accumulate artificats, the in-ear electrode yields a sufficiently different signal containing facial gestures that remain when subtracting both signals from each other and become visible when amplifying the subtracted signal. To our knowledge, previous work did not use differential amplification in this context before, and we seldom encounter it in HCI applications yet.

Implementation

An electric field sensing circuit was designed (*see Figure 4*), which can be used similarly to common EFS sensing circuitry, but also offers signal acquisition by amplifying a differential signal from two separate electrodes. In this mode, the *differential instrumentation amplifier* reduces and even cancels out most environmental noise.

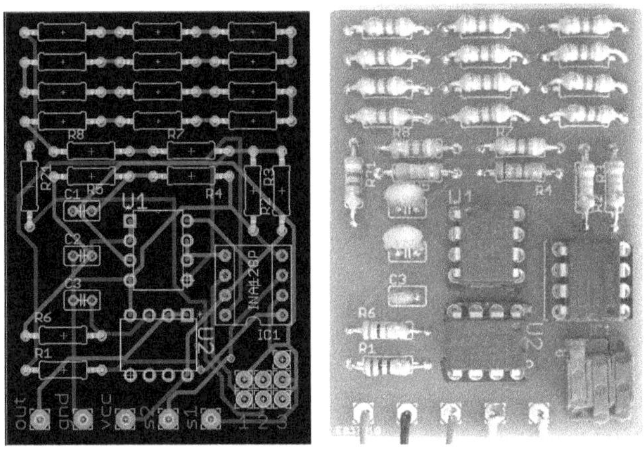

Figure 4. Left: Eagle PCB layout. U1, U2: OPA2705PA; IC1: INA128P. Right: Final *EarFS* PCB. Switches offer two modes (1) ↑↓↓ single electrode / antenna and (2) ↓↑↑ differential electrode / antenna setup.

In order to let other researchers replicate our hardware, we additionally provide the schematics of our sensing circuit (*see Figure 3*). Once the hardware is built, one can easily connect the Signal-Out Pin to the Analogue Input Pin of any microcontroller board, such as A0 on an Arduino board. As most microcontroller boards, our sensing device also runs with 5V DC.

Single Electrode Mode and Differential Mode

Three switches have been included in the circuit to allow the user to choose between (1) single-electrode / antenna setup and (2) differential electrode / antenna setup. (1) The slider switch in Figure 3's top left corner connects PAD2 to PAD1, SW2 is off and SW1 is on. (2) All three switches are being reversed – the slider switch connects PAD2 to PAD3. A pull-up/down resistor was included for single-electrode (S1) usage, so that electric field signals will return to the baseline of half V_{CC} when no change in electric fields is present. Thus, only movements that create field changes are perceivable. Concerning the differential configuration, the instrumentation amplifier was biased to half V_{CC}, so that electric potential changes of either polarity can be sensed.

STUDY 1: TECHNOLOGY PERFORMANCE

In this section, we evaluate the detection of facial-related gestures by a variety of electric sensing technologies.

Research Questions

The goal of this study was to gain an insight into the following research questions while trying to keep all variables as constant as possible (e.g., testing all setups by the same user, only testing one session per day):

Q1: How does our technology perform compared to other electric sensing technologies?

Q2: What would be the best electrode setup providing the highest accuracy rates for each technology?

Q3: Which gestures are the top 5 performing ones with the given technology?

In study 1, we were *not* yet interested in finding out about varying performance levels across users, nor the applicability in mobile scenarios. Therefore, we forfeited on testing all possible setups with multiple users in mobility.

Task and Procedure

To answer these research questions, we performed an extensive study in which we recorded 14,000 gestures (= 7 ear plugs * 2 un/covered * 25 gestures * 10 repetitions * 4 sensing technologies) from a single user. To avoid fatigue effects, we split the recordings into several sessions, which included 1 technology with all earplugs in sequential order. 25 gestures * 10 reps were recorded with each setup before insulating the earplug or taking the next one. Each gesture was recorded in a time window of 1.25s. To prevent invalid data distortion, the earplug was not rearranged during sessions. When the user was not sure about the correct execution, he was enabled to record an additional repetition. The test subject trained steady gesture execution beforehand and triggered the recording manually after being randomly presented with a gesture left in the pool of 250. A complete session contained 250 * 7 = 1750 gestures.

Facial Gesture Set

We compiled a set of 25 facial- and head-related gestures (*see Figure 5*) to compare all technologies based on their performance level. The gesture set covers a broad spectrum of which we are aware that not all of them are subtle or socially acceptable. The set was chosen for straightforward repeatability while it includes gestures involving various muscle groups. The contraction of different muscle groups presumably leads to a distinctive signal in order to identify gestures. Apart from typical gestures, such as 'eye-wink', 'smile', and 'protrude-tongue', simple speech was included as well, because speech is performed highly automated due to it being easy to memorize.

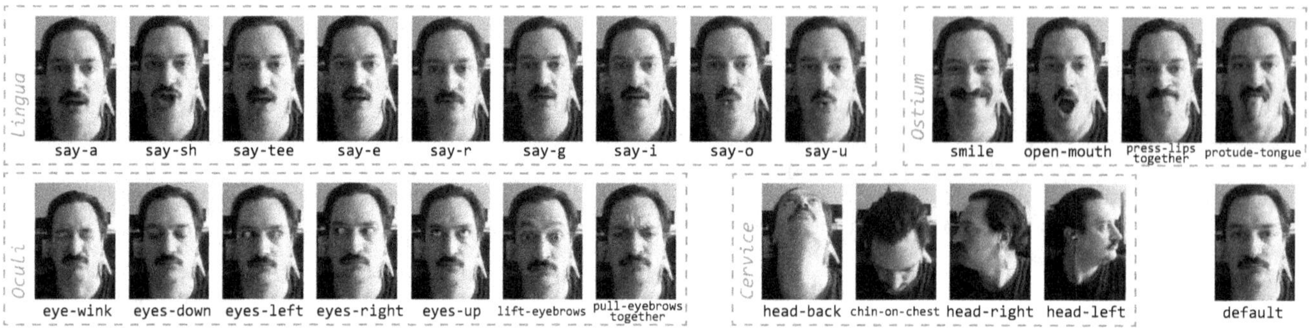

Figure 5. With a set of 25 gestures (including a default gesture) we evaluated four different technologies (EMG, CS, EFS, *EarFS*) .

Apparatus: Electrode Ear Plug

We prepared 7 earplugs which are made out of polyurethane foam and go by the name of OHROPAX Color[3] (*see Figure 6*). #1 is a single electrode wrapped around the earplug. #2h - #4h are two to four increasingly smaller electrodes wrapped horizontally around the earplug in a similar fashion. #2v - #4v have electrodes in decreasing sizes, which are vertically placed alongside the earplug. Accordingly, #2v has two electrodes, #3v has three, and #4v has four electrodes mounted on the earplug.

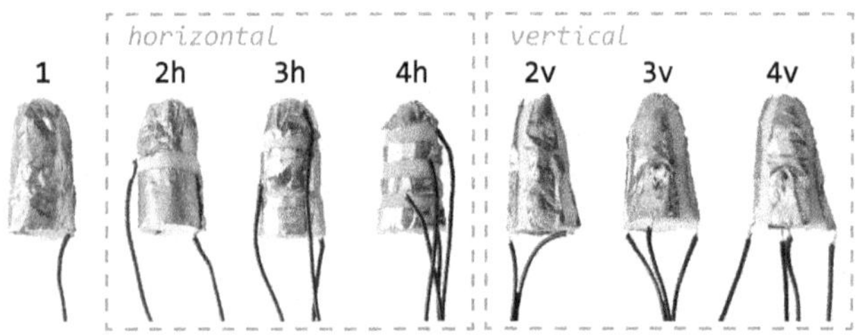

Figure 6. With 7 different electrode layouts we evaluated each technology. For us, it seemed natural arranging the electrodes lengthwise and widthwise alike with varying partitions while we used them blank (as shown), and covered.

All electrodes were cut out from copper foil, soldered to the connecting cables, and subsequently glued onto the earplugs with Pattex superglue. All 7 setups have been tested both with blank electrodes and while being covered with the cut-off tip of a common condom. The lubricant was thoroughly washed off beforehand, and remaining moisture left on the latex was dried off before conducting experiments.

Apparatus: Electromyography (EMG)

EMG is the most common technology to measure *action potentials* stemming from muscle activity, which is usually done invasively by needle electrodes. Nonetheless, the superimposed voltage is also detectable on the surface of the skin while it still shows ranges of up to -100mV [18]. In an interaction scenario, surface electrodes on the skin are typically used [33] for measuring electrical potentials through a relatively thick layer of skin and fat. For classifying gestures one can use not only a clean signal, but also noise [26] and accumulated movement artifacts [24], which occur in the ear canal when performing gestures.

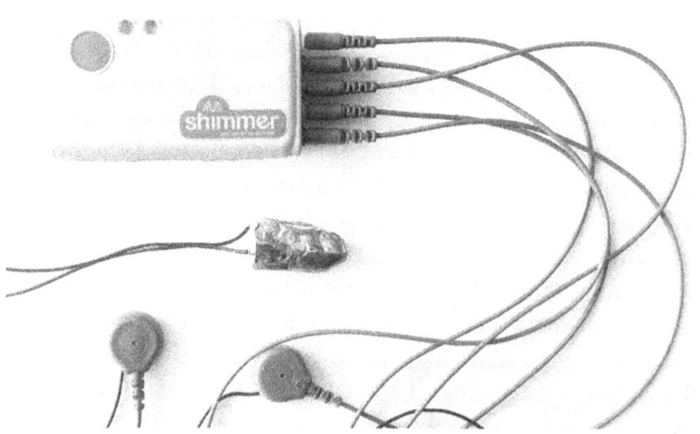

Figure 7. Shimmer3 ECG/EMG Bluetooth device, configured in EMG mode.

In our study, two Shimmer3 EXG units[1] were connected via Bluetooth to a computer (*see Figure 7*). The Shimmer Android/Java API was used to configure the EMG units and to establish communication. A suggested digital filtering (50 Hz noise cancellation and low-pass filtering for signal smoothing) was also implemented. The earplug electrodes were connected to a single channel each in the following way: The earplug-electrode was connected to the positive differential input of the Shimmer3 EMG channel and a clothespin-mounted copper foil reference electrode was clipped to the earlobe of the opposite ear that the earplug was worn in. The reference electrode was connected to the REF input of the up to three Shimmer3 units and connected to all negative differential inputs of active channels.

Apparatus: Capacitive Sensing (CS)

Capacitance describes a body's ability to store an electrical charge when a voltage is applied. The higher the electrical charge a body can store, the higher its' capacitance. As a matter of fact, the human body's cells also have the ability to store electrons and thus a negative electrical charge. Depending on the body part, we can speak of an overall capacitance varying between 50 and 150pF [35]. Excited cells, which accumulate a certain amount of electrons, create the change in capacitance. While this capacitance can be measured invasively, we can also measure it on top of the skin or in distance, such as with an isolated earplug electrode. A typical CS measures the charging time of an electrode. This is also referred to as *loading mode* [38].

[3] OHROPAX Color: http://www.ohropax.de/produkte/color.html

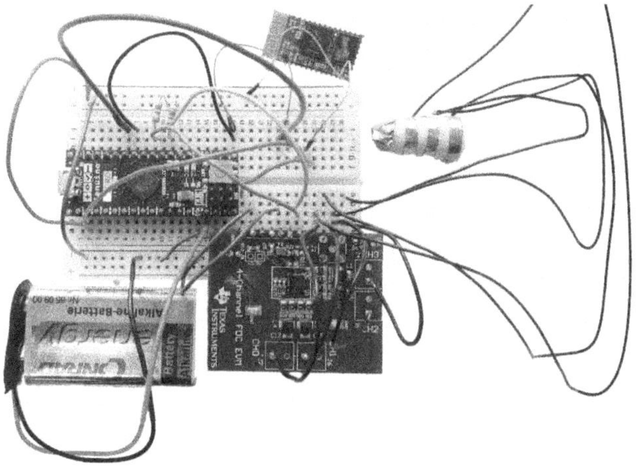

Figure 8. The Capacitive Sensing shield FDC2214 EVM from Texas Instruments was plugged to an Arduino board transmitting the raw data via a Bluetooth 2.0 modem.

The FDC2214[2] also uses capacitive sensing in *loading mode*. We connected it to a Genuino Micro streaming all raw data via an HC05 Bluetooth modem (*see Figure 8*). It is essential to use a battery plus a wireless transmission to avoid irregularities, such as a varying capacitive ground coupling triggered by other hardware components that may also be connected to the computer. To measure each of the four channels in turn, 512 oscillations were used to determine the momentary frequency of the LC oscillator circuit compared to the EVM board's 40 MHz oscillator. After each channel switch, the first 128 oscillations were not considered to allow for the frequency to stabilize.

Apparatus: Electrical Field Sensing (EFS)

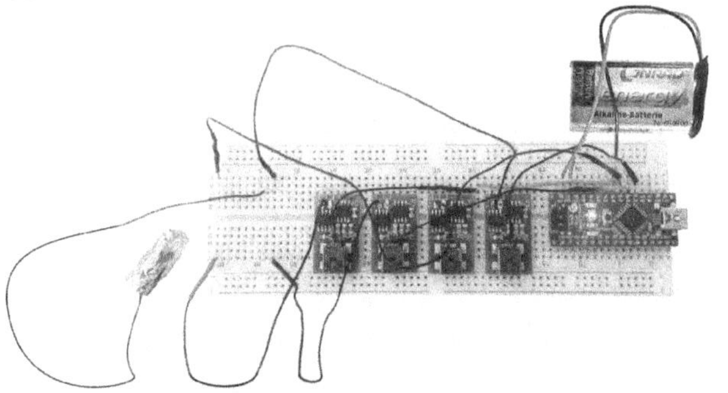

Figure 9. We "hacked" four Loading Mode capacitive sensors from OpenCapSense [14] to act like an Electric Field Sensor.

Electric fields are ubiquitous and exist due to the static electricity of our surroundings. Besides everyday objects, also the human body carries several small electrical fields. Fluctuations in electric fields quickly occur when moving the human body or other charged objects. While we can utilize electrical field changes for a gesture recognition [7], it is also perfectly suitable for an intended facial expression recognition. However, factors such as ambient noise and baseline drift are the most cumbersome obstacles that gesture recognition and classification endeavours face. Anyhow, all that is needed to implement electric field sensing is basically a "passive" electrode (i.e. antenna) with an operational amplifier connected to an analogue-to-digital converter (ADC). To compensate for noise, such as power hum, low-pass filters may apply between op-amp and ADC.

Our EFS setup consists of four „hacked" OpenCapSense *loading mode* sensors, which basically consist of an operational amplifier and an astable Multivibrator that is usually used for a capacitive measurement. However, we only utilize the op-amp whose positive input is connected to the electrode. The op-amp's output is connected to the analogue input of an Arduino Nano (*see Figure 9*), which serves as an ADC and transmits the raw data. It should be particularly noted that here, the op-amps are not connected to an external power source. However, they still output discriminable voltage based on the acquired earplug signal, which also serves as a power supply in a way that the electrode is wired to the op-amp pin right next to the negative supply pin, facilitating a discriminable voltage between the negative and positive op-amp supply pins.

Apparatus: *EarFS*

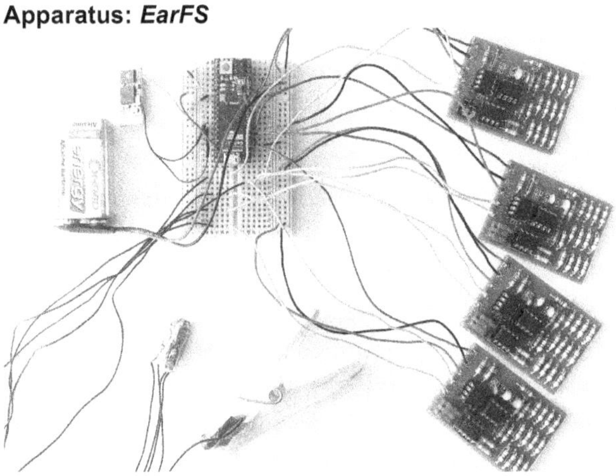

Figure 10. Four EFS shields are connected to an Arduino in order to use a four-electrode ear plug. The data is being streamed via a Bluetooth 2.0 modem to a computer, while the prototype is powered by a 9V battery.

Fluctuations in ambient electric fields can originate both from negative and positive charge balance and thus, a standard single supply op-amp design like seen before would be doomed to miss one of the polarities. Therefore, we introduce a second DC-voltage, keeping the antenna voltage at a proportionally steady and elevated level. It is wise to choose a DC-voltage of half the op-amp's supply voltage, since in this way, incoming antenna signals can deviate from the baseline voltage in the direction of both electrical polarities. When no changing electric field is present, a relatively large resistor pulls up/down the antenna voltage to the baseline voltage eventually. It should be noted that larger resistors cause longer latencies. The addition of such a pull up/down resistor with its tendency to pull the antenna voltage back to half the V_{CC} voltage is the reason that only movements and changes are measurable. In addition, we added a reference electrode (*see Figure 10*) to eliminate extrinsic changes in electrical fields with a differential amp.

		EMG (Shimmer3)			CS (FDC2214 Texas Instruments)			EFS (hacked OpenCapSense)			EarFS		
Electrodes		Average Accuracy (TP)			Average Accuracy (TP)			Average Accuracy (TP)			Average Accuracy (TP)		
blank		all 25	n≥50%	top 5	all 25	n≥50%	top 5	all 25	n≥50%	top 5	all 25	n≥50%	top 5
	1	19.2%	-	-	1.6%	-	-	1.6%	-	-	3.2%	-	-
horizontal	2	11.7%	-	-	16.8%	-	-	35.1%	-	-	5.2%	-	-
horizontal	3	4.8%	-	-	30.8	-	-	40.8%	-	-	8.8%	-	-
horizontal	4	12.8%	-	-	43.2%	-	-	39.5%	-	-	13.2%	-	-
vertical	2	**30.8%**	**4**	**84%**	12%	-	-	43.6%	-	-	13.6%	-	-
vertical	3	10.4%	-	-	34.4%	-	-	**52%**	**11**	**94.5%**	12.4%	-	-
vertical	4	19.2%	-	-	**48.4%**	**13**	**90%**	49%	-	-	**32%**	**5**	**90%**
covered													
	1	**11.6%**	**0**	**64.4%**	9.6%	-	-	4%	-	-	**5.6%**	**0**	**20%**
horizontal	2	5.6%	-	-	**38%**	**11**	**84%**	4.4%	-	-	2.8%	-	-
horizontal	3	6.4%	-	-	35.2%	-	-	5.2%	-	-	4%	-	-
horizontal	4	6.8%	-	-	21.6%	-	-	4.4%	-	-	4.8%	-	-
vertical	2	6.2%	-	-	22.4%	-	-	3.6%	-	-	4%	-	-
vertical	3	6%	-	-	29.6%	-	-	**7.6%**	**1**	**20%**	5.2%	-	-
vertical	4	3.2%	-	-	28%	-	-	5.6%	-	-	2.4%	-	-

Table 1. Performance levels using a J48 DT (C4.5 algorithm). For each technology we can find three columns: 1) true-positive (TP) rates of the complete gesture set, 2) number of gestures yielding at least 50% TP, and 3) TP score of a reduced top 5 gesture set.

Signal Gathering and Data Processing

The aforementioned electrode-earplugs have been combined with all four technologies while we recorded each gesture with a sample rate of 200 Hz and a window-size of 256. Then, we computed 46 state-of-the-art features found in literature on all raw data recordings. Because we are not aware of any library providing them, we implemented them by hand in Java. For analysing the data, we use the Weka data mining tool [11] in order to gain an impression on the performance using five state-of-the-art classifiers (*Bayes Net* - BN, *K-nearest neighbours* - Ibk, *J48 Decision Tree* – J48, *Random Forest* - RF, *Sequential Minimal Optimization* - SMO) while performing a stratified 10-fold-crossvalidation. We have chosen this method, because conducting a manual leave-$k_{instances}$-out method on our huge dataset (14.000 instances) is extremely time consuming and beyond practicality. Nevertheless, we had a quick look (k=5) at a single session (*EarFS*, 4-vertical) and could perceive a marginal accuracy drop of Δ= -1.6 %.

Results

Before presenting the result, it is important to note that we are talking of a theoretical performance level. To make a sophisticated statement on realistic recognition rates, one should have tested users n>10 in ambiguous environments (including critical environments with high level of electric noise, e.g. a server room). In this paper, we decided to keep experiments within reasonable boundaries and share early results of the exact composition with the community.

Classifier & Feature Selection

In order be able to answer our research questions, we first determined the "best" classifier. We compared all five classifiers (BN, J48, Ibk, SMO, RF) by means of an independent samples one-way ANOVA, but which showed no significant differences for EMG ($F_{4,30}$=1.14; p<.357); CS ($F_{4,30}$=0.58; p<.680); *EarFS* ($F_{4,30}$=0.06; p<.993). Nevertheless, the EFS showed strong significant differences ($F_{4,30}$=17.96; p<.0001). Conducting a Tukey HSD Test revealed the J48 (M=43.35; SD=6.25), BN (M=43.47; SD=5.50), and RF (M=37.57; SD=12.12) to perform better than the Ibk (M=20.30; SD=7.53; p<.01). Moreover, the J48 and BN were deemed to significantly perform better than the SMO (M=31.86; SD=8.29; p<.05). Beholding the mean performance over all technologies, we can perceive the J48 and the RF to perform quite well. Because the J48 is most computationally inexpensive and a rather simple classifier, we selected it for further investigations.

Across all best setups, top 5 meaningful features, selected by a *Greedy Stepwise (forwards)* algorithm [5], include: *spectralEnergy, spectralFlux, spectralSignalToNoiseRatio, minMaxDifference, and pairDifference.*

Answering Research Questions

Q1: As seen in *Table 1*, *EarFS* performs similar to other electric sensing technologies, comparing their best setups. A one-way ANOVA ($F_{3,27}$=193.91; p<.001) showed *EarFS* (M=32%) to perform equally to the EMG (M=30.8%) and EFS (M=52%) equally to CS (M=48.4%). Still, a Tukey HSD (p<.01) reveals both EFS and CS to perform significantly better among EMG and *EarFS*.

Q2: The electrode setups providing best performance are indicated in *Table 1*. Generally, we can say that non-insulated, vertically arranged electrodes perform better, because these are more sensitive towards ear-canal deformations (changing skin / electrode contact). Since the vertical electrodes are distributed in circular fashion, an increase in their number leads to higher spatial resolution inside the ear canal.

Q3: We determined a top 5 gesture set for the best setup of each technology *(see Table 2*). In fact, the recognition rates look quite reasonable and foster curiosity: EMG (M=84%), CS (M=90%), EFS (M=94.5%), and *EarFS* (M=90%).

	EMG (Shimmer3)	CS (FDC2214)	EFS (OpenCS)	EarFS
1	eyes-left	head-back	chin-on-chest	eye wink
2	head-back	open-mouth	eye wink	head-right
3	head-left	protrude-tongue	say-u	open-mouth
4	say-e	eye-brows together	eyes-down	say-sh
5	smile	say-a	head-right	smile

Table 2. Top 5 gestures for the best technology setup. We chose to select the number of 5 gestures, because the ability to remember shortcuts, such as gestures, dramatically decreases with larger numbers than 7 in a real scenario. Following cognitive engineering, 5 is also a suggested maximum.

Summary

The analysis revealed all technologies to be capable of a facial-gesture recognition by measuring them inside the ear canal. In our opinion, the classification accuracy is astonishing considering the broad gesture set of 25 facial expressions. Two characteristic 'clusters' of confusions occurred among the gestures. One cluster can be found around gestures of the *Oculi*, and the other around the *Lingua*. Because these gestures are similar in type, the confusion between them is most likely connected to their actual similarity.

STUDY 2: WEARABLE PERFORMANCE

Since the first study was performed in a very controlled environment, we thought it may be interesting to see whether our evaluated technologies could be employed as a wearable technology in a mobile context as well.

Study Setup

Therefore, we conducted an experiment with 3 participants, aged 26, 29, and 30 years. While each technology was tested with all users, the task was to perform all top 5 gestures of each technology (*see Table 2*) with its' best earplug setup for 10 times in a random order.

There was a marginal training phase in which the user had the chance to perform each gesture once or twice. After the study started, the study leader was shouting each gesture out loud while he was triggering the recording. To test the technologies' limits, we instructed each user to randomly walk around within a spot of 10 x 10 meters in a medium-sized lobby with stone-tiled floor.

In summary, we recorded 600 gestures (3 users * 4 technologies * 5 gestures * 10 repetitions). We again calculated 46 state-of-the-art features from the raw data and used a J48 Decision Tree while performing a stratified 10-fold-crossvalidation.

Hypotheses

Since we already know about the theoretical performance in a stationary context, we can establish these hypotheses:

H1: *EarFS* will perform equally or better than other technologies, because it works with a differential amplification. Hence, it should be more robust towards influences from external noise in mobility.

H2: All other technologies will experience a substantial drop in accuracy, because they are heavily affected by environmental noise occurring while moving.

Results

The results confirm our assumption. *EarFS* performs well in context of mobility. *Table 3* shows the performance of *EarFS* in a confusion metrics accumulated over all users:

a	b	c	d	e	<- classified as
96.7%	3.3%	-	-	-	a = eye wink
-	89.7%	3.4%	-	6.9%	b = head right
3.3%	-	80.0%	16.7%	-	c = open mouth
-	-	13.3%	80.0%	6.7%	d = say SH
-	3.3%	6.7%	10.0%	80.0%	e = smile

Table 3. Accumulated confusion matrix of all users showing overall performance of the *EarFS* using a J48 decision tree.

Answering Hypotheses

H1: Looking at *Table 4*, we can see that over all users, *EarFS* (M=85.2%) achieves a substantially higher mean accuracy than EMG (M=76.7%) and CS (M=79.9) when the user walks around randomly. A one-way ANOVA ($F_{3,8}$=6.27; p<.02) also found statistical differences in terms of performance level. A Tukey HSD test confirmed our technology to significantly outperform EFS (M=73.7%). Therefore, we accept this hypothesis: *EarFS* is more robust towards external noise in mobility and yields higher accuracy while it even significantly outperforms EFS.

EMG (Shimmer3)	CS (FDC2214)	EFS (OpenCS)	EarFS	
84%	90%	**94.5%**	90%	sitting
76.7%	79.9%	52.8%	**85.2%**	walking
80.4%	85%	73.7%	**87.6%**	Ø

Table 4. Overall performance (True-Positive rates) of study 1 (sitting) in comparison to study 2 (walking). The setup: top 5 gestures, preferred electrode setup, J48 classifier.

Incidentally, it is even more surprising to see that EFS initially outperformed *EarFS* while sitting. One reason would be because OpenCapSense is a more integrated PCB and does not suffer from small distortions of loose wires like *EarFS*. However, as shown before, it is bound to underperform while walking, since it is not supporting differential measurements.

H2: Running a simple t-Test confirms $CS_{walking}$ (M=79.9%) to be significantly worse than $CS_{sitting}$ (M=90%). Also, $EFS_{walking}$ (M=52.8%) is performing significantly worse than $EFS_{sitting}$ (M=94.5%). We can also see a decrease from $EMG_{sitting}$ (M=84%) to $EMG_{walking}$ (M=76.7%). However, while EMG is generally performing low, it is not yet statistically different. *EarFS* experiences the lowest accuracy drop (Δ= -4.8%) and does not perform significantly worse. Although CS and EFS significantly dropped in accuracy, we have to dismiss this hypothesis, because EMG did not significantly decrease.

Summary

The second study shows *EarFS* to not experience a substantial performance drop in mobility while the user is walking. Moreover, the study reveals that EMG is also not heavily affected by walking artifacts due to the nature of its' sensing method. Therefore, the study indicates that electrical field sensing related technologies may not be the perfect choice for a wearable gesture recognition, unless one applies a differential amplification, such as proposed in *EarFS*.

DISCUSSION

Considering the rather rudimentary electrode setup and the low-cost sensing device, in our opinion, the achieved classification accuracy above 90% with a gesture set of five is astonishing. This is due to the heterogeneous signal, which is a combination of facial-movement-induced ear canal deformations and biopotential processes. Still, a custom six channel *monopolar* EMG, using surface electrodes similar to Zhang et al. [40] but distributed over the entire face, tends to outperform any in-ear setups. We confirmed this in a pilot study where we attached 7 silver/silver chloride gel electrodes to the face in places right above facial muscles of interest (*see Figure 11*).

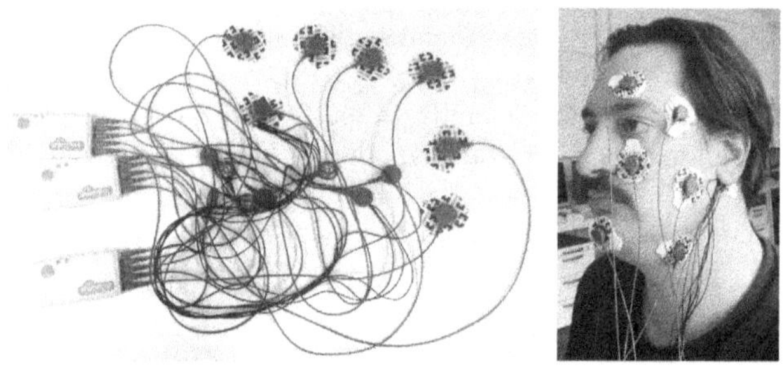

Figure 11. We utilized 3 Shimmer3 EXG sensor devices with 7 Ag/AgCl gel electrodes (6 channels + 1 common ground placed behind the ear, an area that remains relatively unaffected by muscular movement) to detect same gesture set.

We again recorded the complete facial gesture set of 25 with a sampling rate of 200Hz and a window size of 256. A total of 346 features (based on 46 state-of-the-art features) have been extracted from the raw data, whereby the most meaningful features included: *maxAmpFrequency*, *spectralEntropy*, and *logLikelihood*. With this setup, a *RandomForest* classifier performed best while detecting 25 facial gestures with an accuracy of 62%. A reduced set of only 5 facial gestures scored maximum accuracy of 100%.

This pilot clearly highlights the typical trade-off between technology that is obtrusive on the one hand, but on the other hand achieves high accuracy rates. Scoring comparably low precision with an in-ear setup is not surprising, since (1) the maximum number of channels tested with the earplugs was four and (2) sensors cannot directly sense evoking action potentials from the source while resting inside the ear canal. Nevertheless, we expect *EarFS* to technically mature with further iterations (testing different building blocks, EM shielding). However, placing more electrodes inside the ear is not expected to provide significant performance boosts. Instead, a combination of different technologies seems promising and is highly encouraged for further research. While electrodes with direct skin contact could be combined with electrically insulated electrodes, it did not increase performance in our study. In contrast, a future improvement would be to additionally determine the deformations of the ear canal with pressure-activated distance sensors. Another method would be laser-based distance measurements by using modulated laser beams and image-based phase-shift analysis in order to get a distance-to-skin measurement inside the ear canal. Particularly, laser modulation frequencies would have to be very high to cover the sub-millimetre distance range in this approach, and thus suitable hardware would increase the costs of such a sensing device.

CONCLUSION

In this paper, we presented a novel variant of an electrical field sensing (*EarFS*) which provides *hands-free* and partly *eyes-free* interaction for mobile and wearable computing. We introduced our developed sensing circuit in detail so that it can be replicated by any HCI researcher or practitioner. With *EarFS*, we closed an open gap in research while we systematically investigated detecting various facial-related gestures via an electric field sensing inside the ear canal, which has not been done before in this manner. We provided two studies that reveal how electric sensing technologies could possibly perform when using an electrode in-ear plug. On top of that, we were able to show that *EarFS* tends to outperform other electrical sensing approaches when it comes to facial-gesture recognition in mobility while the user is on the go.

FUTURE WORK

Since facial gestures and expressions cannot typically be 'switched off' by users, the field of mobile facial expression recognition still yields great potential as far as implicit interaction is concerned. Based on facial expressions, a future system would be able to know and anticipate the user's intentions before conscious interaction becomes necessary. In terms of apparatus, we believe that in-ear devices, such as earbuds, are much more unobtrusive and socially acceptable than other known hands-free and eyes-free technologies. Therefore, we envision similar sensing approaches to be integrated into in-ear headsets in the near future. Besides headsets, we also see great potential in *EarFS* to be implemented into various other kinds of wearables, since our sensing approach offers a much wider range of recognition capabilities for gestures and activities in mobility than discussed in this paper. Exploring these capabilities in future research could be very beneficial.

ACKNOWLEDGMENTS

We would like to thank all reviewers, in particular Thijs Roumen, for spending their valuable time on providing very valuable feedback. This research is supported by the Federal Republic of Germany under the following grant: BMWi 16KN049121.

REFERENCES

1. Ashbrook, D. (2010). Enabling mobile microinteractions. *PhD Thesis*, Georgia Institute of Technology
2. Ashtiani, B., & MacKenzie, I. S. (2010). BlinkWrite2: an improved text entry method using eye blinks. In *Proceedings of the 2010 Symposium on Eye-Tracking Research & Applications*, 339-345. ACM. http://dx.doi.org/10.1145/1743666.1743742
3. Bartlett, M. S., Littlewort, G., Fasel, I., & Movellan, J. R. (2003, June). Real Time Face Detection and Facial Expression Recognition: Development and Applications to Human Computer Interaction. In *Conference on Computer Vision and Pattern Recognition. CVPRW'03*. (Vol. 5), 53-53. IEEE. http://dx.doi.org/10.1109/CVPRW.2003.10057
4. Bulling, A., Roggen, D., & Tröster, G. (2009). Wearable EOG goggles: eye-based interaction in everyday environments, In *CHI'09 Extended Abstracts on Human Factors in Computing System,* 3259-3264. ACM. http://dx.doi.org/10.1145/1520340.1520468
5. Caruana, R., & Freitag, D. (1994). Greedy Attribute Selection. In *Proceedings of International Conference on Machine Learning*, 28-36.
6. Chai, J. X., Xiao, J., & Hodgins, J. (2003). Vision-based control of 3d facial animation. In *Proceedings of the 2003 ACM SIGGRAPH/Eurographics symposium on Computer animation*, 193-206. ACM.
7. Cohn, G., Gupta, S., Lee, T. J., Morris, D., Smith, J. R., Reynolds, M. S., ... & Patel, S. N. (2012). An ultra-low-power human body motion sensor using static electric field sensing. In *Proceedings of the 2012 ACM Conference on Ubiquitous Computing*, 99-102. ACM. http://dx.doi.org/10.1145/2370216.2370233
8. Ekman, P., & Friesen, W. V. (1977). Facial action coding system. Consulting Psychologists Press, Stanford University, Palo Alto.
9. Fagan, M. J., Ell, S. R., Gilbert, J. M., Sarrazin, E., & Chapman, P. M. (2008). Development of a (silent) speech recognition system for patients following laryngectomy. In *Medical engineering & physics*, 30(4), 419-425. http://dx.doi.org/10.1016/j.medengphy.2007.05.003
10. Fasel, B., & Luettin, J. (2003). Automatic facial expression analysis: a survey. In *Pattern recognition*, 36(1), 259-275. Elsevier. http://dx.doi.org/10.1016/S0031-3203(02)00052-3
11. Gips, J., Olivieri, P., & Tecce, J. (1993). Direct Control of the Computer Through Electrodes Placed Around the Eyes. In *Human-Computer Interaction: Applications and Case Studies,* 630-635. Elsevier.
12. Gips, J. (1998). On building intelligence into EagleEyes. In *Assistive technology and artificial intelligence*, 50-58. Springer Berlin Heidelberg. http://dx.doi.org/10.1007/BFb0055969
13. Grafsgaard, J., Wiggins, J. B., Boyer, K. E., Wiebe, E. N., & Lester, J. (2013). Automatically recognizing facial expression: Predicting engagement and frustration. In *Educational Data Mining 2013*.
14. Grosse-Puppendahl, T., Berghoefer, Y., Braun, A., Wimmer, R., & Kuijper, A. (2013). OpenCapSense: A rapid prototyping toolkit for pervasive interaction using capacitive sensing. In *Proceedings of International Conference on Pervasive Computing and Communications*, 152-159. IEEE. http://dx.doi.org/10.1109/PerCom.2013.6526726
15. Hall, M., Frank, E., Holmes, G., Pfahringer, B., Reutemann, P., & Witten, I. H. (2009). The WEKA data mining software: an update. In *ACM SIGKDD explorations newsletter*, 11(1), 10-18. http://dx.doi.org/10.1145/1656274.1656278
16. Hausen, S. (2014) Peripheral Interaction - Exploring the Design Space, *PhD Thesis*, Faculty of Mathematics, Computer Science and Statistics, University of Munich.
17. Hazlett, R. (2003). Measurement of user frustration: a biologic approach. In *CHI'03 extended abstracts on Human factors in computing systems*, 734-735. ACM. http://dx.doi.org/10.1145/765891.765958
18. Hodgkin, A. L. (1951). The ionic basis of electrical activity in nerve and muscle. In *Biological Reviews*, 26(4), 339-409. http://dx.doi.org/10.1111/j.1469-185X.1951.tb01204.x
19. Ishimaru, S., Kunze, K., Uema, Y., Kise, K., Inami, M., & Tanaka, K. (2014). Smarter eyewear: using commercial EOG glasses for activity recognition. In *Proceedings of the 2014 ACM International Joint Conference on Pervasive and Ubiquitous Computing: Adjunct Publication,* 239-242. ACM. http://dx.doi.org/10.1145/2638728.2638795
20. Majaranta, P., & Räihä, K. J. (2007). Text entry by gaze: Utilizing eye-tracking. In *Text entry systems: Mobility, accessibility, universality*, 175-187.
21. Manabe, H., & Fukumoto, M. (2006). Full-time wearable headphone-type gaze detector. In *CHI'06 Extended Abstracts on Human Factors in Computing Systems,* 1073-1078. ACM. http://dx.doi.org/10.1145/1125451.1125655
22. Manabe, H., Fukumoto, M., & Yagi, T. (2015). Conductive rubber electrodes for earphone-based eye gesture input interface. In *Personal and Ubiquitous Computing,* 19(1), 143-154. Springer. http://dx.doi.org/10.1007/s00779-014-0818-8
23. Mann, S. (1998). Humanistic computing: "WearComp" as a new framework and application for intelligent

signal processing. In *Proceedings of the IEEE*, 86(11), 2123-215. IEEE. http://dx.doi.org/10.1109/5.726784

24. Matthies, D. J. C. (2013). InEar BioFeedController: a headset for hands-free and eyes-free interaction with mobile devices. In *CHI'13 Extended Abstracts on Human Factors in Computing Systems*, 1293-1298. ACM. http://dx.doi.org/10.1145/2468356.2468587
25. Matthies, D. J. C., Antons, J. N., Heidmann, F., Wettach, R., & Schleicher, R. (2012). NeuroPad: use cases for a mobile physiological interface. In *Proceedings of the 7th Nordic Conference on Human-Computer Interaction: Making Sense Through Design*, 795-796. ACM. http://dx.doi.org/10.1145/2399016.2399152
26. Matthies, D. J.C., Perrault, S. T., Urban, B., & Zhao, S. (2015). Botential: Localizing On-Body Gestures by Measuring Electrical Signatures on the Human Skin. In *Proceedings of the 17th International Conference on Human-Computer Interaction with Mobile Devices and Services*, 207-216. ACM. http://dx.doi.org/10.1145/2785830.2785859
27. McFarland, D. J., & Wolpaw, J. R. (2011). Brain-computer interfaces for communication and control. In *Communications of the ACM*, 54(5), 60-66. ACM. http://dx.doi.org/10.1145/1941487.1941506
28. Nguyen, A., Alqurashi, R., Raghebi, Z., Banaei-kashani, F., Halbower, A. C., & Vu, T. (2016). A Lightweight And Inexpensive In-ear Sensing System For Automatic Whole-night Sleep Stage Monitoring. In *Proceedings of the 14th ACM Conference on Embedded Network Sensor Systems 2016*, 230-244. ACM. http://dx.doi.org/10.1145/2994551.2994562
29. Picard, R. W. (1995). Affective computing. *MIT Media Laboratory Perceptual Computing Section Technical Report No. 321*. Cambridge: MIT press.
30. Rantanen, V., Niemenlehto, P. H., Verho, J., & Lekkala, J. (2010). Capacitive facial movement detection for human–computer interaction to click by frowning and lifting eyebrows. In *Medical & biological engineering & computing*,*48*(1), 39-47. http://dx.doi.org/10.1007/s11517-009-0565-6
31. Rantanen, V., Venesvirta, H., Spakov, O., Verho, J., Vetek, A., Surakka, V., & Lekkala, J. (2013). Capacitive measurement of facial activity intensity. In *IEEE Sensors Journal*, 13(11), 4329-4338. http://dx.doi.org/10.1109/JSEN.2013.2269864
32. Sahni, H., Bedri, A., Reyes, G., Thukral, P., Guo, Z., Starner, T., & Ghovanloo, M. (2014). The tongue and ear interface: a wearable system for silent speech recognition. In *Proceedings of the 2014 ACM International Symposium on Wearable Computers*, 47-54. ACM. http://dx.doi.org/10.1145/2634317.2634322
33. Saponas, T. S., Tan, D. S., Morris, D., Balakrishnan, R., Turner, J., & Landay, J. A. (2009). Enabling always-available input with muscle-computer interfaces. In *Proceedings of the 22nd annual ACM symposium on User interface software and technology*, 167-176. ACM. http://dx.doi.org/10.1145/1622176.1622208
34. San Agustin, J., Hansen, J. P., Hansen, D. W., & Skovsgaard, H. (2009). Low-cost gaze pointing and EMG clicking. In *CHI'09 Extended Abstracts on Human Factors in Computing Systems*, 3247-3252. ACM. http://dx.doi.org/10.1145/1520340.1520466
35. Scharfetter, H., Hartinger, P., Hinghofer-Szalkay, H., & Hutten, H. (1998). A model of artefacts produced by stray capacitance during whole body or segmental bioimpedance spectroscopy. In *Physiological measurement*, 19(2), 247. http://dx.doi.org/10.1088/0967-3334/19/2/012
36. Scheirer, J., Fernandez, R., & Picard, R. W. (1999). Expression glasses: a wearable device for facial expression recognition. In *CHI'99 Extended Abstracts on Human Factors in Computing Systems*, 262-263. ACM. http://dx.doi.org/10.1145/632716.632878
37. Smith, E., & Delargy, M. (2005). Locked-in syndrome. *BMJ*, 330(7488), 406-409.
38. Smith, J. R. (1999). Electric Field Imaging. *PhD Thesis*, MIT - Massachusetts Institute of Technology.
39. Yin, E., Zhou, Z., Jiang, J., Chen, F., Liu, Y., & Hu, D. (2013). A novel hybrid BCI speller based on the incorporation of SSVEP into the P300 paradigm. In *Journal of neural engineering,* 10(2), 026012. http://dx.doi.org/10.1088/1741-2560/10/2/026012
40. Zhang, Q., Gollakota, S., Taskar, B., & Rao, R. P. (2014). Non-intrusive tongue machine interface. In *Proceedings of the 32nd annual ACM conference on Human factors in computing systems*, 2555-2558. ACM. http://dx.doi.org/10.1145/2556288.2556981

EchoFlex: Hand Gesture Recognition using Ultrasound Imaging

Jess McIntosh, Asier Marzo, Mike Fraser
Bristol Interaction Group,
University of Bristol,
Bristol, UK
jm0152@bristol.ac.uk

Carol Phillips
Radiology Department
University Hospitals Bristol NHS Foundation Trust, Bristol, UK
Carol.Phillips@UHBristol.nhs.uk

ABSTRACT
Recent improvements in ultrasound imaging enable new opportunities for hand pose detection using wearable devices. Ultrasound imaging has remained under-explored in the HCI community despite being non-invasive, harmless and capable of imaging internal body parts, with applications including smart-watch interaction, prosthesis control and instrument tuition. In this paper, we compare the performance of different forearm mounting positions for a wearable ultrasonographic device. Location plays a fundamental role in ergonomics and performance since the anatomical features differ among positions. We also investigate the performance decrease due to cross-session position shifts and develop a technique to compensate for this misalignment. Our gesture recognition algorithm combines image processing and neural networks to classify the flexion and extension of 10 discrete hand gestures with an accuracy above 98%. Furthermore, this approach can continuously track individual digit flexion with less than 5% NRMSE, and also differentiate between digit flexion at different joints.

Author Keywords
Gesture recognition; interactive ultrasound imaging; machine learning; computer vision

ACM Classification Keywords
H.5.m. Information Interfaces and Presentation (e.g. HCI): Miscellaneous

INTRODUCTION
Our hands are capable of skillful and intricate movements with multiple degrees of freedom, giving us the capacity to manipulate objects and enhance or replace verbal communication through the use of gestures. Gestures play a fundamental role in emerging Human-Computer Interaction (HCI) paradigms, and several wearables have been developed to capture gestures as a way of controlling devices naturally. However, many of these existing technologies and techniques to detect gestures have limitations which make them unsuitable for general applications.

These limitations include inaccurate or variable performance, ergonomic challenges of wearing the devices, and lack of robustness during regular use. Here, we explore the capabilities of ultrasound imaging as a gesture detection mechanism. Ultrasound imaging, or UltraSonography (US), has long been available as a medical technique for safe anatomical inspection for example to see developing fetuses or heart disease. While progress in the medical area has been significant, the use of ultrasound for interactive applications has not been explored within the HCI community.

Ultrasonography allows one to see the musculature within the body in real time. By observing the movement of the muscles, it is possible to infer hand movements. It is unlikely that this technique provides more accuracy than systems which directly measure the moving body parts, such as cameras or data gloves, but US has potential benefits over these existing wearable hand tracking techniques. Directly imaging the muscles is not subject to occlusion, unlike imaging the body parts externally which can be obscured by other body parts or be out of view depending on the mounting of the camera. In contrast to wearing instrumentation on the hand, imaging the muscles leaves the hands free to perform actions unencumbered by devices or sensors. This could be beneficial for sensitive or expert manipulation as in the case of fragile objects, surgical operations, or simply to keep the physical naturalness of a handshake.

Surface electromyography (EMG) captures the electric signals from the muscles with sensors on the skin. EMG is one of the main alternatives for non-invasive hand pose detection, but suffers from cross-talk. That is, it is difficult to differentiate between individual muscles particularly those which lie deeper in the forearm [35]. Techniques that measure wrist shape changes have been shown to work well for small numbers of wrist gestures but there is limited evidence that they are robust to a wide variety of hand movements.

Ultrasound imaging requires a small area of contact with the arm, whereas EMG electrodes are typically placed around the forearm at specific locations selected with a calibration procedure. With ultrasound, the probe that is used to obtain the images is considerably smaller in size, and in contrast with EMG, lends itself well to be integrated with smaller form factors. We discuss this and other wearable hand tracking tech-

CHI 2017, May 06-11, 2017, Denver, CO, USA.
© 2017 ACM. ISBN 978-1-4503-4655-9/17/05 ...$15.00.
DOI: http://dx.doi.org/10.1145/3025453.3025807

niques in related work below and suggest reasons why US is beneficial over existing methods.

In this paper, we analyse the performance of ultrasound to recognise discrete gestures, measure continuous angles of digit flexion and discriminate between different types of digit flexion. Recent work on US for gesture detection has shown very high accuracy. We explore issues of this technology in the context of HCI, and for the first time study the effects of probe location on accuracy, and find that ergonomic mounting positions are viable without significant variation in accuracy. We also provide a simple calibration mechanism to mitigate the effects of cross-session position shift, which is important for day-to-day use. We provide guidelines for the best locations depending on the gesture recognition application. The high recognition accuracy could make several applications possible, including robotic hand control, natural interactions and enhanced sports and musical instrument tuition. Given the trend in reduction of size and cost of ultrasonic imaging devices, we expect to see this approach applied for more interactive scenarios.

RELATED WORK

In this section we describe the different sensing technologies for hand gesture recognition, focusing on non-invasive wearable techniques, and review previous work on ultrasound to support interactive applications.

Optical

Optical methods are based on employing a camera to determine 2D or 3D hand position. The camera can be sensitive to the visible spectrum but alternatives exist in the infra-red or below. A review of these methods can be found in Rautaray et al. work [31]. An example is Digits [23] which uses an IR camera attached to the wrist to sense the distance to the fingers. The sensor is worn on the wrist and as with all optical approaches requires direct line of sight to the fingers, and suffers from occlusions of the fingers by the hand.

Wrist Deformation

When we flex our fingers and wrist the muscles inside our forearm change in size and shift around, causing a deformation of the wrist shape. Measuring this deformation is an indirect method to infer the hand gesture which caused this change in shape. One way of sensing the shape is with pressure sensors, WristFlex [10] uses 15 pressure sensors around the wrist and a Support Vector Machine (SVM) to classify five pinch gestures with an average accuracy of 80%.

Another method for measuring the distance between two parts of a wearable is to use capacitive sensing. The capacitance between two parallel plates is proportional to the distance and material between them. This technique was used by GestureWrist [32] to measure the deformation of the wrist and qualitatively detect some common gestures. Cheng et al. showed that this method can operate with accuracies of 77% for 36 gestures [9]. Electrical impedance tomography is a similar approach that has shown to be more effective in recent work by Zhang et al. [43], reaching accuracies above 94% for a variety of gestures. This technique is close to ultrasound imaging, the key difference is the images formed with IET lack detail of the muscles, meaning they cannot be tracked, but morphological changes of musculature is enough to classify discrete gestures with.

Another way of detecting the wrist shape is with an infra-red distance sensor [17]. Qualitative results suggest that it would be possible to differentiate between 10 gestures.

From these recent findings it is clear that improvements are needed for this to be a sufficiently accurate technique for many applications.

EMG: Electromyography

Electromyography consists of measuring the bioelectric signals produced by the muscles upon contraction. These signals can be measured with surface electrodes on the skin in a non-invasive way.

Tenore et al. [37] showed that with 32 electrodes around the forearm it is possible to detect individual flexion and extension movements of each fingers with an accuracy greater than 90% both in amputees and able-bodied subjects. An interesting and promising result is that detection accuracy between transradial amputees and able-bodied subjects showed no statistical difference. Castellini [7] showed that 10 electrodes is enough to differentiate 4 types of grasps as well as the force applied with an accuracy ranging from 75% to 90%. You et al. used 4 electrodes to detect flexion each of finger with 97.75% accuracy [42].

NASA developed a wearable band for astronaut suits made of 17 electrodes and accelerometers [39]. This wearable represents a way of enhancing communications with other astronauts or vehicles since the accuracy of gesture detection was greater than 96%.

Recent improvements came from using a dense array of 192 EMG electrodes to detect up to 27 gestures with 90% accuracy [2].

EMG tends to suffer from a trade-off between accuracy and the surface area used for measurements. Whilst EMG proves to be highly effective for a high number of electrodes, it performs poorly under placement and surface area restrictions, making it awkward to fit into existing wearable device form factors such as watch straps.

Smith at al. demonstrated that EMG can be used to detect continuous angle of the fingers [36] with an NRMSE of 11%. However, the nature of the biosignal creates particular difficulties regarding continuous angle detection, and so there have been very few attempts to challenge this task using EMG, and is therefore currently more suited to discrete gesture recognition.

Mechanomyography

Mechanomyography is a technique which records vibrations of the muscle fibres after contraction, which oscillate at their resonant frequencies and is characteristic of a specific muscle's activity [28]. Mechanomyography is a useful technique to support prosthesis and switch control since the placement of the sensors does not have to be precise and the change in the skin impedance due to sweating does not affect the performance [21]. Although this technique uses sound, it is not an imaging technique and has been under-explored within the HCI community (with the exception of [40]) despite its simplicity in hardware and robustness to sensor placement or skin condition.

Ultrasound

Sonomyography is the use of ultrasound imaging to create 1-dimensional scans (A-scans). An early study by Hodges et al. [19] proved that muscle contraction of the tibia, biceps and abdomen can be measured with an ultrasound sensor. Later, Zheng et al. [44] showed that it is also possible to infer the wrist angle with an mean error of 7.2%. They defined Sonomyography as measuring the dimensional change of muscles with ultrasound sensors.

Sonomyography has the advantage of using simple hardware because it only needs one transducer element per A-scan; current ultrasonic probes have more than 128 elements and are becoming the standard for ultrasound imaging. Sonomyography can also be used to continuously detect the opening and closing of the hand with an RMS of 12.8% [8] and recently to detect 6 common gestures with an accuracy of 74% [18]. The latter study used a wearable device and a bracelet with five transducers. Comparisons between EMG and sonomyography were favourable for the latter in detecting continuous wrist flexion [15] and hand grasping force [16].

Sonomyography is an appropriate method to detect a reduced set of gestures, but provides limited information and lacks the possibilities offered by modern phased arrays of ultrasound transducers for more detailed imaging.

Mujibiya et al. presented a device that is capable of detecting arm grasps and other on-body touch interactions, using a band of ultrasonic transducers around the forearm and fingers [27]. This device has the advantage of working at much lower frequencies and with fewer transducers than imaging devices, but the drawback is that it can only detect interactions when one hand is touching the arm of the other. Detecting hand movements involving only one hand is a requirement for certain situations [22].

Ultrasound Imaging

Ultrasound imaging has been used previously to infer the position of the foot by tracking the muscle displacement [26]. An image of the muscles and tendons was taken and the insertions of the tendons into the muscle were used as markers to track. A comparison between the estimated position and the ground truth (metallic plate inserted in the tendon) showed errors of less than 10 micrometers or the equivalent of 0.7 degrees on the ankle rotation. Markers were tracked using cross-correlation. Later, this technique was used to track the tendon in the wrist with an error of 80 micrometers [25].

Castellini et al. estimated continuously changing finger angles by analyzing ultrasonic images of the forearm [5] [6], obtaining an NRMSE of approximately 2%. This technique was also extended to determine the force that the fingers were exerting [14]. They captured ultrasound images at the wrist and divided them into regions. Then, the features from each region were used in a linear regressor to establish a relationship between the features and the angle or force of each finger. In more recent work, it was shown that it is possible to recognize 4 different grasps with 80% accuracy, and also 3 levels of strength with 60% accuracy [29].

Sikdar et al. focused their work on recognising discrete hand gestures by imaging the muscles mid-forearm. They divided the image and calculated the average brightness change per region to create different activity patterns for each gesture. A Nearest Neighbour search was able to classify input gestures correctly with 98% accuracy for the flexion of 4 fingers [35] and 91% for 15 gestures [1]. Another group of researchers used an optical flow algorithm to determine the movement of the extensor muscles [34], but they were only able to qualitatively detect different finger flexions.

The results from Castellini and Sikdar demonstrate the capabilities of modern ultrasound imaging in gesture detection, but did not explore probe location or apply recent machine learning techniques. Considering that the anatomy can vary a lot between different locations, there is likely to be some variation in performance. Cross-session accuracies have also not yet been studied, though it is vital for practical use. Given the importance of location to interactive wearables, further research is required to know whether probe location significantly effects the recognition accuracy. We shall also examine the effects of cross-session performance for each of these different locations.

ULTRASOUND IMAGING PRINCIPLES

Sound is a mechanical wave that travels by sequential compression and expansion (rarefaction) of the medium. The frequency describes the number of times the molecules expand and contract per second whereas the amplitude refers to the amount of compression.

Sound travels at a speed that depends on the temperature, pressure and the medium (e.g. 340m/s in air and 1500m/s in water under normal conditions). The product of the density of the medium and the speed of sound through it is called the acoustic impedance. When a sound wave passes from one medium to another with a different acoustic impedance, some of the energy is reflected at the boundary. The proportion that gets reflected is proportional to the mismatch in impedance between the two media. Our forearms are made up of many complex tissues with different acoustic impedances. The reflections from these tissues allow us to see the boundaries between them.

The most basic idea of ultrasonic imaging is to emit a short wave (pulse) and reading back the different reflections from the tissues. The pulse will get partially reflected at different depths of the body, the delay in arrival will be proportional to the distance whereas the intensity will indicate the type of tissue since different tissues have characteristic acoustic impedance.

An ultrasonic transducer or probe is a device which houses one or several piezoelectric elements. The elements can transform an electric pulse into a mechanical pulse to generate a wave. The elements can also transduce the mechanical energy from the reflected pulse into electric signals. These phenomena are referred to as the inverse and forward piezoelectric effect and support pulsing and reading with the same probe by quickly switching the electronic components. Modern ultrasound imaging devices use algorithms to form images, applying beamforming and harmonic imaging to increase resolution.

Ultrasonography typically uses sound waves with frequencies in the order of MHz. The higher the frequency, the better the resolution that can be attained, however the attenuation is higher and therefore imaging depth is reduced. In this paper we image musculoskeletal tissue using transducers with a central frequency ranging from 8 to 12MHz for good resolution and enough image depth.

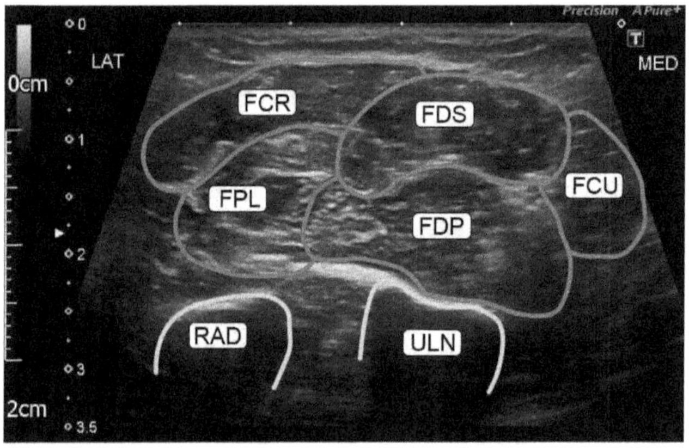

Figure 1: A transversal scan of the mid-forearm, anterior aspect. Labelled in red are the various muscles, and the bones in green.

HAND ANATOMY

The muscles which control the hand can be categorised into extrinsic muscles which originate in the upper/mid forearm, and intrinsic muscles which originate within the hand itself. The extrinsic muscles control wrist motions and some digit movements. The intrinsic muscles are used for finer motor control of the hand, for example pinch gestures and finger adduction/abduction. The extrinsic muscles can be further categorised into flexor and extensor muscles which bend or straighten the digits respectively and, in combination, move the wrist from side to side.

In this paper we exclusively image the extrinsic muscles at positions from the wrist to the forearm. These locations provide a position for the probe that will not interfere with hand movements. However, it will not be possible to capture hand movements that use intrinsic muscles, and this is a tracking limitation for all systems that measure muscle movement at the forearm level.

The muscles that are principally responsible for the flexion and extension of the fingers are the digitorum muscles (Fig. 1, FDS, FDP). These also assist with flexing and extending at the wrist, however the main muscles for the wrist are the carpi radialis/ulnaris (Fig. 1, FCR, FCU). In addition, the carpi radialis and ulnaris assist with adduction and abduction of the wrist. The thumb is controlled by the pollicis muscles (Fig. 1, FPL).

Hand movements change the musculature of the forearm due to contractions of the muscles. These contractions expand the size of the muscles and pull the tendons, and these changes are reflected in the US image. Furthermore, a particular hand movement changes the image at the specific areas where the involved tendons and muscles are located. Depending on the position of the probe (e.g. wrist or forearm) the observed muscles and tendons will be quite different.

STUDY DESIGN AND PILOT

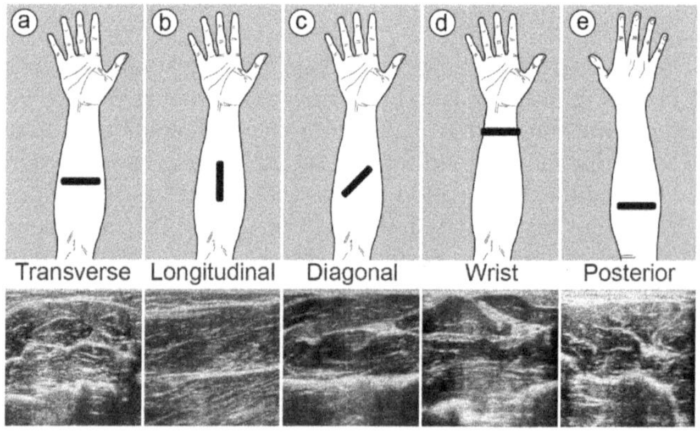

Figure 2: The mounting positions of the probe that were compared with their corresponding ultrasound image. a. Transverse, b. Longitudinal, c. Diagonal, d. Wrist, e. Posterior.

The objective of our study is to analyse the best mounting locations of a wearable device for discrete gesture recognition, cross-session accuracy and detection of continuous flexion angle. The wearable uses ultrasound imaging to track the muscles and tendons inside the forearm and with that infer hand pose. There were several variables to consider in the study; the main ones are locations and gesture sets. In order to make the study feasible we ran a pilot study to discard the options that were clearly inferior or not viable, which is presented after this section.

Locations

There are three parameters to consider when deciding the placement of the probe: orientations, proximity to the elbow, and anterior/posterior placement. The following explains each of these variables in more detail:

Orientation Clinical US scans are usually performed either **Transversally** (Fig. 2a) or **Longitudinally** (Fig. 2b) along the length of the forearm. In transverse mode, a larger range of muscles can be seen, however the muscle fibre displacement cannot be observed as well as in the longitudinal scan. It is medically uncommon to use the probe **Diagonally** (Fig. 2c) but we wanted to test if this position could image a large range of muscles and still observe the displacement of muscle fibres.

Proximal/Distal The muscles are more predominant at the **Proximal** mid-forearm (Fig. 2a), whereas the tendons are more visible at the **Distal** wrist location (Fig. 2d).

Anterior/Posterior The flexor muscles/tendons are located on the **Anterior** (inside) of the forearm and extensors on the **Posterior** (outside) of the forearm (Fig. 2e).

We chose 5 locations to initially test: Transverse, Longitudinal, Diagonal, Wrist and Posterior. These locations are illustrated in Fig. 2, along with their corresponding ultrasound images. The figure shows how different the US images look between positions. Although it cannot be seen from static images, the muscle fibre movement differs greatly with the orientation of the probe. Fig. 5a shows the fibre movement when the probe is oriented perpendicular to the flow of the muscle movement (Transverse), whereas Fig. 5b shows that the general movement is along the axis of the forearm in a Longitudinal scan.

Transverse mounting was used by Sikdar et al. [35] [1], Wrist was the location employed by Castellini et al. [6] [5] and a preliminary study tested Posterior [34]. Here, we compare those locations that were used in previous research and we introduce Longitudinal and Diagonal. Longitudinal is the only image that is completely parallel to the muscle and tendon movement. In a preliminary study for continuously detecting ankle angles it showed good accuracy [26] but we expect it to show poor performance for classifying a variety of gestures since there is less coverage of the muscles. We expected Diagonal to be a good compromise between continuous and discrete tracking.

For the purposes of dynamic assessment, clinical radiologists rarely look at images in the axial plane of the wrist, as it is difficult to identify individual tendons and the movement is not as easily appreciated as in the muscle. This was especially true of the the extensor tendons in the posterior compartment of the wrist, as the tendons here are too compact, and very little motion can be observed when compared to the anterior side. Since the wrist is normally considered to be the most ergonomic location to place a wearable device, we included the transverse distal anterior location to have at least one wrist location. If the tendons provide sufficient information for effective gesture recognition, this technique can be integrated with wrist-worn wearables.

In contrast to EMG, in US imaging we are also able to observe muscle relaxation. This means that it is not crucial to image both the anterior and posterior parts as it is possible to infer motion in both directions by inspecting either the flexor or extensor muscles. Consequently, we did not repeat posterior positions with anterior positions.

Gestures

In ultrasound images it is possible to observe the muscles and tendons which control the fingers, thumb and wrist at all locations, albeit more clearly in some locations than others. Consequently, for our gesture set we mixed a representative collection of single digit flexions, multi-finger flexion, wrist flexion and adduction.

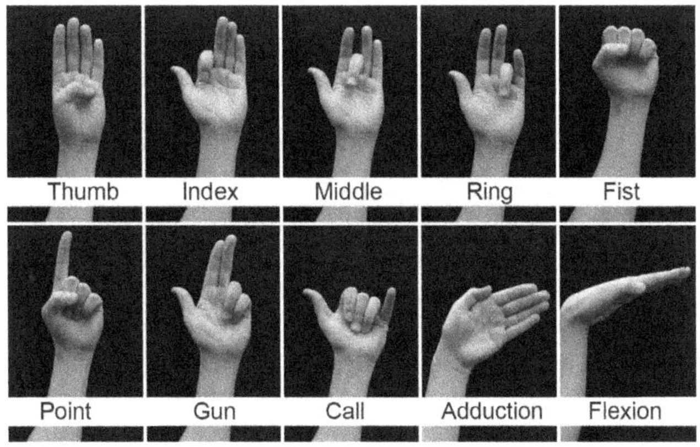

Figure 3: The set of gestures from top to bottom and left to right: thumb, index, middle, ring, fist, point, gun, call, wrist adduction and flexion.

We discarded movements that primarily involve intrinsic hand muscles such as pinch gestures and adduction of the fingers. Perhaps these gestures can be detected in the forearm because they are usually accompanied by other characteristic involuntary movements. However, we decided to remove those gestures from this study and focus on the gestures that involve a unique set of muscle movements that originate in the forearm. Fig. 3 shows the selected gesture set. We split each of these gestures into flexion and extension phases producing a total of 20 discrete movements.

There are numerous ways to flex a digit since they have at least two joints. We instructed the users to perform a natural flexion which usually involves all the joints but with more emphasis on the proximal interphalangeal joint. We thought that this would hinder the angle estimation since the finger is bent at several positions, different to previous studies in which the fingers were held with splints to force flexion at only one joint [6]. We wanted to avoid unnatural or uncomfortable gestures as they would not be used in a real situation. For the same reason, we also discarded individual pinky flexion.

With US imaging it is feasible to see the separation between the deep and the superficial muscles. For instance, the boundary between the flexor digitorum superficialis (FDS) and the flexor digitorum profundus (FDP) can be seen as a bright horizontal line in Fig. 2b . Consequently, it should be possible to differentiate between flexing of the digit at the metacarpophalangeal and the interphalangeal joints (ie different knuckles).

System

Hardware

We used a Toshiba Aplio 80 US imaging machine with a flat, linear probe with an 8MHz central frequency and 12MHz harmonic imaging mode. We used the default musculoskeletal settings with 1 focal point and 4cm of depth imaging for all the positions, except for the Wrist condition where we used 3cm. The machine was an ex-clinical machine but its deficiencies compared to the state of the art reflect the likely limitations of a mobile ultrasound device in resolution and image quality. In order to mount the probe onto the users forearm, we used a 3D printed structure to hold the transducer in place and to strap it around the user's forearm (Fig. 4a). We recorded the images from the US machine via a video capture card (Fig. 4d). Anagel US gel was applied for coupling between the probe and the user's skin.

In order to measure the ground truth of the hand pose, we created a sensor glove (Fig. 4b). We used 5 Spectra Symbol Flex Sensors [12] which were sewn onto each digit of the glove. We used an Arduino to read the resistivity values of each sensor and to transfer the data to the PC. This data was only used for the continuous angle tracking studies. We found that the sensor readings matched the amount of finger flexion linearly.

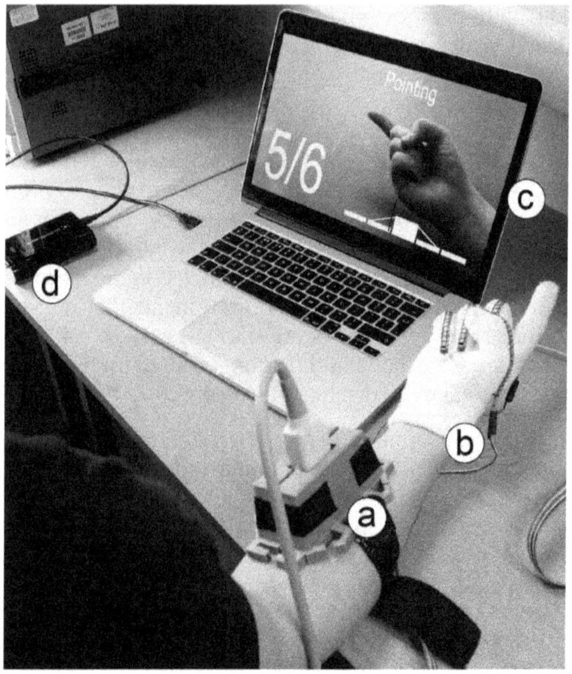

Figure 4: The setup of the experiment: a. Transducer, b. Sensor glove, c. Computer d. Video capture device.

Software

Since a gesture is actuated by a specific set of muscles, the gestures have unique patterns of activity within the US images. The type of motion depends on the location of the probe, and the observed motion is caused by reflections/scattering from the muscle fibres. In a longitudinal scan, the motion is primarily along the main axis of the probe, whereas transversal scans have a variety of different motions including rotations or elevations (Fig. 5). Nevertheless, there are patterns in the images wherever the probe is placed. The motion seemed therefore an appropriate feature to classify discrete gestures with.

Several operations must be performed with the ultrasound videos in order to classify discrete gestures or estimate finger angles. A reduced set of features are extracted from a collection of frames and then used to train a machine learning classifier. Later, this trained classifier determines the gesture or angles from a sample set of features derived from unseen images.

For the discrete classification, the first step is to segment the video stream into either flexions or extensions from the neutral position. Then, we extract features for each of the frames and these features are averaged per segment. In the continuous angle inference, the machine is a regressor that is trained with both the features at each frame and the angles from the data glove.

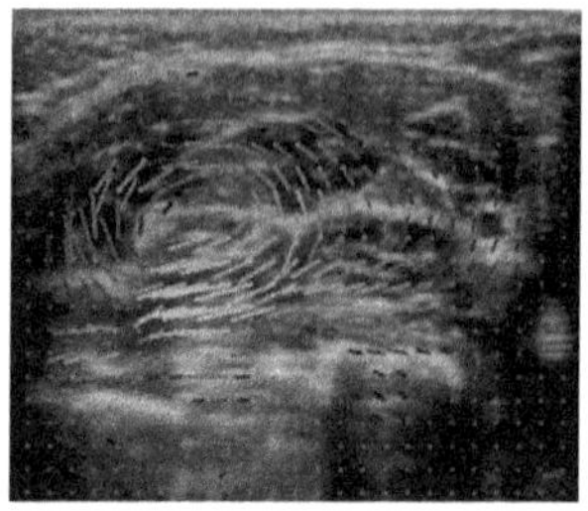

(a) Optical flow for the Transverse position during a thumb gesture.

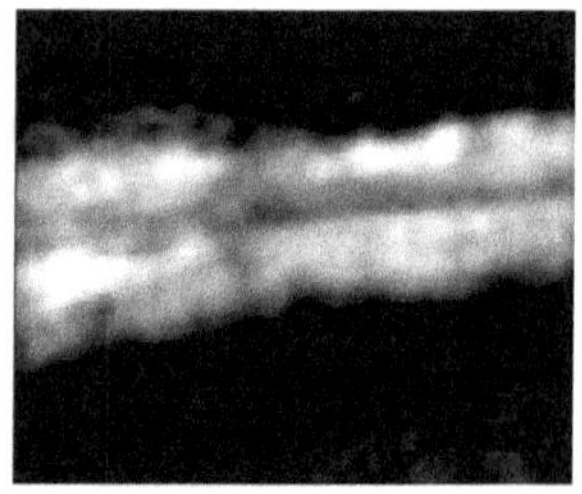

(b) Summation of the magnitudes of the flow vectors representing the activity pattern of the index gesture.

Figure 5: Image processing algorithms.

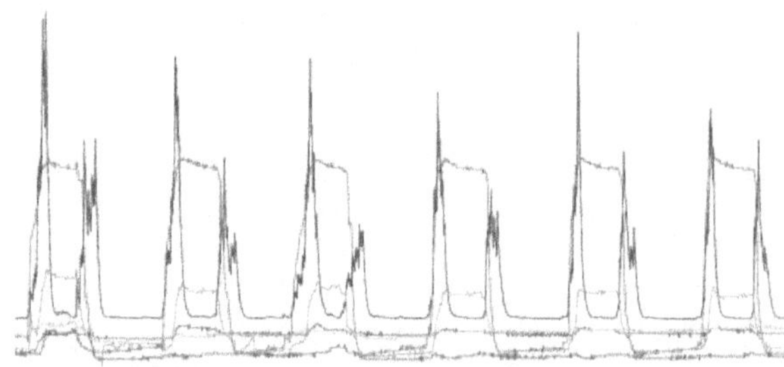

Figure 6: The blue line is a plot of the magnitudes of the flow vectors from an ultrasound video of the index finger repeatedly being flexed. The other lines represent the sensor data from the glove. Each channel is a 1D time signal.

Segmenting the videos for discrete classification was performed by calculating the sum of the magnitudes of the dense optical flow vectors for each pixel of every frame, using Farnebäck's algorithm [11]. A Gaussian blur with a kernel size of 15 pixels was applied beforehand. Fig. 5a shows the sampled points of the optical flow during the index flexing gesture and Fig. 6 plots the magnitude of the optical flow against the data glove values. The latter graph shows that the optical flow produces little or no activity during the period of time when the hand is not moving in the flexion hand pose, unlike EMG signals. The videos were split based on a plot such as this, where each gesture can easily be seen with two peaks at the beginning and end. Each gesture in the training set then has a video clip associated to show participants the gesture.

The machine learning algorithms cannot process all the information contained in an image and thus need a reduced feature set. For the discrete gesture classification, Sikdar et al. used the accumulated difference in brightness level [35] [1]. In our experiments we used the vertical and horizontal components of the optical flow. For each frame of a video clip, the dense optical flow was calculated, and then the horizontal and vertical optical flow values were averaged within each region based on a grid with 20 pixel spacing. Then the optical flow values were accumulated over every frame in the video clip, giving a final feature vector with a length in the order of hundreds of values. In continuous detection of finger angles, Castellini et al. used the first order surface as features [5], we calculated the moments for each frame (m00, m20 and m21-m12) which are equivalent but more standard in the computer vision community. The moments are computed for each frame, and the regressor trained on moments of each frame with the data glove data.

For machine learning in the discrete gesture recognition task, Sikdar et al. used Nearest Neighbour algorithms [35] [1]. We tested Support Vector Machine's (SVM) since it was shown that they gave better results for discrete gesture discrimination in another study [33]. We also tested a type of Neural Network called Multi-Layer Perceptrons (MLP) since they have often shown very good results and have yet to be applied in this technology. In the continuous angle detection, Castellini et al. used Linear Ridge Regression but suggested to use SVMs as they may yield better results [5]. In addition to testing SVMs for the regression task, we also test a multi-layer perceptron regressor. The accuracies of these algorithms are compared in the pilot study.

A shift correction was used to improve the accuracy for cross-session studies. These errors occur because the wearable can be placed slightly differently to the first time it was worn and thus the anatomical features are not in the same position. To correct this shift, we computed the optical flow between the first frame of a training set and the first frame on the current session. The flow was averaged to get a 2D translation and this transformation was applied to the current video to better align the training and sample features.

We used OpenCV [4] for processing the videos and Scikit [30] for the machine learning implementations.

Pilot Study

We eliminated some of the variables from our main experiment through a pilot study, including the least valuable locations, gestures and algorithms. For this pilot, 2 participants performed each of the 10 gestures (with both flexion and extension of each) 20 times at each of the 5 locations. We compared the accuracy of MLP and SVM, with different classifier parameters to find a suitably accurate configuration. We used 10-fold cross validation on the data set in order to have a simple and reliable measure of the accuracy for each case. Table 1 is a table of results for the average cross validation accuracy for each location, given a particular classifier, for the discrete gesture recognition case.

Classifier	Diag.	Long.	Wrist	Trans.	Post.
MLP	99.875	99.5	99.5	99.25	97.875
SVM	99.625	99.125	99.375	98.75	97.5

Table 1: Results for the average discrete gesture classification accuracies for each position, using different classification algorithms.

Classifier	Diag.	Long.	Wrist	Trans.
Participant 1	99.5	97.0	94.0	98.5
Participant 2	98.5	97.0	97.0	98.0
Average	99.0	97.0	95.5	98.25

Table 2: 10-fold cross validation classification accuracies for finger flexing at different joints.

Our initial results demonstrated that MLPs had a slight advantage over SVMs in every location, so our main study used MLPs. Our best MLP configuration had 15 neurons in the hidden layer, alpha=0.001 and BFGS for weight optimization. After initial exploration, it was very difficult to find a position for the posterior location that gave good coverage of all the required muscles. This is due to the arrangement of muscles and bones around the posterior side of the arm and the larger surface area, and is likely to be the reason for the Posterior location's weaker performance.

In our regression tests for this same data set, the same outcome was mirrored: Posterior location showed the worst performance, and the MLP neural network regressor surpassed the SVM. For this reason, we eliminated the Posterior position from our main study. The best MLP regressor configuration we used for this had 15 neurons in the hidden layer, alpha=0.0001 and Adam for weight optimization. The Posterior position is also the usual location for screens and interactive elements of wearables (e.g., watch face). Therefore our decision to ignore this location is appropriate for ergonomics as well as efficiency.

We also asked these participants to perform flexions for each of the 5 digits 10 times, flexing at the metacarpo-phalangeal joint and again at the interphalangeal joints. For each of these 10 video clips, they were again split into flexion and extension gestures. Analysis of this data indicated that it was in fact possible to differentiate between flexing at different joints, with an average accuracy of 97.4% across all positions. The different types of flexing exhibit unique areas of muscle activity across the superficial and deep muscles. This shows the potential for US to detect finer differences in hand pose, a feature that is difficult to achieve with EMG since it is difficult to differentiate between signals from the superficial and the deep flexors.

The ability to differentiate between different levels of pressure has been demonstrated in previous studies with ultrasound imaging [14] [29]. We also found discernible differences in the images and could qualitatively infer the amount of pressure with the changes in the ultrasound images.

USER STUDY

Procedure

12 participants aged between 20 and 50 years were recruited to take part in the user study; 8 were male and 4 female. The participants were asked to sit in front of a computer, wear the sensor glove and the probe mount on the right hand and then to follow the instructions shown on the monitor (Fig. 4c). The arm position was as depicted in (Fig. 4a). The video showed the user which gesture to perform and an indicator at the bottom gave visual cues for the timing of the gestures.

The conditions for the experiment were the locations of the probe: Diagonal, Longitudinal, Wrist and Transverse. Each of the 12 participants were assigned a pair of conditions (there are 12 ways of picking 2 out of 4 with order) and repeated the last condition. Therefore, each participant performed the gestures on three locations, the second and third locations were the same for testing cross-session performance. At each location, the probe was removed and placed again after a short rest, without any attempt to recalibrate using the US images. In this regard, the short time in between may not seem sufficient for a cross-session study. However, we presume the main issue for cross-session performance is sensor misalignment (as is the case with EMG [2]), as the significant changes in the US images are likely to cause classification problems. A short delay between sessions is enough to simulate the misalignment that would occur with extended delays, and this way we focus solely on the calibration mechanism without interferences from other variables.

At each location the participant had to perform a total of 10 gestures, 10 times each. Each 5-second gesture clip prompted the flexion and extension phases, which were then split into those two halves for a total of 10 flexion and extension gestures. Therefore the study involved: 12 participants X 3 locations X 10 gestures X 10 repetitions = 3600 gesture performances. The average study lasted 45 minutes including the time taken to explain the procedure to the participants and to equip the user with the sensors. The data collected from the participants were analysed offline. The data from the pilot study was not used in the main study.

Results

Different measures of accuracy were calculated for discrete recognition and continuous angle detection. All experiments are within-user.

Cross validation was performed on the data, using the MLP classifier described in the pilot study to produce classifications. We employed a 10-fold leave-one-out cross-validation strategy, with each fold containing one instance of every gesture, of which there are 20 of. Since we split gestures into flexion and extension, gestures instances of the same type were not temporally adjacent. The average classification percentages for each location are shown in Fig. 7. The confusion matrix for the Longitudinal location is shown in Fig. 9.

A one-way mixed Analysis of Variance (ANOVA) was conducted to compare the main effect of sensor location on 10-fold MLP classification performance in Diagonal, Longitudinal, Wrist and Traversal conditions. There was a significant effect of location, $F(3,6)=14.44$, $p<0.01$. Post hoc pairwise comparisons used t-tests with Bonferroni corrections to account for multiple comparisons. There was a significant difference between Diagonal (M=99.78, SD=0.09) and Longitudinal (M=97.94, SD=0.38), $t=5.67$, $p<0.01$; Diagonal and Transverse (M=98.94, SD=0.19), $t=4.08$, $p<0.05$; Longitudinal and Wrist (M=99.78, SD=0.12), $t=-4.30$, $p<0.01$; and Wrist and Transverse, $t=4.08$, $p<0.05$. There was no significant difference between Diagonal and Wrist, or Longitudinal and Transverse. From these results we can establish that for classification accuracy the Diagonal and Wrist conditions were best, followed by Transverse, with the Longitudinal condition last.

The cross-session accuracy is shown in Fig. 8 divided by location for both the raw videos and the shift-corrected videos. The cross-session accuracy is obtained by training the classifier with the data from the second session and then classifying the data from the third session which belonged to the same location.

For the continuous detection of finger angles, the main metric was the Normalised Root Mean Square Error (NRMSE) of the predicted angle compared to the real angle. The value was averaged over the five fingers since the errors were similar for all the digits. These values are shown for each location in Fig. 10.

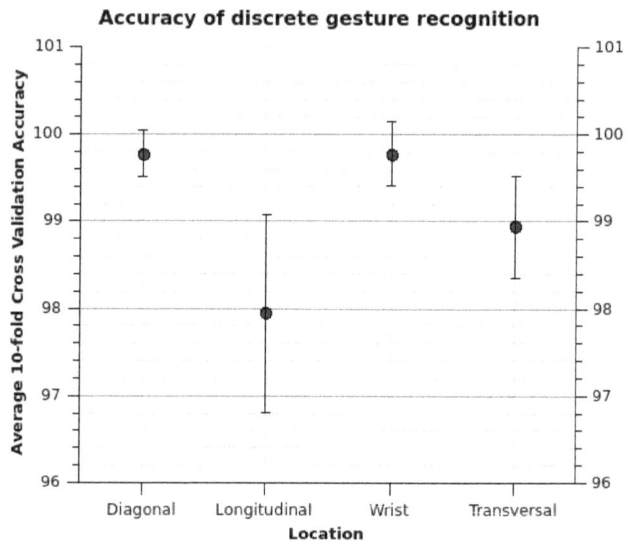

Figure 7: Accuracy of the discrete gesture classification. Average 10-fold cross-validation for each location across all participants.

DISCUSSION

The accuracy in discrete gesture recognition is very high, with the average of all locations being above 99%. The Longitudinal position has been statistically shown to perform the worst for this task. A more limited range of muscles are within the view of the probe at this position, supported by the fact that the gun and ring gestures were usually confused (for both flexion and extension - Fig. 9) since they involve a common

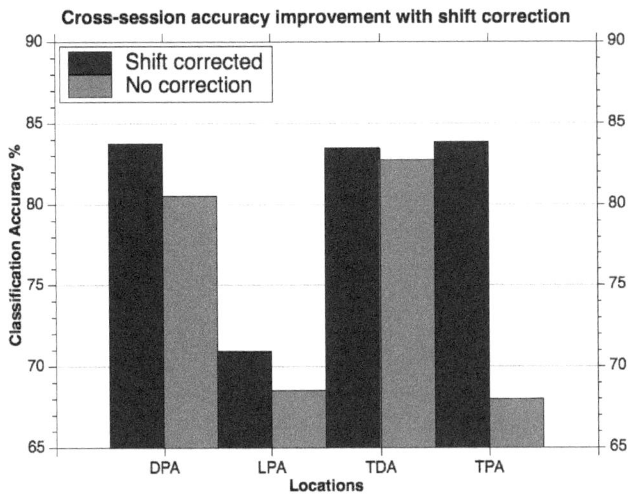

Figure 8: A graph plotting the average classification accuracies for the cross-session data at different locations.

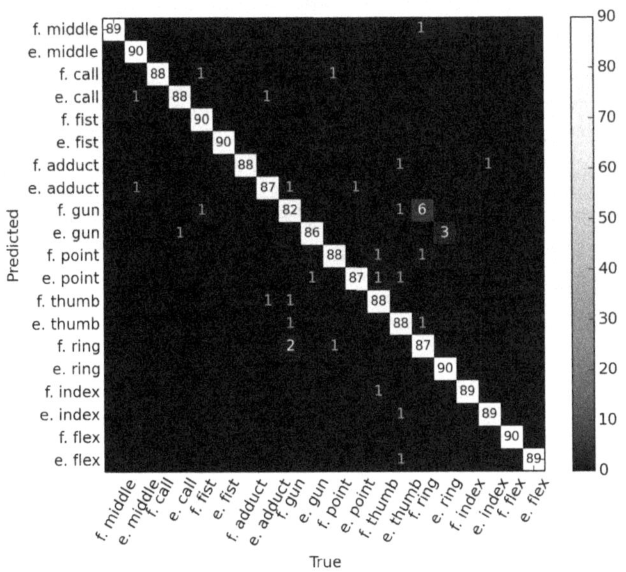

Figure 9: A confusion matrix for the Longitudinal position.

muscle. Other locations showed similar issues, however the issue was more marked in the Longitudinal images. This may also be indicative of inconsistent or insufficient information about the fifth digit muscle across all the locations. In our observations of the images, the thumb and pinky muscles were at the extremities of the images, and it is likely that the pinky could have been out of view. Unexpectedly, the Wrist location offered good results, even when the images seemed to show little movement in comparison to the proximal locations. One possible reason for this is the good coverage of the tendons by the probe, which can easily cover the central part of the wrist due to the smaller surface area. The tendons that move the fingers and wrist have to pass through the carpal tunnel in the wrist making it a concentrated area of information, in contrast

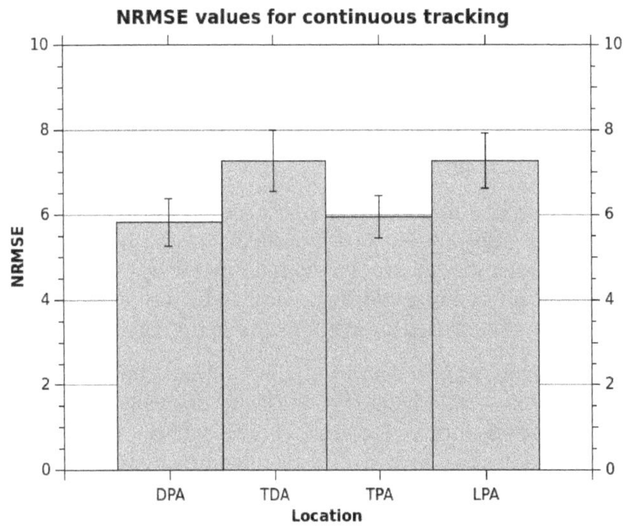

Figure 10: NRMSE values of the continuous digit flexion predictions averaged over all digits and for all participants.

to the proximal locations where the muscles and tendons are spread across a larger area.

The cross-session results show that the loss in accuracy due to probe displacement between sessions affects each location differently. Prior to shift compensation, Transverse and Longitudinal had worse cross-session accuracy when compared to the other locations. This suggests that large shifts occurred between sessions for these positions, and that it may be more difficult to place the probe in the same place between sessions. The shift compensation algorithm improves the cross session accuracy for every location, but this improvement is much larger for Transverse. In contrast, Wrist only improves slightly but that position already offered high cross-session accuracy. This is likely because the smaller size of the wrist allowed less variation in the placement of the probe. Although there were large cross-session errors for Transverse and Longitudinal, the shift can only be compensated well for Transverse. The image shift with Longitudinal cannot be recovered because the image changes differently when the probe shifts laterally, and a simple 2d translation is not enough to correct this change. The other locations are more robust to image changes as displacements perpendicular to the probe do not affect the images significantly.

In summary, the results from the study suggest that there is no significant difference between Diagonal and Wrist in discrete gesture classification, but these are superior to other locations. For ergonomic reasons, Wrist seems like the best location for discrete gestures. For continuous detection of digit angles both Diagonal and Transverse offer the best results. Therefore, the best position for both requirements is Diagonal but if ergonomics is an important factor the Wrist location could be selected for discrete gesture or Transverse for continuous angle detection.

LIMITATIONS AND FUTURE WORK

There are issues with practicality which are yet to be solved before this method is viable as a wearable gesture recognition device. In this section, we will address these limitations and provide information about the current state of research for each of these problems.

Gel is needed to couple the transducer to the skin and facilitate the transmission of ultrasound into the body. It may not be practical to use gel with an everyday wearable, but there have been recent developments which show that hydrogel pads can be used as an alternative coupling medium [20].

Participants were sedentary during our experiments. Different postures will change the muscular disposition inside the forearm and shift the features. There have been some preliminary studies that investigates classification rates for different arm positions, which show that they do not seem to significantly compromise reliability [1]. Further comprehensive research is required to analyse and mitigate the effects of arm movement during everyday activities. It may be possible to use a similar method to our cross-session calibration for this purpose. Also, with inferences of posture from other sensors (e.g. IMU), specific calibration schemes could be applied.

In our experiments, we used a decade old ex-clinical scanner, we are aware of the elevated price and bulky size of these machines. Recently, emergency point of care ultrasonography has created a need for cheaper and smaller pocket-sized scanners; in fact, several portable devices exist [38]. These handheld devices utilise the power of mobile phones to process the raw data. The image quality of these portable devices are comparable to the machine used in our studies. These devices are expensive (>$2k) but will decrease in price with acquisition boards integrated into a chip, and as research in transducer technology progresses [3]. As with most electronics, the cost of the raw materials of these devices is low.

Since the wrist requires a shorter imaging depth, it is possible to use a probe with a higher frequency. This higher frequency may yield better results with the increase in resolution. Higher frequency probes can be smaller in size, making it easier to integrate with wearables.

The probe that was used in this study was large and rigid, hindering its utilization in wearable scenarios. Transducer fabrication research has developed small and flexible thin-film probes, which should help reduce the size. Currently, it is possible to build a flexible probe with multiple elements that can be wrapped around the thumb [41]. This technology may also help to alleviate the aforementioned arm movement artifacts.

The US probe that we used is linear; that is, it has the elements arranged in one dimension. 2D probes that can image 3D volumes without moving them are becoming more available. These probes could improve robustness to shifts in the positioning of the probe, as well as providing more features to classify with.

Always-on gesture detection is desirable for real use. We do not have a dedicated study for proof of gesture spotting, but we found that high levels of activity can be measured by integrating the magnitudes of the optical flow vectors. While we only used this method to split our data, it may also be used as a variable for segmentation. However, this simple approach could be brittle and remains to be tested under realistic conditions, where motion artifacts may cause problems.

Power is a concern for wearable ultrasound imaging devices at the moment. The portable GE Vscan [13] lasts for $\tilde{1}$ hour of continuous use. Battery improvements are expected in the future, but a more interesting approach is to only activate full imaging during gestures, for instance pulsing ultrasound with fewer elements, effectively providing a low-res image to detect gesture onset. A more complete system could have other low-power sensors integrated, such as myoelectric sensors to initially spot the gesture using existing segmentation techniques.

All of the presented experiments are within-user. Much like electromyographic devices, anatomical differences between users creates an interesting challenge for cross-participant use of US wearables. Perhaps a more elaborate classifier and calibration scheme that takes into account the common anatomical features between users, could lead to an effective user-independent system.

Bio identification could be possible with ultrasound imaging. The veins and other anatomical features are detectable with high frequency probes; previously, it has been shown that the structure of the veins can be used as an unique characteristic for identification [24]. This technique could be used to identify the wearer and load their preferences, without the need for external validation.

CONCLUSION

We have presented a solution for detecting discrete gestures and tracking continuous angles of the fingers using ultrasound images captured from a probe mounted on the forearm. Our novel contributions include findings on the variation in performance between different mounting locations. In contrast to previous studies, we provide results for the cross-session accuracy decrease, and show that a simple calibration algorithm can improve the accuracy, and highlights the usefulness for future work. In conclusion, the performance variation across the tested locations vary somewhat insignificantly, meaning that an ergonomic location such as the wrist may be chosen as the desired location for a wearable US device. However, there are some differences in robustness and continuous angle recognition, and depending on the requirements other locations may be more desirable. Wearable applications using ultrasound imaging for gesture detection will become more feasible with the continued decrease in cost and size of US devices, and we hope that this work inspires research in this promising approach.

ACKNOWLEDGMENTS

This research was supported by EPSRC Doctoral Training funding through grant EP/M507994/1. We especially thank members of BIRCH within the UH Bristol NHS Foundation Trust. We also thank Nvidia for facilitating our research by providing hardware and Matthew Sutton for assistance with the video and pictures.

REFERENCES

1. Akhlaghi, N., Baker, C. A., Lahlou, M., Zafar, H., Murthy, K. G., Rangwala, H. S., Kosecka, J., Joiner, W. M., Pancrazio, J. J., and Sikdar, S. Real-time classification of hand motions using ultrasound imaging of forearm muscles. *IEEE Transactions on Biomedical Engineering 63*, 8 (Aug 2016), 1687–1698.
2. Amma, C., Krings, T., Böer, J., and Schultz, T. Advancing muscle-computer interfaces with high-density electromyography. In *Proceedings of the 33rd Annual ACM Conference on Human Factors in Computing Systems*, ACM (2015), 929–938.
3. Bhuyan, A., Choe, J. W., Lee, B. C., Wygant, I. O., Nikoozadeh, A., Oralkan, Ö., and Khuri-Yakub, B. T. Integrated circuits for volumetric ultrasound imaging with 2-d cmut arrays. *IEEE transactions on biomedical circuits and systems 7*, 6 (2013), 796–804.
4. Bradski, G., et al. The opencv library. *Doctor Dobbs Journal 25*, 11 (2000), 120–126.
5. Castellini, C., and Passig, G. Ultrasound image features of the wrist are linearly related to finger positions. In *Intelligent Robots and Systems (IROS), 2011 IEEE/RSJ International Conference on*, IEEE (2011), 2108–2114.
6. Castellini, C., Passig, G., and Zarka, E. Using ultrasound images of the forearm to predict finger positions. *Neural Systems and Rehabilitation Engineering, IEEE Transactions on 20*, 6 (2012), 788–797.
7. Castellini, C., and van der Smagt, P. Surface emg in advanced hand prosthetics. *Biological cybernetics 100*, 1 (2009), 35–47.
8. Chen, X., Zheng, Y.-P., Guo, J.-Y., and Shi, J. Sonomyography (smg) control for powered prosthetic hand: a study with normal subjects. *Ultrasound in medicine & biology 36*, 7 (2010), 1076–1088.
9. Cheng, J., Amft, O., Bahle, G., and Lukowicz, P. Designing sensitive wearable capacitive sensors for activity recognition. *Sensors Journal, IEEE 13*, 10 (2013), 3935–3947.
10. Dementyev, A., and Paradiso, J. A. Wristflex: Low-power gesture input with wrist-worn pressure sensors. In *Proceedings of the 27th annual ACM symposium on User interface software and technology*, ACM (2014), 161–166.
11. Farnebäck, G. Two-frame motion estimation based on polynomial expansion. In *Image analysis*. Springer, 2003, 363–370.
12. Spectra Symbol Flex Sensor 4.5. `http://www.spectrasymbol.com/wp-content/themes/spectra/images/datasheets/FlexSensor.pdf`.
13. GE Vscan. `http://www3.gehealthcare.com/en/products/categories/ultrasound/vscan_portfolio/vscan`.
14. González, D. S., and Castellini, C. A realistic implementation of ultrasound imaging as a human-machine interface for upper-limb amputees. *Frontiers in neurorobotics 7*, 17 (2013).
15. Guo, J.-Y., Zheng, Y.-P., Huang, Q.-H., Chen, X., and He, J.-F. Comparison of sonomyography and electromyography of forearm muscles in the guided wrist extension. In *Medical Devices and Biosensors, 2008. ISSS-MDBS 2008. 5th International Summer School and Symposium on*, IEEE (2008), 235–238.
16. Guo, J.-Y., Zheng, Y.-P., Kenney, L. P., Bowen, A., Howard, D., and Canderle, J. J. A comparative evaluation of sonomyography, electromyography, force, and wrist angle in a discrete tracking task. *Ultrasound in medicine & biology 37*, 6 (2011), 884–891.
17. Hamid Muhammed, H., and Raghavendra, J. Optomyography (omg): A novel technique for the detection of muscle surface displacement using photoelectric sensors. In *10th International Conference on Bioelectromagnetism, ISBEM 2015*, vol. 10 (2015).
18. Hettiarachchi, N., Ju, Z., and Liu, H. A new wearable ultrasound muscle activity sensing system for dexterous prosthetic control. In *Systems, Man, and Cybernetics (SMC), 2015 IEEE International Conference on*, IEEE (2015), 1415–1420.
19. Hodges, P., Pengel, L., Herbert, R., and Gandevia, S. Measurement of muscle contraction with ultrasound imaging. *Muscle & nerve 27*, 6 (2003), 682–692.
20. HydroAid Ultrasound Hydrogel Pad. `http://www.civco.com/mmi/ultrasound/accessories/acoustic-standoffs/Disposable-AquaFlex-Acoustic-Standoff-Pads-610-1322.htm`.
21. Islam, M. A., Sundaraj, K., Ahmad, R. B., and Ahamed, N. U. Mechanomyogram for muscle function assessment: a review. *PloS one 8*, 3 (2013), e58902.
22. Kerber, F., Löchtefeld, M., Krüger, A., McIntosh, J., McNeill, C., and Fraser, M. Understanding same-side interactions with wrist-worn devices. In *Proceedings of the 9th Nordic Conference on Human-Computer Interaction*, NordiCHI '16, ACM (New York, NY, USA, 2016), 28:1–28:10.
23. Kim, D., Hilliges, O., Izadi, S., Butler, A. D., Chen, J., Oikonomidis, I., and Olivier, P. Digits: freehand 3d interactions anywhere using a wrist-worn gloveless sensor. In *Proceedings of the 25th annual ACM symposium on User interface software and technology*, ACM (2012), 167–176.
24. Kono, M., Ueki, H., and Umemura, S.-i. Near-infrared finger vein patterns for personal identification. *Applied Optics 41*, 35 (2002), 7429–7436.

25. Korstanje, J.-W. H., Selles, R. W., Stam, H. J., Hovius, S. E., and Bosch, J. G. Development and validation of ultrasound speckle tracking to quantify tendon displacement. *Journal of biomechanics 43*, 7 (2010), 1373–1379.

26. Loram, I. D., Maganaris, C. N., and Lakie, M. Use of ultrasound to make noninvasive in vivo measurement of continuous changes in human muscle contractile length. *Journal of applied physiology 100*, 4 (2006), 1311–1323.

27. Mujibiya, A., Cao, X., Tan, D. S., Morris, D., Patel, S. N., and Rekimoto, J. The sound of touch: On-body touch and gesture sensing based on transdermal ultrasound propagation. In *Proceedings of the 2013 ACM International Conference on Interactive Tabletops and Surfaces*, ITS '13, ACM (New York, NY, USA, 2013), 189–198.

28. Orizio, C., and Gobbo, M. Mechanomyography. *Wiley Encyclopedia of Biomedical Engineering* (2006).

29. Ortenzi, V., Tarantino, S., Castellini, C., and Cipriani, C. Ultrasound imaging for hand prosthesis control: a comparative study of features and classification methods. In *Rehabilitation Robotics (ICORR), 2015 IEEE International Conference on*, IEEE (2015), 1–6.

30. Pedregosa, F., Varoquaux, G., Gramfort, A., Michel, V., Thirion, B., Grisel, O., Blondel, M., Prettenhofer, P., Weiss, R., Dubourg, V., et al. Scikit-learn: Machine learning in python. *The Journal of Machine Learning Research 12* (2011), 2825–2830.

31. Rautaray, S. S., and Agrawal, A. Vision based hand gesture recognition for human computer interaction: a survey. *Artificial Intelligence Review 43*, 1 (2015), 1–54.

32. Rekimoto, J. Gesturewrist and gesturepad: Unobtrusive wearable interaction devices. In *Wearable Computers, 2001. Proceedings. Fifth International Symposium on*, IEEE (2001), 21–27.

33. Rossi, M., Benatti, S., Farella, E., and Benini, L. Hybrid emg classifier based on hmm and svm for hand gesture recognition in prosthetics. In *Industrial Technology (ICIT), 2015 IEEE International Conference on*, IEEE (2015), 1700–1705.

34. Shi, J., Hu, S.-X., Liu, Z., Guo, J.-Y., Zhou, Y.-J., and Zheng, Y.-P. Recognition of finger flexion from ultrasound image with optical flow: A preliminary study. In *Biomedical Engineering and Computer Science (ICBECS), 2010 International Conference on*, IEEE (2010), 1–4.

35. Sikdar, S., Rangwala, H., Eastlake, E. B., Hunt, I. A., Nelson, A. J., Devanathan, J., Shin, A., and Pancrazio, J. J. Novel method for predicting dexterous individual finger movements by imaging muscle activity using a wearable ultrasonic system. *Neural Systems and Rehabilitation Engineering, IEEE Transactions on 22*, 1 (2014), 69–76.

36. Smith, R. J., Tenore, F., Huberdeau, D., Cummings, R. E., and Thakor, N. V. Continuous decoding of finger position from surface emg signals for the control of powered prostheses. In *Engineering in Medicine and Biology Society, 2008. EMBS 2008. 30th Annual International Conference of the IEEE*, IEEE (2008), 197–200.

37. Tenore, F. V., Ramos, A., Fahmy, A., Acharya, S., Etienne-Cummings, R., and Thakor, N. V. Decoding of individuated finger movements using surface electromyography. *Biomedical Engineering, IEEE Transactions on 56*, 5 (2009), 1427–1434.

38. Wojtczak, J., and Bonadonna, P. Pocket mobile smartphone system for the point-of-care submandibular ultrasonography. *The American journal of emergency medicine 31*, 3 (2013), 573–577.

39. Wolf, M. T., Assad, C., Stoica, A., You, K., Jethani, H., Vernacchia, M. T., Fromm, J., and Iwashita, Y. Decoding static and dynamic arm and hand gestures from the jpl biosleeve. In *Aerospace Conference, 2013 IEEE*, IEEE (2013), 1–9.

40. Yamakawa, S., and Nojima, T. A proposal for a mmg-based hand gesture recognition method. In *Adjunct proceedings of the 25th annual ACM symposium on User interface software and technology*, ACM (2012), 89–90.

41. Yang, Y., Tian, H., Yan, B., Sun, H., Wu, C., Shu, Y., Wang, L.-G., and Ren, T.-L. A flexible piezoelectric micromachined ultrasound transducer. *RSC Advances 3*, 47 (2013), 24900–24905.

42. You, K.-J., Rhee, K.-W., and Shin, H.-C. Finger motion decoding using emg signals corresponding various arm postures. *Experimental neurobiology 19*, 1 (2010), 54–61.

43. Zhang, Y., Xiao, R., and Harrison, C. Advancing hand gesture recognition with high resolution electrical impedance tomography. In *Proceedings of the 29th Annual Symposium on User Interface Software and Technology*, UIST '16, ACM (New York, NY, USA, 2016), 843–850.

44. Zheng, Y.-P., Chan, M., Shi, J., Chen, X., and Huang, Q.-H. Sonomyography: Monitoring morphological changes of forearm muscles in actions with the feasibility for the control of powered prosthesis. *Medical engineering & physics 28*, 5 (2006), 405–415.

Virtuosos on the Screen: Playing Virtual Characters Like Instruments in Competitive Super Smash Bros. Melee

Colin M. Ford
University of California, Irvine
Irvine, CA, United States
Cford1@uci.edu

ABSTRACT

Previous research on virtual sociality in games suggests that players use custom avatars to reflect, alter, and perform new identities in digital spaces. However, this study explores an alternative theory of social performance by analyzing a competitive game, Super Smash Bros. Melee, where players face off in timed matches and interact through pre-designed characters. This study shows how Melee players treat virtual characters as performative instruments, similar to the violin or the piano. In forum posts and player-created media, Melee players emphasize the need to train one's hands, eyes, and mind in order to master a character's complexity and express style and skills in live matches. Instrumental embodiment in a competitive game like Melee thus positions players as virtuosos who perform for perceptive audiences. This research points to a range of ways that players may relate to virtual bodies, connected to distinct kinds of social activities.

Author Keywords

Play; Performance; Avatar; eSports; Player-Character Relationship; Embodiment; Instrument

ACM Classification Keywords

K.8.0 PERSONAL COMPUTING; Games

INTRODUCTION

Researchers have largely studied social interaction online through the lens of the avatar, focusing on virtual world activities like conversation, role play, and team play [8, 15, 39, 51, 64, 91, 95]. These researchers have characterized virtual worlds as stages for assuming new online identities, with the customizable avatar serving as a visual indicator of a player's in-world role [12, 14, 26, 42, 52, 80]. Competitive gaming—or eSports—puts players on stage in a quite different sense, broadcasting high-level matches to crowds of avid spectators. Unlike avatars, competitive games like Super Smash Bros. Melee often feature non-customizable characters, each with a pre-set appearance, backstory, and array of fighting techniques. In an effort to describe the user's relationship with pre-designed characters, some game studies scholars have moved away from the language of the avatar, theorizing virtual characters instead as props, tools, or vehicles for player manipulation of the game world [9, 46, 57]. In contrast to theories of the avatar or the vehicle, I posit that Melee players treat their characters as *performative instruments*, similar to musical instruments like the violin or the piano. This term underscores the expressive potential of a character-instrument as well as the practiced skills necessary to reach that potential. By considering virtual characters as expressive, demanding instruments, it becomes possible to develop an alternative theory of social performance in virtual space, centered not on the management of virtual appearance, but on the virtuoso display of skills and style in the face of challenging activity.

CHI 2017, May 06-11, 2017, Denver, CO, USA
© 2017 ACM. ISBN 978-1-4503-4655-9/17/05…$15.00
DOI: http://dx.doi.org/10.1145/3025453.3026053

Through analysis of Melee tournament broadcasts, online discussions, and edited gameplay videos, I examine the ways in which players discuss, share, and create performances using character-instruments. Melee is a fighting game in which the goal is to knock the other on-screen character out of the play area (called the *stage*) and into the abyss below. Before a match starts, each player selects a fighter from a roster of 25 pre-designed characters, including iconic Nintendo figures like Mario, Fox, Pikachu, Link, and Sheik. Melee boasts a long history of public competition, with recorded matches stretching back to its release in 2001. Apart from recorded tournament matches, the other main video genre in the Melee community is the *combo video*, an edited short-form video that synchronizes energetic music tracks with quick cuts of in-game play sequences. This paper covers the live performances of characters during tournaments, as well as the remixed performances of these characters in edited combo videos.

Figure 1. A combo video. "The GOAT - A MaNg0 M0ntage." 2015. baldcarrots. Youtu.be/Lwh1IsjG05U.

This paper presents the web of musical analogies that Melee players use to describe high-level play. Players repeatedly emphasize the creativity of play sequences, the changing tempos of matches, the importance of practice, and the conversational nature of play [e.g., 5]. Players sometimes even directly compare Melee to art forms like jazz and poetry [36, 48]. Community video makers extend these analogies through combo videos, showcasing players' skilled performances by overlaying them with musical beats. By comparing the ideal—even beautiful—play of combo videos with the clunky play that many describe when they are playing poorly, I examine how players talk about what it is like to perform (or underperform) in competitive games. I also show how existing studies of in-game performance rely on a theatrical model—inspired by Erving Goffman's seminal work, *The Presentation of Self*—but I found that a musical model better fits competitive Melee players' experiences and discussions.

This paper extends existing studies of musician-instrument relationships [28, 32, 58] to the agonistic context of competitive Melee, showing how players train with their favored instruments and develop signature styles of play. Skilled performance has become increasingly important in gaming with the rise of eSports [81]. In response to the growing status of Melee as an eSport, top players in the scene have experienced incredible pressure to perform in order to gain sponsorships, fans, and tournament placings. Like musical performance, high-level Melee is considered both technically impressive and supremely creative. Virtuoso performance in eSports involves the display of personal mastery *with* an instrument, as well as the struggle for interpersonal mastery *between* character-instruments. This struggle may be posited as an important element of the drama and interest of eSports, for both players and spectators. This paper complements existing studies of the player-avatar relationship by outlining key features of the player-character relationship in Melee, showing how character design yields social-interactive possibilities between Melee players and audiences. Drawing on my findings, I also include a series of character design recommendations that may inform the design of eSports games other than Melee.

BACKGROUND

Melee was released on the Nintendo GameCube in 2001, and was the best-selling game on the system, reaching total sales of 7.09 million by 2008 [59]. Each player in Melee directs a single on-screen character with a handheld GameCube Controller, which includes a primary analog stick for movement, five front-facing buttons, a four-way "d-pad," a secondary analog "c-stick," and three top-facing shoulder buttons. During a typical Melee match, competitive players utilize all of these buttons and sticks in rapid succession, spiking to over 400 unique Actions Per Minute [10]. Competitive Melee does not reward "mashing," which simply involves jamming all buttons as quickly as possible, but rather involves a combination of rapid and precise inputs, prizing physical finesse as much as mental decision-making.

The competitive Melee community is relatively small, but growing. While Melee viewer counts peaked at 205,000 in 2015 during the grand finals of Evo 2015 [84], most national tournaments tend to receive a maximum of 50,000 to 100,000 concurrent live-streaming viewers. Competitive Melee is usually played in a one-versus-one format, with the two players sitting side-by-side, looking at the same television screen. As players input moves on their controllers, they attempt to position their characters in order to land decisive blows without getting hit themselves. Successful attacks send opponents careening across the screen, eventually gaining enough strength to knock them out of play entirely. Many attacks also string together into *combos*, where an attacker follows the movement of the defender and lands successive blows. Combos are quite difficult to perform, requiring split-second timing and the ability to read where an opponent will fly after they get hit in order to intercept them with another attack. Due to their difficulty, effectiveness, and flashiness, combos produce a great deal of excitement for players and spectators. Combo videos present a succession of stellar combos from different matches, often performed by a single player in order to showcase that player's style and skill.

Melee is unique due to its exceptional age as a competitive electronic game, lending it a 15-year history of player development, discovery, performance, and organizational change. Players captured the earliest combo videos by pointing handheld recorders at their television screens. Nowadays, they use *capture cards* which they hook up to their machines in order to pull visual data directly from the game itself. For most of its history, Melee has lacked any online functionality. Melee's eSports scene thus revolves around organized tournament events in physical venues, where players gather from across the region, nation, or even the globe, depending on the scale and reputation of the particular event. Nevertheless, competitive players frequently share gameplay videos online, discuss Melee in forums, and spectate live tournament streams. The competitive Melee scene thus extends into digital mediums where high-level play is discussed, analyzed, and enjoyed.

METHODS

This study utilized purposive searching to collect a sample of combo videos and related discussions, ranging from Melee's release in 2001 to 2016. Searches were conducted using search engines on three major sites that Melee community members frequent: Reddit.com, YouTube.com, and Smashboards.com. Search terms included "Melee combo video," "Melee montage," "Melee combo," "Melee tribute," "Melee tournament," "Melee tutorial," "Melee advice," "Melee top player," "high-level Melee," "Melee skill," and "Melee character." Searches were also date-restricted to pull videos from particular years, ensuring that the sample represents Melee's full recorded history. The front page of Reddit.com/r/smashbros was also monitored for a period of 6 months, adding discussions and videos to the sample if they referenced Melee combos, combo videos, characters, tournaments, high-level play, training advice, or the experience of playing Melee. In order to understand how commentators discuss characters, all major tournament broadcasts were observed through the eSports streaming website, Twitch.tv, for a period of 6 months. For this study, a "major tournament" was defined as an event with two or more top-5 players in attendance, using the community's standard player-ranking system [45]. To understand how high-level players narrate their experiences with characters, I also collected samples of interviews, character guides, and forum discussions featuring top players. "Top players" were defined as ranking in the top 100 players worldwide using the community's standard player-ranking system.

To turn gathered data into findings, this study used *Grounded Theory* [76]. Grounded Theory applies coding schema to a body of qualitative data, and then collects codes into concepts and categories. Initial codes were applied by using key terms from the data, and then these codes were iteratively refined. The following codes were applied: "advanced technique," "button input," "control," "fandom," "hype," "practice," "physical challenge," "mental challenge," "relative strength," "style," "tempo," "theorycraft." These codes were the building blocks of my analysis, allowing data to be sorted into my four Findings. Noting the prevalence of musical metaphors across all data, I was able to subsume the categories under a grounded theory of musical performance.

This paper applies *semiotic visual analysis* to interpret the social meanings embedded in combo videos by searching for patterned themes and stylistic choices. According to Giorgia Aiello, the main aim of semiotic analysis is "to look systematically at how textual strategies are deployed to convey certain meanings" [2]. This form of analysis focuses on the *social resources* present in visual media that permit viewers to interpret images. These resources could be rhetorical techniques like the use of perspective or framing, but the term also covers recurrent motifs and symbols that are important to a community [41]. Combo videos are embedded with a variety of social resources that make them resonate with competitive Melee players. Such resources include music choice, editing, game elements, repeated tropes, Melee-specific references, and more. By analyzing these resources, I unpack combo videos as a social medium that attempts both to capture the experience of playing a character and to legitimate the status of particular players, events, and the Melee community as a whole.

This paper also applies *discourse analysis* to interpret player conversations about combo videos, high-level play, and Melee's cast of virtual characters. The form of discourse presented in this article is what James Gee describes as "language-in-use," pointing to the way in which language emerges from particular practices and contexts [34]. By observing discourse that is oriented around a particular activity, it is possible to analyze how people involved in that activity understand it, attempt to change it, and position themselves with respect to others. In this case, I examine discourse produced by Melee community members in order to recognize how Melee players treat virtual characters and competitive performance. Discourse analysis is also useful for following how new players are instructed in learning to play. On forums, experienced players often give newer players advice on how to perform with virtual characters, providing critical insights into how community members understand, practice, and play with their characters in Melee.

FINDINGS

In the following section, I present findings on how Melee players discuss virtual characters and the experience of playing Melee. Specifically, I outline key factors that distinguish character-instruments from avatars, showing how Melee players treat characters not as reflections of themselves, but as instrumental extensions of their creative and effective capacities on-screen. I also show how combo videos represent performative ideals for the Melee community, demonstrating masterful alignment between player and character, as well as mastery over one's opponent.

Qualities of Character-Instruments

I found that Melee players often deploy performative analogies in order to convey the experience of playing a character. Melee players treat characters like fine instruments, praising the manual proficiency and mental prowess of those able to unlock characters' creative potential in live performances. Players sometimes describe good Melee as "art" [96], "jazz" [88], "poetry" [48], or "a conversation" [5], but these metaphors get mixed with sports terminology due to the competitive, goal-oriented nature of Melee. One player sums it up like this: "Melee is two basketball players with saxophones trying to dunk on each other while playing sick jazz solos" [31]. The goal of winning a match is sometimes placed at odds with the goal of giving a beautiful performance, creating a dynamic tension that players navigate between "playing to win" and "playing with heart" [75]. Truly great players are praised for merging the two, with others noting that they have

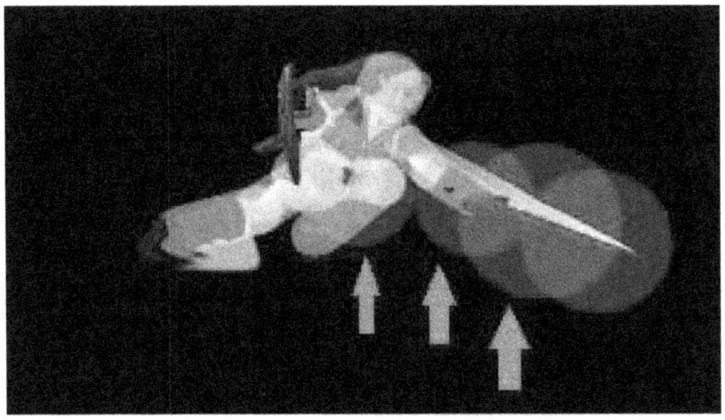

Figure 4. Still of gif showing the character Link's frame data on an attack. Photo Credit: standardtoaster. 2009. "Link Hitboxes and Frame Data." Smashboards.com.

created "their own unique style" that is nevertheless highly effective [88]. This mix of skillful handling, expressiveness, and goal-orientation makes virtual characters a unique kind of instrument, involving the following four qualities:

Rhythm

Melee community members emphasize that playing characters well requires precise timing, and that new players need to learn these timings in order to succeed. Characters are rhythmic in two major senses.

First, characters have certain timings embedded in them as a result of the game's code. In the more technical discussions of Melee, players share knowledge and gifs of characters' *frame data*, a term that refers to the precise number of frames (each frame is 1/60th of a second) a particular in-game action takes to complete. Many advanced techniques in Melee require stringing together inputs with very narrow timing, often allowing only a 1 to 6 frame window for proper execution. For instance, one player outlines the inputs needed to perform an advanced technique called a *multishine* with a character called Fox:

> 1st frame [after pressing B+down] the attack comes out
>
> 2nd and 3rd frames – very slight lag, no attack or reflection, the jump button can be pressed during these frames, but it won't take effect until frame 4
>
> ...
>
> frame 9 – exactly 6 frames into your jump press B+down, this is the most difficult part, you'll have to practice finding the timing to press B exactly 1/12 of a second (5 frames) after pressing Y/X
>
> ...
>
> repeat frames 4-13 as much as you like/can [75]

This technique is not an obscure, unusable trick for Fox players. Rather, top level Fox players execute multishines and other similarly precise skills quite frequently in competitive matches, displaying their bodily attunement to the fine rhythms of in-game action. Extended techniques like *wobbling* have even been specified in terms of Beats per Minute. One player provides an explanation of wobbling: "The rhythmic tapping required to keep an opponent trapped in a wobble is about 200 BPM...if you tap A with the beat you can wobble" [60]. Because different characters have different frame data, each character has a unique rhythmic structure encoded into it. Melee players recognize these rhythms when discussing characters. Fox is a "fast" character that is considered unsuited for newer players who lack a strong sense of the game's precise rhythms. Other characters like Ganon are markedly "slower," meaning that his actions tend to take more frames than Fox's equivalent actions. Frame data thus constitutes a comparative dimension across virtual characters, providing each character its own feel as players experience and respond to differently encoded rhythms [53].

The second way in which characters are rhythmic has less to do with the hard limits of game code, and more to do with how a player chooses to conduct the pace of a match. Like any instrument, characters can be played fast or slow, smoothly or erratically. In discussions of high-level Melee, members sometimes link pacing to a player's mood or energy level, sometimes to skill, and sometimes to strategy. Players can "run over" their opponent with fast play, or they can "slow down" by putting up a defensive "wall" [56]. Top players develop a reputation for playing at a certain pace. For instance, commentators at the Dreamhack Austin tournament noted that top player Hungrybox "likes to establish a slow, deliberate tempo" in order to frustrate his opponents [25]. Players can also decide to "turn it up," a phrase commentators use to describe switching from slow to fast play in order to catch an opponent off guard [73]. Character guides typically advise players to change their rhythms strategically:

> Mixing up your timing, however is often beneficial in order to create a different set of expectations for your opponent [54]

These tempo shifts take advantage of the rhythmic quality of characters, lulling opponents into a false sense of security with a stable rhythm, only to mix it up by changing the timing.

As players tap out new rhythms on their controllers, their characters move to a hidden beat. Good combo videos make these hidden beats explicit, pairing in-game actions with musical tracks that heighten the sense of a player's rhythmic performance. When evaluating combo videos, community members frequently critique the extent to which the video's musical beat fits the beats of selected combos:

> This was actually a legit really good combo video, I was impressed with how well it went along with the song[49]
>
> This was a great combo video. I appreciated how it lined up with the song [85]
>
> I didn't really feel the bits where trying to sync the music to the combos was that, smooth? It felt kind of forced, so I felt it was kind of unnecessary or weird in some way. Especially where you just cut 1 big string of a combo just to match the music's beat. [67]

The latter viewer critiques the maker's choice to distort combos by cutting them into segments, rather than presenting the combo as a continuous whole. The viewer points out that the maker allowed the music's beat to trump the combo's internal beat, forcing the maker to cut up the combo in order to fit the music. Well-received combo videos tend to directly represent the pace at which a player is performing with a character, selecting music and clips that sync up smoothly. Because players set their own unique pace in game, video makers try to choose songs that match the pace at which a player performs. Pacing affords different ways to play the same virtual character, enabling the character to be an instrument attuned to the player's mood, skills, strategies, and desires.

Mechanical Potential

Virtual characters are responsive to a player's inputs. When a player presses a button or moves the control stick, his/her character acts in a predictable manner, according to the game's code. Melee players refer to this predictable player-character relationship as a character's *mechanics*. Skilled players have deep knowledge of mechanics, unlocking a character's mechanical potential to act in the game through practiced hand movements.

In order to perform well, players must work to align their bodily habits with their character's mechanics. Guides for new Melee players typically include sections covering mechanics, writing up exactly what actions the character performs when the player uses different combinations of manual inputs. Experienced players on forums advise newer players to practice until they understand the mechanics that allow them to move around, put out attacks, and block their opponent's attacks:

> You have to get more hours in. Top players have spent countless hours just getting down movement. [61]

> Took me about 4 or 5 months to get all the basic fox tech mostly on lock. It's not hard, you just need to be willing to put in the hours. Think of it like playing an instrument. You need to put in the time to be able to play it. [13]

The latter forum goer links Melee characters specifically to musical instruments, arguing for the importance of sustained practice in order to play well. Similar to how each musical instrument has physical qualities that a novice musician must learn to deal with, each virtual character has a unique set of coded mechanics to master. The goal is for the new player to incorporate a character's mechanics to the extent that in-game action becomes natural. New players must adjust to mechanics through practice, gradually learning how to align their physical bodies with characters' mechanical bodies.

This process of learning is potentially endless; even top players continue to practice, pushing the limits of their characters' mechanical potential. Beyond training with established strategies and mechanical skills, players also talk about experimenting with unorthodox input combinations and tactics. The Melee community's term for this activity is called *labbing*. Players who attempt to figure out new things about characters are "hitting the lab," experimenting with different input combinations, timings, and frame data [44]. Sometimes, this practice even involves delving into Melee's source code [1]. The aim of labbing is to discover new mechanics, advanced techniques, and strategies. Due to continuous player efforts through Melee's 15-year history, community members sense that their knowledge of characters has advanced significantly, and that their ability to control characters has markedly improved, despite the game's actual code remaining unchanged.

Figure 5. Still from in-game tutorial video: "How to Play." Super Smash Bros. Melee. 2001. Nintendo.

Early Melee combo videos showcased the mechanical potential of characters, revealing an unanticipated depth to the game. These videos showed characters performing novel actions that "promised to blow our minds and change the way we thought about Melee forever" [82]. In a discussion on favorite combo videos, one smasher relates the importance of a 2005 video made by the legendary player, Bombsoldier:

> His combo video with that bombs over baghdad song was basically every single smashers intro to competitive melee. He was doing 0-death combos while everyone else was still bumbling around [66]

An article on Bombsoldier's legacy makes the similar claim that his videos changed the way in which Melee was played, showing a new technical level that players could achieve [82]. Another player gives his opinion:

> In a weird way, this article [on Bombsoldier] reminds me a lot of Robert Johnson's impact on blues music. A guy comes out of nowhere, creates something nobody has ever seen before, and then disappears before attaining the success that, in hindsight, should have been his for the taking. [40]

Like great musicians, great players are remembered for making an impact on the scene, showing new ways to play with old mechanics. Combo videos were an early medium for capturing the creativity of Melee's pioneers and sharing knowledge about a character's mechanical potential, especially in an era before streaming video or YouTube. Unlike forum threads, which were limited to pictures and text, combo videos showed mechanics in action, proving not only that advanced techniques were possible, but that they could be performed in a real match. The first recognized combo video in Melee, "The Jarrod Experience"—released in 2003—opens with a clip of Fox performing an extended combo on another character called a *wall shine drill*. This kind of combo is commonplace today, but in 2003 it was unheard of, meriting a full 30 second demonstration of the technique in action [83]. These demonstrations were important for showing the mechanical depth of the game, making the case that Melee characters could be instruments for advanced, technical play. In support of this claim, another early collective of combo video makers opens their trailer by referring to themselves as "A crew dedicated / to high level gameplay / and to proving once & for all / that this is no party game" [84]. Melee's status as a "high level" competitive game, rather than a party game, relies on the ability of skilled players to tap into characters' mechanical potential, distinguishing themselves from "casuals" by performing advanced combos. While party games are considered relatively static over time, competitive Melee is progressive. Like art, new styles and techniques continually replace old ones as players figure out different ways to harness characters' mechanical potential. Exploring mechanical potential is a collective project for Melee players, enabling characters to serve as instruments for the demonstration of novel techniques and performative mastery.

Expressive Potential

Melee players do not treat characters as simple tools for winning in the most efficient way possible. Rather, they use characters' mechanics to express their own style and creativity during competitive matches. Characters are expressive instruments in two main ways:

First, Melee characters permit players to express styles of play, resulting from particular patterns of in-game action. When community members discuss high-level tournament matches, they are quick to point out how each player displays style. Sometimes, members assert that characters themselves have an inherent style that players tap into:

> I just feel that Westballz IS falco, his entire style fits the character like a glove. [50]

> Hungrybox became known as the best puff player because he played patiently (how puff needs to be played). This obviously upset a lot of people...Mang0 for one was very vocal about how much he disliked hbox's playstyle [94]

> S2J is my favorite [Capt.] Falcon hands down...Anything with style, combos, etc. get me hooked. [27]

In each of these comments, forum goers link top players—Westballz, Hungrybox, and S2J—directly to virtual characters: Falco, Jigglypuff, and Captain Falcon. These players are renowned in the Melee community for

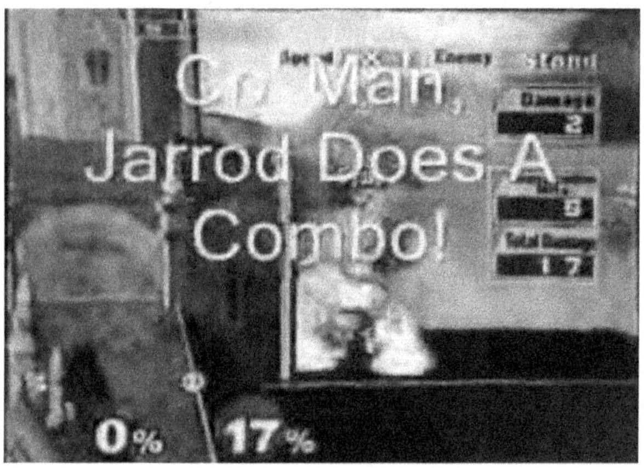

Figure 6. Still from "The Jarrod Experience." 2003. The Punch Crew. Youtu.be/H5ydapVh2VQ.

pioneering a style that harmonizes with their character, finding resonance between their own persona and their characters' mechanics. For example, Westballz has a reputation as an aggressive, flashy, in-your-face player, a style considered to be aligned with his character, Falco. Top players extend characters' expressive potential, revealing that each character is oriented towards a certain style as a result of its mechanics. In this way, mechanics are not only functional, but also expressive, analogous to the timbre of a musical instrument [30]. When player inputs hang together as a playstyle, each character gains a distinctive tone that can be felt and admired by others. On the other hand, Melee players recognize that characters can express a range of styles:

> If you look at Leffen's Fox and compare it to Chillin's Fox, they are vastly different. Not in skill, but in STYLE; this is one of the huge reasons why Melee players love Melee. [37]

Although Leffen and Chillin are playing the same instrument, Fox, they each handle him differently, showing that Fox is a character with deep expressive potential. A character's expressive potential is not treated as a function of in-game appearance. Melee players rarely reference how Fox or any other character looks. Instead, expression is understood as deriving from the range of ways to play, in the same way that the piano's expressive potential results from infinite variations on striking its keys. Fox has high expressive potential because he provides a wide range of effective options for players, allowing for multiple styles to emerge. When Melee players wield instruments with style, they move characters beyond the realm of the purely functional or the purely ornamental, and towards the domain of creative expression.

Second, Melee characters allow players to build shared excitement, or *hype*, by creating impressive moments during matches. In the Melee scene, making hype plays is an ideal goal for top players, helping them gain confidence and acclaim. Commentators of eSports events are quick to recognize hype moments during tournament broadcasts, adopting a particularly feverish pitch and exclaiming disbelief at incredible combos and other "sick" plays [e.g., 78]. Community members share their hype in post-match discussion threads:

> THIS GAME WAS LIKE EATING 700 BIG MACS IN A ROW / MULTIPLE HEART ATTACKS BUT I GOT THROUGH

> GET HYPE!

> AHHHHHHHHHHHHHHHHH

> I NEED TO SLEEP BUT I CAN'T OMG [22]

Stunning performances with characters produce hype, leaving viewers awe-struck. In forum threads, eSports broadcasts, and combo videos, hype game moments are picked up by the community and spread, building a shared sense of excitement and love for the game. Tournament organizers rely on hype to boost attendance and viewership, making special videos that showcase player rivalries and past tournament highlights [e.g., 72, 92]. Top players use hype to win over the crowd, enabling them to receive recognition that can translate into sponsorships and fans. For instance, star play Mang0 is well-known for adding fans to the "Mang0 nation" by making hype plays: "He earns his money stylin'" [680. Not to be confused with playstyle, *styling* refers to showing off for the benefit of an audience through novel, risky, or impressive play. While hype is now popularly broadcast through tournament streams, combo videos set the precedent for styling years earlier. As one veteran player puts it: "The combo video has long been a warning shot to the world, letting people know that you exist and are capable of dropping jaws" [74]. The combo is the quintessential hype moment, where the player and character are completely aligned in action that is both effective and expressive. Hype players are savvy performers who use their characters as instruments that demand attention and appreciation.

Reaching characters' expressive potential is thus a motivating force for competitive Melee players, empowering them to cultivate their own style, capture an audience, and turn them into fans. As expressive instruments, characters allow players to become performers, playing for not only for themselves, but for the benefit of perceptive audiences.

Leverage

Melee players frequently discuss the influence that characters have over other in-game characters, objects, and environments. Characters with the capacity to act on others have *leverage*. In short, leverage is defined as mechanics applied to a particular game situation. Characters with leverage are effective instruments, able to change the present state of a game.

Melee matches are a struggle to gain control over the other player, taking advantage of a character's leverage in order to win. Characters' leverage thus serves as a source of both opportunity and challenge for competitive Melee players, who must apply their own characters' leverage while mitigating their opponent's leverage. Importantly, Melee players recognize leverage as both situational and interactive, delineating situations in which the same character can have more or less leverage. For example, tournament commentators in Melee sometimes relate the strategic importance of "controlling center stage," or positioning one's character in the middle of the stage [73]. This position affords a character maximum leverage, pushing the opponent to the "corner" or edge of the stage, where the cornered character has fewer options to respond or retreat. In this case, leverage is treated as spatial, a function of Melee characters' potential to threaten the space around them and block an opponent's movement.

Figure 7. Top player Axe acknowledges the crowd's applause after a close set with Armada. Evo 2014. Photo Credit: David Zhou. Flickr.com/photos/nodnod/.

Leverage can also be temporal, a result of a sequence of actions that gives one player a relative advantage. For instance, Melee characters block incoming attacks with *shields*, defensive bubbles that form around characters and get smaller as they are attacked until they break. When players use their characters' attacks to catch opponents shielding, they are applying *pressure*. Tournament commentators narrate the effectiveness of this strategy to viewers, explaining how pressure mounts as the defending player's shield shrinks, reducing the defender's options and forcing them to gamble on evasive maneuvers. Good shield pressure is thus a temporal sequence where mechanics are skillfully applied, allowing the aggressor to build leverage and prey on the defender's weaker position. In either case, skillful players manage the challenges of competitive play through leverage, attempting to maintain control of a match and win in a consistent manner. Forum goers recognize the importance of control in Melee:

> I love how once u have the advantage in neutral you really just control the pace of the game until your opponent loses their stock. [65]

> When I watch mid-high level play, the players always feel like they're in 'control' with their characters. When I play I know what I should do, but I'll mess up and completely miss my attack. [6]

As noted in earlier sections, control is partly a function of skill, resulting from: 1. prior training to align one's habits with a character's rhythms; 2. prior experimentation to build deep knowledge of a character's mechanics. However, the current discussion of leverage shows how the struggle for control also occurs in relation to an opposing character. Melee players who maintain absolute control are described as "bodying" their opponents, and many combo videos showcase combo victims "getting bodied" [eg. 43, 47]. Combo videos reflect the important status of control in competitive Melee, marking characters as effective instruments with leverage over others.

While a large portion of controlling a character derives from physical skills like timing and precision, Melee players also spend a good deal of time discussing Melee's "mental game" [93] and theory crafting [62], analyzing specific strategies, character matchups, and in-game scenarios. The Melee community treats rapid, complex thought as an integral part of playing the game at a high level, pointing to the depth of in-game decision-making:

> [At its peak, the] game turns into something incredibly cerebral. The best way to describe the absolute top level of Melee is that it is a super fast-paced chess match.
>
> Basically, the top players are the ones that understand how to play the game, the matchups, and finally the player. [3]
>
> My mind was blown. Not only the depth of the thought process, but how quickly the players have to analyze *and* react to every single situation is just mind-boggling. It's because of this reason and the sheer depth of knowledge they need to have about every attack, what it does, what it beats, etc, that I know that I will *never* be good enough to be this competitive (and really, that's okay). [29]

High-level Melee is considered to involve a constant stream of important decisions and complex thought in order to remain in control of a match. In other words, leverage is not just due to a player's ability to physically execute and exploit mechanics, but to his/her mental capacity to enroll mechanics into effective strategies, mind games, and creative ideas. Players refer to this as the conversational aspect of Melee: "You should think of matches like a conversation with your opponent. If all you think about is beating them then you've only got one side of the conversation" [5]. Here, one player instructs another directly on cultivating mindfulness during a match, listening to the opponent's play as an expression of thoughts, mood, and habits, so that one can respond in kind. Commentators of eSports matches often refer to this activity as "reading" an opponent [e.g., 25], teaching spectators to interpret Melee as a mental battle to "get a read" and figure out the opponent's thought patterns. Conversely, players that stop thinking are interpreted as "going on autopilot" [78], allowing their habits to dominate their play rather than responding to the other's play in a mindful fashion. These examples highlight the deeply interpersonal nature of leverage in competitive games, operating on multiple levels at once: bodily, mechanical, spatial, temporal, and mental. When players attempt to control a Melee match, they do so in direct response to their opponents' actions, demonstrating that competitive players treat characters as responsive instruments, attuned to the emergent play of others.

When players discuss leverage, the musical instrument analogy often gives way to other metaphors like sports, chess, conversation, mind games, and puzzles. Leverage, therefore, makes virtual characters a unique kind of performative instrument due to players' ability to directly respond to and impact other characters. Interactive dynamics like harmony and dissonance are of course present in musical instruments, but virtual characters' interactions often involve more direct forms of control, like combos and cornering. While interactions between traditional instruments are limited by the properties of sound and matter, virtual character-instruments' interactive possibilities are limited by mechanics and code. However, what links traditional instruments and character-instruments is the fact that neither can be reduced to these limiting factors; rather, play emerges from how performers are able handle these instruments in a live situation, creatively working within material and virtual constraints in order to produce beautiful, skillful, readable performances.

DISCUSSION

This study's findings point towards a new understanding of virtual characters in competitive games, based on the model of the performative instrument. The four characteristics delineated here—rhythm, mechanical potential, expressive potential, and leverage—do not exhaust the possibilities of character-instruments, but instead suggest their depth and specific performative qualities in games like Melee. Melee players' experiences with characters show how current models of characters as roles, props, tools [46], vehicles [57], or points of control [9] may not be easily divisible in practice. As instruments, Melee characters combine the expressive potential of props, the leverage of tools, and the mechanical precision of vehicles. This is partly a function of the game's code, but coded qualities would be meaningless without Melee's long history of development by competitive players. Therefore, the four identified qualities of character-instruments should not be thought of as simple technical facts, but rather as potentials that unfold and acquire social meaning through practices like training, discussion, video-making, and competitive performance.

The instrumental model stands in contrast to the standard theatrical model applied to understand virtual bodies like avatars. The theatrical model was established by Erving Goffman's pivotal work *The Presentation of Self*, in which Goffman argues that people act out social roles in public. He observed that people "perform" for others by adopting certain "manners" and "costumes," constructing a "front stage" identity for social interaction [35]. Although Goffman was not writing about virtual life, many avatar researchers explicitly or implicitly reference Goffman in their work, treating avatars as "front stage" identities whose visual properties shape social interaction [8, 12, 17, 39, 42, 64, 90, 91]. Research on avatars has focused on the social impact of visual cues like avatar skin color, gender, shape, age, and dress [14, 26, 38, 51, 52, 80, 87, 95]. Researchers' focus on avatars' visual cues parallels Goffman's analysis of how individuals manage their own appearance in social life. For instance, Katherine Isbister relies on Goffman when she writes that avatars encourage social "role-play," where players take advantage of the flexibility of avatar appearance to construct new online identities [38]. In contrast, this study found that the appearance of characters matters much less to Melee players, who instead focus on characters' mechanics, effective style, hype, and difficulty to control. Because Melee players de-emphasize appearance in favor of other technical capacities, the ways in which they interact do not seem to fit easily with Goffman's theatrical model.

Instead, this paper suggests an alternate theory of performance might be more appropriate for understanding virtual characters. This paper moves away from Goffman's theatrical model—which relies on interaction between "front-stage" identities—and towards a model based on musical performance, which involves interaction between a skilled performer, an instrument, and an audience. Like musicians and other live artists, competitive Melee players are virtuosos who perform for crowds, practice manual techniques, express style, and report feelings of merging with their instruments. The instrumental model emphasizes the creativity and skill required to play a character-instrument, as well as the thought required to respond to other character-instruments. Melee players treat their characters as refined, difficult objects, requiring sustained practice to learn and incorporate. The stakes of this kind of performance are quite high for competitive Melee players, who need to continue to perform well in order to maintain sponsorships, community respect, fans, and tournament winnings. Characters act as smooth *extensions* of self when playing well [16], but these same characters become clunky hindrances when playing poorly. Instrumental embodiment, then, is a skillful practice that involves incorporating a character's rhythms and mechanics, developing the potential for masterful, stylish performance. In contrast, avatar embodiment relies on the player's imaginative capacity to reflect and build on the visual cues provided by avatar bodies [11, 24, 71]. Melee characters still present visual cues, but these are diminished by competitive players in favor of strategic properties like mechanics.

Further studies are needed to determine the extent to which instrumental embodiment is practiced in other games besides Melee, especially in competitive eSports. From this study's findings, it is predicted that similar dynamics may exist in games where players compete with a roster of pre-designed characters, such as League of Legends, Overwatch, and Street Fighter V. Meanwhile, this study suggests an initial, rough division between avatars and characters: avatars are virtual bodies that are *individually* crafted and controlled, representing a relationship between a single unique avatar and a single player. By contrast, characters are virtual bodies that are pre-designed and can be selected by any player, representing a relationship between a *shared* character and an individual player. While avatars point to the uniqueness of the user's physical appearance and the ability to play with that appearance online, characters point to the shared nature of the object being handled by the player, leading to comparisons between different players' skills and styles in handling these characters. According to this schema, virtual worlds like *Second Life* are prime places for avatar embodiment, due to the high ability to customize one's virtual appearance, as well as the cultural emphasis on looks, fashion and identity play in this world. On the other hand, competitive Melee represents the opposite end of the spectrum, with pre-designed characters and a collective emphasis on training, mastery, and signature play styles. This division is overly simplistic, but it helps demonstrate that character-instruments allow for distinctively different kinds of social practice than avatar-selves. Of course, some virtual bodies represent a mix of avatar and character qualities. For instance, in *World of Warcraft*, players operate individual avatar bodies with some ability to choose in-game appearance and dress, but avatars also belong to shared classes like Rogue and Mage, meaning that they share a set of pre-designed fighting abilities. Therefore, virtual bodies in *World of Warcraft* are hybrid avatar-characters, with different kinds of social interaction becoming salient in different play contexts. By making space for characters alongside avatars, this paper calls for further study of the shared design elements of virtual bodies, complementing previous studies of their customizable elements.

Characters are performative foci around which social narratives are built in competitive Melee. These social narratives are quite different from any intended narrative inscribed within the game itself. In fact, when players prioritize a character's intended narrative over the social narrative, the character may cease being a character-instrument altogether. Game designer Toby Gard explores the idea of characters with strong narrative design, identifying them as *actors*:

> The Actor is a character distinct from the player, with its own personality, characteristics, and, to some extent, mind. [33]

While Gard emphasizes the design strategies that help convey a strong sense of personality, ultimately players choose the extent to which they attend to these narrative elements [63]. Players treat characters as actors when they prioritize the game's plot and characterizations, playing the game as a form of interactive fiction [55]. On the other hand, players treat characters as instruments when they prioritize the social narratives afforded by playing with others, playing the game as a challenge to perform acquired skills and style. Actors and instruments thus represent two ways of relating to characters, the former focusing on the character's intended backstory and personality, and the latter highlighting the character's mechanical potential to impact game outcomes. The instrumental side is much more relevant to competitive play, as character mechanics allow for improvised social narratives that derive from live gameplay situations.

This study's findings also demonstrate the importance of mastery in competitive gaming, identifying both personal mastery and interpersonal mastery as integral to player-character relationships in Melee. To master a character's rhythms and mechanics, players devote long hours to practice, much like musicians and other live performers.

The end result is a kind of practical merging with a character-instrument, so that playing the character becomes fluid, creative, and natural, much like playing an instrument [21]. Performance studies scholars have variously written about the performer-instrument relationship as a natural extension of the performer's body [58], as a form of intimacy [32], and as a cyborg hybrid of person and technology [7, 28, 69, 79]. These seem to directly align with this study's findings on the close, cultivated relationship between skilled Melee players and their characters' rhythms and mechanics. Other scholars have rigorously observed the bodily gestures that musicians execute in order to produce sound, as well as the incidental gestures that are a part of live performances [18, 20, 23]. Gesture analysis may be a fruitful avenue for future eSports research, especially to measure differences in performance between live tournament settings and practice at home. However, Melee characters differ from artistic instruments due to the game's agonistic focus on achieving control at the expense of the other player. This struggle for interpersonal mastery colors the relationship between players and character-instruments, emphasizing modes of mindfulness where one actively strategizes by reading the opponent. This paper encourages further explorations of how mental and physical mastery intertwine in play, especially in eSports.

This study joins other researchers of virtual embodiment, who argue that games are mediums that create strong emotional responses [39], establish rhythms of work and play [4], and produce different sensations for differently skilled players [77]. These researchers emphasize the multiple ways in which games affect our bodies, from physiology to emotion to behavioral practice [19]. For example, Steve Swink establishes the concept of "game feel" to describe the tactile sensation of controlling a virtual character in a simulated space [77]. Good game feel is vital for creating a coherent feedback loop between player and game, engaging players and scaffolding skill-building through play [77]. Swink attributes felt characteristics like responsiveness and polish to a game's design as a whole, but this paper's findings suggest that such attributes may vary by character in games like Melee. In fact, rhythm, mechanical potential, expressive potential, and leverage may be seen as the character-specific analogues to Swink's game feel attributes, allowing each character to feel distinct within a single game. As a result, future studies of *character feel* may complement existing research on game feel. But Melee characters do more than establish an embodied connection between player and game; they also mediate between players and perceptive audiences, who judge players through their handling of these characters. Therefore, understanding Melee characters as instruments suggests a new method for looking at the social aspects of play, attentive to the ways in which community members continually compare their own and others' performance as indicative of relative skill, style, knowledge, and focus.

This suggests that designers may think outside of individual relationships like player-to-game and player-to-player, highlighting the need to account for player-to-audience relations as well. I end the discussion with a series of design recommendations for building performative characters:

1) *Eliminate inconsistent outputs*: In Melee, player inputs on the controller consistently translate into specific, predictable outputs by the character. Consistency is the foundation for the player-instrument relationship, allowing players to become skillful by practicing specific timings and move sequences. The predictability of the character-instrument is endangered by designs that translate the same input into different outputs seemingly at random, such as different animations triggered by identical inputs. In addition, designs that alter the cooldown or timing of abilities risk disrupting the chance for players to learn characters' rhythms.

2) *Minimize scripted sequences*: Scripted sequences are those where characters perform pre-determined actions without any input from the player. Many games include lengthy scripted sequences during play, where pressing a single button leads to the character performing complex action sequences that may span several seconds. Long scripted sequences risk breaking the link between player and character-instrument. Melee does have scripted sequences, but these usually last only a matter of frames. Minimizing scripted sequences encourages instrumental mastery and expression, as players have to constantly execute the correct inputs in order to accomplish meaningful game outcomes.

3) *Define power scenarios*: As character-instruments, Melee characters are defined by their relative leverage in different situations, establishing unique power scenarios for each character. Hype occurs when a player executes masterfully during their character's power scenario, but hype also occurs when a player manages to succeed despite being in a disadvantageous power scenario. High-level strategy in Melee involves understanding and anticipating each character's unique strengths. Designing differential strengths for different characters thus encourages both strategic thinking and exciting on-screen performance.

4) *Offer varied move-sets*: Each Melee character has at least 15 simple, unique moves that may be performed at will. This range of options lends high-level Melee its improvisational, "jazz"-like feel. By favoring some moves over others, players express their own unique style. Furthermore, by correctly identifying the best moves from a variety of options, players display skillful decision-making. Varied move-sets offer a range of expressive possibilities to players, encouraging virtuosos to create signature styles.

CONCLUSION

In this paper, I analyzed how community members understand the relationship between player and virtual character in competitive Super Smash Bros. Melee.

Through analysis of forum posts and player-created media, I found that players treat characters as performative instruments, emphasizing the need to practice, train, and incorporate a character's coded rhythms, mechanics, and potentials in order to master it. Character-instruments allow players to express their skill and signature styles in live performance, positioning high-level Melee players as virtuosos who cultivate fans, sponsorships, and collective hype by showing off for crowds. Performance with character-instruments is markedly different from identity play with avatars. This study thus argues for continued exploration of the range and diversity of digital embodiment, enabled by different kinds of virtual constructs, settings, activities, and social milieus.

ACKNOWLEDGEMENTS

I would like to thank Bonnie Nardi, Allison Clark, and the four anonymous reviewers for their comments on this work. Thanks also to the online Smash community, without whom this research would not have been possible.

REFERENCES

1. Achilles1515. 2015. New Global Technique Discovery: V-Canceling! Reduce knockback velocity in select scenarios by 5%. /r/SSBM. URL= Reddit.com/r/SSBM/comments/3n1kgf/new_global_technique_discovery_vcanceling_reduce/
2. Aiello, Giorgia. 2006. Theoretical advances in critical visual analysis: perception, ideology, mythologies and social semiotics. *Journal of Visual Literacy*, *26*(2), 89-102.
3. Anthonygraff24, ympb. 2016. Comments in How good are the top 5 of melee?. /r/Smashbros. URL= Redd.it/4jxi4u
4. Apperley, Tom. 2009. *Gaming rhythms: Play and counterplay from the situated to the global.* Theory on Demand.
5. Astrnght_mike_dexter. 2015. Comment in Is using Fox the only way to truly appreciate everything Melee has to offer?. /r/SSBM. URL= Reddit.com/r/SSBM/comments/3p7u31/is_using_fox_the_only_way_to_truly_appreciate/
6. AstrooooHp. 2015. Tips on how to "control" your character?. /r/Smashbros. URL= Redd.it/366duv
7. Curtis Bahn, Tomie Hahn, and Dan Trueman. 2001. Physicality and feedback: a focus on the body in the performance of electronic music. In *Proceedings of the International Computer Music Conference* (Vol. 2001), 44-51.
8. Jeremy N. Bailenson., Nick Yee, Dan Merget, and Ralph Schroeder. 2006. The effect of behavioral realism and form realism of real-time avatar faces on verbal disclosure, nonverbal disclosure, emotion recognition, and copresence in dyadic interaction. *Presence: Teleoperators and Virtual Environments*, *15*(4), 359-372.
9. Bayliss, Peter. 2007. Beings in the game-world: characters, avatars, and players. In *Proceedings of the 4th Australasian conference on Interactive entertainment*, 4.
10. Beefy Smash Doods. 2015. Melee – How fast is Westballz?. URL= Youtu.be/8vyBV94K4SE
11. Steve Benford, John Bowers, Lennart Fahlen, Chris Greenhalgh, and Dave Snowdon. 1995. User Embodiment in Collaborative Virtual Environments. In *Proceedings of the SIGCHI conference on Human factors in computing systems*, 242-249.
12. Katherine Bessiere, Fleming Seay, and Sara Kiesler. 2007. The ideal elf: identity exploration in World of Warcraft. *CyberPsychology & Behavior* 10.4: 530-535.
13. Big_D_Squirrels. 2015. Comment in Is it hard to be a new Fox main? /r/SSBM. URL= Reddit.com/r/SSBM/comments/39dajx/is_it_hard_to_be_a_new_fox_main/
14. Max Birk, Cheralyn Atkins, Jason Bowey, and Regan Mandryk. 2016. Fostering Intrinsic Motivation through Avatar Identification in Digital Games. In *Proceedings of the SIGCHI conference on Human factors in computing systems*, 2982-2995.
15. Boellstorff, Tom. 2008. *Coming of age in Second Life: An anthropologist explores the virtually human.* Princeton University Press.
16. Brey, Philip. 2000. Technology as extension of human faculties. In Carl Mitcham (ed.), *Metaphysics, Epistemology, and Technology*. Jai 19.
17. Liam Bullingham and Ana C. Vasconcelos. 2013. 'The presentation of self in the online world': Goffman and the study of online identities. *Journal of Information Science*, *39*(1), 101-112.
18. Claude Cadoz and Marcelo M. Wanderley. 2000. Gesture-music. *Trends in gestural control of music*, *12*, 101.
19. Eduardo Calvillo-Gamez, Paul Cairns, and Anna Cox. 2015. Assessing the Core Elements of the Gaming Experience. In *Games User Experience Evaluation*, 37-62. Springer International.
20. Delphine Chadefaux, Marcelo Wanderley, Jean-Loic Le Carrou, Benoit Fabre, and Laurent Daudet. 2012. Experimental study of the musician/instrument interaction in the case of the concert harp. In *Acoustics 2012*, 1645-1650.
21. Custodero, Lori A. 2002. Seeking challenge, finding skill: Flow experience and music education. *Arts Education Policy Review*, *103*(3), 3-9.

22. DangerDamage, Plamore, Tropius2, ClassicalGuitar. 2015. Comments in Mew2King vs Hungrybox. /r/Smashbros. URL= Redd.it/3jxz3k
23. Davidson, Jane W. 2001. The role of the body in the production and perception of solo vocal performance: A case study of Annie Lennox. *Musicae Scientiae*, *5*(2), 235-256.
24. Ignacio Dominguez, Rogelio Cardona-Rivera, James Vance, and David Roberts. 2016. The Mimesis Effect: The Effect of Roles on Player Choice in Interactive Narrative Role-Playing Games. In *Proceedings of the SIGCHI conference on Human factors in computing systems*, 3438-3449.
25. Dreamhacksmash. 2016. SMASH Championship – Dreamhack Austin. URL= Twitch.tv/dreamhacksmash
26. Nicolas Ducheneaut, Ming-Hui Wen, Nicholas Yee, and Greg Wadley. 2007. Body and Mind: A Study of Avatar Personalization in Three Virtual Worlds. In *Proceedings of the SIGCHI conference on Human factors in computing systems*, 445-448.
27. Dynosaur50. 2016. Comment in Johnny B. Goode: An S2J Combo Video. /r/Smashbros. URL= Redd.it/3tilc5
28. Echard, William. 2006. Sensible virtual selves: Bodies, instruments and the becoming-concrete of Music. *Contemporary Music Review*, *25*(1-2), 7-16.
29. Erekai. 2015. Comment in Axe's in-depth look at his 1 minute Silent Wolf 4 stock from Evo 2014. /r/Smashbros. URL= Redd.it/2kqg1m
30. Fales, Cornelia. 2002. The paradox of timbre. *Ethnomusicology*, *46*(1), 56-95.
31. Fashion. 2014. Melee as Art: Basketball, Execution Barriers, and Jazz. Smashboards: Melee Discussion. URL= smashboards.com/threads/melee-as-art-basketball-execution-barriers-and-jazz.379239/
32. Fels, Sidney. 2000. Intimacy and embodiment: implications for art and technology. In *Proceedings of the 2000 ACM workshops on Multimedia*, 13-16.
33. Gard, Toby. 2000. Building character. *Game Developer*, 29-37.
34. Gee, James Paul. 2005. *An introduction to discourse analysis: Theory and method.* Routledge.
35. Goffman, Erving. 1978. *The presentation of self in everyday life*. Harmondsworth.
36. Caleb Goss. 2016. Musical Melee. URL= Youtu.be/D1wLshtOWsg
37. Goose_Choi. 2015. Why Melee is Competitive (Regarding Amount of Characters). /r/Smashbros. URL= Redd.it/2vytol
38. Isbister, Katherine. 2006. *Better Game Characters by Design*. Morgan Kaufmann.
39. Isbister, Katherine. 2016. *How Games Move Us*. The MIT Press.
40. JacoIII. 2015. Comment in Why Bombsoldier is one of the most influential Melee players of all time. /r/Smashbros. Redd.it/3p2g87
41. Jewitt, Carey and Rumiko Oyama. 2001. Visual meaning: A social semiotic approach. *Handbook of visual analysis*, 134-156.
42. Yasmin Kafai, Deborah Fields, and Melissa Cook. 2007. Your Second Selves: Avatar Designs and Identity Play in a Teen Virtual World. In *Proceedings of DiGRA conference*.
43. Karnage. 2015. BAWZ – A Westballz Combo Video. URL= Youtu.be/IvFE6OcXLhc
44. Kuyalicious. 2016. What does 'hitting the lab' actually look like? /r/Smashbros. URL= Redd.it/40q9hr
45. Lee, Daniel "Tafokints". 2016. SSBMRank 2015. Melee It On Me. URL= meleeitonme.com/ssbmrank2015/
46. Linderoth, Jonas. 2005. Animated game pieces. Avatars as roles, tools and props. In *Aesthetics of Play Conference Proceedings*, 14-15.
47. LOAZeus. 2016. Comment in What is the difference between a low level, mid level, and high level player? /r/Smashbros. URL= Redd.it/4cjjro
48. Looperman. 2016. Comment in Thoughts on Hungrybox. /r/Smashbros. URL= Redd.it/4b86jv
49. M120j. 2016. Comment in Johnny B. Goode: An S2J Combo Video. /r/Smashbros. URL= Redd.it/3tilc5
50. ManlierThanGaston. 2016. Comment in C9 | Mango vs. Tempo | Circusballz – Winners Round 1 – Battle of the Five Gods. /r/Smashbros. URL= Redd.it/4b4acg
51. Rosa Mikael Martey and Mia Consalvo. 2011. Performing the looking-glass self: Avatar appearance and group identity in Second Life. *Popular Communication*, *9*(3), 165-180.
52. Victoria McArthur, Robert Teather, and Jennifer Jenson. 2015. The Avatar Affordances Framework: Mapping Affordances and Design Trends in Character Creation Interfaces. In *Proceedings of the Annual Symposium on Computer-Human Interaction in Play.*
53. Meleed. 2015. Comment in Why it's Okay to Start as a Fox Main. /r/SSBM. URL= Redd.it/3j6mrb
54. Muhanna, Sami "Druggedfox". 2015. Sheik Shield Pressure. Melee It On Me. URL= Meleeitonme.com/sheik-shield-pressure/

55. Murray, Janet Horowitz. 1997. *Hamlet on the holodeck: The future of narrative in cyberspace*. Simon and Schuster.

56. MyHooks. 2015. How to approach defensive players?. /r/SSBM. URL= Redd.it/2t2rjv

57. Newman, James. 2002. The myth of the ergodic videogame. *Game studies*, *2*(1), 1-17.

58. Luc Nijs, Micheline Lesaffre, and Marc Leman. 2009. The musical instrument as a natural extension of the musician. In *the 5th Conference of Interdisciplinary Musicology*, 132-133.

59. Nintendo.com. 2008. At Long Last, Nintendo Proclaims: Let the Brawls Begin on Wii! URL= http://web.archive.org/web/20080413125121/http://www.nintendo.com/whatsnew/detail/1u0FthaPxTSSeJelWm4Jt8TI0VJlTt5j

60. Oddishguy. 2015. Comment in Learning to wobble? Try listening to this song!. /r/Smashbros. URL= Redd.it/3iuzik

61. Oddishguy. 2015. Comment in Tips on how to "control" your character? /r/Smashbros. URL= Redd.it/366duv

62. Paul, Christopher A. 2011. Optimizing play: How theorycraft changes gameplay and design. *Game Studies*, *11*(2).

63. Pearce, Celia. 2004. Towards a game theory of game. *First person: New media as story, performance, and game*, *1*, 143-153.

64. Pearce, Celia. 2006. Seeing and being seen: Presence and play in online virtual worlds. *Position paper for Online, Offline & The Concept of Presence When Games and VR Collide, USC's Centers for Creative Technologies, Los Angeles, California.*

65. Phoenixwang. 2015. Comment in Santiago (Lil Fumi) AMA. /r/Smashbros. URL= Redd.it/3jff1x

66. Phoenixwang. 2015. Comment in Who has had the biggest impact on competitive smash that most people have never heard of?. /r/Smashbros. URL= Redd.it/2muy0j

67. Popmycherryyosh. 2015. Comment in A-Punk: A PPMD Combo Video. /r/Smashbros. URL= Redd.it/3tpj0x

68. RegalKillager. 2016. Comment in Close-up of mango's controller during the final moments of mango vs plup. /r/Smashbros. URL= Redd.it/41ewud

69. Reybrouck, Mark. 2006. Music cognition and the bodily approach: Musical instruments as tools for musical semantics. *Contemporary Music Review*,*25*(1-2), 59-68.

70. Rtelly. 2016. I'd like some input from the community on a discussion I had with a friend. What is all of melee about, fundamentally. /r/SSBM. URL= Reddit.com/r/SSBM/comments/4i3304/id_like_some_input_from_the_community_on_a/d2v7hj8

71. Sangseok You and S. Shyam Sundar. 2013. I Feel For My Avatar: Embodied Perception in VEs. In *Proceedings of the SIGCHI conference on Human factors in computing systems*, 3135-3138.

72. Showdowngg. 2016. Genesis Salty Suite – S2J vs Abate. URL= Youtu.be/_dMKnBDaskM

73. ShowdownSmash. 2016. Genesis 3 – Melee Top 8. URL= Twitch.tv/showdownsmash/

74. Smith, Wynton "Prog". 2015. MIOM Bounty #1: Return of the Combo Video. Melee It On Me. URL= meleeitonme.com/miom-bounty-1-return-of-the-combo-video/

75. Stratocaster. 2010. Multishine: an extensive guide – updated 8/13/10. Smashboards: Falco. URL= smashboards.com/threads/multishine-an-extensive-guide-updated-8-13-10.214549/

76. Anselm Strauss and Juliet Corbin. 1998. *Basics of qualitative research: Techniques and procedures for developing grounded theory.* Sage.

77. Swink, Steve. 2009. *Game Feel: A game designer's guide to virtual sensation.* Morgan Kaufmann.

78. SXSWGamingEsports. 2016. SXSW Gaming: March 17 – 19, 2016 in Austin, Texas. URL= Twitch.tv/sxswgamingesports

79. Tanaka, Atau. 2000. Musical performance practice on sensor-based instruments. *Trends in Gestural Control of Music*, *13*(389-405), 284.

80. Taylor, T.L., 2002. Living digitally: Embodiment in virtual worlds. In *The social life of avatars*, 40-62.

81. Taylor, T.L. 2012. *Raising the Stakes: E-sports and the Professionalization of Computer Gaming*. MIT Press.

82. The Phantom Shine. 2015. Retrospective: Bombsoldier and His Understated Impact on the Modern Meta. The Phantom Hit. URL= Phantomhit.com/2015/10/bombsoldier/

83. The Punch Crew. 2003. The Jarrod Experience. URL= Youtu.be/H5ydapVh2VQ

84. The Punch Crew. 2006. DBR Evolution trailer. URL= Youtu.be/YNE_2lEPIkc

85. TheGravyTrainTTK. 2016. Comment in Summit 1.5 – The Combo Video. /r/Smashbros. URL= Redd.it/4fqw9j

86. Thrillahspillah. 2016. Melee is Free Form Jazz. /r/Smashbros. URL= Redd.it/4gr51m

87. Turkle, Sherry. 1995. *Life on the Screen*. Simon and Schuster.

88. Tuttle, Lucas. Sheikh vs. the World. URL= People.rit.edu/lxt9055/320/project3/homepage.html

89. Van Winkle, Dan. 2015. *Smash Bros. Melee* Demonstrates eSports' Power with Record-Breaking Fighting Game Viewership at Evo Tournament. The Mary Sue. URL= themarysue.com/melee-stream-record-broken/

90. Asimina Vasalou, Adam N. Joinson, and Jeremy Pitt. 2007. Constructing my online self: avatars that increase self-focused attention. In *Proceedings of the SIGCHI conference on Human factors in computing systems*, 445-448.

91. Asimina Vasalou and Adam Joinson, 2009. Me, myself and I: The role of interactional context on self-presentation through avatars. *Computers in Human Behavior* 25:510-520.

92. VGBootCamp. 2015. The Big House 5 trailer #4 – October 2-4, 2015 – Dearborn, MI. URL= Youtu.be/nQuDcl3t_eU

93. Victra. 2014. Mango talks about improving at Melee from the Melee It On Me Podcast (link and summary notes in description). /r/Smashbros. URL= Redd.it/1so93m

94. WaluiJ. 2015. Comment in Why does HBox receive hate?. /r/Smashbros. URL= Redd.it/3e7f57

95. Nick Yee, Nicolas Ducheneaut, Mike Yao, and Les Nelson. 2011. Do Men Heal More When in Drag? Conflicting Identity Cues Between User and Avatar. In *Proceedings of the SIGCHI conference on Human factors in computing systems*, 773-776.

96. YungBonesVillain. 2014. Super Smash Brothers Melee is art. Smashboards: Melee Discussion. URL= Smashboards.com/threads/super-smash-brothers-melee-is-art.381937/

Designing Leaderboards for Gamification: Perceived Differences Based on User Ranking, Application Domain, and Personality Traits

Yuan Jia, Yikun Liu, Xing Yu
School of Informatics and Computing
Indiana University–Indianapolis (IUPUI)
Indianapolis, IN 46202 USA
{jiayuan, yikliu, yu64}@umail.iu.edu

Stephen Voida
Department of Information Science
University of Colorado Boulder
Boulder, CO 80309 USA
svoida@colorado.edu

ABSTRACT
Leaderboards, a common gamification technique, are used to enhance engagement through social comparisons. Prior research has demonstrated the overall utility of leaderboards but has not examined their effectiveness when individuals are ranked at particular levels or when the technique is applied in different application domains, such as social networking, fitness, or productivity. In this paper, we present a survey study investigating how preferences for leaderboards change based on individual differences (personality traits), ranking, social scoping, and application domains. Our results show that a respondent's position on the leaderboard had important effects on their perception of the leaderboard and the surrounding app, and that participants rated leaderboards most favorably in fitness apps and least favorably in social networking contexts. More extraverted people reported more positive experiences with leaderboards despite their ranking or the application domain. We present design implications for creating leaderboards targeted at different domains and for different audiences.

Author Keywords
Gamification; leaderboards; motivational affordances; personality; user interface design.

ACM Classification Keywords
H.5.m. Information interfaces and presentation (e.g., HCI): Miscellaneous.

INTRODUCTION
In the past few years, the trend of using gamification to provide gameful, engaging and fun experiences has proliferated into a variety of domains, such as education, health, social networking, fitness, and workplace productivity [22, 26]. Gamification is broadly defined as "using game elements in non-game contexts" [8]. By displaying ranks of comparisons of users' performances, *leaderboards* are one of the most widely used game elements in gamification [12].

Previous research has shown that leaderboards are an effective way to motivate users through competition [5, 12, 23]. Additionally, leaderboards have been identified as one of the ten key "ingredients" in game design [25], one of the "seven primary game mechanics" [31], and one of the "twelve things people like" from gamification [31]. However, studies have revealed that leaderboards were only effective in motivating some users; for some other users, they could actually become a demotivating factor [5, 12, 13]. For example, Codish and Ravid found that extraverted people perceived leaderboards as being less playful than people who were more introverted, based on their experiences in the education domain [5]. In contrast, Jia et al.'s survey study found that more extraverted people reported higher preferences for leaderboards in personal informatics systems [16]. Together, the results of these studies suggest that personality influences people's perceived preference for leaderboards and also implied that people are motivated differently by leaderboards when applied in different domains.

Zichermann et al. summarized multiple ways of presenting leaderboards in gamified applications, such as displaying the user in the middle of what they term a "no-disincentive" leaderboard, in or using a multilayered leaderboard when the space of leaderboard participants is infinite [31]. In game design, a study of leaderboards in the Olympic Games showed that bronze medalists reported higher levels of happiness with their performance than did silver medalists [14]. In studies on digital games, researchers also tested how players were motivated differently by appearing at different leaderboard positions. For example, Butler's study showed that players were more likely to re-play a game when they attained positions at the top or bottom of leaderboards [4]. Another study from Sun and colleagues identified an association between leaderboard positions and players' satisfaction ratings of a digital game. Players in this study reported higher levels of satisfaction when they appeared in the second, fourth or seventh position [27]. These studies demonstrated that people's perceived

CHI 2017, May 06–11, 2017, Denver, CO, USA

ACM 978-1-4503-4655-9/17/05…$15.00
DOI: http://dx.doi.org/10.1145/3025453.3025826

preference for leaderboards was also influenced by how their performance was reflected by their positions on the leaderboards in digital games. However, there have been no studies of which we are aware on the topic of leaderboard positions in gamification.

In this study, we explored how people perceive leaderboards differently when they are ranked at different positions and when this technique is applied in different domains. We selected three positions on the leaderboard to study—top, middle and bottom—and three domains in which leaderboards have been widely applied but studied little—— social networking, fitness, and productivity. We also examined the relations between personality traits and people's preferences for leaderboards. Our three main research questions for this study are:

RQ1: *Are users' subjective perceptions of leaderboards in gamified systems different when they are ranked at different positions on the leaderboard?*

RQ2: *Do these perceptions differ when gamification has been applied to different domains?*

RQ3: *What are the relations (if any) between users' personality traits and their perceived preferences for leaderboards, and are these relations affected by position or application domain?*

RELATED WORK

Leaderboards in Games and Gamification

Gamification has been defined in the research literature as "the use of game design elements in non-game contexts" [8]. Deterding and colleagues defined "game elements" to include those elements used in most games, that are readily associated with games, and that play a significant role in gameplay [8]. From the literature on games and gamification, *leaderboards* were identified as one of the basic ingredients for designing a great game [25]; they were also one of the most-used game elements in gamification approaches [12]. Moreover, Reeves and Read listed leaderboards among "ten ingredients of a great game" in the context of massive multiplayer online (MMO) games. One of the "ingredients" was "competition under rules that are explicit and enforced," which elicited an underlying motivation. Leaderboards also brought a sense of fairness for players during the competition [25].

In their book "Gamification in Design," Zichermann and Cunningham list seven primary game mechanics drawn from the literature and existing gamified applications, including points, levels, leaderboards, badges, challenges/quests, onboarding, and engagement loops [31]. In addition to these core game elements, the authors noted that "feedback" critically influences players' motivation and potentially ties in with many other elements, such as points and leaderboards. It implied that leaderboards can serve as a type of "feedback," rather than an outcome of their own accord [31]. Based on the 42 different "fun" interactions listed by Radoff [24], Zichermann and Cunningham categorized "12 things people like from gamification" [31]. Three of these 12 were associated with leaderboards. The book also proposed three underlying reasons why people were motivated by leaderboards: leading others, getting attention, and gaining status.

Mekler et al. conducted an empirical analysis to examine whether leaderboards affect users' behavior and intrinsic motivation. Their findings indicated that leaderboard did not affect users' intrinsic motivation, but it was one of the effective factors in increasing short-term performance in an image annotation task [18].

Other research categorized leaderboards into two types: "no-disincentive" and "infinite" leaderboards [27, 31]. Leaderboards, when used in social network websites like Facebook, aim to create social incentives rather than disincentives. One way to realize these kind of leaderboards are to organize the names such that the user appears in the middle, with better- and worse-performing individuals bracketing his or her position. These instantiations of leaderboards also often show the user how close he or she is to attaining the next best score. Infinite leaderboards are designed around the premise that a user's score will be beaten by another player sooner or later. Since it would be impossible to allow every user to exist on the leaderboard forever, these kinds of leaderboards are designed to present rankings with multiple layers. For example, the mobile gaming app Doodle Jump includes a leaderboard with a local view, a friends view, and a global view [31].

Leaderboards in Different Domains

Leaderboards are widely used across multiple domains, including social network websites, fitness tracking, and productivity applications. To increase users' engagement on social network websites, leaderboards are usually designed to present the rank of profile views or the number of online activities undertaken. For example, Klout, a popular social leaderboard, ranks its users according to their online social influence via Klout score [2, 31]. Farzan et al. conducted a study to understand the effects that a point-based incentive system (i.e., points, "status" levels, and a leaderboard) played in a social network site, and found that some users were driven by leaderboards to keep up with others—an effect that did not suffer significant decay even after the leaderboard was removed. Their findings suggest that the usage of leaderboards could play a role in transferring extrinsic incentives to intrinsic motivations—at least for some users [9].

Leaderboards are also popular in fitness applications (e.g., Fitbit's companion app). In Wong and Kwok's mobile health app, a leaderboard displayed all users' and groups' step records and rankings [30]. Anderson et al.'s study found that leaderboards introduced a sense of playfulness and indirectly induced participants to walk more [1].

Finally, some workplaces use gamification as a way of improving productivity within the organization, namely Enterprise Gamification [28]. Costa et al. found that

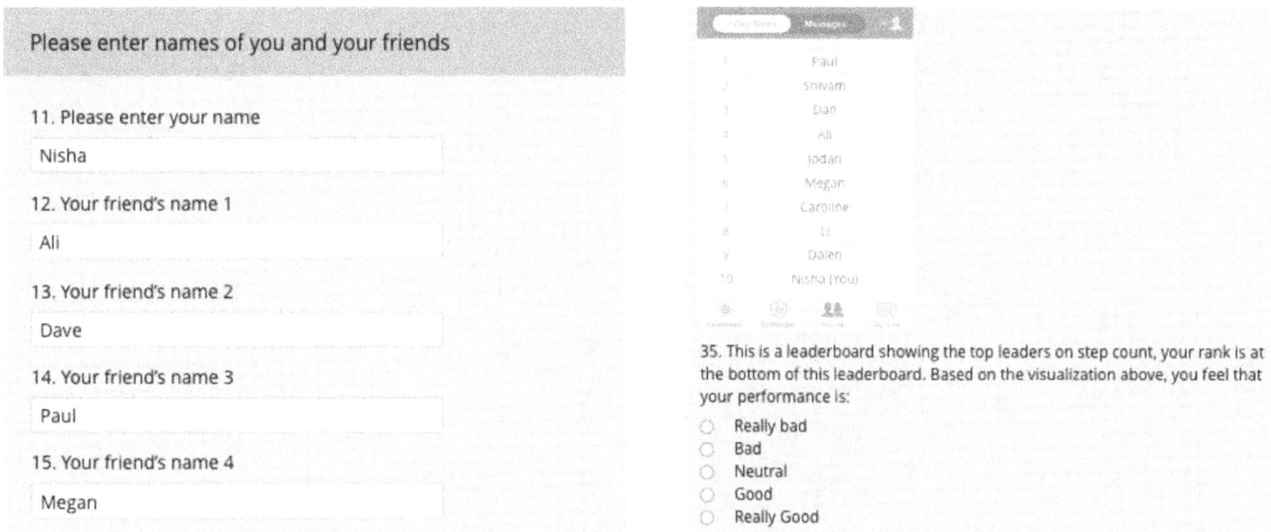

(a) (b)

Figure 1. The respondents' experience of the mockups showing leaderboards applied to the fitness domain from our survey. (a) Each respondent was asked to enter his/her name and 10 names of his/her friends. (b) A screenshot of the survey illustrating the display configuration of the mock-up for the situation of bottom position in the Fitness domain and our survey questions.

leaderboards were effective for improving some employees' punctuality to regularly-scheduled work meetings [6]. However, several studies have also shown that leaderboards could reduce work performance rather than enhance it because they make the performance public for all to see in the workplace [28]. For example, Mollick and Rothbard's study used leaderboards to motivate employees when performing tedious and cumbersome tasks at work [21]. Their results showed that the usage of a leaderboard turned work into a more pleasurable activity and enhanced productivity when employees had provided consent to interact with the leaderboard. But the effects from the leaderboard were reversed in the no-consent condition [21].

Personality differences

Previous studies on gamification have found that leaderboards might only be effective for "some" users [5, 9, 16]. Some researchers studied personality differences and their influences on users' motivation and behaviors. Kaptei and Eckles studied personality and people's online purchasing behavior for e-commerce [15]. Arteaga et al. applied personality differences in app interface redesign [3]. Nov and Arazy found significant relations between conscientiousness and people's participation in online communities [23]. In a study of gamification applied to an educational context, researchers found that personality differences played a role in affecting people's preferences for leaderboards. For example, a learning-management system that featured leaderboards motivated some students to take extra courses and seek out more additional opportunities to demonstrate achievement [20]. Codish and Ravid found that extraverts reported a lack of playfulness in leaderboards when applied to a course setting [5]. In a more recent study by Jia and her colleagues, an online survey study of personality and peoples' preference on 10 types of motivational affordances in gamification, results showed that more extraverted people tended to prefer leaderboards in the context of a habit-tracking application [16].

HCI studies on personality traits often use the "Big-Five factors" as a primary scale [5, 16, 19]. The Big-Five is a descriptive model of personality, which includes *conscientiousness* (people actively organize and carry out tasks), *agreeableness* (people who help others and expect help in return), *neuroticism/emotional stability* (people who have difficulty managing stress), *extraversion* (people who seek out new opportunities and excitement), and *imagination/openness* (people who devise novel ideas) [19].

STUDY DESIGN AND METHODS

This study investigates the relations among people's self-reported preferences both on leaderboards and the corresponding applications when: 1) the user's name is shown at different positions on the leaderboard—namely at the top, near the middle, or at the bottom; 2) these leaderboards are applied to different domains, such as social networking, fitness, and productivity systems within organizations. We conducted a large-scale online survey with 286 participants by using dynamic leaderboard mockups, created with respondents' self-reported names and 10 of their friends' names. The survey was hosted via SurveyMonkey[1] and Amazon Mechanical Turk (AMT)[2].

Survey Design

The survey contained four sections. The first section featured a series of multiple-choice questions about the participant's demographic background, such as gender, age, educational

[1] https://www.surveymonkey.com/home/

[2] https://requester.mturk.com/

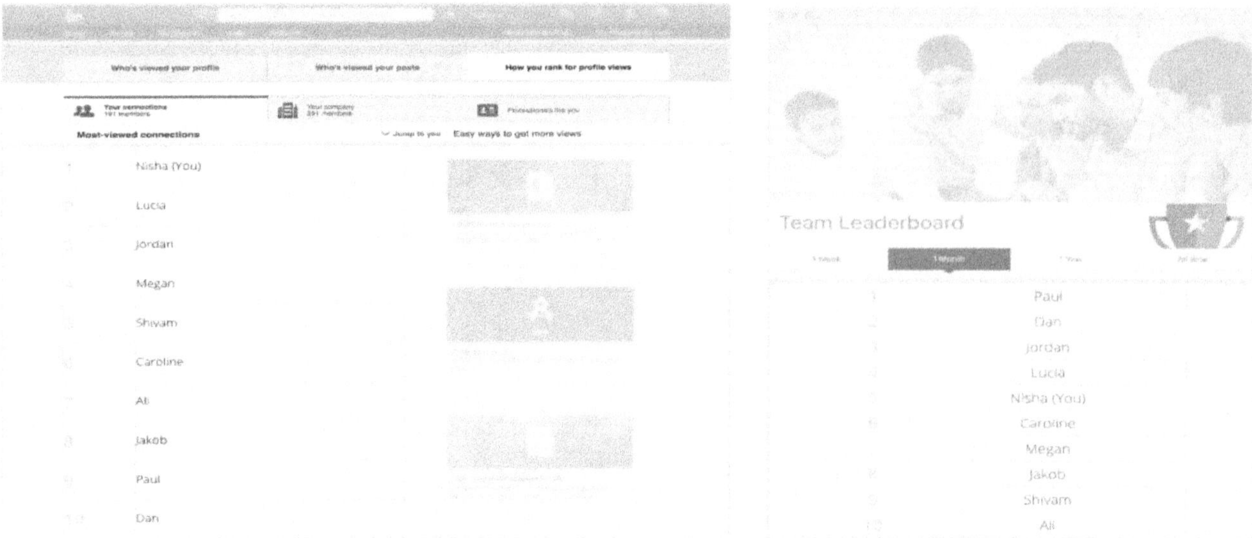

Figure 2. The interface of leaderboard mockups for social network and productivity domains in the survey.

background, occupation, and ethnicity. Next, we asked participants to complete an assessment of the Big-Five factors of personality [7, 17]. We used the 50-item set of IPIP Big-Five Factor Markers, which is a free and research community-developed inventory.

The third part of the survey was designed to elicit feedback regarding different leaderboards with the participant's name appearing at three different positions on leaderboards situated within three domains. At the beginning, each respondent was asked to enter his/her name and the names of ten of his/her close friends (Figure 1a). To help respondents understand the purpose of collecting names and how these names were going to be used (and protected), the following message was shown to all respondents:

> *In the following, you will be asked to give feedback on 9 different leaderboards. To generate leaderboards with names that you are familiar with, you will be asked to enter your name and any 10 of your friends' names in the next page. These names won't be saved or shared with researchers, and they are only used to generate the interface mockups for the rest of this survey.*

Based on these names, we automatically generated 9 interface mockups of various leaderboards for the subsequent survey questions (Figure 1b). Specifically, each respondent's name was displayed in 3 positions on each leaderboard (top, middle, bottom), with leaderboards applied to one of three domains (social networking, fitness, and productivity). These dynamic leaderboard interfaces were generated by a SurveyMonkey feature called "Piping". We used the Latin Square method to counterbalance and avoid any potential ordering effects in the study.

After viewing each leaderboard, each respondent was asked to respond to questions that were designed to collect information regarding the respondents' opinions on (1) self-assessed performance (based solely on the leaderboard display), (2) the perceived enjoyment that the leaderboard might impart, (3) the perceived feeling of motivation provided by the leaderboard, (4) the participants' willingness to use an application like the ones illustrated by the mockups, and 5) the participant's perceived willingness for recommending this application to their friends. Among these 5 questions, question 2 and 3 were designed to elicit feedback about the leaderboard, and questions 4 and 5 were designed to elicit feedback about the corresponding application domains. These questions were adapted from survey questions in previous research on people's preferences for game elements in gamification [16, 27].

At the end of each domain section (each containing 3 leaderboards), we asked 4 questions to elicit respondents' opinions on: (1) for what reasons (if any) that the leaderboards in that particular domain appeal to them, (2) for what reasons (if any) that their positions on the leaderboard appeal to them, (3) whether the inclusion of their friends' names on the leaderboard matters, and (4) whether the inclusion of their own names are on the leaderboard matters. The fourth part of the survey consisted of only one open-ended question: it was designed to gather respondents' opinions on: 1) whether they felt that leaderboards appealed to them differently in different domain, and, if so, why. The survey took approximately 12 minutes to complete. The full list of survey questions is included in the supplementary materials.

Participant Recruitment

We recruited 286 respondents through Amazon Mechanical Turk (MTurk). We chose to use MTurk for our study due to the need for a large participant sample, the efficiency of survey distribution, and its relatively low cost. Participants were paid USD $1.00, the payment rate suggested by the AMT platform for survey studies of this duration.

	Total Participants (n = 286)
Age	18–24 (17.8%) 25–34 (50.3%) 35–44 (21.7%) 45–54 (8.0%) 55 and older (2.1%)
Gender	Female (47.2%) Male (52.8%)
Educational Level	Some high school (0.3%) High school graduate/GED (10.1%) Vocational/Associate degree (6.3%) Some college (24.8%) Bachelor degree (40.6%) Some graduate school (2.8%) Master degree (13.6%) Ph.D., law, or medical degree (1.4%)
Occupation	Employed for wages (60.5%) Self-employed (22.8%) Student (7.3%) Retired (0.7%) Other (9.8%)
Ethnicity	White (65.4%) Asian/Pacific Islander (19.2%) Hispanic or Latino (5.6%) Black or African American (7.3%) Native American or American Indian (0.3%) Other (2.1%)

Table 1. Participant Demographics

RESULTS

Participant Demographics

To summarize the demographic information of the respondents, we present their responses (expressed as percentages of the overall sample population) to questions regarding their age, gender, educational level, occupation, and ethnicity (see Table 1). To support our subsequent correlation analyses, respondents' demographic responses were coded into numerical variables. For age, 18–24 was coded as 1, 25–34 as 2, and so on. For gender, male was coded as 1 and female as 2; for educational level, the eight response levels were coded from 1 to 8 from lowest completed education level to the highest.

Before processing to our regression analysis, we used zero-order correlations to test for correlations among independent variables and respondents' demographic variables (Table 2). The independent variables of interest, i.e., the five IPIP personality traits, were positively correlated with one another. This result was consistent with prior literature [10]. The strongest correlation that we saw was between conscientiousness and emotional stability (r = .481, p < .01). This means that our participants who reported high levels of emotional stability also tended to be more conscientious. Participants with higher agreeableness levels also tended to be more open to new experiences (r = .384, p < .01).

For gender, there was a positive correlation between the coded gender variable and agreeableness (r = .271, p < .01) and a negative correlation between the coded gender variable and emotional stability (r = -.212, p < .01). This result shows that for our sample (n = 286), males were more emotionally stable but less agreeable than females. We found no correlation between respondents' personality characteristics and their age, educational levels or ethnicity.

Positions on Leaderboards

A two-way ANOVA (repeated measure) with sphericity corrections for each perception (enjoyment, motivation, desire to use, and recommend to friends) was conducted. The results show that position and domain, as two factors, did play a role, individually, to affect people's perceived perceptions significantly on leaderboard and the corresponding application (Table 4). The results also show that the interaction between the two factors is significant for each perception. Thus, to further determine the difference between people's perception at each level of each factor, we conducted several t-tests. The detail of the ANOVA and t-test results are presented in the supplementary materials.

Across 9 types of leaderboards, 3 positions × 3 domains, respondents consistently reported significantly higher preference for the leaderboards when their names appeared in the "top" positions than when they appeared in the "middle" positions, which were also consistently and significantly higher than when they appeared in the "bottom" positions, regardless of the application domain. This suggests that respondents were able to understand each mockup presented in the survey.

	Mean	Std. Deviation	1	2	3	4	5	6	7
1. Extraversion	29.30	9.16							
2. Agreeableness	38.19	7.05	.293**						
3. Conscientiousness	36.26	6.85	.167**	.285**					
4. Emotional Stability	32.86	8.62	.315**	.229**.	.481**				
5. Imagination/Openness	38.40	5.86	.287**	.384**	.299**	.198**			
6. Age	2.26	0.91	.033	.114	.080	.070	.012		
7. Gender	1.47	.50	-.036	.271**	.044	-.212**	.120*	-.034	

Table 2. Correlation matrix and descriptive statistics (n = 286). * indicates cells with p < .05 (2-tailed), ** indicates p < .01.

	TopSoc	TopFit	TopPro	TopAvg
Performance	4.3 (0.9)	4.5 (0.9)	4.6 (0.7)	4.5 (0.9)
Enjoyment	3.3 (1.4)	**3.9 (1.2)**	3.8 (1.3)	3.7 (1.3)
Motivation	3.3 (1.4)	**4.0 (1.2)**	3.9 (1.2)	3.7 (1.3)
DesiretoUse	3.3 (1.4)	**3.9 (1.2)**	3.7 (1.3)	3.6 (1.3)
Recommend	3.2 (1.4)	**3.8 (1.2)**	3.6 (1.4)	3.5 (1.3)
	MidSoc	**MidFit**	**MidPro**	**MidAvg**
Performance	3.2 (0.6)	3.3 (0.7)	3.2 (0.7)	3.2 (0.7)
Enjoyment	**2.9 (1.2)**	3.6 (1.1)	3.2 (1.2)	3.2 (1.2)
Motivation	3.0 (1.3)	3.6 (1.2)	3.5 (1.2)	3.4 (1.3)
DesiretoUse	**2.9 (1.3)**	3.6 (1.2)	3.2 (1.2)	3.2 (1.3)
Recommend	**2.8 (1.3)**	3.5 (1.2)	3.1 (1.3)	3.1 (1.3)
	BotSoc	**BotFit**	**BotPro**	**BotAvg**
Performance	2.1 (1.2)	2.0 (1.2)	1.7 (1.1)	1.9 (1.2)
Enjoyment	**2.5 (1.4)**	3.1 (1.4)	**2.5 (1.4)**	2.7 (1.4)
Motivation	**2.6 (1.4)**	3.4 (1.4)	3.0 (1.5)	3.0 (1.4)
DesiretoUse	**2.5 (1.4)**	3.2 (1.4)	**2.6 (1.4)**	2.8 (1.4)
Recommend	**2.5 (1.4)**	3.2 (1.4)	**2.6 (1.4)**	2.8 (1.4)

Table 3. Descriptive results—reported as *mean* (*SD*)—for respondents' perceptions of leaderboards based on their name appearing at three positions (top, middle, and bottom) within three domains (social, fitness, and productivity).

Leaderboards in Different Domains

We found some interesting results when comparing the differences in reported preference based on position results across domains. To be more specific, respondents rated leaderboards highest in fitness apps and lowest in the social networking context. From Table 3, on a scale from 1 to 5 (1 indicating strong disagreement and 5 indicating strong agreement), we can see that when respondents' names were shown on the top or in the middle of the leaderboards, participants provided significantly higher ratings for their perceptions of *Enjoyment*, *Motivation*, *Desire to Use* the application, and would *Recommend* to friends in the Fitness and Productivity domains than they did for leaderboards in the Social network domain. In addition, the only negative perceptions (i.e., given a score below 3.0) that the respondents reported when appearing in the middle position were in the Social Network domain. This suggests that for social network websites, people were only positively affected by leaderboards when can readily interpret their rank relative to other users.

People's perceptions became much more negative when they saw their names at the bottom of the leaderboards. However, respondents still rated perceived *Enjoyment*, *Motivation*, *Desire to Use*, and *Recommend* to friends positively for leaderboards in the Fitness domain even when their perceived performance was low. These results indicate that people have positive experiences of leaderboards in the fitness domain, regardless of their ranking.

Perception	Factor	F value	p value
Enjoyment	Domain	0.97	3.29e-19 *
	Position	0.68	6.18e-42 *
	Domain: Position	0.88	2.39e-11 *
Motivation	Domain	0.94	1.33e-21*
	Position	0.71	3.23e-26*
	Domain: Position	0.92	8.93e-03*
Desire to use the app	Domain	0.96	1.26e-19*
	Position	0.72	2.54e-36*
	Domain: Position	0.89	7.22e-07*
Recommend to a friend	Domain	0.95	6.03e-20*
	Position	0.67	4.15e-29*
	Domain: Position	0.92	6.76e-08*

Table 4. Results from ANOVA. Significant codes (with Greenhouse-Geisser correction): p< .05 '*'

Respondents were also asked about their opinions about whether they would like to see their name on leaderboards and whether they prefer competing only with their friends. Figure 3 summarizes the results from these questions. This figure illustrates that 1) showing users' name on the leaderboard was very important in both the fitness and productivity domains; 2) people had even higher preferences for seeing their names among the top three entries for leaderboards in productivity domain; 3) respondents generally rated leaderboards highly when competing among their friends; and 4) compared to the other two domains, respondents thought that the leaderboard feature in social networking websites was least appealing, regardless of whether their name or their friends' names appeared in the list.

Personality Type and Leaderboard Preferences

To explore the relationship between personality and users' perception, we used structural equation modeling (SEM), a mediational analysis, to test our proposed models. We developed two measurement models showing the relationship between exogenous variables and endogenous variables as well as a structural model showing the relationship between the latent personality traits and latent users' perception. For the measurement model of personality, we used the test scores of the 50 questions from the Big-Five personality inventory as the exogenous variables. We assumed five latent variables (extraversion, agreeableness, conscientiousness, emotional stability, and imagination) for them. As to users' perception, we assumed a latent variable (perception) for the 4 measurements (enjoyment, motivation, desire to use app, and recommend to friend) that we used in our survey.

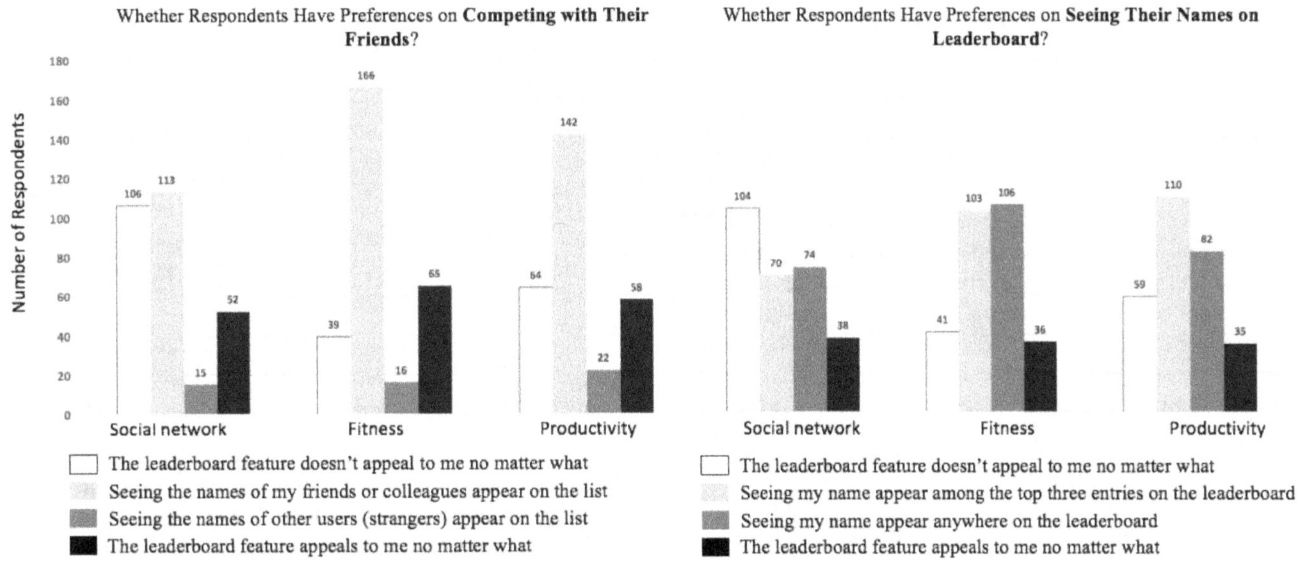

Figure 3. Summarized results of respondents' opinions on whether they would like to see their names on leaderboards and whether they have preferences on competing only with their friends.

For all the paths in the model, we estimated the path parameters based on maximum likelihood, and the process converged normally after 72 iterations. The overall badness-of-fit of our model is significant (Chi-square < 0.001). Based on examination of the path parameters, while the two measurement models showed strong factor loadings, the path parameters of the paths from the Big-Five personality traits to users' perception are fairly small, which suggests a weak impact of personality on users' perception of leaderboards. Thus, from the SEM analysis, we find no statistically significant casual relationships between personality traits and perception on leaderboard. The detailed results from the SEM analysis is included in the supplementary materials.

We also conducted a multiple regression analysis. All individual Beta (β) values from 36 regressions (4 perception types × 3 positions × 3 domains) are summarized, and the significant ($p < .05/36 = .001$) results presented in the supplementary materials. Overall, more extraverted people tended to have more positive perceptions of leaderboards in the domains of social networking and productivity; people with higher levels of agreeableness tended to express greater enjoyment of leaderboards in the fitness domain. We found no significant results for the personality traits of conscientiousness, emotional stability, or imagination.

In the remainder of this section, we report significant differences among perceptions (i.e., enjoyment, motivation, desire to use the application, and would recommend to friends) for each type of leaderboard. In addition, we also report the qualitative results from our open-ended survey questions.

For leaderboards in the **social networking domain,** when respondents' names were shown in the **middle** position, the more extraverted people expressed more desire to use the social networking websites ($\beta = .216$, $p = .001$) and were more likely to recommend the websites to their friends ($\beta = .218$, $p = .001$). When respondents' names were at the **bottom** of the leaderboard on social networking websites, the more extraverted people reported stronger likelihood of being motivated by the leaderboard ($\beta = .218$, $p = .001$); in addition, for more extraverted people, they expressed more desired to use the websites ($\beta = .219$, $p = .001$) and were more likely to recommend it to their friends ($\beta = .232$, $p = .001$).

Our qualitative results from the open-ended questions show that leaderboards on social websites provide another mode of connection, help monitor social influence status, and increase communication among friends:

> *"Leaderboards on social networks help me assess the reputation of people I may not know all that well." (P146)*

> *"I like the leaderboard just for the purpose of being able to identify who I am staying in contact with, and who wants to stay in contact with me." (P224)*

However, respondents reported that they use social media to communicate with others rather than for competition, and the social influence showed from the leaderboard does not reflect reality since their social connections are not derived solely from social websites:

> *"It doesn't appeal to me because I don't see the point in such a ranking, specially between friends. Feels like added competition where there shouldn't be any." (P25)*

> *"If I'm being honest, I don't think I care for the ranking system when it comes to a social network site. It doesn't seem like it belongs on a social site." (P105)*

> *"The leaderboard feature in social networking websites doesn't appeal to me because it doesn't reflect*

my real connections that I have people rather than on some networking websites." (P172)

With regards to leaderboards in the **fitness domain,** when respondents' names were shown at the **bottom** of the leaderboards in fitness apps, the more agreeable respondents rated *Enjoyment* of the leaderboard more highly (β = .227, p = .001). From our qualitative results, respondents reported that fitness itself can be competitive in nature. They also reported feeling a sense of motivation from leaderboards in this domain because leaderboards turn fitness activities into a more fun competition. The leaderboard can also be seen as a type of progress tracking, which is a good match to this domain. Some sample comments from the open-ended survey questions included:

"I always wanted to use a fitness app like this. It's addicting to keep watching your rank go up as you work towards your fitness goals. It's like when you work for hours leveling on a video game only with real life results." (P118)

Consistent with the quantitative results, one reason that respondents reported enjoying the leaderboards was that people enjoy engaging in competition with their friends or families on fitness activities:

"I like the competitive nature of it, plus, having friends and family on the leaderboard is an extra incentive to do well." (P207)

"I have a Fitbit on my hand right now and I look at the leaderboard from time to time to make sure my steps don't get too low. It really does motivate me because I know my mom will get worried if she sees my numbers go too low." (P 32)

"It's just interesting to know how well my performance is compared to my friends. It makes doing activities more exciting and motivating, to me. It motivates me to compete." (P256)

The results of leaderboards in the **productivity domain** reveal that when respondents' names were at the **top** of the leaderboard, people who are more extraverted were more likely to have positive perceptions of the leaderboards (β = .222, p = .001) and the surrounding system (β = .233, p = .000); for the personality traits of agreeableness, emotional stability and imagination, people rated leaderboards in this domain negatively, but this was not a statistically significant difference. When respondents' names were shown in the **middle** of the leaderboard in productivity applications, the more extraverted people still provided positive ratings of the leaderboard and the application. From our qualitative results, our respondents reported that they liked the idea of incorporating leaderboards into team work because it offers an incentive for doing a good job, it provides a visual representation of work performance, and it might be especially valuable when a deadline is approaching:

"This leaderboard lets me know how well I am doing within my team and if I need to improve my performance." (P10)

"Gives real, easily quantifiable feedback on my performance." (P175)

"It is fun to see how well you are doing and makes work feel a little more like a game which makes it a little easier to enjoy what you are doing and feel motivated." (P148)

"I really do like to know how my output and quality of work (of any kind) measures up to my peers. It's good to know whether I need to work harder or if I can relax a bit and maintain." (P192)

On the other hand, many negative comments from respondents mentioned that the competition derived from a leaderboard in a working environment reads more like a "name-and-shame" feature instead of a "game-like" feature since employees don't have other options. They also felt that employees should cooperate to reach a common goal instead of competing with one another, that leaderboards might foster animosity at work, and that some work cannot be judged in a fair and objective manner upon which a leaderboard visualization could be built:

"when I am down at the list I will have a motive to work better, it's a job, it's not optional..." (P12)

"This leaderboard does not appeal to me as I do not feel my work can be judged adequately through it." (P74)

"It does not appeal to me because I feel that productivity in the workplace should be a matter between each employee and their employer and not a public matter between employees." (P47)

DISCUSSION

In this section, we discuss the link between differences in a person's position on a leaderboard and their preferences for leaderboards. We also delve into the relations between their rank or position and their preferences for leaderboards across different domains. Finally, we discuss how personality differences could help to inform the design of leaderboards in gamified applications.

Leaderboard Position and Domain Differences

In the gaming literature, leaderboard position was found to be a factor that affects players' game experiences. In the example of leaderboards in Olympic games, researchers explained the finding that bronze medalists reported higher levels of happiness than silver medalists because of the notion of "what could have been," which implies that silver medalists framed their thinking about the fact that they *could* have won a gold medal, while and bronze medalists understood their ranking as being better than not having received any medal at all [14]. For leaderboards in digital games, in the example of Gold Mine, Sun and colleagues found that players reported higher satisfaction when they appeared in positions 2, 4, and 7 [27].

Our results showed that respondents rated leaderboards differently when they are ranked differently in different domains. It indicates that unlike event-based competitions like the Olympics or short-time-repetitive competitions in digital games, leaderboards in gamified applications typically present long-term competitions of various types of domain-related activities. Thus, to design leaderboards in gamified contexts, in addition to leaderboard position, designers should also consider the impact of domain differences.

For rankings on leaderboards, our results show that respondents reported positive perceptions of leaderboards only when they appeared in the top positons of the leaderboard in the social-networking domain. However, the results from the fitness and productivity domains revealed that people liked leaderboards in fitness applications no matter what their rank; and people had only negative perceptions of leaderboards when ranked in the bottom of leaderboards in the productivity domain. From our qualitative results, one of the key differences among these domains is the perceived fairness of the leaderboard in the social and productivity domains. Unlike step count, the metric typically used to determine ranking on fitness-oriented leaderboards, respondents reported that their social influence cannot be quantifiably reflected by the leaderboard on social websites since not all of their contacts occurred in a single social network application; and for productivity domain, respondents reported that significant facets of their work are simply not rank-able. In the research literature, a design guide for leaderboards in game design mentioned about that competition under rules should be fair and explicit [25]. Thus, we suggest that **the competitive activity used to seed the leaderboard should be designed to bring a sense of fairness for users.**

In our results, respondents provided the lowest ratings for leaderboards in the social networking domain. From our qualitative results, respondents expressed a common concern that they use social network sites primarily for communication instead of a site for competition with others. This finding is consistent with the findings from previous studies of people's experiences with social network games. Wohn et al. mentioned that competition in social games indirectly facilitate social interaction: people passively obtained information about others' performance from leaderboards and treated this interaction as a "friendly competition" [29]. Leaderboards introduce the concept of competition to gamified systems, but social network domains tend to emphasize an ultimate goal of facilitating interaction among friends. It appears that among members of a close social circle, it is not easy to encourage serious competition; rather, competition manifests as friendly banter or a lighthearted game. Thus, we suggest that **leaderboards in social networking contexts should be intentionally designed to serve the purpose of facilitating communication rather than just showing results of a metricized competition**. For example, leaderboards could be designed to be less competition-oriented and instead focus on expanding one's social circle; showing long-time, no-contact friends or shared-interest strangers on the board might be a more effective use of these features than when they simply display the performance of a close, stable group of friends.

We also found that respondents rated leaderboards positively in the fitness domain regardless of their position on those leaderboards. Additionally, respondents reported significantly higher preference for seeing their friends or colleagues on these leaderboards and the lowest preference for seeing strangers on them. Our qualitative results reinforce these quantitative findings: people expressed more enjoyment and motivation when competing against people with whom they were familiar, such as family, friends, or close colleagues. One reason is that the activity people are competing with in this domain is almost always reflective of their personal, daily routines. This may be why people are more comfortable competing with their closer friends and family members in this context. Competing with close acquaintances leverages people's universal desire to interact with and be involved in the lives of their friends and family members; additionally, it provides motivation for improving one's fitness levels because making unhealthy decisions can in some ways be perceived as "letting down" those close friends and family members. This duality is unique in the fitness domain because fitness activities are both deeply personal and influenced by the behavior of others. The finding is consistent with the previous study from Hamari and Koivisto, which found that users felt more attached to gamified applications when they have more friends participating in the gamified system [11]. Our finding also supports Wong and Kwok's hypothesis that people's fitness- or exercise-related motivation could be positively satisfied through human-relatedness needs, such as social recognition and affiliation [30]. People care more about who the individuals are on these leaderboards than his/her own ranking. Thus, we suggest that when designing a leaderboard for a fitness app, **designers should first understand *who* should appear on the leaderboard rather than *where* to position the user, focusing on supporting constructive competitions among a small circle of close friends.**

The results from the findings about productivity-oriented leaderboards reveal that it is very important for respondents to see their name on the leaderboard in this domain. And people have even higher preferences for seeing their names among the top three entries of these leaderboards. From our qualitative results, respondents expressed the most negative perceptions of these leaderboards when their names appeared towards the bottom of the ranked list. Instead of introducing a sense of "fun," respondents thought that the competitive tasks used to seed the rankings on productivity-oriented leaderboards spur serious competition. They also expressed concern that appearing at a low rank might have negative consequences for how they were perceived among their colleagues, or even to strain their relationship with their employer. Our finding is consistent with the study by Mollick and Rothbard, which found that employees experienced less positive affect from leaderboards at work in the "no-consent" condition [21]. Werbach and Hunter also noted the negative effects of leaderboards in working environments, pointing out that leaderboards can play a role in "reducing the richness of a game to a zero-sum struggle for supremacy [and] therefore inherently turns off some people and makes them behave in less desirable ways" [28, p76]. This might due to the sensitivity associated with introducing (additional) competitiveness into workplaces. On the other hand, in those successful documented examples of using leaderboards in the productivity domain, the competitive tasks around which rankings were based were usually repetitive and boring [28]. For example, to reduce the death rate from hospital-acquired infections, leaderboards have been successfully applied in hospitals to motivate staff to compete with one another in washing their hands often and well, which turns hand washing into a competitive game. Thus, we suggest that **when designing leaderboards for the productivity domain, the competitive tasks should be selected from the set of simple and repetitive tasks associated with the job.** Additionally, designers might strive to **avoid showing the lowest-ranking employees on workplace leaderboards**. It is desirable that at workplaces the design of the leaderboard should consider the dynamics among co-workers and the impact that their introduction might have on the overall office culture.

Personality-targeted Leaderboards

Our results show that more extraverted people tended to have more positive perceptions of leaderboards. This finding is consistent with previous studies by Jia et al. [16] and Nov & Arazy [23]. Werbach and Hunter also mentioned that leaderboards have the capability of showing progress that other motivational affordances like *points* and *levels* cannot [28]. One reason for extraverted people to prefer leaderboards is because of their dynamic nature—they reflect the ever-changing social landscape constituted by the gamified system's participants. Thus, we suggest, to **appeal to more extraverted users, designers should not only design leaderboards as a way of showing rankings, but also emphasizing changes**.

In summary, based on the findings from our study, we can provide several concrete suggestions for the design of leaderboards in gamified applications. For these interfaces, we propose that there are five questions that designers should consider:

1. In what domain is the leaderboard going to be applied?
2. Does the competitive task on the leaderboard feature rules that are fair and equally applicable to all participants?
3. What are the relationships among the participant-competitors?
4. Where should the active user be displayed on the leaderboard — at the top, middle, or bottom of the list, or does it not matter? In other words, how should the user's performance be communicated relative to the other users of the system?
5. Will the task or activity that will be measured to seed the leaderboard provide a dynamic enough competitive landscape?

Limitations

Our study used regression results from an online survey. The mockup leaderboards did not capture the wide range of possible leaderboards application domains. Leaderboards could be used in multiple domains and the social dynamics between leaderboard players could vary among these domains. Additionally, the results were gathered from a one-time survey and thus our findings might not reflect actual "after-use" user experiences. In order to constrain the number of questions in our survey, we manipulated the user's ranking on the generated leaderboards to be at the top, in the middle, and at the bottom, which does not reflect a person's real relationship to the domain or the task, given that he/she did not put real effort into improving his/her ranking. Finally, this study uses personality traits as indicator of preference on leaderboard designs. In reality, other factors might play a larger role in determining perceptions of gamification designs.

CONCLUSION AND FUTURE WORK

Overall, this study contributes to the understanding of how leaderboard positions affect people's experiences of leaderboards across different domains. We discovered that for leaderboards in gamified applications, competition is a media rather than purpose. We found that one primary personality trait affect people's perceived preferences on leaderboards by a small amount—and did so in different ways: *extraversion*. We developed several design guidelines for leaderboards in specific domains and for specific personality types.

In future work, we plan to explore the relations between the dynamism of different leaderboard implementations and people's perceptions of those leaderboards. We anticipate that this research will continue to guide the application of motivational affordances to enhance users' experiences with a variety of gamified applications across many potential domains.

ACKNOWLEDGEMENTS

We would like to thank our respondents for their time and effort. We would also like to thank our anonymous reviewers and PC members for their valuable suggestions in improving our data analysis methods and effectively communicating the results of this complex study.

REFERENCES

1. Ian Anderson, Julie Maitland, Scott Sherwood, Louise Barkhuus, Matthew Chalmers, Malcolm Hall, Barry Brown, and Henk Muller. 2007. Shakra: Tracking and sharing daily activity levels with unaugmented mobile phones. *Mobile Networks and Applications* 12, 2–3: 185–199.
2. Isabel Anger and Christian Kittl. 2011. Measuring influence on Twitter. In *Proceedings of the 11th International Conference on Knowledge Management and Knowledge Technologies*, 31.
3. Sonia M. Arteaga, Mo Kudeki, and Adrienne Woodworth. 2009. Combating obesity trends in teenagers through persuasive mobile technology. *SIGACCESS Accessibility and Computing* 94: 17–25. http://doi.acm.org/10.1145/1595061.1595064
4. Charles Butler. 2013. The effect of leaderboard ranking on players' perception of gaming fun. In *International Conference on Online Communities and Social Computing*, 129–136.
5. David Codish and Gilad Ravid. 2014. Personality based gamification-educational gamification for extroverts and introverts. In *Proceedings of the 9th CHAIS Conference for the Study of Innovation and Learning Technologies: Learning in the Technological Era*, 36–44.
6. João P. Costa, Rina R. Wehbe, James Robb, and Lennart E. Nacke. 2013. Time's up: Studying leaderboards for engaging punctual behaviour. In *Proceedings of the First International Conference on Gameful Design, Research, and Applications*, 26–33.
7. Paul T. Costa, Jr. and Robert R. McCrae. 1992. *NEO Personality Inventory–Revised (NEO-PI-R) and NEO Five-Factor Inventory (NEO-FFI) Professional Manual.* Psychological Assessment Resources, Odessa, FL.
8. Sebastian Deterding, Dan Dixon, Rilla Khaled, and Lennart Nacke. 2011. From game design elements to gamefulness: Defining "gamification". In *Proceedings of the 15th International Academic MindTrek Conference: Envisioning Future Media Environments*, 915. http://doi.acm.org/10.1145/2181037.2181040
9. Rosta Farzan, Joan M. DiMicco, David R. Millen, Casey Dugan, Werner Geyer, and Elizabeth A. Brownholtz. 2008. Results from deploying a participation incentive mechanism within the enterprise. In *Proceedings of the SIGCHI Conference on Human Factors in Computing Systems*, 563–572.
10. Samuel D. Gosling, Peter J. Rentfrow, and William B. Swann. 2003. A very brief measure of the Big-Five personality domains. *Journal of Research in personality* 37, 6: 504–528.
11. Juho Hamari and Jonna Koivisto. 2015 "Working out for likes": An empirical study on social influence in exercise gamification. *Computers in Human Behavior* 50: 333–347.
12. Juho Hamari, Jonna Koivisto, and Harri Sarsa. 2014. Does gamification work?: A literature review of empirical studies on gamification. In *Proceedings of the 47th Hawaii International Conference on System Sciences (HICSS '14)*, 3025–3034.
13. Juho Hamari. 2013. Transforming homo economicus into homo ludens: A field experiment on gamification in a utilitarian peer-to-peer trading service. *Electronic Commerce Research and Applications* 12, 4: 236–245.
14. Victoria Husted Medvec, Scott F. Madey and Thomas Gilovich. 1995. When less is more: Counterfactual thinking and satisfaction among Olympic medalists. *Journal of Personality and Social Psychology* 69, 4, 603.
15. Maurits Kaptein and Dean Eckles. 2012. Heterogeneity in the effects of online persuasion. *Journal of Interactive Marketing* 26, 3: 176–188.
16. Yuan Jia, Bin Xu, Yamini Karanam, and Stephen Voida. 2016. Personality-targeted gamification: A survey study on personality traits and motivational affordances. In *Proceedings of the 2016 CHI Conference on Human Factors in Computing Systems*. 2001–2013.
17. Oliver P. John, Laura P. Naumann, and Christopher J. Soto. 2008. Paradigm shift to the integrative Big Five trait taxonomy: History, measurement, and conceptual issues. In *Handbook of Personality: Theory and Research* (3rd ed.), Oliver P. John, Richard W. Robbins, and Lawrence A. Pervin (eds.). Guilford Press, New York, NY, 114–158.
18. Elisa D. Mekler, Florian Brühlmann, Klaus Opwis, and Alexandre N. Tuch. 2013. Do points, levels and leaderboards harm intrinsic motivation?: An empirical analysis of common gamification elements. In *Proceedings of the First International Conference on Gameful Design, Research, and Applications*, 66–73.
19. Robert R. McCrae, and Paul T. Costa. 1989. Reinterpreting the Myers-Briggs type indicator from the perspective of the Five Factor model of personality. *Journal of Personality* 57, 1: 17–40.
20. Rudy McDaniel, Robb Lindgren, and Jon Friskics. 2012. Using badges for shaping interactions in online learning environments. In *Proceeding of IEEE International Professional Communication Conference*, 1–4.

21. Ethan R. Mollick and Nancy Rothbard. 2014. *Mandatory fun: Consent, gamification and the impact of games at work*. The Wharton School research paper series.
22. Mark J. Nelson. 2012. Soviet and American precursors to the gamification of work. In *Proceedings of the 16th International Academic MindTrek Conference*, 23–26.
23. Oded Nov and Ofer Arazy. 2013. Personality-targeted design: Theory, experimental procedure, and preliminary results. In *Proceedings of the 2013 ACM Conference on Computer Supported Cooperative Work* (CSCW '13), 977–984. http://doi.acm.org/10.1145/2441776.2441887
24. Jon Radoff. 2011. *Game on: Energize your business with social media games*. John Wiley & Sons.
25. Byron Reeves and J. Leighton Read. 2009. *Total engagement: Using games and virtual worlds to change the way people work and businesses compete*. Harvard Business School Press, Boston, MA.
26. Katie Seaborn and Deborah I. Fels. 2015. Gamification in theory and action: A survey. *International Journal of Human-Computer Studies* 74, 14–31.
27. Emily Sun, Brooke Jones, Stefano Traca, and Maarten W. Bos. 2015. Leaderboard position psychology: counterfactual thinking. In *Extended Abstracts of the 33rd Annual ACM Conference on Human Factors in Computing Systems*, 1217–1222.
28. Kevin Werbach and Dan Hunter. 2012. *For the win: How game thinking can revolutionize your business*. Wharton Digital Press.
29. Donghee Yvette Wohn, Cliff Lampe, Rick Wash, Nicole Ellison, and Jessica Vitak. 2011. The "s" in social network games: Initiating, maintaining, and enhancing relationships. In *Proceedings of the 44th Hawaii International Conference on System Sciences* (HICSS 2011), 1–10.
30. Clara Choi-Ki Wong and Ron Chi-Wai Kwok. 2016. The effect of gamified mHealth app on exercise motivation and physical activity. In *Proceedings of Pacific Asia Conference on Information Systems (PACIS)*, 389.
31. Gabe Zichermann and Christopher Cunningham. 2011. *Gamification by design: Implementing game mechanics in web and mobile apps*. O'Reilly Media.

Inferring Motion Direction using Commodity Wi-Fi for Interactive Exergames

Kun Qian†**, Chenshu Wu**†**, Zimu Zhou**‡**, Yue Zheng**†**, Zheng Yang**†**, Yunhao Liu**†
†School of Software and TNLIST, Tsinghua University, China
‡Computer Engineering and Networks Laboratory, ETH, Switzerland
{qiank10, wucs32, cczhengy, hmilyyz, yunhaoliu}@gmail.com, zimu.zhou@tik.ee.ethz.ch

ABSTRACT
In-air interaction acts as a key enabler for ambient intelligence and augmented reality. As an increasing popular example, exergames, and the alike gesture recognition applications, have attracted extensive research in designing accurate, pervasive and low-cost user interfaces. Recent advances in wireless sensing show promise for a ubiquitous gesture-based interaction interface with Wi-Fi. In this work, we extract complete information of motion-induced Doppler shifts with only commodity Wi-Fi. The key insight is to harness antenna diversity to carefully eliminate random phase shifts while retaining relevant Doppler shifts. We further correlate Doppler shifts with motion directions, and propose a light-weight pipeline to detect, segment, and recognize motions without training. On this basis, we present *WiDance*, a Wi-Fi-based user interface, which we utilize to design and prototype a contactless dance-pad exergame. Experimental results in typical indoor environment demonstrate a superior performance with an accuracy of 92%, remarkably outperforming prior approaches.

ACM Classification Keywords
H.5.2. Information Interfaces and Presentation: User InterfacesInput devices and strategies; C.2.1. Computer-Communication Networks: Network Architecture and DesignWireless communication

Author Keywords
Motion Direction Recognition; Wireless Sensing; Off-the-shelf Wi-Fi; Exergame

INTRODUCTION
Exergames, where players are compelled to get up and exercise (*e.g.*, dance, kick-boxing, sports moves), bring more than just fun [8, 15]. Researchers find that exergames can improve the fitness, health and social involvement of players [20, 27]. Due to their health benefits, various exergame interfaces have been developed in both the industries (*e.g.* Kinect Sports and Wii Fit) and academia [7, 24]. Most interfaces for exergames are based on computer vision, dedicated sensors or sonic technology. Despite their high accuracy in tracking motions of players, they suffer from limitations such as sensitivity to lighting condition and line-of-sight condition, requirement of device attachment and high-cost installation and instrumentation. We argue that a more ubiquitous exergame interface with fewer environment constraints is essential to fit in the fragmented free time and space in modern life. For instance, a white-collar worker may play a 5-min exergame in the office to refresh. A housekeeper may take a quick workout during the waiting time when preparing dishes in the kitchen.

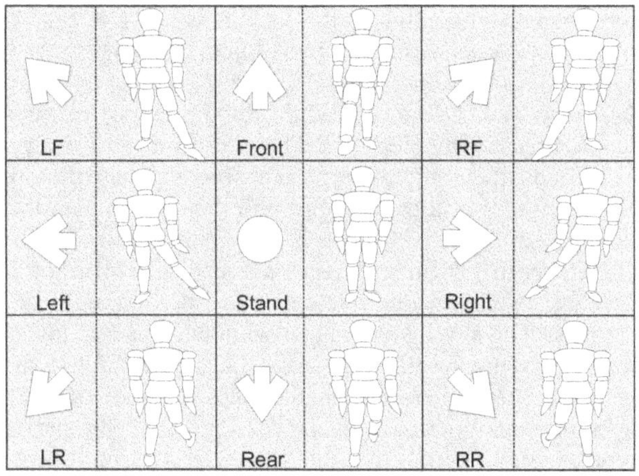

Figure 1. Human-computer interaction interface of *WiDance*

The need for a low-cost, non-invasive, and ubiquitous user interface has triggered extensive research on in-air human sensing, especially using the almost-everywhere Wi-Fi infrastructure [4, 18, 31, 6, 28]. The main idea is to model and extract motion induced variations on Wi-Fi signals to infer human activities. In principle, it is possible to obtain all parameters of incident signals, including amplitudes, phases, frequency shifts, and relate these parameters with human actions. Pioneer works [4, 22, 12] extract accurate signal parameters to derive motion-induced Doppler shift and time-of-flight, which are used to estimate the speed and distance of motions. However, they require specialized hardware because commodity Wi-Fi devices suffer from random phase shifts caused by lack of synchronization, limited frequency bandwidth and multipath effect. Other works [31, 6, 28, 30] apply machine learning to coarse-grained signal parameters available on commodity Wi-Fi devices to infer user activities. Yet the training efforts

CHI 2017, May 06-11, 2017, Denver, CO, USA
 ISBN 978-1-4503-4655-9/17/05...$15.00
DOI: http://dx.doi.org/10.1145/3025453.3025678

involved and the less interpretable features extracted make them unfavorable as a robust and light-weight user gesture interface.

This paper seeks to advance the state-of-the-art in wireless interaction interfaces by accurately deriving motion-induced Doppler shifts using Channel State Information (CSI) available on unmodified Wi-Fi devices, and further extracting motion directions for exergame designs. As a proof-of-concept, we present *WiDance*, a dance-pad like exergame with commercial Wi-Fi devices. As shown in Figure 1, it tracks the leg moving directions of players by monitoring the minute Doppler shifts in the received CSI of Wi-Fi signals, and recognizes the estimated directions as the ones shown on a screen. Technically, *WiDance* addresses two critical challenges. (1) *How to obtain full information of Doppler shifts from off-the-shelf imperfect Wi-Fi devices?* While some previous works [30] have extracted Doppler-related features from commodity Wi-Fi devices, they only extract the absolute values of Doppler shifts without arithmetic signs, and thus fail to identify the *direction* of motions. Instead, *WiDance* extracts accurate and comprehensive Doppler shifts with direction information from CSI by leveraging multiple antennas on commodity Wi-Fi devices. The key insight is that while antennas at the same receiver experience different channel distortions due to spatial diversity, they suffer from the same noise sources. Therefore, we propose a series of signal processing steps to properly manipulate signals from multiple antennas, making it possible to eliminate random noises while retaining Doppler shifts of interests. (2) *How to detect, segment and recognize complex player actions from Doppler shifts series?* To robustly recognize player motions without training, we first verify that single link is insufficient for tracking player actions, and solve inherent ambiguities with minimum cost by adopting one more link. An effective light-weight model is proposed to relate Doppler shifts observed from joint two wireless links with player actions, and a series of data processing steps are developed to achieve robust detection, segmentation and finally recognition of player actions.

We prototype *WiDance* with commodity Wi-Fi infrastructure and evaluate its performance in various indoor environments. Experimental results show that *WiDance* yields accuracies for recognizing player actions of 92%. Compared with the state-of-the-art, the Doppler shifts features obtained by *WiDance* can differentiate all eight actions required by dancing games, while those in existing approaches [30, 6] can only classify actions into three coarse categories. The motion recognition accuracy of *WiDance* is comparable to popular classifiers such as HMM, even without training. We envision *WiDance* as a promising step towards practical wireless human-computer interaction interface, which underpins new insights for future wireless sensing applications.

In summary, the main contributions are as follows:

- We design a novel algorithm to extract complete information of motion-induced Doppler shifts (both absolute values and signs) leveraging antenna diversity on commodity Wi-Fi devices. As far as we are aware of, it is the first work that obtains accurate arithmetic signs of Doppler shifts on Wi-Fi infrastructure without modification.
- We model the relations between Doppler shifts with motion directions, and develop a wireless interactive exergame, *i.e.*, a dance pad with eight types of inputs. It operates via a light-weight yet effective signal processing pipeline to detect, segment and recognize player actions from Doppler shift series without prior training. In addition to interactive exergames, the core techniques in *WiDance* are applicable in various gesture recognition applications, including, but not limited to, fall detection for the elderly, and gait recognition for user identification.
- We implement *WiDance* on commodity Wi-Fi devices and validate its effectiveness with various indoor settings. Experimental results demonstrate that *WiDance* achieves recognition accuracy of 92%. By exploiting complete information of Doppler shifts for motion recognition, *WiDance* outperforms previous feature-based approaches, which fail to derive the direction of motions.

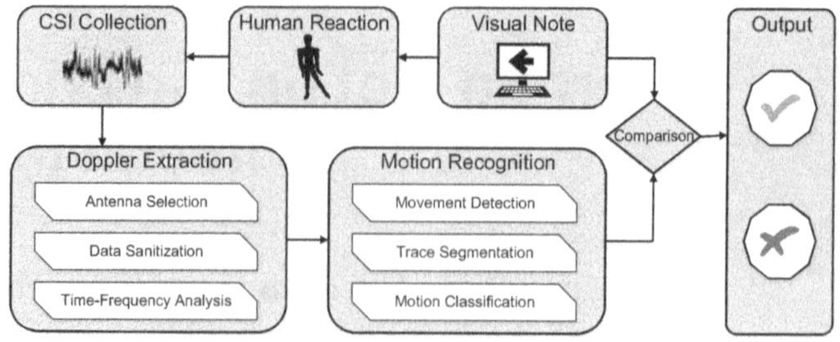

Figure 2. ***WiDance*** **logic flow**

The rest of the paper is organized as follows. We first provide the overview of *WiDance*, followed by the principles of Doppler shifts extraction and player actions recognition. Then, performance evaluation and user study of *WiDance* are provided. Finally, related works are reviewed and conclusion is drawn.

WIDANCE OVERVIEW

WiDance is a passively interactive dancing pad-like exergame using off-the-shelf Wi-Fi devices. Figure 2 shows the logic process of *WiDance*. The game starts by selecting a piece of music. For each note in the music, *WiDance* rhythmically displays an arrow of certain direction on the screen. The player follows visual notes and moves his/her legs along the directions indicated by the notes. *WiDance* continuously records and processes CSI for recognizing the player reactions over the whole gaming period. Each recognized reaction is compared with the corresponding visual note, and the comparison result is displayed on the screen and the reaction is scored.

The main technical challenge for *WiDance* is to promptly and robustly recognize player reactions from noisy CSI data. Towards this goal, *WiDance* leverages the motion-induced Doppler effect observed in CSI and propose a two-step reaction recognition procedure. As shown in Figure 2, the first step is to extract Doppler effect from CSI. It recovers a spectrogram of Doppler frequency shifts in presence of random

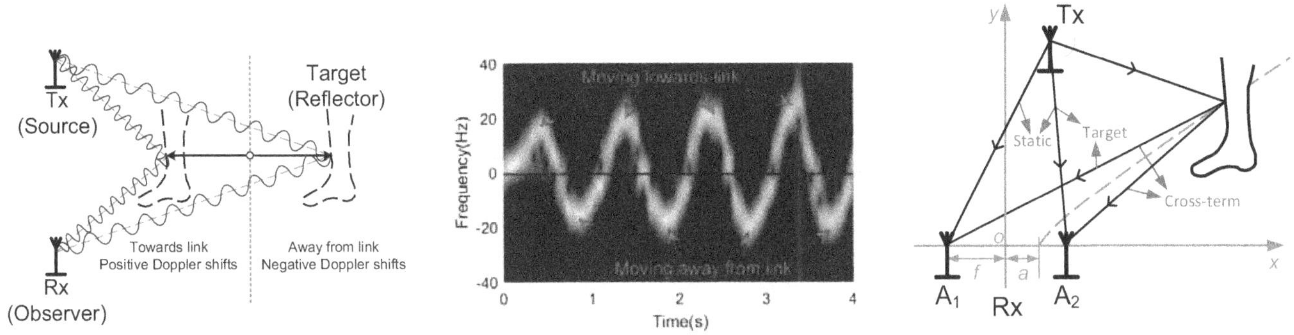

(a) Illustration of Doppler effect (b) Spectrogram of Doppler effect (c) Doppler effect with multiple antennas

Figure 3. Modeling Doppler effect in multipath scenarios.

phase offsets, burst noise and interferences using a series of signal processing techniques including antenna selection, data sanitization and time-frequency analysis. The second step is to recognize player reactions from the spectrogram of Doppler frequency shifts. The challenge for this step is to robustly recognize each individual player reaction from continuous Doppler frequency shifts that may consist of multiple reactions. Operations adopted in this step include movement detection, trace segmentation and motion classification. The output of this step is reaction series recognized by *WiDance*.

DOPPLER EFFECT IN WI-FI

WiDance extracts Doppler effect from Wi-Fi signals to recognize dancing actions of players. This section provides the technical preliminaries, fundamental model and practical issues of identifying Doppler frequency shifts from noisy Wi-Fi signals on commercial devices.

Doppler Effect

Doppler shift is the change in the frequency of a wave for observers. It is caused by change in relative locations of sources, observers and reflectors. In the context of contactless sensing, both transmitters (sources) and receivers (observers) are statically deployed, while target objects (reflectors) move and alter the wireless transmission. As shown in Figure 3a, when the target object moves towards the transmitter and the receiver, the crests and troughs of the reflected signals arrive at the receiver at a faster rate. Conversely, when an object moves away from the receiver, the crests and troughs arrive at a slower rate. In general, for a point object, the Doppler frequency shift of the signal reflected off the object is:

$$f_D = -\frac{1}{\lambda}\frac{\mathrm{d}}{\mathrm{dt}}d(t), \tag{1}$$

where λ is the wavelength of the signal and $d(t)$ is the length of the reflected path.

As an illustrative example, we prototype a wireless transceiver system using two USRPs synchronized by an external clock. The two USRPs are placed together near the ground, and a participant strides with his right leg at moderate rate, at the direction orthogonal to the link, as in Figure 3a. The Doppler effect caused by striding is obtained by tracking the phase of the received signal. Figure 3b shows the spectrogram of Doppler effect of striding. Clearly, positive Doppler shifts appear as the user strides towards the link, while negative Doppler shifts appear as the user strides away from the link. Thus, it is possible to track target motion (both speed and direction) by exploiting Doppler effect.

Doppler Effect in CSI

In reality, instead of single path as the reflected path in Figure 3a, there are multiple paths where signal propagates from the transmitter to the receiver. The phenomenon is known as multipath. As a result, the response of the wireless channel at frequency f and time t is the superimposition of responses of each individual path [21]:

$$H(f,t) = \sum_{k=1}^{K} \alpha_k(t)e^{-j2\pi f\tau_k(t)}, \tag{2}$$

where K is the total number of multipath, and $\alpha_k(t)$ and $\tau_k(t)$ are the complex attenuation factor and time of flight for the k-th path, respectively.

For the k-th path, the time of flight $\tau_k(t)$ is the time for light to travel at a distance of path length of $d_k(t)$, i.e. $d_k(t) = c\tau_k(t)$, where c is the speed of light. Thus, according to Equation 1, the channel response can be represented by Doppler frequency shift on each path and further divided into two categories:

$$H(f,t) = H_s(f) + \sum_{k\in P_d} \alpha_k(t)e^{j2\pi\int_{-\infty}^{t} f_{D_k}(u)\mathrm{du}}, \tag{3}$$

where $H_s(f)$ is the sum of responses of all static path ($f_D = 0$), and P_d is the set of dynamic path ($f_D \neq 0$).

Assuming that $\alpha_k(t)$ and $f_{D_k}(t)$ are nearly constant during short time interval, Doppler frequency shifts can be obtained from spectrogram with time-frequency analysis:

$$\mathscr{H}(f,t) \approx H_s(f) + \sum_{k\in P_d} \alpha_k(t)B(f_{D_k}(t)), \tag{4}$$

where $B(\cdot)$ is the window function for cutting out the signal segment of interest.

CSI is the sampled version of the channel response in Equation 2 and 3. It is available from upper layers on off-the-shelf

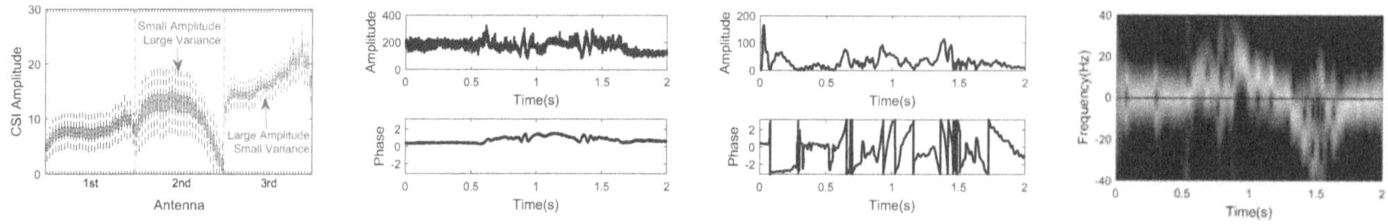

(a) Antenna selection (b) Raw CSI (c) Data sanitization (d) Spectrogram of CSI

Figure 4. Extraction of Doppler frequency shifts from CSI of multiple antennas

Wi-Fi Network Interface Cards with only slight driver modification [9]. However, lack of synchronization between Wi-Fi NICs induces unknown phase shifts in raw CSI:

$$\hat{H}(f,t) = H(f,t)e^{-j2\pi(\Delta_t f+\Delta_f t)}, \tag{5}$$

where $2\pi(\Delta_f t + \Delta_t f)$ is phase shift caused by carrier frequency and timing offset. Therefore, it is infeasible to directly extract Doppler components from actual CSI measurements.

Prior works [30, 6] eliminates phase noises by calculating CSI power, *i.e.* $|\hat{H}(f,t)|^2 = |H(f,t)|^2$. However, this process meanwhile eliminates the imagery part of CSI, and thus loses the information of signs of Doppler shifts. That is, with only CSI power, we have no idea whether reflectors moves towards or away from the link. As a result, CSI power can only be used to recognize *what target does* (*e.g.* activity types), but not *how target does* (*e.g.* activity directions), through an upper-layer learning-based framework.

Doppler Effect by Multiple Antennas

To remove unknown phase shifts while still retain complete Doppler frequency shifts, *WiDance* uses multiple antennas available on Wi-Fi NICs. Since all antennas on the same NIC experience the same phase shifts, calculating conjugate multiplication of CSI of one pair of antennas also eliminates the phase offset. Specifically, denote the CSI of the i-the antenna as $H^{(i)}(f,t)$, we have the following product:

$$\begin{aligned} H^{(1)}(f,t)H^{(2)}(f,t)^* &\approx H_s^{(1)}(f)H_s^{(2)}(f)^* \\ &+ \sum_{k\in P_d^{(1)}} \alpha_k^{(1)}(t)H_s^{(2)}(f)^* e^{j2\pi\int_{-\infty}^{t} f_{D_k}^{(1)}(u)\mathrm{du}} \\ &+ \sum_{k\in P_d^{(2)}} H_s^{(1)}(f)\alpha_k^{(2)}(t)^* e^{-j2\pi\int_{-\infty}^{t} f_{D_k}^{(2)}(u)\mathrm{du}} \\ &+ \sum_{k\in P_d^{(1)}, l\in p_d^{(2)}} \alpha_k^{(1)}(t)\alpha_l^{(2)}(t)^* e^{j2\pi\int_{-\infty}^{t} f_{D_k}^{(1)}(u)-f_{D_l}^{(2)}(u)\mathrm{du}}. \end{aligned} \tag{6}$$

As in Figure 3c, by closely placing antennas A_1 and A_2 of the receiver (e.g., $2f \leq \lambda$), CSI of two antennas may contain the same major multipaths (i.e., $P_d^{(1)} = P_d^{(2)}$) with different complex attenuation factors but similar Doppler shifts. Then the terms in Equation 6 can be divided into three categories:

Static terms. The static term $H_s^{(1)}(f)H_s^{(2)}(f)^*$ are calculated by multiplication of static responses (e.g., LOS) of two antennas. This term does not contain Doppler shifts and can be filtered out with a high-pass filter.

Target terms. Target terms are calculated by multiplication of static responses of one antenna and responses that contain target Doppler shifts of the other antenna. They contain Doppler shifts of interest and their arithmetic opposite numbers. A sufficient condition for extracting Doppler shifts instead of their opposite numbers is that terms containing Doppler shifts have larger amplitudes. Specifically, for the k-th path, following condition should be fulfilled:

$$\left|\frac{H_s^{(1)}(f)}{\alpha_k^{(1)}(t)}\right| < \left|\frac{H_s^{(2)}(f)}{\alpha_k^{(2)}(t)}\right|. \tag{7}$$

Although it is unable to separate static and dynamic responses from CSI and directly verify the condition, there still exist some clues in CSI, which can guide us to obtain multiplication results that satisfy the condition. Note that the issues of antenna selection will be discussed later in this section.

Cross terms. Cross terms are products of dynamic responses of antennas. They only contain difference of Doppler shifts and may obfuscate real Doppler shifts. Fortunately, the static responses indoors are likely to dominate dynamic responses, due to strong LOS signals or large static reflectors like walls. As a result, the cross terms are orders weaker than target terms. Furthermore, in *WiDance*, only one player moves his legs in the monitor area at any time. And the difference of Doppler shifts caused by different body parts are usually small, and can be filtered out with high-pass filter. Thus, the negative effect of cross terms can be tolerated.

Extraction of Doppler Effect

To convert noisy CSI to spectrogram of Doppler frequency shifts, *WiDance* introduces a series of processing steps.

Antenna Selection. Recall that to correctly extract Doppler frequency shift, the condition in Equation 7 should be satisfied. Thus, we should properly select pairs of antennas and assign the order of antennas in conjugated multiplication. Despite of the mixture of static and dynamic responses, CSI itself reveals some clues that help verify the condition.

Observation I: CSI with higher amplitude is likely to possess larger static responses. This is because the amplitude of static responses are orders of magnitude larger than that of dynamic responses, due to existence of strong LOS signals

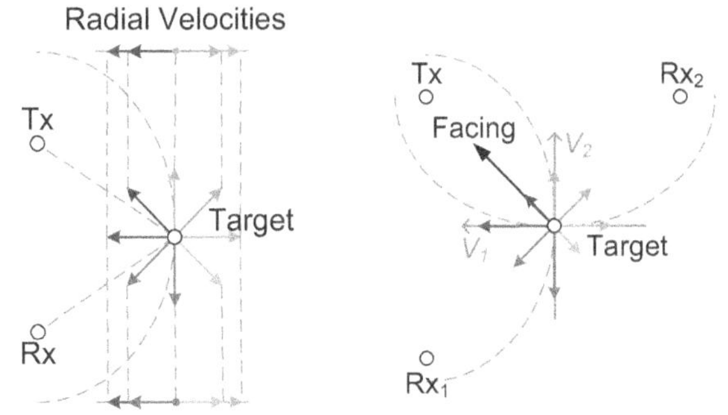

(a) Single link (b) Orthogonal two links

Figure 5. Translation between Doppler effect and player reaction

and larger static reflectors like walls. Consequently, even if slightly disturbed by dynamic responses, the averaged CSI can be used to approximate the static response in Equation 7.

Observation II: CSI with higher variance is likely to possess larger dynamic responses. This is because only dynamic responses contributes to variation of CSI. As a result, the standard deviation of CSI can be used to indicate the dynamic responses in Equation 7.

Figure 4a illustrates the criterion for selection of pair of antennas. The boxes show distributions of CSI of different antennas and across subcarriers over time. In this example, the 2nd antenna has the largest variances with relative small amplitudes, while the 3rd antenna has the largest amplitudes with relative small variances. By comparing the ratio of amplitudes and standard deviations of CSI, the 3rd and 2nd antennas are orderly selected.

Data Sanitization. As noted in Equation 6, raw CSI contains significant static components, low-frequency interferences and burst noises, which obfuscate Doppler shifts of interest. Thus, it is natural to remove these signal components with filters. Specifically, we adopt Butterworth bandpass filter for its flat amplitude response in the pass band, and apply the filter to the multiplication series of each CSI subcarrier. The upper and lower cutoff frequencies of Butterworth filter are set to 40Hz and 2Hz respectively. The upper cutoff frequency is decided by the experimental observation that normal human striding velocities are no more than v_m =1m/s. For Wi-Fi devices working at 5.8GHz, the upper bound of Doppler frequency of PLCR is $f = \frac{2v_m}{\lambda} \approx \frac{2\times 1\text{m/s}}{0.05\text{m}} = 40\text{Hz}$. The lower cutoff frequency is decided by trade-off between fully eliminating interference and loss of low-frequency components of Doppler effect. However, such loss has minor impact on *WiDance*, since *WiDance* can still leverage high-frequency components that are more stable against burst noises for motion recognition.

Figure 4b and 4c show the amplitude and phase of CSI series before and after filtering. Clearly, burst noises and low-frequency interferences are removed. Moreover, the cyclic phase changes that correspond to the target Doppler shifts at time 1 and 1.5 second are signified.

Time-frequency analysis. To further denoise and compress CSI data for time-frequency analysis, we perform Principle Component Analysis (PCA) on all CSI subcarriers and select the first principle component that contains major and consistent power variations caused by target motions. Then, short-term Fourier transform (STFT) is applied to the first principle component to obtain the spectrogram of Doppler frequency shifts. Specifically, a Gaussian window with length shorter than 0.15s is applied in STFT to meet the assumption of nearly constant amplitudes and Doppler shifts in Equation 4. A zero padding is further applied in order to generate finer-grained spectrogram. Finally, the non-overlapping spectrograms of all CSI segments are spliced together to generate the whole spectrogram.

Note that there is lower bound on range of actions that can be detected by *WiDance*, due to the well-known uncertainty principle. Specifically, suppose the time length of the data window of STFT is T, then the frequency resolution of the spectrum is $\Delta_f = \frac{1}{T}$. To correctly identify the signal of the frequency shift, the amplitude of the frequency shift must fall into the non-DC bins, which correspond to a minimum frequency of $\frac{2}{T}$. For a signal segment with constant frequency shift, the frequency shift should fulfil $F = \frac{V}{\lambda} \geq \frac{2}{T}$, where V is the change rate of the reflecting signal path and λ is the wave length of the signal. Thus the sensitivity of action range R is:

$$R > \frac{1}{2}VT \geq \lambda \qquad (8)$$

In reality, the sensitivity of *WiDance* is worse than the theoretical bound due to complex stride actions including acceleration and deceleration and existence of environmental noises.

Figure 4d illustrates the spectrogram of Doppler shifts induced by striding (first towards and then away from the link), from noisy CSI provided by commercial Wi-Fi NIC. Though fluctuating, the spectrogram clearly reflects the trend of *signed Doppler effect* (first positive and then negative), which we use to recognize the reaction performed by the player.

MOTION RECOGNITION

This section details the principles and practical issues to recognize player reactions from spectrogram of Doppler shifts.

Player Reaction in Doppler Effect

We first derive the relation between movements of reflector (player) and Doppler shifts. As shown in Figure 5a, given constant length of the reflecting path, the reflector is on an ellipse with the transceivers as focuses. Based on the impact on the ellipse, the velocity of the reflector can be divided into the tangential velocity along the tangent and the radial velocity along the norm. Specifically, the tangential velocity guides the target moving along the ellipse while the radial velocity drives the target moving off the ellipse. Evidently, the radial velocity is the only cause of change in the length of the reflected path, and thus the Doppler frequency shift. That is, if the reflector moves along various directions with the same speed, the link will experience different changes in the length of the reflected path, according to the radial velocities projected on the norm direction. As a result, it is possible to obtain the moving direction of the reflector with the level of radial velocity derived from Doppler effect.

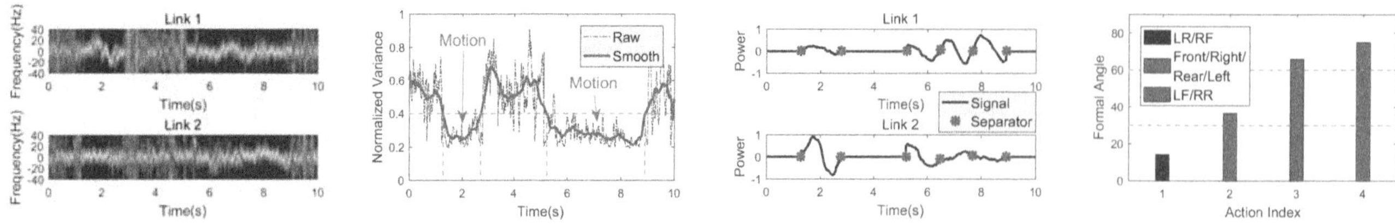

(a) Spectrogram (b) Detection (c) Segmentation (d) Classification

Figure 6. Motion recognition process from Doppler shifts

However, it is insufficient to use one link to estimate the moving direction for the following two reasons. First, the distribution of radial velocity is symmetric about the norm. So it is unable to distinguish any two symmetric directions using Doppler effect of a single link only. Second, recognition using a single link assumes that the player performs reactions at constant speed to consistently map the level of radial velocity to moving direction. However, such assumption will not hold in practice due to diverse actions performed by players.

To address the above challenges, we propose a recognition scheme to solve the symmetric ambiguities with minimum cost by adding one additional link. As shown in Figure 5b, two links are placed orthogonal with each other. As the player stands at the intersection of midnormals of the two link, for any direction where the player reacts, the velocity can be projected on the 2D $V_1 - V_2$ plane, where V_i is the speed of the radial velocity for the i-th link. Even if the player performs reactions at various speeds, the moving direction is reserved by radial velocities of the two orthogonal links, making it possible to recognize player reactions.

Motion Recognition Workflow

Figure 6 shows an illustrative process of motion recognition in *WiDance*. In this example, a player stands at the intersection of midnormals of the two link, facing towards the transmitter. The player first halts for $1s$, then moves the leg in left-rear direction within $2s$, and halts again for another $2s$. Next, the player moves forward, continuously followed by two left-front movements, which takes $6s$ in total. Finally, the player halts for $1s$. The corresponding spectrogram is shown in Figure 6a.

Movement Detection. During the game, the player may occasionally halt, due to *e.g.* long waiting intervals between successive visual action notes (arrow) or tiredness. Periods during which the player halts do not contain valid actions, and should be skipped for efficiency. Thus, it is necessary to perform movement detection before motion recognition.

WiDance conducts movement detection based on the following intuition. When a player is static, no Doppler effect will be observed and the spectrogram contains only noises. As a result, the power of spectrogram spreads out across the whole frequency band. In contrast, when a player moves, the spectrogram is dominated by Doppler effect, and the power of spectrogram concentrates on the frequency of interest. Therefore, *WiDance* calculates and smooths variances of power distribution in frequency domain for movement detection. Note that only the filter of CSI sanitization affects the variance, as the filter decides to which extent the out-of-band components are filtered out. Therefore, regarding a fixed filter, it is feasible to use a predefined threshold. Player movement is detected when the variance falls below the threshold, as shown in Figure 6b.

Trace Segmentation. During an exergame, a player may frequently perform continuous actions, as in Figure 6. Thus, it is necessary for *WiDance* to correctly segment them into individual ones for recognition.

WiDance leverages the characteristics of action patterns performed by players. Specifically, for each action, the player first stretches one of his/her legs in some direction, and then retracts the leg back to stand. As a result, the player action causes a pair of peaks or valleys in Doppler frequency shifts with significantly different amplitudes, depending on the player's moving direction, as illustrated in Figure 6c. For each action, by orthogonally placing two links, at least one link experiences large fluctuations no matter at which direction the player moves. Thus, *WiDance* computes the average sum of absolute values of Doppler frequency shifts of the two links, and detects the prominent peaks. Then two adjacent peaks are grouped as the spectrum of one complete action. An illustrative segmentation result is shown in Figure 6c.

Motion Classification. Finally, *WiDance* applies the recognition model in Figure 5b to Doppler frequency segments to identify the corresponding actions. As Doppler frequency shifts vary even within one segment, due to acceleration and deceleration of human motions, simply estimating moving direction corresponding to each time sample may suffer from significant noises. Hence we propose a two-level rule-based classification scheme, which comprehensively takes advantage of all data available within the Doppler frequency segments.

In the first step, *WiDance* classifies movement directions based on the ratio of accumulative absolute values of Doppler frequency shifts of two links, as shown in Figure 6d. For clarity, we represent the ratio with its arctangent value, which range in $[0, 90^\circ]$. Clearly, the movement directions can be classified into three coarse categories: LR/RF, front/right/rear/left, LF/RR. The theoretical ratios of three categories are 0°, 45° and 90°, respectively. However, due to noises and variations of player positions, non-zero Doppler frequency shifts can still be observed even if the player moves in parallel with the link, which leads to practical ratios slightly larger than 0° for LR/RF category, and smaller than 90° for LF/RR category. Thus, we slightly adjust the thresholds to 30° and 60°, respectively.

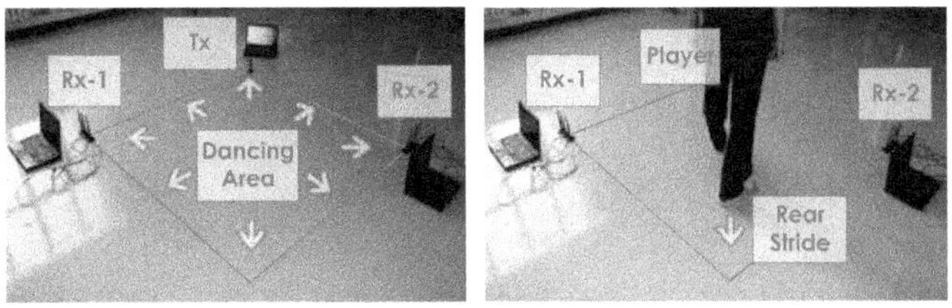

(a) *WiDance* (b) User action

Figure 7. Experiment setup

In the second step, *WiDance* further differentiates movement directions in each coarse categories, based on the order of appearances of the positive and negative Doppler frequency shifts in the segment. Specifically, for any link, if the positive Doppler shift firstly appears, the player stretches his leg towards the link. In contrast, if the negative Doppler shift firstly appears, the player stretches his leg away from the link. Thus, the directions in each coarse directions can be further classified with the knowledge of whether the player stretches his leg towards or away from the two links. With the two-step scheme above, the movement directions of actions can be identified.

EVALUATION

This section presents the experimental settings and the detailed performance of *WiDance*.

Experiment Methodology

Evaluation Setup. *WiDance* consists of one transmitter and two receivers equipped with wireless cards. As shown in Figure 7a, three ThinkPad T-series laptops equipped with Intel 5300 wireless NICs are used to establish orthogonal links. For easier deployment, we connect the devices with external antennas. Specifically, the transmitter has one antenna, and each receiver has three antennas. The links are set up to work on Channel 165 at 5.825GHz. CSI are collected with modified network driver [9], and then passed to processing computer via TCP/IP protocol. The processing computer uses a Intel i7-5600U 2.6GHz CPU, and processes CSI data using MATLAB. The antennas of each receiver are placed loosely in a line, with a spacing distance of about one wavelength (5.2cm). And the packet transmission rate is set to 1024Hz, which is later decimated for study of the impact of sampling rates. The transmission power are set to 15dBm by default.

All experiments are conducted in rooms in academic buildings, where experimental areas are surrounded with desks, chairs and other equipments. Players are asked to stand at the intersection of midnormals of the two links, facing towards the transmitter. To interact with players, we write a program that randomly displays visual notes on the screen, guiding players to perform dancing actions. An action of rear stride is illustrated in Figure 7b. To make sure that players concentrate on the experiment, no music is incorporated in the current version.

To fully understand the variations in user diversity, we recruit 30 participants and ask them to play dancing games with *WiDance*. For preparation, we demonstrate the usage of *WiDance*. Then, participants are asked to individually practice dancing. During experiment, each participant is asked to play 2-minute

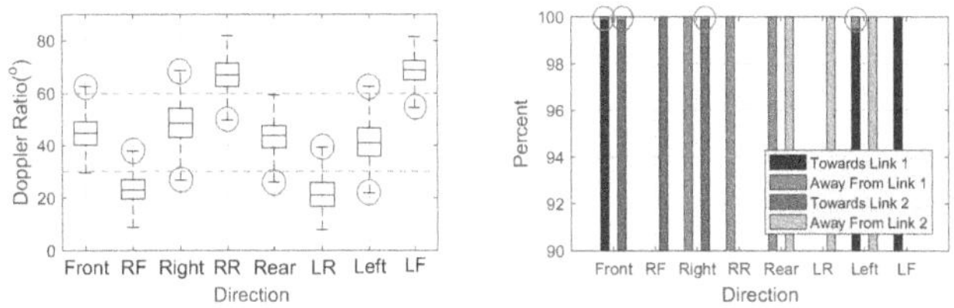

(a) (b)

Figure 10. Criterions and errors. (a) The ratio of Doppler shifts and errors between adjacent directions. (b) The moving directions and errors between non-adjacent directions.

dancing game for 4 times. Games are played in turns to ensure that participants get enough rest before each game. All participants are rewarded after the experiment. The total experiment lasts totally for 2 days and 8 hours each day, and over 10,000 actions are recorded during the experiment.

Baselines. To fairly demonstrate the performance of *WiDance*, we implement *WiDance* and two learning-based schemes, HMM-*WiDance* and CARM [30], for comparison. On one hand, HMM-*WiDance* uses Doppler frequency shifts as *WiDance* does, yet trains HMM for all eight actions. We compare *WiDance* with HMM-*WiDance* to evaluate the non-learning recognition scheme. On the other hand, CARM uses only absolute values of Doppler frequency shifts that is obtained from CSI power, and trains HMMs using this truncated features. We compare *WiDance* with CARM to evaluate the extraction of Doppler frequency shifts. The HMMs implemented in both schemes are similar to those in [30].

Performance

Overall performance. Taking all parameters into consideration, *WiDance* yields an overall accuracy of 92%. As the confusion matrix in Figure 8a shows, *WiDance* achieves consistently high recognition accuracy for all actions.

Yet, there still exist errors for some directions. Based on the root causes, we divide errors into two categories: *errors between adjacent directions* and *errors between non-adjacent errors*. Recall that *WiDance* recognizes actions with two criterions: the amplitude ratio of Doppler shifts and the appearance order of positive and negative Doppler shifts. As shown in Figure 10a, errors in Doppler ratios make *WiDance* confuse actions with adjacent directions, while in Figure 10b, errors in moving directions make *WiDance* confuse actions with non-adjacent directions. Most errors come from misclassification between actions with adjacent directions. For example, about 10.6%, 10.2% and 8.7% actions with right-front, right-rear and left directions are misclassified to their adjacent directions: right, rear and left-rear, respectively. In contrast, errors in moving directions only cause negligible errors, which is about only 0.52% for actions with left direction and 0.14% for actions with front and right direction. The result demonstrates that the condition in Equation 7 can be almost always fulfilled to correctly recognize the true Doppler shifts. Also, it means that compared with signs of Doppler shifts, amplitudes of Doppler shifts is more difficult to estimate, due to environmental noises.

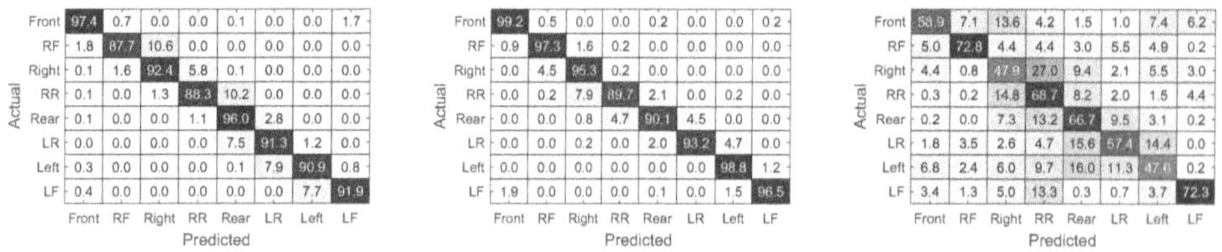

(a) *WiDance* (overall 92%) (b) HMM-*WiDance* (overall 95%) (c) CARM (overall 50%)

Figure 8. Confusion matrices of various methods.

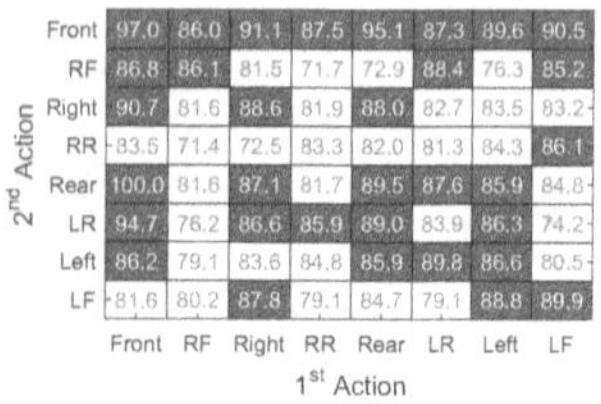

Figure 9. Performance of successive actions. (overall 85%)

Further, the confusion matrix reveals that *WiDance* statistically outperforms in straight directions (front, right, rear, left) than in oblique directions (right-front, right-rear, left-rear, left front). Note that the oblique directions are parallel with one of two links. For simplicity of modelling, *WiDance* assumes that movement in parallel with the link causes zero Doppler shifts to signals of that link. However, such assumption holds only when the player moves strictly at the intersection of mid-normals of two links. In reality, as the player strides within a small range, the link may experience significant Doppler shifts even if the player moves in parallel with the link, which may lead to errors in Doppler amplitude ratios and thus incorrect recognition outputs. Such issues can be solved by further modelling positions of legs, in addition to movement directions in current model, which we leave for future work.

Performance of recognition scheme. To evaluate the performance of non-learning recognition scheme implemented in *WiDance*, we compare *WiDance* with HMM-*WiDance*, which applies Doppler shifts feature to HMM for modelling of eight actions. By carefully tuning the HMM parameters, HMM-*WiDance* merely achieves an accuracy of 95%, which is slightly higher than that of *WiDance*. Thus, we claim that the non-learning recognition scheme can achieve high accuracy comparable with the complex learning method.

Different from *WiDance* which exhibits slightly different performance for different directions, HMM-*WiDance* achieve mild accuracy for all directions. The accuracies of oblique directions and straight directions achieved by HMM-*WiDance* are comparable. As trained with real samples, HMM-*WiDance* is able to differentiate directions at global scale, while modeling small deviations at local scale. Specifically, the fluctuations of Doppler shifts when the player moves in parallel with the link are successfully modelled by HMM. However, HMM-*WiDance* suffers from the common over-fitting problem. For example, the accuracy of actions with rear direction decreases when applying HMM-*WiDance* instead of *WiDance*.

Performance of extraction scheme. To demonstrate the uniqueness and evaluate the performance of extraction of Doppler frequency shifts in *WiDance*, we compare *WiDance* with CARM. Note that we can omit the impact of difference of recognition methods used by *WiDance* and CARM, as these methods have comparable performance, as indicated by the comparison between *WiDance* and HMM-*WiDance* above.

Figure 8c shows the confusion matrix for CARM. CARM fails to recognize actions in several directions, and achieves only 60% accuracy even after carefully tuning the HMM parameters. This is because CARM is based on CSI power and only obtains the absolute values of Doppler shifts, due to loss of imagery part of the signal. Theoretically, if we just use absolute values of Doppler shifts in the non-learning recognition scheme, then only Doppler ratio can be calculated. As a result, only the first step in non-learning recognition scheme can be carried out, and actions can be classified into three coarse categories: LR/RF, front/right/rear/left, LF/RR. However, there is no more clue to differentiate actions in each category. Clearly, some directions are more confused with directions in the same category, besides the large adjacent errors. For example, the right direction is statistically more confused with the front, rear and left direction, and the left-front direction is more confused with the right-rear direction. However, in practice, directions in the same coarse categories are not totally confused by CARM. For all directions, most actions can be correctly classified by CARM. It is because the actions involve movements of whole body rather than only feet and legs, which can be incomprehensively captured by learning method used in CARM to correctly recognize the majority of actions. However, even with these features cannot CARM fully outline the moving directions of actions, which leads to low recognition accuracy.

Performance of compound gestures. Currently, we choose 9 motion directions as the gesture set to fit the dance game. A natural way to scale the gesture set to enable more HCI applications is to construct compound gestures from the 9 motion directions as primitives, e.g. double-left, front-right. Figure 9 shows the performance of *WiDance* in recognizing compound gestures that composes two primitive actions. *WiDance* achieves an overall accuracy of 85%, which is slightly lower than that of recognizing primitive actions. And the accuracy of recognizing compound gestures ranges from 71.4% to 100%. Such diversity in accuracy shows the bias of gesture recognition of *WiDance*. As a result, it is better for real users to conduct pre-training operations to select gestures with high recognition accuracy for practical use. For example, as shown in Figure 9, 33 out of 64 gestures have recognition accuracy higher than 85%, which can be selected to form a larger gesture set than that of 9 primitive actions.

Parameter Study

Impact of user diversity. To evaluate the robustness of *WiDance* for various users, we recruit 30 participants (17 males, 13 females) to test *WiDance*. Figure 12 shows the statistics of participants. The participants have various heights, weight-

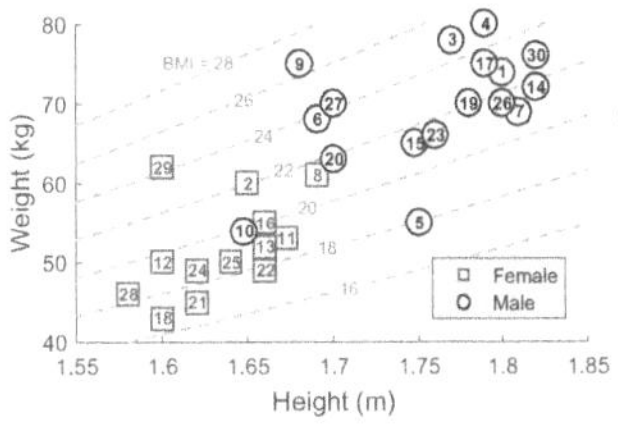

Figure 11. Statistics of participants.

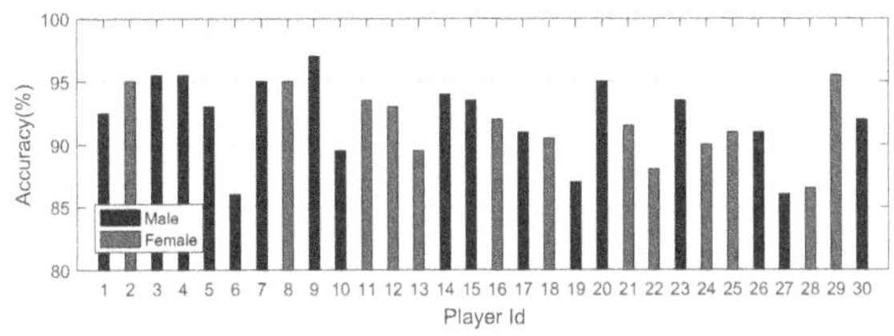

Figure 12. Impact of user diversity.

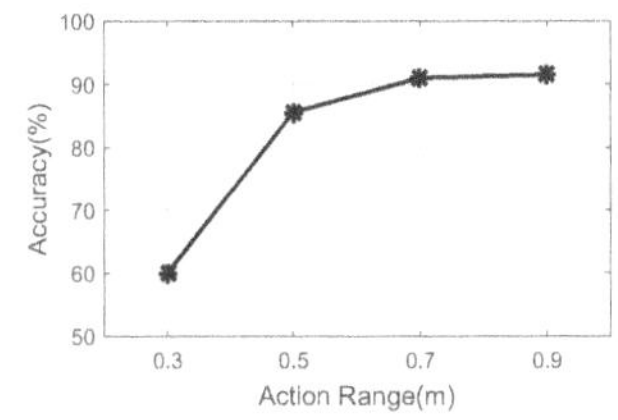

Figure 13. Impact of action range.

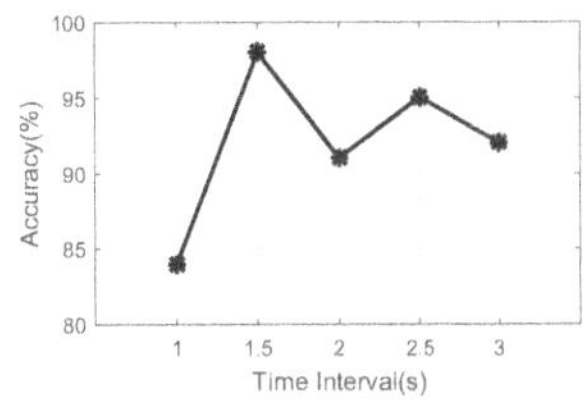

Figure 14. Impact of interval.

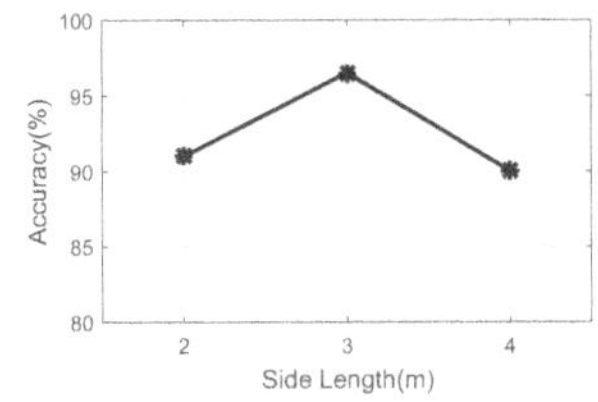

Figure 15. Impact of area size.

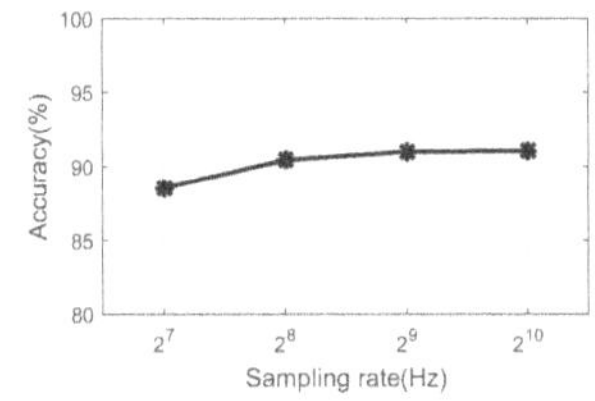

Figure 16. Impact of packet rate.

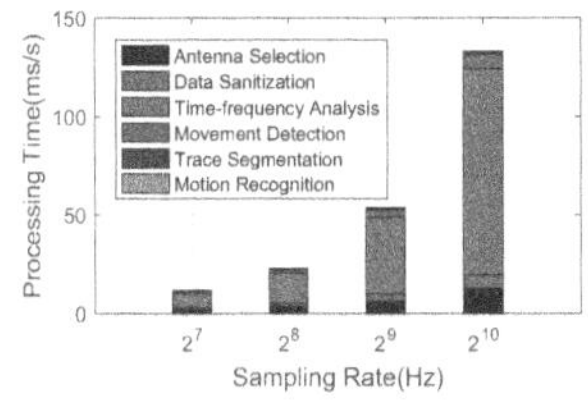

Figure 17. Computation overhead.

s and somatotype, as indicated by Body Mass Index (BMI). Note that the participants also have different levels of body coordination and familiarity with dancing games. Figure 12 shows the performance of *WiDance* with different participants. *WiDance* recognizes actions of all participants with accuracy higher than 85%, without any beforehand per-person learning. However, the result shows no clear correlation between user types and performance of *WiDance*, the further study of which is leaved as future work.

Impact of action range. We evaluate the sensitivity of *WiDance* by asking participants to perform actions with various ranges from 0.3m to 0.9m. Note that a range of 0.3m is comparable to the working range of dancing mats, and a range of 0.9m is almost the extreme range that participants can achieve with the limit of both leg length and note interval length. As shown in Figure 13, *WiDance* maintains consistent high accuracy of 92% when the action range is larger than 0.6m, and slightly degrades to 86% when the range decreases to 0.5m. However, with further decreasing of action range, the accuracy dramatically decreases. It is consistent with the analysis that smaller action ranges leads to shorter actions time and smaller action speed, making it harder to extract Doppler frequency shifts from spectrogram.

Impact of note interval. In real dancing exergames, visual notes appear with various intervals. To evaluate the performance of *WiDance* with different note intervals, we conduct experiments with intervals from 1s to 3s. Note that most novices need repetitive practices to catch up with notes with interval less than 2s. For notes with about 1s interval, users have to perform actions promptly in natural amplitudes without stop to catch up with the notes. As shown in Figure 14, *WiDance* achieves the highest accuracy of 97% with an interval of 1.5s. When the note interval is set to 1s, the accuracy sharply decreases to 84%. The reason is that the interval is too short for players to complete each individual action. Instead, they struggle to catch up with the fast visual notes, and stride with their bodies in an uncontrolled way, which interferes the Doppler frequency shifts of interest. Conversely, when the time interval is longer than 1.5s, the accuracy slightly decreases to about 92%. It is because with a larger interval, players are able to slowly stride during the interval, causing a smaller Doppler frequency shifts that may be interfered with noises.

Impact of area size. We evaluate *WiDance* in monitoring areas with sizes of 2m×2m, 3m×3m, 4m×4m. Figure 15 plots the performance of *WiDance*. As shown, even with an area of as large as $16m^2$, *WiDance* still achieves an accuracy of 90%. While the size of existing dancing pads is only about 1m×1m, *WiDance* enables a large exercising area for players. Players can perform macro actions in the area, which is more helpful for their fitness and health.

Impact of transmission rates. As *WiDance* requires packets transmission for sensing actions, which may occupy channels and interfere normal communication links, we evaluate the performance of *WiDance* with different transmission rates. Initially, we set the transmission rate to 1024Hz and decimate the CSI series to 512, 256, 128Hz. As shown in Figure 16, with decreasing of transmission rate, the performance of *WiDance* slightly degrades, as the high-frequency noises aliases with Doppler frequency of interest. However, *WiDance* still achieves acceptable performance at the transmission rate of 256Hz. Since only the CSIs of packets are used, *WiDance* can transmit even short packets (*e.g.* RTS/CTS) to further reduce the impact on the normal communication channel.

A side effect of using lower transmission rate is reduction of processing time cost. Figure 17 plots the per-second computation cost of each step in *WiDance*. As shown, the major time cost comes from generating spectrogram in the step of time-frequency analysis. By reducing the transmission rate by half, the data amount and thus the processing time reduce by half. With a practical transmission rate of 256Hz, the processing time for a single action is only 25ms, thus enabling real-time processing and reaction of *WiDance*.

LIMITATIONS AND DISCUSSION

Multiple moving objects. Targeting single-player dancing, *WiDance* is unfortunately vulnerable to movements nearby, since reflections from both dancer and intruder are superimposed at receiver. WiTrack [2] enables multiple human tracking by successive silhouette cancellation using FMCW signals. However, it relies on separation of distance and azimuth of multiple objects, which is not feasible for *WiDance*, in that the Doppler shift of the dancer is obfuscated by the similar shift of the intruder. Enabling recognition of multiple objects still remains an open and challenging problem in future.

Dependency on particular hardware cards. CSI is formulated in 802.11 standards for OFDM and MIMO operations. However, accessing CSI is limited to certain NICs with modified drivers (e.g. Intel 5300). An alternative to reduce specific devices is to configure a Wi-Fi device with Intel 5300 NIC as a hotspot and send ICMP packets to collect CSIs from multiple other normal Wi-Fi clients [16]. In this way, only one device with specific NIC is needed. Moreover, as CSI-based Wi-Fi sensing applications continue to explode and mature, we envision future NIC manufacturers will expose CSI to upper layers on most NICs in 3-5 years.

Detection range. While *WiDance* supports up to 4m×4m interaction range, achieving whole-home coverage is not an easy task. As the operation distance increases, (1) The reflected power attenuates exponentially while the interference from static signals and noises remains unchanged; (2) The field of directions with Doppler shifts over the sensitivity continuously narrows. Given the lowest SINR and sensitivity of an NIC, these two factors determines the maximum coverage of the system. Nevertheless, whole-home can still be achieved by deploying more systems in the area of interest, or by sensing actions with larger Doppler frequency shifts (e.g. walking).

Potential applications. The core technology of *WiDance* is to derive motion directions in a device-free manner, which can be applied to various scenarios. In addition to games, it facilitates smart home applications such as remote device selection and control. For example, a user can select a lamp by moving his/her arm towards it, and he/she can control the volume of a speaker by pushing towards or polling away from it. It also benefits localization to eliminate ambiguity in walking directions [17], which enables a range of location-based services such as emergency evacuation, virtual reality and activity tracking. We leave the study on these applications for future work.

RELATED WORK

Wireless Sensing Systems. As an alternative of computer vision in NLOS or dark environments, contactless sensing using wireless signals has attracted extensive interests in recognizing location [4, 3, 2, 25], body activities [22, 32, 12], and vital signs [5, 19, 29, 33]. These systems mainly adopt a radar principle by associating motions with physical measurements such as time-of-flight and Doppler effects, and enable fine-grained and interpretable motion tracking using specialized hardware. For instance, mTrack [32] accurately locates and tracks finger movement using customized millimeter signals. WiSee [22] is the closest to our work, which extracts Doppler shifts in wide-band OFDM signals using USRPs. *WiDance* also recognizes motion directions by modeling and interpreting motion-induced Doppler effects. However, *WiDance* advances the state-of-the-art by extracting Doppler shifts on commercial multi-antenna Wi-Fi devices without any modification.

Wi-Fi-based Gesture Sensing Systems. To bring gesture recognition to commodity Wi-Fi devices, both modeling [1, 30] and pattern matching based principles [31, 28] have been adopted. E-eyes [31] exploits subcarriers of CSI to recognize household activities such as washing dishes and taking a shower. WiGest [1] maps changes in Wi-Fi RSSI into motion primitives, upon which a family of gestures are defined and accurately recognized for device interaction. WiDir [34] proposes to recognize human motion direction by calculating phase differences between CSI subcarriers. In contrast, *WiDance* directly extract Doppler frequency shift with multiple antennas available on commercial Wi-Fi devices, which may serves a wide range of sensing applications than human motion direction. CARM [30] extracts speed-related features from CSI and proposes an effective machine learning framework for CSI-based activity recognition. *WiDance* is built upon this trend of research, and makes one step further by modeling motion directions and extracting the corresoponding Doppler features from noisy CSI, enabling contactless dancing exergame without the need of prior machine learning.

Interfaces for Exergames. Exergame enables physical interaction with users for exercise benefits [26, 10]. Mainstream exergame interfaces are based on either computer vision [24, 11] or controller embedded with sensors [14, 7]. Kinect Sports and Wii Fit are the leading gaming consoles for indoor exergames. ACW [13] combines computer vision and interactive projected graphics for motivating and instructing indoor wall climbing. RetroFab [23] leverages 3D printing technique to agilely adapt physical controllers to arbitrary use. In contrast, wireless sensing with off-the-shelf devices complements shortages of vision-based and sensor-based sensing. We develop a new wireless based exergame interface that tracks body movements and reactions through Doppler effect, and validate the efficiency of the interface by prototyping a dancing game on it. While preliminary, we believe that *WiDance* opens up a new direction for design and development of exergame interfaces.

CONCLUSION

In this paper, we propose *WiDance*, a Wi-Fi-based user interface for contactless dance-pad exergame. First, we design a novel algorithm to extract motion-induced Doppler shifts leveraging antenna diversity on commodity Wi-Fi devices. Then, we model the relation between Doppler shifts and motion directions, and propose a light-weight yet effective signal processing pipeline to translate the model into the interactive dancing exergame. Extensive experimental results show that *WiDance* achieves an overall recognition accuracy of 92% in various indoor environments. Requiring no hardware modifications, *WiDance* is envisioned as a promising step towards practical wireless human-computer interface, which underpins new insights for future wireless sensing applications.

ACKNOWLEDGEMENTS

This work is supported in part by the NSFC under grant 61522110, 61332004, 61672319, 61632008, National Key Research Plan under grant No. 2016YFC0700100.

REFERENCES

1. Heba Abdelnasser, Moustafa Youssef, and Khaled A Harras. 2015. Wigest: A ubiquitous wifi-based gesture recognition system. In *Proc. of IEEE INFOCOM*.
2. Fadel Adib, Zachary Kabelac, and Dina Katabi. 2015. Multi-person localization via rf body reflections. In *Proc. of USENIX NSDI*.
3. Fadel Adib, Zach Kabelac, Dina Katabi, and Robert C Miller. 2014. 3d tracking via body radio reflections. In *Proc. of USENIX NSDI*.
4. Fadel Adib and Dina Katabi. 2013. See through walls with wifi!. In *Proc. of ACM SIGCOMM*.
5. Fadel Adib, Hongzi Mao, Zachary Kabelac, Dina Katabi, and Robert C Miller. 2015. Smart homes that monitor breathing and heart rate. In *Proc. of ACM CHI*.
6. Kamran Ali, Alex Xiao Liu, Wei Wang, and Muhammad Shahzad. 2015. Keystroke recognition using wifi signals. In *Proc. of ACM MobiCom*.
7. Meng-Chieh Chiu, Shih-Ping Chang, Yu-Chen Chang, Hao-Hua Chu, Cheryl Chia-Hui Chen, Fei-Hsiu Hsiao, and Ju-Chun Ko. 2009. Playful bottle: a mobile social persuasion system to motivate healthy water intake. In *Proc. of ACM Ubicomp*.
8. Stefan Göbel, Sandro Hardy, Viktor Wendel, Florian Mehm, and Ralf Steinmetz. 2010. Serious games for health: personalized exergames. In *Proc. of ACM MM*.
9. Daniel Halperin, Wenjun Hu, Anmol Sheth, and David Wetherall. 2011. Predictable 802.11 packet delivery from wireless channel measurements. In *Proc. of ACM SIGCOMM*.
10. Hamilton A Hernandez, Zi Ye, TC Graham, Darcy Fehlings, and Lauren Switzer. 2013. Designing action-based exergames for children with cerebral palsy. In *Proc. of ACM CHI*.
11. Leo Holsti, Tuukka Takala, Aki Martikainen, Raine Kajastila, and Perttu Hämäläinen. 2013. Body-controlled trampoline training games based on computer vision. In *Proc. of ACM CHI*.
12. Kiran Joshi, Dinesh Bharadia, Manikanta Kotaru, and Sachin Katti. 2015. Wideo: Fine-grained device-free motion tracing using rf backscatter. In *Proc. of USENIX NSDI*.
13. Raine Kajastila, Leo Holsti, and Perttu Hämäläinen. 2016. The Augmented Climbing Wall: High-Exertion Proximity Interaction on a Wall-Sized Interactive Surface. In *Proc. of ACM CHI*.
14. Dagmar Kern, Mark Stringer, Geraldine Fitzpatrick, and Albrecht Schmidt. 2006. Curball–A Prototype Tangible Game for Inter-Generational Play. In *Proc. of IEEE WETICE*.
15. Mallory Ketcheson, Luke Walker, and TC Graham. 2016. Thighrim and Calf-Life: a study of the conversion of off-the-shelf video games into exergames. In *Proc. of ACM CHI*.
16. Mengyuan Li, Yan Meng, Junyi Liu, Haojin Zhu, Xiaohui Liang, Yao Liu, and Na Ruan. 2016. When CSI Meets Public WiFi: Inferring Your Mobile Phone Password via WiFi Signals. In *Proc. ACM SIGSAC CCS*.
17. Alex T Mariakakis, Souvik Sen, Jeongkeun Lee, and Kyu-Han Kim. 2014. SAIL: single access point-based indoor localization. In *Proc. of ACM MobiSys*.
18. Pedro Melgarejo, Xinyu Zhang, Parameswaran Ramanathan, and David Chu. 2014. Leveraging directional antenna capabilities for fine-grained gesture recognition. In *Proc. of ACM Ubicomp*.
19. Phuc Nguyen, Xinyu Zhang, Ann Halbower, and Tam Vu. 2016. Continuous and Fine-grained Breathing Volume Monitoring from Afar Using Wireless Signals. In *Proc. of IEEE INFOCOM*.
20. Wei Peng, Jih-Hsuan Lin, and Julia Crouse. 2011. Is playing exergames really exercising? A meta-analysis of energy expenditure in active video games. *Cyberpsychology, Behavior, and Social Networking* 14, 11 (2011), 681–688.
21. John G Proakis. 1995. Digital communications. *McGraw-Hill, New York* (1995).
22. Qifan Pu, Sidhant Gupta, Shyamnath Gollakota, and Shwetak Patel. 2013. Whole-home gesture recognition using wireless signals. In *Proc. of ACM MobiCom*.
23. Raf Ramakers, Fraser Anderson, Tovi Grossman, and George Fitzmaurice. 2016. Retrofab: A design tool for retrofitting physical interfaces using actuators, sensors and 3d printing. In *Proc. of ACM CHI*.
24. Kyle Rector, Cynthia L Bennett, and Julie A Kientz. 2013. Eyes-free yoga: an exergame using depth cameras for blind & low vision exercise. In *Proc. of ACM SIGACCESS*.
25. Longfei Shangguan, Zheng Yang, Alex X Liu, Zimu Zhou, and Yunhao Liu. 2016. STPP: Spatial-Temporal Phase Profiling-Based Method for Relative RFID Tag Localization. *IEEE/ACM Transactions on Networking* (2016).
26. Mike Sheinin and Carl Gutwin. 2014. Exertion in the small: improving differentiation and expressiveness in sports games with physical controls. In *Proc. of ACM CHI*.
27. Amanda E Staiano and Sandra L Calvert. 2011. Exergames for physical education courses: Physical, social, and cognitive benefits. *Child development perspectives* 5, 2 (2011), 93–98.
28. Sheng Tan and Jie Yang. 2016. WiFinger: leveraging commodity WiFi for fine-grained finger gesture recognition. In *Proc. of ACM MobiHoc*.
29. Hao Wang, Daqing Zhang, Junyi Ma, Yasha Wang, Yuxiang Wang, Dan Wu, Tao Gu, and Bing Xie. 2016. Human Respiration Detection with Commodity WiFi Devices: Do User Location and Body Orientation Matter?. In *Proc. of ACM Ubicomp*.

30. Wei Wang, Alex X Liu, Muhammad Shahzad, Kang Ling, and Sanglu Lu. 2015. Understanding and modeling of wifi signal based human activity recognition. In *Proc. of ACM MobiCom*.

31. Yan Wang, Jian Liu, Yingying Chen, Marco Gruteser, Jie Yang, and Hongbo Liu. 2014. E-eyes: device-free location-oriented activity identification using fine-grained wifi signatures. In *Proc. of ACM MobiCom*.

32. Teng Wei and Xinyu Zhang. 2015. mtrack: High-precision passive tracking using millimeter wave radios. In *Proc. of ACM MobiCom*.

33. Chenshu Wu, Zheng Yang, Zimu Zhou, Xuefeng Liu, Yunhao Liu, and Jiannong Cao. 2015. Non-invasive detection of moving and stationary human with wifi. *IEEE Journal on Selected Areas in Communications* (2015).

34. Dan Wu, Daqing Zhang, Chenren Xu, Yasha Wang, and Hao Wang. 2016. WiDir: Walking Direction Estimation Using Wireless Signals. In *Proc. of ACM Ubicomp*.

Be Me, or Be Mii?: A Study of Self-Presentation and Interaction in the Miitomo Mobile Application

Anna Kasunic
Carnegie Mellon University
Pittsburgh, PA, USA
akasunic@andrew.cmu.edu

Geoff Kaufman
Carnegie Mellon University
Pittsburgh, PA, USA
gfk@cs.cmu.edu

ABSTRACT
In this study, we consider what Nintendo's widely downloaded Miitomo mobile application, which simultaneously promotes non-idealized self-fictionalization and authentic self-presentation, can suggest to us about self-presentation and technology design. Ten groups of four friends each (N=40), all novice users, engaged with Miitomo for one week, and completed supplementary pre- and post-use surveys. The data were analyzed to assess the extent to which participants' engagement in Miitomo reflected their "real life" selves and correlated with in-app and "real life" features, respectively. Although most participants believed that their behaviors within the app accurately reflected their "true selves," we found that *in-app* traits generally correlated more strongly with Miitomo engagement patterns than did users' "real life" traits and qualities. We discuss implications for social network and online community design, and propose future plans to study authenticity and self-distancing in online self-presentation.

Author Keywords
Self-presentation; self-distancing; fantasy; authenticity; personality; mobile application; social networks.

ACM Classification Keywords
H.5.m. Information interfaces and presentation (e.g., HCI): Miscellaneous.

INTRODUCTION
Miitomo, the game company Nintendo's first mobile app, first launched in Japan and then gradually released worldwide in the Spring of 2016, enjoyed high early success, quickly becoming the 13th most popular social app in Japan and, as of April 2016, had more than 10 million users [12]. It also showed early evidence of success, with average retention exceeding the 3-7 days typical of mobile apps [9]. With its juxtaposition of fantastic and realistic elements, and its simultaneous pull for fictionalized self-distancing and authentic, non-idealized self-disclosure, the app merits further observation from an HCI perspective.

CHI 2017, May 06-11, 2017, Denver, CO, USA

DOI: http://dx.doi.org/10.1145/3025453.3025934

In Miitomo, each user is represented by and interacts through an animated, talking "Mii," a free-form digital avatar. Users begin by setting up their own Mii and answering a series of questions about themselves; other users can later see/hear one another's responses when their Miis "converse." The app allows users to answer questions posed by their own Miis or others' Miis, hear responses to questions from other Miis, comment on or "heart" (i.e., "like") these responses, and change their Miis' clothing.

As we will discuss in more depth momentarily, some elements of the app encourage users to self-fictionalize, but others pull for more authentic self-presentation. In this study, we sought to understand how this interplay of authenticity and fantasy/self-distancing plays out in novice Miitomo users' self-presentation and interactions. Our two primary research questions were:

- To what extent are participants' Miis distinct from their "real selves"?
- To what extent do app-specific and "real life" features correlate with engagement in the app?

RELATED LITERATURE
Miitomo's design lies somewhere between a social network and a game, and we therefore consider literature about self-presentation in a) social networks and b) avatar game contexts. Research of presentation online has consistently found that people are motivated to self-present authentically. For example, in online social settings that involve avatar representation, such as instant messaging, people generally self-present to show their authentic personality and/or appearance [6]. Research has shown that we can reliably predict people's personality from their Facebook profile photos [4], that friend groups present their actual, non-idealized selves in social networks [2], and that individuals self-disclose differently on social media depending on their personality [10]. In fact, people may express their true (not ideal) selves better online than face-to-face [3], although CMC may increase self-awareness and perceiving others as self-centered [7]. Sstudies have explored authenticity versus self-fictionalization via self-idealization. In one study, users that engaged with avatars representing their ideal future physical selves engaged in more healthy behaviors [5], but other studies have shown that idealized self-fictionalization can impede expression of the "true self," such as in online dating contexts, where there is pressure to present oneself positively [14]. Due to

the unique design features of Miitomo, in the present study we depart from previous work by focusing on authenticity versus *non-idealized* self-fictionalization.

As suggested by theory and research on the Proteus Effect, [16], users assume the characteristics or traits of their avatars. For example, those embodying a reportedly more attractive avatar were more willing to self-disclose, and those with taller avatars self-presented more confidently. Avatar choices may not align with authentic personality or appearances; examples from the literature on role-playing games have found that players often purposefully choose characters with traits and appearances that diverge from their "real life" selves [17], but that in taking on "other" roles, players also incorporate aspects of their true selves, or, conversely, the role-playing and true selves merge as players assume aspects of their characters in their daily lives [15]. Yet Miitomo differs from such examples in that 1) the "role" you assume is intended to be your own self and 2) while still remaining "me," users are urged to present themselves in fictional, largely non-idealized ways.

AUTHENTICITY AND FANTASY IN MIITOMO

We present here a more detailed discussion of the Miitomo platform to abet understanding of the dynamic between the authentic self and the non-idealized fictionalized self in Miitomo's design. The Miitomo platform encourages you to view your Mii as the *you* in many respects. As a new Miitomo user, you can allow the app to automatically create a Mii for you based on their photo, and are instructed, "Choose from a wide library of facial features to make your Mii look just like you" [18]. The app prompts you to set profile features, including five voice dimensions (speed, pitch, depth, accent, and energy) and five personality dimensions (manners, movement, individuality, attitude and expression), chosen using sliders on an 8-point scale.

Yet in the app, it is often unclear whether you should view your Mii as self or other. When you first encounter your Mii, it walks up to you and greets you with, "Oh, hi! How'd you get in? Oh, you're me! Or I'm you—same thing." As you continue with the app, your Mii speaks with other users as your representative, but also communicates with you. You may observe your Mii talking to another Mii, ostensibly without your control, but when you click on the Mii, you assume its role and engage directly with the other user.

The 546 distinct questions that users encountered in our study encompassed a variety of questions about the self, including food preferences (25 questions), and interests in movies, books, music or television (44 questions). Some questions seem designed to elicit more intimate or meaningful information about an individual, such as "What's the biggest adventure you've ever had?" or "Tell me about the most nervous time of your life!" Of the 36 questions promoted by researcher Arthur Aron [1] to promote interpersonal closeness, we found 15 questions in our Miitomo dataset that were highly similar. For example, where Aron asks, *Would you like to be famous? In what way?* Miitomo asks, *If you became a celebrity, what would you want to be famous for?* These questions seem to encourage users to sincerely self-present in the app.

However, questions also incorporate elements of fantasy; 56 of the 546 questions in our study were conditional questions, asking users to consider future or hypothetical circumstances. Several of these involved fantastical scenarios, such as freezing time, combining any two animals into the perfect pet, or being sucked into the TV. Users can also dress their Mii in various outfits, including bizarre options like hot dog costumes and banana suits. The Miis are also cartoonish in both appearance and action, with desexualized bodies that do not vary by gender. When relating a response or comment involving love or affection, a Mii's eyes might suddenly transform into hearts. When expressing excitement, the Mii may produce a shower of confetti out of thin air. Similarly, the customizable voice options are cartoonish and robotic rather than lifelike. Where prior literature has studied contexts in which users may feel persuaded to present idealized selves, the Miitomo app could be said to *discourage* idealization, leading users to self-present in surreal or even downright ridiculous ways.

Figure 1. Photos of the authors' Miitomo Miis

Nintendo's Miitomo design intentions seem purposefully ambiguous, flirting equally with authenticity and playful self-distancing. As producer Sakamoto explained in an interview [11], "It's a combination of this feeling that you can speak indirectly, and this realistic feeling that this is the real person…" It is not immediately clear to what extent the Mii is intended to be the "real self" or some playful, fictionalized version of oneself.

METHOD

For this study, we recruited 10 groups of four novice Miitomo users each (N=40) to engage with the Miitomo application for one week on their mobile devices. We recruited undergraduate and graduate students (aged 18+) to sign up in friend groups of four. We focused on novice users so as to understand emergent usage patterns in Miitomo; high Miitomo attrition rates [19] further informed this decision, suggesting that few Miitomo users reach "expert" status. Participants ranged in age from 20 to 30, with 20 females and 20 males. Thirty-seven were university students, and English was not a primary language for 27. Twenty-seven participants came from India, 6 from the US, 5 from China, and 1 each from Colombia and Indonesia. Groups tended towards country homogeneity; only 2 of the

10 groups represented more than one native country. However, most groups' participants did not share the same primary language; there were only 2 language-homogenous groups. Groups were mostly gender diverse, with 2 all-female groups and 1 all-male group.

After signing consent forms in person, participants completed the Interpersonal Solidarity Scale [13] for each of the other three participants in their group. This 20-item validated scale measures interpersonal closeness, and asks users to rate statements on a 7-point Likert scale, from strongly disagree (1) to strongly agree (7). It includes statements such as, *This person has a great deal of influence over my behavior*, *I trust this person completely*, and *I dislike this person*. Each participant received a custom study ID, group ID, and login email for the Miitomo app, which we had pre-linked to the mynintendo.com website. Each participant downloaded Miitomo, created their Miis using the camera feature, and "friended" one another. They were required to log into the Miitomo app at least once a day (no time limit was imposed) during the weeklong study, and were forbidden from adding friends outside the four-person study group, sharing activity on social media, and making paid in-app purchases.

After one week of app usage, participants deleted the Miitomo app from their devices, and completed an online post-questionnaire. This questionnaire again included the Interpersonal Solidarity Scale, as well as the Big Five Inventory [8]. The Big Five are a set of dimensions accepted and referenced widely in psychology research to describe the key characteristics of personality: openness to experience, conscientiousness, extraversion, agreeableness, and neuroticism. This inventory asks users to characterize themselves according to 44 different Likert scale items, from 1 (disagree strongly) to 5 (agree strongly). Examples include *I am someone who… is outgoing, sociable; tends to find fault with others; is inventive.* Participants also filled out a short demographic questionnaire and answered follow-up questions—both numeric and open-ended—about their experience in Miitomo, including to what extent they felt their responses in Miitomo showed their personality and values. Upon completion of the survey, participants retrieved their study compensation ($25 cash).

Miitomo does not yet offer a data download feature for users, so we set up a simple mySQL database and entered all the app information. Our participants encountered a total of 546 distinct questions, and gave 1,591 answers, 1,227 comments, and 438 hearts. We obtained scores for the Big Five and the Interpersonal Solidarity Scale by summing Likert scale answers, reverse coding when necessary, following the instructions in [8,13]. We used the Miitomo scale sliders to score Miitomo personality and voice traits, and translated both in-app Miitomo traits and the Big Five to a scale of 0-10 for smoother comparison and inference.

FINDINGS

To What Extent are Participants' Miis their "Real" Selves?

Miis as Reflective of True Selves

For the most part, participants reported that their Miis authentically reflected their "true" personality and values. We asked participants two questions: "To what extent did your responses in Miitomo show your true personality [values]," using a 5-point Likert scale from 1 (not at all true) to 5 (extremely true). On average, participants reported that they answered questions honestly, in a way that showed their personality (average = 3.9; SE = 0.1), and to a still relatively high, but slightly lesser extent, their values (average = 3.4; SE=0.2). In open-ended questions about how similar or dissimilar to their Miis, 36 of 40 participants felt their Miis were quite similar in appearance, personality, or both, and 38 of 40 admitted to modifying their Mii over the course of the week to increase similarity. As one participated stated, "For an animated avatar, I feel like my Mii looks fairly similar to how I look in real life, albeit a bit exaggerated. I set my Mii's personality to what I believe is fairly accurate of my actual personality, so presumably we're fairly close there" (p2303).

Distance Between Self and Mii

At the same time, participants engaged in aspects of fantasy or fiction that created a separation between their Mii self and their "true" self. Several spoke of choices in the app that were completely contradictory of their "true" selves. For example, one participant said he aimed for authentic skin color and personality, but "For voice and delivery I just picked something that was ridiculously opposite to my avatar (just for fun)" (p2304). Within self-fictionalizing choices, we saw hints of playfulness and even self-ridicule rather than self-idealization. Many participants chose outlandish clothing, and sometimes engaged in fantasy even when responding to straightforward questions. For example, one participant answered "Where are you from?" with, "Planet where unicorns live!" (p2504). Fantasy appears to have coexisted with sentiments and perceptions of authenticity and honesty.

Lack of Connection Between Miitomo Traits and Big Five

Despite reports of authenticity, we did not find significant correlations between the Big Five personality traits (openness to experience, conscientiousness, extraversion, agreeableness, and neuroticism) and the "Miitomo Five" personality traits (manners, movement, individuality, attitude and expression). Although these two sets of traits are not identical, we might expect to see positive correlations between extraversion and either expression, attitude, or individuality, or openness and expression, and a negative correlation between agreeableness and attitude. However, running a series of simple linear regressions, we found no significant results. Thus, despite participants' perceptions of Mii-self similarity and authenticity, it appears there may have been a separation between the "true" self and the Miitomo self. We explore this phenomenon further in the following section.

To What Extent do App-Specific and "Real Life" Features Correlate with Engagement in the App?

We ran simple linear regressions to investigate whether any of the independent "real life" and in-app traits were significantly correlated with in-app engagement outcomes (number of and average length of answers given, number of comments and hearts made on other participants' responses, and number of clothing changes). From Table 1, it appears Miitomo-specific voice and personality traits (expression, individuality, speed and openness) may better predict levels of app engagement (e.g. number of questions answered, comments given, and outfit changes made) than "real life" traits. The only Big Five trait that emerged as a significant predictor—openness—correlated counter to intuition, with more open individuals expected to provide *shorter* answers.

	outcome	trait	coeff	p-val	F-stat	adj R^2
BFI	ans length	open	-4.31	0.03*	5.23	0.10
Mii. 5; Voice	# answers	expr	7.88	0.03*	5.21	0.10
	answer length	speed	3.01	0.04*	4.64	0.09
	# comment	speed	17.41	0.00*	14.77	0.26
	# outfit changes	indiv	1.02	0.03*	4.99	0.09
		expr	1.26	0.02*	5.51	0.10

Table 1. SLR results, 38 dF, for Big 5 (BFI) & Miitomo-specific traits. Traits normalized to 0-10 scale.

We also looked at interpersonal closeness to see if this real world quality affected app usage. Although we did not see any effects looking at either average closeness per person or per group, we found a significant effect in dyadic relationships, but not in the direction anticipated. For both the number of comments and hearts given to specific individuals within a group, we found a small but significant negative correlation with the Interpersonal Solidarity Scale (ISS) score (COMMENTS: coeff: -0.13; p = 0.025*. HEARTS: coeff: -0.095; p = 0.002*). This suggests that participants were *more* likely to comment and heart in their weaker friendships. To further explore this finding, we compared relationship closeness from the pre- and post-surveys. We found that average group closeness actually decreased after one week of Miitomo use. However, this finding was moderated by the level of initial closeness; those groups for which average closeness declined over the week had, on average, higher initial closeness than those groups for which closeness increased (confirmed with a Welch 2-sample t-test, t=-2.67, df=116.7, p = 0.009). Thus, introducing elements of self-fictionalization may have greater intimacy benefits for less well-acquainted groups.

DISCUSSION

In line with the Proteus Effect, participants appeared to assume certain attributes of their Miis while engaging with the app, with in-app traits emerging more often as significant predictors of app engagement than "real life" traits. At the same time, most participants reported that their Miis accurately represented their true personalities and values, and that they felt quite similar in appearance and personality. We also saw that relationship closeness had a moderating effect, with less close groups and individuals engaging more actively with one another and growing closer to each other after using the app.

These findings contribute to existing bodies of research on the Proteus Effect and online self-presentation, and offers insight into how people engage in technology-mediated circumstances that ask users to present themselves using authenticity as well as fantasy/self-distancing. Where previous research has illuminated the dynamic between authenticity and self-idealization in online context, this study has shown that users can feel they are authentically self-presenting while simultaneously actively engaging in non-idealizing self-fictionalization. It also suggests new directions for online social design. For example, elements of playful fantasy and self-distancing might assist with online community onboarding, or meeting new people (e.g., online dating). "Pop-up" sub-networks specifically designed for short-term, immersive use might serve a need to stimulate self-disclosure and intimacy among little-acquainted individuals in larger networks. We might also think in terms of guided self-disclosure that includes elements of fantasy or self-distancing, or self-presentation "leveling," in which the context in which one self-presents depends on how close one is to other users in a network or how new one is to a community. This suggests that elements of playful, non-idealizing self-fictionalization may aid in increasing the comfort of new acquaintances to self-disclose authentically. In sum, the present study enriches existing bodies of literature on self-presentation and avatar embodiment, and suggests viable techniques and targets for incorporating elements of fantasy and self-distancing in the design of online social environments.

Future work in this domain should include studying more experienced Miitomo users, as well as conducting more in-depth analyses of group dynamics in Miitomo. We also deem it important to conduct follow-up studies with a larger pool of diverse participants to explore differences in how cultural factors such as country, language, race/ethnicity and gender affect authentic vs. fictionalizing self-presentation under the Miitomo context. This would build upon but also diverge from extant research, which has not sufficiently explored cultural factors (e.g. language, country) and has not studied non-idealized fictionalization in online self-presentation.

ACKNOWLEDGEMENTS

A special thanks to all the study participants; to the eHeart lab members; to Fannie Liu, who had the initial idea to conduct a study of Miitomo; to Xu Wang and Anhong Guo for their help and support; to CMU HCII faculty for their feedback; and to Queenie Kravitz, our Miitomo muse.

REFERENCES

1. Arthur Aron and Barbara Fraley. 1999. Relationship Closeness as Including Other in the Self: Cognitive Underpinnings and Measures. *Social Cognition 17*, 140–160. http://doi.org/10.1521/soco.1999.17.2.140
2. Mitja D Back, Juliane M Stopfer, Simine Vazire, et al. 2010. Facebook Profiles Reflect Actual Personality, Not Self-Idealization. *Source: Psychological Science* 21, 3: 372–374. http://doi.org/10.1177/0956797609360756
3. John A. Bargh, Katelyn Y. A. McKenna, and Grainne M. Fitzsimons. 2002. Can You See the Real Me? Activation and Expression of the "True Self" on the Internet. *Journal of Social Issues* 58, 1: 33–48. http://doi.org/10.1111/1540-4560.00247
4. Fabio Celli, Elia Bruni, and Bruno Lepri. 2014. Automatic Personality and Interaction Style Recognition from Facebook Profile Pictures. *Proceedings of the ACM International Conference on Multimedia - MM '14*: 1101–1104. http://doi.org/10.1145/2647868.2654977
5. Youjeong Kim and S. Shyam Sundar. 2012. Visualizing ideal self vs. actual self through avatars: Impact on preventive health outcomes. *Computers in Human Behavior* 28, 4: 1356–1364. http://doi.org/10.1016/j.chb.2012.02.021
6. Kristine L. Nowak. 2013. Choosing Buddy Icons that look like me or represent my personality: Using Buddy Icons for social presence. *Computers in Human Behavior* 29, 4: 1456–1464. http://doi.org/10.1016/j.chb.2013.01.027
7. Bradley M. Okdie, Rosanna E. Guadagno, Frank J. Bernieri, Andrew L. Geers, and Amber R. Mclarney-Vesotski. 2011. Getting to know you: Face-to-face versus online interactions. *Computers in Human Behavior* 27, 1: 153–159. http://doi.org/10.1016/j.chb.2010.07.017
8. John P. Oliver and Sanjay Srivastava. 1999. Big Five Inventory (BFI). *Handbook of personality: Theory and research* 2: 102–138. http://doi.org/10.1525/fq.1998.51.4.04a00260
9. Joseph Schwartz. 2016. Trending US Apps- March 2016. *Digital Vision.*
10. Gwendolyn Seidman. 2013. Self-presentation and belonging on Facebook: How personality influences social media use and motivations. *Personality and Individual Differences* 54, 3: 402–407. http://doi.org/10.1016/j.paid.2012.10.009
11. Itoi Shigesato. 2016. Miitomo's Potential: Yoshio Sakamoto and Shigesato Itoi. *Miitomo website.* Retrieved from https://miitomo.com/en/talk/
12. Aaron Souppouris. 2016. Nintendo's "Miitomo" app passes 10 million users. *Engadget.*
13. Lawrence R. Wheeless. 1978. A Follow-Up Study of the Relationships Among Trust, Disclosure, and Interpersonal Solidarity. *Human Communication Research* 4, 2: 143–157. http://doi.org/10.1111/j.1468-2958.1978.tb00604.x
14. Monica T. Whitty. 2008. Revealing the "real" me, searching for the "actual" you: Presentations of self on an internet dating site. *Computers in Human Behavior* 24, 4: 1707–1723. http://doi.org/10.1016/j.chb.2007.07.002
15. D. Williams, T. L. M. Kennedy, and R. J. Moore. 2011. Behind the Avatar: The Patterns, Practices, and Functions of Role Playing in MMOs. *Games and Culture* 6: 171–200. http://doi.org/10.1177/1555412010364983
16. Nick Yee and Jeremy Bailenson. 2007. The proteus effect: The effect of transformed self-representation on behavior. *Human Communication Research* 33, 3: 271–290. http://doi.org/10.1111/j.1468-2958.2007.00299.x
17. Nick Yee and Jn Bailenson. 2006. Walk a mile in digital shoes: The impact of embodied perspective-taking on the reduction of negative stereotyping in immersive virtual environments. *Proceedings of PRESENCE*: 147–156.
18. Miitomo | Nintendo. Retrieved from https://miitomo.com/en/talk/03.html
19. The rise and fall of Nintendo's Miitomo: Massive downloads don't mean success. Retrieved January 5, 2017 from http://venturebeat.com/2016/05/28/the-rise-and-fall-of-nintendos-miitomo-massive-downloads-dont-mean-success/

Why Players use Pings and Annotations in Dota 2

Jason Wuertz
University of New Brunswick
Fredericton, NB, Canada
jason.wuertz@unb.ca

Scott Bateman
University of New Brunswick
Fredericton, NB, Canada
scottb@unb.ca

Anthony Tang
University of Calgary
Calgary, AB, Canada
tonyt@ucalgary.ca

ABSTRACT
Groupware research has long focused on representing gestures as a means to facilitate collaboration. However, this work has not led to wide support of gesturing in commercial groupware systems. In contrast, Dota 2, a popular MOBA game, provides two frequently-used gesturing tools: *annotations* – freely drawn lines on top of the gamespace – and *pings* – a combination of animation and sound indicating a point of interest. While gesturing tools are important for quickly coordinating with teammates in Dota 2, there is little information about how and why people use them. To gather this information, we performed two complementary studies: an interaction analysis of eight game replays, and a survey of 167 experienced players. Our findings include: six distinct motivations for the use of gesturing tools; when and how frequently gesture motivations occur during games; and, that players find pings an essential tool for winning, but not annotations. Our findings provide new directions for the design of gesturing tools in groupware and online games.

Author Keywords
Dota 2; Pings; Annotations; motivation; gestures; MOBAs; online games; groupware; communication tools.

ACM Classification Keywords
H.5.m. Information interfaces and presentation (e.g., HCI): Miscellaneous.

INTRODUCTION
Groupware research has long focused on how to best design tools that facilitate collaboration. One important focus has been on the best way to support gestures – pointing or motioning with the body to communicate – because it is an easy yet effective way to rapidly share information, often used in face-to-face collaboration [12]. While many types of groupware do not natively support gesturing (e.g., Skype or Google Docs), recent online multiplayer games (notably Multiplayer Online Battle Arenas, called *MOBAs*) provide rich support for gestures. MOBAs, such as *Dota 2*, often provide two gesturing tools frequently seen in past groupware research (e.g., [2,3,4,5,11,13,14,15]): *annotations* – freely drawn lines on top of the gamespace that last a few seconds – and *pings* – a combination of animation and sound that indicates a single point of interest.

CHI 2017, May 06 - 11, 2017, Denver, CO, USA

ACM 978-1-4503-4655-9/17/05…$15.00
DOI: http://dx.doi.org/10.1145/3025453.3025967

While MOBA players learn about pings and annotations early on, and use them frequently, no work has yet looked at *why and how people use gesturing tools in a MOBA*, and to what degree they view them as important for coordinating with teammates to win matches. This information is important for groupware and game designers to understand when gestures are needed. Dota 2 provides a concrete context where such gestures are used today.

We conducted two studies to provide this basic understanding. First, we conducted an interaction analysis of eight Dota 2 game replays, identifying why gestures were created. We found six distinct motivations for gesturing: *planning, warning, resource, conflict, help,* and *emoting*. By examining production time, we found that the motivations for gestures change as a match progresses – from primarily warnings early in matches to primarily planning later on. We also observed that pings are used heavily, but annotations were used much less often. Second, to confirm our identified motivations, and to understand the perceived utility and importance of gesturing tools, we conducted an online survey of 167 experienced players. Players reported that pings are a critical tool for winning matches, while annotations are the least important among surveyed tools. The survey also supported and clarified the motivations identified in the first study.

The results of our studies provide new information about why people use gestures in a popular MOBA, along with new findings about when, how often they are used and their subjective importance. Our work provides new directions for the design of gesturing tools; highlighting that although pings are used frequently, they can be improved by allowing them to convey intent, minimizing ambiguity.

BACKGROUND: MOBAS AND DOTA 2
Dota 2, like other MOBAs, is played on a static map by two teams of five. Each team battles for control over resources in order to advance towards and destroy the other team's base. Each player controls one of 112 possible characters, each with unique abilities and strengths. To increase the odds of success, players must master the nuanced game-mechanics and synergize with their teammates playstyles.

In most MOBAs, players can only see a region of the map in detail at any given time, depending on where their camera is

Figure 1. Communication tools in Dota 2: (left) caution pings; (center) an annotation on the minimap; (right) the chat wheel.

currently set. This means that many actions occur around the map at any given time that are not directly visible, increasing the need for information sharing. Dota 2's interface also provides a *minimap* that displays the entire map in low detail, but makes important information salient (e.g., the location of players and other enemies on the map); see Figure 1, center.

MOBAs provide an array of communication tools that attempt to facilitate and streamline team communications. For the purpose of this note, we select several representative examples from different MOBAs; however, this is not an exhaustive list of all communication tools in the genre.

Text chat – text chat is universally available in MOBAs. Text chat allows players to send free text messages.

Chat wheel – some games (e.g., Dota 2, Strife) allow preset text phrases to be entered with shortcut keys and/or using the mouse to select phrases from a pie menu (see Figure 1, right).

Pings - a combination of animation and sound that indicates a single point of interest. Dota 2, has two ping types created by holding a shortcut key and clicking on an open position on the map: exclamation pings (alt + left clicking) appear as an exclamation mark; and, caution pings (ctrl + alt + left clicking) appear as an 'X' (see Figure 1, left). While the meaning of pings is not specific, exclamation pings are context sensitive, with different effects depending on the object that was clicked. For example, an exclamation ping over an enemy tower produces a unique sound and a sword icon. Pings appear on both the gamespace and the minimap.

Annotations – players can create free hand annotations on the minimap, which allows the creation of more detailed gestures to teammates (ctrl + click and drag on the minimap). Annotations and drawings only last for a few seconds and can only be seen on the minimap. See Figure 1, center.

RELATED WORK GESTURES IN GROUPWARE & GAMES

The more relevant information a team shares, the more likely it is to succeed [16]. Hence, groupware research has focused on providing tools that facilitate communication and increase group awareness [4]. Such tools include gesturing support, which has been shown to facilitate shared work [1,2,5,7]. Gestures can be represented in a variety of ways, including telepointers [4,5], push-pins [3], freely drawn annotations [6, 11] or representations of collaborators' arms [11,13]. Toups et al. studied communication mechanics in games, and identified several ways that games support gestures (including pings) and ways that players approximate gestures when they are not supported by a gesturing tool [14].

Recent work has found that League of Legends (LoL) players want and need to collaborate in "every aspect of the game" to have fun and to be successful [9]. Similarly, a recent study of Portal 2, a game with a rich set of gesturing tools, found that the tools were critical to coordinating actions [15]. Work has also recognized the importance of gestures in MOBAs; a large-scale analysis found that using pings correlated with several metrics of player performance [10]. While research has recognized the importance of gesturing tools to support teamwork in games, no work has yet examined why, when and how gesturing tools are used.

STUDIES OF GESTURING IN DOTA 2

Study 1: Analysis of Game Replays

Our first study focused on identifying the communicative intent behind gesture tool use in Dota 2.

Data and Analysis

Public Dota 2 game replays can be downloaded and replayed in the game's client, allowing full exploration of the entire game state at any time during a match. Eight replays were selected from recent amateur matches to cover a range of match lengths and skill levels (5 normal skill matches; 3 high skill matches). Normal matches covers 75% of players (see: http://de.dota2.com/2013/12/ matchmaking-2/).

We used the iterative nature of Interaction Analysis to create content codes for labeling gesture events [8]. Events (annotations or pings) were identified and recorded with contextual details (e.g. creation time, a communicative intent category, map location, etc.). A new category was created when an event did not fit an existing category. Often this would include discussion and re-watching the event multiple times to ensure accuracy and minimize redundant categories.

Overall Results

Our analysis resulted in 756 gesture events in total (mean: 94.5 events/match; sd. 37.6; min: 31; max: 159). Overall, we found that pings were used extremely frequently, accounting for 729 of the events, while annotations accounted for just 27 events over 8 matches. Matches varied in length between 23 and 56 mins. (mean: 35.3 mins/match; sd: 9.4). Because of this we present data related to time as a normalized value (the percentage of time passed to the end of the match). Based on normalized time, the majority of gestures occur just after the midpoint of matches (after 52.33% of the match has elapsed).

Results: Communicative Intents (Gesturing Motivations)

Our analysis resulted in the six communicative intents (referred to as *motivations*) listed below (with the percentage of total events observed). 751 of the 756 events were categorized into the six motivations. Five events were initially omitted, but categorized later (see Discussion).

Planning (37.2%): Indicates a goal, path or objective that the player plans on pursuing or wants others to achieve or perform. For example, a player pings an enemy tower to tell teammates to attack it.

Warning (37%): When players notice that a teammate is in that an enemy is unaccounted for (i.e., missing), that an area of the map is unsafe, or that an enemy is searching for engagement they may produce warning events.

Resource (8.0%): Makes teammates aware of a resources that are available, such as wards, neutral stacks or runes.

Conflict (8.7%): Draws attention to areas of conflict. For example, a player is ambushed by enemies so they notify their teammates of the ensuing conflict.

Help (1.0%): Sometimes players know that they will require help to complete a task (such as safely farming in a lane), they will request help from other teammates. For example, if a player knows they will need healing from a teammate in the future, they may request help from a healer.

Frustration (*Emoting*) (8.1%): Players often experience frustration, as a result of their own mistakes, the mistakes of teammates, or due to conflict with teammates or enemies. We also observed ignoring warnings and reckless playstyle as causes for frustration in players. Frustration is commonly expressed by creating (spamming) pings in rapid succession. *Note*: Study 1 only uncovered Frustration as a motivation. However, the results of Study 2, caused us to broaden Frustration to *Emoting*. See Discussion for a description.

Results Based on Analysis of Motivations

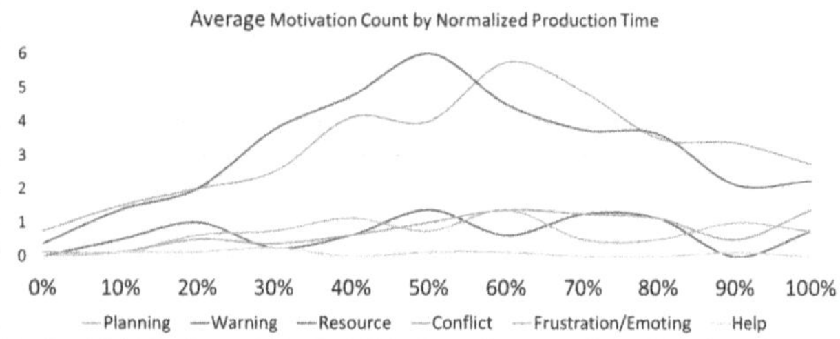

Figure 2. Average Motivation Count by Normalized Production Time

Overall, we observed relatively few uses of the annotation tool; 27 events overall, with coverage in only three of six categories: planning (21 events), warning (4), emoting (2). Figure 2 shows the average count of each motivation type by normalized production time in the match. We can see that most motivations remain relatively stable throughout the match averaging between 0-1.5 uses. However, both warning and planning rise sharply mid-match, with warnings peaking just before the midpoint and planning just after.

Study 2: Survey

Design and Participants

Our online survey collected player's perceived importance of gesturing tools to winning as compared to other available communication tools, the utility of annotation and pings for expressing our six identified motivations from Study 1, and to identify any other motivations for ping and annotations together. To simplify the survey, all of our questions asked participants to consider pings and annotations together.

We advertised our survey on the online forums r/dota2 (reddit) and the LiquidDota forum, in addition to the authors' Twitter accounts. 179 respondents could optionally be entered into a draw for one of five 20USD Steam gift cards.

Participants were from 40 different countries – the top 3 countries were US (47), UK (28), Canada (16) – 63% spoke English as a first language, had an average age of 20.5 (sd. 4.9, min. 14, max. 39), and were predominantly male (175 male; 4 female). Participants were very experienced, the average number of time in game was 2406 hours (s.d. 1757, min. 227, max. 11,050); only 22 participants reported playing fewer than 10 hours/week.

Data and Analysis

Our survey asked a series of Likert-style (on a 5-point scale). Response data was analyzed using a Friedman test and pairwise comparisons were conducted using Wilcoxan, with Bonferonni adjustments. Participant responses to optional free-text questions are used selectively to support findings.

Results

There was an effect of communication tool type on participants rating of the tool helping them win (see Figure 3); $\chi^2(3) = 62.734, p < .001$. Overall, participants rated pings, text chat and the chat wheel significantly more helpful for winning than annotations (all $p < .001$), but there were no other differences between the communication tools.

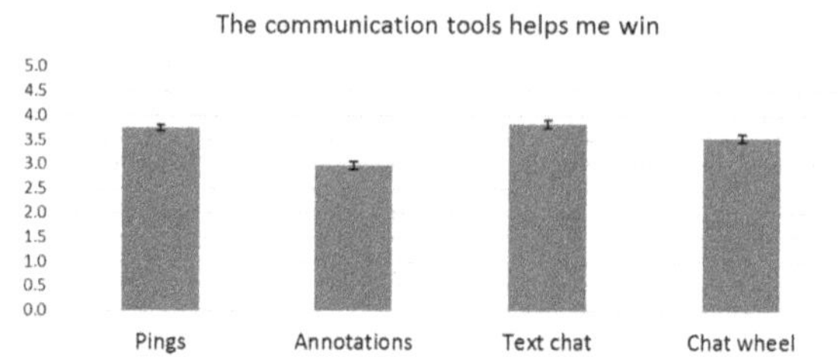

Figure 3. Agreement ratings for the utility of different communications for winning matches.

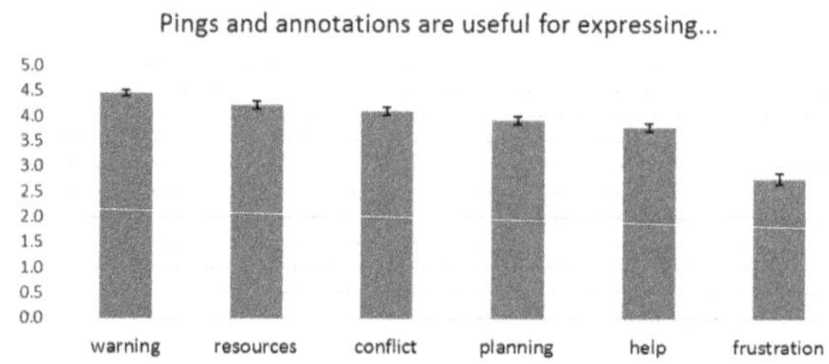

Figure 4. Agreement with the usefulness of tools for expressing six different motivations identified in Study 1.

There was a significant difference between the usefulness of gesturing tools for communicative intents (see Figure 4); $\chi^2(6) = 185.934, p < .001$). Overall, there was a difference between all motivation types ($p<.001$) with the exception of there being no difference between danger and resources, and planning and conflicts. This means that participants felt that pings and annotations are most useful for communicating warnings and resources, followed by planning and conflicts. They were rated least useful for expressing frustration.

We also asked participants to describe why they use pings and annotations. Of the 179 participants, 44 described uses. Two authors looked at these individually and agreed that most mapped to our categories; for example, "Notify a teammate of who to target" maps to 'planning'. However, 10 uses did not fit in our motivation. For example, one participant would cheer for teammates using pings: "Awe at execution of skill or luck in an event." Participants also described using pings and annotations for "flaming" and for "comedic value". These comments led us to broaden Frustration to Emoting (see Discussion).

DISCUSSION

Frustration becomes Emoting

Study 1 originally uncovered only 'Frustration' as a motivation. However, after Study 2, we broadened this category to include other types of 'Emoting' including the expression of joy, praise, pride, playfulness or to flame. This resulted in the only 5 (0.6%) events for which we could not find a category in Study 1, to be recoded as Emoting. For example, these five events included two instances of players expressing pride in making big plays by pinging rapidly, and two instances of a player drawing penises on the minimap; a relatively common act that is meant to be playful.

Why Are Pings More Popular than Annotations?

We were surprised that annotations were not used more frequently; however, we can speculate about two possible reasons for their lack of use, which should be investigated in future work. First, pings are likely enough in many situations. Although, pings carry low information content, drawing attention to a single point only [14], the addition of contextual use (e.g., different behavior for pings when clicking objects like towers) and player's deep knowledge and experience with the game might allow pings to carry much more information that can be inferred rapidly by players. Second, annotations take more time and effort to create. Annotations must be created on the minimap; targeting, clicking and dragging the mouse on this small area can be challenging and might take too much time in the heat of a battle. Further, unlike pings (which appear on the gamespace), annotations only appear on the minimap; meaning they are much less visible.

To address these limitations, we believe that annotations might be used more often if they were more salient and more easily created. For example, annotations could be created and viewed directly on the gamespace rather than the minimap. There is some evidence that such a change could work, as Dota 2 provides exactly this in widely used tools for commentators and casters to describe matches to spectators.

Why Do Motivations Occur at Different Times?

The results relating to production time for the different motivations provide valuable new information regarding the dynamics and different stages of matches. During the early stages of a Dota 2 match players actively engage in well understood activities (e.g., laning, jungling, etc.); however, in the middle of the match players start to form a game plan to try and gain the upper hand. Initially, teammates try to jockey for an advantage (e.g., by pushing lanes, trying to gank enemies), which results in warning pings being created. As this is happening, teams start to plan offensive and defensive tactics, leading to planning pings. This opens up interesting direction for work that looks at how communications can help explain game behavior and dynamics in MOBAs and other games.

Enriching Gestures with More Information

Games like Smite and LoL have recognized that providing a pre-defined type with pings can make them more effective; via an interface similar to the chat wheel, called the ping wheel. Four ping types are provided: danger, enemy missing, on my way, and assistance. At least two of these, map clearly to our motivations (danger & missing >warning, assistance > help). The other messages are available in Dota 2 through the chat wheel, which allows reports of "missing" with a general location (e.g., "top" or "bottom"), and on my way. However, we have identified six motivations and each of these motivations might warrant its own ping wheel (e.g., the planning chat wheel could have pings for "attack", "push", "gank", "hide"). We will explore this in our future work.

Deictic references (the combination of speech and gestures to communicate detail quickly) are common in collaboration [12]. Ping wheels enable a form of deixis; however, it is also likely that voice and pings are often used together in Dota 2. Studying voice chat and their use in combination with pings and annotations was not possible through our study methodology, and would be a complex undertaking. Therefore, our work focused exclusively on non-verbal tools. Future work should start to examine the use of voice in MOBAs and how it is combined with gesturing and other communication tools.

CONCLUSIONS

Our two studies were the first to identify six distinct communicative intents for the use of gesturing tools (planning, warning, resource, conflict, help, and emoting). We found that use of pings for most motivation types are fairly stable throughout matches, with the exception of warning and planning gestures, which peak around the middle of matches. We also found that players clearly view pings as an important tool; players used them extremely frequently and rated them as important to winning. However, annotations were neither used frequently nor felt to be particularly helpful for winning.

Based on these results we have suggested several promising directions for the improvement and future study of gesturing tools in Dota 2 and MOBAs. Given the success and importance of gesturing tools in MOBAs, other genres, such as MMOs and FPSs, might consider them as new ways to support collaboration. Further, we believe that groupware research more generally might learn from some of the communication tools that have successfully been employed in MOBAs (and other games), and provide designers with new directions to support collaborative work tasks.

REFERENCES

1. Herbert H. Clark. 1996. *Using Language*. Cambridge University Press.
2. Susan R. Fussell, Leslie D. Setlock, Jie Yang, Jiazhi Ou, Elizabeth Mauer, and Adam D. I. Kramer. 2004. Gestures over video streams to support remote collaboration on physical tasks. Hum.-Comput. Interact. 19, 3 (September 2004), 273-309. http://dx.doi.org/10.1207/s15327051hci1903_3
3. Steffen Gauglitz, Benjamin Nuernberger, Matthew Turk, and Tobias Höllerer. 2014. World-stabilized annotations and virtual scene navigation for remote collaboration. *In Proceedings of the 27th annual ACM symposium on User interface software and technology* (UIST '14). ACM, New York, NY, USA, 449-459. http://doi.acm.org/10.1145/2642918.2647372
4. Carl Gutwin and Saul Greenberg. 2002. A Descriptive Framework of Workspace Awareness for Real-Time Groupware *Computer Supported Cooperative Work (CSCW)*, 11,3. 411-446. http://dx.doi.org/10.1023/A:1021271517844
5. Carl Gutwin, Mark Roseman, and Saul Greenberg. 1996. A usability study of awareness widgets in a shared workspace groupware system. In *Proceedings of the 1996 ACM conference on Computer supported cooperative work (CSCW '96)*, 258-267. http://dx.doi.org/10.1145/240080.240298
6. Hiroshi Ishii, Minoru Kobayashi, and Jonathan Grudin. 1993. Integration of interpersonal space and shared workspace: ClearBoard design and experiments. *ACM Transactions on Information Systems* 11, 4: 349–375. http://doi.org/10.1145/159764.159762
7. Brennan Jones, Anna Witcraft, Scott Bateman, Carman Neustaedter, and Anthony Tang. 2015. Mechanics of Camera Work in Mobile Video Collaboration. *In Proceedings of the 33rd Annual ACM Conference on Human Factors in Computing Systems* (CHI '15). ACM, New York, NY, USA, 957-966. http://doi.acm.org/10.1145/2702123.2702345
8. Brigitte Jordan, and Austin Henderson. 1995. Interaction Analysis: Foundations and Practice. *Journal of the Learning Sciences. 4,* 1, 39-103. http://dx.doi.org/10.1207/s15327809jls0401_2
9. Yubo Kou and Xinning Gui. 2014. Playing with strangers: understanding temporary teams in league of legends. *In Proceedings of the first ACM SIGCHI annual symposium on Computer-human interaction in play (CHI PLAY '14)*, 161-169. http://dx.doi.org/10.1145/2658537.2658538
10. Alex Leavitt, Brian C. Keegan, and Joshua Clark. 2016. Ping to Win?: Non-Verbal Communication and Team Performance in Competitive Online Multiplayer Games. *In Proceedings of the 2016 CHI Conference on Human Factors in Computing Systems (CHI '16).* 4337-4350. http://dx.doi.org/10.1145/2858036.2858132
11. John C. Tang and Scott L. Minneman. 1991. Videodraw: a video interface for collaborative drawing. *ACM Transactions on Information Systems* 9, 2: 170–184. http://doi.org/10.1145/123078.128729
12. John C. Tang. Findings from observational studies of collaborative work. *International Journal of Man-machine studies* 34, 2 (1991): 143-160.
13. Anthony Tang, Carman Newstaedter and Saul Greenberg. 2006. VideoArms: Embodiments for Mixed Presence Groupware. *In Proceedings of the 20th British HCI Group Annual Conference (HCI 2006)*, 85-102.
14. Zachary O. Toups, Jessica Hammer, William A. Hamilton, Ahmad Jarrah, William Graves, and Oliver Garretson. 2014. A framework for cooperative communication game mechanics from grounded theory. In Proceedings of the first ACM SIGCHI annual symposium on Computer-human interaction in play (CHI PLAY '14). ACM, New York, NY, USA, 257-266. http://dx.doi.org/10.1145/2658537.2658681
15. Deepika Vaddi, Zachary Toups, Igor Dolgov and Rina Wehbe and Lennart Nacke. 2016. Investigating the Impact of Cooperative Communication Mechanics on Player Performance in Portal 2. *In Proceedings of Graphics Interface (GI 2016)*, 41-48. http://doi.org/10.20380/GI2016.06
16. Paul Ward and Eccles, (2006). A commentary on "Team cognition and expert teams: Emerging insights into learning and performance for exceptional teams". *International Journal of Sport and Exercise Psychology* 4: 463-483.

Author Index

NOTES

NOTES

NOTES

NOTES

NOTES

NOTES

NOTES

NOTES

NOTES

NOTES

NOTES

NOTES

NOTES

NOTES

NOTES

NOTES

NOTES

NOTES

NOTES

NOTES

NOTES

NOTES

www.ingramcontent.com/pod-product-compliance
Lightning Source LLC
LaVergne TN
LVHW080105011026
849160LV00013B/1033